Fodor's 97

NOV 21 19

"For practical details...Fodor's can't be beat."
—Gannett News Service

"When it comes to information on regional history, what to see and do, and shopping, these guides are exhaustive."

—USAir Magazine

"Provides a good once-over for the continent's high spots."

—San Diego Magazine

"The easiest of the guides to read, with uncluttered pages, reasonably eclectic restaurant and hotel listings, excellent, simple maps and generally clear prose."

—The New York Times

"Usable, sophisticated restaurant coverage, with an emphasis on good value."
—Andy Birsh, Gourmet Magazine columnist

"Valuable because of their comprehensiveness."
—Minneapolis Star-Tribune

"Fodor's always delivers high quality...thoughtfully presented...thorough."

—Houston Post

"An excellent choice for those who want everything under one cover."

—Washington Post

Visit us on the Web at http://www.fodors.com/

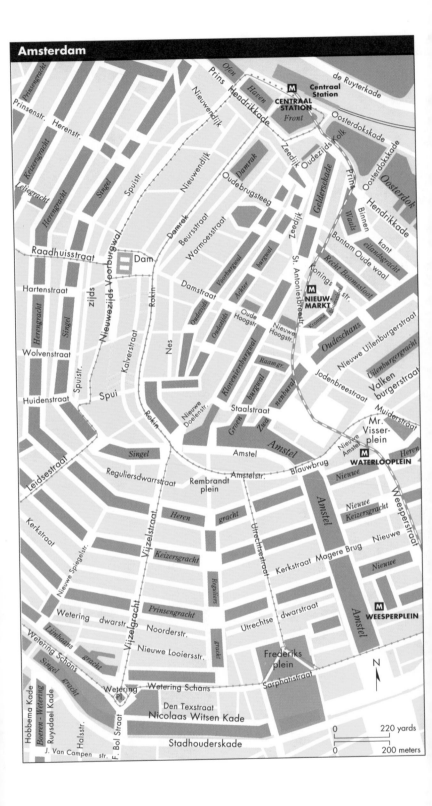

Amsterdam

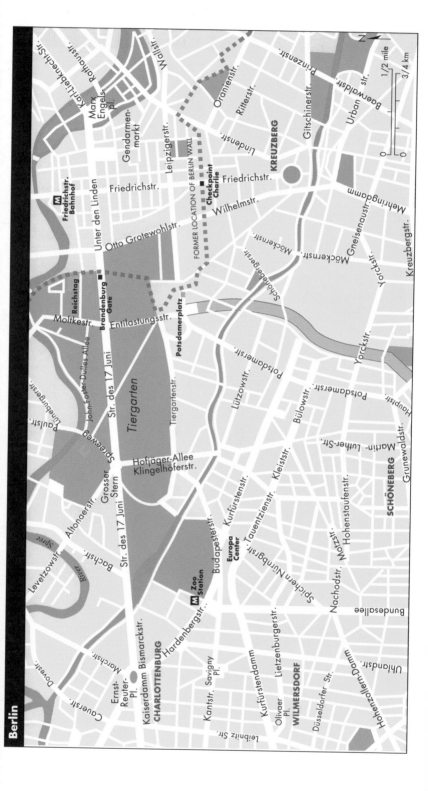

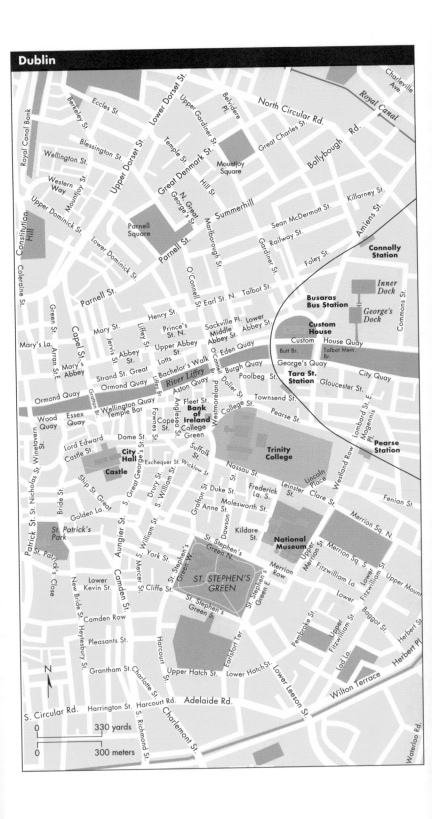

Dublin

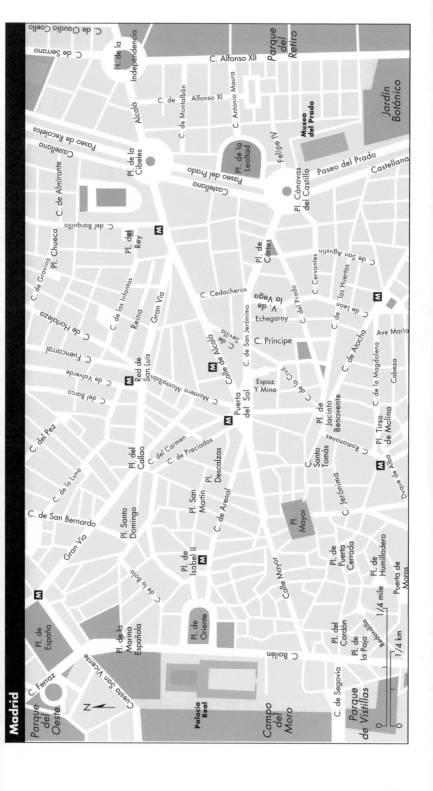

Madrid

Parque del Oeste

Parque del Retiro

Jardín Botánico

Museo del Prado

Palacio Real

Campo del Moro

Parque de Vistillas

C. de Claudio Coello
C. de Serrano
Pl. de la Independencia
C. Alfonso XII
Alcalá
C. de
Alfonso XI
C. de Montalbán
C. Antonio Maura
Felipe IV
Pl. de la Lealtad
Pl. de la Cibeles
Paseo del Prado
Paseo del Prado
Castellana
Pl. Cánovas del Castillo
Castellana
Paseo del Prado
Castellana
Pl. del Rey
C. del Barquillo
C. de Almirante
Pl. Chueca
C. de Gravina
Pl. de Cortes
C. Cervantes
C. de San Agustín
C. de las Infantas
Gran Vía
Reina
C. Cedaceros
V. de la Vega
C. del Prado
C. de las Huertas
C. de San Jerónimo
Echegaray
Sevilla
C. de León
Ave María
C. de Hortaleza
C. Fuencarral
C. de Valverde
C. del Barco
C. del Pez
C. de la Luna
Red de San Luis
C. Montalbán
Calle de Alcalá
C. Príncipe
Espoz Y Mina
C. de Atocha
C. de la Magdalena
Cabeza
Puerta del Sol
C. de la Cruz
Pl. de Jacinto Benavente
Pl. Tirso de Molina
C. de San Bernardo
Gran Vía
Pl. del Callao
C. del Carmen
C. de Preciados
Pl. Descalzas
Pl. San Martín
C. de Arenal
Pl. Mayor
C. Romanones
C. Santo Tomás
C. Jerónima
Duque de Alba
Pl. Santo Domingo
Pl. de Isabel II
C. de la bola
Pl. de la Marina Española
Pl. de España
C. Ferraz
Cuesta San Vicente
Pl. de Oriente
Bailén
Calle Mayor
Pl. de Puerta Cerrada
Pl. de Humilladero
Puerta de Moros
Pl. del Cordón
Pl. de la Paja
Redondilla
C. de Segovia

1/4 mile
1/4 km

London

Regent's Park

Inner Circle

Euston Station

Eversholt St.

Hampstead Rd.

Outer Circle

Chester Rd.

Albany St.

Euston Rd.

Telecom Tower

Tottenham C

Gow

Outer Circle

Park Rd.

Dorset Square

Balcombe St.

Marylebone Rd.

Baker St.

Gloucester Pl.

Marylebone High St.

Harley St.

Portland Pl.

Gt. Portland St.

Berners St.

Abbey Rd.

Grove End Rd.

Wellington Rd.

Prince Albert Rd.

Circus Rd.

Abercorn Pl.

Hall Rd.

St. John's Wood Rd.

Maida Vale

Lisson Grove

Clifton Rd.

Bloomfield Rd.

Edgware Rd.

Harrow Rd.

Marylebone Flyover

Bishop's Bridge Rd.

Paddington Station

Praed St.

Sussex Gdns.

Edgware Rd.

Seymour Pl.

Manchester Square

Wigmore St.

Oxford Oxford Circus

Oxford

SOHO

BAYSWATER

Craven Hill

Bayswater Rd.

N. Carriage Dr.

Oxford St.

Grosvenor Square

Duke St.

Brook St.

New Bond St.

Regent St.

Brewer

Queensway

Bayswater Rd.

U.S. Embassy

Grosvenor St. St.

Berkeley Square

Royal Academy

Piccad Circ

Jermyn St.

Kensington Gardens

Round Pond

Hyde Park

Park Lane

Sth. Audley St.

Curzon St.

Dover St.

St. James's St.

Pall M

The Serpentine

Piccadilly

Green Park

St. Jame Park

Kensington Palace

W. Carriage Dr.

Constitution Hill

Birdcage

Kensington Rd.

Kensington Gore

Kensington Rd.

S. Carriage Dr.

Knightsbridge

Grosvenor Pl.

Buckingham Palace

Palace Gate

Gloucester Rd.

Prince Consort Rd.

Exhibition Rd.

Queen's Gate

Royal Albert Hall

KNIGHTSBRIDGE

Brompton Rd.

Sloane St.

Pont St.

Belgrave Square

Cadogan Pl.

Eaton Square

Buckingham Palace Rd.

Victoria Station

Victoria

Wilton Rd.

Cromwell Rd.

South Kensington Museums

SOUTH KENSINGTON

Old Brompton Rd.

Fulham Rd.

Sloane Ave.

CHELSEA

Pimlico Rd.

Warwick Way

Vau

Belgrave

Redcliffe Gdns.

Finborough Rd.

Fulham Rd.

Old Church St.

Sydney St.

King's Rd.

Oakley St.

Royal Hospital Rd.

Chelsea Br. Rd.

Lupus St.

Cheyne Walk

Beaufort St.

Albert Br.

Battersea Br.

Chelsea Embankment

River Thames

Chelsea Br.

Grosvenor

Battersea Park

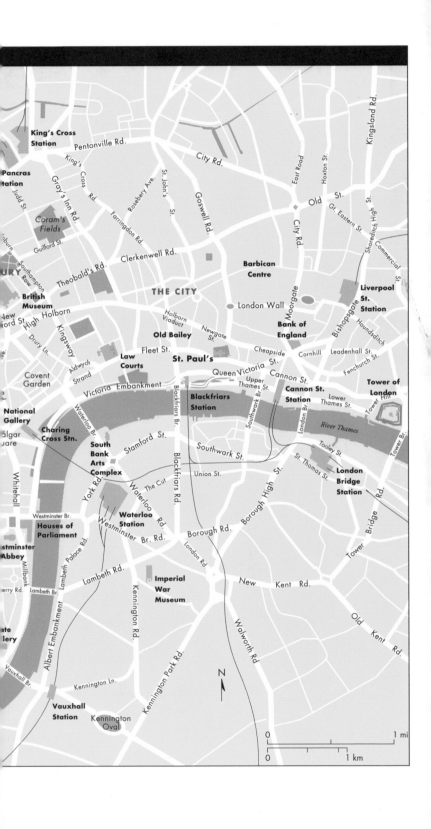

Munich

KEY

i Tourist Information

Englischer Garten

Lerchenfeld Str.
Oettingenstr.
Sternstr.
Maximilians Br.
Isar
Liebigstr.
Unsoldstr.
St.-Anna-Str.
St. Anna Pl.
Christophstr.
Bürkleinstr.
Maximilianstr.
Knöbelstr.
Steinsdorfstr.
Thier.-Wimmer-Ring
Isartorpl.
Kanalstr.
Prinzregentenstr.
Königinstr.
Kaulbachstr.
Schönfeldstr.
V. D. Tannstr.
Ludwigstr.
K.-Scharnagl-Ring
Marstallstr.
Am Kosttor
Am Platzl
Tal
Galeriestr.
Hofgarten
Hofgartenstr.
Residenz
National theater
Pfisterstr.
Burgstr.
Dienerstr.
Odeons- pl.
Max-Joseph- pl.
Residenzstr.
Theatinerstr.
Weinstr.
Rosental
Oberanger
Oscar V. Miller Ring
Türkenstr.
Briennerstr.
Kard.-Faulhaber-Str.
Salvatorpl.
Maffeistr.
Frauen- pl.
Augustinerpl.
Kaufingerstr.
Marien- markt
Rindermarkt
Rosenstr.
Gabelsbergerstr.
Max Joseph- str.
Barerstr.
Ottostr.
Maximilianspl.
Prannerstr.
Pacellistr.
Promenadepl.
Neuhauserstr.
Hotterstr.
Brunnstr.
Karolinenpl.
Lenbachpl.
Glyptothek
Königspl.
Meiserstr.
Luisenstr.
Sophienstr.
Alter Botanischer Garten
Elisenstr.
Sonnenstr.
Prielmayerstr.
Schützenstr.
Karlspl.
Schlosserstr.
Briennerstr.
Augustenstr.
Karlstr.
Dachauerstr.
Seidlstr.
Marsstr.
Bahnhofpl.
Hauptbahnhof
Bayerstr.
Goethestr.
Schillerstr.
Schwanthalerstr.
Landwehrstr.

1/4 mile
1/4 km

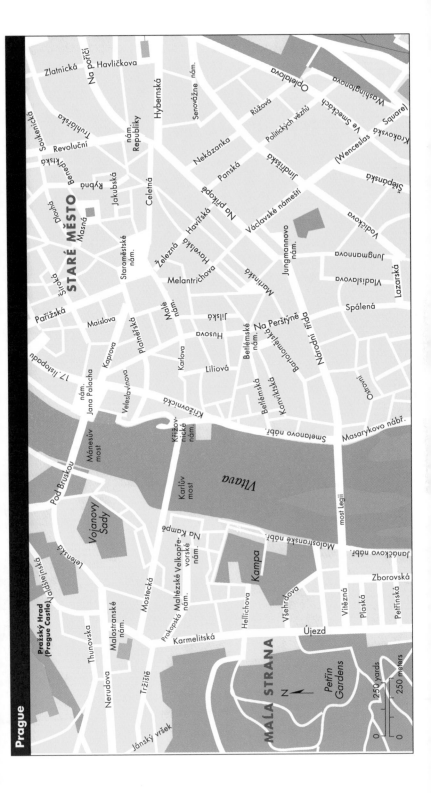

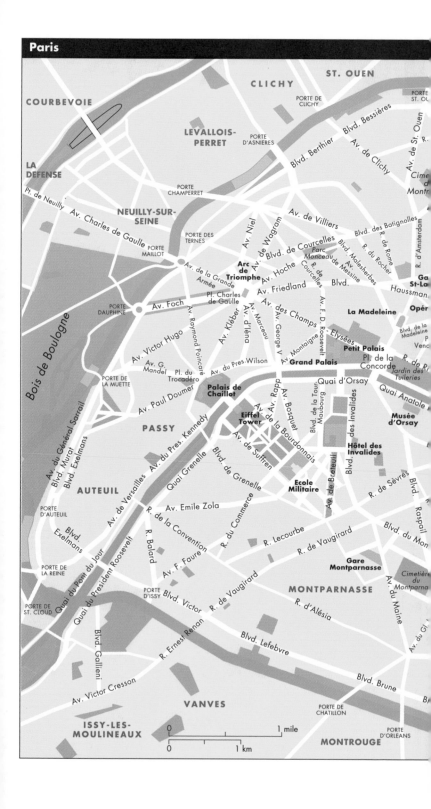

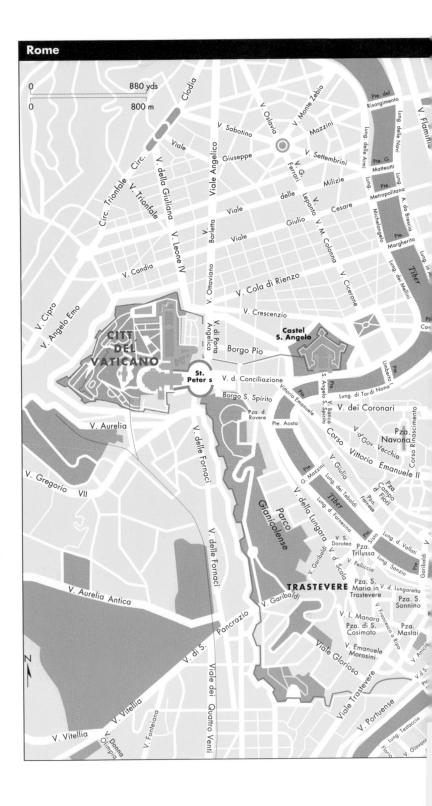

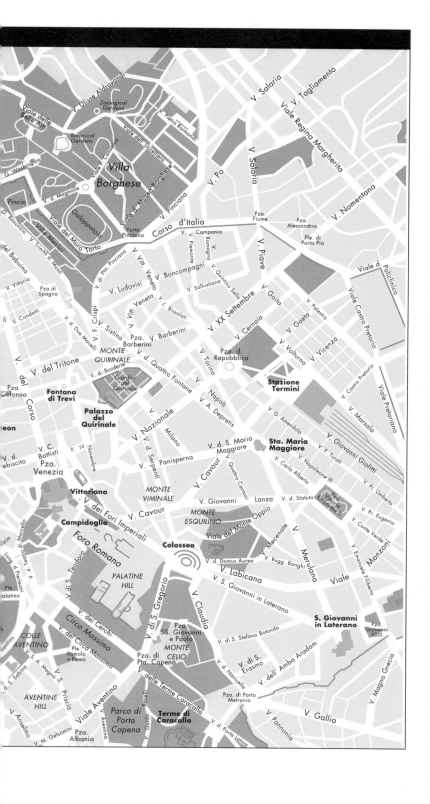

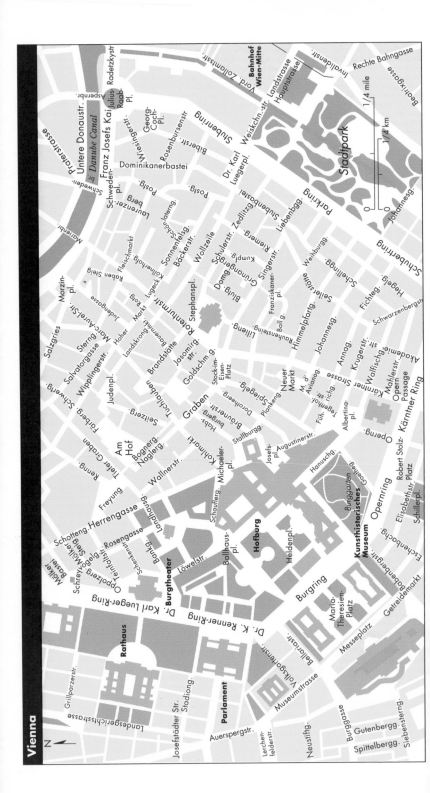

Fodor's 97

Europe

"When it comes to information on regional history, what to see and do, and shopping, these guides are exhaustive."

—*USAir Magazine*

"Usable, sophisticated restaurant coverage, with an emphasis on good value."

—Andy Birsh, *Gourmet Magazine* columnist

"Valuable because of their comprehensiveness."

—*Minneapolis Star-Tribune*

"Fodor's always delivers high quality...thoughtfully presented...thorough."

—*Houston Post*

"An excellent choice for those who want everything under one cover."

—*Washington Post*

Fodor's Travel Publications, Inc.
New York • Toronto • London • Sydney • Auckland
http://www.fodors.com/

Fodor's Europe '97

Editor: Linda Cabasin

Editorial Contributors: Steven Amsterdam, Robert Andrews, Barbara Walsh Angelillo, Robert Blake, Toula Bogdanos, Rodney Bolt, David Brown, Jules Brown, Andrew Collins, Nancy Coons, Cross Publications, Fionn Davenport, Giuliano Davenport, Chris Drake, Mario Falzon, Nigel Fisher, Robert I. C. Fisher, Brent Gregston, George Hamilton, Emma Harris, Nancy Hennessey, Simon Hewitt, Alannah Hopkin, Anto Howard, Dennis Jaffe, Gareth Jenkins, L. M. Kidder, Ky Krauthamer, Leon Lazaroff, Natasha Lesser, Deborah Luhrman, Daniel Mangin, Chelsea Mauldin, Amy McConnell, Caroline Merz, Rebecca Miller, Jason Oliver Nixon, Shelley Panill, Jennifer Paull, Conrad Little Paulus, Karina Porcelli, Kathryn Sampson, Heidi Sarna, Jürgen Scheunemann, Helayne Schiff, Mary Ellen Schultz, M. T. Schwartzman (Gold Guide editor), Bernard Scudder, Kate Sekules, George Semler, Eric Sjogren, Timea Spitka, Dinah Spritzer, Katherine Tagge, Robert Tilley, Julie Tomasz, Ivanka Tomova, William Vasquez, Angela Walker, Daniel Williams, Amanda Wunder.

Creative Director: Fabrizio La Rocca
Associate Art Director: Guido Caroti
Photo Researcher: Jolie Novak
Cartographer: David Lindroth
Cover Photograph: BKA/Network Aspen
Design: Between the Covers

Copyright

Special Sales

Fodor's Travel Publications are available at special discounts for bulk purchases for sales promotions or premiums. Special editions, including personalized covers, excerpts of existing guides, and corporate imprints, can be created in large quantities for special needs. For more information, contact your local bookseller or write to Special Markets, Fodor's Travel Publications, 201 East 50th Street, New York, NY 10022. Inquiries from Canada should be directed to your local Canadian bookseller or sent to Random House of Canada, Ltd., Marketing Department, 1265 Aerowood Drive, Mississauga, Ontario L4W 1B9. Inquiries from the United Kingdom should be sent to Fodor's Travel Publications, 20 Vauxhall Bridge Road, London, England SW1V 2SA.

PRINTED IN THE UNITED STATES OF AMERICA

10 9 8 7 6 5 4 3 2 1

CONTENTS

*Italic entries are maps.

Contents

ON THE ROAD WITH FODOR'S

WE'RE ALWAYS THRILLED to get letters from readers, especially one like this:

It took us an hour to decide what book to buy and we now know we picked the best one. Your book was wonderful, easy to follow, very accurate, and good on pointing out eating places, informal as well as formal. When we saw other people using your book, we would look at each other and smile.

Our editors and writers are deeply committed to making every Fodor's guide "the best one"—not only accurate but always charming, brimming with sound recommendations and solid ideas, right on the mark in describing restaurants and hotels, and full of fascinating facts that make you view what you've traveled to see in a rich new light.

New this Year

A number of expanded sections on popular destinations appear in this edition. Look for a new tour of the highlights of Provence, the magical southern region of France that inspired the paintings of Cézanne and van Gogh. Great Britain adds a tour of the Lake District, with its craggy mountains and stunning blue lakes. In Spain, we've included an excursion to northern Morocco for the many travelers who can't resist making the short journey to north Africa. The historic town of Ghent is now covered in Belgium, and there's more sightseeing information on several of Greece's Aegean islands. Eastern Europe appeals to an increasing number of adventurous visitors; in response, we've expanded the sections on Prague in the Czech Republic and Warsaw and Kraków in Poland, and added a look at Transylvania in Romania.

On the Web

Also check out Fodor's Web site (http://www.fodors.com/), where you'll find travel information on major destinations around the world and an ever-changing array of travel-savvy interactive features.

How to Use this Book

Organization

Chapter 1 is the **Gold Guide.** Its first section, **Important Contacts A to Z,** gives addresses and telephone numbers of organizations and companies that offer destination-related services and detailed information and publications. **Smart Travel Tips A to Z,** the Gold Guide's second section, gives specific information on how to accomplish what you need to in Europe as well as tips on savvy traveling. Both sections are in alphabetical order by topic.

Chapters in *Europe '97* are in alphabetical order by country. Each covers exploring, shopping, dining, lodging, and arts and nightlife in cities and regions, and begins with a section called Essential Information, which tells you how to get there and get around and gives you important local addresses and telephone numbers.

Icons and Symbols

★ Our special recommendations
✕ Restaurant
🏠 Lodging establishment
✕🏠 Lodging establishment whose restaurant warrants a detour
☺ Rubber duckie (good for kids)
☞ Sends you to another section of the guide for more info
✉ Address
☎ Telephone number
FAX Fax number
☉ Opening and closing times
💰 Admission prices (those we give apply only to adults; substantially reduced fees are almost always available for children, students, and senior citizens)

Numbers in black circles—❷, for example—that appear on the maps and in the margins within the tours correspond to one another.

Dining and Lodging

The restaurants and lodgings we list are the cream of the crop in each price range. Price charts appear in the Essential Information section at the beginning of each chapter.

Hotel Facilities

We always list the facilities that are available—but we don't specify whether they cost extra: When pricing accommodations, always ask what's included.

Restaurant Reservations and Dress Codes

Reservations are always a good idea; we note only when they're essential or when they are not accepted. Book as far ahead as you can, and reconfirm when you get to town. Unless otherwise noted, the restaurants listed are open daily for lunch and dinner. We mention dress only when men are required to wear a jacket or a jacket and tie. Look for an overview of local habits under What to Wear in the Essential Information section at the beginning of each country chapter.

Credit Cards

The following abbreviations are used: **AE**, American Express; **DC**, Diners Club; **MC**, MasterCard; and **V**, Visa. The Discover card is not accepted in most places in Europe.

Please Write to Us

You can use this book in the confidence that all prices and opening times are based on information supplied to us at press time; Fodor's cannot accept responsibility for any errors. Time inevitably brings changes, so always confirm information when it matters—especially if you're making a detour to visit a specific place. In addition, when making reservations be sure to mention if you have a disability or are traveling with children, if you prefer a private bath or a certain type of bed, or if you have specific dietary needs or any other concerns.

Were the restaurants we recommended as described? Did our hotel picks exceed your expectations? Did you find a museum we recommended a waste of time? If you have complaints, we'll look into them and revise our entries when the facts warrant it. If you've discovered a special place that we haven't included, we'll pass the information along to our correspondents and have them check it out. So send your feedback, positive *and* negative, to the Europe Editor at 201 East 50th Street, New York, New York 10022—and have a wonderful trip!

Karen Cure
Editorial Director

WHAT'S NEW IN EUROPE '97

THE PERENNIAL ATTRACTIONS of Europe, from unspoiled historic villages to grand cosmopolitan capitals, continue to draw travelers eager to experience everything from a hike in the Alps to some of the world's most glittering nightlife. There's good news for anyone keeping an eye on fluctuating currencies, too: Whether you want to visit a castle in Bohemia or explore a secret corner of Paris, you can take advantage of an increasing array of special airfares, rail passes, advance hotel-booking deals, and fly-drive packages that make the most of your travel dollars. The tips in Chapter 1, the Gold Guide, and the advice in individual chapters will help you plan your trip.

By late 1994, super sleek Eurostar passenger trains—serving London, Paris, and Brussels—and car-carrying Le Shuttle trains were operating through the long-anticipated Channel Tunnel between Great Britain and France. The resulting competition with traditional air, ferry, and even bus services has been good news for travelers. To boost ridership and revenues, both Eurostar and Le Shuttle cut fares during 1996 and offered a number of promotional deals. In addition, Eurostar introduced additional service on the Continent, allowing passengers to buy tickets from London through to Bordeaux or Marseille in southern France, or to Köln in Germany. Direct service from London's Waterloo Station to Disneyland Paris is another option, and more are sure to follow throughout 1997.

As a result of the Maastricht Treaty that went into effect in 1993, the European Community changed its name to the European Union (EU) and removed all trade barriers between the member states, turning much of Europe into one huge tariff-free market, the largest economic grouping in the world. Austria, Finland, and Sweden joined the EU in 1995, bringing the number of countries to 15. Turkey, Cyprus, and Malta, all of which have applied (and were initially turned down for membership), should join the EU by the year 2000. Several Eastern European countries have or are negotiating association agreements.

In spring 1995, 7 of the 15 EU nations (Belgium, France, Germany, Luxembourg, the Netherlands, Portugal, and Spain), known as the Schengen group, officially agreed to lift border controls on land, so that people can travel among the countries and use special lines at airports without showing passports. Italy, Greece, and Austria signed the agreement in 1996 but do not plan to implement it for several years. Travelers from the United States and countries outside the Schengen group will be required to produce passports only on initial entry into one of the Schengen countries. At that time, their names will be checked against a computer database. However, because airlines or various authorities can require proof of identity, it's always advisable to carry a passport. In some ways, the agreement merely confirms practices that have evolved over time in the EU. But the reluctance of some nations (notably Great Britain) to join the Schengen group highlights the separation of forces supporting the integration of Europe and those opposing it.

The collapse of communism in Eastern Europe has had tragic consequences in areas of the former Yugoslavia, notably Bosnia-Herzegovina. A brutal war left tens of thousands of people dead and forced millions to flee their homes. The signing of the Dayton Peace Accords in December 1995 has led to the establishment of a cease-fire in Bosnia-Herzegovina. However, a U.S. State Department travel warning remained in effect for the country because of the extremely volatile situation. At press time there were no travel advisories for other former republics, but anyone planning a visit to the area should check with the State Department.

Austria

As usual, the new year begins with the globally televised New Year's concert from Vienna's Musikverein concert hall, with other cities, including Salzburg and Innsbruck, fielding their own concerts of Strauss waltzes. In 1997, however, Strauss will take a backseat to another Austrian musical genius, for it is the **200th anniversary of the birth of Franz Schubert.** The Biedermeier-era composer was born in 1797 and died (from typhoid) in 1828 at the age of 31. Schubert's music reflects the soul of Vienna as Mozart's does that of Salzburg, so the capital, fittingly, will lead the festivities with its annual **Schubertiade.** Along with a major Schubert show in the Historical Museum of the City of Vienna, there will be an international choral competition in November and special concerts at the city's two major summer music festivals—the Festwochen (mid-May–late June) and the Klangbogen/Musikalischer Sommer (July–September). Other focal points for special commemorative concerts (small, given the spaces involved) will be Schubert's birthplace in Nudorfer Strasse and his brother's house, where Franz died, in Kettenbruckengasse.

Austria's membership in the European Union is taking longer to be digested than most officials in Vienna had hoped. The public had been promised instantly lower prices that have not materialized—a fact travelers will notice at every turn. A recent austerity budget extends into 1997 and has served to hold the government together and, at least, to keep the lid on inflation. Austria remains, however, one of Europe's most expensive countries to visit.

Belgium

The **Europalia** festival has become an important cultural showcase, conveying a deeper understanding of the country it focuses on than is the case with less broad-based initiatives. This year Turkey will be highlighted, with major exhibitions, concerts, and theatrical performances from September to December, in Brussels and other major cities.

This is also **Paul Delvaux year,** marked by a retrospective at Brussels's Musée d'Art Moderne of the painter who, along with Magritte, was a standard bearer of Belgian modern art. Delvaux, who died recently, was a surrealist whose paintings often showed an odd assemblage of vacantly staring nudes, skeletons, and railroad stations.

Bulgaria

For more than five years Bulgaria has been going through a painful transition from a state-controlled economy to a market-driven one, yet it has remained a peaceful island in the Balkans. In the past, the country was a popular destination for citizens of other Eastern European states; now the rest of the world can discover it. A well-developed tourist industry is eager to adjust to the new realities.

Mountainous Bulgaria is appealing to ski lovers but can also claim beautiful beaches. Summertime is rich in cultural events along the Black Sea coast. The biggest art festival, **Varna's Summer,** includes ballet and performances of classical and popular music. In early September, **Sozopol** hosts Apollonia, with musical shows, plays, and poetry readings. Visitors interested in modern Bulgarian art can check out the increasing number of galleries in **Sofia** and **Plovdiv.**

The Czech Republic

Like all of Eastern Europe, the Czech Republic is changing rapidly as the country pursues economic and cultural revitalization, aiming for membership in the EU by the year 2000. In increasing numbers, tourists are rediscovering **Prague** and its freshly restored Baroque churches and Art Nouveau hotels.

In the late 16th and early 17th centuries, Emperor Rudolf II brought many artists, builders, scholars, and charlatans to Prague, his capital. A major exhibition, **"Rudolf II and Prague,"** to be held in and around Prague Castle from May 30 through September 7, will assemble every kind of Rudolfine creation amid the city's superb Renaissance palaces, gardens, and town houses.

Denmark

The venerable **Carlsberg Brewery,** one of the largest supporters of the arts in Denmark, will celebrate its 150th anniversary in 1997. There will be festive beer-based events as well as cultural exhibits highlighting Carlsberg-supported institutions such as the Ny Carlsberg Glyptotek, Royal Copenhagen Porcelain, and even Tivoli.

The $1 billion expansion of **Copenhagen Airport** will continue until the year 2005, but it has been organized to keep traffic flowing conveniently. A new expressway linking the center of the island of Amager to the airport should be open by the middle of the year. Completion of the high-speed rail link between the airport and Copenhagen center is expected by 1998.

The **Great Belt,** linking the island of Fyn to Zealand, is due to be ready for train traffic by mid-1997 and auto traffic by mid-1998. When completed, it will be the world's longest suspension bridge. Dredging of the sea bed has also begun, in anticipation of the long-awaited bridge that will link Denmark and Sweden by the year 2000.

Finland

Finland's decision to join the EU in 1995 and the signing of a cooperation agreement with NATO are two of the most important steps the country has taken since it declared independence from Russia in 1917. As a result of the revaluation of the Finnish mark in May 1993 and changes in the tax laws required by EU membership, Finland is now more affordable than in the past, although still not one of Europe's cheaper destinations. Helsinki has also become a popular base for those tourists wishing to visit the newly independent Baltic states, especially Estonia.

France

François Mitterrand, who altered the face of France during his 14-year presidency, died in January 1996, a few months after the opening of the penultimate project of his ambitious building campaign, the post-modern **Cité de la Musique** at La Villette in Paris. This giant music academy has state-of-the-art concert facilities. Another Mitterrand legacy in Paris, the massive **Bibiothèque de France,** is due to open in eastern Paris in 1997.

Exterior cleaning of the **Louvre** is almost over, and free admission on the first Sunday of the month was introduced in 1996. The replanting and redesign of the adjacent **Tuileries Gardens** continues apace.

As France prepares to host the 1998 Soccer World Cup, a giant new stadium, the **Stade de France,** was scheduled to open at the end of 1997 in the northern Paris suburb of St-Denis.

There's good transportation news in France, besides the lower ticket price for **Eurostar** train travel through the Channel Tunnel. A new fleet of **super-rapid boats** traveling between Corsica and Marseille, Toulon, Nice, and Genoa was introduced in 1996. **Air Inter** has increased the number of domestic flights in France, and the result is convenience and cheaper fares.

Finally, because of a need for more telephone lines, **two digits were added to all French phone numbers in October 1996.** The country chapter has details.

Germany

Berlin, which will take its historic place as capital from Rhineland Bonn by the year 2000, is adjusting slowly to its new role, but many of the projected new government buildings are still under construction. The future parliamentary seat, the 19th-century **Reichstag,** is currently being reconstructed and modernized. Anyone staying in Berlin should pay a visit to the **Potsdamer Platz** (Potsdam Square), the former downtown city center and now Europe's largest construction site. At the **Infobox,** a futuristic-looking information center high above the square, the major investors provide a closer look at how the city is being rebuilt.

A number of celebrations will mark musical anniversaries. In March and April, the Brahms Festival in **Hamburg** will commemorate the 100th anniversary of the composer's death. Concerts in **Leipzig** in April will mark the 150th anniversary of the death of Felix Mendelssohn.

Great Britain

The so-called **"mad cow disease"** and its possible link with Cruetzfeld-Jakob disease (a degenerative disease of the human central nervous system) was one of the major stories out of the United Kingdom in 1996. Many natives have looked to Scottish beef, which is usually grass-fed and (comparatively) disease-free. Because of the disease, at least part of the British cattle population will be slaughtered. In spite of the fact that no one will say that all beef is absolutely safe, there are plenty of locals eating quality beef. Considering the other gustatory riches Great Britain has to offer—from wild game to seafood—no traveler should feel deprived dining out.

With the dawn of the new century a few years away, much is being done to revamp **London's megaliths of the arts.** The South Bank Centre will be canopied in undulating glass by Sir Richard Rogers (architect of the Pompidou Center in Paris), and the Tate Gallery is to be split in two with the opening of the new Tate Gallery of Modern Art. The Royal Opera House has been allotted £80 million to bring the theater up to snuff, improve the nearby Covent Garden Piazza, and build a brand-new home for the Royal Ballet. Kensington Palace is undergoing a three-year refurbishment of its state rooms to make them appear just as they did when young Princess Victoria was growing up. In the City, the Museum of London has added the Roman London Gallery, complete with Roman street and several Roman interiors.

London's most anticipated attraction, the reconstruction of **Shakespeare's Globe,** has put off its official opening until summer 1997. Until then, visitors can tour the theater site under construction for a fascinating behind-the-scenes look.

Reports that the privatization of **BritRail** has led to chaos at ticket counters have been greatly exaggerated. The government has largely come through on its promises to retain through-ticketing and an integrated timetable. Travelers who avail themselves in advance of BritRail's passes can avoid any confusion. The latest package is the BritRail Pass + Eurostar combination, which allows transport via the Channel Tunnel plus a four- or eight-day Flexipass in Britain. Also, travelers can now travel for Paris via Eurostar from cities throughout England, in addition to London.

The spectacular **Tall Ships Race** returns to Aberdeen in Scotland during July 12–15, 1997. The gathering of the world's finest and largest sailing vessels culminates in a grand parade of ships before they begin their race to Trondheim in Norway across the North Sea.

Greece

Athens has set up a new tourism board modeled on the successful examples of Paris and Vienna, as part of the new mayor's campaign to improve the Greek capital. To ease pollution, the city banned traffic in the historic commercial center, purchased new buses to supplement the metro's extension (to be completed in 1998), and instigated a Keep Athens Clean program.

In some neighborhoods, air pollution has decreased by 25%. At night Athens sparkles under a new lighting program that showcases neoclassical buildings, the national gardens, and ancient monuments.

In the north, **Thessaloniki** has been designated Europe's Cultural Capital for 1997. In preparation for numerous artistic and cultural events, the city has broken ground for a new concert hall—the Megaron Mousikis—and upgraded facilities like the railway station. Among the historic buildings being refurbished is one of the city's grander hotels, the Macedonia Palace.

Traveling between **Greek islands** is easier than ever with new vessels called Supercats that can carry 1,500 passengers and 250 cars at speeds of 25 miles per hour. Ports of call for the catamarans include Piraeus, Andros, Tinos, Mykonos, Paros, Naxos, and Amorgos. Ships on the Greece–Italy route now make the trip in only 22 hours, with improved services for 1,500 passengers and 1,000 cars.

To compensate for the lack of mooring facilities for yachts in Attica, Olympic Marina will build a **marina** near Lavrio, a town south of Athens where the Aegean Sea meets the Saronic Gulf. The marina will offer boaters a hotel, restaurant, and cafe. Plans are also underway to build at least 15 new marinas throughout Greece, including a deluxe facility on Mykonos and one in Rhodes.

Hungary

Last year marked Hungary's **1,100th birthday**—the anniversary of the Magyar settlement of the Carpathian Basin. In the wake of celebratory sprucings-up and restorations, many museums have updated historical exhibits, and monuments sparkle like new. Riding the millecentennial momentum, improvements and restoration work on important sites will continue through the year 2000, when Hungary celebrates the 1,000 anniversary of its founding as a state.

Slowly but surely, Hungary is **improving its infrastructure,** helping it fill its increasingly important role as a link between eastern and western Europe. Over the next several years, major highways will be upgraded and extended, the airport in

Budapest will undergo a major expansion, and the antiquated telephone system will be overhauled. Travelers may witness these changes taking place but should not expect to reap their full benefits for some time to come.

Travelers will still find Hungary a bargain compared to Western Europe, but strictly rock-bottom prices are a thing of the past. Restaurant and hotel rates are steadily creeping upward, and at press time, the annual inflation rate was at more than 25% and still rising.

Iceland

The number of tourists to Iceland is still rising—tourism is now second only to fishing as a source of foreign revenue. As such, the need to foster it year-round has come more to the attention of politicians and professionals alike. A severe recession in the early 1990s led to very attractive prices, and efforts have been made to keep them that way, even as the country has recovered. Iceland now offers a greater selection than ever of **less expensive accommodations,** including farmhouses, guest houses and camping holidays. Restaurants have also tried to hold the line on prices. When considering costs in Iceland, bear in mind not only its remote island location, but also a hefty tax system that supports an impressive contemporary society.

Iceland has advanced from a rich Viking existence, with its explorers and classic sagas, to a diverse modern nation that is more appreciative of its natural resources and attractions. Steps are being taken to prevent over-development of the fragile wild highlands. At the same time, Europe's most sparsely populated country is improving its lowland road system for better safety and to reduce erosion caused by rural traffic.

Ireland

Ireland used to rely on its unspoiled countryside and friendly, hospitable people to attract visitors. In the past six years, over IR £500 million has been invested in tourism, and the number of visitors is projected to double from 2 million to 4 million by 1997. Travelers can expect **upgraded accommodations** at all levels (most hotels and many bed-and-breakfasts now offer rooms with private bath, TV, and direct-dial phone), a wider choice of restaurants, better-organized cultural tourism, and greatly improved sporting facilities. **Twenty-five new golf courses** have been built, and as many again are in the making. Water sports, walking routes, fishing, cycling, and equestrian holidays have also been successfully developed.

In **Dublin,** fans of James Joyce can visit the **restored James Joyce Centre** at 35 North Great George's Street, housed in a classic Georgian town house. Besides a coffee shop, there are exhibits, a library for browsing, and a Joyce-themed book and gift shop. The center also sponsors a week of celebrations leading up to Bloomsday, June 16, when even those who have never read Joyce dress up in Edwardian attire and parade around the areas detailed in *Ulysses.*

Italy

There's good news for those who plan to travel by rail or plane. FS, the Italian state railway, now provides **high-speed trains** for more destinations at reasonable rates. The ETR 460 Pendolino trains serve Rome, Florence, Milan, Venice, and other major cities. The Milan–Rome route, for instance, offers a shorter travel time and more affordable fares than traveling by plane. In the air, Alitalia's former monopoly on domestic travel has been shattered by some new airlines such as **Air One** and **Meridiana.** As a result, passengers are finding a wider range of bargain fares.

In 1997 **Rome** will be in the throes of constructing new viaducts, a new subway line, and various other infrastructural repairs to get ready for the **Jubilee** celebrations in the year 2000. The main inconveniences to visitors will probably be traffic snarls around the Vatican.

Restoration work on the **Colosseum** will continue, and if Rome's superintendent of monuments has his way, visitors will have to pay. He has proposed a prepaid pass for admission to the city's numerous classical attractions; the idea is being considered for nationwide adoption. Structural renovations of the **Galleria Borghese** in Rome should be largely completed by 1997, and it is expected that the refurbished main floor will be fully reopened.

Also in Rome, it has finally become possible to buy a new pair of socks or some milk and crackers at 2 AM. Several of what are called "drugstores" opened in 1996. These convenience stores are stocked with food and a range of other basic articles but do not sell medicines. One is in Termini train station, and another will open in Tiburtina Station.

To reduce visitor congestion, **Florence** is considering a number of measures, including restricting the number of tour buses that can enter the city center at one time. The **Torre dei Pulci,** the 15th-century tower adjacent to the Uffizi that was gutted by a terrorist bomb in 1993, has been almost completely restored. Take a look at the tower, on a side street of Piazza degli Uffizi: Demolition work revealed that the exterior was originally painted to look like brickwork, and restorers have reproduced the original effect.

The 1997–98 season at **Milan's La Scala** will be operagoers' last chance to attend performances in the splendid theater at the heart of the city before it is temporarily closed for restoration. In fall 1998, La Scala will move to a modern, 2,300-seat concert hall in Bicocca-Tecnocity, in the postindustrial outskirts of Milan.

Naples will continue to offer **special packages** and **tours** as part of its highly successful efforts to attract tourists. The Capodimonte Museum has reopened after restoration, and many more of the city's historic churches and palaces are being opened on a regular basis.

The most popular after-dinner drink in 1997 will almost surely be the lemon-flavored liqueur called *limoncello,* available under many brand names. Unknown to most until about a year ago, it is now the rage. The best comes from the Capri–Sorrento–Amalfi area, where it was originally made.

Luxembourg

The tremendous efforts put into creating the infrastructure for Luxembourg's year as European City of Culture in 1995 are yielding lasting benefits, as visitors discover that the Grand Duchy is more than a tax haven with a pretty face.

Below the cliffs of **Luxembourg City**'s old castle, in the region known as the Grund, the old Neumünster Abbey, which was used for many years as a prison, is becoming

a very different kind of center. The women's prison has become the Museum of Natural History; the workshop, or Tutesall, has been transformed into an attractive exhibition space; and work is underway to convert the men's prison into the city's new Cultural Center.

Malta

The number of visitors to Malta now exceeds 1 million each year, and the country is establishing itself as one of the top cruise destinations in the Mediterranean. The island has become a leading yachting center and a mecca for scuba divers.

The 5,000-year-old **Hypogeum,** a system of underground burial chambers that is one of Malta's three World Heritage Sites, is scheduled to reopen to the public after almost three years of restoration.

The Netherlands

At the beginning of 1997 you'll be able to catch the final weeks of the blockbuster exhibition at Amsterdam's **Rijksmuseum** of works by **Jan Steen,** best known for his anarchic tavern scenes and pictures of chaotic households. It's still officially "Jan Steen Year," so there are likely to be other lectures and events centered on the tipsy tavernkeeper and painter.

Also in **Amsterdam,** a new science and technology museum will open near Centraal Station in early 1997, and the Rijksmuseum's revamped south wing may be on view at last. A multimedia "Holland Experience" that uses large-screen technology will open in the city before the start of the year.

This is the celebration of the 300th anniversary of the visit of **Peter the Great** to the Netherlands. He spent his time in Amsterdam studying, absorbing Dutch knowledge of shipping. Russia and the Netherlands are making the most of this opportunity to strengthen cultural and business links. Besides conferences and seminars, most cities will have something to offer; precious works of art are coming from the Kremlin and Hermitage museums.

Norway

The heated debate about joining the EU ended in November 1994 when Norway narrowly rejected membership. Despite the decisions of its close neighbors, Sweden and Finland, in favor of the EU, the country has remained steadfast in its refusal to join, rendering it a Eurosceptics' mecca. Norway is a member of the European Economic Area, which has begun to exert a downward pressure on prices, including hotel and restaurant charges.

Trondheim celebrates its 1,000th anniversary in 1997. Events throughout the year will commemorate the city's history since its founding by King Olav Tryggvason. Some highlights are the Nordic World Ski Championships, a festival week with concerts and parades, and the Cutty Sark Tall Ship Race.

In June, **Stavanger** will hold an Emigration Festival, with entertainment and activities focusing on emigration to the United States.

Poland

Upgrading of tourist facilities will continue in 1997, as more new hotels are opened and old ones are refurbished. The ongoing privatization of Orbis hotels should bring more variety in prices and types of accommodations. Poles are getting used to their **new currency,** introduced in 1995; it is certainly easier for the tourist to handle than the old złoty, which had prices running into the millions. Prices, however, continue to rise, particularly for visitor facilities at the upper end of the market.

The Baltic seaport of **Gdańsk** will celebrate its 1,000th anniversary. Highlights will be a major exhibition in May about the city's heritage, a June celebration of the region, and art fairs and entertainment throughout the summer. The history of Solidarity, the anti-Communist union movement born in Gdańsk's shipyards, will also be a focus. It's hoped that a museum on the fall of Communism will open in 1997.

Portugal

Although prices are moving upward, Portugal remains one of Europe's more affordable countries to visit. Lisbon, particularly, offers very good values if visited during the winter, when even top-rated hotels reduce their room rates considerably. Some of the best values can be found at an increasing number of **rural establishments**—particularly in the Sintra area and in the north, where old manors, farmhouses, and even water mills have been converted into superior bed-and-breakfasts. Most of these are run within official programs, existing under a variety of names; local tourist offices can provide brochures and specific information.

Be aware: In advance of the 1998 Expo, **Lisbon is improving its roads** and transportation system; it always pays to request a room off main avenues and thoroughfares to avoid the sound of construction. If you plan to visit Lisbon during the Expo, you might start arranging your trip during 1997. Central hotels, in particular, are sure to be very busy, and early reservations are recommended.

Romania

Romania, and especially the city of Bucharest, has experienced great change since 1989. Just a few years ago the country was marked by bread lines, food shortages, empty store shelves, and a lack of stores, restaurants, and tourist facilities. Throughout Bucharest there are now many new restaurants, as well as shops sporting vast quantities of imported and locally made items. Private enterprise has introduced a number of service-oriented hotels and facilities. There is still much more to be accomplished, but it can no longer be said that Romania is ground in inertia.

Outside Bucharest, Romania is developing at a slower pace. In some areas state-run hotels and restaurants are still the rule, although in outlying cities like Sibiu, new private hotels and restaurants have finally begun to be introduced.

This year is the centennial of the publication of Bram Stoker's vampire novel *Dracula*. Visitors interested in **vampire theme tours** will find a number available in Transylvania.

Slovakia

Since its separation from the Czech Republic in 1993, Slovakia has been undergoing a metamorphosis. Although haunted by the politics of the past, the nation has taken positive strides economically. Tourist facilities continue to be upgraded, with new hotels and restaurants opening and old ones receiving necessary face-lifts. The **peaks of the High Tatras** remain uncharted territory for most tourists from Western Europe and beyond, but they offer sights comparable with the Swiss Alps at rising but still relatively bargain prices.

Spain

In **Madrid,** the construction clutter is due to come down around the Plaza de Oriente in front of Madrid's Royal Palace. A new tunnel and parking garage beneath the plaza should alleviate many traffic problems, leaving the palace with an exhaust-free pedestrian zone in front, rather than the busy street that used to run between the palace and the plaza.

Art is always news in **Barcelona,** but the opening of the Barcelona Museum of Contemporary Art and the Center for Contemporary Culture of Barcelona, along with the reopening of the National Museum of Catalonian Art and the new Catalonian History Museum, will make Barcelona even more exciting in 1997.

The Al-Andalus Express, a luxurious train comprising five exquisitely restored vintage 1920s coaches, winds its way through the dramatically beautiful southwestern region of **Andalucía** on six- and seven-day journeys. This alternative to driving the area's challenging mountain roads allows riders to enjoy constantly changing views of Granada, Córdoba, and Seville while being shamelessly pampered.

In the Canaries, a new conference and convention center is set to open in Playa de las Américas on **Tenerife** at the start of 1997, bringing with it several big new hotels in a complex called Mare Nostrum. As part of a downtown beautification program in Puerto de la Cruz, traffic through the business district has been rerouted, trees planted, and store fronts given a face-lift.

Sweden

Stockholm continues to gear up for its turn as Cultural Capital of Europe in 1998. Accordingly, the Museum of Modern Art, which remains in temporary quarters through 1997, will reopen in its former, refurbished home on January 1, 1998.

With the dollar weaker against the krona than it was three years ago, Sweden has become a relatively expensive country to visit. Hotel and restaurant costs are high, as are most museum admission prices. However, thanks to government subsidies of theater, art, and music institutions, entertainment remains a relative bargain.

Sweden's travel industry, historically geared toward Swedes and other Scandinavians, has in recent years been making a bigger push for international visitors. English-language printed material is increasingly available in museums and visitor information offices, and Stockholm is advertising its year-round attractions instead of focusing only on the usual sun-and-water-worshiping activities.

Switzerland

In consistently voting against joining the **EU,** Switzerland has once more positioned itself apart from the countries that surround it. The decision has had little impact on the traveler, aside from the increased presence of customs and immigration officials, which are rapidly disappearing at the border crossing between EU member countries.

Thanks to the country's political stability, the **Swiss franc** has been steadily rising against the United States dollar, the British pound, and even the mighty Deutschmark. With the exception of Scandinavia, Switzerland now ranks among Europe's most expensive countries to visit, especially since the Swiss voted to add a new value-added tax of 6.5% on all services, including hotels and restaurants. The tourist industry is eager—even anxious—to accommodate, however, offering weekend packages and modest bistro menus. Before booking a trip, check the calendar carefully: Since hotels structure their prices by time of year, it's considerably cheaper to visit during the off-season—summer for ski resorts and winter for lake resorts, or the shoulder season for either.

On the athletic front, the Swiss are beginning to embrace a number of new winter sports, most notably **snowboarding.**

Turkey

Turkey moved closer to Europe following the introduction of a free trade agreement in January 1996, but in the inconclusive general elections a month earlier, the pro-Islamic and anti-European Welfare Party emerged as the largest party. Once again, Turkey demonstrated the ambivalent identity of a country never quite sure whether it belongs in the East or the West.

Still, Turkey remains one of the cheapest and most popular holiday destinations in the Mediterranean, with the number of visitors setting new records in 1995. All political parties recognize the importance of tourism, and the government continues to invest in infrastructure projects. Turkey's telecommunications are now on a par with most other European countries. In Istanbul, design work has begun on a **tunnel under the Bosphorus** that will supplement the bridges already linking its Asian and European shores. The city is also readying a bid to host the Olympic games in 2004.

More and more Turks are taking up **sports.** Istanbul's first golf club opened in 1995, and the city's Eurasian marathon, the only one in the world to be run on two continents, attracted a record number of local and international participants. Many local tour operators have begun to organize walking, mountaineering, and rafting vacations for foreign visitors.

World Time Zones

MONDAY
SUNDAY

International Date Line

+12 +13   -9
-10
3
7
-11   4   -7   -5   -4
-10   5 -8   8   -6   9   13 14 15   -3:30
6   10 11   17 16
2   12   18
-4
19   22
-5   -4   -3
+11   20
+12   21   -3   23
1   24

+11   +12 -   -11   -10   -9   -8   -7   -6   -5   -4   -3   -2

Numbers below vertical bands relate each zone to Greenwich Mean Time (0 hrs.).
Local times frequently differ from these general indications,
as indicated by light-face numbers on map.

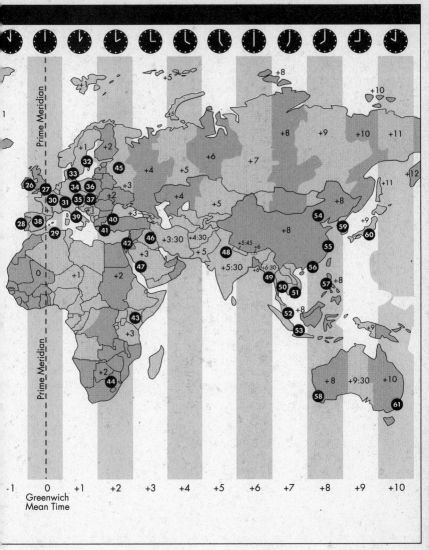

1 The Gold Guide

Important Contacts A to Z

Smart Travel Trips A to Z

IMPORTANT CONTACTS A TO Z

An Alphabetical Listing of Publications, Organizations, and Companies that Will Help You Before, During, and After Your Trip

A

AIR TRAVEL

CARRIERS

U.S. airlines that serve major European cities include **American Airlines** (☎ 800/433–7300); **Continental** (☎ 800/231–0856); **Delta** (☎ 800/241–4141); **Northwest** (☎ 800/447–4747); **TWA** (☎ 800/892–4141); and **United** (☎ 800/538–2929).

European national airlines that fly directly from the United States: **Austria:** Austrian Airlines (☎ 800/843–0002); **Belgium:** Sabena Belgian World Airlines (☎ 800/955–2000); **Bulgaria:** Balkan Airlines (☎ 212/573–5530); **Cyprus:** Cyprus Airways (☎ 212/714–2190 or 800/333–2977); **Czech Republic and Slovakia:** Czech Airlines (ČSA, ☎ 212/765–6022); **Denmark:** Scandinavian Airlines (SAS, ☎ 800/221–2350); **Finland:** Finnair (☎ 800/950–5000); **France:** Air France (☎ 800/237–2747); **Germany:** Lufthansa (☎ 800/645–3880); **Great Britain:** British Airways (☎ 800/247–9297); Virgin Atlantic (☎ 800/862–8621); **Greece:** Olympic Airways (☎ 212/838–3600 or 800/223–1226 outside NY); **Hungary:** Malév Hungarian Airlines (☎ 212/757–6446 or 800/223–6884); **Iceland:** Icelandair (☎ 800/223–5500); **Ireland:** Aer Lingus (☎ 800/223–6537); **Italy:** Alitalia (☎ 800/223–5730); **Malta:** Air Malta (☎ 415/362–2929); **Netherlands:** KLM Royal Dutch Airlines (☎ 800/777–5553); **Norway:** Scandinavian Airlines (SAS, ☎ 800/221–2350); **Poland:** LOT Polish Airlines (☎ 212/869–1074); **Portugal:** TAP Air Portugal (☎ 800/221–7370); **Romania:** Tarom Romanian Airlines (☎ 212/687–6013); **Spain:** Iberia Airlines (☎ 800/772–4642); **Sweden:** Scandinavian Airlines (☎ 800/221–2350); **Switzerland:** Swissair (☎ 800/221–4750); **Turkey:** THY Turkish Airlines (☎ 212/339–9650).

FROM THE U.K.➤ **British Airways** (✉ 156 Regent St., London W1R 5TA, ☎ 0181/897–4000; outside London, 0345/222–111), **British Midland** (☎ 0181/745–7321 or 0345/554–554), **Air UK** (☎ 0345/666–777), or for charter flights **Britannia Airways** (☎ 0181/759–1818).

COMPLAINTS

To register complaints about charter and scheduled airlines, contact the U.S. Department of Transportation's **Aviation Consumer Protection Division** (✉ C-75, Washington, DC 20590, ☎ 202/366–2220). Complaints about lost baggage or ticketing problems and safety concerns may also be logged with the **Federal Aviation Administration (FAA) Consumer Hotline** (☎ 800/322–7873).

CONSOLIDATORS

For services that will help you find the lowest airfares, *see* Discounts & Deals, *below.*

PUBLICATIONS

For general information about charter carriers, ask for the Department of Transportation's free brochure **"Plane Talk: Public Charter Flights"** (✉ Aviation Consumer Protection Division, C-75, Washington, DC 20590, ☎ 202/366–2220). The Department of Transportation also publishes a 58-page booklet, **"Fly Rights,"** available from the Consumer Information Center (✉ Supt. of Documents, Dept. 136C, Pueblo, CO 81009; $1.75).

For other tips and hints, consult the Consumers Union's monthly **"Consumer Reports Travel Letter"** (✉ Box 53629, Boulder, CO 80322, ☎ 800/234–1970; $39 1st year) and the newsletter **"Travel Smart"** (✉ 40 Beechdale Rd., Dobbs Ferry, NY 10522, ☎ 800/327–3633; $37 per year).

For information on how to avoid jet lag, there are two publications: *Jet Lag, A Pocket*

Guide to Modern Treatment by Peter Casano M.D. (✉ MedEd Publications, Box 12415, Columbus, OH 43212, ☎ 614/488–9457; $5.95) and *How to Beat Jet Lag* (✉ Henry Holt, 115 W. 18th St., New York, NY 10011, ☎ 800/288-2131; $14.95).

B
BETTER BUSINESS BUREAU

For local contacts in the hometown of a tour operator you may be considering, consult the **Council of Better Business Bureaus** (✉ 4200 Wilson Blvd., Suite 800, Arlington, VA 22203, ☎ 703/276–0100, FAX 703/525–8277).

BUS TRAVEL

DISCOUNT PASSES
Eurobus (☎ 800/EUROBUS in the United States; ☎ 0181/991–1021) in the United Kingdom), a year-old company, operates "hop-on, hop-off" service on their buses, which travel along one-way circuits on a number of routes, taking in a total of 23 cities on the Continent. Unlimited-travel passes are available for periods from two weeks to three months. A one-month pass costs $260 ($199 for those under 27). A London link is also available, as is a bus pass for Great Britain.

The new **Eurolines Pass** allows unlimited travel between 16 European cities from London to Rome on scheduled bus services. A 30-day pass costs $339 ($299 for those under 26 or over 60); a 60-day pass costs

$409 ($369). Passes can be bought from Eurolines offices and travel agents throughout Europe. For brochures, write the Eurolines Organization (✉ Keizersgracht 317, 1016 EE Amsterdam; ☎ 020/625–3010, FAX 020/420–6904.

FROM THE U.K.
Eurolines (✉ 23 Crawford Rd., Luton LU1 1HX, ☎ 01582/404511, FAX 01582/400694 for general information) links London with 280 Continental destinations from Scandinavia to Turkey. All are via Calais, using either ferry services or Le Shuttle under the English Channel. You can also book passage on individual legs of long-haul routes, as long as they are between points in different countries. Buses leave from Victoria Coach Station (adjoining the railway station). Services can be booked by calling or writing Eurolines (✉ 52 Grosvenor Gardens, London SW1 OAU, ☎ 0171/730–8235, FAX 0171–8721). **Citysprint** uses the 30-minute Calais-to-Dover hovercraft service en route to Amsterdam, Brussels, Paris and Berlin. Additional destinations are about to be added, including Lyon and Perpignan. Reservations can be made at Victoria Coach Station or by calling 01304/240241.

WITHIN EUROPE
Cityzap, a new (1996) budget express service, links London, Paris, and Amsterdam with service twice a day. The London–Paris (six hours)

and London–Amsterdam (seven hours) routes will use the Channel Tunnel. One-way fare between two cities is $49 per person; round-trip fare is $86. All three cities can be visited for $135, or $100 per person if two or more tickets are purchased together. The U.S. agent for Cityzap is Thomas McFerran, Inc. (✉ 118 S. Bellevue Ave., Langhorne, PA 19047, ☎ 215/741–5154 or 800/430–9070, FAX 215/741–5156). For information in the United Kingdom, call 0800/968504.

The **Eurolines Group** now comprises 35 motor-coach operators of international scheduled services. The 19-nation network serves 750 cities with services ranging from twice-weekly to three times daily. Services depart from railway stations or bus terminals, with the exception of Paris, where Eurolines has its own coach station at 28 avenue du Général de Gaulle at Bagnelot (Métro: Gallieni) and Brussels, where the coach station is at 80 rue du Progrès, adjoining the Gare du Nord. The most comprehensive international timetable is published by the Deutsche Touring Gesellschaft (DTG, ✉ Am Römerplatz 17, 60486 Frankfurt, ☎ 069/79030).

C
CAR RENTAL

The major car-rental companies represented in Europe are **Alamo** (☎ 800/327–9633; in the U.K., 0800/272–2000),

THE GOLD GUIDE / IMPORTANT CONTACTS

Avis (☎ 800/331–1084; in Canada, 800/879–2847), **Budget** (☎ 800/527–0700; in the U.K., 0800/181181), **Dollar** (☎ 800/800–4000; in the U.K., 0990/565656, where it is known as Eurodollar), **Hertz** (☎ 800/654–3001; in Canada, 800/263–0600; in the U.K., 0345/555888), and **National InterRent** (sometimes known as Europcar InterRent outside North America; ☎ 800/227–3876; in the U.K., 01345/222–525).

Car rental prices vary considerably throughout Europe, as does tax. Rates in London begin at $25 a day and $103 a week for an economy car with unlimited mileage (plus 17.5% tax). Rates in Paris begin at $29 a day and $165 a week for an economy car with unlimited mileage (plus 15% tax). In Madrid, rates start at $65 a day and $151 a week (plus 16% tax). In Rome, rates begin at $54 a day and $190 a week for an economy car with unlimited mileage (plus 19% tax). Many car rental agencies in Rome impose mandatory theft insurance on all rentals. Coverage costs $10–$15 a day.

RENTAL WHOLESALERS

Contact **Auto Europe** (☎ 207/828–2525 or 800/223–5555), **Europe by Car** (☎ 800/223–1516; in CA, 800/252–9401),or the **Kemwel Group** (☎ 914/835–5555 or 800/678–0678).

CHANNEL TUNNEL

For information about Eurostar and Le Shuttle service, *see* Train Travel, *below.*

CHILDREN & TRAVEL

FLYING

Look into **"Flying with Baby"** (✉ Third Street Press, Box 261250, Littleton, CO 80163, ☎ 303/595–5959; $4.95 includes shipping), cowritten by a flight attendant. **"Kids and Teens in Flight,"** free from the U.S. Department of Transportation's Aviation Consumer Protection Division (✉ C-75, Washington, DC 20590, ☎ 202/366–2220), offers tips on children flying alone. Every two years the February issue of *Family Travel Times* (☞ Know-How, *below*) details children's services on three dozen airlines. **"Flying Alone, Handy Advice for Kids Traveling Solo"** is available free from the American Automobile Association (AAA) (✉ send stamped, self-addressed, legal-size envelope: Flying Alone, Mail Stop 800, 1000 AAA Dr., Heathrow, FL 32746).

KNOW-HOW

Family Travel Times, published quarterly by Travel with Your Children (✉ TWYCH, 40 5th Ave., New York, NY 10011, ☎ 212/477–5524; $40 per year), covers destinations, types of vacations, and modes of travel.

RESORTS

Club Med (✉ 40 W. 57th St., New York, NY 10019, ☎ 800/258–2633) has "Baby Clubs" (from age four months), "Mini Clubs" (for ages four to six or eight, depending on the resort), and "Kids Clubs" (for ages eight and up during school holidays) at many of its resort villages in France, Italy, Switzerland, and Spain.

TOUR OPERATORS

Contact **Grandtravel** (✉ 6900 Wisconsin Ave., Suite 706, Chevy Chase, MD 20815, ☎ 301/986–0790 or 800/247–7651), which has tours for people traveling with grandchildren ages 7–17; **Families Welcome!** (✉ 4711 Hope Valley Rd., Durham, NC 27707, ☎ 919/489–2555 or 800/326–0724); or **Rascals in Paradise** (✉ 650 5th St., Suite 505, San Francisco, CA 94107, ☎ 415/978–9800 or 800/872–7225).

If you're outdoorsy, look into family-oriented programs run by the **American Museum of Natural History** (✉ 79th St. and Central Park W, New York, NY 10024, ☎ 212/769–5700 or 800/462–8687).

CUSTOMS

IN THE U.S.

The **U.S. Customs Service** (✉ Box 7407, Washington, DC 20044, ☎ 202/927–6724) can answer questions on duty-free limits and publishes a helpful brochure, "Know Before You Go." For information on registering foreign-made articles, call 202/927–0540.

COMPLAINTS➣ Note the inspector's badge number and write to the commissioner's office

(⊠ 1301 Constitution Ave. NW, Washington, DC 20229).

CANADIANS

Contact **Revenue Canada** (⊠ 2265 St. Laurent Blvd. S, Ottawa, Ontario K1G 4K3, ☎ 613/993–0534) for a copy of the free brochure **"I Declare/Je Déclare"** and for details on duty-free limits. For recorded information (within Canada only), call 800/461–9999.

U.K. CITIZENS

HM Customs and Excise (⊠ Dorset House, Stamford St., London SE1 9NG, ☎ 0171/202–4227) can answer questions about U.K. customs regulations and publishes a free pamphlet, **"A Guide for Travellers,"** detailing standard procedures and import rules.

D

DISABILITIES & ACCESSIBILITY

COMPLAINTS

To register complaints under the provisions of the Americans with Disabilities Act, contact the U.S. Department of Justice's **Disability Rights Section** (⊠ Box 66738, Washington, DC 20035, ☎ 202/514–0301 or 800/514–0301, FAX 202/307–1198, TTY 202/514–0383 or 800/514–0383). For airline-related problems, contact the U.S. Department of Transportation's **Aviation Consumer Protection Division** (☞ Air Travel, *above*). For complaints about surface transportation, contact the

Department of Transportation's **Civil Rights Office** (☎ 202/366–4648).

ORGANIZATIONS

TRAVELERS WITH HEARING IMPAIRMENTS➤ The **American Academy of Otolaryngology** (⊠ 1 Prince St., Alexandria, VA 22314, ☎ 703/836–4444, FAX 703/683–5100, TTY 703/519–1585) publishes a brochure, "Travel Tips for Hearing Impaired People."

TRAVELERS WITH MOBILITY PROBLEMS➤ Contact the **Information Center for Individuals with Disabilities** (⊠ Box 256, Boston, MA 02117, ☎ 617/450–9888; in MA, 800/462–5015; TTY 617/424–6855); **Mobility International USA** (⊠ Box 10767, Eugene, OR 97440, ☎ and TTY 541/343–1284, FAX 541/343–6812), the U.S. branch of a Belgium-based organization (☞ *below*) with affiliates in 30 countries; **MossRehab Hospital Travel Information Service** (☎ 215/456–9600, TTY 215/456–9602), a telephone information resource for travelers with physical disabilities; the **Society for the Advancement of Travel for the Handicapped** (⊠ 347 5th Ave., Suite 610, New York, NY 10016, ☎ 212/447–7284, FAX 212/725–8253; membership $45); and **Travelin' Talk** (⊠ Box 3534, Clarksville, TN 37043, ☎ 615/552–6670, FAX 615/552–1182) which provides local contacts worldwide for travelers with disabilities.

TRAVELERS WITH VISION IMPAIRMENTS➤ Contact the **American Council of**

the **Blind** (⊠ 1155 15th St. NW, Suite 720, Washington, DC 20005, ☎ 202/467–5081, FAX 202/467–5085) for a list of travelers' resources or the **American Foundation for the Blind** (⊠ 11 Penn Plaza, Suite 300, New York, NY 10001, ☎ 212/502–7600 or 800/232–5463, TTY 212/502–7662), which provides general advice and publishes "Access to Art" ($19.95), a directory of museums that accommodate travelers with vision impairments.

IN THE U.K.

Contact the **Royal Association for Disability and Rehabilitation** (⊠ RADAR, 12 City Forum, 250 City Rd., London EC1V 8AF, ☎ 0171/250–3222) or **Mobility International** (⊠ rue de Manchester 25, B-1080 Brussels, Belgium, ☎ 00–322–410–6297, FAX 00–322–410–6874), an international travel-information clearinghouse for people with disabilities.

PUBLICATIONS

Several publications for travelers with disabilities are available from the **Consumer Information Center** (⊠ Box 100, Pueblo, CO 81009, ☎ 719/948–3334). Call or write for its free catalog of current titles. The Society for the Advancement of Travel for the Handicapped (☞ Organizations, *above*) publishes the quarterly magazine **"Access to Travel"** ($13 for 1-year subscription).

The 500-page **Travelin' Talk Directory** (⊠ Box

3534, Clarksville, TN 37043, ☎ 615/552–6670, FAX 615/552–1182; $35) lists people and organizations who help travelers with disabilities. For travel agents worldwide, consult the *Directory of Travel Agencies for the Disabled* (✉ Twin Peaks Press, Box 129, Vancouver, WA 98666, ☎ 360/694–2462 or 800/637–2256, FAX 360/696–3210; $19.95 plus $3 shipping).

TRAVEL AGENCIES & TOUR OPERATORS

The Americans with Disabilities Act requires that all travel firms serve the needs of all travelers. That said, you should note that some agencies and operators specialize in making travel arrangements for individuals and groups with disabilities, among them **Access Adventures** (✉ 206 Chestnut Ridge Rd., Rochester, NY 14624, ☎ 716/889–9096), run by a former physical-rehab counselor.

Travelers with Mobility Problems➤ Contact **Accessible Journeys** (✉ 35 W. Sellers Ave., Ridley Park, PA 19078, ☎ 610/521–0339 or 800/846–4537, FAX 610/521–6959), a registered nursing service that arranges vacations; **Flying Wheels Travel** (✉ 143 W. Bridge St., Box 382, Owatonna, MN 55060, ☎ 507/451–5005 or 800/535–6790), a travel agency specializing in European cruises and tours; **Hinsdale Travel Service** (✉ 201 E. Ogden Ave., Suite 100, Hinsdale, IL 60521, ☎ 708/325–1335), a travel agency that benefits from the

advice of wheelchair traveler Janice Perkins; and **Wheelchair Journeys** (✉ 16979 Redmond Way, Redmond, WA 98052, ☎ 206/885–2210 or 800/313–4751), which can handle arrangements worldwide.

Travelers with Developmental Disabilities➤ Contact the nonprofit **New Directions** (✉ 5276 Hollister Ave., Suite 207, Santa Barbara, CA 93111, ☎ 805/967–2841) and **Sprout** (✉ 893 Amsterdam Ave., New York, NY 10025, ☎ 212/222–9575), which specializes in custom-designed itineraries for groups but also books vacations for individual travelers.

TRAVEL GEAR

The **Magellan's** catalog (☎ 800/962–4943, FAX 805/568–5406), includes a range of products designed for travelers with disabilities.

DISCOUNTS & DEALS

AIRFARES

For the lowest airfares to Europe, call 800/FLY–4–LES.

CLUBS

Contact **Entertainment Travel Editions** (✉ Box 1068, Trumbull, CT 06611, ☎ 800/445–4137; $28–$53, depending on destination), **Great American Traveler** (✉ Box 27965, Salt Lake City, UT 84127, ☎ 800/548–2812; $49.95 per year), **Moment's Notice Discount Travel Club** (✉ 7301 New Utrecht Ave., Brooklyn, NY 11204, ☎ 718/234–6295; $25 per year, single or

family), **Privilege Card** (✉ 3391 Peachtree Rd. NE, Suite 110, Atlanta, GA 30326, ☎ 404/262–0222 or 800/236–9732; $74.95 per year), **Travelers Advantage** (✉ CUC Travel Service, 49 Music Sq. W, Nashville, TN 37203, ☎ 800/548–1116 or 800/648–4037; $49 per year, single or family), or **Worldwide Discount Travel Club** (✉ 1674 Meridian Ave., Miami Beach, FL 33139, ☎ 305/534–2082; $50 per year for family, $40 single).

HOTEL ROOMS

For discounts on hotel rates, contact the **Hotel Reservations Network** (☎ 800/964–6835). For hotel room rates guaranteed in U.S. dollars, call **Steigenberger Reservation Service** (☎ 800/223–5652).

PASSES

See Bus Travel, *above*, and Train Travel, *below*.

STUDENTS

Members of Hostelling International–American Youth Hostels (☞ Students, *below*) are eligible for discounts on car rentals, admissions to attractions, and other selected travel expenses.

PUBLICATIONS

Consult *The Frugal Globetrotter,* by Bruce Northam (✉ Fulcrum Publishing, 350 Indiana St., Suite 350, Golden, CO 80401, ☎ 800/992–2908; $15.95). For publications that tell how to find the lowest prices on plane tickets, *see* Air Travel, *above*.

Also see Fodor's **Affordable Europe** (available in

bookstores, or ☎ 800/
533–6478; $18.50).

AUTO CLUBS

In the United Kingdom,
the **Automobile Association** (✉ Fanum House,
Basing View, Basingstoke, Hampshire
RQ21 2EA, ☎ 01256/
20123); and the **Royal
Automobile Club** (RAC
House, Bartlett St., Box
10, Croydon CR2
6XW, ☎ 0181/686–
2525) operate on-the-
spot breakdown and
repair services across
Europe. U.S. citizens
cannot use these ser-
vices on the Continent.

To become a member of
the **Automobile Association of America** (AAA),
call 800/564–6222. In
the United Kingdom,
contact the Automobile
Association (AA) or the
Royal Automobile Club
(RAC).

F

Ferry service from the
United Kingdom to
many European coun-
tries is provided by:
Brittany Ferries (Millbay
Docks, Plymouth PL1
3EW, ☎ 01752/
227941; to France,
Spain); **Color Line** (International Ferry Termi-
nal, Royal Quays,
North Shields NE29
6EE, ☎ 01912/961313;
to Norway); **Eurolink
Ferries** (Ferry Terminal,
Sheerness, Kent ME12
1RX, ☎ 01795/
581000; to the Nether-
lands); **Hoverspeed**
(International Hover-
port, Marine Parade,
Dover, Kent CT17 9TG,
☎ 01304/240241; to
France); **Irish Ferries**
(Reliance House, Water
St., Liverpool L2 8TP,

☎ 0151/227–3131; to
Ireland); **North Sea
Ferries** (King George
Dock, Hedon Rd., Hull
HU9 5QA, ☎ 01482/
795141; to Belgium, the
Netherlands); **P&O
European Ferries** (Chan-
nel House, Channel
View Rd., Dover, Kent
CT17 9TJ, ☎ 01304/
203388; to France,
Spain, Northern Ire-
land); **Sally Line Ltd.**
(Argyle Centre, York
St., Ramsgate, Kent
CT11 9DS, ☎ 01843/
595522; to Belgium,
France); **Scandinavian
Seaways** (Scandinavia
House, Parkeston Quay,
Harwich, Essex CO12
4QG, ☎ 01255/
240240; to Denmark,
Germany, Sweden);
Sealink (Charter House,
Park St., Ashford, Kent
TN24 8EX, ☎ 01233/
647047; to France,
Germany, Ireland, the
Netherlands); and
Swansea Cork Ferries
(Kings Dock, Swansea
SA1 8RU, ☎ 01792/
456116; to Ireland).

G

ORGANIZATIONS

The **International Gay
Travel Association** (✉
Box 4974, Key West,
FL 33041, ☎ 800/448–
8550, FAX 305/296–
6633), a consortium of
more than 1,000 travel
companies, can supply
names of gay-friendly
travel agents, tour
operators, and accom-
modations.

PUBLICATIONS

The premier interna-
tional travel magazine
for gays and lesbians is
Our World (✉ 1104 N.
Nova Rd., Suite 251,
Daytona Beach, FL

32117, ☎ 904/441–
5367, FAX 904/441–
5604; $35 for 10
issues). The 16-page
monthly **"Out & About"**
(☎ 212/645–6922 or
800/929–2268, FAX
800/929–2215; $49 for
10 issues and quarterly
calendar) covers gay-
friendly resorts, hotels,
cruise lines, and airlines.

TOUR OPERATORS

Cruises and resort
vacations for gays are
handled by **R.S.V.P.
Travel Productions** (✉
2800 University Ave.
SE, Minneapolis, MN
55414, ☎ 612/379–
4697 or 800/328–
7787). **Olivia** (✉ 4400
Market St., Oakland,
CA 94608, ☎ 510/
655–0364 or 800/631–
6277) specializes in
such bookings for
lesbians. For mixed gay
and lesbian travel,
contact **Hanns Ebensten
Travel** (✉ 513 Fleming
St., Key West, FL
33040, ☎ 305/294–
8174), one of the na-
tion's oldest operators
in the gay market, and
Toto Tours (✉ 1326 W.
Albion Ave., Suite 3W,
Chicago, IL 60626, ☎
312/274–8686 or 800/
565–1241), which
offers group tours to
worldwide destinations.

TRAVEL AGENCIES

The largest agencies
serving gay travelers
are **Advance Travel**
(✉ 10700 Northwest
Fwy., Suite 160, Hous-
ton, TX 77092, FAX
713/682–2002 or 800/
292–0500), **Islanders/
Kennedy Travel** (✉ 183
W. 10th St., New York,
NY 10014, ☎ 212/
242–3222 or 800/
988–1181), **Now
Voyager** (✉ 4406 18th
St., San Francisco, CA
94114, ☎ 415/626–

1169 or 800/255–6951), and **Yellowbrick Road** (✉ 1500 W. Balmoral Ave., Chicago, IL 60640, ☎ 312/561–1800 or 800/642–2488). **Skylink Women's Travel** (✉ 2460 W. 3rd St., Suite 215, Santa Rosa, CA 95401, ☎ 707/570–0105 or 800/225–5759) serves lesbian travelers.

H

HEALTH ISSUES

FINDING A DOCTOR

For its members, the **International Association for Medical Assistance to Travellers** (✉ IAMAT, membership free; 417 Center St., Lewiston, NY 14092, ☎ 716/754–4883; 40 Regal Rd., Guelph, Ontario N1K 1B5, ☎ 519/836–0102; 1287 St. Clair Ave., Toronto, Ontario M6E 1B8, ☎ 416/652–0137; 57 Voirets, 1212 Grand-Lancy, Geneva, Switzerland, no phone) publishes a worldwide directory of English-speaking physicians meeting IAMAT standards.

MEDICAL ASSISTANCE COMPANIES

The following companies are concerned primarily with emergency medical assistance, although they may provide some insurance as part of their coverage. For a list of full-service travel insurance companies, *see* Insurance, *below.*

Contact **International SOS Assistance** (✉ Box 11568, Philadelphia, PA 19116, ☎ 215/244–1500 or 800/523–8930; Box 466, Pl. Bonaven-

ture, Montréal, Québec H5A 1C1, ☎ 514/874–7674 or 800/363–0263; 7 Old Lodge Pl., St. Margarets, Twickenham TW1 1RQ, England, ☎ 0181/744–0033), **Medex Assistance Corporation** (✉ Box 5375, Timonium, MD 21094, ☎ 410/453–6300 or 800/537–2029), **Traveler's Emergency Network** (✉ 3100 Tower Blvd., Suite 3100A, Durham, NC 27702, ☎ 919/490–6065 or 800/275–4836, FAX 919/493–8262), **TravMed** (✉ Box 5375, Timonium, MD 21094, ☎ 410/453–6380 or 800/732–5309), or **Worldwide Assistance Services** (✉ 1133 15th St. NW, Suite 400, Washington, DC 20005, ☎ 202/331–1609 or 800/821–2828, FAX 202/828–5896).

WARNINGS

The hot line of the **National Centers for Disease Control** (✉ CDC, National Center for Infectious Diseases, Division of Quarantine, Traveler's Health Section, 1600 Clifton Rd., M/S E-03, Atlanta, GA 30333, ☎ 404/332–4559, FAX 404/332–4565) provides information on health risks abroad and vaccination requirements and recommendations. You can call for an automated menu of recorded information or use the fax-back service to request printed matter.

I

INSURANCE

IN CANADA

Contact **Mutual of Omaha** (✉ Travel Division, 500 University Ave., Toronto, Ontario

M5G 1V8, ☎ 800/465–0267 in Canada or 416/598-4083).

IN THE U.S.

Travel insurance covering baggage, health, and trip cancellation or interruptions is available from **Access America** (✉ 6600 Broad St., Richmond, VA 23230, ☎ 804/285–3300 or 800/334–7525), **Carefree Travel Insurance** (✉ Box 9366, 100 Garden City Plaza, Garden City, NY 11530, ☎ 516/294–0220 or 800/323–3149), **Near Travel Services** (✉ Box 1339, Calumet City, IL 60409, ☎ 708/868–6700 or 800/654–6700), **Tele-Trip** (✉ Mutual of Omaha Plaza, Box 31716, Omaha, NE 68131, ☎ 800/228–9792), **Travel Guard International** (✉ 1145 Clark St., Stevens Point, WI 54481, ☎ 715/345–0505 or 800/826–1300), **Travel Insured International** (✉ Box 280568, East Hartford, CT 06128, ☎ 203/528–7663 or 800/243–3174), and **Wallach & Company** (✉ 107 W. Federal St., Box 480, Middleburg, VA 22117, ☎ 540/687–3166 or 800/237–6615).

IN THE U.K.

The **Association of British Insurers** (✉ 51 Gresham St., London EC2V 7HQ, ☎ 0171/600–3333) gives advice by phone and publishes the free pamphlet **"Holiday Insurance,"** which sets out typical policy provisions and costs.

L

LODGING

For information on hotel consolidators, *see*

Discounts & Deals, *above*.

APARTMENT & VILLA RENTAL

Among the companies to contact are **At Home Abroad** (⊠ 405 E. 56th St., Suite 6H, New York, NY 10022, ☎ 212/421–9165, FAX 212/752–1591), **Europa-Let** (⊠ 92 N. Main St., Ashland, OR 97520, ☎ 541/482–5806 or 800/462–4486, FAX 541/482–0660), **Hometours International** (⊠ Box 11503, Knoxville, TN 37939, ☎ 423/588–8722 or 800/367–4668), **Interhome** (⊠ 124 Little Falls Rd., Fairfield, NJ 07004, ☎ 201/882–6864, FAX 201/808–1742), **Property Rentals International** (⊠ 1008 Mansfield Crossing Rd., Richmond, VA 23236, ☎ 804/378–6054 or 800/220–3332, FAX 804/379–2073), **Rental Directories International** (⊠ 2044 Rittenhouse Sq., Philadelphia, PA 19103, ☎ 215/985–4001, FAX 215/985–0323), **Rent-a-Home International** (⊠ 7200 34th Ave. NW, Seattle, WA 98117, ☎ 206/789–9377 or 800/488–7368, FAX 206/789–9379), **Vacation Home Rentals Worldwide** (⊠ 235 Kensington Ave., Norwood, NJ 07648, ☎ 201/767–9393 or 800/633–3284, FAX 201/767–5510), **Villas and Apartments Abroad** (⊠ 420 Madison Ave., Suite 1003, New York, NY 10017, ☎ 212/759–1025 or 800/433–3020, FAX 212/755–8316), and **Villas International** (⊠ 605 Market St., Suite 510, San Francisco, CA 94105, ☎ 415/281–0910 or 800/221–2260,

FAX 415/281–0919). Members of the travel club **Hideaways International** (⊠ 767 Islington St., Portsmouth, NH 03801, ☎ 603/430–4433 or 800/843–4433, FAX 603/430–4444; $99 per year) receive two annual guides plus quarterly newsletters and arrange rentals among themselves.

HOME EXCHANGE

Some of the principal clearinghouses are **HomeLink International/Vacation Exchange Club** (⊠ Box 650, Key West, FL 33041, ☎ 305/294–1448 or 800/638–3841, FAX 305/294–1148; $70 per year), which sends members three annual directories, with a listing in one, plus updates; and **Intervac International** (⊠ Box 590504, San Francisco, CA 94159, ☎ 415/435–3497, FAX 415/435–7440; $65 per year), which publishes four annual directories.

M
MONEY

ATMS

For specific foreign **Cirrus** locations, call 800/424–7787; for foreign **Plus** locations, consult the Plus directory at your local bank.

CURRENCY EXCHANGE

If your bank doesn't exchange currency, contact **Thomas Cook Currency Services** (☎ 800/287–7362 for locations). **Ruesch International** (☎ 800/424–2923 for locations) can also provide you with foreign banknotes before you leave home and publishes a number of useful

brochures, including a "Foreign Currency Guide" and "Foreign Exchange Tips."

TAXES

VAT➤ For information about value-added tax (VAT) refunds, *see* the individual country chapters. You can also obtain a refund before leaving Europe if you've shopped at the 90,000 stores affiliated with the refund service Europe Tax-free Shopping (ETS, 233 S. Wacker Dr., Chicago, IL, ☎ 312/382–1101). You ask for a check at the store, have it validated at customs at the airport, and claim a cash refund (minus 20% handling) at an ETS booth.

WIRING FUNDS

Funds can be wired via **MoneyGram℠** (for locations and information in the U.S. and Canada, ☎ 800/926–9400) or **Western Union** (for agent locations or to send money using MasterCard or Visa, ☎ 800/325–6000; in Canada, 800/321–2923; in the U.K., 0800/833833; or visit the Western Union office at the nearest major post office).

P
PACKING

For strategies on packing light, get a copy of *The Packing Book,* by Judith Gilford (⊠ Ten Speed Press, Box 7123, Berkeley, CA 94707, ☎ 510/559–1600 or 800/841–2665, FAX 510/524–4588; $7.95).

PASSPORTS & VISAS

U.S. CITIZENS

For fees, documentation requirements, and other

information, call the State Department's **Office of Passport Services** information line (☎ 202/647–0518).

CANADIANS

For fees, documentation requirements, and other information, call the Ministry of Foreign Affairs and International Trade's **Passport Office** (☎ 819/994–3500 or 800/567–6868).

U.K. CITIZENS

For fees, documentation requirements, and to request an emergency passport, call the **London Passport Office** (☎ 0990/210410).

The **Kodak Information Center** (☎ 800/242–2424) answers consumer questions about film and photography. The **Kodak Guide to Shooting Great Travel Pictures** (available in bookstores; or contact Fodor's Travel Publications, ☎ 800/533–6478; $16.50) explains how to take expert travel photographs.

S

"**Trouble-Free Travel**," from the AAA, is a booklet of tips for protecting yourself and your belongings when away from home. Send a stamped, self-addressed, legal-size envelope to Flying Alone (✉ Mail Stop 75, 1000 AAA Dr., Heathrow, FL 32746).

EDUCATIONAL TRAVEL

The nonprofit **Elderhostel** (✉ 75 Federal St., 3rd Floor, Boston, MA

02110, ☎ 617/426–7788), for people 60 and older, has offered inexpensive study programs since 1975. Courses cover everything from marine science to Greek mythology and cowboy poetry. Costs for two- to three-week international trips—including room, board, and transportation from the United States—range from $1,800 to $4,500.

For people 50 and over and their children and grandchildren, **Interhostel** (✉ University of New Hampshire, 6 Garrison Ave., Durham, NH 03824, ☎ 603/862–1147 or 800/733–9753) runs 10-day summer programs that feature lectures, field trips, and sightseeing. Most last two weeks and cost $2,125–$3,100, including airfare.

ORGANIZATIONS

Contact the **American Association of Retired Persons** (✉ AARP, 601 E St. NW, Washington, DC 20049, ☎ 202/434–2277; annual dues $8 per person or couple). Its Purchase Privilege Program secures discounts for members on lodging, car rentals, and sightseeing.

Additional sources for discounts on lodgings, car rentals, and other travel expenses, as well as helpful magazines and newsletters, are the **National Council of Senior Citizens** (✉ 1331 F St. NW, Washington, DC 20004, ☎ 202/347–8800; annual membership $12) and Sears's **Mature Outlook** (✉ Box 10448, Des Moines, IA 50306, ☎

800/336–6330; annual membership $9.95).

Cunard Line (✉ 555 5th Ave., New York, NY 10017, ☎ 800/221–4770) operates four ships that make transatlantic crossings. The **Queen Elizabeth 2** (**QE2**) makes regular crossings April–December, between Southampton, England, and Baltimore, Boston, and New York City. Arrangements for the QE2 can include one-way airfare. Cunard Line also offers fly/cruise packages and pre- and post-land packages. For other ships that sail to Europe, **check the travel pages of your Sunday newspaper.**

GROUPS

The major tour operators specializing in student travel are **Contiki Holidays** (✉ 300 Plaza Alicante, Suite 900, Garden Grove, CA 92640, ☎ 714/740–0808 or 800/466–0610) and **AESU Travel** (✉ 2 Hamill Rd., Suite 248, Baltimore, MD 21210-1807, ☎ 410/323–4416 or 800/638–7640).

HOSTELING

In the United States, contact **Hostelling International–American Youth Hostels** (✉ 733 15th St. NW, Suite 840, Washington, DC 20005, ☎ 202/783–6161 or 800/444–6111 for reservations at selected hostels, FAX 202/783–6171); in Canada, **Hostelling International–Canada** (✉ 205 Catherine St., Suite 400, Ottawa, Ontario K2P

1C3, ☎ 613/237–7884); and in the United Kingdom, the **Youth Hostel Association of England and Wales** (⊠ Trevelyan House, 8 St. Stephen's Hill, St. Albans, Hertfordshire AL1 2DY, ☎ 01727/855215 or 01727/845047). Membership (in the U.S., $25; in Canada, C$26.75; in the U.K., £9.30) gives you access to 5,000 hostels in 77 countries that charge $5–$30 per person per night.

ORGANIZATIONS

A major contact is the **Council on International Educational Exchange** (⊠ mail orders only: CIEE, 205 E. 42nd St., 16th Floor, New York, NY 10017, ☎ 212/822–2600). The **Educational Travel Centre** (⊠ 438 N. Frances St., Madison, WI 53703, ☎ 608/256–5551 or 800/747–5551, FAX 608/256–2042) offers rail passes and low-cost airline tickets, mostly for flights that depart from Chicago.

In Canada, also contact **Travel Cuts** (⊠ 187 College St., Toronto, Ontario M5T 1P7, ☎ 416/979–2406 or 800/667–2887).

PUBLICATIONS

Check out the *Berkeley Guide to Europe* (available in bookstores; or contact Fodor's Travel Publications, ☎ 800/533–6478; $18.95).

T
TELEPHONE
MATTERS

For local access numbers abroad, contact **AT&T** USADirect (☎ 800/874–4000), **MCI**

Call USA (☎ 800/444–4444 or automated hot line at ☎ 800/444–4141), or **Sprint** Express (☎ 800/793–1153).

TOUR OPERATORS

Among the companies that sell tours and packages to Europe, the following are nationally known, have a proven reputation, and offer plenty of options.

GROUP TOURS

SUPER-DELUXE➤ **Abercrombie & Kent** (⊠ 1520 Kensington Rd., Oak Brook, IL 60521-2141, ☎ 708/954–2944 or 800/323–7308, FAX 708/954–3324) and **Travcoa** (⊠ Box 2630, 2350 S.E. Bristol St., Newport Beach, CA 92660, ☎ 714/476–2800 or 800/992–2003, FAX 714/476–2538).

DELUXE➤ **Globus** (⊠ 5301 S. Federal Circle, Littleton, CO 80123, ☎ 303/797-2800 or 800/221–0090, FAX 303/795–0962), **Maupintour** (⊠ Box 807, 1515 St. Andrews Dr., Lawrence, KS 66047, ☎ 913/843–1211 or 800/255–4266, FAX 913/843–8351), and **Tauck Tours** (⊠ Box 5027, 276 Post Rd. W, Westport, CT 06881, ☎ 203/226–6911 or 800/468–2825, FAX 203/221–6828).

FIRST CLASS➤ **Brendan Tours** (⊠ 15137 Califa St., Van Nuys, CA 91411, ☎ 818/785–9696 or 800/421–8446, FAX 818/902–9876), **Caravan Tours** (⊠ 401 N. Michigan Ave., Chicago, IL 60611, ☎ 312/321–9800 or 800/227–2826), **Collette Tours** (⊠ 162 Middle St., Pawtucket, RI 02860, ☎ 401/728–3805 or 800/

832–4656, FAX 401/728–1380), **Gadabout Tours** (⊠ 700 E. Tahquitz Canyon Way, Palm Springs, CA 92262, ☎ 619/325–5556 or 800/952–5068), **Insight International Tours** (⊠ 745 Atlantic Ave., #720, Boston, MA 02111, ☎ 617/482-2000 or 800/582–8380, FAX 617/482–2884 or 800/622–5015), and **Trafalgar Tours** (⊠ 11 E. 26th St., New York, NY 10010, ☎ 212/689–8977 or 800/854–0103, FAX 800/457–6644).

BUDGET➤ **Cosmos** (☞ Globus, *above*) and **Trafalgar** (☞ Group Tours, *above*).

PACKAGES

Just about every airline that flies to Europe sells independent vacation packages that include round-trip airfare and hotel accommodations. Among U.S. carriers, contact **American Airlines Fly AAway Vacations** (☎ 800/321–2121), **Continental Vacations** (☎ 800/634–5555), **Delta Dream Vacations** (☎ 800/872–7786), and **United Vacations** (☎ 800/328–6877). Independent packages are also available from leading tour operators. Contact **Celtic International Tours** (⊠ 1860 Western Ave., Albany, NY 12203, ☎ 518/463–5511 or 800/833–4373), **CIE Tours** (⊠ Box 501, 100 Hanover Ave., Cedar Knolls, NJ 07927-0501, ☎ 201/292–3899 or 800/243–8687), **DER Tours** (⊠ 11933 Wilshire Blvd., Los Angeles, CA 90025, ☎ 310/479–4140 or 800/782–2424), **Five Star Touring** (⊠ 60 E.

42nd St., #612, New York, NY 10165, ☎ 212/818–9140 or 800/792–7827, FAX 212/818–9142), **4th Dimension Tours** (✉ 7101 S.W. 99th Ave., #105, Miami, FL 33173, ☎ 305/279–0014 or 800/877–1525, FAX 305/273–9777), and **Jet Vacations** (✉ 1775 Broadway, New York, NY 10019, ☎ 212/474–8740 or 800/538–2762). **Funjet Vacations,** based in Milwaukee, Wisconsin, and **Gogo Tours,** based in Ramsey, New Jersey, sell Europe packages only through travel agents.

For independent self-drive itineraries, contact **Budget WorldClass Drive** (☎ 800/527–0700; in the U.K., 0800/181181).

THEME TRIPS

Travel Contacts (✉ Box 173, Camberley, GU15 1YE, England, ☎ 011/44/1/27667–7217, FAX 011/44/1/2766–3477), which represents 150 tour operators, can satisfy just about any special interest in Europe.

ADVENTURE➤ From rafting on Turkey's Coruh River to climbing the Austrian Alps, adventure travel in Europe can mean hiking, walking, skiing, cycling—you name it. Contact **Adventure Center** (✉ 1311 63rd St., #200, Emeryville, CA 94608, ☎ 510/654–1879 or 800/227–8747, FAX 510/654–4200), **Himalayan Travel** (✉ 112 Prospect St., Stamford, CT 06901, ☎ 203/359–3711 or 800/225–2380, FAX 203/359–3669), **Mountain Travel-Sobek**

(✉ 6420 Fairmount Ave., El Cerrito, CA 94530, ☎ 510/527–8100 or 800/227–2384, FAX 510/525–7710), **Uniquely Europe** (✉ 2819 1st Ave., #280, Seattle, WA 98121-1113, ☎ 206/441–8682 or 800/426–3615, FAX 206/441–8862), and **Wilderness Travel** (✉ 801 Allston Way, Berkeley, CA 94710, ☎ 510/548–0420 or 800/368–2794, FAX 510/548–0347).

ART AND ARCHITECTURE➤ For a variety of programs, contact **Archeological Tours** (✉ 271 Madison Ave., New York, NY 10016, ☎ 212/986–3054, FAX 212/370–1561), **Endless Beginnings Tours** (✉ 9825 Dowdy Dr., #105, San Diego, CA 92126, ☎ 619/566–4166 or 800/822–7855, FAX 619/549–9655), **Esplanade Tours** (✉ 581 Boylston St., Boston, MA 02116, ☎ 617/266–7465 or 800/426–5492, FAX 617/262–9829), **Five Star Touring** (☞ Packages, *above*), and **Smithsonian Study Tours and Seminars** (✉ 1100 Jefferson Dr. SW, Room 3045, MRC 702, Washington, DC 20560, ☎ 202/357–4700, FAX 202/633–9250).

BALLOONING➤ **Buddy Bombard European Balloon Adventures** (✉ 855 Donald Ross Rd., Juno Beach, FL 33408, ☎ 407/775–0039 or 800/862–8537, FAX 407/775–7008) operates balloon holidays in France, Italy, Austria, Turkey, the Czech Republic, and Switzerland.

BARGE/RIVER CRUISES➤ Contact **Abercrombie &**

Kent (✉ 1520 Kensington Rd., Oak Brook, IL 60521-2141, ☎ 708/954–2944 or 800/323–7308, FAX 708/954–3324), **Alden Yacht Charters** (✉ 1909 Alden Landing, Portsmouth, RI 02871, ☎ 401/683–1782 or 800/662–2628, FAX 401/683–3668), **European Waterways** (✉ 140 E. 56th St., #4C, New York, NY 10022, ☎ 212/688–9489 or 800/217–4447, FAX 212/688–3778 or 800/296–4554), **KD River Cruises of Europe** (✉ 2500 Westchester Ave., Purchase, NY 10577, ☎ 914/696–3600 or 800/346–6525, FAX 914/696–0833), **Kemwel's Premier Selections** (✉ 106 Calvert St., Harrison, NY 10528, ☎ 914/835–5555 or 800/234–4000, FAX 914/835–5449), and **Le Boat** (☎ 201/342–1838 or 800/922-0291).

BICYCLING➤ Bike tours are available from **Backroads** (✉ 1516 5th St., Berkeley, CA 94710-1740, ☎ 510/577–1555 or 800/462–2848, FAX 510/527–1444), **Butterfield & Robinson** (✉ 70 Bond St., Toronto, Ontario, Canada M5B 1X3, ☎ 416/864–1354 or 800/678–1147, FAX 416/864–0541), **Classic Adventures** (✉ Box 153, Hamlin, NY 14464-0153, ☎ 716/964–8488 or 800/777–8090, FAX 716/964–7297), **Euro-Bike Tours** (✉ Box 990, De Kalb, IL 60115, ☎ 800/321–6060, FAX 815/758–8851), and **Rocky Mountain Worldwide Cycle Tours** (✉ Box 1978, Canmore, Alberta, Canada TOL

OMO, ☎ 403/678–6770 or 800/661–2453, FAX 403/678–4451).

CRUISING➤ **EuroCruises** (✉ 303 W. 13th St., New York, NY 10014, ☎ 212/691–2099 or 800/688–3876) represents more than 20 European-based cruise lines with ship of all sizes available.

FOOD AND WINE➤ For a culinary adventure, try **Annemarie Victory Organization** (✉ 136 E. 64th St., New York, NY 10021, ☎ 212/486–0353, FAX 212/751–3149) or **Travel Concepts** (✉ 62 Commonwealth Ave., #3, Boston, MA 02116, ☎ 617/266–8450). To attend a cooking school in England, France, or Italy, contact **Cuisine International** (✉ Box 25228, Dallas, TX 75225, ☎ 214/373–1161 or FAX 214/373–1162). If you want to learn French cooking, **Le Cordon Bleu** (✉ 404 Irvington St., Pleasantville, NY 10570, ☎ 800/457–2433 in U.S.), one of the world's best-known cooking schools, has courses for beginners and connoisseurs.

GOLF➤ **Golf International** (✉ 275 Madison Ave., New York, NY 10016, ☎ 212/986–9176 or 800/833–1389, FAX 212/986–3720) has golf packages in several European countries. **Francine Atkins' Scotland Ireland** (✉ 2 Ross Court, Trophy Club, TX 76262, ☎ 817/491–1105 or 800/742–0355, FAX 817/491–2025) and **ITC Golf Tours** (✉ 4134 Atlantic Ave., #205, Long Beach, CA 90807, ☎ 310/595–6905 or 800/257–4981)

arrange customized itineraries. Packages including accommodations, confirmed tee times, and golfing fees and lessons are offered by **Stine's Golftrips** (✉ Box 2314, Winter Haven, FL 33883-2314, ☎ 813/324–1300 or 800/428–1940, FAX 941/325–0384).

HISTORY➤ History buffs should contact **Herodot Travel** (✉ 775 E. Blithedale, Box 234, Mill Valley, CA 94941, ☎ FAX 415/381–4031).

HORSEBACK RIDING➤ **FITS Equestrian** (✉ 685 Lateen Rd., Solvang, CA 93463, ☎ 805/688–9494 or 800/666–3487, FAX 805/688–2943) has tours for every level of rider.

HORTICULTURE➤ Amateur and professional gardeners alike should contact **Expo Garden Tours** (✉ 101 Sunrise Hill Rd., Norwalk, CT 06851, ☎ 203/840–1441 or 800/448–2685, FAX 203/840–1224).

LEARNING➤ Contact **Smithsonian Study Tours and Seminars** (☞ Art and Architecture, *above*).

MOTORCYCLE➤ **Beach's Motorcycle Adventures** (✉ 2763 W. River Pkwy., Grand Island, NY 14072-2053, ☎ 716/773–4960, FAX 716/773–5227) can take you on Alpine adventures through Germany, Austria, Italy, France, and Switzerland.

NATURAL HISTORY➤ **Questers** (✉ 381 Park Ave. S, New York, NY 10016, ☎ 212/251–0444 or 800/468–8668, FAX 212/251–0890) explores the wild side of

Europe in the company of expert guides. **Earthwatch** (✉ Box 403, 680 Mount Auburn St., Watertown, MA 02272, ☎ 617/926–8200 or 800/776–0188, FAX 617/926–8532) recruits volunteers to serve in its EarthCorps as short-term assistants to scientists on research expeditions.

PERFORMING ARTS➤ **Dailey-Thorp Travel** (✉ 330 W. 58th St., #610, New York, NY 10019-1817, ☎ 212/307–1555 or 800/998–4677, FAX 212/974–1420) specializes in classical music and opera programs throughout Europe.

SINGLES AND YOUNG ADULTS➤ Travelers 18–35 looking to join a group should try **Club Europa** (✉ 802 W. Oregon St., Urbana, IL 61801, ☎ 217/344–5863 or 800/331–1882, FAX 217/344–4072) and **Contiki Holidays** (✉ 300 Plaza Alicante, #900, Garden Grove, CA 92640, ☎ 714/740–0808 or 800/266–8454, FAX 714/740–0818). **Trafalgar Tours** (☞ Group Tours, *above*) has a "Club 21" program of escorted bus tours through Europe and Great Britain for travelers ages 21 to 35.

SPAS➤ Contact **Custom Spa Vacations** (✉ 1318 Beacon St., Brookline, MA 02146, ☎ 617/566–5144 or 800/443–7727, FAX 617/731–0599), **Great Spas of the World** (✉ 211 E. 43rd St., #1404, New York, NY 10017, ☎ 212/599–0382 or 800/826–8062), **Spa-Finders** (✉ 91 5th Ave., #301, New York, NY 10003-3039, ☎ 212/924–

6800 or 800/255–7727), and **Spa Trek Travel** (475 Park Avenue South., New York, NY 10016, ☎ 212/779–3480 or 800/272–3480, FAX 212/779–3471).

SPORTS➤ **Championship Tennis Tours** (✉ 7350 E. Stetson Dr., #106, Scottsdale, AZ 85251, ☎ 602/990–8760 or 800/468–3664, FAX 602/990–8744) has packages to the French Open, Wimbledon, the Italian Open, and the Swiss Open. **Francine Atkins' Scotland Ireland** (☞ Golf, *above*) arranges fishing, golfing, shooting, and hunting tours. **Sportstours** (✉ 2301 Collins Ave., #A1540, Miami Beach, FL 33139, ☎ 800/879–8647, FAX 305/535–0008) arranges a variety of tennis and golf packages. **Travel Concepts** (☞ Food and Wine, *above*) packages prestigious sporting events.

TRAIN TOURS➤ **Abercrombie & Kent** (☞ Group Tours, *above*) operates luxury tours aboard the legendary transcontinental Venice–Simplon *Orient Express*. Less costly packages travel by regularly scheduled trains with stays in first-class and deluxe hotels, accompanied by a traveling bellboy so you don't have to lug your bags from train to hotel.

VILLA RENTALS➤ Contact **Eurovillas** (✉ 1398 55th St., Emeryville, CA 94608, ☎ FAX 707/648–0266) and **Villas International** (✉ 605 Market St., San Francisco, CA 94105, ☎ 415/281–0910 or 800/221–2260, FAX 415/281–0919).

WALKING➤ For walking and hiking tours throughout Europe contact **Abercrombie & Kent** (☞ Group Tours, *above*), **Above the Clouds Trekking** (✉ Box 398, Worcester, MA 01602, ☎ 508/799–4499 or 800/233–4499, FAX 508/797–4779), **Backroads** and **Butterfield & Robinson** (☞ Bicycling, *above*), **Country Walkers** (✉ Box 180, Waterbury, VT 05676-0180, ☎ 802/244–1387 or 800/464–9255, FAX 802/244–5661), and **Euro-Bike Tours** (☞ Bicycling, *above*).

YACHT CHARTERS➤ Contact **Huntley Yacht Vacations** (✉ 210 Preston Rd., Wernersville, PA 19565, ☎ 610/678–2628 or 800/322-9224, FAX 610/670–1767), **Lynn Jachney Charters** (✉ Box 302, Marblehead, MA 01945, ☎ 617/639–0787 or 800/223–2050, FAX 617/639–0216), **The Moorings** (✉ 19345 U.S. Hwy. 19 N, 4th floor, Clearwater, FL 34624-3193, ☎ 813/530–5424 or 800/535–7289, FAX 813/530–9474), **Ocean Voyages** (✉ 1709 Bridgeway, Sausalito, CA 94965, ☎ 415/332–4681, FAX 415/332–7460), **Russell Yacht Charters** (✉ 404 Hulls Hwy., Southport, CT 06490, ☎ 203/255–2783 or 800/635–8895), and **SailAway Yacht Charters** (✉ 15605 S.W. 92nd Ave., Miami, FL 33157-1972, ☎ 305/253–7245 or 800/724–5292, FAX 305/251–4408).

U.K. OPERATORS

Among the companies that sell tours and packages originating in the United Kingdom, the following are nationally known, have a proven reputation, and offer plenty of options.

ADVENTURE➤ **Top Deck Travel** (✉ 131–135 Earl's Court Rd., London SW5 9RH, ☎ 0171/244–8641) has tours to Europe with activities including flotilla sailing and a variety of water sports, such as rafting.

BALLOONING➤ **Virgin Balloon Flights** (✉ 17 Linhope St., London NW1 6HT, ☎ 0171/706–1021) acts as clearinghouse for balloon activities.

MUSIC➤ **Travel for the Arts** (✉ 117 Regent's Park Rd., London NW1 8UR, ☎ 0171/483–2290) leads groups to the musical highlights of regions throughout Europe. **Prospect Music & Art Tours Ltd.** (✉ 454–458 Chiswick High Rd., London W4 5TT, ☎ 0181/995–2151) and has tours to many of the famous annual festivals—Savonlinna, Prague, Bregenz, and Munich among them.

NATURAL HISTORY➤ **Ramblers Holidays Ltd.** (✉ Box 43, Welwyn Garden City, Hertfordshire AL8 6PQ, ☎ 01707/331–133) arranges walking tours within Europe with guides who point out natural features of interest.

SPAS➤ **Moswin Tours Ltd.** (✉ 21 Church St., Oadby, Leicester LE2 5DB, ☎ 0116/271–9922) counts visits to health farms among its programs.

SPORTS➤ **Green Card Golf Holidays** (✉ 11A Queensdale Rd., London W11 4QF, ☎ 0171/727–7287) arranges visits throughout Western Europe to greens and amateur tournaments suitable for every level of handicap. Companies offering Alpine skiing packages include **Top Deck Ski** (✉ 131 Earls Court Rd., SW5 9RH, ☎ 0171/244–8641) and **Crystal Holidays** (✉ Arlington Rd., Surbiton KT6 6BW, ☎ 0181/399–5144), both with a range of resorts at competitive prices.

WINE AND FOOD➤ **Winetrails** (✉ Greenways, Vann Lake, Ockley, Dorking RH5 5NT, ☎ 01306/712–111) has leisurely walks through wine regions of Europe, with accommodations in family hotels, wine estates, and chateaux.

ORGANIZATIONS

The **National Tour Association** (✉ NTA, 546 E. Main St., Lexington, KY 40508, ☎ 606/226–4444 or 800/755–8687) and the **United States Tour Operators Association** (✉ USTOA, 211 E. 51st St., Suite 12B, New York, NY 10022, ☎ 212/750–7371) can provide lists of members and information on booking tours.

PUBLICATIONS

Contact the USTOA (☞ Organizations, *above*) for its **"Smart Traveler's Planning Kit."** Pamphlets in the kit include the "Worldwide Tour and Vacation Package Finder," "How to Select a Tour or Vacation Package," and information on the organization's consumer protection plan. Also get copy of the Better Business Bureau's **"Tips on Travel Packages"** (✉ Publication 24-195, 4200 Wilson Blvd., Arlington, VA 22203; $2).

TRAIN TRAVEL

A good rail timetable is indispensable if you're doing extensive rail pass traveling. The **Thomas Cook Timetables,** available either for all Europe or for Britain, France, and the Benelux countries, are the most complete (U.S. distributor: Forsyth Travel Library, ✉ Box 2975, Shawnee Mission, KS 66201-1375, ☎ 913/384–3553; $19.95.)

DISCOUNT PASSES

Eurail and EuroPasses are available through travel agents and **Rail Europe** (226-230 Westchester Ave., White Plains, NY 10604, ☎ 914/682–5172 or 800/438–7245; 2087 Dundas E., Suite 105, Mississauga, Ontario L4X 1M2, ☎ 416/602–4195, **DER Tours** (Box 1606, Des Plaines, IL 60017, ☎ 800/782–2424, FAX 800/282–7474), or **CIT Tours Corp.** (342 Madison Ave., Suite 207, New York, NY 10173, ☎ 212/697–2100 or 800/248–8687 or 800/248–7245 in western U.S.).

Rail Europe also sells single-country passes for Austria, Bulgaria, the Czech Republic, Finland, France, Germany, Greece, Hungary, Norway, Poland, Portugal, Romania, Russia, Spain, and Switzerland, as well as multicountry passes.

BritRail Passes can be purchased from **BritRail Travel International** (1500 Broadway, New York, NY 10036, ☎ 212/575–2667 or 800/677–8585 or 94 Cumberland St., Toronto, Ontario, Canada M5R 1A3, ☎ 416/482–1777).

FROM THE U.K.

For information about train service through the Channel Tunnel, contact **Le Shuttle** (in the U.S., ☎ 800/388–3876,; in the U.K., 0990/353535), which transports cars and buses, or **Eurostar** (in the U.S., ☎ 800/942–4866; in the U.K., 0345/881881), the high-speed train service between London (Waterloo) and Paris (Gare du Nord) and London and Brussels (Gare du Midi). Eurostar tickets are available in the U.K. through **InterCity Europe,** the international wing of BritRail (✉ Victoria Station, London, ☎ 0171/834–2345 or 0171/828–0892 for credit-card bookings), and in the United States through **Rail Europe** (☎ 800/942–4866) and **BritRail Travel** (☎ 800/677–8585).

TRAVEL GEAR

For travel apparel, appliances, personal-care items, and other travel necessities, get a free catalog from **Magellan's** (☎ 800/962–4943, FAX 805/568–5406), **Orvis Travel** (☎ 800/541–3541, FAX 703/343–7053), or **TravelSmith** (☎ 800/950–1600, FAX 415/455–0554).

ELECTRICAL CONVERTERS

Send a self-addressed, stamped envelope to the **Franzus Company** (⊠ Customer Service, Dept. B50, Murtha Industrial Park, Box 142, Beacon Falls, CT 06403, ☎ 203/723–6664) for a copy of the free brochure "Foreign Electricity Is No Deep, Dark Secret."

TRAVEL AGENCIES

For names of reputable agencies in your area, contact the **American Society of Travel Agents** (⊠ ASTA, 1101 King St., Suite 200, Alexandria, VA 22314, ☎ 703/739–2782), the **Association of Canadian Travel Agents** (⊠ Suite 201, 1729 Bank St., Ottawa, Ontario K1V 7Z5, ☎ 613/521–0474, FAX 613/521–0805) or the **Association of British Travel Agents** (⊠ 55-57 Newman St., London W1P 4AH, ☎ 0171/637–2444, FAX 0171/637–0713).

U

U.S. GOVERNMENT TRAVEL BRIEFINGS

The U.S. Department of State's American Citizens Services office (⊠ Room 4811, Washington, DC 20520; enclose SASE) issues **Consular Information Sheets** on all foreign countries. These cover issues such as crime, security, political climate, and health risks as well as listing embassy locations, entry requirements, currency regulations, and providing other useful information. For the latest information, stop in at any U.S. passport office, consulate, or embassy; call the interactive hot line (☎ 202/647–5225, FAX 202/647–3000); or, with your PC's modem, tap into the department's computer bulletin board (☎ 202/647–9225).

V

VISITOR INFORMATION

AUSTRIAN NATIONAL TOURIST OFFICE

IN THE UNITED STATES> Telephone inquiries only, ⊠ 500 5th Ave., Suite 2022, New York, NY 10110, ☎ 212/944–6880, FAX 212/730–4568; ⊠ 11601 Wilshire Blvd., Suite 2480, Los Angeles, CA 90025, ☎ 310/477–3332, ☎ 310/477–5141.

IN CANADA> ⊠ 2 Bloor St. E, Suite 3330, Toronto, Ontario M4W 1A8, ☎ 416/967–3381, FAX 416/967–4101. In the United Kingdom: Telephone inquiries only, ⊠ 30 St. George St., London W1R 0AL, ☎ 0171/629–0461, FAX 0171/499–6038.

IN THE U.K.> ⊠ 30 St. George St., London W1R 0AL, ☎ 0171/629–0461.

BELGIAN NATIONAL TOURIST OFFICE

IN THE UNITED STATES AND CANADA> ⊠ 780 3rd Ave., New York, NY 10017, ☎ 212/758–8130, FAX 212/355–7675; in Canada: ⊠ Box 760 NDG, Montréal, Québec H4A 3S2, ☎ 514/584–3594, FAX 514/489–89650. In the United Kingdom: ⊠ 29 Princes St., London W1R 7RG, ☎ 0171/629–0230, FAX 0171/629–0454.

IN THE U.K.> ⊠ 29 Princes St., London W1R 7RG, ☎ 0891/887–799, FAX 0171/629–0454. Calls cost 49p per minute peak rate or 39p per minute cheap rate.

BRITISH TOURIST AUTHORITY

IN THE UNITED STATES> ⊠ 551 5th Ave., Suite 701, New York, NY 10176, ☎ 212/986–2200, FAX 212/986–1188; ⊠ 625 N. Michigan Ave., Suite 1510, Chicago, IL 60611, ☎ 312/787–0490, FAX 312/787–7746; ⊠ World Trade Center, 350 S. Figueroa St., Suite 450, Los Angeles, CA 90071, ☎ 213/628–3525, FAX 213/687–6621; ⊠ 2850 Cumberland Pkwy., Suite 470, Atlanta, GA 30339, ☎ 404/432–9635, FAX 404/432–9641).

IN CANADA> ⊠ 111 Avenue Rd., Suite 450, Toronto, Ontario M5R 3J8, ☎ 416/925–6326.

IN THE U.K.> ⊠ British Travel Centre, 12 Regent St., London SW1 4PQ.

BULGARIAN NATIONAL TOURIST OFFICE

IN THE UNITED STATES AND CANADA> Balkan Holidays (authorized agent), ⊠ 41 E. 42nd St., Suite 508, New York, NY 10017, ☎ 212/573–5530, FAX 212/573–5538. In the United Kingdom: ⊠ 18 Princes St., London W1R 7RE, ☎ 0171/499–6988.

IN THE U.K.➤ Contact Balkan Holidays (✉ 19 Conduit St., London W1R 9TD, ☎ 0171/491–4499).

CYPRUS TOURIST OFFICE

IN THE UNITED STATES AND CANADA➤ ✉ 13 E. 40th St., New York, NY 10016, ☎ 212/683–5280, FAX 212/683–5282.

IN THE U.K.➤ Cyprus Tourist Office (✉ 213 Regent St., London W1R 8DA, ☎ 0891/887–744). Calls cost 49p per minute peak rate or 39p per minute cheap rate.

CZECH TRAVEL BUREAU AND TOURIST OFFICE (ČEDOK)

IN THE UNITED STATES➤ ✉ Central European Tours and Travel, 10 E. 40th St., New York, NY 10016, ☎ 212/689–9720, FAX 212/481–0597.

IN CANADA➤ ✉ Czech Tourist Authority, Box 198, Exchange Tower, 2 First Canadian Pl., 14th Floor, Toronto M5X 1A6, Ontario, ☎ 416/367–3432, FAX 416/367–3492.

IN THE U.K.➤ Czech Centre (✉ 30 Kensington Palace Gardens, London W8 4QY, ☎ 0171/243–7981, FAX 0171/727–9589).

DANISH TOURIST BOARD

IN THE UNITED STATES➤ ✉ Box 4649 Grand Central Station, New York, NY 10163–4649, ☎ 212/949–2333, FAX 212/983–5260.

IN THE U.K.➤ ✉ 55 Sloane St., London SW1X 9SY, ☎ 0891/

600–109. Calls cost 49p per minute peak rate or 39p per minute cheap rate.

FINNISH TOURIST BOARD

IN THE UNITED STATES AND CANADA➤ ✉ Box 4649 Grand Central Station, New York, NY 10163–4649, ☎ 212/949–2333, FAX 212/983–5260; ✉ 1900 Ave. of the Stars, Suite 1070, Los Angeles, CA 90067, ☎ 310/277–5226 or 800/346–4636.

IN THE U.K.➤ ✉ 30 Pall Mall, London, SW1Y 5LP, ☎ 0171/839–4048, FAX 0171/321–0696.

FRENCH GOVERNMENT TOURIST OFFICE

IN THE UNITED STATES➤ Nationwide, ☎ 900/990–0040 (costs 95¢ per minute); ✉ 610 5th Ave., New York, NY 10020, ☎ 212/315–0888 or 212/757–1125, FAX 212/247–6468; ✉ 676 N. Michigan Ave., Chicago, IL 60611, ☎ 312/751–7800; ✉ 9454 Wilshire Blvd., Beverly Hills, CA 90212, ☎ 310/271–2358, FAX 310/276–2835.

IN CANADA➤ ✉ 1981 McGill College Ave., Suite 490, Montréal, Québec H3A 2W9, ☎ 514/288–4264, FAX 514/845–4868; ✉ 30 St. Patrick St., Suite 700, Toronto, Ontario M5T 3A3, ☎ 416/593–4723, FAX 416/979–7587.

IN THE U.K.➤ ✉ 178 Piccadilly, London W1V 0AL, ☎ 0891/244–123. Calls cost 49p per minute peak rate or 39p per minute cheap rate.

GERMAN NATIONAL TOURIST OFFICE

IN THE UNITED STATES➤ ✉ 122 E. 42nd St., New York, NY 10168, ☎ 212/661–7200, FAX 212/661–7174; ✉ 11766 Wilshire Blvd., Suite 750, Los Angeles, CA 90025, ☎ 310/575–9799, FAX 310/575–1565.

IN CANADA➤ ✉ 175 Bloor St. E, Suite 604, Toronto, Ontario M4W 3R8, ☎ 416/968–1570.

IN THE U.K.➤ ✉ Nightingale House, 65 Curzon St., London W1Y 7PE, ☎ 0891/600–100. Calls cost 49p per minute peak rate or 39p per minute cheap rate.

GIBRALTAR GOVERNMENT TOURIST OFFICE

IN THE UNITED STATES AND CANADA➤ ✉ 1155 15th St. NW, Room 710, Washington, DC 20005, ☎ 202/452–1108, FAX 202/872–8543.

IN THE U.K.➤ ✉ Arundel Great Ct., 179 The Strand, London WC2R 1EH, ☎ 0171/836–0777, FAX 0170/240–6612.

GREEK NATIONAL TOURIST ORGANIZATION

IN THE UNITED STATES➤ ✉ 645 5th Ave., New York, NY 10022, ☎ 212/421–5777, FAX 212/826–6940; ✉ 611 W. 6th St., Suite 2198, Los Angeles, CA 90017, ☎ 213/626–6696, FAX 213/489–9744; ✉ 168 N. Michigan Ave., Suite 600, Chicago, IL 60601, ☎ 312/782–1084, FAX 312/782–1091.

IN CANADA➤ ✉ 1233 Rue de la Montagne,

Suite 101, Montréal, Québec H3G 1Z2, ☎ 514/871–1535, FAX 514/871–1498; ✉ 1300 Bay St., Toronto, Ontario M5R 3K8, ☎ 416/968–2220, FAX 416/968–6533.

IN THE U.K.➤ ✉ 4 Conduit St., London W1R 0DJ, ☎ 0171/734–5997).

HUNGARIAN TOURIST BOARD

IN THE UNITED STATES AND CANADA➤ ✉ 150 E. 58th St., New York, NY 10155, ☎ 212/355–0240, FAX 212/207–4103.

IN THE U.K.➤ ✉ Box 4336, London, SW18 4XE, ☎ 0891/171–200. Calls cost 49p per minute peak rate or 39p per minute cheap rate.

ICELAND TOURIST BOARD

IN THE UNITED STATES AND CANADA➤ ✉ Box 4649 Grand Central Station, New York, NY 10163–4649, ☎ 212/949–2333, FAX 212/983–5260.

IN THE U.K.➤ ✉ 172 Tottenham Court Rd., 3rd floor, London W1P 9LG, ☎ 0171/388–7550.

IRISH TOURIST BOARD

IN THE UNITED STATES➤ ✉ 345 Park Ave., New York, NY 10154, ☎ 212/418–0800 or 800/223–6470, FAX 212/371–9052.

IN CANADA➤ ✉ 160 Bloor St. E, Suite 1150, Toronto, Ontario M4W 1B9, ☎ 416/929–2777, FAX 416/929–6783.

IN THE U.K.➤ ✉ Ireland House, 150 New Bond St., London W1Y 0AQ, ☎ 0171/493–3201.

ITALIAN GOVERNMENT TRAVEL OFFICE (ENIT)

IN THE UNITED STATES➤ ✉ 630 5th Ave., Suite 1565, New York, NY 10111, ☎ 212/245–4822, FAX 212/586–9249; ✉ 12400 Wilshire Blvd., Suite 550, Los Angeles, CA 90025, ☎ 310/820–0098, FAX 310/820–6357.

IN CANADA➤ ✉ 1 Pl. Ville Marie, Suite 1914, Montréal, Québec H3B 3M9, ☎ 514/866–7667.

IN THE U.K.➤ ✉ 1 Princes St., London W1R 8AY, ☎ 0171/408–1254.

LUXEMBOURG TOURIST INFORMATION OFFICE

IN THE UNITED STATES AND CANADA➤ ✉ 17 Beekman Pl., New York, NY 10022, ☎ 212/935–8888, FAX 212/935–5896.

IN THE U.K.➤ ✉ 122 Regent St., London W1R 5FE, ☎ 0171/434–2800.

MALTA NATIONAL TOURIST OFFICE

IN THE UNITED STATES AND CANADA➤ ✉ 350 5th Ave., Suite 4412, New York, NY 10118, ☎ 212/695–9520, FAX 212/695–8229.

IN THE UNITED KINGDOM➤ ✉ 36 Piccadilly, London W1V 0PP, ☎ 0171/292–4900.

MONACO GOVERNMENT TOURIST AND CONVENTION BUREAU

IN THE UNITED STATES AND CANADA➤ ✉ 845 3rd Ave., New York, NY 10022, ☎ 212/759–5227, FAX 212/754–9320.

IN THE U.K.➤ ✉ 3–18 Chelsea Garden Market, Chelsea Harbour, London SW10 0XE, ☎ 0171/352–9962, FAX 0171/352–2103.

NETHERLANDS BOARD OF TOURISM

IN THE UNITED STATES➤ ✉ 225 N. Michigan Ave., Suite 326, Chicago, IL 60601, ☎ 312/819–0300, FAX 312/819–1740.

IN CANADA➤ ✉ 25 Adelaide St. E, Suite 710, Toronto, Ontario M5C 1Y2, ☎ 416/363–1577, FAX 416/363–1470.

IN THE U.K.➤ ✉ 25–28 Buckingham Gate, London SW1E 6LD, ☎ 0891/200–277. Calls cost 49p per minute peak rate or 39p per minute cheap rate.

NORWEGIAN TOURIST BOARD

IN THE UNITED STATES AND CANADA➤ ✉ Box 4649 Grand Central Station, New York, NY 10163–4649, ☎ 212/949–2333, FAX 212/983–5260.

IN THE U.K.➤ ✉ Charles House, 5–11 Lower Regent St., London SW1Y 4LR, ☎ 0171/839–6255.

POLISH NATIONAL TOURIST OFFICE

IN THE UNITED STATES AND CANADA➤ ✉ 275 Madison Ave., Suite 1711, New York, NY 10016, ☎ 212/338–9412, FAX 212/338–9283; and ✉ 333 N. Michigan Ave., Suite 224, Chicago, IL 60601, ☎ 312/236–9013, FAX 312/236–

1125. Also contact Orbis Polish Travel Bureau, ✉ 342 Madison Ave., Suite 1512, New York, NY 10173, ☎ 212/867–5011, FAX 212/682–4715.

IN THE U.K.➤ ✉ 310–312 Regent St., London W1R 5AJ, ☎ 0171/580–8811, FAX 0171/580–8866.

PORTUGUESE NATIONAL TOURIST OFFICE

IN THE UNITED STATES➤ ✉ 590 5th Ave., 4th Floor, New York, NY 10036, ☎ 212/354–4403, FAX 212/764–6137.

IN CANADA➤ ✉ 60 Bloor St. W, Suite 1005, Toronto, Ontario M4W 3BS, ☎ 416/921–7376, FAX 416/921–1353.

IN THE U.K.➤ ✉ 22–25A Sackville St., London W1X 1DE, ☎ 0171/494–1441.

ROMANIAN NATIONAL TOURIST OFFICE

IN THE UNITED STATES AND CANADA➤ ✉ 342 Madison Ave., Suite 210, New York, NY 10173, ☎ 212/697–6971, FAX 212/697–6972.

IN THE U.K.➤ ✉ 83A Marylebone High St., London W1M 3DE, ☎ 0171/224–3692.

SLOVAKIA

IN THE UNITED STATES AND CANADA➤ ✉ Viktor Corporation, 10 E. 40th St., Suite 3601, New York, NY 10016, ☎ 212/213–3862, FAX 212/213–4461.

IN THE U.K.➤ ✉ Embassy of the Slovak Republic, Information Dept., 25 Kensington Palace Gardens, London

W8 4QY, ☎ 0171/243–0803, FAX 0171/727–5821.

SPANISH NATIONAL TOURIST OFFICE

IN THE UNITED STATES➤ ✉ 666 5th Ave., 35th fl., New York, NY 10103, ☎ 212/265–8822, FAX 212/265–8864; ✉ 845 N. Michigan Ave., Chicago, IL 60611, ☎ 312/642–1992, FAX 312/642–9817; ✉ San Vicente Plaza Bldg., 8383 Wilshire Blvd., Suite 960, Beverly Hills, CA 90211, ☎ 213/658–7188, FAX 213/658–1061; ✉ 1221 Brickell Ave., Suite 1850, Miami, FL 33131, ☎ 305/358–1992, FAX 305/358–8223.

IN CANADA➤ ✉ 102 Bloor St. W, Suite 1400, Toronto, Ontario M5S 1M8, ☎ 416/961–3131, FAX 416/961–1992.

IN THE U.K.➤ ✉ 57–58 St. James's St., London SW1A 1LD, ☎ 0891/669–920. Calls cost 49p per minute peak rate or 39p per minute cheap rate.

SWEDISH TRAVEL AND TOURISM COUNCIL

IN THE UNITED STATES AND CANADA➤ ✉ Box 4649 Grand Central Station, New York, NY 10163–4649, ☎ 212/949–2333, FAX 212/983–5260.

IN THE U.K.➤ ✉ 73 Welbeck St., London W1M 8AN, ☎ 0171/935–9784, FAX 0171/935–5853.

SWITZERLAND TOURISM

IN THE UNITED STATES➤ ✉ 608 5th Ave., New

York, NY 10020, ☎ 212/757–5944, FAX 212/262–6116; ✉ 222 N. Sepulveda Blvd., Suite 1570, El Segundo, CA 90245, ☎ 310/335–5980, FAX 310/335–5982; ✉ 150 N. Michigan Ave., Suite 2930, Chicago, IL 60601, ☎ 312/630–5840, FAX 312/630–5848.

IN CANADA➤ ✉ 154 University Ave., Suite 610, Toronto, Ontario M5H 3Y9, ☎ 416/971–9734, FAX 416/971–6425.

IN THE U.K.➤ ✉ Swiss Centre, 1 New Coventry St., London W1V 8EE, ☎ 0171/734–1921.

TURKISH TOURIST OFFICE

IN THE UNITED STATES AND CANADA➤ ✉ 821 UN Plaza, New York, NY 10017, ☎ 212/687–2194, FAX 212/599–7568; ✉ 1717 Massachusetts Ave. NW, Suite 306, Washington, DC 20036, ☎ 202/429–9844, FAX 202/429–5649. In Canada: ✉ c/o Turkish Embassy, 197 Wurtemburg St., Ottawa, Ontario K1N 8L9, ☎ 613/789–4044.

IN THE U.K.➤ ✉ 170–173 Piccadilly, 1st floor, London W1V 9DD, ☎ 0171/629–7771, FAX 0171/491–0773.

W
WEATHER

For current conditions and forecasts, plus the local time and helpful travel tips, call the **Weather Channel Connection** (☎ 900/932–8437; 95¢ per minute) from a Touch-Tone phone.

THE GOLD GUIDE / IMPORTANT CONTACTS

The *International Traveler's Weather Guide* (✉ Weather Press, Box 660606, Sacramento, CA 95866, ☎ 916/974–0201 or 800/972–0201; $10.95 includes shipping), written by two meteorologists, provides month-by-month information on temperature, humidity, and precipitation in more than 175 cities worldwide.

SMART TRAVEL TIPS A TO Z

Basic Information on Traveling in Europe and Savvy Tips to Make Your Trip a Breeze

A
AIR TRAVEL

If time is an issue, **always look for nonstop flights,** which require no change of plane. If possible, **avoid connecting flights,** which stop at least once and can involve a change of plane, even though the flight number remains the same; if the first leg is late, the second waits.

Many American airlines have code-sharing agreements with European partners. You travel the first leg with one airline and the second with another, so you may not know that you will transfer to another carrier not of your choosing. The main advantage is that you **get boarding passes and seat assignments for both legs when you check in.** The airline partners also honor one another's frequent flyer programs.

CUTTING COSTS

The Sunday travel section of most newspapers is a good place to look for deals.

MAJOR AIRLINES➤ The least-expensive airfares from the major airlines are priced for round-trip travel and are subject to restrictions. Usually, you must **book in advance and buy the ticket within 24 hours** to get cheaper fares, and you may have to **stay over a Saturday night.** The lowest fare is

subject to availability, and only a small percentage of the plane's total seats is sold at that price. It's smart to **call a number of airlines, and when you are quoted a good price, book it on the spot**—the same fare may not be available on the same flight the next day. Airlines generally allow you to change your return date for a $25 to $50 fee. If you don't use your ticket, you can apply the cost toward the purchase of a new ticket, again for a small charge. However, most low-fare tickets are nonrefundable. To get the lowest airfare, **check different routings.** If your destination has more than one gateway, **compare prices to different airports.**

FROM THE U.K.➤ To save money on flights, **look into an APEX or Super-Pex ticket.** APEX tickets must be booked in advance and have certain restrictions. Super-PEX tickets can be purchased right at the airport.

CONSOLIDATORS➤ Consolidators buy tickets for scheduled flights at reduced rates from the airlines, then sell them at prices below the lowest available from the airlines directly—usually without advance restrictions. Sometimes you can even get your money back if you need to return the ticket. Carefully read the fine

print detailing penalties for changes and cancellations. If you doubt the reliability of a consolidator, **confirm your reservation with the airline.**

CHARTER FLIGHTS➤ Charters usually have the lowest fares and most restrictions. Departures are infrequent and seldom on time, and you can lose all or most of your money if you cancel. (The closer to departure you cancel, the more you lose, although sometimes you can pay only a small fee if you supply a substitute passenger.) The flight may be canceled for any reason up to 10 days before departure (after that, only if it is physically impossible to operate). The charterer may also revise the itinerary or increase the price after you have bought the ticket, but only if the new arrangement constitutes a "major change" do you have the right to a refund. Before buying a charter ticket, **read the fine print** regarding the company's refund policies. Money for charter flights is usually paid into a bank escrow account, the name of which should be on the contract, and if you don't pay by credit card, **make your check payable to the carrier's escrow account** (unless you're dealing with a travel agent, in which case his or her check should be made payable to the escrow account). The U.S. Department of Transportation's Aviation Consumer Protection Division has jurisdiction over charters.

Charter operators may offer flights alone or with ground arrangements that constitute a charter package. Normally, you must book charters through a travel agent.

ALOFT

AIRLINE FOOD➤ If you hate airline food, **ask for special meals when booking.** These can be vegetarian, low-cholesterol, or kosher, for example; commonly prepared to order in smaller quantities than standard fare, they can be tastier.

JET LAG➤ To avoid this syndrome, which occurs when travel disrupts your body's natural cycles, try to maintain a normal routine. At night, **get some sleep.** By day, move about the cabin to **stretch your legs, eat light meals, and drink water—not alcohol.** After you arrive, **wait until evening to catch up on sleep.**

SMOKING➤ Smoking is not allowed on flights of six hours or less within the continental United States. Smoking is also prohibited on flights within Canada. For U.S flights longer than six hours or international flights, **contact your carrier regarding the smoking policy.** Some carriers have prohibited smoking throughout their system; others allow smoking only on certain

routes or even departures of that route.

Foreign airlines are exempt from these rules but do provide no-smoking sections; British Airways has banned smoking, as has Virgin Atlantic on most international flights. Some countries have banned smoking on all domestic flights, and others may not allow smoking on some flights. Talks continue on the feasibility of broadening no-smoking policies.

WITHIN EUROPE

The deregulation of European air travel, begun in 1988, has been a slow process, and consumers have not experienced much of its expected benefits. Full-fare tickets are the only kind available for one-way trips and restriction-free round-trips on national carriers, and they are prohibitively expensive for leisure travelers—roughly double the price you pay to fly the same distance in the United States. For the most reasonable fares, **look for non-refundable and non-transferable round trips (APEX fares),** which almost always require a Saturday night at the destination.

Before booking, **compare different modes of transportation.** Many city pairs are so close together that flying hardly makes sense. For instance, it may take just half an hour to fly between London and Paris, but you must factor in time spent getting to and from the airports, plus check-in time. A 3-hour train

ride from city center to city center seems a better alternative.

It makes sense to **save air travel for longer distances**—say, between London and Rome, Paris and Vienna, Brussels and Stockholm—using round-trip APEX fares, and do your local traveling from these hubs. To date, there exists no such thing as a European air pass.

Before you travel, **check out what each airline has to offer by way of fixed-price flight coupons** (priced at $100–$120) to destinations from their respective hubs and/or domestic or area air passes. These must be bought before leaving home. If you're young, **ask about youth standby fares,** which are available on a number of domestic and some international services.

To find lower fares, **consider the new airlines that have emerged in Europe.** Most frequently they concentrate on key city pairs, where they offer a money-saving alternative to national carriers; occasionally they also serve previously overlooked secondary destinations. Among such carriers are Britain's Air U.K., France's TAT and Air Liberté, Sweden's Transwede and Malmoe Aviation, and Spain's Spanair.

If you're flying between countries, **look into the few no-frills international airlines,** notably Ireland's Ryanair and Britain's Virgin Express, both of which compete successfully with national carriers on high-density routes.

European airfares are nowhere near as complex as U.S fares. Even so, you are likely to spend more than you have to if you do your own shopping around rather, so **think about using a well-informed travel agent.** Best deals are often a well-kept secret, known only to on-the-spot agents. If you wish to deal with a travel agency that has offices in all major European cities, **consider American Express and Carlson/Wagonlit.**

On most European flights, your choice is between business class and economy (coach). Some flights are all economy. First class has ceased to exist in Europe.

AIRPORT PROCEDURES> Most European airport terminals have been modernized and up-graded in recent years to relieve congestion. For scheduled international flights, **arrive in time to check in one hour before departure**; for charter flights, allow two hours. Travelers with just hand luggage may be able to check in as late as 30 minutes before takeoff. If you're traveling business class, **ask about special deals**, such as check-in at designated hotels, or telephone check-in.

Passport control has become a perfunctory affair within most of the European Union, with the exception of Great Britain. When a number of flights from the U.S. arrive at Heathrow or Gatwick close together

in the morning, **be prepared for a longish wait** (though rarely as long as Europeans have to wait at JFK in New York).

The Green Channel/Red Channel customs system in operation at most western European airports and other borders is basically an honor system. If you have nothing to declare, walk through the Green Channel, where there are only spot luggage checks; if in doubt, go through the Red Channel. If you fly between two EU-member countries, go through the new Blue Channel, where there are no customs officers except the one who glances at baggage labels to make sure only people off EU flights get through. In a number of airports, unlicensed "taxi drivers" may accost you in the arrival hall; avoid them like the plague. On average, you need to **count on at least half an hour from deplaning to getting out of the airport.**

AIRPORT SHOPPING> If you're looking for good deals associated with duty-free airport shopping, **check out booze and beauty products,** although prices vary considerably. The amount of liquor you may buy is restricted, generally to two bottles. This form of shopping is will be phased out within the EU, possibly starting in 1999, but will continue in non-EU destinations.

Some airport concourses, notably in Amsterdam, Copenhagen, and Shannon,

have practically been transformed into shopping malls, selling everything from electronics and chocolates to fashion and furs. These are tax-free rather than duty-free shops; if this is your last stop before leaving the EU there's no VAT and you can **avoid the tax-refund rigmarole.**

B
BICYCLING

Some ferry lines transport bicycles free, but others charge a nominal fee, so **shop around.** You can also transport your bicycle by air as checked baggage—you usually won't have to pay extra as long as you are within the 44-pound total baggage allowance.

Most European rail lines will transport bicycles free of charge or for a nominal fee, but **book ahead.** Check with the main booking office.

Local and regional tourist information offices will have information about renting bicycles. (For bike tours of Europe, ☞ Tour Operators *in* Important Contacts A to Z, *above.*

BUS TRAVEL

International bus travel is rapidly expanding in Europe, thanks to changing EU rules and the Channel Tunnel, but it still has some way to go before it achieves the status of a natural choice like Greyhound. Favored by budget travelers and low-income immigrants visiting their home countries, buses remain the most inexpensive form of transportation. Before your trip, **compare the new services and passes** (☞ Bus Travel *in* Important Contacts A to Z, *above*). In northern Europe, the most highly developed domestic bus networks are those of Britain and Germany. In most other northern European countries, bus services exist mostly to supplement railroads.

In several southern European countries—including Portugal, Greece, parts of Spain, and Turkey—the bus has supplanted the train as the main means of public transportation, and is often quicker and more comfortable, with more frequent service, than the antiquated national rolling stock. Unless there is a particular scenic rail route you want to see, **choose the bus over the train in southern Europe**—but be prepared to discover that the bus is more expensive. Competition among lines is keen, so **ask about air-conditioning and reclining seats** before you book.

National or regional tourist offices have information about bus services. For reservations on major lines before you go, **contact your travel agent at home.**

C

CAMERAS, CAMCORDERS, & COMPUTERS

IN TRANSIT

Always **keep your film, tape, or disks out of the sun;** never put them on a car dashboard. Carry an extra supply of batteries, and **be prepared to turn on your camera, camcorder, or laptop computer for security personnel** to prove that it's real.

X-RAYS

Always **ask for hand inspection at security.** Such requests are virtually always honored at U.S. airports, and are usually accommodated abroad. Photographic film becomes clouded after successive exposure to airport x-ray machines. Videotape and computer disks are not harmed by X-rays, but **keep your tapes and disks away from metal detectors.**

CUSTOMS

Before departing, **register your foreign-made camera or laptop with U.S. Customs.** If your equipment is U.S.-made, call the consulate of the country you'll be visiting to find out whether it should be registered with local customs upon arrival.

CAR RENTAL

The decision to rent a car depends not only on cost but also on where and how you want to travel in Europe. Cost-wise, you should **consider renting a car only if you are with at least one other person;** single travelers pay a tremendous premium. Car rental costs vary from country to country; rates in Scandinavia and Eastern Europe are particularly high. If you're visiting a number of countries with varying rates, it may be possible to **rent a vehicle in the cheapest country.**

In cities like London and Paris, a car can be more burden than asset. It is often more relaxing to **rent a car specifically for touring around a country or area,** using public transportation for in-city and inter-city travel.

Picking up a car at an airport is convenient but often costs extra (up to 10%) as rental companies pass along the fees charged to them by airports. Also, **decide if getting into an unfamiliar car right after a transatlantic flight is advisable for you.**

CUTTING COSTS

To save money, don't wait to arrive in Europe; instead, **reserve in advance at a guaranteed dollar rate.** For the best deal, **book through a travel agent who is willing to shop around.** Ask your agent to **look for fly-drive packages,** which also save you money, and **ask if local taxes, including value-added tax (VAT), are included** in the rental or fly-drive price. These can be as high as 20% in some destinations. Don't forget to find out about required deposits, cancellation penalties, drop-off charges, and the cost of any required insurance coverage.

Also **ask your travel agent about a company's customer-service record.** How has it responded to late plane arrivals and vehicle mishaps? Are there often lines at the rental counter, and—if you're traveling during a holiday period—does a confirmed reservation guarantee you a car?

Always **find out what equipment is standard** at your destination before specifying what you want; automatic transmission and air-conditioning are usually optional—and very expensive. When renting in Great Britain or Ireland, however, you may consider paying extra for an automatic if you are unfamiliar with manual transmissions. Driving on the "wrong" side of the road will probably be enough to worry about. Many travelers prefer a midsize car, which typically rents for about $40 more than a subcompact.

Be sure to **look into wholesalers**—companies that do not own their own fleets but rent in bulk from those that do and often offer better rates than traditional car-rental operations. Prices are best during off-peak periods; rentals booked through wholesalers must be paid for before you leave the United States.

INSURANCE

When driving a rented car, you are generally responsible for any damage to or loss of the rental vehicle. Before you rent, **see what coverage you already have** under the terms of your personal auto insurance policy and credit cards.

If you do not have auto insurance or an umbrella insurance policy that covers damage to third parties, purchasing CDW or LDW is highly recommended.

Collision policies that car-rental companies sell for European

rentals typically do not cover stolen vehicles. Before you buy additional coverage for theft, find out if your credit card or personal auto insurance will cover the loss. All car-rental companies operating in Italy mandate the purchase of theft-protection policies.

LICENSE REQUIREMENTS

Your own driver's license is acceptable virtually everywhere. An International Driver's Permit is a good idea; it's available from the American or Canadian automobile associations, or, in the United Kingdom, from the AA or RAC.

SURCHARGES

Before you pick up a car in one city and leave it in another, **ask about drop-off charges or one-way service fees,** which can be substantial. Note, too, that some rental agencies charge extra if you return the car before the time specified on your contract. The best deals are weekly rates, but **be sure to keep a car on weekly rental at least 5 days** or you may be charged higher daily rates. To avoid a hefty refueling fee, **fill the tank just before you turn in the car**—but be aware that gas stations near the rental outlet may overcharge.

CHANNEL TUNNEL

The "Chunnel" is the fastest way to cross the English Channel short of flying—35 minutes from Folkestone to Calais, 60 minutes from motorway to motorway, or 3 hours from

Waterloo, London, to Paris's Gare du Nord, and 3¼ hours from London to Brussels's Gare du Midi. It consists of two large 50-kilometer- (31-mile-) long train tunnels, and a smaller service tunnel running between them. For further information, *see* Train Travel, *below.*

CHILDREN & TRAVEL

When traveling with children, **plan ahead** and **involve your youngsters** as you outline your trip. When packing, **include a supply of things to keep them busy** en route (☞ Children & Travel *in* Important Contacts A to Z). On sightseeing days, try to **schedule activities of special interest to your children,** like a trip to a zoo or a playground. If you **plan your itinerary around seasonal festivals,** you'll never lack for things to do. In addition, **check local newspapers for special events** mounted by public libraries, museums, and parks.

BABY-SITTING

For recommended local sitters, **check with your hotel desk.**

DRIVING

If you are renting a car, don't forget to **arrange for a car seat when you reserve.** Sometimes they're free.

FLYING

Always **ask about discounted children's fares.** On international flights, infants under 2 not occupying a seat generally travel free or for 10% of the accompanying adult's fare; the fare for children ages

2–11 is usually half to two-thirds of the adult fare. On domestic flights, children under 2 not occupying a seat travel free, and older children are charged at the lowest applicable adult rate.

BAGGAGE➤ In general, the adult baggage allowance applies to children paying half or more of the adult fare. If you are traveling with an infant, **ask about carry-on allowances** before departure. In general, for infants charged 10% of the adult fare you are allowed one carry-on bag and a collapsible stroller; you may be limited to less if the flight is full.

SAFETY SEATS➤ According to the FAA, it's a good idea to **use safety seats aloft** for children weighing less than 40 pounds. Airline policies vary. U.S. carriers allow FAA-approved models but usually require that you buy a ticket, even if your child would otherwise ride free, since the seats must be strapped into regular seats. Foreign carriers may not allow infant seats, may charge a child rather than an infant fare for their use, or may require you to hold your baby during takeoff and landing—defeating the seat's purpose.

FACILITIES➤ When making your reservation, **request for children's meals or freestanding bassinets** if you need them; the latter are available only to those seated at the bulkhead, where there's enough legroom. If you don't need a bassinet,

think twice before requesting bulkhead seats—the only storage space for in-flight necessities is in inconveniently distant overhead bins.

GAMES

In local toy stores, **look for travel versions of popular games** such as Trouble, Sorry, and Monopoly ($5–$8).

LODGING

Most hotels allow children under a certain age to stay in their parents' room at no extra charge; others charge them as extra adults. Be sure to **ask about the cutoff age.**

CUSTOMS & DUTIES

To speed your clearance through customs, **keep receipts for all your purchases abroad.** If you feel that you've been incorrectly or unfairly charged a duty, you can **appeal assessments in dispute.** First ask to see a supervisor. If you are still not satisfied, **write to the port director** at your point of entry, sending your customs receipt and any other appropriate documentation. The address will be listed on your receipt. If you still don't get satisfaction, you can take your case to customs headquarters in Washington.

IN EUROPE

See individual country chapters for limits on imports.

IN THE U.S.

You may bring home $400 worth of foreign goods duty-free if you've been out of the country for at least 48 hours and haven't already used the

$400 allowance, or any part of it, in the past 30 days.

Travelers 21 or older may bring back 1 liter of alcohol duty-free, provided the beverage laws of the state through which they reenter the United States allow it. In addition, regardless of their age, they are allowed 100 non-Cuban cigars and 200 cigarettes. Antiques and works of art more than 100 years old are duty-free.

Duty-free, travelers may mail packages valued at up to $200 to themselves and up to $100 to others, with a limit of one parcel per addressee per day (and no alcohol or tobacco products or perfume valued at more than $5); on the outside, the package should be labeled as being either for personal use or an unsolicited gift, and a list of its contents and their retail value should be attached. Mailed items do not affect your duty-free allowance on your return.

IN CANADA

If you've been out of Canada for at least seven days, you may bring in C$500 worth of goods duty-free. If you've been away for fewer than seven days but more than 48 hours, the duty-free allowance drops to C$200; if your trip lasts between 24 and 48 hours, the allowance is C$50. You cannot pool allowances with family members. Goods claimed under the C$500 exemption may follow you by mail; those claimed under the lesser exemptions must accompany you.

Alcohol and tobacco products may be included in the seven-day and 48-hour exemptions but not in the 24-hour exemption. If you meet the age requirements of the province or territory through which you reenter Canada, you may bring in, duty-free, 1.14 liters (40 imperial ounces) of wine or liquor *or* 24 12-ounce cans or bottles of beer or ale. If you are 16 or older, you may bring in, duty-free, 200 cigarettes, 50 cigars or cigarillos, and 400 tobacco sticks or 400 grams of manufactured tobacco. Alcohol and tobacco must accompany you on your return.

An unlimited number of gifts with a value of up to C$60 each may be mailed to Canada dutyfree. These do not affect your duty-free allowance on your return. Label the package "Unsolicited Gift— Value Under $60." Alcohol and tobacco are excluded.

IN THE U.K.

If your journey was wholly within European Union (EU) countries, you no longer need to pass through customs when you return to the United Kingdom. If you plan to bring back large quantities of alcohol or tobacco, check in advance on EU limits.

From countries outside the EU, you may import, duty-free, 200 cigarettes, 100 cigarillos, 50 cigars, or 250 grams of tobacco; 1 liter of spirits or 2 liters of fortified or sparkling wine or liqueurs; 2 liters of still table wine; 60 milliliters of perfume; 250 milliliters of toilet water; plus £136 worth of other goods, including gifts and souvenirs.

D
DISABILITIES & ACCESSIBILITY

When discussing accessibility with an operator or reservationist, **ask hard questions.** Are there any stairs, inside *or* out? Are there grab bars next to the toilet *and* in the shower/tub? How wide is the doorway to the room? To the bathroom? For the most extensive facilities, **opt for newer accommodations,** which more often have been designed with access in mind. Older properties or ships must usually be retrofitted and may offer more limited facilities as a result. Be sure to **discuss your needs before booking.**

DISCOUNTS & DEALS

You shouldn't have to pay for a discount. In fact, you may already be eligible for all kinds of savings. Here are some time-honored strategies for getting the best deal.

LOOK IN YOUR WALLET

When you **use your credit card to make travel purchases,** you may get free travel-accident insurance, collision damage insurance, medical or legal assistance, depending on the card and bank that issued it. Visa and MasterCard provide one or more of these services, so **get a copy of your card's travel benefits.** If you are a member of the AAA or an oil-company-sponsored road-assistance plan, always **ask hotel or car-rental reservationists for auto-club discounts.** Some clubs offer additional discounts on tours, cruises, or admission to attractions. And don't forget that auto-club membership entitles you to free maps and trip-planning services.

DIAL FOR DOLLARS

To save money, **look into "1-800" discount reservations services,** which often have lower rates. These services use their buying power to get a better price on hotels, airline tickets, and sometimes even car rentals. When booking a room, always **call the hotel's local toll-free number** (if one is available) rather than the central reservations number—you'll often get a better price. Ask the reservationist about special packages or corporate rates, which are usually available even if you're not traveling on business.

JOIN A CLUB?

Discount clubs can be a legitimate source of savings, but you must use the participating hotels and visit the participating attractions in order to realize any benefits. Remember, too, that you have to pay a fee to join, so **determine if you'll save enough to warrant your membership fee.** Before booking with a club, make sure the hotel or other supplier isn't offering a better deal.

GET A GUARANTEE

When shopping for the best deal on hotels and car rentals, **look for guaranteed exchange rates,** which protect you against a falling dollar. With your rate locked in, you won't pay more even if the price goes up in the local currency.

SENIOR CITIZENS & STUDENTS

As a senior-citizen traveler, you may be eligible for special rates, but you should mention your senior-citizen status up front. If you're a students or under 26 can also get discounts, especially if you have an official ID card (☞ Senior-Citizen Discounts *and* Students on the Road, *below*).

DRIVING

ADD-ON COSTS

Be prepared: Gasoline costs three to four times as much as in the United States, due to heavy taxes. The better fuel economy of European cars offsets the higher price to some extent.

Motorway tolls can easily add $25 a day to your costs in driving through France, and there are toll roads throughout southern Europe, as well as charges for many tunnels. To get a handle on costs, **ask the national tourist office or car rental firm before you travel.**

BORDERS

Ten of the countries of the European Union are signatories to the so-called Schengen Agreement abolishing border controls. The border posts are still standing, but drivers whiz through them without slowing down. Truck traffic is generally routed to separate checkpoints. However, individual countries can temporarily suspend the accord, and traffic backups can result.

DOCUMENTATION

If you are driving a rented car, **be sure to carry the necessary papers provided by the rental company.** For U.K. citizens, if the vehicle is your own, you will need proof of ownership, a certificate of roadworthiness (known as a Ministry of Transport, or MOT, road vehicle certificate), up-to-date vehicle registration or tax, and a Green Card proof of insurance, available from your insurance company (fees vary depending on destination and length of stay).

ROADS AND RULES

Establishing a speed limit for German motorways has proved a tougher nut than any successive government could crack. On the rest of the Continent, the limit is generally 130 kph (80 mph), but the cruising speed is mostly about 140 kph (about 87 mph). In the United Kingdom, the speed limit is 70 mph (112 kph), but there, too, passing at considerably higher speed is not uncommon. For safe driving, **go with the flow, stay in the slower lane unless you want to pass, and make way for faster cars wanting to pass you.** Much of the time traffic is heavier than is common on U.S. freeways outside major city rush hours.

Most visitors will find it rewarding to **avoid the freeways and use the alternative and toll-free main routes.** Wherever you're driving, **be sure to carry a good road map.** You can purchase maps in book shops and many newsstands at home and throughout Europe.

In the United Kingdom, the Republic of Ireland, Malta, Cyprus, and Gibraltar, cars drive on the left. In other European countries, traffic is on the right. If you're coming off ferries from Britain or Ireland to the Continent (and vice versa), **beware the transition.**

Drivers traveling between Great Britain and the Continent can now **consider using the Channel Tunnel** as well as ferries. Le Shuttle trains carry cars, trucks, buses, and motorbikes. For further information, *see* Train Travel *in* Important Contacts A to Z, *above,* and *below.*

TRAFFIC

During peak vacation periods, main routes can be jammed with holiday traffic. In the United Kingdom, **try to avoid driving during any of the long bank-holiday (public holiday) weekends,** when motorways can be clogged. The tunnels carrying traffic between Italy and the countries to the north are often overburdened with truck traffic; cross the Alps on a

Sunday. In France, Spain, and Italy, huge numbers of people still take a fixed one-month vacation in August, so **avoid driving during le départ,** the first weekend in August, when vast numbers of drivers head south; or *le retour,* when they head back.

F

FERRY TRAVEL

Ferry routes for passengers and vehicles link the countries surrounding the North Sea, the Irish Sea, and the Baltic; Italy with Greece; and Spain, France, Italy and Greece with their respective islands in the Mediterranean. Longer ferry routes—between, for instance, Britain and Spain or Scandinavia—can help you **reduce the amount of driving and often save time.** Prices can be appealing, as companies respond to the opening of the Channel Tunnel and the fierce competition on many routes. A number of modern ships offer improved comfort and entertainment ranging from one-armed bandits to gourmet dining. They also have well-stocked duty-free shops. Improved safety procedures and systems have been introduced on most roll-on, roll-off ships. For ferry operators, *see* Important Contacts A to Z, *above.*

I

INSURANCE

Travel insurance can protect your monetary investment, replace your luggage and its contents, or provide for medical coverage should you fall ill

during your trip. Most tour operators, travel agents, and insurance agents sell specialized health-and-accident, flight, trip-cancellation, and luggage insurance as well as comprehensive policies with some or all of these coverages. Comprehensive policies may also reimburse you for delays due to weather—an important consideration if you're traveling during the winter months. Some health-insurance policies do not cover preexisting conditions, but waivers may be available in specific cases. Coverage is sold by the companies listed in Important Contacts A to Z; these companies act as the policy's administrators. The actual insurance is usually underwritten by a well-known name, such as The Travelers or Continental Insurance.

Before you make any purchase, **review your existing health and homeowner's policies** to find out whether they cover expenses incurred while traveling.

BAGGAGE

Airline liability for baggage is limited to $1,250 per person on domestic flights. On international flights, it amounts to $9.07 per pound or $20 per kilogram for checked baggage (roughly $640 per 70-pound bag) and $400 per passenger for unchecked baggage. Insurance for losses exceeding the terms of your airline ticket can be bought directly from the airline at check-in for about $10 per $1,000 of coverage;

note that it excludes a rather extensive list of items, shown on your airline ticket.

COMPREHENSIVE

Comprehensive insurance policies include all the coverages described above plus some that may not be available in more specific policies. If you have purchased an expensive vacation, especially one that involves travel abroad, comprehensive insurance is a must; **look for policies that include trip delay insurance,** which will protect you in the event that weather problems cause you to miss your flight, tour, or cruise. A few insurers will also sell you a waiver for preexisting medical conditions. Some of the companies that offer both these features are Access America, Carefree Travel, Travel Insured International, and TravelGuard (☞ Important Contacts A to Z).

FLIGHT

You should **think twice before buying flight insurance.** Often purchased as a last-minute impulse at the airport, it pays a lump sum when a plane crashes, either to a beneficiary if the insured dies or sometimes to a surviving passenger who loses his or her eyesight or a limb. Supplementing the airlines' coverage described in the limits-of-liability paragraphs on your ticket, it's expensive and basically unnecessary. Charging an airline ticket to a major credit card often automatically provides you with coverage that may also extend to travel by bus, train, and ship.

HEALTH

Medicare generally does not cover health care costs outside the United States; nor do many privately issued policies. If your own health insurance policy does not cover you outside the United States, **consider buying supplemental medical coverage.** It can reimburse you for $1,000–$150,000 worth of medical and/or dental expenses incurred as a result of an accident or illness during a trip. These policies also may include a personal-accident, or death-and-dismemberment, provision, which pays a lump sum ranging from $15,000 to $500,000 to your beneficiaries if you die or to you if you lose one or more limbs or your eyesight, and a medical-assistance provision, which may either reimburse you for the cost of referrals, evacuation, or repatriation and other services, or automatically enroll you as a member of a particular medical-assistance company. (☞ Health Issues *in* Important Contacts A to Z.)

U.K. TRAVELERS

You can buy an annual travel insurance policy valid for most vacations during the year in which it's purchased. If you are pregnant or have a preexisting medical condition make sure you're covered before buying such a policy.

TRIP

Without insurance, you will lose all or most of your money if you cancel your trip regardless of the reason. Especially if your airline ticket, cruise, or package tour is nonrefundable and cannot be changed, it's essential that you **buy trip-cancellation-and-interruption insurance.** When considering how much coverage you need, look for a policy that will cover the cost of your trip plus the nondiscounted price of a one-way airline ticket should you need to return home early. Read the fine print carefully, especially sections that define "family member" and "preexisting medical conditions." Also **consider default or bankruptcy insurance,** which protects you against a supplier's failure to deliver. Be aware, however, that if you buy such a policy from a travel agency, tour operator, airline, or cruise line, it may not cover default by the firm in question.

L

LODGING

APARTMENT & VILLA RENTAL

If you want a home base that's roomy enough for a family and comes with cooking facilities, **consider taking a furnished rental.** This can also save you money, but not always—some rentals are luxury properties (economical only when your party is large). Home-exchange directories list rentals—often second homes owned by prospective house swappers—and some services search for a house or apartment for you (even a castle if that's your fancy) and handle the paperwork. Some send an illustrated catalog; others send photographs only of specific properties, sometimes at a charge; up-front registration fees may apply.

HOME EXCHANGE

If you would like to find a house, an apartment, or some other type of vacation property to exchange for your own while on holiday, **become a member of a home-exchange organization,** which will send you its updated listings of available exchanges for a year, and will include your own listing in at least one of them. Arrangements for the actual exchange are made by the two parties involved, not by the organization.

M

MEDICAL ASSISTANCE

No one plans to get sick while traveling, but it happens, so **consider signing up with a medical assistance company.** These outfits provide referrals, emergency evacuation or repatriation, 24-hour telephone hot lines for medical consultation, cash for emergencies, and other personal and legal assistance. They also dispatch medical personnel and arrange for the relay of medical records.

MONEY

ATMS

CASH ADVANCES➤ Before leaving home, **make sure that your**

credit cards have been programmed for ATM use in Europe. Note that Discover is accepted mostly in the United States. Local bank cards often do not work overseas either; ask your bank about a Global Access debit card, which works like a bank card but can be used at any ATM displaying a Visa Logo.

TRANSACTION FEES> On credit-card cash advances you are charged interest from the day you receive the money, whether from a teller or an ATM. Although fees charged for ATM transactions may be higher abroad than at home, Cirrus and Plus exchange rates are excellent, because they are based on wholesale rates offered only by major banks.

EXCHANGING CURRENCY

For the most favorable rates, change money at banks. You won't do as well at exchange booths in airports or rail and bus stations, in hotels, in restaurants, or in stores, although you may find their hours more convenient. To avoid lines at airport exchange booths, get a small amount of the local currency before you leave home.

TAXES

VAT> If you shop in Europe, get a value-added tax (VAT) refund. For EU countries, have tax-refund forms from the store stamped at customs as you leave your final EU country; send the stamped form back to the store. For information about value-added tax (VAT)

refunds, *see* the individual country chapters (also ☞ Money *in* Important Contacts A to Z, *above*).

TRAVELER'S CHECKS

Whether or not to buy traveler's checks depends on where you are headed; take cash to rural areas and small towns, traveler's checks to cities. The most widely recognized checks are issued by American Express, Citicorp, Thomas Cook, and Visa. These are sold by major commercial banks for 1%–3% of the checks' face value—it pays to shop around. Both American Express and Thomas Cook issue checks that can be countersigned and used by either you or your traveling companion, and they both provide checks, at no extra charge, valued in various non-U.S. currencies. So you won't be left with excess foreign currency, buy a few checks in small denominations to cash toward the end of your trip. Before leaving home, contact your issuer for information on where to cash your checks without incurring a transaction fee. Record the numbers of all your checks, and keep this listing in a separate place, crossing off the numbers of checks you have cashed.

WIRING MONEY

For a fee of 3%—10%, depending on the amount of the transaction, you can have money sent to you from home through Money-Gram^{SM} or Western

Union (☞ Money Matters *in* Important Contacts A to Z). The transferred funds and the service fee can be charged to a Master-Card or Visa account.

P

PACKING FOR EUROPE

What you pack depends more on the season than on any particular dress code. In general, northern and central Europe have cold, snowy winters, and the Mediterranean countries have mild winters, though parts of southern Europe can be bitterly cold, too. In the Mediterranean resorts you may need a warm jacket for mornings and evenings, even in summer. The mountains usually are warm on summer days, but the weather is unpredictable, and the nights are generally cool.

For European cities, pack as you would for an American city; formal outfits for first-class restaurants and nightclubs, casual clothes elsewhere. Jeans are perfectly acceptable for sightseeing and informal dining. Sturdy walking shoes are appropriate for the cobblestone streets and gravel paths that fill many of the parks and surround some of the historic buildings. For visits to churches, cathedrals, and mosques, avoid shorts and revealing outfits. In Italy, women cover their shoulders and arms (a shawl will do). Women, however, no longer need to cover their heads in Roman Catholic churches. In

Turkey, though, women must have a head covering; a long-sleeved shirt and a long skirt or slacks are required.

To discourage purse snatchers and pickpockets, **take a handbag with long straps** that you can sling across your body, bandolier-style, and with a zippered compartment for money.

If you stay in budget hotels, **take your own soap.** Bring an extra pair of eyeglasses or contact lenses in your carry-on luggage, and if you have a health problem, **pack enough medication** to last the trip or have your doctor write you a prescription using the drug's generic name, because brand names vary from country to country (you'll then need a duplicate prescription from a local doctor). It's important that you **don't put prescription drugs or valuables in luggage to be checked,** for it could go astray. To avoid problems with customs officials, carry medications in the original packaging. Also, don't forget the addresses of offices that handle refunds of lost traveler's checks.

ELECTRICITY

To use your U.S.-purchased electric-powered equipment, **bring a converter and an adapter.** The electrical current in Europe is 220 volts, 50 cycles alternating current (AC); wall outlets in most of Europe take plugs with two round prongs; Great Britain (also Malta) uses plugs with three oblong prongs.

If your appliances are dual-voltage, you'll need only an adapter. Hotels sometimes have 110-volt outlets for low-wattage appliances near the sink, marked FOR SHAVERS ONLY; don't use them for high-wattage appliances like blow-dryers. If your laptop computer is older, carry a converter; new laptops operate equally well on 110 and 220 volts, so you need only an adapter.

LUGGAGE

Airline baggage allowances depend on the airline, the route, and the class of your ticket; **ask in advance.** In general, on domestic flights and on international flights between the United States and foreign destinations, you are entitled to check two bags. A third piece may be brought on board, but it must fit easily under the seat in front of you or in the overhead compartment. In the United States, the FAA gives airlines broad latitude regarding carry-on allowances, and they tend to tailor them to different aircraft and operational conditions. Charges for excess, oversize, or overweight pieces vary.

If you are flying between two foreign destinations, note that baggage allowances may be determined not by piece but by weight—generally 88 pounds (40 kilograms) in first class, 66 pounds (30 kilograms) in business class, and 44 pounds (20 kilograms) in economy. If your flight between two cities abroad *connects* with

your transatlantic or transpacific flight, the piece method still applies.

SAFEGUARDING YOUR LUGGAGE➤ Before leaving home, **itemize your bags' contents** and their worth, and label them with your name, address, and phone number. (If you use your home address, cover it so that potential thieves can't see it readily.) Inside each bag, **pack a copy of your itinerary.** At check-in, **make sure that each bag is correctly tagged** with the destination airport's three-letter code. If your bags arrive damaged—or fail to arrive at all—file a written report with the airline before leaving the airport.

PASSPORTS & VISAS

If you don't already have one, **get a passport.** It is advisable that you **leave one photocopy of your passport's data page** with someone at home and keep another with you, separated from your passport, while traveling. If you lose your passport, promptly call the nearest embassy or consulate and the local police; having the data page information can speed replacement.

U.S. CITIZENS

All U.S. citizens, even infants, need a valid passport to enter the countries covered in this guide; visitors to Turkey also need a visa. See the individual country chapters for any visa requirements or limits on the length of your stay. Application forms for both first-time and renewal passports are available at any of the 13 U.S. Passport Agency offices and at some post offices and courthouses. Passports are usually mailed within four weeks; allow five weeks or more in spring and summer.

CANADIANS

You need a valid passport to enter the countries covered in this guide. See the individual country chapters for any visa requirements or limits on the length of your stay. Passport application forms are available at 28 regional passport offices, as well as post offices and travel agencies. Whether for a first or a renewal passport, you must apply in person. Children under 16 may be included on a parent's passport but must have their own to travel alone. Passports are valid for five years and are usually mailed within two to three weeks of application.

U.K. CITIZENS

Citizens of the United Kingdom need a valid passport to enter the countries covered in this guide. See the individual country chapters for any visa requirements or limits on the length of your stay. Applications for new and renewal passports are available from main post offices and at the passport offices in Belfast, Glasgow, Liverpool, London, Newport, and Peterborough. You may apply in person at all passport offices, or by mail to all except the London office. Children under

16 may travel on an accompanying parent's passport. All passports are valid for 10 years. Allow a month for processing.

S

SENIOR-CITIZEN DISCOUNTS

To qualify for age-related discounts, **mention your senior-citizen status up front** when booking hotel reservations, not when checking out, and before you're seated in restaurants, not when paying the bill. Note that discounts may be limited to certain menus, days, or hours. When renting a car, **ask about promotional car-rental discounts**—they can net even lower costs than your senior-citizen discount.

Radisson SAS Hotels in Europe offer a restriction-free 65+ discount. Customers aged 65 and more qualify for a discount equal to their age in percentage points.

STUDENTS ON THE ROAD

To save money, **look into deals available through student-oriented travel agencies.** To qualify, you'll need to have a bona fide student ID card. Members of international student groups are also eligible (☞ Students *in* Important Contacts A to Z).

T

TELEPHONES

LONG-DISTANCE

The long-distance services of AT&T, MCI, and Sprint make calling

home relatively convenient, but in many hotels you may find it impossible to dial the access number. The hotel operator may also refuse to make the connection. Instead, the hotel will charge you a premium rate—as much as 400% more than a calling card—for calls placed from your hotel room. To avoid such price gouging, travel with more than one company's long-distance calling card—a hotel may block Sprint but not MCI. If the hotel operator claims that you cannot use any phone card, ask to be connected to an international operator, who will help you to access your phone card. You can also dial the international operator yourself. If none of this works, try calling your phone company collect in the United States. If collect calls are also blocked, call from a pay phone in the hotel lobby. Before you go, **find out the local access codes** for your destinations.

TOUR OPERATORS

A package or tour to Europe can make your vacation less expensive and more hassle-free. Firms that sell tours and packages reserve airline seats, hotel rooms, and rental cars in bulk and pass some of the savings on to you. In addition, the best operators have local representatives available to help you at your destination.

A GOOD DEAL?

The more your package or tour includes, the better you can predict the ultimate cost of your vacation. Make sure you know exactly what is covered, and **beware of hidden costs.** Are taxes, tips, and service charges included? Transfers and baggage handling? Entertainment and excursions? These can add up.

Most packages and tours are rated deluxe, first-class superior, first class, tourist, or budget. The key difference is usually accommodations. If the package or tour you are considering is priced lower than in your wildest dreams, **be skeptical.** Also, **make sure your travel agent knows the accommodations** and other services. Ask about the hotel's location, room size, beds, and whether it has a pool, room service, or programs for children, if you care about these. Has your agent been there in person or sent others you can contact?

BUYER BEWARE

Each year a number of consumers are stranded or lose their money when operators—even very large ones with excellent reputations—go out of business. To avoid becoming one of them, take the time to **check out the operator**—find out how long the company has been in business and ask several agents about its reputation. Next, **don't book unless the firm has a consumer-protection program.** Members of the USTOA and the NTA are required to set aside funds for the sole purpose of covering your payments and travel arrangements in case of

default. Nonmember operators may instead carry insurance; look for the details in the operator's brochure— and for the name of an underwriter with a solid reputation. Note: When it comes to tour operators, **don't trust escrow accounts.** Although there are laws governing those of charter-flight operators, no governmental body prevents tour operators from raiding the till.

Next, **contact your local Better Business Bureau and the attorney general's offices** in both your own state and the operator's; have any complaints been filed? Finally, **pay with a major credit card.** Then you can cancel payment, provided that you can document your complaint. Always **consider trip-cancellation insurance** (☞ Insurance, *above*).

Big vs. Small➢ Operators that handle several hundred thousand travelers per year can use their purchasing power to give you a good price. Their high volume may also indicate financial stability. But some small companies provide more personalized service; because they tend to specialize, they may also be more knowledgeable about a given area.

USING AN AGENT

Travel agents are excellent resources. In fact, large operators accept bookings made only through travel agents. But it's good to **collect brochures from several agencies** because some agents' suggestions may be skewed by promo-

tional relationships with tour and package firms that reward them for volume sales. If you have a special interest, **find an agent with expertise in that area;** ASTA can provide leads in the United States. (Don't rely solely on your agent, though; agents may be unaware of small-niche operators, and some special-interest travel companies only sell direct.)

SINGLE TRAVELERS

Prices are usually quoted per person, based on two sharing a room. If traveling solo, you may be required to pay the full double-occupancy rate. Some operators eliminate this surcharge if you agree to be matched up with a roommate of the same sex, even if one is not found by departure time.

TRAIN TRAVEL

DISCOUNT PASSES

You can **use Eurail-Passes** in 17 European countries: Austria, Belgium, Denmark, Finland, France, Germany, Greece, Hungary, the Irish Republic, Italy, Luxembourg, the Netherlands, Norway, Portugal, Spain, Sweden, and Switzerland (but not England, Scotland, Northern Ireland, or Wales). EurailPasses provide unlimited first-class rail travel, in all of the participating countries, for the duration of the pass. If you plan to rack up the miles, get a standard pass. These are available for 15 days ($522), 21 days ($678), one month ($838), two months ($1,148), and 3 months ($1,468). If your plans call for only limited train travel, **look into a Europass,** which costs less money than a EurailPass. Unlike EurailPasses, however, you get a limited number of travel days, in a limited number of countries, during a specified time period. For example, a two-month Europass ($316) allows between five and fifteen days of rail travel, but costs $200 less than the least expensive EurailPass. Keep in mind, however, that the Europass is good only in France, Germany, Italy, Spain, and Switzerland, and the number of countries you can visit is further limited by the type of pass you buy. For example, the basic two-month EuroPass allows you to visit only three of the five participating countries.

In addition to standard EurailPasses, **ask about special rail-pass plans.** Among these are the Eurail Youthpass (for those under age 26), the Eurail Saverpass (which gives a discount for two or more people traveling together), a Eurail Flexipass (which allows a certain number of travel days within a set period), the Euraildrive Pass and the Europass Drive (which combines travel by train and rental car).

Whichever EurailPass or Europass you choose, remember that you must **purchase your pass before you leave** for Europe.

If you're planning to travel in just one country, **look into single-country rail passes.** Some are available in the United States and may be sold in the destination as well.

Many travelers assume that rail passes guarantee them seats on the trains they wish to ride. Not so. You need to **book seats ahead even if you are using a rail pass**; seat reservations are required on some European trains, particularly high-speed trains, and are a good idea on trains that may be crowded—particularly in summer on popular routes. You will also need a reservation if you purchase sleeping accommodations.

European nationals and others who have resided in Europe for at least six months and under 27 qualify for the **Inter Rail Pass.** This entitles you to unlimited second-class travel within up to seven zones you have preselected. One zone for 15 days, for instance, costs $280; all zones for one month, $415. Inter Rail Passes can be bought only in Europe at main rail stations.

FROM THE U.K.

CHANNEL TUNNEL➤ Le Shuttle, a special car, bus, and truck train, operates continuously through the Channel Tunnel. Reservations are not needed, but tickets may be bought in advance from travel agents.

Eurostar train service uses the Channel Tunnel to link London (Walterloo) with Paris (Gare du Nord) in 3 hours and with Brussels (Gare du Midi) in 3¼ hours. If you'll be traveling in France, **ask about high-speed (TGV)**

connections to other cities in France. On the British side, Eurostar train service from Manchester and Birmingham to Paris, bypassing London, is to start in summer 1996, and service from Glasgow and Edinburgh by early 1997.

Intense competition with the ferry companies has inspired a multitude of promotional rates, both on the ships and the train, so **always check for special prices and deals.** Over time, it is likely that early reservations (8 to 30 days in advance) will be rewarded, rather than weekend stays.

FERRIES➤ Conventional boat trains timed to meet ferries at Channel ports leave London and connect with onward trains at the main French and Belgian ports. Calais and Boulogne have the best quick connections for Paris (total journey time about six to seven hours using the cross-Channel Hovercraft); the Ramsgate–Oostende Jetfoil provides the fastest rail-sea connection to Brussels (about 6 hours, station to station), with good rail connections to Germany and points east.

Boat trains connecting with ferries from Harwich to the Dutch and Danish North Sea ports leave from London/Liverpool Street; there are good rail connections from the Dutch ports to Amsterdam and onward to Germany and Belgium and south to France. For the Republic of Ireland, trains connecting with the

THE GOLD GUIDE / SMART TRAVEL TIPS

ferry services across the Irish Sea leave from London/Euston and London/Paddington.

WITHIN EUROPE

If you're at all time- and cost-conscious, **take a serious look at train travel.** High-speed trains have started to challenge air travel on both short and medium-length distances, and even first-class train travel is consistently 60%–75% cheaper than the lowest available one-way airline fare. French TGV trains now serve virtually all major cities in France and also extend southeast to Geneva and Lausanne, north to Brussels and (from summer 1996) Amsterdam and Lièe. Germany's equally fast ICE trains run on special track from Hamburg to Frankfurt and Munich, and on conventional track to Basel and Zurich. Italy's Pendolino trains are scheduled to cut an hour off the journey from Milan to Switzerland, starting the summer of 1996. Similarly, Sweden's X2000 and Spain's AVE trains have made rail competitive with air in these countries. Because of the number of new trains, **ask about any new trains on your route.**

Britain has chosen not to participate in this development. The new rail line that will permit Eurostar trains to travel at full speed from Dover to London has not begun to be built.

Most European systems operate a two-tier class system. If you're considering first class, **be aware that it costs**

substantially more and is usually a luxury rather than a necessity. Some of the poorer European countries retain a third class, but avoid it unless you are on a rock-bottom budget.

Customs and, where applicable, passport formalities are generally completed onboard international trains.

For additional information on rail services and special fares, contact the national tourist office of the country (☞ Visitor Information *in* Important Contacts A to Z; *also* ☞ Train Travel *in* Important Contacts A to Z).

TRANSPORTATION IN EUROPE

Planning the trip is half the fun. Getting around Europe may mean evaluating a variety of transportation methods, so equip yourself with maps, timetables, and brochures and **plan your itinerary using the mix of means of transportation that suits your budget and the amount of time you have.** Even the best-informed travel agents may not have the time to outline all the options, but seek out their advice on your final choice. To help you evaluate your options, take a look at Air Travel, Bus Travel, Car Rental, Driving, Ferry Travel, and Train Travel in this section, *in* Important Contacts A to Z, *above,* and in individual country chapters, *below.*

TRAVEL GEAR

Travel catalogs specialize in useful items that

can **save space when packing** and make life on the road more convenient. Compact alarm clocks, travel irons, travel wallets, and personal-care kits are among the most common items you'll find. They also carry dual-voltage appliances, currency converters and foreign-language phrase books. Some catalogs even carry miniature coffeemakers and water purifiers.

U

U.S. GOVERNMENT

The U.S. government can be an excellent source of travel information. Some of this is free and some is available for a nominal charge. When planning your trip, **find out what government materials are available.** For a small charge, you can **order publications from the Consumer Information Center** in Pueblo, Colorado. Free brochures are available from the Department of Transportation, the U.S. Customs Service, and other government agencies. For specific titles, *see* the appropriate entry in Important Contacts A to Z, *above.*

W

WHEN TO GO

For information about travel seasons and for the average daily maximum and minimum temperatures of the major European cities, *see* Essential Information *in* each country chapter.

2 Andorra

Andorra la Vella and Beyond

THE 191-SQUARE-MILE MOUNTAIN REDOUBT, tax haven, and commercial oasis known as the co-principality of Andorra drafted a constitution—somewhat grandly titled the Carta Magna—and held elections in 1993, converting Europe's last bastion of feudalism into a full-fledged democratic state. The bishop of Urgell and the president of France assumed even more symbolic roles as the co-princes of this unique Pyrenean country. The area originally fell through the cracks between France and Spain when Charlemagne founded Andorra as an independent entity during his 8th-century battles with the Moors. In the 9th century, his heir, Carles el Calb (Charles the Bald), made the bishop of Urgell overlord of Andorra, a role contested by the French counts of Foix until a treaty providing joint suzerainty was agreed upon in 1278. The French monarchy inherited these rights and passed them on to the modern-day presidents of France, and the bishop of Urgell's claim has remained rock-solid for the past thousand years. This dual protection has allowed Andorra to thrive as a virtual no-man's-land and a low-tax, duty-free haven. Europe's new semi-borderless unity, however, is threatening this special status, and the new Andorra is in the process of developing an improved tourist industry and a more legitimate and above-board economy. thought of as the shopping and fiscal paradise for which it has acquired fame.

Winter sports, mountain climbing and hiking, and the architectural and cultural heritage represented by its many Romanesque chapels, bridges, and medieval farm and town houses are Andorra's once and future stock in trade, although numbered bank accounts will surely not be disappearing anytime soon.

ESSENTIAL INFORMATION

Before You Go

When to Go

Winter brings a huge influx of skiing buffs, though any time of year has always attracted consumers wishing to take advantage of Andorra's tax- and duty-free shopping. Andorra is a paradise for lovers of the outdoors. In winter there is reliable snowfall from December to early April, and there are efficient ski resorts at Soldeu, Arinsal, Pas de la Casa, and La Massana. In summer, hikers will find magnificent trails on the Grande Randonnée (GR) network and a score of shorter but still demanding routes. Botanists and bird-watchers should arrive by early April, in time for the bird migrations from Africa and the first flush of spring flowers on the slopes and in the valleys. Be warned that even in summer the nighttime temperatures can drop to freezing.

CLIMATE
The following are the average daily maximum and minimum temperatures for Andorra.

Jan.	43F	6C	May	62F	17C	Sept.	71F	22C
	30	1		43	6		49	10
Feb.	45F	7C	June	73F	23C	Oct.	60F	16C
	30	1		39	4		42	6
Mar.	54F	12C	July	79F	26C	Nov.	51F	10C
	35	2		54	12		35	2
Apr.	58F	14C	Aug.	76F	24C	Dec.	42F	6C
	39	4		53	12		31	1

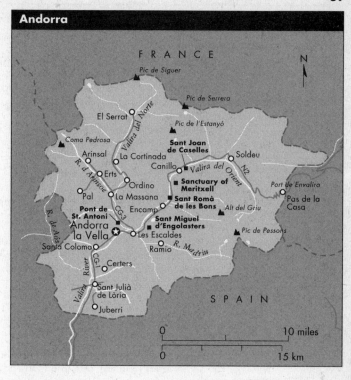

Currency

The Spanish peseta (pta.) is the major Andorran currency, but French francs are equally acceptable, and all prices are quoted in both currencies. For exchange rates and coinage information, ☞ Currency *in* Chapter 10, France, and Chapter 26, Spain.

What It Will Cost

Prices in Andorra are similar to those in neighboring France and Spain. The only bargains still available are products subject to state tax, such as tobacco, alcohol, perfume, and gasoline. Staples such as butter, cheese, and milk sold as surplus by member countries of the European Union (EU) are also cheaper in Andorra.

SAMPLE PRICES
Coca-Cola, 150 ptas.; cup of coffee, 100 ptas.; 1-mile taxi ride, 350 ptas.; ham sandwich, 350 ptas.

Customs

Andorra has traditionally been famous for its liberality regarding customs, duties, and visas. Non-Europeans need a passport to cross the border; Europeans enter with only an identity card. Now that the French–Spanish border is virtually a wave-by, Andorra's is less than a formality. Crossing out of Andorra, however, can be a problem. The French customs officers between Pas de la Casa and the Puymorens Tunnel sporadically stage mammoth roadblocks and may search anything. Spanish customs between Andorra le Vella and Seu d'Urgell can also be tricky. The established limits for all varieties of goods are specified in "Franquicias dels Viatgers," a leaflet in French, Catalan, and Spanish that is distributed by the Andorra National Tourist Office in Barcelona or Andorra la Vella (☞ Visitor Information *in* Important Addresses and Numbers, *below*). No one seems to mind how often you pass customs on a given day, however. So one way to score significant savings is to stay in a hotel on the Spanish side and make half a dozen trips through.

Language

Andorran nationalism is in the process of being invented. Although 82% of the country's population of 61,599 are not native speakers of Catalan, it is the co-principality's official language. Spanish, French, and English are also commonly spoken by merchants and service personnel. The establishment of Catalan as the area's first language has become a fact in the school system as well, and Andorra will join the more than 6 million Catalan-speakers on both sides of the Pyrenees.

Getting Around

By Car

Road maintenance varies. The one main artery from France into Spain via Andorra la Vella is excellent and handles the heaviest traffic. Also superior is the spur north toward the ski resorts at La Massana and Ordino. Elsewhere, roads are narrow, winding, and best suited to four-wheel-drive vehicles or, higher up, mules. In winter, snow tires or chains are essential. Although the Puymorens Tunnel does not surface in Andorra, it does eliminate the switchbacks of the Puymorens mountain pass. This pass is either dangerous or closed in bad weather and adds an extra 30 minutes to the Barcelona–Pas de la Casa trip. In good weather, though, don't miss this spectacularly scenic drive.

By Bus

Minibuses connect the towns and villages, and fares are low; 100 ptas. will take you 5 kilometers (3 miles). Details on fares and services are available at hotels and from tourist offices.

On Foot

Mountainous Andorra is a mecca for hikers, hill-walkers, and backpackers. The mountains are high and the terrain is wild, so a degree of care and experience is advisable. There are two long-distance trails: the GR7, which runs from Portello Blanca on the French frontier to Les Escaldes on the road to Spain; and the GR75, also called the Ordino Route, a magnificent, high-mountain trail that stretches across the central range. Get details on treks and walks from tourist offices.

Staying in Andorra

Telephones

LOCAL CALLS

For local directory assistance, dial 111. There are no regional area codes in Andorra. Most pay phones take phone cards issued by the telephone company; these may be purchased at *tabacs* (stores that sell tobacco and stamps).

INTERNATIONAL CALLS

For assistance, call the local operator at 111. To call Andorra from Spain, dial 07376 and the six-digit local number; from France, dial 19376.

COUNTRY CODE

The country code for Andorra is 376.

Mail

You can buy Andorran stamps with French francs or Spanish pesetas, though the postal service within the country is free. The Spanish post office in Andorra la Vella is at Carrer Joan Maragall 10; the French post office is at 1 rue Père d'Urg. There are no postal codes in Andorra but be sure to write "Principat d'Andorra" to distinguish the country from the Spanish town of the same name.

Opening and Closing Times

Banks are open weekdays 9–1 and 3–5, and Saturday 9–noon. They are closed Sunday.

Churches. Andorra is predominantly Catholic. Most chapels and churches are kept locked around the clock, the key being left at the closest house. Check with the local tourist office for additional details.

Shops are open daily 9–8, though many are closed between 2 and 4.

National Holidays

January 1; March 31 (Easter Monday); May 1 (Labor Day); May 19 (Pentecost Monday); June 23 (St. John); September 8 (La Verge de Meritxell); November 1 (All Saints' Day); December 25.

LOCAL HOLIDAYS

At Canillo, the third Saturday in July and the following Sunday and Monday; at Les Escaldes, July 25–27; at Sant Julià de Lòria, the last Sunday in July and the following Monday and Tuesday; at Andorra la Vella, the first Saturday, Sunday, and Monday in August; at Encamp and La Massana, August 15–17; at Ordino, September 16, 17.

Dining

Andorra is not known as a gastronomic paradise, but the quality of the food is improving. There are good restaurants serving French, Spanish, or Catalan cuisine and plenty of spots where the visitor will eat hearty Pyrenean fare at no great cost. Local dishes worth trying are *truite de carreroles* (a type of omelet with wild mushrooms); *trinchat*, a typical country specialty of potatoes and cabbage with bacon; *estofat d'isard* (stewed mountain goat); local cheeses, such as *formatge de tupí*; and *rostes amb mel* (ham baked with honey). Although most restaurants offer prix-fixe menus, a number of more expensive establishments are only à la carte.

MEALTIMES

True to the co-principality's predominantly Spanish culture, Andorrans eat late: Dinners don't usually get under way until 8:30 or 9, and lunch is a substantial meal served between 1 and 3:30.

WHAT TO WEAR

Casual dress is acceptable in all restaurants in Andorra, regardless of price category.

RATINGS

The following ratings are for a three-course meal for one person, not including wine.

CATEGORY	COST
$$$$	over 5,000 ptas.
$$$	3,500 ptas.–5,000 ptas.
$$	1,500 ptas.–3,500 ptas.
$	under 1,500 ptas.

Lodging

The number of Andorran hotels continues to increase, and standards are rising. The decor is usually functional, but service is friendly and the facilities are excellent.

Most hotels are open year-round. Reservations are necessary during July and August. Hotel rates often include at least two meals.

RATINGS

The following price ratings apply for two people in a double room.

CATEGORY	COST
$$$$	over 9,000 ptas.
$$$	6,000 ptas.–9,000 ptas.
$$	4,000 ptas.–6,000 ptas.
$	2,500 ptas.–4,000 ptas.

Tipping

Restaurants and cafés almost always tack on a 10%–15% service charge; it's customary to leave a similar amount in addition to the charge, but this is optional.

Arriving and Departing

By Plane

The nearest international airports are at Barcelona (200 km/125 mi) and, in France, at Perpignan (136 km/85 mi) and Toulouse-Blagnac (180 km/112 mi).

By Train

From Barcelona, take the train to Puigcerdà, then the bus to La Seu d'Urgell and Andorra la Vella; from Madrid, take the train to Lleida and then a bus to La Seu d'Urgell and Andorra la Vella. From Toulouse, take the train to Ax-les-Thermes and L'Hospitalet, where the bus to Pas de la Casa and Andorra la Vella meets the morning train. Alternatively, go on to Latour-de-Carol and take the bus from Puigcerdà to La Seu d'Urgell and Andorra la Vella.

By Bus

A bus service runs twice daily from Barcelona (✉ Ronda Universidad 4). In summer there are direct buses from Perpignan and Toulouse to Andorra. The ride from Barcelona, Perpignan, or Toulouse to Andorra la Vella takes about three hours.

By Car

The fastest, most direct route from Barcelona to Andorra la Vella—with the fewest curves and the most tolls (around 4,000 ptas. in all)—runs through the Tunel del Cadí and the Cerdanya Valley via Bellver and La Seu d'Urgell. Slightly longer but cheaper, more beautiful, and often free of hold-ups is the western approach to La Seu d'Urgell via N-II to Igualada, then through Cervera, Pons, and Oliana on C-1311. Andorra is 620 kilometers (385 miles) from Madrid via Zaragoza, Lleida, and the C-1311, a six- to seven-hour drive. The roads from Toulouse and Perpignan are beautiful but tortuous, entering Andorra at eastern Pas de la Casa on the French border.

Important Addresses and Numbers

Consulates

U.S. (✉ Pg. Reina Elisenda 23, Barcelona, Spain, ☎ 93/2802227).
Canadian (✉ Nuñez de Balboa 35, Madrid, Spain, ☎ 91/2259119).
U.K. (✉ Apartado de Correos 12111, Barcelona, Spain, ☎ 93/3222151).

Emergencies

Doctor (☎ 118). **Police** (☎ 110). **Ambulance and Fire** (☎ 118).

Travel Agency

Relax Travel Agency/American Express (✉ Roc dels Escolls 2, Andorra la Vella, ☎ 822044, FAX 827055).

Visitor Information

Andorra La Vella. Sindicat d'Iniciativa (National Tourist Office, ✉ Carrer Dr. Vilanova, ☎ 820214, FAX 825823. ☉ Mon.–Sat. 10–1 and

3–7, Sun. and holidays 10–1). City tourist office (✉ Plaça de la Rotonda, ☎ 827117).

Barcelona (✉ Carrer Marià Cubí 159, 08021, ☎ 93/200–0655 or ☎ 93/200–0787).

Canillo (Unió Pro-Turisme, ✉ Caseta Pro-Turisme, ☎ and ⒻⒶⓍ 851002).

Encamp (Unió Pro-Foment i Turisme, ✉ Plaça Consell General, ☎ 831405, ⒻⒶⓍ 831878).

Escaldes-Engordany (Unío Pro-Turisme, ✉ Plaça dels Co-Prínceps, ☎ 820963).

La Massana (Unió Pro-Turisme, ✉ Plaça del Quart, ☎ 835693).

Ordino (Oficina de Turisme, ✉ Cruïlla d'Ordino, ☎ 836963).

Pas de la Casa (Unió Pro-Turisme, ✉ C. Bernat III, ☎ 855292).

Sant Julià de Lòria (Unió Pro-Turisme, ✉ Plaça de la Germandat, ☎ 841352).

Guided Tours

Tours of Andorra la Vella and the surrounding countryside are offered by several firms; check with the tourist office for details or call **Excursion Nadal** (☎ 821138) or **Solineu Excursion** (☎ 823653).

EXPLORING ANDORRA

Exploring Andorra takes time. The roads are narrow and steep, the views compel frequent stops, and every village is worth examining. If possible, do as much sightseeing on foot as time permits.

Overlooking **Andorra la Vella's** main square is the stone bulk of the **Casa de la Vall** (House of the Valley), a medieval-looking building constructed in 1580 and the seat of the Andorran government in the capital city. Charmingly rustic, the Casa contains many noted religious frescoes, some of which were carefully moved here from village churches high in the Pyrenees. The kitchen is particularly interesting, with a splendid array of ancient copper pots and other culinary implements. ✉ *Carrer de la Vall s/n.* ⊙ *Tours weekdays 10–1 and 3–7, Sat. 3–7.*

★ Barely a kilometer (½ mile) from the center of Andorra la Vella is **Caldea,** an elaborate thermal spa complex that has attracted all sorts of celebrity visitors, from Montserrat Caballé to Barcelona soccer players, eager to frolic and cavort, chill out in snow patios, and steam in the Turkish baths. There are three restaurants, boutiques, an art gallery and a cocktail bar open until 2 in the morning. Charges for the treatments vary; a 5-day Andorra ski ticket will get you in for free. ✉ *Parc de la Mola 10, Les Escaldes,* ☎ *865777,* ⒻⒶⓍ *865656.*

The spa town of **Les Escaldes** is about a 15-minute walk from Andorra
★ la Vella. The Romanesque church of **Sant Miquel d'Engolasters** stands on a ridge northeast of the capital and can be reached on foot—allow half a day for the round-trip—or by taxi up a mountain road. The views are well worth the climb. Just beyond Encamp, 6 kilometers (4 miles)
★ northeast, is the 12th-century church of **Sant Romà de les Bons,** in a particularly picturesque setting combining medieval buildings and mountain scenery.

Midway between Encamp and Canillo on CG-2 is the **Sanctuary of Meritxell,** the focal point of the country's religious life. The Blessed Virgin of Meritxell is the principality's patron saint, yet oddly enough for such a religious country, her patronage wasn't declared until the late 19th century. The original sanctuary was destroyed by fire in 1972; the new gray-stone building that replaced it looks remarkably like a factory, but the mountain setting is superb. ▦ *Free.* ⊙ *Wed.–Mon. 9–1 and 3–7.*

Another 3 kilometers (2 miles) farther, just before the town of Canillo, you will see a Gothic, seven-arm stone cross (actually it has six arms, as one has broken off). A mile or so beyond is the Romanesque church of **Sant Joan de Caselles,** whose ancient walls have turned a lovely dappled brown over the centuries. The bell tower is stunning: three stories of weathered stone punctuated by rows of round-arched windows. Inside the main building there is a fine reredos (a wall or screen positioned behind an altar). It dates from 1525 and depicts the life of St. John the Evangelist.

Retrace your way back to Andorra la Vella, and this time take CG-3 due north out of the capital. After just 3 kilometers (2 miles) you'll come to a Romanesque stone bridge spanning a narrow river, the **Pont de Sant Antoni.** Three kilometers (2 miles) beyond is the picturesque mountain town of **La Massana.** Take some time to stroll about in its rustic streets. Another 5 kilometers (3 miles) brings you to the tiny village of **Ordino.** Its medieval church is exceptionally appealing; to see it properly, go at night between 7 and 8, when mass is celebrated.

In **La Cortinada,** a mile or so to the northwest, is the **Can Pal,** another fine example of medieval Andorran architecture. It is a privately owned manor house (strictly no admittance) with a dovecote attached. Note the turret perched high on the far side.

Backtrack once more to Andorra la Vella, then take CG-1 south. In 4 kilometers (2½ miles) you'll come to the pre-Romanesque church of **Santa Coloma,** in the village of the same name; parts of the church date from the 9th and 10th centuries, and there are Romanesque frescoes on the interior walls.

Shopping

Visitors to Andorra have traditionally listed shopping as one of the main attractions, but be careful: Not all the goods displayed are at bargain prices. The French and Spanish come to buy cigarettes, liquor, household items, and foodstuffs, but they often find electrical goods and cameras either flawed or lacking warranties and no cheaper than at home. Good buys are consumables such as gasoline, perfume, butter, cheese, cigarettes, wine, whiskey, and gin. For cameras, tape recorders, and other imported items, compare prices and models carefully. Ask for the *precio último* (final price) and insist politely on *el descuento,* the 10% discount to which you are entitled as a visitor to Andorra.

The main shopping area is **Andorra la Vella,** but there are stores in all the new developments and in the towns close to the frontiers, namely **Pas de la Casa** and **Sant Julià de Lòria.** The **Punt de Trobada** center (⌷ Ctra. d'Espanya, ☎ 843433), 2 kilometers (1¼ miles) from the Spanish border, is bright, modern, and immense. **La Casa del Formatge** in Les Escaldes (⌷ Av. Carlemany s/n, ☎ 821689) has over 500 different kinds of cheeses from all over the world. Tasting is encouraged.

DINING AND LODGING

For details and price-category definitions, *see* Dining *and* Lodging *in* Staying in Andorra, *above.*

Andorra la Vella

$$$ ✕ **Chez Jaques.** The varied menu has both classical and nouvelle French dishes, though other international cuisines are handled with flair. With good food and a cozy ambience, it's very popular with the locals. ⌷ *Av. Tarragona, Edificio Terra Vella,* ☎ *820325. AE, DC, MC, V. Lunch only. Closed July and Aug.*

$$$ ✕ **El Rusc.** A smallish hideaway 1 kilometer (½ mile) from La Massana is one of Andorra's best new options for fine dining. Chef Antoni Garrallá serves both Basque cuisine and French and international specialties. Try the foie gras with onions or *besugo* (baked sea bream), a standard treat from the Basque country. This flower-covered chalet normally seats only 50 diners. ✉ *Ctra. d'Arinsal,* ☎ *838200,* FAX *835180. Reservations essential. AE, DC, MC, V.*

$$$ ✕ **Molí dels Fanals.** This quiet restaurant occupies an antique *borda*, a
★ typical stone Andorran mountain refuge with a fireplace and wooden paneling. The predominantly Catalan cuisine here features consistently high-quality ingredients. Try the *magret de canard* (breast of duck) with grapes and port. ✉ *Carrer Dr. Vilanova, 9 (Borda Casadet),* ☎ *821381. AE, DC, MC, V. Closed Sun. night, Mon., and last 2 wks in Aug.*

$$$ ✕ **1900.** This small, beautifully decorated restaurant serves some of
★ the best food in the co-principality, a blend of French, Spanish, and Andorran cuisines. It's fairly expensive for Andorra, but Chef Alain Despretz's inventive dishes are often worth it. ✉ *11 Plaça de la Unío,* ☎ *826716. AE, DC, MC, V. Closed Mon. and July.*

$$–$$$ ✕ **Borda Estevet.** Another borda with a very Pyrenean feel, this simple spot offers a selection of Spanish and Andorran dishes, beef cooked and served *a la llosa* (on hot slabs of slate), and three private dining rooms in addition to the main dining room. ✉ *Ctra. Comella 2,* ☎ *864026. AE, DC, MC, V. Closed Sun. in Aug.*

$$–$$$ ✕ **Versailles.** A tiny and authentic French bistro with only ten tables,
★ the Versailles is nearly always packed. The cuisine is primarily French with occasional Andorran specialties such as *escudella barrejada*, a thick vegetable and meat soup, or *civet de jabali*, stewed wild boar. ✉ *Cap del Carrer 1,* ☎ *821331. AE, DC, MC, V.*

$$$$ 🏨 **Andorra Palace.** The large, modern Palace is widely considered one
★ of the capital's best hotels. The rooms are spacious and the furnishings smartly contemporary. The outdoor terrace is a pleasant spot to relax and watch the bustle below. ✉ *Carrer de la Roda,* ☎ *821072,* FAX *828195. 140 rooms with bath. Restaurant, bar, pool, sauna, exercise room. AE, DC, MC, V.*

$$$$ 🏨 **Andorra Park.** The Park ranks with the Palace (☞ *above*) as one of Andorra la Vella's two top hotels. It's a grand building away from the city's congestion of traffic and pedestrians. The American Bar is a popular watering hole for local society. There's a pretty garden, as well as a terrace, and the deluxe guest rooms have private balconies. ✉ *Carrer Les Canals 24,* ☎ *820979,* FAX *820983. 40 rooms with bath. Restaurant, bar, pool, tennis courts, croquet. AE, DC, MC, V.*

$$$$ 🏨 **Hotel Eden Roc.** Besides having all the amenities of larger hotels, the smaller Eden Roc offers an exceptional dining room, a terrace, and attentive personal service. ✉ *Av. Dr. Mitjavila 1,* ☎ *821000,* FAX *860319. 56 rooms with bath. Restaurant, bar. AE, V.*

$$ 🏨 **Florida.** For good value, try this cheerful hotel. There's no in-house restaurant, but there are several nearby. ✉ *Carrer La Llacuna 15,* ☎ *820105,* FAX *861925. 52 rooms with bath. Bar, lobby lounge. AE, DC, MC, V.*

$$ 🏨 **Hotel La Mola.** This friendly spot, midway between the ski slopes and the brightish lights of Andorra la Vella, is a comfortable choice that has all the basic facilities at half the price of some of the better-known Andorran hotels. ✉ *Av. Co-Princep Episcopal 62,* ☎ *831181,* FAX *833046. 48 rooms with bath. Restaurant, pool, tennis courts. AE, DC, MC, V.*

Les Escaldes

$$$$ ✕🏨 **Roc Blanc.** Sleek, modern, and luxurious trappings—and a wealth
★ of facilities to pamper the body, from mud baths to acupuncture—are

what the Roc Blanc is all about. The rooms are large, there's a terrace, and the hotel's restaurant, El Pi, is consistently good. ⊠ *Plaça Co-Princeps 5,* ☎ *821486,* 𝖥𝖠𝖷 *860244. 250 rooms with bath. Restaurant, piano bar, 2 pools, beauty salon, mineral baths, sauna, tennis courts, health club. AE, DC, MC, V.*

Ordino

$$ 🏨 **Hotel Coma.** Surrounded by woods and meadows, this Swiss chalet–style hideaway just outside the village offers scenery, silence, and simple Andorran fare at affordable prices. ⊠ *Carretera General,* ☎ *835116,* 𝖥𝖠𝖷 *837909. 48 rooms with bath. Restaurant, bar, pool. AE, DC, MC, V.*

Pas de la Casa

$ ✕ **Le Grizzly.** This is a popular French restaurant for lunch or dinner, especially during the ski season. The food, simple but well prepared, is a good value, with a choice of four prix-fixe menus from 800 ptas. to 1,300 ptas. Try the *entrecôte roquefort* (steak) and the thick Provençal soups. ⊠ *Av. d'Encamp,* ☎ *855227. AE, DC, MC, V.*

Sant Julià de Lòria

$$$ 🏨 **Pol.** Gracefully modern surroundings and friendly staff are just two
★   reasons why this hotel is so popular. A garden and terrace are part of the Pol's appeal, and its dance club is a popular spot at night. ⊠ *Av. Verge de Canólich 52,* ☎ *841122,* 𝖥𝖠𝖷 *841852. 80 rooms with bath. Restaurant, bar. AE, MC, V.*

Santa Coloma

$$ ✕ **El Bon Racó.** This eatery is exactly what the name says it is: a good corner, nook, or retreat. A traditional borda in design, it turns out good local cuisine at encouraging prices. Try to arrive early; the place is popular and fills quickly, especially on weekends. ⊠ *Av. Salou 86,* ☎ *822085. AE, DC, MC, V.*

3 Austria

Vienna

Danube Valley

Salzburg

Innsbruck

AN OFT-TOLD STORY CONCERNS AN AIRLINE PILOT whose prelanding announcement advised: "Ladies and gentlemen, we are on the final approach to Vienna Airport. Please make sure your seat belts are fastened, please refrain from smoking until you are inside the terminal, and please set your watches back 100 years." Apocryphal or not, the pilot's observation suggests the allure of a country where tourists can sense something of what Europe was like before the pulse of the 20th century quickened to a beat that would have dizzied our great-grandfathers. Today, uniformed bus drivers still bow to you as if saluting a Hapsburg prince, and Lippizaner stallions still dance to Mozart minuets—in other words, Austria is a country that has not forgotten how to work, as well as waltz, in three-quarter time.

Look beyond the white horses, the zither strains, and the singing of the Vienna Choir Boys, however, and you'll find a conservative-mannered, remarkably wealthy country that has a steady eye on the future. Vienna may have its sumptuous palaces, but it is also home to the World Trade Center, a super-modern facility featuring a global satellite-communication network. Next to storybook villages are giant plants, one turning out millions of compact disks for Sony. The world's largest penicillin producer is hidden away in a Tirolean valley. By no means is the country frozen in a time warp: Rather, it is the juxtaposition of the old and the new—seeing Andrew Lloyd Webber's *Phantom of the Opera* performed in the theater where Mozart's *Magic Flute* premiered—that makes Austria such a fascinating place to visit.

So, too, does the fact that, poised as it is between East and West, Austria shares a culture with Europe but also has deep affinities with the lands that lie beyond. It was Metternich who insisted that "Asia begins at the Landstrasse," referring to Vienna's crucial role as the meeting place of East and West for two thousand years. Today, Vienna's spectacular historical and artistic heritage—exemplified by the legacies of Beethoven, Freud, and Klimt—lures travelers to this grande dame of a city. It's a unique confection of operetta and psychoanalysis, Apfelstrudel and marble staircases, Strauss waltzes and Schubert melodies, and one that retains a definite Old World charm that natives would be the last to underplay.

But, as with most countries, the capital is only a small part of what Austria has to offer. A grand tour of the country reveals almost as many Austrias as there are drops on the crystal chandelier in a Viennese ballroom: Salzburg—home every summer to the world's snobbiest music festival—is a departure point for the Salzkammergut lake country and the mountains of Land Salzburg; as the hub of the Alps, Innsbruck beckons skiers to explore the resorts of Lech, St. Anton, and Kitzbühel; finally, there's the Wachau, a stretch of the valley of the Danube that easily rivals the scenery of the Rhine.

In the end, the way to get the most out of Austria is to come armed with a taste for history, an appreciation for the quirks in human nature, and a thirst for art and wonderful music. A thirst for good wine comes in handy, too—as you'll discover when you're sitting in the deep wine cellar of some medieval castle enjoying a goblet of regal Trockenbeerenauslesen while listening to a quartet play Mozart.

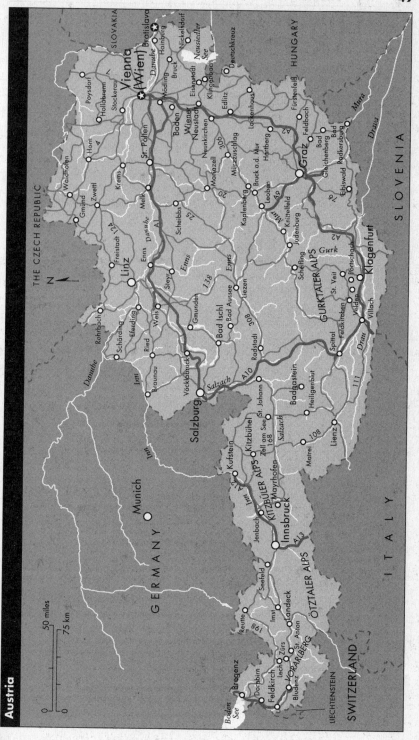

ESSENTIAL INFORMATION

Before You Go

When to Go

Austria has two tourist seasons. The summer season technically starts around Easter, reaches its peak in July, and winds down in September. Aside from a few overly humid days when you may wish for wider use of air-conditioning, even Vienna is pleasant in summer, when the city literally moves outdoors. May, June, September, and October are the most temperate months, and the most affordable. The winter cultural season starts in October and runs into June; winter sports get under way in December and last until the end of April, although you can ski in certain areas well into June and on some of the highest glaciers year-round. Some events—the Salzburg Festival is a prime example—occasion a substantial increase in hotel and other costs.

CLIMATE

Summer can be warm; winter, bitterly cold. The southern region is usually several degrees warmer in summer, several degrees colder in winter. Winters north of the Alps can be overcast and dreary, whereas the south basks in winter sunshine.

The following are the average daily maximum and minimum temperatures for Vienna.

Jan.	34F	1C	May	67F	19C	Sept.	68F	20C
	25	– 4		50	10		53	11
Feb.	38F	3C	June	73F	23C	Oct.	56F	14C
	28	– 3		56	14		44	7
Mar.	47F	8C	July	76F	25C	Nov.	45F	7C
	30	– 1		60	15		37	3
Apr.	58F	15C	Aug.	75F	24C	Dec.	37F	3C
	43	6		59	15		30	– 1

Currency

The unit of currency is the Austrian schilling (AS), divided into 100 groschen. There are AS20, 50, 100, 500, 1,000, and 5,000 bills; AS1, 5, 10, and 20 coins; and 1-, 2-, 5-, 10-, and 50-groschen coins. The 1-, 2-, and 5-groschen coins are rare, and the AS20 coins are unpopular, though useful for some cigarette machines. The 500- and 100-schilling notes look similar; confusing the two can be an expensive mistake.

At press time (spring 1996), the exchange rate was AS10.1 to the dollar, AS7.2 to the Canadian dollar, and AS15.6 to the pound sterling.

Credit cards are widely used throughout Austria, although not all establishments that accept plastic take all cards. Some may require a minimum purchase if payment is to be made by card. Many restaurants take cash only. American Express has money machines in Vienna at its main office, Kärntnerstrasse 21-23 and at the airport. Many of the Bankomat money dispensers will also accept Visa cards if you have an encoded international PIN.

Exchange traveler's checks at a bank, the post office, or the American Express office to get the best rate. All charge a small commission; some smaller banks or "change" offices may give a poorer rate *and* charge a higher fee. All change offices at airports and at main train stations in major cities cash traveler's checks. In Vienna, bank-operated change offices in Vienna with extended hours are found on Stephansplatz and at the main rail stations. The Bank Austria machines on Stephansplatz and at Kärntnerstrasse 51 (to the right of the Opera) and at the Raiffeisenbank on Kohlmarkt (at Michaelerplatz) change bills from other currencies into schillings, but rates are poor and a hefty commission is automatically deducted.

You may bring in any amount of either foreign currency or schillings and take out any amount with you.

What It Will Cost

Austria is not inexpensive, but since inflation is relatively low, costs remain fairly stable. Vienna and Salzburg are the most expensive cities, along with fashionable resorts at Kitzbühel, Seefeld, Badgastein, Velden, Zell am See, Pörtschach, St. Anton, Zürs, and Lech. Many smaller towns near these resorts offer virtually identical facilities at half the price.

Drinks in bars and clubs cost considerably more than in cafés or restaurants. Austrian prices include service and tax.

SAMPLE PRICES
Cup of coffee, AS25; half-liter of draft beer, AS27–AS40; glass of wine, AS35; Coca-Cola, AS25; open sandwich, AS25; theater ticket, AS200–AS300; concert ticket, AS250–AS500; opera ticket, AS600 and up; 1-mile taxi ride, AS35.

Customs on Arrival

Austria's duty-free allowances are as follows: 200 cigarettes or 100 cigars or 250 grams of tobacco; 2 liters of wine and 1 liter of spirits; 1 bottle of toilet water (about 300-milliliter size); and 50 milliliters of perfume for those ages 18 and over arriving from other European countries. Although Austria is a member of the European Union (EU), these limits may apply to EU citizens as well. Visitors arriving from the United States, Canada, or other non-European points may bring in twice the above amounts.

Language

German is the official national language. In larger cities and most resort areas you will have no problem finding English speakers; hotel and restaurant employees, in particular, speak English reasonably well. Most younger Austrians speak at least passable English, and fluency is increasing.

Getting Around

By Car

ROAD CONDITIONS
The highway system is excellent, and all roads are well maintained and well marked. Secondary mountain roads may be narrow and winding, but traffic is generally light. Check the condition of mountain roads in winter before starting out (☎ 0222/711–99–7). Many mountain passes are closed, though tunnels are kept open.

RULES OF THE ROAD
Drive on the right. Seat belts are compulsory in front. Children under 12 must sit in the back, and smaller children must have a restraining seat. Speed limits are as posted; otherwise, 130 kph (80 mph) on expressways, 100 kph (62 mph) on other main roads, 50 kph (31 mph) in built-up areas. Some city-center areas have speed limits of 30 kph (19 mph). The right-of-way is for those coming from the right (especially in traffic circles) unless otherwise marked. A warning triangle—standard equipment in rental cars—must be set up in case of breakdown.

PARKING
Observe signs; tow-away in cities is expensive. In winter, overnight parking is forbidden on city streets with streetcar lines. Vienna, Salzburg,

and Innsbruck have inner-city zones in which overnight parking is restricted to those with resident stickers; check before you leave a car on the street.

GASOLINE

Prices—AS11–AS12 per liter—are fairly consistent throughout the country. Only *bleifrei* (unleaded) fuel—regular and premium—is sold, and smaller filling stations may not carry diesel.

BREAKDOWNS

Emergency road service is available from **ARBÖ** (☎ 123 nationwide) or **ÖAMTC** (☎ 120) auto clubs. Special phones are located along autobahns and major highways.

By Train

Trains in Austria are fast and efficient, and most lines have been electrified. Hourly express trains run on the Vienna–Salzburg route. All principal trains have first- and second-class cars, as well as smoking and no-smoking sections. Overnight trains have sleeping compartments, and most trains have dining cars. Dining-car service and quality are highly variable; value for your money is rare, although the railroads have pledged improvement. If you're traveling at peak times, a reserved seat—available for a small additional fee—is always a good idea.

FARES

If you're visiting other European countries, a **Eurail Pass** (☞ Rail Travel *in* Chapter 1), valid throughout most of Europe, is the best deal. Austria has only two discount tickets, but half-price fares are available to families, with children up to 15 traveling free. Adults need a passport photo to get the family pass at rail stations. A **Bundesnetzkarte** allows unlimited travel for a month and costs AS5,400 for first class and AS3,600 for second class. The alternative is a **Domino** ticket, which is valid for unlimited travel on any three, five, or ten days within a one-month period. For five days, a first-class Domino ticket costs AS2,240, second-class AS1,630. If you're 26 or under, the Domino Junior ticket costs AS1,220 second class. Full details are available from travel agents or from the Austrian National Tourist Office. Prices are likely to be higher in 1997, and a number of changes to special tickets are planned.

By Plane

Domestic service is expensive. **Austrian Airlines** flies between Vienna and Linz, Salzburg, Graz, and Klagenfurt. **Tyrolean Airlines** has service from Vienna to Innsbruck. **Rheintalflug** flies between Vienna and Altenhausen, just over the border in Switzerland, with bus connections to Feldkirch, Bregenz, and Bludenz in the Vorarlberg.

By Bus

Service is available to virtually every community accessible by highway. Winter buses have ski racks. Vienna's central bus terminal (Wien-Mitte/Landstrasse Hauptstrasse, opposite the Hilton) is the arrival/departure point for international bus routes. In most other cities the bus station is adjacent to the train station. Bus services are run by both the post office and the railroads; tourist offices can help you resolve consequent confusions.

By Boat

Boats ply the Danube from Passau in Germany all the way to Vienna, and from Vienna to Bratislava (Slovakia), Budapest (Hungary), and the Black Sea. Only East European boats run beyond Budapest. Overnight boats have cabins; all have dining. The most scenic stretches in Austria are from Passau to Linz and through the Wachau, or Danube Valley (Melk, Krems). From Vienna, there are day trips you can take upstream to the Wachau and downstream to Bratislava and Budapest. There are also special moonlight dancing and jazz excursions. Make reservations from the **DDSG/Blue Danube Schiffahrt** (Danube Steamship Company, ☎ 0222/727–50–0, FAX 0222/727–50–440) in Vienna or travel agents. The company was reorganized last year, so verify schedules and connections.

By Bicycle

Bicycles can be rented at many train stations and returned to any of them. Most trains and some postal buses will take bikes as baggage. Bikes can be taken on the Vienna subway, with the exception of the U-6, year-round all day Sundays and holidays, from 9 to 3 and after 6:30 on weekdays, and, from May through September, after 9 AM Saturday. You'll need a half-fare ticket for the bike (☞ Getting Around *in* Vienna, *below*). Marked cycling routes parallel most of the Danube.

Staying in Austria

Telephones

LOCAL CALLS

Pay telephones take AS1, 5, 10, and 20 coins. A three-minute local call costs AS1. Emergency calls are free. Instructions are in English in most booths. Insert AS1 or more to continue the connection when you hear the tone warning that your time is up. If you will be making frequent phone calls, get a phone card at a post office. These work in all phones marked *Wertkartentelefon.* The cost of the call will be deducted from the card automatically. Cards cost AS190 for AS200 worth of calls, AS95 for AS100 worth, and AS48 for calls totaling AS50.

Phone numbers throughout Austria are currently being changed. A sharp tone indicates either no connection or that the number has been changed. Calls to Vienna from *outside* Austria use the city prefix 01 or 1; from *inside* Austria, 0222. The switch to the 01 Vienna prefix for internal calls will take place in January 1997.

INTERNATIONAL CALLS

It costs more to telephone *from* Austria than it does *to* Austria. Calls from post offices are least expensive. To avoid hotel charges, call overseas and ask to be called back; use an international credit card, available from AT&T, Sprint, MCI, and others; or use access codes to reach operators for **AT&T** (022/903–011) or **MCI** (022/903–012). To make a collect call—you can't do this from pay phones—dial the operator and ask for an R-Gespräch (pronounced air-ga-*shprayk*). For international information, dial 1611 for European numbers, or 1614 for overseas numbers. Most operators speak English; if yours doesn't, you'll be passed along to one who does.

COUNTRY CODE

The country code for Austria is 43.

Mail

POSTAL RATES

Airmail letters to the United States and Canada cost AS11.50 minimum; postcards cost AS8.50. Letters to the United Kingdom cost AS7, postcards AS6, and both automatically go by air. An aerogram costs AS12.

RECEIVING MAIL

American Express offices in Vienna, Linz, Salzburg, and Innsbruck will hold mail at no charge for those carrying an American Express credit card or American Express traveler's checks.

VAT Refunds

A value-added tax (VAT) of 20% is charged on all sales and is automatically included in prices. If you purchase goods worth AS1,000 or more and are not a citizen of an EU country, you can claim a refund of the tax either as you leave or after you've returned home. Ask the store clerk to fill out the necessary papers. Get them stamped at the airport or border crossing by customs officials (who may ask to see the goods). You can get an immediate refund of the VAT, less a service charge, at international airports or at main border crossings, or you can return the papers by mail to the shop(s). The VAT refund can be credited to your credit card account or remitted by check.

Opening and Closing Times

Banks are open weekdays 8–noon or 12:30, and 1:30–3 or 4. Hours vary from one city to another. Principal offices in cities stay open during lunch.

Museums. Opening days and times vary considerably from one city to another and depend on the season, the museum's size, budgetary constraints, and assorted other factors. Monday is often a closing day. Your hotel or the local tourist office will have current details.

Shops are open weekdays from 8 or 9 until 6, and Saturday until noon or 1 only, except the first Saturday of every month, when they stay open until 5. Some shops in larger cities are open on Thursday evening until 8. Many smaller shops close for one or two hours at midday.

National Holidays

January 1; January 6 (Epiphany); March 30–31 (Easter); May 1 (May Day); May 8 (Ascension); May 18–19 (Pentecost); May 29 (Corpus Christi); August 15 (Assumption); October 26 (National Day); November 1 (All Saints' Day); December 8 (Immaculate Conception); December 25–26. On the Dec. 8 holiday, banks and offices are closed but most shops are open.

Dining

Take your choice among sidewalk *Wurstl* (frankfurter) stands, *Imbissstuben* (quick-lunch stops), cafés, *Heuriger* (wine restaurants), self-service restaurants, modest *Gasthäuser* (neighborhood establishments featuring local specialties), and full-fledged restaurants in every price category. Most places post their menus outside. Shops (such as Eduscho) that sell coffee beans also offer coffee by the cup at prices considerably lower than those in cafés. Many Anker bakery shops also offer tasty *Schmankerl* (snacks) and coffee. *Fleischer* or *Fleischhauer* (butchers) may also offer soup and a main course at noon. A growing number of shops and snack bars offer pizza by the slice. We recommend reservations for dinner.

MEALTIMES

Austrians may take up to five meals a day: a very early Continental breakfast of rolls and coffee; *Gabelfrühstück,* a slightly more substantial breakfast with eggs or cold meat—possibly even a small goulash—at mid-morning (understood to be 9, sharp); a main meal at noon; afternoon *Jause* (coffee with cake) at teatime; and, unless dining out, a light supper to end the day.

WHAT TO WEAR

A jacket and tie are generally advised for restaurants in the top price categories. Otherwise casual dress is acceptable, although in Vienna formal dress (jacket and tie) is preferred in some $$ restaurants at dinner. When in doubt, it's best to dress up.

Prices are per person and include soup and a main course, usually with salad, and a small beer or glass of wine. Meals in the top price categories will include a dessert or cheese with coffee. Prices include taxes and service (but adding another 5%–7% to the bill as a tip is customary).

CATEGORY	MAJOR CITY	OTHER AREAS
$$$$	over AS800	over AS600
$$$	AS500–AS800	AS400–AS600
$$	AS200–AS500	AS170–AS400
$	under AS200	under AS170

Lodging

Austrian hotels and pensions are officially classified using from one to five stars. These grades broadly coincide with our own four-point rating system. No matter what the category, standards for service and cleanliness are high. All hotels in the upper three categories have either a bath or shower in the room; even the most inexpensive accommodations provide hot and cold water. Accommodations include castles and palaces, conventional hotels, *Gasthöfe* (country inns), motels (considerably more sparse), and the more modest pensions.

All prices quoted here are for two people in a double room. Although exact rates vary, a single room generally costs more than half the price of a comparable double. Breakfast—which can be anything from a simple roll and coffee to a full and sumptuous buffet—is usually included. In top five-star hotels, however, it is extra (and expensive).

CATEGORY	MAJOR CITY	OTHER AREAS
$$$$	over AS2,700	over AS1,800
$$$	AS1,200–AS2,700	AS1,000–AS1,800
$$	AS950–AS1,200	AS700–AS1,000
$	under AS950	under AS700

Tipping

Railroad porters get AS10 per bag. Hotel porters or bellhops get AS10–AS20 per bag. Doormen get AS20 for hailing a cab and assisting. Room service gets AS20 for snacks and AS20–40 for full meals; in more expensive establishments, expect to tip on the higher side. Maids get no tip unless you stay a week or more, or unless special service is rendered. In restaurants, 10% service is included. Add anything from AS5 to AS50, depending on the restaurant and the size of the bill, or about 5%–7%.

VIENNA

Arriving and Departing

By Plane

All flights use Schwechat Airport (☎ 0222/7007–2231), about 16 kilometers (10 miles) southwest of Vienna.

Buses leave the airport for the city air terminal, Wien-Mitte/Landstrasse Hauptstrasse (☎ 0222/5800–33369), by the Hilton, on every half hour from 5 to 6:30 AM and every 20 minutes from 6:50 AM to 11:30 PM; after that, buses depart every hour until 5 AM. Trains shuttle every half hour between the rail terminal at the airport and Wien-Mitte/Landstrasse Hauptstrasse; the fare is AS34. Check schedules and fares, as a projected new rail service may mean a change in bus service. Buses also run every hour (every half hour on weekends and holidays

Apr.–Sept.) from the airport to the Westbahnhof (West Train Station) and the Südbahnhof (South Train Station). Be sure you get on the right bus! The one-way fare for all buses is AS70. A taxi from the airport to downtown Vienna costs about AS330–AS350; agree on a price in advance. Cabs (legally) do not meter this drive, as airport fares are more or less fixed (legally again) at about double the meter fare. The cheapest cab service is C+K Airport Service (☎ 0222/60808), charging about AS270–AS300. A seat in a limousine costs less; book at the airport. **Mazur** (☎ 0222/7007–6422 or 7007–6491) offers cheaper pickup and delivery service by arrangement. If you are driving from the airport, follow signs to ZENTRUM.

By Train

Vienna has four train stations. The principal station, the Westbahnhof, is for trains to and from Linz, Salzburg, and Innsbruck, and arriving trains from Germany and France. The Südbahnhof is for trains to and from Graz, Klagenfurt, Villach, and Italy. The Franz-Josefs-Bahnhof, or Nordbahnhof, is for trains to and from Prague, Berlin, and Warsaw. Go to Wien-Mitte (Landstrasse) for local trains to and from the north of the city. Budapest trains use both the Westbahnhof and Südbahnhof, and Bratislava trains both Wien-Mitte and the Südbahnhof, so check.

By Bus

If you arrive by bus, it will probably be at the central bus terminal, Wien-Mitte, opposite the city air terminal (and the Hilton).

By Boat

All Danube riverboats dock at the DDSG terminal on Mexikoplatz. There's an awkward connection with the U-1 subway from here. Some boats also make a stop slightly upstream at Heiligenstadt, Nussdorf, from which there is an easier connection to the U-4 subway line.

By Car

Main access routes are the expressways to the west and south (Westautobahn, Südautobahn). Routes leading to the downtown area are marked ZENTRUM.

Getting Around

Vienna is fairly easy to explore on foot; as a matter of fact, much of the heart of the city—the area within the Ring—is a pedestrian zone. The Ring itself replaced the city ramparts, torn down just over a century ago to create today's broad, tree-lined boulevard.

Public transportation is comfortable, convenient, and frequent, though not cheap. Tickets for buses, subways, and streetcars are available in subway stations and from dispensers on buses and streetcars. Tickets in multiples of five are sold at cigarette shops—look for the sign TABAK-TRAFIK—or at the window marked VORVERKAUF at central stations such as Karlsplatz or Stephansplatz. A block of five tickets costs AS85, a single ticket AS20. If you plan to use public transportation frequently, get a **24-hour ticket** (AS50), a **three-day tourist ticket** (AS130), or an **eight-day ticket** (AS265). Tariffs could be slightly higher in 1997. Maps and information in English are available at the Stephansplatz, Karlsplatz, and Praterstern U-Bahn stations.

By Bus or Streetcar

Inner-city buses are numbered 1A through 3A and operate weekdays until about 7:40 PM, Saturday until 2 PM. Reduced fares are available for these routes (buy a **Kurzstreckenkarte;** it allows you four trips for AS34) as well as designated shorter stretches (roughly two to four stops) on all other bus and streetcar lines. Streetcars and buses are numbered or lettered according to route, and they run until about midnight. Night buses marked N follow 22 special routes every half hour between 12:30 AM and 4:30 AM. Get a route plan from any of the public transport or VORVERKAUF offices. The fare is AS25, payable on the bus unless you have a 24-hour, three-day, or eight-day ticket; then you need only pay an AS10 supplement. The central terminus is Schwedenplatz. Streetcars 1 and 2 run the circular route around the Ring, clockwise and counterclockwise, respectively.

By Subway

Subway (U-Bahn) lines—stations are marked with a huge blue U—are designated U-1, U-2, U-3, U-4, and U-6, and are clearly marked and color-coded. Trains run daily until about 12:30 AM. Additional services are provided by fast suburban trains, the S-Bahn, indicated by a stylized blue *S* symbol. Both are tied into the general city fare system.

By Taxi

Cabs can be flagged on the street if the FREI (free) sign is lit. You can also dial 1718, 60160, 31300, or 40100 to request one. All rides around town are metered. The initial fare is AS26, but expect to pay AS65–70 for an average city ride. There are additional charges for luggage, and a surcharge of AS16 is added at night, on Sunday, and for telephone orders. Tip the driver AS5–AS8 by rounding up the fare.

Important Addresses and Numbers

Visitor Information

City Tourist Office (⊠ Kärntnerstr. 38, behind the Opera, ☎ 0222/513–8892. ☉ Daily 9–7).

Embassies

The **U.S. embassy** is at Boltzmanngasse 16; the **consulate** at Gartenbaupromenade, Parkring 12A, in the Marriott building; the telephone number for both is 0222/313–39. The **Canadian embassy** is at Fleischmarkt 19, ☎ 0222/53138–3321. The **U.K. embassy and consulate** are at Jauresgasse 12; embassy ☎ 0222/713–1575, consulate ☎ 0222/714–6117.

Emergencies

Police (☎ 133), **Ambulance** (☎ 144), **Doctor:** ask your hotel, or in an emergency, phone your embassy or consulate (☞ *above*). **Pharmacies:** in city center, open weekdays 8–6, Saturday 8–noon; in neighborhoods, weekdays 8–noon, 2–6.

English-Language Bookstores

Big Ben Bookshop (⊠ Porzellang. 24, ☎ 0222/319–6412), **British Bookshop** (⊠ Weihburgg. 24–26, ☎ 0222/512–1945), **Shakespeare & Co.** (⊠ Sterng. 2, ☎ 0222/535–5053).

Travel Agencies

American Express (⊠ Kärntnerstr. 21–23, ☎ 0222/515–4040); **Austrian Travel Agency** (⊠ Opernring 3–5, ☎ 0222/588628); **Carlson-Wagons-Lits** (⊠ Kärntner Ring 2, ☎ 0222/501600).

Guided Tours

Orientation

Vienna Sightseeing Tours (☎ 0222/712–4683–0) offers a short highlights tour or a lengthier one to the Vienna Woods, Mayerling, and other sights near Vienna. Tours start in front of or beside the Opera. **Cityrama** (☎ 0222/534130) provides city tours with hotel pickup; tours assemble opposite the Inter-Continental Hotel. **Citytouring Vienna**

(☎ 0222/894–1417–0), with hotel pickup, starts from the city air terminal behind the Hilton Hotel. Prices are similar, but find out whether admission fees are included, especially to the Schönbrunn and Belvedere palaces.

Special-Interest

Tours are available to the Spanish Riding School, performances by the Vienna Boys Choir, operettas and concerts, the wine suburb of Grinzing, nightclubs, and Vienna by night. Check with the City Tourist Office or your hotel for details.

Walking

Vienna from A to Z (in English) is available for AS60 at most bookstores and tourist information offices; it explains the numbered plaques attached to all major buildings in Vienna. *In Search of Vienna: Walking Tours in the City,* by Henriette Mandl, outlines suggested routes and provides information on sights.

Excursions

Day bus trips are organized to the Danube Valley, the Hungarian border, the Alps south of Vienna, Salzburg, and Budapest; get information from the city tourist office.

Exploring Vienna

Vienna has been characterized as an "old dowager of a town"—an Austro-Hungarian empress, don't forget, widowed by the Great War. It's not just the aristocratic and courtly atmosphere, with monumental doorways and facades of former palaces at every turn. Nor is it just that Vienna (Wien in German) has a higher proportion of middle-aged and older citizens than any other city in Europe, with a concomitant air of stability, quiet, and respectability. Rather, it's this factor—combined with a love of music; a discreet weakness for rich food (especially cakes); an adherence to old-fashioned and formal forms of address; a high, if unadventurous, regard for the arts; and a gentle mourning for lost glories—that preserves the stiff elegance of Old World dignity.

The Vienna Card, available for AS180 at tourist and transportation information offices and most hotels, will give you unlimited travel for 72 hours on city buses, streetcars and the subway plus tips and discounts on various attractions and selected shopping throughout the city.

The Heart of Vienna

Most main sights are in the inner zone, the oldest part of the city, encircled by the Ring, once the route of the city walls and today a broad boulevard. Carry a ready supply of AS10 coins; many places of interest have coin-operated tape-recording machines that provide English commentaries. As you wander around, train yourself to look upward; some of the most memorable architectural delights are found on upper stories and along roof lines.

Numbers in the margin correspond to points of interest on the Vienna map.

Vienna's role as a hub of empire is preserved in the complex of buildings that make up the former imperial palace. Start your tour at Albertinaplatz, behind the Opera. Head down Augustinerstrasse. To the right is the "Memorial to Victims of Fascism," disputed in part because the sculptor was once an admitted Communist. On your left is
❶ the **Albertina,** home to the world's largest collection of drawings, sketches, engravings, and etchings. There are works here by Dürer (these are perhaps the highlight of the collection), Rembrandt, Michelangelo, Correggio, and many others. The holdings are so vast that only a lim-

ited number can be shown at one time. Some of the original works are so delicate that they can be shown only in facsimile. ⊠ *Augustinerstr. 1,* ☎ *0222/534830. Closed for renovations, but check to see whether parts of collection are being shown elsewhere.*

❷ Beethoven was a regular visitor at the Palais Lobkowitz across the street on Lobkowitzplatz. The renovated palace now houses the **Theater Museum.** Exhibits cover the history of theater in Vienna and the rest of Austria. A children's museum in the basement—alas, open only by appointment—is reached by a slide! ⊠ *Lobkowitzpl. 2,* ☎ *0222/512–8800.* ☎ *AS40.* ☉ *Tues.–Sun. 10–5.*

❸ Go back to Augustinerstrasse to the 14th-century **Augustinerkirche,** a favorite on Sundays, when the 11 AM mass is sung in Latin. The Hapsburg rulers' hearts are preserved in a chamber here. Nearby is the **★ ❹** **Nationalbibliothek** (National Library), with its stunning Baroque great hall—one of Europe's most magnificently decorated spaces. Don't overlook the fascinating collection of globes on the third floor. ⊠ *Josefspl. 1,* ☎ *0222/534–10–397.* ☎ *AS30.* ☉ *Hours may vary, but are generally May–Oct., Mon.–Sat. 10–4; Nov.–Apr., Mon.–Sat. 10–noon. Globe museum:* ☎ *0222/534–10–297.* ☎ *AS15.* ☉ *Mon.–Wed. and Fri. 11–noon, Thurs. 2–3.*

Josefsplatz is where much of *The Third Man* was filmed, specifically in and around the Palais Pallavicini across the street. The usual entrance **★ ❺** to the **Spanische Reitschule** (Spanish Riding School) is also here, though the famed white horses are actually stabled on the other side of the square. During renovations, the entrance to the school has been moved to the main courtyard next to the Swiss Gate, beyond the Michaelertor rotunda dome. For tickets, write to the Spanische Reitschule (⊠ Hofburg, A-1010 Vienna) or the Austrian Tourist Office (⊠ Friedrichstr. 7, A-1010 Vienna) *at least* three months in advance. There are generally performances on Sunday at 10:45 AM from March through June, and from September through October. Evening performances are occasionally given on Wednesdays at 7. Tickets for the few short training performances on Saturday mornings at 10 AM are available only from ticket offices and travel agencies. You can watch the 10 AM–noon training sessions Tuesday to Saturday during much of the performance season; tickets are available only at the door (Hofburg, inner court; ☎ AS80).

★ ❻ From here you're only a few steps from Michaelerplatz, the square that marks the entrance to the **Hofburg,** or imperial palace. On one side of the square, opposite the entrance, at the intersection of Herrengasse and Kohlmarkt, is the **Loos Building** (1911), designed by Adolf Loos. Step inside—it's now a bank—to see the remarkable restoration of the foyer. Outside, it's no more than a simple stucco-and-glass structure, but architectural historians point to it as one of the earliest "modern" buildings—with style determined by function—in Europe. In striking contrast is the Baroque **Michaelertor,** opposite, the principal gateway to the Hofburg.

NEED A BREAK? Some insist that no visit to Vienna is complete without a visit to **Demel** (☎ 0222/535–1717), on the left just down the Kohlmarkt. The pastries and lunches here are expensive even by Viennese standards, but new management has sought to bring back quality and service to match the elegant tradition.

❼ Head through the domed gateway of the Michaelertor to visit the **imperial apartments** of Emperor Franz Josef and Empress Elisabeth. Among the exhibits is the exercise equipment used by the beautiful empress. Here, too, is the dress she was wearing when she was stabbed

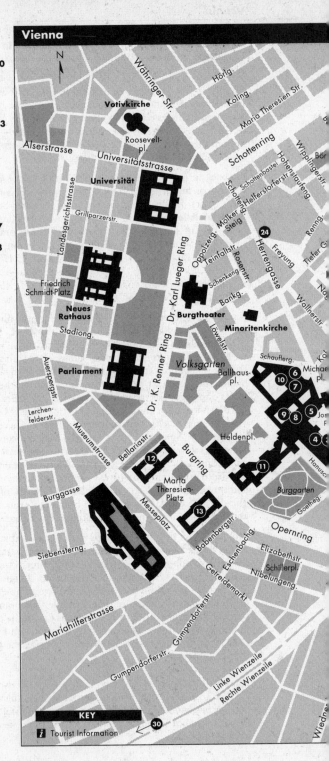

Vienna

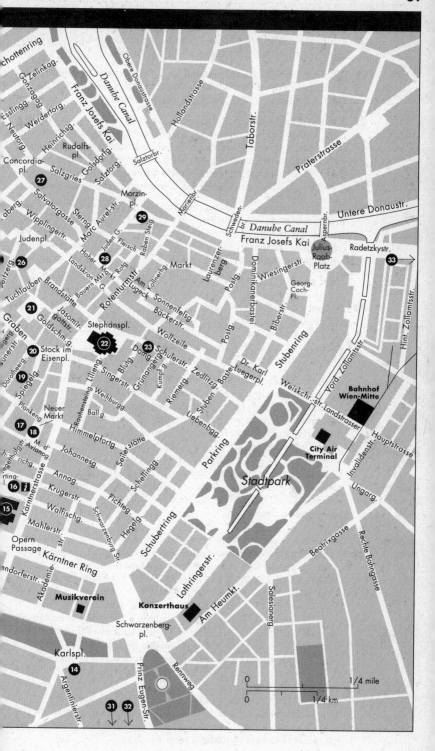

to death in 1898 by a demented Italian anarchist on the shore of Lake Geneva; the dagger marks are visible. ⊠ *Michaelerpl. 1,* ☎ *0222/587–5554–515.* ▣ *AS70; combined admission with Court Silver and Table-ware Museum: AS90.* ⊘ *Daily 9–5.*

⑧ Be sure to see the **Schatzkammer,** the imperial treasury, home of the magnificent crown jewels. ⊠ *Hofburg, Schweizerhof,* ☎ *0222/533–7931.* ▣ *AS60.* ⊘ *Wed., Fri.-Mon. 10–6, Thurs. 10–9.*

⑨ The **Hofburgkapelle,** or court chapel, is where the Vienna Boys Choir sings mass at 9:15 AM on Sunday mid-September through June. You'll need tickets; they are available at the chapel from 5 PM Friday (queue up by 4:30 and expect long lines) or by writing two months in advance to the Hofmusikkapelle, Hofburg, Schweizerhof, A-1010 Vienna. The City Tourist Office can sometimes help with ticket applications.

⑩ Diagonally across the main courtyard is the new **Court Silver and Tableware Museum,** a brilliant showcase of imperial table settings sparkling with light and mirrors reflecting period elegance. ⊠ *Burghof inner court,* ☎ *0222/533-1044.* ▣ *AS70; combined admission with imperial apartments: AS90.* ⊘ *Daily 9–5.*

Head south to Heldenplatz, the vast square punctuated with oversize equestrian statues of Prince Eugene and Archduke Karl, which stand
⑪ in front of the **Neue Hofburg.** This ponderously ornate 19th-century edifice—Hitler announced the annexation of Austria from its balcony in 1938—now houses a series of museums, ranging from archeology to weapons. ⊠ *Neue Hofburg, Heldenpl. 1,* ☎ *0222/521770.* ▣ *AS30.* ⊘ *Wed.–Mon. 10–6. Ethnological Museum* ⊘ *Wed.–Mon. 10–4.*

Walk west again under the unornamented Hero's Monument archway
⑫ and across the Ring. The **Naturhistorisches Museum** (Natural History
★ **⑬** Museum) is on your right, the **Kunsthistorisches Museum** (Art History Museum) on your left. The latter is one of the great art museums of the world, and is not to be missed. Among the highlights of its collec-tions are the old master paintings, including the legendary collection of paintings by Pieter Brueghel the Elder, plus celebrated works by Cranach, Titian, Canaletto, Rubens, and Velázquez. But there are im-portant Egyptian, Greek, Etruscan, and Roman exhibits, too. ⊠ *Bur-gring 5,* ☎ *0222/521770.* ▣ *AS45.* ⊘ *Tues.–Sun. 10–6, selected galleries also Thurs. 10–9.*

NEED A BREAK?   Across the Messeplatz from the museums stretches the Messepalast, the former court stables and now a fair and exhibition space. Inside is one of Vienna's better-kept secrets, the **S'Glacis-Beisl** restaurant (☎ 0222/526–6795). Wine and local specialties have to be experienced in the garden under its vine-clad arbors.

Head east down the Getreidemarkt, with the Kunsthistorisches Museum on your left. Looming up ahead is the gilt cauliflower dome of the Se-cession, with a structure that looks like a huge yellow and blue con-tainer beyond it. Both are art museums with changing exhibits. Beyond
★ **⑭** them, across Karlsplatz, is the heroic **Karlskirche** (Church of St. Charles), its facade and dome flanked by vast twin columns. The church was built around 1715 by Fischer von Erlach. Its oval interior is surprisingly small, given the monumental exterior: One expects something more on the scale of St. Peter's in Rome. The ceiling has airy frescoes, and stiff shafts of gilt radiate like rays of sunlight from the altar.

Take the pedestrian underpass back under the Ring to Opernplatz. This
⑮ is the site of the **Staatsoper,** one of the best opera houses in the world and a focus of Viennese social life. Tickets are expensive and scarce,

so you may have to settle for a backstage tour. The tour schedule for the day is usually posted beside the door under the right front arcade, on the Kärntnerstrasse side, and will depend on the activities inside.

★ **16** Head up Kärntnerstrasse, Vienna's main thoroughfare, now a busy pedestrian mall. On your left is the creamy facade of the **Sacher Hotel.** Take a look inside at the plush red-and-gilt decor, a fin de siècle masterpiece. The hotel is also the home of the original Sachertorte—the ultimate chocolate cake. Back on Kärntnerstrasse, around the corner from the Sacher, is the City Tourist Office. Leading off Kärntnerstrasse, to the left, is the

17 narrow Marco d'Aviano-Gasse. Follow it to the **Kapuzinerkirche,** in whose crypt, called the **Kaisergruft,** or imperial vault, you can stroll among the sarcophagi of long-dead Hapsburgs. The oldest tomb is that of Ferdinand II; it dates from 1633. The most recent one is that of Empress Zita, widow of the last of the kaisers, who died in 1989. ✉ *Neuer Markt 1,* ☎ *0222/512–6853–12.* ✆ *AS40.* ☉ *daily 9:30–4.*

18 In the center of the square is the ornate 18th-century **Donner Brunnen** (Donner Fountain). Sculpted figures represent the main rivers that flow into the Danube. Empress Maria Theresa thought the figures were obscene, and wanted to have them either removed or properly clothed.

NEED A BREAK? Coffee or tea and what are said even by the French and Belgians to be the best pastries in the world are available at the **Konditorei Oberlaa** (✉ Neuer Markt 16).

19 Turn down Plankengasse to Dorotheergasse. On your right, in the former Eskeles palace, is the **Jewish Museum.** Now that its expansion and renovation are complete, its permanent and changing exhibits at last adequately portray the richness of the Jewish culture and heritage that contributed so much to Vienna and Austria. ✉ *Dorotheerg. 11,* ☎ *0222/535–0431.* ✆ *AS70.* ☉ *Sun.–Wed., and Fri. 10–6, Thurs. 10–9.*

20 Continue north through Dorotheergasse to reach the pedestrians-only Graben. The **Pestsäule,** or Plague Column, shoots up from the middle of the broad street like a geyser of whipped cream touched with gold. It commemorates the Black Death of 1697. A small turn to the right,

21 just past the column, leads to the Baroque **Peterskirche** (St. Peter's Church). This little church, erected by Johann Lukas von Hildebrandt in about 1730, has what is probably the city's most theatrical interior. The pulpit is especially fine, with a highly ornate canopy, but florid and swirling decoration is everywhere. Many of the decorative elements are based on the tent form, a motif suggested by the encampment of Turkish forces beyond the city walls during the great siege of Vienna at the end of the 17th century.

22 Walk down Goldschmiedgasse to Stephansplatz, the great square surrounding the **Stephansdom** (St. Stephen's Cathedral). The cathedral's towering Gothic spires and gaudy 19th-century tile roof still dominate the Vienna skyline. The oldest part of the structure is the 13th-century entrance, the soaring **Riesentor,** or Giant Doorway. Inside, the church is mysteriously shadowy, filled with an array of monuments, tombs, sculptures, paintings, and pulpits. Despite extensive wartime damage—and numerous Baroque additions—the atmosphere seems authentically medieval. Climb up the 345 steps of the south tower—the **Alte Steffl,** or Old Steven—for a stupendous view over the city. An elevator goes up the north tower to the **Pummerin,** the Boomer, a 22-ton bell cast in 1711 from cannons captured from the Turks. Take a 30-minute tour of the crypt to see the copper jars in which the entrails of the Hapsburgs are carefully preserved.

23 On a narrow street just east of the cathedral is the house where Mozart lived from 1784 to 1787. Today it contains the **Mozart Erinnerungsräume** (Mozart Museum). It was here that the composer wrote *The Marriage of Figaro* (hence the nickname Figaro House), and, some claim, spent the happiest years of his life. ⊠ *Domg. 5,* ☎ *0222/513–6294.* ⊠ *AS25.* ☺ *Tues.–Sun. 9–12:15 and 1–4:30.*

Other Corners of Vienna

Walk back down the Graben and the narrow Naglergasse and turn left into the Freyung. On your left is the **Palais Ferstl,** now a stylish shopping arcade. At the back is the skillfully restored **Café Central,** once frequented by Vienna's leading literary figures. Next door to the Palais Ferstl is the **Palais Harrach,** part of which is now an outpost of the Museum of Fine Arts, presenting special exhibits and the overflow of tapestries and paintings from the main house.

24 Cross the Freyung to the imposing **Schottenkirche** (Scottish Church). Despite its name, the monks who founded this church were actually Irish, not Scots. The Benedictines have set up a small but worthwhile museum of mainly religious art, including a late-Gothic winged altarpiece removed from the church when the interior was given a Baroque overlay in the mid-1600s. The entrance is in the courtyard to the left. ⊠ *Freyung 6,* ☎ *0222/534–98–600.* ⊠ *AS40.* ☺ *Thurs.–Sat. 10–5, Sun. 12–5.*

Turn back through the Freyung to **Am Hof,** a remarkable square with what is possibly the most ornate fire station in the world. You'll find occasional flea markets here on Thursday and Friday in summer and **25** seasonal markets at other times. Cross the square to the **Kirche am Hof.** The interior is curiously reminiscent of those of many Dutch churches.

NEED A BREAK?

For a tasty thick soup or snack, or just a glass of wine or beer or a coffee, proceed down Drahtgasse and turn into the tiny Ledererhof to discover **Bretzl G'wölb** (⊠ Ledererhof 9, ☎ 0222/533–8811), once a pretzel bakery and now a minicafé charmingly decorated with antiques.

26 Continue to Judenplatz and turn right into Parisergasse to the **Uhrenmuseum** (Clock Museum), housed in a lovely Renaissance structure. Try to be there when the hundreds of clocks strike the noon hour. ⊠ *Schulhof 2,* ☎ *0222/533–2265.* ⊠ *AS50.* ☺ *Tues.–Sun. 9–4:30.*

Turn down Kurrentgasse and, via Fütterergasse, cross the Wipplinger-**27** strasse into Stoss im Himmel (literally, "thrust to heaven"). To your left down Salvatorgasse is **Maria am Gestade,** originally a church for fishermen from the nearby canal. Note its ornate "folded hands" spire. Re-**28** turn along Wipplingerstrasse, across Marc Aurel-Strasse, to **Hoher Markt,** with its central monument celebrating the betrothal of Mary and Joseph. Underground are **Roman ruins,** remains of the 2nd-century Roman legion encampment. ⊠ *Hoher Markt 3,* ☎ *0222/535–5606.* ⊠ *AS25; free on Fri. morning.* ☺ *Tues.–Sun. 9–12:15 and 1–4:30.*

On the north side of Hoher Markt is the amusing **Anker-Uhr,** a clock that marks the hour with a parade of moving figures. The figures are identified on a plaque at the lower left of the clock; it's well worth pass-**29** ing by at noon to catch the show. Go through Judengasse to **Ruprechts-kirche** (St. Rupert's). This oldest church in Vienna, dating from the 11th century, is small, damp, dark, and—unfortunately—most often closed, though you can peek through a window.

Vienna Environs

It's a 15-minute ride from the city center on the U-4 subway line to **★ 30** **Schönbrunn Palace** (stop at either Schönbrunn or Hietzing), the magnificent Baroque residence and formal gardens built for the Hapsburgs between 1696 and 1713. Kaiser Franz Josef I was born and died here. His "office" (kept as he left it in 1916) is a touching reminder of his spartan life. Other rooms, by contrast, are filled with imperial elegance. The ornate reception rooms are still used for state occasions. A guided tour leads through 40–45 of the palace's 1,441 rooms, and is the best way to see inside the palace. Among the many curiosities are the Chinese Room and the gym fitted out for Empress Elisabeth, where she exercised daily to keep her trim figure. Other rooms are occasionally open independent of tours. ⊠ *Schönbrunner Schlosstr.,* ☎ *0222/81113–238.* ⊠ *AS140 with guided tour; AS110 without tour (40 rooms).* ☉ *Nov.–Mar., daily 9–4:30; Apr.–Oct., daily 8:30–5.*

Once on the palace grounds, don't overlook the **Tiergarten** (zoo). It's Europe's oldest menagerie, established in 1752 to amuse and educate the court. It houses an extensive assortment of animals, some of them in their original Baroque enclosures. ☎ *0222/877–9294.* ⊠ *AS90.* ☉ *Nov.–Jan., daily 9–4:30; Feb. and Oct., daily 9–5; Mar., daily 9–5:30; Apr., daily 9–6; May–Sept., daily 9–6:30.*

Follow the pathways up to the **Gloriette,** a Baroque folly on the rise behind Schönbrunn, to enjoy superb views of the city. The palace was originally planned to occupy this site, but the additional construction costs were considered too high. The restored edifice again incorporates a café, as it did when first erected. ⊠ *AS20.* ☉ *May–Sept., daily 9–6; Oct., daily 9–5.*

The **Wagenburg** (Carriage Museum), near the entrance to the palace grounds, displays splendid examples of bygone conveyances, from ornate children's sleighs to the pompous carriages built to carry the coffins of deceased emperors in state funerals. ☎ *0222/877–3244.* ⊠ *AS30.* ☉ *May–Sept., daily 9–6; Apr. and Oct., daily 9–5; Nov.–Mar., Tues.–Sun. 10–5.*

❸❶ Take Streetcar D toward the Südbahnhof to reach **Schloss Belvedere** (Belvedere Palace), a Baroque complex often compared to Versailles. It was commissioned by Prince Eugene of Savoy and built by Johann Lukas von Hildebrandt in 1721–22. The palace consists of two separate buildings, one at the foot of a hill and the other at the top. The lavish gardens are considered among the finest showpieces of the Baroque taste in landscaping found anywhere. Two outstanding art museums are now found here: The Upper Belvedere houses a gallery of 19th-and 20th-century Viennese art, featuring works by Klimt (including his world-famous painting, *The Kiss*), Kokoschka, Schiele, Waldmüller, and Markart; the Lower Belvedere has a Baroque museum together with exhibits of Austrian art of the Middle Ages. ⊠ *Prinz-Eugen-Str. 27,* ☎ *0222/798–4158–0.* ⊠ *AS60.* ☉ *Tues.–Sun. 10–5.*

❸❷ Continue across the Gürtel from the Upper Belvedere southward to the **20th Century Museum,** containing a small but extremely tasteful modern art collection. ⊠ *Schweizer Garten,* ☎ *0222/799–6900–0.* ⊠ *AS45.* ☉ *Tues.–Sun. 10–6.*

You can reach a small corner of the **Vienna Woods** by streetcar and bus: Take a streetcar or the U-2 subway line to Schottentor/University and, from there, Streetcar 38 (Grinzing) to the end of the line. Grinzing itself is a village out of a picture book. Unfortunately, much of the wine offered in its wine taverns, or Heuriger, is less than enchanting. (For better wine and ambience, try the area around Pfarrplatz and Probusgasse in Hohe Warte—Streetcar 37, Bus 39A—or the suburb of Nussdorf—Streetcar D.) To get into the woods, change in Grinzing to Bus 38A. This will take you to the Kahlenberg, which provides a superb view out over the Danube and the city. You can take the bus or hike to the Leopoldsberg, the promontory over the Danube from which Turkish invading forces were repulsed in the 16th and 17th centuries.

Off the Beaten Path

Vienna's **Bermuda Triangle** (around Judengasse/Seitenstettengasse) is jammed with everything from good bistros to jazz clubs. Also check the tourist office's museum list carefully: There's something for everyone, ranging from Sigmund Freud's apartment to the Funeral and Burial Museum. The **Hundertwasserhaus** (⊠ Kegelgasse/Löwengasse; Streetcar N), an astonishing apartment complex designed by artist Friedenreich Hundertwasser, with turrets, towers, unusual windows, and uneven floors, will be of interest to those who do not think that architectural form has to follow function. The nearby Hundertwasser-designed **KunstHaus Wien** art museum offers Hundertwasser plus changing exhibits of other modern works. ⊠ *Untere Weissbergerstr. 13,* ☎ *0222/712–0491.* ☞ *AS80; half-price on Mon.* ☉ *daily 10–7.*

Children and adults alike will enjoy the charming **Doll and Toy Museum,** next door to the Clock Museum (☞ Exploring Vienna, *above*). It's filled with trains, dollhouses, and troops of teddy bears. ⊠ *Schulhof 4,* ☎ *0222/535–6860.* ☞ *AS60.* ☉ *Tues.–Sun. 10–6.*

Shopping

Boutiques

Name brands are found along the **Kohlmarkt** and **Graben** and their respective side streets, and the side streets off the **Kärntnerstrasse.**

Folk Costumes

A good selection at reasonable prices is offered by the **NÖ Heimatwerk** (⊠ Herreng. 6); also try **Trachten Tostmann** (⊠ Schotteng. 3a) or **Loden-Plankl** (⊠ Michaelerpla. 6).

Shopping Districts

Tourists gravitate to the **Kärntnerstrasse,** but the Viennese do most of their shopping on the **Mariahilferstrasse.**

Food and Flea Markets

The **Naschmarkt** (foodstuffs market; ⊠ Between the Rechte and Linke Wienzeile; weekdays 6 AM–mid-afternoon, Sat. 6–1) is a sensational open-air market offering specialties from around the world. The **Flohmarkt** (flea market) operates year-round beyond the Naschmarkt (subway U-4 to Kettenbrückeng.; Sat. 8–4) and is equally fascinating. An **Arts and Antiques Market** with better offerings operates on Saturday (2–6) and Sunday (10–6) alongside the Danube Canal near the Salztorbrücke. From late spring to early fall, check the square Am Hof for antiques and collectibles on Thursday and Friday. Also look for the seasonal markets in the Freyung square opposite Palais Ferstal.

Dining

In recent years Vienna, once a culinary backwater, has produced a new generation of chefs willing to slaughter sacred cows and create a *Neue Küche,* a new Vienna cuisine. The movement is well past the "less is more" stage that nouvelle cuisine traditionally demands (and to which most Viennese vociferously objected), relying now on lighter versions of the old standbys and clever combinations of such traditional ingredients as liver pâtés and sour cream.

In a first-class restaurant you will pay as much as in most other Western European capitals. But you can still find good food at refreshingly low prices in the simpler restaurants, particularly at neighborhood

Gasthäuser in the suburbs. Happily, some of the most delicious taste treats in Austria are gentle on the wallet, such as *Bosner Wurst* (a hot dog with Balkan spice), one of Salzburg's enduring favorites, or the simple *Stelze* (roast knuckle of pork), which can be elevated to cuisine if its crunchy crust is done right. Remember if you eat your main meal at noon (as the Viennese do), you can take advantage of the luncheon specials. For details and price-category definitions, *see* Dining *in* Staying in Austria, *above.*

$$$$ ✕ **Korso.** You'll find outstanding food and atmosphere at this gourmet
★ temple of new Vienna cuisine. Chef Reinhard Gerer produces exquisite variations on Austrian standards such as pork and beef by borrowing accents from Asian traditions. ⊠ *Mahlerstr. 2,* ☎ *0222/51516–546. AE, DC, MC, V. Closed 3 wks in August. No lunch Sat.*

$$$$ ✕ **Palais Schwarzenberg.** The glassed-in restaurant with a view into the palace gardens is a perfect setting for the excellent fillet of beef, lamb in herb crust, or souffléed turbot. Wine prices are high, although special offers can be outstanding and reasonable. The house wines are good. ⊠ *Schwarzenbergpl. 9,* ☎ *0222/798–4515. Reservations essential. AE, DC, MC, V.*

$$$$ ✕ **Steirereck.** Acclaimed as Austria's best restaurant, the Steirereck successfully espouses the lighter new Vienna cuisine, with service that cannot be faulted. You dine handsomely in classical elegance, joining businesspeople at noon, personalities at night. Tables are set with flower arrangements and elegant crystal, with a flair that matches the food. Try Styrian venison, turbot crepes with asparagus, rack of wild boar with tiny sausages, or even a schnitzel. The noontime prix-fixe lunch offers choices and is a good value. ⊠ *Rasumofskyg. 2,* ☎ *0222/713–3168. Reservations essential. AE, DC, MC, V. Closed weekends and holidays.*

$$$$ ✕ **Zu den Drei Husaren.** This is one of Vienna's enduring monuments to tradition, complete with candlelight and live piano music (except on Sunday). Casual visitors (as opposed to regulars) may have to settle for more atmosphere than service, but the food—mainly Viennese standards such as variations on rump steak—is of top quality. A dip into the enticing but pricey hors d'oeurve trolley can easily double the lunch or dinner bill. ⊠ *Weihburgg. 4,* ☎ *0222/512–1092. Reservations essential. AE, DC, MC, V. Closed mid-July–mid-Aug.*

$$$ ✕ **Plachutta.** The feature here is superb *Tafelspitz* (boiled beef), served in its own delicious soup, for which you can order the day's "supplement"—*Frittaten* (thin pancake strips), perhaps, or *Leberknödel* (liver dumpling). You choose the cut or type of beef you prefer (all are outstanding) or select a steak or grilled fish, and finish with a rhubarb strudel. The house wines are fine; service occasionally less so. ⊠ *Wollzeile 38,* ☎ *0222/512–1577. Dinner reservations essential. AE, MC, V.*

$$$ ✕ **Vier Jahreszeiten.** This restaurant effortlessly manages to achieve
★ that delicate balance between food and atmosphere. The service is attentive without being overbearing. The lunch buffet offers both excellent food and value. Evening dining includes grill specialties and live piano music. ⊠ *Hotel Inter-Continental, Johannesg. 28,* ☎ *0222/71122–143. AE, DC, MC, V. Closed weekends and 2 wks in June.*

$$$ ✕ **Zum Kuckuck.** Wood paneling and the patina of years mark this intimate restaurant, candlelit at night. Specials change daily but tend toward regional variations on pork, venison, or lamb. The fig cake with rum sauce is a house classic. ⊠ *Himmelpfortg. 15,* ☎ *0222/512–8470. Reservations essential. AE, DC, MC, V. Closed weekends.*

$$ ✕ **Bei Max.** The decor is somewhat bland, but the tasty Carinthian specialties—*Käsnudeln* and *Fleischnudeln* (cheese and meat ravioli) in particular—keep this friendly restaurant packed. ⊠ *Landhausg. 2/Her-*

rengasse, ☎ *0222/533–7359. No credit cards. Closed Sat., Sun., last wk in July, first 3 wks in Aug.*

$$ ✕ **Figlmüller.** Known for its schnitzel, Figlmüller is always packed. Guests share the benches, the long tables, and the experience. Food choices are limited, but nobody seems to mind. Only wine is offered to drink, but it is good. The small "garden" is now enclosed and is just as popular as the inside rooms. ⊠ *Wollzeile 5 (passageway),* ☎ *0222/512–6177. No credit cards.*

$$ ✕ **Melker Stiftskeller.** This is one of the city's half-dozen genuine *Weinkeller* (cellar wine taverns). The food selection is limited but good, featuring pig's knuckle. House wine from the Wachau is excellent. ⊠ *Schotteng. 3,* ☎ *0222/533–5530. MC. Dinner only; closed Sun.*

$$ ✕ **Ofenloch.** This place is always packed, which speaks well not only of
★ the excellent specialties from some Viennese grandmother's repertory but also of the atmosphere. Waitresses are dressed in turn-of-the-century costume, and the furnishings add to the color. At times the rooms may be too smoky and noisy for some tastes. If you like garlic, try *Vanillerostbraten,* a rump steak with as much garlic as you request. ⊠ *Kurrentg. 8,* ☎ *0222/533–8844. Reservations essential. AE, DC, MC, V.*

$$ ✕ **Stadtbeisl.** Good standard Austrian fare is served at this popular eatery, which is comfortable without being pretentious. The service gets uneven as the place fills up, but if you are seated outside in summer, you probably won't mind. ⊠ *Naglerg. 21,* ☎ *0222/533–3507. Reservations essential. V.*

$$ ✕ **Zu den drei Hacken.** This is one of the few genuine Viennese Gasthäuser in the city center; like the place itself, the fare is solid if not elegant. Legend has it that Schubert dined here; if so, the ambience probably hasn't changed much since then. There are tables outside in summer, although the extra seating capacity strains both the kitchen and the service. ⊠ *Singerstr. 28,* ☎ *0222/512–5895. AE, DC, MC, V. Closed Sun.*

$$ ✕ **Zu ebener Erde und erster Stock.** Ask for a table upstairs in this
★ exquisite, tiny, utterly original Biedermeier house, which serves excellent Austrian fare; the downstairs space is really more for snacks. ⊠ *Burgg. 13,* ☎ *0222/523–6254. AE. No lunch Sat. Closed Sun., Mon., and late July–late Aug.*

$ ✕ **Brezlg'wölb.** Casual food–soups in mini-tureen portions and salad plates—and a cozy, friendly atmosphere draw the crowds here. If you sit in the quiet courtyard between Am Hof and Judenplatz, you look up at classical facades; inside, small, brick-vaulted rooms offer diners a comfortable interlude. Many come just to enjoy the excellent wine, beer, and coffee in the candlelit cellar rooms. ⊠ *Ledererhof 9,* ☎ *0222/533–8811. No credit cards.*

$ ✕ **Gigerl.** It's hard to believe you're right in the middle of the city at
★ this imaginative and charming wine restaurant that serves hot and cold buffets. The rooms are small and cozy but may get smoky and noisy when the place is full—which it usually is. The food is typical of wine gardens on the fringes of the city: roast meats, casserole dishes, cold cuts, salads. The wines are excellent. The surrounding narrow alleys and ancient buildings add to the charm of the outdoor tables in summer. ⊠ *Rauhensteing. 3,* ☎ *0222/513–4431. AE, DC, MC, V. No lunch Sun.*

$ ✕ **Königsbacher bei der Oper.** Its spaces are intimate and its tables close,
★ but portions are generous and the daily special (listed for the week) could be anything from roast pork to a ham-and-noodle casserole. Shaded outdoor tables are delightful in summer. ⊠ *Walfischg. 5,* ☎ *0222/513–1210. No credit cards. No dinner Sat. Closed Sun.*

Cafés

A quintessential Viennese institution, the coffeehouse, or café, is club, pub, and bistro all rolled into one. To savor the atmosphere of the coffeehouses you must take your time; set aside an afternoon, a morning, or at least a couple of hours, and settle down in one of your choice. There is no need to worry about overstaying your welcome, even over a single small cup of Mokka—of course in some of the more opulent coffeehouses, this cup of coffee can cost as much as a meal.

Here's a sampling of the best of the traditional cafés: **Alte Backstube** (⊠ Lange G. 34, ☎ 0222/406–1101; AE, MC, V; closed Mon. and Aug.), in a gorgeous Baroque house—with a café in front and restaurant in back—was once a bakery and is now a museum as well; **Café Central** (⊠ Herreng. 14, ☎ 0222/535–4176–0; AE, DC, MC, V; closed Sun.) is where Stalin and Trotsky played chess; **Haag** (⊠ Schotteng. 2, ☎ 0222/533–1810; closed Sat. evening and Sun. in July and Aug.), with crystal chandeliers and a shaded courtyard garden in summer, serves snacks and desserts; **Museum** (⊠ Friedrichstr. 6, ☎ 0222/586–5202), with its original interior by the architect Adolf Loos, draws a mixed crowd and has lots of newspapers. Whole books have been written at and about the **Café Hawelka** (⊠ Dorotheerg. 12, ☎ 0222/512–8230; closed Tues., Sun. noon). Its international clientele ranges from artists to politicians. Hawelka is jammed any time of day, so you share a table (and the smoky atmosphere). In a city noted for fine coffee, Hawelka's is superb, even more so when accompanied by a freshly baked *Buchterln* (sweet roll; evenings only).

Lodging

Vienna's inner city is the best base for visitors because it's so close to most of the major sights, restaurants, and shops. This accessibility translates, of course, into higher prices. Try bargaining for discounts at the larger international chain hotels during the off season. For details and price-category definitions, *see* Lodging *in* Staying in Austria, *above.*

$$$$ ★ 🏨 **Bristol.** Opposite the Opera, the Bristol is classic Viennese, preferred by many for the service as well as the location. The bar is comfortable, though not overly private, and the restaurants associated with the hotel are outstanding, especially the Korso. Rear and upper guest rooms are quieter. ⊠ *Kärntner Ring 1,* ☎ *0222/515160,* 🖷 *0222/515–16550. 146 rooms with bath. 2 restaurants, bar. AE, DC, MC, V.*

$$$$ ★ 🏨 **Imperial.** This former palace represents elegant old and new Vienna at its best, with such features as heated towel racks in some rooms. The location could hardly be better, although being on the Ring sometimes makes the front and lower rooms a bit noisy. The bar is intimate and pleasant. Lunch in the café is both reasonable and good; the hotel restaurant is still searching for its identity. ⊠ *Kärntner Ring 16,* ☎ *0222/501100,* 🖷 *0222/501–10410. 128 rooms with bath or shower. Restaurant, café, bar, beauty parlor, conference rooms. AE, DC, MC, V.*

$$$$ ★ 🏨 **Inter-Continental.** Vienna's modern Inter-Continental has the reputation of being one of the chain's very best. The rooms are a cut above standard; the main restaurant, exceptional. But whereas the hotel succeeds in acquiring some Viennese charm, the bar is impersonal, as is the less formal Brasserie. Rooms in front overlooking the park are quieter, particularly in winter when the ice-skating rink at the back is in operation. ⊠ *Johannesg. 28,* ☎ *0222/711220,* 🖷 *0222/713–4489. 492 rooms with bath. 2 restaurants, bar, barbershop, sauna, health club, laundry service, parking (fee). AE, DC, MC, V.*

$$$$ ▦ **Marriott.** The only Viennese aspect here is the service; all else is global modern. The atrium lobby, although pleasant, is anything but intimate. The restaurants are satisfactory if not quite up to the level of those of other top hotels, although Sunday brunch at the Marriott has become immensely popular (book at least a week in advance). ⊠ *Parkring 12A,* ☎ *0222/515180,* ⅀ *0222/515–186722. 304 rooms with bath. 2 restaurants, café, bar, pool, sauna, health club, shops, parking (fee). AE, DC, MC, V.*

$$$$ ▦ **Palais Schwarzenberg.** The rooms are furnished with antiques and appropriately incorporated into a quiet wing of this Baroque palace a 10-minute walk from the Opera. The restaurant enjoys a good reputation; the view out over the formal gardens is glorious. ⊠ *Schwarzenbergpl. 9,* ☎ *0222/798–4515,* ⅀ *0222/798–4714. 38 rooms with bath. Restaurant, bar, parking. AE, DC, MC, V.*

$$$$ ▦ **Sacher.** The hotel's reputation has varied considerably during recent years, but it remains one of the legendary addresses in Europe, with its opulent decor highlighted by original oil paintings, sculptures, and objets d'art. The Blue and Red bars are intimate and favored by nonguests as well, as is the café, particularly in summer when tables are set up outside. Guest rooms are spacious and elegantly appointed. ⊠ *Philharmonikerstr. 4,* ☎ *0222/514560,* ⅀ *0222/514–57810. 116 rooms with bath or shower. Restaurant, 2 bars, coffee shop. AE, DC, MC, V.*

$$$ ▦ **Altstadt.** You're one streetcar stop or a short walk from the main museums in this newly renovated Old Vienna residential building. Each of the spacious rooms is decorated individually, though the predominant scheme involves fine wood period furniture set against light blue-gray walls. The upper rooms have views out over the city rooftops. ⊠ *Kircheng. 41,* ☎ *0222/526–33990,* ⅀ *0222/423–4901. 25 rooms with bath or shower. Bar. AE, DC, MC, V.*

$$$ ▦ **Astoria.** Though the Astoria is one of Vienna's traditional old hotels, the rooms have been modernized considerably. The paneled lobby, however, has been preserved and retains an unmistakable Old World patina. The location is central, but because of the street musicians and late-night crowds in the pedestrian zone, rooms overlooking the Kärntnerstrasse tend to be noisy in summer. ⊠ *Fürichg. 1,* ☎ *0222/515770,* ⅀ *0222/515–7782. 108 rooms with bath or shower. Restaurant. AE, DC, MC, V.*

$$$ ▦ **König von Ungarn.** This utterly charming centrally located hotel is tucked away in the shadow of the cathedral. Its historic facade belies the efficient modernity of the interior, from the atrium lobby to the guest rooms themselves. Insist on written confirmation of bookings. ⊠ *Schulerstr. 10,* ☎ *0222/515840,* ⅀ *0222/515848. 32 rooms with bath or shower. Restaurant, bar. DC, MC, V.*

$$$ ▦ **Mailberger Hof.** This is a favorite of opera stars, conductors, and others who want a central but quiet location. Some rooms have limited kitchenette facilities. The arcaded courtyard is very pretty. ⊠ *Annag. 7,* ☎ *0222/512–0641,* ⅀ *0222/512–064110. 40 rooms with bath or shower. Restaurant. AE, MC, V.*

$$$ ▦ **Opernring.** Spacious and homelike front rooms are less quiet but have great views across the Ring to the Opera. Unusually personal attention and helpful management are added features in this Best Western affiliate. ⊠ *Opernring 11,* ☎ *0222/587-5518,* ⅀ *0222/587-5518-29. 35 rooms with bath. AE, DC, MC, V.*

$$ ▦ **Austria.** This older hotel is on a quiet side street in a historic area.
★   It is popular with tourists. Rooms with shower rather than bath are cheapest. ⊠ *Wolfeng. 3/Fleischmarkt,* ☎ *0222/51523,* ⅀ *0222/515–23506. 46 rooms, 42 with bath or shower. Bar, free parking. AE, DC, MC, V.*

$$ ⊞ **Kärntnerhof.** Though tucked away in a tiny, quiet side street, the
★ Kärntnerhof is nevertheless centrally located. It's known for its par-
ticularly congenial staff. The rooms are functionally decorated but clean
and serviceable. Rooms with shower only are in the $ category. ⊠
Grashofg. 4, ☎ *0222/512–1923,* FAX *0222/513–222833. 43 rooms,
41 with bath or shower. AE, DC, MC, V.*

$$ ⊞ **Pension Zipser.** This 1904 house, with an ornate facade and gilt-
★ trimmed coat of arms, has become a favorite with regular visitors to
Vienna. It is slightly less central than some others, but very comfortable. ⊠ *Lange Gasse 49,* ☎ *0222/404–5400,* FAX *0222/408–526613.
46 rooms with bath or shower. Bar. AE, DC, MC, V.*

$$ ⊞ **Post.** Taking its name from the city's main post office, opposite, this
is an older but updated hotel that offers a fine location, a friendly staff,
and a good café. ⊠ *Fleischmarkt 24,* ☎ *0222/515830,* FAX *0222/515–
83808. 107 rooms, 77 with bath or shower. AE, DC, MC, V.*

$$ ⊞ **Wandl.** The house is old and some of the rooms are small, but the
Wandl's location and reasonable prices compensate for most of its de-
ficiencies. Baths with tub rather than shower put prices into the $$$
category. ⊠ *Peterspl. 9,* ☎ *0222/534550,* FAX *0222/534–5577. 134
rooms with bath or shower. Bar. No credit cards.*

$ ⊞ **Kugel.** This older but freshly redecorated hotel is halfway between
the Westbahnhof and the city center. Rooms are small but well furnished
and the staff is helpful. ⊠ *Siebensterng. 43,* ☎ *0222/523-3355,* FAX
0222/523-1678. 38 rooms, 17 with bath or shower. No credit cards.

$ ⊞ **Rathaus.** The spacious rooms are furnished in contemporary style.
Management, the same people who run the nearby Zipser, is particu-
larly accommodating. ⊠ *Lange Gasse 13,* ☎ *0222/406-4302,*
FAX *0222/408-4272. 43 rooms with bath or shower. No credit cards.*

The Arts

Theater and Opera

Check the monthly program published by the city; posters also show
opera and theater schedules. The **Staatsoper,** one of world's great opera
houses, features major stars in its almost-nightly original-language per-
formances. The **Volksoper** offers lighter operas, operettas, and musi-
cals, all in German. Performances at the **Burgtheater** and **Akadamietheater**
are also in German. Tickets for the Staatsoper, the Volksoper, and the
Burg and Akademie theaters are available at the central ticket office to
the left rear of the Staatsoper (**Bundestheaterkassen,** ⊠ Hanuschg. 3,
☎ 0222/514–44–2959, FAX 0222/514–44–2969; ☉ weekdays 8–6, Sat.,
Sun., and holidays 9–noon). Tickets go on sale a month before per-
formances. Unsold tickets can be obtained at the evening box office.
Plan to be there at least one hour before the performance; students can
buy remaining tickets at lower prices, so they are usually out in force.
Tickets can be ordered three weeks or more in advance in writing (or
by fax) or a month in advance from anywhere in the world by phone
(☎ 0222/513–1513; AE, DC, MC, V). Theater is offered in English at
the **Vienna English Theater** (⊠ Josefsg. 12, ☎ 0222/402–1260) and the
International Theater (⊠ Porzellang. 8, ☎ 0222/319–6272).

Music

Most classical concerts are held in either the **Konzerthaus** (⊠ Lothringer-
str. 20, ☎ 0222/712–1211, FAX 0222/712–2872) or the **Musikverein**
(⊠ Dumbastr. 3, ☎ 0222/505–8190, FAX 0222/505–9409). Tickets can
be bought at their box offices or ordered by phone (AE, DC, MC, V).
Pop concerts are scheduled from time to time at the **Austria Center** (⊠
Am Hubertusdamm 6, ☎ 0222/236–9150; U-1 subway to Vienna In-
ternational Center stop). Tickets to various musical events are sold
through **Vienna Ticket Service** (☎ 0222/587–9843, FAX 0222/587–9844),

or at the Salettl gazebo ticket office on the Kärntnerstrasse next to the Opera (☎ 0222/588–85–81, ✆ daily 10–7). At the same office, same-day half-price tickets to many musical events—*but not the Staatsoper, Volksoper, or symphony concerts*—go on sale at 2 PM.

Film

Films are shown in English at **Burg Kino** (✉ Opernring 19, ☎ 0222/587–8406), **de France** (✉ Schottenring 5, ☎ 0222/317–5236), **English Cinema Haydn** (✉ Marihilfer Str. 57, ☎ 0222/587–2262), **Top Kino** (✉ Rahlg. 1, ☎ 0222/587–5557), **Votiv Kino** (✉ Währinger Str. 12, ☎ 0222/317–3571), and the **Film Museum** (✉ Augustinerstr. 1, ☎ 0222/533–7054). To find English-language movies, look for "OF" (original version) or "OmU" (original with subtitles) in newspaper listings.

Nightlife

Cabarets

Most cabarets are expensive and unmemorable. Two of the best are **Casanova** (✉ Dorotheerg. 6, ☎ 0222/512–9845), which emphasizes striptease, and **Moulin Rouge** (✉ Walfischg. 11, ☎ 0222/512–2130).

Discos

Atrium (✉ Schwarzenbergpl. 10, ☎ 0222/505–3594) is open Thursday through Sunday and draws a lively younger crowd. **Queen Anne** (✉ Johannesg. 12, ☎ 0222/512–0203) is central, popular, and always packed. The **U-4** (✉ Schönbrunnerstr. 222, ☎ 0222/858307) ranks high among the young set, as does **P 1** (✉ Rotg. 9, ☎ 0222/535–9995). Live bands, dancing, and snacks are offered at **Chattanooga** (✉ Graben 29, ☎ 0222/533–5000).

Nightclubs

A casual '50s atmosphere pervades the popular **Café Volksgarten** (✉ Burgring 1, ☎ 0222/533–0518), situated in the city park of the same name; tables are set outdoors in summer. The more formal **Eden Bar** (✉ Lilieng. 2, ☎ 0222/512–7450) is considered one of Vienna's classiest nightspots; don't expect to be let in unless you're dressed to kill.

Wine Taverns

For a traditional Viennese night out, head to one of the city's atmospheric wine taverns, some of which date from as far back as the 12th century. You can often have full meals at these taverns, but the emphasis is mainly on drinking. The **Melker Stiftskeller** (☞ *Dining, above*) is one of the friendliest and most typical. Other well-known ones are the **Augustinerkeller** (✉ Augustinerstr. 1, ☎ 0222/533–1026), open at lunchtime as well as evenings, in the same building as the Albertina collection; the **Esterházykeller** (✉ Haarhof 1, ☎ 0222/533–3482), a particularly mazelike network of rooms, with excellent wines; and the **Zwölf Apostelkeller** (✉ Sonnenfelsg. 3, ☎ 0222/512–6777), near St. Stephen's and down, down, down underground.

THE DANUBE VALLEY

Austria contains some of the most beautiful stretches of the Danube (Donau), extending about 88 kilometers (55 miles) west of Vienna. The river rolls through the celebrated Wachau—a seriously scenic valley that is enjoyed by many as part of an excursion from the country's capital. What the Wachau (note that it's redundant to refer to the Wachau Valley since *au* means valley) offers is magnificent countryside, some of Austria's best food and wine, and comfortable—in some cases elegant—accommodations. Above the river are the ruins of ancient castles. The abbeys at Melk and Göttweig, with their magnificent libraries, dominate their settings. Vineyards sweep down to the river, which is lined with fruit trees that burst into blossom every spring. People here live close to the land, and at certain times of year vintners open their homes to sell their own wines and produce. Roadside stands offer flowers, fruits, vegetables, and wines. And this is an area of legend: The Danube shares with the Rhine the story of the mythical Nibelungen, defenders of Siegfried, hero of German myth.

Getting Around

By Car

If you're pressed for time, take the Autobahn to St. Pölten, turn north onto Route S-33, and follow the signs to Melk. For a more scenic route, leave Vienna along the south shore of the Danube via Klosterneuburg and Greifenstein, taking Routes 14, 19, 43, and 33. Cross the Danube at Melk, then return to Vienna along the north bank of the river (Route 3).

By Train

Depart from the Westbahnhof for Melk, then take the bus along the north bank of the Danube to Dürnstein and Krems. Side bus trips can be made from Krems to Göttweig.

By Boat

Travel upstream, with stops at Krems, Dürnstein, Melk, and points between. Return to Vienna by boat or by train from Melk (combination tickets available).

Guided Tours

Vienna travel agencies offer tours of the Wachau. These range from one-day outings to longer excursions. For details, contact the **Lower Austria Tourist Office** (⊠ Heidenschuss 2, ☎ 0222/533–3114–0, FAX 0222/535–0319).

Visitor Information

Dürnstein (⊠ Parkpl. Ost, ☎ 02711/219 or 02711/200, FAX 02711/442).
Klosterneuburg (⊠ Niedermarkt 4, Postfach 6, ☎ 02243/32038, FAX 02243/86773).
Krems (⊠ Undstr. 6, ☎ 02732/82676, FAX 02732/70011—also covers **Stein an der Donau**).
Melk (⊠ Babenbergerstr. 1, ☎ 02752/2307–32, FAX 02752/2307–37).
Tulln (⊠ Albrechtsg. 32, ☎ 02272/5836, FAX 02272/5838).

Exploring the Danube Valley

North of Vienna lies **Klosterneuburg,** whose huge **abbey** dominates this market town. The abbey is a major agricultural landowner in the region and its extensive vineyards produce excellent wines. *Guided tours every hour (winter schedule may vary) Mon.–Sat. 9–11 and 1:30–4:30, Sun. 11 and 1:30–4:30.*

If you are driving, you have the choice of either following the riverbank or heading up over the village of St. Andrae and down again to the river plain. At **Tulln,** the **town hall** dominates the town square.

You will see **Stift Göttweig** long before you reach it. This impressive 11th-century Benedictine abbey affords sensational views of the Danube Valley; walk around the grounds and view the impressive chapel. *Rte. 303, on south bank of Danube, opposite Krems.*

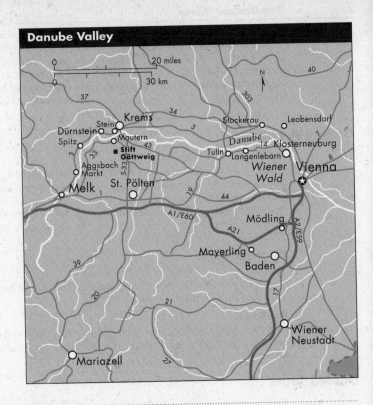

Danube Valley

Have lunch at the abbey's **Stiftskeller.** If the weather is clear, sit out on the open terrace and enjoy the magnificent views of the Danube in the distance. The local wines are excellent. ⊗ *Daily Apr.–Oct.*

Farther along the valley is the abbey of **Melk,** commandingly situated above the Danube. Its library is rich in art as well as books; the ceiling frescoes are particularly memorable. ☎ 02752/2312. ✉ AS50; with *guided tour AS65. ⊗ May–Sept., daily 9–5; Apr. and Oct., daily 9–4; Nov.–Mar., daily 11 and 2.*

Cross to the north bank of the river and head back downstream. The beautiful medieval town of **Dürnstein** is associated with Richard the Loin-Hearted, who was imprisoned in its now-ruined castle for 13 months. The town is also known for its fine hotels, restaurants, and wines. Virtually next door is **Stein,** with its former **Imperial Toll House** and 14th-century **Minoritenkirche,** a church that now serves as an exhibition showcase. Stein and Krems sit at the center of Austria's foremost wine-growing region.

The road back to Vienna now wanders away from the Danube, crossing through some attractive woodlands. When you reach Leobensdorf, you'll spot **Burg Kreuzenstein,** perched to the left upon a nearby hilltop. The 19th-century castle includes a small museum of armor. ⊗ *Mid-Mar.–mid-Nov. Tours daily 9–4, according to demand.*

Dining and Lodging

For details and price-category definitions, *see* Dining and Lodging *in* Staying in Austria, *above.*

Dürnstein

$$$$ ✕⊡ **Richard Löwenherz.** This former cloister sits above the Danube.
★ Room furnishings include antiques and every comfort. The restaurant is excellent, as are the house wines. ✉ *Dürnstein 8,* ☎ *02711/222,* FAX *02711/22218. 40 rooms with bath or shower. Restaurant, bar, outdoor pool, parking. AE, DC, MC, V. Closed Nov.–mid-Mar.*

Krems

$$ ⊡ **Alte Post.** A 16th-century house with an arcaded courtyard, the Alte Post is conveniently positioned right in the center of town. In good weather the courtyard is used for dining. ✉ *Obere Landstr. 32,* ☎ *02732/82276,* FAX *02732/84396. 26 rooms, most with bath. Restaurant (closed Wed.), bicycle rental. No credit cards. Closed Jan.–mid-Mar.*

Langenlebarn

$$$$ ✕ **Zum Roten Wolf.** This outstanding, elegant country restaurant serves
★ traditional local foods and superb wines. ✉ *Bahnstr. 58,* ☎ *02272/2567. Reservations essential. AE, DC, MC, V. Closed Mon. and Tues.*

Mautern

$$$$ ✕ **Landhaus Bacher.** This is one of Austria's best restaurants, elegant
★ but entirely lacking in pretension. Dining in the garden during the summer adds to the experience. ✉ *Südtirolerpl. 208,* ☎ *02732/82937–0,* FAX *02732/74337. Reservations essential. DC, V. Closed Mon., Tues. Nov.–Apr., and mid-Jan.–mid-Feb. No lunch Mon. and Tues. May–Oct.*

SALZBURG

Salzburg is best known as the birthplace of Wolfgang Amadeus Mozart, and receives its greatest number of visitors every summer during the annual Music Festival, the world-famous Salzburger Sommerfestspiele. Dominated by a fortress on one side and the Kapuzinerberg, a small mountain, on the other, this Baroque city is best explored on foot, for many of its most interesting areas are pedestrian precincts. Whereas Mozart rules over the festival months of July and August, visitors have long known that the city has innumerable other attractions as well. Art lovers call Salzburg the Golden City of the High Baroque; thanks to the powerful prince-archbishops of the Hapsburg era, few other places offer an equivalent abundance of Baroque splendor. Visitors also tour the city to the strains of music from the film that made Salzburg a household name in the United States; from Winkler Terrace to Nonnberg Convent, it's hard to go exploring without hearing someone humming "How Do You Solve a Problem like Maria?" No matter what season you visit, be sure to bring an umbrella: Salzburg is noted for sudden, brief downpours.

Arriving and Departing

By Plane

For information, phone Salzburg airport, ☎ 0662/8580. For passenger service and information about arrivals and departures, ☎ 0662/8580-251, FAX 0662/8580-260.

BETWEEN THE AIRPORT AND DOWNTOWN
Buses leave for the Salzburg train station at Südtirolerplatz every 15 minutes during the day, every half hour at night to 10 PM. Journey time is 18 minutes. Taxi fare runs about AS150–AS170.

By Train

Salzburg's main train station is at Südtirolerplatz. For train information, call 0662/1717; for telephone ticket orders and seat reservations, call 0662/1700.

By Bus

The central bus terminal (postal bus information: ☎ 0662/167; railway bus information: ☎ 0662/872150) is in front of the train station, although during construction of a new underground garage, bus stops may be moved to various points around the square.

By Car

Salzburg has several autobahn exits; study the map and decide which one is best for you. Parking is available in the cavernous garages under the Mönchsberg and in other garages around the city; look for the large blue P signs.

Getting Around

By Bus and Trolleybus

Service is frequent and reliable; route maps are available from the tourist office or your hotel. Save money by buying an **Umweltkarte** (available only in blocks of five), a 24-hour ticket that is good on all trolley and bus lines. For local transportation information, call 0662/620551–31.

By Taxi

At festival time, taxis are too scarce to hail on the street, so order through your hotel porter or phone 0662/8111 or 0662/1716.

By Fiaker

Fiakers, or horse-drawn cabs, are available on the Residenzplatz (☎ 0662/844772).

By Car

Don't even think of it! The old part of the city is a pedestrian zone. Many parts of the city have restricted parking (indicated by a blue pavement stripe), either reserved for residents with permits, or for a restricted period. Get parking tickets from coin-operated dispensers on street corners; instructions are also in English.

Guided Tours

Guided bus tours of the city and its environs are given by **Salzburg Sightseeing Tours** (✉ Mirabellpl. 2, ☎ 0662/881616), **Salzburg Panorama Tours** (✉ Mirabellpl./St. Andrä Church, ☎ 0662/874029), and **Bob's Special Tours** (✉ Chiemseeg. 1/Kaig., ☎ 0662/849511–0, FAX 0662/849512). Many tour operators offer special *Sound of Music* excursions through the city; those given by Bob's are highly rated. All tour operators can organize chauffeur-driven tours for up to eight people. Your hotel will have details.

Visitor Information

Salzburg's official tourist office, the **Stadtverkehrsbüro,** has **information centers** at Mozartplatz 5 (☎ 0662/847568 and 0662/88987–330) and at the main train station (☎ 0662/871712). The main office is at Auerspergstrasse 7 (☎ 0662/889870).

Exploring Salzburg

Numbers in the margin correspond to points of interest on the Salzburg map.

The Salzach River separates Salzburg's old and new towns; for the best perspective on the old, climb the **Kapuzinerberg** (follow pathways from Linzergasse or Steingasse). Once back down at river level,

❶ walk across the Markartplatz to the **Landestheater,** where operas, operettas, ballet, and dramas are staged during winter months; the larger houses used by the festival are closed most of the year. Diagonally across from the theater is the reconstructed **Mozart Wohnhaus** (residence), where the family lived for some years. The building includes a small recital hall, the Mozart Audio and Film Museum, and a specialist CD shop for classical music. Wander through the Baroque

★ **Mirabell Gardens** behind the theater and enjoy a dramatic view of the Old City, with the fortress in the background. And at least look

❷ in on the **Baroque Museum.** ✉ AS40. ⏱ Tues.–Sat. 9–noon and 2–5, Sun. 9–noon.

❸ Be sure to step inside **Schloss Mirabell,** which now houses public offices, including that of the city's registrar; many couples come here for the experience of being married in such a sumptuous setting. The foyer and staircase, decorated with cherubs, are good examples of Baroque excess. ✉ Mirabellpl., ☎ 0662/8072–2380. ⏱ Mon.–Thurs. 8–4, Fri. 8–1.

Head left down Schwarzstrasse, back toward the center of the city. On

❹ your left is the famed **Mozarteum.** Inside are the Music Academy (☎ 0662/88908) and the International Mozarteum Foundation (Schwarzstr. 26, ☎ 0662/88940), whose courtyard contains the summerhouse (accessible only during concert intermissions, weather permitting) in which Mozart wrote *The Magic Flute.* Cross the Makartsteg footbridge to the Old City side of the Salzach. Turn right and walk a short dis-

❺ tance up the quay to the **Carolino Augusteum Museum.** This is the city museum, devoted to art, archaeology, and musical instruments. ✉ Museumspl. 1, ☎ 0662/843145. ✉ AS40; combined ticket with toy museum in the Bürgerspital (see below), cathedral excavations, and Folklore Museum: AS60. ⏱ Tues. 9–8, Wed.–Sun. 9–5.

NEED A BREAK? From the Carolinum, as the museum is commonly called, turn the corner into Gstättengasse. On your right is the Mönchsberg elevator, which will take you to the top of the promontory. Once here, follow the signs and path south to **Burgerwehr-Einkehr** (✉ Am Mönchsberg 19c, ☎ 0662/ 841729, closed mid-Oct.–Apr.), a café-restaurant with superb views of the city—the fortress is in the background. It's a delightful hike over the ridge to the fortress from here (making the trip in reverse, however, will save you an uphill climb).

❻ Returning to city level, follow the Gstättengasse to the **Bürgerspital,** which houses a toy and musical instruments museum within its Renaissance arcades. ✉ Bürgerspitalpl. 2, ☎ 0662/847560. ✉ AS30; combined ticket with the Carolino Augusteum, cathedral excavation, and Folklore Museum, AS60. ⏱ Tues.–Sun. 9–5.

Ahead is Herbert-von-Karajan-Platz, most notable for its central **Pferdeschwemme** (Horse Fountain). Built into the side of the mountain itself

❼ is the **Festspielhaus** (Festival Hall), a huge complex where many of the events of Salzburg's annual summer festival are staged. ✉ Hofstallg. 1, ☎ 0662/80450. Ticket office, ☎ 0662/844501, FAX 0662/848424.

78

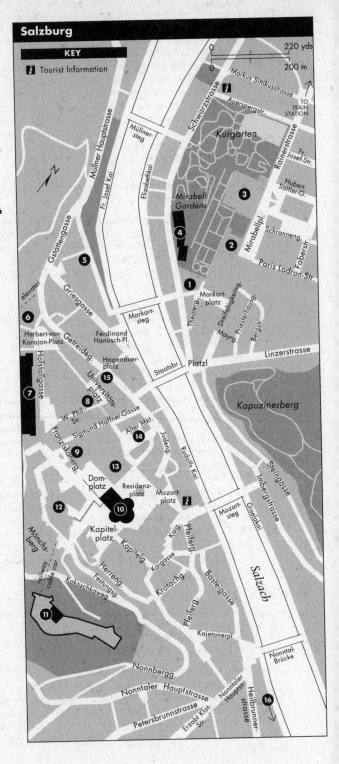

Salzburg

KEY

i Tourist Information

0 — 220 yds
0 — 200 m

TO TRAIN STATION

Kurgarten

Mirabell Gardens

Markus Sittikusstrasse

Auerspergstr.

Schwarzstrasse

Rainerstrasse

Fr. Josef-Str.

Hubert Sattler-G.

Mirabellpl.

Schranneng.

Faberstr.

Paris Lodron-Str.

Linzerstrasse

Kapuzinerberg

Steingasse

Imbergstrasse

Giselakai

Salzach

Müllner Hauptstrasse

Fr. Josef Kai

Müllner-steg

Elizabethkai

Gstättengasse

Griesgasse

elevator

Herbert-von-Karajan-Platz

Getreideg.

Hofstallgasse

Franziskanerg.

Universitäts-platz

W.-Phil.-Str.

Sigmund Haffner-Gasse

Hagenauer-platz

Ferdinand Hanusch-Pl.

Markart-steg

Staatsbr.

Platzl

Markart-platz

Theaterg.

Dreifaltigkeitsg.

Mayrg.

Priesterhausg.

Bergstr.

Alter Mkt.

Judeng.

Rudolfs Kai

Dom-platz

Residenz-platz

Mozart-platz

Kapitel-platz

Mozart-steg

Kapitelg.

Kaig.

Pfeiferg.

Kaigasse

Herreng.

Festungsg.

Kokoschkaweg

Mönchs-berg

railway cable car

Krotachg.

Pfeiferg.

Basteigasse

Kajetanerpl.

Nonntal-Brücke

Nonntaler Hauptstrasse

Petersbrunnstrasse

Erzabt Klot-Str.

Nonntaler Hauptstr.

Heilbrunner-strasse

Nonnbergg.

1
2
3
4
5
6
7
8
9
10
11
12
13
14
15
16

From the Festspielhaus, turn left into Wiener-Philharmoniker-Strasse.
⑧ The **Kollegienkirche** (University Church) on the left is the work of Fischer von Erlach and one of the best examples of Baroque architecture anywhere; be sure to look inside. Cut under the covered passageway and turn right into Sigmund-Haffner Gasse. At the corner on the left
⑨ stands the 13th-century **Franziskanerkirche** (Franciscan Church), an eclectic mix of architectural styles with Romanesque and Gothic accents. Nearby, on the Domplatz, stands the magnificently propor-
⑩ tioned Salzburg **Dom** (Cathedral). Don't overlook the great bronze doors as you enter.

To reach the fortress on the hill above, walk under the arcade to the right side of the church and up the narrow Festungsgasse at the back end of Kapitalplatz. From here, you can either follow the footpath up the hill or take a five-minute ride on the funicular, or Festungsbahn. On a sunny day, a far more pleasurable—and strenuous!—route is to hike up Festungsgasse, turning frequently to enjoy the changing panorama of the city below.

NEED A
BREAK?
Stieglkeller (⊠ Festungsg. 10, ☏ 0662/842681) offers a wide choice of good Austrian fare, served outdoors in summer. The local beer is superb. Try *Salzburger Nockerln,* a meringue dessert. Stop here during the day; in the evenings they hold a *Sound of Music* dinner theater.

★ ⑪ Once you've reached the **Festung Hohensalzburg** itself, you can wander around on your own (⊠ AS35 adults) or take a tour (AS35, in addition to admission). The views from the 12th-century fortress are magnificent in all directions. A main attraction is **St. George's Chapel,** built in 1501. A year later, in 1502, the chapel acquired the 200-pipe barrel organ, which is played daily in summer at 7 AM, 11 AM, and 6 PM. ⊠ Mönchsberg, ☏ 0662/8042–2133. ☉ *Daily Nov.–May 10–4:30; Apr.–June, Sept.–Oct. 9:30–5; July–Aug. 9:30–5:30. Guided tour schedule varies.*

⑫ Back down in the city, follow the wall to **Stiftskirche St. Peter** (St. Peter's Abbey). The cemetery lends an added air of mystery to the monks' caves cut into the cliff. The catacombs attached to the church can be visited by guided tour. ⊠ *Just off Kapitalpl.,* ☏ 0662/845748. ⊠ AS12. *Tours daily at 10:30, 11:30, 1:30, 2:30 and 3:30.*

Head around the cathedral to the spacious Residenzplatz, a vast and
⑬ elegant square. The **Residenz** itself includes the prince-archbishops' living quarters and ceremonial rooms. ⊠ *Residenzpl. 1,* ☏ 0662/8042–2690. ⊠ AS45. *Tours Sept.–June, weekdays at 10, 11, noon, 2, and 3; July–Aug., daily every 30 mins from 10 to 4:30.*

The **Residenzgalerie,** in the same building complex, has an outstanding collection of 16th- through 19th-century European art. ⊠ Residenzpl. 1, ☏ 0662/8042–2270. ⊠ AS50. *Combined ticket with state rooms: AS80.* ☉ *Daily 10–5. Closed on Wed. Oct.–Mar.*

⑭ From the lower end of Residenzplatz, cut across into the **Alter Markt.** Salzburg's narrowest house is squeezed into the north side of the square. Turn left into Getreidegasse, a narrow street packed with boutiques and fascinating shops. At the head of the tiny Hagenauerplatz
★ ⑮ is **Mozart's Birthplace,** now a museum. ⊠ Getreideg. 9, ☏ 0662/844313. ⊠ AS65. ☉ *Daily 9–6; during festival, daily 9–7.*

Wander along Getreidegasse, with its ornate wrought-iron shop signs and the Mönchsberg standing sentinel at the far end. Don't neglect the warren of interconnecting side alleys: These shelter a number of fine shops and often open onto impressive inner courtyards that are guaranteed to be filled with flowers in summer.

⑯ One popular excursion from Salzburg is to **Schloss Hellbrunn,** about 5 kilometers (3 miles) outside the city. Take Bus 55. The castle was built during the 17th century, and its rooms have some fine trompe l'oeil decorations. To entertain Salzburg's great prince-archbishops, its gardens feature an ingenious system of **Wasserspiele**—hidden jets of water conceived by someone with an impish sense of humor: expect to get sprinkled by surprise. ☎ 0662/820372. ⌸ AS60. *Tours Apr. and Oct., daily 9–4:30; May–Sept., daily 9–5. Evening tours July–Aug. on the hour 6–10.*

� The Hellbrunn complex also includes the **Tiergarten,** which is outstanding because of the way in which the animals have been housed in natural surroundings. You can also visit the small **folklore museum** in the Monatsschlössl. *Zoo:* ☎ 0662/820176. ⌸ AS70. ☉ *Oct.–Mar., daily 8:30–4; Apr.–Sept., daily 8:30–6. Folklore museum* ⌸ *AS15.* ☉ *May 15–Oct. 15., daily 9–5.*

Dining

Some of the city's best restaurants are in the leading hotels. This is a tourist town, and popular restaurants are always crowded, so make reservations well ahead, particularly during festival time. For details and price-category definitions, *see* Dining *in* Staying in Austria, *above.*

$$$ ✕ **Goldener Hirsch.** The return to more traditional Austrian and international cuisine suits the preferences of the musical and theater celebrities who regularly dine in these chic rooms. But don't overlook such specialties as fillet of catfish in anchovy sauce or game in season. The same kitchen serves the cheaper **s'Herzl** next door. ⊠ *Getreideg. 37,* ☎ *0662/8084–861. Reservations essential. AE, DC, MC, V.*

$$$ ✕ **Mirabell.** Although it's housed in a chain hotel (the Sheraton), the Mirabell is among the city's top restaurants. The menu mixes international dishes with adventurous versions of such local specialties as Wienerschnitzel and *Wildschwein* (wild boar). ⊠ *Auerspergstr. 4,* ☎ *0662/889995. AE, DC, MC, V.*

$$$ ✕ **Zum Eulenspiegel.** Ignore the Salzburgers who turn up their noses
★ at the mention of this charming restaurant, and go both for the food and the unique setting. The house is hundreds of years old and full of wonderful nooks and crannies reached by odd staircases. This isn't kitsch; it's genuine Old World. ⊠ *Hagenauerpl. 2,* ☎ *0662/843180. MC, V. Closed Sun. except during festival, and early Jan.–mid-Mar.*

$$ ✕ **St. Peter Stiftskeller.** This is allegedly Europe's oldest restaurant. Among the offerings in its network of paneled rooms are the excellent St. Peter's fish and traditional grill and roast specialties. Finish with Salzburger Nockerln, light-as-a-cloud meringues. ⊠ *St. Peter District I/4,* ☎ *0662/848481. Reservations essential. AE, DC, MC, V.*

$$ ✕ **Zipfer Bierhaus.** Such standards as tasty roast pork with bread dumplings seem appropriate in this informal setting of arched ceilings and brick floors, one of the oldest Gasthäuser in town. ⊠ *Sigmund-Haffner-Gasse 12/Universitätspl. 19,* ☎ *0662/840745. No credit cards. Closed Sun.*

$$ ✕ **Zum Mohren.** Arched ceilings in the lower rooms add atmosphere
★ to this historic house. Duck and venison are specialties. ⊠ *Judeng. 9,* ☎ *0662/842387. AE. Closed Sun. and holidays.*

$ ✕ **Sternbräu.** If you're not looking for anything too fancy, try the hearty sausages and roasted meats at this vast complex, which has a pleasant garden in summer. ⊠ *Griesg. 23/Getreideg. 34,* ☎ *0662/842140. No credit cards.*

$ × **Wilder Mann.** The atmosphere may be too smoky for some (choose
★ the outside courtyard in summer), but the beamed ceiling and antlers
are genuine, as are the food and value. Try the *Tellerfleisch* (boiled beef)
or game in season. ⊠ *Getreideg. 20/Griesg. 17 (passageway)*,
☎ *0662/841787. No credit cards. Closed Sun.*

Lodging

Reservations are always advisable and are essential at festival times (both
Easter and summer). For details and price-category definitions, *see* Lodging *in* Staying in Austria, *above*.

$$$$ ⊞ **Altstadt Radisson.** Rooms and suites are elegant and no two are alike
in this handsomely converted Old City hostelry, dating from 1377, with
splendid views across the river or up to the fortress. Furnishings are
individual and include antiques. The Symphony restaurant is excellent
and offers stunning panoramas. ⊠ *Judeng. 15/Rudolfskai 28*, ☎
0662/848571–0, ⅢX *0662/848571–6. 60 rooms with bath. Restaurant.
AE, DC, MC, V.*

$$$$ ⊞ **Goldener Hirsch.** This old-timer—800 years old and an inn since
★ 1564—is conveniently set right in the heart of the Old City. Arched
corridors, vaulted stairs, rustic furniture, and antiques provide a medieval atmosphere; the essential modern appliances stay ingeniously
hidden. The restaurant (☞ Dining, *above*) is excellent. ⊠ *Getreideg.
35–37*, ☎ *0662/8084*, ⅢX *0662/843349. 75 rooms with bath. Restaurant, garage. AE, DC, MC, V.*

$$$$ ⊞ **Österreichischer Hof.** The grande dame of Salzburg's hotels occupies
a lovely riverside location, and the favored rooms give views of the fortress
and the Old City. The house restaurants are disappointing. ⊠ *Schwarzstr.
5–7*, ☎ *0662/88977–0*, ⅢX *0662/88977–14. 120 rooms, 118 with bath
or shower. 4 restaurants, garage. AE, DC, MC, V.*

$$$$ ⊞ **Schloss Mönchstein.** If you're a romantic with money to spend,
look no further. With its sensational castle location overlooking the
city, this is a top hotel. The restaurant is one of the best in the city. ⊠
Mönchsberg 26, ☎ *0662/848555*, ⅢX *0662/848559. 17 rooms with
bath. Restaurant, tennis court, garage. AE, DC, MC, V.*

$$$$ ⊞ **Sheraton.** A Sheraton is a Sheraton, but this one has one of Salzburg's
best restaurants. Favored rooms at the back overlook the Mirabell Gardens. ⊠ *Auerspergstr. 4*, ☎ *0662/889990*, ⅢX *0662/881776. 165
rooms with bath. Restaurant, indoor pools, health club, laundry services, parking. AE, DC, MC, V.*

$$$ ⊞ **Elefant.** This 12th-century structure, right in the middle of the Old
★ City, has been a hotel for four hundred years, and has an atmosphere
of traditional comfort rather than merely old age. The public areas and
the high-ceilinged private rooms are well decorated with Persian car-
pets and Biedermeier furniture in dark woods. ⊠ *Sigmund-Haffner-
G. 4*, ☎ *0662/843397*, ⅢX *0662/840109–28. 36 rooms with bath or
shower. Restaurant, garage. AE, DC, MC, V.*

$$ ⊞ **Markus Sittikus.** This hotel is reasonably priced and more than rea-
★ sonably comfortable. The train station is within walking distance un-
less you're loaded with luggage. ⊠ *Markus-Sittikus-Str. 20*, ☎
0662/871121–0, ⅢX *0662/871121–58. 41 rooms with bath or shower.
AE, DC, MC, V.*

$$ ⊞ **Wolf.** The family touch reigns in this intimate, well-situated hotel
★ with spotless rooms in country decor. Book well ahead. ⊠ *Kaig. 7*,
☎ *0662/843453–0*, ⅢX *0662/842423–4. 12 rooms with bath. AE.*

The Arts

Festivals
It is difficult but no longer impossible to obtain tickets for festival performances once you are in Salzburg. It's best to write or fax ahead to **Salzburger Festspiele**, Postfach 140, A-5010 Salzburg, FAX 0662/846682.

Opera, Music, and Art
Theater and opera are presented in the **Festspielhaus** (☞ Exploring, *above*), opera, operettas, ballet, and drama at the **Landestheater** (✉ Schwarzstr. 22, ☎ 0662/871–5120), and concerts at the **Mozarteum** (✉ Schwarzstr. 26, ☎ 0662/873154). Chamber music is performed in **Schloss Mirabell**. Special art exhibitions in the **Rupertinum** (✉ Wiener-Philharmoniker-Gasse 9) or in the **Galerie Welz** (✉ Sigmund-Haffner-Gasse 16) are often outstanding.

☺ Children of all ages will delight in the celebrated **Salzburg Marionettentheater,** which performs in its own theater next door to the Mozarteum. The company travels all over the world, but it will be in Salzburg around Christmas, during the late-January Mozart Week, Easter, and from May to September (schedule subject to change). The skilled puppetry, the lovely costumes, the rollicking versions of Mozart's opera—all add up to an enchanting experience. ✉ *Schwarzst. 24,* ☎ *0662/872406–0.* 🎟 *AS250–AS400.*

INNSBRUCK

Squeezed by mountains and sharing the valley with the Inn River, Innsbruck is compact and very easy to explore on foot. The medieval city—it received its municipal charter in 1239—no doubt owes much of its fame and charm to its unique situation. To the north, the steep, sheer sides of the Alps rise like a shimmering blue-and-white wall from the edge of the city, an awe-inspiring backdrop for the mellow green domes and red roofs of the picturesque Baroque town.

Arriving and Departing

By Bus
The terminal is to the right of the main train station.

By Car
Exit from the east–west autobahn or from the Brenner autobahn running south to Italy. Much of the downtown area is a pedestrian zone or paid-parking only; get parking vouchers at tobacco shops, coin-operated dispensers, or the city tourist office at Burggraben 3.

By Plane
The airport is 4 kilometers (2 miles) to the west of the city. For flight information, phone 0512/22525–304.

BETWEEN THE AIRPORT AND DOWNTOWN

Buses (Line F) to the city center (✉ Maria-Theresien-Str.) run every 20 minutes and take about 20 minutes. Get your ticket from the bus driver; it costs AS18. Taxis should take no more than 10–15 minutes into town, and the fare is about AS120–AS150.

By Train
All trains stop at the city's main station at Südtiroler-Platz. Train connections are available to Munich, Vienna, Rome, and Zurich. For train information, phone 0512/1717. For ticket reservations, call 0512/1700.

Getting Around

By Bus and Streetcar

Most bus and streetcar routes begin or end at Südtiroler-Platz, in front of the main train station. The bus is the most convenient way to reach the six major ski areas outside the city. Many hotels offer free transportation with direct hotel pickup; for those staying in the Old City, the buses leave from in front of the Landestheater.

By Taxi

Taxis are not much faster than walking, particularly along the one-way streets and in the Old City. To order a radio cab, phone 0512/1718, 0512/5311, or 0512/45500.

Guided Tours

Sightseeing

Bus tours lasting two hours cover the city's highlights and leave from the hotel information office at the railroad station (Südtiroler-Pl.) daily at noon. In summer, additional buses are scheduled at 10 and 2, and there are shorter tours Monday through Saturday at 10:15, noon, 2, and 3:15. Your hotel or tourist office will have tickets and details.

Visitor Information

The **City Tourist Office** is at Burggraben 3 (☎ 0512/5356, FAX 0512/535643; daily 8–7); the **Tirol Tourist Office** at Wilhelm-Greil-Strasse 17 (☎ 0512/5320–170, FAX 0512/5320–174; weekdays 8:30–6, Sat. 9–noon). Pick up a Club-Innsbruck card at your hotel for discounts. **American Express** (✉ Brixnerstr. 3, ☎ 0512/582491, FAX 0512/573385). **Wagons-Lits Travel** (✉ Brixnerstr. 2, ☎ 0512/520790, FAX 0512/520–7985).

Exploring Innsbruck

Numbers in the margin correspond to points of interest on the Innsbruck map.

Modern-day Innsbruck retains close associations with three historical figures: Emperor Maximilian I and Empress Maria Theresa, one or both of whom was responsible for much of the city's architecture, and Andreas Hofer, a Tirolean patriot. You will find repeated references to

★ ❶ these names as you tour the city. A good starting point is the **Goldenes Dachl** (Golden Roof), which has made the ancient mansion with its balcony a landmark. (It's actually made of copper tiles gilded with 31 pounds of gold.) The building now houses an **Olympic Museum,** which runs videotapes of the Innsbruck winter Olympic Games. A combined admission ticket also gives you entry to the **Stadtturm,** a nearby 15th-century city tower with 148 steps to the top. ✉ *Herzog Friedrich-Str. 15,* ☎ *0512/536–0575.* ▣ *AS22.* ☉ *daily 9:30–5:30. Closed on Mon. Nov.–Feb.*

❷ A walk up Hofgasse brings you to the **Hofburg,** the Rococo imperial palace with an ornate reception hall decorated with portraits of Maria Theresa's ancestors. ✉ *Rennweg 1,* ☎ *0512/587186.* ▣ *AS50.* ☉ *May–Oct., daily 9–5; Nov.–Apr., Mon.–Sat. 10–5.*

❸ Go north on Pfarrgasse to the Baroque **Domkirche,** Innsbruck's cathedral, built in 1722 and dedicated to St. James. The main attraction here, aside from the interior with its dramatic painted ceilings, is the high-altar painting of the Madonna by Lucas Cranach the Elder, dating from about 1520. *Sat.–Thurs. 6–noon and 2–5, Fri. 2–5.*

Innsbruck

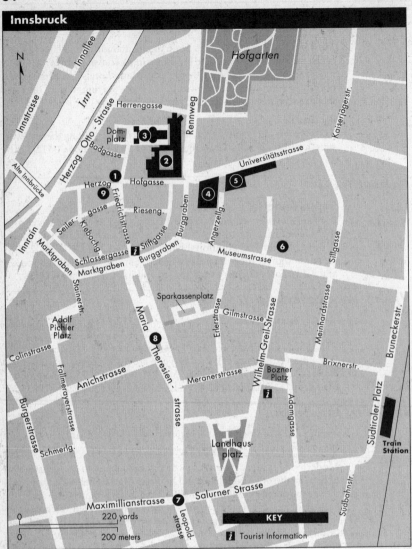

Annasäule, **8**

Domkirche, **3**

Ferdinandeum, **6**

Goldenes Dachl, **1**

Hofburg, **2**

Hofkirche, **4**

Tiroler Volkskunst-
museum, **5**

Triumphpforte, **7**

Helblinghaus, **9**

★ **④** Close by, the **Hofkirche** (Court Church) was built as a mausoleum for Maximilian. The emperor is surrounded by 24 marble reliefs portraying his accomplishments, as well as 28 oversize bronze statues of his ancestors, including the legendary King Arthur. Andreas Hofer is also buried here. Don't miss the ornate altar of the 16th-century Silver Chapel. The fascinating **Tiroler Volkskunstmuseum** (Tirolean Folk Art Museum) is housed in the Hofkirche as well. It exhibits costumes, rustic furniture, and farmhouse rooms decorated in styles ranging from Gothic to Rococo. ⊠ *Universitätsstr. 2,* ☎ *0512/584302.* ☞ *AS20 (Hofkirche), AS40 (Volkskunstmuseum); combined ticket: AS50.* ☉ *Hofkirche Sept.–June, daily 9–5; July–Aug. daily 9–5:30;* ☉ *Volkskunstmuseum Sept.–June, Mon.–Sat. 9–5, Sun. 9–noon; July–Aug., Mon.–Sat. 9–5:30, Sun. 9–noon.*

⑥ Follow Museumstrasse to the **Ferdinandeum,** which houses Austria's largest collection of Gothic art as well as paintings from the 19th and 20th centuries. ⊠ *Museumstr. 15,* ☎ *0512/594–8987.* ☞ *AS50.* ☉ *May–Sept., daily 10–5, Thurs. eve. 7–9; Oct.–Apr., Tues.–Sat. 10–noon and 2–5, Sun. and holidays 10–1.*

NEED A BREAK?
Relax over coffee, excellent pastries, and a newspaper in just about any language you want under the crystal chandeliers at **Café Central** (⊠ Gilmstr. 5, ☎ 0512/5920–0), in the Hotel Central, just off Wilhelm-Greil-Strasse.

⑦ Cut back down Wilhelm-Greil-Strasse to the **Triumphpforte** (Triumphal
⑧ Arch), built in 1765, and walk up Maria-Theresien-Strasse past the **Annasäule** (Anna Column) for a classic view of Innsbruck with the Alps in the background.

⑨ Arriving back near the starting point of our tour, note the dramatic and beautiful blue-and-white **Helblinghaus** on Herzog Friedrich-Strasse, a Gothic structure (1560) to which ornate Rococo decorations were added in 1730.

Dining

For details and price-category definitions, *see* Dining *in* Staying in Austria, *above.*

$$$ ✕ **Europastüberl.** Regional specialties and the resplendent setting are two reasons why the restaurant in the Europa hotel (☞ Lodging, *below*) is highly regarded by locals and visitors alike. ⊠ *Brixnerstr. 6,* ☎ *0512/593–1648. AE, DC, MC, V.*

$$$ ✕ **Schwarzer Adler.** This place drips with atmosphere. Its massive-beamed rooms are a perfect backdrop for typical Austrian dishes like Tafelspitz and *Knödeln* (dumplings). ⊠ *Kaiserjägerstr. 2,* ☎ *0512/587109. AE, DC, MC, V. Closed Sun. and mid-Jan.*

$$ ✕ **Goethe-Stube.** The wine tavern of the city's oldest inn, the Goldener Adler (☞ Lodging, *below*), is one of Innsbruck's best. It was here that Goethe (who lent his name to the tavern) sipped quantities of red South Tirolean wine during his stays in 1786 and 1790. ⊠ *Herzog Friedrich-Str. 6,* ☎ *0512/586334. Dinner only. AE, DC, MC, V.*

$$ ✕ **Hirschenstuben.** Old-fashioned hospitality and dark-wood trim are
★ found here at this charming local favorite. Game is particularly good here. ⊠ *Kiesbachg. 5,* ☎ *0512/582979. Reservations essential. AE, DC, MC, V. Closed Sun.*

$$ ✕ **Ottoburg.** A warren of rooms in a 13th-century building, the Ot-
★ toburg is exactly right for an intimate, cozy lunch or dinner. It's packed with Austriana and is 100% genuine. Go for the trout if it's

available. ⊠ *Herzog Friedrich-Str. 1,* ☎ *0512/574652. Reservations essential. AE, DC, MC, V.*

$ ✕ **Gasthaus Steden.** The substantial portions and unassuming (if occasionally smoky) atmosphere attract visiting businesspeople as well as many local regulars to this thoroughly genuine Gasthaus. Roast pork is particularly tasty and daily specials are a good value. ⊠ *Anichstr. 15,* ☎ *0512/580890. No credit cards. Closed Sun.*

$ ✕ **Schnitzelparadies.** Generous schnitzels are the feature in this spacious restaurant, although daily specials may include turkey or pasta. Cakes and desserts are homemade. ⊠ *Innrain 25,* ☎ *0512/572972. Dinner reservations required. No credit cards. Closed Sun.*

Lodging

Most hotels offer or can arrange transport to ski areas. For details and price-category definitions, *see* Lodging *in* Staying in Austria, *above.*

$$$$ 🏨 **Europa.** The Europa is a postwar building blessed with a surprising amount of charm. Some rooms have period furnishings; others are 20th-century modern. ⊠ *Südtiroler-Pl. 2, A-6020,* ☎ *0512/5931,* ℻ *0512/587800. 132 rooms with bath. Restaurant, bar, beauty salon, sauna, garage. AE, DC, MC, V.*

$$$$ 🏨 **Goldener Adler.** The Golden Eagle has been an inn since 1390, and
★   over the centuries it has welcomed nearly every king, emperor, duke, or poet passing through the city. The facade looks suitably medieval, and inside, passages and stairs twist romantically and rooms crop up where least expected. The several restaurants offer well-prepared seasonal and local dishes. ⊠ *Herzog Friedrich-Str. 6, A-6020,* ☎ *0512/586334,* ℻ *0512/584409. 40 rooms with bath or shower. 2 restaurants, bar. AE, DC, MC, V.*

$$$$ 🏨 **Schwarzer Adler.** Rooms are individual, warm, and inviting in this traditional Romantik Hotel. It's an easy stroll to the Old City. ⊠ *Kaiserjägerstr. 2, A-6020* ☎ *0512/587109,* ℻ *0512/561697. 27 rooms. 2 restaurants, bar, garage. AE, DC, MC, V.*

$$$ 🏨 **Alpotel Tirol.** Abundant space, comfort, and modern style are the keys in this new hotel on the edge of the Old City. The staff is particularly helpful. Many rooms have balconies with splendid views. The Tiroler Stuben restaurant is very good. ⊠ *Innrain 13 (Ursulinenpassage), A-6020,* ☎ *0512/577931,* ℻ *0512/577931–15. 75 rooms with bath. Restaurant, bar, café, sauna, parking. AE, DC, MC, V.*

$$$ 🏨 **Scandic Crown.** Innsbruck's newest major hotel belongs to the leading Scandinavian chain. The rooms are modern plush; the facilities, including sauna, are extensive. The buffet lunch is good value and abundant. The train station is nearby. ⊠ *Salurnerstr. 15, A-6020,* ☎ *0512/59350,* ℻ *0512/593–5220. 176 rooms with bath. 2 restaurants, bar, pool, sauna, health club, garage. AE, DC, MC, V.*

$$ 🏨 **Weisses Kreuz.** Occupying an honored position just steps away
★   from the famous Goldenes Dachl (☞ Exploring, *above*), the White Cross is a lovely inn that dates from 1465. Mozart stayed here in 1769. ⊠ *Herzog Friedrich-Str. 31, A-6020,* ☎ *0512/594790,* ℻ *0512/59479–90. 39 rooms, 28 with bath or shower. Restaurant. AE, V.*

$ 🏨 **Binder.** A short streetcar trip (Line 3) from the center of town shouldn't be too high a price to pay for less-costly comfort at this small, friendly, family-run hotel. ⊠ *Dr.-Glatz-Str. 20, A-6020,* ☎ *0512/33436–0,* ℻ *0512/33436–99. 32 rooms, most with bath or shower. Café-bar, parking. AE, DC, MC, V.*

$ 🏨 **Riese Haymon.** You're outside the center in this onetime cloister (take Bus J, K, or S south to Grassmayrstr.). The furnishings are eclectic, but the rooms are neat. ⊠ *Haymong. 4, A-6020,* ☎ *0512/589837,*

FAX *0512/586190. 22 rooms, 7 with shower. Restaurant, parking. No credit cards.*

The Arts

Most hotels have a monthly calendar of events (in English). Tickets to most events are available at the City Tourist Office (⊠ Burggraben 3, ☎ 0512/5356, FAX 0512/535643). Operas, musicals, and concerts are presented at the **Tiroler Landestheater** (⊠ Rennweg 2, ☎ 0512/520744) and the **Kongresshaus** (⊠ Rennweg 3, ☎ 0512/5936–0).

4 Belgium

Brussels

Antwerp

Ghent

Brugge

BELGIUM PACKS JUST OVER 5 MILLION DUTCH-speaking Flemings and almost as many French-speaking Walloons into a country the size of Vermont. The presence of two language cultures enriches its cultural heritage but also creates constant political tension, even though the country has recently become a federation of three largely self-governing regions—Flanders, Wallonia, and the City of Brussels, which is bilingual and multicultural.

In many ways, Belgium is a country for connoisseurs. This is the land of Brueghel and Van Eyck, Rubens and Van Dyck, Ensor and Magritte, and this is where their best work can be seen. Feudal lords built Belgium's many castles, and prelates its splendid churches, but merchants and craftsmen are responsible for the guild houses and sculpture-adorned town halls of Brussels, Antwerp, Ghent, and Brugge, and those of other towns almost equally rewarding, like Mechelen, Leuven, and Lier. Merchants were also the patrons who commissioned the great works of art in Belgium's churches and museums.

This small country offers surprising variety, from the beaches and dunes of the North Sea coast and the tree-lined canals and big sky of the "platte (flat) land" to the rolling Brueghel country around Brussels and the sheer cliffs and dense woods of the Ardennes. It has been fought over for centuries by invaders from all points of the compass. Julius Caesar called the Belgians the bravest of the tribes that defied the Roman legions. His conquerors were followed by Huns, Vikings, the Spanish and the French. The Battle of the Golden Spurs, in 1302, when mounted French knights were defeated by Flemish foot soldiers, is still commemorated in Flanders. The greatest battleground, though, was Waterloo, just south of Brussels, where Napoléon was defeated in 1815.

Independence came in 1830, and Belgium was able to start forging a national identity. The Belgians are inveterate individualists —witness the endless variations of Art Nouveau in the town houses of the Belle Epoque that line many a prosperous street. The art of living well has been cultivated in Belgium since the days of its great Burgundian feasts, and the country continues to claim an amazing number of gourmet restaurants, some of them world-renowned. Even in places that cater to an expense-account clientele, whole families can often be seen celebrating a first communion, an engagement, or a birthday. That generosity of spirit is also manifested in the comfortable proportions of private homes and the spaciousness of public spaces and avenues.

Belgium's neutrality was violated during both world wars, when much of its architectural heritage was destroyed and great suffering was inflicted by the occupying forces. This may be why Belgium staunchly supports the European Union (EU), which, if it has done nothing else, has guaranteed peace in Western Europe for the past 50 years. As the home of most EU institutions, Brussels has to some become a synonym for a faceless bureaucracy, but this is unfair to both the city and its civil servants. The European Union is strong enough to shrug off temporary unpopularity, but its longer-term survival depends on its success in fashioning unity out of diversity. Exactly the same thing applies to the kingdom of Belgium.

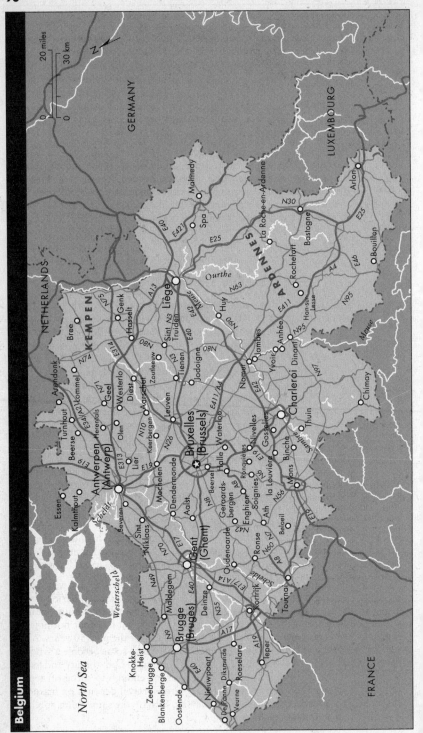

ESSENTIAL INFORMATION

Before You Go

When to Go

The tourist season runs from early May to late September, and peaks in July and August, when the weather is warmest. May and September offer the advantage of generally clear skies and smaller crowds.

CLIMATE

Temperatures range from around 65°F in May to an average of 73°F in July and August. In winter, they drop to an average of about 40°F to 45°F. Snow is unusual except in the mountains of the Ardennes, where cross-country and alpine skiing are popular.

The following are the average daily maximum and minimum temperatures for Brussels.

Jan.	40F	4C	May	65F	18C	Sept.	69F	21C
	30	– 1		46	8		51	11
Feb.	44F	7C	June	72F	22C	Oct.	60F	15C
	32	0		52	11		45	7
Mar.	51F	11C	July	73F	23C	Nov.	48F	9C
	36	25		4	12		38	3
Apr.	58F	14C	Aug.	72F	22C	Dec.	42F	6C
	41	5		54	12		32	0

Currency

The unit of currency in Belgium is the franc (BF). There are bills of 100, 200, 500, 1,000, 2,000, and 10,000 francs, and coins of 1, 5, 20, and 50 francs. At press time (spring 1996), the exchange rate was about BF30 to the dollar, BF21 to the Canadian dollar, and BF46 to the pound sterling.

What It Will Cost

Brussels is a considerably less expensive city than Paris, Zürich, or Frankfurt and on a par with London and New York. Deluxe hotels are very expensive but offer substantially discounted weekend and summer rates. There is also a wide selection of reasonably priced establishments, and hotels away from the capital are generally less costly. Top restaurants are in the $100 range, but you can eat very well in this land of gourmets for a third of that sum. Note that all taxes and service charges are included in hotel and restaurant bills. Gasoline prices conform to the high European average, but the highways are toll-free.

SAMPLE PRICES

A cup of coffee in a café will cost BF45–BF60; a glass of beer, BF35–BF85; and a glass of wine, about BF100. Train travel averages BF7 per mile, the average bus/metro/tram ride costs BF50, theater tickets cost about BF500, and movie tickets about BF250.

Customs on Arrival

Since the EU's 1992 agreement on a unified European market, the limits to what visitors from EU countries may bring in have become generous to the point of being meaningless. For example, travelers from EU nations may import 120 bottles of wine, 10 liters of alcohol, and 800 cigarettes. Duty-free amounts, however, remain unchanged: 300 cigarettes, 5 liters of wine, and 1½ liters of spirits. Visitors from non-EU countries can bring in 200 cigarettes, or 50 cigars, or 250 grams of tobacco; 2 liters of still wine and 1 liter of spirits or 2 liters of aperitif wine; and 50 grams of perfume. Other goods from non-EU countries may not exceed a total value of BF2,000. There are no restrictions on the import or export of currency.

Language

Language is a sensitive subject that leads to frequent political crises. There are three national languages in Belgium: French, spoken primarily in the south of the country (Wallonia); Flemish, spoken in the north; and German, spoken in a small area in the east. Brussels is bilingual, with both French and Flemish officially recognized, though French predominates. Many people speak English in Brussels and in the north (Flanders). When addressing a Fleming, you're likely to get more cooperation if you speak English rather than French. In Wallonia you may have to muster whatever French you possess, but in tourist areas you will be able to find people with at least basic English.

Getting Around

By Car

ROAD CONDITIONS

Belgium has an excellent system of expressways, and the main roads are generally very good. Road numbers for main roads have the prefix *N*; expressways, the prefix *A* or *E*.

RULES OF THE ROAD

Drive on the right and pass on the left; passing on the right is forbidden. Seat belts are compulsory in both front and rear seats. Each car must have a warning triangle to be used in the event of a breakdown or accident. At intersections, traffic on the right has right-of-way. Adhere strictly to this rule, as there are few stop or yield signs. In Brussels, the system of tunnels and ring roads is generally effective. Cars within a traffic circle have priority over cars entering it, but be careful; not all drivers obey this new rule. Buses and streetcars have priority over cars. Maximum speed limits are 130 kph (80 mph) on highways, 90 kph (55 mph) on major roads, and 50 kph (30 mph) in cities.

ROAD SIGNS

Road signs are written in the language of the region, so you need to know that Antwerp is Antwerpen in Flemish and Anvers in French; likewise, Bruges and Brussels are Brugge and Brussel (Flemish) and Bruges and Bruxelles (French); Ghent is Gent (Flemish) and Gand (French). Even more confusing, Liège and Luik are the same place, as are Louvain and Leuven, and Namur and Namen. Even more difficult is Mons (French) and its Flemish equivalent, Bergen, or Tournai (French), which becomes Doornik in Flemish.

PARKING

Most cities have metered on-street parking (meters take 5- or 20-franc coins) and parking lots.

By Train

Fast and frequent trains connect all main towns and cities. If you intend to travel frequently, buy a **Benelux Tourrail Ticket,** which allows unlimited travel throughout Belgium, Luxembourg, and the Netherlands for any five days during a one-month period. The cost of the five-day pass is BF6,320 first class and BF4,220 second class. For those under 26, the pass costs BF3,160 second class (first class is not available). The **Belgian Tourrail Ticket** allows unlimited travel for five days in a one-month period at a cost of BF2,995 first class and BF1,995 second class. Young people from 12 to 26 can purchase a **Go Pass** for BF1,290, valid for 10 one-way trips in a six-month period on the Belgian rail network. These passes are sold at any Belgian train station. The Benelux Tourrail is also available at home (☞ Train Travel *in* Chapter 1).

Special weekend round-trip tickets are valid from Friday morning to Monday night: A 40% reduction is available on the first traveler's ticket and a 60% reduction on companions' tickets. Sample full-price round-trip fares from Brussels are: to Antwerp, BF370; to Brugge, BF710; and to Ghent, BF450.

By Bus

Intercity bus service is almost nonexistent. Details of services are available at train stations and tourist offices.

By Bicycle

You can rent a bicycle from Belgian Railways at 48 stations throughout the country; train travelers get reduced rates. Bicycling is especially popular in the flat northern and coastal areas. There are bicycle lanes in many Flemish cities, but bicycling in Brussels takes a lot of guts.

Staying in Belgium

Telephones

LOCAL CALLS

Pay phones work mostly with telecards, available in a number of denominations; some phones are coin-operated and take 5- and 20-franc coins. The telecards can be purchased at any post office and at many newsstands. Most phone booths that accept telecards have a list indicating where these cards are sold. An average local call costs BF20.

INTERNATIONAL CALLS

The least expensive method is to buy a high-denomination telecard and make a direct call from a phone booth. A five-minute phone call to the United States at a peak time will cost about BF750. For credit card and collect calls, dial **AT&T** (☎ 0800–10010), **MCI** (☎ 0800–10012), or **Sprint** (☎ 0800–10014).

COUNTRY CODE

The country code for Belgium is 32.

Mail

POSTAL RATES

First-class (airmail) letters and postcards to the United States cost BF34, second-class (surface) BF18. Airmail letters and postcards to the United Kingdom cost BF16.

RECEIVING MAIL

You can have mail forwarded to your hotel. Another option is to have mail sent in care of **American Express** (✉ Pl. Louise 1, 1000 Brussels). Cardholders are spared the BF50 per-letter charge.

Shopping

SALES-TAX REFUNDS

When you buy goods for export, you can ask most shops to fill out forms covering VAT or sales tax. An itemized invoice showing the amount of VAT will also do. When you leave Belgium, you must declare the goods at customs and have the customs officers stamp the documents. Once you're back home, you simply send the stamped forms back to the shop and your sales tax will be refunded. This method covers most purchases of more than BF2,000. There's a simpler option, but it requires trust. At the time of purchase by credit card, you pay only the price without VAT, but you also sign, with your card, a guarantee in the amount of the sales tax. Have the invoice stamped by customs when you leave the last EU country on your itinerary. You have three months to return the stamped invoice to the store, where the guarantee is then disposed of. If you fail to do so, you forfeit the guarantee.

Opening and Closing Times

Banks are open weekdays from 9 to 4; some close for an hour at lunch. Exchange facilities are usually open on weekends, but you'll get a better rate during the week.

Museums are generally open from 10 to 5 six days a week. Closing day is Monday in Brussels and Antwerp, Tuesday in Brugge.

Shops are open weekdays and Saturdays from 10 to 6 and generally stay open later on Friday. Some shops close for lunch. Bakeries and some groceries are open Sunday and closed Monday.

National Holidays

January 1; March 31 (Easter Monday); May 1 (May Day); May 8 (Ascension); May 19 (Pentecost Monday); July 21 (National Holiday); August 15 (Assumption); November 1 (All Saints' Day); November 11 (Armistice); December 25.

Dining

Nearly all Belgians take eating seriously and are discerning about fresh produce and innovative recipes. They will spend a considerable amount on a celebratory meal. At the top end of the scale, the *menus de dégustation* offer a chance to sample a large selection of the chef's finest dishes. Prix-fixe menus are widely available and often represent considerable savings. Menus and prices are always posted outside.

Belgian specialties include *lapin à la bière* (rabbit in beer), *faisan à la brabançonne* (pheasant with chicory), *waterzooi* (a rich chicken or fish hot pot), and *carbonnades* (chunky stews). Belgians love *frites* (french fries) so much that they think they invented them. *Steack et frites* can be found everywhere. For the best cut of beef, ask for *filet pur.* Some local specialties are the marvelous asparagus from Mechelen, at its best in May; *salade Liègeoise,* a hot salad with beans and bacon (Liège); strawberries and freshwater fish from the Meuse (Namur); different permutations of sprouts, chicory, and pheasant (Brussels); and oysters, mussels, and tiny, sweet shrimps (Flanders).

Belgian snacks are equally appetizing. The *gaufre/wafel* (waffle) has achieved world fame, but *couques* (sweet buns), *speculoos* (spicy gingerbread biscuits), and *pain d'amandes* (nutty after-dinner biscuits) are less well known. For lunch, cold cuts, *croque-monsieur* (toasted ham-and-cheese sandwiches), and *jambon d'Ardennes* (Ardennes ham) are popular, as is creamy *fromage blanc* (similar to cottage cheese) with radishes and spring onions on rye.

MEALTIMES

Most hotels serve breakfast until 10. Belgians usually eat lunch between 1 and 3, some making it quite a long, lavish meal. However, the main meal of the day is dinner, which most Belgians eat between 7 and 10; peak dining time used to be about 8 but is now creeping closer to 9.

WHAT TO WEAR

Belgians tend to be fairly formal and dress conservatively when dining out in the evenings. Generally speaking, though, a jacket and tie are required only in the most expensive establishments. Younger Belgians favor stylish, casual dress in most restaurants.

RATINGS

Prices are per person and include a first course, main course, dessert, 16% service and 21% sales tax, but no wine. Restaurant prices are roughly the same in Brussels and other cities.

CATEGORY	COST
$$$$	over BF3,500
$$$	BF2,500–BF3,500
$$	BF1,500–BF2,500
$	under BF1,500

Lodging

You can trust Belgian hotels, almost without exception, to be clean and of a high standard. The more ritzy hotels in city centers can be very expensive, but smaller, well-appointed hotels, some of them newly built, offer lodging at less than $100 per night for a double room. The family-run establishments in out-of-the-way spots, such as the Ardennes, can be surprisingly inexpensive, especially out of season.

PENSIONS

Pensions offer a double room with bath or shower and full board from BF2,500 to BF3,500 in Brussels and from BF2,000 to BF3,000 elsewhere. These terms are often for a minimum stay of three days.

YOUTH HOSTELS

For information about youth hostels in Brussels and Wallonia, contact **Les Auberges de Jeunesse** (⊠ Rue Van Oost 52, 1030 Brussels, ☎ 02/215–3100); for Flanders, contact **Vlaamse Jeugdherbergcentraal** (⊠ Van Stralenstraat 40, 2060 Antwerp, ☎ 03/232–7218).

CAMPING

Belgium is well supplied with camping and caravan (trailer) sites. For details regarding Wallonia, contact **C.G.T.** (⊠ Pl. de Wallonie 1, 5100 Jambes, ☎ 081/334066, FAX 081/334022); for Flanders, contact **C.K.V.B.** (⊠ Wapenplein 10, 8400 Oostende, ☎ 059/506969, FAX 059/708843).

RATINGS

Hotel prices include a 16% service charge and 6% sales tax, and are usually listed in each room. All prices are for two people in a double room.

CATEGORY	BRUSSELS	OTHER CITIES
$$$$	over BF9,000	over BF7,500
$$$	BF6,500–BF9,000	BF5,500–BF7,500
$$	BF3,500–BF6,500	BF2,500–BF5,500
$	under BF3,500	under BF2,500

Tipping

Tipping has been losing its hold because a service charge is almost always figured into the bill. For example, a tip of 16% is included in all restaurant and café bills. The tip is also included in taxi fares. If you want to give more, round the amount up to the nearest BF50 or BF100. Railway porters expect a minimum of BF60 per suitcase. For bellhops and doormen, BF100 is adequate. Give movie ushers BF20, whether or not they show you to your seat. In theaters, tip BF50 for programs. Tip washroom attendants in public places BF10.

BRUSSELS

Arriving and Departing

By Plane

All international flights arrive at Brussels National Airport at Zaventem (which is sometimes called simply Zaventem), about a 30-minute drive or a 16-minute train trip from the city center. For flight information, call 0900–00747.

BETWEEN THE AIRPORT AND DOWNTOWN

Train service from the airport to the Gare du Nord (North Station) and the Gare Centrale (Central Station) leaves every 20 minutes. The trip takes 16 minutes and costs BF110 (first class) and BF85 (second class). The first train from the airport runs at 5:24 AM and the last leaves at 11:46 PM. A taxi to the city center takes about half an hour and costs about BF1,000. You can save up to 25% on Autolux airport taxi fares by buying a voucher for the return trip at the same time. Beware freelance taxi drivers who offer their services in the arrival hall.

By the Channel Tunnel

Drivers can now piggyback on **Le Shuttle,** a special car, bus, and truck train, between Dover and Calais in 35 minutes. Several **Eurostar** passenger trains a day link London's Waterloo station with Brussels's Gare du Midi in 3¼ hours. A one-way trip costs BF5,210 in first class, BF3,680 in second; cheaper advance-purchase fares are also available. For Le Shuttle information in Brussels, call 02/512–7999 (reservations 02/512–6661); for Eurostar, call 02/203-3640 (reservations 02/224–8856).

By Train and Boat/Jetfoil

Conventional train services from London connect with the Ramsgate–Oostende ferry or Jetfoil (a hydrofoil), and from Oostende the train takes you to Brussels. The Channel crossing takes about two hours by Jetfoil, 4½ hours by ferry. Total train time on both sides of the Channel is close to three hours. For more information, call **British Rail International** in London (☎ 0171/834–2345) or **Sally Line** (☎ 01843/595522). In Belgium, tickets are available at railway stations and from travel agents; for information call 02/203–3640.

By Bus and Hovercraft

Eurolines (☎ 02/538–2049; in the United Kingdom, ☎ 01582/404511) operates one daily and one overnight service by bus and ferry. The Brussels terminal is at Gare du Nord. From London, the Hoverspeed City Sprint bus connects with the Dover–Calais Hovercraft, and the bus then takes you on to Brussels. The journey takes 6½ hours; for reservations and times, contact **Hoverspeed** (☎ 01304/240241) in Great Britain.

Getting Around

By Metro, Tram, and Bus

The metro (subway), trams (streetcars), and buses run as part of the same system. All are clean and efficient, and a single ticket costs BF50. The best buy is a 10-trip ticket for BF320, or a one-day card costing BF125. Stamp your ticket in the appropriate machine on the bus or tram; in the metro, your card is stamped as you pass through the automatic barrier. Tickets are sold in any metro station or at newsstands. Single tickets can be purchased on the bus.

Detailed maps of the Brussels public transportation network are available in most metro stations and at the Brussels tourist office in the Grand' Place (☎ 02/513–8940). You get a map free with a **Tourist Passport** (also available at the tourist office), which for BF220 allows you a one-day transport card and BF1,000 worth of museum admissions.

By Taxi

To call a cab, phone (or have the restaurant or hotel call) **Taxis Verts** (☎ 02/349–4949) or **Taxis Oranges** (☎ 02/513–6200), or catch one at a cab stand. Distances are not great in Brussels, and typical downtown rides cost BF250–BF500. Tips are included in the fare.

Important Addresses and Numbers

Embassies

U.S. (✉ Blvd. du Régent 27, 1000 Brussels, ☎ 02/513–3830). **Canadian** (✉ Av. de Tervuren 2, 1040 Brussels, ☎ 02/741–0611). **U.K.** (✉ Rue d'Arlon 85, 1040 Brussels, ☎ 02/287–6211).

Emergencies

Police (☎ 101). **Accident and Ambulance** (☎ 100). **Doctor** (☎ 02/479–1818). **Dentist** (☎ 02/426–1026). **Pharmacy:** To find out which one is open on a particular night or on weekends, call 02/479–1818.

English-Language Bookstores

House of Paperbacks (✉ Chaussée de Waterloo 813, Uccle, ☎ 02/343–1122) is open Tuesday–Saturday 10–6. **Librairie de Rome** (✉ Av. Louise 50b, ☎ 02/511–7937) is open Monday–Saturday 8 AM–10 PM, Sunday 9–6; the bookshop sells U.S. and U.K. newspapers and periodicals. **W. H. Smith** (✉ Blvd. Adolphe Max 71–75, ☎ 02/219–2708), which carries hardbacks, paperbacks, and periodicals, is open Monday–Saturday 9–6. The *International Herald Tribune* and *Wall Street Journal* are sold by almost all newsdealers.

Travel Agencies

American Express (✉ Pl. Louise 2, 1000 Brussels, ☎ 02/512–1740). **Carlson Wagonlit Travel** (✉ Blvd. Clovis 53, 1040 Brussels, ☎ 287–8110).

Visitor Information

The **Tourist Information Brussels** (TIB) office (☎ 02/513–8940) is in the Hôtel de Ville on the Grand' Place, open daily 9–6 during the main tourist season (off-season, Sun. 10–2; Dec.–Feb., closed Sun.) The main tourist office for the rest of **Belgium** is near the Grand' Place (✉ Rue Marché-aux-Herbes 63, ☎ 02/504–0390) and is open weekdays 9–7, weekends 9–1 and 2–7. In winter the office closes at 6 PM and is closed Sun. morning. There is a tourist office at **Waterloo** (✉ Chaussée de Bruxelles 149, ☎ 02/354–9910); it is open April–November 15, daily 9:30–6:30 and November 16–March, daily 10:30–5.

Guided Tours

Orientation

De Boeck Sightseeing (✉ Rue de la Colline 8, Grand' Place, ☎ 02/513–7744) operates city tours (💺 BF750) with multilingual cassette commentary. Passengers are picked up at major hotels and at the tourist office in the town hall. More original are the tours run by **Chatterbus** (✉ Rue des Thuyas 12). For reservations, call the Brussels tourist office at 02/513–8940. Tours include visits on foot or by minibus to the main sights (💺 BF600) and a walking tour that includes a visit to a bistro (💺 BF250). Tours are operated early June–September.

Special-Interest Bus Tours

ARAU organizes thematic city bus tours from March through November, including "Brussels 1900: Art Nouveau," "Alternative Brussels," and "Brussels 1930: Art Deco." Tours begin in front of Rue du Midi 2 (next to the Bourse); call 02/513–4761 for times and bookings. The cost is BF500 for a half-day tour.

Regional Tours

De Boeck Sightseeing Tours (☞ Orientation, *above*) visits Antwerp, the Ardennes, Brugge, Ghent, Ieper, and Waterloo.

Exploring Brussels

Brussels (Bruxelles to the French and Brussel to the Flemish) remains at heart a comfortable provincial city, where the principle of live-and-let-live has become a way of life. It is remarkably unaffected by its status as "the capital of Europe" and the influx of international experts who staff the institutions of the European Union and NATO. A stone's throw away from steel and glass towers are cobbled streets where the demands of modern life have made little impact. Away from the winding alleys of the city center, parks and squares are plentiful, and the Bois de la Cambre at the end of fashionable Avenue Louise leads straight into a forest as large as the city itself. In Brussels, Art Nouveau flourished as nowhere else, and its spirit lives on. Town houses are gloriously different from one another, which makes walking down most any residential street a joyous adventure.

The Grand' Place to the Place Royale

Numbers in the margin correspond to points of interest on the Brussels map.

★ ❶ The **Grand' Place** is the jewel of Brussels, one of the most sumptuous market squares in Europe. There is a daily flower market and a Sunday-morning bird market. On summer nights, music and colored light flood the entire square. The Grand' Place also comes alive during local pageants, such as the *Ommegang,* a magnificent historical pageant recreating Emperor Charles V's reception in the city (first Tuesday and Thursday in July); the biennial *Tapis de Fleurs,* when the square is covered by a carpet of flowers (next, mid-August 1998); and the Christmas illumination, when there is also a life-size crèche and real animals.

❷ The bombardment of the city by Louis XIV's troops in 1695 left only the **Hôtel de Ville** (town hall) standing. Civic-minded citizens started rebuilding the Grand' Place immediately, but the highlight of the square remains the Gothic town hall. The central tower, combining boldness and light, is topped by a statue of St-Michel, the patron saint of Brussels (currently hidden by scaffolding). ⊠ Grand' Place, ☎ 02/279–4365. ☞ BF80. *English-speaking tours Tues. 11:30 and 3:15, Wed. 3:15, Sun. 12:15. No individual visits.*

The ornate Baroque guild houses of the Grand' Place, with their burnished facades, were built shortly after the French bombardment. They are topped by gilded statues of saints and heroes so vividly rendered that they seem to call out to each other. Shops and taverns occupy most ground floors, but one serves its original purpose. This is the **Maison des Brasseurs,** which houses the Brewery Museum, appropriately enough in a country that still brews 400 different beers. ⊠ Grand' Place 10, ☎ 02/511–4987. ☞ BF100. ☼ *Daily 10–5.*

❸ Opposite the town hall is the **Maison du Roi** (King's House)—though no king ever lived there—a 16th-century palace housing the **City Museum.** In its collections are important ceramics and silverware—Brussels is famous for both—church sculpture, and statues removed from the facade of the town hall. There are also a number of paintings including Brueghel's *Marriage Procession,* as well as an extravagant collection of costumes for Manneken Pis (☞ *below*). ⊠ Grand' Place, ☎ 02/279–4355. ☞ BF80. ☼ *Mon.–Thurs. 10–12:30 and 1:30–5 (Oct.–Mar. until 4), weekends 10–1.*

NEED A BREAK?   **La Rose Blanche** (Grand' Place 11, ☎ 02/513–6479) is in a town house beside the town hall. Try a *fondue au parmesan* (cheese in batter) with a strong Chimay or a light *bière blanche* (ale). A sweeter combination is coffee and a *dame blanche* (vanilla ice cream with hot chocolate sauce).

Southwest of the town hall, on the corner of the Rue de l'Etuve and Rue du Chêne, stands the famous **Manneken Pis,** originally one of many public fountains. This small bronze statue of a chubby little boy peeing was made by Jerome Duquesnoy in 1619. The statue is known as "Brussels's Oldest Citizen" and is often dressed in one of the 518 costumes that are kept in the City Museum. The present Manneken is a copy; the original was kidnapped by 18th-century French soldiers.

On the opposite side of the Grand' Place, the alley next to the Maison du Roi leads into the **Petite rue des Bouchers,** the main restaurant street in the heart of the tourist maelstrom. Each establishment advertises its wares by means of large signs and carts packed with food. As a rule, remember that the more lavish the display, the poorer the cuisine. From here, explore the network of galleries called **Galeries St-Hubert,** also known as the Galeries Royales, built in 1847. Diffused daylight penetrates the gallery from the glassed arches high above, and neoclassical gods and heroes in their sculpted niches look down on the crowded shopping scene below.

Place Royale to the Bourse

It's a bit of an uphill hike to reach the splendid, neoclassical **Place Royale.** From the gallery entrance closest to the Grand' Place, walk up the Rue de la Madeleine, past the formal Mont des Arts park and up Coudenberg. The Place Royale is the site of the Coudenberg palace, where the sovereigns once lived, and in the center of the square stands the equestrian statue of Godefroy de Bouillon, leader of the First Crusade. Here you have a superb view over the lower town. At the northern corner of the square stands the former Old England department store, an Art Nouveau building now being renovated to house the vast collections of the **Musical Instrument Museum.**

The **Musée d'Art Moderne** (Museum of Modern Art) is housed in an exciting feat of modern architecture that descends seven floors into the ground around a central light well. There are some excellent paintings by modern French artists, but the surprise lies in the quality of Belgian modern art: Magritte's luminous fantasies, James Ensor's masks and still lifes, and Spilliaert's coastal scenes. Do not miss Permeke's deeply brooding *Fiancés* or Delvaux's Surrealist works. ⌧ *Pl. Royale 1,* ☎ *02/508–3211.* ⌧ *Free.* ☉ *Tues.–Sun. 10–1 and 2–5.*

Next door is the **Musée Royale d'Art Ancien** (Royal Museum of Ancient Art), with a collection of Flemish and Dutch paintings from the 15th to the 19th century. Most visitors head straight for the Brueghel Room, which has one of the finest collections of his works, including *The Fall of Icarus;* the next stop is often the Rubens Room. There are many other masterpieces by Hieronymus Bosch, Matsys, Van Dyck, and others. ⌧ *Rue de la Régence 10,* ☎ *02/508–3211.* ⌧ *Free.* ☉ *Tues.–Sun. 10–12 and 1–5.*

If you decide to divide your exploration of Brussels into two walks, this is a good place to break. You can pick up again at the same spot on the Place Royale. The Rue de la Régence runs from this square toward the gigantic Palais de Justice. The Sablon slopes down to the right from this street. The **Grand Sablon,** the city's most sophisticated square, is alive with cafés, restaurants, art galleries, and antiques shops. At the upper end of the square stands the church of **Notre Dame du Sablon,** built in flamboyant Gothic style. The stained-glass windows are illuminated from within at night, creating an extraordinary effect of kindly

100

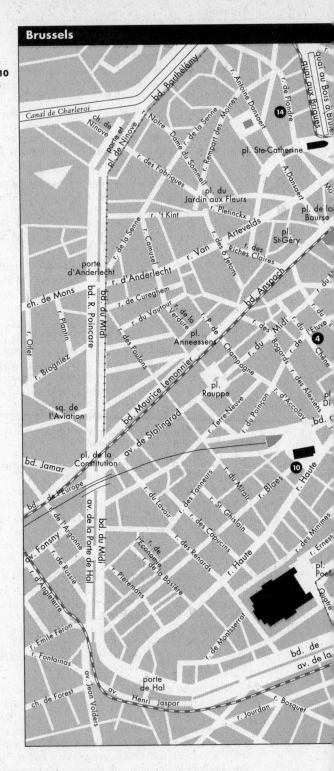

Brussels

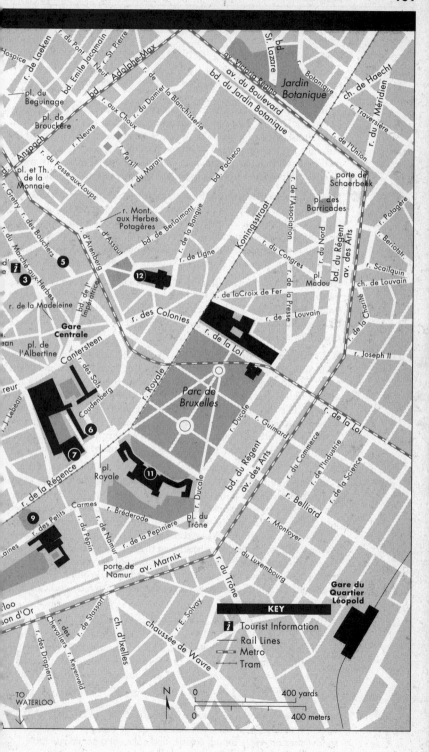

r. de Laeken   r. du Pont   r. Neuf   r. St. Pierre   bd   St. Lazare   bd   ch. de Haecht

hospice   bd. Emile Jacqmain   Adolphe-Max   av. Victoria Regina   av. du Boulevard   Botanique   ch. de Haecht

pl. du Beguinage   de   r. du Damier la Blanchisserie   av. du Jardin Botanique   **Jardin Botanique**   r. du Méridien

pl. de Brouckère   r. aux Choux   r. de la Traversière

Anspach   r. Neuve   r. de l'Union

r. du Fosse-aux-Loups   Persil   bd. Pacheco   porte de Schaerbeek   r. de l'Association

pl. et Th. de la Monnaie   r. du Marais   pl. des Barricades   r. Potagère

Gréty   r. des Bouchers   r. Mont. aux Herbes Potagères   bd. de Berlaimont   r. de Ligne   r. du Nord   r. du Régent   av. des Arts   r. Potagère

5   d'Arenberg   r. d'Assaut   r. de Ligne   r. du Congres   pl. Madou   Bertoldi

i   bd. de l'Impératrice   **12**   r. de la Presse   ch. de Louvain   r. Scailquin

3   r. du Marché-aux-Herbes   r. de laCroix de Fer   r. de Louvain   ch. de Louvain

r. de la Madeleine   r. des Colonies   r. de la Loi   r. de la Charité

Gare Centrale   Cantersteen   r. Joseph II

pl. de l'Albertine   r. des Sols   **Parc de Bruxelles**   r. Ducale   r. de la Loi

reur   Coudenberg   r. Royale   r. Guimard   r. du Commerce   r. de la Loi

6   bd. du Régent   av. des Arts   r. de l'Industrie   r. de la Science

7   r. de la Régence   pl. Royale   **11**   r. Ducale   r. Belliard

Carmes   r. Bréderode   pl. du Trône   r. Montoyer

9   r. des Petits   r. du Pépin   r. de Namur   r. de la Pépinière   r. du Luxembourg

aines   porte de Namur   av. Marnix   r. du Trône   **Gare du Quartier Léopold**

loo   r. des Chevaliers   r. de Stassart   r. F. Solvay   **KEY**

son d'Or   r. des Drapiers   r. Keyenveld   ch. d'Ixelles   chaussée de Wavre   *i* Tourist Information

TO WATERLOO   N   Rail Lines

0   400 yards   Metro

0   400 meters   Tram

warmth. Saturdays and Sunday mornings more than 100 stall holders participate in a lively antiques market below the church.

Wittamer (Grand Sablon 12, ☎ 02/512–3742) is the finest of Brussels's many excellent pastry shops. An attractive upstairs restaurant serves breakfast, light lunches, and Wittamer's unbeatable pastries.

❾ South of the church lies a peaceful garden square, the **Petit Sablon.** Statues of the counts Egmont and Hoorn, executed by the Spanish in 1568, hold pride of place. The square is surrounded by a magnificent wrought-iron fence, topped by 48 small statues representing Brussels's medieval guilds. Each craftsman carries an object that reveals his trade: The furniture maker holds a chair; the wine merchant, a goblet.

❿ Downhill from the Grand Sablon stands the splendidly restored **Eglise de la Chapelle.** The church dates from 1134 and combines Romanesque, Gothic, and Baroque elements. This was Brueghel's local church, and he is buried here in an imposing marble tomb. From the church, head back to the Sablon via the cobbled Rue Rollebeek, lined with restaurants and chic designer shops. ⊠ *Pl. de la Chapelle.*

Return via the Sablon to the Place Royale. Directly ahead is the **Parc de Bruxelles** (Brussels Park). At the end closer to you is the massive ⓫ **Palais Royal** (Royal Palace), rebuilt in 1904 to suit the expansive tastes of Leopold II. ⊠ *Pl. des Palais,* ☎ *02/551–2020.* ⊡ *Free.* ☉ *July 22 to end Sept., Tues.–Sun. 9:30–3:30.*

Walk through the formal park—laid out in 1787 so that the paths form a Masonic compass—or along the elegant Rue Royale to the end of the park. Turn down the Rue des Colonies toward the downtown area and ⓬ a short right-hand detour brings you to the **Cathédrale St-Michel et Ste-Gudule.** The cathedral's chief treasures are the beautiful stained-glass windows designed by Bernard van Orley, an early 16th-century painter at the royal court. In summer the great west window is floodlighted from inside to reveal its glories. In the crypt are remnants of the original 12th-century church.

Continue downhill, past the **Théâtre de la Monnaie** (⊠ Pl. de la Monnaie), the only opera house to have started a revolution. During a performance of a patriotic opera in 1830, members of the audience dashed into the street and started a riot that led to independence from the Dutch. Crossing the busy Boulevard Anspach, you come upon the **Tour Noire** on the left, a much-neglected vestige of the city's original fortifications. ⓭ Next comes the **Vismet** (Fish Market), which still serves its original purpose, although the river has been channeled underground. The area is lined with fish restaurants that have terraces on which you can dine alfresco in summertime.

Walk through the **Place Sainte-Catherine,** a busy market, and turn into the Rue de Flandre. A block away is the entry to a courtyard where ⓮ you'll find the **Maison de la Bellone.** This handsome, 18th-century patrician house has a particularly fine Baroque facade; inside there's a theater museum. Plays, concerts, and exhibitions are often staged here. ⊠ *Rue de Flandre 46,* ☎ *02/513–3333.* ⊡ *Free.* ☉ *Tues.–Fri. 10–6.*

Le Pain Quotidien (⊠ Rue Antoine Dansaert 16, ☎ 02/502–23612) is open from morning to late afternoon and serves superior croissants, sandwiches on crusty bread, salads, and cakes at a communal table.

The **Rue Antoine Dansaert** is home to galleries and trendy boutiques that sell Belgian-designed men's and women's fashions. It leads to the

⑮ Bourse (Stock Exchange), an amply decorated 1871 edifice in neo-Renaissance style; some of the statues are by Rodin.

Next to the Bourse, on Rue de la Bourse, what looks like major road-works is an in-situ archaeological museum, **Bruxella 1238,** where you can inspect the excavation of a 13th-century church. ⊠ *Rue de la Bourse,* ☎ *02/279–4355.* ☎ *BF80.* ☉ *Guided visits only start from the town hall Wed. at 10, 10:45, and 11:30; Fri. at 1:45, 2:30, and 3:15.*

Waterloo

No history buff can visit Brussels without making the pilgrimage to **Waterloo,** where Napoléon was finally defeated by the British and German armies on June 18, 1815. It lies 19 km (12 mi) to the south of the city; take a bus from Place Rouppe or a train from Gare Centrale to Waterloo station.

The **Waterloo Tourist Office** (⊠ Ch. de Bruxelles 149, ☎ 02/354–9910) is in the center of town. Next door is the **Wellington Museum,** in the building where the general established his headquarters. The collections include maps and models of the battle and military memorabilia. ⊠ *Ch. de Bruxelles 147,* ☎ *02/354–7806.* ☎ *BF70.* ☉ *Apr.–Oct., daily 9:30–6:30; Nov.–Mar., daily 10:30–5.*

Just south of town is the actual battlefield. Start at the **Visitors' Center,** which has an audiovisual presentation that shows scenes of the battle. You can also book expert guides to take you around the battlefield. ⊠ *Rte. du Lion 252–254,* ☎ *02/385–1912.* ☎ *BF300.* ☉ *Apr.–Oct., daily 9:30–6:30; Nov.–Mar., daily 10:30–4. Guides 1815:* ⊠ *Rte. du Lion 250,* ☎ *02/385–0625.* ☎ *1 hr, BF1,400; 3 hrs, BF2,200.*

Overlooking the battlefield is the **Butte de Lion,** a pyramid-shape monument erected by the Dutch. After climbing 226 steps, you will be rewarded with a great view of the site, especially the quadrangular fortified farms where British troops broke the French assault.

NEED A BREAK?
For a lunch of authentic Belgian cuisine, try the **Bivouac de l'Empereur** (Rte. de Lion 315, ☎ 02/384–6740), a 1720s farmhouse close to the Butte de Lion.

Off the Beaten Path

The **Atomium** is the trademark of Brussels, visible from all over the city. Erected in the hopeful 1950s as a symbol of science, it is an iron crystal molecule magnified 160 billion times. From the top you have a panoramic view of Brussels. ⊠ *Blvd. du Centenaire,* ☎ *02/477–0977.* ☎ *BF160.* ☉ *Daily 9:30–6 (July and Aug. until 9:30). Metro: Heysel.*

In the same area are the **Brussels Trade Mart** and **Stade Roi Baudouin,** formerly the Heysel Stadium. Here, too, is Bruparck, including **Kinepolis** (a 26-cinema complex) and **Mini-Europe,** a great family attraction comprising 300 models (on a 1:25 scale) of famous European buildings and monuments. ⊠ *Blvd. du Centenaire 20,* ☎ *02/478–0550.* ☎ *BF370.* ☉ *Daily 10–6 (July–Aug. until 8).*

The **Maison d'Erasme** is a beautifully restored 15th-century house where Erasmus, the great humanist, lived in 1521. Every detail is authentic, with period furniture, paintings by Holbein, Dürer, and Hieronymus Bosch, and early editions of Erasmus's works, including *In Praise of Folly.* ⊠ *Rue du Chapitre 31,* ☎ *02/521–1383.* ☎ *BF50.* ☉ *Wed.–Thurs. and Sat.–Mon., 10–noon and 2–5. Metro: Saint-Guidon.*

The **Centre Belge de la Bande Dessinée** (Belgian Comic-Strip Center) celebrates the comic strip, emphasizing such famous Belgian graphic artists as Hergé, Tintin's creator, and many others. There's also a lending library and bookshop. The display is housed in Victor Horta's splendid Art Nouveau building, once a warehouse. ⊠ *Rue des Sables 20,* ☎ *02/219–1980.* ⊴ *BF150.* ⊙ *Tues.–Sun. 10–6.*

For vintage car aficionados, the new **Autoworld** has an outstanding collection of more than 400 cars. ⊠ *Parc du Cinquantenaire 11,* ☎ *02/736–4165.* ⊴ *BF150.* ⊙ *Daily 10–6 (Nov.–March until 5).*

The **Musée Horta** (Horta Museum) was until 1919 the home of the Belgian master of Art Nouveau, Victor Horta. From attic to cellar, every detail of the house displays the exuberant curves of the Art Nouveau style. Horta, who designed the house for himself, wanted to put nature back into daily life. Here his floral motifs give a sense of opulence and spaciousness where little space exists. ⊠ *Rue Américain 25,* ☎ *02/537–1692.* ⊴ *BF100.* ⊙ *Tues.–Sat. 2–5:30.*

The **European Union institutions** are centered on Rond Point Schuman. At press time, the landmark, star-shaped Berlaymont building is closed for renovation. Meanwhile, the **European Commission** has temporary headquarters at Rue de Trèves 120, while the **European Council of Ministers** is at Rue de la Loi 170. The new **European Parliament** building is at Rue Wiertz 43. Its central element, a rounded glass summit, looms behind the Gare de Luxembourg.

Shopping

Gift Ideas

CHOCOLATE

For "everyday" chocolate, try the Côte d'Or variety, available at any newsdealer or food shop. For delicious pralines—rich chocolates filled with a creams, liqueur, or nuts—try **Godiva, Neuhaus,** or the lower-priced **Leonidas,** available at shops throughout the city. Exclusive handmade pralines can be bought at **Wittamer** (⊠ Grand Sablon 16, ☎ 02/512–3742) and **Nihoul** (⊠ Av. Louise 300, ☎ 02/648–3796).

CRYSTAL

Only the Val-St-Lambert mark guarantees handblown, hand-carved lead crystal tableware. Many stores sell it, including **Art and Selection** (⊠ Rue Marché-aux-Herbes 83, ☎ 02/511–8448) near the Grand' Place.

LACE

Be sure to ask the store assistant outright whether the lace is handmade Belgian or made in the Far East. As preparation, visit the **Musée du Coustume et de la Dentelle** (Lace Musuem, ⊠ Rue de la Violette 6, near the Grand' Place, ☎ 02/512–7709). **La Maison F. Rubbrecht** (⊠ Grand' Place, ☎ 02/512–0218) sells authentic Belgian lace. For a large choice of old and modern lace, try **Manufacture Belge de Dentelles** (⊠ Galerie de la Reine 6–8, ☎ 02/511–4477).

Shopping Districts

For boutiques and stores, the main districts are in the old downtown. **Galeries St-Hubert** has luxury goods or gift items. **Rue Neuve** is good for less expensive boutiques and department stores like Innovation, C&A, and Marks & Spencer. **City 2** and the **Anspach Center** are large shopping malls. Avant-garde clothes by the recently famous Antwerp Six and their followers are sold in boutiques in the **Rue Antoine Dansaert.**

Uptown, **Avenue Louise,** with the arcades **Galerie Louise** and **Espace Louise,** counts a large number of shops selling expensive men's and women's wear, accessories, leather goods, and jewelry. The **Boulevard**

de Waterloo is home to the same fashion names as Bond Street or Rodeo Drive. The **Grand Sablon** is as expensive as Boulevard de Waterloo but has more charm. This is the center for antiques, small art galleries, and oriental carpets.

Markets

On Saturday (9–5) and Sunday (9–1), the upper end of the Grand Sablon square becomes an **antiques market.** The **flower market** (Tues.–Sun. 8–4) on the Grand' Place is a colorful diversion. The Sunday-morning **bird market** draws shoppers to the Grand' Place. **Midi Market,** by the Gare du Midi train station, offers a look at another culture. On Sunday (5 AM–1 PM) the whole area becomes a souk as the city's large North African community gathers to buy and sell exotic foods and household goods. The **Vieux Marché** (Old Market) in Place du Jeu de Balle is a flea market worth visiting for the authentic atmosphere of the working-class Marolles district. The market is open daily 7–2. To make real finds, get there early in the morning.

Dining

It is *always* advisable to check out prix-fixe menus, which can cost only half of what you would pay dining à la carte. Lunch menus are an even better buy. Prices in the city's many Vietnamese, Chinese, and Indian restaurants are generally attractive and the food quality high.

For details and price-category definitions, *see* Dining *in* Staying in Belgium, *above.*

$$$$ ✕ **Comme Chez Soi.** Pierre Wynants, the perfectionist owner-chef, has
★ decorated his bistro-size restaurant in art nouveau style. Superb cuisine, excellent wines, and attentive service complement the warm decor. Wynants's earlier creations are quickly relegated to the back page of the menu, from which they can be ordered 24 hours in advance. One all-time favorite, fillets of sole with a white wine mousseline and shrimp, is always on the current menu. A new creation is sautéed duck's liver and quail wings with rhubarb. Many dishes are served for a minimum of two persons. Tables for two are very close together. Make dinner reservations two months in advance, lunch one month. ✉ *Pl. Rouppe 23,* ☎ *02/512–2921,* 𝖥𝖠𝖷 *02/511–8052. Reservations essential. Jacket and tie. AE, DC, MC, V. Closed Sun., Mon., July, and Christmas–New Year's.*

$$$$ ✕ **L'Ecailler du Palais Royal.** This fish-only restaurant just off the Grand Sablon seems more like a comfortable club, and many patrons seem to have known each other and the staff for years. Risotto of prawns in champagne, baked lobster custard, and superb turbot are among the delicacies on offer. There's no prix-fixe menu. ✉ *Rue Bodenbroek 18,* ☎ *02/512–8751. Reservations essential. Jacket and tie. AE, DC, MC, V. Closed Sun., Easter wk, and Aug.*

$$$$ ✕ **Maison du Cygne.** With decor to match its classical cuisine, this restaurant is set in a 17th-century guildhall on the Grand' Place. The formal dining room upstairs features paneled walls hung with old masters, and a small room on the mezzanine floor contains two priceless Brueghels. Service is flawless in the grand old manner. Typical French-Belgian dishes include *lotte aux blancs de poireaux,* a monkfish-and-leeks specialty. ✉ *Rue Charles Buyls 2,* ☎ *02/511–8244. Reservations essential. Jacket and tie. AE, DC, MC, V. Closed Sun. and 3 wks in Aug. No lunch Sat.*

$$$ ✕ **Castello Banfi.** On the Grand Sablon, in beige-and-brown post-modern surroundings, you can enjoy classic French-Italian dishes with small added refinements such as toasted pine nuts with the pesto. Carpaccio with Parmesan and celery is excellent, as is the red mullet with ratatouille. The quality of the ingredients (sublime olive oil, milk-fed veal imported from France) is very high. ⊠ *Rue Bodenbroek 12,* ☎ *02/512–87–94. Jacket and tie. AE, DC, MC, V. Closed Mon. and July. No dinner Sun.*

$$$ ✕ **Ogenblik.** With green-shaded lamps over marble-top tables, saw-
★ dust on the floor, ample servings, and a great ambience, Ogenblik is a true bistro. The long and imaginative menu changes frequently but gen-erally includes such specialties as mille-feuille with lobster and salmon, and saddle or leg of lamb with fresh, young vegetables. ⊠ *Galerie des Princes 1,* ☎ *02/511–6151. Reservations not accepted after 8 PM. AE, DC, MC, V. Closed Sun.*

$$ ✕ **Aux Armes de Bruxelles.** This restaurant is one of the few to escape the "tourist trap" label in this hectic little street. The three rooms have a lively atmosphere: The most popular section overlooks the street the-ater outside, but locals prefer the cozy rotunda. Among the specialties are tomatoes stuffed with freshly peeled shrimps, waterzooi, and mus-sels in white wine. ⊠ *Rue des Bouchers 13,* ☎ *02/511–2118. AE, DC, MC, V. Closed Mon. and June.*

$$ ✕ **Aux Marches de la Chapelle.** Opposite the Eglise de la Chapelle near the Grand Sablon is this attractive restaurant serving high-quality brasserie fare, including traditional cassoulet and sauerkraut. One of the Belle Epoque rooms is dominated by a splendid old bar, the other by an enormous open fireplace. ⊠ *Pl. de la Chapelle 5,* ☎ *02/512–6891. AE, DC, MC, V. Closed Sun. and Aug. No lunch Sat.*

$ ✕ **Au Vieux Saint Martin.** When neighboring eateries on Grand Sablon
★ are empty, this one remains busy, and you're equally welcome whether you order a full meal or a cup of coffee. Belgian specialties dominate the menu, and portions are huge. The restaurant claims to have in-vented the now ubiquitous *filet américain,* the well-seasoned Belgian version of steak tartare. The walls are hung with bright contempo-rary paintings, and picture windows front on the pleasant square. ⊠ *Grand Sablon 38,* ☎ *02/512–6476. Reservations not accepted. No credit cards.*

$ ✕ **Cappuccino.** This sleek, Italian-chic café-cum-bar, in the heart of the uptown shopping area, serves coffee, cocktails, ice cream, sandwiches, and a few Italian standards such as pizza and lasagna. It's open from 8 AM to 8 PM (Sun. from 10 AM). ⊠ *Av. Louise 35,* ☎ *538–5232. Reser-vations not accepted. AE, DC, MC, V.*

$ ✕ **Falstaff.** Some things never change, and Falstaff is one of them. This
★ huge tavern, with an Art Nouveau interior, fills up for lunch and keeps going until 5 AM, with an ever-changing crowd from students to pen-sioners. Cheerful waitresses take your orders for onion soup, filet mignon, salads, and other straightforward dishes. Falstaff II at No. 25 has the same food but not the ambience. The jury is still out on the latest, more upscale addition to this empire, Falstaff-Gourmand (around the corner at ⊠ Rue des Pierres 38, ☎ 02/512–1761). ⊠ *Rue Henri Maus 19,* ☎ *02/511–8789. AE, DC, MC, V.*

$ ✕ **Léon de Bruxelles.** For reasons known only to themselves, the pro-prietors of the old Chez Léon, as it was known to every Bruxellois for the past hundred years, have changed the restaurant's name. Even though prices have been edging upward lately, it continues to do a land-office business and has over the years expanded into a row of eight old houses. Heaping plates of mussels and other Belgian specialties, like eels in a green sauce, are served nonstop from noon to midnight, accompanied by what may be the best french fries in town. ⊠ *Rue des Bouchers 18,* ☎ *02/511–1415. No reservations. AE, DC, MC, V.*

Lodging

The annual hotel guide published by Tourist Information Brussels provides reliable information on prices and services. It does not, however, include American Express on the list of credit cards accepted. You can obtain a copy by writing to TIB (⊠ Hôtel de Ville, 1000 Brussels). In general, finding accommodations is not difficult; there has been a boom in construction. Weekend and summer rebates are available in almost all hotels; be sure to check when you book. The main hotel districts are in the Grand' Place area and around the Avenue Louise shopping district. Avoid the cheap hotel districts near the Gare du Midi and Gare du Nord train stations. Hotels can be booked at the tourist office on the Grand' Place (☎ 02/513−8940); a deposit is required (deductible from the final hotel bill).

For details and price-category definitions, *see* Lodging *in* Staying in Belgium, *above.*

$$$$ ⊞ **Brussels Hilton.** The 27-story Hilton was one of the first high-rises in Brussels back in the '60s and remains a distinctive landmark. Corner rooms are the most desirable. The second-floor Maison du Boeuf restaurant is outstanding, and the Café d'Egmont (open around the clock) is highly popular. Centrally located, the hotel is next to the main luxury shopping area and overlooks the Parc d'Egmont. ⊠ *Blvd. de Waterloo 38, 1000,* ☎ *02/504−1111,* ℻ *02/504−2111. 450 rooms with bath. 2 restaurants, bar, sauna, health club. AE, DC, MC, V.*

$$$$ ⊞ **Conrad.** Opened in 1993, the Conrad seeks to combine the European grand hotel tradition with American tastes and amenities and does a fine job. Rooms come in many different shapes but are uniformly spacious, with three telephones, bathrobes, and in-room checkout. The Maison de Maître restaurant maintains the same high standard, and the large bar is pleasantly clublike. ⊠ *Av. Louise 71, 1050,* ☎ *02/542−4242,* ℻ *02/542−4342. 268 rooms with bath. 2 restaurants, bar, meeting rooms. AE, DC, MC, V.*

$$$$ ⊞ **Radisson SAS.** This 1990 hotel, a few minutes' walk through the
★ Galerie de la Reine from Grand'Place, has guest rooms decorated in different styles: Scandinavian, Asian, Italian, and art deco. A portion of the city wall from 1134 forms part of the atrium. The Sea Grill has become one of the city's top seafood restaurants; the Atrium serves Danish open-face sandwiches. Travelers age 65 or older qualify for discounts of at least 65%; children under 15 stay free. ⊠ *Rue du Fossé-aux-Loups 47, 1000,* ☎ *02/219−2828,* ℻ *02/219−6262. 281 rooms with bath. 2 restaurants, 2 bars, exercise room, business services, meeting rooms. AE, DC, MC, V.*

$$$ ⊞ **Amigo.** Although it was built in the 1950s, this famous, family-owned
★ hotel off the Grand' Place has the charm of an older age. Each room is individually decorated, often in silk, velvet, and brocades. The bar is very pleasant, but the restaurant is not memorable. Room rates vary considerably, with the less expensive options on the lower floors. ⊠ *Rue d'Amigo 1, 1000,* ☎ *02/547−4747,* ℻ *02/513−5277. 183 rooms with bath. Restaurant, bar. AE, DC, MC, V.*

$$$ ⊞ **Metropole.** A major restoration has returned the Metropole to the palace it was during the Belle Epoque. The lobby sets the tone, with its high coffered ceiling, chandeliers, and Oriental rugs. The theme extends seamlessly to the bar with its deep leather sofas, to the gourmet restaurant, and to the café, which opens onto a heated terrace on the busy Place Brouckère. Most guest rooms have been discreetly done over in pastel shades and art deco style, but the very high ceilings take getting used to. ⊠ *Place de Brouckère 31, 1000,* ☎ *02/217−2300,* ℻

02/218–0220. 410 rooms with bath. Restaurant, bar, café, exercise room, meeting rooms, airport shuttle. AE, DC, MC, V.

$$$ 🏨 **Sofitel.** Opened in 1989, the six-floor Sofitel has a great location in the heart of a chic shopping district. There's even a boutique-lined arcade on the ground floor; you reach the lobby on an escalator. Public rooms and bedrooms are decorated in warm brown and beige tones, and bathroom telephones and bathrobes are standard. There's a buffet breakfast and good room service. ⊠ *Av. de la Toison d'Or 40, 1050,* ☎ *02/514–2200,* FAX *02/514–5744. 171 rooms with bath. Bar, breakfast room. AE, DC, MC, V.*

$$ 🏨 **Le Dixseptième.** This stylish 18th-century hotel was originally the residence of the Spanish ambassador. Suites are up a splendid Louis XV staircase, and the standard rooms surround an interior courtyard. Whitewashed walls, bare floors, exposed beams, and colorful textiles are the style here. Some rooms have kitchenettes; suites have working fireplaces and FAX machines, and there's one with a separate office. ⊠ *Rue de la Madeleine 25, 1000,* ☎ *02/502–5744,* FAX *02/502–6424. 12 rooms with bath, 13 suites. Bar, breakfast room. AE, DC, MC, V.*

$$ 🏨 **Manos Stéphanie.** The Louis XV furniture, marble lobby, and plentiful antiques set a standard of elegance rarely encountered in a hotel
★   in this price category. Even the corridors are decorated with paintings and mirrors. This 1992 hotel occupies a converted town house, and most rooms have good-sized sitting areas. Avenue Louise is just a few minutes' walk away. ⊠ *Chaussée de Charleroi 28, 1060,* ☎ *02/539–0250,* FAX *02/537–5729. 55 rooms with bath. Restaurant, bar. AE, DC, MC, V.*

$ 🏨 **Matignon.** Only the Belle Epoque facade of this family-owned-and-operated hotel opposite the Bourse was preserved when it was converted into a hotel in 1993. The lobby is tiny to make room for the large café/brasserie. Rooms are small but have large beds. The five duplex suites are good value for families. ⊠ *Rue de la Bourse 10, 1000,* ☎ *02/511–0888,* FAX *02/513–6927. 17 rooms with bath, 5 suites. Café (closed Mon.), bar. AE, DC, MC, V.*

$ 🏨 **Mozart.** The entrance to the Mozart, which opened in 1993, is between two Greek pita joints; the reception is up a flight of stairs. The lack of an elevator is a drawback, but the spacious, oak-beam rooms, in shades of salmon, are attractive; each has a refrigerator and a shower. Complimentary breakfast is served in a cozy nook. The owners also run the inexpensive restaurant Boccaccio across the street. ⊠ *Rue Marché aux Fromages 15a, 1000,* ☎ *02/502–6661,* FAX *02/502–7758. 23 rooms with bath. Breakfast room. AE, DC, MC, V.*

$ 🏨 **Orion.** This former residential hotel is now operating as a regular hotel. The whitewashed surfaces are enlivened by bright red details. Rooms have pull-out twin beds, and junior suites sleep four; all have fully equipped kitchenettes. Rooms on the courtyard are the quietest. ⊠ *Quai au Bois-à-Brûler 51, 1000,* ☎ *02/221–1411,* FAX *02/221–1599. 169 rooms. Breakfast room, meeting room. AE, DC, MC, V.*

$ 🏨 **Welcome Hotel/Truite d'Argent.** Among the charms of the smallest
★   hotel in Brussels are the young owners, Michel and Sophie Smeesters. The six rooms, with king- or queen-size beds, are as comfortable as those in far more expensive establishments; plans to add four more rooms are well under way. This hotel is much in demand, so book early. There's a charming breakfast room, and around the corner on the fish market Michel doubles as chef of the excellent seafood restaurant La Truite d'Argent. ⊠ *Rue du Peuplier 5, 1000* ☎ *02/219–9546,* FAX *02/217–1887. 6 rooms with bath. 2 restaurants, meeting rooms. AE, DC, MC, V.*

The Arts

The best way to find out what's going on is to buy a copy of the English-language weekly magazine *The Bulletin*. It's published every Thursday and sold at newsstands for BF85.

Music

Major symphony concerts and recitals are held at the **Palais des Beaux-Arts** (⊠ Rue Ravenstein 23, ☎ 02/507–8200). Chamber music is best enjoyed at the intimate **Conservatoire Royal de Musique** (⊠ Rue de la Régence 30, ☎ 02/507–8200). There are free Sunday morning and lunch-time concerts at various **churches,** including the Cathédrale St-Michel et Ste-Gudule and the Petite Église des Minimes (⊠ Rue des Minimes 62). Rock and pop concerts are given at **Forest National** (⊠ Av. du Globe 36, ☎ 02/347–0355).

Opera and Dance

The national opera company, based at the **Théâtre Royal de la Monnaie** (⊠ Pl. de la Monnaie, ☎ 02/218–1202), stages productions of international quality. Tickets cost from BF500 to BF2,000 and are hard to come by. Touring dance and opera companies often play at the **Cirque Royal** (⊠ Rue de l'Enseignement 81, ☎ 02/218–2015).

Theater

At Brussels's 30-odd theaters, actors perform mostly in French, occasionally in Flemish, and rarely in English. The loveliest theater is the **Théâtre Royal du Parc** (in Parc de Bruxelles at ⊠ Rue de la Loi 3, ☎ 02/512–2339), which has productions of Molière and other French classics. Avant-garde theater is performed at the enterprising **Théâtre Varia** (⊠ Rue du Sceptre 78, ☎ 02/640–8258). **Théâtre de Poche** (in Bois de la Cambre at ⊠ Chemin du Gymnase, ☎ 02/649–1727) favors the avant-garde. **Puppet theater** is a Belgian experience not to be missed. In Brussels, visit the intimate **Théâtre Toone VII** (⊠ Impasse Schuddeveld, No. 21, off the Petite Rue des Bouchers, ☎ 02/511–7137). In this atmospheric medieval house, satirical plays are performed in a Bruxellois dialect.

Film

Movies are mainly shown in their original language, so many are in English. Complete listings are published in *The Bulletin* and in newspapers. **The Acropole** (⊠ Galeries de la Toison d'Or), the new **UCG** complex (⊠ Place de Brouckère), and the multiscreen **Kinepolis** (⊠ Av. du Centenaire 1) feature comfortable armchairs and first-run movies. For unusual movies or screen classics, visit the **Musée du Cinéma** (Cinema Museum; ⊠ Rue Baron Horta 9, ☎ 02/507–8370). Five movies are shown daily (⊠ BF80 each, BF50 if you buy tickets 24 hours in advance).

Nightlife

Dance Clubs

In all the clubs, the action starts at midnight. **Griffin's** (⊠ Rue Duquesnoy 5, ☎ 02/505–5555, ☉ Mon.–Sat.) at the Royal Windsor Hotel appeals to young adults and business travelers. The trendy favor **Jeux d'Hiver** (⊠ Chemin du Croquet 1A, ☎ 02/649–0864, ☉ Thurs. and Fri.), a members-only club in the Bois de la Cambre; you'll be admitted if you look the part. **Le Garage** (⊠ Rue Duquesnoy 16, ☎ 02/512–6622, ☉ Daily; Sun. gays only) draws a young crowd. **Le Mirano Continental** (⊠ Chaussée de Louvain 38, ☎ 02/218–5772, ☉ Fri. and Sat.) attracts a self-styled jet set.

Bars

There's a café on virtually every corner in Brussels, and all of them serve beer from morning to late at night. Some of the most authentic, with old-style Flemish wooden furniture and fittings, are around the Grand' Place. **Le Cerf,** recently reopened, is particularly pleasant (⊠ Grand' Place 20, ☎ 02/511–4791). An appealing uptown outpost is **Nemrod** (⊠ Boulevard de Waterloo 61, ☎ 02/511–1127). **La Fleur en Papier Doré** (⊠ Rue des Aléxiens 53, ☎ 02/511–1659) is a quiet bar with surrealist decor that attracts an artistic crowd. **Cirio** (⊠ Rue de la Bourse 18, ☎ 02/512–1395) is a pleasant old Art Nouveau bar. **Rick's Café Américain** (⊠ Av. Louise 344, ☎ 02/647–7530), a favorite with the American and British expat community, packs them in three deep at the bar at lunch. It serves great burgers and similar fare. **Henry J. Bean's** (⊠ Rue du Montagne-aux-Herbes-Potagères 40, ☎ 02/219–2828) is a 1950s-style bar and grill.

Jazz

Blues Corner (⊠ Rue des Chapeliers 12, ☎ 02/511–9794), so anonymous you might pass it by, delivers blues—and potent applejack—straight. **New York Café Jazz Club** (⊠ Chausseace de Charleroi 5, ☎ 02/534–8509) is an American restaurant by day and a modern jazz hangout by night. **Preservation Hall** (also known as La Houblonnière, ⊠ Pl. de Londres 4, ☎ 02/502–1597) is pure New Orleans. **Sounds** (⊠ Rue de la Tulipe 28, ☎ 02/512–9250), a big café, emphasizes jazz rock and other modern trends. **Travers** (⊠ Rue Traversière 11, ☎ 02/218–4086), a café cum jazz club, has sounds from swing to modern jazz.

ANTWERP

Arriving and Departing

By Plane

Antwerp International Airport is 3 km (2 mi) southeast of the city. For flight information, call 03/218–1211. There are a limited number of flights from the United Kingdom and the Netherlands. Most passengers arrive via Brussels National Airport (Zaventem), which is linked with Antwerp by hourly bus service (50 minutes one-way).

BETWEEN ANTWERP AIRPORT AND DOWNTOWN
Buses to Antwerp's Centraalstation leave about every 20 minutes; travel time is around 15 minutes. Taxis are readily available, too.

By Train

Express trains run between Antwerp and Brussels; the trip takes 35 minutes. There are four trains an hour in both directions. The Centraalstation is at Koningin Astridplein 27 (☎ 03/233–3915).

By Car

Several major highways converge on Antwerp's inner-city ring expressway. It's a 10-lane racetrack, so be sure you maneuver into the correct lane well before you exit. Antwerp is an easy 45-kilometer (28-mile) drive from Brussels on the E19.

Getting Around

By Streetcar

In the downtown area, the streetcar (or tram) is the best, and most common, means of transportation. Some lines have been rebuilt underground (look for signs marked M); the most useful line runs between Centraalstation (metro stop Diamant) and the Groenplaats (for the cathe dral). A single ride costs BF40, a 10-ride ticket BF250, and a day pass BF100. For detailed transportation maps, stop at the tourist office.

Guided Tours

The tourist office operates a **Guide's Exchange** and, with a week's notice, is able to meet most requests for city guides. Guides charge BF600 an hour, with a minimum of two hours.

Visitor Information

The **Toerisme Stad Antwerpen** (Antwerp City Tourist Office) is near the cathedral (⊠ Grote Markt 15, ☎ 03/232–0103, FAX 03/231–1937). It is open Monday–Saturday 9–5:45, Sunday 9–4:45. Ask for its booklet on self-guided tours, which includes the famous "Rubens Walk." Various other popular walks are signposted throughout the city. The office will also help with accommodations (☞ Lodging, *below*).

Exploring Antwerp

Antwerp, lying on the Scheldt River 50 kilometers (31 miles) north of Brussels, is the world's fifth-largest port and Rotterdam's main competitor as a container-traffic transit point. Its name, according to legend, is derived from *handwerpen*, or "hand throwing." A Roman soldier allegedly cut off the hand of a giant and flung it into the river. In the 16th century, Emperor Charles V made Antwerp the world's most important trading center, and a hundred years later Rubens and his contemporaries made their city an equally important center of the arts. Craftsmen began practicing diamond-cutting at about this time, and the city is still a world leader in the diamond trade. Antwerp is the principal city of Flanders, and the Antwerpers, convinced that they are a cut above most others, don't mind at all their Spanish-derived nickname: they are known as the *Sinjoren* (señores).

Numbers in the margin correspond to points of interest on the Antwerp map.

❶ Antwerp's **Centraalstation** (Central Station) is a good place to start exploring the city. This elegant, mostly neo-Baroque building, impeccably restored, was built early in this century as a virtual "railway cathedral." To the east of the station is **Antwerp Zoo,** a huge, well-designed complex that includes a winter garden, a planetarium, a good restaurant, and other attractions. ⊠ *Koningin Astridplein 26,* ☎ *03/202–4540.* ☜ *BF425.* ☉ *July–Aug., daily 8:30–6:30; Sept.–Feb., daily 9–5; Mar.–June, daily 8:30–6.*

Near Centraalstation, along the Pelikaanstraat and the streets running off it, lies the **Diamond Quarter.** You can visit the spectacular showrooms of **Diamondland** to see both rough and polished diamonds, slide shows and films illustrating the history of the industry, and diamond cutters at work. Stones purchased here are certified with a Diamond High Council guarantee. ⊠ *Appelmansstraat 33a,* ☎ *03/234–3612.* ☜ *Free.* ☉ *Mon.–Sat. 9:30–5:30.*

The **Provinciaal Diamantmuseum** (Provincial Diamond Museum), farther along the same street, has three floors of maps, models, and videos about the diamond trade, besides a treasure room of jewelry. ⊠ *Lange Herentalsestraat 31-33,* ☎ *03/202–4890.* ☜ *Free (except special exhibitions).* ☉ *Daily 10–5; cutting demonstrations Sat. afternoon.*

❹ The broad De Keyserlei leads west from the train station to the main shopping area, the **Meir.** South of the Meir, on Wapper, is the **Rubenshuis** (Rubens's House). The artist lived here from 1610 until his death

Antwerp

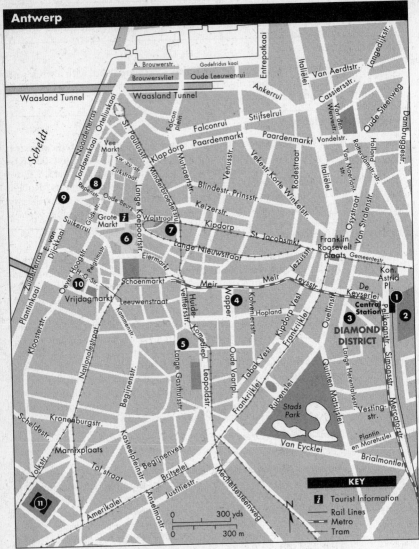

Antwerp Zoo, **2**
Centraalstation, **1**
Diamondland, **3**
Hendrik
Conscienceplein, **7**
Koninklijk Museum
voor Schone
Kunsten, **11**
Museum Mayer
van den Bergh, **5**

Onze-Lieve-
Vrouwekathedraal, **6**
Plantin-Moretus
Museum, **10**
Rubenshuis, **4**
Steen, **9**
Vleeshuis, **8**

in 1640. It is a patrician home, enriched with paintings by Rubens and his contemporaries. ⊠ *Wapper 9,* ☎ *03/232–4751.* ⊠ *BF75.* ☉ *Tues.– Sun. 10–4:45.*

At the western end of the Meir, turn left and you're in a shopping area that the Antwerp Six have made second only to Milan for the fashion-conscious. Ready-to-wear by Ann Demeulemeester and Dirk Bikkenbergs can be found at **Louis** (⊠ Lombardenstraat 2, ☎ 03/232–9872), and **Dries Van Nooten** has his own beautiful new boutique (⊠ Kammenstraat 18, ☎ 03/233–9437).

⑤ A few blocks south is the **Museum Mayer van den Bergh,** whose masterpiece is Brueghel's *Dulle Griet* (referred to in English as *Mad Meg*), an antiwar allegory that may be his greatest work. ⊠ *Lange Gasthuisstraat 19,* ☎ *03/232–4237.* ⊠ *BF75.* ☉ *Tues.–Sun. 10–4:45.*

★ ⑥ Turn back, and head for the recently restored **Onze-Lieve-Vrouwekathedraal** (Cathedral of Our Lady), Antwerp's Gothic masterpiece; you'll see its white, 400-foot spire. Among the cathedral's many art treasures are four Rubens altarpieces. His *Descent from the Cross* is flanked by panels showing Mary's visit to Elizabeth and the presentation of Jesus in the Temple; these are among the most tender and delicate Biblical scenes ever painted. ⊠ *Handschoenmarkt,* ☎ *03/231–3033.* ⊠ *BF60.* ☉ *Weekdays 10–5, Sat. 10–3, Sun. 1–4.*

A few steps north of the cathedral, the triangular **Grote Markt** is flanked on one side by the Renaissance **Stadhuis** (City Hall). It was built in the 1560s during the city's golden age, when only Antwerp and Paris had more than 100,000 inhabitants. Guild houses and a large number of restaurants surround the square.

<table>
<tr><td>NEED A
BREAK?</td><td>**Het Elfde Gebod** (The Eleventh Commandment; ⊠ Torfbrug 10, ☎ 03/ 212–3611) nestles at the cathedral's foot. This café, crammed with plaster saints, serves excellent beer and cheese.</td></tr>
</table>

⑦ The very attractive **Hendrik Conscienceplein** is a short distance east of the Grote Markt. On two sides of the square stand the harmonious Renaissance buildings of the Jesuit convent, now the city library. The Jesuits' splendidly Baroque church, **St. Carolus Borromeus,** stands on the third side. The facade, resembling a richly decorated high altar, is attributed to Rubens.

⑧ Wolstraat and its continuation, Oude Beurs, are lined with the houses of wealthy merchants. These streets lead to the imposing **Vleeshuis** (Meat Hall), a redbrick and sandstone masterpiece of late Gothic secular architecture that dates from 1503. Meat counters occupied the ground floor, and upstairs there were a conference room, chapel, and bridal suite. ⊠ *Vleeshouwersstraat 38–40,* ☎ *03/233-6404.* ⊠ *BF75.* ☉ *Tues.–Sun. 10–5.*

⑨ On the nearby waterfront is the **Steen,** the oldest building in Antwerp. This 9th-century fortress was used as a prison for centuries and is now a maritime museum. From the terraces around the Steen, you can watch the river traffic along with the many Antwerpers out for a stroll. ⊠ *Steenplein,* ☎ *03/232–0850.* ⊠ *BF75.* ☉ *Tues.–Sun. 10–5.*

For a look at the port installations, a 2½-hour **boat excursion** (from Easter weekend to late Sept.) leaves from Quay 13 on weekdays and from the Steen landing stage on Sunday. *Information from N.V. Flandria,* ⊠ *Steenplein 1,* ☎ *03/231–3100.* ⊠ *BF375.*

South of Grote Markt, explore Hoogstraat, Reyndersstraat, Pelgrimsstraat, and the adjoining alleys, an area of old Antwerp that is full of

★ ⑩ shops, authentic bars, and excellent restaurants. Following Helig Geeststraat, you'll reach Vrijdagmarkt and the **Plantin-Moretus Museum,** a famous printing works founded in the 16th century. Among its treasures are many first editions, engravings, and a copy of the Gutenberg Bible. Plantin was printer to the very Catholic King Philip II of Spain, and his workshop produced thousands of liturgical books for distribution in South America. The presses are still in working order, and you can purchase a copy of Plantin's "Ode to Happiness" printed on one of them. ⊠ *Vrijdagmarkt 22,* ☎ *03/233–0294.* ▢ *BF75.* ☯ *Tues.– Sun. 10–4:45.*

⑪ The **Koninklijk Museum voor Schone Kunsten** (Royal Museum of Fine Arts), in the southern part of the Old City, is a short tram ride away. It contains more than 1,500 paintings by old masters, including magnificent works by Rubens, Van Dyck, Hals, and Brueghel. The second floor houses one of the best collections of Flemish paintings from the 15th and 16th centuries; the first floor has more modern paintings. ⊠ *Leopold de Waelplaats 1–9,* ☎ *03/238–78–09.* ▢ *BF150.* ☯ *Tues.–Sun. 10–4:45.*

Dining

For details and price-category definitions, *see* Dining *in* Staying in Belgium, *above.*

$$$$ ✕ **'t Fornuis.** In the heart of Old Antwerp, this old and cozy restaurant, decorated in traditional Flemish style, serves arguably the best food in the city at the steepest prices. Suckling lamb is one specialty, sweetbreads with green cabbage and truffles another. ⊠ *Reyndersstraat 24,* ☎ *03/233–9903. Reservations essential. Jacket and tie. AE, DC, MC, V. Closed weekends and 3 wks in Aug.*

$$$ ✕ **De Matelote.** The gifted chef at this tiny restaurant down a narrow
★ street concocts inventive dishes such as grilled asparagus with fresh morels and a poached egg, or langoustines in a light curry sauce. Local gourmets consider this the best fish restaurant in town. For dessert, try the outstanding crème brûlée. ⊠ *Haarstraat 9,* ☎ *03/231–3207. Jacket and tie. AE, DC, MC, V. Closed Sun. and July. No lunch Mon.*

$$$ ✕ **Petrus.** One specialty of this small establishment opposite the Bourla Theater is a terrine of duck's liver interleaved with *filet d'Anvers* (lightly smoked beef). The sliced, sautéed sea scallops on potato pancakes with olive oil and white truffles are a dream. ⊠ *Kelderstraat 1,* ☎ *03/225–2734. Jacket and tie. AE, DC, MC, V. Closed Mon. and 2 wks in July. No lunch on weekends.*

$$ ✕ **Neuze Neuze.** Five tiny houses have been cobbled together to cre-
★ ate a handsome, split-level restaurant with whitewashed walls, dark brown beams, and a blazing fireplace. Warm smoked salmon with endive and a white beer sauce, scallops with rhubarb preserve, and monkfish rolls with caviar are some of the dishes executed with the flair of pricier establishments. ⊠ *Wijngaardstraat 19,* ☎ *03/232–5783. AE, DC, MC, V. Closed Sun. and 2 wks in summer. No lunch Sat.*

$ ✕ **Foyer.** This very stylish café also serves a buffet lunch and snacks from noon to midnight. It occupies the rotunda of the Bourla Theater, a marvelous 150-year old playhouse. ⊠ *Komedieplaats 18,* ☎ *03/253– 5517. Reservations not accepted. No credit cards.*

$ ✕ **'t Hofke.** Here's one place that's worth visiting for its location alone, in the Vlaeykensgang alley, where time has stood still. The dining room has the look and feel of a private home. There's a large selection of inexpensive salads, omelets, and more substantial fare. ⊠ *Oude Koornmarkt 16,* ☎ *03/233-8606. No credit cards. Closed Mon*

$ ✕ **Zuiderterras.** A stark glass-and-black-metal construction, this river-side café and restaurant was designed by avant-garde architect bOb (his spelling) Van Reeth. Here you can have a light meal for about $15 and enjoy seeing the river traffic on one side and, on the other, a view of the cathedral and the Old Town. ⊠ *Ernest Van Dijckkaai 37,* ☎ *03/234–1275. Reservations not accepted. AE, DC, MC, V.*

Lodging

The Antwerp City Tourist Office (☞ Visitor Information, *above*) maintains a list of some 25 recommended bed-and-breakfast accommodations from BF1,200 to BF2,000. It also keeps track of the best hotel prices and can make reservations for you up to a week in advance. Write or fax for a reservation form. For details and price-category definitions, *see* Lodging *in* Staying in Belgium, *above*.

$$$$ 🏨 **Antwerp Hilton.** The newest contender among luxury hotels in Antwerp opened in 1993, but its five stories are architecturally compatible with the much older buildings on Groenplaats. Rooms are equipped with three telephones, safes, and desks. Afternoon tea is served in the marble-floor lobby, and if you want to throw a party, there's a ballroom for 1,000 guests. The restaurant, Het Vyfde Seizoen, will satisfy gourmets. ⊠ *Groenplaats, 2000,* ☎ *03/204–1212,* FAX *03/204–1213. 211 rooms with bath. 2 restaurants, bar, no-smoking floors, sauna, exercise room, meeting rooms. AE, DC, MC, V.*

$$$$ 🏨 **De Rosier.** A 17th-century mansion provides discreet luxury for the
★ privileged few. Its presence announced only by a small brass plaque, De Rosier focuses instead on the aristocratic garden court and lavishly furnished interiors. Rooms vary from skylighted, modernized garrets to the beamed and leaded-glass Renaissance suite. ⊠ *Rosier 21–23, 2000,* ☎ *03/225–0140,* FAX *03/231–4111. 12 rooms with bath. Breakfast room, indoor pool. AE, DC, MC, V.*

$$$ 🏨 **Classic Hotel Villa Mozart.** This well-situated hotel is in an old building next door to the cathedral. The totally refurbished interior is entirely modern. The rooms seem smaller than they are because of the generously proportioned beds. ⊠ *Handschoenmarkt 3, 2000,* ☎ *03/231–3031,* FAX *03/231–5685. 25 rooms with bath. Brasserie/bar, sauna. AE, DC, MC, V.*

$$ 🏨 **Firean.** An Art Deco gem built in 1929, Firean offers the personal
★ service of a family-operated hotel. Rooms are decorated in pastels, offset by rich fabrics. There's a tiny bar-cum-breakfast room, where eggs are served in floral-print cozies. The location is not central, but there's a tram to the Old Town outside the door. ⊠ *Karel Oomsstraat 6, 2018,* ☎ *03/237–0260,* FAX *03/238–1168. 11 rooms plus 6 in annex next door, all with bath. Bar/breakfast room. AE, DC, MC, V. Closed first half of Aug., and Dec. 24–first Mon. in Jan.*

$$ 🏨 **Prinse.** Opened in 1990, this hotel occupies a 400-year-old building with an interior courtyard. Rooms are modern in decor; those on the top floor have exposed beams and more character. The peaceful Prinse is close to both sightseeing and shopping districts. ⊠ *Keizerstraat 63, 2000,* ☎ *03/226–4050,* FAX *03/225–1148. 30 rooms with bath. Breakfast room, meeting rooms. AE, DC, MC, V.*

$ 🏨 **Pension Cammerpoorte.** In this simple but pleasant hotel, the rooms (some with a view of the cathedral) are decorated in bright pastels and sad-clown art. A buffet breakfast, included in the price, is served in the tidy brick-and-lace café downstairs. There's no elevator. ⊠ *Steenhouwersvest 55, 2000,* ☎ *03/231–2836,* FAX *03/226–2968. 9 rooms with toilet and shower. Breakfast room. AE, DC, MC, V.*

GHENT

Arriving and Departing

By Train
Nonstop trains depart on the hour and 27 minutes past the hour from Gare du Midi in Brussels. Travel time to Ghent is 28 minutes. For train information, call 02/203–3640 or 09/221–4444.

By Car
Ghent lies 55 kms (34 mi) west of Brussels on the six-lane E40, which continues to Brugge and the coast. Traffic can be bumper-to-bumper on summer weekends.

Getting Around
Most of the sights are within a radius of half a mile from the Town Hall, and by far the best way to see them is on foot. You can rent bikes at the train station, but car traffic is fairly heavy.

Guided Tours

Boat Trips
Sightseeing boats depart from landing stages at Graslei and Korenlei for 35-minute trips (☎ *09/282–9418.* ✉ *BF150.* ☉ *Easter–Oct.*).

Guided Walks
Your Ghent experience can be much enhanced by a personal guide. Call **Gidsenbond van Gent** (Association of Ghent Guides; ☎ 09/233–0772). The charge is BF1,500 for the first two hours; BF600 per additional hour.

Visitor Information
The **Dienst voor Tourisme** (Tourist Service) is at Predikherenlei 2 (☎ 09/225-3641) with a satellite office in the Town Hall (✉ Botermarkt, ☎ 09/266–5232).

Exploring Ghent
Ghent—spelled Gent in Flemish—is the home of one of the world's greatest oil paintings, Van Eyck's *Adoration of the Mystic Lamb*. This dynamic modern city has a center straight out of the Middle Ages. It was weavers from Ghent, joined by others from Brugge, who took up arms to defeat the French cavalry in 1302. England's John of Gaunt was born in this city, hence his name. Emperor Charles V was born here, too, but when the townspeople rebelled against Spanish rule, his troops meted out harsh punishments to the city. Centuries later, a weaver saved Ghent from decline by stealing a newfangled spinning mule from England and starting Ghent's industrial revolution. Later, socialists battled here for workers' rights, and Ghent became the site of Belgium's first Flemish-speaking university.

The best spot to start a walk around the center is **Sint-Michielsbrug** (St. Michael's Bridge), with its view of Ghent's three glorious medieval steeples. The closest is that of the early Gothic **Sint Niklaaskerk** (St. Nicholas' Church); behind it is the **Belfort** (Belfry) from 1314. In the background rises the honey-colored tower of **Sint-Baafskathedraal** (St. Bavo's Cathedral) in Brabant Gothic.

From the Korenlei, on the far side of the River Leie, you can look across at the **Graslei,** with its row of Baroque guild houses and other buildings, among them the 12th-century **Koornstapelhuis** (Granary), used for 600 years. These and many other historic buildings are lit up every night from May to October (and Friday and Saturday nights the rest of the year), making an evening walk a memorable experience.

Continuing north on Jan Breydelstraat, the **Groot Vleeshuis** (Great Meat Hall), dating from the 15th century, can be seen on the right, near the confluence of the Leie with the Lieve Canal, the 700-year old waterway that links the city with Brugge. Nearby, the ancient castle of the ★ counts of Flanders, the **Gravensteen,** hulks up like an enormous battleship. First erected in 1180 by Philip of Alsace, it has been rebuilt a number of times, most recently in the 19th century. Its display of torture instruments and its dungeon indicate how feudal justice was meted out. The spinning mules that made Ghent a textile center to rival Manchester were first installed here. ⊠ *Sint-Veerleplein,* ☎ *09/225-9306.* 💰 *BF100.* ⊙ *Apr.-Sept., daily 9–6; Oct.-Mar., daily 9–5.*

NEED A BREAK? | **Café Evaluna** (⊠ Kraanlei 27, ☎ 09/233-3033), in a Renaissance building, serves excellent cakes and inexpensive lunches.

Two Baroque houses on **Kraanlei** (Nos. 77 and 79) have facades decorated with allegorical themes. Behind is **Patershol,** a former workers' quarter turned chic residential area. Back across the Leie is the **Vrijdagmarkt** (Friday Market), which still functions. The people of Ghent have assembled here since the Middle Ages to take up arms against the French, against local counts, or in defense of workers' rights.

The **Stadhuis** (Town Hall) is built in two distinct styles. The older Gothic section, with its lacelike tracery, was begun early in the 16th century. The structure was finished at the end of the century in a more sober Renaissance style. ⊠ *Botermarkt,* ☎ *09/223–9922.* 💰 *BF100.* ⊙ *Guided visits only, April–Oct., Mon.–Thurs. at 3.*

The proud **Belfort** (Belfry), 300 feet high, symbolizes the power of the guilds in the 14th century. The spire was added in 1913, based on the original plans. A 52-bell carillon hangs on the fifth floor. ⊠ *Sint-Baafsplein,* ☎ *09/233–3954.* 💰 *BF80.* ⊙ *Apr.–early Nov., daily 10–12:30 and 2–5:30. Guided visits (BF100) at 10 minutes past the hour.*

★ **Sint-Baafskathedraal** (St. Bavo's Cathedral) contains, in the De Villa Chapel, the stupendous polyptych *The Adoration of the Mystic Lamb,* completed on May 6, 1432, by Jan Van Eyck, who is said to have invented the art of painting with oil. His brother Hubert worked on the painting for four years until his death in 1426, and Jan was brought from Brugge to finish it. Its central panel is based on Revelation 14:1: "And I looked, and, lo, a Lamb stood on Mt. Sion, and with him a hundred forty and four thousand." Van Eyck used a miniaturist technique to express the universal; realism, to portray spirituality. To the medieval viewer, the painting was a theological summation of all things revealed about the relationship between God and the world. The cathedral has several other treasures, notably a Rubens masterpiece, *Saint Bavo's Entrance into the Monastery.* ⊠ *Sint-Baafsplein. Cathedral:* 💰 *Free.* ⊙ *Daily 8:30–6. No visits during services. Chapel:* 💰 *BF60.* ⊙ *Apr.–Sept., Mon.–Sat. 9:30–noon and 2–6, Sun. 1–6; Oct.–Mar., Mon.–Sat., 10:30–noon and 2:30–4, Sun. 2–5.*

Dining

For details and price-category definitions, *see* Dining *in* Staying in Belgium, *above.*

$$$ ✕ **Waterzooi.** Named for Ghent's contribution to Belgian gastronomy, a creamy fish and vegetable stew, this tiny restaurant in the

shadow of Gravensteen serves such specialties as turbot with three pepper sauces and lobster-filled ravioli with tarragon. ⊠ *Sint-Veerleplein 2,* ☎ *09/225–0563. Reservations essential. Jacket and tie. AE, DC, MC, V. Closed Wed., Sun., and late July–mid-Aug.*

$$ ✕ **Buikske Vol.** Probably the best among nouveau-chic Patershol's trendy eateries, the Buikske Vol surprises diners with combinations such as filet of Angus beef with onion confit, or crispy sweetbreads with rabbit. ⊠ *Kraanlei 17,* ☎ *09/225–1880. Jacket required. AE, MC, V. Closed Wed. evening, Sat. lunch, Sun., Easter wk and first ½ Aug.*

$$ ✕ **Het Cooremetershuis.** One flight up from the Graslei in an ancient
★ guild house is this venturesome little restaurant. It's noted for well-executed contemporary dishes like langoustine-and-basil salad, fillet of lamb with lentils, and John Dory with a parsley coulis. ⊠ *Graslei 12,* ☎ *09/223–4971. Reservations essential. Jacket and tie. AE, DC, MC, V. Closed Wed., Sun. and July 15–Aug. 15.*

$ ✕ **Taverne Keizershof.** Touristy taverns are much the same all over Belgium, but this one is popular with locals—always a good sign. The daily plates are large portions of good, solid foods, and all-day snacks include toasted sandwiches and spaghetti. ⊠ *Vrijdagmarkt 47,* ☎ *09/223–4446. MC, V. Closed Sun.*

Lodging

For details and price-category definitions, *see* Lodging *in* Staying in Belgium, *above.*

$$$ 🏨 **Sofitel.** The Ghent outpost of this comfortable, top-of-the-line French hotel chain, decorated in warm brown and beige, is excellently situated in the heart of the Old City. ⊠ *Hoogpoort 63, 9000,* ☎ *09/233–3331,* FAX *09/233–1102. 127 rooms with bath. Restaurant, bar, exercise room, meeting rooms. AE, DC, MC, V.*

$$ 🏨 **Gravensteen.** This handsome 19th-century mansion has been refurbished in Second Empire style. The grand public spaces compensate, perhaps, for the small but personalized rooms. The canal-front location, close to the castle of the counts, is a great plus. ⊠ *Jan Breydelstraat 35, 9000,* ☎ *09/225–1150,* FAX *09/225–1850. 17 rooms with bath. Bar, breakfast room, lobby lounge. AE, DC, MC, V.*

$$ 🏨 **Sint Jorishof.** Napoléon stayed here; so did Mary of Burgundy and Emperor Charles V, for this is the oldest hotel in Europe. Much of its Gothic spirit has been preserved, especially in the reception area and the restaurant, which serves classic French fare. Rooms are fresh and attractive, with peach-tinted wood and Florentine printed textiles. ⊠ *Botermarkt 2, 9000,* ☎ *09/224–2424,* FAX *09/224–2640. 28 rooms with bath (some in annex across the street). Restaurant, meeting rooms. AE, DC, MC, V.*

$ 🏨 **Erasmus.** From the flagstone and wood-beam library/lounge to the
★ stone mantels in the bedrooms, every inch of this noble 16th-century home has been scrubbed, polished, and bedecked with period ornaments. Even the tiny garden has been carefully manicured. ⊠ *Poel 25, 9000,* ☎ *09/224–2195,* FAX *233–4241. 11 rooms with bath. Breakfast room. AE, DC, MC, V. Closed mid-Dec.–mid-Jan.*

BRUGGE

Arriving and Departing

By Train

Trains run hourly at 28 and 59 minutes past the hour from Brussels (Gare du Midi) to Brugge. The station is south of the canal that circles the downtown area; for train information, call 050/382406. Travel time from Brussels is 53 minutes.

By Car

Brugge lies 97 kilometers (61 miles) northwest of Brussels on the E40 motorway to the coast. Holiday weekend traffic is often heavy.

Getting Around

The center of Brugge is best explored on foot, as car and bus access is restricted. This makes for bicycle heaven; ask the tourist office for information on where to rent one.

Guided Tours

Boat Trips

Boat trips along the city canals are run by several companies and depart from five separate landings. Boats ply the waters March–November, daily 10–6. They leave every 10 to 15 minutes, and a 30-minute trip costs BF170.

By Horse-Drawn Cab

The horse-drawn carriages that congregate in the Burg square are an expensive way of seeing the sights. They are available March–November, daily 10–6; a 35-minute trip will cost BF800. The carriages take up to four people.

Orientation Tours

Fifty-minute minibus tours of the city center leave every hour on the hour from the Market Square in front of the post office. Tours are given in seven languages (individual headphones) and cost BF330.

Visitor Information

Toerism Brugge (Brugge Tourist Office) is in the heart of Brugge (✉ Burg 11, ☎ 050/448686, 🖷 050/448600).

Exploring Brugge

Brugge (also well-known by its French name, Bruges) is an exquisitely preserved medieval town. It had the good fortune to be linked with the sea by a navigable waterway, and the city became a leading member of the Hanseatic League in the 13th century, when the town established Europe's first stock exchange. Splendid marriage feasts were celebrated here; that of Charles the Bold to Margaret of York in 1468 is commemorated in the annual Holy Blood Procession. Disaster struck when the Zwin silted up in the 15th century, but this past misfortune is responsible for Brugge's present glory. Little has changed in this city of interlaced canals overhung with humpback bridges.

Numbers in the margin correspond to points of interest on the Brugge map.

❶ Start a walking tour at the **Markt** (Market Square). From the top of the
❷ **Belfort** (Belfry) there's a panoramic view of the town. The belfry has a carillon notable even in Belgium, where they are a matter of civic pride. On summer evenings, the Markt is brightly lighted. ✉ Belfort: 🖾 BF100. ☉ Apr.–Sept., daily 9:30–5; Oct.–Mar., 9:30–12:30 and 1:30–5. Carillon concerts: ☉ Oct.–mid-June, Wed. and weekends 2:15–3; mid-June–Sept., Mon., Wed., and Sat. 9–10 PM, Sun. 2:15–3.

★ ❸ On the eastern side of the Market Square stands the **Provinciaal Hof,** the neo-Gothic provincial government building. Walk east from the square along Breidelstraat to the **Burg,** a magic, medieval square that

Brugge

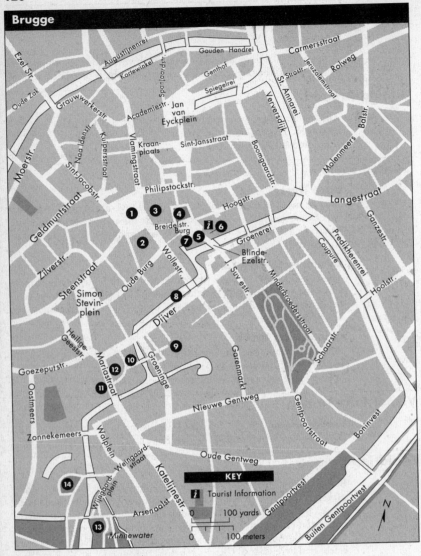

Begijnhof, **14**

Belfort, **2**

Dijver, **8**

Groeninge
Museum, **9**

Gruuthuse
Museum, **10**

Heilig–Bloed
Basiliek, **7**

Markt, **1**

Memling
Museum, **11**

Minnewater, **13**

Onze-Lieve-
Vrouwekerk, **12**

Oude Griffie, **6**

Proosdij, **4**

Provinciaal Hof, **3**

Stadhuis, **5**

4 is the focal point of ancient Brugge. On the left is the **Proosdij** (Provost's House), built in 1665. Across the square is a row of magnificent build-
5 ings. The **Stadhuis** (City Hall), dating from the 14th century, has a won-
6 derfully ornate facade covered with statues; and the **Oude Griffie,** the former Recorder's House from the 1530s, is ornamented with impressive windows. *Stadhuis:* ☜ *BF60.* ⊘ *Apr.–Sept., daily 9:30–5; Oct.–Mar., daily 9:30–12:30 and 2–5.*

7 Here, too, is the **Heilig-Bloed Basiliek** (Basilica of the Holy Blood). Little has changed in the Romanesque 12th-century crypt, but the upper chapel, rebuilt in Gothic style in the 15th century, has been decorated with 19th-century murals. In this chapel the relic of the Holy Blood is worshiped every Friday. The **Heilig-Bloed Museum** (Museum of the Holy Blood) has a reliquary and exhibits of vestments and paintings. The Procession of the Holy Blood on Ascension Day (May 8 in 1997) is a major pageant that combines religious and historical elements. *Museum:* ☜ *BF40.* ⊘ *Apr.–Sept., daily 9:30–noon and 2–6; Oct.–Mar., daily 10–noon and 2–4. Closed Wed. afternoon.*

8 Walk through a passage between the town hall and the Oude Griffie and you'll come to the **Dijver,** the city canal. Heading south along the canal, you'll soon reach a group of museums. The first is the attrac-
★ **9** tively small and manageable **Groeninge Museum,** set back from the canal in a diminutive park. It has an extremely rich, wide-ranging collection, with masterpieces by Van Eyck, Memling, Bosch, and Brueghel, among many others, plus more recent and contemporary works. ⊠ *Dijver 12,* ☏ *050/448711.* ☜ *BF200; combination ticket, BF400, also covers the Gruuthuse and Memling museums (☞ below).* ⊘ *Apr.–Sept., daily 9:30–5; Oct.–Mar., Wed.–Mon. 9:30–12:30 and 2–5.*

10 The **Gruuthuse Museum,** on the other side of the park, was a palace of the aristocratic Gruuthuse family in the 15th century. It has archaeological exhibitions and Flemish sculpture, paintings, furniture, and tapestries. ⊠ *Dijver 17,* ☏ *050/339911.* ☜ *BF130.* ⊘ *Apr.–Sept., daily 9:30–5; Oct.–Mar., Wed.–Mon. 9:30–12:30 and 2–5.*

★ **11** A block away is the **Memling Museum,** housed in the former Sint Janshospitaal, where the sick were nursed for seven centuries and very little has changed since the 13th century. The museum is dedicated to the work of one of Brugge's most famous sons, the painter Hans Memling (?1440–94), perhaps the greatest and certainly the most spiritual of all early Flemish painters. Masterpieces in the museum include the altarpiece *St. John the Baptist and St. John the Evangelist* and the fabulous miniatures adorning the St. Ursula shrine. ⊠ *Mariastraat 38,* ☏ *050/448770.* ☜ *BF100.* ⊘ *Apr.–Sept., daily 9:30–5; Oct.–Mar., Thurs.–Tues. 9:30–12:30 and 2–5.*

12 Across from the Memling Museum is the **Onze-Lieve-Vrouwekerk** (Church of Our Lady), with a 381-foot tower that is Belgium's tallest, a notable collection of paintings and carvings—including Michelangelo's small *Madonna and Child*—and splendid tombs with the effigies of Charles the Bold and Mary of Burgundy. *Mausoleum:* ☜ *BF60.* ⊘ *Apr.–Sept., weekdays 10–11:30 and 2:30–5 (Sat. until 4), Sun. 2:30–5; Oct.–Mar., weekdays 10–11:30 and 2:30–4:30 (Sat. until 4), Sun. 2:30–4:30. Closed Sun.* AM *except to worshipers.*

| NEED A BREAK? | A few blocks to the south, on Walplein, one of Brugge's many charming squares, treat yourself to a **Straffe Hendrik** (Strong Henry) beer—crystal clear, natural, and indeed quite strong—at the eponymous brew pub (⊠ Walplein 26, ☏ 050/332697). |

⓭ Continue south to the enchanting **Minnewater**, once the city harbor and more recently and romantically known as the Lake of Love. From the Minnewater visit the adjoining 16th-century lockkeeper's house, usually surrounded by white swans, the symbol of the city.

⓮ Beside Minnewater, a small bridge leads to the **Begijnhof**, a serene close of small, whitewashed houses. The Beguines were a sisterhood founded in 1245; many early members were widows of fallen crusaders. These women took partial vows and lived a devout life while serving the community. Although the last Beguines left in 1930, a Benedictine community has replaced them.

Dining

For details and price-category definitions, *see* Dining *in* Staying in Belgium, *above*.

$$$$ ✕ **De Karmeliet.** Owner-chef Geert Van Hecke, one of Belgium's best,
★ works in this lovely 18th-century house. His inventive, elaborate kitchen serves a festival of flavors: scallops of goose liver with truffled potatoes, turbot with bacon, and crisp potato nests with langoustines. ⊠ *Langestraat 19,* ☎ *050/338259. Reservations essential. Jacket and tie. AE, DC, MC, V. Closed Mon. and 2 wks in June–July. No dinner Sun.*

$$$ ✕ **'t Boergoensche Cruyce.** Claiming a romantic canal-side setting, this restaurant has salmon-and-copper decor that is reflected in the water. The cuisine is equally romantic: lamb lightly flavored with fennel and cinnamon, delicate smoked halibut, saddle of hare. The establishment now has eight hotel rooms. ⊠ *Wollestraat 41,* ☎ *050/337926,* FAX *050/ 341968. Jacket and tie. AE, DC, MC, V. Closed Tues., Wed., and mid-Nov.–mid-Dec.*

$$ ✕ **De Castillion.** This restaurant and hotel was the residence of 18th-century bishop Jean-Baptiste de Castillion. Predinner drinks and post-prandial coffee are served in a handsome Art Deco salon. Fillet of venison in a Pomerol stock, duck's liver, and a fricassée of turbot and wild salmon are among the offerings. The hotel side comprises 18 rooms and 2 suites. ⊠ *Heilige Geeststraat 1,* ☎ *050/343001,* FAX *050/339475. Jacket and tie. AE, DC, MC, V. No dinner Sun., no lunch Mon. and Tues.*

$ ✕ **Taverna Curiosa.** You have to descend a short but steep staircase to arrive at the cross-vaulted crypt. Snacks include omelets, sandwiches, and a smoked fish plate. ⊠ *Vlamingstraat 22,* ☎ *050/342334. Reservations not accepted. AE, MC, V. Closed Mon.*

$ ✕ **Tom Pouce.** This old tearoom has a superb location, right on the Burg. It serves lunch but is better known for warm apple strudel, airy waffles, and light, eggy pancakes. ⊠ *Burg 16–17,* ☎ *050/330336. Reservations not accepted. AE, DC, MC, V. Closed Mon.*

Lodging

In proportion to its size, Brugge has a large number of hotels, many of them romantic, canal-side residences. Prices are relatively high, but so are the standards. Check with the Brugge Tourist Office (☞ Visitor Information, *above*) for money-saving deals. For details and price-category definitions, *see* Lodging *in* Staying in Belgium, *above*.

$$$ 🏨 **De Tuileriëen.** A stately mansion with Venetian glass windows was
★ converted into this patrician hotel and decorated with discreet antique reproductions. The breakfast room has a coffered ceiling. Canal-side rooms have great views; courtyard rooms are quieter. ⊠ *Dijver 7, 8000,* ☎ *050/343691,* FAX *050/340400. 26 rooms with bath. Bar, breakfast room, indoor pool, hot tub, sauna. AE, DC, MC, V.*

$$$ ☷ **Holiday Inn Crowne Plaza.** This well-situated hotel has been successfully integrated into the heart of the city. Large, modern rooms are decorated in muted colors; the best have dark-wood ceiling beams. In the basement are remnants of the walls of a Romanesque church and a small museum with objects found during construction. ⊠ *Burg 10, 8000,* ☎ *050/345834,* ℻ *050/345615. 96 rooms with bath. Restaurant, bar, pool, sauna, exercise room. AE, DC, MC, V.*

$$ ☷ **Egmond.** Every room in this manorlike inn on Minnewater has garden views, as well as parquet floors and the odd fireplace or dormer ceiling. The hotel is a pleasant retreat from the bustle of the center, 10 minutes away. ⊠ *Minnewater 15, 8000,* ☎ *050/341445,* ℻ *050/342940. 9 rooms with bath. Breakfast room. No credit cards.*

$ ☷ **De Pauw.** At this spotless, family-run hotel, the warmly furnished rooms have names rather than numbers, and breakfast comes with six different kinds of bread, cold cuts, and cheese. The two rooms that share a shower down the hall are a super value. ⊠ *St. Gilliskerkhof 8, 8000,* ☎ *050/337118,* ℻ *050/345140. 8 rooms, 6 with bath. Breakfast room. AE, DC, MC, V.*

$ ☷ **Fevery.** In this friendly, comfortable hotel you are made to feel like a personal guest. ⊠ *Collaert Mansionstraat 3, 8000,* ☎ *050/331269,* ℻ *050/331791. 11 rooms with bath. Bar. AE, DC, MC, V.*

5 Bulgaria

Sofia

The Black Sea Golden Coast

Inland Bulgaria

BULGARIA, A LAND OF MOUNTAINS AND SEASCAPES, of austerity and rustic beauty, lies in the eastern half of the Balkan peninsula. From the end of World War II until recently, it was the closest ally of the former Soviet Union and presented a rather mysterious image to the Western world. This era ended in 1989 with the overthrow of Communist party head Todor Zhivkov. Since then, Bulgaria has gradually opened itself to the West as it struggles toward democracy and a free-market economy.

Endowed with long Black Sea beaches, the rugged Balkan range in its interior, and fertile Danube plains, Bulgaria has much to offer the visitor year-round. Its tourist industry is quite well developed and is being restructured to better shield visitors from the old legacies of rigid central planning.

The Black Sea coast along the country's eastern border is particularly attractive, with secluded coves and old fishing villages, as well as wide stretches of shallow beaches that have been developed into self-contained resorts. The interior landscape offers great scenic beauty, and the traveler who enters it will find a tranquil world of forested ridges, spectacular valleys, and small villages.

Founded in 681, Bulgaria was a crossroads of civilization even before that date. Archaeological finds in Varna, on the Black Sea coast, give proof of civilization from as early as 4600 BC. Bulgaria was part of the Byzantine Empire from AD 1018 to 1185 and was occupied by the Turks from 1396 until 1878. The combined influences are reflected in Bulgarian architecture, which has a truly Eastern feel. Five hundred years of Muslim occupation and nearly half a century of communist rule did not wipe out Christianity, and there are many lovely, icon-filled churches to see. The country's 120 monasteries, with their icons and many frescoes, provide a chronicle of the development of Bulgarian cultural and national identity.

The capital, Sofia, is picturesquely situated in a valley near Mt. Vitosha. There is much of cultural interest here, and the city has good hotels and restaurants. Other main towns are Veliko Târnovo, the capital from the 12th to the 14th century and well worth a visit for its old, characteristic architecture; Plovdiv, southeast of Sofia, which has a particularly interesting old quarter; and Varna, the site of one of Europe's first cultural settlements and the most important port in Bulgaria.

ESSENTIAL INFORMATION

Before You Go

When to Go

The ski season lasts from mid-December through March; the Black Sea coast season runs from May to October, reaching its crowded peak in July and August. Fruit trees blossom in April and May; in May and early June the blossoms are gathered in the Valley of Roses (you have to be up early to watch the harvest); fruit is picked in September, and in October the fall colors are at their best.

CLIMATE

Summers are warm, winters are crisp and cold. The coastal areas enjoy considerable sunshine, though March and April are the wettest months inland. Even when the temperature climbs, the Black Sea breezes and the cooler mountain air prevent the heat from being overpowering.

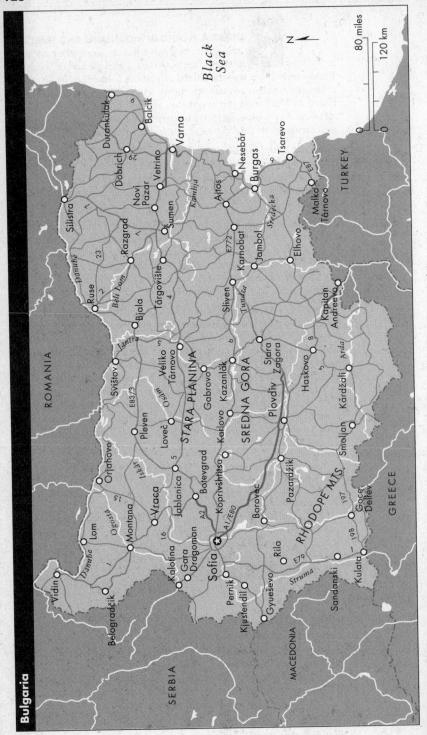

Bulgaria

The following are the average daily maximum and minimum temperatures for Sofia.

Jan.	35F	2C	May	69F	21C	Sept.	70F	22C
	25	– 4		50	10		52	11
Feb.	39F	4C	June	76F	24C	Oct.	63F	17C
	27	– 3		56	14		46	8
Mar.	50F	10C	July	81F	27C	Nov.	48F	9C
	33	1		60	16		37	3
Apr.	60F	16C	Aug.	79F	26C	Dec.	38F	4C
	42	5		59	15		28	– 2

Currency

The unit of currency in Bulgaria is the lev (plural leva), divided into 100 stotinki. There are bills of 1, 2, 5, 10, 20, 50, 100, 200, 500, 1,000, and 2,000 leva; coins of 1, 2, 5, and 10 leva; and coins of 10, 20, and 50 stotinki. At press time (spring 1996), as part of efforts at economic reform, hard-currency payments for goods and services are no longer permitted. These services include air, train, and bus travel; accommodations, from camping to hotels; and car rentals and Balkantourist (the national tourist agency) package tours. You may import any amount of foreign currency, including traveler's checks, and exchange it at branches of the Bulgarian State Bank, commercial banks, Balkantourist hotels, airports, border posts, and other exchange offices, all of which quote their daily selling and buying rates. At press time (spring 1996), the rate quoted by the Bulgarian State Bank is 75 leva to the U.S. dollar, 53 leva to the Canadian dollar, and 112 leva to the pound sterling.

It is forbidden either to import or to export Bulgarian currency. Unspent leva must be exchanged at frontier posts on departure before you go through passport control. You will need to present your official exchange slips to prove that the currency was legally purchased.

The major international credit cards are accepted in some of the larger stores, hotels, and restaurants.

What It Will Cost

Prices in Bulgaria have been low for years, but this is changing as the government tries to revive the economy and open the country up to the West. If you choose the more moderate hotels, accommodations won't be very expensive. It is possible to cut costs even more by staying in a private hotel or private room in a Bulgarian house or apartment, or by camping. The favorable cash exchange rate, linked to foreign-currency fluctuations, makes such expenses as taxi and public transport fares, museum and theater admissions, and meals in most restaurants seem comparatively low by international standards. A little hard currency, exchanged at this rate, goes a long way. Because of fluctuating exchange rates, the following price list, correct as of spring 1996, can be used only as a rough guide.

SAMPLE PRICES

Trip on a tram, trolley, or bus, 10 leva; theater ticket, 80 leva–150 leva; coffee in a moderate restaurant, 10 leva–20 leva; bottle of wine in a moderate restaurant, 150 leva–250 leva.

MUSEUMS

Museum admission is 50 leva (less than $1), except at the National History Museum where it is 150 leva.

Visas

All visitors need a valid passport. Those traveling in groups of six or more do not require visas, and many package tours are exempt from the visa requirement. Americans do not need visas when traveling as tourists. Other tourists, traveling independently, should inquire about visa requirements at a Bulgarian embassy or consulate before entering the country.

Customs on Arrival

You may import duty-free into Bulgaria 250 grams of tobacco products, plus 1 liter of hard liquor and 2 liters of wine. Travelers are advised to declare items of greater value—cameras, tape recorders, etc.—so there will be no problems with Bulgarian customs officials on departure.

Language

The official language, Bulgarian, is written in Cyrillic and is close to Old Church Slavonic, the root of all Slavic languages. English is spoken in major hotels and restaurants. It is essential to remember that in Bulgaria a nod of the head means "no" and a shake of the head means "yes."

Getting Around

By Car

ROAD CONDITIONS

Main roads are generally well engineered, although some routes are poor and narrow for the volume of traffic they have to carry. A large-scale expressway construction program has begun to link the main towns. Completed stretches run from Kalotina—on the Serbian border—to Sofia and from Sofia to Plovdiv. Highway tolls of some $20 total are paid at the border; be prepared for delays during the summer season at border points (open 24 hours) while documents are checked and stamped.

RULES OF THE ROAD

Drive on the right, as in the United States. The speed limits are 50 or 60 kph (31 or 36 mph) in built-up areas, 80 kph (50 mph) elsewhere, except on highways, where it is 120 kph (70 mph). The limits for a car towing a trailer are 50 kph (31 mph), 70 kph (44 mph), and 100 kph (62 mph), respectively. Balkantourist recommends that you take out collision, or Casco, insurance. You are required to carry a first-aid kit, fire extinguisher, and breakdown triangle in the vehicle. Front seat belts must be worn. The drunk-driving laws are strict—you are expected not to drive after you have had more than one drink.

PARKING

Park only in clearly marked parking places. If you are in doubt, check with the hotel or restaurant.

GASOLINE

Stations are regularly spaced on main roads but may be few and far between off the beaten track. All are marked on Balkantourist's free motoring map and sell unlimited quantities of fuel. For motorist information contact the main office of the **Bulgarian Automobile Touring Association** at 3 Pozitano Street, Sofia (☎ 2/86–15–1) or **Shipka Tourist Agency** at 18 Lavele Street, Sofia (☎ 2/88–38–56).

BREAKDOWNS

In case of breakdown, telephone 146. The **SBA** (Bulgarian Automobile Touring Association) trucks carry essential spares. Fiat, Ford, Volkswagen, Peugeot, and Mercedes-Benz all have car-service operations in Bulgaria that offer prompt repairs by skilled technicians.

CAR RENTAL

The **Balkan Holidays/Hertz Rent-a-Car** organization has offices in most of the major hotels and at Sofia Airport (☎ 2/72–01–57). Its main headquarters in Sofia is at 8 Pozitano Street (☎ 2/86–08–64 or 2/31–80–45). Rental cars and fly/drive arrangements can be booked through Balkantourist agents abroad. These agents can also provide you with a driver for a small extra charge. **Avis** (☎ 2/87–34–12 or 2/73–80–23) and **Europe Car** (☎ 2/72–01–57) also have offices in Sofia.

By Train
Buy tickets in advance at a ticket office—there is one in each of the major centers—and avoid long lines at the station. Trains are very busy; seat reservations are obligatory on expresses. All medium- and long-distance trains have first- and second-class carriages and limited buffet services; overnight trains between Sofia and Black Sea resorts have first- and second-class sleeping cars and second-class couchettes. From Sofia there are six main routes—to Varna or Burgas on the Black Sea coast, to Plovdiv and on to the Turkish border, to Dragoman and the Serbian border, to Kulata and the Greek border, and to Ruse on the Romanian border. The main lines are powered by electricity.

By Plane
Balkanair (Balkan Bulgarian Airlines) has regular services to Varna and Burgas, the biggest ports on the Black Sea. Group-travel and air-taxi services are available through privately run Hemus Air and Air Via. Business flights to other destinations in the country are also arranged by Hemus Air.

By Bus
Although bus routes are mainly planned to link towns and districts not connected by rail, there are many bus services run by private companies that connect all major cities. Within the cities, a regular system of trams and trolley buses operates for a single fare of 5–10 leva. Ticket booths, at most bus stops, sell single or season tickets; you can also pay the driver.

By Boat
Modern luxury vessels cruise the Danube from Passau in Austria to Ruse. Hydrofoils link main communities along the Bulgarian stretches of the Danube and the Black Sea, and there are coastal excursions from some Black Sea resorts. A ferry from Vidin to Calafat links Bulgaria with Romania.

Staying in Bulgaria

Telephones
In Bulgaria, calls can be made from public telephones in the post office in each major town or resort or, at a surcharge, from hotels. To place a call to the United States via an **AT&T USADirect** international operator, dial 00–1800–0010; for **Sprint Express,** dial 00–800–0877. There is a new system of international direct-dial phones that operate only with special cards paid for in leva.

COUNTRY CODE
For international calls to Bulgaria, the country code is 359. The access code for Sofia is 2.

Mail
Letters and postcards to North America cost 70 leva; to the United Kingdom, 60 leva.

Opening and Closing Times
Banks are open weekdays 9–3. **Museums** are usually open 9–6, but are often closed on Monday or Tuesday. **Shops** are open Monday–Saturday 9–7. Many shops are open on Sunday, and most grocery stores are open round-the-clock.

National Holidays

January 1; March 3 (Independence Day); April 27–28 (Orthodox Easter); May 1 (Labor Day); May 24 (Bulgarian Culture Day); November 1 (Day of the Leaders of the Bulgarian National Revival); December 24–26.

Dining

Visitors may choose between hotel restaurants with their international menus, Balkantourist restaurants, or privately run restaurants and cafeterias. The best bets are the small folk-style restaurants that serve national dishes and local specialties. Standards have improved, but food is still rarely served piping hot, and visitors should be prepared for loud background music.

Bulgarian national dishes are closely related to their Greek and Slav counterparts: basic Balkan cooking includes lamb and potatoes, pork, sheep cheese, peppers, eggplant, tomatoes, onions, carrots, and spices. Bulgarian melons, apples, and pears are in a class by themselves, as are the rich, amber-colored *bolgar* grapes and orange-red apricots. Bulgaria invented *kiselo mleko* (yogurt), with its promise of good health and longevity, and there are excellent *tarator* (cold yogurt soups) during the summer. *Banitsa*—rich cakes with fruit or cheese—and syrupy baklava are served to round out a meal.

Bulgarian wines are good, usually full-bodied, dry, and inexpensive. The national drink is *rakia*—either *slivova* (plum) or *grozdova* (grape) brandy—but vodka is popular, too. Coffee is strong and is often drunk along with a cold beverage, such as cola or a lemon drink. Tea is taken with lemon instead of milk.

WHAT TO WEAR

In Sofia, formal dress (jacket and tie) is customary at $$$ and $$$$ restaurants. Casual dress is appropriate elsewhere.

RATINGS

Prices are per person and include a first course, main course, dessert, and tip, but no alcohol.

CATEGORY	COST
$$$$	over 1000 leva
$$$	600 leva–1000 leva
$$	300 leva–600 leva
$	under 300 leva

CREDIT CARDS

More and more restaurants are now accepting credit cards, although the list of cards they take may not always be correctly posted. Before you place an order, check to see whether you can pay with your card.

Lodging

There is a wide choice of accommodations, ranging from hotels—most of them dating from the '60s and '70s—to apartment rentals, rooms in private homes, and campsites. Although hotels are improving, they still tend to suffer from temperamental wiring and erratic plumbing, and it is a good idea to pack a universal drain plug, as plugs are often missing in bathrooms. Power failures are not uncommon, so you might want to pack a flashlight and other battery-powered gadgets.

HOTELS

Until recently, most hotels used by Western visitors were owned by Balkantourist and Interhotels. At press time, many of the government-owned or -operated hotels listed below were on the verge of privatization. The conversion is expected to take up to five years. Hotels may be closed for renovation for extended periods or may be permanently shut down. Visitors are strongly urged to call ahead to hotels to get the latest information. Most hotels have restaurants and bars; the large modern ones have swimming pools, shops, and other facilities.

RENTED ACCOMMODATIONS

Rented accommodations are a growth industry, with planned modern complexes as well as picturesque cottages. Cooking facilities tend to be meager, and meal vouchers are included in the deal. An English-speaking manager is generally on hand.

PRIVATE ACCOMMODATIONS

Staying in private homes, with arrangements made by the national tourist agency, is becoming a popular alternative to hotels; it not only cuts costs but also means increased contact with Bulgarians. Balkantourist ranks private accommodations with from one to three stars. Booking offices are located in most main tourist areas. In Sofia, contact **Balkantourist** at 1 Vitosha Boulevard (☎ 2/43–331), or go to the private accommodations office at 27 Stambolijski Boulevard (☎ 2/88–52–56 or 2/88–44–30).

CAMPSITES

There are more than 100 campsites, many near the Black Sea coast. These are also ranked by Balkantourist with from one to three stars, and the best of them offer hot and cold water, grocery stores, and restaurants. Balkantourist provides a map.

RATINGS

Prices are for two people in a double room with half board (breakfast and a main meal). At the leading hotels you can pay in either Western or local currency; many lesser establishments will only accept leva. Foreign currency can be exchanged for leva at the receptionist desk in all hotels. Note that you must save your exchange slips in case you need to prove that the money was legally changed.

CATEGORY	SOFIA	OTHER AREAS
$$$$	over 9,000 leva	over 6,000 leva
$$$	6,000 leva–9,000 leva	4,000 leva–6,000 leva
$$	2,500 leva–6,000 leva	2,000 leva–4,000 leva
$	under 2,500 leva	under 2,000 leva

Tipping

Tipping is not frowned on. Tips are given to waiters, taxi drivers, and hotel employees, but only tips on restaurant bills are more or less determined. You can round up your bill by 10%.

SOFIA

Arriving and Departing

By Plane

All international flights arrive at Sofia airport. For information on international flights, call 2/79–80–35 or 2/72–06–72; for domestic flights, 2/79–32–21–16 or 2/72–24–14.

BETWEEN THE AIRPORT AND DOWNTOWN

Bus 84 serves the airport. Fares for taxis taken from the airport taxi stand run about 150 leva for the 10-kilometer (6-mile) ride into Sofia. Avoid the taxi touts; they tend to overcharge or to insist on payment in hard currency.

By Train

The central station is at the northern edge of the city. For information, call 2/3–11–11 or 2/843–33–33. The ticket offices in Sofia are in the underpass below the National Palace of Culture (✉ 1 Bulgaria Sq., ☎ 2/843–42–92) or at the Rila International Travel Agency (✉ 5 Gurko St., ☎ 2/87–07–77 or 2/87–59–35). There is a taxi stand at the station.

By Car

Heading to or from Serbia, the main routes are E80, going through the border checkpoint at Kalotina on the Niš-Sofia road, or E871 going through the checkpoint at Gyueshevo. Traveling from Greece, take E79, passing through the checkpoint at Kulata; from Turkey, take E80, passing through checkpoint Kapitan-Andreevo. Border crossings to Romania are at Vidin on E79 and at Ruse on E70 and E85.

Getting Around

By Bus

Buses, trolleys, and trams run fairly often. Buy a ticket from the ticket stand near the streetcar stop and punch it into the machine as you board. (Watch how the person in front of you does it.) For information, call 2/312–42–63 or 2/88–13–53.

By Taxi

It is easy to find cabs in Sofia. Hail them in the street or at a stand—or ask the hotel to call one. At press time, daytime taxi rates run about 12 leva per kilometer; it will cost about 14 leva per kilometer after 10 PM. There is a 10-leva surcharge for taxis ordered by phone. To order by phone, call 2121, 1280, 1282, or 1284. To tip, round out the fare by 5%–10%.

By Rental Car

You can rent a car, with or without driver, through Balkantourist, at the airport and at hotel reception desks.

On Foot

The main sights are centrally located, so the best way to see the city is on foot.

Important Addresses and Numbers

Since late 1990, a national commission has been working on renaming cities, streets, and monuments throughout the country. Names given in the following sections were correct as of spring 1996, but are subject to change.

Embassies

U.S. (✉ 1 Suborna St., ☎ 2/88–48–01). **Canadian,** c/o Canadian Embassy in Budapest, Budakeszi u. 32, 1121 Hungary (☎ 36/1–1767–312). **U.K.** (✉ 38 Levski Blvd., ☎ 2/88–53–61).

Emergencies

Police: Sofia City Constabulary (☎ 166); **Ambulance** (☎ 150); **Fire** (☎ 160); **Doctor:** Pirogov Emergency Hospital (☎ 2/5–15–31); **Pharmacies** (☎ 178 for information about all-night pharmacies).

Visitor Information

The main **Balkantourist** office is at 1 Vitosha Boulevard (☎ 2/4–33–31); its tourist and accommodations office is at 27 Stambolijski Boulevard (☎ 2/88–52–56, 2/87–72–33, or 2/88–06–55). It also has offices or desks in all the main hotels. **Pirin** is at 30 Stambolijski Boulevard (☎ 2/88–41–22).

Guided Tours

Orientation

Guided tours of Sofia and environs are arranged by Balkantourist from either of the main Sofia offices or from its desks at the major hotels. Among the possibilities are three- to four-hour tours of the principal city sights by car or minibus or a longer four- to five-hour tour that goes as far as Mt. Vitosha.

Excursions

Balkantourist offers special-interest tours of various lengths, using Sofia as the point of departure. There are trips to the most beautiful monasteries, such as Rila Monastery, 118 kilometers (74 miles) south of Sofia; to museum towns, such as Nesebâr and Koprivshtitsa; to sports areas and spas; to the Valley of Roses; and to other places of exceptional scenic or cultural interest.

Exploring Sofia

Sofia is set on the high Sofia Plain, ringed by mountain ranges: the Balkan range to the north; the Lyulin Mountains to the west; part of the Sredna Gora Mountains to the southeast; and, to the southwest, Mt. Vitosha—the city's playground—which rises to more than 7,600 feet. The area has been inhabited for about 7,000 years, but the visitor's first impression is of a modern city with broad streets, heavy traffic, spacious parks, and open-air cafés. As recently as the 1870s it was part of the Turkish Empire, and one mosque still remains. Most of the city, however, was planned after 1880. There are enough intriguing museums and high-quality musical performances to merit a lengthy stay, but if time is short, you need only two days to see the main sights and another day, at least, for Mt. Vitosha.

Numbers in the margin correspond to points of interest on the Sofia map.

❶ **Ploshtad Sveta Nedelya** (St. Nedelya Square) is a good starting point for an exploration of the main sights. The south side of the square is ❷ dominated by the 19th-century **Tzarkva Sveta Nedelya** (St. Nedelya Church). Go behind it to find Vitosha Boulevard, a lively pedestrian street with plenty of stores, cafés, and dairy bars.

The first building along this boulevard, on the west side of the street, ★ ❸ is the former Courts of Justice, now the **Natzionalen Istoricheski Musei** (National History Museum). Its vast collections, vividly illustrating the art history of Bulgaria, include priceless Thracian treasures, Roman mosaics, enameled jewelry from the First Bulgarian Kingdom, and glowing religious art that survived the years of Ottoman oppression. ✉ *2 Vitosha Blvd.,* ☎ *2/88–41–60.* ◫ *150 leva.* ⊙ *Weekdays 9:30–4:30.*

Return to the northeast side of St. Nedelya Square, and in the court- ❹ yard of the Sheraton Sofia Balkan Hotel you will see the **Rotonda Sveti Georgi** (Rotunda of St. George). Built in the 4th century as a Roman temple, it has served as both a mosque and a church, and recent restoration has revealed medieval frescoes. It is not open to the public. Head east to the vast Alexander Batenberg Square, which is dom- ❺ inated by the **Partiyniyat Dom** (the former headquarters of the Bulgarian Communist party).

Facing the square, but entered via Alexander Stambolijski Boulevard, ❻ is the former Great Mosque, which now houses the **Natzionalen Archeologicheski Musei** (National Archaeological Museum). The 15th-cen-

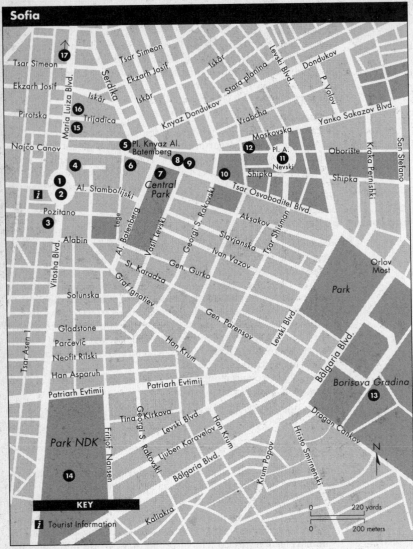

KEY

ℹ️ Tourist Information

0 — 220 yards
0 — 200 meters

Banya Bashi
Djamiya, **16**

Borisova Gradina, **13**

Hram-pametnik
Alexander Nevski, **11**

Mavsolei Georgi
Dimitrov, **7**

Natzionalen
Archeologicheski
Musei, **6**

Natzionalen Dvoretz
na Kulturata, **14**

Natzionalen
Etnografski Musei, **8**

Natzionalen
Istoricheski Musei, **3**

Natzionalna
Hudozhestvena
Galeria, **9**

Partiyniyat Dom, **5**

Ploshtad Sveta
Nedelya, **1**

Rotonda Sveti
Georgi, **4**

Tsentralen
Universalen
Magazin, **15**

Tsentralni Hali, **17**

Tzarkva Sveta
Nedelya, **2**

Tzarkva Sveta
Sofia, **12**

Tzarkva Sveti
Nikolai, **10**

tury building itself is as fascinating as its contents, which illustrate the cultures of the different peoples who inhabited Bulgaria up to the 19th century. ⊠ *2 Suborna St.,* ☎ *2/88–24–06.* ☉ *Tues.–Sun. 10–6.*

❼ On the next block to the east is the former **Mavsolei Georgi Dimitrov** (Georgi Dimitrov Mausoleum), which until 1990 contained the embalmed body of the first general secretary of the Bulgarian Communist party, who died in Moscow in 1949. His remains have been moved to the Central Cemetery, and there is talk of either converting the mausoleum into a museum or razing it.

❽ Across from the mausoleum is the former palace of the Bulgarian tsar, which currently houses the **Natzionalen Etnografski Musei** (National Ethnographic Museum), with displays of costumes, handicrafts, and tools illustrating the life of the country's rural areas up into the 19th century. ⊠ *1 Alexander Batenberg Sq.,* ☎ *2/87–41–91.* 🔳 *50 leva.* ☉ *Wed.–Sun. 10–noon and 1:30–5:30.*

❾ In the west wing of the same building is the **Natzionalna Hudozhestvena Galeria** (National Art Gallery). It houses a collection of outstanding Bulgarian works and also has a section devoted to foreign art. ⊠ *1 Alexander Batenberg Sq.,* ☎ *2/89–28–41.* 🔳 *50 leva.* ☉ *Tues.–Sun. 10:30–6.*

❿ Nearby stands the ornate Russian **Tzarkva Sveti Nikolai** (Church of St. Nicholas), erected 1912–14.

From here you'll enter Tsar Osvoboditel Boulevard, with its monument to the Russians topped by the equestrian statue of Russian Tsar Alexander II. The monument stands in front of the National Assembly. Behind the National Assembly, just beyond Shipka Street, you'll be confronted by the neo-Byzantine structure with glittering onion domes whose image you may recognize from almost every piece of tourist literature, and which really does dominate the city. This is the **Hram-pametnik Alexander Nevski** (Alexander Nevski Memorial Church), built by the Bulgarian people at the beginning of this century as a mark of gratitude to their Russian liberators. Inside are decorations in alabaster, onyx, and Italian marble, Venetian mosaics, magnificent frescoes, and space for a congregation of 5,000. Attend a service to hear the superb choir, and, above all, don't miss the fine collection of icons in the **Crypt Museum.** ⊠ *Alexander Nevski Sq.,* ☎ *2/87–76–97.* 🔳 *50 leva.* ☉ *Wed.–Mon. 10:30–5.* ★ **⓫**

⓬ Cross the square to the west to pay your respects to the much older **Tzarkva Sveta Sofia** (Church of St. Sofia), which dates from the 6th century. Its simplicity contrasts sharply with its much newer and more glamorous neighbor.

★ **⓭** Return to Tsar Osvoboditel Boulevard and continue east to the **Borisova Gradina** (Boris's Garden), with its lake and fountains, woods and lawns, huge sports stadium, and open-air theater. From the park, briefly take Dragan Tsankov west (back toward St. Nedelya Square), then turn left on Patriarh Evtimij, toward Južen Park. The formal gardens and extensive woodlands here are to be extended as far as Mt. Vitosha.

⓮ At the entrance to the park stands a large modern building, the **Natzionalen Dvoretz na Kulturata** (National Palace of Culture), with a complex of halls for conventions and cultural activities. Its multilevel underpass is equipped with a tourist information office, shops, restaurants, discos, and a bowling alley. ⊠ *1 Bulgaria Sq.,* ☎ *2/5–15–01.*

⓯ Back at St. Nedelya Square, follow Knyaginya Maria-Luiza Boulevard to the train station. The large building on the right is the recently refurbished **Tsentralen Universalen Magazin** (Central Department

Store, known as Tsum). ⊠ *2 Knyaginya Maria-Luiza Blvd.* ☉ *Mon.–Sat. 8–8.*

Just beyond is a distinctive building that is a legacy from the centuries of Turkish rule, the **Banya Bashi Djamiya** (Banja Basi Mosque); it is closed to visitors. Across the boulevard is the busy **Tsentralni Hali** (Central Market Hall), which is currently closed for renovations.

⑯
⑰

NEED A BREAK?

Anyone doing the full tour is going to need at least one refreshment stop. Many cafés line the northern length of Vitosha Boulevard. A café huddles near the 14th-century church of **Sveta Petka Samardzijska** (St. Petka of the Saddles), in the underpass leading to the Central Department Store. Or take a break in a café in the underpass at the National Palace of Culture or along Patriarh Evtimij Blvd.

Off the Beaten Path

The little medieval church of **Boyana,** about 10 kilometers (6 miles) south of the city center, is well worth a visit, as is the small, elegant restaurant of the same name, next door. The church itself is closed for restoration, but a replica, complete with copies of the exquisite 13th-century frescoes, is open to visitors.

The **Dragalevci Monastery** stands in beech woods above the nearby village of Dragalevci. The complex is still used as a convent, but you can visit the 14th-century church with its outdoor frescoes. From here take the chairlift to the delightful resort complex of **Aleko,** and another nearby chairlift to the top of Malak Rezen. There are well-marked walking and ski trails in the area. Both Boyana and Dragalevci can be reached by taking Bus 64.

Shopping

Gifts and Souvenirs

There is a good selection of arts and crafts at both the shop of the **Union of Bulgarian Artists** (⊠ 6 Shipka St.) and the **Bulgarian Folk Art Shop** (⊠ 14 Vitosha Blvd.). You will find a range of souvenirs at **Sredec** (⊠ 7 Lege St.) and **Prizma Store** (⊠ 1 Vasil Levski St.). If you are interested in furs or leather, try the shops along Vitosha Boulevard, Levski Boulevard, and Tsar Osvoboditel Boulevard. For recordings of Bulgarian music, go to the **National Palace of Culture** (☞ Exploring Sofia, *above*).

Shopping Districts

The newest shopping center is in the underpass below the modern **National Palace of Culture,** where stores sell fashions, leather goods, and all forms of handicrafts. The pedestrian-only area along **Vitosha Boulevard** features many new, privately owned shops. The colorful small shops along **Graf Ignatiev Street** also merit a visit.

Department Stores

Sofia's biggest department store is the newly renovated **Central Department Store** (⊠ 2 Knyaginya Maria-Luiza Boulevard).

Dining

Eating in Sofia can be enjoyable and even entertaining if the restaurant has a nightclub or folklore program. Be prepared to be patient and make an evening of it, as service can be slow at times. Or try a *mehana*, or tavern, where the atmosphere is informal and the service sometimes a bit quicker. For details and price-category definitions, *see* Dining *in* Staying in Bulgaria, *above.*

$$$$ ✕ **Deva Helios.** With an orchestra serenading diners most evenings, the Deva Helios—across from Alexander Nevski Memorial Church—is one of the more elegant establishments in Sofia. Expect no epicurean revolutions, just fine service and traditional Bulgarian, Italian, and Spanish food. ✉ *95 Vasil Levski Blvd.,* ☎ *2/88–03–85. No credit cards. Closed Sun.*

$$$$ ✕ **Dionyssos.** This club and restaurant above Tsum (the large Central Department Store), opposite the Sheraton Hotel, provides a rich selection of international and Bulgarian cuisine spiced with a three-hour floor show. Specialties include *kavarma* (highly seasoned fried pork). ✉ *2 Knyaginya Maria-Luiza Blvd.,* ☎ *2/81–37–26. DC, MC, V.*

$$$$ ✕ **Krim.** This Russian restaurant serves the best beef Stroganoff in town. ✉ *17 Slavjanska St.,* ☎ *2/87–01–31. AE.*

$$$$ ✕ **Valimpex.** There are wonderful days and nights of wine and roses here, and splendid food. Try the Italian specialties, which have been recently added to the menu of game, fish, and fowl. ✉ *31–33 Vitosha Blvd.,* ☎ *2/87–94–65. Reservations essential. AE, DC, MC, V.*

$$$ ✕ **Mexicano (Casa del Arquitecto).** Mexican food and music make this place popular, but it also serves traditional Bulgarian dishes, including a spicy moussaka (baked minced meat and potatoes). ✉ *11 Krakra St.,* ☎ *2/44–65–98 or 2/44–17–24. No credit cards.*

$$$ ✕ **Budapest.** This place enjoys a reputation as one of the best restaurants in Sofia for good food, wine, and live music. As the name suggests, Hungarian food takes center stage—including a fine *kebap* (stewed meat with garlic and red peppers). ✉ *145 G. S. Rakovski St.,* ☎ *2/87–27–50. No credit cards.*

$$$ ✕ **Party Club.** This restaurant features international and Chinese cuisines. ✉ *3 Vasil Levski Blvd.,* ☎ *2/81–05–44 or 2/81–43–43. AE, DC, MC, V.*

$$ ✕ **Boyansko Hanche.** Local and national specialties are the main features in this restaurant and folklore center, 8 kilometers (6 miles) from downtown (take Bus 64 or 107). ✉ *Near Bojanska Church,* ☎ *2/56–30–16. No credit cards.*

$$ ✕ **The Golden Dragon.** This new, centrally located restaurant is very popular for its wide selection of Chinese dishes. ✉ *86 Rakovski St.,* ☎ *2/87–34–00. No credit cards.*

$$ ✕ **Phenyan.** This place is known for its Far Eastern ambience and Korean specialties. ✉ *24 Assen Zlatarov St.,* ☎ *2/44–34–36. No credit cards.*

$$ ✕ **Vodeničarski Mehani.** The English translation is "Miller's Tavern," which is appropriate, since it's made up of three old mills linked together. It is at the foot of Mt. Vitosha and features a folklore show and a menu of Bulgarian specialties. Try the *giuvech* (potatoes, tomatoes, peas, and onions baked in an earthenware pan). ✉ *Dragalevci district (Bus 64),* ☎ *2/67–10–21 or 2/67–10–01. No credit cards.*

$ ✕ **Chepishev.** At the foot of Mt. Vitosha, this spot offers Bulgarian specialities and live folk music in the evenings. ✉ *Boyana district, 23 Kumata St.,* ☎ *2/55–08–88. No credit cards.*

$ ✕ **Zheravna.** This is a small, cozy place with a homey atmosphere. It serves tasty Bulgarian food. ✉ *67 Levski Blvd.,* ☎ *2/87–21–86. No credit cards.*

Lodging

The following hotels maintain a high standard of cleanliness and are open year-round unless otherwise stated. If you arrive in Sofia without reservations, go to the Interhotels Central Office (✉ 2 Sveta Sofia St.), Balkantourist (✉ 1 Vitosha Blvd.), the Bureau of Tourist Information and Reservations (✉ 22–24 Lavele St.), the National Palace of Culture (✉ 1 Bulgaria Sq.), or the central rail station. For details and price-category definitions, *see* Lodging *in* Staying in Bulgaria, *above.*

$$$$ 🏨 **Novotel Europa.** This member of the prestigious French Novotel chain is on one of Sofia's main boulevards, near the train station, and not far from the center of the city. Among its many facilities are a conference center and casino. ✉ *131 Knyaginya Maria-Luiza Blvd., 1202,* ☎ *2/3–12–61,* ℻ *2/32–00–11. 600 rooms with bath. 2 restaurants, bar, coffee shop, shops. AE, DC, MC, V.*

$$$$ 🏨 **Sheraton Sofia Hotel Balkan.** The former Grand Hotel Balkan has
★ recently been done up to Sheraton standards. It is now a first-class hotel with a central location that is hard to match. It also has excellent restaurants. ✉ *5 St. Nedelya Sq., 1000,* ☎ *2/87–65–41,* ℻ *2/87–10–38. 188 rooms with bath. 3 restaurants, 2 bars, hot tub, exercise room, nightclub. AE, DC, MC, V.*

$$$$ 🏨 **Vitosha.** There is a distinctly Asian flavor to this towering, trim
★ Interhotel—not surprising, as it was designed by a Japanese firm. With audiovisual and simultaneous translation facilities available, this is a prime option for business conferences. The Vitosha also has a shopping arcade and a superb Japanese restaurant. ✉ *100 James Boucher Blvd., 1407,* ☎ *2/6–25–18,* ℻ *2/68–12–25. 454 rooms with bath. 5 restaurants, 6 bars, pool, sauna, tennis courts, health club, shops, nightclub, business services. AE, DC, MC, V.*

$$$ 🏨 **Grand Hotel Sofia.** This five-story, centrally located Interhotel conveys an atmosphere of relative intimacy, compared with some of its larger rivals in the capital. Its Panorama Restaurant provides a fine view of Sofia. ✉ *4 Narodno Sobranie Sq., 1000,* ☎ *2/87–88–21,* ℻ *2/88–13–08. 204 rooms with bath. 3 restaurants, bar, coffee shop, folk tavern, nightclub, shops. AE, DC, MC, V.*

$$$ 🏨 **Park Hotel Moskva.** Twenty stories high, this hotel is equipped with the latest in technical services, including satellite television and a video channel for guest information. The pleasant park setting makes up for the fact that it's not as central as some comparable hotels. An excellent restaurant is hidden away on the rooftop. ✉ *25 Nezabravka St., 1113,* ☎ *2/7–12–61,* ℻ *2/65–67–45. 390 rooms with bath. 4 restaurants, bar, coffee shop, health club, nightclub. AE, DC, MC, V.*

$$$ 🏨 **Rodina.** Sofia's tallest building is not far from the city center. As one of the finest hotels in Sofia, the Rodina features the latest in modern facilities, including a sports center (pool, sauna, and solarium) and CNN news. Besides the main restaurant—complete with evening floor show—there is a Chinese eatery and Grill Room. ✉ *8 Tsar Boris III Blvd., 1606,* ☎ *2/5–16–31,* ℻ *2/54–32–25. 536 rooms with bath. 3 restaurants, bar, coffee shop, pool, shops, nightclub. AE, DC, MC, V.*

$$ 🏨 **Bulgaria.** Despite its central location, this small hotel is quiet and a bit old-fashioned. ✉ *4 Tsar Osvoboditel Blvd., 1000,* ☎ *2/87–19–77 or 2/87–01–91,* ℻ *2/88–05–85. 85 rooms with bath or shower. Restaurant, 2 bars, coffee shop. AE, DC, MC, V.*

$$ 🏨 **Deva-Spartak.** A small hotel behind the National Palace of Culture, the Deva-Spartak offers guests convenient access to the adjoining Spartak sports complex, which includes indoor and outdoor pools. ✉ *4 Arsenalski Blvd., 1421,* ☎ *2/66–12–61,* ℻ *2/66–25–37. 13 rooms with bath. Restaurant, shop. No credit cards.*

$$ 🏨 **Hemus.** Guests here can save money while availing themselves of the myriad facilities—including casino and nightclub—of the grander

Vitosha Hotel, located within easy walking distance. ⊠ *31 Cherni Vrah Blvd., 1421,* ☎ *2/6–39–51 or 2/66–13–19,* FAX *2/66–13–18. 240 rooms with bath or shower. Restaurant, folk tavern, shops, nightclub. AE, DC, MC, V.*

$$ 🏨 **Pliska-Cosmos.** Part of the Balkan Airlines hotel chain, the Pliska-Cosmos, at the entrance to Sofia, has been recently renovated. ⊠ *87 Tsarigradsko Shose Blvd., 1113,* ☎ *2/7–12–81,* FAX *2/72-39-52. 200 rooms with shower. Restaurant, bar, shops, casino. DC, MC, V.*

$$ 🏨 **Rila.** A convenient central downtown location makes the Rila a low-cost alternative to the Sheraton. ⊠ *6 Kaloyan St., 1000,* ☎ *2/88–18–61,* FAX *2/65–01–06. 120 rooms with bath or shower. Restaurant, coffee shop, folk tavern, exercise room. AE, DC, MC, V.*

$ 🏨 **Serdika.** Just opposite the Vasil Levski Monument, the central Serdika has a handy feature for travelers: a bureau for tourist services located on the premises. The restaurant serves some of the best German specialties in Sofia. ⊠ *2 Yanko Sakazov Blvd., 1504,* ☎ *2/44–34–11,* FAX *2/46–52–96. 140 rooms, most with shower. Restaurant, coffee shop. DC, MC, V.*

The Arts

The standard of music in Bulgaria is high, whether in opera houses, symphony halls, or concerts of folk music, which has just broken into the international scene with its close harmonies and colorful stage displays. Contact Balkantourist or the **Concert Office** (⊠ 2 Tsar Osvoboditel Blvd., ☎ 2/87–15–88) for general information.

There are a number of fine art galleries: The art gallery of the **Sts. Cyril and Methodius International Foundation** has a collection of Indian, African, Japanese, and Western European paintings and sculptures (⊠ Alexander Nevski Sq., ☎ 2/88–49–22; ☉ Wed.–Mon. 10:30–6). The art gallery of the **Union of Bulgarian Artists** has exhibitions of contemporary Bulgarian art (⊠ 6 Shipka St., ☎ 2/44–61–15; ☉ Daily 10:30–6). The **City Art Gallery** has both permanent exhibits of 19th-century and modern Bulgarian paintings as well as changing exhibits by contemporary artists (⊠ 1 Gen. Gurko St., ☎ 2/87–21–81).

The following movie theaters show recent foreign films in their original languages with Bulgarian subtitles: **Odeon** (⊠ 1 Patriarh Evtimij Blvd., ☎ 2/87–62–02), **Serdika** (⊠ Pametnik V. Levski Sq., ☎ 2/43–17–97), and **Vitosha** (⊠ 62 Vitosha Blvd., ☎ 2/88–58–78).

Nightlife

Nightclubs

The following hotel bars have floor shows and a lively atmosphere: **Bar Sofia** (⊠ Grand Hotel Sofia, 4 Narodno Sobranie Sq., ☎ 2/87–88–21); **Bar Variety Ambassador** (⊠ Vitosha Hotel, 100 James Boucher Blvd., ☎ 2/6–25–11); **Bar Variety** (⊠ Park Hotel Moskva, 25 Nezabravka St., ☎ 2/7–12–61); **Bar Fantasy** (⊠ Sheraton Sofia Hotel Balkan, 5 St. Nedelya Sq., ☎ 2/87–65–41).

Discos

The **National Palace of Culture** (⊠ 1 Bulgaria Sq.) has a disco, nightclub, and bowling alley. **Orbylux** (⊠ 76 James Boucher Blvd., ☎ 2/6–39–39) is known as the classiest disco in town. **Excalibur** (no phone) is a new popular disco in the underpass of Sofia University. **Yalta Club** (⊠ 21 Aksakov St., ☎ 2/88–12–97) is another popular dance spot.

Casinos

Gamblers can try their luck at the casino in the **Sheraton Sofia Hotel** (⌧ 5 St. Nedelya Sq., ☎ 2/80–55–74) or at **Pliska Cosmos** (⌧ 87 Tsarigradsko Shose Blvd., ☎ 2/7–12–81). There is also a new casino at the **Grand Hotel Sofia** (⌧ 4 Narodno Sobranie Sq., ☎ 2/87–88–21).

THE BLACK SEA GOLDEN COAST

Bulgaria's most popular resort area attracts visitors from all over Europe. Its sunny, sandy beaches are backed by the easternmost slopes of the Balkan range and by the Strandja Mountains. Although the tourist centers tend to be huge state-built complexes with a somewhat lean feel, they have modern amenities. Slânčev Brjag (Sunny Beach), the largest of the resorts, with more than 100 hotels, has plenty of children's amusements and play areas.

The historic port of Varna is a good center for exploration. It is a focal point of land and sea transportation and has museums, a variety of restaurants, and some nightlife. The fishing villages of Nesebâr and Sozopol are more attractive. Lodgings tend to be scarce in these villages. Private accommodations are arranged on the spot or by Balkantourist. Whatever resort you choose, all offer facilities for water sports. Tennis and horseback riding are also available.

Getting Around

Buses make frequent runs up and down the coast. **Cars** and **bicycles** can be rented. A **hydrofoil** service links Varna, Nesebâr, Burgas, and Sozopol. A regular **boat** service travels the Varna–Sveti Konstantin (St. Konstantin)–Zlatni Pjasâci (Golden Sands)–Albena–Balčik route.

Guided Tours

A wide range of excursions can be arranged from all resorts. There are bus excursions to Sofia from Golden Sands, Sveti Konstantin, Albena, and Sunny Beach; a one-day bus and boat trip along the Danube from Golden Sands, Sveti Konstantin, and Albena; and a three-day bus tour of Bulgaria, including the Valley of Roses, departing from Golden Sands, Sveti Konstantin, and Albena. All tours are run by Balkantourist (☞ Visitor Information, *below,* or check with your hotel information desk).

Visitor Information

There is a Balkantourist office in most towns and resorts. Many resort areas, however, do not have regular street names or numbers.

Albena (☎ 05722/27–21).
Burgas (⌧ Hotel Primorets, 1 Knyaz Batenberg St., ☎ 056/4–54–96).
Golden Sands (☎ 052/85–53–02 or 052/85–54–14).
Nesebâr (☎ 0554/58–30 or 0554/58–33).
Sunny Beach (☎ 0554/21–06 or 0554/25–10).
Sveti Konstantin (☎ 052/86–10–45).
Varna (⌧ 3 Moussala Sq., ☎ 052/22–34–84 or 052/22–22–72).

Exploring the Black Sea Golden Coast

Varna

Varna, Bulgaria's third-largest city, is easily reached by rail (about 7½ hours by express) or road from Sofia. If you plan to drive, allow time to see the Stone Forest (Pobiti Kammani) just off the Sofia–Varna road between Devnya and Varna. The unexpected groups of monumental petrified tree trunks are thought to have been formed when the area was inundated by the Lutsian Sea. The ancient city, named Odessos by the Greeks, became a major Roman trading center and is now an important shipbuilding and industrial city. The main sights can be linked by a planned walk.

Begin with the **Archeologicheski Musei,** one of the great—if lesser known—museums of Europe. The splendid collection includes the world's oldest gold treasures from the Varna necropolis of the 4th millennium BC, as well as Thracian, Greek, and Roman treasures, and richly painted icons. ⊠ *41 Osmi Primorski Polk Blvd.,* ☎ *052/23–70–57.* ⊙ *Tues.–Sat. 10–5.*

Near the northeastern end of Osmi Primorski Polk Boulevard are numerous shops and cafés; the western end leads to Mitropolit Simeon Square and the monumental **cathedral** (1880–86), whose lavish murals are worth a look. Running north from the cathedral is Vladislav Varnenchik Street, with shops, movie theaters, and eateries. Opposite the cathedral, in the city gardens, is the **Old Clock Tower,** built in 1880 by the Varna Guild Association. On the south side of the city gardens, on Nezavisimost Square, stands the magnificent Baroque **Stoyan Buchvarov National Theater.**

Leave the square to the east and walk past the Moussala Hotel. Nearby, on the corner of Knyaz Boris I Boulevard and Shipka Street, are the remains of the **Roman fortress wall.**

Walk south along Odessos Street to Han Krum Street. Here you'll find the 1602 Church of the Holy Virgin and substantial remains of the **Roman baths,** dating from the 2nd to the 3rd century AD.

Not far from the baths as you walk west is old Drazki Street, recently restored and comfortingly lined with restaurants, taverns, and coffeehouses.

Head toward the sea and November 8 Street. Continue to Primorski Boulevard and follow it, with the sea on your right, to No. 2 for the **Naval Museum** (☎ 052/22–26–55; ⊙ Weekdays 8–4), with its displays of the early days of navigation on the Black Sea and the Danube. The museum is at the edge of the extensive and luxuriant **Marine Gardens.** In the gardens there are restaurants, an open-air theater, and the fascinating **Copernicus Astronomy Complex** (☎ 052/22–28–90; ⊙ Weekdays 8–noon and 2–5) near the main entrance.

Sveti Konstantin

Eight kilometers (5 miles) north along the coast from Varna is **Sveti Konstantin,** Bulgaria's oldest Black Sea resort. Small and intimate, it spreads through a wooded park near a series of sandy coves. Warm mineral springs were discovered here in 1947, and the five-star **Grand Hotel Varna,** the most luxurious on the coast, offers all kinds of hydrotherapy under medical supervision (☞ Dining and Lodging, *below*).

In contrast to the sedate atmosphere of Sveti Konstantin is lively Zlatni Pjasâci, better known as **Golden Sands,** another 8 kilometers (5 miles) to the north, with its extensive leisure amenities, mineral-spring medical centers, and sports and entertainment facilities. Just over 4 kilometers (2 miles) inland from Golden Sands is **Aladja Rock Monastery,** one of Bulgaria's oldest, cut out of the cliff face and made accessible to visitors by sturdy iron stairways.

From Sveti Konstantin, take a trip 16 kilometers (10 miles) north to **Balčik.** Part of Romania until just before World War II, it is now a re-

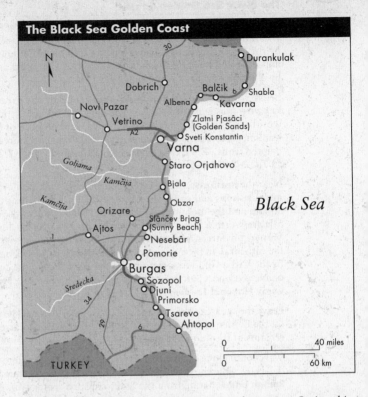

The Black Sea Golden Coast

laxed haven for Bulgaria's writers, artists, and scientists. On its white cliffs are crescent-shaped tiers sprinkled with houses, and by the Balčik ★ Palace, the beautiful **Botanical Gardens** contain some curious buildings, including a small Byzantine-style church.

Albena, the newest Black Sea resort, is located between Balčik and Golden Sands. It is well known for its long, wide beach and clean sea. The most luxurious of its 35 hotels is the **Dobrudja,** with extensive hydrotherapy facilities.

Sunny Beach
Another popular resort, this one 36 kilometers (22.5 miles) south of Varna, is Slâncev Brjag, more familiarly known as **Sunny Beach.** It is enormous, and offers safe beaches, gentle tides, and facilities for children. Sunny Beach has a variety of beachside restaurants, kiosks, and playgrounds.

★ **Nesebâr** is 5 kilometers (3 miles) south of Sunny Beach and accessible by regular buses. It would be hard to find a town that exudes a greater sense of age than this ancient settlement, founded by the Greeks 25 centuries ago on a rocky peninsula reached by a narrow causeway. Among its vine-covered houses are richly decorated medieval churches. Don't miss the frescoes and the dozens of small, private, cozy pubs all over Nesebâr.

Continue traveling south along the coast. The next place of any size is **Burgas,** Bulgaria's second main port on the Black Sea. Burgas is rather industrial, with several oil refineries, though it does have a pleasant **Maritime Park** with an expansive beach below.

For a more appealing stopover, continue another 32 kilometers (20 ★ miles) south to **Sozopol,** a fishing port with narrow cobbled streets leading down to the harbor. This was Apollonia, the oldest of the Greek colonies in Bulgaria. It is now a popular haunt for Bulgarian and, increasingly, foreign writers and artists who find private accommodations in the rustic Black Sea–style houses, so picturesque with their rough stone foundations and unpainted wood slats on the upper stories. It is also famous for the Apollonia Arts Festival, held each September.

Ten kilometers (6 miles) farther south is the vast, modern resort village of **Djuni,** where visitors can stay in up-to-date cottages, in the modern Monastery Compound, or in the Seaside Settlement. The wide range of amenities—cafés, folk restaurants, a sports center, a shopping center, a yacht club, and a marina—make it another attractive vacation spot for families.

Dining and Lodging

For details and price-category definitions, *see* Dining and Lodging *in* Staying in Bulgaria, *above.*

Albena

$$ ✕ **Bambuka.** This open-air restaurant serves international and Bulgarian cuisines and seafood. ⊠ *Albena Resort,* ☎ *05722/24–04. No credit cards.*

$$ ⊞ **Dobrudja Hotel.** The mineral-water health spa is a main attraction at this big, comfortable hotel. ⊠ *Albena Resort, 9620,* ☎ *05722/20– 20,* FAX *05722/22–16. 272 rooms with bath. 2 restaurants, 2 bars, coffee shops, indoor and outdoor pools, exercise room, shops, nightclub. DC, MC, V.*

Burgas

$$ ✕ **Starata Gemia.** The name of this restaurant translates to "old boat," appropriate for a beachfront restaurant that features fish specialties. ⊠ *Next to the Primorets Hotel,* ☎ *056/4–57–08. No credit cards.*

$$ ⊞ **Bulgaria.** The Bulgaria is a high-rise Interhotel in the center of town. It features its own nightclub with floor show and a restaurant set in a winter garden. ⊠ *21 Aleksandrovska St., 8000,* ☎ *056/4–28– 20,* FAX *056/4–72–91. 200 rooms with bath or shower. DC, MC, V.*

Sunny Beach (Slânčev Brjag)

$$ ✕ **Hanska Šatra.** In the coastal hills above the sea, this combination restaurant and nightclub has been built to resemble the tents of the *Hans* (Bulgarian rulers) of old. It has entertainment well into the night. ⊠ *4.8 km (3 mi) west of Slânčev Brjag,* ☎ *0554/28–11. No credit cards.*

$$ ✕ **Ribarska Hiza.** This lively beachside restaurant specializes in fish and has music until 1 AM. ⊠ *Northern end of Slânčev Brjag Resort,* ☎ *0554/21–86. No credit cards.*

$$ ⊞ **Burgas.** Large and comfortable, this hotel lies at the southern end of the resort. ⊠ *Slânčev Brjag Resort, 8240,* ☎ *0554/23–58,* FAX *0554/25–24. 250 rooms with bath or shower. Restaurant, bar, coffee shop, 2 pools, exercise room. AE, DC, MC, V.*

$$ ⊞ **Čajka.** For its price category, this hotel offers the best location. ⊠ *Slânčev Brjag Resort, 8240,* ☎ *0554/23–08. 36 rooms with bath or shower. No credit cards.*

$$ ★ ⊞ **Globus.** Considered by many to be the best in the resort, this hotel combines a central location with modern facilities. ⊠ *Slânčev Brjag Resort, 8240,* ☎ *0554/23–08,* FAX *0554/29–21. 100 rooms with bath or shower. Restaurant, bar, coffee shop, indoor pool, exercise room. AE, DC, MC, V.*

$$ ▥ **Kuban.** Near the center, this large establishment is just a short stroll from the beach. ⊠ *Slânčev Brjag Resort, 8240,* ☎ *0554/23–09,* FAX *0554/25–24. 216 rooms with bath or shower. 2 restaurants, 2 coffee shops. AE, DC, MC, V.*

Sveti Konstantin

$$ ✕ **Bulgarska Svatba.** This folk-style restaurant with dancing is on the outskirts of the resort; charcoal-grilled meats are especially recommended. ⊠ *Sveti Konstantin Resort,* ☎ *052/86–12–83. No credit cards.*

$$ ✕ **Manastirska Izba.** Centrally located, this is a modest but pleasant eatery with a sunny terrace. ⊠ *Sveti Konstantin Resort,* ☎ *052/86–20–36. No credit cards.*

$$$ ▥ **Grand Hotel Varna.** This Swedish-built hotel is just 450 feet from
★ the beach and offers a wide range of hydrotherapeutic treatments featuring the natural warm mineral springs. ⊠ *Sveti Konstantin Resort, 9000,* ☎ *052/86–14–91,* FAX *052/86–19–20. 325 rooms with bath. 3 restaurants, 2 bars, coffee shop, 2 swimming pools, tennis courts, bowling, exercise room, shops, nightclub. AE, DC, MC, V.*

$$ ▥ **Čajka.** Čajka means "seagull" in Bulgarian, and this hotel has a bird's-eye view of the entire resort from its perch above the northern end of the beach. ⊠ *Sveti Konstantin Resort, 9000,* ☎ *052/86–13–32. 130 rooms with bath or shower. No credit cards.*

Varna

$$ ✕ **Orbita.** This cheap hole-in-the-wall is extremely popular with the locals, who come here for the lentil soup, grilled kebabs with potatoes, or Bulgarian sausage in a pot. ⊠ *25 Tsar Osvoboditel, in Hotel Orbita, off Knyaz Boris I Blvd.,* ☎ *052/22–52–75. No credit cards.*

$ ✕ **Horizont.** This restaurant near the Delphinerium has a good selection of seafood as well as a view of the Black Sea from its outside tables. It's not too busy during the day, but at night the live music draws a crowd. ⊠ *Morska Gradina,* ☎ *052/88–45–30. No credit cards.*

$$$ ▥ **Černo More.** One of the more modern hotels in Varna, the Černo
★ More offers panoramic vistas from the top floors of its 22-story-high tower. ⊠ *33 Slivnitza Blvd., 9000,* ☎ *052/23–21–15. 230 rooms with bath or shower. 3 restaurants, bar, café with terrace, nightclub. AE, DC, MC, V.*

INLAND BULGARIA

Inland Bulgaria is not as well known to tourists as the capital and the coast, but an adventurous traveler willing to put up with limited hotel facilities and unreliable transportation will find plenty to photograph, paint, or simply savor. Wooded and mountainous, the interior is dotted with attractive "museum" villages (entire settlements listed for preservation because of their historic cultural value) and ancient towns. The foothills of the Balkan Range, marked Stara Planina ("old mountains") on most maps, lie parallel with the lower Sredna Gora Mountains, with the verdant Rozova Dolina (Valley of Roses) between them. In the Balkan range is the ancient capital of Veliko Târnovo; south of the Sredna Gora stretches the fertile Thracian plain and Bulgaria's second-largest city, Plovdiv. Between Sofia and Plovdiv is the enchanting old town of Koprivshtitsa. To the south, in the Rila Mountains, is Borovec, first of the mountain resorts. A round-trip covering all these towns, with a side excursion to Rila Monastery, could be made in four or five days.

Getting Around

Rail and bus services cover all parts of inland Bulgaria, but the best bet is to rent a car. You may also prefer to hire a driver; Balkantourist can arrange this.

Guided Tours

Organized tours set out from Sofia, each covering different points of interest. Check with your Sofia hotel information desk or with Balkantourist for specific information.

Visitor Information

Plovdiv (⊠ 106 Bulgaria Blvd., ☏ 032/55–38–48).
Veliko Târnovo (⊠ 2 Al. Penchev St., ☏ 062/3–05–71).

Exploring Inland Bulgaria

Koprivshtitsa

★ **Koprivshtitsa,** one of Bulgaria's showpiece villages, is set in mountain pastures and pine forests, about 3,050 feet up in the Sredna Gora range. It is 105 kilometers (65 miles) from Sofia, reached by a minor road south from the Sofia–Kazanlak expressway. Founded in the 14th century, it became a prosperous trading center with close ties to Venice during the National Revival period 400 years later. The architecture of this period, also called the Bulgarian Renaissance, features carved woodwork on broad verandas and overhanging eaves, brilliant colors, and courtyards with studded wooden gates. Throughout the centuries, artists, poets, and wealthy merchants have made their homes here, and many of the historic houses can be visited. The town has been well preserved and revered by the Bulgarians as a symbol of freedom since April 1876, when the rebellion that led to the end of Turkish occupation was sparked here.

After your visit, return to the Sofia–Kazanlak Expressway and turn right. After 15 kilometers (9 miles) you'll reach **Klisura** and the beginning of the Valley of Roses. Here the famous Bulgarian rose water and attar, or essence, are produced. Each May and June, the whole valley is awash in fragrance and color. After another 17 kilometers (11 miles), turn at the village of Karnare. Take the winding scenic road north over the Balkan range to the town of Trojan, and a few miles away you'll see the **Trojan Monastery,** built during the 1600s in the heart of the mountains. The Trojan Monastery Church was painstakingly remodeled during the 19th century, and its icons, wood carvings, and frescoes are classic examples of National Revival art. Back at Trojan, continue north on the mountain road until it meets highway E771, where you turn right for Veliko Târnovo, 82 kilometers (50 miles) away.

Veliko Târnovo

Veliko Târnovo, a town of panoramic vistas, rises up against steep mountain slopes through which the River Jantra runs its jagged course. From the 12th to the 14th century, this was the capital of the Second Bulgarian Kingdom. Damaged by repeated Ottoman attack, and again by an earthquake in 1913, it has been reconstructed and is now a museum city of marvelous relics. Ideally, you should begin at a vantage point above the town in order to get an overview of its design and character. Next, seek out **Tsarevec** to the west, protected by a river loop. This is where medieval tsars and patriarchs had their palaces. The area is under restoration, and steep paths and stairways now provide opportunities to view the extensive ruins of the royal palace.

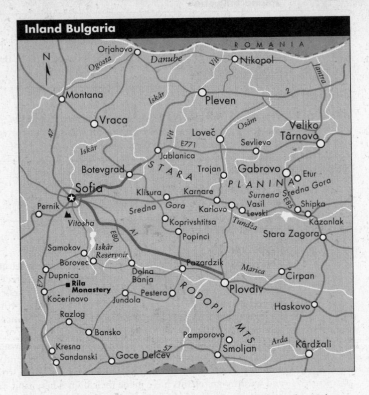

Inland Bulgaria

The prominent feature to the south is **Baldwin's Tower,** the 13th-century prison of Baldwin of Flanders, onetime Latin emperor of Constantinople. Nearby are three important churches: the 13th-century **Church of the Forty Martyrs,** with its Târnovo-school frescoes and two inscribed columns, one dating from the 9th century; the **Church of Sts. Peter and Paul,** with vigorous murals both inside and out; and, across the river, reached by a bridge near the Forty Martyrs, the restored **Church of Saint Dimitrius,** built on the spot where the Second Bulgarian Kingdom was proclaimed in 1185.

Back toward the center of town, near the Jantra Hotel, is Samovodene Street, lined with restored crafts workshops—a fascinating place to linger and a good place to find souvenirs, Turkish candy, or a charming café. On nearby Rakovski Street are a group of buildings of the National Revival period. One of the finest is **Hadji Nikoli,** a museum that was once an inn. ⊠ *17 Georgi Sava Rakovski. Closed for renovations at press time.*

Moving east from Veliko Târnovo toward Varna on E771, you can go back farther in time by visiting the ruins of the two capitals of the First Bulgarian Kingdom in the vicinity of **Šumen.** The first ruins are the fortifications at **Pliska,** 23 kilometers (14 miles) southeast of Šumen, and date from 681. At **Veliki Preslav,** 21 kilometers (13 miles) southwest of Šumen, there are ruins from the second capital that date from 893 to 927. The 8th- to 9th-century **Madara Horseman,** a bas-relief of a rider slaying a lion, appears 18 kilometers (11 miles) east of town on a sheer cliff face.

If you leave Veliko Târnovo by E85 and head south toward **Plovdiv,** you can make three interesting stops en route. The first, near the industrial center of Gabrovo—is the museum village of **Etur,** 8 kilometers (5 miles) to the southeast. Its mill is still powered by a stream, and local craftsmen continue to be trained in traditional skills. The second is **Shipka Pass,** with its mighty monument on the peak to the 200,000 Russian soldiers and Bulgarian volunteers who died here in 1877 during the Russian-Turkish Wars. The third is **Kazanlak,** at the eastern end of the Valley of Roses, where you can trace the history of rose cultivation, Bulgaria's oldest industry. There is also a highly decorated replica of a Thracian tomb of the 3rd or 4th century BC, set near the original, which remains closed for its preservation.

Plovdiv

★ From Kazanlak, take the road west through the **Valley of Roses** to either Vasil Levski or Karlovo, another rose festival town. Then turn south for **Plovdiv,** Bulgaria's second-largest city, one of the oldest cities in Europe and a major industrial center. The old town, on the hillier southern side of the Marica River, is worth a visit.

Begin at the **National Ethnographical Museum** in the House of Arghir Koyumdjioglu, an elegant example of the National Revival style that made its first impact in Plovdiv. The museum is filled with artifacts from that fertile period. ⊠ 2 Čomakov St., ☎ 032/22–56–56. ⊙ Tues.–Sun. 9–noon and 1:30–5.

Below the medieval gateway of Hissar Kapiya are the attractive **Georgiadi House,** on Starinna Street, and the steep, narrow **Strumna Street,** lined with workshops and boutiques, some reached through little courtyards. Follow Saborna Street westward to its junction with the pedestrians-only Knyaz Alexander I Street; here you'll find the remains of a **Roman stadium.** Nearby, the **Kapana District** has many restored and traditional shops and restaurants. Turn east off Knyaz Alexander I Street and walk to the fine hilltop **Roman amphitheater,** sensitively renovated and frequently used for dramatic and musical performances. On the other side of the old town, toward the river, is the **National Archaeological Museum,** which holds a replica of the 4th-century BC Panagjuriste Gold Treasure, the original of which is in Sofia. ⊠ 1 Suedinenie Sq. ⊙ Tues.–Sun. 9–12:30 and 2–5:30.

Travel west along the E80 Sofia road. At Dolna Banja, turn off to **Borovec,** slightly more than 4,300 feet up the northern slopes of the Rila Mountains. This is an excellent walking center and winter sports resort, well equipped with hotels, folk taverns, and ski schools. The winding mountain road leads back to Sofia, 70 kilometers (44 miles) from here, past Lake Iskar, the largest in the country.

★ On the way back to Sofia, you should consider a visit to the **Rila Monastery,** founded by Ivan of Rila in the 10th century. Cut across to E79, travel south to Kočerinovo, and then turn east to follow the steep forested valley past the village of Rila. The monastery has suffered so frequently from fire that most of it is now a grand National Revival reconstruction, although a rugged 14th-century tower has survived. The atmosphere in this mountain retreat, populated by many storks, is still heavy with a sense of the past—although part of the complex has been turned into a museum and some of the monks' cells are now guest rooms. The visitor can see 14 small chapels with frescoes from the 15th and 17th centuries, a lavishly carved altarpiece in the new Church of the Assumption, the sarcophagus of Ivan of Rila, icons, and ancient manuscripts—a reminder that this was a stronghold of art and learning during the centuries of Ottoman rule.

Dining and Lodging

For details and price-category definitions, *see* Dining and Lodging *in* Staying in Bulgaria, *above.*

Koprivshtitsa

$$ ✕ **Djedo Liben Inn.** This attractive folk restaurant with a bar and nightclub is built in the traditional style of the area—with half-timbering above high stone walls. The menu reflects similar attention to traditional detail. ☎ 07184/21–09. *No credit cards.*

$ ⛭ **Barikadite.** This small hotel is set on a hill 15 kilometers (9 miles) from Koprivshtitsa. *No phone; ask Balkantourist for information. 20 rooms with shower. Restaurant, bar, nightclub. No credit cards.*

$ ⛭ **Koprivshtitsa.** This good-value hotel is popular with vacationing Bulgarians and is just across the river from the center of town. ✉ *12 G. Benkovski St., 2090,* ☎ *07184/21–82. 30 rooms with bath or shower. No credit cards.*

Plovdiv

$$$ ✕ **Puldin.** This is an attractive folk restaurant in the center of town. A video presentation in the lobby highlights the city's past. ✉ *3 Knyaz Tseretelev St.,* ☎ *032/23–17–20. AE, DC, MC, V.*

$$ ✕ **Alafrangite.** This charming folk-style restaurant is in a restored 19th-century house with carved wood ceilings and a vine-covered courtyard. One of the specialities is *kiopolu* (vegetable pureé of baked eggplant, peppers, and tomatoes). ✉ *17 Nektariev St.,* ☎ *032/22–98–09 or 032/26–95–95. No credit cards.*

$ ✕ **Filipopol.** This is an elegant folk-style restaurant with a menu that combines traditional Bulgarian, Greek, and international cuisine (including seafood); the food is served by candlelight to the accompaniment of a jazz piano. Try the rich salads and *chushka byurek* (baked green peppers stuffed with cheese and eggs). ✉ *56 Stamat Matanov St.,* ☎ *032/22–52–96. No credit cards.*

$ ✕ **Rhetora.** This coffee bar is in a beautifully restored old house near the Roman amphitheater in the old part of the city. ✉ *8A T. Samodoumov St.,* ☎ *032/22–20–93. No credit cards.*

$$$ ⛭ **Novotel Plovdiv.** The large, modern, and well-equipped Novotel is across the river from the main town, near the fairgrounds. ✉ *2 Zlatju Boyadjiev St., 4000,* ☎ *032/55–51–71 or 032/5–58–92. 322 rooms with bath. Restaurant, bar, folk tavern, pools, exercise room, shops, nightclub. AE, DC, MC, V.*

$$$ ⛭ **Trimontium.** This central Interhotel built in the 1950s is comfortable and ideal for exploring the old town. ✉ *2 Kapitan Raico St., 4000,* ☎ *032/2–34–91. 163 rooms with bath or shower. Restaurant, bar, folk tavern, shop. AE, DC, MC, V.*

$ ⛭ **Marica.** This is a large, modern hotel, a less expensive alternative to its neighbor, the Novotel. ✉ *42 Vazrazhdane Blvd., 4000,* ☎ *032/55–27–35. 171 rooms with bath or shower. Restaurant, bar. AE, DC, MC, V.*

Veliko Târnovo

$$ ✕ **Boljarska Izba.** In the center of the busy district just north of the river, this is a popular place with the locals, many of whom order the house *sarmi* (vine leaves stuffed with pork). ✉ *St. Stambolov St., no phone. No credit cards.*

$$$ ⛭ **Veliko Târnovo.** Located right in the middle of the most historic part of the town, this modern Interhotel boasts some of the best facilities for this class of hotel. ✉ *2 Al. Penchev St., 5000,* ☎ *062/3–05–71. 195 rooms with bath or shower. 2 restaurants, bar, coffee shop, indoor pool, exercise room, shops, dance club. AE, DC, MC, V.*

$ ⛭ **Etur.** This moderate-size hotel is not far from the more expensive Veliko Târnovo, and is also a good base for sightseeing within town.

✉ *1 Ivailo St., 5000,* ☎ *062/2–18–3851. 80 rooms with shower. Restaurant, bar, coffee shop. AE, DC, MC, V.*

$ 🏨 **Jantra.** The Jantra has some of the best views in town, looking across the river to Tsaravec. ✉ *1 Velchova Zavera Sq., 5000,* ☎ *062/2–03–91. 60 rooms, most with shower. Restaurant, bar, coffee shop. DC, MC, V.*

6 Cyprus

The Republic of Cyprus

Northern Cyprus

THE MEDITERRANEAN ISLAND of Cyprus was once a center for the cult of Aphrodite, the Greek goddess who is said to have emerged naked and perfect from the sea near what is now the beach resort of Paphos. Wooded and mountainous, with a 751-kilometer-long (466-mile-long) coastline, Cyprus lies just off the southern coast of Turkey. Oranges, olives, lemons, grapes, and cherries grow here, and fish are plentiful. The summers are hot and dry, the springs gentle. Snow covers the Troodos Mountains in winter, making it possible to ski in the morning and sunbathe on a beach in the afternoon.

Cyprus's strategic position in the eastern Mediterranean has made it subject to regular invasions by powerful empires. Greeks, Phoenicians, Assyrians, Egyptians, Persians, Romans, and Byzantines—all have ruled here. In the Middle Ages, King Richard I of England took Cyprus from the Byzantine Empire by force and gave it to Guy of Lusignan. Guy's descendants ruled the island until the late 15th century, when it was annexed by the Venetians. From the 16th century to the 19th century it was ruled by the Turks. It became a British colony in 1914.

The influence of diverse cultures adds to the island's appeal to tourists. Many fortifications built by the Crusaders and the Venetians still stand. The tomb of the prophet Muhammad's aunt (Hala Sultan Tekke), on the shores of the great salt lake near Larnaca, is one of Islam's most important shrines. A piece of the true cross is said to be kept in the monastery of Stavrovouni, and Paphos has the remains of a pillar to which St. Paul was allegedly tied when he was beaten for preaching Christianity.

The upheavals are not over. Following independence in 1960, the island became the focus of contention between Greeks and Turks. Currently nearly 80% of the population are Greek and 18% Turkish. Since 1974 Cyprus has been divided by a thin buffer zone—occupied by United Nations (UN) forces—between the Turkish Cypriot north and the Greek Cypriot south. The zone cuts right through the capital city of Nicosia. Talks aimed at uniting the communities into one bizonal federal state have been going on for years, lately under the auspices of the UN's secretary-general. The U.S. government is now involved in trying to resolve the dispute, and with the Republic of Cyprus anxious to join the European Union, governments from its member countries are taking a greater interest, too. Both communities have comfortable tourist facilities, but entry through the northern part, which is recognized only by Turkey, makes access to the south impossible.

ESSENTIAL INFORMATION

Before You Go

When to Go

The tourist season runs throughout the year, though prices tend to be lower from November through March. Spring and fall are best, usually warm enough for swimming but not uncomfortably hot.

CLIMATE

The rainy season is in January and February, and it often snows in the highest parts of the Troodos Mountains from January through March. January and February can be cold and wet; July and August are al-

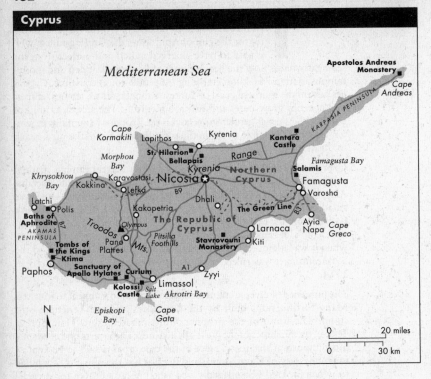

ways very hot and dry. The following are the average daily maximum and minimum temperatures for Nicosia.

Jan.	59F	15C	**May**	85F	29C	**Sept.**	92F	33C
	42	5		58	14		65	18
Feb.	61F	16C	**June**	92F	33C	**Oct.**	83F	28C
	42	5		65	18		58	14
Mar.	66F	19C	**July**	98F	37C	**Nov.**	72F	22C
	44	7		70	21		51	10
Apr.	75F	24C	**Aug.**	98F	37C	**Dec.**	63F	17C
	50	10		69	21		45	7

Visas

No visas are necessary for holders of valid passports from the United States, Canada, the United Kingdom, or mainland European countries.

Customs on Arrival

Duty-free allowances are: 250 grams of tobacco, 1 liter of spirits, 750 milliliters of wine, 300 milliliters of perfume, and up to C£50 in other goods.

The export of antiques and historical artifacts is strictly forbidden unless a license is obtained from the Ministry of Tourism in Nicosia.

Language

Greek is the main language, but English is widely spoken in hotels, tavernas, and other tourist haunts. Off the beaten path, sign language may have to do.

THE REPUBLIC OF CYPRUS

Currency

The monetary unit in the Republic of Cyprus is the Cyprus pound (C£), which is divided into 100 cents. There are notes of C£20, C£10, C£5, and C£1 and coins of 50, 20, 10, 5, 2, and 1 Cyprus cents. At press time (spring 1996) the rate of exchange was C£0.45 to the U.S. dollar, C£0.32 to the Canadian dollar, and C£0.70 to the pound sterling.

What It Will Cost

A cup of coffee or tea costs Cyprus 60¢–C£1; a glass of beer 75¢–C£1; a kebab around C£1.25–C£1.75; a bottle of local wine C£1–C£3. Admission to museums and galleries costs 50¢–C£1.

Arriving and Departing

By Plane

There are now direct flights between Larnaca and New York via **Gulf Air. Cyprus Airways** and **British Airways** fly direct from London, Birmingham, and Manchester to Larnaca and Paphos. Cyprus Airways also operates from Athens, Amsterdam, Brussels, Frankfurt, Munich, Paris, Vienna, and Zurich. **Alitalia** flies from Rome. **United Airlines** and **Swiss Air** have good connections.

By Boat

Passenger ships connect Cyprus (Limassol and Larnaca) with various Greek, Egyptian, Italian, and Middle Eastern ports.

Getting Around

By Car

An international or national license is acceptable in Cyprus. Drive on the left. Main roads between large towns are good. Minor roads can be unsurfaced, narrow, and winding. Gas costs 37¢ per liter. Cars may be rented from C£20 per day; lower rates are available off season.

By Bus

This is the cheapest form of transportation in urban areas; the fare is 40¢. Buses operate every half hour and cover an extensive network. In Nicosia, buses run until 7:30 PM (6:30 PM in winter). In tourist areas during the summer, services are extended until midnight.

Intercity bus fares range between C£2 and C£3. For information on the Nicosia–Limassol–Paphos route, call 02/464636; or for the Limassol–Larnaca–Ayia Napa route, dial 05/351031.

By Service Taxi

Shared taxis accommodate four to seven passengers and are a cheap, fast, and comfortable way of traveling between towns. Taxis operate between the main towns—Nicosia, Limassol, Larnaca, and Paphos. Tariffs are from C£1.65 to C£4.25. Seats must be booked by phone, and passengers may embark/disembark anywhere within the town boundaries. The taxis run every half hour (⊘ Mon.–Sat. 5:45 AM–6:30 PM). Sunday service is less frequent and rides must be booked one day ahead. Contact the **Kypros Taxi Office** (☎ 02/464811), **Karydas** (☎ 02/463126), or **Kyriakos** (☎ 02/444141).

By Private Taxi

Private taxis operate 24 hours throughout the island. They are generally very cheap within towns but far more expensive than service taxis between towns. Telephone from your hotel or hail one in the street.

Urban taxis have an initial charge of 59¢ and charge 23¢ per kilometer (.6 mile) in the daytime, more at night. Drivers are bound by law to display and run a meter. Ask the driver what it will cost before you depart, and don't be afraid to barter. In-town journeys range from C£1.50 to about C£3.

Staying in the Republic of Cyprus

Telephones

LOCAL CALLS
Pay phones take 2¢, 10¢, and 20¢ coins. Some newer pay phones also take 5¢ coins, and others take telecards of C£2, C£5, and C£10, which can be purchased at post offices, souvenir shops, and kiosks. Cheaper rates apply from 10 PM to 8 AM and all day Sunday. For telephone information, dial 192 in all towns.

INTERNATIONAL CALLS
To reach an **AT&T** long-distance operator, dial 080–90010; for **MCI**, 080–90000; for **Sprint**, 080–90001. Public phones may require the deposit of a coin or use of a phone card when you call these services.

COUNTRY CODE
The country code for Cyprus is 357.

Mail

A 20-gram letter to the United States costs 36¢, a postcard, 26¢. To Europe, a 20-gram letter costs 31¢, and a postcard 21¢. Post offices are open Mon.–Fri. 7:30 AM–2:30 PM. Stamps are also sold at hotels, newsstands, and kiosks. Every item of mail must carry a separate 1¢ refugee stamp, which is included in the above costs.

Opening and Closing Times

Banks are open weekdays 8:15 AM–12:30 PM during July and August. The rest of the year they are open weekdays 8:30 AM –12:30 PM and on Monday afternoons 3:15 PM–4:45 PM. Some have special afternoon tourist services and will cash traveler's checks weekdays 3–6 in winter, 4–7 in summer, and Saturday 8:30–noon year-round.

Museum hours vary greatly. It pays to check ahead. Generally, museums are closed for lunch and on Sunday. Most ancient monuments are open from dawn to dusk.

Shops are open Monday–Saturday 8–1 and 4–7 PM (summer); 2–5:30 PM (winter). They are closed Wednesday and Saturday afternoons and on Sundays year-round. In tourist areas shops generally maintain longer hours.

National Holidays

January 1; January 6 (Epiphany); March 10 (Green Monday); April 1 (National Day); April 25–28 (Greek Orthodox Easter); May 1 (May Day); June 16 (Pentecost Monday); August 15 (Assumption); October 1 (Cyprus Independence Day); October 28 (Greek National Day); December 25, 26.

Dining

Most hotels have restaurants, but these tend to serve bland international-style food garnished with french fries. Meals in local restaurants or tavernas start with a variety of *mezes* (appetizers). Kebabs are popular, as are dolmas, stews, fresh fish, and various lamb dishes. End with fruit or honey pastries and Greek coffee. Moderate establishments display a menu; in inexpensive ones it is customary to go into the kitchen and choose your meal. Food is cheap in Cyprus, and the quality is good.

WHAT TO WEAR

Casual dress is acceptable in all restaurants in Cyprus, regardless of price category.

RATINGS

Prices are for a three-course meal for one person, not including drinks or tip.

CATEGORY	COST
$$$	over C£12
$$	C£6–C£12
$	under C£6

Lodging

All hotels listed have private bath or shower, but check when making reservations. Most have at least partial air-conditioning. In resort areas, hotel/apartments are a convenient choice for groups or families—many have kitchens.

RATINGS

Prices are for two people sharing a double room and include breakfast.

CATEGORY	COST
$$$$	over C£80
$$$	C£60–C£80
$$	C£40–C£60
$	under C£40

Tipping

A service charge of 10%, a 3% charge by the Cyprus tourist organization, and an 8% VAT are usually added to all bills. If service has been especially good, add 5%.

Important Addresses and Numbers

EMBASSIES OR HIGH COMMISSIONS

U.S. Embassy (⊠ Metochiou Ploutarchou, Box 4536, Engomi, Nicosia, ☎ 02/476100, FAX 02/465944). **Consulate of Canada** (⊠ 15 Them Dervis St., Box 2125, Nicosia, ☎ 02/451630, FAX 02/459096). **British High Commission** (⊠ Alexander Pallis St., Nicosia, ☎ 02/473131–7, FAX 02/367198).

EMERGENCIES

Ambulance, Fire Brigade, and **Police** (☎ 199). **Doctor: Nicosia General Hospital** (☎ 02/451111); **Limassol Hospital** (☎ 05/330333); **Paphos Hospital** (☎ 06/240111). **Pharmacies** (☎ 192 for information about opening times in English). A list with additional opening details appears in the English-language *Cyprus Mail* and *Cyprus Weekly*.

VISITOR INFORMATION

The main **tourist information office** is in Nicosia (⊠ 19 Limassol Ave., ☎ 02/337715, FAX 02/331644). For personal and telephone inquiries, call the other Nicosia office at Laiki Yitonia (☎ 02/444264). There are also local offices at all major resorts.

Guided Tours

Guided tours are often the best way to see Cyprus and learn about its rich history. Try **National Sightseeing Tours** (⊠ c/o Louis Tourist Agency, 54–58 Evagoras Ave., Nicosia, ☎ 02/442114) for half-day and full-day trips—expect to pay C£7–C£12. Night tours are quite popular, and typically include dinner at a local taverna, folk dancing, and bouzouki music. In Limassol, **Laikon Shipping** (⊠ 124 Ayias Paraskevis St., ☎ 05/326108) arranges coastal cruises on the *Lady Thetis*, which usually include lunch on board.

Exploring the Republic of Cyprus

Nicosia

The capital, **Nicosia,** is twice divided. Its picturesque Old City is contained within 16th-century Venetian fortifications that separate it from the wide, tree-lined streets, large hotels, and high-rises of the modern section. The second division is political and more noticeable. The so-called Green Line (set up by the United Nations) divides the island between the Republic of Cyprus and Turkish-occupied Northern Cyprus. It is possible, at press time (spring 1996), to arrange a day trip from the Greek to the Turkish sector through the official checkpoint in Nicosia (Ledra Palace), though it is essential to return by 5 PM. *Visits in the other direction are not permitted.*

★ In the Greek sector a good starting point is **Laiki Yitonia,** at the southern edge of the Old City, an area of winding alleys and traditional architecture that is being completely renovated. Tavernas, cafés, and crafts workshops line the shaded, cobbled streets. Just to the west lies Ledra Street, where modern shops alternate with yet more crafts shops. Head north of the tourist information center (☎ 02/444264) in Laiki Yitonia to visit the tiny **Tripiotis Church.** This Greek Orthodox church, with its ornately carved golden iconostasis and silver-covered icons, dates from 1690.

The **Leventis Museum** in Laiki Yitonia traces the city's history from 3000 BC to the present, with exhibits on crafts and daily life. ⊠ *17 Hippocratous St.,* ☎ *02/451475.* ⊡ *Free.* ☉ *Tues.–Sun. 10–4:30.*

Within the walls to the east of the Old City is a cluster of museums. Housed in a wing of the archiepiscopal palace built in 1960 in neo-Byzantine style, the **Archbishop Makarios III Cultural Foundation** consists of the **Byzantine Art Museum,** with fine displays of icons spanning 1,000 years, and the **Greek War of Independence Gallery,** with a collection of maps, paintings, and mementos of 1821. ⊠ *Archbishop Kyprianou Sq.,* ☎ *02/456781.* ⊡ *C£1.* ☉ *Weekdays 9–1 and 2–5, Sat. 9–1.*

Next door, the **Museum of the National Struggle** has dramatic displays of the Cypriot campaigns against the British during the pre-independence years 1955–59. ⊠ *Archbishop Kyprianou Sq.,* ☎ *02/302465.* ⊡ *25¢.* ☉ *weekdays 8–2.*

★ Close by is the **Cyprus Folk Art Museum** (housed in the 14th-century part of the archiepiscopal palace), which has demonstrations of ancient weaving techniques and displays of ceramics and olive and wine presses. ⊠ *Archbishop Kyprianou Sq.,* ☎ *02/463205.* ⊡ *50¢.* ☉ *Weekdays 8:30–4, Sat. 8:30–1.*

Don't miss **St. John's Cathedral** (Ayios Ioannis), built in 1662 within the courtyard of the archiepiscopal palace. Look for the 18th-century wall paintings illustrating important moments in Cypriot religious history and including a depiction of the tomb of St. Barnabas. The **Famagusta Gate** is just a short walk to the east. Now a cultural center, it houses exhibitions, a lecture hall, and a theater. ⊠ *Athina St.,* ☎ *02/ 430877.* ☉ *Weekdays 8–1 and 4–7.*

★ Outside the city walls near the western Paphos Gate stands the **Cyprus Museum.** It has extensive archaeological displays ranging from Neolithic to Roman times. This stop is essential to an understanding of the island's ancient sites. ⊠ *Museum St.,* ☎ *02/302189.* ⊡ *C£1.* ☉ *Mon.–Sat. 9–5, Sun. 10–1.*

Across the street from the museum are the neoclassical **Municipal Theatre** (1960) and the lush **Municipal Gardens.**

Larnaca

Many visitors stay in seaside resorts. Larnaca and Paphos, each with its own airport, make excellent centers. **Larnaca,** 51 kilometers (32 miles) southeast of Nicosia, is famous as the burial place of Lazarus and for its flamboyant Whitsuntide celebration, *Cataklysmos*. It has fine beaches, palm trees, and a modern harbor and marina, the starting point for boat trips. The tourist office at Democratias Square (☎ 04/654322; ☉ Weekdays, hours vary) is in the marina district, a short walk from **Larnaca Museum** and its displays of treasures including outstanding sculptures and Bronze Age seals. ⊠ *Kimon and Kilkis Sts.,* ☎ *04/630169.* ⌑ *50¢.* ☉ *Weekdays 7:30–2:30, Thurs. 4–7 (winter 3–6).*

A short walk north from the museum, along Kyman Street, will bring you to the site of **Kition,** the old Larnaca of biblical times and one of the most important ancient city-kingdoms. Architectural remains of ancient temples date from the 13th century BC. ⌑ *50¢.* ☉ *Weekdays 7:30–2:30 and 3–5.*

South of the marina is the 17th-century **Turkish fort,** open the same hours as the Larnaca Museum. The fort contains finds from Hala Sultan Tekke (☞ *below*) and Kition. On the way to the ancient fort is the **Pierides Collection,** a private collection of more than 3,000 pieces distinguished by its Bronze Age terra-cotta figures. ⊠ *Paul Zenon Kitieus St. near Lord Byron St.,* ☎ *04/651345.* ⌑ *C£1.* ☉ *Mon.–Sat. 9–1, Sun. 10–1 and 3–6.*

Walk inland from the fort to the town center and to one of the island's more important churches, **Ayios Lazarus,** resplendent with icons. It has a fascinating crypt housing Lazarus's sarcophagus.

★ South of Larnaca on the airport road is the 2½-square-mile **Salt Lake.** In winter it's a refuge for migrating birds. On the lake's edge, a mosque stands in an oasis of palm trees guarding the **Hala Sultan Tekke**—burial place of the prophet Muhammad's aunt and an important Muslim shrine. ⌑ *Free.* ☉ *June–Sept., daily 7:30–7:30; Oct.–May, daily 7:30–5.*

Nearby, the **Panayia Angeloktistos Church,** in Kiti, is famous for its Byzantine wall mosaics, which date from the 6th and 7th centuries.

Ayia Napa

Once a small fishing village, **Ayia Napa,** 30 kilometers (19 miles) east of Larnaca, is anchored by a **16th-century monastery** and renowned for its white, sandy beaches and views of the brilliant sea. Today its many restaurants and hotels reflect the town's transformation into Cyprus's premier vacationland. Ayia Napa maintains the flavor of its historic past, however, and beneath the monastery's 14th-century sycamore tree, you can still enjoy the panoramic view of the Mediterranean.

Paphos

In the west of the island, **Paphos,** 142 kilometers (88 miles) southwest of Nicosia, combines superb sea swimming with archaeological sites and a rich history. This town near the birthplace of Aphrodite—Greek goddess of love and beauty—has a modern center with numerous ancient sights. Begin at the tourist office on Gladstone Street (☎ 06/232841; ☉ Weekdays, hours vary) in Upper Paphos.

The **Paphos District Museum** is famous for its pottery, jewelry, and statuettes from Cyprus's Roman villas. ⊠ *Grivas Dighenis Ave., Ktima,* ☎ *06/240215.* ⌑ *50¢.* ☉ *Weekdays 7:30–2:30 and 4–6 (winter 7:30–2 and 3–5), weekends 10–1.*

★   Nearby there are notable icons in the **Byzantine Museum** (✉ Andreas Ioannou St., ☎ 06/232092) in the archiepiscopal palace and a charming **Ethnographical Museum.** ✉ *1 Exo Vrysi,* ☎ *06/232010.* ☉ *9–1 and 3–7 (winter 9–1 and 2–5).*

Don't miss the elaborate mosaics in the **Roman Villa of Theseus,** the **House of Dionysos,** and the **House of Aion,** all in New Paphos. The mosaics are considered by many to be among the finest in the eastern Mediterranean. The town bus stops nearby. Also worth seeing are the
★   **Tombs of the Kings,** an early necropolis dating from 300 BC. Though the coffin niches are empty, a powerful sense of mystery remains. ✉ C£1 *(mosaics) and 50¢ (Tombs of the Kings).* ☉ *Daily 7:30–sunset (winter 7:30–5:30).*

The legendary **birthplace of Aphrodite** is just off the main road to Limassol at Petra tou Romiou. Signs (not in English) point to the spot. The tourist authority has a coffee shop there and parking.

Limassol

A commercial port and wine-making center on the south coast, **Limassol,** 75 kilometers (47 miles) from Nicosia, is a bustling, cosmopolitan town popular with tourists. Luxury hotels, apartments, and guest houses stretch along 12 kilometers (7 miles) of seafront. The town's nightlife is the liveliest on the island. In central Limassol, the elegant modern shops of Makarios Avenue contrast with those of the old part of town, where you'll discover local handicrafts.

The tourist information office (✉ Spyros Araouzos St., ☎ 05/362756) is open Monday through Saturday; hours vary. A short walk takes you to **Limassol Fort,** near the old port. This 14th-century castle was built on the site of an earlier Byzantine fortification. According to tradition, Richard the Lion-Hearted was married here in 1191. The **Cyprus Medieval Museum** is housed in the castle and displays a variety of medieval armor and relics. ☎ *05/330132.* ✉ *50¢.* ☉ *weekdays 7:30–5, Sat. 9–5, Sun. 10–1.*

For a glimpse of Cypriot folklore, visit the **Folk Art Museum** on St. Andrew's Street. The collection includes national costumes and fine examples of weaving and other crafts. ☎ *05/362303.* ✉ *30¢.* ☉ *Mon. and Wed.–Fri. 8:30–1:30 and 4–7 (winter 3–5:30); Tues. 8:30–1:30.*

At the annual **Limassol Wine Festival** in September, local wineries offer free samples and demonstrate traditional grape-pressing methods. There are open-air music and dance performances. If wine making interests you, try a nice side trip to the **KEO Winery,** just west of the town, which welcomes visitors daily. ✉ *Roosevelt Ave., toward new port,* ☎ *05/362053.* ✉ *Free.* ☉ *Tours weekdays at 10.*

Troodos Mountains

The **Troodos Mountains,** north of Limassol, are popular in summer for their shady cedar and pine forests and their cool springs. Small, painted churches in the Troodos and **Pitsilia Foothills** are rich examples of a rare indigenous art form. **Asinou Church** and **St. Nicholas of the Roof,** south of Kakopetria, are especially noteworthy. Nearby is the **Tall Trees Trout Farm,** an oasis serving delicious meals of fresh fish. In winter, skiers take over. **Platres,** in the foothills of Mt. Olympus, is the principal resort. Be sure to visit the **Kykko Monastery,** whose prized icon of the Virgin is reputed to have been painted by St. Luke.

Off the Beaten Path

Stavrovouni Monastery stands on a mountain west of Larnaca. It was founded by St. Helena (mother of Emperor Constantine) in AD 326, though the present buildings date from the 19th century. The views of the island from here are splendid. Ideally, the monastery should be visited in a spirit of pilgrimage rather than sightseeing, out of respect for the monks. Male visitors are allowed inside the monastery daily from sunrise to sunset, except between noon and 3 (noon and 1 in winter). The monks have decreed that female visitors will be admitted only on Sunday morning.

Phikardou Village, a half-hour drive from Nicosia on the road to Palechori, is being restored to its appearance at the beginning of the century. Many of these rural houses, outstanding examples of folk architecture, have remarkable woodwork; they also contain the household furnishings used a century ago. Official tour guides are available in the village to provide additional information. ☎ 02/337715 in Nicosia for information. ☒ 50¢. ☺ Year-round; hours vary.

Curium (Kourion), west of Limassol, has numerous Greek and Roman ruins. There is an **amphitheater,** where classic and Shakespearean plays are sometimes staged. Next to the theater is the **Villa of Eustolios,** a summer house built by a wealthy Christian. A nearby **Roman stadium** has been partially rebuilt. Three kilometers (2 miles) farther along the main Paphos road is the **Sanctuary of Apollo Hylates** (Apollo of the Woodlands), an impressive archaeological site. ☒ C£1. ☺ Daily 7:30–sunset (winter 7:30–5:30).

★ **Kolossi Castle,** a Crusader fortress of the Knights of St. John, is 15 minutes by car from Limassol. This notable piece of military architecture was constructed in the 13th century and rebuilt in the 15th. ☒ 50¢. ☺ June–Sept., daily 7:30–7:30; Oct.–May, daily 7:30–5.

Also of interest is the fishing harbor of **Latchi,** on the west coast, 32 kilometers (20 miles) north of Paphos. Near Latchi are the **Baths of Aphrodite,** where the goddess is said to have seduced her swains. The wild, undeveloped Akamas Peninsula is perfect for a hike.

Dining

For details and price-category definitions, *see* Dining *in* Staying in the Republic of Cyprus, *above.*

Larnaca

$$ ✕ **Miliges.** This sea-view restaurant attracts both tourists and locals. It is near the old fort and has a typical village ambience. *Kleftico* (lamb and goat meat wrapped in bay leaves) cooked in traditional clay ovens is a specialty. ☒ 42 Bia-Pasha, ☎ 04/655867. AE, DC, MC, V.

$$ ✕ **Monte Carlo.** The outdoor seating at this spot on the road to the airport is on a balcony extending over the sea. Service is efficient, and the dining area is clean. Particularly worthy Cypriot dishes are the fish and meat mezes and casseroles. ☒ 28 Piale Pashia, ☎ 04/653815. AE, DC, MC, V.

Limassol

$$ ✕ **Ladas.** The old port is the site of this pleasant seafood restaurant. All the fish here is fresh; try the tender and sweet fried calamari and grilled *soupies* (ink fish). ☒ 1 Sadi St., ☎ 05/365760. Closed Sunday. AE, DC, MC, V.

$$ ✕ **Porta.** A varied menu of international and Cypriot dishes, such as *foukoudha* barbecue (grilled strips of steak) and trout baked in prawn and mushroom sauce, is served in this restored warehouse. On many nights, you'll be entertained by soft live music. ☒ 17 Yenethliou Mitella, Old Castle, ☎ 05/360339. MC, V.

Nicosia

$$$ ✕ **Plaka Tavern.** One of the oldest eating establishments in the city, in the heart of Engomi, offers up to 30 different meze dishes, including some unusual items such as snails and okra with tomatoes. Although it's mezes only, there's enough variety to satisfy every palate and size of appetite. ⊠ *8 Stylianou Lena,* ☎ *02/446498. AE, DC, MC, V.*

$$ ✕ **Cellari.** This romantic, candlelit inn is lent a festive touch by a pair of guitarists strumming mellow Greek and Cypriot favorites. The highlight of this restaurant is the traditional local cooking, with dishes such as *souvla* (marinated lamb chunks cooked over charcoal). ⊠ *22 Korai St.,* ☎ *02/448338. No credit cards.*

$$ ✕ **Trattoria Romantica.** Close to the Hilton is one of Nicosia's most popular restaurants for both business and pleasure. The fare, like the owner, is Italian, and the atmosphere is distinctly friendly, with no shortage of advice available on any topic relating to Cyprus. There's a roaring fire in winter and service in the courtyard outside during the summer. ⊠ *13 Evagora Pallikaridi,* ☎ *02/376161. AE, DC, MC, V.*

Paphos

$$ ✕ **Chez Alex.** A well-established tavern, Chez Alex serves only fresh fish (which varies with the catch of the day) and fish mezes. ⊠ *7 Constantia St., Kato Paphos,* ☎ *06/234767. AE, DC, MC, V.*

$$ ✕ **Panicos Corallo Restaurant.** Sheltered from the main road by grapevines, this traditional, family-run restaurant is just outside Paphos on the northern coastal road toward Coral Bay. The veal is recommended, as is the swordfish, a house specialty. Meals are served with homegrown vegetables. ⊠ *Peyia,* ☎ *06/621052. DC, MC, V.*

Lodging

For details and price-category definitions, *see* Lodging *in* Staying in the Republic of Cyprus, *above.*

Ayia Napa

$$$ 🏨 **Nissi Beach.** This modern, fully air-conditioned, family-style hotel is set in magnificent gardens overlooking a sandy beach 3 km (2 mi) outside town. Some accommodations are in bungalows, which do not have kitchens. ⊠ *Nissi Ave., Box 10,* ☎ *03/721021,* 🖷 *03/721623. 270 rooms. Restaurant, pool, dance club. AE, MC, DC, V.*

$$ 🏨 **Pernera Beach Sun Hotel.** This budget hotel has a view of the beach. All rooms are air-conditioned. ⊠ *Pernera Beach, Box 38,* ☎ *03/831011,* 🖷 *03/831020. 156 rooms. AE, DC, MC, V.*

Larnaca

$$$$ 🏨 **Golden Bay.** Comfort is high on the list at this beach hotel to the east of the town center. All rooms have balconies and views of the sea. The extensive sports facilities make this an ideal spot for summer or winter vacations. ⊠ *Larnaca-Dhekelia Rd., Box 741,* ☎ *04/645444,* 🖷 *04/645451. 194 rooms. 2 restaurants, indoor and outdoor pools, miniature golf, tennis courts. AE, DC, MC, V.*

$$ 🏨 **Pasithea.** This apartment/hotel near Salt Lake is a short stroll from the sandy beach. The management is friendly, and the apartments are spacious. ⊠ *4 Michael Angelou, Box 309,* ☎ *04/658264,* 🖷 *04/625848. 14 1-bedroom apartments. Baby-sitting. AE, DC, MC, V.*

$ 🏨 **Cactus Hotel.** The Cactus, near the airport in a popular tourist area, has a restaurant and bar. It's 20 minutes from the seafront and Larnaca's tavernas. ⊠ *6–8 Shakespeare St., Box 188,* ☎ *046/27400,* 🖷 *046/26966. 58 rooms. Restaurant, bar, pool. AE, MC, V.*

Limassol

$$$$ ⊞ **Le Meridien.** The striking lobby of this spacious, luxurious hotel is pink marble and glass. You'll find all the amenities expected in a first-class hotel, as well as the island's largest swimming pool. The water-sport options include scuba diving. ⊠ *Old Limassol/Nicosia Rd., Box 6560,* ☎ *05/634000,* FAX *05/634222. 191 rooms and 60 villas. 3 restaurants, pool, sauna, tennis courts, health club, volleyball, meeting rooms. AE, DC, MC, V.*

$$ ⊞ **Azur Beach.** This fine apartment/hotel has a good sandy beach and helpful management. ⊠ *Potamios Yermasoyias, Box 1318,* ☎ *05/322667,* FAX *05/321897. 24 1-bedroom apartments, 12 studios, 60 rooms. 2 restaurants, baby-sitting. DC, MC, V.*

$ ⊞ **Continental.** A great sea view adds to the appeal of this family hotel close to the castle. ⊠ *137 Spyros Araouzos Ave., Box 398,* ☎ *05/362530,* FAX *05/373030. 30 rooms. Baby-sitting. AE, V.*

Nicosia

$$$$ ⊞ **Cyprus Hilton.** The Hilton is among the island's best hotels, with extensive sports facilities, a skylit indoor pool, dancing, and more. An executive wing with 84 rooms offers separate check-in, a business center, a club room, and exercise rooms. ⊠ *Archbishop Makarios Ave., Box 2023,* ☎ *02/377777,* FAX *02/377788. 314 rooms. 2 restaurants, minibars, 2 pools, tennis courts, health club, squash, dance club, meeting rooms. AE, DC, MC, V.*

$$$ ⊞ **Holiday Inn.** Centrally located in the Old City, near commercial and historic districts, this member of the chain opened in 1995. Its amenities include Japanese, Greek, international, and health-food restaurants, and a rooftop pool with a garden. ⊠ *70 Regina St., Box 1212,* ☎ *02/475131,* FAX *02/473337. 140 rooms. 3 restaurants, bar, minibars, 2 pools (1 indoors), sauna, exercise room. AE, DC, MC, V.*

$$ ⊞ **Cleopatra Hotel.** Visitors to the Cleopatra enjoy its convenient location, cordial service, and well-prepared food served at poolside. ⊠ *8 Florina St., Box 1397,* ☎ *02/445254,* FAX *02/452618. 90 rooms. Restaurant, minibars, pool. AE, DC, MC, V.*

Paphos

$$$ ⊞ **Paphos Beach.** There are many facilities at this hotel surrounded by attractive gardens. Water sports are popular here. Accommodations are either in the main hotel or in spacious bungalows on the grounds. ⊠ *Posidonos St., Box 136,* ☎ *06/233091,* FAX *06/242818. 224 rooms. Minibars, pool, sauna, tennis courts, exercise room, meeting rooms. AE, DC, MC, V.*

$$ ⊞ **Amalthea Hotel.** This hotel on the beach amid banana groves has a friendly, personal atmosphere fostered by the resident owner-managers. The impressive, open lobby, furnished with gray leather couches and large plants, overlooks the water, and the rooms have balconies with sea views. ⊠ *Kissonerga Rd., Box 323,* ☎ *06/247777,* FAX *06/245963. 168 rooms. Restaurant, bar, minibars, indoor and outdoor pools, sauna, tennis courts, exercise room, squash, volleyball. AE, DC, MC, V.*

$$ ⊞ **Hilltop Gardens Hotel Apartments.** All apartments have a view of the sea, just 500 yards away. The decor is a pleasant mixture of traditional Cypriot village style, including wooden furniture, and modern touches. ⊠ *Off Tombs of the Kings Rd., Box 185,* ☎ *06/243111,* FAX *06/248229. 48 apartments. Bar, pool. AE, DC, MC, V.*

NORTHERN CYPRUS

Currency

The monetary unit in Northern Cyprus is the Turkish lira (TL). There are bills for 1,000,000, 500,000, 250,000, 100,000, 50,000, 20,000, and 10,000 TL and coins for 10,000, 5,000, 2,500, 1,000, and 500 TL. The Turkish lira is subject to considerable inflation, so most of the prices in this section are quoted in dollars.

What It Will Cost

Prices for food and accommodations tend to be lower than those in the Republic of Cyprus. Wine and spirits, on the other hand, are imported from Turkey, and drinks will be slightly more expensive.

SAMPLE PRICES

A cup of coffee should cost less than a dollar, a glass of beer about $1. Wine is good and cheap at around $3 per bottle. Taxis are also a bargain—an 80-kilometer (50-mile) ride costs about $15. Admission to museums costs less than $1.

Arriving and Departing

Akdeniz Airlines, Cyprus Turkish Airlines, Istanbul Airlines, and **Turkish Airlines** run all flights via mainland Turkey, usually with a change of plane at Istanbul. There are also direct flights from Adana, Ankara, Antalya, and I(dt)zmir to Ercan Airport near Nicosia. Ferries run from Mersin and Tasucu in Turkey to Famagusta and Kyrenia, respectively. *It is not possible to enter Northern Cyprus from the Republic except for a day trip from Nicosia.*

Getting Around

By Car

See Getting Around by Car *in* the Republic of Cyprus, *above.*

By Bus and Dolmuş

Buses and the shared *dolmuş* (taxis) are the cheapest forms of transportation. Service is frequent on main routes. A bus from Nicosia to Kyrenia costs about U.S. 50¢, and to Famagusta about 90¢. A seat in a dolmuş for the same trips would cost about $1.25 and $3.25, respectively.

Exploring Northern Cyprus

The **main visitor information office** is at the Department of Tourism Marketing in Lefkoşa (Nicosia), Selçuklu Caddesi, ☎ 90/392/228–3666, FAX 90/392/228–5625. The postal address is Selçuklu Cad., Lefkoşa-KKTC, Mersin–10, Turkey. There are also regional tourism offices in Gazimagusa, Girne, and Lefkoşa.

In the hot summer months (May–September), weekday museum hours are usually 8–1:30 and 4–6, but check before you visit.

There are two important things to bear in mind in Northern Cyprus. One is to obey the "no photographs" signs wherever they appear. The other is to note that as Turkish is the language used here, Turkish names designate the cities and towns: **Nicosia** is known as **Lefkoşa, Kyrenia** as **Girne,** and **Famagusta** as **Gazimagusa.** A useful map showing these and other Turkish names is available free from tourist offices.

Lefkoşa (Nicosia)

The Turkish half of **Nicosia** is the capital of Northern Cyprus. In addition to Venetian walls (☞ Exploring the Republic of Cyprus, *above*), it contains the **Selimiye Mosque** (⊠ Selimiye St.), originally the 13th-century Cathedral of St. Sophia and a fine example of Gothic architecture to which a pair of minarets has been added. Near the Girne Gate is the **Mevlevi Tekke ve Etnografy Müzesi** (Mevlevi Shrine and Ethnographic Museum), the former home of the Mevlevi Dervishes, a Sufi order popularly known as Whirling Dervishes. The building now houses a museum of Turkish history and culture. ⊠ *Girne St.* ☉ *Mon.–Fri. 8–1 and 2–5, Sat. 8–1, Sun. 10–1.*

A walk around the **Old City**, within the encircling walls, is rich with glimpses from the Byzantine, Lusignan, and Venetian past. A great deal of restoration and reconstruction work is being undertaken, especially in the parts of the city beyond the walls.

Girne (Kyrenia)

Of the coastal resorts, **Girne**, with its yacht-filled harbor, is the most appealing. There are excellent beaches to the east and west of the town. **Girne Castle**, overlooking the harbor, is Venetian. It now houses the **Batık Gemi Müzesi** (Shipwreck Museum), whose prize possession is the remains of a ship that sank around 300 BC. ☉ *Weekdays 8–1 and 2–5, Sat. 8–1, Sun. 10–1.*

Gazimagusa (Famagusta)

The chief port of Northern Cyprus, **Gazimagusa**, has massive and well-preserved Venetian walls and the late-13th-century Gothic Cathedral of St. Nicholas, now **Lala Mustafa Pasha Mosque**. The **Old Town**, within the walls, is the most intriguing part to explore.

Off the Beaten Path

It is well worth making two short excursions from Girne—to **St. Hilarion** and to **Bellapais**. The fantastic ruins of the Castle of St. Hilarion stand on a hilltop 11 kilometers (7 miles) to the southwest. It's a strenuous walk, so take a taxi; the views are breathtaking. The ruins of the former **Abbey of Bellapais**, built in the 12th century by the Lusignans, are just as impressive. They lie on a mountainside 6 kilometers (4 miles) to the southeast.

Salamis, north of Gazimagusa, is an ancient ruined city and perhaps the most dramatic archaeological site on the island. St. Barnabas and St. Paul arrived in Salamis and established a church near here. The present ruins date largely from the 12th-century Lusignan rulers of Cyprus, who came from France, but Salamis does contain relics of earlier civilizations, including Greek and Roman settlements. The setting is beautiful, and some of the ruins are sufficiently overgrown to give the visitor a satisfying sense of discovery.

7 The Czech Republic

Prague

Bohemia's Spas and Castles

FOR ALL ITS HISTORY, THE CZECH REPUBLIC is very young. After a dramatic but peaceful revolution over-threw a Communist regime that had been in power for 40 years, Czechoslovakia split in 1993 as its two constituent republics, Czech and Slovak, parted ways to form independent countries.

To observers from abroad, the rush to split the republics came as something of a surprise. Formed from the ruins of the Austro-Hungarian empire at the end of World War I, Czechoslovakia had been a modern-day success story: a union of two peoples that had overcome divisive nationalism in the interest of stabilizing a potentially volatile region. Popular perceptions were reinforced by a long list of achievements. During the difficult 1930s, the Czechoslovak republic was the model democracy in central Europe. The 1968 Prague Spring, an intense period of cultural renewal, was centered largely on Czech territory, but was led by a courageous Slovak, Alexander Dubček. In 1989 the Communists were brought down by students and opponents of the regime in both Prague and Bratislava.

The forces for separation, however, proved too powerful. For all its successes, Czechoslovakia was ultimately an artificial creation, masking important and longstanding cultural differences between two outwardly similar peoples. The old Czech Lands of Bohemia and Moravia, whose territory makes up most of the Czech Republic, can look to a rich cultural history going back nearly a millenium, and they played pivotal roles in the great religious and social conflicts of European history. Slovakia, by contrast, languished for centuries as an agrarian outpost of the Hungarian empire. Many Slovaks are still stung by the label of cultural inferiority. Given the state of their national ego, independence was probably inevitable.

The two republics still present themselves to the visitor in many respects as one country, however. Combining a visit to Prague with an excursion to Slovakia's breathtaking High Tatras is as easy as it ever was.

Today, travelers have rediscovered Prague, and Prague has rediscovered the world. Not so long ago, the visitor was unhindered by crowds of tourists but had to struggle with a creeping sensation of melancholy and neglect that threatened to eclipse the city's beauty. At least on the surface, the atmosphere is changing rapidly. The revolution has brought enthusiasm, bustle, and such conveniences as English-language newspapers, attentive hotels, and restaurants that will try to find you a seat even if you don't have a reservation. Musicians and writers are finding new inspiration in the city that once harbored Mozart and Kafka. Countering the drab remnants of socialist reality—the lack of public services, the uncared-for buildings, the strange boxy cars with colors from the '60s—are the spectacular Gothic, Baroque, and Art Nouveau treasures to be found all over the city.

Outside the capital, travelers are now exploring regions rarely visited in recent years. The range of sights is startling, from imperial spas to modern industrial cities. Don't pass up the lovely towns and castles of southern Bohemia: many visitors rank the Renaissance river town of Český Krumlov as a must-see. News for the traveler is that more and more services are being privatized, possibly making them better, certainly making them more expensive. On the other hand, your bill is now more likely to come with a smile.

Czech Republic

ESSENTIAL INFORMATION

Before You Go

When to Go

Organized sightseeing tours run from April or May through October (year-round in Prague). Some monuments, especially castles, either close entirely or open for shorter hours in winter. Hotel rates may drop during the off-season except during festivals. May, the month of fruit blossoms, is the time of the Prague Spring Music Festival. Tourists jam Prague in July and August.

CLIMATE

The following are the average daily maximum and minimum temperatures for Prague.

Jan.	36F	2C	May	66F	19C	Sept.	68F	20C
	25	– 4		46	8		50	10
Feb.	37F	3C	June	72F	22C	Oct.	55F	13C
	27	– 3		52	11		41	5
Mar.	46F	8C	July	75F	24C	Nov.	46F	8C
	32	0		55	13		36	2
Apr.	58F	14C	Aug.	73F	23C	Dec.	37F	3C
	39	4		55	13		28	– 2

Currency

The unit of currency in the Czech Republic is the crown, or *koruna* (plural *koruny*), written as Kč, and divided into 100 *haléřů* (hellers). There are bills of 20, 50, 100, 200, 500, 1,000, and 5,000 koruny and coins of 10, 20, and 50 hellers and 1, 2, 5, 10, 20, and 50 koruny. At press time (spring 1996), the rate of exchange was around 23 Kč to the U.S. dollar, 19 Kč to the Canadian dollar, and 40 Kč to the pound sterling. Banks and ATMs give the best rates. Private exchange offices litter Prague's tourist routes; they usually charge a steep fee. In late 1995 the koruna became fully convertible, and can be purchased outside the country and exchanged into other currencies. Ask about current regulations when you change money, and keep your receipts.

What It Will Cost

Costs are highest in Prague and only slightly lower in the main Bohemian resorts and spas, though even in these places you can now find very reasonable accommodations in private rooms. The least expensive area is southern Bohemia.

SAMPLE PRICES

Cup of coffee, 15 Kč; beer (1/2 liter), 10 Kč–25 Kč, Coca-Cola, 20 Kč; ham sandwich, 30 Kč; 1-mile taxi ride, 50 Kč–100 Kč.

MUSEUMS

Admission to museums and castles ranges from 10 Kč to 150 Kč.

Visas

U.S. and British citizens do not need visas to enter the Czech Republic. Visa requirements have been temporarily reintroduced for Canadian citizens; check whether this is still the case with the consulate. Apply to the Embassy of the Czech Republic, 541 Sussex Drive, Ottawa, Ontario K1N 6Z6, ☎ 613/562–3875, FAX 613/562–3878.

Customs

ON ARRIVAL

Valuable items should be entered on your customs declaration. You can bring in 200 cigarettes, 50 cigars, 1 liter of spirits, 2 liters of wine, and gifts with a total value of 1,000 Kč.

ON DEPARTURE

Antiques may be exported only when certified as not of historical value. Reputable dealers can advise. To be safe, save receipts.

Language

English is spoken fairly widely by the young and those associated with the tourist industry. You will also come across English speakers elsewhere, though not frequently. German is generally understood throughout the country.

Getting Around

By Car

ROAD CONDITIONS

Main roads are usually good, if sometimes narrow, and traffic is light, especially away from the main centers. An expressway links Plzeň, Prague, Brno, and Bratislava. Other highways are single-lane only.

RULES OF THE ROAD

Drive on the right. Speed limits are 60 kph (37 mph) in urban areas, 90 kph (55 mph) on open roads, and 110 kph (68 mph) on expressways. Seat belts are compulsory outside urban areas; drinking and driving is strictly prohibited. A permit is required to drive on expressways and other four-lane highways. They cost 400 Kč and are sold at border crossings and some service stations.

PARKING

Except for hotel guests, parking on the street is banned in much of the center of Prague. A few small lots are within walking distance of the historic center; an underground lot is at Nám. Jana Palacha, near Old Town Square. Don't park in a no-parking area; your car is likely to be towed away. Elsewhere in the country there's little problem.

GASOLINE

At about 81 Kč ($3) a gallon, gasoline is expensive. Look for service stations along main roads on the outskirts of towns and cities. Lead-free gasoline, known as "natural," is now much easier to find.

BREAKDOWNS

The Yellow Angels (☎ 123 or 02/773455) operate a patrol service on main highways. The emergency number for motorists is 154.

By Train

There is an extensive rail network throughout the country. As elsewhere in Eastern Europe, fares are relatively low and trains can be crowded. You have to pay a small supplement on all express trains. Most long-distance trains have dining cars; overnight trains between main centers have sleeping cars.

By Plane

Good internal air service links Prague with several other towns, including Ostrava in Moravia and Bratislava and Poprad (for the High Tatras) in Slovakia. Prices are reasonable. Make reservations at Čedok (tourist agency) offices or directly at **ČSA,** Czech Airlines (☎ 02/2431–4271).

By Bus

A wide-ranging bus network provides quicker service than trains at somewhat higher prices (though they are still very low by Western standards).

Buses are always full, and, on long-distance routes especially, reservations are advisable.

Staying in the Czech Republic

Telephones

LOCAL CALLS

To use a public phone, buy a phone card at a newsstand or tobacconist. Cards cost 100 Kč for 50 units or 190 Kč for 100 units. Local calls cost one unit, and international rates vary according to destination. To place a call, lift the receiver, insert the card, and dial.

INTERNATIONAL CALLS

Automatic dialing is available to many parts of the world, including North America and the United Kingdom. Special international pay booths in central Prague will take 5 Kč coins, and booths that accept phone cards often allow automatic dialing, but your best bet is to go to the main post office at Jindřišská 14, near Václavské náměstí (Wenceslas Square). The international dialing code is 00. For international inquiries, dial 0132 for the United States, Canada, or the United Kingdom. To place a call via an **AT&T** USADirect international operator, dial 0042–000101; for **MCI**, dial 0042–000112; for **Sprint**, dial 0042–087187.

COUNTRY CODE

The country code for the Czech Republic is 42.

Mail

POSTAL RATES

Airmail letters to the United States and Canada cost 11 Kč up to 20 grams, postcards 6 Kč. Airmail letters to the United Kingdom cost 8 Kč up to 20 grams, postcards 5 Kč.

RECEIVING MAIL

Mail can be labeled "poste restante" and sent to the main post office in Prague (✉ Jindřišská 14, window 28) or to any other main post office. There's no charge. The American Express office in Prague's Wenceslas Square will hold letters to cardholders or holders of American Express traveler's checks for up to a month free of charge.

Opening and Closing Times

Banks are open weekdays 8–5 with a one-hour lunch break. **Museums** are usually open Tues.–Sun. 10–5. **Shops** are generally open weekdays 9–6; some close for lunch between noon and 2. Many are also open till noon or later on Saturdays.

National Holidays

January 1; Easter Monday; May 1 (Labor Day); May 8 (Liberation Day); July 5 (Saints Cyril and Methodius); July 6 (Jan Hus); October 28 (Czech National Day); December 24, 25, 26.

Dining

Dining options include restaurants, the *vinárna* (wine cellar), which covers anything from inexpensive wine bars to swank restaurants; the more down-to-earth *pivnice* or *hospody* (beer taverns); cafeterias; and a growing number of coffee shops and snack bars. Eating out is popular, and in summer you must make reservations. Part of privatization's legacy is more culinary variety, especially in Prague.

Prague ham makes a favorite first course, as does soup, which is less expensive. The most typical main dish is roast pork (or duck or goose) with sauerkraut. Trout, carp, and other freshwater fish are also widely enjoyed. Crêpes, here called *palačinky,* are ubiquitous and may come with savory or sweet fillings. Dumplings in various forms, generally with a rich gravy, accompany many dishes.

MEALTIMES

Lunch is usually from 11:30 to 2 or 3; dinner from 6 to 9:30 or 10. Some places are open all day, and you might find it easier to get a table during off-hours.

WHAT TO WEAR

A jacket and tie are recommended for $$$$ and $$$ restaurants. Informal dress is appropriate elsewhere.

RATINGS

Prices are reasonable by American standards, even in the more expensive restaurants. Czechs don't normally go for three-course meals, and the following prices apply only if you're having a first course, main course, and dessert (prices are per person, excluding wine and tip).

CATEGORY	PRAGUE	OTHER AREAS
$$$$	over 800 Kč	over 400 Kč
$$$	350 Kč–800 Kč	250 Kč–400 Kč
$$	200 Kč–350 Kč	100 Kč–250 Kč
$	under 200 Kč	under 100 Kč

Lodging

Visitors may choose between hotels, motels, private accommodations, hostels, and campsites. Many older properties have been renovated, and the best have great character and style. There is still an acute shortage of hotel rooms during the peak season, so make reservations well in advance. Many private room agencies offer a variety of lodgings. The standards of facilities and services hardly match those in the West, so don't be surprised by faulty plumbing or indifferent reception clerks.

HOTELS

These are officially graded with from one to five stars, using the international classification system. Many hotels used by foreign visitors are affiliated with Čedok and are mainly in the three- to five-star categories. These will have all or some rooms with bath or shower. Čedok can also handle reservations for some non-Čedok hotels.

Bills can be paid in koruny (check to see if your hotel insists on hard currency; some hotels refuse to accept credit cards).

PRIVATE ACCOMMODATIONS

Prague is full of travel agencies that offer accommodation in private homes. Such rooms are invariably cheaper and often more comfortable than those in hotels, though you may have to sacrifice some privacy. The largest room-finding service is probably **AVE** in the main and Holešovice train stations (☉ Until 10 PM) and at the airport (☉ 7 AM– 9 PM). The central number for reservations is 02/2422–3226. Insist on a room in the city center, however, or you may find yourself in a dreary, far-flung suburb. Another helpful agency is **City of Prague Accommodation Service** (⊠ Haštalské nám. 8, ☎ 02/231–0202). Elsewhere, look for signs that read ROOM FREE, or in German, ZIMMER FREI or PRIVATZIMMER, along main roads. Čedok and Prague Information Service (PIS) offices can also help in locating private accommodations.

HOSTELS

A few hostels operate all year in Prague. One is **Hostel Estec,** Vaníčkova 5, Prague 6, ☎ 02/527344, FAX 02/527343. Dozens more spring up every summer in university dormitories and schools. Ask at accommodation agencies for details. Rates start at 200 Kč per person.

Campsites are run by a number of organizations. A free map and list are available from Čedok.

RATINGS

Prices are for double rooms, generally including breakfast. Prices at the lower end of the scale apply to low season. At certain periods, such as Easter or during festivals, there may be an increase of 15%–25%.

CATEGORY	PRAGUE	OTHER AREAS
$$$$	over 5,400 Kč	over 2,700 Kč
$$$	2,700–5,400 Kč	1350–2,700 Kč
$$	1350–2,700 Kč	675–1,350 Kč
$	under 1,350 Kč	under 675 Kč

Tipping

Reward good service in restaurants with a few koruny, given directly to the waiter on paying your bill. As a rule of thumb, round up to the nearest multiple of 10 (i.e., if the bill comes to 83 Kč, give the waiter 90 Kč). Give 10% on big or group tabs. For taxis, add up to 10 percent if the fare is reasonable. In the better hotels, doormen should get 5 Kč for each bag they carry to the check-in desk; bellhops get up to 10 Kč for taking them up to your rooms. In $$ or $ hotels, you'll have to lug baggage yourself.

PRAGUE

Arriving and Departing

By Plane

All international flights arrive at Prague's Ruzyně Airport, about 20 kilometers (12 miles) from downtown. For arrival and departure times, call 02/367814 or 02/367760.

BETWEEN THE AIRPORT AND DOWNTOWN

The private Cedaz minibus shuttle links the airport and Náměstí Republiky, a downtown square near the Old Town. Shuttles run in both directions every 30–60 minutes between 5:30 AM and 9 PM daily. The trip costs 60 Kč one-way and takes about 30 minutes. The cheapest way to get into Prague is by regular Bus 119; the cost is 6 Kč, but you'll need to change to the subway at the Dejvická station to reach the center. By taxi, expect to pay 300 Kč.

By Train

The main station for international and domestic routes is Hlavní Nádraží, Wilsonova, not far from Wenceslas Square. Some international trains arrive at and depart from Nádraží Holešovice (☎ 02/2461–5865), on the same metro line (C) as the main station. Call 02/2422–4200 for domestic and international schedules.

By Bus

The main bus station is Florenc (at Na Florenci, ☎ 02/2421–1060), near the main train station. Take Metro B or C to Florenc station.

Getting Around

Public transportation is a bargain. *Jízdenky* (tickets) can be bought at hotels, newsstands, and from dispensing machines in metro stations. The price of a ticket is planned to increase in 1996 from 6 Kč to 10 Kč, and the new tickets will permit one hour's travel on the Metro, tram, and bus network. For the Metro, punch the ticket in the station before getting onto the escalators; for buses and trams, punch the

ticket inside the vehicle. You can also buy one-day passes allowing unlimited use of the system for 50 Kč, two-day for 85 Kč, three-day for
110 Kč, and five-day for 170 Kč. The passes can be purchased at the
main Metro stations and at some newsstands.

Understanding addresses is relatively simple once you know the basic
street sign words: *ulice* (street, abbreviated to ul.; note that common
usage often drops ulice in a printed address), *náměstí* (square, abbreviated to nám.), and *třída* (avenue). In most cases, the blue tags on buildings mark the street address.

By Subway

Prague's three modern Metro lines are easy to use and relatively safe.
They provide the simplest and fastest means of transportation, and most
new maps of Prague mark the routes. The Metro runs from 5 AM to
midnight, seven days a week.

By Tram/Bus

You need to buy a new ticket every time you change vehicles. Trams
are often more convenient than the Metro for short hops. Most bus
lines connect outlying suburbs with the nearest Metro station. Trams
50–59 and Buses 500 and above run all night, after the Metro shuts
down at midnight.

By Taxi

Taxi scams are common. Avoid taxi stands in heavily touristed areas.
Instead, hail cabs from the street or order them in advance by telephone.
Reputable firms include **AAA** (☎ 02/3399) and **Profitaxi** (☎ 02/6104–
5555). The basic charge is 10 Kč, increased by 12 Kč per kilometer.
Be warned: Many drivers don't turn on the meter. Either agree on a
price beforehand (no more than 100 Kč within the city) or ask the driver
to start the meter. Some larger hotels have their own fleets, which are
a little more expensive.

Important Addresses and Numbers

Embassies

U.S. (✉ Tržiště 15, Malá Strana, ☎ 02/2451–0847). **Canadian** (✉ Mick-
iewiczova 6, Hradčany, ☎ 02/2431–1108). **U.K.** (✉ Thunovská 14,
Malá Strana, ☎ 02/2451–0439).

Emergencies

Police (☎ 158). **Ambulance** (☎ 155). **Foreigners' Department of Na
Homolce Hospital** (✉ Roentgenova 2, Prague 5, weekdays ☎ 02/5292–
2146, evenings and weekends ☎ 02/520022); **First Medical Clinic of
Prague** (✉ Vyšehradská 35, Prague 2, ☎ 02/292286, 298978; 24-hr
emergency ☎ 02/0601–225050, mobile phone). Be prepared to pay
in cash for medical treatment, whether you are insured or not. **24-Hour
Pharmacies** (two close to the center are ✉ Štefánikova 6, Prague 5, ☎
02/537039, and ✉ Belgická 37, Prague 2, ☎ 02/258189). **Lost credit
cards:** American Express (02/2421–9992); Diners Club, Visa (02/2412–
5353); MasterCard (02/2442–3135).

English-Language Bookstores

The best selections are at the **Globe Bookstore and Coffeehouse** (✉
Janovského 14, Prague 7) and **U Knihomola** (✉ Mánesova 79, Prague
2). For hiking maps and atlases, try **Orbis** (✉ Václavské nám. 42).

Travel Agencies

American Express (✉ Václavské nám. 56, ☎ 02/2422–9883, FAX
02/2422–7708); **Thomas Cook** (✉ Národní třída 28, ☎ 02/2110–5272).

Visitor Information

The main **Čedok** office (⊠ Na příkopě 18, ☎ 02/2419–7111) is close
to Wenceslas Square. Their other downtown branches are at Rytířská
16 and Pařížská 6. The recently privatized travel agency has offices
throughout the country and also arranges guided tours. **Prague Information Service** (PIS) has two offices in the city (⊠ Na příkopě 20 and
Staroměstské náměstí [Old Town Square] 22, ☎ 02/544444). Information on tourism outside Prague is dispensed by the **Czech Tourist Authority** (⊠ Národní třída 37, ☎ /FAX 02/2421–1458). The
English-language weekly *Prague Post* prints news and information of
interest to long-term residents and tourists alike.

Guided Tours

Čedok arranges a variety of tours in and around Prague; they can be
arranged either before you leave home or during your stay in Prague.

Orientation

Čedok offers a daily three-hour tour of the city, starting at 10 AM from
the Čedok offices at Na příkopě 18 and Pařížská 6 (☎ 02/231–8255).
Contact any Čedok office for the current schedule and itinerary. From
April to October, the organization also operates an afternoon tour, starting at 2. Both tours cost about 500 Kč.

Martin-Tour (☎ 02/2421–2473) offers a similar but cheaper tour departing from Náměstí Republiky and three other Old Town points four
times daily. **PIS** arranges guided tours at its Na příkopě and Old Town
Square locations (☎ 02/2421–2844).

Special-Interest

For cultural tours, call Čedok (☞ *above*). These include visits to the
Jewish quarter, performances of folk troupes, Laterna Magika (☞ The
Arts, *below*), opera, and concerts. You can save money by buying
tickets—if available—at box offices.

Excursions

Čedok's one-day tours out of Prague cover principal historic and scenic
sights and include lunch. The "Treasures of Bohemian Gothic" tour
includes an excursion to the lovely medieval town of Kutná Hora; "Bohemian Paradise" features the bizarre sandstone and rock formations
of northern Bohemia. Other tours include visits to famous spa towns
and castles, wineries, and the Terezín ghetto.

Personal Guides

Contact Čedok or PIS (☞ *above*) to arrange a personal walking tour
of the city. Prices start at around 400 Kč per hour.

Exploring Prague

Poets, philosophers, and the Czech-in-the-street have long sung the praises
of *Praha* (Prague), also referred to as the "Golden City of a Hundred
Spires." Like Rome, Prague is built on seven hills, which slope gently
or tilt precipitously down to the Vltava (Moldau) River. The riverside
location, enhanced by a series of graceful bridges, makes a great setting for two of the city's most notable features: its extravagant, fairy-tale architecture and its memorable music. Mozart claimed that no one
understood him better than the citizens of Prague, and he was only one
of several great masters who lived or lingered here.

It was under Charles IV (Karel IV), during the 14th century, that
Prague briefly became the seat of the Holy Roman Empire—virtually
the capital of western Europe—and acquired its distinctive Gothic imprint. At times you'll need to look quite hard for this medieval inher-

itance; it's still here, though, under the overlays of graceful Renaissance and exuberant Baroque.

Prague escaped serious wartime damage, but it didn't escape neglect. Because of the long-term restoration program now under way, some part of the city is always under scaffolding. But when restoration is undertaken—nearly all of the structures described in the following itineraries have undergone it—it is generally sensitive and painstaking.

Nové Město and Staré Město (New Town and Old Town)

Numbers in the margin correspond to points of interest on the Prague map.

① **Václavské náměstí** (Wenceslas Square) is the Times Square of Prague. This is where hundreds of thousands voiced their disgust for the Communist regime in November 1989, at the outset of the "Velvet Revolution." Confusingly, it's not actually a square at all but rather a broad **②** boulevard that slopes down from the **Národní muzeum** (National Mu- **③** seum) and the equestrian **statue of St. Václav** (Wenceslas). The lower end is where all the action is. Na příkopě, once part of the moat surrounding the Old Town, is now an elegant pedestrian mall. Čedok's main office is here, on your way to Náměstí Republiky (Republic **④** Square) and its centerpiece, the **Obecní dům**, Prague's most lavish Art Nouveau building, which is set to reopen in March 1997. Completed in 1911, its rich allegorical sculptures and luscious facade are being **⑤** restored to their original modern elegance. A bridge links it to the **Prašná brána** (Powder Tower), a 19th-century neo-Gothic restoration of the medieval original.

⑥ Turn into Celetná and you're on the old **Royal Route,** once followed by coronation processions. This will lead you past the Gothic spires of the Týn Church through **Staroměstské náměstí** (Old Town Square), down **Karlova**, across **Karlův most** (Charles Bridge), and up to the castle. As you explore this route, you can study every variety of Romanesque, Gothic, Renaissance, and Baroque architecture. First, **⑦** however, look at the Cubist **Dům U černé Matky Boží** (House of the Black Madonna). Yes, Cubist! In the second decade of this century several leading Czech architects boldly applied Cubism's radical reworking of visual space to structures. The Black Madonna, designed by Josef Gočár, is unflinchingly modern yet topped with an almost Baroque tiled roof. An exhibition of Czech Cubist art and design occupies the top two floors. ⊠ *Celetná at Ovocný trh.* 🕾 *20 Kč.* ⊙ *Tues.–Sun. 10–6.*

★ ⑧ **Staroměstské náměstí** is a remarkably harmonious public space. Looming over it, the twin towers of **Kostel Panny Marie před Týnem** (the Church of the Virgin Mary before Týn) still inspire foreboding even now that their grimy stones have been cleaned and Disneyesque lighting has been installed in the spires. In the dim interior some valuable Gothic carvings remain amid the Baroque fittings. The large Secession-style sculptural group in the square's center commemorates the martyr Jan Hus, whose followers completed the Týn Church in the 15th century. The white, Baroque **Kostel svatého Mikuláše** (Church of St. Nicholas) is tucked into the square's northwest angle. It was built by Kilian Ignatz Dientzenhofer, co-architect also of the Lesser Quarter's church of the same name. Every hour mobs converge on the famous **Clock Tower** of the **Staroměstská radnice** (Old Town Hall) as the clock's 15th-century mechanism activates a procession that includes the twelve apostles. Note the skeleton figure of Death that tolls the bell.

⑨ **Franz Kafka's birthplace** is just north of Old Town Square on U radnice. Since the 1989 revolution, Kafka's popularity has soared, and the works of this German Jewish writer are now widely available in Czech. A fascinating little museum has been set up in the house. ⊠ *U radnice 5.* ☉ *Tues.–Fri. 10–6, Sat. 10–5.*

NEED A BREAK? The dim, cool interior of the wine bar called **U zelené žáby** (the Green Frog) resembles the set of a Hammer horror flick, but the offerings are much more appealing: tasty, if rather expensive, Bohemian wines and excellent cold roast beef and pâté. ⊠ *U Radnice 8.*

★ ❿ In the **Starý židovský hřbitov** (Old Jewish Cemetery) in **Josefov** (Joseph's Town, the former Jewish quarter), ancient tombstones lean and jostle one another; below them, in a dozen layers, are 12,000 graves. Many gravestones—they date from the mid-14th to the late 17th centuries—are carved with symbols indicating the name, profession, and attributes of the deceased. As you stand by the tomb of the scholar Rabbi Löw, who died in 1609, you may see, stuffed into the cracks, scraps of paper bearing prayers and requests. Urban renewal at the turn of the century spared only Josefov's synagogues, cemetery, and Jewish Town Hall, and after the Holocaust only a couple of thousand of Prague's

⓫ Jews survived. A tiny handful worships at the little Gothic **Staronová synagóga** (Old-New Synagogue), one of Europe's oldest surviving houses of Jewish prayer. Its attic was the resting place of the legendary Golem, created by Rabbi Löw to defend the ghetto. The rich collections in the several other synagogues and exhibitions comprising the **Židovské muzeum** (Jewish Museum) were gathered in sadness by Jews forced to fulfill Adolf Hitler's plan to document the lives of the people he was trying to exterminate. They include ceremonial objects, textiles, and displays on the history of Bohemia's and Moravia's Jews. The Pinkas Synagogue has a monument to 77,297 murdered Jewish Czechs. ⊠ *Main ticket office at U starého hřbitova 3a.* ▣ *Museum 150 Kč.* ☉ *Sun.–Fri. 9–6 (9–4:30 in winter; last tour of cemetery at 3 in winter); closed Sat. and religious holidays. Old-New Synagogue: Červená at Pařížská.* ▣ *120 Kč.*

⓬ The pompous **Clam-Gallas Palace** squats on Husova near the intersection with Karlova. It was designed by the great Viennese architect J. B. Fischer von Erlach; the Titans struggling to support the two doorways, like all the sculptures, are the work of one of the great Bohemian Baroque artists, Matthias Braun. Take a peek inside at the superb staircase. ⊠ *Husova 20.*

⓭ The **Betlémská kaple** (Bethlehem Chapel) has been completely reconstructed since Jan Hus thundered his humanitarian teachings from its pulpit in the early 15th century. But the little door through which he came to the pulpit is original, as are some of the inscriptions on the wall. ⊠ *Betlémské nám.* ☉ *Daily 9–6.*

Karlův most and Malá Strana (Charles Bridge and the Lesser Quarter)

★ ⓮ When you stand on busy **Karlův most** (Charles Bridge), you'll see views of Prague that would still be familiar to its 14th-century builder Peter Parler and to the sculptors who added the 30 statues starting in the 17th century (most are copies—the originals have been brought indoors to prevent further deterioration from air pollution). They're worth a closer look, especially the 12th on the left (starting from the Old Town side of the bridge), which depicts St. Luitgarde, sculpted by Matthias Braun, circa 1710, and the 14th on the left, in which a Turk guards suffering saints, by F. M. Brokoff, circa 1714. The eighth on the right side, a bronze of John of Nepomuk, marks the spot where in 1393 King Václav IV's men hurled the saint's tortured corpse into the

Prague

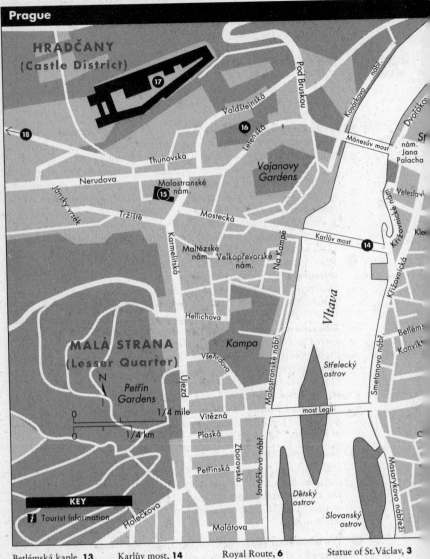

Betlémská kaple, **13**

Chrám svatého
Mikuláše, **15**

Clam Gallas Palace, **12**

Dům U černé Matky
Boží, **7**

Franz Kafka's
Birthplace, **9**

Karlův most, **14**

Loreto, **18**

Národní muzeum, **2**

Obecní dům, **4**

Prašná brána, **5**

Pražský hrad (Prague
Castle), **17**

Royal Route, **6**

Staroměstské
náměstí, **8**

Staronová
synagóga, **11**

Starý
židovský hřbitov, **10**

Statue of St. Václav, **3**

Václavské náměstí, **1**

Valdštejnská
zahrada, **16**

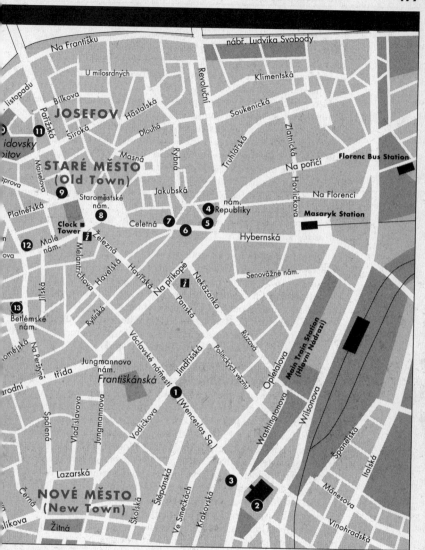

river. The bridge itself is one of King Charles IV's most lasting gifts to
his city.

Cross Charles Bridge and follow Mostecká up to Malostranské náměstí,
the entry to the **Malá Strana** (Lesser Quarter or "Little Town") one of
Prague's most intriguing neighborhoods. Two events above all shaped
this quarter's architectural visage: the fire of 1541, and the expulsions
of Czech nobles and townspeople defeated in the Protestant rebellion
against the Catholic Hapsburgs in 1620. Each of these catastrophes
cleared the way for extensive rebuilding and new construction of
palaces and gardens. On Malostranské náměstí (Lesser Quarter Square),
⑮ you'll find the **Chrám svatého Mikuláše** (Church of St. Nicholas), designed by the architects Dietzenhofer, father and son. Many consider
this the most beautiful edifice of the Bohemian Baroque, an architectural style that flowered in Prague after the turbulence of the Counter-
Reformation at the start of the 17th century. If you're in Prague when
a concert is being given in this church, fight for a ticket. ⊠ Malostranské nám. 🎫 20 Kč. ⊙ Daily 9–4 (9–6 in summer).

On busy Letenská, a small door admits visitors to the large, formal
⑯ **Valdštejnská zahrada** (Wallenstein Gardens), part of the huge palace
built in the 1620s by the Hapsburgs' victorious commander, Albrecht
of Wallenstein. Of the many sumptuous gardens built for the nobility's Lesser Quarter palaces, this is one of the most elegant. A covered
outdoor stage of late-Renaissance style dominates its western end.
Music and theater pieces are occasionally performed here. ⊠ Entrance
at Letenská 10. 🎫 Free. ⊙ May–September, daily 9–7.

Pražský hrad and Hradčany
(Prague Castle and the Castle District)

★ ⑰ The monumental complex of **Pražský hrad** (Prague Castle) has witnessed the changing fortunes of the city for more than 1,000 years. The
castle's physical and spiritual core, **Chrám svatého Víta** (St. Vitus
Cathedral), took from 1344 to 1929 to build, so you can trace the whole
gamut of styles from high Gothic to Art Nouveau. The eastern end,
begun by master architect Matthias of Arras but mostly the work of
Peter Parler, builder of the Charles Bridge, is a triumph of Bohemian
Gothic. "Good King" Wenceslas (in reality a mere prince, later can-
onized) has his own chapel in the south transept, dimly-lit and decorated with fine medieval wall paintings. Four silver angels hover over
the tomb of St. John of Nepomuk, he whose statue adorns many a Central European bridge, including the Charles Bridge. Note the fine 17th-
century carved wooden panels on either side of the chancel. The
left-hand one shows a view of the castle and town in November 1620
and the defeated Czech Protestants fleeing into exile. The three easternmost chapels house tombs of Czech princes and kings of the 11th
to the 13th centuries, while Charles IV and Rudolph II lie in the crypt,
the former in a bizarre modern sarcophagus. 🎫 Free admission to the
cathedral's western part. Chapels, crypt, and tower accessible with a
castle-wide ticket (☞ below).

Behind St. Vitus's, don't miss the miniature houses of "Golden Lane."
Its name, and the apocryphal tale of how King Rudolph II used to lock
up alchemists here until they transmuted lead into gold, may come from
the gold-beaters who once lived here. Knightly tournaments often accompanied coronation ceremonies in the **Královský palác** (Royal
Palace), next to the cathedral, hence the broad Riders' Staircase leading up to the grandiose **Vladislavský sál** (Vladislav Hall), with its
splendid late-Gothic vaulting and Renaissance windows. Oldest of all
the buildings, though much restored, is the complex of **Bazilika svatého
Jiří** (St. George's Basilica and Convent). The basilica's cool Romanesque

lines hide behind a glowing salmon-colored Baroque facade. The ex-convent houses a superb collection of Bohemian art from medieval religious sculptures to Baroque paintings. The castle ramparts afford glorious vistas of Prague's fabled hundred spires rising above the rooftops. To the right are the gardens of Lesser Quarter palaces and the huge leafy **Petřín** park. ✉ *To most castle sites, including St. Vitus Cathedral: 80 Kč, valid for 3 days.* ☉ *Daily 9–5 (9–4 in winter); castle gardens: Apr.–Oct.*

⑱ The Baroque church and shrine of **Loreto** is named for the Italian town to which the Virgin Mary's house in Nazareth was supposedly transported by angels to save it from the infidel. The glory of its fabulous treasury is the monstrance of the *Sun of Prague,* set with 6,222 diamonds. Arrive on the hour to hear the 27-bell carillon. ✉ *Loretánské nám. 7.* ✉ *30 Kč.* ☉ *Tues.–Sun. 9–noon and 1–4:30.*

Off the Beaten Path

Cross the Vltava at the Hotel Inter-Continental (via the Čechův bridge) and climb the steps to the **Letenské sady** (Letná Park) for sweeping views of Prague. The stone platform atop the steps, where skateboarders practice, once supported a gargantuan monument to Joseph Stalin. It was demolished in 1962 and replaced, after the 1989 revolution, with a graceful but eternally stopped metronome.

Almost as old as the oldest parts of Prague Castle, the ruins of **Vyšehrad Castle** crown a rock bluff that rises from the Vltava, about 2 miles upstream from the Old Town. The quiet cemetery adjoining the **Church of Sts. Peter and Paul** is a place to pay homage to some of the nation's cultural giants, among them Bedřich Smetana and the writer Karel Čapek.

Across the river, in the Prague 5 district, is the peaceful **Bertramka Villa,** where Mozart stayed while completing his opera *Don Giovanni.* ✉ *Mozartova ul. 169, Smíchov,* ☎ *02/543893.*

Franz Kafka's grave lies in the overgrown **Židovské hřbitovy** (New Jewish Cemetery) in Vinohrady, a rather depressing part of Prague. Take Metro A to Želivského, turn right at the main cemetery gate, and follow the wall for about 100 yards. Kafka's thin, white tombstone is found at the front of section 21.

Shopping

Shopping Districts

Many of the main shops are in and around Wenceslas Square and Na příkopě, as well as along Celetná and Pařížská. On the Lesser Quarter side, Nerudova has the densest concentration of shops.

Department Stores

The best and biggest department store is **Kotva** (✉ Nám. Republiky 8), which grows classier and more expensive every year. **Bílá Labuť'** (✉ Na poříčí 23) is a good-value option five minutes walk away from the pricier Kotva.

Specialty Shops

Look for the name **Dílo** for objets d'art and prints. **Lidová Řemesla** (folk art) shops in the Old Town stock wooden toys, elegant blue-and-white textiles, and gingerbread Christmas ornaments. **Moser** (✉ Na příkopě 12) is the most famous store for glass and porcelain. Shops specializing in Bohemian crystal, porcelain, ceramics, and antiques abound.

Dining

Eating out in Prague is a very popular pastime, so it's advisable to make reservations whenever possible. For details and price-category definitions, *see* Dining *in* Staying in the Czech Republic, *above*.

$$$$ ✕ **Opera Grill.** Though called a grill, this is one of the most stylish small
★ restaurants in town, complete with antique Meissen candelabra and Czech specialties. ⊠ *K. Světlé 35, Staré Město,* ☎ *02/265508. Reservations essential. AE, DC, V. Dinner only.*

$$$$ ✕ **U Malířů.** This esteemed old restaurant now serves exclusively French food and wines at the highest prices you'll see in the entire country. The specialty of the house is lobster, but the chef prepares a couple of elaborate prix-fixe menus daily. ⊠ *Maltézké nám. 11, Malá Strana,* ☎ *02/2451–0269. AE, DC, MC, V. Dinner only.*

$$$$ ✕ **U Zlaté Hrušky.** Careful restoration has returned this restaurant to its original 18th-century style. It specializes in Moravian wines, which go down well with fillet steaks and goose liver. ⊠ *Nový Svět 3, Hradčany,* ☎ *02/531133. Reservations essential. AE, D, DC, MC, V.*

$$$$ ✕ **V Zátiši.** White walls and casual grace accentuate the subtle flavors of smoked salmon, roast beef, and other non-Czech specialties. It's a favorite spot with the expatriate crowd and visiting businesspeople. ⊠ *Liliová 1, Staré Město,* ☎ *02/2422–8977. AE, MC, V.*

$$$ ✕ **U Mecenáše.** This wine restaurant manages to be both medieval and
★ elegant despite the presence of an ancient gallows. Try to get a table in the back room. The chef specializes in thick, juicy steaks, served with a variety of sauces. ⊠ *Malostranské nám. 10, Malá Strana,* ☎ *02/533881. Reservations essential. AE, DC, MC, V. Dinner only.*

$$$ ✕ **U Modré Kachničky.** The exuberant, eclectic decor is as attractive as the Czech and international dishes served, which include steaks, duck, and game in the autumn, and Bohemian trout and carp specialties. ⊠ *Nebovidská 6, Malá Strana,* ☎ *02/2451–0217. Dinner reservations essential. AE, V.*

$$ ✕ **Myslivna.** The name means "hunting lodge," and the cooks really know their way around pheasant, boar, and quail. The cheaper game dishes can be skimpy on the meat. ⊠ *Jagellonská 21, Prague 3,* ☎ *02/627–0209. AE, MC, V.*

$$ ✕ **Penguin's.** You'd expect to pay more for the setting and service at this popular spot. The muted mauve and matte-black walls make the atmosphere casual yet elegant. ⊠ *Zborovská 5, Prague 5,* ☎ *02/545660. AE, MC, V.*

$$ ✕ **Pezinok.** You'll get good, hearty fare served in a relaxed, no-frills atmosphere at this restaurant behind Národní třída in the New Town. The homemade sausage, accompanied by hearty Slovak wine, is excellent. The large palačinky for dessert are some of the best in Prague. ⊠ *Purkyňova 4, Nové Město,* ☎ *02/291996. AE, MC, V.*

$$ ✕ **U Lorety.** Sightseers will find this an agreeable spot—peaceful except for the welcoming carillon from neighboring Loreto Church. The service here is discreet but attentive, the tables are private, and the food is consistently good. Venison and steak are specialties. ⊠ *Loretánské nám. 8, Hradčany,* ☎ *02/2451–0191. No credit cards.*

$ ✕ **Na Zvonařce.** This bright beer hall serves very good traditional fare at unbeatable prices. In summer, sit on the terrace to escape the noisy crowd. Noteworthy dishes include fried chicken and English roast beef. Fruit dumplings for dessert are a rare treat. Service is slow. ⊠ *Šafaříkova 1, Prague 2,* ☎ *02/254534. No credit cards.*

$ ✕ **U Zlatého Tygra.** This crowded hangout is the last of a breed of authentic Czech pivnice. The smoke and stares preclude a long stay, but it's still worth dropping in for pub staples like ham and cheese plates or roast pork. The service is surly, but the beer is good. ⊠ *Husova 17, Staré Město, no phone. Reservations not accepted. No credit cards.*

$ ✕ **V Krakovské.** This clean pub noted for its excellent traditional fare is the place to try Bohemian duck: It's cooked just right and offered at an excellent price. Wash it down with good light or dark Braník beer. ⊠ *Krakovská 20, Nové Město,* ☎ *02/261537. No credit cards.*

$ ✕ **Vltava.** A riverside retreat with a snug dining room and summertime patio. The specialties, carp and trout, are the classic Bohemian fish dishes, served in big portions and prepared in many ways. ⊠ *On the quay below Ra'ínovo náb'elí, near the Palackého Bridge,* ☎ *02/ 294964. No credit cards.*

Lodging

Many of Prague's older hotels have been renovated, and new establishments in old buildings dot the Old Town and Lesser Quarter. Very few hotel rooms in the more desirable districts go for less than $100 per double room in high season; most less-expensive hotels are scattered far from the center. Private rooms and pensions remain the best deal for budget-minded travelers. For details and price-category definitions, *see* Lodging *in* Staying in the Czech Republic, *above.*

$$$$ ⌆ **Diplomat.** Completed in 1990 as part of a joint venture with an Austrian company, the Diplomat fuses elegance with "Western" efficiency. The effect is marred only by an unfortunate location, a 10-minute taxi or subway ride from the Old Town. ⊠ *Evropská 15, 160 00 Prague 6,* ☎ *02/2439–4111,* FAX *02/2439–4215. 387 rooms with bath. 2 restaurants, sauna, exercise room, nightclub. AE, DC, MC, V.*

$$$$ ⌆ **Forum.** This modern 28-story high-rise is near ancient Vyšehrad Castle, two subway stops south of the city center. The Palace of Culture next door often hosts trade fairs and conferences. ⊠ *Kongresová 1, 140 00 Prague 4,* ☎ *02/6119–1111,* FAX *02/6121–1673. 531 rooms with bath. 3 restaurants, pool, sauna, bowling, exercise room, nightclub. AE, DC, MC, V.*

$$$$ ⌆ **Hoffmeister.** Situated on a picturesque (if a bit busy) corner near the ★ Malostranská metro station, this is one of the most stylish small hotels in the city. The standard double rooms are not large but are decorated with a interior designer's eye. ⊠ *Pod Bruskou 9, 118 00 Prague 1,* ☎ *02/538380,* FAX *02/530959. 42 rooms with bath. Restaurant, bar, parking. AE, DC, MC, V.*

$$$$ ⌆ **Palace Praha.** Beautifully renovated, the Art Nouveau–style Palace ★ is Prague's most elegant and luxurious hotel. Its central location just off Wenceslas Square makes it an excellent choice. ⊠ *Panská 12, 110 00 Prague 1,* ☎ *02/2409–3111,* FAX *02/2422–1240. 125 rooms with bath. Restaurant, café, sauna. AE, DC, MC, V.*

$$$ ⌆ **U Páva.** Some rooms and suites in this refined neoclassical inn on ★ a cobblestone street in the Lesser Quarter have unforgettable views of Prague Castle. The Old World staff is courteous, and the reception and public areas are elegant and discreet. ⊠ *U lužického semináře 32, 118 00 Prague 1,* ☎ *02/2451–0922,* FAX *02/533379. 11 rooms with bath. Restaurant, bar. AE, DC, MC, V.*

$$–$$$ ⌆ **Kampa.** An early Baroque armory-turned-hotel, the Kampa is tucked away in a shady corner of the Lesser Quarter. The rooms are clean, if spare, but the bucolic setting compensates for any discomforts. ⊠ *Všehrdova 16, 118 00 Prague 1,* ☎ *02/2451–0409,* FAX *02/2451–0377. 85 rooms with bath. Restaurant, café. AE, DC, MC, V.*

$$ ⌆ **Karl-Inn.** The neighborhood's nothing much but the rooms, though basic, are comfortable enough and all have televisions and telephones. Two tram lines and a Metro station (Křižkova, line B) provide quick transport to the center and the Florenc bus terminal. ⊠ *Šaldova 54,*

186 00 Prague 8, ☎ *02/2481–1718,* ℻ *02/2481–2681. 168 rooms with bath. Restaurant, meeting rooms. AE, MC, V.*

$$ 🏨 **Central.** Quite conveniently, this hotel lives up to its name, with a site near Celetná and Náměstí Republiky. Rooms are sparely furnished, but all have baths. The Baroque glories of the Old Town are steps away. ⊠ *Rybná 8, 110 00 Prague 1,* ☎ *02/2481–2041,* ℻ *02/232–8404. 62 rooms with bath. Restaurant. MC, V.*

$$ 🏨 **Opera.** Faded glamour without, clean and simple within, the Opera maintains old ways by offering rooms without a private bath. This close to the Old Town, their prices are excellent at around 1,000 Kč in low season and 1,500 Kč at peak times; the more comfortable rooms with bath cost double. The Hotel Merkur across the street offers very similar rooms and rates, and less traffic noise. ⊠ *Opera: Těšnov 13, 110 00 Prague 1,* ☎ *02/231–5609,* ℻ *02/231–1477. 65 rooms, some with bath. Restaurant, bar. AE, DC, MC, V. Merkur:* ⊠ *Těšnov 9, 110 00 Prague 1,* ☎ *02/232–3878,* ℻ *02/232–3906. 63 rooms, some with bath. Restaurant. MC, V.*

$ 🏨 **Balkan.** One of the few central hotels that can compete in cost with private rooms, the spartan Balkan is on a busy street, not far from the Lesser Quarter. ⊠ *Svornosti 28, 150 00 Prague 5,* ☎ ℻ *02/540777. 24 rooms with bath. Breakfast not included. Restaurant. AE.*

The Arts

Prague's cultural life is one of its top attractions—and its citizens like to dress up for it—but performances are usually booked far ahead. You can get a monthly program of events from the PIS, Čedok, or many hotels. The English-language newspaper *The Prague Post* and the glossy magazine *Velvet* carry detailed entertainment listings. The main ticket agencies are **Bohemia Ticket International** (⊠ Salvátorská 6, ☎ 02/2422–7832) and **Tiketpro** (⊠ Main outlet at Štěpánská 61, Lucerna passage, ☎ 02/2481–4020, ℻ 02/2481–4021; credit cards accepted). For major concerts, opera and theater, it's much cheaper, however, to buy tickets at the box office.

Concerts

Performances are held in many palaces and churches. The **churches of St. Nicholas** in both the Old Town Square and in the Lesser Quarter are renowned for their concerts. At **St. James's Church** on Malá Stupartská (Staré Město) cantatas are performed amid a flourish of Baroque statuary. The early-Baroque **Nostic Palace** (Maltézské náměstí) in the Lesser Quarter is a home for music from all periods. At the Prague Castle's **Garden on the Ramparts** the music comes with a view.

The Czech Philharmonic, Prague Symphony, and Czech Radio Orchestra play in the intimate, lavish **Dvořák Hall** in the **Rudolfinum** (⊠ Nám. Jana Palacha, ☎ 02/2489–3111). The other main concert venue, **Smetana Hall,** along with the rest of the Obecní dům building on Náměstí Republiky, is scheduled to reopen in March 1997.

Opera and Ballet

Opera is of an especially high standard in the Czech Republic. One of the main venues in the grand style of the 19th century is the beautifully restored **National Theater** (⊠ Národní třída 2, ☎ 02/24912673). The **State Opera of Prague** (⊠ Wilsonova 4, ☎ 02/265353; formerly the Smetana Theater) is another historic site for opera lovers. The **Theater of the Estates** (⊠ Ovocný trh 1, ☎ 02/2421–5001) hosts opera, ballet, and theater performances. Mozart conducted the premiere of *Don Giovanni* here, and the opera is performed on its stage to this day—although the current version is sung in Czech.

Theater

Theater thrives as a vibrant art form in the Czech Republic. A dozen or so professional companies play in Prague to packed houses. Tourist-friendly, nonverbal theater abounds as well, notably "Black Theater," a melding of live acting, mime, video, and stage trickery that continues to draw crowds despite signs of fatigue. The famous **Laterna Magika** (Magic Lantern) is one of the more established producers of black theater extravaganzas (⊠ Národní třída 4, ☎ 02/2491–4129).

Puppet Shows

This traditional form of Czech entertainment has been given new life thanks to productions at the **National Marionette Theater** (⊠ Žatecká 1) and the **Magic Theater of the Baroque World** (⊠ Celetná 13).

Nightlife

Jazz and Rock Clubs

Jazz clubs are a Prague institution, although foreign customers keep them in business. **Reduta** (⊠ Národní třída 20, ☎ 02/2491–2246), where President Clinton wailed on sax in 1994, features mostly local talent. The same excellent Czech groups play the tiny **Agharta** (⊠ Krakovská 5, ☎ 02/2421–2914); arrive well before the 9 PM show time to get a seat. **Malostranská Beseda** (⊠ Malostranské nám. 21, ☎ 02/539024) is a funky hall for rock, jazz, and folk. Hip locals congregate at **Roxy** (⊠ Dlouhá 33, ☎ 02/2481–0951) for everything from punk to funk to New Age tunes.

Discos and Cabaret

Discos catering to a very young crowd blast sound onto lower Wenceslas Square. A classier act, where the newest dance music plays, is the ever-popular **Radost FX** (⊠ Bělehradská 120, Prague 2, ☎ 02/251210). Try **Variete Praha** (⊠ Vodičkova 30, ☎ 02/2421–5945) for a slightly risqué cabaret starting at 350 Kč.

BOHEMIA'S SPAS AND CASTLES

The Bohemian countryside is a restful world of gentle hills and thick woods. It is especially beautiful during fall-foliage season or in May, when the fruit trees that line the roads are in blossom. Two of the most famous of the Czech Republic's scores of spas lie in such settings: Karlovy Vary (Karlsbad) and Mariánské Lázně (Marienbad). In the 19th and early 20th centuries, European royals and aristocrats came to ease their overindulged bodies (or indulge them even more!) at these spas.

To the south, the higher wooded hills of Šumava, bordering Germany, have their own folklore. Here are the headwaters of the Vltava, and you'll follow its course as you enter South Bohemia, which probably has more castles than any other region of comparable size. The medieval towns of southern Bohemia are exquisite, but be prepared to find them in various stages of disrepair or decay. In such towns the Hussite reformist movement was born in the early 15th century, sparking a series of religious conflicts that embroiled all of Europe.

Getting Around

There are bus or train connections to every corner of this region. The service is cheap and fairly frequent and reliable, though you may be frustrated by incomprehensible small print when trying to decipher timetables. The most convenient way to follow this itinerary is by car.

Guided Tours

Many of the attractions on this itinerary, and some additional ones in Moravia, are covered by one or more of Čedok's many escorted tours out of Prague. Most of the attractions can also be visited on individual day trips from the capital.

Visitor Information

Brno (✉ Nádražní 10/12, ☎ 05/4232–1267).
České Budějovice (✉ Nám. Přem. Otakara II. 39, ☎ 038/52127).
Český Krumlov (✉ Čedok, Latrán 79, ☎ 0337/2189; Infocentrum, Nám. Svornosti 1, ☎ 0337/5670).
Karlovy Vary (✉ Ulice Dr. Bechera 21–23, ☎ 017/322–2994).
Mariánské Lázně (✉ Čedok, Třebízského 2/101, ☎ 0165/2254; City Service, Hlavní 626/1, ☎ 0165/3816).
Plzeň (✉ Prešovská 10, ☎ 019/722–2609).
Tábor (✉ Třída 9 května 1282, ☎ 0361/253563).

Exploring Bohemia's Spas and Castles

If you're traveling by car, the best—though not fastest—route is to head south from Prague on Highway 4, then west along minor roads up the Berounka Valley, taking in the magnificent castles of **Karlštejn** and **Křivoklát.** The former is an admirable restoration of the 14th-century castle built by Charles IV to protect the crown jewels of the Holy Roman Empire, housed in the castle's stunning Chapel of the Holy Rood. Currently being renovated, the chapel—filled with 128 Gothic paintings and encrusted with 2,000 gems—can only be glimpsed from its entrance portal. Karlštejn is also easily reached by a 40-minute train ride from Prague's Smíchovské station. Křivoklát's main attractions are its glorious woodlands, a favorite royal hunting ground in times past. ✉ *Karlštejn,* ☎ *0331/94617.* ⌖ *90 Kč.* ⊙ *Year-round, Tues.–Sun. 9–12 and 1–4 (till 5 Apr. and Oct., till 6 May, June, and Sept., till 7 July and Aug.). Křivoklát,* ⊙ *Apr.–May and Sept.–Dec., Tues.–Sun. 9–4; June–Aug., Tues.–Sun. 9–6.*

★ **Karlovy Vary,** or Karlsbad, was named after Charles IV, who is said to have been led to the main spring of Vřídlo while in pursuit of a fleeing deer during a hunt. Over the years, the spa attracted not only many of the crowned heads and much of the blue blood of Europe, but also leading musicians and writers. For all its later building and more proletarian visitors, Karlovy Vary still has a great deal of elegance. Confident bourgeois architecture, bright facades, and a setting in a deep, forested valley combine to make it as picturesque a town as any in the land. The waters from the spa's 12 springs are uniformly foul-tasting. The thing to do is sip them while nibbling rich Karlovy Vary *oplatky* (wafers), then resort to the "13th spring," Karlovy Vary's tangy herbal liqueur known as Becherovka.

Karlovy Vary and **Mariánské Lázně** have the Czech Republic's two best golf courses—the latter spa hosts a PGA European Tour event. As a spa, Mariánské Lázně (Marienbad) is younger and smaller, yet its more open setting gives it an air of greater spaciousness. It was much favored by Britain's Edward VII, though from all accounts he didn't waste too much time on strict diets and rigorous treatments.

The spas of western Bohemia have long catered to foreign travelers. As you head south to the higher Šumava Mountains bordering Germany, you'll be following much less frequented trails. **Domažlice** is the heart of the region of the Chods, for centuries guardians of Bohemia's frontiers, a function that earned them a number of privileges. Their

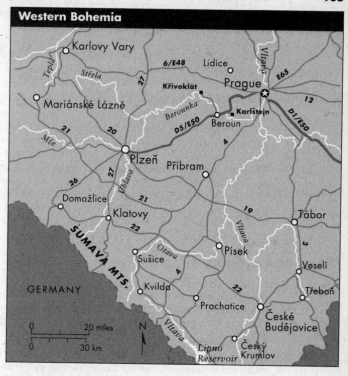

Western Bohemia

special folk culture is still very much alive, not least in their pottery and their infectious dances accompanied by local bagpipes (main festival in mid-August). It is a bustling if neglected little town with a lovely arcaded square, old fortifications, and a castle that houses the **Chod Museum** of local folk culture, scheduled to reopen in 1996.

From Domažlice an intricate but extremely pretty route, mainly along minor roads, runs through Sušice along the upper Otava River and over the hills to Prachatice—another well preserved and pretty town—and back to **Kvilda,** where the road joins the young Vltava River. Downstream, the Vltava has been trapped to form the great reservoir and recreational area of **Lipno.** You skirt part of it before turning northeast to Český Krumlov.

★ This entire section of southern Bohemia has strong associations with such feudal families as the Rožmberks, who peppered the countryside with their castles and created lake-size "ponds" in which to breed highly prized carp, still the main feature of a Czech Christmas dinner. Once the main seat of the Rožmberks, **Český Krumlov** is a magical town dominated by a forbidding Renaissance castle, complete with romantic elevated walkways, a round pastel-hued tower, and a functioning 18th-century theater. The Vltava River snakes through the town, which is steeply stacked on either bank, with flights of steps linking various levels and twisting narrow lanes that converge on **Náměstí Svornosti,** the Old Town's main square. A number of notable Renaissance houses add a more formal feel to the overall effect of this exquisite place. The **Egon Schiele Center** exhibits the work of Schiele, a frequent visitor to the town, and other 20th-century artists. ⊠ *Široká 70–72.* ☎ *100 Kč.* ☉ *Daily 10–6; castle interiors* ☉ *Apr.–Oct. 9–4.*

České Budějovice is on a much larger scale, and here your main stop should be the handsome **Přemysla Otakara II Square** (once called

Žižka Square in honor of the Hussite leader, its name was changed in 1991 to reflect historical reality—the town was firmly on the side of the Catholics). This is the home of the Czech version of Budweiser beer, known in Czech as Budvar and well worth trying. The town is a convenient point from which to head east for the town of Telč, with its Renaissance square, and other Moravian attractions.

Farther north along Highway 3 is **Tábor,** the very cradle of the Hussite movement. After Jan Hus's death at the stake in 1415, his proto-Protestant followers established an egalitarian commune here. Although weakened through doctrinal squabbles, the Táborites were shaped into Europe's most feared army by Jan Žižka, their one-eyed general. The town itself became a weapon of defense: its twisting streets were designed to confuse the enemy. A labyrinth of tunnels and cellars below the town were used both as living quarters and as links with the outer defenses. This unique story is told in the **Hussite Museum,** just off Žižkovo náměstí. ⊠ *Křivkova 31.* ☎ *36 Kč to museum and tunnels.* ⊙ *Apr.–Nov. 8:30–4 (in winter on request).*

Dining and Lodging

In many parts of Bohemia, the only real options for dining are the restaurants and cafés at the larger hotels and resorts; the following list is largely a selection of hotel/restaurants. For details and price-category definitions, *see* Dining and Lodging *in* Staying in the Czech Republic, *above.*

Český Krumlov

$$$ ✕🏠 **Na louži.** Homey wooden shutters on street level set the old-but-
★   cared-for atmosphere that marks the friendly pub restaurant and the five rooms upstairs, which are small, cozily furnished with country-style beds and wardrobes, and immaculate. ⊠ *Kájovská 66, 381 01,* ☎ /FAX *0337/5495. 5 rooms with bath. Restaurant. No credit cards.*

$$$ ✕🏠 **Růže.** This former Renaissance monastery was lovingly restored in 1992. Guest rooms are spacious and well-appointed; some are furnished in period style. Planned reconstruction of the nearby Hotel Krumlov in 1997 will leave the Růže the only full-service hotel in the Old Town. ⊠ *Horní ul. 153, 381 01,* ☎ *0337/2245,* FAX *0337/3881. 50 rooms, most with bath. Restaurant, nightclub. AE, MC, V.*

České Budějovice

$$$ ✕🏠 **Zvon.** Decent rooms, many looking out onto the grand main square, make this one of the better choices for lodging in town. ⊠ *Nám. Přemysla Otakara II 28, 370 01,* ☎ *038/731–1383,* FAX *038/731–1385. 75 rooms with bath. Restaurant. AE, MC, V.*

Karlovy Vary

$$$$ ✕🏠 **Dvořák.** Opened in 1991, this Austrian-built hotel offers imaginative decor, friendly efficiency, and a superb array of facilities. ⊠ *Nova louka 11, 360 21,* ☎ *017/322–4145,* FAX *017/322–2814. 75 rooms with bath. Restaurant, pool, exercise room. AE, DC, MC, V.*

$$$–$$$$ ✕🏠 **Grand Hotel Pupp.** Founded in 1701, the Pupp still has a fine 18th-
★   century hall, the Slavností sál. It's one of the oldest surviving hotels in Europe, with glittering names—past and present—in its guest register. ⊠ *Mírové nám. 2, 360 91,* ☎ *017/209111,* FAX *017/322–4032. 358 rooms with bath. 2 restaurants, sauna, golf, tennis courts, horseback riding, casino, 2 nightclubs. AE, DC, MC, V.*

$$–$$$ 🏠 **Atlantic.** This hotel in the middle of town is run by the nearby Hotel Central. The turn-of-the-century building still bears its landmark (and rather grotesque) porcelain statues on the roof. It may close in low season (November–March); if so, the Central has adequate rooms

in just as excellent a location. ⊠ *Atlantic, Tržiště 23, 360 62;* ⊠ *Central, Divadelní nám. 17, 360 62.* ☎ *For both hotels 017/322–5251,* FAX *017/322–9086. Atlantic: 38 rooms, some with bath. Central: 70 rooms with bath. AE, DC, MC, V.*

Mariánské Lázně

$$$–$$$$ ✕▦ **Palace.** Built in the spa's heyday in 1875, this elegant building is conveniently situated just within the resort center. No-smoking rooms are available. ⊠ *Hlavní třída 67, 353 01,* ☎ *0165/2222,* FAX *0165/4262. 45 rooms with bath. 2 restaurants, café. AE, DC, MC, V.*

$$$ ✕▦ **Bohemia.** Like its neighboring yellow-and-white hotels on Hlavní třída, this one concentrates on providing a full range of hotel services rather than functioning as a spa that also puts up hotel guests; it thus offers more amenities and comforts than some of the spa hotels do. ⊠ *Hlavní třída 100, 353 01,* ☎ *0165/3251,* FAX *0165/2943. 77 rooms with bath. Restaurant, sauna. AE, DC, MC, V.*

$$–$$$ ✕▦ **Pacifik.** Like a *grande dame* gone a bit to seed, this lavishly-fronted spa hotel commands the town's long main avenue. The rooms seem better suited to a strict dieting cure than the self-indulgence Marienbad is famous for, but have plenty of room to move around in. Foregoing a private bath will cut the cost by around 50 percent. ⊠ *Mírové nám. 84, 353 48,* ☎ *0165/3006,* FAX *0165/2645. 75 rooms, some with bath. Restaurant, café. AE, DC, MC, V.*

8 Denmark

Copenhagen

Funen and the Central Islands

Jutland and the Lakes

EBULLIENCE AND A SENSE OF HUMOR have always been Danish trademarks. Though one might expect a country comprising more than 400 islands to develop an island mentality, the Danes are famous for their friendliness. They even have a word—*hyggelig*—for the feeling of well-being that comes from their own brand of cozy hospitality.

The stereotype of melancholic Scandinavia simply doesn't hold here: neither in the café-studded streets of the larger cities, where musicians and fruit vendors hawk their wares to passersby, nor in the tiny coastal towns where the fishing boats are as brightly painted as fire trucks. Even the country's indoor/outdoor museums, where history is brought to life in clusters of reconstructed structures out in the open, indicate that Danes don't choose to keep experience behind glass.

This is a land of well-groomed agriculture, where every available acre is planted in orchards or crops. Nowhere are you far from water as you drive on and off the ferries and bridges linking the three regions of Jylland (Jutland), Fyn (Funen), and Sjælland (Zealand).

The surrounding sea has shaped Denmark's history. The Vikings, unparalleled seafarers, had seen much of the world by the 8th century. Today the Danes remain expert navigators, using their 4,480 kilometers (2,800 miles) of coastline both for sport—there are regattas around Zealand and Funen—and for fishing and trading.

Long one of the world's most liberal countries, Denmark has a highly developed social welfare system. Hefty taxes are the subject of grumbling and jokes, but Danes remain proud of their state-funded medical and educational systems.

The country that gave the world Isak Dinesen, Hans Christian Andersen, and Søren Kierkegaard has a long-standing commitment to culture and the arts. In what other nation does the royal couple translate the writings of Simone de Beauvoir or the queen design costumes for the ballet? The Royal Danish Ballet is world-renowned, and even in the provinces there are numerous theater groups and opera houses.

Perhaps Denmark's greatest charm is its manageable size—about half that of Maine. The ferry journey from Esbjerg, on the western coast of Jutland, to Copenhagen, on the eastern coast of Zealand, takes around five hours. From here you can make comfortable, unhurried expeditions by boat, car, bus, or train to explore one of the world's most civilized countries.

ESSENTIAL INFORMATION

Before You Go

When to Go

Most travelers visit Denmark during the warmest months, July and August, but there are advantages to going in May, June, or September, when sights are less crowded and many establishments offer off-season discounts. However, few places in Denmark are ever unpleasantly crowded, and when the Danes make their annual exodus to the beaches the cities have even more breathing space. Many visitors avoid the winter months, when days are short and dark and when important attractions, including Copenhagen's Tivoli Gardens, are closed for most of the season. It's worth noting, however, that winter holidays are beau-

Denmark

North Sea

Skagerrak

TO GREENLAND

TO FAROE ISLANDS

Skagen

Hirtshals
Hjørring
Frederikshavn
Sæby

Brønderslev

Hanstholm

11

Limfjord

Aalborg

Læsø

Thisted

Limfjord

Aalborg Bugt

Kattegat

Nykøbing

13

Hadsund

Lemvig

Skive

Anholt

Struer

Viborg

Holstebro

16

Jylland

Randers   16

Grenå

Ringkøbing

15

Herning

Silkeborg

Skanderborg

Århus

Ebeltoft

Skjern

Grindsted

Horsens

Samsø

Tisvildeleje

Hornbæk

Vejle

E45

Billund

Samsøbælt

Nykøbing

Helsingør

Frederikssund

Hillerød

Esbjerg

E20

Holsted

Fredericia

Middelfart

Storebælt

Kalundborg

Holbæk

Fanø

Kolding

Kerteminde

Jyderup

Roskilde

Copenhagen

21

Ribe

Odense

Slagelse

E20

Sjælland

Amager

Rømø

Vojens

Assens

Fyn

Ringsted

Køge Bugt

Skærbæk

Haderslev

Nyborg

Fåborg

Korsør

Næstved

Køge

Åbenrå

Lillebælt

Svendborg

Als

Troense

Langeland

Tranekær

Karrebæksminde

St. Heddinge

Tønder

8

Sønderborg

Rudkøbing

Vordingborg

Stege

Ærøskøbing

Nakskov

Møn

Ærø

Marstal

Nykøbing

Rødby

Maribo

Falster

TO BORNHOLM

Lolland

Nysted

E47

Ostsee

GERMANY

SWEDEN

Baltic Sea

Bornholm

Rønne

N

0   50 miles

0   75 km

SWEDEN

tiful and especially cozy—even Tivoli reopens with its special Christmas market.

CLIMATE

The following are the average daily maximum and minimum temperatures for Copenhagen.

Jan.	36F	2C	May	61F	16C	Sept.	64F	18C
	28	– 2		46	8		51	11
Feb.	36F	2C	June	67F	19C	Oct.	54F	12C
	28	– 2		52	11		44	7
Mar.	41F	5C	July	71F	22C	Nov.	45F	7C
	31	– 1		57	14		38	3
Apr.	51F	11C	Aug.	70F	21C	Dec.	40F	4C
	38	3		56	14		34	1

Currency

The monetary unit in Denmark is the krone (kr., DKr, or DKK), which is divided into 100 øre. At press time (spring 1996), the krone stood at about 5.6 kr. to the U.S. dollar, 4.1 kr. to the Canadian dollar, and 8.6 kr. to the pound sterling. Most well-known credit cards are accepted in Denmark, though the American Express card is accepted less frequently than others. Traveler's checks can be changed in banks and in many hotels, restaurants, and shops.

What It Will Cost

Denmark's economy is stable, and inflation remains reasonably low, without wild fluctuations in exchange rates. Although Denmark is slightly cheaper than Norway and Sweden, the standard and the cost of living are nonetheless high, especially for such luxuries as hard liquor and cigarettes. Prices are highest in Copenhagen; the least expensive areas are Funen and Jutland.

SAMPLE PRICES

Cup of coffee, 14 kr.–20 kr.; bottle of beer, 15 kr.–25 kr.; soda, 10 kr.–15 kr.; ham sandwich, 22 kr.–40 kr.; 1-mile taxi ride, 30 kr.

Customs on Arrival

If you have purchased goods in a country that is a member of the European Union (EU) and pay that country's value-added tax (VAT) on those goods, you may import duty-free 1½ liters of liquor; 300 cigarettes or 150 cigarillos or 75 cigars or 400 grams of tobacco.

If you are entering Denmark from a non-EU country or if you have purchased your goods on a ferryboat or in an airport not taxed in the EU, you must pay Danish taxes on any amount of alcoholic beverages greater than 1 liter of liquor or 2 liters of strong wine, plus 2 liters of table wine. For tobacco, the limit is 200 cigarettes or 100 cigarillos or 50 cigars or 250 grams of tobacco. You are also allowed 50 grams of perfume. Other articles (including beer) are allowed up to a maximum of 1,350 kr.

Language

Danish is a difficult tongue for foreigners—except those from Norway and Sweden—to understand, let alone speak. Danes are good linguists, however, and almost everyone, except perhaps elderly people in rural areas, speaks English well.

Getting Around

By Car

Roads here are good and largely traffic-free (except around Copenhagen); you can reach many islands by toll-free bridges.

RULES OF THE ROAD

To drive you will need a valid license, and if you're using your own car it must have a certificate of registration and national plates. A triangular hazard-warning sign is compulsory in every car and is provided with rentals. The driver and all passengers must wear seat belts, and headlights must always be on—even in the daytime. Motorcyclists must always wear helmets and use headlights. All drivers must pay attention to cyclists, who use the outer right lane and have the right-of-way.

Drive on the right and give way to traffic from the left. A red-and-white triangular yield sign, or a line of white triangles across the road, means you must yield to traffic on the road you are entering. Do not turn right on a red light. Speed limits are 50 kph (30 mph) in built-up areas; 100 kph (60 mph) on highways; and 80 kph (50 mph) on other roads. If you are towing a trailer, you must not exceed 70 kph (40 mph). Speeding, and drinking and driving, especially, are punished severely.

PARKING

In areas with signs reading PARKERING/STANDSNING FORBUDT (no parking and no stopping) you are allowed a three-minute grace period to load and unload. In towns, automatic parking-permit machines are used. Drop in coins, push the silver button, and a ticket marked with the expiration time will drop down. Display the ticket clearly on the dash. Parking for an hour costs 6 kr.–15 kr. in Copenhagen, 7 kr. elsewhere. In some areas, signs post parking regulations. All cars have a plastic dial on the inside of their windshields. Set the dial to the time you leave your car.

GASOLINE

Gas costs around 6 kr. a liter.

BREAKDOWNS

Members of organizations affiliated with Alliance International de Tourisme (AIT), including American AAA and British AA, can get technical and legal assistance from the **Danish Motoring Organization** (**FDM,** ⊠ Firskovej 32, DK 2800 Lyngby, ☎ 45/93–08–00). All highways have emergency phones, and you can also phone your car-rental company for help. If you cannot drive your car to a garage for repairs, the rescue corps, **Falck** (☎ 44/92–22–22), can help anywhere, night or day.

By Train and Bus

Traveling by train or bus is easy, since **Danish State Railways (DSB,** ☎ 33/14–17–01) and a few private companies cover the country with a dense network of train services, supplemented in remote areas by buses. Hourly intercity trains connect the main towns in Jutland and Funen with Copenhagen and Zealand, using high-speed diesels, called IC–3s, on the most important stretches. All these trains make the one-hour ferry crossing of the Store Bælt (Great Belt), the waterway separating Funen and Zealand. Seat reservations on intercity trains and IC–3s are optional, but you must have a reservation if you plan to cross the Great Belt. Buy tickets at stations for trains, buses, and connecting ferry crossings (buses allow you to buy tickets on board). For most cross-country trips, children between 4 and 11 accompanied by an adult travel free, though they must have a seat reservation (30 kr.). Ask about discounts for senior citizens and groups.

FARES

The **ScanRail** pass affords unlimited train travel throughout Denmark, Finland, Norway, and Sweden, as well as restricted ferry passage in and beyond Scandinavia. It is available for five days of travel within 15 days ($222 first class, $176 second class); 10 days within a month ($346 first class, $278 second class); or one month ($504 first class,

$404 second class). In the United States, call RailEurope (800/438–7245), or DER (800/782-2424), which also offers a 21-day pass for $400 (first class) or $320 (second class). Buy your tickets in the United States: Though they are available in Denmark, they are more expensive. Children between 4 and 12 pay half-price, and those under 4 travel free. Seniors over 55 receive about a 13 percent discount. Finally, the hotel chains TOP International and Scanclass offer ScanRail pass holders discounts on accommodation. For details, call DER, RailEurope, or your travel agent. DSB also offers other discounts; ask, ask, ask!

By Boat

There is frequent service to Germany, Poland, Sweden, Norway, and the Faroe Islands (in the Atlantic Ocean, north of Scotland), as well as to Britain. Domestic ferries provide service between Jutland, Funen, and Zealand and to the smaller islands, 100 of which are inhabited. Danish State Railways and several private shipping companies publish timetables in English; you should reserve on both domestic and overseas routes. Ask about off-season discounts.

By Bicycle

Some say the Danes have the greatest number of bikes per capita in the world. Indeed, with its flat landscape and uncrowded roads, Denmark is a cyclist's paradise. You can rent bikes at some train stations and many tourist offices, as well as from private firms. Contact the **Danish Cyclists' Association** (Dansk Cyklist Forbund, ⊠ Rømersgade 7, DK 1362 Copenhagen, ☎ 33/32–31–21) for additional information. Danish tourist offices publish the pamphlet "Cycling Holiday in Denmark."

Staying in Denmark

Telephones

LOCAL CALLS

Pay phones take 1-, 5-, and 10-kr. coins. You must use area codes even when dialing a local number. Calling cards, which are sold at DSB stations, post offices, and some kiosks, cost 25, 50, or 100 kr., and may be used at certain phones.

INTERNATIONAL CALLS

Dial 00, then the country code, area code, and the desired number. To reach an **AT&T** long-distance operator, dial 8001–0010; for **MCI**, dial 8001–0022; and for **Sprint**, 8001–0877. Denmark's international telephone country code is 45.

OPERATORS AND INFORMATION

To ask an operator, most of whom speak English, for local assistance, dial 118; for an international operator, dial 113.

Mail

POSTAL RATES

Surface and airmail letters and aerograms to the United States cost 5 kr. for 20 grams; postcards the same. Letters and postcards to the United Kingdom and other EU countries cost 3.75 kr. Stamps are sold at post offices and some shops.

RECEIVING MAIL

If you do not know where you will be staying, your mail can be addressed to "poste restante" and sent to any post office. If no post office is specified, letters will be sent to the main post office in Copenhagen (⊠ Tietgensgade 37, DK 1704). American Express holds mail free of charge for cardholder and those carrying its traveler's checks; others are charged a small fee.

Shopping
VAT REFUNDS

Visitors from a non-EU country can save about 20% on purchases of more than 300 kr. by obtaining a refund of the value-added tax (VAT) at the more than 1,500 shops displaying TAX FREE signs. If the shop sends your purchase directly to your home address, you pay only the sales price, exclusive of VAT. If you want to take the goods home yourself, pay the full price in the shop and get a VAT refund at the Danish duty-free shopping center at the Copenhagen airport. Get a copy of the *Tax-Free Shopping Guide* from the tourist office.

Opening and Closing Times
Banks in Copenhagen are open weekdays 9:30–4 and Thursdays until 6. Several *bureaux de change,* including the ones at Copenhagen's central station and airport, stay open until 10 PM. Outside Copenhagen, banking hours vary.

Museums are generally open 10–3 or 11–4 and closed Mondays. In winter, opening hours are shorter, and some museums close for the season. Check the local papers or ask at tourist offices.

Small shops and boutiques are open weekdays 10–5:30; most stay open Thursday and Friday until 7 or 8 and close on Saturday at 1 or 2. On the first and last Saturday of every month, most shops stay open until 4 or 5. In response to increasingly liberal laws, shop hours keep changing. Check for specifics to avoid disappointment.

National Holidays
January 1; March 30–31 (Easter); April 25 (Common Prayer); May 8 (Ascension); May 18–19 (Pentecost); June 5 (Constitution Day; shops close at noon); and December 24–26.

Dining
Danes take their eating seriously, and Danish food, however simple, is excellent, with an emphasis on fresh ingredients and careful presentation. Fish and meat are both of top quality in this fishing and farming country, and both are staple ingredients of the famous *smørrebrød.* Some smørrebrød are huge meals in themselves: Innocent snackers can find themselves faced with a dauntingly large (but nonetheless delicious) mound of fish or meat, slathered with pickle relish, all atop either *rugbrød* (rye bread) or *franskbrød* (French bread). Another specialty is *wienerbrød,* a confection far superior to anything billing itself "Danish pastry" elsewhere.

All Scandinavian countries have versions of the cold table, but Danes claim that theirs, *det store kolde bord,* is the original and the best. It's a celebration meal; the setting of the long table is a work of art—often with paper sculpture and silver platters—and the food itself is a minor miracle of design and decoration.

In hotels and restaurants the cold table is served at lunch only, though you will find a more limited version at hotel breakfasts—a good bet for budget travelers, since you can eat as much as you like.

Denmark boasts more than 50 varieties of beer, made by as many breweries; the best-known come from Carlsberg and Tuborg. Those who like harder stuff should try *snaps,* the aquavit traditionally drunk with cold food, especially herring. A note about smoking: Danes, like many Europeans, regard smoking as an inalienable right. Militant insistence that they abstain will be regarded as either hysteria or comedy. A polite tone requesting they blow their smoke away from you may prove more effective.

MEALTIMES

The Danes start work early, which means they generally eat lunch at noon. Evening meals are also eaten early, so visitors should make sure they have dinner reservations for 9 at the latest. Bars and cafés stay open later, and most offer at least light fare.

WHAT TO WEAR

The Danes are a fairly casual lot, and few restaurants require a jacket and tie. Even in the chicest establishments, the tone is elegantly casual.

RATINGS

Meal prices vary little between town and country. While approximate gradings are given below, remember that careful ordering can get you a moderate ($$) meal at a very expensive ($$$$) restaurant. Prices are per person and include a first course, main course, and dessert, plus taxes and tip, but not wine.

CATEGORY	COST
$$$$	over 400 kr.
$$$	200 kr.–400 kr.
$$	120 kr.–200 kr.
$	under 120 kr.

Lodging

Accommodations in Denmark range from the spare and comfortable to the resplendent. Even inexpensive hotels offer simple designs in good materials and good, firm beds. Many Danes prefer a shower to a bath, so if you particularly want a tub, ask for it, but be prepared to pay more. Except in the case of rentals, breakfast and taxes are usually included in prices, though this seems to be changing. Check when making a reservation.

HOTELS

Luxury hotels in the city or countryside offer rooms of a high standard, and in a manor-house hotel you may find yourself sleeping in a four-poster bed. Less expensive accommodations, however, are uniformly clean and comfortable.

INNS

A cheaper and charming alternative to hotels are the old stagecoach *kroer*—inns scattered throughout Denmark. You can save money by contacting **Kro Ferie** (✉ Vejlevej 16, DK8700 Horsens, Jutland, ☎ 75/64–87–00) to invest in a book of Inn Checks, valid at 87 inns. Each check costs 375 kr. per person or 575 kr. per couple and includes one overnight stay in a double room with bath, breakfast included. Family checks, for three (650 kr.) and four (725 kr.), are also available. Order a free catalogue from Kro Ferie and choose carefully; the organization includes some chain hotels bereft of even a smidgen of inn-related charm. Some establishments also tack a 125 kr. surcharge on the price of a double.

FARM VACATIONS

These are perhaps the best way to see how the Danes live and work. You stay on a farm and share meals with the family; you can even get out and help with the chores. There's a minimum stay of three nights; bed and breakfast is 175 kr., and half board runs 245. (Full board can be arranged.) Children under 4 get 75% off; ages 4 through 11 get 50%. Contact the **Horsens Tourist Office** (✉ Søndergade 26, DK 8700 Horsens, Jutland, ☎ 70/10-41-90, FAX 75/60–21–90) for details.

YOUTH HOSTELS

The 100 youth hostels in Denmark are open to everyone regardless of age. If you have an International Youth Hostels Association card (obtainable before you leave home), the rate is roughly 65 kr.–85 kr. for a single bed; 150 kr.–250 kr. for a private double room. Without the card, there's a surcharge of 25 kr. For more information, contact **Danmarks Vandrehjem** (⊠ Vesterbrogade 39, DK 1620 Copenhagen V, ☎ 31/31–36–12, ⒡ 31/31–36–26) or American Youth Hostels (☞ Gold Guide).

RENTALS

Many Danes rent out their summer homes—an ideal option for those who wish to see the countryside in a more relaxed way. A simple house with room for four will cost from 1,000 kr. per week to twice as much during the summer high season. Contact the Danish Tourist Board (☞ Important Addresses and Numbers *in* Copenhagen, *below*) for details.

CAMPING

Denmark has more than 500 approved campsites, with a rating system of one, two, or three stars. Campers will need an International Camping Carnet or Danish Camping Pass (available at any campsite and valid for one year). For more details on camping and discounts for groups and families, contact **Campingrådet** (⊠ Hesseløgade 10, DK 2100 Copenhagen 0 ☎ 39/27–88–44).

RATINGS

Prices are for two people in a double room and include service and taxes and usually breakfast.

CATEGORY	COPENHAGEN	OTHER AREAS
$$$$	over 1,100 kr.	over 850 kr.
$$$	800 kr.–1,100 kr.	650 kr.–850 kr.
$$	670 kr.–800 kr.	450 kr.–650 kr.
$	under 670 kr.	under 450 kr.

Tipping

The egalitarian Danes do not expect to be tipped. The exceptions are hotel porters, who get around 5 kr. per bag; you should also leave 1 or 2 kr. for the use of a public toilet, if there is an attendant.

COPENHAGEN

Arriving and Departing

By Plane

The main airport for both international and domestic flights is Copenhagen Airport, 10 kilometers (6 miles) outside of town.

BETWEEN THE AIRPORT AND DOWNTOWN

Bus service to the city is frequent. The airport bus to the central station leaves every 15 minutes: The trip takes about 25 minutes, and the fare is 39 kr. (pay on the bus). Public buses cost 15 kr. and run as often but take longer. Bus 250S takes you to Rådhus Pladsen, the city hall square. A taxi ride takes 15 minutes and costs about 120 kr.

By Train

Copenhagen's clean and convenient central station is the hub of the country's train network. Express trains leave hourly, on the hour, from 6 AM to 10 PM for principal towns in Funen and Jutland. Find out more from **DSB Information** (☎ 33/14–17–01) at the central station. You can make reservations at the central station (☎ 33/14–88–00) as well as most other stations, and through travel agents. Public shower facilities at the central station are open 4:30 AM–2 AM and cost 15 kr.

Getting Around

By Bus and Suburban Train

The best bet for visitors is the **Copenhagen Card,** affording unlimited travel on buses and suburban trains (S-trains), admission to some 60 museums and sights around Zealand, and a reduction on the ferry crossing to Sweden. Buy the card, which costs about 140 kr. (one day), 230 kr. (two days), or 295 kr. (three days)—half price for children 5 to 11—at tourist offices, hotels, or from travel agents.

Buses and suburban trains operate on the same ticket system and divide Copenhagen and environs into three zones. Tickets are validated on the time system: On the basic ticket, which costs 10 kr. for an hour, you can travel anywhere in the zone in which you started. You can buy a clip-card, equivalent to 10 basic tickets, for 75 kr. Call the 24-hour information service for zone information: ☎ 36/45–45–45 for buses, 33/14–17–01 for S-trains. (Wait for the Danish message to end and a live operator will answer.) Buses and S-trains run from 5 AM (6 AM on Sunday) to 12:30 AM.

By Car

Copenhagen is a city for walkers, not drivers. The charm of its pedestrian streets is paid for by a complicated one-way road system and difficult parking. Leave your car in the garage: Attractions are relatively close together, and public transportation is excellent.

By Taxi

Taxis are not cheap, but all are metered. The base charge is 12 kr., plus 8–10 kr. per kilometer. A cab is available when it displays the sign FRI (free); you can either hail a cab (though this can be difficult outside the center), pick one up at a taxi stand, or call 31/35–35–35. If you call, there is a surcharge of 20 kr.; additional fees apply at night.

By Bicycle

More than half the 5 million Danes are said to ride bikes, which are popular with visitors as well. Bike rental costs 30 kr. to 50 kr. a day, with a deposit of 100 kr. to 200 kr. Contact **Danwheel-Rent-a-Bike** (⊠ Colbjørnsensgade 3, ☎ 31/21–22–27) or **Urania Cykler** (⊠ Gammel Kongevej 1, ☎ 31/21–80–88).

Important Addresses and Numbers

Visitor Information

The main tourist information office is the **Danish Tourist Board** (⊠ Danmarks Turistråd, Bernstoffsgade 1, DK 1577 Copenhagen V, ☎ 33/11–13–25). Located on the Tivoli grounds, it is open May, weekdays 9–6, Sat. 9–2, Sun. 9–1; June–Sept., daily 9–6; Oct.–Apr., weekdays 9–5, Sat. 9–noon, closed Sun. There are additional offices in Helsingør, Hillerød, Køge, Roskilde, Gilleleje, Hundersted, and Tisvildeleje. Youth information is available in Copenhagen at **Huset** (⊠ Rådhusstraede 13, ☎ 33/15–65–18).

Embassies

U.S. (⊠ Dag Hammarskjöldsallé 24, ☎ 31/42–31–44). **Canadian** (⊠ Kristen Benikowsgade 1, ☎ 33/12–22–99). **U.K.** (⊠ Kastelsvej 40, ☎ 35/26–46–00).

Emergencies

Police, Fire, Ambulance (☎ 112). **Doctor** (after 4 PM), ☎ 38/88–60–41. (Fees payable in cash only; night fees around 400–500 kr.). **Dentist:** Dental Emergency Service, Tandlægevagten, 14, Oslo Plads, near Østerport station (no phone; emergencies only; cash only). **Pharma-**

cies open 24 hours in central Copenhagen: **Steno Apotek** (⊠ Vester-brogade 6C, ☎ 33/14–82–66); **Sønderbro Apotek** (⊠ Amagerbrogade 158, Amager area, ☎ 31/58–01–40); **Glostrup Apotek** (⊠ Hovedve-gen 101, Glostrup area, ☎ 43/96–00–20). There is a nighttime sur-charge of about 20 kr.

English-Language Bookstores

English-language publications are sold at the central-station news-stand and in most bookstores around town. **Boghallen** (⊠ Rådhus Plad-sen 37) and **Arnold Busck** (⊠ Købmagergade 49) have particularly good selections.

Travel Agencies

American Express (⊠ Amagertorv 18, ☎ 33/12–23–01). **Spies** (⊠ Ny-ropsgade 41, ☎ 33/32–15–00) arranges charter flights and accom-modations all over Europe.

Guided Tours

Orientation

Tours are a good way to get acquainted with Copenhagen. The "Har-bor and Canal Tour" (by boat; May through mid-Sept., daily every ½ hour 10 to 5) leaves from Gammel Strand and the east side of Kon-gens Nytorv. The following bus tours, conducted by **Copenhagen Ex-cursions** (☎ 31/54–06–06), leave from the Lur Blowers' Column in Rådhus Pladsen: "City Tour" (mid-June through mid-Sept., daily at 9:30, 1 and 3); "Grand Tour of Copenhagen" (daily at 11; Apr. through Sept., also at 1:30; Oct. through Mar., Sat. at 1:30); "Royal Tour of Copenhagen" (June through mid-Sept., Tues., Sat. at 10); "City and Harbor Tour" (combined bus and boat; mid-May through mid-Sept., daily at 9:30; mid-June through mid-Sept., also daily at 3). Tickets are available aboard the bus and boat or from travel agencies.

Special-Interest

The "Carlsberg Brewery Tour," which includes a look into the draft-horse stalls, meets at the Elephant Gate (⊠ Ny Carlsbergvej 140) on weekdays at 11 and 2 or by arrangement for groups (☎ 33/27–13–14). The "Royal Copenhagen Porcelain" tour (⊠ Smallegade 45, ☎ 31/86–48–48) is given on weekdays at 9, 10, and 11.

Walking

The Danish Tourist Board supplies maps and brochures and can rec-ommend a walking tour.

Regional

The Danish Tourist Board has full details relating to excursions out-side the city, including visits to castles (such as Hamlet's castle), the Viking Ship Museum, and Sweden.

Personal Guides

The Danish Tourist Board can recommend multilingual guides for in-dividual needs; travel agents have details on hiring a limousine and guide.

Exploring Copenhagen

When Denmark ruled Norway and Sweden in the 15th century, Copen-hagen was the capital of all three countries. Today it is still a lively north-ern capital, with about 1 million inhabitants. It's a city meant for walking, the first in Europe to recognize the value of pedestrian streets in fostering community spirit. As you stroll through the cobbled streets and squares, you'll find that Copenhagen combines the excitement and variety of big-city life with a small-town atmosphere. If there's such a thing as a cozy metropolis, this is it.

Nor are you ever far from water, be it sea or canal. The city itself is built upon two main islands, Slotsholmen and Christianshavn, connected by drawbridges. Walk down Nyhavn Canal, an area formerly haunted by a fairly salty crew of sailors. Now it's gentrified, and the 18th-century houses lining it are filled with chic restaurants. You should linger, too, in the five main pedestrian streets known collectively as Strøget, with their countless shops, restaurants, cafés, street musicians, and vendors. In summer Copenhagen moves outside, and the best views of city life are from sidewalk cafés in the sunny squares.

Numbers in the margin correspond to points of interest on the Copenhagen map.

★ ❶ The best place to start a stroll is Rådhus Pladsen, the hub of Copenhagen's commercial district. The mock-Renaissance building dominating it is the **Rådhus** (City Hall), completed in 1905. A statue of Copenhagen's 12th-century founder, Bishop Absalon, sits atop the main entrance. Inside, you can see the first World Clock, an astrological timepiece invented and built by Jens Olsen and set in motion in 1955. If you're feeling energetic, take a guided tour partway up the 350-foot tower for a panoramic view. ⊠ *Rådhus Pladsen,* ☎ *33/66–25–82.* ⊙ *Mon.–Wed., Fri. 9:30–3, Thurs. 9:30–4, Sat. 9:30–1. Tours in English: weekdays at 3, Sat. at 10. Tower tours: Mon.–Sat. at noon; additional tours June–Sept. at 10 and 2.* ☜ *Tour 20 kr., tower 10 kr.*

❷ On the east side of Rådhus Pladsen is the **Lurblæserne** (Lur Blowers' Column), topped by two Vikings blowing an ancient trumpet called a *lur.* The artist took a good deal of artistic license—the lur dates from the Bronze Age, 1500 BC, whereas the Vikings lived a mere 1,000 years ago. The monument is a starting point for sightseeing tours of the city.

❸ If you continue to the square's northeast corner and turn right, you will be in Frederiksberggade, the first of the five pedestrian streets that make up **Strøget,** Copenhagen's shopping district. Walk past the cafés and trendy boutiques to the double square of **Gammeltorv** and **Nytorv,** where, farther along, the street is paved with mosaic tiles.

❹ Turn down Rådhusstræde toward Frederiksholms Kanal, and continue to Ny Vestergade. Here you'll find the entrance to the **Nationalmuseet** (National Museum), with extensive collections chronicling Danish cultural history to modern times and displays of Egyptian, Greek, and Roman antiquities. Viking enthusiasts may want to see the Runic stones in the Danish cultural history section. ⊠ *Ny Vestergade 10,* ☎ *33/13–44–11.* ☜ *30 kr.* ⊙ *Tues.–Sun. 10–5.*

★ ❺ Cross Frederiksholms Kanal to Castle Island, dominated by the massive gray **Christiansborg Slot** (Christiansborg Castle). The complex, which contains the Folketinget (Parliament House) and the Royal Reception Chambers, is on the site of the city's first fortress, built by Bishop Absalon in 1167. While the castle was being built at the turn of the century, the National Museum excavated the ruins beneath the site. ⊠ *Christiansborg ruins,* ☎ *33/92–64–92.* ☜ *15 kr.* ⊙ *May–Sept., daily 9:30–3:30; closed Oct.–Apr., Mon. and Sat. Folketinget,* ☎ *33/37–55–00.* ☜ *Free.* ⊙ *Tour times vary; call ahead. Reception Chambers:* ☜ *28 kr.* ⊙ *Hours and tour times vary; call ahead. Closed Jan.*

★ ❻ Just north of the castle is the **Thorvaldsen Museum.** The 19th-century Danish sculptor Bertel Thorvaldsen, whose tomb stands in the center of the museum, was greatly influenced by the statues and reliefs of classical antiquity. In addition to his own works, there is a collection of paintings and drawings by other artists illustrating the influence of Italy

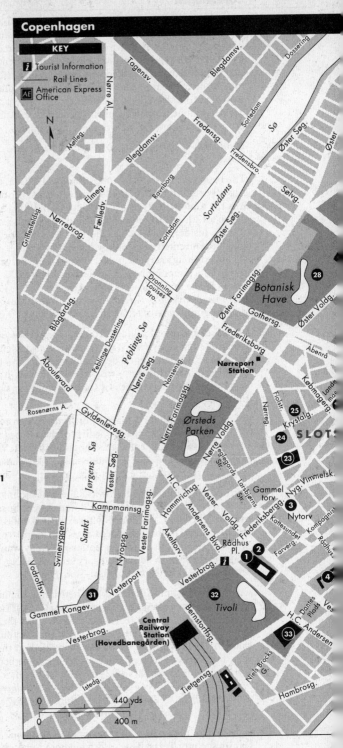

Copenhagen

KEY

🛈 Tourist Information
— Rail Lines
AE American Express
Office

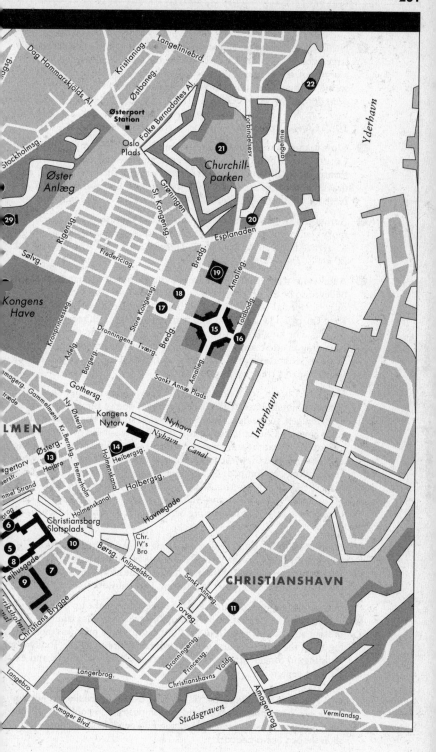

on the artists of Denmark's Golden Age. ⊠ *Porthusgade 2,* ☎ *33/32–15–32.* 🖾 *Free.* ⊘ *Tues.–Sun. 10–5.*

❼ Nearby, the **Kongelige Bibliotek** (Royal Library) houses the country's largest collection of books, newspapers, and manuscripts. Look for early records of the Viking journeys to America and Greenland and the statue of the philosopher Søren Kierkegaard in the garden. ⊠ *Christians Brygge 8,* ☎ *33/93–01–11.* 🖾 *Free.* ⊘ *June–Aug., Mon.–Fri. 9–7, Sat. 10–7; Sept.-May, Mon. 9–7, Tues.–Thurs. 9-9, Fri. 9-7, Sat. 10-7. Closed Sundays.*

❽ Close to the library is the **Teatermuseum** (Theater Museum), in the Royal Court Theater built in 1767. Here you can view extensive exhibits on theater and ballet history, then wander around the boxes, stage, and dressing rooms to see where it all happened. ⊠ *Christiansborg Ridebane 18,* ☎ *33/11–51–76.* 🖾 *20 kr.* ⊘ *Wed. 2–4, weekends noon–4.*

❾ Across the street that bears its name is the **Tøjhusmuseet** (Royal Armory), with impressive displays of uniforms, weapons, and armor in an arched hall 200 yards long. ⊠ *Tøjhusgade 3,* ☎ *33/11–60–37.* 🖾 *20 kr.* ⊘ *Tues.–Sun. 10–4.*

❿ A few steps from the Tøjhusmuseet is the old Stock Exchange, **Børsen,** believed to be the oldest such structure still in use—though it functions only on special occasions. It was built by the 16th-century monarch King Christian IV, a scholar and warrior, and the architect of much of the city. The king is said to have had a hand in twisting the tails of the four dragons that form the structure's distinctive green copper spire. With its steep roofs, tiny windows, and gables, the building is one of Copenhagen's treasures.

⓫ From the Børsen, look east across the drawbridge (Knippelsbro) that connects Slotsholmen with Christianshavn, one of the oldest parts of Copenhagen, to the delicate green-and-gold spire of **Vor Frelsers Kirke** (Our Savior's Church). The Gothic structure was built in 1696. Local legend has it that the staircase encircling it was built curling the wrong way around, and that when its architect reached the top and saw what he had done, he jumped. ⊠ *Skt. Annægade 9,* ☎ *31/57–27–98.* 🖾 *Free.* ⊘ *Mar. 15–May, Mon.–Sat. 9–3:30, Sun. noon–3:30; June–Sept., Mon.–Sat. 9–4:30, Sun. noon–4:30; Oct.–Mar. 14, Mon.–Sat. 10–1:30, Sun. noon–1:30. Closed during services and special functions; call ahead.*

⓬ Head back to Strøget, turning left along the Amagertorv section. Toward the end and to the right (⊠ 5 Niels Hemmingsens Gade) is the 18th-century **Helligånds Kirken** (Church of the Holy Ghost). The choir contains a marble font by the sculptor Thorvaldsen.

⓭ In Østergade, the easternmost of the streets that make up Strøget, you cannot miss the green spire of **Nikolaj Kirke** (St. Nicholas Church). The present structure was built in the 20th century; the previous one, dating from the 13th century, was destroyed by fire in 1728. Today the building no longer functions as a church—it's an art gallery and exhibition center.

NEED A BREAK?   **Café Nikolaj** (⊠ Nikolaiplads, ☎ 33/93–16–26), inside the old Nikolaj Kirke, is a good place to stop for a Danish pastry or a light meal. If you have toddlers, there's a small playground adjacent to the church with a slide shaped like a peacock.

Although Strøget is famous as a shopping area, and elegant stores abound, it's also where Copenhagen comes to stroll. Outside the posh displays of the fur and porcelain shops the sidewalks have the festive aura of a street fair.

Kongens Nytorv (the King's New Market) is the square marking the end of Strøget. The **Kongelig Teater** (Royal Theater), home of Danish opera and ballet as well as theater, sits on the south side. The Danish Royal Ballet remains one of the world's great companies, with a repertoire ranging from classical to modern. On the western side of the square you'll see the stately facade of the D'Angleterre, the grandest of Copenhagen's hotels.

★ The street leading southeast out of Kongens Nytorv is **Nyhavn.** A longtime haunt of sailors, the canal area is one of the most gentrified parts of the city: Restaurants and boutiques outnumber the tattoo shops, but on hot summer nights the area still gets rowdy, with Scandinavians reveling against the backdrop of a fleet of old-time sailing ships and well-preserved 18th-century buildings. Hans Christian Andersen lived at numbers 18 and 20. Nearer the harbor are old shipping warehouses, including two—Nyhavn 71 and the Admiral—that have been converted into comfortable hotels.

Turn left at the end of Nyhavn to see the harbor front, then make an immediate left onto Sankt Annæ Plads. Take the third right onto Amaliegade. Continue straight ahead for the **Amalienborg,** the principal royal residence since 1784. When the royal family is at home here during the fall and winter, the Royal Guard and band march through the city at noon to change the palace guard. Amelienborg's other main attraction is the second division of the Royal Collection, housed inside (the first is at Rosenborg). Among the collection's offerings are the study of King Christian IX (1818–1906) and the drawing room of his wife, Queen Louise. Also included are a set of Rococo banquet silver, highlighted by a bombastic Viking ship centerpiece, and a small costume exhibit. ⊠ *Amalienborg Museum,* ☎ *33/12–21–86.* ⊡ *35 kr.* ☉ *May–late Oct., daily 11–4; late Oct.–Apr., Tues.–Sun. 11–4.*

Rest a moment on the palace's harbor side, enjoying the trees and fountains of **Amaliehavn.** Across the square, it's just a step to Bredgade and the **Marmorkirken** (Marble Church), a 19th-century baroque structure with a dome that looks several sizes too large for its base.

Bredgade is also home to the exotic onion domes of the **Russiske Ortodoks Kirke** (Russian Orthodox Church). Farther north up the street is the **Kunstindustrimuseet** (Museum of Decorative Art), with a large selection of European and Asian handicrafts, as well as ceramics, silver, and tapestries. ⊠ *Bredgade 68,* ☎ *33/14–94–52.* ⊡ *35 kr., more for special exhibits.* ☉ *Permanent exhibition: Tues.–Sun. 1–4; special exhibitions: Tues.–Sat. 10–4, Sun. 1–4.*

Just a short way beyond the museum, turn right onto Esplanaden and you'll come to the **Frihedsmuseet** (Liberty Museum), in Churchillparken. It presents an evocative picture of the heroic Danish Resistance movement during World War II, which managed to save 7,000 Jews from the Nazis by hiding them in homes and hospitals, then smuggling them across to Sweden. ⊠ *Churchillparken,* ☎ *33/13–77–14.* ⊡ *Free.* ☉ *Sept. 16–April, Tues.–Sat. 11–3, Sun. 11–4; May–Sept. 15, Tues.–Sat. 10–4, Sun. 10–5.*

At the park's entrance stands the English church, St. Alban's, and, in the center, the **Kastellet** (Citadel), surrounded by two rings of moats. This was the city's main fortress in the 18th century, but, in a grim reversal during World War II, the Germans used it as their headquarters during their occupation of Denmark. ⊡ *Free.* ☉ *6 AM–sunset.*

㉒ Continue on to the Langelinie, which on Sunday is thronged with promenading Danes, and at last to **Den Lille Havfrue** (the Little Mermaid), the 1913 statue commemorating Hans Christian Andersen's lovelorn creation, and the subject of hundreds of travel posters.

㉓ From Langelinie, take the train or bus from Østerport station to the center or wind back the 2.5 km (1.6 mi) through the pedestrian streets. Walk north from the Strøget on Nørregade until you reach **Vor Frue Kirke** (the Church of Our Lady), Copenhagen's cathedral since 1924. The site itself has been a place of worship since the 13th century, when Bishop Absalon built a chapel here. The spare, neoclassical facade is a 19th-century innovation repairing damage suffered during Nelson's bombing of the city in 1801. If the church is open, you can see Thorvaldsen's marble sculptures of Christ and the Apostles. ⊠ *Nørregade, Frue Plads,* ☎ *33/15–10–78.* ⊙ *Times irregular.*

㉔ Head north up Fjolstræde until you come to the main part of the **Universitet** (University), built in the 19th century on the site of the medieval bishops' palace. Past the university, turn right onto Krystalgade. On the **㉕** left is **Københavns Synagoge** (Copenhagen Synagogue), designed by the contemporary architect Gustav Friedrich Hetsch. Hetsch borrowed from the Doric and Egyptian styles in creating the arklike structure.

㉖ Just across Købmagergade is the **Rundetårn,** a round tower built as an observatory in 1642 by Christian IV. It is said that Peter the Great of Russia drove a horse and carriage up the 600 feet of the inner staircase. You'll have to walk, but the view is worth it. ⊠ *Købmagergade 52A,* ☎ *33/93–66–60.* 🎟 *15 kr.* ⊙ *Sept.–May, Mon.–Sat. 10–5, Sun. noon–4; June–Aug., Mon.–Sat. 10–8, Sun. noon–8.* ⊙ *Observatory and telescope, with astronomer on hand to answer questions, mid-Oct.–mid-Mar., Tues.–Wed. 7–10.*

★ **㉗** Turn right at Rundetårn onto Landemærket, then left onto Åbenrå until you reach Nørre Voldgade, where you turn right and cross Gothersgade to Øster Voldgade, which will bring you to **Rosenborg Slot.** This Renaissance palace—built by jack of all trades Christian IV—houses the Crown Jewels, as well as a collection of costumes and royal memorabilia. Don't miss Christian IV's pearl-studded saddle. ⊠ *Øster Voldgade 4A,* ☎ *33/15–32–86.* 🎟 *40 kr.* ⊙ *Castle: late-Oct.–Apr., Tues., Fri., and Sun. 11–2; treasury: Tues.–Sun. 11–3; both: May, Sept.–late-Oct., daily 11–3; June–Aug., daily 10–4.*

㉘ The palace is surrounded by gardens, and just across Øster Voldgade is the **Botanisk Have,** Copenhagen's 25-acre botanical gardens, with a rather spectacular Palm House containing tropical and subtropical plants. Also on the grounds are an observatory and a geological museum. 🎟 *Free.* ⊙ *May–Aug., daily 8:30–6; Sept.–Apr., daily 8:30–4* ⊙ *Palm House daily 10–3.*

㉙ Leave the gardens through the north exit to get to the **Statens Museum for Kunst** (National Art Gallery), where the collection includes works of Danish art from the Golden Age (early 19th century) to the present, as well as paintings by Rubens, Dürer, and the Impressionists, and other European masters. Particularly fine are the museum's 20 Matisses. ⊠ *Sølvgade 48–50,* ☎ *33/91–21–26.* 🎟 *20 kr. (30 kr. for special exhibitions).* ⊙ *Tues.–Sun. 10–4:30, Wed. until 9 PM.*

NEED A BREAK? | The museum's subterranean **cafeteria** is an excellent place to stop for lunch or coffee. Art posters deck the walls, and a cheerful staff serves hearty lunches.

③⓪ A nearby building houses the **Hirschsprungske Samling** (Hirschprung Collection) of 19th-century Danish art. This cozy museum contains works from the Golden Age, as well as a collection of paintings by the late-19th-century artists of the Skagen school. ⊠ *Stockholmsgade 20,* ☎ *31/42–03–36.* ⌨ *20 kr.; higher for special exhibitions.* ☉ *Thurs.–Mon. 11–4, Wed. 11–9, Tues. closed.*

From Stockholmsgade, turn right onto Sølvgade and then left onto Øster Søgade, just before the bridge. Continue along the canal (the street name will change from Øster Søgade to Nørre Søgade to Vester Søgade) until you reach the head of the harbor.

③① Tucked between St. Jorgens Lake and the main arteries of Vester Søgade and Gammel Kongevej is the **Tycho Brahe Planetarium.** This modern cylindrical building is filled with astronomy exhibits and an Omnimax theater that takes visitors on a simulated journey up into space and down into the depths of the seas. Because these films can be disorienting, planetarium officials do not recommend them for children under 7. ⊠ *Gammel Kongevej 10,* ☎ *33/12–12–24.* ⌨ *Exhibition and theater, 65 kr.; exhibition only, 15 kr. Reservations advised for theater.* ☉ *Daily 10:30–9; films shown 11–9.*

★ ☞ ③② Walk straight ahead and turn left onto Vesterbrogade. On the right lies Copenhagen's best-known attraction, **Tivoli.** In the 1840s, the Danish architect Georg Carstensen persuaded King Christian VIII that an amusement park would be the perfect opiate for the masses, arguing that "when people amuse themselves, they forget politics." In the season from May to September, about 4 million people come through the gates. Tivoli is more sophisticated than a mere funfair: It offers a pantomime theater and an open-air stage, elegant restaurants, and frequent classical, jazz, and rock concerts. On weekends there are elaborate fireworks displays. Try to see Tivoli at least once by night, when the trees are illuminated along with the Chinese Pagoda and the main fountain. ☎ *33/15–10–01.* ⌨ *Mon.–Sat., 11–1, 30 kr.; 1–9:30, 44 kr.; 9:30–midnight, 20 kr; Sun. 11–9:30, 30 kr., 9:30–midnight, 20 kr.* ☉ *May–mid-Sept., daily 11 AM–midnight.*

★ ③③ At the southern end of the gardens, on Hans Christian Andersens Boulevard, is the **Ny Carlsberg Glyptotek** (New Carlsberg Picture Gallery). This elaborate neoclassical building houses a collection of works by Gauguin, Degas, and other Impressionists, as well as Egyptian, Greek, Roman, and French sculpture. ⊠ *Dantes Plads 7,* ☎ *33/41–81–41.* ⌨ *15 kr., free on Wed. and Sun.* ☉ *Sept.–Apr., Tues.–Sat. noon–3, Sun. 10–4; May–Aug., Tues.–Sun. 10–4.*

Excursions from Copenhagen

Shakespeare immortalized both the town and the castle when he chose **Helsingør's Kronborg Castle** as the setting for *Hamlet.* Completed in 1585, the present gabled and turreted structure is about 600 years younger than the fortress we imagine as the setting of Shakespeare's tragedy. Inside are a 200-foot-long dining hall, the luxurious chapel, and the royal chambers. The ramparts and 12-foot-thick walls are a reminder of the castle's role as coastal bulwark—Sweden is only a few miles away. The town—about 29 miles north of Copenhagen—has a number of picturesque streets with 16th-century houses. There is frequent train service to Helsingør station, and then it's a 20-minute walk around the harbor to the castle. ⊠ *Helsingør,* ☎ *49/21–30–78.* ⌨ *30 kr.* ☉ *Easter and May–Sept., daily 10:30–5; Oct. and Apr., Tues.–Sun. 11–4; Nov.–Mar., Tues.–Sun. 11–3.*

★ **Louisiana** is a world-class modern art collection housed in a spectacular building in Humlebæk—part of the "Danish Riviera" on the North Zealand coast. Even if you can't tell a Rauschenberg from a Rembrandt, you should make the 35-kilometer (22-mile) trip to see the setting: It's an elegant, rambling structure set in a large park with views of the sound, and, on a clear day, Sweden. The new children's wing has pyramid-shape chalkboards, kid-proof computers, and weekend activities under the guidance of an artist or museum coordinator. It's a half-hour train ride from Copenhagen to Humlebæk. A 10-minute walk from the station, the museum is also accessible by the E4 highway and the more scenic Strandvejen, or coastal road. ⊠ *Gammel Strandvej 13, Humlebæk,* ☎ *42/19–07–19.* ⊙ *48 kr.; combined train fare (from Copenhagen) and admission 85 kr. available from DSB; prices higher for special exhibitions.* ⊙ *Daily 10–5, Wed. until 10.*

For a look into the past, head 30 kilometers (19 miles) west of Copenhagen to the bustling market town of **Roskilde.** A key administrative center during Viking times, it remained one of the largest towns in northern Europe through the Middle Ages. Today, the legacy of its 1,000-year history lives on in its spectacular cathedral. Built on the site of one of Denmark's first churches, the **Domkirke** (cathedral) has been the burial place of Danish royalty since the 15th century. ⊠ *Domkirkepladsen,* ☎ *46/35–27–00.* ⊠ *6 kr.* ⊙ *Times vary; call ahead.*

★ A 10-minute walk south and through the park takes you to the water and to the **Viking Ship Museum.** Inside are five exquisitely reconstructed Viking ships, discovered at the bottom of Roskilde Fjord in 1962. Detailed placards in English chronicle Viking history. There are also English-language films on the excavation and reconstruction. ⊠ *Strandengen, Roskilde,* ☎ *46/35–65–55.* ⊠ *30 kr.* ⊙ *Apr.–Oct., daily 9–5; Nov.–Mar., daily 10–4.*

About halfway between Copenhagen and Helsingør is **Rungstedlund,** the former home of Karen Blixen. The author of *Out of Africa* and several accounts of aristocratic Danish life, Blixen wrote under the pen name Isak Dinesen. The manor house, where she lived as a child and to which she returned in 1931, was opened as a museum in 1991; it exhibits manuscripts as well as photographs and memorabilia documenting her years in Africa and Denmark. The estate is a half-hour train ride from Copenhagen and a 10-minute walk from Rungsted station. ⊠ *Rungsted Strandvej 111, Rungsted Kyst,* ☎ *42/57–10–57.* ⊠ *30 kr.* ⊙ *May–Sept., daily 10–5; Oct.–Apr., Wed.–Fri. 1–4, weekends 11–4.*

Shopping

Specialty Shops

Strøget's pedestrian streets are synonymous with shopping. For glass, try **Holmegaard** (⊠ Østergade 15, ☎ 33/12–44–77), which carries hand-crafted bowls, glasses, and vases. Just off the street is Pistolstræde, a typical old courtyard that's filled with intriguing boutiques. **Magasin** (⊠ Kongens Nytorv 13, ☎ 33/11–44–33), one of the largest department stores in Scandinavia, offers all kinds of clothing and gifts, and has an excellent grocery department. **Illum** (⊠ Østergade 52, ☎ 33/14–40–02) is similar to Magasin, with another fine basement grocery store and eating arcade. Don't confuse Illum with **Illums Bolighus** (⊠ Amagertorv 10, ☎ 33/14–19–41), where designer furnishings, porcelain, quality clothing, and gifts are displayed in near-gallery surroundings. **Royal Copenhagen Porcelain** (⊠ Amagertorv 6, ☎ 33/13–71–81) carries both old and new china, plus porcelain patterns and figurines. **Georg Jensen** (⊠ Amagertorv 4 and Østergade 40, tel 33/11–

40–80) is one of the world's finest silversmiths and gleams with a wide array of silver patterns and jewelry. Don't miss the **Georg Jensen Museum** (✉ Amagertorv 6, ☎ 33/14–02–29), which showcases glass and silver creations ranging from tiny, twisted-glass shot glasses to an $85,000 silver fish dish.

Off the eastern end of Strøget, **Tin Centret** (✉ Ny Østergade 2, ☎ 33/14–82–00) has a large selection of pewter (*tin* means pewter in Danish), some pieces reminiscent of colonial designs, others fashioned in the simple Scandinavian style. Back along Strøget, at furrier **Birger Christensen** (✉ Østergade 38, ☎ 33/11–55–55) you can ogle chic furs. **A. C. Bang** (✉ Østergade 27, ☎ 33/15–17–26) upholds its Old World, old-money aura with impeccable quality. Mid-summer and after-Christmas fur sales offer real savings. **Otto Madsen** (✉ Vesterbrogade 1, tel 33/13–41–10) features lower prices in a less ritzy, more tourist-oriented shop. **FONA** (✉ Østergade 47, ☎ 33/15–90–55) carries stereo equipment, including the superior design and sound of Bang & Olufsen. **Bang & Olufsen** (✉ Østergade 3–5, ☎ 33/15–04–22) offers reasonable prices in its own upscale shop.

Dining

Food remains one of the great pleasures of a stay in Copenhagen, a city with more than 2,000 restaurants. Traditional Danish fare spans all the price categories: You can order a light lunch of traditional smørrebrød, snack from a store kolde bord, or dine out on lobster and Limfjord oysters. If you are strapped for cash, you can enjoy fast food Danish style, in the form of *pølser* (hot dogs) sold from trucks on the street. Team any of this with some pastry from a bakery (they're the shops displaying an upside-down gold pretzel), and you've got yourself a meal on the go. Most restaurants close for Christmas, roughly from December 24 through December 31.

$$$$ ✕ **Kong Hans Kaelder.** Five centuries ago, this was a Nordic vineyard,
★ but now it's one of Scandinavia's finest restaurants. Chef Daniel Letz's French-inspired cooking is superb. The setting is subterranean and mysterious, with whitewashed arching ceilings, candles, and wood carvings. ✉ *Vingårdstræde 6,* ☎ *33/11–68–68. AE, DC, MC, V. Dinner only. Closed Sun. and July.*

$$$$ ✕ **Krogs.** This elegant canal-front restaurant commands a loyal clientele, both foreign and local; it's decorated with pale green walls, mirrored ceilings, and paintings of old Copenhagen. The menu (printed in five languages) lists such specialties as Canadian lobster flambé and poached Norwegian salmon served with spinach, cranberries, and saffron. ✉ *Gammel Strand 38,* ☎ *33/15–89–15. Reservations essential. AE, DC, MC, V.*

$$$$ ✕ **Skt. Gertrud's Kloster.** The history of this monastery goes back 700
★ years. The dining room is bedecked with hundreds of icons, the only light provided by 2,000 candles. The French menu is extensive, with such specials as fillet of halibut with lobster glacé and duck breast in tarragon sauce. ✉ *Hauser Plads 32,* ☎ *33/14–66–30. Reservations essential. AE, DC, MC, V. Dinner only.*

$$$ ✕ **Els.** When it opened in 1853, the intimate Els was the place to be
★ seen before the theater, and the painted muses on the walls still watch diners rush to make an 8 o'clock curtain. Antique wooden columns and Royal Copenhagen tile tables complement a nouvelle Danish and French menu that changes daily and features game, fish, and market-fresh produce. ✉ *Store Strandstæde 3,* ☎ *33/14–13–41. AE, DC, MC, V.*

$$$ ✕ **L'Alsace.** Set in the cobbled courtyard of Pistolstraede and hung with paintings by Danish surrealist Wilhelm Freddie, this restaurant is peaceful and quiet, attracting such diverse diners as Queen Margrethe and Pope Paul II. The hand-drawn menu includes a hearty *choucroute* (sauerkraut) with sausage and pork, as well as superb fruit tarts and cakes. ⊠ *Ny Østergade 9,* ☎ *33/14–57–43. AE, DC, MC, V. Closed Sun.*

$$$ ✗ **Pakhuskælderen.** Surrounded by thick white walls and raw timbers, the Nyhavn 71 hotel's intimate restaurant attracts a mix of business and holiday guests and is known for its fresh, classically prepared seafood, as well as its Danish-French specialties. ⊠ *Nyhavn 71,* ☎ *33/11–85–85. Reservations essential. AE, DC, MC, V. Dinner only.*

$$ ✗ **Copenhagen Corner.** For a reasonable price, diners get a great view of the Rådhus Pladsen and terrific smørrebrød—both of which compensate for often slack service provided by an overworked staff. Waiters hustle platters of herring, steak, and other Danish and French dishes, and businesspeople clink glasses. In summer you can eat outside—or sit inside, where plants hang from the ceiling. ⊠ *Rådhus Pladsen,* ☎ *33/91–45–45. AE, DC, MC, V.*

$$ ✗ **El Meson.** Ceiling-hung pottery, knowledgeable waiters, and a top-notch menu make this Copenhagen's best Spanish restaurant. Choose carefully for a moderately priced meal, which might include beef spiced with spearmint, lamb with honey sauce, or paella for two. ⊠ *Hauser Plads 12,* ☎ *33/11–91–31. AE, DC, MC, V. Dinner only. Closed Sun.*

$$ ✗ **Havfruen.** A life-size wooden mermaid swings decorously from the ceiling in this small, rustic fish restaurant in Nyhavn. Natives love the maritime-bistro ambience and the daily changing French and Danish menu. ⊠ *Nyhavn 39,* ☎ *33/11–11–38. DC, MC, V. Closed Sun.*

$$ ✗ **Ida Davidsen.** Five generations old, this world-renowned lunch spot
★   has become synonymous with smørrebrød. Choose from creative open-face sandwiches, piled high with such ingredients as pâté, bacon, and steak tartare, or opt for smoked duck served with a beet salad and potatoes. ⊠ *Skt. Kongensgade 70,* ☎ *33/91–36–55. Reservations essential. DC, MC, V. Lunch only. Closed weekends and July.*

$$ ✗ **Peder Oxe.** On a historic square, this lively bistro is countrified, with rustic antiques and 15th-century Portuguese tiles. Grilled steaks and fish—and some of the best burgers in town—come with an excellent salad bar. ⊠ *Gråbrødretorv 11,* ☎ *33/11–00–77. DC, MC, V.*

$$ ✗ **Victor.** This French-style corner café has great people-watching and bistro fare. It's best during weekend lunches, when young and old gather for specialties like rib roast, homemade pâté, smoked salmon, and cheese platters. Careful ordering here can get you an inexpensive meal. ⊠ *Ny Østergade 8,* ☎ *33/13–36–13. AE, DC, MC, V.*

$ ✗ **Flyvefisken.** Silvery stenciled fish swim along blue-and-yellow stenciled walls in this funky Thai eatery. Among the city's more experimental (and spicy) restaurants, it offers chicken with cashews, spicy shrimp soup with lemongrass, and herring shark in basil sauce. There is also a less expensive health-food café in the basement. ⊠ *Larsbjørnsstræde 18,* ☎ *33/14–95–15. AE, DC, MC, V. Closed Sun.*

$ ✗ **Quattro Fontane.** On a corner west of the lakes, one of Copenhagen's best Italian restaurants is a busy, noisy, two-story affair, packed tight with marble-top tables and a steady flow of young Danes. Chatty Italian waiters serve cheese or beef ravioli, cannelloni, linguine with clam sauce, and thick pizza. ⊠ *Guldbersgade 3,* ☎ *31/39–39–31. Weekend reservations essential. No credit cards.*

$ ✗ **Riz Raz.** On a corner off Strøget, this Middle Eastern restaurant hops with young locals who pack it on weekends. The very inexpensive all-you-can-eat buffet is heaped with healthy dishes, including lentils, falafel, bean salads, and occasionally pizza. ⊠ *Kompagnistræde 20,* ☎ *33/15–05–75. Weekend reservations essential. DC, MC, V.*

Lodging

Copenhagen is well served by a wide range of hotels, which are almost always clean, comfortable, and well run. Most Danish hotels include a substantial breakfast in the room rate, but this isn't always the case. Summertime reservations are always recommended, but if you should arrive without one, try the hotel booking service in the tourist office. They can also give you a "same-day, last-minute price," which is about 200–250 kr. for a single hotel room. This service will also locate rooms in private homes, with rates starting at about 140 kr. for a single. Young travelers should head for Use It (Huset) at Rådhusstræde 13 (☎ 33/15–65–18). For details and price-category definitions, *see* Lodging *in* Staying in Denmark, *above.*

$$$$ ⚑ **D'Angleterre.** The grande dame of Copenhagen hotels has under-
★ gone major renovations and changes over the past couple of years, in-cluding the addition of a swimming pool and a nightclub. Luckily, the hotel still retains its Old World, old-money aura. The rooms are done in pinks and blues, with overstuffed chairs and antique escritoires and armoires. Bathrooms shine with brass, mahogany, and marble. ⊠ *Kongens Nytorv 34, DK 1051 KBH K,* ☎ *33/12–00–95,* FAX *33/12–11–18. 130 rooms with bath. 2 restaurants, bar, pool, barbershop, beauty salon, nightclub. AE, DC, MC, V.*

$$$$ ⚑ **Nyhavn 71.** In a 200-year-old warehouse, this quiet hotel is a good choice for privacy-seekers. It overlooks the old ships of Nyhavn, and the maritime interiors have been preserved with their original plaster walls and exposed brick. Rooms are tiny but cozy, with warm woolen spreads, dark woods, soft leather furniture, and crisscrossing timbers. ⊠ *Nyhavn 71, DK 1051 KBH K,* ☎ *33/11–85–85,* FAX *33/93–15–85. 82 rooms with bath. Restaurant, bar. AE, DC, MC, V.*

$$$$ ⚑ **SAS Scandinavia.** Near the airport, this is one of northern Europe's largest hotels and Copenhagen's token skyscraper. The immense lobby is streamlined and modern, as are the rooms—a good choice if you pre-fer convenience to character. ⊠ *Amager Blvd. 70, DK 2300 KBH S,* ☎ *33/11–23–24,* FAX *31/57–01–93. 542 rooms with bath. 4 restaurants, bar, coffee shop, pool, sauna, fitness center, casino. AE, DC, MC, V.*

$$$ ⚑ **Kong Frederik.** West of Rådhus Pladsen, near Strøget, this intimate hotel is a cozy version of its grand sister, D'Angleterre. The sunny Queen's Garden restaurant serves a breakfast buffet; rooms are elegant with Oriental vases, mauve carpets, and plain blue spreads. ⊠ *Vester Voldgade 25, DK 1552 KBH K,* ☎ *33/12–59–02,* FAX *33/93–59–01. 110 rooms with bath, 17 suites. Restaurant, bar, room service, meet-ing rooms, parking. Breakfast not included. AE, DC, MC, V.*

$$$ ⚑ **Neptun.** The centrally situated Neptun has been in business for nearly 150 years and shows no signs of flagging. Guest rooms are decorated with blond wood and are often reserved by American visitors. ⊠ *Skt. Annæ Plads 18, DK 1250 KBH K,* ☎ *33/13–89–00,* FAX *33/14–12–50. 137 rooms with bath, 10 apartments. Restaurant, café, meeting rooms. AE, DC, MC, V.*

$$$ ⚑ **The Phoenix.** This luxury hotel welcomes guests with automatic glass doors, crystal chandeliers, and gilt touches everywhere. The staff switches languages as they register business and cruise guests. Suites and executive-class rooms have Biedermeier-style furniture and 18-karat-gold bathroom fixtures, but the standard rooms are very small, at barely 9′ × 15′. Light sleepers should ask for a room above the second floor to avoid street noise. ⊠ *Bredgade 37, DK 1260 KBH K,* ☎ *33/95–95–00,* FAX *33/33–98–33. 212 rooms with bath, 7 suites. Restaurant, pub (closed Sun.), meeting room. AE, DC, MC, V.*

\$\$ ⛫ **Ascot.** A charming old building downtown, this family-owned hotel has a classically columned entrance and an excellent breakfast buffet. Rooms have colorful geometric-pattern bedspreads and cozy bathrooms. A few have kitchenettes. Repeat guests often ask for their regular rooms. ⊠ *Studiestræde 61, DK 1554 KBH K,* ☎ *33/12–60–00,* FAX *33/14–60–40. 143 rooms with bath, 30 apartments. Restaurant (breakfast only), bar, exercise room, meeting rooms. AE, DC, MC, V.*

\$\$ ⛫ **Copenhagen Admiral.** Overlooking old Copenhagen and Amalienborg, the monolithic Admiral was once a grain warehouse, but now affords travelers no-nonsense accommodations. With massive stone walls broken by rows of tiny windows, it's one of the less expensive top hotels, cutting frills and prices. Guest rooms are spare, with jutting beams and modern prints. ⊠ *Toldbodgade 24–28, DK 1253 KBH K,* ☎ *33/11–82–82,* FAX *33/32–55–42. 365 rooms with bath. Restaurant, bar, café, sauna, nightclub. AE, DC, MC, V.*

\$\$ ⛫ **Triton.** Despite its seedy surroundings, this streamlined hotel attracts a cosmopolitan clientele thanks to a central location in Vesterbro. The large rooms, in blond wood and warm tones, have almost all been updated with new bathrooms and state-of-the-art fixtures. The buffet breakfast is exceptionally generous, the staff friendly. There are also family rooms, each with a separate bedroom and foldout couch. ⊠ *Helgolandsgade 7–11, DK 1653 KBH K,* ☎ *31/31–32–66,* FAX *31/31–69–70. 123 rooms with bath. Restaurant (breakfast only), bar. AE, DC, MC, V.*

\$ ⛫ **Cab-Inn Scandinavia.** Popular with business travelers in winter and kroner-pinching backpackers and families in summer, Copenhagen's answer to Japanese-style hotel minirooms is more cozy than futuristic, with shiplike "berths" brightly decorated. All offer standard hotel furnishings, including a private shower and a small wall-hung desk with chair. Around the corner, on Danasvej 32, is a sister hotel, the Cab-Inn Copenhagen, with 86 rooms. ⊠ *Vodroffsvej 55, DK 1900 FR C,* ☎ *35/36–11–11,* FAX *35/36–11–14. 201 rooms with shower. Café, exercise room. AE, DC, MC, V.*

\$ ⛫ **Missionhotellet Nebo.** This budget hotel is located between the main train station and Istedgade's seediest porn shops. Nonetheless, it's a prim hotel, comfortable and well maintained by a friendly staff. The dormlike guest rooms are furnished with industrial carpeting, polished pine furniture, and gray-striped duvet covers. There are baths, showers, and toilets at the center of each hallway, and downstairs there's a breakfast restaurant with a tiny courtyard. ⊠ *Istedgade 6, DK 1650 KBH V,* ☎ *31/21–12–17,* FAX *31/23–47–74. 96 rooms, 40 with bath. AE, DC, MC, V.*

The Arts

Copenhagen This Week has good information on musical and theatrical happenings, as well as on special events and exhibitions. Concert and festival information is available from the **Dansk Musik Information Center** (⊠ DMIC, Gråbrødretorv 16, ☎ 33/11–20–66). Copenhagen's main theater and concert season runs from September through May, and tickets can be obtained either directly from theaters and concert halls or from ticket agencies; ask your hotel concierge for advice. Billetnet (☎ 35/28-91-83), the post-office box office, has tickets for most major events. Keep in mind that same-day purchases at the box office ARTE (near the Nørreport station) are half price. There is no phone number, so you must show up in person.

Tivoli Concert Hall (⊠ Vesterbrogade 3, ☎ 33/15–10–12) offers more than 150 concerts each summer, featuring a host of Danish and foreign soloists, conductors, and orchestras.

The **Royal Theater** (⌧ Kongens Nytorv, ☎ 33/14–10–02) regularly holds theater, ballet, and opera performances. For English-language theater, call either the professional **London Toast Theatre** (☎ 33/33–80–25) or the amateur **Copenhagen Theatre Circle** (☎ 31/62–86–20).

Copenhagen natives are avid **movie** buffs, and as the Danes rarely dub films or television imports, you can often see original American and British movies and TV shows.

Nightlife

Many of the city's restaurants, cafés, bars, and clubs stay open after midnight, some as late as 5 AM. Copenhagen is famous for jazz, but you'll find night spots catering to musical tastes ranging from bop to ballroom music. Younger tourists should make for the district around the **Nikolaj Kirke,** which has scores of trendy discos and dance spots, with admission ranging between 40 and 50 kr., and beer about half that. **Privé** (⌧ Ny Østergade 14, tel.33/13-75-20) is a trendy, Euro-techno-pop disco, favored by the young and painfully chic. **Rosie McGee's** (⌧ Vesterbrogade 2A, ☎ 33/32-19-23) is hugely popular with a mixed crowd of young and old, who come for the international pop and rock, cavernous English-pub atmosphere, and good-natured rowdiness.

A few streets behind the railway station is Copenhagen's red-light district, where sex shops share space with grocers. Although the area is fairly well lighted and lively, women may feel uncomfortable here alone at night.

Nightclubs

Some of the most exclusive nightclubs are in the biggest hotels. At **Fellini's** in the SAS Royal (⌧ Hammerichsgade 1, ☎ 33/93–32–39), modern, cabaret-style dancers attract lots of Scandinavian businessmen, who come to ogle while downing outrageously priced booze.

Jazz

Many of Copenhagen's sophisticated jazz clubs have closed in the past couple of years. **La Fontaine** (⌧ Kompagnistræde 11) is Copenhagen's quintessential jazz dive, with sagging curtains, impenetrable smoke, crusty lounge lizards and the random barmaid nymph; for jazz lovers, the bordello atmosphere and Scandinavian jazz talent make this a must. **Copenhagen Jazz House** (⌧ Niels Hemmingsensgade 10, ☎ 33/15-26-00) is infinitely more upscale than La Fontaine, attracting European and some international names to its chic, modern barlike ambience. **Jazzhus Slukefter** (⌧ Vesterbrogade 3, ☎ 33/11-11-13) is Tivoli's jazz club, and lures some of the biggest names in the world.

FUNEN AND THE CENTRAL ISLANDS

It was Hans Christian Andersen, the region's most famous native, who dubbed Fyn (Funen) the "Garden of Denmark." Part orchard, part farmland, Funen is sandwiched between Zealand and Jutland, and with its tidy, rolling landscape, seaside towns, manor houses, and castles, it is one of Denmark's loveliest islands. Its capital—1,000-year-old Odense, in the north—is the birthplace of Hans Christian Andersen; his life and works are immortalized here in two museums. Funen is also the site of two of Denmark's best-preserved castles: 12th-century Nyborg Slot, in the east, and 16th-century Egeskov Slot, near Svendborg, in the south. From Svendborg it's easy to hop on a ferry and visit some of the smaller islands, such as Tåsinge, Langeland, and Ærø, whose main town, Ærøskøbing, with its twisting streets and half-timber houses, seems caught in a time warp.

Getting Around

The best starting point is Nyborg, on Funen's east coast, just across the Great Belt from Korsør, on Zealand. (At press time, "the other Chunnel," this one connecting Zealand to Funen, was scheduled to open for rail traffic some time at the end of 1996.) From Nyborg, the easiest way to travel is by car, though public transportation is good. Distances on Funen and its islands are short, but there is much to see and you can easily spend two or three days here, circling the islands from Nyborg or using Odense or Svendborg as a base from which to make excursions.

Guided Tours

There are few organized tours of any area of Denmark outside Copenhagen. However, Odense has a two-hour tour that operates Monday through Saturday during July and August and focuses on native son Hans Christian Andersen.

A day trip to Odense leaves from Copenhagen's city-hall square at 9 AM every Sunday from mid-May to mid-September. Lasting about 11 hours, the trip includes stops at several picturesque villages and a lightning-speed visit to Egeskov Slot.

Visitor Information

Nyborg (⊠ Torvet 9, ☎ 65/31–02–80); **Odense** (⊠ Rådhuset, ☎ 66/12–75–20); **South Fyn Tourist Board** (⊠ Centrumpladsen, Svendborg, ☎ 62/21–09–80).

Exploring Funen and the Central Islands

The 13th-century town of **Nyborg** was Denmark's capital during the Middle Ages, as well as an important stop on a major trading route between Zealand and Jutland. From 1200 to 1413, Nyborg housed the Danehof, the early Danish parliament. Nyborg's major landmark is its 12th-century castle, **Nyborg Slot.** It was here that Erik Glipping granted the first Danish constitution, the Great Charter, in 1282. ⊠ *Slotspladsen,* ☎ *65/31–02–07.* 🎫 *20 kr.* ☉ *Mar.–May, Tues.–Sun. 10– 3; June–Aug., daily 10–5; Sept.–Oct., Tues.–Sun. 10–3.*

Take Route 165 20 kilometers (12½ miles) along the coast to **Kerteminde,** Funen's most important fishing village and a picturesque summer resort. Stroll down Langegade to see its half-timber houses.

If you're a Viking enthusiast, head a few kilometers south to the village of **Ladby.** Stop here to see the **Ladbyskibet,** the 1,100-year-old underground remains of a Viking chieftain's burial, complete with his 72-foot-long ship. The warrior was equipped for his trip to Valhalla (the afterlife) with his weapons, 4 hunting dogs, and 11 horses. ⊠ *Vikingevej 123,* ☎ *65/32–16–67.* 🎫 *20 kr.* ☉ *Mar.–mid-May, daily 10–4; mid-May–mid-Sept., daily 10–6; mid-May–Oct., daily 10–4; Nov.–Feb., weekends 11-3.*

Twenty kilometers (12½ miles) southwest on Route 165 lies **Odense,** Denmark's third-largest city. Plan on spending at least one night here; in addition to its museums and pleasant pedestrian streets, Odense is an especially charming provincial capital.

🕭 If you can't take quaintness, don't go to the **H. C. Andersens Hus** (Hans Christian Andersen Museum). The surrounding area has been carefully preserved, with cobbled pedestrian streets and low houses with lace curtains. Inside, exhibits use photos, diaries, drawings, and let-

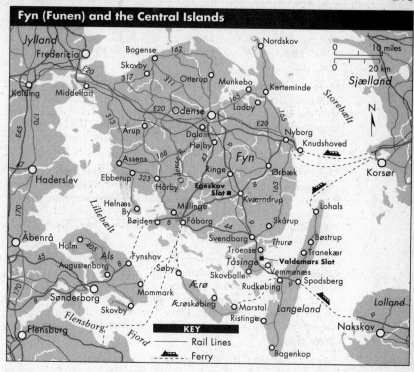

ters to convey a sense of the man and the time in which he lived. Attached to the museum is an extensive library with Andersen's works in more than 127 languages (he was in fact one of the most widely published authors in the history of literature), where you can listen to fairy tales on tape. ⊠ *Hans Jensenstraede 37–45,* ☎ *66/13–13–72.* ☞ *25 kr. adults, 10 kr. children under 14.* ☉ *Sept.–May, daily 10–4; June–Aug., daily 9–6.*

Nearby is the **Carl Nielsen Museum,** a modern structure with multimedia exhibits on Denmark's most famous composer (1865–1931) and his wife, the sculptor Anne Marie Carl-Nielsen. ⊠ *Claus Bergsgade 11,* ☎ *66/13–13–72, ext. 4671.* ☞ *15 kr.* ☉ *Daily 10–4.*

Møntergården, Odense's museum of cultural and urban history, fills four houses representing Danish architectural styles from the Renaissance to the 18th century, all grouped around a shady cobbled courtyard. Inside are dioramas, an extensive coin collection, clothed dummies, toys, and tableaus. ⊠ *Overgade 48–50.* ☞ *15 kr.* ☉ *Daily 10–4.*

Brandt's Passage, off Vestergade, is a heavily boutiqued walking street. At the end of it, in what was once a textile factory, is a four-story art
★ gallery, the **Brandts Klædefabrik,** incorporating the **Museum for Photographic Art,** the **Graphic Museum,** and **Kunst Hallen** (Art Hall), with temporary exhibits for video art. It's well worth the short walk to see Funen's version of a New York Soho loft. ⊠ *37–43 Brandts Passage,* ☎ *66/13–78–97.* ☞ *Photography or graphics museum 20 kr.; Kunst Hallen, 25 kr.; combined 40 kr.* ☉ *Sept.–June, Tues.–Sun. 10–5; July and Aug., daily 10–5.*

Don't neglect **Den Fynske Landsby** (Funen Village), 3 kilometers (2 miles) south; an enjoyable way of getting there is to travel down the Odense River by boat. The open-air museum-village is made up of 20 farm buildings, including workshops, a vicarage, a water mill, and a windmill. There's a theater, too, with summertime adaptations of Andersen's tales. ⊠ *Sejerskovvej 20,* ☎ *66/13–13–72, ext. 4642.* ☎ *20 kr.* ☉ *Apr.–mid-May and mid-Sept.–Oct., daily 10–5; mid-May–mid-Sept., daily 10–7.*

Head 30 kilometers (18 miles) south on Route 43 to **Fåborg,** a lovely little town dating from the 12th century. Four times a day, it echoes with the dulcet chiming of the Klokketårnet's (belfry's) carillon, the largest in Funen. Dating from 1725, the **Gamla Gård** (Old Merchant's House) chronicles the cultural history of Funen. ⊠ *Holkegade 1,* ☎ *62/61–33–38.* ☎ *20 kr.* ☉ *Mid-May–mid-Sept., daily 10:30–4:30.*

Visit the **Fåborg Museum for Fynsk Malerkunst.** This gallery features the compositions—dating mainly from 1880 to 1920—of the Funen Painters, filled with the dusky light that so often illuminates Scandinavian painting. ⊠ *Grønnegade 75,* ☎ *62/61–06–45.* ☎ *25 kr.* ☉ *Apr.–May and Sept.–Oct., daily 10–4; June–Aug., daily 10–5; Nov.–Mar., daily 11–3.*

From Fåborg, take the car ferry to Søby at the northern tip of **Ærø Island,** the "Jewel of the Archipelago," where roads wend through fertile fields and past thatched farmhouses. South from Søby 13 kilometers (8 miles) on Route 16 is the charming town of Ærøskøbing, on the island's north coast. Once you've spent an hour walking through its cobbled 17th- and 18th-century streets, you'll understand its great appeal.

From Ærøskøbing, the ferry takes just over an hour to reach Svendborg, the southernmost town in Funen. Svendborg is also the gateway to the country's southern islands, so leave it for the moment and cross over the bridge onto the tiny island of **Tåsinge.**

On Tåsinge, pretty **Troense** is one of Denmark's best-preserved villages. Once the home port for countless sailing ships, both commercial and Viking, today the harbor is stuffed with pleasure yachts.

Dating from around 1640, **Valdemars Slot,** now a sumptuously furnished home, is one of Denmark's oldest privately owned castles. Upstairs rooms are furnished to the smallest detail. Downstairs is the castle church, illuminated only by candlelight. There's a restaurant (☞ Dining and Lodging, *below*) beneath the church. The café overlooks Lunkebugten, a bay with one of south Funen's best stretches of beach. ⊠ *Slotsalleen 100, Troense,* ☎ *62/22–61–06.* ☎ *45 kr.* ☉ *Times vary greatly; call for details.*

Tåsinge is connected with the island of **Langeland** by a causeway-bridge. The largest island in the southern archipelago, Langeland is rich in relics of the past, and the beaches are worth scouting out.

Head back now, passing through Tåsinge, to Funen's **Svendborg.** Just
★ north of town is **Egeskov Slot,** one of the best-preserved island castles in Europe. Egeskov means "oak forest," and an entire one was felled around 1540 to form the piles on which the rose-stone structure was erected. The park contains noteworthy Renaissance, Baroque, English, and peasant gardens and an antique-car museum. Though this is still a private home, a few rooms, including the trophy-filled hunting room, are open to the public. ⊠ *Egeskovgade 18, Kværndrup,* ☎ *62/27–10–16.* ☎ *To castle and museum, 100 kr.* ☉ *Castle: May–June, Aug.–Sept., daily 10–5; July 10–8; museum: May and Sept., daily 10–5; June and Aug. 9–6, July 9–8.*

Dining and Lodging

Funen has a wide range of hotels and inns, many of which offer off-season (October through May) rates, as well as special weekend deals. The islands are also furnished with numerous campsites and youth hostels, all clean and attractively located. Some, like Odense's youth hostel, are set in old manor houses. Contact the local tourist office for information.

Ærøskøbing

$$ 🏨 **Ærøhus.** A half-timber building with a steep red roof, the Ærøhus looks like a rustic cottage on the outside, and an old aunt's house on the inside. Hanging pots and slanted walls characterize the public areas; pine furniture and cheerful curtains and duvets keep the guest rooms simple and bright. In an annex are apartments, all with kitchenettes. The garden's eight cottages have small terraces. ⊠ *Vestergade 38, 5970,* ☎ *62/52−10−03,* FAX *62/52−21−23. 30 rooms, 18 with bath; 8 cottages; 37 apartments. Restaurant. Closed Jan.*

Fåborg

$$$$ ✕🏨 **Falsled Kro.** Once a smuggler's hideaway, the 500-year-old Falsled Kro is one of Denmark's most elegant inns. A favorite among well-heeled Europeans, it has sumptuously appointed cottages with European antiques and stone fireplaces. The restaurant combines French and Danish cuisines, using ingredients from its own garden and markets in faraway Lyon. ⊠ *Assensvej 513, 5642 Millinge, 13 km (8 mi) northwest of Fåborg on the Millinge–Assens highway,* ☎ *62/68−11−11,* FAX *62/68−11−62. 14 rooms with bath, 3 apartments. Restaurant. AE, DC, MC. Closed Jan.–Feb.*

$$$ ✕🏨 **Steensgård Herregårdspension.** A long avenue of beeches leads to this 700-year-old moated manor house 7 kilometers (4½ miles) northwest of Fåborg. Rooms are elegant, with antiques, four-poster beds, and yards of silk damask. The fine restaurant serves wild game from the manor's own preserve. ⊠ *Steensgård 4, 5642 Millinge,* ☎ *62/61−94−90,* FAX *62/61−78−61. 15 rooms, 13 with bath. Restaurant, tennis, horseback riding. AE, DC, MC, V. Closed Jan.*

Nyborg

$$$ 🏨 **Hesselet.** This modern hotel looks like a brick slab outside, but inside it's a refined English-cum-Oriental sanctuary. The guest rooms are furnished with cushy, modern furniture, and most have splendid views. ⊠ *Christianslundsvej 119, DK 5800 Nyborg,* ☎ *65/31-30-29,* FAX *65/31-29-58. 46 rooms with bath and shower, 4 suites. Restaurant, room service, indoor pool, sauna, 2 tennis courts, meeting rooms. AE, DC, MC, V.*

Odense

$$$ ✕ **Rudolf Mathis.** You'll enjoy delectable fish and seafood specialties and a splendid view of Kerteminde Harbor at this traditional Danish restaurant. ⊠ *Dosseringen 13, Kerteminde, 13 km (8 mi) northeast of Odense on Rte. 165,* ☎ *65/32−32−33. AE, DC, MC, V. Closed Jan.–Mar.; Sun., Oct.–Dec.; Mon. year-round.*

$$ ✕ **Restaurant Provence.** A few minutes from the pedestrian street, this cozy blue-and-white dining room puts a Danish twist on Provençal cuisine, with such specialties as venison in blackberry sauce and duck breast cooked in sherry. ⊠ *Pogstræde 31,* ☎ *66/12−12−96. DC, MC, V.*

$ ✕ **Målet.** A lively crowd calls this sports club its neighborhood bar. Next to steaming plates of schnitzel served in a dozen ways, soccer is the delight of the house. ⊠ *Jernbanegade 17,* ☎ *66/17−82−41. Reservations not accepted. No credit cards.*

$$$$ 🏨 **Grand Hotel.** They don't make spacious, gracious places like this anymore. Dating from 1897, the Grand offers spruced-up fin-de-siè-cle elegance. The decor is cool and green, with a sweeping staircase and a spectacular Pompeiian-red dining room. Guest rooms are ample and comfortable. ⊠ *Jernbanegade 18, 5000 Odense C,* ☎ *66/11–71–71,* 𝔽𝔸𝕏 *66/14–11–71. 137 rooms with bath. Restaurant, bar, sauna, parking (fee). AE, DC, MC, V.*

$ 🏨 **Hotel Ydes.** This bright, colorful hotel is a good bet for students and budget-conscious travelers tired of barracks-type accommodations. The plain, white, hospital-style rooms are clean and comfortable. ⊠ *Hans Tausensgade 11, 5000 Odense C,* ☎ *66/12–11–31. 30 rooms, 24 with shower. Bar and restaurant. AE, DC, MC, V.*

Svendborg

$$ ✕ **Sandig.** This austere white eatery near the harbor is spartan, but food, not decor, is owner-chef-waiter-dishwasher Volkert Sandig's priority. His daily French and Danish menu includes inventive fish and beef specialties. Try cod with mussel and garlic sauce or roast veal in a creamy mushroom ragout. ⊠ *Kullinggade 1b,* ☎ *62/22–92–11. DC, MC, V. Closed Sun.*

Troense

$$$ ✕ **Restaurant Valdemars Slot.** Beneath the castle, this domed restaurant is all romance and prettiness, with pink carpet and candlelight. Fresh ingredients from France and Germany and wild game from the castle's preserve are the essentials for an ever-changing menu, which includes such specialties as wild venison with cream sauce and duck breast à l'orange. A less expensive annex, Den Gråa Dame, serves traditional Danish food. ⊠ *Slotsalleen 100,* ☎ *62/22–59–00. AE, MC, V. Closed Nov.–Mar. except to groups of 4 or more with several days' notice.*

JUTLAND AND THE LAKES

A region of carefully groomed pastures punctuated by stretches of rugged beauty, the peninsula of Jutland (Jylland) is the only part of Denmark that is attached to the mainland of Europe; its southern boundary forms the frontier with Germany. Moors and sand dunes cover a tenth of the peninsula—the windswept landscapes of Isak Dinesen's short stories can be seen in the northwest—and the remaining land is devoted to agriculture and forestry. On the east side of the peninsula, facing Funen, lie well-wooded fjords, which run inland for miles. Besides rustic towns and stark countryside, Jutland has gracious castles, parklands, and the famed Legoland. Ribe, Denmark's oldest town, lies to the south; to the east is Århus, Denmark's second-largest city, with superb museums and a new concert hall.

Getting Around

If you're following this itinerary directly after the tour around Funen, head northwest from Odense through Middlefart and then on to Vejle. By train, either from Odense or Copenhagen, the starting point is Kolding, to the south of Vejle. Although there is good train and bus service between all the main cities, this tour is best done by car. Delightful though they are, the offshore islands are suitable only for those with a lot of time, as many involve an overnight stay.

Guided Tours

Guided tours are scarce in these parts; stop by any tourist office for maps and suggestions for a walking tour. Århus also offers a "Round and About the City" tour, which leaves from the tourist office daily at 10 AM from mid-June to mid-August.

Visitor Information

Aalborg (⊠ Østerå 8, ☎ 98/12–60–22); **Århus** (⊠ Rådhuset, ☎ 86/12–16–00); **Billund** (⊠ c/o Legoland A/S, ☎ 75/33–19–26); **Herning** (⊠ Bredgade 2, ☎ 97/12–44–22); **Kolding** (⊠ Axeltorv 8, ☎ 75/53–21–00); **Randers** (⊠ Tørvebryggen 12, Erhvervens Hus, ☎ 86/42–44–77); **Ribe** (⊠ Torvet 3–5, ☎ 75/42–15–00); **Silkeborg** (⊠ Åhavevej Haven, ☎ 86/82–19–11); **Vejle** (⊠ Søndergade 14, ☎ 75/82–19–55); **Viborg** (⊠ Nytorv 9, ☎ 86/61–16–66).

Exploring Jutland and the Lakes

If **Kolding** is your starting point, don't miss the well-preserved 13th-century **Koldinghus** castle, a royal residence during the Middle Ages. ☎ 75/50–15–00. 🔊 35 kr. ⊙ Daily 10–5.

The **Geografiske Have** (Geographical Garden) has a rose garden with more than 120 varieties, as well as some 2,000 other plants from all parts of the world, arranged geographically. 🔊 30 kr. ⊙ June and Aug., daily 9–7; July, daily 9–8; Sept.–May, daily 10–6.

Vejle, about 20 kilometers (12 miles) to the north of Kolding, is beautifully positioned on the fjord; amid forest-clad hills, the town looks toward the Kattegat, the strait that divides Jutland and Funen. You can hear an old Dominican monastery clock chiming the hours; the clock survives, but the monastery itself was long since torn down to make room for the town's imposing 19th-century city hall.

Leaving Vejle, take the road 10 kilometers (6 miles) north through the Grejs Valley to **Jelling.** Here you'll find two 10th-century burial mounds, all that remains from the court of King Gorm the Old and his wife, Thyra. Between the mounds are the Jelling runic stones, one of which, "Denmark's Certificate of Baptism," is decorated with the oldest known figure of Christ in Scandinavia. The stone was erected by Gorm's son, King Harald Bluetooth, who brought Christianity to the Danes in AD 960.

Head north toward **Silkeborg,** on the banks of the River Gudenå in Jutland's lake district. The region stretches from Silkeborg in the west to Skanderborg in the east and contains some of Denmark's loveliest scenery, as well as one of the country's meager "mountains." The best way to explore the area is by water; the Gudena winds its way some 160 kilometers (100 miles) through lakes and wooded hillsides down to the sea. You can take one of the excursion boats or, better still, a rare old coal-fired paddle steamer, the *Hjejlen,* which runs in summer and is based at Silkeborg. Ever since 1861 it has been paddling its way through narrow stretches of fjord where the treetops meet overhead to the foot of Denmark's highest hill, the Himmelbjerget, which rises all of 438 feet at Lake Julso. You can clamber up the narrow paths through the heather and trees to the top of the hill, where there is an 80-foot tower erected in 1875 in memory of King Frederik VII.

One of Silkeborg's chief attractions can be seen in the **Kulturhistoriske Museum** (Museum of Cultural History). This is the 2,200-year-old Tollund Man, whose corpse was preserved by the natural chemicals in a nearby bog. ⊠ Hovedgaardsvej 7, ☎ 86/82–14–99. 🔊 20 kr. ⊙ Mid-Apr.–late Oct., daily 10–5; late Oct.–mid-Apr., Wed. and weekends noon–4.

Jylland (Jutland)

0   40 miles

0   60 km

N

KEY

Ferry

Skagen

TO SWEDEN

Hirtshals   Tuen

Hjørring   Frederikshavn

Brønderslev   Sæby

Skagerrak

Hanstholm   Nørresundby

Thisted   Limfjord   Limfjord   Aalborg

Mors   Løgstør   Nibe

Nykøbing Mors

Kattegat

Lemvig   Venø Bugt   Skive   Hadsund

Struer   Hobro

Hobro   Mariager   Råsted

Nissum Fjord   Holstebro   Viborg   Randers

Ribe   Gudenå   Auning   Grenå

Ringkøbing   Herning   Silkeborg   Århus   Ebeltoft

Ringkøbing Fjord   Skjern   Skjernå   Brande   Skanderborg

Grindsted   Givskud   Jelling   Horsens   Samsø

Varde   Billund   Vejle   TO KALUNDBORG

Varde Å   Vejle Fjord

Esbjerg   Holsted   Kolding   Fredericia   Fyn   Storebælt

Fanø   Sønderho   Kongeå   Middelfart   Odense

TO HARWICH, NEWCASTLE   Ribe   Christiansfeld

Rømø   Skærbæk   Vojens   Haderslev   Fåborg   Nyborg

Ribe Å   Åbenrå   Svendborg

On the coast, directly east of Silkeborg, is **Århus,** Denmark's second-largest city. The town is at its liveliest during the 10-day Århus Festival in September, which brings together everything from classical concerts to jazz and folk music, clowning, theater, exhibitions, beer tents, and sports. The town's cathedral, the 15th-century **Domkirke,** is Denmark's longest church; it contains a beautifully executed three-panel altarpiece. Look up at the whimsical sketches on the ceiling.

Nearby is the **Vor Frue Kirke,** (Church of Our Lady) formerly attached to a Dominican abbey. Underneath the 13th-century structure is an eerie but interesting crypt church rediscovered in 1955 and dating from 1060, one of the oldest preserved stone churches in Scandinavia. The vaulted space contains a replica of an old Roman crucifix.

Not to be missed is the town's open-air museum, the **Gamle By** (Old Town). A sophisticated version of Disneyland, it features 65 half-timber houses, a mill, and a millstream. The meticulously re-created period interiors range from the 15th to the early 20th century. ✉ *Viborgvej,* ☎ *86/12–31–88.* 🎟 *40 kr.* ☉ *Jan.–Mar. and Nov., daily 11–3; Apr. and Oct., daily 10–4; May and Sept., daily 10–5; June–Aug., daily 9–6; Dec., Mon.–Sat. 10–3, Sun. 10–4. Grounds always open.*

★ Set in a 250-acre forest in a park south of Århus is the indoor/outdoor **Moesgård Prehistoric Museum,** with exhibits on ethnography and archaeology, including the Grauballe Man, an eerie, well-preserved corpse from 2,000 years ago. Take the Prehistoric Trail through the forest, which leads past Stone and Bronze Age displays to some reconstructed houses from Viking times. ✉ *Ny Moesgård Allé 20, Højbjerg,* ☎ *89/42–11–00 or 89/42–45–45.* 🎟 *25 kr.* ☉ *Mid-Sept.–Apr., Tues.–Sun. 10–4; May–mid-Sept., Tues.–Sun. 10–5.*

Heading north 21 kilometers (15 miles), you'll come to the medieval town of **Randers,** where in 1340 the Danish patriot Niels Ebbesen killed the German oppressor Count Gert the Bald of Holstein, whose army then occupied most of Jutland. To the east of Randers is Djursland Peninsula, a popular vacation area, with fine manor houses open to the public. If time is of the essence, choose **Gammel Estrup,** a grand 17th-century manor in the tiny village of **Auning;** it's full of rich period furnishings and includes an alchemist's cellar. ✉ ☎ *86/48–30–01.* 🎟 *20 kr.* ☉ *Manor and farm: May–Oct., daily 10–5; Nov.–Apr., (manor) Tues.–Sun. 11–3, (farm) daily 10–5.*

Aalborg, 71 kilometers (44 miles) north of Randers, guards the narrowest point of the Limfjord, the great waterway of northern Jutland and the gateway between north and south. Here you'll find charming combinations of new and old; twisting lanes filled with medieval houses and, nearby, broad modern boulevards. Jomfru Ane Gade, a tiny cobbled street in the center of Aalborg, is lined with restaurants, inns, and sidewalk cafés. Major sights include the magnificent five-story **Jens Bangs Stenhus** (Jens Bang's Stone House). Dating from 1624, it has an atmospheric restaurant and an excellent wine cellar. The Baroque cathedral, the **Budolfi Kirke,** is consecrated to the English St. Butolph. The 15th-century **Helligandsklosteret** (Monastery of the Holy Ghost), one of Denmark's best-preserved, is now a home for the elderly.

If you have some time to spare, head north to the tip of Jutland, to **Skagen,** whose picturesque streets and luminous light have inspired both painters and writers. Here the Danish artist Holger Drachmann (1846–1908) and his friends founded what has become known as the Skagen school of painting; you can see their work in the **Skagens Museum.** ✉

røndumsvej 4, ☎ *98/44–64–44.* ☜ *30 kr.* ☉ *Apr. and Oct., Tues.–Sun. 11–4; May and Sept., daily 10–5; June–Aug., daily 10–6; Nov.–Mar., Wed.–Fri. 1–4, Sat. 11–4, Sun. 11–3.*

Heading south once more, you'll come next to **Viborg,** a town dating from the 8th century, at which time it was a trading post and a place of pagan sacrifice. Later it became a center of Christianity, with monasteries and its own bishop. The 1,000-year-old **Haervejen,** the old military road that starts near here, was once Denmark's most important connection with the outside world. Legend has it that in the 11th century, King Canute set out from Viborg to conquer England, which he subsequently ruled from 1016 to 1035.

Built in 1130, Viborg's **Domkirke** (cathedral), was once the largest granite church in the world. The crypt, restored and reopened in 1876, is all that remains of the original building. Its 20th-century biblical frescoes were painted by Danish artist Joakim Skovgaard.

There's terrific walking country 8 kilometers (5 miles) south of Viborg, beside **Hald Sø** (Hald Lake) and on the heatherclad **Dollerup Bakker** (Dollerup Hills). Heading southwest 45 kilometers (28 miles) to **Herning,** an old moorland town, you'll find a remarkable circular building with an exterior frieze by Carl-Henning Pedersen; it houses the **Carl-Henning Pedersen and Else Afelt Museum.** Just next door is the **Herning Art Museum.** The concave outer wall of the collar-shape building, a shirt factory until 1977, is lined with another enormous frieze 722 feet long. The two museums are set within a sculpture park. ⊠ *Uldjydevej 3,* ☎ *97/12–10–33.* ☜ *40 kr.* ☉ *Tues.–Sun. 12–5; May–Oct., extended weekend hours 10–5.*

About 100 kilometers (60 miles) to the south is Ribe, Denmark's oldest town, whose medieval center is preserved by the Danish National Trust. From May to mid-September, a night watchman walks around the town telling of its ancient history and singing traditional songs. Visitors can join him in the main square each night at 10.

★ ☖ Before heading back to Vejle, stop off at **Billund** to see one of the country's major tourist attractions. **Legoland** is a park filled with scaled-down versions of cities, towns, and villages, working harbors and airports, a Statue of Liberty, a statue of Sitting Bull, a Mt. Rushmore, a safari park, even a Pirate Land—all constructed of millions of Lego bricks. There are also exhibits of toys from pre-Lego days, including Legoland's showpiece, Titania's Palace, a sumptuous dollhouse built in 1907 by Sir Neville Wilkinson for his daughter. ⊠ *Billund,* ☎ *75/33–13–33.* ☜ *110 kr.* ☉ *April–Sept., daily 10–8, and during the Easter holidays.*

Dining and Lodging

Aalborg

$$ ✕ **Duus Vinkælder.** This amazing cellar is part alchemist's dungeon, ★ part neighborhood bar. Though most people come for a drink before or after dinner, you can also get a light bite. In summer the menu is mostly smørrebrød, but during the winter you can order grilled specialties such as pølser, *frikadeller* (Danish meatballs), *biksemad* (cubed potato, meat, and onion hash) and the restaurant's specialty, pâté. ⊠ *Østerå 9,* ☎ *98/12–50–56. Reservations essential. No credit cards. Closed Sun.*

$$ ✕ **Spisehuset Kniv og Gaffel.** In a 400-year-old building parallel to Jomfru Ane Gade, the busy Knife and Fork is crammed with oak tables balancing on crazy slanting floors and lit by candlelight. Its year-round courtyard is a veritable greenhouse. Young waitresses negotiate the mayhem to deliver inch-thick steaks, the house specialty. ✉ *Maren Turisgade 10,* ☎ *98/16–69–72. DC, MC, V. Closed Sun.*

$$$$ ✕🖬 **Helnan Phønix.** At a central location in a sumptuous old mansion, this hotel is popular with international and business guests. Rooms are luxuriously furnished with plump chairs and polished dark-wood furniture; in some the original raw beams are still intact. The Halling restaurant serves excellent French and Danish cuisines. ✉ *Vesterbro 77, 9000 Aalborg,* ☎ *98/12–00–11,* 🆅🆇 *98/16–31–66. 179 rooms with bath. 2 restaurants, bar, café, sauna. AE, DC, MC, V.*

Århus

$$ ✕ **Medina.** This cozy, casual eatery features hearty Middle-Eastern fare, including hummus, shish kebab, couscous, falafel, and other exotic specialties. ✉ *Vesterbrogade 36,* ☎ *86/13–16–37. AE, DC, MC, V. Dinner only.*

$$$$ 🖬 **Royal Hotel.** Open since 1838, Århus's grand hotel has welcomed such greats as Arthur Rubinstein and Marian Andersen. Guests are welcomed into a stately lobby appointed with Chesterfield sofas, modern paintings, and a winding staircase leading to the accommodations above. The plush rooms vary in style and decor, but all have rich drapery, velour- and brocade-covered furniture, and marble bathrooms. ✉ *Store Torv 4, 8100 Århus C,* ☎ *86/12–00–11,* 🆅🆇 *86/76–04–04. 105 rooms with bath. Restaurant, sauna, casino, nightclub. AE, DC, MC, V.*

$ 🖬 **Youth Hostel Pavilionen.** As in all Danish youth and family hostels, rooms here are clean, bright, and functional, and the secluded, wooded setting near the fjord is downright beautiful. Keep in mind that it does get noisy, with carousing business parties mixed in with budget-conscious backpackers. ✉ *Marienlundsvej 10, 8240 Arhùrhus,* ☎ *86/16–72–98,* 🆅🆇 *86/10–55–60. 30 rooms, 11 with shower; 4 communal showers and toilets. Cafeteria (breakfast only), kitchen, free parking. AE, MC, V. Closed mid-Dec.–mid-Jan.*

Ribe

$$$ ✕🖬 **Hotel Dagmar.** In the middle of Ribe's quaint center, this cozy, half-timber hotel encapsulates the charm of the 16th century, with stained-glass windows, frescoes, sloping floors, and carved chairs. The lavish rooms are all appointed with antique canopy beds, fat armchairs, and chaise longues. The fine French restaurant serves such specialties as fillet of salmon in sorrel cream sauce and marinated *foie gras de canard* (duck liver). ✉ *Torvet 1, 6760 Ribe,* ☎ *75/42–00–33,* 🆅🆇 *75/42–36–52. 50 rooms with bath. Restaurant. AE, DC, MC, V.*

Skagen

$$$ ✕🖬 **Brøndums Hotel.** A few minutes from the beach, this 150-year-old gabled inn is furnished with antiques and Skagen-school paintings. The 21 guest rooms in the main building, without TVs or phones, are old-fashioned, with wicker chairs and Oriental rugs, and pine and four-poster beds. Some are beginning to show their age, but there are also 25 annex rooms that are more modern. The hotel has a fine Danish-French restaurant with a lavish cold table. ✉ *Anchersvej 3, 9990 Skagen,* ☎ *98/44–15–55,* 🆅🆇 *98/45–15–20. 46 rooms, 12 with bath. Restaurant. AE, DC, MC, V.*

Vejle

$$$$ ✕🖬 **Munkebjerg.** Seven kilometers (4 miles) southeast of town, surrounded by a thick beech forest and majestic views of the Vejle Fjord, this elegant hotel attracts guests who prefer privacy. Rooms overlook the forest and are furnished in blond pine and soft green; the lobby is rustic. There are also two top-notch restaurants, one specializing in French cuisine, the other in very Danish fare. ⊠ *Munkebjergvej 125, 7100 Vejle,* ☎ *75/72–35–00,* ℻ *75/72–08–86. 148 rooms with bath. 2 restaurants, café, pool, sauna, golf course, tennis, exercise room, horseback riding, jogging, biking, casino, heliport. AE, DC, MC, V.*

9 Finland

Helsinki

The Lakelands

Finnish Lapland

I F YOU LIKE MAJESTIC OPEN SPACES, fine architecture, and civilized living, Finland is for you. It is a land of lakes—187,888 at the last count—and forests, where nature is so prized that even the designs of urban centers reflect the functional architecture of the countryside.

The music of Sibelius, Finland's most famous son, echoes the mood of this Nordic landscape. Both can swing from the somber nocturne of midwinter darkness to the tremolo of sunlight slanting through pine and bone-white birch, ending with the diminuendo of a sunset as it fades into the next day's dawn. Similarly, the Finnish people reflect the changing moods of their land and climate. Their affinity with nature has produced some of the world's greatest designers and architects. Many American cities have buildings designed by Alvar Aalto and the Saarinens, Eliel and his son Eero. Eliel and his family moved to the United States in 1923 and became American citizens—but it was to a lonely Finnish seashore that Saarinen had his ashes returned.

Until 1917, Finland (the Finns call it *Suomi*) was under the domination of its nearest neighbors, Sweden and Russia, who had fought over it for centuries. Inevitably, after more than 600 years under the Swedish crown and 100 under the czars, the country still bears many traces of these two cultures, among them a small (6%) but influential Swedish-speaking minority and a scattering of onion-domed Russian Orthodox churches.

But the Finns themselves are neither Scandinavian nor Slavic. They are descendants of the wandering Finno-Ugric peoples who probably came from west of the Ural Mountains and settled on the swampy shores of the Gulf of Finland before the Christian era. Finnish is one of the Finno-Ugric languages; it is related to Estonian and, very distantly, to Hungarian.

There is a tough, resilient quality to the Finns. No other people fought the Soviets to a standstill as the Finns did in the Winter War of 1939–40. This resilience, in part, stems from the turbulence of the country's past, but also comes from the people's strength and determination to work the land and survive the long, dark winters. The Finns are in a state of constant confrontation—with the weather, the land, and most recently a huge eastern neighbor engulfed in political and economic turmoil. They are stubborn, self-sufficient, and patriotic, yet not aggressively nationalistic. They mainly take pride in finding ways to live independently and in peace.

The average Finn doesn't volunteer much information, but that's due to reserve, not indifference. Make the first approach and you may have a friend for life. Finns like their silent spaces, though, and won't appreciate back-slapping familiarity—least of all in the sauna, which is regarded by many as a spiritual, as well as a cleansing, experience.

ESSENTIAL INFORMATION

Before You Go

When to Go

The tourist summer season runs from mid-June until mid-August, a magnificently sunny and generally dry time marked by unusually warm temperatures in recent years. Outside this period, many amenities and attractions either close or operate on much-reduced schedules. But there are advantages to visiting Finland off-season, not the least being that you

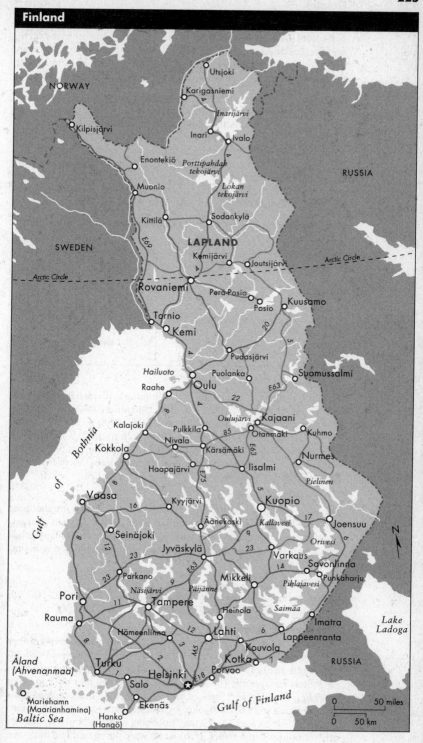

avoid the mosquitoes, which can be fearsome, especially in the north. Fall colors (from early September in the far north, October in the south) are spectacular. January through March (April in the north) is the main cross-country skiing season. Spring is brief but magical: The snow melts, the ice breaks up, and nature explodes into life almost overnight.

CLIMATE

Generally speaking, the spring and summer seasons begin a month earlier in the south of Finland than they do in the far north. You can expect warm (not hot) days in Helsinki from mid-May, and in Lapland from mid-June. The midnight sun can be seen from May to July, depending on the region. For a period in midwinter, magnificent displays of the northern lights almost make up for the fact that the sun does not rise at all. Even in Helsinki, summer nights are brief and never really dark, whereas in midwinter daylight lasts only a few hours.

The following are average daily maximum and minimum temperatures for Helsinki.

Jan.	30F	– 1C	May	64F	18C	Sept.	53F	11C
	26	– 3		48	9		39	4
Feb.	34F	1C	June	60F	16C	Oct.	46F	8C
	24	– 4		48	9		36	2
Mar.	36F	2C	July	68F	20C	Nov.	32F	0C
	26	– 3		55	13		26	– 3
Apr.	46F	8C	Aug.	64F	18C	Dec.	32F	0C
	32	0		53	12		24	– 4

Currency

The unit of currency in Finland is the Finnmark, divided into 100 penniä. There are bills of FIM 20, 50, 100, 500, and 1,000. Coins are 10 and 50 penniä, and FIM 1, FIM 5, and FIM 10. At press time (spring 1996), the exchange rate was about FIM 4.26 to the U.S. dollar, FIM 3.13 to the Canadian dollar, and FIM 6.55 to the pound sterling. Credit cards are widely accepted, even in many taxicabs. Traveler's checks can be cashed only in banks.

What It Will Cost

Prices are highest in Helsinki; otherwise they vary little throughout the country. Taxes are already included in hotel and restaurant charges, and there is no airport departure tax. However, the prices of many goods include an 18% sales tax, less on food (☞ Shopping *in* Staying in Finland, *below*).

SAMPLE PRICES

Cup of coffee, FIM 8; glass of beer, FIM 15–25; soft drink, FIM 10; ham sandwich, FIM 15–FIM 20; 1-mile taxi ride, FIM 30.

Customs on Arrival

Visitors to Finland may import goods for their own use from another European Union (EU) country duty-free, with the exception of tobacco and alcohol. Visitors over age 22 may bring in 1 liter of spirits or 3 liters of aperitifs (over 22% alcohol by volume) or 3 liters of sparkling wines, plus 5 liters of table wine and 15 liters of beer. Spirits containing over 60% alcohol by volume may not be brought into Finland. Visitors ages 18–22 may not bring in spirits, but may import other amounts listed above. If the items were purchased in a duty-free shop at an airport or harbor, or on board an airplane or ship, visitors may bring in 1 liter of spirits, 2 liters of aperitifs or sparkling wines, 2 liters of table wine and 15 liters of beer. Visitors over age 17 may bring in 300 cigarettes, 75 cigars or 400 grams (about 13 oz) of tobacco. If the items were purchased at a duty-free shop, 200 cigarettes, 50 cigars or 250 grams (about 8 oz) of tobacco are allowed.

Language

The official languages of Finland are Finnish and Swedish, though only a small and diminishing minority speaks the latter. English is widely spoken in Helsinki and by young Finns around the country. Nearly all tourist sites and attractions provide texts in English, and English menus are usually available in restaurants. In Finnish Lapland, the native Sami (pronounced Sah-me) population speaks three different dialects of a language distantly related to Finnish.

Getting Around

By Bicycle

Finland's absence of steep hills and heavy traffic make it an ideal place for cyling. Bikes can be rented at some youth hostels. The Finnish **Youth Hostel Association** (⊠ Yrjönkatu 38B, Helsinki, ☎ 09/694–0377) offers accommodation packages to tie in with visitors' cycling tours for FIM 1185 (7 days) or FIM 2165 (14 days). The package includes bike rental, accommodations, and road maps.

By Boat

Helsinki and Turku have regular sea links with the Åland Islands in the Baltic Sea. From mid-June to mid-August you can cruise the labyrinthine lakes of the Finnish interior. Complete timetables are available from the Finnish Tourist Board (☞ Important Addresses and Numbers in Helsinki, *below*).

By Bus

Finland's bus system can take you virtually anywhere. A **Coach Holiday Ticket,** available from bus stations and travel agencies, entitles you to 1,000 kilometers (625 miles) of bus travel within two weeks for FIM 340.

By Car

ROAD CONDITIONS

Finland has no superhighways, but there is an expanding network of efficient major roads, some of which are multilane. In some areas, however, especially in the north, you can expect long stretches of dirt road. These roads are usually adequate to good, although during the spring thaw they become difficult to negotiate. Away from the larger towns, traffic is light, but take moose and reindeer warning signs seriously.

RULES OF THE ROAD

Drive on the right. At intersections, cars coming from the right have right-of-way. Speed limits (usually marked) are 50 kph (30 mph) in built-up areas and between 80 kph and 100 kph (50 mph and 62 mph) in the country and on main roads. Low-beam headlights must be used at all times outside city areas, seat belts are compulsory (on rear as well as front seats), and you must carry a warning triangle in case of a breakdown.

PARKING

Parking is a problem only in some city centers. Major cities offer multistory garages; most towns have on-street meters. In Helsinki, there is no free on-street parking. In areas with no meters, drivers must display *pysäköintlippu* (parking vouchers), for sale at **R-Kiosks** and gas stations, on their dashboard. Illegally parked cars may be towed away.

BREAKDOWNS AND ACCIDENTS

The **Automobile and Touring Club of Finland** (⊠ Autolitto ry, Hämeentie 105 A, Helsinki, ☎ 09/774–761), operates a 24-hour information service (☎ 09/7747–6400) for club members and members of foreign auto clubs. In case of a breakdown over the weekend, dial 9700–8080 from anywhere in Finland. If an accident requires an ambulance or fire squad, call the national emergency number, 112. If you're involved in an accident, report it without delay to the **Finnish Motor Insurers' Bureau** (⊠ Liikennevakuutuskeskus, Bulevardi 28, 00120 Helsinki, ☎ 09/680–401) as well as to the police (10022).

By Plane

Finnair (☎ 09/818–800) operates an elaborate network of flights linking 25 towns in Finland. A **Holiday Ticket** can be purchased outside of Finland for $500 (at press time) and includes 10 flight coupons valid for any domestic Finnair flights. Finnair grants visitors under age 25 a 50-percent **Youth Discount** on flights booked ahead. These tickets are available in most countries, and in Finland they can be purchased at major travel agencies.

By Train

Finland's extensive rail system reaches all main centers of the country and offers high standards of comfort and cleanliness. A special **Finnrail Pass** entitles you to unlimited travel for three, five, or ten days within a four-week period; second-class prices are FIM 505 (three days), FIM 685 (five days), and FIM 945 (10 days); first-class tickets are FIM 760 (three days), FIM 1,030 (five days), and FIM 1,420 (10 days). Children under age 16 pay half fare. These tickets can be purchased both inside and outside the country. In Finland, the Finnrail Pass is available from the Finnish State Railways (☎ 09/010–0127). In the United States and Canada they can be purchased from **Rail Europe** (☎ 800/438–7245), and in the United Kingdom, from **Norvista** (formerly Finlandia Travel) (☎ 0171/409–7334).

Staying in Finland

Telephones

LOCAL CALLS

To avoid exorbitant hotel surcharges on calls, use public pay phones, and have some FIM 1 and FIM 5 coins ready. Some pay phones only accept a phone card, the *Tele Kortti,* available at post offices, R-Kiosks, and some grocery stores. They come in increments of FIM 30, 50, 100, and 150. Note that the Finnish letters *ä* and *ö* and the Swedish *å* come at the end of the alphabet; this may be useful when looking up names in the telephone book. For information about telephone service, call the telephone company HPY/HTF at 6061. For directory assistance, dial 118.

INTERNATIONAL CALLS

You can dial Britain and North America directly from anywhere in Finland. Calls to other countries can be made from a telegraph office; these are marked LENNÄTIN or TELE and are usually found next to the post office. An operator will assign you a private booth and collect payment at the end of the call. To dial the numbers listed in this guide from outside Finland, omit the "0" at the beginning of the city code. To make a direct international phone call from Finland, dial 990, then the appropriate country code and phone number. To reach an **AT&T** long-distance operator, dial 9800–10010; for **MCI**, 9800–10280; for **Sprint**, 9800–10284. For directory assistance abroad, dial 020–208.

COUNTRY CODE

The country code for Finland is 358.

Mail

POSTAL RATES

At press time (spring 1996), airmail rates to North America were FIM 3.40 for postcards or letters weighing up to 20 grams. Letters to the United Kingdom cost FIM 3.20.

RECEIVING MAIL

If you're uncertain about where you'll be staying, be sure that mail sent to you is marked "poste restante" and addressed to the post office in the appropriate town (the address of Helsinki's main post office is Mannerheimintie 11, 00100). American Express offers free mail service to clients and will hold mail for up to one month. Mail should be addressed to Clients' Mail, American Express, Mikonkatu 2D, 00100 Helsinki.

Shopping

SALES TAX REFUNDS

Non-EU residents who purchase goods worth more than FIM 100 in any of the many shops marked "tax free for tourists" can get a 12%–16% refund. Show your passport and the store will give you a check for the appropriate amount, which you can cash at your final point of departure from the EU.

Opening and Closing Times

Banks are open weekdays 9:15–4:15. Opening hours for **Museums** vary considerably, so check individual listings. Many museums in the countryside are open only during the summer months. **Shops** are generally open weekdays 9–6, Saturday 9–2. Department stores and supermarkets stay open until 8 on weekdays. **Sightseeing** schedules are highly varied outside the main tourist season. Check local tourist offices for opening days and hours.

National Holidays

January 1; January 6 (Epiphany); March 28–30 (Good Friday, Easter, and Easter Monday); May 1 (May Day); May 8 (Ascension); May 18–19 (Pentecost); May 25 (Whit Sunday); June 21–22 (Midsummer's Eve and Day); November 1 (All Saints' Day); December 6 (Independence Day); December 25–26.

Dining

You can choose either restaurants, taverns, coffeehouses, or snack bars. As in other parts of Scandinavia, the *voileipäpöytä* (cold table) is often a work of art as well as a feast. Some special Finnish dishes are *poronkäristys* (reindeer casserole); salmon, herring, and various freshwater fish; and *lihapullia* (meatballs with a tasty sauce). Crayfish parties are popular between the end of July and early September. For a delicious dessert, try *lakka* (cloudberries), which grow in the midnight sun above the Arctic Circle and are frequently used in sauces for ice cream. Most restaurants close for major holidays.

MEALTIMES

The Finns eat early; lunch runs from 11 or noon to 1 or 2, dinner from 4 to 7 (a bit later in Helsinki).

WHAT TO WEAR

Except for the most elegant establishments, where a jacket and tie are preferred, casual attire is acceptable for restaurants in all price categories; however, jeans are not allowed in some of the more expensive dining rooms.

RATINGS

Prices are per person and include first course, main course, dessert, and service charge—but not wine. All restaurant checks include a *sisältää palvelupalkkion* (service charge). If you want to leave an additional tip—though it really isn't necessary—it's enough to round the figure off to the nearest FIM 5 or FIM 10.

CATEGORY	HELSINKI	OTHER AREAS
$$$$	over FIM 200	over FIM 170
$$$	FIM 150–FIM 200	FIM 140–FIM 170
$$	FIM 80–FIM 150	FIM 80–FIM 140
$	under FIM 80	under FIM 80

If you select the prix-fixe menu, which usually covers two courses and coffee and is served at certain hours in many establishments, the cost of the meal can be as little as half of the prices shown above.

Lodging

Finland offers a full range of accommodations: hotels, motels, boarding houses, bed and breakfasts, rental chalets and cottages, farmhouses, youth hostels, and campsites. There is no official rating system, but standards are generally high. If you haven't reserved a room before arriving in Helsinki, you can make reservations through a travel agency or at the **Hotel Booking Center** at the railway station (⊠ Rautatieasema, ☎ 09/171–133); the booking service is free if by phone; a fee FIM 12 is charged if you appear in person.

HOTELS

Nearly all hotels in Finland are modern or recently renovated; a few occupy fine old manor houses. Most have rooms with bath or shower. Prices generally include breakfast and often a morning sauna and swim. The **Finncheque** voucher system, subscribed to by many hotels from June through August, offers good discounts. Only the first night can be reserved from outside Finland, but subsequent reservations can be made free from any Finncheque hotel. For additional information, inquire at the Hotel Booking Center or the Finnish Tourist Board (☞ Important Addresses and Numbers in Helsinki, *below*).

SUMMER HOTELS

University students' accommodations are turned into "summer hotels" from June through August; they offer modern facilities at slightly lower-than-average prices. The Finnish Youth Hostel Association publishes "Hostellit," a free brochure listing summer hotels as well as youth hostels across Finland. Copies are available at the Finnish Tourist Board and the YHA (☞ *below*).

BOARDINGHOUSES AND RENTALS

These provide the least expensive accommodations and are found only outside Helsinki. Local tourist offices have lists. The selection is huge, and the chalets and cottages are nearly always in delightful lakeside or seashore settings. For comfortable (not luxurious) accommodations, count on paying FIM 1,000–FIM 3,500 per week for a four-person rental. A central reservations agency is **Lomarengas** (⊠ Malminkaari 23C, 00700 Helsinki, ☎ 09/3516–1321, or Eteläesplanadi 4, 00130 Helsinki, ☎ 09/170–611).

FARMHOUSES

These are located in attractive settings, usually near water. A central reservations agency is **Suomen 4H-liitto** (⊠ Abrahaminkatu 7, 00180 Helsinki, ☎ 09/642–233).

YOUTH HOSTELS

These range from empty schools to small manor houses. The Finnish Tourist Board and the **Finnish Youth Hostel Association** (YHA; ⊠ Yrjönkatu 38B, Helsinki, ☎ 09/694–0377) can provide a list of hostels. There are no age restrictions, and prices range from FIM 50 to FIM 200 per bed, with a discount of FIM 15 for YHA members.

CAMPING

There are about 350 Finnish campsites. All offer showers and cooking facilities, and many include cottages for rent. Lists, with sites graded according to a three-grade system, are available from the Finnish Youth Hostel Association and the Finnish Tourist Board.

RATINGS

Prices are for two people in a double room and include breakfast and service charges. Hotels in Helsinki, particularly in the middle price range of prices, tend to be cheaper in the summer and on weekends.

CATEGORY	HELSINKI	OTHER AREAS
$$$$	over FIM 900	over FIM 700
$$$	FIM 600–FIM 900	FIM 550–FIM 700
$$	FIM 400–FIM 600	FIM 400–FIM 550
$	under FIM 400	under FIM 400

Tipping

The Finns are less tip-conscious than other Europeans. (For tipping in restaurants, ☞ Dining, *above*.) You can give taxi drivers a few small coins, but it's not essential. Train and airport porters have a fixed charge. It's not necessary to tip hotel doormen for carrying bags to the check-in counter, but give bellhops FIM 5–FIM 10 for carrying bags to your room. The obligatory coat-check room fee of about FIM 5 is usually clearly posted; if not, give FIM 5–FIM 10, depending on the number in your party. FIM 5 is a standard tip for all minor services.

HELSINKI

Arriving and Departing

By Plane

All international flights arrive at Helsinki's Vantaa Airport, 20 kilometers (12 miles) north of the city. For arrival and departure information, call 9600–8100.

BETWEEN THE AIRPORT AND DOWNTOWN

Finnair buses make the trip between the Vantaa Airport and the city center two to three times an hour, stopping behind the Inter-Continental hotel (⊠ Töölönkatu 21) and at the Finnair Terminal next to the train station. The ride takes about 30 minutes and costs FIM 24. A local bus service (No. 615) will also take you to the train station and costs FIM 15 for the 40-minute ride. Expect to pay between FIM 100 and FIM 140 for a taxi into the city center. If you are driving, the way is well marked to Highway 137 (Tuusulantie) and KESKUSTA (downtown Helsinki).

By Train

Helsinki's train station (Rautatieasema) is in the heart of the city, off od Kaivokatu. For train information, call 09/010–0121.

By Bus

The main long-distance bus station (Linja-autoasema) is just off Mannerheimintie, between Salomonkatu and Simonkatu. Many local buses arrive and depart from Rautatientori (Railway Station Square). For information on long-distance transport, call 9600–4000.

By Boat

The Silja Line terminal for ships arriving from Stockholm is at Olympialaituri, on the west side of the South Harbor. The Finnjet-Silja and Viking lines terminal for ships arriving from Travemünde and Stockholm is at Katajanokkanlaituri, on the east side of the South Harbor.

Brochures, information, and tickets are also available at the downtown agencies of the **Silja Line** (✉ Mannerheimintie 2, ☎ 9800–74552) and the **Viking Line** (✉ Mannerheimintie 12, ☎ 09/123–577).

Getting Around

The center of Helsinki is compact and best explored on foot. If you want to use public transportation, your best buy is the **Helsinki Card,** which offers unlimited travel on city public transportation, free entry to many museums, a free sightseeing tour, and a variety of other discounts. It's available for one, two, or three days (FIM 105, FIM 135, FIM 165, respectively; about half-price for children). You can buy it at some hotels, travel agencies, Stockmann's department store, and at the Helsinki City Tourist Office.

By Subway
Helsinki's only subway line runs from Ruoholahti, just west of the city center, to Mellunmäki, in the eastern suburbs. It operates Monday through Saturday from 5:25 AM, and Sunday from 6:30 AM, to 11:20 PM. Each ride costs FIM 9; free transfers are available during the first hour of travel. Each trip costs FIM 7.50 if you buy a 10-trip ticket. Tickets may be purchased at subway stations, R-Kiosks, and shops displaying the Helsinki city transport logo (two curving black arrows on a yellow background).

By Streetcar
Helsinki's green "trams" run from 5:45 AM to 1:45 AM, depending on the line. They are easy to use and efficient, and route maps and schedules are posted at most downtown stops. Single tickets are sold on board for FIM 7 (good for one journey by tram without transfers) or FIM 9 (good for one journey with transfers). A 10-trip ticket is available at R-Kiosks for FIM 75. Most of Helsinki's major points of interest, from the Market Square to the Lutheran Cathedral to the Opera House, are located along the 3T tram line; the Helsinki City Tourist Office distributes a free pamphlet called "Helsinki Sightseeing: 3T."

By Taxi
Taxis are all marked TAKSI. Meters start at FIM 30, the fare rising on a kilometer basis. A listing of all taxi companies appears in the white pages—try to choose one that is nearby, since they charge from the point of dispatch. The main phone number for taxi service is 700–700. Be sure to request a cab that accepts credit cards when ordering a taxi by phone. Car services have a minimum charge and should be ordered well in advance.

By Boat
In summer there is regular boat service from the South Harbor Market Square to the fortress island Suomenlinna and to Korkeasaari, site of the Helsinki Zoo. Schedules and prices are listed on signboards at the harbor.

Important Addresses and Numbers

Visitor Information
The **Helsinki City Tourist Office** is near the South Harbor (✉ Pohjoisesplanadi 19, ☎ 09/169–3757 or 09/174–088); open May 2–September, weekdays 8:30–6, weekends 10–3; October 1–April 30, weekdays 8:30–4, closed weekends. The **Finnish Tourist Board's Tourist Information Office,** covering all of Finland, is nearby at Eteläesplanadi 4 (☎ 09/4030–1211 or 09/4030–1300); open June–August, weekdays 8:30–5, Saturday 10–2; September–May, weekdays 8:30–4, closed weekends.

Embassies

U.S. (✉ Itäinen Puistotie 14, ☎ 09/171–931). **Canadian** (✉ Pohjois-esplanadi 25B, ☎ 09/171–141). **U.K.** (✉ Itäinen Puistotie 17, ☎ 09/228–65100).

Emergencies

General (☎ 112); **Police** (☎ 112 or 10022); **Ambulance** (☎ 112); **Doctor** (☎ 10023); **Dentist** (☎ 09/736–166). Twenty-four-hour **Pharmacy:** Yliopiston Apteekki (✉ Mannerheimintie 96, ☎ 09/415–778).

English-Language Bookstores

You'll find a good selection of books, newspapers, and magazines in English at the **Akateeminen Kirjakauppa** (Academic Bookstore; ✉ Keskuskatu 1), and a smaller array at the **Suomalainen Kirjakauppa** (Finnish Bookstore; ✉ Aleksanterinkatu 23).

Travel Agencies

American Express (✉ Area Travel Agency, Mikonkatu 2D, 00100 Helsinki, ☎ 09/628–788). The **Finland Travel Bureau** (Suomen Matkatoimisto; ✉ Kaivokatu 10A, PL 319, 00100 Helsinki, ☎ 09/18261) has several overseas affiliates, including Finnway Inc. in the U.S. (✉ 228 E. 45th St., 14th fl., New York, NY 10017, ☎ 212/818–1198), and Norvista in Great Britain (✉ 227 Regent Street, W1R 8PD London, ☎ 0171/409–7334).

Guided Tours

Orientation

Suomen Turistiauto (☎ 09/588–5166) offers a 1½-hour "City Tour." Tours start from Asema-aukio (the square between the train station and the main post office), Olympia Terminal (South Harbor), or the Havis Amanda (Market Square). In May and September these depart from Asema-aukio at 11:30 and 1:30; from June through August there are three tours a day, at 10:30, 12:30, and 2:30, departing from Havis Amanda, and one at 9:45 beginning at the Olympia Terminal; from October through April there is only a Sunday tour, which leaves Asema-aukio at 11. You can buy tickets on the bus 15 minutes before departure. **Ageba Travel Agency** (☎ 09/669–193) offers a similar tour lasting 2 or 2½ hours. Its tours depart from the Silja Terminal at the Olympic Pier daily at 9:30 and 11, April through October, weekdays at 9:30 and weekends at 11, November through March. Ageba also has boat tours to the old wooden town of Porvoo, with frequent daily departures from the Market Square. The timetables are posted on signboards, and tickets can be purchased on board.

Excursions

To book a guided excursion from Helsinki, contact **Helsingin Matkailuyhdistys,** the Helsinki Tourist Association (✉ Lönnrotinkatu 7B, Helsinki, ☎ 09/645–225). **Finnsov Tours** (☎ 09/694–2011) offers no-visa guided tours to St. Petersburg, Russia, and Tallinn, Estonia. **Atlas Cruising Center** (☎ 09/651–011) also offers visa-free cruises to St. Petersburg and Tallinn.

Exploring Helsinki

Helsinki is a city of the sea, built on the peninsulas and islands of the Baltic shoreline. Streets curve around bays, bridges arch between islands, and ferries carry traffic to islands farther offshore. The smell of the sea hovers over the city, and there is a constant bustle in the city's harbors as the huge ships that ply the Baltic put in and lift anchor.

Helsinki has grown dramatically since World War II, and now accounts for about one-sixth of Finland's population. The city covers a total of 433 square miles and includes 315 islands. Most of Helsinki's sights, hotels, and restaurants, however, are crowded onto a single peninsula, so visitors have no trouble getting around.

Helsinki is relatively young compared to other European capitals. In the sixteenth century, the Swedish king Gustav Vasa, at that time ruler of present-day Finland as well, determined to woo trade away from the Estonian city of Tallinn, hoping to challenge the monopoly of the Hanseatic League. The city was founded next to the rapids of the Vantaa River on June 12, 1550, by a group of Finns who had settled there upon the king's orders.

Over the next three centuries, Helsinki had its ups and downs, suffering several fires and epidemics. Turku, on Finland's west coast, was the country's capital and intellectual center in those years. Helsinki did not take center stage until Sweden ceded Finland to Russia in 1809. The Russian czar, Alexander I, turned Finland into an autonomous grand duchy, proclaiming Helsinki its capital in 1812. About the same time, much of Turku burned to the ground, and the university was forced to move to Helsinki as well. From then on, Helsinki's position as Finland's first city was assured.

Fire also played a role in Helsinki's fortunes. Just before the czar's proclamation, a fire destroyed many of Helsinki's traditional wooden buildings, and it became necessary to build a new city center. The German-born architect Carl Ludvig Engel was entrusted with the project, and thanks to him Helsinki has some of the purest neoclassical architecture in the world. Add to this foundation the stunning outlines of the Jugendstil (Art Nouveau) period of the early 20th century and more modern buildings designed by native Finnish architects, and you have a European capital city as architecturally eye-catching as it is unlike those of its Scandinavian neighbors and the rest of Europe.

Numbers in the margin correspond to points of interest on the Helsinki map.

★ ❶ The **Kauppatori** (Market Square), across from the city tourist office and beside the South Harbor, is frequented by locals and tourists alike. They come to buy freshly cut flowers, fruit and vegetables trucked in from the hinterland, and handicrafts from small country villages—all sold by vendors who set up shop in bright orange tents. In the fruit stalls you will find mountains of strawberries, raspberries, blueberries—and, if you're lucky, cloudberries. Closer to the dock are fresh fish from the waters of the Baltic. You can't miss the **Havis Amanda patsas** (Havis Amanda statue) watching over the busy square.

The open-air market is held year-round, Monday through Saturday from 7 AM to 2 PM. At 3:30 PM in summer the fruit and vegetable stalls give way to stalls featuring arts and crafts, which then close around 8 PM.

❷ ❸ Across the street is the **Pohjoisesplanadi** (North Esplanade), the political center of Finland. The light blue building is the **Kaupungintalo** (City Hall). Standing at the end of Pohjoisesplanadi is the **Presidentinlinna** (President's Palace), which houses the offices of President Martti Ahtisaari and is the scene of official receptions. The President's Palace was built as a private home in 1818 and converted for the use of the czars in 1843. It served as the official residence of Finnish presidents from 1919 to 1993. Across from the palace is the waterfront, where ferries and sightseeing boats can be seen setting out into the bay. On a summer day it's a sailor's dream, with sails hoisted and taut to

★ ④ the wind and island waters to explore. The redbrick edifice that looms over the east side of the market is the Orthodox **Uspenskin Katedraali** (Uspenski Cathedral). ☉ *May–Sept., Mon. and Wed.–Fri. 9:30–4, Tues. 9:30–6, Sat. 10–4, Sun. noon–3; Oct.–Apr., Tues. and Thurs. 9–2, Wed. noon–6, Fri. noon–4, Sun. noon–2, closed Mon. and Sat. Closed on church holidays except for services.*

Tucked in just behind the Orthodox cathedral is the **Katajanokka** district, in which 19th-century brick warehouses are gradually being converted into a complex of boutiques, arts-and-crafts studios, and restaurants. You'll find innovative designs at these shops, and many of the restaurants offer lighter fare, which makes this area a tempting place to stop for lunch. While in Katajanokka, you might enjoy a visit to **Wanha Satama,** on the east side of Kanavakatu, a small, redbrick complex of cafés and specialty food shops attached to an art gallery.

★ ⑤ A one-minute stroll northward from City Hall will take you to the heart of neoclassical Helsinki. **Senaatintori** (Senate Square), designed by Carl Ludvig Engel, is a harmonious ensemble representing the purest styles in European architecture. It is dominated by the domed ⑥ **Tuomiokirkko** (Lutheran Cathedral). ☉ *May–Sept., weekdays 9–7, Sat. 9–6, Sun. noon–6; Oct.–Apr., weekdays 10–4, Sat. 10–6, Sun. noon–6.*

The main building of Helsinki University and the State Council Building also flank the square. Senaatintori has a dignified, stately air, enlivened in summer by the sun-worshipers who gather on the wide steps leading up to Tuomiokirkko and throughout the year by the bustle around the university and **Kiseleff Bazaar Hall,** on the south side of the square.

⑦ Back on the Market Square, head southward on Eteläranta along the western shore of the South Harbor. You'll soon come to the brick **Vanha Kauppahalli** (Old Market Hall)—it's worth taking a look inside at the amazing displays of meat, fish, and other gastronomic delights (open weekdays 8–5, Sat. 8–2). A little farther on are the **Makasiini and Olympia terminals,** where huge ferries from Sweden, Estonia, and Poland dock. Beyond the terminals is **Kaivopuisto** (Well Park), an elegant district much favored by Russian high society in the 19th century. It is now a favored residential area for diplomats and popular strolling ground for Helsinki's citizens.

NEED A BREAK? Coffee drinkers gather on the patio at **Café Ursula** (✉ Ehrenströmintie 3), whose glass walls permit a splendid view of the harbor and its ship traffic.

★ ⑧ You can avoid the long walk back to the Market Square by cutting across Kaivopuisto to Tehtaankatu and catching the 3T tram to the Kauppatori. From here, there's frequent ferry service to the island **Suomenlinna** (Finland's Castle; ☎ 09/668–154). Finnish units of the Swedish army began the construction of this fortress in 1748. Its six islands, known as the "Gibraltar of the North," were Sweden's shield against Russia until a Swedish commander inexplicably surrendered to Russia without a fight during the War of Finland (1808–19). A heavy British naval attack in 1855, during the Crimean War, damaged the fortress.

⑨ Today, though still a military garrison, Suomenlinna is also a collection of museums and parks. In early summer it is awash with purple lilacs introduced from Versailles by the Finnish architect Augustin Ehrensvärd. You may wish to visit the **Pohjoismainen Taidekeskus** (Nordic Arts Center), which exhibits work by Nordic artists. ☎

Helsinki

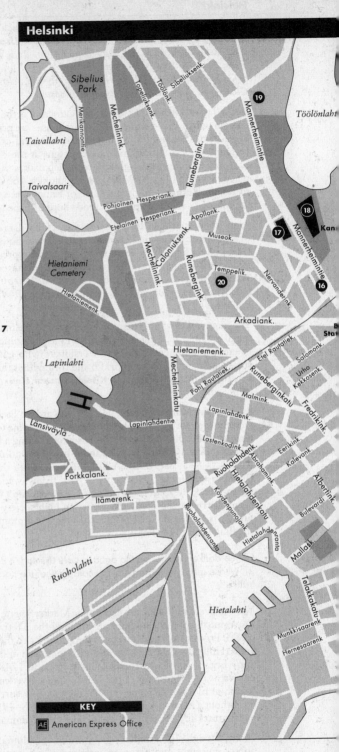

KEY

AE American Express Office

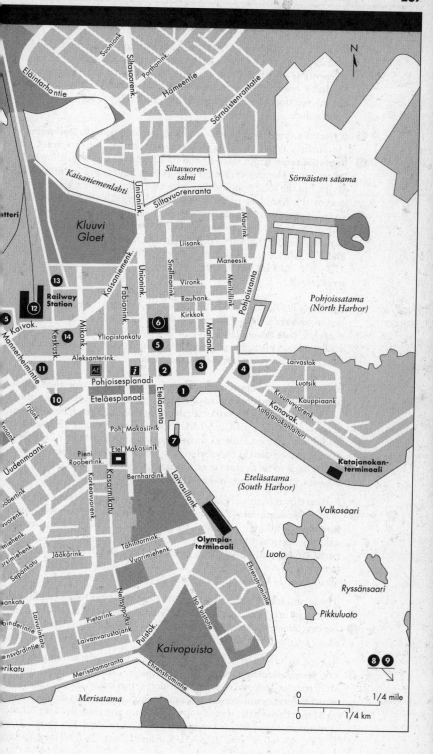

Eläintarhontie

Suónionk.
Porthanink.
Siltasaarenk.
Hämeentie
Sörnäistenrantatie

Kaisaniemenlahti

Unionink.
Siltavuoren-
salmi
Siltavuorenranta

Sörnäisten satama

**Kluuvi
Gloet**

Maurink.

Liisank.

Maneesik.

Kaisaniemenk.
Unionink.
Snellmaninkl.
Vironk.
Rauhank.
Kirkkok.
Meritullink.
Pohjoisranta

Pohjoissatama
(North Harbor)

13

12 Railway
Station

5 Kaivok.
Mikonk.
Keskusk.
14

11 Mannerheimintie

Fabianink.
Yliopistonkatu
Aleksanterink.

6
5

Mariank.

Laivastok.
Luotsik.

AE
i Pohjoisesplanadi
Eteläesplanadi

2
1
3

4

Kauppiaank.
Kruunuvuorenk.
Kanavak.
Katajanokanlaituri

10

Fredrik.

Eteläranta

Pohj Makasiink.

7

**Katajanokan-
terminaali**

Pieni
Roobertink.
Etel Makasiink.

Uudenmaank.

Kalevank.

Roobertink.

Korsimiehenk.
Sepänkatu

Jääkärink.

Bernhardink.

Kasarmikatu
Korkeavuorenk.

Laivasillank.

Eteläsatama
(South Harbor)

Valkosaari

Luoto

Ryssänsaari

Tähtitornink.
Vuorimiehenk.

**Olympia-
terminaali**

Ehrenströmintie

Pikkuluoto

Iso Puistotie

ankatu
Laivurinkatu
ensvärdintie
rikatu

Pietarink.
Laivanvarustajank.
Neitsytpolku
Puistok.

Kaivopuisto

Merisatamaranta
Ehrenströmintie

8 **9**

Merisatama

0   1/4 mile
0   1/4 km

09/668–148. ☎ *Free.* ⊙ *Tues.–Sun. 11–6; galleries closed between exhibits.*

Back on the mainland, head west from Market Square up Pohjoisesplanadi. To your left are the Esplanade Gardens. On your right are the showrooms and boutiques of some of Finland's top designers (☞ Shopping, *below*). The circular **Svenska Teatern** (Swedish Theater) marks the intersection of the Esplanade and Helsinki's main artery, Mannerheimintie.

If you take a right on Mannerheimintie, you soon come to **Stockmann's,** Helsinki's most famous department store. Next comes the **Rautatieasema** (train station) and its square, the city's bustling commuter hub. The station's huge red-granite figures are by Emil Wikström, but the solid building they adorn was designed by Eliel Saarinen, one of the founders of the early-20th-century National Romantic style. The **Suomen Kansallisteatteri** (National Theater) sits on the north side of the square. On the south side, the **Valtion Taidemuseo** (Finnish National Gallery) houses both the Ateneum Museum of Finnish Art and The Museum of Contemporary Art. ⊠ *Kaivokatu 2–4,* ☎ *09/ 173–361.* ☎ *FIM 10.* ⊙ *Tues. and Fri. 9–5, Wed. and Thurs. 9–9, weekends 11–5.*

NEED A
BREAK?

Café Socis (⊠ Kaivokatu 12), in the Seurahuone Hotel opposite the train station, is a restful turn-of-the-century setting for a prix-fixe lunch or afternoon tea. **Café Ekberg** (⊠ Bulevardi 9) is a favorite sipping ground for the literati and the staffs of nearby publishing houses. Its traditional confections and breakfast buffet are unbeatable.

In front of the main post office, west of the station, the equestrian **statue of Marshal Mannerheim** gazes down Mannerheimintie, the major thoroughfare named in his honor. Perhaps no man in Finnish history is so revered as Baron Carl Gustaf Mannerheim, the military and political leader who guided Finland through much of the turbulent 20th century. When he died in Switzerland on January 28, 1951, his body was flown back to lie in state in the cathedral. For three days, young war widows, children, and soldiers filed past his bier.

Farther down Mannerheimintie stands the imposing, colonnaded, red-granite **Eduskuntatalo** (Parliament House). The nearby **Suomen Kansallismuseo** (National Museum) traces Finland's history with diverse exhibits, from medieval church relics to the trappings of Russian imperialism to traditional Sami costumes and dwellings. ⊠ *Mannerheimintie 34,* ☎ *09/405–0470.* ☎ *FIM 15.* ⊙ *June–Aug., Tues. 11–8, Wed.–Sun. 11–5; Sept.–May, Tues. 11–8, Wed.–Sun. 11–4.*

The inland lake Töölönlahti forms the backdrop for two of Helsinki's major cultural sites, Alvar Aalto's **Finlandiatalo** (Finlandia Hall) and the new **Suomen Kansallisooppera** (Finnish National Opera). If you can't make it to an opera, be sure to take a guided tour (☎ 09/4030–2350).

Tucked away in a labyrinth of streets to the west is the strikingly modern **Temppeliaukio Kirkko** (Temple Square Church). Carved out of solid rock and topped with a copper dome, this landmark presents both worship services and concerts. (From here it's only a short distance back to Mannerheimintie, where you can pick up any tram heading for the downtown area.) ⊠ *Lutherininkatu 3,* ⊙ *Weekdays 10–8, Sat. 10–6, Sun. noon–1:45 and 3:15–5:45. Closed Tues. 1–2 PM and during concerts and services.*

Off the Beaten Path

One of Finland's architectural highlights is in Espoo, Helsinki's next-door neighbor. The garden city of **Tapiola** was designed by Alvar Aalto as an urban landscape alternating high and low residential buildings, fountains, gardens, and swimming pools that blend into the natural surroundings. For information on Tapiola, call the Espoo City Tourist Office (☎ 09/460–311).

Akseli Gallen-Kallela (1865–1931) was one of Finland's greatest artists. His studio-home can be seen in Tarvaspää. Take Tram 4 to Munkkiniemi, getting off at the *Laajalahden auto* stop. From there walk straight down the street to the park, then through the woods 1½-mile to the museum. ⊠ *Gallen-Kalleantie 27, Tarvaspää,* ☎ *09/513–388.* ▭ *FIM 35.* ☉ *Mid-May–Aug., Mon.–Thurs. 10–8, Fri.–Sun. 10–5; Sept.–mid-May, Tues.–Sat. 10–4, Sun. 10–5.*

Shopping

Shopping Districts and Specialty Shops

Helsinki's prime shopping districts run along **Pohjoisesplanadi** (North Esplanade) and **Aleksanterinkatu** in the city center. You can find a number of antiques shops in the neighborhood behind Senate Square, called **Kruunuhaka. The Forum** (⊠ Mannerheimintie 20) is a modern, multistory shopping center with a wide variety of stores offering clothing, gifts, books, and toys. You can shop until 10 PM daily in the shops along the Tunneli underpass underneath the train station. The **Kiseleff Bazaar Hall** (⊠ Aleksanterinkatu 22-28) has shops specializing in handicrafts, toys, knitwear, and children's items. **Kaunis Koru,** which sells Finnish-designed jewelry, is next door. **Kalevala Koru** (⊠ Unioninkatu 25) specializes in jewelry based on ancient Finnish designs.

Along Pohjoisesplanadi and Eteläesplanadi, across the gardens, you'll find Finland's design houses. **Hackman Shop Arabia** (⊠ Pohjoisesplanadi 25) sells Finland's well-known Arabia china and Iittala glass. **Pentik** (⊠ Pohjoisesplanadi 27) has artful leather goods. **Aarikka** (⊠ Pohjoisesplanadi 27 and Eteläesplanadi 8) offers wooden jewelry, toys, and gifts. **Artek** (⊠ Eteläesplanadi 18) is known for its Alvar Aalto-designed furniture and ceramics. **Marimekko** (⊠ Pohjoisesplanadi 31 and Eteläesplanadi 14) sells women's clothing, household items, and gifts made from its famous textiles. **Design Forum Finland** (⊠ Eteläesplanadi 8/Fabianinkatu 10), has exhibits and publications on the triumphs of Finnish design.

Department Stores

Stockmann's, a huge store that fills the entire block bordered by Aleksanterinkatu, Keskuskatu, Pohjoisesplanadi, and Mannerheimintie, is your best bet for finding everything under one roof.

Markets

The **Kauppatori** (Market Square) next to the South Harbor (☞ Exploring, *above*) is an absolute must year-round. In good weather you'll find a variety of goods at the **Hietalahti Flea Market,** on Hietalahti at the west end of Bulevardi. ☉ *Mon.–Sat. 7 AM–2 PM; mid-May–Aug.; also open weekdays 3 PM–8 PM.*

Dining

$$$$ ✕ **Alexander Nevski.** In a city famed for having the finest Russian cuisine in Scandinavia, it is hard to stand out as special. But the food, decor, and service at Alexander Nevski have come to be regarded as the best in Finland. Echoing the Russian-French style of 19th-century St. Petersburg

restaurants, the decor is dominated by palm trees and shades of green. Be sure to sample the game specialties—often baked in clay pots—and blinis. ⊠ *Pohjoisesplanadi 17,* ☎ *09/639–610. AE, DC, MC, V.*

\$\$\$\$ ✕ **Amadeus.** In an old town house near the South Harbor, Amadeus specializes in game dishes such as snow grouse, wild duck, and reindeer fillets. ⊠ *Sofiankatu 4,* ☎ *09/626–676. AE, DC, MC, V.*

\$\$\$\$ ✕ **Galateia.** Helsinki's best seafood restaurant is perched on top of the Inter-Continental hotel, with a magnificent view of the lake Töölönlahti. Try the lobster bisque with veal sweetbreads. ⊠ *Inter-Continental, Mannerheimintie 46,* ☎ *09/405–5900 or 09/40551. AE, DC, MC, V. Dinner only. Closed weekends.*

\$\$\$\$ ✕ **Havis Amanda.** Across the street from the Havis Amanda statue, this restaurant specializes in seafood dishes. A variety of prix-fixe menus is available at both lunch and dinner. Don't pass up the flamed cloudberry crepes served with ice cream for dessert. ⊠ *Unioninkatu 23,* ☎ *09/666–882. AE, DC, MC, V. Closed Sun.*

\$\$\$\$ ✕ **Restaurant Palace.** One of Helsinki's top restaurants, the Restau-
★ rant Palace offers elegant surroundings and a splendid view of South Harbor. Chef Markus Maulavirta specializes in Finnish and French fare. Recommended Finnish specialties include jellied roe of *muikku* (a kind of whitefish) with sour-cream dill sauce, and reindeer fillet and tongue with rowanberry sauce. ⊠ *Palace Hotel, Eteläranta 10,* ☎ *09/134– 561. AE, DC, MC, V. Closed weekends; dinner only in July.*

\$\$\$\$ ✕ **Savoy.** In keeping with its reputation as the favorite dining spot of
★ Finnish statesman Baron Carl Gustaf Mannerheim, the Savoy is Helsinki's first choice for business lunches or a festive splurge. The airy 1930s-style dining room with its grand view of the Esplanade Gardens was designed by architect Alvar Aalto. The Savoy still serves *Vorschmack* (appetizers of minced lamb and anchovies) made according to a recipe said to have been introduced by Mannerheim himself. ⊠ *Eteläesplanadi 14,* ☎ *09/176–571. AE, DC, MC, V. Closed weekends.*

\$\$\$ ✕ **Bellevue.** Established in 1917, the Bellevue is one of Helsinki's old-
★ est restaurants. Despite its French name, the restaurant is Russian, both in decor and cuisine. The fillet à la Novgorod (a traditional ox fillet prepared with carrots, barley, and sauerkraut) and chicken à la Kiev are the authentic articles here. ⊠ *Rahapajankatu 3,* ☎ *09/179–560. AE, DC, MC, V. No lunch weekends.*

\$\$\$ ✕ **Sipuli.** Sipuli, at the base of the Russian Orthodox Uspenski Cathedral, takes its name from the golden onion-shape cupolas that adorn the cathedral. In a brick warehouse dating from the late 19th century, French-style food is served with a Finnish flair. The skylight offers a spectacular view of the cathedral. ⊠ *Kanavaranta 3,* ☎ *09/179–900. AE, DC, MC, V. Dinner only. Closed weekends.*

\$\$\$ ✕ **Troikka.** The Troikka takes you back to czarist times in decor, paintings, and music, and offers exceptionally good food and friendly service. Try the Siberian *pelmeny* (small meat pastries). ⊠ *Caloniuksenkatu 3,* ☎ *09/445–229. AE, DC, MC, V. Closed Sun., weekends in July.*

\$\$\$ ✕ **Villa Thai.** This Thai-run kitchen serves authentic Thai food in elegant and comfortable surroundings—patrons have a choice between western and Thai-style seating. One exceptional dish is the curry with coconut milk and pineapple. ⊠ *Bulevardi 28,* ☎ *09/680–2778. AE, DC, MC, V.*

\$\$ ✕ **Asia King.** The Asia King offers generous portions of authentic Indian food in a modest but attractive setting. ⊠ *Sepänkatu 19,* ☎ *09/664–521. AE, DC, MC, V.*

\$\$ ✕ **Omenapuu.** A lunchtime favorite for shoppers and businesspeople, Omenapuu has a varied menu and a central location for a quick stop. The outside elevator in front of the shopping mall will take you up to the restaurant. ✉ *Keskuskatu 6, 2nd floor,* ☎ *09/630–205. AE, DC, MC, V.*

$ ✕ **Café København.** Generous open-face sandwiches are the specialty here; other substantial Scandinavian dishes—chicken with blue cheese sauce, for example—are on the menu as well. ✉ *Tehtaankatu 21,* ☎ *09/633–997. DC, MC, V.*

$ ✕ **Pikku Satama.** The casual Pikku Satama, in the renovated warehouse complex Wanha Satama in the Katajanokka neighborhood, serves a variety of lunch and dinner specialties—pizza, baked potatoes with various toppings, and hot dishes. ✉ *Pikku Satamakatu 3,* ☎ *09/174–093. AE, DC, MC, V. Closed Sun.*

$ ✕ **Ravintola Mechelin.** This is the restaurant associated with Helsinki's catering school. During summer the emphasis is on Finnish food, with myriad salmon options. ✉ *Perhonkatu 11,* ☎ *09/4056–2118. AE, DC, MC, V.*

Lodging

$$$$ 🏨 **Inter-Continental Helsinki.** This is the most popular hotel in the city—
★ at least with American visitors. It's modern and centrally located, close to Finlandia Hall and Finnish National Opera. Restaurant noise may disturb guests staying on the top floor. ✉ *Mannerheimintie 46, 00260,* ☎ *09/40551,* ꜰꜱꜱ *09/405–5255. 552 rooms with bath. 2 restaurants, bar, coffee shop, indoor pool, barbershop, sauna, exercise room. AE, DC, MC, V.*

$$$$ 🏨 **Palace.** The Palace has a splendid location overlooking the South Harbor—but make sure you ask for a room with a view (on the ninth floor). ✉ *Eteläranta 10, 00130,* ☎ *09/134–561,* ꜰꜱꜱ *09/654–786. 50 rooms with bath or shower. 2 restaurants, sauna. AE, DC, MC, V. Closed Dec. 25.*

$$$$ 🏨 **Radisson SAS Hotel Helsinki.** This central luxury hotel is a 10-minute walk from the train station. Its elegant rooms are decorated in four different styles: Scandinavian, Oriental, Italian, and Art Deco. If you want more space and privacy, try the business-class rooms on the hotel's top floors. The Johan Ludvig restaurant specializes in grilled meats. The other restaurant in the house, Ströget, is cheaper and offers buffets of pasta, salads, fish, meat, and fondue. ✉ *Runeberginkatu 2, 00100,* ☎ *09/69580,* ꜰꜱꜱ *09/6958–7100. 260 rooms with bath. 2 restaurants, bar, sauna, health club, meeting rooms. AE, DC, MC, V.*

$$$$ 🏨 **Ramada Presidentti.** In addition to its spacious rooms, the hotel also offers a wide range of facilities that continues to draw repeat visitors. Finland's first international casino was opened here in 1991 and has enjoyed tremendous success. The hotel's main restaurant, the Four Seasons, serves a tasty buffet. ✉ *Eteläinen Rautatiekatu 4, 00100,* ☎ *09/6911,* ꜰꜱꜱ *09/694–7886. 495 rooms with bath. 2 restaurants, bar, coffee shop, pool, sauna, casino, nightclub. AE, DC, MC, V.*

$$$$ 🏨 **Sokos Hotel Hesperia.** Currently undergoing a full renovation and refurnishing, the Hesperia is Finnish with a modern flair and just a short stroll from the center of the city. ✉ *Mannerheimintie 50, 00260,* ☎ *09/43101,* ꜰꜱꜱ *09/431–0995. 383 rooms, 302 with bath, 81 with shower. Restaurant, pool, sauna, golf, nightclub, meeting rooms, helipad. AE, DC, MC, V. Closed Dec. 25.*

$$$$ 🏨 **Strand Inter-Continental.** Adjacent to the Old City on the waterfront,
★ the hotel is both centrally located and tasteful: Granite and marble in the central lobby are accentuated by a soaring atrium and softened by a cozy fireplace. There is a choice of restaurants—Pamir's elegant gourmet dishes of seafood, steak, and game, or the Atrium Plaza's buffet restaurant for light meals. ✉ *John Stenbergin ranta 4, 00530,* ☎

09/39351, FAX 09/393–5255. *200 rooms with bath. 2 restaurants, bar, indoor pool, sauna. AE, DC, MC, V. Closed Dec. 25.*

$$$ ▦ **Airport Hotel Rantasipi.** Rooms here are rather small, but shuttle service is provided to the airport, which is just 3.2 kilometers (2 miles) away. ⊠ *Robert Huberintie 4, 01510 Vantaa,* ☎ 09/87051, FAX 09/822–846. *300 rooms with shower. Restaurant, piano bar, pool, sauna, meeting rooms. AE, DC, MC, V.*

$$$ ▦ **Grand Marina.** This renovated early 19th-century customs warehouse sits in the plush Katajanokka Island neighborhood. Its choice location, as well as friendly service and ample modern facilities, have made the hotel a success. Its congress center across the street—considered the best-equipped in the country—is prized by conventioneers. ⊠ *Katajanokanlaituri 7, 00160,* ☎ 09/16661, FAX 09/664–764. *462 rooms, 60 with bath, 402 with shower. 5 restaurants, bar, pub, sauna. AE, DC, MC, V.*

$$$ ▦ **Lord Hotel.** In a handsome stone castle built in 1903, rooms here offer contemporary furnishings in peaceful blue and gray tones. ⊠ *Lönnrotinkatu 29, 00180,* ☎ 09/615–815, FAX 09/680–1315. *48 rooms with bath or shower (17 rooms with Jacuzzi). Restaurant, bar, sauna, meeting rooms, free parking. AE, DC, MC, V. May be closed Dec. 25.*

$$$ ▦ **Rivoli Jardin.** The small but richly designed rooms in this centrally located town house overlook a quiet courtyard. Breakfast is served each morning in the winter garden. ⊠ *Kasarmikatu 40, 00130,* ☎ 09/177–880, FAX 09/656–988. *53 rooms with shower. Bar, sauna, meeting rooms. AE, DC, MC, V. Closed Dec. 25.*

$$$ ▦ **Seurahuone Socis.** This is a traditional hotel built in 1914 and ren-
★ ovated in 1992. Rooms range from sleek modern to formal classic with crystal chandeliers and brass bedsteads. The street-side rooms that face the train station are not always quiet. ⊠ *Kaivokatu 12, 00100,* ☎ 09/69141, FAX 09/691–4010. *118 rooms, 95 with bath, 23 with shower. Café, pub, sauna. AE, DC, MC, V. Usually closed Dec. 25.*

$$ ▦ **Arthur.** A property of the Helsinki YMCA, the Arthur is on a quiet, central street and is unpretentious and comfortable. ⊠ *Vuorikatu 19, 00100,* ☎ 09/173–441, FAX 09/626–880. *143 rooms with bath or shower. Restaurant, sauna. AE, DC, MC, V.*

$$ ▦ **Aurora.** About a mile from the city center, the Aurora is just opposite the Linnanmäki amusement park. Reasonable prices, cozy rooms, and good facilities have made this hotel a favorite with families. ⊠ *Helsinginkatu 50, 00530,* ☎ 09/717–400, FAX 09/714–240. *70 rooms, 6 with bath, 64 with shower. Restaurant, sauna, spa, squash. AE, DC, MC, V. Closed Dec. 25.*

$$ ▦ **Marttahotelli.** Rooms here are small but pleasantly decorated. The hotel is only a 10-minute walk from the Railway Station. ⊠ *Uudenmaankatu 24, 00120,* ☎ 09/646–211, FAX 09/680–1266. *45 rooms with bath or shower. Sauna. AE, DC, MC, V. Closed Dec. 25, Easter, and Midsummer.*

$$ ▦ **Merihotelli.** Standing right on the seafront, the Merihotelli is a 10-minute walk from the center of town. Rooms are somewhat small and modern; those with a sea view get some traffic noise. ⊠ *John Stenbergin ranta 6, 00530,* ☎ 09/69121, FAX 09/691–2214. *87 rooms with shower. 2 restaurants, coffee shop, sauna. AE, DC, MC, V. Closed Dec. 25.*

$ ▦ **Academica.** Fully renovated in 1992, this summer hotel is a standard student dormitory during the school year. However, its simple, adequate rooms, the 10-minute walk from the town center, and the impressive array of exercise facilities make staying here an excellent value. ⊠ *Hietaniemenkatu 14, 00100,* ☎ 09/402–0206, FAX 09/441–201. *115 rooms with shower and kitchenette. Pool, sauna, tennis court, coin laundry. AE, DC, MC, V. Closed Sept.–May.*

$ 🖼 **Skatta.** In the elegant neighborhood of Katajanokka Island, just 3 kilometers (2 miles) from the Railway Station, the Skatta is modest and practical; each room has a kitchenette. ⊠ *Linnankatu 3, 00160,* ☎ *09/659–233 or 09/669–984,* FAX *09/631–352. 23 rooms with shower and kitchenette. Sauna, exercise room. AE, DC, MC, V. Sometimes closed on Dec. 25.*

The Arts

For a list of events, pick up the free publication *Helsinki This Week,* available in hotels and tourist offices. In summer, the guide lists a telephone number for recorded program information in English. Tickets for all major events are available from **Lippupalvelu** (⊠ Mannerheimintie 5), ☎ 9600–4600 for cultural events, ☎ 9700–4700 for sports, 09/6138–6232 from abroad). Call **Tiketti** (⊠ Yrjönkatu 29C, ☎ 9700–4202) to book tickets for small concerts at clubs and restaurants.

Theater
Although all performances are in Finnish or Swedish, summertime productions in such bucolic settings as **Suomenlinna Island, Kekuspuisto Park, Mustikkamaa Island,** the **Rowing Stadium** (operettas), the **Indoor Ice Rink** (rock concerts), and the **Savoy Theater** (ballet and music performances) make enjoyable entertainment. The splendid **Kansallisooppera** (⊠ National Opera, ☎ 09/4030–2211) opened in 1993 in a waterside park overlooking Töölönlahti, just a few hundred feet from Finlandia Hall.

Concerts
The main concert venues are **Finlandia Hall** (☎ 09/40241), **Temppeliaukio Church** (☎ 09/494–698), and the **Sibelius Academy** (☎ 09/405–441).

Festivals
Many festivals are scheduled throughout the country, especially during the summer months. The **Helsinki Festival** is said to be the biggest in Scandinavia. For more than two weeks during August and September, there are scores of musical happenings and art exhibitions. Contact Helsinki Festival (⊠ Rauhankatu 7E, ☎ 09/135–4522, FAX 09/278–1578). For information on more festivals, call Finland Festivals (⊠ Mannerheimintie 40, B49, ☎ 09/445–686, FAX 09/445–117).

Nightlife

Bars and Lounges
One of Helsinki's most popular nightspots is **Happy Days** (⊠ Pohjoisesplanadi 2, ☎ 09/657–700), known for its hamburgers and outdoor terrace. The historic **Kappeli** (⊠ Eteläesplanadi 1, ☎ 09/179–242) brews its own beer. **Kaarle XII** (⊠ Kasarmikatu 40, ☎ 09/171–312) is located in one of Helsinki's striking German Art Nouveau buildings. **Cantina West** (⊠ Kasarmikatu 23, ☎ 09/622–1500) is a Tex-Mex bar and restaurant with live music nightly.

Jazz Clubs
Try **Storyville** (⊠ Museokatu 8, ☎ 09/408–007), where Finnish and foreign jazz musicians complement New Orleans-style cuisine. Modern jazz brings a hip, young crowd to the **Hot Tomato Jazz Café** (⊠ Annankatu 6, ☎ 09/680–1701).

Nightclubs
Helsinki's largest and most famous club is the **Hesperia Nightclub** (⊠ Hotel Hesperia, Kivelänkatu 2, ☎ 09/43101). **Fennia** (⊠ Mikonkatu 17, ☎ 09/666–355) has dancing and live music on weekends. **Café Adlon** (⊠ Fabianinkatu 14, ☎ 09/664–611) is a well-known disco. **Kaivo-**

huone (Kaivopuisto Park, ☎ 09/177–881) is a summertime favorite in an attractive park setting.

THE LAKELANDS

In southeastern and central Finland, the light has a softness that seems to brush the forests, lakes, and islands, changing the landscape throughout the day. For centuries this beautiful region was a much-contested buffer between the warring empires of Sweden and Russia. The Finns of the Lakelands prevailed by sheer *sisu* (guts), and now their descendants thrive amid the rough beauty of the terrain.

Getting Around

Savonlinna is the most conveniently situated town in the Lakelands and can make a convenient base from which to begin exploring. You can fly to the Savonlinna area from Helsinki in 40 minutes; a connecting bus takes you the remaining 16 kilometers (10 miles) into town. By train, the journey takes 5½ hours; by bus, six hours.

If you travel by car, you can do the lake trips as separate excursions. The alternative is to take advantage of the excellent network of air, rail, bus, and boat transportation. From the end of June through August, you can take the boat from Savonlinna to Kuopio in 11½ hours (**Roll Cruises,** ☎ 971/262–6744). From Kuopio, take the 320-kilometer (200-mile) cross-country bus ride via Jyväskylä to Tampere. Continue by boat to Hämeenlinna for a little more than eight hours (**Finnish Silverline,** ☎ 931/124–803). The final leg by bus or train back to Helsinki takes about 1¼ hours.

Guided Tours

A program of **Friendly Finland Tours,** available through travel agencies in Finland and abroad, offers escorted packages that include stops in the Lakelands. The three-day "Saimaa Lake Tour" and the seven-day "Scenic Tour" both start in Helsinki. Brochures are available from the **Finland Travel Bureau** and its overseas offices (☞ Important Addresses and Numbers *in* Helsinki, *above*).

Visitor Information

Hämeenlinna (⊠ Sibeliuksenkatu 5A, 13100, ☎ 917/621–2388).
Kuopio (⊠ Haapaniemenkatu 17, 70110, ☎ 971/182–584).
Savonlinna (⊠ Puistokatu 1, 57100, ☎ 957/273–492).
Tampere (⊠ Verkatehtaankatu 2, 33211, ☎ 931/212–6652).

Exploring the Lakelands

Savonlinna

The center of **Savonlinna** is a series of islands linked by bridges. First, stop at the tourist office for information; then cross the bridge east to the **open-air market** that flourishes alongside the main passenger quay. In days when ships were the major form of transportation, Savonlinna was the central hub of the passenger fleet serving Saimaa, the largest lake system in Europe. Now lake traffic is dominated by cruise and sightseeing boats.

★ A 10-minute stroll from the quay to the southeast brings you to Savonlinna's most famous sight, the castle **Olavinlinna.** First built in 1475 to protect Finland's eastern border, the castle retains its medieval character and is one of Scandinavia's best-preserved historic monuments. Still surrounded by the water that once made it impregnable, the fortress rises majestically out of the lake. The **Savonlinna Opera Festival** is held in the courtyard each July. Make reservations well in advance for both the opera and hotel rooms; contact the Savonlinna Tourist Service (☎ 957/273–492, FAX 957/514–449) for a current festival schedule and ticket information. ☎ 957/531–164. ✉ *Castle: FIM 20; includes guided tours on the hr. ☉ June–Aug., daily 10–5; Sept.–May, daily 10–3.*

The 19th-century steam schooners **SS Mikko, SS Salama,** and **SS Savonlinna** are three museum ships berthed close to the castle. ✉ *FIM 15. ☉ Aug.–June, Tues.–Sun. 11–5; July, Tues.–Sun. 10–8.*

The most popular excursion from Savonlinna is to **Taidekeskus Retretti** (Retretti Art Center), which you can reach via a two-hour boat ride or a 30-minute, 29-kilometer (18-mile) bus trip. The bus journey takes you along the 8-kilometer (5-mile) ridge of **Punkaharju.** This breathtaking ridge of pine-covered rocks, which rises out of the water and separates the lakes on either side, predates the Ice Age. At times it narrows to only 25 feet, yet it still manages to accommodate a road and train tracks. ☎ 957/644–253. ✉ *FIM 65. ☉ May 24–June 21 and Aug., daily 10–6; June 22–July, daily 10–7.*

Near Retretti is the **Punkaharju National Hotel** (✉ Punkaharju 2, ☎ 957/644–251). The building was constructed as a gamekeeper's lodge for Czar Nicholas I in 1845 but has since been enlarged and restored. Now it's a restful spot for a meal or an overnight visit.

Kuopio

The 11½-hour boat trip from Savonlinna to **Kuopio** is probably the best opportunity you'll get to appreciate the soul of the Finnish Lakelands. Meals are available on board. The boat arrives at Kuopio's passenger harbor, where you'll find a small evening market daily from 3 to 10.

★ Kuopio's tourist office is located close to the **Tori** (marketplace). Called *mualiman napa* ("the belly-button of the world"), Kuopio's market square is one of the most colorful outdoor markets in Finland. ☉ *Apr.–Sept., weekdays 7–5, Sat. 7–2; Oct.–Mar., 7–2.*

The **Ortodoksinen Kirkkomuseo** (Orthodox Church Museum) has one of the most interesting and unusual collections of its kind in the world. When Karelia (the eastern province of Finland) was ceded to the Soviet Union after World War II, religious art was removed from its monasteries and brought to Kuopio. ✉ *Karjalankatu 1, ☎ 971/261–8818. ✉ FIM 15. ☉ May–Aug., Tues.–Sun. 10–4; Sept.–Apr., weekdays noon–3, weekends noon–5.*

Visitors fascinated by the treasures in the museum will want to visit **Valamon Luostari** (Valamo Monastery); a center for Russian Orthodox religious and cultural life in Finland, it holds daily services. Precious 18th-century icons and other sacred objects are housed in the main church and in the icon conservation center, and the Orthodox library—the most extensive in Finland—is open to visitors. On the grounds are a café-restaurant as well as hotel and hostel accommodations. Valamo can be reached by car and by bus from Kuopio, Joensuu, and Varkaus. The Kuopio Tourist Service (✉ Haapaniemenkatu 17, ☎ 017/182–584) provides bus and boat excursions to Valamo; from there it's a short ride by boat, bus, or taxi to **Lintulan Luostari,** the Orthodox convent of Lintula. ✉ *Uusi Valamo, ☎ 972/570–111 (972/570–1501 for hotel reservations). ✉ Free. Guided tours: FIM 20 adults, FIM 5 children. ☉ Daily 8 AM–9 PM; open at 7 AM Mar.–Sept.*

Puijo Näkötorni (Puijo Tower) is best visited at sunset, when the lakes shimmer with reflected light. The slender tower stands 3 kilometers

The Lakelands

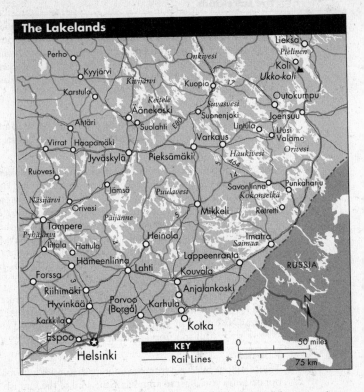

(2 miles) northwest of Kuopio. It has two observation decks and a re-volving restaurant on top from which you can enjoy the marvelous views. ☎ 971/209–103. ☜ FIM 15. *Free Sept.–Apr.* ☉ *May–Sept., daily 11–11; Oct.–Apr., daily 11–10.*

Tampere

The 320-kilometer (200-mile) journey from Kuopio to **Tampere** will take four to five hours, whether you travel by car or bus. Almost every guide will inform you that Tampere, the country's third-largest city, is Finland's Pittsburgh. However, the resemblance begins and ends with the con-centration of industry—the settings themselves have little in common.

From about the year 1000, this part of Finland was a base from which traders and hunters set out on their expeditions to northern Finland. But it was not until 1779 that a Swedish king, Gustav III, founded Tam-pere. One hundred and three years later, a Scotsman by the name of James Finlayson came to the infant city and established a factory for spinning cotton. The firm of Finlayson exists today and is still one of the country's large industrial enterprises.

An isthmus, little more than half a mile wide at its narrowest point, separates the lakes Näsijärvi and Pyhäjärvi, and at one spot the wa-ters of one rush through to the other down the **Tammerkoski Rapids.** Called the "Mother of Tampere," these rapids provide some of the power upon which the town's livelihood depends. Their natural beauty has been preserved despite the presence of the factories on either bank, and the distinctive public buildings of the city grouped around them add to the overall effect. Also in the heart of town is **Hämeensilta Bridge,** with four statues—*The Hunter, The Merchant, The Maid of Finland,* and *The Tax Collector.*

Close to the Hämeensilta Bridge, near the high-rise Hotel Ilves, some old factory buildings have been restored as shops and boutiques. Nearby, at Verkatehtaankatu 2, the city tourist office offers helpful service and sells a 24-hour **Tourist Ticket** (FIM 25 adults, FIM 20 children) that allows unlimited travel on city transportation.

To the west of the Tammerkoski Rapids, the Särkänniemi peninsula holds many attractions, just a 20-minute walk from the city center. On the way there, visit one of Tampere's best museums, the **Amurin Työläismuseokortteli** (Amuri Museum of Workers' Housing). The museum consists of more than 30 wooden houses, plus a sauna, bakery, haberdashery, and more from the 1880s to the 1970s, recounting almost a century of history through glimpses of everyday life. ⊠ *Makasiininkatu 12,* ☎ *931/214–1633.* 💳 *FIM 15.* ☉ *Mid-May–mid-Sept., Tues.–Sat. 9–5, Sun. 11–5.*

Särkänniemen Huvikeskus (Särkäniemi Amusement Center) is a major recreation complex for both children and adults, made up of an amusement park, a children's zoo, a planetarium, and a well-planned aquarium with a separate dolphinarium. Within Särkäniemi, the **Sara Hildénin Taidemuseo** (Sara Hildén Art Museum) is a striking example of Finnish architecture, and displays works by modern Finnish and international artists, among them Chagall, Klee, Miró, and Picasso. ⊠ *Särkänniemi,* ☎ *931/248–8111; Hildén Museum,* ☎ *931/214–3134.* 💳 *Joint admission: FIM 130; Hildén Museum only: FIM 15.* ☉ *Daily 11–6.*

Särkänniemi also includes Finland's tallest structure, the 168-meter (550-foot) **Näsinneula Observation Tower,** which dominates the Tampere skyline. At the top of the tower are an observatory and a revolving restaurant. The views of the lake, the forest, and the town are magnificent—the contrast between the industrial maze of Tampere at your feet and the serenity of the lakes stretching out to meet the horizon is unforgettable. 💳 *FIM 12.* ☉ *June–Aug., daily 10–10; Sept.–May, daily 10–4.*

It was in Tampere that Lenin and Stalin first met, and that fateful meeting is commemorated with displays of photos and mementoes in the **Lenin Museo** (Lenin Museum). ⊠ *Hämeenpuisto 28, 3rd floor,* ☎ *931/212–7313.* 💳 *FIM 15.* ☉ *Weekdays 9–5, weekends 11–4.*

Two of Tampere's major churches are on the east side of town. The modern **Kalevan Kirkko** (Kaleva Church) is a soaring monument to light and space. ⊠ *Lissanpuisto 1.* ☉ *May–Aug., daily 10–5; Sept.–Apr., daily 11–3.*

The **Tuomiokirkko** (cathedral), built in 1907, houses some of the best-known masterpieces of Finnish art, including Magnus Encknell's *The Resurrection* and a few works by Hugo Simberg, including *Wounded Angel* and *Garden of Death.* ⊠ *Tuomiokirkonkatu.* ☉ *May–Aug., daily 10–6; Sept.–Apr., daily 11–3.*

One of the most popular excursions from Tampere is the **"Poet's Way"** boat tour along Lake Näsijärvi. The boat passes through the agricultural parish of Ruovesi, where J. L. Runeberg, Finland's national poet, once lived. Shortly before the boat docks at Virrat, you'll pass through the straits of Visuvesi, where many artists and writers spend their summers. ⊠ *Finnish Silverline and "Poet's Way," Verkatehtaankatu 2,* ☎ *931/212–4804.* 💳 *Round-trip fare: FIM 310.*

Hämeenlinna

★ The Finnish Silverline's white motor ships (☎ 931/212–4804) leave Tampere every morning from the Laukontori harbor for **Hämeenlinna.** If you're traveling by car, take Highway 3 and stop en route at the famous

Iittala Lasikeskus (Iittala Glass Centre), which offers museum tours and has a shop. The magnificent glass is produced by top designers, and the seconds are bargains you won't find elsewhere. ⊠ *14500 Iittala,* ☏ *917/535–6230.* ▨ *FIM 10 (FIM 7 in winter).* ☉ *Museum open May–Aug., daily 10–6; Sept.–Apr., weekdays 10–5, weekends 10–6. Factory shop open May–Aug., daily 10–8; Sept.–Apr., daily 10–6.*

Hämeenlinna's secondary school has educated many famous Finns, among them composer Jean Sibelius (1865–1957). The only surviving timber house in the town center is the **Sibeliuksen syntymäkoti** (Sibelius's birthplace), a modest dwelling built in 1834. The museum staff will play your favorite Sibelius CD as you tour the rooms, one of which houses the harmonium Sibelius played as a child. ⊠ *Hallituskatu 11,* ☏ *917/612–5698.* ▨ *FIM 10.* ☉ *May–Aug., daily 10–4; Sept.–Apr., daily noon–4.*

Hämeen Linna (Häme Castle) is Finland's oldest castle: Swedish crusaders began building it in the thirteenth century to strengthen and defend the Sweden's domination of the region. In modern times the castle has served in turn as a granary and as a prison. It is now restored and open to the public for tours and exhibitions. The castle sits on the lakeshore half a mile north of Hämeenlinna's town center. Guided tours in English are given every hour in the summer and are available every hour in winter by appointment only. ⊠ *Kustaa III: n katu 6,* ☏ *03/675–6820.* ▨ *FIM 15.* ☉ *May–Aug. 14, daily 10–6; Aug. 15–Apr., daily 10–4.*

The **Hattulan Kirkko** (Hattula Church) in nearby Hattula, 6 kilometers (3½ miles) to the north, is the most famous of Finland's medieval churches. The interior has frescoes of biblical scenes in which the vicious little devils and soulful saints are still as vivid as when they were first painted around 1510. ☏ *917/672–3383 during opening hours; 917/637–2477 at all other times.* ▨ *FIM 15.* ☉ *May 14–Aug. 14, daily 11–5; open at other times by previous appointment.*

Rail and bus departures to Helsinki are frequent. If you're traveling by car, take Highway 12. As you pass by **Riihimäki,** you'll see signs to the **Suomen Lasimuseo** (Finnish Glass Museum). Follow them for an outstanding display of the history of glass from early Egyptian times to the present, artfully arranged in an old glass factory. ⊠ *Tehtaankatu 23, Riihimäki,* ☏ *914/741–494.* ▨ *FIM 15.* ☉ *Apr.–Sept., daily 10–6; Oct.–Dec., Feb.–Mar., Tues.–Sun. 10–6.*

Dining and Lodging

Hämeenlinna

$$ ✕ **Bistro Park.** In a renovated old timber building, Bistro Park offers Finnish and international fare. ⊠ *Kirkkorinne 2,* ☏ *917/612–1606. DC, MC, V.*

$$ ✕ **Huviretki.** For light, artful cuisine, try the salmon soup or the smoked reindeer salad in this friendly eatery. They also have a wide range of standard international fare, such as pepper steak and honey chicken—all with an emphasis on presentation. The restaurant is located inside the Cumulus Hotel. ⊠ *Raathuneenkatu 16–18,* ☏ *917/64881. AE, DC, MC, V.*

$$$ 🏨 **Rantasipi Aulanko.** One of Finland's top hotels sits on the lakeshore
★ in a beautifully landscaped park 6.4 kilometers (4 miles) from town. ⊠ *13210 Hämeenlinna,* ☏ *917/658–801,* FAX *917/682–1922. 245 rooms with bath. Indoor pool, sauna, golf, tennis court, horseback riding, boating, nightclub. AE, DC, MC, V.*

Kuopio

$$$ ✕ **Musta Lammas.** Near the passenger harbor, the attractive Musta Lammas occupies what was once a beer cellar, and features Finnish specialties. ⊠ *Satamakatu 4,* ☎ *971/262–3494. AE, DC, MC, V. Closed Sun.*

$$ ✕ **Sampo Vapaasatama.** The specialty here is whitefish. The atmosphere is unpretentious and lively, and the location in the town center is convenient for a quick meal. ⊠ *Kauppakatu 13,* ☎ *971/261–4677. AE, DC, MC, V.*

$$$ ⊞ **Arctia Hotel Kuopio.** The most up-to-date and best equipped of local hotels, the Arctia has all the advantages of a lakefront location while being close to the center of town. ⊠ *Satamakatu 1, 70100,* ☎ *971/195–111,* FAX *971/195–170. 141 rooms with bath or shower. Pool, sauna, boating. AE, DC, MC, V.*

$$ ⊞ **Hotel-Spa Rauhalahti.** Sports-oriented travelers and families flock to this high-energy setting. Close to the lakeshore and 4.8 kilometers (3 miles) from the town center, Rauhalahti offers lively activities and conveniences for all ages and interests. The hotel has three restaurants, including the tavern-style Vanha Apteekkari—a favorite with locals. ⊠ *Katiskaniementie 8, 70700,* ☎ *971/473–111,* FAX *971/473–470. 106 rooms with bath or shower, 13 apartments, and 20 hostel rooms. 3 restaurants, sauna, spa, tennis court, badminton, exercise room, horseback riding, boating, nightclub. AE, DC, MC, V.*

$$ ⊞ **Iso-Valkeinen Hotel.** The rooms are spacious and quiet at this lakeshore property, only 5 kilometers (3 miles) from the town center. ⊠ *Päiväranta, 70420,* ☎ *971/539–6100,* FAX *971/539–6555. 100 rooms with shower. 2 restaurants, pool, sauna, miniature golf, tennis court, beach, boating, fishing, nightclub. AE, DC, MC, V.*

Savonlinna

$$$ ✕ **Rauhalinna.** This romantic turn-of-the-century timber villa was built by a general in the Imperial Russian Army. From town it's 16 kilometers (10 miles) by road, 40 minutes by boat. Both the food and atmosphere are Old Russian, touched by Finnish accents. ⊠ *Lehtiniemi,* ☎ *957/523–119. Festival-season reservations essential. AE, DC, MC, V. Closed Aug. 7–July 3.*

$$ ✕ **Majakka.** Centrally located, Majakka goes in for home cooking and a family atmosphere. ⊠ *Satamakatu 11,* ☎ *957/21456. Festival-season reservations essential. AE, DC, MC, V.*

$ ✕ **Paviljonki.** An affiliate of the Savonlinna restaurant school, this convenient spot just 1 kilometer west of the city serves classic Finnish dishes. ⊠ *Rajalahdenkatu 4,* ☎ *957/520–960. DC, MC, V.*

$$$–$$$$ ⊞ **Seurahuone.** This hotel is near the market and passenger harbor. An open-air summer restaurant has view of the harbor and the market. ⊠ *Kauppatori 4–6, 57130,* ☎ *957/5731,* FAX *957/273–918. 84 rooms with shower. 6 restaurants, bar, sauna, nightclub. AE, DC, MC, V. Closed Dec. 25.*

$$$ ⊞ **Casino Spa.** Built in the 1960s and renovated in 1986, the Casino Spa has a bucolic lakeside setting on an island linked by a pedestrian bridge to the center of town. ⊠ *Kylpylaitoksentie, Kasinosaari, 57130,* ☎ *957/57500,* FAX *957/272–524. 80 rooms with shower. Restaurant, pool, sauna, spa, boating. AE, DC, MC, V.*

$–$$ ⊞ **Vuorilinna Summer Hotel.** Guests at this modern hotel enjoy the same island setting and facilities as guests at the more expensive Casino Spa Hotel nearby. ⊠ *Kasinonsaari, 57130,* ☎ *957/57500,* FAX *957/272–524. 225 rooms, with shower for every 2 rooms. AE, DC, MC, V. Closed Sept.–May.*

Tampere

$$$ ✕ **Tiiliholvi.** Fish, meat, and game dishes are the specialties of this romantic converted cellar. ⊠ *Kauppakatu 10,* ☎ *931/212–1220. AE, DC, MC, V. Closed Sun.*

$$ ✕ **Astor.** Dark wood and red tones create a pleasant ambience in which to try the kitchen's renowned reindeer and snow grouse dishes. In the evening, candlelight and live piano music add still more charm. ⊠ *Aleksis Kivenkatu 26,* ☎ *931/213–3522. AE, DC, MC, V.*

$$ ✕ **Bodega Salud.** Bodega Salud has a well-earned reputation for Spanish specialties, though it also has such unconventional dishes as grilled alligator and stewed kangaroo. ⊠ *Otavalankatu 10,* ☎ *931/223–5996. AE, DC, MC, V.*

$$ ✕ **Silakka.** Despite its casual atmosphere, Silakka (which means Baltic
★   herring) has earned a considerable reputation with its Finnish fish specialties. The restaurant is on the second floor of the Koskikeskus shopping mall. ⊠ *Koskikeskus, Hatanpään valtatie 1,* ☎ *931/214–9740. DC, MC, V.*

$$$$ 🏨 **Sokos Hotel Ilves.** This hotel soars above a newly gentrified area of old warehouses near the city center. It is favored by Americans. ⊠ *Hatanpäänvaltatie 1, 33100,* ☎ *03/262–6262,* 🖷 *03/262–6263. 336 rooms with bath or shower. 4 restaurants, no-smoking floor, pool, sauna, exercise room, nightclub. AE, DC, MC, V. May be closed Dec. 25, Midsummer, Easter.*

$$$ 🏨 **Cumulus Koskikatu.** Overlooking the tamed rapids of Tammerkoski, Cumulus Koskikatu is central and modern. The Finnair terminal is in the same building. ⊠ *Koskikatu 5, 33100,* ☎ *931/242–4399,* 🖷 *931/242–4399. 227 rooms with shower. Restaurant, bar, pool, sauna, nightclub. AE, DC, MC, V.*

$ 🏨 **Domus Summer Hotel.** About 3 kilometers (2 miles) from the center of town in the Kaleva district, this standard hotel represents a good value. ⊠ *Pellervonkatu 9, 33540,* ☎ *931/255–0000,* 🖷 *931/222–5409. 137 rooms, 80 with shower. Pool, sauna. MC, V. Closed Sept.–May.*

FINNISH LAPLAND

Lapland, a region of great silences with endless forests and fells, is often called Europe's last wilderness,. Settlers in Finnish Lapland have walked gently and left the landscape almost unspoiled. Now easily accessible, this Arctic outpost offers visitors all the necessary comforts and the chance to experience an almost primordial solitude.

The oldest traces of human habitation in Finland have been found in Lapland, where hoards of Danish, English, and even Arabian coins indicate active trading many centuries ago. Until the 1930s, Lapland was still largely unexploited, and any trip to the region was an expedition. Its isolation ended when the Canadian-owned Petsamo Nickel Company completed the great road, now known as the Arctic Highway, connecting Rovaniemi with the Arctic Sea.

There are only about 4,500 native Sami still living in Lapland; the remainder of the province's population of 220,000 is Finnish. Though Sami culture has inevitably been influenced by tourism, recent grassroots efforts to preserve its language and traditions have been largely successful. Sami tradition has much of interest to the respectful tourist. Sami craftspeople create beautiful objects and clothing out of the materials readily at hand: wood, bone, and reindeer pelts. The Lady Day church festival in Enontekiö in March is a particularly colorful event, attended by many Sami in their most brilliant costumes and usually featuring reindeer racing or lassoing competitions.

In December and January, Sami and Finnish reindeer owners bring their herds together from all over Lapland and corral them by the thousands. Sometimes dressed in colorful traditional costumes, the herders lasso their reindeer in true Wild West fashion, recognizing their own animals by brand marks on their ears. These roundups are attended by numerous buyers, for reindeer meat is considered a delicacy and is exported to the south of Finland and abroad.

Many reindeer corrals are near the road, especially around Ivalo, Inari, and Enontekiö. To get to some of the more remote roundups, however, you may have to travel by taxi plane. Most Sami and northern Finns get there on the motorized sleds that have almost wholly replaced the traditional and much more attractive reindeer-drawn *pulkka,* boat-shape sleighs on one runner. An increasing number of roundups occur in the fall, especially in southern Lapland. Since roundups depend on the whims of the weather and the herds themselves, it can be difficult to find out exactly when and where they are to take place; check locally.

Though summer offers no reindeer corralling, it does have the blessing of daylight for up to 24 hours, and beautiful weather typically accompanies the nightless days. In early fall the colors are so fabulous that the Finns have a special word for it: *ruskaa.* If you can take the intense but dry cold, winter in Lapland is full of fascinating experiences, from the northern lights to reindeer roundups.

Experienced travelers who wish to roam the wilds for days on end without meeting a fellow human being can still do so with ease in Lapland. Be warned, however, that weather conditions can change quickly and dangerously. Always seek local advice and let your hotel and friends know where you are heading and how long you intend to be gone. If you would rather not strike out on your own, an attractive alternative is to join an organized canoeing or hiking trip spending nights in huts or tents in the wilderness.

Getting Around

Rovaniemi is the best base for traveling around the Arctic area. Road, rail, and air links connect it to Helsinki and the south—there are daily flights from Rovaniemi to Ivalo. There's even a car-train from Helsinki. Driving is the easiest way to get around the Arctic area, although regular bus service connects most regional centers.

Guided Tours

Friendly Finland Tours, operated by the Finland Travel Bureau (✉ Incoming and Incentive Department, PL 319, 00101 Helsinki, ☎ 09/18261), offers an escorted five-day "North Cape" tour in summer and a seven-day "Winter's Tale" tour, both departing from Helsinki.

Visitor Information

Ivalo (✉ Ivalontie 12, 99800, ☎ 9697/662–521).
Rovaniemi (✉ Koskikatu 1, 96200, ☎ 960/346–270). For further information on the region, contact **Lapland Travel** (✉ Koskikatu 1, 96200, ☎ 960/346–052).
Saariselkä (✉ Saariselkätie, PL 22, 99831, ☎ 9697/668–122).
Sodankylä (✉ Jäämerentie 9, 99600, ☎ 9693/613–474).

Exploring Lapland

Rovaniemi

Your best launching point is the town of **Rovaniemi,** almost on the Arctic Circle at the confluence of the Ounas and Kemi rivers. Rovaniemi is the so-called Gateway to Lapland—the province's administrative and communications hub.

If you're expecting an Arctic shanty town, you're in for a surprise. Rovaniemi was nearly razed by the retreating German army in 1944, so what you'll see today is a modern-looking university town and cultural center strongly influenced by Alvar Aalto's architecture. In the process of rebuilding, the city grew from a population of 8,000 to around 34,000, so be prepared to find it a contemporary city on the edge of the wilderness, with a number of amenities and some incredible architecture. One notable structure is the **Lappia-Talo** (Lappia House), an Aalto-designed concert and congress center that houses the world's northernmost professional theater.

After collecting information from the tourist office, find a window table in the restaurant at the nearby **Pohjanhovi Hotel** (⌧ Pohjanpuistikko 2) and contemplate your next move while gazing at the swiftly flowing Ounas rapids.

★ You can get a good instant introduction to the region and its natural history at the **Arktikum** (Arctic Research Center), 1 kilometer (½ mile) north of Lappia-Talo. The Arktikum houses the Museum of the Province of Lapland, with exhibits on Sami culture. Guided tours are available. ⌧ *Pohjoisranta 4,* ☎ *960/317–840.* ▣ *FIM 45.* ☉ *May–Aug., daily 10–6; Sept.–Apr., Tues.–Sun. 10–6.*

You'll also get a feel for the living past of Lapland's hardy inhabitants at the **Pöykkölä Museum,** housed in 19th-century farm buildings just 3 kilometers (2 miles) from the town center. ⌧ *Pöykkölä,* ☎ *016/348–1095.* ▣ *FIM 10.* ☉ *June–Aug., Tues.–Sun. noon–4. Bus service available.*

Arctic Highway

The Arctic Highway (Highway 4) is the main artery through central and northern Lapland; you'll follow it north for most of this tour. Eight kilometers (5 miles) north of Rovaniemi, right on the Arctic Circle,
★ is **Santa Claus Village,** where you can shop for gifts at any time of year and have your purchases shipped and marked with a special Santa Claus Land stamp. For most visitors, the main attractions are Santa Claus himself, the chance to mail postcards home from the special Arctic Circle post office, and seeing the mountains of mail that pour in from all over. Yes, he answers every letter! ⌧ *96930 Arctic Circle,* ☎ FAX *960/356–2096.* ▣ *Free.* ☉ *June–Aug., daily 8–8; Sept.–May, daily 10–5.*

Continue north through the village of Vuotso to **Tankavaaran Kultakylän** (Tankavaara Gold Village), the most accessible and best developed of several gold-panning areas. The **Kultamuseo** (Gold Museum) tells the century-old story of Lapland's hardy fortune seekers. In the summer months authentic prospectors will show you how to wash gold dust and tiny nuggets from the dirt of an ice-cold stream. You can keep what you find, but don't expect an early retirement. ⌧ *Arctic Highway 4, Kultakylä, Tankavaara,* ☎ *9693/626–158.* ▣ *FIM 55 (FIM 25 in winter); summer admission includes gold washing.* ☉ *June–Aug. 15, daily 9–6; Aug. 16–Oct., daily 9–5; Nov.–May, daily 10–4.*

Finnish Lapland

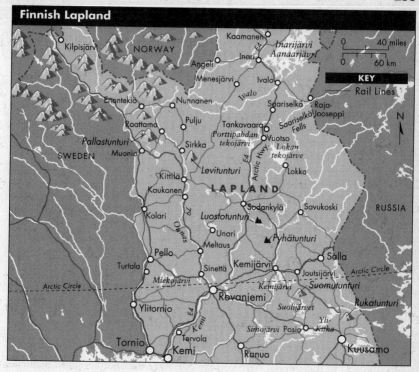

Thirty miles (19 kilometers) north of Tankavaara is the resort center of **Saariselkä**, which has a variety of accommodations. This makes a sensible base from which to set off on a trip into the true wilderness; during the snowy months, it's where you'll find the finest cross-country and downhill skiing in Finland. There are marked trails through forests and over fells where nothing much has changed since the last Ice Age, and where you can experience the timeless silence of the Arctic. More than 2,500 square kilometers (965 square miles) of this magnificent area has been set aside as **Uhrokekkosen Kansallispüisto** (Urho Kekkonen National Park).

Northern Lapland

Just south of the village of Ivalo, the highway passes the **Ivalojoki** (Ivalo River). It is possible to join a canoe trip down its swift waters to Lake Inari, returning by bus. The village of **Ivalo** is the main center for northern Lapland. With a first-class hotel, an airport, and the standard amenities of a modern community, Ivalo is not the place for the tourist in search of a wilderness experience.

The huge island-studded expanses of **Inarijärvi** (Lake Inari), north of Ivalo, offer endless possibilities for wilderness exploration. It is a beautiful 40-kilometer (25-mile) drive northwest from Ivalo, along the lakeshore, to **Inari,** home of the Sámi Parlamenta (parliament). This is a good base for summer boat excursions. The **Saamelaismuseo** (Sami Museum), on the village outskirts, covers all aspects of Sami culture. ✉ Inari, ☎ 9697/671–014. 🎫 FIM 20. ⏰ June 1–Aug. 10, daily 8–10; Aug. 11–31, daily 8–8; Sept. 1–20, daily 9–3:30.

In recent years, a growing number of small holiday villages have blossomed near Inari and to the north, usually offering a small restaurant and attached shop. Conveniences are simple, but the locations are often magnificent and bring you very close to the true pulse of Lapland. In most of these villages you'll have the chance to rent a boat, go fishing, and even prepare your own sauna. From Kaamanen, north of Inari, a side road leads to **Sevettijärvi,** home of the Skolt Sami, and eventually across into Norway.

It is an attractive drive back south from Inari to **Menesjärvi** following a relatively new secondary road that passes through a wilderness of forest and swamps. Take every opportunity to leave your car and do some walking; it's the only way to experience the vastness of these Arctic spaces. The hills get gentler and the ride less dramatic as you continue south to Levitunturi, the last of the gently sloping fells before you reach the banks of the Ounas River and turn onto Highway 79 for the return to Rovaniemi.

Dining and Lodging

Inari

$$ ⊞ **Inari Kultahovi.** This old inn, renovated in 1987, stands on the wooded bank of a swiftly flowing river. ✉ 99870 Inari, ☎ 9697/671–221, FAX 9697/671–250. 29 rooms with shower. Restaurant, sauna. DC, MC, V.

Ivalo

$$ ⊞ **Ivalo.** Modern and fully equipped, the Hotel Ivalo is right on the river about a kilometer (½ mile) from the village center. One of its two restaurants serves Lapland specialties, including *poronkäristys,* a reindeer casserole. ✉ Ivalontie 34, 99800 Ivalo, ☎ 9697/688–111, FAX 9697/661–905. 94 rooms with bath or shower. 2 restaurants, pool, sauna. AE, DC, MC, V.

$ ⊞ **Kultahippu.** Here you can patronize the "northernmost nightclub in Finland." In addition to that facility (and its traffic), you will find cozy guest rooms in this hotel in the heart of Ivalo, next to the Ivalo River. ✉ Petsamontie 1, 99800 Ivalo, ☎ 9697/661–825, FAX 9697/662–510. 30 rooms with bath (7 with saunas). Restaurant, sauna, beach, nightclub. AE, DC, MC, V. Closed Dec. 25.

Levitunturi

$$–$$$ ⊞ **Levitunturi.** Built in traditional log style at the foot of the fells, Levitunturi is a particularly well-equipped and modern tourist complex. ✉ 99130 Sirkka, ☎ 9694/641–301, FAX 9694/641–434. 121 rooms with shower. Restaurant, café, no-smoking floor, pool, sauna, spa, tennis court, exercise room, squash, boating, cross-country skiing. AE, DC, MC, V.

Luostotunturi

$$ ⊞ **Arctia Hotel Luosto.** Set amid the fells southeast of Sodankylä, this small timber hotel has a traditional feel yet is perfectly modern and comfortable. ✉ Luostotunturi, 99550 Aska, ☎ 9693/624–400, FAX 9693/624–410. 54 cabins. Sauna, boating, cross-country skiing. AE, DC, MC, V. Closed in May.

Rovaniemi

$$ ✕ **Fransmanni.** In the Vakunna Hotel in downtown Rovaniemi, the Fransmanni specializes in international, Finnish, and Sami dishes. ✉ Koskikatu 4, ☎ 960/332–211. AE, DC, MC, V.

$$ ✕ **Ounasvaaran Pirtit.** This town favorite serves traditional Finnish and Sami fare. Try the sautéed salmon with cream. ✉ Antinmukka 4, ☎ 960/369–056. Reservations essential; owner recommends that patrons order ahead if possible. MC, V.

$$$ ⊞ **Sky Hotel Ounasvaara.** The views of the town and the surround-
★ ing area are fantastic from this tranquil, full-service hotel. Since the Sky Hotel is perched on a hilltop 3 kilometers (2 miles) from the cen-

ter of town, it's best for those with a car. ⊠ *96400 Rovaniemi,* ☎ *960/ 335–3311,* FAX *960/318–789. 69 rooms with shower, 47 with sauna. Restaurant, sauna, cross-country skiing. AE, DC, MC, V.*

$$$ ⊡ **Sokos Hotel Vaakuna.** Opened in January 1992, the Vaakuna is a welcome addition to the high-class hotel scene. The club here is reportedly the center of Rovaniemi nightlife. ⊠ *Koskikatu 4, 96200 Rovaniemi,* ☎ *960/332–211,* FAX *960/332–2199. 157 rooms (all doubles) with shower, 2 suites. 3 restaurants, pub, sauna, exercise room, nightclub. AE, DC, MC, V.*

$$ ⊡ **Lapponia.** Opened in 1992, Hotel Lapponia is one of the newest luxury hotels in Lapland. ⊠ *Koskikatu 23, 96200 Rovaniemi,* ☎ *960/33661,* FAX *960/313–770. 167 rooms with shower, 9 with sauna, 8 with Jacuzzi. 5 restaurants, bar, pub, sauna, nightclub. AE, DC, MC, V.*

$$ ⊡ **Pohjanhovi.** With its pleasant location overlooking the Kemi River, this hotel is an old favorite with travelers to the north. It has been expanded and modernized over the years. ⊠ *Pohjanpuistikko 2, 96200 Rovaniemi,* ☎ *960/33711,* FAX *960/313–997. 216 rooms with bath or shower. Some rooms in neighboring building. No-smoking floor, pool, sauna, nightclub. AE, DC, MC, V.*

$$ ⊡ **Rudolf.** Completely renovated, renamed, and under new management since spring 1995, the former Gasthof is still a comfortable small hotel with a traditional restaurant. ⊠ *Koskikatu 41, 96100 Rovaniemi,* ☎ *960/342–3222,* FAX *960/342–3226. 41 rooms with shower. Restaurant, no-smoking floor, pool, sauna. AE, DC, MC, V.*

$ ⊡ **Oppipoika.** As a branch of the Hotel School of Rovaniemi, this place focuses on service. Rooms are spacious and comfortable, but the real reason to come here is the food: Chef Tapio Sointu has created the "Lappi à la Carte" program, featuring a variety of Lapland specialties. ⊠ *Korkalonkatu 33, 96200 Rovaniemi,* ☎ *960/338–8111,* FAX *960/346–969. 40 rooms with bath or shower. Restaurant, bar, pool, sauna, exercise room, meeting rooms. AE, DC, MC, V.*

Saariselkä

$$$ ⊡ **Riekonlinna.** This is the most recent and best-equipped addition to the developing tourist complex on the fringes of the wilderness fells. ⊠ *99839 Saariselkä,* ☎ *9697/668–601,* FAX *9697/668–602. 124 rooms with shower. Sauna, squash, boating, cross-country skiing. AE, DC, MC, V.*

Tankavaara

$$ ✕ **Wanha Waskoolimies.** Sami specialties predominate at this attractive café and restaurant; try the gold prospector's reindeer beefsteak with mashed peas and potatoes. ⊠ *Tankavaaran Kultakylän,* ☎ *9693/626–158. DC, V.*

10 France

Paris

Ile-de-France

Normandy

Burgundy and Lyon

The Loire Valley

Provence

The Riviera

LIKE THE NEW 300-KPH TGV TRAINS speeding toward the Channel Tunnel, France is on the move. No other European capital has seen as much pharaonic building in the last two decades as Paris. I. M. Pei's glass pyramid at the Louvre, the postmodern Grande Arche de la Défense, and the soaring Bibliothèque de France are only a few examples of the architecturally dramatic new monuments that have shocked purists and set the city abuzz.

But traditionalists need not worry. France's attachment to its heritage persists, as major restorations of the Champs-Elysées and the Marais in Paris prove. The world's most sumptuous châteaux—Versailles and Fontainebleau near Paris, and Cheverny and Chambord in the Loire Valley—remain testaments to France's illustrious nobility. The spires of Chartres and the gardens of Giverny still demonstrate France's glorious artistic and architectural legacy.

Many French people, too, continue to believe that the essence of French *savoir-vivre* is the enjoyment of daily rituals—eating, drinking, talking, dressing, shopping. Meals are painstakingly planned and prepared, carefully served, and savored. People take pleasure in good food and wine and conversation with friends.

To see France in its most traditional form, you must travel outside of Paris and explore the distinctive charms of each region. The verdant Loire Valley has majestic chateaus. Normandy is home to camembert, calvados, the D-day landings, and dramatic Mont-St-Michel. Burgundy's vineyards produce fine Beaujolais and Côte de Beaune; Dijon and Lyon are gastronomic capitals. Provence conjures warm Mediterranean colors and the sweet smell of lavender, and the sun shines brightly on the star-filled Riviera. If you've spent some time in Paris before heading off to the country's small villages, you'll be surprised at how much more relaxed the pace is and how easy it is to find locals willing to help you find your way, especially if you try a little French.

ESSENTIAL INFORMATION

Before You Go

When to Go

June and September, free of the midsummer crowds, are the best months to be in France. June offers the advantage of long daylight hours, while slightly cheaper prices and frequent Indian summers (often lasting well into October) make September attractive. The second half of July and all of August are spoiled by inflated prices and huge crowds on the beaches, and the heat can be stifling in southern France. Paris, though pleasantly deserted, can be stuffy in August, too.

Anytime between March and November offers a good chance to soak up the sun on the Riviera. The weather in Paris and the Loire is unappealing before Easter. If you're dreaming of Paris in the springtime, May (not April) is your best bet.

CLIMATE

North of the Loire (including Paris), France has a northern European climate—cold winters, pleasant if unpredictable summers, and frequent rain. Southern France has a Mediterranean climate: mild winters, long, hot summers, and sunshine throughout the year. The more Continental climate of eastern and central France is a mixture of these

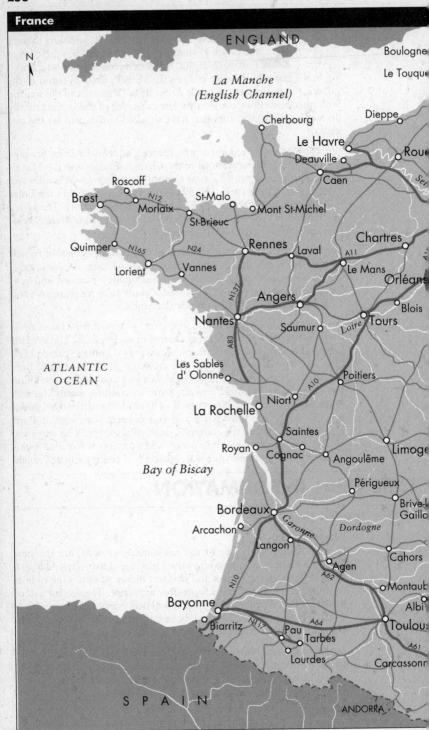

Calais

BELGIUM

A26

Lille

Arras

Amiens

Cambrai
St. Quentin

Beauvais

A1

Laon

Reims

LUXEMBOURG

A4

Paris

A5

A26

Fontainebleau

Troyes

Metz

Châlons-en-
Champagne

Nancy

Strasbourg

Sens

A31

Colmar

Auxerre

Mulhouse

A6

Belfort

Bourges

Dijon

A36

Besançon

Nevers

Beaune

A71

Autun

Saône

SWITZERLAND

Montluçon

Mâcon

Bourg-en-
Bresse

Clermont-
Ferrand

A72

Lyon

Rhône

ITALY

A43

Chambéry

Aurillac

Le Puy

Rhône

Grenoble

Rodez

Millau

Rhône

Montélimar

Gap

Nîmes

Avignon

A9

Montpellier

Aix-en-Provence

A8

Monte Carlo
Nice
Cannes

Narbonne

Marseille

Perpignan

Toulon

0 _____ 50 mi

0 _____ 75 km

Mediterranean Sea

Corsica

Corsica

Calvi

Bastia

Corte

Ajaccio

N198

Bonifacio

GERMANY

two extremes: Winters can be very cold and summers very hot. France's Atlantic coast has a temperate climate even south of the Loire, with the exception of the much warmer Biarritz.

The following are the average daily maximum and minimum temperatures for Paris and Marseille.

Paris

Jan.	43F	6C	May	68F	20C	Sept.	70F	21C
	34	1		49	10		53	12
Feb.	45F	7C	June	73F	23C	Oct.	60F	16C
	34	1		55	13		46	8
Mar.	54F	12C	July	76F	25C	Nov.	50F	10C
	39	4		58	15		40	5
Apr.	60F	16C	Aug.	75F	24C	Dec.	44F	7C
	43	6		58	15		36	2

Marseille

Jan.	50F	10C	May	71F	22C	Sept.	77F	25C
	35	2		52	11		58	15
Feb.	53F	12C	June	79F	26C	Oct.	68F	20C
	36	2		58	14		51	10
Mar.	59F	15C	July	84F	29C	Nov.	58F	14C
	41	5		63	17		41	5
Apr.	64F	18C	Aug.	83F	28C	Dec.	52F	11C
	46	8		63	17		37	3

Currency

The unit of French currency is the franc, subdivided into 100 centimes. Bills are issued in denominations of 50, 100, 200, and 500 francs (frs); coins are 5, 10, 20, and 50 centimes and 1, 2, 5, 10, and 20 francs. The small, copper-color 5-, 10-, and 20-centime coins have considerable nuisance value, but they can be used for tips in bars and cafés.

International credit cards and traveler's checks are widely accepted throughout France, except in rural areas. At press time (spring 1996), the U.S. dollar bought 4.75 francs, the Canadian dollar 4 francs, and the pound sterling 7.49 francs.

What It Will Cost

France can be expensive, but many travel basics—hotels, restaurants, plane and train tickets—are affordable if you plan ahead, take advantage of price-fixed menus, and stay in smaller, family-run places. Prices are highest in Paris and on the Riviera. But even in these areas, you can find pleasant accommodations and excellent food for surprisingly reasonable prices.

All taxes must be included in posted prices in France. The initials TTC (*toutes taxes comprises,* which means taxes included) are sometimes included on price lists, but they are superfluous. Restaurant and hotel prices must *by law* include taxes and service charges: If they are tacked onto your bill as additional items, you should complain.

SAMPLE PRICES

Prices vary greatly depending on the region, proximity to tourist sights, and—believe it or not—whether you're sitting down or standing up in a café! Here are a few samples: cup of coffee, 5–10 francs; glass of beer, 10–20 francs; soft drink, 10–20 francs; ham sandwich, 15–25 francs; 1-mile taxi ride, 35 francs.

Visas

Citizens of the United States, Canada, and Britain do not need a visa for visits to France of less than three months. A valid passport is required.

Customs on Arrival

There are two levels of duty-free allowance for travelers entering France: one for goods obtained (tax paid) within another EU country and the other for goods obtained anywhere outside the EU or for goods purchased in a duty-free shop within the EU.

In the first category, you may import duty-free: 300 cigarettes, or 150 cigarillos, or 75 cigars, or 400 grams of tobacco; 5 liters of table wine and (1) 1½ liters of alcohol over 22% volume (most spirits), (2) 3 liters of alcohol under 22% by volume (fortified or sparkling wine), or (3) 3 more liters of table wine; 90 milliliters of perfume; 375 milliliters of toilet water; and other goods to the value of 2,400 francs (620 frs for those under 15).

In the second category, you may import duty-free: 60 milliliters of perfume; 250 milliliters of toilet water; 200 cigarettes, or 100 cigarillos, or 50 cigars, or 250 grams of tobacco (these allowances are doubled if you live outside Europe); 2 liters of wine and (1) 1 liter of alcohol over 22% volume, (2) 2 liters of alcohol under 22% volume, or (3) 2 more liters of table wine; and other goods to the value of 300 francs (150 frs for those under 15).

Language

The French study English for a minimum of four years at school and, although few are fluent, their English is probably better than the French of most Americans. English is widely understood in major tourist areas, and in most hotels there is likely to be at least one person who can converse with you. Even if your own French is rusty, try to master a few words: People will greatly appreciate that you are at least making an effort to speak their beloved language.

Getting Around

By Car

ROAD CONDITIONS

France's roads are classified into five types, numbered and prefixed *A*, *N*, *D*, *C*, or *V*. Roads marked *A* (Autoroutes) are expressways. There are excellent links between Paris and most French cities, but poor ones between the provinces (the principal exceptions being A62 between Bordeaux and Toulouse and A9/A8 the length of the Mediterranean coast). It is often difficult to avoid Paris when crossing France—just try to steer clear of the rush hours (7–9:30 AM and 4:30–7:30 PM). A *péage* (toll) must be paid on most expressways: The rate varies but can be steep. The *N* (Route Nationale) roads—which are sometimes divided highways—and *D* (Route Départementale) roads are usually wide and fast, and driving along them can be a real pleasure. Don't be daunted by smaller (*C* and *V*) roads, either. The yellow regional Michelin maps—on sale throughout France—are invaluable.

RULES OF THE ROAD

You may use your own driver's license in France, but you must be able to prove you have third-party insurance. Drive on the right and yield to drivers coming from the right. Seat belts are obligatory for all passengers, and children under 12 may not travel in the front seat. Speed limits are 130 kph (80 mph) on expressways, 110 kph (70 mph) on divided highways, 90 kph (55 mph) on other roads, 50 kph (30 mph) in towns. French drivers break these limits and police dish out hefty on-the-spot fines with equal abandon.

PARKING

Parking is a nightmare in Paris and often difficult in other large towns. Meters and ticket machines (pay and display) are common: Make sure you have a supply of 1-franc coins. Parking is free during August in most of Paris, but be sure to check the signs. In smaller towns, parking may be permitted on one side of the street only—alternating every two weeks—so pay attention to signs.

GASOLINE

Gas is expensive, especially on expressways and in rural areas. Don't let your tank get too low—you can go for many miles in the country without passing a gas station—and keep an eye on pump prices as you go. These vary enormously; anything from 5.60 to 6.30 francs per liter.

BREAKDOWNS

If your car breaks down on an expressway, go to a roadside emergency telephone and call the breakdown service. If you have a breakdown anywhere else, find the nearest garage or contact the police (dial 17).

By Train

SNCF, the French national railroad, is generally recognized as Europe's best national train service: fast, punctual, comfortable, and comprehensive. The high-speed TGVs (trains *à grande vitesse*) with a top speed of 190 mph, are the best domestic trains, heading southeast from Paris to Lyon, the Riviera, and Switzerland; west to Nantes; southwest to Bordeaux; and north to Lille. Most TGV trains require passengers to pay a supplement—usually 20–40 francs, but a bit more during peak periods. Also, you need a seat reservation—easily obtained at the ticket window or from a machine. Seat reservations are reassuring but seldom necessary on other French trains, except at holiday times.

You must punch your train ticket in one of the orange machines you'll encounter alongside platforms. Slide your ticket in faceup and wait for a "clink" sound. (The small yellow tickets and automatic ticket barriers used for most suburban Paris trains are similar to those in the métro/RER.) The ticket collectors will present you with an on-the-spot fine of 100 francs if your ticket hasn't been validated before boarding.

On overnight trains, you choose between wagons-lits (private sleeping cars), which are expensive, and *couchettes* (bunks), which sleep six to a compartment in second class and four to a compartment in first class (sheet and pillow provided) and are cheaper (around 90 frs). Ordinary compartment seats do not pull together to enable you to lie down. In summer special night trains from Paris to Spain and the Riviera are geared for a younger market, with discos and bars.

FARES

Various reduced-fare passes are available from major train stations in France and from SNCF travel agents. If you are planning a lot of train travel, buy a special **France Vacances** card (around 1,400 frs for nine days). Families and couples are also eligible for big discounts. So are senior citizens (over 60) and young people (under 26), who qualify for different discount schemes (**Carte Vermeil** and **Carrissimo**). You can get 50% discounts in blue periods (most of the time) and 20% most of the rest of the time (white periods: noon Friday to noon Saturday; 3 PM Sunday to noon Monday). Calendars are available at stations. The **Carte Kiwi 4 x 4** (285 frs) enables children and up to four accompanying adults to make four trips at half price.

By Plane

Domestic flights from Paris, which are on **Air Inter,** leave from Orly. Contact your travel agent or Air Inter (☎ 01–45–46–90–00). Train service may be faster when you consider time spent getting to and from the airport.

By Bus

Because of the excellent train service, long-distance buses are rare; they're found mainly where train service is scarce. Bus tours are organized by the **SNCF.** Long-distance routes to many European cities are covered by **Eurolines** (✉ 28 av. Général-de-Gaulle, Bagnolet; ☎ 01–49–72–51–51; Métro: Galliéni).

By Boat

Canal and river vacations are popular: Visitors can either take an organized cruise or rent a boat and plan their own leisurely route. Contact a travel agent for details or ask for a "Tourisme Fluvial" brochure in any French tourist office. Some of the most picturesque stretches are in Brittany, Burgundy, and the Midi. The Canal du Midi between Toulouse and Sète, constructed in the 17th century, is a historic marvel. Contact the French national tourist offices or **Bourgogne Voies Navigables** (✉ 1 quai de la République, 89000 Auxerre, ☎ 03–86–52–18–99).

By Bicycle

The French are great cycling enthusiasts—witness the Tour de France. For around 45 francs a day bikes can be rented from 260 train stations; you need to show your passport and leave a deposit of about 500 francs (unless you have a Visa or MasterCard). Bikes may be taken as accompanied luggage from any station in France; some trains in rural areas don't even charge for this. Tourist offices supply details on the more than 200 local shops that rent bikes, or you can get the SNCF brochure "Guide du Train et du Vélo" from any station.

Staying in France

Telephones

France-Télécom added two digits to all phone numbers in 1996. The digits are determined by zone: for Paris and Ile-de-France, add 01; the northwest, 02; the northeast, 03; the southeast, 04; and the southwest, 05. Area codes (16 within France, 1 when calling the Paris region from abroad) have been abandoned under the new scheme, and the 19 code used for international calls replaced by 00.

LOCAL CALLS

The French telephone system is modern and efficient. Phone booths are plentiful; they are nearly always available at post offices and cafés. A local call in France costs 80 centimes per three minutes; half-price rates apply between 9:30 PM and 8 AM and between 1:30 PM Saturday and 8 AM Monday.

Some French pay phones take 1-, 2-, and 5-franc coins (1-fr minimum), but most phones are now operated by *télécartes* (phone cards), sold in post offices, métro stations, and cafés sporting a red TABAC (tobacco) sign outside (cost: 40 frs for 50 units; 96 frs for 120 units).

INTERNATIONAL CALLS

Dial 00 and wait for the tone, then dial the country code, area code, and number. To reach an **AT&T** long-distance operator, dial 19–0011; for **MCI,** dial 19–0019; and for **Sprint,** 19–0087. Dial 12 for local operators. France's country code is 33. Note that the 19 code was due to be replaced by 00 in 1996.

Mail

POSTAL RATES

Airmail letters to the United States and Canada cost 4.30 francs for 20 grams. Letters to the United Kingdom cost 2.80 francs for up to 20 grams, as do letters within France. Postcards cost 2.40 francs within France and if sent to EU countries (2.40 frs for surface or 3.80 frs for airmail to North America). Stamps can be bought in post offices and tabacs.

RECEIVING MAIL

If you're uncertain where you'll be staying, have mail sent to American Express (if you're a card member) or Thomas Cook; mail labeled "poste restante" is also accepted at most French post offices.

Precaution

Beware of thieves! Though no one likes to talk about it, burglaries, once confined to major cities, have spread into the countryside.

Shopping

VAT REFUNDS

A number of shops, particularly large stores in cities and holiday resorts, offer value-added tax (VAT) refunds to foreign shoppers. You are entitled to an export discount of 13% or 23%, depending on the item purchased, though this often applies only if your purchases in the same store reach a minimum 2,800 francs (for residents of EU countries) or 2,000 francs (all others).

BARGAINING

Shop prices are clearly marked and bargaining is not a way of life. Still, at outdoor markets, flea markets, and in antiques stores, you can try your luck. If you're thinking of buying several items in these places, you have nothing to lose in cheerfully suggesting to the proprietor, *"Vous me faites un prix?"* ("How about a discount?").

Hours

Banks are open weekdays 9:30–4:30, with variations. Most close for at least an hour at lunch.

Museums are closed one day a week (often Monday or Tuesday) and on national holidays. Usual hours are from 9:30 to 5 or 6. Many museums close for lunch (noon–2); on Sunday many are open afternoons only.

Shops in big towns are open from 9 or 9:30 to 7 or 8 without a lunch break; some also open on Sunday. Smaller shops often open earlier and close later, but take a lengthy lunch break (1–4). This siesta-type schedule is more typical in the south of France. Corner grocery stores frequently stay open until around 10 PM.

National Holidays

January 1; March 31 (Easter Monday); May 1 (Labor Day); May 8 (VE Day and Ascension); May 19 (Pentecost Monday); July 14 (Bastille Day); August 15 (Assumption); November 1 (All Saints' Day); November 11 (Armistice); December 25.

Dining

Eating in France is serious business, at least for two of the three meals each day. For a light meal, try an informal brasserie (steak and french fries remain the classic), a picnic (a baguette with ham, cheese, or pâté is a perfect combination), or one of the fast-food outlets that have sprung up in urban areas during recent years.

French breakfasts are relatively modest—strong coffee, fruit juice if you insist, and croissants. International chain hotels are likely to offer

American or English breakfasts, but in cafés you will probably be out of luck if this is what you want.

Reservations are advised at most restaurants, particularly in summer.

MEALTIMES
Dinner is the main meal and usually begins at 8. Lunch begins at 12:30 or 1.

WHAT TO WEAR
Jacket and tie are recommended for $$$$ and $$$ restaurants, and at some of the more stylish $$ restaurants as well. When in doubt, it's best to dress up. Otherwise casual dress is appropriate.

PRECAUTIONS
Tap water is perfectly safe, though not always very palatable (least of all in Paris). Mineral water is a good alternative; there is a vast choice of *eaux plates* (plain) as well as *eaux gazeuses* (fizzy).

RATINGS
Prices are per person and include a first course, main course, and dessert plus tax (20.6%) and service (which are always included in displayed prices), but not wine.

CATEGORY	MAJOR CITY	OTHER AREAS
$$$$	over 550 francs	over 500 francs
$$$	300–550 francs	250–500 francs
$$	175–300 francs	125–250 francs
$	under 175 francs	under 125 francs

Lodging

France has a wide range of accommodations, from rambling old village inns to stylishly converted châteaus. Prices must, by law, be posted at the hotel entrance and should include taxes and service. Prices are always by room, not per person. Breakfast is not always included, but you are usually expected to have it and often are charged for it whether you partake or not. In smaller rural hotels, you may be expected to have your evening meal at the hotel, too.

The quality of rooms, particularly in older properties, is uneven; if you don't like the room you're given, ask to see another. If you want a private bathroom, state your preference for *douche* (shower) or *baignoire* (tub)—the latter always costing more. Tourist offices in major train stations can reserve hotels for you, and so can tourist offices in most towns.

HOTELS
Hotels are officially classified from one-star to four-star-deluxe. France has—but is not dominated by—big hotel chains: Examples in the upper price bracket are Frantel, Holiday Inn, Novotel, and Sofitel. The Ibis, Campanile, and Climat de France chains are more moderate. Chains, as a rule, lack atmosphere, with these exceptions:

Logis de France. This is a group of small, inexpensive hotels that can be relied on for comfort, character, and regional cuisine. Look for its distinctive yellow and green sign. The Logis de France paperback guide is widely available in bookshops (around 75 frs) or from Logis de France (⌧ 83 av. d'Italie, 75013 Paris, ☎ 01–45–84–83–84, FAX 01–44–24–08–74).

France-Accueil is another chain of friendly low-cost hotels. You can get a free booklet from France-Accueil (⌧ 163 av. d'Italie, 75013 Paris, ☎ 01–45–83–04–22, FAX 01–45–86–49–82).

Relais & Châteaux. You can stay in style at any of the 150 members of this prestigious chain of converted châteaus and manor houses.

Each hotel is distinctively furnished, provides top cuisine, and often has spacious grounds. A booklet listing members is available in bookshops or from Relais & Châteaux (⊠ 15 rue Galvani, 75017 Paris, ☎ 01–45–72–96–50, ℻ 01–45–72–96–69).

RENTALS
Gîtes Ruraux offers families or small groups economical stays in a furnished cottage, chalet, or apartment. These can be rented by the week or month. Contact either the **Fédération Nationale des Gîtes de France** (⊠ 35 rue Godot-de-Mauroy, 75009 Paris, ☎ 01–49–70–75–75, ℻ 01–49–70–75–76; indicate the region that interests you), or the French Government Tourist Office in New York or London (☞ Visitor Information *in* Chapter 1).

BED-AND-BREAKFASTS
Known as *chambres d'hôte,* these are increasingly popular in rural areas and can be a great bargain. Check local tourist offices for details.

YOUTH HOSTELS
With inexpensive hotel accommodations so easy to find, you may think twice before staying in a youth hostel—especially as standards of French hostels don't quite approximate those in neighboring countries. Contact **Fédération Unie des Auberges de Jeunesse** (⊠ 27 rue Pajol, 75018 Paris, ☎ 01–44–89–87–27, ℻ 01–44–89–87–10).

VILLAS
The French Government Tourist Offices in London and New York publish extensive lists of agencies specializing in villa rentals. You can also write to **Rent-a-Villa Ltd.** (⊠ 3 W. 51st St., New York, NY 10019) or, in France, **Interhome** (⊠ 15 av. Jean-Aicard, 75011 Paris).

CAMPING
French campsites have a good reputation for organization and amenities but are crowded in July and August. Many campsites welcome reservations, and in summer, it makes sense to book in advance. A guide to France's campsites is published by the **Fédération Française de Camping et de Caravaning** (⊠ 78 rue de Rivoli, 75004 Paris, ☎ 01–42–72–84–08). They'll send it to you directly for 70 francs, plus shipping.

RATINGS
Prices are for standard double rooms and include tax (20.6%) and service charges.

CATEGORY	MAJOR CITY	OTHER AREAS
$$$$	over 1,200 francs	over 800 francs
$$$	750–1,200 francs	500–800 francs
$$	450–750 francs	250–500 francs
$	under 450 francs	under 250 francs

Tipping
The check in a bar or restaurant will include service, but it is customary to leave some small change unless you're dissatisfied. The amount varies, from 30 centimes for a beer to a few francs after a meal. Tip taxi drivers and hairdressers about 10%. Give ushers in theaters 1–2 francs. Cloakroom attendants will expect nothing if there is a sign saying POURBOIRE INTERDIT (tipping forbidden); otherwise give them 5 francs. Washroom attendants usually get 5 francs—a sum that is often posted. Bellhops should get 10 francs per item.

If you stay in a moderately priced hotel for more than two or three days, it is customary to leave something for the chambermaid—perhaps 10 francs per day. Expect to tip 10 francs for room service—but nothing is expected if breakfast is routinely served in your room.

Service station attendants get nothing for giving you gas or oil, and 5 or 10 francs for checking tires. Train and airport porters get a fixed sum (6–10 frs) per bag. Museum guides should get 5–10 francs after a guided tour. Tip guides (and bus drivers) after an excursion.

PARIS

Arriving and Departing

By Plane
International flights arrive at either Charles de Gaulle Airport (always known in France as Roissy), 24 kilometers (15 miles) northeast of Paris, or at Orly Airport, 16 kilometers (10 miles) south of the city. Both airports have two terminals.

BETWEEN THE AIRPORT AND DOWNTOWN

From Roissy: Buses operated by **Air France** leave every 15 minutes from 5:40 AM to 11 PM. The fare is 55 francs and the trip takes 40 minutes to 1½ hours during rush hour. You arrive at the Arc de Triomphe or Porte Maillot, on the Right Bank by the Hôtel Concorde-Lafayette. Alternatively, the **Roissybus,** operated by Paris Transport Authority (RATP), runs directly to and from rue Scribe by the Opera every 15 minutes and costs 40 francs.

From Orly: Buses operated by **Air France** leave every 12 minutes from 6 AM to 11 PM and arrive at the Air France terminal near Les Invalides on the Left Bank. The fare is 40 francs, and the trip takes between 30 and 60 minutes, depending on traffic. RATP also runs the **Orlybus** to and from Denfert-Rochereau and Orly every 15 minutes for 30 francs; the trip takes around 35 minutes.

Both airports have their own train stations, from which you can take the RER to Paris. The advantages of this are speed, price (45 frs to Paris from Roissy, 52 frs from Orly on the shuttle-train **Orlyval**), and the RER's direct link with the métro system. The disadvantage is having to lug your bags around. Taxi fares from airports to Paris range from 150 to 250 francs, with a 6-franc surcharge per bag. A new **Paris Airports Service** takes you by 8-passenger van to your destination in Paris from de Gaulle: 140 francs (one person) or 170 francs (two); Orly: 110 francs (one), 130 francs (two), less for groups. To book ahead (English-speaking clerks), call ☎ 33–1/49–62–78–78, FAX 33–1/49–11–18–82; on arrival, ☎ 01–09–14–16–93.

By Train
Paris has five international stations: Gare du Nord (for northern France, northern Europe, and England via Calais or the Channel Tunnel); Gare de l'Est (for Strasbourg, Luxembourg, Basle, and central Europe); Gare de Lyon (for Lyon, Marseille, the Riviera, Geneva, and Italy); Gare d'Austerlitz (for the Loire Valley, southwest France, and Spain); and Gare St-Lazare (for Normandy and England via Dieppe). The Gare Montparnasse serves western France (mainly Nantes and Brittany) and is the terminal for the TGV Atlantic service from Paris to Bordeaux. For train information, call ☎ 01–45–82–50–50. You can reserve tickets at any Paris station regardless of the destination. Go to the Grandes Lignes counter for travel within France or to the Billets Internationaux desk if you're heading out of France.

By Bus

Long-distance bus journeys within France are uncommon, which may be why Paris has no central bus depot. The leading Paris-based bus company is **Eurolines** (✉ 28 av. du Général-de-Gaulle, Bagnolet, ☎ 01–49–72–51–51).

By Car

The highway system fans out from Paris. You arrive from the north (England/Belgium) via A1; from Normandy via A13; from the east via A4; from Spain and the southwest via A10; and from the Alps, the Riviera, and Italy via A7. Each of these expressways connects with the *périphérique* (beltway). Exits are named by "Porte" and are not numbered. The "Périphe" can be fast—and gets very busy; it is best avoided between 7:30 and 10 AM and between 4:30 and 7:30 PM.

Getting Around

Paris is relatively small as capital cities go, and most of its prize monuments and museums are within walking distance of one another. A river cruise is a pleasant way to get an overview. The most convenient form of public transportation is the métro; buses are a slower alternative, though they do allow you to see more of the city. Taxis are not expensive but are not always easy to hail. Car travel within Paris is best avoided because finding parking is difficult.

By Métro

There are 13 métro lines crisscrossing Paris and the nearby suburbs, and you are seldom more than a five-minute walk from the nearest station. It is essential to know the name of the last station on the line you take, since this name appears on all signs within the system. A connection (you can make as many as you please on one ticket) is called a *correspondance*. At junction stations, illuminated orange signs bearing the names of each line terminus appear over the corridors that lead to the various correspondances.

The métro runs from 5:30 AM to 1:15 AM. Some lines and stations in the seedier parts of Paris are a bit risky at night—in particular, Line 2 (Porte-Dauphine–Nation) and the northern section of Line 13 from St-Lazare to St-Denis/Asnières. The long, bleak corridors at Jaurès and Stalingrad are a haven for pickpockets and purse snatchers. But the Paris métro is relatively safe, as long as you don't walk around with your wallet hanging out of your back pocket or travel alone (especially women) late at night.

The métro connects at several points in Paris with RER trains that race across Paris from suburb to suburb: RER trains are a sort of supersonic métro and can be great time-savers. All métro tickets and passes are valid for RER and bus travel within Paris. Métro tickets cost 7.50 francs each, though a *carnet* (10 tickets for 44 frs) is a far better value. If you're staying for a week or more, the best deal is the *coupon jaune* (weekly) or *carte orange* (monthly) ticket, sold according to zone. Zones 1 and 2 cover the entire métro network (67 frs per week or 230 frs per month). If you plan to take a suburban train to visit monuments in the Ile de France, you should consider a four-zone ticket (Versailles, St-Germain-en-Laye; 119 frs per week) or a six-zone ticket (Rambouillet, Fontainebleau; 158 frs per week). For these weekly or monthly tickets, you need a pass (available from train and major métro stations), and you must provide a passport-size photograph.

Alternatively there are one-day (Formule 1) and two-, three- and five-day (Paris Visite) unlimited travel tickets for the métro, bus, and RER. Unlike the coupon jaune, which is good from Monday morning to Sunday evening, the latter are valid starting any day of the week and give you admission discounts to a limited number of museums and tourist attractions. The prices are 40, 70, 105, and 165 francs for Paris only; 100, 170, 220, and 315 francs for the suburbs including Versailles, St-Germain-en-Laye, and Disneyland Paris.

Access to métro and RER platforms is through an automatic ticket barrier. Slide your ticket in flat and pick it up as it pops up farther along. Keep your ticket; you'll need it again to leave the RER system. Sometimes green-clad métro authorities will ask to see it when you enter or leave the station: be prepared—they aren't very friendly.

By Bus

Most buses run from around 6 AM to 8:30 PM; some continue until midnight. Noctambus (night buses) operate from 1 AM to 6 AM between Châtelet and nearby suburbs. They can be stopped by hailing them at any point on their route. You can use your métro tickets on the buses, or you can buy a one-ride ticket on board. You need to show weekly/monthly/special tickets to the driver; if you have individual tickets, state your destination and be prepared to punch one or more tickets in the red and gray machines on board the bus.

By Taxi

There is no standard vehicle or color for Paris taxis, but all offer good value. Daytime rates (7 to 7) within Paris are about 2.80 francs per kilometer, and nighttime rates are around 4.50 francs, plus a basic charge of 12 francs. Rates outside the city limits are about 40% higher. Ask your hotel or restaurant to call for a taxi, since cruising cabs can be hard to find. There are numerous taxi stands, but you have to know where to look. Taxis seldom take more than three people at a time.

Important Addresses and Numbers

Visitor Information

Paris Tourist Office (⊠ 127 av. des Champs-Elysées, ☎ 01–49–52–53–54). Open daily 9–8 (except Dec. 25, Jan 1.) Offices in major train stations are open daily 8–8.

Embassies

U.S. (⊠ 2 av. Gabriel, 75008 Paris, ☎ 01–42–96–12–02). **Canadian** (⊠ 35 av. Montaigne, 75008 Paris, ☎ 01–44–43–29–00). **U.K.** (⊠ 35 rue du Faubourg-St-Honoré, 75008 Paris, ☎ 01–42–66–91–42).

Emergencies

Police: dial 17 for emergencies. Automatic phone booths can be found at various main crossroads for use in police emergencies (Police-Secours) or for medical help (Services Médicaux). **Ambulance:** ☎ 01–15 or 43–78–26–26. **Doctor:** ☎ 01–47–07–77–77. **Hospitals: American Hospital** (⊠ 63 blvd. Victor-Hugo, Neuilly, ☎ 01–47–45–71–00); **British Hospital** (⊠ 3 rue Barbès, Levallois-Perret, ☎ 01–47–58–13–12) **Dentist:** ☎ 01–43–37–51–00; ⊙ 24 hours. **Pharmacies: Dhéry** (⊠ Galerie des Champs, 84 av. des Champs-Elysées, ☎ 01–45–62–02–41; ⊙ 24 hours); **Pharmacie des Arts** (⊠ 106 blvd. Montparnasse, 6ᵉ, ☎ 01–43–35–44–88; ⊙ Until midnight).

English-Language Bookstores

W. H. Smith (⊠ 248 rue de Rivoli); **Galignani** (⊠ 224 rue de Rivoli); **Brentano's** (⊠ 37 av. de l'Opéra); **Shakespeare & Co.** (⊠ rue de la Bûcherie). Most newsstands in central Paris sell *Time, Newsweek,* and the *International Herald Tribune,* as well as the English dailies.

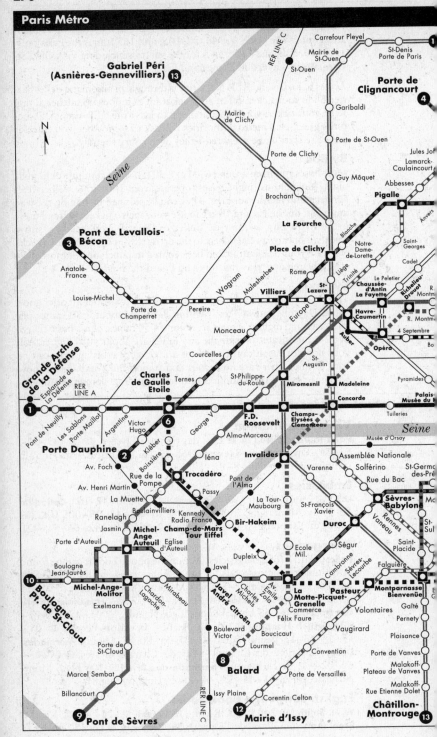

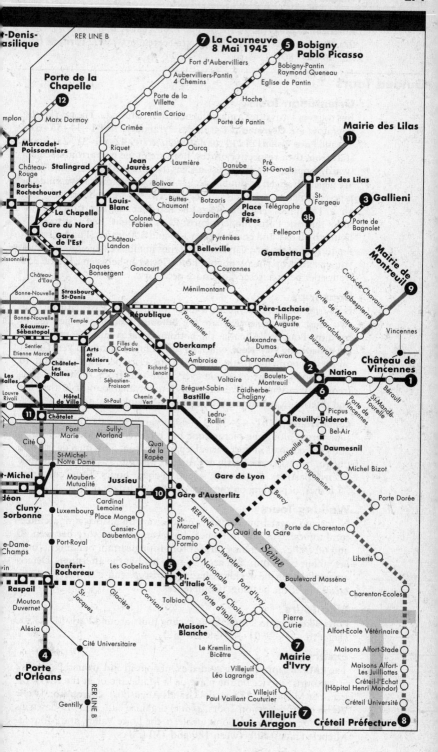

Travel Agencies

American Express (⊠ 11 rue Scribe, 75009 Paris, ☎ 01–47–77–77–07). **Wagons-Lits** (⊠ 32 rue du Quatre-Septembre, 75002 Paris, ☎ 01–42–66–15–80).

Guided Tours

Orientation Tours

Bus tours of Paris offer a good introduction to the city. The two largest operators are **Cityrama** (⊠ 4 pl. des Pyramides, ☎ 01–44–55–61–00) and **Paris Vision** (⊠ 214 rue de Rivoli, ☎ 01–42–60–31–25). Tours start from their respective offices. Both are in the first arrondissement (ward), opposite the Tuileries Gardens (toward the Louvre end). Tours are generally given in double-decker buses with either a live guide or tape-recorded commentary. They last two to three hours and cost about 150 francs. The same operators also offer a variety of other theme tours (historic Paris, modern Paris, Paris by night) that last from 2½ hours to all day and cost between 120 and 300 francs. For a more intimate tour of the city, Cityrama also runs minibus excursions that pick you up and drop you off at your hôtel Costs run between 210 and 350 francs per person; reservations are necessary.

Boat Trips

Boat trips along the Seine are a must for first-time Paris visitors. The two most famous services are the **Bâteaux Mouches,** which leaves from the Pont de l'Alma, at the bottom of the avenue George-V, and the **Vedettes du Pont-Neuf,** which sets off from the square du Vert-Galant on the western edge of the Ile de la Cité. Price per trip is around 40 francs. Boats depart in season every half hour from 10:30 to 5 (less frequently in winter). Evening cruises are available most of the year and offer unexpected views of Paris's riverbanks.

Canauxrama (☎ 01–42–39–15–00) organizes canal tours in flat-bottom barges along the picturesque but relatively unknown St-Martin and Ourcq canals in East Paris. Departures from 5 bis quai de la Loire (métro: Jaurès), or the Bassin de l'Arsenal, opposite 50 blvd. de la Bastille (métro: Bastille). Times vary, so call to check hours. Tours cost from 75 francs, depending on the time of day and length of trip.

Walking Tours

Numerous special-interest tours concentrate on historical or architectural topics. Most are in French, however. Charges vary between 40 and 60 francs, depending on fees for visiting certain buildings. Tours last about two hours and are generally held in the afternoon. Details are published in the weekly magazines *Pariscope* and *L'Officiel des Spectacles* under the heading "Conférences."

Bike Tours

Paris Bike organizes three-hour cycling tours around Paris (⊠ 83 rue Daguerre, 14ᵉ, ☎ 01–45–38–58–58).

Excursions

The **RATP** organizes many guided excursions in and around Paris. Ask at its tourist service on the place de la Madeleine or at the RATP office at St-Michel (⊠ 53 quai des Grands-Augustins). **Cityrama** and **Paris Vision** (☞ Orientation Tours, *above*) organize half- and full-day trips to Chartres, Versailles, Fontainebleau, the Loire Valley, and Mont St-Michel at a cost of between 180 and 750 francs.

Personal Guides

International Limousines (⊠ 182 blvd. Pereire, 17ᵉ, ☎ 01–53–81–14–00) and **Paris Bus** (⊠ 22 rue de la Prévoyance, Vincennes, ☎ 01–43–

65–55–55) have limousines and minibuses that take up to seven passengers around Paris or to surrounding areas for a minimum of three hours. The cost starts at about 250 francs per hour. Call for details.

Exploring Paris

Paris is a compact city. With the exceptions of the Bois de Boulogne and Montmartre, you can easily walk from one sight to the next. Paris is divided in two by the River Seine, with two islands (Ile de la Cité and Ile St-Louis) in the middle. The south—or Left—Bank has a more intimate, bohemian flavor than the haughtier Right Bank. The east–west axis from Châtelet to the Arc de Triomphe, via the rue de Rivoli and the Champs-Elysées, is the principal thoroughfare for sightseeing and shopping on the Right Bank.

A special **Carte Musées et Monuments** pass, allowing access to most Paris museums and monuments, can be obtained from museums or métro stations (one-day pass, 70 frs; three days, 140 frs; five days, 200 frs).

Though attractions are grouped into four logical touring areas, there are several "musts." If time is a problem, explore Notre-Dame and the Latin Quarter; head to place de la Concorde and enjoy the vista from the Champs-Elysées to the Louvre; then take a boat along the Seine for a waterside rendezvous with the Eiffel Tower. You could finish off with dinner in Montmartre and consider it a day well spent.

Notre-Dame and the Left Bank
Numbers in the margin correspond to points of interest on the Paris map.

★ ❶ The most enduring symbol of Paris, and its historic and geographic heart, is **Notre-Dame,** around the corner from Cité métro station. This is the logical place from which to start any tour of the city—especially as the tour starts on the **Ile de la Cité,** one of the two islands in the middle of the Seine, where Paris's first inhabitants settled around 250 BC. Notre-Dame has been a place of worship for more than 2,000 years; the present building is the fourth on this site. It was begun in 1163, making it one of the earliest Gothic cathedrals, but not finished until 1345. The facade seems perfectly proportioned until you notice that the north (left) tower is wider than the south. The interior is at its lightest and least cluttered in the early morning. Bay-by-bay cleaning is gradually revealing the original honey color of the stone. Window space is limited and filled with shimmering stained glass; the circular rose windows in the transept are particularly delicate. The 387-step climb up the towers is worth the effort for a perfect view of the famous gargoyles and the heart of Paris. *Cathedral:* ▨ *Free. Towers:* ▨ *27 frs.* ⊘ *Daily 10–5. Treasury (religious and vestmental relics)* ▨ *15 frs.* ⊘ *Mon.–Sat. 10–6, Sun. 2–6.*

The pretty garden to the right of the cathedral leads to a bridge that crosses to the city's second and smaller island, the **Ile St-Louis,** barely 600 meters (650 yards) long and an oasis of inner-city repose.

❷ Head down rue St-Louis-en-l'Ile, then right onto rue des Deux-Ponts and cross Pont de la Tournelle. To your left is the **La Tour d'Argent,** one of the city's most famous restaurants (☞ Dining, *below*).

❸ Continue right along quai de la Tournelle past Notre-Dame, then turn left at rue St-Jacques. A hundred yards ahead, on the right, is the back end of the **Eglise St-Séverin,** an elegant 16th-century church. Note the spiraling column among the forest of pillars behind the altar.

274

Paris

KEY

i Tourist Information

| 0 | 1 mile |
| 0 | 1 km |

Turn left out of the church, cross the bustling boulevard St-Germain,
❹ and take rue de Cluny to the left. This leads to the **Hôtel de Cluny,** which
houses the **Musée National du Moyen-Age,** a museum devoted to the
late Middle Ages and Renaissance. Look for the *Lady with the Unicorn* tapestries and the beautifully displayed medieval statues. ⊠ *6 pl.
Paul-Painlevé.* ☒ *27 frs; Sun. 18 frs.* ☾ *Wed.–Mon. 9:30–5:45.*

❺ Head up rue de la Sorbonne to the **Sorbonne,** Paris's ancient university. Students used to listen to lectures in Latin, which explains why the
surrounding area is known as the Quartier Latin (Latin Quarter). The
Sorbonne is one of the oldest universities in Europe, and has for centuries been one of France's principal institutions of higher learning.

❻ Walk up rue Victor-Cousin and turn left onto rue Cujas to the **Panthéon.** Its huge dome and elegant colonnade are reminiscent of St. Paul's
in London but date from a century later (1758–89). The Panthéon was
intended to be a church, but during the Revolution it was earmarked
as a secular hall of fame. Its crypt contains the remains of such national
heroes as Voltaire, Rousseau, and Zola. The interior is empty and austere, with principal interest centering on Puvis de Chavannes's late 19th-century frescoes, relating the life of Geneviève, patron saint of Paris.
☒ *32 frs.* ☾ *Daily 10–5:30.*

Behind the Panthéon is **St-Etienne du Mont,** a church with two claims
to fame: its ornate facade and its curly Renaissance rood-screen (1521–
35), the only one of its kind in Paris. Don't forget to check out the fine
17th-century glass in the cloister at the back of the church.

Take the adjoining rue Clovis, turn right onto rue Descartes, then left
at the lively place de la Contrescarpe down rue Rollin. Cross rue
❼ Monge to rue de Navarre. On the left is a Gallo-Roman arena, the **Arènes
de Lutèce,** rediscovered only in 1869 (☒ Free; ☾ Always open during
daylight hours); it has since been landscaped and excavated to reveal
parts of the original amphitheater, but remains one of the lesser-known
points of interest in Paris.

☙ ❽ Rue de Navarre and rue Lacépède lead to the **Jardin des Plantes** (Botanical Gardens), which have been on this site since the 17th century. The
gardens have what is reputedly the oldest tree in Paris, an *acacia Robinia*
(allée Becquerel) planted in 1636, several natural history museums,
plus a zoo, an alpine garden, hothouses, an aquarium, and a maze. Natural science enthusiasts will be in their element at the various museums,
devoted to insects (Musée Entomologique), fossils and prehistoric animals (Musée Paléontologique), and minerals (Musée Minéralogique).
The **Grande Galerie de l'Evolution** has a mind-blowing collection of stuffed
and mounted animals (some now extinct). ☒ *12–25 frs for museums
and zoo.* ☾ *Museums: Wed.–Mon. 9–11:45, 1–4:45.*

Head back up Rue Lacépède from the Jardin des Plantes. Turn left onto
rue Gracieuse, then right onto rue Ortolan, which soon crosses the rue
Mouffetard—site of a colorful market and many restaurants. Continue
along rue du Pot-de-Fer and rue Rataud. At rue Claude-Bernard, turn
right; then make your first left up rue St-Jacques.

❾ Set slightly back from the street is the **Val de Grâce,** a domed church
designed by François Mansart and Jacques Lemercier and erected in
1645–67 (after the Sorbonne church but before the Invalides). Its
two-tiered facade, with capitals and triangular pedestals, was inspired
by the Counter-Reformation Jesuit architectural style found more
often in Rome than in Paris. The Baroque style of the interior is epitomized by the huge twisted columns of the baldachin (ornamental
canopy) over the altar.

10 Head up rue du Val-de-Gráce for an enticing view down the tree-lined avenue de l'Observatoire toward the **Palais du Luxembourg.** The palace was built by Queen Maria de' Medici at the beginning of the 17th century in answer to Florence's Pitti Palace. It now houses the French Senate and is not open to the public. In the surrounding gardens, mothers push their baby carriages along tree-lined paths among the majestic fountains and statues.

11 Head through the gardens to the left of the palace, cross rue de Vaugirard and head down rue Férou to the enormous 17th-century church of **St-Sulpice.** Stand back and admire the impressive, though unfinished, 18th-century facade, with its unequal towers. The interior is overwhelmingly impersonal, but the wall paintings by Delacroix, in the first chapel on the right, are worth a visit.

12 Rue Bonaparte descends to boulevard St-Germain. You can hardly miss the sturdy pointed tower of **St-Germain-des-Prés,** the oldest church in Paris (begun around 1160, though the towers date from the 11th century). Note the colorful nave frescoes by the 19th-century artist Hippolyte Flandrin, a pupil of Ingres.

NEED A BREAK? The spirit of writers Jean-Paul Sartre and Simone de Beauvoir still haunts the **Café de Flore** opposite the church, though it (and neighboring Les Deux Magots) has more tourists than literary luminaries these days. Still, you can linger over a drink while watching what seems to be all of Paris walking by. ✉ *172 Blvd. St-Germain.*

Rue de l'Abbaye runs along behind St-Germain-des-Prés to rue de Furstemberg, broadening into a charming square where fiery Romantic artist Eugène Delacroix (1798–1863) had his studio. Turn left into rue Jacob and continue along rue de l'Université. You are now in the heart of the Carré Rive Gauche, the Left Bank's district of art dealers and galleries.

★ **13** About a quarter of a mile along rue de l'Université, turn down rue de Poitiers. Ahead is the sandstone bulk of the **Musée d'Orsay.** Follow it around to the left to reach the main entrance. The Musée d'Orsay is one of Paris's star attractions, thanks to its imaginatively housed collections of the arts (mainly French) spanning the period 1848–1914. Exhibits take up three floors, but the visitor's immediate impression is one of a single, vast hall. This is not surprising: The museum was originally built in 1900 as a train station.

The chief artistic attraction is the Impressionist collection, transferred from the inadequate Jeu de Paume across the river. Other highlights include Art Nouveau furniture, a faithfully restored Belle Epoque restaurant, and a model of the Opéra quarter beneath a glass floor. ✉ *1 rue Bellechasse,* ☎ *01–40–49–48–14.* 🎟 *35 frs.* ☉ *Tues., Wed., Fri., Sat. 10–5:30; Thurs. 10–9:30; Sun. 9–5:30.*

14 Farther along on rue de l'Université is the 18th-century **Palais Bourbon,** home of the French National Legislature (Assemblée Nationale). The colonnaded facade commissioned by Napoléon is a sparkling sight. There is a fine view across to place de la Concorde and the Madeleine.

★ **15** Follow the Seine down to the exuberant **Pont Alexandre III.** The Grand and Petit Palais are to your right, across the river. To the left, the silhouette of the **Hôtel des Invalides** soars above expansive if hardly manicured lawns. The Invalides was founded by Louis XIV in 1674 to house wounded (or "invalid") war veterans. Although only a few old soldiers live here today, the military link remains in the form of the **Musée de l'Armée**—a vast, albeit musty, collection of arms, armor, uniforms, banners, and pictures. The **Musée des Plans-Reliefs** contains a fascinating collection of scale models of French towns made by the military architect Vauban in the 17th century.

The museums are far from being the only reason to visit the Invalides. It is an outstanding Baroque ensemble, designed by Bruand and Mansart, and its church possesses the city's most elegant dome as well as the tomb of Napoléon, whose remains are housed in a series of no less than six coffins within a tomb of red porphyry. ▨ *Museums and church: 35 frs.* ☉ *Daily 10–6 (10–5 in winter).*

16 Alongside is the **Musée Rodin.** Together with the Picasso Museum in the Marais, this is the most charming of Paris's individual museums, consisting of an old house (built 1728) with a pretty garden, both filled with the sculptures of Auguste Rodin (1840–1917). The garden also has hundreds of rosebushes, with dozens of different varieties. ⊠ *77 rue de Varenne.* ▨ *27 frs, 18 frs Sun.* ☉ *Tues.–Sun. 10–5.*

★ 17 Take avenue de Tourville to avenue de La Motte-Picquet. Turn left, and in a few minutes you will come face-to-face with the **Eiffel Tower.** It was built by Gustave Eiffel for the World Exhibition of 1889. Restorations haven't made the elevators any faster—long lines are inevitable—but decent shops and two good restaurants were added. In the evening, every girder is lit in glorious detail. Such was Eiffel's engineering precision that even in the fiercest winds the tower never sways more than a few centimeters. Today, of course, it is the best-known Parisian landmark. Standing beneath it, you may have trouble believing that it nearly became 7,000 tons of scrap-iron when its concession expired in 1909. Only its potential use as a radio antenna saved the day; it now bristles with a forest of radio and television transmitters. The view from 1,000 feet up will enable you to appreciate the city's layout and proportions. ▨ *On foot, 12 frs; by elevator, 20–55 frs, depending on the level.* ☉ *July–Aug., daily 9 AM–midnight; Sept.–June, Sun.–Thurs. 9 AM–11 PM, Fri., Sat. 9 AM–midnight.*

West Paris and the Louvre

18 Our second itinerary starts at the **Musée Marmottan.** To get there, take the métro to La Muette, then head down chaussée de la Muette, through the small Ranelagh park to the corner of rue Boilly and avenue Raphaël. The museum is a sumptuous early 19th-century mansion and may be the most underestimated museum in Paris. It houses a magnificent collection of paintings by Claude Monet, along with other Impressionist works and some illustrated medieval manuscripts. ⊠ *2 rue Louis-Boilly.* ▨ *35 frs.* ▨ *Tues.–Sun. 10–5:30.*

☾ 19 Continue along rue Boilly and turn left on boulevard Suchet. The next right takes you into the **Bois de Boulogne.** Class and style have been associated with "Le Bois" (The Wood) ever since it was landscaped into an upper-class playground by Haussmann in the 1850s. The attractions of this sprawling 2,200-acre wood include cafés, restaurants, gardens, waterfalls, and lakes. Pass Auteuil racetrack on the left and then walk to the right of the two lakes. An inexpensive ferry crosses frequently to an idyllic island. Rowboats can be rented at the far end of the lake. Just past the boathouse, turn right on the route de Suresnes and follow it to Porte Dauphine, a large traffic circle.

Cross over to avenue Foch, with the unmistakable silhouette of the Arc de Triomphe in the distance. Notice the original Art Nouveau iron-and-glass entrance to Porte Dauphine métro station, on the left. Continue along avenue Foch, the widest and grandest boulevard in Paris, **20** to the **Arc de Triomphe.** This 164-foot arch was planned by Napoléon to celebrate his military successes. Yet when Empress Marie-Louise entered Paris in 1810, it was barely off the ground and an arch of painted canvas was strung up to save appearances. Napoléon had been dead for 15 years when the Arc de Triomphe was finished in 1836.

Place Charles-de-Gaulle, referred to by Parisians as **L'Etoile** (The Star), is one of Europe's most chaotic traffic circles. Short of a death-defying dash, your only way to get over to the Arc de Triomphe is to take the pedestrian underpass from either the Champs-Elysées (to your right as you arrive from avenue Foch) or avenue de la Grande-Armée (to the left). France's Unknown Soldier is buried beneath the archway; the flame is rekindled every evening at 6:30.

From atop the Arc you see the "star" effect of Etoile's 12 radiating avenues and admire two vistas: one down the Champs-Elysées toward place de la Concorde and the Louvre, and the other down avenue de la Grande-Armée toward the **Grande Arche de La Défense,** a severe modern arch surrounded by imposing glass and concrete towers. Halfway up the Arc is a small museum devoted to its history. ⊡ *Museum and platform: 32 frs.* ⊙ *Daily 10–5:30 (10–5 in winter).*

★ The **Champs-Elysées** is the site of colorful national ceremonies on July 14 and November 11; its trees are often decked with French tricolors and foreign flags to mark visits from heads of state. It is also where the cosmopolitan pulse of Paris beats strongest. The gracefully sloping 2-kilometer (1¼-mile) boulevard was originally laid out in the 1660s by André Le Nôtre as a garden sweeping away from the Tuileries. There is not much sign of its pastoral past as you stroll past the cafés, restaurants, airline offices, car showrooms, movie theaters, and chic arcades that occupy its upper half, although the avenue was spruced up in the early 1990s, with wider sidewalks and an extra row of trees. Farther down, on the right, is the striking glass roof of the **㉑** **Grand Palais.** It traditionally hosts Paris's major art exhibitions, but the spectacular main hall was closed for major repairs and will not reopen until 1998.

☾ One wing of the Grand Palais houses the **Palais de la Découverte,** with scientific and mechanical exhibits and a planetarium. Entrance is in the avenue Franklin-D.-Roosevelt. ⊡ *25 frs; additional 15 frs for planetarium.* ⊙ *Tues.–Sat. 9:30–6, Sun. 10–7.*

㉒ Directly opposite the main entrance to the Grand Palais is the **Petit Palais,** built at the same time (1900) and now home to an attractively presented collection of French paintings and furniture from the 18th and 19th centuries. ⊡ *26 frs.* ⊙ *Tues.–Sun. 10–5:40.*

Continue down the Champs-Elysées to **place de la Concorde,** built around 1775 and the scene of more than 1,000 deaths at the guillotine, including those of Louis XVI and Marie Antoinette. The obelisk, a gift from the viceroy of Egypt, originally stood at Luxor and was shipped here in 1833.

㉓ Across place de la Concorde lies the **Jardin des Tuileries:** formal gardens with trees, ponds, and statues, recently renovated as part of the Grand Louvre project. Standing guard on either side are the **Jeu de Paume** and the **Orangerie,** identical buildings erected in the mid-19th century. The Jeu de Paume, home of an Impressionist collection before its move to the Musee d' Orsay, has been completely transformed. Its spacious, austere, white walls now hold exhibits of contemporary art. The Orangerie contains fine early 20th-century French works by Monet (including some of his *Water Lilies*), Renoir, Marie Laurencin, and others. ⊡ *Jeu de Paume: 35 frs.* ⊙ *Tues. noon–9:30, Wed.–Fri. noon–7, weekends 10–7.* ⊡ *Orangerie: 27 frs, 18 frs Sun.* ⊙ *Wed.–Mon. 9:45–5:45.*

★ ㉔ Pass through the Tuileries to the **Arc du Carrousel,** a dainty triumphal arch erected more quickly (1806–08) than its big brother at the far end of the Champs-Elysées. Towering before you is the **Louvre,** with its glass pyramids. The Louvre, originally a royal palace, is today the world's largest and most famous museum. I. M Pei's pyramids are the highlight of a major modernization program begun in 1984. The museum now occupies the Richelieu wing, the facades have been cleaned, and the gardens between the Louvre and the Tuileries relaid. In the course of construction of an underground garage and shopping arcade, the **Carrousel du Louvre,** the medieval foundations of the palace were unearthed and are now displayed as an integral part of the museum's collection.

The Louvre was begun as a fortress in 1200 (the earliest parts still standing date from the 1540s) and completed under Napoléon III in the 1860s. The Louvre used to be even larger; a wing facing the Tuileries Gardens was razed by rampaging revolutionaries during the bloody Paris Commune of 1871. Whatever the aesthetic merits of Pei's new Louvre, the museum has emerged less cramped and more rationally organized. Yet its sheer variety can seem intimidating. The main tourist attraction is Leonardo da Vinci's *Mona Lisa* (known in French as *La Joconde*), painted in 1503. The latest research, based on Leonardo's supposed homosexuality, suggests that the subject was actually a man! The *Mona Lisa* may disappoint you: It's smaller than most imagine, it's kept behind glass, and it's invariably encircled by a mob of tourists.

Turn your attention to some less-crowded rooms and galleries nearby, where Leonardo's fellow Italians are strongly represented: Fra Angelico, Giotto, Mantegna, Raphael, Titian, and Veronese. El Greco, Murillo, and Velázquez lead the Spanish; Van Eyck, Rembrandt, Frans Hals, Brueghel, Holbein, and Rubens underline the achievements of northern European art. English paintings are highlighted by works of Lawrence, Reynolds, Gainsborough, and Turner. Highlights of French painting include works by Poussin, Fragonard, Chardin, Boucher, and Watteau—together with David's *Coronation of Napoléon,* Géricault's *Raft of the Medusa,* and Delacroix's *Liberty Guiding the People.*

Famous statues include the soaring *Victory of Samothrace,* the celebrated *Venus de Milo,* and the realistic Egyptian *Seated Scribe.* New rooms for sculpture were opened in the Denon Wing's former imperial stables in 1994. Be sure to inspect the Gobelins tapestries, the Crown Jewels (including the 186-carat Regent diamond), and the 9th-century bronze statuette of Emperor Charlemagne. 🖼 *40 frs, 20 frs after 3* PM *and Sun.* ☉ *Mon. and Wed. 9–9:45* PM, *Thurs.–Sun. 9–6.*

Montmartre

If you start at the Anvers métro station and head up rue de Steinkerque, with its budget clothing shops, you will be greeted by the most familiar and spectacular view of the Sacré-Coeur basilica atop the Butte Mont-
㉕ martre. The **Sacré-Coeur** was built in a bizarre, mock-Byzantine style between 1876 and 1910; although no favorite with aesthetes, it has become a major Paris landmark. It was built as an act of national penitence after the disastrous Franco-Prussian War of 1870—a Catholic show of strength at a time of bitter church-state conflict.

㉖ Around the corner is the **place du Tertre,** full of would-be painters and trendy, overpriced restaurants. The painters will plead with you to do your portrait.

Despite its eternal tourist appeal and ever-growing commercialization, Montmartre has not lost all its traditional bohemian color. Walk down rue Norvins and descend the bustling rue Lepic to place Blanche and

㉗ one of the favorite haunts of Toulouse-Lautrec and other luminaries of the Belle Epoque—the legendary **Moulin Rouge** cabaret.

Montmartre is some distance from the rest of the city's major attractions, so go left up boulevard de Clichy as far as **place Pigalle,** then take the métro to Madeleine.

Central Paris

㉘ The **Eglise de la Madeleine,** with its uncompromising array of columns, looks like a Greek temple. The only natural light inside comes from three shallow domes; the walls are richly but harmoniously decorated, with plenty of gold glinting through the dim interior. The church was designed in 1814 but not consecrated until 1842, after futile efforts to turn the site into a train station. The portico's majestic Corinthian colonnade supports a pediment with a sculptured frieze of the *Last Judgment*. From the steps you can admire the vista down rue Royale across the Seine. Another vista leads up boulevard Malesherbes to the dome of **St-Augustin,** a mid-19th-century church noted for its innovative use of iron girders as structural support.

㉙ ㉚ Place de la Madeleine is in the heart of Paris's prime shopping district: Jewelers line rue Royale; **Fauchon** and **Hédiard,** behind the Madeleine, are delightful *epiceries* (gourmet food shops). Alongside the Madeleine is a **ticket kiosk** (☉ Tues.–Sat. 12:30–8) that sells tickets for same-day theater performances at greatly reduced prices.

Continue down boulevard de la Madeleine and turn right into rue des Capucines. This nondescript street leads to rue de la Paix. Immediately
㉛ to the right is **place Vendôme,** one of the world's most opulent squares: A rhythmically proportioned example of 17th-century urban architecture that shines in all its golden-stone splendor since being sandblasted several years ago. Other things shine here, too, in the windows of jewelry shops that are even more upscale (and understated) than those in rue
㉜ Royale—fitting neighbors for the top-ranking **Ritz** hotel. The square's central column, topped by a statue of Napoléon, is made from the melted bronze of 1,200 cannons captured at the Battle of Austerlitz in 1805.

NEED A
BREAK?

Rue de la Paix leads, logically enough, to the **Café de la Paix** in front of the Opéra. There are few grander cafés in Paris, and fewer places where you can perch with as good a tableau before you. ✉ *5 pl. de l'Opéra.*

㉝ Dominating the northern side of the square is the imposing **Opéra,** the first great work of the architect Charles Garnier, dating from the 1860s. He used elements of neoclassical architecture—bas-reliefs on facades and columns—in an exaggerated combination that borders on parody. The lavishly upholstered auditorium, with its delightful ceiling painted by Marc Chagall in 1964, seems small—but this is because the stage is the largest in the world, accommodating up to 450 players. It was the Opéra Garnier that inspired Gaston Leroux's **The Phantom of the Opera,** as it was rumored that a diabolical genius who lived in the cellar lured the opera singers down to his murky chambers. ☎ *01–47–42–57–50.* ✏ *30 frs.* ☉ *Daily 10–4:30.*

㉞ Behind the Opéra are *les grands magasins,* Paris's most venerable department stores. The **Galeries Lafayette** is perhaps the more outstanding because of its elegant turn-of-the-century glass dome. But **Printemps,** farther along boulevard Haussmann to the left, is better organized and has an excellent view from its rooftop cafeteria.

Take the métro at Chaussée d'Antin, near the Galeries Lafayette, and
㉟ travel three stops (direction Villejuif) as far as **Palais-Royal.** This for-

mer royal palace, built in the 1630s, has a charming garden bordered by arcades and boutiques that many visitors overlook.

㊱ On the square in front of the Palais-Royal is the **Louvre des Antiquaires,** a chic shopping mall full of antiques dealers. It deserves a browse whether you intend to buy or not. Afterward, head east along rue St-Honoré and left into rue du Louvre. Skirt the circular **Bourse du Commerce** (Commercial Exchange) and head toward the imposing church
㊲ of **St-Eustache** (1532–1637), an invaluable testimony to the stylistic transition between Gothic and Classical architecture. It is also the
㊳ "cathedral" of **Les Halles**—the site of the central market of Paris until the much-loved glass-and-iron sheds were torn down in the late '60s. The area has since been transformed into a trendy—and already slightly seedy—shopping complex, Le Forum.

Head across the topiary garden and left down rue Berger. Pass the square des Innocents, with its Renaissance fountain, to boulevard de Sébastopol.
㊴ Straight ahead lies the futuristic, funnel-topped **Centre Pompidou**—a must for lovers of modern art. The Pompidou Center—known to Parisians as Beaubourg, after the surrounding district—was built in the mid-1970s and named in honor of former French president Georges Pompidou (1911–74). This "cultural Disneyland" is always crowded with visitors to the **Musée National d'Art Moderne,** the huge library, experimental music and industrial design sections, the children's museum, and the variety of activities and exhibitions. Musicians and other street performers fill the large forecourt that slopes down to the entrance. ⊠ *Pl. Georges-Pompidou,* ☎ *01–44–78–12–33.* ⊠ *Free; art museum: 35 frs, Sun. 24 frs; 20–50 frs for special exhibitions; 50 frs for daily pass covering all sectors of the center.* ☉ *Mon., Wed.–Fri. noon–10; weekends 10–10. Guided tours in English in summer and the Christmas season: weekdays 3:30 PM and weekends 11 AM.*

Note, on the right side of the Pompidou Center, the large digital clock, dubbed the **Genitron,** which counts down the seconds to the year 2000 at what seems like an apocalyptic pace. Peek into the café-lined **place Igor-Stravinsky** just to the right; kids will delight in the lively fountain animated by the colorful and imaginative sculptures and aquatic mechanisms by French artists Niki de Saint-Phalle and Jean Tinguely. Then continue east into the **Marais,** one of the most historic quarters of Paris. The spacious affluence of its 17th-century mansions, many of them beautifully restored, contrasts with narrow winding streets full of shops and restaurants. Rue de Rambuteau leads from Beaubourg into rue des Francs-Bourgeois. Turn left on rue Elzévir—via the **Musée Cognacq-Jay** (devoted to the arts of the 18th century)—to rue Thorigny, where
★ **㊵** you will find the Hôtel Salé and its **Musée Picasso.** This is a convincing experiment in modern museum layout, whether you like Picasso or not. Few of his major works are here, but many fine, little-known paintings, drawings, and engravings are on display. ⊠ *5 rue Thorigny,* ☎ *01–42–71–25–21.* ⊠ *27 frs, Sun. 18 frs.* ☉ *Wed.–Mon. 9:30–6.*

Double back down rue Elzévir and turn left along rue des Francs-Bour-
★ **㊶** geois until you reach the **place des Vosges.** Built in 1605, this is the oldest square in Paris. Its harmonious proportions, soft pink brick, and cloisterlike arcades give it an aura of calm. In the far corner is the **Maison de Victor Hugo,** containing souvenirs of the great poet's life and many of his surprisingly able paintings and ink drawings. ⊠ *6 pl. des Vosges.* ⊠ *27 frs.* ☉ *Tues.–Sun. 10–5:45.*

Rue Birague leads from the middle of the place des Vosges down to
㊷ rue St-Antoine. To the left is the **place de la Bastille.** Unfortunately, there are no historic vestiges here; not even the soaring column, topped

by the figure of Liberty, commemorates the famous storming of the Bastille in 1789 (the column stands in memory of Parisians killed in the uprisings of 1830). Only the new **Opéra de la Bastille,** which opened in 1989, can be said to mark the bicentennial.

Retrace your steps down rue St-Antoine as far as the large Baroque
㊸ church of **Saint-Paul-Saint-Louis** (1627–41). Then continue down rue
㊹ de Rivoli to the **Hôtel de Ville.** This magnificent city hall was rebuilt in its original Renaissance style after being burned down in 1871, during the violent days of the Paris Commune. The vast square in front of its many-statued facade has fountains and bronze lamps.

㊺ Avenue de Victoria leads to place du Châtelet. On the right is the **Tour St-Jacques.** This richly worked 170-foot stump is all that remains of a 16th-century church destroyed in 1802.

From Châtelet take the pont-au-Change over the Seine to the Ile de la
㊻ Cité and the **Palais de Justice** (law courts). Visit the turreted **Conciergerie,** a former prison with a superb vaulted 14th-century hall (Salles des Gens d'Armes) that often hosts temporary exhibitions. The **Tour de l'Horloge** (clock tower) near the entrance on the quai de l'Horloge has a clock that has been ticking off time since 1370. Around the corner in the boulevard du Palais, through the imposing law court gates, is the **Sainte-Chapelle,** built by St-Louis (Louis IX) in the 1240s to house the Crown of Thorns he had just bought from Emperor Baldwin of Constantinople. The building's lead-covered wood spire, rebuilt in 1854, rises 246 feet. The somewhat garish lower chapel is less impressive than the upper one, whose walls consist of little else but dazzling 13th-century stained glass. ▦ *Conciergerie and Sainte-Chapelle: 40 frs (joint ticket), 27 frs (single ticket).* ☉ *Daily 9:30–6:30 (winter 10–5).*

From boulevard du Palais turn right on quai des Orfèvres. This will
㊼ take you past the quaint place Dauphine to the **square du Vert-Galant** at the westernmost tip of the Ile de la Cité. Here, above a peaceful garden, you will find a statue of the Vert Galant himself: gallant adventurer Henry IV, king from 1589 to 1610.

Off the Beaten Path

☽ Few tourists venture into East Paris, but there are several points of interest tucked away here. The largest is the **Bois de Vincennes,** a less touristy version of the Bois de Boulogne, with several cafés and lakes. Rowboats can be taken to the two islands in Lac Daumesnil or to the three in Lac des Minimes. There is also a zoo, a cinder racetrack (the hippodrome), and an extensive flower garden (Parc Floral, route de la Pyramide). The **Château de Vincennes** (av. de Paris) is an imposing, high-walled castle surrounded by a dry moat and dominated by a 170-foot keep. It contains a replica of the Sainte-Chapelle on Ile de la Cité and two elegant classical wings added in the mid-17th century. *Bois de Vincennes (métro: Porte Dorée). Parc Floral and Château de Vincennes (métro: Château de Vincennes).* ▦ *Garden and castle: 27 frs.* ☉ *Daily 10–6 in summer, Wed. only, 10–noon and 2–5 in winter.*

Cemeteries aren't every tourist's idea of the ultimate attraction, but **Père Lachaise** is the largest and most interesting in Paris. It forms a veritable necropolis with cobbled avenues and tombs competing in pomposity and originality. Steep slopes and lush vegetation contribute to a powerful atmosphere; leading incumbents include Frédéric Chopin, Molière, Marcel Proust, Oscar Wilde, Sarah Bernhardt, Jim Morrison, Gertrude Stein and Alice B. Toklas (in the same grave), and Edith Piaf. Get a map at the entrance and track them down. Some people even bring a picnic lunch! ⊠ *Av. du Père-Lachaise, 20ᵉ. Métro: Gambetta.* ☉ *Daily 8–6, winter 8–5.*

The **Canal St-Martin** starts life just south of the place de la Bastille but really comes into its own during the 1,500-meter (1-mile) stretch north across the 10ᵉ arrondissement. It has an unexpected flavor of Amsterdam, thanks to its quiet banks, locks, and footbridges. *Métro: Jaurès to the north or Jacques-Bonsergent to the south.*

Hidden away in a grid of narrow streets, not far from the Opéra, is Paris's central auction house, the **Hôtel Drouot.** It is open six days a week (except at Christmas, Easter, and midsummer), and its 16 salesrooms make a fascinating place to browse, with absolutely no obligation to bid. Everything from stamps and toy soldiers to Renoirs and 18th-century commodes is available. The mixture of ladies in fur with money to burn, penniless art lovers desperate to unearth an unidentified masterpiece, and scruffy dealers trying to look anonymous makes up Drouot's unusually rich social fabric. ⊠ *9 rue Drouot. Métro: Richelieu-Drouot.* ☉ *Viewing 11–noon and 2–6, auctions start at 2.*

Some of Paris's less-frequented arrondissements afford great walks. The **Bercy** section of the 12ᵉ arrondissement (Métro: Bercy) is the focus of a massive renovation project scheduled for completion in 1997. Once filled with warehouses for the storing of wine from the provinces, the neighborhood has seen a total transformation, which was kicked off in the mid-'80s with the creation of the **Palais Omnisports,** the strangely grassy-walled, pyramid-shape sports complex, and the installation of the **French Finance Ministry** in quayside glass-and-steel offices. These buildings serve as cornerstones for the **Parc de Bercy,** which is also bordered by a large food and wine business complex and the **American Center,** a venue for American art and cultural events (but for sale at press time due to lack of funds) designed by architect Frank Gehry. On the other side of the Seine is the new **Bibliothèque Nationale,** late President Mitterrand's last major project.

Enjoy an afternoon stroll along the tree-lined streets of Paris's so-called **Beaux Quartiers,** which are in the 16ᵉ arrondissement (Métro: Eglise d'Auteil, Ranelagh, La Muette) and are punctuated with some superb examples of 20th-century architecture. Of greatest interest are the Art Nouveau buildings built by **Hector Guimard** (who designed the métro entrances)—particularly 34 rue Boileau; 8 av. de la Villa-de-la-Réunion; and 14, 17, and 19 rue de la Fontaine); and **Le Corbusier's** first private houses, featuring Villa La Roche (1923), on a small cul-de-sac off rue du Docteur-Blanche.

Finally, for those weary of monument gazing, Paris's **Chinatown**—concentrated between the high-rises of rue Tolbiac, avenue de Choisy, and boulevard Massena (Métro: Tolbiac) in the 13ᵉ—has a delightful array of Chinese restaurants, supermarkets, and clothing stores.

Shopping

Gift Ideas

Old prints are sold by *bouquinistes* (second-hand booksellers) in stalls along the banks of the Seine. **Guerlain** (⊠ 47 rue Bonaparte, métro Mabillon) sells legendary French perfumes. The **Musée des Arts Décoratifs** (⊠ 107 rue de Rivoli, 1ᵉʳ, métro Palais-Royal) has state-of-the-art home decorations. **Fauchon** (⊠ 30 pl. de la Madeleine, 8ᵉ, métro Madeleine) is an upscale grocery with regional specialty foods, herbs, and pâtés. **Hédiard** (⊠ 21 pl. de la Madeleine, 8ᵉ, métro Madeleine) is a super deluxe delicatessen with a wide choice of French specialties.

Antiques

Dealers proliferate in the **Carré Rive Gauche** between St-Germain-des-Prés and the Musée d'Orsay. There are also several around the **Drouot** auction house near the Opéra (corner of rue Rossini and rue Drouot, métro Richelieu-Drouot). The **Louvre des Antiquaires** (⊠ pl. du Palais-Royal, 1ᵉʳ, métro Palais-Royal) is a stylish shopping mall dominated by antiques (☞ Exploring, *above*). At the **Village Suisse** (⊠ 78 av. de Suffren, 15ᵉ, métro La Motte-Picquet-Grenelle), near the Champ de Mars, over 100 dealers are grouped around an outdoor mall.

Boutiques

Only Milan can compete with Paris for the title of Capital of European Chic. The top shops are along the Champs-Elysées, along avenue Montaigne and rue du Faubourg-St-Honoré, and at place des Victoires. St-Germain-des-Prés, rue de Grenelle, and rue de Rennes on the Left Bank are centers for small specialty shops and boutiques. Search for bargains along the streets around the foot of Montmartre (☞ Exploring, *above*), or in the designer discount shops (Cacharel, Rykiel, Dorotennis) along rue d'Alésia in Montparnasse. The streets to the north of the Marais, close to Arts-et-Métiers métro, are historically linked to the cloth trade, and some shops offer garments at wholesale prices.

Department Stores

Au Bon Marché (⊠ 22 rue de Sèvres, 7ᵉ, métro Sèvres-Babylone) is the leading department store on the Left Bank. **Galeries Lafayette** (⊠ 40 blvd. Haussmann, 9ᵉ, métro Chaussée-d'Antin) has a comprehensive array of fashionable goods beneath its shimmering turn-of-the-century glass cupola. **Printemps** (⊠ 64 blvd. Haussmann, 9ᵉ, métro Havre-Caumartin) is perhaps the most famous Paris department store; its distinctive narrow domes add an art nouveau touch to boulevard Haussmann. **La Samaritaine** (⊠ 19 rue de la Monnaie, 1ᵉʳ, métro Pont-Neuf) occupies several buildings near the Louvre, including an airy Art Deco store overlooking the Seine.

Food and Flea Markets

Marché aux Puces de St-Ouen (🕐 Sat.–Mon., métro Porte de Clignancourt), just north of Paris, is one of Europe's largest flea markets. Best bargains are to be had early in the morning. There are smaller flea markets at the Porte de Vanves and Porte de Montreuil (weekends only).

Every *quartier* (neighborhood) has at least one open-air food market. Sunday morning till 1 PM is usually a good time to go; Monday they are likely to be closed.

Dining

Eating out in Paris should be a pleasure, and there is no reason why choosing a less expensive restaurant should spoil the fun. After all, Parisians themselves eat out frequently and cannot afford haute cuisine every night, either. For details and prices-category definitions, *see* Dining *in* Staying in France, *above*.

Left Bank

$$$$ ✕ **L'Arpège.** With its curving, hand-crafted wood panels and wrought-★ iron window frames, the decor of this small, striking restaurant near the Rodin museum is unusually minimalist. Young chef-owner Alain Passard's cuisine is both original (lobster/turnip starter in a sweet-sour vinaigrette, stuffed sweet tomato) and classic (beef Burgundy, pressed duck). The problem here is inconsistency: one sublime meal can be followed by a mediocre experience. The prix-fixe lunch is a steal. ⊠ 84 *rue de Varenne, 7ᵉ,* ☎ *45–51–47–33. AE, DC, MC, V. Closed Sat. and Aug. No lunch Sun. Métro: Varenne.*

$$$$ ✕ **La Tour d'Argent.** Dining at this temple of haute cuisine is an event—
★   from apéritifs in the ground-floor bar to dinner in the top-floor din-
     ing room, with its view of Notre-Dame. The food, unfortunately, does
     not reach the same heights. La Tour classics such as *caneton Tour d'Ar-
     gent* (pressed duck) and *filets de sole Cardinal* have been lightened and
     contemporary creations added. You can visit the cellars before or after
     your meal. The lunch menu is relatively affordable. ⊠ *15 quai de la
     Tournelle,* ☎ *01–43–54–23–31. Reservations essential at least 1 wk
     in advance. Jacket and tie at dinner. AE, DC, MC, V. Closed Mon. Métro:
     Cardinal Lemoine.*

$$–$$$ ✕ **La Timonerie.** Only a few steps along the quai from La Tour d'Ar-
★   gent, this small, elegant restaurant offers fine cooking with no theatrics.
     Philippe de Givenchy works with a small staff and his creations are
     consistently interesting and well-executed. In his hands, a simple dish
     such as rosemary and lemon mackerel reaches new levels of refinement.
     ⊠ *35 quai de la Tournelle, 5ᵉ,* ☎ *01–43–25–44–42. Jacket and tie.
     MC, V. Closed Sun. and Mon. Métro: Maubert-Mutalité.*

$$ ✕ **Les Bookinistes.** Talented chef Guy Savoy's cheery postmodern din-
★   ing room, painted peach with red, blue, and yellow wall sconces, has
     a view of the Seine. The French country menu changes seasonally, and
     might include mussel and pumpkin soup or baby chicken roasted in a
     casserole with root vegetables. The somewhat pricey wine list contrasts
     with the reasonable prices. Service is friendly and efficient. ⊠ *53 quai
     des Grands-Augustins, 6ᵉ,* ☎ *01–43–25–45–94. AE, DC, MC, V.
     Closed Sun, lunch Sat. Métro: St-Michel.*

$$ ✕ **Campagne et Provence.** On the quai across from Notre-Dame, this
★   very pleasant little restaurant with rustic Provençal fabrics and blue
     grass-cloth wallpaper has a Provençal menu that includes grilled John
     Dory with preserved fennel, and peppers stuffed with cod and eggplant.
     In season, try the roasted figs with shortbread and black currant sauce,
     an outstanding dessert. ⊠ *25 quai de la Tournelle, 5ᵉ,*☎ *01–43–54–
     05–17. MC, V. Closed Mon. lunch, Sat. lunch, Sun. Métro: Maubert-
     Mutalité.*

$ ✕ **Le Petit Plat.** This popular bistro in a quiet residential area is small,
     but the feel is intimate rather than crowded. Try the generous portions
     of urbanized French country cooking that Parisians are currently mad
     about: terrine of rabbit in tarragon aspic, sausage with potato salad
     in shallot vinaigrette, and roast chicken with sautéed mushrooms. The
     excellent wine list was selected by Henri Gault of Gault-Millau, the
     famous French food guide (his daughter is one of the three owners).
     ⊠ *45 av. Emile-Zola, 15ᵉ,* ☎ *01–45–78–24–20 V. Closed Mon., Tues.
     lunch. Métro: Charles-Michel.*

$ ✕ **La Régalade.** Yves Camdeborde's cooking is worth the trip to a re-
★   mote, colorless neighborhood. A veteran of the Crillon, he has kept
     prices remarkably low—$37 for a three-course feast. Tables need to
     be booked at least one month in advance, but service continues until
     midnight, and you can often sneak in late in the evening. ⊠ *49 av. Jean-
     Moulin, 14ᵉ,* ☎ *01–45–45–68–58. MC, V. Closed Sat. lunch, Sun.,
     Mon., Aug. Métro: Alesia.*

$ ✕ **La Rôtisserie d'Armaillé.** Admire the handsome oak paneling, cran-
     berry and green upholstery, and the *très* Parisian crowd at star-chef
     Jacques Cagna's third restaurant. The prix-fixe menu has many tempt-
     ing choices, among them pastilla of guinea hen and a terrific choco-
     late cake. Wines are a little pricey. ⊠ *6 rue d'Armaillé, 17ᵉ,* ☎
     01–42–27–19–20 AE, MC, V. Closed Sat. lunch, Sun. Métro: Argentine.

West Paris

$$$$ ✕ **Guy Savoy.** Top chef Guy Savoy's other five bistros have not dis-
★ tracted him too much from his handsome luxury restaurant near the
Arc de Triomphe. The oysters in aspic, sea bass with spices, and
poached and grilled pigeon reveal the magnitude of his talent. His mille-
feuille is a contemporary classic. ⊠ *18 rue Troyon, 17ᵉ, ☎ 01–43–
80–40–61. AE, MC, V. Closed Sat. lunch, Sun. Métro: Charles de
Gaulle–Etoile.*

$$$$ ✕ **Taillevent.** Many say it's the best restaurant in Paris. Dining in the
★ paneled rooms of this mid-19th-century mansion is certainly a sublime
experience. Service is exceptional, the wine list stellar, and the classical French cuisine perfect. Among the signature dishes are cream of
watercress soup with caviar and truffled tart of game. Desserts are also
superb, especially the creamy chocolate tart served with thyme ice
cream. ⊠ *15 rue Lamennais, 8ᵉ, ☎ 01–45–63–39–94. Reservations
3–4 wks in advance essential. Jacket and tie. AE, MC, V. Closed weekends, Aug. Métro: Charles de Gaulle–Etoile.*

$$$ ✕ **Le Cercle Ledoyen.** This luxury brasserie is below the landmark
restaurant Ledoyen. For about $50 a dinner—wine included—you
can sample chef Ghislaine Arabian's cooking, including the specials
served at Ledoyen. The handsome curved dining room with a view of
the surrounding park is a pleasure year-round, and the terrace is a spe-
cial treat in warm weather. ⊠ *1 av. Dutuit, 8ᵉ, ☎ 01–47–42–23–23.
AE, DC, MC, V. Closed Sun. Métro: Champs-Elysées–Clemenceau.*

$ ✕ **Le Petit Yvan.** Yvan's annex near his eponymous restaurant is a stylish
spot for lunch. The decor and the menu are simpler than at Yvan's star-
studded outpost. But the cuisine is also very good: the best option is
the reasonable prix-fixe menu that might include lemon-marinated
salmon or steak tartare. ⊠ *1 bis rue Jean-Mermoz, 8ᵉ, ☎ 01–42–89–
49–65. MC, V. Closed Sun., Sat. lunch. Métro: St-Philippe-du-Roule.*

Central and Eastern Paris

$$$$ ✕ **Le Grand Véfour.** Luminaries from Napoléon to Colette to Jean
Cocteau have frequented this intimate address under the arcades of the
Palais-Royal; you can request to be seated at their preferred tables. This
sumptuously decorated restaurant, with its mirrored ceiling and painted
glass panels, is perhaps the prettiest in Paris, and its 18th-century ori-
gins make it one of the oldest. Chef Guy Martin impresses with his
unique blend of sophisticated yet rustic dishes, including roast lamb
in a juice of herbs. Reservations at least one week in advance are ad-
vised. ⊠ *17 rue Beaujolais, 1ᵉ, ☎ 01–42–96–56–27. Jacket and tie.
AE, DC, MC, V. Closed weekends, Aug. Métro: Palais-Royal.*

$$–$$$ ✕ **Pile ou Face.** Housed on two floors in a narrow building, this restau-
rant offers an intimate setting for discussing big business and the most
interesting and creative food around the Stock Exchange. Try the rab-
bit paté or the scrambled eggs with mushrooms, then move on to the
sweetbreads and the exquisite roast chicken. Service is attentive. ⊠ *52
bis rue de Notre-Dame des Victoires, 2ᵉ, ☎ 01–42–33–64–33. MC,
V. Closed weekends, Aug. Métro: Bourse.*

$$ ✕ **Chardenoux.** A bit off the beaten path but well worth the effort,
★ this cozy neighborhood bistro with etched-glass windows, dark bent-
wood furniture, tile floors, and a long zinc bar attracts a cross section
of savvy Parisians. The traditional cooking is first-rate: start with one
of the delicious salads, such as the green beans and foie gras, then try
the veal chop with morels or a game dish. Savory desserts and a nicely
chosen wine list with several excellent Côtes-du-Rhônes complete the
dining experience. ⊠ *1 rue Jules-Valles, ☎ 01–43–71–49–52, 11ᵉ.
AE, V. Closed weekends, Aug. Métro: Charonne.*

$ ✕ **Les Zygomates.** This handsome old butcher's shop, converted into a bistro, is very popular. Since it's in a part of the city few tourists venture to, it's mostly filled with Parisians. Experience delicious modern bistro food like a terrine of rabbit with tarragon, chicken in cream with chives, and a very fairly priced catch-of-the-day selection. ⊠ *7 rue Capri 12e, ☎ 01–40–19–93–04. V. Closed Sun., Sat. lunch Oct.–May, Sat. June–Sept., first 3 wks Aug. Métro: Michel-Bizot or Daumesnil.*

Lodging

For details and price-category definitions, *see* Lodging *in* Staying in France, *above.*

Left Bank

$$$$ 🏨 **L'Hôtel.** Rock idols and movie stars adore this expensive and eccentric Left Bank hôtel. Oscar Wilde died here in room 16 ("I am dying beyond my means," he wrote). The decor is over the top at times; one small double is decorated entirely in leopard skin; another handsome suite features the mirrored Art Deco boudoir furniture that belonged to vaudeville star Mistinguett. Many rooms are extremely small. The hotel's fine restaurant, Le Bélier, has a fountain and a live tree. The piano bar, open until 1 AM, is popular with a well-heeled international crowd. ⊠ *13 rue des Beaux-Arts, 75006, ☎ 01–44–41–99–00, FAX 01–43–25–64–81. 15 rooms with bath, 10 with shower, 2 suites with bath. Restaurant, bar, air-conditioning, in-room safes, meeting rooms. AE, DC, MC, V. Métro: St-Germain-des-Prés.*

$$ 🏨 **Grandes Ecoles.** It's hard to find a quieter, more charming hotel for ★ the price; just ask the loyal American clientele of this delightfully intimate 2-star place that looks like a country cottage. It is off the street and occupies three buildings on a beautiful, leafy garden, where breakfast is served in summer. Parquet floors, Louis-Philippe furnishings, lace bedspreads, and the absence of TV all add to the rustic ambience. ⊠ *75 rue du Cardinal Lemoine, 75005, ☎ 01–43–26–79–23, FAX 01–43–25–28–15. 45 rooms with bath, 6 with shower. No-smoking rooms. MC, V. Métro: Cardinal Lemoine.*

$$ 🏨 **Jardin des Plantes.** Across the street from the lovely Jardin des Plantes, this pleasant 2-star hotel has very reasonable prices and botanical-theme decor. There's a fifth-floor terrace where you can breakfast or sunbathe in summer, and a sauna in the cellar. ⊠ *5 rue Linné, 75005, ☎ 01–47–07–06–20, FAX 01–47–07–62–74. 29 rooms with bath, 4 with shower. Restaurant, bar, in-room safes, no-smoking rooms, sauna, meeting room. AE, DC, MC, V. Métro: Jussieu.*

West Paris

$$$$ 🏨 **Le Bristol.** Luxury and discretion are its trump cards. The understated facade on rue du Faubourg St-Honoré might mislead the unknowing, but the Bristol ranks among Paris's top four hotels. Some of the spaciously elegant rooms have authentic Louis XV and Louis XVI furniture and magnificent marble bathrooms. The public areas are filled with Old Master paintings, sculptures, sumptuous carpets, and tapestries. There's an enclosed pool on the roof, complete with solarium and sauna for guests. Service throughout is impeccable. ⊠ *112 rue du Faubourg St-Honoré, 75008, ☎ 01–42–66–91–45, FAX 01–42–66–68–68. 155 rooms and 45 suites, all with bath. Restaurant, bar, air-conditioning, in-room safes, room service, health club, laundry service, meeting rooms. AE, DC, MC, V. Métro: St-Philippe du Roule.*

$$$$ 🏨 **Crillon.** The Crillon is the crème de la crème of Paris's "palace" ho- ★ tels. It is in two 18th-century town houses on the place de la Concorde, site of the French Revolution's infamous guillotine. Marie Antoinette took singing lessons at the Hôtel de Crillon, where one of the original

grands appartements, now sumptuous salons protected by the French National Historic Landmark Commission, has been named after her. Rooms are decorated with Rococo and Directoire antiques, crystal and gilt wall sconces, and gold fittings. Most doubles have separate sitting rooms. The sheer quantity of marble downstairs—especially in the top-rated Les Ambassadeurs restaurant—is staggering. ⊠ *10 pl. de la Concorde, 75008,* ☎ *01–44–71–15–00,* FAX *01–44–71–15–02. 118 rooms and 45 suites, all with bath. 2 restaurants, 2 bars, tea shop, air-conditioning, in-room safes, no-smoking rooms, room service, meeting rooms. AE, DC, MC, V. Métro: Concorde.*

$$$$ 🏨 **Grand Hôtel Inter-Continental.** Open since 1862, Paris's biggest
★ luxury hotel has a facade that seems as long as the Louvre. The grand salon's Art Deco dome and the restaurant's painted ceilings are registered landmarks. The Art Deco rooms are spacious and light. The famed Café de la Paix is one of the city's great people-watching spots. ⊠ *2 rue Scribe, 75009,* ☎ *01–40–07–32–32,* FAX *01–42–66–12–51. 514 rooms and 60 suites, all with bath. 3 restaurants, 2 bars, air-conditioning, in-room safes, no-smoking rooms, room service, health club, laundry service, meeting rooms. AE, DC, MC, V. Métro: Opéra.*

$$$$ 🏨 **Ritz.** Surrounded by the city's finest jewelers, the Ritz is the crowning gem of the sparkling place Vendôme. Festooned with gilt and ormolu, dripping with crystal chandeliers and swathed in heavy silk and tapestries, this dazzling hotel, which opened in 1896, is the epitome of fin-de-siècle Paris. Yet, it's surprisingly intimate. The lack of a lobby discourages paparazzi and sightseers who might annoy the privileged clientele. Legendary suites are named after former residents like Marcel Proust and Coco Chanel. Don't miss the famous Hemingway Bar (which the writer claimed to have "liberated" in 1944). ⊠ *15 pl. Vendôme, 75001,* ☎ *01–43–16–30–30,* FAX *01–43–16–36–68. 142 rooms and 45 suites, all with bath. 3 restaurants, 2 bars, air-conditioning, in-room safes, room service, indoor pool, beauty salon, health club, laundry service, meeting rooms. AE, DC, MC, V. Métro: Opéra.*

$$$ 🏨 **Etoile-Pereire.** If you want a welcoming, personally run place, few
★ can beat this one. The owner has created a unique, intimate hotel behind a quiet, leafy courtyard in a chic residential district. It consists of a fin-de-siècle building on the street and a 1920s annex overlooking an interior courtyard. Rooms and duplexes are decorated in soothing pastels with Laura Ashley curtains and upholstery. The copious breakfast is legendary, featuring 40 assorted jams and jellies. The bar is always busy in the evening. ⊠ *146 blvd. Pereire, 75017,* ☎ *01–42–67–60–00,* FAX *01–42–67–02–90. 23 rooms, 4 duplexes and 1 suite, all with bath, 3 rooms with shower, Bar, air-conditioning, no-smoking rooms, laundry service. AE, DC, MC, V. Métro: Pereire.*

$$–$$$ 🏨 **Gaillon-Opéra.** One of the most charming in the Opéra neighbor-
★ hood, this hotel has such character that you would never guess that it's part of the Best Western chain. It still has its old oak beams, stone walls, marble tiles, and leafy patio. ⊠ *9 rue Gaillon, 75002,* ☎ *01–47–42–47–74, (US: 800/528-1234)* FAX *01–47–42–01–23. 17 rooms and 9 suites, all with bath. Air-conditioning, in-room safes, room service, laundry service. AE, DC, MC, V. Métro: Opéra.*

$$ 🏨 **Keppler.** Near the Champs-Elysées, on the edge of the 8th and 16th arrondissements, this small 2-star hotel in a 19th-century building has some 3-star features (room service, small bar) and extremely reasonable prices. The spacious, airy rooms are simply decorated. ⊠ *12 rue Keppler, 75116,* ☎ *01–47–20–65–05,* FAX *01–47–23–02–29. 31 rooms with bath, 18 with shower. Bar. AE, MC, V. Métro: George V.*

$ 🏨 **Argenson.** This friendly, family-run hotel provides good value in the swanky 8th arrondissement, just a 10-minute walk from the Champs-Elysées. Chimneys, corniced ceilings, and large mirrors recall its fin-de-siècle roots. Reserve well in advance for a room with full bath. Breakfast is included. ⊠ *15 rue d'Argenson, 75008,* ☏ *01–42–65–16–87,* ℻ *01–47–42–02–06. 5 rooms with bath, 21 with shower, 2 with shared bath. In-room safes. MC, V. Métro: Miromesnil.*

Montmartre and Central Paris

$$$$ ⊞ **Pavillon de la Reine.** This magnificent mansion, reconstructed from
  ★ original plans, is on the 17th-century place des Vosges. It's filled with Louis XIII fireplaces and antiques. Ask for a duplex with French windows overlooking the first of two flower-filled courtyards behind the historic Queen's Pavilion. Breakfast is in a vaulted cellar. ⊠ *28 pl. des Vosges, 75003,* ☏ *01–42–77–96–40,* ℻ *01–42–77–63–06. 30 rooms and 25 suites, all with bath. Bar, air-conditioning, room service, laundry service. AE, DC, MC, V. Métro: Bastille.*

$$$ ⊞ **Deux-Iles.** This converted 17th-century mansion on the Ile St-Louis
  ★ has long won plaudits for charm and comfort. Flowers and plants are scattered around the stunning main hall. The delightful rooms, blessed with exposed beams, are small but fresh and airy. Ask for a room overlooking the little garden courtyard. In winter, a roaring fire warms the bar-lounge. ⊠ *59 rue St-Louis-en-l'Ile, 75004,* ☏ *01–43–26–13–35,* ℻ *01–43–29–60–25. 8 rooms with bath, 9 with shower. Bar, air-conditioning. V. Métro: Pont-Marie.*

$ ⊞ **Castex.** This 2-star Marais hotel in a Revolution-era building is a
  ★ real find. Rooms are squeaky clean, the owners are extremely friendly, and the prices are rock-bottom, which ensures that the hotel is often booked months ahead by a largely American clientele. There's no elevator, and the only TV is in the ground-floor lobby. ⊠ *5 rue Castex, 75004,* ☏ *01–42–72–31–52,* ℻ *01–42–72–57–91. 4 rooms with bath, 23 with shower. No-smoking rooms. MC, V. Métro: Bastille.*

$ ⊞ **Place des Vosges.** A loyal American clientele swears by this small, historic 2-star hotel on a charming street just off the exquisite Place des Vosges. The Louis XIII reception area and rooms with oak-beamed ceilings and rough-hewn stone evoke the old Marais. Ask for the top-floor room, the hotel's largest, for its view over Right Bank rooftops; others are the size of walk-in closets, and are less expensive. There's a welcoming little breakfast room. ⊠ *2 rue de Birague, 75004,* ☏ *01–42–72–60–46,* ℻ *01–42–72–02–64. 11 rooms with bath, 5 with shower. AE, DC, MC, V. Métro: Bastille.*

$ ⊞ **Regyn's Montmartre.** Despite its small rooms, this owner-run hotel on Montmartre's charming place des Abbesses provides simple, comfortable accommodations. Ask for a room on one of the top two floors, for great views of either the Eiffel Tower or Sacré Coeur. Courteous service and a relaxed atmosphere make this an attractive choice. ⊠ *18 pl. des Abbesses, 75018,* ☏ *01–42–54–45–21,* ℻ *01–42–52–74–22. 8 rooms with bath, 14 with shower. In-room safes. AE, MC, V. Métro: Abbesses.*

The Arts

The weekly magazines *Pariscope, L'Officiel des Spectacles,* and *Figaroscope* give detailed entertainment listings. The Paris Tourist Office has a **24-hour English-language hot line** (☏ 01–49–52–53–56) with information about weekly events. Buy tickets at the place of performance; otherwise, try hotels, travel agencies (such as **Paris-Vision** at 214 rue de Rivoli), and special ticket counters (in the **FNAC** stores in the Forum des Halles or at 26 av. des Ternes, near the Arc de Triomphe). Half-price tickets for same-day theater performances are available at the ticket stand at the west side of the Eglise de la Madeleine.

Theater

There is no Parisian equivalent to Broadway or the West End, although a number of theaters line the grand boulevards between the Opéra and République. Shows are mostly in French. **Comédie Française** (✉ 2 rue de Richelieu, 1ᵉʳ, métro Palais-Royal) hosts distinguished classical drama by Racine, Molière, and Corneille. **Théâtre de la Huchette** (✉ 23 rue de la Huchette, 5ᵉ, métro St-Michel) is a tiny venue where Ionesco's short plays *La Canatatrice Chave* and *La Leçon* make a deliberately ridiculous mess of the French language.

Concerts

Inexpensive organ or chamber music concerts proliferate in churches throughout the city. **Salle Pleyel** (✉ 252 rue du Faubourg-St-Honoré, 8ᵉ, métro Ternes), remains the principal venue for symphonic music. **Théâtre Musical de Paris** (✉ pl. du Châtelet, 1ᵉʳ, métro Chatelet) regularly hosts orchestral concerts.

Opera

Getting a ticket for an opera or ballet performance is not always easy, and may require luck, preplanning, or a well-connected hotel receptionist. **Opéra Bastille** (✉ pl. de la Bastille, 12ᵉ, ☎ 01–47–42–53–71, métro Bastille) has replaced the 19th-century Opéra Garnier as the main Paris operatic venue since opening in 1989. It has a spectacular, steeply-tiered auditorium. **Opéra Comique** (✉ 5 rue Favart, 2ᵉ, métro Richelieu-Drouot, ☎ 01–42–44–45–46) is the French term for opera with spoken dialogue, and stages light-hearted musical dramas.

Dance

Occasional venues include the **Théâtre de la Ville** (☎ 01–42–74–22–77) at Châtelet and the **Palais des Congrès** (☎ 01–40–68–22–22) at Porte Maillot. **Opéra Garnier** (✉ pl. de l'Opéra, 9ᵉ, métro Opéra), or the "old Opéra", now concentrates on dance: in addition to being the sumptuous home of the well-reputed Paris Ballet, it also bills dozens of major foreign troupes ranging from classical to modern.

Film

There are hundreds of movie theaters in Paris, and some of them, especially in principal tourist areas such as the Champs-Elysées and the boulevard des Italiens near the Opéra, run English films marked *"version originale"* (VO, i.e., not dubbed). Admission is around 40–50 francs, with reduced rates on Monday. Movie fanatics should check out the **Centre Pompidou** and the **Musée du Cinéma** at Trocadéro, where old and rare films are often screened.

Nightlife

Cabaret

Paris's nightclubs are household names—more so abroad than in France, it would seem, judging by the hefty percentage of foreigners present at most shows. Prices range from 200 francs (basic admission plus one drink) to 750 francs (dinner included). For 400–500 francs, you can get a good seat plus half a bottle of champagne.

Crazy Horse (✉ 12 av. George V, 8ᵉ, ☎ 01–47–23–32–32, métro Alma-Marceau) is one of the best known clubs for pretty girls and raunchy dance routines: lots of humor and lots fewer clothes. **Folies Bergère** (✉ 32 rue Richer, 9ᵉ, ☎ 01–44–79–98–98, métro Cadet), a legend since the days of Manet, has a new-and-improved show that returns to its music hall origins, helped by ornate costumes and masterful lighting. **Lido** (✉ 116 bis av. des Champs-Elysées, 8ᵉ, ☎ 01–40–76–56–10, métro George V) stars the famous Bluebell Girls; the owners claim that no show in Las Vegas can rival it for special effects. **Moulin Rouge**

(✉ pl. Blanche, 18ᵉ, ☎ 01–46–06–00–19, métro Blanche), the old
favorite at the foot of Montmartre, mingles the Doriss girls, crocodiles,
and the Can-Can in an extravagant spectacle.

Bars and Nightclubs

Upscale nightclubs are usually private, so unless you have a friend who
is a member, forget it. The Pigalle area in Montmartre is becoming the
place to go, despite its reputation as a seedy red-light district. Nightlife
is still hopping in and around the Bastille, and the Left Bank boasts a
bit of everything. The Champs-Elysées is making a comeback, though
the clientele remains predominantly foreign.

Le Casbah (✉ 18 rue de la Forge-Royale, 11ᵉ, ☎ 01–43–71–71–89,
métro Faidherbe-Chaligny) is a bar and dance club with a touch of
Casablanca. **China Club** (✉ 50 rue de Charenton, 12ᵉ, ☎ 01–43–43–
82–02, métro Ledru-Rollin) is a trendy bar with a colonial Orient theme.
Pistou Pélican (15 rue de Bagnolet, 20ᵉ, ☎ 01–43–70–93–98, métro
Alexandre-Dumas), a favorite with Beaux-Arts students, has a laid-back
ambience and occasional live music.

Le Dépanneur (✉ 27 rue Fontaine, 9ᵉ, ☎ 01–40–16–40–20, métro
Blanche) caters to a gin- and tequila-drinking yuppie crowd. **Lili la Ti-
gresse** (✉ 98 rue Blanche, 9ᵉ, ☎ 01–48–74–08–25, métro Blanche)
is a sexy, velvet-lined lounge with bar-top dancers and a trendy crowd.
Moloko (26 rue Fontaine, 9ᵉ, ☎ 01–48–74–50–26, métro Blanche),
a smoky late-night bar with several rooms, a mezzanine, a jukebox,
and a small dance floor, is a popular spot. **Châo-Bâ** (✉ 22 blvd. de Clichy,
18ᵉ, ☎ 01–46–06–72–90, métro Pigalle), a spacious, two-tiered café
with Oriental decor and mock-bamboo furniture.

Niel's (27 av. Ternes, 17ᵉ, ☎ 01–47–66–45–00, métro Ternes) numbers top models and showbiz glitterati among its regulars; music ranges
from rap to techno to mainstream disco. **The Forum** (✉ 4 blvd.
Malesherbes, 8ᵉ, ☎ 01–42–65–37–86, métro Madeleine), a discreet,
archetypal French cocktail bar, has one of the best selections of cocktails and whiskies in Paris. **Harry's Bar** (✉ 5 rue Daunou, 2ᵉ, ☎ 01–
42–61–71–14, métro Opéra), a cozy, wood-paneled hangout popular
with expatriates, is haunted by the ghosts of Ernest Hemingway and
F. Scott Fitzgerald. **Rosebud** (✉ 11 bis rue Delambre, 14ᵉ, ☎ 01–43–
20–44–13, métro Vavin) is a jazzy cult spot for the *jeunesse dorée* (young
and fashionable) of Montparnasse.

Gay and Lesbian

Gay and lesbian bars and clubs are mostly concentrated in the Marais
and include some of the most happening addresses in the city.

MOSTLY MEN

The **Banana Café** (✉ 13 rue de la Ferronnerie, 1ᵉʳ, ☎ 01–42–33–35–
31, métro Les Halles) attracts a trendy and scantily clad mixed crowd;
dancing on the tables is the norm. **Club 18** (✉ 18 rue de Beaujolais, 1ᵉʳ,
☎ 01–42–97–52–13, métro Pyramides), the oldest gay disco in Paris,
is as popular and casual as ever. **Quetzal** (✉ 10 rue de la Verrerie, 4ᵉ,
☎ 01–48–87–99–07, métro Hôtel-de-Ville) gleams with chrome, blue
lighting, and pick-me-up smiles; it's packed and smoky on weekends.
Subway (✉ 35 rue St-Croix-de-la-Bretonnerie, 4ᵉ, ☎ 01–42–77–41–
10, métro Hôtel de Ville) looks like a roadside dive, has a pool table
and cellar bar, and caters to a middle-aged, tight-jeaned crowd.

MOSTLY WOMEN

Champmeslé (✉ 4 rue Chabanais, 2ᵉ, ☎ 01–42–96–85–20, métro
Bourse) is the hub of lesbian nightlife with a dusky back room reserved
exclusively for ladies. **Memorie's** (✉ 2 pl. de la Porte-Maillot, 17ᵉ, ☎

01–40–68–22–22, métro Porte Maillot), though situated in a staid neighborhood beneath the bunkerlike Palais des Congrés, is Paris's most renowned lesbian dance club. **El Scandalo** (✉ 21 rue Keller, 11ᵉ, ☎ 01–47–00–24–59, métro Ledru-Rollin) has a circular bar, blackjack table, and cellar dance floor; things swing loud and late.

Discos

Les Bains (✉ 7 rue du Bourg-l'Abbé, 3ᵉ, métro Etienne-Marcel, closed Mon.), an always trendy hot spot, is hard to get into; it helps to be famous—or look like a model. **Balajo** (✉ 9 rue de Lappe, 11ᵉ, métro Bastille) is an old Java ballroom that specializes in salsa and techno; entry is free for women on Thursday. **Palace** (✉ 8 rue du Faubourg-Montmartre, 9ᵉ, métro Rue Montmartre) is a legendary, two-story haunt that saw its heyday come and go in the '80s, but is still fun for a night out; music ranges from techno to pop to African beat. **Zed Club** (✉ 2 rue des Anglais, 6ᵉ, métro Maubert-Mutualité, closed Sun.–Tues.) is a prime rock-and-roll and bebop venue for all ages.

Jazz Clubs

The French take jazz seriously, and Paris is one of the great jazz cities of the world. Remember that nothing gets going till 10 or 11 PM, and that entry prices can vary widely from about 40 francs to over 100 francs.

Caveau de la Huchette (✉ 5 rue de la Huchette, 5ᵉ, ☎ 01–43–26–65–05, métro St-Michel) is a smoke-filled shrine to the Dixieland beat. **Duc des Lombards** (✉ 42 rue des Lombards, 1ᵉʳ, ☎ 01–42–33–22–88, métro Les Halles), an ill-lit, romantic, bebop venue, has decor inspired by the Paris métro. **Montana** (✉ 28 rue Saint-Benoît, 6ᵉ, ☎ 01–45–48–93–08, métro St-Germain-des-Prés), in a restored Art Deco building, concentrates on traditional jazz with occasional forays into country and blues. **New Morning** (✉ 7 rue des Petites-Ecuries, 10ᵉ, ☎ 01–45–23–51–41, métro Château-d'Eau) is a premier spot for serious fans of avant-garde jazz—as well as folk and world music; decor is spartan, the mood reverential. **Petit Journal** (✉ 71 blvd. St-Michel, 5ᵉ, ☎ 01–43–26–28–59, RER Luxembourg), opposite the Luxembourg gardens, serves up good food and has long attracted leading exponents of New Orleans jazz. The **Slow Club** (✉ 130 rue de Rivoli, 1ᵉʳ, ☎ 01–42–33–84–30, métro Châtelet), one of the few Paris jazz clubs with a dance floor, plays swing, bebop, and Dixieland—and sometimes rock'n'roll.

Rock Clubs

Bataclan (✉ 50 blvd. Voltaire, 11ᵉ, ☎ 01–47–00–30–12, métro Oberkampf) is a good spot to hear live rock in an intimate setting. **Sunset** (✉ 60 rue des Lombards, 1ᵉʳ, ☎ 01–40–26–46–60, métro Châtelet) is a small, whitewashed cellar with first-rate live music.

ILE-DE-FRANCE

The region surrounding Paris is called the Ile de France, although it isn't actually an island (île). If you are visiting Paris—and France—for the first time, this is an area where you can get a taste of French provincial life, with its slower pace and fierce devotion to the soil. Parts of the area are fighting a losing battle against the encroaching capital, but you can still see the countryside that was the inspiration for the Impressionists and other 19th-century painters, and is home to a wealth of architecture dating from the Middle Ages. The most famous buildings are Chartres—one of the most beautiful of French cathedrals—and Versailles, the monumental château of Louis XIV, the Sun King. Before the completion of Versailles, king and court resided in the delightful château of St-Germain-en-Laye, west of Paris. This is also an easy day trip from Paris, as are the châteaus of Vaux-le-Vicomte, Rambouillet, and Fontainebleau, and Disneyland Paris.

Getting Around

The region is reached easily from Paris by car and by regular suburban train services. But you might find it convenient to group some sights together: Versailles, Rambouillet, and Chartres are all on the Paris–Chartres train line; Fontainebleau, Barbizon, and Vaux-le-Vicomte are all within a few miles of each other.

By Train

Three lines connect Paris with Versailles; on each the trip takes about 30 minutes. The best is RER-C5 to Versailles Rive Gauche station. Trains from Gare St-Lazare go to Versailles Rive Droite. Trains from Gare Montparnasse go to Versailles Chantiers and then on to Rambouillet and Chartres. Fontainebleau is served by 20 trains a day from Gare de Lyon; buses for Barbizon leave from the main post office in Fontainebleau. The RER-A4 line will take you to Disneyland Paris.

By Car

Expressway A13, from the Porte d'Auteuil, links Paris to Versailles. You can get to Chartres on A10 from Porte d'Orléans. For Fontainebleau, take A6 from Porte d'Orléans or, for a more attractive route through the Forest of Sénart and the northern part of the Forest of Fontainebleau, take N6 from Porte de Charenton via Melun. Vaux-le-Vicomte is 6 kilometers (4 miles) northeast of Melun via N36 and D215. The 32-kilometer (20-mile) drive along the A4 expressway from Paris to Disneyland Paris takes about 30 minutes, longer in heavy traffic. Disneyland is 4 kilometers (2½ miles) off the A4; follow the signs for the park.

Guided Tours

Two private companies, **Cityrama** and **Paris Vision,** organize regular half-day and full-day tours from Paris with English-speaking guides. Times and prices are identical. Tours are subject to cancellation, and reservations are suggested. Cityrama leaves from 4 pl. des Pyramides, 1er (☎ 01–44–55–61–00). Paris Vision leaves from 214 rue de Rivoli, 1er (☎ 01–42–60–31–25).

Versailles. Daily excursions starting at 9:30 include a complete tour of Paris in the morning followed by an afternoon at Versailles. Half-day excursions of Versailles leave mornings and afternoons daily (9:30 and 2:30, 300 frs) and include a guided tour of the château, Hall of Mirrors, and Queen's Suite. On Thursday only, you can extend the morning tour (450 frs) to include an afternoon visit (starting 1:30) to the Trianons, or take a separate afternoon trip there (1:30; 220 frs).

Chartres. Both companies organize half-day tours to Chartres on Tuesday, Thursday, and Saturday afternoons (1:30, 270 frs), but if you're short of time or cash, you'd be better off taking the **Versailles–Chartres** day trips on Tuesday and Saturday (9:30, 450 frs).

Fontainebleau and Barbizon. Half-day trips (1:30, 310 frs) on Wednesday, Friday, and Sunday run to Fontainebleau and nearby Barbizon (which is otherwise difficult to reach), but can be linked to a Versailles tour leaving at 9:30 on the same days.

Visitor Information

Barbizon (✉ 55 Grande Rue, ☎ 01–60–66–41–87).
Chartres (✉ pl. de la Cathédrale, ☎ 02–16/37–21–50–00).

Disneyland Paris (✉ B.P. 100, 77777 Marne-la-Vallée cedex 4, ☎ 01–60–30–60–30).
Fontainebleau (✉ 31 pl. Napoléon-Bonaparte, ☎ 01–64–22–25–68).
Rambouillet (✉ 8 pl. de la Libération, ☎ 01–34–83–21–21).
Versailles (✉ 7 rue des Réservoirs, ☎ 01–39–50–36–22).

Exploring the Ile-de-France

Versailles

★ **Versailles** is the location of one of the world's grandest palaces and one of France's most popular attractions. Wide, tree-lined avenues, broader than the Champs-Elysées and bordered by massive 17th-century mansions, lead directly to the Sun King's château. From the imposing place d'Armes, you enter the Cour des Ministres, a sprawling cobbled forecourt. Right in the middle, the statue of Louis XIV stands triumphant, surveying the town that he built from scratch to house those of the 20,000 noblemen, servants, and hangers-on who weren't lucky enough to get one of the 3,000 beds in the château.

The château took 50 years to complete. Hills were flattened, marshes drained, forests transplanted, and water for the magnificent fountains was channeled from the Seine several miles away. Visit the **Grands Appartements,** the six salons that made up the royal living quarters, and the famous **Galerie des Glaces** (Hall of Mirrors). Both can be visited without a guide, but you can get a cassette in English. There are also guided tours of the **Petits Appartements,** where the royal family and friends lived in relative intimacy, and the miniature opera house—one of the first oval rooms in France, built on the *aile nord* (north wing) for Louis XV in 1770. *Château:* ☎ 01–30–84–74–00. 🎫 *40 frs.* ☉ *Tues.–Sun. 9–6:30 (9–5:30 in winter).*

The château's vast grounds are masterpieces of formal landscaping. At one end of the Petit Canal, which crosses the Grand Canal at right angles, is the **Grand Trianon,** a scaled-down pleasure palace built in the 1680s. The **Petit Trianon,** nearby, is a sumptuously furnished 18th-century mansion, commissioned by Louis XVI for Marie Antoinette, who would flee here to avoid the stuffy atmosphere of the court. Nearby, she built the village, complete with dairy and mill, where she and her companions led a make-believe bucolic life. *Château grounds:* 🎫 *Free.* ☉ *7–dusk. Grand Trianon:* 🎫 *21 frs.* ☉ *June–Sept., daily 10–6:30, Oct.–May, daily 10–12:30 and 2–5:30. Petit Trianon:* 🎫 *12 frs.* ☉ *June–Sept., daily 10–6:30; Oct.–May, daily 2–5:30.*

Rambouillet

A little more than 20 kilometers (12 miles) southwest of Versailles is the small town of **Rambouillet,** home of a château, an adjoining park, and 34,000 acres of forest. Since 1897, the château has been a summer residence of the French president; today, it is also used as a site for international summits. You can visit the château only when the president is not in residence—fortunately, he's not there very often.

French kings have lived in the château since it was built in 1375. Highlights include the **Appartements d'Assemblée,** decorated with finely detailed wood paneling, and Napoléon's bathroom, with its Pompeii-inspired frescoes. The park stretches way behind the château. Beyond the **Jardin d'Eau** (Water Garden) lies the English-style garden and the **Laiterie de la Reine** (Marie Antoinette's Dairy). This was another of her attempts to "get back to nature." *Château:* ☎ 01–34–94–28–00; 🎫 *27 frs.* ☉ *Wed.–Mon. 10–11:30 and 2–5:30. Park:* 🎫 *Free.* ☉ *Sunrise–sunset. Marie Antoinette's Dairy:* 🎫 *13 frs.* ☉ *Same hrs as château; closes at 4 in winter.*

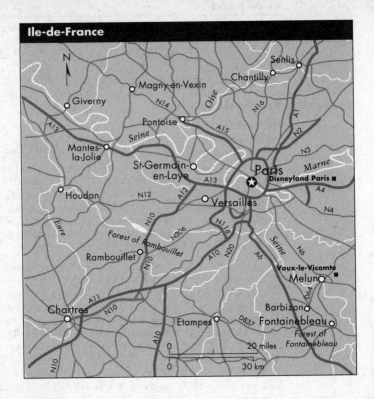

Ile-de-France

(Map showing Ile-de-France region with locations including Senlis, Chantilly, Magny-en-Vexin, Giverny, Pontoise, Mantes-la-Jolie, St-Germain-en-Laye, Paris, Disneyland Paris, Versailles, Houdan, Forest of Rambouillet, Rambouillet, Vaux-le-Vicomte, Melun, Chartres, Barbizon, Etampes, Fontainebleau, Forest of Fontainebleau, and roads N14, Oise, N16, A1, A13, Seine, A15, N2, N3, Marne, A4, N4, A13, N12, A12, N10, N306, N118, Seine, N6, A10, N20, A6, D64, A11, N10, D837, A10, N10)

Chartres

From Rambouillet, N10 will take you straight to **Chartres.** Long before you arrive you will see its famous cathedral towering over the plain of the Beauce, France's granary. The attractive old town, steeped in religious history and dating from before the Roman conquest, is still laced with winding medieval streets.

★ Today's Gothic cathedral, **Notre-Dame de Chartres,** is the sixth Christian church on the site; despite a series of fires, it has remained virtually the same since the 12th century. The **Royal Portal** on the main facade, presenting "the life and triumph of the Savior," is one of the country's finest examples of Romanesque sculpture. Inside, the 12th- and 13th-century rose windows, many of which have been restored over the past decade, come alive even in dull weather, thanks to the deep Chartres blue of the stained glass: Its formula remains a mystery to this day. *Cathedral tours available. Ask at the Maison des Clercs, 18 rue du Cloître-Notre-Dame.* ☺ *Tours in English daily noon and 2:45.*

Since the rest of the tour is on another side of Paris, it is probably easier to return to the capital to continue (☞ Getting Around Ile-de-France, *above*).

Fontainebleau

In the early 16th century, the flamboyant François I transformed the
★ medieval hunting lodge of **Fontainebleau** into a magnificent Renaissance palace. His successor, Henry II, covered the palace with his initials, woven into the *D* for his mistress, Diane de Poitiers. When he died, his queen, Catherine de' Medici, carried out further alterations, later continued under Louis XIV. Napoléon preferred the relative intimacy of Fontainebleau to the grandeur of Versailles. Before he was exiled to Elba, he bade farewell to his Old Guard in the courtyard now known as the **Cour des Adieux** (Farewell Court). The emperor also ha-

rangued his troops from the **Horseshoe Staircase.** Ask the curator to let you see the **Cour Ovale** (Oval Court), the oldest and perhaps most interesting courtyard. It stands on the site of the original 12th-century fortified building, but only the keep remains.

The **Grands Appartements** (royal suites and ballroom) are the main attractions of any visit to the château. The **Galerie de François I** is really a covered bridge (built 1528–30) looking out over the Cour de la Fontaine. The overall effect inside the Galerie is one of classical harmony and proportion, combining to create a sense of Renaissance lightness and order. François I appreciated the Italian Renaissance, and the ballroom is decorated with frescoes by Primaticcio (1504–70) and his pupil, Niccolò dell'Abbate. If you're here on a weekday, you will also be able to join a guided tour of the Petits Appartements, used by Napoléon and Josephine. ⊠ *Pl. du Général-de-Gaulle,* ☎ *01–64–22–27–40.* 🎟 *31 frs.* ⊙ *Wed.–Mon. 9:30–5.*

Barbizon

The **Rochers des Demoiselles,** a rocky outcrop just south of town, are good for an afternoon stroll. The **Gorges d'Apremont,** which offer the best views of the rocks, are near **Barbizon,** on the edge of the forest, 10 kilometers (6 miles) northwest of Fontainebleau. This delightful little village is scarcely more than a main street lined with restaurants and boutiques, but a group of landscape painters put it on the map in the mid-19th century. Théodore Rousseau and Jean-François Millet both had their studios here. Sculptor Henri Chapu's bronze medallion, sealed to one of the famous sandstone rocks in the forest nearby, pays homage to the two leaders of what became known as the Barbizon group.

Drop in at the **Auberge du Père Ganne** (⊠ 92 Grande Rue), where most of the landscape artists ate and drank while in Barbizon. They painted on every available surface, and even now you can see some originals on the walls and in the buffet.

Next to the church, in a barn that Rousseau used as a studio, you'll find the **Musée de l'Ecole de Barbizon** (Barbizon School Museum), containing documents of the village as it was in the 19th century as well as a few original works. ⊠ *55 Grande Rue,* ☎ *01–60–66–22–38.* 🎟 *25 frs.* ⊙ *Apr.–Sept., Wed.–Sun. 10:30–12:30 and 2–6; Oct.–Mar., Wed.–Sun. 10:30–12:30 and 2–5.*

★ From Barbizon, D64 runs to Melun, where N36 heads north-east toward the château of **Vaux-le-Vicomte,** one of the greatest monuments of 17th-century France. Nicolas Fouquet, superintendent of finances under Louis XIV, intended it to be his pride and joy. It turned out to be his downfall. The jealous Sun King accused Fouquet—on flimsy evidence—of siphoning off state resources for this grandiose architectural project, and hurled him into the slammer. From the visitor's point of view, though, Fouquet's *folie de grandeur* is a treat. He hired the era's leading architectural super group (Louis Le Vau for design, André Le Nôtre in the gardens, and Charles Le Brun on all lead murals); the Sun King was so sold on their performance that he employed them all when he built Versailles. Don't forget to visit the basement kitchens and the restored gardens. 🎟 *Château: 56 frs.* 🎟 *Gardens and stables only: 30 frs.* ⊙ *Apr.–Oct., daily 10–6; closed Nov.–Feb. Candlelight visits:* 🎟 *70 frs.* ⊙ *May–Sept., Sat. 8:30–11:30.*

Disneyland Paris

Now you can get a dose of American pop culture in between visits to the Louvre and the Left Bank. In April 1992 the **Disneyland Paris** (formerly Euro Disney) complex opened in Marne-la-Vallée, just 32 kilometers (20 miles) east of Paris, much to the consternation of French cultural partisans. The resort is on A4 (Exit 14—PARC DISNEYLAND PARIS). From Paris, the RER-A4 (40 min, 74 frs round-trip) runs directly to Marne-la-Vallée, a short walk from the theme park entrance; as of June 1994 a new TGV line connects Disneyland to Lille and Lyon.

The complex is divided into several areas, including the theme park that is the main reason for coming here. Occupying 136 acres, the park is less than half a mile across and ringed by a railroad with whistling steam engines. Smack in the middle of the park is the soaring Sleeping Beauty Castle, which is surrounded by a plaza from which you can enter the four "lands" of Disney: **Frontierland, Adventureland, Fantasyland,** and **Discoveryland.** In addition, Main Street U.S.A. connects the castle to the entrance, under the pointed pink domes of the Disneyland Hotel. ☎ 01–60–30–60–30. 🎫 *120–195 frs (prices vary according to season).* ☉ *Mid-June–mid-Sept., daily 9 AM–10 PM; mid-Sept.–mid-June, daily 10–6; Dec. and spring school holidays, daily 10–9.*

There are six hotels in the 4,800-acre Disneyland Paris complex, just outside the theme park. The resort also comprises parking lots, a train station, and the Festival Disney entertainment center, with restaurants, a theater, dance clubs, shops, a post office, and a tourist office. Cheaper accommodations—log cabins and campsites—are available at Camp Davy Crockett, farther from the theme park.

Dining and Lodging

For details and price-category definitions, *see* Dining *and* Lodging *in* Staying in France, *above.*

Barbizon

$–$$ ✕ **Le Relais.** Enjoy the large portions of the delicious specialties—particularly the beef and the game (in season). The selection of prix-fixe menus is very good. Walls are covered with paintings and hunting trophies, and there is a big open fireplace. In summer, you can eat in the shade of lime and chestnut trees on the large terrace. Expect crowds in July. ⊠ *2 av. Charles-de-Gaulle,* ☎ *01–60–66–40–28. Weekend reservations essential. MC, V. Closed Tues. dinner, Weds.*

$$ ✕🏨 **Les Alouettes.** This delightful 19th-century inn is on two acres of grounds. The interior has been decorated in '30s style, but many rooms still have their original oak beams. The restaurant, on a large open terrace, features nouvelle cuisine in sizable portions. ⊠ *4 rue Antoine-Barye, 77630,* ☎ *01–60–66–41–98,* FAX *01–60–66–20–69. 22 rooms with bath or shower. Restaurant, tennis court, parking. Weekend dinner reservations essential. AE, DC, MC, V.*

Chartres

$$$ ✕ **Vieille Maison.** In a refitted 14th-century building a stone's throw from the cathedral, the Vieille Maison serves both excellent nouvelle cuisine and traditional dishes. Try the regional *menu beauceron* for the homemade foie gras and duck dishes. ⊠ *5 rue au Lait,* ☎ *02–01–37–34–10–67. AE, MC, V. Closed Mon., dinner Sun.*

$$ ✕ **Buisson Ardent.** Almost within sight of the cathedral's south portal, in an attractive old oak-beam building, is this popular restaurant that offers a prix-fixe menu and dishes with imaginative sauces. Try chicken ravioli with leeks or rolled beef with spinach. ⊠ *10 rue au Lait,* ☎ *02–37–34–04–66. AE, DC, MC, V. Closed Sun. dinner.*

$$$ ✕🏨 **Grand Monarque.** The most popular rooms in this 18th-century coaching inn are in a separate turn-of-the-century building overlooking a garden. The hotel also has an excellent, reasonably priced restaurant.

✉ *22 pl. des Epars, 28000,* ☎ *02–37–21–00–72,* ℻ *02–37–36–34– 18. 54 rooms with bath or shower. Restaurant. AE, DC, MC, V.*

Disneyland Paris

$–$$ ✕ **Disneyland** is peppered with places to eat, ranging from snack bars and fast-food joints to full-service restaurants—all with a distinguishing theme. In addition, Disney hotels have restaurants that are open to the public. These are outside the theme park, so you may not want to waste time going to them for lunch. ☎ *01–60–45–65–40. Sit-down restaurants: AE, DC, MC, V; counter-service restaurants: no credit cards.*

$$–$$$$ ▥ The resort has 5,000 rooms in six hotels, all a short distance from the park, ranging from the luxurious Disneyland Hotel to the not-so-rustic Camp Davy Crockett. ✉ *Disneyland Paris, Central Reservations Office, Box 105, 77777 Marne-la-Vallée cedex 4,* ☎ *01–60–45–65– 40,* ℻ *01–49–41–49–49.*

Fontainebleau

$$ ✕ **La Table des Maréchaux.** Two good-value prix-fixe menus (130 frs and 180 frs) are available at this elegant restaurant on the town's main street, five minutes from the château. Traditional French dishes include gizzard salad and lamb with béarnaise sauce. ✉ *9 rue Grande,* ☎ *01–64–22–20–39. AE, MC, V.*

$$ ▥ **Londres.** The balconies of this tranquil hotel look out over the palace and the Cour des Adieux; the 1830 facade is preserved by government order. Inside, the decor is dominated by Louis XV furniture. ✉ *1 pl. du Général-de-Gaulle, 77300,* ☎ *01–64–22–20–21,* ℻ *01– 60–72–39–16. 22 rooms with bath or shower. Restaurant, bar, tea shop. AE, DC, MC, V. Closed mid-Dec.–early Jan.*

Rambouillet

$ ✕ **La Poste.** Traditional, unpretentious cooking is the attraction of this former coaching inn. The restaurant's two dining rooms are often packed with a lively crowd. The service is good, as is the selection of inexpensive prix-fixe menus. ✉ *101 rue du Général-de-Gaulle,* ☎ *01–34–83–03–01. AE, MC, V. Closed Mon., dinner Sun.*

Versailles

$$$$ ✕ **Trois Marches.** Don't miss Gerard Vié's nouvelle cuisine at the best-known restaurant in town—and one of France's best. Try the bisque of lobster or salmon with fennel. The view of the château park and the setting—in the sumptuous Trianon Palace Hotel—add to the experience. ✉ *1 blvd. de la Reine,* ☎ *01–39–50–13–21. Reservations essential. Jacket and tie. AE, DC, MC, V. Closed Sun., Mon., Aug.*

$$ ✕ **La Grande Sirène.** The 154-franc lunch menu (wine included), served every day but Sunday, makes this pretty spot near the château a popular noontime choice. Zesty simmered snails and well-prepared fish are good options. ✉ *25 rue du Maréchal-Foch,* ☎ *01–39–53– 08–08. AE, MC, V. Closed Mon.*

$$ ✕ **Quai No. 1.** Barometers, sails, and model boats fill this small, charming seafood restaurant. During the summer you can enjoy your meal on the terrace. Home-smoked salmon is a specialty; any dish on the two fixed-price menus is a good value. ✉ *1 av. de St-Cloud,* ☎ *01– 39–50–42–26. MC, V. Closed Sun. dinner and Mon.*

NORMANDY

Jutting out into the Channel, Normandy has had more connections with the English-speaking world than any other part of France, from William the Conqueror to D-Day. Visitors flock here not only to see historic monuments but to relax in the rich countryside amid apple orchards, lush meadows, and sandy beaches.

The historic cities of Rouen and Caen, capitals of Upper and Lower Normandy, respectively, are full of churches, well-preserved buildings, and museums. The Seine Valley is lined with abbeys and castles from all periods: St-Wandrille, for example, dates from the 7th century. Richard the Lionhearted's 12th-century Château Gaillard, at Les Andelys, is still imposing, and memories of the D-Day landings are still fresh. Normandy also has one of France's most enduring tourist attractions: Mont St-Michel, a remarkable Gothic abbey perched on a rocky mount off the Cotentin peninsula.

Etretat and Fécamp on the Alabaster Coast and Deauville, Trouville, and Honfleur on the Côte Fleurie (Flowered Coast) are among Normandy's many seaside resorts. Hotels, restaurants, and beaches cater to the simpler pleasures of life, while casinos make the rich poor—and sometimes the other way around, too. Normandy is also recognized as one of France's finest gastronomic regions for its excellent cheeses, cider, calvados, and wide range of seafood dishes.

Getting Around

Normandy is best visited by car. Trains leave regularly from Paris to Rouen, Caen, and Bayeux, but limited train connections make crosscountry traveling difficult. Also visiting many of the historic monuments and towns—such as Honfleur, which has no train station—means using buses, which don't always run so frequently.

Guided Tours

Paris Vision (⊠ 214 rue de Rivoli, 75001 Paris, 1ᵉʳ, ☎ 01–42–60–31–25) and **Cityrama** (⊠ 4 pl. des Pyramides, Paris, 1ᵉʳ, ☎ 01–44–55–61–00) organize identical one-day excursions (990 frs) to Mont St-Michel from Paris, leaving at 7:15 Saturday morning and taking you by bus to Mont St-Michel in time for lunch at Terrasses Poulard (☞ Dining and Lodging, *below*). After a guided tour of the mount and the abbey, you return by first-class train from Laval to Gare Montparnasse.

Visitor Information

Regional Centers
Caen (⊠ Lower Normandy, pl. du Canada, ☎ 02–31–86–53–30).
Rouen (⊠ Upper Normandy, 2 bis rue du Petit-Salut, ☎ 02–35–88–61–32).

Local Offices
Les Andelys (⊠ rue Philippe Auguste, ☎ 02–32–54–41–93).
Bayeux (⊠ Pont St-Jean, ☎ 02–31–92–16–26).
Caen (⊠ 12 pl. St-Pierre, ☎ 02–31–27–14–14).
Deauville (⊠ pl. de la Mairie, ☎ 02–31–88–21–43).
Etretat (⊠ pl. de la Mairie, ☎ 02–35–27–05–21).
Fécamp (⊠ pl. Bellet, ☎ 02–35–28–20–51).
Honfleur (⊠ 9 rue de la Ville, ☎ 02–31–89–23–30).
Mont St-Michel (⊠ Corps de Garde des Bourgeois, ☎ 02–33–60–14–30).
Rouen (⊠ 25 pl. de la Cathédrale, ☎ 02–35–08–32–40).

Exploring Normandy

Take Expressway A13 from Paris (Porte d'Auteuil) as far as Meulan or Mantes and cross the Seine to the right bank. Then follow D913 or

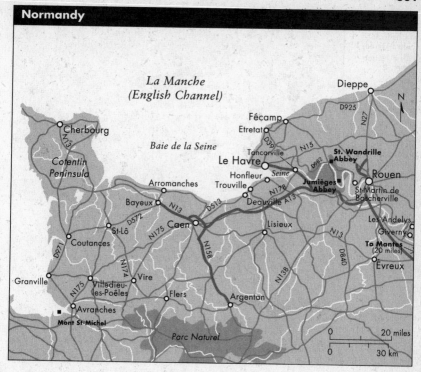

La Manche
(English Channel)

★ make a short stop in the village of **Giverny,** where you can visit the house and gardens in which Claude Monet lived and worked. 🖾 *38 frs (garden only, 30 frs).* ⊘ *Tues.–Sun. 10–noon and 2–6.*

D313 goes to **Les Andelys,** a small town on the Seine, dominated by the imposing **Château Gaillard,** the fortress built in 1196 by Richard the Lionhearted, king of England and duke of Normandy. 🖾 *15 frs.* ⊘ *Mid-Mar.–mid-Nov., Thurs.–Mon. 10–12:30 and 2–5, Wed. 2–5.*

Rouen

Numbers in the margin correspond to points of interest on the Rouen map.

① Rouen, the capital of Upper Normandy, has many historic churches, from the city's **Cathédrale Notre-Dame,** dating from the 12th century,
② to the modern, fish-shaped **Eglise Jeanne d'Arc** on the old market square, where Joan of Arc was burned at the stake in 1431. The tourist office organizes a guided tour leaving from place de la Cathédrale. Cov-
③ ered are the city's main churches, the **Palais de Justice,** and the lively old quarter around the rue du Gros-Horloge, where you can see a giant Renaissance clock built in 1527. The most noteworthy churches can
④ be visited on foot. Make sure to visit **Eglise St-Maclou,** with its five-
⑤ gable facade; **Abbaye St-Ouen,** a beautifully proportioned 14th-cen-
⑥ tury abbey; and the **Eglise St-Godard,** with well-preserved stained-glass windows.

⑦ Rouen's leading museum is the **Musée des Beaux Arts** (Fine Arts Museum), near Eglise St-Godard (on Square Vedral). It specializes in 17th- and 19th-century French painting, with an emphasis on works by local artists. There is an outstanding collection of macabre paintings by Romantic painter Géricault (🖾 20 frs, ⊘ Wed.–Mon. 10–6). Other
⑧ museums include the **Musée Le Secq des Tournelles** (⊠ in the Eglise

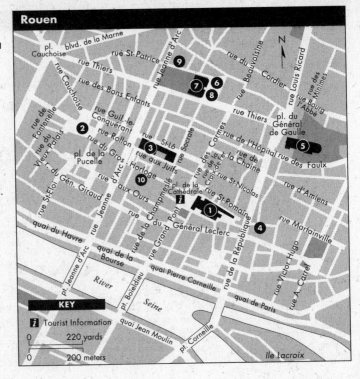

Rouen

St-Laurent, rue Jacques Villon, ▦ 13 frs, ⊘ Wed.–Mon. 10–1 and 2–
6), which has an unusual collection of wrought iron; the **Musée de la
Céramique** (⊠ rue Faucon, ▦ 13 frs, ⊘ Wed.–Mon. 10–1 and 2–6),
which houses Rouen's porcelain collections; and the **Musée du Gros-
Horloge,** where you can study the mechanism of the Renaissance clock
that gives its name to the museum. ⊠ *Rue du Gros-Horloge.* ▦ *10
frs.* ⊘ *Wed.–Mon. 10–1 and 2–6.*

Follow D982 across the Forest of Roumare and along the Seine via St-
Martin de Boscherville, with its mighty 12th-century Romanesque
abbey church of St-Georges, to **Jumièges Abbey,** once a powerful Benedictine center, founded in the 7th century. The abbey was dismantled
during the Revolution, but you can visit the remains of the chapter house
and several chapels. ▦ *24 frs.* ⊘ *Apr.–Sept., daily 10–noon and 2–6;
Oct.–Mar., weekdays 10–noon and 2–4, weekends 2–5.*

The nearby **St-Wandrille Abbey,** off D982, founded in 649, still has a
Benedictine community. Arrive early in the morning to hear the Gre-
gorian chants at Mass. *Mass: Mon.–Sat. 9:30* AM; *Sun. and holidays
at 10. Guided tours (18 frs) weekdays 3 and 4* PM.

Fécamp

Fécamp, at the foot of the highest cliffs in Normandy, was the region's
first place of pilgrimage. Legend has it that in the first century, an abandoned boat washed ashore here with a bottle containing Christ's blood.
The 11th-century **Eglise de la Trinité** was built to accommodate all the
pilgrims. ⊘ *Guided tours May–Oct., Sun. at 11, 3, and 5.*

Fécamp is also home of the famous Bénédictine liqueur. The **Musée de
la Bénédictine,** devoted to its production and rebuilt in 1892 after a
fire, is one of the most popular attractions in Normandy. ⊠ *110 rue
Alexandre-le-Grand,* ☏ *02–35–28–00–06.* ▦ *30 frs.* ⊘ *Easter–mid-*

Nov., daily 9:30–noon and 2–6; mid-Nov.–Easter, daily 10–1:30 and 3:30–4:30.

Follow the pretty coast road about 12 kilometers (7 miles) to **Etretat,** where the sea has cut into the cliff to create two immense archways that lead to the neighboring beaches at low tide. For a view over the bay and the **Aiguille,** which is an enormous rock towering in the middle, take the little path up the Falaise d'Aval cliff.

To avoid doubling back to Fécamp, take D39 to the Tancarville Bridge, which links Upper and Lower Normandy; there's a toll. Turn right on N178 and drive south for 14 kilometers (9 miles) to a major crossroads. Turn right and drive the same distance to Honfleur.

Honfleur

Once an important port for maritime expeditions, **Honfleur** became a favorite spot for painters, including the Impressionists. Today, Honfleur's lively cobbled streets, harbors full of colorful yachts, and the **Eglise Ste-Catherine**—a little 15th-century wooden church—make it the most picturesque town on the north coast. In summer or on weekends, be prepared for lines at restaurants and cafés.

The popular resorts of **Trouville** and **Deauville** are 16 kilometers (10 miles) along the Côte de Grâce, on D513. Deauville is the swankier of the two, with its palaces, casino, horse racing, and film festival. Its more modest neighbor, Trouville, with its active fishing fleet, is easier to relax in and less damaging to the wallet.

Caen, slightly inland from these resorts, is the capital of Lower Normandy. It was badly bombed in 1944 but has been rebuilt with care. William the Conqueror was responsible for Caen's large **fortress** perched on a hill behind the town: Its ramparts now encircle the public garden. William and his queen, Mathilde, also built Caen's "his and hers" abbeys—**Abbaye aux Hommes** and **Abbaye aux Dames.** The city hall is alongside the Abbaye aux Hommes, which has hourly guided tours (☎ 10 frs); Abbaye aux Femmes is now a hospital, and only the church is open to visitors. The **Mémorial,** a museum in the north of the city, has videos, photos, arms, paintings, and prints that detail the Normandy landings, the Battle of Normandy, and France's liberation, within a historical context from the 1930s to the 1960s. ⊠ *Esplanade Général Eisenhower.* ☎ *61 frs.* ☉ *Wed.–Mon. 9–7.*

Bayeux

Bayeux, a few miles inland from the D-Day beach via N13, was the first French town freed by the Allies in June 1944. But it is known primarily as the home of **La Tapisserie de la Reine Mathilde** (the Bayeux Tapestry), which tells the epic story of William's conquest of England in 1066. It is on show at the **Centre Culturel Guillaume le Conquérant** (William the Conqueror Cultural Center). ⊠ *13 bis, rue de Nesmond,* ☎ *02–31–92–05–48.* ☎ *35 frs.* ☉ *May–mid-Sept., daily 9–6:30; mid-Sept.–Apr., daily 9:30–12:30 and 2–6.*

Head up rue de Nesmond to rue Larchet, turning left into lovely place des Tribuneaux, where you'll find the **Musée Baron Gérard:** it has a fine collection of Bayeux porcelain and lace, ceramics from Rouen, a marvelous array of apothecary jars from the 17th and 18th centuries, and furniture and paintings from the 16th to 19th centuries. ⊠ *1 rue la Chaine,* ☎ *02–31–92–14–21.* ☎ *20 frs.* ☉ *June–mid-Sept., daily 9–7; mid-Sept.–May, 10–12:30 and 2–6. Last visits to be 30 min before closing. Closed 2 wks in Jan.*

Behind the museum sits Bayeux's most important historic building, the **Cathédrale Notre-Dame,** a harmonious mixture of Norman and Gothic architecture. Note the portal on the south side of the transept, which depicts the assassination of English Archbishop Thomas à Becket in Canterbury Cathedral in 1170.

The **Musée de la Bataille de Normandie** (Museum of the Battle of Normandy) traces the history of the Allied advance against the Germans in 1944. It overlooks the British Military Cemetery. ⊠ *Blvd. Général-Fabian-Ware.* ☎ *02–31–92–93–41.* ☜ *30 frs.* ☉ *May–mid-Sept., daily 9–6:30; mid-Sept.–Apr., daily 10–noon and 2–6.*

Bayeux is a good base for excursions up the Cotentin coast, to Mont-St-Michel, and the D-Day beaches. In **Arromanches** harbor, you can see the remains of **Mulberry B,** an artificial port built for the British D-Day landings. Mulberry A, where American troops landed farther up the coast on **Omaha Beach,** was destroyed by a storm a few months after the landings. The **Musée du Débarquement** (Landings Museum) on Arromanches's seafront shows the landing plan and a film (in English) about the operation. ⊠ *Pl. du 6-Juin,* ☎ *02–31–22–34–31.* ☜ *32 frs.* ☉ *May–Sept., daily 9–7; Oct.–Apr., 9:30–4:30.*

Mont-St-Michel

Drive among the rolling hills and orchards that produce calvados and cider: Take D972 to **St-Lô** and then D999 to **Villedieu-les-Poêles,** a town famous for its kitchen copperware. Join N175 and continue to **Avranches,** where you will have your first view of **Mont-St-Michel,** the Gothic abbey and village rising up from the sea. The mount's fame comes not just from its location—until the causeway was built, it was cut off from the mainland at high tide—but from the dramatic nature of its construction in the 8th century, when tons of granite were brought from the nearby Chausey Islands and Brittany and hauled up the 265-foot peak. It has been a pilgrimage center ever since.

★

For most of the year, Mont-St-Michel is surrounded by sandy beach. The best time to see it is during the high tides of spring and fall, when the sea comes pounding in—dangerously fast—and encircles the mount. **La Merveille** (the Wonder) is the name given to the collection of Gothic buildings on top. What looks like a fortress is in fact a series of architectural layers that trace the evolution of French architecture from Romanesque to late-Gothic. You can join a guided tour (in English). ☎ *02–33–60–14–14.* ☜ *36 frs.* ☉ *Mid-May–Sept., daily 9:30–11:30 and 1:30–6; Oct.–mid-May, Wed.–Mon. 9–11 and 1:30–4.*

Dining and Lodging

For details and price-category definitions, *see* Dining *and* Lodging *in* Staying in France, *above.*

Bayeux

$ ✕ **L'Amaryllis.** This small, simply decorated restaurant with fewer than 15 tables offers good Norman fare at very reasonable prices. For 98 francs you can get a three-course dinner that might include a half dozen oysters, sole with a cider-based sauce, and pastries for dessert. ⊠ *32 rue St-Patrice,* ☎ *02–31–22–47–94. AE, DC, MC, V. Closed Mon. and Dec. 20–Jan. 15.*

$$$ ✕▥ **Le Chenevière.** This elegant hotel is in a late 19th-century grand manor in parkland between Bayeux and the coast. The rooms have modern furnishings, with plain draperies on the floor-to-ceiling windows and flowered bedspreads that add a splash of color. Chef Claude Espraben's Norman dishes, are worth the detour: The roasted scampi with sesame seed and fresh chanterelles is delicious, as is the justifiably famous rack of lamb with truffle sauce. ⊠ *Escures-Commes, 14520 Port-*

en-Bressin, ☎ 02–31–21–41–96, FAX 02–31–21–47–98. *19 rooms with bath. Restaurant. AE, MC, V.*

\$\$ ✕⍓ **Grand Hôtel du Luxembourg.** Rooms at this fairly run-of-the-mill hotel are adequate; all but two face the courtyard garden away from any street noise. But Les Quatre Saisons, the restaurant, has the best kitchen in town. Chef Daniel Rivière's classical repertoire from Normandy includes a galette of salmon, chicken roasted with cider, and veal in a sauce strongly scented with calvados. ✉ *25 rue des Bouchers, 14403,* ☎ *02–31–92–54–26,* FAX *02–31–92–54–26. 19 rooms with bath, 3 suites. Restaurant, bar. AE, DC, MC, V.*

\$–\$\$ ⍓ **Churchill.** This friendly, family-run inn is within walking distance of Bayeux's major attractions. Rooms in this old town house vary in shape and size. Furnishings are modest and functional; bathrooms are compact. Hearty breakfasts are served in the veranda café. ✉ *14 rue St-Jean, 14400,* ☎ *02–31–21–32–80,* FAX *02–31–21–41–66. 32 rooms with bath or shower. AE, DC, MC, V. Closed mid-Nov.–mid-Mar.*

Caen

\$\$\$ ✕ **Bourride.** Michel Bruneau, owner and chef of this famous restaurant on one of the town's oldest streets, bases his inventive recipes almost exclusively on local and regional produce. Specialties include skate caramelized in honey and cider and meat pastry cooked in cider vinegar. ✉ *15 rue du Vaugueux,* ☎ *02–31–93–50–76. AE, DC, MC, V. Closed Sun., Mon., first three weeks in Jan., and Aug. 15–31.*

\$\$ ✕⍓ **Le Dauphin.** Rooms in this old priory are small but clean. Many of them overlook a quiet courtyard. The restaurant serves excellent Norman dishes, emphasizing seafood topped with unusually light sauces. ✉ *29 rue Gémare, 14000,* ☎ *02–31–86–22–26,* FAX *02–31–86–35–14. 21 rooms with bath or shower. Restaurant (closed Sat.). AE, DC, MC, V. Closed part of Feb. and mid-July–mid-Aug.*

Deauville

\$\$ ✕ **Spinnaker.** This is a convenient, affordable, informal restaurant in the center of Deauville. Dishes are based on local seafood recipes: the fresh pasta and crab salad is particularly delicious. ✉ *52 rue Mirabeau,* ☎ *02–31–88–24–40. MC, V. Closed Wed. off-season, Thurs., and mid-Jan.–mid-Feb.*

Etretat

\$\$ ✕ **Roches Blanches.** Just off the beach, this family-owned restaurant is a concrete post–World War II eyesore. But the views and the superbly fresh seafood are another story. Be sure to try the veal escalope with mushrooms and flambéed in calvados, and the mussels. ✉ *Rue Abbé Cochet,* ☎ *02–35–27–07–34. Reservations essential. MC, V. Closed Wed. in summer, Tues.–Thurs. in winter, Oct., and Jan.*

\$\$ ✕⍓ **Le Donjon.** This charming little château, in a park overlooking the town, has a lovely view of the bay. Rooms are individually furnished, spacious, comfortable, and quiet. Reliable French cuisine is served with flair in the cozy, romantic restaurant. ✉ *Chemin de St-Clair, 76790,* ☎ *02–35–27–08–23,* FAX *02–35–29–92–24. 8 rooms, 6 with bath. Restaurant, pool. AE, DC, MC, V.*

Fécamp

\$\$ ✕⍓ **Auberge de la Rouge.** This quaint inn is in a little hamlet a mile or so south of Fécamp. Classic and modern dishes include many local specialties such as *coquilles St-Jacques* (scallops in the shell in a sherry cream sauce) and pressed duck. ✉ *Commune de St-Léonard, 76400,*

☎ 02–35–28–07–59, FAX 02–35–28–70–55. *8 rooms with bath.
Restaurant. AE, DC, MC, V. Closed Mon., no dinner Sun.*

Honfleur

$$$ ✕ **Absinthe.** A magnificent 17th-century dining room is the setting for
nouvelle and traditional cuisine, with an accent on seafood. In warm,
sunny weather, dine on the quayside terrace. There's also a pub, the
Ivanhoe. ⊠ *10 quai de la Quarantaine,* ☎ *02–31–89–39–00. AE,
DC, MC, V. Closed Mon. evening (except in midsummer), Tues., and
mid-Nov.–late 20.*

$$–$$$ ✕ **L'Assiette Gourmande.** When Chef Gérard Bonnefoy comes into the
dining room at Honfleur's unsung top restaurant, he decides what the
diners would enjoy after only a few minutes of culinary conversation.
You may be lucky enough in fall to have the superb coquilles St-
Jacques grilled with sautéed asparagus in a raspberry vinaigrette and
orange sauce. Or roast lamb *pré-salé,* lamb that has grazed on the salt
marshes around Mont-St-Michel. ⊠ *2 quai des Passagers,* ☎ *02–31–
89–24–88. AE, DC, MC, V. Closed Mon.*

$$ ⊞ **Le Cheval Blanc.** Owners Alain Petit and his wife run this friendly
★ inn in a renovated 15th-century building on the harbor front. Rooms
offer fine views of the port; Room 34 (slightly more expensive than
the others) has gabled ceilings supported by cross beams pegged together, a small sitting area, and a whirlpool bath. ⊠ *2 quai des Pas-
sagers, 14600,* ☎ *02–31–81–65–00,* FAX *02–31–89–52–80. 35
rooms, 14 with bath. Breakfast room. MC, V. Closed Jan.*

Mont-St-Michel

$$$ ✕⊞ **Terrasses Poulard.** This collection of town houses, while still
overpriced, is the less expensive sister hotel to the exorbitant Mère
Poulard. Each room is named after a famous Norman personality and
is decorated accordingly; several have breathtaking views of the bay;
others look out onto a little garden. The restaurant, crowded with Amer-
ican, British, and Canadian tourists, has its best views upstairs. ⊠ *Grande
Rue, 50116,* ☎ *02–33–60–14–09,* FAX *02–33–60–37–31. 29 rooms
with bath. Restaurant. AE, DC, MC, V.*

$$ ✕⊞ **Le Manoir de la Roche Turin.** Only 9 kilometers (6 miles) away
from Mont-St-Michel, this small ivy-clad manor house is an appeal-
ing alternative to high-priced hotels. Rooms are pleasantly old-fashioned, but the bathrooms are modern. The owners run a delightful dining
room. The local lamb is superb; lobster and fresh fish are also available on the 150-franc and 200-franc menus. ⊠ *50220 Courtils,* ☎ *02–
33–70–96–55,* FAX *02–33–48–35–20. 11 rooms with bath, 1 suite.
Restaurant (closed Mon.). MC, V. Closed mid-Nov.–mid-Mar.*

Rouen

$$$ ✕ **La Couronne.** Built in 1345, La Couronne is supposedly the oldest
inn in France. Amid the oak beams, leather upholstery, and woodwork,
there's a sculpture collection. The traditional cuisine features home-
made foie gras and turbot in flaky pastry. Keep to the "menu Normand,"
for 180 francs, or expect a hefty bill. ⊠ *31 pl. du Vieux-Marché,* ☎
02–35–71–40–90. Reservations essential. AE, DC, MC, V.

$$–$$$ ⊞ **Mercure Rouen Centre.** In the jumble of narrow streets of Rouen
center, near the cathedral, this modern hotel offers small, comfortable
rooms that are breezily furnished in pastels. It's not particularly charm-
ing, but its location makes it ideal and there's a bar for an evening aper-
itif. ⊠ *Rue Croix-de-Fer, 76000,* ☎ *02–35–52–69–52,* FAX
02–35–89–41–46. 125 rooms with bath. Bar. AE, DC, MC, V.

$–$$ ✕ **Hôtel de la Cathédrale.** This appealing hotel is in a medieval building on a narrow pedestrian street behind the cathedral. Rooms are petite, but neat and comfortable. Guests can sleep soundly: the cathedral bells do not boom out the hour at night. Breakfast is served in a wonderful beamed dining room. The extremely cordial owner, on hand at the desk, gives tips on exploring and dining in Rouen. ✉ *12 rue St-Romain, 76000,* ☎ *02–35–71–57–95,* FAX *02–35–70–15–54. 25 rooms with bath or shower. Breakfast room. MC, V.*

BURGUNDY AND LYON

For a region whose powerful medieval dukes held sway over large tracts of Western Europe and whose current image is closely allied to its expensive wine, Burgundy is a place of surprisingly rustic, quiet charm. Its leading religious monument is the Romanesque basilica at Vézelay, once an important pilgrimage center, and today a tiny village hidden in rolling hills.

The heart of Burgundy is the dark, brooding Morvan Forest. Dijon, the region's only city, retains something of its medieval opulence, but its present reputation is essentially gastronomic. Top restaurants abound, and local industries produce mustard, cassis, snails, and—of course—wine. The vineyards leading down toward Beaune are among the world's most distinguished and picturesque.

The vines continue to flourish as you head south along the Saône Valley, through the Mâconnais and Beaujolais, toward Lyon, one of France's most appealing cities. The combination of frenzied modernity and unhurried joie de vivre gives Lyon a sense of balance. The only danger is a temptation to overindulge in its rich, robust cuisine.

Getting Around

Burgundy is best visited by car. Its meandering country roads invite leisurely exploration. There are few big towns, and traveling around by train is unrewarding, especially as the infrequent cross-country trains steam along at the speed of a legendary Burgundy snail.

Guided Tours

The Dijon branch of the regional tourism office organizes a series of tours using Dijon as a base. These include wine tastings and historic tours of the famous religious centers. Write to Comité Régional de Tourisme (✉ 21 blvd. Brosses, 21000 Dijon).

Visitor Information

Auxerre (✉ 1 quai de la République, ☎ 03–86–52–06–19).
Beaune (✉ rue de l'Hôtel-Dieu, ☎ 03–80–26–31–30).
Dijon (✉ 29 pl. Darcy, ☎ 03–80–30–35–39).
Lyon (✉ pl. Bellecour, ☎ 04–78–42–25–75).
Sens (✉ pl. Jean-Jaurès, ☎ 03–86–65–19–49).

Exploring Burgundy and Lyon

It makes sense for **Sens** to be your first stop on the way down to Burgundy, as it is just 120 kilometers (75 miles) from Paris on N6—a fast, pretty road that hugs the Yonne Valley south of Fontainebleau. Sens is home to France's senior archbishop and is dominated by the 12th-century **Cathédrale St-Etienne.** This is one of the oldest cathedrals in France and has a foursquare facade topped by towers and an incon-

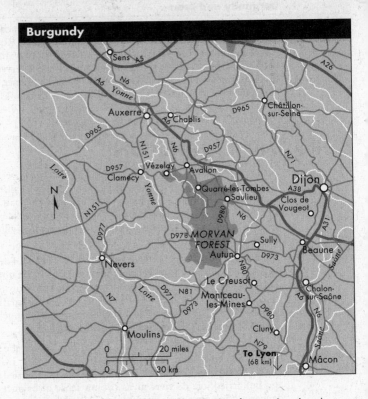

Burgundy

gruous little Renaissance campanile. The vast, harmonious interior contains outstanding stained glass of various periods.

The 13th-century **Palais Synodal** alongside, with six grand windows and a vaulted hall, provides a first encounter with Burgundy's multicolored tiled roofs; from its courtyard, there is a fine view of the cathedral's south transept, constructed in the fluid Flamboyant Gothic style of the 16th century. It's now a museum with statues, mosaics, and tapestries. ⊠ *Rue des Déportés de la Résistance.* 🖭 *18 frs.* ☉ *Mar.–mid-Dec., daily 10–noon and 2–5; mid-Dec.–Feb., Thurs.–Tues. 2–4:30.*

Auxerre

N6 continues to **Auxerre,** a small, peaceful town with its own **Cathédrale St-Etienne,** perched on a steepish hill overlooking the Yonne. The muscular cathedral, built between the 13th and 16th centuries, has a powerful north tower similar to that at Clamecy. The former **abbey of St-Germain** nearby contains a crypt dating from the 9th century. ⊠ *Rue Cochois.* 🖭 *25 fr covers St-Germain and crypt, and the treasury at St-Etienne.* ☉ *Wed.–Mon. 10–noon and 2–5.*

Chablis, famous for its dry white wine, makes an attractive excursion 16 kilometers (10 miles) to the east of Auxerre, along N65 and D965. Beware of village tourist shops selling local wines at unpalatable prices. The surrounding vineyards are dramatic: Their steeply banked hills stand in contrast to the region's characteristic gentle slopes.

Clamecy

From Auxerre, take N151 43 kilometers (27 miles) south along the Yonne to **Clamecy.** This sleepy town is not on many tourist itineraries, but its tumbling alleyways and ancient houses epitomize *la France profonde*—classic rural France. The many-shaped roofs of Clamecy, dominated by the majestic square tower of the **church of St-Martin,** are best viewed from the banks of the Yonne. The river played a crucial role in Clamecy's development: Trees from the Morvan Forest were cut down and floated in huge convoys to Paris. The history of this curious form of transport—called *flottage*—now extinct, is detailed in the town museum, in two mansions, the **Musée d'Art et d'Histoire Romain Rolland,** named for a native son, a Nobel laureate for literature in 1915. ⊠ *Av. de la République,* ☎ *03–86–27–17–99.* ⊡ *15 frs.* ⊙ *Nov.–Easter, Mon. and Wed.–Sat. 10–noon and 3–6; Easter–Oct., Wed.–Mon. 10–noon and 2–6.*

Vézelay lies 24 kilometers (15 miles) east of Clamecy along D957. The **Basilica** is perched on a rocky crag, with commanding views of the surrounding countryside. It rose to fame in the 11th century as the resting place of the relics of St. Mary Magdalene and became a departure point for the great pilgrimages to Santiago de Compostela in northwest Spain. The church was rescued from decay by the 19th-century Gothic Revival architect Eugène Emmanuel Viollet-le-Duc and counts as one of the foremost Romanesque buildings in existence. Its interior is long and airy, with superbly carved column capitals; the facade boasts an equally majestic tympanum.

Avallon is 13 kilometers (8 miles) farther along from Vézelay, via D957. Its location, on a promontory, is spectacular, and the old streets and ramparts are great places to stroll. The imagination of medieval stone carvers ran riot at the portals of the venerable church of **St-Lazarus.**

The expressway passes near Avallon and can whisk you to Dijon, 96 kilometers (60 miles) away, in less than an hour. If you're in no rush, take time to explore the huge **Morvan Regional Park;** the road twists and turns through lakes, hills, and forests. Take D944 out of Avallon ★ and then turn left on D10 to reach **Quarré-les-Tombes**—so called because of the empty prehistoric stone tombs discovered locally, and eerily arrayed around the church—before continuing southeast toward Saulieu. The **Rocher de la Pérouse,** 8 kilometers (5 miles) from Quarré-les-Tombes, is an outcrop worth climbing for the view of the Cousin Valley. Continue to **Saulieu** via the N6, D264, and D977.

Saulieu's reputation belies its size (just 3,000 inhabitants). It is renowned for good food (Rabelais, that 16th-century authority, extolled its hospitality) and Christmas trees (a million are harvested each year). The **Basilica of St-Andoche** is almost as old as Vézelay's, though less imposing and more restored. The adjoining town **museum** (⊡ 20 frs.; ⊙ Wed.–Mon., 10–noon and 2–5) contains a room devoted to François Pompon, the sculptor of art deco animals.

Dijon
N6 and then D977 link Saulieu to the Dijon-bound A38 to the east. **Dijon** is capital of both Burgundy and gastronomy. Visit its restaurants ★ and the **Palais des Ducs** (Ducal Palace), testimony to bygone splendor and now one of France's leading art museums (⊠ Pl. de la Ste-Chapelle, ☎ 03–80–74–52–70, ⊡ 15 frs, ⊙ Wed.–Mon. 10–6., closed holidays). The tombs of Philip the Bold and John the Fearless head a rich collection of medieval objects and Renaissance furniture.

Highlights of the city's old churches are the stained glass of **Notre-Dame,** the austere interior of the **cathedral of St-Bénigne,** and the chunky Renaissance facade of **St-Michel.** Don't miss the exuberant 15th-century gateway at the **Chartreuse de Champmol**—all that remains of a former charterhouse—or the adjoining **Puits de Moïse,** the so-called Well of Moses, with six large, realistic medieval statues.

Beaune

A31 connects Dijon to **Beaune,** 40 kilometers (25 miles) to the south,
but you may prefer a leisurely trip through the vineyards. Take D122,
then N74 at Chambolle-Musigny; just to the south is the Renaissance
Château du Clos de Vougeot, famous as the seat of Burgundy's elite
company of wine tasters, the Confrérie des Chevaliers du Tastevin, who
gather here in November at the start of the three-day festival Les Trois
Glorieuses—which includes a wine auction at the Hospices de Beaune.
⊠ *Château du Clos de Vougeot.* ☎ *03–80–62–86–09.* 🎟 *17 frs.* ☉
*Apr.–Sept., weekdays and Sun. 9–7, Sat. 9–6:30; Oct.–Mar., weekdays
and Sun. 9–11:30 and 2–5:30, Sat. 9–5.*

★ The **Hospices de Beaune** (or Hôtel Dieu), founded in 1443 as a hospital, owns some of the region's finest vineyards. Its history is retraced
in a **museum** that also has Roger van der Weyden's medieval Flemish
masterpiece *The Last Judgment,* plus a collection of tapestries. Other
tapestries, relating the life of the Virgin, hang in Beaune's main church,
the **Collégiale Notre-Dame,** dating from 1120. ⊠ *Hospices de Beaune,*
☎ *03–80–24–45–00.* 🎟 *29 frs.* ☉ *Apr.–mid-Nov., daily 9–6:30; mid-
Nov.–Mar., daily 9–11:30 and 2–5:30.*

The history of local wines can be explored at the **Musée du Vin de Bourgogne** (🎟 *10 frs;* ☉ *Apr.–Oct., daily 9–noon and 1:30–6; Nov.–Mar.,
daily 10–noon and 2–5:30*), housed in a mansion built in the 15th and
16th centuries. You can taste as much as you please in the candlelit
★ cellars of the **Marché aux Vins** (wine market), on rue Nicolas Rolin,
beginning with whites and fruity Beaujolais, and ending with big reds
such as Gevrey-Chambertin, including the new vintage of Grands Vins
des Hospices de Beaune. ⊠ *7 rue Nicolas Rolin,* ☎ *03–80–22–27–
69.* 🎟 *50 frs, with tasting.* ☉ *Easter–third weekend in Nov., daily 9:30–
noon and 3:30–6; 3rd wk in Nov.–Easter, daily 9:30–noon and 2:30–6.*

Autun

Autun is 48 kilometers (30 miles) west of Beaune along D973. But it's
worth the detour and on the way you can visit the Renaissance **château
of Sully** (☎ *03–85–82–10–27,* ☉ Summer afternoons for 45-min guided
tours, 🎟 35 frs, call for precise times; ☉ Grounds daily 10–noon and
2–6, 🎟 15 frs.). Autun's importance dates back to Roman times, as
you can detect at the **Porte St-André,** a well-preserved archway, and
the **Théâtre Romain,** once the largest arena in Gaul. The leading mon-
★ ument in Autun is the church of **St-Lazarus,** a curious Gothic cathedral redone in the Classical style by 18th-century clerics trying to
follow fashion. Note the majestic picture by Ingres, the *Martyrdom of
St-Symphorien,* in one of the side chapels. Across from the cathedral
is the **Musée Rolin** with several fine paintings from the Middle Ages.
⊠ *Pl. St-Louis,* ☎ *03–85–52–09–76.* 🎟 *16 frs.* ☉ *Nov.–Mar., Mon.
and Wed.–Sat. 10–noon and 2–6, Sun. 10–noon and 2–5; Apr.–Sept.,
Wed.–Mon. 9:30–noon and 1:30–6; Oct., Mon. and Wed.–Sat. 10–
noon and 2–5, Sun. 10–noon and 2:30–5.*

Cluny

From Autun, head southeast along N80 and D980, via industrial
Montceau-les-Mines, to **Cluny,** 80 kilometers (50 miles) away. The **Abbey**
of Cluny, founded in the 10th century, was the largest church in Europe until St. Peter's was built in Rome in the 16th century. The ruins
give an idea of its original grandeur. Note the **Clocher de l'Eau-Bénite,**
a majestic bell tower, and the 13th-century **farinier** (flour mill) with
its fine chestnut roof and collection of statues. ☎ *03–85–59–12–79.*
🎟 *31 frs. Museum only: 15 frs.* ☉ *Nov.–Mar., daily 10:30–11:30 and
2–4; Apr.–June, daily 9:30–noon and 2–6; July–Sept., daily 9–7;
Oct., daily 10–noon and 2–5. Museum closed Tues.*

A model of the original abbey can be seen in the **Musée Ochier,** the 15th-century abbot's palace. ⊠ *Rue Conant.* ☜ *8 frs.* ⊘ *Wed.–Mon. 10–noon and 2–5. Closed Jan. 1–15.*

Cluny is a mere 28 kilometers (16 miles) northwest of **Mâcon,** a bustling town best known for its wine fair in May and for its stone bridge across the Saône; the low arches are a headache for large river barges. At Mâcon take N6 or A6 due south to Lyon, where the River Rhône runs parallel to the Saône before the two converge south of the city center.

Lyon

In recent years, **Lyon** has solidified its role as a commercial center, thanks to France's policy of decentralization and the TGV train. Much of the city has an enchanting air of untroubled prosperity and the dining choices are plentiful. A human-size town, you can easily walk its pedestrian streets, explore Old Lyon and Presqu'Ile (almost island), lying between the two rivers, and visit all its seductive sights in a few days.

The clifftop silhouette of **Notre Dame de Fourvière** is the city's most striking symbol: The 19th-century basilica is an exotic mishmash of styles with an interior that's pure overkill. Climb the Fourvière heights for the view, instead, and then go to the nearby Roman remains. ⊠ *Théâtres Romains.* ☜ *Free.* ⊘ *Daily 8–noon and 2–6.*

The best Lyon museum is the **Musée des Beaux-Arts.** It houses sculpture, classical relics, and an extensive collection of Old Masters and Impressionists. Don't miss local artist Louis Janmot's 19th-century mystical cycle *The Poem of the Soul,* 18 canvases that took nearly 50 years to complete. ⊠ *20 pl. des Terreaux,* ☏ *04–72–10–17–40.* ☜ *20 frs.* ⊘ *Wed.–Sun. 10:30–6.*

Dining and Lodging

For details and price-category definitions *see* Dining *and* Lodging *in* Staying in France, *above.*

Auxerre

$$ Jardin Gourmand. As its name implies, the Jardin Gourmand has a pretty garden where you can eat *en terrasse* in warm weather. The interior, accented by light-colored oak, is equally congenial. The cuisine is innovative—try the ravioli and foie gras or the duck with black currants. Service is unobtrusive. ⊠ *56 blvd. Vauban, 89000,* ☏ *03–86–51–53–52. MC, V. Closed Mon. No lunch Tues.*

$ 🏨 Normandie. This picturesque creeper-covered hotel with a garden is right in the town center. The well-equipped rooms are unpretentious. ⊠ *41 blvd. Vauban, 89000,* ☏ *03–86–52–57–80,* ⅎ⅄ *03–86–51–54–33. 47 rooms, some with bath or shower. AE, DC, MC, V.*

Avallon

$$ ✗🏨 Moulin des Ruats. Housed in an old flour mill just southwest of Avallon along D427, this popular hotel has rustic rooms. Many have their own balcony and most look out onto the sparkling River Cousin. In summer you can eat on the riverbank. At other times, traditional dishes are served in the wood-paneled restaurant: try the coq au vin. Make a reservation in July or August. ⊠ *Vallée du Cousin, 89200,* ☏ *03–86–34–07–14,* ⅎ⅄ *03–86–31–65–47. 27 rooms, some with bath or shower. Restaurant. AE, DC, MC, V. Closed winter.*

Beaune

$$ ✗ L'Ecusson. Despite its unimpressive exterior, L'Ecusson is a friendly, comfortable, thick-carpeted restaurant with four prix-fixe menus offering outstanding value. For around 200 francs, you can have rabbit terrine with tarragon followed by leg of duck in oxtail sauce, then cheese, and dessert. ⊠ *2 rue du Lieutenant-Dupuis,* ☎ *03–80–24–03–82. AE, DC, MC, V. Closed Sun., mid-Feb.–mid-Mar.*

$$ ✕ **La Grilladine.** Chef Pierre Lenko's fare at this small, warm restau-
★   rant is not elaborate, but it is good, hearty Burgundy cooking: sample the beef bourguignonne and *oeufs en meurette* (eggs poached in a red wine and bacon sauce). One of the two dining rooms has rose-pink tablecloths, exposed stone walls, and a mammoth, ancient wood beam supporting the ceiling's center; the other is less rustic and more spacious. ⊠ *17 rue Maufoux,* ☎ *03–80–22–22–36. MC, V. Closed Mon., and 2 weeks in the winter usually end of Nov.–mid-Dec.*

$$ ✕📷 **Central.** A well-run establishment with several enlarged and modernized rooms, the Central is around the corner from the Hospices de Beaune. The restaurant is cozy—some might say cramped—and the consistently good cuisine is popular with the local gentry. Dinner is obligatory in July and August. ⊠ *2 rue Victor-Millot, 21200,* ☎ *03–80–24–77–24,* FAX *03–80–22–30–40. 20 rooms, most with bath. Restaurant (closed Wed. and Sun. dinner, Nov.–June). MC, V. Closed Dec.–Jan.*

$$$ 📷 **Le Cep.** This top hotel in two old town houses (the oldest is circa
★   1547) is only five minutes from the main square. The spacious rooms are tastefully furnished with antiques and have large tile bathrooms; the ones facing the courtyard are quieter. The ground floor has large exposed beams. Service can become a little harried when tour groups, albeit of fairly small size, check in and out. ⊠ *27 rue Maufoux, 21200,* ☎ *03–80–22–35–48,* FAX *03–80–22–76–80. 52 rooms with bath. Restaurant (closed Mon., no lunch Tues.). AE, DC, MC, V.*

Chablis

$$–$$$ ✕📷 **Hostellerie des Clos.** Guest rooms at this inn are ordinary, but are
★   made colorful by the cheerful floral curtains and quilts on the beds. Michel Vignaud's superb culinary art is the main attraction. Experience his *sandre* (perchlike freshwater fish) served in a chicken-based sauce, a tasty juxtaposition to the fish; the robust hare casserole (autumn only); or the *huîtres d'Isigny* (small oysters) in a dill-and-chablis sauce. ⊠ *Rue Jules-Rathier, 89800,* ☎ *03–86–42–10–63,* FAX *03–86–42–17–11. 26 rooms with bath. Restaurant. AE, DC, MC, V.*

Cluny

$$$ ✕📷 **Bourgogne.** You can get into the medieval mood of Cluny at this old-fashioned hotel, right next door to the famous abbey. There is a small garden and an atmospheric restaurant with sober pink decor and refined cuisine: foie gras, snails, and fish with ginger are specialties. ⊠ *Pl. de l'Abbaye, 71250,* ☎ *03–85–59–00–58,* FAX *03–85–59–03–73. 14 rooms with bath or shower. Restaurant. AE, DC, MC, V. Closed Wed. lunch, Mon., and mid-Nov.–mid-Feb.*

$ ✕📷 **Hôtel de l'Abbaye.** This modest, simple hotel is just five minutes from Cluny center. Request one of the three rooms to the right of the dining room: they were redecorated more recently than the others and are an especially good value. The restaurant offers fresh, local cuisine: the chicken fricassee in a white Macon sauce, and the confit of rabbit are particularly rich, hearty fare. Prices—for example, 98 francs for the three-course prix-fixe menu—are very reasonable. ⊠ *Av. Charles-de-Gaulle, 71250,* ☎ *03–85–59–11–14,* FAX *03–85–59–09–76. 16 rooms, 9 with bath. Restaurant (closed Mon., Tues. lunch, and Jan.–mid-Feb.). MC, V. Closed Jan.–mid-Feb.*

Dijon

$$$ ✕ **Jean-Pierre Billoux.** M. Billoux's restaurant is reputedly the best in this most gastronomic of French cities. It is in a magnificent, spacious, restored town house with a garden, a bar, and stone-vaulted rooms. Specialties include steamed frogs' legs served with cress pancakes, and guinea fowl with foie gras. Service is charming. ⊠ *14 pl. Darcy,* ☎ *03–80–30–11–00. Reservations essential. MC, V. Closed Mon., part of Feb., and first half Aug. No dinner Sun.*

$$–$$$ ✕🏨 **Chapeau Rouge.** If you want to be sure of getting a quiet, tasteful room in the center, close to Dijon cathedral, this is a good choice. The restaurant is renowned as a haven of regional cuisine. Snails, pigeon, and veal in mustard top the list of specialties. ⊠ *5 rue Michelet, 21000,* ☎ *03–80–30–28–10,* 𝔽𝔸𝕏 *03–80–30–33–89. 29 rooms with bath or shower. Restaurant (reservations essential). AE, DC, MC, V.*

$ ✕🏨 **Hostellerie du Sauvage.** In a courtyard off a busy street in Dijon's old quarter is this small, charming hotel. Rooms are old-fashioned and far from stylish, but they offer a quiet night's sleep. Prices depend on the size of the bed. The restaurant, which has sunken beams and open fireplaces, attracts both guests and locals. ⊠ *64 rue Mange, 21000,* ☎ *03–80–41–31–21,* 𝔽𝔸𝕏 *03–80–42–06–07. 23 rooms with bath or shower. Restaurant. MC, V.*

Lyon

$$$ ✕ **Léon de Lyon.** A mix of traditional fare (dumplings, hot sausages) ★ and eye-opening innovation keep Léon de Lyon at the forefront of restaurants. It occupies two floors of an old house full of alcoves and wood paneling. The blue-aproned waiters melt into the old-fashioned decor. Dishes such as fillet of veal with celery or leg of lamb with fava beans are memorable. ⊠ *1 rue Pléney,* ☎ *04–78–28–11–33. Reservations essential. MC, V. Closed Aug. No dinner Sun., no lunch Mon.*

$$ ✕ **A Ma Vigne.** This restaurant is popular because you can get a straightforward meal that is a break from gourmet Lyonnais dining. French fries, *moules* (mussels), roast ham, and tripe lead the menu. Get there early, especially for lunch. ⊠ *23 rue Jean-Larrivé,* ☎ *04–78–60–46–31. MC, V. Closed Sun., Aug.*

$$$$ 🏨 **La Cour des Loges.** Four Renaissance mansions have been transformed into this stylish hotel. The sand-color stone, immense courtyard, spiral stone staircases, and exposed roof beams lend a courtly ambience. Rooms, varying in size and price, have contemporary or modern classic decor (Room No. 62 is particularly attractive, with windows looking down on the street). Service is exemplary. ⊠ *6 rue du Boeuf, 69005,* ☎ *04–78–42–75–75,* 𝔽𝔸𝕏 *04–72–40–93–61. 63 rooms with bath. Bar, breakfast room, indoor pool, hot tub, sauna, health club, library, meeting room. AE, DC, MC, V.*

$$$ 🏨 **Royal.** The Royal is on the spacious and elegant place Bellecour in the heart of Lyon. Beware of the huge range in room prices (590–890 frs); some of the most expensive (with their own Jacuzzi) are positively luxurious. ⊠ *20 pl. Bellecour, 69002,* ☎ *04–78–37–57–31,* 𝔽𝔸𝕏 *04–78–37–01–36. 80 rooms, most with bath or shower. Restaurant. AE, DC, MC, V.*

Sens

$$ ✕🏨 **Paris et Poste.** This hotel, a former staging post, is a pleasant stop ★ on the way from Paris to Burgundy. Rooms are comfortably large and have modern tiled bathrooms; the quietest are on the inner courtyard. The helpful staff and sumptuous breakfasts (rare in France) create a sense of well-being, confirmed by the robust dinner. The prix-fixe menus include duck, snails, and steak. ⊠ *97 rue de la République, 89100,*

☎ *03–86–65–17–43,* 𝔽𝔸𝕏 *03–86–64–48–45. 25 rooms with bath or shower. Restaurant, bar. AE, DC, MC, V.*

Vézelay

$$$$ ✕⊞ **L'Espérance.** In St-Père-sous-Vézelay, a neighboring village, you can enjoy renowned chef Marc Meneau's subtle and original cuisine at one of France's premier restaurants. Reservations and jacket and tie are essential here (closed Tues., Wed. lunch, and Feb.). A second restaurant in a modern building, Le Pré des Marguerites, offers simpler, more traditional, less expensive fare. L'Espérance also has 40 luxurious rooms. The 13 rooms in the main house are pretty, but rather small; the others, in nearby buildings, are slightly larger. ⊠ *St-Père-sous-Vézelay, 89450,* ☎ *03–86–33–20–45,* 𝔽𝔸𝕏 *03–86–33–26–15. 40 rooms. Restaurant.*

THE LOIRE VALLEY

The Loire is the longest river in France, rising near Le Puy in the east of the Massif Central and pursuing a broad northwest curve on its 1,000-kilometer (620-mile) course to the Atlantic near Nantes. The meandering Loire offers two distinct faces: fast-flowing and spectacular in spring, sluggish and sandy in summer. Château country, the region encompasses the 225-kilometer (140-mile) stretch to Orléans, the 113 kilometers (70 miles) south of Paris, and Angers, 96 kilometers (60 miles) from the Atlantic coast. Thanks to its mild climate and lush meadowland, this area is known as the Garden of France.

To the north lies the vast grain plain of the Beauce; to the southeast the marshy, forest-covered Sologne, renowned for mushrooms, asparagus, and game. The star attractions along the rocky banks of the Loire and its tributaries—the Rivers Cher, Indre, Vienne, and Loir—are the famous châteaus: stately houses, castles, and fairy-tale palaces. Renaissance elegance is often combined with fortresslike medieval mass. The Loire Valley was fought over by France and England during the Middle Ages. It took the example of Joan of Arc, the "Maid of Orléans" (scene of her most rousing military successes), for the French to finally expel the English.

The Loire Valley's golden age came under François I (1515–47), France's flamboyant contemporary of England's Henry VIII. He hired Renaissance craftsmen from Italy and hobnobbed with the aging Leonardo da Vinci, his guest at Amboise. You can see his salamander emblem in many châteaus.

Getting Around

The easiest way to visit the Loire châteaus is by car; N152 hugs the riverbank and offers excellent sightseeing possibilities. Trains run along the Loire Valley every two hours, supplemented by local bus services. A peaceful way to explore the region is to rent a bicycle at one of the SNCF train stations (some trains even transport bikes for free).

Guided Tours

Bus tours for the main châteaus leave daily in summer from Tours, Blois, Angers, Orléans, and Saumur: Ask at the relevant tourist office for latest times and prices. Most châteaus insist that visitors follow one of their tours; try to get a booklet in English before joining the tour, as most are in French only.

The Loire Valley

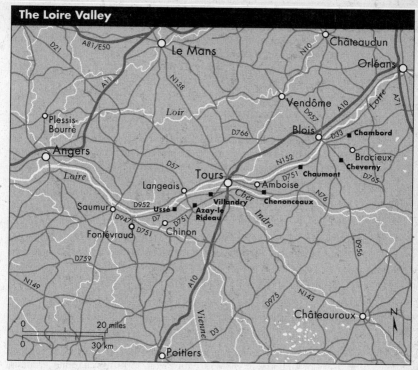

Visitor Information

Angers (✉ pl. du Président-Kennedy, ☎ 02–41–23–15–11).
Blois (✉ 3 av. du Dr-Jean-Laigret, ☎ 02–54–74–06–49).
Orléans (✉ pl. Albert-Ier, ☎ 02–38–53–05–95).
Tours (✉ 78 rue Bernard-Palissy, ☎ 02–47–70–37–37).

Exploring the Loire Valley

Châteaudun

Orléans, little more than an hour away by expressway (A10) or train, is the most obvious gateway to the Loire Valley if you're coming from Paris. Apart from its art museum and majestic Sainte-Croix cathedral, however, Orléans has little of interest. Instead take the expressway from Paris to Chartres, then N10 to **Châteaudun,** where a colossal château, resplendent on a steep promontory, contains graceful furniture and lavish tapestries. In its chapel are 15 statues produced locally in the 15th century. ☎ 02–37–45–22–70. 🎫 27 frs. ☉ Daily, mid-Mar.–Sept., 9:30–11:45 and 2–6; Oct.–mid-Mar., 10–11:30 and 2–4.

★ Continue along N10 to **Vendôme,** 40 kilometers (25 miles) southwest, where the Loir River (not to be confused with the larger and more famous Loire to the south) splits into many arms, giving the town a canal-like charm that harmonizes with its old streets and bridges. The large but little-known main church, **Eglise de la Trinité,** an encyclopedia of different styles, with brilliantly carved choir stalls and an exuberant west front, is the work of Jean de Beauce, best known for his spire at Chartres Cathedral. Vendôme also has a ruined **castle** with ramparts and pleasant, uncrowded gardens. 🎫 Free. ☉ 9–dusk.

Blois

★ **Blois** lies 32 kilometers (20 miles) southeast of Vendôme along D957. It is the most attractive of the major Loire towns, with its tumbling alleyways and its **château,** a mixture of four different styles: Feudal (13th century); Gothic-Renaissance transition (circa 1500); Renaissance (circa 1520); and Classical (circa 1635). ☎ 02–54–74–16–06. ▨ 32 frs. ☉ May–Aug., daily 9–6:30; Sept.–Apr., daily 9–noon and 2–5.

★ ☙ Blois makes an ideal launching pad for a visit to the châteaus of Chambord and Cheverny. **Chambord** (begun in 1519) is 20 kilometers (11 miles) east of Blois along D33, near Bracieux. It is in a vast forest and game park. There's another forest on the roof: 365 chimneys and turrets, representing architectural self-indulgence at its least squeamish. Grandeur or a mere 440-room folly? Judge for yourself, and don't miss the superb spiral staircase or the chance to saunter over the rooftop terrace. ☎ 02–54–50–40–28. ▨ 35 frs. ☉ July–Aug., daily 9:30–6:30; Sept.–June, daily 9:30–5:15.

About 20 kilometers (12 miles) south of Blois, along D751, stands the sturdy château of **Chaumont,** built between 1465 and 1510—well before Benjamin Franklin became a regular visitor. There is a magnificent Loire panorama from the terrace, and the stables—where purebreds dined like royalty—show the importance attached to fine horses, for hunting or just prestige. ☎ 02–54–20–98–03. ▨ 27 frs. ☉ Apr.–Sept., daily 9:30–6; Oct.–Mar., daily 10–4:30.

Amboise

★ Downstream (westward) another 16 kilometers (10 miles) is the bustling town of **Amboise.** Its **château,** dating from 1500, has charming grounds, a rich interior, and fine views of the river from the battlements. But it wasn't always so peaceful: In 1560, more than 1,000 Protestant "conspirators" were hanged from these battlements during the Wars of Religion. ☎ 02–47–57–00–98. ▨ 33 frs. ☉ July–Aug., daily 9–6:30; Sept.–June, daily 9–noon and 2–5.

☙ The nearby **Clos-Lucé,** a 15th-century brick manor house, was the last home of Leonardo da Vinci, who was invited to stay here by François I. Leonardo died here in 1519, and his engineering genius is illustrated by models based on his plans and sketches. ✉ 2 rue du Clos-Luce, ☎ 02–47–57–62–88. ▨ 35 frs. ☉ Daily 9–6.

★ The early 16th-century château of **Chenonceau,** 16 kilometers (10 miles) south of Amboise along D81 and then D40, straddles the tranquil River Cher like a bridge. It is surrounded by elegant gardens and plane trees. Inside, note the fine paintings, colossal fireplaces, and richly worked ceilings. A waxworks museum (separate admission, 10 frs) lurks in an outbuilding. ☎ 02–47–23–90–07. ▨ 40 frs. ☉ Mid-Mar.–mid-Sept., daily 9–7; mid-Sept.–mid-Mar., daily 9–5.

Tours

Tours, 25 kilometers (15 miles) farther on, is the unofficial capital of the Loire. It retains a certain charm despite its sprawling size (250,000 inhabitants) and extensive postwar reconstruction. The attractive old quarter around place Plumereau, Le Vieux Tours, has been tastefully ★ restored, and the **Cathédrale St-Gatien** (1239–1484) numbers among France's most impressive churches. The influence of local Renaissance sculptors and craftsmen is evident on the ornate facade. The stained glass in the choir is particularly delicate; some of it dates from 1320.

★ The château of **Villandry,** 16 kilometers (10 miles) southwest of Tours along the River Cher, is known for its painstakingly relaid 16th-century gardens, with long avenues of 1,500 manicured lime trees. The château interior, restored, like the gardens, in the mid-19th century, is equally beguiling. Note the painted and gilded ceiling from Toledo and the collection of Spanish pictures. ☎ 02–47–50–02–09. 🖃 *Château and gardens: 40 frs; gardens only: 27 frs.* ⊘ *June–Sept., 9–6, gardens 9–8; Oct.–May, daily 9–5, gardens 9–dusk.*

Langeais

Langeais is just 14 kilometers (9 miles) west of Villandry: Keep on D7 to Lignières before turning right onto D57 and crossing the Loire. A massive **castle,** built in the 1460s and never altered, dominates this small town. Its apartments contain a superb collection of tapestries, chests, and beds. ☎ 02–47–96–72–60. 🖃 *35 frs.* ⊘ *Easter–Oct., daily 9–6:30; Nov.–Easter, Tues.–Sun. 9–noon and 2–5. Closed Mon.*

★ **Azay-le-Rideau** (1518–29), one of the prettiest of the Loire châteaus, lies on the River Indre 10 kilometers (6 miles) south of Langeais along D57. Its high roof and cheerful corner turrets are reflected in the river that surrounds the château like a lake. This graceful ensemble compensates for the château's spartan interior, as does the charm of the surrounding village. ☎ 02–47–45–42–04. 🖃 *32 frs.* ⊘ *Apr.–Oct., daily 9:30–6; Nov.–Mar., daily 9:30–12:30 and 2–5:30.*

A short ride down the Indre Valley (on D17 and D7) from Azay will help you judge whether the château of ⊘ **Ussé**—actually in the village of Rigny-Usse—really is, as the brochures claim, the castle that inspired *Sleeping Beauty.* Its bristling turrets, terraces, and forest backcloth are undeniably romantic. Don't forget the **chapel** in the park, built 1520–38 in Renaissance proportions. ☎ 02–47–95–54–05. 🖃 *59 frs.* ⊘ *Mar.–mid-Nov., daily 9–noon and 2–6.*

Chinon

Chinon, 13 kilometers (8 miles) from Ussé via D7 and D16, is an ancient town nestled by the River Vienne, with a rock-of-ages **castle** patrolling the horizon. This 12th-century fortress, with walls 370 meters (400 yards) long, is mainly in ruins, though small museums are installed in the Royal Chambers and sturdy Tour de l'Horloge (clock tower). The views from the ramparts of Chinon of the Vienne Valley are excellent. ☎ 02–47–93–13–45. 🖃 *23 frs.* ⊘ *Nov.–mid-Mar., daily 9–noon and 2–5; mid-Mar.–June and Sept., daily 9–6; July and Aug., daily 9–7; Oct., daily 9–5.*

Just south of Chinon, D751 heads up the Vienne Valley toward **Fontevraud,** 21 kilometers (13 miles) away. This quiet village is dominated by its medieval **abbey,** where English kings Henry II and Richard the Lionhearted are buried. The church, cloisters, Renaissance chapter house, long-vaulted refectory, and octagonal kitchen are all still standing. The guided tours are in French, but you can get a brochure in English. ☎ 02–41–51–71–41. 🖃 *27 frs.* ⊘ *May–mid-Sept., daily 9–noon and 2–6:30; mid-Sept.–Apr., daily 9:30–noon and 2–5.*

★ **Saumur,** 16 kilometers (10 miles) west along the Loire from Fontevraud via D947, is a prosperous town famous for its riding school, wines, and **château**—a white 14th-century castle that towers above the river. The château contains two outstanding museums: the **Musée des Arts Décoratifs** (Decorative Arts Museum), featuring porcelain and enamels, and the **Musée du Cheval** (Horse Museum), with saddles, stirrups, skeletons, and Stubbs engravings. ☎ 02–41–51–30–46. 🖃 *33 frs.* ⊘ *July–Sept., daily 9–6:30; Oct. and Apr.–June, daily 9–11:30 and 2–6; Nov.–Mar., Wed.–Mon. 9:30–noon and 2–5:30.*

Angers

Angers is an historic city on the River Maine just north of the Loire. D952 runs along the Loire Valley from Saumur, 45 kilometers (28 miles)
★ away. The feudal **château** was built by St-Louis (1228–38) and has a dry moat, drawbridge, and 17 round towers along its ½-mile-long walls. A gallery houses an exquisite tapestry collection, notable for the blockbuster *Tapestry of the Apocalypse*, woven in Paris around 1380 and restored to almost pristine glory in 1996. ☎ 02–41–87–43–47. ▨ *32 frs.* ☉ *July–Aug., daily 10–7; Sept.–June, daily 9:30–12:30 and 2–5:30.*

Dining and Lodging

For details and price-category definitions, *see* Dining *and* Lodging *in* Staying in France, *above.*

Amboise

$–$$ ✕▦ **Le Blason.** This delightful small hotel, with enthusiastic owners, is behind the château, a four-minute walk from the center of town. Room 229, with exposed beams and a cathedral ceiling, is especially charming; Room 109 is comfortably spacious and has a good view of the square. The pretty little restaurant has a seasonal menu that begins at 95 francs and might include an appetizer of air-dried duck breast with herbs and spices, followed by roast lamb with garlic or medallions of pork. ⊠ *11 pl. Richelieu, 37400,* ☎ *02–47–23–22–41,* ℻ *02–47–57–56–18. 29 rooms with bath. Restaurant. MC, V.*

Angers

$ ✕ **La Treille.** For traditional, simple fare, try this small two-story mom-and-pop restaurant just off the place Ste-Croix (next to the cathedral). The prix-fixe menu may start with a *salade au chèvre chaud* (warm goat cheese salad), followed by confit of duck, and an apple tart. A bottle of local wine completes the meal. The upstairs dining room has a party atmosphere; downstairs is better for quiet conversation. ⊠ *12 rue Montault,* ☎ *02–41–88–45–51. MC, V. Closed Sun.*

$$$ ✕▦ **Le Quéré.** Paul Le Quéré's luxurious hotel complements his fine restaurant in a mansion off the main avenue. Rooms, decorated by his wife, Martine, in classic modern style, have flashy marble bathrooms. The chef happily juggles tradition and modern innovations, be it roast lobster tails or diced beef with mussels. The opulent dining room in the glass rotunda is splendid for lunch; the formal dining room with a Charles X fireplace sets a classic tone for dinner. ⊠ *3 blvd. du Maréchal-Foch, 49100,* ☎ *02–41–20–00–20,* ℻ *02–41–20–06–20. 6 rooms with bath, 4 suites. Restaurant. AE, DC, MC, V.*

Blois

$$ ✕ **Au Rendez-vous des Pêcheurs.** On the right bank of the Loire below the castle, this extremely modest restaurant offers excellent value. Chef Eric Reithler creates inventive fish-based specialties. ⊠ *27 rue de Foix,* ☎ *02–54–74–67–48. MC, V. Closed Sun., dinner Mon.*

$$ ✕▦ **Le Médicis.** Your best bet in Blois, this smart, friendly hotel, 1,000 yards from the château, has comfortable, air-conditioned rooms that are soundproofed from the main avenue. They are each furnished differently, but share the same joyous color scheme. The restaurant itself is worth the stay. Chef-owner Christian Garanger's cooking is innovative classical—coquille St-Jacques with a pear fondue, and thin slices of roast hare with black currant sauce, for example. ⊠ *2 allée François-1ᵉʳ, 41000,* ☎ *02–54–43–94–04,* ℻ *02–54–42–04–05. 12 rooms* *with bath, 1 suite with whirlpool. Restaurant (no dinner Sun. in low season). AE, DC, MC, V. Closed early-late Jan.*

Chambord

$$ ⊞ **Grand St-Michel.** Considering its location across from the château, the St-Michel is reasonable. Some of the rooms have splendid views of the château, its lawns, and the forest backdrop, as does the terrace, an ideal place for summer morning coffee before the tourist hordes arrive. ⊠ *Pl. St-Michel, 41250 Chambord,* ☎ *02–54–20–31–31,* FAX *02–54–20–36–40. 38 rooms, some with bath or shower. Restaurant, tennis court, parking. MC, V. Closed mid-Nov.–late Dec.*

Chenonceaux

$$ ✕⊞ **Bon Laboureur et Château.** In 1882, it won Henry James's praise
★ as a simple, rustic inn. Since then, through four generations of the Jeudi family, it has become an elegant hotel. Rooms in the old house are comfortably traditional; those in the former stables are larger and more modern; the biggest are in the converted manor house across the street; there's a "honeymoon" room in the garden. You can dine on excellent turbot with hollandaise or braised rabbit with dried fruit. The *poêlée de St-Jacques* (sautéed scallops) with fresh wild mushrooms is a must in the autumn. Reserve early for a table in the dining room rather than in the annex. ⊠ *6 rue du Dr-Bretonneau, 37150,* ☎ *02–47–23–90–02,* FAX *02–47–23–82–01. 36 rooms with bath. Restaurant, heated pool. AE, DC, MC, V. Closed Dec.–mid-Mar.*

Chinon

$$$ ✕⊞ **Château de Marçay.** In this 15th-century château 6 km (4 miles) south of Chinon by D49 and D116, Pascal Bodin prepares excellent cuisine—try the carpaccio of duck or the tournedos of salmon in a Chinon wine sauce. Rooms are furnished with antiques, space is generous, beams and gables add warmth, and bathrooms are marbled. Those on the ground floor in the west wing have private patios; the ones in the pavilion near the château, though pleasantly furnished, have less charm. ⊠ *37500 Marçay,* ☎ *02–47–93–03–47,* FAX *02–47–93–45–33. 35 rooms with bath (27 in château). Restaurant, pool, tennis court. AE, DC, MC, V. Closed 2nd wk of Jan.–mid-Mar.*

Saumur

$$ ⊞ **Anne d'Anjou.** Close to the center of town, this hotel facing the river has a view of the château (floodlit at night) perched above. Inside the 18th-century building is a staircase with wrought-iron banisters that circle up to the top floor. The simple rooms are filled with both old furniture and contemporary decor; Room 102 has wood panel paintings and Empire furnishings. The restaurant, Les Ménestrels, serves traditional cuisine. ⊠ *32 quai Mayaud, 49400,* ☎ *02–41–67–30–30,* FAX *02–41–67–51–00. 50 rooms. Restaurant. AE, DC, MC, V.*

Tours

$$$ ✕⊞ **Domaine de la Tortinière.** This turreted mid-19th century man-
★ sion stands proudly on a hill amid vast fields and woodland, 10 kilometers (6 miles) south of Tours, near Montbazon along N10. Rooms vary in styles, ranging from conventionally old-fashioned to brashly modern. The spacious restaurant looks out over the gardens. Salmon, pigeon, and rabbit with truffles are menu highlights. ⊠ *10 rte de Ballan, 37250 Veigné,* ☎ *02–47–26–00–19,* FAX *02–47–65–95–70. 14 rooms with bath. Restaurant (closed Tues. in Nov., Dec., Mar., Wed. lunch.). MC, V. Closed mid-Dec.–Feb.*

$$$ ⊞ **Univers.** Rooms in this old hotel are all slightly different and all cleverly designed; most look onto the garden. Wood paneling and soft colors give them warmth. Bathrooms are spacious. The lobby has murals depicting some famous guests, among them Winston Churchill, Rudyard Kipling, and Maurice Chevalier. ⊠ *5 blvd. Heurteloup, 37000,* ☎ *02–47–05–37–12,* FAX *02–47–61–51–80. 89 rooms with bath, 10 suites. Restaurant, bar. AE, DC, MC, V.*

PROVENCE

As you approach Provence, there is a magical moment when the north is finally left behind: Cypresses and red-tile roofs appear; you hear the screech of cicadas and catch the scent of wild thyme and lavender—and all of this is against a backdrop of harsh, brightly lit landscapes that inspired the paintings of Paul Cézanne and Vincent van Gogh. Roman remains litter the ground in well-preserved profusion. The theater and triumphal arch at Orange, the amphitheater at Nîmes and Arles (both are still used for spectacles that include bullfighting), the aqueduct at Pont-du-Gard, and the mausoleum at St-Rémy-de-Provence are considered the best of their kind in existence.

A number of towns have grown up along the Rhône Valley owing to its historical importance as a communications artery. The biggest is bustling Marseille; Orange, Avignon, Tarascon, and Arles have more picturesque charm. The Camargue, on the other hand, is the marshy realm of birds and beasts. North of Marseille lies Aix-en-Provence, with an old-time elegance that reflects its former role as regional capital. Extending the traditional boundaries of Provence westward, historic Nîmes has been included. The Riviera is also part of this region, but there is so much to see that an entire section has been devoted to it.

Getting Around

Provence's key attractions are not far apart. Traveling by car is by far the most rewarding way to get around, especially if you want to go to the smaller villages and explore the landscapes that have inspired artists. If you're limited to public transportation, Avignon makes the best base for both train and bus connections.

Guided Tours

The regional tourist offices' "52 Week" program pools 52 tours offered by various agencies throughout the year, touching on wine tasting, sailing, hang gliding, golfing, gastronomy, and cultural exploration. Contact **Loisirs-Acceuil** (⊠ Domaine de Vergon, 13370 Mallemort, ☎ 01–90–59–18–05) for details.

Visitor Information

Aix-en-Provence (⊠ 2 pl. du Général-de-Gaulle, ☎ 04–42–16–11–61).
Arles (⊠ Esplanade Charles-de-Gaulle, ☎ 04–90–18–41–21).
Avignon (⊠ 41 cours Jean-Jaurès, ☎ 04–90–82–65–11).
Marseille (⊠ 4 La Canebière, ☎ 04–91–13–89–00).
Montpellier (⊠ Pl. René-Devic, ☎ 04–67–58–67–58).
Nîmes (⊠ 6 rue Auguste, ☎ 04–66–67–29–11).

Exploring Provence

Orange

Traveling south down the autoroute A7 from Lyon, **Orange** will be your
★ first stop. The magnificent, semicircular **Théâtre Antique,** in the center of town, is the best-preserved remains of a theater from the ancient world. It was built just before the birth of Jesus and still accommodates seven

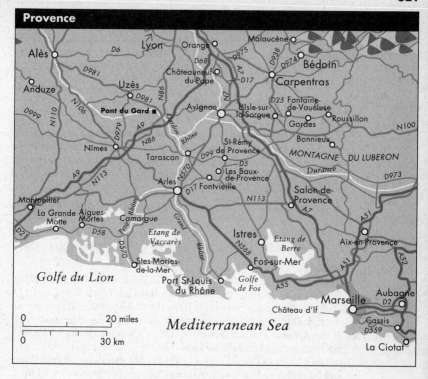

Provence

thousand spectators for open-air concerts and operatic performances. The **Parc de la Colline St-Eutrope,** the banked garden behind the theater, yields a fine view of the theater and the 6,000-foot Mont Ventoux to the east. Orange also boasts the third-highest Roman arch still standing. The 70-foot **Arc de Triomphe** was probably built around AD 25 in honor of the Gallic Wars. ⊠ *Pl. des Frères-Mounet,* ☎ 04–90–34–70–88. 🎫 *Theater: 30 frs; this is a joint ticket with Musée Municipal.* ⊙ *Apr.–Oct., daily 9–6:30; Nov.–Mar., daily 9–noon and 1:30–5.*

South of Orange pass through the hillside village of **Châteauneuf-du-Pape,** founded by the popes in the 14th century—the vineyard is still regarded as the best of the southern Rhône.

Avignon

A warren of medieval alleys nestling behind a protective ring of stocky towers, **Avignon** is where seven exiled popes camped between 1309 and 1377 after fleeing from the corruption of Rome. The most dominant building within the town walls is the colossal **Palais des Papes.** It's really two buildings: the severe **Palais Vieux** (Old Palace), built between 1334 and 1342 by Pope Benedict XII, a member of the Cistercian order, which frowned on frivolity, and the more decorative **Palais Nouveau** (New Palace), built in the following decade by the arty, lavish Pope Clement VI. The Great Court, where visitors arrive, links the two. ⊠ *Pl. du Palais-des-Papes,* ☎ 04–90–27–50–73. 🎫 *35 frs.* ⊙ *Mar.–Oct., daily 9–7; Nov.–Mar. daily 9–12:45 and 2–6.*

Nearby, the 12th-century **cathedral** contains the Gothic tomb of Pope John XII. Beyond is the **Rocher des Doms,** a large, attractive garden offering fine views of Avignon, the Rhône, and the 12th century **Pont St-Bénezet** of "Sur la Pont d'Avignon" fame. Only half the bridge now remains. ☎ 04–90–85–60–16. 🎫 *10 frs.* ⊙ *Apr.–Sept., daily 9–6:30; Oct.–Mar., Tues.–Sun. 9–1 and 2–5.*

The medieval **Petit Palais,** between the bridge and the Rocher des Doms garden, was once home to cardinals and archbishops. Nowadays it contains an outstanding collection of Old Masters, led by the Italian schools of Venice, Siena, and Florence. ✉ *21 pl. du Palais,* ☎ *04–90–86–44–58.* ☞ *20 frs.* ☉ *Wed.–Mon. 9:30–noon and 2–6.*

In the shop-lined streets of old Avignon is the **Musée Lapidaire,** with a variety of archaeological finds. ✉ *27 rue de la République,* ☎ *04–90–85–75–38.* ☞ *5 frs.* ☉ *Wed.–Mon. 10–noon and 2–6.*

A few minutes' walk away is the **Musée Calvet,** an 18th-century town house featuring an extensive collection of mainly French paintings from the 16th century on. Greek, Roman, and Etruscan statuettes are also displayed. ✉ *65 rue Joseph-Vernet,* ☎ *04–90–86–33–84.* ☞ *20 frs.* ☉ *Wed.–Mon. 10–noon and 2–6.*

West of Avignon is the well-preserved **Pont du Gard,** a huge, three-tiered aqueduct, erected 2,000 years ago as part of a 30-mile canal supplying water to Roman Nîmes. Its setting, spanning a rocky gorge 150 feet above the River Gardon, is nothing less than spectacular.

Nîmes

Nîmes lies 20 km (12½ mi) southwest of the Pont du Gard (via N86). Few towns have preserved such visible links with their Roman past. A 60-franc "passport," available from the tourist office, admits you to the town's museums and monuments and is valid for three days. Start
★ at the **Arènes.** The amphitheater, with a seating capacity of 21,000, has been restored and almost looks like the original. An inflatable roof covers it in winter, when various exhibits and shows occupy the space, and bullfights and tennis tournaments are held in it in summer. ✉ *Blvd. Victor-Hugo,* ☎ *04–66–67–45–76.* ☞ *22 frs; joint ticket to Arènes and Tour Magne: 30 frs.* ☉ *May–Oct., 9–6:30; Nov.–Mar., daily 9–noon and 2–5.*

Take rue de la Cité-Foulc, behind the Arènes, to the **Musée des Beaux-Arts** (Fine Arts Museum), where you can admire a vast Roman mosaic, as well as works by Nicolas Poussin, Pieter Brueghel, Peter Paul Rubens, and Auguste Rodin. ✉ *Rue de la Cité-Foulc,* ☎ *04–66–67–38–21.* ☞ *22 frs.* ☉ *Tues.–Sat. 11–6.*

Find time to visit the **Musée Archéologique et d'Histoire Naturelle,** rich in local archaeological finds. ✉ *Blvd. de l'Amiral-Courbet,* ☎ *04–66–67–25–57.* ☞ *22 frs.* ☉ *Tues.–Sun. 11–6.*

The **cathedral** in Nîmes, an uninspired 19th-century reconstruction, is of less interest than either the surrounding pedestrian streets or the **Musée du Vieux Nîmes** (Museum of Old Nîmes) in a 17th-century Bishop's Palace. Embroidered garments and woolen shawls fill the rooms in an exotic and vibrant display. ✉ *Pl. aux Herbes,* ☎ *04–66–36–00–64.* ☞ *22 frs.* ☉ *Tues.–Sun. 11–6.*

★ North of the cathedral is **Maison Carrée.** This former Roman temple, dating from the 1st century AD, is now a museum that contains an imposing statue of Apollo and other antiquities. ✉ *Blvd. Victor-Hugo.* ☞ *Free.* ☉ *May–Oct. daily 9–7; Nov.–Apr. daily 9–6.*

Other delights include the formal garden **Jardin de la Fontaine** and the shattered remnant of a Roman ruin, known as the **Temple of Diana.** At the far end of the jardin is the **Tour Magne**—a stumpy tower that provides fine views of Nîmes. ✉ *Quai de la Fontaine,* ☎ *04–66–67–65–56.* ☞ *Tour Magne: 12 frs; joint ticket with the Arènes: 30 frs.* ☉ *May–Oct. daily 9–7; Nov.–Apr. daily 9–12:30 and 1:30–6.*

The Camargue and Arles

Turning south, head for **Aigues-Mortes,** hemmed in by sturdy walls sprouting towers at regular intervals. Aigues-Mortes was originally a port, created at the behest of Louis IX for a base for his Crusades to the Holy Land. The sea has long since receded, though, and Aigues-Mortes's size and importance have decreased with it. Further east is the haunting, desolate **Camargue:** a marshy wilderness of endless horizons, vast pools, low flat plains, and innumerable species of migrating birds overhead. While away an hour at **Stes-Maries-de-la-Mer,** a commercialized resort and home to a tiny, dark fortress-church that guards caskets containing relics of the "Holy Maries" after whom the town was named.

On the northern border of Carmague is Roman **Arles.** For 55 frs you can purchase a joint ticket to all the monuments and museums. Its most notable sight is the 26,000-capacity **Arènes,** built in the 1st century AD for circuses and gladiator combats. The amphitheater is 150 yards long and as wide as a football field, with each of its two stories composed of 60 arches. ⊠ *Rond-Point des Arènes,* ☎ *04–90–96–03–70.* ▦ *15 frs, or use joint ticket.* ☉ *June–Sept., daily 8:30–7; Nov.–Mar., daily 9–noon and 2–4:30; Apr.–May and Oct., daily 9–12:30 and 2–6:30.*

Close by are the scanty remains of Arles's **Théâtre Antique** (Roman theater); the bits of marble column scattered around the grassy enclosure hint poignantly at the theater's onetime grandeur. ⊠ *Rue du Cloître,* ☎ *04–90–96–93–30 for ticket information.* ▦ *15 frs, or use joint ticket.* ☉ *June–Sept., daily 8:30–7; Nov.–Mar., daily 9–noon and 2–4:30; Apr.–May and Oct., daily 9–12:30 and 2–6:30.*

Opposite the 11th–12th century church of **St-Trophime** is the **Musée d'Art Païen** (Museum of Pagan Art), housed in a former church next to the 17th-century Hôtel de Ville. The "pagan art" displays encompass Roman statues, busts, mosaics, and a white marble sarcophagus. ⊠ *Pl. de la République.* ▦ *12 frs, or use joint ticket.* ☉ *June–Sept., daily 8:30–7; Nov.–Mar., daily 9–noon and 2–4:30; Apr.–May and Oct., 9–12:30 and 2–6:30.*

The **Muséon Arlaten** is housed next door in a 16th-century mansion. The charming displays include costumes and headdresses, puppets, and waxworks, lovingly assembled by the great 19th-century Provençal poet, Frédéric Mistral. ⊠ *29 rue de la République,* ☎ *04–90–96–08–23.* ▦ *15 frs, or use joint ticket.* ☉ *June–Sept., daily 8:30–7; Nov.–Mar., Tues.–Sun. 9–noon and 2–4:30; Apr.–May and Oct., Tues.–Sun. 9–12:30 and 2–6:30.*

Be sure to visit the **Musée d'Art Chrétien** (Museum of Christian Art). One of the highlights is a magnificent collection of sculpted marble sarcophagi, second only to the Vatican's, that date from the 4th century on. ⊠ *Rue Balze.* ▦ *12 frs, or use joint ticket.* ☉ *June–Sept., daily 8:30–7; Nov.–Mar., daily 9–noon and 2–4:30; Apr.–May and Oct., daily 9–12:30 and 2–6:30.*

At the east end of the **boulevard des Luces** is the **Jardin d'Hiver,** a public garden whose fountains figure in several of Van Gogh's paintings. Firebrand Dutchman Vincent van Gogh produced much of his best work—and chopped off his ear—in Arles during a frenzied 15-month spell (1888–90) just before his suicide at 37. Cross the gardens to the **Alyscamps,** where empty Roman tombs and sarcophagi line the allée des Sarcophages. ☎ *04–90–49–36–87.* ▦ *12 frs.* ☉ *Daily 9–5.*

Les Baux to Tarascon

★ East of Arles is the striking medieval village of **Les Baux-de-Provence** perched high above the surrounding countryside of vines, olive trees, and bauxite quarries. Hilly D5 heads north from Les Baux to the small
★ town of **St-Rémy de Provence,** founded in the 6th century BC and known as Glanum to the Romans. Its **Roman Mausoleum** was erected around AD 100 to the memory of Caius and Lucius Caesar, grandsons of the emperor Augustus. The nearby **Arc Municipal** is a few decades older and has suffered heavily; the upper half has crumbled away, although you can still make out some of the stone carvings. Excavations of **Glanum** began in 1921, and a tenth of the original Roman town has now been unearthed. The remains are less spectacular than the arch and mausoleum, but can be fascinating for students of archaeology. ☎ 04–90–92–23–79. ☞ 32 frs. ⊘ Apr.–Sept., daily 9–noon and 2–6; Oct.–Mar., daily 9:30–noon and 2–5.

Many of the finds from Glanum—statues, pottery, and jewelry—can also be examined at the town museum, **Le Musée Archéologique,** in the center of St-Rémy. ⊠ Hôtel de Sade, rue Parage, ☎ 04–90–92–64–04. ☞ 15 frs. ⊘ June–Oct., daily 9–noon and 2–6; Apr.–May and Oct., weekends 10–noon, weekdays 3–6; closed Nov.–Mar.

Take D99 16 km (10 mi) west from St-Rémy to **Tarascon.** The town has a formidable 12th-century **castle** with massive stone walls, towering 150 feet above the Rhône, among the most daunting in France. ☎ 04–90–91–01–93. ☞ 26 frs. ⊘ July–Aug., daily 9–7; Sept.–June, daily 9–noon and 2–6 (2–5 Oct.–Mar.).

The Luberon

Venture into the Luberon Mountains to visit **L'Isle-sur-la-Sorgue,** where the River Sorgue once turned the waterwheels of the town's silk factories. Some of the waterwheels are still in place. Tiny D25 leads east from L'Isle-sur-la-Sorgue to **Fontaine-de-Vaucluse,** where the Sorgue emerges from underground imprisonment: Water shoots up from a cavern as the emerald-green river sprays and cascades at the foot of steep cliffs. Wend your way to **Gordes,** a golden-stone village perched dramatically on its own hill. Two other nearby picturesque hilltop villages are **Roussillon,** whose houses are built with a distinctive orange- and pink-colored stone, and neighboring **Bonnieux.**

Aix-en-Provence

Few towns are as well preserved as the traditional capital of Provence:
★ elegant **Aix-en-Provence,** birthplace of the Impressionist Paul Cézanne (1839–1906) and the novelist Émile Zola (1840–1902). The celebrated, graceful, lively avenue **cours Mirabeau** is the town's nerve center. It divides Old Aix into two, with narrow medieval streets to the north and sophisticated, haughty 18th-century mansions to the south. To see these, go to rue Espariat. The sumptuous Hôtel Boyer d'Eguilles at No. 6, erected in 1675, is worth a visit for its fine woodwork, sculpture, and murals, but is best known as the **Muséum d'Histoire Naturelle.** The highlight is the rare collection of dinosaur eggs, accompanied by life size models of the dinosaurs that roamed locally 65 million years ago. ⊠ 6 rue Espariat, ☎ 04–42–26–23–67. ☞ 15 frs. ⊘ Mon.–Sat. 10–noon and 2–6, Sun. 2–6.

At No. 10 rue Espariat see the sculpted facade of the Hôtel d'Albertas (built in 1707), then turn right onto rue Aude, lined with ancient town houses. Notice the **Hôtel de Ville** and the 16th-century **Tour de l'Horloge** (former town belfry) next to it. Toward the far end of the street (now known as rue Gaston-de-Saporta) stands the **Cathédrale St-Sauveur** with a remarkable 15th-century triptych by Nicolas Froment, entitled Tryptique du Buisson Ardent (Burning Bush). The adjacent Archbishop's Palace is home to the **Musée des Tapisseries** (Tapestry Museum). Its highlight is a magnificent suite of 17 tapestries made in Beauvais that date, like the palace itself, from the 17th and 18th centuries. Nine woven panels illustrate the adventures of the bumbling Don Quixote. ⊠ *28 pl. des Martyrs de la Résistance,* ☎ *04–42–23–09–91.* ⊡ *14 frs.* ⊘ *Wed.–Mon. 10–noon and 2–5:45.*

Drop into the **Musée-Atelier de Paul Cézanne** (Cézanne's studio). No major pictures are on display here, but his studio remains as he left it at the time of his death in 1906. ⊠ *9 av. Paul-Cézanne,* ☎ *04–42–21–06–53.* ⊡ *15 frs.* ⊘ *Wed.–Mon. 10–noon and 2–5.*

The **Musée Granet** has several of Cézanne's oils and watercolors. ⊠ *13 rue Cardinale, pl. St-Jean de Malte,* ☎ *04–42–38–14–70.* ⊡ *18 frs.* ⊘ *Wed.–Mon. 10–noon and 2–6.*

Marseille

From Aix head down the toll-free A51 expressway to **Marseille,** Mediterranean's largest port and a melting pot where different peoples have mingled for centuries. The picturesque old harbor, the **Vieux Port,** is the heart of Marseille; Avenue Canebière leads to the water's edge. A short way down the quay on the right (as you look out to sea) is the elegant 17th-century **Hôtel de Ville** (Town Hall). Just behind, on rue de la Prison, is the Maison Diamantée, a 16th-century mansion housing the **Musée du Vieux Marseille,** which displays costumes, pictures, and figurines. ⊠ *2 rue de la Prison,* ☎ *04–91–55–10–19.* ⊡ *12 frs.* ⊘ *Tues.–Sun. 11–6 in summer; 10–5 in winter.*

Marseille's pompous, striped neo-Byzantine **cathedral** stands around the corner, its various domes looking utterly incongruous against the backdrop of industrial docks.

The grid of narrow, tumbledown streets leading off rue du Panier is called simply *Le Panier* (The Basket). Apart from the colorful, sleazy ambience, the Panier is worth visiting for the elegantly restored 17th-century hospice now known as the **Musée de la Vieille-Charité.** Excellent art exhibitions are held here. ⊠ *2 rue de la Charité,* ☎ *04–91–56–28–38.* ⊡ *12 frs (25 frs for exhibitions).* ⊘ *Tues.–Sun. 11–6 in summer; 10–5 in winter.*

Make the climb up to **Notre-Dame de la Garde** with its great gilded statue of the Virgin standing sentinel over the old port, 500 feet below. The church's interior is generously endowed with bombastic murals, mosaics, and marble. ⊠ *Pl. du Colonel-Edon,* ☎ *04–91–13–40–80.* ⊘ *Daily 7–5:30.*

Take time to drive the scenic 5-km (3-mi) coast road (corniche du Président-J.-F.-Kennedy) which links the Vieux Port to the newly created **Prado beaches** in the swanky parts of southern Marseille. There are breathtaking views across the sea toward the rocky **Frioul Islands,** which can be visited by ferries that leave from Vieux Port. On one of these is Château d'If, to which Alexandre Dumas condemned his fictional hero, the count of Monte Cristo.

Dining and Lodging

For details and price-category definitions, *see* Dining *and* Lodging *in* Staying in France, *above.*

Aix-en-Provence

$$$ × **Le Clos de la Violette.** Aix's best restaurant is in a residential dis-
★ trict north of the old town. You can eat under chestnut trees or in the

charming, airy pink-and-blue dining room. Chef Jean-Marc Banzo uses only fresh, local ingredients in both his nouvelle and traditional recipes. Try the *saumon vapeur* (aromatic steamed salmon) or the oyster and calamari salad. The weekday lunch menu is moderately priced and well worth the trek uptown. ⊠ *10 av. de la Violette,* ☎ *04–42–23–30–71. Jacket required. AE, MC, V. Closed Sun., Mon. lunch, early Nov., and most of Mar.*

$$–$$$ 🏨 **Nègre-Coste.** An elegant 18th-century town house has been mod-
★ ernized but features a luxurious old-world decor in rooms and public areas. The front rooms are noisier, but they are sunnier, larger, and better furnished, and have a view. ⊠ *33 cours Mirabeau, 13100,* ☎ *04–42–27–74–22,* 🗚 *04–42–26–80–93. 37 rooms with bath. AE, DC, MC, V.*

Arles

$$ ✕ **Le Vaccarès.** In this elegant restaurant overlooking place du Forum, Bernard Dumas serves Provençal classics with a touch of inventiveness. His seafood creations are particularly good: Try the mussels dressed in herbs and garlic. ⊠ *11 rue Favorin,* ☎ *04–90–96–06–17. MC, V. Closed mid-Jan.–mid-Feb., Sun. dinner, and Mon.*

$$$ 🏨 **Arlatan.** Follow the signposts from place du Forum to the pic-
★ turesque street where this 15th-century house is built on the site of a 4th-century basilica (tiled flooring dating from this period is visible below glass casing). Antiques, pretty fabrics, sumptuous tapestries, and elegant furniture lend it a gracious atmosphere. The garden is lovely. ⊠ *26 rue du Sauvage, 13200,* ☎ *04–90–93–56–66,* 🗚 *04–90–49–68–45. 51 rooms with bath. Bar. AE, DC, MC, V.*

Avignon

$$$ ✕ **Hiély-Lucullus.** According to most authorities, this restaurant is one
★ of the top 50 in France. The dining room, run with aplomb by Mme. Hiély, is charmingly quiet and dignified. Traditional delicacies include crayfish tails in scrambled eggs hidden inside a puff-pastry case. Save room for the extensive cheese board. ⊠ *5 rue de la République,* ☎ *04–90–86–17–07. Reservations essential. AE, V. Closed most of Jan., last 2 wks in June, Mon. and Tues. lunch.*

$$$ ✕🏨 **Europe.** This noble 16th-century town house became a hotel in Napoleonic times. The spacious guest rooms, filled with period furniture, have lavishly appointed modern bathrooms. The restaurant, La Vieille Fontaine, serves respectable regional cuisine, which you can eat outside in the stone courtyard. ⊠ *12 pl. Crillon, 84000,* ☎ *04–90–82–66–92,* 🗚 *04–90–85–43–66. 47 rooms with bath. Restaurant (closed Sat. lunch and Sun.). AE, DC, MC, V.*

Fontaine-de-Vaucluse

$$ ✕🏨 **Le Parc.** In the heart of the village is this comfortable hotel with a terrace overlooking the Sorgue. The restaurant has a good choice of prix-fixe menus. Specialties range from pasta with foie gras to duckling with berries. ⊠ *Rue de Bourgades, 84800,* ☎ *04–90–20–31–57,* 🗚 *04–90–20–27–03. 12 rooms with bath or shower. Restaurant. AE, DC, M, V. Closed Wed. and Jan.–mid-Feb.*

Gordes

$$$ ✕ **Comptoir du Victuailler.** There are only 10 tables at this tiny restaurant in the village center. Elegantly simple meals are served using only the freshest local capon, guinea fowl, asparagus, and truffles. The fruit sorbets are a revelation. ⊠ *Place du Château,* ☎ *04–90–72–01–31.*

Reservations essential. MC, V. Closed mid-Nov.–mid-Dec., mid-Jan.–mid-Mar., Tues. dinner, and Wed. Sept.–May.

Marseille

\$\$ ✕ **Chez Madie.** Every morning Madie Minassian, the colorful *pa-*
★ *tronne*, trades insults with the fishwives at the Vieux Port—and scours
their catch for the freshest specimens. They end up in her bouillabaisse,
fish soup, *favouilles* sauce (made with tiny crabs), and other savory
dishes. ⊠ *138 quai du Port*, ☎ *04–91–90–40–87. AE, DC, MC, V.
Closed Mon., Sun. dinner, and most of Aug.*

\$\$\$ ▥ **Grand Hôtel Beauvau.** Right on the Vieux Port, a few steps from
★ the end of La Canebière, the Beauvau is ideal. The 200-year-old former coaching inn has charming old-world opulence, enhanced by
wood paneling, designer fabrics, fine paintings, antique furniture, and
exceptional service. The best rooms look out onto the Vieux Port. ⊠
4 rue Beauvau, 13001, ☎ *04–91–54–91–00 (U.S. reservations,
800/223–9868; in the U.K., 0171/621–1962)*, ⊞ *04–91–54–15–76.
71 rooms with bath. Bar, breakfast room. AE, DC, MC, V.*

Nîmes

\$ ✕ **Nicolas.** Locals have long known about this homey place, which is
★ always packed. A friendly, frazzled staff serves up delicious *bourride*
and other local specialties—all at unbelievably low prices. ⊠ *1 rue Poise*,
☎ *04–66–67–50–47. MC, V. Closed Mon., first 2 wks in July, and
mid-Dec.–first wk in Jan.*

\$\$–\$\$\$ ✕▥ **Impérator.** This little palace-hotel, just a few minutes' walk from
★ the Jardin de la Fontaine, is totally modernized, but most rooms retain a quaint Provençal feel. All are cozy and spacious. The fine restaurant, L'Enclos de la Fontaine, is Nîmes's most fashionable eating place.
The price-fixed menus are bargains. ⊠ *15 rue Gaston-Boissier, 30900*,
☎ *04–66–21–90–30*, ⊞ *04–66–67–70–25. 59 rooms with bath.
Restaurant (closed Sat. lunch). AE, DC, MC, V.*

\$\$ ✕▥ **Lisita.** There's a Spanish feel to this cozy hotel near the Arènes.
It's a favored haunt of matadors whenever they're in town for a bullfight. Rooms are smallish; most are tastefully decorated with regional
furniture. The restaurant specializes in classic French fish and meat dishes.
⊠ *2 bis blvd. des Arènes, 30000*, ☎ *04–66–67–66–20*, ⊞ *04–66–
76–22–30. 30 rooms with bath or shower. Restaurant (closed Sat. and
first half of Aug.). AE, DC, MC, V.*

Orange

\$\$–\$\$\$ ✕ **Le Pigraillet.** One of Orange's best lunch spots is Le Pigraillet, at
★ the far end of the gardens behind the theater. You may want to eat outside, but most diners seek shelter from the mistral in the glassed-in terrace. The modern cuisine includes crab ravioli, foie gras in port, and
duck breast in muscat wine. ⊠ *Chemin de la Colline St-Eutrope*, ☎
04–90–34–44–25. MC, V. Closed Jan.–Feb. and Mon.

\$\$ ▥ **Arène.** This stylish old hotel, on a venerable, shady square lined with
plane trees, prides itself on providing a warm welcome, attentive service, and large, air-conditioned rooms. ⊠ *Pl. de Langes, 84100*, ☎ *04–
90–34–10–95*, ⊞ *04–90–34–91–62. 30 rooms with bath or shower.
Air-conditioning. AE, DC, MC, V. Closed Nov.–mid-Dec.*

St-Rémy-de-Provence

\$\$\$–\$\$\$\$ ✕▥ **Vallon de Valrugues.** This luxurious villa is fast making a name
for itself. Rooms are large and have marble bathrooms. Some have a
view of the rocky Alpilles hills, while others look out across olive
groves. Chef Joël Guillet specializes in imaginative regional dishes like

sea bass with calamari, pigeon roasted in lavender honey, and fricassee of scallops with cauliflower and parsley. ⊠ *Chemin Canto-Cigalo, 13210,* ☎ *04–90–92–04–40,* FAX *04–90–92–44–01. 34 rooms and 17 suites with bath. Restaurant, pool, hot tub, sauna. AE, MC, V.*

Tarascon

$$ ✕▨ **Saint-Jean.** A dozen cozy, spacious, rustic rooms are hidden behind the austere facade. In the wood-beamed dining room, regional dishes, including steak with shallot butter, salade niçoise, scallops, and chicken in basil, are served. ⊠ *24 blvd. Victor-Hugo, 13150,* ☎ *04–90–91–13–87,* FAX *04–90–91–32–42. 12 rooms with shower or bath. Restaurant (closed Fri. and Sat. lunch in winter). AE, DC, MC, V. Closed mid-Dec.–mid-Jan.*

THE RIVIERA

Few places in the world have the same pull on the imagination as France's fabled Riviera, the Mediterranean coastline stretching from St-Tropez in the west to Menton on the Italian border. Cooled by the Mediterranean in the summer and warmed by it in winter, the climate is almost always pleasant. Avoid the area in July and August, however, unless you love crowds.

While the Riviera's coastal resorts seem to live exclusively for the tourist trade and have often been ruined by high-rises, the hinterlands remain relatively untarnished. The little villages perched high on the hills behind medieval ramparts seem to belong to another century. One of them, St-Paul-de-Vence, is the home of the Maeght Foundation, one of the world's leading museums of modern art. Artists have played a considerable role in popular conceptions of the Riviera, and their presence is reflected in the number of art museums: the Musée Picasso at Antibes, the Musée Renoir and the Musée d'Art Moderne Mediterranée at Cagnes-sur-Mer, and the Musée Jean Cocteau near the harbor at Menton. Wining and dining are special treats on the Riviera; bouillabaisse, a spicy fish stew, is the most popular regional specialty.

The tiny principality of Monaco, which lies between Nice and Menton, is included in this section despite the fact that it is a sovereign state. Although Monaco has its own army and police force, its language, food, and way of life are French.

Getting Around

By Car

Expressway A8 is the only way to get around the Riviera quickly. For the drama of mountains and sea, take one of the famous Corniche roads, which traverse the coastline at various heights over the Mediterranean.

By Train

The train line follows the coast from Marseille to the Italian border, providing excellent access to the seaside resorts. You have to take local buses (marked GARE ROUTIÈRE) or guided tours to visit Grasse and the perched villages.

Guided Tours

SNCF runs many organized tours (contact the Nice Tourist Office) to areas otherwise hard to reach: St-Paul-de-Vence, Upper Provence, and the Verdon Gorges. Boats operate from Nice to Marseille; from St-Tropez to the charming Hyères Islands; and from Antibes, Cannes, and Juan-les-Pins to the Lérins Islands.

The Riviera

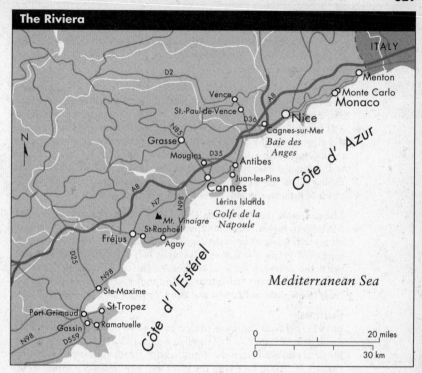

Visitor Information

Antibes (✉ 11 pl. Général-de-Gaulle, ☎ 04–92–90–53–00).
Cagnes-sur-Mer (✉ 6 blvd. du Mal-Juin, ☎ 04–93–20–61–64).
Cannes (✉ Palais des Festivals La Croisette, ☎ 04–93–39–24–53).
Fréjus (✉ 325 rue Jean-Jaurès, ☎ 04–94–17–19–19).
Grasse (✉ 22 cours Honoré-Cresp, ☎ 04–93–36–03–56).
Juan-les-Pins (✉ 51 blvd. Charles-Guillaumont, ☎ 04–93–61–04–98).
Menton (✉ Palais de l'Europe, Av. Boyer, ☎ 04–93–57–57–00).
Monaco (✉ 2a blvd. des Moulins, ☎ 04–92–16–61–16).
Nice (✉ av. Thiers, ☎ 04–93–87–07–07; 5 av. Gustave-V, ☎ 01–93876060).
St-Paul-de-Vence (✉ Maison Tour, rue Grande, ☎ 04–93–32–86–95).
St-Tropez (✉ quai Jean-Jaurès, ☎ 04–94–97–45–21).
Vence (✉ pl. du Grand-Jardin, ☎ 04–93–58–06–38).

Exploring the Riviera

St-Tropez

★ **St-Tropez** was just another pretty fishing village until it was "discovered" in the 1950s by the "beautiful people," a fast set of film stars, starlets, and others who scorned bourgeois values while enjoying bourgeois bank balances. Today, its summer population swells from 6,000 to 60,000, and the top hotels and nightclubs are jammed. In the winter, it's hard to find a restaurant open. The best times to visit, therefore, are early summer or fall. May and June are perhaps the best months, when the town lets its hair down during two local festivals.

The **old port** is the liveliest part of town. You can kill time here on a café terrace, watching the rich and famous on their gleaming yachts. Between the old and new ports is the **Musée de l'Annonciade,** set in a cleverly converted chapel, which houses paintings by artists drawn to St-Tropez between 1890 and 1940, including Signac, Matisse, Derain, and Van Dongen. ✉ *Quai de l'Épi,* ☎ *04–94–97–04–01.* 🔳 *25 frs.* ☉ *June–Sept., Wed.–Mon. 10–noon and 3–7; Oct.–May, Wed.–Mon., 10–noon and 2–6.*

Across the place de l'Hôtel de Ville lies the old town, where twisting streets, designed to break the impact of the terrible mistral (the cold, dry, northerly wind common to this region), open onto tiny squares and fountains. A long climb up to the **citadel** is rewarded by a splendid view across the gulf to **Ste-Maxime,** a quieter, more working-class family resort with a decent beach and reasonably priced hotels. St-Tropez is also a good base for visiting **Port Grimaud,** a pastiche of an Italian fishing village (take D558), and nearby hilltop villages: the old Provençal town of **Ramatuelle** and the fortified village of **Gassin.**

The **Corniche des Issambres** (N98) runs along the coast from Ste-Maxime to **Fréjus,** a Roman town built by Caesar in 49 BC, standing on a rocky plateau between the Maures and Estérel hills. Two main roads link Fréjus and Cannes. Tortuous N7, originally a Roman road, skirts the northern flank of the rugged Estérel hills. Look for an intersection called the "carrefour du Testannier" and follow the signs to **Forêt Domaniale de l'Estérel** and **Mont Vinaigre** for a magnificent view.

Cannes

In 1834, a chance event was to change the town of **Cannes** forever. Lord Brougham, Britain's lord chancellor, was en route to Nice when an outbreak of cholera forced the authorities to freeze all travel. Trapped in Cannes, he fell in love with the place and built himself a house to use as an annual refuge from the British winter. The English aristocracy, czars, kings, and princes soon caught on, and Cannes became a community for the international elite. Grand palace hotels were built to cater to them, and Cannes came to symbolize dignified luxury. Today, Cannes is also synonymous with the **International Film Festival.**

Cannes is ideal for strolling along the seafront on the **Croisette** and tanning on the beaches. Almost all the beaches are private, but that doesn't mean you can't use them, only that you must pay for the privilege. The Croisette offers splendid views of the **Napoule Bay.** Only a few steps inland is the old town, known as the **Suquet,** with its steep, cobbled streets and its 12th-century watchtower.

Grasse is perched in the hills behind Cannes. Take N85 or just follow your nose to the town that claims to be the perfume capital of the world. A good portion of its 40,000 inhabitants work at distilling and extracting scent from the tons of roses, lavender, and jasmine produced here every year. The various perfumers are only too happy to guide visitors around their fragrant establishments. Fragonard is the best known (✉ 20 blvd. Fragonard, ☎ 04–93–36–44–65). The old town is attractive, with its narrow alleys and massive, somber **cathedral.** Three of the paintings inside the cathedral are by Rubens and one is by Fragonard, who lived here for many years.

Take N85 back down to the coast, but fork left at **Mougins,** an attractive fortified hilltop town, famous for one of France's best restaurants, Le Moulin de Mougins (☞ Dining and Lodging, *below*). D35 takes you to **Antibes** and **Juan-les-Pins,** originally two villages that now form one town on the west side of the **Baie des Anges** (Angels' Bay).

Antibes

Antibes, an older village, dates back to the 4th century BC, when it was a Greek trading port. Until recently, the town was renowned throughout Europe for its commercial flower and plant production, today somewhat diminished. Every morning except Monday, the market on the Cours Masséna comes alive with the colors of roses, carnations, anemones, and tulips. The Grimaldis, the family that rules Monaco, built **Château Grimaldi** here in the 12th century on the remains of a Roman camp. Today, the château's main attraction is the **Musée Picasso,** a bounty of paintings, ceramics, and lithographs inspired by the sea and Greek mythology. ⊠ *Pl. du Château,* ☎ *04–92–90–54–20.* ▣ *25 frs.* ⊙ *Dec.–Oct., Wed.–Mon., 10–noon and 2–6.*

Nice

With a population of 350,000, its own university, a new congress hall, and a nearby science park, Nice is the undisputed capital of the Riviera. Founded by the Greeks as Nikaia, it has lived through several civilizations and was attached to France only in 1860. It consequently boasts a profusion of Greek, Italian, British, and French styles. Tourism may not be the main business of Nice, but it is a deservedly popular center. There is an eclectic mixture of old and new architecture, an opera house, museums, flourishing markets, and regular concerts and festivals, including the Mardi Gras festival and the Battle of Flowers.

Numbers in the margin correspond to points of interest on the Nice map.

❶ The **place Masséna** is the logical starting point for an exploration of Nice. This fine square was built in 1815 to celebrate a local hero: one of Napoléon's most successful generals. Just west of it are the foun-
❷ tains and gardens of the **Jardin Albert I**ᵉʳ**.** A short stroll brings you to
❸ the **Promenade des Anglais,** built by the English community here in 1824. The promenade is very busy, but it's a pleasant strand between town and sea with fine views of the Baie des Anges.

❹ Just up rue de Rivoli is the **Palais Masséna,** a museum concerned with the Napoleonic era. ⊠ *65 rue de France,* ☎ *04–93–88–11–34.* ▣ *30 frs.* ⊙ *Dec.–Oct., Tues.–Sun., 10–noon and 2–5 (3–6 May–Sept.).*

Further west, along rue de France, and right up avenue des Baumettes
❺ is the **Musée des Beaux-Arts Jules-Chéret,** Nice's fine arts museum, built in 1878 as a palatial mansion for a Russian princess. The rich collection has works by Renoir, Degas, Monet; Oriental prints; sculptures by Rodin; and ceramics by Picasso. ⊠ *33 av. des Baumettes,* ☎ *04–93–44–50–72.* ▣ *30 frs.* ⊙ *May–Sept., Tues.–Sun., 10–noon and 3–6; Oct.–April, Tues.–Sun., 10–noon and 2–5.*

The Cours Saleya flower market and the narrow streets in the old town
★ ❻ are the prettiest parts of Nice: Take the rue de l'Opéra to see **St-François-**
❼ **de-Paule** church (1750) and the **opera house.** At the northern extremity of the old town lies the vast place Garibaldi—all yellow-ocher buildings and formal fountains. Nearby, along the boulevard Jean-Jau-
❽ rès, is the **Musée d'Art Contemporain,** with an outstanding collection of French and international abstract and figurative art from the late 1950s onward: Martial Ryasse, Yves Klein, Frank Stella, and pop-art popes such as Rauschenberg and Lichtenstein. ⊠ *Promenade des Arts,* ☎ *04–93–62–61–62.* ▣ *Free.* ⊙ *Wed.–Mon. 11–6 (Fri. 11–10).*

❾ The **Musée Chagall** is off the boulevard de Cimiez, near the Roman ruins. The museum houses the Chagall collection, including the 17 huge canvases of *The Message of the Bible,* which took 13 years to complete. ⊠ *Av. du Dr-Ménard,* ☎ *04–93–81–75–75.* ▣ *30 frs.* ⊙ *July–Sept., Wed.–Mon. 10–7; Oct.–June, Wed.–Mon. 10–12 and 2–5:30.*

Nice

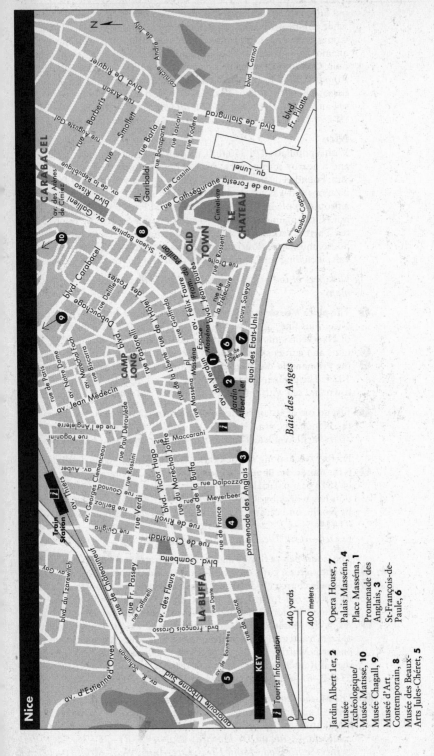

KEY

ⓘ Tourist Information

0   440 yards

0   400 meters

Jardin Albert 1er, **2**
Musée
Archéologique/
Musée Matisse, **10**
Musée Chagall, **9**
Museé d'Art
Contemporain, **8**
Musée des Beaux-
Arts Jules-Chéret, **5**

Opera House, **7**
Palais Masséna, **4**
Place Masséna, **1**
Promenade des
Anglais, **3**
St-François-de-
Paule, **6**

A 17th-century Italian villa amid the Roman remains contains two museums: the **Musée Archéologique,** with a plethora of ancient objects, and the renovated **Musée Matisse,** with paintings and bronzes by Henri Matisse (1869–1954). ⊠ *164 av. des Arènes-de-Cimiez,* ☎ *04–93– 81–08–08. Musée Matisse* 🎫 *30 frs.* ☉ *Apr.–Sept., Wed.–Mon., 11– 7; Oct.–Mar., Wed.–Mon., 10–5. Musée Archéologique,* 🎫 *30 frs.* ☉ *Dec.–Oct., Tues.–Sat. 10–noon and 2–5, Sun. 2–5.*

Monaco

Numbers in the margin correspond to points of interest on the Monaco map.

Sixteen kilometers (10 miles) along the coast from Nice is **Monaco.** For more than a century Monaco's livelihood was centered beneath the copper roof of its splendid **casino.** The oldest section dates from 1878 and was conceived by Charles Garnier, architect of the Paris opera house. It's as elaborately ornate as anyone could wish, bristling with turrets, gold filigree, and masses of interior frescoes and bas-reliefs. The main activity is in the American Room, where beneath the gilt-edged ceiling busloads of tourists feed the one-armed bandits. ⊠ *Pl. du Casino,* ☎ *04–92–16–21–21. Persons under 21 not admitted.* 🎫 *50 frs (American Room free).* ☉ *Daily noon–4 AM. Closed May 1.*

The **Musée National des Automates et Poupées d' Autrefois** (Museum of Antique Dolls and Automatons) has 18th- and 19th-century dolls and mechanical figures, the latter shamelessly showing off their complex inner workings. It's magically set in a 19th-century seaside villa (designed by Garnier). ⊠ *17 av. Princesse-Grace,* ☎ *04–93–30–91– 26.* 🎫 *30 frs.* ☉ *Daily 10–12:15 and 2:30–6:30.*

Monaco Town, the principality's old quarter, has many vaulted passageways and exudes an almost tangible medieval feel. The magnificent **Palais du Prince** (Prince's Palace), a grandiose Italianate structure with a Moorish tower, was largely rebuilt in the last century. Here, since 1297, the Grimaldi dynasty has lived and ruled. The spectacle of the **Changing of the Guard** occurs each morning at 11:55; inside, guided tours take visitors through the state apartments and a wing containing the **Palace Archives** and **Musée Napoléon** (Napoleonic Museum). ⊠ *Pl. du Palais,* ☎ *04–93–25–18–31. Palace:* 🎫 *40 frs.* ☉ *June–Oct., daily 9:30–12:30 and 2–6:30. Musée Napoléon and Palace Archives:* 🎫 *30 frs.* ☉ *Tues.–Sun. 9:30–6:30.*

Monaco's **cathedral** (⊠ 4 rue Colonel Bellando de Castro) is a late-19th-century neo-Romanesque confection in which Philadelphia-born Princess Grace lies entombed in splendor along with past members of the Grimaldi dynasty.

Next to the **St-Martin Gardens**—which contain an evocative bronze monument in memory of Prince Albert I (Prince Rainier's great-grandfather, the one in the sou'wester and flying oilskins, benignly guiding a ship's wheel)—is the **Musée Océanographique** (Oceanography Museum and Aquarium). This museum is also an internationally renowned research institute founded by the very Prince Albert who is remembered outside as an eminent marine biologist; the well-known underwater explorer Jacques Cousteau is the present director. The aquarium is the undisputed highlight, however, where a collection of the world's fish and crustacea—some colorful, some drab, some the stuff of nightmares— live out their lives in public. ⊠ *Av. St-Martin,* ☎ *04–93–15–36–00.* 🎫 *70 frs.* ☉ *Sept.–Oct. and May–June, daily 9:30–7; Nov.–Apr., daily 9:30–6; July and Aug., daily 9–8.*

Monaco

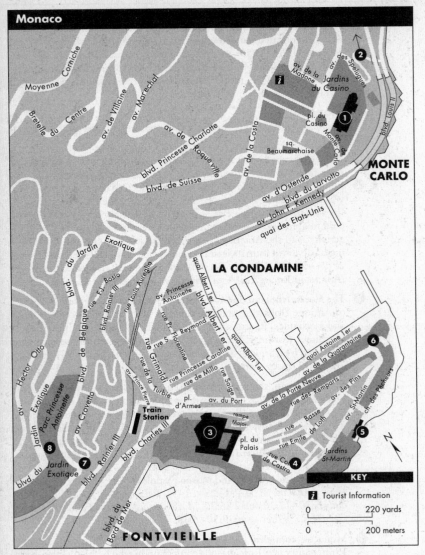

Casino, **1**

Cathedral, **4**

Fort Antoine
Theater, **6**

Jardin Exotique, **7**

Musée National des
Automates et Poupées
d'Autrefois, **2**

Musée
Océanographique, **5**

Museum of Prehistoric Anthropology, **8**

Palais du Prince, **3**

6 Before heading back inland, take a stroll to the eastern tip of the rock, to the **Fort Antoine Theater** (⊠ av. de la Quarantaine, ☎ 04–93–30–19–21), a converted 18th-century fortress that is covered in ivy and flowering myrtle and thyme. In summer, this is an open-air theater that seats 350.

7 The Moneghetti area is the setting for the **Jardin Exotique** (Garden of Exotic Plants), where 600 varieties of cacti and succulents cling to the rock face. Your ticket also allows you to explore the **caves** next to the **8** gardens, and to visit the adjacent **Museum of Prehistoric Anthropology.** ⊠ *Blvd. du Jardin Exotique,* ☎ *04–93–15–80–06.* ⌷ *40 frs.* ⊙ *Mid-May–mid-Sept., daily 9–7; mid-Sept.–mid-May, daily 9–6. Closed 19 Nov. and 25 Dec.*

Menton

Menton once also belonged to the Grimaldis and, like Nice, became part of France only in 1860. Because of its popularity among British visitors, the western side of the town was developed at the turn of the century to cater to the influx of the rich and famous, with spacious avenues, first-class hotels, and the inevitable casino. The eastern side of town long remained the domain of the local fishermen but has been developed to cater to the needs of tourists. A large marina was built and the **Sablettes,** once a tiny beach, has been artificially extended.

Down by the harbor stands a small 17th-century fort, where Jean Cocteau, the artist, writer, and filmmaker, once worked. It now houses the **Musée Jean Cocteau,** with a collection of his work. ⊠ *111 quai Napoléon,* ☎ *04–93–57–72–30.* ⌷ *Free.* ⊙ *Apr.–Oct., Wed.–Sun. 10–noon and 2–6; Nov.–Mar., Wed.–Sun. 10–noon and 3–6.*

Dining and Lodging

For details and price category definitions, *see* Dining *and* Lodging *in* Staying in France, *above.*

Antibes

$$ ✕⊞ **Auberge Provençale.** Rooms in this one-time abbey, complete
★ with beams and canopied beds, seem straight out of a romantic Victor Hugo novel. The dining room and the covered garden are decorated with the same impeccable taste. Cuisine includes fine bouillabaisse, fresh seafood, and lamb and duck specialties grilled over wood coals. ⊠ *61 pl. Nationale, 06600.* ☎ *04–93–34–13–24,* ℻ *04–93–34–89–88. 6 rooms with bath. AE, DC, MC, V. Restaurant (closed Mon., no lunch Tues.).*

Cagnes

$$$ ✕⊞ **Le Cagnard.** This hotel and restaurant occupies a 14th-century building once part of the ramparts of a medieval fortress. The restaurant—formerly the Grimaldi Château Guards Room—is a lovely beamed and vaulted space with an immense fireplace. The hotel has several suites in two houses in the garden and a third up the road. The view of the Cap d'Antibes is memorable. ⊠ *Haut-de-Cagnes, rue Pontis Long, 06800.* ☎ *04–93–20–73–22,* ℻ *04–93–22–06–39. 19 rooms and suites with bath. Restaurant (closed Nov.–mid-Dec., no lunch Thurs.). AE, DC, MC, V.*

Cannes

$$$ ✕ **Mirabelle.** For many, this is a favorite restaurant in the Suquet. The cuisine is inventive, the sauces light, and the desserts special. ⊠ *24 rue St-Antoine,* ☎ *04–93–38–72–75. MC, V. Closed Tues., 2nd half Feb., and Dec. 1–20.*

$$ ★ ✕ **Au Bec Fin.** This busy family-run bistro, always crowded with a boisterous crowd of ecstatic diners, is clearly *the* spot to dine in Cannes year round. Do not miss the fish soup *allioli.* ✉ *12 rue du 24–Août,* ☎ *04–93–38–35–86. AE, DC, MC, V. Closed Sat. dinner, Sun., and Dec. 20–Jan.*

$$$ ✕ 🏨 **Majestic.** Unlike most luxury hotels lining the La Croisette promenade, the Majestic has a less blatantly luxurious charm. Rooms are spacious and traditional, but refreshingly decorated in pastels. The restaurant offers a reasonably priced evening meal in winter. ✉ *14 La Croisette, 06400,* ☎ *04–92–98–77–00,* FAX *04–93–38–97–90. 283 rooms with bath. Air-conditioning, pool, golf, tennis court, horseback riding, beach. AE, DC, MC, V. Closed Nov.–mid-Dec.*

$–$$ 🏨 **Beverly.** The Beverly (formerly the Bristol) offers a wallet-friendly contrast to the big names nearby on La Croisette. Prices start at around 180 francs, but are higher for one of the 10 (quieter) rooms with a balcony at the back of the building. The beach, train station, and Palais des Festivals are within a three-minute walk. ✉ *14 rue Hoche, 06400,* ☎ *04–93–39–10–66,* FAX *04–92–98–65–63. 19 rooms, 15 with bath or shower. AE, MC, V. Closed Dec.–mid-Jan.*

$–$$ 🏨 **Touring Hotel.** This simple but elegant little hotel is five minutes from the beach. It manages to retain a distinct traditional flavor thanks to its floor-to-ceiling windows and small balconies overlooking red-tiled rooftops. ✉ *11 rue Hoche, 06400.* ☎ *04–93–38–34–40;* FAX *04–93–38–7–34. 30 rooms with bath. AE, MC, DC, V.*

Grasse

$$ 🏨 **Panorama.** Most rooms have excellent views of the Massif de l'Estérel and Cannes (thus the name) in this modern, well-run hotel. There's ample parking, too. ✉ *2 pl. du Cours, 06130,* ☎ *04–93–36–80–80,* FAX *04–93–36–92–04. 36 rooms with bath. MC, V.*

Menton

$$ 🏨 **Princesse et Richmond.** This classic hotel on the promenade is an excellent standby. It's nothing fancy, but rooms are sunny and cheery; most have terraces looking out on the sea. As a peaceful alternative to the often jam-packed beach, you can enjoy the roof-top terrace on the eighth floor, complete with a whirlpool bath. ✉ *617 prom. du Soleil, 06500,* ☎ *04–93–35–80–20,* FAX *04–93–57–40–20. 44 rooms with bath. Breakfast room. AE, DC, MC, V. Closed Nov.–early Dec.*

Monaco

$$$$ ★ ✕ **Louis XV.** A strong contender for the best-in-Monaco award, Louis XV's opulent decor and chef Alain Ducasse's beautifully conceived dishes, such as ravioli with foie gras and truffles, contribute to the formal atmosphere. ✉ *Hôtel de Paris, pl. du Casino,* ☎ *04–92–16–30–01.* FAX *04–92–16–69–21. Reservations essential. AE, DC, MC, V.*

$$–$$$ ✕ **Port.** Harbor views from the terrace and top-notch Italian food make Port a good choice. A large, varied menu includes shrimp, pasta, fish risotto, and veal with ham and cheese. ✉ *Quai Albert Ier,* ☎ *04–93–50–77–21. AE, DC, MC, V. Closed Mon. and Nov.*

$$$$ ★ 🏨 **Hôtel de Paris.** At this exceptional establishment, elegance, luxury, dignity, and old-world charm are the watchwords. Built in 1864, it still exudes the gold-plated splendor of an era when kings and grand dukes stayed here. ✉ *Pl. du Casino, 98000,* ☎ *04–92–16–30–00,* FAX *04–93–15–90–03. 245 rooms with bath. 2 restaurants, bar, pool, tennis court, health club, shops. AE, DC, MC, V.*

$$ ⊡ **Balmoral.** Despite the name, there's nothing even vaguely Scottish about this somewhat old-fashioned hotel overlooking the harbor. Rooms are reasonably sized, if bland; many have balconies. ⊠ *12 av. de la Costa, 98000,* ☎ *04–93–50–62–37,* FAX *04–93–15–08–69. 75 rooms with bath or shower, half with air-conditioning. Restaurant (closed Nov.). AE, DC, MC, V.*

Mougins

$$$$ ✕⊡ **Le Moulin de Mougins.** Roger Vergé has created one of France's finest restaurants in a converted mill a short distance west of Mougins along D3. The cuisine ranges from seemingly simple salads to rich, complicated sauces for lobster, salmon, or turbot. The atmosphere is surprisingly informal. There are five elegantly rustic guest rooms as well. ⊠ *Quartier Notre-Dame-de-Vie, 424 Chemin du Moulin, 06250,* ☎ *04–93–75–78–24,* FAX *04–93–90–18–55. Restaurant (Reservations essential; AE, DC, MC, V; closed Thurs. lunch and Mon.). Hotel and restaurant closed Feb.–Mar.*

Nice

$$$ ✕ **Ane-Rouge.** Popular with locals, this tiny, family-run restaurant has been *the* place for Nice's best fish and seafood for generations. ⊠ *7 quai des Deux-Emmanuel,* ☎ *04–93–89–49–63. MC, V. Closed weekends, mid-July–end of Aug.*

$$ ✕ **La Mérenda.** For some of the finest local cooking Nice has to offer, this tiny gem is worth squeezing into. Although rumors suggest that chef Jean Giusti may retire, they also indicate that a like-minded successor is waiting in the wings. Everything on the menu is good. Try the stockfish or the *boeuf en daube.* ⊠ *4 rue de la Terrasse. No telephone. No credit cards. Closed Sat.–Mon., Feb. and Aug.*

$$$$ ✕⊡ **Négresco.** Opened in 1912, the Négresco is officially listed as a ★ historic monument and is a byword for old-world elegance. The public rooms have antique coffered ceilings and magnificent fireplaces. No two bedrooms are alike, but they all have antique furniture and paintings. The main restaurant, Le Chantecler, is without doubt the best in Nice. ⊠ *37 promenade des Anglais, 06000,* ☎ *04–93–16–64–00,* FAX *04–93–88–35–68. 148 rooms with bath. 2 restaurants (reservations essential, closed mid-Nov.–mid-Dec.). AE, DC, MC, V.*

St-Tropez

$$$$ ✕⊡ **Byblos.** This hotel is unique. Its luxury rooms and suites are built around tiled courtyards, fragrant with magnolia and orange trees, like a miniature Provençal village. Each one is differently decorated with amusing touches and subtle lighting. Les Caves du Roy, one of two nightclubs, and Les Arcades, a restaurant run by Philipe Audibert, are considered among the best in town. ⊠ *Av. Paul Signac, 83990,* ☎ *04–94–56–68–00,* FAX *04–94–56–68–01. 58 rooms with bath, 48 suites. Restaurant, pool, beauty salon, sauna, exercise room, nightclub. AE, DC, MC, V. Closed mid-Oct.–mid-Mar.*

11 Germany

Munich

Frankfurt

Hamburg

The Rhine

The Black Forest

Berlin

Saxony and Thuringia

AREUNITED GERMANY OFFERS THE TRAVELER a unique experience. Today one country exists where there used to be two, and although the 40-year division was an artificial one, the differences that developed will take many years to even out. Technically, Germany is already one country: the same language, the same currency, the same federal political structure. But some of the differences can be quirky.

Rapid reunification—critics said it was too hasty—has had a damaging effect on the German economy, which had previously been unaffected by the recession in other parts of the Western world. The bid to quickly rejuvenate former East Germany and provide its 17 million inhabitants with better standards of living has so far proved difficult, while costing western German taxpayers billions of Deutschmarks. By the end of 1992, the effects of reunification had virtually stopped the great German economic locomotive, resulting in higher prices and the threat of higher taxes—and causing much grumbling in the west. Inflation had been cut to less than 2% by 1996, but there had been a parallel drop in the country's growth rate. Germany is again in recession, with little hope of improvement by 1997.

In the eastern part of the country, Germans still earn less than their fellow countrymen in the west. But many basic costs of living are lower. Overall, eastern German shops are less numerous and elegant, but they are filled with the sort of material goods that were unobtainable under the Communist regime.

Eastern Germany's emergence from communism has not so much inspired a new sense of nationhood as it has revived regional traditions and identities. The villages south of Leipzig and Dresden have more in common with their neighbors in northern Bavaria, from whom they were cut off for four decades, than with Berlin bureaucrats.

Germans tend to rise very early; they may be found hammering away at a building site by 7 AM or seated at an office desk by 8 AM, but they take their leisure time just as seriously. Annual vacations of up to six weeks are the norm, and secular and religious festivals occupy at least another 12 days. Every town and village, and many city neighborhoods, manages at least one "Fest" a year, when the beer barrels are rolled out and sausages are thrown on the grill. The seasons have their own festivities: Fasching (carnival) heralds the end of winter, countless beer gardens open up with the first warm rays of sunshine; fall is celebrated with the Munich Oktoberfest; and Advent brings Christkindlmärkte, colorful pre-Christmas markets held in town and city squares.

The great outdoors has always been an important escape hatch for Germans. A Bavarian mountain inn, the glow of its lights reflected on the blanket of snow outside, may be only a short drive from Munich. The busy industrial city of Stuttgart lies at the gateway to the Schwarzwald (Black Forest), the popular region of spas, hiking trails, and tempting cake. Berlin is surrounded by its own lakes and green parklands.

The transportation system that links these various regions is a godsend to the visitor. German trains are fast, clean, and punctual; a drive on a speed limit–free autobahn will give you an idea of just how fast all those BMW and Mercedes sports cars are meant to go.

ESSENTIAL INFORMATION

Before You Go

When to Go

The main tourist season in Germany runs from May to late October, when the weather is best. In addition to many tourist events, there are hundreds of folk festivals during this period. Winter-sports season in the Bavarian Alps runs from Christmas to mid-March. Prices are generally higher in summer, so you may find considerable advantages in visiting off season. Most resorts have *Zwischensaison* (between season) and *Nebensaison* (edge-of-season) rates, and tourist offices can provide lists of hotels offering *Pauschalangebote* (special low-price inclusive weekly packages). Similarly, many winter resorts lower their rates for the periods immediately before and after the Christmas and New Year high season (*weisse Wochen*, or "white weeks"). On the other hand, the colder months are often marred by gloomy weather, and, except at ski resorts and in the larger cities, many attractions are closed.

CLIMATE

Germany's climate is generally temperate. Winters vary from mild and damp to very cold and bright. Summers are usually sunny and warm, though you should be prepared for a few cloudy and wet days. In Alpine regions, spring often comes late, with snow flurries well into April. Fall is sometimes spectacular in the south: warm and soothing. Only in southern Bavaria (Bayern) will you find strikingly variable weather, which is caused by the *Föhn*, a warm Alpine wind that brings sudden barometric changes and gives rise to clear but oppressive conditions in summer and causes snow to disappear overnight in winter.

The following are the average daily maximum and minimum temperatures for Munich.

Jan.	35F	1C	May	64F	18C	Sept.	67F	20C
	23	− 5		45	7		48	9
Feb.	38F	3C	June	70F	21C	Oct.	56F	13C
	23	− 5		51	11		40	4
Mar.	48F	9C	July	74F	23C	Nov.	44F	7C
	30	− 1		55	13		33	0
Apr.	56F	14C	Aug.	73F	23C	Dec.	36F	2C
	38	3		54	12		26	− 3

Currency

The unit of currency in Germany is the Deutschmark, written DM and generally referred to as the mark. It is divided into 100 pfennige. There are bills of 5 (rare), 10, 20, 50, 100, 200, 500, and 1,000 marks and coins of 1, 2, 5, 10, and 50 pfennige and 1, 2, and 5 marks. At press time (spring 1996), the mark stood strong at DM 1.34 to the U.S. dollar, DM 1.01 to the Canadian dollar, and DM 2.19 to the pound sterling.

The Deutschmark is legal tender throughout Germany. The cost of living is still somewhat lower in the former German Democratic Republic (DDR), and some of these lower costs benefit tourists. But a growing number of places that cater specifically to visitors are now charging Western rates.

Major credit cards are widely, though not universally, accepted in Germany. Most hotels, many restaurants, the most popular car-rental agencies, Lufthansa, and the Deutsche Bahn (the German railway company) accept credit cards. All department stores and a growing number of smaller shops also honor them, but don't be surprised if you are offered a discount for cash.

What It Will Cost

Inflation has crept up in the 1990s (although at press time, the annual rate of inflation was around 2%). The most expensive areas to visit are the major cities, notably Berlin, Frankfurt, Hamburg, and Munich.

SAMPLE PRICES
Cup of coffee in a café, DM 3.50, in a stand-up snack bar DM 1.80; mug of beer in a beer hall, DM 4.50, a bottle of beer from a supermarket, DM 1.50; soft drink, DM 2; ham sandwich, DM 4; 2-mile taxi ride, DM 13.

Visas

To enter Germany, only passports are required of visitors from the United States, Canada, and the United Kingdom, although U.S. citizens must obtain a visa if they plan to stay longer than three months.

Customs

The establishment in 1993 of a single, unrestricted market within the European Union (EU) means that there no longer are any restrictions on importing items duty-free for citizens of the 12 member countries.

If you are entering Germany as a citizen of a country that does not belong to the EU, you may import duty-free: (1) 200 cigarettes, or 50 cigars, or 250 grams of tobacco; plus (2) 1 liter of spirits more than 22% proof or 2 liters of spirits less than 22% proof, and 2 liters of still wine; plus (3) 50 grams of perfume and ¼ liter of toilet water; plus (4) other goods with a total value of up to DM 115.

Tobacco and alcohol allowances are for visitors ages 17 and over. Other items intended for personal use may be imported and exported freely. There are no restrictions on the import and export of German currency.

Language

English has long been taught in high schools in the western part of Germany. Consequently, many people under age 40 speak some English, although the level of understanding varies considerably. Older people in rural areas are less familiar with English, but a substantial number have retained some basic words of communication from the immediate postwar years when American and British forces occupied the country.

For a visitor attempting to practice his or her German, the country's many dialects pose the biggest problem. Probably the most difficult to comprehend is Bavaria's, which is like another language. Nonetheless, except for older people in remote, rural districts, virtually everyone can also speak *Hochdeutsch,* the German equivalent of Oxford English. Hochdeutsch is always used on TV and radio.

Getting Around

By Car
ROAD CONDITIONS
The autobahn system in western Germany is of the highest standard. These roads are marked either A (on blue signs), meaning inter-German highways, or E (on green signs), meaning they form part of the Europe-wide *Europastrasse* network. All autobahns are toll-free. Local roads are called *Bundesstrassen* and are marked by their number on a yellow sign. All local roads are single lane and slower than autobahns. In eastern Germany many roads have been repaired and new autobahns are being added.

Germany

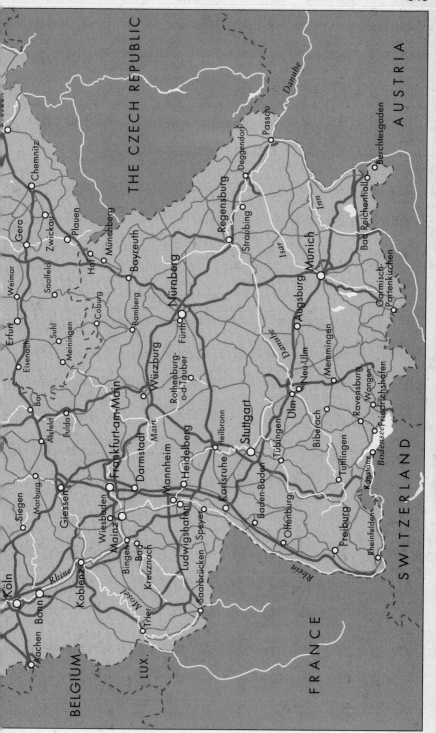

Officially, there's no speed limit on autobahns, although you'll find signs recommending that motorists stay below 130 kph (80 mph). You'll also find blue signs on autobahns stating the recommended minimum speed on that stretch. Germans are fast drivers, and autobahn speeds of more than 160 kph (100 mph) are common. Unless you're driving at that speed, stay in the right-hand lane on autobahns, using the faster-paced left-hand lanes only for passing. There are speed limits on other roads—100 kph (60 mph) on Bundesstrassen, 80 kph (50 mph) on country roads, between 30 kph (18 mph) and 60 kph (36 mph) in built-up urban areas. Fines for exceeding the speed limit can be heavy. Penalties for driving under the influence of alcohol are even more severe, so make sure to keep within the legal limit—equivalent to the consumption of two small beers or a glass of wine.

PARKING

Daytime parking in cities is very difficult. If you can find a parking lot, use it or you'll risk having your car towed. Parking restrictions are not always clearly marked and can be hard to understand when they are. At night, parking-meter spaces are free.

GASOLINE

Leaded and unleaded gas and diesel are generally available all over Germany. At press time (spring 1996), the price of a liter of gas ranged from DM 1.10 to DM 1.65, depending on the grade.

BREAKDOWNS

The **ADAC,** the major German automobile organization, gives free help and advice to tourists, though you have to pay for any spare parts and labor you need. All autobahns have regularly spaced telephones with which you can call for help. The contact address for the ADAC is Am Westpark 8, D-81373 Munich (☎ 089/76760).

By Train

The German railway system is being privatized, so routes and timetables may still change in some areas. The two separate rail networks of the former East and West Germany merged in 1994 into one entity known as **Deutsche Bahn** (DB), or German Rail, bringing Berlin and the cities of the old DDR much closer to the main railheads of the west.

InterCity (IC) and EuroCity services were improved and expanded, and the regional InterRegio network was extended nationwide. Train travel times were reduced so dramatically that journeys between many cities—Munich–Frankfurt, for example—can be completed faster by rail than by plane. All overnight InterCity services and the slower D-class trains have sleepers, with a first-class service that includes breakfast in bed. All InterCity and InterCity Express trains have restaurant cars, and the Hamburg–Berchtesgaden service has introduced an onboard McDonald's as an experiment. A DM 6 surcharge is added to the one-way ticket price on all InterCity and EuroCity journeys irrespective of distance (DM 8 if you pay on board instead of at the ticket office), while InterCity Express fares are about 20% more expensive than normal ones. Seat reservations (highly advisable on InterCity, EuroCity, and InterCity Express trains) cost DM 3. Bikes cannot be transported on InterCity Express services, but InterCity, EuroCity, and most D-class trains have onboard storage, and InterRegio trains even have compartments where cyclists can travel next to their bikes.

FARES

The **German Rail Pass,** not available to Germans, allows travel over the entire German rail network for 5, 10, or 15 days within a single month. It can be purchased for first- or second-class travel. A **Twin Pass** discounts these rates for two people traveling together. A **Youth Pass,** sold to those age 12–25, is for second-class travel. These passes are also valid on all buses operated by the Deutsche Bahn, as well as on tour routes along the Romantic and Castle roads served by **Deutsche Touring Gesellschaft** (DTG, ✉ Am Römerhof 17, D-60486 Frankfurt/Main, ☎ 069/79030) and Rhine, Main, and Mosel river cruises operated by the **Köln-Düsseldorfer (KD) German Rhine Line** (☞ *By Boat, below*). Passes are sold by travel agents and DER Tours (✉ Box 1606, Des Plaines, IL 60017, ☎ 800/782–2424) in the U.S. and by Deutsche Bahn in Germany.

In 1995 a new and more comprehensive version of the popular **Inter Rail** ticket became available. It's complicated, but there are big savings for young travelers (26 years old or younger) touring just one area of Europe. Young travelers intending to tour only Germany can get an even better deal with a **Euro Domino** ticket, but you must purchase the ticket outside of Germany and in local currency. No age limit is linked to other special deals, such as the **Sparpreis** and **ICE-Super Sparpreis** which offer big savings on return journeys made on off-peak days.

Travelers under 26 who do not have a rail pass should inquire about discount travel fares available under the **Billet International Jeune** (BIJ) scheme. The special one-trip tariff (also known as a **twen-tickets** fare) is offered by EuroTrain International, which has offices in 22 European cities. You can buy a EuroTrain ticket at one of these offices or at travel agencies, mainline rail stations, and youth-travel operators.

One tip: There is very little difference in comfort between first- and second-class compartments in the newer InterCity trains and all InterCity Express trains but there's a big difference in fares.

By Bus

Long-distance bus services in Germany are part of the Europe-wide Europabus network. Services are neither as frequent nor as comprehensive as those on the rail system, so make reservations. Be careful in selecting the service you travel on: All Europabus services have a bilingual hostess and offer small luxuries that you won't find on the more basic, though still comfortable, regular services. For details and reservations, contact DTG (☞ *By Train, above*). Reservations can also be made at any of the Deutsche Touring offices in Cologne, Hannover, Hamburg, Munich, Nürnberg, and Wuppertal, and at travel agents.

Rural bus services are operated by local municipalities and some private firms, as well as by Deutsche Bahn and the post office. Services are variable, however, even when there is no other means to reach your destination by public transportation.

By Plane

Germany's national airline, **Lufthansa** (in the U.S., ☎ 800/645–3880; in Great Britain ☎ 0171/495–2044; in Germany ☎ 068/6907–1222), serves all major cities. **LTU International Airways** (in the U.S., ☎ 800/546–7334; in Germany, ☎ 0211/941–8888) has connections between Düsseldorf and Munich and between Frankfurt and Munich. Regular fares are high, but you can save up to 40% with *Flieg und Spar* (fly-and-save) specials; several restrictions apply, such as a DM 100 penalty for changing flights. A British Airways subsidiary, **Deutsche BA** (based at Munich's Franz Josef Strauss Airport, ☎ 089/9759–1500), competes with Lufthansa on many domestic routes, including those between Berlin and Munich and Köln/Bonn and Düsseldorf.

By Boat

For a country with such a small coastline, Germany is a surprisingly nautical nation: You can cruise rivers and lakes throughout the country. The biggest fleet belongs to the Cologne-based KD line. It operates services on the Rivers Rhine, Mosel, Elbe, and Main. For details, contact **KD River Cruises of Europe** (Rhine Cruise Agency, ✉ 2500 Westchester Ave., Purchase, NY 10577, ☎ 914/696–3600) or **KD German Rhine Line** (✉ Frankenwerft 15, D-50667 Köln, ☎ 0221/208–8288).

Services on the 160-kilometer (100-mile) stretch of the Danube (Donau) between the spectacular Kelheim Gorge and Passau on the Austrian border are operated by **Donauschiffahrt Wurm & Köck** (✉ Höllgasse 26, D-94032 Passau, ☎ 0851/929–292). The company has daily summer cruises on the Danube, Inn, and Ilz, which meet at Passau; some two-day cruises into Austria are also offered. The Bodensee (Lake Constance), the largest lake in Germany, located at the meeting point of Germany, Austria, and Switzerland, has up to 40 ships crisscrossing it in summer. **Deutsche Bahn** (✉ Bodensee-Schiffsbetriebe, Hafenstr. 6, D-78462 Konstanz) also has information on cruises. Bavaria's five largest lakes—Ammersee, Chiemsee, Königsee, Tegernsee, and Starnbergersee—have regular summer cruises and excursions. Details are available from local tourist offices.

By Bicycle

Bicycles can be rented at more than 130 train stations throughout Germany from April 1 to October 31. The cost is DM 11 or DM 13 (with gears) per day, DM 7 or DM 9 if you have a valid rail ticket. You can pick up a bike at one station and return it to another, provided both stations rent bikes. Mountain bikes can be rented for DM 20 a day at the Garmisch-Partenkirchen station and three other Alpine stations (Immenstadt, Oberstdorf, and Sonthoten). You will need to buy a *Fahrradkarte,* or bicycle ticket (DM 8.60 per journey), to take your bike on the train; InterCity Express trains do not carry bikes. Full details are given in German Rail's brochure "Radler-Bahn." Most cities also have companies that rent bikes for about DM 15 per day or DM 80–DM 90 a week.

Staying in Germany

Telephones

LOCAL CALLS

Since reunification, all phones in the east and west use the same coins: 10 pf, DM 1, and DM 5 for long-distance calls. A local call from a call-box costs 30 pf and lasts six minutes. Card phones are rapidly replacing coin-operated phones: Cards cost DM 12 or DM 50 (the latter good for DM 60 worth of calls) and can be purchased at all post offices and many exchange places. If you need an operator, dial 010.

INTERNATIONAL CALLS

These can be made from public phones bearing the sign INLANDS UND AUSLANDSGESPRÄCHE. Using DM 5 coins is best for long-distance dialing; a four-minute call to the United States costs DM 15. To avoid weighing yourself down with coins, however, make international calls from post offices; even those in small country towns will have a special booth for international calls. You pay the clerk at the end of your call. To reach an **AT&T** long-distance operator, dial 0130–0010; for **MCI,** dial 0130–0012; for **Sprint,** 0130–0013. Dial 0010 for a local operator who handles international calls.

COUNTRY CODE

Germany's country code is 49.

Mail

Airmail letters to the United States and Canada cost DM 3; postcards cost DM 2. Airmail letters to the United Kingdom cost DM 1; postcards cost 80 pf.

You can arrange to have mail sent to you in care of any German post office; have the envelope marked "Postlagernd." This service is free. Alternatively, if you have an American Express card or have booked a vacation with American Express you can have mail sent to any American Express office in Germany. There's no charge.

Shopping

VAT REFUNDS

German goods carry a 15% value-added tax (VAT). You can claim this back either as you leave the country or once you've returned home. When you make a purchase, ask the shopkeeper for a form known as an *Ausfuhr-Abnehmerbescheinigung*; he or she will help you fill it out. As you leave the country, present the form, plus the goods and receipts, to German customs, which will give you an official export certificate or stamp. In the unlikely event that there's a branch of the Deutsche Bank near customs, you can take the stamped form to it, where you will receive the refund on the spot. Otherwise, send the form back to the shop, and it will send the refund.

Opening and Closing Times

Banks. Times vary from state to state and city to city, but banks are usually open weekdays from 8:30 or 9 to 2 or 3 (5 or 6 on Thursday). Some banks close from 12:30 to 1:30. Branches at airports and main train stations open as early as 6:30 AM and close as late as 10:30 PM.

Museums are generally open Tuesday to Sunday 9–5. Some close for an hour or more at lunch, and some are open on Monday. Many stay open until 9 on Thursday.

Legislation has been proposed recently to allow **shops** to stay open until 8 PM, but the idea has been met by some resistance, especially from the shop workers' unions. The legislation seems likely to pass, however, so by 1997 department stores and larger shops may be open weekdays from 9:30 to 8, and on Saturdays from 9:30 AM to 2 PM.

National Holidays

January 1; January 6 (Epiphany—Bavaria, Baden-Württemberg, and Sachsen-Anhalt only); March 28 (Good Friday); March 31 (Easter Monday); May 1 (Worker's Day); May 8 (Ascension); May 19 (Pentecost Monday); May 29 (Corpus Christi—south Germany only); August 15 (Assumption Day—Bavaria and Saarland only); October 3 (German Unity Day); November 1 (All Saints' Day); December 24–26.

Dining

It's hard to generalize about German food beyond saying that standards are high and portions are large. In fact, the range of dining experiences is vast: everything from highly priced nouvelle cuisine to plenty of sausages. Seek local restaurants if atmosphere and regional specialties are your priority. Beer restaurants in Bavaria, *Apfelwein* (alcoholic apple cider) taverns in Frankfurt, and *Kneipen*—the pubs-cum-local-cafés on the corner—in Berlin nearly always offer the best value and atmosphere. But throughout the country you'll find *Gaststätten, Gasthäuser,* and/or *Gasthöfe*—local inns—where atmosphere and regional specialties are always available. Likewise, just about every town will have a *Ratskeller,* a cellar restaurant in the town hall, where exposed beams, huge fireplaces, sturdy tables, and immense portions are the rule.

The natural accompaniment to German food is either beer or wine. Munich is the beer capital of Germany, though there's no part of the country where you won't find the amber nectar. Say *"Helles"* or *"Export"* if you want light beer; *"Dunkles"* if you want dark beer. In Bavaria, try the sour but refreshing beer brewed from wheat, called *Weissbier*.

Germany is also a major wine-producing country, and much of it is of superlative quality. You will probably be happy with the house wine in most restaurants or with one of those earthenware pitchers of cold Mosel wine. If you want something more expensive, remember that all wines are graded in one of three basic categories: *Tafelwein* (table wine); *Qualitätswein* (fine wine); and *Qualitätswein mit Prädikat* (top-quality wine).

MEALTIMES

Breakfast, served from 6:30 to 10 (in some cafés and Kneipen, until as late as 2 or 4 PM), is often a substantial meal, with cold meats, cheeses, rolls, and fruit. Many city hotels offer Sunday brunch, and the custom is rapidly catching on. Lunch is served from around 11:30 (especially in rural areas) to around 2; dinner is generally from 6 until 9:30, or earlier in some quiet country areas. Big-city hotels and popular restaurants serve later. Lunch tends to be the main meal, a fact reflected in the almost universal appearance of a lunchtime *Tageskarte*, or suggested menu; try it if you want maximum nourishment for minimum outlay.

WHAT TO WEAR

Jacket and tie are advised for restaurants in the $$$$ and $$$ categories. Casual dress is appropriate elsewhere.

RATINGS

Prices are per person and include a first course, main course, dessert, and tip and tax.

The following chart gives price ranges for restaurants in the western part of Germany. Food prices in the territory of former East Germany are still somewhat unstable, although in the bigger cities many of the better-quality restaurants already mimic "western" rates. Generally speaking, the prevailing price structure in the eastern part of the country, except for restaurants in the priciest hotels, falls into the $ to $$$ categories listed below. Bills in simple restaurants in country areas of the eastern region will, however, still come well below DM 35.

CATEGORY	MAJOR CITIES AND RESORTS	OTHER AREAS
$$$$	over DM 100	over DM 90
$$$	DM 75–DM 100	DM 55–DM 90
$$	DM 50–DM 75	DM 35–DM 55
$	under DM 50	under DM 35

Lodging

The standard of German hotels, from top-notch luxury spots (of which the country has more than its fair share) to the humblest pension, is excellent. You can expect courteous service; clean and comfortable rooms; and, in rural areas especially, considerable old-German atmosphere.

In addition to hotels proper, the country has numerous *Gasthöfe* or *Gasthäuser* (country inns); pensions or *Fremdenheime* (guest houses); and, at the lowest end of the scale, *Zimmer*, meaning, quite simply, rooms, normally in private houses. Look for the sign ZIMMER FREI (rooms free) or ZU VERMIETEN (for rent). A red sign reading BESETZT means there are no vacancies.

Lists of hotels are available from the German National Tourist Office
(✉ Beethovenstr. 69, D-60325 Frankfurt/Main 1, ☎ 069/75720), and
from all regional and local tourist offices. Tourist offices will also
make reservations for you—they usually charge a nominal fee—but may
have difficulty doing so after 4 PM in peak season and on weekends.
The German National Tourist Office also operates a reservations service (Allgemeine Deutsche Zimmer-reservierung, ✉ Cornelius-str. 34,
D-60325 Frankfurt/Main, ☎ 069/740–767; ⊙ Mon.–Fri. 9–5), which
is free of charge.

Most hotels have restaurants, but those describing themselves as *Garni*
will provide breakfast only. Many larger hotels offer no-smoking
rooms, and some even offer no-smoking floors, so ask.

Tourist accommodations in eastern Germany are beginning to blossom
under free enterprise. The formerly state-owned Interhotel chain (34
hotels with several thousand rooms) has been dismantled, its components sold individually. The addition of new properties is also moder-
ating the high room rates, which have been the rule in the in the east.
Accommodations remain fairly scarce at the top- and middle-quality
levels. This can't be stressed enough: if you want to stay in good hotels in eastern Germany, book well in advance (Berlin is the notable
exception). Hotel rooms in the cities are in demand year-round because
of the high rate of business travel. Traditional inn accommodations have
become run-down during the past 40 years—still, you may well come
across the odd gem.

ROMANTIK HOTELS

Among the most delightful places to stay and eat in Germany are the
aptly named Romantik Hotels and Restaurants. All are in historic
buildings—this is a precondition of membership—and are personally
run by the owners. The emphasis generally is on solid comfort, good
food, and style. A detailed listing of all Romantik Hotels is available
in the United States for $5 from **Harm Meyer Romantik Hotels** (✉ Box
1278, Woodinville, WA 98072, ☎ 206/486–9394 or 800/826–0015,
reservations only).

CASTLE HOTELS

Gast im Schloss is a similar hotel association, though some of the simpler establishments lack a little in the way of comfort, and furnishings
can be basic. On the whole, they're delightful, with antiques, imposing interiors, and out-of-the-way locations. Prices are mostly moderate. Ask the German National Tourist Office or your travel agent for
the "Gast im Schloss" brochure that lists nearly 60 castle hotels in Germany; they can also advise on a number of good-value packages.

RINGHOTELS

This association groups 130 individually owned and managed hotels
in the medium price range. Many are in the countryside or in pretty
villages. Package deals of 2–3 days are available. Contact **Ringhotels**
(✉ Belfortstr. 8, D-81667 Munich, ☎ 089/448–9206).

RENTALS

Apartments and hotel homes, most accommodating from two to eight
guests, can be rented throughout Germany. Rates are low, with reductions
for longer stays. Charges for gas and electricity, and sometimes water,
are usually added to the bill. Local and regional tourist offices have
lists of apartments in their areas; otherwise contact the German National Tourist Office (☞ *Above*).

FARM VACATIONS

Taking an *Urlaub auf dem Bauernhof,* as the Germans put it, has increased dramatically in popularity over the past four or five years. Almost every regional tourist office has listings of farms, by area, offering bed and breakfast, apartments, or whole farmhouses to rent. Alternatively, contact the **German Agricultural Association** (DLG, ✉ Eschborner Landstr. 122, D–60489 Frankfurt/Main, ☎ 069/247–880). It produces an annual listing of more than 1,500 farms, all of them inspected and graded, that offer accommodations. The brochure costs DM 14.

CAMPING

There are 2,600 campsites in Germany, about 1,600 of which are listed by the **German Camping Club** (DCC, ✉ Mandlstr. 28, D-80802 Munich, ☎ 089/380–1420). The German National Tourist Office also publishes a listing of sites. Most are open from May through October, with about 400 staying open year-round. They tend to become crowded during the summer, so it's always worthwhile to make reservations a day or two ahead. Prices range from DM 15 to DM 20 per night for two adults, a car, and trailer (less for tents).

YOUTH HOSTELS

Germany's *Jugendherberge* (youth hostels) are probably the most efficient and up-to-date in Europe. There are 600 in all, many located in castles, adding a touch of romance to otherwise utilitarian accommodations. There's an age limit of 27 in Bavaria; elsewhere, there are no restrictions, though those under 20 take preference if space is limited. You'll need a Hostelling International (HI) card to stay in a German youth hostel; write **American Youth Hostels Association** (✉ Box 37613, Washington, DC 20013) or **Canadian Hostelling Association** (✉ 333 River Rd., Ottawa, Ontario K1L 8H9). In Great Britain, contact the **Youth Hostels Association** (✉ 22 Southampton St., London WC2). The HI card can also be obtained from the **Deutsches Jugendherbergswerk Hauptverband** (✉ Bismarckstr. 8, D-32754 Detmold, ☎ 05231/74010, or one of their regional offices), which provides a complete list of German hostels for DM 6.50.

Hostels must be reserved well in advance for midsummer, especially in eastern Germany. Bookings for hostels can only be made by calling the hostels directly; telephone numbers are listed in the Deutsches Jugendherbergswerk's listings (☞ *Above*).

RATINGS

Service charges and taxes are included in all quoted room rates. Similarly, breakfast is usually, but not always, included, so check before you book. Major hotels in cities often have lower rates on weekends or in other periods when business is quiet. If you're lucky, you can find reductions of up to 60%. Likewise, rooms reserved after 10 PM will often carry a discount. Although it's worthwhile to ask if your hotel will give you a reduction, don't count on finding rooms at lower rates late at night, especially in the summer. Prices are for two people in a double room.

The following chart is for hotels throughout Germany. In Berlin, hotel price categories are about DM 50 higher than those for major cities indicated below.

CATEGORY	MAJOR CITIES AND RESORTS	OTHER AREAS
$$$$	over DM 300	over DM 200
$$$	DM 200–DM 300	DM 160–DM 200
$$	DM 140–DM 200	DM 100–DM 160
$	under DM 140	under DM 100

Tipping

The Germans are as punctilious about tipping as they are about most facets of life. Overtipping is as frowned upon as not tipping at all. In restaurants, service is included (under the heading *Bedienung,* at the bottom of the check), and it is customary to round out the check to the next Mark or two, a practice also commonplace in cafés, beer halls, and bars. For taxi drivers, also round out to the next mark or two: for DM 11.20, make it DM 12; for DM 11.80, make it DM 13. Railway and airport porters (if you can find any) have their own scale of charges, but round out the requested amount to the next mark. Hotel porters get DM 1 per bag. Doormen are tipped the same amount for small services, such as calling a cab. Room service should be rewarded with at least DM 2 every time you use it. Maids should get about DM 1 per day. Double all these figures at luxury hotels. Service-station attendants get 50 pf or DM 1 for checking oil and tires or cleaning windshields.

MUNICH

Arriving and Departing

By Plane

Munich's Franz Josef Strauss (FJS) Airport, named after a former state premier, opened in 1992. It is 28 kilometers (17½ miles) northeast of the city center.

BETWEEN THE AIRPORT AND DOWNTOWN

The S-8 S-Bahn (suburban train line) links FJS Airport with the city's main train station (Hauptbahnhof). Trains depart in both directions every 20 minutes from 3:55 AM to 12:55 AM daily. Intermediate stops are made at the Ostbahnhof (good for hotels located east of the River Isar) and city-center stations such as Marienplatz. The 38-minute trip costs DM 10.40 if you purchase a multi-use strip ticket (☞ Getting Around, *below*) and use 8 strips; otherwise an ordinary one-way ticket is DM 12.80 per person. A tip for families: Up to five people (maximum of two adults) can travel to or from the airport for only DM 24 by buying a Tageskarte (☞ Getting Around, *below*). This is particularly advantageous if you are arriving in Munich in the morning, because you can continue to use the Tageskarte in the city for the rest of the day. The only restriction is that you cannot use this special day ticket before 9 AM weekdays.

Bus service was reintroduced in 1994, but it's slower and more expensive (DM 15) than the S-Bahn; only use it if you're carrying a great deal of luggage. A taxi will cost between DM 80 and DM 100. If you are driving from the airport into the city, follow the MÜNCHEN autobahn signs to A92 and A9. Once on the A92, watch carefully for the signs to Munich; a relatively high number of motorists miss the sign and end up headed toward Stuttgart!

By Train

All long-distance services arrive at and depart from the main train station, the Hauptbahnhof. Trains to and from destinations in the Bavarian Alps usually use the adjoining Starnbergerbahnhof. For information on train times, call 089/19419. For tickets and information, go to the station or to the ABR travel agency right by the station on Bahnhofplatz.

By Bus

Munich has no central bus station. Long-distance buses arrive at and depart from the north side of the train station on Arnulfstrasse.

By Car

From the north (Nürnberg, Frankfurt), leave the autobahn at the Schwabing exit and follow the STADTMITTE signs. The autobahn from Stuttgart and the west ends at Obermenzing; again, follow the STADT-MITTE signs. The autobahns from Salzburg and the east, from Garmisch and the south, and from Lindau and the southwest all join up with the city beltway, the Mittlerer Ring. The city center is well posted.

Getting Around

Downtown Munich is only about 1 mile square, so it can easily be explored on foot. Other areas—Schwabing, Nymphenburg, the Olympic Park—are best reached on the efficient and comprehensive public transportation network, which incorporates buses, streetcars, U-Bahn (subways), and S-Bahn (suburban trains). Tickets are good for the entire network, and you can break your trip as many times as you like using just one ticket, provided you travel in one direction within a given period of time. If you plan to make only a few trips, buy strip tickets (Streifenkarten)—blue for adults, red for children. An adult ticket of 10 strips costs DM 13; children get the same number for DM 8. For adults, short rides that span up to 4 stations cost 1 strip; trips spanning more than 4 stations cost 2 strips. Children pay 1 strip per ride. All tickets must be validated by time-punching them in the automatic machines at station entrances and on all buses and streetcars. The best buy is the Tageskarte: Up to two adults and three children can use this ticket for unlimited journeys between 9 AM and the end of the day's service (about 2 AM). It costs DM 12 for the inner zone, which covers central Munich. A Tageskarte for the entire system, extending to the Starnbergersee and Ammersee lakes, costs DM 24. Holders of a Eurail Pass, a Youth Pass, an InterRail Card, or a DB Tourist Card travel free on all S-Bahn trains.

By Taxi

Munich's cream-color taxis are numerous. Hail them in the street or call 089/21610 (there's an extra charge for the drive to the pickup point). Rates start at DM 5 and rise by DM 2.20 per kilometer (about DM 4 per mile). There are additional charges of DM 2 if a taxi is ordered by telephone and DM 1 per piece of luggage. Plan to pay about DM 13 for a short trip within the city.

Important Addresses and Numbers

Consulates

U.S. Consulate General (⊠ Königinstr. 5, ☎ 089/28880). **Canadian Consulate** (⊠ Tal 29, ☎ 089/290–650). **U.K. Consulate General** (⊠ Bürkle-instr. 10, ☎ 089/211–090).

Emergencies

Police (☎ 110). **Fire Department and Paramedical Aid** (☎ 112), **Ambulance** and **emergency medical attention** (☎ 089/19222). **Dentist** (☎ 089/723–3093). **Pharmacies: Internationale Ludwigs-Apotheke** (⊠ Neuhauserstr. 11, ☎ 089/260–3021); **Europa-Apotheke** (⊠ Schützen-str. 12, near the Hauptbahnhof, ☎ 089/595–423) ☉ Weekdays 8–6, Sat. 8–1; outside these hours, call 089/594–475.

English-Language Bookstores

The **Anglia English Bookshop** (⊠ Schellingstr. 3, ☎ 089/283–642) has the largest selection of English-language books in Munich. Also try the **Hugendubel** bookshops at Marienplatz and Karlsplatz. A library of English-language books is kept in **Amerika Haus** (⊠ Karolinenpl. 3, ☎ 089/5525–3721).

Travel Agencies
American Express (⊠ Promenadepl. 6, ☎ 089/21990). **ABR**, the official Bavarian travel agency, has outlets all over Munich; ☎ 089/12040 for information.

Visitor Information
The address to write to for information in advance of your visit is **Fremdenverkehrsamt München**, 80310 München. This address also deals with lodging questions and bookings. Two other offices provide on-the-spot advice: at the Hauptbahnhof (☎ 089/233–0300, ☾ Mon.–Sat. 8 AM–10 PM, Sun. and public holidays 11–7) and at the corner of Rindermarkt and Pettenbeckstrasse, behind Marienplatz (☎ 089/233–0300, ☾ Mon.–Thurs. 8:30–4, Fri. 8:30–2).

Guided Tours

Orientation
City bus tours are operated by **Panorama Tours** (⊠ Arnulfstr. 8, ☎ 089/591–504). Tours run daily and take in the city center, the Olympic Park, and Nymphenburg. Departures are at 10 AM and 2:30 PM (and 11:30 AM in midsummer) from outside the Hertie department store across from the train station, and the cost is between DM 15 and DM 27 per person, depending on the duration of the tour.

Walking and Cycling Tours
A walking-tour (cost: DM 10) of central Munich starts daily at 9:30 at the Mariensäule column in the center of the Marienplatz. Bike tours of the city, including bike rentals, are offered through **City Hopper Touren** (☎ 089/272–1131). Charges run from DM 40 per person in a group of two to DM 20 for larger groups. Tours on foot, by bicycle, and by streetcar are organized by **Radius Touristik** (⊠ Arnulfstr. 3, north side of Hauptbahnhof, ☎ 089/596–113).

Excursions
Panorama Tours (⊠ Arnulfstr. 8, ☎ 089/591–504) organizes bus trips to most leading tourist attractions outside the city, including the "Royal Castles Tour" (Schlösserfahrt) of "Mad" King Ludwig's dream palaces. This tour, which takes in Neuschwanstein, costs DM 75.

Exploring Munich

People who live in other parts of Germany sometimes refer to Munich (München in German) as the nation's "secret capital." Flamboyant, easygoing Munich, city of beer and Baroque, is starkly different from the sometimes stiffly Prussian-influenced Berlin; the gritty and industrial Hamburg; or the hard-headed, commercially driven Frankfurt. This is a city to visit for its good-natured and relaxed charm—*Gemütlichkeit,* they call it here.

Munich is a crazy mix of high culture (witness its world-class opera house and art galleries) and wild abandon (witness the vulgar frivolity of the Oktoberfest). Its citizenry seems determined to perpetuate the lifestyle of the 19th-century king Ludwig I, the Bavarian ruler who brought so much international prestige to his home city after declaring: "I want to make out of Munich a town that does such credit to Germany that nobody knows Germany unless he has seen Munich." He kept his promise with an architectural and artistic renaissance—before abdicating because of a wild romance with a half-caste Irish-born dancing girl, Lola Montez (who died in exile in New York).

The Historic Heart

Numbers in the margin correspond to points of interest on the München (Munich) map.

❶ Begin your tour of Munich at the **Hauptbahnhof,** the main train station and an important orientation point. The city tourist office is here, too, ready with information and maps. Cross the street and you're at the start of a kilometer (½ mile) of pedestrian shopping malls, the first being Schützenstrasse. Facing you are **Hertie,** Munich's leading department store, and **Karlsplatz** square, known locally as the "Stachus."

❷ The huge, domed building on your left is the late-19th-century **Justizpalast** (Palace of Justice). It's one of Germany's finest examples of the *Gründerzeit* style, 19th-century versions of medieval and Renaissance architecture.

❸ Head down into the pedestrian underpass—it's another extensive shopping area—to reach the other side and one of the original city gates, the **Karlstor.** The city's two principal shopping streets—**Neuhauserstrasse** and **Kaufingerstrasse**—stretch away from it on the other side. Two of

❹ ❺ the city's major churches are here, too: the **Bürgersaal** and the **Michaelskirche.** The latter is one of the most magnificent Renaissance churches in Germany, a spacious and handsome structure decorated throughout in plain white stucco. It was built for the Jesuits in the late 16th century and is closely modeled on their church (Il Gesù) in Rome. The highly decorated Rococo interior of the Bürgersaal makes a startling contrast with the simplicity of the Michaelskirche. Guided tours of the Michaelskirche are given every Wed. at 2 PM and cost DM 5.

★ ❻ A block past the Michaelskirche to your left is Munich's late-15th-century cathedral, the **Frauenkirche,** or Church of Our Lady. Towering above it are two onion-shape domes, symbols of the city (perhaps because they resemble brimming beer mugs, cynics claim). Step inside and you'll be amazed at the stark simplicity of the church. The crypt houses the tombs of numerous Wittelsbachs, the family that ruled Bavaria for seven centuries until forced to abdicate in 1918.

★ ❼ From the Frauenkirche, walk to the **Marienplatz** square, the heart of the city, surrounded by shops, restaurants, and cafés. It takes its name from the 300-year-old gilded statue of the Virgin in the center. The square

❽ is dominated by the 19th-century **Neues Rathaus,** the New Town Hall,

❾ built in the fussy, turreted style so loved by Ludwig II. The **Altes Rathaus,** or Old Town Hall, a medieval building of great charm, sits, as if forgotten, in a corner of the square. At 9 AM and 11 AM daily (also May–Oct. at 5 PM and 9 PM), the **Glockenspiel,** or chiming clock, in the central tower of the New Town Hall, swings into action. Two tiers of dancing and jousting figures perform their ritual display. It can be worth while to schedule your day to catch the clock. April through October, an elevator whisks visitors to an observation point near the top of one of the towers. On a clear day the view is spectacular. The elevator operates Monday–Saturday 10–5; the fare is DM 2.

NEED A BREAK?
On the western, arcaded side of the square, you'll find one of Munich's oldest hostelries, the **Donisl** (✉ Weinstr. 1, ☎ 089/220–184), whose restaurant is open practically 24 hours daily—an ideal place for morning coffee, a lunchtime beer, afternoon tea, evening supper, or a predawn shake-awake. The menu is basic Bavarian and cheap, and the steaming soups are the best deal in the area.

Heading south along Rosenstrasse to Sendlingerstrasse, you come to
❿ the **Asamkirche** on your right. Some consider the Asamkirche a preposterously overdecorated jewel box; others find it one of Europe's finest

late-Baroque churches. It was built around 1730 by the Asam brothers—Cosmas Damian and Egid Quirin—next door to their home, the Asamhaus. They dedicated it to St. John Nepomuk, a 14th-century. Inside, there is a riot of decoration: frescoes, statuary, rich rosy marbles, billowing clouds of stucco, and gilding everywhere.

★ ⑪ Go back to Marienplatz and turn right for the **Viktualienmarkt,** the open-air food market. Stalls sell cheese, wine, sausages, fruit, and flowers. Fortified with Bavarian sausage and sauerkraut, walk a few blocks north on Dienerstrasse and plunge into local history with a visit
★ ⑫ to the **Residenz,** home of the Wittelsbachs from the 16th century on. From Max-Joseph-Platz you'll enter the great palace, with its glittering Schatzkammer, or treasury, and glorious Rococo theater, designed by court architect François Cuvilliès. Also facing the square is the
⑬ stern Neoclassical portico of the **Nationaltheater,** built at the beginning of the 19th century and twice destroyed. ⊠ *Residenz and Schatzkammer, Max-Joseph-Pl. 3:* 🎫 *To each DM 4.* ☺ *Tues.–Sun. 10–4:30 PM. Cuvilliès Theater:* 🎫 *DM 2.50.* ☺ *Mon.–Sat. 2–5, Sun. 10–5.*

⑭ To the north of the Residenz is the **Hofgarten,** the palace park. Dominating the east side of the Hofgarten is the Bavarian state chancellery.

NEED A BREAK?

Munich's oldest café, the **Annast,** is on Odeonsplatz, right by the west entrance to the Hofgarten. In warm weather, sit at an outside table and watch the bustle of Odeonsplatz or choose a quieter table under the chestnut trees behind the café.

Odeonsplatz itself is dominated by two striking buildings. One is the
⑮ **Theatinerkirche,** built for the Theatine monks in the mid-17th century, though its handsome facade, with twin eye-catching domes, was added only in the following century. Despite its Italian influences, the interior,
⑯ like that of the Michaelskirche, is austerely white. The other notable building here is the **Feldherrnhalle,** built by Ludwig I and modeled on the Loggia dei Lanzi in Florence, and later used by the Nazis as a speakers' rostrum.

The Feldherrnhalle looks north along one of the most imposing boulevards in Europe, the **Ludwigstrasse,** which in turn becomes the **Leopoldstrasse.** The state library and the university are located along it; halfway
⑰ up it is the **Siegestor,** or Arch of Victory, modeled on the Arch of Constantine in Rome. Beyond this is **Schwabing,** once a student and artist quarter but now much glossier, with a mix of bars, discos (☞ Nightlife, *below*), trendy cafés, and boutiques.

Back on Leopoldstrasse, wander down to the university, turn on to Professor-Huber-Platz (he was a Munich academic executed by the Nazis for his support of an anti-Hitler movement), and take Veterinärstrasse
★ ⑱ to Munich's largest park, the magnificent **Englischer Garten.** You can rent a bike (☎ 089/282–500) at the entrance to the park on summer weekends (May–Oct.). The cost is DM 5 per hour and DM 25 for the day.

The Englischer Garten, 4½ kilometers (3 miles) long and more than ½ kilometer (¼ mile) wide, was laid out by Count Rumford, a refugee from the American War of Independence. He was born in England, but it wasn't his English ancestry that determined the park's name as much as its open, informal nature, a style favored by 18th-century English aristocrats. You can rent boats, visit beer gardens—the most famous is at the foot of a Chinese Pagoda—ride your bike (or ski in winter), or simply stroll around. Ludwig II loved to wander incognito along

356

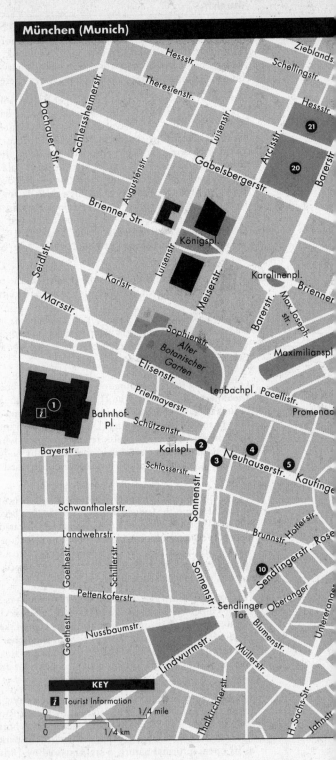

München (Munich)

KEY

_i_ Tourist Information

0 ___ 1/4 mile

0 ___ 1/4 km

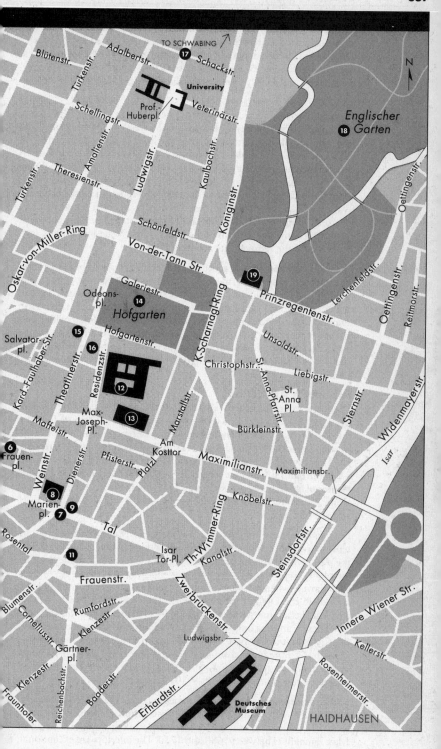

TO SCHWABING

Blütenstr.

Türkenstr.

Adalbertstr.

Schackstr.

Schellingstr.

University

Prof.-Huberpl.

Veterinärstr.

Amalienstr.

Theresienstr.

Ludwigstr.

Kaulbachstr.

Königinstr.

Englischer Garten

Türkenstr.

Oskar-von-Miller-Ring

Schönfeldstr.

Von-der-Tann Str.

Prinzregentenstr.

Lerchenfeldstr.

Oettingenstr.

Reitmorstr.

Galeriestr.

Odeons-pl.

Hofgarten

Hofgartenstr.

K.-Scharnagl-Ring

Unsöldstr.

Salvator-pl.

Kard.-Faulhaber-Str.

Theatinerstr.

Residenzstr.

Christophstr.

St.-Anna-Pfarrstr.

Liebigstr.

St. Anna Pl.

Sternstr.

Widenmayerstr.

Max-Joseph-Pl.

Marstallstr.

Bürkleinstr.

Isar

Maffeistr.

Am Kosttor

Maximilianstr.

Maximiliansbr.

Frauen-pl.

Weinstr.

Dienerstr.

Pfisterstr.

Plazl

Knöbelstr.

Marien-pl.

Tal

Th.-Wimmer-Ring

Kanalstr.

Steinsdorfstr.

Rosental

Isar Tor-Pl.

Frauenstr.

Zweibrückenstr.

Innere Wiener Str.

Blumenstr.

Rumfordstr.

Klenzestr.

Ludwigsbr.

Kellerstr.

Corneliusstr.

Gärtner-pl.

Rosenheimerstr.

Klenzestr.

Reichenbachstr.

Baaderstr.

Erhardtstr.

Deutsches Museum

Fraunhofer

HAIDHAUSEN

⑲ the serpentine paths. A large section of the park right behind the **Haus der Kunst**—Munich's leading modern art gallery and a surviving example of Third Reich architecture—has been designated a nudist area. The building, which underwent major renovations in 1992, also houses one of the city's most exclusive discos, the P1. ⊠ *Haus der Kunst, Prinzregentenstr. 1.* 🎫 *DM 5; Sun. and holidays free.* ⊙ *Tues.–Sun. 10–5, Thurs. until 8.*

Munich's two leading picture galleries, the Alte (old) and the Neue (new) Pinakothek, are on Barerstrasse, just to the west of the university. The ★ **⑳** **Alte Pinakothek** is traditionally the repository of some of the world's most celebrated old master paintings; it is also an architectural treasure in its own right, though much scarred from wartime bomb damage. It was built by Leo von Klenze at the beginning of the 19th century to house Ludwig I's collections. In 1994, the museum closed for renovations scheduled to take at least three years. Its most famous paintings (including most of the Dürers, Rembrandts, Rubenses, and two celebrated Murillos) are now on display at the Neue Pinakothek (☞ *Below*) until the renovations are completed.

㉑ The **Neue Pinakothek** was another of Ludwig I's projects, built to house his "modern" collections, meaning, of course, 19th-century works. The building was destroyed during World War II, and today's museum opened in 1981. The low, brick structure—some have compared it with a Florentine palazzo—is an unparalleled setting for one of the finest collections of 19th-century European paintings and sculpture in the world. ⊠ *Barerstr. 29.* 🎫 *DM 6; free Sun. and holidays.* ⊙ *Tues.–Sun. 9–5, Tues. and Thurs. till 8 PM. Take Streetcar 27, bus 53, or the U-2 subway to Königspl. from Karlspl.*

Suburban Attractions

There are a number of trips you can take to worthwhile sights not far from the city center. One is to the **Olympic Park,** a 10-minute U-Bahn ride (U-3); another is to **Nymphenburg,** 6 kilometers (4 miles) northwest and reached by the U-1 subway to Rotkreuzplatz, then Streetcar 12. The town of Dachau is a 20-minute ride from Marienplatz on the S-2 suburban railway line. To get to the **Dachau Concentration Camp Memorial** from the stop, take Bus 722 to Robert-Boschstrasse and walk along Alte Römerstrasse for 100 yards, or board Bus 720 and get off at Ratiborer Strasse.

Perhaps the most controversial buildings in Munich are the circus tent–shape roofs of the **Olympic Park.** Built for the 1972 Olympics, the park, with its undulating, transparent tile roofs and modern housing blocks, represented a revolutionary marriage of technology and visual daring when first unveiled. Sports fans might like to join the crowds in the Olympic Stadium when the local soccer team, Bayern Munich, has a home game. Call 089/699–310 for information and tickets. There's an amazing view of the stadium, the Olympic Park, and the city from the Olympic Tower. An elevator speeds you to the top in seconds. ⊠ *Take the U-3 subway.* 🎫 *DM 5 (tower); DM 7 (combined tower and park tour, until 5 PM); DM 1 (stadium).* ⊙ *Tower daily 9 AM–midnight; stadium daily 9–4:30.*

★ **Schloss Nymphenburg** was the summer palace of the Wittelsbachs. The oldest parts date from 1664, but construction continued for more than 100 years, the bulk of the work undertaken during the reign of Max Emmanuel between 1680 and 1730. The interiors are exceptional, especially the Banqueting Hall, a Rococo masterpiece in green and gold. Make a point of seeing the Schönheits Galerie, the **Gallery of Beauties.** It contains more than 100 portraits of women who had caught the eye of Ludwig I; duchesses rub shoulders with butchers' daughters. Among them is Lola Montez. Seek out the **Amalienburg,** or Hunting Lodge, on the grounds. It was built by Cuvilliès, architect of the Residenz-Theater in Munich. The palace also contains the **Marstallmuseum** (Museum of Royal Carriages), containing a sleigh that belonged to Ludwig II, among the opulently decorated vehicles, and, on the floor above, the **Nymphenburger Porzellan,** with examples of the porcelain produced here between 1747 and the 1920s. ⊠ *Schloss Nymphenburg. Take Streetcar 12 or Bus 41.* ▣ *DM6 (all Nymphenburg attractions); DM 2.50 (Schloss, Gallery of Beauties, Amalienburg, and Marstallmuseum; DM 1.50 (botanic gardens).* ⊙ *Apr.–Sept., Tues.–Sun. 9–12:30 and 1:30–5; Oct.–Mar., Tues.–Sun. 10–12:30 and 1:30–4; gardens daily year-round.*

A recent addition to the north wing of the Schloss Nymphenburg has nothing to do with the Wittelsbachs but has fast become a major attraction. The **Museum Mensch und Natur** (Museum of Man and Nature) concentrates on three areas: the history of humans, the variety of life on Earth, and our place in the environment. ▣ *DM 3; free Sun. and holidays.* ⊙ *Tues.–Sun. 9–5.*

Although the 1,200-year-old town of **Dachau** attracted hordes of painters and artists from the mid-19th century until World War I, most people remember it as the site of Germany's first **concentration camp.** From its opening in 1933 until its capture by American soldiers in 1945, the camp held more than 206,000 political dissidents, Jews, homosexuals, clergy, and other "enemies" of the Nazis; more than 32,000 prisoners died here. Photographs, contemporary documents, the few remaining cell blocks, and the grim crematorium create a somber and moving picture of the vicious living and working conditions at the camp. ▣ *Free.* ⊙ *Tues.–Sun. 9–5; documentary (in English) shown at 11:30 and 3:30.*

Shopping

Gift Ideas

Munich is a city of beer, and beer mugs and coasters make an obvious gift to take home. Many shops specialize in beer-related souvenirs, but **Ludwig Mory** (Marienplatz 8) is about the best. Munich is also the home of the famous Nymphenburg porcelain factory; its major outlet is on Odeonsplatz. You can also buy direct from the factory, which is on the half moon–shape road—Schlossrondell—in front of Nymphenburg Palace. ⊠ *Nördliche Schlossrondell 8,* ☎ *089/1791–9710.* ⊙ *Mon.–Fri. 8:30–noon and 12:30–5 (salesroom).*

Shopping Districts

From Odeonsplatz you are poised to plunge into the heart of the huge pedestrian mall that runs through the center of town. The first street you come to, **Theatinerstrasse,** is also one of the most expensive. In fact, it has only one serious rival in the money-no-object stakes: **Maximilianstrasse,** the first major street to your left as you head down Theatinerstrasse. Both are lined with elegant shops selling desirable German fashions and other high-price goods from around the world. Leading off to the right of Theatinerstrasse is **Maffeistrasse,** where **Loden-Frey** has Bavaria's most complete collection of traditional wear, from green "loden" coats to lederhosen. Maffeistrasse runs parallel to Munich's principal shopping streets: **Kaufingerstrasse** and **Neuhauserstrasse,** the one an extension of the other.

Department Stores

All the city's major department stores—other than **Hertie** (☞ Exploring, *above*)—are along Maffeistrasse, Kaufingerstrasse, and Neuhauserstrasse. **Kaufhof** and **Karstadt-Oberpollinger** are probably the best. Both have large departments stocking Bavarian arts and crafts, as well as clothing, household goods, jewelry, and other accessories.

Antiques

Antique hunters should visit **Blumenstrasse, Ottostrasse, Türkenstrasse, and Westenriederstrasse.** Also try the open-air Auer Dult fairs held on Mariahilfplatz at the end of April, July, and October (Streetcar 25), or the Friday and Saturday markets at the old Riem airport (take the S-6 to Riem).

Dining

Münchners love to eat just as much as they love to drink their beer, and the range of food is as varied and rich as the local breweries' output. Some of Europe's best chefs are here, purveyors of French nouvelle cuisine in some of the most noted—and pricey—restaurants in Germany. For those in search of local cuisine, the path leads to Munich's tried-and-true, wood-paneled, flagstone beer restaurants and halls where the food is as sturdy as the large measure of beer that comes to your table almost automatically.

For details and price-category definitions, *see* Dining *in* Staying in Germany, *above.*

$$$$ ✕ Königshof. On the second floor of the postwar Königshof Hotel and
★ overlooking the Karlstor at the northern entrance to the pedestrian-only center, the Königshof is without doubt Munich's most opulent restaurant. The neo-baroque style includes ceiling frescoes, subdued chandelier lighting, and heavy drapery. Nouvelle cuisine is served—breast of goose with truffles, for example, or veal in basil cream and mushroom sauce. ⊠ *Karlspl. 25,* ☎ *089/551–360. AE, DC, MC, V.*

$$$ ✕ Käferschänke. Daily imported seafood—including lobster, crab, salmon, trout, and halibut—is the attraction here. Try the grilled prawns in a sweet-and-sour sauce. The rustic decor, complemented by some fine antique pieces, is also sure to delight. The restaurant is in the classy Bogenhausen suburb, a 10-minute taxi ride from downtown. ⊠ *Prinzregentenstr. 73,* ☎ *089/416–8247. AE, DC, MC. Closed Sun. and holidays.*

$$$ ✕ Le Gourmet. Imaginative combinations of French and Bavarian spe-
★ cialties have made this small bistro a local favorite. Try chef Otto Koch's soufflé of sole in lemongrass sauce, or filled marrowbones with *Rösti* (Swiss-style panfried potatoes). ⊠ *Hartmannstr. 8,* ☎ *089/212–0958. AE, DC, MC. Closed Sun., Mon., and first 10 days of Jan.*

$$$ ✕ Preysing Keller. Devotees of all that's best in modern German cook-
★ ing—food that's light and sophisticated but with recognizably Teutonic touches—will love the Preysing Keller, a hotel-restaurant. It's in a 16th-century cellar, though it has been so over-restored that there's practically no sense of its age or original character. Never mind; it's the food, the extensive wine list, and the perfect service that make this place special. ⊠ *Innere-Wiener-Str. 6,* ☎ *089/481–015. Reservations essential. No credit cards. Closed Sun., Christmas, and New Year's Day.*

$$ ✕ Augustiner Keller. This 19th-century establishment is the flagship beer restaurant of one of Munich's oldest breweries, Augustiner. The decor emphasizes wood—from the refurbished parquet floors to the wooden barrels from which the beer is drawn. A full range of Bavarian specialties comprises the daily changing menu, but try to order *Tellerfleisch*—cold roast beef with lashings of horseradish, served on a big wooden board. The communal atmosphere of the two baronial hall–like rooms makes this a better place to meet locals than to attempt a quiet meal for two. ✉ *Arnulfstr. 52,* ☎ *089/594–393. AE, MC, V.*

$$ ✗ **Bamberger Haus.** This historic villa on the edge of Schwabing's Luitpold Park renovated its rambling, vaulted beer-cellar last year but thankfully retained the slightly faded decor of the upstairs dining room. You still dine beneath crystal chandeliers and under the gaze of baroque statuary. The imaginative menu is not as expensive as the surroundings suggest, and some of the vegetarian dishes, such as finely prepared vegetables au gratin, are incredibly cheap and filling. ✉ *Brunnerstrasse 2, tel 089/308–8966. AE, DC, MC, V.*

$$ ✗ **Dürnbräu.** A fountain plays outside this picturesque old Bavarian inn. Inside, it's crowded and noisy. Expect to share a table; your fellow diners will range from business sorts to students. The food is resolutely traditional. Try the cream of spinach soup and the boiled beef. ✉ *Dürnbräug. 2,* ☎ *089/222–195. AE, DC, MC, V.*

$$ ✗ **Grüne Gans.** This small, chummy restaurant near the Viktualienmarkt is popular with local entertainers, whose photographs clutter the walls. International fare with regional German influences dominates the menu, although there are a few Chinese dishes. Try the chervil cream soup, followed by calves' kidneys in tarragon sauce. ✉ *Am Einlass 5,* ☎ *089/266–228. Reservations essential. MC. Closed lunch and Sat.*

$$ ✗ **Weinhaus Neuner.** Originally a seminary, this early 18th-century building houses Munich's oldest surviving wine hostelry, in the Neuner family since 1852. There is a timeless atmosphere in the high-ceilinged dining rooms lined with dark oak paneling. Look for the herb-filled pork fillets with noodles, and veal with Morchela mushroom sauce. ✉ *Herzogspitalstr. 8,* ☎ *089/260–3954. Reservations essential. AE, DC, MC, V. Closed Sun. and holidays.*

$ ✗ **Altes Hackerhaus.** This upscale beer restaurant on one of Munich's
★ ritziest shopping streets is full of bric-a-brac and mementos that harken back to its origins as a medieval brewery and one-time home of the Hacker family. Since 1570, beer has been brewed or served here, the birthplace of one of the city's largest breweries—Hacker-Pschorr. On a cold day, duck into one of the cozy little rooms and choose from the selection of hearty soups, then try a plate of *Käsespätzle* (egg noodles with melted cheese). ✉ *Sendlingerstr. 14,* ☎ *089/260–5026. No credit cards.*

$ ✗ **Brauhaus zur Brez'n.** This hostelry is bedecked in the blue and white of the Bavarian flag. The eating and drinking are spread over three floors and enjoyed by a broad clientele—from local business lunchers to hungry night owls emerging from Schwabing's bars looking for a bite at 2 AM. Brez'n offers a big all-day menu of traditional roasts, to be washed down with a choice of three draft beers. ✉ *Leopoldstr. 72,* ☎ *089/390–092. MC.*

$ ✗ **Franziskaner.** Vaulted archways, cavernous rooms interspersed with intimate dining areas, bold blue frescoes on the walls, and long wooden tables create a spic-and-span medieval atmosphere. Aside from the late-morning *Weisswurst,* a delicate white sausage, look out for *Ochsenfleisch* (boiled ox meat) and dumplings. ✉ *Perusastr. 5,* ☎ *089/231–8120. Reservations not accepted. No credit cards.*

$ ✗ **Hofbräuhaus.** The heavy stone vaults of the Hofbräuhaus contain the most famous of the city's beer restaurants. Crowds of singing, shouting, swaying beer drinkers fill the cavernous, smoky hall. The menu is strictly Bavarian. If you're not here solely to drink, try the more subdued upstairs restaurant, where the service is not so brusque and less beer gets spilled. It's between Marienplatz and Maximilianstrasse. ✉ *Platzl 9,* ☎ *089/221–676. Reservations not accepted. No credit cards.*

$　✕ **Hundskugel.** History practically oozes from the crooked walls at this tavern, Munich's oldest, which dates from 1440. If *Spanferkel*—roast suckling pig—is on the menu, make a point of ordering it. This is simple Bavarian fare at its best. ⊠ *Hotterstr. 18,* ☎ *089/264–272. No credit cards. Closed Sun.*

$　✕ **Pfälzer Weinprobierstube.** A warren of stone-vaulted rooms of various sizes, wooden tables, glittering candles, dirndl-clad waitresses, and ★　a vast range of wines add up to an experience as close to your picture of timeless Germany as you're likely to get. The food is reliable rather than spectacular. Local specialties predominate. ⊠ *Residenzstr. 1,* ☎ *089/225–628. Reservations not accepted. No credit cards.*

Lodging

Though Munich has a vast number of hotels in all price ranges, many are full year-round. If you plan to visit during the "fashion weeks" (Mode Wochen) in March and September or during the Oktoberfest at the end of September, make reservations at least several months in advance. Munich's tourist offices will handle only written or personal requests for reservations assistance. Write/fax: Fremdenverkehrsamt, Sendlingerstr. 1, D-80313 Munich, ⨎ 089/239–1313. Your best bet for finding a room if you haven't reserved one is the tourist office at the Hauptbahnhof, by the Bayerstrasse entrance. There is a small fee.

Consider staying in a suburban hotel—where rates are often, but not always, lower—and taking the U-Bahn or S-Bahn into town. A 15-minute train ride is no obstacle to serious sightseeing. Check out the city tourist office "Key to Munich" packages. These include reduced-rate hotel reservations, sightseeing tours, theater admissions, and low-cost travel on the U- and S-Bahn. Write to the tourist office (☞ Important Addresses and Numbers in Munich, *above*).

For details and price-category definitions, *see* Lodging *in* Staying in Germany, *above*.

$$$$　▥ **Bayerischer Hof.** This is one of Munich's most traditional luxury hotels. Public rooms are decorated with antiques, fine paintings, marble, and painted wood. Old-fashioned comfort and class abound in the older rooms; some of the newer rooms are less ornate but functional. ⊠ *Promenadepl. 2–6, D-80333,* ☎ *089/21200,* ⨎ *089/212–0906. 383 rooms with bath, and 45 apartments. 3 restaurants, bars, pool, barbershop, massage, sauna, nightclub, parking (fee). AE, DC, MC, V.*

$$$$　▥ **Kempinski Hotel Vier Jahreszeiten.** The Vier Jahreszeiten—Four Sea- ★　sons—has been playing host to the world's wealthy and titled for more than a century. It has an unbeatable location on Munich's premier shopping street and is only a few minutes' walk from the heart of the city. Elegance and luxury set the tone throughout; many rooms have handsome antique pieces. ⊠ *Maximilianstr. 17, D-80539,* ☎ *089/21250,* ⨎ *089/2125–2000. (Reservations in the U.S.,* ☎ *800/426–3135.) 268 rooms with bath, 30 suites, presidential suite, 17 apartments. 2 restaurants, piano bar, pool, sauna, nightclub, travel services, car rental, parking (fee). AE, DC, MC, V.*

$$$$　▥ **Rafael.** A character-laden lodging in the heart of the Old Town (close ★　to the Hofbräuhaus), the Rafael, which opened in 1989, retains many of the architectural features of its building's late-19th-century origins, including a sweeping staircase and stucco ceilings. The hotel staged a coup in 1995 by attracting the patronage of Britain's Prince Charles, who broke with royal tradition and elected to stay here during a visit to Germany. Rooms are individually furnished and extravagantly decorated. The hotel restaurant, Mark's, has made a name for itself with its new German cuisine. ⊠ *Neuturmstr. 1, D-80331,* ☎ *089/290–980,*

FAX 089/222–539. *54 rooms and 19 suites with bath. Restaurant, bar, indoor pool, sauna. AE, DC, MC, V.*

$$$–$$$$ 🏨 **Eden Hotel Wolff.** Chandeliers and dark wood paneling in the public rooms underline the old-fashioned elegance of this downtown favorite. It's directly across the street from the train station and the airport bus terminal. The rooms are comfortable, and most are spacious. Dine on excellent Bavarian specialties in the intimate Zirbelstube restaurant. ⊠ *Arnulfstr. 4, D-80335,* ☎ *089/551–150,* FAX *089/5511–5555. 209 rooms and 2 suites with bath. Restaurant, bar, cafe, parking (fee). AE, DC, MC, V.*

$$$–$$$$ 🏨 **Torbräu.** You'll sleep in the shadow of one of Munich's ancient city gates—the 14th-century Isartor—if you stay here. This snug hotel offers comfortable rooms decorated in plush and ornate Italian style, and has an excellent location between the Marienplatz and the Deutsches Museum (and around the corner from the Hofbräuhaus). There's an Italian restaurant and a coffee shop that bakes its own cakes. ⊠ *Tal 41,* ☎ *089/225–016,* FAX *089/225–019. 97 rooms with bath, 3 suites. Restaurant, coffee shop, bowling. AE, MC, V.*

$$$ 🏨 **Pannonia Hotel Königin Elisabeth.** Housed in a 19th-century neo-
★ classical building that was completely restored and opened for the first time as a hotel in 1989, the Elisabeth is modern and bright, with an emphasis on the color pink. The restaurant offers Hungarian specialties. The Elisabeth is a 15-minute streetcar ride northwest of the city center en route to Nymphenburg. ⊠ *Leonrodstr. 79, D-80636,* ☎ *089/126–860,* FAX *089/1268–6459. 80 rooms with bath. Restaurant, bar, beer garden, hot tub, sauna, steam room, exercise room. AE, DC, MC, V.*

$$–$$$ 🏨 **Amba.** Families get an especially good deal at the Amba, a member of a hotel group that prides itself on being child-friendly. A modern, brightly furnished double room comes for as low as DM 140, and additional beds cost DM 35. The hotel is across the street from the main railway station and has its own porter service. A hotel bus collects guests from the airport. ⊠ *Arnulfstr. 20, D-80335,* ☎ *089/545–140,* FAX *089/5451–4555. 86 rooms, 74 with bath. Restaurant, coffee shop, parking (fee). AE, DC, MC, V.*

$$–$$$ 🏨 **Hotel Carlton.** This is a diplomats' favorite—a small, elegant, discreet hotel on a quiet side street in the best area of downtown Munich. The American and British consulates are nearby, as are some of the liveliest Schwabing bars and restaurants. Art galleries, museums, and cinemas are also in the neighborhood. Rooms, some of them decorated in romantic baroque style, are on the small side, but there are also four apartments with cooking facilities. ⊠ *Fürstenstr. 12, D-80333,* ☎ *089/282–061,* FAX *089/284–391. 49 rooms with bath, 4 apartments. AE, DC, MC, V.*

$$ 🏨 **Adria.** This modern, comfortable hotel is ideally located in the upscale area of Lehel, in the middle of Munich's museum quarter. Rooms are large and tastefully decorated, with old prints on the pale-pink walls, Oriental rugs on the floors, and flowers beside the large double beds. A spectacular breakfast buffet (including a glass of sparking wine) is included in the room rate. There's no hotel restaurant, but the area is rich in good restaurants, bistros, and bars. ⊠ *Liebigstr. 8a,* ☎ *089/293–081,* FAX *089/227–015. 46 rooms, 43 with bath. AE, MC, V.*

$$ 🏨 **Tele-Hotel.** This modern, well-appointed hotel on the outskirts of Munich is close to the television studios (hence the name) at Unterföhrung, and is conveniently located along the airport S-8 line, only a 15-minute ride from downtown. TV types escape their studio cafeteria's drab fare by popping into the hotel's Bavarian Hackerbräu restaurant, where a lunchtime menu for less than DM 30 is a favorite. Rooms are furnished stylishly in cherry wood. ⊠ *Bahnhofstr. 15, Unter-*

föhring. D-85774, , ☎ 089/950–146, 𝐅𝐀𝐗 089/950–6652. 60 rooms with bath, 1 apartment. Restaurant, bar, bowling, free parking. AE, DC, MC, V.

$ 🏨 **Hotel-Pension Beck.** American and British guests receive a particularly warm welcome from the Anglophile owner of the rambling, friendly Beck. Rooms are furnished in pinewood. The pension has a prime location in the heart of fashionable Lehel—handy for museums and the Englischer Garten. ✉ *Thierschstr. 36, D-80538, ☎ 089/220–708 or 089/225–768, 𝐅𝐀𝐗 089/220–925. 44 rooms, 5 with shower. No credit cards.*

$ 🏨 **Mariandl.** Large families are catered to at this rambling, friendly pension with huge rooms furnished in a variety of homey styles. The ground floor is taken up by a Viennese-style restaurant, with Biedermeier furnishings and a menu featuring every variety of Wienerschnitzel. The large grand piano isn't in here just for decoration—soirees in the style of those once enjoyed by Franz Schubert and his friends in Vienna are held here Monday through Friday (portraits of the composer adorn the walls). If you like your schnitzel with Lieder, then you'll love this place. ✉ *Goethestr. 51, D-80336, ☎ 089/534–108 or 089/535–158. 30 rooms, 4 with shower. AE, V.*

The Arts

Details of concerts and theater performances are available from the "Vorschau" or "Monatsprogramm" booklets obtainable at most hotel reception desks. Some hotels will make ticket reservations; otherwise use one of the ticket agencies in the city center: **Hieber Konzertkasse** (✉ Liebfrauenstr. 1, ☎ 089/290–080) or the **Residenz Bücherstube** (✉ Residenzstr. 1, concert tickets only, ☎ 089/220–868). You can also book tickets at the two kiosks on the concourse below Marienplatz.

Concerts

Munich's Philharmonic Orchestra performs in Germany's biggest concert hall, the **Gasteig Cultural Center** (✉ Rosenheimerstr, on a hill above the Ludwig Bridge, ☎ 089/5481–8181). Tickets can be bought at the box office. The Bavarian Radio Orchestra performs Sunday concerts here. In summer, concerts are held at two Munich palaces, **Nymphenburg** and **Schleissheim,** and in the open-air interior courtyard of the **Residenz.**

Opera

Munich's **Bavarian State Opera** company is world-famous, and tickets for major productions in its permanent home, the State Opera House, are difficult to obtain. Book far in advance for the annual opera festival held in July and August; contact the tourist office for the schedule of performances and ticket prices. The opera house box office (✉ Maximilianstr. 11, ☎ 089/2185–1920) takes reservations one week in advance only. It's open weekdays 10–1 and 2–6, Saturday 10–1.

Dance

The ballet company of the Bavarian State Opera performs at the State Opera House. Ballet productions are also staged at the attractive late-19th-century **Gärtnerplatz Theater** (☎ 089/201–6767).

Film

Munich hosts a film festival each June. English-language films are shown regularly at several downtown cinemas: **Ricks and Hollywood** (✉ Schwantalerstr. 2–6), **Cinema** (✉ Nymphenburgerstr. 31), the **Film Museum** (✉ St. Jakobs Pl.), and the **Museum Lichtspiele** (✉ Ludwigsbrücke).

Theater

There are two state theater companies, one of which concentrates on the classics. More than 20 other theater companies (some of them performing in basements) are to be found throughout the city. Regular English-language productions, featuring an American cast and director, are staged at **America House** and the **Theater an der Leopold-strasse** (⊠ Leopoldstr. 17, ☎ 089/343–803).

Nightlife

Although it lacks the racy reputation of Hamburg, Munich has something for just about all tastes.

Bars, Cabaret, Nightclubs

Schumann's (⊠ Maximilianstr. 36) has a shabby New York bar look but the clientele is Munich chic. Munich's media types have turned the **Alter Simpl** (⊠ Turkenstr. 57) into an unofficial press club. Television contracts are shoved across the tables here like menus. But don't venture in before midnight.

Irish pubs are springing up in Munich like wild shamrocks, and one of the best has staked a claim in the city's most expensive mile, fashionable Maximilianstrasse, where **O'Reilly's Irish Cellar Pub** offers escape from the German bar scene and serves genuine Irish Guinness. Great Caribbean cocktails and a powerful Irish-German Black and Tan (Guinness and strong German beer) are served at the English, nautical-style **Pusser's** bar (⊠ Falkenturmstr. 9; it replaced Munich's own Harry's Bar). The **Havana** (⊠ Herrnstr. 3) does its darnedest to look like a run-down Cuban dive, although the chic clientele spoils such pretensions.

Jazz

The **Scala Music Bar** (⊠ Oscar-von-Miller Ring 3), is difficult to find and unpromisingly located in a barren office block, but it's worth searching out. The **Unterfahrt** (⊠ Kirchenstr. 96), in Munich's latest "quartier Latin", Haidhausen, has a regular program of traditional and mainstream jazz. Munich's longest-established jazz haunt, the **Podium** (⊠ Wagnerstr. 1), has taken to offering rock 'n' roll as well as traditional jazz; it's a highly popular place, packed nightly.

Discos

Discos abound in the side streets off Freilitzschstrasse surrounding Münchener Freiheit in Schwabing. **Babalu** (⊠ Leopoldstr. 19) is among the best—a real old-timer on Munich's changing disco scene. **Nachtcafe** (⊠ Maximilianspl. 5), open all night on weekends, is more upscale than most. Ritzy in every sense is the **Skyline** at the top of the Hertie building at Münchner Freiheit. **P1** (⊠ In the Haus der Kunst, Prinzregenstr. 1) is the queen of them all, a place to see and be seen, with a series of tiny dance floors and a great sound system.

For Singles

Every Munich bar is singles territory. Making contact at the **Wunderbar** (⊠ Hochbrückenstr. 3) is made easier on Tuesday nights when telephones are installed on the tables and at the bar, and the place hums like a stygian switchboard. Munich's gay scene is found between Sendlingertorplatz and Isartorplatz. Its most popular bars are **Together** (⊠ Rumfordstr. 2), **Nil** (⊠ Hans-Sachs-Str. 2), **Ochsengarten** (⊠ Müllerstr. 47), and **Pimpernel** (Müllerstr. 56). For the student, beard, and pipe scene, try **Türkenstrasse,** behind the university (Cafe Puck, No. 33, and La Boheme, No. 79, are typical of the scene).

FRANKFURT

Arriving and Departing

By Plane
Frankfurt's airport, the busiest in mainland Europe, is about 10 kilometers (6 miles) southwest of the city.

BETWEEN THE AIRPORT AND DOWNTOWN
Getting into Frankfurt from the airport is easy. The S-8 (S-Bahn) runs from the airport to downtown, stopping at the Hauptbahnhof (main train station) and then at the centrally located Hauptwache Square. Trains run every 15 minutes and the ride takes about as long; the one-way fare is DM 5.50. InterCity and InterCity Express (ICE) trains to and from most major West German cities also stop at the airport. City Bus 61 also serves the airport, with service to the Südbahnhof, the train station south of downtown. The trip takes about 30 minutes; the fare is DM 5.50. Taxis from the airport downtown take about 20 minutes (double that in rush hour); the fare averages DM 40. If driving, take the B43 main road, following signs for STADTMITTE.

By Train
EuroCity and InterCity trains connect Frankfurt with all other German cities and many major European ones. The new InterCity Express line links Frankfurt with Hamburg, Munich, and several other major German cities. All long-distance trains arrive at and depart from the Hauptbahnhof. For information, call **Deutsche Bahn** (German Railways, ☎ 069/19419) or ask at the information office in the station.

By Bus
Long-distance buses connect Frankfurt with more than 200 other European cities. Buses leave from the south side of the Hauptbahnhof. Tickets and information are available from **Deutsche Touring GmbH** (✉ Am Römerhof 17, ☎ 069/79030).

By Car
Frankfurt is the junction of many major autobahns, of which the most important are the A-3, running south from Köln and then on to Würzburg, Nürnberg, and Munich; and the A-5, running south from Giessen and then on to Mannheim, Heidelberg, Karlsruhe, and the Swiss-German border at Basel. A complex series of beltways surrounds the city. If you're driving to Frankfurt on the A-5 from either north or south, exit at Nordwestkreuz and follow A-66 to the Nordend district, just north of downtown. Driving south on A-3, exit onto A-66 and follow the signs to Frankfurt-Höchst and then the Nordend district. Driving north on A-3, exit at Offenbach onto A-661 and follow the signs for FRANKFURT-STADTMITTE.

Getting Around

By Public Transportation
Frankfurt's efficient, well-integrated public transportation system consists of the U-Bahn (subway), S-Bahn (suburban railway), and Strassenbahn (streetcars). Fares for the entire system are uniform but based on a complicated zone system that can be hard to figure out. A day ticket for unlimited travel in the inner zone costs DM 8.50. The Frankfurt tourist office sells a two-day ticket, the Frankfurt Card, for DM 13, entitling you to unlimited inner-zone travel and half-off admission to 14 museums. Buy tickets at newspaper kiosks or from blue dispensing machines. For further information or assistance, call 069/269–462.

By Taxi

Fares start at DM 2.50 and increase by DM 2.15–DM 2.53 per kilometer, depending on the time of day. Count on paying DM 10 to DM 12 for a short city ride. There's an extra charge for each piece of baggage you carry. You can hail taxis in the street or call them (☎ 069/250–001, 069/230–033, or 069/545–011); there's an extra charge if you phone ahead to be picked up.

Important Addresses and Numbers

Consulates

U.S. (✉ Siesmayerstr. 21, ☎ 069/75350). **Canadian** (✉ Friedrich–Wilhelm Str. 18, D-53113 Bonn, ☎ 0228/968–3903). **U.K.** (✉ Bockenheimer Landstr. 42, ☎ 069/170–0020).

Emergencies

Police (☎ 110). **Fire** (☎ 112). **Medical Emergencies** (☎ 069/7950–2200 or 069/19292). **Pharmacies** (☎ 069/11500). **Dental Emergencies** (☎ 069/660–7271).

English-Language Bookstores

The **British Bookshop** (✉ Börsenstr. 17, ☎ 069/280–492) and the **American Book Center** (✉ Jahnstr. 36, ☎ 069/552–816) carry English-language titles.

Travel Agencies

American Express (✉ Kaiserstr. 8, ☎ 069/210–548). **DER Deutsches Reisebüro** (✉ Emil-von-Behring Str. 6, ☎ 069/9588–3560).

Visitor Information

For information, write to the **Verkehrsamt Frankfurt/Main** (✉ Kaiserstr. 52, D-60329 Frankfurt, ☎ 069/2123–8800). The main tourist office is at Römerberg 27 (☎ 069/2123–8708), in the heart of the Old Town. It's open daily 9–6. A secondary office is at the Hauptbahnhof opposite Track 23 (☎ 069/2123–8849). This branch is open weekdays 8 AM–9 PM, Saturday–Sunday 9–6. Both offices can help you find accommodations, as can two additional information offices at the airport: the **FAG Flughafen-Information,** on the first floor of Arrivals Hall B (☉ Daily 6:45 AM–10:15 PM) and the **DER Deutsches Reisebüro,** in Arrivals Hall B-6 (☉ Daily 8 AM–9 PM).

Guided Tours

Orientation

Two-and-a-half-hour bus tours that take in all the main sights with English-speaking guides are offered throughout the year. March through October, tours leave from outside the main tourist information office at Römerberg 27 daily at 10 AM and 2 PM; these buses leave from the train-station tourist office (opposite Track 23) 15 minutes later. In winter (November–February), tours leave on weekends and holidays at 1 PM from the Römer office, stopping at 1:15 at the train-station tourist office. The cost is DM 39. **Gray Line** (☎ 069/230–492) offers two-hour city tours four times a day; the price (☎ DM 50) includes a typical Frankfurt snack. The city transit authority (☎ 069/2132–2425) runs a brightly painted old-time streetcar—the **Ebbelwei Express** (Cider Express)—on Saturday, Sunday, and holidays every 40 minutes between 1:32 and 5:32. Departures are from the Bornheim-Mitte U- and S-Bahn station and the fare is DM 4. Special tours are offered by the tourist office by prior arrangement. For further information, call 069/2123–8953. For DM 12, visitors can buy a cassette (in English) of a one-hour walking tour at the tourist office at the Römer and rent a Walkman for a DM 50 deposit.

Excursions

Bus tours of the surrounding countryside, as far as the Rhine, are offered by **Noblesse Limousine Service** (☎ 06101/12055) in Bad Vilbel, **Deutsche Touring GmbH** (✉ Am Römerhof 17, ☎ 069/790–3268), and **Gray Line** (☞ *Above*). One-day excursions are also offered by German Railways, the Deutsche Bahn. These are described in a brochure, "Der Schöne Tag," obtainable from the main train station and the DER tourist office. Pleasure boats of the **Primus Line** cruise the Main and Rhine rivers from Frankfurt, sailing as far as the Lorelei and back in a day; for schedules and reservations, contact **Frankfurter Personenschiffahrt** (✉ Mainkai 36, ☎ 069/281–884).

Exploring Frankfurt

Numbers in the margin correspond to points of interest on the Frankfurt map.

At first glance, Frankfurt-am-Main doesn't seem to offer much to the tourist. Virtually flattened by bombs during the war, it now bristles with skyscrapers, the visible signs of the city's role as Germany's financial capital.

Originally a Roman settlement, Frankfurt later served as one of Charlemagne's two capitals (the other being Aachen). Still later, the electors of the Holy Roman Empire met here to choose and crown the emperor. It was also the birthplace of the poet and dramatist Johann Wolfgang von Goethe (1749–1832).

Although the true center of Frankfurt is its ancient **Römerberg Square,** where the election of Holy Roman Emperors was traditionally proclaimed and celebrated, this tour of the city begins slightly to the north, at the

❶ **Hauptwache,** an 18th-century guardhouse that today serves a more peaceful purpose as a café. The ground floor houses Intertreff, an information office that assists young visitors with such tasks as finding moderately priced accommodations. ☉ *Weekdays 10–6, Sat. 10–1.*

❷ Head south along Kornmarkt, passing on the left the **Katerinenkirche** (Church of St. Catherine), the historic center of Frankfurt Protestantism and the church in which Goethe was confirmed. After cross-

❸ ing Berlinerstrasse, still heading south, you'll pass the **Paulskirche** (Church of St. Paul). It was here that the first all-German parliament convened in 1848. Continue down Buchgasse, and within a few minutes you're on the north bank of the River **Main.** Turn left toward the iron footbridge known as the **Eiserner Steg** and, at the **Rententurm,** one of the city's medieval gates, bear left again and you'll arrive at the spa-

❹ cious **Römerberg Square,** center of Frankfurt civic life over the centuries. In the center of the square stands the 16th-century **Fountain of Justice:** At the coronation of Emperor Matthias in 1612, wine spouted from the stonework instead of water. Not long ago, city officials started restaging this momentous event for festive occasions, among them the annual Main Fest.

❺ Compared with many city halls, Frankfurt's **Römer** is a modest affair, with a gabled Gothic facade. It occupies most of one side of the square and is actually three patrician houses. The Römer's most important function, however, was as the site of elections of Holy Roman Emperors. The **Kaisersaal** (Imperial Hall) was last used for that purpose in 1792, when the victor was Emperor Francis II. Today, visitors can admire the impressive full-length 19th-century portraits of the 52 emperors of the Holy Roman Empire that line the walls of the reconstructed banquet hall. ⊟ *DM 3.* ☉ *Tues.–Sun. 11–3. Closed during official functions.*

Charlemagne's son, Ludwig the Pious, established a church on the present site of the Römerberg in AD 850. His church was replaced by a much grander Gothic structure, one used for imperial coronations; it became

6 known as the **Kaiserdom,** the Imperial Cathedral. The cathedral suffered only superficial damage during World War II, and it still contains many of its original treasures, including a fine 15th-century altar.

7 On the south side of the square stands the 13th-century **Nikolaikirche** (St. Nicholas Church). It's worth trying to time your visit to the square to coincide with the chiming of the Glockenspiel. ☉ *Carillon chimes daily at 9, noon, and 5; Nikolaikirche Mon–Sat. 10–5.*

From the Römerberg, stroll south toward the river, but this time turn

8 right. Walk past the riverside **Leonhardskirche** (St. Leonard's Church), which is filled with wonderful things, including a fine 13th-century porch and a beautifully carved Bavarian altar from about 1500, and then fol-

9 low the narrow Karmelitergasse to the **Karmeliterkloster** (Carmelite church and monastery). The secularized and renovated church houses the **Museum für Vor- und Frühgeschichte** (Museum of Prehistory and Ancient History); next door, the main cloister contains the largest religious fresco north of the Alps, a 16th-century representation of the birth and death of Christ. The cloister also hosts rotating exhibitions of modern art. *Museum:* ▨ *DM 5.* ☉ *Tues.–Sun. 10–5 (until 8 on Wed.). Art gallery in cloister:* ▨ *DM 3.* ☉ *Tues.–Sun. 11–6.*

★ **10** From here, it's only a short way to the **Goethehaus und Goethe Museum** (Goethe House and Museum). The poet was born here in 1749, and though the house was destroyed by Allied bombing, it has been carefully restored and is furnished with pieces from Goethe's time, some belonging to his family. The adjoining museum is closed for renovations. ⊠ *Grosser Hirschgraben 23–25,* ☏ *069/282–824.* ▨ *DM 4.* ☉ *Apr.–Sept., Mon.–Sat. 9–5:30, Sun. 10–1; Oct.–Mar., Mon.–Sat. 9–4, Sun. 10–1.*

From the Goethehaus, retrace your steps to the Hauptwache via Rossmarkt. From here, take a window-shopping stroll past the elegant boutiques of Goethestrasse, which ends at Opernplatz and Frankfurt's

11 reconstructed opera house, the **Alte Oper.**

Looking out from the Alte Oper, you'll see the skyscrapers—many of them housing the nation's biggest and wealthiest banks—that have earned Frankfurt the nickname "Mainhattan." Cross Opernplatz and bear left down Grosse Bockenheimer Strasse (known locally as Fressgasse—literally "Pig Out Alley"—because of its abundance of gourmet shops and restaurants), turn left into Börsenstrasse, and you'll hit the center of the financial district. Just around the corner from Fressgasse is the

12 Frankfurt **Börse,** Germany's leading stock exchange and a financial powerhouse. It was founded by Frankfurt merchants in 1558 to establish some order in their often chaotic dealings. Today's dealings can also be quite hectic; see for yourself by slipping into the visitors' gallery. ▨ *Free.* ☉ *Gallery weekdays 9:30–1:30.*

From the Börse, turn right into Schillerstrasse, and within two minutes you're once again back at the Hauptwache. Here begins Frankfurt's main shopping street, the **Zeil.** Resist, if you can, the temptations in the shop windows on both sides of this crowded pedestrian zone and head eastward to the nearby point where it is crossed by Hasengasse. Turn right into Hasengasse and you'll see the striking wedge of Frankfurt's newest museum rising straight ahead of you. This is the

13 **Museum für Moderne Kunst** (Museum of Modern Art), which was opened in 1991 and contains an important collection of works by such artists as Siah Armajani, Joseph Beuys, Walter de Maria, and Andy

Frankfurt

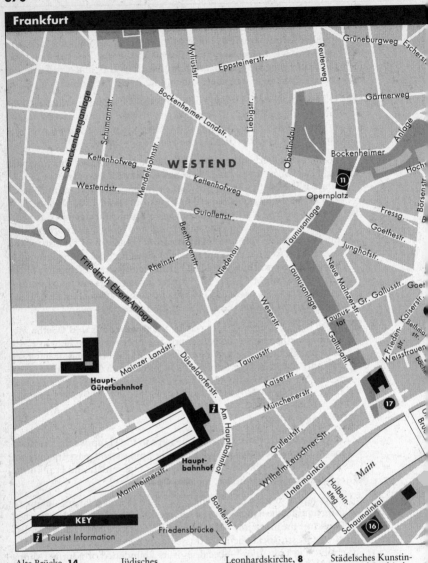

KEY

ⓘ Tourist Information

Alte Brücke, **14**
Alte Oper, **11**
Börse, **12**
Goethehaus und
Goethe Museum, **10**
Hauptwache, **1**

Jüdisches
Museum, **17**
Kaiserdom, **6**
Karmeliterkloster, **9**
Katerinenkirche, **2**
Kuhhirtenturm, **15**

Leonhardskirche, **8**
Museum für Moderne
Kunst, **13**
Nikolaikirche, **7**
Paulskirche, **3**
Römer, **5**
Römerberg Square, **4**

Städelsches Kunstin-
stitut und Städtische
Galerie, **16**

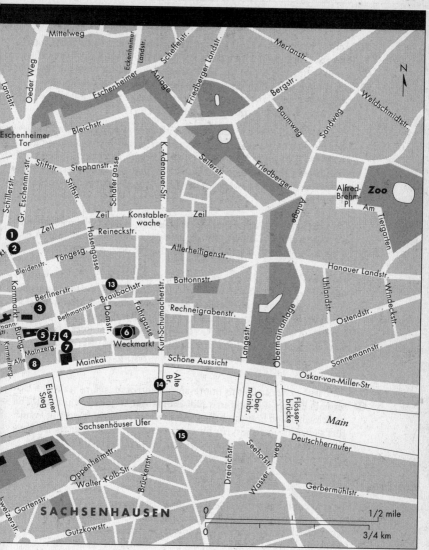

Warhol. ⊠ *Domstr. 10,* ☎ *069/2123–8819.* ⌷ *DM 7.* ☉ *Tues.–Sun. 10–5 (until 8 on Wed.)*

★ Across the Main lies the district of **Sachsenhausen.** It's said that Charlemagne arrived here with a group of Saxon families in the 8th century.
⑭ Cross to Sachsenhausen over the **Alte Brücke.** Along the bank to your
⑮ left you'll see the 15th-century **Kuhhirtenturm,** the only remaining part of Sachsenhausen's original fortifications. The composer Paul Hindemith lived and worked in the tower from 1923 to 1927.

The district still has a medieval air, with narrow back alleys and quiet squares that have escaped the destructive tread of city development. Here you'll find Frankfurt's famous Ebbelwei taverns. A green pine wreath over the entrance tells passersby that a freshly pressed—and alcoholic—apple wine or cider is on tap. You can eat well in these little inns, too.

NEED A   The main street in Sachsenhausen, **Neuer Wall,** is lined with atmospheric
BREAK?   old taverns offering home-brewed apple wine and solid local fare. A favorite is Dauth-Schneider (⊠ *Neuer Wall 7,* ☎ *069/613–533*).

No fewer than eight top-ranking museums line the Sachsenhausen side of the Main, on **Schaumainkai** (known locally as the **Museumsufer**
★ ⑯ or Museum Bank). The **Städelsches Kunstinstitut und Städtische Galerie** (Städel Art Institute and Municipal Gallery) has one of the most significant art collections in Germany, with fine examples of Flemish, German, and Italian old masters, plus a sprinkling of French Impressionists. ⊠ *Schaumainkai 63.* ⌷ *DM 8 (free on Wed.).* ☉ *Tues.–Sun. 10–5 (Wed. until 8).*

Across the river from this impressive lineup of museums (take the Un-
⑰ termain Bridge) is Frankfurt's **Jüdisches Museum** (Jewish Museum). The fine city mansion houses a permanent exhibit tracing the history of Frankfurt's Jewish community; its library is Germany's main registry for Jewish history. ⊠ *Untermainkai 14–15,* ☎ *069/2123–5000.* ⌷ *DM 5.* ☉ *Tues–Sun. 10–5 (Wed. until 8).*

Dining

Several Frankfurt restaurants close for the school summer vacation break, a six-week period that falls between mid-June and mid-September. Always check to avoid disappointment. For details and price-category definitions, *see* Dining *in* Staying in Germany, *above.*

$$$ ✕ **Brückenkeller.** This establishment offers magnificent German spe-
★ cialties in the sort of time-honored vaulted cellar that would have brought a lump to Bismarck's throat. What's more, though the food may be unmistakably Teutonic, it's light and delicate. In addition to the antiques-strewn surroundings (the restaurant has been in business since 1652) and the classy food, there's a phenomenal range of wines: The cellars—don't be shy about asking to see them—hold around 85,000 bottles. ⊠ *Schützenstr. 6,* ☎ *069/284–238. AE, DC, MC, V. Dinner only. Closed Sun.*

$$$ ✕ **Erno's Bistro.** Small, chic, and popular with visiting power brokers, Erno's has become something of a Frankfurt institution. The menu features classy nouvelle specialties, with fish—flown in daily, often from France—predominating. The waiters speak English and are both able and happy to choose your meal for you. ⊠ *Liebigstr. 15,* ☎ *069/721– 997. Reservations essential. AE, DC, MC, V. Closed weekends and mid-June–mid-July.*

$$ ✗ **Altes Zollhaus.** In this beautiful, 200-year-old half-timber house, you can sample very good versions of traditional German specialties. Try a game dish. In summer, you can eat in the beautiful garden. ✉ *Friedberger Landstr. 531,* ☎ *069/472–707. AE, DC, MC, V. Dinner only. Closed Mon.*

$$ ✗ **Börsenkeller.** Solid Germanic food, with just a hint of French style, is served here to fortify the business community from the nearby stock exchange. Soft lighting, heavy arches, and high-back booths establish the mood; steaks are a specialty. ✉ *Schillerstr. 11,* ☎ *069/281–115. AE, DC, MC, V. Closed Sun. No dinner Sat.*

$$ ✗ **Charlot.** The French cuisine of this very popular restaurant acquired an Italian touch with the arrival of chef Mario, but it survived the transition well. The Alte Oper is just across the street, so after the curtain falls you'll be fighting with the music buffs for a place in the French bistro–style dining rooms, spread over two floors. But you might also be sharing a table with Luciano Pavarotti. ✉ *Opernpl. 10,* ☎ *069/287–007. AE, DC, MC, V. No lunch Sun.*

$$ ✗ **Jaspers.** This is technically a French restaurant, but the many Al-
★ satian specialties give it a German flair. Some better dishes include fish soup with croutons, and snails in Calvados sauce over spinach. The high level of service and cooking puts many better known and more expensive restaurants to shame, and there's a great wine list, too. In summer, consider dining in the small courtyard outback. ✉ *Schifferstr. 8 (just off Affentorpl.), Sachsenhausen,* ☎ *069/614–117. AE, DC, V. Closed Sun.*

$ ✗ **Café GegenwART.** "Gegenwart" means "the present," and the accent on ART means there are always works of local artists exhibited in this friendly, bustling café. The cuisine is also artfully presented; the menu changes often. In summer, the tables spill out onto the sidewalk. Try the freshly caught angler fish or the tomato fondue when available. ✉ *Bergerstr. 6,* ☎ *069/497–0544. No credit cards.*

$ ✗ **Germania.** This noisy, smoky, apple-cider tavern, one of Sachsen-
★ hausen's most authentic, is filled with long wooden tables at which locals rub—and bend—elbows. Good traditional grub and great cider, but absolutely no beer! ✉ *16 Textorstr.,* ☎ *069/613–336. No credit cards. Closed Mon.*

$ ✗ **Melange.** This festive, largely vegetarian restaurant is typically packed with students and professors from the nearby university. ✉ *Jordanstr. 19,* ☎ *069/701–287. No credit cards.*

$ ✗ **Zum Gemalten Haus.** This is the real thing: a traditional wine tav-
★ ern in the heart of Sachsenhausen. Its name means "at the painted house," a reference to the frescoes that cover the place inside and out. In the summer and on fine spring and autumn days, the courtyard is the place to be (the inner rooms can get a bit crowded). But if you can't at first find a place at one of the bench-lined long tables, order an apple wine and hang around until someone leaves: It's worth the wait. ✉ *Schweizerstr. 67,* ☎ *069/614–559. No credit cards. Closed Mon. and Tues.*

Lodging

For details and price-category definitions, *see* Lodging *in* Staying in Germany, *above.*

$$$$ ☖ **Gravenbruch Kempinski.** The atmosphere of the 16th-century manor
★ house that this elegant, sophisticated hotel was built around still remains at this parkland sight in leafy Neu Isenburg (a 15-minute drive south of Frankfurt). Some of its luxuriously appointed rooms and suites are arranged as duplex penthouse apartments. Make sure you get a room overlooking the lake. ✉ *D-63243 Neu Isenburg,* ☎ *06102/5050,* 𝕱𝕬𝕏 *06102/505–445. 287 rooms with bath. 2 restaurants,*

indoor and outdoor pools, tennis courts, health spa, hairdresser, conference center, limo service to airport and city (both 15 mins away). AE, DC, MC, V.

$$$$ 🏨 **Hessischer Hof.** This former palace is still owned by a prince of Hesse, and fine antiques are deftly positioned in many guest rooms. One of the two bars, Jimmy's, numbers among Frankfurt's best, and the hotel restaurant, Sevres, is prized for its gourmet cuisine and refined ambience. ⊠ Friedrich-Ebert-Anlage 40, D-60235, ☎ 069/75400, FAX 069/754–0924. 117 rooms with bath. Restaurant, 2 bars, garage. AE, DC, MC, V.

$$$$ 🏨 **Steigenberger Hotel Frankfurter Hof.** The Victorian Frankfurter
★ Hof is one of the city's oldest hotels. The atmosphere throughout is one of old-fashioned, formal elegance, with burnished woods, fresh flowers, and thick-carpeted hush. Kaiser Wilhelm once slept here. ⊠ Am Kaiserpl., D-60311, ☎ 069/21502, FAX 069/215–900. 347 rooms with bath, 10 suites. 4 restaurants, café, 2 bars. AE, DC, MC, V.

$$$ 🏨 **Dorint Hotel.** A palm-fringed rooftop pool beckons after a day of touring downtown Frankfurt, which is a short walk across the river from this stylish member of the Dorint group. The hotel has all the comfort and facilities expected from this respected hotel chain. ⊠ Hahnstr. 9, D-60492, ☎ 069/663–060, FAX 069/6630–6600. 183 rooms with bath, 8 suites, 29 no-smoking rooms. Restaurant, 2 bars, indoor pool, sauna, parking. AE, DC, MC, V.

$$ 🏨 **Hotel Ibis Frankfurt Friedensbrücke.** This modern hotel on the north bank of the Main River is just a five-minute walk from the train station. It is owned by the Ibis chain, known for providing modern comfort at affordable prices. ⊠ Speicherstr. 3–5, D-60327, ☎ 069/273–030, FAX 069/237–024. 233 rooms with bath. Restaurant, bar, parking. AE, DC, MC, V.

$$ 🏨 **Maingau.** This excellent-value hotel is in the city's Sachsenhausen
★ district, within easy reach of the downtown area and just a stone's throw from the lively Altstadt quarter. The rooms are spartanly furnished, though clean and comfortable, and all have TV. The breakfast buffet is substantial. Families with children are welcome. ⊠ Schifferstr. 38–40, D-60594, ☎ 069/617–001, FAX 069/620–790. 100 rooms with bath. Restaurant, garage. AE, MC.

$ 🏨 **Hotel-Schiff Peter Schlott.** Watch your step when returning to this unusual hotel after a night out in Frankfurt—it's a hotel ship, moored on the Main River in the suburb of Höchst, a 15-minute train or tram ride from the city center. Guest cabins are predictably on the small side, but the marvelous river views more than compensate. ⊠ Mainberg, D-65929, ☎ 069/315–480, FAX 069/307–671. 19 rooms, about half with shower. Restaurant, parking. AE, MC.

HAMBURG

Arriving and Departing

By Plane

Hamburg's international airport, Fuhlsbüttel, is 11 kilometers (7 miles) northwest of the city. Lufthansa connects Hamburg with all other major German cities and European capitals.

BETWEEN THE AIRPORT AND DOWNTOWN

An Airport-City-Bus runs between the airport and Hamburg's Hauptbahnhof (main train station) daily at 20-minute intervals. Along the way, buses stop at the hotels Reichshof, Atlantic, and Hamburg-Plaza, the central bus station at Adenauerallee 78, and at the fairgrounds. Buses run from 5:40 AM to 10:30 PM. Tickets are DM 8 per person. The Airport-Express (Bus 110) runs every 10 minutes between the airport and the Ohlsdorf U- and S-Bahn stations, a 17-minute ride from the main train station. The fare is DM 3.60. If you're picking up a rental car at the airport, follow the signs to STADTZENTRUM (downtown).

By Train

Hamburg is a terminus for main line service to northern Germany. There are two principal stations: the Hauptbahnhof and Hamburg-Altona. For information, call 040/19419.

By Bus

Hamburg's bus station, the Zentral-Omnibus-Bahnhof, is located right behind the Hauptbahnhof (Adenauerallee 78). For information call 040/247–575, or contact the **Deutsche Touring-Gesellschaft** (⊠ Am Römerhof 17, D-60486 Frankfurt/Main, ☎ 069/79030).

By Car

Hamburg is easier to handle by car than are many other German cities, and relatively uncongested by traffic. Incoming autobahns connect with Hamburg's three beltways, which then take you easily to the downtown area. Follow the signs for STADTZENTRUM.

Getting Around

By Public Transportation

The comprehensive city and suburban transportation system includes a U-Bahn network, which connects efficiently with S-Bahn lines, and an exemplary bus service. Tickets cover travel by all three, as well as by harbor ferry. The one- and three-day **Hamburg CARD** allows free travel on all public transportation within the city, free admission to state museums, and discounts of approximately 30% on most bus, train, and boat tours. For information about this card, inquire at tourist offices (☞ *below*). Information on the public-transportation system can be obtained directly from the **Hamburg Passenger Transport Board** (HVV, ⊠ Steinstr.1, ☎ 040/322–911; ⊙ Daily 7 AM–8 PM).

By Taxi

Taxi meters start at DM 3.60, and the fare is DM 2.20 per kilometer, plus 50 pfennigs for each piece of luggage. To order a taxi, call 040/441–011, 040/686–868, or 040/611–061.

Important Addresses and Numbers

Consulates

U.S. (⊠ Alsterufer 28, ☎ 040/411–710). **U.K.** (⊠ Harvestehuder Weg 8a, ☎ 040/448–0320).

Emergencies

Police (☎ 110). **Ambulance** and **Fire Department** (☎ 112). **Medical Emergencies** (☎ 040/228–022). **Dentist** (⊙ 040/11500).

English-Language Bookstores

Try **Frensche** (⊠ Spitalerstr. 26e, ☎ 040/327–585) for a selection of English-language newspapers and books.

Travel Agencies

American Express (⊠ Rathausmarkt 5, ☎ 040/331–141). **Hapag-Lloyd** (⊠ Verkehrspavillon Jungfernstieg, ☎ 040/3258–5640).

Visitor Information

The principal Hamburg tourist office is at **Bieberhaus,** at Hachmannplatz (⊠ Next to the Hauptbahnhof, ☎ 040/3005–1244; ⊙ Weekdays 7:30 AM–6 PM, Saturday 8 AM–3 PM). There's also an information center inside the **Hauptbahnhof** (☎ 040/300–51230; ⊙ Daily 7 AM–11

PM) and in the arrivals hall of **Hamburg airport** (☎ 040/300–51240; ⊙ Daily 8 AM–11 PM). Other tourist offices can be found in the Hanse-Viertel shopping arcade (☎ 040/3005–1220; ⊙ Weekdays 10–6:30, Thurs. 10–8:30), Saturday 10–3 (10–6 on the first Sat. of the month) and at the **Landungbrücken** (☎ 00/300–51200, ⊙ Daily 9:30–5:30). All centers will reserve hotel accommodation.

Guided Tours

Orientation

Bus tours of the city, with an English-speaking guide, leave from Kirchenallee (in front of the Hauptbahnhof) at regular intervals (six times daily in summer). The 1¾-hour tour costs DM 26. A 2½-hour tour, taking in more of the city, starts at 10 and 2 daily from the same place. The fare is DM 32. For an additional DM 12, either tour can be combined with a one-hour boat trip.

Boat Tours

Tours of the harbor leave every half hour in summer, less frequently during the winter, from Piers (Landungsbrücken) 1–7. The one-hour tour costs DM 15. A special harbor tour with an English-speaking guide leaves Pier 1 at 11:15 daily from March 1 to November 30 (same price). The Störtebeker line has a special party boat on which you can wine, dine (a six-course banquet), and dance. The boat casts off from Pier 6 every evening at 8. The all-inclusive cost of the four-hour cruise is DM 111, and reservations can be made by calling 040/2274–2375. Fifty-minute cruises of the Binnenalster and Aussenalster leave from the Jungfernstieg every half hour between 10 and 6 April-October, less frequently the rest of the year. The fare is DM 14.

Exploring Hamburg

The comparison that Germans like to draw between Hamburg and Venice is somewhat exaggerated. Nevertheless, Hamburg, like Venice, is a city on water: the great River Elbe, which flows into the North Sea; the smaller River Alster, which has been dammed to form two lakes, the Binnenalster and Aussenalster; and many canals. Once a leading member of the Hanseatic League, which dominated trade on the North Sea and the Baltic during the Middle Ages, the city is a major port, with 33 individual docks and 500 berths for oceangoing vessels, and Germany's gateway to the world.

Within the remaining traces of its old city walls, Hamburg combines the seamiest, steamiest streets of dockland Europe with sleek avenues. During World War II, Hamburg was wrecked by fire, then by Allied bombing raids. The following itinerary includes a few detours, some by boat, that will enhance your enjoyment of Hamburg.

Numbers in the margin correspond to points of interest on the Hamburg map.

❶ Hamburg's main train station, the **Hauptbahnhof,** is not only the start of the city tour but very much part of it. It's not often you are tempted to linger at a train station, but this is an exception. Originally built in 1906 and completely renovated earlier this decade, it has a remarkable spaciousness and sweep, accentuated by a 486-foot-wide glazed roof, the largest unsupported construction of its kind in Europe. Ride one stop on the S-Bahn to the Dammtor station and compare this Art Nouveau–style building (built in 1903) with the one you've just left.

From the Dammtor station you emerge at the northern end of the **Wall-ringpark,** a stretch of parkland that runs for more than a kilometer

★ ❷
❸ alongside what was once the western defense wall of the city. The first two sections of the park—the **Alter Botanischer Garten** (Old Botanical Garden) and the **Planten un Blom**(Plants and Flowers)—have lots to attract the attention of gardeners and flower lovers.

❹ The **Grosse Wallanlagen** section of the park—to the southwest—is interrupted abruptly by the northern edge of the **St. Pauli** district and its most famous—or infamous—thoroughfare, the **Reeperbahn** (☞ Nightlife, *below*). Unlike other business sections of Hamburg, this industrious quarter works around the clock; although it may seem quiet as you stroll down its tawdry length in broad daylight, any tourist who stops at one of its bars will discover that many of the girls who work this strip are on a day shift.

★ ❺ If it's Sunday morning, join the late revelers and early joggers and dog-walkers for breakfast and shopping at the **Fischmarkt** (fish market), down at the Elbe riverside between the St. Pauli Landungsbrücken (the piers where the excursion boats tie up) and Grosse Elbstrasse. ⊠ *Fish market held Sun. 5 AM–10 AM, 7 AM–10 AM in winter.*

❻ The nearby **Landungsbrücken** (piers) are the start of the many boat trips of the harbor that are offered throughout the year (☞ Guided Tours, *above*).

❼ Along the north bank of the Elbe is one of the finest walks Hamburg has to offer. The walk is a long one, about 13 kilometers (8 miles) from the St. Pauli Landungsbrücken to the attractive waterside area of **Blankenese,** and that's only three-quarters of the route. But there are S-Bahn stations and bus stops along the way, to give you a speedy return to the downtown area.

Blankenese is another of Hamburg's surprises—a city suburb that has the character of a quaint fishing village. By all means attempt an exploratory prowl through some of its tiny lanes.

❽
❾ A ferry connects Blankenese with Hamburg's St. Pauli, although the S-Bahn ride back to the city is much quicker. Back at St. Pauli, resume your tour at the riverside and head back toward the downtown area through Elbpark, crossing Helgoländer Allee to the **Bismarck-Denkmal** (Bismarck Memorial)—an imposing statue of the Prussian "Iron Chancellor." Cross the square ahead of you and make for the **Museum für Hamburgische Geschichte** (Museum of Hamburg History) at Holstenwall 24. A visit to this museum is highly recommended—it gives an excellent overall perspective of the forces that have guided Hamburg from its origins in the 9th century to the present. ⊠ *Holstenwall 24,* ☎ *040/3504–2360.* ☒ *DM 6.* ☉ *Tues.–Sat. 10–5, Sun. 10–6.*

★ ❿ Cross Holstenwall to Peterstrasse, where you'll find a group of finely restored, 18th-century, half-timber houses. Turn right down Neanderstrasse and cross Ludwig-Erhard-Strasse to Hamburg's principal Protestant church, the **St. Michaliskirche** (St. Michael's Church), the finest Baroque church in northern Germany. ⊠ *Krayenkamp 4c,* ☎ *040/376–780.* ☉ *Apr.–Sept., daily 9–6, Thurs. until 10; Oct.–March, daily 10–5, Thurs. until 10. Tower (elevator or staircase of 449 steps):* ☒ *DM 4* ☉ *Apr.–Sept., daily 9–6, Sun. 11:30–6; Oct.–March, daily 10–5.*

⓫ From the St. Michaeliskirche, return to Ludwig-Erhard-Strasse, turn right, then left down Brunnenstrasse to Wexstrasse. Follow Wexstrasse to Grosse Bleichen, turn right down Heugberg, and cross the Bleichenbrücke and Adolphsbrücke over two of Hamburg's canals (known as the Fleete). Make a left into Alter Wall, and you'll come to the **Rathaus-**

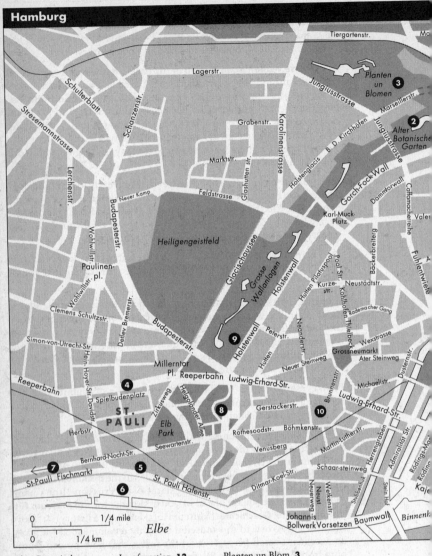

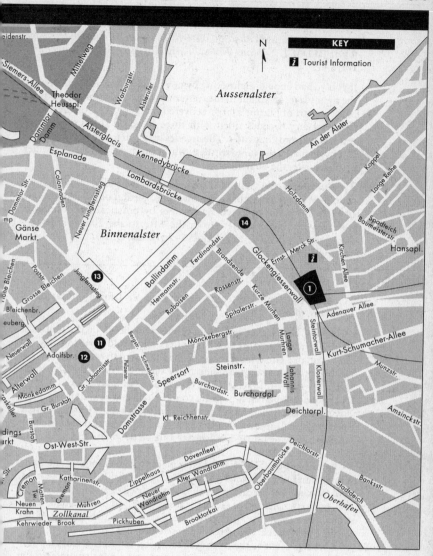

N

Aussenalster

Siemers-Allee

Mittelweg

Theodor
Heusspl.

Warburgstr.

Alsterufer

Dammtor Damm

Alsterglacis

Esplanade

Kennedybrücke

An der Alster

Koppel

Lange Reihe

Dammtor Str.

Colonnaden

Lombardsbrücke

Holzdamm

Spadteich

Baumeisterstr.

mp

Gänse
Markt.

Neuer Jungfernstieg

Binnenalster

14

Glockengiesserwall

Ernst Merck Str.

Kirchen Allee

Hansapl.

Hohe Bleichen

Poststr.

Jungfernstieg

13

Ballindamm

Hermannstr.

Ferdinandstr.

Brandsende

Rossenstr.

Kurze Mühren

_i_

1

Grosse Bleichen

Raboisen

Spitalerstr.

Steintorwall

Adenauer Allee

Bleichenbr.

euberg

Bergstr.

Mönckebergstr.

Lange Mühren

Kurt-Schumacher-Allee

Neuerwall

Alterwall

11

Adolfsbr.

12

Gr. Johannisstr.

Plazerin

Schmiedstr.

Speersort

Steinstr.

Burchardstr.

Johannis Wall

Klosterwall

Munzstr.

Mönkedamm

Gr. Burstah

Domstrasse

Burchardpl.

Deichtorpl.

Amsinckstr.

dings
arkt

Burstah

Kl. Reichhenstr.

Ost-West-Str.

Doventfleet

Deichtorstr.

Bansstr.

Str.

Cremon

Matten Tw.

Cremon

Katharinenstr.

Zippelhaus

Neuer
Wandrahm

Alter Wandrahm

Oberbaumbrücke

Stadtdeich

Oberhafen

Neuen
Krahn

Zollkanal

Mühren

Pickhuben

Brooktorkai

Kehrwieder

Brook

★ ⑫ **markt** (Town Hall Square). The 100-year-old **Rathaus** (Town Hall) has 647 rooms, six more than Buckingham Palace. Only the state rooms are open to visitors. ⊠ *Rathauspl.*, ☎ *040/3681–2470. English-language tours:* ⌑ *DM 1.* ☉ *Mon.–Thurs. hourly 10:15–3:15, Fri.–Sun. hourly 10:15–1.*

If you've had enough sightseeing by now, you've finished your tour at the right place; an arcade at the western edge of the Rathausmarkt signals the start of Europe's largest covered shopping area, nearly a kilometer of airy arcades filled with three hundred shops, expensive restaurants, and cozy cafés. The arcades lead you to the wide, seaside-
⑬ like promenade, the **Jungfernstieg,** which borders Hamburg's smaller artificial lake, the **Binnenalster.**

⑭ The **Kunsthalle** (Art Gallery) is well placed at the end of our Hamburg tour, next to the Hauptbahnhof, and its collection of paintings is one of Germany's finest. You'll find works by practically all the great northern European masters from the 14th to the 20th century. ⊠ *Glockengiesserwall 1,* ☎ *040/2486–2612.* ⌑ *DM 6.* ☉ *Tues.–Sun. 10–6 (Thurs. until 9).*

Dining

For details and price-category definitions, *see* Dining *in* Staying in Germany, *above.*

$$$ ✕ **La Mer.** The elegant restaurant of the Hotel Prem, on the southeast bank of the Aussenalster, La Mer offers a fine and varied menu. Try the marinated enoki mushrooms with imperial oysters and salmon roe or the spring venison with elderberry sauce. ⊠ *An der Alster 9,* ☎ *040/245–454. AE, DC, MC, V. Closed Sat. No lunch Sun.*

$$$ ✕ **Landhaus Scherrer.** A popular, country house–style restaurant in the
★ city's Altona district, Landhaus Scherrer fuses sophisticated nouvelle specialties with more down-to-earth local dishes and prides itself on its extensive wine list. ⊠ *Elbchaussee 130,* ☎ *040/880–1325. AE, DC, MC, V. Closed Sun.*

$$$ ✕ **Peter Lembcke.** There's no better place to eat eel soup or the tradi-
★ tional Hamburg *Labskaus*—a stew made from pickled meat, potatoes, and (sometimes) herring, garnished with a fried egg, sour pickles, and lots of beets. The best of German cuisine is served in this small, traditional restaurant just north of the train station. ⊠ *Holzdamm 49,* ☎ *040/243–290. AE, DC, MC, V. Closed Sun. No lunch Sat.*

$$ ✕ **Ahrberg.** Next to the river in Blankenese, the Ahrberg has a pleasant terrace for summer dining, and a cozy, wood-paneled dining room for colder days. The menu features a range of traditional German dishes and seafood specialties—often served together. Try the shrimp and potato soup and the fresh carp in season. ⊠ *Strandweg 33,* ☎ *040/860–438. AE, MC. Closed Sun.*

$$ ✕ **Fischerhaus.** Hamburg's famous fish market is right outside the door of this traditional old restaurant, which accounts for the variety and quality of fish dishes on its menu. Meat-eaters are also catered to, and the soups are legendary; fish soup is understandably the pride of the house. It's always busy, so be sure to reserve a table and arrive on time. ⊠ *St. Pauli Fischmarkt 14,* ☎ *040/314–053. No credit cards.*

$ ✕ **At Nali.** This is one of Hamburg's oldest and most popular Turkish restaurants. A plus is that it's open till 1 AM, handy if you're hankering after a late-night kebab. Prices are low, service is reliable and friendly, and the menu is extensive. ⊠ *Rutschbahn 11,* ☎ *040/410–3810. AE, DC, MC, V.*

Lodging

For details and price-category definitions, *see* Lodging *in* Staying in Germany, *above.*

$$$$ ☆ **Kempinski Hotel Atlantic Hamburg.** The sumptuous Atlantic has been ★ a focal point of Hamburg's social scene since it opened in 1909. Rooms, whether traditionally furnished or more modern, exude an understated luxury, and suites are just short of palatial; the service is swift and hushed. ⊠ *An der Alster 72-79, D-20099,* ☎ *040/28880,* FAX *040/2163–297. 243 rooms with bath, 13 suites. 2 restaurants, bar, snack bar, room service, indoor pool, beauty salon, massage, sauna, boutique, garage. AE, DC, MC, V.*

$$$$ ☆ **Vier Jahreszeiten.** This handsome 19th-century town-house hotel ★ offers scenic views of the Binnenalster and is rated, with its old-style rooms, impeccable service, and excellent food, among the world's best. ⊠ *Neuer Jungfernstieg 9–14, D-20354,* ☎ *040/34940,* FAX *040/349–4602. 158 rooms and 23 apartments, all with bath. 4 restaurants, bar, patisserie, wine shop, room service, beauty salon, boutique, garage. AE, DC, MC, V.*

$$$ ☆ **Aussen Alster.** Crisp and contemporary in design, this boutique hotel prides itself on giving personal attention to its guests. Rooms are compact; most have a full bathroom, and a few have a shower only. The cool, modern decor is given warmth by a fireplace and friendly bar. ⊠ *Schmilinskystr. 11, D-20099,* ☎ *040/241–557,* FAX *040/280–3231. 27 rooms with bath or shower. Restaurant, bar, sauna, boating, bicycles. AE, DC, MC, V.*

$$ ☆ **Hotel Graf Moltke.** The sturdy old Count Moltke rules majestically over central Steindamm street (a short walk from the main railway station). All rooms are equipped with soundproofing. Special weekend deals are offered for families. ⊠ *Steindamm 1, D-20099,* ☎ *040/280–1154,* FAX *040/280–2562. 97 rooms with bath or shower. Bar, boutiques. AE, DC, MC, V.*

$$ ☆ **Kronprinz.** For its down-market location (on a busy street opposite the railway station) and its moderate price, the Kronprinz is a surprisingly attractive hotel, with a whiff of five-star flair. Rooms are individually styled, modern but homey; ask for Number 45, with its mahogany and red-plush decor. ⊠ *Kirchenallee 46, D-20099,* ☎ *040/243–258,* FAX *040/280–1097. 69 rooms with bath or shower. Restaurant. AE, DC, MC, V.*

$ ☆ **Alameda.** The Alameda offers guests good, basic accommodations. The upstairs rooms are more spacious, but all rooms have TV, radio, and minibar. ⊠ *Colonnaden 45, D-20354,* ☎ *040/344–000,* FAX *040/343–439. 18 rooms with shower. AE, DC, MC, V.*

Nightlife

Few visitors can resist taking a look at the **Reeperbahn,** if only by day. From about 10 PM on, however, the place really shakes into life, and *everything* is for sale. Among the Reeperbahn's even rougher side streets, the most notorious is the Grosse Freiheit, which means "Great Freedom." The Reeperbahn area is not just a red-light district, however. Side streets are rapidly filling up with a mixture of yuppie bars, restaurants, and theaters that are somewhat more refined than the seamen's bars and sex shops. The **Hans-Albers-Platz** is a center of this revival; here the stylish bar La Paloma provides contrast to the Hans-Albers-Ecke, an old sailors' bar. The **Theater Schmidt** (⊠ Spielbudenplatz 23, ☎ 040/311–231) presents variety shows most evenings to a packed house.

THE RHINE

None of Europe's many rivers is so redolent of history and legend as the Rhine. For the Romans, who established forts and colonies along its western bank, the Rhine was the frontier between civilization and the barbaric German tribes. Roman artifacts can be seen in museums throughout the region. Throughout the Middle Ages, the river's importance as a trade artery made it the focus of conflict between princes, noblemen, and archbishops. Many of the picturesque castles that crown its banks were the homes of robber barons who held up passing ships and exacted tolls to finance even grander fortifications.

For poets and composers, the Rhine—or *Vater Rhein* (Father Rhine), as the Germans call it—has been an endless source of inspiration. As legend has it, the Lorelei, a treacherous, craggy rock, was home to a beautiful and bewitching maiden who lured sailors to a watery grave. The Rhine does not belong to Germany alone, but the German span of it has the most spectacular scenery—especially the stretch between Mainz and Köln (Cologne) known as the Middle Rhine. This is the "typical" Rhine: a land of steep and thickly wooded hills, vineyards, tiny villages hugging the banks, and a succession of brooding castles.

Getting Around

By Train
One of the best ways to visit the Rhineland in very limited time is to take the scenic train journey from Mainz to Köln along the western bank of the river. The views are spectacular, and the entire trip takes less than two hours. Contact **Deutsche Bahn** (German Railways) (⊠ Friedrich-Ebert-Anlage 43, Frankfurt, ☏ 069/19419), or get details at any central train station travel office.

By Boat
Köln-Düsseldorfer Rheinschiffahrt (⊠ Frankenwerft 15, D-50667 Köln, ☏ 0221/208–8288), **JFO CruiseService Corp.** (⊠ 2500 Westchester Ave., Purchase, NY 10577, ☏ 914/696–3600 or ☏ 800/346-6525), and **KD River Cruises of Europe** (⊠ 323 Geary St., Suite 603, San Francisco, CA 94102, ☏ 415/392–8817 or 800/346-6525) have daily cruises between Cologne and Frankfurt, from Easter to late October. The last-named company also offers trips up the Mosel as far as Trier. From March through November, the **Hebel-Line** (☏ 06742/2420) in Boppard cruises the Lorelei Valley; night cruises have music and dancing. For information about Neckar River excursions, contact **Neckar Personen Schiffahrt** (☏ 0711/541–073 or 0711/541–074).

By Car
If you choose to drive, you'll take in some of the region's most spectacular scenery on the Rhineland's comprehensive highway network. For information about routes, contact the **German Automobile Club** (AVD, ⊠ Lyonerstr. 16, D-60528 Frankfurt-am-Main, ☏ 069/66060).

By Bicycle
Tourist offices in all the larger towns will provide information and route maps. Deutsche Bahn rents bikes at numerous stations. For information, call 069/19419 or ask for the *"Fahrrad am Bahnhof"* ("Bikes for Rent") brochure at any station.

Visitor Information

For general information on the region, contact the Fremdenverkehrsverband Rheinland-Pfalz (⊠ Löhrstr. 103, D-00000 Koblenz, ☏ 0261/915–200).

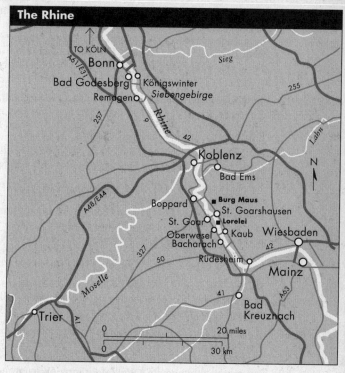

The Rhine

TO KÖLN

Bonn

Bad Godesberg — Königswinter
Remagen — Siebengebirge
Sieg

255

Rhine

42

Koblenz
Bad Ems

Lahn

N

Boppard
■ Burg Maus
St. Goarshausen
St. Goar ■ Lorelei
Oberwesel ○ Kaub
Bacharach
Wiesbaden

42

Rüdesheim

Mainz

Moselle

41

Bad
Kreuznach

Trier

A63

0   20 miles
0   30 km

Bacharach (Fremdenverkehrsamt, ✉ Oberstr. 1, ☎ 06743/2968).
Boppard (Verkehrsamt, ✉ Karmeliterstr. 2, ☎ 06742/10319).
Koblenz (Fremdenverkehrsamt Pavillon am Hauptbahnhof, ☎ 0261/31304).
Köln (Verkehrsamt, ✉ Unter Fettenhennen 19, ☎ 0221/221–3340).
Mainz (Verkehrsverein, ✉ Bahnhofstr. 15, ☎ 06131/286–210).
Rüdesheim (Verkehrsamt, ✉ Rheinstr. 16, ☎ 06722/2962).
St. Goarshausen (Verkehrsamt, ✉ Bahnhofstr. 8, ☎ 06771/427).

Guided Tours

In addition to a number of special-interest cruises, **KD River Cruises of Europe** (☞ Getting Around, *above*) operates a series of guided excursions covering the towns along its routes. A host of local shipping lines do the same, including **Personenschiffahrt Merkelbach** (✉ Emserstr. 87, Koblenz-Pfaffendorf, ☎ 0261/76810) or **Rhein und Moselschiffahrt Gerhard Collee-Holzbein** (✉ Rheinzollstr. 4, Koblenz, ☎ 0261/37744). The tourist offices in Mainz, Köln, and Koblenz also offer tours (in English) of their respective cities.

Exploring the Rhine

Köln

The largest German city on the Rhine is **Köln** (Cologne), first settled by the Romans in 38 BC. The Franks and Merovingians followed the Romans before Charlemagne restored the city's fortunes in the 9th century, appointing its first archbishop and ensuring its ecclesiastical prominence for centuries.

By the Middle Ages, Köln was the largest city north of the Alps, and, as a member of the powerful Hanseatic League, it was more important commercially than either London or Paris. Ninety percent of the city was destroyed in World War II, and the rush to rebuild it after the war shows in some of the blocky, uninspired architecture. Still, attempts were made to restore many of its old buildings. Whatever the city's aesthetic drawbacks, the Altstadt (Old Town), within the line of the medieval city walls, has great charm, and at night it throbs with life.

★ Towering over the Old Town is the extraordinary Gothic cathedral, the **Kölner Dom,** dedicated to St. Peter and the Virgin. It's comparable to the best French cathedrals; a visit to it may prove a highlight of your trip to Germany. At 515 feet high, the two western towers of the cathedral were by far the tallest structures in the world when they were finished. The length of the building is 469 feet; the width of the nave is 148 feet; and the highest part of the interior is 139 feet.

The cathedral was built to house what were believed to be the relics of the Magi, the three kings or wise men who paid homage to the infant Jesus. Today the relics are kept just behind the altar, in the same enormous gold-and-silver **reliquary** in which they were originally displayed. The other great treasure of the cathedral is the **Gero Cross,** a monumental oak crucifix dating from 971. Impressive for its simple grace, it's in the last chapel on the left as you face the high altar.

Still more treasures can be seen in the **Schatzkammer,** the cathedral treasury, including the silver shrine of Archbishop Engelbert, who was stabbed to death in 1225. ▦ *DM 3.* ☉ *Mon.–Sat. 9–5, Sun. 1–5.*

Outside again, you have the choice of either more culture or commerce. Köln's **shopping district** begins at nearby **Wallrafplatz.** Grouped around the cathedral is a collection of superb museums. If your priority is painting, try the ultramodern ★**Wallraf-Richartz-Museum** and **Museum Ludwig** complex. Together, they form the largest art collection in the Rhineland. The Wallraf-Richartz-Museum's pictures span the years 1300 to 1900, with Dutch and Flemish schools particularly well represented (Rubens, who spent his youth in Köln, has a place of honor). The Museum Ludwig is devoted exclusively to 20th-century art. A new, all-Picasso museum will be constructed for its Picasso collection in the near future. ⊠ *Bischofsgartenstr. 1,* ☎ *0221/221–2379 or 3491.* ▦ *Both museums: DM 10.* ☉ *Tues.–Fri. 10–6, weekends 11–6.*

Opposite the cathedral is the **Römisch-Germanisches Museum,** built from 1970 to 1974 around the famous Dionysus mosaic that was uncovered at the site during the construction of an air-raid shelter in 1941. The huge mosaic, more than 300 feet square, once covered the dining-room floor of a wealthy Roman trader's villa. ⊠ *Roncallipl. 4,* ☎ *0221/221-4438.* ▦ *DM 5.* ☉ *Tues.–Fri. 10–4, weekends 11–4.*

Now head south to the nearby **Alter Markt** and its **Altes Rathaus,** the oldest town hall in Germany. The square has a handsome ensemble of buildings—the oldest dating from 1135—in a range of styles. There was a seat of local government here in Roman times, and directly below the current Rathaus are the remains of the Roman city governor's headquarters, the Praetorium. Go inside to see the 14th-century **Hansa Saal,** whose tall Gothic windows and barrel-vaulted wooden ceiling are potent expressions of medieval civic pride. The figures of the prophets, standing on pedestals at one end, are all from the early 15th century.

Cross Unter Käster to get to the river and one of the most outstanding of Köln's 12 Romanesque churches, the **Gross St. Martin.** Its massive 13th-century tower, with distinctive corner turrets and an imposing central spire, is another landmark of Köln. Gross St. Martin is the parish church of Köln's colorful old section, the **Martinsviertel,** an attractive combination of reconstructed, high-gabled medieval buildings, winding alleys, and tastefully designed modern apartments and business quarters. Head here at night—the place comes alive at sunset.

To complete your daytime Köln tour, however, leave the Martinsviertel along Martinstrasse and turn right into Gürzenichstrasse, passing the crenellated Gothic-style Gürzenich civic reception/concert hall. Take a left turn into Hohestrasse and another right turn into Cäcilienstrasse. At Number 29, you'll find the 12th-century St. Cecilia Church, and within its cool, well-lighted interior one of the world's finest museums of medieval Christian art, the **Schnütgen Museum.** Although the main emphasis of the museum falls on early and medieval sacred art, the collection also covers the Renaissance and Baroque periods. ⊠ *Cäcilienstr. 29,* ☎ *0221/221–2310.* ☎ *DM 5.* ☉ *Tues.–Fri. 10–4, weekends 11–4. Guided tours (in German) Sun. at 11.*

Around the corner, on Leonhard-Tietz-Strasse, is **St. Peter's Church,** where the painter Peter Paul Rubens was christened. There's a fine Rubens painting in the altar recess, joined recently by a modern triptych by the British painter Francis Bacon.

A few steps away is the expansive **Neumarkt** square, at whose western end is one of Köln's finest Romanesque basilicas, **St. Aposteln.** The Neumarkt was an early trading center; the church was built in the 11th century amid the hustle and bustle of a daily market.

Bonn

Not far south of Köln is the staid city of **Bonn,** the former capital of West Germany, now preparing to hand most of its legislative and administrative functions over to Berlin. The **Beethovenhaus** (Beethoven Museum, ⊠ Bonngasse 20, ☎ 0228/635–188; ☎ DM 8) displays scores, a grand piano, and an ear trumpet or two in the house where the composer was born. The city also has a respectable **Münster** (cathedral) and a trio of new museums, including the **Federal Kunsthalle,** which brings Bonn more into the swing of things, culturally speaking.

The diplomats' ghetto of **Bad Godesberg,** just south of Bonn, is across the river from **Königswinter,** site of one of the most visited castles on the Rhine, the **Drachenfels.** Its ruins crown the highest hill in the **Siebengebirge** (Seven Hills), commanding a spectacular view of the river. The castle was built during the 12th century by the archbishop of Köln.

Koblenz

The city of **Koblenz** began as a Roman camp more than 2,000 years ago. The vaults beneath **St. Florin's Church** contain an interesting assortment of Roman remains. A good place to begin your tour of Koblenz is the **Deutsches Eck,** or "Corner of Germany," the tip of the sharp peninsula separating the two rivers. On summer evenings, concerts are held in the nearby **Blumenhof Garden.** Most of the city's historic churches are also within walking distance of the Deutsches Eck. The **Liebfrauenkirche** (Church of Our Lady), completed in the 13th century but later much modified, incorporates Romanesque, Late Gothic, and Baroque elements. **St. Florin,** a Romanesque church built around 1100, was remodeled in the Gothic style in the 14th century. Gothic windows and a vaulted ceiling were added in the 17th century. The city's most important church, **St. Kastor,** also combines Romanesque and Gothic elements and features some unusual altar tombs and rare Gothic wall paintings.

Much of the **Old Town** of Koblenz is now a pedestrian district, an attractive area for a leisurely stroll. Many of the ancient cellars beneath the houses have been rediscovered and now serve as wine bars and jazz clubs.

Across the river, on the Rhine's east bank, towers the city's most spectacular castle, **Ehrenbreitstein.** The fortifications of this vast structure date from the 1100s, although the bulk of it was built much later, in the 16th and 17th centuries. To reach the fortress, take the *Sesselbahn* (cable car) or, if you're in shape, try walking up.

One of Koblenz's two noteworthy art galleries, the **Ludwig Museum** presents rotating exhibitions of contemporary art, much of it from the enormous collection of Koblenz-born tycoon Peter Ludwig. *DM 5. ⊘ Tues.–Sat. 10–5 (Wed. 11–8) and Sun. 10–6.*

The other gallery, the **Mittelrhein Museum,** features Rhenish art and artifacts from the Middle Ages to the present day. ⊠ *15 Florinsmarkt. DM 5. ⊘ Tues.–Sat. 10–5 (Wed. 11–8) and Sun. 10–6.*

Rhine Gorge

Between the cities of Koblenz and Mainz, the Rhine flows through the 64-kilometer (40-mile) stretch known as the **Rhine Gorge.** It is here that the Rhine lives up to its legends and lore and where in places the river narrows to a mere 200 yards. Today, vineyards occupy every inch of available soil on the steep, terraced slopes. High above, ancient castles crown the rocky shelves.

South of Koblenz, at a wide, western bend in the river, lies the quiet old town of **Boppard,** once a bustling city of the Holy Roman Empire. Now the remains of its Roman fort and castle are used to house a museum of Roman artifacts and geological specimens. There are also several notable churches, including the **Carmelite Church,** with its fine Baroque altar, and the Romanesque church of **St. Severus.** From Boppard there is a wonderful view across the Rhine to the ruined castles of **Liebenstein** and **Sterrenberg.**

Continuing south from Boppard, you come to the little town of **St. Goar,** crowded against the steep gorge cliff and shadowed by the imposing ruin of **Rheinfels Castle.** Rheinfels was built in the mid-13th century by Count Dieter von Katzenelnbogen (whose name means "cat's elbow"). The count's enormous success in collecting river tolls provoked the other river barons to unite and lay siege to his castle. The ruins are now being restored, and a luxury hotel has been built on the site (☞ Dining and Lodging, *below*). DM 5. ⊘ *Apr.–Oct., daily 9–5.*

On the east bank of the river, just across from the town of St. Goar, lies its sister village, **St. Goarshausen.** An hourly ferry service links the two. St. Goarshausen is dominated by **Burg Katz** (Cat Castle), a massive fortress built by a later count von Katzenelnbogen. Tourists are not permitted inside, but the top of the cliff offers a lovely view of the famous Lorelei rock. About 3.2 kilometers (2 miles) north of St. Goarshausen is **Burg Maus,** or Mouse Castle.

Many tourists visit St. Goarshausen for its location—only a few kilometers from the legendary **Lorelei rock.** To get to the Lorelei, follow the road marked with LORELEI-FELSEN signs. Here the Rhine takes a sharp turn around a rocky, shrub-covered headland. This is the narrowest and shallowest part of the Middle Rhine, full of treacherous currents. According to legend, the beautiful maiden, Lore, sat on the rock here, combing her golden hair and singing a song so irresistible that passing sailors forgot the navigational hazards and were swept to their deaths.

One of the most photographed sites of the Middle Rhine region is the medieval village of **Kaub,** south of the Lorelei on the east side of the river. Its unusual castles are well worth a visit. The **Pfalzgrafenstein,** on a tiny island in the middle of the Rhine, bristles with sharp-pointed towers and has the appearance of a small sailing ship. In the 14th century, the resident *Pfalzgraf,* or count Palatine, was said to have strung chains across the Rhine to stop riverboats and collect his tolls. A special boat takes visitors to the island. *Ferry:* ⊠ *DM 2.50;* ⊙ *Trips every ½-hour 9–1 and 2–5 (in season). Castle:* ⊠ *DM 4.*

On a hillside above Kaub hovers another small castle, **Burg Gutenfels.** Built in the 13th century, Gutenfels was renovated completely at the end of the 18th century and is now an exquisite hotel (☞ Dining and Lodging, *below*).

The picturesque little village of **Bacharach,** encircled by 15th-century walls, is the best-preserved town of the Middle Rhine. The town's name has become associated with wine, as it is an important trading center for the region's vintages.

Farther south, on the Rhine's east bank and at the center of the Rhine Gorge region, lies another famous wine town. According to legend, **Rüdesheim**'s first vines were planted by Charlemagne. More recent vintages can be enjoyed in the many taverns lining **Drosselgasse,** a narrow, colorful street in the heart of town. Rüdesheim is a tourist magnet—about the most popular destination on the Rhine—so if you plan to stay overnight, be sure to reserve well in advance.

Mainz

On the west bank of the Rhine, at the mouth of the Main River, stands the city of **Mainz.** Once the seat of powerful archbishops, this is where, around 1450, the printing pioneer Johannes Gutenberg first experimented with moveable type. He is commemorated by a monument and square bearing his name and a museum containing his press and one of the Bibles he printed. ⊠ *Liebfrauenpl. 5.* ⊠ *DM 5.* ⊙ *Tues.–Sat. 10–6, Sun. and holidays 10–1. Closed Jan.*

★ Today, Mainz is a bustling, modern city of nearly 200,000 inhabitants. A focal point is the city's **Dom** (cathedral), one of the finest Romanesque churches in Germany. On **Gutenbergplatz** in the **Old Town** stand two fine Baroque churches, the **Seminary Church** and **St. Ignatius.** The Old Town also claims the country's oldest Renaissance fountain— the **Marktbrunnen**—and the **Dativius-Victor-Bogen,** an arch dating from Roman times. The **Römisch-Germanisches Museum,** in the **Kurfürstliches Schloss** (Elector's Palace), contains a notable collection of archaeological finds. ⊠ *Rheinstr.* ⊠ *Free.* ⊙ *Tues.–Sun. 10–6.*

A newer touch is provided in the Gothic church of **St. Stephan,** standing on a hilltop to the south of the Old Town; in its choir are six stained-glass windows by French artist Marc Chagall.

Dining and Lodging

When it comes to cuisine, the Rhineland offers a number of regional specialties. Be sure to sample the wide variety of sausages available, the goose and duck dishes from the Ahr Valley, and Rhineland sauerbraten—accepted by many as the most succulent of pot roasts. During the peak summer season and in early autumn—wine festival time—accommodations are scarce, so reserve well in advance.

For details and price-category definitions, *see* Dining *and* Lodging *in* Staying in Germany, *above.*

Bacharach

$$ ✕⊡ **Altkölnischer Hof.** This small but cozy half-timber hotel was built at the turn of the century. Its rustic restaurant serves typical local dishes and some excellent wines. ⊠ *Blücherstr. 2, D-55422,* ☎

06743/1339, FAX 06743/2793. *18 rooms with bath. Restaurant, parking. AE, V. Closed Nov.–Mar.*

Bonn

$$ ✕ **Haus Daufenbach.** The stark white exterior of the Daufenbach, near the church of St. Remigius, conceals one of the most distinctive restaurants in Bonn. The mood is rustic, with simple wooden furniture and antlers on the walls. Specialties include Spanferkel and a range of imaginative salads. Wash them down with wines from the restaurant's own vineyards. ⊠ *Brüderg. 6,* ☎ *0228/637–944. No credit cards. Closed Mon. No dinner Sun. in summer.*

$ ✕ **Em Höttche.** Travelers have been dining at this tavern since the late 14th century; today, it offers one of the best-value lunches in town. The tone is rustic, the food hearty, and the portions are large. ⊠ *Markt 4,* ☎ *0228/690–009. Reservations not accepted. No credit cards.*

$$$$ 🏨 **Domicil.** A group of buildings around a quiet central courtyard has been stylishly converted into a hotel of great charm and comfort. The rooms are decorated in styles from fin-de-siècle romantic to Italian modern. ⊠ *Thomas-Mann-Str. 24-26, D-53115,* ☎ *0228/729–090,* FAX *0228/691–207. 42 rooms with bath. Restaurant, coffee bar, sauna, hairdresser. AE, DC, MC, V. Closed Christmas–New Year's Day.*

$$ 🏨 **Rheinland.** This modest lodging has the advantage of being a short walk from the center of the Old Town. Rooms are comfortable, and although there is no restaurant, a good buffet breakfast greets the day. ⊠ *Berliner Freiheit 11, D-53111,* ☎ *0228/658–096,* FAX *0228/472–844. 31 rooms with bath. AE, MC.*

$$ 🏨 **Sternhotel.** For good value, solid comfort, and a central location in the Old Town, the family-run "Star" is tops. Rooms can be small, but all are pleasantly furnished. There's no restaurant, but snacks are available at the bar. ⊠ *Markt 8, D-53111,* ☎ *0228/72670,* FAX *0228/726–7125. 81 rooms with bath. Bar. AE, DC, MC, V.*

Boppard

$$$ 🏨 **Bellevue Rheinhotel.** This is one of the Rhineland's most majestic hotels, an imposing turn-of-the-century building whose elegant white-and-yellow facade, under steep slate eaves, faces directly onto the river. ⊠ *Rheinallee 41–42, D-54156,* ☎ *06742/1020,* FAX *06742/102–602. 94 rooms with bath. Restaurant, beer cellar, bar, indoor pool, sauna, Turkish bath, tennis courts, health club. AE, DC, MC, V.*

Kaub

$$$–$$$$ 🏨 **Burg Gutenfels.** The terrace of this luxurious castle hotel offers one
★   of the finest views in the Rhine Valley (☞ Exploring, *above*). Guests can also enjoy wine from the hotel's own vineyard. Be sure to reserve well in advance. ☎ *06774/220,* FAX *06774/1760. 10 rooms with bath. Restaurant, private chapel. AE, DC, MC, V.*

Koblenz

$$ ✕ **Wacht am Rhein.** The name of this attractive riverside restaurant, Watch on the Rhine, sums it up. In summer, take a table on the terrace and watch the river traffic pass by; in winter, choose a window table and dine with the Rhine outside and the atmospheric warmth of the fin-de-siècle fittings and furnishings inside. Fish is the basis of the extensive menu. ⊠ *Adenauer-Ufer 6,* ☎ *0261/15313. AE.*

$$$$ 🏨 **Scandic Crown.** This modern, somewhat charmless hotel stands directly on the bank of the Rhine; most rooms have fine views of the river and the Ehrenbreitstein fortress. A lovely garden and terrace also overlook the river. ⊠ *Julius-Wegeler-Str. 6, D-56068,* ☎ *0261/1360,* FAX

0261/136–1199. *159 rooms with bath. 2 restaurants, bar, sauna, whirlpool. AE, DC, MC, V.*

$$–$$$ ⊞ **Kleiner Reisen.** This is a well-run, straightforward hotel that gives value for the money. Another plus is the quiet riverside location that's still within walking distance of the train station and Old Town. There's no restaurant. ⊠ *Kaiserin-Augusta-Anlagen 18, D-56068,* ☎ *0261/32077,* FAX *0261/160–725. 27 rooms with bath. Parking. AE, DC, MC, V.*

Köln

$$$ ✕ **Weinhaus im Walfisch.** The black-and-white gabled facade of this
★ 400-year-old restaurant lets you know what to expect inside—though the local offerings are spruced up for an upmarket clientele. The menu presents quasi-traditional dishes with a French accent: fine fare at corresponding prices, and a wide range of wines. The restaurant is tucked away between the Heumarkt (Haymarket) and the river. ⊠ *Salzg. 13,* ☎ *0221/258–0397. AE, DC, MC, V. Closed weekends and holidays.*

$$ ✕ **Früh am Dom.** For real down-home German food, there are few places to compare with this time-honored former brewery. Bold frescoes on the vaulted ceilings establish the mood, and such dishes as *Hämmchen* (pork shank) provide an authentically Teutonic experience. The beer garden is delightful for summer dining. ⊠ *Am Hof 12–14,* ☎ *0221/258–0389. No credit cards.*

$$$$ ✕⊞ **Dom-Hotel.** The Dom is in a class of its own. Old-fashioned, for-
★ mal, and gracious, with a stunning location right by the cathedral, it offers the sort of elegance and discreetly efficient service few hotels even aspire to these days. Enjoy views of the cathedral from the glassed-in Atelier am Dom, where you can dine on anything from wild boar served with chanterelle ragout to tofu piccata with curried rice. ⊠ *Domkloster 2A, D-50667,* ☎ *0221/20240,* FAX *0221/202–4444. 126 rooms with bath. 2 restaurants, bar, café, parking. AE, DC, MC, V.*

$$$$ ✕⊞ **Excelsior Hotel Ernst.** The Empire-style lobby in sumptuous royal
★ blue, bright yellow, and gold is striking, and a similar, boldly conceived grandeur extends to all the public rooms in this 1863 hotel. Old master paintings (including a Van Dyck) are everywhere; you'll be served breakfast in a room hung with Gobelin tapestries. Guest rooms are appropriately more intimate in scale, with spectacular marble bathrooms and ultramodern fixtures. The lacquered-wood-paneled restaurant serves classic French cuisine imaginatively prepared. ⊠ *Trankg. 1-5, D-50667,* ☎ *0221/2701,* FAX *0221/135–150. 160 rooms with bath. Restaurant, piano bar, beauty salon, massage, exercise room. AE, DC, MC, V.*

$$ ✕⊞ **Stapelhäuschen.** One of the few houses along the riverbank to have survived World War II bombings, this is one of the very oldest buildings in Köln. You can't beat the location, overlooking the river and right by Gross St. Martin; yet rooms are reasonably priced, making up in quaintness for what they lack in luxury. ⊠ *Fischmarkt 1-3, D-50667,* ☎ *0221/257–7862,* FAX *0221/257–4232. AE, DC, MC, V.*

$$ ⊞ **Altstadt.** Close to the river and in the Old Town, this is the place
★ for charm and low rates. Each room is furnished differently, and the service is impeccable—both welcoming and efficient. There's no restaurant. ⊠ *Salzg. 7, D-50667,* ☎ *0221/257–7851,* FAX *0221/257–7853. 28 rooms with bath. Sauna. AE, DC, MC, V. Closed Christmas–New Year's Day.*

Königswinter

$$ ✕⊞ **Gasthaus Sutorius.** Just across from the church of St. Margaretha, this wine tavern serves refined variations on traditional German dishes, along with an intelligent selection of local wines. In summer, food is served outdoors beneath the lime trees. ⊠ *Oelinghovener Str. 7, D-*

53639 Stieldorf, ☎ *02244/4749. No credit cards. Closed two weeks in Jan., all of Sept. No lunch except Sun.*

Mainz

$$ ✕ **Rats- und Zunftstuben Heilig Geist.** Although the decor is predominantly modern, this popular restaurant also incorporates some Roman remains and offers a traditional atmosphere. The cuisine is hearty German fare. ✉ *Renteng. 2,* ☎ *06131/225–757. Reservations essential. AE, DC, MC, V. Closed Sun.*

$ ✕ **HDW.** The abbreviated name stands for "House of German Wine," a German bistro with a modern approach to traditional food. The Mainz Spuntekäse is excellent as are the salad with fish and the venison ragout with Späetzle (homemade noodles). Near the Gutenberg museum. ✉ *Gutenbergplatz 3,* ☎ *06131/228–676. No credit cards.*

$$$ ☒ **Hilton International.** A terrific location by the Rhine and high standards of service and comfort make the Hilton the top accommodation choice in Mainz. Don't come looking for too much in the way of old German atmosphere, however. The hotel has a casino and two restaurants. ✉ *Rheinstr. 68, D-55116,* ☎ *06131/2450,* FAX *06131/245–589. 433 rooms with bath. 2 restaurants, beauty salon, sauna, exercise room. AE, DC, MC, V.*

$ ☒ **Hotel Stadt Coblenz.** In the heart of the town, this attractive hotel offers budget rooms (bath in the hall) at budget prices—ask for a room facing the back. The rustic restaurant serves local and German specialties. ✉ *Rheinstr. 49, D-55116,* ☎ *0631/227–602. Restaurant. No credit cards.*

Rüdesheim

$$–$$$ ✕ **Krone.** The extensive restoration work recently carried out on the 450-year-old Krone included a complete renovation of its restaurant, which now ranks among the most outstanding in the region. Chef Herbert Pucher's terrines and pâtés draw regular customers from as far away as Frankfurt. His fish dishes are supreme, and the Rhine wines are the best. ✉ *Rheinuferstr. 10, Assmannshausen,* ☎ *06722/4030. AE, DC, MC, V.*

$$$–$$$$ ☒ **Hotel Jagdschloss Niederwald.** This is not so much a place to overnight as a luxury resort hotel where you might want to spend your entire vacation. It's set in the hills 5 kilometers (3 miles) outside of Rüdesheim, with predictably good views over the Rhine and the Rhine Gorge. The former hunting lodge of the dukes of Hesse, it has a lavish, baronial atmosphere. ✉ *Auf dem Niederwald 1, D-65383,* ☎ *06722/1004,* FAX *06722/47970. 52 rooms with bath. Restaurant, bar, indoor pool, sauna, exercise room, tennis courts, horseback riding. AE, DC, MC, V. Closed Jan. 1–Feb. 14.*

$$ ☒ **Rüdesheimer Hof.** For a taste of Rhein Gorge hospitality, try this typical inn. There's a terrace for summer dining on excellent local specialties, which you can enjoy along with any of the many wines offered. ✉ *Geisenheimerstr. 1, D-65385,* ☎ *06722/2011,* FAX *06722/48194. 42 rooms with bath. Restaurant, parking. AE, DC, MC, V. Closed mid-Nov.–mid-Feb.*

St. Goar, St. Goarshausen

$$ ✕ **Roter Kopf.** This is a historic wine restaurant brimming with rustic Rhineland atmosphere. ✉ *Burgstr. 5, St. Goarshausen,* ☎ *06771/ 2698. No credit cards.*

$$$ ☒ **Schlosshotel-Burg Rheinfels.** High above St. Goar, on a hill commanding spectacular river views, the Schlosshotel-Burg Rheinfels rises

from the ruins of the adjacent castle (☞ Exploring, *above*). ⊠ *Schloss-berg 47, D-56329 St. Goar,* ☎ *06741/8020,* FAX *06741/7652. 58 rooms with shower. Restaurant, pool, sauna. AE, DC, MC, V.*

$ 🏨 **Hermannsmühle.** This rustic, chalet-style hotel just outside of town has heavy furniture decorated with painted floral patterns. Herr Hermann, the host, extends a warm welcome to all, and his place offers good value at low prices. ⊠ *Forstbachstr. 46, D-56346 St. Goar-shausen,* ☎ *06771/7317. 10 rooms with bath. Restaurant. MC, V. Closed mid-Nov.–Feb.*

THE BLACK FOREST

Only a century ago, the Black Forest (Schwarzwald) was one of the wildest stretches of countryside in Europe. But then, the deep hot springs first enjoyed by the Romans were rediscovered, and small forgotten villages became wealthy spas. Today, the region is friendly and hospitable, still extensively forested but with large, open valleys and stretches of verdant farmland.

The Black Forest is the southernmost German wine region and the custodian of some of the country's best traditional foods. Black Forest smoked ham and Black Forest cake are world-famous. The region retains its vibrant clock-making tradition, and local wood-carvers haven't yet died out.

Getting Around

The Rhine Valley autobahn, the A5, runs the entire length of the Black Forest and connects at Karlsruhe with the rest of the German expressway network. Well-paved, single-lane highways traverse the region. A main north–south train line follows the Rhine Valley, carrying EuroCity and InterCity trains that call at hourly intervals at Freiburg and Baden-Baden, connecting those two centers directly with Frankfurt and many other German cities. Local lines connect most Black Forest towns, and two local east–west services, the Black Forest Railway and the Höllental Railway, are spectacular scenic runs. The nearest airports are in Stuttgart; Strasbourg, in the neighboring French Alsace; and the Swiss border city of Basel, just 64 kilometers (40 miles) from Freiburg.

Visitor Information

Baden-Baden (⊠ Augustapl. 8, ☎ 07221/275–200).
Freiburg (⊠ Rotteckring 14, ☎ 0761/368–9090).
Freudenstadt (⊠ Promenadenpl. 1, ☎ 07741/8640).
Pforzheim (⊠ Marktpl. 1, ☎ 07231/39900).

Guided Tours

There are guided bus tours of the Black Forest that begin in Freiburg; contact the visitor information office (☞ Above). A choice of 25 one-day tours includes the French Alsace region, the Swiss Alps, and various attractions in the Black Forest itself. Prices start at DM 32 and include English-speaking guides.

Exploring the Black Forest

The regional tourist authority has worked out a series of scenic routes covering virtually every important attraction (contact the **Fremden-verkehrsverband,** ⊠ Bertoldstr. 45, D-79098 Freiburg, ☎ 0761/31317). The following itinerary is accessible by all means of transportation and

The Black Forest

takes in parts of the Black Forest High Road, Low Road, Spa Road, Wine Road, and Clock Road.

The ancient Roman city of **Pforzheim** is the starting point here, accessible either from the Munich–Karlsruhe autobahn or by train from Karlsruhe, Frankfurt, or Stuttgart. Pforzheim has the world's finest museum collection of jewelry in the **Schmuckmuseum** (Jewelry Museum) in the **Reuchlinhaus** (✉ Jahnstr. 42, ☎ 07231/392–126; ☞ DM 5; ☉ Tues.–Sun. 10–5). Pforzheim was almost completely destroyed by wartime bombing and is a fine example of careful reconstruction.

Bad Liebenzell, our first stop on B463, is one of the Black Forest's oldest spas, with the remains of 15th-century installations. Visitors are welcome to take the waters at the **Paracelsus Baths** on the Nagold riverbank. ☎ 07052/408–250. ☞ DM 12 for 3 hours. ☉ Apr.–Oct., Tues., Wed., Fri.–Sun. 7:30 AM–9 PM, Mon., Thurs. 7:30 AM–5 PM; Nov.–Mar., Tues., Wed., Fri.–Sun. 8:30 AM–8 PM, Mon., Thurs. 8:30 AM–5 PM.

Take some time to explore **Calw** (pronounced calve), the next town on the road south. Its famous native son, the novelist and poet Hermann Hesse, called it the "most beautiful [town] of all I know."

Back on the main road south, turn off at Talmühle for the **Neubulach silver mine.** Once the most productive workings of the Black Forest, the mine closed in 1924 but is now open to visitors. ☞ DM 4 (includes entry to mineral museum). ☉ Apr.–Oct., daily 10–4:15.

| NEED A BREAK? | In the town of **Nagold,** visit the half-timber **Alte Post** inn at Bahnhofstrasse 2, built in 1697. Kings and queens have taken refreshment here. Enjoy the local beer and a plate of Black Forest smoked ham or a pot of strong coffee and a slice of delectable Black Forest cake. |

From Nagold, the road travels on through lush farmland to **Freuden-stadt,** another war-flattened German city that has been painstakingly restored. Don't miss Freudenstadt's **Protestant parish church,** just off the square. Its L-shaped ground plan was a daring innovation in the early 17th century, when this imposing church was built.

★ From here, take B294 to **Wolfach** and visit the Dorotheen-Glashütte, one of the last Black Forest factories where glass is blown by centuries-old techniques once common throughout the region. ⊠ *Glashütten-weg 4,* ☎ *07834/751.* ⊒ *DM 4 (includes tour).* ☉ *Weekdays 9–4:30, Sat. 9–2.*

The valley of **Gutachtal,** south of Wolfach, is famous for its traditional costumes, and if you're here at the right time (holidays and some Sundays), you'll see the married women sporting black pom-poms on their hats to denote their matronly status (red pom-poms are for the unmarried). At the head of the valley, at **Triberg,** are Germany's high-
★ est waterfalls, plunging nearly 509 feet. This is also cuckoo-clock country. The **Uhrenmuseum** (Clock Museum) at Furtwangen is the largest in Germany. Its collection includes an astronomical timepiece weighing more than a ton. ⊠ *Gerwigstr. 11,* ☎ *07723/920–117.* ⊒ *DM 4.* ☉ *Apr.–Oct., daily 9–5; Nov.–Mar., daily 10–5.*

From Furtwangen, the road leads to the lakeland of the Black Forest. The two largest lakes, **Titisee** and **Schluchsee,** are beautifully set amid fir-clad mountains, but try to avoid them at the height of the summer holidays, when they are quite crowded.

Perched on the western slopes of the Black Forest, **Freiburg,** now one of the Black Forest's largest and loveliest cities, was founded as a free market town in the 12th century. Towering over the rebuilt medieval
★ streets of the city is its most famous landmark, the cathedral, or **Mün-ster.** The cathedral took three centuries to build and has one of the finest spires in the world. Tours: ⊒ *DM 8.* ☉ *Mon. and Fri. 2:30, Wed., Thurs., Sat., Sun. 10:30.*

On weekdays, the square in front of the cathedral becomes a mass of color and movement; it's the town market, where you can buy everything from herbs to hot sausage. A fitting backdrop is provided by the **Kaufhaus,** a 16th-century market house.

NEED A BREAK?	Stroll up to Oberlinden Square and stop in at **Zum Roten Bären** (The Red Bear), reputedly Germany's oldest inn; it has a documented history dating from 1091. Order a *Viertel* of the local wine and a plate of locally smoked ham—and if you like the atmosphere, why not stay the night?

Staufen, which claims the inquisitive Dr. Faustus as one of its early burghers, is some 19 kilometers (12 miles) south of Freiburg.

From Staufen, turn northward to Baden-Baden along the **Wine Road,** skirting the French border to your left, through the southernmost vineyards of Germany. These produce the prized Baden wine.

All the vineyards along the Wine Road offer tastings, so don't hesitate to drop in and try one or two. To continue on our tour, leave the Wine Road at the town of Lahr and head inland, on B415, through the narrow Schuttertal valley to Zell, and from there to the Black Forest **High Road.** This is the land of fable and superstition, and if you're here during the misty days of autumn, stop off at the mystery-shrouded lake called the **Mummelsee.**

★ From the Mummelsee, it's downhill all the way to fashionable **Baden-Baden,** idyllically set in a wooded valley of the northern Black Forest and sitting atop the extensive underground hot springs that gave the city its name (*Bad* means baths). The Romans first exploited the springs, which were then rediscovered by wealthy travelers a couple of centuries ago. By the end of the 19th century, there was scarcely a crowned head of Europe who had not dipped into the healing waters of Baden-Baden.

One of the grand buildings of Baden-Baden's Belle Epoque is the pillared **Kurhaus,** home of Germany's first casino, which opened its doors in 1853. It costs a modest DM 5 to get in, though visitors are required to sign a declaration that they enter with sufficient funds to settle subsequent debts! ☺ *Sun.–Fri. 2 PM–2 AM, Sat. 2 PM–3 AM. Tours:* ☒ *DM 3.* ☺ *Apr.–Sept., daily 9:30–noon; Oct.–Mar., 10–noon. Jacket and tie. Passport necessary as proof of identity.*

Although jackets and ties are de rigueur at the casino, no clothes at all are expected at Baden-Baden's famous Roman baths, the **Friedrichsbad.** You take the waters here just as the Romans did nearly 2,000 years ago—nude. The remains of the Roman baths that lie beneath the Friedrichsbad can be visited (☒ DM 2) from April through October. ☒ *Römerpl. 1,* ☎ *07221/275–920.* ☒ *DM 28 for 3 hours (DM 48 with massage).* ☺ *Mon.–Sat. 9 AM–10 PM, Sun. 2–10 PM. Children under 18 not admitted.*

NEED A BREAK?	Step into the warm elegance of the **Café König** in the nearby Lichtentalerstrasse pedestrian zone. Order a pot of coffee and a wedge of Black Forest cake and listen to the hum of contentment from the monied spa crowd that has made this quiet corner a favorite haunt.

The attractions of the Friedrichsbad are rivaled by the neighboring **Caracalla Baths,** renovated and enlarged in 1985. The huge, modern complex has five indoor pools, two outdoor ones, numerous whirlpools, a solarium, and what is described as a "sauna landscape"—you look out through windows at the countryside while you bake. ☒ *Römerpl. 11,* ☎ *07221/275–940.* ☒ *DM 18 for 2 hours, DM 24 for 3 hours.* ☺ *Daily 8 AM–10 PM.*

Dining and Lodging

For details and price-category definitions, *see* Dining *and* Lodging *in* Staying in Germany, *above.*

Baden-Baden

$$$ ✕ **Stahlbad.** The Gallo-Germanic menu here is echoed by the restaurant's furnishings—19th-century French oils adorn the walls, and French and German china are reflected in the mahogany gleam of antique tables and sideboards. An abundance of green velvet catches the tone of the parklike grounds of the stately house that accommodates this elegant restaurant. ☒ *Augustapl. 2,* ☎ *07221/ 24569. AE, DC, MC, V. Closed Sun. and Mon.*

$$$ ✕▣ **Der Kleine Prinz.** Each room of this beautifully modernized 19th-
★ century mansion is decorated in a different style, from romantic Art Nouveau to Manhattan modern. Chef Berthold Krieger is in charge of the kitchen, and by combining nouvelle cuisine flair with unmistakable German thoroughness, he has elevated the restaurant to a leading position in demanding Baden-Baden. ☒ *Lichtentalerstr. 36, D-76530,* ☎ *07221/3464,* ℻ *07221/38264. 39 rooms with bath. Restaurant (closed first 2 wks of Jan.). AE, DC, MC, V.*

\$\$ ✕🏨 **Gasthaus zur Traube.** Regional specialties such as smoked bacon and homemade noodles take pride of place in this cozy inn, south of the city center in the Neuweier district. If you like the food, you can also spend the night in one of the 18 neatly furnished and moderately priced rooms. ⊠ *Mauerbergstr. 107,* ☎ *07223/57216. MC, V. Closed Wed.*

\$\$\$\$ 🏨 **Brenner's Park Hotel.** This exceptional, stately mansion is set in spacious private grounds. All rooms are luxuriously furnished and appointed—as they should be for the price. ⊠ *Schillerstr. 6, D-76530,* ☎ *07221/9000,* 🅵🅰🅶 *07221/38772. 68 rooms with bath and balcony, 32 suites. 2 restaurants, indoor pool, beauty salon, sauna, bridge room, bicycles. AE, DC, MC.*

\$\$ 🏨 **Etol.** This centrally located, established hotel, a few minutes' stroll from the Kurhaus, offers fresh, comfortable rooms at reasonable prices in an otherwise expensive town. The family that owns the Etol also runs the Merkur (☎ 07221/3030) and the Sterntaller restaurant across the street. ⊠ *Merkurstr. 7, D-76530,* ☎ *07221/36040,* 🅵🅰🅶 *07221/360444. 18 rooms with bath. Bar, wine and beer tavern, bicycles. AE, DC, MC, V.*

\$ 🏨 **Hotel am Markt.** The Bogner family has run the place for more than three decades—a relatively short amount of time for this 250-plus-year-old building. It's friendly, popular, and right in the center of town. ⊠ *Marktpl. 17–18, D-76530,* ☎ *07221/22747,* 🅵🅰🅶 *07221/391–887. 28 rooms, 14 with bath. Restaurant. AE, DC, MC, V.*

Bad Liebenzell

\$\$\$ ✕🏨 **Kronen Hotel.** This is a comfortable hotel with a large modern wing. The kitchen, which provides the food for the hotel's three different restaurants, prides itself on serving healthful cuisine with lots of fresh vegetables and herbs, whole-grain products, and fruit. ⊠ *Badweg 7, D-75378,* ☎ *07052/4090,* 🅵🅰🅶 *07052/409–420. 3 restaurants, café. AE, DC, V.*

\$\$–\$\$\$ ✕🏨 **Waldhotel Post.** This spa hotel has a fine view of town and of the surrounding Black Forest. The spacious rooms range from comfortable to luxurious; some have south-facing balconies. The Black Forest creeps to the very edge of the garden. The hotel's Restaurant Krieg is one of the best in the region. ⊠ *Hölderlinstr. 1, D-75378,* ☎ *07052/4070,* 🅵🅰🅶 *07052/40790. Restaurant, café, indoor pool, sauna, massage. AE, V.*

Baiersbronn

\$\$\$\$ ✕🏨 **Bareiss.** The beautiful mountain resort of Baiersbronn is blessed
★ with two of Germany's leading restaurants. The most notable is the Bareiss, in the luxury hotel of the same name. Its dark wood furniture and tapestry-papered walls are warmly lighted by candles and traditional lamps. Guests are lured by the light, classic cuisine and carefully selected wines (30 vintages of champagne alone). ⊠ *Gärtenbühlweg 14, D-07442 Mitteltal/Baiersbronn,* ☎ *07442/470,* 🅵🅰🅶 *07442/47320. 51 rooms with bath, 42 apartments, 7 suites. 2 restaurants, bar, 3 swimming pools, sauna, solarium, tennis, exercise room, bowling, bicycles, billiards. AE, DC, MC, V.*

\$\$\$\$ ✕🏨 **Traube Tonbach.** Baiersbronn's second world-class restaurant, the
★ Schwarzwaldstube, is also part of a luxurious hotel, the Traube Tonbach. If the fabulous Schwarzwaldstube is full or too pricey, then the Köhlerstube is an acceptable alternative. In both, you dine beneath beamed ceilings at tables bright with fine silver and glassware. The hotel is a harmonious blend of old and new furnishings and decor, each room enjoying sweeping views of the Black Forest. ⊠ *Tonbachstr. 237, D-72270,* ☎ *07442/4920,* 🅵🅰🅶 *07442/492–692. 134 rooms with bath, 38*

apartments, 8 suites. 2 restaurants, bars, cafeteria, 3 swimming pools, sauna, tennis, exercise room, bowling, bicycles. AE, DC, MC, V.

$$ ×🏨 **Hotel Lamm.** The half-timber exterior of this 200-year-old building presents a clear picture of the traditional Black Forest hotel within. Rooms are furnished with heavy oak fittings and some fine antiques. In its beamed restaurant, you can order fish taken from the hotel's trout pools. ✉ *Ellbacherstr. 4, D-07442 Mitteltal/Baiersbronn,* ☎ *07442/4980,* FAX *07442/49878. Restaurant, indoor pool, sauna, billiards, table tennis. AE, DC, MC, V.*

Calw

$$$ ×🏨 **Hotel Kloster Hirsau.** This country-house hotel on the wooded outskirts of Calw stands on the site of a 900-year-old monastery, whose Gothic cloisters are still largely intact. The hotel prides itself on its restaurant, where owner-chef Joachim Ulrich's menu changes daily. The emphasis is on regional dishes enhanced with a French touch: featured are Swabian farmhouse noodles along with truffle vinaigrette. ✉ *Wildbaderstr. 2, D-75365,* ☎ *07051/5621,* FAX *07051/51795. 43 rooms with bath. Restaurant, bar, indoor pool, parking. DC, MC, V.*

$$ ×🏨 **Ratsstube.** Most of the original features, including 16th-century beams and brickwork, are intact at this historic house in the center of Calw. Rooms aren't spacious but they are brightly decorated, with pastel colors and floral patterns. The restaurant offers sturdy, traditional German fare, such as marinated beef and noodles, thick soups, and Black Forest sausage. ✉ *Marktpl. 12, D-75365,* ☎ *07051/1864,* FAX *07051/70826. 13 rooms with bath. Restaurant, parking. No credit cards.*

Freiburg

$$–$$$ × **Oberkirchs Weinstuben.** Located right across from the Gothic cathedral and next to the Renaissance Kaufhaus, this wine cellar is a bastion of tradition and local Gemütlichkeit. Approximately 20 Baden wines are served by the glass, from white Gutedel to red Spätburgunder. The proprietor personally bags some of the game that ends up in the kitchen. Fresh trout is another specialty. In summer, the dark-oak dining tables spill onto a garden terrace. ✉ *Münsterpl. 22,* ☎ *0761/31011. V. Closed Sun., public holidays, and Jan. 10–Feb. 2.*

$$ × **Kleiner Meyerhof.** Weinstube atmosphere with more places to sit. A good place to try regional specialties at comfortable prices. In the fall and winter, they serve goose and wild game. ✉ *Rathausg. 27,* ☎ *0761/26941. MC. Closed Sunday between June and August.*

$$ × **Kühler Krug.** Venison dominates the proceedings at this restaurant, which has even given its name to a distinctive saddle-of-venison dish. Those who prefer fish shouldn't despair: There's an imaginative range of freshwater varieties available. ✉ *Torpl. 1,* ☎ *0761/29103. MC. Closed Wed., Thurs., and 3 wks in June.*

$ × **Freiburger Salatstuben.** Healthy vegetarian food is prepared in creative ways—try the homemade whole-wheat noodles with cauliflower in a pepper cream sauce—and served cafeteria style. And all that nutrition and fiber costs no more than a meal at the McDonald's around the corner. Crowded at peak hours with students from the university up the street. ✉ *Am Martinstor-Löwenstr. 1,* ☎ *0761/35155. No credit cards. Closed Sat. dinner, Sun., public holidays.*

$$$–$$$$ ×🏨 **Colombi.** Freiburg's most luxurious hotel also has the city's finest
★ and most original restaurant and two reconstructed 18th-century farmhouse guest cottages, now luxuriously furnished and decorated with antiques. In the rustic section of the restaurant, you can order hearty local dishes, such as lentil soup and venison, while its more elegant section's menu goes decidedly upscale, combining traditional meat and fish dishes with innovative sauces. The hotel is centrally located and

quiet. ⊠ *Am Colombi Park/Rotteckring 16, D-79098,* ☎ *0761/21060,* FAX *0761/31410. 80 rooms with bath, 12 suites. Restaurant (reservations essential; closed Sun). AE, DC, MC, V.*

$$$ ✗⊞ **Zum Roten Bären.** Now a showpiece of the Ring group, this inn, which dates from 1311, has retained its character with very comfortable lodging and excellent dining in a cozy warren of four restaurants and taverns. A tour of the two basement floors of cellars, dating from the original 12th-century foundation of the town of Freiburg and now well stocked with fine wines, is also recommended. ⊠ *Oberlinden 12, D-79098,* ☎ *0761/36913,* FAX *0761/36916. 19 rooms with bath, 3 apartments. Restaurant, wine tavern, sauna, parking. AE, DC, MC, V.*

$$ ✗⊞ **Markgräfler Hof.** Even the French make the pilgrimage to dine in Hans Leo Kempchen's restaurant in this traditional old hotel in Freiburg's quaint pedestrian zone. Kempchen rewards travelers with special gourmet menus and unbeatable two-day deals that include accommodations, a wine tasting, and a guided tour of the city. Call well in advance to reserve rooms. ⊠ *Gerberau 22, D-79098,* ☎ *0761/32540,* FAX *0761/37947. 18 rooms with bath or shower. Restaurant, parking. AE, DC, MC, V.*

$$ ⊞ **Rappen Hotel.** The Rappen is in the center of the traffic-free Old Town overlooking the marketplace and the cathedral (and overhearing the bustle of the former and the bells of the latter). A farmhouse theme dominates here, with rustic furnishings in every room. In the countrified but comfortable restaurant, patrons have the choice of more than 200 regional wines. ⊠ *Am Münsterpl. 13, D-79098,* ☎ *0761/31353,* FAX *0751/382–252. 25 rooms, 13 with bath. Restaurant. AE, DC, MC, V.*

Freudenstadt

$$ ✗ **Ratskeller.** If it's cold outside, ask for a place near the Ratskeller's *Kachelofen,* a large, traditional, tiled stove. Swabian dishes and venison are prominent on the menu, but if the homemade trout roulade with crab sauce is available, go for it. ⊠ *Marktpl. 8,* ☎ *07441/2693. MC, V. Closed Mon.*

$$–$$$ ✗⊞ **Bären.** The sturdy old Gasthof Bären has been owned by the same family since 1878, and it strives to maintain tradition and service with a personal touch. Rooms are modern but with homey touches such as farmhouse-style bedsteads and cupboards. The beam-ceiling restaurant is a favorite with the locals; its menu combines heavy German dishes (roasts and hearty sauces) and lighter international fare. ⊠ *Langestr. 33, D-72250,* ☎ *07441/2779,* FAX *07441/2887. 23 rooms with bath. Restaurant, parking. MC.*

$$ ✗⊞ **Luz Posthotel.** This old coaching inn in the heart of town has been managed by the same family since 1809. But there's nothing old-fashioned about the rooms, which are both modern and cozy. The restaurant offers Swabian delicacies. In summer there's a coffee terrace. ⊠ *Stuttgarterstr. 5, D-72250,* ☎ *07441/8970,* FAX *07441/ 84533. 45 rooms with bath, some with balcony. Wine bar, library. AE, DC, MC, V. Closed Nov.*

Gutach

$$–$$$ ⊞ **Romantik Hotel Stollen.** The flower-bedecked balconies and low roofs
★ of this hotel disguise a distinctive and luxurious interior, where understated comfort—some rooms have four-poster beds—is combined with attentive service. The restaurant, complete with a roaring log fire, serves regional food with nouvelle touches. The hotel is 21 kilometers (15 miles) northeast of Freiburg. ⊠ *D-79261 Gutach im Elztal,* ☎ *07685/207,* FAX *07685/1550. 11 rooms with bath and balcony, 1 suite. AE, MC, V.*

Hinterzarten

$$$$ 🏨 **Park Hotel Adler.** Since 1446, when an early ancestor of the hotel's
   ★   present owners paid 17 schillings for the original property, it has been
developing into one of Germany's finest hotels. The hotel complex stands
on nearly 10 acres of grounds ringed by the Black Forest. Among the
seven rooms devoted to eating and drinking are a French restaurant
and a paneled 17th-century dining room. An orchestra accompanies
dinner and later moves to the bar for dancing. ✉ *Adlerpl. 3, D-79854,*
☎ *07652/1270,* ℻ *07652/127–717. 84 rooms with bath. 2 restaurants, bar, pool, beauty salon, sauna, solarium, tennis (indoor/outdoor),
horseback riding, bicycles, library. AE, DC, MC, V.*

Nagold

$$–$$$ ✗ **Romantik Restaurant Alte Post.** At this centuries-old half-timber inn,
   ★   the menu ranges from Swabian traditional to pricey French, so stay
with the local dishes (veal in a rich mushroom sauce or, in season, venison in the Baden-Baden style) and you won't be shocked by the bill.
✉ *Bahnhofstr. 2,* ☎ *07452/4048. Reservations essential. AE, DC, MC,
V. Closed two wks in Jan. and two wks in July–Aug. No lunch Fri.*

$$–$$$ 🏨 **Hotel Post Gästehaus.** Run by the former proprietors of the adja-
cent Alte Post restaurant, this hotel is made up of an old coaching inn
and modern additions. It offers a high degree of comfort—and homemade preserves for breakfast. ✉ *Bahnhofstr. 3, D–72202,* ☎
07452/4048, ℻ *07452/4040. 24 rooms with bath. English-language
cable TV. AE, DC, MC, V.*

Pforzheim

$ ✗ **Silberburg.** This is a rustic restaurant offering classic and regional
cooking at bargain prices. For best value, ask to see the *Tage-
sempfehlungen*—the chef's daily recommendations. ✉ *Dietlingerstr. 27,*
☎ *07231/41159. Reservations essential. AE, DC, MC, V. Closed Mon.
and 3 wks in Aug. No lunch Tues.*

Titisee

$$ ✗🏨 **Romantik Hotel Adler Post.** This hotel is in the Neustadt district of
Titisee, about 4½ kilometers (3 miles) from the lake. The solid old build-
ing has been in the possession of the Ketterer family for more than 140
years. The guest rooms are comfortably and traditionally furnished.
The hotel's restaurant, the Rôtisserie zum Postillon, is noted for its re-
gional cuisine. ✉ *Hauptstr. 16, D-79822 Titisee–Neustadt,* ☎ *07651/5066,*
℻ *07651/3729. 24 rooms, 4 apartments, all with bath. Restaurant, pool,
sauna, library. AE, DC, MC, V. Closed mid-Mar.–early Apr.*

Triberg

$$–$$$ ✗🏨 **Park Hotel Wehrle.** The Wehrle family has owned this enchant-
ing building in the center of town since 1707; its vine-covered facade
dominates the marketplace. The comfortable rooms are individually
furnished, the service is impeccable, the restaurant is outstanding, and
the prices are surprisingly low for this kind of luxury. ✉ *Am Mark-
tpl. 1, D-78098,* ☎ *07722/86020,* ℻ *07722/860–290. 52 rooms, 2
apartments, 2 suites, all with bath. Indoor/outdoor pools, sauna, fit-
ness room, parking. AE, DC, MC, V.*

BERLIN

Berlin is now a united metropolis and only four small sections of the
Wall have been left in place to remind visitors and residents of the hideous
barrier that divided the city for nearly 30 years. However, there's still
a strong feeling of passing from one world into another when cross-
ing the scar that marks the line where the Wall once stood. It's not just

the very visible differences between the glitter of western Berlin and the relative shabbiness of the former eastern section. Somehow the historical heritage of a long-divided city permeates the place and penetrates the consciousness of every visitor.

Arriving and Departing

By Plane

Tegel (☎ 030/410–2306) airport is only 7 kilometers (4 miles) from downtown. Delta, United, Air France, British Airways, Deutsche BA, Lufthansa, and some charter specialists regularly fly to Tegel. Because of increased air traffic at Tegel following unification, the former military airfield at **Tempelhof** (☎ 030/691–510), even closer to downtown, is being used more and more. **Schönefeld** (☎ 030/60910) airport is about 24 kilometers (15 miles) outside the downtown area.

BETWEEN THE AIRPORTS AND DOWNTOWN
Buses 109 and X09 run every 10 minutes between Tegel airport and downtown. The journey takes 30 minutes and the fare is DM 3.90 for adults, DM 2.50 for children, and covers all public transportation throughout Berlin. A taxi will cost about DM 25. If you're driving from the airport, follow signs for the STADTAUTOBAHN highway. Tempelhof is right on the U-6 subway line, in the center of the city. A shuttle bus leaves Schönefeld airport every 10–15 minutes for the nearby S-Bahn station. S-Bahn trains leave every 20 minutes for the Friedrichstrasse and Zoologischer Garten stations. The trip takes about 30 minutes, and you can get off at whatever stop is nearest your hotel. The fare for this trip is DM 3.90. Taxi fare to your hotel will be about DM 40– DM 55, and the trip will take about 40 minutes. By car, follow the signs for BERLIN— ZENTRUM.

By Train

There are six major rail routes to Berlin from the western part of the country (from Hamburg, Hannover, Köln, Frankfurt, Munich, and Nürnberg), and the network has expanded considerably, making the rest of eastern Germany more accessible. For information call **Deutsche Bahn** (☎ 030/19419) or inquire at the local main train station.

By Bus

Long-distance bus services link Berlin with numerous other German and European cities. For travel details, if you're in Berlin, call the main bus station (✉ Messedam, ☎ 030/301–8028); if you're in other parts of Germany, inquire at the local tourist office.

By Car

The eight former "transit corridor" roads linking the western part of Germany with Berlin have been incorporated into the country-wide autobahn network, but be prepared for large traffic jams, particularly on weekends.

Getting Around

By Public Transportation

Berlin is surprisingly large, and only the center can be explored comfortably on foot. Fortunately, the city has an excellent public transportation system: a combination of U-Bahn and S-Bahn lines, buses, and streetcars (in eastern Berlin only). For DM 3.90 (DM 2.60 children) you can buy a ticket that covers travel on the entire system for 2 hours. If you are just making a short trip, buy a **Kurzstreckentarif.** It allows you to ride six bus stops or three U-Bahn or S-Bahn stops for DM 2.50 (DM 2.00 children). A multiple ticket, valid for four trips on the entire system, costs DM 13 (DM 9 children). Or, you can pay DM 15 for a **Day Card** (no children's discount), good for 30 hours of unlimited public-transportation travel. The **Group Day Card,** for DM 24, offers the same benefits for two adults and as many as three children. If you're staying for more than a few days, the **Tourist Pass,** valid for a week and costing DM 40, is the best bargain. The **BerlinWelcomeCard,** at DM 16 for a day (or DM 29 for two days), entitles one adult and up to three children to unlimited travel as well as free or reduced sightseeing trips and admission to museums, theaters, and other events and attractions. If you're caught without a ticket, the fine is DM 60. Tickets are available from vending machines at U-Bahn and S-Bahn stations or from bus drivers. For information, call the **BVG** (☎ 030/752–7020) or go to the information office on Hardenbergplatz, directly in front of the Bahnhof Zoo train station.

By Taxi
The base rate is DM 4, after which prices vary according to a complex tariff system. If your ride will be short, ask in advance for their special Kurzstreckentarif, which is DM 5 for rides of less than two kilometers or five minutes. Figure on paying around DM 15 for a ride the length of the Ku'damm. Hail cabs in the street or at taxi stands, or order one by calling 030/9644, 030/210–202, 030/691–001, or 030/261–026. U-Bahn employees will call a taxi for passengers after 8 PM.

Important Addresses and Numbers

Consulates
U.S. (⊠ Clayallee 170, ☎ 030/819–7454). **Canadian** (⊠ International Trade Center, Friedrichstr. 95, ☎ 030/261–1161). **U.K.** (⊠ Unter den Linden 32–34, ☎ 030/201–8401). **Ireland** (⊠ Ernst-Reuter-Pl. 10, ☎ 030/3480-0822).

Emergencies
Police (☎ 030/110). **Ambulance and emergency medical attention** (☎ 030/310–031). **Dentist** and **emergency pharmaceutical assistance** (☎ 030/01141).

English-Language Bookstores
Marga Schoeller (⊠ Knesebeckstr. 33, ☎ 030/881–1112) and **Buchhandlung Kiepert** (⊠ Hardenbergstr. 4–5, ☎ 030/311–0090) sell English-language publications.

Visitor Information
The main tourist office, **Verkehrsamt Berlin,** is at the Europa Center (⊠ Budapesterstr., ☎ 030/262–6031). It's open Monday–Saturday 8 AM–10:30 PM, Sunday 9–9. There are other offices at the main hall of **Tegel** airport (☎ 030/4101–3145, ⊙ Daily 8 AM–11 PM); at the **Zoologischer Garten,** (☎ 030/313–9063, ⊙ Mon.–Sat. 8 AM–11 PM); and at the **Hauptbahnhof** (☎ 030/279–5209, ⊙ Daily 8–8) in east Berlin.

Accommodations can be reserved at all offices, which also issue a free English-language information brochure, "Berlin Turns On." Pretravel information on Berlin can be obtained by writing to the Verkehrsamt Berlin (⊠ Martin-Luther-Str. 105, D-10825 Berlin).

TIPS FOR TRAVELERS WITH DISABILITIES
Many S- and U-Bahn stations have elevators and a few buses have hydraulic lifts. Check the public transportation maps or call the **BVG** (☞ *Above*). **Service-Ring-Berlin e.V.** (☎ 030/859–4010 or 030/9389–2410) and **Verband Geburts- und anderer Behinderter e.V.** (☎ 030/341–1797) provide information and van and wheelchair rentals.

Guided Tours

By Bus

Severin & Kühn (⊠ Kurfürstendamm 216, ☎ 030/883–1015); **Berliner Bären Stadtrundfahrt** (BBS, ⊠ Rankestr. 35, corner of Kurfürstendamm, ☎ 030/214–8790); **Berolina Stadtrundfahrten** (⊠ Kurfürstendamm 22, corner Meinekestr., ☎ 030/882–2091); and **Bus Verkehr Berlin (BVB,** ⊠ Kurfürstendamm 225, ☎ 030/885–9880) offer more or less identical tours in English, covering all the major sights in Berlin, as well as day tours to Potsdam and Dresden. The Berlin tours cost DM 25–DM 45, those to Potsdam and Sanssouci Palace, the favorite residence of Frederick the Great, DM 54.

By Boat

Berlin is a city of waterways, and boat trips can be made on the Spree River, on the canals that connect the city's network of big lakes, and on the lakes themselves. For details, contact the main city tourist office.

Exploring Berlin

Visiting Berlin is still a bittersweet experience, as so many of the triumphs and tragedies of the past are tied up with the bustling present. The result can be either dispiriting or exhilarating. By European standards, Berlin isn't too old. Although already a royal residence in the 15th century, Berlin really came into its own three centuries later, under the rule of King Friedrich II—Frederick the Great—whose liberal reforms and artistic patronage led the way as the city developed into a major cultural capital.

What Berlin was forced to endure in the 20th century would have crushed the spirit of most other cities. Hitler and his supporters destroyed the city's reputation for tolerance and plunged Berlin headlong into the war that led to the wholesale destruction of monuments and houses. And after World War II, Berlin was still to face the bitter division of the city and the construction of the infamous Wall in 1961. But a storm of political events, beginning in 1989, brought the downfall of the East German communist regime; finally, in October 1990, there was a reunification of Berlin and of all Germany.

Downtown Berlin

Numbers in the margin correspond to points of interest on the Downtown Berlin map.

The **Kurfürstendamm,** or Ku'damm as the Berliners call it, is one of Europe's busiest thoroughfares, throbbing with activity day and night. ★ ❶ At its origin is the **Kaiser Wilhelm Gedächtniskirche** (Kaiser Wilhelm Memorial Church). This landmark had come to symbolize West Berlin, and it still is a dramatic reminder of the futile destructiveness of war. The shell of the tower is all that remains of the church that was built at the end of the 19th century and dedicated to Kaiser Wilhelm I. Surrounding the tower are the new church and bell tower. ⊠ *Breitscheidpl.,* ☎ *030/218–5023.* 🎟 *Free.* ⊙ *Tues.–Sat. 10–5. Closed holidays.*

★ ❷ Cross Budapesterstrasse to enter the **Zoologischer Garten,** Berlin's zoo. It has the world's largest variety of individual types of fauna along with a fascinating aquarium. ⊠ *Budapesterstr. 34,* ☎ *030/254–010.* 🎟 *Zoo only, DM11; aquarium only, DM 10; combined, DM 17.* ⊙ *Zoo daily 9–6:30, or until dusk in winter; aquarium daily 9—6.*

Downtown Berlin

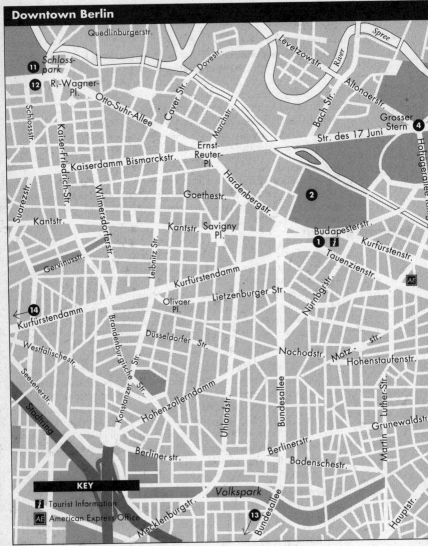

KEY

i Tourist Information

AE American Express Office

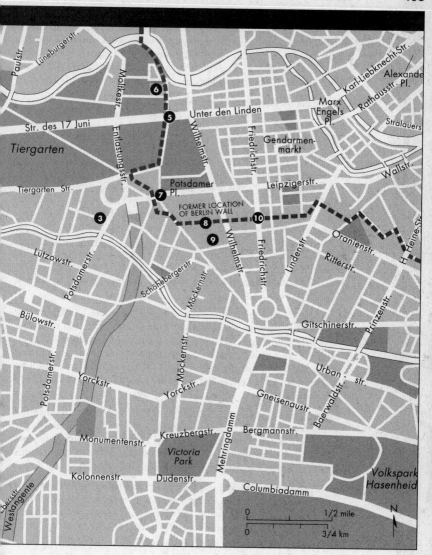

Double back across Breitscheidplatz and take Tauentzienstrasse to Wittenbergplatz to catch Bus 129 to Potsdamer Brücke. Among the museums, buildings, and galleries that comprise the **Kulturforum** (Cultural Forum) on the large square is the **Philharmonie** (Philharmonic Hall), home of the famous Berlin Philharmonic orchestra. ⊠ *Matthäikirchstr. 1,* ☎ *030/2548—8132.* ⊙ *Box office, weekdays 3:30–6, weekends 11–2.*

Opposite is the **Kunstgewerbemuseum** (Museum of Decorative Arts), part of the Cultural Forum, which displays arts and crafts of Europe from the Middle Ages to the present day. ⊠ *Matthäikirchpl. 6,* ☎ *030/266–291. Admission: DM 4; free Sun. Open Tues.–Fri. 9–5, weekends 10–5.*

Leave the museum and walk south past the mid-19th-century church of St. Matthew to the **Neue Nationalgalerie** (New National Gallery), a modern glass-and-steel building designed by Mies van der Rohe and built in the mid-1960s. The gallery's collection consists of paintings, sculptures, and drawings from the 19th and 20th centuries, with an accent on works by the Impressionists. ⊠ *Potsdamer Str. 50,* ☎ *030/266–2662.* 🎫 *DM 4, free Sun and holidays.* ⊙ *Tues.–Fri. 9–5, weekends 10–5. A Tageskarte (day pass) covers 1-day admission to this and all other museums at the Cultural Forum.* 🎫 *DM 8. Card is available at each museum.*

The Kulturforum is adjacent to the 630-acre **Tiergarten** (Animal Park), the former hunting grounds of the Great Elector. The column in the center of a large traffic circle in the park is the **Siegessäule** (Victory Column), erected in 1873 to commemorate four Prussian military campaigns. Climb the 285 steps to its 213-foot summit, and you'll be rewarded with a fine view of Berlin. ⊠ *Am Grossen Stern,* ☎ *030/391—2961.* 🎫 *DM 1.50.* ⊙ *Mon. 1–6, Tues.–Sun. 9–6.*

Moving along Strasse des 17. Juni (June 17th Street), you'll reach the **Brandenburger Tor** (Brandenburg Gate), built in 1788 to celebrate the triumphant Prussian armies. The monumental gate was cut off from West Berlin by the Wall, and it became a focal point of celebrations marking the reunification of Berlin and of all Germany.

Just north of the Brandenburg Gate is the **Reichstag,** which served as Germany's parliament building from its completion in 1894 until 1933, when it was gutted by fire under suspicious circumstances. When the federal government relocates to Berlin (scheduled for 2000), the Bundestag, the lower house of parliament, will convene here.

Walk south along where the Wall used to stand to **Potsdamer Platz** (Potsdam Square). It was one of prewar Berlin's busiest squares.

Follow farther along the Wall's former course to see the real thing, one of four still-standing segments of the famous **Berliner Mauer** (Berlin Wall), just north of the **Prinz-Albrecht-Gelände** (Prince Albrecht Grounds) along Niederkirchnerstrasse. Buildings that once stood here housed the headquarters of the Gestapo and other Nazi security organizations from 1933 until 1945. After the war, they were leveled and remained so until 1987, when what was left of the buildings was excavated and an exhibit, "Topography of Terrors," documenting their history and Nazi atrocities was opened. ⊠ *Stresemannstr. 110,* ☎ *030/2548–6703.* 🎫 *Free.* ⊙ *Daily 10–6. Tours by appointment only.*

The history of the frontier fortification can be followed in the museum that arose at its most famous crossing point, at Friedrichstrasse, the second cross street heading east. Checkpoint Charlie, as it was known, disappeared along with the Wall, but the **Haus am Checkpoint Charlie** (House at Checkpoint Charlie–The Wall Museum) is still there. ⊠ *Friedrichstr. 44,* ☎ *030/251–1031.* 🎫 *DM 7.50.* ☯ *Daily 9 AM–10 PM.*

NEED A
BREAK?
Try to visualize the former Checkpoint Charlie crossing and the Wall from a window seat at **Café Adler** (⊠ Friedrichstr. 206, ☎ 030/251—8965), which bumped right up against the Wall here. The soups and salads are all tasty and cheap.

⭐ ⑪ Take the U-Bahn south two stops from the Kochstrasse station and change to the U-7 line for 14 stops, to Richard-Wagner-Platz station. From the station, walk east along Otto-Suhr-Allee to the handsome **Schloss Charlottenburg** (Charlottenburg Palace) and its beautiful, calming grounds. Built at the end of the 17th century by King Frederick I for his wife, Queen Sophie Charlotte, the palace was progressively enlarged for later royal residents. ⊠ *Luisenpl.,* ☎ *030/320–911.* 🎫 *DM 4, free Sun.* ☯ *Tues.–Fri. 9–5, weekends 10–5.*

⭐ ⑫ Opposite the palace is the **Ägyptisches Museum** (Egyptian Museum), home of perhaps the world's best-known portrait sculpture, the beautiful head of Nefertiti. The 3,300-year-old queen is the centerpiece of a fascinating collection of Egyptian antiquities that includes some of the finest preserved mummies outside Cairo. ⊠ *Schlosstr. 70,* ☎ *030/320–911.* 🎫 *DM 4.50, free Sun. and holidays.* ☯ *Mon.–Thurs. 9–5, weekends 10–5. A Tageskarte (day pass), available at the Ägyptisches Museum and the nearby Antikensammlung and Museum für Vor- and Frühgeschichte covers 1-day admission to all three museums and includes a guided tour of Schloss Charlottenburg.* 🎫 *DM 8.*

⑬ Take U-Bahn line U-7 back toward Schöneberg to Fehrbelliner Platz, where you change to line U-1 southwest for five stops to Dahlem-Dorf station. This is the stop for the magnificent **Dahlem museums,** chief of which is western Berlin's leading picture gallery, the **Gemäldegalerie.** The collection includes many works by the great European masters, with 26 pieces by Rembrandt and 14 by Rubens. ⊠ *Arnimallee 23/27,* ☎ *030/83011.* 🎫 *DM 4 (combined day pass to 7 Dahlem museums, DM 8), free Sun.* ☯ *Tues.–Fri. 9–5, weekends 10–5.*

⑭ No visit to west Berlin is complete without an outing to the city's outdoor playground, the **Grunewald** (Green Forest). Bordering the Dahlem district to the west, the park is a vast green space, with meadows, woodlands, and lakes.

Historic Berlin
Numbers in the margin correspond to points of interest on the Historic Berlin map.

⑮
⑯ For a sense of times past, enter the historic part of Friedrichstrasse and turn right onto Mohrenstrasse and you'll arrive at the **Gendarmenmarkt,** with its beautifully reconstructed **Schauspielhaus**—built in 1818, and now one of the city's main concert halls—and twin **Deutscher** (German) and **Französischer** (French) cathedrals.

⑰ Continue east along Französische Strasse and turn left into Hedwigskirchgasse to reach Bebelplatz. The peculiar round shape of **St. Hedwigs-Kathedrale** (St. Hedwig's Cathedral) calls to mind Rome's Pantheon.

⑱ Walk north across Bebelplatz to Unter den Linden, the elegant central thoroughfare of Old Berlin. On your right is the **Staatsoper Unter den Linden** (German State Opera), the great opera house of Berlin.

Historic Berlin

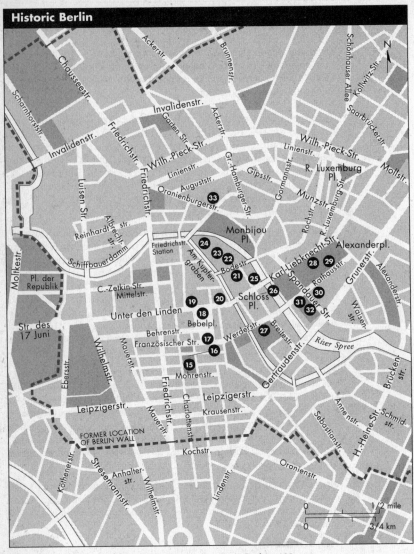

⑲ Cross Unter den Linden and look into the courtyard of **Humboldt Universität** (Humboldt University): It was built as a palace for the brother of Friedrich II of Prussia but became a university in 1810. Marx and Engels were its two most famous students. Beyond the war memorial,
⑳ housed in a onetime arsenal (built 1695–1730), is the **Deutsches Historisches Museum** (German Historical Museum), which has an exhibit tracing German history from the Middle Ages to the present. ⊠ *Unter den Linden 2,* ☎ *030/215–020.* ⊡ *Free.* ☉ *Thurs.–Tues. 10–6.*

Turning left along the Spree Canal (following Am Zeughaus and Am Kupfergraben) will bring you to east Berlin's museum complex, at the northern end of what is known as **Museumsinsel** (Museum Island). The
㉑ first of the Big Four that you'll encounter is the **Altes Museum** (entrance on Lustgarten), an austere neoclassical building just to the north of Schlossplatz. The collections here include postwar art from some of Germany's most prominent artists and numerous etchings and draw-
㉒ ings from the old masters. Next comes the **Alte Nationalgalerie,** on Bodestrasse, which displays 19th- and 20th-century paintings and sculptures.
★ ㉓ The **Pergamon Museum,** on Am Kupfergraben, is one of Europe's greatest museums. It takes its name from the museum's principal exhibit, the Pergamon Altar, a monumental Greek altar dating from 180
㉔ BC that occupies an entire city block. To the north is the **Bodemuseum** (also on Am Kupfergraben, but with its entrance on Monbijoubrücke), with an outstanding collection of early Christian, Byzantine, and Egyptian art. ⊠ *Museumsinsel,* ☎ *030/203–550 for all museums.* ⊡ *DM 4 each (combined day pass to 4 museums, DM 8), free Sun.* ☉ *Tues.–Sun. 9–5.*

From the museum complex, follow the Spree River south to Unter den
㉕ Linden and the vast **Berliner Dom** (Berlin Cathedral). The cathedral's impressive nave was reopened in June 1993 after a 20-year renovation. The hideous modern building in bronze mirrored glass just across from
㉖ it is the **Palast der Republik** (Palace of the Republic), a postwar monument to socialist progress. The building at the south end of Schloss-
㉗ platz used to house East Germany's **Staatsratsgbäude** (State Senate).

Head east on Karl-Liebknecht-Strasse for a closer look at the 13th-cen-
㉘ tury **St. Marienkirche** (Church of St. Mary), especially noting its late-Gothic *Dance of Death* fresco. You are now at the lower end of
㉙ Alexanderplatz. Just ahead is the massive **Fernsehturm** (TV Tower), 1,198 feet high (not accidentally, 710 feet *taller* than West Berlin's broadcasting tower). Its observation deck affords the best view of Berlin; the city's highest café, which revolves, is also up there. ⊠ *Alexanderpl.,* ☎ *030/242–3333.* ⊡ *6 DM.* ☉ *Daily 9 AM–midnight.*

㉚ The red building southwest of the tower is the **Rotes Rathaus** (Red City
㉛ Hall). The area adjacent to the Rathaus, known as the **Nikolaiviertel** (Nikolai Quarter), has been handsomely rebuilt and is now filled with delightful shops, cafés, and restaurants. On the quarter's Niko-
㉜ laikirchplatz is Berlin's oldest building, the **Nikolaikirche** (St. Nicholas Church), dating from 1230.

Take the U-2 subway from Märkisches Museum station three stops to Stadtmitte, then change to the U-6, traveling three stops to Oranienburger Tor. Walk a few blocks down Oranienburger Strasse to reach
㉝ the **Neue Synagoge.** Completed in 1866, in Middle Eastern style, the synagogue was one of Germany's most beautiful until it was seriously damaged on *Kristallnacht,* November 9, 1938, when synagogues and Jewish stores across Germany were vandalized, looted, and burned. Today, the outside is perfectly restored, and the interior is connected

to the Centrum Judaicum (Jewish Center)—an institution of Jewish culture and learning.

Shopping

Fine porcelain is still produced at the former Royal Prussian Porcelain Factory, now called **Staatliche Porzellan Manufaktur,** or KPM. This delicate, handmade, hand-painted china is sold at KPM's store at Kurfürstendamm 26A (☎ 030/2292–691), but it may be more fun to visit the factory salesroom at Wegelystrasse 1. It sells seconds at reduced prices. If you long to have the Egyptian queen Nefertiti on your mantlepiece at home, try the **Gipsformerei der Staatlichen Museen Preussicher Kulturbesitz** (⌧ Sophie-Charlotte-Str. 17, ☎ 030/321–7011, ⊙ Weekdays 9–4). It sells plaster casts of this and other museum treasures.

Shopping Districts
The liveliest and most famous shopping area in west Berlin is the **Kurfürstendamm** and its side streets, especially between **Breitscheidplatz** and **Olivaer Platz.** The **Europa Center** at Breitscheidplatz encompasses more than 100 stores, cafés, and restaurants—but this is not a place to bargain-hunt. Running east from Breitscheidplatz is **Tauentzienstrasse,** another shopping street. Eastern Berlin's chief shopping areas are along the **Friedrichstrasse, Unter den Linden,** and in the area around **Alexanderplatz.**

Department Stores
The classiest department store in Berlin is the Kaufhaus des Westens, or **KaDeWe,** Europe's largest consumer's paradise, at Wittenbergplatz. Be sure to check out the food department, which occupies the whole sixth floor. The other main department store downtown is **Wertheim,** on the Ku'damm. Neither as big nor as attractive as KaDeWe, Wertheim nonetheless has a large selection of fine wares. The main department store in eastern Berlin is **Kaufhof,** at the north end of Alexanderplatz.

Antiques
On Saturday and Sunday from 10 to 5, the colorful and lively antiques and handicrafts fair on Strasse des 17. Juni swings into action. Not far from Wittenbergplatz, several streets are strong on antiques, including Eisenacher Strasse, Fuggerstrasse, Keithstrasse, Kalckreuthstrasse, Motzstrasse, and Nollendorfstrasse.

Dining

Dining in Berlin can mean sophisticated nouvelle creations in upscale restaurants or hearty local specialties in atmospheric and inexpensive inns. The range is as vast as the city. Typical specialties are *Eisbein* (knuckle of pork) *mit Sauerkraut,* Spanferkel, *Berliner Schüsselsülze* (potted meat in aspic), and *Schlachterplatte* (mixed grill). *Currywurst* is a chubby and very spicy frankfurter that's sold at wurst stands citywide.

For details and price-category definitions, *see* Dining *in* Staying in Germany, *above.*

$$$$ ✕ **Bamberger Reiter.** Considered by Berliners to be one of the city's ★ best restaurants, Bamberger Reiter is the pride of its chef, Tyrolean Franz Raneburger. He relies heavily on fresh market produce for his *neue deutsche Küche* (new German cuisine), so the menu changes from day to day. Fresh flowers, too, abound in his attractive, oak-beamed restaurant. ⌧ *Regensburger Str. 7,* ☎ *030/218–4282. Reservations essential. AE, DC, V. Dinner only. Closed Sun., Mon., Jan. 1–15.*

$$$$ ✕ **Ermeler Haus.** The rococo grandeur of this wine restaurant reflects ★ the elegance of the restored patrician home whose upper floors it occupies. The restaurant's atmosphere is subdued and formal, the wines are imported, and the service and German cuisine are excellent. ⊠ *Märkisches Ufer 12,* ☎ *030/279–4028. AE, DC, MC, V. Closed Mon.*

$$$ ✕ **Borchardt.** This fashionable meeting place has columns, red plush
★ benches, and an Art Nouveau mosaic, all of which help create the impression of a 1920s salon. The restaurant serves entrées that are prepared with a French accent, and it's also well known for its luscious seafood platter. ⊠ *Französische Str. 47,* ☎ *030/229–3144. AE, V.*

$$$ ✕ **Paris Bar.** This top-class restaurant in Charlottenburg attracts a polyglot clientele of film stars, artists, entrepreneurs, and executives. The cuisine is high-powered, medium-quality French. ⊠ *Kantstr. 152,* ☎ *030/313–8052. AE.*

$$ ✕ **Blockhaus Nikolskoe.** Prussian King Frederick Wilhelm III built this Russian-style wooden lodge for his daughter Charlotte, wife of Russia's Czar Nicholas I. In character with its history and appearance, the Blockhaus features game dishes. It's in the southwest of the city, on the eastern edge of Glienicke Park, with an open terrace (in summer) overlooking the Havel River. ⊠ *Nikolskoer Weg 15,* ☎ *030/805–2914. AE, DC, MC, V. Closed Thurs.*

$$ ✕ **Reinhard's.** This restaurant in the Nikolai Quarter is one of the city's
★ newer popular eating establishments. Berliners of all stripes meet here to enjoy the carefully prepared entrées and to sample spirits from the amply stocked bar. The honey-glazed breast of duck is one of the house specialties. ⊠ *Poststr. 28,* ☎ *030/242–5295. AE, DC, MC, V.*

$$ ✕ **Turmstuben.** Tucked away below the cupola of the French Cathedral, which sits on the north side of the beautiful Gendarmenmarkt, this restaurant is approached by a long, winding staircase. The reward at the top of the stairs is a table in one of Berlin's most original and attractive restaurants. The menu is as short as the stairway is long, but there's an impressive wine list. ⊠ *Gendarmenmarkt 5,* ☎ *030/229–9313. Weekend reservations essential. AE, MC, V.*

$ ✕ **Alt-Cöllner Schankstuben.** A tiny restaurant and Kneipe are contained within this charming, historic Berlin house. The menu is relatively limited, but the quality, like the service, is good. ⊠ *Friedrichsgracht 50,* ☎ *030/242–5972. AE, DC, MC, V.*

$ ✕ **Zur Letzten Instanz.** Established in 1621, Berlin's oldest restaurant combines the charming atmosphere of Old-World Berlin with a limited (but tasty) choice of dishes. The emphasis here is on beer, both in the recipes and in the mug. Service can be erratic, though engagingly friendly. ⊠ *Waisenstr. 14–16,* ☎ *030/242–5528. AE, DC, MC, V.*

Lodging

Add DM 50 to the price chart categories given in Lodging *in* Staying in Germany, *above.*

$$$$ 🏨 **Bristol Hotel Kempinski.** This grand hotel in the heart of the city has
★ the best of Berlin's shopping on its doorstep. All the rooms and suites are luxuriously decorated and equipped, with marble bathrooms, air-conditioning, and cable TV. English-style furnishings give the "Kempi" an added touch of class. Children under 12 stay for free if they share their parents' room. ⊠ *Kurfürstendamm 27, D-10719,* ☎ *030/884–340,* FAX *030/883–6075. 315 rooms with bath, 52 suites. 3 restaurants, bar, room service, indoor pool, beauty salon, massage, sauna, fitness room, boutiques, limousine service. AE, DC, MC, V.*

$$$$ 🏨 **Grand Hotel Esplanade.** The Grand Hotel Esplanade exudes luxury.
★ Uncompromisingly modern architecture, chicly styled rooms, and works of art by some of Berlin's most acclaimed artists are some of its outstanding visual delights. ⊠ *Lützowufer 15, D-10785,* ☎ *030/254–780,* FAX *030/265–1171. 369 rooms with bath, 33 suites. 2 restaurants, pub,*

bar, room service, pool, beauty salon, massage, sauna, whirlpool, steam room, solarium, health club, boutique, bicycles. AE, DC, MC, V.

$$$$ 🏨 **Inter-Continental Berlin.** In conjunction with the recent addition of a major conference center, the whole hotel was substantially improved. Rooms and suites are all of the highest standard and their decor shows exquisite taste. The lobby is a quarter the size of a football field, opulently furnished, and just the place for afternoon tea and pastries. ⊠ *Budapester Str. 2, D-10787,* ☎ *030/26020,* FAX *030/2602–80760. 511 rooms with bath, 70 suites. 3 restaurants (including rooftop garden), 2 bars, no-smoking floor, indoor pool, whirlpool, sauna, room service, boutiques. AE, DC, MC, V.*

$$$$ 🏨 **Schlosshotel Vier Jahreszeiten.** This newcomer to Berlin's high-end
★ hotel scene has a lush green setting in the Grunewald forest. The palatial building is all style, the interior was done by renowned designer Karl Lagerfeld. ⊠ *Brahmsstr. 10, D-14193,* ☎ *030/895-840,* FAX *030/8958–4800. 52 rooms with bath, 12 suites. 2 restaurants, bar, in-room safes, minibars, no-smoking rooms, room service, indoor pool, beauty salon, massage, sauna, exercise room. AE, DC, MC, V.*

$$$ 🏨 **Forum Hotel.** With its 40 stories, the Forum Hotel competes with the nearby TV tower for the title of premier downtown landmark. As the city's largest hotel, it is understandably somewhat impersonal, although a recent renovation of all public areas has made the atmosphere more welcoming. The high-level dining room, Panorama 37, has good food, good service, and stunning views; reservations are essential. ⊠ *Alexanderpl., D-10178,* ☎ *030/23890,* FAX *030/2389–4305. 943 rooms with bath, 14 suites. 2 restaurants, bar, no-smoking floors, exercise room, casino, parking. AE, DC, MC, V.*

$$ 🏨 **Märkischer Hof.** All of downtown Berlin is within walking distance of this small hotel conveniently located just off Friedrichstrasse. The rooms are fairly large and cheerfully furnished. ⊠ *Linienstr. 133, D-10115,* ☎ *030/282-7155,* FAX *030/282-4331. 20 rooms, most with bath. AE, MC, V.*

$$ 🏨 **Riehmers Hofgarten.** A few minutes' walk from the Kreuzberg hill
★ and surrounded by the colorful district's bars and restaurants, this hotel also has fast connections to the center of town. The 19th-century building's high-ceiling rooms are elegantly furnished. ⊠ *Yorckstr. 83, D-10965,* ☎ *030/781–011,* FAX *030/786–6059. 21 rooms with bath or shower. Restaurant, bar. AE, DC, MC, V.*

$ 🏨 **Gendarm Garni Hotel.** This well-run hotel is also near the Gendar-
★ menmarkt. All the rooms are neat and pleasantly furnished. Ask for the corner suite facing the square; the view and the large living room make it one of the better deals in town (DM 225). ⊠ *Charlottenstr. 60, D-10117,* ☎ *030/200–4180,* FAX *030/208–2482. 25 rooms with bath, 4 suites. Lobby bar. AE, MC, V.*

The Arts

The quality of opera and classical concerts in Berlin is high. Tickets are available at the theaters' own box offices, either in advance or an hour before the performance, at many hotels, and at numerous ticket agencies, including **Ticket Counter** (⊠ Europa Center, ☎ 030/264–1138); **Hekticket** (⊠ Ratshausstr. 1, at Alexanderpl., ☎ 030/883–6010); **Theaterkasse Centrum** (⊠ Meinekestr. 25, ☎ 030/882–7611); and the **Top Ticket** branches (in all major stores, such as Hertie, Wertheim, and KaDeWe). Check the monthly publication *Berlin Programm* for a detailed guide to what's going on in the arts while you're here.

Concerts

The Berlin Philharmonic, one of the world's leading orchestras, performs in the **Philharmonie** (⊠ Matthäikirchstr. 1, ☎ 030/261–4383).

A more historic venue is the **Konzerthaus Berlin** (⊠ Gendarmenmarkt, ☎ 030/2030–92100).

Opera and Ballet

The **Deutsche Oper** (⊠ Bismarckstr. 35, ☎ 030/341–0249), by the U-Bahn stop of the same name, is home to both opera and ballet. Other performances are given at **Staatsoper Unter den Linden** (⊠ Unter den Linden 7, ☎ 030/2035–4555) and the **Komische Oper** (⊠ Behrenstr. 55–57, ☎ 030/2026–0360).

Musicals

Check the **Metropol-Theater** (⊠ Friedrichstr. 101, ☎ 030/20246–6117) and **Theater des Westens** (⊠ Kantstr. 12, ☎ 030/882–2888).

Nightlife

With more than 6,000 Kneipen (pubs), bars, and clubs, nightlife in Berlin is no halfhearted affair. It starts late (from 9 PM) and runs until breakfast. Almost 50 Kneipen have live music of one kind or another, and there are numerous small cabaret clubs and discos. The heart of this nocturnal scene used to be the Kurfürstendamm, but today most of the best bars and Kneipen can be found around Savignyplatz, in Charlottenburg, Nollendorfplatz and its side streets in Schöneberg, and along Oranienstrasse and Wienerstrasse in Kreuzberg. In eastern Berlin, nighthawks come together around Kollwitzplatz in the Prenzlauer Berg district and along Oranienburger Strasse in Mitte.

Berlin is a major center for jazz in Europe. If you're visiting in the fall, call the tourist office for details on the annual international Jazz Fest. Throughout the year a variety of jazz groups appears at the **A-Trane** (⊠ Pestalozzistr. 105), **Eierschale** (⊠ Podbielskiallee 50), and **Quasimodo** (⊠ Kantstr. 12a).

During the past few years, Berlin has become Germany's prime hot spot for variety shows. A must for circus buffs is the world's largest show at the **Friedrichstadtpalast** (⊠ Friedrichstr. 107, ☎ 030/2326–2474). Smaller but classier in style is the **Wintergarten** (⊠ Potsdamer Str. 96, ☎ 030/2627–070), a romantic homage to the twenties. Equally intimate and intellectually entertaining is the **Bar jeder Vernuft** (⊠ Schaperstr. 24, ☎ 030/8831–582). More than hilarious and constantly sold out are the shows at the **Chamäleon Varieté** (⊠ Rosenthaler Str. 40/41, ☎ 030/2827–118).

SAXONY AND THURINGIA

Saxony and Thuringia—the names alone conjure up images of kingdoms and forest legends, of cultural riches and booming industrial enterprises. Since German reunification, Saxony has thrown open its doors to visitors. Tourists are proudly conducted around the world-famous porcelain factory in Meissen. Leipzig may be renowned for its East–West trade fairs, but its true fame lies in its music and literary tradition, proudly upheld by the internationally famous Gewandhaus Orchestra and by its annual book fair.

Back in the 14th century, Thuringia was known as the Rynestig or Rennsteig (literally, "fast trail"), when it attracted traders from the dark forested depths of the Thüringer Wald (forest) to the prospering towns of Erfurt (today the state capital), Eisenach, and Weimar, then already 600 years old. It was in Weimar in 1777 that the privy councillor and poet Johann Wolfgang von Goethe was inspired by the pristine beauties of the 168 kilometers (104 miles) of the Rennsteig to write that "tranquillity crowns all its peaks."

Getting Around

By Car

Some 1,600 kilometers (1,000 miles) of autobahn and 11,300 kilometers (7,000 miles) of secondary roads crisscross the five new federal states in the east. Resurfacing of some of the communist-built highways has now resulted in the lifting of the previous strictly enforced 100 kph (62 mph) speed limits on autobahns. Gas stations can be scarce on back roads, so be careful not to let fuel reserves get too low.

By Train

InterCity, EuroCity, and InterCity Express trains connect Dresden and Leipzig with Berlin and other major German cities, with InterRegio services completing the express network; older and slower D- and E-class trains connect smaller towns.

Leipzig has an S-Bahn system. Tickets must be obtained in advance, at various prices according to the number of rides in a block. Get S-Bahn tickets at the main railway station.

By Bus and Streetcar

Within Saxony and Thuringia, most areas are accessible by bus, but service is infrequent and serves chiefly to connect with rail lines. Check schedules carefully. In Dresden, Leipzig, and Weimar, public buses and streetcars are cheap and efficient.

By Taxi

Taxis in Dresden are inexpensive, but the city is small and walking is the best way to discover its hidden surprises. Leipzig has more cabs than any other eastern German city because of the number needed to cope with peak traffic at fair time. Weimar's chief attractions are within walking distance, but you may want to take a taxi from the main train station, which is somewhat removed from the city center.

By Boat

The **Weisse Flotte** (White Fleet) of inland boats, including paddle side-wheelers, ply the River Elbe, starting in Dresden or at the beautiful forested border town of Bad Schandau and proceeding on into the Czech Republic. **KD River Cruises of Europe** (⊠ 2500 Westchester Ave., Purchase, NY 10577, ☎ 914/696–3600; ⊠ 323 Geary St., Suite 603, San Francisco, ☎ 415/392–8817) operates luxury cruises in both directions on the Elbe from May to October.

Visitor Information

Dresden (⊠ Pragerstr. 10–11, ☎ 0351/495–5025).
Leipzig (⊠ Sachsenpl. 1, ☎ 0341/71040).
Weimar (⊠ Marktstr. 4, ☎ 03643/24000).

Guided Tours

The visitor information office in **Leipzig** leads regularly scheduled bus and tram tours of the city. Daily two-hour bus tours leave from near the tourist office at Am Brühl at 1:30 PM (additional tours in summer at 10 AM); reservations are advised (☎ 0341/79590). The cost is DM 20. Walking tours start from the Thomaskirche at 4 and 7, and cost DM 10.

In **Dresden,** every day there are 10 guided tours by bus, tram, or open carriage, at least two steamer trips on the Elbe, and four tours of the

Saxony and Thuringia

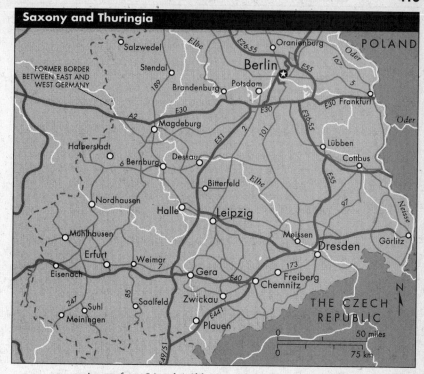

city on foot. It's advisable to consult the tourist office before setting off. Costs range from DM 12 for a walking tour to DM 55 for a 2½-hour deluxe expedition. The tourist office also sells a one-day Dresden Card (DM 11, or DM 20 for 48 hours) covering various museum admissions and transportation.

Walking tours of **Weimar** start from outside the tourist office, daily at 11 and 4. The cost is DM 5. The tourist office can also arrange individual tours of the city.

Exploring

Dresden

Dresden, superbly located on the banks of the River Elbe, suffered appalling damage during World War II but has been lovingly rebuilt. Italianate influences are everywhere, most pronounced in the glorious Rococo and Baroque buildings in pastel shades of yellow and green.

The **Semper Opera House** at Theaterplatz, in the center of Dresden, is a mecca for music lovers. Named after its architect, Gottfried Semper, the sumptuous theater saw the premieres of Wagner's *The Flying Dutchman* and *Tannhäuser* (conducted by the composer) and nine operas by Richard Strauss. Tickets are in great demand at the Semper (☎ 0351/49110, 0351/491–1716, or 0351/491–1717); try booking through your travel agent before you go or ask at your hotel. As a last resort, line up at the Abendkasse (evening box office) half an hour before the performance begins. Tours of the opera house are included in one of the daily guided tours of the city.

★ From Theaterplatz, stroll down the Sophienstrasse to the largely 18th-century **Zwinger** palace complex, which remains one of the city's cultural wonders, in the heart of the Altstadt. Completely enclosing a central courtyard of lawns and pools, the complex consists of six linked pavilions decorated with a riot of garlands, nymphs, and other Baroque ornamentation and sculpture, all created under the direction of Matthäus Daniel Pöppelmann.

The Zwinger complex is the home of the world-renowned **Sempergalerie** (Gemäldegalerie Alte Meister) collection of old master paintings, among them works by Dürer, Holbein the Younger, Rembrandt, Vermeer, Raphael, Correggio, and Canaletto. The Zwinger's other treasures include the Porzellansammlung (porcelain collection)—famous for its Meissen pieces—the Zoological Museum, and the Mathematisch-Physikalischer Salon, which displays marvelous old scientific instruments. ⊠ *Zwinger,* ☎ *0351/484–0620.* 🎫 *Art gallery, DM 7; porcelain collection, DM 3; scientific collection, DM 3; Zoological Museum, DM 2.* ☉ *Art gallery, Tues.–Sun. 10–6; porcelain collection, Fri.–Wed. 10–6; scientific collection, Fri.–Wed. 9:30–5; Zoological Museum, Sept.–May, Tues.–Sun. 9–4, June–August, daily 9–5.*

After leaving the Zwinger, head eastward along Ernst-Thälmann-Strasse and turn into the **Neumarkt** (New Market), which is, despite its name, the historic heart of old Dresden. The ruined shell on the right is all that remains of the mighty Baroque **Frauenkirche,** once Germany's greatest Protestant church. The church, destroyed in the bombing raids of February 1945, is being rebuilt.

Behind the Frauenkirche looms Dresden's leading art museum, the **Albertinum.** Permanent exhibits at the Albertinum include the **Gemäldegalerie Neue Meister** (New Masters Gallery), which displays outstanding 19th- and 20th-century European pictures.

Despite the rich array of paintings, it is the **Grünes Gewölbe** (Green Vault) that invariably attracts most attention. Named after a green room in the palace of August the Strong, this part of the Albertinum (entered from Georg-Treu-Platz) contains an exquisite collection of unique objets d'art fashioned from gold, silver, ivory, amber, and other precious and semiprecious materials. Next door is the **Skulpturensammlung** (sculpture collection), which includes ancient Egyptian and classical objects and Italian Mannerist works. ☎ *0351/495–3056.* 🎫 *DM 7, includes all three galleries.* ☉ *Fri.–Wed. 10–6.*

The southern exit from the Albertinum, at Augustus-Strasse, brings you back to the Neumarkt and leads you to another former royal building now serving as a museum, the 16th-century **Johanneum,** once the royal stables. Instead of horses, the Johanneum now houses the **Verkehrsmuseum** (Transport Museum), a collection of historical vehicles, including vintage automobiles and engines. ⊠ *Am Neumarkt,* ☎ *0351/495–3002.* 🎫 *DM 4, half-price on Fri.* ☉ *Tues.–Sun. 10–5.*

On the outside wall of the Johanneum is a prime example of Meissen porcelain art: a 335-foot-long mural of a royal procession. Follow this procession to the end and you arrive at the former royal palace, the **Herzogschloss.** Standing next to the Herzogschloss is the **Katholische Hofkirche,** also known as the Cathedral of St. Trinitas, Saxony's largest church. In the cathedral's crypt are the tombs of 49 Saxon rulers and a precious vessel containing the heart of August the Strong.

Moving away from the treasures near the river, along the St. Petersburger Strasse, make a left into Lingnerplatz. The **Deutsches Hygiene-Museum** (German Health Museum) reflects Dresden's important role in the history of medicine. ⊠ *Lingnerpl. 1,* ☎ *0351/48460.* 🎫 *DM 5.* ☉ *Tues.–Sun. 9–5.*

Leipzig

With a population of about 560,000, Leipzig is the second-largest city (after Berlin) in eastern Germany. Since the Middle Ages, it has been an important market town and a center for printing, book publishing, and the fur industry. Nowadays, its twice-yearly fairs, staged in March and September, maintain Leipzig's position as a commercial center. Yet it is music and literature that most people associate with Leipzig. Johann Sebastian Bach (1685–1750) was the organist and choir director at St. Thomas's church. The composer Richard Wagner was born in Leipzig in 1813. The writers Johann Wolfgang von Goethe (1749–1832) and Friedrich von Schiller (1759–1805) are also closely associated with the city and its immediate area. Trade and the arts are just two aspects of the city's fame. One of the greatest battles of the Napoleonic Wars, and one that led to the ultimate defeat of the French general—the Battle of the Nations—was fought here in 1813.

Railroad buffs may want to start their tour of Leipzig at the **Hauptbahnhof,** the main train station. With its 26 platforms, majestic staircase, and great arched ceiling, it is Europe's largest and is unique among German railway stations.

Cross the Platz der Republik to the pedestrian area, leading to Sachsenplatz and the **Markt,** the old market square. Here, in the rebuilt 12th-century marketplace, you will find the **Altes Rathaus,** the Renaissance town hall. It now houses the municipal museum, where Leipzig's illustrious past is well documented. ✉ *Markt 1,* ☎ *0341/70921.* 🎟 *DM 3.* ⊘ *Tues–Fri. 10–6, weekends 10–4.*

Small streets leading off from the Markt on all sides attest to Leipzig's rich trading past. Tucked in among them are glass-roofed arcades of surprising beauty and elegance. At the **Apotheke** at Hainstrasse 9, you enter surroundings that haven't changed for 100 years or more, redolent of powders and perfumes, home cures and foreign spices. It's spectacularly Jugendstil, all stained glass and rich mahogany. Nearby, on Grimmaischestrasse, is Leipzig's finest arcade, the **Mädlerpassage.** Here, at Number 2, you'll find the **Auerbachs Keller** restaurant (☞ Dining and Lodging, *below*), built in 1530 and immortalized in Goethe's *Faust.*

★ Continuing west, Grimmaischestrasse becomes Thomasgasse, site of the **Thomaskirche,** where Johann Sebastian Bach worked for 27 years; he composed most of his cantatas for the church's boys' choir. The great composer's burial place, the church is to this day the home of the Thomasknabenchor (St. Thomas Boys' Choir) and a center of Bach tradition.

★ Another church of more than historic interest is the **Nikolaikirche,** behind Grimmaischestrasse on Nikolaistrasse. The church, more impressive inside than outside, has an ornate 16th-century pulpit and an unusual diamond-pattern ceiling supported by classical pillars that are crowned with palm-tree-like flourishes.

Looming above the Nikolaikirche in the city center is the 470-foot-high **Leipzig University Tower,** dubbed the "Jagged Tooth" by students. Using the university skyscraper as a landmark, you come to **Augustus-Platz,** on which stand the modernistic **Opera House** and the **Neues Gewandhaus** concert hall, both centers of Leipzig's musical life. By heading across the Ring and up the Grimmaisch Steinweg, you reach the **Grassimuseum** complex (✉ Johannespl. 5–11), built in the late 1920s in striking Art Deco style. It includes the **Museum of Arts and Crafts** (☎ 0341/214-2114; 🎟 DM 4; ⊘ Tues.–Fri. 10–6, Wed. until 8, weekends 10–5), the **Geographical Museum** (🎟 DM 5; ⊘ Tues.–Fri. 10–5:30, weekends

10–4), and the **Musical Instruments Museum** (enter from Taubchenweg 2; ☎ DM 3; ☉ Tues.–Fri. 9–5, Sat. 10–5, Sun. 10–1).

Back on the Ring and heading clockwise (west), turn left into Harkorstrasse. You'll come to the city's most outstanding museum, the **Museum der Bildenden Künste,** an art gallery of international stature that is especially strong in German and Dutch painting. ☒ *Georgi-Dimitroff-Pl. 1,* ☎ *0341/216–9914.* ☎ *DM 5, free Sun.* ☉ *Tues. and Thurs.–Sun. 9–5, Wed. 1–9:30.*

Weimar

Weimar sits prettily on the Ilm River between the Ettersberg and Vogtland hills, and has a place in German political and cultural history out of all proportion to its size (population 63,000). Goethe and the poet and dramatist Friedrich von Schiller were neighbors here, Carl Maria von Weber wrote some of his best music here, and later it was here that Liszt presented the first performance of Wagner's *Lohengrin.* Walter Gropius founded his famous Bauhaus design school in Weimar in 1919, and it was here in 1919–20 that the German National Assembly drew up the constitution of the Weimar Republic. After the collapse of the ill-fated Weimar government, Hitler chose the city as the site for the first national congress of his new Nazi Party.

Weimar owes much of its greatness to the widowed Countess Anna Amalia, who in the late-18th century set about attracting cultural figures to enrich the glittering court her Saxon forebears had established in the town. One of these was Goethe, who as councilor advised the countess on financial matters and town design; Schiller was another. In front of the National Theater, on **Theaterplatz,** there is a statue of the famous pair, showing Goethe placing a patronizing hand on the shoulder of the younger Schiller.

Adjacent to the National Theater is the Baroque **Wittumspalais,** once the home of Countess Anna Amalia. ☒ *Theaterpl. 9.* ☎ *DM 6.* ☉ *Mar.–Oct., Tues.–Sun. 9–noon and 1–5; Nov.–Feb., Tues.–Sun. 9–noon and 1–4.*

★ Goethe spent 57 years in Weimar, 47 of them in the house that has since become a place of pilgrimage for millions of visitors. The **Goethehaus** is two blocks south of Theaterplatz on a street called the Frauenplan. The museum it contains is testimony not only to the great man's literary might but also his interest in the sciences, particularly medicine, and his administrative skills (and frustrations) as Weimar's exchequer. Here you find the desk at which Goethe stood to write (he liked to work standing up), some of his own paintings (he was an accomplished watercolorist), and the modest bed in which he died. ☒ *Frauenplan 1,* ☎ *03643/ 62041.* ☎ *DM 8.* ☉ *Mar.–Oct., Tues.–Sun. 9–5; Nov.–Feb., Tues.–Sun. 9–4.*

On a tree-shaded square around the corner from Goethe's house is the green-shuttered **Schillerhaus,** in which Friedrich Schiller and his family spent an all-too-brief but happy three years (the poet died here in 1805). His study, dominated by the desk at which he probably completed *William Tell,* is tucked up underneath the mansard roof. ☒ *Schillerstr. 17,* ☎ *03643/62041.* ☎ *DM 6.* ☉ *Mar.–Oct., Wed.–Mon. 9–5; Nov.–Feb., Wed.–Mon. 9–4.*

Another historic house worth visiting stands on the **Marktplatz,** the central town square. It was the home of the painter Lucas Cranach the Elder, who spent his last years (1552–53) in Weimar.

Around the corner and to the left is Weimar's 16th-century castle, the **Stadtschloss,** with its restored classical staircase, festival hall, and falcon gallery. The castle's impressive art collection includes several fine paintings by Cranach the Elder and many early 20th-century works by such artists as Böcklin, Liebermann, and Beckmann. ⊠ *Burgpl.* 🎫 *DM 3.* ⊙ *May–Sept., Tues.–Sun. 9–6; Oct.–Apr., Tues.–Sun. 9–5.*

In Weimar's old, reconstructed town center stands the late-Gothic **Herderkirche,** with its large winged altarpiece started by Lucas Cranach the Elder and finished by his son in 1555.

Just south of the city (take Bus 1 from Goetheplatz) is the lovely 18th-century hunting and pleasure palace, **Schloss Belvedere,** which now houses a museum of Baroque art and an exhibition of coaches and other old vehicles. The formal gardens were in part laid out according to Goethe's concepts. ☎ *0621/661–831.* 🎫 *DM 4.* ⊙ *Apr.–Oct., Tues.–Sun. 10–6. Closed Nov.–Mar.*

North of Weimar, in the Ettersberg Hills, is a blighted patch of land that contrasts cruelly with the verdant countryside that so inspired Goethe: ★ **Buchenwald,** where, between 1937 and 1945 some 65,000 men, women, and children from 35 countries met their deaths from disease, starvation, or gruesome medical experiments. Buses to the camp depart at least hourly between 9 and 3:30 from the main railway station, or you can take the more frequent Bus 6 to Ettersburg. *Contact Weimar Visitor Information,* ☎ *03643/24000.* 🎫 *Free.* ⊙ *Tues.–Sun. 8:45–4:30.*

Dining and Lodging

Many of the best restaurants in Saxony and Thuringia are in the larger hotels. Roast beef, venison, and wild boar are often on Saxon menus, and in the Vogtland you'll find *Kaninchentopf* (rabbit stew). In Thuringia, regional specialties include *Thüringer Rehbraten* (roast venison); roast mutton served in a delicate cream sauce; tasty grilled Thuringian sausages; *Thüringer Sauerbraten mit Klössen* (marinated beef with dumplings); *Börenschinken* (cured ham); and roast mutton shepherd-style, with beans and vegetables. The light wine from the Meissen region, Meissner Wein, is splendid.

Dining out in Saxony and Thuringia can still be relatively inexpensive. Hotel prices, which have been high because of a shortage of quality accommodations, are beginning to drop because of new hotel construction. Cheap but clean accommodation can be found in the lists of private bed-and-breakfasts available at most tourist offices.

For details and price-category definitions, *see* Dining *and* Lodging *in* Staying in Germany, *above.*

Dresden

$$ ✕ **Italienisches Dörfchen.** This picturesque baroque structure on the Elbe, opposite the opera house, was built to house Italian craftsmen working on the nearby Hofkirche. It has been cleverly and tastefully converted into a restaurant and café, with a shady beer garden and fine river views. The Italian influence is still in evidence—in the decor and on the menu, where pasta dishes are heavily favored. ⊠ *Theaterplatz 3,* ☎ *0351/498160. AE, DC, MC, V.*

$$ ✕ **Pfund's.** Often dubbed the world's most beautiful dairy, Pfund's has a delightful restaurant that serves a bit more than milk, cream, and butter. Hearty Saxon specialties are the norm. This 1880 building is furnished with hand-painted Villeroy & Boch tiles from floor to ceiling. ⊠ *Bautzner Str. 79,* ☎ *0351/808080. No credit cards.*

$–$$ ✕ **Haus Altmarkt.** The choice of cuisine in this busy corner of the colonnaded Altmarkt is enormous—from the McDonald's that has wormed itself into the landscape to the upscale Amadeus restaurant on the first floor. In between are a jolly, bistrolike café and, downstairs, a vaulted restaurant, Zum Humpen, with a secluded bar. The restaurant offers good value, with midday menus under DM 20. In warm weather you can eat outside on a terrace and watch the marketplace's bustle. ⊠ *Am Altmarkt 1,* ☎ *0351/495–1212. No credit cards.*

$$$$ 🏨 **Maritim Hotel Bellevue.** Across the river from the Zwinger palace, the opera, and main museums, this modern hotel cleverly incorporates an old restored mansion. The hotel views of the historic center are terrific, the rooms luxurious, and the service is good. Its Cafe Pöppelmann is especially recommended for its atmosphere and hearty dishes. ⊠ *Grosse-Meissner-Str. 15, D-01097,* ☎ *0351/56620,* FAX *0351/55997. 328 rooms with bath. 5 restaurants, bar, café, taproom, sauna, jogging, shops, nightclub, free parking. AE, DC, MC, V.*

$$ 🏨 **Hotelschiff Florentina.** From your cabin window in this cleverly-converted "hotel ship" you have a better view of the Elbe and Dresden than from many of the luxury hotels along the riverbanks. Accommodation is understandably a bit cramped, although all the cabins have bathrooms with showers, and satellite TV. The public rooms and the deck-terrace, however, are unusually spacious. ⊠ *Terrassenufer, D-01069,* ☎ *0351/459–0169,* FAX *0351/459–5036. 63 cabins with shower. AE, DC, MC, V.*

Leipzig

$$ ✕ **Auerbachs Keller.** This most famous of Leipzig's restaurants was
★   closed in early 1996 when the owners went bankrupt, but it's expected to reopen by the start of 1997. Established in 1530, it was made famous by Goethe's *Faust* and became an indispensable part of Leipzig life. ⊠ *Mädler-Passage 2–4,* ☎ *0341/216–1040. Reservations essential. Jacket and tie. AE, DC, MC, V.*

$$ ✕ **Paulaner Palais.** Munich's Paulaner brewery has transformed a his-
★   toric corner of Leipzig into a vast complex combining a restaurant, banquet hall, café; and beer garden. There's something for everybody here, from intimate dining to noisy Bavarian-style tavern-table jollity. The Paulaner beer is a perfect accompaniment. ⊠ *Klosterg. 3–5,* ☎ *0341/211–3115. AE, MC, V.*

$$ ✕ **Zill's Tunnel.** The tunnel refers to the barrel-vaulted ground-floor restaurant, where foaming glasses of excellent local beer are cheerily served by the friendly staff, which can also help you decipher the menu's Old Saxon descriptions of traditional dishes. Upstairs there's a larger wine restaurant, with a welcoming open fireplace. Goose in a variety of forms is a staple here and among the soups is a potent mixture of vegetables, beer, and gin. ⊠ *Barfussgässchen 9,* ☎ *0341/200–446. No credit cards.*

$ ✕ **Thüringer Hof.** This fine old tavern-restaurant has been in business for centuries, and its dark-paneled walls have history carved deep into the wood. The roast wild boar is served just as Leipzigers would have ordered it in ages past, and the other traditional Thuringian dishes couldn't be more authentic—marinated beef, dumplings, and red cabbage sweetened with apple, to name just one. ⊠ *Burgstr. 19–23,* ☎ *0341/209–884. No credit cards. Closed Fri. No dinner. Sat.*

$$$$ 🏨 **Hotel Inter-Continental Leipzig.** The city's most luxurious accommodation is imposing for its high-rise profile as well as its Japanese restaurant and garden. Rooms have every comfort, including bathrooms with marble walls and floors and air-conditioning. The hotel is close to the main rail station. ⊠ *Gerberstr. 15, D-04105,* ☎ *0341/9880,* FAX *0341/988–1229. 429 rooms with bath, 18 suites. 4 restaurants, 2 bars, coffee shop, taproom, indoor pool, sauna, bowling, exercise room, jogging, billiards, casino, nightclub. AE, DC, MC, V.*

$$$ 🏨 **Holiday Inn Garden Court.** The former, and slightly seedy, Hotel Zum Löwen has undergone two successive transformations and is now a smart and very comfortable hotel. Unchanged is the excellent location, across the street from Leipzig's main railway station. Rooms still tend to be small but lack nothing in terms of comfort and facilities. ⊠ *Rudolf-Breitscheid-Str. 3, D-04103,* ☎ *0341/12510,* FAX *0341/125–1100. 108 rooms, 14 suites. Restaurant, bar, sauna, exercise room, parking (fee). AE, DC, MC, V.*

$$$ 🏨 **Hotel Garni Silencium.** This newly opened hotel is part of the Silencium group, which guarantees its guests a peaceful night's sleep. So although it's on a busy thoroughfare, a hush permeates this beautifully restored old city mansion. The hotel is about 3 kilometers (2 miles) from the city center, but tram stops are nearby. The modern, comfortable rooms have satellite TV and fax/modem outlets. ⊠ *Georg-Schumann-Str. 268, D-04105 Leipzig-Möckern,* ☎ *0341/901–2990,* FAX *0341/901–2991. 34 rooms with bath. AE, DC, MC, V.*

Weimar

$$$ ✕ **Weisser Schwan.** This historic restaurant in the center of town, right by the Goethehaus, dates from 1500. It offers high-quality international cuisine and Thuringian specialties, particularly fish and grilled meats. A squabble over post-reunification ownership closed the restaurant in early 1996, but it was hoped that the historic house would reopen before the end of the year. ⊠ *Frauenstorstr. 23,* ☎ *03643/61715. Reservations essential. AE, DC, MC, V. Closed Mon.*

$$ ✕ **Hotel Thüringen.** The plush elegance of the Thüringen's restaurant, complete with velvet drapes and chandeliers, makes it seem expensive, but there's a pleasant surprise in store: The menu of international and regional dishes is remarkably moderately priced. An excellent Thüringer roast beef, for instance, costs less than DM 20. ⊠ *Brennerstr. 42,* ☎ *03643/3675. AE, DC, MC, V.*

$ ✕ **Scharfe Ecke.** Thuringia's traditional *Knödeln* (dumplings) are best here. But be patient; they are made to order and take at least 20 minutes to prepare. The Knödeln come with just about every dish, from roast pork to venison stew. And the ideal accompaniment to any of the choices here is the locally brewed beer. ⊠ *Eisfeld 2,* ☎ *03643/202–430. Reservations not accepted. Closed Mon. No dinner Sun. No credit cards.*

$$$$ 🏨 **Flamberg Hotel Elephant.** The historic Elephant, dating from 1696, is now a member of the Flamberg group, which has, thankfully, kept the original charm that made the hotel one of Germany's most famous, even in the communist years. Goethe, Schiller, and Liszt (after whom the friendly hotel bar is named) are some of the illustrious names in the hotel register. If you want to share the "Elephant" experience, book well in advance. ⊠ *Am Markt 19, D-99423,* ☎ *03643/8020,* FAX *03643/65310. 102 rooms with bath, 5 suites. 2 restaurants, bar, sauna, nightclub, free parking. AE, DC, MC, V.*

$$$ 🏨 **Hotel Russischer Hof.** Franz Liszt, Hector Berlioz, Richard Wagner, and a group of other well-known friends founded a Weimar cultural society here in 1848. The rooms are furnished and decorated in pastel shades, light woods, and floral prints. The restaurant has a reputation far beyond Weimar; an airy, enclosed garden-terrace and a beer tavern in the vaulted cellar are two other favorite meeting places. ⊠ *Goethepl. 2, D-99423,* ☎ *03643/7740,* FAX *03643/62331. 87 rooms with bath. 2 restaurants, bar, taproom, parking (fee). AE, DC, MC, V.*

12 Great Britain

London

Windsor to Bath

Cambridge

York and Environs

Lake District

Edinburgh

GREAT BRITAIN IS A SMALL COUNTRY WITH A LONG history. Two factors have helped to ensure the preservation of so much of the nation's past. The first is the absence of fighting on British soil. Although for centuries Britain's armies crossed the Channel to take part in European wars and during the 18th and 19th centuries the nation won for itself an extensive worldwide empire, the physical fact of the English Channel has kept Britain's shores free from invasion for more than 900 years, blocking the process of destruction and reconstruction seen throughout the rest of Europe. In addition, the nation's internal conflicts, though bloody, have generally been brief. The second factor is the innate sense of history (some would call it conservatism) of the British, who generally prefer the old to the new and are often reluctant to contemplate change, especially in their physical surroundings.

All this means that Great Britain is an ideal holiday destination for anyone with a feel for the past. Here you'll find soaring medieval cathedrals, tributes to the faith of the churchmen and masons who built them; grand country mansions of the aristocracy filled with treasures—paintings, furniture, tapestries—and set in elegantly landscaped grounds; and grim fortified castles, whose gray-stone walls held fast against all challengers.

But Britain is not merely a historical theme park, and the visitor who concentrates solely on such traditional sights misses the essence of the land and the people. Many of the pleasures of exploration away from the main tourist routes derive from the ever-changing variety of the countryside. A day's drive from York, for example, will take you through stretches of wild, heather-covered moorland, ablaze with color in the fall; or past the steep, sheep-dotted mountainsides of the Dales, cut by deep valleys and scattered with isolated stone-built hamlets.

Wandering off the beaten track will also allow you to discover Britain's many distinctive country towns and villages, which move at a notably slower pace than the metropolitan centers. A medieval parish church, a high street of 18th-century buildings accented by occasional survivors from earlier centuries, and perhaps a grandiose Victorian town hall, all still in use today, help to convey a sense of a living past.

This direct continuity of past into present can be generously experienced in such a celebrated place as Stratford-upon-Avon, but even more in such communities as the little town of Chipping Campden, set in the rolling Cotswold Hills, or Bury St. Edmunds, in the gentle Suffolk countryside east of Cambridge. In such places, the visitor's understanding is often aided by small museums devoted to local history, full of intriguing artifacts and information on trade, traditions, and social life. These towns are likely places to look for specialty goods, such as knitwear, pottery, glass, and pictures, the result of a 1980s renaissance in craftsmanship.

In contrast is the hectic—at times aggressive—pace of life in London. This is a city with a vibrant artistic, cultural, and commercial life. Yet here, too, the links with the past are plain for all to see. For instance, despite all the recent rebuilding, the basic street pattern of the City (the financial quarter between St. Paul's Cathedral and the Tower of London) is still the one that evolved in the Middle Ages, more than 600 years ago, and still standing is much of the work of Christopher Wren, the master architect chiefly responsible for reconstruction after the disastrous Great Fire of 1666. Most notable of these works is St. Paul's

Great Britain

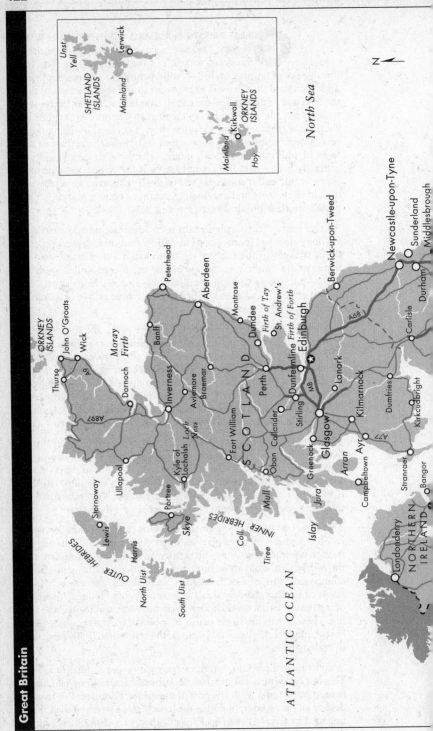

N

North Sea

SHETLAND ISLANDS

Unst
Yell
Lerwick
Mainland

Mainland
Kirkwall
ORKNEY ISLANDS
Hoy

Newcastle-upon-Tyne
Sunderland
Middlesbrough

Berwick-upon-Tweed
Durham

ORKNEY ISLANDS
John O'Groats
Wick
Moray Firth
Thurso
A9
Dornoch
A897

Peterhead
Aberdeen
Montrose
Dundee
Firth of Tay
St. Andrew's
Firth of Forth
Edinburgh

Banff
Inverness
Aviemore
Braemar
S C O T L A N D
Perth
Dunfermline
M8
Stirling
Glasgow
Lanark
A68
Carlisle

Fort William
Oban
Callander
Greenock
Kilmarnock
Dumfries
Kirkcudbright

Kyle of
Lochalsh
Loch Ness

Ullapool
Portree
Skye
INNER HEBRIDES
Coll
Mull
Tiree
Jura
Islay
Arran
Ayr
A77
Campbeltown
Stranraer
Bangor

Stornoway
Lewis
Harris
North Uist
South Uist
O U T E R   H E B R I D E S

Londonderry
NORTHERN IRELAND

A T L A N T I C   O C E A N

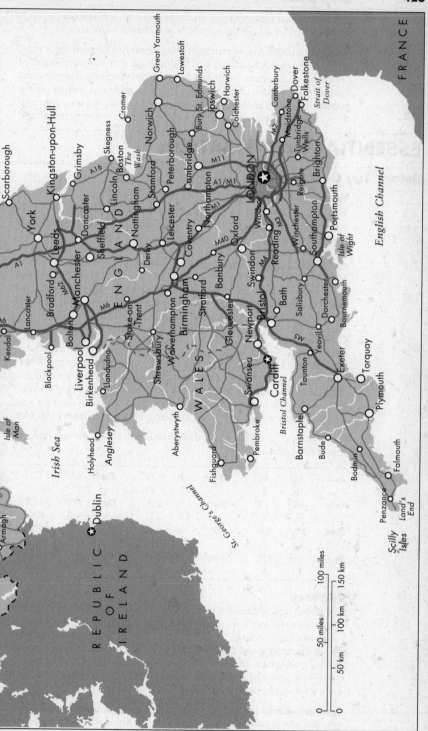

itself. Here again, exploration off the beaten path will reward you with the discovery of a London relatively untouched by tourists.

Finally, it is important to remember that Great Britain consists of three nations—England, Scotland, and Wales—and that 400 miles north of London lies the capital city of Edinburgh, whose streets and monuments bear witness to the often turbulent and momentous history of the Scottish people. Cardiff, 170 miles west of London, is a busy port and the focal point of two of the famous Welsh passions—singing and rugby.

ESSENTIAL INFORMATION

Before You Go

When to Go

The main tourist season runs from mid-April to mid-October. In recent years, however, parts of the winter—especially December—have been almost as busy. Winter is also the height of London's theater, ballet, and opera season. Springtime reveals the countryside at its most verdant and beautiful, while fall offers soft vistas of muted, golden color. May, September, and October are the months to visit the northern moorlands and Scottish highlands, while June is best for Wales and the Lake District. Most British people take their vacations during July and August, when costs are high and accommodations at a premium.

CLIMATE

On the whole, Britain's winters are rarely bitter, except in northern Scotland. Recent summers have been scorchers all over the country. Wherever you are, and whatever the season, be prepared for sudden changes. What begins as a brilliant, sunny day often turns into a damp and dismal one by lunchtime. Take an umbrella and raincoat wherever you go, particularly in Scotland, where the temperatures are somewhat cooler.

The following are the average daily maximum and minimum temperatures for London.

Jan.	43F	6C	May	62F	17C	Sept.	65F	19C
	36	2		47	8		52	11
Feb.	44F	7C	June	69F	20C	Oct.	58F	14C
	36	2		53	12		46	8
Mar.	50F	10C	July	71F	22C	Nov.	50F	10C
	38	3		56	13		42	6
Apr.	56F	13C	Aug.	71F	22C	Dec.	45F	7C
	42	6		56	13		38	3

Currency

The British unit of currency is the pound sterling, divided into 100 pence (p). Bills are issued in denominations of 5, 10, 20, and 50 pounds (£). Coins are £1, 50p, 20p, 10p, 5p, 2p, and 1p; the 10p and 5p are the size of a quarter and a dime, respectively. Scottish banks issue Scottish currency, of which all coins and notes—with the exception of the £1 notes—are accepted in England. At press time (spring 1996), exchange rates were approximately 61p to the U.S dollar.

Traveler's checks are widely accepted in Britain, and many banks, hotels, and shops offer currency-exchange facilities. You will probably lose from 1¢ to 4¢ on the dollar, however, depending on where you change them; banks offer the best rates. In London and other big cities, *bureaux de change* abound, but it definitely pays to shop around: They usually have a minimum charge of £1 and often a great deal more.

Credit cards are universally accepted, too. The most commonly used are MasterCard and Visa.

What It Will Cost

In general, transportation in Britain is expensive in comparison with other countries. You would be well advised to take advantage of the many reductions and special fares available on trains, buses, and subways. Always ask about these when buying your ticket. Gasoline prices are about the same as those on the Continent.

London now ranks with Tokyo as one of the world's most expensive hotel capitals. Finding budget accommodations—especially during July and August—can be difficult; you should try to book well ahead if you are visiting during these months. Many London hotels offer special off-season (October–March) rates, however. Dining out, even in moderate restaurants, can be prohibitively expensive, but a large number of pubs and ethnic restaurants offer excellent food at reasonable prices, and fast-food facilities are widespread.

Remember that the gulf between prices in the capital and outside is wide. Be prepared to pay a value-added tax (VAT) of 17½% on almost everything you buy; in nearly all cases it is included in the advertised price.

SAMPLE PRICES

For London: cup of coffee, £1–£2; pint of beer, £1.70–£2.20; glass of wine, £2–£5; soda, 60p; 1-mile taxi ride, £2.50; ham sandwich, £1.75.

Customs on Arrival

There are two levels of duty-free allowance for people entering the United Kingdom: one, for goods bought outside the European Union (EU) or for goods bought in a duty-free shop within the EU; two, for goods bought in an EU country.

In the first category, you may import duty-free 200 cigarettes or 100 cigarillos or 50 cigars or 250 grams of tobacco (*note:* If you live outside Europe, these allowances are doubled), plus 1 liter of alcoholic drinks over 22% volume or 2 liters of alcoholic drinks not over 22% volume or fortified or sparkling wine, plus 2 liters of still table wine, plus 60 cc/ml of perfume, plus 250 cc/ml of toilet water, plus other goods to the value of £136.

In the second category, you may import duty-free a considerable amount of liquor and tobacco—800 cigarettes, 400 cigarillos, 200 cigars, 1 kilogram of pipe tobacco, 10 liters of spirits, 90 liters of wine, 110 liters of beer, and other goods to the value of £71.

In addition, no animals or pets of any kind may be brought into the United Kingdom without a six-month quarantine. Penalties for evading this regulation are severe and strictly enforced.

Getting Around

By Car

ROAD CONDITIONS

Britain has superhighways (called motorways) running almost the length of the country, with links connecting them in the South, Midlands, and North. Motorways, given the prefix *M* on maps and road signs, have two or three lanes in each direction and are designed for high-speed rather than scenic travel.

The main north–south road between London and Leeds is M1. Other principal routes are M5, running from the Midlands to the Southwest, and M6, from the Midlands north to Scotland. M4 covers the route from London to Wales via Bristol. Encircling London is M25, which provides access to the countryside and southeast coast. It is, however, heavily traveled and not capable of supporting the volume of traffic it sees. Be ready for lengthy traffic jams.

Divided A roads are usually shown on maps as thick, red lines and, except for occasional traffic lights, are similar to motorways. Most other major routes are the 19th-century coach and turnpike roads designed for horses and carriages. Although they—and the even narrower, winding village roads—will allow you to see much more of the real Britain, your journey could end up taking twice the time. In remote country areas, road travel can be slow, especially in an icy winter. Good planning maps are available from the **AA** (Automobile Association) and the **RAC** (Royal Automobile Club); for in-depth exploring, try the Ordnance Survey 1:50,000-series maps. These show every road, track, and footpath in the country. You might also consult the very useful Ordnance Survey *Motoring Atlas*.

RULES OF THE ROAD

You can use either your driver's license or an International Driving Permit in Britain. Drive on the left-hand side of the road and pay close attention to the varying—and abruptly changing—speed limits. Seat belts are obligatory for front-seat passengers (and back-seat ones when the cars are fitted with them). In general, speed limits are 30 mph in the center of cities and built-up areas, 40 mph in suburban areas, 70 mph on motorways and divided highways, and 60 mph on all other roads.

PARKING

Parking in London and other large cities can be a nightmare. On-street meters are hard to find and can be very expensive. Cheaper pay-and-display lots (the driver inserts money into a machine to receive a sticker for the car with the amount of time allowed for parking) are common in smaller towns and suburban areas. But wherever you are, in town or city, beware of yellow or red lines. A single yellow line denotes no parking during the daytime. Double yellow lines or red lines indicate a more extensive prohibition on stopping. The exact times can always be ascertained from nearby signs, usually attached to lamp posts. Illegal parking can result in having your vehicle removed or wheel clamped, which can lead to a great deal of inconvenience as well as a hefty fine. Be sure to check street signs carefully before parking. In central London, where there is good bus and underground service and taxis are plentiful, the use of a car is not recommended. If you must drive, a useful reference book is the *London Parking Guide* (Two Heads Publications).

GASOLINE

In Britain gas (called petrol) comes in three grades; the price difference among them is negligible. Though most gas stations advertise prices by the gallon, pumps actually measure in liters. A British Imperial gallon is larger than its American equivalent—four of the former equal five of the latter. At press time (spring 1996), the price of gasoline was about £2.60 per gallon, less for lead-free. A recent campaign to promote lead-free gas has been fairly successful, helped by the fact that it's slightly cheaper (£2.05 per gallon) than the leaded variety.

By Train

Britain's rail system is somewhat overpriced, but it no longer deserves its reputation for being unreliable. All in all, it is one of the fastest, safest, and most comfortable rail services in the world. At press time (spring 1996), trains were still run by the state-owned **British Rail (BR)**, although this is due to change, as various routes are sold off to private operators.

The country's principal—and most efficient—service is the InterCity network, linking London with every major city in the country. The most modern high-speed trains travel up to 140 mph and offer comfortable, fully air-conditioned cars, both first- and second-class, with restaurant or buffet facilities. Local train services are not quite as reliable, particularly around congested city centers such as London. In general, seat reservations are not necessary except during peak vacation periods and on popular medium- and long-distance routes. Reserving a standard-class seat costs £1.

FARES

British Rail fares are high when compared with those in other countries. However, the network does offer a wide, and often bewildering, range of ticket reductions, and these can make a tremendous difference. The information office in each station is generally the most reliable source of information. Information and tickets can also be obtained from British Rail Travel Centers within the larger train stations and from selected travel agents displaying the double-arrow British Rail logo.

One of the best bargains available to overseas visitors is the **BritRail Pass** or the **BritRail Youth Pass,** the U.K. equivalent of the Eurail ticket. It provides unlimited standard and first-class travel over the entire British Rail network for periods of 8, 15, or 22 days, or one month. The cost of a **BritRail adult pass** for 8 days is $235 standard and $325 first-class; for 15 days, $365 standard and $525 first-class; for 22 days, $465 and $665; and for a month, $545 and $765. The **Youth Pass,** for those aged 16 to 25, provides unlimited second-class travel and costs $189 for 8 days, $289 for 15 days, $369 for 22 days, and $435 for one month. The **Senior Citizen Pass,** for passengers over 60 and first class seating only, costs $275 for 8 days, $445 for 15 days, $399 for 22 days, and $650 for one month. There is also a **Flexi Pass,** which allows 4, 8, or 15 days' travel in one month. These passes can be purchased only outside Britain, either in the United States, before you leave, or in one of 46 other countries. British Rail has its own information offices in New York, Los Angeles, Chicago, Dallas, Vancouver, and Toronto. The quoted prices are in U.S. dollars. Canadian tickets are slightly higher-priced.

If you are planning to travel only short distances, be sure to buy inexpensive same-day return tickets ("cheap day returns"). These cost only slightly more than ordinary one-way ("single"), standard-class tickets but can be used *only* after 9:30 AM and on weekends. Other special offers are regional **Rover** tickets, giving unlimited travel within local areas, and **Saver** returns, allowing greatly reduced round-trip travel during off-peak periods. For information about routes and fares, contact the **British Travel Centre** (⊠ 12 Regent St., London SW1Y 4PQ, no information given by phone). Also inquire at main rail stations for details about reduced-price tickets to specific destinations.

By Plane

For a comparatively small country, Britain offers an extensive network of internal air routes. These are run by about six different airlines. Hourly shuttle services operate every day between London and Glasgow, Edinburgh, Belfast, and Manchester. Seats are available on a no-reservations basis, and you can generally check in about half an hour before flight departure time. Keep in mind, however, that Britain's internal air services are not as competitive as those in the United States. And with modern, fast trains and relatively short distances, it is often much cheaper—and not much more time-consuming—to travel by train.

By Bus

Buses provide the most economical form of public transportation in Britain. Prices are invariably half those of train tickets, and the network is just as extensive. In recent years, both short- and long-distance buses have improved immeasurably in speed, comfort, and frequency. There is one important semantic difference to keep in mind when discussing bus travel in Britain. **Buses** (either double- or single-decker) are generally part of the local transportation system in towns and cities and make frequent stops. **Coaches,** on the other hand, are comparable to American Greyhound buses and are used only for long-distance travel.

National Express offers the largest number of routes of any coach operator in Britain. It also offers a variety of discount tickets, including the **BritExpress Card** and the **Tourist Trail Pass** for overseas visitors. The BritExpress Card (£7) is a discount card that provides a 30% reduction on journeys made within a year and is only available to students and those under 25 years or over 50. The Tourist Trail Pass costs £49 for 3 consecutive days' travel, £79 for 5 days' travel out of 10 consecutive days, £119 for 8 days out of 16, and £179 for 15 days out of 30. Passes can be bought from travel agents in the United States; in London, at the Victoria Coach Station (⊠ Buckingham Palace Rd., SW1 9TP) or at main train stations in Edinburgh and Glasgow. Information about all services can be obtained from the National Express Information Office at Victoria Coach Station (☎ 0990/808080) or from **SMT** (⊠ St. Andrew Sq., ☎ 0131/556–8464) in Edinburgh.

By Boat

Britain offers more than 1,500 miles of navigable inland waterways—rivers, lakes, canals, locks, and loughs—for leisure travel. Particular regions, such as the Norfolk Broads in East Anglia, the Severn Valley in the West Country, and the sea lochs and canals of Scotland, are especially popular among the nautically minded. Although there are no regularly scheduled waterborne services, hundreds of yachts, canal boats, and motor cruises are available throughout the year. The **British Tourist Authority's** booklet "U.K. Waterway Holidays" is a good source of information. You can also contact the **Inland Waterways Association** (⊠ 114 Regents Park Rd., London NW1 8UQ, ☎ 0171/586–2510) or the **British Waterways Board** (⊠ Willow Grange, Church Lane, Watford WD1 3QA, ☎ 01923/226422).

By Bicycle

Cycling provides an excellent way to see the countryside, and most towns—including London—offer bike-rental facilities. Any bike shop or tourist information center should be able to direct you to the nearest rental firm. Rental fees generally start at £15 per day, plus a fairly large deposit, though this can often be put on your credit card. If you're planning a tour and would like information on rental shops and special holidays for cyclists, contact a British Tourist Authority office in the United States before you leave home. In Britain, contact the **Cyclists' Touring Club** (⊠ Cotterell House, 69 Meadrow, Godalming, Surrey GU7 3HS, ☎ 01483/417217).

On Foot

Many organizations conduct group walking holidays during the summer months. These are especially popular in the Welsh mountains, the Lake District, Dartmoor, and Exmoor. Details are available from the British Tourist Authority.

Staying in Great Britain

Telephones

In spring 1995, an extra digit was added to area codes nationwide. This may not yet be reflected on every business card or listing, so if a phone number doesn't work, try adding a "1" after the initial "0."

Your passport around the world.

- Worldwide access
- Operators who speak your language
- Monthly itemized billing

MCI Calling Card

415 555 1234 2244
J.D. SMITH

Use your MCI Card® and these access numbers for an easy way to call when traveling worldwide.

Austria (CC)♦†	022-903-012
Belarus	
From Gomel and Mogilev regions	8-10-800-103
From all other localities	8-800-103
Belgium (CC)♦†	0800-10012
Bulgaria	00800-0001
Croatia (CC)★	99-385-0112
Czech Republic (CC)♦	00-42-000112
Denmark (CC)♦†	8001-0022
Finland (CC)♦†	9800-102-80
France (CC)♦†	0800-99-0019
Germany (CC)†	0130-0012
Greece (CC)♦†	00-800-1211
Hungary (CC)♦	00▼800-01411
Iceland (CC)♦†	800-9002
Ireland (CC)†	1-800-55-1001
Italy (CC)♦†	172-1022
Kazakhstan (CC)	1-800-131-4321
Liechtenstein (CC)♦	155-0222
Luxembourg†	0800-0112
Monaco (CC)♦	800-90-19

Netherlands (CC)♦†	06-022-91-22
Norway (CC)♦†	800-19912
Poland (CC)✣†	00-800-111-21-22
Portugal (CC)✣†	05-017-1234
Romania (CC)✣	01-800-1800
Russia (CC)✣♦	747-3322
For a Russian-speaking operator	747-3320
San Marino (CC)♦	172-1022
Slovak Republic (CC)	00-42-000112
Slovenia	080-8808
Spain (CC)†	900-99-0014
Sweden (CC)♦†	020-795-922
Switzerland (CC)♦†	155-0222
Turkey (CC)♦†	00-8001-1177
Ukraine (CC)✣	8▼10-013
United Kingdom (CC)†	
To call to the U.S. using BT ■	0800-89-0222
To call to the U.S. using Mercury ■	0500-89-0222
Vatican City (CC)†	172-1022

To sign up for the MCI Card, dial the access number of the country you are in and ask to speak with a customer service representative.

http://www.mci.com

(CC) Country-to-country calling available. May not be available to/from all international locations. (Canada, Puerto Rico, and U.S. Virgin Islands are considered Domestic Access locations.) ♦ Public phones may require deposit of coin or phone card for dial tone. † Automation available from most locations. ★ Not available from public pay phones. ▼ Wait for second dial tone. ✣ Limited availability. ■ International communications carrier.

We think about your holiday as much as you do.

The moment you choose a British Airways Holiday, you can start anticipating a well-deserved break. Our expertise and experience mean we can offer you the best value in the widest range of worldwide destinations. For more information and a free brochure, call your travel agent or 1-800-AIRWAYS.

BRITISH AIRWAYS
HOLIDAYS®

LOCAL CALLS

Public telephones are plentiful in British cities, especially London, and you will find fewer out of order these days than in years past. Other than on the street, the best place to find a bank of pay phones is in a hotel or large post office; pubs usually have a pay phone, too. As part of British Telecom's modernization efforts, the distinctive red phone booths are gradually being replaced by generic glass and steel cubicles, but the red boxes still remain in more remote areas of the country. The workings of coin-operated telephones vary, but there are usually instructions in each unit. Most take 10p, 20p, 50p, and £1 coins. A Phonecard is also available; it comes in denominations of 10, 20, 40, and 100 units and can be bought in a number of retail outlets. Cardphones, which are clearly marked with a special green insignia, will not accept coins.

A local call before 6 PM costs 15p for three minutes. A daytime call to the United States will cost 47p a minute. Each large city or region in Britain has its own numerical prefix, which is used only when you are dialing from outside the city. In provincial areas, the dialing codes for nearby towns are often posted in the booth.

INTERNATIONAL CALLS

The cheapest way to make an overseas call is to dial it yourself. But be sure to have plenty of coins or Phonecards close at hand. After you have inserted the coins or card, dial 00 (the international code), then the country code—for the United States, it is 1—followed by the area code and local number. To reach an **AT&T** long-distance operator, dial 0500890011; for **MCI,** dial 0800890202 , and for **Sprint,** dial 0800890877 (from a British Telecom phone) or 0500890877 (from a Mercury Communications phone). To make a collect or other operator-assisted call, dial 155.

COUNTRY CODE

When you're dialing overseas, the United Kingdom's country code is 44.

OPERATORS AND INFORMATION

For information anywhere in Britain, dial 192. For the operator, dial 100. For assistance with international calls, dial 155.

Mail

POSTAL RATES

Airmail letters to the United States and Canada cost 41p for 10 grams; postcards, 35p; aerograms, 36p. Letters and postcards to Europe weighing up to 20 grams cost 30p (25p to EU-member countries). Letters within the United Kingdom: first-class, 25p; second-class and postcards, 19p. These rates are likely to have risen by early 1996.

RECEIVING MAIL

If you're uncertain where you'll be staying, you can arrange to have your mail sent to American Express (✉ 6 Haymarket, London SW1Y 4BS). The service is free to cardholders and Amex travelers' check holders; all others pay a small fee. You can also collect letters at London's main post office. Ask to have them addressed to "poste restante" and mailed to the Main Post Office, Trafalgar Square, London. The point of collection is 24-28 William IV Street, London WC2N 4DL. Hours are Monday–Saturday 8–8. You'll need your passport or other official form of identification.

Shopping

VAT REFUNDS

Foreign visitors can avoid Britain's crippling 17½% value-added tax (VAT) by taking advantage of a variety of special refund and export schemes. The easiest and most common way of getting a refund is the Over-the-Counter method. To qualify for this, you must buy goods worth £75 or more (stores vary; if you are from the EU, it can be as much as £420). The shopkeeper will attach a special paper—Form VAT 407—to the invoice, and upon leaving the United Kingdom, you present the goods, form, and invoice to the customs officer. Allow plenty of time to do this at the airport; there are often long lines. The form is then returned to the store, and the refund forwarded to you, minus a small service charge. The Direct Export method is another option. With this method, you are also issued Form VAT 407, but your purchases are sent home separately, and upon returning home, you must have the form certified by customs or a notary public. You then return the form to the store, and your money is refunded. For enquiries, call Customs and Excise at 01895/842200.

Opening and Closing Times

Banks. Most banks are open weekdays 9:30–4:30. Some have extended hours on Thursday evenings, and a few are open on Saturday mornings.

Museums. Museum hours vary considerably from one part of the country to another. In large cities, most are open Tuesday–Saturday 10–5; many are also open on Sunday afternoons. The majority close one day a week. Be sure to double-check the opening times of historic houses, especially if the visit involves a difficult trip.

Shops. Usual business hours are Monday–Saturday 9–5:30, but many shops are now open Sundays. Outside the main centers, most shops observe an early closing day once a week, often Wednesday or Thursday; they close at 1 PM and do not reopen until the following morning. In small villages, many also close for lunch. In large cities—especially London—department stores stay open for late-night shopping (usually until 7:30 or 8) one day midweek.

National Holidays

England and Wales: January 1; March 28 (Good Friday); March 31 (Easter Monday); May 1 (May Day); May 6, 27 (Spring Bank Holidays); August 26 (Summer Bank Holiday); December 25–26. Scotland: January 1–2; March 28, 31; May 27 (Spring Bank Holiday); August 26; December 25–26.

Dining

In days past, British food was condemned the world over for its plainness and mediocrity. Today, with great strides made in most restaurants, the problem is not so much bad food as expensive food—you might want to check prices on the menu, which by law must be displayed outside the restaurant, before committing yourself. The best of traditional British cooking relies on top-quality, fresh local ingredients: wild salmon, spring lamb, orchard apples, and countless varieties of seasonal vegetables. Nearly all restaurant menus also include some vegetarian dishes, and interesting ethnic cuisines, especially Asian, provide variety even in quite small towns. In the capital, restaurants have taken such giant steps during the past decade that London is now one of the world's greatest cities for dining out.

MEALTIMES

These vary somewhat, depending on the region of the country you are visiting. But in general, breakfast is served between 7:30 and 9 and lunch between noon and 2. Tea—a famous British tradition and often a meal in itself—is generally served between 4 and 5:30. Dinner or supper is served between 7:30 and 9:30, sometimes earlier, but rarely later outside the metropolitan areas. High tea, at about 6, replaces dinner in some areas—especially in Scotland—and in large cities, after-theater suppers are often available.

WHAT TO WEAR

Jacket and tie are suggested for the more formal restaurants in the top price categories, but, in general, casual chic or informal dress is acceptable in most establishments.

RATINGS

Prices quoted here are per person and include a first course, a main course, and dessert, but not wine or service.

CATEGORY	LONDON AND SOUTHERN ENGLAND	OTHER AREAS
$$$$	over £50	over £40
$$$	£30–£50	£25–40
$$	£20–£30	£15–25
$	under £20	under £15

Lodging

Britain offers a wide variety of accommodations, ranging from enormous, top-quality, top-price hotels to simple, intimate farmhouses and guest houses.

HOTELS

British hotels vary greatly, and there is no reliable official system of classification. Most have rooms with private bathrooms, although there are still many—usually older hotels—that offer some rooms with only wash basins; in this case, showers and bathtubs (and toilets) are usually just down the hall. Many also have "good" and "bad" wings. Be sure to check the room before you take it. Generally, British hotel prices include breakfast, but beware: Many offer only a Continental breakfast—often little more than tea and toast. A hotel that includes a traditional British breakfast in its rates is usually a good bet. Hotel prices in London can be significantly higher than in the rest of the country, and sometimes the quality does not reflect the extra cost. Tourist information centers all over the country will reserve rooms for you, usually for a small fee. A great many hotels offer special weekend and off-season bargain packages.

BED-AND-BREAKFASTS

In Britain these are small, simple establishments, not the upscale option Americans know by this name. They offer modest, inexpensive accommodations, usually in a family home. Few have private bathrooms, and most offer no meals other than breakfast. Guest houses are a slightly larger, somewhat more luxurious, version. Both provide the visitor with an excellent glimpse of everyday British life.

FARMHOUSES

Farmhouses rarely offer professional hotel standards, but they have a special appeal: the rustic, rural experience. Prices are generally very reasonable. Ask for the British Tourist Authority booklets "Farmhouse Vacations" and "Stay on a Farm." A car is vital for a successful farmhouse stay. The **Farm Holiday Bureau** (⊠ National Agricultural Centre, Stoneleigh, Kenilworth, Warwickshire CV8 2LZ, ☎ 01203/696909), a network of farming and country people who offer B&B accommodation, is a good source for regional tourist board inspected and approved properties.

HOLIDAY COTTAGES

Furnished apartments, houses, cottages, and trailers are available for weekly rental in all areas of the country. These vary from quaint, cleverly converted farmhouses to brand-new buildings set in scenic surroundings. For families and large groups, they offer the best value for the money. Lists of rental properties are available free of charge from the British Tourist Authority. Discounts of up to 50% apply during the off-season (October to March). A useful publication on the subject is the *Good Holiday Cottage Guide* (Swallow Press).

HISTORIC BUILDINGS

Do you dream of spending your vacation in a gothic banqueting house, an old lighthouse, or maybe in a gate house that sheltered Mary, Queen of Scots, in 1586? There are some half-dozen organizations in Great Britain that have specially adapted historic buildings to rent. Most of them have cooking facilities, so for a short while you can pretend to have lived there all your life. Two of the leading charities that have such buildings for rent are **The Landmark Trust** (⊠ Shottesbrooke, Maidenhead, Berkshire SL6 3SW, ☎ 01628/825925) and the **National Trust** (⊠ Box 101, Western Way, Melksham, Wiltshire SN12 8EA, ☎ 01225/705676). All the buildings have been adapted and modernized, with due respect to their historic status, so you don't have to worry about medieval plumbing or Tudor kitchens. There are, however, no TVs in the Landmark Trust properties. Other organizations are **Portmeirion Cottages** (⊠ Portmeirion, Gwynedd, Wales LL48 6ET, ☎ 01766/770228) and the rather upscale **Rural Retreats** (⊠ Retreat House, Station Rd., Blockley, Moreton-in-Marsh, Gloucestershire GL56 9DZ, ☎ 01386/701177).

UNIVERSITY HOUSING

In larger cities and in some towns, certain universities offer their residence halls to paying vacationers. The facilities available are usually compact sleeping units, and they can be rented on a nightly basis. For information, contact the **British Universities Accommodation Consortium** (⊠ Box 1315, University Park, Nottingham NG7 2RD, ☎ 01159/504571).

YOUTH HOSTELS

There are more than 350 youth hostels throughout England, Wales, and Scotland. They range from very basic to very good. Many are located in remote and beautiful areas; others can be found on the outskirts of large cities. Despite the name, there is no age restriction. The accommodations are inexpensive and generally reliable and usually include cooking facilities. For additional information, contact the **YHA Headquarters** (⊠ Trevelyan House, 8 St. Stephen's Hill, St. Albans, Hertfordshire AL1 2DY, ☎ 01727/855215).

CAMPING

Britain offers an abundance of campsites. Some are large and well equipped; others are merely small farmers' fields, offering primitive facilities. For information, contact the British Travel Authority in the United States or the **Camping and Caravan Club, Ltd.** (⊠ Greenfields House, Westwood Way, Coventry CV4 8JH, ☎ 01203/694995).

RATINGS

Prices are for two people in a double room and include all taxes.

CATEGORY	LONDON AND SOUTHERN ENGLAND	OTHER AREAS
$$$$	over £150	over £110
$$$	£80-£150	£60-£110
$$	£60-£80	£50-£60
$	under £60	under £50

Tipping

Some restaurants and most hotels add a service charge of 10%–15% to the bill. If this has been done, you're under no obligation to tip further. If no service charge is indicated, add 10%–15% to your total bill. Taxi drivers should also get 10%–15%. You are not expected to tip theater or cinema ushers, elevator operators, or bartenders in pubs. Hairdressers and barbers should receive 10%–15%.

LONDON

Arriving and Departing

By Plane

International flights to London arrive at either Heathrow Airport, 12 miles west of London, or at Gatwick Airport, 25 miles south of the capital. Most flights from the United States go to Heathrow. Gatwick generally serves European destinations. American Airlines flights from Chicago and AirTransit flights from Toronto and Vancouver land at a third airport, Stansted.

BETWEEN THE AIRPORT AND DOWNTOWN

The Piccadilly Line serves Heathrow (all terminals) with a direct Underground (subway) link. The 40-minute ride costs £3.10 at press time (spring 1996). Three special buses also serve Heathrow: A1 leaves every 30 minutes for Victoria Station and takes about an hour; A2 goes to Euston Station every 30 minutes and takes 80 minutes. The one-way cost for either bus is £6. Bus 390 runs to Victoria eight times daily and costs £5 one-way.

From Gatwick, the quickest way to London is the nonstop rail Gatwick Express, costing (at press time) £8.90 one-way and taking 30 minutes to reach Victoria Station. Regular bus services are provided by Greenline Coaches, including the Flightline 777 to Victoria Station. This takes about 70 minutes and costs £6 one-way.

Cars and taxis drive into London on M4; the trip can take more than an hour, depending on traffic. The taxi fare is about £25, plus tip. From Gatwick, the taxi fare is at least £35, plus tip; traffic can be very heavy.

By Train

London is served by no fewer than 15 train stations, so be absolutely certain of the station for your departure or arrival. All have Underground stops either in the train station or within a few minutes' walk from it, and most are served by several bus routes. The principal routes that connect London to other major towns and cities are on an InterCity network. Seats can be reserved by phone only with a credit card. You can, of course, apply in person to any British Rail Travel Centre or directly to the station from which you depart. Below is a list of the major London rail stations and the areas they serve.

Charing Cross (☏ 0171/928–5100) serves southeast England, including Canterbury, Margate, Dover/Folkestone.

Euston/St. Pancras (☏ 0171/387–7070) serves East Anglia, Essex, the Northeast, the Northwest, and North Wales, including Coventry, Stratford-upon-Avon, Birmingham, Manchester, Liverpool, Windermere, Glasgow, and Inverness.

King's Cross (☏ 0171/278–2477) serves the east Midlands; the Northeast, including York, Leeds, and Newcastle; and north and east Scotland, including Edinburgh and Aberdeen.

Liverpool Street (☏ 0171/928–5100) serves Essex and East Anglia.

Paddington (☎ 0171/262–6767) serves the south Midlands, west and south Wales, and the west country, including Reading, Bath, Bristol, Oxford, Cardiff, Swansea, Exeter, Plymouth, and Penzance.

Victoria (☎ 0171/928–5100) serves southern England, including Gatwick Airport, Brighton, Dover/Folkestone (from May), and the south coast.

Waterloo (☎ 0171/928-5100) serves the southwestern United Kingdom, including Salisbury, Bournemouth, Portsmouth, Southampton, Isle of Wight, Jersey, and Guernsey.

FARES

The fare structures are slowly changing as the formerly nationalized British Rail is sold off to various independent operators. Generally speaking, though, it is less expensive to buy a return (round-trip) ticket, especially for day trips not far from London, and you should always inquire at the information office to find out what discount fares are available for your route. You can hear a recorded summary of timetable and fare information to many destinations by calling the appropriate "dial and listen" numbers listed under British Rail in the telephone book.

Via the Channel Tunnel

If you're combining a trip to Great Britain with stops on the Continent, you can either drive your car onto a Le Shuttle train through the Channel Tunnel (35 minutes from Folkestone to Calais), or book a seat on the Eurostar high-speed train service that zips through the tunnel (3 hours from London's Waterloo Station to Paris, 3¼ hours from London to Brussels). For details, *see* the Channel Tunnel *in* Chapter 1.

By Bus

The **National Express** coach service has routes to more than 1,000 major towns and cities in the United Kingdom. It's considerably cheaper than the train, although the trips usually take longer. National Express offers two types of service: an ordinary service, which makes frequent stops for refreshment breaks, and a Rapide service, which has hostess and refreshment facilities on board. Day returns are available on both, but booking is advised on the Rapide service. National Express coaches leave Victoria Coach Station (Buckingham Palace Rd.) at regular intervals, depending on the destination. For travel information and credit card reservations, dial 0171/730–0202.

Getting Around

By Underground

Known as "the tube," London's extensive Underground system is by far the most widely used form of city transportation. Trains run both beneath and above ground out into the suburbs, and all stations are clearly marked with the London Underground circular symbol. (A SUBWAY sign refers to an under-the-street crossing.) Trains are all one class; smoking is *not* allowed on board or in the stations.

There are 10 basic lines—all named—plus the East London line, which runs from Shoreditch and Whitechapel across the Thames south to New Cross, and the Docklands Light Railway, which runs from Stratford in London's East End to Greenwich, with an extension to the Royal Docks to be completed. The Central, District, Northern, Metropolitan, and Piccadilly lines all have branches, so be sure to note which branch is needed for your particular destination. Electronic platform signs tell you the final stop and route of the next train, and most signs also indicate how many minutes you'll have to wait for the train to arrive.

London Underground

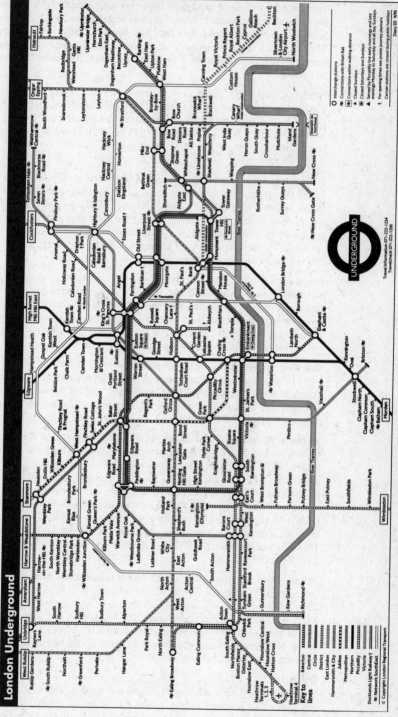

From Monday to Saturday, trains begin running around 5:30 AM; the last services leave central London between midnight and 12:30 AM. On Sundays, trains start two hours later and finish about an hour earlier. The frequency of trains depends on the route and the time of day, but normally you should not have to wait more than 10 minutes in central areas.

A pocket map of the entire tube network is available free from most Underground ticket counters. There should also be a large map on the wall of each platform, and the new computerized database, "Routes," is available at 14 London Transport (LT) Travel Information Centres (☞ *below*).

FARES

For both buses and tube fares, London is divided into six concentric zones; the fare goes up the farther afield you travel. Ask at Underground ticket counters for the LT booklet "Tickets," which gives details of all the various ticket options and bargains for the tube; after some experimenting, you'll soon know which ticket best serves your particular needs. Till then, here is a brief summary of the major ticket categories, but note that these prices are subject to increases.

Singles and Returns. For one trip between any two stations, you can buy an ordinary single (one-way ticket) for travel anytime on the day of issue; if you're coming back on the same route the same day, then an ordinary return (round-trip ticket) costs twice the single fare. Singles vary in price from 70p in the central zone to £3.10 for a six-zone journey—not a good option for the sightseer who wants to make several journeys.

One-Day Travelcards. These allow unrestricted travel on the tube, most buses, and British Rail trains in the Greater London zones and are valid weekdays after 9:30 AM, weekends, and all public holidays. They cannot be used on airbuses, night buses, or for certain special services. The price is £2.80–£3.80.

Visitor's Travelcard. These are the best bet for visitors, but they must be bought before leaving home (they're available in both the United States and Canada). They are valid for periods of three, four, or seven days ($25, $32, $49 adults; $11, $13, $21 children) and can be used on the tube and virtually all buses and British Rail services in London. One-day Visitor's Travelcards can be bought at hotels in London for £3.90. All these cards also include a set of money-saving discounts to many of London's top attractions. Apply to travel agents or to BritRail Travel International (✉ 1500 Broadway, New York, NY 10036, ☎ 212/382–3737).

For more information, there are **LT Travel Information Centres** at the following tube stations: Euston (⊘ Sat.–Thurs. 7:15–6, Fri. to 7:30); King's Cross (⊘ Sat.–Thurs. 8:15–6, Fri. to 7:30); Oxford Circus (⊘ Mon.–Sat. 8:15–6); Piccadilly Circus (⊘ Mon.–Sun. 8:15–6); Victoria (⊘ Mon.–Sun. 8:15–9:30); and Heathrow (⊘ Mon.–Sun. to 9, or 10 PM in Terminals 1 and 2). For information on all London bus and tube times, fares, and so on, dial 0171/222–1234.

By Bus

London's bus system consists of bright red double- and single-deckers, plus other buses of various colors. Destinations are displayed on the front and back, with the bus number on the front, back, and side, though not all buses run the full length of their route at all times. Some buses are still operated with a conductor whom you pay after finding a seat, but these days you will more often find one-person buses, in which you pay the driver upon boarding.

Buses stop only at clearly indicated stops. Main stops—at which the bus should stop automatically—have a plain white background with a red LT symbol on it. There are also request stops with red signs, a white symbol, and the word REQUEST added; at these you must hail the bus to make it stop. Smoking is not allowed on any bus. Although you can see much of the town from a bus, *don't* take one if you want to get anywhere in a hurry; traffic often slows travel to a crawl, and during peak times you may find yourself waiting at least 20 minutes for a bus and not being able to get on it once it arrives. If you intend to go by bus, ask at a Travel Information Centre for a free "Londonwide Bus Map."

FARES

Single fares start at 50p for short distances (90p in the central zone). Travelcards are good for tube, bus, and British Rail trains in the Greater London Zones. There are also a number of bus passes available for daily, weekly, and monthly use, and prices vary according to zones. A photograph is required for weekly or monthly bus passes; this also applies to children and older children who may need a child-rate photocard to avoid paying the adult rate.

By Taxi

London's black taxis are famous for their comfort and for the ability of their drivers to remember the mazelike pattern of the capital's streets. Hotels and main tourist areas have ranks (stands) where you wait your turn to take one of the taxis that drive up. You can also hail a taxi if the flag is up or the yellow FOR HIRE sign is lighted. Fares start at £1 and increase by units of 20p per 291 yards or 1 minute. A surcharge of 60p is added in the evenings until midnight, on Sundays, and on holidays.

By Car

The best advice is to avoid driving in London because of the illogical street patterns and the chronic parking shortage. A constantly changing system of one-way streets adds to the confusion.

Important Addresses and Numbers

Visitor Information

The main **London Tourist Information Centre** at Victoria Station Forecourt provides details about London and the rest of Britain, including general information; tickets for tube and bus; theater, concert, and tour bookings; and accommodations (☉ Apr.–Oct., daily 9–8:30; Nov.–Mar., Mon.–Sat. 9–7, Sun. 9–5). Other information centers are located in **Selfridges** (✉ Oxford St., W1A 2LR) and is open store hours only; at **Tower of London** (✉ West Gate, EC3W 4AB), open summer months only; and **Heathrow Airport** (Terminals 1, 2, and 3). **Visitorcall** is the London Tourist Board's phone service—a premium-rate (49p per minute; 39p off-peak) recorded information line, with different numbers for theater, events, museums, sports, getting around, and so on. To access the list of options, call 01839/123456, or see the display advertisement in the phone book.

Embassies and Consulates

American Embassy (✉ 24 Grosvenor Sq., W1A 1AE, ☎ 0171/499–9000).

Canadian High Commission (✉ McDonald House, 1 Grosvenor Sq., W1X 0AB, ☎ 0171/258–6600).

Emergencies

For **police, fire brigade**, or **ambulance**, dial 999.

The following **hospitals** have 24-hour emergency rooms: **Charing Cross** (✉ Fulham Palace Rd., W6, ☎ 0181/846–1234); **Guys** (✉ St. Thomas

St., SE1, ☎ 0171/955–5000); **Royal Free** (✉ Pond St., Hampstead, NW3, ☎ 0171/794–0500); and **St. Thomas's** (✉ Lambeth Palace Rd., SE1, ☎ 0171/928–9292).

Pharmacies

Chemists (drugstores) with late opening hours include **Bliss Chemist** (✉ 5 Marble Arch, W1, ☎ 0171/723–6116, ⊘ Daily 9 AM–midnight) and **Boots** (✉ 44 Piccadilly Circus, W1, ☎ 0171/734–6126, ⊘ Mon.–Sat. 8:30–8, also the branch at 439 Oxford St., W1, ☎ 0171/409–2857, ⊘ Thurs. 8:30–7).

Travel Agencies

American Express (✉ 6 Haymarket, SW1, ☎ 0171/930–4411; 89 Mount St., W1, ☎ 0171/499–0288; and other branches). **Thomas Cook** (✉ 4 Henrietta St., WC2, ☎ 0171/240–4872; 1 Marble Arch, W1, ☎ 0171/706–4188; and branches).

Credit Cards

Should your credit cards be lost or stolen, here are some numbers to dial for assistance: **Access (MasterCard,** ☎ 0181/450–3122); **American Express** (☎ 0171/222–9633, 24 hours, or 0800/521313 for traveler's checks); **Barclaycard (Visa,** ☎ 01604/230230); **Diners Club** (☎ 01252/516261).

Guided Tours

Orientation Tours

BY BUS

The **Original London Sightseeing Tour** (☎ 0181/8777–1722) offers passengers a good introduction to the city from double-decker buses (seating capacity 64–72). Tours run daily every half hour or so, departing from Marble Arch, Haymarket, Baker Street, or Victoria. There are about 21 stops, where you may board and alight to view the sights and then get back on the next bus. Tickets cost £10 (£5 for those under 16 years old) and can be bought from the driver. Other reputable agencies offering bus tours include **Evan Evans** (☎ 0171/930–2377), **Frames Rickards** (☎ 0171/837–3111), and **The Big Bus Company** (☎ 0181/944–7810). These tours have a smaller seating capacity of approximately 50 passengers and include stops at places such as St. Paul's Cathedral and Westminster Abbey. Prices and pick-up points vary according to the sights visited, but many pick-up points are at major hotels.

BY RIVER

From April to October, boats cruise up and down the Thames, offering a different view of the London skyline. Most leave from Westminster Pier (☎ 0171/930–4097), Charing Cross Pier (☎ 0171/839–3572), or Tower Pier (☎ 0171/488–0344). Downstream routes go to the Tower of London, Greenwich, and Thames Barrier; upstream destinations include Kew, Richmond, and Hampton Court. Most of the launches seat between 100 and 250 passengers, have a public-address system, and provide a running commentary on passing points of interest. Depending upon the destination, river trips may last from one to four hours. For more information, call **Catamaran Cruisers** (☎ 0171/839–3572), or **Tidal Cruises** (☎ 0171/928–9009).

BY CANAL

During summer, narrow boats and barges cruise London's two canals, the Grand Union and Regent's Canal; most vessels (seating about 60) operate on the latter, which runs between Little Venice in the west (the nearest tube is Warwick Ave. on the Bakerloo Line) and Camden Lock (about 200 yards north of Camden Town tube station). **Jason's Trip** (☎ 0171/286–3428) operates one-way and round-trip narrow boat cruises on this route. During April, May, and September, there are two cruises per day; from June to August there are four. Trips last 1½ hours. **Canal Cruises** (☎ 0171/485–4433) also offers cruises from March to October on the *Jenny Wren* and all year on the cruising restaurant *My Fair Lady*.

Walking Tours

One of the best ways to get to know London is on foot, and there are many guided walking tours from which to choose. **The Original London Walks** (☎ 0171/624–3978), **City Walks** (☎ 0171/700–6931), and **Citisights** (☎ 0181/806–4325) are just a few of the better-known firms, but your best bet is to peruse a variety of leaflets at the London Tourist Information Centre at Victoria Station. The duration of the walks varies (usually 1–3 hours), and you can generally find one to suit even the most specific of interests—Shakespeare's London, say, or a Jack the Ripper tour. Prices are around £4 for adults.

If you'd rather explore on your own, then the City of London Corporation has laid out a **Heritage Walk** that leads through Bank, Leadenhall, and Monument; follow the trail by the directional stars set into the sidewalks. A map of this walk can be found in *A Visitor's Guide to the City of London,* available from the City Information Centre across from St. Paul's Cathedral. Another option is to follow the **Silver Jubilee Walkway,** created in 1977 in honor of the 25th anniversary of the reign of the present queen. The entire route covers 10 miles and is marked by a series of silver crowns set into the sidewalks; Parliament Square makes a good starting point. Several guides offering further London walks to follow are available in bookshops.

Excursions

LT, Evan Evans, and Frames Rickards (☞ Orientation Tours, *above*) all offer day excursions (some combine bus and boat) to places of interest within easy reach of London, such as Windsor, Hampton Court, Oxford, Stratford–upon–Avon, and Bath. Prices vary and may include lunch and admission prices or admission only.

Personal Guides

British Tours (☎ 0171/629–5267) will pick you up from your hotel and take you anywhere in the United Kingdom. Tour prices include car and driver-guide expenses and range from £100 for two people in a medium-size car going on a three-hour tour of London to £295 for four people in a large car taking in Bath and Stonehenge (10 hours). A good choice of tours, for one to six people, is available all year. Details of similar private operators can be found at the London Tourist Information Centre in Victoria Station or at Heathrow.

Exploring London

Traditionally London has been divided between the City, to the east, where its banking and commercial interests lie, and Westminster to the west, the seat of the royal court and of government. Today the distinction between the two holds good, and even the briefest exploration will reveal each area's distinct atmosphere. It is also in these two areas that you will find most of the grand buildings that have played a central role in British history: the Tower of London and St. Paul's Cathedral, Westminster Abbey and the Houses of Parliament, Buckingham Palace, and the older royal palace of St. James's.

These sights are natural magnets for visitors to London, as the crowds of people and the ubiquitous tourist coaches demonstrate. But visitors who restrict their sightseeing to these well-known tourist areas miss much of the best the city has to offer. Within a few minutes' walk of

Buckingham Palace, for instance, lie St. James's and Mayfair, two neighboring quarters of elegant town houses built for the nobility in the 17th and early 18th centuries and now notable for the shopping opportunities they house. The same lesson applies to the City, where, tucked away in quiet corners, stand many of the churches Christopher Wren built to replace those destroyed during the Great Fire of 1666.

Other parts of London worth exploring include Covent Garden, a former fruit and flower market converted into a lively shopping and entertainment center where you can wander for hours enjoying the friendly bustle of the streets. Hyde Park and Kensington Gardens, by contrast, offer a great swathe of green parkland across the city center, preserved by past kings and queens for their own hunting and relaxation. A walk across Hyde Park will bring you to the museum district of South Kensington, with three major national collections: the Natural History Museum, the Science Museum, and the Victoria and Albert Museum, which specializes in costume and the fine and applied arts.

The south side of the River Thames has its treats as well. A short stroll across Waterloo Bridge brings you to the South Bank Arts Complex, which includes the National Theatre, the Royal Festival Hall, the Hayward Gallery (with changing exhibitions of international art), the National Film Theatre, and the Museum of the Moving Image (MOMI)—a must for movie buffs. Here also are the exciting reconstruction of Shakespeare's Globe theater and its sister museum, and the future home, at Bankside Power Station, of the Tate Gallery of Modern Art—due for completion for the millenium. The views from the South Bank are stunning—to the west are the Houses of Parliament and Big Ben; to the east the dome of St. Paul's is just visible on London's changing skyline.

London, although not simple of layout, is a rewarding walking city, and this remains the best way to get to know its nooks and crannies. The infamous weather may not be on your side, but there's plenty of indoor entertainment to keep you amused if you forgot the umbrella. More than in most cities, though, London's centuries of history are revealed as much in the quotidian street life and residential districts as in the grand national monuments, so keep your eyes peeled, and discover it for yourself.

Westminster

Numbers in the margin correspond to points of interest on the London map.

Westminster is the royal backyard—the traditional center of the royal court and of government. Here, within a kilometer or so of each other, are virtually all London's most celebrated buildings (St. Paul's Cathedral and the Tower of London excepted), and there is a strong feeling of history all around you. Generations of kings and queens have lived here since the end of the 11th century—including the current monarch. The Queen resides at Buckingham Palace through most of the year; during summer periods when she visits her country estates, the palace is partially open to visitors.

❶ Start at **Trafalgar Square,** which is on the site of the former Royal Mews. Both the square's name and its present appearance date from about 1830. A statue of Admiral Lord Nelson, victor over the French in 1805 at the Battle of Trafalgar, at which he lost his life, stands atop a 145-foot granite column. Huge stone lions guard the base of the column, which is decorated with four bronze panels depicting naval battles against France and cast from French cannons captured by Nelson. The bronze equestrian statue on the south side of the square is of the unhappy Charles

I; he is looking down Whitehall toward the spot where he was executed in 1649.

★ ❷ In the **National Gallery**, which occupies the long neoclassical building on the north side of the square, is one of the world's greatest museums, generally ranked right after the Louvre. It contains works by virtually every famous artist and school from the 14th to the 19th century and its galleries are overflowing with legendary masterpieces, including Jan van Eyck's *Arnolfini Marriage,* Leonardo da Vinci's *Burlington Virgin and Child,* Velasquez's *Rokeby Venus,* and Constable's *Hay Wain.* The gallery is especially strong on Flemish and Dutch masters, Rubens and Rembrandt among them, and on Italian Renaissance works. The Sainsbury Wing houses the early Renaissance collection. ⊠ *Trafalgar Sq.,* ☎ *0171/839–3321; 0171/839–3526 (recorded information).* ⊠ *Free; charge for Sainsbury Wing exhibitions.* ⊙ *Mon.–Sat. 10–6, Sun. 2–6; June–Aug., Wed. until 8.*

❸ Around the corner, at the foot of Charing Cross Road, is a second major art collection, the **National Portrait Gallery,** which contains portraits of well-known (and not so well-known) Britons, including monarchs, statesmen, and writers. ⊠ *2 St. Martin's Pl.,* ☎ *0171/930–1552.* ⊠ *Free.* ⊙ *Weekdays 10–5, Sat. 10–6, Sun. 2–6.*

❹ The Gallery's entrance is opposite the distinctive neoclassical church of **St. Martin-in-the-Fields,** built in about 1730. Regular lunchtime music recitals are held here.

| NEED A BREAK? | Both **The Brasserie** in the Sainsbury Wing of the National Gallery and **Café in the Crypt** in St. Martin's serve ambitious hot meals at lunchtime, as well as sandwiches, salads, snacks, cakes, and coffee. |

❺ **Admiralty Arch** guards the entrance to **The Mall,** the great ceremonial way that leads alongside **St. James's Park** to Buckingham Palace. The Mall takes its name from a game called *palle maille,* a version of croquet that James I imported from France, and Charles II popularized in the late 1600s. The park—with its duck-filled lake, deck chairs, bandstand, and perfectly maintained flower beds—was developed by successive monarchs, most recently by George IV in the 1820s, having originally been used for hunting by Henry VIII. Join office workers relaxing with a lunchtime sandwich, or stroll here on a summer's evening when the illuminated fountains play and Westminster Abbey and the Houses of Parliament beyond the trees are floodlit.

❻ On the other side of the Mall, you'll pass along the foot of the imposing
❼ **Carlton House Terrace,** built in 1827–32 by John Nash. A right turn up Marlborough Road brings you to **St. James's Palace.** Although the earliest parts of this lovely brick building date from the 1530s, it had a relatively short career as the center of royal affairs—from the destruction of Whitehall Palace in 1698 until 1837, when Victoria became queen and moved the royal household down the road to Buckingham Palace. Today, the Palace is closed to the public, although a number of royal functionaries have offices here, and important visitors to London are still accredited to the Court of St. James's.

❽ At the end of Marlborough Road, beyond the open-sided **Friary Court,** turn left along **Cleveland Row,** and walk past **York House,** the London home of the duke and duchess of Kent. Another left turn into **Stable**
❾ **Yard Road** takes you to **Lancaster House,** built for the duke of York by Nash in the 1820s and used today for government receptions and
❿ conferences. On the other side of Stable Yard is **Clarence House,** designed and built by Nash in 1825 for the duke of Clarence, who later

London

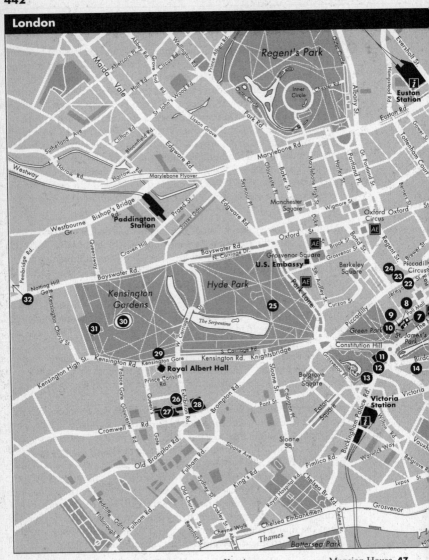

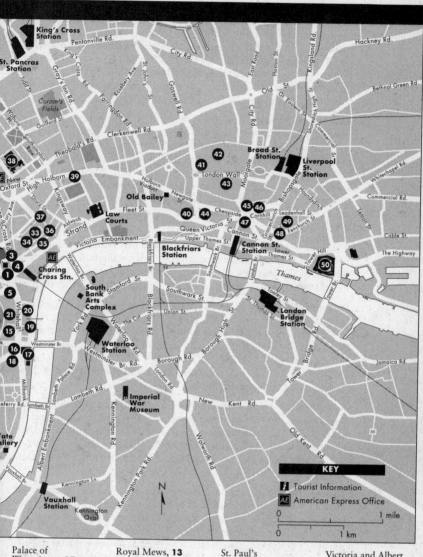

KEY

i Tourist Information

AE American Express Office

0   1 mile

0   1 km

Palace of
Westminster, **17**

Parliament
Square, **16**

Portobello Road, **32**

Queen's Gallery, **12**

Round Pond, **30**

Royal Academy, **23**

Royal Exchange, **46**

Royal Mews, **13**

Royal Opera
House, **37**

St. James's
Church, **22**

St. James's Palace, **7**

St. Martin-in-the-
Fields, **4**

St. Mary-le-Bow, **44**

St. Paul's
Cathedral, **40**

St. Paul's Church, **34**

Science Museum, **26**

Sir John Soane's
Museum, **39**

Theatre Museum, **36**

Tower of London, **50**

Trafalgar Square, **1**

Victoria and Albert
Museum, **28**

Wellington
Barracks, **14**

Westminster
Abbey, **18**

York House, **8**

became King William IV. It was restored in 1949 and is now the home of the Queen Mother. Inside the palace is the **Chapel Royal,** said to have been designed for Henry VIII by the painter Holbein; it was heavily redecorated in the mid-19th century. The ceiling still has the initials *H* and *A*, intertwined, standing for Henry VIII and his second wife, Anne Boleyn, the mother of Elizabeth I and the first of his wives to lose her head. The public can attend Sunday morning services here between the first week of October and Good Friday.

⓫ **Buckingham Palace,** at the end of the Mall, is the London home of the queen and the administrative hub of the entire royal family. When the queen is in residence (normally on weekdays except in January, August, September, and part of June), the royal standard flies over the east front. Inside there are dozens of ornate 19th century-style state rooms used on such formal occasions as banquets for visiting heads of state. The private apartments of Queen Elizabeth and Prince Philip are in the north wing. Behind the palace lie some 40 acres of private gardens, a wildlife haven.

The ceremony of the **Changing of the Guard** takes place in front of the palace at 11:30 daily, May through July, and on alternate days during the rest of the year. It's advisable to arrive early, since people are invariably stacked several deep along the railings, whatever the weather.

Parts of Buckingham Palace are open to the public during August and September; the former chapel, bombed during World War II, rebuilt ⓬ in 1961, and now the **Queen's Gallery,** shows paintings from the vast royal art collections from March through December. ⊠ *Buckingham Palace Rd.,* ☎ *0171/493–3175.* ☞ *£8.50. Queen's Gallery,* ☎ *0171/799–2331.* ☞ *£3.50.* ☉ *Tues.–Sat. and bank holidays 10–5, Sun. 2–5; closed between exhibitions.*

Just along Buckingham Palace Road from the Queen's Gallery is the ⓭ **Royal Mews,** where some of the queen's horses are stabled and the elaborately gilded state coaches are on view. ☎ *0171/799–2331.* ☞ *£3.50. Combined ticket with Queen's Gallery: £6.* ☉ *Oct.–Mar., Wed. noon–4; April–Sept., Tues.–Thurs. noon–4; closed March 25–30, Oct. 1–6, Dec. 23–Jan. 5.*

Birdcage Walk, so called because it was once the site of the royal ⓮ aviaries, runs along the south side of St. James's Park, past the **Wellington Barracks.** These are the regimental headquarters of the Guards Division, the elite troops that traditionally guard the sovereign and mount the guard at Buckingham Palace. The **Guards Museum** relates the history of the Guards from the 1660s to the present; paintings of battle scenes, uniforms, and a cat-o'-nine-tails are among the items on display. ☎ *0171/414–3428.* ☞ *£2.* ☉ *Sat.–Thurs. 10–4.*

⓯ The **Cabinet War Rooms,** between the Foreign Office and the Home Office, are the underground offices used by the British High Command during World War II. Among the rooms on display are the Prime Minister's Room, from which Winston Churchill made many of his inspiring wartime broadcasts, and the Transatlantic Telephone Room, from which he spoke directly to President Roosevelt in the White House. ⊠ *Clive Steps, King Charles St.,* ☎ *0171/930–6961.* ☞ *£4.* ☉ *daily 10–5:15.*

⓰ **Parliament Square** is flanked, on the river side, by the Palace of Westminster, better known in its current incarnation as the Houses of Parliament. The statues around the square include bronzes of Churchill, Abraham Lincoln, Richard the Lionheart, and Oliver Cromwell, the Lord Protector of England during the country's brief attempt at being a republic (1648–60).

⓱ The **Palace of Westminster** was the monarch's main residence from the 11th century until 1512, when the court moved to the newly built White-hall Palace. The only parts of this building to have survived are the Jewel Tower and **Westminster Hall,** which has a fine hammer-beam roof. Westminster Hall is used only on rare ceremonial occasions. The rest was destroyed in a disastrous fire in 1834 and was rebuilt in the newly popular mock-medieval Gothic style with ornate interior decorations. The architect, Augustus Pugin, provided many delightful touches, such as Gothic umbrella stands. This newer part of the palace contains the debating chambers and committee rooms of the two Houses of Parliament—the Commons (whose members are elected) and the Lords (whose members are appointed or inherit their seats). There are no tours of the palace, but the public is admitted to the Public Gallery of each House; expect to wait in line for several hours (the line for the Lords is generally much shorter than that for the Commons).

The most famous features of the palace are its towers. At the south end is the 341-foot **Victoria Tower.** At the other end is **St. Stephen's Tower,** better known, but inaccurately so, as Big Ben; that name properly belongs to the 13-ton bell in the tower on which the hours are struck. Big Ben himself was probably Sir Benjamin Hall, commissioner of works when the bell was installed in the 1850s. A light shines from the top of the tower during a night sitting of Parliament.

★ ⓲ **Westminster Abbey** is the most ancient of London's great churches and the most important, for it is here that Britain's monarchs are crowned. It is unusual for a church of this size and national importance not to be a cathedral. The abbey dates largely from the 13th and 14th centuries, although **Henry VII's Chapel,** an exquisite example of the heavily decorated late-Gothic style, was not built until the early 1600s, and the twin towers over the west entrance are an 18th-century addition. There is much to see inside, including the touching tomb of the Unknown Warrior, a nameless World War I soldier buried, in memory of the war's victims, in earth brought with his corpse from France; and the famous Poets' Corner, where England's great writers—Milton, Chaucer, Shakespeare, et al—are memorialized, and some are actually buried. Behind the high altar are the royal tombs, including those of Queen Elizabeth I; Mary, Queen of Scots; and Henry V. In the Chapel of Edward the Confessor stands the Coronation Chair. Among the royal weddings that have taken place here are those of the present queen and most recently, in 1986, the (ill-starred) duke and duchess of York.

It is all too easy to forget, swamped by the crowds trying to see the abbey's sights, that this is a place of worship. Early morning is a good moment to catch something of the building's atmosphere. Better still, take time to attend a service. ✉ *Broad Sanctuary,* ☎ *0171/222–5152.* 🎫 *Free admittance to the nave; £4 to Poets' Corner and Royal Chapels (chapels free Wed. 6–7:45 PM).* ☉ *Mon., Tues., Thurs., and Fri. 9–4, Wed. 9–8; Sat. 9–2 and 3:45–5; Sun. all day for services only; museum and cloisters open Sun.; closed weekdays to visitors during services; chapels closed Sun. No photography except Wed. 6–8 PM.*

The Norman **Undercroft,** off the original monastic cloisters, houses a small museum with exhibits on the abbey's history. In the **Pyx Chamber** next door, the original strongroom, the Abbey's treasure is housed. The nearby **Chapter House** was where the English Parliament first met. ☎ *0171/222–5152.* 🎫 *£2.50 (joint).* ☉ *daily 10:30–1:45.*

From Parliament Square, walk up **Parliament Street** and **Whitehall** (this is a single street—its name changes), past government offices, toward **⓳** Trafalgar Square. The **Cenotaph,** in the middle of the road, is the national memorial to the dead of both world wars. On the left is the entrance to **Downing Street,** a row of unassuming 18th-century houses. The prime minister's office is at No. 10 (he has a private apartment on the top floor). The chancellor of the exchequer, the finance minister, occupies No. 11.

20 On the right side of Whitehall is the **Banqueting House,** built by the architect Inigo Jones in 1625 for court entertainments. This is the only part of Whitehall Palace, the monarch's principal residence in the 16th and 17th centuries, that was not burned down in 1698. It has a magnificent ceiling by Rubens, and outside there is an inscription that marks the window through which King Charles I stepped to his execution. ☎ 0171/930–4179. 💷 £3. ⊙ Tues.–Sat. 10–5, Sun. 2–5.

21 Opposite is the entrance to **Horse Guards Parade,** the former tiltyard of Whitehall Palace. This is the site of the annual ceremony of Trooping the Colour, when the queen takes the salute in the great military parade that marks her birthday on the second Saturday in June (her real one is on April 21). There is also a daily guard-changing ceremony outside the guard house, at 11 AM (10 on Sunday).

St. James's and Mayfair

After such a concentrated dose of grand, historical buildings, it's time to explore two of London's elegant shopping areas. Start by walking west from Piccadilly Circus along **Piccadilly,** a busy street lined with some grand and very English shops (including **Hatchards,** the booksellers; **Swaine, Adeney Brigg,** the equestrian outfitters; and **Fortnum and Mason,** the department store that supplies the queen's groceries).

22 **St. James's Church** was designed by the 17th-century architect Christopher Wren and contains beautiful wood carvings by Grinling Gibbons.

NEED A BREAK?	**The Wren** at St. James's is a friendly café in the church precincts. Coffee, pastries, and light lunches are served.

Jermyn Street, south of Piccadilly, is famous for upscale shops that sell accessories for the gentleman's wardrobe, from handmade shoes to bespoke hats (his suits come from nearby Savile Row). Shops along **Duke Street** and **Bury Street** specialize in paintings, the former in old masters, the latter in early English watercolors. Don't be put off by the exclusive appearance of these establishments—anyone is free to enter, and there is no obligation to buy. **King Street** is home to **Christie's,** the fine arts auctioneer, and to **Spink and Son,** renowned for Oriental art.

23 On the north side of Piccadilly, **Burlington House** contains the offices of many learned societies and the headquarters of the **Royal Academy.** The RA, as it is generally known, stages major visiting art exhibitions. The best known is the Summer Exhibition (May–Aug.), featuring a chaotic hodgepodge of works by living British artists.

Burlington Arcade, beside the RA, is a covered walkway that dates from 1819, where quaint shops sell luxury items: cashmere sweaters, silk scarves, handmade chocolates, leather-bound books. A uniformed beadle is on duty to ensure that no one runs, whistles, or sings here.

24 The **Museum of Mankind,** behind the RA, contains the British Museum's ethnographic collection, though this will shortly be transferred to the British Museum when the British Library moves to its new premises in St. Pancras. There are displays on the South Seas, the Arctic, and other regions of the world. ✉ 6 Burlington Gardens, ☎ 0171/323–8043. 💷 Free. ⊙ Mon.–Sat. 10–5, Sun. 2:30–6.

There are three special shopping streets in this section of Mayfair, each with its own specialties. **Savile Row** is the home of gentlemen's tailors. Nearby **Cork Street** has many dealers in modern and classical art. **Bond Street** (divided into two parts, Old and New, though both are some 300 years old) is the classiest shopping street in London, the home of haute couture, with such famous names as **Gucci, Hermès,** and **Chanel,** and costly jewelry from such shops as **Asprey, Tiffany,** and **Cartier.**

Some of the original 18th-century houses survive on the west side of **Berkeley Square** (currently being renovated). Farther along is **Curzon Street,** which runs along the northern edge of **Shepherd Market,** a maze of narrow streets full of antiques shops, restaurants, and pubs.

NEED A BREAK? **L'Artiste Musclé** (⊠ 1 Sheperd Market) is a popular bistro serving French food with a few picturesque tables outside in summer.

Hyde Park and Beyond

25 A great expanse of green parkland begins at **Hyde Park Corner** and cuts right across the center of London. **Hyde Park,** which covers about 340 acres, was originally a royal hunting ground, while **Kensington Gardens,** which adjoins it to the west, started life as part of the royal Kensington Palace. These two parks contain many fine trees and are a haven for wildlife. The sandy track that runs along the south edge of the parks has been a fashionable riding trail for centuries. Though it's called **Rotten Row,** there's nothing rotten about it. The name derives from *route du roi* (the King's Way)—the route William III and Queen Mary took from their home at Kensington Palace to the court at St. James's. There is boating and swimming in the **Serpentine,** the S-shaped lake formed by damming a stream that used to flow here. Refreshments can be had at the lakeside tearooms, and the **Serpentine Gallery** (☎ 0171/402–6075) holds noteworthy exhibitions of modern art.

26 Leave the park at **Exhibition Road** and visit three of London's major museums. The **Science Museum** is the leading national collection of science and technology, with extensive hands-on exhibits on outer space, astronomy, computers, transportation, and medicine. ☎ *0171/938–8000 or 0171/938–8123 (recorded information).* 🎟 *£5.* 🕑 *Mon.–Sat. 10–6, Sun. 11–6.*

27 The **Natural History Museum** is housed in an ornate late-Victorian building with striking modern additions. As in the Science Museum, its displays on topics such as human biology and evolution are designed to challenge visitors to think for themselves. ⊠ *Cromwell Rd.,* ☎ *0171/938–9123 or 0142/692–7654 (recorded information).* 🎟 *£5.50; free weekdays 4:30–5:50.* 🕑 *Mon.–Sat. 10–6, Sun. 2:30–6.*

★ **28** The **Victoria and Albert Museum** (or V&A) originated in the 19th century as a museum of the decorative arts and has extensive collections of costumes, paintings, jewelry, and crafts from every part of the globe. The collections from India, China, and the Islamic world are especially strong. ⊠ *Cromwell Rd.,* ☎ *0171/938–8500 or 0171/938–8441 (recorded information).* 🎟 *£4.50 (suggested contribution).* 🕑 *Mon.–Sat. 10–5:50, Sun. 2:30–5:50.*

NEED A BREAK? The **V&A restaurant** has morning coffee, hot lunchtime dishes, Sunday brunch, and afternoon tea.

29 Back in Kensington Gardens, the **Albert Memorial** commemorates Queen Victoria's much-loved husband, Prince Albert, who died in 1861 at the age of 42. The monument, itself the epitome of high Victorian taste, commemorates the many socially uplifting projects of the prince, among them the Great Exhibition of 1851, whose catalog he is holding. The Memorial, which has been badly eroded by pollution, is currently being restored. A small exhibit in front of it explains the conservation effort.

From the **Flower Walk,** behind the Albert Memorial—carefully planted so that flowers are in bloom virtually throughout the year—strike out ③⓪ across Kensington Gardens to the **Round Pond,** a favorite place for children to sail toy boats.

③① **Kensington Palace,** across from the Round Pond, has been a royal home since the late 17th century. From the outside it looks less like a palace than a country house, which it was until William III bought it in 1689. Inside, however, are state rooms on a grand scale, mostly created in the early 18th century. Such distinguished architects as Wren, Hawksmoor, Vanbrugh, and William Kent were all employed here. Queen Victoria spent a less-than-happy childhood at Kensington Palace, moving to Buckingham Palace as soon as she was crowned. Of its current occupants (many members of the royal family reside here), the most famous is Princess Diana. Kensington Palace has recently been refurbished, with its state apartments restored to how they were in Princess Victoria's day. ☎ 0171/937–9561. ☒ £5.50. ⏱ 9:45 AM–5 PM.

North of Kensington Gardens is the lively **Notting Hill** district, full of restaurants and cafés where young people gather. The best-known at- ③② traction in this area is **Portobello Road,** where the lively antiques and bric-a-brac market is held each Saturday (arrive early in the morning for the best bargains). The street is also full of regular antiques shops that are open most weekdays.

NEED A BREAK? **Geales** (☒ 2 Farmer St.) is a superior Notting Hill fish-and-chips restaurant, popular with locals and visitors alike.

Covent Garden

You could easily spend a half day exploring the block of streets north ③③ of the Strand known as **Covent Garden.** The heart of the area is a former wholesale fruit and vegetable market—made famous as one of Eliza Doolittle's haunts in *My Fair Lady*—established in 1656. The market moved to more modern and accessible premises only in 1974. **The Piazza,** the Victorian Market Building, is now a vibrant shopping center, with numerous boutiques, crafts shops, and cafés. On the south side of the market building is the **Jubilee market,** with crafts and clothing stalls.

③④ Look for the open-air entertainers performing under the portico of **St. Paul's Church**—you can enjoy an excellent show for the price of a few coins thrown into the hat that's passed among the onlookers. The church, entered from Bedford Street, is known as the Actors' Church, and inside are numerous memorials to theater people. The **Royal Opera House** and the **Theatre Royal Drury Lane,** two of London's oldest theaters, are close by.

NEED A BREAK? Around here, you can scarcely move for restaurants jostling to feed you. Try **Maxwell's,** on James Street near the tube station, for one of London's best burgers, or **Crank's** in the Piazza for vegetarian alternatives.

For interesting specialty shops, head north of the Market Building. Shops on **Long Acre** sell maps, art books and materials, and clothing; shops on **Neal Street** sell clothes, pottery, jewelry, tea, housewares, and goods from the Far East.

⟡ ㉟ The collection of vehicles at the **London Transport Museum** includes a steam locomotive, a tram, a subway car, and an Underground train simulator. Visitors are encouraged to operate many of the vehicles, and the museum is among the most surprising in town—because it's so interesting! Take care of your gift buying in the excellent shop, too. ✉ *The Piazza (southeast corner),* ☎ *0171/379–6344.* 🎫 *£4.25.* ☉ *Daily 10–5:15.*

㊱ The **Theatre Museum** contains a comprehensive collection of material on the history of the English theater—not merely the classic drama but also opera, music hall, pantomime, and musical comedy. Scripts, playbills, costumes, and props are displayed; there is even a re-creation of a dressing room filled with memorabilia of former stars. ✉ *Russell St.,* ☎ *0171/836–7891.* 🎫 *£3 adults.* ☉ *Tues.–Sun. 11–7.*

㊲ On **Bow Street** is the **Royal Opera House,** home of the Royal Ballet and the Royal Opera Company. The plush interior captures the richness of Victorian England.

Bloomsbury

Bloomsbury is a semiresidential district to the north of Covent Garden that contains some spacious and elegant 17th- and 18th-century squares. It could claim to be the intellectual center of London, since both the British Museum and the University of London are here. The area also gave its name to the Bloomsbury Group, a clique of writers and painters who thrived here in the early 20th century. The antiquarian and specialist bookshops, publishing houses, restaurants, and pubs frequented by the local literati add to the academic-cum-bohemian ambience of the area.

★ ㊳ The **British Museum** houses a vast and priceless collection of treasures, including Egyptian, Greek, and Roman antiquities; Renaissance jewelry; pottery; coins; glass; and drawings from virtually every European school since the 15th century. It's best to pick out one section that particularly interests you—to try to see everything would be an overwhelming and exhausting task. Some of the highlights are the **Elgin Marbles,** sculptures that formerly decorated the Parthenon in Athens; the **Rosetta Stone,** which helped archaeologists to interpret Egyptian script; a copy of the **Magna Carta,** the charter signed by King John in 1215 to which is ascribed the origins of English liberty; and the **Mildenhall treasure,** a cache of Roman silver found in East Anglia in 1842. ✉ *Great Russell St.,* ☎ *0171/636–1555 or 0171/580–1788 (recorded information).* 🎫 *Free.* ☉ *Mon.–Sat. 10–5, Sun. 2:30–6.*

★ ㊴ On the border of London's legal district, **Sir John Soane's Museum** is an eccentric and delightful 19th-century collection of art and artifacts in the former home of the architect of the Bank of England. Soane's great sense of humor and keen eye for visual perspective are equally apparent. ✉ *13 Lincoln's Inn Fields,* ☎ *0171/405–2107.* 🎫 *Free.* ☉ *Tues.–Sat. 10–5.*

The City

The **City,** the commercial center of London, is the most ancient part of the capital, having been the site of the great Roman city of Londinium. Since those days, the City has been rebuilt several times. The wooden buildings of the medieval City were destroyed in the Great Fire of 1666. There were further waves of reconstruction in the 19th century, and then again after World War II to repair the devastation wrought by air attacks. The 1980s saw the construction of many mammoth office developments, some undistinguished, others incorporating adventurous and exciting ideas.

Throughout all these changes, the City has retained its unique identity and character. The lord mayor and Corporation of London are still responsible for the government of the City, as they have been for many centuries. Commerce remains the lifeblood of the City, which is a world financial center rivaled only by New York City, Tokyo, and Zurich. The biggest change has been in the City's population. Until the first half of the 19th century, many of the merchants and traders who worked in the City lived there, too. Today, despite its huge daytime population, scarcely 8,000 people live in its 677 acres. Try, therefore, to explore the City on a weekday morning or afternoon. On weekends its streets are deserted, and many of the shops and restaurants, even some of the churches, are closed.

★ ④⓪ Following the Great Fire, **St. Paul's Cathedral** was rebuilt by Sir Christopher Wren, the architect who was also responsible for designing 50 City parish churches to replace those lost in that disaster. St. Paul's is Wren's greatest work. Fittingly, he is buried in the crypt under a simple Latin epitaph, composed by his son, which translates as: "Reader, if you seek his monument, look around you." The cathedral has been the site of many famous state occasions, including the funeral of Winston Churchill in 1965 and the ill-fated marriage of the prince and princess of Wales in 1981. Note the fine choir stalls by the great 17th-century wood-carver Grinling Gibbons, a rare decorative flourish in an otherwise surprisingly restrained interior, with relatively few monuments and tombs. In the ambulatory (the area behind the high altar) is the American Chapel, a memorial to the 28,000 U.S. servicemen and women stationed in Britain during World War II who lost their lives while on active service.

The greatest architectural glory of the cathedral is the dome. This consists of three distinct elements: an outer, timber-frame dome covered with lead; an interior dome built of brick and decorated with frescoes of the life of St. Paul by the 18th-century artist Sir James Thornhill; and, in between, a brick cone that supports and strengthens both. There is a good view of the church from the **Whispering Gallery,** high up in the inner dome. The gallery is so called because of its remarkable acoustics, whereby words whispered on one side can be clearly heard on the other, almost 115 feet away. Above this gallery are two others, both external, from which there are fine views over the City and beyond. ☎ *0171/248–2705.* ✏ *Free to cathedral; £3 to ambulatory (American Chapel), Crypt, and Treasury; £2.50 to galleries; £5 combined ticket.* ⊙ *Cathedral: Mon.–Sat. 7:30–6, Sun. 8–6; ambulatory, crypt, and galleries: weekdays 10–4:15, Sat. 11–4:15; tours weekdays 11, 11:30, 2, 2:30.*

A short walk north of the cathedral, to **London Wall,** so called because it follows the line of the wall that surrounded the Roman settlement,
④① brings you to the **Museum of London.** Its displays enable you to get a real sense of what it was like to live in London at different periods of history, from Roman times to the present day. Among the highlights are the Lord Mayor's Ceremonial Coach, an imaginative reconstruction of the Great Fire, and the Cheapside Hoard, jewelry hidden during an outbreak of plague in the 17th century and never recovered by its owner. ✉ *London Wall,* ☎ *0171/600–3699.* ✏ *£3.50.* ⊙ *Tues.–Sat. 10–6, Sun. 2–6.*

④② The **Barbican** is a vast residential complex and arts center built by the City of London. It takes its name from the watchtower that stood here during the Middle Ages, just outside the City walls. The arts center contains a concert hall, where the London Symphony Orchestra is based, two theaters, an art gallery, a cinema, and several restaurants. The theaters are the London home of the Royal Shakespeare Company.

43 On the south side of London Wall stands **Guildhall,** the much reconstructed home of the Corporation of London; the lord mayor of London is elected here each year with ancient ceremony. ✉ *King St.,* ☎ *0171/606–3030.* ✒ *Free.* ⊙ *weekdays 10–5.*

Now walk south to **Cheapside.** This was the chief marketplace of medieval London (the word *ceap* is Old English for "to barter"), as the street names hereabouts indicate: Milk Street, Ironmonger Lane, etc. Despite rebuilding, many of the streets still run on the medieval pat-
44 tern. The church of **St. Mary-le-Bow** in Cheapside was rebuilt by Christopher Wren after the Great Fire; it was built again after being bombed during World War II. It is said that to be a true Cockney, you must be born within the sound of Bow bells.

NEED A BREAK? **The Place Below** (✉ St Mary-le-Bow, Cheapside) serves a very high standard of meatless soup-quiche-salad lunches.

45 A short walk east along Cheapside brings you to a seven-way intersection. The **Bank of England,** which regulates much of Britain's financial life, is the large windowless building on the left. At the northern side
46 of the intersection, perpendicular to the bank, is the **Royal Exchange,** originally built in the 1560s as a trading hall for merchants. The present building, opened in 1844 and the third on the site, is now occupied by the **London International Financial Futures Exchange.** ☎ *0171/623–0444.* ✒ *Free.* ⊙ *Visitors' Gallery by appointment to groups from relevant organizations.*

47 The third major building at this intersection, on its south side, is the **Mansion House,** the official residence of the lord mayor of London.

48 Continue east along **Cornhill,** site of a Roman basilica and of a medieval grain market. Turn right into Gracechurch Street and then left into **Leadenhall Market.** There has been a market here since the 14th century; the present building dates from 1881.

49 Just behind the market is one of the most striking pieces of contemporary City architecture: the headquarters of **Lloyd's of London,** built by the modernist architect Richard Rogers, whose other famous work is Paris's Pompidou Center; Rogers' firm has also won the competition to redesign the South Bank arts complex. The underwriters of Lloyd's provide insurance for everything imaginable, from oil rigs to a pianist's fingers, though they suffered a crash in 1993, with most of the so-called Names, whose millions formed the Lloyd's backbone, losing major money. ✉ *1 Lime St.,* ☎ *0171/623–7100.* ✒ *Free.* ⊙ *By appointment to groups from recognized organizations.*

★ ☪ **50** From here it's a short walk east to the **Tower of London,** one of London's most famous sights and one of its most crowded, too. Come as early in the day as possible and head for the Crown Jewels so you can see them before the crowds arrive.

The tower served the monarchs of medieval England as both fortress and palace. Every British sovereign from William the Conqueror in the 11th century to Henry VIII in the 16th lived here, and it remains a royal palace, in name at least. The **History Gallery,** south of the White Tower, is a walk-through display designed to answer questions about the inhabitants of the tower and its evolution over the centuries.

The **White Tower** is the oldest and also the most conspicuous building in the entire complex. Inside, the **Chapel of St. John** is one of the few unaltered parts. The **Royal Armories,** England's national collection of arms and armor, occupies the rest of the White Tower. Among other buildings worth seeing is the **Bloody Tower.** The little princes in the tower—the boy-king Edward V and his brother Richard, duke of York, supposedly murdered on the orders of the duke of Gloucester, later crowned Richard III—certainly lived in the Bloody Tower, and may well have died here, too. Another bloody death is alleged to have occurred in the **Wakefield Tower,** when Henry VI was murdered in 1471 during England's medieval civil war, the Wars of the Roses. It was a rare honor to be beheaded in private inside the tower; most people were executed outside, on **Tower Hill,** where the rabble could get a much better view.

The **Crown Jewels** are a breathtakingly beautiful collection of regalia, precious stones, gold, and silver. The Royal Scepter contains the largest cut diamond in the world. The Imperial State Crown, made for the 1838 coronation of Queen Victoria, contains some 3,000 precious stones, largely diamonds and pearls. The Jewels are housed in the Duke of Wellington's Barracks. Look for the ravens whose presence at the tower is traditional. It is said that if they leave, the tower will fall and England will lose her greatness. ⊠ *Tower Hill,* ☎ *0171/709–0765.* ▦ *£8.30; small additional admission charge to Fusiliers Museum only.* ☉ *Mar.–Oct., Mon.–Sat. 9:30–6, Sun. 10–6; Nov.–Feb., Mon.–Sat. 9–5; Sun 10–5. Yeoman Warder guides conduct tours daily from Middle Tower, no charge, but a tip is always appreciated. Subject to weather and availability of guides, tours are conducted about every 30 mins until 3:30 in summer, 2:30 in winter.*

Off the Beaten Path

Hampstead

Hampstead is a village within the city, where many famous poets and writers have lived. Today it is a fashionable residential area, with a main shopping street and some rows of elegant 18th-century houses. The heath is one of London's largest and most attractive open spaces. In **Keats Grove,** on the southern edge of the heath, is the house where the Romantic poet John Keats (1795–1821) lived. ⊠ *Wentworth Pl.,* ☎ *0171/435–2062.* ▦ *Free.* ☉ *Call in advance for exact times.*

Standing alone in its own landscaped grounds on the north side of the heath is **Kenwood House,** built in the 17th century and remodeled by Robert Adam, the talented exponent of classical decoration, at the end of the 18th century. The house contains a collection of superb paintings by such masters as Rembrandt, Vermeer, Turner, Reynolds, Van Dyck, and Gainsborough, which gain enormously from being displayed in the grand country-house setting for which they were originally intended. The lovely landscaped grounds, with lake, provide the setting for symphony concerts in summer. ⊠ *Hampstead La.,* ☎ *0181/348–1286.* ▦ *Free.* ☉ *Apr.–Oct., weekdays 2–6, Sat. 10–1 and 2–5, Sun. 2–5; Nov.–Mar., weekdays 1–5, Sat. 10–1 and 2–5 , Sun. 2–5.*

Greenwich

The historical and maritime attractions at **Greenwich,** on the Thames, some 5 miles east of central London, make it an ideal destination for a day out. You can get to Greenwich by riverboat from Westminster and Tower Bridge piers, by ThamesLine's high-speed river buses, or by train from Charing Cross station. You can also take the Docklands Light Railway from Tower Gateway to Island Gardens and walk a short distance along a pedestrian tunnel under the river.

Visit the **National Maritime Museum,** a treasure house of paintings; maps; models; sextants; and, best of all, ships from all ages, including the ornate royal barges. ⊠ *Romney Rd.,* ☎ *0181/858–4422.* ▦ *£5.50* *(joint admission with observatory).* ☉ *late-Mar.–late-Oct., Mon.–Sat. 10–6, Sun. 2–6; late-Oct.–late-Mar., Mon.–Sat. 10–5, Sun. 2–5.*

Two ships now in dry dock are the glorious 19th-century clipper ship **Cutty Sark** and the tiny **Gipsy Moth IV,** which Sir Francis Chichester sailed single-handed around the world in 1966. ✉ *Cutty Sark, King William Walk,* ☎ *0181/858–3445.* ✇ *£3.25.* ☉ *late-Mar.–Sept., Mon.–Sat. 10–5:30, Sun. noon–5:30; Oct.–late-Mar., Mon.–Sat. 10–4:30, Sun. noon–4:30. Gipsy Moth IV,* ✉ *King William Walk,* ☎ *0181/853–3589.* ✇ *50p.* ☉ *Apr.–Oct., Mon.–Sat. 10–5:30, Sun. noon–5:30.*

The **Royal Naval College** was built in 1694 as a home, or hospital, for old sailors. You can see the magnificent **Painted Hall,** where Nelson's body lay in state following the Battle of Trafalgar, and the College Chapel. ☎ *0181/858–2154.* ✇ *Free.* ☉ *Fri.–Wed. 2:30–4:30.*

Behind the museum and the college is **Greenwich Park,** originally a royal hunting ground and today an attractive place in which to wander and relax. On top of the hill is the **Old Royal Observatory,** founded in 1675, where original telescopes and other astronomical instruments are on display. The prime meridian—zero degrees longitude—runs through the courtyard of the observatory. ✉ *Greenwich Park,* ☎ *0181/858–4422.* ✇ *Joint admission with National Maritime Museum. Open Apr.–Oct., Mon.–Sat. 10–6, Sun. 2–6; Nov.–Mar., Mon.–Sat. 10–5, Sun. 2–5.*

Shopping

Shopping is one of London's great pleasures. Different areas retain their traditional specialties, as described below, but there are also numerous pockets of local shops to explore, and it's fun to seek out the small crafts, antiques, and gift stores, designer clothing resale outlets, and national department-store chains.

Shopping Districts

Chelsea centers on the King's Road, once synonymous with ultrafashion; it still harbors some designer boutiques, plus antiques and home furnishings stores.

Covent Garden is a something-for-everyone neighborhood, with clothing chain stores and top designers, stalls selling crafts, and shops selling gifts of every type—bikes, kites, herbs, beads, hats, you name it.

Crowded **Oxford Street** is past its prime and lined with tawdry discount shops. Selfridges, John Lewis, and Marks and Spencer are good department stores, though, and there are interesting boutiques secreted off Oxford Street, just north of the Bond Street tube stop, in little St. Christopher's Place and Gees Court.

Perpendicular to Oxford Street lies **Regent Street,** with possibly London's most pleasant department store, Liberty's, as well as Hamley's, the capital's toy mecca. Shops around once-famous **Carnaby Street** stock designer youth paraphernalia and at least 57 varieties of T-shirt.

In **Mayfair** is Bond Street, Old and New, with desirable dress designer and jewelry outposts, plus fine art. South Molton Street offers high-price high-style fashion—especially at Browns—and the tailors of Savile Row are of worldwide repute.

In **St. James's,** the English gentleman buys the rest of his gear: handmade hats, shirts, and shoes, silver shaving kits, and hip flasks. Here is also the world's best cheese shop, Paxton & Whitfield. Nothing in this neighborhood is cheap, in any sense.

Kensington's main drag, Kensington High Street, is a smaller, classier version of Oxford Street, with Barkers department store, and a branch of Marks & Spencers at the eastern end. Try Kensington Church Street for expensive antiques, plus a little fashion.

Neighboring **Knightsbridge** has Harrods, of course, but also Harvey Nichols, the top clothes stop, and many expensive designers' boutiques along Sloane Street, Walton Street, and Beauchamp Place.

Markets

Street markets are one aspect of London life not to be missed. Here are some of the more interesting markets:

Bermondsey. Arrive as early as possible for the best treasure—that's what the dealers do. ⊠ *Tower Bridge Rd., SE1.* ⊘ *Fri. 4:30 AM–noon. Take tube to London Bridge and walk, or take Bus 15 or 25 to Aldgate and then Bus 42 over Tower Bridge to Bermondsey Square.*

Camden Lock. The youth center of the world, apparently, and good for cheap clothes and boots. The canal-side antiques, crafts, and junk markets are also picturesque in their fashion, and very crowded. ⊠ *Chalk Farm Rd., NW1.* ⊘ *Sat.–Sun. 9:30–5:30. Take tube or Bus 24 or 29 to Camden Town.*

Camden Passage. The rows of little antiques shops are a good hunting ground for silverware and jewelry. Stalls open Wednesday and Saturday, a books and prints market opens Thursdays, and shops open the rest of the week. ⊠ *Islington, N1.* ⊘ *Wed.–Sat. 8:30–3. Take tube or Bus 19 or 38 to Angel.*

Petticoat Lane. Look for budget-priced leather goods, gaudy knitwear, and fashions, plus cameras, videos, stereos, antiques, books, and bric-a-brac. ⊠ *Middlesex St., E1.* ⊘ *Sun. 9–2. Take tube to Liverpool Street, Aldgate, or Aldgate East.*

Portobello Market. Saturday is the best day for antiques, though this neighborhood is London's melting pot, becoming more vibrant every year. Find fabulous small shops, the city's trendiest restaurants, and a Friday and Saturday flea market at the far end. ⊠ *Portobello Rd., W11.* ⊘ *Fri. 5–3, Sat. 8–5. Take tube or Bus 52 to Notting Hill Gate or Ladbroke Grove, or Bus 15 to Kensington Park Rd.*

Dining

For details and price-category definitions, *see* Dining *in* Staying in Great Britain, *above.*

Bloomsbury

$$ ✕ **Chez Gerard.** This purveyor of *steak-frîtes* (steak and french fries) and similarly simple Gallic offerings is reliable, relaxed, and usefully located near Oxford Street. ⊠ *8 Charlotte St.,* ☎ *0171/636–4975. Reservations essential. AE, DC, MC, V. Closed Dec. 25. Tube: Goodge St.*

$$ ✕ **Museum Street Café.** Convenient for British Museum lunches, and worth a special trip in the evening, the Mediterranean-tinged home cooking (spinach-and-olive tart; char-grilled leg of lamb; Valrhona chocolate cake), and minimalist white-wall decor in this little place are satisfying. ⊠ *47 Museum St.* ☎ *0171/405–3211. AE, MC, V. Closed first week in August, Dec 25. Tube: Holborn.*

Chelsea

$$$$ ✕ **La Tante Claire.** This spot is justly famous for Pierre Koffmann's superb haute cuisine: hot foie gras on shredded potatoes with a sweet wine and shallot sauce or his famous signature dish of pig's trotter stuffed with sweetbreads and wild mushrooms. The set-price lunch is a relative bargain. ⊠ *68 Royal Hospital Rd.,* ☎ *0171/352–6045. Reservations*

essential, 3–4 wks in advance. AE, DC, MC, V. Closed weekends, 10 days at Easter and Christmas, 3 wks in Aug.–Sept. Tube: Sloane Sq.

$$$ ✕ **Chutney Mary.** London's only Anglo-Indian restaurant provides a fantasy version of the British Raj, with colonial cocktails and authentic re-creations of comforting, rich dishes like Country Captain (chicken with almonds, raisins, chilis, and spices). ⊠ *535 King's Rd.,* ☎ *0171/351–3113. AE, DC, MC, V. Closed Dec. 26. No dinner Dec. 25. Tube: Fulham Broadway.*

$ ✕ **Henry J. Bean's.** Hamburgers and Tex-Mex food are served to American oldies music. Order food at the bar, then wait—in the big patio garden if you're lucky. ⊠ *195–197 King's Rd.,* ☎ *0171/352–9255. Reservations not accepted. No credit cards. Closed Dec. 25–26, 31. Tube: Sloane Sq.*

The City

$$$ ✕ **St John.** Resembling a stark monks' refectory crossed with an art gallery, this modern British innovator has equally uncompromising menus. Some loathe bone marrow and parsley salad, huge servings of braised pheasant with "black cabbage," or deviled crab, or organ meats any which way, with English puddings and Malmsey wine to follow, but newspaper journalists and swank architects love it to bits. ⊠ *26 St John St.,* ☎ *0171/251–0848. Closed Sun. dinner, Dec. 25. Tube: Farringdon.*

$$ ✕ **Sweetings.** City gents stand in line to lunch at this tiny, basic Victorian restaurant where nothing has changed for years, let alone the menu, which is fish cooked however you want (it's best grilled or as fish cakes), served with potatoes and peas. The service is old-world courteous, the food comforting and well prepared. ⊠ *39 Queen Victoria St.,* ☎ *0171/248–3062. Reservations not accepted. No credit cards. Lunch only. Closed weekends, Dec. 25, and holidays. Tube: Cannon St.*

Covent Garden

$$$$ ✕ **The Savoy Grill.** Continuing to attract more than its fair share of
★ mostly male power brokers, from newspaper editors to tycoons, this paneled French-English salon exudes comfort, from the avuncular yet deferential service to the traditional British food, which most choose over the more modern, more French side of the menu. The daily dish is the way to go—or something British, like jugged hare (a stew of hare, with blood), or the omelet Arnold Bennett (with cheese and smoked fish), invented here for that novelist. ⊠ *Strand,* ☎ *0171/836–4343. Reservations essential for lunch and Thurs.–Sat. dinner. AE, DC, MC, V. No lunch Sat. Closed Sun. and Aug. Tube: Aldwych.*

$$$ ✕ **The Ivy.** The epitome of style without pretentiousness, this restau-
★ rant beguiles everybody, including media, literary, and theatrical movers and shakers. The menu's got it all—fish-and-chips, sausage-and-mash, squid-ink risotto, bang-bang chicken, sticky toffee pudding—and all are good. ⊠ *1 West St.,* ☎ *0171/836–4751. Reservations essential. AE, DC, MC, V. Closed Dec. 25–26. Tube: Covent Garden.*

$$$ ✕ **Rules.** This city's oldest restaurant (it has been here since 1798) is traditional from soup to nuts, or rather, from venison (disconcertingly listed on the menu as "deer") and Dover sole to trifle and Stilton. Nowadays there's the odd nod to newer cuisines, but the clientele of expense-accounters and tourists in search of olde London Towne remains. ⊠ *35 Maiden La.,* ☎ *0171/836–5314. Reservations essential. AE, DC, MC, V. Closed Sun., Dec. 25. Tube: Covent Garden.*

$$ ✕ **Christopher's.** New Yorkers missing the food of The Palm and the feel of Café des Artistes can have comfort on both counts here, with the Met Opera's soundtrack thrown in. It's a palatially good-looking slice of überurban USA, with a vaguely famous face at the neighboring table. Great shrimp, Maryland crab cakes, and steaks of course. ⊠ *18 Wellington St.,* ☎ *0171/240–4222. Reservations essential. AE, DC, MC, V. Closed Sun. dinner, Sat lunch, Dec. 25. Tube: Covent Garden.*

$–$$ ✕ **Joe Allen.** This basement restaurant behind the Strand Palace Hotel
★ follows the style of its New York counterpart, is descended on by packs of theatrical types after curtain, and is forever noisy. The menu, too, is straight from the Manhattan parent—Caesar salad, barbecue ribs with black-eyed peas and wilted greens, brownies with ice cream—and it's open late. ⊠ *13 Exeter St.,* ☎ *0171/836–0651. Reservations essential. No credit cards. Closed Dec. 25. Tube: Covent Garden.*

$ ✕ **Food for Thought.** This is a simple downstairs vegetarian restaurant,
★ with seats for only 50. The menu—stir-fries, casseroles, salads, and dessert—changes daily, and each dish is freshly made. No alcohol is served. ⊠ *31 Neal St.,* ☎ *0171/836–0239. Reservations not accepted. No credit cards. Closed Sun., Sat. after 4:30 PM, weekdays after 8 PM, 2 wks at Christmas, holidays. Tube: Covent Garden.*

Kensington

$$$$ ✕ **Bibendum.** Upstairs in the renovated 1911 Michelin building, this
★ excellent restaurant has survived the departure of superstar chef Simon Hopkinson, and continues to delight with a menu as Gallic and gorgeous as ever. From the scallops in citrus sauce to the passion-fruit *bavarois* (Bavarian cream), all the dishes are unpretentious but perfectly done every time. The separate Oyster Bar, downstairs, is another way to go. ⊠ *81 Fulham Rd.,* ☎ *0171/581–5817. Reservations essential, 2–3 wks in advance. MC, V. Closed Dec. 25 and holidays. Tube: South Kensington.*

$$ ✕ **Bistrot 190.** Chef-restaurateur Antony Worral-Thompson seems to
★ know exactly what the people want, which, in this case, is big plates of happy, hearty food from southern Europe (liver and wild mushroom terrine; grilled squid with red and green salsa; lemon tart). The decor incorporates hardwood floors and art-laden walls. Next door is **Downstairs at 190**—similar, but offering fish and seafood. ⊠ *190 Queensgate,* ☎ *0171/581–5666. Reservations not accepted. AE, DC, MC, V. No lunch Sat. Closed Sun., Dec. 25–26, Jan. 1. Tube: Gloucester Rd.*

$$ ✕ **Wodka.** This modern Polish restaurant in a quiet back street serves
★ stylish food to a fashionable group and often has the relaxed atmosphere of a dinner party. Try herring blinis, roast duck with figs and port, and the several flavored vodkas. ⊠ *12 St. Albans Grove,* ☎ *0171/937–6513. AE, DC, MC, V. No lunch weekends. Closed Dec. 25–26. Tube: Kensington High St.*

Knightsbridge

$$ ✕ **St. Quentin.** This is a popular French spot just a few blocks west of Harrods. Every inch of the Gallic menu is explored—Gruyère quiche, escargots, cassoulet, lemon tart—in the bourgeois provincial comfort so many London chains (the Dômes, the Cafés Rouges) try hard, yet fail, to achieve. ⊠ *243 Brompton Rd.,* ☎ *0171/589–8005. Reservations essential. AE, DC, MC, V. Closed Dec. 25. Tube: South Kensington.*

$ ✕ **Stockpot.** Speedy service is the mark of this large, jolly restaurant full of students and shoppers. The food is filling and wholesome; try the homemade soups, the Lancashire hot pot, and the apple crumble. Breakfast is also served Monday–Saturday. ⊠ *6 Basil St.,* ☎ *0171/589–8627. No credit cards. Closed Dec. 25, Jan. 1. Tube: Knightsbridge.*

Mayfair

$$$$ ✕ **Chez Nico at Ninety Park Lane.** Those with refined palates and very deep pockets should not miss Nico Ladenis's exquisite gastronomy. He is one of the world's great chefs, and is famous for knowing it. Nowhere is food taken more seriously; the menu is in French (untranslated); vegetarians and children are not welcome. ⊠ *90 Park La.,* ☎ *0171/409–1290. Reservations essential. AE, DC, MC, V. Closed weekends, public holidays, 3 wks in Aug. Tube: Marble Arch.*

$$$$ ✕ **Le Gavroche.** Long regarded as a top temple of haute cuisine, this
★ dark and rich dining room lost a bit of its lustre when its famed chef, Albert Roux, passed the torch to his son, Michel. But dining here is still an unashamedly sybaritic and costly experience, punctuated with foie gras, oysters, and lobster, but one that becomes accessible with the three-course lunch for £37, inclusive of coffee, wine, and service. ⊠ *43 Upper Brook St.,* ☎ *0171/408–0881. Reservations essential at least 1 wk in advance. AE, DC, MC, V. Closed weekends, 10 days at Christmas, holidays. Tube: Marble Arch.*

$$$ ✕ **Mulligans.** At this friendly and relaxing slice of Dublin, the cook-
★ ing is unpretentious and satisfying—London's finest black pudding served with calvados and spiced apples; steak, Guinness, and kidney pie; and, of course, a sublime Irish stew. ⊠ *13–14 Cork St.,* ☎ *0171/409–1370. AE, DC, MC, V. No lunch Sat., no dinner Sun. Closed Dec. 25–26, Jan. 1. Tube: Green Park.*

$–$$ ✕ **Criterion.** A spectacular neo-Byzantine palace of gold mosaic, Christo-size turquoise drapes, and white tablecloths is under the aegis of Marco Pierre White, big-mouthed, big-headed wunderchef, and features his style of haute-bistro French food: a rich, black squid-ink risotto; intricate assemblies of fish, and delicate salads. This has become one of the city's see-and-be-seen glamour houses. ⊠ *Piccadilly Circus,* ☎ *0171/930–0488. Reservations essential. AE, DC, MC, V. Closed Dec. 25. Tube: Piccadilly Circus.*

$ ✕ **The Chicago Pizza Pie Factory.** Huge pizzas with salad and garlic bread are served at reasonable prices in this loud basement. These pies are American-style with a thick chewy base and a somewhat limited choice of toppings. ⊠ *17 Hanover Sq.,* ☎ *0171/629–2669. No credit cards. Closed Dec. 25–26. Tube: Oxford Circus.*

Notting Hill

$$$ ✕ **Clarke's.** There's no choice of dishes at dinner (and only a limited choice at lunch); chef Sally Clarke plans the meal according to what is freshest and best in the market each day. Her style is natural and unfussy West Coast cuisine. ⊠ *124 Kensington Church St.,* ☎ *0171/221–9225. MC, V. Closed weekends, 10 days at Christmas, Easter, 3 wks in Aug. Tube: Notting Hill Gate.*

$$$ ✕ **Kensington Place.** Trendy and loud, this ever-popular place features enormous plate-glass windows through which to be seen, and plenty of fashionable food. Try the foie gras with sweet-corn pancake, rack of lamb, and baked tamarillo with vanilla ice cream. ⊠ *201 Kensington Church St.,* ☎ *0171/727–3184. Reservations essential. MC, V. Closed Aug. bank holiday, Dec. 25–26. Tube: Notting Hill Gate.*

$$ ✕ **192.** A noisy, buzzy wine bar-restaurant just off the Portobello
★ Road, this is a social hangout for the local media mafia, and the food is always ahead of fashion. The best part of the menu is the appetizer list; also try the risottos, the seasonal salad, or whatever sounds unusual. ⊠ *192 Kensington Park Rd.,* ☎ *0171/229–0482. Reservations essential. AE, MC, V. Closed holidays. Tube: Notting Hill Gate.*

$ ✕ **The Cow.** Slightly tucked away in the backwaters of trendy Portobello-land, this is the nicest of a trio of foodie pubs that feed the neighborhood arty hipsters and media stars. The Cow is the child of Tom Conran, son of Sir Terence (who owns half of London's restaurants), and pretends to be a pub in County Derry, serving oysters, crab salad, and other seafood with the beer, and heartier food in the cozy restaurant upstairs. (Try the Westbourne or the Prince Bonaparte if it's full here.) ⊠ *89 Westbourne Park Rd.,* ☎ *0171/221–0021. MC, V. Closed 2 wks in August, Dec 25. Tube: Westbourne Park.*

$ ✕ **Tootsies.** A useful burger joint characterized by loudish rock and vintage advertisements on the walls, Tootsies serves some of London's better burgers, as well as chili, chicken, BLTs, taco salad, apple pie, fudge cake, and ice cream. There are five other branches. ⊠ *120 Holland Park Ave.,* ☎ *0171/229–8567. MC, V. Tube: Holland Park.*

St. James's

$$$$ ✕ **The Ritz.** The British menu here hasn't always lived up to its setting, but since this Louis XVI marble, gilt, and trompe l'oeil treasure, with its view over Green Park, is known as London's most magnificent dining room, that's not such a crime. The latest chef retains the French accent and ingredients as rich as the decor (foie gras terrine with fig preserve; lobster thermidor), and also offers British specialties—Irish stew, braised oxtail, steak-and-kidney pie, and a daily roast. Prix-fixe menus make the check more bearable, but the wine list is pricey. ⊠ *Picadilly,* ☎ *0171/493–8181. Jacket and tie. Reservations essential. AE, DC, MC, V. Tube: Green Park.*

$$$ ✕ **Le Caprice.** Fabulously dark and glamorous, with its black walls and
★ stark white tablecloths, Caprice is a perennial that does nothing wrong, from its kind, efficient, non-partisan (famous folk eat here often) service to its pan-European menu (salmon fish cake with sorrel sauce; confit of goose with prunes). ⊠ *Arlington House, Arlington St.,* ☎ *0171/629–2239. Reservations essential. AE, DC, MC, V. Closed 10 days at Christmas. Tube: Green Park.*

Soho

$$–$$$ ✕ **Atlantic Bar and Grill.** This is the late-night hangout of Piccadilly— a huge, subterranean Art Deco boîte, which has come through its too-trendy-to-live bar scene phase, and is primarily a young and buzzy, somewhat cliquey late night restaurant, with bars attached. Menus are big on grazing food, but something like "hot meat platter of pot roasted pheasant with creamed woodland mushroom and oak smoked beef fillet with rosemary" will appear alongside. ⊠ *20 Glasshouse St.,* ☎ *0171/734–4888. AE, MC, V. Closed Sun lunch. Tube: Piccadilly Circus.*

$$ ✕ **Bistrot Bruno.** Although nearby L'Odeon is much larger, swankier, and pricier, this—young star chef Bruno Loubet's first restaurant—is still charming the crowds. Here are big, fat flavors in large portions: smoked fish cannelloni, salt cod on minestrone vegetables, and sautéed rabbit with Swiss chard, olives, and rosemary. Next door is the bargain Café Bruno. ⊠ *63 Frith St.,* ☎ *0171/734–4545. Reservations essential. AE, D, MC, V. No lunch Sat. Closed Sun., Dec. 25, Jan. 1. Tube: Leicester Sq.*

$–$$$ ✕ **Mezzo.** Sir Terence Conran's restaurants are like bookends propping up the London dining scene. This one is more like the bookcase, though—it's Europe's largest restaurant and you could decant most of Soho inside its three levels. Downstairs is Mezzo, where the soaring, glass-walled kitchen abuts a bustling ocean liner of a dining room; here, the food is French-ish, with the usual Conran seafood platters, and there's a nifty jazz trio and dance floor. Upstairs, the "Mezzonine" and bar is informal, and less expensive, with Thai-inspired dishes prominent. Finally, a separate café/newsstand stays open for drop-in trade till the wee hours. ⊠ *100 Wardour St.,* ☎ *0171/314–4000. AE, DC, MC, V. Tube: Leicester Square.*

$–$$ ✕ **dell'Ugo.** At this three-story Mediterranean café-restaurant from the Antony Worral-Thompson stable (☞ *Bistrot 190, above*), heartwarming country food is the style—spaghetti with roasted peppers, anchovy, and chili; tuna tartare with spicy gazpacho; and bruschetta with pears, watercress, and Gorgonzola. ✉ *56 Frith St.,* ☎ *0171/734–8300. Reservations essential for restaurant. AE, MC, V. Closed Sun., Dec. 25. Tube: Leicester Sq.*

$ ✕ **Crank's.** This restaurant belongs to a popular vegetarian chain that has weathered the storms of food fashion since the '60s, despite a certain worthiness of menu—mixed salads and thick soups; dense, grainy breads; and sugarless cakes. It is self-service, and many branches, though not this one, close at 8 PM. ✉ *8 Marshall St.,* ☎ *0171/437–9431. AE, DC, MC, V. Closed Sun., Dec. 25. Tube: Leicester Sq.*

$ ✕ **Lee Ho Fook.** You may as well go to this representative of London's compact Chinatown as any, immortalized as it was by Warren Zevon in *Werewolves of London.* Order the beef chow mein. ✉ *15 Gerrard St W1.,* ☎ *0171/494–1200. AE, MC, V. Closed Dec. 25–26. Tube: Leicester Sq.*

Lodging

Although British hotels traditionally included breakfast in their nightly tariff, these days many of London's most expensive establishments charge extra for breakfast. For details and price-category definitions, *see* Lodging *in* Staying in Great Britain, *above.*

Bayswater

$$$$ 🏨 **Whites.** This cream-face Victorian "country mansion" has a wrought-iron portico that looks especially grand when floodlit at night. Thick carpets, gilt and mirrors, marble balustrades, swagged silk draperies, and Louis XV-style furniture all help to give a sense of deep luxury. Some of the bedrooms have balconies with a wonderful view of Kensington Gardens, across the road; all have seating areas and personal safes. Colors are muted: powder blue, old rose, and pale green. ✉ *90–92 Lancaster Gate, W2 3NR,* ☎ *0171/262–2711,* 𝔽𝔸𝕏 *0171/262–2147. 54 rooms with bath. Restaurant, lobby lounge. AE, DC, MC, V. Tube: Lancaster Gate.*

$$ 🏨 **Columbia.** The public rooms in these five joined Victorians are as big as museum halls, painted in icy hues of powder blue and buttermilk, or paneled in dark wood. At one end of the day they contain the most hip band du jour doing alcohol; at the other, there are sightseers sipping coffee. Rooms are clean, high-ceilinged, and sometimes very large (especially those with three or four beds), boasting park views and balconies; all have hair dryers, tea/coffeemakers, TVs, and direct-dial telephones. It's just a shame that teak veneer, khaki-beige-brown color schemes, and avocado bathroom suites haven't made it back into the style bible yet. ✉ *95–99 Lancaster Gate, W2 3NS,* ☎ *0171/402–0021,* 𝔽𝔸𝕏 *0171/706–4691. 103 rooms with bath. Restaurant, bar, lobby lounge, meeting rooms. AE, MC, V.*

$ ★ 🏨 **Commodore.** This peaceful hotel of three converted Victorians has some amazing (especially for the price) rooms—as superior to the regular ones (which usually go to package tour groups) as Harrods is to Woolworths. Twenty are mini duplexes, with sleeping gallery, and all have the full deck of tea/coffemakers, hair dryers, and TV with pay movies. One (Number 11) is a real duplex, entered through a secret mirrored door, with a thick-carpeted *very* quiet bedroom upstairs and its toilet below. ✉ *50 Lancaster Gate W2 3NA,* ☎ *0171/402–5291,* 𝔽𝔸𝕏 *0171/262–1088. 90 rooms with bath. Bar, lobby lounge. AE, MC, V.*

$ 🏨 **London Elizabeth.** Steps from Hyde Park, Lancaster Gate tube, and from rows of depressing cheap hotels, is this family-owned gem. Foyer and lounge are crammed with coffee tables and chintz drapery, lace antimacassars, and little chandeliers, and this country sensibility persists through the freshly decorated bedrooms. Some rooms have TV, direct-dial phone, and hair dryer, and all are serviced by an exceptionally charming Anglo-Irish staff. ✉ *Lancaster Terrace, W2 3PF,* ☎ *0171/402–6641,* FAX *0171/224–8900. 55 rooms with bath. Restaurant, bar, lobby lounge, room service. AE, DC, MC, V.*

Bloomsbury

$$–$$$ 🏨 **Morgan.** This charming family-run hotel in an 18th-century terrace house has rooms that are small and comfortably furnished, but friendly and cheerful. The tiny paneled breakfast room is straight out of a doll's house. The back rooms overlook the British Museum. ✉ *24 Bloomsbury St., WC1B 3QJ,* ☎ *0171/636–3735. 14 rooms with bath or shower. No credit cards. Tube: Russell Sq.*

$$ 🏨 **Ridgemount.** The kindly owners, Mr. and Mrs. Rees, make you feel at home in this tiny hotel by the British Museum. There's a homey, cluttered feel in the public areas and some bedrooms overlook a leafy garden. ✉ *65 Gower St., WC1E 6HJ,* ☎ *0171/636–1141. 15 rooms, none with bath. Lobby lounge. No credit cards. Tube: Russell Sq.*

Chelsea, Kensington, and Holland Park

$$$$ 🏨 **Blakes.** Patronized by musicians and film stars, this hotel is one of
★   the most exotic in town. Its Victorian exterior contrasts with the rather 1980s ultrachic interior, with its arty mix of Biedermeier and bamboo, four-poster beds, and chinoiserie, all lit as dramatically as film noir. The bedrooms have individual designs ranging from swaths of black moiré silk to an entirely pink suite. ✉ *33 Roland Gardens, SW7 3PF,* ☎ *0171/370–6701. 52 rooms with bath. Restaurant, bar. AE, DC, MC, V. Tube: Gloucester Rd.*

$$$$ 🏨 **Halcyon.** Discretion, decadent decor, and disco divas make this ex-
★   pensive enormous wedding cake Edwardian desperately desirable. Many hotels lie when they claim "individual" room decor; not this one. The Blue Room has moons and stars, the famous Egyptian Suite is canopied like a bedouin tent; one room has a Jacuzzi and mint green stripes, another has heraldic motifs, black and red walls, a four-poster and creaky floorboards. All are large, with the high ceilings and big windows of the Holland Park vernacular. ✉ *81 Holland Park, W11 3RZ,* ☎ *0171/727–7288,* FAX *0171/229–8516. 44 rooms with bath. Restaurant. AE, DC, MC, V.*

$$$ 🏨 **Abbey Court.** A short walk from Kensington Gardens brings you to this luxury bed-and-breakfast establishment in a historic 1850 building, with a sweet garden. Each bedroom is individually designed with 19th-century French furniture, Venetian mirrors, and oil portraits; some have four-poster beds. ✉ *20 Pembridge Gardens, W2 4DU,* ☎ *0171/221–7518,* FAX *0171/792–0858. 22 rooms with bath. Hot tub. AE, DC, MC, V. Tube: Notting Hill Gate.*

$$$ 🏨 **The Gore.** Every wall of every room in this very friendly and quiet
★   hotel near the Albert Hall is smothered in prints and etchings, and antiques pepper the rooms. Some of these are spectacular follies—like Tudor-style Room 101, with its minstrel gallery and four-poster, or Room 211, with its ceramic Greek goddess mural. Despite all that, it manages to remain most elegant, and certainly unique. ✉ *189 Queen's Gate, SW7 5EX,* ☎ *0171/584–6601,* FAX *0171/589–8127. 54 rooms with bath. Lobby lounge. AE, DC, MC, V. Tube: Gloucester Rd.*

$$$ 🏨 **Portobello.** A faithful core of visitors returns again and again to this eccentric hotel in a Victorian terrace near the Portobello Road antiques market. Some rooms are tiny, but the ambience of Sixties swinging London, the ecclesiastical antiques, and the peaceful vista of the gardens in back make up for it. ✉ *22 Stanley Gardens, W11 2NG,* ☎ *0171/727–2777,* FAX *0171/792–9641. 25 rooms with bath or shower. Restaurant, 24-hr bar. AE, DC, MC, V. Closed 10 days at Christmas. Tube: Ladbroke Grove.*

$ ☎ **Abbey House.** Standards are high (some rooms even feature orthopedic beds) and the rooms unusually spacious in this hotel in a fine residential block near Kensington Palace and Gardens. ✉ *11 Vicarage Gate, W8 4AG,* ☎ *0171/727–2594. 15 rooms without bath. No credit cards. Tube: Kensington High St.*

$ ☎ **Vicarage Hotel.** This genteel establishment, run by the same husband/wife team for the past 40 years, has high standards of cleanliness throughout. Bedrooms are traditional and comfortable with solid English furniture. It attracts many repeat visitors from the United States and welcomes single travelers. ✉ *10 Vicarage Gate, W8 4AG,* ☎ *0171/229–4030. 20 rooms without bath. No credit cards. Tube: Kensington High St.*

Knightsbridge, Belgravia, and Victoria

$$$$ ☎ **Berkeley.** This is a luxurious, spacious, air-conditioned modern building into which a period country mansion has been decanted. One very special feature is the penthouse health club, with a pool whose roof opens in good weather. Bedrooms are elegant and sophisticated and there are some spectacular suites, including one with a sauna. The restaurant is the glamorous Euro-Thai Vong, a copy of the one in New York. ✉ *Wilton Pl., SW1X 7RL,* ☎ *0171/235–6000. 160 rooms with bath. Two restaurants, bar, lobby lounge, beauty salon, health club, cinema. AE, DC, MC, V. Tube: Knightsbridge.*

$$$$ ☎ **Halkin.** This peaceful, ultramodern haven for the design-conscious has many high-tech features in the bedrooms, like personal fax, video player, two phone lines, and a keypad for operating lights and TV. Everything is cool and beautiful, from the charcoal gray curved corridors to the Armani staff uniform. But it's surprisingly friendly. ✉ *Halkin St., SW1X 7DJ,* ☎ *0171/333–1000. 41 rooms with bath. Restaurant. AE, DC, MC, V. Tube: Hyde Park Corner.*

$$$$ ☎ **The Lanesborough.** Brocades and Regency stripes, moiré silks and fleurs-de-lis, antiques, oils, and reproductions in gilded splendor—everything undulates with richness in this multimillion-pound conversion of the old St. George's Hospital at Hyde Park Corner. To register you just sign the book, then retire to your room to find a personal butler, business cards with your in-room fax and phone numbers, VCR and CD player, umbrella, robe, huge flacons of unguents for bath time, and a drinks tray. Such a palace should be nearer the shops. ✉ *1 Lanesborough Pl., SW1X 7TA,* ☎ *0171/259–5599,* FAX *0171/259–5606. 95 rooms with bath. Two restaurants, bar. AE, DC, MC, V. Tube: Hyde Park Corner.*

$$$ ☎ **Basil Street.** Family-run for some 80 years, this is a gracious Edwardian hotel on a quiet street. The rooms are filled with antiques, as are the various lounges, hushed like libraries with polished wooden floors and Oriental rugs. It sounds swanky, but Basil Street is more like home. ✉ *Basil St., SW3 1AH.* ☎ *0171/581–3311. 96 rooms, 72 with bath. Two restaurants, wine bar, lobby lounge. AE, DC, MC, V. Tube: Knightsbridge.*

$$$ ★ ☎ **Beaufort.** "Hotel" would be a misnomer for this elegant pair of country house-style Victorian houses; there's a sitting room instead of a reception area, and guests have a front door key. The rates include drinks, breakfast, and anything from the 24-hour service menu, plus membership at a local health club. ✉ *33 Beaufort Gardens, SW3 1PP,* ☎ *0171/584–5252,* FAX *0171/589–2834. 29 rooms with bath. Access to health club. AE, DC, MC, V. Tube: Knightsbridge.*

$$$ ☎ **The Pelham.** Eighteenth-century pine paneling in the drawing room, glazed chintz and antique lace, four-posters in some rooms, fireplaces in others—this is another hotel that feels more like an elegant home. It's opposite South Kensington tube, near the big museums, and 24-

hour room service plus business services are available. ⊠ *15 Cromwell Pl., SW7 2LA,* ☎ *0171/589–8288,* FAX *0171/584–8444. 37 rooms with bath. Restaurant. AE, MC, V. Tube: South Kensington.*

West End

$$$$ ⛫ **Brown's.** Close to Bond Street, Brown's is like a country house in the middle of town, with wood paneling, grandfather clocks, and large fireplaces. Both Roosevelts used to stay here and it has remained popular with Anglophile Americans ever since. ⊠ *34 Albemarle St., W1A 4SW,* ☎ *0171/493–6020,* FAX *0171/493–9381. 133 rooms with bath. Restaurant, bar, lobby lounge. AE, DC, MC, V. Tube: Green Park.*

$$$$ ⛫ **Claridges.** This legendary hotel has one of the world's classiest
★   guest lists. The liveried staff are friendly, not at all condescending, and the rooms are luxurious. The hotel was founded in 1812, but present decor is either 1930s Art Deco or country-house style. Have a drink or afternoon tea in the Foyer and hear the Hungarian mini-orchestra. The rooms are spacious, the sweeping staircase grand. ⊠ *Brook St., W1A 2JQ,* ☎ *0171/629–8860,* FAX *0171/499–2210. 200 rooms with bath. Two restaurants, lobby lounge, beauty salon. AE, DC, MC, V. Tube: Bond St.*

$$$$ ⛫ **Savoy.** This grand, historic late-Victorian hotel has been the byword
★   for luxury for just over a century. Spacious bedrooms have antiques and cream plasterwork, and the best ones overlook the Thames. More than a hint of 1920s style remains, not least in the bathrooms with their original splendid fittings. The Fitness Gallery is a more recent addition, situated on top of the freshly restored historic Savoy Theatre. ⊠ *Strand, WC2R 0EU,* ☎ *0171/836–4343,* FAX *0171/240–6040. 202 rooms with bath. Three restaurants, 2 bars, coffee shop, health club. AE, DC, MC, V. Tube: Aldwych.*

$$$–$$$$ ⛫ **Duke's.** This small Edwardian hotel in a cul-de-sac in St. James's recently underwent a change of ownership and a top-to-toe refurbishment, raising its popularity rating several notches. Top floor suites are among the finds of London for peace, views, antiques, and hominess. ⊠ *35 St. James's Pl., SW1A 1NY,* ☎ *0171/491–4840,* FAX *0171/493–1264. 62 rooms with bath. Restaurant, bar. AE, DC, MC, V. Tube: Green Park.*

$$$ ⛫ **Dorset Square.** The same husband (architect) and wife (interior de-
★   signer) team who own the Pelham (☞ *above*) created this stunning, comfortable small hotel in a fine pair of Regency town houses north of Oxford Street almost a decade ago, but it remains fresh. Service is personal and charming; there's an "honesty bar" in the parlor, where you help yourself and own up later, and you can be chauffeured in the owner's vintage Bentley on request. ⊠ *39–40 Dorset Sq., NW1 6QN,* ☎ *0171/723–7874,* FAX *0171/724–3328. 37 rooms with bath. Restaurant. AE, MC, V. Tube: Baker St.*

$$$ ⛫ **Hazlitt's.** Still Soho's sole hotel, this, the last home of Hazlitt the essayist (1778–1830), is crammed with prints on every wall, Victorian claw-foot baths, assorted antiques, plants, and bits of art. There's no elevator, the sitting room is minuscule, floors can be creaky and bedrooms tiny, but Hazlitt's legion of devotees don't mind. And who needs room service when you live on Restaurant Row? ⊠ *6 Frith St., W1V 5TZ,* ☎ *0171/434–1771,* FAX *0171/439–1524. 23 rooms with bath. AE, DC, MC, V. Tube: Tottenham Court Rd.*

$$–$$$ ⛫ **Bryanston Court.** Three 18th-century houses have been converted into a traditional English family-run hotel with open fires and comfortable armchairs; the bedrooms are more contemporary. ⊠ *56–60 Great Cumberland Pl., W1H 7FD,* ☎ *0171/262–3141,* FAX *0171/262–7248. 56 rooms with bath or shower. Restaurant, bar, lobby lounge. AE, DC, MC, V. Tube: Marble Arch.*

$$–$$$ 🛏 **The Fielding.** Tucked away in a quiet alley, steps from the Royal Opera House, this funny little place is so adored by its regulars, you'd better book ahead. It's shabby-homey in decor and attitude—there's no elevator, only one room with a bathtub (most have showers), and no room service or restaurant, but it's cute and so handy for the theater. ⊠ *4 Broad Ct., Bow St., WC2B 5OZ,* ☎ *0171/836–8305,* FAX *0171/497–0064. 26 rooms, 1 with bath, 23 with showers. Bar, breakfast room. AE, DC, MC, V. Tube: Covent Garden.*

$$ 🛏 **Edward Lear.** The former home of Edward Lear, the artist and writer of nonsense verse, this hotel has barely anything in the way of amenities, but it's a good value for the area, which is very central. The peacefulness of the rooms varies—ask for a quieter room to the rear—as does their size (Room 14 is the smallest). ⊠ *28–30 Seymour St., W1H 5WD,* ☎ *0171/402–5401,* FAX *0171/706–3766. 32 rooms, 12 with bath or shower. V. Tube: Marble Arch.*

The Arts

For a list of events in the London arts scene, visit a newsstand or bookstore to pick up the weekly magazine *Time Out.* The city's evening paper, the *Evening Standard,* carries listings, as do the major Sunday papers; the daily *Independent* and *Guardian;* and, on Friday, *The Times.* The London Tourist Board's *Visitor Call* service (calls cost 49p/min. ☎ 0891/505440 for what's on this week) also offers listings for theater and other arts events.

Theater

London's theater life can more or less be divided into three categories: the government-subsidized national companies; the commercial, or "West End," theaters; and the fringe.

The **Royal National Theatre Company** (NT) and the **Royal Shakespeare Company** (RSC) are the two main national companies (*box office: NT,* ☎ *0171/928–2252; RSC,* ☎ *0171/638–8891*). Each has its own custom-designed facilities, in the South Bank arts complex and in the Barbican Arts Centre, respectively. Each presents a variety of plays by writers of all nationalities, ranging from the classics of Shakespeare and his contemporaries to specially commissioned modern works.

The West End theaters largely stage musicals, comedies, whodunits, and revivals of lighter plays of the 19th and 20th centuries, often starring television celebrities. Occasionally there are more serious productions, including successful productions transferred from the subsidized theaters, such as RSC's *Les Liaisons Dangereuses* and *Les Misérables.*

The two dozen or so established fringe theaters, scattered around central London and the immediate outskirts, frequently present some of London's most intriguing productions, if you're prepared to overlook occasional rough staging and uncomfortable seating.

Most theaters have an evening performance at 7:30 or 8 daily, except Sunday, and a matinee twice a week (Wednesday or Thursday and Saturday). Expect to pay from £7 to £10 for a seat in the upper balcony and at least £20 for a good seat in the stalls (orchestra) or dress circle (mezzanine)—more for musicals. Tickets may be booked in person at the theater box office; over the phone by credit card; or through ticket agents, such as **First Call** (☎ 0171/497–9977). In addition, the ticket booth in Leicester Square sells half-price tickets on the day of performance for about 45 theaters; there is a small service charge. Beware of unscrupulous ticket agents who sell tickets at four or five times their box-office price (a small service charge is legitimate) and scalpers, who stand outside theaters offering tickets for the next performance; they've been known to charge £200 for a sought-after show.

Concerts

Ticket prices for symphony orchestra concerts are still relatively moderate—between £5 and £15, although you can expect to pay more to hear big-name artists on tour. If you can't book in advance, arrive half an hour before the performance for a chance at returns.

The London Symphony Orchestra is in residence at the **Barbican Arts Centre** (☎ 0171/638–8891), although other top symphony and chamber orchestras also perform here. The **South Bank arts complex** (☎ 0171/928–8800), which includes the **Royal Festival Hall** and the **Queen Elizabeth Hall,** is another major venue for choral, symphonic, and chamber concerts. For less expensive concert going, try the **Royal Albert Hall** (☎ 0171/589–8212) during the summer Promenade season; special tickets for standing room are available at the hall on the night of performance. **The Wigmore Hall** (☎ 0171/935–2141) is a small auditorium, ideal for recitals. Inexpensive lunchtime concerts take place all over the city in smaller halls and churches, often featuring string quartets, vocalists, jazz ensembles, and gospel choirs. **St. John's, Smith Square** (☎ 0171/222–1061), a converted Queen Anne church, is one of the more popular venues. It has a handy crypt cafeteria.

Opera

The **Royal Opera House** ranks alongside the New York Met. Prices range from £3 (for standing room in the upper balconies, from which only a tiny portion of the stage is visible) to more than £300 for a box in the Grand Tier. Bookings are best made at the box office (☎ 0171/240–1066). The **Coliseum** (☎ 0171/836–3161) is the home of the English National Opera Company; productions are staged in English and are often innovative and exciting. The ticket price range is about £8 to £50.

Ballet

The Royal Opera House also hosts the **Royal Ballet.** The prices are slightly more reasonable than for the opera, but be sure to book well ahead. The **English National Ballet** and visiting companies perform at the Coliseum from time to time, especially during the summer. **Sadler's Wells Theatre** (☎ 0171/278–8916) hosts regional ballet and international modern dance troupes. Prices here are reasonable.

Film

Most West End cinemas are in the area around Leicester Square and Piccadilly Circus. Tickets run from £6 to £8. Matinees and Monday evenings are cheaper. Cinema clubs screen a wide range of films: classics, Continental, underground, rare, or underestimated masterpieces. A temporary membership fee is usually about £1. One of the best clubs is the **National Film Theatre** (☎ 0171/928–3232), part of the South Bank arts complex.

Nightlife

London's night spots are legion, and there is only space here to list a few of the best known. For up-to-the-minute listings, buy *Time Out* magazine.

Jazz

Blue Note (✉ 1 Hoxton Sq., ☎ 0171/729–8440), situated in an out-of-the-way warehouse on the northern edge of the City (the nearest tube is Old Street), is a cool jazz and worldbeat club for youth, on two floors, with restaurant. **Ronnie Scott's** (✉ 47 Frith St., ☎ 0171/439–

0747) is the legendary Soho jazz club where international performers regularly take the stage.

Nightclubs

The Wag (⊠ 33–35 Wardour St., ☎ 0171/437–5534) is a tenacious entry in Soho's notoriously fickle club circuit—it's still hip, though it changes according to who's hosting and which DJ is spinning. Be under 30. Glitzy **Stringfellows** (⊠ 16 Upper St. Martin's Lane, ☎ 0171/240–5534) has an art deco upstairs restaurant, mirrored walls, and a dazzling light show in the downstairs dance floor. **The Limelight** (⊠ 136 Shaftesbury Ave., ☎ 0171/434–0572), in a converted church, is one of London's enduringly popular nightspots, with lots of one-nighter shows.

Casinos

By law, you must apply in person for membership in a gaming house; in many cases, clubs prefer an applicant's membership to be proposed by an existing member. Approval usually takes about two days.

Crockford's (⊠ 30 Curzon St., ☎ 0171/493–7771) is a civilized and unflashy 150-year-old club with a large international clientele; American roulette, punto banco, and blackjack are played. **Sportsman Club** (⊠ 3 Tottenham Court Rd., ☎ 0171/637–5464) has a dice table as well as punto banco, American roulette, and blackjack.

Discos

Camden Palace (⊠ 1A Camden High St., ☎ 0171/387–0428) is perennially popular with both Londoners and visiting youth. This multitier place, following a recent overhaul, has two major dance floors, plus at least three bars and a colorful light show. American-style food is served. The **Hippodrome** (⊠ Cranbourn St., ☎ 0171/437–4311) is a hugely popular and lavish disco with an exciting sound-and-laser light system, live bands and dancing acts, a video screen, bars, and a restaurant.

Rock

The Forum (⊠ 9–17 Highgate Rd., Kentish Town, ☎ 0171/284–0303), a little out of the way, is a premier venue for medium-to-big acts. **The Shepherds Bush Empire** (Shepherds Bush Green W12, ☎ 0181/740–7474) is a similar idea in West London. **100 Club** (⊠ 100 Oxford St., W1, ☎ 0171/636–0933) is a basement dive that's always been there for r&b, rock, jazz, and beer.

Cabaret

The best comedy in town can be found in the bigger, brighter, new-look **Comedy Store** (⊠ Haymarket House, Oxendon St., near Piccadilly Circus, ☎ 01426/914433). There are shows at 8 and midnight on Friday and Saturday, at 8 only Tuesday to Thursday. **Madame Jo Jo's** (⊠ 8 Brewer St., ☎ 0171/734–2473) is possibly the most fun of any London cabaret, with its outrageous, glittering drag shows. The place is luxurious and civilized. There are two shows, at 12:15 and 1:15 AM.

WINDSOR TO BATH

The Thames, England's second-longest river, winds its way toward London through an accessible and gracious stretch of countryside. An excursion west from the capital, roughly following the river toward its source in the Cotswold Hills, allows you to explore historic townships such as Windsor, where the castle is still regularly used by the royal family; Oxford, home of the nation's oldest university; and Stratford-upon-Avon, Shakespeare's birthplace. Traveling south, you come to Bath, whose 18th-century streets recall an age more elegant than our own.

Getting Around

By Train

Suburban services run from London (Waterloo and Paddington stations) to Windsor. Regular fast trains run from Paddington to Oxford and Bath, and less frequent and slower services requiring at least one change, to Stratford. For information, call 0171/262–6767. An alternative route to Stratford is from London's Euston Station to Coventry, from which there are hourly bus connections on the Stratford Blue line; call 01788/535555 for details.

By Bus

Regular long-distance services leave from Victoria Coach Station. For information, call **National Express** (☎ 0990/808080); **Green Line** (☎ 0181/668-7261), or **Oxford Bus Company** (☎ 0181/668–7261).

By Car

M4 and M40 are the main highways out of London serving Oxford, the Cotswolds, and Bath. Once you're clear of London, take to the country roads and explore tiny villages and the best of the English countryside.

Visitor Information

Bath (⊠ The Colonnades, 11–13 Bath St., ☎ 01225/462831). **Oxford** (⊠ The Old School, Gloucester Green, ☎ 01865/726871). **Stow-on-the-Wold** (⊠ Hollis House, The Square, ☎ 01451/831082). **Stratford** (⊠ Bridgefoot, next to the canal bridge, ☎ 01789/293127). **Warwick** (⊠ The Court House, Jury St., ☎ 01926/492212). **Windsor** (⊠ 24 High St., ☎ 01753/852010).

Guided Tours

National Holidays operates five-day trips in the Cotswolds, some in Bath. There are agents throughout the country. **Frames Rickards** (☎ 0171/837–3111) runs full-day sightseeing tours to Windsor, Stratford-upon-Avon, Oxford, and Bath. **Guide Friday** (Windsor: ☎ 01753/855755; Oxford: ☎ 01865/790522; and Stratford: ☎ 01789/294466) offers excellent open-top bus tours of Windsor, Oxford, and Shakespeare country.

Exploring Windsor to Bath

Windsor

★ **Windsor,** 25 miles west of London, has been a royal citadel since the days of William the Conqueror in the 11th century. In the 14th century, Edward III revamped the old castle, building the Norman gateway, the great round tower, and new apartments. Almost every monarch since then has added new buildings or improved existing ones; over the centuries, the medieval fortification has been transformed into the lavish royal palace the visitor sees today.

The following are some of the highlights of the castle: **St. George's Chapel,** more than 230 feet long with two tiers of great windows and hundreds of gargoyles, buttresses, and pinnacles, is one of the noblest buildings in England. Inside, above the choir stalls, hang the banners, swords, and helmets of the Knights of the Order of the Garter, the most senior Order of Chivalry. The many monarchs buried in the chapel include Henry VIII and George VI, father of the present queen. (Note that St. George's Chapel is closed to the public on Sundays.) The magnificent art collection at Windsor contains paintings by such masters as Rubens, Van Dyck, and Holbein; drawings by Leonardo da Vinci;

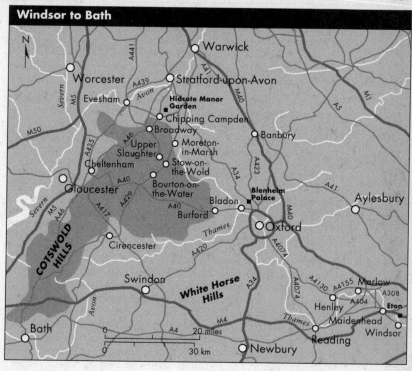

Windsor to Bath

and Gobelin tapestries. There are splendid views across to Windsor Great Park, the remains of a former royal hunting forest. Make time to view **Queen Mary's Dolls' House,** a charming toy country house with every detail complete, including electricity, running water, and miniature books on the library shelves. It was designed in 1921 by the architect Sir Edwin Lutyens for the present queen's grandmother.

The terrible fire of November 1992, which started in the Queen's private chapel, completely destroyed some of the **State Apartments.** Miraculously, a swift rescue effort meant that hardly any works of art were lost. Repairs are scheduled to last until 1997, though all but the Great Hall and two of the state rooms previously visitable were open at press time (spring 1996), along with all the other public areas. ⊠ *Windsor Castle,* ☎ *01753/868286.* 🎟 *£8.50, £19.50 family ticket; Dolls' House £1 extra (£2 extra for family ticket), or separately (including entry to the precincts) £3.50. Ticket prices are £1–2 less on Sun., when St. George's Chapel is closed.*🕙 *Daily Mar.–Oct. 10–4 (last admissions at 3); Nov.–Feb. 10–5:30 (last entrance at 4).*

After seeing the castle, stroll around the town and enjoy the shops; antiques are sold in cobbled Church Lane and Queen Charlotte Street.

NEED A BREAK?

The **Adam and Eve** pub, opposite the walls of Windsor Castle on Thames St., serves light meals and ploughman's lunches, while **The Slug and Lettuce** café/restaurant, also on Thames St., is an inviting spot for soups, puddings, or just a cup of tea or coffee.

A short walk over the river brings you to **Eton,** Windsor Castle's equally historic neighbor and home of the famous public school. (In Britain, so-called public schools are private and charge fees.) Classes still take place in the distinctive redbrick Tudor-style buildings; the oldest are grouped around a quadrangle called School Yard. The **Museum of Eton Life** has displays on the school's history, and a guided tour is also available. ⊠ *Brewhouse Yard,* ☎ *01753/671177.* 🖾 *£2.50; with tour: £3.50.* ⊙ *Daily 2–4:30 during term, 10:30–4:30 on school holidays; guided tours Apr.–Sept., daily at 2:15 and 3:30.*

A brand new attraction to delight children (of all ages) is a **Legoland** set in woodland 3½ (2 miles) outside Windsor on the B3202 Bracknell/Ascot road. Hands-on activities both indoors and out include building, driving, and boating. For more information, ask at Windsor tourist office, or call 01753/636364.

A relatively uncrowded route from Windsor to Oxford is along the river through Marlow and Henley on A308, then A4094, and A4155. In **Marlow,** there are some stylish 18th-century houses on Peter and West streets, and several princes of Wales have lived in Marlow Place on Station Road, which dates from 1721. Mary Shelley completed her celebrated horror story *Frankenstein* in the town.

Henley has been famous since 1839 for the rowing regatta it holds each year around the first Sunday in July. The social side of the regatta is as entertaining as the races themselves; elderly oarsmen wear brightly colored blazers and tiny caps, businessmen entertain wealthy clients, and everyone admires the ladies' fashions. The town is worth exploring for its small but good selection of specialty shops. The Red Lion Hotel near the 200-year-old bridge has been visited by kings, dukes, and writers; the duke of Marlborough stayed there while Blenheim Palace was being built. St. Mary's Church has a 16th-century "checkerboard" tower made of alternate squares of flint and stone, and the **Chantry House,** built in 1420 as a school for poor boys, is an unspoiled example of the rare overhanging timber-frame design. ⊠ *Hart St.,* ☎ *01491/577062.* 🖾 *Free.* ⊙ *For church services or by appointment.*

Oxford

Numbers in the margin correspond to points of interest on the Oxford map.

Continue along A4130 and A4074 northwest to **Oxford.** The surest way to absorb Oxford's unique blend of history and scholarliness is to wander around the tiny alleys that link the honey-color stone buildings topped by elegant "dreaming" spires, exploring the colleges where the undergraduates live and work. Oxford University, like Cambridge University, is not a single building but a collection of 35 independent colleges; many of their magnificent chapels and dining halls are open to visitors—times and (in some cases) entry charges are displayed at the entrance lodges. **Magdalen College** (pronounced maudlin) is one of the most impressive, with cloisters more than 500 years old and lawns leading down to a deer park and the River Cherwell. **St. Edmund Hall,** the next college up the High Street, has one of the smallest and most picturesque quadrangles, with an old well in the center. **Christ Church,** on St. Aldate's, has the largest quadrangle, known as Tom Quad; hanging in the medieval dining hall are portraits of former pupils, including John Wesley, William Penn, and no fewer than 14 prime ministers. The doors between the inner and outer quadrangles of **Balliol College,** on Broad Street, still bear the scorch marks from the flames that burned Archbishop Cranmer and Bishops Latimer and Ridley at the stake in 1555 for their Protestant beliefs.

The **Oxford Story** on Broad Street is a dramatic multimedia presentation of the university's 800-year history, in which visitors travel through depictions of college life. ⊠ *Broad St.,* ☎ *01865/790055.* 🖾 *£4.50.*

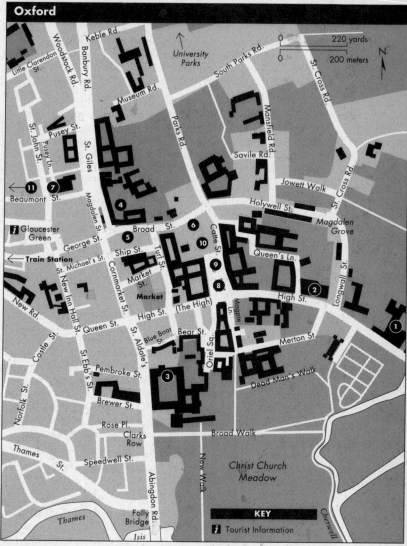

Oxford

Ashmolean Museum, **7**
Balliol College, **4**
Bodleian Library, **10**

Christ Church, **3**
Magdalen College, **1**
Oxford Story, **5**
Radcliffe Camera, **9**
St. Edmund Hall, **2**

Sheldonian Theatre, **6**
University Church (St. Mary's), **8**
Worcester College, **11**

☉ *Apr.–June and Sept.–Oct., daily 9:30–5; Jul.–Aug., daily 9:30–7; Nov.–Mar., daily 10–4.*

❻ Also on Broad Street is the **Sheldonian Theatre,** which St. Paul's architect Christopher Wren designed to look like a semicircular Roman amphitheater. Graduation ceremonies are held here. ✉ *Broad St.,* ✆ *01865/277299.* ❎ *50p.* ☉ *Mon.–Sat. 10–12:45 and 2–4:45; closes at 3:45 mid-Nov.–Feb.*

❼ The **Ashmolean Museum,** which you encounter by turning right out of Broad Street into Magdalen Street, then taking the first left, is Britain's oldest public museum, holding priceless collections of Egyptian, Greek, and Roman artifacts; Michelangelo drawings; and European silverware. ✉ *Beaumont St.,* ✆ *01865/278000.* ❎ *Free.* ☉ *Tues.–Sat. 10–4, Sun. 2–4.*

❽ Back near the center of Oxford, the 14th-century tower of the **University Church** (St. Mary the Virgin) provides a splendid panoramic view of the city's famous skyline—the pinnacles, towers, domes, and spires spanning every architectural style since the 11th century. The interior of the church is crowded with 700 years of funeral monuments, including one belonging to Amy Robsart, the wife of Dudley, Elizabeth I's favorite. ✆ *01865/243806.* ❎ *£1.40 (tower).* ☉ *Daily 9:15–7, 9:15–4:30 in winter (tower).*

❾ Immediately opposite the church is the **Radcliffe Camera,** a striking English Baroque structure adorned with marble urns and massive columns and topped by one of the largest domes in Britain. The Camera con-
❿ tains the reading room of the **Bodleian Library,** begun in 1602 and one of the oldest libraries in the world, with an unrivaled collection of manuscripts. Limited sections of the Bodleian can be visited on a tour (☉ *Mon.–Fri., 2 PM and 3 PM; Sat., 10:30 AM and 11:30 AM; tickets £3—for more information, call 01865/277165). Otherwise, the general public can only visit the former Divinity School, a superbly vaulted room with changing exhibitions of manuscripts and rare books.

⓫ Beaumont Street leads on **Worcester College** (1714), noted for its wide lawns, colorful cottage garden, and large lake. It was built on the site of a former college, founded in 1283.

For a relaxing walk, make for the banks of the River Cherwell, either through the University Parks area or through Magdalen College to Addison's Walk, and watch the undergraduates idly punting a summer's afternoon away, or rent one of these narrow flat-bottom boats yourself. But be warned: Navigating is more difficult than it looks!

NEED A BREAK?   The **St. Aldate's Coffee House** (✉ 94 St. Aldate's) is run by the church next door and is a great place for lunch or coffee. The **Eagle and Child** is a historic pub on St. Giles. On the outskirts of the city are two excellent pubs, the **Perch** at Binsey and the **Trout** at Godstow.

★ **Blenheim Palace,** about 8 miles north of Oxford on A44 (Woodstock Road), is the most spectacular house in England, even beating Buckingham Palace and Windsor Castle for sheer grandeur and majesty. A vast pile of towers, colonnades, and porticoes, Blenheim was built in neoclassical style in the early 18th century by the architect Sir John Vanbrugh; it stands in 2,500 acres of beautiful gardens landscaped later in the 18th century by "Capability" Brown, the famous English landscape gardener. Soldier and statesman John Churchill, first duke of Marlborough, built the house on land given to him by Queen Anne and with money voted him by Parliament on behalf of a "grateful nation" as a reward for his crushing defeat of the French at the Battle of Blenheim in 1704. The house is filled with fine paintings—don't miss the grand John Singer Sargent portrait of the 9th Duke and his wife, Consuelo Vanderbilt—tapestries, and furniture. Winston Churchill, a descendant of Marlborough, was born in the palace; some of his paintings are on display, and there is an exhibition devoted to his life. A restaurant and cafeteria are on the grounds. ⊠ *Woodstock,* ☎ *01993/811091.* ✆ *Free to grounds; £7.30 to house.* ☉ *Mid-Mar.–Oct., 10:30–4:45; grounds open year-round 9–4:45.*

Sir Winston Churchill (1874–1965) is buried in the nearby village of **Bladon.** His grave in the small tree-lined churchyard is all the more touching for its simplicity.

Stratford-upon-Avon

A34 runs northwest from Oxford and Blenheim across the Cotswold Hills to **Stratford-upon-Avon,** the home town of William Shakespeare. Even without its most famous son, Stratford would be worth visiting. The town's timbered buildings bear witness to its prosperity in the 16th century, when it was a thriving craft and trading center, and attractive 18th-century buildings are also of note.

Numbers in the margin correspond to points of interest on the Stratford-upon-Avon map.

The main places of Shakespearean interest are run by the **Shakespeare Birthplace Trust.** They all have similar opening times (mid-Mar.–mid-Oct., Mon.–Sat. 9–5:30, Sun. 10–5:30; mid-Oct.–mid-Mar., Mon.–Sat. 9:30–4, Sun. 10–4; last entry always 30 mins before closing) and you can get a combination ticket for them all—£9—or pay separate entry fees if you want to visit only one or two. The **Shakespeare Centre** and **Shakespeare's Birthplace** contain the costumes used in the BBC's versions of the plays and an exhibition of the playwright's life and work. ⊠ *Henley St.,* ☎ *01789/204016. A Shakespeare Birthplace Trust property.*

❶ ★ ❷

NEED A BREAK? **Mistress Quickly** (⊠ 59–60 Henley St.) serves light refreshments and meals throughout the day; an unusual feature is the jigsaw tree sculpture on the stairs. The **Black Swan**—better known locally as the Dirty Duck— is a riverside pub beside the theater, serving good ales and bar meals.

Two very different attractions reveal something of the times in which Shakespeare lived. Originally a farmhouse, the girlhood home of Shakespeare's mother, **Mary Arden's House,** is now an extensive museum of farming and country life. It was built in the 16th century and many of the original outbuildings are intact, together with a 600-nesting-hole dovecote. There is a garden planted with trees mentioned in Shakespeare's plays. ⊠ *Wilmcote (5.5 km/3½ mi northwest of Stratford, off A3400 and A46),* ☎ *01789/204016. Also reachable by train in a few minutes from Stratford. A Shakespeare Birthplace Trust property.*

❸

❹ **Anne Hathaway's Cottage,** in Shottery on the edge of the town, is the early home of the playwright's wife. ☎ *01789/292100. A Shakespeare Birthplace Trust property.*

❺ A complete contrast is **Hall's Croft,** a fine Tudor town house that was the home of Shakespeare's daughter Susanna and her doctor husband; it is furnished in the decor of the day, and the doctor's dispensary and consulting room can also be seen. ⊠ *Old Town,* ☎ *01789/292107. A Shakespeare Birthplace Trust property.*

❻ Continue down the main thoroughfare of Church Street to note poorhouses, on the left-hand side, built by the Guild of the Holy Cross in the early 15th century. Farther along, on the second floor of the **Guild-**

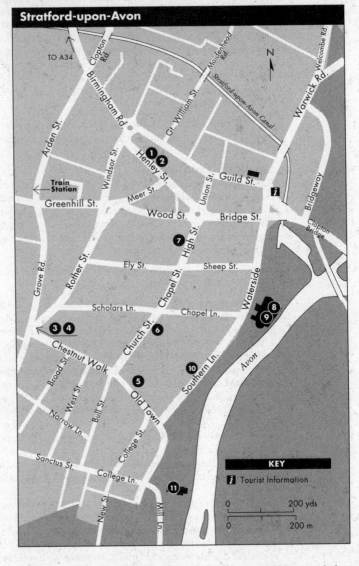

Stratford-upon-Avon

hall is the **Grammar School,** which Shakespeare probably attended as a boy and which is still used as a school. ☎ 01789/293351. ⊙ *Easter and summer school vacations, daily 10–6.*

⑦ On High Street, next to the Garrick Inn, you'll find **Harvard House,** a half-timbered 16th-century structure that was home to Catherine Rogers, mother of the John Harvard who founded Harvard University in 1636. Unfortunately, the house is virtually unfurnished. ⊙ *May—Sept. Contact the Shakespeare Centre for hours.*

⑧ The **Royal Shakespeare Theatre** occupies a perfect position on the banks of the Avon—try to see a performance if you can. The company (always referred to as the RSC) performs several Shakespeare plays each season, as well as plays by a wide variety of other playwrights, between March and January. For a fascinating insight into how the theater operates, join one of the backstage tours, led twice daily (four times on

⑨ Sundays). Beside the main theater there is the smaller **Swan,** the gift of an Anglophile American, Frederick Koch. Modeled on an Elizabethan theater, the Swan provides a very exciting auditorium for in-the-round staging. The Swan also provides entry to the RSC Collection, comprising paintings, props, and memorabilia; visit it either on one of the backstage tours or on your own. A new auditorium for experimental productions, **The Other Place,** is located just down the street. It's best to book well in advance for RSC productions, but a very few tickets for the day of performance are always available, and it is also worth asking if there are any returns. *Programs are available starting in February from* ✉ *The Royal Shakespeare Theatre, Stratford-upon-Avon, Warwickshire CV37 6BB,* ☎ *01789/295623; call 01789/412602 for details on backstage tours and RSC Collection.*

⓫ It is in **Holy Trinity Church,** close to the Royal Shakespeare Theatre, that Shakespeare and his wife are buried.

Warwick

Warwick, some 8 miles north of Stratford along A46, is an unusual mixture of Georgian redbrick and Elizabethan half-timber buildings, although some unattractive postwar developments have spoiled the town center. **Warwick Castle** is one of the finest medieval structures of its kind in England, towering on a precipice above the River Avon. Most of the present buildings date from the 14th century. The interior contains magnificent collections of armor, paintings, and furniture and a waxworks display by Madame Tussaud's, while outside, peacocks strut in the 60 acres of landscaped riverside gardens. A restored Victorian boathouse has a flora-and-fauna exhibition and a nature walk. ✉ *Castle Hill,* ☎ *01926/495421.* ≋ *£8.25.* ⊙ *Apr.–mid-Oct., daily 10–6; mid-Oct.–Mar., daily 10–5 (last entry 30 mins before closing); open until 7 PM. Closed Aug. bank holiday.*

NEED A BREAK? The paneled bar in the **Zetland Arms** (✉ 11 Church St.) serves good local beer and simple meals. There is also a quiet, attractive little garden.

The Cotswolds

From Stratford take an easy detour via A3400 and B4632 into the **Cotswolds**—high, bare hills patterned by patches of ancient forest and stone walls that protect the sheep that have grazed here from the earliest times. In the Middle Ages, English wool commanded high prices, and the little towns and villages nestling in valleys and on hillsides grew in prosperity. Although the wool trade has now dwindled in importance, the legacy of those days remains in the solid, substantial churches, cottages, and manor houses built of the mellow, golden-gray local stone. Burford, Stow-on-the-Wold, Upper Slaughter, Bourton-on-the-Water, Broadway, and Moreton-in-Marsh are just a few of the picturesque towns connected by pleasant country roads.

If you have time to visit only one Cotswold town, make it **Chipping Camden.** Its broad High Street is lined with houses in an attractive disarray of styles, many dating from the 17th century. Look for the group of almshouses built in 1624 and raised above street level and for the gabled **Market Hall** built three years later for the sale of local produce. One of the town's earliest buildings, dating from the 14th century, is the **Woolstaplers Hall,** which contains a museum of local history; besides material on the wool trade, there is a 1920s cinema and collections of medical equipment. ✉ *High St.,* ☎ *01386/840101.* ≋ *£2.50.* ⊙ *Apr.–Oct., daily 10–5.*

★ Four miles outside Chipping Campden is **Hidcote Manor Garden,** a 20th-century garden created around a Cotswold manor house (not open to the public). The lovely garden—which some connoisseurs consider the finest in Britain—consists of a series of open-air rooms divided by walls and hedges, each in a different style. ✉ *Hidcote Bartrim,* ☎ *01386/438333.* 🎫 *£5.20.* ☉ *Apr.–May and Aug.–Sept., Sat.–Mon., Wed., Thurs. 11–7; June–July, Sat.–Thurs. 11–7; Oct. Sat.–Mon., Wed., Thurs. 11–6. Last entrance 6 PM or 1 hr before sunset.*

B4632 runs along the western edge of the gently rolling Cotswold Hills as far as **Cheltenham,** once the rival of Bath in its Georgian elegance. Although it's now marred by modern developments, there are still some fine examples of the Regency style in its graceful secluded villas, lush gardens, and leafy crescents and squares.

Bath

Bath lies at the southern end of the Cotswolds (at the end of A46), some 70 miles from Stratford. A perfect 18th-century city, perhaps the best preserved in all Britain, it is a compact place, easy to explore on foot; the museums, elegant shops, and terraces of magnificent town houses are all close to one another.

Numbers in the margin correspond to points of interest on the Bath map.

It was the Romans who first took the waters at Bath, building a temple in honor of their goddess Minerva and a sophisticated series of baths to make full use of the curative hot springs. To this day, these springs gush from the earth at a constant temperature of 115.7°F (46.5°C). In the **Roman**

❶ **Baths Museum,** underneath the 18th-century Pump Room, you can see the excavated remains of almost the entire baths complex. ✉ *Abbey Churchyard,* ☎ *01225/477785.* 🎫 *£5.60; £7.50 combined ticket for Roman Baths and Museum of Costume.* ☉ *Apr.–July and Sept., daily 9–6; Aug. 8 PM–10 PM; Oct.–Mar., Mon.–Sat. 9:30–5, Sun. 10:30–5.*

❷ Next to the Pump Room is the **Abbey,** built in the 15th century. There are superb fan-vaulted ceilings in the nave.

In the 18th century, Bath became the fashionable center for taking the waters. The architect John Wood created a harmonious city from the mellow local stone, building beautifully executed terraces, crescents, and villas. The heart of Georgian Bath is the perfectly proportioned

❸ ★ ❹ **Circus** and the Royal Crescent. On the corner, **No. 1 Royal Crescent** is furnished as it might have been when Beau Nash, the master of ceremonies and arbiter of 18th-century Bath society, lived in the city. ☎ *01225/428126.* 🎫 *£3.50.* ☉ *Mid-Feb..–Oct., Tues.–Sun. 10:30–5; Nov., Tues.–Sun. 10:30–4.*

❺ Also near the Circus are the **Assembly Rooms,** frequently mentioned by Jane Austen in her novels of early 19th-century life. This neoclassical villa now houses a Museum of Costume that displays dress styles from Beau Nash's day to the present. ✉ *Bennett St.,* ☎ *01225/477000, ext. 2785.* 🎫 *£3.50.* ☉ *Mon.–Sat. 10–5, Sun. 11–5.*

❻ The **Theatre Royal** opened in 1805 and was restored in 1982. Next door, the former home of Richard "Beau" Nash—the dictator of fashion for mid-18th-century society in Bath—and his mistress Juliana Popjoy, is now a restaurant called Popjoy's (☞ Dining, *below*).

❼ One of the most charming and picturesque sights in Bath is the **Pulteney Bridge,** an 18th-century span which was based on the Ponte Vecchio of Florence. Lined with little shops, the bridge is the only work of Robert Adam in the city. At the western end is the Victoria Art Gallery.

❽ Across the Avon, in an elegant 18th-century building, is the **Holburne Museum and Crafts Study Centre,** which houses a superb collection of 17th- and 18th-century fine art and decorative arts. ✉ *Great Pulteney*

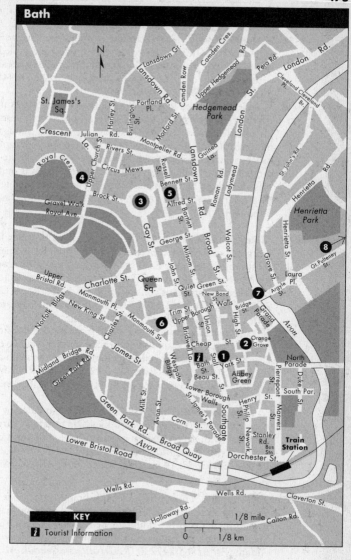

Bath

KEY

ℹ Tourist Information

St., ☎ 01225/466669. ✉ £3.50. ⊗ Mid-Feb.–Easter, Tues.–Sat. 11–5, Sun. 2:30–5:30; Easter–mid-Dec., Mon.–Sat. 11–5, Sun. 2:30–5:30.

NEED A BREAK?	Try the **Pump Room** (✉ Abbey Churchyard) for morning coffee or afternoon tea in grand surroundings, perhaps listening to the music of a string quartet, or, in nearby North Parade Passage, **Sally Lunn's,** where the famous Sally Lunn bun is still baked.

Dining and Lodging

For details and price-category definitions, *see* Dining *and* Lodging *in* Staying in Great Britain, *above.*

Bath

$$ ✕ **Popjoy's Restaurant.** Beau Nash entertained the best of 18th-century society here, and Popjoys retains its air of elegance. Diners can top off meals with coffee and petits fours served upstairs in a lovely

Georgian drawing room. ✉ *Sawclose,* ☎ *01225/460494. Reservations essential. AE, MC, V. Closed Sun.*

$–$$ ✕ **Number Five.** This candlelit bistro off Pulteney Bridge has a relaxed ambience and offers simple pasta with olive oil and grilled eggplant or more elaborate dishes such as confit of duck or roast breast of chicken with sun-dried tomatoes. ✉ *5 Argyle St.,* ☎ *01225/444499. AE, DC, MC, V. Closed Sun. No lunch Mon.*

$ ✕ **Rascals.** Located in a mazelike cellar of interconnecting rooms just south of the abbey, Rascals is a cheerful bistro-style restaurant offering excellent food, fine wines at low prices, and a noisy, relaxed atmosphere. Chef and proprietor Nick Anderson provides an international range of dishes, such as chicken casserole with white-wine sauce, though the menu changes regularly. The emphasis is on fresh vegetables and salads, and homemade ice cream features among the desserts. ✉ *8 Pierrepoint Pl.,* ☎ *01225/330201. Reservations essential. MC, V. No lunch Sun.*

$$$–$$$$ 🏨 **Royal Crescent.** The Royal Crescent is the ultimate in luxury living, in a gracious, lavishly converted building, situated on one of England's most famous terraces. Each bedroom has been individually designed to recapture the elegance of Bath's heyday. The hotel's formal Dower House restaurant wins consistent praise. ✉ *16 Royal Crescent, BA1 2LS,* ☎ *01225/739955,* 🖷 *01225/339401. 29 rooms with bath, 17 suites. Restaurant. AE, DC, MC, V.*

$$$ 🏨 **Pratt's.** Just a few minutes' walk from the center of town and the main sights, Pratt's is a fine Georgian house. Once the home of novelist Sir Walter Scott, it is now a comfortable hotel with an innovative restaurant. ✉ *South Parade, BA2 4AB,* ☎ *01225/460441,* 🖷 *01225/448807. 46 rooms with bath. Restaurant, bar, meeting rooms. AE, DC, MC, V.*

$$ 🏨 **Tasburgh Hotel.** This Victorian house, surrounded by gardens with beautiful views over the Avon Valley, has tastefully furnished rooms complete with every modern comfort. It's a mile from city center. ✉ *Warminster Rd., Bathampton, BA2 6SH,* ☎ *01225/425096,* 🖷 *01225/463842. 14 rooms, 10 with bath. AE, DC, MC, V.*

Oxford

$$$ ✕ **Elizabeth's.** These small, elegant dining rooms in a 16th-century bishop's palace overlook Christ Church and have the best views of any restaurant in Oxford. Salmon quenelles and roast lamb are among the Spanish chef's specialties, and there are outstanding wines. ✉ *82 St. Aldates,* ☎ *01865/242230. Reservations essential. AE, DC, MC, V. Closed Mon.*

$$ ✕ **Fifteen North Parade.** Just outside the city center, this is an intimate, stylish restaurant with cane furniture and a bright, open feeling. The menu changes regularly and may feature crab au gratin, guinea fowl, or vanilla and lychee panna cotta. ✉ *15 North Parade,* ☎ *01865/513773. Reservations essential. MC, V. Closed Sun. eve and Mon.*

$ ✕ **Munchy Munchy.** A constantly changing menu of spicy Malaysian dishes and a good selection of fresh fruit and vegetables make this a refreshing and popular spot. The surroundings are unpretentious and the prices are reasonable. ✉ *6 Park End St.,* ☎ *01865/245710. MC, V. Closed Sun., Mon., 2 wks in Aug.–Sept and 2 wks in Dec.–Jan.*

$$$$ 🏨 **The Randolph.** Oxford's only large central hotel has undergone extensive restoration of its elaborate Victorian Gothic interior. It's across from the Ashmolean Museum. ✉ *Beaumont St., OX1 2LN,* ☎ *01865/247481,* 🖷 *01865/791678. 105 rooms with bath, 4 suites. Restaurant, bar. AE, DC, MC, V.*

$$$ ⊞ **Eastgate Hotel.** This welcoming hotel has the traditional style of an inn. Its bar is a favorite with undergraduates and is a good place for getting an insight into university life. ⊠ *The High, OX1 4BE,* ☎ *01865/248244,* ℻ *01865/791681. 43 rooms with bath. Restaurant, bar. AE, DC, MC, V.*

$$$ ⊞ **Old Parsonage.** It's rare to find an attractive country house-hotel, with stone gables and mullion windows, in the middle of a city, but that is just what awaits at the Old Parsonage. Just a few yards behind St. Giles church, close to Somerville and Keble colleges, the Old Parsonage was established in 1660 and was completely restored and refurbished in 1991. Open fires, fascinating pictures, comfortable rooms, and immaculate service make this a hotel to remember. The rates put it at the top of its price category. ⊠ *1 Banbury Rd., OX2 6NN,* ☎ *01865/310210,* ℻ *01865/311262. 30 rooms with bath. Restaurant, bar. AE, DC, MC, V.*

Stratford

$$$ ✕ **Box Tree Restaurant.** In the Royal Shakespeare Theatre, this elegant restaurant overlooks the river and is a favored spot for pre- and post-theater dining. Specialties include roast rack of lamb and grilled Scotch beef fillet. ⊠ *Waterside,* ☎ *01789/293226. Reservations essential. AE, MC, V. Closed when theater is closed.*

$$ ✕ **The Opposition.** Located near the Royal Shakespeare Theatre, the Opposition caters to the pre- and post-theater dining crowd (as do all sensible restaurants in Stratford). It is extremely popular with the locals, so book in advance. The American and Continental dishes change constantly—if you're lucky there'll be Cajun chicken or mushrooms and asparagus served in a cream sauce. ⊠ *13 Sheep St.,* ☎ *01789/269980. Reservations essential. MC, V.*

$ ✕ **The Slug and Lettuce.** Don't let the name put you off—this pine-paneled pub serves excellent meals. Long-standing favorites are chicken breast baked in avocado and garlic, and poached cushion of salmon. ⊠ *38 Guild St.,* ☎ *01789/299700. Reservations essential. MC, V.*

$$$ ⊞ **Falcon Hotel.** Licensed as an alehouse since 1640, it still has a friendly inn atmosphere. The heavily beamed rooms in the older part are small and quaint; those in the modern extension are in standard international style. ⊠ *Chapel St., CV37 6HA,* ☎ *01789/279953,* ℻ *01789/414260. 73 rooms with bath. Restaurant, 2 bars. AE, DC, MC, V.*

$$$ ⊞ **Shakespeare Hotel.** For a touch of typical Stratford, stay at this timbered Elizabethan town house in the heart of the town, close to the theater and to most of the attractions. It has been luxuriously modernized while still retaining its Elizabethan character. ⊠ *Chapel St., CV37 6ER,* ☎ *01789/294771,* ℻ *01789/415411. 63 rooms with bath. AE, DC, MC, V.*

$$ ⊞ **Caterham House.** Built in 1830, this elegantly furnished building is in the center of town, within an easy walk of the theater. You may spot an actor or two among the guests. ⊠ *58 Rother St., CV37 6LT,* ☎ *01789/267309,* ℻ *01789/414836. 10 rooms with bath or shower. Restaurant. MC, V.*

Windsor and Eton

$$–$$$ ✕ **The Cockpit.** Cockfighting once took place in the courtyard of this smart 500-year-old inn with oak beams located on Eton's quiet main street. Now a restaurant with a strong Italian flavor, its specialties include calves' liver and fresh fish. ⊠ *47–49 High St., Eton,* ☎ *01753/860944. Reservations essential. AE, DC, MC, V. Closed Mon.*

$ ✕ **The Courtyard.** This little snack bar tucked away near the river and castle is a convenient spot for light lunches, teas, and a little peace and quiet. ⊠ *8 King George V Pl.,* ☎ *01753/858338. No credit cards.*

$$$–$$$$ 🏨 **Oakley Court.** This Victorian mansion is set in leafy grounds beside the river, just outside Windsor. Most of the bedrooms are in a bright wing of converted stables. It has the excellent Oak Leaf Room restaurant. ✉ *Windsor Rd., Water Oakley, SL4 5UR,* ☎ *01628/609988,* FAX *01628/37011. 92 rooms with bath. Two restaurants, putting green, tennis court, health club, croquet, helipad. AE, DC, MC, V.*

$$$ 🏨 **Sir Christopher Wren's House.** As the name suggests, this house was built by the famous architect, though modern additions have been made to convert it into a hotel. There is a strong period flavor, though the Baroque frills and flounces can be wearing. The restaurant overlooks the river, and cream teas are served on the terrace. ✉ *Thames St., Windsor, SL4 1PX,* ☎ *01753/861354,* FAX *01753/860172. 42 rooms with bath. Restaurant. AE, DC, MC, V.*

CAMBRIDGE

Cambridge, home of England's second-oldest university, is an ideal place to explore. There have been students here since the late 13th century, and virtually every generation since then has produced fine buildings, often by the most distinguished architects of its day. The result is a compact gallery of the best of English architecture. There is also good shopping in the city, and you can enjoy relaxing riverside walks.

Getting Around

By Train

Half-hourly trains from London's Liverpool Street Station and King's Cross Station run to Cambridge. For information call 0990/468468. Average journey time varies from 50 minutes to 1½ hours, depending on the day of week or time of day.

By Bus

There are 14 buses daily from Victoria Coach Station that take just under two hours. Call 0990/808080.

By Car

M11 is the main highway from London to Cambridge. The main car-rental companies have offices in Cambridge.

Visitor Information

Cambridge (✉ Wheeler St., off King's Parade, ☎ 01223/322640). FAX 01223/463385.

Guided Tours

The **Cambridge Tourist Information Centre** offers two-hour guided walking tours of the city and the colleges daily; tickets (£3.50) are available up to 24 hours in advance (☎ 01223/463290). Various theme tours are also offered, including combined walking/punting tours and 1½-hour evening pub tours. Booking is essential—the tours are very popular. **Guide Friday** (tel.01223/362444), in Cambridge, operates a city open-top bus tour every 15 minutes throughout the day (Oct.–May, half-hourly); tickets (£7) can be bought from the driver or the office at Cambridge train station. You can join the tours at the station or at any of the specially-marked bus stops throughout the city.

Exploring Cambridge

The university is in the very heart of **Cambridge.** It consists of a number of colleges, each of which is a separate institution with its own distinct character and traditions. Undergraduates join an individual college and are taught by dons attached to the college, who are known as "fellows." Each college is built around a series of courts, or quadrangles; because students and fellows live in these quadrangles, access is sometimes restricted, especially during examination weeks (April to mid-June). Visitors are not normally allowed into college buildings other than chapels and halls. It is best to check first with the city tourist office to find out which colleges may be visited.

Numbers in the margin correspond to points of interest on the Cambridge map.

① ★ **King's College,** off King's Parade, is possibly the best known of all the colleges. Its **chapel,** started by Henry VI in 1446, is a masterpiece of late-Gothic architecture, with a great fan-vaulted ceiling supported only by a tracery of soaring side columns. Behind the altar hangs Rubens's painting *Adoration of the Magi.* Every Christmas Eve the college choir sings the Festival of Nine Lessons and Carols, which is broadcast all over the world. King's runs down to the "Backs," the tree-shaded grounds on the banks of the River Cam, which is the background of many of the colleges. From King's make your way along the river and
② **③** **④** through the narrow lanes past **Clare College** and **Trinity Hall** to **Trinity.** This is the largest college, established by Henry VIII in 1546. It has a handsome 17th-century Great Court, around which are the chapel, hall, gates, and a library by Christopher Wren. In the massive gate house is Great Tom, a large clock that strikes each hour with high and low notes. The novelist E. M. Forster, who wrote *Howards End* and *A Passage to India,* studied at King's, as did the war poet Rupert Brooke. Prince Charles was an undergraduate here during the late 1960s.

⑤ Beyond Trinity lies **St. John's,** the second-largest college. The white crenellations of the enormous mock-Gothic **New Building** of 1825 have earned it the nickname "the wedding cake." To reach it, cross a bridge that's a facsimile of Venice's Bridge of Sighs. Among St. John's build-
⑥ ings is one of the oldest houses in Cambridge, **Merton Hall,** with its origins in the 12th century (although the building itself largely dates from the 16th century).

⑦ Up Northampton and across **Magdalene Street** you come to **Magdalene College,** with its pretty redbrick courts. The **Pepys Library** contains the 17th-century diarist's own books and desk. ▭ *Free.* ◷ *Oct.–Mar., daily 2:30–3:30; Apr.–Sept., daily 11:30–12:30 and 2:30–3:30.*

⑧ Beyond Magdalene is **Kettle's Yard.** Originally a private house owned by a connoisseur of modern art, Kettle's Yard is home to a fine permanent collection of 20th-century art, sculpture, furniture and decorative arts. A separate gallery provides space for a regular program of exhibitions on modern arts and crafts. ⊠ *Castle St.,* ☎ *01223/352124.* ▭ *Free.* ◷ *House: Tues.–Sun. 2–4; gallery: Tues.–Sat. 12:30–5:30, Sun. 2–5:30.*

Returning the way you've just come, along the Backs from King's, you'll
⑨ see **Queen's College,** where Isaac Newton's **Mathematical Bridge** crosses the river. This arched wooden structure was originally held together by gravitational force; when it was taken apart to see how Newton did it, no one could reconstruct it without using nails. Back from the
⑩ river, on Trumpington Street, sits **Pembroke College,** which contains
⑪ some 14th-century buildings and a chapel by Wren, and **Peterhouse,** the oldest college, dating from 1281. Next to Peterhouse is the
⑫ **Fitzwilliam Museum,** which contains outstanding art collections (including paintings by Constable, Gainsborough, and the French Im-

Cambridge

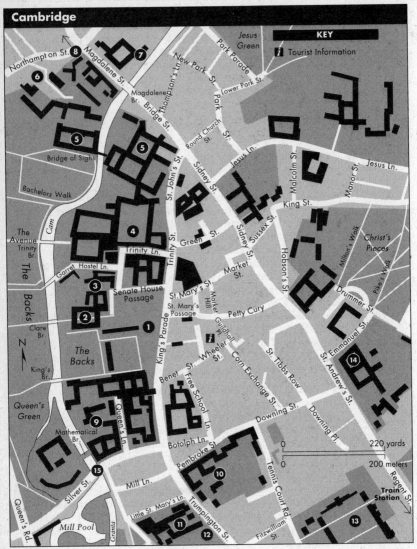

pressionists) and antiquities (especially from ancient Egypt). ✉ *Trumpington St.*, ☎ *01223/332900.* 🖼 *Free.* ⏰ *Tues.–Sat. 10–5; Sun. 2:15–5; guided tours Sun. at 2.30,* 🖼 *£2.*

⓲ Other colleges worth visiting include **Downing College,** which has a unique collection of neoclassical buildings dating from 1800, and **⓳ Emmanuel College,** in whose chapel—designed by Christopher Wren—lies a memorial to John Harvard, founder of Harvard University.

⓴ If you have time, hire a punt at **Silver Street Bridge** or at **Magdalene Bridge** and navigate down past St. John's or upstream to **Grantchester,** the pretty village made famous by the Edwardian poet Rupert Brooke. On a sunny day, there's no better way to absorb Cambridge's unique atmosphere.

NEED A BREAK?	The coffee shop in the **Fitzwilliam Museum** is an excellent choice for a pastry or a light lunch. So is **The Copper Kettle** (✉ King's Parade), a traditional students' hangout. The **Fort St. George**, on Jesus Green, is a riverside pub with plenty of outdoor space for summer drinking, or try **The Orchard** at Grantchester for a peaceful afternoon tea beneath the apple trees.

Dining

For details and price-category definitions, *see* Dining *in* Staying in Great Britain, *above.*

\$\$–\$\$\$ ✕ **Midsummer House.** A classy restaurant set beside the River Cam,
★ Midsummer House is lovely in summer. There's a comfortable conservatory. Set-price menus for lunch and dinner offer a selection of robust yet sophisticated European and Mediterranean dishes. Opt for a shell of foie gras with sweetbreads and scallops, followed by tender noisettes of lamb served on a confit of garlic with artichokes. ✉ *Midsummer Common, Cambridge,* ☎ *01223/69299. Reservations essential. AE, DC, MC, V. No lunch Sat., no dinner Sun. Closed Mon.*

\$\$ ✕ **Three Horseshoes.** This is an early 19th-century thatched cottage. The menu in the busy—sometimes crowded—pub restaurant and conservatory sets out a tempting range of beautifully presented dishes. The emphasis is on modern British cuisine, for example pan-fried mallard with rosti, green cabbage, and wild mushrooms. ✉ *Madingley,* ☎ *01954/210221 (3 mi southwest of Cambridge). Reservations essential. AE, DC, MC, V.*

\$–\$\$ ✕ **Brown's.** This huge, airy French-American style brasserie-diner was converted from the outpatient department of the old Addenbrooke's Hospital opposite the Fitzwilliam Museum. Large fans still keep things cool in the pale yellow dining room. The wide-ranging menu runs from toasted tuna sandwiches, steak-mushroom-and-Guinness pie, hamburgers, and salads to venison or gigot of lamb; check the daily specials, too—there's usually fresh fish. ✉ *23 Trumpington St.,* ☎ *01223/461655. Reservations not accepted. AE, MC, V. Closed Dec. 25–26.*

\$ ✕ **Hobbs Pavilion.** Housed in an old cricket pavilion on the western edge of Parker's Piece, this modest but cheery creperie has wooden walls decorated with cricketing memorabilia and a small terrace ideal for watching players in summer. Three-course set-price menus, including vegetarian and vegan options, are a special bargain. ✉ *Park Terrace, Cambridge,* ☎ *01223/67480. No credit cards. Closed Sun. and Mon.*

Lodging

For details and price-category definitions, *see* Lodging *in* Staying in Great Britain, *above.*

$$$$ ⚑ **Garden House Hotel.** Set among the colleges, this luxurious, mod-
★   ern hotel makes the most of its peaceful riverside location—it even rents
out its own punts. Its gardens, lounge, cocktail bar, and conservato-
ries all have river views, as do most of the guest rooms—if you want
one, make it clear when you make your reservation, as some of the
rooms at the rear of the L-shaped hotel have less desirable views. The
recently refurbished guest rooms are comfortable, with minibars, TVs,
and fine bathrooms. Plans for a leisure center incorporating indoor swimming pool, gym, sauna, and steam room have been announced as we
go to press. ⊠ *Granta Pl., Mill La., Cambridge CB2 1RT*, ☎
01223/63421, 🖷 *01223/316605. 118 rooms with bath. Restaurant,
bar. AE, DC, MC, V.*

$$$–$$$$ ⚑ **De Vere University Arms Hotel.** Respectfully modernized, this is an
elegant 19th-century hotel, conveniently sited in the city center. Guest
rooms are comfortable and well-appointed without being large, though
views of Parker's Piece from many rooms compensate. The central lounge
provides a comfortable place for afternoon tea, where you can sit by
the fire enjoying a pot of Darjeeling and smoked salmon sandwiches.
⊠ *Regent St., Cambridge CB2 1AD*, ☎ *01223/351241*, 🖷
*01223/315256. 115 rooms with bath. Restaurant, 3 bars, room ser-
vice. AE, DC, MC, V.*

$$ ⚑ **Arundel House.** This hotel occupies a converted terrace of Victorian houses overlooking the river Cam and open parkland. The bed-
rooms are comfortably furnished with locally made mahogany furniture.
⊠ *53 Chesterton Rd., Cambridge CB4 3AN*, ☎ *01223/67701*, 🖷
*01223/67721. 105 rooms with bath or shower. Restaurant, bar. AE,
DC, MC, V.*

YORK AND ENVIRONS

Once England's second city, the ancient town of York has survived the
ravages of time, war, and industrialization to remain one of northern
Europe's few preserved walled cities. It was King George VI, father of
the present queen, who remarked that the history of York is the history of England. Even in a brief visit to the city, you can see evidence
of life from every era since the Romans, not only in museums but also
in the very streets and houses.

York is surrounded by some of the grandest countryside England has
to offer. A fertile plain dotted with ancient abbeys and grand aristocratic mansions leads westward to the hidden valleys and jagged,
windswept tops of the Yorkshire Dales and northward to the brooding mass of the North York Moors. This is a land quite different from
the south of England—it's friendlier, emptier, and less aggressively
materialistic. No visitor to Britain should overlook it.

Getting Around

By Train
Regular fast trains run from London's King's Cross Station to York.
The trip takes two hours. For information, call 0171/278–2477.

By Bus
Regular Rapide buses leave from Victoria Coach Station daily. The trip
takes 4½ hours. For information, call 0171/730–0202.

By Car
Take A1, the historic main route from London to the north, which
branches east onto A64 near Tadcaster for the final 12 miles to York.
Alternatively, take M1, then M18, and finally A1. The drive from Lon-

don takes a minimum of four hours. The main car-rental companies have offices in York.

The best way to explore the area around York is by car—although it's inadvisable, and sometimes impossible, to take a car into the crowded city center. Bus tours (☞ Guided Tours, *below*) visit most of the nearby attractions.

Visitor Information

There is a tourist information office at **De Grey Rooms** (⊠ Exhibition Square, North Yorkshire Y01 2HB, ☎ 01904/621756) and smaller ones at the **York railway station** (☎ 01904/621756) and 6 Rougier Street (☎ 01904/620557).

Guided Tours

Guide Friday (⊠ De Grey Rooms, Exhibition Square, ☎ 01904/640896) runs frequent city tours that allow you to get on and off the bus as you please (£6.50). They also conduct tours of the surrounding country-side, including Fountains Abbey and Castle Howard. The **York Association of Voluntary Guides** (⊠ in De Grey Rooms, Exhibition Square, ☎ 01904/640780) arranges short walking tours around the city (free, but a gratuity is appreciated) each morning at 10:15, with additional tours at 2:15 PM from April through October, and one at 7 PM from July through August.

Exploring York

Numbers in the margin correspond to points of interest on the York map.

★ ❶ York's greatest glory is the **Minster,** the largest Gothic church in England and one of the finest in Europe. Take time to gaze at the soaring columns and intricate tracery of the 14th-century nave, the choir screen portraying whimsical images of the kings of England, and the imposing tracery of the mighty rose window—just one of 128 stained-glass windows in the Minster—which commemorates the marriage of Henry VII and Elizabeth of York. Visit the exquisite 13th-century **Chapter House** and the Roman and Saxon remains in the **Undercroft Museum and Treasury.** Climb the 275 steps of the **Central Tower** for an unrivaled view of the city and the countryside beyond. The **Crypt** features some of the cathedral's oldest and most valuable treasures, among them the Romanesque 12th-century statue of a heavy-footed Virgin Mary. ⊠ *Duncombe Place, York Minster Undercroft Museum and Treasury, Chapter House, Central Tower, and Crypt,* ☎ *01904/624426.* ☜ *Minster free (£1.50 donation appreciated); foundations £1.80; Chapter House 70p; Central Tower £2; Crypt 60p.* ☉ *Minster: summer daily 7–8:30; winter 7–6; Undercroft, Chapter House, Central Tower, and Crypt: summer Mon.–Sat. 10–5:30, Sun. 1–5:30, winter Mon.–Sat. 10–4:30, Sun. 1–4:30.*

❷ At the **Jorvik Viking Centre,** south of the Minster through tiny medieval streets, you can take another journey into history—whisked back in little "time cars" to the sights, sounds, and even the smells of a Viking street, which archaeologists have re-created in astonishing detail. ⊠ *Coppergate,* ☎ *01904/643211.* ☜ *£4.25.* ☉ *Apr.–Oct., daily 9–7; Nov.–Mar., daily 9–5:30.*

★ ❸ Walk south down Castlegate and onto Tower Street, where you'll find the **Castle Museum,** housed in an 18th-century prison. It has a series of realistic period displays that bring the past to life. Highlights include

York

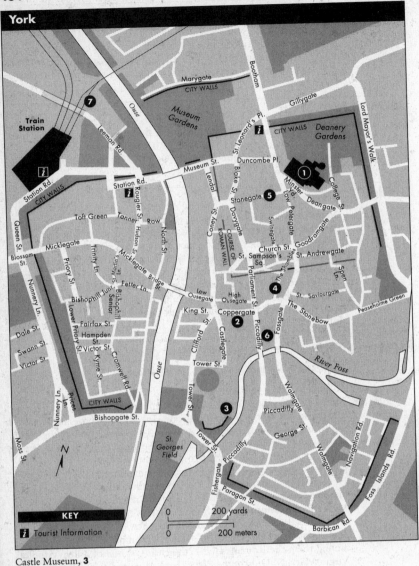

Castle Museum, **3**
Jorvik Viking
Centre, **2**
Merchant
Adventurers' Hall, **6**
Minster, **1**
National Railway
Museum, **7**
Shambles, **4**
Stonegate, **5**

a Victorian street scene, an 18th-century dining room, and a moorland farmer's cottage. Don't miss the Coppergate Helmet, one of only three Anglo-Saxon helmets ever found. The welcoming tearoom serves drinks and simple snacks. ✉ *Clifford St.,* ☎ *01904/653611.* ☎ *£4.20.* ⊙ *Apr.–Oct., Mon.–Sat. 9:30–5:30, Sun. 10–5:30; Nov.–Mar., Mon.–Sat. 9:30–4, Sun. 10–4.*

Even more than the wealth of museums, it is the streets and city walls that bring York's past to life. A walk along the **walls**, most of which date from the 13th century, though with extensive restoration, provides delightful views across rooftops and gardens and the Minster itself. The narrow paved path winds between various fortified gates where the old roads ran out of the city.

★ ❹ Within the walls, the narrow streets still follow the complex medieval pattern. The **Shambles,** in the heart of this walled city, is a well-preserved example; the half-timbered shops and houses have such large overhangs that you can practically reach from one second-floor win-
❺ dow to another. **Stonegate** is a narrow pedestrian street of 18th-century (and earlier) shops and courts. Along a narrow passage off Stonegate, at 52A, you will find the remains of a 12th-century Norman stone house—one of the very few surviving in England.

❻ The **Merchant Adventurers' Hall** is a superb medieval building (1357–68) built and owned by one of the richest medieval guilds; it contains the largest timber-framed hall in York. ✉ *Fossgate,* ☎ *01904/654818.* ☎ *£1.80.* ⊙ *Mid-Mar.–mid-Nov., daily 8:30–5; mid-Nov.–mid-Mar., Mon.–Sat. 8:30–3.*

❼ One very different attraction is the **National Railway Museum,** the largest railway museum in the world, just outside the city walls, by the train station. This houses Britain's national collection of railway locomotives, including such giants of the steam era as *Mallard,* holder of the world speed record for a steam engine (126 mph), early rolling stock, and pioneer diesel and electric locomotives. ✉ *Leeman Rd.,* ☎ *01904/621261.* ☎ *£4.20.* ⊙ *Apr.–Oct., Mon.–Sat. 10–6, Sun. 11–6; Nov.–Mar.,Mon.–Sat. 10–5, Sun. 11–5.*

| NEED A BREAK? | In St. Helens Square, **Betty's** has been a York institution since 1912, serving teas with mouth-watering cakes and desserts as well as light meals and a splendid selection of exotic coffees. |

Outside York

Traveling west on A59, once a Roman road, you soon reach the **Yorkshire Dales,** made world-famous by the writings of a local veterinarian, the late James Herriot, and inspiration for, among others, the poet William Wordsworth and the quintessentially English painter J. M. W. Turner. The fertile river valleys of the Dales are separated from one another by areas of wild, high moorland that offer many opportunities for exhilarating walks and drives. At **Bolton Abbey,** about 36 miles
★ west of York, the ruins of a 13th-century priory lie on a grassy embankment contained within a great curve of the River Wharfe. (There's unrestricted access during daylight.) Explore the ruins and walk through some of the most romantic woodland scenery in England, past the legendary **Strid,** where the river plunges through a rocky chasm only a few yards wide.

Northwest from Bolton Abbey, off B6160, is **Grassington,** a village of stone houses with an ancient, cobbled marketplace—a convenient center from which to explore the wild landscapes of Upper Wharfedale. The **National Park Centre** has a wide choice of guidebooks, maps, and

York Environs

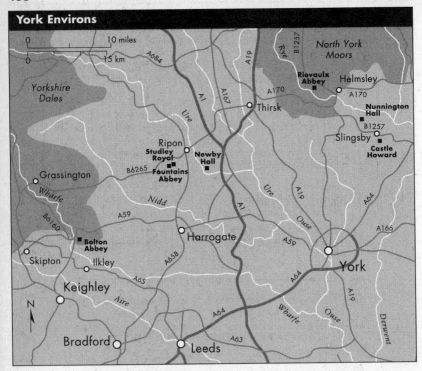

bus schedules to help you enjoy a day in the Dales. Organized tours depart from the center with qualified guides who explain the botanical and geological features of the area. ⊠ *Colvend, Hebdon Rd.,* ☎ *01756/752748.* ⊘ *Apr.–Oct., daily 9:30–5:30; Nov.–Mar., Fri. 1–4:30, weekends 10–12:30 and 1–4:30, Mon. 10–1.*

About 15 miles east from Grassington, along B6265, across the moors, is **Fountains Abbey and Studley Royal,** on the very edge of the hills. Here, the extensive ruins of a 12th-century monastery are set beside an 18th-century landscaped water garden and deer park, complete with lakes, half-moon ponds, statuary, and pseudo-Greek temples. ☎ *01765/601002.* ⊠ *£4,* ⊘ *Jan.–Mar. daily 10–5 or dusk; Apr.–Sept., daily 10–7; Oct.–Dec. daily 10–5 or dusk; closed Fri Nov.–Jan. Guided tours daily Apr.–Oct. at 2:30.*

Nearby **Newby Hall**—3 miles due east of Fountains Abbey along pleasant country roads—has some restored interiors by the 18th-century master architect Robert Adam and some equally celebrated gardens with a collection of rare roses. There is a handy restaurant. ⊠ *Skelton-on-Ure,* ☎ *01423/322583.* ⊠ *£5.40; gardens only, £3.80.* ⊘ *Apr.–Sept., Tues.–Sun., grounds 11–5:30, house noon–5.*

To the northeast, across the Vale of York, lie the **North York Moors,** dominated by a vast expanse of dense woodland and heather moorland that in late summer turns a rich blaze of crimson and purple. Nestled in deep valleys are charming villages built of brownstone—a contrast with the gray stone of the Dales.

Helmsley is a pleasant market town on the southern edge of the Moors. The old cross in the market square marks the start of the long-distance, moor-and-coastal footpath known as the Cleveland Way; not far from ★ the path's origin, it passes the famous ruins of **Rievaulx Abbey.** An hour's walk from town, or two miles by road (B1257 north), this medieval seat of Cistercian monastic learning sports graceful arches, cloisters, and associated buildings which occupy a dramatic riverside setting. Having wandered among the ruins, you might also like to climb (or drive) up to the **Rievaulx Terraces,** a long grassy walkway on the hillside above, terminating in the remains of several classical temples. The views of the abbey from here are magnificent. ⊠ *Rievaulx Abbey, B1257* ☎ *01439/798228.* ⊡ *£2.50.* ◷ *Apr.–Sept., daily 10–6; Oct.–Mar., daily 10–4. Rievaulx Terrace,* ☎ *01439/798340.* ⊡ *£2.30.* ◷ *Apr.–Oct., daily 10:30–6.*

Returning south to York, stop off at **Nunnington Hall** (off B1257), a largely late-17th-century manor house set on the River Rye containing a paneled hall with a carved chimneypiece, fine tapestries and china, and a superb collection of miniature rooms with intricate dollhouse furniture of different periods. ⊠ *Nunnington,* ☎ *01439/748283.* ⊡ *£3.50; gardens only, £1.* ◷ *Apr.–June and Sept.–Oct., Tues.–Thurs. and weekends 2–6; July–Aug., Tues.–Fri. 2–6, weekends noon–6.*

NEED A BREAK?	Teas (and light lunches on summer weekends) can be enjoyed at Nunnington Hall's excellent tearoom.

★ In marked contrast to Nunnington is the palatial majesty of **Castle Howard** (south off B1257 at Slingsby), one of the leading monuments of the English Baroque style and known to TV viewers as the setting for the series *Brideshead Revisited.* The great central domed tower, flanked by two huge and richly decorated wings, took 60 years—from 1699 to 1759—to build. The central hall, with its painted ceiling, leads to a series of grand state rooms and galleries, filled with paintings, sculpture, and furniture. The house is surrounded by one of the most beautiful parks in Britain, which is landmarked with the "follies"— marble pavilions, temples, and pyramids—so beloved by 18th-century aristocrats. ⊠ *Coneysthorpe,* ☎ *01653/648333.* ⊡ *Castle: £5.50; grounds only: £3.* ◷ *House mid-Mar.–Oct. daily 11–4:30. Grounds mid-Mar.–Oct., daily 10–4:30; Nov.–mid-Mar. Sun. 10–4.*

Dining

For details and price-category definitions, *see* Dining *in* Staying in Great Britain, *above.*

$$–$$$ ✕ **Melton's.** Just 10 minutes from the Minster, this unpretentious restaurant has local art on the walls and an open kitchen. The seasonal menu proves to be highly imaginative, a legacy of chef Michael Hjort's former stint at the Roux brothers' establishments, and offers modern English, Continental, and fish dishes. ⊠ *7 Scarcroft Rd., York,* ☎ *01904/634341. Reservations essential. MC, V. No dinner Sun., no lunch Mon. Closed 3 wks at Christmas and 1 wk in Sept.*

$$–$$$ ✕ **19 Grape Lane.** The narrow, slightly cramped restaurant is housed ★ in a typically leaning timbered York building in the heart of town. Hugely popular, it serves modern English food from a blackboard of specials such as medallions of hare with field mushrooms in a red wine sauce. ⊠ *19 Grape La., York,* ☎ *01904/636366. Reservations essential. MC, V. Closed Sun. and Mon., 2 wks in Feb., 2 wks in Sept.*

$$ ✕ **Kites.** Climb a steep, narrow staircase to find an innovative restaurant serving a changing menu of offbeat, health-conscious food. Influences in the entrées might be Italian or Thai, and you can always rely on the desserts: the creamy banofi pie is a perennial favorite. ⊠ *13 Grape La., York,* ☎ *01904/640750. AE, DC, MC, V. Closed Sun.*

$$ ✕ **Partners.** The restaurateur is Polish, so you'll find the occasional Eastern European dish among the modern English cuisine in this simple, elegant restaurant, tucked well off the road and arranged around a pretty paved courtyard. Try the traditional Polish pork *kotley* (a mixture of ground pork with mushrooms, onion, and garlic). ✉ *13a High Ousegate, York,* ☎ *01904/627929. Reservations essential. AE, DC, MC, V. Closed Sun.*

$–$$ ✕ **Pierre Victoire.** Saunter in to this airy brasserie at lunchtime and you can feast on three courses of simple French food for just £5, one of the city's best bargains. At dinner, prices increase, but not outrageously so, while the dishes become more elaborate: try the roast pheasant on a bed of sweet red cabbage or that old brasserie standby, *moules mariniere* (mussels). ✉ *2 Lendal, York,* ☎ *01904/655222. MC, V.*

$ ✕ **Pizza Express.** The successful London chain has set up shop in the regal River House at Lendal Bridge, now delightfully renovated. You eat in the grand salons of what used to be the York Gentleman's Club; a piano serenades evening diners from the lounge; even the rest rooms are fancy. The pizzas are not always all they could be, but lap up the good house wine and the upscale ambience and all is forgiven. ✉ *River House, 17 Museum St., York,* ☎ *01904/672904. MC, V.*

Lodging

For details and price-category definitions, *see* Lodging *in* Staying in Great Britain, *above.*

$$$$ 🏨 **Middlethorpe Hall.** This handsome, superbly restored 18th-century
★ mansion is located on the edge of the city, about 1½ miles from the center, beside the racetrack. The individually decorated rooms, some in cottage-style accommodations around an 18th-century courtyard, are filled with antiques, paintings, and fresh flowers, and the extensive grounds boast a lake, a 17th-century dovecote, and "ha-ha's"— drops in the garden level that create cunning views. ✉ *Bishopthorpe Rd., York YO2 1QB,* ☎ *01904/641241, from the U.S. toll-free 800/260–8338,* FAX *01904/620176. 30 rooms with bath. Restaurant (reservations essential; jacket and tie), croquet. AE, DC, MC, V.*

$$$–$$$$ 🏨 **Mount Royale Hotel.** Two elegant town houses dating from the 1830s have been furnished in a traditional English country-cottage style to make a very attractive hotel about 15 minutes from the town center. The open-plan "garden suites" open out onto the hotel's lovely grounds; semitropical plants, including oranges and figs, decorate the approach to these suites. ✉ *119 The Mount, York YO2 2DA,* ☎ *01904/628856,* FAX *01904/611171. 23 rooms with bath. Restaurant, pool, sauna, steam room. AE, DC, MC, V. Closed Dec. 24–31.*

$$$ 🏨 **Dean Court.** This large Victorian house once provided accommodation for the clergy of York Minster, the imposing cathedral which looms just across the road. The house has had a model renovation and now features comfortably furnished rooms with plump sofas, TVs, and fine views overlooking the Minster. Parking is a few minutes from the hotel, but there is a valet parking service. The restaurant serves good English cuisine, including a hearty Yorkshire breakfast. ✉ *Duncombe Place, York, YO1 2EF,* ☎ *01904/625082,* FAX *01904/620305. 40 rooms with bath. Restaurant, bar, coffee shop. AE, DC, MC, V.*

$$–$$$ 🏨 **Curzon Lodge and Stable Cottages.** This attractive white 17th-century house was once owned by York's famous Terry chocolate family. It sits on the edge of town, near the racetrack, a mile or so from the train station. The house itself is beautifully furnished with antiques, four-poster beds, and Victorian brass bedsteads; delightful oak-beam

"cottages," in the old coach house and stables, offer two-room family suites. Breakfast is served in the cozy, rustic dining room. ⊠ *23 Tadcaster Rd., Dringhouses, YO2 2QG,* ☎ *01904/703157. 10 rooms with bath or shower. Dining room. MC, V.*

$$–$$$ 🏨 **Savages.** Despite its name, this small hotel on a leafy road near the town center is eminently refined, with a reputation for attentive service. Once a Victorian home, it has a stylish and comfortable interior, and there's a bar in which to relax. ⊠ *15 St. Peter's Grove, York, YO3 6AQ,* ☎ *01904/610818,* FAX *01904/627729. 18 rooms with bath or shower. Restaurant, bar. AE, DC, MC, V.*

$ 🏨 **Abbey Guest House.** This quaint, pretty no-smoking guest house is a 10-minute walk from the train station and town center. Although small, it's very clean and friendly, with a peaceful garden right on the river. Picnic lunches and evening meals can be arranged on request. ⊠ *14 Earlsborough Terr., Marygate, YO3 7BQ,* ☎ *01904/627782. 7 rooms, 2 with bath. Breakfast room. AE, MC, V.*

THE LAKE DISTRICT

The poets Wordsworth and Coleridge can probably be held responsible for the development of the Lake District as a tourist mecca. They, and other English men of letters, found it an inspiring setting for their work—and fashion, and thousands of visitors, have followed. The lakeland district, created in the 1970s as a national park from parts of the old counties of Cumberland, Westmoreland, and Lancashire, combines so much that is magnificent in mountain, lake, and dales that new and entrancing vistas open out at each corner of the road. There are most certainly higher mountains in Britain, but none that are finer in outline or which give a greater impression of majesty; deeper and bluer lakes can be found, but none that fit so readily into the surrounding scene. There are more than 100 lakes here, ranging from tiny mountain pools (called, in the local dialect, tarns) to England's largest lake, 11-mile-long Lake Windemere.

Perhaps it is only natural that an area so blessed with natural beauties should have become linked with so many prominent figures in English literature. In addition to Wordsworth and Coleridge, other literary figures who made their homes in the region include De Quincey, Southey, Ruskin, Arnold, and later, Walpole, and the children's writer Beatrix Potter. Today, travelers—especially hikers, rock climbers, and painters—find this region one of England's most peaceful destinations. Needless to say, walking is perhaps the best way to discover the delights of this area.

Getting Around

By Train

Take an InterCity train from London's Euston Station (☎ 0171/387–7070) bound for Carlisle, Edinburgh, or Glasgow and change at Oxenholme for service to Kendal and Windermere. Average travel time to Windermere (including the change) is 4½ hours. The **Lakeside & Haverthwaite Railway Co.** (☎ 015395/31594) runs vintage steam trains in summer (and at Christmas) between Lakeside and Haverthwaite along Lake Windermere's southern tip.

By Bus

National Express (☎ 0171/730–0202) buses serve the region from London's Victoria Coach Station. Average travel time to Kendal is just over seven hours; to Windermere, 7½ hours; and to Keswick, 8¼ hours. **Cumberland Motor Services** (☎ 01946/63222) operates year-round throughout the Lake District, with reduced service on Saturday, Sunday, and bank holidays. In summer, **Mountain Goat** (Victoria St., Windermere, ☎ 015394/45161) runs a minibus service linking Keswick, Grasmere, Ambleside, Windermere, and Kendal.

By Car

Take M1 north from London to M6, leaving at exit 36 and joining A590/A591 west (around the Kendal bypass to Windermere) or at exit 40, joining A66 direct to Keswick and the northern lakes. Travel time to Kendal is about four hours, to Keswick five to six hours. Car-rental companies are few and far between in the Lakes; rent in London or York before your trip.

Roads within the region are generally good, although many of the minor routes and mountain passes can be steep and narrow. Warning signs are normally posted if snow has made a road impassable. In July and August and during public holiday weekends, expect heavy traffic.

By Boat

Bowness Bay Boating Co. (☎ 015394/43360) runs small vessels around Lake Windermere, particularly to Ambleside and Brockhole National Park Centre. **Windermere Iron Steamboat Co.** (☎ 015395/31188) employs its fleet of vintage cruisers in a regular service between Ambleside, Bowness, and Lakeside on Lake Windermere.

By Walking

Every hamlet, village, and town provides scores of walking opportunities and stores throughout the region stock the right equipment, books, and maps; always check on weather conditions before setting out, since mist or rain can roll in without warning. For short, local walks consult the tourist information centers, which can provide maps, guides, and advice. The other main source of information is the **Lake District National Park Visitor Information Centre** (☞ Windermere, *below*).

Visitor Information

The **Cumbria Tourist Board** (✉ Ashleigh, Holly Rd., Windermere, Cumbria LA23 2AQ, ☎ 015394/44444) has information about the entire region. There are local offices in **Ambleside** (✉ The Old Courthouse, Church St., ☎ 015394/32582); **Grasmere** (✉ Red Bank Rd., ☎ 015394/35245); **Kendal** (✉ Town Hall, Highgate, ☎ 01539/725758); **Keswick** (✉ Moot Hall, Market Sq., ☎ 017687/72645); and **Windermere** (✉ The Gateway Centre, Victoria St., ☎ 015394/46499).

Guided Tours

From Easter until October, the **National Park Authority** (☎ 015394/46601) at Brockhole, near Windermere, arranges half-day or full-day walks introducing you to the history and natural beauties of the Lake District. **Mountain Goat Holidays** (☎ 015394/45161) provides half- and full-day minibus sightseeing tours with skilled local guides.

Exploring the Lake District

The two tours in this chapter divide the Lake District into two compact areas. The first takes in the southern lakes along with some of the most historic houses of the lakeland, including Wordsworth's Rydal Mount and Dove Cottage, John Ruskin's Brantwood estate, and Beatrix Potter's Hill Top. The second tour ventures north through some of the most quintessential countryside of the district, passes Derwentwater—one of England's finest lakes—and ends up in Cockermouth, Wordsworth's birthplace.

The Lake District

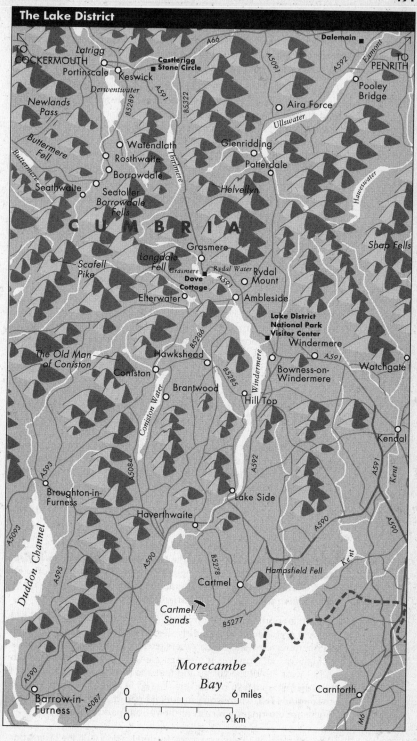

TO COCKERMOUTH

Latrigg

Portinscale

Keswick

Derwentwater

Newlands Pass

Buttermere Fell

Buttermere

Seathwaite

Watendlath

Rosthwaite

Borrowdale

Seatoller

Borrowdale Fells

Castlerigg Stone Circle

A66

A5091

Dalemain

A592

Eamont

TO PENRITH

Pooley Bridge

Aira Force

Ullswater

Glenridding

Patterdale

Helvellyn

Haweswater

C U M B R I A

Shap Fells

Scafell Pike

Langdale Fell

Grasmere

Grasmere

Rydal Water

Rydal Mount

Dove Cottage

Elterwater

Ambleside

The Old Man of Coniston

Hawkshead

Coniston

Brantwood

Coniston Water

Hill Top

Lake District National Park Visitor Center

Windermere

Bowness-on-Windermere

Watchgate

Kendal

Kent

Broughton-in-Furness

Haverthwaite

Lake Side

A5092

A5093

A5095

A5087

A590

B5278

B5277

Hampsfield Fell

Cartmel

Cartmel Sands

Duddon Channel

Morecambe Bay

Barrow-in-Furness

Carnforth

M6

Thirlmere

B5289

B5322

A591

A592

A590

A591

B5286

B5285

A5084

0   6 miles

0   9 km

Kendal to Coniston—the Southern Lakes

The ancient town of **Kendal** was one of the most important textile centers in northern England before the Industrial Revolution. Away from the busy main road, you'll discover narrow, winding streets and charming courtyards, many dating from medieval times.

Take a stroll along the River Kent, where—close to the Parish Church—you can visit the 18th-century **Abbott Hall.** Here the **Museum of Lakeland Life and Industry** offers interesting exhibits on blacksmithing, wheelwrighting, farming, weaving, printing, local architecture, and regional customs. ⊠ *Kirkland,* ☏ *01539/722464.* ▣ *£2.50; entrance to other associated museums at Abbott Hall costs an extra £1.* ☉ *Apr.–Oct., daily 10:30–5; Nov.–Mar., daily 10:30–4; various days closed in winter, call for details.*

At the northern end of town the **Kendal Museum** details splendidly the flora and fauna of the Lake District, and also contains displays on Alfred Wainwright, the region's most avid chronicler of countryside matters, who died in 1991. His multivolume Lake District walking guides are famous the world over; you'll see them in every local book and gift shop. ⊠ *Station Rd.,* ☏ *01539/721374.* ▣ *£2.60.* ☉ *Apr.–Oct. daily 10:30–5; Nov.–Mar., daily 10:30–4.*

★ It's an easy road or rail ride northwest to **Windermere**—a natural touring base for the southern half of the Lake District—split between the part of town around the station (known as Windermere) and the prettier lakeside area ½ miles away, called **Bowness-on-Windermere.** A minibus (hourly service), leaving from outside Windermere train station, links the two.

NEED A
BREAK?

At the **Hole in t'Wall** (⊠ Fallbarrow Rd., Bowness), sample traditional Cumbrian ales and tasty pub lunches in authentic 19th-century surroundings. There's a spitting log fire in winter.

Although Windermere's marinas and piers have some charm, you can bypass the busier stretches of shoreline by walking beyond the boathouses, from where there's a fine view across the lake. A ferry crosses the water at this point to reach Far Sawrey and the road to Hawkshead; the crossing takes just a few minutes. ▣ *Cars £1.60, foot passengers 30p.* ☉ *Ferries run every 20 mins Mon.–Sat. 6:50 AM–9:50 PM, Sun. 9:10 AM–9:50 PM; winter until 8:50.*

Three miles northwest from Windermere station on A591, a magnificent lakeside mansion houses the **Lake District National Park Visitor Centre,** which offers a fine range of exhibitions about the Lake District. ⊠ *Ambleside Rd., near Windermere,* ☏ *015394/46601.* ▣ *Free (£2 parking fee each car).* ☉ *Easter–late Oct., daily 10–4.*

Four miles north of Brockhole along A591 at the head of the lake is the town of **Ambleside,** a handsomely sited town, but—as with much of this southern region—one which suffers terribly from tourist overcrowding in high season. However, it's easy enough to escape the crowds. Follow A593 west out of the village and take the turning for the village of **Elterwater,** a popular stop for hikers. The B5343 continues west from here to **Langdale Fell,** where you can attempt one of several excellent walks: There are information boards at the various parking places.

NEED A
BREAK?

After a hard walk, there's no more comforting stop than the hiker's bar of the **Old Dungeon Ghyll Hotel** (⊠ on B5343, west of Elterwater), where the roaring fireplace rapidly dries out wet walking gear.

In case you want to see the world.

At American Express, we're here to make your journey a smooth one. So we have over 1,700 travel service locations in over 120 countries ready to help. What else would you expect from the world's largest travel agency?

do more

http://www.americanexpress.com/travel

Travel

In case you want to be welcomed there.

We're here to see that you're always welcomed at establishments everywhere. That's why millions of people carry the American Express® Card – for peace of mind, confidence, and security, around the world or just around the corner.

do more

Cards

In case you're running low.

We're here to help with more than 118,000 Express Cash locations around the world. In order to enroll, just call American Express before you start your vacation.

do more

Express Cash

And just in case.

We're here with American Express® Travelers Cheques and Cheques *for Two.*® They're the safest way to carry money on your vacation and the surest way to get a refund, practically anywhere, anytime.
Another way we help you...

do more

Travelers Cheques

Continuing north along A591 from Ambleside toward Grasmere (a journey of around 3 miles), you'll come to **Rydal Mount,** where William Wordsworth lived from 1813 until his death 37 years later. The poet and his family moved to these grand surroundings when he was nearing the height of his career, and his descendants still live here, surrounded by his furniture, portraits, and the 4½-acre garden laid out by Wordworth himself. ⊠ *Rydal, Ambleside,* ☎ *015394/33002.* ▨ *£3.* ☉ *Mar.–Oct., daily 9:30–5; Nov.–Feb., Wed.–Mon. 10–4; closed 3 wks. in Jan.*

★ A little further on, just before reaching Grasmere, **Dove Cottage** is the leading literary shrine of the Lake District. This was Wordworth's earlier home, from 1799 until 1808, and the tiny house still contains many personal belongings. Dove Cottage is also headquarters of the **Centre for British Romanticism,** which documents the literary contributions made by Wordsworth and his sister Dorothy, Samuel Taylor Coleridge, Thomas De Quincey, and Robert Southey. ⊠ *The Wordsworth Trust, Dove Cottage, Grasmere LA22 9SH,* ☎ *015394/35544.* ▨ *Dove Cottage and museum: £4.10; museum only £2.25.* ☉ *Mid-Feb.–mid-Jan., daily 9:30–5.30.*

Although Wordsworth was born in Cockermouth, northwest of Keswick, it is the town of **Grasmere** that is most closely associated with him. Grasmere, too, is overwhelmed in summer by tourists and cars, but it is worth exploring the crooked lanes. Wordsworth, his wife Mary, his sister Dorothy, and his daughter Dora are buried in Grasmere churchyard.

☝ Take the minor road out of Grasmere, skirting Rydal Water, and follow the signs south about 8 miles to **Hawkshead,** another enclave of narrow, cobbled streets and little bow-fronted stores. Two miles south of here on B5285 stands **Hill Top,** home of children's author and illustrator Beatrix Potter, most famous for her Peter Rabbit stories. Nearby is an easily reached summit, Orrest Head or Cat Bells, the imaginary home of Mrs. Tiggy-Winkle; the Lake District is an ideal place to introduce children to hiking. ⊠ *Near Sawrey, Ambleside,* ☎ *015394/36269.* ▨ *£3.30.* ☉ *Apr.–Oct., Sat.–Wed. 11–4:30.*

From Hawkshead, continue west along B5285 for about 3 miles until you come to **Coniston,** a small lake resort and boating center, wonderfully sited at the foot of the peak called **The Old Man of Coniston** (2,635 feet). Tracks lead up from the village past an old mine to the peak, which you can reach in about two hours.

★ Just outside Coniston is **Brantwood,** the home of Victorian artist, critic, and social reformer John Ruskin (1819–1900). You can reach it by boat, either taking the Ruskin Ferry (☉ Apr.–Jan., hourly service from Coniston Pier or Waterhead), or the steam yacht *Gondola* (☉ 4–5 trips daily) from Coniston Pier. Here, in the rambling white 18th-century house, you'll find a collection of Ruskin's own paintings, drawings, and books. The extensive grounds were laid out by Ruskin himself. ☎ *015394/41396.* ▨ *House and grounds £3.50; grounds only £1.* ☉ *Mid-Mar.–mid-Nov., daily 11–5:30; mid-Nov.–mid-Mar., Wed.–Sun. 11–4.*

Penrith to Cockermouth—the Northern Lakes

The northern lakeland contains some of the longest and wonderously bleak stretches of the Lake District, but it also contains some fascinating sights. The attractive, red-sandstone-built town of **Penrith** was the capital of the semi-independent kingdom of Cumbria in the 9th and 10th centuries. The evocative remains of the 14th-century redbrick **castle** (▨ Free, ☉ 9–6) are set in a little park across from the train station. To find out more about Penrith's history, stop in at the **Penrith**

Museum on Middlegate. Ask at the museum about the historic "town trail" route, which includes the King Street plague stone, where food was left for the plague-stricken. ✉ *Robinson's School, Middlegate, Penrith,* ☎ *01768/64671, ext. 228.* 🎫 *Free.* ☉ *Mon.–Sat. 10–5, Sun. 1–5; June–Sept., stays open Mon.–Sat. until 7, Sun. until 6; Nov.–Easter, closed Sun.*

Follow A592 southwest along the River Eamont to **Ullswater,** the region's second-largest lake, hemmed in by towering hills. Some of the finest views are from A592 as it sticks to the lake's western shore, through **Glenridding** and Patterdale at the southern end. Here, you're at the foot of **Helvellyn** (3,118 feet), which lies to the west. Arduous footpaths run from the road between Glenridding and Patterdale and pass by **Red Tarn,** at 2,356 feet the highest Lake District tarn.

Aira Force, 5 miles north of Patterdale, is a spectacular series of waterfalls pounding through a wooded ravine to feed into Ullswater. From the parking lot (parking fee charged), it's a 20-minute walk to the falls—bring sturdy shoes in wet weather. Just above Aira Force in the woods of Gowbarrow Park, William Wordsworth and his sister Dorothy were walking on April 15, 1802. Dorothy remarked that she had never seen "daffodils so beautiful." Two years later Wordworth was inspired by his sister's words to write one of the best-known lyric poems in English, "I Wandered Lonely as a Cloud."

Leaving Aira Force, follow A5091 north and when you hit A66, 5 miles farther on, follow the signs west to **Keswick** (pronounced "Kezzick") on the scenic shores of Derwentwater. The great Lakeland mountains of Skiddaw and Blencathra brood over Keswick's gray slate houses and since many of the best hiking routes radiate from the town, it is more of a touring base than a tourist destination. People stroll the congested, narrow streets in boots and hiking trousers, and there are mountaineering shops in addition to hotels, guest houses, pubs, and restaurants.

All the interesting sights lie within easy walking distance of the central streets: Market Place, Main Street, and Lake Road. The town received its market charter in the 13th century, and its Saturday market is still going strong. The handsome 19th-century **Moot Hall** (assembly hall) on Market Place has served as both the Keswick town hall and the local prison. Now it houses the main **tourist information center** for the region.

★ To understand why **Derwentwater** is considered one of England's finest lakes, take a short walk from the town center to the lake shore, and follow the **Friar's Crag** path—about 15 minutes' level walk from the center. This pine-tree-fringed peninsula is a favorite vantage point, with its view over the lake, the surrounding ring of mountains, and many tiny wooded islands. Ahead you will see the crags that line the **Jaws of Borrowdale** and overhang a dramatic mountain ravine—the perfect setting for a Romantic painting or poem. Between late March and November, cruises set off every hour in each direction from a wooden dock at the lake shore.

To explore the area by car, follow B5289 from Keswick along the eastern edge of Derwentwater to **Borrowdale,** heart of the **Borrowdale Valley,** whose varied landscape of green valley floor and surrounding crags has long been considered one of the region's most magnificent spots. Two miles farther south along the main road lies **Seatoller,** behind which rise the vaultingly steep **Borrowdale Fells.** To the south, you can also see England's highest mountain, **Scafell** (pronounced "Scarfell") **Pike** (3,210 ft.).

Beyond Seatoller, B5289 turns westward. It's a superb drive along one of the most dramatic of the region's roads, which is lined with huge boulders and at times channels through soaring rock canyons. The road sweeps down from the pass to the village of Buttermere and then heads on through charming flatland countryside to **Cockermouth,** an attractive little town at the confluence of the Derwent and Cocker rivers. Slightly larger than Keswick, Cockermouth has a maze of narrow streets that's a delight to wander, and a brisk market-town atmosphere. It was the birthplace of William Wordsworth (and his sister Dorothy), whose childhood home, **Wordsworth House,** is a typical 18th-century north-country gentleman's home, now owned by the National Trust. ⊠ *Main St.,* ☎ *01900/824805.* ▣ *£2.50.* ☉ *Apr.–Oct., weekdays 11–5; also open Sat. 11–5, July–Aug.*

Dining and Lodging

For details and price category definitions, *see* Dining *and* Lodging in Staying in Great Britain, *above.*

Ambleside

$$ ★ ✕▥ **Britannia Inn.** The Britannia is a friendly inn in the heart of splendid walking country, with quaint little rooms and hearty homemade English food served in the bar. There's also a very popular four-course table d'hote dinner served nightly (weekends only from November to mid-March). ⊠ *Elterwater LA22 9HP, on B5343, 4 mi west of Ambleside,* ☎ *015394/37210,* ℻ *015394/37311. 13 rooms, 7 with shower. Restaurant, bar. MC, V.*

Grasmere

$$$ ★ ✕▥ **The Swan.** The flower-decked 300-year-old Swan, a former coaching inn just outside Grasmere, was mentioned in Wordsworth's poem "The Waggoner"; Coleridge and Sir Walter Scott were both guests here. Then, as now, the inn's watchword was comfort—a fire in the lounge grate, an oak-beam restaurant serving lakeland specialties, and elegant guest rooms. ⊠ *A591, Grasmere, LA22 9RF,* ☎ *015394/35551,* ℻ *015394/35741. 36 rooms with bath. Restaurant (reservations essential), bar. AE, DC, MC, V.*

Kendal

$–$$ ✕ **The Moon.** The good reputation here has been won with quality homemade dishes on a menu that changes monthly. There's always a strong selection of vegetarian dishes, and the cooking uses Mediterranean and Asian flourishes at times. The Moon is open only for dinner. ⊠ *129 Highgate,* ☎ *01539/729254. MC, V. Closed Dec. 25, Jan. 1, and mid-Jan.–mid-Feb.*

$$$ ▥ **The Woolpack.** The town's best hotel is ideally placed, right on the main street. Formerly a coaching inn, the building dates back to the 17th century, and the public rooms—bar, restaurant, and carvery—retain a whiff of bygone days, with their oak beams and stone walls. ⊠ *Stricklandgate LA9 4ND,* ☎ *01539/723852,* ℻ *01539/728608. 54 rooms with bath. Restaurant, bar. AE, MC, V.*

Keswick

$ ✕ **Four in Hand.** This is a typical Cumbrian pub—once a stagecoach inn on the route between Keswick and Borrowdale—with a 19th-century paneled bar decorated with horse brasses and banknotes. The imaginative touches in its menu include hot asparagus rolled in ham; traditional dishes are steaks, meat pies, and Cumberland sausage. ⊠ *Lake Rd.,* ☎ *017687/72069. No credit cards.*

\$\$\$ ✕🖼 **Keswick Hotel.** Built to serve railroad travelers in the 19th century, the Keswick has all the grandeur and style of that age, although it has been modernized. The room rate includes dinner, as well as breakfast, though you can opt for a stay without dinner if you wish. ⊠ *Station Rd., CA12 4NQ,* ☎ *017687/72020,* 🅵🅰🆇 *017687/71300. 66 rooms with bath. Restaurant, bar, putting green, croquet. AE, DC, MC, V.*

Penrith

\$\$ ✕🖼 **The George.** This rambling coaching inn, in the center of Penrith, has been hosting guests for over 300 years. Either stay overnight in one of the modernized rooms, or just stop in for morning coffee or lunch. The lounges are full of wood paneling, copper and brass fixtures, old paintings, and comfortable chairs; the attractive restaurant serves extremely good-value set meals. ⊠ *Devonshire St., CA11 7SH,* ☎ *01768/862696,* 🅵🅰🆇 *01768/868223. 30 rooms with bath or shower. Restaurant, bar, lobby lounge. MC, V.*

Seatoller

\$\$ ✕ **Yew Tree Restaurant.** One of the best of the Lakes' hidden restau-
★ rants, the Yew Tree, at the foot of Honister Pass, has been converted from two 17th-century cottages. The inventive menu is based largely on local produce and country dishes, including venison, hare, eel, and salmon, are seasonally available. ⊠ *Seatoller, Borrowdale,* ☎ *017687/77634. Reservations essential. MC, V. Closed Mon., and Jan.–mid-Feb.*

Windermere

\$\$ ✕ **Porthole Eating House.** Located in an intimate 18th-century house
★ in the center of Bowness, the small restaurant has an Italian menu featuring homemade pasta and excellent meat and fish dishes. In winter, a large open fire adds to the ambience. The place is only open for dinner. ⊠ *3 Ash St., Bowness-on-Windermere,* ☎ *015394/42793. AE, DC, MC, V. Closed Tues. and mid-Dec.–late Feb.*

\$\$\$\$ ✕🖼 **Miller Howe.** This small, white Edwardian country house hotel is
★ beautifully situated, with views across Windermere to the Langdale Pikes. The bedrooms have exceptional individual style, and fresh and dried flowers are everywhere. The outstanding restaurant serves an imaginative set menu that has been masterminded by John Tovey, renowned for his experimental British cuisine. Note that the room rate includes breakfast and dinner. ⊠ *Rayrigg Rd., Bowness-on-Windermere LA23 1EY,* ☎ *015394/42536,* 🅵🅰🆇 *015394/45664. 13 rooms with bath. Restaurant (reservations essential, jacket and tie). AE, DC, MC, V. Closed Dec.–Feb.*

\$\$ 🖼 **Mortal Man.** This converted 17th-century inn lies in a valley about 3 miles north of Windermere; there are magnificent views all around. Guest rooms are fairly simple, but pleasantly decorated, and there's a relaxing atmosphere to the place, helped along by a log fire crackling away in winter. ⊠ *Troutbeck, LA23 1PL,* ☎ *015394/33193,* 🅵🅰🆇 *015394/31261. 12 rooms with bath. Restaurant, bar. No credit cards. Closed mid-Nov.–mid-Feb.*

EDINBURGH

Scotland and England *are* different—and let no Englishman tell you otherwise. Although the two nations have been united in a single state since 1707, Scotland retains its own marked political and social character, with, for instance, legal and educational systems quite distinct from those of England. And by virtue of its commanding geographic position, on top of a long-dead volcano, and the survival of a large number of outstanding stone buildings carrying echoes of the nation's history, Edinburgh ranks among the world's greatest capital cities.

Getting Around

By Train

Regular fast trains run from London's King's Cross Station to Edinburgh Waverley; the fastest journey time is just over four hours. For information in London, call 0171/278–2477; in Edinburgh, 0131/556–2451 (recorded information lines: weekday service 0131/557–3000; Saturday service 0131/557–2737; Sunday service 0131/557–1616).

By Plane

British Airways operates a shuttle service from London's Heathrow Airport to Edinburgh; reservations are not necessary, and you are guaranteed a seat. Flying time from London is one hour, 15 minutes. For information, call 0181/759–2525 or 0345/222111. **British Midland** also flies from Heathrow (☎ 0181/745–7321 or 0345/554554). **Air UK** flies from Gatwick (☎ 01293/535353) and Stansted (☎ 01279/662816)— both airports are far less crowded than Heathrow, and are as easy to reach by rail. From Edinburgh, call 0345/666777 for Air UK flights to both Gatwick and Stansted. Transatlantic flights direct to Scotland use Glasgow Airport, from which there are regular rail connections to Glasgow city center and on to Edinburgh.

By Bus

Regular services are operated by **National Express** between Victoria Coach Station, London, and St. Andrew's Square bus station, Edinburgh, three times a day. The 405-mile journey takes approximately eight hours.

By Car

London and Edinburgh are 405 miles apart; allow a comfortable nine hours for the drive. The two principal routes to the Scottish border are A1 (mostly a small but divided road) or the eight-lane M1, then M6. From there, the choice is between the four-lane highway A74, which can be unpleasantly busy, followed by A701 or A702, or the slower but much more scenic A7 through Hawick. All the main car-rental agencies have offices in Edinburgh.

Visitor Information

The **Edinburgh and Scotland Information Centre** (3 Princes St., ☎ 0131/557–1700) gives expert advice on what to see and do in Edinburgh and throughout Scotland. Services include information and literature, accommodation reservations, route planning, coach tour tickets, entertainment reservations, a Scottish bookshop, and currency exchange. Visitors can also buy National Trust, Historic Scotland, and Great Britain Heritage passes.

Guided Tours

Both **Lothian Region Transport** (dark red and white buses) and **SMT** (green buses) operate tours in and around the city. For information, call 0131/555–6363 (Lothian) or 0131/313–1515 (SMT). Tickets allowing unlimited travel on city buses for various periods are also available.

The Cadies and **Witchery Tours** (352 Castlehill, 3rd floor, ☎ 0131/225–6745) offer a highly popular murder and mystery tour, and historical and other special-interest tours.

Exploring Edinburgh

The key to understanding Edinburgh is to make the distinction between the Old and New Towns. Until the 18th century, the city was confined to the rocky crag on which its castle stands, straggling between the fortress at one end and the royal residence, the Palace of Holyroodhouse, at the other. In the 18th century, during a civilizing time of expansion known as the "Scottish Enlightenment," the city fathers fostered the construction of another Edinburgh, one a little to the north. This is the mostly residential New Town, whose elegant squares, classical facades, wide streets, and harmonious proportions remain largely intact and lived-in today.

The Royal Mile

Numbers in the margin correspond to points of interest on the Edinburgh map.

★ ❶ **Edinburgh Castle,** the brooding symbol of Scotland's capital and the nation's martial past, dominates the city center. The castle's attractions include the city's oldest building—the 11th-century **St. Margaret's Chapel;** the **Crown Room,** where the Regalia of Scotland are displayed; **Old Parliament Hall;** and **Queen Mary's Apartments,** where Mary, Queen of Scots, gave birth to the future King James VI of Scotland (who later became James I of England). In addition, military features of interest include the **Scottish National War Memorial** and the **Scottish United Services Museum.** ☎ *0131/244–3101.* ⊡ *£5.50.* ☉ *Apr.–Sept., daily 9:30–5:15; Oct.–Mar., daily 9:30–4:15.*

❷ The **Royal Mile,** the backbone of the Old Town, starts immediately below the **Castle Esplanade,** the wide parade ground that hosts the annual Edinburgh Military Tattoo—a grand military display staged during a citywide festival every summer (☞ *below*). The Royal Mile consists of a number of streets, running into each other—**Castlehill, Lawnmarket, High Street,** and **Canongate**—leading downhill to the Palace of Holyroodhouse, home to the Royal Family when they visit Edinburgh. Tackle this walk in leisurely style; the many original Old Town "closes," narrow alleyways enclosed by high tenement buildings, are rewarding to explore and give a real sense of the former life of the city.

❸ In Lawnmarket, the six-story tenement known as **Gladstone's Land** dates from 1620. It has an arcaded front and first-floor entrance typical of the period and is furnished in the style of a merchant's house of the time; there are magnificent painted ceilings. ⊠ *747B Lawnmarket,* ☎ *0131/226–5856.* ⊡ *£2.60.* ☉ *Apr.–Oct., Mon.–Sat. 10–5, Sun. 2–5 (last entrance 4:30).*

❹ Close by is **The Writers' Museum,** housed in Lady Stair's House, a town dwelling of 1622 that recalls Scotland's literary heritage with exhibits on Sir Walter Scott, Robert Louis Stevenson, and Robert Burns. ⊠ *Lady Stair's Close, Lawnmarket,* ☎ *0131/225–2424, ext. 4901.* ⊡ *Free.* ☉ *June–Sept., Mon.–Sat. 10–6; Oct.–May, Mon.–Sat. 10–5, Sun. 2–5 during the festival.*

A heart shape set in the cobbles of the High Street marks the site of the
❺ **Tolbooth,** the center of city life until it was demolished in 1817. Nearby
❻ stands the **High Kirk of St. Giles,** Edinburgh's cathedral; parts of the church date from the 12th century, the choir from the 15th. ⊠ *High St.* ⊡ *Free.* ☉ *Mon.–Sat. 9–5 (7 in summer), Sun. 2–5 and for services.*

NEED A BREAK?	At the **Internet Café,** located on Coburn Street around the corner from St. Giles, sip a traditional cup of tea while plugging into tomorrow at one of the computers offered for customers' use.

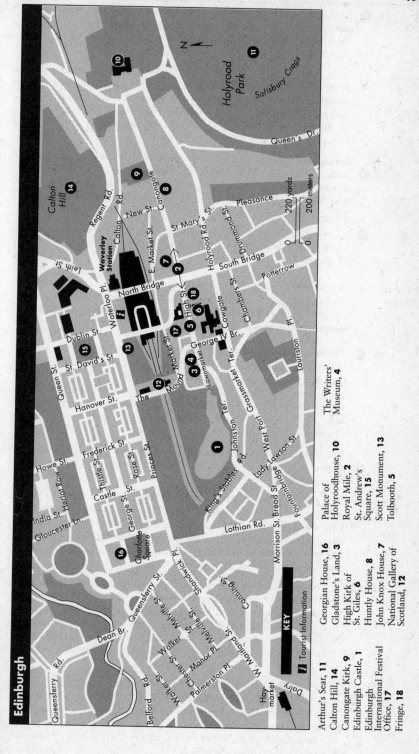

Edinburgh

KEY

i Tourist Information

Arthur's Seat, **11**
Calton Hill, **14**
Canongate Kirk, **9**
Edinburgh Castle, **1**
Edinburgh
International Festival
Office, **17**
Fringe, **18**

Georgian House, **16**
Gladstone's Land, **3**
High Kirk of
St. Giles, **6**
Huntly House, **8**
John Knox House, **7**
National Gallery of
Scotland, **12**

Palace of
Holyroodhouse, **10**
Royal Mile, **2**
St. Andrew's
Square, **15**
Scott Monument, **13**
Tolbooth, **5**

The Writers'
Museum, **4**

❼ Farther down High Street you'll see **John Knox House.** Its traditional connections with Scotland's celebrated religious reformer are tenuous, but it gives a flavor of life in the Old Town during Knox's time. ✉ *45 High St.,* ☎ *0131/556–2647.* 🎟 *£1.75.* ☉ *Mon.–Sat. 10–5.*

Next door is the ☾ **Netherbow Arts Centre** (phone and opening hours as for John Knox House), with a theater, an art gallery, and a café. Opposite the Centre is the **Museum of Childhood,** a celebration of toys that even adults may well enjoy. ✉ *42 High St.,* ☎ *0131/225–2424.* 🎟 *Free.* ☉ *June–Sept., Mon.–Sat. 10–6, Sun. during festival 2–5; Oct.–May, Mon.–Sat. 10–5.*

❽ **Canongate** was formerly an independent burgh, or trading community, outside the city walls of Edinburgh. **Huntly House,** built in 1570, is a museum featuring Edinburgh history and social life. ✉ *142 Canongate,* ☎ *0131/225–2424, ext. 4143.* 🎟 *Free.* ☉ *June–Sept., Mon.–Sat. 10–6; Oct.–May, Mon.–Sat. 10–5, Sun. 2–5 during the festival.*

❾ Some notable Scots are buried in the graveyard of the **Canongate Kirk** nearby, including the economist Adam Smith and the poet Robert Fergusson.

NEED A BREAK?	Two places that serve a good cup of tea and a sticky cake (a notable Scottish indulgence) are **The Elephant Cafe** on George the Fourth Bridge, complete with fabulous views of the Castle, and the **Abbey Strand Tearoom,** near the palace gates.

★ **❿** The **Palace of Holyroodhouse,** still the Royal Family's official residence in Scotland, was founded by King James IV at the end of the 15th century and was extensively remodeled by Charles II in 1671. The state apartments, with their collections of tapestries and paintings, can be visited. ☎ *0131/556–7371.* 🎟 *£5.* ☉ *Apr.–Oct., Mon.–Sat. 9:30–5:15, Sun. 10:30–4:30; Nov.–Mar., Mon.–Sat. 9:30–3:45, Sun. 10–3:45; closed during royal and state visits.*

⓫ The open grounds of **Holyrood Park** enclose Edinburgh's distinctive, originally volcanic minimountain, **Arthur's Seat,** with steep slopes and miniature crags.

In 1767, the competition to design the New Town was won by a young and unknown architect, James Craig. His plan was for a grid of three east–west streets, balanced at each end by a grand square. The plan survives today, despite all commercial pressures. Princes, George, and Queen streets are the main thoroughfares, with St. Andrew Square at one end and Charlotte Square at the other.

★ **⓬** The **National Gallery of Scotland,** on the Mound, the street that joins the Old and New Towns, contains works by the old masters and the French Impressionists and has a good selection of Scottish paintings. This is one of Britain's best national galleries, and is small enough to be taken in easily on one visit. ☎ *0131/556–8921.* 🎟 *Free; charge for special exhibitions.* ☉ *Mon.–Sat. 10–5, Sun. 2–5. Print Room, weekdays 10–noon and 2–4 by arrangement.*

⓭ To the east along Princes Street is the unmistakable soaring Gothic spire of the 200-foot-high **Scott Monument,** built in the 1840s to commemorate the celebrated novelist of Scots history. There is a statue of Sir Walter and his dog within. The views from the top are well worth the 287-step climb. ☎ *0131/549–4143.* 🎟 *£1.* ☉ *Apr.–Sept., Mon.–Sat. 9–6; Oct.–Mar., Mon.–Sat. 9–3.*

★ **⓮** There are more splendid views from **Calton Hill:** north across the Firth (or estuary) of Forth to the Lomond Hills of Fife and to the Pentland

Hills that enfold the city from the south. Among the various monuments on Calton Hill are a partial reproduction of the **Parthenon,** in Athens, begun in 1824 but left incomplete because the money ran out; the **Nelson Monument;** and the **Royal Observatory.**

15 Make your way to **St. Andrew's Square,** then along George Street, where there is a wide choice of shops, and on to **Charlotte Square,** whose north side was designed by the great Scottish neoclassical architect Robert **16** Adam. The rooms of the elegant **Georgian House** are furnished to show the domestic arrangements of a prosperous late-18th-century Edinburgh family. ⊠ *7 Charlotte Sq.,* ☎ *0131/225–2160.* 🖼 *£3.* ☉ *Apr.–Oct., Mon.–Sat. 10–5, Sun. 2–5 (last admission 4:30).*

NEED A BREAK?	**Bianco's,** in Hope Street, close to the Georgian House, is good for coffee and croissants.

Finally, a word about the **Edinburgh International Festival,** the celebration of music, dance, and drama that the city stages each summer (the 1997 dates are Aug. 10–30), featuring international artists of the highest caliber. The **Festival Fringe,** the unruly child of the official festival, spills out of halls and theaters all over town, offering visitors a cornucopia of theatrical and musical events of all kinds—some so weird that they defy description. Although the official festival is the place to see top-flight performances by established artists, at a Fringe event you might catch a new star, or a new art form, or a controversial new play. Advance information, programs, and ticket sales for the **17** festival are available from the **Edinburgh International Festival Office 18** (21 Market St., ☎ 0131/226–4001), and for the **Fringe** from its office (180 High St., ☎ 0131/226–5257 or 5259).

Dining

For details and price-category definitions, *see* Dining *in* Staying in Great Britain, *above.*

$$$$ ✕ **Le Pompadour.** The decor in this Caledonian Hotel restaurant is inspired by the France of Louis XV, with ornate gilts and reds prevailing. A sophisticated French menu is accented with Scottish delicacies. The Caledonian has a second, just refurbished and less pricey restaurant, **Carriages,** which offers a Scottish menu. ⊠ *Caledonian Hotel, Princes St.,* ☎ *0131/459–9988. Reservations essential. Jacket and tie. AE, DC, MC, V.*

$$$ ✕ **Jackson's Restaurant.** Intimate and candlelit in a historic Old Town close halfway down the Royal Mile, Jackson's offers good Scots fare. Aberdeen Angus steaks and Border lamb are excellent; there are vegetarian and seafood specialties, too. ⊠ *2 Jackson Close, 209–213 High St.,* ☎ *0131/225–1793. Reservations essential. AE, MC, V. No lunch weekends.*

$$$ ✕ **Martin's.** This very small spot is good for imaginative vegetarian dishes, game, and fresh seafood. Try the succulent halibut with leeks and carrot-and-basil coulis, or the breasts of mallard and pigeon with red cabbage and raisins. There's a good-value set-price lunch. ⊠ *70 Rose St., North La. (between Castle and Frederick Sts.),* ☎ *0131/225–3106. Reservations essential. Jacket and tie. AE, DC, MC, V. No lunch Sat. Closed Sun., Mon.*

$$ ✕ **Howie's.** Howie's is a simple, neighborhood bistro, unlicensed, so you have to bring your own bottle. The steaks are tender Aberdeen beef, the Loch Fyne herring are sweet-cured to Howie's own recipe, and the clientele's lively. ⊠ *75 St. Leonard's St.,* ☎ *0131/668–2917, and 63 Dalry Rd., Edinburgh,* ☎ *0131/313–3334. MC, V. No lunch Mon.*

$ ✕ **Pierre Victoire.** An Edinburgh success story with five in-town branches and franchises as far as London and Bristol, this bistro chain serves tasty unpretentious French cuisine in excellent set menus, with especially good value at lunch. ✉ *38 Grassmarket,* ☎ *0131/226–2442; 10 Victoria St.,* ☎ *0131/225–1721 (closed Sun.); 8 Union St.,* ☎ *0131/557–8451 (closed Mon.); 17 Queensferry Street,* ☎ *0131/225–1890; 5 Dock Pl., Leith,* ☎ *0131/556–6178 (closed Sun.) MC, V.*

Lodging

For details and price-category definitions, *see* Lodging *in* Staying in Great Britain, *above.*

$$$$ 🏨 **Caledonian Hotel.** Popularly known as "the Caley," this hotel echoes the days of the traditional great railway hotel, though its neighbor station has long since been demolished. The imposing Victorian decor has been lovingly preserved and embellished. There are also two excellent restaurants (☞ *Le Pompadour, above*). ✉ *Princes St. EH1 2AB,* ☎ *0131/459–9988,* ℻ *0131/225–6632. 239 rooms with bath. Two restaurants. AE, DC, MC, V.*

$$$$ 🏨 **George Hotel.** This imposing and extensively refurbished 18th-century building in the heart of the New Town retains some elegant Georgian features in its public areas, while the bedrooms are up-to-date and moderately luxurious. Though busy, the staff takes time to be helpful. ✉ *19 George St., EH2 2PB,* ☎ *0131/225–1251,* ℻ *0131/226–5644. 195 rooms with bath. Two restaurants, bar. AE, DC, MC, V.*

$$$ 🏨 **Mount Royal Hotel.** This modern hotel is ideally located for sightseeing and shopping. The front rooms have views of the castle. It has a friendly staff. ✉ *53 Princes St., EH2 2DG,* ☎ *0131/225–7161,* ℻ *0131/220–4671. 156 rooms with bath. AE, DC, MC, V.*

$$ 🏨 **Brunswick Hotel.** This totally no-smoking bed-and-breakfast, close to the city center and near the Playhouse Theatre, prides itself on its fine Georgian building. Two of the guest rooms have four-posters. ✉ *7 Brunswick St., EH7 5JB,* ☎ ℻ *0131/556–1238. 10 rooms with shower. AE, MC, V.*

$$ 🏨 **Dorstan Private Hotel.** A Victorian villa in a quiet area, the Dorstan has been lately refurbished providing smart, cottage-style bedrooms. ✉ *7 Priestfield Rd., EH16 5HJ,* ☎ *0131/667–6721,* ℻ *0131/668–4644. 14 rooms, 9 with bath or shower. MC, V.*

13 Greece

Athens

The Northern Peloponnese

Mainland Greece

The Aegean Islands

IN GREECE, YOU CANNOT TRAVEL FAR ACROSS THE LAND without meeting the sea or far across the sea without meeting one of its roughly 2,000 islands. About the size of New York State, Greece has 15,019 kilometers (9,312 miles) of coastline, more than any other country of its size. The sea is everywhere, not on three sides only but at every turn, reaching through the shoreline like a probing hand. The land itself is stunning, dotted with cypress groves, vineyards, and olive trees, carved into gentle bays or dramatic coves with startling white sand, rolling hills, and rugged mountain ranges that plunge into the sea. This natural beauty and the sharp, clear light of sun and sea, combined with plentiful archaeological treasures, make Greece one of the world's most inviting countries.

Poetry, music, architecture, politics, medicine, law—all had their Western birth here in Greece centuries ago. Among the great mountains of mainland Greece are the cloud-capped peak of Mt. Olympus, fabled home of the Greek gods, and Mt. Parnassus, favorite haunt of the sungod Apollo and the nine Muses, goddesses of poetry and science. Romantic and beautiful remains of the ancient past—the Acropolis and the Parthenon, the temples of Delphi, the Tombs of the Kings in Mycenae—and a later procession of Byzantine churches, Crusader castles and fortresses, and Turkish mosques are spread throughout the country.

Of the hundreds of islands and islets scattered across the Aegean Sea in the east and the Ionian Sea in the west, fewer than 250 are still inhabited. This world of the farmer, fisherman, and seafarer has largely been replaced by the world of the tourist. More than 10 million vacationers visit Greece each year, almost as many as the entire native population; in fact, tourism has overtaken shipping as the most important element in the nation's economy. Once-idyllic beaches have become overcrowded and noisy, and fishing harbors have become flotilla-sailing centers. On some of the islands, the impact of the annual influx of visitors has meant the building of a new Greece, more or less in their image. But traditional Greece survives: Pubs and bars stand next door to *ouzeri, kfeneia* are as popular as discos, and pizza and hamburger joints must compete with tavernas.

Although mass tourism has transformed the main centers, it is still possible to strike out and find your own place among the smaller islands and the miles of beautiful mainland coastline. Except for some difficulty in finding accommodations (Greek families on vacation tend to fill the hotels in out-of-the-way places during high summer), this is the ideal way to see traditional Greece. Those who come only to worship the classical Greeks and gaze at their temples, seeing nothing but the glory that was, miss today's Greece. If you explore this fascinating country with open eyes, you'll enjoy it in all its forms: its slumbering cafés and buzzing tavernas; its elaborate religious rituals; its stark, bright beauty; and the generosity, curiosity, and kindness of its people.

ESSENTIAL INFORMATION

Before You Go

When to Go

Although the tourist season runs from May through October, the heat can be unpleasant in July and August, particularly in Athens. On the islands, a brisk northwesterly wind, the *meltemi,* can make life more comfortable. Less crowded months are May, June, and September. The winter months tend to be damp and cold virtually everywhere.

The following are the average daily maximum and minimum temperatures for Athens.

Jan.	55F	13C	May	77F	25C	Sept.	84F	29C
	44	6		61	16		67	19
Feb.	57F	14C	June	86F	30C	Oct.	75F	24C
	44	6		68	20		60	16
Mar.	60F	16C	July	92F	33C	Nov.	66F	19C
	46	8		73	23		53	12
Apr.	68F	20C	Aug.	92F	33C	Dec.	58F	15C
	52	11		73	23		47	8

Currency

The Greek monetary unit is the drachma (dr.). Banknotes are in denominations of 50, 100, 500, 1,000, 5,000, and 10,000 dr.; coins, 5, 10, 20, 50, and 100. At press time (spring 1996), there were approximately 234 dr. to the U.S. dollar, 361 dr. to the pound sterling, and 170 dr. to the Canadian dollar. Daily exchange rates are prominently displayed in banks.

What It Will Cost

Inflation in Greece is rather high—just under 10% a year—and fluctuations in currency make it impossible to do accurate budgeting long in advance, so watch the exchange rates. On the whole, Greece offers good value compared with many other European countries.

There are few regional price differences for hotels and restaurants. A modest hotel in a small town will charge only slightly lower rates than a modest hotel in Athens, with the same range of amenities. The same is true of restaurants. The spread of tourism has made the range of hotels and restaurants on Rhodes, Corfu, and Crete as affordable as many other islands. Car rentals are expensive in Greece, but taxis are inexpensive even for long-distance runs.

SAMPLE PRICES

At a central-city café, you can expect to pay about 500 dr. for a cup of coffee, 400 to 800 dr. for a bottle of beer, 400 dr. for a soft drink, and around 500 dr. for a grilled cheese sandwich. A 1½-kilometer (1-mile) taxi ride costs about 300 dr.

Customs on Arrival

You may take in one carton of cigarettes or cigars or ¼ pound of smoking tobacco; 1 liter of alcohol, or 2 liters of wine; and gifts up to a total value of 51,000 dr. There's no duty on articles for personal use. The only restrictions applicable to tourists from European Union (EU) countries are those for cigarettes, cigars, and tobacco. Foreign bank notes amounting to more than $2,500 must be declared for re-export. There are no restrictions on traveler's checks. Foreign visitors may take in 100,000 dr. in Greek currency and export up to 40,000 dr.

Language

English is widely spoken in hotels and elsewhere, especially by young people, and even in out-of-the-way places someone is always happy to lend a helping hand.

In this guide, names are given in the Roman alphabet according to the Greek pronunciation except when there is a familiar English form, such as "Athens."

FORMER YUGOSLAV
REPUBLIC OF
MACEDONIA

BULGARIA

ALBANIA

Sidirókastro
Séres
Philippi
Stavroupoli
Eleftheroupoli
Amfipoli
Ka

Kilkis

Edessa
Florina
Gianitsa
Alexandria
Veria
Thessaloniki
Thérmi
E90
Nea
Apolonia
Polygyros
Ormylia
Vatope
Ivi
Dafni
Athos

Kastoria
Ptolemaïda
Kozani
Siatista
Grevena
Katerini
Gulf of
Thermaikos
Kalithea
Palioúri

Gulf of Kassandra

Mount
Olympus

Konitsa
Delvinakio
Metsovo
Elassona
Kalambaka
Tirnavos
Agia
Ioanina
Trikala
Larissa
Karditsa
Volos
Stavros
Farsala
Almiros
Skiathos

Kerkira
Corfu

Igoumenitsa
Paramythia
Arta
Aliki
Karpenissi
Lamia
Skopelos
Skyros

S P O R A D

Parga

Preveza

N

Lefkas
Vassiliki

Agrinio
Orhomenos
E75
EVIA
Kymi

Kephalonia
Ithaki
E55
Nafpaktos
Itea
Delphi
Livadia
Halkida

Lixouri
Sami
Messolongi
Patras
Galaxidi
Thebes
Rafina

Gulf of Corinth
Diakofto
Megara
Piraeus
Athens

Killini
Loutra
Amalias
Corinth
Nemea
Aegina
Glyfada
Voula
Lavrio

Zakynthos
Pyrgos
Olympia
Argos
Nauplion
Poros
Sounio

Zakynthos
Kaiafas
Andritsena
Tripoli
Toló
Ermioni
Ydra
Kythnos

Kyparissia
PELOPONNESE
Spetses

Gargaliani
Messini
Sparta
Leonidio
Serife

Ionian Sea

Pilos
Kalamata
Mystras
Geraki
Kyparissi
Mirtoan
Sea

Methoni
Koroni
Skala
Gythio
Monemvassia
Milc

Areopoli

Agia Pelagia

Kythira
Kythira

Mediterranean Sea

Hania

0 ——— 100 miles
0 ——— 150 km

CRET

Black Sea

THRACE

Kastanies

Didymotiho

Xanthi

Avdira

Makri

Alexandroupoli

Thassos

Samothrace

Limnos

TURKEY

Istanbul

Sea of
Marmara

Troy

Lesvos

Mytilini

Plomari

TURKEY

Aegean Sea

Hios

Mesta

Pirgi

Hios

Izmir (Smyrna)

Ephesus

Andros

Andros

Tinos

Ikaria

Samos

Samos

rmoupoli

Tinos

Agios
Kirykos

Pythagorio

Syros

Mykonos

Delos

Patmos

Paros

Naxos

Leros

Bodrum
(Halicarnassus)

CYCLADES

Amorgos

Kos

Kos

Ios

Astypalea

Nissyros

Symi

Oia

Fira

Tilos

Kameiros

Rhodes

Santorini

Anafi

DODECANESE

Halki

Rhodes

Lindos

Sea of Crete

Karpathos

Heraklion

Mallia

Knossos

Siteia

Kassos

Ayios Nikolaos

Phaestos

Ierapetra

Getting Around

By Car
ROAD CONDITIONS
Driving in cities is not recommended unless you have iron nerves. Red traffic lights are frequently ignored; motorists pass on hills and while rounding corners. For the ratio of collisions to the number of cars on the road, Greece has one of the worst records in Europe. This is due, in part, to varied road conditions. Motorways tend to be good; tolls run between 200 dr. and 1,200 dr. and are charged according to distance. Many country roads are narrow but free of traffic.

RULES OF THE ROAD
Unless you are a citizen of an EU country, you must have an international driver's license. The **Automobile and Touring Club of Greece**, known as ELPA (☞ Breakdowns, *below*), no longer issues these, so non-EU members should arrange for a license through their local automobile association before leaving home. ELPA can help with tourist information for drivers (call ☎ 174). Driving is on the right, and although the vehicle on the right has the right-of-way, don't expect this or any other driving rule to be obeyed. The speed limit is 120 kph (74 mph) on the National Road, 90 kph (54 mph) outside built-up areas, and 50 kph (31 mph) in town. Seat belts are compulsory, as are helmets for motorcyclists, though many natives ignore the laws. In downtown Athens do not drive in the bus lanes marked by a yellow divider.

PARKING
In Greece's half-dozen large cities, parking is hard to find. In Athens or Thessaloniki, you can pay to use one of the temporary parking areas set up in vacant lots, but it's better to leave your car in the hotel garage and walk or take a cab. Elsewhere, parking is easy.

GASOLINE
At press time gas cost about 182 dr.–201 dr. a liter. Gas pumps and service stations are everywhere, and lead-free gas is widely available. Be aware that many stations close at 7 PM.

BREAKDOWNS
The **Automobile and Touring Club of Greece** (ELPA, ⊠ Athens Tower, Messoghion 2–4, Athens, ☎ 01/748–8800; in an emergency, ☎ 104) assists tourists with breakdowns free of charge if they belong to AAA or to ELPA (19,700 dr. per year); otherwise, there is a charge.

By Motorcycle and Bicycle
Dune buggies, bicycles, mopeds, and motorcycles can be rented on the islands. Use extreme caution. Helmets, technically compulsory for motorcyclists, are not usually available, and injuries are common.

By Train
Few tourists use the trains because they are slow and railway networks are limited. The main line runs north from Athens to the former Yugoslavia. It divides into three lines at Thessaloniki. The main line continues on to Belgrade, a second line goes east to the Turkish border and Istanbul, and a third line heads northeast to Bulgaria. The Peloponnese in the south is served by a narrow-gauge line dividing at Corinth into the Mycenae–Argos section and the Patras–Olympia–Kalamata section. For information, call 01/524–0601.

By Plane
Olympic Airways (⊠ Syngrou 96, Athens, ☎ 01/966–6666) has service between Athens and several cities and islands. Thessaloniki is also linked to the main islands, and there are several interisland con-

nections. Reservations can be made by telephone daily from 7:30 AM to 9:30 PM. For information on arrivals and departures for Olympic Airways flights (West Terminal), call 01/936–3363 through 01/936–3366; for other carriers (East Terminal), call 01/969–4466 or 01/969–4467. In summer, call for information on American-based charters at 01/969–4686; 01/969–4240 for other charters.

By Bus

Travel by bus is inexpensive, usually comfortable, and relatively fast. The journey from Athens to Thessaloniki takes the same time as the slow train, though the express covers the distance 1¼ hours faster. In the Peloponnese, however, buses are much faster than trains. Bus information and timetables are available at tourist information offices. Make reservations at least one day before your planned trip, earlier for holiday weekends. Railway-operated buses leave from the Peloponnisos railway station in Athens. All other buses leave from one of two bus stations: Liossion 260, for central and eastern Greece and Evia; Kifissou 100, for the Peloponnese and northwestern Greece.

By Boat

There are frequent car ferries and hydrofoils from Piraeus, the port of Athens, to the central and southern Aegean islands and Crete. Nearby islands are also served by hydrofoils and ferries from Rafina, east of Athens. Ships to the Ionian islands sail from ports nearer to them, such as Patras. Travel agents and shipping offices in Athens and Piraeus and in the main towns on the islands have details. Buy your tickets two or three days in advance, especially if you are traveling in summer or taking a car. Reserve your return journey or continuation soon after you arrive. Timetables change frequently, and boats may be delayed by weather conditions, so your plans should be flexible.

Staying in Greece

Telephones

LOCAL CALLS

Many curbside kiosks have pay telephones for local calls only. You pay the kiosk owner 20 dr. per call after you've finished. It's easier, though, to buy a phone card from the Telecommunications Office (OTE), kiosks, or convenience shops and use it at the now-ubiquitous card phones. If you're calling within Greece, the price is reduced by 30% weekdays 3 PM–5 PM and 10 PM–9 AM, and on weekends from 3 PM Saturday to 9 AM Monday.

INTERNATIONAL CALLS

Although you can buy phone cards with up to 10,000 dr. credit, if you plan to make and pay for several international phone calls, go to an OTE office for more convenience and privacy. There are several branches in Athens. There is a three-minute minimum charge for operator-assisted station-to-station calls, a four-minute minimum for person-to-person connections. For an **AT&T** long-distance operator, dial 00/800–1311; **MCI**, 00/800–1211; **Sprint**, 00/800–1411.

OPERATORS AND INFORMATION

There are English-speaking operators on the International Exchange. Dial 161 or 162. It may take up to an hour to place an international collect call.

COUNTRY CODE

The country code for Greece is 30.

Mail

POSTAL RATES

Airmail letters and postcards for delivery within Europe cost 120 dr. for 20 grams and 200 dr. for 50 grams; for outside Europe, 150 dr. for 20 grams and 240 dr. for 50 grams. For parcels, you must bring whatever you are mailing with your wrapping materials to the post office so it can be inspected. In Athens, parcels that weigh more than two kilograms must be brought to the station at Mitropoleos 60 or to the Spiromiliou arcade off Voukourestiou Street.

RECEIVING MAIL

Except for the main offices at **Aeolou 100** and on **Syntagma Square** (⊙ Weekdays 7:30 AM–8 PM, Sat. 7:30–2, Sun. 9–1:30), most post offices are open weekdays 8–2. You can have your mail addressed to "poste restante" and sent to Aeolou 100, Athens 10200 (take your passport when you pick up your mail), or to American Express (⊠ Ermou 2, Athens, 10225). Holders of American Express cards or traveler's checks pay nothing for the service; others pay 400 dr. for each pickup.

Shopping

Prices quoted in shops include the value-added tax (VAT). There are no VAT refunds. Prices in large stores are fixed. Bargaining may take place in small, owner-managed souvenir and handicrafts shops and in antiques shops. In flea markets, bargaining is expected.

EXPORT PERMITS

Antiques and Byzantine icons require an export permit (not normally given if the piece is of any value), but replicas can be bought fairly cheaply, although even these require a certificate stating they are copies.

Opening and Closing Times

Office and shopping hours vary considerably. Check with your hotel for up-to-the-minute information on opening and closing times.

Banks are open weekdays 8–2, except Friday, when they close at 1:30; they are closed weekends and public holidays. ATM machines are becoming more numerous in most cities.

Museums and archaeological sites are open 8:30–3, with longer summer hours. Many museums are closed on Monday. Admission is free on Sunday from mid-November to March. EU students enjoy free admission, students from other countries pay half the fee, and senior citizens often get a discount. Hours vary; check with tourist offices or travel agencies before visiting.

Shops are usually open Tuesday, Thursday, and Friday 9–2 and 5:30–8; Monday, Wednesday, and Saturday 9–2. Supermarkets are open Monday–Saturday 8–8.

National Holidays

January 1; January 6 (Epiphany); March 10 (Clean Monday); March 25 (Independence Day); April 25 (Good Friday); April 27 (Greek Easter Sunday); April 28 (Greek Easter Monday); May 1 (Labor Day); June 15 (Pentecost); August 15 (Assumption); October 28 (Ochi Day); December 25–26.

Dining

The principal elements of Greek cuisine are such fresh vegetables as eggplants, tomatoes, and olives, inventively combined with lots of olive oil and seasoned with lemon juice, garlic, and oregano. Meat dishes are limited (pork, lamb, and chicken being the most common); fish is often the better, though more expensive choice, particularly on the coast. Your best bet is to look for tavernas and *estiatoria* (restaurants) and choose the one frequented by the most Greeks. The estiatorio serves oven-baked dishes called *magirefta*, precooked and served at room temperature; tavernas offer similar fare plus grilled meats and fish. Another alternative is an *ouzeri* or *mezedopolion*, where you order plates of appetizers instead of an entrée. The decor of these establishments may range from simple to sophisticated, with prices to match.

Traditional fast food in Greece consists of the gyro (slices of grilled lamb with tomato and onions in pita bread), souvlakia (shish kebab), and pastries filled with a variety of stuffings (spinach, cheese, or meat)—but hamburgers and pizzas are found everywhere.

MEALTIMES

Lunch in Greek restaurants is served from 12:30 until 3. Dinner begins at about 9 and is served until 1 in Athens and until midnight outside Athens.

PRECAUTIONS

Tap water is safe to drink everywhere, but it is often heavily chlorinated. Bottled mineral water (Loutraki, for example) is widely available.

WHAT TO WEAR

Throughout the Greek islands you can dress informally for dinner, even at expensive restaurants; in Athens, jackets are appropriate at the top-price restaurants.

RATINGS

Prices are per person and include a first course, main course, dessert, VAT, and the 16% service charge. They do not include drinks or tip.

ATHENS/CATEGORY	THESSALONIKI	OTHER AREAS
$$$$	over 11,000 dr.	over 8,000 dr.
$$$	7,000 dr.–11,000 dr.	6,000 dr.–8,000 dr.
$$	4,000 dr.–7,000 dr.	3,000 dr.–6,000 dr.
$	under 4,000 dr.	under 3,500 dr.

Lodging

Most accommodations are in standard hotels, sometimes called motels. There are a number of "village" complexes, especially at the beaches and as part of some hotels. On islands and at beach resorts, large hotels are complemented by family-run pensions and guest houses—usually clean, bright, and recently built—and self-catering apartment and bungalow complexes. In a very few places, there are state-organized "traditional settlements"—houses with guest accommodations in buildings that are representative of the local architecture.

Greek hotels are classified by the government as Luxury (L) and A–E. Within each category, quality varies greatly, but prices usually don't. Still, you may come across an A-class hotel that charges less than a B-class, depending on facilities. In this guide, hotels are classified according to price. All $$$$ and $$$ hotels are assumed to have air-conditioning, so listings in these categories mention only when it is absent. If a $$ or $ hotel is air-conditioned, this is indicated. All have been built or completely renovated during the past 20 years, and, unless indicated, all have private baths.

Prices quoted by hotels usually include service, local taxes, and VAT; many include breakfast. At certain times, you can negotiate the price, sometimes by eliminating breakfast. The official price should be posted on the back of the door or inside a closet. Booking a room through a travel agency may reduce the price substantially. Seaside hotels, especially those in the $$$$ and $$$ categories, frequently insist that guests take half board (lunch or dinner included in the price).

RATINGS

Prices quoted are for a double room in high season, including taxes and service, but not breakfast unless noted.

CATEGORY	COST
$$$$	over 40,000 dr.
$$$	23,000 dr.–40,000 dr.
$$	15,000 dr.–23,000 dr.
$	under 15,000 dr.

Tipping

In restaurants, cafés, and tavernas, leave a tip of around 10%. In hotels, tip porters 100 dr. per bag for carrying your luggage—more in a top hotel. For taxi drivers, Greeks usually round off the fare. Hairdressers usually get 10% or slightly more. In legitimate theaters, tip ushers 100 dr. if you are shown to your seat. In movie theaters, tip about 50 dr. if you receive a program from the usher. On cruises, cabin and dining-room stewards get about 500 dr. per day; guides receive about the same.

ATHENS

Arriving and Departing

By Plane

Most visitors arrive by air at **Ellinikon Airport,** about 10 kilometers (6 miles) from the city center. All Olympic Airways flights, international and domestic, use the West Terminal. All other flights arrive and depart from the East Terminal on the opposite side of the airport.

BETWEEN THE AIRPORT AND DOWNTOWN

A bus service connects the two air terminals, Syntagma Square, Omonia Square, and Piraeus. Between the terminals and Athens, the express bus (No. 91) runs every 35 minutes 7 AM–12:30 AM. You can catch the bus to the airport on Syntagma Square in front of the Bank of Macedonia-Thrace or off Omonia Square on Stadiou. From the terminals to Karaiskaki Square in Piraeus, the express bus (No. 19) runs hourly 7 AM–11:10 PM. The night express buses for both lines run irregularly; ask for a schedule from a Greek National Tourist Organization office (☞ Important Addresses and Numbers, *below*).The fare is 160 dr., 200 dr. after 11:30 PM. It's easier to take taxis: about 1,800 dr. to Piraeus; 1,000 dr. between terminals; 1,600 dr. to the center. The price goes up by about two-thirds between midnight and 5 AM.

By Train

Athens has two railway stations, side by side, not far from Omonia Square. International trains from the north arrive at, and depart from, **Stathmos Larissis** (☎ 01/823–7741). Take Trolley 1 from the terminal to Omonia Square. Trains from the Peloponnese use the marvelously ornate and old-fashioned **Stathmos Peloponnisos** (☎ 01/513–1601) next door. To Omonia and Syntagma squares, take Bus 57. Since the phones are almost always busy and agents often don't speak English, it's easier to get information and buy tickets at a railway office downtown (✉ Sina 6, ☎ 01/362–4402 through 01/362–4406; ✉ Filellinon 17, ☎ 01/323–6747 and 01/323–6273; or ✉ Karolou 1, ☎ 01/524–0646 through 01/524–0648).

By Bus

Greek buses arrive either at **Terminal A** (✉ 100 Kifissou, ☎ 01/512–4910) or **Terminal B** (✉ Liossion 260, ☎ 01/831–7153). From Terminal A, take Bus 51 to Omonia Square; from Terminal B, take Bus 24 downtown. To get to the stations, catch Bus 51 at Zinonos and Menandrou off Omonia Square and Bus 24 on Amalias Avenue in front of the National Gardens. International buses drop their passengers off on the street, usually in the Omonia or Syntagma Square areas or at Stathmos Peleponnisos.

By Car

Whether you approach Athens from the Peloponnese or from the north, you enter by the National Road (as the main highways going north and south are known) and then follow signs for the center. Leaving Athens, routes to the National Road are well marked; signs usually name Lamia for the north and Corinth or Patras for the southwest.

By Ship

Except for cruise ships, few passenger ships from other countries call at Piraeus, the port of Athens, 10 kilometers (6 miles) from Athens's center. If you do dock at the main port in Piraeus, you can take the nearby metro right into Omonia Square. The trip takes 20 minutes and costs 100 dr. Alternatively, you can take a taxi, which may well take longer because of traffic and will cost around 1,300 dr. If you arrive by hydrofoil in the smaller port of Zea Marina, take Bus 905 or Trolley 20 to the metro.

Getting Around

Many of the sights and most of the hotels, cafés, and restaurants are within a fairly small central area. It's easy to walk everywhere.

By Metro

An electric (partially underground) railway runs from Piraeus to Omonia Square and then on to Kifissia. It is not useful for getting around the central area. The standard fare is 75 dr. or 100 dr., depending on the distance. There are no special fares or day tickets for visitors. Validate your ticket by stamping it in the orange machines at the entrance to the platforms, or you may be fined 1,500 dr.

By Bus

The fare on blue buses and the roomier yellow trolley buses is 75 dr. Purchase tickets beforehand at a curbside kiosks, or from booths at the main terminals. Validate your ticket when you board to avoid a fine. You may continue from a trunk line (A1–A16) to a connecting bus on the same ticket, and the mini "shopping" buses that serve the downtown historical triangle are free. Buses run from the center to all suburbs and suburban beaches until about midnight. For suburbs beyond central Kifissia, change at Kifissia. Attica has an efficient bus network. Most buses to the east Attica coast, including those for Sounion (☎ 01/823–0179; 1,050 dr.) and Marathon (☎ 01/821–0872; 650 dr.), leave from the KTEL terminal, Platia Aigyptiou on Mavromateon, at the corner of Patission and Alexandras avenues.

By Taxi

Although you will eventually find an empty taxi, it's often faster to call out your destination to one carrying passengers; if the taxi is going in that direction, the driver will pick you up. Most drivers speak basic English. The meter starts at 200 dr., and even if you join other passengers, you must add this amount to your final charge. There is a basic charge of 58 dr. per kilometer; this increases to 113 dr. between midnight and 5 AM. There are surcharges for holidays (100 dr.), pick-ups from, not to, the airport (300 dr.) and from the port, train stations, and bus terminals (160 dr.) There is also a 55 dr. charge for each suitcase over 10 kilograms. Waiting time is 2,000 dr. per hour. Some drivers overcharge foreigners; make sure they turn on the meter and use the high tariff ("Tarifa 2") only after midnight. You can also call a radio taxi, which charges an additional 200 dr.–300 dr. for the pickup. Some reliable companies are **Kosmos** (☎ 01/420–7244, 01/420–7261 or 01/420–7247) and **Parthenon** (☎ 01/581–1809).

Important Addresses and Numbers

Visitor Information

There are **Greek National Tourist Organization (EOT)** offices at Karageorgi Servias 2, in the National Bank of Greece, 01/322–2545; at the East Terminal of Ellinikon Airport, 01/961–2722; and at Piraeus, EOT Building, 1st Floor, Zea Marina, 01/413–5716.

Embassies

U.S. (✉ Vasilissis Sofias 91, ☎ 01/721–2951); **Canadian** (✉ Gennadiou 4, ☎ 01/725–4011); **U.K.** (✉ Ploutarchou 1, ☎ 01/723–6211).

Emergencies

Police: Tourist police (☎ 171); for auto accidents, call the city police (☎ 100). **Fire:** (☎ 199). **Ambulance:** ☎ 166, but a taxi is often faster. Not all hospitals are open nightly; dial ☎ 106 (in Greek) or check the English-language *Athens News,* which lists emergency hospitals daily. **Doctors:** Any hotel will call one for you. You can also call your embassy. **Dentist:** Ask your hotel or embassy. **Pharmacies:** Many pharmacies in the central area have someone who speaks English. Try **Marinopoulos** (✉ Kanari 23, ☎ 01/361–3051). For information on late-night pharmacies, dial 07 (Greek) or check the *Athens News.*

English-Language Bookstores

Pantelides (✉ Amerikis 9–11, ☎ 01/362–3673); **Eleftheroudakis** (✉ Nikis 4, ☎ 01/322–9388) and their newest, larger store (✉ Panepistimiou 17, ☎ 01/331–4180); **Compendium** (✉ Nikis 28, upstairs, ☎ 01/322–1248); **Reymondos** (✉ Voukourestiou 18, ☎ 01/364–8188). Daily listings of cultural events are published in English year-round in *The Athens News,* available in hotels and at newsstands. Both it and the weeklies *Athenscope* and *Greek News* list concerts, exhibitions, and showings of films in English.

Travel Agencies

American Express (✉ Ermou 2, ☎ 01/324–4975, FAX 01/322—7893); **CHAT Tours** (✉ Stadiou 4, ☎ 01/322–2886, FAX 01/323–5770); **Condor Travel** (✉ Stadiou 43, off Omonia Sq., ☎ 01/321–2453, FAX 01/321–4296); **Key Tours** (✉ Kallirois 4, ☎ 01/923–3166, FAX 01/923–2008); **Travel Plan** (✉ Christou Lada 9, ☎ 01/323–8801 through 01/323–8804 and 01/324–0224 through 01/324–0225, FAX 322–2152).

Guided Tours

Orientation Tours

All tour operators offer a four-hour morning bus tour of Athens, including a guided tour of the Acropolis, for around 8,400 dr. Make reservations at your hotel or at a travel agency; besides those agents already mentioned, there are hundreds of others, many situated around Filellinon and Nikis streets off Syntagma Square.

Special-Interest Tours

Those interested in folk dancing can take a four-hour evening tour (April–Oct.; 8,200 dr.) that begins with a sound-and-light show of the Acropolis from Filopappou Hill and then goes on to a performance of Greek folk dances in the open-air theater nearby. Another tour offers a dinner show at a taverna in the Plaka area, after the sound and light, for around 11,300 dr. Any travel agency can arrange these tours—and the excursions below—for you, but go first to **CHAT Tours** (☞ Important Addresses and Numbers, *above*) for efficient service.

Excursions

The choice is almost unlimited. A one-day tour to Delphi will cost up to 17,900 dr., with lunch included, 15,900 without lunch; a two-day tour to Corinth, Mycenae, Nauplion, and Epidaurus, around 29,500 dr., including half board in first-class hotels, and a full-day cruise from Piraeus, visiting the islands of Aegina, Poros, and Hydra costs around 16,000 dr. (including buffet lunch on the ship). *See also* Guided Tours in Mainland Greece, *below*.

Personal Guides

All the major tourist agencies can provide English-speaking guides for personally organized tours. Hire only those licensed by the EOT.

Exploring Athens

Athens is essentially a village that outgrew itself, spreading outward from the original settlement at the foot of the Acropolis. Back in 1834, when it became the capital of modern Greece, the city had a population of fewer than 10,000. Now it houses more than a third of the Greek population—around 4 million. A modern concrete city has engulfed the old village and now sprawls for 388 square kilometers (244 square miles), covering almost all the surrounding plain from the sea to the encircling mountains.

The city is crowded, dusty, and overwhelmingly hot during the summer. It also has an appalling air-pollution problem, caused mainly by traffic fumes; in an attempt to lessen the congestion, it is forbidden to drive private cars in central Athens on alternate workdays. Still, Athens is an experience not to be missed. Its tangible vibrancy makes it one of the most exciting cities in Europe, and the sprawling cement has failed to overwhelm the few astonishing reminders of the ancient town.

The central area of modern Athens is small, stretching from the Acropolis to Mt. Lycabettus, with its small white church on top. The layout is simple: Three parallel streets—Stadiou, Venizelou (a.k.a. Panepistimiou), and Akademias—link two main squares—Syntagma and Omonia. Try to wander off this beaten tourist track: Seeing the Athenian butchers in the central market near Monastiraki sleeping on their cold marble slabs during the heat of the afternoon siesta may give you more of a feel for the city than seeing hundreds of fallen pillars.

Keep in mind that most museums and archaeological sites are free on Sunday. In summer, closing times often depend on the site's available personnel, but throughout the year, arrive at least 30 minutes before the official closing time to ensure you can buy a ticket. Flash photography is forbidden in museums.

The Historic Heart

Numbers in the margin correspond to points of interest on the Athens map.

1 At the center of modern Athens is **Syntagma (Constitution) Square.** It has several leading hotels, airline and travel offices, and numerous cafés.

2 Along one side of the square stands the **Parliament Building,** completed in 1838 as the royal palace for the new monarchy. In front of the palace, you can watch the changing of the vividly costumed Evzone guard at the Tomb of the Unknown Soldier. On Sunday there is a more elaborate ceremony that begins at 11 AM from the barracks and ends in front

516

Athens

of Parliament at 11:15 AM. Amalias Avenue, leading out of Syntagma, will take you to the National Gardens.

❸ Across Vasilissis Olgas, at the far end of the National Gardens, are the columns of the once-huge **Temple of Olympian Zeus.** This famous temple was begun in the 6th century BC, and, when it was finally completed 700 years later, it exceeded in magnitude all other temples in Greece. It was destroyed during the invasion of the Goths in the 4th century, and only a few towering sun-browned columns remain. ✉ *Vas. Olgas 1,* ☎ *01/922–6330.* 🎫 *500 dr.* 🕙 *Tues.–Sun. 8:30–3.*

❹ Nearby stands **Hadrian's Arch,** built at the same time as the temple by the Roman emperor. It consists of a Roman archway, with a Greek superstructure of Corinthian pilasters. Visiting heads of state are officially welcomed here.

❺ About three-quarters of a kilometer (a half mile) east, down Vasilissis Olgas, you'll come to the white marble **Panathenaic Stadium,** built for the first modern Olympic Games in 1896. This reconstruction of the ancient Roman stadium of Athens can seat 80,000 spectators.

❻ From Hadrian's Arch, take Dionysiou Areopagitou a few blocks west to the **Theater of Dionysos,** built during the 6th century BC. Here the famous ancient dramas and comedies were originally performed in conjunction with bacchanalian feasts. ☎ *01/322–4625.* 🎫 *500 dr.* 🕙 *Daily 8:30–sunset (8:30–3 in winter).*

❼ A little farther along, on the right, is the back wall of the much better preserved **Odeon of Herod Atticus,** built by the Romans in the 2nd century AD. Here, on pine-scented summer evenings, the Athens Festival takes place. It includes opera, ballet, drama, and concerts (☞ The Arts, *below). It is not otherwise open to the public.*

★ ❽ Beyond the theater, a steep, zigzag path leads to the **Acropolis.** After a 30-year building moratorium at the time of the Persian wars, the Athenians built this complex during the 5th century BC to honor the goddess Athena, patron of the city. It is now undergoing conservation as part of an ambitious 20-year rescue plan launched with international support in 1983 by Greek architects. The first ruins you'll see are the **Propylaea,** the monumental gateway that led worshipers from the temporal world into the spiritual world of the sanctuary; now only the columns of Pentelic marble and a fragment of stone ceiling remain. Above, to the right, stands the graceful **Temple of Athena Nike,** called the Wingless Victory because the sculptor depicted the goddess Athena as a victory without wings, thus unable to fly away. The elegant and architecturally complex **Erechtheion** temple, most sacred of the shrines of the Acropolis and later turned into a harem by the Turks, has now emerged from extensive repair work. Dull, heavy copies of the Caryatids (draped maidens) now support the roof. The Acropolis Museum houses five of the six originals, their faces much damaged by acid rain; only four are on display, since one is being restored. The sixth is in the British Museum in London.

★ ❾ The **Parthenon** dominates the Acropolis and indeed the Athens skyline. Designed by Ictinus, with Phidias as master sculptor, it was completed in 438 BC and is the most architecturally sophisticated temple of that period. Even with hordes of tourists wandering around the ruins, you can still feel a sense of wonder. The architectural decorations were originally picked out in vivid red and blue paint, and the roof was of marble tiles, but time and neglect have given the marble pillars their golden-white shine, and the beauty of the building is all the more stark and striking. The British Museum houses the largest remaining part of the original 532-foot frieze (the Elgin Marbles). The building has 17 fluted columns along each side and 8 at the ends, and these were cleverly made to lean slightly inward and to bulge, counterbalancing the natural optical distortion. The Parthenon has had a checkered history: It was made into a brothel by the Romans, a church by the Christians, and a mosque by the Turks. The Turks also stored gunpowder in the Propylaea, and when this was hit by a Venetian bombardment in 1687, a fire raged for two days and 28 columns of the Parthenon were blown out, leaving the temple in its present condition. ☎ 01/321–0219. ✉ 2,000 dr., joint ticket to Acropolis and museum. ☉ Weekdays 8–6:30 (8–4:30 in winter), weekends 8:30–3.

★ ⑩ The **Acropolis Museum,** just below the Parthenon, contains superb sculptures from the Acropolis, including the Caryatids and a collection of colored korai (statues of women dedicated by worshipers to Athena, patron of the ancient city). ☎ 01/323–6665. ✉ 2,000 dr., joint ticket to the Acropolis. ☉ Mon. 11:30–6:30 (10:30–4:30 in winter), Tues.–Fri. 8–6:30 (8–4:30 in winter), weekends 8:30–3.

On **Areopagus,** the rocky outcrop facing the Acropolis, St. Paul preached to the Athenians; the road leading down between it and the hill of Pnyx is called Agiou Pavlou (St. Paul). To the right stands the ⑪ **Agora,** which means "marketplace," the civic center and focal point of community life in ancient Athens. The sprawling confusion of stones, slabs, and foundations is dominated by the best-preserved tem- ⑫ ple in Greece, the **Hephaisteion** (often wrongly referred to as the Theseion), built during the 5th century BC. Nearby, the impressive Stoa of Attalos II, reconstructed by the American School of Classical Studies in Athens with the help of the Rockefeller Foundation, houses the ⑬ **Museum of the Agora Excavations.** ☎ 01/321–0185. ✉ 1,200 dr. ☉ Tues.–Sun. 8:30–3.

★ ⑭ Stretching east from the Agora is **Plaka,** almost all that's left of 19th-century Athens. In the 1950s and '60s, the area became garish with neon as nightclubs moved in and residents moved out. Renovation has preserved Plaka, with its winding lanes, neoclassical houses, and sights like the **Greek Folk Art Museum** (✉ Kidathineon 17), the **Tower of the Winds** (a first-century BC water clock near the Roman agora), and the **Monument of Lysikrates** (in a park off Lysikratous). Above Plaka, at ★ the base of the Acropolis and climbing up its northeast side, is **Anafiotika,** the closest thing you'll find to a village in Athens. Take time to wander among its whitewashed, bougainvillea-framed houses and tiny churches, away from the city's bustle.

Below Plaka, in Cathedral Square, stands a 12th-century Byzantine ⑮ church known as the Old or **Little Cathedral,** whose outer walls are covered with reliefs. It nestles below the vast structure of the 19th-century Cathedral of Athens. From here, a short walk up Mitropoleos will take you back to Syntagma.

NEED A BREAK?   Visit the **De Profundis Tea Room** (✉ Hatzimichali 1), in an old mansion, for pastries and tea. **Byzantino,** on the main square in Plaka (✉ Kidathineon 18), is good for a Greek lunch—wild greens, roast chicken, *imam* (a spicy eggplant dish). Go around the corner to **Glikis** (✉ Aggelou Geronta 2) for an inexpensive Greek coffee or ouzo and a *mikri pikilia* (appetizers, including cheese, sausage, olives, and dips).

16 **17** **18** If you walk along Venizelou Avenue (Panepistimiou) from Syntagma, you will pass, on the right, three imposing buildings in classical style: the **Academy,** the **Senate House** of the University, and the **National Library.** When you reach Omonia Square, a bedlam of touts and tourists, you are in the heart of downtown Athens.

★ **19** It is essential to make time for the **National Archaeological Museum,** though it's somewhat off the tourist route, a good 10-minute walk north of Omonia Square. It houses one of the most exciting collections of antiquities in the world, including sensational archaeological finds made by Heinrich Schliemann at Mycenae; 16th-century BC frescoes from the Akrotiri ruins on Santorini; and the 6½-foot-tall bronze sculpture *Poseidon,* an original work of circa 470 BC, possibly by the sculptor Kalamis, which was found in the sea off Cape Artemision in 1928. ⊠ *28 Oktovriou (Patission) 44,* ☎ *01/821–7717.* ☜ *2,000 dr.* ⊙ *Mon. 12:30–7 (11–5 in winter), Tues.–Fri. 8–7 (8–5 in winter), weekends and holidays 8:30–3.*

20 **21** From Syntagma you can take Vasilissis Sofias along the edge of the National Gardens to reach the **Evzone Guards' barracks.** From here you can turn right onto Herod Atticus, which leads to the **Presidential Palace,** used by Greece's kings after the restoration of 1935 and now by the head of state.

★ **22** Or you can cross the street and turn up Neofytou Douka to the **Museum of Cycladic Art.** The collection spans 5,000 years, with nearly 100 exhibits of the Cycladic civilization (3000–2000 BC), including many of the slim marble figurines that so fascinated artists like Picasso and Modigliani. ⊠ *Neofytou Douka 4 or Irodotou 1,* ☎ *01/722–8321.* ☜ *400 dr.* ⊙ *Mon. and Wed.–Fri. 10–4, Sat. 10–3.*

★ **23** A little farther along Vasilissis Sofias is the **Byzantine Museum,** housed in an 1848 mansion built by an eccentric French aristocrat. Since the museum is undergoing renovation, not all its pieces are on display, but it has a unique collection of icons and the very beautiful 14th-century Byzantine embroidery of the body of Christ, in gold, silver, yellow, and green. Sculptural fragments provide an excellent introduction to Byzantine architecture. ⊠ *Vasilissis Sofias 22,* ☎ *01/721–1027.* ☜ *500 dr.* ⊙ *Tues.–Sun. 8:30–3.*

24 Kolonaki, a chic shopping district and fashionable residential area, occupies the lower slopes of **Mt. Lycabettus** and is only a 10-minute walk northeast of Syntagma; it's worth a stroll around if you enjoy window-shopping and people-watching. Three times the height of the Acropolis, Lycabettus can be reached by funicular railway from the top of Ploutarchou; Minibus 60 from Kolonaki Square drops you at the station. The view from the top—pollution permitting—is the finest in Athens. You can see all Athens, Attica, the harbor, and the islands of Aegina and Poros. *Funicular* ☜ *800 dr. round-trip.* ⊙ *Fri.–Wed. 8:45 AM–12, Thurs. 10:30 AM–12).*

NEED A
BREAK?   Take a cappuccino break at one of the many trendy but friendly cafés such as **Da Capo,** in the pedestrian zone off Kolonaki Square, or walk northeast a few minutes to the popular **Dexameni,** with its tables along a tree-lined pedestrian zone of the same name. Sip an ouzo with your *mezedes* (appetizers) on **Mt. Lycabettus** at I Prasini Tenta (the Green Awning), with its resplendent view of the city. To get there, take the funicular to the top and walk back down the road about 10 minutes.

Off the Beaten Path

★ Outside central Athens, on the slopes of Mt. Ymittos (ancient Mt. Hymettus), stands the **Kaisariani monastery,** one of the city's most evocative Byzantine remains. Take a taxi or Bus 224 from the terminal on Akademias (across from the Municipal Cultural Center) for 6 kilometers (4 miles) east of central Athens until you pass through the working-class suburb of Kaisariani. The monastery is an additional 30-minute walk along the paved road that climbs Mt. Ymittos. The well-restored 11th-century church, built on the site of a sanctuary of Aphrodite, has some beautiful frescoes dating from the 17th century. If you feel particularly energetic, you can continue walking up Mt. Ymittos—the roads wind for 19 kilometers (12 miles)—and take your pick of the many picnic spots. ☎ 01/723–6619. 🎫 800 dr. ⊘ Tues.–Sun. 8:30–3.

Mikrolimano, beyond the port of Piraeus, is famous for its many seafood restaurants—22 at last count—but has lost favor with some Athenians because its pretty, crescent-shape harbor suffers from pollution. The delightful atmosphere remains intact, however, and the harbor is crowded with elegant yachts. While it's not a particularly cheap place to eat, the quality of the seafood matches that of any in Greece. If you don't like seafood, you'll still be enchanted by the terraces of lovely houses tucked up against the hillsides. From Athens, take the metro from Omonia Square to Neo Faliron or a bus from Filellinon to the Neo Faliron train station; it's only five minutes' walk from there.

Shopping

Gift Ideas

Better tourist shops sell copies of traditional Greek jewelry, silver filigree, enamel, Skyrian pottery, onyx ashtrays and dishes, woven bags, attractive rugs (including flokatis—shaggy wool rugs, often brightly colored), worry beads in amber or silver called *koboloi,* good leather items, and furs. Natural sponges from Kalymnos also make good gifts, as do boxes of dried fruit, packaged pistachios, and canned olives. Some museums sell replicas of small items that are in their collections. The **National Welfare Organization** shop (⊠ Ypatias 6) near the Cathedral of Athens sells the best handicrafts. **The Center of Hellenic Tradition** (⊠ Pandrossou 36, in Monastiraki), which also has a café on the upper floor, is an excellent source of handmade goods.

Antiques

Pandrossou is especially rich in shops selling small antiques and icons. Keep in mind that there are many fakes, and that you must have permission from the government to export genuine objects from the Greek, Roman, or Byzantine periods.

Shopping Areas

The central shopping area lies between Syntagma and Omonia; **around Syntagma** you'll find good jewelers, shoe shops, and handicrafts and souvenir shops, especially along Voukourestiou. **Stadiou** is the best bet for men's clothing. Try **Ermou** for shoes and the fascinating small streets that lead off it for fabrics and housewares. Go to **Mitropoleos** for rugs and moderately priced fur shops, including **Hydra** (⊠ Mitropoleos 3–5) and **Voula Mitsakou** (⊠ Mitropoleos 7). At **Karamichos Flokati** (⊠ Voulis 31–33) you'll find a large selection of flokatis. Ermou runs west to **Monastiraki,** a crowded market area popular with Athenians. **Pandrossou,** below the cathedral, has antiques, sandals (an especially good buy), and inexpensive souvenirs. **Kolonaki** has the most expensive shops: You'll find unique jewelry here at the famous **LALAoUNIS** (⊠ Panepistimiou 6), at **La Chrysoteque Zolotas** (⊠ Panepistimiou 10), and at **PentheRoudakis** (⊠ Voukourestiou 19, in a pedestrian zone lined with jewelry shops). In Kolonaki you'll also find such designer boutiques as **Gianni Versace** (⊠ Anagnostopoulou 3), **DKNY** (⊠ Tsakalof 34), **Armani** (at Morel ⊠ Leventi 2), and the more modestly priced **Emporio Armani** (⊠ Milioni 8), as well as Greek designers **Aslanis** (⊠ Anagnostopoulou 16) and **Makis Tselios** (⊠ Solonos 2). For a broad selection, try **Sotris** (⊠ Anagnastopoulou 30), which has designs by Dolce & Gabbana, Prada, and Jil Sanders; **Linea Piu** (⊠ Sekeri 6), featuring Mizrahi, Dior, and Lagerfeld; and **Carouzos** (⊠ Kanari 12), with a large collection of menswear.

Flea Market

The **Sunday morning flea market** (⊠ based on Pandrossou and Ifestou streets) sells almost anything: secondhand clothes, old books, guitars, and backgammon sets. Pontians—Greeks who lived in the former Soviet Union—sell Russian caviar, vodka, and table linens. However little it costs, you should haggle. **Ifestou,** where coppersmiths have their shops, is interesting on weekdays; you can pick up copper wine jugs, candlesticks, cooking ware, and more for next to nothing.

Dining

Search for places with at least half a dozen tables occupied by Athenians—they're discerning customers. You can also pick up the weekly English-language magazine *Athenscope,* available at most central kiosks, for a list of ethnic restaurants. For details and price-category definitions, *see* Dining *in* Staying in Greece, *above.*

$$$$ ✕ **Bajazzo.** If you can splurge only once in Greece, this is the place.
★   Chef Klaus Feuerbach changes the menu often, creating imaginative, beautifully presented dishes. The beef fillets layered with foie gras and served with cognac-cream sauce; the fillet of sole with smoked-salmon mousse, mascarpone, and chive sauce; and the venison with bitter chocolate sauce are mouth-watering. ⊠ *Anapafseos 14, Mets,* ☎ *01/921–3013. Reservations essential. AE, DC, V. Closed Sun.*

$$$ ✕ **Melrose.** An anomaly in the student neighborhood of Exarchia, Melrose serves up the only Pacific Rim cuisine in Athens, in an understated setting punctuated with striking modern art. Popular dishes include salmon *ponsu* (seared and served with a saki-soy-scallion dipping sauce), duck with kumquats, and a Japanese salad—fresh spinach drizzled with rice wine vinegar and toasted sesame oil and topped with shrimp and scallops. ⊠ *Zosimadou 16, at top of stairs off Kallidromiou 68, Exarchia,* ☎ *01/825–1627. AE, V. Closed Aug. No lunch.*

$$$ ✕ **Symposio.** After a show at the nearby Odeon of Herod Atticus, sit in the glass-enclosed dining room and enjoy prawns and caviar with vodka dressing, or breast of duck with cassis sauce. The menu changes weekly. ⊠ *Erecthiou 46, Makriyanni,* ☎ *01/922–5321, 01/996–0501 and 093/235–203 for reservations. AE, DC, MC, V. Closed Sun., Greek Easter, and Aug. 12–17. No lunch.*

$$ ✕ **Apotsos.** This famous ouzerie, close to Syntagma Square but hidden away down an arcade, is an echoing barn of a place—truly Athenian in atmosphere. Politicians, journalists, and artists gather here at lunchtime. As well as ouzo, wine and beer are served, along with dishes of mezedes—three or four of these will add up to a substantial meal. ⊠ *Panepistimiou 10 in the arcade, Syntagma,* ☎ *01/363–7046. No credit cards. Closed Sun. and 2 wks in Aug. Lunch only (11–5).*

$$ ✗ **Kostoyiannis.** One of the oldest and most popular tavernas in the area, this authentic establishment behind the Archaeological Museum has an impressively wide range of Greek dishes—including excellent shrimp salads, stuffed mussels, rabbit *stifado* (a stew), and sautéed brains. ⊠ *Zaimi 37, Exarchia,* ☎ *01/821–2496. No credit cards. Closed Sun. and July 20–Aug. 20. No lunch.*

$$ ✗ **Socrates' Prison.** Amiable owner Socrates declares, "This is my prison; I'm here every day." He eschews run-of-the-mill taverna fare for his own creations: pork rolls stuffed with carrots and celery in lemon sauce or zucchini with ham and bacon topped with béchamel. It's ideal for dinner after a show at the nearby Herod Atticus theater. ⊠ *Mitseon 20, Makriyanni,* ☎ *01/922–3434. Weekend reservations essential. V. Closed Sun. and latter half of Aug. No lunch.*

$$ ✗ **Ta Tria Tetarta.** A bit more upscale than most mezedopolia, Ta Tria Tetarta serves a large variety of appetizers in a tri-level stone and wood setting, decorated with Greek knicknacks. Try the spicy feta sprinkled with red pepper and roasted in foil, cheese bread, skewered *seftalies* (seasoned meat dumplings), seafood pie, and Turkish dishes like yogurt and sausage salad. ⊠ *Oikonomou 25, Exarchia, tel 01/823–0560. Reservations essential. No credit cards. No lunch.*

$$ ✗ **Vlassis.** Relying on recipes from Thrace, Roumeli, Thessaly, and the
★ islands, the cooks whip up Greek home cooking in generous portions that more than make up for the daunting noise level. Order several appetizers for a meal: Musts are the *pastitsio* (baked minced lamb and macaroni) with bits of liver and the octopus stifado, tender and sweet with lots of onions. Also good are the spicy cheese salad, oven-baked pork or lamb, marinated eggplant, and *katsiki ladorigani* (goat with oil and oregano). The *galaktobouriko* (custard in phyllo) is a delicious dessert. In summer, the restaurant moves to Athos in northern Greece. ⊠ *Armatolon and Klefton 20, Ambelokipi,* ☎ *01/642–5337. Reservations essential. DC, MC, V. Closed Sun. and July–Sept. No lunch.*

$$ ✗ **Xynos.** Enter a time warp in this Plaka taverna: Athens in the '50s. The excellent food is still the same. Start with stuffed grape leaves, then move on to cooked dishes like lamb *yiouvetsi,* made with tiny noodles called *kritharakia,* and *tsoutsoukakia,* spicy meat patties with cinnamon. Roving musicians charm the crowd of regulars. ⊠ *Aggelou Geronta 4, Plaka (entrance down walkway next to kafenion Glikis),* ☎ *01/322–1065. No credit cards. Closed weekends and part of July. No lunch.*

$ ✗ **Karavitis.** A neighborhood favorite, this taverna near the Olympic Stadium has warm-weather garden seating and a winter dining room decorated with huge wine casks. The classic Greek cuisine is well prepared, including pungent *tzatziki* (yogurt-garlic dip), *bekri meze* (lamb chunks in a spicy red sauce), and *stamnaki* (beef baked in a clay pot). ⊠ *Arktinou 35 and Pausaniou 4, Pangrati,* ☎ *01/721–5155. No credit cards. Closed a few days around Greek Easter. No lunch.*

$ ✗ **O Platanos.** One of Plaka's oldest tavernas has a shady courtyard
★ for outdoor dining. Don't miss the oven-baked potatoes, roast lamb, and exceptionally cheap but delicious barrel retsina. Although the place is very friendly, not much English is spoken. ⊠ *Diogenous 4, Plaka,* ☎ *01/322–0666. No credit cards. Closed Sun.*

$ ✗ **Sigalas.** Run by the Bairaktaris family for more than a century, this
★ is the best place to eat in Monastiraki Square. Go to the window case to view the day's magirefta or sample the gyro platter. Appetizers include small cheese pies with sesame seeds, tender mountain greens, and

fried zucchini with garlicky dip. ⊠ *Platia Monastiraki 2, Monastiraki,* ☎ *01/321–3036. No credit cards.*

Lodging

It's always advisable to reserve a room ahead. Both traditional and modern hotels can be found in the center of town and out along the seacoast toward the airport. Modern hotels are more likely to be air-conditioned, and look for double-glazed windows; the center of Athens can be so noisy that it's hard to sleep. Except where noted, breakfast is not included in the rate, though it is often provided—sometimes in the form of a lavish buffet. For details and price-category definitions, *see* Lodging *in* Staying in Greece, *above.*

$$$$ 🏨 **Andromeda Athens Hotel.** Athens's newest luxury hotel caters to business travelers. The spacious rooms have a salmon color scheme, with quilted headboards, wall-to-wall carpeting, minibars, and TVs (computers and fax machines are available on request). The hotel is on a quiet street near the U.S. Embassy, and the bedrooms have double-glazed windows. The White Elephant Polynesian restaurant is excellent. ⊠ *Timoleondos Vassou 22, Mavili Sq., 11521,* ☎ *01/643–7302 through 01/643–7304,* 𝖥𝖠𝖷 *01/646–6361. 23 rooms with bath, 4 suites, 3 penthouses. 2 restaurants, meeting rooms, business services, convention center. AE, DC, MC, V.*

$$$$ 🏨 **Athenaeum Inter-Continental.** The plush Inter-Continental has a marble atrium lobby that displays a private art collection. Its spacious rooms have sitting areas and marble bathrooms; ask for one with an Acropolis view. All floors were recently redone except for the eighth and ninth, which are still undergoing renovation–one will become an executive floor. In the morning a shuttle takes guests to the airport, and the rest of the day until 9:30 PM it travels hourly between the hotel and Syntagma Square, 15 minutes away. ⊠ *89–93 Syngrou Ave., Neos Kosmos, 11745,* ☎ *01/902–3666,* 𝖥𝖠𝖷 *01/924–3000. 520 rooms with bath, 38 suites. 3 restaurants, 2 bars, outdoor pool, health club, meeting rooms. AE, DC, MC, V.*

$$$$ 🏨 **Athens Hilton.** A 200-year-old olive tree with a Turkish cannonball in its branches stands near what is still one of the city's top hotels after nearly 30 years. It is about a 20-minute walk to Syntagma, but a shuttle takes guests downtown and to the airport. The spacious rooms all have balconies and double-glazed windows, as well as fine views of either the Acropolis or Mt. Ymittos. The executive floor has private check-in and checkout, business facilities, and a private lounge. ⊠ *Vasilissis Sofias 46, 11528,* ☎ *01/725–0201,* 𝖥𝖠𝖷 *01/725–3110. 434 rooms with bath, 19 suites. 3 restaurants, 2 bars, outdoor pool, massage, sauna, health club, meeting rooms. AE, DC, MC, V.*

$$$$ 🏨 **Grande Bretagne.** The G. B., as it is known, is centrally located on Syntagma Square. An internationally famous landmark and the hub of Athenian social life, this distinguished hotel had a face-lift in 1992. Ask for an inside room overlooking the courtyard to escape the noise of the traffic, or try one of the coveted Syntagma rooms with large balconies and Acropolis views. ⊠ *Syntagma Square, 10563,* ☎ *01/331–4444,* 𝖥𝖠𝖷 *01/322–8034. 341 rooms with bath, 23 suites. Restaurant, 2 bars, meeting rooms. AE, DC, MC, V.*

$$$ 🏨 **Electra Palace.** At the edge of Plaka, this hotel offers cozy rooms in warm hues—with TVs, hair dryers, balconies, and minibars—for comparatively low prices. Rooms from the fifth floor up are smaller but have bigger balconies. The best feature is the rooftop pool, where you can spend hours sunning, sipping a cool drink, and gazing at the nearby Acropolis. American breakfast is included in the price. ⊠ *Nikodimou 18, Plaka, 10557,* ☎ *01/324–1401 through 01/324–*

1410, FAX 01/324–1875. *101 rooms with bath, 5 suites. Restaurant, bar, pool, meeting rooms. AE, DC, MC, V.*

$$$ ☷ **Novotel Athenes.** Although not central, this hotel is just a 10-minute walk to the rail station or the national museum. One of the city's better values, it has an elegant lobby and quiet rooms with minibars and TVs. The rooftop pool is beside a Greek restaurant from which, in summer, you can watch the sun set behind the Acropolis. ⊠ *M. Voda 4–8, Vathis Sq., 10439,* ☎ *01/825–0422,* FAX *01/883–7816. 190 rooms with bath, 5 suites. 2 restaurants, bar, 2 pools, meeting rooms. AE, DC, MC, V.*

$$ ☷ **Acropolis View Hotel.** This hotel in a quiet neighborhood below the
★ Acropolis has agreeable rooms, about half with Parthenon views; most floors have been renovated in the last two years. Staff members in the homey lobby are efficient and friendly, and major sights lie a stone's throw away. American breakfast (cornflakes, egg, ham, cheese) is included in the price. ⊠ *Webster 10, Acropolis, 11742,* ☎ *01/921–7303 through 01/921–7305,* FAX *01/923–0705. 32 rooms with bath. Bar (summer), roof garden (summer), air-conditioning. AE, MC, V.*

$$ ☷ **Astor.** The no-frills Astor is a good choice if you want to stay very close to Syntagma Square and enjoy the standard amenities—TV, air-conditioning, room service—without paying a fortune. In 1995 new air-conditioning and elevators were installed, and rooms were outfitted with more modern furniture. If possible, request a room on the sixth floor or higher for a memorable view of the Acropolis (also visible from the roof garden, where breakfast is served). Continental breakfast is included in the price. ⊠ *Karageorgi Servias 16, Syntagma, 10562,* ☎ *01/325–5111,* FAX *01/325–5115. 131 rooms with bath. Restaurant, bar, air-conditioning. AE, DC, V.*

$$ ☷ **Austria.** This small, unpretentious hotel on Filopappou Hill, opposite the Acropolis, is ideal as a base for exploring the heart of ancient Athens. Although it has no restaurant, it is at the bottom of its category's price range and is well worth considering. Continental breakfast is included in the quoted rate but is not required (700 dr. per person). ⊠ *Mouson 7, Filopappou, 11742,* ☎ *01/923–5151 or 01/922–0777,* FAX *01/924–7350. 37 rooms with bath. Breakfast room, air-conditioning, TV room. AE, DC, MC, V.*

$$ ☷ **Plaka Hotel.** Convenient for sightseeing and the Monastiraki Square metro, this hotel has a roof garden with a view to the Parthenon. Double-glazed windows cut down the noise; the highest floors are the quietest. All rooms have TV and are simply furnished; those in back from the fifth floor up have the best Acropolis views. ⊠ *Kapnikareas 7, Plaka, 10556,* ☎ *01/322–2096 through 01/322–2098,* FAX *01/322–2412. 67 rooms with bath. Air-conditioning. AE, DC, MC, V.*

$ ☷ **Aphrodite Hotel.** Near Syntagma and perfectly comfortable, the Aphrodite has quiet and tidy, if rather spare, rooms. With all the facilities of more costly hotels, it offers excellent value, with rates at the low end of the category. The gleaming white marble lobby ends in a bar, where guests often relax in the evenings. ⊠ *Apollonos 21, Syntagma, 10557,* ☎ *01/323–4357 through 01/323–4359,* FAX *01/322–5244. 84 rooms with bath. Bar, air-conditioning. AE, DC, MC, V.*

$ ☷ **Art Gallery Pension.** On a quiet side street near the Acropolis, this
★ friendly place is prized by students and single travelers. The handsome house has an old-fashioned look, with family paintings on the muted white walls, comfortable beds, and hardwood floors. Most rooms have balconies with views of Filopappou or the Acropolis. ⊠ *Erecthiou 5, Koukaki, 11742,* ☎ *01/923–8376,* FAX *01/923–3025. 21 rooms with bath. Bar. No credit cards. Closed Nov.–Feb.*

$ ☒ **Attalos Hotel.** The market area, where the Attalos is located, is full
of life and color by day, but deserted at night. The hotel has a rooftop
garden and fine views of the Acropolis; rooms from the third floor up
have balconies. Try to get a room on the fifth or sixth floor in the rear,
where street noise is less, though it's also reduced by double-glazed windows. Most rooms have air-conditioning. ☒ *Athinas 29, Monastiraki,
10554,* ☎ *01/321–2801 through 01/231–2803,* FAX *01/324–3124. 80
rooms with bath. Bar. V.*

$ ☒ **Marble House.** This friendly, popular pension, in a cul-de-sac about
15 minutes' walk from the Acropolis, has a steady clientele—even in
winter, when it offers low monthly and weekly rates. Rooms are clean
and quiet, with ceiling fans. The courtyard is a lovely place to relax.
Take Trolleys 1, 5, or 9 from Syntagma and get off at the Zinni stop.
☒ *A. Zinni 35, Koukaki, 11741,* ☎ *01/923–4058 or 01/922–6461.
16 rooms, 11 with bath. Breakfast room. No credit cards.*

The Arts

The **Athens Festival** runs from late June through September with concerts, opera, ballet, folk dancing, and drama. Performances are in various locations, including the theater of Herod Atticus below the
Acropolis and Mt. Lycabettus. Tickets range from 2,000 dr. to 15,000
dr. and are available a few days before the performance from the box
office (☒ In the arcade at Stadiou 4, ☎ 01/322–1459).

Though rather corny, the **sound-and-light shows** beautifully display the
Acropolis with dramatic lighting and a brief narrated history. Performances are given nightly from April through October, in English, at 9
PM (the time is subject to change), and admission is 1,200 dr. The entrance is on Dionysiou Areopagitou, opposite the Acropolis.

The lively **Dora Stratou Troupe** performs Greek and Cypriot folk dances
from mid-May through mid-September at its theater (☒ Atop Filopappou Hill, ☎ 01/921–4650; ⊘ Daily at 10:15 PM, also at 8:15 PM Wed.
and Sun.). Tickets, which range from 2,500 to 3,000 dr. can be purchased at the box office before the show. For information, call the theater or the troupe's offices at 01/324–4395, FAX 01/324–6921.

Concerts and Operas

Concerts are given September through June by Greek and world-class
international orchestras at the **Megaron Athens Concert Hall** next to
the U.S. embassy (☒ Vasilissis Sofias and Kokkali, ☎ 01/728–2333).
Information and tickets are available from the Megaron weekdays 10–
4; prices range from 2,500 dr. to 20,000 dr. Tickets go on sale a few
weeks in advance but many events sell out within hours. On the first
day of sales, they can be purchased by credit card in person at the
Megaron; sales begin at 8 AM, but try to arrive an hour before. Tickets remaining the next day may be purchased by phone with a credit
card. From the second day on, tickets are also sold at the Megaron's
downtown box office (☒ In the arcade at Stadiou 4).

Films

Almost all **Athens cinemas** now show foreign films; *The Athens News,
Athenscope,* and *Greek News* list them in English. Downtown cinemas are the most comfortable. Near Syntagma try the **Astor** (☒ Stadiou 28, ☎ 01/323–1297), the **Apollon Renault** (☒ Stadiou 19, ☎
01/323–6811) or the **Attikon Renault** (☒ Stadiou 19, ☎ 01/322–
8221). The **Ideal** near Omonia, (☒ Panepistimiou 46, ☎ 01/362–6720)
has the best seats in Athens. Unless they have air-conditioning, most
cinemas close June–September, giving way to wonderful **outdoor movie
theaters,** such as the **Thission** (☒ Pavlou 7, ☎ 01/342–0864 or 01/347–

0980) near the Acropolis and **Cine Paris** (✉ Kidathineon 22, ☎ 01/322–2071) in Plaka. At both, the films change every few days, and you can order drinks from the bar during the screening.

Nightlife

Athens has an active nightlife: even at 3 AM the central squares and streets are crowded with revelers. In summer, many places downtown move to the seaside. Ask your hotel for recommendations or see listings in *Athenscope*, and check ahead for summer closings. For a uniquely Greek evening, try a taverna with a floor show (most are in Plaka) or the *bouzoukia* (clubs with live bouzouki music). In the bigger clubs, where the food tends to be overpriced and second-rate, there is usually a per-person minimum or a prix-fixe menu; a bottle of whiskey costs about 24,000 dr.–29.000 dr.

Bars

Balthazar (✉ Tsoha 27, Ambelokipi, ☎ 01/644–1215), in a neoclassical house, has a lush garden courtyard where Athenians come to escape the summer heat.

To enjoy Greek *kefi* (high spirits) without the formalities of a big bouzouki club, visit **Karpouzi** (✉ Politechniou and 34 Syntagmatos, Piraeus, ☎ 01/412–6074), especially on a Sunday afternoon, when DJs spin Greek music and the audience dances on the tabletops.

Of the new bars for the under-40 crowd, **Lobby** (✉ Ermou 110 and Avliton 6–8, Psirri, ☎ 01/323–6975) is the most interesting, an ode to kitsch, with two dance floors and rooms done as a "boardroom," a "classroom," and a "bedroom" (complete with bed and fake fur pillows).

Stavlos (✉ Hraklidou 10, Thission, ☎ 01/345–2502), in the former royal stables, often features live music, art shows, and Sunday afternoon jazz in its restaurant-bar-gallery complex.

Strofilia (✉ Karitsi 7, Kolokotronis Square, ☎ 01/323–4803, closed May–Aug.) is one of the city's few wine bars; it offers vintages from about 50 small Greek producers, about 20 of them by the glass.

Live Rock, Jazz, Blues

Most big names in popular music perform at the informal **Rodon** (✉ Marni 24, Platia Vathis, ☎ 01/524–7427). Smaller jazz groups play the cozy **Half Note** (✉ Trivonianou 17, Mets, ☎ 01/923–2460).

Bouzoukia

Diogenes Palace (✉ Syngrou 259, Nea Smyrni, ☎ 01/942–4267) is currently the "in" place with Athenians who want to hear Greece's most popular singers, such as Leftheris Pantazis, Iannis Parios, and Katerina Kouka; it's also the most expensive.

Decadence reigns at **Posidonio** (✉ Posidonios 18, Elliniko, ☎ 01/894–1033) as diners dance the seductive *tsifteteli* with enthusiasm and order flower vendors to shower gardenias on their favorite singers.

Rembetika Clubs

Rembetika, the blues sung by Asia Minor refugees who came to Greece in the 1920s, still enthralls Greeks. At **Ennea** Ogdoa (✉ Leof. Alexandras 40, Pedion Areos, ☎ 01/823–5841), which features the "forbidden" rembetika (lyrics refer to hashish), the band usually starts off slowly, but by 1 AM is wailing to a packed dance floor. Closed Sun.

Amid the bars of Exarchia, **Frangosyriani** (✉ Arachovis 57, Exarchia, ☎ 01/380–0693) has a band specializing in the songs of rembetika great Markos Vamvakaris. Closed Tues.–Wed.

Tavernas

At **Stamatopoulou Palia Plakiotiki Taverna** (✉ Lysiou 26, ☏ 01/322–8722), in an 1822 Plaka house, you'll find good food along with an acoustic band of three guitars and bouzouki playing old Athenian songs. In summer the show moves to a cool garden.

THE NORTHERN PELOPONNESE

Suspended from the mainland of Greece like a large leaf, the ancient land of Pelops offers beautiful scenery—rocky coasts, sandy beaches, mountains—and a fascinating variety of ruins: temples, theaters, mosques, churches, palaces, and medieval castles built by crusaders. Legend and history meet a few miles south of the isthmus of Corinth, in Mycenae, where Agamemnon, Elektra, and Orestes played out their grim family tragedy. This city dominated the entire area from the 18th to the 12th century BC, and may even have conquered Minoan Crete. According to Greek mythology, Paris, son of the king of Troy, in Asia Minor, abducted the beautiful Helen, wife of Menelaus, king of Sparta. Agamemnon, king of Mycenae, was Menelaus's brother. This led to the Trojan War and the defeat of Troy—the story is told in Homer's *Iliad*. After Heinrich Schliemann's excavations in 1874 uncovered gold-filled graves and a royal palace, Mycenae became a world-famous archaeological site.

Sparta, once a powerful city-state, is today, unfortunately, devoid of charm or character. Like Corinth, once the largest, richest, and most pleasure-loving city of ancient Greece, Sparta now appears sadly lifeless and unattractive. Corinth, in fact, was destroyed by earthquakes in 1858 and 1928, and each time underwent a more practical and banal reconstruction, the last of which left it 5 kilometers (3 miles) from its original site.

During the Middle Ages, the Peloponnese was conquered by leaders of the Fourth Crusade and held as a feudal state by French and Italian nobles. It formed the cornerstone of Latin (Christian) power in the eastern Mediterranean during the 13th and 14th centuries. In 1821, the Peloponnese played a key role in the Greek War of Independence. Nauplion was, for a short time during the 1800s, the capital of Greece. Among the region's many contributions to humanity are the Olympic Games, begun in 776 BC in Olympia.

Getting Around

The best way to see the sights of the Peloponnese at your own pace is by car. If you take the car ferry from Italy to Patras, capital of the Peloponnese, or if you rent a car in Patras, you can tour them on the way to Athens. Or you can begin your tour, as we do, in Athens.

Guided Tours

CHAT Tours (✉ 4 Stadiou, Athens, ☏ 01/322–2886, FAX 01/323–5770) and **Key Tours** (✉ Kallirois 4, Athens, ☏ 01/923–3166, FAX 01/923–2008) both organize tours in the Peloponnese. A four-day tour of the Peloponnese and Delphi, including the sites, a qualified guide, and half-board accommodations at first-class hotels, costs around 97,000 dr. A two-day tour, again including accommodations, to Corinth, Mycenae, and Epidauros, will cost around 29,500 dr. A six-day grand tour of the Peloponnese, offered less frequently, costs around 145,000 dr.

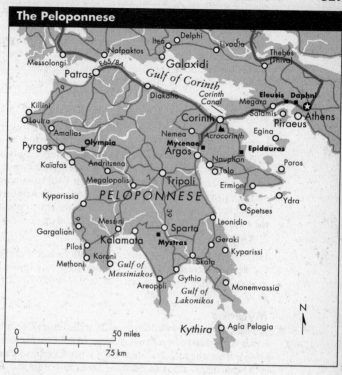

The Peloponnese

Visitor Information

In **Patras,** visit the Greek National Tourist Organization (⊠ Iroon Polytechniou 110, Glyfada, ☎ 061/653–358 through 061/653–360) or the American Express representative at Albatros Travel (⊠ Othonos 48, ☎ 061/220–993, 𝖥𝖠𝖷 061/623–113); Albatros can assist with all travel arrangements. The Tourist Police are in the welcome station on the harbor (⊠ Norman-Iroon Politechniou, Glyfada, ☎ 061/651–833 and 061/651–893). The Olympic Airlines office is at Aratou 17–19 (☎ 061/222–901). The Automobile and Touring Club of Greece (ELPA) has an office at Patroon Athinon 18 (☎ 061/425–141 and 061/426–416). In **Olympia** you'll find the Municipal Tourist Office at Kondili 75 (☎ 0624/23–100). The Tourist Police are at Spiliopoulou 5 (☎ 0624/22–550). **Nauplion** also has a Municipal Tourist Office (⊠ 25th Martiou across from OTE, ☎ 0752/24–444); its Tourist Police are at 25th Martiou and Anapafseos (☎ 0752/28–131).

Exploring the Northern Peloponnese

Daphni

Eleven kilometers (7 miles) northwest of Athens, after you have passed the last houses of the Athenian urban sprawl, you'll come to the 6th-century monastery of **Daphni.** It was sacked in 1205 by Frankish crusaders, who later installed Cistercian monks from Burgundy to rebuild it. The monastery has superb mosaics. ⊠ *End of Iera Odos,* ☎ *01/581–1558.* 🎟 *800 dr.* ☉ *Daily 8:30–2:45.*

Eleusis

Descending from Daphni to the sea, you face the narrow straits of Salamis, where the Persian fleet of Xerxes was defeated in 480 BC by Athens and its allies. Beyond are the ruins of **Eleusis,** site of antiquity's most important harvest celebrations, the Eleusinian Mysteries. Here participants underwent rites in honor of Demeter, goddess of grain. There is almost nothing left of ancient Eleusis but a few fallen pillars and overgrown pathways, and the area is surrounded by factories. Admission to the site includes entrance to a small museum. ⊠ *Iera Odos 2,* ☎ *01/554–6019.* ⊠ *500 dr.* ☼ *Tues.–Sun. 8:30–3.*

Corinth

★ When you cross the **Corinth Canal,** about 84 kilometers (52 miles) from Athens, you will have entered the Peloponnese. Modern Corinth lies by the sea; the ancient Greek city stood higher up. You'll see an important ruin, that of the Doric **Temple of Apollo,** built in the 6th century BC and one of the few buildings that still stood when Julius Caesar decided to restore Corinth. In AD 51, St. Paul fulminated against the sacred prostitutes who served Aphrodite on the **Acrocorinth,** the peak behind the ancient city. A museum beside the ruins contains finds from the excavations. ☎ *0741/31–207.* ⊠ *1,200 dr.* ☼ *weekdays 8–7 (8–5 in winter), Sat.–Sun. 8:30-3.*

Drive from the square of ancient Corinth or hire a taxi to take you to the **Fort of Acrocorinth,** then continue on to explore the imposing Franco-Turkish fortifications. ☎ *0741/31–207.* ⊠ *free.* ☼ *Daily 8:30–5.*

Mycenae

★ Ancient **Mycenae,** 44 kilometers (28 miles) from Corinth, was the fabulous stronghold of the Achaean kings of the 13th century BC. Destroyed in 468 BC, it was forgotten until 1874 when German archaeologist Heinrich Schliemann, who had discovered the ruins of ancient Troy, uncovered the remains of this fortress city. Mycenae was the seat of the doomed House of Atreus—of King Agamemnon and his wife, Clytemnestra (sister of Helen of Troy), and of their tragic children, Orestes and Elektra. When Schliemann uncovered six shaft graves (so named because the kings were buried standing up) of the royal circle, he was certain that one was the tomb of Agamemnon. The gold masks and diadems, daggers, jewelry, and other treasures found in the graves are now in the National Archaeological Museum in Athens; the new local museum is dedicated to archaeological studies. You'll also see the monumental **Lion Gate,** dating to 1250 BC, the castle ruins crowning the bleak hill, and the astounding beehive tomb (the so-called **Treasury of Atreus,** or Agamemnon's Tomb) built into the hillside outside the massive fortification walls, all remnants of the first great civilization in continental Europe. The tombs, the acropolis, the palace, and the museum can all be explored for the cost of admission. ☎ *0751/76–585.* ⊠ *1,500 dr.* ☼ *Daily 8–7 (8–5 in winter).*

Argos

Moving south, 11 kilometers (7 miles) from Mycenae, you'll pass **Argos,** prominent during the 8th century BC, and the Cyclopean ramparts (huge, irregular stones) of **Tiryns.** One version of the legend has Tiryns as the birthplace of Hercules, and the present remains, including the walls, date mostly from the 13th century BC when Tiryns was one of the most important Mycenaean cities.

Nauplion

★ Farther on is **Nauplion,** a picturesque town on a peninsula in the Gulf of Argos, below brooding Venetian fortifications. Modern Greece's first king lived for a year or two within the walls of the high fortress when Nauplion was capital of Greece. His courtiers had to climb 999 steps to reach him; you can still climb the long staircase or drive up to the fortress. ☎ 0752/28–036. ⊠ 800 dr. ⊙ weekdays 8:30–7 (8–2:45 in winter), weekends.

Wander for at least a few hours through the narrow streets and shady squares, admiring the mix of Venetian, Turksh, Frankish, and Byzantine buildings, and having a leisurely meal. The Venetian naval arsenal on the town square houses an **Archaeological Museum** with Mycenaean finds, including a 7th-century BC gorgon mask from Tiryns. ☎ 0752/27–502. ⊠ 500 dr. ⊙ Tues.–Sun. 8:30–3.

Epidauros

★ **Epidauros,** 24 kilometers (15 miles) east of Nauplion, was the sanctuary of Asklepios, the Greek god of healing. You can visit the foundations of the temples and ancient hospital, but the site you must not miss is the ancient **open-air theater,** which seats 14,000. In summer, during the Festival of Ancient Drama, plays are staged here (☞ The Arts, below), but it merits a visit at any time of year. The acoustics are so good that you can sit in the top row and hear a whisper on stage. ☎ 0753/22–009. ⊠ 1,500 dr. ⊙ Theater: daily 8–7 (8–5 in winter); museum: same hours, except Mon., when it opens at 12.

Olympia

★ From Epidauros you can return to Athens along the coast, a lovely drive, or continue on to Olympia by way of the rugged mountains of Arcadia. The site of **ancient Olympia** lies a few kilometers from the sea, northwest of Megalopolis, where a huge assembly hall was built to hold the Ten Thousand representatives of the Arcadian League. The Olympic Games were first held in 776 BC and continued to be celebrated every four years until AD 393, when the Roman emperor Theodosius I, with his Christian sensibility, banned these "pagan rites." Women were excluded from watching the games under penalty of death, although no one was ever executed. They always held their own games a few weeks earlier. Archaeologists still uncover statues and votive offerings among the pine trees surrounding **Olympic Stadium** and the imposing ruins of the **temples of Zeus and Hera** within the sacred precinct. ⊠ Stadium ☎ 0624/22–517, museum ☎ 0624/22–742. ⊠ 1,200 dr. museum; 1,200 dr. stadium. ⊙ Stadium: weekdays 7:30–7 (7:30–5 in winter), weekends 8:30–3; museum: same schedule except that it opens at 10:30 on Mon., 8 on Tues.–Fri.

The International Olympic Academy, 6.4 kilometers (4 miles) east, houses a **Museum of the Olympic Games,** which has a collection of commemorative postage stamps and mementos. ☎ 0624/22–544. ⊠ 500 dr. ⊙ weekdays 8–3:30, weekends 9–4:30.

Patras

North of Olympia, 122 kilometers (76 miles) away, lies **Patras,** the third-largest city in Greece, its main western port, and the hub of business in the Peloponnese. Walk up to the **Byzantine kastro,** built on the site of the ancient acropolis, to take a look at the fine view along the coast. The **Cathedral of St. Andrew's,** reputedly the largest in Greece and built on the site of the crucifixion of St. Andrew, is also worth exploring. It's on the far west side of the harbor at the end of Ayios Andreou. Its treasure is the saint's silver-mounted skull, returned to Patras in 1964 after 500 years in St. Peter's, Rome. Apart from the kastro and cathedral, there is little of interest here. The city's prettiest features are its arcaded streets and its squares, surrounded by neoclassical buildings.

The shortest route back to Athens follows the National Road along the shore of the Gulf of Corinth, an exceptionally beautiful drive. You could instead cross the entrance to the gulf and visit Delphi (☞ Exploring Mainland Greece, below) on your way back to Athens.

Dining and Lodging

Many of the hotels in the Peloponnese have good dining rooms, so try these as well as the local tavernas. For details and price-category definitions, *see* Dining and Lodging *in* Staying in Greece, *above.*

Nauplion

$$ ✕ **O Arapakos.** Settle in on the waterfront and start with grilled octopus and *bourekakia* (cheese pastries); then move on to lamb with homemade noodles or *arnaki exohiko* (lamb stuffed with feta and potatoes). Fresh fish is also available, including charcoal-grilled sea bream. ⊠ *Bouboulinas 81,* ☎ *0752/27–675. V.*

$$ ✕ **Savouras.** Fresh seafood is served in this unpretentious taverna overlooking the bay; it is generally regarded as one of the area's best fish restaurants. Specialties are red mullet and dorado. ⊠ *Bouboulinas 79,* ☎ *0752/27–704. No credit cards.*

$ ✕ **Karamanlis.** This taverna near the courthouse is crowded at lunch with civil servants who come for its tasty magirefta. The fish soup makes a good appetizer, followed by *yiouvelakia* (meat-rice balls) with egg-lemon sauce, baked potatoes, and wild greens. Fresh fish is also available. ⊠ *Bouboulinas 1,* ☎ *0752/27–668. No credit cards.*

$ ✕ **Ta Fanaria.** Sit at one of the tables in the narrow alley beside the
★ restaurant and ask what's best that night. The restaurant is known for its *ladera* (vegetables cooked in olive oil), but equally delicious are the mini cheese pies, charcoal-grilled lamb ribs, and lamb baked with okra or green beans. ⊠ *Staikopoulos 13,* ☎ *0752/27–141. V.*

$$$ 🏨 **Candia House.** This beautifully decorated hotel 17 kilometers (10½
★ miles) south of Nauplion on Candia Beach weds good taste with comfort. Fresh flowers, antiques, paintings by Greek artists, and handcrafted mirrors are just some of the special touches. All suites have balconies, sitting rooms, television, and a refrigerator. Buffet breakfast is included in the price. ⊠ *Candia-Irion, 21100,* ☎ *0752/94–060 through 0752/94–063,* ℻ *0752/94–480. Off-season call the Athens office,* ☎ *01/347–1503,* ℻ *01/347–4732. 10 suites. Restaurant, pool, exercise room. AE, DC, MC, V.*

$$$ 🏨 **Amalia.** The Amalia occupies a fine neoclassical building in large gardens 3 kilometers (2 miles) outside town, on the sea, near ancient Tiryns. The public rooms are spacious and comfortable, and service is attentive. The beach nearby makes this ideal for a relaxing stay; a buffet breakfast is included. ⊠ *National Road to Argos outside Nauplion, 21100,* ☎ *0752/24–401,* ℻ *0752/24–400. For reservations, call the Athens office at* ☎ *01/323–7201,* ℻ *01/323–8792. 171 rooms with bath. 3 restaurants, cafeteria, bar, pool, meeting rooms. AE, DC, MC, V.*

$–$$ 🏨 **Byron.** This lovely hotel is in a rose and blue 18th-century house. The owners have now added another building (yellow with green shutters), with four rooms that have Jugendstil furniture, minibars, and air-conditioning. Guests eat breakfast on a terrace overlooking the town and the gulf. ⊠ *Platonos 2, Platia Agios Spiridonos,* ☎ *0752/22–351,* ℻ *0752/26–338. 18 rooms with bath. Courtyard. Closed Nov.–mid-Dec. MC, V.*

$ 🏨 **Dioscouri.** This family-run hotel above the old town, with a fine view across the gulf of Nauplion, is cool and quiet, and Continental breakfast is included. ⊠ *Zigomala 6, 21100,* ☎ *0752/28–550 and 0752/28–644,* ℻ *0752/21–202. 51 rooms with bath. Restaurant, bar. V.*

Olympia

$$ ✕ **O Kladeos.** Named for the river it borders, this cozy spot is big with
★ locals. Sit near the fireplace in winter, in the shade of the plane tree in

summer. The food is simple but classic Greek: codfish with garlic dip, mountain greens, charcoal grilled lamb chops, and *patsa,* a tripe soup that is said to cure all ills. ⊠ *Ancient Olympia next to the river,* ☎ *0624/23–322. No credit cards.*

\$\$ ✕ Taverna Praxitelis. This taverna offers tasty appetizers: Order the pikilia (variety) plate, which includes zucchini fritters, *bourekakia tirolates* (ham and cheese fingers), marinated red peppers, stuffed grape leaves, tzatziki, and meatballs. The prix-fixe Greek menu includes a variety plate, rabbit stifado, beef in lemon sauce, or souvlaki, and a dessert like baklava. ⊠ *Spiliopoulou 7,* ☎ *0624/23–570. V.*

\$\$ ✕ Thraka. This family-run taverna has a large variety of home-cooked food including *lahanokeftedes* (fried vegetable balls), *arnaki giouvetsi* (lamb with bite-size noodles), and beef stifado made with vinegar and garlic. The two kinds of baklava are from the family's pastry shop. Off-season, the cook (and family matriarch) will still prepare meals for you; just call. ⊠ *Vasiliou Bakopanou and Praxitelis Kondili,* ☎ *0624/22– 575; off-season, 0624/22–475. AE, DC, MC, V. Closed Dec.–Mar.*

\$ ✕ Vakhos. If you're at the ancient site and want to break for lunch, follow signs to the nearby village of Miraka. You can try hearty dishes like rooster with noodles, charcoal-broiled chicken, and goat in oregano sauce. ⊠ *3 km (2 mi) outside Olympia on Tripolis road in Miraka,* ☎ *0624/22–498. No credit cards. Closed Dec.–Feb.*

\$\$\$ ⊞ Hotel Europa. Run by the friendly Spiliopoulos family, this Best Western hilltop hotel overlooks ancient Olympia, the mountains of Arcadia, Alfios Valley, and the distant sea. Rooms have flokati rugs, hair dryers, and marble bathrooms. Most rooms face the pool, but try to book one of the six that look onto the archaeological site. Buffet breakfast is included. ⊠ *Off the road to ancient Olympia, at Oikismou Drouba, 27065,* ☎ *0624/22–650 or 0624/22–700,* FAX *0624/23–166. 42 rooms with bath. Restaurant, bar, taverna (summer), pool, tennis court. AE, DC, MC, V.*

\$\$ ⊞ Altis. The Altis is opposite the old museum and near the archaeological site. The rooms have balconies and plenty of light, and the garden is ideal for enjoying the restaurant's hearty *spesiota* (perch baked with onion). Continental breakfast is included in the price. ⊠ *Platia Dimarchiou (town hall sq.), 27065,* ☎ *0624/23–101, 0624/23–102, and 0624/22–459,* FAX *0624/22–525. 61 rooms with bath. Restaurant, air-conditioning. AE, DC, MC, V. Closed Nov.–Mar.*

\$ ⊞ Pelops. The Australian owner has taken a standard '60s Greek hotel and decked the rooms in chintz and lace curtains, for an old-fashioned feel. This fairly quiet hotel across from the main church has rooms with orthopedic mattresses and telephones; most have balconies. Guests without a balcony can use those at the end of each floor or sit on the vine-shaded terrace. ⊠ *Varela 2, 27065,* ☎ *0624/22–543,* FAX *0624/22– 213. 25 rooms with bath. Restaurant, bar. AE, MC, V. Closed Oct.–Feb.*

Patras

\$\$ ✕ Kalypso. In the beach area of Porto Rio about 10 kilometers (6 miles) from Patras, Kalypso offers fresh grilled red mullet and dorado; its specialty, *mides saganaki* (mussels with fried cheese); and a lemon-fish soup, in addition to grilled meats and the usual magirefta. ⊠ *Posidonios 21, Porto Rio,* ☎ *061/994–739. AE, DC, MC, V.*

\$\$ ✕ Majestic. Diners choose from an eclectic mix of Greek, French, and Italian dishes at this restaurant on one of Patras's main squares. Besides fresh seafood like dorado and swordfish, reliable options are pork chops simmered in wine and octopus marinated in vinaigrette. ⊠ *Agiou Nikolaou 2, Platia Trion Simmachon,* ☎ *061/222–792 and 061/272–243. AE, DC, MC, V.*

$$ ✕ **Trikoyia.** The Trikoyia family cooks delicious food in its traditional
★ taverna, where a typical menu showcases *kalofaga* (beef baked with
ham) and fresh grilled fish. Enjoy the ocean view as you complete your
meal with a piece of kaidaifi with whipped cream. ⊠ *Amalias 46,*
☏ *061/279–421. AE, DC, MC, V.*

$ ✕ **Faros.** During the day, the owner is out hauling in his catch, which
he serves up to locals that night. This is a bare-bones, often noisy place,
without a menu, but it serves the freshest fish at the lowest prices. No-
body speaks English, but just point (you pay by weight). Round out
your meal with a Greek salad. ⊠ *Othonos-Amalias 101,* ☏ *061/336–
500. No credit cards. No lunch.*

$$$ ⛉ **Astir.** This large hotel enjoys an excellent location on the waterfront
near the center of town. Spacious and pleasant, it looks out on the busy
harbor and to the mountains across the gulf. All rooms have color TVs.
⊠ *Ag. Andreou 16, 26223,* ☏ *061/277–502 and 061/276–311,* ⅎⅩ
*061/271–644. 120 rooms with bath. 2 restaurants, bar, roof garden,
pool, sauna, conference rooms. AE, DC, MC, V.*

$$$ ⛉ **Porto Rio.** There's a varied selection of rooms and cottages with a
★ wide range of prices at this hotel complex on the sea at Rion, about 8
kilometers (5 miles) from Patras. Most rooms have outstanding views
across the narrow entrance to the Gulf of Corinth. American break-
fast is included. ⊠ *National Road, 26500,* ☏ *061/992—212,* ⅎⅩ
*061/992–115. 218 rooms with bath, 7 suites, 42 cottages. 2 restau-
rants, indoor and outdoor pools, sauna, 2 tennis courts, exercise room,
casino, playground. AE, DC, MC, V.*

$ ⛉ **Adonis.** For its price and location, Adonis has very good rooms, with
TV and air-conditioning. Rooms have balconies, all with gulf and
Adriatic views. Because the hotel is by the bus terminal, some rooms
may be noisy during the day. The price includes buffet breakfast. ⊠
Zaimi and Kapsali 9, ☏ *061/226–715 or 061/224–235,* ⅎⅩ *061/226–
971. 56 rooms with bath. Bar, air-conditioning. AE, MC, V.*

The Arts

The **Festival of Ancient Drama** in the theater at Epidauros takes place
from mid-July to mid-September, weekends only, at 9 PM. Tickets can
be bought at the theater before performances or in advance from the
festival box office in Athens (⊠ Stadiou 4, ☏ 01/322–1459). Patras
also stages a **summer arts festival** July through August. Check with
the Patras International Festival office (⊠ Koryllon 2, Old Municipal
Hospital, Old Town, ☏ 061/279–008, 061/276–540 and 061/278–
730) for details. A few weeks before Greek Orthodox Lent Patras holds
masquerade balls, and, on the last Sunday, the Grand Parade, with en-
trants competing for the best costume. Buy tickets for seats at the Grand
Parade (around 5,500 dr.) at the kiosk in Vas. Georgiou square or at
the Carnival office in the Municipal Cultural Center (⊠ Koryllon 2,
Old Municipal Hospital, Old Town ☏ 061/226–063).

MAINLAND GREECE

The dramatic rocky heights of mainland Greece provide an appropriate
setting for man's attempt to approach divinity. The ancient Greeks
placed their gods on snowcapped Mt. Olympus and chose the pre-
cipitous slopes of Parnassus, "the navel of the universe," as the site
for Delphi, their most important religious center. Many centuries
later, pious Christians built a great monastery (Hosios Loukas) in a
remote mountain valley. Others settled on the rocky peninsula of
Athos, the Holy Mountain. Later, devout men established themselves

precariously on top of strange, towerlike rocks and, to be closer to God, built monasteries like those at Meteora. In fact, many of mainland Greece's most memorable and interesting sites are closely connected with religion—including the remarkable Byzantine churches of Thessaloniki.

In this land of lonely mountain villages, narrow defiles, and dark woods, bands of *klephts* (a cross between brigands and guerrillas) earned their place in folk history and song during the long centuries of Turkish rule. The women of Souli, one of the mountain strongholds of the klephts, threw themselves dancing and singing over a cliff rather than be captured by the Turks. During the German occupation of World War II, guerrilla bands descended from these same mountains to the valleys and plains to harry and attack the enemy.

Since Greece joined the EU farmers have flourished, and few villages, even those tucked away in the hills, are still poor and isolated. But despite the arrival of video clubs and discos, the traditional way of life still survives. The mainland Greeks see fewer tourists and have more time for those they do see; hotels are unlikely to be full, and the sights—steep, wooded mountains, cypress trees like candles, narrow gorges, the soaring monasteries of Meteora—are bold and beautiful.

Getting Around

This proposed itinerary begins in Athens. It can be done by public transportation, car, or guided tour. A one-day trip to Delphi is rushed; two days will give you more leisure time. Your best bet is a three-day trip that includes Delphi and Meteora. The five-day tour takes in more remote parts of western Greece, and other main sights. A longer trip through the mainland should include Hosios Loukas. Thessaloniki is usually included only in lengthy guided tours of northern Greece, but special arts events will attract visitors during 1997, when it is the Cultural Capital of Europe. If you don't have a car, you can leave the Delphi–Meteora tour at Trikala, take the train to Thessaloniki, and return to Athens by plane or train. In September, during the Thessaloniki International Trade Fair, make hotel reservations well in advance.

Guided Tours

For travel agencies in Athens that have tours of mainland Greece, *see* Important Addresses and Numbers *in* Athens, *above*. American Express also has a representative in Thessaloniki at Memphis Travel (⊠ Nikis 23, ☎ 031/222–745 or 031/281–217, ᴬˣ 031/281–508) that can arrange tours in northern Greece. A three-day trip to Delphi and Meteora with half board (hotel, breakfast, and lunch or dinner) costs 73,000 dr. A nine-day tour of northern and central Greece, including Delphi, Meteora, Thessaloniki, Philippi, Kavala, Pella, and Vergina costs around 220,000 dr. with half-board accommodations. Athens travel agencies can also arrange a four-day Thessaloniki tour via plane (about 116,500 dr. and airfare).

Visitor Information

In **Delphi,** visit the municipal tourist office on Vas. Pavlou and Friderikis 12 for helpful service (☎ 0265/82–900); the tourist police are at Apollonos 46 (☎ 0265/82–220). At **Kalambaka,** the tourist police can be found at Hatzipetrou 10–11 (☎ 0432/22–813). In **Thessaloniki,** visit the Greek National Tourist Organization (⊠ Mitropoleos 34 on Platia Aristotelous, ☎ 031/222–935, or at the airport, ☎ 031/471–

Mainland Greece

170); the Thessaloniki tourist police are at Dodekanissou 4 (☎ 031/254–871). ELPA, Greece's Automobile Club, is at Vas. Olgas and Aigaiou (☎ 031/426–319 and 031/426–310).

Exploring Mainland Greece

Thebes and Livadia

To get from Athens to Delphi, take the National Road toward Thessaloniki and turn off to **Thebes** (Thiva), the birthplace of the legendary Oedipus, who unwittingly fulfilled the prophecy of the Delphic Oracle by slaying his father and marrying his mother. Little now remains of the ancient city. At **Livadia,** 45 kilometers (28 miles) farther along the road, are the ruins of a medieval fortress tower above the springs of Lethe (Oblivion) and Mnemosyne (Remembrance). Halfway between Livadia and Delphi is the crossroads where, according to mythology, Oedipus killed his father.

★ The road to the left leads to a serene upland valley and the **Monastery of Hosios Loukas,** a fine example of Byzantine architecture and decoration. Built during the 11th century to replace the earlier shrine of a local saint, it has some of the world's finest Byzantine mosaics. ☎ 0267/22–797. ⌲ 800 dr. ⊙ Daily 8–2 and 4–7 (8–6 in winter).

Arahova

Back on the road to Delphi, you'll climb a spur of Mt. Parnassus to reach the village of **Arahova,** 32 kilometers (20 miles) from Livadia, known for handmade items in brightly colored wools, especially rugs. From Arahova, a short, spectacular drive down to Delphi will take you across the gorge of the Pleistos. You'll see the twin cliffs called the Phaedriades split by the Castalian spring, which gushes with cool, pure water. It was here that pilgrims to the Delphic Oracle came for purification.

Delphi

★ To the ancient Greeks **Delphi** was the center of the universe because two eagles released by the gods at opposite ends of earth met here. For hundreds of years, the worship of Apollo and the pronouncements of the Oracle here made Delphi the most important religious center of ancient Greece. As you walk up the Sacred Way to the **Temple of Apollo,** the **theater,** and the **stadium,** you'll see Mt. Parnassus above; silver-green olive trees below; and, in the distance, the blue Gulf of Itea. This is one of the most rugged and lonely sites in Greece, and one of the most striking; if you can get to the site in the early morning or evening, avoiding the busloads of tourists, you will feel the power and beauty of the place. First excavated in 1892, most of the ruins date from the 5th to the 3rd century BC. ☎ 0265/82–312. ▦ 1,200 dr. ☉ Mon.–Fri. 7:30–7:30 (7:30–5:30 in winter), weekends 8:30–3.

Don't miss the famous bronze charioteer (early 5th century BC) in the **Delphi Museum.** Other works of art here include a statue of Antinoüs, Emperor Hadrian's lover; fragments of a 6th-century BC silver-plated bull, the largest example of an ancient statue in precious metal; the stone *omphalos,* representing the navel of the earth; and fragments from the site's Sifnian Treasury, depicting scenes from the Trojan War. Also note the statues of Kleobis and Viton, who, according to legend, pulled their mother 50 miles by chariot to the Temple of Hera, then died when the goddess rewarded them with eternal sleep. It was said of them, "Those whom the gods love die young." ☎ 0265/82–312. ▦ 1,200 dr. ☉ Tues.–Fri. 7:30–7:30 (7:30–5:30 in winter), Mon. 12–6:30 (11–5:30 in winter), weekends 8:30–3.

Meteora

Past Delphi, the road descends in sharp bends past groves of gnarled, ancient olive trees. Continue 17 kilometers (11 miles) to Amfissa and over the Pournaraki (Bralos) Pass 90 kilometers (56 miles) to the town of Lamia. Follow the road northwest to Karditsa and around the Thessalian plain, past Trikala to **Kalambaka** (139 kilometers, or 86 miles, from Lamia). This will be your base for visits to the monasteries of

★ **Meteora,** which sit atop gigantic pinnacles that tower almost 1,000 feet above the plain. Monks and supplies once reached the top on ladders or in baskets; now steps are cut into the rocks, and some of the monasteries can easily be reached by car. Of the original 24 monasteries, only six can now be visited. Females should wear skirts to the knee, not shorts, and men should wear long pants.

The fortresslike **Varlaam monastery** is easy to reach and has beautiful Byzantine frescoes. To get a better idea of what living in these monasteries was like 300 years ago, climb the steep rock steps to the **Megalo Meteoron,** the largest of them. Make sure that you allow time for the trek up if it's nearing midday or evening closing time. ☎ 0432/22–277 (Varlaam), ☎ 0432/22–278 (Megalo Meteoron). ▦ 400 dr. each. ☉ Daily 9–1 and 3–6 (3–5 in winter). Varlaam closed Fri. (Thurs.–Fri. in winter); Megalo Meteoron closed Tues. (Tues.–Wed. in winter).

Thessaloniki

En route to Thessaloniki, the road east from Trikala crosses the plain of Thessaly (one of Europe's hottest places in summer) and joins the National Road at Larissa. Eventually you will see Mt. Olympus, Greece's highest mountain. The road runs for 154 kilometers (96

★ miles) through the valley of Tempe and up the coast to **Thessaloniki—**

Greece's second-largest city, its second port after Piraeus, and the capital of northern Greece. It is the cocapital of the country as a whole; as a shopping center it is possibly superior to Athens.

Although Thessaloniki still has some remains from the Roman period, it is best known for its fine Byzantine churches. The city is compact enough for you to see the main sights on foot. Start at the 15th-century grayish **White Tower,** landmark and symbol of Thessaloniki, previously named "Tower of Blood," referring to its use as a prison. Now it houses a museum, with an exhibition that includes pottery, mosaics, and ecclesiastical objects relating to the history and art of Byzantine Thessaloniki. ⊠ *Pavlou Mela and Nikis,* ☎ *031/267–832.* ⊡ *800 dr.* ⊙ *Mon. 12:30–7 (11–5 in winter), Tues.–Fri. 8–7 (8–5 in winter), weekends 8:30–3.*

Next, walk up Pavlou Mela toward Tsimiski, the elegant tree-lined shopping street, and cut across to the green-domed basilica-style church of ★ **Agia Sophia,** which dates from the 8th century and has beautifully preserved mosaics.

Walk to Egnatia, which partially traces the original Roman road leading from the Adriatic to the Bosporus. Continue north along the **Roman Agora** (town center) to **Agios Dimitrios,** the principal church. Though it is only a replica of the original 7th-century church that burned down in 1917, it is adorned with many 8th-century mosaics that were in the original building. Follow Aghiou Dimitriou east to **Agios Georgios,** a rotunda built in the 4th century by Roman emperor Galerius as his tomb. His successor, Constantine the Great, the first Christian emperor, turned it into a church. If the current restoration has been completed, have a look at the 4th-century mosaics of flowers, birds, and fish.

Return to Egnatia and the **Arch of the Emperor Galerius,** built shortly before he built the rotunda, to commemorate his victories over forces in Persia, Armenia, and Mesopotamia. A short walk downhill to ★ Tsimiski, where you turn left, brings you to the **Archaeological Museum.** Among its many beautiful objects are a huge bronze vase and a delicate, gold myrtle wreath from Derveni, as well as precious artifacts from the royal tombs of Vergina, including an exquisite gold casket thought to contain the bones of Philip II of Macedon, father of Alexander the Great. ⊠ *Manoli Andronikou 6, Platia Hanth,* ☎ *031/830–538.* ⊡ *1,500 dr.* ⊙ *Mon. 12:30–7 (10:30–5 in winter), Tues.–Fri. 8–7 (8–5 in winter), weekends 8:30–3.*

Dining and Lodging

Visitors to Thessaloniki should note that during the two weeks of the International Trade Fair in September, many room prices increase by about 40%. For details and price-category definitions, *see* Dining and Lodging *in* Staying in Greece, *above.*

Delphi

$$ ✕ **Topiki Gefsi.** This excellent restaurant offers many local specialties, with an emphasis on appetizers: zucchini and eggplant croquettes, roast feta. In winter, warm yourself at the fireplace; in summer, dine on the veranda overlooking Delphi. Try the *kokkora krasato* (rooster stewed in wine), pork with celery, *hortopites* (vegetable pies), and mides saganaki. ⊠ *Vas. Pavlou and Friderikis 19,* ☎ *0265/82–710,* 🖷 *0265/83–186. Reservations essential. AE, DC, MC, V.*

$ ✕ **Vakhos.** From the large terrace decorated with murals of Bacchus (for whom the restaurant is named), you have a view of the Gulf of Itea; enjoy it with the local retsina, kokkora krasato, vegetable pies, souvlakia, and for the adventurous, boiled goat. There are also several fixed-price menus. ⊠ *Apollonos 31,* ☎ *0265/82–448. Closed Sun.–Thurs. mid-Nov.–mid-Mar., except holidays. V.*

$$ ✕⊞ **Kastalia.** Fedriades's (☞ *below*) sister hotel has simple rooms with paintings of the area and views over Mt. Parnassus or to the Gulf of Itea. The restaurant serves traditional Greek food, sometimes with a twist; lamb fricassee, for example, has lettuce rather than the typical cabbage. The price includes Continental breakfast. ⊠ *Vas. Pavlou and Friderikis 13, 33054,* ☎ *0265/82–205 through 0265/82–207,* ℻ *0265/82–208. 26 rooms with bath. Restaurant, bar, TV lounge. AE, DC, MC, V. Closed weekdays Nov.–Mar.*

$$$ ⊞ **Hotel Vouzas.** The hotel sits on the edge of a gorge and has won-
★ derful views from every room. There's a cozy living room with a fire-place, which fills up on winter weekends with Athenians who come to ski Mt. Parnassus. American breakfast is included. ⊠ *Vas. Pavlou and Friderikis 1, 33054,* ☎ *0265/82–232 and 0265/82–234,* ℻ *0265/82–033. 51 rooms with bath, 8 suites. Restaurant. MC, V.*

$$ ⊞ **Apollo.** The *saloni* (living room) here has traditional wall hangings and old prints among its carefully selected furnishings. The light wood furniture in the cheerful bedrooms is set off by blue quilts and striped curtains. Many rooms have views and balconies with iron railings; all have hair dryers, minibars, and TVs. A full breakfast is included. ⊠ *Vas. Pavlou and Friderikis 59B, 33054,* ☎ *0265/82–580 or 0265/82–244,* ℻ *0265/82–455. 21 rooms with bath. Bar, breakfast room, air-conditioning. DC, MC, V. Closed weekdays Nov.–Mar. except during Christmas and Carnival (before Lent).*

$$ ⊞ **Fedriades.** Named after Delphi's famous rocks, this hotel has a neo-classical exterior that gives way to a light, airy lobby and rooms done in marble and wood with views of the Gulf of Itea. Continental break-fast is included in the price. ⊠ *Vas. Pavlou and Friderikis 38, 33054,* ☎ *0265/82–919 or 0265/82–370,* ℻ *0265/82–208. 22 rooms with bath. Cafeteria, bar. MC, V. Closed Mon.–Thurs. Nov.–Mar.*

$ ⊞ **Acropole.** This friendly, family-run hotel has a garden and a spec-
★ tacular view—bare mountainside and a sea of olive groves—so that guests feel as though they're completely secluded. The most romantic rooms–decorated with carved Skyrian furniture–are on the fifth floor. Some rooms have minibars and air-conditioning. ⊠ *Filellinon 13,* ☎ *0265/82–675,* ℻ *0265/83–171. 42 rooms with bath. Bar, breakfast room, air-conditioning, TV lounge. AE, DC, MC, V.*

Kalambaka

$ ✕ **Restaurant Meteora.** A local favorite since 1925, this family restau-
★ rant on the main square relies on the cooking of matriarch Ketty Gert-zos, who prepares such dishes as tsoutsoukakia lamb fricassee, and chicken or pork in wine with green peppers and garlic. The restau-rant closes early; it's best to arrive before 8 PM. ⊠ *Ekonomou 4, on Platia Dimarchou,* ☎ *0432/22–316. No credit cards. Closed Nov.–Mar.*

$ ✕ **Vachos.** This traditional taverna is decorated with ceramics and iron-work; its flower-filled garden has a view of Meteora. Try the mince-meat-stuffed squash with egg-lemon sauce, baked perch, or *pilino Vachos* (baked beef and vegetables topped with cheese). ⊠ *Platia Riga Fereou,* ☎ *0432/24–678. Closed Nov.–Feb. except for Christmas. No credit cards.*

$$$ 🏨 **Amalia.** The area's best hotel is about 4 kilometers (2½ miles) out-
★ side Kalambaka. The low-lying complex has spacious, handsomely dec-
orated public rooms: The sitting room has floral murals; the poolside
bar has glistening blue tiles and rustic rafters. Rooms are done in sooth-
ing colors and have large beds and art prints. Buffet breakfast is included.
✉ *Trikalon 14, Theopetra, 42200,* ☎ *0432/72–216 and 0432/72–217,*
FAX *0432/72–457. 171 rooms with bath, 2 suites. 2 restaurants, bar, cafe-
teria, pool, TV room, meeting rooms. AE, DC, MC, V.*

$$$ 🏨 **Motel Divani.** In spite of its name, this is actually an A-class hotel
priced at the low end of its range. In 1996 the older wing was com-
pletely renovated with new furnishings; also, TVs were added to all
rooms. The hotel's advantage over the Amalia is that half the rooms
have views of the pinnacles. The professional reception staff can arrange for a taxi driver to take you to the various monasteries. Buffet
breakfast is included (half board is available for another 4,500 dr. per
person). ✉ *Trikalon 1, 42200,* ☎ *0432/22–583 and 0432/23–230,*
FAX *0432/23–638. 165 rooms with bath. Restaurant, snack bar, pool.
AE, DC, MC, V.*

$$ 🏨 **Hotel Antoniadi.** After its recent extension, the hotel has many more
pastel-hued rooms with carpeting, minibars, color TVs, and hair dry-
ers; about half view the Meteora rocks. Guests are treated to a wel-
come ouzo upon arrival. Buffet breakfast is included. ✉ *Trikalon 148,
42200,* ☎ *0432/24–387,* FAX *0432/24–319. 70 rooms with bath.
Restaurant, air-conditioning, pool, TV room. AE, V.*

Thessaloniki

$$$ ✗ **Oinanthi.** One of the city's newest, this restaurant quickly became
★ a favorite with visitors for such flawless dishes as duck liver flambé
with Armagnac, salmon and beef carpaccio, and homemade tagli-
atelle. The wine list has several rare vintages. ✉ *Kalapothaki 16,* ☎
031/271–074. AE, V. Closed mid-June–Aug. No lunch.

$$ ✗ **Krikelas.** A Thessaloniki landmark, this family-run taverna has
been serving classic Greek dishes for more than half a century. Its home-
made eggplant dip has a faint smoky taste, and its gyros are heaped
high with succulent lamb. In winter, Krikelas specializes in game like
wild pig and venison; fresh fish is served year-round. ✉ *Ethnikis An-
tistasis 32, Kalamaria,* ☎ *031/451–690 or 031/451–289. AE, DC, MC,
V. Closed June–Aug.*

$$ ✗ **O Ragias.** Known for Macedonian cooking, this small restaurant
decorated with old prints provides a respite from the city's bustle. Un-
usual dishes include *yiaourtlou ragias* (veal topped with tomato and
yogurt-garlic sauces) and *hungar begiendi* (veal with eggplant purée).
Other crowd-pleasers are grilled mussels with butter and garlic and seasonal dishes: beef with leeks and cream, and chicken with plums.
There is piano music nightly, and the restaurant is open throughout
the day for coffee. ✉ *Nikis 13,* ☎ *031/279–993 or 031/227–468. AE,
DE, MC, V. Closed Sun. and national holidays. No lunch.*

$$ ✗ **Ta Nissia.** This restaurant near the White Tower is ideal for any oc-
casion: a business lunch or family celebration. Once you're seated
(amid embroidered curtains, paintings of boats, handicrafts), take
some time to choose from a menu with more than 150 dishes, includ-
ing unbeatable seafood appetizers. Try the boned sardines with onion
and parsley, or squid stuffed with feta and regato. Entrées range from
wild boar to grilled swordfish to beef cassoulet. ✉ *Proxenou Ko-
romila 13,* ☎ *031/285–991 and 031/224–277. Reservations essential.
AE, V. Closed July–Aug.*

$ ✗ **O Kipos ton Pringipon.** The Milos enclave, a former mill complex
★ in the city's slaughterhouse area, is now a nightlife center, with a café
and bars playing everything from light jazz to Greek music. This ouzeri

has a large selection of appetizers—croquettes made with *kasseri* cheese, grilled mushrooms, pastries with shrimp or a cured beef called *pastourma*—and such specialties as diced beef in a mushroom and red-wine sauce topped with cheese and fried *athirina* (a delicious small fish). ✉ *Andrea Georgiou 56, Sfagia,* ☎ *031/516–945. No credit cards.*

$$$$ 🏨 **Makedonia Palace.** The city's only deluxe-category hotel has re-opened after several years' refurbishing. The seaside location is within walking distance of the archaeological museum, International Exhibition Center, and White Tower. All rooms have balconies, minibars, satellite TV with pay movie channels, individual voice mail system, and personal safes. No-smoking and business rooms are also available. ✉ *Megalou Alexandrou 2, 54640,* ☎ *031/861–400,* FAX *868–942. 272 rooms with bath, 16 suites. 2 restaurants, 3 bars, pool, children's pool, beauty salon, health club, meeting rooms. AE, DC, MC, V.*

$$$ 🏨 **Capsis.** A few blocks from the rail station, this hotel is popular with Greek business travelers for its convenient downtown location. There's a roof garden, and recently the hotel added a new floor with more conference space, shops, and a snack bar. Buffet breakfast is included. ✉ *Monastiriou 18, 54629,* ☎ *031/521–321 or 031/521–421,* FAX *031/510–555. 421 rooms with bath, 7 suites. Restaurant, bar, pool, meeting rooms. AE, DC, MC, V.*

$$$ 🏨 **Electra Palace.** This hotel is built in a neo-Byzantine style to match
★ the other buildings on Thessaloniki's grand square in the center of town. There is a no-smoking floor, and rooms have hair dryers, refrigerators, and TV; those with a view run about 3,000 dr. more. Buffet breakfast is included. ✉ *Platia Aristotelous 9, 54624,* ☎ *031/232–221 through 031/232–230,* FAX *031/235–947. 125 rooms with bath, 6 suites. Restaurant, bar, meeting rooms. AE, DC, MC, V.*

$$$ 🏨 **Panorama.** If you don't mind taking a taxi or the shuttle downtown, this is a delightful hotel tucked into the wealthy, foothill suburb of Panorama, about 10 kilometers (6 miles) from downtown. Rooms have Italian lighting and furniture, TVs, and three telephones, including one in the bathroom. On the terrace you can enjoy the city view unhurriedly with an iced coffee or frozen sherbet. ✉ *Analipseos 26, Panorama, 55236,* ☎ *031/341–123,* FAX *031/341–229. 47 rooms with bath, 3 suites. Restaurant, bar, minibar. AE, DC, MC, V.*

$$ 🏨 **Pella.** The owners of this quiet hotel between city hall and the Ministry of Northern Greece are always making improvements to their small but spotless rooms. Prices are quite low (except for September), so book early. ✉ *Ionos Dragoumi 63, 54630,* ☎ *031/524–221, 031/524–222, or 031/524–224,* FAX *031/524–223. 79 rooms with bath. Breakfast room, meeting rooms. AE, MC, V.*

$ 🏨 **Hotel Tourist.** One block from the main square, this extremely modest hotel is a dignified high-ceilinged building from the turn of the century. It has absoutely no frills, but for those on a budget, it's one of the best in the city. ✉ *Mitropoleos 21, 54624,* ☎ *031/276–335,* FAX *031/226–865. 37 rooms, 32 with bath. No credit cards.*

THE AEGEAN ISLANDS

The islands of the Aegean have colorful legends of their own—the Minotaur in Crete; the lost continent of Atlantis, which some believe was Santorini; and the Colossus of Rhodes, to name a few. Each island has its own personality. Mykonos has windmills, dazzling white-washed buildings, hundreds of tiny churches and chapels on golden hillsides, and small fishing harbors. Visitors to volcanic Santorini sail into what was once a vast volcanic crater and anchor near the island's forbidding cliffs. Crete, with its jagged mountain peaks, olive orchards, and vineyards, contains the remains of the Minoan civilization. In Rhodes, a bustling modern town surrounds a walled town with a medieval castle.

Getting Around

The simplest way to visit the Aegean Islands is by cruise ship. You might consider a three-day cruise to the four most popular islands—Mykonos, Rhodes, Crete, and Santorini. Car and passenger ferries sail to these main destinations from Piraeus, the port of Athens, and to Mykonos also from Rafina, 32 kilometers (20 miles) north of Athens. If you sail from Piraeus, you will be able to see one of the great sights of Greece: the Temple of Poseidon looming on a hilltop at Cape Sounion, at the tip of mainland Greece. There is also frequent air service from Athens, and most flights are full, especially in summer. It's vital to book well in advance and to reconfirm.

Guided Tours

Aegean Cruises

From April through October many cruises go to the Aegean Islands from Piraeus. Try **Hydrodynamic Cruises** (⊠ Xenofontos 14, Athens, 10557, ☎ 01/323–4292) or **Sun Line-Epirotiki** (⊠ Iasonas 3, Piraeus, 18537, ☎ 01/429–0700 for reservations or 800/872–6400 in the U.S.). They offer cruises ranging from one to seven days. In the United Kingdom, contact **Epirotiki** (⊠ Westmoreland House, 127-131 Regent St., London WIR 7HA, ☎ 0171/734–0805 through 734/0806).

Visitor Information

There are **Greek National Tourist Organization** offices on **Crete,** at Kriari 40, Hania (☎ 0821/92–624 or 0821/92–943), Xanthoudidou 1, across from the archaeological museum in Heraklion (☎ 081/244–462 and 081/228–203), and on the El. Venizelou beach road in Rethymnon (☎ 0831/29–148); on **Rhodes,** at Archbishop Makarios and Papagou, Rhodes town (☎ 0241/23–655, 0241/21–921, or 0241/27–466). Friendlier and closer to the Old Town is the **Rhodes Municipal Tourism Office** off Platia Rimini (☎ 0241/35–945; closed Nov.–Apr.) The **tourist police** can be of help in **Mykonos** (⊠ at the port, ☎ 0241/22–482) and **Santorini** (⊠ on Thira's main road 600 ft. from the square, ☎ 0286/22–649).

Exploring the Aegean Islands

Mykonos

Mykonos is the name of the island and also of its chief village—a colorful maze of narrow, paved streets lined with whitewashed houses, many with bright blue doors and shutters. Every morning, women scrub the sidewalks and streets in front of their homes, undaunted by the donkeys that pass by each day. During the 1960s, the bohemian jet set discovered Mykonos, and many old houses along the waterfront are now restaurants, nightclubs, bars, and discos—both gay and straight—all blaring music until early morning; a quiet café or taverna is hard to find. Mykonos is a favorite anchorage with the international yacht set, as well as being *the* holiday destination for the young, lively, and liberated—finding yourself alone on any of its beaches is unlikely.

The Aegean Islands

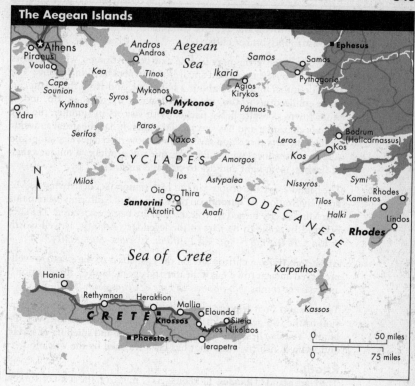

Those staying more than a day should pay a quick visit to the **archaeological museum** to get a sense of the island's history; the most significant local find is a 7th-century BC pithos, or storage jar, showing the Greeks emerging from the Trojan Horse. ⊠ *North end of port,* ☎ *0289/22–325.* ⊡ *500 dr.* ☼ *Tues.–Sun. 8:30–3.*

From the museum stroll down to the esplanade, where islanders promenade in the evening, or meander through the town, whose confusing layout was designed to foil attacking pirates. In a much-visited neighborhood called **Little Venice,** at the southwest end of the port, a few of the old houses have been turned into stylish bars and colorful balconies hang over the water. In the distance, lined up like toy soldiers on the high hill, are the famous **Mykonos windmills,** vestiges of a time when wind power was used to grind the island's grain.

Mykoniots claim that 365 churches and chapels dot their landscape, one for each day of the year. The best known of these is the **Church of Paraportiani** on Anargon Street. The whitewashed mix of Byzantine and vernacular idiom has been described as a confectioner's dream gone mad.

Delos

About 30–40 minutes by boat from Mykonos is the ancient isle of **Delos,** the legendary sanctuary of Apollo. Its **Terrace of the Lions,** a remarkable group of nine Naxian marble sculptures from the 7th century BC, is worth the trip. Another highlight is some of the houses of the Roman period, with their fine floor mosaics. The best of these mosaics are in the **Archaeological Museum.** ☎ *0289/22–259.* ⊡ *1,200 dr. (archaeological site and museum).* ☼ *Tues.–Sun. 8:30–3.*

Santorini

The best way to approach **Santorini** is to sail into its harbor, once the vast crater of the volcano, and dock beneath its black and red cliffs, rising up to 1,000 feet above the sea. The white houses and churches of the main town, **Thira** (Fira), cling inside the rim in dazzling white contrast to the somber cliffs.

Most passenger ferries now use the new port, Athinios, where visitors are met by buses, taxis, and small-hotel owners hawking rooms. The bus ride into Thira takes about a half hour, and from there you can make connections to **Oia,** the serene town at the northern tip, and to other towns. Despite being packed with visitors in summer, the tiny town is charming and has spectacular views. It has the usual souvenir and handicrafts shops and several reasonably priced jewelry shops. Be sure to try the local wines. The volcanic soil produces a unique range of flavors, from light and dry to rich and aromatic.

The island's volcano erupted in the 15th century BC, destroying its Minoan civilization. At **Akrotiri,** on the south end of Santorini, the remains of a Minoan city buried by volcanic ash are being excavated. The site, believed by some to be part of the legendary Atlantis, is well worth visiting. ☎ 0286/81–366. ▣ 1,200 dr. ☉ Tues.–Sun. 8:30–3.

At **Ancient Thira,** a clifftop site on the east coast of the island, a well-preserved ancient town has a theater and agora, houses, fortifications, and ancient tombs. *No phone.* ▣ *Free.* ☉ *Tues.–Sun. 8:30–3.*

Take a short boat trip for an enjoyable but slightly unnerving excursion to the still-active volcanic islands called the **Kamenes** (Burnt Islands). You can descend into a small crater, hot and smelling of sulfur, and swim in nearby water that has been warmed by the volcano.

Rhodes

The large island of **Rhodes,** 11 kilometers (7 miles) off the coast of Turkey, is the chief island of the group of 12 called the Dodecanese. The northern end is one of Greece's major vacation centers, and the **old walled city** is full of crooked cobbled streets and echoes of antiquity. It's also full of the trappings of tourism, mainly evident in pubs and bars that cater to the large European market. The island as a whole is not so beautiful, but it has fine beaches and an excellent climate. It makes a good base for visiting other islands of the Dodecanese, with their mixture of Aegean and Turkish architecture.

The town of Rhodes has an attractive harbor with fortifications; the gigantic bronze statue of the Colossus of Rhodes, once supposed to have straddled the entrance, was one of the wonders of the ancient world. The fascinating Old Town of Rhodes was built by crusaders—the Knights of St. John—on the site of an ancient city. The knights ruled the island from 1309 until they were defeated by the Turks in

★ 1522. On the Street of the Knights stands the **Knights' Hospital,** now the Archaeological Museum, with ancient pottery and sculpture, including two famous statues of Aphrodite. ☎ 0241/27–657. ▣ 800 dr. ☉ Tues.–Fri. 8–7 (8:30–3 in winter), weekends and holidays 8:30–3.

Another museum that deserves your attention is the restored medieval **Palace of the Grand Master.** Destroyed in 1856 by a gunpowder explosion, the palace was renovated by the Italians as a summer retreat for Mussolini. Note its splendid Hellenistic and Roman floor mosaics. ✉ *Street of the Knights,* ☎ 0241/23–359. ▣ 1,200 dr. ☉ Tues.–Fri. 8–7 (8:30–3 in winter), weekends and holidays 8:30–3.

★ The **walls** of Rhodes's Old Town are among the greatest medieval monuments in the Mediterranean. For 200 years the knights strengthened them, making them up to 40 feet thick in places and curving the surfaces to deflect cannon balls. You can take a walk on part of the 4-

kilometer (2½-mile) road along the top of the walls. ☎ 0241/23–359 for information. ▦ 1,200 dr. ⊘ Tues., Sat. at 2:40.

★ From the town of Rhodes, drive about 60 kilometers (37 miles) down the east coast to the enchanting village of **Lindos.** Put on your comfortable shoes and walk up the steep hill to the ruins of the ancient **Acropolis of Lindos.** The sight of its beautiful colonnade with the sea far below is unforgettable. Look for little St. Paul's Harbor, beneath the cliffs of the acropolis; seen from above, it appears to be a lake, as the entrance from the sea is obscured by rocks. ☎ 0244/31–258. ▦ 1,200 dr. ⊘ Tues.–Sun. 8:30–6:40 (8:30–2:40 in winter).

Crete

Greece's largest island, situated in the south Aegean, was the center of Europe's earliest civilization, the Minoan, which flourished from about 2000 BC to 1200 BC. **Crete** was struck a mortal blow in about 1450 BC by an unknown cataclysm, now thought to be political. The most im-

★ portant Minoan remains are in the **Archaeological Museum** in Heraklion, Crete's largest (and least attractive) city. The museum's treasures include some sophisticated frescoes and ceramics depicting Minoan life. ✉ Plateia Eleftherias, ☎ 081/226–092. ▦ 1,500 dr. ⊘ Mon. 12:30–7 (12:30–5 in winter), Tues.–Sun. 8–7 (8–5 in winter).

★ Not far from Heraklion is the partly reconstructed **Palace of Knossos.** Note the simple throne room, which contains the oldest throne in Europe, and the bathrooms with their efficient plumbing. The palace was the setting for the legend of the Minotaur, a monstrous offspring of Queen Pasiphae and a bull, which King Minos confined to the labyrinth under the palace. ☎ 081/231–940. ▦ 1,500 dr. ⊘ Daily 8–7 (8–5 in winter).

Crete belonged to Venice from 1210 until 1669, when it was conquered by the Turks. The island became part of Greece early in this century. The **Venetian ramparts** that withstood a 24-year Turkish siege still surround Heraklion. In addition to archaeological treasures, Crete boasts beautiful mountain scenery and many beach resorts along the north coast. One is **Mallia,** which contains the remains of another Minoan palace and has good sandy beaches. Two other beach resorts, **Ayios Nikolaos** and the nearby **Elounda,** lie farther east.

Western Crete, with soaring mountains, deep gorges, and rolling olive orchards, is much less overrun by tourists. The region is rich in Byzantine churches, Venetian monasteries, and interesting upland villages. A worthwhile detour is to **Arkadi Monastery,** off the old Heraklion-Hania road, one of the island's most stunning pieces of Renaissance architecture and a place of pilgrimage for Cretans. In 1866, the monastery was besieged during a rebellion against the Turks, and the abbot, together with several hundred rebels and their families, refused to surrender. When the Turkish forces broke though the gate, the defenders set the gunpowder store afire, killing themselves and many Turks. ☎ 0831/71–216. ▦ 200 dr. (museum). ⊘ Daily 8–5.

The town of ★**Rethymnon** is dominated by the Venetian castle at its western end, the Fortezza. Wandering through the town's **old section,** you will come across carved-stone Renaissance doorways belonging to vanished mansions, fountains, wooden Turkish houses, and one of the few surviving minarets in Greece. It belongs to the Neratzes mosque, now a concert hall, and you can climb its 120 steps for a panoramic view. Don't miss the carefully restored Venetian loggia, the clubhouse of the local nobiity. The small Venetian harbor, with its 13th-century lighthouse, comes to life in summer, with restaurant tables cluttering the quayside.

★ **Hania** is one of the most attractive towns in Greece. Work your way through the covered market, then through the maze of narrow streets to the waterfront. Walk along the inner harbor, past the Venetian arsenals and around to the old lighthouse, for a magnificent view of the town with the White Mountains looming beyond. Behind the outer harbor, Theotokopoulou and Zambeliou streets lead you into the alleys where almost all the houses are Venetian or Turkish, and to the **archaeological museum.** The finds come from all over western Crete: The painted Minoan clay coffins and elegant Late Minoan pottery indicate the wealth of the region during the Bronze Age. ⊠ *Halidos 24,* ☏ *0821/20–334.* ▣ *500 dr.* ☉ *Tues–Sun. 8:30–3.*

In summer, boat service operates along the southwest coast, stopping at **Paleochora,** the area's main resort. **Elafonissi** islet has white sand beaches and black rocks set in a turquoise sea (to get there, you wade across a narrow channel). A good road on the west coast from Elafonissi north accesses beaches that are rarely crowded even in summer,

★ including **Falasarna,** near Crete's northwest tip.

Dining and Lodging

For details and price-category definitions, *see* Dining *and* Lodging *in* Staying in Greece, *above.*

Crete

$$ ✕ **Vassilis.** Watch the boats bobbing along the jetty at this classic tav-
★ erna. Don't miss the fish roe dip and Cretan dishes like *koukouvayia* (a local roll soaked in wine, tomato, oil, and herbs) and lamb fricassee stewed with lettuce. The owners also make their own wine. ⊠ *Nearchou 10, old harbor, Rethymnon,* ☏ *0831/22–967 or 0831/26–920. AE, DC, MC, V. Closed an occasional Sun. in winter.*

$ ✕ **Kyriakos.** This popular taverna, with pink tablecloths and green chairs, offers fish and such Cretan specialties as snail stew with *pligouri* (cracked wheat), artichokes with broad beans, roast lamb with yogurt, baked vegetable omelette, and *tiropitakia* (pies with honey and creamy, mild Cretan cheese). ⊠ *Leoforos Dimokratias 53, Heraklion,* ☏ *081/224–649. AE, DC, V. Closed Wed. and June 15–July 15.*

$ ✕ **Minos Taverna.** Specialties at this outdoor restaurant include lamb in yogurt, stifado, fresh seafood, stuffed squash blossoms (spring only), and homemade *rizogalo* (rice pudding made from sheep's milk). Service is prompt and attentive. ⊠ *Daedalou 10, Heraklion,* ☏ *081/244–827, 081/220–339, or 081/246–466. Closed Nov.–Jan. AE, MC, V.*

$$ ✕▥ **Doma.** This converted 19th-century mansion on the outskirts of Hania has the welcoming atmosphere of a private house: The sitting room has a fireplace, armchairs with embroidered scarlet bolsters, and artifacts such as marble fragments with Ottoman inscriptions. The dining room, where the owner serves dinner on request (lamb cooked with white wine and Cretan mountain herbs, for example), has a memorable view across the bay to the old town. Many rooms have air-conditioning; ask for one overlooking the garden to reduce street noise. Continental breakfast is included. ⊠ *E. Venizelou 124, Hania, 73100,* ☏ *0821/51–772,* ☏ *0821/41–578. 25 rooms with bath, 3 suites. Dining room, air-conditioning. MC, V. Closed Nov.–Mar.*

$$$$ ▥ **Elounda Beach.** This is one of Greece's most renowned seaside resorts, 9 kilometers (7 miles) north of Ayios Nikolaos. The complex,
★ set in beautiful grounds—the pool is cleverly landscaped among

carob trees—includes a miniature Greek village, complete with kafeneion and church. Buffet breakfast is included in the hefty price. ✉ *Elounda Beach, 72053,* ☎ *0841/41–812 or 0841/41–412,* ⅋ *0841/41–373. 121 rooms with bath, 85 bungalows, 58 suites and suite-bungalows. 5 restaurants, 3 bars, outdoor pool, miniature golf, 2 tennis courts, health club, 2 beaches, dance club. AE, DC, MC, V. Closed Nov.–Mar.*

$$$ ⚇ **Casa Delfino.** This tranquil hotel in the heart of Hania's old town
★ was once part of a Venetian Renaissance palace. Rooms (most on two levels) are decorated in cool pastel colors with modern furniture and are set around a courtyard. By early 1997 the owners will have added four apartments with hydromassage bathtubs and satellite TVs. A full breakfast is included. ✉ *Theofanous 9, Palio Limani, Hania, 73131,* ☎ *0821/93–098 or 0821/87–400,* ⅋ *0821/96–500. 12 rooms with bath. Kitchenettes. DC, MC, V.*

$$$ ⚇ **Porto Rethymno.** To escape street noise, ask for a room high up, with a view across the bay to the Venetian fortress. This strikingly designed waterfront hotel, though only five minutes from the center, has its own beach. Tennis and other sports are available at the Grecotel Rithymna Beach. ✉ *Paralia, Rethymno, 74100,* ☎ *0831/50–432 through 0831/50–436,* ⅋ *0831/27–825. 197 rooms with bath, 3 suites. Restaurant, snack bar, pool, sauna, steam room, exercise room. AE, DC, MC, V. Closed Nov.–Mar.*

$$ ⚇ **Atrion.** Tucked away in a quiet street behind Heraklion's historical museum is this well-run hotel. All rooms, done in shades of blue with heavy wood furniture, are air-conditioned, with sea or courtyard views and TVs. Drinks are served in the evening in the tiny patio-garden, and a generous breakfast buffet is included in the price. ✉ *Chronaki 9, Hania, 71202,* ☎ *081/229–225,* ⅋ *081/223–292. 65 rooms with bath. Restaurant, air-conditioning. AE, DC, MC, V.*

$$ ⚇ **Mediterranean.** This comfortable hotel is in the center of Heraklion, 5 kilometers (3 miles) from the beach. More than half the rooms have air-conditioning, and full breakfast is included. Half-board is available (4,000 dr.). ✉ *Smyrnis 1, Platia Daskaloyianni, Heraklion, 71201,* ☎ *081/289–331 through 081/289–334,* ⅋ *081/289–335. 55 rooms with bath. Restaurant, air-conditioning. AE, DC, MC, V.*

Mykonos

$$$ ✕ **Chez Cat'rine.** This restaurant's splendid interior combines the
★ whitewashed walls and archways of the Cyclades with the feeling of a French chateau. Among the superbly cooked French and Greek dishes are baby squid stuffed with rice, cheese souffle, leg of lamb, and tournedos langoustine. ✉ *Delos and Drakopoulou, opposite St. Gerasimos's church,* ☎ *0289/22–169. Reservations essential. AE, MC, V. Closed Nov.–Apr. No lunch.*

$$ ✕ **Pilafas.** This friendly taverna just behind the waterfront (follow the signs) is patronized by locals for its good grilled dishes, salads, and seafood. ✉ *Chora,* ☎ *0289/24–120. No credit cards. No lunch.*

$$$$ ⚇ **Cavo Tagoo.** This medley of cream cubical suites perched above a
★ small beach has been recognized for its unique architecture in several international competitions. The hotel is about ten minutes' walk from the port; all rooms have balconies or terraces with sea views. American breakfast is included. ✉ *Tourlou Beach off Polykandrioti St., 84600,* ☎ *0289/23–692 through 0289/23–695,* ⅋ *0289/24–923; in Athens* ☎ *01/643–0233,* ⅋ *01/644–5237. 67 rooms with bath, 5 maisonettes. Restaurant, 2 bars, saltwater pool, baby-sitting. AE, DC, MC, V. Closed Nov.–Mar.*

$$ **⊞ Kamari.** This hotel looks like new and is 4 kilometers (2½ miles) from Mykonos town, between two sheltered sandy beaches that are each a five-minute walk away. The hotel has added 12 upscale rooms, with TV, refrigerator, and air-conditioning. Buffet breakfast is included. ⊠ *Platy Gialos, 84600,* ☎ *0289/23–424, 0289/23–982, or 0289/25–054,* FAX *0289/24–414. 55 rooms with bath. Breakfast room, bar, air-conditioning, pool. AE, MC, V. Closed Nov.–Mar.*

$$ **⊞ Kouneni Hotel.** The Kouneni is a casual, family-run hotel in the town center that's quieter than most. It is set in a cool green garden, the ideal place to linger over the full breakfast that's included in the price. Rooms are fairly large and look out on the garden. ⊠ *Tria Pigadia, across from public school, 84600,* ☎ *0289/22–301 and 0289/23–311,* FAX *0289/26–559. 20 rooms with bath. Bar. No credit cards.*

Rhodes

$$$–$$$$ **✕ Ta Kioupia.** Antique farm implements hang on the walls at this
★ Rhodes landmark, and tables are elegantly set with linens, fine china, and crystal. Food arrives on large platters, and for a fixed price you select what pleases your eye: carrot bread, pine-nut salad, oven-baked meatballs with leeks, *tiropites* (four-cheese pie), and rooster kebab. ⊠ *Tris, about 7 km (4¼ mi) from Rhodes town,* ☎ *0241/91–824. Reservations essential. AE, V. Closed Sun. and Jan. No lunch.*

$$$ **✕ Alexis.** The owner spares effort to bring his enthusiastic clientele
★ the very best seafood—whether fresh lobster, sea bream, or red mullet, or specialties such as sea urchin and sea snail. A side dish might be delicate sautéed squash with greens such as *vlita* (notchweed) and *glistrida* (purslane). Finish your meal on the shady terrace with *hilli,* a kind of baklava with ice cream. ⊠ *Sokratous 18, Old Town,* ☎ *0241/29–347. AE, MC, V. Closed Christmas, New Year's, and Easter.*

$$ **✕ Dinoris.** Set in a great hall built in 1530 as a stable for the knights, this establishment has long specialized in fish. For mezedes, try the variety platter, which includes their famous *psarokeftedakia* (fish balls made from a secret recipe) as well as mussels, shrimp, and lobster. Other savory dishes are the bourekakia with shrimp and the coquilles St. Jacques. ⊠ *Platia Mouseou 14A, Old Town,* ☎ *0241/25–824 or 0241/35–530. Reservations essential for garden. AE, MC, V.*

$$ **✕ Palia Istoria.** Ensconced in an old house with genteel murals, this
★ mezedopolion is a visual treat. Begin your meal with a few appetizers such as feta saganaki dusted with the potent red pepper *bukova* or plump mussels served with *tsouska* peppers. Entrées include pork tenderloin in wine sauce and shrimp ouzo with orange juice. ⊠ *Mitropoleos 108 and Dendrinou, Ayios Dimitrios area (about 600 dr. by taxi from center),* ☎ *0241/32–421. MC, V. No lunch.*

$ **✕ Taverna Nissiros.** Once the home of an Aga, this simple taverna serves traditional Greek dishes in the large courtyard or the cozy interior decorated with sheep bells and kilims. Besides fresh fish, the owner serves good charcoal-grilled meats and strong barrel wine. ⊠ *Ayiou Fanouriou 44–47 between Sokratous and Omirou sts, Old Town,* ☎ *0241/31–471. AE, MC, V. Closed Nov.–Mar.*

$$$–$$$$ **⊞ Rhodos Imperial.** The buildings of this Grecotel establishment zigzag
★ down the hillside like stacked red, blue, and yellow boxes. Linked by a pedestrian tunnel to the beach, the hotel offers excellent value for a resort set just 4 kilometers (2½ miles) from Rhodes town. The crisp, modern rooms are in shades of peach and gray or blue and sea green; all have balconies, about two-thirds with sea views (it's the extra cost for the view that bumps the price category up another notch). Buffet breakfast is included. ⊠ *Ialyssou Ave, P.O. Box 316, Ixia, 85100,* ☎

0241/75–000, FAX 0241/76–691. *357 rooms with bath, 49 suites. 3 restaurants, 3 pools (1 indoor), sauna, 4 tennis courts, exercise room, 2 squash courts, children's programs, meeting rooms. AE, DC, MC, V. Closed mid-Nov.–mid-Mar.*

$$$ 🏨 **Grand Hotel Summer Palace.** This resort hotel in Rhodes town offers easy access to the beach across the street and the casino next door, the Old Town (20 minutes on foot), and the New Town's vibrant nightlife. The best rooms are in the new wings, with their pink marble floors and paintings of nymphs and goddesses. Rooms have either a sea or a garden view. American breakfast is included. ✉ *Akti Miaouli 1, Rhodes, 85100,* ☎ *0241/26–284,* FAX *0241/35–589; in Athens* ☎ *01/291–7027,* FAX *01/291–7672. 350 rooms with bath, 18 suites. Restaurant, bar, 4 pools (1 indoor, 1 children's), tennis court, sauna, exercise room, nightclub, meeting rooms. AE, DC, MC, V.*

$$ 🏨 **S. Nikolis Hotel.** This small hotel within the Old Town is away from the most crowded tourist area. The rooms, renovated in 1995, are outfitted with dark, rustic furniture, air-conditioning, TVs, and refrigerators; they look out toward the spacious courtyard or the old city walls. A roof terrace lets you enjoy the included buffet breakfast with a view over the entire town. ✉ *Ippodamou 61, Rhodes, 85100,* ☎ *0241/34–561, 0241/36–238, 0241/34–747,* FAX *0241/32–034. 10 rooms with bath, 4 apartments, 4 honeymoon suites. Restaurant, bar, breakfast room, air-conditioning. AE, DC, MC, V.*

$ 🏨 **Spartalis Hotel.** Many rooms in this simple but lively hotel near the city's port have balconies overlooking the bay. Note that the rooms on the street are noisy. ✉ *Plastira 2, Rhodes, 85100,* ☎ *0241/24–371 and 0241/24–372,* FAX *0241/20–406. 79 rooms with bath. Breakfast room, bar. AE, DC, MC, V. Closed Nov.–Mar.*

Santorini

$$$ ✕ **Alexandria.** Island specialties are served in this remodeled private house with high ceilings and a great veranda, set on the rim of the caldera. Especially good are the stuffed lamb cutlets with cumin, mushrooms, and wine. ✉ *S. end of Hypapantis walkway, Thira,* ☎ *0286/22510. V. Closed Nov.–Mar.*

$$ ✕ **Camille Stefani.** At one of the island's best restaurants, you can enjoy
★ the seafood and the Greek and Continental cuisine with a view of the sea. Try the mushrooms in cream and garlic, followed by one of the 16 versions of beef fillet, and at least a glass of the mellow Santorini Lava red wine. ✉ *Beach road, Kamari,* ☎ *0286/31–716. Reservations essential. AE, MC, V. Closed Mon.–Thurs. mid-Nov.–Mar.*

$ ✕ **Nikolas.** You can't go wrong at this simple, congenial taverna, one
★ of the few places in town that stays open in winter. The menu, which changes daily, offers a limited but delicious choice of classic Greek dishes, including stifado, stuffed cabbage rolls, and mountain greens. ✉ *Erithrou Stavrou, Thira, no phone. No credit cards.*

$$$$ 🏨 **Perivolas.** Built into the cliffside at the outskirts of beautiful Oia village, these traditional houses are individually designed in Cycladic style. They overlook the sea and the volcano and offer comfortable accommodations complete with a sculptured fresh water pool and terrace bar. Buffet breakfast is included. ✉ *Oia, 84702,* ☎ *0286/71–308,* FAX *0286/71–309. 14 houses, each with 2 rooms and bath. Bar, kitchenettes, pool. No credit cards. Closed Nov.–Mar.*

$$$ 🏨 **Hotel Kavalari.** This inviting hotel is built into the cliffside facing
★ the caldera. Each room is different; some resemble small caves, with colorful blankets and interesting local handicrafts. All have access to flower-decked terraces. Continental breakfast is included. ✉ *Follow signs from Hypapantis walkway, Box 17, Thira, 84700,* ☎ *0286/22–*

455 or 0286/22–347, FAX *0286/22–603. 18 rooms with bath. Some rooms with kitchenettes. MC, V. Closed Nov.–mid.-April.*

$$ ☷ **Matina.** Near the beach at Kamari, this pleasant family-run hotel is set among vineyards. Prices are at the bottom of the category; half the rooms have air-conditioning, and the owners are now building a swimming pool. ⊠ *Kamari, 84700,* ☎ *0286/31–491 or 0286/32–295,* FAX *0286/31–860. 27 rooms with bath. Bar, air-conditioning. AE, DC, MC, V. Closed mid-Nov.–mid-Mar.*

14 Hungary

Budapest

The Danube Bend

Lake Balaton

HUNGARY SITS, PROUDLY BUT PRECARIOUSLY, at the crossroads of Central Europe, having somehow retained its own identity despite countless invasions and foreign occupation by great powers of the East and West. Its industrious, resilient people have a history of brave but doomed uprisings: against the Turks in the 17th century, the Hapsburgs in 1848, and the Soviet Union in 1956. Each has resulted in a period of readjustment, a return to politics as the art of the possible.

The '60s and '70s saw matters improve politically and materially for most Hungarians. Communist party leader János Kádár remained relatively popular at home and abroad, allowing Hungary to improve trade and relations with the West. The bubble began to burst in the 1980s, however, when the economy stagnated and inflation escalated. The peaceful transition to democracy began when young reformers in the party shunted aside the aging Mr. Kádár in 1988 and began speaking openly about multiparty democracy, a market economy, and cutting ties with Moscow. Events quickly gathered pace, and by spring 1990, as the Iron Curtain fell, Hungarians went to the polls in the first free elections in 40 years. A center-right government took office, sweeping away the communists and their renamed successor party, the Socialists, who finished fourth. Ironically, four years later, in the nation's next elections, Hungarians voted out the ailing center-right party in favor of none other than the Hungarian Socialist party, which now rules in coalition with the Free Democrats. *Plus ça change . . .*

In bald mathematical terms, the total area of Hungary (Magyarország) is less than that of Pennsylvania, but every square foot is packed with natural beauty. Two rivers cross the country: the Duna (Danube) flows from the west through Budapest on its way to the southern frontier, the smaller Tisza from the northeast across the Great Plain (Nagyalföld). Western Hungary is dominated by the largest lake in Central Europe, Lake Balaton. Although overdevelopment is creeping up, the northern lakeshore is still dotted with Baroque villages and Old World spas, and the surrounding hills are covered with vineyards. In eastern Hungary, the Nagyalföld is steeped in the romantic culture of the Magyars (the Hungarians' name for themselves), with its spicy food, strong wine, and proud *csikós* (horsemen).

However, it is Budapest, a city of more than 2 million people, that draws travelers from all over the world. Bisected by the Danube, the city has a split personality; villas and government buildings cluster in the hills of Buda to the west, whereas an imposing array of hotels, restaurants, and shopping areas crowd the flatlands of Pest.

Hungarians are known for their hospitality and love talking to foreigners, although their unfamiliar language, which has almost no links to Indo-European tongues, can be a problem. Today, however, everyone seems to be learning English, especially young people. Older people, on the other hand, tend to be more familiar with German. Hungarians of all ages share a deep love of music, and wherever you go you will hear it, whether it's opera performed at Budapest's imposing opera house or simply gypsy violins serenading you at dinner.

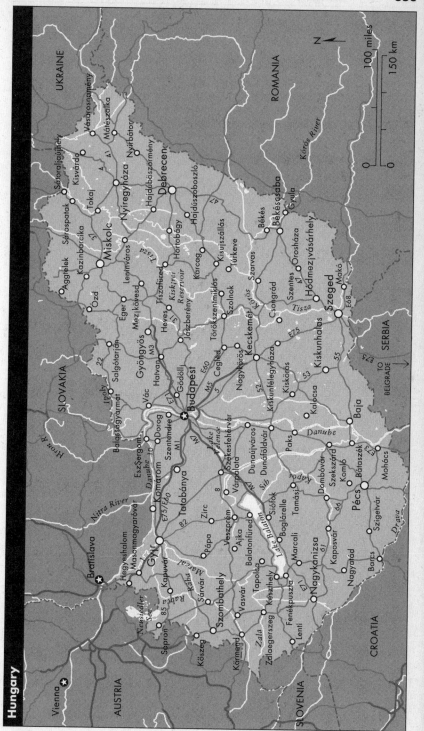

ESSENTIAL INFORMATION

Before You Go

When to Go

Many of Hungary's major fairs and festivals take place in the spring and fall. During July and August, Budapest can be hot and the resorts at Lake Balaton crowded, so spring (May) and the end of summer (September) are the ideal times to visit.

CLIMATE

The following are average daily maximum and minimum temperatures for Budapest.

Jan.	34F	1C	May	72F	22C	Sept.	73F	23C
	25	– 4		52	11		54	12
Feb.	39F	4C	June	79F	26C	Oct.	61F	16C
	28	– 2		59	15		45	7
Mar.	50F	10C	July	82F	28C	Nov.	46F	8C
	36	2		61	16		37	3
Apr.	63F	17C	Aug.	81F	27C	Dec.	39F	4C
	45	7		61	16		30	– 1

Currency

The unit of currency is the forint (Ft.), divided into 100 fillérs (f.). There are bills of 50, 100, 500, 1,000, and 5,000 forints; coins of 10, 20, and 50 fillérs and 1, 2, 5, 10, and 20 forints. A newly designed series of the forint coins—including new but rare 100- and 200-forint pieces—was introduced into the system in late 1993, precipitating general frustration with pay phones and other coin-operated machines that still accept only the old coins. At press time (spring 1996) the exchange rate was approximately 145 Ft. to the U.S. dollar, 105 Ft. to the Canadian dollar, and 217 Ft. to the pound sterling. Note that official exchange rates are adjusted at frequent intervals.

Most credit cards are accepted, but don't rely on them in smaller towns or less expensive accommodations and restaurants. Eurocheque holders can cash personal checks in all banks and in most hotels. Many banks now also cash American Express and Visa traveler's checks. American Express has a full-service office in Budapest (⌧ V, Deák Ferenc u. 10, ☎ 1/267–2020, 1/267–2313, or 1/266–8680; ℻ 1/267–2029), which also dispenses cash to its cardholders. Hungary's first Citibank (⌧ V, Vörösmarty tér 4) opened in 1995, offering full services to account holders, including a 24-hour ATM.

Hundreds of other ATMs have recently appeared throughout the capital and in other major towns. Some accept Plus network bank cards and Visa credit cards, others Cirrus and MasterCard. You can withdraw forints only (automatically converted at the bank's official exchange rate) directly from your account; most levy a 1 percent or $3 service charge. For those without plastic, many cash-exchange machines, into which you feed paper currency for forints, have also sprung up.

There is still a black market in hard currency, but changing money on the street is risky and illegal, and the bank rate almost always comes close. Stick with banks and official exchange offices.

What It Will Cost

Hungary continues to struggle through the transition from communism to a market economy. The forint, which is expected to be convertible by 1997, was significantly devalued over the last two years, and inflation rages on at an annual rate of more than 25%. Tourists receive more forints for their dollar, but will find that prices have risen to keep up with inflation. However, even with inflation and the 25% value-added tax (VAT) in the service industry, enjoyable vacations with all the trimmings remain less expensive than in nearby western European cities like Vienna.

SAMPLE PRICES

Cup of coffee, 80 Ft.; bottle of beer, 150 Ft.–200 Ft.; soft drinks, 80 Ft.; ham sandwich, 100 Ft.; 1-mile taxi ride, 130 Ft.; museum admission, 80 Ft.–200 Ft.

Visas

Only a valid passport is required of U.S., British, and Canadian citizens. For additional information, contact the Hungarian Embassy in the United States (⊠ 3910 Shoemaker St. NW, Washington, DC 20008, ☎ 202/362–6730), in Canada (⊠ 299 Waverley St. Ottawa, Ontario K2P 0V9 ☎ 613/230–9614), or in London (⊠ 35b Eaton Pl., London SW1X 8BY, ☎ 0171/235–7191).

Customs

ON ARRIVAL

Objects for personal use may be imported freely. If you are over 16, you may also bring in 250 cigarettes or 50 cigars or 250 grams of tobacco, plus 2 liters of wine, 1 liter of spirits, and .25 liters of perfume. A customs charge is made on gifts valued in Hungary at more than 8,000 Ft.

ON DEPARTURE

Take care when you leave Hungary that you have the right documentation for exporting goods. Keep receipts of any purchases from Konsumtourist, Intertourist, or Képcsarnok Vállalat. A special permit is needed for works of art, antiques, or objects of museum value. You are entitled to a VAT refund on new goods (i.e., not works of art, antiques, or objects of museum value) valued at more than 25,000 Ft. (VAT inclusive). But applying for the refund may result in more frustration than money: cash refunds are given only in forints, and you may find yourself in the airport with a handful of soft currency, of which no more than 1,000 forints may be taken out of the country. If you made your purchases by credit card, you can file for a credit to your card or to your bank account (again in forints), but this process is slow at best. If you intend to apply for the credit, make sure you get customs to stamp the original purchase invoice before you leave the country. For more information, pick up a tax refund brochure from any tourist office or hotel, or contact the APEH Budapest Directorate Foreigners' Refund Office (⊠ V, Sas u. 2, ☎ 1/118–1910) or Intel Trade Rt. (⊠ I, Csalogány u. 6-10, ☎ 1/201–8120 or 1/156–9800).

For further customs information, inquire at the **National Customs and Revenue Office** (⊠ VI, Rózsa u. 89, ☎ 1/131–3536). If you have trouble communicating, ask **Tourinform** (☎ 1/117–9800) for help.

Getting Around

By Car

DOCUMENTATION

To drive in Hungary, U.S. and Canadian visitors are supposed to have an International Driver's License—although their domestic licenses are usually accepted—and U.K. visitors may use their own domestic licenses.

ROAD CONDITIONS

There are three classes of roads: highways (designated by the letter M and a single digit), secondary roads (designated by a two-digit number), and minor roads (designated by a three-digit number). Highways and secondary roads are generally well-maintained. The condition of minor roads varies considerably; keep in mind that tractors and horse-drawn carts may slow you down in rural areas. At press time (spring 1996), Hungary was continuing massive upgrading of many of its motorways. To help fund the project, tolls on major highways were introduced in January 1996. The recently completed M1 from Budapest to Vienna became, at 940 Ft. per car, the most expensive road to travel in Europe. Other toll roads are the M5, from Budapest to Serbia, and the M3 (incomplete at press time), from Budapest to Ukraine.

RULES OF THE ROAD

Hungarians drive on the right. Unless otherwise noted, the speed limit in developed areas is 50 kph (30 mph), on main roads 90 kph (55 mph), and on highways 120 kph (75 mph). Seat belts are compulsory and drinking alcohol is prohibited—the penalties are very severe.

GASOLINE

Gas stations are plentiful in and around major cities, and major chains have opened modern full-service stations on highways in the provinces. A gallon of *ólommentes benzin* (unleaded gasoline) costs about $4.50, and is usually available at all stations, as is diesel.

BREAKDOWNS

The **Hungarian Automobile Club** runs a 24-hour "Yellow Angels" breakdown service from Budapest (⊠ XIV, Francia út 38/B, ☎ 1/252–8000; when outside Budapest, ☎ 088).

By Train

Travel by train from Budapest to other large cities or to Lake Balaton is cheap and efficient. Remember to take a *gyorsvonat* (express train) and not a *személyvonat* (local), which can be extremely slow. A *helyjegy* (seat reservation), which costs about 55 Ft. (200 Ft. for Inter-City trains) and is sold up to 60 days in advance, is advisable for all express trains, especially for weekend travel in summer.

FARES

Only Hungarian citizens are entitled to student discounts; non-Hungarian senior citizens (men over 60, women over 55), however, are eligible for a 20% discount. InterRail cards are available for those under 26, and the Rail Europe Senior Travel Pass entitles senior citizens to a 30% reduction on all train fares. For more information about rail travel, contact the **MÁV Passenger Service** (⊠ VI, Andrássy út 35, ☎ 1/322–8275).

By Bus

Long-distance buses link Budapest with many main cities in Eastern and Western Europe. Services to the eastern part of the country leave from Népstadion station (☎ 1/252–4496). Buses to the west and south leave from the main Volán bus station at Erzsébet tér in the Inner City (☎ 1/117–2318). Buses are inexpensive and tend to be crowded, so reserve your seat.

By Boat

Boat travel is possible in many parts of Hungary. Budapest, of course, straddles a major international waterway—the Danube. Vienna is six hours away by hydrofoil, and many Hungarian resorts are accessible by either hydrofoil or boat. For information about excursions or pleasure cruises, contact **MAHART Tours** (⊠ V, Belgrád rakpart, ☎ 1/118–1704 or 1/118–1743).

By Bicycle

A land of rolling hills and flat plains, Hungary lends itself to bicycling. In Budapest, a rental outfit on Margaret Island (⊠ Hajós Alfréd sétány

1, across from Thermal Hotel, ☎ 1/269–2747) offers popular, four-wheeled pedalled contraptions called *Bringóhintós*, as well as traditional two-wheelers; standard bikes cost about 400 Ft. per hour, 1,450 Ft. for 24 hours. For more information about renting in Budapest, contact **Tourinform** (✉ V, Sütő u. 2, ☎ 1/117–9800). For brochures and general information on bicycling conditions and suggested routes, try Tourinform or contact the **National Society of Bicycle Commuters** (✉ III, Miklós tér 1, ☎ 1/250–0420 or 1/250–0424, ext. 28 on both) or the **Bicycle Touring Association of Hungary** (✉ V, Bajcsy-Zsilinszky út 31, 2nd floor, apt. 3, ☎ 1/111–2467). The **IBUSZ Travel Riding and Hobbies** department provides a variety of guided bicycle tours (✉ V, Ferenciek tere 10, ☎ 1/118–2967).

Staying in Hungary

Telephones

LOCAL CALLS

Pay phones use 10 Ft. coins—the cost of a three-minute local call—and also accept 20 Ft. and 50 Ft. coins. At press time (spring 1996), most pay phones had been converted to accept Hungary's new coins. Most towns in Hungary can be dialed direct—dial 06 and wait for the buzzing tone, then dial the local number. It is unnecessary to use the city code, 1, when dialing within Budapest.

Gray card-operated telephones outnumber coin-operated phones in Budapest and the Balaton region. The cards—available at post offices and most newsstands and kiosks—come in units of 50 (500 Ft.) and 120 (1,100 Ft.) calls. Don't be surprised if a flock of kids gathers around your pay phone while you talk—collecting and trading used phone cards is a raging fad.

As Hungary's telephone system is being modernized, phone numbers are subject to change—sometimes without forewarning. Thousands of phone numbers in Budapest alone will be changed over the next few years; if you're having trouble getting through, ask your concierge to check the number (or if the number begins with a 1, try dialing it starting with a 3 instead—many changes will be of this type).

INTERNATIONAL CALLS

Direct calls to foreign countries can be made from Budapest and all major provincial towns by dialing 00 and waiting for the international dialing tone; on pay phones the initial charge is 40 Ft. To reach an **AT&T** long-distance operator, dial 00–800–01111; for **MCI**, dial 00–800–01411; for **Sprint,** dial 00–800–01877.

OPERATORS

International calls can be made through the operator by dialing 09; for operator-assisted calls within Hungary, dial 01. Be patient: Though continuously improving, the telephone system is still antiquated, especially in the countryside.

Dial 1/117–0170 for Budapest directory assistance, 1/267–3333 for assistance in rural areas. Depending on their mood, some operators may assist you in English. A safer bet is to consult *The Phone Book,* an English-language yellow pages-style telephone directory that also has cultural and tourist information; it's provided in guest rooms of most major hotels and is sold at many English-language bookstores.

COUNTRY CODE

The country code for Hungary is 36.

Mail

The post offices near two of Budapest's main train stations, Keleti (Eastern; ⊠ VII, Baross tér 11c) and Nyugati (Western; ⊠ VI, Teréz körút 51), are open 24 hours.

POSTAL RATES

All airmail postcards and letters to the United States, the United Kingdom, and the rest of Western Europe cost 10 Ft. per 10 grams; an airmail postcard will cost about 70 Ft., a letter from 100 Ft. Surface-mail postcards to the United Kingdom and the rest of Western Europe cost 60 Ft., letters from 75 Ft.

RECEIVING MAIL

General delivery service is available through any post office in Budapest. The address of the main downtown branch is ⊠ Magyar Posta 4. sz., H-1052 Budapest, Városház utca 18; the envelope should have your name written on it, as well as "posta maradó" (poste restante) in big letters. The roman numeral prefix listed in a Budapest address refers to one of the city's 22 districts.

Opening and Closing Times

Banks are generally open weekdays 8–3, often with a one-hour lunch break at around noon; most close at noon on Fridays.

Museums are generally open daily from 10 to 6 and are closed on Mondays. Many have free admission one day a week; see individual listings in tours below, but double-check, as the days tend to change.

Department stores are open weekdays 10 to 5 or 6, Saturday until 1.

Grocery stores are generally open weekdays from 7 to 6 or 7, Saturday until 1 PM; **"non-stops"** or *éjjeli-nappali* are (theoretically) open 24 hours.

National Holidays

January 1; March 15 (Anniversary of 1848 Revolution); March 30–31 (Easter and Easter Monday); May 1 (Labor Day); May 18–19 (Pentecost); August 20 (St. Stephen's and Constitution Day); October 23 (1956 Revolution Day); December 24–26.

Dining

Although prices are steadily increasing, there are plenty of good, affordable restaurants offering a variety of Hungarian dishes. Meats, rich sauces, and creamy desserts predominate, but the health-conscious will also find salads, even out of season. Bypass the usual red-or-white question and order *Egri Bikavér,* or "bull's blood," Hungary's best-known red wine, with any meal. A regular restaurant is likely to be called either a *vendéglő* or an *étterem.* But you also have the option of choosing to eat in an *önkiszolgáló étterem* (self-service restaurant), a *bistró étel bár* (sit-down snack bar), a *büfé* (snack counter), an *eszpresszó* (café), or a *söröző* (pub). Be sure to visit a *cukrászda* (pastry shop).

One caveat: many restaurants have a fine-print policy of charging for each slice of bread consumed from the bread basket. General overcharging is not unheard of either.

MEALTIMES

Hungarians eat early—you risk offhand service and cold food after 9 PM. Lunch, the main meal for many, is served from noon to 2.

WHAT TO WEAR

At most moderately priced and inexpensive restaurants, casual but neat dress is acceptable.

RATINGS

Prices are per person and include a first course, main course, and dessert, but no wine or tip. Prices in Budapest tend to be a good 30% higher than elsewhere in Hungary.

CATEGORY	COST
$$$$	over 2,400 Ft.
$$$	1,700 Ft.–2,400 Ft.
$$	1,000 Ft.–1,700 Ft.
$	under 1,000 Ft.

Lodging

HOTELS

There are few expensive hotels outside Budapest, but the moderately priced hotels are generally comfortable and well-run. Inexpensive establishments—more numerous every year as Hungarians convert unused rooms or second apartments into rental units for tourists—seldom have private baths, but plumbing is adequate almost everywhere.

RENTALS

Apartments in Budapest and cottages at Lake Balaton are available for short- and long-term rental, and can make the most economic lodging for families. Rates and reservations can be obtained from tourist offices in Hungary and abroad. A Budapest apartment might cost anywhere from 5,000 Ft. to 10,000 Ft. a day; a luxury cottage for two on Lake Balaton costs about the same. Bookings can be made in Budapest at the **IBUSZ Welcome Hotel Service** at ⊠ Apáczai Csere János u. 1 (☏ 1/118–3925 or 1/118–5776, FAX 1/117–9099), which is open 24 hours a day, or through IBUSZ offices in the United States and Great Britain (☞ Visitor Information *in* Chapter 1). Although some enterprising locals stand outside the IBUSZ office and offer tourists their apartments for lower than official rates, it's less risky if you go the official route. Other rental agencies in Budapest are IBUSZ's main office (⊠ V, Ferenciek tere 10, ☏ 1/118–6866) and **Cooptourist** (⊠ I, Attila u. 107, ☏ 1/175–2846 or 1/175–2937). **Charles Apartments** (⊠ I, Hegyalja út 23, ☏ 1/201–1796 or 1/212–3830) offers apartment accommodations in its own building for about $60 per night. **Amadeus Apartments** (Üllői út 197, ☏ 30/422–893, FAX 1/177–2871) oversees five apartments that cost roughly $55 a night.

GUEST HOUSES AND PRIVATE ROOMS

Also called *panziók* (pensions), small guest houses lying just outside the heart of the city or town provide simple accommodations, well-suited to people on a budget. These usually include a private bathroom and many also offer breakfast. A room for two in Budapest with breakfast and private bath will run around 4,500 Ft. to 6,000 Ft. Arrangements can be made through local tourist offices or travel agents abroad.

In the provinces it is safe to accept rooms that you are offered directly: They will almost always be clean and in a relatively good neighborhood, and the prospective landlord will probably not cheat you. Look for a placard reading either SZOBA KIADÓ or—in German—ZIMMER FREI (room for rent). The rate per night for a double room in Budapest or at Lake Balaton is around 2,000 Ft.–2,500 Ft., which usually includes the use of a bathroom but not breakfast. Reservations can also be made by any tourist office.

CAMPING

Most of the over 100 campsites in Hungary are open from May through September. As rates are no longer regulated, prices vary. An average rate is about 700 Ft. a day per site in Budapest, slightly less elsewhere. There's usually a small charge for hot water, electricity, and parking, plus an accommodations fee—around 250 Ft. per person per night. Children under 14 often get a 50% reduction. Camping is forbidden except in designated areas. Information can be obtained through travel agencies, the **Hungarian Camping and Caravanning Club** (✉ VIII, Üllői út 6, ☎ 1/133–6536), and **Tourinform** (☞ Visitor Information, *below*).

RATINGS

The following price categories are for a double room with bath and breakfast, VAT included, during the peak season; rates are lower off-season and in the countryside, sometimes under 1,500 forints for two. For single rooms with bath, count on about 80% of the double-room rate. Most large hotels require payment in hard currency.

CATEGORY	BUDAPEST	BALATON AND DANUBE BEND
$$$$	over 30,000 Ft.	over 11,000 Ft.
$$$	20,000 Ft.–30,000 Ft.	9,000 Ft.–11,000 Ft.
$$	10,000 Ft.–20,000 Ft.	5,000 Ft.–9,000 Ft.
$	under 10,000 Ft.	under 5,000 Ft.

During the peak season (June through August), full board may be compulsory at some of the Lake Balaton hotels. During the off-season (in Budapest, September through March; at Lake Balaton and the Danube Bend, in May and September), rates can be considerably lower than those given above.

Tipping

Four decades of socialism didn't alter the Hungarian habit of tipping generously. Cloakroom and gas-pump attendants, hairdressers, waiters, and taxi drivers all expect tips. At least 10% should be added to a restaurant bill or taxi fare. If a gypsy band plays exclusively for your table, you can leave 100 Ft. in the discreetly provided plate.

BUDAPEST

Arriving and Departing

By Plane

The only nonstop service between Budapest and the United States is aboard **Malév** (☎ 1/266–9033, 1/267–2911, or 1/267–4333 for tickets). Flights depart New York City's JFK International Airport aboard Boeing 767s.

Hungary's international airport, **Ferihegy** (☎ 1/157–9123), is about 22 kilometers (14 miles) southeast of the city. All **Lufthansa** and **Malév** flights operate from the newer Terminal 2; other airlines use Terminal 1. For same-day flight information, call the airport authority (☎ 1/157–7155), where operators theoretically speak some English.

BETWEEN THE AIRPORT AND DOWNTOWN

Minibuses marked LRI CENTRUM-AIRPORT-CENTRUM leave every half hour from 5:30 AM to 9:30 PM for the Erzsébet tér station (Platform 1) in downtown Budapest. The trip takes 30–40 minutes and costs around 300 Ft. The modern minivans of the reliable LRI Airport Shuttle service (☎ 1/157–8555) take you to any destination in Budapest, door to door, for around 1,000 Ft., even less than the least expensive taxi—and most employees speak English. At the airport, buy tickets at the LRI counter in the arrivals hall near baggage claim; for your return trip, just call ahead for a pick-up. There are also approved taxi stands outside both terminals.

By Train

There are three main train stations in Budapest: Keleti (Eastern), Nyugati (Western), and Déli (Southern). Trains for Vienna usually depart from Keleti station, those for Balaton from Déli.

By Bus

Most buses to Budapest from the western region of Hungary, including those from Vienna, arrive at **Erzsébet tér** station downtown.

By Car

The main routes into Budapest are the newly-completed M1 from Vienna (via Győr), the M3 from near Gyöngyös, the M5 from Kecskemét, and the M7 from the Balaton; the latter three are being upgraded in the next few years and extended to Hungary's borders with Ukraine, Serbia, and Slovenia, respectively.

Getting Around

Budapest is best explored on foot. The maps provided by tourist offices are not very detailed, so arm yourself with one from any of the bookshops in Váci utca or from a stationery shop or newsstand.

By Public Transportation

The Budapest Transportation Authority (BKV) runs the public transportation system—a metro (subway) with three lines, buses, streetcars, and trolleybuses—and it's cheap, efficient, and simple to use, but most of it closes down around 11:30 PM. Certain trams and buses run on a limited schedule all night. A *napijegy* (day ticket) costs 400 Ft. (three-day, 800 Ft.) and allows unlimited travel on all services within the city limits. You can also buy tickets for single rides for 50 Ft. at metro stations or newsstands. You can travel on all trams, buses, and on the subway with this ticket, but you can't change lines or direction.

Bus, streetcar, and trolleybus tickets must be canceled on board—watch how other passengers do it; metro tickets are canceled at station entrances. Don't get caught without a canceled ticket: Spot checks by plainclothes agents wearing red arm bands are frequent, often targeting tourists, and you can be fined several hundred forints.

By Taxi

Taxis are plentiful and are a good value, but make sure that they have a working meter. The average initial charge is 40 Ft.–60 Ft., to which is added 80 Ft.–90 Ft. per kilometer plus 16 Ft.–20 Ft. per minute of waiting time. There are too many taxis in Budapest, but some drivers try to charge outrageous prices. Avoid unmarked "freelance" taxis; stick with those affiliated with an established company. Your safest bet is to do what the locals do and order a taxi by phone. Simply provide the phone number you're calling from and they will know where you are; a car will arrive in about 5 to 10 minutes. The best rates are offered by **Fötaxi** (☎ 1/222–2222), **6 X 6** (☎ 1/266–6666), **Citytaxi** (☎ 1/211–1111), and **Teletaxi** (☎ 1/155–5555).

By Boat

In summer the BKV runs a not-so-regular boat service linking the north and south ends of the city and stopping at points on both banks of the river and on Margit-sziget (Margaret Island); at press time (spring 1996), details were uncertain—contact Tourinform for current schedules. From May through October boats leave from the quay at Vigadó tér on 1½-hour cruises between the railroad bridges north and south of the Árpád and Petőfi bridges, respectively. The trip, organized by **MAHART** (☎ 1/118–1223), runs twice a day and costs around 500 Ft.; from mid-June through August, the evening cruise features live music and costs about 100 Ft. more. In April, cruises operate on Saturday and Sunday only.

Important Addresses and Numbers

Embassies

U.S.: ⊠ V, Szabadság tér 12 (☎ 1/267–4400). **Canadian:** ⊠ XII, Budakeszi út 32 (☎ 1/275–1200). **U.K.:** ⊠ V, Harmincad u. 6 (☎ 1/266–2888).

Emergencies

Police (☎ 07). **Ambulance** (☎ 04); or call **SOS** (⊠ XI, Fraknó u. 32, ☎ 1/204–5500 or 1/204–5501), a 24-hour private ambulance service with English-speaking personnel. **Doctor:** Ask your hotel or embassy for recommendations or visit the **R-Clinic** (⊠ II, Felsőzöldmáli út 13, ☎ 1/250–3488, 1/250–3489, 1/250–3490), a private clinic staffed by English-speaking doctors and offering 24-hour medical and ambulance service. The clinic accepts major credit cards and prepares full reports for your insurance company. U.S. and Canadian visitors are advised to take out full medical insurance. U.K. visitors are covered for emergencies and essential treatment.

English-Language Bookstores

Bestsellers (⊠ V, Október 6 u. 11) sells exclusively English-language books, as does its smaller, more academically-focused branch at the Central European University (⊠ V, Nádor u. 9). Other stores with good selections of books in English are **Libri International Bookstore** (⊠ V, Váci u. 32), **Idegennyelvű Könyvesbolt** (⊠ V, Petőfi Sándor u. 2), **Longman ELT** (⊠ VIII, Kölcsey u. 2), **Litea Bookshop and Tea Salon** (⊠ I, Hess András tér 4), and **Atlantisz Book Island** (⊠ V, Váci u. 31–33). Foreign publications—including those in English—can be bought at the reception desks of major hotels and at newsstands at major traffic centers.

Travel Agencies

American Express (⊠ V, Déak Ferenc u. 10, ☎ 1/266–8680, ℻ 1/267–2028). **Getz International** (⊠ V, Falk Miksa u. 5, ☎ 1/312–0645 or 1/312–0649, ℻ 1/112–1014). **Vista** (⊠ VII, Károly körút 21, ☎ 1/269–6032, 1/342–9316, or 1/342–1534, ℻ 1/269–6031).

Visitor Information

Tourinform (⊠ V, Sütő u. 2, ☎ 1/117–9800) is open April–October, daily 8–8, and November–March, weekdays 8–8, weekends 8–3. **IBUSZ Welcome Hotel Service** (⊠ V, Apáczai Csere János u. 1, ☎ 1/118–3925 or 1/118–5776) is open 24 hours. **IBUSZ's** main branch (⊠ V, Ferenciek tere 10, ☎ 118–6866) and **Budapest Tourist** (⊠ V, Roosevelt tér 5, ☎ 1/117–3555) are also helpful. *The Budapest Sun,* an English-language weekly newspaper that covers news, business, and culture, carries general orientation tips for tourists. *Budapest Week* is a similar weekly publication. Both are sold at newsstands, bookstores, and hotels.

Guided Tours

Orientation

Year-round, **IBUSZ** (☞ Important Addresses and Numbers, *above*) sponsors three-hour bus tours of the city that cost about 2,200 Ft. Starting from Erzsébet tér, they take in parts of both Buda and Pest. **Gray Line Cityrama** (⊠ V, Báthori u. 22, ☎ 1/132–5344) also offers a three-hour city bus tour (about 2,400 Ft. per person).

Special-Interest Tours and Excursions

IBUSZ, Cityrama, and **Budapest Tourist** organize a number of unusual tours, including trips to the Buda Hills and goulash parties as well as visits to the National Gallery and Parliament and other traditional sights. These tour companies will provide personal guides on request. Some tour operators now offer oddities such as day trips to former Soviet army bases and historical excursions focusing on Budapest's remaining communist monuments. Also check at your hotel's reception desk.

The Chosen Tours (⊠ XII, Zolyomi lépcső 27, ☎ 1/319–3427 or ☎ FAX 1/319–6800) offers a three-hour bus tour ($17), "Budapest Through Jewish Eyes," and a two-hour walking tour ($11) highlighting the sights and cultural life of the city's important Jewish community. Bus tours run three times a week, walking tours twice a week, from April (after Passover) through October; arrangements can also be made, however, for unscheduled and off-season tours for groups of four or more.

Excursions farther afield include day-long trips to the *Puszta* (another term for the Great Plain), the Danube Bend, and Lake Balaton. **IBUSZ's Travel Riding and Hobbies** department (☞ Getting Around *in* Essential Information, *above*) offers a variety of excellent special-interest tours, including horseback riding, bicycling, and angling, as well as special stays in many of Hungary's historic castles and mansions.

Exploring Budapest

Budapest, situated on both banks of the Danube, unites the hills of Buda and the wide boulevards of Pest. Though it was the site of a Roman outpost in the 1st century AD, the modern city was not actually created until 1873, when the towns of Óbuda, Pest, and Buda were joined. The resulting capital is the cultural, political, intellectual, and commercial heart of the nation; for the 20% of the nation's population who live here, anywhere else is just "the country."

Much of the charm of a visit to Budapest consists of unexpected glimpses into shadowy courtyards and long vistas down sunlit cobbled streets. Although some 30,000 buildings were destroyed during World War II and in 1956, the past lingers on in the often crumbling architectural details of the antique structures that remain and in the memories and lifestyles of Budapest's citizens.

The principal sights of the city fall roughly into three areas, each of which can be comfortably covered on foot. The Budapest hills are best explored by public transportation. Note that many street names have been changed to purge all reminders of the communist regime. If the street you're looking for seems to have disappeared, ask any local—though he or she may well be as bewildered as you are.

Castle Hill

Numbers in the margin correspond to points of interest on the Budapest map.

❶❷ If you're starting from Pest, take a bus or taxi from **Erzsébet tér** across the Danube to **Dizs tér,** at the top of **Várhegy** (Castle Hill), where painstaking reconstruction work has been in progress since World War II. Having made their final stand in the Royal Palace itself, the Nazis left this section of Castle Hill a blackened wasteland. Under the rubble, archaeologists discovered the medieval foundations of the palace of King Matthias Corvinus, who in the 15th century presided over one of the most splendid courts in Europe.

★ ❸ The rebuilt **Királyi Palota** (Royal Palace), a vast museum complex and cultural center, is easily reached on foot from Dísz tér. The **Ludwig**

564

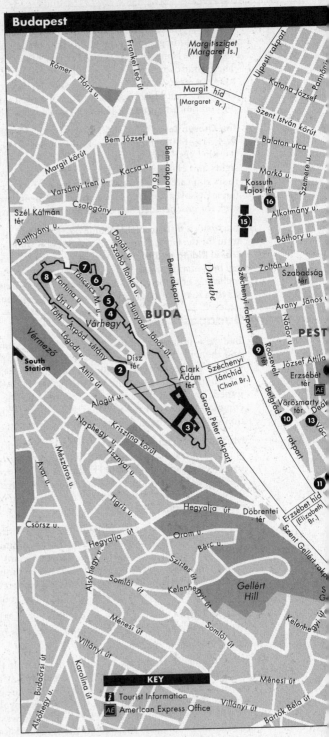

Budapest

KEY

🛈 Tourist Information

AE American Express Office

Múzeum (Ludwig Museum), with a collection of more than 200 pieces of Hungarian and contemporary world art, including works by Picasso and Lichtenstein, fills the castle's northern wing. The central section houses the **Magyar Nemzeti Galeria** (Hungarian National Gallery), exhibiting a wide range of Hungarian fine art. Names to look for are Munkácsy, a 19th-century Romantic painter, and Csontváry, an early Surrealist admired by Picasso. *Ludwig Museum:* ✉ *Buda Castle (Wing A), Dísz tér 17,* ☎ *1/175–7533.* 🎫 *100 Ft.; free Tues.* ☉ *Tues.–Sun. 10–6. Hungarian National Gallery:* ✉ *Buda Castle (Wing C), Dísz tér 17,* ☎ *1/175–7533.* 🎫 *100 Ft.; free on Wed.; tour for up to 5 people with English-speaking guide (book in advance), 1000 Ft.* ☉ *Mar.–Nov., Tues.–Sun. 10–6; Dec.–Feb., Tues.–Sun. 10–4; closed Mon.*

The southern block of the palace contains the **Budapesti Történeti Múzeum** (Budapest History Museum), displaying a fascinating new permanent exhibit of the city's history from Buda's liberation from the Turks in 1686 through the 1970s. Viewing the 19th- and 20th-century photos and videos of the castle, the Chain Bridge, and other Budapest monuments here—and seeing them as the backdrop to the horrors of World War II and the 1956 Revolution—can be a helpful orientation for later sightseeing. To complete the sensation of time telescoping, look out a window toward the Danube. Down in the cellars are the original medieval vaults of the palace, a palace chapel, and more royal relics. ✉ *Buda Castle (Wing E), Szt. György tér 2,* ☎ *1/175–7533.* 🎫 *100 Ft.* ☉ *Mar.–Nov., Wed.–Mon. 10–6; Dec., Wed.–Mon. 10–4; Jan.–Feb., Wed.–Mon. 10–5.*

★ ❹ The **Mátyás templom** (Matthias Church), northeast of Dísz tér, with its distinctive roof of colored, diamond-patterned tiles and skeletal Gothic spire, dates from the 13th century. Built as a mosque by the occupying Turks, it was destroyed and reconstructed in the 19th century, only to be bombed during World War II. Only the south porch survives from the original structure. The Hapsburg emperors were crowned kings of Hungary here, the last of them, Charles IV, in 1916. High mass is held every Sunday at 10 AM with an orchestra and choir, and organ concerts are often held in the summer on Friday at 8 PM. Tourists are asked to remain at the back of the church during services (it's best to come after 10 AM Mon.–Fri. and after 1 PM Sun. and holidays). ✉ *I, Szentháromság tér 2,* ☎ *1/155–5657.* ☉ *Daily 7–8.* 🎫 *Free, except during concerts. Treasury:* 🎫 *50 Ft.* ☉ *Daily 9–5:30.*

★ ❺ The turn-of-the-century **Halászbástya** (Fishermen's Bastion) is on your left as you leave the church. It was built as a lookout tower to protect what was once a thriving fishing settlement. Its neo-Romanesque columns and arches frame views over the city and the river. Near the church, in Hess András tér, are the remains of the oldest church on Castle Hill, built by Dominican friars in the 13th century. These have now been tastefully integrated into the modern Hilton hotel.

Many of the town houses lining the streets of the Castle district are occupied by offices, restaurants, and diplomatic residences; however, the handsome, 18th-century gray-stone palace that once belonged to ❻ the noble Erdődy family is now the **Zenetörténeti Múzeum** (Museum of Music History), which hosts intimate recitals of classical music and displays rare manuscripts and antique instruments. ✉ *I, Táncsics Mihály u. 7,* ☎ *1/175–9011.* 🎫 *60 Ft.* ☉ *Tues.–Sun. 10–6.*

❼ The remains of Castle Hill's **medieval synagogue** are open to the public, and display a number of objects relating to the Jewish community, including religious inscriptions, frescoes, and tombstones dating from the 15th century. ✉ *Táncsics Mihály u. 26,* ☎ *1/155–8849.* 💰 *50 Ft.* ☉ *May–Oct., Tues.–Fri. 10–2, weekends 10–6.*

8 The **Hadtörténeti Múzeum** (Museum of Military History) is at the far end of Castle Hill. The collection includes uniforms and regalia, many belonging to the Hungarian generals who took part in the abortive uprising against Austrian rule in 1848. Other exhibits trace the military history of Hungary from the original Magyar conquest in the 9th century up to the middle of this century. ✉ *I, Tóth Árpád sétány 40,* ☎ *1/156–9522.* 💰 *100 Ft.; Sat free. English-language tours (arrange in advance) 500 Ft.* ☉ *Mar.–Oct., Tues.–Sat. 10–5, Sun. 10–6; Nov.–Feb., Tues.–Sat. 10–4, Sun. 10–5.*

The Heart of the City

★
9 Cross the **Széchenyi lánchíd** (Chain Bridge) from Clark Ádám tér to reach **Roosevelt tér** in Pest, with the 19th-century neoclassical Academy of Sciences on your left, and directly in front, the 1907 Gresham Palace, a crumbling temple to the age of Art Nouveau. Pest fans out from the **Belváros** (Inner City), which is bounded by the **Kiskörút** (Little Ring Road). The **Nagykörút** (Grand Ring Road) describes a wider semicircle from the Margaret Bridge to the Petőfi Bridge. To your
★ right, an elegant promenade, the **Korzó,** runs south along the river, providing postcard views of Castle Hill, the Chain Bridge, and Gellért Hill on the other side of the Danube.

NEED A BREAK? The **Bécsi Kávéház** (Viennese Café) in the Fórum Hotel serves the best *isler* (giant chocolate-covered cookies filled with apricot or raspberry jam) and cream pastries in town. ✉ *V, Apáczai Csere János u. 12–14,* ☎ *1/117–8088.* ☉ *Daily 9–9.*

10 The square known as **Vigadó tér** is dominated by the Danube view and the Vigadó concert hall, built in an eclectic mix of Byzantine, Moorish, and Romanesque styles; the façade even draws upon the ceremonial knots from the uniforms of the Hungarian hussars. Liszt, Brahms, and Bartók all performed here. Completely destroyed during World War
11 II, it has been faithfully rebuilt. Another square, **Március 15 tér,** commemorates the 1848 struggle for independence from the Hapsburgs with a statue of the poet Petőfi Sándor, who died in a later uprising. On March 15, the national holiday commemorating the revolution, the square is packed with patriotic Hungarians. Behind the square is
12 the 12th-century **Belvárosi plébánia templom** (Inner-City Parish Church), the oldest church in Pest. The structure incorporates a succession of Western architectural styles, and even preserves a Muslim prayer niche from the time when the Turks ruled the country. Liszt, who lived only a few yards away, often played the organ here.

★ **13** Running parallel to the Korzó is Budapest's most upscale shopping street, **Váci utca,** for pedestrians only. It originates at **Vörösmarty tér,** a handsome square in the heart of the Inner City. Street musicians and sidewalk cafés make the square one of the liveliest places in Budapest and a good spot to sit and relax.

NEED A BREAK? **Gerbeaud,** an elegant pastry shop founded in 1857, always seems crowded with people devouring the rich chocolate cake known as *dobos torta,* their pleasure undiminished by the surliness of the waitresses. ✉ *V, Vörösmarty tér 7,* ☎ *1/118–1311.* ☉ *Daily 9–8.*

14 A slight detour back down the river and deeper into Pest brings you to the steps of the stern, Classical edifice of the **Magyar Nemzeti Múzeum** (Hungarian National Museum), built between 1837 and

1847. On these steps, on March 15, 1848, Petőfi Sándor recited his revolutionary poem, the *"Nemzeti Dal"* ("National Song"), declaring "By the God of Magyar, / Do we swear, / Do we swear, chains no longer / Will we wear." This poem, along with the "12 Points," a formal list of political demands by young Hungarians, called upon the people to rise up against the Hapsburgs. Celebrations of the national holiday—long banned by the communist regime—are now held here (and throughout the city) every year on March 15. You'll find the museum's most sacred treasure, the Szent Korona (Holy Crown)—it's the one that looks like a great golden soufflé resting on a Byzantine band of enamel, pearls, and other gems—with a host of other royal relics in the domed Hall of Honor. The museum's epic Hungarian history exhibition, reopened in August 1996, has been updated with exhibits chronicling the end of communism and the much-celebrated exodus of the Russian troops. ⊠ *IX, Múzeum körút 14–16,* ☎ *1/138–2122.* 🎫 *200 Ft.* ☼ *Mid-Mar.–mid-Oct., Tues.–Sun. 10–6; mid-Oct.–mid-Mar., Tues.–Sun. 10–5.*

⑮ North of Roosevelt tér is the riverfront's most striking landmark, the imposing neo-Gothic **Parliament,** now minus the red star on top (open for tours only; call IBUSZ, ☎ 1/118–5776 or 1/118–3925, or Budapest Tourist, ☎ 1/117–3555). To its left sits an expressive statue of József Attila (1905–37), who, in spite of his early death, became known as one of Hungary's greatest poets.

⑯ Across from the Parliament is the majestic **Néprajzi Múzeum** (Museum of Ethnography), with impressive, exhaustive exhibits—captioned in English—of folk costumes and traditions. These are the authentic pieces you can't see in tourist shops. ⊠ *V, Kossuth Lajos tér 12,* ☎ *1/132–6340.* 🎫 *100 Ft.; Tues. free.* ☼ *Tues.–Sun. 10–6.*

⑰ Dark and massive, the 19th-century **Szent István Bazilika** (St. Stephen's Basilica) is one of the chief landmarks of Pest. It was planned early in the 19th century as a neoclassical building, but turned out to be in the neo-Renaissance style by the time it was completed more than 50 years later. During World War II, the most precious documents from the municipal archives were placed in the basilica's cellar—one of the few available bombproof sites. The mummified right hand of St. Stephen, Hungary's first king and patron saint, is preserved in the Szent Jobb chapel; the guard will illuminate it for you for about 50 Ft. Extensive restorations have been underway for years, with a target completion date of 2010, and some part of the structure is likely to be under scaffolding when you visit. ⊠ *V, Szt. István tér,* ☎ *1/117–2859.* 🎫 *Free. Church:* ☼ *Mon.–Sat. 7–7, Sun 1–5. Szt. Jobb Chapel:* ☼ *Apr.–Sept., Mon.–Sat. 9–5, Sun. 1–5; Oct.–Mar., Mon.–Sat. 10–4.*

★ ⑱ Andrássy út runs 3.2 kilometers (2 miles) from the basilica to **Hősök tere** (Heroes' Square). About a fourth of the way, on the left, at Hajós utca, is the **Állami Operaház** (State Opera House), with its statues of the Muses in the second-floor corner niches. Completed in 1884, it was the crowning achievement of architect Miklós Ybl. It has been restored to its original ornate glory—particularly inside—and has been spared attempts at modernization. Foreign-language tours (45 minutes) are held daily at 3 PM and 4 PM; they meet in front of the opera house, but call ahead to confirm that there is a tour on the day you want to visit (☎ 1/131–2550 ext. 156). The cost is about 500 Ft. The best way to view the inside is to attend a ballet or opera, but there are no performances in summer, except for the week-long BudaFest international opera and ballet festival in mid-August.

Heroes' Square and Városliget

⑲ In the center of Heroes' Square stands the 120-foot bronze **Millenniumi Emlékmű** (Millennium Monument), begun in 1896 to commemorate the 1,000th anniversary of the Magyar Conquest, and now newly shining in celebration of yet another 100 years. Statues of Prince Árpád and six other founders of the Magyar nation occupy the base of the monument, while Hungary's greatest rulers and princes stand between the columns on either side.

⑳ The **Szépművészeti Múzeum** (Fine Arts Museum) stands on one side of the square. An entire section is devoted to Egyptian, Greek, and Roman artifacts, including many rare pieces of Greco-Roman ceramics. The institution's collection of Spanish paintings is considered the best of its kind outside of Spain. ⊠ *XIV, Dózsa György út 41,* ☎ *1/343–9759.* ⊡ *200 Ft.* ⊙ *Tues.–Sun. 10–5:30; usually closed Jan.–Mar.*

★ **㉑** The striking 1895 **Műcsarnok** (Palace of Exhibitions), on the other side of the square, schedules exhibitions of contemporary Hungarian and international art and a rich series of films, plays, and concerts. ⊠ *XIV, Dózsa György út 37,* ☎ *1/343–7401.* ⊡ *200 Ft.; Tues. free.* ⊙ *Tues.–Sun. 10–6.*

☾ The **Városliget** (City Park) extends beyond the square; on the left as you enter it are the zoo, the state circus, an amusement park, and the outdoor swimming pool of the Széchenyi mineral baths. On the right is **Vajdahunyad Castle,** an art historian's Disneyland, created for the millennial celebration in 1896 and incorporating architectural elements typical of various periods of Hungary's history all in one complex. In one wing is the surprisingly interesting **Mezőgazdasági Múzeum**
㉒ (Agricultural Museum), with displays on animal husbandry, forestry, and horticulture. ⊠ *XIV, Városliget, Széchenyi Island,* ☎ *1/343–3198.* ⊡ *60 Ft.* ⊙ *Mar.–Nov., Tues.–Sat. 10–5, Sun. 10–6; Dec.–Feb., Tues.–Fri. 10–4, weekends 10–5.*

Off the Beaten Path

A **libegő** (chairlift) will take you to the highest point in Budapest, **Jánoshegy** (János Hill), where you can climb a lookout tower for the best view of the city. ⊠ *Take Bus 158 from Moszkva tér to last stop, Zugligeti út,* ☎ *1/156–7975 or 1/176–3764.* ⊡ *100 Ft. one-way, 150 Ft. round-trip.* ⊙ *Mid-May–mid-Sept., daily 9–5; mid-Sept.–mid-May (depending on weather), daily 9:30–4. Closed alternate Mons.*

For a look at Budapest's too-recent Iron Curtain past, make the 30-minute trip out to **Szobor Park** (Statue Park), to which 42 of the communist statues and memorials that once dominated the city have been exiled since the political changes in 1989. Here you can wander among mammoth figures of Lenin and Marx while listening to songs from the Hungarian and Russian workers' movement blaring from loudspeakers. ⊠ *XXII, Balatoni út, corner of Szabadkai út,* ☎ ℻ *1/227–7446.* ⊡ *150 Ft.* ⊙ *Mid-Apr.–Oct., daily 10–6; Nov.–mid-Apr., Sat.–Sun. 10–dusk, weather permitting.*

Shopping

You'll find plenty of expensive boutiques, folk art and souvenir shops, and classical record shops on or around **Váci utca,** Budapest's famous, pedestrian-only promenade. However, browsing among some of the smaller, less touristy, more typically Hungarian shops in Pest—on the **Kiskörút** (Small Ring Boulevard) and **Nagykörút** (Great Ring Boulevard), and **Kossuth Lajos utca**—may prove more interesting and less pricey. The popular, modern **Skála-Metro** department store near the

Nyugati train station sells a little bit of not entirely everything. You'll also encounter Transylvanian women dressed in colorful folk costume standing on busy sidewalks, selling their own handmade embroideries and ceramics at rock-bottom prices. Look for them at **Moszkva tér, Jászai Mari tér,** outside the **Kossuth tér** metro, and around **Váci utca.**

The magnificent **Vásárcsarnok,** or Central Market Hall (⊠ IX, Vámház körút 1–3), was reopened in late 1994 after years of renovation (and disputes over who would foot the bill). The cavernous, three-story hall once again teems with shoppers browsing among stalls packed with salamis and red paprika chains, crusty bread, fresh fish, and other enticements. Upstairs you can buy folk embroideries and souvenirs. The market opens bright and early at 6 AM and closes at 5 on Monday, at 6 Tuesday through Friday, and at 2 on Saturday; it's closed Sunday.

A good way to find bargains (and adventure) is to make an early-morning trip out to **Ecseri Piac** (⊠ IX, Nagykőrösi út—take Bus 54 from Boráros tér), a vast, colorful, chaotic flea market on the outskirts of Budapest. The place is a cornucopia of secondhand goods of every conceivable form and function, including frayed Russian military fatigues, authentic (and counterfeit) Herend and Zsolnay porcelain, and single—that is, half a pair of—cowboy boots. It's open weekdays 8–4, Sat. 8–3, but the best selection is on Saturday mornings. Foreigners are a favorite target for overcharging, so prepare to be tough when bargaining.

Dining

Private restaurateurs are breathing excitement into the Budapest dining scene. You can choose from Chinese, Mexican, Italian, French, Indian, or various other "ethnic" cuisines—there is even a vegetarian restaurant. Or you can stick to solid, traditional Hungarian fare. Be sure to check out the less expensive spots favored by locals. Our selection is primarily Hungarian and Continental, but if you get a craving for sushi or tortellini, consult the restaurant listings in *The Budapest Sun* (☞ Important Addresses and Numbers *in* Visitor Information, *above*). For price-category definitions, *see* Dining *in* Staying in Hungary, *above*.

$$$$ ✕ **Gundel.** Kings, prime ministers, and Communist party bosses have ★ dined in this turn-of-the-century palazzo in City Park since it was founded in 1894, but its elegance dissipated under state control. Now relaunched by New York-based restaurateur George Lang, it showcases all that's best in Hungarian cuisine. The interior is one of the most handsome in Budapest, with dark-wood paneling, navy-blue upholstered seating, and tables set with Zsolnay porcelain. Waiters in black tie serve traditional favorites such as tender veal in a paprika-and-sour-cream sauce and carp *Dorozsma* (panfried with mushrooms), to the accompaniment of gypsy music led by one of Hungary's legendary gypsy violinists. ⊠ XIV, Allatkerti út 2, ☎ 1/321–3550, FAX 1/342–2917. *Reservations essential. Jacket and tie. AE, DC, MC, V.*

$$$$ ✕ **Vadrózsa.** The name means "wild rose," and there are always fresh ones on the table at this restaurant in an old villa in Buda's exclusive Rózsadomb district. It's elegant to the last detail—even the service is white-glove—and the garden is delightful in summer. ⊠ II, Pentelei Molnár u. 15, ☎ 1/135–1118. *Reservations essential. Jacket and tie. AE, DC, MC, V.*

$$$ ✕ **Kacsa.** Hungarian and international dishes with a focus on duck are done with a light touch and served by candlelight, with quiet traditional Hungarian music in the background, in this small, celebrated restaurant just a few steps from the river. Try the crisp wild duck stuffed with plums. ⊠ *II, Fő u. 75,* ☏ *1/201–9992. Reservations essential. AE, DC, MC, V. Dinner only.*

$$$ ✕ **Kisbuda Gyöngye.** This Budapest favorite, hidden away on a small street in Óbuda, is filled with mixed antique furniture, and its walls are covered with a patchwork of antique carved wooden cupboard doors. A Mozart-inclined violin-piano duo sets a romantic mood. Try the fresh trout smothered in a cream sauce with mushrooms and capers. In warm weather, guests can dine outdoors in the cozy back garden. ⊠ *III, Kenyeres u. 34,* ☏ *1/168–6402 or 1/168–9246. Reservations essential 2 days ahead. AE. Closed Sun. July–Aug. No dinner Sun.*

$$$ ✕ **Múzeum.** Fans swear that this elegant salon with mirrors, mosaics, and swift-moving waiters has the best dining in Budapest. The salads are generous, the Hungarian wines excellent, and the chef dares to be creative. ⊠ *VIII, Múzeum körút 12,* ☏ *1/267–0375. AE. Closed Sun.*

$$–$$$ ✕ **Náncsi Néni.** "Aunt Nancy's" restaurant is a perennial favorite, de-
★ spite its out-of-the-way location. Irresistibly cozy, the dining room feels like a country kitchen: Chains of paprikas and garlic dangle from the low wooden ceiling and shelves along the walls are crammed with jars of home-pickled vegetables, which you can purchase to take home. On the homestyle Hungarian menu (large portions!), turkey dishes are given a creative flair, such as breast fillets stuffed with apples, peaches, mushrooms, cheese, and sour cream. Special touches include a popular outdoor garden in summer, and free champagne for all couples in love. ⊠ *II, Ördögárok út 80,* ☏ *1/176–5809. AE, MC, V.*

$$ ✕ **Tabáni Kakas.** Just below Castle Hill, this popular restaurant has a distinctly warm and friendly atmosphere. It specializes in large helpings of poultry dishes, particularly goose. Try the catfish *paprikás* (fresh catfish fried in the powder of crushed, sun-dried red peppers) or the roast duck with steamed cabbage. A pianist entertains every evening except Monday. ⊠ *I, Attila út 27,* ☏ *1/175–7165. AE, MC.*

$ ✕ **Bohémtanya.** There's always a wait for a table at this lively hangout, but it pays to be patient. The reward: heaping plates of stuffed cabbage, fried pork chops filled with goose liver, and other Hungarian specialties. The quadrilingual menu is extra budget-conscious. ⊠ *VI, Paulay Ede u. 6,* ☏ *1/122–1453. No credit cards.*

$ ✕ **Fészek.** Hidden away inside the nearly 100-year-old Fészek Artists' Club in downtown Pest is this large, neoclassical dining room. In summer, guests dine outdoors in a Venetian-style courtyard. The extensive, almost daunting menu is shared with the sister restaurant Kispipa (☞ *below*), and features all the Hungarian classics such as turkey stuffed with goose liver and a variety of game dishes. Guests must pay a 150-Ft. Artists' Club cover charge upon entering the building; if you've reserved a table in advance, it will be charged to your bill instead. ⊠ *VII, Dob u. 55 (corner of Kertész u.),* ☏ *1/322–6043. AE.*

$ ✕ **Kispipa.** The street outside, a lane full of crumbling old buildings, makes this restaurant's gleaming brass fixtures, nightly piano music, and convivial crowd seem that much more polished. On the extensive menu, the game dishes stand out, and the venison stew with tarragon is outstanding. ⊠ *VII, Akácfa u. 38,* ☏ *1/342–2587. Reservations essential. AE, MC. Closed Sun. and holidays.*

$ ✕ **Tüköry Söröző.** Hearty Hungarian fare comes in big portions at this
★ popular downtown restaurant close to Parliament. Best bets are pork cutlets stuffed with savory liver or apples and cheese, washed down with a big mug of inexpensive beer. Courageous carnivores can sample the beefsteak tartar, topped with a raw egg; many say it's the best in town. ⊠ *V, Hold utca 15,* ☏ *361/269–5027. No credit cards. Closed Sat. and Sun.*

Lodging

Some 30 million tourists come to Hungary every year, and the boom has encouraged hotel building; yet there is sometimes a shortage of rooms, especially in summer. If you arrive in Budapest without a reservation, go to the 24-hour IBUSZ Welcome Hotel Service (⊠ V, Apáczai Csere János u. 1, ☎ 1/118–3925 or 1/118–5776) or to one of the tourist offices at any of the train stations or at the airport. For details and price-category definitions, *see* Lodging *in* Staying in Hungary, *above*.

$$$$ 🏨 **Budapest Hilton.** Built in 1977 around a 13th-century monastery
★ adjacent to the Matthias Church, this perfectly integrated architectural wonder overlooks the Danube from the best site on Castle Hill. Every ample, contemporary room has a remarkable view; service and facilities are of the highest caliber. ⊠ *I, Hess András tér 1–3, H-1014 Budapest,* ☎ *1/214–3000,* FAX *1/156–0285; in U.S. and Canada,* ☎ *800/445–8667. 295 rooms with bath, 27 suites. 3 restaurants, 2 bars, café, beauty salon, sauna, exercise room, shops, casino, laundry service and dry cleaning, business services, meeting rooms, travel services, parking (free and fee). AE, DC, MC, V.*

$$$$ 🏨 **Fórum Hotel.** This boxy, modern riverside hotel consistently wins applause for its gracious appointments, friendly service, and gorgeous views across the Danube to Castle Hill. Half the rooms look onto the street, so be sure to request one facing the river (more expensive), if that's your preference. The Fórum has some of the most modern hotel fitness facilities in the country, and the central location makes it popular with businesspeople. Note: breakfast is not included in the room rates. ⊠ *V, Apáczai Csere János u. 12–14, Box 231, H-1368 Budapest,* ☎ *1/117–9111,* FAX *1/117–9808. 376 rooms with bath, 24 suites. 2 restaurants, bar, café, no-smoking floors, health club, business services, meeting rooms, car rental, parking (fee). AE, DC, MC, V.*

$$$$ 🏨 **Gellért.** Built in 1918 in the *Jugendstil* (Art Nouveau style), this grand old lady with its double-deck rotunda sits regally at the foot of Gellért Hill. One of Hungary's most prized spa hotels, it also houses wonderfully ornate thermal baths. Rooms range from palatial suites to awkward, tiny spaces and have either early-20th-century furnishings, including some authentic Jugendstil pieces, or newer, more basic contemporary pieces. Avoid the rooms that face the building's inner core. ⊠ *XI, Gellért tér 1, H-1111 Budapest,* ☎ *1/185–2200,* FAX *1/166–6631. 233 rooms with bath, 13 suites. Restaurant, bar, brasserie, café, indoor pool, outdoor wave pool, beauty salon, spa, shops, baby-sitting, business services, meeting rooms, parking (fee). AE, DC, MC, V.*

$$$$ 🏨 **Kempinski Hotel Corvinus Budapest.** Afternoon chamber music sets
★ the tone at this sleek luxury hotel, a favorite of visiting VIPs. Rooms are spacious, with elegant contemporary decor featuring geometric blond-and-black Swedish inlaid woods. Large, sparkling bathrooms, most with tubs and separate shower stalls, are the best in Budapest. ⊠ *V, Erzsébet tér 7–8, H-1051 Budapest,* ☎ *1/266–1000; in the U.S. and Canada,* ☎ *800/426–3135,* FAX *1/266–2000. 339 rooms with bath, 28 suites. 2 restaurants, bar, lobby lounge, pub, indoor pool, barbershop, beauty salon, massage, health club, shops, laundry service and dry cleaning, business services, meeting rooms, travel services, parking (fee). AE, DC, MC, V.*

$$$ 🏨 **Astoria.** Revolutionaries and intellectuals once gathered in the marble-and-gilt Art Deco lobby here. Rooms are Empire-style and renovations have not obscured their charm; rather, they added comforts—most notably soundproofing, essential since the Astoria is located at a busy downtown intersection. ⊠ *V, Kossuth Lajos u. 19–21, H-1053 Budapest,* ☎ *1/117–3411,* FAX *1/118–6798. 123 rooms* *with bath or shower, 5 suites. Restaurant, bar, café, nightclub, business services, meeting rooms, free parking. AE, DC, MC, V.*

$$$ ★ 🏨 **Budapest Marriott.** At this sophisticated yet friendly hotel near downtown Pest, every detail sparkles, including the marble floors, brass lamps, and dark-wood paneling in the lobby. Rooms feature expansive beds, floral bedspreads, and etched glass. Stunning vistas are provided from every guest room, the ballroom, and even the swimming pool. Most rooms have a balcony. ⊠ *V, Apáczai Csere János u. 4, H-1364 Budapest,* ☎ *1/266–7000,* 🆉 *1/266–5000; in U.S. and Canada,* ☎ *800/831–4004. 362 rooms with bath, 20 suites. 3 restaurants, bar, no-smoking rooms, indoor pool, health club, squash, shops, baby-sitting, laundry service and dry cleaning, business services, meeting rooms, travel services, parking (fee). AE, DC, MC, V.*

$$$ 🏨 **Ramada Grand Hotel.** Set on a car-free island in the Danube and connected to a bubbling thermal spa, the Ramada feels removed from the city, but is still only a short taxi- or bus-ride away. This venerable hotel, built in 1873, has been completely modernized, yet retains its period look, with high ceilings and Old World furnishings. Choose either a view across the Danube at a less attractive, industrial section of Pest or one out onto a tranquil park. ⊠ *XIII, Margit-sziget, H-1138 Budapest,* ☎ *1/311–1000,* 🆉 *1/153–3029; for reservations,* ☎ *1/131–7769; in the U.S. and Canada,* ☎ *800/228–9898. 164 rooms with bath, 10 suites. Restaurant, ice cream parlor, indoor pool, beauty salon, massage, spa, exercise room, bicycles, meeting rooms, travel services, free parking. AE, DC, MC, V.*

$$$ 🏨 **Thermal Hotel Helia.** Sleek Scandinavian design and a less hectic location upriver make this spa hotel on the Danube a change of pace from its Pest peers. Its neighborhood is nondescript, but guests can be in town in minutes or stay and take advantage of the thermal baths and special health packages—including anything from Turkish baths to electrotherapy and fitness tests. ⊠ *XIII, Kárpát u. 62–64, H-1133 Budapest,* ☎ *1/270–3277,* 🆉 *1/270–2262; in the U.S. and Canada,* ☎ *800/223–5652. 254 rooms with bath; 8 suites, 4 with sauna. 2 restaurants, bar, café, indoor pool, beauty salon, massage, sauna, spa, steam room, tennis courts, exercise room, shops, business services, meeting rooms, free parking. AE, DC, MC, V.*

$$ 🏨 **Alba Hotel.** Tucked behind an alleyway at the foot of Castle Hill, this spotless, modern gem of a hotel is a short walk via the Chain Bridge from business and shopping districts. Rooms are snug and quiet, with clean white and pale-gray contemporary decor and quintessentially Budapestian views over rooftops and chimneys. Half have bathtubs and air-conditioning. ⊠ *I, Apor Péter u. 3, H-1011 Budapest,* ☎ *1/175–9244,* 🆉 *1/175–9899. 95 rooms with bath. Bar, breakfast room, no-smoking rooms, meeting room, parking (fee). AE, DC, MC, V.*

$$ 🏨 **Hotel Centrál.** Relive history—stay in this hotel, well-situated in a leafy diplomatic quarter just a block from Heroes' Square, as visiting communist dignitaries once did. The architecture and furnishings are straight out of the 1950s, but rooms are comfortable and most have unusually large bathrooms. Suites are classically elegant, with eclectic turn-of-the-century Hungarian furnishings; ask for Rudolf Nureyev's favorite. ⊠ *VI, Munkácsy Mihály u. 5–7, H-1063 Budapest,* ☎ *1/321–2000,* 🆉 *1/322–9445. 36 rooms with bath, 6 suites. Restaurant (no dinner), free parking. AE, DC, MC, V.*

$$ ★ 🏨 **Victoria.** The stately Parliament building and city lights across the river can be seen from every room at this relatively young establishment right on the Danube. The absence of conventioneers is a plus, and the location—an easy walk from Castle Hill and downtown Pest—couldn't be better. ⊠ *I, Bem rakpart 11, H-1011 Budapest,* ☎ *1/201–*

8644, FAX 1/201–5816. *24 rooms with bath, 2 with balcony; 1 suite. Bar, sauna, meeting room, parking (fee). AE, DC, MC, V.*

$ 🏨 **Kulturinnov.** One wing of a magnificent 1902 neo-Baroque castle
★   now houses basic budget accommodations. Rooms come with two or three beds and are clean and delightfully peaceful. The neighborhood—one of Budapest's most famous squares in the luxurious castle district—is magical. ⊠ *I, Szentháromság tér 6, H-1014 Budapest,* ☎ *1/155–0122 or 1/175–1651,* FAX *1/175–1886. 16 rooms with shower. Snack bar, library, meeting rooms. AE, DC, MC, V.*

$ 🏨 **Medosz.** The Medosz provides a central location near the Oktogon, a major transport hub, and lovely Andrássy út; the opera house is a block away. Rooms are neat but very basic, with small, low beds, worn upholstery, and a depressing leftover 1950s institutional feel. Rooms have no TVs or telephones. ⊠ *VI, Jókai tér 9, H-1061 Budapest,* ☎ *1/153–1700 or 1/153–1434,* FAX *1/132–4316. 63 rooms with bath, 7 suites. Restaurant (for groups only). No credit cards.*

$ 🏨 **Molnár Panzió.** Fresh air, peace, and quiet await at this immaculate guest house nestled high above Buda on Széchenyi Hill. Rooms in the octagonal main house are polyhedral, clean and bright; most have distant views of Castle Hill and Gellért Hill, and some have balconies. Service is at once friendly and professional, and the restaurant is first-rate. Rooms in a new addition are due to be completed by 1997. ⊠ *XII, Fodor u. 143, H-1124 Budapest,* ☎ *1/209–2974,* ☎ FAX *1/209–2973. 25 rooms with bath. Restaurant, bar, sauna, exercise room, playground, travel services, free parking. AE, DC, MC, V.*

The Arts

Budapest's English-language newspapers are the most up-to-date sources for arts information in English. The "Style" section of *The Budapest Sun* maps out the week's entertainment and cultural events. *The Sun* is sold for about $1 at many newsstands in well-trafficked areas. Hotels and tourist offices will provide you with a copy of the monthly publication *Programme*, which contains details of all cultural events in the city. Tickets can be bought at venue box offices, your hotel desk, many tourist offices, or any of several ticket agencies, the biggest of which are the **National Philharmonic Ticket Office** (⊠ V, Vörösmarty tér 1, ☎ 1/117–6222) and the **Central Theater Booking Office** (⊠ VI, Andrássy út 18, ☎ 1/112–0000).

There are two opera houses, the **Magyar Állami Operaház** or Hungarian State Opera (⊠ VI, Andrássy út 22) and the **Erkel Színház** or Erkel Theater (⊠ VIII, Köztársaság tér), for which dress can be informal. Concerts are given all year at the **Academy of Music** on Liszt Ferenc tér, at the **Pesti Vigadó** on Vigadó tér, and at the **Old Academy of Music** on Vörösmarty utca. The 1896 **Vígszínház** or Comedy Theater (⊠ XIII, Pannónia út 1), sparkling inside and out after its recent overhaul, hosts primarily musicals, as does the **Operett Színház** (Operetta Theater) on Nagymező utca. Displays of Hungarian folk dancing are presented at the **Cultural Center** on Corvin tér, and regular participatory folk-dance evenings—with instructions for beginners—are held at district cultural centers.

Arts festivals begin to fill the calendar in early spring. The season's first and biggest, the **Budapest Spring Festival** (early to mid-March), showcases Hungary's best opera, music, theater, fine arts, and dance, as well as visiting foreign artists. It's followed by the smaller annual **Jazz Festival** (April), and, after the opera season ends, by the week-long **BudaFest** opera and ballet festival (mid-August) at the opera house. Information and tickets are available from the ticket sources listed above.

Nightlife

Budapest is a lively city by night. Establishments stay open well past midnight and Western European–style drink-bars have sprung up all over the city. For quiet conversation, there are such bars in most hotels, but beware of the inflated prices. Hotel nightclubs are convenient but pricey, and not usually among the "in" places to be. Although a few places do accept credit cards, it's best to expect to pay cash for your night on the town.

Bars and Clubs

The **Jazz Café** (⊠ V, Ballasi Bálint u. 25, ☎ 1/269–5506) hosts local jazz bands several nights a week in a small basement space of blue neon lights and funky papier-mâché statues. The most popular of Budapest's Irish pubs and a favorite ex-pat watering hole is **Becketts** (⊠ V, Bajcsy-Zsilinszky út 72, ☎ 1/111–1035), where Guinness flows freely in a polished-wood and brass decor. A hip, low-key crowd mingles at the stylish **Cafe Incognito** (⊠ VI, Liszt Ferenc tér 3, ☎ 1/267–9428), with low lighting and funky music kept at a conversation-friendly volume by savvy DJs.

Made Inn (⊠ VI, Andrássy út 112, ☎ 1/111–3437) is a prime example of the nearly schizophrenic atmosphere of many new Budapest clubs. Housed in an old stone mansion near Heroes' Square, it has an elaborate decor modeled after an underground mine shaft, a kitchen specializing in Mediterranean foods, a large outdoor bar, and a disco dance floor packed with local and international Beautiful People. (It's closed Mon. and Tues. Nov.–Apr.). Classy and just a touch pretentious, **Piaf** (⊠ VI, Nagymező u. 20, ☎ 1/112–3823) is popular with arts sophisticates. Red velvet chairs and low, candlelit tables crowd together in cozy brick rooms. Open only from 10 PM, it often is still serving enthusiasts at 6 and 7 in the morning. You have to ring the bell to get in. **Picasso Point** (⊠ V, Hajós u. 31, ☎ 1/269–5544), a very popular, spacious bar with a hip, coffeehouse feel and Pablo-themed decor, hosts local art exhibits and live jazz and rock bands. **Café Pierrot** (⊠ I, Fortuna u. 14, ☎ 1/175–6971), an elegant café and piano bar on a small street on Castle Hill, is well suited for a secret rendezvous.

Casinos

Most casinos are open daily from 2 PM until 4 or 5 AM, and offer gambling in hard currency—usually dollars—only. Sylvester Stallone is alleged to be an owner of the popular **Las Vegas Casino** (⊠ V, Roosevelt tér 2, ☎ 1/117–6022), in the Atrium Hyatt Hotel. The **Gresham Casino** (⊠ V, Roosevelt tér 5, ☎ 1/117–2407) is located in the famous Gresham Palace at the Pest end of the Chain Bridge. In an 1879 building designed by prolific architect Miklós Ybl, who also designed the State Opera House, the **Várkert Casino** (⊠ I, Miklós Ybl tér 9, ☎ 1/202–4244) is the most attractive one in the city.

THE DANUBE BEND

About 40 kilometers (25 miles) north of Budapest, the Danube abandons its eastward course and turns abruptly south toward the capital, cutting through the Börzsöny and Visegrád hills. This area is called the Danube Bend, and features the Baroque town of Szentendre, the hilltop castle ruins and town of Visegrád, and the cathedral town of Esztergom. The attractive combination of hillside and river should dispel any notion that Hungary is one vast, boring plain.

Here, in the heartland, are traces of the country's history—the remains of the Roman empire's frontiers, the battlefields of the Middle Ages, and relics of the Hungarian Renaissance. Although the area can be covered by car in a day—the round-trip from Budapest is only 124 kilometers (78 miles)—two days, with a night in Visegrád or Esztergom, would be a better way to savor its charms.

Getting Around

The best way to get around is by boat or hydrofoil on the Danube. The three main centers—Szentendre, Esztergom, and Visegrád—all have connections with one another and with Budapest. Contact MAHART (☎ 1/118–1704) for schedules. There is also regular bus service connecting all three with one another and with Budapest. Szentendre can also be reached by HÉV commuter rail, departing from the Batthyány tér metro; the trip takes about 40 minutes and costs around 130 Ft.

Guided Tours

IBUSZ (☎ 1/118–1139 or 1/118–1043) organizes daylong bus trips from Budapest along the Danube stopping in Esztergom, Visegrád, and Szentendre on Tuesday and Friday from May through October, and Saturday only from November through April: the cost, including lunch, is about 6,500 Ft. Full-day boat tours to Szentendre and Visegrád run May through October on Wednesday and Saturday and cost about 7,000 Ft., including lunch and a cocktail.

Visitor Information

Budapest (Dunatours, ⊠ VI, Bajcsy-Zsilinszky út 17, ☎ 1/131–4533 or 1/111–4555, 𝙵𝙰𝚇 1/111–6827).

Esztergom (Grantours, ⊠ Széchenyi tér 25, ☎ 𝙵𝙰𝚇 33/313–756; IBUSZ, ⊠ Lőrinc u. 1, ☎ 33/312–552; Komtourist, ⊠ Lőrinc u. 6, ☎ 33/312–082).

Szentendre (Tourinform, ⊠ Dumsta J. u. 22, ☎ 𝙵𝙰𝚇 26/317–965; Dunatours, ⊠ Bogdányi út 1, on the quay, ☎ 26/311–311).

Exploring the Danube Bend

Heading north from Budapest toward Szentendre, 19 kilometers (12 miles) by car on Road 11, or by train, look to your right for the reconstructed remains of **Aquincum**, capital of the Roman province of Pannonia. Careful excavations have unearthed a varied selection of artifacts and mosaics, giving a tantalizing inkling of what life was like on the northern fringes of the Roman empire. The on-site **Aquincum Museum** displays the dig's most notable finds. ⊠ *Szentendre út 139*, ☎ *1/250–1650.* 🎟 *100 Ft.* ⏱ *Apr.–Oct., Tues.–Sun. 10–5; May–Sept., Tues.–Sun. 10–6.*

Szentendre, now a flourishing artists' colony with a lively Mediterranean atmosphere, was first settled by Serbs and Greeks fleeing the advancing Turks in the 14th and 17th centuries. The narrow cobbled streets are lined with cheerfully painted houses. Part of the town's artistic reputation can be traced to the ceramic artist Margit Kovács, whose work blended Hungarian folk art traditions with motifs from modern art. The **Margit Kovács Pottery Museum,** devoted to her work, is housed in a small 18th-century merchant's house with an attractive courtyard. ⊠ *Vastag György u. 1*, ☎ *26/310–244.* 🎟 *200 Ft.* ⏱ *Mid-Mar.–Oct., Tues.–Sun. 10–6; Nov.–mid-Mar., Tues.–Sun. 10–4.*

A short drive up Szabadság Forrás út, or a bus ride from the train station, will take you to the **Szabadtéri Néprajzi Múzeum** (Open-Air Ethnography Museum), where a collection of buildings show Hungarian

Danube Bend

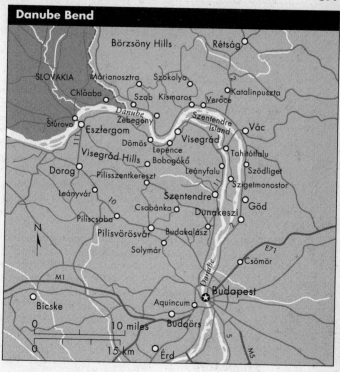

peasant life and folk architecture in the 19th century. Regular crafts demonstrations are held in summer. ✉ *Szabadság Forrás út*, ☎ *26/312–304.* 🎫 *200 Ft.* 🕐 *Apr.–Oct., Tues.–Sun. 10–5.*

Visegrád, 23 kilometers (14 miles) from Szentendre, was the seat of the kings of Hungary in the 14th century. The ruins of the palace of King Matthias on the main street have been excavated and reconstructed; there are jousting tournaments on the grounds in June and a medieval festival in July. A winding road leads up to a haunting late-medieval fortress, from which you have a fine view of the Danube Bend.

Esztergom, 21 kilometers (13 miles) farther upriver, stands on the site of a Roman fortress. St. Stephen, the first Christian king of Hungary, was crowned here in the year 1000. The kings are long gone, but Esztergom is still the home of the archbishop of Esztergom, the cardinal primate, head of the Catholic church in Hungary.

★ Thousands of pilgrims visit the imposing **bazilika** (basilica), the largest in Hungary, which stands on a hill overlooking the town. It was here, in the center of Hungarian Catholicism, that the famous anti-communist cleric, Cardinal József Mindszenty, was finally reburied in 1991, ending an era of religious intolerance and prosecution. The cathedral also houses a valuable collection of ecclesiastical art. Below it are the streets of Viziváros (Watertown), lined with Baroque buildings. The **Keresztény Múzeum** (Museum of Christian Art) is in the Primate's Palace. It is the finest art gallery in Hungary, with a large collection of early Hungarian and Italian paintings. The Italian collection, coupled with the early Renaissance paintings from Flanders and the Lower Rhine, provides insights into the transition of European sensibilities from medieval Gothic to the humanistic Renaissance. ✉ *Mindszenty tér 2*, ☎ *33/313–880.* 🎫 *100 Ft.* 🕐 *Mid-Mar.–Sept., Tues.–Sun. 10–6; Oct.–Dec. and Mar.–mid-Mar., Tues.–Sun. 10–5.*

Dining and Lodging

For details and price-category definitions, *see* Dining *and* Lodging *in* Staying in Hungary, *above.*

Esztergom

$$ ✕ **Primáspince.** Vaulted ceilings and exposed brick walls make a charming setting for refined Hungarian fare at this restaurant just below the cathedral. Try the tournedos Budapest style, tender beef with sautéed vegetables and paprika, or the thick stuffed turkey breast Fiaker style (stuffed with ham and melted cheese). ⊠ *Szent István tér 4,* ☎ *33/313–495. AE, DC, MC, V. Lunch only Jan.–Feb.*

$ ✕ **Fili Falatozó.** The hearty German fare is heavy on meat and potatoes. The location is on Esztergom's most pleasant old cobblestone street, just a short stroll from the Danube. ⊠ *Pázmány Péter u. 1,* ☎ *33/312–534. Reservations not accepted. No credit cards. Closed Jan. and Mon., Oct.–Mar.*

$–$$ 🏠 **Ria Panzió.** In this small, friendly guest house near the cathedral, all rooms face a garden courtyard. The very reasonable room rates include breakfast. ⊠ *Batthyány u. 11, H-2500 Esztergom,* ☎ *33/313–115. 13 rooms with bath. Breakfast room. No credit cards.*

$ 🏠 **Alabárdos Panzió.** Conveniently situated downhill from the basilica, this cozy, remodeled home provides an excellent view of Castle Hill, topped by the oldest royal castle in Hungary. All rooms (doubles and quads) are large. ⊠ *Pázmány Péter u. 49, H-2500 Esztergom,* ☎ FAX *33/312–640. 21 rooms with bath. Breakfast room. No credit cards.*

Szentendre

$$ ✕ **Rab Ráby.** This popular restaurant, decorated with wood beams and equestrian decorations, is the source for fish soup and fresh grilled trout. ⊠ *Péter Pál u. 1,* ☎ *26/310–819. No credit cards.*

$$ 🏠 **Bükkös Panzió.** Impeccably clean, this stylishly modernized old house is on a small canal just a few minutes' walk from the town center. The narrow staircase and small rooms give it a homey feel. ⊠ *Bükkös part 16, H-2000 Szentendre,* ☎ *26/312–021 or* ☎ FAX *26/310–782. 16 rooms with bath. Restaurant. MC, V.*

Visegrád

$$$ 🏠 **Silvanus.** Set high up on Fekete hill, this hotel is renowned for its spectacular views. Located at the end of a long, steep road, it's recommended for motorists (though the bus from town does stop here) and offers hiking trails through the forest. Rooms are bright and clean. ⊠ *Fekete-hegy, H-2025 Visegrád,* ☎ FAX *26/398–311 or 26/398–170. 66 rooms with bath, 4 suites. Restaurant, terrace café, pub, tennis court, bowling, mountain bikes, shop. AE, MC, V.*

$ 🏠 **Haus Honti.** This intimate, alpine-style pension, named after its owner, József Honti, is situated in a quiet residential area far from the main highway but close to the Danube ferry. A stream running close to the house amplifies the country atmosphere. ⊠ *Fő u. 66, H-2025 Visegrád,* ☎ *26/398–120. 7 rooms with bath. Breakfast room. No credit cards.*

LAKE BALATON

Lake Balaton, the largest lake in Central Europe, stretches 80 kilometers (50 miles) across western Hungary. It is within easy reach of Budapest by any means of transportation. Sometimes known as the nation's playground, it goes some way toward making up for Hungary's much-lamented lack of coastline. On its hilly northern shore, ideal for growing grapes, is **Balatonfüred,** the country's oldest and most famous spa town.

The national park on the Tihany Peninsula is just to the south, and regular boat service links Tihany and Balatonfüred with Siófok on the southern shore. This shore is not as attractive as the northern one, being flatter and more crowded with resorts, cottages, and high-rise hotels once used as communist trade-union retreats. Still, it is worth visiting as its shallower—you can walk out for nearly 2 kilometers (1¼ miles) before it deepens—and warmer waters make it a better choice for swimming than other locations.

A circular tour taking in Veszprém, Balatonfüred, and Tihany could be managed in a day, but two days, with a night in Tihany or Balatonfüred, would be more relaxed and allow for detours to Herend and its porcelain factory, or to the castle at Nagyvázsony.

The region gets more crowded every year (July and August are the busiest times) but a few steps along any side road will still lead you to a serene landscape of vineyards and old stone houses.

Getting Around

Trains from Budapest serve all the resorts on the northern shore; a separate line links the resorts of the southern shore. Road 71 runs along the northern shore; M7 covers the southern. Buses connect most resorts. Regular ferries link the major ones. On summer weekends, traffic can be heavy and driving slow around the lake, and bus and train tickets should be booked in advance. In winter, note that schedules are curtailed, so check before making plans.

Guided Tours

IBUSZ has several tours to Balaton from Budapest; inquire at the main office in Budapest (☞ Important Addresses and Numbers *in* Budapest, *above*). Other tours more easily organized from hotels in the Balaton area include boat trips to vineyards and folk music evenings.

Visitor Information

Budapest (Balatontourist, ⊠ V. Váci u. 7, ☎ 1/267–2726).
Balatonfüred (Balatontourist, ⊠ Blaha L. u. 5, ☎ 87/343–471 or 87/342–822, FAX 87/343–435).
Tihany (Balatontourist, ⊠ Kossuth u. 20, ☎ 87/448–519).
Veszprém (Balatontourist, ⊠ Kossuth Lajos u. 21, ☎ 88/429–630).

Exploring Lake Balaton

Hilly **Veszprém** is the center of cultural life in the Balaton region. ★ **Várhegy** (Castle Hill) is the most attractive part of town, north of Szabadság tér. **Hősök Kapuja** (Heroes' Gate), at the entrance to the Castle, houses a small exhibit on Hungary's history. Just past the gate and down a little alley to the left, is the **Tűztorony** (Fire Tower); note that the lower level is medieval while the upper stories are Baroque. There is a good view of the town and surrounding area from the balcony. ☉ *May–Oct., Tues.–Sun. 10–6.*

Vár utca, the only street in the castle area, leads to a small square in front of the **Püspök Palota** (Bishop's Palace) and the **cathedral**; outdoor concerts are held here in the summer. Vár utca continues past the square up to a terrace erected on the north staircase of the castle. Stand beside the modern statues of St. Stephen and his queen, Gizella, for a far-reaching view of the old quarter of town.

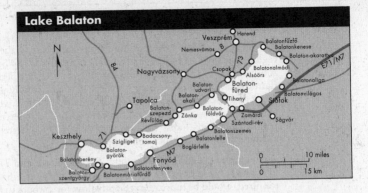

Lake Balaton

If you are traveling by car, go 5 kilometers (3 miles) west to the village of **Nemesvámos,** where you'll find the **Vámosi Betyár Csárda** (Highwayman's Inn). This 18th-century Baroque building takes its name from Savanyu Jóska ("Sour Joe"), an infamous 19th-century highwayman who claimed it as one of his bases. Go down to the cellar to see the tables and seats made from tree trunks—a local architectural feature.

Herend, 16 kilometers (10 miles) northwest of Veszprém on Road 8, is the home of Hungary's renowned hand-painted porcelain. The factory, founded in 1839, displays many valuable pieces in its **museum.** ☎ 88/361–144. ☒ 150 Ft. ☉ May–Oct., daily 8:30–4; Nov.–Dec. and Mar., weekdays 10–3; Apr., Mon.–Sat. 8:30–4.

From Veszprém, take Road 73 about 20 kilometers (12 miles) south to **Balatonfüred,** a spa and resort with good beaches. It is also one of the finest wine-growing areas of Hungary. In the main square of town, medicinal waters bubble up under a colonnaded pavilion; drinking the water alledgedly combats fatigue and cardiac conditions—if you can stand its strong smell. Down at the shore, the Tagore sétány (Tagore Promenade) is a wonderful place to stroll and watch the local swans glide by.

A short boat trip takes you from Balatonfüred to the **Tihany Peninsula,** a national park rich in rare flora and fauna. From the ferry port, follow green markers to the springs (Oroszkút) or red ones to the top of **Csúcs-hegy,** a hill from which there is a good view of the lake.

★ The village of **Tihany,** with its famous **abbey,** is on the eastern shore. The abbey building houses a **museum** with exhibits related to the Balaton area. Also worth a look are the pink angels floating on the ceiling of the abbey church. Detour to the Rege pastry shop (open Apr.–Oct.) at ☒ Első András tér 2, just below the abbey. ☒ Első András tér 1, ☎ 87/448–405. ☒ 100 Ft. ☉ May–Sept., daily 9–5:30; Nov.–Mar., daily 10–3; Apr. and Oct., daily 10–4:30; Sun. and holidays year-round, open from 11 (after mass).

The castle of **Nagyvázsony,** about 20 kilometers (12 miles) northwest of Balatonfüred, dates to the early 15th century. The 92-foot-high keep is the oldest part, and its upper rooms now house the **Kinizsi vár műzeum** (Kinizsi Castle Museum). Try to get to the highest balcony in late afternoon for the best view. The surrounding buildings are preserved in their original style. ☎ 88/364–318. Castle and museum: ☒ 150 Ft. ☉ Nov.–Mar. Tues.–Sun. 10–6; Apr.–Oct. daily 10–6.

Dining and Lodging

For details and price-category definitions, ☞ Dining *and* Lodging *in* Staying in Hungary, *above*. Note that off-season lodging is significantly cheaper at Lake Balaton.

Balatonfüred

$$$ ✕ **Tölgyfa Csárda.** A prime hilltop location gives the Oak Tree Tavern breathtaking views over the steeples and rooftops of Balatonfüred and the Tihany peninsula. The menu and decor are worthy of a first-class Budapest restaurant, and there's live gypsy music in the evenings. ⊠ *Meleghegy (walk north on Jókai Mór út and turn right on Mérleg út)*, ☎ 87/343–036. AE. *Closed late-Oct.–mid-Apr.*

$$ ✕ **Baricska Csárda.** From its perch atop a hill at the southwestern end of town, this rambling, reed-thatched inn overlooks a smooth carpet of vineyards toward the river. The hearty yet ambitious fare includes roasted trout and *fogas* (a freshwater fish particular to the Balaton region), and desserts crammed with sweet poppy seed filling. In summer, colorful Gypsy wedding shows are held nightly under the grape arbors. ⊠ *Baricska dülő, off Rd. 71 (Széchenyi út) behind Shell station*, ☎ 87/343–105. AE, V. *Closed mid-Nov.–mid-Mar.*

$$$ 🏨 **Annabella.** The cool, spacious guest quarters in this Miami-style high rise are especially pleasant during summer. Overlooking the Tagore Promenade and Lake Balaton, it has access to excellent water-sports facilities and is just around the corner from the main square in town. ⊠ *Deák Ferenc u. 25, H-8230 Balatonfüred*, ☎ 87/342–222, 🖷 87/343–084. *390 rooms with bath. Restaurant, bar, brasserie, café, indoor and outdoor pool, barbershop, sauna, shop, nightclub, laundry service.* AE, DC, MC, V. *Closed mid-Oct.–mid-Apr.*

$$$ 🏨 **Margaréta.** This attractive apartment-hotel stands across the street from the lakefront Hotel Marina and, unfortunately, behind a large gas station. It is smaller and more intimate than most of its neighbors, and its restaurant is popular locally. Each room has a minifridge, a balcony, a phone, a TV, and a radio. ⊠ *Széchenyi út 29, H-8230 Balatonfüred*, ☎ 🖷 87/343–824. *51 rooms with bath, 1 suite. Restaurant, bar, laundry service.* AE, DC, MC, V. *Closed mid-Nov.–mid-Mar.*

$ 🏨 **Blaha Lujza.** This sober summer house in the historic section of town, built in classic Roman-villa style, was formerly owned by legendary Hungarian actress Blaha Lujza. Today it's a friendly, unassuming bed-and-breakfast inn with clean, functional rooms. ⊠ *Blaha Lujza u. 4, H-8230 Balatonfüred*, ☎ 🖷 87/343–094. *17 rooms with bath, 2 with shared bath. Restaurant. No credit cards.*

Tihany

$$ ✕ **Halásztanya.** The location on a twisting, narrow street and evening gypsy music help contribute to the popularity of the Halásztánya, which specializes in fish. ⊠ *Visszhang u. 11*, ☎ 87/448–771. *Reservations not accepted. No credit cards. Closed Nov.–Mar.*

$$ ✕ **Pál Csárda.** Two thatched cottages tucked away off a narrow street house this simple restaurant, where cold fruit soup and fish stew are the specialties. You can eat in the garden, which is decorated with gourds and strands of peppers. ⊠ *Visszhang u. 19*, ☎ 87/448–605. *Reservations not accepted. No credit cards. Closed Dec.–Mar.*

$$$–$$$$ 🏨 **Kastely and Park Hotel.** Lush landscaped gardens surround this stately
★ mansion on the water's edge. Inside, it's all understated elegance; rooms have balconies, views, and crisp sheets. A newer, less attractive building houses the Kastely's sister, the Park Hotel, with 60 less expensive rooms. ⊠ *Fürdötelepi út 1, H-8237 Tihany*, ☎ 87/448–611,

FAX *87/448–409. 25 rooms with bath, 1 suite. Restaurant, bar, café, sauna, miniature golf, tennis courts, beach, laundry service. AE, DC, MC, V. Closed mid-Oct.–mid-Apr.*

$$ ⊞ **Kolostor.** The cozy, wood-paneled rooms are built into an attic above a popular restaurant and brewery in the heart of Tihany village. ⊠ *Kossuth u. 14, H-8237 Tihany,* ☎ FAX *87/448–009. 7 rooms with bath. Breakfast room. No credit cards.*

Veszprém

$ ✕ **Diana.** The Diana is just a little southwest of the town center, but
★ worth the trip if you want to experience the old-fashioned charm of a small provincial Hungarian restaurant. The fish and game specialties are perennial favorites. There is also a 10-room pension on the premises. ⊠ *József Attila u. 22,* ☎ *88/421–061. No credit cards.*

$ ✕ **Club Skorpio.** This city-center eatery might look like an Alpine hut, but the menu is excellent and features grilled meats and specialties such as pheasant soup and steamed wild duck. ⊠ *Virág Benedek út 1,* ☎ *88/420–319. No credit cards.*

$ ⊞ **Veszprém.** This modern, comfortable hotel in the center of town is in one of the less attractive buildings in Veszprém, but is convenient to all the major sights and to the bus station. ⊠ *Budapest u. 6, H-8200 Veszprém,* ☎ *88/424–677,* FAX *88/424–076. 52 rooms with bath, 10 with shower and toilet, and 10 with sink that share a toilet. Restaurant, bar, beauty salon. No credit cards.*

15 Iceland

Reykjavík

The Icelandic Countryside

CELAND IS ANYTHING BUT ICY. Though glaciers cover about 10% of the country, summers in Iceland are relatively warm, and the winter climate is milder than New York's. Coastal farms lie in green, pastoral lowlands where cows, sheep, and horses graze alongside raging streams. Distant waterfalls plunge from heather-covered mountains with great spiked ridges and snowcapped peaks. If you're looking for more than landscapes, the people are warm, too, and seem to take a delight in meeting visitors from other countries.

Iceland's chilly name can be blamed on Hrafna-Flóki, a 9th-century Norse settler who failed to store up enough fodder to see his livestock through their first winter. Leaving in a huff, he passed a fjord filled with pack ice and cursed the country with a name that's kept tourism in cold storage for 1,100 years.

The second-largest island in Europe, Iceland is in the middle of the North Atlantic, where the warm Gulf Stream from the south meets cold currents from the north, providing a choice environment for the fish on which the nation depends for 80% of its export revenue. Iceland itself was pushed up from the bed of the Atlantic Ocean by volcanic activity, which is still going on. Every five years on average, this fire beneath the earth breaks the surface in the form of an eruption, sometimes even below glaciers. No one needs to wait for an eruption to be reminded of the fiery forces' presence, because they also heat the hot springs and geysers that bubble and spout in many parts of the country. The springs, in turn, provide heating for most homes and buildings, and hot water for public swimming pools, helping to keep the air smogless. Furthermore, hydropower generated by harnessing the country's many waterfalls is another main energy source, so pollution from fossil fuels is at a minimum. Except for fish and agricultural products, almost all consumer goods are imported, making the cost of living high. Economic stability and reforms in recent years, however, have been bringing prices down to make them competitive with the rest of Scandinavia and not so different from those of Europe in general.

The first permanent settlers arrived from Norway in 874, though some Irish monks had arrived a century earlier. In 1262, the country came under foreign rule, by Norway and later Denmark, and did not win complete independence until 1944. Today nearly three-fifths of the country's 267,000 people live in Reykjavík and its suburbs.

ESSENTIAL INFORMATION

Before You Go

When to Go

The best time to visit is from May through November; from June through July, the sun never sets. Weather is unpredictable: In June, July, and August, sunny days alternate with spells of rain showers and driving winds. Winter weather fluctuates bewilderingly, with temperatures as high as 50°F (10°C) or as low as −14°F (−10°C.). In December the sun shines for only three hours a day, but on a clear and cold evening any time from September to March you can see the Northern Lights dancing among the stars.

CLIMATE

Iceland enjoys a temperate ocean climate with cool summers and mild winters. In the northern part of the country, the weather is more sta-

Iceland

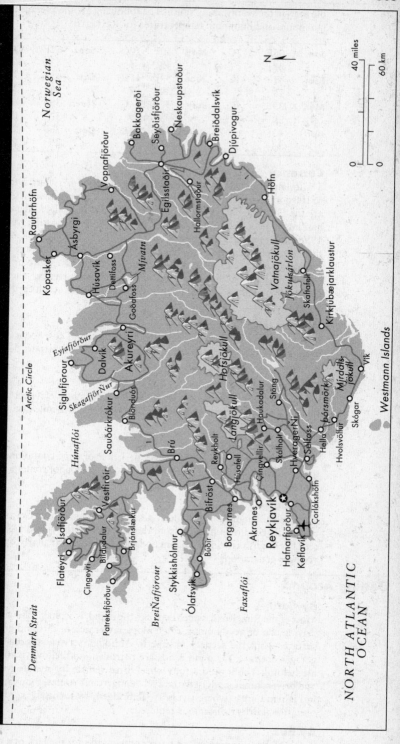

ble than in the windy, rainy south. The following are the average daily maximum and minimum temperatures for Reykjavík.

Jan.	35F	2C	May	50F	10C	Sept.	52F	11C
	28	– 2		39	4		43	6
Feb.	37F	3C	June	54F	12C	Oct.	45F	7C
	28	– 2		34	7		38	3
Mar.	39F	4C	July	57F	14C	Nov.	39F	4C
	30	– 1		48	9		32	0
Apr.	43F	6C	Aug.	56F	14C	Dec.	36F	2C
	33	1		47	8		29	– 2

Currency

The Icelandic monetary unit is the króna (plural krónur), which is equal to 100 aurar, and is abbreviated kr. locally and ISK internationally. Coins are the ISK 1, 5, 10, 50, and 100. There are krónur bills in denominations of 100, 500, 1,000, 2,000, and 5,000. At press time (spring 1996), the rate of exchange was ISK 67 to the U.S. dollar, ISK 49 to the Canadian dollar, and ISK 101 to the pound sterling, but some fluctuation occurs. No limitations apply to import and export of currency, and you may bring any amount of foreign currency, which is easily exchanged for krónur at Icelandic banks. Major credit cards are widely accepted.

What It Will Cost

Iceland is on the expensive side. Hotels and restaurants cost about 20% more in Reykjavík than elsewhere in the country. The airport departure tax is ISK 1,340.

SAMPLE PRICES

A cup of coffee or soft drink costs about ISK 150; a bottle of beer costs ISK 300; a sandwich or snack about ISK 400; and a 2-mile taxi ride, about ISK 500.

Customs on Arrival

Tourists can bring in 6 liters of beer or 1 liter of wine containing up to 21% alcohol, 1 liter of liquor with up to 47% alcohol content, and 200 cigarettes.

Language

The official language is Icelandic, a highly inflected North Germanic tongue that is little changed from that spoken by the island's Norse settlers. English is widely understood and spoken, particularly by the younger generation.

Getting Around

By Car

Most of the Ring Road, which encircles the island, is asphalt. Elsewhere, driving can be very bumpy, often along lava track or dirt and gravel surfaces—but the scenery is superb. Although service stations and garages are rare, the main roads are patrolled, and fellow motorists are helpful. You'll need a four-wheel-drive vehicle for remote roads, and drivers are not advised to travel "dangerous" routes, for example in highland areas where rivers are unbridged, by themselves. An international driver's license is required.

By Bus

A comprehensive network of buses compensates for the lack of a railway system. A good buy, if you want to explore extensively, is the **Omnibus Passport,** which permits you to travel on all scheduled bus routes for one to four weeks for ISK 13,500–ISK 28,500. The **Full Circle Pass-**

port, which costs ISK 12,500 and is valid for a trip around Iceland on the Ring Road, will take you to some of the most popular attractions, but to see even more, you'll have to pay extra for the scheduled bus tours. For further information, contact **Reykjavík Central Bus Terminal** (BSÍ; ⊠ Vatnsmýrarvegur 10, ☎ 552–2300, 🆉 552–9973).

By Plane

Icelandair, Íslandsflug, Norlandair, and a few other airlines have domestic flights to some 50 towns and villages. Special discounts are available on certain combinations of domestic air routes.

Staying in Iceland

Telephones

INTERNATIONAL CALLS

For collect calls and assistance with overseas calls, dial 115; for direct international calls dial 00. To reach a long-distance operator in the United States from Iceland, use the following international access codes: **AT&T** (800–9001), **MCI** (999–002), **Sprint** (800–9003).

LOCAL CALLS

All phone numbers in Iceland contain seven digits; there are no city codes. Pay phones take ISK 10 and ISK 50 coins and are found in hotels, shops, bus stations, and post offices. There are few outdoor telephone booths in the towns and villages. Phone cards cost ISK 500 and are sold at post offices, hotels, etc. For operator assistance with local calls dial 119; for information dial 118.

COUNTRY CODE

The country code for Iceland is 354.

Mail

POSTAL RATES

Airmail letters to the United States cost ISK 55; ISK 35 to Europe.

RECEIVING MAIL

You can have your mail sent to the post office in any town or village in Iceland. In Reykjavík, have mail sent to the downtown post office (⊠ R/O Pósthússtræti, 101 Reykjavík).

Opening and Closing Times

Banks are open weekdays 9:15–4. Some branches are also open Thursdays 5–6. The bank at Hotel Loftleiðir in Reykjavík is open weekends for foreign exchange only. **The Change Group** (⊠ Bankastræti 2, ☎ 552–3735), which handles exchanges only, is open seven days a week, May through September 8:30AM–8PM and October through April 8:30AM–6PM. **Museums** are usually open 1–4:30, but some open as early as 10 and others stay open until 7. **Shops** are open weekdays 9–6 and Saturdays 9–noon (shopping malls 9–4). Grocery stores are open later, including Sunday afternoons.

National Holidays

January 1; March 27–31 (Easter); April 24 (first day of summer); May 1 (Labor Day); May 8 (Ascension); May 18–19 (Pentecost); June 17 (National Day); August 5 (public holiday); December 24–26; December 31.

Dining

Seafood and lamb are local specialties. Don't miss the fresh fish served in this country—it's surely some of the best you'll ever have. Restaurants are small and varied—Asian, Lebanese, Indian, French, and Italian. Many are located in interesting old buildings. Although pizzas and hamburgers are widely available, the favorite local snack food is a tasty version of a hot dog, served with fried onions.

Dinner, served between 6 and 9, is the main meal; a light lunch is usually served between noon and 2. Most restaurants are open from mid-morning until midnight.

WHAT TO WEAR
Casual dress is acceptable in all but the most expensive restaurants, where a jacket and tie are recommended.

RATINGS
The following ratings are for a three-course meal for one person. Prices include taxes and service charges but not wine or cocktails.

CATEGORY	REYKJAVÍK	OTHER AREAS
$$$	over ISK 4,000	over ISK 3,500
$$	ISK 3,000–ISK 4,000	ISK 2,500–ISK 3,500
$	under ISK 3,000	under ISK 2,500

Lodging

Hotels are clean, quiet, and friendly. Reykjavík and most villages also have guest houses and private accommodations. Hostels are few and only functional. Lodging in farmhouses is highly recommended: Around 120 participating farms are listed with **Icelandic Farm Holidays** (⊠ Bændahöllin, Hagatorg, 101 Reykjavík, ☎ 562–3640, 562–3642, or 562–3643, 𝔉𝔞𝔵 562–3644), and many offer fishing, guided tours, and horseback riding. Outside Reykjavík, the **Icelandic Touring Club** (⊠ Mörkin 6, ☎ 568–2533, 𝔉𝔞𝔵 568–2535) operates a number of huts for mountaineers and hikers in remote areas, available all year except spring; club members have priority.

If you tour Iceland on your own, get a list of hotels and guest houses in the regions from the **Tourist Information Center** (⊠ Bankastræti 2, ☎ 562–3045, 𝔉𝔞𝔵 562–3057). The **Iceland Tourist Bureau (ITB)** (⊠ Skógarhlíð 18, ☎ 562–3300, 𝔉𝔞𝔵 562–5895) offers additional information on where to stay. The ITB actually operates its own chain of tourist-class hotels called EDDA. However, many are open in summer only. A Sleep-As-You-Please voucher is available from **Samvinn Travel** (⊠ Austurstræti 12, ☎ 569–1010 or 569–1070), entitling holders to stay at a selection of hotels and guest houses all over Iceland; it costs ISK 10,000 for seven nights.

RATINGS
Prices are for two people sharing a double room.

CATEGORY	REYKJAVÍK	OTHER AREAS
$$$	over ISK 11,000	over ISK 9,000
$$	ISK 8,000–ISK 11,000	ISK 6,000–ISK 9,000
$	under ISK 8,000	under ISK 6,000

Tipping
Tipping is not customary in Iceland.

REYKJAVÍK

Arriving and Departing

By Boat
During summer, the North Atlantic ferry **Norröna** sails from the Faroe Islands, Denmark, and Norway to Seyðisfjörður, one of the magnificent fjords on the east side of Iceland, 720 kilometers (450 miles) from Reykjavík. From Seyðisfjörður, Reykjavík is a 10-hour drive; the nearest airport to Seyðisfjörður is 32 kilometers (20 miles) away in Egilsstaðir, and the flight from there to Reykjavík takes one hour. For informa-

tion, contact **Smyril Line Passenger Department** (⊠ Box 370, FR-110 Torshavn, Faroes) or **Norræna ferðaskrifstofan** (⊠ Laugavegur 3, Reykjavík; ☎ 562–6362, 𝔽𝔸𝕏 552–9450).

By Plane

Flights from the United States and Europe arrive at Keflavík Airport (☎ 505–0500), 50 kilometers (30 miles) from Reykjavík.

BETWEEN THE AIRPORT AND DOWNTOWN

Buses connect with all flights to and from Keflavík. The drive takes 45 minutes and costs ISK 600. **Flybus,** from **Reykjavík Excursions,** has terminals at Scandic Hótel Loftleiðir and Scandic Hótel Esja. Taxis are also available, but they cost at least ISK 4,500.

Getting Around

Most interesting sights are in the city center, within easy walking distance of one another. Sightseeing tours are also recommended.

By Bus

Buses run from 7 AM to around midnight, some slightly later on weekends. The flat fare for Reykjavík and suburbs is ISK 120 for adults and ISK 25 for children under 13. Exact change is required. Strips of tickets are available from bus drivers and at bus stations. If you need to change buses (once, within half an hour), ask for a free transfer ticket.

By Taxi

Rates start at about ISK 300; few taxi rides exceed ISK 700. The best taxis to call are: **Hreyfill** (☎ 588–5522), **BSR** (☎ 561–0000, 561–1720), and **Bæjarleiðir** (☎ 553–3500).

Important Addresses and Numbers

Embassies

U.S. (⊠ Laufásvegur 21, ☎ 562–9100). **Canadian Consulate** (⊠ Suður-landsbraut 10, ☎ 568–0820). **U.K.** (⊠ Laufásvegur 49, ☎ 551–5883).

Emergencies

The general emergency number for **police, ambulance,** and **fire** is 112, nationwide. **Doctors and dentists:** weekdays 8 AM–5 PM, ☎ 569–6600; weekdays 5 PM–8 AM and weekends, ☎ 552–1230. **Pharmacies** operate in shifts at night and on weekends; for information, ☎ 551–8888.

English-Language Bookstores

Eymundsson-Penninn (⊠ Austurstræti 18, ☎ 511–1130 or 511–1140). **Mál og menning** (⊠ Laugavegur 18, ☎ 552–4240).

Travel Agencies

Iceland Tourist Bureau (⊠ Skógarhlíð 18, ☎ 562–3300, 𝔽𝔸𝕏 562–5895); **Samvinn Travel** (⊠ Austurstræti 12, ☎ 569–1010, 569–1070, 𝔽𝔸𝕏 569–1095, 552–7796; **Úrval–Útsýn Travel** (⊠ Lágmúli 4, ☎ 569–9300, 𝔽𝔸𝕏 588–0202).

Visitor Information

The **Tourist Information Center** (⊠ Bankastræti 2, ☎ 562–3045, 𝔽𝔸𝕏 562–3057) is adjacent to the main shopping district. It's open June through August, weekdays 8:30–6, Sat. 8:30–2, Sun. 10–2; September–May, weekdays 9–5, Sat. 10–2.

Exploring Reykjavík

Reykjavík has a small, safe city center, clean air, and plenty of open spaces. Dining on fresh local seafood from the pollution-free waters is something most visitors welcome. For a city of 100,000, Reykjavík offers an astonishingly wide range of artistic events—the main cultural season is winter, but there's always plenty going on in summer as well. Reykjavík hosts a two-week arts festival in June (biennially, in even-numbered years), with a strong international flavor. Most nightlife is in or near the city center; it's liveliest on weekends—crowds hang around long after bars close at 3AM.

Numbers in the margin correspond to points of interest on the Reykjavík map.

① The heart of Reykjavík is **Austurvöllur,** a small square in the city cen-
★ ter. The 19th-century **Alþingi** (Parliament building), one of the oldest stone buildings in Iceland, faces the square. Notice the statue of Jón Sigurðsson (1811–79), the national hero who led Iceland's process towards independence, which it achieved fully in 1944.

② **Dómkirkjan** (Lutheran cathedral) is a small, charming stone church on
③ the corner of Austurvöllur square. Behind it is **Tjörnin,** a natural lake next to **Reykjavík City Hall,** which has a tourist information office, a large-scale model of Iceland, and a coffee shop. Modern architecture and nature meet here—notice the moss growing on the stone walls. One corner of the pond does not freeze; it is fed by warm water, making it an attraction for birds year-round. The stately white building overlooking
④ Tjörnin is the **National Gallery** (Fríkirkuvegur 7, ☎ 562–1000. ☉ Tues.– Sun. noon–6), which houses a collection of Icelandic art.

Lækjargata is the main street linking the natural environment of Tjörnin lake with the busier city center. Overlooking it is the **Bern-höftstorfa** district, a small hill with colorful two-story preserved or restored wooden houses from the mid-19th century. Here you'll find the
⑤ oldest educational institution in the country, **Menntaskólinn í Reykjavík,** a college whose graduates have from the early days dominated political and social life in Iceland.

NEED A BREAK?	**Kaffi París** (⊠ Austurstræti 14, ☎ 551–1020) on the corner of Austurvöllur square and Pósthússtræti, is a cozy, Parisian-style bistro with sidewalk dining in the summer.

⑥ **Lækjartorg** (literally "Brook square"—a brook here used to drain the lake into the sea) is a focal point in Reykjavík's otherwise rambling city center. It opens onto Austurstræti, a semipedestrian shopping street, which is intersected by Pósthússtræti, a short street that runs from the main post office to Austurvöllur square. The main shopping street starts out from Lækjartorg square, too, up the hill to Bankastræti and along Laugavegur. On the seaward side of Bankastræti is an
⑦ 18th-century white building, the **Government House,** which houses the offices of Iceland's president and prime minister.

Stroll down Laugavegur to Hlemmtorg, a square where Hlemmur, the
⑧ city's main bus station, is located. Here you'll find the **Náttúrufræðistofnun** (Museum of Natural History), with one of the last great auks on display and several exhibits that focus on Icelandic natural history. ⊠ Hlemmtorg, ☎ 562–9822. ☞ Free. ☉ Tues., Thurs., and weekends. 1:30–4:00.

From Hlemmur bus station you can take Bus 10 for a 20-minute ride
⑨ to the **Árbæjarsafn** (Open-Air Folk Museum), a "village" of 18th-and 19th-century houses. ⊠ Árbær, ☎ 577–1111. ☞ ISK 300 ☉ June–Aug., Tues.–Sun. 10–6 and by appointment.

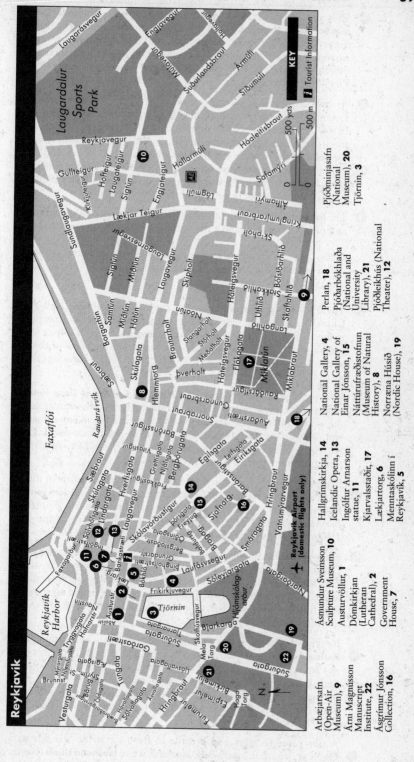

Reykjavik

KEY
i Tourist Information

Árbæjarsafn (Open-Air Museum), **9**

Árni Magnússon Manuscript Institute, **22**

Ásgrímur Jónsson Collection, **16**

Ásmundur Sveinsson Sculpture Museum, **10**

Austurvöllur, **1**

Dómkirkjan (Lutheran Cathedral), **2**

Government House, **7**

Hallgrímskirkja, **14**

Icelandic Opera, **13**

Ingólfur Arnarson statue, **11**

Kjarvalsstaðir, **17**

Lækjartorg, **6**

Menntaskólinn í Reykjavík, **5**

National Gallery, **4**

National Gallery of Einar Jónsson, **15**

Náttúrufræðistofnun (Museum of Natural History), **8**

Norræna Húsið (Nordic House), **19**

Perlan, **18**

Þjóðarbókhlaða (National and University Library), **21**

Þjóðleikhús (National Theater), **12**

Þjóðminjasafn (National Museum), **20**

Tjörnin, **3**

⑩ Only a five-minute ride from Hlemmur on Bus 5 is the **Ásmundur Sveins-son Sculpture Museum.** Some originals by this sculptor, depicting ordinary working people, myths, and folktale episodes, are in the surrounding garden, which is accessible at all times free of charge. ✉ *v/Sigtún,* ☎ *553–2155.* ⌹ *ISK 200.* ◷ *June–Sept., daily 10–4; Oct.–May, daily 1–4.*

⑪ Arnarhóll hill is dominated by a statue of Viking **Ingólfur Arnarson,** Iceland's first settler, who arrived in 874. From here there's a fine view of Reykjavík's architectural melange, from 18th-century houses to the modern, futuristic-looking black glass building to the north, which is the **Seðlabanki** (Central Bank). This area was once the cultural heart of Reykjavík; prominent structures are the **Þjóðleikhús** (National The-⑫ ater), built during the 1940s, and the old **National Library** building, which dates from the beginning of the 20th century.

⑬ The **Icelandic Opera** building looks like an old-fashioned movie house, and in fact, it was Iceland's first cinema before it was converted.

....

NEED A   A bar, light snacks, art shows, live music, and intimate theater are the
BREAK?   draws at **Café Sólon Íslandus** (✉ Bankastræti 7A, ☎ 551-2666), a
          great place to rest your tired feet.

....

⑭ The 210-foot gray stone tower of the **Hallgrímskirkja** (Hallgrim's Church), which took more than 40 years to build and was completed in the '80s, is visible from almost anywhere in the city. It's open to the public and from the top you can enjoy a panoramic view of the city and its spacious suburbs. ☎ *551–0745.* ⌹ *ISK 200* ◷ *May–Sept., daily 9–6; Oct.–Apr., daily 10–6 .*

⑮ Looking almost like a fortress, the **National Gallery of Einar Jónsson** is devoted to the works of Iceland's leading early-20th-century sculptor, whose monumental works have a strong symbolic and mystical content. ✉ *Njarðargata.* ⌹ *ISK 200.* ◷ *Mid-June–Sept, Tues.–Sun 1:30–4; mid-Sept.–Nov. and Feb.–May, weekends only; closed Dec.–Jan. Sculpture garden open at all times.*

Everywhere in the city you'll find art galleries, many of them tucked away in old houses overlooking downtown. The **Ásgrímur Jónsson Col-**⑯ **lection** features works by this popular post-Impressionist painter. ✉ *Bergstaðastræti 74,* ☎ *551–3644.* ⌹ *Free.* ◷ *June–Aug., Tues.–Sun. 1:30– 4; Sept.–Nov. and Feb.–May, weekends 1:30–4; closed Dec.–Jan.*

⑰ **Kjarvalsstaðir,** a municipal art museum named after Jóhannes Kjarval (1885–1972), the nation's best-loved painter, stands in the spacious park **Miklatún.** Works by Icelandic and international artists are featured, as well as paintings, many of them of lava landscapes and mystical beings, from the museum's Kjarval collection. ✉ *Flókagata,* ☎ *552–6131.* ⌹ *ISK 300.* ◷ *Daily 10–6.*

Reykjavík is by no means all timber and concrete. The gleaming glass ⑱ **Perlan** dome perches like a space station high on a hill atop six huge hot-water reservoirs that heat the capital area. The wooded slopes of the hill are especially popular with strollers and joggers. There's a fine restaurant here (☞ *in* Dining, *below*), a coffee shop, an ice cream bar, and a balcony with splendid views. ✉ *Öskjuhlíð,* ☎ *562–0200.* ⌹ *Free.* ◷ *Daily 11:30 AM–10 PM.*

A fine place to relax and breathe in fresh air is the lakeside park ⑲ Hljómskálagarður. Nearby, the blue-and-white **Norræna Húsið** (Nordic House), designed by Finnish architect Alvar Aalto, is a Scandinavian cultural center with exhibitions, lectures, concerts, and a coffee shop.

✉ *Sæmundargata,* ☎ *551–7030.* ☉ *Coffee shop, daily 9–5; exhibitions, daily 2–7.*

⑳ On the edge of the campus of the **University of Iceland,** to the north and west of Nordic House, stands the superb **Þjóðminjasafn** (National Museum). On display are Viking artifacts, national costumes, weavings, carvings, and silver works. ✉ *Suðurgata 41,* ☎ *552–8888.* ✉ *ISK 200.* ☉ *Mid-May–mid-Sept., Tues.–Sun 11–5; late Sept.–early May, Tues., Thurs., and weekends noon–5.*

㉑ It's hard to miss the red aluminum-clad **Þjóðarbókhlaða** (National and University Library) on the corner of Suðurgata and Hringbraut. This fortresslike structure was completed in 1994. ✉ *Arngrímsgata,* ☎ *563–5600.* ☉ *Weekdays 9–7, Sat. 10–5.*

㉒ Arguably, the greatest treasure trove in Iceland is housed on the University of Iceland campus at the **Árni Magnússon Manuscript Institute:** priceless manuscripts containing most of the sagas and mythical poetry that have established medieval Icelandic literature as one of the great literatures of the world are found here. ✉ *Suðurgata,* ☎ *552–5540.* ☉ *Mid-June–Sept., Mon.–Sat. 2–6 or by appointment.*

Shopping

Many of the shops that sell the most attractive Icelandic woolen goods and arts and crafts are on Aðalstræti, Hafnarstræti, and Vesturgata streets. The **Icelandic Handcrafts Center** (✉ Falcon House, Hafnarstræti 3, ☎ 551–1785) stocks Icelandic woolens, knitting and tapestry materials, pottery, glassware, and jewelry. At the **Handknitting Association of Iceland,** (✉ Skólavörðustígur 9, ☎ 552–1890) you can buy high-quality hand-knits through a knitters' cooperative. **Rammagerðin** (✉ Hafnarstræti 19, ☎ 551–7910) stocks a wide range of Icelandic-made clothes and souvenirs. **Álafoss** (✉ Pósthússtræti 13, ☎ 551–3404) sells mainly woolens. On weekends between 11AM and 5PM, try the harborside **Kolaportið** flea market in the rear of the Customs House on Geirsgata.

Dining

Most Reykjavík restaurants feature excellent seafood dishes as well as lamb specialties. Reservations are vital on weekends in the better restaurants. Jacket and tie are rarely required. Most restaurants are open from noon to midnight, and most take major credit cards. Some offer discount lunch or tourist menus. For details and price-category definitions, *see* Dining *in* Staying in Iceland, *above.*

$$$ ✕ **Gallery at Hótel Holt.** The walls of this dark hotel dining room are covered with Icelandic art from the owner's private collection. Diners here indulge in mouthwatering seafood such as gravlax and grilled halibut, and there's a fabulous wine list to match. ✉ *Holt Hotel, Bergstaðastræti 37,* ☎ *552–5700. AE, DC, MC, V.*

$$$ ✕ **Perlan.** In this slightly formal revolving restaurant under the Per-
★ lan dome, you may pay a bit more for the food—including Icelandic fish and lamb dishes—but the splendid view, especially at sunset, more than compensates for the expense. ✉ *Öskjuhlíð,* ☎ *562–0200. No lunch. AE, DC, MC, V.*

$$ ✕ **Hornið.** Pizzas and pasta are the draw, but good meat and fish dishes are also served at this cosmopolitan bistro. ✉ *Hafnarstræti 15,* ☎ *551–3340. AE, DC, MC, V.*

$$ ✕ **Við Tjörnina.** The imaginative Icelandic seafood cuisine here in-
★ cludes marinated cod cheeks and *tindabikkja* (starry ray) with grapes, capers, and Pernod. It's on the second floor of a typical corrugated-

iron-clad early 20th-century house. ⊠ *Templarasund 3,* ☎ *551–8666. AE, MC, V.*

$ ✕ **Kaffivagninn (Coffee Wagon).** Here, on the waterfront in West Reykjavík, local fishermen enjoy hearty, inexpensive lunches. ⊠ *Grandagarði 10,* ☎ *551–5932. MC, V.*

$ ✕ **Oðinsvé.** On the ground floor of a hotel with the same name, this cozy restaurant serves up Scandinavian-French–style fare, mostly seafood and lamb. Don't miss the fish chowder or the hot apple strudel. ⊠ *Oðinstorg,* ☎ *552–5090. AE, DC, MC, V.*

$ ✕ **Potturinn og Pannan.** The service at this small restaurant on the edge of the downtown area is efficient and friendly. Lamb and fish dishes and American-style salads are the specialties. ⊠ *Brautarholt 22,* ☎ *551–1690. AE, MC, V.*

$ ✕ **Þrír Frakkar Hjá Úlfari.** An interesting selection of seafood includes whale meat. Beef dishes are also recommended. ⊠ *Baldursgata 14,* ☎ *552–3939. DC, MC, V.*

Lodging

For details and price-category definitions, *see* Lodging *in* Staying in Iceland, *above.*

$$$ 🏨 **Hótel Borg.** The refurbished Art Deco interior is comfortable and el-
★ egant. Built in 1930, this magnificent hotel retains its old style, yet provides rooms with all of today's modern conveniences, including CD players and coffeemakers. ⊠ *Pósthússtræti 11, Box 200, 121 Reykjavík,* ☎ *551–1440,* FAX *551–1420. 26 rooms, 4 suites all with bath. Restaurant, bar, minibars, in-room VCRs, meeting rooms. AE, D, MC, V.*

$$$ 🏨 **Hótel Holt.** One of Reykjavík's finest hotels, the Holt is in a central residential district. Many of the rooms are adorned with Icelandic art. The restaurant (☞ Dining, *above*) is especially good. ⊠ *Bergstaðastræti 37,* ☎ *552–5700,* FAX *562–3025. 40 rooms with bath or shower, 14 suites. Restaurant, lobby lounge. AE, DC, MC, V.*

$$$ 🏨 **Hótel Saga.** All the rooms of this business-oriented hotel are above
★ the fourth floor and have spectacular views. It's within walking distance of most museums, shops, and restaurants. There's live music and dancing here on weekends. ⊠ *Hagatorg,* ☎ *552–9900,* FAX *562–3980. 216 rooms with bath. Restaurant, 6 bars, grill, in-room VCRs, sauna, health club, meeting rooms. AE, DC, MC, V.*

$$$ 🏨 **Scandic Loftleiðir.** Conveniently near the domestic airport, and only 15 minutes from the town center, this hotel is popular with both tourists and conventioneers. ⊠ *Reykjavík Airport,* ☎ *552–2322,* FAX *505–0905. 218 rooms with bath. 2 restaurants, indoor pool, sauna. AE, DC, MC, V.*

$$ 🏨 **City Hotel.** On a quiet street, this comfortable hotel is in the center of town. ⊠ *Ránargata 4A,* ☎ *551–8650,* FAX *552–9040. 31 rooms with bath or shower. Restaurant. AE, DC, MC, V.*

$$ 🏨 **Hotel Leifur Eiriksson.** Adjacent to the hilltop church, Hallgrímskirkja, this plain hotel is an easy walk from all the city's main attractions. ⊠ *Skólavörðustígur 45,* ☎ *562–0800,* FAX *562–0804. 29 rooms with shower. Restaurant, bar. AE, DC, MC, V.*

$$ 🏨 **Lind.** Near the Hlemmur bus station and a 10-minute walk from downtown, the Lind offers few frills but plenty of clean rooms. ⊠ *Rauðarárstígur 18,* ☎ *562–3350,* FAX *562–3351. 44 rooms with bath. Restaurant, lobby lounge, meeting rooms. AE, DC, MC, V.*

$$ 🏨 **Garður.** This student residence is open as a hotel only in summer, when students are on vacation. Its basic but comfortable, modernized rooms are adequate for travelers on a tight budget. It's within easy reach of the National Museum, downtown and other attractions. ⊠ *Hring-*

braut, ☎ 551–5656. *44 rooms without bath. AE, DC. MC, V. Closed in winter (bookings through Hótel Örk),* ☎ *483–4700).*

$ ⊞ **Smárar Guest House.** The rooms are basic but clean, and all have washbasins. The main bus station is close by. ⊠ *Snorrabraut 52,* ☎ *551–6522. 18 rooms without bath. MC, V.*

THE ICELANDIC COUNTRYSIDE

The real beauty of Iceland is in the countryside: the fjords of the east, the stark mountains of the north, the sands of the south, the rough coastline of the west, and the lava fields of the interior.

Getting Around

There are daily flights to most of the large towns. Although flights are expensive, special family fares and vacation tickets are available. There are car-rental agencies in Reykjavík and in many towns. The few scheduled ferries travel mainly to the Vestmannaeyjar (Westman Islands), from Þorlákshöfn on the south coast, and to Akranes, from Reykjavík. If you do not have your own car, consider buying one of the special bus tickets that cover scheduled routes throughout the country (☞ Getting Around *in* Staying in Iceland, *above*).

Guided Tours

Many people prefer guided bus tours to driving on the rough roads; both day excursions and longer journeys are available. Such tours are an excellent way to relax and enjoy Iceland's spectacular scenery. Most longer tours operate between June and September and cost from ISK 25,000 to ISK 150,000 per person, including accommodations and three meals a day. On some tours you'll stay in hotels; on others you'll sleep in tents. Tours typically last from 3 to 19 days and can be booked from abroad through **Icelandair** or travel agencies. For information on tour operators, contact the **Icelandic Tourist Board** (⊠ Gimli, Lækjargata 3, Reykjavík, ☎ 552–7488, FAX 562–4749).

Day Tours
THE NORTH

The **Iceland Tourist Bureau** (☎ 562–3300) operates a 12-hour day-trip package daily June through mid-September including return flight from Reykjavík to Akureyri and bus trip to Mývatn; the cost is ISK 16,700. Tours to Lake Mývatn from Akureyi take about 10 hours; the cost is ISK 4,500 per person. A 12-hour round trip to Ásbyrgi from Akureyri costs 4,600 per person.

THE SOUTH

Glacier Tours (⊠ Hafnarbraut, ☎ 478–1000, FAX 478–1901) offers a 9-hour bus tour from Höfn in Hornafjörður; the tour includes a snowmobile or Sno-Cat ride and a visit to a glacier lagoon. The trip costs ISK 8,750 per person. Ask about other available tours, such as skiing on Vatnajökull.

Boat tours can be arranged on arrival at the **Jökulsárlón** glacial lagoon for about ISK 1,000. Information is available from Fjölnir Torfason (☎ 478–1065) and at Skaftafell National Park (☎ 478–1627).

The enthusiastic Páll Helgasson from **Westman Islands Travel Service** (⊠ Herjólfsgötu 4, Westman Islands ☎ 481–2922, FAX 481–2007) offers informative, reasonably priced sightseeing trips by boat and bus in the Westman Islands; if you call ahead, he will meet you at the airport.

THE WEST
Eyjaferðir (☎ 438–1450) has boat tours departing from Stykkishól-
mur in West Iceland. Tours of western fjords also run from Isafjörður
(☎ 456–3155 or 456–4655); **Snjófell** (☎ 435–6783, FAX 435–6795)
at Arnarstapi offers trips to the top of the Snæfellsnes glacier by snowmobile for ISK 3,500 per person; **West Tours** (☎ 456–5111) gives hiking and mountaineering trips to the inhabitable parts of Strandasýsla.

Visitor Information

Akureyri: Tourist Center (✉ Hafnarstræti 82, ☎ 462–7733, FAX 461–
1817). **Egilsstaðir:** Tourist Information at Egilsstaðir Campsite, ☎
471–2320. **Höfn:** Tourist Information at Höfn Campsite (✉ Hafnarbraut, ☎ 478–1701). **Ísafjörður:** Tourist Information Center (✉ Hafnarstræti 6, ☎ 456–5121, FAX 456–5122). **Lake Mývatn:** Eldá Travel
(✉ Mývatnssveit, ☎ 464–4220, FAX 464–4321); for information June
through August contact ✉ Reykjahlíðarskóli school, ☎ 464–4390,
🕘 9 AM–10 PM. **Ólafsvík:** Gamla pakkhúsið, ☎ 436–1543. **Seyðisfjörður:**
Austfar (✉ Fjarðargata 8, ☎ 472–1111).

Exploring the Icelandic Countryside

How much of the countryside you explore naturally depends on the
amount of time you have. Day-trips from Reykjavík can easily be expanded with a few rewarding days in the neighboring southern or western regions. To cover the whole country along the Ring Road (Road
1), you should allow at least a week—this will give you time to explore the many spectacular attractions along the way. The following
itinerary takes the Ring Road from Reykjavík in the southwest corner
of Iceland and heads east. There can be up to 80 kilometers (50 miles)
between tourist accommodations, so you must be prepared for some
considerable traveling every day.

The South

In **Hveragerði**, about 40 kilometers (25 miles) east of Reykjavík, there
are some interesting hot springs and greenhouses where fruits and
vegetables are grown. Once you've passed **Selfoss**, 8 kilometers (5 miles)
farther south, you'll be in the heartland of Icelandic farming, and soon
you'll cross the longest river in the country, the Þjórsá. For an overnight
stop in this area, there is lodging in a school dormitory (summer only)
in **Skógar**, 120 kilometers (75 miles) east of Selfoss, and in a year-round
hotel in **Kirkjubæjarklaustur**, 80 kilometers (50 miles) farther east on
Road 205 (☞ Dining and Lodging, *below*).The landscape around
Kirkjubæjarklaustur is shaped by 200-year-old lava deposits. When the
volcano Laki erupted in 1783, it produced the greatest amount of lava
from a single eruption in recorded history.

The south coast's landscape is a major tourist attraction. Don't miss
★ the **Skaftafell National Park** (☎ 478–1627), where you can put down
your tent for ISK 400 a night. The park is at the foot of the glacier Sví-
nafellsjökull; farther up is the highest peak in Iceland, Hvannadalsh-
njúkur, rising to 6,950 feet. About 32 kilometers (20 miles) east of the
★ park is the adventure world of the **Jökulsárlón** glacial lagoon; you can
tour its eerie ice floes by boat (☞ Guided Tours, *above*).

The **Vatnajökull Glacier** is not only Iceland's largest but is equal in size
to all the glaciers on the European mainland put together. One-day downhill skiing and snowmobiling tours of great nature spots in Vatnajökull
are scheduled from June through September (☞ Guided Tours, *above*).

The East

From Höfn the journey continues to Djúpivogur, Road 98, and along the east coast, where one fjord lies beside another. From **Breiðdalsvík** there are two alternative routes. The coastal one runs through the fishing villages of **Stöðvarfjörður, Fáskrúðsfjörður,** and **Reyðarfjörður,** which can be reached via Roads 97, 96, and 92, respectively.

From Reyðarfjörður the Ring Road continues for 32 kilometers (20 miles) to **Egilsstaðir.** If you decide not to follow the coastline from Breiðdalsvík, you'll reach Egilsstaðir across Breiðdalsheiði, which, at approximately 2,500 feet, is the highest mountain road in Iceland. The road is steep and badly engineered. In Egilsstaðir you are about 768 kilometers (480 miles) from Reykjavík, or halfway around the island, so you can either turn back or continue north. The Egilsstaðir campsite has a tourist information center (☎ 471–2320).

Some 24 kilometers (15 miles) south of Egilsstaðir on Road 931 is **Hallormsstaðarskógur,** the largest forest in Iceland. Here you can stop for the night at an Edda hotel (☞ Lodging, *below*) or pitch a tent by the Lögur lagoon, home of Iceland's equivalent of the Loch Ness monster.

From here you can travel around the **Hérað district** and to **Seyðisfjörður,** 48 kilometers (30 miles) from Egilsstaðir on Road 93. Here the Faroese ferry *Norröna* docks weekly on its North Atlantic summer sailing route. Check with the tourist office for information on such activities as boat trips and pony trekking.

★ From Egilsstaðir the Ring Road continues for more than 160 kilometers (100 miles) across remote highlands to **Lake Mývatn.** On this day-long journey through a remote area, you will pass the highest inhabited farm in the country, Möðrudalur, approximately 1,350 feet above sea level. Lake Mývatn, with its incredibly rich variety of waterfowl, is a mecca for bird lovers and also offers fantastic geological formations. Information about bike rentals, fishing, and other activities is available at Hótel Reynihlíð (☎ 464–4170) and Eldá Travel (☎ 464–4220).

From Lake Mývatn there are two possible routes. One is to go directly along Road 1 to **Akureyri,** the capital of the north, a journey of 96 kilometers (60 miles). A key attraction on this route is the graceful waterfall **Goðafoss.**

The other alternative is to go to **Húsavík** (Road 87) and **Tjörnes** (Road 85) for a day or so, a detour of more than 160 kilometers (100 miles).
★ The major attractions in this area are the thundering waterfall **Detti-**
★ **foss** (Road 864) and the great rocky haven of **Ásbyrgi,** which legend says is a giant hoofprint left by Sleipnir, the eight-legged horse of the ancient Norse god Odin.

The North and the West

The natural surroundings in **Akureyri** are unequaled by any other Icelandic town. Late-19th-century wooden houses give the city center a sense of history, as well as architectural variety. **Lystigarðurinn** (Arctic Botanic Gardens) has more than 400 species of arctic flora native to Iceland. ☒ *Eyrarlandsvegur.* ☒ *Free.* ☉ *Daily 8 AM–11 PM.*

Akureyri has the northernmost 18-hole golf course in the world, host of the **Midnight Sun Open Golf Tournament** each year around midsummer. For information, call the Iceland Tourist Bureau (☎ 562–3300, 𝖥𝖠𝖷 562–5895).

From Akureyri you can take an evening tour along the coast of **Eyjafjörður** (Road 82) to see the midnight sun; June and July are the brightest months. Information for traveling in the north is available at the Akureyri tourist center and Nonni Travel (☎ 461–1841 or 461–1843).

Driving from Akureyri to Reykjavík, a journey of 400 kilometers (250 miles) takes an entire day, so if there is time to spare, a stay in **Sauðárkrókur** (Roads 75 and 76), **Blönduós,** or **Borgarnes** can be both pleasant and peaceful. Holders of the Omnibus Passport (☞ Getting Around in Iceland, *above*) should not miss the 320-kilometer (200-mile) detour to the peninsula of **Snæfellsnes,** via Roads 54 and 57. A night near the glacier Snæfellsjökull, where Jules Verne's *Journey to the Center of the Earth* begins, is recommended.

Trips to the top of the glacier by snowmobile can be arranged from **Ólafsvík,** north of the glacier, or **Arnarstapi,** to the south. Information is available from Snjófell (☞ Guided Tours, *above*).

Another interesting detour, which can take up to a week, is to **Vestfirðir** (the West Fjords; Roads 68, 69, and 61). From Ísafjörður, guided trips to the inhabitable parts of Strandasýsla may be of interest to hikers and mountaineers (☞ Guided Tours, *above*).

Dining and Lodging

Most restaurants outside Reykjavík are in hotels. Accordingly, there are no separate restaurant listings in the following selection. For details and price-category definitions, *see* Dining *and* Lodging *in* Staying in Iceland, *above*.

Akureyri

$$$ ✕🍽 **Hótel KEA.** Here you'll receive first-class service at reasonable
★   prices. In addition to the rooftop restaurant that serves Danish haute cuisine, there's an inexpensive cafeteria on the ground floor. ⊠ *Hafnarstræti 97, 600 Akureyri,* ☎ *462–2200,* FAX *461–2285. 72 rooms with shower. Restaurant, cafeteria, minibars. AE, DC, MC, V.*

$$$ ✕🍽 **Hótel Norðurland.** Rooms here are pleasantly decorated with floral prints and Danish furniture. On the ground floor are a dining room for hotel guests and the separately run Pizza 67 restaurant. There's also a sitting room with a panoramic view. ⊠ *Geislagata 7, 600 Akureyri,* ☎ *462–2600,* FAX *462–7962. 38 rooms with bath. Restaurant, minibars. AE, DC, MC, V.*

$$ ✕🍽 **Hótel Edda.** This summer hotel in a school dormitory is known for its quality service. ⊠ *Menntaskólinn, 600 Akureyri,* ☎ *461–1434. 79 rooms, 7 with bath. Restaurant. AE, MC, V. Closed Sept.–mid-June.*

$ 🍽 **Lónsá Farm Holidays.** It's the bare basics, but kitchen facilities are available. ⊠ *Glæsibæjarhreppur, 601 Akureyri,* ☎ FAX *462–5037. 14 rooms without bath. Kitchen. MC, V.*

Blönduós

$$ ✕🍽 **Sveitasetrið, Blönduós.** This small hotel, in the old center of town, is a stone's throw from the seashore. It is no coincidence that fresh trout and salmon are specialties at the hotel's large restaurant. ⊠ *Aðalgata 6, 540 Blönduós,* ☎ *452–4126,* FAX *452–4989. 18 rooms, 11 with shower. Restaurant. AE, MC, V.*

Borgarnes

$$$ ✕🍽 **Hótel Borgarnes.** This is one of the largest and most popular hotels on the west coast. The restaurant is rather elegant. ⊠ *Egilsgata 14–16, 310 Borgarnes,* ☎ *437–1119,* FAX *437–1443. 75 rooms with shower. Restaurant, bar, cafeteria. AE, DC, MC, V.*

Breiðdalsvík

$$ ✗🏨 **Hótel Bláfell.** This small hotel in a fishing village on Route 96 has a cozy, rustic interior and an award-winning seafood restaurant. ✉ *Sólvellir 14, 760 Breiðdalsvík,* ☎ *475–6770,* FAX *475–6668. 15 rooms, 7 with bath. Restaurant. AE, MC, V.*

Búðir

$$ ✗🏨 **Hótel Búðir.** Under the magical glacier Snæfellsjökull and close to a beach of black lava and golden sand, this rustic hotel has an excellent restaurant. ✉ *Staðarsveit, 355 Snæfellsnes,* ☎ *435–6700,* FAX *435–6701. 22 rooms without bath, 4 with bath. Restaurant, horseback riding. MC, V. Closed Oct.–April.*

Djúpivogur

$ ✗🏨 **Hótel Framtíð.** In an old fishing village where 19th-century Danish merchant houses still stand, this small hotel by the harbor has a friendly dining room where home-style food is served. ✉ *Vogaland 4, 765 Djúpivogur,* ☎ *478–8887,* FAX *478–8187. 10 rooms without bath. Restaurant. AE, MC, V.*

$ 🏨 **Berunes Youth Hostel** This small summer hostel offers lodging for 25 people in 2-, 3-, and 4-person rooms. There is a separate house for up to 5 people. ✉ *Beruneshreppur, 765 Djúpivogur,* ☎ FAX *478–8988. No credit cards. Closed mid-Sept.–mid-May.*

Egilsstaðir

$$$ ✗🏨 **Hótel Valaskjálf.** There is dancing on the weekends at this large, practical hotel. Breakfast is included in the room rate. ✉ *Skógarlönd, 700 Egilsstaðir,* ☎ *471–1500,* FAX *471–1501. 71 rooms, 66 with shower. Restaurant, cafeteria, minibars. AE, MC, V.*

$ 🏨 **Húsey Youth Hostel.** Many visitors opt for longer stays at this farm 30 km (18 miles) northeast of Egilsstaðir. ✉ *Hróarstunga, Tunguhreppur, 701 Egilsstaðir,* ☎ *471–3010,* FAX *471–3009. Horseback riding, fishing. No credit cards.*

Hallormsstaður

$$ ✗🏨 **Hótel Edda.** The hotel is merely adequate, but the harmony of forest, lake, and quiet bays is the real attraction. A good restaurant is on the premises. ✉ *707 Hallormsstaður,* ☎ *471–1705,* FAX *471-2197. 17 rooms without bath. Restaurant. AE, MC, V. Closed Sept.–May.*

Höfn

$$$ ✗🏨 **Hótel Höfn.** This clean and comfortable hotel has a restaurant with good service and tasty food; try the lobster. Fast food is also available at the grill. ✉ *780 Hornafjörður,* ☎ *478–1240,* FAX *478–1996. 40 rooms, most with shower. Restaurant, grill. AE, DC, MC, V.*

Húsavík

$$ ✗🏨 **Hótel Húsavík.** This comfortable hotel is popular with skiers during winter. The restaurant serves up delicious seafood dishes. ✉ *Ketilsbraut 22, 640 Húsavík,* ☎ *464–1220,* FAX *464–2161. 33 rooms with shower. Restaurant, cafeteria. MC, V.*

Hveragerði

$$$ ✗🏨 **Hótel Örk.** The rooms here are expensive, but meals in the ground-floor restaurant are reasonable. Three- to seven-day "spa cure" retreat packages are available. ✉ *Breiðamörk 1, 810 Hveragerði,* ☎ *483–4700,* FAX *483–4775. 81 rooms with shower. Restaurant, pool, spa, sauna, 9-hole golf course, tennis court. AE, DC, MC, V.*

$ ⊞ **Ból Youth Hostel.** A standard youth hostel, rooms here have one to five beds, and kitchen facilities. There's a new guest house with double rooms and a shower. ⊠ *Hveramörk 14, 810 Hveragerði,* ☎ *483–4198,* FAX *483–4088. 20 beds. MC, V. Closed mid-Sept.–mid-May.*

Ísafjörður

$$$ ✕⊞ **Hótel Ísafjörður.** This is a good family hotel. All rooms are decorated differently with old-fashioned furnishings and floral fabrics. The restaurant offers a great variety of tasty seafood. ⊠ *Silfurtorg 2, 400 Ísafjörður,* ☎ *456–4111,* FAX *456–4767. 32 rooms with shower. Restaurant, minibars. AE, MC, V.*

Kirkjubæjarklaustur

$$ ✕⊞ **Hótel Edda.** This standard Edda facility, in a modern building with a restaurant and a swimming pool, is open all year round. ⊠ *880 Kirkjubæjarklaustur,* ☎ *487–4799,* FAX *487–4614. 73 rooms, 57 with shower. Restaurant, pool. AE, MC, V.*

Mývatn

$$ ✕⊞ **Hótel Reykjahlíð.** This small hotel and restaurant has a prime lakeside location. ⊠ *660 Reykjahlíð,* ☎ *464–4142,* FAX *464–4336. 9 rooms with bath. Restaurant. MC, V.*

$$$ ✕⊞ **Hótel Reynihlíð.** This popular hotel offers a helpful tourist information service. ⊠ *660 Reykjahlíð,* ☎ *464–4170,* FAX *464–4371. 41 rooms with shower. Restaurant. AE, DC, MC, V.*

Ólafsvík

$$ ✕⊞ **Höfði Guesthouse.** This family-style, harborside hotel has a small restaurant that offers fresh local delicacies such as trout and halibut. ⊠ *Ólafsbraut 20, Ólafsvík,* ☎ *436–1650,* FAX *436–1651. 14 rooms without bath. Restaurant. AE, MC, V.*

Sauðárkrókur

$ ✕⊞ **Hótel Mælifell.** This attractive hotel has a restaurant, plus dancing on weekends. ⊠ *Aðalgata 7, 550 Sauðárkrókur,* ☎ *453–5265,* FAX *453–5640. 16 rooms, 2 with bath. Restaurant. MC, V.*

Seyðisfjörður

$$ ✕⊞ **Hótel Snæfell.** This hotel, in an old wooden house, has a glassed-
★   in restaurant with a dramatic view of the fjord. ⊠ *Austurvegur 3, 710 Seyðisfjörður,* ☎ *472–1460,* FAX *472–1570. 9 rooms with shower. Restaurant. AE, MC, V.*

Skaftafell

$$ ⊞ **Hótel Skaftafell.** This guest house, adjacent to Skaftafell National Park, has a travel shop, gas station, and campsite. ⊠ *Skaftafell, 785 Fagurhólsmýri,* ☎ *478–1945,* FAX *478–1946. 21 rooms with bath, (plus 20 for sleeping bags, with self-catering). Restaurant. MC, V.*

Skógar

$$ ✕⊞ **Hótel Edda.** Close to the waterfall Skógafoss, this summer hotel has views of the sea, mountains, and glaciers. ⊠ *Skógar, 861 Hvolsvöllur,* ☎ *487–8870,* FAX *187–8870. 34 rooms without bath. Restaurant. AE, MC, V. Closed Sept.–May.*

16 Ireland

Dublin

Dublin to Cork

Cork to Galway

The Northwest

FOR A SMALL ISLAND COUNTRY (just over half the size of New York state) isolated on the westernmost extreme of the continent, Ireland has always managed to strut a large part on the European stage. Economically it is a mere understudy to the great European powers, politically its influence is minimal, and yet everyone knows of the Irish, and they all cast a slightly envious eye at this mysterious island of romance.

One reason for this fame has been, of course, the "troubles" in Northern Ireland, which remains part of the United Kingdom. A fragile peace and a movement toward a political solution has sparked a certain renaissance in tourism to the North, and Belfast, the battered capital and old industrial giant, is rumored to be making a comeback.

In the Republic of Ireland to the south, independent since 1921, a new influx of funds from the European Union has led to a substantial program of urban renewal centered on the capital city of Dublin. One-third of the country's very young population lives in the city, giving it a vibrant, lively atmosphere. Galleries, art-house cinemas, juice bars, coffeehouses, and vegetarian restaurants are springing up on every street, transforming the provincial capital that suffocated Joyce into a city every bit as cosmopolitan as the Paris to which he fled.

But the center of Dublin culture remains the public house, where the Irish can be found at their sharpest and most convivial, while seated in fast-talking, welcoming circles around tables supporting the almost sacred black stout, Guinness. Even if you do not usually frequent bars at home, attendance at the ritual of the Irish hostelry will add greatly to your visit.

Dublin's small city center is easy to navigate and strikingly beautiful, with recent renovations to Trinity College, Dublin Castle, and many of the magnificent granite public buildings and distinctive Georgian squares adding to its grandeur.

The pace of life outside the capital is even more relaxed. When a local was asked for the Irish-language equivalent of *mañana,* the reply came that there is no word in Irish to convey quite the same sense of urgency. An exaggeration, of course, but the farther you travel from the metropolis, the more you will be inclined to linger. Apart from such sporting attractions as championship golf, horse racing, angling, and the native games of hurling and Gaelic football, the thing to do in Ireland is to stop, take a deep breath of the best air in the western world, and look around you.

The lakes of Killarney—a chain of azure lakes surrounded by wild, boulder-strewn mountains—are justifiably among the country's most famous attractions. The Ring of Kerry is a gift from the gods to the touring motorist, an out-and-back, daylong adventure through lush green mountain and valley, and on down to the sea. By contrast the lunar landscape of County Clare's eerie limestone desert, the Burren, must be explored on foot if you're to enjoy its rare alpine and Mediterranean flowers. Likewise, if you want to stand on the summit of the Cliffs of Moher to watch the Atlantic breakers bite into the ancient rocks 712 feet below, you'll have to get out of your car, even in the rain, and it often rains in Clare. The history buff will delight in the castles and great stately houses peppered along the banks of the old River Shannon, the spine of the nation. Throughout the country, prehistoric and early Christian ruins and remains hint at the awesome age of civilization on this ancient island. Alternatively you could just visit a bookstore and pick up anything by the great writers of Ireland; let James Joyce, William Butler Yeats, John Millington Synge, and Seamus Heaney be your travel guides, as you seek the places made famous in their works.

ESSENTIAL INFORMATION

Before You Go

When to Go

The main tourist season runs from June to mid-September. The attractions of Ireland are not as dependent on the weather as those in most other northern European countries, and the scenery is just as attractive in the off-peak times of fall and spring. Accommodations are more economical in winter, although some of the smaller attractions are closed from October through March. In all seasons the visitor can expect to encounter rain.

CLIMATE

Winters are mild though wet; summers can be warm and sunny, but there's always the risk of a sudden shower. No one ever went to Ireland for a suntan.

The following are the average daily maximum and minimum temperatures for Dublin.

Jan.	46F	8C	May	60F	15C	Sept.	63F	17C
	34	1		43	6		48	9
Feb.	47F	8C	June	65F	18C	Oct.	57F	14C
	35	2		48	9		43	6
Mar.	51F	11C	July	67F	19C	Nov.	51F	11C
	37	3		52	11		39	4
Apr.	55F	13C	Aug.	67F	19C	Dec.	47F	8C
	39	4		51	11		37	3

Currency

The unit of currency in Ireland is the pound, or punt (pronounced poont), written as IR£ to avoid confusion with the pound sterling. The currency is divided into the same denominations as in Britain, with IR£1 divided into 100 pence (written *p*). There is likely to be some variance in the rates of exchange between Ireland and the United Kingdom (which includes Northern Ireland). Change U.K. pounds at a bank when you get to Ireland (pound coins not accepted); change Irish pounds before you leave.

Although the Irish pound is the only legal tender currency in the Republic, U.S. dollars and British currency are often accepted in large hotels and shops licensed as bureaux de change. Banks give the best rate of exchange. The rate of exchange at press time (spring 1996) was 65 pence to the U.S. dollar, 50 pence to the Canadian dollar, and 95 pence to the British pound sterling.

What It Will Cost

Dublin is one of Europe's most expensive cities—an unfortunate state of affairs that manifests itself most obviously in hotel and restaurant rates. You can generally keep costs lower if you visit Ireland on a package tour. Alternatively, consider staying in a guest house or one of the multitude of bed-and-breakfasts; they provide an economical and atmospheric option (☞ Lodging *in* Staying in Ireland, *below*). The rest of the country—with the exception of the better-known hotels and restaurants—is less expensive than Dublin. That the Irish themselves complain bitterly about the high cost of living is partly attributable to

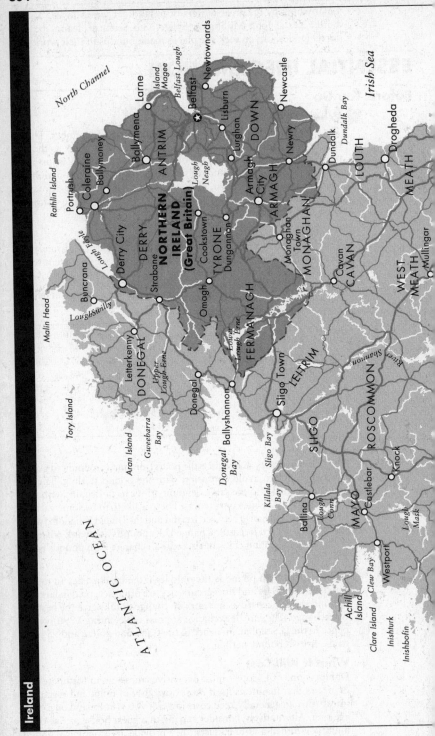

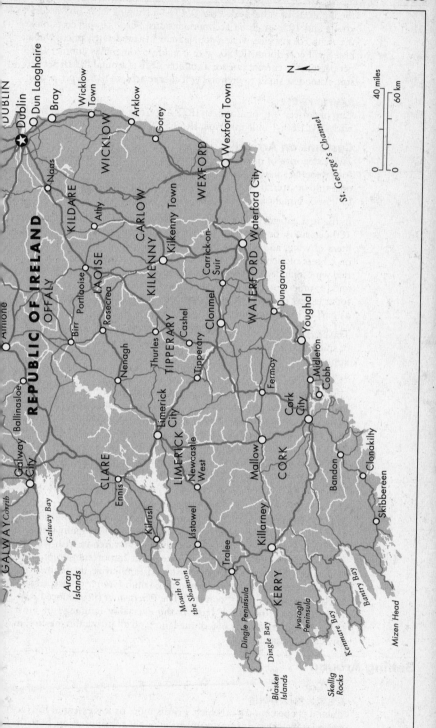

the high rate of value-added tax (VAT)—a stinging 21% on "luxury" goods and 10% on hotel accommodations. Some sample costs make the point. For instance, while a double room in a moderately priced Dublin hotel will cost about IR£90, with breakfast sometimes another IR£9 per person, the current rate for a country B&B is around IR£16 per person. A modest small-town hotel will charge around IR£25 per person.

SAMPLE PRICES
Cup of coffee, 70p; pint of beer, IR£2.10; Coca-Cola, 95p; ham sandwich, IR£1.80; 1-mile taxi ride, IR£3.50.

Customs on Arrival

Two categories of duty-free allowance exist for travelers entering the Irish Republic: one for goods obtained outside the European Union (EU), on a ship or aircraft, or in a duty-free store within the EU; and the other for goods bought in the EU, with duty and tax paid.

In the first category, you may import duty-free: (1) 200 cigarettes, or 100 cigarillos, or 50 cigars, or 250 grams of smoking tobacco; (2) 2 liters of wine, and either 1 liter of alcoholic drink over 22% volume or 2 liters of alcoholic drink under 22% volume (sparkling or fortified wine included); (3) 50 grams of perfume and ¼ liter of toilet water; and (4) other goods to a value of IR£34 per person (IR£17 per person for travelers under 15 years of age); you may import 12 liters of beer as part of this allowance.

Travelers are now entitled to purchase (1) 800 cigarettes, (2) 10 liters of spirits, (3) 45 liters of wine, and (4) 55 liters of beer. The allowances apply only to goods bought in shops in EU countries, including Britain and Northern Ireland, which already have the duty paid.

Goods that cannot be freely imported include firearms, ammunition, explosives, drugs (e.g., narcotics, amphetamines) and drug paraphernalia, indecent or obscene books and pictures, oral smokeless tobacco products, meat and meat products, poultry and poultry products, plants and plant products (including shrubs, vegetables, fruit, bulbs, and seeds), domestic cats and dogs from outside the United Kingdom, and live animals from outside Northern Ireland.

Language

Officially, Irish (Gaelic) is the first language of the Republic, but the everyday language of the vast majority of Irish people is English. Except for the northwest and parts of Connemara, where many signs are not translated, most signs in the country are written in Irish with an English translation underneath. There is one important exception to this rule, with which all visitors should familiarize themselves: FIR (pronounced fear) and MNÁ (pronounced muh-*naw*) translate, respectively, into "men" and "women." The *Gaelteacht* (pronounced *gale-tocked*)—areas in which Irish *is* the everyday language of most people—comprises only 6% of the land, and all its inhabitants are, in any case, bilingual.

Getting Around

By Car

ROAD CONDITIONS
Ireland is one country in which a car is more or less essential for successful travel. Despite improvements in public transportation, both the train and bus networks are limited, and many of the most intriguing areas are accessible only by car. Roads are reasonable, though the absence of turnpikes means that trip times can be long; on the other hand, you'll soon find that driving past an ever-changing and often dramatic

series of unspoiled landscapes can be very much part of the fun. There's a bonus in the fact that traffic is normally light, though you can easily find yourself crawling down country lanes behind an ancient tractor or a flock of sheep. This is not a country for those with a taste for life in the fast lane.

All principal roads are designated by the letter N, meaning National Primary Road. Thus, the main highway north from Dublin is N1, the main highway northwest is N2, and so on. Road signs are usually in both Irish and English; in the northwest and Connemara, most are in Irish only, so make sure you have a good road map. Distances on the new green signposts are in kilometers; the old white signposts give distances in miles.

RULES OF THE ROAD

Driving is on the left. There is a general speed limit of 96 kph (60 mph) on most roads; in towns, the limit is 48 kph (30 mph). In some areas, the limit is 64 kph (40 mph); this is always clearly posted. At traffic circles, traffic from the right takes priority.

Seat belts must be worn by the driver and front-seat passengers. Children under 12 must ride in the back. The new (and controversial) drunk-driving laws are strict, restricting the driver to less than one pint of beer.

PARKING

Despite the relative lack of traffic, parking in towns is a real problem. Signs with the letter P indicate parking lots, but if there's a stroke through the P, keep away or you'll collect a stiff fine, normally around IR£25. After 6 PM, restrictions are lifted. Give lot attendants about 50p when you leave.

By Train

Iarnód Eireann (Irish Rail) and **Bus Eireann** (Irish Bus) are independent components of the state-owned public transportation company **Coras Iompair Eireann** (CIE). The rail network, although much cut back in the past 25 years, is still extensive, with main routes radiating from Dublin to Cork, Galway, Limerick, Tralee, Killarney, Westport, and Sligo; there is also a line for the north and Belfast. All trains are diesel; cars on principal expresses have air-conditioning. There are two classes on many trains—Super Standard (first class) and Standard (second class). Dining cars are carried on main expresses. There are no sleeping cars.

Speeds are slow in comparison with those of other European trains. Dublin, however, has a modern commuter train—the DART (Dublin Area Rapid Transit)—that runs south from the suburb of Howth through the city to Bray on the Wicklow coast and makes many stops along the way.

FARES

There is a **Rambler** ticket (rail and bus) for IR£78, valid for any eight days in a 15-day period. One- and four-day round-trip train tickets are also available at discounted rates. The **Irish Rover** ticket includes travel in Northern Ireland via rail, bus, and Ulsterbus; it costs IR£70 for five days' travel out of 15 consecutive days.

By Plane

Distances are not great in Ireland, so airplanes play only a small role in internal travel. There are daily flights from Dublin to Shannon, Cork, Waterford, Kerry, Knock, and Galway; all flights take around 30 minutes. There is frequent service to the Aran Islands, off Galway Bay, from Connemara Airport, Galway. The flight takes five minutes.

By Bus

For the strictly independent traveler, the 15-day **Rambler** ticket gives unlimited travel by bus and is an excellent value at IR£95. It can be purchased from any city bus terminal and is valid for travel on any 15 days in a 30-day period. The provincial bus system operated by Bus Eireann is widespread—more so than the train system—although service can be infrequent in remote areas. But the routes cover the entire country and are often linked to the train services. *See* By Train, *above*, for details of combined train and bus discount tickets.

By Boat

Exploring Ireland's lakes, rivers, and canals is a delightful, offbeat way to get to know the country. Motor cruisers can be chartered on the Shannon, the longest river in the British Isles. Bord Fáilte (the Irish Tourist Board, pronounced Board *Fall*-cha) has details of the wide choice of trips and operators available.

For drifting through the historic Midlands on the Grand Canal and River Barrow, contact **Celtic Canal Cruisers,** 24th Lock, Tullamore, County Offaly, ☎ 0506/21861.

By Bicycle

Biking can be a great way to get around Ireland. Details of bicycle rentals are available from the Bord Fáilte. Rates average IR£7.50 per day or IR£35 per week. You must pay a IR£30 deposit. Be sure to make reservations, especially in July and August. If you rent a bike in the Republic, you may *not* take it into Northern Ireland; nor may you take a bike rented in Northern Ireland into the Republic.

Staying in Ireland

Telephones

LOCAL CALLS

There are pay phones in all post offices and most hotels and bars, as well as in street booths. Local calls cost 20p for three minutes, calls within Ireland cost about 50p for three minutes, and calls to Britain cost about IR£1.75 for three minutes. Telephone cards are available at all post offices and most newsagents. Prices range from IR£2 for 10 units to IR£8 for 50 units. Card booths are as common as coin booths. Rates go down by about a third after 6 PM and all day Saturday and Sunday.

INTERNATIONAL CALLS

For calls to the United States and Canada, dial 001 followed by the area code. For calls to the United Kingdom, dial 0044 followed by the number, dropping the beginning zero. To reach an **AT&T** long distance operator, dial 1–800/550–000; for **MCI,** dial 1–800/551–001; and for **Sprint,** dial 1–800/552–001.

COUNTRY CODE

The country code for the Republic of Ireland is 353.

Mail

POSTAL RATES

Airmail rates to the United States, Canada, and the Commonwealth are 52p for the first 10 grams, air letters 45p, and postcards 38p. Letters to Britain and continental Europe cost 32p, postcards 28p.

RECEIVING MAIL

A general delivery service is operated free of charge from Dublin's General Post Office (✉ O'Connell St., Dublin 1, ☎ 01/872–8888).

Shopping

Visitors from outside Europe can take advantage of the "cash-back" system on value-added tax (VAT) if their purchases total more than IR£50. A cash-back voucher must be filled out by the retailer at the point of sale. The visitor pays the total gross price, including VAT, and receives green and yellow copies of the invoice; both must be retained. These copies are presented to and stamped by customs, as you leave the country. Take the stamped form along to the cashier, and the VAT will be refunded.

Opening and Closing Times

Banks are open weekdays 10–4, and until 5 on selected days. In small towns they may close for lunch from 12:30–1:30.

Museums are usually open weekdays 10–5, Saturday 10–1, Sunday 2–5. Always make a point of checking, however, as hours can change unexpectedly.

Shops are open Monday–Saturday 9–5:30, closing earlier on Wednesday, Thursday, or Saturday, depending on the locality. Most shops will, however, remain open until 9 PM on Thursdays for late shopping.

National Holidays

January 1 (New Year's); March 17 (St. Patrick's Day); March 28 (Good Friday); March 31 (Easter Monday); May 1 (May Day); May 19 (Whit Monday); August 5 (August Holiday); October 28 (October Holiday); and December 25–26 (Christmas). If you're planning a visit at Easter, remember that theaters and cinemas are closed for the last three days of the preceding week.

Dining

When it comes to food, Ireland has some of the best raw materials in the world: prime beef, locally raised lamb and pork, free-range poultry, game in season, abundant fresh seafood, and locally grown seasonal vegetables. Despite the near-legendary awfulness of much Irish cooking in the recent past, times are definitely changing, and a new generation of chefs is beginning to take greater advantage of this abundance of magnificent produce. In almost all corners of the country, you'll find a substantial choice of restaurants, many in hotels, serving fresh local food that is imaginatively prepared and served.

If your tastes run toward traditional Irish dishes, there are still a few old-fashioned restaurants serving substantial portions of excellent, if plain, home cooking. Look for boiled bacon and cabbage, Irish stew, and colcannon (cooked potatoes diced and fried in butter with onions and either cabbage or leeks and covered in thick cream just before serving). The best bet for daytime meals is "pub grub"—a choice of soup and soda bread, two or three hot dishes of the day, salad platters, or sandwiches. Most bars serve food, and a growing number offer coffee and tea as an alternative to alcohol. Guinness, a dark ale (also known as "stout") brewed with malt, is the Irish national drink. Even if you never go out for a drink at home, you should visit at least one or two pubs in Ireland. The pub is one of the pillars of Irish society, worth visiting as much for entertainment and conversation as for drinking.

Breakfast is served between 8 and 10—earlier by special request only— and is a substantial meal of cereal, bacon, eggs, sausage, and toast. Lunch is eaten between 12:30 and 2. The old tradition of "high tea" taken around 5, followed by a light snack before bed, is still encountered in many Irish homes, including many B&Bs. Elsewhere, however, it is generally assumed that you'll be eating between 7 and 9:30 and that this will be your main meal of the day.

WHAT TO WEAR

A jacket and tie or upscale casual dress are suggested for expensive restaurants. Otherwise casual dress is acceptable.

RATINGS

Prices are per person and include a first course, a main course, and dessert, but no wine or tip. Sales tax at 10% is included in all Irish restaurant bills. Some places, usually the more expensive establishments, add a 12% or 15% service charge, in which case no tip is necessary; elsewhere a tip of 10% is adequate.

CATEGORY	COST
$$$	over IR£28
$$	IR£16–IR£28
$	under IR£16

Lodging

Accommodations in Ireland range all the way from deluxe castles and renovated stately homes to thatched cottages and farmhouses to humble B&Bs. Standards everywhere are high, and they continue to rise. Pressure on hotel space reaches a peak between June and September, but it's a good idea to make reservations in advance at any time of the year, particularly at the more expensive spots. Rooms can be reserved directly from the United States; ask your travel agent for details. Bord Fáilte has a Central Reservations Service (⊠ 14 Upper O'Connell St., Dublin 1, ☎ 01/874–7733, FAX 01/874–3660) that can make reservations, as can local tourist board offices.

Bord Fáilte has an official grading system and publishes a detailed price list of all approved accommodations, including hotels, guest houses, farmhouses, B&Bs, and hostels. No hotel may exceed this price without special authorization from Bord Fáilte; prices must also be displayed in every room. Don't hesitate to complain either to the manager or to Bord Fáilte, or both, if prices exceed this maximum.

In general, hotels charge per person. In most cases (but not all, especially in more expensive places), the price includes a full breakfast. VAT is included, but some hotels—again, usually the more expensive ones—add a 10%–15% service charge. This should be mentioned in their price list. If it's not, a tip of between 10% and 15% is customary—if you think the service is worth it. In $$ and $ hotels, be sure to specify whether you want a private bath or shower; the latter is cheaper. Off-season (October–May) prices are reduced by as much as 25%.

GUEST HOUSES

Some smaller hotels are graded as guest houses. To qualify, they must have at least five bedrooms. A few may have restaurants; those that do not will often provide evening meals by arrangement. Few will have a bar. Otherwise these rooms can be as comfortable as those of a regular hotel, and in major cities they offer very good value for the money, compared with the $ hotels.

BED-AND-BREAKFASTS

Bed-and-breakfast means just that. The bed can vary from a four-poster in the wing of a castle to a feather bed in a whitewashed farmhouse or the spare bedroom of a modern cottage. Rates are generally around IR£16 per person, though these can vary significantly. Although many larger B&Bs offer rooms with bath or shower, in some you'll have to use the bathroom in the hall and, in many cases, pay 50p–IR£1 extra for the privilege.

CAMPING

There are a variety of beautifully sited campgrounds and trailer parks, but be prepared for wet weather! All are listed in *Guest Accommodation* (IR£4), available from Bord Fáilte.

RATINGS

Prices are for two people in a double room, based on high season (June–September) rates.

CATEGORY	COST
$$$$	over IR£160
$$$	IR£120–IR£160
$$	IR£80–IR£120
$	under IR£80

Tipping

Other than in upscale hotels and restaurants, the Irish are not really used to being tipped. Some hotels and restaurants will add a service charge of about 12% to your bill, so tipping isn't necessary unless you've received particularly good service.

Tip taxi drivers about 10% of the fare if the taxi has been using its meter. For longer journeys, where the fare is agreed in advance, a tip will not be expected unless some kind of commentary (solicited or not) has been provided. In luxury hotels, porters and bellhops will expect IR£1; elsewhere, 50p is adequate. Hairdressers normally expect a tip of about IR£1. You don't tip in pubs, but if there is waiter service in a bar or hotel lounge, leave about 20p.

DUBLIN

Arriving and Departing

By Plane

All flights arrive at Dublin Airport, 10 kilometers (6 miles) north of town. For information on arrival and departure times, call individual airlines.

BETWEEN THE AIRPORT AND DOWNTOWN

Buses leave every 20 minutes from outside the Arrivals door for the central bus station in downtown Dublin. The ride takes about 30 minutes, depending on the traffic, and the fare is IR£2.50. A taxi ride into town will cost from IR£10 to IR£14, depending on the location of your hotel.

By Train

There are three main stations. Heuston Station (⊠ at Kingsbridge) is the departure point for the south and southwest; Connolly Station (⊠ At Amiens St.), for Belfast, the east coast, and the west; Pearse Station (⊠ On Westland Row), for Bray and connections via Dun Laoghaire to the Liverpool/Holyhead ferries. Call 01/836–6222 for information.

By Bus

The central bus station, Busaras, is at Store Street near the Custom House. Some buses terminate near O'Connell Bridge. Call 01/873–4222 for information on city services (Dublin Bus); dial 01/836–6111 for express buses and provincial services (Bus Eireann).

By Car

The main access route from the north is N1; from the west, N4; from the south and southwest, N7; from the east coast, N11. On all routes there are clearly marked signs indicating the center of the city: AN LÁR.

Getting Around

Dublin is small as capital cities go—the downtown area is positively compact—and the best way to see the city and soak in the full flavor is on foot.

By Train

An electric train commuter service, DART, serves the suburbs out to Howth, on the north side of the city, and to Bray, County Wicklow, on the south side. Fares are about the same as for buses. Street-direction signs to DART stations read STAISIUM/STATION. The **Irish Rail** office is at 35 Lower Abbey Street; for rail inquiries, call 01/836–6222.

By Bus

Most city buses originate in or pass through the area of O'Connell Street and O'Connell Bridge. If the destination board indicates AN LÁR, that means that the bus is going to the city center. Timetables (IR£2.50) are available from the **Dublin Bus** office (⊠ 59 Upper O'Connell St., ☎ 01/873–4222) and give details of all routes, times of operation, and price codes. The minimum fare is 65p.

By Taxi

Taxis do not cruise, but are located beside the central bus station, at train stations, at O'Connell Bridge, at St. Stephen's Green, at College Green, and near major hotels. They are not of a uniform type or color. Make sure the meter is on. The initial charge is IR£2; the fare is displayed in the cab. A one-mile trip in city traffic costs about IR£3.50.

Important Addresses and Numbers

Visitor Information

There is a visitor information office in the entrance hall of the **Bord Fáilte** headquarters (⊠ Baggot St. Bridge, ☎ 01/676–5871; ⊙ Weekdays 9–5). More conveniently located is the office at 14 Upper O'Connell Street (☎ 01/874–7733); open weekdays 9–5:30, Saturday 9–1. There is also an office at the airport (☎ 01/844–5387). From mid-June to September, there is an office at the Ferryport, Dun Laoghaire (☎ 01/280–6984).

Embassies

U.S. (⊠ 42 Elgin Rd., Ballsbridge, ☎ 01/688–8777), **Canadian** (⊠ 65 St. Stephen's Green, ☎ 01/478–1988), **U.K.** (⊠ 29 Merrion Rd., ☎ 01/205–3700).

Emergencies

Police (☎ 999), **Ambulance** (☎ 999), **Doctor** (☎ 01/679–0700), **Dentist** (☎ 01/679–4311), **Pharmacy** (⊠ Hamilton Long, 5 Upper O'Connell St., ☎ 01/874–8456).

Travel Agencies

American Express (⊠ 116 Grafton St., ☎ 01/677–2874), **Thomas Cook** (⊠ 118 Grafton St., ☎ 01/677–1721).

Guided Tours

Orientation Tours

Both **Bus Eireann** (☎ 01/836–6111) and **Gray Line Sightseeing** (☎ 01/661–9666) offer bus tours of Dublin and its surrounding areas. Both also offer three- and four-hour tours of the main sights in the city center. In summer **Dublin Bus** (☎ 01/873–4222) has a daily three-hour city-center tour using open-top buses in fine weather (IR£7). From mid-April through September Dublin Bus runs a continuous guided open-top bus tour (IR£5) that allows you to hop on and off the bus as often as you wish and visit some 15 sights along its route.

Special-Interest Tours

Bus Eireann has a "Traditional Irish Music Night" tour. **Elegant Ireland** (☎ 01/475–1665) organizes tours for groups interested in architecture and the fine arts; these include visits with the owners of some of Ireland's stately homes and castles.

Walking Tours

Most tourist offices have leaflets giving information on a selection of walking tours, including "Literary Dublin," "Georgian Dublin," and "Pub Tours." **Bord Fáilte** has a "Tourist Trail" walk, which takes in the main sites of central Dublin and can be completed in about three hours.

Excursions

Bus Eireann (☎ 01/836–6111) and **Gray Line Sightseeing** (☎ 01/661–9666) offer day-long tours into the surrounding countryside and longer tours elsewhere; price includes accommodations, breakfast, and admission costs. **CIE Tours International** offers vacations lasting from one to 10 days that include touring by train or bus, accommodations, and main meals. Costs range from around IR£240 (IR£345, including round-trip airfare from London) to IR£370 (IR£410 from London) for an eight-day tour in July and August.

Exploring Dublin

Numbers in the margin correspond to points of interest on the Dublin map.

Dublin is a small city with a population of just over 1 million. For all that, it has a distinctly cosmopolitan air, one that complements happily the individuality of the city and the courtesy and friendliness of its inhabitants. Originally a Viking settlement, Dublin is situated on the banks of the River Liffey. The Liffey divides the city north and south, with the more lively and fashionable spots, such as the Grafton Street shopping area, to be found on the south side. Most of the city's historically interesting buildings date from the 18th century, and, although many of its finer Georgian buildings disappeared in the overenthusiastic redevelopment of the '70s, enough remain, mainly south of the river, to recall the elegant Dublin of the past. The slums romanticized by writers Sean O'Casey and Brendan Behan have virtually been eradicated, but literary Dublin can still be recaptured by those who want to follow the footsteps of Leopold Bloom's progress, as described in James Joyce's *Ulysses*. And Trinity College, alma mater of Oliver Goldsmith, Jonathan Swift, and Samuel Beckett, among others, still provides a haven of tranquillity.

O'Connell Street

① Begin your tour of Dublin at **O'Connell Bridge,** the city's most central landmark. Look closely and you will notice a strange feature: The bridge is wider than it is long. The north side of O'Connell Bridge is dominated by an elaborate memorial to Daniel O'Connell, "The Liberator," erected as a tribute to the great 19th-century orator's achievement in securing Catholic Emancipation in 1829. Today **O'Connell Street** is the city's main shopping area. Turn left just beyond the General Post Office and take a look at Henry Street. This pedestrian-only shopping area leads to the colorful **Moore Street Market,** where street vendors recall their most famous ancestor, Molly Malone, by singing their wares—mainly flowers and fruit—in the traditional Dublin style.

614

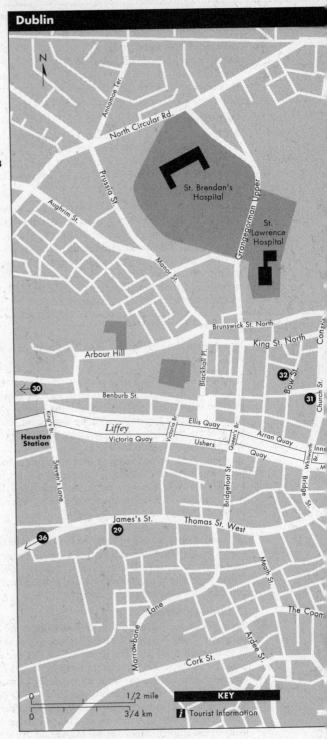

Dublin

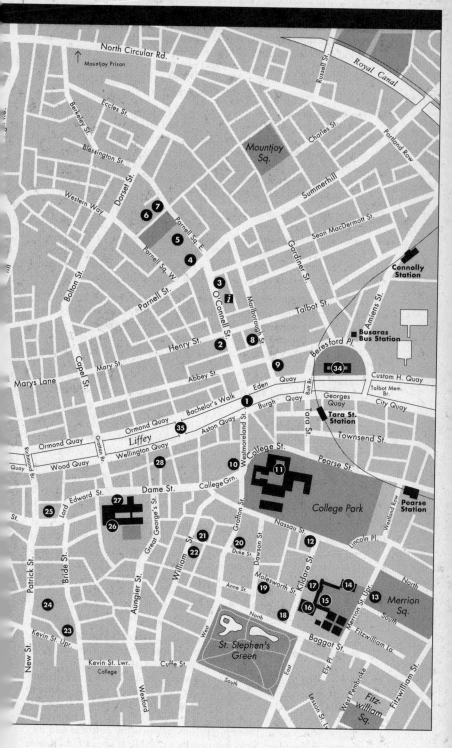

❷ The **General Post Office,** known as the GPO, occupies a special place in Irish history. It was from the portico of its handsome classical facade that Padraig Pearse read the Proclamation of the Republic on Easter Monday, 1916. You can still see the scars of bullets on its pillars from the fighting that ensued. The GPO remains the focal point for political rallies and demonstrations and is used as a viewing stand for VIPs during the annual St. Patrick's Day parade.

❸ **The Gresham Hotel** has played a part in Dublin's history since 1817, although, along with the entire O'Connell Street area, it is less fashionable now than it was during the last century. Just south of the Gresham is the Bord Fáilte information office; drop in for a free street map, shopping guides, and information on all aspects of Dublin tourism. Opposite is the main office of Bus Eireann, which can supply bus timetables and information on excursions.

❹ At the top of O'Connell Street is the **Rotunda,** the first maternity hospital in Europe, opened in 1755. Not much remains of the once-elegant Rotunda Assembly Rooms, a famous haunt of fashionable Dubliners until the mid-1800s. The **Gate Theater,** housed in an extension of the Rotunda Assembly Rooms, however, continues to attract crowds to its fine repertoire of classic Irish and European drama.

❺ Beyond the Rotunda, you will have a fine vista of **Parnell Square,** one of Dublin's earliest Georgian squares. You will notice immediately that the first-floor windows of these elegant brick-face buildings are much larger than the others and that it is easy to look in from street level. This is more than simply the result of the architect's desire to achieve perfect proportions on the facades: These rooms were designed as reception rooms, and fashionable hostesses liked passersby to be able to peer in and admire the distinguished guests at their luxurious, candlelighted receptions.

★ ❻ **Charlemont House,** whose impressive Palladian facade dominates the top of Parnell Square, now houses the **Hugh Lane Municipal Gallery of Modern Art.** Sir Hugh Lane, a nephew of Lady Gregory, who was Yeats's curious, high-minded aristocratic patron, was a keen collector of Impressionist paintings. The gallery also contains some interesting works by Irish artists, including Yeats's brother Jack. ⊠ *Parnell Sq.,* ☎ *01/674–1903.* ▨ *Free.* ⊙ *Tues.–Fri. 9:30–6, Sat. 9:30–5, Sun. 11–5.*

❼ The Parnell Square area is rich in literary associations. They are explained and illustrated in the **Dublin Writers Museum,** which opened in 1991 in two carefully restored 18th-century buildings. Paintings, letters, manuscripts, and photographs relating to Joyce, O'Casey, Shaw, Yeats, Behan, Synge, and others are on permanent display. There are also temporary exhibitions, lectures, and readings, as well as a bookshop. ⊠ *18–19 Parnell Sq. N,* ☎ *01/872–2077.* ▨ *IR£2.25.* ⊙ *Mon.–Sat. 10–5, Sun. 1–5.*

❽ Return to O'Connell Street, where a sign on the left will direct you to **St. Mary's Pro Cathedral,** the main Catholic church of Dublin. Try to catch the famous Palestrina Choir on Sunday at 11 AM. John McCormack is one of many famous voices to have sung with this exquisite ❾ ensemble. Turn right, down Marlborough Street, to get to the **Abbey,** Ireland's national theater. Founded by W. B. Yeats and Lady Gregory in 1904, the original building was destroyed in a fire in 1951; the present theater was built in 1966. It has some noteworthy portraits and mementos in the foyer. Seats are usually available at about IR£12, and with luck you may just have a wonderful evening.

On Westmoreland Street is **Bewley's Coffee House** (there's another one nearby on Grafton Street), an institution that has been supplying Dubliners with coffee and buns since 1842. The aroma of coffee is irresistible, and the dark interior—with marble-top tables, original wood fittings, and stained-glass windows—evokes a more leisurely Dublin of the past. ⊠ *12 Westmoreland St. and 78 Grafton St.* ⊙ *Mon.–Sat. 9–5:30.*

Trinity and Stephen's Green

⑩ It is only a short walk across O'Connell Bridge to **Parliament House.** Today this stately, early 18th-century building is no more than a branch of the Bank of Ireland; originally, however, it housed the Irish Parliament. The original House of Lords, with its fine coffered ceiling and 1,233-piece Waterford glass chandelier, is open to the public during banking hours (⊙ Weekdays 10–12:30 and 1:30–3). It's also worth taking a look at the main banking hall, whose judicial character—it was previously the Court of Requests—has been sensitively maintained.

★ ⑪ Across the road is the facade of **Trinity College,** whose memorably atmospheric campus is a must for every visitor. Trinity College, Dublin (familiarly known as TCD) was founded by Elizabeth I in 1592 and offered a free education to Catholics—provided that they accepted the Protestant faith. As a legacy of this condition, right up until 1966, Catholics who wished to study at Trinity had to obtain a dispensation from their bishop or face excommunication. Today more than 70% of Trinity's students are Catholics, a clear indication of how far away those days seem to today's generation.

The facade, built between 1755 and 1759, consists of a magnificent portico with Corinthian columns. The design is repeated on the interior, so the view from outside the gates and from the quadrangle inside is the same. On the sweeping lawn in front of the facade are statues of two of the university's illustrious alumni—statesman Edmund Burke and poet Oliver Goldsmith. Other famous students include the philosopher George Berkeley (who gave his name to the San Francisco-area campus of the University of California), Jonathan Swift, Thomas Moore, Oscar Wilde, John Millington Synge, Henry Grattan, Wolfe Tone, Robert Emmet, Bram Stoker, Edward Carson, Douglas Hyde, and Samuel Beckett.

The 18th-century building on the left, just inside the entrance, is the chapel. There's an identical building opposite, the Examination Hall. The oldest buildings are the library in the far right-hand corner and a row of redbrick buildings known as the Rubrics, which contain student apartments; both date from 1712.

Ireland's largest collection of books and manuscripts is housed in the **Trinity College Library.** There are 3 million volumes gathering dust here; about half a mile of new shelving has to be added every year to keep pace with acquisitions. The library is entered through the library shop.

★ Its principal treasure is the **Book of Kells,** a beautifully illuminated manuscript of the Gospels dating from the 8th century. Because of the beauty and the fame of the Book of Kells, at peak hours you may have to wait in line to enter the library; it's less busy early in the day. Apart from the many treasures it contains, the aptly named **Long Room** is impressive in itself, stretching for 213 feet and housing 200,000 of the library's volumes, mostly manuscripts and old books. Originally it had a flat plaster ceiling, but the perennial need for more shelving resulted in a decision to raise the level of the roof and add the barrel-vaulted ceiling and the gallery bookcases. ☎ *01/677–2941.* 🎫 *IR£2.50.* ⊙ *Mon.–Sat. 9:30–4:45, Sun. noon–5.*

In the Thomas Davis Theatre in the Arts Building, The **"Dublin Experience"** is an audiovisual presentation devoted to the history of the city over the last 1,000 years. ☎ 01/677–2941. ▨ IR£2.75 (IR£5 with library). ☉ May–Oct., daily 10–5; shows every hr on the hr.

Leave Trinity by the Nassau Street exit, a covered way beside the Arts Block. Shoppers will find a detour along Nassau Street in order here. **⑫** As well as being well endowed with bookstores, it contains the **Kilkenny Design Workshops,** which, besides selling the best in contemporary Irish design for the home, also holds regular exhibits of exciting new work by Irish craftsmen. ⊠ Nassau St. ☉ Mon.–Sat. 9–5.

NEED A BREAK?   The **Kilkenny Kitchen,** a self-service restaurant on the first floor of the Kilkenny Design Workshops, overlooking the playing fields of Trinity, is an excellent spot for a quick, inexpensive lunch in modern, design-conscious surroundings. The emphasis is on natural fresh foods and home baking. ⊠ Nassau St. ☉ Mon.–Sat. 9–5.

★ **⑬** Nassau Street will lead you into **Merrion Square,** past a distinctive corner house that was the home of Oscar Wilde's parents. Merrion Square is one of the most pleasant in Dublin. Its flower gardens are well worth a visit in summer. Note the brightly colored front doors and the intricate fanlights above them—a distinctive feature of Dublin's domestic architecture.

★ **⑭** The **National Gallery** is the first in a series of important buildings on the west side of the square. It is one of Europe's most agreeable and compact galleries, with more than 2,000 works on view, including a major collection of Irish landscape painting, 17th-century French works, paintings from the Italian and Spanish schools, and a collection of Dutch masters. ⊠ Merrion Sq., ☎ 01/661–5133. ▨ Free. ☉ Mon.–Sat 10–5:30, Thurs. until 8:30, Sun. 2–5.

⑮ Next door is **Leinster House,** seat of the Irish Parliament. This imposing 18th-century building has two facades: Its Merrion Square facade is designed in the style of a country house, while the other facade, in Kildare Street, is in the style of a town house. Visitors may be shown the house when Dáil Eireann (pronounced dawl Erin), the Irish Parliament, is not in session.

NEED A BREAK?   A half-block detour to your left, between Merrion Square and Stephen's Green, will bring you to the door of **Doheny & Nesbitt's,** an old Victorian-style bar whose traditional "snugs"—individual wood-panel booths—are popular any time. Usually noisy and smoky, but always friendly, it is one of the few authentic pubs left in the city.

Stephen's Green, as St. Stephen's Green is always called by Dubliners, suffered more from the planning blight of the philistine '60s than did its neighbor, Merrion Square. An exception is the magnificent **Shelbourne Hotel,** which dominates the north side of the green. It is still as fashionable—and as expensive—as ever. Still, even budget-conscious visitors can dress up and try afternoon tea in the Lord Mayor's Room. You can experience its old-fashioned luxury for around IR£9 (including sandwiches and cakes) per head.

Around the corner on Kildare Street, the town-house facade of Leinster House is flanked by the **National Museum** (▨ Free; ☉ Tues.–Sat. **⑯** 10–5, Sun. 2–5) and the **National Library,** each featuring a massive **⑰** colonnaded rotunda entrance built in 1890. The museum houses a remarkable collection of Irish treasures from 6000 BC to the present, including the Tara Brooch, the Ardagh Chalice, and the Cross of Cong.

Every major figure in modern Irish literature, from James Joyce onward, studied in the National Library at some point. In addition to a comprehensive collection of Irish authors, it contains extensive newspaper archives. ⊠ *Kildare St.,* ☎ *01/661–8811.* ⊠ *Free.* ◷ *Mon. 10–9, Tues.–Wed. 2–9, Thurs.–Fri. 10–5, Sat. 10–1.*

(18) The **Genealogical Office**—the starting point for ancestor-tracing—also incorporates the **Heraldic Museum,** which features displays of flags, coins, stamps, silver, and family crests that highlight the uses and development of heraldry in Ireland. ⊠ *2 Kildare St.,* ☎ *01/661–8811. Genealogical Office:* ◷ *Weekdays 10–5. Heraldic Museum:* ⊠ *Free.* ◷ *Weekdays 10–12:30 and 2:30–4. Guided tours Mar.–Oct.,* ⊠ *IR£1.*

(19) The **Royal Irish Academy,** on Dawson Street, is the country's leading learned society; it has many important manuscripts in its unmodernized 18th-century library (◷ *Weekdays 9:30–5:15).* Just below the academy is **Mansion House,** the official residence of the Lord Mayor of Dublin. Its Round Room was the location of the first assembly of Dáil Eireann in January 1919. It is now used mainly for exhibitions.

Grafton Street, which runs between Stephen's Green and Trinity College, has inherited O'Connell Street's reputation as the city's premier
(20) shopping street. Check out **Brown Thomas,** Ireland's most elegant and old-fashioned department store; it has an extremely good selection of sporting goods and Waterford crystal—an odd combination. Many of the more stylish boutiques are just off the main pedestrian-only areas, so be sure to poke around likely—and unlikely— corners. Don't miss
(21) the **Powerscourt Town House,** an imaginative shopping arcade installed in and around the covered courtyard of an impressive 18th-cen-
(22) tury building. Nearby is the **Civic Museum,** which contains drawings, models, maps of Dublin, and other civic memorabilia. ⊠ *58 S. William St.,* ☎ *01/679–4260.* ⊠ *Free.* ◷ *Tues.–Sat. 10–6, Sun. 11–2.*

(23) A short walk from Stephen's Green will bring you to one of the smaller and more unusual gems of old Dublin, **Archbishop Marsh's Library.** It was built in 1701, and access is through a tiny but charming cottage garden. Its interior has been unchanged for more than 300 years and still contains "cages" into which scholars who wanted to peruse rare books were locked. (The cages were to discourage students who, often impecunious, may have been tempted to make the books their own.) ⊠ *St. Patrick's Close,* ☎ *01/454–8511.* ◷ *Mon., Wed., and Fri. 10–12:45 and 2–4, Sat. 10:30–12:45.*

(24) Opposite, on Patrick Street, is **St. Patrick's Cathedral.** Legend has it that St. Patrick baptized many converts at a well on the site of the cathedral in the 5th century. The building dates from 1190 and is mainly early English Gothic in style. At 305 feet, it is the longest church in the country. Its history has not always been happy. In the 17th century, Oliver Cromwell, dour ruler of England and no friend of the Irish, had his troops stable their horses in the cathedral. It wasn't until the 19th century that restoration work to repair the damage was begun. St. Patrick's is the national cathedral of the Protestant Church of Ireland and has had many illustrious deans. The most famous was Jonathan Swift, author of *Gulliver's Travels,* who held office from 1713 to 1745. Swift's tomb is in the south aisle, and Dean Swift's corner at the top of the north transept contains his pulpit, his writing table and chair, his portrait, and his death mask. Memorials to many other celebrated figures from Ireland's past line the walls of St. Patrick's. ⊠ *Patrick St.,* ☎ *01/475–4817.* ⊠ *IR£1.*

★ **(25)** St. Patrick's originally stood outside the walls of Dublin. Its close neighbor, **Christ Church Cathedral** (⊠ Christ Church Rd.), on the other hand, stood just within the walls and belonged to the See of Dublin.

It is for this reason that the city has two cathedrals so close to one another. Christ Church was founded in 1172 by Strongbow, a Norman baron and conqueror of Dublin for the English crown, and it took 50 years to build. Strongbow himself is buried in the cathedral beneath an impressive effigy. The vast, sturdy **crypt** is Dublin's oldest surviving structure and should not be missed.

26 Signs in the Christ Church area will lead you to **Dublin Castle.** Guided tours of the lavishly furnished state apartments are offered every half hour and provide one of the most enjoyable sightseeing experiences in town. Only fragments of the original 13th-century building survive; the elegant castle you see today is essentially an 18th-century building. The state apartments were formerly the residence of the English viceroys and are now used by the president of Ireland to entertain visiting heads of state. The state apartments are closed when in official use, so phone first to check. ⊠ *Off Dame St.,* ☎ *01/677-7129.* 🎟 *IR£2.50.* ☉ *Weekdays 10–12:15 and 2–5, weekends 2–5.*

27 Step into the **City Hall** on Dame Street to admire the combination of grand classical ornament and understated Georgian simplicity in its circular main hall. It also contains a good example of the kind of gently curving Georgian staircase that is a typical feature of most large town houses in Dublin.

28 Between Dame Street and the River Liffey is a new semipedestrianized area known as **Temple Bar,** the city's version of the Latin Quarter, which should interest anyone who wants to discover "young Dublin." The area is chock-full of small, imaginative shops; innovative art galleries; and inexpensive restaurants.

★ **29** The **Guinness Brewery,** founded by Arthur Guinness in 1759 and covering 60 acres, dominates the area to the west of Christ Church. Guinness is proud of its brewery and invites visitors to attend a 30-minute film shown in a converted hops store next door to the brewery itself. After the film, you can sample the famous black beverage. ⊠ *Guinness Hop Store, Crane St.,* ☎ *01/453-6700.* 🎟 *IR£2.50.* ☉ *Weekdays 10–3.*

Phoenix Park and the Liffey

★ **30** Across the Liffey is **Phoenix Park,** 1,760 acres of green open space. Though the park is open to all, it has only two residents: the president of Ireland and the American ambassador. The park is dominated by a 210-foot-tall obelisk, a tribute to the first duke of Wellington. Sunday is the best time to visit: Games of cricket, soccer, polo, baseball, hurling—a combination of lacrosse, baseball, and field hockey—or Irish football will be in progress.

31 Returning to the city's central area along the north bank of the Liffey, you pass through a fairly run-down section that's scheduled for major redevelopment. A diversion up Church Street to **St. Michan's** will be relished by those with a macabre turn of mind. Open coffins in the vaults beneath the church reveal mummified bodies, some more than 900 years old. The sexton, who can be found at the church gate on weekdays, will guide you around the church and crypt.

32 **Irish Whiskey Corner** is just behind St. Michan's. A 90-year-old warehouse has been converted into a museum to introduce visitors to the pleasures of Irish whiskey. There's an audiovisual show and free tasting. ⊠ *Bow St.,* ☎ *01/872-5566.* 🎟 *IR£3.* ☉ *Tours weekdays at 3:30 or by appointment.*

The Liffey has two of Dublin's most famous landmarks, both of them the work of 18th-century architect James Gandon and both among the city's finest buildings. The first is the **Four Courts,** surmounted by a massive copper-covered dome, giving it a distinctive profile. It is the seat of the High Court of Justice of Ireland. The building was completed between 1786 and 1802, then gutted in the Civil War of the '20s; it has since been painstakingly restored. You will recognize the same architect's hand in the **Custom House,** farther down the Liffey. Its graceful dome rises above a central portico, itself linked by arcades to the pavilions at either end. Behind this useful and elegant landmark is an altogether more workaday structure, the central bus station, Busaras.

Midway between Gandon's two masterpieces is the Metal Bridge, otherwise known as the **Ha'penny Bridge,** so called because, until early in this century, a toll of a half-penny was charged to cross it. The poet W. B. Yeats was one among many Dubliners who found this too high a price to pay—more a matter of principle than of finance—and so made the detour via O'Connell Bridge. Today no such high-minded concern need prevent you from marching out to the middle of the bridge to admire the view up and down the Liffey as it winds its way through the city.

★ ③⑥ The **Royal Hospital Kilmainham** is a short ride by taxi or bus from the center; it's well worth the trip. The hospital is considered the most important 17th-century building in Ireland and has recently been renovated. It was completed in 1684 as a hospice—the original meaning of the term "hospital"—for veteran soldiers. Note especially the chapel with its magnificent Baroque ceiling. It also houses the **Irish Museum of Modern Art,** which opened in 1991. Parts of the old building, used as a national cultural center, are occasionally closed to the public. ✉ *District of Kilmainham,* ☎ *01/671–8666.* ⊙ *Exhibitions: Tues.–Sat. 10–5:30, Sun. noon–5:30; tours: Sun. noon–5 and holidays 2–5; cost IR£2.*

Off the Beaten Path

★ It is all too easy for the visitor to forget how close Dublin is to the sea: Take advantage of fine weather and visit the fishing village of **Howth**— it's easily reached on the DART train—and watch the fishermen mending their nets on the pier. Or take the DART in the opposite direction to **Sandycove,** where intrepid all-weather swimmers brave the waves at the men-only **Forty Foot** bathing beach.

Devotees of James Joyce may find Sandycove a worthwhile detour, for it was here, in a Martello tower (a circular fortification built by the British as a defense against possible invasion by Napoléon at the beginning of the 19th century), that the maverick Irish genius lived for some months in 1904. It now houses the **Joyce Museum.** ✉ *Sandycove Coast.* ⌨ *IR£1.50.* ⊙ *Apr.–Oct., Mon.–Sat. 10–1 and 2–5, Sun. 2:30–6. Also by appointment,* ☎ *01/280–8571.*

The **Irish Jewish Museum** was opened in 1985 by Chaim Herzog, former president of Israel and an ex-Dubliner himself, and displays memorabilia of the Irish-Jewish community covering approximately 120 years of history. ✉ *3–4 Walworth Rd.,* ☎ *01/453–1797.* ⊙ *Sun. 10:30–2:30. Also by appointment,* ☎ *01/676–0737 or 01/455–5452.*

Shopping

Although the rest of the country is well supplied with crafts shops, Dublin is the place to seek out more specialized items—antiques, traditional sportswear, haute couture, designer ceramics, books and prints, silverware and jewelry, and designer hand-knit items.

Shopping Districts

Grafton Street is the most sophisticated shopping area in Dublin city center.

The new **St. Stephen's Green Center** contains 70 stores, large and small, in a vast Moorish-style glass-roof building. ⊠ *St. Stephen's Green,* ☎ *478–0888.* ⊙ *9–7, Mon–Sat, Sun 11–6*

Molesworth and **Dawson streets** are the places to browse for antiques.

Nassau and **Dawson streets** are for books; the smaller cross side streets for jewelry, art galleries, and old prints.

The pedestrianized **Temple Bar** area, with its young, offbeat ambience, has a number of small art galleries, specialty shops (including music and books), and inexpensive and adventurous clothes shops. The area is further enlivened by buskers (street musicians) and street artists.

Department Stores

The shops north of the river tend to be less expensive and less design-conscious; chain stores and lackluster department stores make up the bulk of them.

The **ILAC Shopping Center** (⊠ Henry St.) is worth a look with several department stores inside.

Clery's (⊠ O'Connell St., directly opposite the GPO) was once the city's most fashionable department store and is still worth a visit, despite its rapidly aging decor.

Brown Thomas (⊠ Grafton St.) is Dublin's most elegantly decorated department store, with many international fashion labels on sale.

Arnotts (⊠ Henry St.) is Dublin's largest department store and has a good range of cut crystal.

Visit **Kilkenny Design Workshops** (⊠ Nassau St.) for the best selection of Irish designs for the home.

Tweeds and Woolens

Kevin and Howlin (⊠ Nassau St.) makes ready-made tweeds for men.

Cleo Ltd. (⊠ Kildare St.) also makes tweeds and woolens.

The **Blarney Woollen Mills** (⊠ Nassau St.) has a good selection of tweed, linen, and woolen sweaters in all price ranges.

The **Woolen Mills** (⊠ Liffey St.) at Ha'penny Bridge, has a good selection of hand-knit and other woolen sweaters at competitive prices.

Dining

The restaurant scene in Dublin has improved beyond recognition in recent years. Though no one is ever likely to confuse the place with, say, Paris, the days of chewy boiled meats and soggy, tasteless vegetables are long gone. Food still tends to be substantial rather than subtle, but more and more restaurants are at last taking advantage of the magnificent livestock and fish that Ireland has in such abundance. For details and price-category definitions, *see* Dining *in* Staying in Ireland, *above.*

$$$ ✕ **Celtic Mews.** This long-established oasis of calm is in a Georgian mews off Baggot Street. A deep wine-color interior is the backdrop for a collection of fine antiques, and tuxedo-clad waiters provide full silver service at polished or white-cloth tables. Despite the elegance of the setting, the atmosphere is cozy and informal. The chefs have successfully blended classical French and Irish cooking styles, with cuisine ranging from the very rich—Celtic filet mignon, cooked at the table and served in a whiskey-and-cream sauce—to upscale versions of traditional dishes such as Irish stew made with center loin chops. ⊠ *109A Lower Baggot St.,* ☎ *01/676–0796. AE, DC, MC, V. Closed Sun. and holidays. No lunch Sat.*

$$$ ✕ **The Commons Restaurant.** In the basement of the Georgian showplace Newman House, you will find this elegantly modern restaurant, where the cream-and-dark-blue walls are hung with specially commissioned Irish art, and French windows open onto a patio used for al fresco lunches. The menu is international with French and Middle-Eastern influences; main courses lean toward fish, but other favorites include lamb cutlets roasted in garlic and thyme. ⊠ *85–86 St. Stephen's Green,* ☎ *01/478–0530. Reservations essential. AE, DC, MC, V. Closed Sun. and holidays. No lunch Sat.*

$$$ ✕ **Ernie's.** This luxurious place is built around a small floodlighted courtyard shaded by an imposing mulberry tree. The rustic interior's granite walls and wood beams are adorned by 135 paintings of Kerry, where, for generations, the late Ernie Evans's family ran the famous Glenbeigh Hotel. The Evans family serves generous portions of the very best seafood—try scallops Mornay or prawns in garlic butter—and steaks. ⊠ *Mulberry Gardens, Donnybrook,* ☎ *01/269–3300. AE, DC, MC, V. Closed Sun., Mon. No lunch Sat.*

$$$ ✕ **King Sitric.** Owner-chef Aidan MacManus's quay-side restaurant in
★ the fishing village-cum-suburb of Howth is a 20-minute ride north of Dublin by DART or cab. It's worth the journey to taste the succulent selection of locally caught seafood; try the turbot with saffron or the wild Irish salmon steaks with Hollandaise sauce. You eat in the quietly elegant Georgian dining room of the former harbormaster's house. ⊠ *East Pier, Howth,* ☎ *01/832–5235. AE, DC, MC, V. Dinner only. Closed Sun., holidays, Dec. 24–Jan. 1, and wk preceding Easter.*

$$$ ✕ **Le Coq Hardi.** Award-winning owner-chef John Howard is noted for
★ his wine cellar and for such specialties as Coq Hardi smokies (smoked haddock marbled with tomato, cream, and cheese) and, in season, roast loin of venison with fresh cranberries and port wine. The seriousness of the cooking is complemented by the polished wood and brass and the gleaming mirrors of the sumptuous interior. ⊠ *35 Pembroke Rd., Ballsbridge,* ☎ *01/268–9070. Reservations essential. AE, DC, MC, V. Closed Sun.*

$$$ ✕ **Patrick Guilbaud.** This is an authentic, rather formal French restaurant with a consistently good reputation, decked out in a refreshing combination of pink, white, and green with hanging plants. The emphasis is firmly on traditional bourgeois cuisine; the Gallic connection is reinforced by the all-French staff. ⊠ *46 James Pl.,* ☎ *01/676–4192. AE, DC, MC, V. Closed Sun., Mon., and holidays.*

$$ ✕ **Elephant & Castle.** American visitors may be familiar with the New York cousin of this "Left Bank" restaurant. Traditional American food on an eclectic and flavorful menu incorporates everything from spicy nachos to ginger-laced stir fry and a wide assortment of tasty omelets. The diner-style decor is sparse, the noise level high, and the portions large—but this suits the typically voracious clientele. The central location attracts a young crowd. ⊠ *18 Temple Bar,* ☎ *01/679–3121. Reservations not accepted. AE, DC, MC, V.*

$$ ✕ **La Pigalle.** This is a charming, unpretentious French restaurant in an old and crooked building that forms part of the archway leading to the Ha'penny Bridge. It is in the heart of, and very much part of, the Temple Bar area scene. The decor is old-fashioned and well-worn, the atmosphere relaxed and the food authentically French, with a menu that changes daily. Typical dishes include fresh asparagus tart, sea trout fillet with sorrel and muscadet, and duck breast with apples and calvados. ⊠ *14 Temple Bar,* ☎ *01/671–9262. MC, V. No lunch Sat. Closed Sun.*

$$ ⨉ **Le Caprice.** This Italian restaurant with busy decor and white linen ★ tablecloths is right in the city center. The menu includes traditional Continental dishes such as prawn cocktail, deep-fried scampi, and roast duckling a l'orange, as well as an interesting selection of authentic Italian dishes including pasta and veal. This place can develop a real party atmosphere later in the evening if the pianist is in the right mood. ⊠ *12 St. Andrew's St.,* ☎ *01/679–4050. AE, DC, MC, V. Closed for lunch Mon.–Sun.*

$ ⨉ **Bad Ass Café.** Definitely one of Dublin's loudest restaurants, this barnlike place in the trendy Temple Bar area, between the Central Bank and the Ha'penny Bridge, is always a fun place to eat. American-style fast food—burgers, chili, and pizzas—and the pounding rock music attract a lively crowd, both the young and the young at heart. Look out for the old-fashioned cash shuttles whizzing around the ceiling! ⊠ *9–11 Crown Alley,* ☎ *01/671–2596. AE, MC, V. Closed Good Fri., and Dec. 25–26.*

$ ⨉ **Cornucopia Wholefoods.** This recently refurbished vegetarian restaurant above a health-food shop provides good value for the money in simple rustic surroundings. It's popular with students from nearby Trinity College. The menu includes red lentil soup, avocado quiche, vegetarian spring rolls, and vegetarian curry—all of them regular favorites. ⊠ *19 Wicklow St.,* ☎ *01/677–7583. Reservations not accepted. No credit cards. Closed Sun.*

$ ⨉ **Gallagher's Boxty House.** Located behind the Central Bank in the lively Temple Bar area, this highly original Irish eatery has a country cottage ambience, with antique pine furniture complementing the dark green decor. Boxty is a traditional Irish potato bread or cake that is served here as a pancake thin enough to wrap around savory fillings such as bacon and cabbage, chicken with leeks, and smoked fish. Follow these with "Bailey's and brown bread" ice cream or the superb bread-and-butter pudding. ⊠ *20 Temple Bar,* ☎ *01/677–2762. Reservations not accepted. V.*

$ ⨉ **Pizzeria Italia.** This tiny, one-room pizza-bar and restaurant is decorated in the red, white, and green of the Italian flag and adorned by a nostalgia-provoking collection of Italian travel posters. It is all delightfully cheap and cheerful: Either take a place at the one large central table or perch on a bar stool at a wall-side counter. The delicious herbal aromas signal a good selection of freshly prepared pizzas and classic pasta dishes, but there is also a choice of light snacks, steaks, ribs, and chicken at very reasonable prices. ⊠ *22 Temple Bar,* ☎ *01/677–8528. Reservations not accepted. No credit cards. Closed Sun. and Mon.*

Pub Food

All the pubs listed here serve food at lunchtime; some also have food in the early evening. They form an important part of the dining scene in Dublin and make a pleasant and informal alternative to a restaurant meal. In general, a one-course meal should not cost much more than IR£4–IR£5, but a full meal will put you in the lower range of the $$ category. In general, credit cards are not accepted.

⨉ **Barry Fitzgerald's.** Salads and a freshly cooked house special are available in the upstairs bar at lunch on weekdays. Pretheater dinners are served in the early evening. ⊠ *90 Marlborough St.,* ☎ *01/677–4082.*

✕ **Davy Byrne's.** James Joyce immortalized Davy Byrne's in his sprawling novel *Ulysses*. Nowadays it's more akin to a cocktail bar than a Dublin pub, but it's good for fresh and smoked salmon, salads, and a hot daily special. Food is available at lunchtime and in the early evening. ⊠ *21 Duke St.,* ☎ *01/671–1298.*

✕ **Kitty O'Shea's.** Kitty O'Shea's cleverly, if a little artificially, re-creates the atmosphere of old Dublin. ⊠ *23–25 Grand Canal St.,* ☎ *01/660–9965.*

✕ **Thomas Read's.** This new Continental-style bar serves a wide variety of atypical pub grub, including hot bagels, danishes, and Parma ham. The coffees, especially the megaccino (a jumbo-size cappuccino), are particularly good. ⊠ *Corner of Dame and Parliament Sts.,* ☎ *677–2504.*

✕ **Old Stand.** Located conveniently close to Grafton Street, the Old Stand offers grilled food, including steaks. ⊠ *37 Exchequer St.,* ☎ *01/677–0821.*

Lodging

Although only a few major hotels have opened in Dublin in the past few years, considerable investment in redevelopment, updating of facilities, and refurbishing of some of the older establishments is taking place. As in most major cities, there is a shortage of mid-range accommodations. For value-for-the-money, try one of the registered guest houses; in most respects they are indistinguishable from small hotels. Most economical of all is the B&B. Both guest houses and B&Bs tend to be in suburban areas—generally a 10-minute bus ride from the center of the city. This is not in itself a great drawback, and savings can be significant.

Bord Fáilte (⊠ 14 Upper O'Connell St.) can usually help if you find yourself without reservations.

For details and price-category definitions, *see* Lodging *in* Staying in Ireland, *above.*

$$$$ 🏨 **Berkeley Court.** The most quietly elegant of Dublin's large modern hotels, Berkeley Court is located in Ballsbridge—a leafy suburb about a 10-minute cab ride from the center of town. Its new conservatory gives freshness and spaciousness to the atmosphere of the public rooms; among the other new features are five luxury suites, each with its own Jacuzzi. ⊠ *Lansdowne Rd., Ballsbridge, Dublin 4,* ☎ *01/660–1711,* FAX *01/661–7238. 157 rooms with bath, 29 suites. 2 restaurants, bar, conference center, parking (free). AE, DC, MC, V.*

$$$$ 🏨 **Conrad.** A subsidiary of Hilton Hotels, the Conrad is firmly aimed at the international business executive. The seven-story redbrick and smoked-glass building is well located just off Stephen's Green. The spacious rooms are decorated in light brown and pastel shades of green, and the bathrooms are fitted in Spanish marble. Alfie Byrne's, the main bar, attempts to re-create the traditional Irish pub atmosphere in spite of its high-powered clientele. ⊠ *Earlsfort Terrace, Dublin 2,* ☎ *01/676–5555,* FAX *01/676–5076. 190 rooms with bath. Restaurant, 2 bars, coffee shop, sauna, sporting facilities available by arrangement, parking (fee). AE, DC, MC, V.*

$$$$ 🏨 **Shelbourne.** The Shelbourne is one of Europe's grand old hotels whose ★ guest book contains names ranging from the Dalai Lama and Princess Grace to Laurel and Hardy, Richard Burton, and Peter O'Toole. In the bustling open lobby, the blazing open fire—flanked by two huge rose brocade sofas—is proof that the Shelbourne has not lost the sense of grandeur of its past. Between 1986 and 1988, IR£7 million was lavished on major refurbishment, which included restoring many original Georgian features and emphasizing them with luxurious drapes and

a prominently displayed collection of fine antiques and heirlooms. A supplement is charged for rooms overlooking the leafy but busy green; the back bedrooms without views are far quieter, however. ⊠ *27 Stephen's Green, Dublin 2,* ☎ *01/676–6471,* FAX *01/661–6006. 165 rooms with bath. 2 bars, restaurant, sporting facilities available by arrangement. AE, DC, MC, V.*

$$$ 🏨 **Burlington.** Dublin's largest hotel is popular with American tour groups and Irish and European business travelers. It is about five minutes by car from the city's central area. At night the Burlington's disco and Irish cabaret turn it into a lively spot for overseas visitors. Bedrooms are the usual modern plush in neutral tones. ⊠ *Upper Leeson St., Dublin 4,* ☎ *01/660–5222,* FAX *01/660–8496. 477 rooms with bath. Restaurant, 2 bars, cabaret dance club. AE, DC, MC, V.*

$$$ 🏨 **Hibernian.** An early 20th-century Edwardian nurses' home was converted into this hotel in 1993. The distinctive red-and-amber brick facade has been retained, and every room is a different shape, decorated in light pastel shades with deep-pile carpets. The public rooms are slightly small, but are attractively done in cheerful chintz and stripes. There is a library off the lobby and a small restaurant that provides intimate dinners and lunches. ⊠ *Eastmoreland Pl., off Upper Baggot St., Dublin 4,* ☎ *01/668–7666,* FAX *01/660–2655. 30 rooms with bath. Restaurant, bar. AE, DC, MC, V.*

$$$ 🏨 **Jury's.** This lively, fashionable spot has more atmosphere than most comparable modern hotels. It's a short cab ride from the center of town. Bedrooms are relatively spacious, and each comes with a picture-window view of town. Exclusive facilities for businesspeople are provided in the 100-room Towers annex. ⊠ *Ballsbridge, Dublin 4,* ☎ *01/660– 5000,* FAX *01/660–5540. 390 rooms with bath. 3 restaurants, 2 bars, indoor/outdoor pool, cabaret May–Oct., hot tub. AE, DC, MC, V.*

$$$ 🏨 **Westbury.** This comfortable, modern hotel has an excellent location right off the fashionable shopping mecca of Grafton Street. The spacious main lobby on the mezzanine level is furnished with attractive antiques and large sofas, on which guests sit to take afternoon tea. Bedrooms are rather utilitarian with pastel color schemes; the suites, which combine European decor with Japanese prints and screens, are more inviting. The flowery Russell Room serves formal lunches and dinners; the Sandbank, a ground floor seafood bar, is less enticing. ⊠ *Grafton St., Dublin 2,* ☎ *01/679–1122,* FAX *01/679–7078. 195 rooms with bath, 8 suites. 2 restaurants. AE, DC, MC, V.*

$$ 🏨 **Ariel Guest House.** This is Dublin's leading guest house, just a block
★ from the elegant Berkeley Court and a 10-minute walk from Stephen's Green. The lobby lounge and restaurant of this Victorian villa are furnished with leather and mahogany heirlooms, as are most of the spacious bedrooms, 13 of which were added to the house in 1991. This is a good bet if you're in town for a leisurely, relaxing holiday. ⊠ *52 Lansdowne Rd., Dublin 4,* ☎ *01/668–5512,* FAX *01/668–5845. 27 rooms with bath. Parking (fee). MC, V. Closed Dec. 21–Jan. 31.*

$$ 🏨 **Lansdowne.** In the leafy suburb of Ballsbridge, convenient to the city center, this small establishment offers a very friendly ambience. The cozy, modest rooms are painted in pastel shades, and have all the basics. The basement bar is a popular hangout for local businesspeople and fans of the international rugby matches held at nearby Lansdowne Road; photos of sporting personalities hang on the walls. Parker's Restaurant is better than the average hotel spot and specializes in steaks and seafood. ⊠ *27 Pembroke Rd., Dublin 4,* ☎ *01/688–4079,* FAX *01/688– 5585. 28 rooms. Restaurant, bar. AE, DC, MC, V.*

$$ 🏨 **Temple Bar.** Previously a city center bank, these premises were converted into this well-appointed hotel in 1993. Although the decor is unexceptional, the triangular shape of the building on the corner of

two streets makes the layout rather interesting. It is just around the corner from Trinity College and on the edge of the lively Temple Bar district. Busker's Pub is a popular street-level bar, and there is also a quieter lounge bar and a conservatory-style restaurant and coffee shop. ⊠ *Fleet St., Temple Bar, Dublin 2,* ☎ *01/677–3333,* FAX *01/677– 3088. 108 rooms with bath. Restaurant, 2 bars. AE, DC, MC, V.*

$ 🏠 **Dublin International Youth Hostel.** Housed in a converted convent, it offers dormitory accommodations (up to 25 people per room) and also family-size rooms that can take up to four people. This is a spartan, low-cost alternative to hotels. Nonmembers of the youth hostelling organization can stay for a small extra charge. The hostel is north of Parnell Square, near the Mater Hospital. ⊠ *51 Mountjoy St., Dublin 1,* ☎ *01/ 830–1766,* FAX *01/830–1600. 500 beds. Restaurant. No credit cards.*

$ 🏠 **Isaac Tourist Hotel.** This cheap cheerful alternative for budget travelers provides either bunk beds in small dormitories or private rooms from about IR£6 per person. At the top of the range here—about IR£17 per night—there are eight rooms en suite available for singles and doubles. ⊠ *2 Frenchman's La., Dublin 1,* ☎ *01/836–3877,* FAX *01/874– 1574. 21 private rooms, 16 dormitory rooms. Restaurant. No credit cards.*

$ 🏠 **Jury's Christchurch Inn.** Jury's has now introduced functional budget hotels into its hitherto upscale hotel chain. There are very few frills, but this hotel does offer good value for sharers, with a fixed room rate for up to three adults or two adults and two children. The main advantage is the pleasant location, facing Christ Church Cathedral and within walking distance of most city center attractions. The rooms are decorated in pastel colors with utilitarian furniture. A bar offers a pub lunch, and the restaurant serves breakfast and dinner. ⊠ *Christchurch Pl., Dublin 8,* ☎ *01/475–0111,* FAX *01/475–0488. 183 rooms. Restaurant, bar, parking (fee). AE, DC, MC, V.*

$ 🏠 **Kilronan House.** This guest house, a five-minute walk from St. Stephen's Green, is a favorite with vacationers. The large, late-19th-century terraced house is well converted, and the decor and furnishings are updated each year by the Murray family, who have run the place for the past 30 years. The bedrooms are pleasantly furnished with plush carpeting and pastel colored walls. ⊠ *70 Adelaide Rd., Dublin 2,* ☎ *01/475–5266,* FAX *01/478–2841. 12 rooms with bath. Restaurant. MC, V. Closed Dec. 21–Jan. 1.*

$ 🏠 **Mount Herbert Guest House.** Located close to the swank luxury hotels in the tree-lined inner suburb of Ballsbridge, a 10-minute bus ride from Dublin's center, the Mount Herbert is popular with budget-minded American visitors in the high season. Bedrooms are small, but all have 10-channel TVs and hair dryers. There is no bar on the premises, but there are plenty to choose from nearby. ⊠ *7 Herbert Rd., Ballsbridge, Dublin 4,* ☎ *01/668–4321,* FAX *01/660–7077. 135 rooms with bath. Restaurant. AE, DC, MC, V.*

The Arts

The fortnightly magazine *In Dublin* contains comprehensive details of upcoming events, including ticket availability. In peak season, consult the free Bord Fáilte leaflet "Events of the Week."

Theaters

Ireland has a rich theatrical tradition. The **Abbey Theatre** (⊠ Marlborough St., ☎ 01/478–7222) is the home of Ireland's national theater company, its name forever associated with J. M. Synge, W. B. Yeats, and Sean O'Casey. The **Peacock Theatre** (same address) is the Abbey's more experimental small stage. The **Gate Theatre** (⊠ Cavendish Row, Parnell Sq., ☎ 01/874–4045) is an intimate spot for modern drama and plays by Irish writers. The **Gaiety Theatre** (✉ South King St., ☎ 01/677–1717) features musical comedy, opera, drama, and revues.

The **Olympia Theatre** (✉ Dame St., ☎ 01/677–8962) has seasons of comedy, vaudeville, and ballet. The **Project Arts Centre** (✉ 39 E. Essex St., ☎ 671–2321) is an established fringe theater. The **National Concert Hall,** just off Stephen's Green, (✉ Earlsfort Terrace, ☎ 01/671–1888) is the place to go for classical concerts.

Nightlife

Dublin does not have sophisticated nightclubs in the international sense. Instead, there is a choice of discos (often billed as nightclubs) and cabarets, catering mainly to visitors. There is also a very animated bar-pub scene—some places with live music and folksinging. No visit to this genial city will be complete without spending at least one evening exploring them.

Discos
Annabels (✉ Mespil Rd., ☎ 01/660–5222) is a popular late-evening spot. **The Pink Elephant** (✉ S. Frederick St., ☎ 01/677–5876) is still a favorite with the stars.

Cabarets
The following all offer Irish cabaret, designed to give visitors a taste of Irish entertainment:

Burlington Hotel (✉ Upper Leeson St., ☎ 01/660–5222. ◷ May–Oct.).
Jury's Hotel (✉ Ballsbridge, ☎ 01/660–5000. ◷ May–mid-Oct.).
Abbey Tavern (✉ Howth, Co. Dublin, ☎ 01/839–0307).

Pubs
Check advertisements in evening papers for "sessions" of folk, ballad, Irish traditional, or jazz music. Listings below with telephone numbers offer some form of musical entertainment.

The **Bailey** (✉ 2 Duke St.) is mentioned in *Ulysses* (under its original name, Burton's) and retains something of its Edwardian character. The **Brazen Head** (✉ 20 Lower Bridge St., ☎ 01/677–9549)—Dublin's oldest pub, dating from 1688—has music almost every night. **Henry Grattan** (✉ 47–48 Lower Baggot St.) is popular with the business and sporting crowd. In the **Horseshoe Bar** (✉ Shelbourne Hotel, St. Stephen's Green) you can eavesdrop on Dublin's social elite and their hangers-on. Locals and visitors bask in the theatrical atmosphere of **Neary's** (✉ Chatham St.). **O'Donoghue's** (✉ 15 Merrion Row, ☎ 01/661–4303) features some form of musical entertainment on most nights. **O'Neill's Lounge Bar** (✉ 37 Pearse St.) is always busy with students and faculty from nearby Trinity College. The **Palace Bar** (✉ 21 Fleet St.) is a journalists' haunt. **William Ryan's** (✉ 28 Parkgate St.) is a beautifully preserved Victorian gem.

For details on pubs serving food, *see* Dining *in* Staying in Ireland, *above.*

DUBLIN TO CORK

Ireland can be covered in three itineraries that, taken together, form a clockwise tour of the country, starting and ending in Dublin. Distances in Ireland seem short—the total mileage of the three itineraries combined is less than 960 kilometers (600 miles)—but roads are small and often twisty and hilly, and side attractions are numerous, so you should aim for a daily mileage of no more than 240 kilometers (150 miles). The consistently dazzling scenery, intriguing ruins, and beguiling villages will lead to many impromptu stops and explorations along the way. (We have tried to provide full addresses for hotels, restaurants, and sights, though many of Ireland's villages and towns are so tiny they barely have street names, much less numbers. If in doubt, just ask for directions.)

The first tour takes you southwest from Dublin to hilly Cork, the Republic's second-largest city. On the way, you'll see the lush green fields of Ireland's famous stud farms and imposing Cashel, where Ireland built its reputation as the "Land of Saints and Scholars" while most of Europe was slipping into the Dark Ages.

Getting Around

By Train
The terminal at Cork is Kent Station. There are direct services from Dublin and Tralee and a suburban line to Cobh; call 021/506766 for information.

By Bus
The main bus terminal in Cork is at Parnell Place (☎ 021/508188).

By Car
All the main car-rental firms have desks at Cork Airport. Be sure to get a map of Cork's complicated one-way street system.

By Bicycle
Bicycles can be rented from **Isaac's** (⊠ 48 MacCurtain St., Cork, ☎ 021/505399).

Guided Tours

Bus Eireann operates a number of trips from Parnell Place in Cork (☎ 021/506066).

Visitor Information

Tourist House (⊠ Grand Parade, Cork, ☎ 021/273251, FAX 021/273504).

Exploring Dublin to Cork

Leaving Dublin by N7 for **Naas** (pronounced *nace*), you will pass through the area known as The Pale—that part of Ireland in which English law was formally acknowledged up to Elizabethan times. Beyond Naas, the road takes you to the center of the Irish racing world. **Goff's Kildare Paddocks** at Kill sells more than 50% of all Irish-bred horses. Naas has its own racecourse and lies just 4.8 kilometers (3 miles) from Punchestown, famous for its steeplechases. The **Curragh** begins just after Newbridge and is the biggest area of common land in Ireland, containing about 31 square kilometers (12 square miles). You will see the **Curragh Racecourse,** home of the Irish Derby, on your right-hand side; to your left is the training depot of the Irish army.

If you are interested in horses, **Kildare,** the traditional home of St. Brigid, is not to be missed. The main attraction is the **National Stud and Horse**
★ **Museum** and its **Japanese Gardens.** ☎ *045/21617.* ⊡ *IR£4.* ☉ *Feb–Nov., daily 9:30-6. Tours on request.*

At Portlaoise (pronounced *portleash*)—the location of Ireland's top-security prison—follow N8 to **Cashel.** Your first glimpse of the famous
★ **Rock of Cashel** should be an unforgettably majestic sight: It rises imposingly to a height of 200 feet above the plains and is crowned with a magnificent group of gray-stone ruins. The kings of Munster held it as their seat for about seven centuries, and it was here that St. Patrick

reputedly plucked a shamrock from the ground, using it as a symbol to explain the mystery of the Trinity, giving Ireland, in the process, its universally recognized symbol. The central building among the ruins is a 13th-century Gothic cathedral; next to it is the Romanesque Cormac's chapel. ☎ 062/61437. 🖃 IR£2.50. ☉ June–Sept., daily 9–7:30; mid-Mar.–May, daily 9:30–5:30; Oct.–mid-Mar., daily 9:30–4.30.

Cashel and the next town, **Cahir** (pronounced *care*), are both popular stopping places to break the Dublin–Cork journey. In the center of Cahir, you will discover a formidable **medieval fortress** with a working portcullis, the gruesome barred gate that was lowered to keep out attackers. An audiovisual display can be seen in the castle complex. ☎ 052/41011. 🖃 IR£2. ☉ Apr.–June and late Sept., daily 10–6; June–mid-Sept., daily 9–7:30; Nov.–Mar., daily 10–1 and 2–4; closed Oct.

The road continues through Mitchelstown and Fermoy, both of them busy market towns serving Cork's dairy farmers. A short detour at Mitchelstown will allow you to visit former President Reagan's ancestral home, **Ballyporeen,** a pretty little village with wide streets built to accommodate the open-air cattle markets held there until the '60s.

The road enters **Cork City** along the banks of the River Lee. In the center of Cork, the Lee divides in two, giving the city a profusion of picturesque quays and bridges. The name Cork derives from the Irish *corcaigh* (pronounced *corky*), meaning a marshy place. The city received its first charter in 1185 and grew rapidly in the 17th and 18th centuries with the expansion of its butter trade. It is the major metropolis of the south, and, with a population of about 133,250, the second-largest city in Ireland.

The main business and shopping center of Cork lies on the island created by the two diverging channels of the Lee, and most places of interest are within walking distance of the center. **Patrick Street** is the focal point of Cork. Here, you will find the city's most famous statue, that of **Father Theobald Mathew** (1790–1856), who led a nationwide temperance crusade, no small feat in a country as fond of a drink (or two) as this one. In the hilly area to the north of Patrick Street is the famous 120-foot **Shandon Steeple,** the bell tower of **St. Anne's Church.** It is shaped like a pepper pot and houses the bells immortalized in the song "The Bells of Shandon." Visitors can climb the tower; read the inscriptions on the bells; and, on request, have them rung over Cork. 🖃 IR£1, with bell tower IR£1.50. ☉ May–Oct., Mon.–Sat. 9:30–5; Nov.–Apr., Mon.–Sat. 10–3:30.

Patrick Street is the main shopping area of Cork, and here you will find the city's two major department stores, **Roches** and **Cash's.** Cash's has a good selection of Waterford crystal. The liveliest place in town to shop is just off Patrick Street, to the west, near the city center parking lot, in the pedestrian-only **Paul Street** area. **Meadows & Byrne** of Academy Street stocks the best in modern Irish design, including tableware, ceramics, knitwear, hand-woven tweeds, and high fashion. The **Donegal Shop** in Paul Street Piazza specializes in made-to-order tweed suits and rainwear. At the top of Paul Street is the **Crawford Art Gallery,** which has an excellent collection of 18th- and 19th-century views of Cork and mounts adventurous exhibitions by modern artists. ⊠ Emmet Pl., ☎ 021/273377. 🖃 Free. ☉ Weekdays 10–5, Sat. 9–1.

One of Cork's most famous sons was William Penn (1644–1718), founder of the Pennsylvania colony. He is only one of thousands who sailed from Cork's port, the Cove of Cork, on Great Island, 24 kilometers (15 miles) down the harbor. **Cobh** (pronounced *cove*), as it is known nowadays, can be reached by train from Kent Station, and the

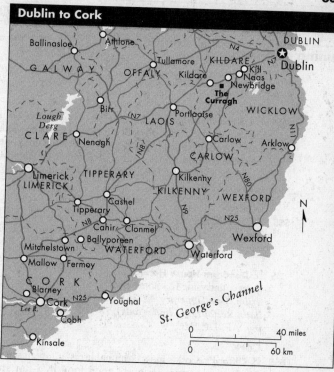

Dublin to Cork

trip provides excellent views of the magnificent harbor. Cobh is an attractive hilly town dominated by its 19th-century **cathedral.** It was the first and last European port of call for transatlantic liners, one of which was the ill-fated *Titanic.* Cobh has other associations with shipwrecks: It was from here that destroyers were sent out in May 1915 to search for survivors of the *Lusitania,* torpedoed by a German submarine with the loss of 1,198 lives. Cobh's maritime past and its links with emigration are documented in a new IR£2 million heritage center known as **The Queenstown Project,** which opened in the town's old railway station in 1993. ☎ 021/813591. ⊠ IR£3.50. ⊗ Feb.–Nov., daily 10–6.

Fota Island, midway between Cork and Cobh, is a recent and very welcome addition to Cork's tourist attractions. The Royal Zoological Society has created a 238-square-kilometer (70-acre) wildlife park here. ☎ 021/812678. ⊠ IR£3.10. ⊗ Mar. 17–Sept. 30, daily 10–6. Parking: IR£1 per car.

Most visitors to Cork want to kiss the famous **Blarney Stone** in the hope of acquiring the "gift of the gab." Blarney itself, 8 kilometers (5 miles) from Cork City, should not, however, be taken too seriously as an excursion. All that is left of **Blarney Castle** is its ruined central keep containing the celebrated stone. This is set in the battlements, and to kiss it, you must lie on the walk within the walls, lean your head back, and touch the stone with your lips. Nobody knows how the tradition originated, but Elizabeth I is credited with giving the word *blarney* to the language when, commenting on the unfulfilled promises of Cormac MacCarthy, Lord Blarney of the time, she remarked, "This is all Blarney; what he says, he never means." In Blarney village there are several good crafts shops, and the outing provides a good opportunity to shop around for traditional Irish goods at competitive prices. ☎ 021/385252. ☞ *IR£3.* ⊙ *Mon.–Sat. 9 to sundown, Sun. 9–5:30.*

Dining and Lodging

For details and price-category definitions, *see* Dining *and* Lodging *in* Staying in Ireland, *above.*

Cahir

$$ ✕⊞ **Kilcoran Lodge Hotel.** Set on its own grounds on the main road, Kilcoran Lodge Hotel is an ideal place to break the journey with coffee or a plainly cooked lunch. It occupies a bucolic country setting on the southern slope of the Galtee Mountains. ⊠ *Cahir, Co. Tipperary, on N8,* ☎ *052/41288,* 🆉 *052/41994. 23 rooms with bath. Indoor pool, sauna. AE, DC, MC, V.*

Cashel

$$$ ✕ **Chez Hans.** Fresh local produce cooked with a French accent is served in this converted chapel at the foot of the famous rock. ⊠ *Rockside,* ☎ *062/61177. MC, V. Dinner only. Closed Sun., Mon., first 3 wks in Jan.*

$$ ⊞ **Dundrum House Hotel.** This magnificent Georgian house is set in quiet countryside 12 kilometers (7 ½ miles) outside busy Cashel. ⊠ *Dundrum, Co. Tipperary.* ☎ *062/71116,* 🆉 *062/71366. 55 rooms with bath. Restaurant (dinner only), 18-hole golf course, tennis court, fishing. AE, DC, MC, V.*

Cork

$$$ ✕ **Clifford's.** Cork's most fashionable restaurant, just a short walk from Jury's hotel, serves seriously good food in a fun atmosphere. The ground floor of a Georgian house has been strikingly modernized and decorated in black and white. Choose from the owner-chef's small set menu (four or five choices for each course), which includes items such as black sole and prawns in a pepper and lime sauce or medallions of veal garnished with apples and walnuts. ⊠ *18 Dyke Parade,* ☎ *021/ 275333. AE, DC, MC, V. Closed Sun. and Mon. No lunch Sat.*

$ ✕ **Isaac's.** In an old warehouse with cast-iron pillars, this popular
★ brasserie-style spot has a Continental atmosphere echoed by the food, which combines Mediterranean influences with excellent local produce. Worth a try, whatever your budget. ⊠ *48 MacCurtain St.,* ☎ *021/ 503805. MC, V.*

$$$ ✕⊞ **Arbutus Lodge.** This exceptionally comfortable hotel has an out-
★ standing restaurant and panoramic views of the city and the river. The restaurant is acclaimed throughout Ireland, not least for its excellent wine list. ⊠ *Middle Glanmire Rd., Montenotte,* ☎ *021/501237,* 🆉 *021/502893. 20 rooms with bath. Restaurant, bar, tennis court. AE, DC, MC, V. Closed 1 wk at Christmas.*

$$$ ✕⊞ **Ballymaloe House.** This rambling house on 400 acres has been
★ developed into an informal, easygoing hotel over the past few years. Each guest room is decorated elegantly in variations on the country-house style. The restaurant—run by Myrtle Allen, a world expert on Irish cookery—is outstanding. ⊠ *Shanagarry, Midleton,* ☎ *021/652531,* 🆉 *021/652–021. 30 rooms with bath. Restaurant (jacket and tie), bar, outdoor heated pool, tennis court, deep-sea fishing by arrangement. AE, DC, MC, V.*

$$$ ⊞ **Fitzpatrick's Silver Springs.** On its own grounds overlooking the River Lee and only five minutes' drive from the town center, this modern low rise reopened in 1989 after major refurbishment. A popular choice for tour groups, it also has the most up-to-date leisure facilities in town.

    ✉ *Tivoli,* ☎ *021/507533,* 🖷 *021/507641. 110 rooms with bath. 2 restaurants, 2 bars, indoor pool, sauna, gym, 9-hole golf course, tennis courts (1 outdoor, 2 indoor),bowling, squash. AE, DC, MC, V.*

$$$ 🏨 **Jury's.** This modern two-story hotel has a lively bar and occupies a riverside location a five-minute walk from the downtown area. ✉ *Western Rd.,* ☎ *021/276622,* 🖷 *021/274477. 185 rooms with bath. 2 restaurants, indoor and outdoor pools, sauna, 2 tennis courts, health club, squash. AE, DC, MC, V. Closed Dec. 25–26.*

$ 🏨 **Jury's Cork Inn.** Opened in 1994, the newest member of Jury's budget chain provides modern, well-equipped rooms in the city center that can accommodate three adults or two adults and two children. ✉ *Anderson's Quay,* ☎ *021/276444,* 🖷 *021/276144. 133 rooms with bath. AE, DC, MC, V.*

$ 🏨 **Victoria Lodge.** Originally built in the early 20th century as a Capuchin monastery, this exceptionally well-appointed B&B is a five-minute drive from the town center; it is also on several bus routes. The rooms are simple but comfortable, with views over the lodge's own grounds. Breakfast is served in the spacious old refectory. ✉ *Victoria Cross,* ☎ *021/542233,* 🖷 *021/542572. 20 rooms with bath. Restaurant (wine license only), TV lounge. MC, V.*

CORK TO GALWAY

The trip from Cork to Galway is about 300 kilometers (188 miles) and includes stops in Killarney and Limerick. Killarney and the mysterious regions of the Burren are two very different areas of outstanding natural beauty. The Shannon region around Limerick is littered with castles, both ruined and restored.

Getting Around

By Train

Trains run from Cork to Tralee, via Killarney, and from Cork to Limerick, changing at Limerick Junction.

By Bus

Buses offer more flexible service than do trains; details are available from local visitor information offices.

By Car

All major rental companies have facilities at Shannon Airport. **Killarney Autos Ltd.** (✉ Park Rd., ☎ 064/31355) is the major firm in Killarney. Taxis do not operate on meters; agree on the fare beforehand.

By Bicycle

You can rent bicycles from **Killarney Rent-A-Bike,** (✉ Market Cross, Killarney, ☎ 064/32578). **D. O'Neill** (✉ Plunkett St., Killarney, ☎ 064/31970), and **Emerald Cycles** (✉ 1 Patrick St., Limerick, ☎ 061/416–983).

Guided Tours

Bus Eireann offers day tours by bus from Killarney and Tralee train stations; check with the tourist office or rail station for details. **Shannon Castle Tours** (☎ 061/61788) and **Destination Killarney** (☎ 064/32638) also operate tours.

Visitor Information

All visitor information offices are open weekdays 9–6, Sat. 9–1.

Killarney (✉ Town Hall, ☎ 064/31633, 🖷 064/34506).
Limerick (✉ Arthur's Quay, ☎ 061/317522, 🖷 061/317939).

Shannon Airport (☎ 061/471-664).
Tralee (✉ Ashe Memorial Hall, ☎ 066/21288).

Exploring Cork to Galway

Beyond Macroom, the main Cork–Killarney road passes through the west-Cork **Gaelteacht**—a predominantly Irish-speaking region—and begins its climb into the Derrynasaggart Mountains. A detour to the left at Macroom will take you to the lake of **Gougane Barra,** source of the River Lee and now a national park. The 6th-century monk St. Finbarr, founder of Cork, had his cell on an island in the lake; this island can now be reached by causeway.

Killarney itself is an undistinguished market town, well developed to handle the tourist trade that flourishes here in the peak season. To find the famous scenery, you must head out of town toward the lakes that lie in a valley running south between the mountains. Part of Killarney's

★ lake district is within **Killarney National Park.** At the heart of the park is the 10,000-acre **Muckross Estate** (open daily, daylight hours). Cars are not allowed in the estate, so if you don't want to walk, rent a bicycle in town or take a trip in a jaunting car—a small two-wheeled horse-drawn cart whose operators can be found at the gates to the estate and in Killarney. At the center of the estate is **Muckross House,** a 19th-century manor that contains the **Kerry Country Life Experience.** On the adjoining grounds is an Old World farm. ☎ 064/31440. ✉ *IR£2.50; combined farm and house: IR£3.50. ⊙ Sept.–June, daily 9–5:30; July and Aug., daily 9–7. Closed 1 wk. at Christmas.*

To get an idea of the splendor of the lakes and streams—and of the massive glacial sandstone and limestone rocks and lush vegetation that characterize the Killarney district—take one of the day-long tours

★ of the **Gap of Dunloe, the Upper Lake, Long Range, Middle** and **Lower lakes,** and **Ross Castle.** The central section, the Gap of Dunloe, is not suitable for cars, but horses and jaunting cars are available at **Kate Kearney's Cottage,** which marks the entrance to the gap.

★ The **Ring of Kerry** will add about 176 kilometers (110 miles) to your trip, but in good weather it provides a pleasant experience. Leave Killarney by the Kenmare Road. **Kenmare** is a small market town 34 kilometers (21 miles) from Killarney at the head of Kenmare Bay. Across the water, as you drive out along the Iveragh Peninsula, will be views of the gray-blue mountain ranges of the Beara Peninsula. **Sneem,** on the estuary of the River Ardsheelaun, is one of the prettiest villages in Ireland. Beyond the next village, Caherdaniel, is **Derrynane House,** home of the 19th-century politician and patriot Daniel O'Connell, "The Liberator," and completed by him in 1825. It still contains much of its original furniture. ☎ 066/75113. ✉ *IR£1. ⊙ Mid-June–Sept., daily 10–1 and 2–7; Oct.–mid-June, Tues.–Sat. 10–1, Sun. 2–5. Park: ✉ Free. ⊙ Year-round.*

The village of **Waterville** is famous as an angling center; it also has a fine sandy beach and a championship golf course. Charles de Gaulle, the French statesman, used to come to Waterville for the fishing; he intended to retire here, but died before ever taking up residence. Off-

★ shore, protruding in conical shapes from the Atlantic, are the **Skellig Rocks,** which contain the cells of early Christian monks. To learn more about the history and bird life of these islands, visit **The Skellig Experience,** an interpretative center situated where the bridge joins Valentia Island. Landing is prohibited on the Skelligs without a special permit, but the 1½-hour boat cruise (weather permitting) offered at the center is a good substitute. ☎ 064/31633. ✉ *IR£3; with cruise: IR£15*

Cork to Galway

⊙ *Apr.–June and Sept., daily 9:30–5; July–Aug., daily 9:30–7. Call to confirm cruise times.*

Beyond Cahirciveen, you are on the other side of the Ring, with views across Dingle Bay to the rugged peaks of the Dingle Peninsula. At the head of the bay is **Killorglin,** which has a three-day stint of unbridled merrymaking the first weekend in August—including the crowning of a goat as monarch of the town—known as Puck Fair.

If time and the weather are on your side, turn off the main Killorglin–Tralee road and make a tour of the **Dingle Peninsula**—one of the wildest and least spoiled regions of Ireland—taking in the **Connor Pass, Mount Brandon, the Gallarus Oratory,** and stopping at **Dunquin** to hear some of Ireland's best traditional musicians. For an adventure off the beaten path, arrange for a boat ride to the **Blasket Islands** and spend a few blissful hours wandering along the cliffs. Dingle town is a handy touring base, with a surprisingly wide choice of good restaurants, open Easter–October.

Tralee is the commercial center of Kerry, and home to the **Kerry County Museum,** which traces the history of Kerry's people from 5000 BC to the present day. ☎ 066/27777. ⊡ IR£3.50. ⊙ Mon.–Sat. 10–6, 10–8 in August.

In September, the "Rose of Tralee" is selected from an international lineup of young women of Irish descent. Listowel is similarly transformed during its race week in October. From **Tarbert** (where a ferry provides a handy shortcut directly to County Clare and the Burren), the road skirts the estuary of the River Shannon. **Limerick** is the fourth-largest city in the Republic, with a population of 60,000; it's also arguably the least attractive city in Ireland. Its Newtown area, however, is dominated by handsome Georgian buildings.

★ **Bunratty Castle** is a famous landmark midway between Limerick and Shannon Airport. It is one of four castles in the area that offer nightly medieval banquets, which, though as fake as they come, at least offer some fairly uninhibited fun. The castle was the stronghold of the princes of Thomond and is the most complete and—despite its ye-Olde-World banquets—authentic medieval castle in Ireland, restored in such a way as to give an idea of the 15th- and 16th-century way of life. The **Folk Park** on its grounds has farm buildings and crafts shops typical of the 19th century. ☎ 061/361511. ⌨ IR£4.50. ⊙ Daily 9:30–dusk (last entry 1 hr before closing).

NEED A BREAK? Drop in to **Durty Nelly's**, beside Bunratty Castle—it's one of Ireland's most popular old-time bars.

There is an incredible number of castles—almost 900—in the Shannon area, ranging from such fully restored examples as **Knappogue** at Quin, 14 kilometers (9 miles) from Bunratty, to the multitude of crumbling ruins that loom up all over the area.

Beyond Shannon Airport is County Clare and its principal town, **Ennis,** the campaigning base of Eamon de Valera, the New York–born politician whose character and views dominated the Republic from independence until the mid-'50s. Just beyond Ennis, a detour to **Corofin** will take you to the **Clare Heritage Center,** which explains the traumatic story of Ireland in the 19th century, a story of famines and untold misery that resulted in the mass emigrations of the Irish to England and the United States. ☎ 065/37955. ⌨ IR£1.75. ⊙ Apr.–Oct., daily 10–6; Nov.–Mar. by appointment.

Ennistymon and Lisdoonvarna, both quiet villages with an old-fashioned charm, make excellent bases for touring the Burren. **Lisdoonvarna** has developed something of a reputation over the years as a matchmaking center, with bachelor farmers and single women converging here each year around harvesttime for a **Bachelors' Festival.** This strange, rocky, limestone district is a superb nature reserve, with a profusion of unique wildflowers that are at their best in late May. Huge colonies of puffins, kittiwakes, shags, guillemots, and razorbills nest along its coast. The **Burren Display Center** at **Kilfenora** explains the extraordinary geology and wildlife of the area in a simple audiovisual display. ☎ 065/88030. ⌨ IR£2. ⊙ Mid-Mar.–May and Sept.–Oct., daily 10–5; June–Aug., daily 10–6.

★ The dramatic **Cliffs of Moher** are a must: They rise vertically out of the sea in a wall that stretches 8 kilometers (5 miles) and varies in height from 710 to 1,440 feet, with **O'Brien's Tower** at their highest point. There is a visitor center beside the parking lot (⊙ Mar.–Oct., daily 10–6). On a clear day, the **Aran Islands** are visible from the cliffs, and in summer there are regular day trips to them from **Doolin,** a small village popular with young travelers and noted for its spontaneous traditional music sessions.

At **Ailwee Cave** near Ballyvaughan, you can take a guided tour into the underworld of the Burren, where 3,415 feet of cave, formed millions of years ago, can be explored. ☎ 065/77036. ⌨ IR£3.95. ⊙ Early Mar.–June and Sept.–early Nov., daily 10–6 (last tour 5:30); July and Aug., daily 10–7 (last tour 6:30).

The coast road continues into County Galway, through the pretty fishing village of Kinvara. Galway City itself is approached through **Clarinbridge,** the village that hosts Galway's annual Oyster Festival, which is held in September and features the superlative products of the village's oyster beds.

Dining and Lodging

For details and price-category definitions, *see* Dining *and* Lodging *in* Staying in Ireland, *above.*

Ballyvaughan

$$ ✕▥ **Hyland's Hotel.** They have been looking after travelers for 250
★ years at this comfortable, family-run coaching inn in a seaside village in the heart of the Burren. The cheerful, unpretentious dining room specializes in local seafood and lamb. ⊠ *Co. Clare,* ☎ *065/77037.* ℻ *065/77131. 31 rooms with bath. Restaurant, bar. Closed Jan.*

Clarinbridge

$ ✕ **Moran's of the Weir.** This waterside traditional thatched cottage is one of Ireland's simplest yet most famous seafood eateries. The specialty here is oysters, but they also serve crab, prawns, mussels, and smoked salmon. ⊠ *The Weir, Kilcolgan, Co. Galway,* ☎ *091/96113. AE, MC, V.*

Dingle

$$ ✕ **Beginish.** The best of several small but sophisticated restaurants in town, this relaxing place serves local meat and seafood in a generous version of nouvelle cuisine. ⊠ *Green St.,* ☎ *066/51588. AE, DC, MC, V. Closed Mon. and Nov. 1–Mar.*

$$ ✕ **Doyle's Seafood Bar.** This is Dingle's best-known seafood restaurant, specializing in simply prepared local fish and shellfish. ⊠ *John St.,* ☎ *066/51174. DC, MC, V. Closed Sun. and mid-Nov.–early Mar.*

$ ▥ **Greenmount House.** This impeccably–kept, modern B&B a short walk from the town center is renowned for its imaginative breakfasts. ⊠ *Gortanora, Dingle, Co. Kerry,* ☎ *066/51974. 12 rooms with bath.*

Ennis

$$$ ▥ **Old Ground.** This rambling creeper-clad building in the town center, dating from the early 18th century with much added to over the years, is a comfortable, well-established hotel that has retained its past elegance. The lodging serves as a popular base for Americans, especially golfers. ⊠ *O'Connell St.,* ☎ *065/28127,* ℻ *065/28112. 60 rooms with bath. Restaurant, bar. AE, DC, MC, V.*

Kenmare

$$$$ ✕▥ **Park.** A guest feels truly pampered at this antique-laden hotel, widely
★ considered to be one of Ireland's best. Be sure to sample the seafood on the sophisticated menu of the renowned restaurant (jacket and tie). ☎ *064/41200,* ℻ *064/41402. 50 rooms with bath. Restaurant, 18-hole golf course, tennis court, horseback riding, fishing, bicycles. TV in rooms on request. AE, DC, MC, V.*

Killarney

$$ ✕ **Gaby's.** For simple and fresh seafood, Gaby's can't be beat. ⊠ *17 High St.,* ☎ *064/32519. AE, DC, MC, V. Closed Sun. and Dec.–mid-Mar. No lunch Mon.*

$$$$ ✕▥ **Aghadoe Heights.** This luxury hotel overlooks the lakes and has
★ the most romantic view of all the hotels in Killarney. The restaurant is outstanding. ⊠ *Aghadoe Heights,* ☎ *064/31766,* ℻ *064/31345. 57 rooms with bath. Restaurant, bar, indoor heated pool, hot tub, sauna, tennis court, fishing. AE, DC, MC, V.*

$$$$ ✕▥ **Europe.** This large, luxurious, modern hotel has a secluded lakeside location, a large panoramic restaurant and excellent sporting facilities. ⊠ *Killorglin Rd., Fossa,* ☎ *064/31900,* ℻ *064/32118. 205 rooms with bath. Restaurant, bar, indoor pool, sauna, tennis court, exercise* *room, horseback riding, fishing, bicycles. AE, DC, MC, V. Closed Nov.–Feb.*

$$ ✕▥ **Foley's.** This popular eatery specializes in seafood, steaks, and Kerry mountain lamb. Foley's also offers well-appointed Victorian–style town rooms in the center of town. ⊠ *23 High St.,* ☎ *064/31217,* ℻ *064/34683. 12 rooms with bath. Closed Nov.–April. AE, DC, MC, V.*

$$ ▥ **Arbutus.** Newly refurbished and centrally located, Arbutus benefits from a lively bar and an old-world atmosphere. ⊠ *College St.,* ☎ *064/31037,* ℻ *064/34033. 35 rooms with bath. AE, DC, MC, V.*

Lahinch

$$ ▥ **Aberdeen Arms.** Golfers abound among the clientele of this com-
★ fortably refurbished Victorian seaside hotel. ⊠ *Lahinch, Co. Clare,* ☎ *065/81100,* ℻ *065/81228. 55 rooms with bath. 2 restaurants, 2 bars, hot tub, sauna, 10 tennis courts, snooker, bicycles. AE, DC, MC, V.*

Limerick

$$ ✕ **De La Fontaine.** The French owner-chef uses only the best local produce to present imaginative "cuisine moderne" creations in this intimate hideaway. ⊠ *12 Gerald Griffin St.,* ☎ *061/414–461. Reservations advised. AE, DC, MC, V. Closed Sun. Lunch served only on Fri.*

$$$$ ▥ **Castletroy Park.** High standards of comfort are the rule at this well-
★ designed modern hotel on the outskirts of town. ⊠ *Dublin Rd.,* ☎ *061/335566,* ℻ *061/331117. 107 rooms with bath. 2 restaurants, bar, indoor pool, hot tub, sauna, steam room, exercise room. AE, DC, MC, V.*

$$ ▥ **Greenhills.** This suburban, modern low rise is convenient for Shannon Airport and also makes a good touring base. The friendly owner-manager welcomes families. ⊠ *Ennis Rd.,* ☎ *061/453033,* ℻ *061/453307. 55 rooms with bath. Restaurant, bar, coffee shop, indoor heated pool, hot tub, sauna, steam room, tennis court, exercise room. AE, DC, MC, V.*

Lisdoonvarna

$ ▥ **Ballinalacken Castle.** It's not a castle, but a converted Victorian shooting lodge on the very edge of the Burren that commands a breathtaking view of the Atlantic. Rooms are modest but full of character. ⊠ *Co. Clare,* ☎ *065/74025,* ℻ *065/74025. 12 rooms with bath. Restaurant, bar. MC, V. Closed early Nov.–Easter.*

$ ▥ **Sheedy's Spa View.** This is a friendly, family-run establishment with open turf fires and an excellent restaurant. ⊠ *Lisdoonvarna,* ☎ *065/74026,* ℻ *065/74555. 11 rooms with bath. Restaurant, tennis. AE, DC, MC, V.*

THE NORTHWEST

This route from Galway to Sligo and then back to Dublin, via Kells, takes you through the rugged landscape of Connemara to the fabled Yeats country in the northwest and then skirts the borders of Northern Ireland before returning to Dublin. The entire trip is about 400 kilometers (250 miles) and passes through some of the wildest and loneliest parts of Ireland.

Getting Around

By Train

Trains to Galway, Westport, and Sligo operate from Dublin's Heuston or Connolly (Sligo) stations. There is no train service north of Sligo.

By Bus

Travel within the area is more flexible by bus; details are available from local visitor information offices.

By Car

In Galway, cars can be rented from **Avis** (☎ 091/68886), **Budget** (☎ 091/66376), or **Murray's** (☎ 091/62222). Taxis do not operate on meters; agree on the fare beforehand.

By Bicycle

You can rent bikes from **Celtic Cycles** (⊠ Victoria Place, Galway City, ☎ 091/66606), **John Mannion** (⊠ Railway View, Clifden, ☎ 095/21160), or **Gary's Cycles** (⊠ Quay St., Sligo, ☎ 071/45418).

Guided Tours

CIE Tours International operates day tours of Connemara out of Galway City and bus tours into the Donegal highlands from Sligo train station; details are available from local tourist offices. **CIE/Bus Eireann** (☎ 01/830–2222) and **Gray Line** (☎ 01/661–9666) offer tours of the Boyne Valley and County Meath out of Dublin.

Visitor Information

All are open weekdays 9–6, Sat. 9–1.

Galway (⊠ off Eyre Sq., ☎ 091/63081, FAX 091/65201).
Sligo (⊠ Temple St., ☎ 071/61201, FAX 071/60360).
Westport (⊠ The Mall, ☎ 098/25711, FAX 098/26709).

Exploring the Northwest

Galway City is the gateway to the ancient province of Connacht, the most westerly seaboard in Europe. Galway City was well established even before the Normans arrived in the 13th century, rebuilding the city walls and turning the little town into a flourishing port. Later its waterfront was frequented by Spanish grandees and traders. The salmon fishing in the River Corrib, which flows through the lower part of the town, is unsurpassed. In early summer, you can stand on the **Weir Bridge** beside the town's cathedral and watch thousands of salmon as they leap and twist through the narrow access to the inner lakes. **Lynch's Castle** on Shop Street, now a bank, is a good example of a 16th-century fortified house—fortified because the neighboring Irish tribes persistently raided Galway City, whose commercial life excluded them. Nowadays the liveliest part of town is around the area between **Eyre Square** (the town's center) and the **Spanish Arch**.

NEED A BREAK?
Drop in at **Noctan's** pub on the corner of Abbeygate Street for food at lunchtime and the latest news of what's on in town.

On the west bank of the Corrib estuary, just outside of the Galway town walls, is **Claddagh,** said to be the oldest fishing village in Ireland. **Salthill Promenade,** with its lively seaside amenities, is the traditional place "to sit and watch the moon rise over Claddagh, and see the sun go down on Galway Bay"—in the words of the city's most famous song.

Connemara is a land of romantic, underpopulated landscapes, and rugged craggy coastlines, where the Irish language is still used by many people. **Rossaveale,** a port on the coast road beyond Spiddal, is the handiest port for a trip to the Aran Islands, 48 kilometers (30 miles) off the coast, where J. M. Synge drew the inspiration for his play *Riders to the Sea.* The islands are still 100% Irish speaking and retain an at-

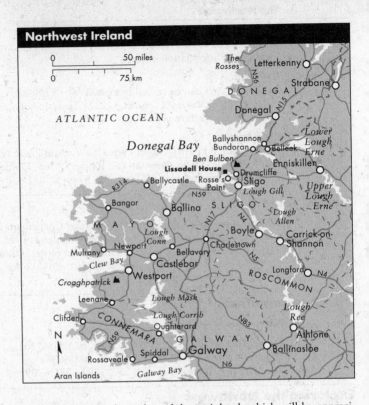

Northwest Ireland

mosphere distinct from that of the mainland, which will be appreciated by those in search of the peace and quiet of a past century. **Inishmaan,** the middle island, is considered the most unspoiled of the three and will delight botanists, ornithologists, and walkers. ☯ *Sailings daily from Rossaveale and less frequently from Galway.* 🖾 *Round-trip fare about IR£12. Details from Galway Tourist Information Office. Also accessible by air from Connemara Airport (☎ 091/93034).* ☯ *Daily flights.* 🖾 *Round-trip fare about IR£32.*

Oughterard is an important angling center on Lough Corrib. Boats can be rented for excursions to the lake's many wooded islands. The road to Clifden runs between the Maamturk and the Cloosh Mountains beside a string of small lakes. **Clifden,** the principal town of Connemara, has an almost alpine setting, nestling on the edge of the Atlantic with a spectacular mountain backdrop. Just beyond Clifden is the **Connemara National Park,** with its many nature trails offering views of sea, mountain, and lake. Its visitor center features an audiovisual presentation and a collection of farm furniture. ☎ *095/41054.* 🖾 *Free to park,* 🖾 *£1.50 to visitor center.* ☯ *Apr.–Oct., daily 10–6.*

Westport is a quiet, mainly 18th-century town overlooking Clew Bay—a wide expanse of water studded with nearly 400 islands. The distinctive silhouette of **Croaghpatrick,** a 2,540-foot mountain, dominates the town. Today some 25,000 pilgrims climb it on the last Sunday in July in honor of St. Patrick, who is believed to have spent 40 days fasting on its summit in AD 441. Whether he did or not, the climb is an exhilarating experience and can be completed in about three hours; it should be attempted only in good weather, however.

County Sligo is noted for its seaside resorts, the famous golf course at Rosse's Point (just outside Sligo Town), and its links with Ireland's most famous 20th-century poet, W. B. Yeats, who is buried just north of **Sligo**

Town at Drumcliffe. An important collection of paintings by the poet's brother, Jack B. Yeats, can be seen in the **Sligo Museum** (✉ Stephen St., ☎ 071/42212), which also has memorabilia of Yeats, the poet. Take
★ a boat from Sligo up to **Lough Gill** and see the **Lake Isle of Innisfree** and other places immortalized in Yeats's poetry. His grave is beneath the slopes of Ben Bulben, just north of the town. Nearby is **Lissadell House,** a substantial mansion dating from 1830 that features prominently in his writings. It was the home of Constance Gore-Booth, later Countess Markeviecz, who took part in the 1916 uprising. ☎ 071/63150. ⊡ IR£2. ☉ June–Sept., Mon.–Sat. 10:30–noon, 2–4:30.

Bundoran, the southernmost town of Donegal, is one of Ireland's major seaside resorts, with excellent sandy beaches. From **Donegal Town,** you can set off to tour the ever-changing landscape of Donegal's rugged coastline and highlands, visiting the "tweed villages" on the coast at the Rosses, where the famous Donegal tweed is woven.

This route heads back to Dublin through **Belleek,** on the borders of Counties Donegal and Fermanagh, known for its fragile, lustrous china; a factory visit can be arranged (☎ 08036/565–501). For the remaining towns on this tour, *see* the Ireland country map. Belleek is a frontier post on an approved road that skirts the shores of Lower Lough Erne in Northern Ireland, passing through Enniskillen and reemerging in Belturbet, County Cavan, on the main N3 Dublin road. The N3 continues across a beautiful patchwork of lakes, the heart of the low-lying lakelands. In **Cavan** you may want to visit the **Crystal Factory,** which runs daily tours of the premises, showing visitors the techniques for blowing and cutting glass. ✉ *Dublin Rd.,* ☎ *049/31800.* ⊡ *Free.* ☉ *Guided tours weekdays 9:30, 10:30, 11:30, 12:30, 2:30.*

The N3 returns you to Dublin by way of **Kells,** in whose 8th-century abbey the Book of Kells was completed; a facsimile can be seen in **St. Columba's Church.** Among the remains of the abbey is a well-preserved round tower and a rare example of a stone-roof church dating from the 9th century. There are five richly sculptured stone crosses in Kells. Just south of **Navan** is the **Hill of Tara,** the religious and cultural capital of Ireland in ancient times. Its importance waned with the arrival of Christianity in the 5th century, and today its crest is, appropriately enough, crowned with a statue of the man who brought Christianity to Ireland—St. Patrick.

Dining and Lodging

For details and price-category definitions, *see* Dining *and* Lodging *in* Staying in Ireland, *above.*

Cashel Bay

$$$$ ⊞ **Cashel House.** One of Ireland's outstanding country-house hotels,
★ luxurious and secluded, Cashel House attracts an affluent outdoor-loving international clientele as well as Ireland's elite. ✉ *Cashel Bay, Connemara, Co. Galway,* ☎ *095/31001,* 𝖥𝖠𝖷 *095/31077. 32 rooms with bath. Restaurant, bar, tennis court, horseback riding, beach, fishing, bicycles. AE, MC, V.*

Clifden

$$ ⊞ **Abbeyglen Castle.** This comfortable hotel is quietly set about 1 kilometer (½ mile) west of town, featuring panoramic views over the rolling green hillsides. The secluded garden is a haven for travel-weary souls. ✉ *Sky Rd.,* ☎ *095/21201,* 𝖥𝖠𝖷 *095/21797. 39 rooms with bath. Heated pool, 9-hole golf course, tennis court, horseback riding, bicycles. AE, DC, MC, V. Closed Jan.*

\$\$\$ **Rock Glen Manor House.** Dating from 1815, this converted hunt-
★   ing lodge is 1½ kilometers (1 mile) south of town in exceptionally peaceful surroundings. ☎ 095/21035, FAX 095/21737. *29 rooms with bath.
AE, DC, MC, V. Closed Oct.–mid-Mar.*

Collooney

\$\$\$ ✕ **Markree Castle.** This magnificent 17th-century castle, which also
★   houses the renowned Knockmuldowney Restaurant, is situated on a
1,000-acre estate. The host family offers bed and breakfast, delectable
home-cooked French food at dinner, and a traditional Sunday lunch.
⊠ *11 km (7 mi) south of Sligo Town on N4, Co. Sligo,* ☎ 071/67800,
FAX 071/67840. *14 rooms with bath. AE, DC, MC, V.*

Cong

\$\$\$\$ ✕ **Ashford Castle.** This imposing castle is set in its own park on the
★   edge of Lough Corrib and has a superb restaurant, the Connaught Room.
President Reagan stayed here in 1984. ⊠ *Co. Mayo.* ☎ 092/46003,
FAX 092/46260. *83 rooms with bath. 2 restaurants, 2 bars, 9-hole golf
course, 2 tennis courts, horseback riding, fishing, jaunting car, bicycles, clay-target shooting. AE, DC, MC, V.*

Galway City

\$\$\$ ✕ **Drimcong House.** The chef-owner prepares his award-winning meals
★   in a 300-year-old lakeside house, 13 kilometers (8 miles) from Galway
City. ⊠ *Northwest on N59,* ☎ 091/85115. *AE, DC, MC, V. Open
Tues.–Sat., dinner only. Closed Christmas–mid-Mar.*

\$\$ ✕ **de Burgos.** This Old World basement restaurant serves an extensive French-influenced menu focused around local seafood and char-
grilled steaks. ⊠ *15 Augustine St.,* ☎ 091/62188. *AE, DC, MC, V.
Closed Sun.*

\$\$ ✕ **Noctan's.** This excellent small French restaurant is above a popular pub. ⊠ *17 Cross St.,* ☎ 091/66172. *MC, V. Dinner only. Closed
Sun.–Mon.*

\$\$\$ **Great Southern.** Recently refurbished, this old-style town hotel en-
joys a convenient central location. ⊠ *Eyre Sq.,* ☎ 091/64041, FAX
091/66704. *115 rooms with bath. Rooftop heated pool, sauna, health
complex. AE, DC, MC, V.*

\$\$ **Ardilaun House.** This hotel is set in pleasant grounds midway between Galway City and the seaside suburb of Salthill. ⊠ *Taylors Hill,*
☎ 091/21433, FAX 091/21546. *89 rooms with bath. AE, DC, MC, V.*

Oughterard

\$\$\$ **Connemara Gateway.** This modern low rise makes a convenient tour-
ing base and has relatively spacious rooms with views of the Connemara
hills. ⊠ *Oughterard, Co. Galway,* ☎ 091/82328, FAX 091/82332. *62
rooms with bath. Restaurant, indoor pool, tennis court, sauna. AE,
DC, MC, V. Closed Dec. and Jan.*

Sligo Town

\$\$\$ ✕ **Ballincar House Hotel.** Just outside of town, this converted coun-
★   try house with gardens has a highly recommended restaurant that specializes in fresh seafood. ⊠ *Rosses Point Rd.,* ☎ 071/45361, FAX
071/44198. *25 rooms with bath. Restaurant, sauna, tennis court,
squash. AE, DC, MC, V.*

\$\$ **Silver Swan Hotel.** In the town center overlooking the Garavogue
River, this '60s-style hotel has recently been refurbished, with quite effective results. ⊠ *Hyde Bridge,* ☎ 071/43231, FAX 071/42232. *29
rooms with bath. Restaurant, bar. AE, DC, MC, V.*

$$ ⊞ **Sligo Park.** This is a modern two-story building, set on spacious grounds. ⊠ *Pearse Rd.,* ☎ *071/60291,* FAX *071/69556. 89 rooms with bath. Restaurant, indoor pool, tennis court. AE, DC, MC, V.*

Westport

$$ ✗ **Asgard.** The Asgard is a pub with award-winning food in both its bar and second-floor restaurant. ⊠ *The Quay,* ☎ *098/25319. AE, DC, MC, V.*

$$ ⊞ **Hotel Westport.** A modern low rise, this quiet hotel is five minutes' walk from the town center and overlooks the grounds of Westport House. ⊠ *Newport Rd.,* ☎ *098/25122,* FAX *098/26739. 49 rooms with bath.*

17 Italy

Rome

Florence

Tuscany

Milan

Venice

Campania

WHERE ELSE IN EUROPE CAN YOU FIND the blend of great art, delicious food and wine, and sheer verve that awaits you in Italy? This Mediterranean country has made a profound contribution to Western civilization, producing some of the world's greatest thinkers, writers, politicians, saints, and artists. Impressive traces of their lives and works can still be seen in Italy's great buildings and lovely countryside.

The whole of Italy is one vast attraction, but the triangle of its most-visited cities—Rome (Roma), Florence (Firenze), and Venice (Venezia)—gives a good idea of the great variety to be found here. In Rome and Florence, especially, you can feel the uninterrupted flow of the ages, from the Classical era of the ancient Romans to the bustle and throb of contemporary life being lived in centuries-old settings. Venice, by contrast, seems suspended in time, the same today as it was when it held sway over the eastern Mediterranean and the Orient. Each of these cities presents a different aspect of the Italian character: the Baroque exuberance of Rome, Florence's serene stylishness, and the dreamy sensuality of Venice.

The uninhibited Italian lifestyle can be entertaining or irritating, depending on how you look at it. Rarely do things run like clockwork here; you are more likely to encounter unexplained delays and incomprehensible complications. Relax: There's usually something you can smile about even in the most trying circumstances.

Trying to soak in Italy's rich artistic heritage is a great challenge. The country's many museums and churches draw hordes of visitors, all wanting to see the same thing at the same time. From May through September, the Sistine Chapel, Michelangelo's *David,* St. Mark's Square, and other key sights are more often than not swamped by mobs of tourists. Try to see the highlights at off-peak times. If they are open during lunch—and many are not—that is often a good time. Again, relax: Seeing some attractions—such as the scrubbed facades of Rome's glorious Baroque churches—entails no opening hours and no lines at all.

Along with hordes of tourists, large Italian cities are plagued by automobiles. Recent regulations barring some traffic from the centers of Rome and Florence have made them less noisy in spots, but air pollution remains a serious problem. Plans are now afoot to curtail the auto traffic that swirls around the Colosseum, sparing it some of the pollution and vibration it has suffered as perhaps the world's most extravagant *spartitraffico* (traffic circle).

Even in the major tourist cities, Italians generally take a friendly interest in their visitors. Only the most blasé waiters and salespeople will be less than courteous and helpful. However, the persistent attention some Italian Casanovas pay to foreign females can be oppressive and annoying. If you're not interested, the best tactic is to ignore them. It's important to be attentive to matters of personal security in certain parts of the country; always be on guard against pickpockets and purse snatchers in the main tourist cities and in Naples. Especially in Rome and Florence, watch out for bands of gypsy children, expert at lifting wallets. Small cities and towns are usually safe.

Making the most of your time in Italy doesn't mean rushing through it. To gain a rich appreciation for Italy, don't try to see everything all at once. Do what you really want to do, and if that means skipping a museum to sit at a table in a pretty café, enjoying the sunshine and a cappuccino, you're getting into the Italian spirit. Art—and life—are to be enjoyed, and the Italians can show you how.

ESSENTIAL INFORMATION

Before You Go

Visitor Information

Contact the **Italian Government Travel Office** (**ENIT,** ✉ 630 5th Ave., Suite 1566, New York, NY 10111, ☎ 212/245–4822, FAX 212/586–9249; 500 N. Michigan Ave., Chicago, IL 60611, ☎ 312/644–0990, FAX 312/644–3019; 12400 Wilshire Blvd., Suite 550, Los Angeles, CA 90025, ☎ 310/820–0098, FAX 310/820–6357). In Italy, regional and local agencies, either the **Azienda di Promozione Turismo (APT or AST)** or the **Ente Provinciale per il Turismo (EPT),** as well as municipal tourist offices and others known as **Pro Loco** in small towns, provide helpful information. Allow plenty of time for return mail.

When to Go

The main tourist season in Italy runs from April to mid-October. It follows that for serious sightseers the best months are from fall to early spring. The so-called low season may be cooler and inevitably rainier, but it has its rewards: less time waiting on lines and closer, less hurried views of what you want to see. Foreign tourists crowd the major cities at Easter, when Italians flock to resorts and the countryside. Avoid traveling in August, when the heat can be oppressive and when vacationing Italians cram roads, trains, and planes, as well as beach and mountain resorts. Especially around the August 15 holiday, such cities as Rome and Milan are deserted, and many restaurants and shops close. Except for such year-round resorts as Taormina and a few on the Italian Riviera, coastal resorts close up tight from October or November to April. The best time for resorts is June and September, when the weather is usually fine and everything is open but not crowded.

The hottest months are July and August, when brief afternoon thunderstorms are common in inland areas. Winters are relatively mild in most places on the tourist circuit, but there are always some rainy spells.

Low-season rates do not officially apply in Rome, Florence, and Milan, but you can usually bargain for discounted rates in Rome and Milan in summer (when business travelers are few) and in Florence in winter. Ask for *"la tariffa scontata."* You can save on hotel accommodations in Venice and in such resorts as Sorrento and Capri during their low seasons—the winter, early spring, and late-autumn months.

CLIMATE

The following are average daily maximum and minimum temperatures for Rome.

Jan.	52F	11C	**May**	74F	23C	**Sept.**	79F	26C
	40	5		56	13		62	17
Feb.	55F	13C	**June**	82F	28C	**Oct.**	71F	22C
	42	6		63	17		55	13
Mar.	59F	15C	**July**	87F	30C	**Nov.**	61F	16C
	45	7		67	20		49	9
Apr.	66F	19C	**Aug.**	86F	30C	**Dec.**	55F	13C
	50	10		67	20		44	6

The following are average daily maximum and minimum temperatures for Milan.

Jan.	40F	5C	May	74F	23C	Sept.	75F	24C
	32	0		57	14		61	16
Feb.	46F	8C	June	80F	27C	Oct.	63F	17C
	35	2		63	17		52	11
Mar.	56F	13C	July	84F	29C	Nov.	51F	10C
	43	6		67	20		43	6
Apr.	65F	18C	Aug.	82F	28C	Dec.	43F	6C
	49	9		66	16		35	2

Currency

The unit of currency in Italy is the lira (plural, lire). There are bills of 1,000, 2,000, 5,000, 10,000, 50,000, and 100,000 lire; coins are worth 50, 100, 200, and 500 lire. At press time (spring 1995), the exchange rate was about 1,621 lire to the U.S. dollar; 1,157 to the Canadian dollar; and 2,575 lire to the pound sterling.

When your purchases run into hundreds of thousands of lire, beware of being shortchanged, a dodge that is practiced at ticket windows, toll booths, and cashiers' desks, as well as in shops and even in banks. *Always count your change before you leave the counter.*

Always carry some smaller-denomination bills for sundry purchases; you're less likely to be shortchanged, and you won't have to face the eye-rolling dismay of cashiers chronically short of change.

Credit cards are generally accepted in shops and hotels, but may not always be welcome in restaurants, so always look for those little signs in the window or ask when you enter to avoid embarrassing situations. When you wish to leave a tip beyond the 15% service charge that is usually included with your bill (☞ Tipping *in* Staying in Italy, *below*), leave it in cash rather than adding it to the credit card slip.

What It Will Cost

Rome, Milan, and Venice are the more expensive Italian cities to visit. Taxes are usually included in hotel bills; a cover charge may appear as a separate item in restaurant checks, as does the service charge, usually about 15%, if added. There is a 19% tax on car rentals.

SAMPLE PRICES

A cup of espresso consumed while standing at a bar costs from 1,200 lire to 1,400 lire, the same cup served at a table triple that. A bottle of beer costs from 2,500 lire to 3,800 lire, a soft drink about 2,200 lire. A *tramezzino* (small sandwich) costs about 2,200 lire, a more substantial one about 3,500. You will pay about 10,000 lire for a short taxi ride in Rome and Florence, more in Milan. Admission to a major museum is about 12,000 lire; a three-hour sightseeing tour, about 45,000 lire.

Customs on Arrival

Two still cameras and one movie camera can be brought in duty-free. Travelers arriving in Italy from a European Union (EU) country are allowed, duty-free, a total of 800 cigarettes (or 400 cigarillos or 400 cigars), 10 liters of spirits plus 90 liters of still wine, if duty and taxes have been paid on them at the time of purchase. Visitors traveling directly from non-EU countries are allowed 200 cigarettes and cigars or tobacco not exceeding 250 grams, 1 liter of spirits, and 2 liters of still wine. Not more than 20 million lire in Italian bank notes may be taken into or out of the country.

Language

Italy is accustomed to English-speaking tourists, and in major cities you will find that many people speak at least a little English. In smaller hotels and restaurants, a smattering of Italian comes in handy.

Italy

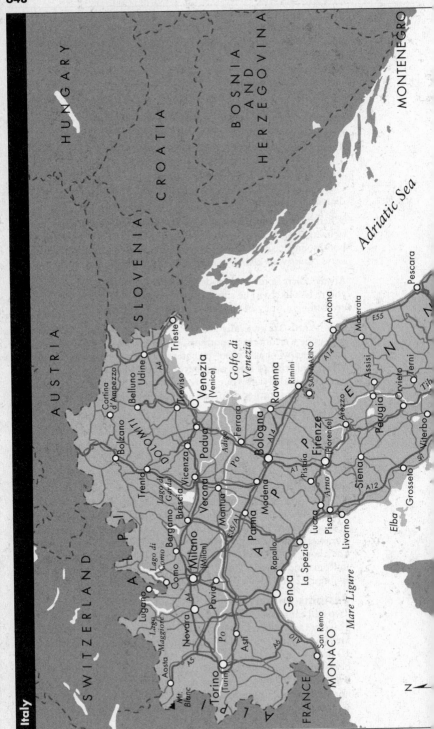

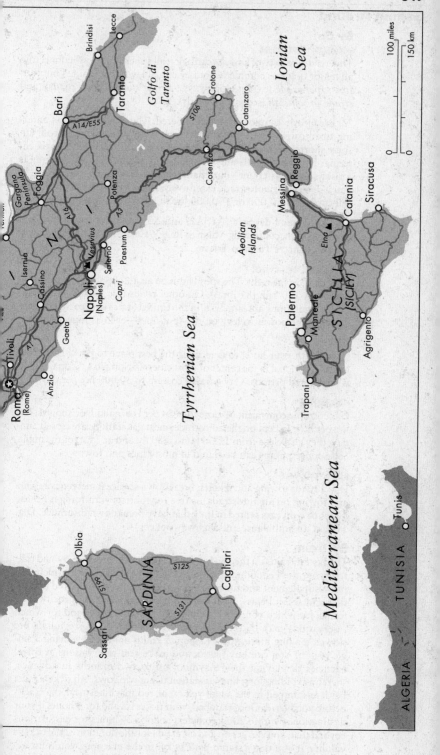

Ionian Sea

100 miles
150 km

Lecce
Brindisi
Golfo di Taranto
Crotone
Bari
Taranto
A14/E55
S106
Catanzaro
Foggia
Potenza
Cosenza
Gargano Peninsula
A16
Reggio
Messina
A3
Catania
Vesuvius
Paestum
Salerno
Aeolian Islands
Siracusa
Isernia
Napoli (Naples)
Etna
Cassino
Capri
SICILIA (SICILY)
Gaeta
Palermo
Tivoli
A1
Monreale
Agrigento
Roma (Rome)
Anzio
Trapani

Tyrrhenian Sea

Mediterranean Sea

Olbia
S199
SARDINIA
S125
Sassari
S131
Cagliari

Tunis
TUNISIA
ALGERIA

Getting Around

By Car

ROAD CONDITIONS

The extensive network of *autostrade* (toll superhighways) connecting all major towns is complemented by equally well-maintained but toll-free *superstrade* (express highways), *strade statali* (main roads), and *strade provinciali* (secondary roads).

All are clearly signposted and numbered. The ticket issued on entering an autostrada must be returned on leaving, along with the toll. On some shorter autostrade, mainly connections, the toll is payable on entering. Have small bills and change handy for tolls; shortchanging is a risk, so always count your change before leaving the toll booth. If you will be using autostrade extensively, buy a Viacard—an automatic toll card—for 50,000 or 100,000 lire at autostrada locations.

The Autostrada del Sole (A1, A2, and A3) crosses the country from north to south, connecting Milan to Reggio Calabria. The A4 from west to east connects Turin to Trieste.

RULES OF THE ROAD

Driving is on the right. The speed limit on an autostrada for a medium-size car is 130 kph (81 mph). On other roads it is 90 kph (56 mph). Other regulations are largely as in the United States except that the police have the power to levy on-the-spot fines—even as high as $500!

PARKING

Check with your hotel to determine the best place to park. Parking is greatly restricted in the center of most cities. Parking in a "Zona Disco" is for limited periods. City garages cost up to 30,000 lire per day.

GASOLINE

Gas costs the equivalent of more than $4 per U.S. gallon, or about 1,700 lire per liter. Except on the autostrade, most gas stations are closed Sunday; they also close from 12:30 PM to 3:30 PM and at 7 PM for the night. Self-service pumps can be found in most cities and towns.

BREAKDOWNS

Dial 116 for towing and repairs; breakdown service (emergency repairs and towing on an autostrada) is free for tourists with foreign license plates or with cars rented in Italy that have breakdown insurance. Dial 113 for an ambulance and highway police.

By Train

The fastest trains on the FS (Ferrovie dello Stato), the state-owned railroad, are the Pendolino Eurostar or ETR 460 trains, for which you pay a supplement and for which seat reservations are required in both first and second class. Also fast are Intercity (IC) and Eurocity (EC) trains, for which you pay a supplement in both classes and for which reservations may be required. Trains designated *Interregionale* are slower, making more stops. *Regionale* trains are locals, serving a single region. You can buy tickets and make seat reservations at travel agencies displaying the FS symbol up to two months in advance, thereby avoiding long lines at station ticket windows. All tickets must be date-stamped in the small yellow or red machines near the tracks before you board. Once stamped, your ticket is valid for 6 hours if your destination is within 200 kilometers and for 24 hours for destinations beyond that; you can get on and off at will for the duration of the ticket's validity. If you don't stamp your ticket in the machine, you must actively seek out a conductor to validate the ticket on the train, paying an extra 10,000 lire for the service. If you merely wait in your seat for him to collect your ticket, you must pay a 30,000 lire fine. You will pay a hefty surcharge if you purchase your ticket on board the train. Tickets for destinations within a 100-kilometer (62-mile) range can be purchased at any *tabacchi* (tobacconist's). There is a refreshment service on all long-distance trains. Tap water on trains is not drinkable. Carry compact bags for easy overhead storage. Trains are very crowded at holiday times; always reserve.

By Plane

Alitalia and its domestic affiliate **ATI,** plus some privately owned companies such as **Meridiana** and **Airone,** provide service throughout Italy. Alitalia offers several types of discount fares; inquire at travel agencies or at Alitalia agencies in major cities.

By Bus

Regional bus companies provide service over an extensive network of routes throughout Italy. Route information and timetables are usually available at tourist information offices and travel agencies, or at bus company ticket offices. One of the interregional companies providing long-distance service is **SITA** (⊠ Viale Cadorna 105, Florence, ☎ 055/47821).

By Boat

Ferries connect the mainland with all the major islands. Car ferries operate to Sicily, Sardinia, Elba, Ponza, Capri (though taking a car here is not advised), and Ischia, among others. Lake ferries connect the towns on the shores of the Italian lakes: Como, Maggiore, and Garda.

Staying in Italy

Telephones

LOCAL CALLS

Most local calls cost 200 lire. Pay phones take either 100-, 200- or 500-lire coins or *schede telefoniche* (phone cards), which can be purchased in bars, tobacconists, post offices and TELECOM offices, in either 5,000- or 10,000-lire denominations. Local calls cost 200 lire for a minimum of 2 minutes. For *teleselezione* (long-distance direct dialing), place several coins in the slot; unused coins are returned when you push the return button. For information and operators in Europe and the Mediterranean area, dial 15; for intercontinental service, dial 170.

INTERNATIONAL CALLS

To place international calls, many travelers go to the TELECOM telephone exchange, where the operator assigns you a booth, can help place your call, and will collect payment when you have finished. TELECOM exchanges are found in all cities. To place an international call, insert a phone card, dial 00, then the country code, area code, and phone number. The cheaper and easier option, however, will be to use your AT&T, MCI, or Sprint calling card. For **AT&T,** dial access number 172–1011; for **MCI,** access number 172–1022; for **Sprint,** access number 172–1877. You will be connected directly with an operator in the United States.

COUNTRY CODE

The country code for Italy is 39.

Mail

The Italian mail system has been notoriously erratic and occasionally excruciatingly slow. Until a trend toward greater efficiency is confirmed, allow up to 15 days for mail to and from the United States and Canada, almost as much to and from the United Kingdom, and much longer for postcards.

POSTAL RATES
Airmail letters to the United States cost 1,250 lire for up to 20 grams; postcards with a short greeting and signature cost 1,000 lire, but are charged at the letter rate if the message is lengthy. Airmail letters to the United Kingdom cost 750 lire, postcards 650 lire.

RECEIVING MAIL
You can have mail sent to American Express offices or to Italian post offices, marked "fermo posta" and addressed to you c/o Palazzo delle Poste, with the name of the city in which you will pick it up. In either case you must show your passport and pay a small fee.

Shopping
SALES-TAX REFUNDS
Italy's value-added tax, known as the IVA-refund system, is complicated. Foreign tourists who have spent more than 300,000 lire (before tax) in one store can take advantage of it, however. At the time of purchase, with passport or ID in hand, ask the store for an invoice describing the article or articles and the total lire amount. If your destination when you leave Italy is a non-EU country, you must have the invoice stamped at customs upon departure from Italy; if your destination is another EU country, you must obtain the customs stamp upon departure from that country. Once back home—and within 90 days of the date of purchase—you must send the stamped invoice back to the store, which should forward the IVA rebate directly to you. If the store participates in the Europe Tax-Free Shopping System (those that do display a sign to the effect), things are simpler. The invoice provided is a Tax-Free Cheque in the amount of the tax refund, which can be cashed at the Tax-Free Cash Refund window in the transit area of major airports and border crossings.

BARGAINING
Most shops now have *prezzi fissi* (fixed prices), but you may be able to get a discount on a large purchase. Always bargain with a street vendor or at a market (except for food).

Opening and Closing Times
Banks. Banks are open weekdays 8:30–1:30 and 2:45–3:45.

Churches. Churches are usually open from early morning to noon or 12:30, when they close for about two hours or more, opening again in the afternoon until about 7 PM.

Museums. National museums are usually open from 9 AM until 2 and are often closed on Monday, but there are many exceptions. Non-national museums have entirely different hours, which may vary according to season. Most major archaeological sites are open every day, except some holidays. At all museums and sites, ticket offices close an hour or so before official closing time. Always check with the local tourist office for current hours and holiday closings.

Shops. Shops are open, with individual variations, from 9 to 1 and from 3:30 or 4 to 7 or 7:30. They are open from Monday through Saturday, but close for a half day during the week; for example, in Rome most shops (except food shops) are closed on Monday morning (also Saturday afternoon in July and August), though a 1995 ordinance allows greater freedom. Some tourist-oriented shops—in downtown Rome, Florence, and Venice—are open all day, every day.

National Holidays
Offices, shops, and most museums are closed on the following dates: January 1; January 6 (Epiphany); March 30-31 (Easter Sunday and Monday); April 25 (Liberation Day); May 1 (May Day); August 15 (the re-

ligious feast of the Assumption, known as Ferragosto); November 1 (All Saints Day); December 8 (Immaculate Conception); December 25-26. In major cities, services are also closed on local feast days: in Venice the feast of St. Mark (April 25), in Florence that of John the Baptist (June 24), and in Rome that of Sts. Peter and Paul (June 29).

Dining

Generally speaking, a *ristorante* pays more attention to decor, service, and menu than does a *trattoria*, which is simpler and often family-run. An *osteria* used to be a lowly tavern, though now the term may be used to designate a chic and expensive eatery. A *tavola calda* offers hot dishes and snacks, with seating. A *rosticceria* offers the same to take out.

The menu is always posted in the window or just inside the door of an eating establishment. Check to see what is offered, and note whether there are charges for *coperto* (cover) and *servizio* (service), which will increase your check. The coperto charge has been abolished in many eating places. Many restaurants offer a *menu turistico,* usually a complete dinner, limited to a few entrées, at a reasonable price (including taxes and service, with beverages extra).

MEALTIMES

Lunch hour in Rome lasts from 1 to 3, dinner from 8 to 10. Service begins and ends a half hour earlier in Florence and Venice, later in the south. Practically all restaurants close one day a week; some close for winter or summer vacations.

PRECAUTIONS

Tap water is safe in large cities and almost everywhere else unless noted *non potabile.* Bottled mineral water is available everywhere, *gassata* (with bubbles) or *non gassata* (without). If you prefer tap water, ask for *acqua semplice.*

WHAT TO WEAR

Except for restaurants in the $$$$ and occasionally in the $$$ categories, where jacket and tie are advisable, casual attire is acceptable.

RATINGS

Prices are per person and include first course, main course, dessert or fruit, and house wine, where available.

CATEGORY	ROME, MILAN*	OTHER AREAS
$$$$	over 120,000 lire	over 80,000 lire
$$$	65,000 lire–120,000 lire	45,000 lire–80,000 lire
$$	40,000 lire–65,000 lire	25,000 lire–45,000 lire
$	under 40,000 lire	under 25,000 lire

Note that restaurant prices in Venice are slightly higher than those in Rome and Milan; in small cities prices are usually lower.

Lodging

Italy, especially its main tourist capitals Rome, Florence, and Venice, offers a good choice of accommodations. Room rates are on a par with those of most European capitals, although porters, room service, and in-house laundering are disappearing in all but the most elegant hotels. Taxes and service are included in the room rate. Although breakfast is usually quoted in the room rate, it's actually an extra charge that you can decline. The desk might not be happy about it, but make your preference clear when booking or checking in. Air-conditioning also may be an extra charge. In older hotels, room quality may be uneven; if you don't like the room you're given, ask for another. This applies to noise, too; some front rooms are bigger and have views but get street noise. Specify if you care about having either a bathtub or shower, as not all rooms have both. In $$ and $ places, showers may be the drain-in-the-floor type guaranteed to flood the bathroom. Rail stations in major cities have hotel-reservation service booths.

HOTELS

Italian hotels are classified by regional tourist boards from five-star (deluxe) to one-star (modest hotels and small inns). The established price of the room appears on a rate card on the back of the door of your room or inside the closet door, though you may be able to get a lower rate by asking. Any variations above the posted rate should be cause for complaint and should be reported to the local tourist office. CIGA, Jolly, Space, Atahotels, Best Western, Holiday Inn, and Italhotels are among the reliable chains or groups operating in Italy, with CIGA among the most luxurious. Sheraton hotels are having a major impact in Italy, though most, located in Rome, Florence, Bari, Padua, and Catania, tend to be geared toward convention and business travel. There are a few Relais et Châteaux hotels that are noted for individual atmosphere, personal service, and luxury; they are also expensive. The AGIP chain is found mostly on main highways. The Family Hotels group, composed mostly of small $$ and $ family-run hotels, offers good value, reliability, and special attention to families.

Standards in one-star hotels are very uneven. At best, rooms are usually spotlessly clean but basic, with shower and toilets down the hall.

AGRITOURISM

Recent years have seen a boom in Agritourism—short or long stays on rural estates or farms. Popular in Tuscany, Umbria, and other rural areas throughout Italy, many options are near art towns and cities. Agritourism accommodations range in style from rustic simplicity to country chic, and prices vary accordingly. They are ideal if you're traveling with children, as there's always plenty to see and do on the farm; a car or bicycle is mandatory, as most places are some distance from towns. ENIT, the Italian tourist board, and local APT tourist offices can provide information.

RENTALS

An option for families or groups of up to eight people looking for a bargain–or just independence–is renting a town apartment or country house in Italy. Availability is subject to change, so it is best to ask your travel agent or the nearest branch of ENIT, the Italian tourist board, about rentals.

CAMPING

Italy has a wide selection of campgrounds, and the Italians themselves have taken to camping by the thousands, which means that beach or mountain sites will be crammed in July and August. It's best to avoid these peak months. An international camping *carnet* (permit) is required; get one from your local association before leaving home. You can buy a campsite directory such as the detailed guide published by the Touring Club Italiano (available in bookstores) or obtain the free directory of campsites published by the Federazione Italiana del Campeggio in tourist information offices or by mail from the organization (Casella Postale 23, 50041 Calenzano, Florence, FAX 055/882–5918) if you send three international reply coupons.

RATINGS

The following price categories are determined by the cost of two people in a double room.

CATEGORY	ROME, MILAN*	OTHER AREAS
$$$$	over 450,000 lire	over 350,000 lire
$$$	280,000 lire–450,000 lire	200,000 lire–350,000 lire
$$	160,000 lire–280,000 lire	120,000 lire–200,000 lire
$	under 160,000 lire	under 120,000 lire

As with restaurant prices, the cost of hotels in Venice may be slightly more than those shown here.

Tipping

Tipping practices vary depending on where you are. Italians tip smaller amounts in small cities and towns, often not at all in cafés and taxis north of Rome. The following guidelines apply in major cities.

In restaurants, a 15% service charge is usually added to the total, but it doesn't all go to the waiter. In large cities and resorts it is customary to give the waiter a 5% tip in addition to the service charge made on the check.

Charges for service are included in all hotel bills, but smaller tips to staff members are appreciated. In general, in a **$$** hotel, chambermaids should be given about 1,000 lire per room per day, 4,000 lire–5,000 lire per week; bellhops 1,000 lire–2,000 lire. Tip a minimum of 1,000 lire for room service and valet service. Tip breakfast waiters 500 lire–1,000 lire per day per table (at end of stay). These amounts should be increased by 40% in **$$$** hotels, doubled in **$$$$** hotels. Give the concierge about 15% of his bill for services. Tip doormen about 500 lire for calling a cab.

Taxi drivers are happy with 5%–10%. Porters at railroad stations and airports charge a fixed rate per suitcase; tip an additional 500 lire per person, more if the porter is very helpful. Service-station attendants are tipped 500 lire–1,000 lire if they are especially helpful. Tip guides about 2,000 lire per person for a half-day tour, more if they are very good.

ROME

Arriving and Departing

By Plane

Rome's principal airport is at Fiumicino, 29 kilometers (18 miles) from the city. Though its official name is Leonardo da Vinci Airport, everybody calls it Fiumicino. For flight information, call 06/659–53640. The smaller airport of Ciampino is on the edge of Rome and is used as an alternative by international and domestic lines, especially for charter flights. For flight information, call 06/794941.

BETWEEN THE AIRPORT AND DOWNTOWN

To get to downtown Rome from Fiumicino Airport you have a choice of two trains. Ask at the airport (at EPT or train information counters) which one takes you closest to your hotel. The nonstop Airport-Termini express takes you directly to Track 22 at Termini Station, Rome's main train terminal, well served by taxis and the hub of Metro (subway) and bus lines. The ride to Termini takes 30 minutes; departures are hourly, beginning at 7:50 AM, with the final departure at 10:05 PM. Tickets cost 13,000 lire. The other airport train (FM1) runs to Rome and beyond to Monterotondo, a suburban town to the east. The main stops in Rome are at the Trastevere, Ostiense, and Tiburtina stations. At each of these you can find taxis and bus and/or Metro connections to various parts of Rome. This train runs from 6:35 AM to 6:15 PM, with departures every 20 minutes. The ride to Tiburtina takes 40 minutes. Tickets cost 7,000 lire. For either train you buy your ticket at an automatic vending machine (you need Italian currency). There are ticket counters at some stations (Termini Track 22, Trastevere, Tiburtina). Remember to date-stamp your ticket in one of the yellow machines near the track.

A taxi to or from Fiumicino costs about 65,000 lire, including supplements. At a booth inside the terminal you can hire a four-or five-passenger car with driver for a little more. If you decide to take a taxi, use only the yellow or the newer white cabs, which must wait outside the terminal; make sure the meter is running. Gypsy cab drivers solicit your business as you come out of customs; they're not reliable, and their rates may be rip-offs.

Ciampino is connected with the Anagnina Station of the Metro A by bus (every half hour). A taxi between Ciampino and downtown Rome costs about 35,000 lire.

By Train

Termini Station is Rome's main train terminal, although the Tiburtina and Ostiense stations serve some long-distance trains, many commuter trains, and the FM1 line to Fiumicino Airport. For train information, try the English-speaking personnel at the Information Office in Termini, or at any travel agency. Tickets and seats can be reserved and purchased at travel agencies bearing the FS (Ferrovie dello Stato) emblem. Tickets can be purchased up to two months in advance. Short-distance tickets are also sold by tobacconists and from ticket machines (instructions in English) in the stations.

By Bus

There is no central bus station in Rome; long-distance and suburban buses terminate either near Tiburtina Station or near strategically located Metro stops.

By Car

The main access routes from the north are the Autostrada del Sole (A1) from Milan and Florence, and the Aurelia highway (SS 1) from Genoa. The principal route to or from points south, such as Naples, is the southern leg of the Autostrada del Sole (A2). All highways connect with the GRA (Grande Raccordo Anulare), a beltway that encircles Rome and funnels traffic into the city. Markings on the GRA are confusing; take time to study in advance which route into the center best suits you.

Getting Around

The best way to see Rome is to choose an area or a sight that you particularly want to see, reach it by bus or Metro, then explore the area on foot, following one of our itineraries or improvising one to suit your mood and interests. Wear comfortable, sturdy shoes, preferably with thick rubber soles to cushion you against the cobblestones. Heed our advice on security, and try to avoid the noise and polluted air of heavily trafficked streets, taking parallel byways wherever possible.

You can buy transportation route maps at newsstands and at ATAC (bus company) information and ticket booths.

Metrebus

Rome's integrated Metrebus transportation system includes buses and trams (ATAC), Metro and suburban trains and buses (COTRAL), and some other suburban trains (FS) run by the state railways. A ticket valid for 75 minutes on any combination of buses and trams and one admission to the Metro costs 1,500 lire (date-stamp your ticket when boarding the first vehicle and stamp it again when boarding for the last time). Tickets are sold at tobacconists', newsstands, some coffee bars, automatic ticket machines in Metro stations, some bus stops, and at ATAC and COTRAL ticket booths. A BIG tourist ticket, valid for one day on all public transport, costs 6,000 lire. A weekly ticket (Settimanale, also known as CIS) costs 24,000 lire and can be purchased only at ATAC and Metro booths.

By Metro

The Metro provides the easiest and fastest way to get around. It opens at 5:30 AM, and the last train leaves each terminal at 11:30 PM. Metro A runs from the eastern part of the city to Termini Station and past Piazza di Spagna and Piazzale Flaminio to Ottaviano, near St. Peter's and the Vatican Museums. Metro B serves Termini, the Colosseum, and Tiburtina Station (where the FM1 Fiumicino Airport train stops).

By Bus

Orange ATAC (☎ 06/4695–4444) city buses (and a few streetcar lines) run from about 6 AM to midnight, with night buses (indicated N) on some lines (night service may be eliminated entirely; check locally). When entering a bus, remember to board at the rear and exit at the middle. Bus line 119, with compact electric vehicles, makes a circuit of a limited but scenic route from Piazza del Popolo to the Pantheon and Piazza di Spagna. It can save lots of steps, and you can get on and off as you please with a regular 75-minute or BIG ticket.

By Taxi

Taxis wait at stands and, for a small extra charge, can also be called by telephone. The meter starts at 6,400 lire; there are supplements for service after 10 PM, on Sundays and holidays, and for each piece of baggage. Use the yellow or the newer white cabs only, and be very sure to check the meter. To call a cab, phone 06/3570, 06/3875, 06/4994, or 06/88177.

By Bicycle

Bikes provide a pleasant means of getting around when traffic isn't heavy. There are bike-rental shops at Via di Porta Castello 43, near St. Peter's, and at Piazza Navona 69, next to Bar Navona. Rental concessions are at the Piazza di Spagna and Piazza del Popolo Metro stops, and at Largo San Silvestro and Largo Argentina. There are also some in Villa Borghese (at Sector III of the underground parking lot) and at Viale della Pineta and Viale del Bambino on the Pincio.

By Moped

You can rent a moped or scooter and mandatory helmet at **Scoot-a-Long** (⊠ Via Cavour 302, ☎ 06/678–0206) or **St. Peter Moto** (⊠ Via di Porta Castello 43, ☎ 06/687–5714).

Important Addresses and Numbers

Consulates

U.S. (⊠ Via Veneto 121, ☎ 06/46741). **Canadian** (⊠ Via Zara 30, ☎ 06/445981). **U.K.** (⊠ Via Venti Settembre 80a, ☎ 06/482–5441).

Emergencies

Police (☎ 06/4686; the Polizia Statale) and **Carabinieri** (☎ 06/112; militarized police corps): call either for theft, general crimes; **Polizia Municipale** (☎ 06/67691; city police): for traffic violations. **Ambulance** (☎ 06/5510). **Doctor:** for a recommendation call your consulate, the private **Salvator Mundi Hospital** (☎ 06/588961), or the **Rome American Hospital** (☎ 06/22551), which has English-speaking staff members. **Pharmacies:** You will find American and British medicines (or their equivalents) and English-speaking personnel at **Farmacia Internazionale Capranica** (⊠ Piazza Capranica 96, ☎ 06/679–4680), **Farmacia Internazionale Barberini** (⊠ Piazza Barberini 49, ☎ 06/482–5456), and **Farmacia Cola di Rienzo** (⊠ Via Cola di Rienzo 213, ☎ 06/324–3130), among others. They are open 8:30–1 and 4–8; some stay open all night.

English-Language Bookstores

You'll find English-language books and magazines at newsstands in the center of Rome, especially on Via Veneto. Also try the **Economy Book and Video Center** (⊠ Via Torino 136, ☎ 06/474–6877), the **Anglo-American Bookstore** (⊠ Via della Vite 102, ☎ 06/679–5222), or the **Lion Bookshop** (⊠ Via del Babuino 181, ☎ 06/322–5837).

Travel Agencies

American Express (⊠ Piazza di Spagna 38, ☎ 06/67641). **CIT** (⊠ Piazza della Repubblica 64, ☎ 06/482–7052). **CTS** (youth and budget travel, discount fares; Via Genova 16, ☎ 06/46791; for information ☎ 06/467–9271).

Visitor Information

The main **EPT** (Rome Provincial Tourist) office is at Via Parigi 5, 00185 (☎ 06/488–99253; ⊙ Weekdays 8:15–7:15, Sat. 8:15–1:15). There are also EPT booths at Termini Station and Fiumicino Airport. A booth on the main floor of the **ENIT** (National Tourist Board) building at Via Marghera 2 (☎ 06/497–1293; ⊙ Mon., Wed., Fri. 9–1 and 4–6; Tues., Thurs. 9–1) can provide information on destinations in Italy outside Rome.

Municipal tourist information booths are located at Largo Goldoni (⊠ Corner of Via Condotti and Via del Corso in the Spanish Steps area), Via dei Fori Imperiali (⊠ Opposite the entrance to the Roman Forum) and Via Nazionale (⊠ At Palazzo delle Esposizioni). They're open Tuesday–Saturday 10–6, Sunday 10–1.

Guided Tours

Orientation

American Express (☎ 06/67641), **CIT** (☎ 06/47941), and **Appian Line** (☎ 06/488–4151) offer three-hour tours in air-conditioned buses with English-speaking guides, covering Rome with four separate itineraries: "Ancient Rome" (including the Roman Forum and Colosseum), "Classic Rome" (including St. Peter's Basilica, Trevi Fountain, and the Janiculum Hill, with its panorama of the city), "Christian Rome" (some major churches and the Catacombs), and the "Vatican Museums and Sistine Chapel." Most tours cost about 53,000 lire, though the Vatican Museums tour is about 60,000 lire. American Express tours depart from Piazza di Spagna, CIT from Piazza della Repubblica, and Appian Line picks sightseers up at their hotels. The continuous-service Roma Trolley Tour bus makes a circuit of the major sights, with 11 stops. You get on and off as you please; a ticket is valid for 24 hours and costs about 26,000 lire. The bus runs 9:30–6 daily. The least expensive organized bus tour is run by **ATAC,** the municipal bus company, and lasts three hours. Book tours for about 15,000 lire at the ATAC information booth in front of Termini Station. There is at least one tour daily, departing at 2:30 (3:30 in summer).

Almost all operators offer "Rome by Night" tours, with or without dinner and entertainment. Reservations can be made through travel agents.

Special-Interest

You can make your own arrangements (at no cost) to attend a public papal audience in the Vatican or to be at the Sunday blessing at the

Pope's summer residence at Castel Gandolfo, or do it through **CIT** (☎ 06/47941), **Appian Line** (☎ 06/488–4151), or **Carrani** (☎ 06/488–0510). **Secret Walks** (☎ 06/397–28728) conducts small groups on theme walks led by English-speaking connoisseurs of the city.

Excursions

Most operators offer half-day excursions to Tivoli to see the Villa d'Este's spectacular fountains and gardens; Appian Line's and CIT's half-day tours to Tivoli also include Hadrian's Villa and its impressive ancient ruins. Most operators have all-day excursions to Assisi, to Pompeii and/or Capri, and to Florence.

Personal Guides

Visitors can arrange for a personal guide through **American Express** (☎ 06/67641), **CIT** (☎ 06/47941), or the main **EPT** tourist office (☎ 06/488–3748).

Exploring Rome

Antiquity is taken for granted in Rome, where successive ages have piled the present on top of the past—building, layering, and overlapping their own particular segments of Rome's 2,500 years of history to form a remarkably varied urban complex. Most of the city's major sights are located in a fairly small area known as the *centro*. At its heart lies ancient Rome, site of the Forum and Colosseum. It was around this core that the other sections of the city grew up through the ages: medieval Rome, which covered the horn of land that pushes the Tiber toward the Vatican and extended across the river into Trastevere; and Renaissance Rome, which was erected upon medieval foundations and extended as far as the Vatican, with beautiful villas created in what was then the outskirts of the city.

The layout of the centro is highly irregular, but several landmarks serve as orientation points to identify the areas that most visitors come to see: the Colosseum, the Pantheon and Piazza Navona, St. Peter's, the Spanish Steps, and Villa Borghese. You'll need a good map to find your way around; newsstands offer a wide choice. Energetic sightseers will walk a lot, a much more pleasant way to see the city now that some traffic has been barred from the centro during the day; others might choose to take taxis, buses, or the Metro. The important thing is to relax and enjoy Rome. Don't try to see everything, but do take time to savor its pleasures. If you are in Rome during a hot spell, do as the Romans do: Start out early in the morning, have a light lunch and a long siesta during the hottest hours, then resume sightseeing in the late afternoon and end your evening with a leisurely meal outdoors, refreshed by cold Frascati wine and the *ponentino,* the cool evening breeze.

Ancient Rome

Numbers in the margin correspond to points of interest on the Roma (Rome) map.

❶ Start your first tour at the city's center, in **Piazza Venezia.** Behind the enormous marble monument honoring the first king of unified Italy,
❷ Victor Emmanuel II, stands the **Campidoglio** (Capitol Square) on the
★ **Capitoline Hill**. The majestic ramp and beautifully proportioned piazza are Michelangelo's handiwork, as are the three palaces. **Palazzo Senatorio** at the center is still the ceremonial seat of Rome's city hall; it was built over the Tabularium, where ancient Rome's state archives were kept.

The palaces flanking the Palazzo Senatorio contain the **Capitoline Museums.** On the left, the **Museo Capitolino** holds some fine classical sculp-
❸

660

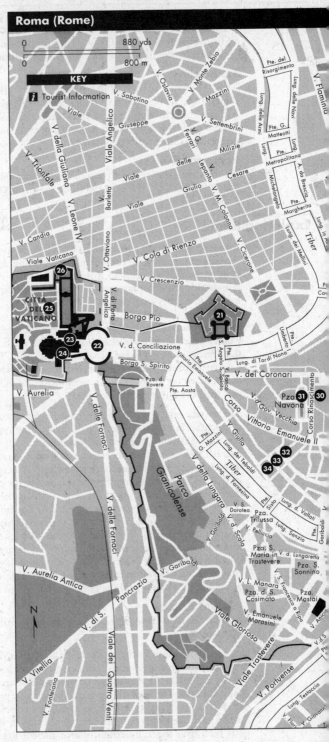

Roma (Rome)

tures, including the gilded bronze equestrian statue of Marcus Aure-lius that once stood on the pedestal in the piazza, as well as the *Dying Gaul,* the *Capitoline Venus,* and a fascinating series of portrait busts

❹ of ancient philosophers and emperors. In the courtyard of the **Palazzo dei Conservatori,** on the right of the piazza, you can use the mammoth fragments of a colossal statue of the emperor Constantine as amusing props for snapshots. Inside you will find splendidly frescoed salons, as well as sculptures and paintings. ⊠ *Piazza del Campidoglio,* ☎ *06/671–002475.* ☞ *10,000 lire, free last Sun. of month.* ☉ *May–Sept., Tues. 9–1:30 and 5–8, Wed.–Fri. 9–1:30, Sat. 9–1:30 and 8–11, Sun. 9–1; Oct.–Apr., Tues. and Sat. 9–1:30 and 5–8; Wed.–Fri. 9–1:30, Sun. 9–1.*

❺ The Campidoglio is also the site of the very old church of the **Aracoeli,** which you can reach by way of the stairs on the far side of the Museo Capitolino. Stop in to see the medieval pavement; the Renaissance gilded ceiling that commemorates the victory of Lepanto; some Pinturicchio frescoes; and a much-revered wooden statue of the Holy Child. The Campidoglio gardens offer some good views of the heart of ancient Rome, the Imperial Fora, built when the original Roman Forum be-came too small for the city's burgeoning needs.

❻ In the valley below the Campidoglio, the **Foro Romano** (Roman Forum), once only a marshy hollow, became the political, commercial, and so-cial center of Rome, studded with public meeting halls, shops, and temples. As Rome declined, these monuments lost their importance and were eventually destroyed by fire or the invasions of barbarians. Rub-ble accumulated (though much of it was carted off later by medieval home-builders as construction material), and the site reverted to marshy pastureland; sporadic excavations began at the end of the 19th century.

You don't really have to try to make sense of the mass of marble frag-ments scattered over the area of the Roman Forum. Just consider that 2,000 years ago this was the center of the Mediterranean world. Wan-der down the Via Sacra and climb the Palatine Hill, where the emper-ors had their palaces and where 16th-century cardinals strolled in elaborate Italian gardens. From the belvedere you have a good view of the Circus Maximus. ⊠ *Entrances on Via dei Fori Imperiali, Piazza Santa Maria Nova, and Via di San Gregorio,* ☎ *06/699–0110.* ☞ *12,000 lire.* ☉ *Apr.–Sept., Mon.–Sat. 9–6, Sun. 9–1; Oct.–Mar., Mon.–Sat. 9–3, Sun. 9–1.*

Leave the Forum from the exit at Piazza Santa Maria Nova, near the
★ ❼ Arch of Titus, and head for the **Colosseum,** inaugurated in AD 80 with a program of games and shows that lasted 100 days. On opening day alone some 5,000 wild animals perished in the arena. The Colosseum could hold more than 50,000 spectators; it was faced with marble, dec-orated with stuccos, and had an ingenious system of awnings to pro-vide shade. Try to see it both in daytime and at night, when yellow floodlights make it a magical sight. The Colosseum, by the way, takes its name from a colossal, 118-foot statue of Nero that stood nearby. You must pay a fee to explore the upper levels. Some sections of the amphitheater may be closed off during ongoing restorations. ⊠ *Piazza del Colosseo,* ☎ *06/700–4261.* ☞ *8,000 lire to upper levels.* ☉ *Apr.–Sept., Mon., Tues., and Thurs.–Sat. 9–7, Sun. and Wed. 9–1; Oct.–Mar., Mon., Tues., and Thurs.–Sat. 9–3.*

NEED A
BREAK?

For delicious *gelati* (ice creams) try **Ristoro della Salute** (⊠ Piazza del Colosseo 2a), one of Rome's best *gelaterie*.

8 Stroll past the **Arch of Constantine.** The reliefs depict Constantine's victory over Maxentius at the Milvian Bridge. Just before this battle in AD 312, Constantine had a vision of a cross in the heavens and heard the words: "In this sign thou shalt conquer." The victory led not only to the construction of this majestic marble arch but also to a turning point in the history of Christianity: Soon afterward a grateful Constantine decreed that it was a lawful religion and should be tolerated throughout the empire.

9 A fairly long but pleasant walk takes you to the **Baths of Caracalla,** which numbered among ancient Rome's most beautiful and luxurious such establishments, inaugurated by Caracalla in 217 and used until the 6th century. An ancient version of a swanky athletic club, the baths were open to the public; citizens could bathe, socialize, and exercise in huge pools and richly decorated halls and libraries, now towering ruins. ✉ *Via delle Terme di Caracalla.* 🎫 *8,000 lire.* ⊙ *Apr.–Sept., Tues.–Sat. 9–6, Sun. and Mon. 9–1; Oct.–Mar., Tues.–Sat. 9–3, Sun.–Mon. 9–1.*

Piazzas and Fountains

10 **Piazza del Popolo** is one of the largest and airiest squares in Rome, but for many years it was just an exceptionally beautiful parking lot with a 3,000-year-old obelisk in the middle. Now most traffic has been **11** barred, and the piazza is open to strollers. The church of **Santa Maria del Popolo** over in the corner of the piazza near the arch stands out more, now that it has been cleaned, and is rich in art, including two stunning Caravaggios in the chapel to the left of the main altar.

12 If you're interested in antiques, stroll along **Via del Babuino.** If trendy fashions and accessories suit your fancy, take Via del Corso and turn into **13** **Via Condotti,** Rome's most expensive shopping street. Here you can ogle fabulous jewelry, designer fashions, and accessories in the windows of Buccellati, Ferragamo, Valentino, Gucci, and Bulgari.

NEED A
BREAK?

The more-than-200-year-old **Antico Caffè Greco** (✉ Via Condotti 86; closed Sun.) is the haunt of writers, artists, and well-groomed ladies toting Gucci shopping bags. With its small marble-topped tables and velour settees, it's a nostalgic sort of place—Goethe, Byron, and Liszt were regulars here, and even Buffalo Bill stopped in when his road show came to town. Table service is expensive.

Via Condotti gives you a head-on view of the Spanish Steps in **Piazza 14** **di Spagna,** and of the church of **Trinità dei Monti.** In the center of the piazza is Bernini's **Fountain of the Barcaccia** (Old Boat), around which Romans and tourists cool themselves on hot summer nights. The 200-★ **15** year-old **Spanish Steps,** named for the Spanish Embassy to the Holy See, opposite the American Express office, are a popular rendezvous, especially for the young people who throng this area. On weekend afternoons, Via del Corso is packed with wall-to-wall teenagers, and McDonald's, tucked away in a corner of Piazza di Spagna beyond the American Express office, is a mob scene. **Babington's Tea Room,** by contrast, to the left of the Spanish Steps, is a stylish institution that caters to an upscale clientele.

To the right of the Spanish Steps is the **Keats and Shelley Memorial House.** Keats died in the rooms he rented here, and the building is now a museum. ✉ *Piazza di Spagna 26,* ☎ *06/678–4235.* 🎫 *5,000 lire.* ⊙ *June–Sept., weekdays 9–1 and 3–6; Oct.–May, weekdays 9–1 and 2:30–5:30.*

★ ⑯ Head for Via del Tritone and cross this heavily trafficked shopping street into narrow Via della Stamperia, which leads to the **Fontana di Trevi** (Trevi Fountain), a spectacular fantasy of mythical sea creatures and cascades of splashing water. Legend has it that visitors must toss a coin into the fountain to ensure their return to Rome, but you'll have to force your way past crowds of tourists and aggressive souvenir vendors to do so. The fountain as you see it was completed in the mid-1700s, but there had been a drinking fountain on the site for centuries. Pope Urban VIII almost sparked a revolt when he slapped a tax on wine to cover the expenses of having the fountain repaired.

⑰ At the top of Via del Tritone, **Piazza Barberini** boasts two fountains by Bernini: the jaunty **Triton** in the middle of the square and the **Fountain of the Bees** at the corner of Via Veneto. Decorated with the heraldic Barberini bees, this latter shell-shaped fountain bears an inscription that was immediately regarded as an unlucky omen by the superstitious Romans, for it erroneously stated that the fountain had been erected in the 22nd year of the reign of Pope Urban VIII, who commissioned it, whereas in fact the 21st anniversary of his election was still some weeks away. The wrong numeral was hurriedly erased, but to no avail: Urban died eight days before the beginning of his 22nd year as pontiff.

⑱ A few steps up Via delle Quattro Fontane is the **Palazzo Barberini,** Rome's most splendid 17th-century palace, now surrounded by rather unkempt gardens and occupied in part by the **Galleria Nazionale di Arte Antica.** Visit the latter to see Raphael's *Fornarina*, many other fine paintings, some lavishly frescoed ceilings, and a charming suite of rooms decorated in 1782 on the occasion of the marriage of a Barberini heiress. ✉ *Via delle Quattro Fontane 13,* ☎ *06/481–4591.* 🎫 *8,000 lire.* ☉ *Tues.–Sat. 9–2, Sun. 9–1.*

⑲ One of Rome's oddest sights is the **crypt** of the **Church of Santa Maria della Concezione** on Via Veneto, just above the Fountain of the Bees. In four chapels beneath the main church, the skeletons and scattered bones of some 4,000 dead Capuchin monks are arranged to form decorative designs, a macabre practice peculiar to the Baroque age. ✉ *Via Veneto 27,* ☎ *06/462850.* 🎫 *Free (donations encouraged).* ☉ *Daily 9–noon and 3–6.*

The lower reaches of Via Veneto are quiet and sedate, but at the intersection with Via Bissolati, otherwise known as "Airline Row," the avenue comes to life. The big white palace on the right is the U.S. Embassy, and the even bigger white palace beyond it is the luxurious **Hotel Excelsior.** Together with next-door Doney's and the Café de Paris across the street, the Excelsior was a landmark of La Dolce Vita, that effervescent period during the 1950s when movie stars, playboys, and exiled royalty played hide-and-seek with press agents and paparazzi, ducking in and out of nightclubs and hotel rooms along the Via Veneto. The atmosphere of Via Veneto is considerably more sober now, and its cafés cater more to tourists than to the rich and famous.

Via Veneto ends at **Porta Pinciana,** a gate in the 12-mile stretch of defensive walls built by Emperor Aurelian in the 3rd century; 400 years later, when the Goths got too close for comfort, Belisarius reinforced the gate with two massive towers. Beyond is **Villa Borghese,** most famous of Rome's parks, studded with tall pines that are gradually dying off as pollution and age take their toll. Inside the park, strike off to

⑳ the right toward the **Galleria Borghese,** a pleasure palace created by Cardinal Scipione Borghese in 1613 as a showcase for his fabulous sculpture collection. In the throes of structural repairs for several years, the now-public gallery is, at press time, only partially open to visitors. It's still worth a visit to see the seductive reclining statue of Pauline Borghese by Canova and some extraordinary works by Bernini, among them the unforgettable *Apollo and Daphne,* in which marble is transformed into flesh and foliage. With restorations dragging on, perhaps into 1997, a few of the best works, including the Caravaggios, have been moved from the upstairs picture gallery, which is closed, to the San Michele complex in Trastevere, where they are on view (Via di San Michele, ☎ 06/581–6732; ☑ 4,000 lire; ☉ Tues.–Sat. 9–7, Sun. 9–1). During reconstruction, the entrance to Galleria Borghese is on Via Raimondi, reached from Via Pinciana. ✉ *Via Pinciana (Piazzale Museo Borghese–Villa Borghese),* ☎ *06/854–8577.* ☑ *4,000 lire.* ☉ *May–Sept., Tues.–Sat. 9–7, Sun. 9–1; Oct.–Apr., Tues.–Sat. 9–1:30, Sun. 9–1.*

Castel Sant'Angelo–St. Peter's

Ponte Sant'Angelo, an ancient bridge spanning the Tiber, is decorated with lovely Baroque angels designed by Bernini. From the bridge there are fine views of St. Peter's, in the distance, and of the **Castel Sant'Angelo,** ㉑ a formidable fortress that was originally built as the tomb of Emperor Hadrian in the 2nd century AD. In its early days, it looked much like the **Augusteo,** or Tomb of Augustus, which still stands in more or less its original form across the river. Hadrian's Tomb was incorporated into the city's walls and served as a military stronghold during the barbarian invasions. According to legend it got its present name in the 6th century, when Pope Gregory the Great, passing by in a religious procession, saw an angel with a sword appear above the ramparts to signal the end of the plague that was raging. Enlarged and fortified, the castle became a refuge for the popes, who fled to it along the **Passetto,** an arcaded passageway that links it with the Vatican. Inside the castle you see ancient corridors, medieval cells, and Renaissance salons, a museum of antique weapons, courtyards piled with stone cannonballs, and terraces with great views of the city. There's a pleasant bar with outdoor tables on one level. The highest terrace of all, under the newly restored bronze statue of the legendary angel, is the one from which Puccini's heroine Tosca threw herself to her death. ✉ *Lungotevere Castello 50,* ☎ *06/687–5036.* ☑ *8,000 lire.* ☉ *Mon.–Sat. 9–2, Sun. 9–noon. Closed 2nd and 4th Tues. of month.*

Via della Conciliazione, the broad avenue leading to St. Peter's Basilica, was created by Mussolini's architects by razing blocks of old houses. This opened up a vista of the basilica, giving the eye time to adjust to its mammoth dimensions, and thereby spoiling the effect Bernini sought when he enclosed his vast, oval-shaped square in the embrace ㉒ of huge quadruple colonnades. In **Piazza San Pietro** (St. Peter's Square), which has held up to 400,000 people at one time, look for the stone disks in the pavement halfway between the fountains and the obelisk. From these points the colonnades seem to be formed of a single row of columns all the way around.

When you enter St. Peter's Square (completed in 1667), you are entering Vatican territory. Since the Lateran Treaty of 1929, **Vatican City** has been an independent and sovereign state, which covers about 108 acres and is surrounded by thick, high walls. Its gates are watched over by the Swiss Guards, who still wear the colorful dress uniforms designed by Michelangelo. Sovereign of this little state is John Paul II, 264th pope of the Roman Catholic Church. At noon on Sunday, the ㉓ pope appears at his third-floor study window in the **Vatican Palace,** to the right of the basilica, to bless the crowd in the square. (Note: Entry to St. Peter's, the Vatican Museums, and all other sites within Vatican City, including the Gardens, is barred to those wearing shorts, miniskirts, sleeveless T-shirts, and otherwise revealing clothing. Women should carry scarves to cover bare shoulders and upper arms or wear blouses that come to the elbow. Men should dress modestly, in slacks and shirts.) Free 90-minute tours of St. Peter's Basilica are offered in English daily (usually starting about 10 AM and 3 PM) by volunteer guides. They start at the information desk under the basilica portico.

★ ㉔ **St. Peter's Basilica** is one of Rome's most impressive sights. It takes a while to absorb the sheer magnificence of it, however, and its rich decoration may not be to everyone's taste. Its size alone is overwhelming, and the basilica is best appreciated when it is being used as the lustrous background for ecclesiastical ceremonies thronged with the faithful. The original basilica was built in the early 4th century AD by the emperor Constantine, above an earlier shrine that supposedly marked the burial place of St. Peter. After more than a thousand years, the old basilica was so decrepit it had to be torn down. The task of building a new, much larger one took almost 200 years, and employed the architectural genius of Alberti, Bramante, Raphael, Peruzzi, Antonio Sangallo the Younger, and Michelangelo, who died before the dome he had planned could be completed. The structure was finally finished in 1626.

The basilica is full of extraordinary works of art. Among the most famous is Michelangelo's *Pietà* (1498), seen in the first chapel on the right just as you enter the basilica. Michelangelo carved four *Pietà*s; this one is the earliest and best known, two others are in Florence, and the fourth, the *Rondanini Pietà,* is in Milan.

At the end of the central aisle is the bronze statue of **St. Peter,** its foot worn by centuries of reverent kisses. The bronze throne above the altar in the apse was created by Bernini to contain a simple wood and ivory chair once believed to have belonged to St. Peter. Bernini's bronze baldachin over the papal altar was made with metal stripped from the portico of the Pantheon at the order of Pope Urban VIII, one of the powerful Roman Barberini family. His practice of plundering ancient monuments for material with which to carry out his grandiose schemes inspired the famous quip, *"Quod non fecerunt barbari, fecerunt Barberini"* ("What the barbarians didn't do, the Barberini did").

As you stroll up and down the aisles and transepts, observe the fine mosaic copies of famous paintings above the altars, the monumental tombs and statues, and the fine stucco work. Stop at the **Treasury** (Historical Museum), which contains some priceless liturgical objects.

Vatican Grottoes

The entrance to the so-called **Vatican Grottoes,** or crypt, is in one of the huge piers at the crossing. It's best to leave this visit for last, as the crypt's only exit takes you outside the church. The crypt contains chapels and the tombs of many popes. It occupies the area of the original basilica, over the necropolis, the ancient burial ground where evidence of what may be St. Peter's burial place has been found. You can book special tours of the necropolis. To see the roof and dome of the basilica, take the elevator or climb the stairs in the courtyard near the exit from the Vatican Grottoes. From the roof you can climb a short interior staircase to the base of the dome for an overhead view of the basilica's interior. Only if you are in good shape should you attempt the very long, strenuous, and claustrophobic climb up the narrow stairs to the balcony of the lantern atop the dome, where you can look down on the Vatican Gardens and out across all of Rome. ⊠ *St. Peter's Basilica,* ☎ 06/6988–4466. ☉ *Apr.–Sept., daily 7–7; Oct.–Mar., daily 7–6. Treasury (Museo Storico-Artistico; entrance in Sacristy).* 🎟 *3,000* *lire.* ☼ *Apr.–Sept., daily 9–6:30; Oct.–Mar., daily 9–5:30. Roof and Dome (entrance in courtyard to the left as you leave basilica).* 🖃 *6,000 lire if you wish to use the elevator, 5,000 lire if you climb the spiral ramp on foot.* ☼ *Apr.–Sept., daily 8–6; Oct.–Mar., daily 8–5. Vatican Grottoes (Tombs of the Popes; entrance alternates from one or the other of the piers at the crossing).* 🖃 *Free.* ☼ *Apr.–Sept., daily 7–6; Oct.–Mar., daily 7–5. Necropolis: Apply a few days in advance to Ufficio Scavi, left beyond Arco delle Campane entrance to Vatican, or try in morning for the same day,* ☎ *06/6988–5318.* 🖃 *10,000 lire for 2-hr guided visit, 6,000 lire with tape cassette.* ☼ *Ufficio Scavi office hrs: Mon.–Sat. 9–5; closed Sun. and religious holidays.*

For many visitors, a **papal audience** is the highlight of a trip to Rome. Mass audiences take place on Wednesday morning in a modern audience hall (capacity 7,000) off the left-hand colonnade or in St. Peter's Square. Tickets are necessary, but you can also see the Pope when he appears at the window of the **Vatican Palace** to bless the crowd in the square below at noon on Sunday. He also blesses the public on summer Sundays when he's at the papal residence at **Castel Gandolfo.** ⊠ *For audience tickets, write well in advance to Prefettura della Casa Pontificia (00120 Vatican City), indicating the date you prefer, language you speak, and hotel in which you will stay. Pick up free tickets from 4–6 PM at North American College, Via dell 'Umiltà 30 (*☎ *06/678–9184), or apply to Papal Prefecture (Prefettura), which you reach through a bronze door in right-hand colonnade,* ☎ *06/6988–4466;* ☼ *Mon. and Tues. 9–1. Or arrange for tickets through a travel agent: Carrani Tours, Via V. E. Orlando 95,* ☎ *06/488–0510; Appian Line, Via Barberini 109,* ☎ *06/488–4151.* 🖃 *About 40,000 lire (including transportation) if booked through an agent or hotel concierge.*

㉕ Guided tours through the **Vatican Gardens**—an hour by bus and an hour on foot—show you some attractive landscaping, a few historical monuments, fountains, and the lovely 16th-century house of Pius IV designed by Pirro Ligorio. These tours give you a different perspective of the basilica itself. ⊠ *Tickets at information office, on left side of St. Peter's Square,* ☎ *06/6988–4466.* ☼ *Mon.–Sat. 8:30–7. Garden tour cost: 16,000 lire. Available Mon., Tues., and Thurs.–Sat.*

From the St. Peter's Square information office you can take a shuttle bus (cost: 2,000 lire) directly to the Vatican Museums. This operates every morning, except Wednesday and Sunday, gives you a glimpse of the Vatican Gardens, and saves you the 15-minute walk that goes left from the square and continues along the Vatican walls.

㉖ The collections in the **Vatican Museums** cover nearly 8 kilometers (5 miles) of displays. If you have time, allow at least half a day for Castel Sant'Angelo and St. Peter's, and another half day for the museums. Posters at the museum entrance plot out a choice of four color-coded itineraries; the shortest takes about 90 minutes, the longest more than four hours, depending on your rate of progress.

Sistine Chapel

★ No matter which tour you take, it will include the famed **Sistine Chapel.** In 1508, Pope Julius II commissioned Michelangelo to paint in fresco the more than 10,000 square feet of the chapel's ceiling. For four years Michelangelo dedicated himself to painting over fresh plaster, and the result was a masterpiece. Recent cleaning, now completed, has removed centuries of soot and revealed the ceiling's original and surprisingly brilliant colors.

You can try to avoid the tour groups by going early or late, allowing yourself enough time before the closing hour. In peak season, the crowds definitely detract from your appreciation of this outstanding artistic achievement. To make sense of the figures on the ceiling, buy an illustrated guide or rent a taped commentary. A pair of binoculars also helps.

The Vatican collections are so rich that unless you are an expert in art history you will probably want to merely skim the surface, concentrating on pieces that strike your fancy. If you really want to see the museums thoroughly, you will have to come back again and again. Some of the highlights that might be of interest on your first tour are the newly re-organized Egyptian collection and the *Laocoön*, the *Belvedere Torso*, which inspired Michelangelo, and the *Apollo Belvedere*. The Raphael Rooms are decorated with masterful frescoes, and there are more Raphaels in the *Pinacoteca* (Picture Gallery). At the Quattro Cancelli, near the entrance to the Picture Gallery, a rather spartan cafeteria provides basic nonalcoholic refreshments. ⊠ *Viale Vaticano,* ☎ *06/6988–3332.* 🎫 *15,000 lire, free on last Sun. of the month.* 🕙 *Easter period and July–Sept., weekdays 8:45–5, Sat. 8:45–2; Oct.–June, Mon.–Sat. 8:45–2. Ticket office closes 1 hr before museums close. Closed Sun., except last Sun. of the month, and religious holidays: Jan. 1, Jan. 6, Feb. 11, Mar. 19, Easter Sun. and Mon., May 1, Ascension Thurs., Corpus Christi, June 29, Aug. 15–16, Nov. 1, Dec. 8, Dec. 25–26.*

NEED A BREAK?	Near the Vatican are many good trattorias that are preferable to the touristy eateries opposite the Vatican Museums entrance. At moderately priced **La Caravella** (⊠ Via degli Scipioni 32, corner of Via Vespasiano, off Piazza Risorgimento; closed Thurs.) you can lunch on pizza or try the homemade pasta and other specialties of Roman and Abruzzo cooking. **Dino e Toni** (⊠ Via Leone IV 60, near Largo Trionfale; closed Sun.) is a typical Roman trattoria, hospitable and moderately priced. There are also several others on and around Borgo Pio.

Old Rome

㉗ Take Via del Plebiscito from Piazza Venezia to the huge **Church of the Gesù.** This paragon of Baroque style is the tangible symbol of the power of the Jesuits, who were a major force in the Counter-Reformation in Europe. Encrusted with gold and precious marbles, the Gesù has a fantastically painted ceiling that flows down over the pillars, merging with painted stucco figures to complete the three-dimensional illusion.

㉘ On your way to the Pantheon you will pass **Santa Maria Sopra Minerva,** a Gothic church built over a Roman temple. Inside there are some beautiful frescoes by Filippo Lippi; outside there is a charming elephant by Bernini with an obelisk on its back.

㉙ Originally built in 27 BC by Augustus's general Agrippa and rebuilt by Hadrian in the 2nd century AD, the **Pantheon** is one of Rome's finest, best-preserved, and perhaps least appreciated ancient monuments. Romans and tourists alike pay little attention to it, and on summer evenings it serves mainly as a backdrop for all the action in the square in front. It represents a fantastic feat of construction, however. The huge columns of the portico and the original bronze doors form the entrance to a majestic hall covered by the largest dome of its kind ever built, wider even than that of St. Peter's. In ancient times the entire interior was encrusted with rich decorations of gilt bronze and marble that were plundered by later emperors and popes. ⊠ *Piazza della Rotonda.* 🕙 *Mon.–Sat. 9–2, Sun. 9–1.*

NEED A BREAK?	There are several sidewalk cafés on the square in front of the Pantheon, all of which are good places to nurse a cappuccino while you observe

the scene. Serious coffee drinkers also like **Tazza d'Oro** (⌧ Via degli Orfani 84), just off Piazza della Rotonda. And for a huge variety of ice creams in natural flavors, **Giolitti** (⌧ Via Uffici del Vicario 40; closed Mon.) is generally considered by gelato addicts to be the best in Rome. It also has good snacks and a quick-lunch counter.

30 On Via della Dogana Vecchia, stop in at the church of **San Luigi dei Francesi** to see the three paintings by Caravaggio in the last chapel on the left; have a few hundred-lire coins handy for the light machine. The clergy of San Luigi considered the artist's roistering and unruly lifestyle scandalous enough, but his realistic treatment of sacred subjects was just too much for them. They rejected his first version of the altarpiece and weren't particularly happy with the other two works either. Thanks to the intercession of Caravaggio's patron, an influential cardinal, they were persuaded to keep them—a lucky thing, since they are now recognized to be among the artist's finest paintings. ☉ *Fri.–Wed. 7:30–12:30 and 3:30–7, Thurs. 7:30–12:30.*

★ **31** Just beyond San Luigi is **Piazza Navona,** an elongated 17th-century piazza that traces the oval form of the underlying Circus of Diocletian. At the center, Bernini's lively **Fountain of the Four Rivers** is a showpiece. The four statues represent rivers in the four corners of the world: the Nile, with its face covered in allusion to its then unknown source; the Ganges; the Danube; and the River Plate, with its hand raised. And here we have to give the lie to the legend that this was Bernini's mischievous dig at Borromini's design of the facade of the church of **Sant'Agnese in Agone,** from which the statue seems to be shrinking in horror. The fountain was created in 1651; work on the church's facade began some time later. The piazza dozes in the morning, when little groups of pensioners sun themselves on the stone benches and children pedal tricycles around the big fountain. In the late afternoon the sidewalk cafés fill up for the aperitif hour, and in the evening, especially in good weather, the piazza comes to life with a throng of street artists, vendors, tourists, and Romans out for their evening *passeggiata* (promenade).

NEED A BREAK?
The sidewalk tables of the **Tre Scalini** café (⌧ Piazza Navona 30; closed Wed.) offer a grandstand view of this gorgeous piazza. Treat yourself to a *tartufo,* the chocolate ice-cream specialty that was invented here. The restaurant is also a pleasant place for a moderately priced lunch. For a salad or light lunch, go to **Cul de Sac** (⌧ Piazza Pasquino 73, just off Piazza Navona) or to **Insalata Ricca** (⌧ Via del Paradiso, next to the church of Sant'Andrea della Valle). Both are informal and inexpensive.

32 Across Corso Vittorio is **Campo dei Fiori** (Field of Flowers), the site of a crowded and colorful daily morning market. The hooded bronze figure brooding over the piazza is philosopher Giordano Bruno, who was **33** burned at the stake here for heresy. The adjacent **Piazza Farnese,** with fountains made of Egyptian granite basins from the Baths of Caracalla, **34** is an airy setting for **Palazzo Farnese,** now the French Embassy, one of the most beautiful of Rome's many Renaissance palaces. There are several others in the immediate area: **Palazzo Spada,** a Wedgwood kind of palace encrusted with stuccos and statues; **Palazzo della Cancelleria,** a massive building that is now the Papal Chancellery, one of the many Vatican-owned buildings in Rome that enjoy extraterritorial privileges; and the fine old palaces along Via Giulia.

This is a section to wander through, getting a feel for the daily life in a centuries-old setting, and looking into the dozens of antiques shops. Stroll along Via Arenula into a rather gloomy part of Rome bounded by Piazza Campitelli and Lungotevere Cenci, the ancient Jewish ghetto. Among the most interesting sights here are the pretty **Fountain of the Tartarughe** (Turtles) on Piazza Mattei, the **Via Portico d'Ottavia,** with medieval inscriptions and friezes on the old buildings, and the **Teatro di Marcello,** a theater built by Julius Caesar to hold 20,000 spectators.

35 A pleasant place to end your walk is on **Tiberina Island.** To get there,
36 walk across the ancient **Fabricio Bridge,** built in 62 BC, the oldest bridge in the city.

Off the Beaten Path

If the sky promises a gorgeous sunset, head for the **Terrazza del Pincio** above Piazza del Popolo, a vantage point prized by Romans.

For a look at a real patrician palace, see the **Galleria Doria Pamphili,** still the residence of a princely family. You can visit the gallery housing the family's art collection and also some of the magnificently furnished private apartments. ⊠ *Piazza del Collegio Romano 1/a, near Piazza Venezia,* ☎ *06/679–7323.* 🎫 *10,000 lire; additional 5,000 lire for guided visit of private rooms.* ☉ *Mon., Tues., and Fri.–Sun. 10–1.*

Make an excursion to **Ostia Antica,** the well-preserved Roman port city near the sea, as rewarding as an excursion to Pompeii and much easier to get to from Rome. There's a regular train service from the Ostiense Station (Piramide Metro stop). ⊠ *Via dei Romagnoli, Ostia Antica,* ☎ *06/565–1405.* 🎫 *8,000 lire.* ☉ *Daily 9–1 hr before sunset.*

Delve into the world of the Etruscans, who inhabited Italy even in pre-Roman times and have left fascinating evidence of their relaxed, sensual lifestyle. Visit the **Museo Nazionale di Villa Giulia,** in a gorgeous Renaissance mansion with a full-scale Etruscan temple (and a small coffee bar) in the garden. You'll see smiles as enigmatic as that of the Mona Lisa on deities and other figures in terra cotta, bronze, and gold. Ask especially to see the **Castellani collection of ancient jewelry** (and copies) hidden away on the upper floor. ⊠ *Piazza di Villa Giulia 9,* ☎ *06/320–1951.* 🎫 *8,000 lire.* ☉ *Tues.–Sat. 9–7, Sun. 9–1.*

Shopping

Shopping is part of the fun of being in Rome, no matter what your budget. The best buys are leather goods of all kinds, from gloves to handbags and wallets to jackets; silk goods; and high-quality knitwear. Shops are closed on Sunday and on Monday morning; in July and August, they close on Saturday afternoon as well.

Antiques

A well-trained eye will spot some worthy old prints and minor antiques in the city's fascinating little shops. For prints, browse among the stalls at **Piazza Fontanelle Borghese** or stop in at **Casali** (Piazza della Rotonda 81a), at the Pantheon, or at **Tanca** (Salita dei Crescenzi 10), also near the Pantheon. For minor antiques, **Via dei Coronari** and other streets in the **Piazza Navona** area are good. The most prestigious antiques dealers are situated in **Via del Babuino** and its environs.

Boutiques

Via Condotti, directly across from the Spanish Steps, and the streets running parallel to Via Condotti, as well as its cross streets, form the most elegant and expensive shopping area in Rome. Lower-price fashions may be found on display at shops on **Via Frattina** and **Via del Corso.**

Shopping Districts

Romans themselves do much of their shopping along **Via Cola di Rienzo** and **Via Nazionale.** Among the huge new shopping malls dotting Rome's outskirts, CinecittàDue is easiest to reach; just take Metro A to the Subaugusta stop. The complex has 100 shops, as well as snack bars and cafés.

Religious Articles

These abound in the shops around St. Peter's, on **Via di Porta Angelica** and **Via della Conciliazione,** and in the souvenir shops tucked away on the roof and at the crypt exit in St. Peter's itself.

Food and Flea Markets

The open-air markets at **Campo dei Fiori** and in many neighborhoods throughout the city are colorful sights. The flea market held at **Porta Portese** on Sunday morning is stocked mainly with new or secondhand clothing. If you go, beware of pickpockets and purse snatchers.

Dining

There are plenty of fine restaurants in Rome serving various Italian regional cuisines and international specialties with a flourish of linen and silver, as well as a whopping *conto* (check) at the end. If you want family-style cooking and prices, try a trattoria, a usually smallish and unassuming, often family-run place. Fast-food places and Chinese restaurants are proliferating in Rome. Prix-fixe tourist menus can be scanty and unimaginative. Brunch is catching on. The Hassler, Hilton, and De La Ville hotels started a Sunday trend that has now filtered down to less pricy levels. On weekdays, try brunch at the Jazz Café, (⊠ Via Zanardelli 12), the Replay Café, (⊠ Piazza delle Coppelle 43), or Be Vi (⊠ Piazza Ricci 140). During August many restaurants close for vacation. For details and price-category definitions, *see* Dining *in* Staying in Italy, *above.*

$$$$ ✕ **El Toulà.** On a little byway off Piazza Nicosia in Old Rome, El Toulà has the warm, welcoming atmosphere of a 19th-century country house, with white walls, antique furniture in dark wood, heavy silver serving dishes, and spectacular arrangements of fruits and flowers. There's a cozy little bar off the entrance where you can sip a *prosecco,* the aperitif best suited to the chef's Venetian specialties, among them the classic *pasta e fagioli* (pasta-and-bean soup), risotto with radicchio, and *fegato alla veneziana* (calves' liver with onions). ⊠ *Via della Lupa 29/b,* ☎ *06/687–3750. Reservations essential. AE, DC, MC, V. No lunch Sat. Closed Sun., Aug., and Dec. 24–26.*

$$$$ ✕ **La Pergola.** A fabulous view of Rome whets your appetite for imag-
★ inatively prepared cuisine in this rooftop restaurant atop the Hilton on Monte Mario, one of the highest of the hills surrounding the city. If you take your eyes off the splendid vista, you will find what might be called a Tuscan garden ambience—potted lemon trees and discreet floral motifs, fresh herbs and candles on every table. The menu is fresh and changes with the seasons. It might include pasta with shrimp and *rucola* (arugula) or breast of guinea hen on a red-wine onion confit. A special three-course menu is priced at about 65,000 lire, a four-course menu at 90,000. ⊠ *Cavalieri Hilton. Via Cadlolo 101,* ☎ *06/35091. Jacket and tie. AE, DC, MC, V. Dinner only. Closed Sun., Mon.*

$$$ ✕ **Andrea.** Ernest Hemingway and King Farouk both ate here; FIAT supremo Gianni Agnelli and other Italian power brokers still do. A half block off Via Veneto, Andrea offers classic Italian cooking in an intimate, clubby ambience in which snowy table linens gleam against a discreet background of dark green paneling. The menu features delicacies such as homemade *tagliolini* (thin noodles) with shrimp and spinach sauce, spaghetti with seafood, and mouthwatering *carciofi al-l'Andrea* (artichokes simmered in olive oil). ⊠ *Via Sardegna 26,* ☎ *06/482–1891. AE, DC, MC, V. No lunch Sat. Closed Sun. and most of Aug.*

$$$ ✕ **Coriolano.** The only tourists who find their way to this classic restaurant near Porta Pia are likely to be gourmets looking for quintessential Italian food—that means light homemade pastas, choice olive oil, and market-fresh ingredients, especially seafood. Although seafood dishes vary, tagliolini *all'aragosta* (with lobster sauce) is usually on the menu, as are porcini mushrooms (in season) cooked to a secret recipe. The wine list is predominantly Italian but also includes some French and Californian wines. ⊠ *Via Ancona 14,* ☎ *06/442–49863. AE, DC, MC, V. Closed Sun. and Aug. 1–25.*

$$$ ✕ **Ranieri.** On a quiet street off fashionable Via Condotti near the Spanish Steps, this historic restaurant was founded by a former chef of Queen Victoria's. It remains a favorite with tourists for its traditional atmosphere and decor, with damask-covered walls, velvet banquettes, crystal chandeliers, and old paintings. Among the many specialties on the vast menu are gnocchi *alla parigina* (souffléed gnocchi with cheese sauce) and *mignonettes alla Regina Vittoria* (veal with pâté and an eight-cheese sauce). ⊠ *Via Mario dei Fiori 26,* ☎ *06/678–6505. AE, DC, MC, V. Closed Sun.*

$$ ✕ **Colline Emiliane.** Near Piazza Barberini, the Colline Emiliane is an unassuming trattoria offering exceptionally good food. Behind an opaque glass facade there are a couple of plain little dining rooms where you are served light homemade pastas, a very special chicken broth, and meats ranging from pot roast to *giambonetto di vitello* (roast veal) and *cotoletta alla bolognese* (veal cutlet with cheese and tomato sauce). ⊠ *Via degli Avignonesi 22,* ☎ *06/481–7538. No credit cards. Closed Fri. and Aug.*

$$ ✕ **La Campana.** An inconspicuous trattoria off Via della Scrofa, this is a place with a long tradition of hospitality; there has been an inn on this spot since the 15th century. The atmosphere is now that of a classic Roman eating place, with friendly but businesslike waiters and a menu that offers Roman specialties such as *vignarola* (sautéed fava beans, peas, and artichokes), rigatoni with prosciutto and tomato sauce, and *olivette di vitello* (tiny veal rolls, served with mashed potatoes). ⊠ *Vicolo della Campana 18,* ☎ *06/686–7820. AE, DC, MC, V. Closed Mon. and Aug.*

$$ ✕ **Paris.** Off Piazza Santa Maria in Trastevere, Paris is reassuring and
★ understated, with none of the flamboyant folklore of so many eateries in Trastevere, a characteristically colorful but clearly gentrified neighborhood. "Paris" is a traditional man's name in Rome, and this restaurant remains true to classic Roman cuisine, serving, among other things, homemade fettuccine and delicate fritto misto. Before or after your meal, take a stroll through the neighborhood. ⊠ *Piazza San Callisto 7/a,* ☎ *06/581–5378. AE, DC, MC, V. Closed Sun. eve, Mon. and Aug.*

$$ ✕ **Pierluigi.** In the heart of Old Rome, this is a longtime favorite. On busy evenings it's almost impossible to find a table, so make sure you reserve well in advance. Seafood predominates, but traditional Roman dishes are offered, too, such as *orecchiette con broccoli* (disk-shaped pasta with greens) and *abbacchio* (roast lamb). In warm weather ask for a table in the piazza. ⊠ *Piazza dei Ricci 144,* ☎ *06/687–8717. AE. Closed Mon. and 2 wks in Aug.*

$$ ✕ **Romolo.** Generations of Romans have enjoyed the romantic garden
★ courtyard and historic dining room of this charming Trastevere haunt, reputedly once home of Raphael's ladylove, *La Fornarina*. In the evening, a guitarist serenades diners. The cuisine is appropriately

Roman; specialties include mozzarella *alla fornarina* (deep-fried with ham and anchovies) and *braciolette d'abbacchio scottadito* (grilled baby lamb chops). Alternatively, try one of the vegetarian pastas featuring artichokes or radicchio. ⊠ *Via di Porta Settimiana 8,* ☏ *06/581–8284. AE, DC, V. Closed Mon. and Aug. 2–23.*

$ ✗ **Baffetto.** Rome's best-known inexpensive pizza restaurant is plainly decorated and *very* popular; you'll probably have to wait in line outside on the *sampietrini*—the cobblestones. The interior is mostly given over to the ovens, the tiny cash desk, and the simple paper-covered tables. *Bruschetta* (toast) and *crostini* (canapés) are the only variations on the pizza theme. Expect to share a table. ⊠ *Via del Governo Vecchio 114,* ☏ *06/686–1617. Reservations not accepted. No credit cards. Dinner only. Closed Sun. and Aug.*

$ ✗ **Fratelli Menghi.** A neighborhood trattoria that has been in the same family as long as anyone can remember, Fratelli Menghi consists of several modest dining rooms off the busy kitchen, which produces typical Roman fare for faithful customers, many of whom work nearby. There's usually a thick, hearty soup such as minestrone, pasta *e ceci* (with chick peas), and other Roman standbys including *involtini* (meat roulades). ⊠ *Via Flaminia 57,* ☏ *06/320–0803. Reservations not accepted. No credit cards. Closed Sun.*

$ ✗ **Grappolo d'Oro.** Off Campo dei Fiori and close to Piazza Navona, this trattoria has been a favorite for decades with locals and foreign residents, one of whom immortalized it in a *New Yorker* profile not so many years ago. This measure of notoriety has not spoiled the place at all. The graying owners are still friendly and patient, and the menu still leans heavily on Roman classics such as pasta all'amatriciana and scaloppini any way you want them. ⊠ *Piazza della Cancelleria 80,* ☏ *06/686–4118. AE, MC, V. Closed Sun.*

$ ✗ **Pollarola.** Near Piazza Navona and Campo dei Fiori, this typical Roman trattoria has flowers (artificial) on the tables and an antique Roman column embedded in the rear wall, evidence of its long history. You can eat outdoors in fair weather. Try a pasta specialty such as fettuccine *al gorgonzola* (with creamy Gorgonzola sauce) and a mixed plate from the temptingly fresh array of antipasti. The house wines, white or red, are good. ⊠ *Piazza della Pollarola 24 (Campo dei Fiori),* ☏ *06/6880–1654. AE, V. Closed Sun.*

Lodging

The list below covers mostly those hotels that are within walking distance of at least some sights and handy to public transportation. Those in the $$ and $ categories do not have restaurants but serve Continental breakfast. Rooms facing the street get traffic noise throughout the night, and few hotels in the lower price categories have double glazing. Ask for a quiet room—or bring earplugs.

We strongly recommend that you always make reservations, even if only a few days in advance, by phone or fax. Always inquire about special low rates. Should you find yourself in the city without reservations, however, contact **HR,** a hotel reservation service (☏ 06/699–1000; English-speaking operator available daily 7 AM–10 PM), with desks at Termini Station and Fiumicino Airport, or one of the following **EPT** offices: at Fiumicino Airport (☏ 06/650–10255); Termini Station (☏ 06/487–1270); or the main information office at Via Parigi 5 (☏ 06/488–3748), which is near Piazza della Repubblica. The Rome municipal tourist information booths also will help you find a room. For details and price-category definitions, *see* Lodging *in* Staying in Italy, *above.*

$$$$ **Cavalieri Hilton.** Though it is outside the main part of Rome and a taxi or courtesy shuttle-bus ride to wherever you are going, this is a large, comfortable, elegant hotel, fresh from a stylish renovation and set in its own park, with two excellent restaurants. ✉ *Via Cadlolo 101, 00136,* ☎ *06/35091,* FAX *06/315–12241. 378 rooms with bath. 2 restaurants, pool. AE, DC, MC, V.*

$$$$ ★ **Eden.** Totally renovated and reopened in 1994 under the aegis of the Forte hotel group, the historic Eden, a haunt of Hemingway, Ingrid Bergman, and Fellini, merits superlatives for dashing elegance and stunning vistas of Rome from the rooftop restaurant and bar (also from some of the most expensive rooms). Precious but discreet antique furnishings, sensuous Italian fabrics, fine linen sheets, and marble baths contribute to an atmosphere of understated opulence. ✉ *Via Ludovisi 49, 00187,* ☎ *06/478–121,* FAX *06/482–1584. 112 rooms and suites with bath. Restaurant, bar, fitness center. AE, DC, MC, V.*

$$$$ **Hassler-Villa Medici.** Guests can expect a cordial atmosphere and magnificent service at this hotel, just at the top of the Spanish Steps. The public rooms have an extravagant, somewhat dated decor, especially the first-floor bar (a chic city rendezvous), and the glass-roof lounge, with gold marble walls and hand-painted tile floors. The elegant bedrooms are decorated in a variety of classic styles (the best feature frescoed walls). The restaurant has a panoramic view of Rome. ✉ *Piazza Trinità dei Monti 6, 00187,* ☎ *06/678–2651,* FAX *06/678–9991. 100 rooms with bath. 2 restaurants, bar. AE, MC, V.*

$$$ ★ **Farnese.** A turn-of-the-century mansion, the Farnese is in a quiet but central residential district. Furnished in art deco style, with charming fresco decorations, it has compact rooms, plenty of lounge space, and a roof garden. It also serves a banquet-size breakfast. ✉ *Via Alessandro Farnese 30, 00184,* ☎ *06/321–2553,* FAX *06/321–5129. 24 rooms with bath. Bar, parking. AE, DC, MC, V.*

$$$ **Victoria.** Oriental rugs, oil paintings, welcoming armchairs, and fresh flowers add charm to the slightly dated public rooms of this hotel, a favorite of American businesspeople who prize the personalized service and restful atmosphere. Some upper rooms and the roof terrace overlook the Villa Borghese. ✉ *Via Campania 41, 00187,* ☎ *06/473931,* FAX *06/487–1890. 110 rooms with bath. Restaurant, bar. AE, DC, MC, V.*

$$ ★ **Britannia.** A quiet location off Via Nazionale is only one of the attractions of this small and special hotel, where guests are coddled with luxury touches such as English-language dailies and local weather reports delivered to their room each morning. The well-furnished rooms (two with a rooftop terrace), frescoed halls, and lounge (where a rich breakfast buffet is served) indicate that the management really cares about giving guests superior service and value. ✉ *Via Napoli 64, 00184,* ☎ *06/488–3153,* FAX *06/488–2343. 32 rooms with bath. Bar. AE, DC, MC, V.*

$$ **D'Este.** Within hailing distance of Santa Maria Maggiore and close to Termini Station, the hotel occupies a roomy 19th-century building. The fresh, pleasing decor evokes turn-of-the-century comfort with brass bedsteads and lamps and walnut furniture. Rooms are quiet, light, and spacious; many can be adapted to suit families. The attentive owner-manager makes sure everything works, and he encourages inquiries about special rates, particularly during the slack summer months. ✉ *Via Carlo Alberto 4/b, 00185,* ☎ *06/446–5607,* FAX *06/446–5601. 37 rooms with bath. Bar, garden. AE, DC, MC, V.*

$$ **La Residenza.** A converted town house near Via Veneto, this hotel offers good value and first-class comfort at reasonable rates. Public areas are spacious and furnished nicely and have a private-home atmosphere. Guest rooms are comfortable and have large closets and TVs. The hotel's clientele is mainly American, and rates include a generous buffet breakfast. ✉ *Via Emilia 22, 00187,* ☎ *06/488–0797,* FAX *06/485721. 27 rooms with bath. Bar, air-conditioning, refrigerators, roof terrace, parking. No credit cards.*

$ ⊞ **Amalia.** Near the Vatican and the Cola di Rienzo shopping district, this small, former *pensione* is owned and operated by the Consoli family—Amalia and her brothers. On several floors of a 19th-century building, it has 21 newly renovated rooms with TV sets, direct-dial telephones, and gleaming marble bathrooms (hair dryers included). The Ottaviano stop of Metro A is a block away. ✉ *Via Germanico 66, 00192,* ☎ *06/397–23354,* FAX *06/397–23365. 25 rooms, 21 with bath or shower. Bar. AE, MC, V.*

$ ⊞ **Margutta.** Near the Spanish Steps and Piazza del Popolo, this small
★ hotel has an unassuming lobby but bright, attractive bedrooms with wrought-iron bedsteads and modern baths. ✉ *Via Laurina 34, 00187,* ☎ *06/322–3674. 21 rooms with bath. AE, DC, MC, V.*

$ ⊞ **Romae.** Near Termini Station, this mid-size hotel has clean, spacious rooms with light-wood furniture and small but bright bathrooms. The cordial, helpful management offers special winter rates and welcomes families. TVs and hair dryers in the rooms plus low rates that include breakfast make this a good value. ✉ *Via Palestro 49, 00185,* ☎ *06/446–3554,* FAX *06/446–3914. 20 rooms with bath. AE, MC, V.*

The Arts

You will find information on scheduled events and shows at EPT and municipal tourist offices or booths. The biweekly booklet "Un Ospite a Roma," free from concierges at some hotels, is another source of information, as is "Wanted in Rome," available at newsstands. There are listings in English in the back of the weekly "Roma c'è" booklet, with handy bus information for each listing; it is sold at newsstands. If you want to go to the opera, the ballet, or a concert, it's best to ask your concierge to get tickets for you. They are sold at box offices only, just a few days before performances.

Opera

The **Teatro dell'Opera** is on Via del Viminale (☎ 06/481–7003; toll-free in Italy 167-016665); its summer season from May through August is famous for spectacular open-air performances. After having been evicted from the ancient ruins of the Baths of Caracalla, performances may be held in Villa Pepoli, a parklike area adjacent to the ruins of the Baths. Tickets are sold at the opera box office.

Concerts

The main concert hall is the **Accademia di Santa Cecilia** (✉ Via della Conciliazione 4, ☎ 06/6880–1044). There are many concerts year-round; look for posters or for schedules in the publications mentioned above.

Film

The only English-language movie theater in Rome is the **Pasquino** (Vicolo del Piede, just off Piazza Santa Maria in Trastevere, ☎ 06/580–3622). The program is listed in Rome's daily newspapers. Several other movie theaters show films in English on certain days of the week; the listings in "Roma c'è" are reliable.

Nightlife

Rome's "in" nightspots change like the flavor of the month, and many fade into oblivion after a brief moment of glory. The best places to find an up-to-date list are the weekly entertainment guide "Trovaroma," published each Thursday in the Italian daily *La Repubblica,* and "Roma c'è."

Bars

Jacket and tie are in order in the elegant **Blue Bar** of the Hostaria dell'Orso (⊠ Via dei Soldati 25, ☎ 06/686–4250). One of the grandest places for a drink in well-dressed company is **Le Bar** of Le Grand Hotel (⊠ Via Vittorio Emanuele Orlando 3, ☎ 06/482931). **Jazz Club** (⊠ Via Zanardelli 12, ☎ 06/686–1990), near Piazza Navona, is an upscale watering hole open from 7 PM to 2 AM, with a happy hour from 7 to 10 and Sunday brunch from noon to 3. **Flann O'Brien** (⊠ Via Napoli 29, ☎ 06/488–0418) has the look and atmosphere of a good Irish pub but also serves cappuccino.

Informal wine bars are popular with young Romans and offer snacks or light meals. Near the Pantheon is **Spiriti** (⊠ Via Sant'Eustachio 5, ☎ 06/689–2499). **Enoteca Roffi** (⊠ Via della Croce 76/a, ☎ 06/679–0896) invites weary shoppers in the Condotti area. **Trimani Wine Bar** (⊠ Via Cernaia 37/b, ☎ 06/446–9630) has an extensive choice of Italy's best wines. **Birreria Marconi** (⊠ Via di Santa Prassede 9c, ☎ 06/486636), near Santa Maria Maggiore, is a beer-hall pizzeria. Near the Pantheon, a hub of fashionable after-dark activity is **Antico Caffè della Pace** (⊠ Via della Pace 3, ☎ 06/686–1216). Brazilian music is big in Rome; Trastevere has several Carioca clubs. **Clarabella** (⊠ Piazza San Cosimato 39, ☎ 0337/801772) features live music and is open from 10 PM to 4 AM. **Mambo** (⊠ Via dei Fienaroli 30/a, ☎ 06/589–7196) lives up to its name with lively Latin music and dancing.

Discos and Nightclubs

There's deafening disco music for an under-30 crowd at **Smile** (⊠ Entrance at Via Luciani 52, ☎ 06/322–1251). Special events such as beauty pageants and theme parties are a feature, and there's a restaurant on the premises. **Gilda** (⊠ Via Mario dei Fiori 97, ☎ 06/678–4838) is a combination supper club–disco–piano bar, often featuring theme parties and special events. **Spago** (⊠ Via di Monte Testaccio, ☎ 06/574–4999) has a trendier atmosphere, with late-night dining, piano bar, and dancing to disco music, funk, and soul; it's not easy to find, so take a taxi.

Singles Scene

Locals and foreigners of all ages gather at Rome's cafés in **Piazza della Rotonda** in front of the Pantheon, in **Piazza Navona,** and in **Piazza Santa Maria in Trastevere.** The cafés on **Via Veneto** and the bars of the big hotels draw mainly tourists, and are good places to meet other travelers in the over-thirty age group. Rome's many pubs draw an easygoing crowd of students and youngish career people. In fair weather, under-thirties will find crowds of contemporaries on the **Spanish Steps,** where it's easy to strike up a conversation.

FLORENCE

Arriving and Departing

By Plane

The airport that handles most arrivals is Galileo Galilei Airport—more commonly known as Pisa-Galilei Airport—at Pisa (☎ 050/500707), connected with Florence by train direct to the Santa Maria Novella station. Service is hourly throughout the day and takes about 60 minutes. When departing, you can buy train tickets for the airport and check in for all flights leaving from Pisa-Galilei Airport at the Florence Air Terminal at Track 5 of Santa Maria Novella station (flight information ☎ 055/216073). Some domestic and European flights use Florence's Vespucci Airport at Peretola (☎ 055/333498), connected by SITA bus to the downtown area.

By Train

The main train station is Santa Maria Novella, abbreviated SMN on signs. There is an Azienda Transporti Autolinee Fiorentine (ATAF) city bus information booth across the street from the exit on the left side of the station (⊠ Also at Piazza del Duomo 57/r). Inside the station is an Informazioni Turistiche Alberghiere (ITA) hotel association booth, where you can get accommodations information and bookings. The booking fee is from 3,000 to 10,000 lire, depending on the category.

By Bus

The SITA bus terminal is on Via Santa Caterina da Siena, near the Santa Maria Novella station. The CAP bus terminal is at Via Nazionale 13, also near the station.

By Car

The north–south access route to Florence is the Autostrada del Sole (A1) from Milan or Rome. The Florence–Mare autostrada (A11) links Florence with the Tyrrhenian coast, Pisa, and the A12 coastal autostrada.

Getting Around

On Foot

You can see most of Florence's major sights on foot, as they are packed into a relatively small area. It's best not to plan to use a car in Florence; most of the center is off-limits and ATAF buses will take you where you want to go. Wear comfortable shoes and wander to your heart's content. It is easy to find your way around in Florence. There are so many landmarks that you cannot get lost for long. The system of street addresses is unusual, with commercial addresses (those with an *r* in them, meaning *rosso,* or red) and residential addresses numbered separately (32/r might be next to or a block away from plain 32).

By Bus

ATAF city buses run from about 5:15 AM to 1 AM. Buy tickets before you board the bus; they are on sale singly or in books of eight at many tobacco shops and newsstands. The cost is 1,400 lire for a ticket good for 60 minutes on all lines, 1,900 lire for 120 minutes, and 5,400 lire for a book of four 60-minute tickets, called a *multiplo.* An all-day ticket (*turistico*) costs 5,000 lire.

By Taxi

Taxis wait at stands. Use only authorized cabs, which are white with a yellow stripe or rectangle on the door. The meter starts at 3,200 lire. To call a taxi, phone 055/4798 or 055/4390.

By Bicycle

You can rent a bicycle at **Alinari** (⊠ Via Guelfa 85/r, ☎ 055/280500), which has several locations in Florence; **Motorent** (⊠ Via San Zanobi 9/r, ☎ 055/490113); and at city concessions in several locations, including Piazza della Stazione, Piazza Pitti, and Fortezza da Basso.

By Moped

For a moped, go to **Alinari** or **Motorent** (☞ By Bicycle, *above*), or to **Ciao e Basta** (⊠ Lungarno Pecori Girardi 1, ☎ 055/234–2726).

Important Addresses and Numbers

Visitor Information

The municipal tourist office is at Via Cavour 1/r (☎ 055/276–0382; ⏰ 8:30–7), with a branch next to the train station and another information office near Piazza della Signoria, at Chiasso dei Baroncelli 17/r (☎ 055/230–2124). The **Azienda Promozione Turistica (APT)** tourist board has its headquarters and an information office at Via Manzoni 16, 50121 (☎ 055/234–6284; ⏰ Mon.–Sat. 8:30–1:30).

Consulates

U.S. (✉ Lungarno Vespucci 38, ☎ 055/239–8276). **Canadian** (citizens should refer to their consulate in Rome). **U.K.** (✉ Lungarno Corsini 2, ☎ 055/284133).

Emergencies

Police (☎ 113). **Ambulance** (☎ 118 or 055/212222). **Doctor:** Call your consulate for recommendations, or call the **Tourist Medical Service** (☎ 055/475411), associated with IAMAT, for English-speaking medical assistance 24 hours a day. **Pharmacies:** There are 24-hour pharmacies at Via Calzaiuoli 7/r (☎ 055/289490); Piazza San Giovanni 20/r (☎ 055/284013); and at the train station (☎ 055/289435).

English-Language Bookstores

You'll find English-language magazines and paperbacks on the newsstands in Piazza della Repubblica. **The Paperback Exchange** (✉ Via Fiesolana 31/r, ☎ 055/247–8154), in the Santa Croce area, has new and used paperbacks for sale. **The BM Bookshop** (✉ Borgo Ognissanti 4/r, ☎ 055/294575) has a good selection of books.

Travel Agencies

American Express (✉ Via Guicciardini 49/r, ☎ 055/288751; branch at Via Dante Alighieri 20/r, ☎ 055/50981). **CIT** (✉ Via Cavour 54/r, ☎ 055/294306). **Wagons-Lits** (✉ Via del Giglio 27/r, ☎ 055/218851).

Guided Tours

Orientation

A bus consortium (through hotels and travel agents) offers three-hour tours in air-conditioned buses. Two tours cover most of the important sights: The morning itinerary gives you a look at the outside of the cathedral, baptistry, and bell tower, takes you to the Accademia to see Michelangelo's *David,* to Piazzale Michelangelo for the view, and perhaps then to the Palazzo Pitti to visit the Palatine Gallery; the afternoon tour includes Piazza della Signoria, a visit to the Uffizi Gallery and to Santa Croce, and an excursion to Fiesole. The cost is about 48,000 lire for a three-hour tour, including entrance fees, and bookings can be made through travel agents.

Special-Interest

Inquire at travel agents or at **Agriturist Regionale** (✉ Piazza San Firenze 3, ☎ 055/287838) for visits to villa gardens around Florence from April through June, or for visits to farm estates during September and October.

Personal Guides

American Express (☎ 055/288751) can arrange for limousine or minivan tours and personal guide services. **Europedrive** (✉ Via Bisenzio 35, ☎ 055/422–2839) will provide cars with English-speaking drivers.

Excursions

Operators offer a half-day excursion to Pisa, usually in the afternoon, costing about 48,000 lire, and a full-day excursion to Siena and San

Gimignano, costing about 68,000 lire. Pick up a timetable at ATAF information offices near the train station, at SITA (✉ Via Santo Caterina da Siena 17, ☎ 055/214721), or at the APT tourist office (☞ Visitor Information *in* Important Addresses and Numbers, *above*).

Both ATAF and tourist information offices may offer a free booklet containing information on interesting excursions in the vicinity of Florence, complete with timetables of local bus and train services.

Exploring Florence

Founded by Julius Caesar, Florence has the familiar grid pattern common to all Roman colonies. Except for the major monuments, which are appropriately imposing, the buildings are low and unpretentious. It is a small, compact city of ocher and gray stone and pale plaster; its narrow streets open unexpectedly into spacious squares populated by strollers and pigeons. At its best, it has a gracious and elegant air, though it can at times be a nightmare of mass tourism. Plan, if you can, to visit Florence in late fall, early spring, or even in winter, to avoid the crowds.

A visit to Florence is a visit to the living museum of the Italian Renaissance. The Renaissance began right here in Florence, and the city bears witness to the proud spirit and unparalleled genius of its artists and artisans. In fact, there is so much to see that it is best to savor a small part rather than attempt to absorb it all in a muddled vision.

For 10,000 lire you can purchase a special museum ticket valid for six months at seven city museums, including the Palazzo Vecchio, the Museum of Firenze Com'Era (museum of Florentine history), and the Museum of Santa Maria Novella. Inquire at any city museum.

Numbers in the margin correspond to points of interest on the Firenze (Florence) map.

Piazza del Duomo and Piazza della Signoria

The best place to begin a tour of Florence is the **Piazza del Duomo**, where the cathedral, bell tower, and baptistry stand on the rather

★ ❶ cramped square. The lofty **Cathedral of Santa Maria del Fiore** is one of the longest in the world. Begun by master sculptor and architect Arnolfo di Cambio in 1296, its construction took 140 years to complete. Gothic architecture predominates; the facade was added in the 1870s but is based on Tuscan Gothic models. Inside, the church is cool and austere, a fine example of the architecture of the period. Among the sparse decorations, take a good look at the frescoes of equestrian figures on the left wall; the one on the right is by Paolo Uccello, the one on the left by Andrea del Castagno. The dome frescoes by Vasari take second place to the dome itself, Brunelleschi's greatest architectural and technical achievement. It was also the inspiration behind such later domes as the one Michelangelo designed for St. Peter's in Rome and even the Capitol in Washington. You can climb to the cupola gallery, 463 fatiguing steps up between the two skins of the double dome for a fine view of Florence and the surrounding hills. ✉ *Dome entrance is in left aisle of cathedral.* 🎟 *8,000 lire.* ☉ *Mon.–Fri. 9:30–5:30, Sat. 9:30–5. Cathedral* ☉ *Mon.–Fri. 9–6, Sat. 8:30–5, Sun. 1–5.*

❷ Next to the cathedral is Giotto's 14th-century **bell tower,** richly decorated with colored marbles and sculpture reproductions (the originals are in the Museo dell'Opera del Duomo). The 414-step climb to the top is less strenuous than that to the cupola. ✉ *Piazza del Duomo.* 🎟 *8,000 lire.* ☉ *Mar.–Oct., daily 9–7; Nov.–Feb., daily 9–4:30.*

★ ❸ In front of the cathedral is the **baptistry** (☉ Mon.–Sat. 1:30–6, Sun. 9–1:30), one of the city's oldest and most beloved edifices, where

680

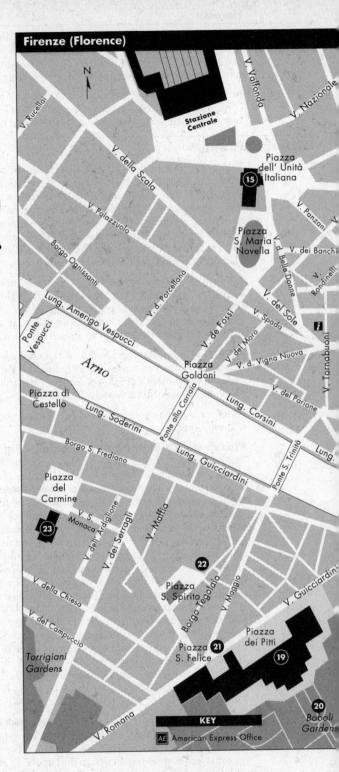

Firenze (Florence)

KEY

AE American Express Office

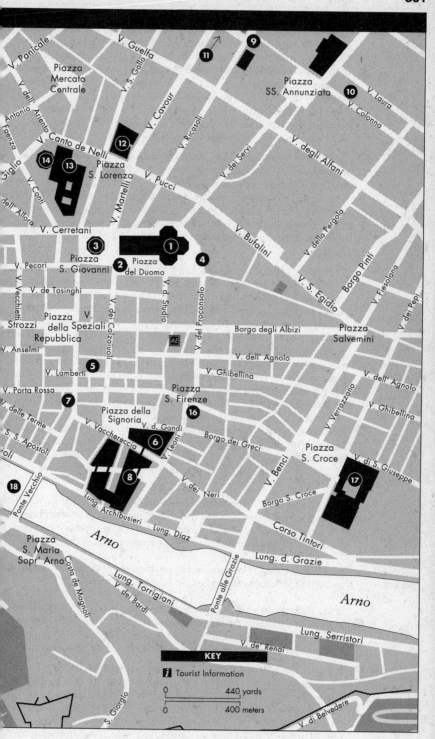

since the 11th century Florentines have baptized their children. The most famous of the baptistry's three portals are Ghiberti's east doors (facing the Duomo), dubbed the "gates of Paradise" by Michelangelo; gleaming copies now replace the originals, which have been removed

★ ❹ to the **Museo dell'Opera del Duomo** (Cathedral Museum). The museum contains some superb sculptures by Donatello and Luca della Robbia—especially their *cantorie,* or singers' galleries—as well as an unfinished *Pietà* by Michelangelo, which was intended for his own tomb. ⊠ *Piazza del Duomo 9,* ☎ *055/230–2885.* ⊯ *8,000 lire.* ☉ *Mar.–Oct., Mon.–Sat. 9–6:50; Nov.–Feb., Mon.–Sat. 9–5:30.*

❺ Stroll down fashionable Via Calzaiuoli to the church of **Orsanmichele,** for centuries an odd combination of first-floor church and second-floor granary. The statues in the niches on the exterior (many of which are now copies) constitute an anthology of the work of eminent Renaissance sculptors, including Donatello, Ghiberti, and Verrocchio, while the tabernacle inside is an extraordinary piece by Andrea Orcagna. Some of the original statues can be seen in the Bargello and the Palazzo della Signoria.

Continuing another two blocks along Via Calzaiuoli you'll come upon the **Piazza della Signoria,** the heart of Florence and the city's largest square. During the long and controversial process of replacing the paving stones over the past few years, well-preserved remnants of Roman and medieval Florence came to light and were thoroughly examined and photographed before being buried again and covered with the new paving. In the center of the square a slab marks the spot where Savonarola, the reformist monk who urged the Florentines to burn their pictures, books, musical instruments, and other worldly objects, was hanged and then burned at the stake as a heretic in 1498. The square, the **Neptune Fountain** by Ammanati, and the surrounding cafés are popular gathering places for Florentines and for tourists who come to ad-

❻ mire the massive **Palazzo della Signoria** (better known as the **Palazzo Vecchio**), the copy of Michelangelo's *David* outside its entrance, and the frescoes and art in its impressive salons. ⊠ *Piazza della Signoria,* ☎ *055/276–8465.* ⊯ *10,000 lire; Sun. free.* ☉ *Mon.–Wed., Fri.–Sat. 9–7, Sun. 8–1.*

The statues in the 14th-century **Logia dei Lanzi,** to the left as you're looking at the Palazzo Vecchio, include Cellini's famous bronze *Perseus Holding the Head of Medusa;* even the pedestal is superbly executed (although the statuettes in its niches are recent copies of the originals).

NEED A BREAK? | Stop in at **Rivoire,** a Florentine institution, for some of its delectable ice cream and/or chocolate goodies. ⊠ *Piazza della Signoria 5/r.*

If you'd like to do a little shopping, make a brief detour off Piazza della ❼ Signoria to the **Loggia del Mercato Nuovo** on Via Calimala. It's crammed with souvenirs and straw and leather goods at reasonable prices; bargaining is acceptable here. ☉ *Mon.–Sat. 8–7 (closed Mon. AM).*

★ ❽ If time is limited, this is your chance to visit the **Uffizi Gallery,** which houses Italy's most important collection of paintings. (Try to see it at a leisurely pace, though—it's too good to rush through!) The Uffizi Palace was built to house the administrative offices of the Medici, one-time rulers of the city. Later their fabulous art collection was arranged in the Uffizi Gallery on the top floor, which was opened to the public in the 17th century—making this the world's first modern public gallery. The emphasis is on Italian art of the Gothic and Renaissance periods. Make sure you see the works by Giotto, and look for the Botticellis in Rooms X–XIV, Michelangelo's *Holy Family* in

Room XXV, and the works by Raphael next door. In addition to its art treasures, the gallery offers a magnificent close-up view of the Palazzo Vecchio tower from the little coffee bar at the end of the corridor. Authorities have done wonders in repairing the damage caused by a bomb in 1993. ⊠ *Loggiato Uffizi 6,* ☎ *055/23885.* ▦ *12,000 lire.* ⊙ *Tues.–Sat. 9–7, Sun. 9–2.*

Accademia, San Marco, San Lorenzo, Santa Maria Novella

★ ❾ Start at the **Accademia Gallery,** and try to be first in line at opening time so you can get the full impact of Michelangelo's *David* without having to fight your way through the crowds. Skip the works in the exhibition halls leading to the *David;* they are of minor importance and you'll gain a length on the tour groups. Michelangelo's statue is a tour de force of artistic conception and technical ability, for he was using a piece of stone that had already been worked on by a lesser sculptor. Take time to see the forceful *Slaves,* also by Michelangelo; their roughhewn, unfinished surfaces contrast dramatically with the highly polished, meticulously carved *David.* Michelangelo left the *Slaves* "unfinished" as a symbolic gesture, to accentuate the figures' struggle to escape the bondage of stone. He simply abandoned them because his patrons changed their minds about the tomb monument for which they were planned. ⊠ *Via Ricasoli 60,* ☎ *055/214375.* ▦ *12,000 lire.* ⊙ *Tues.–Sat. 9–7, Sun. 9–2.*

❿ You can make a detour down Via Cesare Battisti to Piazza Santissima Annunziata to see the arcade of the **Ospedale degli Innocenti** (Orphans' Hospital) by Brunelleschi, with charming roundels by Andrea della Robbia, and the **Museo Archeologico** (Archaeological Museum) on Via della Colonna, under the arch. The latter has some fine Etruscan and Roman antiquities and a pretty garden. ⊠ *Via della Colonna 36,* ☎ *055/247–8641.* ▦ *8,000 lire.* ⊙ *Tues.–Sat. 9–2, Sun. 9–1.*

⓫ Retrace your steps to Piazza San Marco and the **Museo di San Marco,** housed in a 15th-century Dominican monastery. The unfortunate Savonarola meditated on the sins of the Florentines here, and Fra Angelico decorated many of the otherwise austere cells and corridors with brilliantly colored frescoes on religious subjects. (Look for his masterpiece, *The Annunciation.*) Together with many of his paintings arranged on the ground floor, just off the little cloister, they form a fascinating collection. ⊠ *Piazza San Marco 1,* ☎ *055/238–8608.* ▦ *8,000 lire.* ⊙ *Tues.–Sat. 9–2, Sun. 9–1.*

★ ⓬ Lined with shops, Via Cavour leads to the **Palazzo Medici Riccardi,** a massive Renaissance mansion (☞ Off the Beaten Path, *below*). Turn
⓭ right here to the elegant **Church of San Lorenzo,** with its Old Sacristy designed by Brunelleschi, and two pulpits by Donatello. Rounding the church, you'll find yourself in the midst of the sprawling **San Lorenzo Market,** dealing in everything and anything, including some interesting leather items. ⊠ *Piazza San Lorenzo, Via dell'Ariento.* ⊙ *Tues.–Sat. 8–7.*

NEED A BREAK? In the big covered food market near San Lorenzo, **Nerbone** is a favorite with market workers for a quick sandwich or plate of pasta, which they usually eat standing at the counter. You can sit at the tables across the way, too. It's impossibly crowded between 1 and 1:30. ⊠ *Mercato Centrale. Closed Sun.*

★ ⓮ Enter the **Medici Chapels** from Piazza Madonna degli Aldobrandini, behind San Lorenzo. These remarkable chapels contain the tombs of practically every member of the Medici family, and there were a lot of them, for they guided Florence's destiny from the 15th century to 1737. Cosimo I, a Medici whose acumen made him the richest man in Europe, is buried in the crypt beneath the Chapel of the Princes, and Donatello's tomb is next to that of his patron. The chapel upstairs is decorated in a dazzling array of colored marbles. Michelangelo's tombs of Giuliano and Lorenzo de' Medici are adorned with the justly famed sculptures of *Dawn* and *Dusk*, *Night* and *Day*. ⊠ *Piazza Madonna degli Aldobrandini*, ☎ *055/213206*. 🔲 *10,000 lire*. ☉ *Tues.–Sun. 9–2.*

⑮ You can take either Via Panzani or Via del Melarancio to the large square next to the massive church of **Santa Maria Novella,** a handsome building in the Tuscan version of the Gothic style. See it from the other end of Piazza Santa Maria Novella for the best view of its facade. Inside are some famous paintings, especially Masaccio's *Trinity*, a Giotto crucifix in the sacristy, and Ghirlandaio's frescoes in the apse. ⊠ *Piazza Santa Maria Novella*, ☎ *055/210113*. ☉ *Daily 7–11:30 and 3:30–6.*

Next door to the church is the entrance to the **Museum of Santa Maria Novella,** worth a visit for its serene atmosphere and the restored Paolo Uccello frescoes in the Green Cloister. ⊠ *Piazza Santa Maria Novella 19*, ☎ *055/282187*. 🔲 *5,000 lire*. ☉ *Mon.–Thurs., Sat. 9–2, Sun. 8–1.*

★ ⑯ Only a few blocks behind the Piazza della Signoria is the **Bargello,** a fortresslike palace that served as residence of Florence's chief magistrate in medieval times and later as a prison. Don't be put off by its grim look, for it now houses Florence's **Museo Nazionale** (National Museum), a treasure-house of Italian Renaissance sculpture. In this historic setting, it displays masterpieces by Donatello, Verrocchio, Michelangelo, and other major sculptors, amid an eclectic array of arms and ceramics. For Renaissance art lovers, this museum is on a par with the Uffizi. ⊠ *Via del Proconsolo 4*, ☎ *055/238–8606*. 🔲 *8,000 lire*. ☉ *Tues.–Sun. 9–2.*

NEED A BREAK?	From Piazza San Firenze follow Via degli Anguillara or Borgo dei Greci toward Piazza Santa Croce. Don't miss the chance to taste what's held by many to be the best ice cream in Florence, at **Vivoli,** on a little side street, the second left off Via degli Anguillara as you head toward Santa Croce. ⊠ *Via Isole delle Stinche 7/r. Closed Mon.*

★ ⑰ The mighty church of **Santa Croce** was begun in 1294; inside, Giotto's frescoes brighten two chapels and monumental tombs of Michelangelo, Galileo, Machiavelli, and other Renaissance luminaries line the walls. In the adjacent museum, you can see what remains of a Giotto crucifix, irreparably damaged by a flood in 1966, when water rose to 16 feet in parts of the church. The **Pazzi Chapel** in the cloister is an architectural gem by Brunelleschi. ⊠ *Piazza Santa Croce*, ☎ *055/244619*. ☉ *Church: Apr.–Sept., Mon.–Sat. 8–6:30, Sun. 8–12:30 and 3–6:30; Oct.–Mar., Mon.–Sat. 8–12:30 and 3–6:30, Sun. 3–6. Opera di Santa Croce (Museum and Pazzi Chapel)*, ☎ *055/244619*. 🔲 *3,000 lire*. ☉ *Mar.–Sept., Thurs.–Tues. 10–12:30 and 2:30–6:30; Oct.–Feb., Thurs.–Tues. 10–12:30 and 3–5.*

The monastery of Santa Croce houses a leather-working school and showroom, with entrances at Via San Giuseppe 5/r and Piazza Santa Croce 16. The entire Santa Croce area is known for its leather workshops and inconspicuous shops selling gold and silver jewelry at prices much lower than those of the elegant jewelers near Ponte Vecchio.

NEED A
BREAK? You have several eating options here. For ice cream, the **bar** on Piazza Santa Croce has a tempting selection. If it's a snack you're after, the **Fiaschetteria** (⊠ Via dei Neri 17/r) makes sandwiches to order and has a choice of antipasti and a hot dish or two. And if you're homesick for brownies and chocolate chip cookies, head for **Carlie's American Bakery** (⊠ Via delle Brache, also called Via dei Legnaioli, 12/r, a narrow street off Via dei Neri between Via dei Benci and Via dei Rustici; ⊘ 10–1:30 and 3:30–7:30).

★ ⑱ Now head for the **Ponte Vecchio,** Florence's oldest bridge. It seems to be just another street lined with goldsmiths' shops until you get to the middle and catch a glimpse of the Arno below. Spared during World War II by the retreating Germans (who blew up every other bridge in the city), it also survived the 1966 flood. It leads into the **Oltrarno district,** which has its own charm, still preserves much of the atmosphere of old-time Florence, and is full of fascinating craft workshops.

⑲ But for the moment you should head straight down Via Guicciardini to **Palazzo Pitti,** a 15th-century extravaganza that the Medici acquired from the Pitti family shortly after the latter had gone deeply into debt to build the central portion. The Medici enlarged the building, extending its facade along the immense piazza. Solid and severe, it looks like a Roman aqueduct turned into a palace. The palace houses several museums: One displays the fabulous Medici collection of objects in silver and gold; another is the **Gallery of Modern Art.** The most famous museum, though, is the **Palatine Gallery,** with an extraordinary collection of paintings, many hung frame-to-frame in a clear case of artistic overkill. Some are high up in dark corners, so try to go on a bright day. ⊠ *Piazza dei Pitti,* ☎ *055/210323. Gallery of Modern Art:* ▦ *4,000 lire; Palatine Gallery:* ▦ *12,000 lire; Monumental Royal Apartments:* ▦ *8,000 lire; Silver Museum:* ▦ *8,000 lire (includes entry to Historical Costume Gallery and Porcelain Museum at top of the Boboli Gardens, if open).* ⊘ *Tues.–Sun. 9–2.*

⑳ Take time for a refreshing stroll in the **Boboli Gardens** behind Palazzo Pitti, a typical Italian garden laid out in 1550 for Cosimo de' Medici's wife, Eleanor of Toledo. ⊠ *Piazza dei Pitti,* ☎ *055/213440.* ▦ *4,000 lire.* ⊘ *Daily, except first and last Mon. of the month. Apr., May, and Sept., 9–6:30; June–Aug., 9–7:30; Oct. and Mar.–Apr., 9–5:30; Nov.–Feb., 9–4:30.*

㉑ In the far corner of Piazza dei Pitti, poets Elizabeth Barrett and Robert Browning lived in the **Casa Guidi,** facing the smaller Piazza San Felice. ⊠ *Piazza San Felice 6.* ▦ *Free.* ☎ *055/212594 (British Consulate) for hours.*

NEED A
BREAK? From Piazza San Felice it's not far to the **Caffè Notte,** a wine and sandwich shop featuring a different salad every day (⊠ Corner of Via delle Caldaie and Via della Chiesa; closed Mon.). For more substantial sustenance, go to the **Cantinone del Gallo Nero** (⊠ Via Santo Spirito 6/r. Closed Mon.), an atmospheric wine cellar where Chianti is king and locals lunch on soups, pastas, and salads. A block from the church of Santo Spirito, **Casalinga** (⊠ Via dei Michelozzi 9; closed weekends) is a large, popular trattoria, fine for a hearty, inexpensive lunch.

㉒ The church of **Santo Spirito** is important as one of Brunelleschi's finest architectural creations, and it contains some superb paintings, including a Filippino Lippi *Madonna.* Santo Spirito is the hub of a colorful neighborhood of artisans and intellectuals. An **outdoor market** enlivens the square every morning except Sunday; in the afternoon, pigeons, pet owners, and pensioners take over. An arts and crafts fair is held in the square on the second Sunday of the month. The area is definitely on an upward trend, with new cafés, restaurants, and upscale shops opening every day.

㉓ Walk down Via Sant'Agostino and Via Santa Monaca to the church of **Santa Maria del Carmine,** of no architectural interest but of immense significance in the history of Renaissance art. It contains the celebrated frescoes painted by Masaccio in the **Brancacci Chapel,** unveiled not long ago after a lengthy and meticulous restoration. The chapel was a classroom for such artistic giants as Botticelli, Leonardo da Vinci, Michelangelo, and Raphael, since they all came to study Masaccio's realistic use of light and perspective and his creation of space and depth. ⊠ *Piazza del Carmine,* ☏ *055/212331.* ☑ *5,000 lire.* ☉ *Mon. and Wed.–Sat. 10–5, Sun. 1–5.*

Off the Beaten Path

Few tourists get to see one of Florence's most precious works of art, Benozzo Gozzoli's glorious frescoes in the tiny chapel on the second floor of the **Palazzo Medici Riccardi,** representing the journey of the Magi as a spectacular cavalcade with Lorenzo the Magnificent on a charger. ⊠ *Via Cavour 1,* ☏ *055/276–0340.* ☑ *6,000 lire.* ☉ *Mon.–Tues., Thurs.–Sat. 9–1 and 3–6, Sun. 9–1.*

The **English Cemetery** is on a cypress-studded knoll in the middle of heavily trafficked Piazza Donatello, not far from the botanical garden. Here you can walk with the shades of Elizabeth Barrett Browning, Algernon Swinburne, and other poets. You will need to ask the custodian to let you into the cemetery, which is kept locked. ⊠ *Piazza Donatello. Ring bell at entrance for admission.*

See some of Florence's smaller museums. The **Davanzati Museum** is a dusky and imposing medieval palazzo furnished with antiques from as early as the 14th century on. ⊠ *Via Porta Rossa 13,* ☏ *055/238–8610. (Closed for restorations in 1996, it should be open in 1997; check hours locally).*

Casa Buonarroti, which was Michelangelo's home from 1508 until his death in 1564 and subsequently belonged to his heirs, highlights the artist's early works and drawings in evocative surroundings. ⊠ *Via Ghibellina 70,* ☏ *055/241752.* ☑ *8,000 lire.* ☉ *Wed.–Mon. 9:30–1:30.*

The **Stibbert Museum,** a Victorian mansion full of objets d'art and armor, was donated to Florence by 19th-century collector Frederick Stibbert. This is the city's most eclectic and bizarre museum. ⊠ *Via Stibbert 26,* ☏ *055/486049.* ☑ *5,000 lire.* ☉ *Mon.–Wed., Fri., and Sat. 9–2, Sun. 9–12:30.*

Take Bus 12 or 13 from the train station or cathedral up to Piazzale Michelangelo, then walk along Viale dei Colli and climb to **San Miniato al Monte,** a charming green-and-white marble Romanesque church full of artistic riches.

Visit the **synagogue** on Via Farini and the **Jewish Museum** next door, which contains antique scrolls and ritual objects. ⊠ *Via Farini 4,* ☏ *055/245252. Call in morning for hrs.*

Shopping

Florence offers top quality for your money in leather goods, linens and upholstery fabrics, gold and silver jewelry, and cameos. Straw goods, gilded wooden trays and frames, hand-printed paper desk accessories, and ceramic objects make good inexpensive gifts. Many shops offer fine old prints.

Shopping Districts

The most fashionable streets in Florence are **Via Tornabuoni** and **Via della Vigna Nuova.** Goldsmiths and jewelry shops can be found on and around the **Ponte Vecchio** and in the **Santa Croce area,** where there is also a high concentration of leather shops.

Antiques

Most of Florence's many antiques dealers are located in **Borgo San Jacopo** and **Borgo Ognissanti,** but you'll find plenty of small shops throughout the center of town.

Department Stores

Principe, in Piazza Strozzi, is a high-quality apparel store that incorporates several designer boutiques. At the low end of the price range, **UPIM,** in Piazza della Repubblica and various other locations, has inexpensive goods of all types.

Markets

The big food market at **Piazza del Mercato Centrale** is open in the morning (Mon.–Sat.) and is worth a visit. The **San Lorenzo market** on Piazza San Lorenzo and Via dell'Ariento is a fine place to browse for buys in leather goods and souvenirs (⊙ Tues. and Sat. 8–7; also Sun. in summer). The **Mercato Nuovo,** Via Calimala, which is sometimes called the **Mercato del Porcellino** because of the famous bronze statue of a boar at one side, is packed with stalls selling souvenirs and straw goods (⊙ Tues.–Sat. 8–7; closed Sun. and Mon. mornings in winter). There's a colorful neighborhood market at **Sant'Ambrogio,** Piazza Ghiberti (⊙ Mon.–Sat. mornings). A permanent flea market can be found at **Piazza Ciompi** (⊙ Mon.–Sat. 9–1 and 4–7, Sun. 9–1 in summer). A huge weekly market takes over Viale Lincoln in the Cascine park every Tuesday morning.

Dining

Mealtimes in Florence are 12:30 to 2 and 7:30 to 9 or later. Many $$ and $ places are small, and you may have to share a table. Reservations are always advisable; to find a table at inexpensive places, get there early. For details and price-category definitions, *see* Dining *in* Staying in Italy, *above.*

$$$$ ✕ **Enoteca Pinchiorri.** In the beautiful Renaissance palace and its charm-
★ ing garden courtyard that was home to Giovanni da Verrazano (a 15th-century Florentine navigator), husband-and-wife team Giorgio Pinchiorri and Annie Feolde have created an exceptional restaurant that ranks as one of Italy's best. Guests can enjoy Annie's rediscoveries of traditional Tuscan dishes, or her own brand of imaginatively creative nouvelle cuisine, while Giorgio oversees the extraordinary wine cellar. At upward of 150,000 lire per person, meals here are for real connoisseurs; a prix-fixe menu costs about 95,000 lire. ⊠ *Via Ghibellina 87,* ☏ *055/242777. Reservations essential. AE, MC, V. Closed Sun., Aug., and 10 days at Christmas. No lunch Mon. or Wed.*

$$$ ✕ **Terrazza Brunelleschi.** The rooftop restaurant of the hotel Baglioni
★ has the best view in town. The dining room, decorated in pale blue and creamy tones, has big picture windows; the summer-dining terrace is charming, with tables under arbors and turrets for guests to climb to get an even better view. The menu offers such traditional Tuscan dishes as *minestra di fagioli* (bean soup) and other more innovative choices, such as a pâté of peppers and tomato. ⊠ *Hotel Baglioni, Piazza Unità Italiana 6,* ☏ *055/215642. AE, DC, MC, V.*

$$ ✕ **Alle Murate.** Between the Duomo and Santa Croce, this sophisticated but informal restaurant features creative versions of classic Tuscan food, along with such specialties of other regions as the Calabrian *cavatelli con broccoli* (pasta with broccoli and cheese). In a smaller room called the *vineria*, the menu and service are simpler and prices lower. ✉ *Via Ghibellina 52/r,* ☎ *055/240618. No credit cards. Dinner only. Closed Mon.*

$$ ✕ **Angiolino.** This bustling little trattoria has a real charcoal grill and
★ an old wood-burning stove to keep its customers warm on nippy days. Glowing with authentic atmosphere, Angiolino offers such specialties as *ribollita* (a Tuscan version of minestrone) and juicy *bistecca alla fiorentina* (T-bone steak basted in olive oil and black pepper). The bistecca will push the bill up, as you pay by weight (order one for two). ✉ *Via Santo Spirito 36/r,* ☎ *055/239–8976. No credit cards. No dinner Sun. Closed Mon. and first 3 wks in July.*

$$ ✕ **Cavallini.** It makes sense that this restaurant, with its outdoor café, is touristy, particularly since it's situated right on Piazza della Signoria. But it is also consistently good, it's open on Sundays, and it's so handy for collapsing in after a hard day at the Uffizi. The cooking is pure Tuscan, with broad *pappardelle* (pasta), bean soup, and grilled meat on the menu. ✉ *Via delle Farina 6/r,* ☎ *055/215818. AE, DC, MC, V. No dinner Tues. Closed Wed. and Aug. 1–22.*

$$ ✕ **Il Cibreo.** The young chefs of this upscale trattoria near the San-
★ t'Ambrogio market prepare updated versions of traditional Florentine dishes and present them with flair, as in *passato di peperoni gialli* (yellow-pepper soup) and *anatra farcita* (boned duck with a meat, raisin, and pine-nut stuffing). Tables are set outdoors in June and July. It has a café annex across the street and an inexpensive tavern annex around the corner. ✉ *Via dei Macci 118/r,* ☎ *055/234–1100. AE, DC, MC, V. Closed Sun., Mon., July 25–Sept. 5, and Dec. 31–Jan. 7.*

$$ ✕ **La Giostra.** A five-minute walk from the back of the cathedral or from Santa Croce, the Giostra has the typically unpretentious and rustic look of a Florentine trattoria, but with a difference: the gourmet touch of the courteous owner-chef. Try his ravioli or veal *agli agrumi* (with an unusual and delicate citrus sauce) or *spianata di carne* (a generous portion of thinly sliced beef redolent of herbs). Like the menu, the wine list offers good value. Service is informal. ✉ *Borgo Pinti 10/r,* ☎ *055/241341. AE, MC, V.*

$$ ✕ **Le Fonticine.** This roomy restaurant near Santa Maria Novella has a warm, rustic atmosphere, with paintings and ceramics covering the walls. Owner Silvano Bruci and his staff are cordial, the homemade pasta is exquisite (try the tortellini or *tortelli,* with meat or cheese stuffing), and the menu offers a good choice of main courses. ✉ *Via Nazionale 79/r,* ☎ *055/282106. AE, DC, MC, V. Closed Sun., Mon., and July 25–Aug. 25.*

$ ✕ **La Maremmana.** A lavish display of produce at the entrance holds promise of what's in store at this typical Florentine trattoria near Santa Croce. The prix-fixe menu includes generous servings of local favorites such as ribollita and *stracotto* (stew with meat and potatoes). There is an à la carte menu, too, and there are tables in the garden. ✉ *Via dei Macci 77/r,* ☎ *055/241226. MC, V. Closed Sun.*

$ ✕ **Za-Za.** Near the San Lorenzo market, this is an informal but trendy trattoria with posters of movie stars on the walls and a lively Italian clientele. The food is classic Florentine: ribollita, fagioli served several ways, and good steaks, with everything fresh from the market. ✉ *Piazza Mercato Centrale 16/r,* ☎ *055/215411. AE, DC, MC, V. Closed Sun. and Aug.*

Lodging

What with mass tourism and trade fairs, rooms are at a premium in Florence for most of the year. Make reservations well in advance. If you arrive without a reservation, the ITA office in the railway station (☉ 8:20 AM–9 PM) can help you, but there may be a long line. Now that much traffic is banned in the downtown area, many central hotel rooms are quieter. Local traffic and motorcycles can still be bothersome, however, so check the decibel level before you settle in. From November through March ask for special low winter rates. For details and price-category definitions, *see* Lodging *in* Staying in Italy, *above*.

$$$$ 🏨 **Grand.** A Florentine classic with Old World elegance and truly luxurious amenities. Smaller and more intimate than the Excelsior, its sis-
★ ter hotel across the square, the Grand has public areas and most rooms decorated in rich Renaissance style. Some rooms have balconies overlooking the Arno. ⊠ *Piazza Ognissanti 1, 50123,* ☎ *055/288781,* FAX *055/217400. 107 rooms with bath. Restaurant, bar, winter garden, parking. AE, DC, MC, V.*

$$$$ 🏨 **Regency.** One of the Ottaviani family's small, select hotels, the Regency has the intimate and highly refined atmosphere of a private villa, luxuriously furnished with antiques and decorated with great style. Just outside the historic center of the city, it has a charming garden and the pleasant Le Jardin restaurant. ⊠ *Piazza Massimo d'Azeglio 3, 50121,* ☎ *055/245247,* FAX *055/234–2938. 33 rooms with bath. Garage. AE, DC, MC, V.*

$$$$ 🏨 **Villa Cora.** In a residential area on a hill overlooking the Oltrarno section of Florence and across the Arno to the Duomo and bell tower, the Villa Cora is a converted private villa. Furnishings are exquisite and the atmosphere is quietly elegant. There are gardens in which to stroll, a pool in which to wallow, and a formal but charming restaurant in which to dine. There is a Mercedes shuttle service between the hotel and the center of Florence. ⊠ *Viale Machiavelli 18, 50125,* ☎ *055/229–8451,* FAX *055/229086. 48 rooms with bath. Restaurant, bar, pool, garden. AE, DC, MC, V.*

$$$ 🏨 **Baglioni.** Spacious, elegant, and a favorite of businesspeople, the Baglioni has well-proportioned rooms tastefully decorated in antique Florentine style. The hotel also has a charming roof terrace, and the splendid Terrazza Brunelleschi restaurant (☞ Dining, *above*), which has the best view in all Florence. ⊠ *Piazza Unità Italiana 6, 50123,* ☎ *055/23580,* FAX *055/235–8895. 197 rooms with bath. Restaurant, garage. AE, DC, MC, V.*

$$$ 🏨 **Brunelleschi.** This unique hotel in the heart of Florence encom-
★ passes a Byzantine tower, a medieval church, and an 18th-century palazzo. Sections of ancient stone walls and brick arches set off the tasteful contemporary decor in the public rooms. Bedrooms are decorated with textured, coordinated fabrics in soft colors; the beige marble bathrooms are luxurious. ⊠ *Piazza Sant'Elisabetta (Via dei Calzaiuoli), 50122,* ☎ *055/562068,* FAX *055/219653. 94 rooms with bath. Restaurant, bar. AE, DC, MC, V.*

$$$ 🏨 **Monna Lisa.** Staying here is like living in an aristocratic palace in
★ the heart of Florence. American visitors in particular are fond of its smallish but homey bedrooms and sumptuously comfortable sitting rooms. Ask for a room on the quiet 17th-century courtyard, especially the one with the delightful balcony. A lavish buffet breakfast is included in the price. Reserve well in advance. ⊠ *Borgo Pinti 27, 50121,* ☎ *055/247–9751,* FAX *055/247–9755. 30 rooms with bath. Bar, garden, parking. AE, DC, MC, V.*

$$ ⛻ **Hermitage.** Comfort and charm are the attributes of this hotel occupying the top two floors of a palazzo next to the Ponte Vecchio and the Uffizi. In the inviting living room overlooking the Arno, the bright breakfast room, the flowered roof terrace, and the well-lighted bedrooms, decor, and atmosphere are those of a well-kept Florentine home. Double glazing, air conditioning, and attentive maintenance sustain the relaxing ambience. (The hotel is served by an elevator located at the top of a short flight of stairs). ⊠ *Vicolo Marzio 1 (Piazza del Pesce–Ponte Vecchio), 50122,* ☎ *055/287216,* FAX *055/212208. 30 rooms with bath. Breakfast room, roof terrace. AE, MC, V.*

$$ ⛻ **Loggiato dei Serviti.** You'll find the Loggiato dei Serviti tucked
★ under an arcade in one of the city's quietest and most attractive squares. Vaulted ceilings and tasteful furnishings (some of them antiques) go far toward making this hotel a real find for those who want to get the genuine Florentine feel and who will appreciate the 19th-century townhouse surroundings while enjoying modern creature comforts. ⊠ *Piazza Santissima Annunziata 3, 50122,* ☎ *055/239–8280,* FAX *055/289595. 29 rooms with bath. Bar. AE, DC, MC, V.*

$$ ⛻ **Morandi alla Crocetta.** This charming and distinguished residence
★ near Piazza Santissima Annunziata was once a monastery, and access is up a flight of stairs. It is furnished in the classic style of a gracious Florentine home, and guests feel like privileged friends of the family. Small and exceptional, it is also a good value and must be booked well in advance. ⊠ *Via Laura 50, 50121,* ☎ *055/234–4747,* FAX *055/248–0954. 9 rooms with bath. Bar. AE, DC, MC, V.*

$$ ⛻ **Villa Azalee.** In a residential area about five minutes from the train station, this century-old mansion is set in a large garden. It has a private-home atmosphere and comfortable living rooms. Bedrooms are decorated individually and are air-conditioned. ⊠ *Viale Fratelli Rosselli 44, 50123,* ☎ *055/214242,* FAX *055/268264. Air-conditioning, garden. 24 rooms with bath. AE, DC, MC, V.*

$ ⛻ **Apollo.** A hospitable Italian-Canadian couple owns and manages this conveniently located hotel near the station, offering good value in spacious rooms decorated in Florentine style, with gleaming new bathrooms that, though compact, have such amenities as hair dryers. The staff is helpful and attentive to guests' needs. ⊠ *Via Faenza 77, 50123,* ☎ *055/284119,* FAX *055/210101. 15 rooms with bath. Bar. AE, DC, MC, V.*

$ ⛻ **Bellettini.** Very centrally located, this small hotel occupies two floors
★ of an old but well-kept building near the Church of San Lorenzo, in an area with many inexpensive eating places. Rooms are ample, with Venetian or Tuscan decor, and bathrooms are modern. The management is friendly and helpful. ⊠ *Via dei Conti 7, 50123,* ☎ *055/213561,* FAX *055/283551. 27 rooms, 23 with bath. Bar, lounge. AE, DC, MC, V.*

The Arts

For a list of events, pick up a "Florence Concierge Information" booklet from your hotel desk, or the monthly information bulletin published by the **Comune Aperto** city information office (⊠ Via Cavour 1/r). This bulletin is also available at information offices at the station, at Via Cavour 1/r, and at Chiasso dei Baroncelli.

Music and Ballet

Most major musical events are staged at the **Teatro Comunale** (⊠ Corso Italia 16, ☎ 055/277–9236). The box office (closed Sun. and Mon.) is open from 9 to 1, and a half hour before performances. It's best to order your tickets by mail, however, as they're difficult to come by at the last minute. You can also order concert and ballet tickets through **Universalturismo** (⊠ Via degli Speziali 7/r, ☎ 055/217241).

Amici della Musica (Friends of Music) puts on a series of concerts at the **Teatro della Pergola** (⊠ Box office, Via della Pergola 10a/r, ☎ 055/247–9651). For program information, contact the Amici della Musica directly at Via Sirtori 49 (☎ 055/608420).

Film

English-language films are shown at the **Cinema Astro,** on Piazza San Simone near Santa Croce. There are two shows every evening, Tuesday through Sunday. It closes in July.

Nightlife

Bars

Many of the top hotels have piano bars; that of the **Plaza Lucchesi** (⊠ Lungarno della Zecca Vecchia 38, ☎ 055/264141) is particularly spacious and pleasant. The terrace of the hotel **Baglioni** (☞ Lodging, *above*) has no music but has one of the best views in Florence, candlelit tables, and a wonderful atmosphere. Music is on tape at the **Champagneria** (⊠ Via Lambruschini 15/r, ☎ 055/490804; closed Sun.), a bistro-type meeting place for a fairly sophisticated mélange of young Florentines and internationals. **Caffè Voltaire** (⊠ Via della Scala 9/r, ☎ 055/218255; closed Mon.) serves Brazilian food and drink and plays Latin music to a lively crowd.

Nightclubs

The River Club (⊠ Lungarno Corsini 8, ☎ 055/282465) has winter-garden decor and a large dance floor (closed Mon.). **Meccanò** (⊠ In the Cascine park at Viale degli Olmi 1, ☎ 055/331371; closed Mon.) offers a multimedia experience, with videos, art, and music, in a high-tech disco with a late-night restaurant, the Pomodoro d'Acciaio.

Discos

Jackie O (⊠ Via dell'Erta Canina 24a, ☎ 055/234–2442; closed Wed.) is a glittering art deco disco with lots of mirrors and marble and a trendy clientele. **Space Electronic** (⊠ Via Palazzuolo 37, ☎ 055/239–3082; closed Mon., except Mar.–Sept., when it's open every night) is exactly what its name implies: ultramodern and psychedelic. **Yab** (⊠ Via Sassetti 5/r, ☎ 055/282018) is another futuristic-style disco popular with the young international set. It's closed Sunday and Monday.

TUSCANY

Tuscany is a blend of rugged hills, fertile valleys, and long stretches of sandy beach that curve along the west coast of central Italy and fringe the pine-forested coastal plain of the Maremma. The gentle, cypress-studded green hills may seem familiar: Leonardo and Raphael often painted them in the backgrounds of their masterpieces. The cities and towns of Tuscany were the cradle of the Renaissance, which during the 15th century saw its greatest flowering in nearby Florence. Come to Tuscany to enjoy its unchanged and gracious atmosphere of good living, and, above all, its unparalleled artistic treasures, many still in their original settings in tiny old churches and patrician palaces.

Getting Around

By Train

The main train network connects Florence with Arezzo and Prato. Another main line runs to Pisa, while a secondary line goes from Prato to the coast via Lucca. Trains also connect Siena with Pisa, a two-hour ride.

By Bus

The region is crisscrossed by bus lines, good alternatives to trains, especially from Florence to Prato, a half-hour trip, and from Florence to Siena, which can take from 1¼ (by express bus) to 2 hours. Use local buses to tour the many pretty hill towns around Siena, such as San Gimignano, and then take a Tra-In or Lazzi bus from Siena to Arezzo, where you can get back onto the main Rome–Florence train line.

By Car

The main autostrade run parallel to the train routes. Roads throughout Tuscany are in good condition, though often narrow.

Guided Tours

A local bus consortium (book through travel agencies and hotels) operates one-day excursions to Siena and San Gimignano out of Florence. **American Express** (⊠ Via Guicciardini 49/r, ☎ 055/288751) also can arrange for cars, drivers, and guides for special-interest tours in Tuscany. **CIT** (⊠ Via Cavour 54/r, ☎ 055/294306) has regional tours, too.

Visitor Information

Arezzo (⊠ Piazza della Repubblica 28, ☎ 0575/377678).
Cortona (⊠ Via Nazionale 72, ☎ 0575/630352).
Lucca (⊠ Piazza Guidiccione 2, tel.. 0583/419689).
Pisa (⊠ Piazza del Duomo 8, ☎ 050/560464).
Pistoia (⊠ Palazzo dei Vescovi, ☎ 0573/21622).
Prato (⊠ Via Cairoli 48, ☎ 0574/24112).
San Gimignano (⊠ Piazza del Duomo, ☎ 0577/940008).
Siena (⊠ Via di Città 43, ☎ 0577/42209; Piazza del Campo 55, ☎ 0577/280551).

Exploring Tuscany

Starting from Florence, you can go west to Prato and Pistoia, workaday cities with a core of fine medieval buildings, then to the historic cities of Lucca and Pisa. Lucca makes a good base for an excursion to Pisa, which is only about a half hour away by car, bus, or train. Heading south from Florence you can explore the Chianti district by car. You can make Siena your base for excursions by car or local bus to some picturesque hill towns: San Gimignano, Montepulciano, and Pienza.

Prato

Since the Middle Ages, **Prato,** 21 kilometers (13 miles) northwest of Florence, has been Italy's major wool-producing center, and it remains one of the world's largest manufacturers of cloth. Ignore the drab industrial outskirts and devote some time to the fine old buildings in the downtown area, crammed with artwork commissioned by Prato's wealthy merchants during the Renaissance. The **Duomo** (cathedral), erected during the Middle Ages, was decorated with paintings and sculptures by some of the most illustrious figures of Tuscan art, among them Fra Filippo Lippi, who took 12 years to complete the frescoes in the apse (perhaps because in the meantime he was being tried for fraud and was also wooing a nun with whom he then eloped). Look in particular for his passionate portrayals of *Herod's Feast* and *Salome's Dance.* ⊠ *Piazza del Duomo.* ☽ *Daily May–Oct. 6:30–noon and 4–7; Nov.–Apr. 7:30–noon and 4–6.*

In the former bishop's palace, now the **Museo dell'Opera del Duomo,** you can see the original reliefs by Donatello for the Pulpit of the Holy Girdle (Mary's belt, supposedly given to Doubting Thomas as evidence

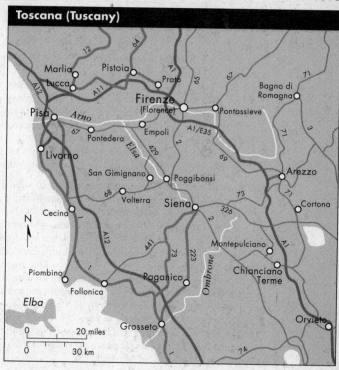

Toscana (Tuscany)

of her assumption; the relic is kept in a chapel of the cathedral). ⊠ *Piazza del Duomo 49,* ☎ *0574/29339.* ☎ *5,000 lire (ticket valid for other Prato museums).* ⊙ *Mon. and Wed.–Sat. 9:30–12:30 and 3–6:30, Sun. 9:30–12:30.*

Architects and architecture buffs rhapsodize over the church of **Santa Maria delle Carceri,** off Via Cairoli. Built by Giuliano Sangallo in the 1490s, it was a landmark of Renaissance architecture. Next to it, the formidable **castle** built for Frederick II of Hohenstaufen is another impressive sight, the only castle of its type to be seen outside southern Italy. ⊠ *Piazza Santa Maria delle Carceri.* ☎ *Free.* ⊙ *Mon. and Wed.–Sat. 9:30–11:30 and 3:30–5:30, Sun. 9:30–11:30.*

Pistoia

Pistoia lies about 15 kilometers (9 miles) northwest of Prato. A floricultural capital of Europe, it's surrounded by greenhouses and plant nurseries. Flowers aside, Pistoia's main sights are all in the downtown area, so you can easily see them on the way to Lucca. The Romanesque **Duomo** (cathedral) is flanked by a 13th-century bell tower, while in its side chapel dedicated to San Jacopo (St. James) there's a massive **silver altar** that alone makes the stop in Pistoia worthwhile. Two hundred years in the making, it's an incredible piece of workmanship, begun in 1287. ⊠ *Piazza del Duomo.* ☎ *Illumination of altarpiece: 2,000 lire.*

Take a look at the unusual Gothic baptistry opposite the Duomo, then follow Via delle Pappe (to the left behind the Duomo) to admire the superb frieze by Giovanni della Robbia on the Ospedale del Ceppo. Continue on to the church of **Sant'Andrea** (⊠ Via Sant'Andrea) to see Pistoia's greatest art treasure, Giovanni Pisano's powerfully sculpted 13th-century **pulpit.** Heading back toward the train station and bus terminal, stop on the way to take in the green-and-white marble church of **San Giovanni Fuorcivitas** (Via Francesco Crispi, off Via Cavour). Highlights here include a *Visitation* by Luca della Robbia, a painting by Taddeo Gaddi, and a holy-water font by Giovanni Pisano.

Lucca

★ Your next destination is **Lucca,** a city well loved by sightseers who appreciate the careful upkeep of its medieval look. Though it hasn't the number of hotels and other tourist trappings that, say, Pisa does, for that very reason it's a pleasant alternative. You can easily make an excursion to Pisa from here—it's only 22 kilometers (14 miles) away. First enjoy the views of the city and countryside from the tree-planted 16th-century ramparts. Then explore the city's marvelously elaborate Romanesque churches, fronted with tiers and rows of columns, and looking suspiciously like oversize marble wedding cakes.

From vast **Piazza Napoleone,** a swing around the Old Town will take
★ you past the 11th-century **Duomo** on Piazza San Martino, with its 15th-century tomb of Ilaria del Carretto by Jacopo della Quercia. Don't neglect a ramble through the **Piazza del Mercato,** which preserves the oval form of the Roman amphitheater over which it was built, or the three surrounding streets that are filled with atmosphere: **Via Battisti, Via Fillungo,** and **Via Guinigi.** In addition to the Duomo, Lucca has two other fine churches. **San Frediano** (Piazza San Frediano) is graced with an austere facade ornamented by 13th-century mosaic decoration. Inside, check out the exquisite reliefs by Jacopo della Quercia in the last chapel on the left. **San Michele in Foro** (⊠ Piazza San Michele) is an exceptional example of the Pisan Romanesque style and decorative flair peculiar to Lucca: Note its facade, a marriage of arches and columns crowned by a statue of St. Michael.

The **Villa Reale** is 8 kilometers (5 miles) outside town, at Marlia. Once the home of Napoléon's sister, and recently restored by the Counts Pecci-Blunt, this villa is celebrated for its spectacular gardens, laid out in the 18th and 19th centuries. Gardening buffs adore the legendary *teatro di verdura,* a theater carved out of hedges and topiaries; concerts are occasionally offered there. ⊠ *Marlia,* ☎ *0583/30108.* ☜ *8,000 lire.* ☉ *Guided visits on the hr., July–Sept., Tues.–Sun. at 10, 11, 4, 5, and 6; Oct.–Nov. and Mar.–June, Tues.–Sun. at 10, 11, 3, 4, and 5. Closed Dec.–Feb.*

Pisa

As you drive southwest, the next Tuscan town of note you'll come to is **Pisa,** a dull, overcommercialized place, though even skeptics have to admit that the **Torre Pendente** (Leaning Tower) really is one of the world's more amazing sights. Designed by Bonanno Pisano (the first of three architects to work on the structure), the tower began to tilt even before it was finished, as its foundations shifted under its weight. A 294-step staircase spirals its way up the tower, and now that the tower has been firmly anchored to the earth to keep it from tilting too far, it may be reopened to visitors on a limited basis. If you want a two-foot marble imitation of the Leaning Tower, perhaps even illuminated from within, this is your chance to grab one at a souvenir stand. ⊠ *Campo dei Miracoli.*

Pisa's **Duomo** is elegantly simple, its facade decorated with geometric and animal shapes. The cavernous interior is supported by a series of 68 columns, while the pulpit is a prime example of Giovanni Pisano's work and one of the major monuments of the Italian Gothic style. Be sure to note the suspended lamp that hangs across from the pulpit; known as Galileo's Lamp, it's said to have inspired his theories on pendular motion. ⊠ *Piazza del Duomo.* ☜ *2,000 lire.* ☉ *Mon.–Sat. 10–5, Sun. 1–5.*

Also in Campo dei Miracoli are the **Baptistry** and the **Camposanto** (cemetery), with important frescoes. Adjacent are the Museo dell'Opera del Duomo, full of medieval sculpture, and the Museo delle Sinopie, the latter—comprising examples of wall sketches preparatory to the painting of frescoes—of limited interest to most visitors. The baptistry was begun in 1153 but not completed until 1400; the celebrated Pisano family did most of its decoration. Test out the excellent acoustics (occasionally the guard will slam the great doors shut and then sing a few notes—the resulting echo is very impressive, and costly, too, since he'll expect a tip). ☒ *To any two: 10,000 lire; to any four: 15,000 lire.* ⊙ *Baptistry and Camposanto: Apr.–Sept., daily 8–7:40; Oct.–Mar., daily 9–5:40. Museo delle Sinopie, Piazza del Duomo,* ☎ *050/560547.* ⊙ *Daily 9–5:40.*

Visitors may find it more convenient to take a train back to Florence and get a bus or train there for the nearly 1½-hour trip to Siena. For a more leisurely look at the Tuscan countryside, investigate the possibility of taking local trains from Pisa to Siena, changing trains at Empoli and then passing through **Certaldo,** a pretty hill town that's the birthplace of Giovanni Boccaccio, 14th-century author of the *Decameron*.

Siena

One of Italy's best-preserved medieval towns, **Siena** is rich both in works of art and in expensive antique shops. The famous **Palio** is held here, a breakneck, 90-second horse race that takes place twice each year in the Piazza del Campo, on July 2 and August 16. Built on three hills, Siena is not an easy town to explore, for everything you'll want to see is either up or down a steep hill or stairway. But it is worth every ounce of effort. Siena really gives you the chance of seeing and feeling what the Middle Ages must have been like: dark stone palaces that look like fortresses, Gothic church portals, and narrow streets opening out into airy squares.

Siena was a center of learning and art during the Middle Ages, and almost all the public buildings and churches in the town have enough artistic or historical merit to be worth visiting. Unlike most churches, Siena's **Duomo** has a mixture of religious and civic symbols ornamenting both its interior and exterior. The cathedral museum in the unfinished transept contains some fine works of art, notably a celebrated *Maestà* by Duccio di Buoninsegna. The animated frescoes of papal history in the Piccolomini Library (with an entrance off the left aisle of the cathedral) are credited to Pinturicchio and are worth seeking out. ☒ *Piazza del Duomo. Cathedral Museum:* ☒ *5,000 lire.* ⊙ *Mar. 12–Sept., daily 9–7:30; Oct.1–31, daily 9–6:30; Nov.–Dec., daily 9–1:30; Jan. 2–Mar. 12, daily 9–1:30. Library:* ☒ *2,000 lire.* ⊙ *Mid-Mar.–Oct. 31, daily 9–7:30; Nov.–Dec., and Jan.2 – mid-Mar., daily 10–1 and 2–5.*

★ Nearby, the fan-shaped **Piazza del Campo** is Siena's main center of activity, with 11 streets leading into it. Farsighted planning has preserved it as a medieval showpiece, containing the 13th-century **Palazzo Pubblico** (City Hall) and the **Torre del Mangia** (Bell Tower). Try to visit both these buildings, the former for Lorenzetti's frescoes on the effects of good and bad government, the latter for the wonderful view (you'll have to climb 503 steps to reach it, however). ☒ *Piazza del Campo,* ☎ *0577/292111. Bell Tower:* ☒ *5,000 lire.* ⊙ *Mar. 15–Nov. 15, daily 10–1 hr before sunset; Nov. 16–Mar. 14, daily 10–1. Palazzo Pubblico (including the Civic Museum):* ☒ *6,000 lire.* ⊙ *Mar. 15–Nov. 15, Mon.–Sat. 9–7, Sun. 9–1:30; Nov.–Mar., daily 9–1:30.*

There are several **gelaterie** on Piazza del Campo, but if you need
something more substantial, walk east from the square to **Verrocchio**
(✉ Logge del Papa 2; closed Wed.), a restaurant serving local fare.

San Gimignano

★ From Siena, **San Gimignano** is only about a half hour away by car and
an hour by Tra-In bus (change buses in Poggibonsi). San Gimignano-
of-the-Beautiful-Towers—to use its original name—is perhaps the most
delightful of the Tuscan medieval hill towns. There were once 79 tall
towers here, symbols of power for the wealthy families of the Middle
Ages. Thirteen are still standing, giving the town its unique skyline.
The bus stops just outside the town gates, from which you can stroll
down the main street to the picturesque Piazza della Cisterna.

Just around the corner is the church of the **Collegiata.** Its walls, and
those of its chapel dedicated to Santa Fina, are decorated with radiant
frescoes (have plenty of 100-lire coins at hand for the light machines;
to get a closer look at the chapel frescoes, buy a ticket for the Municipal Museum in Palazzo del Popolo; ✎ 5,000 lire). From the steps of
the church you can observe the town's countless crows as they circle
the tall towers. In the pretty courtyard on the right as you descend the
church stairs, there's a shop selling Tuscan and Deruta ceramics, which
you'll also find in other shops along the Via San Giovanni. The excellent San Gimignano wine could be another souvenir of your visit; it's
sold in gift cartons from just about every shop in town.

If you have a car, you can drive northeast of Siena on Route 222, through
hilly Chianti country, or southeast of Siena to the Abbey of Monte Oliveto
Maggiore and the hill towns of Montepulciano and Pienza, each worth
seeing and much less crowded than San Gimignano. You can also
reach Montepulciano and Pienza by bus from Siena, though service is
often haphazard.

Arezzo

A local bus takes you from Siena to **Arezzo,** about 48 kilometers (30
miles) east. The route meanders around thickly wooded hills, past
vineyards and wheat fields, and across the broad ribbon of the Autostrada
del Sole in the fertile Chiana Valley, known for its pale beef cattle that
provide the classic bistecca alla fiorentina. Arezzo is not a particularly
beautiful town, though the old, upper town still has a good assortment
of medieval and Renaissance buildings. What makes Arezzo worth a
visit, however, is its fine array of Tuscan art treasures, including frescoes, stained glass, and ancient Etruscan pottery.

The **Museo Archeologico** (Archaeological Museum) is near the train station, next to what's left of an ancient **Roman amphitheater.** The museum has a rich collection of Etruscan art, artifacts, and pottery. The
latter has been copied by contemporary Arezzo artisans and is sold in
the local ceramic shops. ✉ *Via Margaritone 10,* ☎ *0575/20882.* ✎
8,000 lire. ☉ *Tues.–Sat. 9–2, Sun. 9–1.*

Via Guido Monaco, named after the 11th-century originator of the mu-
★ sical scale, leads to the church of **San Francesco,** which holds some of
the town's main attractions, namely the famous frescoes by Piero della
Francesca depicting the Legend of the True Cross. Due for restoration
after intensive studies of suitable methods, these frescoes may be at least
partially hidden for a few years. Though faded, they still rank among
the outstanding examples of Renaissance painting, and art lovers are
looking forward to seeing them in renewed splendor. ✉ *Via Cavour.
Push button on black box for light.*

Now you enter the old part of Arezzo, where the poet Petrarch (1304–74), the artist Vasari (1511–74), and the satirical author Pietro Aretino (1492–1556) all lived. Climb Via Cesalpino uphill to the fine Gothic **cathedral** (Piazza del Duomo), then stroll past **Petrarch's House** to **Piazza Grande,** an attractive, sloping square where an extensive open-air fair of antiques and old bric-a-brac is held the first weekend of every month. The shops around the piazza also specialize in antiques, with prices lower than those you will encounter in Florence. The colonnaded apse and bell tower of the Romanesque church of **Santa Maria della Pieve** grace one end of this pleasant piazza.

Cortona

A full day may be enough for you to get the feel of Arezzo, but you may wish to stay overnight, especially during the antiques fair, or if you want to use the town as a base for an excursion to **Cortona,** about 30 kilometers (18 miles) south. This well-preserved, unspoiled medieval hill town is known for its excellent small art gallery and a number of fine antiques shops, as well as for its colony of foreign residents. Cortona has the advantage of being on the main train line, though you will have to take a local bus from the station up into the town, passing the Renaissance church of **Santa Maria del Calcinaio** on the way.

The heart of Cortona is formed by **Piazza della Repubblica** and the adjacent **Piazza Signorelli.** Wander into the courtyard of the picturesque **Palazzo Pretorio,** and, if you want to see a representative collection of Etruscan bronzes, climb its centuries-old stone staircase to the **Museo dell'Accademia Etrusca** (Gallery of Etruscan Art). ⊠ *Piazza Signorelli 9,* ☎ *0575/630415.* ⊡ *5,000 lire.* ⊙ *Apr.–Sept., Tues.–Sun. 10–1 and 4–7; Oct.–Mar., Tues.–Sun. 9–1 and 3–5.*

The nearby **Museo Diocesano** (Diocesan Museum) houses an impressive number of large and splendid paintings by native son Luca Signorelli, as well as a beautiful *Annunciation* by Fra Angelico, a delightful surprise to find in this small, eclectic town. ⊠ *Piazza del Duomo 1,* ☎ *0575/62830.* ⊡ *5,000 lire.* ⊙ *Apr.–Sept., Tues.–Sun. 9–1 and 3–6:30; Oct.–Mar., Tues.–Sun. 9–1 and 3–5.*

Dining and Lodging

For details and price-category definitions, *see* Dining *and* Lodging *in* Staying in Italy, *above.*

Arezzo

$$ ✕ **Buca di San Francesco.** Travelers and passing celebrities come to this
★ rustic and historic cellar restaurant for the 13th-century cantina atmosphere, but locals love it for the food, especially ribollita and *sformato di verdure* (vegetable pie). ⊠ *Piazza San Francesco 1,* ☎ *0575/23271. AE, DC, MC, V. No dinner Mon. Closed Tues. and July.*

$$ ✕ **Tastevin.** Arezzo's purveyor of creative bistrot cooking serves traditional Tuscan dishes as well, in two attractive rooms in warm Tuscan provincial style and one in more sophisticated art deco. At the cozy bar the talented owner plays and sings Sinatra songs in the evening. Specialties are risotto Tastevin, with cream of truffles, and *tagliata* Tastevin (sliced beef with olive oil and rosemary). ⊠ *Via dei Cenci 9,* ☎ *0575/28304. AE, MC, V. Closed Mon., (Sun. in summer), and Aug. 1-25.*

$ ✕ **Spiedo d'Oro.** Cheery red-and-white tablecloths add a colorful touch to this large, reliable trattoria near the Archaeological Museum. The menu offers such Tuscan home-style specialties as *zuppa di pane* (bread soup), pappardelle *oll'ocio* (with duck sauce), and osso buco *aretina* (sautéed veal shank). ⊠ *Via Crispi 12,* ☎ *0575/22873. No credit cards. Closed Thurs. and first 2 wks in July.*

$$ ▣ **Continental.** The circa-1950 Continental has fairly spacious rooms decorated in white and bright yellow, gleaming bathrooms, and the advantage of a central location within walking distance of all major sights. ⊠ *Piazza Guido Monaco 7, 52100,* ☎ *0575/20251,* ℻ *0575/340485. 74 rooms with bath. Restaurant. AE, DC, MC, V.*

Cortona

$$ ✕ **Tonino.** The place to eat in Cortona, it's known for its delicious an-
★   tipasto and for succulent steaks of Chiana Valley beef. It's best on week-days, when it's quieter. Both service and food have a touch of class. The dining rooms, on two floors, have large picture windows overlooking the valley. ⊠ *Piazza Garibaldi,* ☎ *0575/630500. AE, DC, MC, V. No dinner Mon. Closed Tues.*

Lucca

$$–$$$ ✕ **La Mora.** You'll need a car or a taxi to take you to this charming old way station 10 kilometers (6 miles) outside Lucca, but its authentic local cooking is worth every effort. It is widely considered to be one of the best regional restaurants in Italy. ⊠ *Via Sesto di Moriano 1748, Ponte a Moriano,* ☎ *0583/406402. AE, DC, MC, V. Closed Wed., Oct. 10–30.*

$$ ✕ **Buca di Sant'Antonio.** A Lucca favorite, near the church of San
★   Michele, Buca di Sant'Antonio was around more than two centuries ago, and it still retains something of its rustic look. It specializes in traditional local dishes, some unfamiliar but well worth trying, among them ravioli *di ricotta alle zucchine* (with cheese and zucchini) and kid or lamb roasted with herbs. ⊠ *Via della Cervia 3,* ☎ *0583/55881. AE, DC, MC, V. No dinner Sun. Closed Mon. and July 7–31.*

$$ ✕ **Il Giglio.** Off vast Piazza Napoleone, Il Giglio has a quiet, turn-of-the-century charm and a dignified atmosphere. In the summer the tables outdoors have a less formal air. The menu is classic: *crostini di fegatini* (savory Tuscan chicken liver pâté on small pieces of toast), steaks, and seafood, as well. ⊠ *Piazza del Giglio 3,* ☎ *0583/494058. AE, DC, MC, V. No dinner Tues. Closed Wed.*

$$$–$$$$ ▣ **Villa La Principessa.** This pretty 19th-century country mansion, 3½
★   kilometers (2 miles) outside Lucca, is an exclusive hotel with a deluxe annex, Principessa Elisa. All rooms are individually and tastefully decorated. Antique floors, furniture, and portraits set the tone, and the restaurant is known for its fine Tuscan dishes. ⊠ *Massa Pisana, 55050,* ☎ *0583/370037,* ℻ *0583/379019. 44 rooms with bath. Restaurant, pool, park. AE, DC, MC, V. Closed Nov. 1–Mar. 31.*

$ ▣ **La Luna.** There's an aura of Old World charm in this family-run hotel on one of Lucca's most central and historic streets. Recent, extensive renovations have endowed the establishment with gleaming modern bathrooms, leaving the atmosphere intact. A plus for anyone touring by car is the hotel's own garage and parking area. ⊠ *Corte Compagni 12 (corner of Via Fillungo), 55100,* ☎ *0583/493634,* ℻ *0583/490021. 30 rooms with bath. AE, DC, MC, V. Closed Jan. 1–31.*

$ ▣ **Ilaria.** This small, family-run hotel sits in a pretty location on a minuscule canal within easy walking distance of the main sights. The rooms are smallish but fresh and functional. ⊠ *Via del Fosso 20, 55100,* ☎ *0583/47558. 17 rooms, 13 with bath or shower. AE, DC, MC, V.*

Montepulciano

$ ✕ **Cittino.** A few plants outside the door mark this plain, family-run trattoria off one of the town's main streets. *Pici* (homemade spaghetti) with meat sauce and local pecorino cheese are good choices. The house wine is local, too. ⊠ *Vicolo Via Nuovo 2 (Via Voltaia),* ☎ *0578/757335. Reservations not accepted. No credit cards. Closed Wed.*

Pievescola (Casola d'Elsa)

$$$ ✕🏨 **La Suvera.** In this luxurious hotel in the Tuscan countryside, 27 kilometers (17 miles) from Siena and 56 kilometers (35 miles) from Florence, you can savor living on an aristocratic estate that was once owned by Pope Julius II. Rooms and suites are magnificently furnished with antiques and fitted with up-to-the-minute comforts. With salons, a library, Italian garden, swimming pool, and L'Oliviera restaurant (serving estate wines) to enjoy, guests find it hard to tear themselves away. ✉ *Pievescola (Casola d'Elsa), off Rte. 541, 53030,* ☎ *0577/960300,* FAX *0577/960220. 19 rooms with bath, 13 suites. Restaurant, bar, park, heated pool, garden, sauna, tennis court, horseback riding, meeting rooms, helipad. AE, DC, MC, V. Closed Nov. 1–Mar. 31.*

Pisa

$$ ✕ **Bruno.** A country-inn look, with beamed ceilings and soft lights, makes Bruno a pleasant place to lunch on classic Tuscan dishes, from *zuppa alla pisana* (vegetable soup) to *baccalà con porri* (cod with leeks). It's just outside the old city walls and only a short walk from the bell tower and cathedral. ✉ *Via Luigi Bianchi 12,* ☎ *050/560818. AE, DC, MC, V. No dinner Mon. Closed Tues.*

$$ ✕ **Osteria dei Cavalieri.** Just off Piazza dei Cavalieri, in Pisa's medieval center, this popular tavern/wine cellar occupies the ground floor of a centuries-old tower. It offers a one-course lunch menu, prix-fixe dinner menus and a wide range of vegetarian, meat, and fish dishes à la carte, including freshly made *tagliolini* (noodles) and tagliata *di manzo* (sliced steak, usually served with mushrooms). ✉ *Via San Frediano 16,* ☎ *050/580858. AE, DC, MC, V. No lunch Sat. Closed Sun. and Aug.*

Pistoia

$$ ✕ **La Casa degli Amici.** The name means "the house of friends," and that's the atmosphere that the two industrious ladies who own it succeed in creating in this restaurant located outside Pistoia's old walls, on the road toward the A11 autostrada exit. They offer homey specialties, such as ribollita, pasta e fagioli, and *coniglio alla Vernaccia* (rabbit in white wine). There's a terrace for outdoor dining in the summer. ✉ *Via Bonellina 111,* ☎ *0573/380305. AE, DC, MC, V. No dinner Sun. Closed Tues. and Aug.*

$$ ✕ **Leon Rosso.** To find this little restaurant, take Via Roma off Piazza del Duomo, and walk straight ahead to Via Panciatichi. Usually crowded with locals, it serves typical Tuscan specialties, among them appetizing crostini served with liver pâté. For dessert, try *panna cotta* (milk custard). ✉ *Via Panciatichi 4,* ☎ *0573/29230. AE, DC, MC, V. Closed Sun., Aug.*

Prato

$$ ✕ **Stefano.** At the lower end of the moderate price range, this trattoria is popular with the locals. A simple place, it serves regional dishes such as ribollita, fagioli laced with local olive oil, and grilled meat. ✉ *Via Pomeria 23,* ☎ *0574/34665. Reservations not accepted. No credit cards. Closed Sun.*

San Gimignano

$$$ ✕ **Bel Soggiorno.** Bel Soggiorno is attached to a small hotel. It has fine views, refectory tables set with linen and candles, and leather-covered chairs. Specialties are *zuppa medioevale* (soup of mushrooms, truffle, grain, and potatoes) and *sorpresa in crosta* (spicy rabbit stew in a bread crust). ✉ *Via San Giovanni 91,* ☎ *0577/940375. AE, DC, MC, V. Closed Mon. and Jan.–Feb.*

$$ 🏠 **Pescille.** This rambling stone farmhouse, about 3 kilometers (2 miles) outside San Gimignano, with a good view of the town, has been restored as a hotel and furnished in attractive rustic-chic style. ☒ *Località Pescille, 53037,* ☎ *0577/940186,* ℻ *0577/940186. 40 rooms with bath. Bar, garden, pool, tennis court. AE, DC, MC, V. Closed Nov. 15–Feb. 28.*

Siena

$$$ ✕ **Ai Marsili.** In a medieval palace near the Duomo, Ai Marsili is a spa-
★ cious, brick-vaulted wine cellar with refectory tables and excellent Tuscan cuisine; it's a place for a leisurely meal accompanied by classic Chianti wines. Specialties include pici with mushroom sauce, and beef with fresh estragon sauce. ☒ *Via del Castoro 3,* ☎ *0577/47154. AE, DC, MC, V. Closed Mon.*

$$ ✕ **Osteria Le Logge.** Just off Piazza del Campo, this is a fine choice for an informal but memorable meal. Get there early to claim a table. Among the specialties are *malfatti all'Osteria* (ricotta and spinach dumplings in cream sauce) and tagliata *alla rucola* (sliced steak with arugula). ☒ *Via del Porrione 33,* ☎ *0577/48013. DC, MC, V. Closed Sun., 2 wks in June and in Nov.*

$$ ✕ **Tullio Tre Cristi.** To find this historic trattoria, take Via dei Rossi from Via Banchi di Sopra. Even though it was discovered by tourists long ago, it remains true to typical Sienese cooking and atmosphere. Try spaghetti *alle briciole,* a poor-man's pasta with bread crumbs, tomato, and garlic. ☒ *Vicolo di Provenzano 1,* ☎ *0577/280608. MC, V. No dinner Sun. Closed Mon., and Jan.*

$ ✕ **Le Tre Campane.** Boasting a convenient location between Piazza del Campo and the Duomo, this small trattoria displays the colorful banners of Siena's 17 districts. Popular with the locals, it specializes in Tuscan fare and a *trittico* (trio) of pastas. ☒ *Piazzetta Bonelli 5,* ☎ *0577/286091. No credit cards. Closed Tues. and Jan.–Feb.*

$$$$ 🏠 **Certosa di Maggiano.** A 14th-century Carthusian monastery less than a mile southeast of Siena has been converted into a sophisticated oasis furnished in impeccable style. The bedrooms have every comfort, and the atmosphere is that of an aristocratic family villa. ☒ *Strada di Certosa 82, 53100,* ☎ *0577/288180,* ℻ *0577/288189. 18 rooms with bath. Restaurant, garage, pool, tennis court. AE, DC, MC, V.*

$$$$ 🏠 **Park Hotel.** Just outside the walls of the old city, this is a handsome
★ 15th-century villa on its own well-equipped grounds. The furnishings strike an elegant balance between antique charm and sybaritic comfort. Immersed in this warm but sophisticated ambience, you can pretend you're a houseguest of the Medici. There's a fine restaurant and garden terrace. ☒ *Via di Marciano 18, 53100,* ☎ *0577/44803,* ℻ *0577/49020. 80 rooms with bath. Restaurant, pool, tennis court, 6-hole practice golf course, garden. AE, DC, MC, V.*

$$ 🏠 **Antica Torre.** A cordial young couple runs this hotel in a restored centuries-old tower a 10-minute walk from Piazza del Campo. Rooms are smallish and are furnished sparingly but in good taste. Beamed ceilings throughout and original brick vaults here and there are reminders of the tower's venerable history. ☒ *Via Fieravecchia 7, 53100,* ☎ *0577/222255,* ℻ *0577/222255. 8 rooms with bath. AE, MC, V.*

$–$$ 🏠 **Duomo.** Occupying the top floor of a 17th-century building in the
★ center of Siena, near Piazza del Campo, the hotel is quiet and is furnished in a neat contemporary style, with traces of the past showing in the artfully exposed brickwork in the breakfast room. Many rooms have superb views of the city's towers and the hills beyond. Two rooms are endowed with balconies. ☒ *Via Stalloreggi 38, 53100,* ☎ *0577/289088,* ℻ *0577/43043. 23 rooms with bath. AE, DC, MC, V.*

MILAN

Arriving and Departing

As Lombardy's capital and the most important financial and commercial center in northern Italy, Milan is well connected with Rome and Florence by fast and frequent rail and air service, though the latter is often delayed in winter by heavy fog.

By Plane

Linate Airport, 11 kilometers (7 miles) outside Milan, handles mainly domestic and European flights (☏ 02/7485–2200). Malpensa, 50 kilometers (30 miles) from the city, handles intercontinental flights (☏ 02/7485–2200).

BETWEEN THE AIRPORT AND DOWNTOWN

Buses connect both airports with Milan, stopping at both the central station and at the Porta Garibaldi station. Fare from Linate is 4,000 lire on the special airport bus or 1,400 lire on municipal Bus 73 (to Piazza San Babila); from Malpensa, 12,000 lire. A taxi from Linate to the center of Milan costs about 30,000 lire; from Malpensa, about 120,000 lire.

By Train

The main train terminal is the central station in Piazzale Duca d'Aosta (☏ 02/67500). Several smaller stations handle commuter trains. There are several fast Intercity trains daily between Rome and Milan, stopping in Florence. A nonstop Intercity leaves from Rome or Milan morning and evening, taking about four hours to go between the two cities.

By Car

From Rome and Florence, take the A1 Autostrada. From Venice, take the A4. With bans on parking throughout the center of Milan, it's easier to park on the outskirts and use public transportation.

Getting Around

By Subway

Milan's subway network, the Metropolitana, is modern, fast, and easy to use. MM signs mark Metropolitana stations. There are, at present, three lines. The ATM (city transport authority) has an information office on the mezzanine of the Duomo Metro station (☏ 02/875495). Tickets are sold at newsstands at every stop, and in ticket machines *for exact change only.* The fare is 1,400 lire, and the subway runs from 6:20 AM to midnight.

By Bus and Streetcar

Buy tickets at newsstands, tobacco shops, and bars. The fare is 1,400 lire. One ticket is valid for 75 minutes on all surface lines and one subway trip. Daily tickets valid for 24 hours on all public transportation lines are sold at the Duomo Metro station ATM information office, and at Stazione Centrale Metro station. Twenty-four-hour tickets cost 4,800 lire; 48-hour tickets 8,000 lire.

By Taxi

Use yellow cabs only. They wait at stands or can be telephoned in advance (☏ 6767, 8585, or 8388).

Important Addresses and Numbers

Consulates

U.S. (✉ Via Principe Amedeo 2, ☏ 02/290351). **Canadian** (✉ Via Pisani 19, ☏ 02/669–7451). **U.K.** (✉ Via San Paolo 7, ☏ 02/723001).

Emergencies

Police, ☎ 02/113; **Carabinieri,** ☎ 02/112; **Ambulance,** ☎ 02/7733; **Medical Emergency,** Fatebenefratelli Hospital, Corso di Porta Nuova 23, ☎ 02/63631.

Travel Agencies

Compagnia Italiana Turismo (CIT) (✉ Galleria Vittorio Emanuele, ☎ 02/866661); **American Express Travel Agency** (✉ Via Brera 3, ☎ 02/809645).

Visitor Information

The main **APT Tourist Offices** are at Stazione Centrale (☎ 02/669–0532; ⊙ Mon.–Sat. 8–7, Sun. 9–12:30 and 1:30–6), and in the Palazzo del Turismo at Via Marconi 1, Piazza del Duomo (☎ 02/809662; ⊙ Mon.–Sat. 8–8, Sun. 9–12:30 and 1:30–5).

Guided Tours

Orientation

Three-hour morning or afternoon sightseeing tours depart Tuesday–Sunday from Piazzetta Reale, next to the Duomo; the cost is about 50,000 lire and tickets can be purchased from APT offices (☞ Visitor Information, *above*) or aboard the bus.

Excursions

From April through September the **Autostradale** bus company (✉ Via Pompeo Marchesi 55, ☎ 02/4820–3177) and **Autostradale Viaggi** (✉ Piazza Castello 1, ☎ 02/801161) offer an all-day tour of Lake Maggiore, including a boat trip to the Borromean Islands and lunch. The cost is about 105,000 lire.

Exploring Milan

Milan, capital of all that is new in Italy, has a history that goes back at least 2,500 years. Its fortunes ever since, both as a great commercial trading center and as the object of regular conquest and occupation, are readily explained by its strategic position at the center of the Lombard Plain. Virtually every invader in European history—Gaul, Roman, Goth, Longobard, and Frank—as well as every ruler of France, Spain, and Austria, has taken a turn at ruling the city and the region. So if you are wondering why so little seems to have survived from Milan's antiquity, the answer is simple—war. Thanks to the great family dynasties of the Visconti and the Sforza, however, there are still great Gothic and Renaissance treasures to be seen, including Leonardo's unforgettable *Last Supper*. And thanks to new names—Valentino, Versace, and Armani among them—the city now dazzles as the design and fashion center of the world. Old and new come together at Milan's La Scala—Europe's most important opera house—where audiences continue to set sail for passion on the high C's.

Numbers in the margin correspond to points of interest on the Milano (Milan) map.

★ ❶ The center of Milan is the Piazza del Duomo. The massive **Duomo** is one of the largest churches in the world, a mountain of marble fretted with statues, spires, and flying buttresses. The interior is a more solemn Italian Gothic. Take the elevator or walk up 158 steps to the roof, from which—if it's a clear day—you can see over the city to the Lombard Plain and the Alps beyond, all through an amazing array of spires and statues. The **Madonnina,** a gleaming gilt statue on the highest spire, is a Milan landmark. ✉ *Piazza del Duomo. Entrance to elevator and stair-*

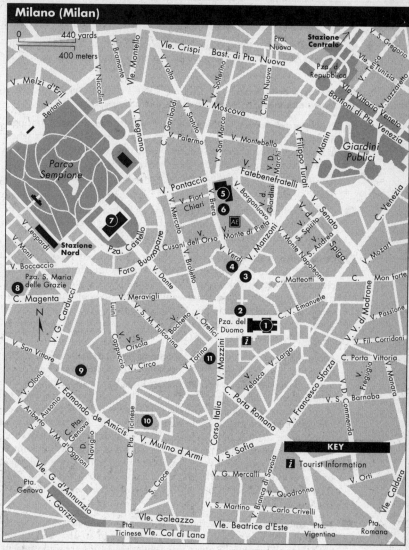

Milano (Milan)

Castello Sforzesco, **7**
Duomo, **1**
Galleria, **2**
Jamaica, **6**
Piazza della Scala, **3**
Pinacoteca di Brera, **5**
San Lorenzo
Maggiore, **10**

San Satiro, **11**
Santa Maria delle
Grazie, **8**
Sant'Ambrogio, **9**
Teatro alla Scala, **4**

way outside cathedral, to the right. ▣ *Stairs, 5,000 lire; elevator, 7,000 lire.* ☉ *Mar.–Oct., daily 9–5:45; Nov.–Feb., daily 9–4:30.*

★ ❷ The **Galleria,** just off the Piazza del Duomo, is where the Milanese and visitors stroll, window-shop, and sip pricey cappuccinos at trendy cafés.

❸ In **Piazza della Scala,** you will find Milan's city hall on one side and
❹ **Teatro alla Scala,** the world-famous opera house, opposite.

★ ❺ **Pinacoteca di Brera** houses one of Italy's great collections of paintings. Most are of a religious nature, confiscated in the 19th century when many religious orders were suppressed and their churches closed. Most interesting among these are works by Mantegna, Raphae, and Titian. ▣ *Via Brera 28,* ☎ *02/862634.* ▣ *8,000 lire.* ☉ *Tues.–Sat. 9–5:30, Sun. 9–12:45.*

❻ Once a bohemian hangout, **Jamaica** is an offbeat café in the heart of the Brera neighborhood, which is dotted with art galleries and chic little restaurants. ▣ *Via Brera 26,* ☉ *7:30–2:30AM.*

❼ **Castello Sforzesco** is a somewhat sinister 19th-century reconstruction of the imposing 15th-century fortress built by the Sforzas, who succeeded the Viscontis as lords of Milan in the 15th century. Surrounded by a moat, it now houses wide-ranging collections of sculptures, antiques, and ceramics, including Michelangelo's *Rondanini Pietà,* his last work, left unfinished at his death. ▣ *Piazza Castello,* ☎ *02/620–8391.* ▣ *free* ☉ *Tues.–Sun. 9:30–5:30.*

★ ❽ Although portions of the church of **Santa Maria delle Grazie** were designed by Bramante, it plays second fiddle to the **Refectory** next door, where, over a three-year period, Leonardo da Vinci painted his megafamous fresco, *The Last Supper.* The fresco has suffered more than its share of disaster, beginning with the experiments of the artist, who used untested pigments that soon began to deteriorate. *The Last Supper* is now a mere shadow of its former self, despite meticulous restoration that proceeds at a snail's pace. To save what is left, visitors are limited in time and number, and you may have to wait in line to get a glimpse of this world-famous work. ▣ *Piazza Santa Maria delle Grazie 2,* ☎ *02/498–7588.* ▣ *6,000 lire.* ☉ *Tues.–Sun. 8–2; hrs may vary, call to confirm.*

❾ **Sant'Ambrogio** is for those interested in medieval architecture. The medieval church was consecrated by St. Ambrose in AD 387, and it's the model for all Lombard Romanesque churches. Inside are some ancient works of art, including a remarkable 9th-century altar in precious metals and enamels and some 5th-century mosaics. On December 8, the day after the feast day of St. Ambrose, the streets around the church are the scene of a lively flea market. ▣ *Piazza Sant'Ambrogio.*

❿ **San Lorenzo Maggiore** has 16 ancient Roman columns in front and some 4th-century mosaics in the Chapel of St. Aquilinus. ▣ *Corso di Porta Ticinese.*

⓫ The church of **San Satiro** is another architectural gem in which Bramante's perfect command of proportion and perspective, characteristic of the Renaissance, made a small interior seem extraordinarily spacious and airy. ▣ *Via Torino.*

NEED A
BREAK?   Only a few steps from the church of San Satiro are two Peck shops, one a gourmet delicatessen, the other with a tempting array of snacks to eat on the premises. ▣ *Via Spadari 9; Via Cantù 3.*

Shopping

Milan's most elegant shopping streets are as follows: **Via Monte Napoleone, Via Manzoni, Via della Spiga,** and **Via Sant'Andrea.**

Head for **Corso Buenos Aires,** near the central train station, if the chic goods of other areas are a shock to your purse.

Dining

For details and price-category definitions, *see* Dining *in* Staying in Italy, *above.*

$$$ ✕ **Biffi Scala.** The elegant Biffi Scala caters mainly to the after-opera crowd that pours in around midnight. Built in 1861, it features a high ceiling and polished wood walls. Specialties include *crespelle alle erbette* (pancakes stuffed with wild mushrooms and other vegetables) and *carpaccio alla Biffi Scala* (thin slices of cured raw beef with a tangy sauce). ⊠ *Piazza della Scala,* ☎ *02/866651. AE, DC, MC, V. Closed Sun., Aug. 10–20, and Dec. 24–Jan. 6. No lunch Sat.; no dinner Sat. mid-June–mid-July.*

$$$ ✕ **Boeucc.** Milan's oldest restaurant is situated not far from La Scala
★ and is subtly lighted, with fluted columns, chandeliers, thick carpet, and a garden for warm-weather dining. In addition to the typical Milanese foods, it also serves such exotica as penne *al branzino e zucchine* (with sea bass and zucchini sauce) and gelato *di castagne con zabaglione caldo* (chestnut ice cream with hot zabaglione). ⊠ *Piazza Belgioioso 2,* ☎ *02/760–20224. Reservations essential. Closed Sat., Dec. 24–Jan. 2, Easter, and Aug. No lunch Sun. AE.*

$$$ ✕ **Don Lisander.** This 17th-century chapel has been drastically redecorated, and now features designer lighting, abstract prints, and a modern terra-cotta tile floor, creating an uncompromisingly contemporary effect. Try the *scaloppe di fegato con menta* (calves' liver scaloppini with fresh mint leaves) or else go for the branzino *al timo* (sea bass with thyme). ⊠ *Via Manzoni 12A,* ☎ *02/760–20130. Reservations essential. AE, DC, MC, V. Closed Sun., 2 wks in mid-Aug., and 2 wks at Christmas. No dinner Sat.*

$$$ ✕ **Savini.** Red carpets and cut-glass chandeliers characterize the classy
★ Savini, a typical Old World Milanese restaurant whose dining rooms spread over three floors. There's also a "winter garden" from which patrons can people-watch shoppers in the Galleria. The risotto *al salto* (rice cooked as a pancake, tossed in the pan, a Milanese specialty) is excellent here, as is the *cotoletta di vitello* (breaded veal cutlets). ⊠ *Galleria Vittorio Emanuele,* ☎ *02/720–03433. AE, DC, MC, V. Closed Sun., 10 days in Aug., and 1 wk at Christmas.*

$$ ✕ **Antica Trattoria della Pesa.** Though the management has changed, the turn-of-the-century decor and atmosphere, dark wood paneling, and old-fashioned lamps still look much as they must have when this eatery opened one hundred years ago. This is authentic Old Milan, and the menu is right in line, with risotto, minestrone, and osso buco. ⊠ *Viale Pasubio 10,* ☎ *02/655–5741. AE, DC, MC, V. Closed Sun. and 2 wks in Aug.*

$$ ✕ **Nabucco.** This is a smart restaurant in the Brera district, tastefully furnished. Highlights on the menu include risotto con porcini, an excellent range of salads, and homemade pastries and desserts. The prix-fixe lunches are particularly good values. ⊠ *Via Fiori Cjoaoro 10,* ☎ *02/860663. AE, DC, MC, V. Closed Sun. No lunch Mon.*

$$ ✕ **Trattoria Milanese.** Situated between the Duomo and the Basilica of Sant'Ambrogio, this small, popular trattoria has been run by the same family for more than 80 years. It's invariably crowded, especially at dinner, when the regulars love to linger. Food is classic regional in approach, with risotto and cotoletta *alla milanese* (veal milanese-style) good choices. ⊠ *Via Santa Marta 11,* ☎ *02/864-51991. AE, D, MC, V. Closed Tues., Aug., and Dec. 25.*

$ ✕ **Al Cantinone.** Operagoers still come to the Cantinone bar for a drink after the final curtain, just as they did a century ago. The decor is basic, the atmosphere lively, the service fast, and the food reliable. The proprietor stocks 240 different wines. Try the cotoletta *al Cantinone* (veal cutlets with mushrooms, olives, and a cream and tomato sauce). ⊠ *Via Agnello 19,* ☎ *02/864−61338. AE, MC, V. No lunch Sat. Closed Sun., Aug., and Dec. 25.*

$ ✕ **Birreria-Bistro San Tomaso.** A popular lunch spot for trendy Milanese, this place has the informal atmosphere of an old beer hall. At the self-service counter you can have a salad made to order, a cheese platter, or other light fare. It's usually quieter at night, and the kitchen stays open until 1 AM. ⊠ *Via San Tomaso 5,* ☎ *02/874510. No credit cards. Closed Sun.*

$ ✕ **La Bruschetta.** A winning partnership of Tuscans and Neapolitans runs this tiny, busy, and first-class pizzeria near the Duomo. It features the obligatory wood-burning oven, so you can watch your pizza being cooked, though there are plenty of other dishes to choose from as well— try the spaghetti *alle cozze e vongole* (with clams and mussels). ⊠ *Piazza Beccaria 12,* ☎ *02/869−2494. No credit cards. Closed Mon., 3 wks in Aug, a few days at Christmas and Easter.*

$ ✕ **La Giara.** At this tavern with bare wooden tables and benches, the menu offers a limited selection of southern Italian specialties, notably a varied vegetable antipasto. Meat is grilled on a range at the front of the restaurant and served with crusty bread and dense olive oil from the Puglia region. It is located in the vicinity of Piazzale Loreto. You may be asked to share a table. ⊠ *Viale Monza 10,* ☎ *02/261−43835. No credit cards. Closed Wed.*

Lodging

For details and price-category definitions, *see* Lodging *in* Staying in Italy, *above.*

$$$$ 🏨 **Duomo.** Just 20 yards from the cathedral, this hotel's first-, second-,
★ and third-floor rooms all look out onto the church's Gothic gargoyles and pinnacles. The rooms are spacious and snappily furnished in contemporary style. ⊠ *Via San Raffaele 1, 20121,* ☎ *02/8833,* FAX *02/864−62027. 160 rooms with bath. Restaurant, bar. AE, DC, MC, V. Closed Aug.*

$$$$ 🏨 **Four Seasons.** The elegant restoration of a 14th-century monastery on an exclusive shopping street in the center of Milan has produced a gem, and a precious one, at the highest rates in the city. The hotel blends European class with American comfort. Individually furnished rooms have opulent marble bathrooms; most rooms face the quiet courtyard. Downstairs is the hotel's Il Teatro restaurant. ⊠ *Via Gesù 8, 20121,* ☎ *02/77088,* FAX *02/770−85000. 98 rooms with bath. Restaurant, bar, convention facilities. AE, DC, MC, V.*

$$$$ 🏨 **Pierre.** Luxury keynotes rooms individually furnished with elegant fabrics and an assortment of modern and antique furniture. Electronic gadgetry controls curtains and lights. The Pierre is near the medieval church of Sant'Ambrogio. ⊠ *Via De Amicis 32, 20123,* ☎ *02/720−00581,* FAX *02/805−2157. 47 rooms with bath. Restaurant, bar. AE, DC, MC, V.*

$$$$ 🏨 **Principe di Savoia.** The most fashionable and glitzy hotel in Milan, this is where fashion buyers and expense-account businesspeople stay. Dark wood paneling and period furniture, brass lamps, and a stucco

lobby are all reminiscent of early 1900s Europe. ✉ *Piazza della Re-pubblica 17, 20124,* ☎ *02/6230,* FAX *02/659–5838. 287 rooms with bath. Restaurant, bar. AE, DC, MC, V.*

$$$ ⊞ **Carlton-Senato.** This hotel is in the heart of Milan's chic shopping district. The atmosphere is light and airy, and there are lots of little touches (such as complimentary chocolates and liqueurs in the rooms) to make up for the rather functional furnishings. ✉ *Via Senato 5, 20121,* ☎ *02/760–15535,* FAX *02/783–300. 79 rooms with bath. Restaurant, bar, parking. AE, MC, V. Closed Aug.*

$$ ⊞ **Canada.** This friendly, small hotel is close to Piazza del Duomo on the edge of a district full of shops and restaurants. Recently renovated, it offers good value; all rooms have TV, air-conditioning, and minifridge. ✉ *Via Santa Sofia 16, 20122,* ☎ *02/583–04844,* FAX *02/583–00282. 35 rooms with bath. Bar. AE, DC, MC, V.*

$$ ⊞ **Casa Svizzera.** A faithful clientele considers this one of Milan's best moderately priced small hotels, so it's advisable to make early reser-vations. The location, adjacent to the Duomo and a few yards from the Galleria, is central and handy to Metro and bus lines. The hotel has been totally renovated and soundproofed. Rooms have air condi-tioning, TV, and minifridge, and they are decorated in cheery floral-printed fabric. ✉ *Via San Raffaele 3, 20123,* ☎ *02/869–2246,* FAX *02/7200–4690. 45 rooms with bath. Bar. AE, DC, MC, V. Closed Aug.*

$$ ⊞ **Gritti.** This bright, clean hotel has a cheerful atmosphere. Rooms are adequate, with picturesque views from the upper floors over the tiled roofs to the gilt Madonnina atop of the Duomo, only a few hun-dred yards away. ✉ *Piazza Santa Maria Beltrade 4 (north end of Via Torino), 20123,* ☎ *02/801056,* FAX *02/890–1099. 48 rooms with bath. Bar. AE, DC, MC, V.*

$ ⊞ **Città Studi.** Near the University and Piazzale Susa, this hotel is mod-ern and functionally furnished, undistinguished but with a reputation as a reliable, reasonably comfortable place to stay. Most rooms have private showers. ✉ *Via Saldini 24, 20133,* ☎ *02/744666,* FAX *02/713122. 45 rooms, 38 with shower. AE, MC, V.*

$ ⊞ **London.** Close to the Duomo, the London has clean, good-size, simply furnished rooms and an English-speaking staff. It also has an arrangement with the Opera Prima restaurant in the same building, where guests may take their meals if they wish. ✉ *Via Rovello 3, 20121,* ☎ *02/720–20166,* FAX *02/805–7037. 29 rooms with shower. Bar. MC, V. Closed Dec. 25–Jan. 3, Aug.*

$ ⊞ **San Francisco.** In a residential area between the central station and the university, this medium-size pension is handy to subway and bus lines. It also has the advantages of a friendly management, rooms that are bright and clean, and a charming garden. ✉ *Viale Lombardia 55, 20131,* ☎ *02/236–1009,* FAX *02/266–80377. 31 rooms with bath or shower. Bar, garden. AE, DC, MC, V.*

The Arts

The most famous spectacle in Milan is **La Scala,** which presents some of the world's most impressive operatic productions. The opera sea-son begins December 7 (St. Ambrose Day) and ends in May. The con-cert season runs from May to the end of June and from September through November. There is a brief ballet season in September. Pro-grams are available at principal travel agencies and tourist informa-tion offices in Italy and abroad. Tickets are usually hard to come by, but your hotel may be able to help obtain them. For information on schedules, ticket availability, and how to buy tickets, there is an Info-tel Scala Service in operation (with English-speaking staff) at the ticket office. Telephone bookings are not accepted, but travelers from abroad can book in advance—within a short specified period before each presentation (these dates are published at the beginning of the season)—through postal bookings, for which a certain percentage of tickets are set aside, allocated on a first-come, first-served basis. Apply for a reservation by mail or fax (transmitted 9–6 local time, with time and date of transmission, and sender's fax number). You may also be able to book at CIT or other travel agencies (no more than 10 days before performance). There is a 15% advance booking charge. ⊠ *Teatro alla Scala, Ufficio Biglietteria, Via Filodrammatici 2, 20121,* ☎ *02/720–03744,* FAX *02/877–996, or 805–1625* ☉ *Daily, 10–7.*

Nightlife

Bars
El Brellin (⊠ Vicolo Lavandai at the corner of Alzaia Naviglio Grande, ☎ 581–01351, closed Sun.) is one of many bars in the Navigli district.

In the Brera quarter, **Momus** (⊠ Via Fiori Chiari 8, ☎ 02/805–6227) is upscale and intimate.

Jazz
Le Scimmie (⊠ Via Ascanio Sforza 49, ☎ 02/894–02874, closed Tues.) is a good spot for cool jazz in a relaxed atmosphere.

NIGHTCLUBS
The following clubs are good bets for an evening of dinner and dancing, but don't expect this entertainment to come cheap: **Stage** (⊠ Galleria Manzoni, off Via Monte Napoleone, ☎ 02/760–21071, closed Sun., dinner served on Tues. only) and **Charly Max** (⊠ Via Marconi 2, ☎ 02/871801, closed Sun.).

VENICE

Arriving and Departing

By Plane
Marco Polo International Airport is situated about 10 kilometers (6 miles) northeast of the city on the mainland. For flight information, call 041/260–9260.

BETWEEN THE AIRPORT AND DOWNTOWN
Blue ATVO buses make the 25-minute trip in to Piazzale Roma, where the road to Venice terminates; the cost is around 5,000 lire. From Piazzale Roma visitors will most likely have to take a vaporetto (water bus) to their hotel (☞ Getting Around, *below*). The Cooperative San Marco motor launch (fare 20,000 lire) can be a more convenient way to reach the city, depending on where your hotel is located. It runs from the airport via the Lido, dropping passengers across the lagoon at Piazza San Marco. (It runs on a limited schedule in winter.) Land taxis are available, running the same route as the buses; the cost is about 50,000 lire. Water taxis (slick high-power motorboats) are very expensive: Negotiate the fare in advance, usually upward of 100,000 lire (the official scale of tariffs is published in the "Guest in Venice" booklet; ☞ The Arts, *below*).

By Train
Make sure your train goes all the way to the Santa Lucia station in Venice's northwest corner; some trains leave passengers at the Mestre Station on the mainland. All trains traveling to and from Santa Lucia stop at Mestre, so to get from Mestre to Santa Lucia, or vice versa (a journey of about 10 minutes), take the first available train, remembering there is a *supplemento* (extra charge) for traveling on Intercity and Eu-

rocity trains, and that if you board one of these trains without having paid in advance for this part of the journey, you are subject to a hefty fine. For train information, call 041/715555, 7:15 AM–9:30 PM. Since most tourists arrive in Venice by train, tourist services are conveniently located at Santa Lucia, including an APT information booth (☎ 041/719078; ☉ Daily 8–8) and baggage depot. If you need a hotel room, the station has a Venetian Hoteliers Association (AVA) desk (☉ Apr.–Oct., daily 8 AM–10 PM; Nov.–Mar., daily 8 AM–9:30 PM), with others at the airport and at the city garage at Piazzale Roma. Directly outside the train station are the main vaporetto landing stages; from here, vaporetti can transport you to your hotel's general neighborhood. It's easy to lose your way in Venice, so it's best to get advance telephone instructions from the hotel. A good map of Venice will also prove useful. When all else fails, however, the staff at the railroad station and central vaporetti stops can help.

By Car

If you bring a car to Venice, you will have to pay for a garage or parking space during your stay. Do not on any account allow yourself to be waylaid by illegal touts, often wearing fake uniforms, who will try to flag you down and offer to arrange parking and hotels; keep driving until you reach the automatic ticket machines. Parking at Piazzale Roma (in the Autorimessa Comunale, run by the city) costs between 15,000 and 25,000 lire, depending on the size of the car; at the private Garage San Marco next door rates are between 30,000 and 45,000 lire for 24 hours, also depending on the size of the car. Parking at the Tronchetto parking area (privately run) costs around 35,000 lire per day under cover, and 18,000 outside. (Do not leave valuables in your car. There is a left-luggage office next door to the Pullman Bar on the ground floor of the municipal garage in Piazzale Roma.) The AVA has arranged a discount of around 40% for hotel guests who use the official Tronchetto parking facility. Ask for a voucher on checking into your hotel. Present the voucher at Tronchetto when you pay the parking fee.

There is a vaporetto (currently No. 82) from Tronchetto to Piazzale Roma and Piazza San Marco (also to the Lido in summer). In thick fog or when tides are extreme, a bus runs instead to Piazzale Roma, where you can pick up a vaporetto.

Getting Around

First-time visitors find that getting around Venice presents some unusual problems: the complexity of its layout (the city is made up of more than 100 islands, all linked by bridges); the bewildering unfamiliarity of waterborne transportation; the apparently illogical house numbering system and duplication of street names in its six districts; and the necessity of walking whether you enjoy it or not. It's essential to have a good map showing all street names and water bus routes; buy one at any newsstand.

By Vaporetto

ACTV water buses run the length of the Grand Canal and circle the city. There are several lines, some of which connect Venice with the major and minor islands in the lagoon. **Line 1** is the Grand Canal local, calling at every stop, and continuing via San Marco to the Lido. (It takes about 45 minutes from the station to San Marco.) As the result of recent (extremely confusing and unpopular) rerouting, there are now two **Line 52** routes: one running from the railway station to San Zaccaria, skirting the north of the city, via Fondamente Nove (where boats leave for the islands of the northern lagoon) and Murano, and continuing via the Arsenal; the other acting as a fast service via Zattere on the Giudecca Canal, south of the city, to San Marco and the Lido. There are also two **Line 82** routes from the Tronchetto: One goes via Piazzale Roma, the railway station, and Rialto, and continues during the day down the Grand Canal, with fewer stops than the Line 1, to San Marco and, in the summer, on to the Lido. The other takes the southern route through the Giudecca Canal, via Zattere and also stopping on Giudecca, to San Marco, and in the summer, continues to the Lido. The fare is 3,500 on most lines. A 24-hour tourist ticket costs 14,000 lire and a 3-day tourist ticket 20,000 lire; these are especially worthwhile if you are planning to visit the islands. Timetables are posted at every landing stage, but there is not always a ticket booth operating. You may get on a boat without a ticket, but you will have to pay a higher fare on the boat. For this reason, it may be useful to buy a *blochetto* (book of tickets) in advance. Landing stages are clearly marked with name and line number, but check before boarding, particularly with the 52 and 82, to make sure the boat is going in your direction.

By Water Taxi

Known as *motoscafi,* or "taxi," these are excessively expensive, and the fare system is as complex as Venice's layout. A minimum fare of about 50,000 lire gets you nowhere, and you'll pay three times as much to get from one end of the Grand Canal to the other. *Always agree on the fare before starting out.* It's probably worth considering taking a water taxi only if you are traveling in a small group.

By Traghetto

Few tourists know about the two-man gondolas that ferry people across the Grand Canal at various fixed points. It's the cheapest and shortest gondola ride in Venice, and it can save a lot of walking. The fare is 600 lire, which you hand to one of the gondoliers when you get on. Look for TRAGHETTO signs.

By Gondola

Don't leave Venice without treating yourself to a gondola ride, preferably in the quiet of the evening when the churning traffic on the canals has died down, the palace windows are illuminated, and the only sounds are the muted splashes of the gondolier's oar. Make sure he understands that you want to see the *rii,* or smaller canals, as well as the Grand Canal. There's supposed to be a fixed minimum rate of about 50,000 lire for 50 minutes. (Official tariffs are quoted in the "Guest in Venice" booklet; ☞ The Arts, *below.*) Come to terms with your gondolier *before* stepping into his boat.

On Foot

This is the only way to reach many parts of Venice, so wear comfortable shoes. Invest in a good map that names all the streets, and count on getting lost more than once.

Important Addresses and Numbers

Consulates

There is no U.S., Canadian, or U.K. consular service in Venice. The nearest consulates for all three countries are in Milan (☞ Important Addresses and Numbers *in* Milan, *above.*)

Emergencies

Police (☎ 113). **Carabinieri** (☎ 112). English-speaking officers are available 24 hours a day to deal with any kind of emergency. **Ambulance** (☎ 041/523–0000). **Doctor:** Try the emergency room at Venice's hospital (☎ 041/529–4517). **Red Cross First Aid Station** (⊠ Piazza San

Marco 55, near Caffè Florian, ☎ 041/5228–6346; ⊘ Mon.–Sat. 8:30–1). **Pharmacies: Farmacia Italo-Inglese** (⊠ Calle della Mandola, ☎ 041/522–4837); **Farmacia Internazionale** (⊠ Calle Larga XXII Marzo, ☎ 041/522–2311). Pharmacies are open weekdays 9–12:30 and 4–7:45; Saturday 9–12:45; a notice telling where to get late-night and Sunday service is posted outside every pharmacy.

Travel Agencies

American Express (⊠ San Moisè 1471, ☎ 041/520–0844, FAX 041/522–9937). **Wagons-Lits Travel** (⊠ Piazzetta dei Leoncini 289, ☎ 041/522–3405, FAX 041/522–8508).

Visitor Information

The main Venice **APT Tourist Office** (☎ 041/522–6356, FAX 041/529–8730) is at Palazzetto Selva, on the waterfront near the San Marco vaporetto stop. Open in summer and during Carnival every day (except public holidays) 9:30–1 and 2–5; in winter, Mon.–Sat. 9–1 and 2–4. There are APT information booths at the Santa Lucia station (☎ 041/719078) and on the Lido (Gran Viale S. M. Elisabetta 6A, ☎ 041/526–5721, FAX 041/529–8720).

Guided Tours

Orientation

American Express and other operators offer two-hour walking tours of the San Marco area, taking in the basilica and the Doge's Palace. The cost is about 35,000 lire. American Express also has an afternoon walking tour from April through October that ends with a gondola ride. The cost is about 35,000 lire.

Special-Interest

Some tour operators offer group gondola rides with a serenade. The cost is about 40,000 lire. During the summer, free guided tours of the Basilica di San Marco are offered by the Patriarchate of Venice; information is available at a desk in the atrium of the church (☎ 041/520–0333). There are several tours daily, except Sunday, and some tours are in English, including one at 11 AM.

Excursions

The Cooperativa San Marco organizes tours of the islands of Murano, Burano, and Torcello, with daily departures at 9:30 and 2:30 from the landing stage in front of Giardini Reali near Piazza San Marco; tours last about three hours and cost about 25,000 lire. However, tours tend to be annoyingly commercial and emphasize glass factory showrooms where you are pressured to buy, often at higher than standard prices. You can visit these islands on your own if you have a little more time and are feeling a bit more adventuresome. To get to Burano and Torcello, take Vaporetto 52 to Fondamente Nuove and change to Vaporetto 12. For Murano, take Vaporetto 52 all the way to Murano. (You can also pick up the Vaporetto 12 at Murano to continue to Burano and Torcello.) In summer there is a Line 23 from San Zaccaria (near Piazza San Marco) to Murano, circling back to Venice via Sant'Elena around the eastern end of the city. **American Express** offers a day trip by car to the Venetian villas, Padua, and Asolo, available all year round. The cost is about 140,000 lire per person, and bookings need to be made the day before.

Personal Guides

American Express can provide guides for walking or gondola tours of Venice, or cars with driver and guide for excursions on the mainland. Pick up a list of licensed guides and their rates from the main **APT** Information Office at Calle dell'Ascensione 71C (☎ 041/522–6356, FAX 041/529–8730).

Exploring Venice

Venice—La Serenissima, the Most Serene—is disorienting in its complexity, an extraordinary labyrinth of narrow streets and waterways, opening now and again onto an airy square or broad canal. The majority of its magnificent palazzi are slowly crumbling; though this sounds like a recipe for a down-at-the-heels slum, somehow in Venice the shabby, derelict effect is magically transformed into one of supreme beauty and charm, rather than horrible urban decay. The place is romantic, especially at night when the lights from the vaporetti and the stars overhead pick out the gargoyles and arches of the centuries-old facades. For hundreds of years Venice was the unrivaled mistress of trade between Europe and the Orient, and the staunch bulwark of Christendom against the tide of Turkish expansion. Though the power and glory of its days as a wealthy city-republic are gone, the art and exotic aura remain.

To enjoy the city, you will have to come to terms with the crowds of day trippers, who take over the center around San Marco from May through September. Hot and sultry in summer, Venice is much more welcoming in early spring and late fall. Romantics like it in the winter, when prices are much lower, the streets are often deserted, and the sea mists impart a haunting melancholy to the *campi* (squares) and canals. Piazza San Marco (St. Mark's Square) is the pulse of Venice, but after joining with the crowds to visit the Basilica di San Marco and the Doge's Palace, strike out on your own and just follow where your feet take you—you won't be disappointed.

A new program, called "Dal Museo alla Città" (from Museum to City) was begun in 1995 to encourage visitors to seek out artwork not only in museums but also within the city itself—primarily in the churches and *scuole* (charitable confraternity halls) for which they were originally commissioned. More than a dozen places selected for their artistic importance now have fixed visiting hours, when tourists can be sure of admission and of not intruding on church services. At these times, given below as "Special visiting hours," information, a free leaflet, and an opportunity to purchase souvenirs and booklets will be available. New lighting systems have been installed, taking 500-lire coins. Churches in this program—and many other churches—are also usually open 10–12 AM and 4–6 PM in winter (5–7 PM in summer).

Piazza San Marco and the Accademia

Numbers in the margin correspond to points of interest on the Venezia (Venice) map.

★ ❶ Even the pigeons have to fight for space on **Piazza San Marco,** the most famous piazza in Venice, and pedestrian traffic jams clog the surrounding byways. Despite the crowds, San Marco is the logical starting place of each of our various itineraries. The short side of the square, opposite the Basilica of San Marco, is known as the Ala Napoleonica, a wing built by order of Napoléon to complete the much earlier palaces on either side of the square, enclosing it to form what he called "the most beautiful drawing room in all of Europe." Upstairs

❷ is the **Museo Correr,** with eclectic collections of historical objects and a picture gallery of fine 13th–17th-century paintings. ⊠ *Piazza San Marco, Ala Napoleonica,* ☎ *041/522–5625.* ▣ *8,000 lire.* ☉ *Apr.–Oct., Wed.–Mon. 10–5; Nov.–Mar., Wed.–Mon. 9–4.*

★ ❸ The **Basilica di San Marco** (St. Mark's Basilica) was begun in the 11th century to hold the relics of St. Mark the Evangelist, the city's patron saint, and its richly decorated facade is surmounted by copies of four famous gilded bronze horses (the originals are in the basilica's upstairs museum). Inside, golden mosaics cover walls and vaults, lending an extraordinarily exotic aura, half Christian church, half Middle Eastern mosque. Be sure to see the **Pala d'Oro,** an eye-filling 10th-century altarpiece in gold and silver studded with precious gems and enamels. From the atrium, climb the steep stairway to the museum: The bronze horses alone are worth the effort. ☉ *Basilica: Mon.–Sat. 9:30–5, Sun. 2–5. Pala d'Oro and Treasury:* ☎ *041/522–5205.* ☒ *3,000 lire.* ☉ *Apr.–Sept., Mon.–Sat. 9:30–5, Sun. 2–5; Oct.–Mar., Mon.–Sat. 10–4, Sun. 2–4, although these times may vary slightly. Gallery and Museum:* ☒ *3,000 lire.* ☉ *Apr.–Sept., daily 9:30–5; Oct.–Mar., daily 10–4.*

★ ❹ During Venice's heyday, the **Palazzo Ducale** (Doge's Palace) was the epicenter of its great empire. More than just a palace, it was a combination White House, Senate, Supreme Court, torture chamber, and prison. The building's exterior is striking; the lower stories consist of two rows of fragile-seeming arches, while above rests a massive pink-and-white marble wall whose solidity is barely interrupted by its six great Gothic windows. The interior is a maze of vast halls, monumental staircases, secret corridors, and sinister prison cells. The palace is filled with frescoes, paintings, and a few examples of statuary by some of the Renaissance's greatest artists. Don't miss the famous view from the balcony, overlooking the piazza and St. Mark's Basin and the church of San Giorgio Maggiore across the lagoon. ☒ *Piazzetta San Marco,* ☎ *041/522–4951.* ☒ *10,000 lire.* ☉ *Apr.–Oct., daily 9–7; Nov.–Mar., daily 9–4. Last entry 1 hr before closing time.*

★ ❺ The **Campanile di San Marco** (St. Mark's bell tower) is ideal for a pigeon's-eye view of Venice. You can now take the elevator up to the top, as this is a reconstruction of the 1,000-year-old tower that collapsed one morning in 1912, practically without warning. Fifteenth-century clerics found guilty of immoral acts were suspended in wooden cages from the tower, sometimes to live on bread and water for as long as a year, sometimes to die of starvation and exposure. Look for them in Carpaccio's paintings of the square that hang in the Accademia. ☒ *Piazza San Marco,* ☎ *041/522–4064.* ☒ *5,000 lire.* ☉ *Easter–Sept., daily 9:30–7; Oct., daily 10–6; Nov.–Easter, daily 10–4:30. Closed most of Jan.*

NEED A BREAK? **Caffè Florian** a Venetian landmark is a great place to nurse a Campari or a cappuccino. The pleasure of relaxing amid so much history does not come cheap. A pot of hot chocolate indoors runs about $6—and there's an extra charge if you're served when the orchestra is playing. If you drink sitting at the bar, there is no service charge. ☒ *Piazza San Marco. Closed Wed.*

Armed with a street map, head west out of Piazza San Marco (with the facade of the basilica to your back), making your way past the Amer-
❻ ican Express office, across the bridge in front of **San Moisè's** elaborate Baroque facade, and on to Calle Larga 22 Marzo. Continue on
❼ to the church of **Santa Maria del Giglio,** behind the **Gritti Palace** hotel. Across the bridge behind the church, **Piazzesi** on Campiello Feltrina is famous for its hand-printed paper and desk accessories. Join the stream of pedestrians crossing the Grand Canal on the wooden Accademia Bridge, and head straight on for the Galleria dell'Accademia (Accademia Gallery), Venice's most important gallery.

Venezia (Venice)

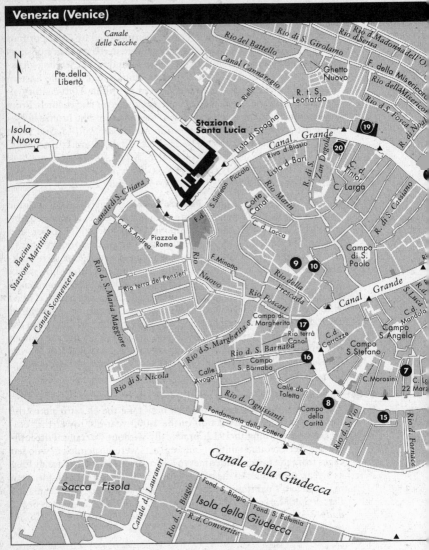

Basilica di San
Marco, **3**
Ca' d'Oro, **18**
Ca' Foscari, **17**
Ca' Rezzonico, **16**
Campanile di San
Marco, **5**
Fondaco dei
Turchi, **20**
Frari, **10**

Galleria
dell'Accademia, **8**
Museo Correr, **2**
Palazzo Ducale, **4**
Palazzo Vendramin
Calergi, **19**
Peggy Guggenheim
Museum, **15**
Piazza San Marco, **1**
Rialto Bridge, **14**

San Moisé, **6**
San Zanipolo, **13**
Santa Maria
Formosa, **11**
Santa Maria dei
Miracoli, **12**
Santa Maria del
Giglio, **7**
Scuola di
San Rocco, **9**

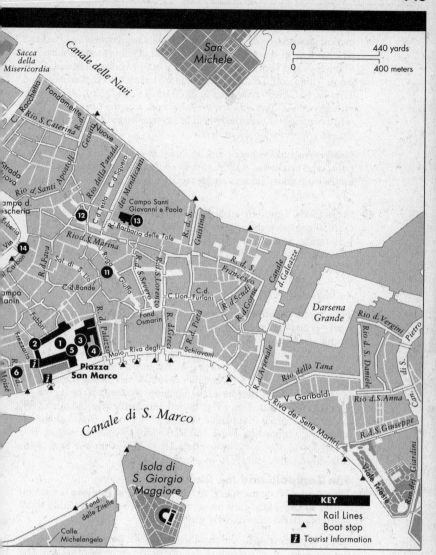

Sacca
della
Misericordia

Canale delle Navi

San
Michele

0   440 yards

0   400 meters

Rocchetta

Fondamente
Nuove

Rio S. Caterina

C. d.

Gesuiti

Rio d. Santi Apostoli

Strada
Nuova

Rio d. Panada

C. d. Squero

ampo d.
escheria

Erbería

C. d. Testa

R. d. Mendicanti

Campo Santi
Giovanni e Paolo

R. d. S.
Giustina

12

13

Vin

Rio d. S. Marina

R. Barbaria delle Tole

14

R. d. Fava

Sal. di S. Lio

Rugo Giuffa

R. d. S. Severo

R. d. S.
Lorenzo

R. d. S.
Francesco

Canale d. Galeazze

l Carbon

C. d. Bonde

11

C. Lion

C. d.
Furlani

R. d. Scudi

R. d. Gorne

Darsena
Grande

Rio d. Vergini

ampo
anin

Fabbri

R. d. Palazzo

Fond.
Osmarin

R. d. Greci

R. d. Pietà

Rio d. S. Daniele

di S.
Pietro

Frezzeria

2   **1**   **3**

5   **4**

i

Molo

Riva degli

Schiavoni

R. d. Arsenale

Rio della Tana

Canale

di S.

6

R. d.
Moisè

i

**Piazza
San Marco**

V. Garibaldi

Rio d. S. Anna

R. d. S. Giuseppe

Riva dei Sette Martiri

Canale di S. Marco

Viale Trieste

Rio dei Giardini

Isola di
S. Giorgio
Maggiore

i

Fond.
delle Zitelle

Calle
Michelangelo

KEY	
——	Rail Lines
▲	Boat stop
i	Tourist Information

★ **8** **Galleria dell'Academia** is Venice's most important picture gallery and a must for art lovers. Try to spend at least an hour viewing this remarkable collection of Venetian art, which is attractively displayed and well lighted. Works range from 14th-century Gothic to the Golden Age of the 15th and 16th centuries, including oils by Giovanni Bellini, Giorgione, Titian, and Tintoretto, and superb later works by Veronese and Tiepolo. ⊠ *Campo della Carità,* ☎ *041/522–2247.* ▣ *12,000 lire.* ◷ *Fri.–Mon. 9–2, Tues.–Thurs. 9–7. Entry to recently opened top floor (displaying works previously held in storage) by guided visit only. For details, telephone or ask at desk.*

Mondonovo ranks as one of the city's most interesting mask shops (Venetians, who originated Italy's most splendid carnival, love masks of all kinds, from gilded lions to sinister death's heads). ⊠ *Rio Terra Canal.* ◷ *9–1 and 2–7.*

9 In the 1500s, Tintoretto embellished the **Scuola di San Rocco** with more than 50 canvases; they are an impressive sight, dark paintings aglow with figures hurtling dramatically through space amid flashes of light and color. *The Crucifixion* in the Albergo (the room just off the great hall) is held to be his masterpiece. ⊠ *Campo di San Rocco,* ☎ *041/523–4864.* ▣ *8,000 lire.* ◷ *Weekdays 9–5:30, weekends 10–4 in winter, 9–5:30 in summer.*

The church of **Santa Maria Gloriosa dei Frari**—known simply as the **10** **Frari**—is one of Venice's most important churches, a vast and soaring Gothic structure of brick. Since it is the principal church of the Franciscans, its design is austere, suitably reflecting the order's vows of poverty. Paradoxically, however, it contains a number of the most sumptuous pictures in any Venetian church. Chief among them are the magnificent Titian altarpiece, the immense *Assumption of the Virgin* over the main altar. Titian was buried here at the ripe old age of 88, the only one of 70,000 plague victims to be given a personal church burial. ⊠ *Campo dei Frari.* ▣ *1,000 lire.* ◷ *Special visiting hrs: Mon.–Sat. 2:30–6.* ◷ *Apr.–Oct., Mon.–Sat. 9–noon, Sun. 3–6; Nov.–Mar., Mon.–Sat. 9:30–noon, Sun. 3–5:30.*

San Zanipolo and the Rialto

11 The graceful white marble church of **Santa Maria Formosa** is right on a lively square (of the same name) with a few sidewalk cafés and a small vegetable market on weekday mornings.

12 Perfectly proportioned and sheathed in marble, **Santa Maria dei Miracoli** embodies all the classical serenity of the early Renaissance. The interior of this late-15th-century building is decorated with marble reliefs by the church's architect, Pietro Lombardo, and his son Tullio. ⊠ *Campo dei Miracoli, beside Calle Castelli.*

13 The massive Dominican church of Santi Giovanni e Paolo—**San Zanipolo,** as it's known in the slurred Venetian dialect—is the twin (and rival) of the Franciscan Frari. The church is a kind of pantheon of the doges (25 are buried here), and contains a wealth of artwork. Outside in the campo stands Verrocchio's magnificent equestrian statue of Colleoni, who fought for the Venetian cause in the mid-1400s. ⊠ *Calle delle Erbe.* ▣ *Special visiting hrs: Mon.–Sat. 9–12 and 3–6.*

Cross the canal in front of the church and continue along Calle Larga Giacinto Gallina, crossing a pair of bridges to Campillo Santa Maria Nova. Take Salizzada San Canciano to Salizzada San Giovanni Crisostomo to find yourself once again in the mainstream of pedestrians ★ **14** winding their way to the **Rialto Bridge.** Street stalls hung with scarves and gondolier's hats signal that you are entering the heart of Venice's shopping district. Cross over the bridge, and you'll find yourself on the edge of the famous market. Try to visit the Rialto market when it's in full swing (Tues.–Sat. mornings; Mondays are quiet because the fish market is closed), with fruit and vegetable vendors hawking their wares in a colorful and noisy jumble of sights and sounds. Not far beyond is the fish market, where you'll probably find sea creatures you've never seen before (and possibly won't want to see again). Ruga San Giovanni and Ruga del Ravano, beside the market, will bring you face to face with scores of shops. Start from the Salizzada S. Giovanni side of the bridge.

At **La Scialuppa** (⊠ Calle Saoneri 2695) you'll find hand-carved wooden models of gondolas and their graceful oar locks known as *forcole.*

The Grand Canal

Set off on a boat tour along the **Grand Canal,** which serves as Venice's main thoroughfare. The canal winds in the shape of an S for more than 3½ kilometers (2 miles) through the heart of the city, past some 200 Gothic and Renaissance palaces. Although restrictions have been introduced to diminish the erosive effect of wash on buildings, this is still the route taken by vaporetti, gondolas, water taxis, mail boats, police boats, fire boats, ambulance boats, barges carrying provisions and building materials, bridal boats, and funeral boats. Your vaporetto tour will give you an idea of the opulent beauty of the palaces and a peek into the side streets and tiny canals where the Venetians go about their daily business. ⊠ *Just off Piazzetta di San Marco (the square in front of the Doge's Palace) you can catch Vaporetto 1 at either the San Marco or San Zaccaria landing stages (on Riva degli Schiavoni).* ▭ *3,500 lire.*

Soon after leaving the San Marco landing, the Vaporetto 1 tour passes
⑮ the **Accademia Gallery** (described above). Next comes the **Peggy Guggenheim Museum,** an exceptional modern art collection (☞ Off the Beaten Path, *below*) housed in the incomplete Palazzo Venier dei Leoni.

★ ⑯ The **Ca' Rezzonico**—the most spectacular palace in all of Venice—was built between the mid-17th and 18th centuries and is now a museum of sumptuous 18th-century Venetian paintings and furniture. It offers the best glimpse of true Venetian splendor and is a must-see. ⊠ *Ca' Rezzonico,* ☎ *041/522–4543.* ▭ *8,000 lire.* ☉ *Apr.–Oct., Sat.–Thurs. 10–5; Nov.–Mar., Sat.–Thurs. 10–4.*

⑰ **Ca' Foscari** is a 15th-century Gothic structure that was once the home of Doge Foscari, who was unwillingly deposed and died the following day! Today it's the headquarters of Venice's university. ⊠ *Ca' Foscari.*

⑱ **Ca' d'Oro** is the most flowery palace on the canal; it now houses the Galleria Franchetti. ⊠ *Ca' d'Oro,* ☎ *041/523–8790.* ▭ *4,000 lire.* ☉ *Daily 9–2.*

⑲ The **Palazzo Vendramin Calergi** is a opulent Renaissance structure noted for the fact that Wagner died here in 1883. It's also the winter home of the municipal casino. ⊠ *Ca' Calergi.*

⑳ The **Fondaco dei Turchi** was originally the home and warehouse of a wealthy Venetian merchant, but suffered some fanciful remodeling during the 19th century. It is now the Natural History Museum. ⊠ *Fondaco dei Turchi,* ☎ *041/524–0885.* ▭ *5,000 lire.* ☉ *Tues.–Sat. 9–1.*

Off the Beaten Path

Explore the **Ghetto,** where Venice's Jewish community lived in cramped quarters for many centuries, being sure to visit the **Museo Ebraico** and the Ghetto's several synagogues. ⊠ *Jewish Museum, Campo del Ghetto*

Nuovo, ☎ *041/715359.* 🎫 *4,000 lire; with tour, every half hr from 10:30–3:30, 10,000 lire.* ☉ *June–Sept., Sun.–Fri. 10–7; Oct.–May, Sun.–Fri. 10–4:30.*

Visit late heiress Peggy Guggenheim's house and collection of modern art at the **Palazzo Venier dei Leoni** on the Grand Canal. ✉ *Entrance: Calle San Cristoforo, Dorsoduro,* ☎ *041/520–6288.* 🎫 *10,000 lire.* ☉ *Sun.–Mon., Wed.–Sat. 11–6.*

In the **Palazzo Labia** you'll find the prettiest ballroom in Venice, magnificently adorned with Giambattista Tiepolo's 18th-century frescoes of Anthony and Cleopatra. This palace, once the home of Venice's most ostentatiously rich family, is now the Venetian headquarters of RAI, Italy's National Broadcasting Corporation, which occasionally hosts concerts in the Tiepolo ballroom. ✉ *Campo San Geremia, Cannaregio,* ☎ *041/524–2821.* 🎫 *Free to ballroom Mon., Thurs., and Fri. 3– 4; tour of ballroom and other rooms (available in English) 10,000 lire, by prior arrangement, Mon.–Fri. 10–4.*

Torcello. Discover the Venetian equivalent of World's End on this magical island in the Venetian lagoon. Settled 1,500 years ago and a thriving city during the Byzantine era, the island is now deserted, but art lovers still make pilgrimages to it because of its two great 11th-century churches. The cathedral of Santa Maria Assunta has a world-famous mosaic of the Virgin. Locanda Cipriani, a restaurant favored by Hemingway and the Duke of Windsor, still lures gourmands. Katherine Hepburn and Rossanzo Brazzi fell in love during a picnic on Torcello in the film classic *Summertime.* ✉ *To get to Torcello, take Vaporetto 12 from Venice.*

Shopping

Glass
Venetian glass is as famous as the city's gondolas, and almost every shop window displays it. There's a lot of cheap glass for sale; if you want something better, try **l'Isola,** where Carlo Moretti's chic, contemporary designs are on display. ✉ *Campo San Moisè 1468, near Piazza San Marco.*

Domus has a good selection of glass and is on the island of Murano, where prices are generally no lower than in Venice. ✉ *Fondamenta dei Vetrai.*

Fabrics
Norelene has stunning hand-painted fabrics that make wonderful wall-hangings or elegantly styled jackets and chic scarves. ✉ *Calle della Chiesa 727, in Dorsoduro, near the Guggenheim.*

Venetia Studium is famous for Fortuny-inspired lamps, furnishings, clothes, and accessories. ✉ *Calle Larga XXII Marzo 2430.*

Shopping District
Merceria, one of Venice's busiest streets and, with the **Frezzeria** and **Calle dei Fabbri,** part of the shopping area that extends across the Grand Canal into the **Rialto district.**

Dining

Venetians love seafood, and it figures prominently on most restaurant menus, sometimes to the exclusion of meat dishes. Fish is generally expensive, however, and you should bear this in mind when ordering: The price given on menus for fish as a main course is often per 100 grams, not the total cost of what you are served, which could be two or three times that amount. This is not sharp practice, but a conventional way of pricing fish in Italy. Venice is not a particularly inexpensive place to eat, but there are good restaurants huddled along Venice's squares and seemingly endless canals. City specialties include pasta e fagioli; risotto, and all kinds of seafood—also the delicious fegato alla veneziana served with grilled polenta. For details and price-category definitions, *see* Dining *in* Staying in Italy, *above*.

$$$$ ✕ **Da Fiore.** Long a favorite with Venetians, Da Fiore has been discovered
★ by tourists, so reservations are imperative. It's known for its excellent seafood dinners, which might include such specialties as *pasticcio di pesce* (fish pie) and *seppioline* (little cuttlefish). Not easy to find, it's just off Campo San Polo. ⊠ *Calle dello Scaleter 2202, San Polo,* ☎ *041/721308. Reservations essential. AE, DC, MC, V. Closed Sun., Mon., Aug. 10–early Sept., and Dec. 25–Jan. 15.*

$$$$ ✕ **Grand Canal.** The Hotel Monaco's restaurant is a favorite with Vene-
★ tians, who enjoy eating on the lovely canal-side terrace on sunny days, looking across the mouth of the Grand Canal to the island of San Giorgio Maggiore, and in the cozy dining room in winter. All the pasta is made fresh daily on the premises, and the smoked and marinated salmon are also produced in the restaurant's kitchen. The traditional Venetian dishes are very well prepared; the chef, Fulvio De Santa, also offers delicious meat and fish dishes, such as scampi *alla Ca' d'Oro* (in cognac sauce, served with rice). ⊠ *Calle Vallaresso 1325, San Marco,* ☎ *041/520–0211. Jacket required. AE, DC, MC, V.*

$$$$ ✕ **La Caravella.** La Caravella is decorated like the dining saloon of an old Venetian sailing ship, with lots of authentic touches, and has a pretty garden courtyard used during summer. The menu is long and slightly intimidating, though the highly competent mâitre d' will advise you well. The *granseola* (crab) is marvelous in any of several versions. ⊠ *Calle Larga XXII Marzo 2397, San Marco,* ☎ *041/520–8901. AE, DC, MC, V. Closed Wed. Nov.–Apr.*

$$$ ✕ **Da Arturo.** The tiny Da Arturo is a refreshing change from the numerous seafood restaurants of which Venetians are so fond. The cordial proprietor prefers, instead, to offer varied and delicious seasonal vegetable and salad dishes, or tasty, tender and generous meat courses like *braciola alla veneziana* (pork chop schnitzel with vinegar). ⊠ *Calle degli Assassini 3656, San Marco,* ☎ *041/528–6974. Reservations essential. No credit cards. Closed Sun., 3 wks in Aug.*

$$$ ✕ **Fiaschetteria Toscana.** Once the storehouse of a 19th-century wine merchant from Tuscany, this popular restaurant has long been a favorite of Venetians and visitors from terra firma, especially in the summer, when they can sit under the arbor out front. Courteous, cheerful waiters serve such specialties as *rombo* (turbot) with capers and an exceptionally good pasta *alla buranella* (with shrimp, au gratin). ⊠ *Campo San Giovanni Crisostomo 5719, Cannaregio,* ☎ *041/528–5281. AE, DC, MC, V. Closed Tues. and first 2 wks in July.*

$$ ✕ **Al Mondo Novo.** This fish restaurant is owned by a fish wholesaler in the Rialto market, so you can be sure that everything is absolutely fresh. Specialties prepared by Signora Trevisan, the owner's wife, include *cape sante* (pilgrim scallops) and *cape longhe* (razor clams), risotto and pasta dishes, and charcoal-grilled fish. Meat dishes are also available. ⊠ *Salizzada San Lio 5409, Castello,* ☎ *041/520–0698. AE, MC, V. Closed Wed. Feb.–Mar.*

$$ ✕ **Da Gigio.** Just off the Strada Nuova, this is an attractive, friendly, family-run trattoria on the quayside of a canal. Da Gigio is popular with those who appreciate the affable service and excellently cooked, homemade pasta, fish and meat dishes, and high-quality draft wine. Its barroom makes a pleasant, informal setting for simple lunches.

⊠ *Fondamenta de la Chiesa 3628A, Cannaregio,* ☎ *041/528–5140.*
AE, DC, MC, V. No dinner Sun. Closed Mon., 2 wks in mid-Jan., and
2 wks in Aug.

$ ✕ **L'Incontro.** This trattoria has a faithful clientele attracted by good
food (excellent meat, no fish) at reasonable prices. Menu choices include freshly made Sardinian pastas, juicy steaks, wild duck, boar, and
(with advance notice) roast suckling pig. L'Incontro is between San Barn-
aba and Campo Santa Margherita. ⊠ *Rio Terra Canal 3062A, Dorsoduro,* ☎ *041/522–2404. MC, V. Closed Mon.*

$ ✕ **Metropole Buffet.** Here at the Hotel Metropole's buffet, in a charm-
ing, comfortable room overlooking the waterfront by the Pietà Church,
you can eat a substantial and tasty lunch or dinner, helping yourself
from a varied selection of starters, soup, pastas, hot and cold fish and
meat dishes, and desserts, all for around 50,000 lire. The price even
includes a highly drinkable Bianco di Custoza (a light white wine from
the Veneto region) on draft. ⊠ *Riva degli Schiavoni 4149, Castello,*
☎ *041/520–5044. AE, DC, MC, V.*

$ ✕ **Montin.** Peggy Guggenheim used to wine and dine the greatest artists
of the 20th century here after showing them the collection at her
nearby Palazzo Venier dei Leoni. Since those days, Montin has become
more of an institution, less a bohemian hang-out. Service can sometimes be erratic, but crowds still pack the place to enjoy the rigatoni
ai quattro formaggi (with four cheeses, mushrooms, and tomato) and
antipasto Montin (seafood antipasto). ⊠ *Fondamenta di Borgo 1147,
Dorsoduro,* ☎ *041/522–7151. AE, DC, MC, V. No dinner Tues.
Closed Wed., 15 days in Jan., and 15 days in Aug.*

Lodging

Venice is made up almost entirely of time-worn buildings, so it stands
to reason that the majority of hotels are in renovated palaces. However, space is at a premium in this city, and even in the best hotels rooms
can be small and offer little natural light. Preservation restrictions on
buildings often preclude the installation of such things as elevators, air-
conditioning systems, and satellite dishes (if any of these amenities is
of paramount importance to you, check on their availability before booking). So don't come to Venice expecting to find the standard modern
hotel room—you will almost certainly be disappointed. On the other
hand, Venice's luxury hotels can offer rooms of fabulous opulence and
elegance, and even in the more modest hotels you can find comfortable rooms of great charm and character, sometimes with stunning views.

Venice attracts visitors all year round, although the winter months are
generally much quieter, and most hotels offer lower rates during this
period. It is always worth booking in advance, but if you haven't, the
AVA desk at the railway station (☎ 041/715016 and 041/715288. ☉
Apr.–Oct., daily 8 AM–10 PM; Nov.–Mar., daily 8 AM–9:30 PM), at the
airport (☉ Apr.–Oct., daily 10–9; Nov.–Mar., daily 10:30–6:30), or
at the municipal parking garage at Piazzale Roma (☉ Apr.–Oct., daily
9 AM–10 PM; Nov.–Mar., daily 9–9) will help you find a room after
your arrival in the city. For details and price-category definitions, *see*
Lodging *in* Staying in Italy, *above.*

$$$$ 🏨 **Cipriani.** A sybaritic oasis of stunningly decorated rooms and suites
with marble baths and Jacuzzis, the Cipriani is located across St. Mark's
Basin on the island of Giudecca, offering a panorama of romantic views
of the entire lagoon. The hotel launch whisks guests back and forth to
Piazza San Marco at any hour of the day or night. Cooking courses and
fitness programs are offered as special programs to occupy the guests.
Some rooms have pretty garden patios. The newly restored Palazzo Ven-

dramin annex of the Cipriani (with 7 suites and 3 double rooms) is open all year. ✉ *Giudecca 10,* ☎ *041/520–7744,* 𝔽𝔸𝕏 *041/520–3930. 104 rooms with bath. Restaurant, bar, air-conditioning, pool, tennis court, health club. AE, DC, MC, V. Closed Dec.–mid-Mar.*

$$$$ 🏨 **Danieli.** Parts of this rather large hotel are built around a 15th-century palazzo bathed in sumptuous Venetian colors, though the Danieli also has several modern annexes that some find bland and impersonal, and the lower-price rooms can be exceedingly drab. Still, it's a favorite with celebrities and English-speaking visitors, and the dining terrace does have a fantastic view of St. Mark's Basin. ✉ *Riva degli Schiavoni 4196, Castello,* ☎ *041/522–6480,* 𝔽𝔸𝕏 *041/520–0208. 231 rooms with bath. Restaurant, bar, roof terrace, air-conditioning, access to tennis court and pool at the Hotel Exclesior and/or Hotel des Bains on the Lido. AE, DC, MC, V.*

$$$$ 🏨 **Gritti Palace.** The atmosphere of an aristocratic private home is what
★ the management is after here, and they succeed beautifully. Fresh flowers, fine antiques, sumptuous appointments, and Old World service make this a terrific choice for anyone who wants to be totally pampered. The dining terrace overlooking the Grand Canal is best in the evening when boat traffic dies down. ✉ *Campo Santa Maria del Giglio 2467, San Marco,* ☎ *041/794611,* 𝔽𝔸𝕏 *041/520–0942. 88 rooms with bath. Restaurant, bar, air-conditioning, canal-side terrace, access to tennis court and pool at Hotel Excelsior and/or Hotel des Bains on Lido. AE, DC, MC, V.*

$$$ 🏨 **Londra Palace.** You get the obligatory view of San Giorgio and St. Mark's Basin at this distinguished hotel whose rooms are decorated in dark paisley prints, with such sumptuous touches as canopied beds. French chefs preside over Les Deux Lions restaurant, now a haven of *cuisine française,* and the piano bar is open late. The hotel offers a complimentary Mercedes for one-day excursions and free entrance to the casino. ✉ *Riva degli Schiavoni 4171, Castello,* ☎ *041/520–0533,* 𝔽𝔸𝕏 *041/522–5032. 69 rooms with bath. Restaurant, piano bar, air-conditioning, solarium. AE, DC, MC, V.*

$$$ 🏨 **Metropole.** Guests can step from their water taxi or gondola into
★ the lobby of this small, very well-run hotel, rich in precious antiques, just five minutes from Piazza San Marco. Many rooms have a view of the lagoon, others overlook the garden at the back, but all are furnished with style. ✉ *Riva degli Schiavoni 4149, Castello,* ☎ *041/520–5044,* 𝔽𝔸𝕏 *041/522–3679. 73 rooms with bath. Restaurant (☞ Dining, above), bar, air-conditioning. AE, DC, MC, V.*

$$ 🏨 **Accademia.** Hidden within the heart of Venice, this miniature Pal-
★ ladian villa—complete with canal-side garden—is the city's most enchanting hotel. There's plenty of atmosphere here, with just a touch of romance, though there are indications that it may be becoming a little too well-worn: Readers have reported chairs with broken springs. Many rooms overlook the gardens, where you can sit in warm weather. ✉ *Fondamenta Bollani 1058, Dorsoduro,* ☎ *041/523–7846,* 𝔽𝔸𝕏 *041/523–9152. 27 rooms, most with bath. Bar, air-conditioning, gardens. AE, DC, MC, V.*

$ 🏨 **Alboretti.** This small hotel is simply but attractively furnished. Despite its size and central location, it has a little garden courtyard off the breakfast room and a lounge upstairs from the tiny lobby and bar area. There is no elevator. Together with its moderately priced restaurant, the Alboretti is a good value. ✉ *Rio Terra Sant'Agnese 882, Dorsoduro,* ☎ *041/523–0058,* 𝔽𝔸𝕏 *041/521–0158. 19 rooms with bath. Restaurant, bar, air-conditioning. AE, MC, V.*

$ 🏨 **Bucintoro.** Whistler once stayed here, and today the Bucintoro is still favored by artists, drawn by the lagoon views from every room. Slightly off the tourist track, this friendly, family-run hotel has clean and simple rooms. The price is unbeatable for such spectacular vistas. ⊠ *Riva San Biagio 2135, Castello,* ☎ *041/522–3240,* FAX *041/523–5224. 28 rooms, 18 with bath. Restaurant, bar. No credit cards. Closed Jan.–mid-Feb.*

$ 🏨 **La Residenza.** A Gothic palace makes a delightful setting for this charming hotel, set on a an attractive square off the waterfront and just a 10-minute walk from San Marco. Breakfast is served in a real antique-furnished Venetian salon. With a decidedly subdued atmosphere, this is not the place for children or for the high-spirited. Make reservations well in advance. ⊠ *Campo Bandiera e Moro 3608, Castello,* ☎ *041/528–5315,* FAX *041/523–8859. 17 rooms, 14 with bath. AE, DC, MC, V. Closed mid-Jan.–mid-Feb., mid-Nov.–early Dec.*

$ 🏨 **Locanda Fiorita.** Just off Campo Sant Stefano, near the Accademia Bridge, you'll find this welcoming, newly refurbished hotel tucked away in a sunny little square (where breakfast is served in summer). The location is a big plus: it's very central for sightseeing. The rooms have beamed ceilings and are simply furnished. ⊠ *Campiello Novo 3457, San Marco,* ☎ *041/523–4754,* FAX *041/522–8043. 10 rooms, 7 with shower. AE, MC, V. Closed 2 wks Nov.–Dec.*

$ 🏨 **Paganelli.** The lagoon views here so impressed Henry James that he wrote the Paganelli up in the preface to his *Portrait of a Lady*. This charming, small hotel on the waterfront near Piazza San Marco has an annex on the quiet square of Campo San Zaccaria, and is tastefully decorated in the Venetian style. Three rooms overlook the lagoon, and six have good views over the square. ⊠ *Riva degli Schiavoni 4182, Castello,* ☎ *041/522–4324,* FAX *041/523–9267. 22 rooms, 19 with bath or shower. Bar. AE, DC, MC, V.*

The Arts

For a program of events, pick up the free "Un Ospite di Venezia" ("Guest in Venice") booklet, available from the Assessorato al Turismo (⊠ Ca' Giustinian, 2nd Floor, Calle del Ridotto), near Piazza San Marco, or at most hotel desks. Your hotel may also be able to get you tickets for some events.

Concerts

There are regular concerts at the Pietà Church, with an emphasis on Vivaldi, and at San Stae and San Barnaba. Concerts, sometimes free, are also held by visiting choirs and musicians in other churches. For information on these often short-notice events, ask at the APT office, and look for posters on walls and in restaurants and shops. For more information contact: *The Kele e Teo Agency,* ⊠ *Piazza San Marco 4930,* ☎ *041/520–8722 (Box Office,* ⊠ *Calle Loredan 4127, off Salizzada San Luca,* ☎ *041/988369.)*

Opera

Because of the devastating fire that destroyed **Teatro La Fenice** in January 1996, opera and concert performances were rescheduled in various venues. At press time, plans for 1997 were uncertain. For the latest information, call the Italian Government Tourist Board (☞ Visitor Information *in* Chapter 1).

Nightlife

The bars of the top hotels stay open as long as their customers keep on drinking. Dedicated nighthawks should get a copy of "Fuori Orario: di Notte a Venezia e Mestre" ("Out of Hours: By Night in Venice and Mestre"), a guide to live music venues, discos, and late bars in and around Venice, published by the Assessorato alla Gioventù, the municipality's Youth Department (Corte Contarini 1529, 4th Floor, near Piazza San

Marco). It's available free at APT information offices, at present only in Italian, but with useful maps and easy-to-follow notes.

The **Martini Scala Club** is an elegant piano bar with late-night restaurant. ✉ *Calle delle Veste, near Teatro La Fenice,* ☎ *041/522–4121.*

Ai Canottieri is popular with young people, and has live music on Thursday and Saturday. ✉ *Fondamenta San Giobbe 690, Cannaregio,* ☎ *041/71548.* ☉ *closed Sun. and in summer.*

Paradiso Perduto is another hangout for the younger set, with live music on most weekends. ✉ *Fondamenta Misericordia 2540, Cannaregio,* ☎ *041/720581. Closed Wed. and first half of Aug.*

CAMPANIA

Campania, the region that includes Naples, the Amalfi coast, and other well-known tourist destinations, is where most people's preconceived ideas of Italy become a reality. You'll find lots of sun, good food that relies heavily on tomatoes and mozzarella, acres of classical ruins, and gorgeous scenery. The exuberance of the locals doesn't leave much room for efficient organization, however, and you may have to revise your concept of real time; here minutes dilate into hours at the drop of a hat.

Once a city that rivaled Paris as a brilliant and refined cultural capital, Napoli (Naples) is afflicted by acute urban decay and chronic delinquency. You need patience, stamina, and a healthy dose of caution to visit Naples on your own, but it's worth it for those who have a sense of adventure and the capacity to discern the enormous riches the city has accumulated in its 2,000-year history.

On the other hand, if you want the fun without the hassle, head for Sorrento, Capri, and the Amalfi coast, legendary haunts of the sirens who tried to lure Odysseus off course. Sorrento is touristy but has some fine old hotels and beautiful views; it's a good base for a leisurely excursion to Pompeii. Capri is a pint-size paradise, though sometimes too crowded for comfort, and the Amalfi coast offers enchanting towns and spectacular scenery.

Getting Around

By Plane

There are several daily flights between Rome and Naples's Capodichino Airport (☎ 081/081/789–6111), 8 kilometers (5 miles) north of the downtown area. During the summer months there's a direct helicopter service between Capodichino, Capri, and Ischia; for information, call 081/789–6273 or 081/584–4355.

By Train

A great number of trains run between Rome and Naples every day; Intercity trains make the journey in less than two hours. There are several stations in Naples, and a network of suburban trains connects the city with diverse points of interest in Campania—most usefully the **Circumvesuviana** line, which runs to Herculaneum (Ercolano), Pompeii, and Sorrento. The central station is at Piazza Garibaldi. For train information, call 081/554–3188. Naples has a Metropolitana (subway); though it's old and trains are infrequent, it beats the traffic. The fare is 1,500 lire.

By Bus

For bus information, call **SITA** (☎ 081/552–2176) or the Naples Transport Board (☎ 081/700–5091).

By Car

The Naples–Pompeii–Salerno toll road has exits at Herculaneum and Pompeii, and connects with the tortuous coastal road to Sorrento and the Amalfi coast at the Castellammare exit. Parking within Naples is not recommended: Window smashing and robbery are not uncommon.

By Boat

Most boats and hydrofoils for the islands, the Sorrento peninsula, and the Amalfi coast leave from the Molo Beverello, near Naples's Piazza Municipio. **Caremar** (☎ 081/551–3882), **Navigazione Libera del Golfo** (☎ 081/552–7209), and **Lauro** (☎ 081/551–3236) operate frequent passenger and car ferry services, while hydrofoils of the Caremar, Navigazione Libera del Golfo, and **Alilauro** (☎ 081/552–2838) lines leave from both Molo Beverello and the hydrofoil station at Mergellina pier, from which **SNAV** (☎ 081/761–2348) also operates.

Guided Tours

One-, two-, or three-day guided tours of the area, departing from Rome, are offered by **American Express** (☎ 06/67641), **Carrani** (☎ 06/488–0510 and 06/474–2501), **Appian Line** (☎ 06/488–4151) and other operators. **Tourcar** (⊠ Piazza Matteotti 1, ☎ 081/552–3310) and **STS** (⊠ Piazza Medaglie d'Oro 41, ☎ 081/578–9292) in Naples have a wide range of half-day and all-day tours on the mainland and to the islands.

Visitor Information

Capri (⊠ Marina Grande pier, ☎ 081/837–0634; Piazza Umberto I, Capri town, ☎ 081/837–0686).
Naples. EPT Information Offices (⊠ Piazza dei Martiri 58, ☎ 081/405311; central station, ☎ 081/268779; hydrofoil station, Mergellina, summer only, ☎ 081/761–4585; ⊠ Capodichino Airport, ☎ 081/780–5761). Azienda Autonoma di Soggiorno, Cura e Turismo Information Office (AASCT, ⊠ Piazza del Gesù, ☎ 081/552–3328).
Sorrento (⊠ Via De Maio 35, ☎ 081/807–4033).

Exploring Campania

Naples

Founded by the Greeks, **Naples** became a playground of the Romans and was ruled thereafter by a succession of foreign dynasties, all of which left traces of their cultures in the city and its environs. The most splendid of these rulers were the Bourbons, who were responsible for much of what you will want to see in Naples, starting with the 17th-century **Palazzo Reale** (Royal Palace), still furnished in the lavish Baroque style that suited them so well. ⊠ *Piazza del Plebiscito,* ☎ *081/413888.* 🎫 *8,000 lire.* ☉ *Apr.–Oct., Tues.–Sun. 9–7:30; Nov.–Mar., Tues.–Wed. 9–2, Thurs.–Sat. 9–2, 4–7:30, Sun. 9–1, 4–7:30.*

Across the way is the massive stone **Castel Nuovo,** which was built by the city's Aragon rulers in the 13th century; some rooms recently opened to the public contain sculptures and frescoes that date from the 14th and 15th centuries. 🎫 *6,000 lire.* ☉ *Weekdays 9–7, Sat. 9–1:30.*

Walk up Via Toledo, keeping an eye on the antics of the Neapolitans, whose daily lives are fraught with theatrical gestures and fiery speeches. They all seem to be actors in their own human comedy.

NEED A BREAK? | For an authentic Neapolitan pizza in a genuine pizzeria, stop in at **Brandi's,** just off Via Chiaia (between Palazzo Reale and Piazza dei Mártiri), which claims to be the birthplace of the Pizza Margherita,

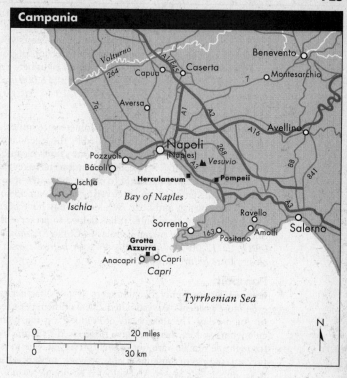

Campania

Volturno
264
Capua
Caserta
Benevento
Montesarchio
7
Aversa
7a
Avellino
A16
Pozzuoli
Napoli
(Naples)
Vesuvio
268
Bácoli
Herculaneum
Pompeii
Ischia
Bay of Naples
88
841
Ischia
Ravello
Sorrento
163
Amalfi
Salerno
Grotta
Azzurra
Positano
Anacapri
Capri
Capri

Tyrrhenian Sea

0   20 miles
0   30 km

N

named in honor of Queen Margherita of Savoy. ⊠ *Salita Sant'Anna di Palazzo 1 (off Via Chiaia),* ☎ *081/416928. Closed Mon.*

Continue along Via Toledo, also known as Via Roma, and make a detour to the right to see the oddly faceted stone facade and elaborate Baroque interior of the church of the **Gesù** (Via Benedetto Croce) and, directly opposite, the church of **Santa Chiara,** built in the early 1300s in Provençal Gothic style. A favorite Neapolitan song celebrates the quiet beauty of its cloister, decorated in delicate floral tiles.

Another detour off Via Toledo, to the left this time, takes you from **Piazza Dante** to the Montesanto funicular, which ascends the Vomero hill, where you can see the bastions of **Castel Sant'Elmo** (⊠ 4,000 lire, ☉ Tues.–Sun. 9–2) and visit the museum in the **Certosa di San Martino,** a Carthusian monastery restored in the 17th century. It contains an eclectic collection of Neapolitan landscape paintings, royal carriages, and *presepi* (Christmas crèches). Check out the view from the balcony off Room 25. ⊠ *Certosa di San Martino,* ☎ *081/578–1769.* ⊠ *8,000 lire.* ☉ *Tues.–Sun. 9–2.*

Return to Piazza Dante and follow Via Pessina (an extension of Via Toledo) ★ to the **Museo Archeologico Nazionale.** Dusty and unkempt, the museum undergoes perpetual renovations, but it holds one of the world's great collections of antiquities. Greek and Roman sculptures, vividly colored mosaics, countless objects from Pompeii and Herculaneum, and an equestrian statue of the Roman emperor Nerva are all worth seeing. ⊠ *Piazza Museo,* ☎ *081/440166.* ⊠ *12,000 lire.* ☉ *Aug.–Sept., Mon.–Sat. 9–7, Sun. 9–1; Oct.–July, Mon.–Sat. 9–2, Sun. 9–1.*

About a mile north on the same road (take a bus or a taxi), you'll come ★ to the **Museo di Capodimonte,** housed in an 18th-century palace built by Bourbon king Charles III, and surrounded by a vast park that must have been lovely when it was better cared for. In the picture gallery are some fine Renaissance paintings; climb the stairs to the terrace for a magnificent view of Naples and the bay. Downstairs you can visit the State Apartments and see the extensive collection of porcelain, much of it produced in the Bourbons' own factory right here on the grounds. ⊠ *Parco di Capodimonte,* ☎ *081/744–1307.* ☑ *8,000 lire.* ☉ *Apr.–Oct., Tues.–Sun. 9–7:30; Nov.–Mar., Tues.–Fri. 10–6, Sat. 10–9, Sun. 9–3.*

Herculaneum

★ **Herculaneum** (Ercolano) lies 10 kilometers (6 miles) southeast of Naples. Reputed to have been founded by the legendary Hercules, the elite Roman resort was devastated by the same volcanic eruption that buried Pompeii in AD 79. Recent excavations have revealed that many died on the shore in an attempt to escape, as a slow-moving mud slide embalmed the entire town by covering it with an 36-foot-deep blanket of volcanic ash and ooze. While that may have been unfortunate for Herculaneum's residents, it has helped to preserve the site in pristine detail for nearly two millennia. ⊠ *Corso Ercolano,* ☎ *081/739–0963.* ☑ *12,000 lire.* ☉ *Daily 9–1 hr before sunset (ticket office closes 2 hrs before sunset).*

Pompeii

★ **Pompeii,** a community 12 kilometers (8 miles) farther to the east, lost even more residents. An estimated 2,000 of them perished on that fateful August day. The ancient city of Pompeii was much larger than Herculaneum, and excavations have progressed to a much greater extent (though the remains are not as well preserved, due to some 18th-century scavenging for museum-quality artwork, most of which you are able to see at Naples's Museo Archeologico Nazionale; ☞ *above*). This prosperous Roman city had an extensive forum, lavish baths and temples, and patrician villas richly decorated with frescoes. It's worth buying a detailed guide of the site to gain an understanding of the ruins and their importance. Be sure to see the **Villa dei Misteri,** whose frescoes are in mint condition. Perhaps that is a slight exaggeration, but the paintings are so rich with detail and depth of color that one finds it difficult to believe that they are 1,900 years old. Have lots of small change handy to tip the guards at the more important houses so they will unlock the gates for you. ⊠ *Pompeii Scavi,* ☎ *081/861–0744.* ☑ *12,000 lire.* ☉ *Daily 9–1 hr before sunset (ticket office closes 2 hrs before sunset).*

Sorrento

Another 28 kilometers (18 miles) southwest is **Sorrento,** in the not-too-distant past a small, genteel resort for a fashionable elite. Now the town has spread out along the crest of its fabled cliffs. Once this was an area full of secret haunts for the few tourists who came for the beauty of this coastline. Now, it has been "discovered" and the secret haunts are the playground for package tours. In Sorrento's case, however, the change is not as grim as it sounds, since nothing can dim the delights of the marvelous climate and view of the Bay of Naples. For the best views go to the **Villa Comunale,** near the old church of **San Francesco** (in itself worth a visit), or to the terrace behind the **Museo Correale.** The museum, an attractive 18th-century villa, houses an interesting collection of decorative arts (furniture, china, and so on) and paintings of the Neapolitan school. ⊠ *Via Correale.* ☑ *8,000 lire; gardens only, 2,000 lire.* ☉ *Apr.–Sept., Mon. and Wed.–Sat. 9–12:30 and 4–6, Sun. 9–12:30; Oct.–Dec. and Feb.–Mar., Mon. and Wed.–Sat. 9–12 and 3–5, Sun. 9–8. Closed Jan.*

Capri

Sorrento makes a convenient jumping-off spot for a boat trip to **Capri.** No matter how many day-trippers crowd onto the island, no matter how touristy certain sections have become, Capri remains one of Italy's loveliest places. Incoming visitors disembark at Marina Grande, from where you can take some time out for an excursion to the **Grotta Azzurra** (Blue Grotto). Be warned that this must rank as one of the country's all-time great rip-offs: Motorboat, rowboat, and grotto admissions are charged separately, and if there's a line of boats waiting, you'll have little time to enjoy the grotto's marvelous colors. At Marina Grande you can also embark on a boat excursion around the island.

A cog railway or bus service takes you up to the town of Capri, where you can stroll through the **Piazzetta,** a choice place from which to watch the action, and window-shop expensive boutiques or browse in souvenir shops along Via Vittorio Emanuele on your way to the **Gardens of Augustus,** which have gorgeous views. The town of Capri is deliberately commercial and self-consciously picturesque. To get away from the crowds, hike to **Villa Jovis,** one of the many villas that Roman emperor Tiberius built on the island, at the end of a lane that climbs steeply uphill. The walk takes about 45 minutes, with pretty views all the way and a final spectacular vista of the entire Bay of Naples and part of the Gulf of Salerno. ⊠ *Villa Jovis, Via Tiberio.* ☎ *4,000 lire.* ☉ *Daily 9–1 hr before sunset.*

Or take the bus or a jaunty open taxi to **Anacapri** and look for the little church of **San Michele,** off Via Orlandi, where a magnificent hand-painted majolica tile floor shows you an 18th-century vision of the Garden of Eden. ☉ *Easter–Oct., daily 7–7; Nov.–Easter., 10–3.*

From Piazza della Vittoria, picturesque Via Capodimonte leads to **Villa San Michele,** charming former home of Swedish scientist-author Axel Munthe. ⊠ *Via Axel Munthe.* ☎ *6,000 lire.* ☉ *May–Sept., daily 9–6; Nov.–Feb., daily 10:30–3:30; Mar., daily 9:30–4:30; Apr. and Oct., daily 9:30–5.*

Amalfi and Positano

From Sorrento, the coastal drive down to the resort town of Amalfi provides some of the most dramatic and beautiful scenery you'll find in all of Italy. **Positano's** jumble of pastel houses, topped by whitewashed cupolas, clings to the mountainside above the sea. The town—the prettiest along this stretch of coast—attracts a sophisticated group of visitors and summer residents who find that its relaxed and friendly atmosphere more than compensates for the sheer effort of moving about this exhaustingly vertical town, most of whose streets are stairways. This former fishing village has now opted for the more regular and lucrative rewards of tourism and commercialized fashion. Practically every other shop is a boutique displaying locally made casual wear. The beach is the town's main focal point, with a little promenade and a multitude of café-restaurants.

Amalfi itself is a charming maze of covered alleys and narrow byways straggling up the steep mountainside. The piazza just below the cathedral forms the town's heart—a colorful assortment of pottery stalls, cafés, and postcard shops grouped around a venerable old fountain. The cathedral's exterior is its most impressive feature, so there's no need to climb all those stairs unless you really want to.

Ravello

Do not miss **Ravello,** 8 kilometers (5 miles) north of Amalfi. Ravello is not actually on the coast, but on a high mountain bluff overlooking the sea. The road up to it is a series of switchbacks, and the village itself clings precariously on the mountain spur. The village flourished during the 13th century and then fell into a tranquillity that has remained unchanged for the past six centuries. The center of the town is **Piazza Duomo,** with its cathedral, founded in 1087. Note the fine bronze 12th-century doors and, inside, two pulpits richly decorated with mosaics: one depicting the story of Jonah and the whale; the other—more splendid—carved with fantastic beasts and resting on a pride of lions.

To the right of the cathedral is the entrance to the 11th-century **Villa Rufolo.** The composer Richard Wagner once stayed in Ravello, and there is a Wagner festival every summer on the villa's garden terrace. There is a Moorish cloister with interlacing pointed arches, beautiful gardens, an 11th-century tower, and a belvedere with a fine view of the coast. ⊠ 4,000 lire. ☉ Summer, daily 9–8; winter, daily 9–6 or sunset.

Across the square from the cathedral is a lovely walk leading to the **Villa Cimbrone.** At the entrance to the villa complex is a small cloister that looks medieval but was actually built in 1917, with two bas-reliefs: one representing nine Norman warriors, the other illustrating the seven deadly sins. Then, the long avenue leads through peaceful gardens scattered with grottoes, small temples, and statues to a belvedere and terrace where, on a clear day, the view stretches out over the Mediterranean Sea. ⊠ 5,000 lire. ☉ Daily 8:30–1 hr before sunset.

Dining and Lodging

For details and price-category definitions, see Dining and Lodging in Staying in Italy, above.

Amalfi

$$ ✕ **La Caravella.** Tucked away under some arches lining the coast road, the Caravella has a nondescript entrance but a pleasant interior decorated in a medley of colors and with paintings of old Amalfi. It's small and intimate, and proprietor Franco describes the cuisine as "sfiziosa" (taste-tempting). Specialties include scialatielli (homemade pasta with shellfish sauce) and pesce al limone (fresh fish with lemon sauce). ⊠ Via M. Camera 12, ☎ 089/871029. AE, DC, MC, V. Closed Tues. and Nov. 10–30.

$$$$ 🏨 **Santa Caterina.** A large mansion perched above terraced and flow-
★ ered hillsides on the coast road just outside Amalfi proper, the Santa Caterina is one of the best hotels on the entire coast. The rooms are tastefully decorated, and most have small terraces or balconies with great views. There are lounges and terraces for relaxing, and an elevator whisks guests down to the seaside saltwater pool, bar, and swimming area. Amid lemon and orange groves, there are two romantic villa annexes. ⊠ Strada Amalfitana 9, ☎ 089/871012, ﬀﬞAX 089/871351. 70 rooms with bath. Restaurant, bar, pool, beach bar, parking. AE, DC, MC, V.

Capri

$$–$$$ ✕ **La Capannina.** Only a few steps away from Capri's social center, the Piazzetta, La Capannina has a delightful vine-hung courtyard for summer dining and a reputation as one of the island's best eating places. Antipasto features fried ravioli and eggplant stuffed with ricotta, and house specialties include chicken, scaloppini, and a refreshing, homemade lemon liqueur. ⊠ Via Botteghe 14, ☎ 081/837–0732. AE, MC, V. Closed Wed. (except during Aug.) and Nov.–mid-Mar.

$$ ✕ **Al Grottino.** This small family-run restaurant, with a handy loca-
★ tion near the Piazzetta, displays autographed photographs of celebrity customers. House specialties are gnocchi with mozzarella and linguine con gamberini (with shrimp sauce). ⊠ Via Longano 27, ☎ 081/837–0584. AE, MC, V. Closed Tues. and Nov. 3–Mar. 20.

$$ **✕ Da Gemma.** One of Capri's favorite places for a homey atmosphere and a good meal, Da Gemma features pappardelle all'aragosta and fritto misto. If you're on a budget, forgo the fish that you pay for by weight—it's always expensive. Pizza makes a great starter in the evening. ✉ *Via Madre Serafina 6,* ☎ *081/837–0461. AE, DC, MC, V. Closed Mon. and Nov.*

$$$$ **⊞ Quisisana.** One of Italy's poshest hotels is right in the center of the town of Capri. The rooms are spacious, and many have arcaded balconies with views of the sea; the decor is traditional or contemporary, with some antique accents. From the small terrace at the entrance you can watch all Capri go by, but the enclosed garden and pool in the back are perfect for getting away from it all. The bar and restaurant are casual in a terribly elegant way. ✉ *Via Camerelle 2,* ☎ *081/837–0788,* 🖷 *081/837–6080. 143 rooms with bath. Restaurant, pool, tennis court. AE, DC, MC, V. Closed Nov.–mid-Mar.*

$$$ **⊞ Villa Brunella.** The glassed-in bar of this family-run hotel is on the
★ lane leading to Punta Tragara and the Faraglioni. From that level you descend to the restaurant, with the rooms and the swimming pool all on lower levels. Furnishings are tastefully casual and comfortable, and the views from all levels are wonderful. Be prepared to climb stairs; there's no elevator. ✉ *Via Tragara 24,* ☎ *081/837–0122,* 🖷 *081/837–0430. 18 rooms with bath. Restaurant, bar, pool. AE, DC, MC, V. Closed Nov.–Mar.*

$$$ **⊞ Villa Sarah.** Just a 10-minute walk from the Piazzetta, the Sarah is a whitewashed Mediterranean villa with bright, simply furnished rooms. There's a garden and small bar, but no restaurant. ✉ *Via Tiberio 3/A,* ☎ *081/837–7817,* 🖷 *081/837–7215. 20 rooms with bath. Bar, garden. AE, MC, V. Closed Nov.–Mar.*

Naples

$$$ **✕ La Sacrestia.** This lovely restaurant is in an elevated position, above Mergellina, with a fine view and a delightful summer terrace. The menu offers traditional Neapolitan cuisine; among the specialties are sea bass, either steamed or baked, and linguine in *salsa di scorfano* (scorpionfish sauce). ✉ *Via Orazio 116,* ☎ *081/761–1051. AE, DC, MC, V. Closed Mon. Sept.–June, Sun. in July, and Aug.*

$$ **✕ Ciro a Santa Brigida.** Centrally located off Via Toledo near the Castel Nuovo, this no-frills restaurant is a favorite with businesspeople, artists, and journalists. Tables are arranged on two levels, and the decor is classic trattoria. This is the place to try traditional Neapolitan *sartù di riso* (a rich rice dish with meat and peas) and *melanzane alla parmigiana* or scaloppe *alla Ciro* (eggplant or veal with prosciutto and mozzarella). There's pizza, too. ✉ *Via Santa Brigida 71,* ☎ *081/552–4072. AE, DC, MC, V. Closed Sun. and 2 wks in Aug.*

$$ **✕ La Bersagliera.** This restaurant has been making tourists happy for years, with a great location on the Santa Lucia waterfront, cheerful waiters, mandolin music, and good spaghetti *alla disgraziata* (with tomatoes, capers, and black olives) and fried mozzarella in *carrozza* (batter). ✉ *Borgo Marinaro 10,* ☎ *081/764–6016. AE, DC, MC, V. Closed Tues.*

$$$$ **⊞ Excelsior.** Splendidly situated on the shore drive, the Excelsior has views of the bay from its front rooms. The spacious bedrooms are well furnished in informal floral prints or more formal Empire style; all have a comfortable, traditional air. The salons are formal, with chandeliers and wall paintings, and the excellent Casanova restaurant is elegant. ✉ *Via Partenope 48,* ☎ *081/764–0111,* 🖷 *081/764–9743. 102 rooms with bath. Restaurant, bar, sauna, parking. AE, DC, MC, V.*

$$–$$$ 🏨 **Jolly Ambassador.** This hotel occupies the top 14 floors of a down-
★ town skyscraper, and its rooms and roof restaurant have wonderful
views of Naples and the bay. It's furnished in the functional, modern
style typical of this reliable chain, which promises comfort and efficiency in a city where these are scarce commodities. ✉ *Via Medina 70,*
☎ *081/416000,* 📠 *081/551–8010. 251 rooms with bath. Restaurant,*
bar, parking. AE, DC, MC, V.

$$ 🏨 **Rex.** This hotel occupies a fairly quiet location near the Santa Lucia
waterfront. It is situated on the first two floors of an Art Nouveau build-
ing and lacks an elevator. The decor ranges from 1950s modern to fake
period pieces and even some folk art, haphazardly combined. Al-
though it has no restaurant, there are many in the area. ✉ *Via Pale-*
poli 12, ☎ *081/764–9389,* 📠 *081/764–9227. 37 rooms with bath*
or shower. Bar, parking. AE, DC, MC, V.

Positano

$$ ✕ **Capurale.** Among all the popular restaurants on the beach promenade, Capurale (just around the corner) has the best food and lowest
prices. Tables are set under vines on a breezy sidewalk in the summer,
upstairs and indoors in winter. Spaghetti con melanzane and crepes al
formaggio are good choices here. ✉ *Via Regina Giovanna 12,* ☎ *089/*
875374. AE, DC, MC, V. Closed Tues. Nov.–Mar. and 4 wks Jan.–Feb.

$$$$ 🏨 **Le Sirenuse.** The most fashionable hotel in Positano, this renovated
18th-century villa has been in the same family for eight generations.
The hotel is set into the hillside about 200 feet above Positano's harbor. Most of the bedrooms face the sea—these are the best. Because
of the hotel's location, the dining room is like a long, closed-in terrace
overlooking the village of Positano—a magnificent view. The cuisine
varies from acceptable to excellent. ✉ *Via Cristoforo Colombo 30,* ☎
089/875066, 📠 *081/811798. 60 rooms with bath or shower. Restau-*
rant, bar, pool, sauna. AE, DC, MC, V.

$$$$ 🏨 **San Pietro.** Situated on the side of a cliff, this is quite possibly one
of the world's most attractive hotels because of its magnificent views
of the sea and the Amalfi coast. The decor of the hotel is eclectic, with
unusual antiques and, everywhere, hanging bougainvillea. The furnishings are perfectly arranged to give a sense of openness and create
a feeling of opulence. The guest rooms are decorated with an eye to
detail but the window views steal the show. Verdant with plants, the
light, open dining room offers fine Italian cuisine. An elevator takes
guests to the hotel's small beach area. ✉ *Via Laurito 2,* ☎ *089/875455,*
📠 *089/811449. 60 rooms with bath. Restaurant, pool, tennis court,*
beach. AE, DC, MC, V. Closed Nov.–Mar.

$$$ 🏨 **Palazzo Murat.** The location is perfect, in the heart of town, near
the beachside promenade and set within a walled garden. The old wing
is a historic palazzo, with tall windows and wrought-iron balconies;
the newer wing is a whitewashed Mediterranean building with arches
and terraces. Guests can relax in antiques-strewn lounges or on the
charming vine-draped patio. ✉ *Via dei Mulini 23,* ☎ *089/875177,* 📠
089/811419. 28 rooms with bath. Bar, garden. AE, DC, MC, V. Closed
Nov. 5–Mar.

$ 🏨 **Santa Caterina.** There is more to this newly refurbished hotel than
meets the eye, with rooms descending on three levels down the steep
slope. The exquisite view over the town and seashore can be relished
from each of the somewhat cramped rooms as well as the generous bal-
conies and terraces. On street level (the top floor), there is also a good
fish restaurant, well patronized by the locals. It's quite a hike down to
the beach—a good 15 minutes down the steps—but that's nothing new

in Positano. ⊠ *Via Pasitea 113.* ☎ *089/857019. 10 rooms with bath or shower. Restaurant, bar. AE, DC, MC, V. Closed Nov.–Mar.*

Ravello

$$$$ ⊞ **Hotel Palumbo.** Of all the hotels on the Amalfi coast, the Hotel Palumbo is the most genteel—and one of the most costly. Occupying a 12th-century patrician palace furnished with antiques and provided with modern comforts, this hotel has an elegant, warm atmosphere. With lovely garden terraces, breathtaking views, and a sumptuous upstairs dining room, the hotel is a memorable one. Some of the bedrooms are small, but they are full of character. The rooms facing the sea are the choice ones—and the more expensive. With the greatest of ease, guests quickly come to view the Hotel Palumbo as their private palazzo. ⊠ *Via Toro 28,* ☎ *089/857244,* FAX *089/858133. 30 rooms with bath. Restaurant, bar, garden. AE, DC, MC, V.*

Sorrento

$$ ✕ **Antica Trattoria.** This is a homey, hospitable place with a garden for summer dining. The specialties of the house are a classic pennette *al profumo di bosco* (with a creamy mushroom and ham sauce), fish (which can be expensive), and *gamberetti freschi* Antica Trattoria (shrimp in a tomato sauce). ⊠ *Via Giuliani 33,* ☎ *081/807–1082. No credit cards. Closed Mon., Jan. 10–Feb. 10.*

$$ ✕ **La Belle Epoque.** Occupying a 19th-century villa perched on the edge of the vine-covered gorge of the Mulini, this is an elegant veranda restaurant. Try the scialatielli *alla siciliana* (with mozzarella and eggplant). ⊠ *Via Fuorimura 7,* ☎ *081/878–1216. AE, DC, MC, V. Closed Mon.*

$$ ✕ **Parrucchiano.** One of the town's best and oldest, Parrucchiano features greenhouse-type dining rooms dripping with vines and dotted with plants. Among the antipasti, try the *panzarotti* (pastry crust filled with mozzarella and tomato), and for a main course, the scaloppe *alla sorrentina*, again with mozzarella and tomato. ⊠ *Corso Italia 71,* ☎ *081/878–1321. MC, V. Closed Wed. Nov.–May.*

$$$$ ⊞ **Cocumella.** In a lovely cliff-side garden in a quiet residential area just outside Sorrento, this historic old villa (it features a 17th-century chapel) has been totally renovated for comfort. Furnishings are a tasteful blend of antique and modern; there are vaulted ceilings and archways, a dining veranda, and stunning tiled floors. Cocumella has an exclusive, elegant atmosphere without being stuffy. ⊠ *Via Cocumella 7,* ☎ *081/878–2933,* FAX *081/878–3712. 60 rooms with bath. Restaurant, pool, garden, tennis court. AE, DC, MC, V. Closed Jan.–Feb.*

$$$$ ⊞ **Excelsior Vittoria.** In the heart of Sorrento, but removed from the main square by an arbored walk, the Excelsior Vittoria is right on the cliff and has Art Nouveau furnishings, some very grand, though faded. Tenor Enrico Caruso's bedroom is preserved as a relic; guest bedrooms are spacious and elegant in a turn-of-the-century way. It overlooks the bay and is recommended for those who like a lot of atmosphere with their views. ⊠ *Piazza Tasso 34,* ☎ *081/807–1044,* FAX *081/877–1206. 106 rooms with bath. Restaurant, pool, garden. AE, DC, MC, V.*

$$$ ⊞ **Imperial Hotel Tramontano.** Incorporating the birthplace of the poet Torquato Tasso—the first of an impressive list of literary credentials— this palatial villa lies within a semitropical garden in the center of Sorrento. The sumptuous furnishings and Belle Epoque tone are set off by the spectacular views out to sea. ⊠ *Via Veneto 1,* ☎ *081/878–2588,* FAX *081/807–2344. 120 rooms with bath or shower. Restaurant, bar, garden, private beach, meeting rooms. Closed Dec.–Mar. AE, DC, MC, V.*

$$ ⊞ **Eden.** The Eden occupies a fairly quiet but central location, with a garden. The bedrooms are bright but undistinguished; the lounge and lobby have more character. It's an unpretentious but friendly hotel, although it can get crowded in high season. ⊠ *Via Correale 25,* ☏ *081/878–1909,* 🖷 *081/807–2016. 60 rooms with bath. Restaurant, bar, pool. AE, MC, V. Closed Nov.–Feb.*

$ 🏨 **City.** The central location and excellent value for money are the best reasons to stay in this modest establishment, close to the bus and train stations. Bedrooms are small and functional, but the atmosphere is relaxed and the management always ready with information and advice. ⊠ *Corso Italia 221,* ☏ *081/877–2210,* 🖷 *081/877–2210. 13 rooms with shower. AE, MC, V.*

18 Luxembourg

Luxembourg City

Excursions from Luxembourg City

ARRIVING IN THE CAPITAL OF LUXEMBOURG from the airport, visitors crossing the Grand Duchess Charlotte Bridge are greeted by an awe-inspiring panorama of medieval stonework fortifications and massive gates. Then a simple left turn and they're back in the 20th century. The boulevard Royal, crowded with luxury automobiles, glitters with glass-and-concrete office buildings. Luxembourg, until recently little more than a cluster of meager farms and failing mines, flaunts new wealth, new political muscle, and the highest per capita income in the world.

One of the smallest countries in the United Nations, Luxembourg comprises only 2,587 square kilometers (999 square miles), less than Rhode Island. It is dwarfed by its neighbors—Germany, Belgium, and France—yet from its history of invasion, occupation, and siege, you might think those square miles were built over solid gold. In fact, it was Luxembourg's very defenses against centuries of attack that rendered it all the more desirable: From AD 963, when Siegfried built a castle on the high promontory of the Bock, the duchy encased itself in layer upon layer of fortifications until by the mid-19th century its very impregnability was considered a threat. After successive invasions—by the Burgundians, the Spanish, the French, the Austrians, the French again, the Dutch, and the Prussians—Luxembourg was ultimately dismantled in the name of peace, its neutrality guaranteed by the 1867 Treaty of London and its function reduced to that of a buffer zone. What remains of its walls, while impressive, is only a reminder of what was one of the strongholds of Europe—the "Gibraltar of the North."

Luxembourg is currently being besieged again, this time by bankers and Eurocrats. It now bristles with international banks—enough to rival Switzerland—and just outside the old city, a new colony has been populated by *functionnaires* of the European Union (EU), the successor to the Common Market. Fiercely protecting its share in the expanding bureaucracy against raids by its co-capitals Strasbourg and Brussels, Luxembourg digs its heels in once again, vying not only for political autonomy but also for continued prosperity and clout. In this it will be helped by the new president of the EU's powerful European Commission, Jacques Santer, who served for a decade as Luxembourg's prime minister. The national motto, *Mir wëlle bleiwe wat mir sin* ("We want to stay what we are"), thus takes on new meaning; the country wishes to remain a viable grand duchy in the heart of modern Europe.

Visitors will find evidence of the grand duchy's military past scattered around its luxurious countryside: There are castles by the dozen, set in the densely wooded hills of La Petite Suisse (Little Switzerland) to the east, in the crests and valleys of the Ardennes to the north, and along the banks of the Our and the Moselle rivers.

ESSENTIAL INFORMATION

Before You Go

When to Go

The main tourist season in Luxembourg is the same as Belgium's—early May to late September, with spring and fall the nicest times. But temperatures in Luxembourg tend to be cooler than those in Belgium, particularly in the hilly north, where there is frequently snow in winter.

Luxembourg

CLIMATE

In general, temperatures in Luxembourg are moderate. Drizzling rain is common, so be sure to bring a raincoat. The following are the average daily maximum and minimum temperatures for Luxembourg.

Jan.	37F	3C	**May**	65F	18C	**Sept.**	66F	19C
	29	– 1		46	8		50	10
Feb.	40F	4C	**June**	70F	21C	**Oct.**	56F	13C
	31	– 1		52	11		43	6
Mar.	49F	10C	**July**	73F	23C	**Nov.**	44F	7C
	35	1		55	13		37	3
Apr.	57F	14C	**Aug.**	71F	22C	**Dec.**	39F	4C
	40	4		54	12		32	0

Currency

In Luxembourg, as in Belgium, the unit of currency is the franc (abbreviated Flux). Luxembourg issues its own currency in bills of 100, 1,000 and 5,000 francs and coins of 1, 5, 20, and 50 francs. Belgian currency can be used freely in Luxembourg, however, and the two currencies have exactly the same value. Luxembourg's currency is not valid in Belgium. At press time (spring 1996), the exchange rate was Flux 26 to the U.S. dollar, Flux 20 to the Canadian dollar, and Flux 46 to the pound sterling.

What It Will Cost

Luxembourg is a highly developed and sophisticated country with a high standard and cost of living. Luxembourg City is an international banking center, and a number of European institutions are based there, which tends to push prices slightly higher in the capital.

Cup of coffee, Flux 50–Flux 60; glass of beer, Flux 40–Flux 60; movie ticket, Flux 200–Flux 220; 3-mile taxi ride, Flux 600.

Customs on Arrival

For information on customs regulations, *see* Essential Information *in* Chapter 4, Belgium.

Language

Native Luxembourgers speak three languages fluently: Luxembourgish, German, and French. Many also speak English.

Staying in Luxembourg

Telephones

LOCAL CALLS

You can find public phones on the street and in city post offices. A local call costs a minimum of Flux 5 from a public phone (slightly more from restaurants and gas stations). No area codes are needed when you call within the grand duchy. Post offices also sell a Telekaart, in units of Flux 50 and Flux 150, that can be used in nearly half the country's phone booths. For operator-assisted calls, dial 0010.

INTERNATIONAL CALLS

The cheapest way to make an international call is to dial direct from a public phone; in a post office, you may be required to make a deposit before the call. To reach an **AT&T** long-distance operator, dial 0800–0111; for **MCI**, dial 0800–0112; for **Sprint**, dial 0800–0115.

COUNTRY CODE

The country code for Luxembourg is 352.

Mail

POSTAL RATES

Airmail postcards and letters to North America weighing less than 20 grams cost Flux 25. Letters and postcards to the United Kingdom cost Flux 16.

RECEIVING MAIL

Holders of American Express cards or traveler's checks can have mail sent in care of American Express (✉ Av. de la Porte-Neuve 34, L-2227 Luxembourg).

Shopping

SALES TAX REFUNDS

Purchases of goods for export may qualify for a sales tax (TVA) refund of 12%. Ask the shop to fill out a refund form. You must then have the form stamped by customs officers on leaving either Luxembourg, Belgium, or the Netherlands by air for a non-EU country.

Opening and Closing Times

Banks are generally open weekdays 8:30–noon and 1:30–4:30, though more and more are remaining open through the lunch hour.

Museums. Opening hours vary, so check individual listings. Many close on Monday, and most also close for lunch between noon and 2.

Shops. Large city department stores and shops are generally open weekdays, except Monday morning, and Saturday 9–noon and 2–6. A few small family businesses are open Sunday morning from 8 to noon.

National Holidays

January 1; February 10–11 (Carnival); March 31 (Easter Monday); May 1 (May Day); May 8 (Ascension); May 19 (Pentecost Monday);

June 23 (National Day); August 15 (Assumption); November 1 (All Saints' Day); November 2 (All Souls' Day); December 25–26.

Dining

Restaurants in Luxembourg combine French quality with German quantity. The best deals are at lunch, when you can find a *plat du jour* (one-course special) or *menu* (two or three courses included in price) at bargain rates. Pizzerias offer an inexpensive alternative.

MEALTIMES

Most hotels serve breakfast until 10. Luxembourgers drop their tools and shut down their computers at noon to rush home for a 2-hour lunch. Businesspeople entertaining guests, tourists, and partying young people populate restaurants for dinner between 7 and 10.

WHAT TO WEAR

Stylish, casual dress is generally acceptable in most restaurants, but when in doubt, err on the formal side. In expensive French restaurants, formal dress (jacket and tie) is taken for granted.

RATINGS

Prices quoted are per person and include a first course, main course, and dessert, but not wine. Service (10%) and a reasonable sales tax of 3% (compared to Belgium's 21%) are included in quoted prices.

CATEGORY	COST
$$$$	over Flux 3,000
$$$	Flux 1,500–3,000
$$	Flux 750–1,500
$	under Flux 750

Lodging

HOTELS

Most hotels in Luxembourg City are relatively modern and range from the international style, mainly near the airport, to family-run establishments in town. Outside the capital, many hotels are housed in more picturesque buildings. Prices vary considerably between town and country. Luxembourg City is host to countless business travelers, and many of its hotels offer reduced rates on weekends.

YOUTH HOSTELS

Inexpensive youth hostels are plentiful; many are housed in ancient fortresses and castles. For information, contact **Centrale des Auberges de Jeunesse** (⊠ Pl. d'Armes 18, L-1136 Luxembourg, ☎ 225588).

CAMPING

The grand duchy is probably the best-organized country in Europe when it comes to camping. It offers some 120 sites, all with full amenities. Listings are published annually by the National Tourist Office (☞ Important Addresses and Numbers *in* Luxembourg City, *below.*)

RATINGS

Price categories are for a double room. Service (10%) and sales tax (3%) are included in posted rates. Check for special rates when making reservations.

CATEGORY	COST
$$$$	over Flux 8,000
$$$	Flux 5,000–8,000
$$	Flux 2,500–5,000
$	under Flux 2,500

Tipping

In hotels and restaurants, taxes and service charges are included in the bill. If you wish to tip, round off the sum to the nearest Flux 50 or Flux 100. Bellhops and doormen should receive between Flux 50 and Flux 100, depending on the grade of the hotel. At the movies, tip the usher Flux 20 if you are seated personally. In theaters, tip about Flux 20 for checking your coat and the same to the program seller. Public washroom attendants receive between Flux 5 and 10. Taxi drivers expect a tip; add about 15% to the amount on the meter.

LUXEMBOURG CITY

Arriving and Departing

By Plane

All international flights arrive at Luxembourg's Findel Airport, 6 kilometers (4 miles) from the city.

BETWEEN THE AIRPORT AND DOWNTOWN

Bus 9 leaves the airport at regular intervals for the city center; it then continues to the main bus depot, next to the train station. Tickets cost Flux 40. A taxi will cost you Flux 700–Flux 800. If you are driving, follow the signs for the CENTRE VILLE (city center).

By Train

Luxembourg is served by frequent direct trains from Paris and Brussels. From Paris, travel time is about four hours; from Brussels, just under three hours. From Amsterdam, the journey is via Brussels and takes about six hours. There are connections from most German cities via Koblenz. Outside Luxembourg City, three major train routes extend to the north, south, and east into the Moselle Valley. For all train information, phone 492424. All service is from the Gare Centrale.

Getting Around

One of the best transportation options is the **Oeko-Carnet,** a block of five one-day tickets good for unlimited transportation on trains and buses throughout the country. In Luxembourg City, these cards, costing Flux 600, are sold at the Gare Centrale and at the Aldringen Center, located underground in front of the central post office.

By Bus

Luxembourg City has a highly efficient bus service. The blue-and-white buses outside the train station go all around the city and also to some outlying areas. Get details about services at the information counter in the station arrivals hall. Fares are low, but the best bet is to buy a 10-ride ticket (Flux 300), available from banks or from the bus station in the Aldringen Center. Other buses, connecting Luxembourg City with towns throughout the country, leave from the Gare Centrale.

By Car

A car is a liability in this small, walkable city. You can see the rest of the country in a day or two, and you may wish to rent a car for this purpose. Major highways and smaller roads are excellent and fairly uncrowded. Speed limits are 120 kph (75 mph) on highways, 90 kph (55 mph) on major roads, and 50 kph (30 mph) in built-up areas.

On-street parking in Luxembourg City is difficult. Make use of one of the underground parking lots, or park at the sizable Parking Glacis next to the Municipal Theater, five minutes' walk from the city center.

By Bicycle

Bicycling is an excellent way to see the city and outlying areas. A brochure, "Cycling Tracks," is available from the National Tourist Office (⊠ Box 1001, L-1010 Luxembourg, ☎ 481199). Bikes can be rented in Luxembourg City at **Luxembourg DELTA** (⊠ Bisserwee 8, ☎ 4796–2383) from March 30 through October 31. In Reisdorf, Diekirch, and Echternach, rent bikes at the tourist office (**Syndicat d'Initiative**). Maps are available from the local tourist offices.

By Taxi

There are taxi stands near the Gare Centrale and the main post office; it is almost impossible to hail one in the street. To call a taxi, phone 480058 or 482233.

Important Addresses and Numbers

Embassies

U.S. (⊠ Blvd. Emmanuel Servais 22, ☎ 460123). **Canadian:** The embassy in Belgium (⊠ Av. de Tervuren 2, B-1040 Brussels, ☎ 00322/741–06–11) serves Luxembourg. **U.K.** (⊠ Blvd. F. D. Roosevelt 14, ☎ 229864).

Emergencies

Police (☎ 113). **Ambulance, Doctor, Dentist** (☎ 112). **Pharmacies** in Luxembourg stay open nights on a rotation system. Signs listing late-night facilities are posted outside each pharmacy.

English-Language Books

For books and magazines in English, try **Magasin Anglais** (⊠ Allée Scheffer 13, ☎ 224925).

Travel Agencies

American Express (⊠ Av. de la Porte-Neuve 34, ☎ 228555). **Carlson/Wagonlit** (⊠ Grand'rue 99, ☎ 460315). **CIT** (⊠ Pl. de la Gare, ☎ 485102). **Emile Weitzel** (⊠ Rue Notre-Dame 15, ☎ 222931). **Keiser Tours** (⊠ Rue Philippe II 34, ☎ 472717). **Sotour** (including youth travel; ⊠ Pl. du Theatre 15, ☎ 461514).

Visitor Information

The main **National Tourist Office** (ONT; ⊠ Gare Centrale, ☎ 481199) is open daily (except Sun., Nov.–Mar.) 9–noon and 2–6:30 (July–mid-Sept., 9–7). A branch at the airport (☎ 4008–0821) is open the same hours. The **Luxembourg City Tourist Office** (⊠ Pl. d'Armes, ☎ 222809) is open mid-September–mid-June, Monday–Saturday 9–1 and 2–6; mid-June–mid-September, weekdays 9–7, Saturday 9–1 and 2–7, Sunday 10–noon and 2–6.

Guided Tours

Orientation

Sales-Lentz (⊠ Rue du Curé 26, ☎ 461818) offers tours every morning from April through October. Tours leave from Platform 5 of the bus station (next to the railway station) or from the war memorial in place de la Constitution and cost Flux 290. They include the historic sights of the center, the area housing various branches of the EU, and some of the villas on the city's outskirts. Another tour takes in the monuments of Luxembourg City, the war cemeteries, and the castle of Bourglinster (Apr., May, and Oct., weekends 2:30–5:45; June–Sept., Tues., Thurs., Sat., and Sun. 2:30–5:45; Flux 320).

From April through October, guided minitrain tours of the Old Town and the Pétrusse Valley start from the place de la Constitution (☎ 461617; Flux 230.)

Walking

You can rent headphones and a cassette with a self-guided city tour at the bus booth on the place de la Constitution for Flux 180 (a refundable deposit of Flux 1,000 is required).

The new **Wenzel Walk** allows visitors to experience 1,000 years of history in 100 minutes. It is named for Wenceslas II, Duke of Luxembourg and Holy Roman Emperor (no relation to the good king of the Christmas carol), who played an important part in fortifying the city. The walk starts at the Bock promontory and leads into the valley, over medieval bridges, and past ancient ruins and exact reconstructions (labeled as such), with two audiovisual presentations along the way. Good walking shoes are required. There are explanations at each sight. A descriptive leaflet is available from the City Tourist Office (☞ Visitor Information, *above*), which can provide a guide (Flux 1,600, per group).

For information on weekend walking tours, contact the tourist office or the **Fédération Luxembourgeoise des Marches Populaires** (✉ Boite Postale 794, L-2018 Luxembourg). Also consult the *Agenda Touristique,* published by the ONT.

Excursions

Pick up the booklet "Circuits Auto-Pedestres," available at newsstands and bookstores (Flux 895), for information on combination driving-walking tours outside the city.

Exploring Luxembourg City

This walk takes in the military fortifications and the Old Town, with its cobbled streets and inviting public squares. In 1994 the United Nations Educational, Scientific, and Cultural Organization (UNESCO) declared these areas part of the world's architectural heritage.

Numbers in the margin correspond to points of interest on the Luxembourg City map.

❶ Start on the **Passerelle,** a 19th-century road bridge that links the station with the valley of the Pétrusse. The Pétrusse is more of a brook than a river and is now contained by concrete, but the valley has become a beautiful park. From here you'll see the rocky ledges—partly natural, partly human-made—on which the city was founded.

❷ At the cathedral end of the Passerelle, on the right, take the steps and curving sidewalk up to the **Monument de la Solidarité Nationale** (Monument to National Unity) and admire its perpetual flame. It was erected in 1971 to commemorate the citizens of Luxembourg who died during World War II.

❸ To the right of the monument, follow the road along the remains of the old city fortifications, known as the **Citadelle du St-Esprit** (Citadel of the Holy Spirit). This 17th-century citadel was built by Vauban, the French military engineer, in the typical style of thrusting wedges. From the end you can see the three spires of the cathedral, the Alzette, and the incongruous white tower of the European Parliament secretariat.

★ ❹ Retrace your steps along the old city fortifications, cross boulevard F. D. Roosevelt, and continue on to the **place de la Constitution,** marked by a war memorial, the striking gilt *Gëlle Fra,* or "Golden Woman." Here you'll find the entrance to the ancient **Pétrusse casemates,** military tunnels carved into the bedrock. During the many phases of the fortress's construction, the rock itself was hollowed out to form a honeycomb of underground passages, some 24 kilometers (15 miles) of them

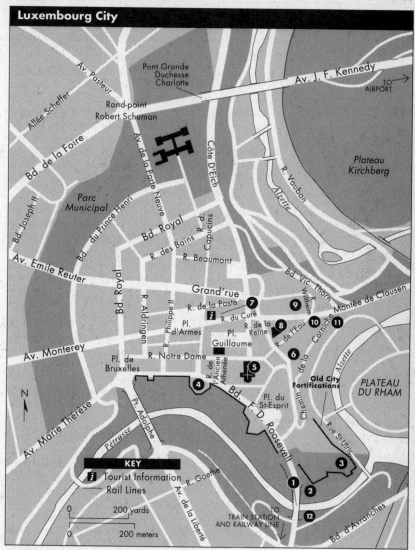

Luxembourg City

KEY

ℹ Tourist Information
— Rail Lines

0   200 yards

0   200 meters

Bock, **11**
Cathédrale
Notre-Dame, **5**
Chapelle de
St-Quirin, **12**
Citadelle du
St-Esprit, **3**
Grand Ducal
Palace, **8**
Maquette, **7**

Monument de la
Solidarité
Nationale, **2**
Musée d'Histoire de
la Ville de
Luxembourg, **6**
Musée National, **9**
Passerelle, **1**
Place de la
Constitution, **4**
St-Michel, **10**

in all. These were used for storage and as a place of refuge. Two sections of the passages are open to the public. These contain a former barracks, cavernous abattoirs, bakeries, and a deep well. ⊠ *Place de la Constitution.* ⌚ *Flux 50.* ☉ *July–Sept.*

Take rue de l'ancien Athénée alongside the former Jesuit college, now the National Library. To your right in rue Notre-Dame is the entrance to the 17th-century **Cathédrale Notre-Dame,** with its Baroque organ gallery and crypt. In the crypt are the tombs of John the Blind, the gallant 14th-century king of Bohemia and count of Luxembourg who fell at the Battle of Crécy in France in 1346, and members of the present ruling dynasty. The valley side of the church was rebuilt in 1935; the main tower was reroofed in 1985. ⊠ *Rue Notre-Dame.* ☉ *Easter–Oct., weekdays 10–5, Sat. 8–6, Sun. 10–6; Nov.–Easter, weekdays 10–11:30 and 2–5, Sat. 8–11:30 and 2–5, Sun. 10–5.*

★ ❻ Just east of the cathedral and past place Clairefontaine with its graceful statue of Grand Duchess Charlotte is the new **Musée d'Histoire de la Ville de Luxembourg** (Luxembourg City Historical Museum), which opened in mid-1996. This interactive multimedia museum traces the development of the city over 1,000 years and is partially underground, with the lowest five levels showing the town's preserved ancient stonework. A glass-wall elevator provides a wonderful view of the ravine from the upper floors. ⊠ *Rue du St-Esprit 14,* ☎ *4796–2766.* ⌚ *Flux 250.* ☉ *Tues.–Sun. 10–6, Thurs. until 8.*

A couple of blocks northwest via the rue du Fossé is **place Guillaume,** also known as the Knuedler. In the morning on market days (Wednesday and Saturday) the square is noisy and colorful. The lively place d'Armes, with its cafés and restaurants, lies just beyond place Guillaume. Open-air concerts are held here every evening in summer. The City Tourist Office is on the square, and on rue du Curé a small museum displays ❼ the **Maquette,** a fascinating model of the fortress at various stages of its construction. ⊠ *Rue du Curé,* ☎ *4796–2496.* ⌚ *Flux 40.* ☉ *July–Aug. only, daily 10–12:30 and 2–6.*

❽ From place Guillaume, rue de la Reine leads to the glorious **Grand Ducal Palace,** containing the offices of Grand Duke Jean. It dates from the 16th century, and a distinct Spanish-Moorish influence is obvious in its elaborate facade. Official receptions are held in the ceremonial hall on the second floor. The extensive art collection was dispersed during World War II, but was recovered afterward. ⊠ *Rue du Marché-aux-Herbes.* ⌚ *Flux 200; tickets sold only at the City Tourist Office (early booking recommended).* ☉ *Guided tours only; mid-July–early Sept., in English at 4 PM daily except Wed. and Sun.*

Behind the palace is the oldest part of town, the Marché-aux-Poissons, site of the old fish market and originally the intersection of two Roman roads. On the left is the **Musée National** (National Museum), set in an ❾ attractive row of 16th-century houses. The art gallery has a fine Cranach and two Turner watercolors of the Luxembourg fortress. The major discovery awaiting visitors in the modern art collection is the work of the Expressionist Joseph Kutter, probably Luxembourg's greatest artist. The museum also hosts the spectacular Bentinck-Thyssen collection of 15th- to 19th-century art, with works by Brueghel, Rembrandt, and other masters. ⊠ *Marché-aux-Poissons,* ☎ *479330.* ⌚ *Free.* ☉ *Tues.–Fri. 10–4:45, Sat. 2–5:45, Sun. 10–11:45 and 2–5:45.*

NEED A
BREAK?

In the rue Wiltheim, which runs alongside the National Museum, is the **Welle Man** (⊠ 12 rue Wiltheim, ☎ 471783), the quintessentially Luxembourgish museum bar. Sit on the tiny terrace and enjoy the view.

10 At the bottom of rue Wiltheim is the gate of **St-Michel** and its Trois Tours (Three Towers), the oldest of which was built around 1050. During the French Revolution, a guillotine was set up in these towers. From here you can clearly appreciate Luxembourg's strength as a fortress.

11 To your right is the **Bock** promontory, the site of the earliest castle (from AD 963) and always the grand duchy's most heavily fortified point. From the Bock, steep cliffs plunge to the Alzette Valley. At the entrance to the casemates, the **Archaeological Crypt** offers an excellent audiovisual presentation covering Luxembourg's history from the 10th to the 15th century. ☒ *Crypt: Flux 70; casemates: Flux 50.* ☉ *Both: Mar.–Oct., daily 10–5.*

The scenic ramparts of the Bock's **corniche** provide a view over the lower town, known as the Grund. Many of the houses on the right were refuges, used in times of danger by nobles and churchmen from the surrounding area. The massive towers on the far side of the valley were part of the fortifications Wenceslas erected in 1390 to extend the protected area, and the blocklike *casernes* (barracks) were built in the 17th century by the French.

At the place du Saint-Esprit, take the elevator down to the Grund, formerly a workers' district but today a chic residential area with many pubs and popular restaurants. To the left across the small bridge is the new **Musée des Sciences Naturelles** (Museum of Natural History), housed in a former women's prison. ☒ *Rue Munster. Opening late 1996; no further details at press time.*

Opposite, on a leafy square, stands the Baroque **Eglise de St-Jean Baptise.** This was a Benedictine church until the order was expelled from the city during the French Revolution. Among its treasures are a Way of the Cross made of Limoges enamel and a Black Madonna once thought to provide protection against the plague. The riverside passageway outside the church has a view of the cliffs and the towering fortifications on the other side of the Alzette. ☒ *Rue Munster.*

12 A right turn from the elevator exit leads into the green Pétrusse Valley park. On the left, the little **Chapelle de St-Quirin** (St. Quirin's Chapel) is hollowed out of the rock near the Passerelle. The original cave is said to have been carved by the Celts; a chapel has stood on the site since at least the 4th century.

At Pont Adolphe, walk back up to city level. The boulevard Royal, once the main moat of the fortress, is now Luxembourg's Wall Street, packed with the famous names of the international banking scene; there are 230 foreign banks doing business in the duchy. Take the **Grand'rue** to the right. It widens to become an upscale pedestrian shopping street, with boutiques bearing the same names as those on Fifth Avenue or Bond Street, sidewalk cafés, and tempting pastry shops.

Off the Beaten Path

The **Plateau Kirchberg,** reached by the Grand Duchess Bridge, is a center for EU institutions, including the European Court of Justice. The most prominent structure—at 23 stories, Luxembourg's only skyscraper—is home to the secretariat of the European Parliament. Among the new sculptures in the area are a work by Henry Moore near the Court of Justice, a replica of Carl Fredrik Reutersward's *Nonviolence* by the Jean Monnet Building, and a sculpture by Frank Stella in front of Frank Meier's Hypo Bank on rue Alphonse Weicker. Note also German architect Gottfried Boehm's Deutsche Bank Building on boule-

vard Konrad Adenauer. There are usually art exhibitions in its atrium.
For loop tour, take Bus 18 (Domaine du Kiem) from the boulevard Royal.

Shopping

Luxembourg City's principal shopping area comprises the **Grand'rue**
and its side streets. Jewelry and designer fashions are particularly well
represented. Luxembourg chocolates, called *knippercher,* are popular
purchases available at the best pastry shops. Luxembourg's most famous product is **Villeroy and Boch porcelain.** Feast your eyes on their
tableware, crystal, and cutlery at the glitzy main shop at rue du Fossé
2, then buy—at a 20% discount—at the excellent second-quality factory outlet to the northwest of the city center (⊠ rue Rollingergrund
330, ☎ 4682–1216).

Excursions from Luxembourg City

Diekirch

The Luxembourg countryside is both peaceful and scenic. To see the
Ardennes, take Route N7 north to **Diekirch,** which has a church dating from the 7th century; there are Frankish tombs in its crypt. The
Musée National d'Histoire Militaire (National Military History Museum)
mainly commemorates the Battle of the Bulge, with very realistic dioramas, military equipment, and uniforms. Other exhibits illustrate
Luxembourg's military history since the Congress of Vienna, which
brought an end to the Napoleonic wars. ⊠ *Bamertal 10,* ☎ *808908.*
🖭 *Flux 120.* ☾ *Easter–Oct., Wed.–Mon. 10–noon and 2–6.*

South of town there are traces of ancient civilizations. As you climb
the switchbacks, you will find a sign leading to the **Diewelsalter** (Devil's
Altar), an impressive dolmen attributed to the Celts. No one knows
who erected this ancient arch or why they did it.

Petite Suisse and Echternach

In order to emphasize the region's attractions, Luxembourgers long ago
★ took to calling the **Müllerthal** their **"Petite Suisse,"** and the name has
stuck. It's a hilly area of leafy woods, rushing brooks, and old farms,
ideal for hikes and picnics. Visitors following routes E27 and 121
climb to vantage points for panoramas of the River Sûre at Perekop
and Bildscheslay, peer down the crevices at Werschrumsluff and Zick-
zackschluff, and squeeze between the cliffs of the Gorge du Loup
(Wolf's Gorge) before arriving, via 364, at the small town of **Echternach,** much in favor with German tourists from across the river. Here
St. Willibrord, a 7th-century English missionary, founded a Benedictine abbey. The magnificent quadrant of the present abbey buildings
dates from the 18th century. On the Tuesday after Pentecost some 15,000
pilgrims participate in a dancing procession ending at the basilica near
the abbey. The basement **Musée de l'Abbaye** (Abbey Museum) displays
painstaking reproductions of the illuminated manuscripts that were once
the abbey's pride. ⊠ *Place du Marché.* 🖭 *Flux 40.* ☾ *April.–Oct., daily
10–noon and 2–6; Nov.–Mar., weekends 2–5.*

Northeast to Vianden and Clervaux

To take in some of Luxembourg's best castles, allow a full day. First
follow E27 and N30 north to **Larochette,** still inhabited, but whose owners permit visitors to explore the older ruins out back. Routes 118 and
128 take you to **Beaufort,** a dramatic mix of ruins and restored cham-
★ bers. Then follow the German border north (364 and N10) to visit **Vianden,** perhaps the most spectacular of all. Until recently, Vianden was
owned by the grand ducal family. Continue north (322, E240, and N18)
to **Clervaux,** dominated on one side by the vast Benedictine abbey and

on the other by its castle, which has become the permanent home for Luxembourg-born Edward Steichen's "Family of Man," arguably the greatest photographic exhibit ever put together. ⊠ *Grand Rue,* ☎ *522–4241.* ⊡ *Flux 150.* ☉ *Mar.–Dec., Tues.–Sun. 10–6.*

On the way back south via E240, detour at Lipperscheid via 308 to ★ **Bourscheid,** whose castle looms 500 feet above the Sûre, commanding three valleys. There are magnificent views from the ramparts.

Dining

Luxembourg has more star-studded restaurants per capita than any other European country. Many restaurants offer a more reasonably priced menu at lunch. Crisp, fruity white wines range from the humble El-bling and Rivaner to fine Pinot Gris and Riesling. For details and price-category information, *see* Dining *in* Staying in Luxembourg, *above.*

$$$$ ✕ **Clairefontaine.** This lavish but dignified dining spot on the city's most
★ attractive square attracts government ministers and visiting dignitaries as well as real gourmets. Chef/owner Tony Tintinger's inspirations include a showcase of foie gras specialties, innovative fish dishes (soufflé of langoustines perfumed with aniseed), and game novelties (tournedos of doe with wild mushrooms). ⊠ *Pl. de Clairefontaine 9,* ☎ *462211. Reservations essential. Jacket and tie. AE, DC, MC, V. Closed Sun., 3 wks in Aug., and 1st wk in Nov. No lunch Sat.*

$$$ ✕ **Am Pays.** Seriously good fish, such as grilled sea bass infused with
★ basil and saffron-flavored monkfish, is served in this bandbox bistro, which has booths downstairs and a more formal dining room up a winding staircase. In August, Am Pays is virtually the only ambitious restaurant in town to stay open. ⊠ *Rue du Curé 20,* ☎ *222618. AE, DC, MC, V. Closed Sun. and Feb. No lunch Sat.*

$$$ ✕ **Bouzonviller.** The modern, airy dining room, with a magnificent view over the Alzette valley, is a pleasure in itself. Over the years Christian Bouzonviller has built up a following with dishes like sea scallops in a wild mushroom bouillon, loin of veal with olive *rissole* (a small filled pastry), and original desserts such as a coffee-and-whisky tart. ⊠ *Rue Albert-unden 138,* ☎ *472259. Reservations essential. Jacket and tie. MC, V. Closed Sat., Sun. and 3 wks in Aug.*

$$$ ✕ **La Lorraine.** Outstanding seafood is the specialty of this restaurant strategically placed on the place d'Armes. A retail shop around the corner shows off the freshness of their wares. Baked skate (in hazelnut butter with capers) and puff pastry with sole and morels are good bets. ⊠ *Pl. d'Armes 7,* ☎ *474620. Jacket required. AE, DC, MC, V. Closed Sun. and second half of Aug. No lunch Sat.*

$$ ✕ **Ancre d'Or.** This tidy, friendly brasserie, just off place Guillaume, has a wide variety of old-time Luxembourgish specialties. Try their *judd mat gardebounen* (smoked pork with broad beans) or *treipen* (blood pudding). The apple tart (Luxembourgish style, with custard base) is house-made. Portions are generous, service is friendly, and the clientele is local. ⊠ *Rue du Fossé 23,* ☎ *472973. MC, V. Closed Sun.*

$$ ✕ **Mousel's Cantine.** Right next to the great Mousel brewery, this fresh, comfortable café serves up heaping platters of local specialties— braised and grilled ham, sausage, broad beans, and fried potatoes— to be washed down with crockery steins of creamy *Gezwickelte Béier* (unfiltered beer). The front café is brighter, but the tiny, fluorescent-lighted dining room has windows opening into the brewery. ⊠ *Mon-tée de Clausen 46,* ☎ *470198. MC, V. Closed Sun.*

$$ ✕ **Times.** On a pedestrian street of art galleries and boutiques you'll
★   also find excellent-value food. The narrow dining room is lined with
glass and Canadian cherrywood and often filled with artists and jour-
nalists. The cuisine features ambitious creations like fillet of suckling
pig cooked with tea, and three variations on the carpaccio theme (beef,
tuna and salmon). ⊠ *Rue Louvigny 8,* ☎ *222722. AE, DC, MC, V.*

$ ✕ **Ems.** This lively establishment with vinyl booths draws a loyal,
local crowd for its vast portions of mussels in a rich wine-and-garlic
broth, accompanied by french fries and a bottle of sharp, cold, and in-
expensive Auxerrois or Rivaner. Ems is open until 1 AM. ⊠ *Pl. de la
Gare 30,* ☎ *487799. Reservations not accepted. AE, DC, MC, V. No
lunch Sat.*

$ ✕ **Taverne Bit.** In this cozy local pub, you can drink a *clensch* (stein)
of draft Bitburger beer (from just across the German border) and have
a plate of sausage with good potato salad, a plate of cold ham, or
kachkeis, the pungent local cheese spread, served with baked potatoes.
It's just off the Parking Glacis. ⊠ *Allée Scheffer 43,* ☎ *460751. No
credit cards. Closed Sun. No lunch Sat.*

$ ✕ **Oberweis.** Luxembourg's most famous patisserie also serves light
lunches. You select your meal at the counter (quiche lorraine, spinach
pie, and the like), and it is served at your table. Beer and wine are avail-
able. ⊠ *Grand'rue 19–20,* ☎ *470703. Reservations not accepted. AE,
DC, MC, V. Closed Sun.*

Lodging

Hotels in the city center are preferable to those clustered around the
train station. There are also large, modern hotels near the airport and
on the Plateau Kirchberg. For details and price-category definitions,
see Lodging *in* Staying in Luxembourg, *above.*

$$$$ 🏨 **Le Royal.** On Luxembourg's Wall Street and within steps of parks,
★   shopping, and the Old Town, Le Royal is the best choice for luxury.
It's solid, modern, and sleek, with a great deal of lacquer, marble, and
glass, and pleasant lobbies on each floor. Opt for a quiet back room
facing the park. The main restaurant, Le Relais Royal, is *the* place for
power dining. ⊠ *Blvd. Royal 12, L-2449,* ☎ *416161,* FAX *225948. 180
rooms with bath. Restaurant, brasserie/breakfast room, piano bar,
pool, beauty salon, sauna, tennis court. AE, DC, MC, V.*

$$$ 🏨 **Parc Belair.** This privately owned, family-run hotel a few blocks from
the city center stands on the edge of the Parc de Merl, which also has
an attractive playground. Rooms are a warm beige; those on the park
are the quietest. The complex includes a separate restaurant with outdoor café. A substantial buffet breakfast is included. ⊠ *Av. du X
Septembre 109, L-2551,* ☎ *442323,* FAX *444484. 45 rooms with bath.
Restaurant, breakfast room, meeting rooms. AE, DC, MC, V.*

$$$ 🏨 **Cravat.** This charming Luxembourg relic—moderately grand, mod-
estly glamorous—straddles the valley and the Old Town in the best lo-
cation in the city. Though corridors have a dated air, rooms are fresh
and welcoming in a variety of tastefully retro styles. The art deco cof-
fee shop has been freshened up but despite its younger look still draws
fur-hatted ladies of a certain age. The prime minister and his cabinet
can be found in the hotel tavern most Friday afternoons. ⊠ *Blvd. F.
D. Roosevelt 29, L-2011,* ☎ *221975,* FAX *226711. 60 rooms with
bath. Restaurant, bar, breakfast room/taproom. AE, DC, MC, V.*

$$ 🏨 **Auberge le Châtelet.** At the edge of a quiet residential area but within
easy reach of the train station and Old Town, this pleasant hotel has
stone and terra-cotta floors, double windows, Oriental rugs, and tropical plants. Rooms are freshly furnished in knotty pine and have new
tile baths. There's a French restaurant and a comfortable oak-and-stone

bar. The nine rooms in the annex down the street cost slightly less. ✉ *Blvd. de la Pétrusse 2, L-2320,* ☎ *402101,* FAX *403666. 32 rooms with bath. Restaurant, bar. AE, DC, MC, V.*

$$ ☉ **Romantik Hotel/Grunewald.** The Grunewald is just outside the city
★ and at the high end of this category. The old-fashioned lounge is crammed with wing chairs, knickknacks, and old prints; rooms have Oriental rugs, rich fabrics, and Louis XV–style furniture. Garden-side rooms are worth booking ahead, although street-side windows are triple-glazed. There's a garden terrace, and the pricey restaurant serves rich, classic French cuisine. ✉ *Rte. d'Echternach 10–14, L-1453 Dommeldange,* ☎ *431882,* FAX *420646. 26 rooms with bath. Restaurant (closed Sun., no lunch Sat.). AE, DC, MC, V.*

$$ ✗ **Italia.** This is a find: a former private apartment house converted into hotel rooms, some with plaster details and cabinetry left behind. Rooms are solid and freshly furnished, all with tile bathrooms; Italia also has a garden. The restaurant downstairs is one of the city's better Italian eateries. ✉ *Rue d'Anvers 15-17, L-1130,* ☎ *486626,* FAX *480807. 20 rooms with bath. Restaurant, bar. AE, DC, MC, V.*

$$ ☉ **La Cascade.** A turn-of-the-century villa has been converted into a hotel of considerable charm and elegance. There's a good Italian restaurant and a lovely terrace, overlooking the Alzette River. A bus stops outside to take you to the city center, just over a mile away. ✉ *Rue de Pulvermuhl 2, L-2356,* ☎ *428736,* FAX *4287–8888. 9 rooms with bath. Restaurant, garden. AE, DC, MC, V.*

$$ ☉ **Sieweburen.** At the northwestern end of the city is this attractively rustic hotel, opened in 1991; the clean, large rooms have natural-wood beds and armoires. There's a playground in front and woods in the back. The brasserie-style tavern, older than the rest of the property, is hugely popular, especially when its terrace is open. ✉ *Rue des Septfontaines 36, L-2534,* ☎ *442356,* FAX *442353. 13 rooms with bath. Restaurant, playground. AE, DC, MC, V.*

$ ☉ **Carlton.** In this vast 1918 hotel near the train station, budget travelers will find roomy, quiet quarters. The beveled glass, oak parquet, and terrazzo floors are original—but so are the toilets, all down the hall. Each room has antique beds, floral-print comforters, and a sink; wooden floors, despite creaks, are white-glove clean. ✉ *Rue de Strasbourg 9, L-2561,* ☎ *484802,* FAX *486480. 50 rooms without toilet, 8 with shower. Bar, breakfast room. No credit cards.*

$ ☉ **Cottage.** Modern budget hotels are few and far between; the one closest to the city (a 15-minute train ride away) is the motel-style but pleasant Cottage. ✉ *Rue Auguste Liesch, L-3474 Dudelange,* ☎ *520591,* FAX *520576. 45 rooms with bath. Restaurant/bar.*

19 Malta

Valletta

Around the Islands

THE MEDITERRANEAN ISLAND OF MALTA and its two sister islands, Gozo and Comino, enjoy a mild, sunny climate and have attractive bays and beaches—a fitting setting for the festive and hospitable people who live here. For those interested in history and archaeology, tiny Malta—with only 28 kilometers (17 miles) between its two farthest points—displays the remains of a long and eventful past. Among the most fascinating ruins are Neolithic temples and stone megaliths left by prehistoric inhabitants. In AD 60, St. Paul, shipwrecked here, converted the people to Christianity. Other less welcome visitors, attracted by Malta's strategic position, conquered and ruled. These included the Phoenicians, Carthaginians, Romans, Arabs, Normans, and Aragonese.

The Knights of the Order of St. John of Jerusalem arrived here in 1530, after having been driven from their stronghold on the island of Rhodes by the Ottoman emperor Suleyman the Magnificent. In 1565, with only a handful of men, the knights held Malta against the Ottoman Turks in a dramatic and bloody siege. They left massive fortifications and rich architecture—including Valletta, Malta's capital—and ruled the islands until Napoléon arrived in 1798.

The British drove the French out in 1800 and gave the island a distinctive British feel, which it retains today. In 1942, during World War II, King George VI awarded the Maltese people the George Cross for their courage in withstanding repeated German and Italian attacks, especially from the air. Malta gained independence from Britain in 1964 and was declared a republic within the Commonwealth in 1974. On December 2–3, 1989, the island hosted the first Bush–Gorbachev summit, marking the beginning of improved relations between the two superpowers. Today an increasing number of visitors, many on cruises, are discovering these islands; in response, museums are being renovated, hotel construction continues apace, and water-sports facilities are being upgraded in this diving and yachting center.

ESSENTIAL INFORMATION

Before You Go

When to Go

The archipelago is a year-round delight, but May through October is the main tourist season. April and May are the months for spring freshness. Summer is the time for *festas*, joyous village religious festivals. August is just too hot for touring. In winter, you'll find the climate mild, but you may encounter sudden rainstorms.

CLIMATE

The following are the average daily maximum and minimum temperatures for Valletta.

Jan.	58F	14C	May	71F	22C	Sept.	81F	27C
	50	10		61	16		71	22
Feb.	59F	15C	June	79F	26C	Oct.	75F	24C
	51	10		67	19		66	19
Mar.	61F	16C	July	84F	29C	Nov.	67F	20C
	52	11		72	22		60	16
Apr.	65F	18C	Aug.	85F	29C	Dec.	61F	16C
	56	13		73	23		54	12

Malta

Mediterranean Sea

Currency

The unit of currency is the Maltese lira (Lm), also sometimes referred to as the pound; it's divided into 100 cents. There are Lm 2, 5, 10, and 20 bills. The 1¢ coin is bronze, and other coins—2¢, 5¢, 10¢, 25¢, 50¢, and Lm 1—are silver. At press time (spring 1996), the exchange rate was Lm .34 to the U.S. dollar, Lm .25 to the Canadian dollar, and Lm .55 to the pound sterling.

What It Will Cost

Malta is one of the cheapest holiday destinations in Europe, though with the rapid development of tourism, prices are inevitably rising. Prices tend to be uniform, except in Sliema and Valletta, the capital, where they are slightly higher. There is a value-added tax (VAT) of 15% on most services and goods; restaurant meals have a 10% VAT.

SAMPLE PRICES
Cup of coffee, 25¢ (Maltese); bottle of beer, 25¢; Coca-Cola, 20¢.

Customs on Arrival

You may bring into Malta, duty-free, 200 cigarettes, one bottle of liquor, one bottle of wine, and one bottle of perfume. Up to Lm 50 in currency may be brought in.

Language

The spelling of many Maltese words can be bewildering. Fortunately, both Maltese and English are the official languages on the island, so you shouldn't experience any problems. Italian is widely spoken, too.

Getting Around

By Car

The roads around Valletta are busy most mornings, but a new road network has made it easier to reach Sliema and St. Julian's from the airport. Road conditions are fairly good, but driving around the island can be a trial. Driving is on the left-hand side of the road. Speed limits are 40 kph (25 mph) in towns, 65 kph (40 mph) elsewhere. International and British driving licenses are acceptable. Be careful at roundabouts, or traffic circles.

By Bus

Most routes across the island pass through Valletta, which facilitates travel out of the capital but makes cross-country trips a bit longer. Public transportation is inexpensive. Though some of the old yellow buses show their age, they are usually on time. Plans are in the works to upgrade the fleet and the shabby terminal at Valletta.

By Boat

Daily car and passenger ferries operate year-round from Cirkewwa to Mgårr on Gozo. Telephone 243964 in Malta; 571884 in Cirkewwa; and 556114 or 556743 in Gozo for details. The crossing from Marfa to Mgårr in Gozo takes 25 minutes, with shuttle service in summer and departures every hour in winter. The round-trip fare is Lm 1.50. There is also one service weekdays from Pietà (near Valletta) to Gozo, leaving in the morning and taking an hour and 15 minutes each way. The round-trip fare from Mgårr (passenger plus car) is Lm 4.50. A daily ferry service links the tourist resort town of Sliema to Valletta.

By Helicopter

Malta Air Charter (☎ 557905 or 662211) flies to and from Gozo several times daily and offers helicopter sightseeing tours. Flight time to Gozo from Luqa Airport is 10 minutes and costs Lm 25 round-trip (open return date) and Lm 20 (same-day return). Twenty- and 40-minute tours cost Lm 22 and Lm 30, respectively.

By Taxi

There are plenty of metered taxis, and fares are reasonable compared with those in other European countries. Be sure the meter is switched on when your trip starts, or bargain first. Tip the driver 10%.

Staying in Malta

Telephones

LOCAL CALLS

There are no regional area codes in Malta. For a time check, dial 195; for flight inquiries, dial 662211.

INTERNATIONAL CALLS

There is direct dialing to most parts of the world from Malta. The overseas operator is 194; the international dialing access code is 00. You may place calls from the Overseas Telephone Division of Telemalta at St. Julian's, Qawra, St. Paul's Bay, Sliema, Valletta, and Luqa International Airport. For an **AT&T** long-distance operator, dial 0800–890110; public phones are operated by phone cards, which may be purchased at many shops.

COUNTRY CODE

The country code for Malta is 356.

Mail

Airmail letters to the United States and Canada cost 20¢; postcards cost 20¢. Airmail letters to the United Kingdom cost 14¢; postcards 14¢.

Opening and Closing Times

Banks are open weekdays 8:30–12:45, Tuesday and Friday 2:30–4, Saturday 8:30–noon (11:30 in summer). Banks in tourist areas are also open in the afternoon. The currency-exchange booth at the airport is open 24 hours, and there are ATMs in tourist areas.

Museums run by the Museums Department are generally open mid-June through September, Monday, Wednesday, and Friday 8:30–5, Tuesday, Thursday, and Saturday 8:15–1:30; October through mid-June, Monday–Saturday 8:15–5 and Sunday 8:15–4:15; closed on holidays. Valletta's museums are closed on Sunday in August and September but are open in the afternoon on Monday, Wednesday, and Friday. Other museums' hours may vary slightly, so check locally. At many museums, there is no entrance fee for people under 19 or over 65.

Shops are open Monday–Saturday 9–1 and 4–7.

National Holidays

January 1; February 10 (St. Paul's Shipwreck); March 19 (St. Joseph's Day); March 31 (Freedom Day); March 28 (Good Friday); May 1 (Workers' Day); June 7 (Sette Giugno); June 29 (Sts. Peter and Paul); August 15 (Assumption, or Santa Marija); September 8 (Our Lady of Victories); September 21 (Independence Day); December 8 (Immaculate Conception); December 13 (Republic Day); December 25.

Dining

There is a good choice of restaurants, ranging from expensive hotel restaurants to fast-food hamburger joints. Local specialties include *torta tal-lampuki* (dorado fish pie), *dentici* (sea bream), and tuna. *Minestra* is the local variant of minestrone soup, and the *timpana* (baked macaroni and meat) is filling. Rabbit, stewed or fried, is a national dish. Accompany your meal with the locally produced red, white, or rosé wine—*marsovin* or *lachryma vitis*—and sample the house wines, too. Maltese beers are excellent; highly popular are Cisk Lager and Hop Leaf. Löwenbräu recently began brewing in Malta, as well. Another choice is Kinnie, a refreshing local nonalcoholic citrus and herb drink.

PRECAUTIONS

The water in Malta is safe to drink, the only drawback being its salty taste: Many prefer bottled mineral water.

WHAT TO WEAR

A jacket and tie are suggested for higher-priced restaurants and the casino. Otherwise, casual dress is acceptable.

RATINGS

Prices are per person for a three-course meal, not including wine, VAT, and tip.

CATEGORY	COST*
$$$	over Lm 9
$$	Lm 6–Lm 9
$	under Lm 6

10% VAT is charged on meals; 15% VAT on beverages

Lodging

Choices range from luxurious modern hotels to modest guest houses. Some self-contained complexes are geared to package tours.

RATINGS

Prices are for two people sharing a double room and exclude the 15% VAT.

CATEGORY	COST
$$$$	over Lm 35
$$$	Lm 22–Lm 35
$$	Lm 12–Lm 22
$	under Lm 12

Tipping

A tip of 10% is expected when a service charge is not included.

VALLETTA

Arriving and Departing

By Plane

There is a weekly direct flight from New York every Monday. This is run by **Balkan Airlines** in conjunction with Air Malta. Several airlines, including **Air Malta,** fly from London, Paris, Frankfurt, Athens, and Rome to Luqa Airport, 6 kilometers (4 miles) south of Valletta.

BETWEEN THE AIRPORT AND DOWNTOWN

There is local bus service (Bus 8) that passes through the town of Luqa on its way to Valletta, with a stop in front of the airport. It operates every 10 or 15 minutes from 6 AM to 11 PM; the trip takes about 30 minutes, and the fare is about 10¢. Taxis are also available and prices are posted on a board at the taxi stand.

By Boat

The **Gozo Channel Co.** (☎ 243964) operates weekly car and passenger ferries from Catania, Sicily, during the summer. **Euro Malta Express** (⌧ Flagstone Wharf, Marsa, ☎ 25994213) operates ferries year-round via Otranto, Catania, and Syracusa in Italy. **Island Seaway** (⌧ Republic St., Valletta, ☎ 232211) also runs year-round, with service from Reggio Calabria and Catania.

Every Sunday, **Grimaldi Lines** (☎ 231689) has service between Genoa, Tunis and Malta. **Virtu** (☎ 318854) runs express passenger ferry service from Catania (Tuesday, Thursday, Saturday, Sunday); Pozzallo (Monday, Thursday, Sunday); and Licata (Wednesday, Sunday).

Important Addresses and Numbers

Embassies and High Commissions

U.S. Development House (⌧ St. Anne St., Floriana, ☎ 235960).
Canadian Embassy (in Rome; ⌧ Via G. B. de Rossi 27, ☎ 06/445981).
British High Commission (⌧ 7 St. Anne St., Floriana, ☎ 233134).

Emergencies

Police (☎ 191). **Ambulance** (☎ 196). **Fire Brigade** (☎ 199). **Hospital:** St. Luke's (Gwardamangia, ☎ 241251) or Craig Hospital (on Gozo, ☎ 561600).

Travel Agencies

American Express (representative) (⌧ Brockdorff, 14 Zachary St., Valletta, ☎ 232141). **Thomas Cook** (⌧ Il-Pjazzetta, Tower Rd., Sliema, ☎ 344225).

Visitor Information

Gozo (⌧ Mġarr Harbor, ☎ 553343; Victoria, ☎ 558106).
St. Julian's (⌧ Balluta Bay, ☎ 342671 or 342672).
Sliema (⌧ Bisazza St., ☎ 313409).
Valletta (⌧ 1 City Gate Arcade, ☎ 237747; ⌧ Luqa Airport, ☎ 249600; or ⌧ 280 Republic St., ☎ 224444 or 228282).

Guided Tours

Orientation

Sightseeing tours are arranged by local travel agents and the large hotels. There are half-day, full-day, and "Malta by Night" coach tours;
rates vary. Contact the tourist offices (☞ Important Addresses and Numbers, *above*) for details. Beware of cheap tours: These usually turn out
to be rip-offs, the guide being the driver himself, who is far from qualified. Officially licensed guides should wear an identification tag.

One-hour boat tours of the harbor of Valletta leave regularly from Sliema
jetty. Prices vary; buy tickets at most travel agencies.

Personal Guides

Licensed guides can be hired through local travel agencies represented
at most hotels.

Exploring Valletta

The minicity of **Valletta,** with ornate palaces and museums, protected
by massive fortifications of honey-color stone, was built by the knights
of the Order of St. John, who occupied the island from 1530 to 1798.
The main entrance is through the **City Gate** (where all bus routes end),
which leads onto Republic Street, the spine of the city and the main
shopping street. From Republic Street, other roads are laid out on a
grid pattern; some are stepped. Houses along the narrow streets have
overhanging wooden balconies, which visiting artists love to paint.

Valletta's small size makes it ideal to explore on foot. Before setting
out along Republic Street, stop at the tourist information office for maps,
brochures, and a copy of *What's On*. Two blocks farther, on your left,
is the Auberge de Provence (the hostel of the knights from Provence),
★ which now houses the **National Museum of Archaeology.** Its collection
includes finds from Malta's many prehistoric sites—Tarxien, Hagar Qim,
and the Hypogeum at Paola. You'll see pottery, statuettes, temple carvings, and, on the upper floor, finds from Punic and Roman tombs. ⊠
Republic St., ☎ *225577.* ☒ *Lm 1.* ☉ *Oct.–mid-June, Mon.–Sat. 8:15–
4:15, Sun. 8:15–4:15; mid-June–Sept., Mon. and Wed. 8:30–5, Tues.,
Thurs., Sat. 8:15–1:30, Fri., 8:15–8; closed holidays.*

From Republic Street, turn right at the Inter-Flora kiosk and head to
★ St. John's Square. Dominating the square is **St. John's Co-Cathedral.**
This was the Order of St. John's own church, completed in 1578. It is
by far Malta's most important treasure. A side chapel was given to each
national group of knights, who decorated it in their own distinctive
way. The cathedral *museum* includes the oratory in which hangs *The
Beheading of St. John,* the masterpiece painted by Caravaggio when
he stayed on Malta in 1608. In the museum, you'll find a rich collection of Flemish tapestries based on drawings by Poussin and Rubens,
antique embroidered vestments, and illuminated manuscripts. ☒ *Museum: Lm 1.* ☉ *Weekdays 9:30–12:30 and 1:30–4:55, Sat. 9:30–1.*

While in St. John's Square, visit the **Government Craft Center** for traditional handmade goods. ☉ *Weekdays 8:30–12:30 and 2–5.*

★ Continue along Republic Street to the **Grand Master's Palace,** where
Malta's parliament sits. You can walk through the shady courtyards.
Inside, friezes in the sumptuously decorated state apartments depict
scenes from the history of the knights. There is also a gallery with Gobelin tapestries. At the back of the building is the **Armoury of the Knights,**
with displays of arms and armor down through the ages. ☒ *State apartments and Armoury: Lm 1 each.* ☉ *Oct.–mid-June, Mon.–Sat. 8:15–*

4:15; mid-June–Sept., Mon., Wed. 8:30–5, Tues., Thurs., Sat. 8:15–1:30, Fri. 8:15–8; closed holidays.

Also on Republic Street, spend some time at **Casa Rocca Piccola,** a traditional 16th-century Maltese house. Continue to **Ft. St. Elmo,** built by the knights to defend the harbor. Though completely destroyed during the siege of 1565, it was rebuilt by succeeding military leaders. Today part of the fort houses the **War Museum,** with its collection of military objects largely related to World War II. Here you can see an Italian E-boat and *Faith,* one of three Gloster Gladiator biplanes that defended the island. The other two, *Hope* and *Charity,* were shot down in the air battles of 1940–1941. ⊠ *Ft. St. Elmo.* 🖾 *Free.* ☾ *Sat. 1–5, Sun. 9–5. War Museum.* 🖾 *Lm 1.* ☾ *Oct.–mid-June, Mon.–Sat. 8:15–4:15; mid-June–Sept., Mon., Wed. 8:30–5, Tues., Thurs., Sat. 8:15–1:30, Fri. 8:15–8; closed holidays.*

Continue along the seawall to the **Hospital of the Order** at the end of Merchants Street. This gracious building has been converted into the Mediterranean Conference Center. For an excellent introduction to the island, see the "Malta Experience," a multimedia presentation (🖾 Lm 2.50) on the history of Malta that is given here daily. 🖾 *Center: Lm 1.* ☾ *Weekdays 9–4.*

Walk along the seawall past the siege bell memorial and climb up to the **Upper Barrakka Gardens.** Once part of the city's defenses, they're now a pleasant area from which to watch the comings and goings in
★ the Grand Harbour. The **War Rooms** below, from which World War II operations were planned, are open to the public. 🖾 *Lm 1.45.* ☾ *Weekdays 9:30–4:30, weekends 9:30–1.*

Next, stroll down to this end of Merchants Street, which is dominated by an open-air market. Here, with some haggling, you may snap up a good bargain. Then cut along South Street, across Republic Street, to the **National Museum of Fine Art.** The 18th-century palace has paintings that date from the 15th century to the present, including works by Tintoretto, Preti, and de Favray, as well as local artists. ⊠ *South St.,* ☎ *225769.* 🖾 *Lm 1.* ☾ *Oct.–mid-June, Mon.–Sat. 8:15–4:15; mid-June–Sept., Mon., Wed. 8:30–5, Tues., Thurs., Sat. 8:15–1:30, Fri., 8:15–8; closed holidays.*

Valletta's neighboring towns of **Sliema** and **St. Julian's** have seaside resort facilities and nightlife. The casino at St. Julian's is in an elegant early-20th-century palazzo. **Ta' Xbiex** is equipped for yachts.

Dining

For details and price-category definitions, *see* Dining *in* Staying in Malta, *above.*

$$$ ✕ **San Giuliano.** St. Julian's and Sliema are Malta's smartest seaside
★ resorts and main entertainment districts. The San Giuliano has terrace dining in a harborside setting. On the menu are Maltese-Italian dishes, as well as pasta, steak, lobster, prawns, and squid. ⊠ *Spinola Bay, St. Julian's,* ☎ *332000. Reservations essential. AE, DC, MC, V.*

$$ ✕ **Barracuda.** This old house perched precariously on columns—thus
★ commanding a superb view of St. Julian's Bay—is one of Malta's most delightful and efficiently run restaurants. Seafood, not surprisingly, is the drawing card here, with dentici and baked barracuda as options. ⊠ *194/5 Main St., St. Julian's,* ☎ FAX *337370. AE, DC, MC, V.*

$$ ✕ **Bologna.** This restaurant in the heart of the city specializes in Italian cuisine, including lobster dishes and avocado with seafood. ⊠ *59 Republic St.,* ☎ *246149. AE, DC, MC, V.*

$$ ✕ **Giannini.** Atop Valletta's mighty bastions, this is one of the city's
★ most elegant restaurants. Leading local politicians and the fashionable
set dine here on Maltese-Italian cuisine, especially seafood, while en-
joying the marvelous view. ⊠ *23 Windmill St.,* ☎ *237121 or 236575.*
Reservations essential. AE, DC, MC, V.

$$ ✕ **Pappagall.** This friendly restaurant is popular with locals and vis-
★ itors. Specialties include fillet of beef with green peppercorns and
spinach-and-shrimp ravioli. ⊠ *Melita St.,* ☎ *236195. AE, DC, MC,*
V. Closed Sun.

$$ ✕ **Scalini.** An attractive cellar restaurant with walls of Malta's golden
limestone, it features seafood and Italian-style pastas. The prix-fixe menu
is a good value. ⊠ *32B South St.,* ☎ *246221. AE, DC, MC, V.*

$$ ✕ **Ta' Kolina.** This waterfront restaurant overlooking Malta's casino
specializes in Maltese food and fish, including *bragioli* (rolled slices of
beef stuffed with mincemeat and stewed in tomato sauce) and swordfish. ⊠ *151 Tower Rd., Sliema,* ☎ *335106. AE, DC, MC, V.*

$ ✕ **Lantern.** Two brothers run this friendly spot. The 18th-century
town-house location may not win any design awards, but the food is
delicious and served in a traditional Maltese atmosphere. ⊠ *20 Sap-
pers St.,* ☎ *237521. Closed Sun.*

$ ✕ **Pizzeria Bologna.** A street-level pizza house beside the Grand Mas-
ter's Palace serves delicious pizzas with an interesting choice of ingredients. ⊠ *59B Republic St.,* ☎ *238014.*

Lodging

For details and price-category definitions, *see* Lodging *in* Staying in
Malta, *above.*

$$$$ ▥ **Holiday Inn Crowne Plaza.** This large resort hotel is in Sliema, close
to the sea and the major shopping area. It has activities from swimming and windsurfing to dining and dancing. ⊠ *Tigne St., Sliema*
SLM 11, ☎ *341173,* ℻ *311292. 182 rooms with bath. Restaurant,*
bar, pool, sauna, tennis courts, health club. AE, DC, MC, V.

$$$ ▥ **Grand Hotel les Lapins.** A modern building on the banks of the Ta'
Xbiex seafront, this hotel has contemporary decor and overlooks a yacht
marina. It's popular with businesspeople but has resort facilities, too.
⊠ *Ta' Xbiex Seafront, MSD 11,* ☎ *342551,* ℻ *343902. 191 rooms*
with bath. Restaurant, bar, pool, tennis courts. AE, DC, MC, V.

$$ ▥ **Castille.** For a touch of old Malta, stay at the Castille in what used
to be a 16th-century palazzo. This is a gracious, comfortable, Old World
hotel with a friendly, relaxed ambience. The central location is ideal,
close to the museums and the bus terminal. There's a sun terrace and
a good rooftop restaurant with an excellent prix-fixe menu. A pianist
plays most evenings during dinner, and the views across the harbor are
stunning. ⊠ *St. Paul St., VLT 07,* ☎ *243677 or 243678,* ℻ *243677.*
38 rooms with bath. Bar/coffee shop. AE.

$$ ▥ **Osborne.** The centrally located Osborne has spacious rooms but undis-
tinguished decor. Spend a few minutes in the rooftop lounge and enjoy
the view. ⊠ *50 South St., VLT 11,* ☎ *243656,* ℻ *232120. 60 rooms*
with bath. Restaurant. AE, DC, MC, V.

AROUND THE ISLANDS

It is impractical to attempt a tour of Malta and Gozo in one day. Allow
at least two days for the main island—three to include Valletta—and
one full day for Gozo. The rest of Malta has much to offer, from unique
prehistoric sites to richly decorated churches.

The Southeast

★ Leaving Valletta, head first for the **Hypogeum** at **Paola**, 6 kilometers (3½ miles) south of the capital. This massive area of underground chambers was used for burials more than 4,000 years ago. Built on three levels, the chambers descend to 40 feet beneath the ground, and there are examples of fine carving to be seen. ▨ *Lm 1.* ☉ *Closed for restoration at press time but slated to reopen by mid-1996; check with tourist office in Valletta.*

Nearby is **Tarxien,** an ordinary suburban town with extraordinary megalithic monuments. The **Tarxien Temples** are three interconnecting temples with curious carvings, oracular chambers, and altars, all dating from about 2800 BC. There are also remains of an earlier temple from about 4000 BC. ▨ *Lm 1.* ☉ *mid-June–Sept., Mon., Wed., Fri. 8:30–5, Tues., Thurs., weekends 8:15–1:30; Oct.–mid-June, Mon.–Sat. 8:15–5, Sun. 8:15–4:15; closed holidays.*

Northeast of Paola, across the Grand Harbour from Valletta, lie evidences of the reign of the Knights of St. John: the **Cottonera Lines**—massive defensive walls—and the city of **Vittoriosa,** dominated by the looming Fort St. Angelo and site of a 17th-century church as well as the Inquisitor's Palace built by the knights.

Turning southward, you can visit the fishing and resort towns of **Marsaskala** and **Marsaxlokk** on the southeast coast and then head west to **Ghar Dalam.** A cave here was found to contain the semifossilized remains of long-extinct species of dwarf elephants and hippopotamuses that roamed the island when it was still joined to Europe, about 125,000 years ago. You can visit the cave and see the fossils on display in the small museum. ▨ *Lm 1.* ☉ *Mid-June–Sept., Mon., Wed., Fri. 8:30–5, Tues., Thurs., weekends 8:15–1:30; Oct.–mid-June, Mon.–Sat. 8:15–5, Sun. 8:15–4:15; closed holidays.*

Follow the coast first south through **Birzebbugia,** a beach town, and **Kalafrana,** where the U.S. and Russian leaders met in 1989, and then west to the **Blue Grotto,** near Wied-iz-Zurrieq. This is part of a group of water-filled caves made vivid by the phosphorescent marine life that colors the water a distinctive, magical blue. You can reach the grotto only by sea. Boatmen will take you there for Lm 2.50.

★ Nearby, within walking distance of each other, are the imposing prehistoric temples of **Hagar Qim** and **Mnajdpa.** Some of the stones weigh as much as 20 tons. ▨ *Lm 1.* ☉ *Mid-June–Sept., daily 8:30–1:30; Oct.–mid-June, daily 8:30–5; closed holidays.*

Central Malta and the Northwest

Take the northwest route to Rabat and Mdina, visiting **Buskett,** a very old and colorful garden, along the way. This trip is best in the spring when the orange and lemon trees are in blossom. In **Rabat,** visit the beautiful **St. Paul's Church,** built above a grotto where St. Paul is said to have taken refuge when he was shipwrecked on Malta in AD 60. Also of interest are the 4th-century **catacombs** of St. Paul and St. Agatha, unusual for their rock tables where mourners held celebratory meals for the dead. ▨ *Lm 1.* ☉ *Mid-June–Sept., Mon., Wed., Fri. 8:30–5, Tues., Thurs., weekends 8:15–1:30; Oct.–mid-June, Mon.–Sat. 8:15–5, Sun. 8:15–4:15; closed holidays.*

The Crafts Village in nearby **Ta' Qali** is geared mainly toward tourists. Browse through the shops, but be cautious when buying. Here, in this converted World War II aerodrome, you can see filigree silver, gold jewelry, and handblown Mdina glass being made using age-old methods.

There are also leather workshops and pottery shops selling gaily colored items. Some of the seconds in the glass workshops are good buys.

Adjoining Rabat is **Mdina,** Malta's ancient walled capital. The Maltese have a special love for what is often called the Silent City. It certainly lives up to its sobriquet: Traffic here is limited to residents' cars, and the noise of the busy world outside somehow doesn't penetrate the thick, golden walls. Visit the serene Baroque cathedral of **St. Peter and St. Paul** for a look at Preti's 17th-century wall painting, *The Shipwreck of St. Paul,* and the **Cathedral Museum** nearby to see the Dürer woodcuts and illuminated manuscripts. ☎ 454697. ☜ *Lm 1.* ☉ *Mon.–Sat. 9–1 and 1:30–4:30.*

On your way out of the city you can visit the **National Museum of Natural History** (✉ Vilhena Palace, ☎ 455951) and the **Mdina Dungeons** (✉ St. Publius Sq., ☎ 450267) for a feel of Old Malta.

Continue to **Mosta** to see the **Church of St. Mary.** The Rotunda, as it is also known, has the third-largest unsupported dome in Europe, after St. Peter's in Rome and Hagia Sophia in Istanbul. You can also see a replica of the bomb that crashed through the dome during a service in 1942 and fell to the ground without exploding.

On the northwest tip of the island, there are beach and water-sports centers near **Qawra** and **St. Paul's Bay** and along Mellieha Bay.

Gozo and Comino

Ferries leave from Cirkewwa for **Gozo,** Malta's lusher, quieter sister island. The capital, **Victoria,** is a charming old town with attractive cafés and bars around the main square. In it stands the massive hilltop citadel of **Gran Castello,** with an impressive Baroque cathedral famous for a trompe l'oeil ceiling that makes the flat roof appear to be a dome. The museum here offers displays of ceremonial silver and manuscripts. ☜ *Lm 1.* ☉ *Mon.–Sat. 10:30–4:30; closed holidays.*

The town also has a **Folklore Museum** (✉ Milite Bernardo St.) and a collection of objects from various periods in the **Archaeological Museum** (✉ Cathedral Sq.). ☜ *To each: Lm 1.* ☉ *Daily 8:30–5.*

★ On Xaghra plateau stands the extraordinary pair of megalithic **Ggantija Prehistoric Temples,** dating from 3500 BC. ☜ *Lm 1.* ☉ *Daily 8:30–5.*

In the town of **Xaghra** itself, there are two underground alabaster caves with delicately colored stalagmites and stalactites. Visit the parish church of St. Mary, famous for its alabaster interiors. In the cliffs nearby is the cave where the sea nymph Calypso, mentioned in Homer's *Odyssey,* is said to have lived; with such stunning views and the sandy beach, it's easy to imagine that the myth might be true.

At the southwestern end of the island, **Dwerja point** is a beautiful spot that is a paradise for scuba divers.

From Mgårr, you can take a ferry for a day trip to the tiny (1 square mi) island of **Comino;** there are also connections from Cirkewwa on Malta. The attractions here are quiet (no cars), water sports, and intense natural beauty. Club Nautico (☎ 529821), on a bay, has rooms and bungalows; call ahead for day use of facilities or for lunch reservations.

Dining and Lodging

For details and price-category definitions, *see* Dining *and* Lodging *in* Staying in Malta, *above.*

Gozo

$$$$ ⊞ **Ta' Çenç.** Surprisingly, the little island of Gozo harbors one of the best hotels in this part of the Mediterranean. The Ta' Çenç is a luxurious paradise, and its location on the coast about 6 kilometers (4 miles) out of Victoria ensures guests' privacy and accommodates a full range of water sports. ⊠ *Ta' Çenç, near Sannat, VCT 112,* ☎ *561522 or 561525,* FAX *558199. 82 rooms with bath. Restaurant, bar, 2 pools, tennis court, dance club. AE, DC, MC, V.*

$$ ⊞ **Calypso.** This modern hotel has so many services and facilities—from a boutique and a bank to a rooftop splash pool—that it's almost like a small town in itself. Among the dining spots is a Chinese restaurant. The rooms are comfortably furnished and have balconies, most with sea views. ⊠ *Marsalforn, XRA 105,* ☎ *562000,* FAX *562012. 92 rooms with bath. Restaurant, coffee shop, tennis courts, squash, nightclub. AE, DC, MC, V.*

$$ ⊞ **Cornucopia.** For pleasant, personal service and a restful vacation, try this lovingly restored farmhouse near the village of Xaghra—it's an ideal base for exploring the island, and the sea is just a short drive away. There's a good restaurant, with barbecues in the summer. ⊠ *10 Gnien Imrik St., Xaghra XRA 102,* ☎ *556486 or 553866,* FAX *552910. 52 rooms with bath. Restaurant, pool. AE, DC, MC, V.*

Marsaxlokk

$$ ✕ **Pisces.** Diners can enjoy a superb view across Malta's largest fishing village. Seafood specialties include *aljotta* (a soup with chunks of fish), *pagell* (red bream, baked or grilled), and risotto with mussels. ⊠ *49/50 Xatt is-Sajjieda,* ☎ *684956. MC, V.*

Qawra

$$$$ ⊞ **Suncrest Hotel.** At this modern, seven-story turquoise-and-white complex overlooking Salina Bay in the northern part of the island, the atmosphere is relaxed and informal. Rooms have fresh white walls and marble-tile floors that are covered with rugs in winter. ⊠ *Qawra Coast Rd.,* ☎ *577101,* FAX *575478. 427 rooms with bath. Café, 3 restaurants, bar, pool, sauna, tennis courts, health club, beach, meeting room. AE, DC, MC, V.*

Rabat

$$ ⊞ **Medina.** This is a good value near Medina. It is not luxurious but is quite comfortable. ⊠ *Labour Ave.,* ☎ *450953,* FAX *450952. 40 rooms with bath. Restaurant, indoor pool, exercise room. MC, V.*

20 The Netherlands

Amsterdam

Historic Holland

The Hague, Delft, and Rotterdam

I **F YOU COME TO THE NETHERLANDS** expecting to find its residents shod in wooden shoes, you're years too late; if you're looking for windmills at every turn, you're looking in the wrong place. The bucolic images that brought tourism here in the decades after World War II have little to do with the Netherlands of the '90s. Sure, tulips grow in abundance in the bulb district of Noord and Zuid Holland provinces, but today's Netherlands is no backwater operation: This tiny nation has an economic strength and cultural wealth that far surpass its size and population. Sophisticated, modern Netherlands has more art treasures per square mile than any other country on earth, as well as a large number of ingenious, energetic citizens with a remarkable commitment to quality, style, and innovation.

The 41,526 square kilometers (15,972 square miles) of the Netherlands are just about half the number of the state of Maine, and its population of 15 million is slightly less than that of the state of Texas. Size is no measure of international clout, however: The Netherlands is second only to Great Britain and Japan as an investor in the American economy. The country encourages internal accomplishments as well, particularly of a cultural nature. Within a 120-kilometer (75-mile) radius are 10 major art museums and several smaller ones that together contain the world's richest and most comprehensive collection of art masterpieces from the 15th to the 20th centuries, including the majority of paintings by Rembrandt and Vincent van Gogh. In the same small area are half a dozen performance halls offering music, dance, and internationally known performing arts festivals.

The marriage of economic power and cultural wealth is nothing new to the Dutch; in the 17th century, for example, money raised through their colonial outposts overseas was used to buy or commission portraits and paintings by young artists such as Rembrandt, Hals, Vermeer, and van Ruisdael. But it was not only the arts that were encouraged: The Netherlands was home to the philosophers Descartes, Spinoza, and Comenius; the jurist Grotius; the naturalist van Leeuwenhoek, inventor of the microscope; and others like them who flourished in the country's enlightened tolerance. The Netherlands continues to subsidize its artists and performers, and it supports an educational system in which creativity in every field is respected, revered, and nourished.

The Netherlands is the delta of Europe, located where the great Rhine and Maas rivers and their tributaries empty into the North Sea. Near the coast, it is a land of flat fields and interconnecting canals; in the center it is surprisingly wooded, and in the far south are rolling hills. The country is too small for there to be vast natural areas, and it's too precariously close to sea level, even at its highest points, for there to be dramatic landscapes. (In fact, about half of the Netherlands is below sea level.) Instead, the country is what the Dutch jokingly call a big green city. Amsterdam is the focal point of the nation; it also is the beginning and end point of a 60-kilometer (37½-mile) circle of cities that includes The Hague (the Dutch seat of government and the world center of international justice), Rotterdam (the industrial center of the Netherlands and the world's largest port), and the historic cites of Haarlem, Leiden, Delft, and Utrecht. The northern and eastern provinces are rural and quiet; the southern provinces that hug the Belgian border are lightly industrialized and sophisticated. The great rivers that cut through the heart of the country provide both geographical and sociological borders. The area "above the great rivers," as the Dutch phrase it, is peopled by tough-minded and practical Calvinists; to the south are more ebullient Catholics. A tradition of tolerance pervades this densely populated land; aware that they cannot survive alone, the Dutch are bound by common traits of ingenuity, personal honesty, and a bold sense of humor.

ESSENTIAL INFORMATION

Before You Go

When to Go

The prime tourist season in the Netherlands runs from April through October and peaks during school vacation periods (Easter, July, and August), when hotels may impose a 20% surcharge. Dutch bulb fields bloom from late March to the end of May—not surprisingly, the hotels tend to fill up then, too. June is the ideal time to catch the warm weather and miss the crowds, but every region of the Netherlands has its season. Delft is luminous after a winter storm, and fall in the Utrecht countryside can be as dramatic as in New England.

CLIMATE

Summers are generally warm, but beware of sudden showers and blustery coastal winds. Winters are chilly and wet but are not without clear days. After a cloudburst, notice the watery quality of light that inspired Vermeer and other great Dutch painters. The following are the average daily maximum and minimum temperatures for Amsterdam.

Jan.	40F	4C	May	61F	16C	Sept.	65F	18C
	34	1		50	10		56	13
Feb.	41F	5C	June	65F	18C	Oct.	56	13C
	34	1		56	13		49	9
Mar.	47F	8C	July	70F	21C	Nov.	47F	8C
	38	3		59	15		41	5
Apr.	52F	11C	Aug.	68F	20C	Dec.	41F	5C
	43	6		59	15		36	2

Currency

The unit of currency in the Netherlands is the guilder, written as NLG (for Netherlands guilder), Fl., or simply F. (from the centuries-old term for the coinage, florin). Each guilder is divided into 100 cents. Bills are in denominations of 10, 25, 50, 100, 250, and 1,000 guilders. Denominations over Fl. 100 are rarely seen, and many shops refuse to change them. Coins are 1, 2.5, and 5 guilders and 5, 10, and 25 cents. Be careful not to confuse the 1- and 2.5-guilder coins and the 5-guilder and 5-cent coins. Bills have a code of raised dots that can be identified by touch; this is for people who have vision impairments.

At press time (spring 1996), the exchange rate for the guilder was Fl. 1.56 to the U.S. dollar, Fl. 1.12 to the Canadian dollar, and Fl. 2.47 to the pound sterling.

What It Will Cost

The Netherlands is a prosperous country with a high standard of living, so overall costs are similar to those in other northern European countries. Prices for hotels and services in major cities are 10%–20% higher than those in rural areas. Amsterdam and The Hague are the most expensive. Hotel and restaurant service charges and the 6% value-added tax (VAT) are usually included in the prices quoted.

The cost of eating varies widely, from a snack in a bar or a modest restaurant offering a *dagschotel* (day special) or "tourist menu" at around

The Netherlands

North Sea

W a d d e n I s l a n d s

Schiermonnikoog

Ameland

Terschelling

Delfzijl

Dokkum

Groningen

Winschoten

Vlieland

Leeuwarden

Drachten

Assen

A7/E22

N41

N34

Harlingen

Texel

Bolsward

Sneek

Emmen

A32

N371

A28/E232

Waddenzee

Den Helder

IJsselmeer

Enkhuizen

Meppel

Hoogeveen

Zwolle

Almelo

Hengelo

A7/E22

A50

N34

N48

N36

Alkmaar

Hoorn

Lelystad

N35

Enschede

Purmerend

Deventer

A6

A28/E232

Zaanstad

Apeldoorn

A1/E30

Haarlem

Amsterdam

Bussum

Amersfoort

Winterswijk

A9

Hilversum

Arnhem

Doetinchem

A5/N14

A3

Leiden

Utrecht

A12/E35

Rhine

Den Haag
(The Hague)

Oude Rijn

Rijn

Nijmegen

GERMANY

E30

Lek

Tiel

A12

A25

Delft

Oss

A50

Rotterdam

Waal

's Hertogenbosch

A27

A15/E31

Dordrecht

Maas

Veghel

Maas

A59

Haringvliet

Overflakkee

Grevelingen

A16/E22

*Schouwen/
Duiveland*

Breda

Tilburg

Eindhoven

A67/E34

Steenbergen

A2/E25

Tholen

Oosterschelde

Bergen op Zoom

Weert

Roermond

Walcheren

Goes

A58

Beveland

Middelburg

Westerschelde

Breskens

Terneuzen

Schelde

Sittard

Antwerp

Maastricht

Aachen

Vaals

KEY

Ferry

BELGIUM

Liège

0 ——— 40 miles

0 ——— 60 km

Brussels

N

Fl. 25 to the considerable expense of gourmet cuisine. A traditional Dutch breakfast is usually included in the overnight hotel price.

One cost advantage the Netherlands has over other European countries is that because it is so small, traveling around is inexpensive—especially if you take advantage of money-saving transportation deals.

SAMPLE PRICES
Half bottle of wine, Fl. 25; glass of beer, Fl. 3.50; cup of coffee, Fl. 2.75; ham and cheese sandwich, Fl. 5; 1-mile taxi ride, Fl. 10.

MUSEUMS
The **Museumkaart,** which can be purchased from some museums and all tourist offices, provides a year's free admission to about 350 museums. It costs Fl. 45, Fl. 32.50 if you're over 65, and Fl. 15 if you're under 18. A photo and passport are required for purchase. If your time is limited, check the list; not all museums participate.

Customs on Arrival
For travelers arriving from a country that is not a member of the European Union (EU) or those coming from an EU country who have bought goods in a duty-free shop, the allowances are (1) 200 cigarettes, or 50 cigars, or 100 cigarillos, or 250 grams of tobacco, (2) 1 liter of alcohol more than 22% by volume and 2 liters of wine less than 15% by volume; or 2 liters of sparkling wine and 2 liters of wine less than 15% by volume, (3) 50 grams of perfume or 25 centiliters of toilet water, and (4) other goods with a total value of Fl. 380.

Since January 1, 1993, allowances for travelers within the EU have been effectively removed, provided that goods have been bought duty-paid (i.e., not in a duty-free shop) and are for personal use. All personal items are considered duty-free, provided you take them with you when you leave the Netherlands. Tobacco and alcohol allowances are for those 17 and older. There are no restrictions on the import and export of Dutch currency.

Language
Dutch is a difficult language for foreigners, but luckily the Dutch are fine linguists, so almost everyone speaks at least some English, especially in larger cities and tourist centers.

Getting Around

By Car
ROAD CONDITIONS
The Netherlands has one of the best road systems in Europe, and even the longest trips between cities take only a few hours. Multilane expressways (toll-free) link major cities, but the smaller roads and country lanes provide more varied views of the Netherlands. In towns many of the streets are narrow, and you'll have to contend with complex one-way systems and cycle lanes. Information about weather and road conditions can be obtained by calling 06/9622.

RULES OF THE ROAD
The speed limit on expressways is 120 kph (75 mph); on city streets and in residential areas it is 50 kph (30 mph) or less, according to the signs. Driving is on the right.

PARKING
Parking in the larger towns is difficult and expensive, with illegally parked cars quickly towed away or subject to a wheel clamp. Fines for recovery can reach Fl. 300. So consider parking on the outskirts of a town and using public transportation to get to the center.

Gas, *benzine* in Dutch, costs around Fl. 1.88 per liter for regular, Fl. 1.94 for super, Fl. 2.04 for leaded, and Fl. 1.34 for diesel.

BREAKDOWNS

Experienced, uniformed mechanics of the **Wegenwacht** patrol the highways in yellow cars 24 hours a day. Operated by the Royal Dutch Touring Club (ANWB), they will help if you have car trouble. On major roads, ANWB also maintains phone boxes from which you can call for assistance. To use these services, you may be asked to take temporary membership in ANWB.

By Train

Fast, frequent, comfortable trains operate throughout the country. All trains have first- and second-class cars, and many intercity trains have buffet or dining-car services. Intercity trains run every 30 minutes and regular trains run to the smaller towns at least once an hour. Sometimes one train contains two separate sections that divide during the trip, so be sure you are in the correct car for your destination. Trains have specially designed entryways for people using wheelchairs.

At railway stations, look for blue columns marked REISWIJZER ("Route Finder"). For Fl. 1.25, paid with a telephone card, you can get a printout in English with door-to-door travel information that includes stops and connections on trains, buses, and trams.

FARES

To get the best value out of rail travel it is advisable to purchase one of the available passes. The Benelux Tourrail can be bought abroad, but the others are available only in the Netherlands. The **Benelux Tourrail** gives you unlimited travel throughout the Netherlands, Belgium, and Luxembourg on any five days within one month ($217 first class, $155 second class). A **Holland Rail Pass** (known in the Netherlands as a EuroDomino Holland) ticket allows unlimited travel throughout the Netherlands for 3, 5, or 10 days within any 30-day period (first class: 3-day $88, 5-day $140, 10-day $260; second class: 3-day $68, 5-day $104, 10-day $184). A **Transport Link** ticket, which offers free travel on buses and trams as well, may be bought in conjunction with the Holland Rail Pass (3-day $14, 5-day $23, 10-day $36). Your rail pass is also valid on **Interliner,** a fast bus network that operates 16 intercity lines. Other options are a one-day **Dagkaart** and, from June to August, a **Zomertoer** (summer tour) ticket for 3 days' travel in a 10-day period. The Netherlands Board of Tourism's (NBT) offices abroad have information on train services, as do overseas offices of Netherlands Railways. Your passport may be needed when you purchase these tickets. **Dagtochtkaartjes** are special combined tickets covering train, boat, and bus trips. Ask about these fares at railway information bureaus or local tourist offices.

By Plane

KLM Royal Dutch Airlines, under the banner of CityHopper, operates several domestic services connecting major cities. In this small country, however, you'd probably travel just as fast by car or train.

By Bus

The Netherlands has an excellent bus network between towns that are not connected by rail and also within towns. Bus excursions can be booked on the spot and at local tourist offices. In major cities, the best buy is a **strippenkaart** ticket (Fl. 11), which can be used for all bus, tram, and metro services. Each card has 15 strips, which are canceled either by the driver as you enter the buses or by the stamping machine at each door of the trams. More than one person can travel on a strippenkaart—it just gets used up more quickly. A strippenkaart with 45 strips is available for Fl. 32.25. You can buy it at train stations, post offices, and some tourist offices, or in Amsterdam at the national bus system (GVB) ticket office in the plaza in front of the central railway station and at many newsagents. A **dagkaart,** a travel-anywhere ticket, covers all urban bus/streetcar routes and costs Fl. 12 for one day, Fl. 16 for two days, and Fl. 19.75 for three days.

By Bicycle

The Netherlands is a cyclist-friendly country with specially designated cycle paths, signs, and picnic areas. Bikes can usually be rented at train stations in most cities and towns, and Dutch trains are cycle-friendly, too, with extra-spacious entryways designed to accommodate bicycles. You will need an extra ticket for the bike, however. There are some restrictions on carrying bicycles on trains, so check first. The flat-rate single fare for a bike to anywhere in the country is Fl. 10, but this can rise to Fl. 25 depending on the day of the week, the season, and what kind of ticket you hold. (It's most expensive to transport a bike on Monday and Friday in July or August.) Rental costs for bicycles are around Fl. 10 per day or from Fl. 40 per week, plus a deposit of Fl. 50–Fl. 200. Many larger railway stations rent bicycles to holders of valid train tickets at Fl. 6 per day and Fl. 24 per week. Advice on rentals and routes is available from offices of the Netherlands Board of Tourism in North America or in the Netherlands, or from local tourist offices; cycling packages can be booked at the larger offices.

Staying in The Netherlands

Telephones

LOCAL CALLS

The telephone system is excellent and reliable. All towns and cities have area codes that are used only when you are calling from outside the area. Most pay phones take 25¢ or Fl. 1 coins, though newer ones also accept other denominations. Public phone booths are being converted to a phone-card system. Phone cards may be purchased from post offices, railway stations, and some newsagents for Fl. 5, Fl. 10, or Fl. 25. Lines at coin-operated boxes tend to be longer, so a phone card is worth the investment, especially if you intend to make international calls. Dial 06/0410 for an English-speaking operator.

INTERNATIONAL CALLS

Direct-dial international calls can be made from any phone booth. Lower rates to the United States are charged from 7 PM to 10 AM weekdays, and from 7 PM Friday to 10 AM Monday. The average cost per minute to the U.S. is Fl. 1.70 (Fl. 1.50 nights and weekends). To reach an **AT&T** long-distance operator, dial 06/022–9111; for **MCI,** dial 06/022–9122; for **Sprint,** dial 06/022–9119.

COUNTRY CODE

The country code for the Netherlands is 3l.

Mail

POSTAL RATES

The Dutch postal system is as efficient as the telephone network. Airmail letters to the United States cost Fl. 1.60 for the first 20 grams; postcards cost Fl. 1; aerograms cost Fl. 1.30. Airmail letters to the United Kingdom cost Fl. 1 for the first 20 grams; postcards cost 80¢; aerograms cost Fl. 1.30.

RECEIVING MAIL

If you're uncertain where you'll be staying, have mail sent to "poste restante, Hoofd Postkantoor" in major cities along your route (making sure that your name and initials are clear and correctly spelled), or to American Express offices, where a small fee is charged on collection to non-American Express customers.

Shopping

VAT REFUNDS

Purchases of goods in one store on one day amounting to Fl. 300 or more qualify for a value-added tax (VAT) refund of 17.5%, which can be claimed at the airport or main border crossing when you leave the Netherlands, or by mail. This arrangement is only valid if you export the goods within 30 days. Ask the salesperson for a VAT refund form when you buy anything that may qualify.

BARGAINING

The prices in most shops and markets are fixed, but you can try to bargain for secondhand items in flea markets.

Opening and Closing Times

Banks are open weekdays from 9 to 4. You can also change money at GWK Border Exchange Offices at major railway stations and Schiphol Airport, which are open Monday–Saturday 8–8 and Sunday 10–4. GWK offices in major cities or at border checkpoints are open 24 hours. Many tourist offices exchange funds, too.

Museums now close on Monday, but there are exceptions, so check with local tourist offices. In rural areas, some museums close or operate shorter hours during winter. Usual hours are 10–5.

Shops are open weekdays and Saturdays from 8:30 or 9 to 5:30 or 6, but outside the cities, some close for lunch. Department stores and most shops, especially in shopping plazas (in The Hague and Amsterdam) do not open on Monday until 1 PM, and a few close one afternoon a week on whichever day they choose. Late-night shopping usually can be done until 9 PM on Thursday or Friday. Certain shops are open Sunday from noon to 5; this varies from city to city. In larger cities, major department stores and chain and mall stores will probably be open, but most stores still close on Sunday.

National Holidays

January 1; March 28–31 (Easter); April 30 (Queen's Day; shops are open unless it falls on Sunday); May 5 (Liberation); May 8 (Ascension); May 18–19 (Pentecost); December 25–26.

Dining

Of the many earthly pleasures in which the Dutch indulge, eating probably heads the list. There is a wide variety of cuisines from traditional Dutch to Indonesian—the influence of the former Dutch colony. Breakfast is hearty and substantial—including several varieties of bread, butter, jam, ham, cheese, chocolate, boiled eggs, juice, and steaming coffee or tea. Dutch specialties for later meals include *erwtensoep* (a rich, thick pea soup with pieces of tangy sausage or pigs' knuckles) and *hutspot* (a meat, carrot, and potato stew); both are usually served only in winter. *Haring* (herring) is particularly popular, especially the "new herring" caught between May and September and served raw in brine, garnished with onions. If Dutch food begins to pall, try an Indonesian restaurant, where the chief item is rijsttafel, a meal made up of rice and 20 or more small meat, seafood, or vegetable dishes, many of which are hot and spicy.

The indigenous Dutch liquor is potent and warming *jenever* (gin), both "old" and "new." Dutch liqueurs and beers are also popular.

Eating places range from snack bars, fast-food outlets, and modest local cafés to gourmet restaurants of international repute. Of special note are the "brown cafés," traditional pubs of great character that normally serve snack-type meals.

MEALTIMES

The Dutch tend to eat dinner at around 6 or 7 PM, especially in the country and smaller cities, so many restaurants close at about 10 PM and accept final orders at 9. In larger cities dining hours vary, and some restaurants stay open until midnight.

WHAT TO WEAR

Jacket and tie are advised for restaurants in the $$$$ and $$$ categories. The tolerant Dutch accept casual outfits in most eateries.

RATINGS

Prices are per person including three courses (appetizer, main course, and dessert), service, and sales tax but not drinks. For budget travelers, many restaurants offer a tourist menu at an officially controlled price, currently Fl. 25.

CATEGORY	AMSTERDAM/ MAIN CITIES	OTHER AREAS
$$$$	over Fl. 100	over Fl. 85
$$$	Fl. 70–Fl. 100	Fl. 55–Fl. 85
$$	Fl. 40–Fl. 70	Fl. 35–Fl. 55
$	under Fl. 40	under Fl. 35

Lodging

The Netherlands has a wide range of accommodations, from the luxurious Dutch-owned international Golden Tulip hotel chain to traditional, small-town hotels and family-run guest houses. For young or adventurous travelers, the provinces abound with modest hostels, campgrounds, and rural bungalows. Travelers with modest budgets may prefer bed-and-breakfast establishments; these are in short supply and must be booked well ahead at local tourist offices.

HOTELS

Dutch hotels are generally clean, if not spotless, no matter how modest their facilities, and service is normally courteous and efficient. There are many moderate and inexpensive hotels, most of which are relatively small. In the provinces, the range of accommodations is more limited, but there are friendly, inexpensive family-run hotels that are usually centrally located. Some have good—if modest—dining facilities. English is spoken or understood almost everywhere. Hotels generally quote room prices for double occupancy, and rates often include breakfast, service charges, and VAT.

To book hotels in advance, you can use the free **Netherlands Reservation Center** (⊠ Box 404, 2260 AK Leidschendam, ☎ 070/3202500, FAX 070/3202611; ☯ Weekdays 8–8, Sat. 8–2). Alternatively, for a small fee, tourist offices can usually make reservations at short notice. Bookings must be made in person, however.

RATINGS

Prices are for two people sharing a double room.

CATEGORY	AMSTERDAM/ MAIN CITIES	OTHER AREAS
$$$$	over Fl. 500	over Fl. 350
$$$	Fl. 300–Fl. 500	Fl. 200–Fl. 350
$$	Fl. 200–Fl. 300	Fl. 150–Fl. 200
$	under Fl. 200	under Fl. 150

Tipping

Hotels and restaurants almost always include 10%–15% service and 6% VAT in their charges. Give a doorman Fl. 3 for calling a cab. Bell-hops in first-class hotels should be tipped Fl. 2 for each bag they carry. Hat-check attendants expect at least Fl. 1, and washroom attendants get 50¢. Taxis in almost every town have a tip included in the meter charge, but you round the fare to the nearest guilder nevertheless.

AMSTERDAM

Arriving and Departing

By Plane

Most international flights arrive at Amsterdam's Schiphol Airport, one of Europe's finest. Immigration and customs formalities on arrival are relaxed, with no forms to be completed.

BETWEEN THE AIRPORT AND DOWNTOWN

The best transportation between the airport and the city center is the direct rail link to the central train station, where you can get a taxi or tram to your hotel. The train runs every 10 to 15 minutes throughout the day and takes about half an hour. Second-class fare is Fl. 5.75.

Taxis from the airport to central hotels cost about Fl. 60.

By Train

The city has excellent rail connections with the rest of Europe. Fast services link it to Paris, Brussels, Luxembourg, and Cologne. Centraal Station is conveniently located in the center of town.

Getting Around

By Bus, Tram, and Metro

A zonal fare system is used. Tickets (starting at Fl. 3) are bought from automatic dispensers on the metro or from the drivers on trams and buses; or buy a money-saving **strippenkaart** (☞ Getting Around, By Bus, *in* Essential Information, *above*). Even simpler is the **dagkaart,** which covers all city routes for Fl. 12. These discount tickets can be obtained from the main GVB ticket office in front of Centraal Station and from many newsstands, along with route maps of the public transportation system. The **Canalbus,** which travels between the central train station and the Rijksmuseum, is Fl. 22 for a hop-on, hop-off day card.

By Taxi

Taxis are expensive: A short 3-mile ride costs around Fl. 15. Taxis are not usually hailed on the street but are picked up at stands near stations and other key points. Alternatively, you can dial 020/6777777. Water taxis (☎ 020/6222181) are even more expensive: Standard-size water taxis—for up to eight people—cost Fl. 150 for an hour, including pick-up charge, with a charge of Fl. 30 per 15 minutes thereafter, and a minimum charge of Fl. 90 for a half hour.

By Car

Parking in Amsterdam has always been difficult. Frequent attempts to ban cars from the city center are scuppered by the opposition of local big business. The city's concentric ring of canals, one-way systems, and lack of parking facilities continue to plague drivers. It's best to put your car in one of the parking lots on the edge of the old center and abandon it for the rest of your stay.

By Bicycle

Rental bikes are widely available for around Fl. 10 per day with a Fl. 50–Fl. 200 deposit. Bikes are an excellent and inexpensive way to explore the city. Several rental companies are close to the central train station, or ask at tourist offices for details. Lock your bike at all times, preferably to something immovable. Also, check with the rental company to see what your liability is under their insurance terms.

By Boat

The **Museum Boat** (☞ Guided Tours, *below*), which makes seven stops near major museums, is Fl. 22.

On Foot

Amsterdam is a small city of narrow streets, ideal for exploring on foot. The tourist office issues seven excellent guides that detail walking tours around the center. The best are "The Jordaan," a stroll through the lively canal-side district, and "Jewish Amsterdam," a walk past the symbolic remains of Jewish housing and old synagogues.

Important Addresses and Numbers

Consulates

U.S. (⊠ Museumplein 19, ☎ 020/6645661). **Canadian** (⊠ 7 Sophialaan, The Hague, ☎ 070/3614111). **U.K.** (⊠ Koningslaan 44, ☎ 020/6764343).

Emergencies

The general number for emergencies is 06/112, but note direct numbers. **Police** (☎ 020/6222222). **Ambulance** (☎ 020/5555555). For emergency medical service, call **Academisch Medisch Centrum** (⊠ Meibergdreef 9, ☎ 020/5669111). **Central Medical Service** (☎ 06/35032042) will give you names of pharmacists and dentists as well as doctors.

English-Language Bookstores

American Book Center (⊠ Kalverstraat 185, ☎ 020/6255537). **Athenaeum Boekhandel** (⊠ Spui 14, ☎ 020/6233933). **English Bookshop** (⊠ Lauriergracht 71, ☎ 020/6264230). **W.H. Smith** (⊠ Kalverstraat 152, ☎ 020/6383821).

Travel Agencies

American Express (⊠ Damrak 66, ☎ 020/5207777; ⊠ Van Baerlestraat 39, ☎ 020/6738550); **Holland International** (⊠ Leidseplein 23, ☎ 020/6262660); **Key Tours** (⊠ Dam 19, ☎ 020/6235051); **Reisburo Arke** (⊠ Damrak 90, ☎ 020/5550888); **Thomas Cook** (Bureau de Change, ⊠ Leidseplein 31a, ☎ 020/6267000; ⊠ Damrak 1, ☎ 020/6203236).

Visitor Information

There are two locations for the **VVV Amsterdam Tourist Office:** one in front of Centraal Station (⊠ Stationsplein 10, in the Old Dutch Coffee House, ☉ Daily 9–5) and another at Leidseplein 1 (☉ Fall–spring, daily 9–7; summer, daily 9–9). VVV is the acronym for information offices; you'll see it on signposts throughout the country. The general number for telephone inquiries in Amsterdam is 06/34034066, but you are charged 75¢ per minute and kept waiting in an electronic line.

Guided Tours

Boat Tours

The most enjoyable way to get to know Amsterdam is a boat trip along the canals. There are frequent departures from points opposite Centraal Station, along the Damrak, and along the Rokin and Stadhouderskade (near the Rijksmuseum). For a tour lasting about an hour, the cost is around Fl. 12.50, but the student guides expect a small tip for their multilingual commentary. On summer evenings, longer cruises include wine and cheese or a full buffet dinner. A few tours make increasingly drunken stops for wine tastings in canal-side bars. A candlelight dinner cruise costs upward of Fl. 39.50. Trips can be booked through the tourist office.

Alternatively, you may want to rent a pedal boat and make your own canal tour. At **Canal-Bike** (☎ 020/6239886), a pedal boat for four costs FL. 20.50 per hour.

The **Museum Boat** (✉ Stationsplein 8, ☎ 020/6222181) combines a scenic view of the city with seven stops near 20 museums. Tickets, good for the entire day, are Fl. 22.

Bus Tours

Guided bus tours also provide an excellent introduction to Amsterdam. A bus-and-boat tour includes the inevitable trip to a diamond factory. Costing Fl. 25–Fl. 35, the comprehensive three-and-a-half-hour tour can be booked through **Lindbergh** (✉ Damrak 26–27, ☎ 020/6222766) or **Key Tours** (✉ Dam 19, ☎ 020/6235051).

Exploring Amsterdam

Amsterdam is a gem of a city for the visitor. Small and densely packed with fine buildings, many dating from the 17th century or earlier, it is easily explored on foot or by bike. The old heart of the city consists of canals, with narrow streets radiating out like the spokes of a wheel. The hub of this wheel and the most convenient point to begin sightseeing is Centraal Station. Across the street, in the same building as the Old Dutch Coffee House, is a tourist information office. Amsterdam's key points of interest can be covered within two or three days, with each walking itinerary taking in one or two of the important museums and galleries. The following exploration of the city center can be broken up into several sessions.

Around the Dam

Numbers in the margin correspond to points of interest on the Amsterdam map.

❶ Start at **Centraal Station,** the central train station. Designed by P. J. H. Cuijpers and built in 1884–89, it is a good example of Dutch architecture at its most flamboyant. The street directly in front of the station square is Prins Hendrikkade. To the left, a good vantage point for
❷ viewing the station, is **St. Nicolaaskerk** (Church of St. Nicholas), consecrated in 1888.

Around the corner from St. Nicolaaskerk, facing the harbor, is the
❸ **Schreierstoren** (Weepers' Tower), a lookout tower for women whose men were out at sea. The tower was erected in 1480, and a tablet marks the point from which Henrik (a.k.a. Henry) Hudson set sail on the *Half Moon* on April 4, 1609, on a voyage that eventually took him to what is now New York and the river that still bears his name. Today the Weepers' Tower is used as a combined reception and exhibition center, which includes a maritime bookshop.

Three blocks to the southwest along the Oudezijds Voorburgwal is the
★ ❹ **Museum Amstelkring,** whose facade carries the inscription *"Ons Lieve Heer Op Solder"* ("Our Dear Lord in the Attic"). In 1578, Amsterdam embraced Protestantism and outlawed the church of Rome. So great was the tolerance of the municipal authorities, however, that secret Catholic chapels were allowed to exist; at one time there were 62

772

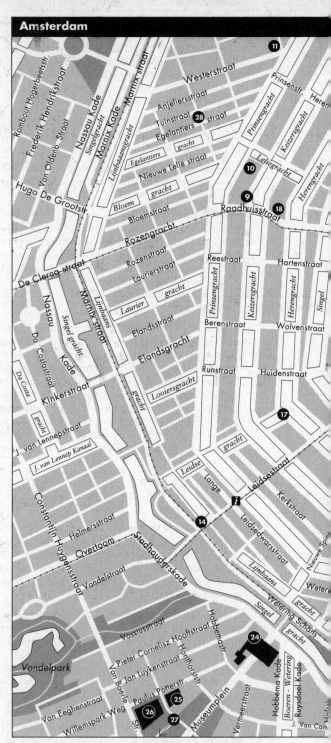

Amsterdam

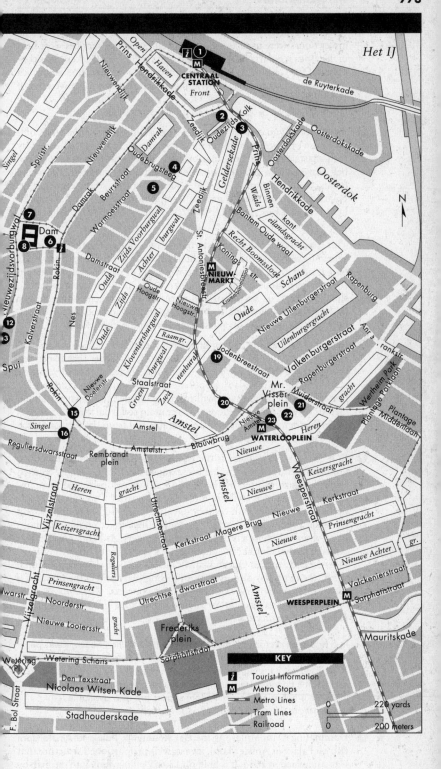

Het IJ

CENTRAAL
STATION
Front

de Ruyterkade

Prins Hendrikkade

Open Haven

Nieuwendik

Singel

Spuistr.

Nieuwendik

Damrak

Oudebrugsteeg

Zeedijk

Oudezijds Kolk

Oosterdokskade

Geldersekade

Prins Hendrikkade

Oosterdokskade

Oosterdok

Binnen kant eilandsgracht

Waals

Bantam Oude waal

Recht Boomssloot

Rapenburg

N

Beursstraat

Warmoesstraat

Damrak

Oudebrugwal

Zeedijk

St. Antoniesbreestr.

Konings str.

Schans

Dam

Zijds Voorburgwal

Achter burgwal

Kromme Waal

Oude

Damstraat

Nieuwe

Ziids Voorburgwal

Oude Hoogstr.

**M NIEUW
MARKT**

Oude

Nieuwe Uilenburgerstraat

Singel

Nieuwezijdsvoorburgwal

Rokin

Kalverstraat

Nes

Oude

Ziids

Oude Hoogstr.

Nieuwe Hoogstr.

Oude

Uilenburgergracht

Rapenburg

Spui

Nieuwe Doelenstr.

Klovenierburgwal

Raamgr.

Nieuwburg

Jodenbreestraat

Valkenburgerstraat

Anna ... ranstr.

Wertheim Park
Plantage Parklaan

Staalstraat

Groen burgwal

Zuid

Mr.
Visserplein

Rapenburgerstraat

Plantage Middenlaan

Singel

Reguliersdwarsstraat

Rokin

Amstel

Amstel

Blauwbrug

Mr.
Visserplein

Muiderstraat

Heren

gracht

WATERLOOPLEIN

Nieuwe
Amstel

Rembrandt
plein

Amstelstr.

Nieuwe

Nieuwe

Keizersgracht

Weesperstraat

Kerkstraat

Vijzelstraat

Heren

gracht

Amstel

Nieuwe

Prinsengracht

Nieuwe Achter

gr.

Keizersgracht

Regliers

Kerkstraat

Magere Brug

Nieuwe

Valckenierstraat

Prinsengracht

Vijzelgracht

Noorderstr.

grach

Utrechtsestraat

Amstel

M WEESPERPLEIN

Sarphatistraat

Nieuwe Looiersstr.

Utrechtse dwarsstraat

Mauritskade

Fredenks
plein

Sarphatistraat

Wetering
Pl.

Wetering Scharrs

Den Texstraat

Nicolaas Witsen Kade

F. Bol Straat

Stadhouderskade

KEY

i Tourist Information
M Metro Stops
Metro Lines
Tram Lines
Railroad

0   220 yards

0   200 meters

in Amsterdam alone. One such chapel was established in the attics of these three neighboring canal-side houses, built around 1661. The lower floors were used as ordinary dwellings, while services were held in the attics regularly until 1888, the year the St. Nicolaaskerk was consecrated for Catholic worship. Of interest are the Baroque altar with its revolving tabernacle, the swinging pulpit that can be stowed out of sight, and the upstairs gallery. ⊠ *Oudezijds Voorburgwal 40,* ☎ *020/ 6246604.* ☜ *Fl. 5.* ⊘ *Mon.–Sat. 10–5, Sun. 1–5.*

⑤ Just beyond, you can see the **Oude Kerk** (Old Church), the city's oldest house of worship. Built in the 14th century but badly damaged by iconoclasts after the Reformation, the church still retains its original bell tower and a few remarkable stained-glass windows. From the tower, there is a typical view of Old Amsterdam stretching from St. Nicolaaskerk to medieval gables. Rembrandt's wife, Saskia, is buried here. ⊠ *Oudekerksplein 23,* ☎ *020/6258284.* ☜ *Fl. 5.* ⊘ *Mon.–Sat. 11–5, Sun. 1–5.*

This area, bordered by Amsterdam's two oldest canals (Oudezijds Voorburgwal and Oudezijds Achterburgwal), is the heart of the *rosse buurt,* or red-light district. In the windows at canal level, women in sheer lingerie slouch, stare, or do their nails. Although the area can be shocking, with its sex shops and porn shows, it is generally safe, but midnight walks down dark side streets are not advised. If you do explore the area, watch for purse snatchers and pickpockets.

⑥ Return to the Damrak and continue to the **Dam** (Dam Square), the broadest square in the old section of the town. It was here that fishermen used to come to sell their catch. Today it is circled with shops and bisected by traffic; it is also a popular center for outdoor performers. At one side of the square you will notice a simple monument to Dutch victims of World War II. Eleven urns contain soil from the 11 provinces of the Netherlands, while a 12th contains soil from the former Dutch East Indies, now Indonesia.

⑦ In a corner of the square is the **Nieuwe Kerk** (New Church). A huge Gothic structure, it was gradually expanded until 1540, when it reached its present size. Gutted by fire in 1645, it was reconstructed in an imposing Renaissance style, as interpreted by strict Calvinists. The superb oak pulpit, the 14th-century nave, the stained-glass windows, and the great organ (1645) are all shown to great effect on national holidays, when the church is bedecked with flowers. As befits The Netherlands' national church, the Nieuwe Kerk is the site of all coronations, most recently that of Queen Beatrix in 1980. But in democratic Dutch spirit, the church is also used as a meeting place and is the home of a lively café, temporary exhibitions, and concerts. ⊠ *Dam,* ☎ *020/ 6268168.* ☜ *Free, except for special exhibitions (from Fl. 12.50).* ⊘ *Daily 11–5; exhibitions daily 10–6.*

NEED A BREAK? In a house on a crooked, medieval street behind the Nieuwe Kerk, **De Drie Fleschjes** (The Three Bottles) is a typical 17th-century *proeflokalen* (wine- and spirit-tasting houses). The tone is set by the burnished wood interior, the candlelit bar, and the profusion of kegs and taps. Although the main emphasis is on drink, light snacks are also available. ⊠ *Gravenstraat 18,* ☎ *020/6248443.* ⊘ *Mon.–Sat. noon–8.*

★ ⑧ Dominating Dam Square is the **Het Koninklijk Paleis te Amsterdam** (Royal Palace at Amsterdam), a vast, well-proportioned structure that was completed in 1655. It is built on 13,659 pilings sunk into the marshy soil. The great pediment sculptures are an allegorical representation of Amsterdam surrounded by Neptune and mythological sea creatures. ⊠ *Dam,* ☎ *020/6248698.* 🎫 *Fl. 5.* ⏱ *Tues.–Thurs. 1–4; daily 12.30–5 in summer. Sometimes closed for state events.*

From behind the palace, Raadhuisstraat leads west across three canals ⑨ to Westermarkt and the **Westerkerk** (West Church), built in 1631. The church's 279-foot tower is the city's highest; it also has an outstanding carillon. Rembrandt and his son Titus are buried in the church. In summer you can climb to the top of the tower for a fine view over the city. ⊠ *Prinsengracht (corner of Westermarkt),* ☎ *020/6247766.* ⏱ *Tower: June–Sept., Tues., Wed. and Fri.–Sat. 2–5.*

Opposite, at Westermarkt 6, is the house where René Descartes, the great 17th-century French philosopher (*"Cogito, ergo sum"*—"I think, therefore I am") lived in 1634. Another more famous house lies far-⑩ ther down Prinsengracht. This is the **Anne Frankhuis** (Anne Frank House), immortalized by the poignant diary kept by the young Jewish girl from 1942 to 1944, when she and her family hid here from the German occupying forces. A small exhibition on the Holocaust can also be seen in the house. ⊠ *Prinsengracht 263,* ☎ *020/5567100.* 🎫 *Fl. 8.* ⏱ *June–Aug., Mon.–Sat. 9–7, Sun. 10–7; Sept.–May, Mon.–Sat. 9–5, Sun. 10–5.*

⑪ Continuing across the Prinsengracht, you'll reach the **Noorderkerk** (North Church), built in 1623. In the square in front of the church, the Noorderplein, a bird market is held every Saturday.

South of the Dam

Turn down Kalverstraat, a shopping street leading from the Royal Palace. You will notice a striking Renaissance gate (1581) that guards a series of tranquil inner courtyards. In medieval times, this area was an island devoted to piety. Today the bordering canals are filled in. The medieval doorway around the corner in St. Luciensteeg leads to the former ★ ⑫ Burgerweeshuis (City Orphanage), now the **Amsterdam Historisch Museum** (Amsterdam Historical Museum). The museum traces the city's history from its origins as a fishing village through the 17th-century Golden Age of material and artistic wealth to the decline of the trading empire during the 18th century. The engrossing story unfolds through a display of old maps, documents, and paintings, often aided by a commentary in English. ⊠ *Kalverstraat 92,* ☎ *020/5231822.* 🎫 *Fl. 7.50.* ⏱ *Weekdays 10–5, weekends 11–5.*

★ ⑬ A small passageway and courtyard link the museum with the **Begijnhof** (Beguine Court), an enchanting, enclosed square of almshouses founded in 1346 that is an oasis of silence beside the hectic Kalverstraat. The Beguines were women who chose to lead a form of convent life, often taking the vow of chastity. The last Beguine died in 1974 and her house, Number 26, has been preserved as she left it. Number 34, dating from the 15th century, is the oldest and the only one to preserve its wooden Gothic facade. ⊠ *Begijnhof 29,* ☎ *020/6233565.* 🎫 *Free.* ⏱ *Weekdays 11–4.*

In the center of the square is a church given to Amsterdam's English and Scottish Presbyterians more than 300 years ago. On the church wall and also in the chancel are tributes to the Pilgrim Fathers who sailed from Delftshaven (present-day Delfshaven, in Rotterdam) to the New World in 1620. Opposite the church is another of the city's secret Catholic chapels, built in 1671.

Continuing along Kalverstraat, you soon come to Spui, a lively square in the heart of the university area. It was a center for student rallies in revolutionary 1968. Now it is busy with bookstores and bars, including the cozy brown cafés.

Beyond is the Singel Canal and, following the tram tracks, Leidsestraat,
⑭ an important shopping street that terminates in the **Leidseplein,** a lively
square that is one of the centers of the city's nightlife.

If you continue straight along Kalverstraat instead of turning at Spui,
⑮ you'll soon reach the **Muntplein,** with its **Munttoren** (Mint Tower, built
in 1620), a graceful structure whose clock and bells still seem to mir-
⑯ ror the Golden Age. Beginning at the Muntplein is the floating **Bloe-
menmarkt** (Flower Market) on the Singel Canal, which is open
Monday–Saturday 9:30–5.

From the Singel, take Leidsestraat to the Herengracht, the city's most
prestigious "Gentlemen's Canal." The stretch of canal from here to
⑰ Huidenstraat is named the **Gouden Bocht** (Golden Bend) for its sumptuous patrician houses with double staircases and grand entrances. Sev-
enteenth-century merchants moved here from the Amstel River to
escape the disadvantageous byproducts of their wealth: noisy warehouses,
unpleasant brewery smells, and the risk of fire in the sugar refineries.
These houses display the full range of Amsterdam facades, from houses
with gables in a variety of shapes to grander Louis XIV–style houses
with elaborate cornices and frescoed ceilings. These houses are best seen
from the east side of the canal. For more gables, turn down Wolven-
straat into the Keizersgracht, the Emperor's Canal. Walk northward
toward Westerkerk and the Anne Frankhuis.

NEED A
BREAK?

On the corner of Keizersgracht and Reestraat is the **Pulitzer Hotel** and
restaurant complex. Inside, you can wander around quiet inner courtyards and a modern art gallery before sitting down in the **Café Pulitzer,**
which overlooks the canal, for a well-deserved apple tart or pastry.
⊠ *Keizersgracht 236,* ☎ *020/5235235.* ⊙ *Daily 11 AM–10 PM.*

⑱ Along Herengracht, parallel to the Westerkerk, is the **Nederlands Theater Instituut.** This theater museum is a dynamic find on such a genteel canal. Two frescoed Louis XIV–style merchants' houses form the
backdrop for a history of the circus, opera, musicals, and drama.
Miniature theaters and videos of stage productions are just two entertaining features. In summer, the large garden is open for buffet
lunches. Major renovations will keep the museum closed until late 1997.
⊠ *Herengracht 168,* ☎ *020/6235104.* ⊡ *Fl. 5.* ⊙ *Tues.–Fri. 11–5,
weekends 1–5.*

Jewish Amsterdam

Take the Museum Boat or the metro from Centraal Station to Waterlooplein and walk east to Jodenbreestraat. This is the heart of **Joden-
buurt,** the old Jewish district and an important area to all Amsterdammers.
The original settlers here were wealthy Sephardic Jews from Spain and
Portugal, later followed by poorer Ashkenazic refugees from Germany
and Poland. At the turn of the century, this was a thriving community
of Jewish diamond polishers, dyers, and merchants. During World War
II, the corner of Jodenbreestraat marked the end of the *Joodse wijk* (Jewish neighborhood), by then an imposed ghetto. Although the character
of the area was largely destroyed by highway construction in 1965, and
more recently by construction of both the metro and the Muziekthe-
ater/Stadhuis complex (☞ *below*), neighboring Muiderstraat has retained
much of the original atmosphere. Notice the gateways decorated with
pelicans, symbolizing great love; according to legend, the pelican will
feed her starving young with her own blood.

From 1639 to 1658, Rembrandt lived at Jodenbreestraat 4, now the
⑲ **Museum Het Rembrandthuis** (Rembrandt's House). For more than 20
years, the ground floor was used by the artist as living quarters; the sunny

upper floor was his studio. It contains a superb collection of his etchings. From St. Antonies Sluis bridge, just by the house, there is a canal view that has barely changed since Rembrandt's time. ⊠ *Jodenbreestraat 4–6,* ☎ *020/6249486.* ☜ *Fl. 7.50.* ☉ *Mon.–Sat. 10–5, Sun. 1–5.*

After visiting Rembrandt's House, walk back to the canal and go left to pass the Waterlooplein flea market. Ahead of you is the Amsterdam ⓴ **Muziektheater/Stadhuis** (Music Theater/Town Hall) complex, which presents an intriguing combination of bureaucracy and art. Amsterdammers come to the town hall section of the building by day to obtain driver's licenses, pick up welfare payments, and get married. They return by night to the rounded part of the building facing the river to see opera and ballet performed by the Netherlands' finest companies. Feel free to wander into town hall for a look at some interesting sculptures and other displays. Opera and ballet fans can go on a tour of the Muziektheater, which takes you around the dressing rooms, dance studios, and even to the wig department. ⊠ *Amstel 3,* ☎ *020/5518054.* ☜ *Fl. 8.50.* ☉ *Guided tours every Wed. and Sat. at 3.*

★ ㉑ Walk through the flea market behind the Muziektheater, and you come to the 17th-century **Portugees Israelitische Synagogue** (Portuguese Israelite Synagogue). As one of Amsterdam's four neighboring synagogues, it was part of the largest Jewish religious complex in Europe. The austere interior is still intact, even if the building itself is marooned on a traffic island. ⊠ *Mr. Visserplein 3,* ☎ *020/6245351.* ☜ *Fl. 5.* ☉ *Apr.–Oct., Sun.–Fri. 10–4; Nov.–Mar., Mon.–Thurs. 10–4, Fri. 10–3, Sun. 10–noon. Closed daily 12:30–1.*

㉒ Jonas Daniël Meijerplein is a square behind the synagogue. In the center is a statue of the **Dokwerker** (Dockworker), a profession that has played a significant part in the city's history. The statue commemorates the 1942 strike by which Amsterdam dockworkers expressed their solidarity with persecuted Jews. A memorial march is held every year on February 25.

㉓ On the other side of the square is the intriguing **Joods Historisch Museum** (Jewish History Museum), set in a complex of three ancient synagogues. These synagogues once served a population of 100,000 Jews, which shrank to fewer than 10,000 after 1945. The new museum, founded by American and Dutch Jews, displays religious treasures in a clear cultural and historical context. Since the synagogues lost most of their treasures in the war, their architecture and history are more compelling than the exhibits. ⊠ *Jonas Daniël Meijerplein 2–4,* ☎ *020/6269945.* ☜ *Fl. 7.* ☉ *Daily 11–5.*

NEED A BREAK?	In the Jewish History Museum (☞ *above*), **Cafeteria Kosher** (☉ Daily 11–5) is built above the former kosher meat halls that later became ritual baths. It still looks like part of a clandestine Catholic church, the original model for the synagogue. Delicacies include fish cakes, cheese tarts, bagels, and spicy cakes with gingerbread and almond cream filling.

Instead of returning on foot, you can catch the Museum Boat from the Muziektheater to Centraal Station or to a destination near your hotel. If you feel like a breath of fresh air, stroll along Nieuwe Herengracht, once known as the "Jewish Gentlemen's Canal." In Rembrandt's day, there were views of distant windjammers sailing into port, but today the canal is oddly deserted.

The Museum Quarter

By crossing the bridge beyond the Leidseplein and walking a short distance to the left on Stadhouderskade, you'll find three of the most distinguished museums in the Netherlands—the Rijksmuseum, the Stedelijk Museum, and the Rijksmuseum Vincent van Gogh. Of the

★ ㉔ three, the **Rijksmuseum** (State Museum) is the most important; allow at least an hour or two to explore the main collection of Dutch paintings, a morning or afternoon if you want to visit other sections. It was founded in 1808, but the current, rather lavish, building dates from 1885. The museum contains significant collections of furniture, textiles, ceramics, sculpture, and prints, as well as Italian, Flemish, and Spanish paintings. Its fame, however, rests on its unrivaled collection of 16th- and 17th-century Dutch masters. Of Rembrandt's masterpieces, make a point of seeing *The Nightwatch,* concealed during World War II in caves in Maastricht. The painting was misnamed because of its dull layers of varnish; in reality it depicts the Civil Guard in daylight. Also worth searching out are Frans Hals's family portraits, Jan Steen's drunken scenes, Van Ruysdael's romantic but menacing landscapes, and Vermeer's glimpses of everyday life bathed in his usual pale light. ✉ *Stadhouderskade 42,* ☎ *020/6732121.* ▣ *Fl. 12.50.* ☉ *Daily 10–5.*

㉕ A few blocks beyond is the **Rijksmuseum Vincent van Gogh** (State Vincent van Gogh Museum). This museum contains the world's largest collection of the artist's works—200 paintings and nearly 500 drawings— as well as works by some 50 of his contemporaries. ✉ *Paulus Potterstraat 7,* ☎ *020/5705200.* ▣ *Fl. 12.50* ☉ *Daily 10–5.*

㉖ Next door is the **Stedelijk Museum** (Municipal Museum), with its neo-Renaissance facade. The museum has a stimulating collection of modern art and ever-changing displays of contemporary artists. Before viewing the works of Cézanne, Chagall, Kandinsky, and Mondrian, check the list of temporary exhibitions in Room 1. Museum policy is to trace the development of the artist rather than merely to show a few masterpieces. Don't forget the museum's restaurant overlooking a garden filled with modern sculptures. ✉ *Paulus Potterstraat 13,* ☎ *020/5732911.* ▣ *Fl. 11.* ☉ *Daily 11–5.*

㉗ Diagonally opposite the Stedelijk Museum, at the end of the broad Museumplein, is the **Concertgebouw,** home of the country's foremost orchestra, the world-renowned Concertgebouworkest. The building has two auditoriums, the smaller of which is used for chamber music and recitals. A block or two in the opposite direction is **Vondelpark,** an elongated rectangle of paths, lakes, and pleasant shade trees. A monument honors the 17th-century epic poet Joost van den Vondel, for whom the park is named. From Wednesday to Sunday in summer, free concerts and plays are performed in the park.

The Jordaan

㉘ One old part of Amsterdam that is worth exploring is the **Jordaan,** the area bordered by Prinsengracht, Lijnbaansgracht, Brouwersgracht, and Raadhuisstraat. The canals and side streets here are named for flowers and plants. Indeed, when this was the French quarter of the city, the area was known as *le jardin* (the garden), a name that over the years has become Jordaan. The best time to explore this area is on a Sunday morning, when there are few cars and people about, or in the evening. The Jordaan has attracted many artists and is something of a bohemian quarter, where run-down buildings are being converted into restaurants, antiques shops, boutiques, and galleries.

NEED A BREAK?

The Jordaan is the best part of Amsterdam for relaxing in a brown café, so named because of the rich wooden furnishings and—some say—the centuries-old pipe-tobacco stains on the ceilings. You can while away a rainy afternoon chatting with friendly strangers over homemade meatballs or apple tarts. Spend an hour or three over a beer or coffee at either **Rooie Nelis** (Laurierstraat 101, ☎ 020/6244167) or **De Gijs** (Lindegracht 249, ☎ 020/6380740).

Off the Beaten Path

Another "see-worthy" district is the burgeoning **Maritime Quarter.** To reach it, walk from Centraal Station along the Prins Hendrikkade and the Eastern Harbor, the hub of shipping activity during the Netherlands' Golden Age. A collection of restored vessels is moored at the **Rijksmuseum Nederlands Scheepvaart** (State Museum of Netherlands Shipping), a former naval complex. ⊠ *Kattenburgerplein 1,* ☎ *020/5232321.* ▣ *Fl. 12.50.* ☉ *Mon.–Sat. 10–5, Sun. 1–5.*

Also in this area, a short stroll farther down the Kattenburgergracht-Wittenburgergracht to the footbridge over the canal leads to the **Museumwerf 't Kromhout** (Museum Wharf, the Kromhout). Many early steamships were built at this wharf, where models and motors are on display. ⊠ *Hoogte Kadijk 147,* ☎ *020/6276777.* ▣ *Fl. 3.50.* ☉ *Weekdays 10–4.*

About three blocks from Centraal Station, at **Haarlemmerstraat 75,** a plaque commemorates the occasion, in 1623, when the directors of the Dutch West India Company planned the founding of Nieuw Amsterdam on the southernmost tip of the island of Manhattan. In 1664, this colony was seized by the English and renamed New York.

An otherwise unremarkable building at **Singel 460** (near Herengracht) has special significance for Americans. In this building John Adams raised the first foreign loan ($2 million) for the United States from the banking house of Van Staphorst in 1782. Additional loans from this and other banks soon followed, for a total of $30 million—a gesture of Dutch confidence in the future of America.

Beer lovers—or anyone with an interest in the production of a world-class product—will want to take time to visit the **Heineken Ontvangstcentrum,** formerly the Heineken Brewery. The guided weekday tours (year-round 9:30 and 11, additional summer tours at 1 and 2:30) take in a slide presentation, the old brewery stables, and, of course, include free beer at the end of the tour. ⊠ *Stadhouderskade 78,* ☎ *020/5239666.* ▣ *Fl. 2. Children under 18 not admitted.*

Shopping

Amsterdam is a cornucopia of interesting markets, quirky specialty shops, antiques, art, and diamonds.

Gift Ideas

Diamonds. Since the 17th century, "Amsterdam cut" has been synonymous with perfection in the quality of diamonds. You can see this craftsmanship at any of the diamond-cutting houses. The cutters explain how the diamond's value depends on the four *c*s—carat, cut, clarity, and color—before encouraging you to buy. There is a cluster of diamond houses on the Rokin.

Porcelain. The Dutch have been producing Delft, Makkum, and other fine porcelain for centuries. **Focke and Meltzer** stores have been selling it since 1823. Available pieces range from affordable, newly painted tiles to expensive Delft blue-and-white pitchers. One store is near the Rijksmuseum (⊠ P. C. Hooftstraat 65–67, ☎ 020/6642311).

Shopping Districts

The Jordaan is a treasure trove of trendy small boutiques and unusual crafts shops, where the locals love to browse. **Leidsestraat, Kalverstraat,** and **Nieuwendijk** are Amsterdam's chief shopping districts, which have largely been turned into pedestrian-only areas. **Magna Plaza** shopping center, built inside the glorious old post office behind the Royal Palace, is *the* place for A-to-Z shopping in a huge variety of stores. **Nieuwe Spiegelstraat,** just a stone's throw from the Rijksmuseum, is Amsterdam's "antiques street," with smart shops for wealthy collectors, as well as old curiosity shops that sell a less expensive range. **P. C. Hooftstraat,** and also Van Baerlestraat and Beethovenstraat, are the homes of haute couture and other fine goods.

The Rokin is hectic with traffic and houses a cluster of boutiques and renowned antiques shops selling 18th- and 19th-century furniture, antique jewelry, Art Deco lamps, and statuettes. **Schiphol Airport** is Europe's best tax-free shopping center, so put aside a little extra time to look around when leaving the Netherlands.

Department Stores

De Bijenkorf (⊠ Dam Square), the city's number-one department store, is excellent for contemporary fashions and furnishings. **Maison de Bonneterie en Pander** (⊠ Rokin 140–142 and ⊠ Beethovenstraat 32) is the Queen Mother of department stores, gracious, genteel and understated. **Vroom and Dreesmann** (⊠ Kalverstraat 201), is a popular store with well-stocked departments carrying all manner of goods.

Markets

Antiekmarkt de Looier (⊠ Elandsgracht 109; Sun.–Wed. 11–5, Thurs. 11–9) is a bustling, bulging covered market that's great for antiques, especially silver and toys. During the summer, art lovers can buy etchings, drawings, and watercolors at the Sunday **art markets** on Thorbeckeplein and the Spui. An unusual **bird market** is held in the Noordermarkt on Saturday, though in recent years the number of participants has shrunk, and the bird vendors have been all but pushed aside by a general market. Amsterdam's lively **flea market** (Mon.–Sat. 9:30–4) on Waterlooplein around the Musiektheater is the ideal spot to search for second-hand clothes, inexpensive antiques, and all sorts of other curiosities. Locals and visitors alike come to the **floating flower market** (Mon.–Sat. 9:30–5) on the Singel to stock up on bulbs and cut flowers. Philatelists will not want to miss the small but choice **stamp market** (Wed. and Sat. 1–4) held on the Nieuwezijds Voorburgwal.

Dining

Amsterdammers are less creatures of habit than are the Dutch in general. Even so, set menus and early dinners are preferred by these health-conscious citizens. For travelers on a diet or a budget, the blue-and-white TOURIST MENU sign guarantees an economical (Fl. 25) yet imaginative set menu created by the head chef. For traditionalists, the NEDERLANDS DIS soup tureen sign is a promise of regional recipes and seasonal ingredients. "You can eat in any language" is the city's proud boast, so when Dutch restaurants are closed, Indonesian, Chinese, and Turkish restaurants are often open. For details and price-category definitions, *see* Dining *in* Staying in The Netherlands, *above.*

$$$$ ✕ **Excelsior.** The Hôtel de l'Europe's renowned restaurant offers a
★ varied menu of French cuisine that is based on local ingredients. There is a splendid array of seafood dishes as well as an elaborate vegetarian menu. Service is discreet and impeccable, and the Excelsior's view over the Amstel River, to the Muntplein on one side and the Music The-

ater on the other, is the best in Amsterdam. ⊠ *Nieuwe Doelenstraat 2–4,* ☎ *020/6234836. Reservations essential. Jacket and tie. AE, DC, MC, V. No lunch Sat.*

$$$$ ✕ **La Rive.** This world-class restaurant in the 125-year-old Amstel
★ Inter-Continental is fit for royalty. The French cuisine, with an awe-inspiring "truffle menu" of dishes prepared with exotic (and expensive) ingredients, can be tailored to meet your every whim. Epicureans should inquire about the "chef's table": With a group of six you can sit at a table alongside the open kitchen and watch chefs describe each of your courses as it is prepared. ⊠ *Professor Tulpplein 1,* ☎ *020/ 6226060. Jacket and tie. AE, DC, MC, V.*

$$$$ ✕ **'t Swarte Schaep.** The Black Sheep is named after a proverbial
★ 17th-century sheep that once roamed the area. With its creaking boards and array of copper pots, the interior is reminiscent of a ship's cabin. The Dutch chef uses seasonal ingredients to create classical French dishes with regional flourishes. Dinner orders are accepted until 11 PM—unusually late even for Amsterdam. ⊠ *Korte Leidsedwarsstraat 24,* ☎ *020/6223021. Reservations essential. Jacket and tie. AE, DC, MC, V.*

$$$ ✕ **De Silveren Spiegel.** In an alarmingly crooked 17th-century house,
★ you can have an outstanding meal while you enjoy the personal attention of the owner at one of just a small cluster of tables. Local ingredients such as Texel lamb and wild rabbit are cooked with subtlety and flair. ⊠ *Kattengat 4–6,* ☎ *020/6246589. Jacket and tie. AE, MC, V.*

$$$ ✕ **Le Tout Court.** This small, meticulously appointed restaurant features seasonal specialties (spring lamb, summer fruits, game during autumn and winter) personally prepared by owner-chef John Fagel, who hails from a well-known Dutch family of chefs. ⊠ *Runstraat 13,* ☎ *020/ 6258637. AE, DC, MC, V.*

$$$ ✕ **Yamazato.** Japanese expatriates laud this as the top Japanese restaurant in town. An award-winning chef blends the freshest local ingredients with exotica flown in daily from the Land of the Rising Sun. The full seasonal set menu will cost you more than Fl. 100, but there are scores of less pricey options. At a separate bar fresh sushi is prepared before your eyes. The adjoining Sazanka Restaurant specializes in *teppan yaki* (food grilled at the table). ⊠ *Hotel Okura, Ferdinand Bolstraat 333,* ☎ *020/6787111. Jacket and tie. AE, DC, MC, V.*

$$–$$$ ✕ **Eerst Klas.** Amsterdam's best-kept secret is in the most obvious of places: the former first-class waiting lounge of the central train station. Classic dark-wood paneling and soft interior lighting create the perfect hideaway from the city's hustle and bustle. Diners munch their way through tasty salads, steaks, and fish dishes. ⊠ *Stationsplein 15, Spoor 2b,* ☎ *020/6250131. Jacket and tie. AE, DC, MC, V.*

$$–$$$ ✕ **Lonny's.** Lonny Gerungan's family have been cooks on Bali for gen-
★ erations–even preparing banquets for visiting Dutch royals. His plush restaurant in Amsterdam, draped in silky fabrics, serves the finest authentic Indonesian cuisine. Even the simplest rijsttafel is a feast of over 15 delicately spiced dishes. ⊠ *Rozengracht 46-48,* ☎ *020/6238950. Reservations essential. AE, DC, MC, V.*

$$–$$$ ✕ **Lucius.** Outstanding fish and seafood are simply served in a plain setting. Choices range from fish burgers with Gorgonzola to grilled lobster. This may not be the place for the queasy, though—as you tuck into your fish, its live cousins eye you from a tank along the wall. ⊠ *Spuistraat 247,* ☎ *020/6241831. AE, DC, MC, V. Closed Sun.*

$$–$$$ ✕ **Oesterbar.** The Oyster Bar specializes in seafood, grilled, baked, or fried. The upstairs dining room is more formal than the downstairs bistro, but prices don't vary. Salmon, monkfish, and halibut are favorite seafood entrées; oysters are a good, if pricey, appetizer. ⊠ *Leidseplein 10,* ☎ *020/6232988. AE, DC, MC, V.*

$$–$$$ ✕ **Pier 10.** Perched on the end of a pier behind Centraal Station is this
★ intimate restaurant built in the '30s as a shipping office. Water laps
gently just beneath the windows, and the harbor lights twinkle in the
distance. The chef's special salads are lavish affairs, and other culinary
adventures might include a handsome platter of dove, duck, and partridge with cranberry sauce. ✉ *De Ruyterkade Steiger 10,* ☎ *020/
6248276. Reservations essential. AE, MC, V.*

$$ ✕ **Haesje Claes.** Traditional Dutch food is served in a traditional
Dutch environment, with prices that are easy on the wallet; it sounds
like a tourist's dream and, in ways, it is. There's a cozy feeling and a
relaxed simplicity. Dining choices can be as basic as *stamppot* (mixed
potatoes and sauerkraut) or as elaborate as filet of salmon with lob-
ster sauce; a tourist menu is an option, too. ✉ *Spuistraat 273–275,*
☎ *020/6249998. Reservations advised. AE, DC, MC, V.*

$$ ✕ **Rose's Cantina.** This perennial favorite of the sparkling set offers
spicy Tex-Mex food, lethal cocktails, and a high noise level. Pop in for
a full meal or a late afternoon drink. ✉ *Reguliersdwarsstraat 38,* ☎
020/6259797. Weekend reservations essential. AE, DC, MC, V.

$$ ✕ **Toscanini.** This cavernous, noisy Italian restaurant has superb cui-
★ sine. Try the pasta with game sauce, the scrumptious selection of an-
tipasti, the rabbit, or the fresh fish dishes. ✉ *Lindengracht 75,* ☎ *020/
6232813. Reservations essential. No credit cards. No lunch.*

$ ✕ **De Keuken van 1870.** "The Kitchen of 1870" was a soup kitchen
through the Great Depression and two world wars and now serves up
hearty Dutch food at unbeatably low prices. Plates are borne from the
steamy kitchen piled high with good, nutritious meat and vegetables
doused in gravy. ✉ *Spuistraat 4,* ☎ *020/6248965. Reservations not
accepted. AE, DC, MC, V.*

$ ✕ **Eettuin.** This "eating garden" in the heart of the arty Jordaan area
has something for everyone—from vegetarian dishes to spare ribs and
the house special, pork. Unusual for Europe is the salad bar. ✉ *Tweede
Tuindwarsstraat 10,* ☎ *020/6237706. No credit cards. No lunch.*

$ ✕ **Pancake Bakery.** Here's a chance to try a traditionally Dutch way
of keeping eating costs down. The name of the game is pancakes—for
every course including dessert, for which the topping can be ice cream,
fruit, or liqueur. The Pancake Bakery is not far from the Anne Frankhuis.
✉ *Prinsengracht 191,* ☎ *020/6251333. Reservations not accepted. AE,
MC, DC, V.*

Lodging

Accommodations are tight from Easter to summer, so early booking
is advised. Since few hotels have parking lots, cars are best abandoned
in a multistory parking ramp for the duration of your stay. Many vis-
itors like to stay inside the concentric ring of canals, an atmospheric
area of historic gable-roof merchants' houses. Others prefer the qui-
eter museum quarter, convenient for the Rijksmuseum and near enough
to the Vondelpark for jogging. For details and price-category defini-
tions, *see* Lodging *in* Staying in The Netherlands, *above.*

$$$$ ▦ **Amstel Inter-Continental.** Amsterdam's grande dame opened in 1867
★ and was spectacularly renovated in late 1992; the completely new in-
terior creates a Dutch atmosphere with a European touch. The spa-
cious rooms have Oriental rugs, brocade upholstery, Delft lamps, and
a color scheme that borrows from the warm tones of Makkum pot-
tery. The Amstel is frequented by many of the nation's top business-
people and visited at times by the royal family. ✉ *Professor Tulpplein
1, 1018 GX,* ☎ *020/6226060,* FAX *020/6225808. 79 rooms with bath.
2 restaurants, pool, exercise room. AE, DC, MC, V.*

$$$$ 🏨 **Golden Tulip Barbizon Palace.** The newest Golden Tulip hotel in Amsterdam combines past and present with fantasy and flair. The exterior blends in with neighboring old houses; inside, a towering atrium stretches across the length of the hotel. Rooms are small but are decorated nicely. ⊠ *Prins Hendrikkade 59–72, 1012 AD,* ☎ *020/5564564,* 𝔽𝔸𝕏 *020/6243353. 263 rooms with bath, 5 suites. 2 restaurants, exercise room. AE, DC, MC, V.*

$$$$ 🏨 **Grand Amsterdam.** In 1991, Amsterdam's former city hall was converted into a luxury hotel. Parts of the building date from the 16th century, but most of it belongs to the early 20th, when the country's best artists and architects were commissioned to create a building the city could be proud of. The rooms are pamperingly luxurious and the kitchens are supervised by the incomparable Albert Roux. ⊠ *Oudezijds Voorburgwal 197, 1001 EX,* ☎ *020/5553111,* 𝔽𝔸𝕏 *020/5553222. 182 rooms with bath. Restaurant, spa. AE, DC, MC, V.*

$$$$ 🏨 **Hôtel de l'Europe.** Behind the stately facade of this 100-year-old hotel
★ is a full complement of modern facilities. The rooms are larger than is usual for Amsterdam, and each is decorated according to its shape and location. Bright rooms overlooking the Amstel are done in pastel colors; others have warm, rich colors and antiques. Apart from its world-renowned Excelsior restaurant (☞ Dining, *above*), the hotel houses a sophisticated leisure complex. ⊠ *Nieuwe Doelenstraat 2–8, 1021 CP,* ☎ *020/6234836,* 𝔽𝔸𝕏 *020/6242962. 100 rooms with bath. Restaurant, pool, sauna, exercise room. AE, DC, MC, V.*

$$$ 🏨 **Grand Hotel Krasnapolsky.** This fine Old World hotel is enhanced by the Winter Garden restaurant, which dates from 1818. During 1995, the hotel expanded into the building next door, increasing its size by half and replacing the bland decor with stylish period furnishings. The cosmopolitan atmosphere carries through all the rooms, with decor ranging from Victorian to Art Deco. ⊠ *Dam 9, 1012 JS,* ☎ *020/5549111,* 𝔽𝔸𝕏 *020/6228607. 429 rooms with bath. Restaurant. AE, DC, MC, V.*

$$$ 🏨 **Pulitzer.** The Pulitzer is one of Europe's most ambitious hotel restora-
★ tions, using the shells of a row of 17th-century merchants' houses. Inside, the refined atmosphere is sustained by the modern art gallery, the lovingly restored brickwork, oak beams, and split-level rooms—no two are alike. Redecoration during 1996 replaced much of the modern furniture with pieces in a more appropriate period style. ⊠ *Prinsengracht 315–331, 1016 GZ Amsterdam,* ☎ *020/5235235,* 𝔽𝔸𝕏 *020/6276753. 213 rooms with bath, 7 suites, 5 apartments. Restaurant, bar. AE, DC, MC, V.*

$$ 🏨 **Ambassade.** With its beautiful canal-side location, its Louis XV–style
★ decoration, and its Oriental rugs, the Ambassade seems more like a stately home than a hotel. Service is attentive and room prices include breakfast. For other meals, the neighborhood has a good choice of restaurants. ⊠ *Herengracht 341, 1016 AZ,* ☎ *020/6262333,* 𝔽𝔸𝕏 *020/6245321. 49 rooms with bath. Lobby lounge. AE, DC, MC, V.*

$$ 🏨 **Atlas Hotel.** Renowned for its friendly atmosphere, this small hotel has moderate-size rooms decorated in art nouveau style. It's also handy for Museumplein, whose museums are within easy walking distance. ⊠ *Van Eeghenstraat 64, 1071 GK,* ☎ *020/6766336,* 𝔽𝔸𝕏 *020/6717633. 23 rooms with bath. Restaurant, bar. AE, DC, MC, V.*

$$ 🏨 **Het Canal House.** The American owners of this canal-side hotel opt for antiques rather than televisions as furnishings. Spacious rooms overlook the canal or the illuminated garden. A hearty Dutch breakfast is included in the price. ⊠ *Keizergracht 148, 1015 CX,* ☎ *020/6225182,* 𝔽𝔸𝕏 *020/6241317. 26 rooms with bath or shower. Breakfast room. AE, DC, MC, V.*

$$ ⊞ **Hotel de Filosoof.** This hotel on a quiet street near Vondelpark attracts artists, thinkers, and people looking for something a little unusual. Each room is decorated in a different cultural motif—there's an Aristotle room, and a Goethe room adorned with texts from *Faust*. ⊠ *Anna van den Vondelstraat 6, 1054 GZ,* ☎ *020/6833013,* FAX *020/6853750. 29 rooms, 25 with bath. Bar. AE, MC, V.*

$–$$ ⊞ **Agora.** The cheerful bustle of the nearby Singel flower market is re-
★ flected in this small hotel in an 18th-century house. Rooms are light and spacious, some decorated with vintage furniture; the best overlook the canal or the university. The Agora has a considerate staff, and a relaxed neighborhood ensures the hotel's popularity. Book well in advance. ⊠ *Singel 462, 1017 AW,* ☎ *020/6272200,* FAX *020/6272202. 15 rooms, 11 with bath or shower. AE, DC, MC, V.*

$–$$ ⊞ **Hotel Seven Bridges.** Named for the scene beyond its front steps, this small canal-house hotel has rooms decorated with individual flair. Oriental rugs are laid on wooden floors, and there are comfy antique armchairs and marble washstands. The Rembrandtsplein is nearby. For a stunning view, request a canal-side room. ⊠ *Reguliersgracht 31, 1017 RK,* ☎ *020/6231329. 6 rooms with bath. AE, MC, V.*

$ ⊞ **Amstel Botel.** This floating hotel moored near Centraal Station is an appropriate place to stay in watery Amsterdam. The rooms are small, but the windows are large, with fine views across the water to the city. Make sure you don't get a room on the land side of the vessel, or you'll end up staring at an ugly postal sorting office. ⊠ *Oosterdokskade 224, 1011 AE,* ☎ *020/6264247,* FAX *020/6391952. 176 rooms with shower. Bar. AE, DC, MC, V.*

$ ⊞ **Quentin Hotel.** A stone's throw from the hectic Leidseplein is the small, family-run Quentin. It is simply decorated with pale colors and modern prints, and flooded with light through large windows. The best rooms are the spacious corner ones that overlook a canal. The overnight price doesn't include breakfast, but there is a 24-hour bar and snack service. ⊠ *Leidsekade 89, 1017 PN,* ☎ *020/6262187,* FAX *020/6220121. 24 rooms, 19 with shower and toilet. AE, DC, MC, V.*

The Arts

The arts flourish in cosmopolitan Amsterdam. The best sources of information about performances are the monthly publications *Time Out Amsterdam* (in English) and *Uit Krant* (in Dutch) and the biweekly *What's On in Amsterdam,* which you can get at the tourist office, where you can also secure tickets for the more popular events. Tickets must be booked in person from Monday to Saturday, 10 to 4. You also can book at the **Amsterdam Uit Buro** (⊠ Stadsschouwburg, Leidseplein 26, ☎ 020/6211211).

Classical Music
Classical music is featured at the **Concertgebouw** (⊠ Concertgebouwplein 2–6), home of one of Europe's finest orchestras. A smaller auditorium in the same building is used for chamber music, recitals, and even jam sessions. While ticket prices for international orchestras are fairly high, most concerts are good values and the Wednesday lunchtime concerts are free. The box office is open from 9:30 to 7; you can make telephone bookings (020/6718345) from 10 to 5.

Opera and Ballet
The Dutch national ballet and opera companies are housed in the new **Muziektheater** (☎ 020/6255455) on Waterlooplein. Guest companies from foreign countries perform here during the three-week Holland Festival in June.

Theater

Young American comedians living in Amsterdam have created **Boomtown Chicago** (⊠ Korte Leidsedwarsstraat 12, ☎ 020/4221776), improvised comedy with a local touch. You can munch pizzas and salad during performances. For experimental theater and colorful cabaret in Dutch, catch the shows at **Felix Meritis House** (⊠ Keizersgracht 324, ☎ 020/6231311).

Film

The largest concentration of movie theaters is around Leidseplein and near Muntplein. Most foreign films are subtitled rather than dubbed, which makes Amsterdam a great place to catch up on movies you missed at home. The **City 1–7** theater (⊠ Kleine Garmanplantsoen 13–25, ☎ 020/6234579) near Leidseplein is the biggest (seven screens) in the city. The Art Deco–era **Tuschinski** (⊠ Reguliersbreestraat 26, ☎ 020/6262633) is the most beautiful cinema house.

Nightlife

Amsterdam has a wide variety of dance clubs, bars, and exotic shows. The more respectable—and expensive—after-dark activities are in and around Leidseplein and Rembrandtsplein; fleshier productions are on Oudezijds Achterburgwal and Thorbeckeplein. Most bars and clubs are open every night from 5 PM to 2 AM or 5 AM. On weeknights, very few clubs charge admission, though the more lively ones sometimes ask for a "club membership" fee of Fl. 20 or more.

Bars

De Jaren (⊠ Nieuwe Doelenstraat 20, ☎ 020/6255771) is a spacious café with a canal-side terrace. The smart young business set comes in for a drink after work; arts and media people use it as a communal sitting room; and the trendy pass through on their way out nightclubbing.

Jazz Clubs

Bimhuis (⊠ Oude Schans 73–77, ☎ 020/6233373, ☉ Thurs.–Sat. from 9 PM), set in a converted warehouse, has long offered the best jazz and improvised music in town. Ticket holders can sit in the adjoining BIM café and enjoy a magical view across the Oude Schans. At the **Joseph Lam Jazz Club** (⊠ Van Diemenstraat 242, ☎ 020/6228086), locals and visitors cram in on Saturday nights for an evening of traditional and Dixieland jazz.

Rock Clubs

Paradiso (⊠ Weteringschans 6–8, ☎ 020/6264521) is an Amsterdam institution; converted from a church, it has become a vibrant venue for rock, New Age, and even contemporary classical music.

Dance Clubs

Mostly only hidden in cellars around the Leidseplein, the dance clubs fill up after midnight. The cavernous **Escape** (⊠ Rembrandtsplein 11–15, ☎ 020/6221111) has shrugged off its mainstream image and taken on a much hipper mantle. **It** (⊠ Amstelstraat 24, ☎ 020/6250111) is generally gay on Friday and Saturday. It's straight on Thursday and Friday—but could never be accused of being straitlaced.

Roxy (⊠ Singel 465, ☎ 020/6200354) is the current hot spot, though you need to be a member or impressively dressed to get in. **Seymour Likely Too** (⊠ Nieuwezijd Voorburgwal 161, ☎ 020/4205663) was opened by a group of artists in the wake of their success with the Seymour Likely Lounge, a popular bar across the road. This club is guaranteed to have a lively, trendy crowd hopping to the latest music.

Casinos

Holland Casino (✉ Max Euweplein 62, ☎ 020/6201006), just off Leidseplein, has blackjack, roulette, and slot machines in elegant, canalside surrounds. You'll need your passport to get in; the minimum age is 18.

Gay and Lesbian Bars

Amsterdam has a vibrant gay and lesbian community, concentrated principally on Warmoesstraat, Reguliersdwarsstraat, Amstelstraat, and Kerkstraat near Leidseplein. The **Gay & Lesbian Switchboard** (☎ 020/6236565) has friendly operators who provide information on the city's nightlife and other advice for gay or lesbian visitors.

HISTORIC HOLLAND

This circular itinerary can be followed clockwise or counterclockwise. Highlights are the historic towns of Leiden and Utrecht and the major museums in Haarlem; in between these towns, you'll see some of the Netherlands' windmill-dotted landscape and pass through centers of tulip growing and cheese production.

Getting Around

The most convenient way to cover the following itinerary is by rented car out of Amsterdam. If you want someone else to do the navigating, then all the towns listed below can be reached by bus or train. From Amsterdam there are, for example, three direct trains per hour to Haarlem, Leiden, and Utrecht. Check with the tourist office in Amsterdam for help in planning your trip, or inquire at Centraal Station.

Guided Tours

Alternatively, these towns are covered, in various combinations, by organized bus tours out of Amsterdam. Brochures for tour operators are available from the **VVV Amsterdam Tourist Offices** at Stationsplein 10 or Leidseplein 1; the central telephone number is 06/34034066.

The VVV office in Utrecht organizes several excursions, including a boat trip along the canals and a sightseeing flight over the city. There are also day trips to country estates, castles, and gardens.

Visitor Information

Amersfoort (✉ Stationsplein 9–11, ☎ 033/4635151).
Apeldoorn (✉ Stationstraat 72, ☎ 06/91681636).
Gouda (✉ Markt 27, ☎ 0182/513666).
Haarlem (✉ Stationsplein 1, ☎ 06/32024043).
Leiden (✉ Stationsplein 210, ☎ 071/5146846).
Lisse (✉ Grachtweg 53a, ☎ 0252/414262).
Utrecht (✉ Vredenburg 90, ☎ 06/34034085).

Exploring Historic Holland

Amersfoort

Traveling southeast from Amsterdam, 90 kilometers (56 miles) along highway A1, you will reach Apeldoorn; but if you have time, stop off at **Amersfoort** en route. Although today it is a major industrial town, Amersfoort still manages to retain much of its medieval character and charm. Starting at the **Koppelport,** the imposing water gate across the Eem that dates from 1400, walk down Kleine Spui. On the right is **St. Pieters-en-Bloklands Gasthuis,** a hospice founded in 1390. Close by is the **Museum Flehite,** with its unusual medieval collections that give a fascinating insight into the history of the town. There's a large model

Historic Holland

of the Old Town. ⊠ *Westsingel 50,* ☎ *033/4619987.* ☞ *Fl. 7.50 summer, Fl. 5 winter.* ⊙ *Tues.–Fri. 10–5, weekends 2–5.*

Continuing along Breestraat, you'll come to the graceful, 335-foot-high **Onze Lieve Vrouwetoren** (Tower of Our Lady). The musical chimes of this Gothic church can be heard every Friday between 10 and 11 AM. Turning left down Langstraat, past the Gothic **St. Joriskerk,** you will come to the **Kamperbinnenpoort,** the turreted land gate dating from the 15th century. Making your way left down Muurhuizen, you'll come to a short canal, the **Hovik,** which was once the old harbor.

Apeldoorn

★ The main attraction at **Apeldoorn** is the **Rijksmuseum Paleis Het Loo.** This former royal palace was built in the late-17th century for William III and has been beautifully restored to illustrate the domestic surroundings enjoyed by the House of Orange for more than three centuries. The museum, which is housed in the stables, has a fascinating collection of royal memorabilia, including cars and carriages, furniture and photographs, silver and ceramics. The formal gardens and the surrounding parkland have attractive walks. ⊠ *Koninklijk Park 1,* ☎ *055/5772400.* ☞ *Fl. 12.50.* ⊙ *Tues.–Sun. 10–5.*

★ From Apeldoorn, travel 5 kilometers (3 miles) on N304 to the **Kröller-Muller Museum.** In the woods in the middle of a national park, the museum displays one of the finest collections of modern art in the world. It possesses 278 works by Vincent van Gogh, as well as paintings, drawings, and sculptures by such masters as Seurat, Redon, Braque, Picasso, and Mondrian. The building, too, is part of the experience; it seems to bring the museum's wooded setting right into the galleries with you. The major sculptures are shown in the garden; don't miss them. ⊠ *National Park De Hoge Veluwe,* ☎ *0318/591041.* ☞ *Fl. 7.50.* ⊙ *Tues.–Sun. 10–5. Sculpture garden closes ½ hr earlier and is closed Nov.–Mar.*

Arnhem

If you have children in tow, consider a visit to the **Nederlands Open-lucht Museum** (Open-Air Museum) in **Arnhem,** 15 kilometers (9 miles) from Apeldoorn on A90. In a 44-acre park, the curators have brought together original buildings and furnishings from all over the Netherlands to establish a comprehensive display of Dutch rural architectural styles and depict traditional ways of living. There are farmhouses and barns, workshops, and windmills—animals, too. ✉ *Schelmseweg 89,* ☎ *026/3576111.* ▭ *Fl. 16.* ☉ *Apr.–Oct., daily 10–5.*

Utrecht

The city of **Utrecht** is 72 kilometers (44 miles) west of Apeldoorn. The gabled houses of Nieuwegracht, the canals with their water gates, the 13th-century wharves and storage cellars of Oudegracht, and the superb churches and museums are just some of the city's key attractions, most of which are on the main cathedral square. The **Domkerk** is a late-Gothic cathedral with a series of fine stained-glass windows. The **Domtoren** (cathedral tower) opposite was connected to the cathedral until a hurricane hit in 1674. The bell tower is the country's tallest, and its 465 steep steps lead to a magnificent view. A guide is essential in the tower's labyrinth of steps and passageways. ✉ *Domplein,* ☎ *030/2310403.* ▭ *Domkerk: free.* ☉ *Tours on the hr (Fl. 2.25); May–Sept., weekdays 10–5, Sat. 10–3:30, Sun. 2–4; Oct.–Apr., weekdays 11–4, Sat. 11–3:30, Sun. 2–4.* ▭ *Domtoren: Fl. 4.* ☉ *Apr.–Oct., weekdays 10–5, weekends noon–5; Nov.–Mar., weekends noon–5.*

★ Not far from the cathedral is the merry **Rijksmuseum van Speelklok tot Pierement** (National Museum of Mechanical Musical Instruments) devoted solely to music machines—from music boxes to street organs and even musical chairs. During the guided tour, music students play some of the instruments. The museum is housed in Utrecht's oldest parish church. ✉ *Buurkerkhof 10,* ☎ *030/2312789.* ▭ *Fl. 7.50.* ☉ *Tues.–Sat. 10–5, Sun. 1–5.*

Behind the museum is **Pieterskerk,** the country's oldest Romanesque church, built in 1048. The grandeur of the city's churches reflects the fact that Utrecht was Holland's religious center during the Middle Ages. Most churches are open in summer and a church concert is held almost every day.

Walk south out of Domplein, down Lange Nieuwstraat. Halfway down is the **Rijksmuseum Het Catharijneconvent.** In addition to its collection of holy relics and vestments, this museum contains the country's largest display of medieval art. ✉ *Nieuwegracht 63,* ☎ *030/2317296.* ▭ *Fl. 6.* ☉ *Tues.–Fri. 10–5, weekends 11–5.*

There are more museums on Agnietenstraat, which crosses Lange Nieuwstraat. The **Centraal Museum** houses a rich collection of contemporary art and other city exhibits. Amid the clutter is a Viking ship (discovered in 1930) and a 17th-century dollhouse with period furniture, porcelain, and miniature old master paintings. ✉ *Agnietenstraat 1,* ☎ *030/2362362.* ▭ *Fl. 6.* ☉ *Tues.–Sat. 10–5, Sun. noon–5.*

An important part of the museum's collection is a house that is a 15-minute walk away in Utrecht's eastern suburbs, the **Rietveld-Schröder House.** In 1924 architect Gerrit Rietveld, working with Truus Schröder, designed what is considered to be the architectural pinnacle of de Stijl (The Style). The use of primary colors (red, yellow, blue) and black and white, as well as the definition of interior space, is unique and innovative even today. The experience of the house is, as one art historian phrased it, "like wandering into a Mondrian painting." ✉ *Prins Hen-*

driklaan 50a, ☎ *030/2362310.* 🖃 *Fl. 9.* ☉ *Wed.–Sat. 11–4.30, Sun. 1.30–4.30. Call for appointment.*

Gouda

West of Utrecht, 36 kilometers (22 miles) along the A12, you'll come to **Gouda,** famous for its cheese. On Thursday mornings in July and August, the cheese market is held in front of the ornate Baroque **Waag,** or Weigh House. Brightly colored farm wagons are loaded high with cheeses. From April to October, the Weigh House is open to visitors.

★ Take a good look at the **Stadhuis** (Town Hall), parts of which date from 1449 (🖃 Fl. 1, ☉ Weekdays 10–noon and 2–4, Sat. 11–3). After trying all five types of Gouda cheese, leave some space for syrup waffles, the city's other culinary specialty.

★ By the side of the market square is **Sint Janskerk** (Church of St. John); what you see today was built in the 16th century. It has the longest nave in the country and 70 glorious stained-glass windows, the oldest of which is from 1555. Around the corner from the cathedral is the Catharina Gasthuis, now the **Stedelijk Museum Het Catharina Gasthuis,** the municipal museum that houses many unusual exhibits, including a fearsome medieval torture chamber and an equally horrific operating room. ✉ *Oosthaven 9, Achter de Kerk 14,* ☎ *0182/588440.* 🖃 *Fl. 4.* ☉ *Mon.–Sat. 10–5, Sun. noon–5.*

Leiden

Heading north on N11, you'll come to the ancient city of **Leiden,** renowned for its spirit of religious and intellectual tolerance and known for its university and royal connections. Start at the **De Lakenhal,** built in 1639 for the city's cloth merchants and now an art gallery and textile and antiques museum. Pride of place in the collection goes to the 16th- and 17th-century Dutch paintings, with works by Steen, Dou, Rembrandt, and, above all, Lucas van Leyden's *Last Judgment*—the first great Renaissance painting executed in what is now the Netherlands. Other rooms are devoted to furniture and to the history of Leiden's medieval guilds: the drapers, tailors, and brewers. ✉ *Oude Singel 32,* ☎ *071/5165361.* 🖃 *Fl. 5.* ☉ *Tues.–Fri. 10–5, weekends noon–5.*

★ ☾ Near the De Lakenhal is the **Molenmuseum de Valk** (Windmill Museum), housed in a windmill built in 1747, which was worked by 10 generations of millers until 1964. The seven floors contain the original workings, an old forge, and living quarters. ✉ *2e Binnenvestgracht 1,* ☎ *071/5165353.* 🖃 *Fl. 5.* ☉ *Tues.–Sat. 10–5, Sun. 1–5.*

Crossing the canal and walking into bustling Breestraat and then down the narrow Pieterskerk-Choorsteeg, you'll come to the imposing **St. Pieterskerk,** with its memories of the Pilgrim Fathers who worshiped here and of their spiritual leader, John Robinson, who is buried here. A narrow street by the **Persijnhofje** almshouse, dating from 1683, takes you downhill to the gracious, tree-lined Rapenburg canal, crossed by triple-arch bridges and bordered by stately 18th-century houses. To the right is the **Rijksmuseum van Oudheden** (National Museum of Antiquities), the country's leading archaeological museum. The prize exhibit is the entire 1st-century AD Temple of Taffeh, donated by the Egyptian government. There is also a floor devoted to finds in the Netherlands. ✉ *Rapenburg 28,* ☎ *071/5163163.* 🖃 *Fl. 5; Fl. 3 surcharge for special exhibitions.* ☉ *Tues.–Sat. 10–5, Sun. noon–5.*

On the other side of the canal, a little farther down, you find the **Academie** (university) and its **Hortus Botanicus** gardens. The university was founded by William the Silent as a reward to Leiden for its victory against the Spanish in the 1573–74 siege. During the war, the dikes were opened and the countryside flooded so that the rescuing navy could sail right up to the city walls. Founded in 1587, the botanical gardens are among the oldest in the world. The highlights are a faithful reconstruction of a 16th-century garden, an herb garden, a colorful orangery, and ancient trees. ⊠ *Rapenburg 73,* ☎ *071/5277249.* ⌑ *Garden: Fl. 5.* ☉ *Apr.–Oct., Mon.–Sat. 10–5, Sun. 11–5; Nov.–Mar., Mon.–Fri. 10–5, Sun. 11–5.*

At press time, the **Pilgrim Fathers Documentatie Centrum** (Vliet 45, ☎ 071/5120191) was closed. This center contained documents and maps related to the Pilgrims during their stay in Leiden, before they went to Delftshaven on the first stage of their arduous voyage to the New World. People interested in the Pilgrims may visit the Public Reading Room of the **City Record Office,** where there are photocopies of documents and other material. ⊠ *Dolhuissteeg 7,* ☎ *071/5120191 or 071/5165355.* ☉ *Weekdays 9:30–5, Sat. 9–12:15.*

Lisse/Aalsmeer

North from Leiden toward Haarlem, you can stop to visit (in spring ★ only) the **Keukenhof,** a 70-acre park and greenhouse complex that is planted each year to create a special exhibition of flowering bulbs. The world's largest flower show draws huge spring crowds to its regimental lines of tulips, hyacinths, and daffodils. (A lazier way to see the flowers is from the windows of the Leiden–Haarlem train.) ⊠ *Lisse,* ☎ *0252/465555.* ⌑ *Fl. 16.* ☉ *Late Mar.–late May, daily 8–7:30.*

During the rest of the year, or as a complement to a spring visit to Keukenhof, you can see how flowers are marketed. Flowers are big business to the Dutch, and the Netherlands has the world's largest complex of flower auction houses. The biggest of these facilities (it also is the single largest in the world) is the **Bloemenveiling** (Flower Auction) in Aalsmeer, near the national airport and not far from Amsterdam. In a building the size of three football fields, there are three auction rooms functioning at the same time. Get there early; it's all over by 10 AM. ⊠ *Legmeerdijk 313,* ☎ *0297/334567.* ☉ *Weekdays 7:30 AM–11:30 AM. Closed weekends and holidays.*

Haarlem

With buildings notable for their secret inner courtyards and pointed gables, **Haarlem** can resemble a 17th-century canvas, even one painted by Frans Hals, the city's greatest painter. The area around the **Grote Markt,** the market square, provides an architectural stroll through the 17th and 18th centuries. Some of the facades are adorned with such homilies as "The body's sickness is a cure for the soul." Haarlem's religious faith can also be sensed in any of its 20 almshouses. The **Stadhuis** was once a hunting lodge. Nearby is the **Vleeshal,** or meat market, which has an especially fine gabled front. This dates from the early 1600s and is now used as an art gallery and a museum of local history. ⊠ *Lepelstraat.* ⌑ *Fl. 4.* ☉ *Mon.–Sat. 11–5, Sun. 1–5.*

★ Across from the Vleeshal is the **Grote Kerk,** dedicated to St. Bavo. The church, built between 1400 and 1550, houses one of Europe's most famous organs. This massive instrument has 5,000 pipes and was played by both Mozart and Handel. It is still used for concerts, and an annual organ festival is held here in July. ⊠ *Grote Markt,* ☎ *023/5330877.* ⌑ *Fl. 250.* ☉ *Apr.–Aug., Mon.–Sat. 10–4; Sept.–Mar., Mon.–Sat. 10–3:30.*

Make your way down Damstraat, behind the Grote Kerk, and turn left ★ at the **Waag** (Weigh House). On the left is the **Teylers Museum,** which claims to be the oldest museum in the country. It was founded by a wealthy merchant in 1778 as a museum of science and the arts; it now houses a fine collection of the Hague school of painting as well as drawings and sketches by Michelangelo, Raphael, and other non-Dutch masters. Since the canvases in this building are shown in natural light, try to see the museum on a sunny day. ⊠ *Spaarne 16,* ☎ *023/5319010.* ☑ *Fl. 6.50.* ۞ *Tues.–Sat. 10–5, Sun. 1–5.*

Follow the Binnen Spaarn and turn right onto Kampervest and then onto Gasthuisvest. On your right, on Groot Heiligland, you'll find the **Frans Hals Museum.** This museum, in what used to be a 17th-century hospice, contains a marvelous collection of the artist's work; his paintings of the guilds of Haarlem are particularly noteworthy. The museum also has works by Hals's contemporaries. ⊠ *Groot Heiligland 62,* ☎ *023/5319180.* ☑ *Fl. 7.50.* ۞ *Mon.–Sat. 11–5, Sun. 1–5.*

Dining and Lodging

In towns such as Apeldoorn and Gouda, which have few good hotels, B&B accommodations, booked through the VVV tourist office, make more interesting choices. Rooms in Utrecht are often in short supply, so book in advance or immediately upon arrival. For details and price-category definitions, *see* Dining *and* Lodging *in* Staying in The Netherlands, *above.*

Apeldoorn

$$$$ ✕ **De Echoput.** Near Het Loo, this delightful restaurant is a member of the Alliance Gastronomique Nederlandaise, a guarantee of an excellent meal. Game from the surrounding forest is a specialty. There is an attractive terrace, overlooking fountains and greenery, for summer dining. ⊠ *Amersfoortseweg 86,* ☎ *055/5191248. Reservations essential. Jacket and tie. AE, DC, MC, V. Closed Mon. No lunch Sat.*

$$$ ▥ **Bilderberg Hotel de Keizerskroon.** A perfect complement to the nearby royal palace is a stay at the Keizerskroon ("Emperor's Crown"). In style and amenities it is a business hotel; in comfort and cordiality, a traveler's hotel; in setting—at the edge of the city on a quiet street leading toward the woods—a weekend getaway inn. ⊠ *Koningstraat 7, 7315 HR,* ☎ *055/5217744,* ☒ *055/5214737. 100 rooms with bath. Restaurant, pool, sauna, exercise room. AE, DC, MC, V.*

Gouda

$$ ✕ **Goudsche Salon.** Wooden floors, a big table of newspapers and magazines, and a friendly atmosphere combine with tasty cuisine to make this an ideal place for lunch or dinner. There are salads and a good-value, seasonally changing set menu that might include such delights as peppery rabbit stew. ⊠ *Wijdstraat 13,* ☎ *0182/512330. MC, V.*

Haarlem

$$ ✕ **Café Restaurant Brinkman.** This elegant, classic grand café overlooks the magnificent Grote Kerk. You can while away the afternoon over a single coffee or choose from a wide menu of casseroles and grills with salad. ⊠ *Grote Markt 9–13,* ☎ *023/5323111. AE, DC, MC, V.*

$$$ ▥ **Golden Tulip Lion d'Or.** Just five minutes from the old city center and conveniently near the railway station, this comfortable but unprepossessing hotel offers all the luxuries associated with a Golden Tulip hotel. Special weekend deals include reduced room rates, gourmet evening meals, and free cocktails. ⊠ *Kruisweg 34–36, 2011 LC,* ☎ *023/5321750,* ☒ *023/5329543. 36 rooms with bath. Restaurant, meeting rooms. AE, DC, MC, V.*

Leiden

$$ ✕ **Jill's.** A delightful, bright restaurant just a few minutes' walk from the De Valk windmill, this spot is ideal for a relaxing meal. A variety of set menus with mainly French flavors but with Italian, Asian, and Dutch influences means that there is something to satisfy almost every palate. Fresh fish is served daily. ⊠ *Morsstraat 6,* ☎ *071/5143722. AE, DC, MC, V.*

$–$$ ✕ **Annie's Verjaardag.** A low, vaulted cellar full of cheery students and a water-level canal-side terrace make Annie's popular in all weather. There is a modest but well-prepared selection of salads and baguettes and usually at least one more substantial daily special, such as mussels or breast of wild goose with chestnuts. ⊠ *Oude Rijn 1a,* ☎ *071/5125737. Reservations not accepted. No credit cards.*

$–$$ ✕🏨 **Nieuw Minerva.** This family-run hotel, a bit worn in places, is a conversion of eight 15th-century buildings. The original part of the hotel is decorated in Old Dutch style; the newer part is better equipped but has slightly less character. Many rooms overlook a quiet tributary of the Rhine. The restaurant caters to most tastes and pockets; the excellent three-course tourist menu has vegetarian as well as meat and fish selections. ⊠ *Boommarkt 23, 2311 EA,* ☎ *071/5126358,* 𝖥𝖠𝖷 *071/5142674. 40 rooms, 30 with bath or shower. Restaurant. AE, DC, MC, V.*

$$ 🏨 **Hotel De Doelen.** The spartan decor of this small hotel is in keeping with its origins as a 15th-century house, but the rooms are comfortable and much sought after. ⊠ *Rapenburg 2, 2311 EV,* ☎ *071/5120527,* 𝖥𝖠𝖷 *071/5128453. 15 rooms with bath or shower. AE, DC, MC, V.*

Utrecht

$$ ✕ **Town Castle Oudaen/"Between Heaven and Earth."** In medieval times Utrecht's Oudegracht (Old Canal) was lined with many "town castles" such as this fine one. You may be confused by the clublike atmosphere as you enter, but you'll find the dining room on the second floor (which may be why it is called "Between Heaven and Earth") and an excellent café at ground level. Another unique feature is that the owners brew their own beer in the basement. ⊠ *Oudegracht 99,* ☎ *030/2311864. AE, DC, MC, V. Lunch in café only.*

$ ✕ **De Soepterrine.** This snug restaurant offers steaming bowls of homemade soups. Ten varieties are made daily, usually including Dutch specialties such as thick erwtensoep. Each bowl comes with crusty bread and herb butter. Quiches and generous salads fill up those extra corners. ⊠ *Zakkendragerssteeg 40,* ☎ *030/2317005. Reservations not accepted. AE, MC, DC, V.*

$$ 🏨 **Malie.** The Malie is in a 19th-century row house on a quiet leafy street a 15-minute walk from the old center. Rooms are brightly decorated though simply furnished. The attractive breakfast room of this small, friendly hotel overlooks a garden and terrace. ⊠ *Maliestraat 2–4, 3581 SL,* ☎ *030/2316424,* 𝖥𝖠𝖷 *030/2340661. 29 rooms with bath or shower. Bar, breakfast room. AE, DC, MC, V.*

THE HAGUE, DELFT, AND ROTTERDAM

Within this itinerary you can visit the Netherlands' most dignified and spacious city—the royal, diplomatic, and governmental seat of Den Haag (better known as The Hague)—and its close neighbor, the leading North Sea beach resort of Scheveningen. Also nearby are Delft, a historic city with many canals and ancient buildings, and the energetic and thoroughly modern international port city of Rotterdam. The lat-

ter is known to the Dutch as "Manhattan on the Maas," for its office
towers as well as its cultural attractions.

Getting Around

The Hague and Delft are each about 60 kilometers (37½ miles) southwest of Amsterdam and can be reached within less than an hour by
fast, frequent trains. The heart of both towns is compact enough to be
explored on foot. Scheveningen is reached from The Hague's center
by bus or tram. Travelers will find public transportation more convenient than driving because of severe parking problems at the resort.
The RET Metro is an easy-to-use option for getting around Rotterdam.
There are two main branches (north–south and east–west), and they
cross in the heart of the business district at a major transfer center.

Guided Tours

Boat Trips

From The Hague, various boat companies run short day trips and longer
candlelight dinner cruises. These can be booked at The Hague tourist
office or through **Rondvaartbedrijf RVH** (✉ Spui 256, ☎ 070/3462473).
In Scheveningen there are fishing-boat tours around the Dutch coast;
contact **Sportsviscentrum Trip 30** (☎ 070/3541122). In Delft, the
tourist office organizes boat tours along the unspoiled canal system.

You can cruise the port of Rotterdam on a basic tour of 1¼ hours (year-
round) or choose one that lasts as long as nine hours (midsummer only).
Spido Havenrondvaarten (✉ Willemsplein, ☎ 010/4135400), the
main boat company, also operates summer-evening music-and-dinner
cruises of the inner harbor. The 1¼-hour tour costs Fl. 17.50. The pier
can be reached by taking the RET Metro blue line toward Spijkenisse
to the Leuvehaven station and walking to the end of the boulevard.

Orientation Tours

City sightseeing tours of The Hague can be arranged by or through
the main VVV tourist office next to the train station. The size and diversity of the city make a bus tour a logical choice. The "Royal Bus
Tour" leaves from outside the office at 1 PM every day between April
and September. The 2½- to 3-hour trip includes background on the royal
family and takes passengers past Queen Beatrix's residences. Book in
advance at the tourist office (cost: Fl. 22).

Scheveningen and Delft are best seen on foot. The VVV Delft Tourist
Office organizes tours, while the Scheveningen office has information
about coastal strolls.

From April through September, there are daily two-hour bus tours of
Rotterdam conducted by the VVV Rotterdam Tourist Office. The
tours leave from the office at 1:30 PM and cost Fl. 25.

Visitor Information

Delft (✉ Markt 83–85, ☎ 015/2126100).
The Hague (✉ Babylon Center, Koningin Julianaplein 30, next to the
train station, ☎ 06/34035051).
Rotterdam (✉ Coolsingel 67, ☎ 06/34034065).
Scheveningen (✉ Gevers Deynootweg 1134, ☎ 06/34035051).

If you're planning to spend a few days in The Hague or Rotterdam,
ask for the VVV brochure on city events and entertainment. Tickets
for concerts and other activities can be reserved in person at the VVV.

Exploring The Hague, Delft, and Rotterdam

The Hague

During the 17th century, when Dutch maritime power was at its zenith, **The Hague** was known as "the Whispering Gallery of Europe" because it was thought to be the secret manipulator of European politics. Although the Golden Age is over, The Hague remains a powerful world diplomatic capital, quietly boastful of its royal connections. It also is the seat of government for the Netherlands.

★ The city's heart is the **Hofvijver** reflecting pool and the complex of gracious **Parliament Buildings.** At the center of it all is the **Ridderzaal** (Knights' Hall). Inside are vast beams spanning a width of 59 feet, flags, and stained-glass windows. A sense of history pervades the 13th-century great hall, now used mainly for ceremonies: Every year the queen's gilded coach brings her here to open Parliament. The two government chambers sit separately in buildings on either side of the Ridderzaal and can be visited by guided tour only when Parliament is not in session. Tours in English are conducted by Stichting Bezoekerscentrum Binnenhof, located just to the right of the Ridderzaal. ⊠ *Binnenhof 8a,* ☎ *070/3646144 (for tours; reservations required).* ☞ *Tour: Fl. 6, Parliament exhibition: Free.* ☉ *Mon.–Sat. 10–4.*

★ On the far side of the **Binnenhof,** the inner court of the complex, is a small, well-proportioned Dutch Renaissance building called the **Mauritshuis,** one of the finest small art museums in the world. This diminutive 17th-century palace contains a feast of art from the same period, including six Rembrandts; of these the most powerful is *The Anatomy Lesson of Dr. Tulp,* a theatrical work graphically depicting a dissection of the lower arm. Also featured are Vermeer's celebrated *Girl Wearing a Turban* and the glistening *View of Delft.* ⊠ *Korte Vijverberg 8,* ☎ *070/3469244.* ☞ *Fl. 10.* ☉ *Tues.–Sat. 10–5, Sun. 11–5.*

Outside the Mauritshuis, follow the Korte Vijverberg past the reflecting pool, which is bordered by patrician houses with revamped 18th- and 19th-century facades, a sign of the area's continuing popularity.

Turn right at Lange Vijverberg and walk a short way until you come to **Lange Voorhout,** a large L-shape boulevard. During the last century, horse-drawn trams clattered along its cobbles and deposited dignitaries outside the various palaces. Apart from the trams, not much has changed. Diplomats still eat in the historic Hotel des Indes (☞ Dining and Lodging, *below*) at Nos. 54–56. For more than 100 years, it has hosted ambassadors and kings, dancers and spies. Memories of famous guests remain in the form of Emperor Haile Selassie's gold chair and the ballerina Anna Pavlova's silver candlesticks. Lange Voorhout 34 once belonged to William I, the first king of the Netherlands, but later it became the royal library; it is now the **Supreme Court.** With its clumsy skewed gable, the headquarters of the Dutch Red Cross at No. 6 seems out of place on this stately avenue. A few doors down, at the corner of Parkstraat, is The Hague's oldest church, the **Kloosterkerk,** built in 1400. In spring, the adjoining square is covered with yellow and purple crocuses; on Thursday in summer it is the setting for a colorful antiques market.

North of Lange Voorhout is the **Panorama Mesdag,** a 400-foot painting-in-the-round that shows the nearby seaside town of Scheveningen as it looked in 1880. Hendrik Mesdag was a late-19th century marine painter, and he used the typically melancholic colors of the Hague school in his calming seascape. Mesdag was assisted by his wife, who painted much of the fishing village, and by a friend, who painted the sky and

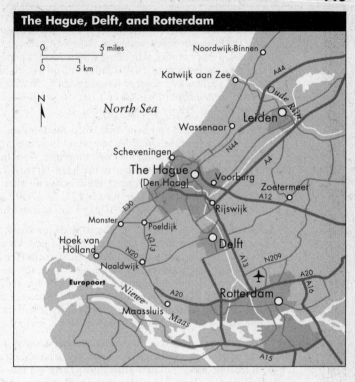

dunes. ⊠ *Zeestraat 65,* ☏ *070/3642563.* ◻ *Fl. 5.* ☉ *Mon.–Sat. 10–5, Sun. noon–5.*

Around the corner in Laan van Meerdervoort is the painter's home, now the **Rijksmuseum H. W. Mesdag.** Paintings by Mesdag and members of the Hague school are hung beside those of Corot, Courbet, and Rousseau. These delicate landscapes represent one of the finest collections of Barbizon School painting outside France. At press time the museum was closed for renovation and was scheduled to reopen late in 1996. ⊠ *Laan van Meerdervoort 7f. For information, contact the Vincent van Gogh Museum in Amsterdam,* ☏ *020/5705200.*

The **Vredespaleis** (Peace Palace), near Laan van Meerdervoort, is a monument to world peace through negotiation. Following the first peace conference at The Hague in 1899, the Scottish-American millionaire Andrew Carnegie donated $1.5 million for the construction of a building to house a proposed international court. The Dutch government donated the grounds, and other nations offered furnishings and decorations. Although it still looks like a dull multinational bank, the building has been improved by such gifts as Japanese wall hangings, a Danish fountain, and a grand staircase presented by The Hague. Today the **International Court of Justice,** consisting of 15 jurists, has its seat here. There are guided tours when the court is not in session. ⊠ *Carnegieplein 2,* ☏ *070/3469680.* ◻ *Fl. 5.* ☉ *June–Sept., weekdays 10–4; Oct.–May, weekdays 10–3. Guided tours at 11, 2, and 3.*

The nearby **Haags Gemeentemuseum** (Hague Municipal Museum) is the home of the largest collection of Mondrians in the world plus two vast collections of musical instruments—European and non-European. The 1935 building itself is fascinating as an example of the International Movement in modern architecture. ⊠ *Stadhouderslaan 41,* ☏ *070/3512873.* ◻ *Fl. 8.* ☉ *Tues.–Sun. 11–5.*

Behind the Gemeentemuseum, overlooking Zorgvliet (the western-most park of the Scheveningse Bosjes, a vast stretch of green that separates The Hague from Scheveningen), is the IMAX theater **Omniversum.** It is housed in a cylindrical building with a 75-foot dome that acts as a screen for the projection of 6–10 daily video presentations about outer space and nature. ⊠ *President Kennedylaan 5,* ☎ *070/3545454 for reservations and show times.* ⊞ *Fl. 17.* ☉ *Shows Tues.–Thurs. hourly 11–4, Fri.–Sun. hourly 11–9 (except 6).*

Between The Hague and Scheveningen is **Madurodam,** a miniature Netherlands where the country's important buildings are duplicated at a scale of 1:52. No detail has been forgotten, from the lighthouse and quay-side cranes in a harbor to the hand-carved furniture in the gabled houses. In July and August, there is also an after-dark sound-and-light presentation. ⊠ *Haringkade 175,* ☎ *070/3520930.* ⊞ *Fl. 19.50.* ☉ *Apr.–Sept., daily 9 AM–10 PM; Oct.–March, daily 9–5.*

Scheveningen is adjacent to The Hague along the North Sea coast. A fishing village since the 14th century, it became popular as a beach resort during the last century, when the grand Kurhaus Hotel, still a focal point of this beach community, was built. The beach itself, protected from tidal erosion by stone jetties, slopes gently into the North Sea in front of a high promenade whose function is to protect the boulevard and everything behind it from winter storms. The surface of the beach is fine sand, and you can bicycle or walk for miles to the north.

At the turn of the century, the **Kurhaus Hotel** stood alone at the center of the beach as a fashionable resort. Now it is modern and bustling, with a casino among its new attractions. There is a fancifully painted ceiling over the large central court and buffet restaurant.

The Kurhaus area includes the Golfbad, a surf pool complete with artificial waves. **The Pier,** completed in 1962, stretches 1,220 feet into the sea. Its four circular end buildings contain a sun terrace and restaurant, an observation tower, an amusement center with a children's play area, and an underwater panorama. At 11 on summer evenings, the Pier is the scene of dramatic fireworks displays.

Also on the beachfront is the **Sea Life Center,** an ingeniously designed aquarium complex with a transparent underwater tunnel. You walk through it as if you were on the sea floor, with sharks, rays, eels, and octopuses swimming inches above your head. ⊠ *Strandweg 13,* ☎ *070/3542100.* ⊞ *Fl. 13.50.* ☉ *Sept.–June, daily 10–6; July–Aug., daily 10–8.*

Delft

Thirteen kilometers (8 miles) along the A13 from The Hague, you'll enter **Delft.** There is probably no town in the Netherlands that is more intimate, more attractive, or more traditional than this minimetropolis, whose famous blue-and-white earthenware is popular throughout the world. Compact and easy to explore despite its web of canals, Delft is best discovered on foot—although canal-boat excursions are available April through October, as are horse-drawn trams that leave from the marketplace. Every street is lined with attractive Gothic and Renaissance houses.

In the marketplace, the only lively spot in this tranquil town, is the **Nieuwe Kerk** (New Church), built in the 14th century, with its tall Gothic spire and a carillon of 48 bells. The mausoleum of Prince William the Silent, a massive, ornate structure of black marble and alabaster, dominates the chancel. Nearby in the floor is a stone that covers the entry to a crypt containing the remains of members of the Orange-Nassau line, including all members of the royal family since King William I ascended the throne in the mid-16th century. ✉ *Markt,* ☎ *015/2123025.* ✑ *Fl. 4, in combination with Oude Kerk (☞ below).* ✑ *Tower: Fl. 2.50. Mar.–Oct., Mon.–Sat. 9–6; Nov.–Feb., Mon.–Sat. 11–4.*

Walk around the right side of the Nieuwe Kerk, then left at the back and along the Vrouwenregt canal for a few steps before taking another left turn into Voldersgracht. To the left, the backs of the houses rise straight from the water as you stroll to the end of the street, which is marked by the sculptured animal heads and outdoor stairs of the old **Meat Market** on the right. Cross the Wijnhaven and turn left along its far side to the Koornmarkt, a stately canal spanned by a high, arching bridge that is one of the hallmarks of Delft.

Turn right at the Peperstraat to reach the **Oude Delft,** the city's oldest waterway. A few blocks farther along the canal is the **Prinsenhof,** formerly the Convent of St. Agatha, founded in 1400. The chapel inside dates from 1471; its interior is remarkable for the wooden statues under the vaulting ribs. Today the Prinsenhof is a museum that tells the story of the liberation of the Netherlands after 80 years of Spanish occupation (1568–1648). For Dutch royalists, the spot is significant for the assassination of Prince William of Orange in 1584; the bullet holes can still be seen in the wall. ✉ *St. Agathaplein 1,* ☎ *015/2602358.* ✑ *Fl. 5.* ☉ *Tues.–Sat. 10–5, Sun. 1–5.*

Across the Oude Delft canal is the **Oude Kerk** (Old Church), a vast Gothic monument from the 13th century. Its beautiful tower, surmounted by a brick spire, leans somewhat alarmingly. ✉ *Heilige Geest Kerkhof,* ☎ *015/2123015.* ✑ *Fl. 4, in combination with the Nieuwe Kerk (☞ above).* ✑ *Mar.–Oct., Mon.–Sat. 9–6.*

Beyond the Prinsenhof on the same side of the Oude Delft canal is the **Lambert van Meerten Museum,** a mansion whose timbered rooms are filled with the country's most complete collection of old Dutch tiles as well as Delft pottery. ✉ *Oude Delft 199,* ☎ *015/2602358.* ✑ *Fl. 3.50.* ☉ *Tues.–Sat. 10–5, Sun. 1–5.*

While in Delft, you will want to see the famous local specialty—Delftware. Decorated porcelain was brought to the Netherlands from China on East India Company ships and was so popular that Dutch potters felt their livelihood was being threatened. They therefore set about creating pottery to rival Chinese porcelain. Only two manufacturers still make hand-painted Delftware: **De Delftse Pauw** and the more famous "Royal" **De Porceleyne Fles.** *De Delftse Pauw:* ✉ *Delftweg 133,* ☎ *015/2124920.* ✑ *Free.* ☉ *Apr.–mid-Oct., daily 9–4.30; mid-Oct.–Mar., weekdays 9–4.30, weekends 11–1. De Porceleyne Fles:* ✉ *Rotterdamsweg 196,* ☎ *015/2560234.* ✑ *Fl. 3.* ☉ *Apr.–Oct., Mon.–Sat. 9–5, Sun. 10–4; Nov.–Mar., weekdays 9–5, Sat. 10–4.*

Rotterdam

One of the few thoroughly modern cities in the Netherlands and the site of the world's largest and busiest port, **Rotterdam** is 13 kilometers (8 miles) south of Delft on the A13. Art lovers know the city for its extensive and outstanding collection of art; philosophers recall it as the city of Erasmus. Rotterdam is a major stop on the rock-and-roll concert circuit, and its soccer team is well known, but the city's main claim to fame is its extraordinary concentration of adventuresome modern architecture. Among the most intriguing buildings are a series of cube-shape apartments, turned to balance on one corner at the top of a tall stem. One of these precarious-looking houses, the **Kijk-Kubus,** just east of the center, is open to the public. ✉ *Overblaak 70,* ☎ *010/4142285.* ✑ *Fl. 3.50.* ☉ *Mar.–Nov., daily 11–5; Dec.–Feb., Fri.–Sun 11–5.*

The biggest surprise in Rotterdam is the remarkable 48-kilometer-long (30-mile-long) **Europoort,** which handles more than 250 million tons of cargo every year and more ships than any other port in the world. It is the delta for three of Europe's most important rivers (the Rhine, the Waal, and the Meuse/Maas) and a seemingly endless corridor of piers, warehouses, tank facilities, and efficiency. You can get to the piers at Willemsplein by tram or Metro (blue line to the Leuvehaven station) from the train station. The 1¼-hour harbor tour (☞ Boat Trips *in* Guided Tours, *above*) illuminates Rotterdam's vital role in world trade.

As an alternative to the boat tour, you also can survey the harbor from the vantage point of the **Euromast** observation tower. Get there via the RET Metro red line to Dijkszicht. ✉ *Parkhaven 20,* ☎ *010/4364811.* ⌖ *Fl. 14.50.* ☉ *Apr.–June and Sept., daily 10–7; July and Aug., Sun. and Mon. 10–7, Tues.–Sat. 10 AM–10:30 PM; Oct.–Mar., daily 10–5.*

After the harbor tour, walk down the boulevard past the Metro station into Leuvehaven. On your right as you stroll along the inner harbor is **IMAX Rotterdam,** a gigantic theater in which films are projected onto a six-story screen. There are earphones for English translation. ✉ *Leuvehaven 77,* ☎ *010/4048844.* ⌖ *Fl. 15.* ☉ *Shows Tues.–Sun. 2, 3, and 4; Mon. also during holiday periods. Non-IMAX films (from the regular commercial circuit) shown daily (times vary).*

Past the theater is a hodgepodge of cranes, barges, steamships, and old shipbuilding machines, even a steam-operated grain elevator. What looks to be a sort of maritime junkyard is a work in progress: Volunteers are restoring these vessels and machines. The whole operation is an open-air museum of shipbuilding, shipping, and communications that is part of the **Prins Hendrik Maritime Museum,** housed in a large gray building at the head of the quay. Also moored in this inner harbor adjacent to the museum is the historic 19th-century Royal Dutch Navy warship *De Buffel.* Within the museum are exhibits devoted to the history and activity of the great port outside. ✉ *Leuvehaven 1,* ☎ *010/4132680.* ⌖ *Fl. 6.* ☉ *Tues.–Sat. 10–5, Sun. 11–5.*

From the nearby Churchillplein Metro station, take the red line toward Marconiplein to the first stop at Eendrachtsplein, where you will walk along the canal toward the Museumpark. As a welcome contrast to the industrial might of the Europoort and the Netherlands' maritime history, the **Boymans–van Beuningen Museum** is an impressive refresher course in Western European art history. There is an Old Arts section that includes the work of Brueghel, Bosch, and Rembrandt and a renowned print gallery with works by artists such as Dürer and Cézanne. Dali and Magritte mix with the Impressionists in the Modern Arts collection. ✉ *Mathenesserlaan 18–20,* ☎ *010/4419400.* ⌖ *Fl. 7.50.* ☉ *Tues.–Sat. 10–5, Sun. 11–5.*

Beside this long-established museum is the spanking-new **Nederlands Architectuurinstituut,** which houses changing exhibitions in the field of architecture and interior design. Across the park is the **Kunsthal,** which hosts all manner of major temporary exhibitions—from Andy Warhol retrospectives to rows of compact cars. *Nederlands Architectuurinstituut:* ✉ *Museumpark 25,* ☎ *010/4401200.* ⌖ *Fl. 7.50.* ☉ *Tues.–Sat. 10–5, Sun. 11–5. Kunsthal:* ✉ *Westzeedijk 341,* ☎ *010/4400300.* ⌖ *Fl. 12.50.* ☉ *Tues.–Sat. 10–5, Sun. 11–5.*

Three stops farther west along the Metro line is **Delfshaven**—spelled Delftshaven back when the Pilgrims set sail from here—the last remaining nook of old Rotterdam. (From the station double back along Schiedamseweg, then turn right down Aelbrechtskolk.) Rows of gabled buildings and a windmill line the waterfront. Today Delfshaven is an up-and-coming area of trendy galleries, cafés, and restaurants.

Dining and Lodging

For details and price-category definitions, *see* Dining *and* Lodging *in* Staying in The Netherlands, *above*.

Delft

$$$ ✕ **L'Orage.** This fresh, classically designed canal-side restaurant serves up delicious fish steeped in tantalizing sauces. The award-winning chef/owner, Jannie Munk, bases many of her dishes on recipes from her native Denmark. ⊠ *Oude Delft 111b,* ☎ *015/2123629. Reservations advised. Jacket and tie. AE, DC, MC, V. Closed Sun.–Mon.*

$–$$ ✕ **Spijshuis De Dis.** Seafood is a house specialty at this favorite neighborhood spot, where a friendly staff serves typically Dutch cuisine. The mussels with garlic sauce are delicious, and you can try such delicacies as roast quail. ⊠ *Beestenmarkt 36,* ☎ *015/2131782. AE, MC, V.*

$ ✕🏨 **Hotel de Plataan.** Converted in 1994 from a rather grand old post
★ office building, Hotel de Plataan was decorated by a local artist in 1950s-style cream and green. Most rooms have a kitchen nook where you can prepare you own breakfast. You can also have meals in Het Establissement, an excellent restaurant with meaty casseroles as well as imaginative vegetarian dishes. ⊠ *Doelenplein 9–10, 2611 BP,* ☎ *015/2126046,* ℻ *015/2157327. 26 rooms with bath or shower. Restaurant (*☎ *015/2121687). AE, DC, MC, V.*

$$–$$$ 🏨 **Hotel De Ark.** This bright, airy hotel in the center of old Delft comprises three canal houses joined so that nearly every room has a view of either the canal or the large garden in back. Rooms are clean and modern. ⊠ *Koornmarkt 59–65, 2611 EC,* ☎ *015/2157999,* ℻ *015/2144997. 16 rooms with bath, 9 apartments. Meeting room. AE, DC, MC, V.*

$$ 🏨 **Hotel Leeuwenbrug.** On one of the prettiest canals in Delft, you'll find this traditional Dutch family-style hotel. There are two buildings, one of which is simpler, with smaller, cheaper rooms; the annex is more contemporary and businesslike. Everyone enjoys breakfast overlooking the canal, however, and rooms on the top floor of the annex overlook the city. ⊠ *Koornmarkt 16, 2611 EE,* ☎ *015/2147741,* ℻ *015/2159759. 38 rooms with bath or shower. Bar, lobby lounge. AE, MC, V.*

The Hague

$$$ ✕ **Da Roberto.** Popular with politicians and The Hague's business elite, Roberto's is a quiet and comfortable restaurant, where all the adventure goes into the cuisine. Italian standards and some ambitious variations are treated to nouvelle cuisine presentation. The garlicky carpaccio and the lasagna are delicious, as is the vegetarian ravioli with orange sauce. ⊠ *Noordeinde 96,* ☎ *070/3464977. AE, DC, MC, V.*

$$–$$$ ✕ **Bistromer.** A notch above most other seafood restaurants in The
★ Hague, Bistromer has a menu that spans from the North Sea to the Mediterranean. Portions are generous, and the food is cooked to perfection. It's probably the only restaurant in the country that is happy to serve its tuna steaks medium rare. There's a wood-paneled dining room for snug winter meals and an attractive glassed-in porch for the summer. ⊠ *Javastraat 9,* ☎ *070/3607389. AE, DC, MC, V.*

$$–$$$ ✕ **Djawa.** Whether or not it is a result of the city's diplomatic heritage is unknown, but The Hague is said to have the Netherlands' highest concentration of Indonesian restaurants. Among them is this cozy,

family-run, neighborhood restaurant located not far from the center.
⊠ *Mallemolen 12a*, ☎ *070/3635763. AE, DC, MC, V. No lunch.*

$$–$$$ ✕ **Le Haricot Vert.** What was built in 1638 as a staff house for the nearby
palace is nowadays an intimate, candlelit restaurant in the city center.
Dishes combine Dutch simplicity with French flair. Succulent meats swimming in sauce appear on large white plates with a colorful tangle of
vegetables. Owner Herman van Overdam can be seen chatting at diners' tables or flitting back into the kitchen to create one of his sinfully
laden dessert platters. Menus change frequently according to what is
in season. ⊠ *Molenstraat 9a–11*, ☎ *070/3652278. No credit cards.*

$$$$ ✕🖼 **Hotel Des Indes.** Standing almost unobtrusively at the end of one
of The Hague's most prestigious squares, the Des Indes is grace and
gentility supreme. Once a private residence, the mansion was built for
grand balls and entertainments. Rooms are spacious and stylish, and
one suite offers a spectacular view across the city to the beach. The
restaurant ($$$) serves memorable haute cuisine amid the glitter of crys-
tal and silver. ⊠ *Lange Voorhout 54-56, 2514 EG*, ☎ *070/3632932*,
FAX *070/3451721. 76 rooms. Restaurant, bar. AE, DC, MC, V.*

$$$ 🖼 **Corona.** Overlooking a charming square in the center of the city is
this pride and joy of The Hague. Rooms are restfully decorated in a
muted scheme of white, cream, and dove gray. The restaurant is one
of the best in town; for less expensive meals, try the brasserie. ⊠
Buitenhof 39–42, 2513 AH, ☎ *070/3637930*, FAX *070/3615785. 26
rooms with bath. 2 restaurants. AE, DC, MC, V.*

$–$$ 🖼 **Hotel Sebel.** In a largely residential district between the city center
and the Peace Palace, Hotel Sebel provides a convenient stopover for
businesspeople and for visitors on vacation. The rooms are invitingly
spacious, and the owners friendly and attentive. ⊠ *Zoutmanstraat 38*,
2518 GR, ☎ *070/3608010*, FAX *070/3455855. 14 rooms with bath. Bar.*
AE, DC, MC, V.

Rotterdam

$$$ ✕ **Miller's.** In Rotterdam's thicket of modern architecture, Delfshaven
is one area that reminds visitors how the old city must have looked.
Miller's makes its home here, in a converted 17th-century warehouse
beside the water. Dine casually in the downstairs bistro or by candle-
light beneath the wooden rafters. The Dutch chef raids other national
cuisines to produce hearty, mainly meat-based meals, with rich, tasty
sauces. ⊠ *Voorhaven 3*, ☎ *010/4775181. AC, DC, MC, V.*

$$ ✕ **Inn the Picture.** This trendy café offers a wide selection of typical
Dutch fare. The salads are especially inviting. In summer, tables offer
a view of passing crowds in the shopping district. ⊠ *Karel Door-
manstraat 294*, ☎ *010/4133204. AE, DC, MC, V.*

$–$$$ ✕ **Heerenhuis De Heuvel.** Resplendent beside a lake in the city's Maas
Park, this airy 19th-century building has one of the most attractive lo-
cations—and the sunniest terrace—in town. In one wing is a restau-
rant serving such tantalizing dishes as monkfish with ginger and saffron.
In the café on the other side of the building, the same kitchen serves
inexpensive, lighter meals. On Sunday the restaurant has live classical
music during breakfast. ⊠ *Baden-Powelllaan 12*, ☎ *010/4364249.*
Reservations not accepted for café. AE, MC, DC, V.

$$–$$$ ✕🖼 **Hotel New York.** For more than 90 years, the twin towers of the
Hotel New York have been a feature of Rotterdam's skyline. Before a
1993 renovation, though, the building was the headquarters of the Hol-
land-America Line. Today some rooms retain the original walnut pan-
eling and restored Art Nouveau carpets, while others are modern in

design. Downstairs, the huge café-restaurant (it seats 400) serves everything from English afternoon tea to a selection of five different types of oysters. The hotel is 15 minutes' walk from the Rijnhaven Metro station, or you can take one of the hotel's water taxis direct from Veerhaven or Leuvehaven. ⊠ *Koninginnenhoofd 1, 3072 AD,* ☎ *010/4390500,* 𝖥𝖠𝖷 *010/4842701. 73 rooms with shower or bath. Restaurant, meeting rooms. AE, DC, MC, V.*

$ 🛏 **Hotel Van Walsum.** This pleasant, family-run hotel is just around the corner from Rotterdam's main museums and has an apartment as one of the options. There's a small restaurant that overflows into the garden in good weather. ⊠ *Mathenesserlaan 199–201, 3014 HC,* ☎ *010/4363275,* 𝖥𝖠𝖷 *010/4364410. 25 rooms and 1 apartment. Restaurant, bar. AE, DC, MC, V.*

21 Norway

NORWAY HAS SOME OF THE MOST REMOTE and dramatic scenery in Europe. Along the west coast, deep fjords knife into steep mountain ranges. Inland, cross-country ski trails follow frozen trout streams and downhill trails career through forests whose floors teem with wildflowers and berries during the summer. In older villages, wooden houses spill down toward docks where Viking ships—and later, whaling vessels—once were moored. Today, oil is Norway's economic lifeblood and the maritime horizon is dominated by tankers and derricks. Fishing and timber, however, still provide many Norwegians with a stable income.

Inhabited since 1700 BC, Norway is today considered a peaceful nation. This was hardly so during the Viking period (the 8th–10th centuries AD), when, apart from vicious infighting at home, the Vikings were marauding as far afield as Seville and the Isle of Man. This fierce fighting spirit remained, despite Norway's subsequent centuries of subjugation by the Danes and Swedes. Independence came early this century but was put to the test during World War II, when the Germans occupied the country. Norwegian Resistance fighters rose to the challenge, eventually quashing Nazi efforts to develop atomic weapons.

The foundations for modern Norwegian culture were laid in the 19th century, during the period of union with Sweden, which lasted until 1905. Oslo blossomed at this time, and Norway produced its three greatest men of arts and letters: composer Edvard Grieg (1843–1907), playwright Henrik Ibsen (1828–1906), and painter Edvard Munch (1863–1944). Other notable Norwegians of this period were the polar explorers Roald Amundsen and Fridtjof Nansen.

All other facts aside, Norway is most famous for its fjords, formed during an ice age a million years ago. The ice cap burrowed deep into existing mountain-bound riverbeds, creating enormous pressure. There was less pressure along the coast, so the entrances to most fjords are shallow, about 500 feet, while inland depths reach as much as 4,000 feet. Although Norway's entire coastline is notched with fjords, the most breathtaking sights are on the west coast between Stavanger and Trondheim, and the northern Helgeland coastline to the Lofoten Islands. Oil-prosperous or fisherman-poor, friendly or taciturn, Norwegians remain outdoor fanatics, firmly in the grip of their country's natural beauty.

ESSENTIAL INFORMATION

Before You Go

When to Go

Cross-country skiing was born in Norway, and the country remains an important winter sports center. Although much of the terrain is dark and impassable through the winter, you can cross-country or downhill ski within Oslo's city limits. January, February, and early March are good skiing months, and hotel rooms are plentiful then. Avoid April, when sleet, rain, and repeated thaws and refreezings may ruin the good skiing snow and leave roads—and spirits—in bad shape. Bear in mind that the country virtually closes down for the five-day Easter holiday, when Norwegians make their annual migration to the mountains. If you plan to visit at this time, reserve well in advance. May is one of the best times to visit—the days are long and sunny, cultural life is still

Norway

North Cape

Vardø

Vadsø

Hammerfest

Kirkenes

*ATLANTIC
OCEAN*

Alta

Masi

Tromsø

Kantokeino

FINLAND

Bardu

Narvik

Svolvoer

*N o r w e g i a n
S e a*

Vestfjorden

Bodø Fauske

Saltdal

Arctic   Circle

Mo i Rana Umbukta

Sandnessjøen

Mosjøen

Brønnøysund

E6

S W E D E N

Gulf of Bothnia

Vikna

Namsos

Steinkjer

Trondheim

Meråker

Støren

Kristiansund N.

70 Oppdal

Ålesund

Røros

E69

Tynset

Dombås

Otta

Nordfjord

Koppang

Florø

Jostedalsbreen

Rena

Lillehammer

Sognefjorden

*Lake
Mjøsa*

Hamar

Voss

E68

Eidsvoll

Bergen

Hønefoss

40

Hardangerfjorden

11

Kongsberg

N

Oslo

Drammen

Sarpsborg

Haugesund

Skien

Oslofjord

Fredrikstad

Baltic Sea

Sandefjord

Stavanger

39

Larvik

Egersund Evje

Arendal

Grimstad

Skagerrak

Mandal Kristiansand S.

Kattegat

0 200 miles
0 300 km

going strong, and *Syttende mai* (Constitution Day, May 17), with all its festivities, is worth a trip in itself.

Summers are generally mild. Then there's the famous midnight sun: Even in the "southern" city of Oslo, night seems more like twilight around midnight, and dawn comes by 2 AM. The weather can be fickle, however, and rain gear and sturdy waterproof shoes are recommended even in the summer. The Norwegians themselves tend to take their vacations in July and the first part of August.

CLIMATE

The following are the average daily maximum and minimum temperatures for Oslo.

Jan.	28F	– 2C	May	61F	16C	Sept.	60F	16C
	19	– 7		43	6		46	8
Feb.	30F	– 1C	June	68F	20C	Oct.	48F	9C
	19	– 7		50	10		38	3
Mar.	39F	4C	July	72F	22C	Nov.	38F	3C
	25	– 4		55	13		31	– 1
Apr.	50F	10C	Aug.	70F	21C	Dec.	32F	0C
	34	1		54	12		25	– 4

Currency

The unit of currency in Norway is the krone, written as Kr. on price tags but officially written as NOK (bank designation), NKr, or kr. The krone is divided into 100 øre. Bills of NKr 50, 100, 200, 500, and 1,000 are in general use. Coins are in denominations of 50 øre and 1, 5, 10, and 20 kroner. Credit cards are accepted in most hotels, stores, restaurants, and many gas stations and garages, but generally not in smaller shops and inns in rural areas. The exchange rate at press time (spring 1996) was NKr 6.42 to the U.S. dollar, NKr 4.63 to the Canadian dollar, and NKr 9.63 to the pound sterling.

What It Will Cost

Norway has a high standard—and cost—of living, but there are ways to save money by taking advantage of special offers for accommodations and travel during the tourist season and on weekends throughout the year.

Hotels in larger towns have special summer rates from late June to early August, and some chains have their own discount offers—see Norway's annual accommodation guide at tourist offices. Discounts in smaller hotels are offered to guests staying several days; meals are then included in the rate. Meals are generally expensive, so take hotel breakfast when it's offered. Alcohol is very expensive and is sold only during strictly regulated hours at state-owned *vinmonopol* stores.

SAMPLE PRICES

Cup of coffee, NKr 12–NKr 25; a half-liter of beer, NKr 35–NKr 50; soft drink, NKr 10–NKr 25; ham sandwich, NKr 20–NKr 50; 1-mile taxi ride, NKr 45 (for night rates, add 15%).

Customs on Arrival

Residents of non-European countries who are over 18 may import duty-free into Norway 200 cigarettes or 500 grams of other tobacco goods, and souvenirs and gifts to the value of NKr 1,200. Residents of European countries who are over 18 may import 200 cigarettes or 250 grams of tobacco or cigars, a small amount of perfume or eau de cologne, and other goods to the value of NKr 1,200. Anyone over 20 may bring in 1 liter of wine and 1 liter of liquor or 2 liters of wine or beer.

Language

In larger cities and in most commercial establishments, people speak English. English is the main foreign language taught in schools, and movies, music, and TV reinforce its popularity.

There are two official forms of the Norwegian language—*bokmål* and *nynorsk*—plus many dialects, so don't be disappointed if you've studied it but find that you can't understand everyone. As is typical of Scandinavian languages, Norwegian's additional vowels—æ, ø, and å—come at the end of the alphabet in the phone book.

Getting Around

By Car

ROAD CONDITIONS

Away from the major routes, roads are narrow and winding, so don't expect to cover more than 240 kilometers (150 miles) a day, especially in fjord country. The climate plays havoc with the roads: Even the best roads suffer from frost, and mountain passes may be closed in winter. Snow tires (preferably studded) are compulsory in winter in many areas; if you're planning to rent a car, choose a smaller model with front-wheel drive.

RULES OF THE ROAD

Driving is on the right. The speed limit is 90 kph (55 mph) on highways, 80 kph (50 mph) on main roads, 50 kph (30 mph) in towns, and 30–40 kph (18–25 mph) in residential areas. The use of headlights at all times is mandatory. For assistance contact **Norges Automobil Forbund (NAF)**—the Norwegian Automobile Association (✉ Storgt. 2, 0155 Oslo, ☎ 22341400). It is important to remember to yield to the vehicle approaching from the right. Passing areas on narrow roads are marked with a white M (for *møteplass*) on a blue background.

PARKING

Street parking in cities and towns is clearly marked. There are also municipal parking lots. You cannot park on main roads or on bends. Details can be found in the leaflet "Parking in Oslo," available free from tourist offices and gas stations.

GASOLINE

Gas costs 8–9 NKr per liter and diesel costs 7.17–7.36 NKr per liter. Gas stations are plentiful and not hard to find in remote areas.

BREAKDOWNS

The NAF patrols main roads and has emergency telephones on mountain roads. For NAF 24-hour service, dial ☎ 22341600.

By Train

Trains are punctual and comfortable, and most routes are scenic. They fan out from Oslo and leave the coastline (except in the south) to buses and ferries. Reservations are required on all *ekspresstog* (express trains) and night trains. The Oslo–Bergen route is superbly scenic, and the Oslo–Trondheim–Bodø route takes you within the Arctic Circle. Do not miss the side trips from Myrdal to Flåm from the Oslo–Bergen line, and Dombås to Åndalsnes from the Oslo–Trondheim line. Trains leave Oslo from Sentralstasjonen (Oslo S or Central Station) on Jernbanetorget (at the beginning of Karl Johans gate).

FARES

In addition to the Europe-wide passes (**Eurail** and **Inter-Rail**), **ScanRail** passes, good in Norway, Sweden, Denmark, and Finland, are also available. ScanRail passes offer unlimited travel in a set numbers of travel days within a specified period. They are available in the United

States through **Rail Europe** (☎ 914/682–2999) and **DER Travel Service** (☎ 310/479–4411), and in Great Britain through **NSB Travel,** the Norwegian State Railway (✉ 21–24 Cockspur St., London SW1Y 5DA, ☎ 0171/930–6666). A **Norway Rail Pass** is available for one or two weeks' unlimited rail travel within Norway. In the United States the ticket is available through **ScanAm** (☎ 201/835–7070 or 800/545–2204), and in London through **NSB Travel.** Reduced fares during off-peak times ("green" routes) are also available if booked in advance.

By Plane

As so much of Norway is remote, air travel is a necessity for many natives. The main Scandinavian airline, **SAS,** operates a network, along with **Braathens SAFE** and **Widerøe.** Fares are high, so be sure to ask about the special rates available year-round within Norway. For longer distances, flying can be cheaper than driving a rented car, given the cost of gas and incidentals. Inquire about "Visit Norway" passes, which give you relatively cheap domestic-flight coupons. Norwegian airlines can be contacted at the following addresses: **SAS** (✉ Oslo City, Stenersgt. 1A, 0184 Oslo, ☎ 81003300); **Braathens SAFE AS** (✉ Haakon VII's gt. 2, 0161 Oslo, ☎ 67597000 or 22834470); **Norsk Air** (✉ Torp Airport, Sandefjord, ☎ 33469000); and **Widerøe** (✉ Mustads vei 1, 0283 Oslo, ☎ 22736600).

By Bus

The Norwegian bus network makes up for some of the limitations of the country's train system, and several of the routes are particularly scenic. For example, the North Norway bus service, starting at Fauske (on the train line to Bodø), goes right up to Kirkenes on the Russian-Norwegian border, covering the 1,000 kilometers (625 miles) in four days. Most buses leave from Bussterminalen (✉ Galleri Oslo, Schweigaardsgt. 10, ☎ 22170166), close to Oslo's Central Station.

By Ferry

Norway's long, fjord-indented coastline is served by an intricate and essential network of ferries and passenger ships. A wide choice of services is available, from simple hops across fjords (saving many miles of traveling) and excursions among the thousands of islands to luxury cruises and long journeys up the coast. Most ferries carry cars. Reservations are required on journeys of more than one day but are not needed for simple fjord crossings. Fares and exact departure times depend on the season and the availability of ships. Contact the main Norwegian travel office, Nortra, or the Norway Information Center (☞ Important Addresses and Numbers *in* Oslo, *below*) for details.

One of the world's great sea voyages is aboard one of the mail-and-passenger *Hurtigruten* ships that run up the Norwegian coast from Bergen to Kirkenes, well above the Arctic Circle. Contact the **Bergen Line** (✉ 405 Park Ave., New York, NY 10022, ☎ 800/323–7436), or the **Tromsø Main Office** (☎ 77686088).

Nortra (✉ Norwegian Travel Association; Postboks 499, Sentrum, 0150 Oslo, ☎ 22925200, FAX 22560505) will answer your queries about long-distance travel.

Staying in Norway

Telephones

Norway's phone system is not as expensive as one might fear. Domestic rates are reduced 5 PM–8 AM weekdays and all day on weekends. Also, avoid using room phones in hotels. Cheap rates for international calls apply only after 10 PM. In public booths, place coins in the phone before dialing. The largest coins generally accepted are NKr 10, although some new phones take NKr 20 coins. Most older phones take only NKr 1 or NKr 5 coins. The minimum deposit is NKr 2 or NKr 3, depending on the phone.

LOCAL CALLS

The cost of calls within Norway varies according to distance: Within Oslo, the cost goes up according to the amount of time used after the three-minute flat fee. Check the Oslo phone book for dialing information.

INTERNATIONAL CALLS

These can be made from any pay phone. For calls to North America, dial 00–1, then the area code and number. When dialing the United Kingdom, omit the initial zero of the area code (for Central London you would dial 00 followed by 44, then 171 and the local number). To reach an **AT&T** long-distance operator, dial 80019011; for **MCI**, 180019912; and for **Sprint,** 180019877.

COUNTRY CODE

The international country code for Norway is 47.

OPERATORS AND INFORMATION

For local information, dial 180. For international information, dial 181. For international collect calls, dial 115.

Mail

Post offices throughout the country are open weekdays 8:30–5 and Saturday 8:30–noon. They cash traveler's checks and exchange foreign currency as well as offering postal services.

POSTAL RATES

Letters and postcards to the United States cost NKr 5.50 for the first 20 grams. For the United Kingdom, the rate is NKr 4.50 for the first 20 grams.

RECEIVING MAIL

If you're uncertain about where you'll be staying, have your mail marked "poste restante" and sent to the town where you plan to pick it up. Your last name should be underlined. The service is free; letters are directed to the nearest main post office, where you'll need your passport to pick up your mail. American Express offices will also hold mail (nonmembers pay a small charge on collection).

Shopping

VAT REFUNDS

Much of the 23% Norwegian value-added tax (VAT) will be refunded to visitors who spend more than NKr 300 in any single store. Ask for a special tax-free check and show your passport to confirm that you are not a resident. All purchases must be sealed and presented together with the tax-free check at the tax-free counter at foreign ferry ports and at airports and border posts. The VAT will be refunded, minus a service charge. General information about the tax-free system is available by calling 67149901.

Opening and Closing Times

Banks are open weekdays 8–3:30, in summer 8:15–3. (All post offices change money.)

Museums are usually open Tuesday to Sunday 10–3 or 4. Many, but not all, are closed on Monday.

Shops are usually open weekdays 9 or 10–5 (Thursday until 7) and Saturday 9–1 or 2, though times vary. Shopping malls are often open until 8 on weeknights.

National Holidays

January 1; March 23 (Palm Sunday); March 30–31 (Easter); May 1 (Labor Day); May 8 (Ascension); May 17 (Constitution Day); May 18–19 (Pentecost); December 24–26.

Dining

The Norwegian diet emphasizes protein and carbohydrates. Breakfast is usually a large buffet of smoked fish, cheeses, sausage, cold meats, and whole-grain breads accompanied by tea, coffee, or milk. Lunch is simple, usually *smørbrød* (open-face sandwiches). Restaurant and hotel dinners are usually three-course meals, often starting with soup and ending with fresh fruit and berries. The main course may be salmon, trout, or other fish; alternatives can include lamb or pork, reindeer, or even ptarmigan. Remember that the most expensive part of eating is drinking (☞ What It Will Cost *in* Before You Go, *above*) and that spirits are not served on Sundays, although beer and wine are available in most establishments. When dining out, take note that laws relating to drinking and driving are very strict; you should never drink without having a designated driver.

MEALTIMES

Lunch is from noon to 3 at restaurants featuring a *koldtbord*. This is a Scandinavian buffet, primarily for special occasions and visitors. Dinner has traditionally been early, but in hotels and major restaurants it is now more often from 6 to 11. In certain smaller communities, however, dinner is still served from 4 to 7.

WHAT TO WEAR

Unless otherwise indicated, jacket and tie or high-fashion casual wear are recommended for restaurants in the $$$$ and $$$ price categories, although during the summer, neat casual dress is acceptable in most places.

RATINGS

Prices are per person and include a first course, main course, and dessert, without wine or tip. Outside the major cities, prices are considerably lower. Service is always included (☞ Tipping, *below*).

CATEGORY	OSLO
$$$$	over NKr 450
$$$	NKr 300–NKr 450
$$	NKr 150–NKr 300
$	under NKr 150

Lodging

HOTELS

Accommodations in Norway are usually spotless, and smaller establishments are often family-run. Service is thoughtful and considerate, right down to blackout curtains to block out the midnight sun. Passes are available for discounts in hotels. The **Scandinavian Bonus Pass,** costing approximately $25 and also valid in Denmark, Sweden, and Finland, gives up to a 50% discount in 120 Norwegian hotels during summer (May 15–Oct. 1). In addition, children under 15 may stay in their parents' room at no extra charge. Contact **Inter Nor Hotels** (✉ Dronningensgt. 40, 0154 Oslo, ☎ 22334200) or **Scandinavia Choice Hotels International** (✉ Lienga 11, 1410 Kolbotn, ☎ 80034444, FAX 66801077; in USA ☎ 800/221–2222; in UK ☎ 800/444444) or consult Norway's accommodations guide, free from any tourist office. The **Fjord Pass** (✉ Fjord Tours, Box 1752, 5024 Bergen, ☎ 55326550), which costs about $11, is valid at 250 establishments.

CAMPING

Camping is a popular way to keep costs down. There are more than 900 authorized campsites in the country, many in spectacular surroundings. Prices vary according to the facilities provided: A family with a car and tent can expect to pay about NKr 100 per night. Some campsites have log cabins available from NKr 250–NKr 600 per night. *Camping Norway* is available from tourist offices and the **NAF** (⊠ Storgt. 2, 0155 Oslo, ☎ 22341400).

YOUTH HOSTELS

There are about 90 youth hostels in Norway; some are schools or farms used for this purpose in the summer. Members of the Youth Hostel Association (YHA) get a discount. Contact **Norske Vandrerhjem (NoVa;** ⊠ Dronningensgt. 26, 0154 Oslo, ☎ 22421410).

International YHA guides are available to members in the United Kingdom and North America. (There are no age restrictions for membership.) In the United States, contact **American Youth Hostels Inc.** (⊠ 733 15th St. NW, Suite 840, Washington, DC 20005, ☎ 202/783–6161, FAX 202/783–6171). In Canada, contact **Canadian Hostelling Association** (⊠ 1600 James Naismith Dr., Suite 608, Gloucester, Ontario K1B 5N4, ☎ 613/748–5638).

RENTALS

Norwegians escape to mountain cabins whenever they have the chance. Stay in one for a week or two and you'll see why—magnificent scenery, pure air, edible wild berries and a chance to hike, fish, or cross-country ski. For information on renting cabins, farms, or private homes, write to Den Norske Hytteformidling A.S. (⊠ Box 3404, Bjølsen, 0406 Oslo, ☎ 22356710), or get the brochure "Norsk Hytteferie" from tourist offices. An unusual alternative is to rent a *rorbu* (fisherman's dwelling) in the northerly Lofoten Islands. Contact Destination Lofoten (⊠ Box 210, 8301 Svolvær, ☎ 76073000).

RATINGS

Prices are summer rates and are for two people in a double room with bath, and include breakfast, service, and all taxes.

CATEGORY	MAJOR CITIES	OTHER AREAS
$$$$	over NKr 1,300	over NKr 1,000
$$$	NKr 1,000–NKr 1,300	NKr 850–NKr 1,000
$$	NKr 800–NKr 1,000	NKr 650–NKr 850
$	under NKr 800	under NKr 650

Tipping

A 10%–12% service charge is added to most bills at hotels and restaurants. If you have had exceptional service, then give an additional 5% tip. Round off a taxi fare to the next higher unit, or a little more if the driver has been particularly helpful with luggage. If a doorman hails a taxi for you, you can give NKr 5. On sightseeing tours, tip the guide NKr 10–NKr 15 if you are satisfied. Tip with local currency only.

OSLO

Arriving and Departing

By Plane

Oslo's Fornebu Airport, about 20 minutes southwest of Oslo, has international and domestic services. Charter flights go to Gardermoen Airport, about 50 minutes north of the city, which will be Oslo's main airport by 1998.

BETWEEN THE AIRPORT AND DOWNTOWN

The **Flybussen** departs from terminals under Galleri Oslo shopping center and from the SAS Scandinavia Hotel every 10 minutes during scheduled hours and stop at both at Jernbanetorget and Nationaltheatret. Flybussene make round-trips to Fornebu, and the fare is NKr 35; call 67596220 for more information. Alternatively, take Bus 31 from Jernbanetorget (at the central station), marked SNARØYA. The fare is NKr 20; the bus makes a round-trip every hour. Buses meet flights to Gardermoen and take passengers to the central station; the fare is NKr 70. Taxis between Fornebu and downtown cost around NKr 130, depending on time of day.

By Train

Trains on international or domestic long-distance and express routes arrive at Oslo's Sentralstasjon—Oslo S (Oslo Central Station). Suburban trains depart from the Sentralstasjonen, Stortinget, and the Nationaltheatret station.

Getting Around

By Public Transportation

The **Oslo Card**—valid for one, two, or three days—entitles you to free entrance to museums, public swimming pools, and the racetrack; unlimited travel on the Oslo transport system and Norwegian Railways commuter trains within the city limits; free parking on the street and in some lots; and discounts at various stores, cinemas, and sports centers. You can get the card at Oslo's tourist information offices and hotels (☞ Important Addresses and Numbers in Oslo, *below*). A one-day card costs NKr 130; two days NKr 200; three days NKr 240.

If using public transportation only occasionally, you can get tickets (NKr 18) at bus and subway (T-bane) stops. For NKr 40, the **Tourist Ticket** gives 24 hours' unlimited travel on all public transportation, including the summer ferries to Bygdøy. The **Flexikort** gives you eight subway, bus, or *trikk* (streetcar) rides for NKr 100, including transfers.

By Taxi

A taxi is available if the roof light is on. There are taxi stands at the Oslo S Station and usually alongside Narvesen newsstands, or call 22388090; during peak hours, though, you may have to wait.

Important Addresses and Numbers

Embassies

U.S. (✉ Drammensvn. 18, ☎ 22448550). **Canadian** (✉ Oscarsgt. 20, ☎ 22466955). **U.K.** (✉ Thos. Heftyesgt. 8, ☎ 22552400).

Emergencies

Police (✉ Grønlandsleiret 44, ☎ 112 or 22669050; 24-hour service). **Ambulance** (☎ 113 or 22117080; 24-hour service). **Emergency Clinic: Oslo Legevakt** (✉ Storgt. 40, ☎ 22117070); **Dentist** (✉ Oslo Kommunale Tannlegevakt, Tøyen Center, Kolstadsgt. 18; for emergencies, 7 PM–11 PM, weekends and holidays 11 AM–2 PM, ☎ 22673000). **Pharmacy: Jernbanetorgets Apotek** (✉ Jernbanetorget 4B, ☎ 22412482; ⊙ 24 hours).

Post Office

The main post office at Dronningensgate 15 is open weekdays 8–6, Saturday 9–3. The **Telegraph Office** is at Kongensgate 21. Mail can be sent to "poste restante," 0101 Oslo, and picked up at the main post office (☞ Mail *in* Staying in Norway *above*).

English-Language Bookstores
Tanum Libris (⊠ Karl Johans gt. 37–41, ☎ 22411100); **Erik Qvist** (⊠ Drammensvn. 16, ☎ 22445269, next to the U.S. Embassy).

Travel Agencies
Winge (⊠ Karl Johans gt. 33/35, ☎ 22004500) is an agent for American Express. **Kilroy Travels Norway** (⊠ Nedre Slottsgt. 23, ☎ 22420120) specializes in student and youth travel. Try also **Bennett** (⊠ Linstowsgt. 6, ☎ 22697100) or **NSB Travel Agency** (⊠ Stortingsgt. 28, ☎ 22838850).

Visitor Information
The main tourist offices are the **Norway Information Center** (⊠ Vestbaneplassen 1, ☎ 22830050), ☉ Oct.–Apr., Mon.–Sat. 9–4; May and Sept., Mon.–Sat. 9–6; June, Mon.–Sat. 9–6, Sun. 9–4; July and Aug., daily 9–8) and the **Oslo Sentralstasjonen** (Walk-in only. ☉ June–Sept., 8AM–11PM, Oct.–May, 8AM–3PM and 4:30PM–11PM. For information on public transportation call **Trafikanten** (⊠ Oslo Sentralstasjon ☎ 22177030 or 177). It's open weekdays 7AM–11PM, weekends 8AM–11PM.

Guided Tours

Orientation
HMK provides three half-day tours and full-day "Oslo Inclusive" tours that combine various half-day tours. The "Oslo Highlights" morning or afternoon tour goes to the Vigeland Sculpture Park, Holmenkollen ski jump, the Viking Ship Museum, and either the polar ship *Fram* in the morning or the *Kon-Tiki* in the afternoon.

The "Vikingland" afternoon tour visits Oslo's newest attraction park to explore Viking handicrafts, cuisine, and superstitions, and experience a Viking-style raid.

The "Tyrifjord" afternoon excursion heads out of Oslo and to the Hadeland Glass Factory, where you can blow your own glass bottles and shop at the glass outlet.

The "Fjordland" tours are one- to three-day excursions to Bergen and back, on a combination of buses, trains, and boats through some of Norway's most untamed and beautiful mountains, valleys, and fjords. Longer trips include hotel stays. Tickets start at Nkr 190 and may cost as much as Nkr 3,130, depending on the tour. Tickets are available from the Norway Information Center (☞ Important Addresses and Numbers, *above*). Call ☎ 22208206 for more information.

Båtservice Sightseeing has eight boat and/or bus tours—from a 40-minute minicruise to an all-day grand tour of Oslo by boat and bus. ⊠ Rådhusbrygge 3, ☎ 22200715. ⊡ *Minicruise: NKr 70; all-day tour: NKr 320.* ☉ *Tours run Mid-May to mid-Sept.*

Walking
The "Oslo Guide" brochure (free from the tourist office) has several walking tours on its map.

Personal Guides
Taxi drivers give sightseeing tours in English for NKr 300 per hour (fewer than 4 people). Call 22388070 for reservations.

Exploring Oslo

Although it's one of the world's largest capital cities in area, Oslo has only about 480,000 inhabitants. In recent years, the city has taken off: shops are open later, and pubs, cafés, and restaurants are crowded at all hours. The downtown area is compact, but the geographic limits of Oslo spread out to include forests, fjords, and mountains, which give the city a pristine airiness that complements its urban dignity. Explore downtown on foot, then venture beyond via bus, streetcar, or train.

Numbers in the margin correspond to points of interest on the Oslo map.

Oslo's main street, **Karl Johans gate,** runs right through the center of town, from the Oslo S Station uphill to the Royal Palace. Half its length is closed to traffic, and it is in this section that you will find many of the city's shops and outdoor cafés.

★ ❶ Start at **Slottet** (the Royal Palace), the royal family's residence. The neoclassical structure, completed in 1848, is as sober, sturdy, and unpretentious as the Norwegian character. The surrounding park is open to the public, though the palace is not. The changing of the guard happens daily at 1:30. When the king is in residence—signaled by a red flag—the Royal Guard strikes up the band.

❷ Walk down Karl Johans gate to what was once Oslo's **Universitet** (University)—now only the law buildings—comprising the three yellow buildings on your left. The university's main hall, the *Aula* (hall), is decorated with murals by the famous Norwegian artist Edvard Munch (1863–1944). It is open only during July and for public concerts and lectures during the rest of the year. ⊠ *Karl Johans gt. 47.* ☜ *Free.* ☽ *July, weekdays 10–2:45.*

❸ Behind the University is **Nasjonalgalleriet** (the National Gallery), Norway's largest public gallery. It has a small but high-quality selection of paintings by European artists and there's an impressive collection of works by Scandinavian Impressionists. Here you can see Edvard Munch's most famous painting, *The Scream;* however, most of his work is in the Munch Museum (☞ *below*), east of the city center. ⊠ *Universitetsgt. 13.* ☎ *22200404.* ☜ *Free.* ☽ *Mon., Wed., Fri., and Sat. 10–4, Thurs. 10–8, Sun. 11–3.*

❹ In addition to displays of daily life and art from the Viking period, the **Historisk Museum** (Historical Museum) has an ethnographic section with a collection related to the great polar explorer Roald Amundsen, the first man to reach the South Pole. ⊠ *Frederiksgt. 2.* ☎ *22859912.* ☜ *Free.* ☽ *Summer, Tues.–Sun. 11–3; winter, Tues.–Sun. noon–3.*

❺ **Nationaltheatret** (the National Theater) is watched over by the statues of Bjørnstjerne Bjørnson and Henrik Ibsen. Bjørnson was the nationalist poet who wrote Norway's anthem. Ibsen, an internationally lauded playwright, wrote *Peer Gynt* (he personally requested Edvard Grieg's musical score for it), *A Doll's House, Hedda Gabler,* and other classics. He worried that his plays, packed with allegory, myth, and sociological and emotional angst, might not have appeal outside Norway. As it happened, they changed the face of modern theater around the world.

NEED A BREAK? Inside the Grand Hotel, the informal **Palmen** (⊠ Karl Johans gt. 31, ☎ 22429390) serves salads and light meals as well as pastries and cakes.

❻ **Stortinget** (the Parliament), a bow-fronted, yellow-brick building stretched across the block, is open to visitors by request when Parliament is not in session. A guide will take you around the frescoed interior and into the debating chamber. ⊠ *Karl Johans gt. 22,* ☎ *22313050.* ☜ *Free.* ☽ *Guided tours July–Aug; public gallery: weekdays when parliament is in session. Call for hrs.*

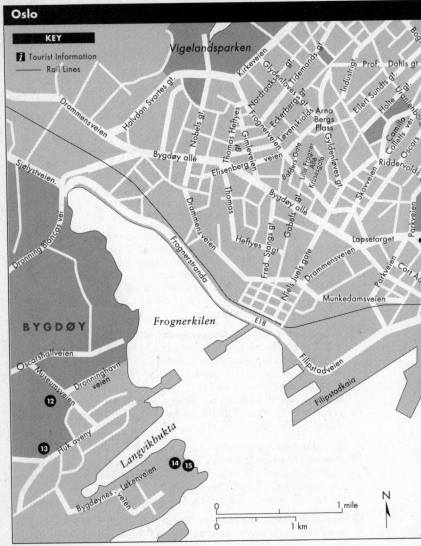

Oslo

KEY

ℹ Tourist Information
—— Rail Lines

Vigelandsparken

Kirkeveien
Nordraaksens gt.
Gyldenløves gt.
Tidemands gt.
Industrigt.
Prof. Dahls gt.

Drammensveien
Halvdan Svartes gt.
Nobels gt.
Thomas Heftyes
Frognerveien
Eckerbergs gt.
Løvenskiolds
Arno Bergs Plass
Eilert Sundts gt.
Holte Gt.
Camillo
Colletts vei
Oscars
Gabels Gate

Bygdøy allé
Gimleveien
veien
Bolders Gate
Lille Frogner Allé
Gyldenløves gt.
Skovveien
Riddervolds
Oscars

Sjølystveien.
Elisenberg
Thomas
Bygdøy allé
Kruses gate

Dronning Blancas vei
Drammensveien
Heftyes
Lapsetorget
Parkveien

Frognerstranda
Fred. Stangs gt.
Niels Juels gate
Drammensveien
Parkveien
Cort Ade

BYGDØY

Frognerkilen
E18
Munkedamsveien

Oscarshallveien
Filipstadveien

Museumsveien
Dronninghavn veien

12

Filipstadkaia

13   Huk aveny

Langvikbukta

14 **15**

Bygdøynes-
Løkenveien
veien

0 ——————— 1 mile
0 ——————— 1 km

N ↑

Seilduksgt.

Helgesens gt.

Grüners gt.

Helgesens gt.

Sofienberggt.

Colletts gt.

Waldemar Thranes gt.

Akersbakken

Maridalsveien

Akerselva

Møllerveien   Nordregt.

Parkveien

Pilestredet

Holbergs gate

Ullevålsveien

Akersveien

Hausmanns gt.

Trondheimsveien

Jens Bjelkes gt.

Wessels gt.

Nordahl Bruns gt.

St. Olavsgt.

Frederiks gate

Universitetsgt.

Rosenkrantz' gt.

Henrik Ibsens gt.

Grubbe

Møllergt.

Torggt.

Urtegt.

Norbygt.

Tøyengt.

1

4   3

2

Karl

5

Johans

gate

Akersgata

Grensen

Youngs-
torget

Storgt.

Brugt.

16

ammensveien

Stortingsgt.

6

Nedre Voll

Slottsgt.

7

Stortorvet

Oslo
Spektrum

Løkkegata

Grønlandsleiret

unkedamsveien

Amundsengt.

11

i

Rådhusgt.

Prinsens gt.

Oslo City

okkveien

10

Nedre Tollbugata

Kirkegata

Dronningens gt.

Skippergt.
Fred Olsens gt.

Strandgt.

Oslo S
Station

Nylandsveien

Schweigaards gt.

Pipervika

Akershusstranda

9

Mynt gt.

Bjørvika

Akerselva

Bispegt.

E18

Bispevika

8

Kongens gate

Skippergt.

SØRENGA

Oslo gt.

Oslofjorden

Mosseveien

Ekebergsletta

❼ Karl Johans gate is closed to traffic near the staid **Oslo Domkirke** (cathedral). The much-renovated cathedral, consecrated in 1697, is modest compared to those of other European capitals, but the interior is rich with treasures, such as the Baroque carved wooden altarpiece and pulpit. The ceiling frescoes by Hugo Lous Mohr were done after World War II. Behind the cathedral is an area of arcades, small restaurants, and street musicians. ⊠ *Stortorvet 1.* 🎫 *Free.* ☉ *Weekdays 10–4.*

❽ **Akershus Slott,** a fortified castle on the harbor, was built during the Middle Ages but restored in 1527 by Christian IV of Denmark (Denmark then ruled Norway) after it was damaged by fire. He then laid out the present city of Oslo (naming it Christiania, after himself) around his new residence; Oslo's street plan still follows his design. Some rooms are open for guided tours, and the grounds form a park around the castle. Also on the grounds are the **Forsvarsmuséet** and **Hjemmefrontmuseum** (Defense and Resistance museums). Both give you a feel for the Norwegian fighting spirit throughout history and especially during the German occupation, when the Nazis set up headquarters on this site and had a number of patriots executed here. ⊠ *Akershus Castle and museums. Entrance from Festningspl.,* ☎ *22412521.* 🎫 *NKr 20.* ☉ *Guided tours of the castle, May–Sept., Mon.–Sat. 11, 1, and 3, Sun. 1 and 3. Forsvarsmuseet and Hjemmefrontmuseum* ☉ *June–Aug., Mon.–Sat. 10–5, Sun. 11–5; May and Sept., Mon.–Sat. 10–4, Sun. 11–4; Oct.–April, Mon.–Sat. 10–3, Sun. 11–4.*

❾ A few blocks behind Akershus Castle, in the direction of the Oslo S Station, is **Muséet for Samtidskunst** (Museum of Contemporary Art), housed in the former Bank of Norway building. ⊠ *Bankpl. 4,* ☎ *22335820.* 🎫 *Free.* ☉ *Tues.–Fri. 11–7, Sat 11–4, Sun. 11–5.*

★ ❿ Walk along Rådhusgate to the waterfront and head toward the central **harbor**—the heart of Oslo and head of the fjord. **Aker Brygge** (Aker Wharf), the quayside shopping and cultural center, with a theater, cinemas, and galleries among the shops, restaurants, and cafés, is a great place to hang out late into summer nights.

⓫ The large redbrick **Rådhuset** (City Hall) is on the waterfront, too. Friezes in the courtyard depict scenes from Norwegian folklore, but its exterior is dull compared to the marble-floored inside halls, where murals and frescoes bursting with color depict daily life, historical events, and Resistance activities in Norway. The elegant main hall has been the venue for the Nobel Peace Prize Ceremony since 1991. ⊠ *Rådhuspl.,* ☎ *22410090.* 🎫 *Free.* ☉ *May–Aug., Mon.–Sat. 9–5, Sun. noon–4; Sept.–Apr., Mon.–Sat. 9–3:30. Tours Mon.–Fri. 10, 12, and 2.*

From **Rådhusbryggen** (the City Hall Wharf) you can board a ferry in summertime for the seven-minute crossing of the fjord to the **Bygdøy** peninsula, where there are several museums and some popular beaches. ☉ *Ferries run May–Sept., daily every half hr 8:15–5:45.*

★ ⓬ The first ferry stop is Dronningen. From here, walk up a well-marked road to the **Norsk Folkemuseum** (Norwegian Folk Museum), a large park where centuries-old historic farmhouses have been collected from all over the country and reassembled. A whole section of 19th-century Oslo was moved here, as was a 12th-century wooden stave church. ⊠ *Museumsvn. 10,* ☎ *22437020.* 🎫 *NKr 50.* ☉ *Summer, daily 9–6; winter, daily 11–3, weekends 11–4.*

⓭ Follow signs to the **Vikingskipshuset** (Viking Ship Museum), which contains 9th-century ships used by Vikings as royal burial chambers. The ships were excavated from the shores of the Oslofjord. Also on display are treasures that accompanied the royal bodies on their last voyage. The ornate craftsmanship evident in the ships and jewelry dispels any notion that the Vikings were skilled only in looting and pillaging. ⊠ *Huk aveny 35.* 🖾 *NKr 30.* ☉ *Nov.–Mar., daily 11–3; Apr. and Oct., daily 11–4; May–Aug., daily 9–6; Sept., daily 11–5.*

★ ⓮ Reboard the ferry or follow signs for the 20-minute walk to the **Kon-Tiki Muséet,** where Thor Heyerdahl's *Kon-Tiki* raft and his reed boat *RA II* are on view. He crossed the Pacific on the former and the Atlantic in the latter. ⊠ *Bygdøynesvn. 36,* ☎ *22438050.* 🖾 *NKr 25.* ☉ *Oct.–Mar., daily 10:30–4; Apr.–May and Sept., daily 10:30–5; June –Aug., daily 9:30–5:45.*

⓯ The **Fram-Muséet,** housed in a triangular building, is a museum devoted to the polar ship *Fram,* the wooden vessel that belonged to polar explorer Fridtjof Nansen. In 1893 Nansen led an expedition that reached latitude 86°14′N, farther north than any European had been at that time. Active in Russian famine-relief work, Nansen received a Nobel Peace Prize in 1922. You can board the ship and imagine yourself in one of the tiny berths, and that outside a force-9 gale is blowing and the temperature is dozens of degrees below freezing. ⊠ *Bygdøynes,* ☎ *22438370.* 🖾 *NKr 20.* ☉ *Mar.–Apr., daily 11–2:45; May, Sept., daily 10–4:45; June–Aug., daily 9–5:45; Oct., daily 10–2:45; Nov., weekends 11–2:45; Dec.–Feb., weekends 11–3:45.*

| NEED A BREAK? | Before catching the ferry back to the center of Oslo, consider a meal or snack at **Lanternen Kro** (⊠ Huk Aveny 2, ☎ 22438125). In summer you can sit on the terrace and enjoy a view of the entire harbor. |

Back at City Hall, board Bus 29 or take the T-bane from the Nationaltheatret to **Tøyen,** an area in northeast Oslo where you'll find the
★ ⓰ **Munch-Muséet** (Munch Museum). In 1940, four years before his death, Edvard Munch bequeathed much of his work to the city; the museum opened in 1963, the centennial of his birth. Although only a fraction of its 22,000 items—books, paintings, drawings, prints, sculptures, and letters—are on display, you can still get a sense of the tortured expressionism that was to have such an effect on European painting. ⊠ *Tøyengt. 53,* ☎ *22673774.* 🖾 *NKr 40.* ☉ *June–mid-Sept., daily 10–6; late Sept.–May, Tues., Wed., Fri, Sat. 10–4, Thurs., Sun., 10–6.*

Off the Beaten Path

Vigelandsparken

Gustav Vigeland's sculptures *Wheel of Life,* a circle in stone depicting the stages of human life, and *Monolith,* nearly 50 feet (15 meters) high and covered with more than 100 linked human forms, are the focal point of **Vigelandsparken,** in northwest Oslo, which is filled with his works. Open-air restaurants, tennis courts, and swimming pools provide additional diversions. To get there, take Trikk 12 or 15 or T-bane trains 1, 2, 3, 4, 5, or 8 and get off at Majorstuen. ⊠ *Kirkevn. and Middelthunsgt.* 🖾 *Free.* ☉ *24 hrs.*

Walk down Frognerveien to Krusesgate and turn left for a view of what Oslo looked like 100 years ago. The decorative gingerbread houses are on the historic preservation list.

Holmenkollen

The **Holmenkollen ski jump,** at 203 feet above ground level, is one of the world's highest and the site of an international contest each March. At the base is a ski museum carved into the rock. To get there, board any Frognerseter/Holmenkollen T-bane train at Nationaltheatret, get off at Holmenkollen, and walk uphill to the jump. The half-hour train ride sweeps from underground up to 1,322 feet above sea level.

The forests within Oslo's vast city limits include 11 sports chalets geared towards exercise and the outdoor life. The areas around **Skullerudstua** and **Skistua** are recommended for their walking and skiing trails. Contact Oslo Kommune (✉ Forestry Services, Skogvesenet, ☎ 22381870) for more information. Or, for winter or summer "safaris" through the forest by Land-Rover, contact the Norway Information Center (☞ Important Addresses and Numbers, *above*).

Ekebergsletta Park
Head east on Trikk 18 or 19 (from Nationaltheatret or Jernbanetorget) to the Sjømannsskolen stop to see 5,000-year-old runic carvings on the stones near **Ekebergsletta park.** They are across the road from the park on Karlsborgveien and marked by a sign reading FORTIDSMINNE. Walk through the park and take Oslogate and then Bispegata to the **Oslo Ladegård,** which has scale models of old Oslo on the site of the 13th-century Bispegård (Bishop's Palace). ✉ *St. Hallvards Plass, Oslogt. 13,* ☎ *22194468.* ⊡ *NKr 20.* ☉ *May–Sept.; guided tours Wed. at 6 and Sun. at 1, and on request. Tours must be booked in advance.*

Lillehammer
Beyond Oslo lies **Lillehammer,** at the top of the long finger of **Lake Mjøsa.** It is reached by train from the Oslo S Station in about two hours. A paddle steamer, **D/S Skibladner,** travels the length of the lake (six hours each way) in summer, making several stops. Site of the 1994 Winter Olympics, Lillehammer is also home of **Maihaugen** (✉ Maihaugvn. 1, ☎ 61288900), one of the largest open-air museums in northern Europe. Why not try out the Olympic bobsled track while you're there? It's in Hunderfossen about 3 miles from town. You can book at the Lillehammer Tourist Office (✉ Lilletorget, ☎ 61259299). There's even a specially adapted sleigh ride for summer fun.

At the southern tip of the lake is **Eidsvoll,** where the Norwegians proclaimed their new constitution in 1814, marking the end of centuries of domination by Denmark. There are limitless possibilities for outdoor activities in the region, all within reach of Oslo.

Shopping

Gift Ideas
Oslo is the best place to do your shopping since prices on handmade articles are government-controlled and selection is widest here: Pewter, silver, glass, sheepskin, leather, painted wood decorations, kitchenware, and knitwear are all appealing.

Shopping Districts
Many of the larger stores are in the area between Stortinget and the cathedral; much of this area is for pedestrians only. The **Basarhallene,** at the back of the cathedral, is an art and handicrafts boutique center just around the corner from the many outdoor vendors and shops that line the pedestrian part of Karl Johans Gate. One of Oslo's newest shopping areas, **Aker Brygge,** was once a shipbuilding wharf. Right on the waterfront, it is a complex of booths, offices, and sidewalk cafés, and is especially lively in summer and spring. Check out the many shops and galleries on **Bogstadveien/Hegdehaugsveien,** which runs from Majorstua to Parkveien. Shops stay open until 5 or 6 on weekdays, 2 or 3 on Saturdays, and 7 or 8 on Thursdays. Stores hold extended hours the first Saturday of the month, known as "Super Saturday."

Department Stores and Malls

Oslo's main department stores are in the shopping district near the cathedral. **Christiania Glasmagasinet** has a smattering of wares, including a fabulous larger-than-life toy shop (Fetter Klovn's), a well-stocked souvenir shop, and lots of silver and pewter jewelry. **Paléet** on Karl Johans gate is an elegant indoor shopping center with 45 shops and 13 restaurants. It has extended shopping hours. Across the street from Oslo's Sentralstasjon you will find Oslo's largest shopping mall—**Oslo City**—with more than 100 stores and businesses including a bank, a travel agency, and a grocery store on the lower level; hours are 9–8 weekdays and 9–6 weekends. Also check out **Grønlands Torg** behind the Oslo Plaza Hotel, a market with produce, jewelry, and nearby discount clothing stores.

Food and Flea Markets

Every Saturday during spring, summer, and fall, there is a flea market at Vestkanttorget, two blocks from Frogner Park at the junction of Professor Dahls gate and Eckerbergs gate. Check the papers for local *loppemarkeder* (flea markets) in schools and outdoor squares around town.

Dining

For details and price-category definitions, *see* Dining *in* Staying in Norway, *above*.

$$$$ ✕ **Bagatelle.** Bagatelle was the first restaurant with a Norwegian chef
★ serving Norwegian food to receive international recognition. Choose the seven-course menu for the full range of chef Hellstrøm's talents. The chairs are comfortable, service is impeccable, and Norwegian contemporary art adorns the walls. ⊠ *Bygdøy allé 3*, ☎ *22446397. AE, DC, MC, V. No lunch. Closed Sun.*

$$$$ ✕ **D'Artagnan.** Among gourmands, D'Artagnan is a favorite. Stellar
★ French-inspired food and excellent service make this a place to remember. Try chef Freddie Nielsen's copious Grand Menu if you're famished. Otherwise, try the beef: you can literally cut it with a fork. **A Touch of France** (☎ *22425697, $$*), downstairs from D'Artagnan, is a French-style brasserie run by the same chef. The bouillabaisse is outstanding. ⊠ *Øvre Slottsgt. 16*, ☎ *22415062. Reservations essential. AE, DC, MC, V. Closed weekends.*

$$$$ ✕ **De Fem Stuer.** Chef Frank Halvorsen prepares food that is even bet-
★ ter than the view. Enjoy modern versions of Norwegian specialties, with the accent on fish and game. ⊠ *Holmenkollen Park Hotel, Kongevn. 26*, ☎ *22922734. AE, DC, MC, V.*

$$$$ ✕ **Feinschmecker.** In the fashionable Frogner area only minutes from the center of town, this restaurant specializes in modern Scandinavian cuisine. ⊠ *Balchensgt. 5*, ☎ *22441777. Reservations essential. AE, DC, MC, V. Closed Sun.*

$$$ ✕ **Babette's Gjestehus.** This warm and intimate restaurant has an international menu with a French accent. ⊠ *Rådhuspassasjen*, ☎ *22416464. Reservations essential. AE, DC, MC, V. Closed Sun. No lunch.*

$$$ ✕ **Theatercafeen.** This Oslo institution is one of the last Viennese-style
★ cafés in northern Europe and is a favorite with the literary and entertainment crowd. Save room for dessert, which the pastry chef also makes for Norway's royal family. ⊠ *Hotel Continental, Stortingsgt. 24/26*, ☎ *22824050. AE, DC, MC, V.*

$$ ✕ **Det Gamle Raadhus.** The "old city hall," Oslo's oldest restaurant, is in a building that dates from 1641. Specialties include stockfish and shellfish casserole. ⊠ *Nedre Slottsgt. 1*, ☎ *22420107. AE, DC, MC, V. Closed Sun.*

$$ ✕ **Dinner.** Though its name is not the best for a restaurant specializ-
★ ing in Szechuan-style cuisine, this is the best place for Chinese food,
both hot and not so pungent. The mango pudding for dessert is won-
derful. ✉ *Stortingsgt. 22,* ☎ *22426890. AE, DC, MC, V. No lunch.*

$$ ✕ **Frognerseteren.** Just above the Holmenkollen ski jump, this restaurant looks down on the entire city. Take the Holmenkollbanen to the
end station and then walk downhill to the restaurant. Follow the signs.
The upstairs room has the same view as the more expensive panorama
veranda. There is also an outdoor café. ✉ *Holmenkollenvn. 200,* ☎
22143736. DC, MC, V.

$$ ✕ **Kastanjen.** The short menu at this stylish neighborhood bistro,
whose name means "the chestnut tree," changes often and features all
seasonal ingredients. The three-course prix-fixe dinner is an excellent
value. ✉ *Bygdøy allé 18,* ☎ *22434467. AE, DC, MC, V. Closed Sun
and 2 wks in July.*

$ ✕ **Lofotstua.** This rustic fish restaurant has a cozy atmosphere and good
food. Typical specialties include fresh cod and seafood from the Lo-
foten Islands in northern Norway. ✉ *Kirkevn. 40,* ☎ *22469396. AE,
DC, MC, V. Closed Sat. and July.*

$ ✕ **Vegeta.** Next to the Nationaltheatret bus and trikk station, this is
a popular spot for hot and cold vegetarian meals and salads. It is a no-
smoking restaurant. The all-you-can-eat specials offer top value. ✉
Munkedamsvn. 3B, ☎ *22834020. Reservations not accepted. AE,
DC, V.*

Lodging

The **tourist office** (☉ June–Sept., 8AM–11PM, Oct.–May, 8AM–3PM and
4:30PM–11PM) in Oslo's Sentralstasjonen has an **accommodations bu-
reau** that can help you find rooms in hotels, pensions, and private homes.
You must apply in person and pay a fee of NKr 20. If you arrive and
need a hotel the same day, ask about last-minute prices, which are gen-
erally discounted. If you are planning your trip from home, call **ScanAm**
(☞ Getting Around *in* Essential Information, *above*) about the Oslo
Package, which combines an Oslo Card with discounted room rates
on almost all of Oslo's better hotels; in the U.K. call **NSB Travel** (☞
Getting Around *in* Essential Information, *above*). For details and price-
category definitions, *see* Lodging *in* Staying in Norway, *above.*

$$$$ ▥ **Grand Hotel.** It's hard to beat the Grand's location on Oslo's main
★ street, opposite Parliament. The hotel has comforts and history to
match its name: Ibsen had a permanent table in Grand Caféen, a fa-
mous Oslo rendezvous. Palmen, just off the lobby, is where Oslo ma-
trons drink their afternoon tea. ✉ *Karl Johans gt. 31, 0159,* ☎
22429390, ℻ *22421225. 289 rooms with bath and shower, 37 suites.
3 restaurants, 2 bars, indoor pool, health club, parking (fee). AE, DC,
MC, V.*

$$$$ ▥ **Holmenkollen Park Rica.** This is probably the best place for anyone
★ hoping to do some skiing. You'll quickly spot this imposing building
in the old romantic folkloric style near the ski jump in Holmenkollen.
The rooms are bright, and most have balconies with excellent views
of the city and the fjord. The hotel runs a shuttle bus for its guests since
it's a 20-minute drive from downtown. ✉ *Kongevn. 26, 0390,* ☎
22922000, ℻ *22141692. 221 rooms with bath. 2 restaurants, bar, in-
door pool, hot tub, sauna, cross-country skiing, nightclub. AE, DC,
MC, V.*

$$$$ ▥ **Hotel Continental.** The Brockmann family, owners since 1900, have
★ succeeded in combining the rich elegance of the turn of the century with
modern, comfortable living. Antique furniture and shiny white porce-
lain fixtures add a distinctive touch to the impeccably decorated rooms.

The adjoining Theatercafeen (☞ Dining, *above*) has for years been a haunt of local celebrities and CEOs—a place to see and be seen. ⊠ *Stortingsgt. 24–26, 0161,* ☎ *22824000,* FAX *22429689. 158 rooms with bath, 12 suites. 3 restaurants, 2 bars, nightclub. AE, DC, MC, V.*

$$$$ 🏨 **SAS Scandinavia Hotel.** The SAS, across from the Royal Palace, is a comfortable business hotel with impeccable service . The airport bus stops right outside. The rooftop lunch bar, Summit 21, has views of the entire city. ⊠ *Holbergs gt. 30, 0166,* ☎ *22113000,* FAX *22113017. 491 rooms with bath, 3 suites. 2 restaurants, 2 bars, indoor pool, health club, shops. AE, DC, MC, V.*

$$$ 🏨 **Ambassadeur.** On a quaint residential street, this hotel has individually
★ designed rooms and personalized service. ⊠ *Camilla Colletts vei 15, 0266,* ☎ *22441835,* FAX *22444791. 41 rooms with bath or shower, 8 suites. Restaurant, bar, indoor pool, sauna, AE, DC, MC, V.*

$$$ 🏨 **Radisson SAS Park Royal Hotel.** Fifteen minutes from Oslo's center, this hotel is clean, efficient, and convenient to Fornebu Airport. The top-class facilities, including direct airport check-in, are well suited to business stays. ⊠ *Fornebuparken, Box 1324, 1324 Lysaker,* ☎ *67120220,* FAX *67120011. 254 rooms with bath, 14 suites. Restaurant, health club, tennis courts, meeting rooms. AE, DC, MC, V.*

$$$ 🏨 **Stefan.** The service is cheerful and accommodating in this hotel in the center of Oslo. One of its main attractions is the popular restaurant on the top floor, where Oslo's best buffet lunch, featuring traditional Norwegian dishes, is served. ⊠ *Rosenkrantz' gt. 1, 0159,* ☎ *22429250,* FAX *22337022. 130 rooms with bath or shower. Restaurant, meeting room. AE, DC, MC, V.*

$$ 🏨 **Bondeheimen.** Established to provide "down-home" accommodations for farmers on business in the big city, this may be Oslo's most Norwegian hotel. The simple rooms are comfortable. ⊠ *Rosenkrantz' gt. 8, 0159,* ☎ *22429530,* FAX *22419437. 76 rooms with shower. Café, meeting rooms. AE, DC, MC, V.*

$$ 🏨 **Cecil Hotel.** Known for its copious breakfast table, this relatively inexpensive hotel is right in the heart of town near the Parliament building. It also claims to have the best air-conditioning in the city. ⊠ *Stortingsgt. 8, 0130,* ☎ *22427000,* FAX *22422670. 110 rooms with bath. Breakfast room, air-conditioning. AE, DC, MC, V.*

$$ 🏨 **Gabelshus Hotel.** Only five minutes from the center of town on an attractive side street in Frogner, Gabelshus has the feel of a large country house. The rooms are spacious and airy. ⊠ *Gabels gt. 16, 0272,* ☎ *22552260,* FAX *22442730. 50 rooms with bath. Restaurant. AE, DC, MC, V.*

$ 🏨 **Haraldsheim.** Oslo's youth hostel is one of Europe's largest. Most of the rooms have four beds, and those in the new wing all have showers. It is about 15 minutes from the city center on Trikk 10 or 11 to Sinsen. Breakfast is included.⊠ *Haraldsheimvn. 4, 0409,* ☎ *22155043,* FAX *22221025. 264 beds. V.*

$ 🏨 **Munch.** This B&B hotel, near the National Gallery, is only a 5-minute walk from city center. The rooms are large, but rather basic. ⊠ *Munchsgt. 5, 0165,* ☎ *22424275,* FAX *22206469. 180 rooms with shower. AE, DC, MC, V.*

$ 🏨 **Rainbow Gyldenløve.** Freshly decorated rooms are offered here at a reasonable price. Just outside the hotel's door are many shops and cafés. ⊠ *Bogstadvn. 20, 0355,* ☎ *22601090,* FAX *22603390. 169 rooms with bath or shower. Breakfast room. AE, DC, MC, V.*

The Arts

Considering the size of the city, Oslo has a surprisingly good arts scene. Consult the "Oslo Guide" or the monthly "What's On in Oslo" for details. Both are available at the Tourist Information Center. Winter is *the* cultural season, with the **Nationaltheatret** featuring modern plays (all in Norwegian), classics, and a good sampling of Ibsen. **Det Norske Teatret** (⊠ Kristian IV's gate 8, ☏ 22424344), one of Europe's most modern theater complexes, has musicals and plays.

Oslo's modern **Konserthuset** (⊠ Munkedamsvn. 14, ☏ 22833200) is the home of the Oslo Philharmonic, famous for its recordings of Tchaikovsky's symphonies. A smaller hall in the same building has folk dancing, held Monday and Thursday at 9 in July and August. The **Museet for Samtidskunst** (☞ Exploring, *above*) has a fine collection of international and Norwegian pieces. The **Henie-Onstad Kunstsenter** displays an impressive collection of important works by Leger, Munch, Picasso, Bonnard, and Matisse (⊠ Høvikodden, ☏ 67543050; ☉ Mon. 11–5, Tue.–Fri. 9–9, weekends, 11–7). The center was a gift from the Norwegian Olympic skater Sonja Henie and her husband, shipowner Niels Onstad, and is about 12 kilometers (7 miles) outside of Oslo. If you want to go to the movies, note that all films are screened in the original language with Norwegian subtitles. Tickets cost NKr 50. If you like alternative and classic films, try **Cinemateket** (⊠ Dronningensgt. 16, ☏ 22474505), the city's only independent cinema.

Nightlife

Karl Johans Gate is a lively and drunken place into the wee hours. There are loads of music cafés and clubs, as well as more conventional nightspots. **Barock** (⊠ Universitetsgt. 26, ☏ 22424420) is where Oslo's young and beautiful people choose to dance, complete with elegant chandeliers, white cloth–clad tables, and blaring techno pop. **Smuget** (⊠ Rosenkrantz' gt. 22, ☏ 22425262) is a combination discotheque and bar with live rock and blues bands almost every night of the week. **Lipp** (⊠ Olav V's gt. 2, ☏ 22414400) is a disco, pre-dinner drinks bar, and popular dinner spot. Media people and students hang out at **Kristiania** (⊠ Kristian IV's gt. 12, ☏ 22425660), a three-story disco with frequent live jazz sessions on the third floor.

THE COAST ROAD TO STAVANGER

This tour follows the Sørlandet coast south of Oslo toward the busy port Kristiansand and then west to Stavanger. It is an area where whaling has given way to canneries, lumber, paper production, and petrochemicals. Yet the beauty of this 608-kilometer (380-mile) route has not been greatly marred, and you'll find seaside towns, rocky headlands, and stretches of forest (fjord country does not begin until north of Stavanger). The route outlined here follows the coast, but it is also possible to reach Stavanger on an inland route through Telemark.

Getting Around

By Car
Driving is recommended because it gives you the chance to stop at coastal villages that are either not served by trains or have only sporadic service. The route is simple: E18 as far as Flekkefjord, then Route 44 to Stavanger.

By Train
The best train service is the Sørland line, which leaves Oslo S Station and goes all the way to Stavanger. The Oslo–Drammen stretch is an engineering feat and features Norway's longest tunnel, an 11-kilometer (7-mile) bore through sheer rock.

By Bus

Local buses cover the entire route, but they take much longer than the train. For details on fares and schedules, check with the tourist offices listed below or the Norway Information Center in Oslo (☞ Important Addresses and Numbers *in* Oslo, *above*).

Guided Tours

In summer there is a daily boat excursion from Oslo to the coastal resorts of Kragerø, Jomfruland, and Risør southwest of the capital. Sightseers return the same day, and refreshments are served on board. The excursion is organized by the Norway Information Center (☞ Important Addresses and Numbers *in* Oslo, *above*).

Visitor Information

Arendal (✉ Friholmsgt. 1, ☎ 37022193); **Drammen** (✉ Rådhuset, ☎ 32806210); **Flekkefjord** (☎ 38321260); **Kristiansand** (✉ Dronningensgt. 2, ☎ 38026065); **Larvik** (✉ Storgt. 48, ☎ 33130100); **Mandal** (✉ Bryggetgt., ☎ 38260820); **Risør** (☎ 37158560); **Stavanger** (✉ Stavanger Kulturhus, Sølvberget, ☎ 51896200); **Tønsberg** (✉ Nedre Langgt. 36B, ☎ 33310220).

Exploring the Coast Road to Stavanger

From Oslo, take E18 west for about 40 kilometers (25 miles) to the bustling port of **Drammen.** At the mouth of a large timber-floating river, Drammen operates as a processing and shipping center for lumber and paper products. Take a short detour west of town on Route 11, turn right on Kongsgate, and climb the mile-long series of spiraling tunnels leading to **Spiraltoppen** at **Bragernes Hill.** During the '50s, locals decided against any further quarrying of building stone and turned instead to tunneling for it. The result is this scenic and dramatic road with panoramic views of **Drammensfjord** and **Oslofjord.**

Return to E18 and continue to the coastal town of **Åsgårdstrand,** an unspoiled summer resort where Edvard Munch painted many of his best works. He spent seven summers in a small yellow frame house, **Munchs lille hus** (✉ Munchsgt. ⊠ NKr 15), which is open to visitors during the summer. Farther along is **Tønsberg,** which inhabitants claim is Norway's oldest town, founded in AD 870. The steep hill, Slottsfjellet, beside the train station leads to the ruins of **Tønsberghus,** an extensive fortress and abbey. The outlook tower, built in 1870 to commemorate the town's millennium, has a good view of the coast. The rise of Oslo as Norway's capital led to the decline of Tønsberg, although it thrived as a whaling port in the 1700s.

Attractive **Sandefjord,** 15 kilometers (9 miles) down E18, is a port that served as the base for the Norwegian whaling fleet until after World War II, when large-scale competition from the Soviet Union and Japan made the operation uneconomical. The port remains a busy depot for timber shipping.

Just beyond Sandefjord, E18 crosses the Lågen, an important lumbering river, and then follows it to the port of **Larvik,** which is the terminus for ferries to Frederikshavn in Denmark. Like Tønsberg and Sandefjord, Larvik once looked to whaling for its livelihood, but it, too, has turned to lumber and ferrying for employment.

The **Maritime Museum,** in the former customs house, chronicles Larvik's seafaring history, and includes Thor Heyerdahl's voyages, with mod-

Coast Road to Stavanger

els of the *Kon-Tiki* and *RA II. Admission charges and opening times vary; check with the tourist office.*

After Larvik, progress is faster, as E18 cuts across some of the narrower peninsulas on its way south. Side roads offer the chance to explore the smaller coastal village of **Kragerø,** where Edvard Munch spent many summers painting. Next is **Risør,** a sailing center with picturesque, white-painted, patrician 19th-century harbor-front houses. If you happen to be here in late summer, don't miss the wooden sailboat festival this town hosts every August. After **Risør** comes **Tvedestrand,** which has charming historic sections.

Arendal, 120 kilometers (75 miles) beyond Larvik, was once called the Venice of Scandinavia, but its canals have now been turned into wide streets. The atmosphere of bygone whaling prosperity in this and other Sørland ports is like that of Nantucket, with tidy cottages and grandiose captains' houses all within shouting distance of the docks. Explore Arendal's **Tyholmen quarter** for a glimpse into this 19th-century world.

Kristiansand is another 50 kilometers (31 miles) along the coast from Arendal. It is the largest town in Sørlandet and has important air, sea, road, and rail links. It was laid out during the 17th century in a grid pattern, with the imposing **Christiansholm Festning** guarding the eastern harbor approach. East of Kristiansand on Route E18 is the open-air **Vest-Agder Fylkesmuseum** (county museum), with 30 old buildings and farms rebuilt in the local style of the 18th and 19th centuries. ⊠ *Kongsgård,* ☎ *38090228.* 🎟 *NKr 20.* ☉ *Late June–late Aug., Mon.–Sat. 10–6, Sun. noon–6; winter, Sun. noon–5 or by appointment.*

Kids love the nearby **Kristiansand Dyrepark** with five separate parks, including a water park, a forested park, an entertainment park, and a zoo. There's also Kardemomme By (Cardamom Town), a replicated village. ☎ 38049700. ✉ *NKr 160 (prices may be discounted off-season).* ☉ *Jan.–mid-June and mid-Aug.–Dec., daily 10–3; mid-June–mid-Aug., daily 9–6.*

Continue along E18 for another 30 kilometers (19 miles) to **Mandal,** Norway's most southerly town, famous for its beach, salmon, and 18th- and 19th-century houses. Every year, seafood lovers flock here for the shellfish festival the second weekend in August. For the next 30 kilometers (19 miles), the road climbs and weaves its way through steep, wooded hills and then descends to the fishing port of **Flekkefjord,** with its charming **Hollenderbyen,** or Dutch Quarter.

E18 heads inland here to Stavanger, but it is more rewarding to follow the coast road (Route 44) past the fishing port of **Egersund,** 40 kilometers (25 miles) ahead, and a little farther to **Ogna,** known for the stretch of sandy beach that has inspired so many Norwegian artists, among them Kitty Kjelland. Here you will find some of the most beautiful and unspoiled beaches in the south of Norway. Camping is an option to consider, available at Brusand and Ogna. For the last hour or so before Stavanger, you will be in the region known as the **Jæren.** Flat and stony, it is the largest expanse of level terrain in this mountainous country. The mild climate and the absence of good harbors caused the people here to turn to agriculture, and the miles of stone walls are a testament to their labor.

★ **Stavanger,** at the end of the tour, is a former trading town that became a focus (some environmentalists say victim) of the oil boom. It is now the fourth-largest city in Norway. Drilling platforms and oil tankers take the place of fishing boats in the harbor. In sharp contrast to the new high-rise complexes, there is an old quarter with narrow, cobbled lanes and clapboard houses at odd angles. The town is believed to date from the 8th century; its Anglo-Norman **Domkirke** (cathedral), next to the central market, was established in 1125 by the English bishop of Winchester. (Trading and ecclesiastical links between Norway and England were strong throughout the Middle Ages.)

Ledaal (✉ Eiganesvn. 45, ☎ 51520618. ✉ NKr 20. ☉ Mid-June–mid Aug., daily 11–4; mid-Aug.–mid-June, Sun. 11–4) is a fine patrician mansion where the royal family resides when it's visiting Stavanger. Across the street is **Breidablikk** manor house (✉ Eiganesvn. 40A, ☎ 51526035. ✉ NKr 20. ☉ Mid-June–mid Aug., daily 11–4; mid-Aug.–mid-June, Sun. 11–4), built by a Norwegian shipping magnate. An outstanding example of what Norwegians call "Swiss style" architecture, it has been perfectly preserved since the 1960s. Nearby **Ullandhaug** (✉ Grannesvn., Ullandhaug, ☎ 51534140. ✉ NKr 20. ☉ Mid-June–Aug., daily noon–5; early May–mid-Sept., Sun. noon–4) is a reconstructed Iron Age farm. The ♨ **Norsk Hermetikkmuseum** (Canning Museum; ✉ Øvre Strandgt. 88A, ☎ 51534989. ✉ NKr 20), in the heart of Old Stavanger, is a reconstructed sardine factory in use between 1890 and 1920; here you'll get a lesson in the production of sardines and fish conserves.

The **Norwegian Emigration Center** specializes in genealogy and family research, helping to bridge the gap between Norway and the families of Norwegians who emigrated to America. ✉ *Bergjelandsgt. 30,* ☎ *51501267,* FAX *51501290.* ☉ *Weekdays 9–3.*

The **Ryfylke fjords** north and east of Stavanger form the southern end of the fjord country. The city is a good base for exploring this region, with the "white fleet" of low-slung sea buses making daily excursions into even the most distant fjords of Ryfylke. Great for a heart-stop-

★ ping view is **Prekestolen** (Pulpit Rock), a huge cube of rock with a vertical drop of 2,000 feet. You can join a tour to get there or you can do

it on your own from mid-June to late August by taking the ferry from Fiskepiren across Hildefjorden to Tau, riding a bus to the Pulpit Rock Lodge, and walking 1½ to 2 hours to the rock. If you're here between January and April, try skiing in Sirdal, 2½ hours from Stavanger. Special ski buses leave the Stavanger bus station weekends at 8:30 AM; contact SOT Reiser (☎ 51556066) for information.

Dining and Lodging

For details and price-category definitions, *see* Dining and Lodging *in* Staying in Norway, *above.*

Arendal

$$ ✕ **Madam Reiersen.** Good, traditional Norwegian food is served in an informal atmosphere at this waterfront restaurant. ⊠ *Nedre Tyholmsvn. 3,* ☎ *37021900. Reservations essential on weekends. AE, DC, MC, V.*

$$ 🔟 **Inter Nor Tyholmen.** This new maritime hotel is in the heart of Tyholmen, Arendal's old town, which is filled with well-preserved, brightly painted houses. The views of the fjord are splendid. ⊠ *Teaterpl. 2, 4801,* ☎ *37026800,* 🅵🅰🆇 *37026801. 60 rooms with bath. 2 restaurants, bar. AE, DC, MC, V.*

Drammen

$$ ✕ **Le Franske Café.** The perfect spot for a romantic lunchtime rendezvous, this café just off Bragernes Plaza serves French and continental dishes. ⊠ *Øvre Torggt.12,* ☎ *32832620. Reservations not accepted. AE, DC, MC, V.*

$$ ✕ **Spiraltoppen Café.** You'll find excellent views and good food at this café atop Bragernes Hill. ⊠ *Bragernesåsen,* ☎ *32837815. Reservations not accepted. AE, DC, MC, V.*

$$ 🔟 **Rica Park Hotel.** This comfortable and central hotel has a traditional Norwegian atmosphere. ⊠ *Gamle Kirkepl. 3, 3019,* ☎ *32838280,* 🅵🅰🆇 *32893207. 103 rooms and 2 suits with bath or shower. 2 restaurants, bar, nightclub. AE, DC, MC, V.*

Kristiansand

$$–$$$ ✕ **Sjøhuset.** Seafood and fish are best bets in this rustic waterfront restaurant. ⊠ *Østre Strandgt. 12a,* ☎ *38026260. Reservations not accepted. AE, DC, MC, V. Closed Oct.–Feb.*

$$ 🔟 **Rica Fregatten.** Only a stone's throw from the town hall and cathedral, this medium-size hotel is right in the center of town. Also nearby is the new harbor beach. ⊠ *Dronningens gt. 66, 4602,* ☎ *38021500,* 🅵🅰🆇 *38020119. 47 rooms with shower. Restaurant, bar. AE, DC, MC, V.*

Larvik

$$ ✕🔟 **Inter Nor Grand Hotel Farris.** Spotless rooms and attentive service are what you'll find at this large hotel overlooking the fjord. Sample the local fish soup and smoked meat platters in the hotel's restaurant, Alexander, which is particularly good for lunch. ⊠ *Storgt. 38–40, 3256,* ☎ *33187800,* 🅵🅰🆇 *33187045. 89 rooms with bath. Restaurant, bar, pub, night club. AE, DC, MC, V.*

Sandefjord

$$–$$$ ✕ **Edgar Ludl's Gourmet.** Enjoy fish specialties prepared by master chef ★ Ludl in the best restaurant outside Oslo. The eight- and five-course menus are an excellent choice. ⊠ *Rådhusgt. 7.,* ☎ *33462741. AE, DC, MC, V. Closed Sun.*

$$$ 🏨 **Rica Park Hotel.** The imposing Rica Park, one of the best hotels in
★   Norway, overlooks Sandefjord's attractive harbor. The rooms are large
and comfortable, and the service is flawless. ⊠ *Strandpromenaden 9,*
3200, ☎ *33465550,* FAX *33467900. 185 rooms with bath or shower.*
2 restaurants, 4 bars, pool, sauna. AE, DC, MC, V.

Stavanger

$$ ✕ **Harry Pepper.** This trendy Mexican restaurant has a popular ad-
joining bar. The color schemes are a fun and gaudy display of tacky
South American souvenirs. ⊠ *Øvre Holmegate 15,* ☎ *51893993. AE,*
DC, V.

$$ ✕ **Sjøhuset Skagen.** A restored 17th-century wharf house, this spot spe-
cializes in seafood plus lots of atmosphere. ⊠ *Skagen 16,* ☎ *51895180,*
FAX *51895181. AE, DC, MC, V.*

$$ ✕ **Straen.** In the oldest part of town, this famous fish restaurant offers a wide selection of delicious fresh seafood. A nightclub, a rock café,
and a pub are on the premises. ⊠ *Nedre Strandgt. 15,* ☎ *51526230,*
FAX *51567798. AE, DC, MC, V. Closed Sun.*

$$–$$$ 🏨 **Skagen Brygge.** This hotel comprises three rehabilitated old sea
houses. Almost all rooms are different, from modern to old-fashioned
maritime with exposed beams and brick-and-wood walls; many have
harbor views. The hotel has an arrangement with 14 restaurants in the
area—it makes the reservations and the tab ends up on your bill. ⊠
Skagenkaien 30, 4006, ☎ *51894100,* FAX *51895883. 106 rooms with*
bath. Bar, pool, Turkish bath, exercise room, meeting rooms. AE, DC,
MC, V.

$–$$ 🏨 **Grand Hotel.** On the edge of the town center, this hotel doesn't aim
to be fancy: Rooms are comfortable and bright, done in pastels and
white. In summer the rates drop significantly. ⊠ *Klubbgt. 3, 4012,* ☎
51895800, FAX *51895710. 92 rooms with bath. Breakfast room, bar.*
AE, DC, MC, V.:

THROUGH TELEMARK TO BERGEN

Bergen is Norway's second-largest city. To get there from Oslo, you
can detour south through the Telemark area. This region is marked by
steep valleys, pine forests, lakes, and fast-flowing rivers full of trout.
Morgedal, the cradle of skiing, is here. You'll go on to Hardangervidda,
a wild mountain area and national park that was the stronghold of
Norway's Resistance fighters during World War II, and then down to
the beautiful Hardangerfjord. Few places on earth match western Norway for spectacular scenic beauty—this is the fabled land of the fjords.

Fjord transportation is good, as crossing fjords is a necessary as well
as scenic way to travel in Norway. Hardangerfjorden, Sognefjord, and
Nordfjord are three of the deepest and most popular fjords.

Guided Tours

Bergen is the gateway to the fjords, and excursions cover most of the
last half of the tour below as well as the fjords farther north. Contact
the tourist information offices (☞ *below*) for details of these constantly changing tours.

Visitor Information

Bergen (⊠ Bryggen 7, ☎ 55321480); **Drammen** (⊠ Rådhuset, ☎
32806210); **Kinsarvik** (⊠ Public library bldg., mid-June–mid–Aug., ☎

53663112); **Kongsberg** (⊠ Storgt. 35, ☎ 32735000); **Røldal** (☎ 53647259).

Exploring Through Telemark to Bergen

Take E18 west from Oslo to nearby Drammen (☞ The Coast Road to Stavanger, *above*). Follow Route 11 through Drammen and continue west for about 40 kilometers (25 miles) to **Kongsberg,** by the fast-flowing Lågen River. Kongsberg was founded in 1624 as a silver-mining town. Although there is no more mining, the old mines at Saggrenda are open for guided tours. The **Norsk Bergverksmuseum** (Norwegian Mining Museum; ⊠ Hyttegt. 3, ☎ 32733260) includes the Silver Mines Collection, the Ski Museum, and the Royal Mint Museum. In the center of town is an 18th-century Rococo church, which reflects the town's former source of wealth—silver.

Kongsberg is one of the gateways to Telemark, which is just beyond Meheia on the county border. Forests give way to rocky peaks and desolate spaces farther into the plateau. **Heddal** is the first stop in Telemark. Norway's largest stave church, the Heddal church, is here. Stave churches are built with wooden planks staked vertically into the ground or base and usually have some carved ornamentation on the doors and around the aisle. These churches date from the medieval period and are found almost exclusively in southern Norway.

Route 11 climbs from Heddal and skirts the large Telemark plateau. You'll see the **Lifjell** area's highest peak, Røydalsnuten (4,235 feet), on the left before you descend toward **Seljord,** on the lake of the same name. The countryside by the lake is richer than that on the plateau; meadows and pastureland run down to the lakefront. The attractive village of Seljord has ornamented wooden houses and a medieval church.

Continue south from Seljord, making sure to stay right (on Route 11) at the Brunkeberg intersection, where the other road continues south to Kristiansand. You are now entering the steep valley of **Morgedal.** It was here in the last century that Sondre Nordheim developed the Telemark method of skiing. You can get the full story on the development of skiing at the **Olav Bjåland's Museum** (⊠ Opposite Morgedal Turisthotell, ☎ 35054250), named for the south polar explorer and ski hero.

Turn left at Høydalsmo for a scenic diversion to mountain-bound **Dalen.** At Dalen is **Tokke I,** one of Europe's largest hydroelectric power stations. From here it's an 8-kilometer (5-mile) drive to **Eidsborg,** where there is a stave church and a dramatic view of the Dalen valley.

Take Route 38 from Dalen along the Tokke valley to **Åmot.** The 305-foot Hyllandfoss Falls were destroyed by the hydroelectric project, but the drive is still spectacular.

Rejoin Route 11 at Åmot. At the next crossroads (**Haukeligrend**), Route 11 really begins to climb, and you'll see why the Norwegians are so proud of keeping this route open all year. Before you leave Telemark, you'll pass through the 6-kilometer (4-mile) Haukeli Tunnel and then begin a long descent to **Røldal,** another lakefront village with a hydroelectric plant.

Turn north on Route 13 a few miles after Røldal, and drive to the **Sørfjord** at Odda. Continue along the fjord to the attractive village of **Kinsarvik.** For the best view of the junction of the Sørfjord and the mighty Hardangerfjord, take the ferry across the Sørfjord to Utne. On the dramatic 30-minute ferry crossing from Utne to Kvanndal, you will know why this area was such a rich source of inspiration for Romantic composer Edvard Grieg.

Through Telemark to Bergen

At Kvanndal, turn left on Route 7. The road follows the fjord west, then veers right to **Norheimsund.** After climbing another coastal mountain spur, it winds through the wild **Tokagjel Gorge** and across the mountains of **Kvamskogen,** then descends tortuously into Bergen, capital of the fjords.

★ **Bergen** was founded in 1070, and has been named the EEC's European Culture Center for the year 2000. Norway's second-largest city, Bergen has a population of 219,000. Before oil brought an influx of foreigners to Stavanger, it was the most international of the country's cities, having been an important trading and military center when Oslo was still an obscure village. Bergen was a member of the medieval Hanseatic League and offered an ice-free harbor and convenient trading location on the west coast. Natives of Bergen still think of Oslo as a dour provincial town.

Despite numerous fires in its past, much of medieval Bergen has survived. Seven surrounding mountains set off the weathered wooden houses, cobbled streets, and Hanseatic-era warehouses of **Bryggen** (the harbor area).

The best way to get a feel for Bergen's medieval trading heyday is to visit the **Hanseatisk Museum.** One of the oldest and best-preserved of Bergen's wooden buildings, it is furnished in 16th-century style. ⊠ *Bryggen,* ☎ *55316710.* ⊡ *NKr 35.* ☯ *June–Aug., daily 9–5; May and Sept., daily 11–2; Oct.–Apr., Mon., Wed., Fri., Sun. 11–2.*

On the western end of the Vågen is **Rosenkrantz tårnet** (the tower), part of the **Bergenhus,** the 13th-century fortress guarding the harbor entrance. The tower and fortress were destroyed during World War II, but were meticulously restored during the '60s and are now rich with furnishings and household items from the 16th century. ⊠ *Bergenhus,* ☎ *55314380.* ⊡ *NKr 15.* ☯ *Mid-May–mid-Sept., daily 10–4; mid-Sept.–mid-May, Sun. noon–3, or upon request.*

From Øvregaten, the back boundary of Bryggen, you can walk through the meandering back streets to the popular **Fløybanen,** a funicular that climbs a steep 1,070 feet to the top of Fløyen, one of the seven mountains guarding the city.

★ **Troldhaugen** manor on Nordås Lake, once home to Edvard Grieg, is now a museum and incorporates a new chamber-music hall. Recitals are held each Wednesday and Sunday at 7:30 PM from late June through early August. ⊠ *Troldhaugsvn, Hop, Bergen,* ☎ *55911791.* ⊡ *NKr 40.* ☯ *May–Sept., daily 9–5:30.*

Dining and Lodging

For details and price-category definitions, *see* Dining and Lodging *in* Staying in Norway, *above.*

Bergen

$$$$ ✕ **Lucullus.** This French-inspired seafood restaurant is, appropriately enough, in the Hotel Neptun. It has an excellent wine cellar, with special emphasis on white wines to go with the fish. ✉ *Walckendorffsgt. 8,* ☎ *55901000,* FAX *55233202. AE, DC, MC, V. Closed Sun.*

$$$ ✕ **Finnegaardstue.** This classic Norwegian restaurant near Bryggen has
★ four small rooms that make for a snug, intimate atmosphere. Some of the timber interior dates from the 18th century. The emphasis here is on seafood, but the venison and reindeer are outstanding. Traditional Norwegian desserts such as cloudberries and cream are irresistible. ✉ *Rosenkrantzgt. 6,* ☎ *55313620,* FAX *55315811. AE, DC, MC, V. Closed Sun.*

$$–$$$ ✕ **Munkestuen Café.** The locals regard this tiny mom-and-pop place
★ as a hometown legend. Try the monkfish with hollandaise sauce or the fillet of roe deer with morels. Reserve a table early; sometimes they're booked up to four weeks in advance. ✉ *Klostergt. 12,* ☎ *55902149. Reservations essential. AE, DC, MC, V. No lunch. Closed Sat., Sun., and 3 wks in July.*

$$–$$$$ 🏨 **Radisson SAS Hotel.** Right on the harbor, this hotel is near a section of old, well-preserved warehouses and buildings. Ravaged by nine fires since 1170, the warehouses have been rebuilt each time in the same style, which SAS has incorporated into its design. ✉ *Bryggen, 5003,* ☎ *55543000,* FAX *55324808. 273 rooms with bath. 2 restaurants, bar, pub, pool, sauna, dance club, convention center. AE, DC, MC, V.*

$–$$ 🏨 **Augustin.** This small but excellent hotel in the center of town has been restored to its original late–Art Nouveau character, complete with period furniture in the lobby. ✉ *C. Sundtsgt. 22–24, 5004,* ☎ *55230025,* FAX *55304010. 38 rooms with bath. AE, DC, MC, V.*

$–$$ 🏨 **Bryggen Orion.** Facing the harbor in the center of town, the hotel is surrounded by Bergen's most famous sights. ✉ *Bradbenken 3, 5003,* ☎ *55318080,* FAX *55329414, 229 rooms with bath. Restaurant, bar, nightclub. AE, DC, MC, V.*

Kinsarvik

$$ 🏨 **Kinsarvik Fjord Hotel.** This handsome hotel near the busy ferry port offers good views of Hardangerfjord and the glacier. The rooms are bright and spacious. ✉ *5780 Kinsarvik,* ☎ *53663100,* FAX *53663374. 70 rooms with bath or shower. Restaurant, bar, dining room. AE, DC, MC, V.*

Kongsberg

$$ ✕ **Gamle Kongsberg Kro.** Hearty Norwegian dishes are served at this café near Nybrofossen (the Nybro waterfall). There's also a mini-golf course nearby. ✉ *Thornesvn. 4,* ☎ *32731633,* FAX *32732603. DC, MC, V.*

Utne

$$ ✕🏨 **Utne Hotel.** The white frame house dates from 1722, and the hotel, one of the oldest in Norway, has been run by the same family since 1787. The dining room is wood paneled and hand painted, and decorated with copper pans, old china, and paintings. The Utne makes a good base for hiking or cycling. ✉ *5797 Utne,* ☎ *53666983,* FAX *53666950. 18 rooms with bath or shower, 5 rooms share bath. AE, DC, MC, V.*

ABOVE BERGEN: THE FAR NORTH

The fjords continue northward from Bergen all the way to Kirkenes, at Norway's border with the Republic of Russia. Norway's north is for anyone eager to hike, climb, fish, bird-watch (seabirds), see Samiland—the land of the Sami ("Lapps")—or experience the unending days of the midnight sun in June and July. The Lofoten Islands present the grand face of the "Lofoten Wall"—a rocky, 96-kilometer-long (60-mile-long) massif surrounded by the sea and broken into six pieces. Svolvær, the most populated island, has a thriving summer artists' colony. It's also known for Lofotfisket, the winter cod fishing.

The major towns north of Bergen are Ålesund, Trondheim, Bodø, Narvik, Tromsø, Hammerfest, and Kirkenes. Cheaper accommodations are the rule in the north, whether you stay in a cabin, campsite, or guest house, or in *rorbuer*—fishermen's huts on the islands that are available for rent outside the January to April fishing season.

Getting Around

By Ship

One of the best ways to travel in northern Norway is by way of the **Hurtigruten,** or coastal steamer, which begins in Bergen and turns around 2,000 nautical kilometers (1,250 miles) later at Kirkenes. Many steamers run this route, so you can stay at any of the ports for any length of time and pick up the next one coming through: Major tourist offices have schedules, and reservations are essential as far in advance as a year (☞ Important Addresses and Numbers in Oslo, *and* Getting Around by Ferry, *above*).

By Car

E6 and its feeder roads are the only route available north of Trondheim, where the country narrows dramatically.

By Train

Major train routes are Oslo–Bergen and Oslo–Trondheim–Bodø (the Trondheim–Bodø leg takes one day). From Bodø there are tours to the Lofoten and Vesterålen islands and to the Væren Islands, two tiny, remote islands at the tail of the Lofoten chain. You can get to Svolvær, the Lofotens' main port, via ferry from Skutvik.

To get all the way to Nordkapp (the North Cape, the northernmost mainland point in Norway and Europe) and the Land of the Midnight Sun, you must continue your trip by bus from Fauske.

Visitor Information

Ålesund (✉ Rådhuset , ☎ 70121202); **Bodø** (✉ Sjøgt. 21, ☎ 75526000); **Hammerfest** (☎ 78412185); **Harstad** (✉ Torvet 8, ☎ 77063235); **Kirkenes** (✉ off E6 in a wooden hut behind Rica Hotel, on Pasvikvn., ☎ 78992544); **Narvik** (✉ Kongensgt. 66, ☎ 76943309); **Svolvær** (✉ Torget 6, ☎ 76073000); **Tromsø** (✉ Storgt. 61, ☎ 77610000); **Trondheim** (✉ Munkegt. 19, ☎ 73929394).

Exploring the Far North

The steamer is probably the best route from Ålesund to Trondheim because no main road connects them directly. **Ålesund,** a much-overlooked coastal city flanked by fjords, is perhaps the only example you'll find of true architectural eccentricity in Norway. After a fire here in the early 1900s, anyone who had any aspirations to architecture designed his or her own new home, and the result is a rich, playful mixture of styles ranging from austere to Art Nouveau. There are excellent tours of the Romsdal, Geiranger, and Hjørund fjords. Pick up the free "Ålesund Guide" and "On Foot in Ålesund" from the tourist office (☞ Tourist Information, *above*).

Trondheim sits at the southern end of Norway's widest fjord, Trondheimsfjord. This water-bound city is the third-largest in the country and is where Norwegian rulers are traditionally crowned. Construction of what is Scandinavia's largest medieval building, **Nidaros Domkirke** (cathedral), started here in 1320 but was not completed until the early 1920s. For centuries this was a pilgrimage church. There is a historic fish market worth seeing. Scandinavia's two largest wooden buildings are in Trondheim. One is the rococo **Stiftsgården,** a royal palace built in 1774, and the other is a student dormitory.

After Trondheim, the country thins into a vertebral cord of land hugging the border with Sweden and hunching over the top of Finland. **Bodø,** the northern terminus of the Nordland railway, is the first major town above the Polar Circle. For those who want boat excursions to **coastal bird colonies** (the Væren Islands), Bodø is the best base. The city was bombed by the Germans in 1940. The stunning, contemporary **Bodø Cathedral,** its spire separated from the main building, was built after the war. Inside are rich modern tapestries; outside is a war memorial. The **Nordland County Museum** (✉ Prinsengt. 116, ☎ 75526128) depicts the life of the Sami, as well as regional history.

If you want to see a real maelstrom—a furious natural whirlpool—ask at the Bodø tourist office (☞ Tourist Information, *above*) about **Saltstraumen.**

| NEED A BREAK? | Alongside the maelstrom is **Saltstraumen Hotel** (✉ Knaplund, 8056 Saltstraumen, ☎ 75587685). Try the poached halibut—delicious! |

Bodø is considered a gateway to the Lofoten and Vesterålen islands; the tourist office will make the necessary arrangements.

★ The **Lofoten** Islands are a 190-kilometer (118-mile) chain of mountaintops rising from the bottom of the sea. During the summer their farms, fjords, and fishing villages make them a major tourist attraction. Between January and March, thousands of fishermen from all over the country head for Lofoten to the annual Lofotfisket, the world's largest annual cod fishing event.

Narvik is a rebuilt city, an "ice-free" seaport, and a major shipping center for iron ore. An excellent railway connects it to the mines across the Swedish border. The **Krigsminnemuseet** (War Memorial Museum) has gripping displays on wartime intrigue and suffering. ✉ *Kongensgt., near the main square,* ☎ 76944426. ☐ *NKr 25.*

Northeast of Lofoten on Hinnøya, Norway's largest island, is **Harstad,** where the population of 22,000 swells to 42,000 during the annual June cultural festival and its July deep-sea fishing festival.

Farther north on the mainland is **Tromsø,** self-dubbed "the Paris of the North" for its nightlife inspired by the midnight sun. Looming over this remote arctic university town are 6,100-foot peaks with permanent snowcaps. Tromsø trails off into the islands: Half the town lives offshore. Its population is about 50,000. Be sure to see the spectacular **Ishavskatedral** (cathedral), with its eastern wall made entirely of stained glass, across the long stretch of **Tromsø bridge.** Coated in aluminum, the bridge's triangular peaks make a bizarre mirror for the midnight sun.

Be sure to walk around old Tromsø along the waterfront and to visit the **Tromsø Museum,** which concentrates on science, the Sami, and northern churches. ⊠ *Lars Thøringsvei 10, Folkeparken; take Bus 27 or 22,* ☎ *77645000.* ⌕ *NKr 10.* ⊙ *June–Aug., daily 9–9; Sept.–May, weekdays 8:30–3:30, Sat. noon–3, Sun. 11–4.*

Hammerfest is the world's northernmost town. It is surrounded by Sami settlements and is home to the **Royal and Ancient Polar Bear Society,** which has taxidermic displays of polar bears and other Arctic animals. The society has several conservation programs to protect some of these endangered species. ⊠ *Town Hall basement.* ⌕ *Free.* ⊙ *June–Aug., weekdays 8–8, weekends 10–5.*

Hammerfest is an elegant, festive-looking port town despite having been razed twice in its history. In the late-19th century the town was leveled by fire. Years later, defeated German troops destroyed the town as they retreated so as to avoid leaving anything to the Russians.

Dining and Lodging

For details and price-category definitions, *see* Dining and Lodging *in* Staying in Norway, *above.*

Ålesund

$$ ✕ **Fjellstua.** This mountaintop restaurant has tremendous views over the surrounding peaks, islands, and fjords. There are several places to eat here, but the main restaurant offers the biggest variety. ⊠ *Fjellstua,* ☎ *70126582. AE, DC, MC, V. Closed Dec.–early March.*

$$ ✕ **Sjøbua.** On an old wharf at Brunholmen, Sjøbua offers an excellent seafood selection. You can even pick your own dinner from a saltwater aquarium. ⊠ *Brunholmgt. 1,* ☎ *70127100. AE, DC, MC, V.*

$$ 🏨 **Bryggen Home Hotel.** This dockside warehouse was converted into a hotel, which has splendid views over the water. ⊠ *Apotekergt. 1– 3, 6004* ☎ *70126400,* FAX *70121180. 65 rooms with bath or shower. Sauna, Turkish bath. AE, DC, MC, V.*

$$ 🏨 **Inter Nor Hotel Scandinavie.** The impressive building with towers and arches dates from 1905. The rooms are decorated in shades of blues, peaches, and greens, with reproduction Biedermeier furniture . ⊠ *Løvenvoldgt. 8, 6002,* ☎ *70123131,* FAX *70132370. 65 rooms with bath. Restaurant, bar, pizzeria. AE, DC, MC, V.*

Bodø

$$–$$$ ✕ **Marlene Restaurant.** A superb seafood buffet is offered in summer at this restaurant in the Radisson SAS hotel. Be sure to try one of the salmon dishes. ⊠ *Storgt. 2,* ☎ *75524100. AE, DC, MC, V.*

$$ ✕ **Blix.** One of the best restaurants in town, you'll find a variety of items on the menu, from open-face sandwiches and lasagna to fresh fish and reindeer. ⊠ *Sjøgata 23, in the Inter Nor Diplomat Hotel,* ☎ *75527000. AE, DC, MC, V.*

$$$ ✕🏨 **Radisson SAS.** Throbbing with life, this grandiose hotel has enough amenities to keep you entertained virtually around the clock. ⊠ *Storgt. 2, 8000,* ☎ *75524100,* FAX *75527493. 190 rooms with bath. Restaurant, bar, sauna, nightclub. AE, DC, MC, V.*

$$ 🏨 **Norrøna.** The Radisson SAS runs this simple yet comfortable budget accommodation. Guests here have access to the facilities of the larger Radisson SAS. ⊠ *Storgt. 4B, 8006,* ☎ *75524118,* FAX *75523388. 106 rooms with bath or shower. Breakfast room. AE, DC, MC, V.*

Narvik

$$$ ✕⊞ **Grand Royal Hotel.** An eager-to-please staff will enhance your stay at this handsome hotel right near the train station. There are many possibilities for skiing and fishing nearby. ⊠ *Kongensgt. 64, 8500,* ☎ *76941500,* FAX *76945531. 108 rooms with bath. 2 restaurants, 3 bars, sauna, nightclub. AE, DC, MC, V.*

Svolvær

$$–$$$ ✕⊞ **Nyvågar Rorbu.** This hotel and recreation complex is a 15-minute drive from the Svolvær airport. Activities include fishing trips, eagle safaris, and deep-sea rafting. ⊠ *Kabelvåg, 8310,* ☎ *76078900,* FAX *76078950. 60 rooms with showers. 2 restaurants, conference rooms. AE, DC, MC, V.*

Tromsø

$$$–$$$$ ✕⊞ **Radisson SAS Hotel Tromsø.** The rooms in this hotel in the center of town have spectacular views over Tromsø's shoreline. ⊠ *Sjøgt. 7, 9001,* ☎ *77600000,* FAX *77685474. 195 rooms with bath. 3 restaurants, bar, nightclub. AE, DC, MC, V.*

$$ ⊞ **Saga Hotel.** On a pretty town square, this hotel is in a convenient location. Its restaurant has affordable, hearty meals, and the rooms—although somewhat basic—are quiet and comfortable. ⊠ *Richard Withs pl. 2, 9008,* ☎ *77681180,* FAX *77682380. 66 rooms and 3 suites with bath. Cafeteria. AE, DC, MC, V.*

Trondheim

$$$ ✕ **Bryggen.** A feast of Norwegian specialties with a Gallic accent are
★ served at this popular restaurant near the Gamle Bybro (Old Town Bridge). They also have a creperie and a wine and cheese room. ⊠ *Ø Bakklandet 66,* ☎ *73520230. AE, DC, MC, V.*

$$ ✕ **Hos Magnus.** The price–value ratio is excellent at this old-fashioned, cozy restaurant in the new part of Bryggen section of town. The menu includes such dishes as rosette of salmon cured and marinated with aquavit and brandy sauce, and lamb roulade stuffed with cheese and mushrooms. ⊠ *Kjøpmannsgt. 63,* ☎ *73524110. AE, DC, MC, V.*

$$ ✕ **Tavern på Sverresborg.** Outside the city, at the open-air Folk Mu-
★ seum, this restaurant serves Norwegian specialties. ⊠ *Sverresborg,* ☎ *73520932. AE, DC, MC, V.*

$$$ ⊞ **Royal Garden Hotel.** Trondheim's finest hotel has excellent facilities for sports and fitness, as well as many features to help guests with disabilities. ⊠ *Kjøpmannsgt. 73, 7010,* ☎ *73521100,* FAX *73531766. 297 rooms with bath. Restaurant, bar, indoor pool, sauna, exercise room. AE, DC, MC, V.*

$$ ⊞ **Bakeriet.** Built as a bakery in 1863, Trondheim's newest hotel
★ opened in March 1991. Few rooms look alike, but all are large and stylish in their simplicity, with natural wood furniture and beige-and-red textiles. Although there's no restaurant, a hot evening meal is included in the room rate. ⊠ *Brattørgt. 2, 7010,* ☎ *73525200,* FAX *73502330. 106 rooms with bath or shower. Sauna, Turkish bath, exercise room. AE, DC, MC, V.*

$–$$ ⊞ **Hotel Ambassadeur.** Take in the panoramic view from the roof terrace of this hotel, about 300 feet from the market square. The deep blue waters of the Trondheimsfjord reflect the dramatic and irregular coastline. The hotel does not have its own dining room, but offers discounts with local restaurants. ⊠ *Elvegt. 18, 7013,* ☎ *73527050,* FAX *73527052. 34 rooms with bath and mini bar. Bar, meeting rooms. AE, DC, MC, V.*

22 Poland

Warsaw

Kraków and Environs

Gdańsk and the North

POLES ARE FOND OF QUOTING, WITH A WRY grimace, the old Chinese saying, "May you live in interesting times." The times are certainly interesting in 1990s Poland, the home of the Solidarity trade union movement that sent shock waves through the Soviet bloc in 1980, and the first Eastern European state to shake off communist rule. But as the grimace implies, being on the firing line of history—something that the Poles are well used to—can be an uncomfortable experience. You will be constantly reminded that the return to free-market capitalism after more than 45 years of state socialism is an experiment on an unprecedented scale that brings inconveniences and surprises as well as benefits.

With 38 million inhabitants living in a territory of 121,000 square miles, Poland in the 1990s is suspended between the Old World and the New, and the images can be confusing. Bright, new, privately owned shops with smiling assistants are in shabby buildings that have not been renovated for decades. Billboards advertise goods that most Poles cannot afford. Public services, such as transportation, are underfunded, and water supplies and central heating can be erratic, as local authorities attempt with insufficient funds to keep the show on the road.

The official trappings of the communist state were quickly dismantled after the Solidarity victory in the 1989 elections. But communism never sat easily with the Poles. It represented yet another stage in their age-old struggle to retain their identity in the face of pressure from the lifestyles of neighbors to the west and east. Founded as a unified state in the 10th century on the great north European plain, Poland lay for a thousand years at the heart of Europe, precisely at the halfway point on a line drawn from the Atlantic coast of Spain to the Ural Mountains. This has never been an enviable position. During the Middle Ages, Poland fought against German advance; in the Golden Age of Polish history during the 16th and 17th centuries—of which you will be reminded by splendid Renaissance buildings in many parts of the country—Poland pushed eastward against her Slavic neighbors, taking Kiev and dreaming of a kingdom that stretched to the Black Sea. By the end of the 18th century, Poland's territories were divided among the Austrian, Prussian, and Russian empires.

In the 20th century, Poland fell victim to peculiarly vicious forms of the old struggle between east and west: the Nazi occupation and Stalin's postwar settlement. Despite this history of hardships, Poland remains a fascinating place for the visitor with an inquiring mind. Its historic cities—Kraków, Warsaw, Gdańsk—tell much of the tale of European history and culture. Its countryside offers unrivaled opportunities to escape from the 20th century. Paradoxically, communism—which after 1956 dropped attempts to collectivize agriculture and left the Polish farmer on his small, uneconomic plot—has preserved rural Poland in a romantic, preindustrial state. Despite pollution, cornflowers still bloom, storks perch atop untidy nests by cottage chimneys, and horsepower still frequently comes in the four-legged variety. While the Poles have a certain wary reserve, they will win you over with their strong individualism—expressed through their well-developed sense of humor and their capacity for conviviality.

Poland

Baltic Sea

Bornholm (Denmark)

LITHUANIA

RUSSIA

Kołobrzeg
Świnoujście E28
Białogard
Koszalin
Szczecin
Stargard
10
Słupsk
Lebork
Gdynia
Gdańsk
Tczew
Starogard
Elbląg
Malbork
Suwałki
Szczecinek
Chojnice
Kwidzyn
Ostróda
Olsztyn
Ełk
Masurian Lakes
Piła
Chełmno
Grudziądz
Nidzica
Gorzów Wielkopolski
Bydgoszcz
Inowrocław
Toruń
Mława
Ciechanów
Płońsk
Łomża
Ostrołęka
Białystok
Narew
Poznań
Gniezno
Włocławek
Plock
Ostrów Mazowiecka
Zielona Góra
Kościan
Konin
Kutno
Warsaw
Siedlce
Głogów
Ozorków
Łowicz
E30
Otwock
Międzyrzec Podlaski
Biała Podlaska
Lubin
Zgierz
Skierniewice
Ostrów Wielkopolski
14
Łódź
Deblin
Bolesławiec
Legnica
Wieluń
Tomaszów Mazowiecki
Radom
17
Lublin
Jelenia Góra
Wrocław
Radomsko
E7/77
Ostrowiec
Chełm
Świdnica
Wałbrzych
Częstochowa
Kielce
Świętokrzyski
Kłodzko
Nysa
Prudnik
Tarnowskie Góry
Zawiercie
Zamość
Zabrze
Sosnowiec
Katowice
A4
Kraków
Rzeszów
Jarosław
Bielsko-Biała
Krosno
Przemyśl
CZECH REPUBLIC
Zakopane
Nowy Sącz
UKRAINE
GERMANY
Odra
Nysa
Vistula
Bug
SLOVAKIA
N

0   100 miles
0   150 km

HUNGARY

ESSENTIAL INFORMATION

Before You Go

When to Go

The official tourist season runs from May through September. The best times for sightseeing are late spring and early fall. Major cultural events usually take place in the cities during the fall. The early spring is often wet and windy.

Below are the average daily maximum and minimum temperatures for Warsaw.

Jan.	32F	0C	May	67F	20C	Sept.	66F	19C
	22	– 6		48	9		49	10
Feb.	32F	0C	June	73F	23C	Oct.	55F	13C
	21	– 6		54	12		41	5
Mar.	42F	6C	July	75F	24C	Nov.	42F	6C
	28	– 2		58	16		33	1
Apr.	53F	12C	Aug.	73F	23C	Dec.	35F	2C
	37	3		56	14		28	– 3

Currency

The monetary unit in Poland is the złoty (zł), which is divided into 100 groszy (gr). Since the currency reform of 1994, there are notes of 10, 20, 50, 100, and 200 złotys, and coins in values of 1, 2, and 5 złotys and 1, 2, 5, 10, and 50 groszys. However, the old, inflated banknotes—the highest of which represented 2 million złotys—remained in circulation until late 1996, and many Poles use the old denominations when they talk about money, referring to zł 2.5 as zł 25,000. This can cause confusion among Poles and visitors alike. At press time (spring 1996), the exchange rate was zł 2.5 to the U.S. dollar, zł 1.8 to the Canadian dollar, and zł 3.8 to the pound sterling.

The złoty is legally exchangeable at a free-market rate in banks (Bank Narodowy and Pekao are the largest) and at *kantory* (private exchange bureaus), which sometimes offer slightly better rates than do banks. If you run out of złotys, Polish taxi drivers, waiters, and porters usually accept dollars or any other Western currency.

CREDIT CARDS

Many credit cards are accepted in all major hotels, in the better restaurants and nightclubs, and for other tourist services. In small cafés and shops, especially in the provinces, credit cards may not be accepted.

What It Will Cost

At press time, it was still illegal to import or export złotys. This may change: Still, don't buy more złotys than you need, or you will have to go to the trouble of changing them back at the end of your trip.

Poland is one of the more expensive countries of Eastern Europe, and inflation is high by Western standards, although the rate is falling. Prices are highest in the big cities, especially Warsaw. The farther you stray from the tourist track, the cheaper your vacation will be.

SAMPLE PRICES

A cup of coffee, zł 1.5–zł 5; a bottle of beer, zł 2–zł 4.5; a soft drink, zł 1–zł 4.5; a ham sandwich, zł 2–zł 5; a 1-mile taxi ride, zł 4.

MUSEUMS

Admission fees to museums and other attractions are rising. They range from zł 1 to zł 15.

Visas

Citizens of the United States and the United Kingdom do not need visas for entry to Poland; Canadian citizens and citizens of other countries that have not yet abolished visas for Poles must pay the equivalent of $35 (more for multiple-entry visas). Apply at any Orbis office (the official Polish tourist agency, ☞ Visitor Information *in* Chapter 1), at an affiliated travel agent, or at the Polish Consulate General in any country. Visitors from Canada and other countries that require visas must complete three application forms and provide two photographs. They should allow about two weeks for processing. Such visas are issued for 90 days but can be extended in Poland, either through the local county police headquarters or through Orbis.

You can contact the **Polish Consulate General** at the following addresses.
United States: 233 Madison Ave., New York, NY 10016, ☎ 212/889–
8360; 1530 N. Lake Shore Dr., Chicago, IL 60610, ☎ 312/337–8166;
2224 Wyoming Ave. NW, Washington DC 20008, ☎ 202/232–4517.
Canada: 1500 Pine Ave West., Montréal, Québec H3G 1B4, ☎ 514/
937–9481; 2603 Lakeshore Blvd. W, Toronto, Ontario M8V 1G5, ☎
416/252–5471. **United Kingdom:** 73 New Cavendish St., London
W1N 7RB, ☎ 0171/580–0475.

Customs on Arrival

Persons over 17 may bring in duty-free: personal belongings, including musical instruments, typewriter, radio, 2 cameras with 24 rolls of
film; up to 250 cigarettes or 50 cigars, ½ liter of spirits and 2 liters of
wine; and goods with a total value of $200. Foreign currency to the
value of $2,500 may be brought in but must be declared on arrival.
Further information can be obtained from Customs Information (☎
022/650–28–73).

Language

Polish is a Slavic language that uses the Roman alphabet but has several additional characters and diacritics. Because it has a much higher
incidence of consonant clusters than English, most English speakers
find it a difficult language to decipher, much less pronounce. Most older
Poles know German; the younger generation usually knows some English. In the big cities you will find people who speak English, especially in hotels, but you may have difficulty in the countryside.

Getting Around

By Car

ROAD CONDITIONS

Despite the extensive road network, driving conditions, even on main
roads, have deteriorated in the 1990s owing to a significant increase
in traffic. Minor roads tend to be narrow and cluttered with horse-
drawn carts and farm animals. Drivers in a hurry should stick to roads
marked E or T.

RULES OF THE ROAD

Driving is on the right, as in the United States. The speed limit on highways is 110 kph (68 mph) and on roads in built-up areas, 60 kph (37
mph). A built-up area is marked by a white rectangular sign with the
name of the town on it.

GASOLINE

The price of gas is between zł 8.5 and zł 12 for 10 liters of high oc-
tane. Filling stations are located every 30 kilometers (20 miles) or so
and are usually open 6 AM–10 PM; there are some 24-hour stations.

BREAKDOWNS

Poland's **Motoring Association** (PZMot) offers breakdown, repair, and
towing services to members of various international insurance organizations; check with Orbis before you leave home. Carry a spare-parts
kit. For emergency road help, call 981.

CAR RENTALS

You can rent cars at international airports or through Orbis offices.
Rates vary according to season, car model, and mileage. Fly-drive vacations are also available through Orbis.

By Train

Poland's PKP railway network is extensive and relatively inexpensive.
Most trains have first- and second-class accommodations, but Western visitors usually prefer to travel first-class. You should arrive at the

station well before departure time. The fastest trains are intercity and express trains, which require reservations. Orbis and other travel agents furnish information, reservations, and tickets. Overnight trains have first- and second-class sleeping cars and second-class couchettes. Most long-distance trains carry buffets, but the quality of the food is unpredictable; you may want to bring your own.

FARES

Polish trains run at three speeds—*ekspresowy* (express), *pośpieszny* (fast), and *osobowy* (slow)—and fares vary accordingly. You pay more for intercity and express, and round-trip tickets are priced at precisely double the one-way far.

By Plane

LOT, Poland's national airline, operates daily flights linking five main cities: **Warsaw, Kraków, Gdańsk, Wrocław,** and **Rzeszów.** Fares begin at about $60 round-trip. Tickets and information are available from LOT, Orbis, or other travel agents. Be sure to book well in advance, especially for the summer season.

By Bus

PKS, the national bus company, offers long-distance service to most cities. Express PKS buses, on which you can reserve seats, are somewhat more expensive than trains but often—except in the case of a few major intercity routes—get to their destination more quickly. For really out-of-the-way destinations, the bus is often the only means of transportation. PKS bus stations are usually near railway stations. Tickets and information are best obtained from Orbis. Warsaw's central bus terminal is located at aleje Jerozolimskie 144. There are also new private operators, some of whom undercut PKS prices. For example, **Polski Express** (☎ 022/630-29-67) runs services to seven major cities.

Staying in Poland

Telephones

LOCAL CALLS

Older public phone booths take *żetony* (tokens) for gr 50 for local calls and zł 1 or zł 2 for long-distance calls, which must be made from special booths, usually in post offices. Place a token in the groove on the side or top of the phone, lift the receiver, and dial the number. Many phones automatically accept the token; in others you push it into the machine when the call is answered. Phone booths taking cards can be used for both local and long-distance calls. Cards, which cost zł 7.5 or zł 15, are sold at post offices and at most newspaper kiosks. When making a long-distance call, first dial 0, wait for the dial tone, then dial the rest of your number. To place a domestic long-distance call to a number without a direct-dial facility, dial 900.

INTERNATIONAL CALLS

Post offices and first-class hotels have booths at which you either use your calling card or pay after the completion of your call. To place a call with an **AT&T** USADirect international operator, dial 0, wait for dial tone, then 010–480–0111; from major hotels in Warsaw, dial 010–480–0111. To place a call with **MCI,** dial 01–04–800–222; for **Sprint,** dial 0010–480–0115.

COUNTRY CODE

The international country code for Poland is 48.

INFORMATION
For local directory information, dial 913; for country-wide directory information, including dialing codes, dial 912; for international information (including international codes), dial 930.

Mail

POSTAL RATES

Airmail letters to the United States or Canada cost zł 1.50; postcards, zł 1. Letters to the United Kingdom or Europe cost zł 1.20; postcards, gr 90. Post offices are open weekdays 8 AM–8 PM. At least one post office is open 24 hours in every major city. In Warsaw the 24-hour post office is at ulica Świętokrzyska 31.

Opening and Closing Times

Banks are open weekdays 8 or 9 AM–3 or 6 PM.

Museum hours vary greatly but are generally Tuesday–Sunday 9–5.

Shops. Food shops are open weekdays 7–7, Saturday 7 AM–1 or 2 PM; many are now open on Sunday, and there are a few all-night stores in most districts. Other stores are open weekdays 11 AM–7 PM and Saturday 9 AM–1 or 2 PM.

National Holidays

January 1; March 30, 31 (Easter Sunday and Monday); May 1 (Labor Day); May 3 (Constitution Day); May 29 (Corpus Christi); August 15 (Assumption); November 1 (All Saints' Day); November 11 (rebirth of Polish state, 1918); December 25, 26.

Dining

Polish food and drink are basically Slavic with Baltic overtones. There is a heavy emphasis on soups and meat (especially pork), as well as freshwater fish. Much use is made of cream, and pastries are rich and often delectable. The most popular soup is *barszcz* (known to many Americans as borscht), a clear beet soup often served with such Polish favorites as sausage, cabbage, potatoes, sour cream, coarse rye bread, and beer. Other typical dishes are pierogi, which may be stuffed with savory or sweet fillings; *gołąbki,* cabbage leaves stuffed with minced meat; *bigos,* sauerkraut with meat and mushrooms; and *flaki,* a select dish of tripe, served boiled or fried. Polish beer is good; vodka is a specialty and is often downed before, during, and after meals.

Zajazdy (roadside inns), which are often less expensive than regular restaurants, serve more traditional food. As elsewhere in central Europe, cafés are a way of life in Poland and are often stocked with delicious pastries and ice cream.

MEALTIMES

At home, Poles eat late lunches (their main meal, usually around 4 PM) and late suppers (a light dinner around 10 PM). Restaurants—especially in major cities—are increasingly operating on an earlier timetable. Many begin service at 2 PM, but more sophisticated restaurants have been opening around noon to offer a luncheon distinct from the late afternoon meal; they then serve dinner between 7–10 PM. Although many restaurants continue to close at 9 PM—especially in the provinces— more cosmopolitan establishments are staying open to 10 or 11 PM or later. Most hotel restaurants serve the evening meal until 10:30.

PRECAUTIONS

Tap water is generally regarded as unsafe, so ask for bottled mineral water. Beware of meat dishes served in cheap snack bars.

WHAT TO WEAR

In Warsaw and Kraków, formal dress is customary at $$$ and $$$$ restaurants. Casual dress is appropriate elsewhere.

RATINGS

Prices are for one person and include three courses and service but not drinks.

CATEGORY	WARSAW	OTHER AREAS
$$$$	over zł 70	over zł 60
$$$	zł 50–70	zł 40–60
$$	zł 25–50	zł 20–40
$	under zł 25	under zł 20

Lodging

HOTELS

The government rates hotel accommodations with from one to five stars. Orbis hotels, owned by the state tourist office and currently undergoing privatization, have almost all been accorded four or five stars and guarantee a reasonable standard of cleanliness and service (although some travelers will find them characterless). Most of them range in price from $$ to $$$$ and include a number of foreign-built luxury hotels. In recent years Orbis hotels have faced competition from a growing number of privately owned lodgings, often part of international chains and mostly in the top price range.

Municipal hotels and Dom Turysty hotels are run by local authorities or the Polish Tourist Association. They are often rather old and can have limited bath and shower facilities. Standards are improving as many undergo renovations; however, prices remain in the $$ category.

ROADSIDE INNS

A number of roadside inns, many of which are very attractive, offer inexpensive food and a few guest rooms at moderate rates.

PRIVATE ACCOMMODATIONS

Rooms can be arranged either in advance through Orbis or on the spot at the local tourist information office. Villas, lodges, rooms, or houses are available, and the prices are often negotiable. Rates vary from about $6 for a room to more than $150 for a villa.

RATINGS

The following chart is based on a rate for two people in a double room, with bath or shower and breakfast. These prices are in U.S. dollars; many hotels in Poland quote prices in American dollars or German marks because of the fluctuations in Polish currency.

CATEGORY	COST
$$$$	over $200
$$$	$100–$200
$$	$50–$100
$	under $50

Tipping

Waiters get a standard 10% of the bill. Hotel porters and doormen should get about zł 2. If you choose to tip in foreign currency (readily accepted), remember that $1 is about an hour's wage.

WARSAW

Arriving and Departing

By Plane

All international flights arrive at Warsaw's Okęcie Airport (Port Lotniczy) just southwest of the city. Terminal 1 serves international flights; Terminal 2 serves domestic flights. For flight information, contact the airlines, or call the airport at ☎ 022/650–42–20.

BETWEEN THE AIRPORT AND DOWNTOWN

LOT operates a regular bus service into Warsaw. Orbis cars and minivans also transport visitors to their hotels. A Warsaw city transport bus, No. 175, runs past almost all major downtown hotels, leaving Okęcie every 10 minutes during peak hours, and every 14 minutes at other times. The trip takes about 15 minutes and the fare is zł 1 . There is also a direct airport–city bus to the main hotels at a fare of zł 3.5 .

Avoid taxi drivers asking for business in the arrivals hall. Take either a taxi from the LOT marked fleet (fare about 20 zł to the city center), or call 919 for a radio taxi (fare about 10 zł to city center).

By Train

Trains to and from Western Europe arrive at Dworzec Centralny (Central Station) on aleje Jerozolimskie in the center of town. For tickets and information, contact Orbis.

By Car

Seven main access routes lead to the center of Warsaw. Drivers heading to or from the West will use the highways E8 or E12.

Getting Around

By Tram and Bus

These are often crowded, but they are the cheapest way of getting around. Trams and buses (including express buses) cost zł 1. The bus fare goes up to zł 2.5 between 11 PM and 5:30 AM. Tickets must be bought in advance from **Ruch** newsstands or certain shops. You must cancel your own ticket in a machine on the tram or bus when you get on; watch how others do it.

By Subway

Warsaw's new subway opened in spring 1995. At present there is only one line, running 11 miles from the southern suburbs to the city center (Natolin to Plac Politechniki); but it is clean, fast, and costs the same as the tram and bus. You use the same tickets, canceling them at the entrance to the station. Trains run every 5 minutes during rush hours, every 15 minutes during off-peak hours.

By Taxi

Taxis are a relatively cheap ride—about zł 4 for the first mile (1.6 km) and then 60 gr per each additional mile—and are readily available at stands downtown; the Marriott and Victoria hotels have their own monogrammed fleets. There is an efficient radio taxi service (☎ 919) that is much cheaper than taxis at stands.

By Buggy

Horse-drawn carriages can be rented at a negotiated price from the Old Town Market Square.

Important Addresses and Numbers

Embassies

U.S. (⊠ Al. Ujazdowskie 29–31, ☎ 022/628–30–41). **Canadian** (⊠ Ul. Matejki 1/5, ☎ 022/629–80–51). **U.K.** (⊠ Al. Róż 1, ☎ 022/628–10–01). **U.K. Consulate** (⊠ Ul. Emilii Plater 28, ☎ 022/625–30–30).

Emergencies

Police (☎ 997). **Ambulance** (☎ 998). **Doctor** (☎ 998 or call your embassy).

Travel Agencies

American Express (⊠ Ul. Bagińskiego 1, ☎ 022/635–20–02; 24-hour ☎ 022/625-40-30). **Thomas Cook** (⊠ Ul. Nowy Świat 64, ☎ 022/26–47–29). **Polish Motoring Association (PZMot)** (⊠ Al. Jerozolimskie 63, ☎ 022/629–45–50).

Visitor Information

The **Center for Tourist Information** (⊠ Plac Zamkowy 1, ☎ 022/635–18–81) is open 9 to 6 weekdays and 11 to 6 weekends. There are **Orbis** offices at ulica Bracka 16 (☎ 022/26–02–71) and ulica Marszałkowska 142 (☎ 022/27–80–31 or 022/27–36–73).

Guided Tours

Bus tours of the city depart in the morning and afternoon from major hotels. **Orbis** also has half-day excursions into the countryside. These usually include a meal and some form of traditional entertainment. Check with your hotel, Orbis, or the tourist information office.

Exploring Warsaw

At the end of World War II, Warsaw lay in ruins, a victim of systematic Nazi destruction. Only one-third of its prewar population survived the German occupation. The experience is visible everywhere in the memorial plaques describing mass executions of civilians and in the bullet holes on the facades of buildings. Against all the odds, Warsaw's survivors have rebuilt their historic city. The old districts have been painstakingly reconstructed according to old prints and paintings. The result, a city of warm pastel colors, is remarkable.

Surrounding the old districts, however, is the modern Warsaw, built since the war in utilitarian Socialist-Realist and later styles. Whether you like it or not is your business, but it is worth noting as a testimony to one approach to urban life. The sights of Warsaw are all relatively close to one another, making most attractions accessible by foot.

The Stare Miasto (Old Town)

Numbers in the margin correspond to points of interest on the Warsaw map.

A walking tour of the old historic district takes about two hours.
❶ Begin in the heart of the city at **plac Zamkowy** (Castle Square), where you will see a slender column supporting the **statue of Zygmunt (Sigismund) III Wasa,** king of Poland and Sweden, who made Warsaw his capital in the early 17th century. It is the city's oldest monument and was the first to be rebuilt after the wartime devastation.

★ **❷** Dominating the square is the **Zamek Królewski** (Royal Castle).The princes of Mazovia first built a residence here in the 14th century; its present Renaissance form dates from the reign of King Sigismund III, who needed a magnificent palace for his new capital. Reconstructed later than the Old Town, in the 1970s, the castle now gleams as it did

POLAND HAS BEEN CONQUERED AND

RECAPTURED AT LEAST SEVENTEEN TIMES.

SEE FOR YOURSELF WHAT ALL THE FUSS

IS ABOUT. AND TO SEE IT EVEN SOONER,

FLY LOT, THE ONLY NONSTOP TO POLAND.

LOT

It helps to be pushy in airports.

Introducing the revolutionary new TransPorter™ from American Tourister® It's the first suitcase you can push around without a fight. TransPorter's™ exclusive four-wheel design lets you push it in front of you with almost no effort–the wheels take the weight. Or pull it on two wheels if you choose. You can even stack on other bags and use it like a luggage cart.

Stable 4-wheel design.

TransPorter™ is designed like a dresser, with built-in shelves to organize your belongings. Or collapse the shelves and pack it like a traditional suitcase. Inside, there's a suiter feature to help keep suits and dresses from wrinkling. When push comes to shove, you can't beat a TransPorter™ For more information on how you can be this pushy, call 1-800-542-1300.

Shelves collapse on command.

Making travel less primitive®

in its earliest years, with gilt, marble, and wall paintings; it houses impressive art collections—including the famous views of Warsaw by Canaletto—and period furniture. ☒ *Plac Zamkowy 4,* ☎ *022/657–23–38.* 🎫 *Tues.–Sat. zł 10; Sun. zł 6.* ☉ *Tues.–Sat. 10–2:30, Sun. 9–2:30; tours leave hourly from side entrance.*

Enter the narrow streets of the **Stare Miasto** (Old Town), with its colorful medieval houses, cobblestone alleys, uneven roofs, and wrought-iron grillwork. On your right as you proceed along ulica Świętojańska

③ is the **Bazylika świętego Jana** (Cathedral of St. John), the oldest church in Warsaw, dating from the 14th century. Several Polish kings were

④ crowned here. Soon you will reach the charming and intimate **Rynek Starego Miasta** (Old Town Market Square). The town hall, which once stood in the middle, was pulled down in the 19th century. It was not replaced, and today the square is full of open-air cafés, tubs of flowering plants, and the inevitable artists displaying their talents for tourists. At night the brightly lighted Rynek is the place to go for good food and atmosphere.

⑤ If you are interested in Polish writers, you might visit the **Adam Mickiewicz Museum of Literature,** on the square at No. 20, which contains manuscripts, mementos, and portraits, particularly from the Romantic period. ☎ *022/31–40–61.* 🎫 *Zł 2.5.* ☉ *Tues.–Sat. 10–2:30.*

Continue along ulica Nowomiejska until you reach the pinnacled red-

⑥ brick **Barbakan**, a fine example of a 16th-century defensive fortification. From here you can see the partially restored wall that was built to enclose the Old Town, and enjoy a splendid view of the Vistula River, with the district of Praga on its east bank.

Follow ulica Freta to Warsaw's **Nowe Miasto** (New Town), founded at the turn of the 15th century. Rebuilt after the war in 18th-century style, this district has a more elegant and spacious feeling to it. Of in-

⑦ terest here is the **Muzeum Marii Skłodowskiej-Curie,** where the woman who discovered radium and polonium was born. ☒ *Ul. Freta 16,* ☎ *022/31–80–92.* 🎫 *Zł 2.* ☉ *Tues.–Sat. 10–4:30, Sun. 10–2:30.*

⑧ One block farther down, ulica Freta opens up into the leafy **Rynek Nowego Miasta** (New Town Square), slightly more irregular and relaxed than its Old Town counterpart. If you cross over the square to ulica Kościelna, passing houses with curiously stark and formalized wall

⑨ paintings, you will see the oldest church in the New Town, the **Kościół Najświętszej Marii Panny** (St. Mary's Church). Built as a parish church for the New Town by the princes of Mazovia in the early 15th century, St. Mary's has been destroyed and rebuilt many times throughout its history. The Gothic bell tower dates from the early 16th century. ☒ *Przyrynek 2.* ☉ *6 AM–10 PM.*

The Royal Route

All towns with kings had their Royal Routes; the one in Warsaw—the Trakt Królewski—stretched south from Castle Square down Krakowskie Przedmieście, through Nowy Świat and on along aleje Ujazdowskie to

⑩ the 18th-century **Pałac Belweder** (Belvedere Palace) and Łazienki Park. Some of Warsaw's finest churches and palaces are along this route, as well as plaques bearing the names of famous Poles.

⑪ On your left, immediately south of plac Zamkowy, is the **Kościół świętej Anny** (St. Anne's Church), originally built in 1454 and rebuilt in high Baroque style in the 17th century; thanks to recent redecoration and regilding, it once again glows in its original splendor. A plaque on the wall outside marks the spot where Pope John Paul II celebrated Mass in 1980, during his first visit to Poland after his election to the

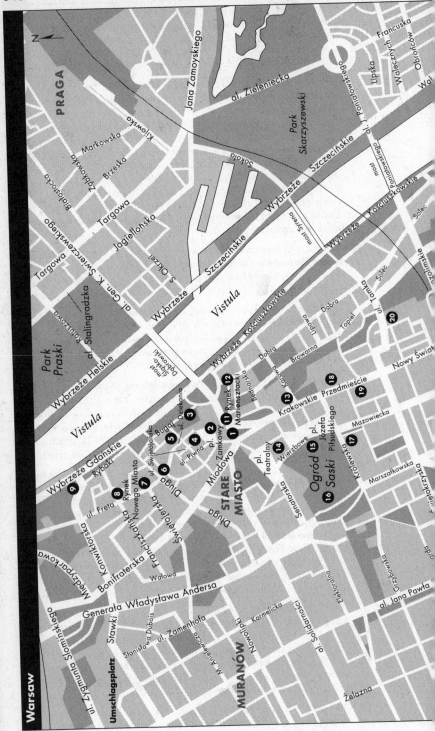

Warsaw

PRAGA

Park
Praski

Umschlagsplatz

MURANÓW

STARE
MIASTO

Park
Skarzyszewski

Vistula

Vistula

Nowy Świat

Krakowskie Przedmieście

Ogród
Saski

N

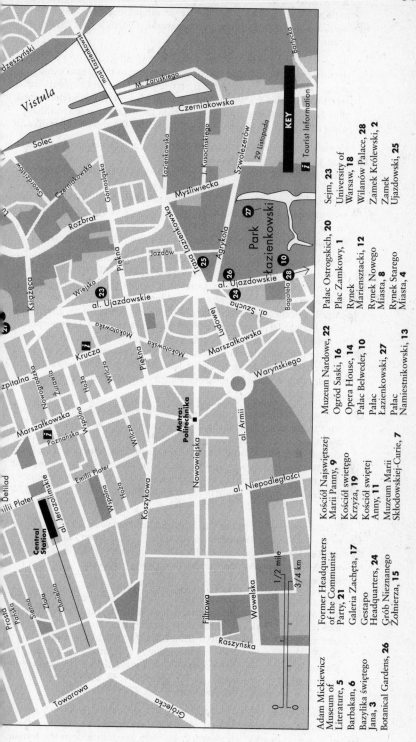

Vistula

KEY

i Tourist Information

Adam Mickiewicz Museum of Literature, **5**

Barbakan, **6**

Bazylika świętego Jana, **3**

Botanical Gardens, **26**

Former Headquarters of the Communist Party, **21**

Galeria Zachęta, **17**

Gestapo Headquarters, **24**

Grób Nieznanego Żołnierza, **15**

Kościół Najświętszej Marii Panny, **9**

Kościół świętego Krzyża, **19**

Kościół świętej Anny, **11**

Muzeum Marii Skłodowskiej-Curie, **7**

Muzeum Nardowe, **22**

Ogród Saski, **16**

Opera House, **14**

Pałac Belweder, **10**

Pałac Łazienkowski, **27**

Pałac Namiestnikowski, **13**

Pałac Ostrogskich, **20**

Plac Zamkowy, **1**

Rynek Mariensztacki, **12**

Rynek Nowego Miasta, **8**

Rynek Starego Miasta, **4**

Sejm, **23**

University of Warsaw, **18**

Wilanów Palace, **28**

Zamek Królewski, **2**

Zamek Ujazdowski, **25**

② papacy. A hundred yards farther, the steeply sloping, cobbled ulica Bed-narska leads down to **Rynek Mariensztacki,** a quiet, leafy 18th-century square that is worth a detour.

Back on Krakowskie Przedmieście, in the small garden to your right opposite ulica Bednarska, stands a monument to the great Polish poet Adam Mickiewicz. It was here that Warsaw University students gathered in March 1968, after a performance of Mickiewicz's hitherto banned play *Forefathers' Eve,* and set in motion the events that led to the toppling of Poland's longtime communist leader Władysław Gomułka.

Continuing along Krakowskie Przedmieście, at number 46–48 you will **⑬** pass the **Pałac Namiestnikowski.** Built in the 17th century by the Radziwiłł family (into which Jacqueline Kennedy's sister, Lee, later married), this palace at one time functioned as the administrative office of the czarist occupiers. In 1955 the Warsaw Pact was signed here, and now the palace serves as the official residence of Poland's president. In the forecourt is an equestrian statue of Prince Józef Poniatowski, a nephew of the last king of Poland, and one of Napoléon's marshals.

If you turn right onto ulica Królewska at this point, you reach plac **⑭** Piłsudskiego. To your right is the **Opera House,** built in the 1820s and **⑮** reconstructed after the war. In front of you is the **Grób Nieznanego Żołnierza** (Tomb of the Unknown Soldier), a surviving fragment of an early 18th-century Saxon Palace. Ceremonial changes of the guard take place here at 10 AM on Sunday; many visitors may be faintly surprised to see that the Polish Army still uses the goose step on occasions of **⑯** this kind. Behind the tomb stretches the palace park, the **Ogród Saski** (Saxon Gardens), designed by French and Saxon landscape gardeners; visitors can still admire the 18th-century sculptures, man-made lake, and sundial.

⑰ Across ulica Królewska stands the **Galeria Zachęta** (Zachęta Gallery), built in the last years of the 19th century by the Society for the Encouragement of the Fine Arts. It was in this building that the first president of the post–World War I Polish Republic, Gabriel Narutowicz, was assassinated by a right-wing fanatic in 1922. It has no permanent collection but organizes thought-provoking special exhibitions (primarily modern art) in high, well-lit halls. ⊠ *Pl. Małachowskiego 3,* ☏ *022/27–69–09.* 🎟 *Varies.* ☉ *Tues.–Sun. 10–6.*

Retrace your steps to the Royal Route, and on your left you'll come **⑱** to the **University of Warsaw** on your left. Farther down, on your right, **⑲** the **Kościoł świętego Krzyża** (Holy Cross Church) contains a pillar in which the heart of the great Polish composer Frédéric Chopin is entombed.

You may wish at this point to make a detour into ulica Tamka to the **⑳** headquarters of the **Chopin Society,** in the 17th-century **Pałac Ostrogskich** (Ostrogski Palace), which towers impressively above the street. The best approach is via the steps from ulica Tamka. In the 19th century the Warsaw Conservatory was housed here (Paderewski was one of its students); now used for Chopin concerts, it has a small museum with mementos of the composer. ⊠ *Ul. Okólnik 1,* ☏ *022/27–54–71.* 🎟 *Free.* ☉ *Mon.–Wed., Fri., and Sat. 10–2; Thurs. noon–6.*

As you enter the busy Nowy Świat thoroughfare, you pass on your left the statue of the great astronomer Nicolaus Copernicus, who was born **㉑** in Poland. On your left as you cross aleje Jerozolimskie is the **former headquarters of the Polish Communist Party.** This large, solid, gray building, erected in the Socialist-Realist architectural style, now houses banks and Poland's new stock exchange.

㉒ Next to this building is the **Muzeum Narodowe** (National Museum of Warsaw), which has an impressive collection of contemporary Polish and European paintings, Gothic icons, and works from antiquity. The famous Canaletto paintings that were used to facilitate the rebuilding of Warsaw after the war are also on display. ⊠ *Al. Jerozolimskie 3,* ☎ *022/621–10–31.* 🎫 *Zł 3.5, free Wed.* 🕑 *Wed., Fri., and Sat. 10–4; Thurs. noon–6; Sun. and holidays 10–5. Closed day after holidays.*

The adjacent **Muzeum Wojska Polskiego** (Polish Army Museum) captures the romance of the military. Exhibits of weaponry, armor, and uniforms trace Polish military history across the past 10 centuries. Heavy armaments are displayed outside. ⊠ *Al. Jerozolimskie 3,* ☎ *022/629–52–71.* 🎫 *Zł 2, free Wed.* 🕑 *Wed. noon–6, Thurs.–Sat. 11–4, Sun. and holidays 10:30–5. Closed day after holidays.*

Aleje Ujazdowskie, the next stage of the Royal Route, is considered by many locals to be Warsaw's finest street. Lined with magnificent buildings, it has something of a French flavor. At ulica Matejki, make ㉓ a detour to the left to see the Polish Houses of Parliament, the **Sejm.** The round, white debating chamber was built during the 1920s, after the rebirth of an independent Polish state.

At plac Na Rozdrożu turn right and head south on aleja Szucha to reach ㉔ the World War II **Gestapo headquarters,** now the Ministry of National Education; a small museum recalls the horrors that took place behind its peaceful facade. ⊠ *Al. Szucha 2,* ☎ *022/629–49–19.* 🎫 *Free.* 🕑 *Tues.–Sat. 10–2.*

㉕ A walk through plac na Rozdrożu brings you to the 18th-century **Zamek Ujazdowski** (Ujazdów Castle), reconstructed in the 1980s. This now hosts a variety of exhibitions by contemporary Polish, European, and North American artists; the building has a terrace at the back looking over formal gardens laid out down to the Vistula. ⊠ *Al. Ujazdowskie 6,* ☎ *022/628–12–71.* 🎫 *Zł 2.5.* 🕑 *Tues.–Sun. 11–5.*

㉖ Just beyond plac Na Rozdrożu lie the **Botanical Gardens,** laid out in 1818, and, at the entrance, the neoclassical **Observatory.** Farther south, before Aleje Ujazdowskie becomes Belwederska, the French-style landscaped **Park Łazienkowski** (Łazienki Park), with pavilions and a royal ★ ㉗ palace, offers a refreshing contrast to the bustling streets. The **Pałac Łazienkowski** (Łazienki Palace), a gem of the Polish neoclassical style, was the private residence of Stanisław August Poniatowski, the last king of Poland. It overlooks a lake stocked with huge carp. At the impressionistic Chopin monument nearby, you can stop for a well-deserved rest and, on summer Sundays, listen to an open-air concert. ☎ *022/621–62–41.* 🎫 *Zł 3.5.* 🕑 *Tues.–Sat. 9:30–3.*

The Royal Route extends along ulica Belwederska, ulica Jana So-★ ㉘ bieskiego, and aleja Wilanowska to the **Wilanów Palace,** 10 km (6 mi) from the town center. Built by King John Sobieski, who in 1683 stopped the Ottoman advance on Europe at the Battle of Vienna, the palace later passed into the hands of Stanisław Kostka Potocki. Potocki amassed a major art collection and was responsible for the layout of the palace gardens. He opened Poland's first public museum here in 1805. Potocki's neo-Gothic tomb can be seen to the left of the driveway as you approach the palace. The palace interiors still hold much of the original furniture; there's also a striking display of 16th- to 18th-century Polish portraits on the first floor.

Outside, to the left of the main entrance, is a Romantic park with pagodas, summerhouses, and bridges overlooking a lake. There's also a **gallery** of contemporary Polish art on the grounds, and the stables to the right of the entrance now house a **poster gallery** that is well worth visiting. ⊠ *Ul. Wiertnicza 1l,* ☎ *022/42–07–95.* ⊠ *Zł 4; guided tour in English from zł 10 per person.* ⊙ *Wed.–Mon. 10–2:30.*

Off the Beaten Path

Some 3 million Polish Jews were put to death by the Nazis during World War II, ending the enormous Jewish contribution to Polish culture, tradition, and achievement. The **Jewish Historical Institute and Museum** has photographic exhibitions and displays of mementoes and artifacts that recall a lost world. ⊠ *Al. Solidarności 79,* ☎ *022/27–18–43.* ⊠ *Free.* ⊙ *Weekdays 9–3.*

A simple monument to the **Heroes of the Warsaw Ghetto,** a slab of dark granite with a bronze bas-relief, stands on ulica Zamenhofa in the Muranów district, the historic heart of the old prewar Warsaw Jewish district and ghetto under the Nazi regime. In April 1943, the Jewish resistance began the Warsaw Ghetto uprising, which was put down by the Nazis with unbelievable ferocity; the Muranów district was flattened. Today there are only bleak gray apartment blocks here. The monument marks the site of the house at **ulica Miła 18,** in which the command bunker of the uprising was situated.

At the corner of ulica Stawki and ulica Dzika was the **Umschlagplatz,** the rail terminus from which tens of thousands of the ghetto's inhabitants were shipped in cattle cars to the extermination camp of Treblinka, about 100 km (60 mi) northeast of Warsaw. The low building to the left of the square was used to detain those who had to wait overnight for transport, and the beginning of the rail tracks survives on the right. At the entrance to the square is a **symbolic gateway,** erected in 1988 as a memorial on the 45th anniversary of the uprising.

Warsaw's **Jewish Cemetery** on ulica Okopowa is an island of continuity amid destruction. The cemetery survived the war, and although badly neglected during the postwar period, it is gradually being restored. Fine 19th-century headstones testify to the Jewish community's role in Polish history and culture. Ludwik Zamenhof, the creator of Esperanto, is buried here.

With ironic humor, locals tell you that the best vantage point from which to admire their city is atop the 37-story **Palace of Culture and Science.** Why? Because it is the only point from which you can't see the Palace of Culture and Science. This wedding-cake-style skyscraper was a personal gift from Stalin. Although Poles dislike it as a symbol of Soviet domination, it does afford a panoramic view and is Warsaw's best example of 1950s "Socialist Gothic" architecture. ⊠ *Plac Defilad,* ☎ *022/656–67–77.* ⊠ *Zł 10 (viewing terrace).* ⊙ *Daily 9–5.*

Shopping

Nowy Świat, Krakowskie Przedmieście, and ulica Chmielna are lined with boutiques selling good-quality leather goods, clothing, and trinkets. Try the **Cepelia** stores (⊠ Plac Konstytucji 5, ☎ 022/621–26–18, and ⊠ Rynek Starego Miasta 8–10, ☎ 022/31–18–05) for handicrafts such as glass, enamelware, amber, and handwoven woolen rugs. Interesting glassware, pottery, and wickerwork can be found at the shop and gallery run by the **Instytut Wzornictwa Przemysłowego** (Institute of Industrial Design; ⊠ Świętojerska 7, ☎ 022/31–04–53), which has the benefit of being open on Sundays from 10 to 4. **Orno** (⊠ Nowy Świat 52, ☎ 022/26–42–81) is good for traditional handmade jewelry and silverware. **Metal Galeria** (⊠ Chmielna 32–34, ☎ 022/27–45–09) has a large range of modern silver and gold jewelry, well displayed in austere glass cases. **Desa** (✉ Marszałkowska 34, ☎ 022/621–66–15) specializes in ornaments and objets d'art. Polish and imported wines and spirits are sold at most large delicatessens.

For the more adventurous there is a flea market, **Bazar Różyckiego,** at ulica Targowa 55, where you can find almost anything. A huge market, where visitors from all over Eastern Europe sell their wares, is open daily at the **Stadion Tysiąclecia,** a sports stadium, near Rondo Waszyngtona.

Dining

More and more interesting restaurants have been opening throughout the city, but some of the best and most atmospheric dining rooms are still to be found on and around the Rynek Starego Miasta in the Old Town. Reservations for dinner can be made by telephone (by your hotel receptionist if you don't speak Polish); in the case of expensive and fashionable restaurants, this is usually necessary. For details and price-category definitions, *see* Dining *in* Staying in Poland, *above.*

$$$$ ✕ **Belvedere.** This restaurant is housed in the elegant, romantic set-
★ ting of the "new"—19th-century—orangery in the Łazienki Park. Tables are set among palms and waterfalls. The food lives up to the setting, with many traditional dishes, such as saddle of hare in nut sauce. ✉ *Łazienki Królewskie, entrance from ul. Parkowa,* ☎ 022/41–48–06. *Reservations essential. AE, DC, MC, V.*

$$$ ✕ **Ambasador.** The updated menu at this good-sized restaurant in Warsaw's diplomatic quarter includes excellent soups, fresh fish, and well-prepared vegetables. The Ambassador's location, near aleje Ujazdowskie, makes it a good place for lunch while exploring the Royal Route. ✉ *Ul. Matejki 4,* ☎ 022/25–99–61. *AE, DC, MC, V.*

$$$ ✕ **Bazyliszek.** Dimly lighted and elegant, the Bazyliszek excels in boar, venison, and duck. A good café and snack bar are downstairs. ✉ *Rynek Starego Miasta 7/9,* ☎ 022/31–18–41. *AE, DC, MC, V.*

$$$ ✕ **Flik.** Light and spacious, Flik has a lantern-lighted terrace overlooking
★ the Morskie Oko park in Mokotów. The proprietors are devoted to serving good food and tend toward nouvelle cuisine. Try the fresh salmon to start. ✉ *Ul. Puławska 43,* ☎ 022/49–43–34. *AE, DC, MC, V.*

$$ ✕ **Kamienne Schodki.** This intimate, candlelit restaurant is in one of the Old Market Square's medieval houses. Its specialty is duck; also be sure to try the pastries. ✉ *Rynek Starego Miasta 26,* ☎ 022/31–08–22. *AE, DC, MC, V.*

$$ ✕ **Menora.** On the poignantly dilapidated, prewar side of Plac Grzybowski, opposite the Jewish Theater and synagogue, is this homey kosher restaurant. Among the traditional dishes are kreplach (pancakes with liver filling) and apple cake. ✉ *Plac Grzybowski 2,* ☎ 022/620–37–54. *AE, DC, MC, V.*

Lodging

Orbis hotels are recommended for convenience and high standards. The rooms are comfortable though standardized, with functional, nondescript carpeting and furniture; some are beginning to show signs of wear. Private accommodations are cheap and hospitable, and are available through Orbis, through the Center for Tourist Information, or Warszawska i Krajowa Informacja Noclegowa (☎ 022/643–95–92). There is no off-season for tourism. For details and price-category definitions, *see* Lodging *in* Staying in Poland, *above.*

$$$$ ▦ **Bristol.** Since reopening in 1992 after a decade of renovation, Warsaw's most famous hotel has tried to reclaim its long traditions of luxury and elegance. Built in 1901 and once owned by Ignacy Paderewski,

the concert pianist who served as Poland's prime minister in 1919–1920, the Bristol was always at the center of Warsaw's social life. ⊠ *Krakowskie Przedmieście 42–44, 00–325,* ☎ *022/625–25–25,* FAX *022/625–25–77. 163 rooms with bath, 43 suites. 2 restaurants, 2 bars, café, pool, health club. AE, DC, MC, V.*

$$$$ 🏨 **Holiday Inn.** This five-story hotel in the center of the city has rooms with color TVs that have four satellite programs. ⊠ *Ul. Złota 2, 00–120,* ☎ *022/620–03–41,* FAX *022/630–05–69. 338 rooms with bath. Restaurant, 2 bars, café, no-smoking floor, sauna, health club, business services. AE, DC, MC, V.*

$$$$ 🏨 **Marriott.** The Warsaw Marriott was completed in late 1989, and at
★ 40 stories (20 make up the hotel; the rest are set aside for office and retail shopping space), it is also the city's tallest building. Luxuries include 24-hour room service and a color TV in every room. ⊠ *Al. Jerozolimskie 65, 00–697,* ☎ *022/630–63–06,* FAX *022/630–52–39. 525 rooms with bath. 11 restaurants, bar, pool, sauna, health club, shops, casino. AE, DC, MC, V.*

$$$$ 🏨 **Victoria Inter-Continental.** Frequented by Western travelers, this is a large 1970s hotel in an ideal location in the center of town. It has a variety of facilities, including a fine restaurant and nightclub. Try to get a room facing Victory Square. ⊠ *Ul. Królewska 11, 00–065,* ☎ *022/657–80–11,* FAX *022/27–98–56. 370 rooms with bath or shower. Restaurant, indoor pool, sauna. AE, DC, MC, V.*

$$$ 🏨 **Hotel Europejski.** This fine old Warsaw hotel, built in the late 19th
★ century, has views over the Royal Route and the Tomb of the Unknown Soldier. Rooms are spacious; the hotel is so well located, and the atmosphere is so friendly, that guests are prepared to accept the slightly shabby appearance of some furnishings. ⊠ *Krakowskie Przedmieście 13, 00–071,* ☎ *022/26–50–51,* FAX *022/26–11–11. 279 rooms with bath or shower. Restaurant. AE, DC, MC, V.*

$$ 🏨 **Dom Chłopa.** After renovation, this 1950s hotel built by the Gromada peasant cooperative has bright, pine–furnished rooms with gleaming bathrooms. It is five minutes on foot from the main shopping streets and the National Philharmonic. It's a good value if you don't mind the noisy clientele of the nightclub on the ground floor. ⊠ *Plac Powstańców Warszawy 2, 00–030,* ☎ *022/27–49–43,* FAX *022/26–14-54. 160 rooms with bath. Restaurant. AE, DC, MC, V.*

$$ 🏨 **Zajazd Napoleoński.** This small, privately owned inn has an excellent
★ restaurant and deluxe facilities. Napoléon reputedly stayed here when his Grand Army passed through Warsaw on its way to Russia. It is about 12.8 km (8 mi) outside of town. Book well in advance. ⊠ *Ul. Płowiecka 83, 04–501,* ☎ *022/15–30–68,* FAX *022/15–22–16. 22 rooms with bath, 3 suites. Restaurant. AE, DC, MC, V.*

The Arts

For information, buy the newspaper *Życie Warszawy* or *Gazeta Wyborcza* at Ruch newsstands; the weekly English-language *Warsaw Voice,* available at most newsstands, also has information. Tickets can be ordered by your Orbis hotel receptionist, through the Center for Tourist Information (☞ *Important Address and Numbers, above*), or at the ticket office at ulica Marszałkowska 104.

Theaters

There are still 17 major theaters in Warsaw, despite cuts in state funding, attesting to the popularity of this art form. **Teatr Narodowy,** opened in 1764 and the oldest in Poland, is on plac Teatralny; after a major fire, it has been closed for repairs and may reopen during 1997. **Współczesny** (⊠ Mokotowska 13, ☎ 25–59–79) presents contemporary works. In addition, two English-language theaters have started up. The **English Theater Company** (✉ Moliera 4, ☎ 022/619–98–17) concentrates on light comedy. The **English Theatre Group** (✉ Czumy 14, ☎ 022/665–50–45) has a varied contemporary repertoire.

Concerts

The **National Philharmonic** (✉ Ul. Sienkiewicza 12, ☎ 022/26–57–12) is regarded as the country's best concert hall. An excellent new concert hall, opened in 1992, is the **Studio Koncertowe Polskiego Radia** (✉ Woronicza 17, ☎ 022/44–32–50). In summer, free Chopin concerts take place both at the Chopin monument in **Łazienki Park** and each Sunday at **Żelazowa Wola,** the composer's birthplace, 58 km (36 mi) outside Warsaw. Call the Chopin Society (✉ ul. Okólnik 1, ☎ 022/27–95–99) for information.

Opera

Teatr Wielki (✉ Pl. Teatralny 1, ☎ 022/26–32–88) hosts the Grand Theater of Opera and Ballet. Its stage is one of Europe's largest.

Nightlife

Cabaret

Orpheus (✉ Al. Jerozolimskie 65/79, ☎ 022/630–54–16), on the top floor of the Hotel Marriott, is elegant and very expensive; hotel guests have priority for admission. **Arena** (✉ Ul. Marsza☎kowska 4, ☎ 022/27–50–91) has boisterous floor shows, including female wrestling. All major hotels have nightclubs that are popular with Westerners and present striptease and jazz. Check listings in the press.

Bars

Gwiazdeczka (✉ Piwna 42, ☎ 022/31–94–63) is a noisy, hip, upscale joint, popular with chic young Warsovians. **Harenda** (✉ Krakowskie Przedmieście 4–6, ☎ 022/26–29–00), with an outdoor terrace in summer, is open until 4 AM. The **John Bull Pub** (✉ Zielna 37, ☎ 022/620–06–56) is open until midnight and serves English draft beers.

Jazz Clubs

Akwarium (✉ Ul. Emilii Platter 49, ☎ 022/620–50–72) and **Wanda Warska's Modern Music Club** (✉ Ul. Wałowa 7, ☎ 022/31–17–39) are popular jazz clubs. **Kawiarnia Literacka** (✉ Krakowskie Przedmieście 87/89, ☎ 022/635–89–95) has classic jazz on weekends.

Discos

Apart from those in the hotels, there is a well-established disco at the student club **Stodoła** (✉ Batorego 10, ☎ 022/25–86–25). **Hades** (✉ Al. Niepodległości 162, ☎ 022/49–12–51) is a popular disco in the basement of the Central School of Economics, with plenty of seating space. **Tango** is a popular upmarket disco, where high entrance charges— zł 85—include a buffet supper (✉ Ul. Smolna 15, ☎ 022/27–86–39).

Cafés

Warsaw is filled with *kawiarnie* (cafés), which move outdoors in summer. They are popular meeting places and usually serve delicious coffee and pastries in the best central European style.

Ambassador (✉ Ul. Matejki 4, ☎ 022/25–99–61) is an elegant, brightly lighted café with a tree-lined terrace that's open in the summer. **Nowe Miasto** (✉ Rynek Nowego Miasta 13–15, ☎ 022/31–43–79), a vegetarian café-cum-restaurant, has cane furniture and a resident harpist. **Nowy Świat** (✉ Nowy Świat 63, ☎ 022/26–58–03), a large and very busy café on the corner of Nowy Świat and Świętokrzyska streets, has a good selection of English-language newspapers for customers. **Le Petit Trianon** (✉ Ul. Piwna 40, ☎ 022/31–73–13) is an intimate 18th-century French-style restaurant and café. **Telimena** (✉

Krakowskie Przedmieście 27, ☎ 022/26–73–63) is a small corner café
with an art gallery on the ground floor.

KRAKÓW AND ENVIRONS

Kraków (Cracow), seat of Poland's oldest university and once the capital of the country (before losing the honor to Warsaw in 1611), is one of the few Polish cities that escaped devastation during World War II. Today Kraków's fine ramparts, towers, facades, and churches, illustrating seven centuries of Polish architecture, make it a major attraction for visitors. Its location—about 270 kilometers (160 miles) south of Warsaw—also makes it a good base for hiking and skiing trips in the mountains of southern Poland. Also within exploring range from Kraków are the famous Polish shrine to the Virgin Mary at Częstochowa, and, at Auschwitz (Oświęcim), a grim reminder of man's capacity for inhumanity.

Getting Around

Kraków is reached by major highways—E7 direct from Warsaw and E82 from Częstochowa. Trains link Kraków with most major destinations in Poland; the station is in the city center near the Old Town, on ulica Pawia. The bus station is across the street.

Guided Tours

Bus or walking tours of Kraków and its environs are provided by **Orbis** and other travel agents. Horse-drawn carriages can be rented at the main market square for a negotiated price.

Visitor Information

Częstochowa. Częstochowa Informacja Turystyczna (⊠ Al. najświętszej Marii Panny 37/39, ☎ 034/24–67–55, ☉ 9:30–4).

Kraków. Orbis (⊠ Al. Marszałka F. Focha 1, ☎ 012/21-98-80) is open 9–5. **Sport Tourist** (⊠ Ul. Pawia 8, ☎ 012/22–95–10) is open 9–5; **Wawel Tour** (⊠ Ul. Swie(rcd)tego Tomasza 26, ☎ 012/22–08–52) is open 10 to 6.

Exploring Kraków

Numbers in the margin correspond to points of interest on the Kraków map.

Kraków's Old Town—listed by UNESCO as one of the 12 great historic cities of the world—is ringed by a park called the **Planty.** The park replaced the old walls of the town, which were torn down in the mid-❶ 19th century. Begin your tour at **Brama Floriańska** (St. Florian's Gate), the beginning of the Royal Route that leads to the Old Town. The gate ❷ is guarded by an imposing 15th-century fortress called the **Barbakan.**

The surviving fragment of the city wall opposite the Barbakan, where students and amateur artists like to hang their paintings for sale in the ❸ summer, contains the Renaissance **Municipal Arsenal,** which now houses part of the National Museum's **Czartoryski Collection,** one of the best art collections in Poland. Highlights include Leonardo da Vinci's *Lady with an Ermine.* ⊠ Ul. Św. Jana 19, ☎ 012/22–55–66. ☒ Zł 5; free Fri. ☉ Fri. noon–5:30, Sat.–Tues. 10–3:30.

NEED A
BREAK?   **Jama Michalikowa** (⊠ Ul. Floriańska 45, ☎ 012/22–15–61), Kraków's most famous café, serves good coffee and excellent ice cream.

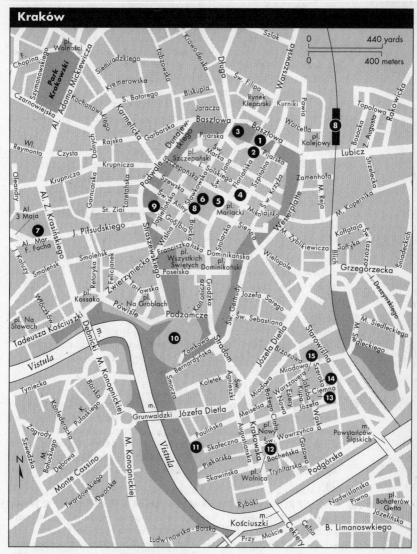

Kraków

Barbakan, **2**

Brama Floriańska, **1**

Collegium Maius, **9**

Kościół Mariacki, **5**

Kościół na Skałce, **11**

Municipal Arsenal, **3**

National Museum, **7**

Ryenk Głowny, **4**

Stara Synagoga, **14**

Sukiennice, **6**

Synagoga R'emuh, **15**

Synagoga Wyoska, **13**

Town Hall of
Kazimierz, **12**

Wawel Castle and
Cathedral, **10**

Wieża Ratuszowa, **8**

❹   Ulica Floriańska leads to the **Rynek Główny** (main market square), one of the largest and finest Renaissance squares in Europe. The calm of this square, with its pigeons and flower stalls, is interrupted every hour

★ ❺   by four short bugle calls drifting down from the spire of the **Kościół Mariacki** (Church of the Virgin Mary). The notes are a centuries-old tradition that honors a trumpeter whose throat was pierced by an enemy arrow as he was warning his fellow citizens of an impending Tartar attack. The square Church of the Virgin Mary contains a 15th-century wooden altarpiece—the world's largest—carved by Veit Stoss. The saints' faces are reputedly those of local burghers.

❻   In the center of the square stands a covered market called the **Sukiennice** (Cloth Hall), built in the 14th century but remodeled during the Renaissance. The ground floor is still in business, selling trinkets and folk art souvenirs. ☉ *Mon.–Sat. 10–6, Sun. 10–5.*

On the second floor of the Cloth Hall, in a branch of the **National Museum,** you can view a collection of 19th-century Polish painting. ▦ *Zł 5; free Thurs.* ☉ *Wed. and Fri.–Sun. 10–3:30, Thurs. noon–5:30.*

❼   You may wish to detour slightly to the west to visit the main building of the **National Museum** (✉ Al. 3 Maja 1, ☎ 012/34–33–37) and then return to the Cloth Hall. Highlights are Polish Art Nouveau and 20th-century painting, as well as historic arms and uniforms.

❽   Across from the Cloth Hall is the **Wieża Ratuszowa** (Town Hall Tower), all that remains of the 16th-century town hall. The tower now houses a branch of the Kraków History Museum and has a panoramic view of the Old Town. ▦ *Zł 3.* ☉ *June–Sept., Fri.–Wed. 9–3, Thurs. noon–5. Closed 2nd weekend of every month.*

★ ❾   From the main market square, turn down ulica świętej Anny to No. 8, the **Collegium Maius,** the oldest building of the famous **Jagiellonian University,** which was founded in 1364. Its pride is the Italian-style arcaded courtyard. A museum here contains the Copernicus globe, the first on which the American continents were shown, as well as astronomy instruments belonging to Kraków's most famous graduate. ▦ *Free.* ☉ *Mon.–Sat. 8–6 (courtyard); museum by appointment only, 10–noon.*

★ ❿   Backtracking on ulica Grodzka and passing on the corner of the square the small Romanesque **Church of St. Adalbert,** will lead you to the **Wawel Castle and Cathedral.** This impressive complex of Gothic and Renaissance buildings stands on fortifications dating from as far back as the 8th century. Inside the castle is a museum with an exotic collection of Oriental tents that were captured from the Turks at the Battle of Vienna in 1683 and rare 16th-century Flemish tapestries. Wawel Cathedral is where, until the 18th century, Polish kings were crowned and buried. Until 1978, the cathedral was the principal church of the see of Archbishop Karol Wojtyła, now Pope John Paul II. ✉ *Ul. Grodzka,* ☎ *012/22–51–55.* ▦ *Castle: zł 8.5.* ☉ *Tues., Thurs., and weekends 9:30–3, Wed. and Fri. noon–6.* ▦ *Cathedral Museum: zł 2.* ☉ *Tues.–Sun. 10–3.*

⓫   From Wawel Hill, make your way via ulica Bernardyńska and the Vistula embankment to the Pauline **Kościół na Skałce** (Church on the Rock). This is the center of the cult of St. Stanisław, an 11th- century bishop and martyr. Starting in the 19th century, it also became the last resting place for well-known Polish writers and artists; among those buried here are the composer Karol Szymanowski and the poet and painter Stanisław Wyspiański.

You are now on the edge of **Kazimierz,** a district of Kraków that was once a town in its own right, chartered in 1335 and named for its founder,

Kazimierz the Great. After 1495, when they were expelled from Kraków by King John Albert, this was the home of Kraków's Jewish community. Following ulica Skałeczna and ulica Krakowska, you will come ⑫ to the market square. The 15th-century **Town Hall of Kazimierz,** now the Ethnographic Museum, displays a well-mounted collection of regional folk art. ⊠ *Pl. Wolnica,* ☎ *012/66–28–63.* ☜ *Zł 5, free Mon.* ☉ *Mon. 10–6, Wed.–Sun. 10–3.*

Leave the square by ulica Bożego Ciała and turn right onto ulica Józefa. ⑬ The late-16th-century **Synagoga Wysoka** (High Synagogue) stands on ⑭ your left at No. 38. On the corner of ulica Szeroka is the **Stara Synagoga** (Old Synagogue), built in the 15th century and reconstructed in Renaissance style following a fire in 1557. Here, in 1775, Tadeusz Kościuszko successfully appealed to the Jewish community to join in the national insurrection. This synagogue now houses the **Museum of the History and Culture of Kraków Jews.** ☎ *012/22–09–62.* ☜ *Free.* ☉ *Mon.–Thurs., weekends 9–3; Fri. 11–6. Closed 1st weekend of month.*

⑮ Also on ulica Szeroka is the 16th-century **Synagoga R'emuh** at No. 40, still used for worship. It is associated with the name of the son of its founder, Rabbi Moses Isserles, who is buried in the cemetery attached to the synagogue. Used by the Jewish community from 1533 to 1799, this is the only well-preserved Renaissance Jewish cemetery in Europe. (The so-called **New Cemetery** on ulica Miodowa, which contains many old headstones, was established in the 19th century).

Schindler's List, Steven Spielberg's award-winning 1993 film, inspired visitors to Kraków to retrace the steps of German industrialist Oskar Schindler, who saved the lives of more than 1,200 Jews during the Holocaust by hiring them to work in his enamel factory at ulica Lipowa 4. "Schindler's List" tours are offered by Orbis (⊠ Al. Marszałka F. Focha 1, ☎ 012/21-98-80) and the Judaica bookstore, Jordan (ul. Szeroka 2, Miodowa 41, ☎ 012/21–71–66). The two-hour minibus tours include the Kazimierz district, the Liban quarry, the Płaszów concentration camp (now a city park), and the Vistula River bridge.

About 50 km (30 mi) west of Kraków is Oświęcim, better known by its German name, **Auschwitz.** Here 4 million victims, mostly Jews, were executed by the Nazis in the Auschwitz and Birkenau concentration camps. Auschwitz is now a museum, with restored crematoria and barracks housing dramatic displays of Nazi atrocities. The buildings at Birkenau, a 15-minute walk away, have been left just as they were found in 1945 by the Soviet Army. Oświęcim itself is an industrial town with good connections from Kraków; buses and trains leave Kraków approximately every hour, and signs in Oświęcim direct visitors to the camp. ⊠ *Ul. Więźniów Oświęcimia 20,* ☎ *0381/321–33.* ☜ *Free.* ☉ *Mar. and Nov., Tues.–Sun. 8–4; Apr. and Oct., Tues.–Sun. 8–5; May and Sept., daily 8–6; June–Aug., daily 8–7; Dec.–Feb., Tues.–Sun. 8–3. Birkenau:* ☜ *Free.* ☉ *Daily, sunrise–sunset.*

★ **Wieliczka,** about 8 km (5 mi) southeast of Kraków, is the oldest salt mine in Europe, in operation since the end of the 13th century. It is famous for its magnificent underground chapel hewn from crystal rock, the **Chapel of the Blessed Kinga** (Queen Kinga was a 14th-century Polish queen, later beatified). ⊠ *Ul. Daniłowicza 10,* ☎ *012/78–26–53.* ☜ *Zł 10.* ☉ *Daily 9–4.*

Częstochowa, 120 km (70 mi) from Kraków and reached by regular trains and buses, is the home of the holiest shrine in a country that is more than 90% Catholic. Inside the 14th-century **Pauline monastery** on Jasna Góra (Light Hill) is the famous *Black Madonna,* a painting of Our Lady of Częstochowa attributed by legend to St. Luke. It was here that an invading Swedish army met heroic resistance from the Poles in 1655. About 25 miles southwest of Kraków is the little town of **Wadowice,** birthplace of Pope John Paul II. ⊠ *Wadowice Museum,* ☎ *033/327–97* 🎫 *Zł 2.* ◷ *Tues.–Sat. 10–3, Sun. 10–5.*

Dining and Lodging

For details and price-category definitions, *see* Dining *and* Lodging *in* Staying in Poland, *above.*

Częstochowa

$ 🏨 **Polonia.** The Polonia makes a good base for exploring the Pauline monastery, and since most of the other guests are pilgrims, the atmosphere is an interesting mixture of piety and good fun. ⊠ *Ul. Piłsudskiego 9,* ☎ *034/24–40–67,* FAX *034/65–11–05. 62 rooms with bath or shower. Restaurant, café. AE, DC, MC, V.*

Kraków

$$$$ ✕ **Wierzynek.** One of the best restaurants in the country serves tradi-
★ tional Polish specialties and excels in soups and game. It was here, after a historic meeting in 1364, that the king of Poland wined and dined the Holy Roman Emperor Charles IV, five kings, and a score of princes. ⊠ *Rynek Główny 15,* ☎ *012/22–14–04. AE, DC, MC, V.*

$$$ ✕ **Pałac Pugetów.** Eat traditional Polish food by candlelight in Baron Konstanty de Puget's dining room, just outside the walls of the Old Town. Besides the restaurant, there's a café in which concerts are occasionally given. ⊠ *Ul. Starowiślna 13, no phone. AE, DC, MC, V.*

$$$ ✕ **Staropolska.** Traditional Polish cuisine is served in a medieval setting. Try the pork, duck, or veal. ⊠ *Ul. Sienna 4,* ☎ *012/22–58–21. AE, DC, MC, V.*

$$$ ✕🏨 **Francuski.** This small, turn-of-the-century hotel is just inside the Old Town's ramparts. It has an intimate atmosphere and friendly service, and the rooms are elegant in a homey, Eastern European way. The excellent restaurant is tranquil and plush and has a café with dancing. ⊠ *Ul. Pijarska 13,* ☎ *012/22–51–22,* FAX *012/22–52–70. 42 rooms with bath or shower. Restaurant, café. AE, DC, MC, V.*

$$ ✕🏨 **Cracovia.** Large and Orbis-run, this five-story 1960s hotel has one
★ of the best restaurants in town. The chef specializes in an internationalized Polish cuisine; try the *krem z pieczarek* (thick and creamy mushroom soup), followed by chateaubriand. ⊠ *Al. Marszałka F. Focha 1,* ☎ *012/22–86–66,* FAX *012/21–95–86. 427 rooms with bath. Restaurant, nightclub. AE, DC, MC, V.*

$$ ✕🏨 **Holiday Inn.** The first Holiday Inn in Eastern Europe is rather bland but comfortable. This high-rise establishment is pleasantly located on the far side of Kraków Common, making it a good choice for those who want to combine sightseeing with a little exercise. ⊠ *Ul. Koniewa 7,* ☎ *012/37–50–44,* FAX *012/37–59–38. 310 rooms with bath. Restaurant, indoor pool, sauna. AE, DC, MC, V.*

$$$ 🏨 **Forum.** Opened in 1988, this Orbis hotel stands on the south bank of the Vistula, commanding a fine view of Wawel Castle. It's a bit farther from the Old Town but has good health and sports facilities. ⊠ *Ul. Marii Konopnickiej 28,* ☎ *012/66–95–00,* FAX *012/66–58–27. 280 rooms with bath. Restaurant, indoor pool, beauty salon, sauna, tennis courts. AE, DC, MC, V.*

$$$ 🏨 **Grand.** An air of Regency elegance predominates at this late-19th-
★ century hotel in the Old Town, although some Art Nouveau stained-glass windows have been preserved on the first floor. Rooms have

reproduction period furniture and modern bathrooms and facilities. ⊠ *Ul. Sławkowska 5–7,* ☎ *012/21–72–55,* 𝖥𝖠𝖷 *012/21–83–60. 50 rooms with bath. Restaurant, café, exercise room. AE, DC, MC, V.*

$ ☷ **Europejski.** This small, older hotel overlooking the Planty park has now been renovated, and most of the rooms have shower or bath. ⊠ *Ul. Lubicz 5,* ☎ *012/22–09–11,* 𝖥𝖠𝖷 *012/22–89–25. 55 rooms, most with bath. AE, DC, MC, V.*

GDAŃSK AND THE NORTH

In contrast to Kraków and the south, Poland north of Warsaw is a land of medieval castles and châteaus, dense forests and lakes, and fishing villages and beaches. If you don't have a car, consider going straight to Gdańsk and making excursions from there.

Getting Around

Gdańsk is a major transportation hub, with an airport just outside town (and good bus connections to downtown) and major road and rail connections with the rest of the country.

Guided Tours

Orbis arranges an eight-day tour of Warsaw, Toruń, Gdańsk, and Poznań. It also handles group and individual tours of Toruń, Gdańsk, and the surrounding areas.

Visitor Information

Gdańsk (⊠ Ul. Heweliusza 8, ☎ 058/31–03–38; Orbis, ⊠ Ul. Heweliusza 22, ☎ 022/31–45–44).
Olsztyn (Orbis, ⊠ Ul. Dąbrowszczaków 1, ☎ 089/27–46–74).
Ostróda (⊠ Ul. Czarnieckiego 10, ☎ 088/46–65–57).
Płock (⊠ Ul. Tuńska 4, ☎ 024/62–94–97; Orbis, ⊠ Al. Jachowicza 47, ☎ 024/62–29–89).
Toruń (⊠ Ul. Kopernika 27, ☎ 056/272–99; Orbis, ⊠ Ul.Mostowa 7, ☎ 056/228–73).

Exploring Gdańsk and the North

From Warsaw, follow routes E81 and 107 through **Płock.** Once you get through Płock's industrial area, you'll find a lovely medieval city that was for a short time the capital of Poland. Worth seeing are the 12th-century cathedral, where two Polish kings are buried, and the dramatic 14th-century Teutonic castle. Continue through Włocławek to Toruń, where an overnight stay is recommended.

Toruń

Toruń, birthplace of Nicolaus Copernicus, is an interesting medieval city that grew wealthy due to its location on the north–south trading route along the Vistula. Its Old Town district is a remarkably successful blend of Gothic buildings—churches, the town hall, and burghers' homes—and Renaissance and Baroque patricians' houses. The town hall's tower (1274) is the oldest in Poland. Don't leave without trying some of Toruń's famous gingerbread and honey cakes.

The route leading north from Toruń to Gdańsk passes through some of the oldest towns in Poland. Along the way are many medieval castles, manor houses, and churches that testify to the wealth and strategic importance of the area. Two short detours are a must: One is to **Kwidzyń,** to see the original 14th-century castle and cathedral complex, which is free and open to the public. The other is to **Malbork.**

Gdańsk and the North

This huge castle, 58 km (36 mi) from Gdańsk, was one of the most powerful strongholds in medieval Europe. From 1308 to 1457, it was the residence of the Grand Masters of the Teutonic Order. The Teutonic Knights were a thorn in Poland's side until their defeat at the Battle of Grunwald in 1410. Inside Malbork Castle is a museum with beautiful examples of amber—including lumps as large as melons and pieces containing perfect specimens of prehistoric insects. ☎ 055/72–33–64. 🎫 Zł 10. ☉ Tues.–Sat. 10–3, Sun. 10–5.

Gdańsk

Gdańsk, once the free city of Danzig, is another of Poland's beautifully restored towns, displaying a rich heritage of Gothic, Renaissance, and Mannerist architecture. This is where the first shots of World War II were fired and where the free trade union Solidarity was born after strikes in 1980. The city's Old Town has a wonderful collection of historic town houses and narrow streets. The city's axis is formed by splendid Długa Street (best for shopping) and Długi Targ Square—great starting points for walks into other districts. The evocative **Solidarity Monument**—erected in honor of workers killed by the regime during strikes in 1970—stands outside the Lenin shipyards. The nearby town of **Sopot** is Poland's most popular seaside resort.

For a different route back to Warsaw, follow highway E81 southeast through Poland's scenic forest and lake district. The area is rich in natural and historic attractions. Recommended is a side trip 42 kilometers (26 miles) east of Ostróda to the medieval town of **Olsztyn.** The Old Town was once administered and fortified by Copernicus.

About 30 km (19 mi) farther south on E81 is **Olsztynek,** where the **Museum of Folk Buildings** has a collection of timber buildings from different parts of the country. They include a small Mazurian thatch-roofed church, an inn, a mill, a forge, old windmills, and thatched cottages, some of which have period-style furnishings. ☎ 089/19–24–64. ✆ Zł 5. ⊙ May–Sept., Tues.–Sun. 9–4; closed Mon.

Another diversion, 17 kilometers (10½ miles) west of Olsztynek, is the **site of the Battle of Grunwald,** possibly the greatest battle of the Middle Ages. Here on July 15, 1410, Władysław Jagiełło and his Polish Lithuanian army annihilated the Grand Master of the Teutonic Order, Ulrich von Jungingen, and thousands of his knights. A small museum on the site (⊙ Summer only, 10–10) graphically explains the course of the battle.

Dining and Lodging

For details and price-category definitions, *see* Dining *and* Lodging *in* Staying in Poland, *above.*

Gdańsk

$$$ ✕ **Pod Łososiem.** The name of this restaurant refers to salmon, which,
★ if available on the day you visit, is highly recommended. Other fish and wild fowl such as duck and pheasant are good choices, too. ⊠ *Ul. Szeroka 51,* ☎ *058/31–76–52. AE, DC, MC, V.*

$$ ✕ **Kaszubska.** The specialties here come from Kashubia, the lake district west of the city. Smoked fish dishes are highly recommended. ⊠ *Ul. Kartuska 76,* ☎ *058/32–06–02. AE, DC, MC, V.*

$$ ✕ **Tawerna.** This well-established restaurant overlooking the river
★ serves traditional Polish and Germanic dishes such as pork cutlets and seafood. Yes, it's touristy, but the food is delicious. ⊠ *Ul. Powroźnicza 19–20, off Długi Targ,* ☎ *058/31–92–48. AE, DC, MC, V.*

$$ ☷ **Hewelius.** This large, modern, high-rise hotel is within walking distance of the Old Town. The spacious, blandly furnished rooms have all the modern conveniences. ⊠ *Ul. Heweliusza 22,* ☎ *058/31–56–31,* ℻ *31 058/31–19–22. 250 rooms with bath. Restaurant, nightclub. AE, DC, MC, V.*

$$ ☷ **Marina.** Built in 1982, this large high-rise, popular with Western
★ businesspeople, is probably the best in town. Upper floors have splendid views. ⊠ *Ul. Jelitkowska 20,* ☎ *058/53–20–79,* ℻ *058/53–04–60. 193 rooms with bath or shower. Restaurant, indoor pool, sauna, tennis courts, bowling, nightclub. AE, DC, MC, V.*

Olsztyn

$$ ☷ **Orbis Novotel.** This standard 1970s hotel is typical of the kind found in Poland. It is, however, the most comfortable lodging in the area, set in beautiful surroundings on the shores of Lake Ukiel. ⊠ *Ul. Sielska 4A,* ☎ *089/27–40–81,* ℻ *089/27–54–03. 98 rooms with bath. Restaurant, pool. AE, DC, MC, V.*

Ostróda

$ ☷ **Panorama Hotel.** This town is not visited by many foreign tourists and lacks good-quality facilities. Still, the architecturally undistinguished but friendly Panorama will provide a pleasant overnight stay. ⊠ *Ul. Krasickiego 23,* ☎ *088/82–22–27. 26 rooms, some with bath. Restaurant. No credit cards.*

Toruń

$$$ ✕ **Pod Kurantem.** Regional cuisine is featured in this attractive old wine
★ cellar. Slow service is the penalty for popularity. ⊠ *Rynek Staromiejski 28. No phone. Reservations not accepted. No credit cards.*

$$ ✕ **Wodnik.** This large café on the bank of the Vistula is very popular with locals. ⊠ *Blwd. Filadelfijski,* ☎ *056/287–55. AE, DC, MC, V.*

$$ ✕ **Zajazd Staropolski.** Excellent meat dishes and soups are served in a restored 17th-century interior. ⊠ *Ul. Żeglarska 10/14,* ☎ *056/260– 60. AE, DC, MC, V.*

$$ ✕🖽 **Helios.** This friendly, medium-size hotel in the city center has a good restaurant (albeit with slow service). ⊠ *Ul. Kraszewskiego 1,* ☎ *056/250–33,* 𝖥𝖠𝖷 *056/235–65. 140 rooms, most with bath or shower. Restaurant, beauty salon, sauna, nightclub. AE, DC, MC, V.*

$$ 🖽 **Kosmos.** A functional 1960s hotel, Kosmos was beginning to show signs of wear and tear before a recent facelift. It is near the river, in the city center. ⊠ *Ul. Portowa 2,* ☎ *056/270–85. 180 rooms, most with bath or shower. AE, DC, MC, V.*

23 Portugal

Lisbon

*The Portuguese Riviera, Sintra,
and Queluz*

The Algarve

CLINGING TO THE WESTERN CUSP of the continent, insulated from Spain's arid plains and burning sun, Portugal springs one of Europe's great surprises. While you'll find similarly fine food and wine, spectacularly sited castles, medieval hilltop villages, and excellent beaches, Portugal is a land of myriad and delightful distinctions. It's far more lush than Spain—the landscape unfolds in astonishing variety to reveal a mountainous, green interior and a sweeping coastline—and Celtic and Moorish influences are evident in the land, its people, and their tongue.

Given its long Atlantic coastline, it isn't surprising that Portugal has been a maritime nation for most of its tumultuous history. From the charting of the Azores archipelago in 1427 to the discovery of Japan in 1542, Portuguese explorers unlocked the major sea routes to southern Africa, India, the Far East, and the Americas. This great era of exploration, known as the *descobrimentos,* reached its height in the 15th century under the influence of Prince Henry the Navigator. The glories of the Portuguese empire were relatively short lived, however, and the next several centuries saw dynastic instability, extravagant spending by feckless monarchs, natural disasters, and foreign invasion. The 20th century brought little change, and not until a bloodless coup in 1974 deposed the ruling rightist dictatorship was democracy established and the process of modernization begun.

Today Portugal is a stable country, its people keen to share in the prosperity offered by developments within the European Union. Given the relatively short time since the revolution, this stability indeed speaks well for the inherent strengths of the Portuguese psyche. Political confidence couldn't have been maintained without improvements in the economy, and there have been great strides forward since 1974. One effect of this regeneration that regular visitors will notice is that Portugal has become more expensive over the last few years, though you're unlikely to find costs prohibitive.

The sections that follow concentrate on the southern part of the country—the region most frequented by visitors—including Lisbon, its coastal and wooded environs, and the beaches and low-lying plains of the southern Algarve. In these areas, the architecture and culture that make Portugal unique now mingle with contemporary styles and lifestyles. Accordingly, the resort towns and cities can no longer claim to be undiscovered: The Algarve coast is one of Europe's most popular vacation areas, and Lisbon, Portugal's sophisticated capital, has rapidly acquired the trappings of a modern commercial center, with skyscrapers wedged in among turn-of-the-century buildings. Take time to get off the beaten track, however, and you'll be rewarded with glimpses of a traditional life and culture shaped by memories of empire and tempered by the experience of revolution.

ESSENTIAL INFORMATION

Before You Go

When to Go

The tourist season runs from spring through autumn, but some parts of the country—especially the Algarve, which boasts 3,000 hours of sunshine annually—are balmy even in winter. Hotel prices are greatly reduced between November and February, except in Lisbon, where business visitors keep prices uniformly high throughout the year.

Portugal

50 miles
50 km

ATLANTIC
OCEAN

N

Minho
Valença
Viana
do Castelo
Lima
Serra do Gerês N103
Chaves
Bragança
Barcelos
Braga
Póvoa de Varzim
Guimarães
Tâmega
N15
Mirandela
Vila do Conde
Amarante
Vila Real
Sabor
Mogadouro
Oporto
Penafiel
Douro
Duoro
Espinho
Douro
Lamego
Oliveira
dos Azeméis
Moimenta
da Beira
Albergaria-a-Velha
Vouga
S. Pedro
do Sul
Aveiro
Viseu
Pinhel
Mealhada
Sta. Comba
Dão
Mira
Cantanhede
Mondego
Guarda
Coimbra
Serra da Estrêla
Figueira
da Foz
Arganil
Covilhã
Fundão
E1/A1
Zêzere
Penamacor
Pombal
N110
Serra da
Gardunha
N233
Leiria
Ourém
Proença-
a-Nova
Castelo
Branco
Nazaré
Batalha
Tomar
Alcobaça
Fátima
Nisa
Caldas
da Rainha
Sra.
do Aire
Abrantes
Tagus N118
Obidos
Torres
Novas
Aveiras de Cima
Santarém
Portalegre
Torres Vedras
Mafra
Tejo
Ponte
de Sor
Vila Franca
de Xira
Sintra
Sorraia
Avis
Cascais
Lisbon
N10
Arraiolos
Estremoz
Elvas
Estoril
Montemor-
o-Novo
Sra. de Ossa
Guadiana
Seixal
A2
Vila
Viçosa
Setúbal
Sado
Évora
Reguengos
Cabo
Espichel
Alcácer
do Sal
N2
TO THE
AZORES
Ferreira do
Alentejo
Moura
Sines
E1
Beja
Cabo de
Sines
Santiago
do Cacem
Vilaverde de Ficalho
Castro
Verde
Serpa
Odemira
Ourique
N122
TO MADEIRA
ISLAND
Mira
Mértola
Chança
N120
Almodôvar
Guadiana
Monchique
ALGARVE
Vila do Bispo
Portimão EN125
Albufeira
S. Brás de Alportel
Cabo de
S. Vicente
Sagres
Lagos
Faro
Tavira
Vila Real de
S. António
Olhão

S P A I N

CLIMATE
Since Portugal's entire coast is on the Atlantic Ocean, the country's climate is temperate year-round. Even in August, the hottest month, the Algarve and the Alentejo are the only regions where the midday heat may be uncomfortable, but most travelers go to the beaches there to swim and soak up the sun. What rain there is falls from November to March; December and January can be chilly outside the Algarve, and very wet to the north, but there is no snow except in the mountains of the Serra da Estrela in the northeast. The almond blossoms and vivid wildflowers that cover the countryside start to bloom early in February.

The following are the average daily maximum and minimum temperatures for Lisbon.

Jan.	57F	14C	May	71F	21C	Sept.	79F	26C
	46	8		55	13		62	17
Feb.	59F	15C	June	77F	25C	Oct.	72F	22C
	47	8		60	15		58	14
Mar.	63F	17C	July	81F	27C	Nov.	63F	17C
	50	10		63	17		52	11
Apr.	67F	20C	Aug.	82F	28C	Dec.	58F	15C
	53	12		63	17		47	9

Currency

The unit of currency in Portugal is the escudo, which can be divided into 100 centavos. Escudos come in bills of 500$00, 1,000$00, 2,000$00, 5,000$00, and 10,000$00. (In Portugal the dollar sign stands between the escudo and the centavo.) Coins come in 1$00, 2$50, 5$00, 10$00, 20$00, 50$00, 100$00, and 200$00.

At press time (spring 1996), the exchange rate was about 150$00 to the U.S. dollar, 115$00 to the Canadian dollar, and 242$00 to the pound sterling. Owing to the complications of dealing in millions of escudos, 1,000$00 is always called a *conto*, so 10,000$00 is referred to as 10 contos. You can change money in hotels and in larger shops and restaurants, but banks and *cambios* (exchange offices) usually give better rates.

What It Will Cost

Although the cost of hotels and restaurants in Portugal is still reasonable, inflation is pushing prices up. The most expensive areas are Lisbon, the Algarve, and the tourist resort areas along the Tagus estuary. The least expensive areas are country towns, which all have reasonably priced hotels and *pensões,* or pensions, as well as numerous café-type restaurants. A sales, or value-added, tax (called IVA) of 17% is imposed on hotel and restaurant bills, car rentals, and services such as car repairs.

SAMPLE PRICES
Cup of coffee, 100–150$00; bottle of beer, 150$00; soft drink, 125–175$00; bottle of house wine, 500$00–750$00; ham sandwich, 225$00; 1-mile taxi ride, 450$00; city bus ride, 150$00; museum entrance, 250$00–450$00.

Customs on Arrival

Non-EU visitors over age 17 are allowed to bring the following items into Portugal duty-free: 200 cigarettes or 250 grams of tobacco, 1 liter of liquor (over 22% volume) or 2 liters (under 22% volume), 2 liters of wine, 100 milliliter of perfume, and a reasonable amount of personal effects (camera, binoculars, etc). No more than 100,000$00 in Portuguese currency or the equivalent of 500,000$00 in foreign currency may be taken out without proof that an equal amount or more was brought into Portugal.

Language

Portuguese is easy to read by anyone with even slight knowledge of a Latin language, but it is difficult to pronounce and understand (most people speak quickly and elliptically). But in large cities and major resorts many people speak English and, occasionally, French.

Getting Around

By Car

ROAD CONDITIONS

The few turnpikes (moderate tolls) and the major highways between Lisbon and the coast, the Algarve, and Oporto are in good shape. For the most part, road conditions in Portugal have greatly improved, but minor roads are often poor and winding with unpredictable surfaces.

New highways have made the once grueling drive between the Algarve and Lisbon a pleasure. EN 125, the principal east–west Algarve highway, has been widened and resurfaced, while construction of the new Algarve highway should be completed by press time (spring 1996). New bridges have eliminated the formerly horrendous bottlenecks at Portimão and replaced the ferry across the Guadiana River from Vila Real de Santo António to Spain.

In the north, the IP5 makes the drive from Aveiro to the border with Spain, near Guarda, a pleasant one, and the IP4 connects Oporto through Vila Real to once-remote Bragança. There's no superhighway from Lisbon leading east to the nearest frontier post at Badajoz, Spain, but the route over the Tagus bridge through Setúbal (turnpike from Lisbon), via Montemor-o-Novo and Estremoz, is good and fast.

RULES OF THE ROAD

Driving is on the right. At the junction of two roads of equal size, traffic coming from the right has priority. Vehicles already in a traffic circle have priority over those entering it from any point. The use of seat belts is obligatory. Horns should not be used in built-up areas, and a reflective red warning triangle, for use in a breakdown, must be carried. The speed limit on turnpikes is 120 kph (72 mph); on other roads it is 90 kph (54 mph), and in built-up areas, 50–60 kph (30–36 mph).

PARKING

Lisbon, Coimbra, and Oporto are experimenting with parking meters, although these are still rare. Parking lots and underground garages abound in major cities, but those in Lisbon and Oporto are no longer cheap. It's often difficult to find a parking space near city-center hotels.

GASOLINE

Gas prices are among the highest in Europe: 185$00 per liter for super and 170$00 for regular. Unleaded gas is now available for 165$00. Many gas stations are self-service, and credit cards are widely accepted.

BREAKDOWNS

All large garages in and around towns have breakdown services. Special orange emergency (SOS) telephones are located at intervals on turnpikes and highways. Motorists in Portugal are very helpful; if your car breaks down, aid from a passing driver is usually forthcoming. The national automobile organization, **Automóvel Clube de Portugal** (⌧ Rua Rosa Araújo 24/26, 1200 Lisbon, ☎ 01/356–3931) provides reciprocal membership with AAA and other European automobile associations, provided the membership is current.

By Train

The Portuguese railway system is surprisingly extensive for such a small country. Trains are clean and leave on time, but there are few express runs except between Lisbon and Oporto, which takes just over three hours for the 210-mile (338-kilometer) journey. Most trains have first-and second-class compartments; some of the Lisbon–Oporto expresses are first-class only; suburban lines around Lisbon have a single class. Tickets should be bought, and seats reserved, at the stations or through travel agents, two or three days in advance. Advance reservations are essential on Lisbon–Oporto express trains. Timetables are generally the same on Saturday and Sunday as on weekdays, except on suburban lines. **Wasteels–Expresso** (⊠ Av. António Augusto Aguiar 88, 1000 Lisbon, ☎ 01/357–9655 or 01/357–9180) is reliable for all local and international train tickets and reservations.

Special **tourist passes** can be obtained through travel agents or at main train stations. These are valid for periods of 7, 14, or 21 days for first-and second-class travel on any domestic train service; mileage is unlimited. At press time (spring 1996), the cost was 17,500$00 for 7 days; 27,500$00 for 14 days; and 38,500$00 for 21 days. Child passes cost exactly half those amounts.

Trains to Madrid, Paris, and other parts of Europe depart from the Santa Apolonia Station in Lisbon and Campanhã in Oporto.

By Plane

The internal air services of **TAP Air Portugal** are good. Lisbon is linked at least four times daily with Oporto and Faro; daily with Funchal (Madeira), more at peak periods; weekly with Porto Santo, an island some way off Madeira; and several times a week with the archipelago of the Azores. TAP (⊠ Praça Marquês de Pombal 3, 1200 Lisbon, ☎ 01/386–1020) also has flights to Viseu, Vila Real and Bragança. Other internal services are provided by LAR, Portugália, and SATA-Air Açores (which flies to the Azores), all of whose schedules change according to season. Any travel agent can provide up-to-date prices and timetables.

By Bus

The main bus company, **Rodoviaria Nacional,** has passenger terminals in Lisbon (⊠ Av. Casal Ribeiro 18, ☎ 01/354–4539), with regular bus services throughout Portugal. Several private companies also offer luxury service between major cities. It is three hours to Oporto and five hours to the Algarve. For information and reservations in Lisbon, contact the main tourist office (☞ Important Addresses and Numbers *in* Lisbon, *below*) or **Marcus & Harting** (⊠ Rossío 45–50, ☎ 01/346–9271). Most long-distance buses have toilet facilities, and the fares are often lower than those for trains.

By Boat

Ferries across the River Tagus (Lisbon) leave from Praça do Comércio, Cais do Sodré, and Belém. From April to October, a two-hour boat excursion leaves the ferry station at Praça do Comércio in Lisbon daily at 2:30 PM. The price is 3,750$00. In the United States, contact **Euro Cruises** (⊠ 303 W. 13th St., New York, NY 10014, ☎ 212/691–2099 or 800/661–1119) about cruises on the Douro River in an 80-cabin vessel, with weekly departures.

One-hour boat trips on the River Douro (Oporto) are organized from May through October by **Porto Ferreira** (⊠ Rua da Cavalhosa 19, Vila Nova de Gaia, Oporto, ☎ 02/300866). Overnight cruises up the River Douro are also available. Contact **Endouro** (⊠ Rua da Reboleira 49, 4000 Oporto, ☎ 02/208–4161, 𝖥𝖠𝖷 02/317260).

By Bicycle

You can rent bicycles at certain Algarve resorts, though heavy traffic on the main roads can make cycling an exhausting experience. There aren't any cycle rental outfits in downtown Lisbon, which is just as well—if the hills don't defeat you, the careering taxis, trams, and buses will. **Tip Tours** (⊠ Av. Costa Pinto 91-A, 2750 Cascais, ☎ 01/483–5150 and 01/483–5159) rents bicycles by the day or half day. **Cycling through the Centuries** (⊠ in U.S., 1925 Wallenberg Dr., Ft. Collins, CO 80526, ☎ 970/484–8489 or 800/685–4565; in Portugal, ⊠ Rua Dra. Iracy Doyle 9, 3-E, 2750 Cascais, ☎ 01/486–2044 offers bicycle tours in the Alentejo, Minho, and the Algarve.

Staying in Portugal

Telephones

LOCAL CALLS

Pay phones take 10$00, 20$00, and 50$00 coins; 10$00 is the minimum payment for short local calls. Pay phones marked CREDIFONE will accept plastic phone cards, which can be purchased at post offices and most tobacconist shops.

INTERNATIONAL CALLS

Long-distance calls cost less from 8 PM to 7 AM. Collect calls can also be made from post offices. In larger towns, you may be able to charge calls costing over 500$00 to your MasterCard or Visa. Some telephone booths accept international calls. Access numbers to reach American long-distance operators are: for **AT&T**, 050–171288; for **MCI**, 0010–480–0112; for **Sprint**, 050–171877.

COUNTRY CODE

The country code for Portugal is 351.

Mail

Main post offices in towns are open weekdays 8:30 to 6. In Lisbon, the post office in the Praça dos Restauradores is open daily from 8 AM until 10 PM. More rural post offices close for lunch and at 6 PM on weekdays; they are not open on weekends.

RECEIVING MAIL

Mail can be sent in care of American Express Star (⊠ **Top Tours,** Av. Duque de Loulé 108, 1000 Lisbon, ☎ 01/315–5877, FAX 01/352–3227); there is no service charge.

Shopping

Bargaining is not common in city stores or shops, but it is sometimes possible in flea markets, antiques shops, and outdoor markets that sell fruit, vegetables, and household goods. The **Centro de Turismo Artesanato** (⊠ Rua Castilho 61, 1200 Lisbon, ☎ 01/353–4879) will ship goods abroad even if they were not bought in Portugal. By air to the United States, parcels take about three weeks; by sea, two months.

IVA REFUNDS

IVA tax on items over a certain value can be reclaimed, although the methods are time-consuming. For non-EU residents, the tax paid on individual items costing more than 10,000$00 can be reclaimed in cash on presentation of receipts and a special *Tax-Free Shopping Cheque* to special departments in airports (in Lisbon, near Gate 23). You can also have the check stamped at any border crossing and receive the refund by mail or credit card. Shops specializing in IVA-refund purchases are clearly marked throughout the country, and shop assistants can help with the forms. For details consult the main tourist office in Lisbon (☞ Important Addresses and Numbers, *below*).

Opening and Closing Times

Banks are open weekdays 8:30 to 3; they do not close for lunch. There are automatic currency-exchange machines in Lisbon (around the Praçado Comércio and Praça dos Restauradores) and in other cities.

Museums are usually open 10–12:30 and 2–5. Most close on Sunday afternoon, and all close Monday. Most palaces close on Tuesday.

Shops are open weekdays 9–1 and 3–7, Saturdays 9–1. Shopping malls and supermarkets in Lisbon and other cities remain open until 10 PM or midnight and are often open on Sunday.

National Holidays

January 1; March 28 (Good Friday); April 25 (Anniversary of the Revolution); May 1 (Labor Day); June 6 (Corpus Christi); June 10 (National Day); August 15 (Feast of the Assumption); October 5 (Day of the Republic); November 1 (All Saints' Day); December 1 (Independence Day); December 8 (Immaculate Conception); December 25.

Dining

Seafood is a staple, and *sardinhas assadas* (fresh-grilled sardines) are a local favorite. There are said to be as many ways to prepare *bacalhau* (cod) as there are days in the year. Freshly caught lobster, crab, shrimp, tuna, sole, and squid are prepared in innumerable ways, and *caldeirada* is a piquant seafood stew made with a little bit of everything. In the Algarve, *cataplana* is a must: It's a mouthwatering mixture of clams, ham, tomatoes, onions, garlic, and herbs, named for the dish in which it is cooked. Meat lovers wax rhapsodic over northern-style *leitão da Bairrada* (roast suckling pig), *coelho á caçadora* (rabbit with potatoes, onions, garlic, and a splash of wine), and the tasty *liguiça* (spiced sausages) and *presunto* (cured) ham. There are some excellent local wines, and in modest restaurants even the *vinho da casa* (house wine) is usually very good. Desserts feature *doces de ovos* (egg and sugar confections), *pudim flan* (egg custard), egg and almond tarts, and always fruit. Water is generally safe, but visitors may want to drink bottled water—*sem gas* for still, *com gas* for fizzy. Unless noted, reservations are not necessary.

MEALTIMES
Lunch usually begins around 1 PM; dinner is served at about 8 PM.

WHAT TO WEAR
Jacket and tie are advised for most restaurants in the $$$ and $$$$ categories, but otherwise casual dress is acceptable.

RATINGS
Prices are per person, without alcohol. Taxes and service are usually included, but a tip of 5%–10% is always appreciated.

CATEGORY	ALL AREAS
$$$$	over 6,000$00
$$$	3,500$00–6,000$00
$$	2,000$00–3,500$00
$	under 2,000$00

Lodging

Visitors have a wide choice of lodging in Portugal, which offers some of the lowest rates in Europe for accommodations. The government grades hotels with one-to-five stars. Smaller inns called *estalagems* or *albergarias,* which usually provide breakfast only, are also rated. Pensões go up to four stars and often include meals (though they don't usually insist that you take them). The state-subsidized *pousadas,* most of which are in castles, old monasteries, or have been built where there is a particularly fine view, are five-star luxury properties. *Residenciais* (between a pensão and a hotel) are in most towns and larger villages; most rooms have private baths or showers, and breakfast is usually included. They are an extremely good value (around 5,000$00–7,000$00), but since they usually have only a few rooms, we don't review many residenciais.

For more information about pousadas, contact **Enatur Pousadas de Portugal** (⊠ Av. Santa Joana Princesa 10, 1700 Lisbon, ☎ 01/848–1221, 🖷 01/805846), or the national tourist organization in your home country. **Marketing Ahead** (⊠ 433 5th Ave., New York, NY 10016, ☎ 212/686–9213 or 800/223–1356), and **Abreu Tours** (⊠ 317 E. 34th St., New York, NY 10016, ☎ 800/223–1580) can make pousada bookings and arrange tailor-made vacations.

A recent innovation is *Turismo no Espaço Rural* (Tourism in the Country), in which private homeowners all over the country offer visitors a room and breakfast (and sometimes provide dinner on request). Details are available from several agencies, including **Associação Portuguesa de Turismo de Habitação** (⊠ Rua João Penha 10, 1200 Lisbon, ☎ 01/690549, 🖷 01/388–8115).

Tourist offices can help with reservations and will provide lists of the local hostelries without charge. In Lisbon, there's a hotel reservations desk at the airport and at the downtown tourist information center.

CAMPING

Camping has become increasingly popular in Portugal in recent years, and there are now more than 150 campsites throughout the country. The best equipped have markets, swimming pools, and tennis courts. For additional information, contact **Federação Portuguesa do Campismo** (⊠ Av. 5 Outubro 15-3, 1000 Lisbon, ☎ 01/315–2715).

RATINGS

Prices quoted are for two people in a double room based on high-season rates, including tax and service.

CATEGORY	COST
$$$$	over 40,000$00
$$$	20,000$00–40,000$00
$$	14,000$00–20,000$00
$	under 14,000$00

Tipping

Modest tips are usually the rule. Service is included in bills at hotels and most restaurants. In luxury hotels, give the porter who carries your luggage 200$00; in less expensive establishments, 100$00. If the maid brings your breakfast, give her 100$00 a day or 500$00 for a stay of a week. If you dine regularly in the hotel, give your waiter between 500$00 and 1,000$00 at the end of your stay; give the wine waiter somewhat less if you order wine with every meal. Otherwise tip 5%–10% on restaurant bills, except at inexpensive establishments, where you may just leave any coins given in change. Taxi drivers get 10%; cinema and theater ushers who seat you, 50$00; train and airport porters, 100$00 per bag; service-station attendants, 50$00 for gas, 75$00 for checking tires and cleaning windshields; hairdressers, around 10%.

LISBON

Arriving and Departing

By Plane

Lisbon's **Portela Airport** (☏ 01/840–2060 or 01/840–2262) is about 20 minutes from the city by car or taxi.

BETWEEN THE AIRPORT AND DOWNTOWN
A special bus, the Aerobus 91, runs every 20 minutes, 7 AM–9 PM, from outside the airport into the city center; tickets, available from the driver, cost 420$00 or 880$00 and provide one and three days' travel respectively on all of Lisbon's buses and trams. Taxis here are so cheap, however, that visitors would be wise to take one straight to their destination. The cost into Lisbon is about 1,500$00–2,000$00, and to Estoril or Sintra, 6,000$00. If you put luggage in the trunk, add on another 300$00. There are no trains or subways between the airport and the city, but there are car-rental desks.

By Train

International trains from Paris and Madrid arrive at **Santa Apolonia Station** (☏ 01/888–4025), just east of the city center. There is a tourist office at the station and plenty of taxis and porters are available, but no car-rental firms. To get to the central Praça dos Restauradores by public transport, take Bus 9, 39, 46, or 90.

Getting Around

Lisbon is a hilly city, and the sidewalks are paved with cobblestones, so walking can be tiring, even when you're wearing comfortable shoes. Fortunately, Lisbon's tram service is one of the best in Europe, and buses go all over the city. A **Tourist Pass** for unlimited rides on the tram or bus costs 420$00 for one day's travel, 880$00 for three days; four-day passes (1,500$00) and seven-day passes (2,120$00) are also valid on the metro and the *elevador* (funicular railway system). Tourist passes can be purchased at the Cais do Sodré Station, Restauradores metro station, and other terminals. Otherwise, you pay a flat fee of 150$00 to the driver every time you ride a bus, tram, or the elevador; it's cheaper to buy your ticket in advance from a kiosk, where it costs just 140$00 and is valid for two journeys.

By Tram and Bus

Buses and trams operate from 6:30 AM to midnight. Try Tram 12 or 28 for an inexpensive tour of the city; Buses 52 and 53 cross the Tagus bridge. In summer, old-fashioned trams run on tours through the city (2,000$00–2,800$00 per person), departing from Praçca do Comércio; call 01/363–9343 for details.

By Subway

The subway, called the **Metropolitano,** operates from 6:30 AM to 1 AM; it is modern and efficient but covers a limited area. Individual tickets cost 70$00; a 10-ticket strip, a *caderneta,* is 500$00. Watch out for pickpockets during rush hour.

By Taxi

Taxis have a lighted sign on their green roofs. There are stands in the main squares, or you can flag one cruising by, though this can be difficult late at night. Taxis are metered and take up to four passengers at no extra charge. Rates start at 300$00, with an extra charge for luggage.

By Ferry

Ferries cross the Tagus River from the Fluvial terminal, adjacent to Praça do Comércio, to the suburb of Cacilhas, famous for its fish restaurants; it's a 10-minute crossing (daily 7 AM–9:30 PM) and costs 95$00. Alternatively, ferries run to Cacilhas all night from the quay at Cais do Sodré. For details about two-hour cruises on the Tagus River, contact **Transtejo** (☎ 01/887–5058).

Important Addresses and Numbers

Embassies

U.S. (✉ Av. Forças Armadas, ☎ 01/726–6600); **Canadian** (✉ Av. da Liberdade 144-3, ☎ 01/347–4892); **U.K.** (✉ Rua S. Domingos à Lapa 37, ☎ 01/396–1191).

Emergencies

SOS Emergencies (☎ 115). **Police** (☎ 01/346–6141). **Ambulance** (☎ 01/301–7777). **Fire Brigade** (☎ 01/606060). **Doctor:** British Hospital (✉ Rua Saraiva de Carvalho 49, ☎ 01/395–5067). **Pharmacies:** Hours at pharmacies are weekdays 9–1 and 3–7, Saturday 9–1. Consult the notice on the door for the nearest one open on weekends or after hours; a similar list appears in Lisbon's daily newspapers.

Travel Agencies

American Express (✉ c/o Top Tours, Av. Duque de Loulé 108, ☎ FAX 01/315–5877). **Marcus & Harting** (✉ Rossío 45–50, ☎ 01/346–9271). **Wagons-Lits** (✉ Av. da Liberdade 103, ☎ 01/346–5344). **Abreu** (✉ Av. da Liberdade 158–160, ☎ 01/347–6441).

Visitor Information

The main **Lisbon Tourist Office** (☎ 01/346–3314; ⏱ Mon.–Sat. 9–8, Sun. 10–6) is in the Palácio Foz, Praça dos Restauradores, at the Baixa (Lower Town) end of the Avenida da Liberdade, the city's main artery of the city. The office at Lisbon airport (☎ 01/849–3689) is open daily 6 AM–2 AM.

Guided Tours

Orientation and Excursions

Various companies organize half-day tours of Lisbon and environs, as well as full-day trips to more distant places of interest. Those listed below are reliable and offer similar trips and prices. Reservations can be made through any travel agent or hotel. A half-day tour of Lisbon will cost about 6,000$00. A full-day trip north to Obidos, Nazaré, and Fatima will run about 13,500$00 (including lunch), as will a full day east along the "Roman Route" to Évora and Monsaraz. Companies are **Citirama** (✉ Av. Praia da Vitória 12-b, ☎ 01/355–8567); **Gray Line Tours** (✉ Av. Fontes Pereira de Melo 14, ☎ 01/352–2594); and **Top Tours** (✉ Av. Duque de Loulé 108, ☎ 01/315–5877).

Personal Guides

Contact the main Lisbon Tourist Office (☞ Important Addresses and Numbers, *above*) or the **Syndicate of Guide Interpreters** (✉ Rua do Telhal 4, ☎ 01/346–7170). The front desk at your hotel may also have a list of bilingual guides. Beware of unauthorized guides who will approach you at popular attractions and try to "guide" you to a particular shop or restaurant.

Exploring Lisbon

Spread out over a string of hills to the north of the Tagus River estuary, Portugal's capital presents unending treats for the eye. Its wide boulevards are bordered by black-and-white mosaic sidewalks made of tiny cobblestones called *calçada*. Modern, pastel-colored apartment blocks vie for attention with Art Nouveau structures faced with decorative tiles. Winding, hilly streets provide scores of *miradouros,* vantage points offering spectacular views of the river and the city.

With a population of around a million, Lisbon is a small capital by European standards. Its center stretches north from the spacious Praça do Comércio, one of the largest riverside squares in Europe, to the Rossío, a smaller square lined with shops and sidewalk cafés. This district is known as the Baixa (Lower Town), and it is one of the earliest examples of town planning on a large scale. The grid of parallel streets between the two squares was built after an earthquake and tidal wave destroyed much of the city in 1755. The Alfama, the old Moorish quarter that survived the earthquake, lies just east of the Baixa, and Belém, a section containing many royal palaces and museums, lies about 5 kilometers (3 miles) to the west.

Lisbon is not easy to explore on foot. The steep inclines of many streets present a tough challenge to the casual tourist, and places that appear to be close to one another on a map are sometimes on different levels. Yet the effort is worthwhile—judicious use of trams, the funicular railway, and the majestic city-center elevador (vertical lift) make walking tours enjoyable even on the hottest summer day.

Castelo de São Jorge and the Alfama

Numbers in the margin correspond to points of interest on the Lisbon map.

The Moors, who imposed their rule on most of the southern Iberian Peninsula during the 8th century, left their mark on Lisbon. Their most visible traces are the imposing castle, set on one of the city's highest hills, and the Alfama, a district of narrow, twisting streets that wind up toward it. The best way to tour this area is to take Tram 28, Bus 37, or a taxi up to the castle and then walk down.

★ ❶ Although the **Castelo de São Jorge** (St. George's Castle) is Moorish in construction, it stands on the site of a fortification used by the Visigoths as early as the 5th century. Today its idyllic calm is disturbed only by the shrieks of the many peacocks that strut around the well-tended grounds, which are also home to swans, turkeys, ducks, ravens, and other birds. The castle walls enclose the ruins of a Muslim palace that served as the residence of the kings of Portugal until the 16th century; there is also a small village inside with a surviving church, a few simple houses, and souvenir shops. The walls offer panoramic views of Lisbon, but visitors should take care, because the footing is uneven and slippery. 🎫 *Free.* ☉ *Apr.–Sept., daily 9–9; Oct.–Mar., daily 9–7.*

❷ After you reemerge through the castle's impressive gate, wander down through the warren of streets that make up the **Alfama.** This jumble of whitewashed houses with flower-laden balconies and red-tile roofs rests on a foundation of solid bedrock. It's notoriously easy to get lost in, however it's relatively compact, and you'll keep coming upon the same main squares and streets.

❸ In the Alfama east of the castle is the **Museu da Marioneta,** a puppet museum that's worth a look. ✉ *Largo Rodrigues de Freitas 19A.* 🎫 *300$00.* ☉ *Tues.–Sun. 10–1 and 2–6.*

❹ From there head south along the Rua de São Tomé to the Largo das Portas do Sol, where you'll find the **Museu de Artes Decorativas** (Museum of Decorative Arts) in a 17th-century mansion that also houses the Fundação Ricardo Espirito Santo. Here more than 20 workshops

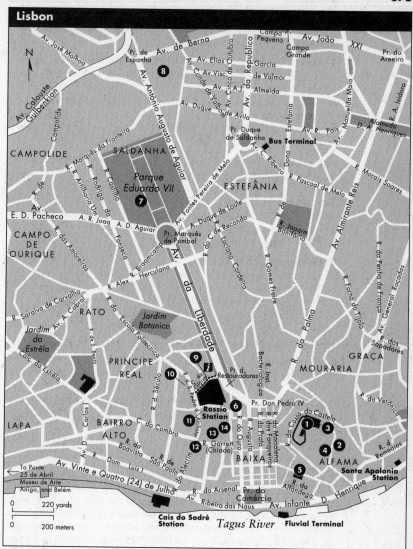

Lisbon

Alfama, **2**

Castelo de São Jorge, **1**

Elevador da Glória, **9**

Elevador de Santa Justa, **14**

Fundação Calouste Gulbenkian , **8**

Igreja do Carmo, **13**

Igreja de São Roque, **11**

Instituto do Vinho do Porto, **10**

Largo do Chiado, **12**

Museu de Artes Decorativas, **4**

Museu da Marioneta, **3**

Parque Eduardo VII, **7**

Rossío, **6**

Sé, **5**

teach threatened handicrafts—bookbinding, ormolu, carving, and cabinetmaking. ⊠ *Largo das Portas do Sol 2.* 🖼 *500$00.* ⊙ *Wed. and Fri.–Sun. 10–5, Tues. and Thurs. 10–6.*

Head southwest past the Largo de Santa Luzia along the Rua do Limoeiro, which eventually becomes the Rua Augusto Rosa. This route takes you **❺** past the **Sé** (cathedral), founded in 1150 to commemorate the defeat of the Moors three years earlier. The Sé's austere Romanesque interior is offset by a splendid 13th-century cloister. ⊠ *Largo da Sé.* 🖼 *Cathedral free, cloister 100$00, sacristy 300$00.* ⊙ *Daily 9–noon and 2–6.*

Continue northwest from the cathedral along the Rua de Santo António da Sé, turn left along the Rua da Conceição, then right and north up the Rua Augusta. A 10-minute stroll along this street takes you through the **Baixa,** one of Lisbon's main shopping and banking districts, where you'll find a small crafts market, some of the best shoe shops in Europe, glittering jewelry stores, and a host of delicatessens selling everything from game birds to *queijo da serra*—a delicious mountain cheese from the Serra da Estrela range north of Lisbon.

Avenida da Liberdade

❻ Rua Augusta leads into the **Rossio** (officially, Praça Dom Pedro IV), Lisbon's principal square, which in turn opens on its northwestern end into the Praça dos Restauradores. This is the beginning of modern Lisbon, for here the broad, tree-lined **Avenida da Liberdade** begins its northwesterly ascent, ending just over 1.6 kilometers (1 mile) away at the **❼** green expanses of the **Parque Eduardo VII.**

A leisurely stroll from the Praça dos Restauradores to the park takes about 30 minutes, though you may want to stop off along the way at one of the open-air cafés in the esplanada that runs down the center of the avenue. You'll also pass a pleasant mixture of ornate 19th-century architecture and Art Deco structures from the 1930s. In the park, rare flowers, trees, and shrubs thrive in both the *estufa fria* (cold greenhouse) and the *estufa quente* (hot greenhouse). ⊠ *Parque Eduardo VII.* 🖼 *Greenhouses 75$00.* ⊙ *Winter, daily 9–5; summer, daily 9–6.*

Walk through to the northeast corner of the park and then head north along the Avenida António Augusto de Aguiar. A 15-minute walk will bring you to the busy Praça de Espanha, to the right of which, in the **★ ❽** Parque de Palhava, is the renowned **Fundação Calouste Gulbenkian,** a cultural trust whose museum houses treasures collected by Armenian oil magnate Calouste Gulbenkian (1869–1955) and donated to the people of Portugal. It presents superb examples of Greek and Roman coins, Persian carpets, Chinese porcelain, and paintings by such old masters as Rembrandt and Rubens, as well as Impressionist and Pre-Raphaelite works. You can also travel here by metro, getting off at Palhavã. ⊠ *Av. de Berna 45,* ☎ *01/795–0236.* 🖼 *200$00, free Sun.* ⊙ *June–Sept., Tues., Thurs., Fri., and Sun. 10–5, Wed. and Sat. 2–7:30; Oct.–May, Tues.–Sun. 10–5; closed Mon. year-round.*

The complex also houses a good modern art museum (same times and price as the main museum) and two concert halls where music and ballet festivals are held during the winter and spring. Modestly priced tickets are available at the box office in the main building. Pick up an events brochure at the reception desk.

Bairro Alto

★ Lisbon's **Bairro Alto** (Upper Town) is largely made up of 18th-and 19th-century buildings that house an intriguing mixture of restaurants, theaters, nightclubs, churches, bars, and antiques shops. The best way to **☝ ❾** start a tour of this area is via the **Elevador da Glória** (funicular railway; ☜ 150$00 or free with Tourist Pass; ☉ Daily 7 AM–midnight) on the western side of Avenida da Liberdade by the Praça dos Restauradores. The ascent takes about a minute and passengers are let out at the São Pedro de Alcântara miradouro, a viewpoint facing the castle and the Alfama.

⑩ The **Instituto do Vinho do Porto** (Port Wine Institute), across the street from the miradouro, has a cozy, clublike lounge where visitors can sample more than 300 types and vintages of Portugal's most famous beverage—from extra-dry white varieties to the older ruby-red vintages. ☒ *Rua S. Pedro de Alcântara 45,* ☎ *01/342–3307.* ☜ *Tastings start at 200$00.* ☉ *Mon.–Sat. 10–10.*

From the institute, turn right and walk down Rua de São Pedro de Alcântara. On your left is the Largo Trindade Coelho, site of the highly **⑪** decorative **Igreja de São Roque** (Church of St. Roque). The church is best known for its flamboyant 18th-century **Capela de São João Baptista** (Chapel of St. John the Baptist), but it is a showpiece in its own right. The **Museu de Arte Sacra** (Museum of Sacred Art) is nextdoor. ☒ *Largo Trindade Coelho.* ☜ *Church free, museum 150$00.* ☉ *Church daily 8:30–6, museum Tues.–Sun. 10–1 and 2–5.*

Continue south down Rua de São Pedro de Alcântara until you reach **⑫** the **Largo do Chiado** on your left. The Chiado, once a chic shopping district, was badly damaged by fire in 1988, but it still houses some of the city's most fashionable shops and department stores.

- - - - - - - - - -

NEED A BREAK? The Chiado's wood-paneled coffee shops attract tourists and locals alike; the most popular of these is the **Brasileira** (☒ Rua Garrett 120, ☎ 01/346–9541; closed Sun.), which features a life-size statue of Fernando Pessoa, Portugal's national poet, seated at one of the sidewalk tables.

- - - - - - - - - -

North of the Chiado, on the Largo do Carmo, lies the partially ruined **⑬** **Igreja do Carmo** (Carmo Church), one of the few structures in the area to have survived the 1755 earthquake. Today its sacristy houses the interesting **Museu Arqueológico** (Archaeological Museum), filled with everything from Roman coins to medieval sarcophagi. ☒ *Largo do Carmo.* ☜ *300$00.* ☉ *Oct.–Mar., Mon.–Sat. 10–1 and 2–5; Apr.–Sept., Mon.–Sat. 10–6.*

⑭ Return directly to the Praça dos Restauradores via the nearby **Elevador de Santa Justa** (St. Just Elevator; ☜ 150$00 or free with Tourist Pass; ☉ Daily 7 AM–midnight.), which is enclosed in a Gothic tower created by Raul Mesnier, a Portuguese protégé of Gustave Eiffel.

Belém

Numbers in the margin correspond to points of interest on the Belém map.

To see the best examples of that uniquely Portuguese, late-Gothic architecture known as Manueline, head for Belém, at the far southwestern edge of Lisbon. If you are traveling in a group of three or four, taxis are the cheapest way to get here; otherwise take Tram 15, 16, or 17 from the Praça do Comércio for a more scenic, if bumpier, journey.

★ **⑮** Trams 15 and 16 stop directly outside the **Mosteiro dos Jerónimos** (Jerónimos Monastery), in the Praça do Império. This impressive structure was conceived and planned by King Manuel I at the beginning of the 16th century to commemorate the discoveries of Vasco da Gama. Construction began in 1502 and was largely financed by treasures brought back from the Portuguese "discoveries" in Africa, Asia, and South Amer-

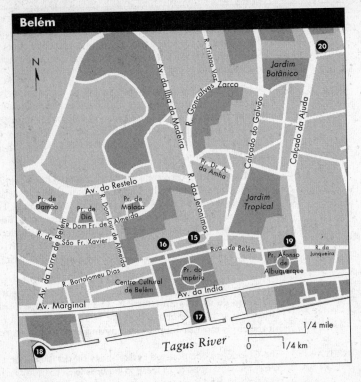

Belém

ica. Don't miss the stunning double cloister, which has arches and pillars heavily sculpted with marine motifs. ☒ *Church free; cloisters 400$00, 250$00 Oct.–May.* ☉ *June–Sept., Tues.–Sun. 10–6:30; Oct.–May, Tues.–Sun. 10–1 and 2:30–5.*

🖐 **16** The **Museu de Marinha** (Maritime Museum) is at the west end of the monastery. Its huge collection reflects Portugal's long seafaring tradition, and its exhibits range from early maps, model ships, and navigational instruments to entire fishing boats and royal barges. ☒ *250$00, free Sun.* ☉ *Tues.–Sun. 10–5.*

NEED A BREAK? | There are a number of small restaurants and inexpensive cafés close to the monastery on Rua de Belém. Stop for coffee at the **Fábrica dos Pasteis de Belém** (Belém Pastry Factory; ☒ Rua de Belém 86–88) to sample the delicious custard pastries served hot with cinnamon and powdered sugar.

---

17 Across from the monastery, at the water's edge, stands the **Monumento dos Descobrimentos,** a tall, white angular slab. Erected in 1960, this modern tribute to the seafaring explorers stands at what was the departure point for many of their voyages. An interesting mosaic, surrounded by an intricate wave pattern of black and white stones, lies at its foot. Take the elevator to the top for river views. ☒ *300$00.* ☉ *Tues.–Sun. 9:30–7.*

★ **18** A 15-minute walk west of the monument brings you to the **Torre de Belém** (Belém Tower), another fine example of Manueline architecture with openwork balconies, a loggia, and domed turrets. Although it was built in the early 16th century on an island in the middle of the River Tagus, the tower now stands near its north bank—the river has changed course over the centuries. ☒ *Av. de India.* ☒ *400$00 June–Sept.,*

250$00 Oct.–May. ☾ *June–Sept., Tues.–Sun. 10–6:30; Oct.–May, Tues.–Sun. 10–1 and 2:30–5.*

☾ **⑲** Away from the Tagus and east of the monastery, on the Praça Afonso de Albuquerque, is the **Museu Nacional dos Coches** (National Coach Museum), which houses one of the largest collections of coaches in the world. The oldest conveyance on display was made for Philip II of Spain in the late 16th century, but the most stunning exhibits are three golden Baroque coaches made in Rome for King John V in 1716. ⊠ *Praça Afonso de Albuquerque,* ☎ *01/363–8022.* ✆ *400$00 June–Sept., 250$00 Oct.–May; free Sun. year-round.* ☾ *June–Sept., Tues.–Sun. 10–1 and 2:30–6:30; Oct.–May, Tues.–Sun. 10–1 and 2:30–5:30.*

⑳ Head north from the coach museum on Calçada da Ajuda to the **Palácio da Ajuda** (Ajuda Palace). Once a royal residence, this impressive building now contains a collection of 18th- and 19th-century paintings, furniture, and tapestries. ⊠ *Largo da Ajuda,* ☎ *01/363–7095.* ✆ *500$00; free Sun. 10–2. Guided tours arranged on request.* ☾ *Thurs.–Tues. 10–5.*

Off the Beaten Path

North of the city, in the suburb of São Domingos de Benfica, is one of the most beautiful private estates in the capital. The **Palácio da Fronteira,** built in the late 17th century, contains splendid reception rooms with 18th-century figurative tiles, furnishings, and paintings, but it is the gardens that are unique. A long rectangular pool is backed by 17th-century tiled panels of heroic-size knights on prancing horses. Stone steps on either side lead up to a terraced walk above, between pyramid-shape pavilions roofed with copper-colored tiles. This beautiful conceit is surrounded by a topiary garden, statuary, fountains, and terraces. ⊠ *Largo de S. Domingos de Benfica 1,* ☎ *01/778–2023.* ✆ *Gardens 300$00, 500$00 on Sat.; palace and gardens 1,000$00, 1500$00 on Sat.* ☾ *June–Sept, Mon.–Sat., 4 daily tours between 10:30 and noon; Oct.–May, Mon.–Sat. tours at 11 and noon.*

In the wealthy district of Lapa, halfway between the Bairro Alto and Belém, the **Museu de Arte Antiga** (Museum of Ancient Art) occupies a 17th-century palace. This is Lisbon's only museum rivaling the Gulbenkian. It has a beautifully displayed collection of Portuguese art, mainly 15th–19th century. Its highlight is undoubtedly the St. Vincent altarpiece (1467–1470), a masterpiece by Nuno Gonçalves. The six panels depict St. Vincent, Lisbon's patron saint, receiving homage from king, court, and citizens, and 60 of the figures can be identified, including Henry the Navigator himself. ⊠ *Rua das Janelas Verdes 95, Lapa. Tram 19 from Praça do Comércio.* ✆ *500$00, free Sun. 10–1.* ☾ *Tues.–Sun. 10–1 and 2–5.*

Shopping

Shopping Districts

Since the fire that destroyed much of the Chiado in 1988, an extensive reconstruction project has made some progress. Another important shopping area is in the **Baixa** quarter (between the Rossío and the River Tagus). On Avenida Engenheiro Duarte Pacheco, west of Parque Eduardo VII, the blue-and-pink towers of the **Amoreiras** (☾ Daily 9 AM–11 PM), a huge shopping center, dominate the Lisbon skyline.

Flea Markets

A **Feira da Ladra** (flea market) is held on Tuesday morning and all day Saturday in the Largo de Santa Clara behind the Church of São Vicente, near the Alfama district.

Gift Ideas

LEATHER GOODS

Fine leather handbags and luggage are sold at **Galeão** (⊠ Rua Augusta 190). Shoe stores abound in Lisbon, but they may have a limited selection of large sizes (the Portuguese have relatively small feet); the better shops can make shoes to order on short notice, however. Leather gloves can be purchased at a variety of specialty shops on Rua do Carmo and Rua Aurea. Visit **Ulisses** (⊠ Rua do Carmo 87) for a fine selection of gloves.

HANDICRAFTS

Viúva Lamego (⊠ Largo Infante P. Manique 28 and Rua do Sacramento 29) has the largest selection of tiles and pottery. **Fábrica Sant'Ana** (⊠ Rua do Alecrim 95), in the Bairro Alto, sells wonderful hand-painted ceramics and tiles. For embroidered goods and baskets from the Azores, try **Casa Regional da Ilha Verde** (⊠ Rua Paiva de Andrade 4). **Casa Quintão** (⊠ Rua Ivens 30, Bairro Alto) has an excellent selection of *arraiolos*, traditional hand-embroidered Portuguese carpets. For fine porcelain, visit **Vista Alegre** (⊠ Largo do Chiado 18 and Rua Ivens 52, Bairro Alto). **Casa Ribeiro da Silva** (⊠ Trav. Fiéis de Deus 69, Bairro Alto) is the place to go for handcrafted pottery.

JEWELRY AND ANTIQUES

Antonio da Silva (⊠ Praça Luis de Camões 40), at the top of the Chiado, specializes in antique silver and jewelry. Most of the antiques shops are along the Rua Escola Politénica, Rua Dom Pedro IV, Rua da Misericórdia, and Rua do Alecrim. Look for characteristic Portuguese gold and silver filigree work at **Sarmento** (⊠ Rua Aurea 251), in the Baixa.

Dining

For details and price-category definitions, *see* Dining *in* Staying in Portugal, *above*.

$$$$ ✕ **António Clara.** Housed in an attractive Art Nouveau building in north Lisbon, this restaurant serves French and international dishes with a flourish. The elegant dining room has a decorated ceiling, heavy draperies, and a huge chandelier. The menu is seasonal, and there's a fine wine list. ⊠ *Av. República 38,* ☎ *01/796–6380. Reservations essential. AE, DC, MC, V. Closed Sun.*

$$$$ ✕ **Aviz.** One of the best and classiest restaurants in Lisbon, Aviz has
★ a Belle Epoque decor—even the rest rooms are impressive—and an excellent French and international menu. The restaurant is hidden on a side street off the Baixa's Rua Garrett. ⊠ *Rua Serpa Pinto 12,* ☎ *01/342–8391. Reservations essential. AE, DC, MC, V. Closed Sun. No lunch Sat.*

$$$$ ✕ **Gambrinus.** One of Lisbon's older restaurants, Gambrinus is noted for its fish and shellfish. Enter through an inconspicuous door off a busy street into one of the restaurant's numerous small dining rooms. ⊠ *Rua das Portas de S. Antão 23–25,* ☎ *01/346–8974 or 01/342– 1466. AE, DC, MC, V.*

$$$$ ✕ **Tagide.** Delicious Portuguese food and wine are served in this fine old tiled house that looks out over the Baixa and the river. Try to secure a window table. ⊠ *Largo Academia das Belas Artes 18–20,* ☎ *01/346–0570. AE, DC, MC, V. Closed weekends.*

$$$$ ✕ **Tavares Rico.** A seasonal, French-inspired menu, an excellent wine
★ list, and handsome Edwardian furnishings have made this dining room (established as a café in the 18th century) one of Lisbon's most famous restaurants. ⊠ *Rua Misericórdia 37,* ☎ *01/342–1112. Reservations essential. AE, DC, MC, V. Closed Sat. No lunch Sun.*

$$$ ✕ **Michel.** Innovative French cooking and an intimate atmosphere can be found in this attractive restaurant in the village inside the walls of St. George's Castle. ⊠ *Largo S. Cruz do Castelo 5,* ☎ *01/886–4338. AE, DC, MC, V. Closed Sun. No lunch Sat.*

$$$ ✕ **O Madeirense.** Lisbon's only Madeiran restaurant, this rustic-style room is inside the Amoreiras shopping center. The *espedata* is famously traditional—a skewer of fillet steak is hung from a stand above the table so that you can serve yourself at will. ⊠ *Loja 3027, Amoreiras Shopping Center, Av. Eng. Duarte Pacheco,* ☎ *01/383–0827. AE, DC, MC, V.*

$$$ ✕ **Solmar.** This large restaurant near the Rossío, Lisbon's main square, is best known for its seafood and shellfish, but try the wild boar or venison in season. ⊠ *Rua das Portas de S. Antão 108,* ☎ *01/342–3371. AE, DC, MC, V.*

$$$ ✕ **Sua Excêlencia.** There's no written menu in this cozy little restau-
★ rant in the Lapa district. The English-speaking owner will personally talk you through the outstanding Portuguese dishes available. ⊠ *Rua do Conde 42,* ☎ *01/603614. MC, V. Closed Wed. and Sept. No weekend lunch.*

$$ ✕ **Cervejaria Trindade.** Prepare for hearty Portuguese cuisine served
★ in a 19th-century Lisbon beer hall adorned with colorful tiles. It specializes in seafood and is open until 2 AM. There's a garden for summer dining, too. ⊠ *Rua Nova da Trindade 20,* ☎ *01/346–3506. AE, DC, MC, V.*

$$ ✕ **Comida de Santo.** Lively Brazilian music and excellent Brazilian food served in an attractive, brightly painted dining room ensure a steady repeat clientele. ⊠ *Calçada Eng. Miguel Pais 39,* ☎ *01/396–3339. AE, DC, MC, V.*

$$ ✕ **Farah's Tandoori.** A small, simple place, Farah's is known as one of the best and friendliest Indian restaurants in Lisbon. All the curries, which are served with Indian bread, are sure bets for a good meal. ⊠ *Rua de Sant'Ana a Lapa 73,* ☎ *01/609219. MC, V. Closed Tues.*

$$ ✕ **O Alexandre.** This tiny restaurant in Belém has outdoor tables from which diners, mostly local, soak up the superb views of the monastery. Try one of the grilled fish dishes, or even the more unusual squid and octopus dishes if they're available. (Note that the restaurant closes at 10 PM.) ⊠ *Rua Vieria Portuense 84, Belém,* ☎ *01/363–4544. Reservations not accepted. MC, V. Closed Sat.*

$$ ✕ **Ribadouro.** This bustling basement restaurant serves notable seafood to a discerning local clientele. The crabs, crayfish, and other shellfish are all excellent. ⊠ *Av. de Liberdade 155,* ☎ *01/354–9411. AE, DC, MC, V.*

$ ✕ **Bonjardim.** Known as "Rei dos Frangos" (King of Chickens), the Bonjardim specializes in the spit-roasted variety. Just off the Restauradores, it gets very crowded at peak hours; you may have to wait in line for a table, but it's worth it. ⊠ *Travessa S. Antão 11,* ☎ *01/342–7424. AE, DC, MC, V.*

$ ✕ **Vá e Volta.** This is a splendid place for one-plate Bairro Alto fare—fried or grilled meat or fish dishes served with gusto and good humor. ⊠ *Rua do Diario de Notícias 100,* ☎ *01/342–7888. MC, V.*

Lodging

Lisbon has a good array of accommodations in all price categories, ranging from some of the major international chain hotels to charming little family-run establishments. During peak season, reservations should be made well in advance. For details and price-category definitions, *see* Lodging *in* Staying in Portugal, *above.*

$$$$ 🏨 **Lisboa Sheraton and Towers.** This is a typical Sheraton hotel with a huge reception area and medium-size rooms. The 79 deluxe units in the Towers section, which has a separate reception desk in the lobby and a private lounge, are about the same size but more luxuriously appointed. The hotel is centrally located and is just across the street from a large shopping center. ⊠ *Rua Latino Coelho 1, 1000 Lisboa,* ☎ *01/357–5757,* ℻ *01/354–7164. 384 rooms with bath. Restaurant, bar, grill, pool, sauna, health club. AE, DC, MC, V.*

$$$$ 🏨 **Meridien Lisboa.** The rooms in this luxury hotel are on the small side, but they are soundproof and attractively decorated; the front ones overlook the Parque Eduardo VII, which means the hotel is ideally situated for downtown exploration. ⊠ *Rua Castilho 149, 1000 Lisboa,* ☎ *01/383–0400,* ℻ *01/383–3231. 331 rooms with bath. 2 restaurants, bar, beauty salon, sauna. AE, DC, MC, V.*

$$$$ 🏨 **Ritz Lisboa.** One of the finest hotels in Europe, the Ritz is renowned
★   for its excellent service. The large, handsomely decorated guest rooms all have terraces, and the public rooms are elegantly appointed with tapestries, antique reproductions, and fine paintings. The best rooms are in the front overlooking Parque Eduardo VII. There's convenient dining at the Varanda restaurant, which has a summer terrace. ⊠ *Rua Rodrigo da Fonseca 88, 1200 Lisboa,* ☎ *01/383–2020,* ℻ *01/383–1783. 304 rooms with bath. Restaurant, bar, snack bar, no-smoking floor, exercise room. AE, DC, MC, V.*

$$$$ 🏨 **Tivoli Lisboa.** Fronting on Lisbon's main avenue, this comfortable,
★   well-run establishment has a large public area furnished with inviting armchairs and sofas. The guest rooms are all pleasant, but the ones in the rear are quieter. There's also a good restaurant, and the grill on the top floor has wonderful views of the city and the Tagus. ⊠ *Av. da Liberdade 185, 1250 Lisboa,* ☎ *01/353–0181,* ℻ *01/357–9461. 327 rooms with bath. Restaurant, 2 bars, coffee shop, grill, pool, 2 tennis courts. AE, DC, MC, V.*

$$$ 🏨 **As Janelas Verdes.** This late-18th-century mansion has marvelously
★   restored, individually furnished guest rooms. There's a lovely ivy-covered patio garden where you can eat breakfast—and you're not far from the Sua Excelência restaurant (☞ Dining, *above*). Reservations are vital at this hotel, since it's as popular as it is small; rates in winter are slightly reduced. ⊠ *Rua das Janelas Verdes 47, 1200 Lisboa,* ☎ *01/396–8143,* ℻ *01/396–8144. 17 rooms with bath. Dining room. AE, DC, MC, V.*

$$$ 🏨 **Lisboa Plaza.** This family-owned hotel behind Avenida da Liberdade is most comfortable. Service is friendly and helpful, while pastel colors, prints on the walls, attractive ornaments, dried flower arrangements, and smart, well-stocked bathrooms all add to the charm. An excellent buffet breakfast is included in the room rate. ⊠ *Travessa do Salitre 7, 1200 Lisboa,* ☎ *01/346–3922,* ℻ *01/347–1630. 106 rooms with bath. Restaurant, bar, no-smoking rooms. AE, DC, MC, V.*

$$$ 🏨 **Sofitel Lisboa.** Tasteful modern architecture and a convenient location make this hotel a favorite with the international business community. Moderately sized guest rooms are comfortably furnished in pleasing colors. Next to the small elegant lobby is an intimate piano bar. ⊠ *Av. da Liberdade 123–125, 1200 Lisboa,* ☎ *01/342–9202,* ℻ *01/342–9222. 170 rooms with bath. Restaurant, bar. AE, DC, MC, V.*

$$$ 🏨 **York House.** This residência, built as a convent in the 17th century,
★   is set in a shady garden at the top of a long flight of steps, near the Museu de Arte Antiga. It has a good restaurant, and full or half board is available. Book well in advance: This atmospheric place is small and has a loyal following. ⊠ *Rua das Janelas Verdes 32, 1200 Lisboa,* ☎ *01/396–2435,* ℻ *01/397–2793. 36 rooms with bath. Restaurant, bar. AE, DC, MC, V.*

$$ ⊞ **Albergaria Senhora do Monte.** The rooms in this unpretentious lit-
★ tle hotel, in the oldest part of town near St. George's Castle, have ter-
races that offer some of the loveliest views of Lisbon, especially at night,
when the castle and Igreja do Carmo ruins in the middle distance are
softly illuminated. The top-floor grill has a picture window. ⊠ *Calçada
do Monte 39, 1100 Lisboa,* ☎ *01/886–6002,* FAX *01/887–7783. 28
rooms with bath. Bar, grill. AE, DC, MC, V.*

$$ ⊞ **Fenix.** At the top of Avenida da Liberdade, this elegant hotel has
largish guest rooms—many with fine views—and a pleasant first-floor
lounge. Its restaurant serves good Portuguese food. ⊠ *Praça Marquês
de Pombal 8, 1200 Lisboa,* ☎ *01/386–2121,* FAX *01/386–0131. 119
rooms with bath. Restaurant, bar. AE, DC, MC, V.*

$$ ⊞ **Flamingo.** A good-value choice near the top of the Avenida da
Liberdade, this hotel has a friendly staff and pleasant guest rooms, though
those in the front tend to be noisy. There's a parking lot right next door
(guests get a 20% discount), which is a bonus in this busy area. ⊠ *Rua
Castilho 41, 1250 Lisboa,* ☎ *01/386–2191,* FAX *01/386–1216. 39
rooms with bath. Restaurant, bar. AE, DC, MC, V.*

$$ ⊞ **Florida.** This centrally located hotel has a restful atmosphere and
guest rooms with marble-clad bathrooms. It's short on facilities but
close to the downtown restaurants. ⊠ *Rua Duque de Palmela 32, 1200
Lisboa,* ☎ *01/357–6145,* FAX *01/354–3584. 112 rooms with bath. Bar,
breakfast room. AE, DC, MC, V.*

$ ⊞ **Duas Nacões.** This basic, noisy pensão has a superb location in the
heart of the Baixa grid. Guest rooms are plain and functional (ask for
one at the rear for minimal street noise), but the impressive dining room
retains its original large dimensions and fine decor. ⊠ *Rua da Vitória
41, 1100 Lisboa,* ☎ *01/346–0710. 66 rooms, 42 with bath. Bar, dining room. No credit cards.*

$ ⊞ **Hotel Borges.** In the heart of the Chiado district, convenient for shop-
ping, this dependable, old-fashioned hotel has good service and a
charm that transcends its limited facilities. You're also only a step away
from the famous Brasileira café, an excellent breakfast spot. ⊠ *Rua
Garrett 108–110, 1200 Lisboa,* ☎ *01/346–1951,* FAX *01/342–6617.
Bar, breakfast room. MC, V.*

The Arts

You'll find listings of music, theater, film, and other entertainment in
the monthly *Agenda Cultural* booklet, available from the tourist office. The Friday editions of the *Diario de Notícias* and *O Independente*
newspapers also contain listings magazines.

Plays are performed in Portuguese at the **Teatro Nacional de D. Maria
II** (⊠ Praça Dom Pedro IV, ☎ 01/342–2210) from August through June.
Classical music, opera, and ballet are presented in the beautiful **Teatro
Nacional de Opera de São Carlos** (⊠ Rua Serpa Pinto 9, ☎ 01/346–
8408). Classical music and ballet are also staged from autumn to summer by the **Fundação Calouste Gulbenkian** (⊠ Av. Berna 45, ☎
01/793–5131). Of particular interest is the annual Early Music and
Baroque Festival staged in churches and museums around Lisbon every
spring. The **Centro Cultural de Belém** (⊠ Av. da India, ☎ 01/301–9606)
also hosts a full range of concerts and exhibitions—pick up a monthly
program of events from the reception desk. Otherwise, free recitals are
regularly presented at the Igreja do Carmo and Igreja de São Roque
in the Bairro Alto, and at the Sé. The **Nova Filarmônica,** one of Portugal's national orchestras, performs concerts around the country
throughout the year; consult local papers for details.

Nightlife

Clubs with Live Music

The most popular nightspots in Lisbon are the *adegas típicas* (wine cellars), where customers dine on Portuguese specialties, drink wine, and listen to the haunting melodies of *fado* (traditional Portuguese folk music). Most of these establishments are scattered throughout the Alfama and Bairro Alto districts. The singing starts at 10 PM, and reservations are advised. The **Adega do Machado** (⊠ Rua do Norte 91, ☎ 01/342–8713; closed Mon.) is a reliable spot in the Bairro Alto. For reasonable food, as well entertaining singing by a number of people, including one of the cooks, visit the **Adega do Ribatejo** (⊠ Rua Diário de Notícias 23, Bairro Alto, ☎ 01/346–8343). In the Alfama, **Parreirinha d'Alfama** (⊠ Beco do Espírito Santo 1, ☎ 01/886–8209) is considered one of the best.

Lisbon's top spot for live jazz is **The Hot Clube** (⊠ Praça da Alegria 39, ☎ 01/346–7369; closed Sun.–Wed.), where sessions don't usually begin until 11 PM.

Dance Clubs and Bars

The main areas for bars and discos are the Bairro Alto or along Avenida 24 de Julho, northwest of Cais do Sodre station. In the Bairro Alto, the best place to start a night's entertainment is the refined **Instituto do Vinho do Porto** (⊠ Rua de São Pedro de Alcântara 45, ☎ 01/347–5707), where you choose drinks from a menu of port wines. **Cena de Copas** (⊠ Rua da Barroca 103–105, ☎ 01/347–3372) is a loud and fashionable bar attracting a youthful clientele. **Pavilhão Chines** (⊠ Rua Dom Pedro V 89, ☎ 01/342–4729) is decorated with extraordinary bric-a-brac from around the world. Along Avenida 24 de Julho, one of the current favorites is **Café Central** (⊠ Av. 24 de Julho 112, ☎ 01/395–6111), which has designer style and rock videos. The **Kapital** (⊠ Av. 24 de Julho 68, ☎ 01/395–5963) continues to attract the trendiest Lisboetas. **Trumps** (⊠ Rua Imprensa Nacional 104b, ☎ 01/397–1059) is the city's biggest gay dance club. **Memorial** (⊠ Rua Gustavo Sequeira 42, ☎ 01/396–8891) is popular with both gay and lesbian visitors.

THE PORTUGUESE RIVIERA, SINTRA, AND QUELUZ

Extending 32 kilometers (20 miles) west of Lisbon is a stretch of coastline known as the Portuguese Riviera. Over the years, the casino at Estoril and the beaches, both there and in Cascais, have served as playgrounds for the wealthy, attracting expatriates and exiled European royalty to find homes here. To the north of Cascais and Estoril lie the lush, green mountains of Sintra and to the northeast, the historic town of Queluz, dominated by its 18th-century rococo palace and formal gardens. The villas, châteaus, and luxury *quintas* (country properties) of Sintra contrast notably with Cascais and Estoril, where life revolves around the sea.

Sporting possibilities abound: golf courses, horseback riding, fishing, tennis, squash, swimming, water sports, grand prix racing, mountain climbing, and country walks. Beaches vary both in quality and cleanliness. Some display the blue Council of Europe flag, which signals a high standard of unpolluted water and sands, but others leave much to be desired. The waters off Cascais and Estoril are calm, though sullied as a result of their proximity to the mouth of Lisbon's Tagus River. To the north, around Guincho's rocky promontory and along the Praia de Maças coast, the Atlantic is often windswept and rough, but provides good surfing and windsurfing.

Getting Around

The area is served by three main roads: the often congested four-lane coastal road (the N6 Avenida Marginal), the N117/N249 to Sintra, and the A5 expressway, which links Lisbon with Cascais. A commuter train leaves every 15 to 30 minutes (5:30 AM–2:30 AM) from Cais do Sodré Station in Lisbon for the trip to Estoril and on to Cascais, four stops farther. The 30-minute journey affords splendid sea views as it traces the shore. A one-way ticket costs 170$00. Trains from Lisbon's Rossío station run every 15 minutes to Queluz (150$00), taking 20 minutes, and on to Sintra (170$00), which takes 40 minutes. For current information about train services, call 01/888–4025.

Guided Tours

Citirama (⊠ Av. Praia de Vitória 12-B, ☎ 01/355–8567) offers a half-day tour that takes in the principal sights; it costs 7,300$00. **Gray Line Tours** (⊠ Av. Fontes Pereira de Melo 14, ☎ 01/352–2594) offers a similar tour at the same price. Both tours have daily departures.

Visitor Information

Cascais (⊠ Rua Visconde da Luz 14, ☎ 01/486–8204).
Estoril (⊠ Arcadas do Parque, ☎ 01/468–0113).
Sintra (⊠ Praça da Republica 3, ☎ 01/923–3919).

Exploring the Portuguese Riviera, Sintra, and Queluz

Leave Lisbon by car via the Estrada Marginal highway (following signs for Cascais/Estoril) and take the curving coastal route (the N6) to Estoril. Both Estoril and Cascais are favored residential areas; thanks to their special microclimate, they enjoy milder winters than nearby Lisbon.

Estoril

Estoril is filled with grand homes and gardens, and many of its large mansions date from the last century, when the town was a favorite with the European aristocracy. People-watching is the favored pastime, and one of the best places for it is on the **Tamariz esplanade,** especially from an alfresco restaurant. A palm-studded coastline, plush accommodations, sports facilities, and restaurants are among Estoril's other attractions, but it is perhaps best known for its **casino** (⊙ 3 PM–3 AM), an excellent gambling hall and nightspot that also offers a restaurant, a bar, a theater, and an art gallery. A major open-air handicrafts and ceramics fair is held here from July to September, and many concerts and ballets are staged here during the Estoril Festival each summer.

NEED A BREAK? The luxurious **Hotel Palácio** (☞ Dining and Lodging, *below*), in Parque do Estoril, is worth a visit simply to take tea in one of its ample salons. During World War II, it was an espionage center, where the Germans and Allies kept watch on each other in neutral Portugal, and where exiled European courts waited out the war.

Cascais and Environs

★ **Cascais** lies less than 3.2 kilometers (2 miles) west of Estoril. A pretty but heavily developed tourist resort, it is packed with shopping centers, cinemas, and hotels. The three beaches are small and crowded,

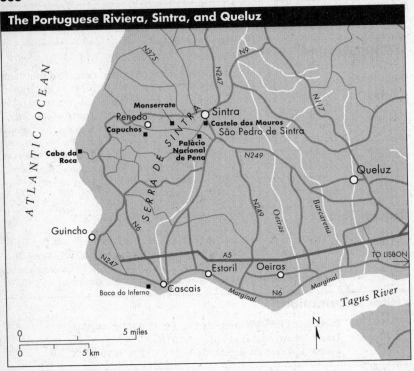

and parking in summer is a headache. Even so, there are a number of sights worth seeing.

The **Igreja de Nossa Senhora da Assunção** (Church of Our Lady of the Assumption) has paintings by Portuguese artist Josefa de Óbidos. ✉ *Largo da Assunção.* 🎫 *Free.* 🕙 *Daily 9–1 and 5–8.*

Opposite the church is one of the entrances to the **Parque do Marachal Carmona** (🕙 Daily 9–6), in which you'll find a shallow lake, a café, and a small zoo. Walk through the park to its southern edge and the **Museu Conde de Castro Guimarães** (Museum of the Count of Castro Guimarães), a large, stately home set on spacious grounds. It displays some good paintings, ceramics, furniture, and local archaeological finds. ✉ *Estrada da Boca do Inferno.* 🎫 *250$00, free Sun.* 🕙 *Tues.–Sun. 11–12:30 and 2–5.*

Continue west from the museum along the coastal road (N247), in the direction of Guincho beach, and it's less than 2 kilometers (about 1¼ miles) to the notorious **Boca do Inferno,** or Hell's Mouth. This rugged section of coastline has numerous stunning tide-swept grottoes.

A scenic 9-kilometer (5½-mile) drive along the coastal road from Boca do Inferno brings you to the superb rocky surfing beach at **Guincho.** From here, the road cuts inland north to the turnoff for **Cabo da Roca,** whose lighthouse marks the westernmost point of land in continental Europe.

Back on the main road, turn into the hills at the end of Praia do Guincho (Guincho Beach). This is the beginning of the **Serra de Sintra** (Sintra Mountains), and here, at **Capuchos,** you can visit a tiny friary built in 1560 by Franciscan monks. Its 12 diminutive cells, hacked out of solid rock, are lined with cork for warmth and insulation—hence its nickname "the Cork Convent." 🎫 *200$00.* 🕙 *June–Sept., daily 10–6; Oct.–May, daily 10–5.*

Return to the main road and follow its winding course through the village of **Penedo**, which offers terrific views of the sea and the surrounding mountains, until you reach the world-renowned gardens of **Monserrate**, 5½ kilometers (3 miles) from the superb Palácio de Seteais hotel (☞ *below*). This botanical wonderland was laid out by Scottish gardeners in the mid-1800s and surrounds an exotic and architecturally extravagant domed Moorish-style palace (closed to visitors). In addition to a dazzling array of other plant species, the gardens have one of the largest collections of fern varieties in the world. ⊠ *Estrada da Monserrate.* ☎ *200$00.* ☉ *June–Sept., daily 10–6; Oct.–May, daily 10–5.*

NEED A
BREAK?

Follow signs to Seteais and stop for a meal at the **Palácio de Seteais** (Seteais Palace), built by the Dutch consul in Portugal in the 18th century. Now a luxury hotel (☞ Dining and Lodging, *below*), the Seteais has an excellent but expensive restaurant, its stately rooms decorated with delicate wall and ceiling frescoes. From here, the main road gently winds down toward Sintra.

Sintra

One of Portugal's oldest towns, **Sintra** is full of history. At the center of the **Old Town** near the Hotel Tivoli Sintra stands the 14th-century ★ **Palácio Nacional de Sintra** (Sintra Palace). This twin-chimneyed building, a combination of Moorish and Gothic architectural styles, was once the summer residence of the House of Avis, Portugal's royal line. Today it's a museum featuring some fine examples of Moorish-Arabic *azulejos* (hand-painted tiles). ⊠ *Praça da Republica.* ☎ *400$00 June–Sept., 200$00 Oct.–May, free Sun. morning year-round.* ☉ *Thurs.–Tue. 10–1 and 2–5.*

If you stand on the steps of the palace and look up toward the Sintra Mountains, you can spot the ruins of the 8th-century **Castelo dos Mouros** (Moors' Castle), which defied hundreds of invaders until it was finally conquered by Dom Afonso Henriques in 1147. Follow the steep, partially cobbled road that leads up to the ruins, or rent one of the horse-drawn carriages outside the palace. From the castle's serrated walls, you can see why its Moorish architects chose the site: The panoramic views falling away on all sides are breathtaking. ⊠ *Estrada da Pena.* ☎ *Free.* ☉ *June–Sept., daily 10–6; Oct.–May, daily 10–5.*

★ ☾ Farther up the same road you'll reach the **Palácio Nacional de Pena** (Pena Palace), a Wagnerian-style extravaganza built by the king consort Ferdinand of Saxe-Coburg in 1840. It is a cauldron of clashing styles, from Arabian to Victorian, and was home to the last kings of Portugal. The nucleus of the palace is a convent commissioned by Dom Fernando, consort to Dona Maria II. The palace is surrounded by a park filled with a variety of trees and flowers brought from every corner of the Portuguese empire by Dom Fernando in the 1840s. ⊠ *Estrada da Pena.* ☎ *Guided tour 400$00 June–Sept.,200$00 Oct.–May, free Sun. 10–2 year-round.* ☉ *Tues.–Sun. 10–5.*

Back in downtown Sintra, the **Museu do Brinquedo** (Toy Museum) houses an enjoyable collection of dolls and traditional toys from this region of Portugal. ⊠ *Largo Latino Coelho 9.* ☎ *200$00.* ☉ *Tues.–Sun. 10–12:30 and 2:30–5.*

If you're in the area on the second or fourth Sunday of the month, visit the **Feira de Sintra** (Sintra Fair) in the nearby village of **São Pedro de Sintra,** 2 kilometers (about 1¼ miles) to the southeast. This is one of the best-known fairs in the country.

Queluz

The town of **Queluz** is accessible by train directly from Lisbon, or by way of the IC19/N249 road, which runs between Lisbon and Sintra.

★ Once you turn off the main road, it's hard to miss the magnificent **Palácio Nacional de Queluz** (Queluz Palace). Inspired in part by Versailles, this salmon pink rococo palace was begun by Dom Pedro III in 1747, and took 40 years to complete. The formal landscaping and waterways surrounding it are the work of the French designer Jean-Baptiste Robillon. Restored after a fire in 1934, the palace is now used for formal banquets, music festivals, and as housing for visiting heads of state. Visitors are permitted to walk through its more elegant rooms, among them the Music Salon, the Hall of the Ambassadors, and the mirrored Throne Room with its crystal chandeliers and gilt trimmings. ☎ *400$00 June–Sept., 200$00 Oct.–May.* ⊙ *Wed.–Mon. 10–1 and 2–5.*

Dining and Lodging

For details and price-category definitions, ☞ Dining *and* Lodging *in* Staying in Portugal, *above.*

Cascais

$$$ ✕ **João Padeiro.** This restaurant in the town center serves the best sole in the region—and other seafood as well—amid cheerful surroundings. ⊠ *Rua Visconde da Luz 12,* ☎ *01/483–0232. AE, DC, MC, V. Closed Tues.*

$$ ✕ **Beira Mar.** This well-established restaurant behind the fish market has a wide variety of fish and meat dishes. The atmosphere is comfortable and unpretentious. ⊠ *Rua das Flores 6,* ☎ *01/483–0152. AE, DC, MC, V. Closed Tues.*

$$$$ ✕🏨 **Hotel Albatroz.** Situated on a rocky outcrop, this attractive old
★ house, converted from an aristocrat's summer residence, is the most luxurious of Cascais's hotels. Though enlarged and modernized, it has retained its character, with charming bedrooms and a pleasant terrace bar. The restaurant boasts superior views of the sea and over the coast toward Lisbon; it specializes in fish dishes. ⊠ *Rua Frederico Arouca 100, 2750 Cascais,* ☎ *01/483–2821,* FAX *01/484–4827. 40 rooms with bath. Restaurant, bar, saltwater pool. AE, DC, MC, V.*

$$ 🏨 **Hotel Baia.** This modern, stone hotel fronted with white balconies overlooks the fishing boats at the quayside. Its small, comfortable rooms are well-appointed; more than half have balconies and sea views. ⊠ *Av. Marginal, 2750 Cascais,* ☎ *01/483–1033,* FAX *01/483–1095. 114 rooms with bath. Restaurant, bar, café, pool. AE, DC, MC, V.*

Estoril

$$$$ ✕ **Restaurant Grill Four Seasons.** This famous, elegant establishment
★ in the Hotel Palácio (☞ *below*) serves buffets around the garden pool in summer and seeks perfection with the freshest of foods. ⊠ *Parque do Estoril,* ☎ *01/468–0400. AE, DC, MC, V.*

$$$ ✕ **A Choupana.** Just outside town toward Lisbon, this restaurant overlooks the beach. You can sample high-quality fresh seafood and other local dishes and dance to a live band until 2 AM. ⊠ *Estrada Marginal, São João de Estoril,* ☎ *01/468–3099. AE, DC, MC, V.*

$$$ ✕ **The English Bar.** This mock-Tudor establishment serves good international cuisine in friendly, comfortable surroundings. There are beautiful views over the beach to Cascais and an excellent wine list. ⊠ *Av. Saboia, off Av. Marginal, Monte Estoril,* ☎ *01/468–0413. AE, DC, MC, V. Closed Sun.*

$$ ✕ **Restaurante Frolic.** Situated next to the Hotel Palácio, the Frolic is a friendly restaurant-bar with a covered, outdoor terrace. Try the delectable cakes, or stop longer for a Portuguese meal or pizza. ⊠ *Av. Clotilde,* ☎ *01/468–1219. AE, DC, MC, V.*

$$$ 🏨 **Hotel Palácio.** During World War II, exiled European aristocrats came
★ here to wait out the war in grand style. The pastel rooms are decorated in Regency style and the hotel contains one of Portugal's most famous restaurants (☞ *above*). It's a two-minute walk to the beach, and golfers can tee off at the nearby Estoril Golf Club, which has special rates for hotel guests. ⊠ *Parque do Estoril, 2765 Estoril,* ☎ *01/468–0400,* ℻ *01/468–4867. 162 rooms with bath. Restaurant, 2 bars, pool, sauna, exercise room. AE, DC, MC, V.*

Queluz

$$$ ✕ **Restaurante de Cozinha Velha.** This restaurant, housed in what
★ were once the great kitchens of the adjoining Queluz Palace, is dominated by an open fireplace. There are some fine wines in the cellar to go with the traditional Portuguese cooking—a spicy dish with salmon, monkfish, clams, and shrimp is just one superb main course. ⊠ *Palácio Nacional de Queluz,* ☎ *01/435–0232. AE, DC, MC, V.*

Sintra

$$$ ✕ **Solar de São Pedro.** Highly recommended by its habitués, this restaurant specializes in Portuguese and French country cooking. Its English-speaking host adds to the warm, friendly atmosphere. ⊠ *Largo da Feira 12, São Pedro de Sintra,* ☎ *01/923–1860. AE, DC, MC, V. Closed Wed.*

$$ ✕ **Alcobaça.** Excellent value for classic Portuguese home cooking is offered at this central restaurant—try the grilled chicken or the *arroz de marisco* (seafood rice). ⊠ *Rua das Padarias 7–11,* ☎ *01/923–1651. MC, V.*

$$$$ ✕🏨 **Palácio de Seteais.** This luxurious former palace set on its own
★ grounds a kilometer from Sintra (☞ Exploring, *above*) houses a splendid restaurant. ⊠ *Rua Barbosa do Bocage 8, 2710 Sintra,* ☎ *01/923–3200,* ℻ *01/923–4277. 30 rooms with bath. Restaurant, bar, pool, tennis courts, horseback riding. AE, DC, MC, V.*

$$$ 🏨 **Tivoli Sintra.** From its perch in the center of Sintra, the Tivoli has excellent views over the nearby valleys. ⊠ *Praça da República, 2710 Sintra,* ☎ *01/923–3505,* ℻ *01/923–1572. 75 rooms with bath. Restaurant, bar. AE, DC, MC, V.*

$$–$$$ 🏨 **Quinta das Sequóias.** Reservations are essential at this lovely old an-
★ tiques-filled manor house (formerly known as the Casa da Tapada), set in its own gardens down a side road. It's just beyond the Palácio de Seteais and makes an excellent touring base. Dinner is served if ordered in advance. ⊠ *Apartado 4, 2710 Sintra,* ☎ *and* ℻ *01/923–0342. 6 rooms with bath. Bar, breakfast room, pool, hot tub. AE, DC, MC, V.*

THE ALGARVE

The Algarve, Portugal's southernmost region, encompasses some 240 sun-drenched kilometers (150 miles) of coastline that are the top destination for foreign visitors to Portugal. During the past three decades, this area has been heavily developed in an effort to create a playground for international sun worshipers. Well known to Europeans as a holiday destination with clean, sandy beaches, championship golf courses, and local color, the Algarve is only now being discovered by Americans. Although some parts of the coastline have been seriously overbuilt, there are still fishing villages and secluded beaches that remain untouched.

Arriving and Departing

Faro, the capital of the Algarve, is only 45 minutes from Lisbon by air. **TAP Air Portugal** has daily service from Lisbon, and there are frequent flights to Faro from London, Frankfurt, and Brussels. Daily bus and rail service connects Lisbon with the major towns in the Algarve; trips take four to six hours, depending on your destination. To reach the Algarve from Lisbon by car, cross the Tagus bridge and take the A2 toll road to Setúbal. From there, the main IP1 (E1) highway runs via Alcácer-do-Sal, Grandola, and Ourique, eventually joining with the east–west N125. Albufeira is straight ahead; head east for Faro and the Spanish border, or west for Lagos. The drive to Albufeira from Lisbon takes about four hours; allow another hour to reach either Faro or Lagos.

Getting Around

The main east–west highway in the Algarve is the two-lane N125, which extends 165 kilometers (100 miles) from Vila Real de Santo António, on the Spanish border, to Vila do Bispo, north of Cabo de São Vicente. This road does not run right along the coast, but turnoffs to beach-side destinations mentioned here are posted along the route. A four-lane motorway, the IP1/E1, is several miles inland and runs parallel to the coast from the suspension bridge at the Spanish border west to Albufeira, where it joins the main road to Lisbon. Local rail and bus services link most of the villages and towns in the Algarve, and organized guided bus tours of some of the more noteworthy villages and towns depart from Faro, Quarteira, Vilamoura, Albufeira, Portimão, and Lagos.

Visitor Information

Local tourist offices can be found in the following towns:

Albufeira (⊠ Rua 5 de Outubro, ☎ 089/512144).
Armação de Pêrá (⊠ Av. Marginal, ☎ 082/312145).
Faro (⊠ Rua da Misericórdia 8/12, ☎ 089/803604.; airport branch, ☎ 089/818582).
Lagos (⊠ Largo Marquês de Pombal, ☎ 082/763031).
Loulé (⊠ Edifico do Castelo, ☎ 089/63900).
Monte Gordo (⊠ Av. Marginal, ☎ 081/44495).
Olhão (⊠ Largo da Lagoa, ☎ 089/713936).
Portimão (⊠ Largo 1° de Dezembro, ☎ 082/23695).
Praia da Rocha (⊠ Av. Tomás Cabreira, ☎ 082/22290).
Quarteira (⊠ Av. Infante de Sagres, ☎ 082/312217).
Silves (⊠ Rua 25 de Abril, ☎ 082/442255).
Tavira (⊠ Praça da República, ☎ 081/22511).
Vila Real de Santo António (⊠ Praça Marquês de Pombal, ☎ 081/44495; ⊠ Frontier Tourist Post, ☎ 081/43272).

Exploring the Algarve

From the Spanish Border to Olhão

Visitors entering the Algarve by car from Spain can drive from Ayamonte, the Spanish frontier town, across a graceful suspension bridge over the River Guadiana to **Vila Real de Santo António.** This showcase of 18th-century Portuguese town planning is laid out on a grid pattern similar to the Baixa section of Lisbon, though there isn't really much to see here. A few miles west of the border, pine woods and

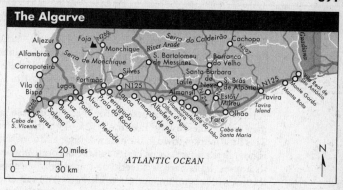

The Algarve

Aljezur · Foja · Serra do Caldeirão · Cachopo
Alfambras · Monchique · River Arade · S. Bartolomeu de Messines · Barranco do Velho
Carrapateira · Serra de Monchique · Santa Bárbara de
Vila do Bispo · Portimão · Silves · Loulé · Nexe · S. Brás de Alportel · N125 · Monte Gordo
Lagos · N125 · Almansil · Estói · Tavira · V. Real de St. António
Burgau · Terragudo · Armação de Pêra · Albufeira · Olhos d'Água · Milreu
Sagres · Luz · Alvor · Praia da Rocha · Quarteira · Vale do Lobo · Faro · Olhão
Salema · Ponta da Piedade · Faro · Tavira Island
Cabo de S. Vicente

0 — 20 miles
0 — 30 km

ATLANTIC OCEAN

N

orchards break up the flat landscape around **Monte Gordo,** a town of brightly colored houses with extensive tourist facilities. The long stretch of beach here slopes steeply, and swimmers quickly find themselves in deep water.

Continuing west past the excellent **Praia Verde** and **Manta Rota** beaches, you come to **Tavira,** which many consider the prettiest town in the Algarve. Situated at the mouth of the River Gilão, it is famous for its figs, cobbled old town streets, a seven-arch Roman bridge, old Moorish defense walls, and interesting churches. There are good sand beaches on nearby **Tavira Island,** which is reached by ferry (☉ May–mid-Oct., every 30–60 min; ☎ 175$00 round-trip) from the jetty at Quatro Águas, 2 kilometers (1¼ mile) east of the town center.

Another 22 kilometers (14 miles) west lies the fishing port and market town of **Olhão.** Founded in the 18th century, Olhão is notable for its North African–style architecture—cube-shaped whitewashed buildings—and some of the best food markets in the Algarve next to the harbor. There are also ferries (☉ July–Aug., 9 daily; Sept.–June, 3–4 daily; ☎ 225$00 round-trip) from Olhão to the nearby sandy islands of **Armona** and **Culatra,** both of which have excellent beaches.

Faro and Environs

From Olhão it's just 9 kilometers (6 miles) to **Faro,** the provincial capital. This city was finally taken by Afonso III in 1249, ending the Arab domination of Portugal. Remnants of the medieval walls and gates that guarded the city at that time can still be seen in the older district, the ★ **Cidade Velha.** One of the gates, the **Arco da Vila,** with a white marble statue of St. Thomas Aquinas in a niche at the top, leads to the grand Largo da Sé. The Gothic **Sé** (☎ Free; ☉ Weekdays 10–noon, 5 PM Sat. for mass, Sun. 8–1) has a stunning interior decorated with 17th-century tiles. There are also several fascinating museums in Faro, notably the **Museu do Etnografia Regional** (Algarve Ethnographic Museum; ☎ 300$00; ☉ Weekdays 9–6) on Rua do Pé da Cruz, with good historical and folkloric displays; and the **Museu Marítimo** (Maritime Museum; ☎ 150$00; ☉ Weekdays 9–12:30 and 3–5:30) next to the Hotel Eva on Rua Comunidade Lusiada, near the yacht basin. The **Museu Municipal** (Municipal Museum; ☎ 110$00; ☉ Weekdays 9–5) on Largo Afonso III has a section devoted to the Roman remains found at Milreu. But the best of the sights is surely the **Capela dos Ossos** (Chapel of the Bones; ☎ 50$00; ☉ Mon.–Sat. 10–1 and 3–5) in the Igreja do Carmo on Largo do Carmo, decorated with human bones taken from the monks' cemetery. There's a large sand beach on Faro Island, the **Praia de Faro,** which is connected by road (Bus 16 from the harbor gardens). Or you can take the ferry from the jetty below the old town to the beach at Farol on Culatra island (☞ Olhão, *above*).

About 9 kilometers (6 miles) north of Faro, a road branches east from the N2 to the village of **Estói,** where you'll find the 18th-century **Palácio do Visconde de Estói** (⊠ Free; ☉ Tues.–Sat. 9–12:30); the palace itself is closed to the public, but visitors can stroll around the gardens. Close by, a 10-minute walk down the main road, there are extensive 1st-century **Roman ruins** (⊠ Free; ☉ Tues.–Sun. 10–12 and 2–5) at **Milreu.**

Another worthwhile excursion from Faro is to **Loulé,** about 17 kilometers (10 miles) away. Take the N125–4 northwest from the N125. This little market town in the hills was once a Moorish stronghold and is now best known for its crafts and the decorative white chimneys of its houses. In its narrow streets you can usually see coppersmiths and leather workers toiling in their workshops. You can also visit the partially restored ruins of a medieval Saracen **castle** (⊠ Largo D. Pedro I; ⊠ Free; ☉ Daily 9–12:30 and 2:30–5), inside of which is the town's museum. The nearby 13th-century **parish church** (⊠ Largo Pr. C. da Silva; ⊠ Free; ☉ Mon.–Sat. 9–12 and 2–5:30), recently restored, is decorated with handsome tiles and wood carvings and features an unusual wrought-iron pulpit.

From Almansil through Albufeira

Back on N125, stop in the town of **Almansil** at the 18th-century Baroque chapel of **São Lourenço,** (⊠ 200$00; ☉ Mon.–Sat. 10–1 and 2–5), with its blue-and-white tile panels and intricate gilt work. The cottages next to the church have been transformed into a lovely art gallery. As you continue westward, look for turnoffs to the south for local beach resorts. The tennis center at **Vale do Lobo,** one of the Algarve's earliest resort developments, is one of the best in Europe. **Quarteira,** once a quiet fishing village, is now a bustling high-rise resort, with golf courses and tennis courts as well as an excellent beach. **Vilamoura** is one of the most highly developed resort centers in the Algarve. In addition to its modern luxury hotels and a casino, it has a large yacht marina, several golf courses, a major tennis center, one of Europe's largest shooting centers, and other sports facilities.

If you continue on N125, you'll soon arrive at the turnoff to **Albufeira.** Once an attractive fishing village, the town long since mushroomed into the Algarve's largest and brashest resort. Even the dried-up riverbed has been turned into a parking lot. But with its steep, narrow streets and hundreds of whitewashed houses clutching the slopes, Albufeira retains a distinctly Moorish flavor. Among its attractions are a lively fish market (held daily), stunning caves and grottoes, and plenty of nightlife. About 14 kilometers (8 miles) west of it is the onetime fishing village of **Armação de Pêra,** now a bustling resort that claims to have the largest beach in the Algarve.

Silves

At **Lagoa,** a market town known for its wine, turn north to **Silves,** 8 kilometers (5 miles) up the N124-1. Once the Moorish capital of the Algarve, Silves ceased to be important after it was almost completely

★ ☾ destroyed by the 1755 earthquake. The 12th-century sandstone **fortress** (⊠ 250$00; ☉ Daily 9–7), with its impressive parapets, was restored in 1835 and still dominates the town. Below the fortress stands the 12th–13th-century **Santa Maria da Sé** (Cathedral of Saint Mary; ⊠ Free; ☉ Mon.–Sat. 8:30–6, Sun. 8:30–1), which was built on the site of a Moorish mosque. The excellent **Museu Arqueológico,** below the cathedral on Rua das Portas de Loulé (⊠ 300$00; ☉ Mon.–Sat. 10–12:30 and 2–6), features artifacts from prehistoric times through the 17th century.

Portimão and Environs

Return to the N125 and continue to **Portimão,** the most important fishing port in the Algarve. There was a settlement here at the mouth of the River Arade even before the Romans arrived. This is a cheerful, busy town and a good place to shop. Although the colorful fishing boats now unload their catch at a modern terminal across the river, open-air restaurants along the quay are pleasant spots in which to sample the local specialty: charcoal-grilled sardines with chewy fresh bread and red wine.

Across the bridge, in **Ferragudo,** are the ruins of a 16th-century castle, and 3 kilometers (about 2 miles) south of Portimão is **Praia da Rocha.** Now dominated by high-rise apartments and hotels, this was the first spot in the Algarve to be developed as a resort. It still has an excellent beach, made all the more interesting by its wall of huge, colored rocks worn into strange shapes by sea and wind.

For a different view, drive north about 24 kilometers (15 miles) from Portimão on routes N124 and 266 into the hills of the Serra de Monchique to the spa town of **Caldas de Monchique.** Here, in addition to charming 19th-century buildings, there's a therapeutic spa in a shady wood that dates from Roman times (though the current spa building is resolutely modern).

Lagos

Return to the N125 and continue your route westward through **Lagos,** a busy fishing port with an attractive harbor, a modern marina, and amazing nearby cove beaches that attract a bustling holiday crowd. Lagos has a venerable history—Henry the Navigator maintained a base here—most evident in its imposing **city walls,** which still survive, and its 17th-century harborside fort at **Ponta da Bandeira** (✆ 200$00; ⊘ Tues.–Sat. 10–1 and 2–6, Sun. 10–1). The 18th-century Baroque **Igreja de Santo António** (Church of Santo Antonio), off Rua General Alberto Silveira, is renowned for its exuberant carved and gilt wood decoration. An amusing regional **museum** (✆ 250$00; ⊘ Tues–Sun. 9:30–12:30 and 2–5) is next door. Lagos is the western terminus of the coastal railway that runs from Vila Real de Santo António.

Sagres

After Lagos, the terrain becomes more rugged as you approach the windy headland at **Sagres,** where some contend that Prince Henry established his famous school of navigation—the first of its kind—in the 15th century. Take the N268 south from the N125 at Vila do Bispo to a promontory hundreds of feet above the sea. From here, a small road ★ ☾ leads through the tunnel-like entrance to the **Fortaleza de Sagres** (Sagres Fortress), destroyed in the great earthquake of 1755 and rebuilt in 1793. The **Rosa dos Ventos** (compass rose), made of stone and earth, was uncovered in this century in the courtyard, but is believed by some to have been used in his calculations by Prince Henry. Inside the fortress, which is always open, are the **Graça Chapel** and a building believed to have been Henry's house. A stark modern structure houses a small **museum** (✆ Free; ⊘ Tues.–Sun. 10-12 and 2-6) with exhibits documenting the region's history.

★ There are spectacular views from **Cabo de São Vicente** (Cape St. Vincent), 6 kilometers (4 miles) to the west, where most historians think Henry the Navigator founded his school. This point, the most southwesterly tip of the European continent, is sometimes called *o fim do mundo* (the end of the world). The lighthouse at Cabo de São Vicente is said to have the strongest reflectors in Europe, casting a beam some 96 kilometers (60 miles) out to sea; it is open to the public. It was at this breathtaking spot that Pedro Álvares Cabral, Vasco da Gama, Ferdinand Magellan, and other great explorers learned their craft 500 years ago.

Dining and Lodging

For details and price-category definitions, *see* Dining *and* Lodging *in* Staying in Portugal, *above*. In winter, particularly January–March, hotel rates are discounted by as much as 40%.

Albufeira

$$$ ✕ **Cabaz da Praia.** This long-established restaurant has a spectacular view of the main beach from its cliffside terrace. There's fine French-Portuguese cooking here—fish soup, imaginatively served fish, and chicken with seafood. ⊠ *Praça Miguel Bombarda 7,* ☎ *089/512137. AE, MC, V. Closed Thurs. No lunch Sat.*

$$–$$$ ✕ **A Ruina.** A rustic restaurant on the beach, built on several levels, this is the place for good views and charcoal-grilled seafood. ⊠ *Cais Herculano, Praia dos Pescadores,* ☎ *089/512094. No credit cards.*

$$$$ ✕🏨 **Estalagem Vila Joya.** One of the most luxurious restaurants and
★   elegant inns in the Algarve also has Moorish-style rooms and suites, all with a sea view. The French-inspired food in the restaurant continues to impress. The inn is 4 kilometers (2½ miles) west of town. ⊠ *Praia da Galé, 8200 Albufeira,* ☎ *089/591839,* 🗏 *089/591201. 14 rooms, 3 luxury suites, all with bath. Restaurant (reservations, jacket and tie required), bar, pool, sauna. AE, DC. Closed Nov. 15–Feb. 15.*

$$$$ 🏨 **Sheraton Algarve.** This new luxury hotel occupies a spectacular cliff-
★   top site 8 kilometers (5 miles) east of town: It overlooks the sea and has access to some of the Algarve's finest beaches. The architecture and decor blend traditional Moorish features with modern elements. ⊠ *Praia da Falésia, 8200 Albufeira.* ☎ *089/501999,* 🗏 *089/501950. 215 rooms with bath. Restaurant, bar, indoor pool, outdoor pool, sauna, 9-hole golf course, tennis courts, exercise room. AE, DC, MC, V.*

$$$ 🏨 **Hotel Cerro Alagoa.** The smartly decorated guest rooms here have private balconies; be sure to request a sea view. It's a 10-minute walk to the town center, but there's courtesy bus service to both Albufeira and the local beaches. ⊠ *Via Rápida, 8200 Albufeira,* ☎ *089/588261,* 🗏 *089/588262. 310 rooms with bath. Restaurant, bar, pool, exercise room. AE, DC, MC, V.*

Alvor

$$$$ 🏨 **Golfe da Penina.** This impressive golf hotel, on 360 well-main-
★   tained, secluded acres off the main road between Portimão and Lagos, has spacious, elegant public rooms, pleasant guest rooms, and attentive service. Most of the guest rooms have balconies; those in the back of the hotel face the Serra de Monchique and have the best views. The excellent golf courses were designed by Henry Cotton, and greens fees are waived for hotel guests. There's a special bus to the beach. ⊠ *Montes de Alvor, 8500 Portimão.* ☎ *082/415415,* 🗏 *082/415000. 192 rooms with bath. Restaurant, bar, grill, pool, sauna, one 18-hole and two 9-hole golf courses, tennis court, horseback riding, beach, water sports, billiards. AE, DC, MC, V.*

$$ 🏨 **Aparthotel Torralta.** This large apartment complex, offering good-size rooms, fully equipped kitchens, and daily maid service, is a very good value and has exceptionally low winter rates. ⊠ *Praia de Alvor, 8500 Portimão.* ☎ *082/459211,* 🗏 *082/459171. 655 units. 2 restaurants, 2 pools, tennis court, horseback riding, dance club. AE, DC, MC, V.*

Armação de Pêra

$$ ✗ **A Santola.** This well-established restaurant overlooking the beach is probably the best in town. Try the excellent *cataplana* (stew of clams, pork, onions, tomatoes, and wine). ⊠ *Largo da Fortaleza,* ☎ *082/312332. MC, V. Closed Sun.*

$$$ ⊞ **Hotel Garbe.** The bar, lounge, and restaurant—all with terraces that provide unhindered views of the sea—take full advantage of the superb location of this squat, white, central hotel. Rooms are modern and smartly furnished, and steps lead from the hotel down to the beach below. ⊠ *Av. Marginal, 8365 Armação de Pêra,* ☎ *082/315187,* ℻ *082/315087. 152 rooms with bath. Restaurant, bar, coffee shop, pool. AE.*

Caldas de Monchique

$ ✗⊞ **Albergaria do Lageado.** Right in the center of this spa town, the Albergaria has rather small guest rooms, but they're attractively furnished and some overlook the lush gardens. The traditionally tiled dining room serves good home cooking, and there's a terrace for summer dining. ⊠ *8550 Caldas de Monchique* ☎ *082/92616. 19 rooms with bath. Bar, dining room, pool. No credit cards. Closed Nov.–Apr.*

Faro

$$$ ✗ **Cidade Velha.** Occupying an 18th-century house within the walls of the Old City, this intimate restaurant serves excellent international cuisine. ⊠ *Rua Domingos Guieiro 19,* ☎ *089/27145. Closed Sun. Dinner only June–Sept. AE, MC, V.*

$$ ✗ **Dos Irmãos.** A friendly staff in this central, cheery setting serves up an array of cataplana dishes. Save room for the homemade *pudim caseiro* (creme caramel). ⊠ *Largo do Terreiro do Bospo 14–15,* ☎ *089/823337. AE, DC, MC, V.*

$$ ⊞ **Hotel Eva.** This well-appointed, modern hotel block on the main square overlooking the yacht basin received a face-lift in 1995. The best rooms face the sea, and there's a courtesy bus to the beach. ⊠ *Av. da República 1, 8000 Faro,* ☎ *089/803354,* ℻ *089/802304. 150 rooms with bath. Restaurant, pool, dance club. AE, DC, MC, V.*

$ ⊞ **Casa de Lumena.** This 150-year-old Faro mansion has been tastefully converted into a small hotel. Each room has a unique ambience, and the courtyard Grapevine Bar is a pleasant place for a drink. ⊠ *Praça Alexandre Herculano 27, 8000 Faro,* ☎ *089/801990,* ℻ *089/804019. 12 rooms with bath. Restaurant, bar. AE, DC, MC, V.*

Lagos

$$$$ ✗ **NO Patio.** This cheerful restaurant with an attractive inner patio serves some of the finest food in Lagos. Run by a Danish couple, Bjarne and Gitte, the fare is international with a Scandinavian accent. Specialties include tenderloin of pork with a Madeira and mushroom sauce. ⊠ *Rua Lançarote de Freitas 46,* ☎ *082/763777. AE, MC, V.*

$$$ ✗ **Dom Sebastião.** Portuguese cooking and charcoal-grilled specials are ★ the main attractions at this cheerful restaurant. It has a wide range of aged Portuguese wines. ⊠ *Rua 25 de Abril 20,* ☎ *082/762795. AE, DC, MC, V. Closed Sun. in winter.*

$$$ ⊞ **Hotel de Lagos.** This modern hotel stretches out at the eastern edge ★ of the old town and is within easy walking distance of all the sights and restaurants. From its terraced rooms one looks down at the pool or out across the river to the coast. Traditional tiles are effectively used throughout, even on lamps and tabletops. A shuttle bus runs to the beach, where the hotel has outstanding club facilities. ⊠ *Rua Nova* *da Aldeia, 8600 Lagos,* ☎ *082/769967,* FAX *082/769920. 317 rooms with bath. Restaurant, bar, pool, tennis court, health club, windsurfing, billiards. AE, DC, MC, V.*

Monchique

$ ✕ **Restaurant Teresinha.** Simply decorated, this modest restaurant
★ serves good country cooking; desserts are particularly outstanding. The terrace overlooks a lovely valley and the coastline. ⊠ *Estrada da Foia,* ☎ *082/92392. MC, V.*

$$ ✕▥ **Estalagem Abrigo da Montanha.** This bucolic inn, noted for its garden of magnolias and camellias, serves excellent regional dishes. It also has guest rooms, for which you'll need a reservation. ⊠ *Estrada da Foia, 8550,* ☎ *082/92131,* FAX *082/93660. 15 rooms with bath. Pool. AE, DC, MC, V.*

Monte Gordo

$ ✕ **Mota.** The Mota is a lively, unpretentious restaurant with a covered terrace right on the ocean. Noted for its seafood and regional cuisine, it has live music in the evenings. ⊠ *On the beach at Monte Gordo,* ☎ *081/42650. No credit cards.*

$$ ▥ **Alcazar.** This is one of the most attractive hotels in town, with unusual architecture and interior design—the sinuous arches and low molded ceilings suggest the inside of a cave or an Arab tent. ⊠ *Rua de Ceuta 9, 8900 Monte Gordo,* ☎ *081/512184,* FAX *081/512242. 95 rooms with bath. Restaurant, bar, pool. AE, DC, MC, V.*

$$ ▥ **Vasco da Gama.** This long, relatively low-lying hotel occupies a choice site next to the broad sandy beach—rooms with sea views cost more but are worth the extra expense. The staff is friendly and helpful. ⊠ *Av. Infante Dom Henrique, 8900 Monte Gordo,* ☎ *081/511321,* FAX *081/511622. 200 rooms with bath. Restaurant, pool, tennis court, bowling, water sports, dance club. AE, DC, MC, V.*

Olhos d'Agua

$$$ ✕ **La Cigale.** Nine kilometers (5½ miles) east of Albufeira, this restaurant—one of the best—offers both French and native Portuguese cuisine. ⊠ *On the beach,* ☎ *089/501637. DC, MC, V. Closed Dec.–Feb.*

Portimão

$$ ✕ **A Lanterna.** This well-run restaurant is just over the bridge at Parchal, on the Ferragudo side. Its specialty is duck, but try the exceptional fish soup or smoked fish. ⊠ *Parchal,* ☎ *082/414429. MC, V. Closed Sun.*

$$ ✕ **A Vela.** A pleasant restaurant decorated in the Moorish style, A Vela has a spacious open kitchen that produces a varied selection of tasty Portuguese and international specialties. ⊠ *Rua Dr. Manuel de Almeida 97,* ☎ *082/414016. AE, DC, MC, V. Closed Sun.*

Praia da Rocha

$$ ✕ **Safari.** This lively Portuguese seafront restaurant has a distinctly African flavor. Seafood and delicious Angolan recipes are the specialties. ⊠ *Rua António Feu,* ☎ *082/23540. AE, DC, MC, V.*

$$$$ ▥ **Algarve.** A luxurious modern hotel, the Algarve is perched on a cliff top. Decorated in Moorish style, it has good-size rooms and a large, attentive staff. Leisure facilities are particularly good here, and there is easy access to the fine beach below. ⊠ *Av. Tomás Cabreira, 8500 Portimão,* ☎ *082/415001,* FAX *082/415999. 220 rooms with bath. Restaurant, bar, grill, 2 pools, 2 tennis courts, health club, dance club. AE, DC, MC, V.*

$$$ ⊞ **Hotel Bela Vista.** A small, tastefully decorated beachfront hotel with magnificent traditional tiles, this is one of the most delightful accommodations on the Algarve. Relax on the terrace and enjoy live music in the summer. ⊠ *Av. Tomás Cabreira, 8500 Portimão,* ☎ *082/24055,* FAX *082/415369. 14 rooms with bath. Bar. AE, DC, MC, V.*

Sagres

$$$ ╳⊞ **Pousada do Infante.** Housed in a sprawling structure with a red-
★   tile roof, this pousada affords spectacular views of the sea and craggy rock cliffs. The moderate-size rooms are well appointed and have small balconies. The restaurant has excellent fresh fish, good desserts, and more marvelous sea views. ⊠ *8650 Sagres,* ☎ *082/64222,* FAX *082/64225. 39 rooms with bath. Restaurant, bar, pool, tennis court. AE, DC, MC, V.*

Santa Barbara de Nexe

$$$$ ╳⊞ **Hotel La Reserve.** This intimate luxury hotel in the hills, 10 kilo-
★   meters (6 miles) inland from Faro and set in a 6-acre park, offers high-class apartment accommodations, including small duplexes with verandas and sea views. Don't pass up the restaurant, which serves elegant cuisine with a French accent; local game is a specialty, and the wine list is very good. ⊠ *Santa Barbara de Nexe, 8000 Faro,* ☎ *089/90234 or 089/90474,* FAX *089/90402. 12 studios with kitchenette, 8 duplexes. Restaurant (dinner only; reservations essential; closed Tues.), bar, pool, tennis court. No credit cards.*

Vale do Lobo

$$$$ ╳⊞ **Dona Filipa.** The Dona Filipa has a lavish and striking interior, pleasant rooms, and first-rate service. Set in extensive, beautifully landscaped grounds near the beach, the hotel houses a chic restaurant that offers an excellent international menu. Greens fees for the nearby 18-hole golf course are included in room rates. ⊠ *Vale do Lobo, 8235 Almansil,* ☎ *089/394141,* FAX *089/394288. 147 rooms with bath. Restaurant, pool, golf privileges, tennis court. AE, DC, MC, V.*

Vilamoura

$$$ ⊞ **Hotel Dom Pedro Golf.** Situated in the heart of this successful vacation complex, the Dom Pedro is close to the casino and not far from the beach. Each room is attractively furnished and has its own balcony. ⊠ *Vilamoura, 8125 Quarteira,* ☎ *089/389650,* FAX *089/315482. 263 rooms with bath. Restaurant, bar, pool, golf privileges, tennis court, health club. AE, DC, MC, V.*

Vila Real de Santo António

$ ╳ **Caves do Guadiana.** Occupying a large, old-fashioned building facing the fishing docks, this restaurant is well known for its seafood and Portuguese specialties. ⊠ *Av. República 90,* ☎ *081/44498. Reservations not accepted. DC, MC. Closed Thurs.*

24 Romania

Bucharest

*The Black Sea Coast
and Danube Delta*

Transylvania

ROMANIA CAN BE A CHALLENGING DESTINATION, but it may well be the most beautiful country in Eastern Europe. Its natural attractions are varied, from the summer resorts on the Black Sea coast to the winter ski resorts in the rugged Carpathian Mountains. There are even greater rewards for the adventurous who explore the many medieval towns and rural villages that are among the most unspoiled in Europe.

Romania is made up of the provinces of Wallachia, Moldavia, and Transylvania, and borders the Ukraine, Moldova, Bulgaria, Serbia, and Hungary. With a population of 23 million, Romania is a "Latin Island" in a sea of Slavs and Magyars—its people are the descendants of the Dacian tribe and of the Roman soldiers who garrisoned this easternmost province of the Roman Empire. Barbarian invasions, struggles against the Turks, the Austro-Hungarian domination of Transylvania, and a strong French cultural influence have all played a part in the evolution of Romanian culture and its folk history. Famous descendants of what is now Romania include Androcles (famed for his care of a lion), writer and Nobel Peace Prize winner Elie Wiesel, and the sculptor Brâncuşi.

The overthrow of the Ceauşescu regime in December 1989 started the country on a slow march toward a Western-style democracy and market economy. Shortages are easing, and the range of available goods and services is increasing, though rising prices have hit many Romanians hard. Still, the many problems that tourists encounter are often outweighed by traditional hospitality.

Most visitors start with Romania's largest metropolis, Bucharest, with its wide, tree-lined avenues, Arcul de Triumf, and lively café life. Other leading attractions are the painted monasteries of Bucovina, and the Romanian Riviera on the Black Sea, with the spectacular wildlife sanctuaries of the nearby Danube Delta. The biggest draw to Transylvania is of course the Dracula legend and its related sites, but the region is also home to a Hungarian and German population with distinctive folk traditions. And, for the truly intrepid traveler, the government sees tourism as such a high priority that it's now easier to explore once inaccessible royal and communist sites all over Romania.

After Albania, Romania is the poorest country in Europe, so travelers should keep certain precautions in mind. Petty theft remains a widespread problem. If you are traveling independently, you may wish to take some food supplies with you. Vegetarians are warned that there is a limited range of produce available (especially in winter) and dairy products remain in short supply. Visitors should use water purification tablets or boil their tap water, since hepatitis is a danger. Alternatively, water fountains in most towns provide natural spring water, and bottled mineral water is available in many restaurants. All visitors should bring an emergency supply of toilet paper, a full first-aid kit, a flashlight for poorly lighted streets and corridors, and, in summer, insect repellent. Since medical facilities do not meet Western standards, it is best to take along your own vitamins and medication (including needles and syringes for injections if you need them).

Romania is likely to remain underexplored until the serious problems caused by the overthrown Ceauşescu regime are resolved, but, in the meantime, whether you're on a controlled package vacation or fearlessly trekking alone, you will experience a part of Europe that has, for better or worse, largely escaped the complexities of modern times.

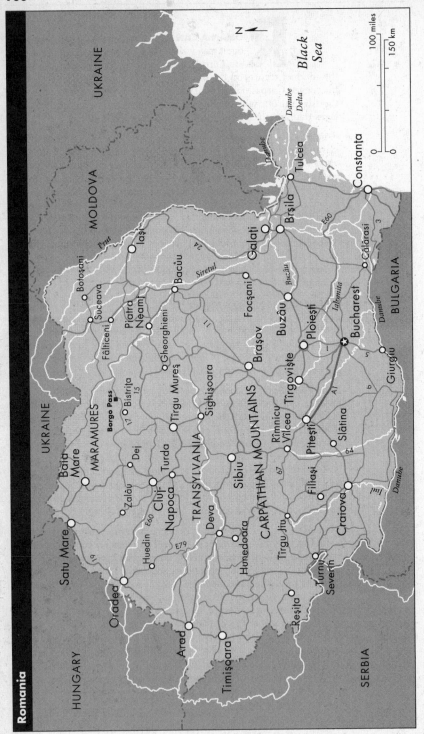

Romania

ESSENTIAL INFORMATION

Before You Go

When to Go

Bucharest is at its best during the spring and fall. The Black Sea resorts open in mid- to late May and close at the end of September. Developed ski resorts in the Carpathians such as Poiana Braşov, Predeal, and Buşeni, are increasingly popular in winter months.

CLIMATE

The Romanian climate is temperate and generally free of extremes, but snow as late as April is not unknown, and the lowlands can be very hot in midsummer.

The following are the average daily maximum and minimum temperatures for Bucharest.

Jan.	34F	1C	May	74F	23C	Sept.	78F	25C
	19	– 7		51	10		52	11
Feb.	38F	4C	June	81F	27C	Oct.	65F	18C
	23	– 5		57	14		43	6
Mar.	50F	10C	July	86F	30C	Nov.	49F	10C
	30	– 1		60	16		35	2
Apr.	64F	18C	Aug.	85F	30C	Dec.	39F	4C
	41	5		59	15		26	– 3

Currency

The unit of currency is the *leu* (plural *lei*). There are coins of 1, 3, 5, 10, 20, 50, and 100 lei. Banknotes come in denominations of 200, 500, 1,000, 5,000, and 10,000 lei. The Romanian currency is expected to continue to drop in value, causing inflation and frequent price increases; costs are therefore best calculated in convertible hard currencies such as U.S. dollars, German marks, or Swiss francs. U.S. dollars are the most readily negotiated currency and it is a good idea to always have some with you, especially in smaller denominations. At press time (spring 1996), the official exchange rate was approximately 2,550 lei to the U.S. dollar, 1,990 lei to the Canadian dollar, and 4000 lei to the pound sterling. Prices of basic items, artificially low from communism, are gradually increasing.

Coins in denominations smaller than 20 and 50 lei are seldom used and not always accepted. There is no longer an obligatory currency exchange, and an increasing number of licensed *casă de schimb* (exchange offices) have been competing to offer rates far higher than official rates. There is no longer any reason for tourists to deal with the black market. Retain all exchange receipts, as you may need to prove your money was changed legally. By law, foreigners must pay for everything except air tickets in lei, though hard currency is widely accepted. The local police—rather than the *garda financiară* (financial police)—are useful if you experience difficulty. You may not import or export lei.

CREDIT CARDS

Major credit cards are welcome in many major hotels and restaurants, but are not accepted in most independent establishments.

What It Will Cost

Independent travelers can find prices of hotels and restaurants as high as those in Western Europe. Those with less flexible but prepaid arrangements may enjoy substantial reductions.

SAMPLE PRICES
Museum admission usually costs less than 50¢; a bottle of imported beer in a restaurant around $2.50 or about 75¢ in a kiosk. A one-mile taxi ride will cost around 60¢.

Visas

Visas are not required for U.S. citizens for stays of less than 30 days. The only requirement is a valid American passport, with an expiration date more than three months beyond the date of departure from Romania. All other visitors entering Romania must have a visa, but no formal application or photograph is needed for British and Canadian citizens. The visa is stamped onto the passport and is valid for a minimum of three months from the date of entry into Romania. This visa can be issued from any Romanian diplomatic or consular office abroad, or at any Romanian customs station at the border when entering the country. Visa fees vary widely. For specifics, contact the relevant office: in **Canada,** Romanian Consulate (⌧ 111 Peter St., Suite 530, Toronto, Ontario M5V 2H1, ☎ 416/585–5802, FAX 416/585–9117), Romanian Consulate (⌧ 1111 Street Urbain, Suite M-01, Montréal, Québec H2Z 1Y6, ☎ 514/876–1793, FAX 514/876–1797), or Embassy of Romania (⌧ 655 Rideau St., Ottawa, Ontario K1N 6A3, ☎ 613/789–3709, FAX 613/789–4365); in the **United Kingdom,** Consular Section of the Romanian Embassy (⌧ 4 Palace Green, London W8 4QD, ☎ 0171/937–9667, FAX 0171/937–8069); in the **United States,** the Embassy of Romania (⌧ 1607 23rd St. NW, Washington, DC 20008, ☎ 202/387–6902, FAX 202/232–4748) or the Romanian Consulate (⌧ 200 E. 38th St., New York, NY 10016, ☎ 212/682–9122, FAX 212/972–8463).

Customs

You may bring in a personal computer and printer, 2 cameras, 10 rolls of film, 1 small camcorder/video camera and VCR, 10 rolls of video film, a typewriter, binoculars, a radio/tape recorder, a small television set, a bicycle, a stroller for a child, 200 cigarettes, 2 liters of liquor, and 4 liters of wine or beer. Gifts are permitted, though you may be charged duty for some electronic goods. Declare video cameras, personal computers, and expensive jewelry on arrival.

Souvenirs and gifts may be taken out of Romania, provided their value does not exceed 50% of the currency you have changed legally—so keep all receipts.

Language

Romanian sounds pleasantly familiar to anyone who speaks a smattering of French, Italian, or Spanish. French is widely spoken and understood in Romanian cities, German and Russian less so. Romanians involved with the tourist industry and the staff in most hotels and major resorts usually speak English.

Getting Around

By Car

ROAD CONDITIONS

An adequate network of main roads covers the country, though the majority only allow for a single lane in each direction. Some roads have many potholes and a few roads have not been paved at all. Progress may be further impeded by farm machinery, slow-moving trucks, horses and carts, or herds of animals. At night, the situation becomes doubly hazardous with poorly lighted or un-lighted roads and vehicles.

RULES OF THE ROAD

Driving is on the right and road signs are the same as in much of Western Europe. Speed limits are 60 kph (37 mph) in built-up areas and 80 kph–90 kph (50 mph–55 mph) on all other roads. Driving after drinking any alcohol is prohibited. Seat belts are compulsory. Spot checks are frequent and police are empowered to levy enormous on-the-spot fines.

GASOLINE

State gas stations, usually found at the edge of towns on main roads, remain scarce, but there are many new private gas stations that charge a bit more money than the state stations. Most gas stations sell regular (90-octane), premium (98-octane), and *motorina* (diesel), but rarely unleaded gas. Prices remain low compared to those of Western Europe, but shortages sometimes cause waits of several hours. The Automobil Clubul Roman (☞ *see below*) and tourist offices can provide visitors with a "Tourist and Motor Car Map" that shows the location of each gas station.

BREAKDOWNS

Automobil Clubul Roman (✉ Str. Tache Ionescu 27, Bucharest, ☎ 01/6502595, ℻ 01/3120434) offers mechanical assistance in case of breakdowns, and medical and legal assistance at fixed rates in case of accidents. (ACR also provides coupons and booking services for various tour and hotel arrangements.) In case of breakdown, dial 927 in Bucharest and 12345 elsewhere. Spare parts are scarce, so carry extras. Thefts of parts from vehicles under repair are common.

CAR RENTALS

A number of international car rental companies have opened offices in Bucharest and other major towns. **Hertz** is in the former ACR building (✉ Str. Cihoski 2, Bucharest, ☎ 01/2120040), and also at Bucharest's Otopeni Airport, (☎ 01/2120122). **Europcar** is in the ONT Carpaţi building (✉ B-dul Magheru 7, ☎ 01/6131540, ℻ 01/3120915).

By Train

Romanian Railways (CFR) operates an extensive network of trains. *Rapid* and *accelerat* trains are the fastest, with limited stops; *Personal* trains are slow and have many stops. *Expres* designates special international express trains, such as the Dacia Expres to Vienna. Note that when the conductor checks tickets, your ticket can occasionally be mixed up with another ticket and destination, so double check that the correct stub is returned to you. First class is worth the extra cost. A *vagon de dormit* (sleeper) or cheap *cuşeta*, with bunk beds, is available on longer journeys. It is always advisable to reserve a seat, but you cannot buy the ticket itself at a train station more than one hour before departure. If your reserved seat is already occupied, it may have been sold twice. If you're in Bucharest and want to buy your ticket ahead of time, contact either a travel agency or the Advance Booking Office (✉ Strada Domniţa Anastasia 10–14, ☎ 01/6132642/3/4) or, for international reservations, contact CFR International (✉ B-dul I. C., Brătianu 44, ☎ 01/6134008). You will be charged a small commission, but the process is less time-consuming than buying your ticket at the station.

By Plane

Tarom operates daily flights to major Romanian cities from Bucharest's Baneasa Airport. In summer, additional flights link Constanţa with major cities, including Cluj and Iaşi. Be prepared for delays and cancellations. Prices average $90 round-trip. For domestic flights, go to Piaţa Victoriei 1 (☎ 01/6594125). International flights can be booked at the central reservations office, Strada Brezoianu 10, and at some major hotels.

By Bus

Bus stations, or *autogara*, are usually near train stations. Buses are generally crowded and far from luxurious. Tickets are sold at the stations up to two hours before departure.

By Boat
Regular passenger services operate on various sections of the Danube; tickets are available at the ports (e.g., Giurgiu, Turnu Severin).

Staying in Romania

Telephones

LOCAL CALLS
The Romanian telephone system is antiquated and overextended: Local calls can be dialed directly, but you may have to order and wait a long time for long-distance calls. Coin-operated telephones at roadsides, airports, and train stations usually work only for local calls: Older phones use a 20-lei coin, newer ones 50- and 100-lei coins. It is less expensive to telephone from the post office than from hotels. Post offices have a waiting system whereby you order your call and pay at the counter. When your call is ready, the name of the town you are phoning is announced, together with the number of the cabin you should proceed to for your call. In some large towns, private business services have opened that offer phone, fax, and telex services.

The area code for Bucharest is 01, and telephone numbers in the city have 2, 3, 6, or 7 as a prefix, followed by a six-digit number. Long-distance calls within Romania should be prefixed with a 0 followed by the area code for the county or region. For information in Romania, your hotel's front desk or phone book is often your best bet, but you can also try dialing the relevant area code, then 11515; in Bucharest, dial 931 (A–L) and 932 (M–Z); for internal long distance, dial 991; for local information, dial 951.

INTERNATIONAL CALLS
Direct-dial international calls can now be made from hotels, the train station, the phone company building on Calea Victoriei, and local post offices (☞ *see* Local Calls, *above*). To place long distance calls out of Romania, dial 00, then country code and number. To place a call from Romania via an **AT&T** USADirect international operator, dial 01–800–4288; for **MCI,** dial 01–800–1800; for **Sprint,** dial 01–800–01–877. For international information, dial 971.

COUNTRY CODE
The country code for Romania is 40.

Mail
The Bucharest central post office is at Matei Millo 10 (☉ Mon.–Thurs. 7:30–7:30, Fri.–Sat. 8 AM–2 PM; telephone service is always available).

POSTAL RATES
Rates increase regularly, so check before you post.

Opening and Closing Times
Banks are open weekdays 9 to 12:30 or 1. Many exchange offices are also open Saturday mornings.

Museums are usually open from 10 to 6, closed on Monday (and sometimes Tuesday); it's best to check with local tourist offices.

Shops are generally open Monday–Friday from 9 or 10 AM to 6 or 8 PM and closed between 1 and 3, though some food shops open earlier. Many shops are closed on Saturday afternoons.

National Holidays
January 1–2 (New Year); April 28 (Orthodox Easter Monday); May 1 (Labor Day); December 1 (National Day); December 25–26 (Christmas); December 31 (New Year's Eve).

Dining

Shortages have eased and standards have improved to a point that more hotels and restaurants can offer reasonable cuisine and menu choices. Traditional Romanian foods are *mamaliga* (corn porridge), *ciorbă* (a soup stock, slightly spicy and sour), and sheep cheeses. Featured meats are usually pork or beef. Away from the bigger restaurants with printed menus, overcharging is a hazard. You can insist on seeing the prices, but small establishments may genuinely not have a menu prepared for just one or two dishes, so you may want to ask before you eat. For snacks, there are always the street vendors and their fragrant offerings such as *covrigi* (giant pretzels), *gogoşi* (fried sugar dough), and roasted chestnuts.

MEALTIMES

Outside Bucharest and the Black Sea and Carpathian resorts, many restaurants will have stopped serving by 9 PM, although an increasing number have begun staying open until 11 PM or later.

PRECAUTIONS

The best bet is often found at the better *cofetarie* (coffee shops). The far less expensive *bufet expres* (beer and snack bar), *lacto vegetarian* snack bars (often serving meat, however), and *autoservire* (cafeteria) cannot always be recommended; the food may be inexpensive but sanitary conditions may be poor. Romanian coffee is served with grounds; instant coffee is called *nes*. Some travelers bring their own coffee creamer, as milk is sometimes in short supply.

WHAT TO WEAR

Jacket and tie are advised for the best restaurants and business lunches and dinners. Casual conservative dress is appropriate at other times.

RATINGS

Prices are per person and include first course, main course, and dessert, plus wine and tip. Because high inflation means local prices frequently change, ratings are given in U.S. dollars, which remain reasonably constant. Your bill will be in lei.

CATEGORY	COST
$$$$	over $30
$$$	$20–$30
$$	$10–$20
$	under $10

Lodging

Prices are highly variable depending on booking arrangements. Prepaid arrangements through travel agencies abroad often benefit from discounted prices. Some schemes, such as fly-drive holidays, come with bed-and-breakfast accommodation vouchers (which cannot be bought in Romania). Most places take vouchers; in deluxe hotels, you have to pay a little extra. Otherwise, book accommodations directly with hotels or through tourist agencies. Some agencies deal only with their local areas; those spawned from the formerly monolithic *agenţis de turism* (national tourism office) now known as ONT, and from the former youth tourism bureau now known as the **Biroul de Turism Şi Tranzacţii** (BTT), offer nationwide services. Travelers staying at less expensive hotels have encountered perilous conditions.

HOTELS

The international star system of hotel classification has recently been introduced in Romania, and now ranks hotels with one to five stars, ranging from inexpensive to deluxe. Standards of facilities, including plumbing and hot water, decline rapidly through the categories and may not be ideal even in expensive accommodations. Ask at the front desk when hot water will be available. In principle, at least, all hotels leave a certain quota of rooms unoccupied until 8 PM for unexpected foreign visitors. Theft seems to be rampant: No matter what class of property you choose, you should not leave valuables in the room and, on departure, you should check your bill for unnecessary charges.

RENTALS

Rustic cottages may be rented at such ski resorts as Sinaia and Predeal. Details are available from Romanian tourist offices abroad (☞ Important Addresses and Numbers *in* Bucharest, *below*).

RATINGS

The following hotel price categories are for two people in a double room. Guests staying in single rooms are charged a supplement. Prices are estimated for high season. Because of inflation, ratings are given according to hard-currency equivalents. (Note that hotels may insist on your buying lei from them to pay your bill, unless you can produce an exchange receipt to prove you changed your money legally.) Rates in Bucharest tend to be much higher than in the rest of the country.

CATEGORY	BUCHAREST	BLACK SEA COAST
$$$$	over $200	over $80
$$$	$125–$200	$50–$80
$$	$70–$125	$30–$50
$	under $70	under $30

Tipping

A 12% service charge is added to meals at most restaurants. Elsewhere, a 10% tip is welcomed and (especially by taxi drivers) expected.

BUCHAREST

Arriving and Departing

By Plane

All international flights to Romania land at Bucharest's Otopeni Airport (☎ 01/6333137), 16 kilometers (9 miles) north of the city.

BETWEEN THE AIRPORT AND DOWNTOWN

Express Bus 783 leaves the airport every 30 minutes between 7 AM and 10 PM, stopping in the main squares before terminating in Piata Unirii. The journey takes an hour and costs 25¢. Your hotel can arrange transport by car from the airport. Taxi drivers at the airport seek business aggressively and usually demand payment in dollars. Note that the "official" fare is in lei, about $12 with tip, so bargain.

By Train

There are five main stations in Bucharest, though international lines operate from Gara de Nord (☎ 01/952). For tickets and information, go to the Advance Booking Office (✉ Str. Domniţa Anastasia 10–14, ☎ 01/6132642). For international trains, go to CFR International (✉ B-dul I. C. Brătianu 44, ☎ 01/6134008).

By Car

There are three main access routes into the city—E70 from the Hungarian border to the west, E60 via Braşov from the north, and E70/E85 from Bulgaria and the south. Bucharest has few street signs and many one-way systems. Learn: *Unde este centrul*? (*oon-*day *yes-*tay *tchen-*trul)—"Where is the town center?"

Getting Around

Bucharest is spacious and sprawling. Though the old heart of the city and the two main arteries running the length of it are best explored on foot, long, wide avenues and vast squares make some form of transportation necessary. It is generally safe on the streets at night, but watch out for unlighted vehicles and hidden potholes.

By Subway

Four subway lines serve the city. Change is available from kiosks inside stations, and, once you have paid your fare, you may travel any distance. The present price is 100 lei (usually paid with two 50-lei coins). The system closes at 11:45 PM.

By Tram, Bus, and Trolley Bus

Surface transit is uncomfortable, crowded, and infrequent, but service is extensive. A ticket valid for two trips of any length can be purchased from kiosks near bus stops or from tobacconists; validate your ticket when you board. There are also *abonaments* (day and week passes) but more expensive *maxi taxis* (minibuses that stop on request) and express buses take fares on board. The system shuts down at midnight.

By Taxi

Hail a cab in the street, or phone 01/953—they speak English. Taxis charge from 35¢ to over $1.00 per kilometer depending on pick-up point. You should agree on a price before the ride begins.

Important Addresses and Numbers

Embassies

American Embassy ⊠ Tudor Arghezi, ☎ 210–4042, 210-0149, FAX 210–0395; **British Embassy** ⊠ Nicolae Iorga, ☎ 312–8345, FAX 312-0366; **Canadian Embassy** ⊠ Jules Michelet 24, ☎ 312–304, FAX 312–0229.

Emergencies

Police (☎ 955). **Ambulance** (☎ 961). **Fire** (☎ 981).

Travel Agencies

Condor (⊠ Str. Luterană 4, Bucharest, ☎ 01/3113449, FAX 01/3113499); **Magellan** (⊠ B-dul. Magheru 12-14, Bucharest, ☎ 01/211-96-50, FAX 01/2104903); **New Frontiers-Simpa Turism** (⊠ Str. Puţu cu Plopi 18, Bucharest, ☎ 01/6666009, FAX 01/3128694).

Visitor Information

There are many new travel agencies in Bucharest and throughout the country. The main branch of **ONT** (formerly the Romanian National Tourist Office, and now privatized) is at 7 Boulevard General Magheru, Bucharest (☎ 01/3122598, FAX 01/3122594) and deals with all inquiries related to tourism (◷ weekdays 8–8 and weekends 8–2). There are also ONT offices at Otopeni Airport (◷ 24 hours) and at the Gara de Nord (◷ Mon.–Sat. 8–8). ONT is currently being broken up and privatized, so its office signs in most Romanian towns now read AGENŢIA DE TURISM.

Guided Tours

Tours are available from the growing number of tourist agencies, many of which maintain desks in the larger hotels. Possibilities range from chauffeured sightseeing drives in Bucharest to excursions to Prince Ştirbei estate at Buftea, to more ambitions expeditions to the Danube Delta.

Travel Agencies

Quest Tours & Adventures (✉ One World Trade Center, 121 SW Salmon, Suite 1100, Portland, OR 97204, ☎ 800/621-8687) offers a wide choice of tours incorporating local lecturers. **Littoral Tours** (✉ 615 Hope Road, Building 2-8B, Eatontown, NJ 07724, ☎ 908/389-2160) has offices throughout the country. **Carpati International** (✉ Gypsy Trail Rd., Carmel, NY 10512, ☎ 914/225–2215 or 800/766–2642, FAX 914/225–2215) provides transportation and itineraries for specialty tours (from Dracula to spas).

Exploring Bucharest

The name Bucureşti was first used officially in 1459 by Vlad Ţepeş, the real-life Dracula (sometimes known as Vlad the Impaler for his blood-thirsty habit of impaling unfortunate victims on wooden stakes). Two centuries later, this citadel on the Dîmboviţa River became the capital of Wallachia, and after another 200 years, it was named the capital of Romania. Bucureşti, which derives from the Romanian word for beautiful, gradually developed into a place of bustling trade and gracious living, with ornate and varied architecture, landscaped parks, busy, winding streets, and wide boulevards. Still a center for expression of popular opinion, the city was known before World War II as the Paris of the Balkans, but its glory now lies under decades of neglect and political turmoil.

The high-rise Hotel Inter-Continental now dominates the main intersection at Piaţa Universităţii; northward, up the main shopping streets Bulevardul Nicolae Bălcescu, Bulevardul General Magheru, and Bulevardul Ana Ipătescu, only the occasional older building survives. However, along Calea Victoriei, a flavor of Bucharest's grander past can be savored, especially at the former royal palace opposite the Romanian Senate (formerly Communist Party headquarters) in Piaţa Revoluţiei. Here, one also sees remains of the domed National Library, gutted by fire. The walls nearby are riddled with bullet holes. These are understated monuments to the more than 1,000 people killed in the 1989 revolution.

South along Calea Victoriei is the busy Lipscani trading district, a remnant of the Old City that used to sprawl farther southward before it was bulldozed in Nicolae Ceauşescu's megalomaniacal drive to redevelop the capital. Piaţa Unirii was the hub of his enormously expensive and impractical vision, which involved the forced displacement of thousands of people and the demolition of many priceless early houses, churches, and synagogues and other irreplaceable buildings. Construction cranes now stand eerily idle above unfinished tower blocks with colonnaded, white marble facades. They flank a lengthy boulevard leading to the enormous, empty, and unfinished Palace of the People (the second largest building in the world, after Washington DC's Pentagon). After such a massive diversion of resources, it is not surprising that the infrastructure is weakened, but the city is currently redirecting its resources to remedying the situation. Happily, Bucharest still has places of historic interest, cafés, cinemas, and performance halls.

Historic Bucharest

Numbers in the margin correspond to points of interest on the Bucharest map.

A tour of this city should start at one of its most fascinating sites, the **Curtea Veche** (Old Princely Court) and the Lipscani District. The
❶ Princely Court now houses **Muzeul Curtea Veche-Palatul Voievodal,** a museum exhibiting the remains of the palace built by Vlad Ţepeş in the 15th century. One section of the cellar wall presents the palace's

history from the 15th century onward. Prisoners were once kept in these cellars, which extend far into the surrounding city; a pair of ancient skulls of two young *boyars* (aristocrats), decapitated at the end of the 17th century, are on ghoulish display. ✉ *Str. Iuliu Maniu 31,* ☎ *01/6140375.* 🎟 *900 lei.* ☉ *Tues.–Sun. 10–6.*

★ ❷ The **Biserica din Curtea Veche** (Curtea Veche Church), beside the Princely Court, was founded in the 16th century and remains an important center of worship in the city. Sunday morning is the best time to view ceremonies. Nearby, **Hanul lui Manuc** (Manuc's Inn), a renovated 19th-century ❸ inn arranged in the traditional Romanian fashion around a courtyard, now houses a small hotel and restaurant. Manuc was a wealthy Armenian merchant who died in Russia—poisoned by a famous French fortune-teller who, having forecast Manuc's death on a certain day, could not risk ruining her reputation. The 1812 Russian-Turkish Peace Treaty was signed here. Some visitors may wish to journey across the river to see **Queen Marie of Romania's Cotroceni Palace** on the Dîmbovița River corniche near the Botanical Gardens. If you make it here, be sure to see the bedroom decorated in her adapted folk style.

Lipscani District

Nearby, **Lipscani** is a bustling bazaar of narrow streets, open stalls, and small artisans' shops. In Hanul cu Tei, off Strada Lipscani, you'll find ❹ many galleries and crafts and gift shops. The **Biserica Stavropoleoš** on the street of the same name is a small, exquisite church combining late-Renaissance and Byzantine styles with elements of the Romanian folk-art style. Go inside to see the superb wood and stone carvings and a richly ornate iconostasis (the painted screen that partitions off the altar). Boxes on either side of the entrance contain votive candles—for the living on the left, for the "sleeping" on the right.

NEED A BREAK? Down the road, at Strada Stavropoleos 3, is the historic—and now shiningly restored—**Carulcu Bere,** serving ½-liter tankards of beer, appetizers, and Turkish coffee.

---

❺ At the end of the street is the **Muzeul Național de Istorie** (National History Museum), which contains a vast collection of exhibits from Neolithic to modern times. The Treasury has a stunning collection of objects in gold and precious stones—royal crowns, weapons, plates, and jewelry—dating from the 4th millennium BC through the 20th century. Op-❻ posite the Treasury is a full-size replica of **Trajan's Column,** in Rome, commemorating a Roman victory over Dacia in AD 2. ✉ *Calea Victoriei 12,* ☎ *01/6157056.* 🎟 *900 lei.* ☉ *Treasury: Tues.–Sun. 10–5; museum: Wed.–Sun. 10–4.*

Turning north along the Calea Victoriei, you'll pass a military club and ❼ academy before reaching the pretty little **Crețulescu Church** on your left. Built in 1722, the church and some of its original frescoes were restored during the 1930s. (As was usual, the frescoes depict the church's donors). Immediately north is a massive building, once the royal palace ★❽ and now the Palace of the Republic. The **Muzeul de Artă al României** (National Art Museum) is housed here, with a fine collection that includes pieces by the world-famous sculptor Brâncuşi, and a marvelous works from the Brueghel school. ✉ *Str. Știrbei Vodă 1,* ☎ *01/6155193.* 🎟 *1,000 lei.* ☉ *Wed.–Sun. 10–6.*

Around Piața Revoluției (Revolutionary Square)

The former headquarters of the Romanian Communist Party was based in Piața Revoluției, opposite the palace. Before the revolution in December 1989, no one was allowed to walk in front of this building. During the uprising the square was a major scene of the fighting

KEY

i Tourist Information

AE American Express Office

Arcul de Triumf, **12**
Ateneul Român, **9**
Biserica din Curtea Veche, **2**
Biserica Stavropoleoş, **4**
Cretulescu Church, **7**
Hanul lui Manuc, **3**

Muzeul Curtea Veche-Palatul Voievodal, **1**
Muzeul de Artă al României, **8**
Muzeul de Ştiinţe Naturale Grigore Antipa, **10**
Muzeul National de Istorie, **5**

Muzeul Satului Romanesc, **13**
Muzeul Ţăranului Român, **11**
Trojan's Column, **6**

⑨ that destroyed the National Library, parts of the Palace, and the Cina restaurant next to the **Ateneul Român** (Romanian Athenaeum Concert Hall). The Ateneul, with its Baroque dome and Greek columns, since 1888 has survived much upheaval and is still home to the George Enescu Philharmonic Orchestra.

⑩ Return to Calea Victoriei and head north past 19th century buildings and some chic new stores for about half an hour until you reach the Piaţa Victoriei. Opposite is the **Muzeul de Ştiinţe Naturale Grigore Antipa** (Natural History Museum), with its exceptional butterfly collection and the skeleton of the dinosaur *Dinotherium gigantissimum.* ⊠ *Şoseaua Kiseleff 1,* ☎ *01/6504710.* ☞ *800 lei.* ☉ *Tues.–Sun. 10–5.*

⑪ Next door, in an imposing redbrick building, is the impressive **Muzeul Ţăranului Român** (Museum of the Romanian Peasant). This museum has costumes, icons, carpets, and other artifacts from rural life, including reconstructed interiors from two 19th-century wooden churches. ⊠ *Şoseaua Kiseleff 3,* ☎ *01/6595655.* ☞ *1,000 lei.* ☉ *Tues.–Sun. 10–6.*

⑫ One and a half miles along Şoseaua Kiseleff, a pleasant tree- and embassy-lined avenue, is the **Arcul de Triumf,** built in 1922 to commemorate the Allied victory in World War I. Originally constructed of wood and stucco, it was rebuilt during the 1930s and carved by some of Romania's most talented sculptors.

★ ⑬ Still farther north lies Herăstrău Park, accommodating the fascinating **Muzeul Satului Romanesc** (Village Museum), as well as Herăstrău Lake. Wander through the more than 300 representations of folk style and architecture taken from peasant villages of different regions and periods in Romania's history. ⊠ *Şoseaua Kiseleff 28,* ☎ *01/6171732.* ☞ *1,000 lei.* ☉ *Winter, daily 8–4; summer, daily 10–7.*

Shopping

Gifts and Souvenirs
New private shops are bringing new style and variety to shopper's Bucharest, but note the customs restrictions (☞ Customs *in* Before You Go, *above*): Keep receipts of all purchases, regardless of their legal export status. The **Apollo** gallery, in the National Theater building next to the Hotel Inter-Continental and the galleries in the fascinating **Hanul cu Tei** off Strada Lipscani sell art that you may legally take home with you. Romanian-made Christmas icons are excellent souvenirs.

Market
A main food market is in Piaţa Amzei, open seven days a week and best visited during the morning. If you decide to visit outlying flea markets such as Piaţa Obor, be careful of inflated prices.

Dining

The restaurants of the pricier hotels are recommended for an assuredly reasonable meal in pleasant surroundings—which sometimes may be tough to find. Some eateries offer a folklore show or live music. Although prices are not exorbitant, it is possible to rack up quite a total. Also note that most places will serve wine only by the bottle and not by the glass. For details and price-category definitions, *see* Dining *in* Staying in Romania, *above*.

$$$$ ✕ **Casa Doina.** Recently refurbished, this historic restaurant—popular with the Bucharest elite between the wars—is once again one of the city's best. It serves Romanian and international cuisine in a relaxing atmosphere. A terrace looks over Kisseleff Park. ⊠ *Şos. Kiseleff 4,* ☎ *01/6176715. AE, DC, MC, V.*

$$$$ ✕ **Darclée, Volubilis.** These two restaurants in the new Hotel Sofitel
★ have excellent French and international cuisine. ✉ *B-dul. Expoziţiei
2,* ☎ *01/2122998. AE, DC, MC, V.*

$$$$ ✕ **La Premiera.** One of Bucharest's most popular restaurants is conveniently located at the back of the National Theatre. It offers a broad
menu, and in summer months you can look out over the Old City from
the terrace. ✉ *Str. Arghezi 9,* ☎ *01/3124397. AE, DC, V.*

$$$$ ✕ **Madrigal.** Situated on the ground floor of the modern Hotel Inter-
Continental, this is a quiet, elegant restaurant with live piano every night.
There is a wide choice of Romanian and international dishes. ✉ *B-dul
Nicolae Bălcescu 4–6,* ☎ *01/6140400. AE, DC, MC, V.*

$$$ ✕ **Bar Grecesc.** A new German-run restaurant is in the basement of a
turn-of-the-century building off Calea Victoriei. It serves mainly in-
ternational cuisine, including a tasty (and thrifty) Sunday brunch of
salami, cheese, and pastries. ✉ *Str. Occidentului 44,* ☎ *01/6596155.
AE, DC, MC, V.*

$$$ ✕ **Hanul lui Manuc.** Lively crowds and classic atmosphere let you for-
give the sometimes cursory service in this restored 19th-century inn,
which circles a courtyard. Try the *Salam de Sibiu.* ✉ *B-dul Iuliu Maniu
30,* ☎ *01/6131415. AE, DC, MC, V.*

$$$ ✕ **Select.** In the Cartierul Primaverii (Primavera District, just south of
Lake Floreasca)—one of the more well-to-do residential areas of
Bucharest—this restaurant offers good food, reasonable prices, and
friendly service. ✉ *Aleea Alexandru 18,* ☎ *01/6794120. No credit cards.*

$$ ✕ **Maramureş.** You'll find this popular spot tucked in a corner behind
the Hotel Bucareşti. You can dine in the garden during the summer and
fall. The restaurant also has a small disco/bar. ✉ *Str. G-ral Berthelot
at corner of Str. T. Aman,* ☎ *01/6644983. No credit cards.*

$$ ✕ **Nan-Jing.** Of the many recently opened Chinese restaurants here,
★ this is may be the best. ✉ *Str. Lemnea 2,* ☎ *01/6506010. No credit
cards.*

$ ✕ **Pani Pat.** If your weakness is delicious pastries, you won't want to
miss the desserts offered by these take-out eateries. The main menu con-
sists of a selection of pizzas. ✉ *Str. C.A. Rosetti 1,* ☎ *01/2107128;* ✉
Ştefan Stefan Cel Mare 4, ☎ *01/2103469;* ✉ *Şoş. Dorobanti,* ☎
01/2103874. No credit cards.

Lodging

Hotels in Bucharest are often heavily booked during the tourist sea-
son. If you don't have reservations, the ONT office will be of help in
suggesting available options. For details and price-category defini-
tions, *see* Lodging *in* Staying in Romania, *above.*

$$$$ 🏨 **Helveţia.** The Helveţia has established itself as one of the capital's
best hotels. This is a small, quiet hotel with an emphasis on individual
service and comfort. It is located a little north of the city center but is
easily accessible by metro or taxi. ✉ *Str. Uruguay 29,* ☎ *01/3110566,*
FAX *01/3110567. 30 rooms. Restaurant, bar, café. AE, DC, MC, V.*

$$$$ 🏨 **Hotel Inter-Continental.** Designed principally for business clients,
the four-star Inter-Continental offers American-style accommodation
in the city's tallest building. Every room is air-conditioned and has a
balcony. ✉ *B-dul N. Bălcescu 4–6,* ☎ *01/6140400,* **FAX** *01/3120486.
423 rooms. 4 restaurants, 3 bars, pool, health club, casino, nightclub.
AE, DC, MC, V.*

$$$$ 🏨 **Sofitel.** Pleasantly set in an area of parks and lakes, this link in the
★ international Sofitel chain offers all the modern conveniences that one
could want in a hotel. ✉ *Free Press Square, B-dul Expoziţiei 2,* ☎
01/6182828, **FAX** *01/2120646. 190 rooms, 13 suites, some wheelchair-
accessible rooms. 2 restaurants, bar, café, nearby "Le Club" sports and*

leisure complex (pool, gym, tennis courts), shops, nightclub, business services, airport shuttle. AE, DC, MC, V.

$$$ **Continental.** This small, turn-of-the-century four-star property recalls Bucharest's more gracious past. Furnishings are traditional, but the rooms have air-conditioning. Located just north of the lively Lipscani district. ⊠ *Calea Victoriei 56,* ☎ *01/6385022,* FAX *01/3120134. 53 rooms. Restaurant, coffee shop, bar. AE, DC, MC, V.*

$$$ **Flora.** The four-star Flora, on the outskirts of the city near Herăstrău Park, offers its mainly cosmopolitan clientele modern facilities for anti-aging treatments. The sun terraces are havens of relaxation. Many find this a quiet, restful refuge, and business travelers may find it an economical (and relaxing) option. ⊠ *B-dul Poligrafiei 1,* ☎ *01/6184640,* FAX *01/3128344. 155 rooms. Restaurant, pool, sauna, spa, health club. AE, DC, MC, V.*

$$ **Ambassador.** The three-star, 13-story Ambassador was built in 1937 and has comfortable rooms, a worthwhile café, a fine central location, and a large Roman Empire pool. ⊠ *B-dul General Magheru 6–8,* ☎ *01/6159080,* FAX *01/3121239. 233 rooms. Restaurant, café, pool. AE, DC, MC, V.*

$$ **Lido.** Conveniently located in the center of the city, this prewar three-star hotel has been recently privatized and renovated to offer comfortable rooms and good facilities. ⊠ *B-dul Magheru 5,* ☎ *01/6144930,* FAX *01/3126544. 92 rooms. Restaurant, bar, pool, nightclub. AE, DC, MC, V.*

$$ **Parc.** Near Herău Park and the Flora Hotel, the modern Parc is convenient to the airport; many stay here before moving on to the Black Sea resorts. There's a good restaurant that has live music every night. ⊠ *B-dul Poligrafiei 3,* ☎ *01/6180950,* FAX *01/3128419. 314 rooms. Restaurant, pool, sauna. AE, DC, MC, V.*

$ **Capitol.** The circa-1900, two-star Capitol is in a lively part of town near Cişmigiu Gardens. In days gone by, it was the stomping ground of Bucharest's mainstream artists and writers. Today the Capitol has modern, comfortable rooms. ⊠ *Calea Victoriei 29,* ☎ *01/6158030,* FAX *01/3124169. 70 rooms. Restaurant. No credit cards.*

$ **Central.** This small, two-star hotel sits on a quiet side street in the middle of town near Cişmigiu Gardens. ⊠ *Strada Brezoianu 13,* ☎ *01/6155637,* FAX *01/6155635. 65 rooms. DC, MC, V.*

$ **Triumf.** This economical, comfortable hotel is on a small park near the Arcul de Triumf. Formerly the President, it used to serve only the communist elite. The more expensive rooms are miniapartments. ⊠ *Şoseaua Kiseleff 12,* ☎ *01/6184110,* FAX *01/3128411. 98 rooms, 49 with bath. Restaurant, bar, tennis. AE, DC, V.*

The Arts

Take advantage of Bucharest's active theater and music scene at prices well below those in the West. Tickets can be bought from the theater or hall or through your hotel. Performances usually begin at 7 PM (6 in winter). **Opera Română** (The Opera House; ⊠ B-dul Mihail Kogălniceanu 70) has some good productions of classic Romanian and other European works. The George Enescu Philharmonic Orchestra holds concerts at the **Ateneul Român** (Romanian Athenaeum in Piaţa Revoluţiei) or at the more modern **Studioul de Concerte al Radioteleviziunii** (Radio Concert Hall; ⊠ Str. General Berthelot 62–64). The **Teatrul de Operetă** (Operetta House) is now at the **Teatrul National** (National Theater; ⊠ B-dul N. Bălcescu 2), which also offers serious drama. For lighter entertainment, try the **Teatrul de Comedie** (Comedy Theater; ⊠ Str. Mandinesti); even if you don't understand the language, there is often enough spectacle to ensure an evening's entertainment. **Teatrul Tăndărică** (Tandarica Puppet Theater; ⊠ Calea Victoriei 50) has an international reputation. The **Teatrul Evreesc de Stat** (State Jewish Theater; ⊠ Str. Barasch 15) stages Yiddish-language performances. Don't miss the fine folklore show at the **Rapsodia Română Artistic Ensemble** (⊠ Str. Lipscani 53). The **Cinematica Romana** (⊠ Str. Eforie 5) runs a daily program of old, undubbed American and English films.

Nightlife

Increasing numbers of bars and restaurants stay open late—which can mean until 6 AM. Coffee shops, however, are usually closed after 8 PM.

Nightclubs
The **Lido, Ambassador,** and **Inter-Continental** hotels have nightclubs with floor shows, and many others are popping up as well. **Vox Maris** (⊠ Piața Victoriei); **Salonul Spaniol** (⊠ 116 Calea Victoriei); and **Club A** (⊠ Str. Blănari) are some late-night discos. **Șarpele Roșu** or "Red Snake" (⊠ Str. Icoanei Piața Galați), has a bohemian atmosphere.

Cafés
Cafés with outdoor terraces remain a feature of the city. Try the **Lido** or, in winter, the excellent indoor **Ana Café** (⊠ Str. Aviator Radu Beller 6), just north of Piața Dorobanți.

THE BLACK SEA COAST AND DANUBE DELTA

The southeastern Dobrogea region, only 45 minutes by air from Bucharest, 210 kilometers (130 miles) by road, has been a focal point of Romania's long history. Within a clearly defined area are the historic port of Constanța; the Romanian Riviera pleasure coast; the Murfatlar vineyards; Roman, Greek, and earlier ruins; and the Danube Delta, which has become one of Europe's leading wildlife sanctuaries. The rapid development of the resorts and increasing interest in the delta region have led to an equally rapid improvement of tourist facilities and transport.

Getting Around

By Bus
Tourist agencies arrange bus trips from the Black Sea resorts and Constanta to the Danube Delta, the Murfatlar vineyards, and Istria.

By Car
Rental cars, with or without drivers, are available through ONT offices, hotels, and specialized agencies.

By Boat
Regular passenger and sightseeing boats operate along the middle and southern arms of the Danube Delta. Motorboats are available for hire, or you can rent one of the quieter (motorless) fishermen's boats.

Visitor Information

Constanța. Societatea Comercială Litoral (⊠ B-dul Tomis 69, ☎ and FAX 041/611429). **BTT** (⊠ Hotel Tineretului, B-dul Tomis 20–26, ☎ 041/613590, FAX 041/616624). Note: Tours in this area involve several hours on the road, so it is better to allow more than one day for a substantive trip.

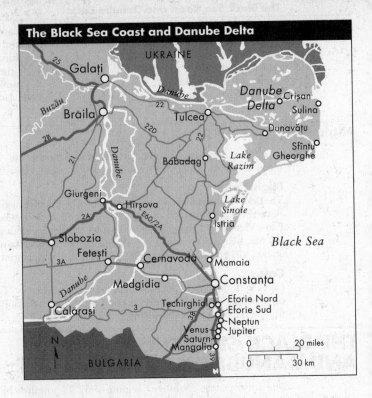

The Black Sea Coast and Danube Delta

Mamaia. Societatea Comercială Mamaia (⊠ Hotel Bucureşti, B-dul Mamaia, ☎ 041/831780).

Tulcea. Societatea Comercială Deltarom (⊠ Hotel Delta, Str. Isaccei 2, ☎ 040/614720, ℻ 040/515776). **BTT** (⊠ Str. Babadag Bloc B1, ☎ 040/512496, ℻ 040/616842).

Exploring the Black Sea Coast and Danube Delta

Tulcea, the main town of the Danube Delta, is the gateway to the region. Built on seven hills and influenced by Turkish styles, this former market town is now an important sea and river port. This is the center of the Romanian fish industry, which is famous for processing caviar-bearing sturgeon. The **Muzeul Deltei Dunării** (Danube Delta Museum) provides a good introduction to the flora, fauna, and way of life of the communities in the area. ⊠ *Str. Progresului 32,* ☎ *040/158666.* ⊡ *700 lei.* ⊙ *Tues–Sun 11–4.*

The Danube Delta

The **Delta Dunării** (Danube Delta) is Europe's largest wetlands reserve, covering 1,676 square miles, with a sprawling, watery wilderness that stretches from the Ukrainian border to a series of lakes north of the Black Sea resorts. This ecosystem allows you to wander through habitats that are endangered throughout the rest of Europe. Romanians have committed themselves to the restoration of this treasure. The Danube Delta is a refuge for hundreds of species of seasonal and migratory birds, and home to natives like the pelican. Living on the reserve is a small population of the Russian sect of "Old Believers."

As it approaches the Delta Dunării, the great Danube divides into three. The northernmost branch forms the border with Ukraine, the middle arm leads to the busy port of Sulina, and the southernmost arm meanders gently toward the little port of Sfintu Gheorghe, a simple holiday spot. From these channels, countless canals widen into tree-fringed lakes, reed islands, and water-lily pools; there are sand dunes and lush forest. More than 300 bird species visit the area; some come from as far away as China and India.

There are good roads to the Black Sea resorts from Tulcea that take you to **Babadag** via the desolate landscape of the eroded Măcin hills. It was here, according to local legend, that Jason and the Argonauts cast anchor in their search for the mythical Golden Fleece. Farther south is **Istria,** founded in 6 BC by Greek merchants from Miletus. Here there are traces of early Christian churches, baths, and even entire neighborhoods.

Istria lies only 60 kilometers (37 miles) from **Mamaia,** the largest of the Black Sea resorts. Mamaia is on a strip of land bordered on one side by the Black Sea and fine beaches and on the other by the fresh waters of Mamaia Lake. All the resorts along this stretch of the coast have high-rise modern apartments, villas, restaurants, nightclubs, and discos. There are cruises down the coast to Mangalia and along the new channel that links the Danube with the Black Sea near Constanţa. Sea-fishing expeditions can also be arranged for early risers, with all equipment provided.

Constanţa

Just a short ride by trolley bus from Mamaia, **Constanţa** is Romania's second-largest city, with the busy, polyglot flavor characteristic of so many seaports. The famous Roman poet Ovid was exiled here from Rome in AD 8; a statue of him presides over a city square. The **Muzeul Naţional de Istorie şi Arheologie** (National History and Archaeological Museum) features statues from the Neolithic Hamangian culture (4000 to 3000 BC) as well as Greek and Roman artifacts. ⊠ *Piaţa Ovidiu 12,* ☎ *041/614562.* 🔳 *500 lei.* ⊙ *Tues.–Sun. 10–6.*

Near the museum is **Edificiu Roman cu Mozaic,** a Roman complex of warehouses and shops from the 4th century AD, including a large mosaic floor (⊠ Piaţa Ovidiu 1). Not far away are remains of the Roman baths from the same period. The **Parcul Arheologic** (Archaeology Park) on Bulevardul Republicii contains items dating from the 3rd and 4th centuries AD. Modern-day attractions include an **Acvariul,** or aquarium (⊠ Str. Februarie 16), and the **Delfinariul,** or dolphinarium (⊠ B-dul Mamaia 265).

★ A string of seaside resorts lies just south of Constanţa. **Eforie Nord** is an up-to-date thermal treatment center. A series of nearby resorts built during the 1960s are named for the coast's Greco-Roman past—**Neptun, Jupiter, Venus,** and **Saturn.** Not in any way typically Romanian, these resorts offer good amenities for relaxed seaside vacations. The old port of **Mangalia** is the southernmost resort.

There are regular excursions from the seaside resorts to the **Podgorile Murfatlar** (Murfatlar vineyards) for wine tastings and to visit the ruins of the Roman town at **Tropaeum Trajani.**

Most of the old Greek city of **Callatis** lies underwater now, but a section of the walls and the remains of a Roman villa are still visible.

Dining and Lodging

For details and price-category definitions, *see* Dining *and* Lodging *in* Staying in Romania, *above.* Expect to pay with cash.

Constanţa

$$$$ ✕ **Cazinou.** A turn-of-the-century former casino close to the aquarium, the Cazinou is decorated in an ornate 20th-century style; there's an ad-

joining bar by the sea. Seafood dishes are the house specialties. ⊠ *Str. Februarie 16,* ☎ *041/617416. No credit cards.*

$$$ 🏨 **Palace.** Near the city's historic center, the large and gracious two-star Palace has recently been renovated. It has a good restaurant and a terrace that overlooks the sea and the port of Tomis. ⊠ *Str. Remus Opreanu 5–7,* ☎ *041/614696. 132 rooms with bath. Restaurant. No credit cards.*

Crişan
$$ 🏨 **Lebăda.** This comfortable two-star hotel is convenient for those who plan to make fishing trips into the more remote parts of the delta. ⊠ *Sulina Canal, mile 14.5,* ☎ *040/514720. 74 rooms. Restaurant, currency exchange. No credit cards.*

Mamaia
$$ ✕ **Insula lui Ovidiu.** This reed-thatched complex of rustic-style buildings has a relaxed, informal atmosphere. Lively music accompanies the delicious seafood dishes every evening. ⊠ *Lake Siutghiol. No phone. No credit cards.*

$$$$ 🏨 **Rex.** One of King Carol's former residences, this four-star hotel is the largest of all the hostelries in Mamaia. Unlike most of the communist-style accommodations one must choose from in the area, the Rex has true grandeur. ⊠ *Staţiunea Mamaia.* ☎ *041/831595,* 𝖥𝖠𝖷 *041/862292. 102 rooms with bath. Restaurant, bar, cafeteria, pool. AE, DC, MC, V.*

$$ 🏨 **Ambasador, Lido, and Savoy.** Among the many modern hotels, these three are all newly built and moderately priced. They are grouped in a horseshoe around open-air pools near the beach at the north end of the resort. Contact them through the Societatea Comercială Mamaia Hotel Bucrureşti (☎ 041/531025).

Tulcea
$$ 🏨 **Delta.** On the bank of the Danube, this spacious, modern hotel has good facilities. ⊠ *Str. Isaacei 2,* ☎ *040/514720,* 𝖥𝖠𝖷 *040/516260. 117 rooms. Restaurant, bar, cafeteria. No credit cards.*

TRANSYLVANIA

Transylvania, Romania's western province, offers travelers the chance to explore some of Europe's most beautiful and unspoiled villages and rural landscapes. The Carpathian Mountains, which separate Transylvania from Wallachia and Moldavia shielded the province from the Turks and Mongols during the Middle Ages. Germans and Hungarians settled in Transylvania during this period, building spectacular castles, towns, and churches. Since the 1980s many ethnic Germans have emigrated, but Transylvania, which was ruled by Hungary until 1920, is still home to a large Hungarian minority and to many of Romania's 2 million ethnic Gypsies. Many of Romania's most beautiful tourist spots can be found in Transylvania, but the lack of amenities outside of the main towns makes traveling difficult. Although private entrepreneurs are developing tourism, standards are not always satisfactory. One solution is to base yourself in a major town like Sibiu, Cluj, or Braşov and take day trips into the countryside.

Visitor Information
Braşov. (⊠ Aro-Palace, B-dul Eroilor 9, ☎ 068/142840).
Cluj. (⊠ Str. Şincai 2, ☎ 064/177778).
Sibiu. (⊠ Str. Cetăţii 1, ☎ 069/411788).

Getting Around

By Bus
Many tour agencies arrange coach trips to Transylvania. Local buses can be crowded and slow.

By Car
Travel by car is perhaps the best way to explore Transylvania's rich rural life. Rental cars, with or without drivers, are available through tourism offices and major hotels.

By Plane
There are regular flights from Bucharest to Cluj, Sibiu, and other major towns. Traveling by plane is a good option for those with limited time, given the slow train and bus services and the relatively inexpensive cost of air travel.

By Train
With many routes and speeds, rail journeys are cheapest for those prepared for their sometimes difficult conditions. To save time, travel by *expres* or *accelerat* services.

Guided Tours

The Romanian National Tourist office (ONT) and the Romanian Automobile Club (ACR) in Bucharest organize tours to Transylvania, as do an increasing number of private companies. The itineraries of "Dracula" tours combine locations figuring in Bram Stoker's *Dracula* with those connected to the primary historical source of the novel.

Exploring Transylvania

The wooded Carpathian mountains provide a scenic backdrop to the medieval town of **Braşov,** the gateway to Transylvania for those starting their journey in Bucharest. Braşov, known as Kronstadt to the Saxon merchants who settled in the city during the 13th century, was keen to exploit trade routes with Turkey and the Orient. Like many Romanian cities, Braşov underwent heavy industrialization during the communist period. Thankfully, however, much of the historic part of the city remains intact. Good amenities and the town's proximity to **Poiana Braşov,** Romania's best ski and mountain resort, and **Dracula's Castle** at **Bran** make it a popular tourist destination. The **Black Church,** the largest church between Vienna and Istanbul, dominates the old part of the town. The church backs onto **Piaţa Sfatului,** a splendid medieval square, with a **Romanian Orthodox Church** at No. 3, a museum in the 15th-century former town hall in the middle, and several pleasant cafés and restaurants. To the east of the square, toward **Mount Timpa** (and its cable car), one can see remnants of the old city wall and its seven towers built to protect the town from Turkish invasion.

Leaving Braşov you can either turn westward, following the spectacular **Fagaraş** range toward the town of **Sibiu,** or you can head northwest to **Sighişoara.** Along the road to Sighişoara you will find some of Transylvania's most enchanting villages. During the 12th and 13th centuries, Romania's Hungarian kings offered Saxon craftsmen land in return for settling in the region and defending it against raiders. Sadly, with the departure of ethnic Germans to Germany since the 1980s, many villages have fallen into disrepair. However, you can still find impressive fortified churches at **Homorod, Rupea,** and **Saschiz.**

Sighişoara's towers and spires can be seen from quite a distance before you reach this enchanting place. Towering above the modern town is a medieval **citadel** and upper town that must be among the least spoiled in Europe. Walking up from the city center, one enters the citadel through the 60-meter-tall **clock tower,** which dates from the 14th century. The tower houses the town's **History Museum,** which includes some moving photographs of the 1989 revolution that led to the execution of dictator Nicolae Ceauşescu and his wife, Elena. From the wooden gallery at the top of the tower, you can look out over the town with its terra-cotta roofs and painted houses. Opposite is a small ocher-colored house where the father of Vlad Ţepes, better known as **Dracula,** once lived. It is now a pleasant restaurant. Behind the restaurant, walking uphill along narrow, cobbled streets lined with faded pink, green, and more ocher houses, you'll come to a covered staircase. This leads to a 14th-century **Gothic church** and a leafy, ivy-filled **German cemetery,** which extends over the hilltop beyond the city walls.

★ **Cluj,** once the capital of Hungarian-ruled Transylvania and known as Kolozsvar to Hungarians, is some 170 kilometers (105 mi) northwest of Sighişoara. Nearly a quarter of Cluj's 320,000 inhabitants are ethnic Hungarians, and this elegant Habsburg city enjoys a rich cultural life, with good theaters, galleries, and concert halls. **Piaţa Unirii,** the main square, is dominated by **St Michael's,** a 14th-century Roman Catholic church with a huge 19th-century spire. In front of it is an imposing statue of **Matthias Corvinus,** the son of a Romanian prince, who became one of Hungary's greatest kings (1458–90). On the east side of the square is the **Art Museum,** which has an interesting permanent collection. To the west of the square is the **Ethnographic Museum,** which has one of Romania's best collections of costumes and carpets. Nearby, you'll find **Babes-Bolyai University,** one of the finest colleges in Romania, and, in the adjoining Piaţas Victoriei and Stefan Cel Mare, are the imposing **Romanian Orthodox Cathedral** (1921–33), a neo-Byzantine building with a huge cupola, the **Opera House,** and the local branch of the **Romanian National Theater.**

Sibiu was the main Saxon town in Transylvania. Like Sighişoara and Braşov, the town still has a distinctly German or Central European feel to it, even though there are few ethnic Germans left. The old part of the town centers around the magnificent **Piaţa Mare** (Great Square) and **Piaţa Mica** (Small Square), with their painted 17th-century town houses. On Piaţa Mare are the **Roman Catholic church,** a splendid high-Baroque building, and the **Brukenthal Museum.** This museum, housed in the palace of its founder, Samuel Brukenthal (Hapsburg governor from 1777 to 1787), has one of the most extensive collections of silver, paintings, and furniture in Romania. Next to Piaţa Mica you'll find the **Lutheran Cathedral,** a massive 14th- to 15th-century edifice with a simple, stark interior in total contrast to the Roman Catholic church just a couple of hundred meters away. On the outskirts of the town there is a large Gypsy community, complete with the ornate homes of their self-proclaimed leaders **King Cioba** and **Emperor Iulian.**

Dining and Lodging

Braşov

$–$$$ ✕ **Stradivari.** This is a new Italian-owned establishment with a pizzeria and a more expensive restaurant that serves pasta and seafood dishes. ✉ *Piaţa Sfatului 1,* ☎ *068/151165. No credit cards. Closed Wed.*

$ ✕ **Gustari.** This simple, bistro-type restaurant serves traditional Romanian dishes such as *ciorbă* (sour soups), *caşcaval pane* (fried cheese), and *clătite* (pancakes). ✉ *Piaţa Sfatului 14,* ☎ *068/150857. No credit cards. Open from 9 AM to 9 PM.*

$ ✕ **Timpa.** A new self-service restaurant located on the pedestrian mall, a couple of minutes from Piaţa Sfatului, Timpa serves pizza, excellent salads, and vegetarian offerings even in winter. This is the best place for a quick and inexpensive meal. ✉ *Str. Republicii. No credit cards. Closed Sun.*

$$$ ⊞ **Aro Palace.** Architecturally a typical communist-era hotel built in the 1950s, the Aro Palace lacks charm but is comfortable, has good facilities, and is close to the main tourist attractions in the town center. ✉ *Bdul Eroilor 27,* ☎ *068/142840,* ⅋ℵ *068/150427. 262 double rooms, 30 single rooms, 15 suites. 2 restaurants, café, pool, barbershop, currency exchange, parking. AE, DC, MC, V.*

$$ ⊞ **Coroana.** This turn-of-the-century two-star hotel, formerly called the Postăvarul, has seen better days. Though shabby, the rooms are clean and spacious and the hotel is only a few minutes' walk from the cafés, restaurants, and attractions of Piaţa Sfatului. ✉ *Str. Republicii 62,* ☎ *068/144330,* ⅋ℵ *068/141505. 319 rooms. 2 restaurants, currency exchange, parking. AE, MC, V.*

Cluj

$$$$ ✕⊞ **Transylvania.** Formerly the Belvedere, the Transylvania is a modern, seven-story hotel situated on top of Cetăţuia Hill just 15 minutes' walk from the city center. It is clean, warm in winter, and offers many facilities, including two good but inexpensive restaurants. The hotel itself lacks charm but has excellent views of the town and the surrounding countryside. ✉ *Str. Călăraşi 1,* ☎ *064/134466,* ⅋ℵ *064/136910. 156 rooms. 2 restaurants, pool, barbershop, beauty salon, sauna, exercise room, currency exchange, parking. AE, DC, MC, V.*

$$$ ✕⊞ **Casa Alba.** This is a small, privately run hotel in a pleasant residential district on Cetăţuia Hill. ✉ *Str. Racoviţa 22,* ☎ *064/132315. 18 rooms. Restaurant, bar, parking.*

$$$ ✕⊞ **Continental.** Right on the central square with views of St. Michael's Cathedral, this turn-of-the-century hotel has gotten dumpy lately, but has preserved some of its former elegance. ✉ *Str. Napoca 1,* ☎ *064/ 111441,* ⅋ℵ *064/111152. 91 rooms. 2 restaurants, currency exchange.*

Sibiu

$$$ ✕⊞ **Împăratul Romanilor.** This turn-of-the-century hotel, conveniently situated in the town center, is considered by many to be Romania's best provincial hotel. Rooms are attractively decorated with paintings and locally made furniture. The restaurant, open to nonresidents, is the best eatery in Sibiu, with a lively floor show and discotheque on weekends. ✉ *Str. Nicolae Bălcescu 4,* ☎ *069/416490,* ⅋ℵ *069/413278. Restaurant, antiques shop, currency exchange. AE, DC, MC, V.*

Sighişoara

$$ ✕ **Casa Vlad Dracul.** Occupying a house where the father of Vlad Ţepes, once lived, this pleasant bar and restaurant is the best place in town for a meal. On the first floor you can drink draft beer from a tankard and sit at wooden tables. Upstairs, you'll find a cozy restaurant with fittingly Gothic-style furniture that serves good soups and traditional Romanian dishes. It closes early, however—9 PM. ✉ *Str. Cositorarilor 5,* ☎ *065/771596.*

$ ⊞ **Steaua.** This 19th-century hotel has seen better days. Though the lobby is worn, the rooms are spacious and clean and the staff is helpful. The restaurant serves reasonably priced local dishes. ✉ *Str. 1 Decembrie 12,* ☎ *065/771954. 121 rooms. Restaurant, bar, nightclub, parking.*

25 Slovakia

Bratislava

Highlights of Slovakia

EVEN IF IT HAD NOT DEVELOPED SEPARATELY for nearly a millennium under Hungarian and Hapsburg rule, the newly independent Slovak Republic would be different from its Czech neighbor (☞ Chapter 7) in many respects. The mountains are higher here; the veneer less sophisticated. The people seem more outgoing, and the folk culture is particularly rich.

Although they speak a language closely related to Czech, the Slovaks have a strong sense of national identity. United in the 9th century as part of the Great Moravian Empire, the Slovaks were conquered a century later by the Magyars and remained under Hungarian domination until 1918. After the Tartar invasions of the 13th century, many Saxons were invited to resettle the land, exploit its rich mineral resources, and develop the economy. In the 15th and 16th centuries, Romanian shepherds migrated from Wallachia through the Carpathians into Slovakia. The merging of these varied groups with the resident Slavs further enriched the native folk culture.

Bratislava, the capital of Hungary for nearly 250 years until 1784, and now the capital of the new republic, was once a city filled with picturesque streets and Gothic churches. Forty years of communist rule left a clear mark on the city, hiding its ancient beauty with hulking, and now dilapidated, futurist structures. Take time, however, to walk the streets of the Old Town, now undergoing frenzied revitalization. The city has many good concert halls, restaurants, and wine bars.

Most visitors head for the great peaks of the High Tatras. The smallest Alpine range in the world—and the reason Slovakia can claim to be the Switzerland of Central Europe—the Tatras rise magnificently from the foothills of northern Slovakia. The tourist infrastructure here is very good, catering especially to hikers and skiers. Visitors who come to admire the peaks, however, often overlook some of the area's subtler attractions. The exquisite medieval towns of the Spiš region below the Tatras and the beautiful 18th-century wood churches farther east are well worth exploring.

ESSENTIAL INFORMATION

Before You Go

When to Go

Organized sightseeing tours run from April or May through October. Many tours are run by Satur Tours and Travel; once a division of Čedok (the government-owned travel agency of former Czechoslovakia), Satur will probably be privatized in the future. Some monuments, especially castles, either close entirely or have shorter hours in winter. Hotel rates drop during the off-season except during festivals. The High Tatra mountains come into their own in winter (Dec.–Feb.), when skiers from all over Eastern Europe crowd the slopes and resorts. If you're not into skiing, visit the mountains in late spring (May or June) or fall, when the hills bloom with flowers, and you'll have the hotels and restaurants pretty much to yourself.

CLIMATE

The following are the average daily maximum and minimum temperatures for Bratislava.

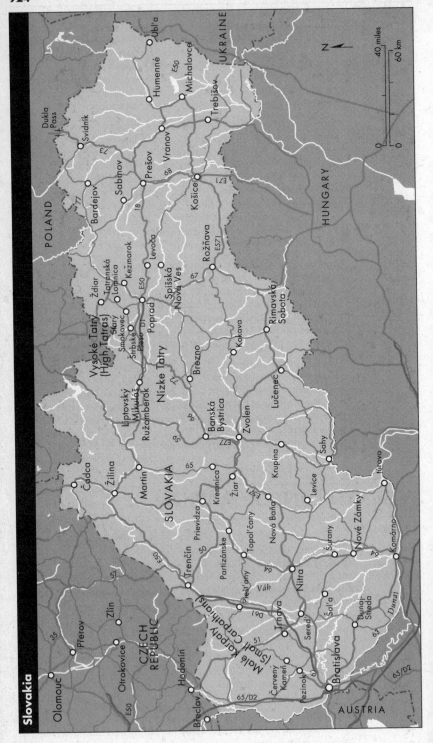

Slovakia

Jan.	36F	2C	**May**	70F	21C	**Sept.**	72F	22C
	27	– 3		52	11		54	12
Feb.	39F	4C	**June**	75F	24C	**Oct.**	59F	15C
	28	– 2		57	14		45	7
Mar.	48F	9C	**July**	79F	26C	**Nov.**	46F	8C
	34	1		61	16		37	3
Apr.	61F	16C	**Aug.**	79F	26C	**Dec.**	39F	4C
	43	6		61	16		32	0

Currency

The unit of currency in Slovakia is the crown, or koruna, written as Sk., and divided into 100 halierov. There are bills of 20, 50, 100, 200, 500, 1,000, and 5,000 Sk., and coins of 10, 20, and 50 halierov and 1, 2, 5, and 10 Sk.

At press time (spring 1996), the rate of exchange was around 30 Sk. to the American dollar, 21 Sk. to the Canadian dollar, and 46 Sk. to the pound sterling.

What It Will Cost

Costs are highest in Bratislava and only slightly less in the High Tatra resorts and main spas, although even in those places you can now find bargain private accommodations. The least expensive areas are central and eastern Slovakia.

SAMPLE PRICES

Cup of coffee, 10 Sk.; beer (½ liter), 15 Sk.; Coca-Cola, 10 Sk.–15 Sk.; ham sandwich, 30 Sk.; 1-mile taxi ride, 100 Sk.

MUSEUMS

Admission fees to museums and castles range from 5 Sk. to 50 Sk.

Visas

U.S. and British citizens do not need visas to enter Slovakia. Visa requirements have been temporarily reintroduced for Canadian citizens; check with the consulate to determine whether this is still the case. Apply to the Consulate of the Slovak Republic (⊠ 50 Rideau Terrace, Ottawa, Ontario K1M 2A1, ☎ 613/749–4442).

Customs

ON ARRIVAL

Valuable items should be entered on your customs declaration. You can bring in 250 cigarettes (or their equivalent in tobacco), 2 liters of wine, 1 liter of spirits, and ½ liter of eau de cologne.

ON DEPARTURE

There is no limit on the amount of goods purchased for non-commercial use, but to be on the safe side, hang on to all receipts. Only antiques bought at specially designated shops may be exported.

Language

Slovak, a western-Slavic tongue closely related to both Czech and Polish, is the official language of Slovakia. English is popular among young people, but German is still the most useful language for tourists.

Getting Around

By Car

ROAD CONDITIONS

Main roads are often narrow but adequate. Traffic is light, especially away from main centers. Outside of **Bratislava**, a car is incredibly useful, especially when exploring central and eastern Slovakia, where many of the interesting sights are difficult to reach by mass transit.

Drive on the right. Speed limits are 60 kph (37 mph) in built-up areas, 90 kph (55 mph) on open roads, and 110 kph (68 mph) on expressways. Seat belts are compulsory; drinking and driving is strictly prohibited.

GASOLINE
Gasoline is expensive, averaging $2.50 a gallon. Service stations are usually located along main roads on the outskirts of towns and cities. Finding a station in Bratislava can be difficult. Fill up on the freeway as you approach the city to avoid frustration. Lead-free gasoline, known as "natural," is still available only at select stations, so tank up when you see it.

BREAKDOWNS
In case of breakdown in Bratislava, contact the 24-hour service (☏ 07/249404). The *Auto Atlas SR* (available at any bookstore) has a list of emergency road-repair numbers in various towns. If you have an accident and need an ambulance, call the emergency number (☏ 155).

By Train
Train service is erratic to all but the largest cities—**Poprad, Prešov, Košice,** and **Banská Bystrica.** Make sure to take the express trains marked R or the fast Intercity trains. Good, if slow, electric rail service, connects Poprad with the resorts of the **High Tatras.** If you're going just to the Tatras, you won't need any other kind of transportation.

By Bus
Bus and tram service in Bratislava is very cheap and reasonably frequent, and you can use it with confidence to reach any of the places in the tours below. The timetables can be confusing, so be sure to confirm your itinerary.

The bus network in Slovakia is dense, linking all the towns on the tours given here. If going this route, however, leave a couple of extra days to compensate for infrequent service to the smaller towns.

Staying in Slovakia

Telephones
LOCAL CALLS
These cost 2 Sk. from a pay phone. Lift the receiver, place the coin in the holder, dial, and insert the coin when your party picks up. Public phones are on street corners; unfortunately, they're often out of order. Try asking in a hotel if you're stuck. If you plan to make several local or out-of-town calls, it would be advisable to consider buying a phone card. They can be bought at most newsstands or at any post office and cost 100 Sk. for 50 local calls.

INTERNATIONAL CALLS
There's automatic dialing to many countries, including North America and the United Kingdom. For international inquiries, dial 0132 for the United States, Canada, or the United Kingdom. To place a call via an **AT&T** USADirect international operator, dial 00–420–00101; for **MCI,** dial 00–42–000112; for **Sprint,** dial 0042–087–187.

COUNTRY CODE
The country code for Slovakia is 42.

Mail
POSTAL RATES
Airmail letters to the United States and Canada cost 11 Sk. up to 10 grams, postcards 6 Sk. Airmail letters to the United Kingdom cost 8 Sk. up to 20 grams, postcards 5 Sk.

Mail can be sent to "poste restante" at any main post office; there's no charge.

Opening and Closing Times

Banks are open weekdays 8–3. **Museums** are usually open Tues.–Sun. 10–5. **Shops** are generally open weekdays 9–6 (Thurs. 9–8); some close between noon and 2. Many are also open Sat. 9–noon (department stores, 9–4).

National Holidays

January 1 (Day of founding of the Slovak Republic); April 4 and 7 (Good Friday and Easter Monday); May 1 (Labor Day); July 5 (Sts. Cyril and Methodius); August 29 (anniversary of the Slovak National Uprising); September 1 (Constitution Day); September 1 (All Saints Day); September 15 (Lady of the Sorrows); December 24–26 (Christmas Holiday).

Dining

The options in Slovakia include restaurants, wine cellars, the more down-to-earth beer taverns, cafeterias, and a growing number of coffee shops and snack bars. Most restaurants are remarkably reasonable, but privatization is beginning to push up prices in a few places.

The most typical main dishes are roast pork, duck, or goose, served with sauerkraut and some type of dumpling or potatoes, generally with a rich gravy. Peppers are frequently used as well to spice up bland entrées. Look for *halušky,* a tasty Slovak noodle dish, usually served with sheep cheese. Fresh green vegetables and salads are still rare, but there are plenty of the pickled variety. Be sure to try *palačinky,* a delicious treat of crepes stuffed with fruit and ice cream or jam.

WHAT TO WEAR

A jacket is suggested for higher-priced restaurants. Otherwise, casual dress is acceptable.

MEALTIMES

Lunch is usually from 11:30 to 2 or 3; dinner from 6 to 9:30 or 10. Some places are open all day, and in Bratislava you might find it easier to find a table during off hours.

RATINGS

Prices are reasonable by American standards, even in the more expensive restaurants. The following prices are for meals made up of a first course, main course, and dessert (excluding wine and tip).

CATEGORY	COST
$$$$	over 600 Sk.
$$$	400 Sk.–600 Sk.
$$	200 Sk.–400 Sk.
$	under 200 Sk.

Lodging

Slovakia's hotel industry has been slow to react to the political and economic changes that have taken place since 1989. Few new hotels have been built, and many of the older hotels are still majority-owned by the state. The good news is that many older properties are gradually being renovated, and the best have great character and style. There is still an acute shortage of hotel rooms during the peak season, so make reservations well in advance. Many private room agencies are now in operation, and as long as you arrive before 9 PM, you should be able to get a room. Brace yourself for faulty plumbing, indifferent reception clerks, and more.

These are officially graded with from one to five stars by Satur, the country's largest travel agency. Many foreign visitors stay at Interhotels—often owned by Satur—which are mainly in the three- to five-star categories. Most of the rooms in these hotels have baths or showers.

Satur and other tourist information services can help you find a private room in Bratislava and other large cities. These accommodations are invariably cheaper (around $20) and often more comfortable than hotels, though you may have to sacrifice some privacy. You can also wander the main roads looking for signs reading ROOM FREE, or more frequently, in German, ZIMMER FREI or PRIVATZIMMER.

Prices are for double rooms, generally not including breakfast. Prices at the lower end of the scale apply to low season. At certain periods, such as Easter or during festivals, there may be an increase of 15%–25%.

CATEGORY	COST
$$$$	over 3,200 Sk.
$$$	1,600 Sk.–3,200 Sk.
$$	480 Sk.–1,600 Sk.
$	under 480 Sk.

Tipping

Although many Slovaks still tip in restaurants by rounding up the bill to the nearest multiple of 10, higher tipping is beginning to catch on. For good service, 10% is considered an appropriate reward on very large tabs. Tip porters 20 Sk. For room service, a 20 Sk. tip is enough. In taxis, round up the bill to the nearest multiple of 10. Give tour guides and helpful concierges between 20 Sk. and 30 Sk. for services rendered.

BRATISLAVA

Arriving and Departing

By Plane

As few international airlines land in Bratislava, the most convenient international airport for Slovakia is Vienna's Schwechat Airport, approximately 50 kilometers (30 miles) from Bratislava. Four buses a day stop at Schwechat en route to Bratislava, or you could even take a taxi; the journey takes just over an hour, depending on the border crossing. From Prague's Ruzyně Airport you can take a Czech Airlines (ČSA) flight to Bratislava; the flight takes about an hour.

If time is a factor during your stay in Slovakia, consider flying to the relatively far-flung Tatras and eastern Slovakia. During peak tourist season, ČSA has reasonably priced flights from Prague and Bratislava to Poprad (the regional airport for the Tatras). For further information, contact the ČSA offices in Prague (☎ 02/20104111) or Bratislava (☎ 07/361042 or 07/361045).

By Train

Reasonably efficient train service connects Prague and Bratislava. Trains leave from Prague's two main stations (Hlavní Nádraží and Nádraží Holešovice). The journey takes from five to six hours depending on the train. Unless you crave adventure, take the Intercity trains for their speed and safety. There are several trains a day to and from Vienna's Wien-Mitte and Südbahnhof stations; the journey takes just over an hour. The train station in Bratislava has a tourist information booth that can be very helpful with traveling tips and finding accommodation in the city.

By Bus

There are many buses from Prague to Bratislava; the trip costs around 200 Sk. and takes about five hours. From Vienna, there are four buses a day from Autobusbahnhof Wien-Mitte. These take between 1½ and two hours. The **Autobus Stanica** (station) in Bratislava is outside the center; take Trolleybus 217 to Mierové námestie or Bus 107 to the castle (Hrad).

By Car

There are good freeways from Prague to Bratislava via Brno (D1 and D2); the 315-kilometer (203-mile) journey takes about 3½ hours. From Vienna, take the A4 and then Route 8 to Bratislava. The 60-kilometer (37-mile) trip will take about 1½ hours.

Getting Around

By Car

Driving can be difficult in Bratislava and parking spaces are at a premium in the city center; hence, for touring the republic's capital, foot power will be the most effective way of seeing the sights. If you do need to rent a car, you can do so either at Satur or at the Hotel Forum. Watch out for no-parking zones or you get the boot, and have to pay a hefty fine to have it removed.

By Bus

Bus and tram service in Bratislava is cheap, fairly frequent, and convenient for getting to the main sights. Buy tickets ahead of time at any newspaper stand or at automatic ticket dispensers for 5 Sk. each and stamp them when you enter the bus or tram.

Important Addresses and Numbers

Embassies

U.S. (✉ Huiezdoslavovo námestie 4, ☎ 07/330861, FAX 07/335439). **U.K.** (✉ Grosslingova 35, ☎ 07/364420, FAX 07/364396). **Canadian.** (✉ Kolarska 4, ☎ 07/361277, FAX 07/361220).

Emergencies

Police (☎ 158). **Ambulance** (☎ 155).

LATE-NIGHT PHARMACIES

Lekárne (pharmacies) take turns staying open late or on Sunday. Look for the list posted on the front door of each pharmacy. For after-hours service, ring the bell; you will be served through a little hatch-door.

Visitor Information

Bratislava has its own information service, **Bratislava Tourist Information** (✉ BIS, Panská 18, ☎ 07/5333715 or 07/5334370). The office is in the Old Town, a few steps down from Hlavné námestie, and can supply visitors with information about accommodations. It's open weekdays 9–5 (8–6 in summer) and Saturday 9–12. **Satur Tours and Travel**—the largest, with 54 offices all around Slovakia—can set you up with a hotel; a tour; and train, rail, and bus tickets. The main office is in Bratislava (✉ Jesenské 5, ☎ 07/367613 or 07/367624, FAX 07/323816; ☉ Weekdays 9–6, Sat. 9–noon). Satur's U.S. representative is **Slovakia Travel Service** (✉ 10 E. 40th St., Suite 3601, New York, NY 10016, ☎ 212/213–3865, FAX 212/213–4461).

Guided Tours

The best tours of Bratislava are offered by **BIS** (☞ Visitor Information, *above*) which can arrange a tour in a vintage coach or a tour with an individual guide for a very reasonable price. Both **BIS** and **Satur** (☞ Visitor Information, *above*) offer worthwhile one-day tours of castles and the Small Carpathian mountains close to Bratislava.

Exploring Bratislava

Expecting a Slovak version of Prague or Vienna, many visitors to Bratislava are disappointed to discover instead a city with more than its fair share of high-rise housing projects, faded supermodern structures, and less-than-inspiring monuments to carefully chosen acts of heroism. But Europe's newest capital city is on the move. Everywhere you look new shops are opening and older buildings are being renovated—as if the city's residents were trying to forget as quickly as possible the past 40 years of playing second fiddle to Prague. Avoid the newer, and shabbier, parts of the city and head toward the Danube River to discover the peace and beauty of the Staré Mesto (Old Town) and its Gothic and Renaissance architectural treasures.

Numbers in the margin correspond to points of interest on the Bratislava map.

❶ Begin your tour of the city at the modern square **Námestie SNP.** An abbreviation for Slovenské Národné Povstanie (Slovak National Uprising), these three letters appear on streets, squares, bridges, and posters throughout Slovakia. This anti-Nazi resistance movement involved partisan fighting, organized partly but not exclusively by the communists, in Slovakia's mountainous areas during the final years of the war. In 1992 this was the center for demonstrations in support of Slovak independence, and you can often see the Slovak flag (red, blue, and white with a double cross) flying from a partisan's gun.

❷ From here walk up to a bustling town square, **Hurbanovo námestie.** Across the road, next to a large shoe store, is the enchanting entrance to the Old Town. A small bridge, decorated with statues of St. John Nepomuk and St. Michael, takes you over the old moat, now blossoming with trees and fountains, into the intricate barbican, a set of gates and houses that were part of the Old Town's medieval fortifications. After passing through the first archway, you come to the narrow **Michalská ulica**
❸ (Michael's Street); in front of you is the **Michalská brána** (Michael's Gate), the last remaining of the city's three original gates.

❹ A little farther down Michalská ulica on the right is the **Palác Uhorskej král'ovskej komory** (Hungarian Royal Chamber), a Baroque palace that housed the Hungarian nobles' parliament from 1802 until 1848; it is now used as the university library. Go through the arched passageway at the back of this building and you'll come to a tiny square dominated
★ by the **Church and Convent of the Poor Clares.**

Follow Farská ulica up to the corner, and turn left on **Kapitulská ulica,** noticing the paving stone depicting two kissing lizards. At the bottom
❺ of the street is the side wall of the **Dóm svätého Martina** (St. Martin's Cathedral). Construction of this massive Gothic church, with its 280-foot steeple twinkling with gold trim, began in the 14th century. Between the 16th and 19th centuries, the cathedral saw the coronation of 17 Hungarian royals.

As you leave the church and walk around to the front, the freeway leads
❻ to the futuristic bridge, **Most SNP.** Follow the steps under the passageway

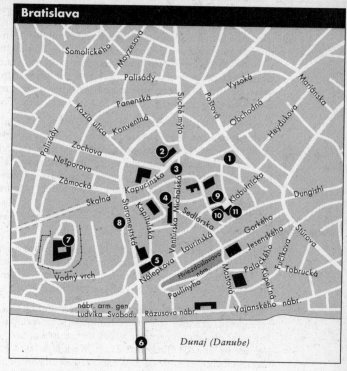

and up the other side in the direction of the historic castle, Bratislavský
Hrad.

NEED A
BREAK?

At the top of the wooden stairs, you come to **Arkadia,** one of
Bratislava's better private establishments, situated in a beautiful old
house. Here you can fuel up before your ascent to the Castle.

---

❼ Continue up the steps, through a Gothic arched gateway built in 1480,
until you reach the **Bratislavský Hrad** (castle) area. The original fortifications date from the 9th century. The Hungarian kings expanded the
castle into a large royal residence, and the Hapsburgs turned it into a
very successful defense against the Turks. Its current design, square with
four corner towers, stems from the 17th century, although the existing
castle had to be completely rebuilt after a disastrous fire in 1811. In the
castle, you'll find the **Slovenské národné múzeum** (Slovak National Museum). The exhibits cover glassmaking, medieval warfare, and minting.
✉ *Zámocká ul.,* ☎ *07/332985.* ✎ *40 Sk.* ⊙ *Tues.–Sun., 10–5.*

❽ Leave the castle by the same route, but instead of climbing the last stairs
by the Arkadia restaurant, continue down the Old World thoroughfare called the **Beblaveho.** Continue along **Židovská ulica.** The name,
Jews' Street, identifies this area as the former Jewish ghetto. Walk up
Židovská until you come to a thin concrete bridge that connects with
the reconstructed city walls across the freeway.

Across the road you'll find steps leading down into the Old Town. Go
through Františkánske námestie into the adjoining square, **Hlavné námestie,** which is lined with old houses and palaces representing the spec-
trum of architectural styles from Gothic (No. 2), through Baroque (No.
4) and Rococo (No. 7), to a wonderfully decorative example of Art Nouveau (No. 10). To your immediate left as you come into the square is

❾ the richly decorated **Jezuitský kostol** (Jesuit Church). Next door is the colorful jumble of Gothic and Renaissance arcades, archways, and au-
❿ dience halls that makes up the **Stará radnica** (Old Town Hall). Walk through the vaulted passageway, still with early Gothic ribbing, into a wonderfully cheery Renaissance courtyard with romantic gables. Toward the back of the courtyard, you'll find the entrance to the **Mestské múzeum** (City Museum), which documents Bratislava's rocky past. ⊠ *Primaciálne nám.,* ☏ *07/5333800.* ▨ *10 Sk.* ⊙ *Tues.–Sun. 10–5.*

Leaving by the back entrance of the Old Town Hall, you come to the **Primaciálne námestie** (Primates' Square), with the glorious pale pink,
⓫ classical elegance of the **Primaciálny palác** (Primates' Palace) taking pride of place. If the building is open, go up to the dazzling Hall of Mirrors. In this room, Napoléon and Hapsburg Emperor Francis I signed the Peace of Bratislava of 1805, following Napoléon's victory at the Battle of Austerlitz.

Shopping

You will find plenty of folk art and souvenir shops along **Obchodná ulica** (shopping street) as well as on **Námestie SNP.** Stores still come and go in the city that is undergoing a metamorphosis, so don't be too surprised if some of those listed have vanished.

There are several **DIELO** stores which feature works by Slovak artists and craftspeople at reasonable prices. Paintings, some creative wooden toys, and great ceramic and pottery pieces are featured at two of these standing side by side (⊠ Obchodná 27, ⊙ Weekdays 10–5 and Sat. 9–12, and ⊠ Obchodná33, MC, ⊙ Weekdays 1–7 and Sat.–Sun. 10-1; these accept Visa). A larger one (⊠ Námestie SNP 12, ⊙ Weekdays 10–1 and 12–6, Sat. 10–12; AE, MC, V) also has designer jewelry and clothing.

Folk, Folk (⊠ Obchodná 10, ☏ 07/5334292) has a large collection of Slovak folk art, including crystal, pottery, hand-woven table cloths, wooden articles, and dolls in folk costumes.

Folk Art (Námestie SNP 12, ☏ 07/323802) has a nice selection of hand-painted table pottery and vases, wooden figures, and folk costumes. Check out the corn-husk figures here; they can be quite beautiful (and dirt cheap), though difficult to transport.

Dining

Prague may have its Slovak rival beat when it comes to architecture, but when it's time to eat, you can thank those lucky red stars you still see around town that you're in Bratislava. The long-shared history with Hungary gives Slovak cuisine an extra fire that Czech cooking—many gourmands will admit—generally lacks. Bratislava's proximity to Vienna, moreover, has lent something of grace and charm to the city's eateries. The happy result is that you'll seldom see plain pork and dumplings on the menu. Instead, prepare for a variety of shish kebabs, grilled meats, steaks, and pork dishes, all spiced to enliven the palate and served (if you're lucky) with those special noodles Slovaks call halušky. Keep in mind that the city's many street stands offer a price-conscious alternative to restaurant dining. In addition to the ubiquitous hot dogs and hamburgers (no relation to their American namesakes), try some *langoš*—flat, deep-fried, and delicious pieces of dough, usually seasoned with garlic.

For details and price-category definitions, *see* Dining *in* Staying in Slovakia, *above.*

$$$$ ╳ **Arkadia.** The elegant setting, at the threshold of Bratislava Castle, sets the tone for a luxurious evening of shish kebobs and steaks. There are several dining rooms to choose from, ranging from intimate to boisterous, all decorated with period 19th-century furnishings. Come here by taxi and enjoy the 15-minute and mostly downhill walk back into town. ✉ *Zámocké schody,* ☎ *07/5335650. Jacket and tie. AE, DC, MC, V.*

$$$ ╳ **Klaštorná Vináreň.** Old Town dining can be a delight in the vaulted
★ cellars of this old monastery. Wash down *čikós tokáň* (a fiery mixture of pork, onions, and peppers) with a glass of mellow red wine and a fire hose. *Bravcové ražníci* is milder, a tender pork shish kebab with fried potatoes. ✉ *Františkánská ul. 1,* ☎ *07/5330430. AE. Closed Sun.*

$$ ╳ **Modrá Hviezda.** The first of a new breed of small, privately owned wine cellars, the "Blue Star" eschews the international standards in favor of regional fare. Try the *bryndza* (baked sheep-cheese) pie and the tasty goulash. ✉ *Beblavého 14,* ☎ *07/332747. No credit cards.*

$ ╳ **Pekná Brána.** With more than 75 main-course meals from which to choose, this is not a place for the indecisive. The menus at this old-fashioned, cozy restaurant include Chinese and vegetarian cuisines, as well as traditional Slovak specialties. You can also sit in the newly added back rooms and the cellar to enjoy a fireplace and various tasty dishes all made on an open roast grill. The restaurant is open daily from 9:30 am to midnight, the cellar until sunrise. ✉ *Obchodná ul. 39,* ☎ *07/323008. AE, MC, V.*

$ ╳ **Stará Sladovňa.** This mammoth beer hall is known lovingly, and fittingly, as "Mamut" to Bratislavans. Locals come here for the Bohemian beer on tap and for inexpensive, filling meals. The place seats almost 2,000, so don't worry about reservations. ✉ *Cintorínska ul. 32,* ☎ *07/321151. No credit cards.*

Lodging

For details and price-category definitions, *see* Lodging *in* Staying in Slovakia, *above.*

$$$$ ▥ **Danube.** Opened in 1992, this French-run hotel on the bank of the
★ Danube has quickly developed a reputation for superior facilities and service. The modern rooms are done in tasteful pastels; the gleaming public areas are everything you expect from an international hotel chain. Of all the hotels in Bratislava, this one wins hands down for location—alongside the river, with a stunning view of the castle out the front door. ✉ *Rybné nám. 1,* ☎ *07/5340833,* FAX *07/5314311. 280 rooms. Restaurants, pool, health club, nightclub. AE, DC, MC, V.*

$$$$ ▥ **Forum Bratislava.** The Forum opened in 1989 in downtown Bratislava, offering top facilities. It houses a French as well as a Slovak restaurant and several cafés and bars. ✉ *Hodžovo nám. 2,* ☎ *07/348111,* FAX *07/314645. 219 rooms. 3 restaurants, 2 bars, café, pool, saunas, health club, nightclub. AE, DC, MC, V.*

$$ ▥ **Hotel Echo.** This small, bright, affordable hotel is near the center of Bratislava. It has a friendly staff, great breakfasts, and rooms that are wheelchair-accessible. ✉ *Presovská ul. 39,* ☎ *07/329170,* FAX *07/329174. 66 rooms. Restaurant. MC, V.*

The Arts and Nightlife

Bratislava does not have a roaring nightlife scene, so stick to the classics. The **Slovak Philharmonic Orchestra** puts on excellent concerts at the Reduta (✉ Medená 3, ☎ 07/333351). **Slovenské Národné Divadlo** (✉ Hviezdoslavo Námestie 1, ☎ 07/321146) offers high quality opera and ballet performances at bargain prices.

For listings of events, including the fall jazz festival, look in Bratislava's English-language newspaper, *The Slovak Spectator,* or ask at **BIS** (☞ Visitor Information, *above*).

HIGHLIGHTS OF SLOVAKIA

Outside of Bratislava, the great peaks of the High Tatras remain the prime destination for most travelers. In this resort region, the hotels are excellent and there are many tours to introduce visitors to some of the most beautiful mountains in Europe. The hills *are* spectacular, but also worth seeing are the brooding medieval towns of the **Spiš region** below the High Tatras and the lovely 18th-century country churches just to east. Away from main centers, these latter areas are short on tourist amenities, so if creature comforts are crucial, stick to the Tatras.

Getting Around

If you want to travel by plane, **ČSA's** 40-minute flights from Bratislava to Poprad connect with services from Prague and are reasonably priced. For information on other transportation in Slovakia, *see* Getting Around *in* Essential Information, *above.*

Guided Tours

Satur's seven-day **Grand Tour of Slovakia,** which leaves from Bratislava every other Saturday from June through September, stops in the High Tatras, Kežmarok, Košice, and Banská Bystrica. The tour includes all meals and accommodations. For more information, contact the Satur office in Bratislava (☎ 07/367613).

Slovair offers a novel biplane flight over the Tatras from Poprad airport. Contact the Satur office in Poprad (☎ 092/23430). The Satur office in Starý Smokovec (☎ 0969/2417) is also helpful in arranging tours of the Tatras and the surrounding area.

Visitor Information

Bardejov (✉ Radnicné nam. 21, ☎ 0935/551064).
Košice (✉ Hlavná 8, ☎ 095/186).
Prešov (✉ Hlavná ul. 42, ☎ 091/731113).
Smokovec (✉ Starý Smokovec V/22, ☎ 0969/3127).
Žilina (✉ Burianová medzierka 4, ☎ 089/23171).

Exploring Slovakia

Despite its charms, there's no denying that Bratislava is intensely industrial. If you're not going on to the mountains and fresh air of the High Tatras, a good one- or two-day natural respite can be had less than an hour north of the city, in the **Malé Karpaty** (Small Carpathians). Drive or take the bus to the dusty wine-making town of **Modra,** and from there, follow the signs to **Zochová Chata,** some 8 kilometers (5 miles) away in the hills. The Chata is really a cozy mountain chalet, with big rooms, plenty of period furniture, and a romantic *koliba* (tavern) that serves the best roast chicken in Slovakia. From here, trails fan out in all directions. For a full day's walk, follow the yellow-marked path about three hours to the Renaissance castle **Červený Kameň** ("Red Rock"). The blue-marked path will take you back to Zochová Chata.

The Spiš Region

Whether you travel by car, bus, or train, your route will follow the Vah Valley for most of the way to **Poprad,** a transit point for Slovakia's most magnificent natural treasure, the High Tatras. Although Poprad itself is a dreary place, its suburb of **Spišská Sobota,** reached by Buses 2, 3, or 4, is a little gem. It was one of 24 small Gothic towns in the medieval region known as **Spiš.** Steep shingled roofs, high timber-framed gables, and arched brick doorways are the main features of Spišská Sobata's historic dwellings. The lovely old square—itself a nearly perfect ensemble of Renaissance houses—features a Romanesque church, **Sv. Juraj** (St. George's), rebuilt in the early 16th century. The church's ornate altar is the work of Pavel of Levoča, one of the great woodcarvers of the 16th century. The **museum** is worth a visit. 🖃 4 Sk. ☉ Mon.–Sat. 9–4.

The High Tatras

Both an electric train network and a winding highway link Poprad with the resorts spread about on the lower slopes of the High Tatras. **Štrbské Pleso** is the highest of the towns and the best launching point for mountain excursions. A rewarding two-hour trek of moderate difficulty leads from here to **Popradské Pleso,** one of dozens of tiny, isolated Alpine lakes that dot the Tatras. **Smokovec** is really three resorts in one (Starý, Nový, and Horný) and has the most varied amenities. For the most effortless high-level trip, though, go to **Tatranská Lomnica,** from which a two-stage cable car will take you via Skalnaté Pleso to Lomnický štít, which at 8,635 feet is the second-highest peak in the range. From Skalnaté Pleso, you can take the red-marked Magistrale Trail down to **Hrebienok,** where you can board a funicular and ride down to Starý Smokovec. The **Museum of the Tatra National Park** at Tatranská Lomnica offers an excellent introduction to the area's natural and human history. 🖃 6 Sk. ☉ Weekdays 8:30–noon and 1–5, weekends 8–noon.

Levoča

Leave Poprad on Highway 18 heading east. Restoration work on
★ **Levoča,** the most famous of the Spiš towns, is well under way, and the overlays of Renaissance on Gothic are extremely satisfying to the eye (note especially Nos. 43, 45, 47, and 49 on the main square). Pavel of
★ Levoča's work on the main altar of **Sv. Jakub** (St. Jacob's) on the main square is monumental in size and exquisite in its detail. The surrounding countryside is dotted with more medieval towns. About 16 kilometers (10 miles) to the east, the massive, partly restored ruins of **Spiš Castle,** above Spišské Podhradie, dominate the surrounding pastures and orchards. Some of **Prešov's** fortifications survive, and its spindle-shape main square is lined with buildings in Gothic, Renaissance, and Baroque styles.

The Šariš Region

You have now left Spiš and entered **Šariš,** a region whose proximity to the Orthodox east has left a unique legacy of both Orthodox and
★ Greek Catholic (Uniate) churches. **Bardejov** is a splendid walled town and makes the best center from which to set out on a journey. Be prepared, though, to get lost along some rough minor roads while seeking out the 17th- and 18th-century wooden churches of **Bodružal, Ladomirová, Mirola,** and **Šemetkovce**—and the right person to open them up for you. You'll find these churches east and northeast of **Svidník,** near the border with Poland (follow the road to Dukla Pass). These churches jostle for attention with the dramatic collection of Nazi and Soviet tanks and planes dotted around this area to commemorate the fighting that took place here in 1944. Easier to find is the 15th-century church of **Hvervartov** (Roman Catholic), 10 kilometers (6 miles) southwest of Bardejov—a fascinating example of timber Gothic with some famous 17th-century frescoes.

The Tatras and Eastern Slovakia

Dining and Lodging

Finding a satisfying meal in the Tatras can be about as tough as making the 1,000- foot climb from Starý Smokovec to Hrebienok, especially in late fall, when some restaurants close completely. Try restaurants with a *koliba,* or open-faced grill, which offer tasty Slovak dishes in a rustic setting. The Grand in Smokovec and the Grandhotel Praha in Tatranská Lomnica have decent restaurants that make up in style for what they might lack in culinary excellence. For lunch, local grocery stores, which stock basic sandwich fixings, are an alternative to restaurants.

If you are looking to splurge on accommodations, you will find no better place than the Tatras. That noted, ask to see several rooms in your hotel before selecting one, as reader reports indicate rooms can be quite quirky.

For details and price-category definitions, *see* Dining *and* Lodging *in* Staying in Slovakia, *above.*

Bardejov

$$ 🏨 **Minerál.** This rather sterile modern hotel lies in a quiet location in the spa town of Bardejovské kúpele, 2¼ kilometers (1½ miles) from Bardejov proper. ⊠ *Bardejovské kúpele,* ☎ *0935/724122,* 𝔽𝔸𝕏 *0935/724124. 60 rooms with shower. Restaurant, bar, tennis courts. No credit cards.*

Levoča

$$ 🏨 **Hotel Satel.** Levoča, the hub of the historic Spiš region, is busily preserving its heritage while building a future based on tourism, and this beautifully renovated hotel is a fine case in point. Housed in an 18th-century mansion, it's centered around a picturesque courtyard that conjures up all the charm of fairy-tale Levoča. The guest rooms are bright

and modern. ☎ *0966/2943,* FAX *0966/4486. 21 rooms, 2 suites. Restaurant. No credit cards.*

Smokovec

$$ ✕ **Restaurant Koliba.** This charming restaurant with rustic decor and an open-faced grill features tasty local cuisine. Try some Slovak specialties such as *brinza* (goat's cheese) and *kapustová polievka* (sauerkraut soup with mushrooms and sausage). If you are lucky, you may get serenaded by the local Gypsy band that plays here most nights. ⊠ *Starý Smokovec,* ☎ *0969/2204. No credit cards. Closed sundays.*

$$$ ▥ **Bellevue.** This modern high-rise with well-appointed rooms lies about 200 yards from the resort center, although a good 15-minute walk away from the city's grocers and bars. Rates include breakfast and dinner. ⊠ *Horný Smokovec,* ☎ *0969/2941,* FAX *0969/2719. 103 rooms, 63 with bath. Restaurant, bar, pool, saunas. AE, DC, MC, V.*

$$$ ▥ **Grand Hotel.** The town's oldest hotel has a wonderful air of faded
★ fin-de-siècle elegance. The location, at the commercial and sports center of the region and the attendant crowds are a mixed blessing. The hotel has a reasonably priced restaurant. Rooms without bath are less expensive. ⊠ *Starý Smokovec,* ☎ *0969/2154,* FAX *0969/2157. 83 rooms, some with bath. Restaurant, pool, sauna, nightclub. AE, DC, MC, V.*

Tatranská Lomnica

$$ ✕ **Zbojnícka Koliba.** This tavern offers a small range of Slovak specialties prepared over an open fire, amid rustic decor and accompanied by folk music. ⊠ *Near Grandhotel Praha,* ☎ *0969/967630. No credit cards. Dinner only.*

$$$ ▥ **Grandhotel Praha.** Housed in a multiturreted turn-of-the-century
★ building often acclaimed as one of the wonders of the Tatras, the Grandhotel Praha offers visitors spacious but slightly shabby guest rooms decorated with a traditional touch. The restaurant still has an air of elegance that is unusual in Slovakia. ☎ *0969/967941,* FAX *0969/967891. 92 rooms. Restaurant, nightclub. AE, DC, MC, V.*

26 Spain

SPAIN IS FLAMENCO GUITAR, WHITE VILLAGES cling-
ing to parched hillsides, bullfighting, and Don
Quixote windmills scattered across an endless plain.
It is also the land of austere castles, walled cities, graceful medieval
churches, and great art—Goya, Velázquez, El Greco, Picasso, and Dalí
are a few of its masters.

As any Spaniard is quick to point out, Spain is really several countries
in one, each with its own proud character, its own distinctive cuisine,
and sometimes even its own language. Andalucía, for example, in the
south, is the part of Spain that comes closest to the traditional images:
rolling hills dotted with white-washed villages and olive trees. Andalucía's
capital, Seville, is known for flamenco music, for the girls dressed in
ruffled polka-dot dresses at its April Fair, and for the solemn processions of penitents during Holy Week or *semana santa*. The region is
also famous for its Moorish heritage, and remnants of its Islamic past
abound, from the red-and-white striped mosque of Córdoba to Spain's
most important monument, the Alhambra Palace of Granada. Andalucía
is known more for its *tapas* (savory tidbits) than for gourmet cuisine;
specialties of the province include mounds of fried fish and shellfish
called *frituras*, olives, cured ham, and the sherries of Jerez. On the Andalucían coast, the famed Costa del Sol, make like the jet set at Marbella or, for the more adventurous, cross the Straits of Gibraltar to explore
the colorful cities of northern Morocco.

The vast center of Spain is still dominated by its onetime role as a great
battlefield for centuries of skirmishes between Moorish and Christian
armies. Turreted castles look out over the bleak plains of Castile-La
Mancha, the land of Don Quixote, and Castile-Leon, which was once
called Old Castile. Castile is home to the religious center of Toledo where,
prior to the reconquest, Jews, Moors, and Christians lived and worked
together. It also boasts medieval jewels like Segovia, the university city
of Salamanca, and the fortress town of Ávila. The people of Castile
are as simple, warm, and hearty as their cuisine—huge portions of roast
lamb or suckling pig washed down with red wine from the Valdepeñas
or Ribera del Duero regions.

At the hub of it all is Madrid, one of the liveliest capitals in Europe. Madrid
is the seat of the government, a media center, and home to dozens of embassies, but its shine of sophistication is just a veneer. Scratch the surface and beyond its designer boutiques and chic restaurants you'll find
a simple Castilian town. Life here is lived in cafés and rustic taverns—
all it takes to become a local is to duck inside.

Madrid is also a mecca for art lovers and boasts three world-class
museums—the Prado, the Reina Sofía, and the Thyssen-Bornemisza—
all within a 1 kilometer (½ mile) stretch of leafy promenade. The capital has good food from all the regions of Spain, but it is probably
best known for its seafood, which arrives daily from the coasts and
has earned landlocked Madrid a reputation as Spain's biggest port.

Catalonia—home to 3 million Catalan-speaking residents—is the richest and most industrial region of Spain. Its capital, Barcelona, rivals
Madrid for power and is generally regarded as the winner in culture
and chic. Barcelona's tree-lined streets, Art Nouveau architecture, and
renovated waterfront still gleam from the scouring they received for
the 1992 Summer Olympics—an event that not only focused worldwide attention on the Mediterranean port but also provided the city
with new museums, sports venues, and restaurants. The spirit of turn-

Bay of Biscay

El Ferrol
La Coruña
Villalba
Luarca
Gijón
Ribadeo
Ribadesella
Santander
Santiago de Compostela
Lugo
Oviedo
Cangas de Onis
Bilbao
Mieres
PICOS DE EUROPA
Muros
CANTABRIAN MTS.
Pontevedra
Ponferrada
León
Vigo
Orense
Astorga
Burgos
Tui/Túy
Benavente
Palencia
Valladolid
Zamora
Tordesillas
Duero
Salamanca
Adanero
Segovia
SIERRA DE GUAD
Ávila
Guado
Ciudad Rodrigo
El Escorial
MADRID

PORTUGAL

SIERRA DE GREDOS
Toledo
Plasencia
Talavera de la Reina
Aranjue:
Tajo
Guadalupe
Alcáza San Ju
Cáceres
Trujillo
Ciudad Real
Mérida
Abenójar
Valdepeñas
Guadiana
Badajoz
Zafra
Almadén
Jerez de los Caballeros
SIERRA MORENA
Fregenal de la Sierra
Bailén
Linares
Córdoba
Aroche
Jaén
Baeza
Seville
Guadalquivir
Ecija
Baena
Guadi
Carmona
Lucena
Granada
Huelva
Loja
SIER
Gulf of Cádiz
Sanlúcar de Barrameda
Antequera
COSTA DE LA LUZ
Ronda
Nerja
Cádiz
Jerez de la Frontera
Torremolinos
Málaga
Motri
ATLANTIC OCEAN
Estepona
Fuengirola
Marbella
COSTA DEL SOL
Algeciras
Gibraltar
Strait of Gibraltar
TO CANARY ISLANDS

of-the-century moderniste architect Antoni Gaudí is still in evidence both in his Sagrada Familia cathedral, which is still under construction, and in the passions that Catalans show for stylish design.

In the 22 years since Franco died and since joining the European Union in 1986, Spain has been forced to modernize—the most obvious improvement for the visitor is a fast new nationwide network of superhighways. But fortunately Spain's uniqueness has not been tossed aside in the headlong rush toward the 21st century. Although fewer Spaniards may take time for a siesta, shops still close at midday and three-hour lunches are commonplace. Young adults still live with their parents until marriage. Bullfight fans show no signs of giving in to animal-rights crusaders. And flamenco is making a comeback with young rock and rollers.

Best of all for those on a holiday in Spain is the way Spaniards put enjoying life ahead of everything else in importance. This may mean strolling in the park with the family on a Sunday afternoon, lingering over a midweek lunch, or socializing with friends all night. A zest for living life to its fullest is Spain's greatest contribution to Europe.

ESSENTIAL INFORMATION

Before You Go

When to Go

The tourist season runs from Easter to mid-October. The best months for sightseeing are May, June, September, and early October, when the weather is usually pleasant and sunny without being unbearably hot. During July and August try to avoid Madrid or the inland cities of Andalucía, where the heat can be stifling and many places close down at 1 PM. If you visit Spain in high summer, the best bet is to head for the coastal resorts or to mountain regions such as the Pyrenees or Picos de Europa. The one exception to Spain's high summer temperatures is the north coast, where the climate is similar to that of northern Europe.

Visitors should be aware of the seasonal events that can clog parts of the country and should reserve in advance if traveling during peak periods. Easter is always a busy time, especially in Madrid, Barcelona, and the main Andalucían cities of Seville, Córdoba, Granada, Málaga, and the Costa del Sol resorts. July and August, when most Spaniards and other Europeans take their annual vacations, see the heaviest crowds, particularly in coastal resorts. Holiday weekends are naturally busy, and major fiestas, such as Pamplona's running of the bulls, cause prices to soar. Off-season travel offers fewer crowds and lower rates in may hotels.

CLIMATE

The following are the average daily maximum and minimum temperatures for Madrid.

Jan.	47F	9C	**May**	70F	21C	**Sept.**	77F	25C
	35	2		50	10		57	14
Feb.	52F	11C	**June**	80F	27C	**Oct.**	65F	18C
	36	2		58	15		49	10
Mar.	59F	15C	**July**	87F	31C	**Nov.**	55F	13C
	41	5		63	17		42	5
Apr.	65F	18C	**Aug.**	85F	30C	**Dec.**	48F	9C
	45	7		63	17		36	2

Currency

The unit of currency in Spain is the peseta (pta.). There are bills of 1,000, 2,000, 5,000, and 10,000 ptas. Coins are 1, 5, 25, 50, 100, 200, and 500 ptas. The 2- and 10-pta. coins and the old 100-pta. bills are rare but still legal tender. Note that pay phones in Spain won't accept the new, smaller 5- and 25-pta. coins first minted in 1991. Following the recent European currency shakeup, which resulted in several devaluations of the peseta, most foreigners find that their currency now goes farther in Spain than it had in recent years. At press time (spring 1996), the exchange rate was about 121 ptas. to the U.S. dollar, 93 ptas. to the Canadian dollar, and 175 ptas. to the pound sterling.

CREDIT CARDS

Most hotels, restaurants, and stores accept payment by credit card. Visa is the most widely accepted piece of plastic, followed by MasterCard (called EuroCard in Spain). More expensive establishments may also take American Express and Diners Club.

CHANGING MONEY

The word to look for is CAMBIO (exchange). Most Spanish banks take a 1½% commission, though some less scrupulous places charge more; always check, as rates can vary greatly. To change money in a bank, you need your passport and a lot of patience, because filling out the forms takes time. Hotels offer rates lower than banks, but they rarely make a commission, so you may well break even. Restaurants and stores, with the exception of those catering to the tour bus trade, do not usually accept payment by dollars or traveler's checks. If you have a credit card with a Personal Identification Number (PIN), you'll be able to make withdrawals or get cash advances at most cash machines at banks.

CURRENCY REGULATIONS

Visitors may take any amount of foreign currency in bills or traveler's checks into Spain as well as any amount of pesetas. When leaving Spain, you may take out only 100,000 ptas. per person in Spanish bank notes and foreign currency up to the equivalent of 500,000 ptas., unless you can prove you declared the excess at customs on entering the country.

What It Will Cost

Prices rose fast during the first decade of Spain's democracy, and Spain's inflation rate was one of the highest in Europe. By the 1990s, however, inflation had been curbed; in spring 1996, it was just a little more than 5%. Generally speaking, the cost of living in Spain is now on a par with that of most other European countries, and the days when Spain was the bargain basement of Europe are truly over, although the weakness of the peseta has somewhat improved the buying power of visitors from North America and the United Kingdom.

TAXES

A value-added tax known as IVA was introduced in 1986 when Spain joined the EU. IVA is levied at 6% on most goods and services, but it's 7% on hotels and restaurants (except in the Canary Islands, where it's 4%), and 16% on car rentals. IVA is always included in the purchase price of goods in stores, but for hotels, restaurants, and car rentals, the tax will be added to your bill. Many restaurants include IVA in their menu prices, but plenty—usually the more expensive ones—do not. Large stores, such as the country-wide Corte Inglés chain, operate a tax refund plan for foreign visitors who are not EU nationals; but to qualify for this refund, you need to spend at least 48,000 ptas. (about $400) in any one store and, in theory, on any one item. There is no airport tax in Spain.

SAMPLE PRICES

A cup of coffee will cost around 125 ptas., a Coca-Cola 150 ptas., bottled beer 150 ptas., a small draught beer 100 ptas., a glass of wine in a bar 100 ptas., an American-style cocktail 400 ptas., a ham sandwich 300 ptas., an ice-cream cone about 150 ptas., a local bus or subway ride 125 ptas., a 1-mile taxi ride about 350 ptas., a foreign newspaper around 225 ptas., and a movie around 500-600 ptas.

Language

In major cities and coastal resorts you should have no trouble finding people who speak English. In such places, reception staff in hotels of three or more stars are required to speak English. Don't expect the person in the street or the bus driver to speak English, although you may be pleasantly surprised.

Getting Around

By Car

ROAD CONDITIONS

Roads marked A (*autopista*) are toll roads. N stands for national or main roads, and C for country roads. A huge road improvement scheme has been largely completed, but many N roads are still single-lane and the going can be slow. Tolls vary but are high; for example, Bilbao–Zaragoza 3,010 ptas., Salou–Valencia 2,150 ptas., Seville–Jerez 610 ptas., and Santiago–La Coruña 510 ptas.

RULES OF THE ROAD

Driving is on the right, and horns and high-beam headlights may not be used in cities. Front seat belts are compulsory. Children under age 10 may not ride in front seats. At traffic circles, give way to traffic coming from the right unless your road has priority. Your home driving license is essential and must be carried with you at all times, along with your car insurance and vehicle registration document. You will also need an International Driving License and a proof-of-insurance Green Card if you are bringing your own car into Spain. Speed limits are 120 kph (74 mph) on autopistas, 100 kph (62 mph) on N roads, 90 kph (56 mph) on C roads, and 60 kph (37 mph) in cities unless otherwise signed.

PARKING

Parking restrictions should be checked locally. In many cities, a blue line on the street indicates residents-only parking; other cars are towed promptly. In other places, curbside signs inform you of legal parking times. Never leave *anything* on view inside a parked car. Thefts are common, and it is safer to leave your car in one of the many staffed parking lots; charges are reasonable.

GASOLINE

At press time (spring 1996), gas cost 115 ptas. a liter for super and 108 ptas. a liter for regular. *Sin plomo* (unleaded) gas is now available at a steadily increasing number of pumps. There is attendant service at most pumps, but there's no need to tip for just a fill-up. Most gas stations accept payment by credit card.

By Train

The Spanish railroad system, known usually by its initials RENFE, has greatly improved in recent years. Air-conditioned trains are now widespread but by no means universal. Most overnight trains have first- and second-class sleeping cars and second-class *literas* (couchettes). Dining, buffet, and refreshment services are available on most long-distance trains. There are various types of trains—*Talgo* (ultramodern), electric unit expresses (ELT), diesel rail cars (TER), and ordinary *expresos* and *rápidos*. Fares are determined by the kind of train you travel on and not just by the distance traveled. Talgos are by far the quickest, most comfortable, and the most expensive trains; expresos and rápidos are the slowest and cheapest of the long-distance services. In 1992, the high-speed Alto Velocidad Español (AVE) began service between Madrid and Seville, reducing travel time between these cities from 6 to 2½ hours (fares vary, but the AVE can cost almost as much as flying). A few lines, such as the narrow-gauge FEVE routes along the north coast from San Sebastián to El Ferrol and on the Costa Blanca around Alicante, do not belong to the national RENFE network, and international rail passes are not valid on these lines.

TICKET PURCHASE AND SEAT RESERVATION

Tickets can be bought from any station (regardless of your point of departure), and from downtown RENFE offices and travel agents displaying the blue and yellow RENFE sign. The latter are often best in the busy holiday season. At stations, buy your advance tickets from the window marked LARGO RECORRIDO, VENTA ANTICIPADA (Long Distance, Advance Sales). Seat reservation can be made up to 60 days in advance and is obligatory on all the better long-distance services.

FARE SAVERS

The **RENFE Tourist Card** is an unlimited-kilometers pass, valid for 3, 5, or 10 days' travel, and can be bought by anyone who lives outside Spain. It is available for first- or second-class travel and can be purchased from selected travel agencies and main railroad stations abroad; and in Spain at RENFE travel offices and major long-distance stations such as those in Madrid, Barcelona, Port Bou, and Irún. At press time (spring 1996) the second-class pass cost 18,350 ptas. for 3 days, 31,222 ptas. for 5 days, and 48,134 ptas. for 10 days. RENFE has no representative in the United States. Contact the Spanish National Tourist Office for a list of agencies or call RENFE in Madrid direct, 011–34/1–563–0202

Prices are determined according to when the train leaves. There are three price categories: *valle* (low), *llano* (regular), and *punto* (high). On the most heavily used runs, Madrid–Barcelona or Madrid–Seville, for example, there is one *valle* and one *punto* train each day. The rest are in the *llano* price category. The cheapest train generally departs early in the morning, while the most expensive leaves at midday.

By Plane

Iberia and its subsidiary **Aviaco** operate a wide network of domestic flights, linking all the main cities and the Balearic Islands. Distances are great and internal airfares are high by U.S. standards, although deregulation is pushing prices lower. Flights from the mainland to the Balearics are heavily booked in summer, and the Madrid–Málaga route is frequently overbooked at Easter and in high season. A frequent shuttle service operates between Madrid and Barcelona. Iberia has its own offices in most major Spanish cities and acts as agent for Aviaco. In Madrid, Iberia headquarters are at Velázquez 130 (☎ 91/411–1011 for domestic reservations, and 91/329–4353 for international, or call Info-Iberia for flight information, ☎ 91/329–5767). Flights can also be booked at most travel agencies. Air Europa (☎ 91/305–8159 and ☎ 91/559–1500) and Spanair (☎ 91/393–6735) offer slightly cheaper service between Madrid and Barcelona as well as flights to the Canary Islands. For information on other airlines' flights to and within Spain, call the airline itself, or call the airport (☎ 91/305–8343, -44, -45, or -46) and ask for your airline.

By Bus

Spain has an excellent bus network, but there is no national or nationwide bus company. The network simply consists of numerous *empresas* (private regional bus companies) and there are therefore no comprehensive bus passes. Some of the buses on major routes are now quite luxurious, although this is not always the case in some of the more rural areas. Buses tend to be more frequent than trains, are sometimes cheaper, and often allow you to see more of the countryside. On major routes and at holiday times it is advisable to buy your ticket a day or two in advance. Some cities have central bus stations, but in many, including Madrid and Barcelona, buses leave from various boarding points. Always check with the local tourist office. Bus stations, unlike train stations, usually provide luggage storage facilities.

Staying in Spain

Telephones

LOCAL CALLS

Pay phones are supposed to work with coins of 25 and either 50 or 100 ptas. (smaller 5- and 25-ptas. coins do not work in the machines). The minimum charge for short local calls is 25 ptas. In the older blue phones, place several coins in the slot, or in the groove on top of the phone, lift the receiver, and dial the number. Coins then fall into the machine as needed. In the newer green phones, place several coins in the slot, watch the display unit and feed as needed. These phones take 100-pta. coins. Area codes always begin with a 9 and are different for each province. In Madrid province, the code is 91; in Cantabria, it's 942. If you're dialing from outside the country, drop the 9.

INTERNATIONAL CALLS

Calling abroad can be done from any pay phone marked TELÉFONO INTERNACIONAL. Use 50-pta. (or 100-pta. if the phone takes them) coins initially, then coins of any denomination to prolong your call. Dial 07 for international, wait for the tone to change, then 1 for the United States, 0101 for Canada, or 44 for England, followed by the area code and number. For calls to England, omit the initial 0 from the area code. For lengthy international calls, go to the *telefónica*, a telephone office found in all sizable towns, where an operator assigns you a private booth and collects payment at the end of the call; this is the least expensive and by far the easiest way of phoning abroad. You can charge calls more than 500 ptas to your Visa or MasterCard.

OPERATORS AND INFORMATION

For the operator and information for any part of Spain, dial 003. If you're in Madrid, dial 008 to make collect calls to countries in Europe; 005 for the rest of the world. Private long-distance companies now have special access numbers: **AT&T** (☎ 900/99–00–11), **MCI** (☎ 900/99–00–14), **Sprint** (☎ 900/99–00–13).

Mail

POSTAL RATES

To the United States, airmail letters up to 15 grams and postcards each cost 90 ptas. (These were the rates at press time, spring 1996). To the United Kingdom and other EU countries, letters up to 20 grams and postcards each cost 45 ptas. To non–EU European countries, letters and postcards up to 20 grams cost 60 ptas. If you wish to expedite your overseas mail, send it *urgente* for 160 ptas. more than the regular airmail cost. Within Spain, letters and postcards each cost 27 ptas.; within a city in Spain, letters and postcards cost 17 ptas. Mailboxes are yellow with red stripes, and the slot marked EXTRANJERO is the one for mail going abroad. Buy your *sellos* (stamps) at a *correos* (post office) or in an *estanco* (tobacco shop).

If you're uncertain where you'll be staying, have mail sent to American Express or addressed to "poste restante" or *lista de correos* and mailed to the local post office. To claim your mail, you'll need to show your passport. American Express has a $2 service charge per letter for non-cardholders.

Shopping

SALES TAX REFUNDS

If you purchase goods up to a value of 48,000 ptas. or more in any one store (and in theory this should be on only one item), you are entitled to a refund of the IVA tax paid (usually 6% but more in the case of certain luxury goods), provided that you leave Spain within three months. You will be given two copies of the sales invoice, which you must present at customs together with the goods as you leave Spain. Once the invoice has been stamped by customs, mail the blue copy back to the store, which will then mail your tax refund to you. If you are leaving via the airports of Madrid, Barcelona, Málaga, or Palma de Mallorca, you can get your tax refund immediately from the Banco Exterior de España in the airport. The above does not apply to residents of EU countries, who must claim their IVA refund through customs in their own countries. The Corte Inglés department stores operate the above system, but don't be surprised if other stores are unfamiliar with the tax-refund procedure and do not have the necessary forms.

BARGAINING

Prices in city stores and produce markets are fixed; bargaining is possible only in flea markets, some antiques stores, and with gypsy vendors, with whom it is *essential,* though you'd do best to turn them down flat as their goods are almost always fake and grossly overpriced.

Opening and Closing Times

Banks are open Monday to Saturday 9–2 from October to June; during the summer months they are closed on Saturdays.

Museums and churches. Opening times vary. Most are open in the morning, and most museums close one day a week, often Monday.

Post offices are usually open weekdays 9–2, but this can vary.

Stores are open weekdays from 9 or 10 until 1:30 or 2, then again in the afternoon from around 5 to 8. In some cities, especially in summer, stores close on Saturday afternoon. The Corte Inglés and other department stores in major cities are open continuously from 10 to 8, and some stores in tourist resorts also stay open through the siesta.

National Holidays

January 1; January 6 (Epiphany); March 28 (Good Friday); May 1 (May Day); July 25 (St. James); August 15 (Assumption); October 12 (National Day); November 1 (All Saints' Day); December 6 (Constitution); December 8 (Immaculate Conception); December 25. Other holidays include May 2 (in the province of Madrid) and March 19 (St. Joseph). These holidays are not celebrated in every region; always check locally.

Dining

Visitors have a choice of restaurants, tapas bars, and cafés. Restaurants are strictly for lunch and dinner; they do not serve breakfast. Tapas bars are ideal for a glass of wine or beer accompanied by an array of tapas. Cafés, called *cafeterías,* are basically coffee shops that serve snacks, light meals, tapas, pastries, and coffee, tea, and alcoholic drinks. They also serve breakfast and are perfect for afternoon tea or a cup of thick, creamy hot chocolate.

MEALTIMES
Mealtimes in Spain are much later than in any other European country. Lunch begins between 1 and 2:30, with 2 being the usual time, and 3 more normal on Sunday. Dinner is usually available from 8:30 onward, but 10 PM is the usual time in the larger cities and resorts. Lunch is the main meal, not dinner. Tapas bars are busiest between noon and 2 and from 8 PM on. Cafés are usually open from around 8 AM to midnight.

PRECAUTIONS
Tap water is safe to drink in all but the remotest villages (in Madrid, tap water, from the surrounding Guadarrama Mountains, is excellent; in Barcelona, it's safe but tastes terrible). However, most Spaniards drink bottled mineral water; ask for either *agua sin gas* (without bubbles) or *agua con gas* (with bubbles). A good paella should be served only at lunchtime and should be prepared to order (usually 30 minutes); beware the all-too-cheap version.

TYPICAL DISHES
Paella—a mixture of saffron-flavored rice with seafood, chicken, and vegetables—is Spain's national dish. Gazpacho, a cold soup usually made of crushed garlic, tomatoes, and olive oil and garnished with diced vegetables, is a traditional Andalucían dish and is served mainly in summer. The Basque country and Galicia are the gourmet regions of Spain, and both serve outstanding fish and seafood; indulge in a *fuente de marisco* (mixed shellfish/seafood platter). Asturias is famous for its *fabadas* (bean stews), cider, and dairy products; Extremadura for its hams and sausages; and Castile for its roasts, especially *cochinillo* (suckling pig), *cordero asado* (roast lamb), and *perdiz* (partridge). The best wines are those from the Rioja and Penedés regions. Valdepeñas is a pleasant table wine, and most places serve a perfectly acceptable house wine; ask for *vino de la casa* (say *tinto* for red and *blanco* for white). Sherries from Jerez de la Frontera make fine aperitifs; ask for a *fino* or a *manzanilla;* both are dry. In summer you can try *horchata,* a sweet white drink made from ground nuts, *granizados de limón* or *de café,* lemon juice or coffee served over crushed ice, or a *blanco y negro,* a splash of cold espresso served with a scoop of vanilla ice milk. *Un café solo* is a small, black espresso coffee, and *café con leche* is coffee with cream, cappuccino-style. Weak, black American-style coffee is hard but not impossible to come by; ask for a *café americano,* a cup of watered-down espresso, or instant coffee.

WHAT TO WEAR
In $$$$ and $$$ restaurants, jacket and tie are the norm. Elsewhere, casual dress is appropriate.

RATINGS
Spanish restaurants are officially classified from five forks down to one fork, with most places falling into the two- or three-fork category. In our rating system, prices are per person and include a first course, main course, and dessert, but not wine or tip. Sales tax (IVA) is usually included in the menu price; check the menu for *IVA incluído* or *IVA no incluído*. When it's not included, an additional 7% will be added to your bill. Most restaurants offer a prix-fixe menu called a *menú del día;* however, this is often offered only at lunch, and at dinner tends to be merely a reheated midday offering. This is usually the cheapest way to eat; à la carte dining is more expensive. Service charges are never added to your bill; leave around 10%, less in $ restaurants and bars. Major centers such as Madrid, Barcelona, Marbella, and Seville tend to be a bit more expensive.

CATEGORY	COST
$$$$	over 9,000 ptas.
$$$	6,000 ptas.–9,000 ptas.
$$	3,000 ptas.–6,000 ptas.
$	under 3,000 ptas.

Lodging

Spain has a wide range of accommodations, including luxury palaces, medieval monasteries, converted 19th-century houses, modern hotels, high rises on the coasts, and inexpensive hostels in family homes. All hotels and hostels are listed with their rates in the annual *Guía de Hoteles* available from bookstores and kiosks for around 1,200 ptas., or you can see a copy in local tourist offices. Rates are always quoted per room, and not per person. Single occupancy of a double room costs 80% of the normal price. Breakfast is rarely included in the quoted room rate; always check. The quality of rooms, particularly in older properties, can be uneven; always ask to see your room *before* you sign the acceptance slip. If you want a private bathroom in a less expensive hotel, state your preference for shower or bathtub; the latter usually costs more though many hotels have both.

HOTELS AND HOSTELS

Hotels are officially classified from five stars (the highest) to one star, hostels from three stars to one star. Hostels—not the youth hostels associated with the word in most countries—are usually family homes converted to provide accommodations that often occupy only part of a building. If an *R* appears on the blue hotel or hostel plaque, the hotel is classified as a *residencia,* and full dining services are not provided, though breakfast and cafeteria facilities may be available. A three-star hostel is usually comparable to a two-star hotel; two- and one-star hostels offer simple, basic accommodations.

The main hotel chains are Barceló, Husa, Iberotel, Meliá Sol, and Tryp, and the state-run *paradores* (tourist hotels; paradors). Holiday Inn, InterContinental, and Forte also own some of the best hotels in Madrid, Barcelona, and Seville; only these, the paradors, and the recently organized Estancias de España, a group of lodgings set in historic buildings, have any special character. The others mostly provide clean, comfortable accommodation in the two- to four-star range.

In many hotels, rates vary fairly dramatically according to the time of year. The hotel year is divided into *temporada alta, media,* and *baja* (high, mid, and low season); high season usually covers the summer and Easter and Christmas periods, plus the major fiestas. IVA is rarely included in the quoted room rates, so be prepared for an additional 6% to be added to your bill. Service charges are never included.

PARADORS

There about 100 state-owned-and-run paradors, many of which are in magnificent medieval castles or convents or in places of great natural beauty. Most of these fall into the four-star category and are priced accordingly. Most have restaurants that specialize in local regional cuisine and serve a full breakfast. The most popular paradors are booked far in advance. For more information or to make reservations, contact **Paradores** (✉ Requena 3, 28013 Madrid, ☎ 91/559–0069, 𝖥𝖠𝖷 91/559–3233), **Keytel International** (✉ 402 Edgware Rd., London, W2 1ED, ☎ 0171/402–8182, 𝖥𝖠𝖷 0171/724–9503), or **Marketing Ahead Inc.** (✉ 433 5th Ave., New York, NY 10016, ☎ 212/686–9213 or 800/223–1356, 𝖥𝖠𝖷 212/686–0271); they also have extensive information about and can make reservations for other fine lodgings in addition to the paradors).

VILLAS

Villas are plentiful all along the Mediterranean coast, and cottages in Cantabria and Asturias on the north coast are available from a few agencies. Several agencies in both the United States and United Kingdom specialize in renting property; check with the Spanish National Tourist Office.

CAMPING

There are approximately 540 campsites in Spain, with the highest concentration along the Mediterranean coast. The season runs from April through October, though some sites are open year-round. Sites are listed in the annual publication *Guía de Campings* available from bookstores or local tourist offices, and further details are available from the Spanish National Tourist Office. Reservations for the most popular seaside sites can be made either directly with the site or through camping reservations at: Federación Española de Campings, ⊠ Príncipe de Vergara 85, 2°-dcha, 28006 Madrid, ☎ 91/562–9994.

RATINGS

Prices are for two people in a double room and do not include breakfast.

CATEGORY	MAJOR CITY	OTHER AREAS*
$$$$	over 20,000 ptas.	over 18,000 ptas.
$$$	14,000 ptas.–20,000 ptas.	12,000 ptas.–18,000 ptas.
$$	9,000 ptas.–14,000 ptas.	7,000 ptas.–12,000 ptas.
$	under 9,000 ptas.	under 7,000 ptas.

In Gibraltar, $$$: £65–£75 ($104–$120); $$: £40–£46 ($64–$74) (not including tax).

Tipping

Spaniards appreciate being tipped, though the practice is becoming less widespread. Restaurants and hotels are by law not allowed to add a service charge to your bill, though confusingly, your bill for both will most likely say *servicios e impuestos incluídos* (service and tax included). Ignore this unhelpful piece of advice, and leave 10% in most restaurants where you have had a full meal; in humbler eating places, bars, and cafés, 5%–10% is enough, or you can round out the bill to the nearest 100 ptas. A cocktail waiter in a hotel will expect at least 50 ptas. a drink, maybe 75 ptas. in a luxury establishment. Tip taxi drivers about 5% to 10% when they use the meter, otherwise *nothing*—they'll have seen to it themselves. Gas station attendants get no tip for pumping gas, but they get about 50 ptas. for checking tires and oil and cleaning windshields. Train and airport porters usually operate on a fixed rate of 60 ptas.–100 ptas. a bag. Coat-check attendants get 25 ptas.–50 ptas., and rest-room attendants get 10 ptas.–25 ptas. In top hotels, doormen get 100 ptas.–150 ptas. for carrying bags to the check-in counter or for hailing taxis, and bellhops get 100 ptas. for room service or for each bag they carry to your room. In moderate hotels about 50 ptas. is adequate for the same services. Leave your chambermaid about 500 ptas. for a week's stay. There's no need to tip for just a couple of nights.

MADRID

Arriving and Departing

By Plane

All international and domestic flights arrive at Madrid's Barajas Airport (☎ 91/305–8343), 16 kilometers (10 miles) northeast of town just off the N-II Barcelona highway. For information on arrival and departure times, call **Info-Iberia** (☎ 91/329–5767) or the airline concerned.

Buses leave the national and international terminals every 15 minutes from 5:40 AM to 2 AM for the downtown terminal at Plaza de Colón just off the Paseo de la Castellana. The ride takes about 20 minutes and the fare at press time (spring 1996) was 360 ptas. Most city hotels are then only a short taxi ride away. The fastest and most expensive route into town (usually about 1,500 ptas., but up to 2,000 ptas. plus tip in traffic) is by taxi. Pay what is on the meter plus 350 ptas. surcharge and 150 ptas. for each suitcase. By car, take the N-II, which becomes Avenida de América, into town, then head straight into Calle María de Molina and left on either Calle Serrano or the Castellana.

By Train

Madrid has three railroad stations. Chamartín, in the northern suburbs beyond the Plaza de Castilla, is the main station, with trains to France and the north (including Barcelona, Segovia, El Escorial, Santiago, and La Coruña). Most trains to Valencia, Alicante, and Andalucía now leave from here, too, but stop at Atocha station, at the southern end of Paseo del Prado on the Glorieta del Emperador Carlos V. Also departing from Atocha are trains to Toledo, Granada, Extremadura, and Lisbon. In 1992, a convenient new metro stop (Atocha RENFE) was opened in Atocha station, connecting it to the city subway system. The old Atocha station, designed by Eiffel, was refurbished and reopened in 1992 as the Madrid terminal for a new high-speed rail service to Seville. Norte (or Príncipe Pío), on Paseo de la Florida, in the west of town below the Plaza de España, is the departure point for local trains to the Madrid suburbs.

For all train information, call RENFE (☎ 91/328–9020, in Spanish and English), or go to its offices at Alcalá 44 (⏰ Weekdays 9:30–8). There's another RENFE office at Barajas Airport in the International Arrivals Hall, or you can purchase tickets at any of the three main stations, or from travel agents displaying the blue and yellow RENFE sign.

By Bus

Madrid has no central bus station. The two main bus stations are the Estación del Sur (✉ Canarias 17, ☎ 91/468–4200), near the metro Palos de la Frontera, for buses to Toledo, La Mancha, Alicante, and Andalucía; and Auto-Rés (✉ Plaza Conde de Casal 6, ☎ 91/551–7200), near the metro Conde de Casal, for buses to Extremadura, Cuenca, Salamanca, Valladolid, Valencia, and Zamora. Auto-Rés has a central ticket and information office at Salud 19 near the Hotel Arosa, just off Gran Vía. Buses to other destinations leave from various points, so check with the tourist office. The Basque country and most of north central Spain is served by Auto Continental (✉ Alenza 20, near the metro Ríos Rosas, ☎ 91/533–0400). For Àvila, Segovia, and La Granja, Empresa La Sepulvedana (☎ 91/527–9537) leaves from Paseo de la Florida 11, next to the Norte station, a few steps from the Norte metro stop. Empresa Herranz (☎ 91/543–8167), serving San Lorenzo de El Escorial and the Valley of the Fallen, departs from the base of Calle Fernández de los Ríos, a few yards from the Moncloa metro stop. La Veloz (✉ Avda. Mediterraneo 49, ☎ 91/409–7602) serves Chinchón.

By Car

The main roads are north–south, the Paseo de la Castellana and Paseo del Prado; and east–west, Calle de Alcalá, Gran Vía, and Calle de la Princesa. The M30 ring road circles Madrid and the M40 is an outer ring road about 12 kilometers (7 miles) further out. For Burgos and France, drive north up the Castellana and follow the signs for the N-I. For Barcelona, head up the Castellana to Plaza Dr. Marañón, then right onto María de Molina and the N-II; for Andalucía and Toledo, head south down Paseo del Prado, then follow the signs to the N-IV and N401, respectively. For Segovia, Ávila, and El Escorial, head west along Princesa to Avenida Puerta de Hierro and onto the N-VI La Coruña.

Getting Around

Madrid is a fairly compact city and most of the main sights can be visited on foot. But if you're staying in one of the modern hotels in the north of town off the Castellana, you may well need to use the bus or subway. As a rough guide, the walk from the Prado to the Royal Palace at a comfortable sightseeing pace but without stopping takes around 30 minutes; from Plaza del Callao on Gran Vía to the Plaza Mayor, it takes about 15 minutes.

By Metro

The metro offers the simplest and quickest means of transport and is open from 6 AM to 1:30 AM. Metro maps are available from ticket offices, hotels, and tourist offices. Fares at press time (spring 1996) were 130 ptas. a ride. Savings can be made by buying a 10-ride ticket for 645 ptas. Keep some change (5, 25, 50, and 100 ptas.) handy for the ticket machines, especially after 10 PM; the machines give change and are handy for beating often long lines for tickets.

By Bus

City buses are red and run from 6 AM to midnight (though check, as some stop earlier). Again there is a flat-fare system, with each ride costing 130 ptas. Route plans are displayed at paradas (bus stops), and a map of the entire system is available from Empresa Municipal de Transportes (EMT) booths on Plaza de la Cibeles, Callao, or Puerta del Sol. Savings can be made by buying a **Bonobus** (645 ptas.), good for 10 rides, from EMT booths or any tobacco shop.

By Taxi

Madrid has more than 18,000 taxis, and fares are low by New York or London standards. The meter starts at 170 ptas. and each additional kilometer costs 70 ptas. The average city ride costs about 500 ptas., and there is a surcharge of 150 ptas. between 11 PM and 6 AM and on holidays from 6 AM to 11 PM. A supplemental fare of 150 ptas. applies to trips to the bullring or soccer matches, and there is a charge of 150 ptas. per suitcase. The airport surcharge is 350 ptas. Cabs available for hire display a LIBRE sign during the day and a green light at night. They hold four passengers. Make sure the driver puts the meter on when you start your ride, and tip from 5% to 10% of the fare.

Important Addresses and Numbers

Visitor Information

The main Madrid tourist office (☎ 91/541–2325) is on the ground floor of the Torre de Madrid in Plaza de España, near the beginning of Calle de la Princesa, and is open weekdays 9–7, Saturdays 9:30–1:30. Another Madrid Provincial Tourist Office (✉ Duque de Medinacelli 2, ☎ 91/429–4951) is on a small street across from the Palace Hotel. The much less useful municipal tourist office is at Plaza Mayor 3 (☎ 91/366–5477) and is open weekdays 10–8, Saturdays 10–2. A third office is in the International Arrivals Hall of Barajas Airport (☎ 91/305–8656) and is open weekdays 8–8, Saturdays 9–1.

Embassies

U.S. (✉ Serrano 75, ☎ 91/577–4000), **Canadian** (✉ Núñez de Balboa 35, ☎ 91/431–4300), **U.K.** (✉ Fernando el Santo 16, ☎ 91/319–0200).

Emergencies

Police: (emergencies, ☎ 091; Municipal Police, ☎ 092 for towed cars or traffic accidents). To report lost passports, go to ✉ Los Madrazos 9 just off the top of Paseo del Prado (☎ 91/521–9350). **Ambulance:** ☎ 91/522–2222 or 91/588–4400. **Doctor:** Your hotel reception will contact the nearest doctor for you. **Emergency clinics:** Hospital 12 de Octubre (✉ Avda. Córdoba, ☎ 91/390–8000) and La Paz Ciudad Sanitaria (✉ Paseo de la Castellana 261, ☎ 91/358–2600). English-speaking doctors are available at British-American Medical Unit (✉ Conde de Aranda 7, ☎ 91/435–1823). **Pharmacies:** A list of pharmacies open 24 hours (farmacias de guardia) is published daily in El País. Hotel receptions usually have a copy. **Company** (✉ Puerta del Sol 14, ☎ 91/521–3625) has English-speaking pharmacists. It does not stock American medicines but will recognize many American brand names.

English-Language Bookstores

Booksellers (✉ José Abascal 48, ☎ 91/442–8104) and **Turner's English Bookshop** (✉ Génova 3, ☎ 91/319–0926) both have large selections of English-language books.

Travel Agencies

American Express (✉ Plaza de las Cortes 2, ☎ 91/322-5445), **Marsans** (✉ Gran Vía 59, ☎ 91/547–7300), **Wagons-Lits** (✉ Alcalá 23, ☎ 91/522–4334).

Airlines

Iberia (✉ Velázquez 130, ☎ 91/411–1011 for domestic reservations or ☎ 91/329–4353 for international flights; for flight information, call Info-Iberia, ☎ 91/329–5767), **British Airways** (✉ Serrano 60, 5th floor, ☎ 91/431–7575), **TWA** (✉ Plaza de Colón 2, ☎ 91/310–1905 or 91/305–4290), and **Continental** (✉ Gran Vía 59, ☎ 91/559–2710).

Guided Tours

Orientation Tours

City sightseeing tours are run by **Julià Tours** (✉ Gran Vía 68, ☎ 91/559–9605), **Pullmantur** (✉ Plaza de Oriente 8, ☎ 91/541–1807), and **Trapsatur** (✉ San Bernardo 23, ☎ 91/302–6039). All three run the same tours, mostly in 48-seat buses and conducted in Spanish and English. Book tours directly with the offices above, through any travel agent, or through your hotel. Departure points are from the addresses above, though in many cases you can be picked up at your hotel. "Madrid Artístico" is a morning tour of the city with visits to the Royal Palace and Prado Museum, entrance fees included. The "Madrid Panorámico" tour includes University City, the Casa del Campo park, and the northern reaches of the Castellana. This is a half-day tour, usually in the afternoon, and makes an ideal orientation for the first-time visitor. Also offered are "Madrid de Noche," a night tour combining a drive around the illuminations, dinner in a restaurant, a flamenco show, and cabaret at La Scala nightclub; and "Panorámico y Toros," on bullfight days only (usually Sunday), a panoramic drive and visit to a bullfight. Trapsatur also runs the Madridvision tourist bus, which makes a one-hour sightseeing tour of the city with recorded commentary in English. No reservation is necessary. Catch the bus in front of the Prado Museum every 1½ hours beginning at 10 AM Tuesday through Sunday; no buses on Sunday afternoon. A round-trip ticket costs 1,500 ptas. and a two-day pass, which allows you to get on or off at various attractions, is 2,200 ptas.

Walking and Special-Interest Tours

Those who understand Spanish can take advantage of a hugely popular selection of tours launched by the **Ayuntamiento** (city hall) under the title "Discubre Madrid." Walking tours are held most mornings year-round and visit many of the capital's hidden corners, as well as the major sights. Special-interest tours include "Madrid's Railroads," "Medicine in Madrid," "Goya's Madrid," and "Commerce and Finance in Madrid." Some tours are by bus, others on foot. Schedules are listed in the "Discubre Madrid" leaflet available from the municipal tourist office and tickets can be purchased at the Patronato de Turismo (C. Mayor 69, 91/588–2906).

Excursions

Julià Tours, Pullmantur, and **Trapsatur** (☞ Orientation Tours, *above*) run full- or half-day trips to El Escorial, Ávila, Segovia, Toledo, and Aranjuez, and in summer to Cuenca and Salamanca; for additional information about these places, *see* Madrid Environs, *below*. The "Tren de la Fresa" (Strawberry Train) is a popular excursion on summer weekends; a 19th-century train carries passengers from the old Delicias Station to Aranjuez (known for its production of strawberries) and back. Tickets can be obtained from RENFE offices, travel agents, and the Delicias Station (Paseo de las Delicias 61). Other one- or two-day excursions by train to such places as Àvila, Cuenca, or Salamanca are available on summer weekends. Contact RENFE for details.

Exploring Madrid

Numbers in the margin correspond to points of interest on the Madrid map.

You can walk the following route in a day, or even half a day if you stop only to visit the Prado and Royal Palace. Two days should give you time for browsing. Begin in the Plaza Atocha, more properly known as the Glorieta del Emperador Carlos V, at the bottom of the Paseo del Prado, and check out what's showing in the **Centro de Arte Reina Sofía** (Queen Sofía Arts Center) opened by Queen Sofía in 1986. This converted hospital, home of art and sculpture exhibitions and symbol of Madrid's cultural pride, is one of Europe's most dynamic venues—a Madrileño rival to Paris's Pompidou Center. It is home to works by Joan Miró and Salvador Dalí as well as Picasso's famed *Guernica*, the horrific painting depicting the April 1937 carpet bombing of the Basque country's traditional capital by Nazi warplanes aiding Franco during the Spanish Civil War (1936–39). ✉ *The main entrance is on C. de Santa Isabel 52.* ☎ *91/467–5062.* ✉ *400 ptas.* ☉ *Mon., Wed.–Sat. 10–9; Sun. 10–2:30. Free Sat. 2:30–9 and Sun.*

Walk up Paseo del Prado to Madrid's number-one sight, the famous **Museo del Prado** (Prado Museum), one of the world's most important art galleries. Plan to spend half a day here, though it will take at least two full days to view its treasures properly. Brace yourself for the crowds. The greatest treasures—the Velázquez, Murillo, Zurbarán, El Greco, and Goya galleries—are all on the upper floor. Two of the best works are Velázquez's *Surrender of Breda* and his most famous work, *Las Meninas*, which occupies a privileged position in a room of its own. The Goya galleries contain the artist's none-too-flattering royal portraits—Goya believed in painting the truth—his exquisitely beautiful *Marquesa de Santa Cruz,* and his famous *Naked Maja* and *Clothed Maja,* for which the 13th duchess of Alba was said to have posed. Goya's most moving works, the *Second* *of May* and the *Fusillade of Moncloa* or *Third of May*, vividly depict the sufferings of Madrid patriots at the hands of Napoléon's invading troops in 1808. Before you leave, feast your eyes on the fantastic flights of fancy of Hieronymus Bosch's *Garden of Earthly Delights* and his triptych *The Hay Wagon*, both on the ground floor. ⊠ *Paseo del Prado s/n,* ☎ *91/420–3662.* ▦ *400 ptas.* ⊙ *Tues.–Sat. 9–7, Sun. 9–2.*

3 Across the street is the **Ritz,** the grand old lady of Madrid's hotels, built in 1910 by Alfonso XIII when he realized that his capital had no hotels elegant enough to accommodate the guests at his wedding. The Ritz garden is a delightfully aristocratic place to lunch in summer.

4 The **Museo Thyssen-Bornemisza** across the plaza Neptuno from the Ritz opened in 1992 in the Villahermosa Palace, which was elegantly renovated to include plenty of airy spaces and natural light. This ambitious collection of 800 paintings attempts to trace the history of Western art with examples from all the important movements beginning with 13th-century Italy. Among the museum's gems are the *Portrait of Henry VIII* by Hans Holbein, purchased from Princess Diana's grandfather, who used the money to buy a new Bugatti sports car. Two halls are devoted to the Impressionists and Post-Impressionists and contain many works by Pissarro as well as canvases by Renoir, Monet, Degas, Van Gogh, and Cézanne. Among the more recent movements represented are terror-filled examples of German Expressionism, but there are also soothing paintings by Georgia O'Keeffe and Andrew Wyeth. ⊠ *Paseo del Prado 8,* ☎ *91/369–0151.* ▦ *600 ptas., under 12 free.* ⊙ *Tues.–Sun. 10–7.*

★ **5** The **Parque del Retiro** (Retiro Park), once a royal retreat, is today Madrid's prettiest park. Visit the beautiful rose garden, **La Rosaleda,** and wander past the many statues and fountains. You can enjoy street musicians and magicians, row a boat on El Estanque, gaze up at the monumental **statue to Alfonso XII,** one of Spain's least notable kings (though you wouldn't think so to judge by its size), or wonder at the **Monument to the Fallen Angel**—Madrid claims the dubious privilege of being the only capital to have a statue dedicated to the Devil. The **Palacio de Velázquez** and the beautiful steel-and-glass **Palacio de Cristal,** built as a tropical plant house in the 19th century, now host occasional art exhibits.

6 Leaving the Retiro via its northwest corner, you come to the Plaza de la Independencia, dominated by the **Puerta de Alcalá,** a grandiose gateway built in 1779 for Charles III. A customs post once stood beside the gate, as did the old bullring until it was moved to its present site at Las Ventas in the 1920s. At the turn of the century, the Puerta de Alcalá more or less marked the eastern limits of Madrid.

7 Continue to the **Plaza de la Cibeles,** one of the great landmarks of the city, at the intersection of its two main arteries, the Castellana and Calle de Alcalá. Peer through the roar and fumes of the thundering traffic to see the **Cibeles Fountain,** the unofficial emblem of Madrid. Cybele, the Greek goddess of fertility, languidly rides her lion-drawn chariot, overlooked by the mighty Palacio de Comunicaciónes, a splendidly pompous cathedral-like post office.

NEED A BREAK? To rest your feet and sip a cup of coffee or a beer, head about one block up the center boulevard of the Paseo Recoletos and pull up a chair on the shady terrace or inside the air-conditioned, stained-glass-windowed bar of **El Espejo** (⊠ Paseo Recoletos 31).

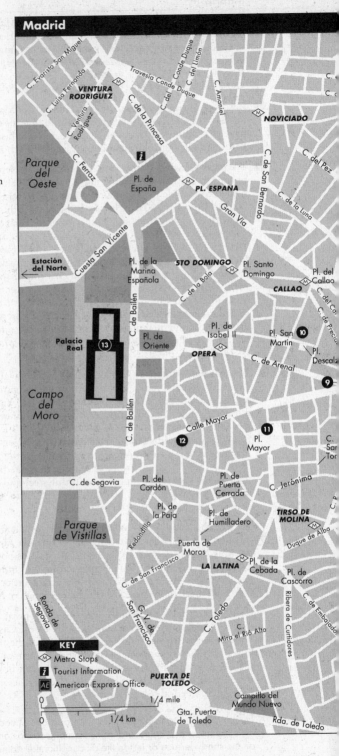

Madrid

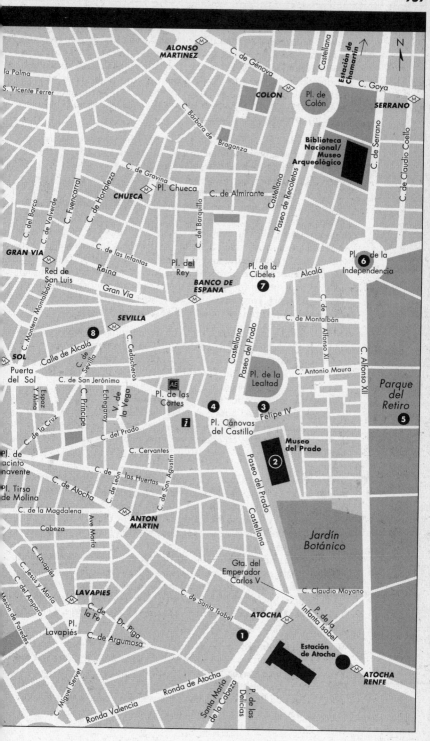

la Palma
S. Vicente Ferrer

ALONSO MARTINEZ

C. de Génova

Estación de Chamartín

C. Goya

COLON

Pl. de Colón

SERRANO

Castellana

C. de Serrano

C. de Claudio Coello

C. de Bárbara de Braganza

Biblioteca Nacional/ Museo Arqueológico

C. de Gravina

Pl. Chueca

C. de Almirante

Castellana

Paseo de Recoletos

CHUECA

C. de Hortaleza

C. Fuencarral

C. de Valverde

C. del Barco

C. del Barquillo

GRAN VIA

C. de las Infantas

Reina

Pl. del Rey

Pl. de la Cibeles

7

Alcalá

Pl. de la Independencia

6

Red de San Luis

C. Montera

Montalbán

Gran Via

BANCO DE ESPAÑA

C. de Montalbán

C. de Alfonso XI

C. Alfonso XII

SEVILLA

8

Calle de Alcalá

C. Cedaceros

Castellana

Paseo del Prado

Pl. de la Lealtad

C. Antonio Maura

Parque del Retiro

SOL

Puerta del Sol

C. de San Jerónimo

C. de Sevilla

C. V. de la Vega

AE

Pl. de las Cortes

4

3

Felipe IV

5

Espoz Y Mina

C. Príncipe

Echegaray

i

Pl. Cánovas del Castillo

C. del Prado

C. de la Cruz

Pl. de acinto navente

C. Cervantes

Museo del Prado

2

Pl. Tirso de Molina

C. de Atocha

C. de las Huertas

C. de León

C. de San Agustín

C. de la Magdalena

ANTON MARTIN

Cabeza

Ave María

Jardín Botánico

C. Lavapiés

C. Jesús y María

LAVAPIES

Gta. del Emperador Carlos V

C. Claudio Moyano

C. del Amparo

Mesón de Paredes

Pl. Lavapiés

C. de la Fe

Dr. Piga

C. de Santa Isabel

ATOCHA

P. de la Infanta Isabel

C. de Argumosa

1

Estación de Atocha

ATOCHA RENFE

C. Miguel Servet

Ronda de Atocha

Santa María de la Cabeza

P. de las Delicias

Ronda Valencia

Now head down the long and busy Calle de Alcalá toward the Puerta del Sol, resisting the temptation to turn right up the Gran Vía, which beckons temptingly with its mile of stores and cafés. Before reaching

8 the Puerta del Sol, art lovers may want to step inside the **Real Academia de San Fernando** at ⊠ Alcalá 13. This fine arts gallery boasts a collection second only to the Prado's and features all the great Spanish masters: Velázquez, El Greco, Murillo, Zurbarán, Ribera, and Goya. ⊠ *Alcalá 13,* ☎ *91/532–1546.* 🎟 *200 ptas., free Sat and Sun.* 🕐 *Tues.–Fri. 9–9; Sat.–Mon. 9–2:30.*

9 The **Puerta del Sol** is at the very heart of Madrid. Its name means Gate of the Sun, though the old gate disappeared long ago. It's easy to feel you're at the heart of things here—indeed, of all of Spain—for the kilometer distances for the whole nation are measured from the zero marker in front of the police headquarters. The square was expertly revamped in 1986 and now accommodates both a copy of **La Mariblanca** (a statue that 250 years ago adorned a fountain here) and, at the bottom of Calle Carmen, the much-loved statue of the **bear and madroño** (strawberry tree). The Puerta del Sol is inextricably linked with the history of Madrid and of the nation. Here, half a century ago, a generation of literati gathered in the long-gone cafés to thrash out the burning issues of the day; and if you can cast your thoughts back almost 200 years, you can conjure up the heroic deeds of the patriots' uprising immortalized by Goya in the *Second of May.*

This is a good place to break the tour if you've had enough sightseeing for one day. Head north up Preciados or Montera for some of the busiest shopping streets in the city or southeast toward Plaza Santa Ana for tavern-hopping in Old Madrid.

NEED A BREAK?	If it's teatime (6–7 PM), don't miss **La Mallorquina** (⊠ C. Mayor 2, ☎ 91/521–1201), an old pastry shop between Calle Mayor and Arenal. Delicious pastries are sold at the downstairs counter; the old-fashioned upstairs tea salon offers an age-old tea ritual and unbeatable views over the Puerta del Sol.

10 Art lovers will want to make a detour to the **Convento de las Descalzas Reales** on Plaza Descalzas Reales just above Arenal. It was founded by Juana de Austria, daughter of Charles V, and is still inhabited by nuns. Over the centuries the nuns, daughters of the royal and noble, endowed the convent with an enormous wealth of jewels, religious ornaments, superb Flemish tapestries, and the works of such great masters as Titian and Rubens. A bit off the main tourist track, it's one of Madrid's better-kept secrets. Your ticket includes admission to the nearby, but less interesting, **Convento de la Encarnación.** ⊠ *Plaza de las Descalzas Reales,* ☎ *91/559–7404.* 🎟 *650 ptas.* 🕐 *Tues.–Thurs., Sat. 10:30–12:30 and 4–5:30; Fri. 10:30–12:30, and Sun. 11–1:30. Guided tours in Spanish only.*

Walk up **Calle Mayor,** the Main Street of Old Madrid, past the shops full of religious statues and satins for bishops' robes, and turn left one

★ **11** block to the **Plaza Mayor,** the capital's greatest architectural showpiece. The square was built in 1617–19 for Philip III—that's Philip on the horse in the middle. The plaza has witnessed the canonization of saints, burning of heretics, fireworks, and bullfights, and is still one of the great gathering places of Madrid.

If you're here in the morning, take a look inside the 19th-century steel-and-glass San Miguel market, a colorful provisions market, before con-

12 tinuing down Calle Mayor to the **Plaza de la Villa.** The square's notable cluster of buildings includes some of the oldest houses in

Madrid. The **Casa de la Villa,** the Madrid city hall, was built in 1644 and has also served as the city prison and the mayor's home. Its sumptuous salons are occasionally open to the public; ask about guided tours, which are sometimes given in English. An archway joins the Casa de la Villa to the **Casa Cisneros,** a palace built in 1537 for the nephew of Cardinal Cisneros, primate of Spain and infamous inquisitor general. Across the square, the **Torre de Lujanes** is one of the oldest buildings in Madrid. It once imprisoned Francis I of France, archenemy of the Emperor Charles V.

NEED A BREAK? | If it's lunchtime, close by is a moderately priced restaurant with turn-of-the-century decor: **Fuente Real** (⊠ C. de las Fuentes 1, ☏ 91/559–6613).

★ **⑬** The last stop on the tour, but Madrid's second most important sight, is the **Palacio Real** (Royal Palace). This magnificent granite and limestone residence was begun by Philip V, the first Bourbon king of Spain, who was always homesick for his beloved Versailles, the opulence and splendor of which he did his best to emulate. His efforts were successful, to judge by the 2,800 rooms with their lavish rococo decorations, precious carpets, porcelain, timepieces, mirrors, and chandeliers. From 1764, when Charles III first moved in, till the coming of the Second Republic and the abdication of Alfonso XIII in 1931, the Royal Palace proved a very stylish abode for Spanish monarchs. Today King Juan Carlos, who lives in the far less ostentatious Zarzuela Palace outside Madrid, uses it only for official state functions. Allow 1½–2 hours for a visit that includes the Royal Pharmacy and other outbuildings. ⊠ *Bailén s/n,* ☏ *91/559–7404.* 🖭 *850 ptas.* ☉ *Mon.–Sat. 9:30–6, Sun. 9–3. Closed during official functions.*

The **Royal Carriage Museum,** which belongs to the palace, has a separate entrance on Paseo Virgen del Puerto. One of its highlights is the wedding carriage of Alfonso XIII and his English bride, Victoria Eugenia, granddaughter of Queen Victoria, which was damaged by a bomb thrown at it in the Calle Mayor during their wedding procession in 1906; another is the chair that carried the gout-stricken old Emperor Charles V to his retirement at the remote monastery of Yuste. The museum has been closed for several years for restoration, so make sure to check at the Royal Palace to find out if it is open.

Shopping

Gift Ideas

There are no special regional crafts associated with Madrid itself, but traditional Spanish goods are on sale in many stores. The **Corte Inglés** department store stocks good displays of Lladró porcelain, as do several specialist shops on the Gran Vía and behind the Plaza hotel on Plaza de España. Department stores stock good displays of fans, but for really superb examples, try the long-established **Casa Diego** in Puerta del Sol. Two stores opposite the Prado on Plaza Cánovas del Castillo, **Artesanía Toledana** and **El Escudo de Toledo,** have a wide selection of souvenirs, especially Toledo swords, inlaid marquetry ware, and pottery. Carefully selected handicrafts from all over Spain—ceramics, furniture, glassware, rugs, embroidery, and more—are sold at **Artespaña** (⊠ Hermosilla 14), a government-run crafts store.

Antiques

The main areas to see are the Plaza de las Cortes, the Carrera San Jerónimo, and the Rastro flea market, along the Ribera de Curtidores and the courtyards just off it.

Boutiques

.Calle Serrano has the largest collection of smart boutiques and designer fashions—think Prada, Gucci, and Cartier. Another up-and-coming area is around Calle Argensola, just south of Calle Génova. Three upscale shopping centers group a variety of exclusive shops stocked with unusual clothes and gifts: **Galerías del Prado** on the lower level of the Palace Hotel, **Los Jardines de Serrano** at the corner of Calle Goya and Claudio Coelho, and the newly opened **Centro ABC** on Calle Serrano. **Loewe,** Spain's most prestigious leather store, has boutiques on ⊠ Serrano 26 and ⊠ Gran Vía 8. **Adolfo Dóminguez,** one of Spain's top designers, has several boutiques in Salamanca, and another on Calle Orense in the north of town.

Shopping Districts

The main shopping area in the heart of Madrid is around the pedestrian streets of **Preciados** and **Montera,** between Puerta del Sol and Plaza Callao on Gran Vía. The smartest and most expensive district is the **Barrio de Salamanca** northeast of Cibeles, centered around Serrano, Velázquez, and Goya. **Calle Mayor** and the streets to the east of **Plaza Mayor** are lined with fascinating old-fashioned stores straight out of the 19th century.

Department Stores

El Corte Inglés is the biggest, brightest, and most successful Spanish chain store. Its main branch is on Preciados, just off the Puerta del Sol. Other branches are on the Paseo de la Castellana, Goya corner of Conde de Peñalver, Serrano and Ortega y Gasset, and at La Vaguada. **Marks and Spencer,** a British department store, is at ⊠ C. Serrano 52 and specializes in woolen goods, underwear, and gourmet foods. All these stores are open Monday–Saturday 10–8, and do not close for the siesta.

Food and Flea Markets

The Rastro, Madrid's most famous flea market, operates on Sundays from 9 to 2 around the Plaza del Cascorro and the Ribera de Curtidores. A **stamp and coin market** is held on Sunday mornings in the Plaza Mayor, and there's a **secondhand book market** most days on the Cuesta Claudio Moyano near Atocha Station.

Bullfighting

The Madrid bullfighting season runs from March to October. Fights are held on Sunday, and sometimes also on Thursday; starting times vary between 4:30 and 7 PM. The pinnacle of the spectacle may be seen during the three weeks of daily bullfights held during the San Isidro festivals in May. The bullring is at Las Ventas (formally known as the Plaza de Toros Monumental), Alcalá 237 (metro Ventas). You can buy your ticket there shortly before the fight, or, with a 20% surcharge, at the agencies that line Calle Victoria, just off Carrera San Jerónimo and Puerta del Sol.

Dining

For details and price-category definitions, *see* Dining *in* Staying in Spain, *above.*

$$$$ ✕ **Horcher.** Housed in a luxurious mansion at the edge of Retiro Park, ★ this classic restaurant is renowned for its hearty but elegant fare, served with impeccable style. Specialties include wild boar, venison, or roast wild duck with almond croquettes. The star appetizer is lobster salad with truffles. Other dishes such as stroganoff with mustard, pork chops with sauerkraut, and a chocolate-covered fruit and cake dessert called *baumkuchen* betray the Germanic roots of this restaurant, which originally opened in Berlin at the turn of the century. The dining room is intimate, with rust brocade fabric on the walls and antique Austrian porcelains. A wide selection of French and German wines rounds out the menu. ⊠ *Alfonso XII 6,* ☎ *91/522–0731. Reservations essential. AE, DC, MC, V. Closed Sun.*

\$\$\$\$ ✕ **Viridiana.** The trendiest of Madrid's gourmet restaurants, Viridiana has the relaxed atmosphere of a bistro and a black-and-white decor highlighted by photograms from Luis Buñuel's classic anti-clerical film of the same name. Iconoclast chef Abraham García says "market-based" is too narrow a description of his creative menu, which changes every two weeks and includes such varied fare as red onions stuffed with *morcilla* (black pudding); soft flour tortillas wrapped around marinated fresh tuna; and filet mignon in white truffle sauce. The tangy grapefruit sherbet for dessert is a marvel. ⊠ *Juan de Mena 14,* ☎ *91/531–5222. Reservations essential. No credit cards. Closed Sun., Easter wk, and Aug.*

\$\$\$\$ ✕ **Zalacaín.** A deep apricot color scheme, set off by dark wood and gleaming silver, gives this restaurant the atmosphere of an exclusive villa. Zalacaín introduced nouvelle cuisine to Spain and continues to set the pace after 20 years at the top. Splurge on dishes such as prawn salad in avocado vinaigrette; scallops and leeks in Albariño wine; and roast pheasant with truffles. Service is somewhat stuffy. A prix-fixe tasting menu allows you to sample the best of Zalacaín for about 6,500 ptas. ⊠ *Alvarez de Baena 4,* ☎ *91/561–5935. Reservations essential. AE, DC, V. No lunch Sat. Closed Sun., Easter wk, and Aug.*

\$\$\$ ✕ **El Cenador del Prado.** The Cenador's innovative menu features
★ French and Oriental touches, as well as exotic Spanish dishes not often found in restaurants. Dine in a baroque salmon-and-gold salon or a less formal plant-filled conservatory. The house specialty is *patatas a la importancia* (sliced potatoes fried in a sauce of garlic, parsley, and clams). Other possibilities include shellfish consommé with ginger ravioli, veal and eggplant in béchamel, or wild boar with prunes. For dessert try the cream-filled pastry called *cañas fritas*—a treat once served only at Spanish weddings. ⊠ *C. del Prado 4,* ☎ *91/429–1561. AE, DC, MC, V. No lunch Sat. Closed Sun., Easter wk, and 1st half of Aug.*

\$\$\$ ✕ **Gure-Etxea.** In the heart of Old Madrid on the Plaza de Paja, this is one of the capital's most authentic Basque restaurants. The ground floor dining room is airy, high-ceilinged, and elegant; brick walls line the cellar eating area, giving it a rustic, farmhouse feel. As in the Basque country, you are waited on by women. Classic dishes include *bacalao pil-pil* (spicy cod fried in garlic and oil, making the "pil-pil" sound), *rape en salsa verde* (monkfish in garlic and parsley sauce), and for dessert *leche frita* (fried custard). On weekdays a hearty and inexpensive plate of the day is added to the lunchtime menu. ⊠ *Plaza de Paja 12,* ☎ *91/365–6149. AE, DC, V. Closed Sun., Easter wk, and Aug.*

\$\$\$ ✕ **La Trainera.** Fresh seafood—the best money can buy—is what La Trainera is all about. For decades this informal restaurant, with its nautical decor and maze of little dining rooms, has reigned as the queen of Madrid's seafood houses. Crab, lobster, shrimp, mussels, and a dozen other types of shellfish are served by weight in *raciones* (large portions). Although many Spanish diners share several plates of these delicacies as their entire meal, the grilled hake, sole, or turbot make an unbeatable second course. Skip the listless house wine and go for a bottle of Albariño from the cellar. ⊠ *Lagasca 60,* ☎ *91/576–8035. AE, MC, V. Closed Sun. and Aug.*

\$\$ ✕ **Casa Botín.** Madrid's oldest and most famous restaurant, just off
★ the Plaza Mayor, has been catering to diners since 1725. Its decor and food are traditionally Castilian, as are the wood-fire ovens used for

cooking. Cochinillo asado and cordero asado are the specialties. It was a favorite of Hemingway's and is somewhat touristy, but fun. Try to be seated in the basement or the upstairs dining room. ⊠ *Cuchilleros 17,* ☎ *91/366–4217. Reservations essential. AE, DC, MC, V.*

$$ ✕ **Casa Vallejo.** With its homey dining room, friendly staff, creative menu, and reasonable prices, this restaurant is the well-kept secret of Madrid's budget gourmets. Try the tomato, zucchini, and cheese tart or artichokes and clams for starters, then follow up with duck breast in prune sauce or meatballs made with lamb, almonds, and pine nuts. Their fudge-and-raspberry pie is worth a trip in itself. ⊠ *San Lorenzo 9,* ☎ *91/308–6158. Reservations essential. AE, MC, V. Closed Sun. No lunch Mon.*

$$ ✕ **La Gamella.** American-born chef Dick Stephens has created a new
★ reasonably priced menu at this hugely popular dining spot. The sophisticated rust-red dining room, batik tablecloths, oversize plates, and attentive service remain the same. But much of the nouvelle cuisine has been replaced by more traditional fare, such as chicken in garlic, beef bourguignonne, or steak tartar à la Jack Daniels. A few signature dishes such as sausage and red pepper quiche and the bittersweet chocolate pâté for dessert remain, and the lunchtime menú del día, at 1,700 ptas., is a great value. ⊠ *Alfonso XII 4,* ☎ *91/532–4509. AE, DC, MC, V. Closed Sun., Mon., and Aug. 15–31.*

$$ ✕ **Mediterraneo.** Flawlessly prepared rice dishes are served day and night in this casual brick and brass paella house conveniently located near the Serrano shopping district. Specialties include a perfect paella *mixta* (with seafood, pork, and vegetables). ⊠ *Jorge Juan 13,* ☎ *91/437–2161. AE, V. Closed Sun. night.*

$$ ✕ **Nicolas.** One of Madrid's hottest restaurants, Nicolas serves updated versions of traditional Spanish classics in a chic brasserie setting at reasonable prices. Specialties include garlic soup, a stew of garbanzos and baby squid, sea bass with shrimp, and red peppers stuffed with pork. ⊠ *Villalar 4,* ☎ *91/431–7737. AE, DC, MC, V. Closed Sun. and Mon.*

$ ✕ **Café La Plaza.** Strategically positioned between the Prado and Thyssen-Bornemisza art museums and open continuously from 10 AM to midnight, the Café La Plaza is an indispensable rest stop for tourists exploring Madrid. It's an upscale, self-service restaurant with a green-and-white garden-party decor, set among the exclusive boutiques of the Galería del Prado shopping center. Food is arranged on several circular tables. There's a salad bar, a pasta bar, and an economical menú del día, which, depending on the day, might be Spanish-style chicken, breaded fish, or beef stew served with vegetables, bread, and wine. ⊠ *Plaza de las Cortes 7,* ☎ *91/429–6537. Reservations not accepted. AE, V. Closed Sun.*

$ ✕ **Casa Mingo.** Resembling an Asturian cider tavern, Casa Mingo is
★ built into a stone wall beneath the Norte train station. It's a bustling place and the only dishes offered are succulent roast chicken, salad, and sausages, all washed down with numerous bottles of *sidra* (hard cider). Inside, you'll share long plank tables with other diners; in summer small tables are set up on the sidewalk. ⊠ *Paseo de la Florida 2,* ☎ *91/547–7918. Reservations not accepted. No credit cards.*

Lodging

For details and price-category definitions, *see* Lodging *in* Staying in Spain, *above.*

$$$$ ▥ **Palace.** This dignified turn-of-the-century hotel opposite parliament and the Prado is a slightly less dazzling stepsister of the nearby Ritz but is full of charm and style. It has long been a favorite of politicians and journalists. Its Belle Epoque decor—especially the glass dome over the lounge—is superb. ⊠ *Plaza de las Cortes 7, 28014,* ☏ *91/429–7551,* FAX *91/429–8266. 436 rooms with bath, 20 suites. Restaurant, bar, hair salon, shops, parking. AE, DC, MC, V.*

$$$$ ⊞ **Ritz.** Spain's most exclusive hotel is elegant and aristocratic with beau-
★ tiful rooms, spacious suites, and sumptuous public salons furnished with antiques and handwoven carpets. Its palatial restaurant is justly famous, and its garden terrace is the perfect setting for summer dining. There are brunches with harp music on weekends, and tea or supper cham-ber-music concerts from February through May. Close to the Retiro Park and overlooking the famous Prado Museum, it offers pure unadul-terated luxury. ⊠ *Plaza Lealtad 5, 28014,* ☏ *91/521–2857,* FAX *91/532–8776. 158 rooms with bath. Restaurant, bar, hair salon, park-ing. AE, DC, MC, V.*

$$$$ ⊞ **Villamagna.** Second in luxury only to the Ritz, the Villamagna's mod-ern facade belies a palatial interior exquisitely furnished with 18th-cen-tury antiques. Set in a delightful garden, it offers all the facilities one would expect in a hotel of international repute. ⊠ *Paseo de la Castel-lana 22, 28046,* ☏ *91/576–7500,* FAX *91/575–9504. 164 rooms with bath, 18 suites. Restaurant, bar, hair salon, sauna, shops, parking. AE, DC, MC, V.*

$$$$ ⊞ **Villa Real.** Aubusson tapestries from the 19th century and English antiques set the tone in the lobby of this very personal hotel. The em-phasis is on service and luxurious details, such as three telephones in every room and teletext service on TV. All rooms have both an upstairs and a downstairs and slightly clubby masculine decor with leather sofas and dark red floral fabrics. The hotel looks over the Plaza de las Cortes and is convenient to almost everything. ⊠ *Plaza de las Cortes 10, 28014,* ☏ *91/420–3767,* FAX *91/420–2547. 94 rooms with bath, 20 suites. Bar, shops, parking. AE, DC, MC, V.*

$$$ ⊞ **El Prado.** Wedged in among the classic buildings of Old Madrid, this skinny hotel is within stumbling distance of the city's best bars and nightclubs. Rooms are soundproofed with double-pane glass and are surprisingly spacious. Decor includes pastel floral prints and gleam-ing marble baths. ⊠ *C. Prado 11, 28014,* ☏ *91/369–0234,* FAX *91/429–2829. 50 rooms with bath. Cafeteria, parking. AE, DC, MC, V.*

$$$ ⊞ **Reina Victoria.** One of Madrid's most historic and best loved ho-
★ tels, the Reina Victoria faces two of the city's liveliest squares. Once a haven for bullfighters, the hotel now attracts a more upscale clien-tele who are treated to large renovated rooms with a comfortable feel and magnificent views. ⊠ *Plaza del Angel 7, 28014* ☏ *91/531–4500,* FAX *91/522–0307. 110 rooms with bath. Bar. AE, DC, MC, V.*

$$$ ⊞ **Tryp Ambassador.** In the refurbished palace of the Dukes of Granada, this hotel sits on a quiet old street near the Royal Palace. A magnifi-cent front door and three-story spiral staircase in the entryway greet visitors. Rooms are large and luxurious with separate sleeping and sit-ting areas. ⊠ *Cuesta de Santo Domingo 5, 28013,* ☏ *91/541–6700,* FAX *91/559–1040. 182 rooms with bath. Restaurant, bar, parking. AE, DC, MC, V.*

$$ ⊞ **Carlos V.** If you like to be right in the center of things, this classic Madrid hotel on a quiet, pedestrians-only street is just a few steps away from the Puerta del Sol and Plaza Mayor. A suit of armor decorates the tiny lobby, and crystal chandeliers add elegance to a second-floor guest lounge. All rooms are bright and carpeted. ⊠ *Maestro Victoria 5, 28013,* ☏ *91/531–4100,* FAX *91/531–3761. 67 rooms with bath. AE, MC, V.*

$$ ⊞ **Inglés.** The exterior may seem shabby, but don't be deterred. The Inglés is a long-standing budget favorite. Its rooms are comfortable—if a bit dreary—and the location is a bonus: You're a short walk from the Puerta del Sol one way, and from the Prado the other; inexpensive restaurants and atmospheric bars are right at hand. ✉ *Echegaray 10, 28014,* ☎ *91/429–6551,* 𝔽𝔸𝕏 *91/420–2423. 58 rooms with bath. Cafeteria, bar, exercise room, parking. AE, DC, MC, V.*

$$ 🏨 **Paris.** Overlooking the Puerta del Sol, the Paris is a stylish hotel full
★ of old-fashioned appeal. It has an impressive turn-of-the-century lobby and a restaurant where you can dine for around 1,500 ptas. Recently refurbished, the hotel has managed to retain its character while adding modern amenities. ✉ *Alcalá 2, 28014,* ☎ *91/521–6496,* 𝔽𝔸𝕏 *91/531–0188. 114 rooms with bath. Restaurant. MC, V.*

$ 🏨 **Lisboa.** Clean, small, and central, the Lisboa is a well-kept secret in the lively bar-and-restaurant neighborhood of Plaza Santa Ana. Rooms have tile floors and are sparsely furnished. They vary greatly in size and quality, so be sure to ask to see your room before taking it. ✉ *Ventura de la Vega 17, 28014,* ☎ 𝔽𝔸𝕏 *91/429–9894. 22 rooms with bath. AE, DC, MC, V.*

$ 🏨 **Mora.** Directly across the Paseo del Prado from the Botanical Gardens, the Mora underwent a complete renovation in 1994 and now offers a sparkling faux marble lobby and bright, carpeted hallways. Rooms are simple, but large and comfortable. Those on the street have great views of the gardens and Prado Museum and have double-pane windows for soundproofing. ✉ *Paseo del Prado 32, 28014,* ☎ *91/420–1569,* 𝔽𝔸𝕏 *91/420–0564. 61 rooms with bath. AE, DC, MC, V.*

Bars and Cafés

Bars

Mesónes. The most traditional and colorful taverns are on Cuchilleros and Cava San Miguel just west of Plaza Mayor, where you'll find a whole array of mesónes with such names as Tortilla, Champiñón, and Boqueron.

Old Madrid. Wander the narrow streets between Puerta del Sol and Plaza Santa Ana, which are packed with traditional tapas bars. Favorites here are the **Cervecería Alemana** (✉ Plaza Santa Ana 6), a beer hall founded more than 100 years ago by Germans and patronized, inevitably, by Hemingway; **Los Gabrieles** (✉ Echegaray 17), with magnificent ceramic decor; **La Trucha** (✉ Manuel Fernández y González 3), with loads of atmosphere; and **Viva Madrid** (✉ Fernández y González 7), a lovely old bar.

Calle Huertas. Fashionable bars with turn-of-the-century decor and chamber or guitar music, often live, line this street. **La Fídula** at No. 57 and El Hecho at No. 56 are two of the best.

Plaza Santa Bárbara. This area just off Alonso Martínez is packed with fashionable bars and beer halls. Stroll along Santa Teresa, Orellana, Campoamor, or Fernando VI and take your pick. The **Cervecería Santa Bárbara** in the plaza itself is one of the most colorful, a popular beer hall with a good range of tapas.

Cafés

If you like cafés with an old-fashioned atmosphere, dark wooden counters, brass pumps, and marble-top tables, try any of the following: **Café Comercial** (✉ Glorieta de Bilbao 7); **Café Gijón** (✉ Paseo de Recoletos 21), a former literary hangout and the most famous of the cafés of old, now one of the many café-terraces that line the Castellana; **Café León** (✉ Alcalá 57), just up from Cibeles; and **El Espejo** (✉ Paseo de Recoletos 31), with art-nouveau decor and an outdoor terrace in summer. For a late night coffee or something stronger, try to stop in at the baroque **Palacio de Gaviria** (✉ Arenal 9) a restored 19th-century palace tucked away on the upper level of a tawdry commercial street. It allegedly once housed an unofficial royal consort.

The Arts

Details of all cultural events are listed in the daily newspaper *El País* or in the weekly *Guía del Ocio*.

Concerts and Opera

The main concert hall is the new **Auditorio Nacional de Madrid** (✉ Príncipe de Vergara 146, ☎ 91/337–0100; metro Cruz del Rayo), which opened at the end of 1988. The old **Teatro Real** on the Plaza de Oriente opposite the Royal Palace is being converted into Madrid's long-needed opera house and was scheduled to reopen in late 1996; inquire at the tourist office.

Zarzuela

Zarzuela, a combination of light opera and dance ideal for non-Spanish speakers, is held at the **Teatro Nacional Lírico de la Zarzuela** (✉ Jovellanos 4, ☎ 91/524–5400). The season runs from October through July.

Theater

If language is no problem, check out the fringe theaters in Lavapiés and the Centro Cultural de la Villa (☎ 91/575–6080) beneath the Plaza Colón, and the open-air events in the Retiro Park. Other leading theaters—you'll also need reasonable Spanish—include the **Círculo de Bellas Artes** (✉ Marqués de Casa Riera 2, just off Alcalá 42, ☎ 91/532–4437); the **Teatro Español** (✉ Príncipe 25 on Plaza Santa Ana, ☎ 91/429–6297) for Spanish classics; and the **Teatro María Guerrero** (✉ Tamayo y Baus 4, ☎ 91/319–4769), home of the Centro Dramático Nacional, for plays by García Lorca. Most theaters have two curtains, at 7 and 10:30 PM, and close on Mondays. Tickets are inexpensive and often easy to come by on the night of performance.

Films

Foreign films are mostly dubbed into Spanish, but movies in English are listed in *El País* or *Guía del Ocio* under "VO," meaning *versión original*. A dozen or so theaters now show films in English; some of the best bets are **Alphaville** and **Cines Renoir,** both in Martín de los Heroes, just off Plaza España, and the **Filmoteca** (✉ Santa Isabel 3), a city-run institution where classic VO films change daily.

Nightlife

Cabaret

Florida Park (☎ 91/573–7805), in the Retiro Park, offers dinner and a show that often features ballet, Spanish dance, or flamenco and is open Monday through Saturday from 9:30 PM, with shows at 10:45 PM. **Berlin** (✉ Costanilla de San Pedro 11, ☎ 91/366–2034) opens at 9:30 for a dinner that is good by most cabaret standards, followed by a show and dancing until 4 AM. **La Scala** (✉ Rosario Pino 7, ☎ 91/571–4411), in the Meliá Castilla hotel, is Madrid's top nightclub, with dinner, dancing, cabaret at 8:30, and a second, less expensive show around midnight. This is the one visited by most night tours.

Flamenco

Madrid offers the widest choice of flamenco shows in Spain; some are good, but many are aimed at the tourist trade. Dinner tends to be mediocre and overpriced, but it ensures the best seats; otherwise, opt for the show and a *consumición* (drink) only, usually starting around 11 PM and costing 3,000 ptas.–3,500 ptas. **Arco de Cuchilleros** (✉ Cuchilleros 7, ☎ 91/266–5867), behind the Plaza Mayor, is one of the better, cheaper ones. **Café de Chinitas** (✉ Torija 7, ☎ 91/547–1502) and **Corral de la Morería** (✉ Morería 17, ☎ 91/365–8446 and 91/265–

1137) are two of the more authentic places where well-known troupes perform. Another choice is **Corral de la Pacheca** (⊠ Juan Ramón Jiménez 26, ☎ 91/359–2660).

Jazz

The city's best-known jazz venue is **Café Central** (⊠ Plaza de Angel 10), followed by **Clamores** (⊠ Albuquerque 14). Others include **Café Jazz Populart** (⊠ Huertas 22) and **Café del Foro** (⊠ San Andrés 38). Excellent jazz frequently comes to Madrid as part of city-hosted seasonal festivals; check the local press for listings and venues.

Casino

Madrid's **Casino** (☎ 91/856–1100) is 28 kilometers (17 miles) out at Torrelodones on the N-VI road to La Coruña. Open 5 PM–4 AM. Free transportation service from ⊠ Plaza de España 6.

MADRID ENVIRONS

The beauty of the historic cities surrounding Madrid and the role they have played in their country's history rank them among Spain's most worthwhile sights. Ancient Toledo, the former capital; the great palace-monastery of El Escorial; the sturdy and picturesque medieval walls of Ávila; Segovia's Roman aqueduct and fairy-tale Alcázar; and the magnificent Plaza Mayor of the old university town of Salamanca all lie within an hour or so from the capital.

All the towns below, with the possible exception of Salamanca, can easily be visited on day trips from Madrid. But if you've had your fill of the hustle and bustle of Spain's booming capital, you'll find it far more rewarding to tour from one place to another, spending a day or two in one or more of these fascinating locales. After the day-trippers have gone home, you can enjoy the real charm of these small provincial towns and wander at leisure through their medieval streets.

Getting There from Madrid

Trains to Toledo leave from Madrid's Atocha Station; to Salamanca from Chamartín station; to Ávila, Segovia, and El Escorial from both stations, although sometimes more frequently from Chamartín. For schedules and reservations call RENFE, (☎ 91/563–0202)

Getting Around

There's a direct train line between El Escorial, Ávila, and Salamanca; otherwise, train connections are poor and you'll do better to go by bus. All places are linked by bus services and the local tourist offices will advise on schedules. Toledo's bus station is on the Ronda de Castilla la Mancha (☎ 925/215850) just off the road from Madrid. Ávila's bus station is on Avenida de Madrid (☎ 920/220154); Segovia's is on Paseo Ezequiel González (☎ 921/427707); and Salamanca's is on Filiberto Villalobos 71 (☎ 923/236717). The N403 from Toledo to Ávila passes through spectacular scenery in the Sierra de Gredos mountains, as does the C505 Ávila–El Escorial route. From El Escorial to Segovia, both the Puerto de León and Puerto de Navacerrada mountain passes offer magnificent views. The N501 from Ávila to Salamanca will take you across the tawny plain of Castile.

Visitor Information

Ávila (⊠ Plaza de la Catedral 4, ☎ 920/211387); ⊘ Weekdays 8–3 and 4–6 (5–7 in summer), Sat. 9–1:30.

El Escorial (✉ Floridablanca 10, ☎ 91/890–1554); ⊘ Weekdays 10–2 and 3–5, Sat. 10–2.
Salamanca (✉ Casa de las Conchas, Rúa Mayor s/n, ☎ 923/268571); ⊘ Weekdays 10–2 and 5–8, Sat. 9–2. There's also an information booth on the Plaza Mayor (market side).
Segovia (✉ Plaza Mayor 10, ☎ 921/460334; ⊘ Mon.–Fri. 10–2 and 5–8, Sat. 10–2; Sun. 10–2 in summer.
Toledo (✉ Puerta de Bisagra, ☎ 925/220843); ⊘ Mon.–Fri. 9–2 and 4–6, Sat. 9–3 and 4–6, Sun. 9–3.

Exploring the Madrid Environs

Toledo

Head south from Madrid on the road to Toledo. About 20 minutes from the capital look left for a prominent rounded hill topped by a statue of Christ. This is the **Hill of the Angels,** which marks the geographical center of the Iberian Peninsula. After 90 minutes of drab, industrial scenery, the unforgettable silhouette of **Toledo** suddenly rises before you, the imposing bulk of the Alcázar and the slender spire of the cathedral dominating the skyline. This former capital, where Moors, Jews, and Christians once lived in harmony, is now a living national monument, depicting all the elements of Spanish civilization in hand-carved, sun-mellowed stone. For a stunning view and to capture the beauty of Toledo as El Greco knew it, begin with a panoramic drive around the Carretera de Circunvalación, crossing over the Alcántara bridge and returning by way of the bridge of San Martín. As you gaze at the city rising like an island in its own bend of the Tagus, reflect how little the city skyline has changed in the four centuries since El Greco painted *Storm Over Toledo.*

Toledo is a small city steeped in history and full of magnificent buildings. It was the capital of Spain under both Moors and Christians until some whim caused Philip II to move his capital to Madrid in 1561. Begin your visit with a drink in one of the many terrace cafés on the central **Plaza Zocodover,** study a map, and try to get your bearings, for a veritable labyrinth confronts you as you try to find your way to Toledo's great treasures. While here, search the square's pastry shops for the typical *mazapanes* (marzipan candies) of Toledo.

Begin your tour with a visit to the 13th-century **Cathedral,** seat of the Cardinal Primate of Spain, and one of the great cathedrals of Spain. Somber but elaborate, it blazes with jeweled chalices, gorgeous ecclesiastical vestments, historic tapestries, some 750 stained-glass windows, and paintings by Tintoretto, Titian, Murillo, El Greco, Velázquez, and Goya. The cathedral has two surprises: a **Mozarabic chapel,** where Mass is still celebrated on Sundays according to an ancient Mozarabic rite handed down from the days of the Visigoths (AD 419–711); and its unique **Transparente,** an ornate Baroque roof that gives a theatrical glimpse into heaven as the sunlight pours down through a mass of figures and clouds. ☎ 925/222241. ✆ 500 ptas. ⊘ Mon.–Sat. 10:30–1 and 3:30–6 (7 in summer), Sun. 10:30–1:30 and 4–6 (7 in summer).

En route to the real jewel of Toledo, the **Chapel of Santo Tomé,** you'll pass a host of souvenir shops on Calle Santo Tomé, bursting with damascene knives and swords, blue-and-yellow pottery from nearby Talavera, and El Greco reproductions. In the tiny chapel that houses El Greco's masterpiece, *The Burial of the Count of Orgaz,* you can capture the true spirit of the Greek painter who adopted Spain, and in particular Toledo, as his home. Do you recognize the sixth man from the left among the painting's earthly contingent? Or the young boy in the left-hand corner? The first is El Greco himself, the second his son

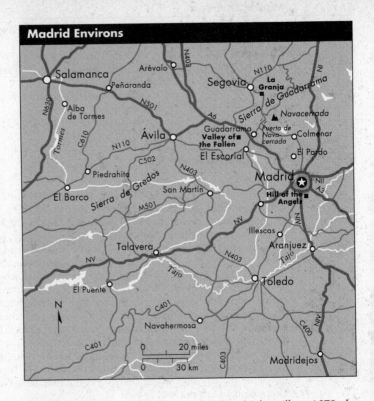

Madrid Environs

Salamanca · Arévalo · Segovia · La Granja · Sierra de Guadarrama · Navacerrada · Peñaranda · Alba de Tormes · Guadarrama · Puerto de Navacerrada · Colmenar · Ávila · Valley of the Fallen · El Pardo · El Escorial · Piedrahita · Madrid · Hill of the Angels · El Barco · San Martín · Illescas · Aranjuez · Talavera · Toledo · El Puente · Navahermosa · Madridejos

0   20 miles
0   30 km

N

Jorge Manuel—embroidered on his handkerchief you'll see 1578, the year of his birth. ☎ 925/210209. 🎟 150 ptas. ☉ Daily 10–1:45 and 3:30–5:45 (6:45 in summer).

Not far away is **El Greco's House,** a replica containing copies of his works. ☎ 925/224046. 🎟 400 ptas. ☉ Tues.–Sat. 10–2 and 4–6, Sun. 10–2.

The splendid **Sinagoga del Tránsito** stands on the corner of Samuel Levi and Reyes Católicos. Commissioned in 1366 by Samuel Levi, chancellor to Pedro the Cruel, the synagogue shows Christian and Moorish as well as Jewish influences in its architecture and decoration—look at the stars of David interspersed with the arms of Castile and León. There's also a small **Sephardic Museum** chronicling the life of Toledo's former Jewish community. ☎ 925/223665. 🎟 400 ptas. ☉ Tues.–Sat. 10–2 and 4–6, Sun. 10–2.

Another synagogue, **Santa María la Blanca** (it was given as a church to the Knights of Calatrava in 1405), is just along the street. Its history may have been Jewish and Christian, but its architecture is definitely Moorish, for it resembles a mosque with five naves, horseshoe arches, and capitals decorated with texts from the Koran. ☎ 925/227257. 🎟 150 ptas. ☉ Daily 10–2 and 3:30–6 (until 7 in summer).

Across the road is **San Juan de los Reyes,** a beautiful Gothic church begun by Ferdinand and Isabella in 1476. Wander around its fine cloisters and don't miss the iron manacles on the outer walls; they were placed there by Christians freed by the Moors. The Catholic Kings originally intended to be buried here, but then their great triumph at Granada in 1492 changed their plans. ☎ 925/223802. 🎟 150 ptas. ☉ Daily 10–1:45 and 3:30–5:45 (6:45 in summer).

Walk down the hill through the ancient **Cambrón Gate** and your visit to Toledo is over. Should you have more time, however, head for the

Museum of Santa Cruz, just off the Zocodover, with its splendid El Grecos. ☎ 925/221036. ☐ 200 ptas. ☉ Mon. 10–2 and 4–6:30, Tues.–Sat. 10–6:30, Sun. 10–2.

Also consider a visit to the **Hospital de Tavera,** outside the walls, where you can see Ribera's amazing *Bearded Woman.* ☎ 925/220451. ☐ 500 ptas. ☉ Daily 10:30–1:30 and 3:30–6.

El Escorial

In the foothills of the Guadarrama Mountains, 50 kilometers (31 miles) to the northwest of Madrid, and 120 kilometers (74 miles) from Toledo, lies **San Lorenzo del Escorial,** burial place of Spanish kings and queens. The **Monastery,** built by the religious fanatic Philip II as a memorial to his father, Charles V, is a vast rectangular edifice, conceived and executed with a monotonous magnificence worthy of the Spanish royal necropolis. It was designed by Juan de Herrera, Spain's greatest Renaissance architect. The **Royal Pantheon** contains the tombs of monarchs since Carlos I save three. Only those queens who bore sons later crowned lie in the same crypt; the others, along with royal sons and daughters who never ruled, lie in the nearby **Pantheon of the Infantes.** The monastery's other highlights are the magnificent **Library of Philip II,** with 40,000 rare volumes and 2,700 illuminated manuscripts, including the diary of Santa Teresa, and the **Royal Apartments.** Contrast the spartan private apartment of Philip II and the simple bedroom in which he died in 1598 with the beautiful carpets, porcelain, and tapestries with which his less austere successors embellished the rest of his somber monastery-palace. ✉ San Lorenzo de El Escorial, ☎ 91/890–5905. ☐ 850 ptas. ☉ Tues.–Sun. 10–6 (7 in summer). Last entry is 45 mins before closing time.

Valley of the Fallen

Eight kilometers (5 miles) along the road to Segovia, the mighty cross of the **Valley of the Fallen** looms up on your left. This vast basilica hewn out of sheer granite was built by General Franco between 1940 and 1959 as a monument to the dead of Spain's Civil War of 1936–39. Buried here are 43,000 war dead and Franco himself, who died in 1975. A funicular to the top of the monument costs 350 ptas. ☎ 91/890–5611. ☐ 650 ptas. ☉ Tues.–Sun. 10–6 (9:30–7 in summer).

A spectacular drive lies ahead for those who use the local road rather than the autoroute, from the resort of Navacerrada up through the Guadarrama Mountains by way of the **Navacerrada pass** at 6,000 feet. The steep descent through pine forests via the hairpin bends of the *Siete Revueltas* (Seven Curves) brings you straight into La Granja.

La Granja

The **Palace of La Granja,** with its splendid formal gardens and fountains, was built between 1719 and 1739 by the homesick Philip V, first Bourbon king of Spain and grandson of France's Louis XIV, to remind him of his beloved Versailles. The whole place is like an exquisite piece of France in a Spanish wood, and it's small wonder that Philip chose to be buried here in the splendor of his own creation rather than in the austerity of El Escorial. The splendid gardens are open until dusk and you can stroll around them for free except when the fountains are running. ☎ 921/470020. ☐ 650 ptas. ☉ Tues.–Sun. 10–6; winter, Tues.–Sat. 10–1:30 and 3–5, Sun. 10–2.

Segovia

From La Granja, a 10-minute drive will bring you to the golden-stone market town of **Segovia.** In front of you rises the majestic **Roman aqueduct,** its huge granite blocks held together without mortar. At its foot is a small bronze statue of Romulus and the wolf, presented by Rome in 1974 to commemorate the 2,000-year history of Spain's most complete Roman monument.

Drive around the base of the rock on which Segovia stands. The Ronda de Santa Lucía leads to the most romantic view of the Alcázar, perched high on its rock like the prow of a mighty ship. Return via the Carretera de los Hoyos for yet another magical view, this time of the venerable cathedral rising from the ramparts. Next, fend off the pestering gypsies around the aqueduct and make for the **Calle Real,** the main shopping street. As you climb, you'll pass the Romanesque church of **San Martín,** with its porticoed outer gallery. Continue to the picturesque **Plaza Mayor** with its colorful ceramic stalls (good bargains) and pleasant cafés set against the backdrop of ancient arcaded houses and one of the loveliest (externally, at least) Gothic cathedrals in Spain.

Segovia **cathedral** was the last Gothic cathedral to be built in Spain (the one in Ávila was the first). Begun in 1525 by order of Charles V, its interior is sadly disappointing, as many of its treasures were carried off by Napoléon's troops in the Peninsular War of the early 1800s. Its museum has the first book printed in Spain (1472). You should also seek out the tomb of Don Pedro, two-year-old son of Henry IV who slipped from his nurse's arms and tumbled to his death over the battlements of the Alcázar. ☎ *911/435325.* ▨ *250 ptas.* ◷ *Daily 9:30–6 in winter, 9–7 in summer.*

The turreted **Alcázar** is largely a fanciful re-creation from the 1880s, the original 13th-century castle having been destroyed by fire in 1862. The view from its ramparts—and, even better, from its tower if you can manage the 156 steps—is breathtaking. The Alcázar served as a major residence of the Catholic Kings. Here Isabella met Ferdinand, and from here she set out to be crowned Queen of Castile. The interior successfully re-creates the era of this dual monarchy that established Spain's Golden Age. ☎ *911/460759.* ▨ *375 ptas.* ◷ *Daily 10–6 in winter, 10–7 in summer.*

Ávila

★ **Ávila,** almost 4,100 feet above sea level, is the highest provincial capital in Spain. Alfonso VI and his son-in-law, Count Raimundo de Borgoña, rebuilt the town and walls in 1090, bringing it permanently under Christian control. It is these walls, the most complete military installations of their kind in Spain, that give Ávila its special medieval quality. Thick and solid, with 88 towers tufted with numerous untidy storks' nests, they stretch for 2½ kilometers (1½ miles) around the entire city and make an ideal focus for the start of your visit. For a superb overall view and photo spot, drive out to the **Cuatro Postes,** ¾ kilometer (½ mile) out on the road to Salamanca.

The personality of Santa Teresa the Mystic, to whom the city is dedicated, lives today as vividly as it did in the 16th century. Several religious institutions associated with the life of the saint are open to visitors, the most popular of which is the **Convent of Santa Teresa,** which stands on the site of her birthplace. There's an ornate Baroque chapel, a small gift shop, and a museum with some of her relics: her rosary, books, walking stick, a sole of her sandal, and her finger wearing her wedding ring. ⊠ *Plaza de la Santa, just inside the southern gate,* ☎ *920/211030.* ▨ *Free.* ◷ *Daily 9:30–1:30 and 3:30–8:30 (until 9 in summer).*

Ávila's other ecclesiastical monuments are far older and more rewarding than those that commemorate the saint. The impregnable hulk of the **cathedral** is in many ways more akin to a fortress than a house of God. Though of Romanesque origin—the Romanesque sections are recognizable by their red-and-white brickwork—it is usually claimed as Spain's first Gothic cathedral. Inside is the ornate alabaster tomb of Cardinal Alonso de Madrigal, a 15th-century bishop whose swarthy complexion earned him the nickname of "El Tostado" (the toasted one). ☎ 920/211641. ☞ *Cathedral free, museum 200 ptas.* ☉ *In summer Tues.–Sun. 9–1:30 and 3:30–6:30, in winter 9–1:30 and 3:30–5.*

The **Basilica of San Vicente,** just outside the walls, is one of Ávila's finest Romanesque churches, standing on the spot where St. Vincent and his sisters Sabina and Cristeta were martyred in AD 306. Here, too, Santa Teresa is said to have experienced the vision that told her to reform the Carmelite order. ☎ 920/255230. ☞ *50 ptas.* ☉ *Tues.–Sun. 10–2 and 4–7:15.*

Before continuing to the **Monastery of Santo Tomás,** you can relax in the pleasant **Plaza de Santa Teresa** with its outdoor cafés and statue of the saint erected for Pope John Paul's visit in 1982. Built between 1482 and 1493 by Ferdinand and Isabella, who used it as a summer palace, the monastery houses the tomb of their only son, Prince Juan—who died at the age of 19 while a student at Salamanca—as well as the tomb of that far less lovable character, the notorious Inquisitor General Tomás de Torquemada. ☞ *Monastery free, cloisters 50 ptas., Museum of Eastern Art 100 ptas.* ☉ *Daily 10–1 and 4–8.*

Alba de Tormes

From Ávila it's straight sailing all the way to Salamanca unless you're a devotee of Santa Teresa and choose to take a small detour to the old ducal town of **Alba de Tormes** to visit the **Carmelite Convent** (☉ Daily 9–2 and 4–8), where the saint is buried.

Salamanca

★ **Salamanca** is an ancient city, and your first glimpse of it is bound to be unforgettable. Beside the road flows the Tormes River and beyond it rise the old houses of the city and the golden walls, turrets, and domes of the Plateresque cathedrals. "Plateresque" comes from *plata* (silver) and implies that the stone is chiseled and engraved as intricately as that delicate metal. A superb example of this style is the facade of the Dominican **Monastery of San Esteban** (☎ 923/215000. ☞ 200 ptas.; ☉ Daily 9–1 and 4–7, 5–8 in summer), which you'll pass on your way to the cathedrals. The **old cathedral** far outshines its younger sister, the **new cathedral.** Inside the sturdy Romanesque walls of the old cathedral is a stunning altarpiece with 53 brightly painted panels. Don't miss the splendid **cloisters,** which now house a worthwhile collection of religious art, and the **Degree Chapel,** where anxious students sought inspiration on the night before their final exams. ☎ 923/217476. ☞ *New cathedral free, old cathedral and cloisters 300 ptas.* ☉ *New cathedral: Daily 10–1 and 4–6; Old cathedral and cloisters: Daily 10–12:30 and 4–5:30.*

Founded by Alfonso IX in 1218, **Salamanca University** is to Spain what Oxford University is to England. On its famous **doorway** in the Patio de las Escuelas, a profusion of Plateresque carving surrounds the medallions of Ferdinand and Isabella. See if you can find the famous frog and skull, said to bring good luck to students in their examinations. Inside, the **lecture room** of Fray Luis de León has remained untouched since the days of the great scholar, and the prestigious **library** boasts some 50,000 parchment and leather-bound volumes. ☎ 923/294400, ext. 1150. ☞ *300 ptas.* ☉ *Mon.–Fri. 9:30–1:30 and 4–7:30, Sat. 9:30–1:30 and 4–7, Sun. 10–1:30.*

Now make for Salamanca's greatest jewel, the elegant 18th-century **Plaza Mayor.** Here you can browse in stores offering typical *charro* jewelry (silver and black flowerheads), head down the steps to the market in search of colorful tapas bars, or simply relax in an outdoor café. In this, the city's crowning glory, and the most exquisite square in Spain, you've found the perfect place to end your tour of Salamanca and Castile.

Dining and Lodging

For details and price-category definitions, see Dining and Lodging in Staying in Spain, above.

Ávila

$$ ✕ **El Fogón de Santa Teresa.** Traditional Castilian roasts, lamb chops, and trout feature on the menu of this attractive restaurant in the vaults of the Palacio de Valderrábaños. ✉ *Alemania 3,* ☎ *920/211023. AE, DC, MC, V.*

$$ ✕ **El Molino de la Losa.** Situated on a spit of land jutting into the Adaja
★ River, this restaurant occupies a restored 15th-century mill and has splendid views of Ávila's walls. During summer, you can have a drink and enjoy some tapas at tables set up alongside the duck pond. Specialties include lamb roasted in a medieval-style wood oven and fresh river trout. ✉ *Bajada de la Losa 12,* ☎ *920/211101. AE, MC, V. Closed Mon. in winter.*

$$ ✕ **Mesón del Rastro.** This ancient inn tucked into the city walls is Ávila's
★ most atmospheric place to dine. Local specialties include *ternera* (veal) and *yemas de Santa Teresa,* a dessert made from candied egg yolks. ✉ *Plaza del Rastro 4,* ☎ *920/211218. AE, DC, MC, V.*

$$$ 🏨 **Meliá Palacio de los Velada.** A beautifully restored palace dating
★ from the 16th century, Ávila's top hotel just opened its doors in April 1995. In its ideal location in the heart of the city beside the cathedral, you can relax between sightseeing excursions in the lovely palace courtyard, which has been enclosed and serves as a popular meeting place for guests and locals alike. The attractive rooms are modern and comfortable; here you'll find all the amenities of home. ✉ *Plaza de la Catedral 10, 05001,* ☎ *920/255100,* 𝔽𝔸𝕏 *920/254900. 85 rooms with bath. Restaurant, bar, meeting rooms. AE, DC, MC, V.*

$$$ 🏨 **Parador Raimundo de Borgoña.** The location of this parador in a 15th-century palace just inside the northern walls of the city is superb. The rooms are decorated in traditional Castilian style and have spacious, well-equipped bathrooms. Some rooms also have four-poster beds and a view of the city walls. Its dining room is atmospheric and serves local Ávilan dishes, including the inevitable yemas, and its garden offers the only access to the walls. Closed for renovation until spring 1996. ✉ *Marqués Canales de Chozas 2, 05001,* ☎ *920/211340,* 𝔽𝔸𝕏 *920/226166. 62 rooms with bath. Restaurant, meeting room. AE, DC, MC, V.*

El Escorial

$$$ ✕ **Charolés.** This elegant restaurant has a terrace above the street for
★ summer dining. Its meat dishes are famous throughout the region. Try the *charolés a la pimienta* (pepper steak). Fresh fish is brought in daily from Spain's north coast. ✉ *Floridablanca 24,* ☎ *91/890–5975. Weekend reservations essential. AE, DC, MC, V.*

$$ ✕ **Mesón de la Cueva.** Founded in 1768, this atmospheric mesón has several small, rustic dining rooms. This inn is a must for ambience, and the food is good, too. ✉ *San Antón 4,* ☎ *91/890–1516. No credit cards. Closed Mon.*

$$ ✕ **El Candil.** One of the best of the many middle-range restaurants in El Escorial, El Candil is situated above a bar on the corner of Plaza San Lorenzo on the village's main street. In summer you can dine outdoors in the square, a delightful spot. ⊠ *Reina Victoria 12,* ☎ *91/890–4103. AE, DC, MC, V.*

$$$ 🏨 **Victoria Palace.** The rooms at the back of this grand old-world hotel close to the monastery have balconies and a splendid view toward Madrid; there's a garden, too. ⊠ *Juan de Toledo 4, 28200,* ☎ *91/890–1511,* ℻ *91/890–1248. 89 rooms with bath. Pool. AE, DC, MC, V.*

$$ 🏨 **Miranda Suizo.** Rooms are comfortable in this charming old hotel, which was undergoing renovations in the beginning of 1996. Located on the main street, the hotel appears to have stepped right out of the 19th century with its dark wood fittings and marble tables in the café. ⊠ *Floridablanca 20, 28200,* ☎ *91/890–4711,* ℻ *91/890–4358. 52 rooms with bath. AE, DC, MC, V.*

Salamanca

$$ ✕ **Chapeau.** This chic spot offers both meat and fish carefully roasted
★ in its wood-fire ovens. Try their *pimientos relleños* (stuffed peppers) and orange mousse for dessert. ⊠ *Gran Vía 20,* ☎ *923/271833. AE, DC, MC, V. No dinner Sun.*

$$ ✕ **El Mesón.** There's plenty of colorful atmosphere and good traditional Castilian food in this typical mesón just off the Plaza Mayor, beside the Gran Hotel. ⊠ *Plaza Poeta Iglesias 10,* ☎ *923/217222. AE, MC, V. Closed Sun. evening.*

$$ ✕ **Río de la Plata.** This small, atmospheric restaurant close to El Mesón and the Gran Hotel serves superb *farinato* sausage; it's a great find. ⊠ *Plaza del Peso 1,* ☎ *923/219005. AE, MC, V. Closed Mon. and the month of July.*

$$$–$$$$ 🏨 **Gran Hotel.** The grande dame of Salamanca's hotels offers stylishly baroque lounges and refurbished yet old-fashioned, oversized rooms just steps from the Plaza Mayor. ⊠ *Poeta Iglesias 5, 37001,* ☎ *923/213500,* ℻ *923/213501. 137 rooms with bath. Restaurant, bar. AE, DC, MC, V.*

$$$ 🏨 **Palacio de Castellanos.** Opened in 1992 in an immaculately restored 15th-century palace, this hotel offers a much-needed alternative to Salamanca's national parador (probably the ugliest of them all). There is an exquisite interior patio and an equally beautiful restaurant. ⊠ *San Pablo 58, 37001,* ☎ *923/261818,* ℻ *923/261819. 63 rooms with bath. Restaurant. AE, DC, MC, V.*

$$–$$$ 🏨 **Las Torres.** Overlooking the Plaza Mayor, this newly renovated hotel overlooks Spain's most beautiful square. The rooms are modern and comfortable; be sure to ask for one with balconies on the plaza. ⊠ *Plaza Mayor 26 and Concejo 4, 37001,* ☎ *923/212100,* ℻ *923/212101. 44 rooms with bath. AE, DC, MC, V.*

Segovia

$$–$$$ ✕ **Casa Duque.** At the end of the main shopping street, this restaurant has several floors of beautifully decorated traditional dining rooms and is the main rival to the famous Cándido. There's plenty of local atmosphere, and the food is pure Castilian—roasts are the house specialty. ⊠ *Cervantes 12,* ☎ *921/430537. AE, DC, MC, V.*

$$–$$$ ✕ **Mesón de Cándido.** Segovia's most prestigious restaurant has seven
★ dining rooms pulsating with atmosphere and decorated with bullfighting memorabilia and photos of the dignitaries who have dined here over the years. Specialties are cochinillo and cordero asado. ⊠ *Plaza Azoguejo 5,* ☎ *921/425911. Sun. lunch reservations essential. AE, DC, MC, V.*

$$ ✕ **La Oficina.** Traditional Castilian dishes are served in two delightful dining rooms that date back to 1893. It's just off the Plaza Mayor. ⊠ *Cronista Lecea 10,* ☎ *921/460286. AE, DC, MC, V.*

$$ ⊞ **Los Linajes.** The advantages of this hotel, which is scheduled for long overdue renovations in 1996, are its central location and the superb views from some of its rooms. ⊠ *Dr. Velasco 9, 40003,* ☎ *921/460475,* FAX *921/460479. 55 rooms with bath. Restaurant, bar, meeting room, disco. AE, DC, MC, V.*

$$ ⊞ **Infanta Isabel.** A recently restored building with a Victorian feel houses this small, centrally located hotel—it's two steps off the Plaza Mayor and offers great views of Segovia's cathedral. Guest rooms are feminine and light, with white-painted furnishings. ⊠ *Isabel la Católica, 40001,* ☎ *921/443105,* FAX *921/433240. 29 rooms with bath. Coffee shop. AE, DC, MC, V.*

$$ ⊞ **Parador.** To the north of town is this modern parador offering
★ comfortable, spacious rooms and pools. The views of the city, especially when illuminated, are magnificent. The restaurant offers superior parador cooking. ⊠ *Carretara de Valladolid s/n (Off the N601 toward Valladolid), 40003,* ☎ *921/443737,* FAX *921/437362. 106 rooms with bath. Restaurant, indoor and outdoor pools, meeting room, business services. AE, DC, MC, V.*

Toledo

$$$ ✕ **Asador Adolfo.** Toledo's most famous restaurant is near the cathe-
★ dral and is well known for its good food, service, and old world charm. The interior features a recently discovered painted wood-beam ceiling which dates from the 14th century. Try the superb roast meat and the pimentos rellenos. ⊠ *C. de la Granada 6 and Hombre de Palo 7,* ☎ *925/227321. AE, DC, MC, V. No dinner Sun.*

$$$ ✕ **Hostal del Cardenal.** Set in the 17th-century palace of Cardinal
★ Lorenzana, up against the city ramparts, this restaurant has five dining rooms and a delightful garden for summer dining. A popular choice for tourists, both food and service are excellent (try the cochinillo asado). ⊠ *Paseo de Recaredo 24,* ☎ *925/220862. Reservations essential in high season. AE, DC, MC, V.*

$$ ✕ **La Abadía.** Perfect for a light lunch, a sandwich, or a round of tapas, this stylish bar-restaurant has vaulted stone ceilings and a huge old wooden door. The dining room downstairs specializes in shish kebabs, grilled meats, and salads. ⊠ *Plaza San Nicolás 3,* ☎ *925/251140. No credit cards. No dinner.*

$$ ✕ **Venta de Aires.** A century-old inn on the edge of town and not far from the Tajo River, this is where Toledanos go to eat partridge. Steaks and lamb are also expertly prepared. ⊠ *Circo Romano 35,* ☎ *925/ 220545. AE, DC, MC, V.*

$$$ ⊞ **Parador Conde de Orgaz.** This is one of Spain's most popular
★ paradores, and the best and most expensive hotel in Toledo (a 15-minute drive from city center). It's a modern parador built in traditional Toledo style and stands on a hill across the river, commanding magnificent views of the city. Book far ahead. ⊠ *Cerro del Emperador s/n, 45001,* ☎ *925/221850,* FAX *925/225166. 77 rooms with bath. Pool. AE, DC, MC, V.*

$$ ⊞ **Hostal del Cardenal.** Built in the 18th century as a summer palace for a cardinal, this quiet and beautiful hotel has some rooms that overlook a wooded garden. It's difficult to believe that the main Madrid road is a short distance away. ⊠ *Paseo de Recaredo 24, 45004,* ☎ *925/224900,* FAX *925/222991. 27 rooms with bath. Restaurant. AE, DC, MC, V.*

$$ ⊞ **Pintor El Greco.** Next door to the famous painter's house-museum, this friendly hotel occupies a building that was once a 17th-century bakery. Extensive renovation has resulted in a light and modern interior, with some antique touches such as exposed brick vaulting. ⊠ *Alamillos del Tránsito 13, 45002,* ☎ *925/214250,* ℻ *925/215819. 33 rooms with bath. AE, DC, MC, V.*

BARCELONA

Arriving and Departing

By Plane
All international and domestic flights arrive at El Prat de Llobregat airport, 14 kilometers (8½ miles) south of Barcelona just off the main highway to Castelldefels and Sitges. For information on arrival and departure times, call the airport (☎ 93/478–5000 or 478–5032) or Info-Iberia (☎ 93/412–5667).

BETWEEN THE AIRPORT AND DOWNTOWN
The airport–city train leaves every 30 minutes between 6:30 AM and 11 PM and, at a cost of 400 ptas., reaches the Barcelona Central (Sants) Station in 15 minutes and Plaça de Catalunya in the heart of the old city at the head of La Rambla in 20-25 minutes. A short taxi hop of 350-500 ptas will take you from Plaça Catalunya to most of central Barcelona's hotels. The Aerobus service connects the airport with Plaça Catalunya every 15 minutes between 6:25 AM and 11 PM; the fare of 450 ptas. can be paid with all international credit cards. RENFE provides a bus service to the Central Station during the night hours. A cab from the airport to your hotel, including airport and luggage surcharges, will cost about 3,500 ptas.

By Train
The old Estació de França on Avenida Marquès de l'Argentera now serves as the main terminal for trains to France and some express trains to points in Spain. The Sants Central Station serves suburban destinations as well as most cities in Spain. Inquire at the tourist office to find out which station you need. Many trains also stop at the Passeig de Gràcia underground station at the junction of Aragó. This station is closer to the Plaça de Catalunya and Rambla area than Sants; though tickets and information are available here, luggage carts and taxi ranks are not. Check with tourist offices for current travel information and phone numbers. For RENFE information, call 93/490–0202 (24 hours).

By Bus
Barcelona has no central bus station, but many buses operate from the old Estació Vilanova (or Norte) at the end of Avenida Vilanova. **Julià,** Ronda Universitat 5, runs buses to Zaragoza and Montserrat; and **Alsina Graëlls,** Ronda Universitat 4, to Lérida and Andorra.

Getting Around

Modern Barcelona, the Eixample—above the Plaça de Catalunya—is built on a grid system, though there's no helpful numbering scheme as in cities such as Manhattan. The Gothic Quarter from the Plaça de Catalunya to the port is a warren of narrow streets. In any case, you'll need a good street map to get around. Almost all sightseeing can be done on foot, but you may need to use taxis, the metro, or buses to link certain sightseeing areas, depending on the time you have.

By Metro
The subway is the fastest way of getting around, as well as the easiest to use. You pay a flat fare of 150 ptas. no matter how far you travel, or purchase a **tarjeta multiviatge,** good for 10 rides (750 ptas.). Plans

of the system are available from main metro stations or from branches of the Caixa savings bank.

By Bus

City buses run from about 5:30 or 6 AM to 10:30 PM, though some stop earlier. There are also night buses to certain destinations. Again, there's a flat fare system (150 ptas.). Plans of the routes followed are displayed at bus stops. A reduced rate **tarjeta multiviatge,** good for 10 rides, can be purchased at the transport kiosk on Plaça de Catalunya (700 ptas.).

By Taxi

Taxis are black and yellow, and when available for hire show a LIBRE sign in the daytime and a green light at night. The meter starts at 400 ptas., and there are small supplements for luggage (100 ptas. per case); Sundays and fiestas; rides from the airport, a station, or the port (varies according to zone); and for going to or from the bullring or a soccer match. There are cab stands all over town; cabs may also be flagged down on the street. Don't be paranoid about taxi drivers in Barcelona; they are nearly always pleasant, helpful, and fair, and they don't care much about tips one way or the other.

By Cable Car and Funicular

Montjuïc Funicular is a cog railroad that runs from the junction of Avenida Parallel and Nou de la Rambla to the Miramar Amusement Park on Montjuïc. It runs only when the amusement park is open (11– 8:15 in winter, noon–2:45 and 4:30–9:25 in summer). A *teleferic* (cable car) then runs from the amusement park up to Montjuïc Castle (noon–8 daily in summer; winter, weekends only, 11–7:30).

A **Transbordador Aeri Harbor Cable Car** runs from Miramar on Montjuïc across the harbor to the Torre de Jaume I on Barcelona *moll* (quay), and on to the Torre de Sant Sebastià at the end of Passeig Joan de Borbó in Barceloneta. You can board at either stage; the fare is 850 ptas. (1000 ptas. round-trip). Operates Oct. to June, weekdays noon to 5:45, weekends noon to 6:15; June to Oct., daily 11 to 9.

To reach Tibidabo summit, take either Bus 58 or the Ferrocarrils de la Generalitat train from Plaça de Catalunya to Avenida Tibidabo, then the *tramvía blau* (blue tram) to Peu del Funicular, and the Tibidabo Funicular from there to the Tibidabo Fairground. The funicular runs every half hour from 7:15 AM to 9:45 PM.

By Boat

Golondrinas harbor boats operate short harbor trips from the Portal de la Pau near the Columbus Monument between 10 AM and 1:30 PM weekends only in winter, daily in summer between 10 and 8. A one-way ticket lets you off at the end of the breakwater for a 2½-mile stroll, surrounded by the Mediterranean, back into Barceloneta.

Important Addresses and Numbers

Visitor Information

The city's three main tourist offices are at the **Central (Sants)** train station (☎ 93/491–4431; ☉ Daily 8–8), the **França** train station (☎ 93/319–5758; ☉ Daily 8–8), and at the **airport** (☎ 93/478–4704; ☉ Mon.–Sat. 9:30–8).

Information on the province and city can be found at the office at ⊠ **Gran Via 658** (☎ 93/301–7443; ☉ Weekdays 9–7, Sat. 9–2, closed holidays).

During special events and conferences, a tourist office is open at the **Palau de Congressos** (⊠ Avda. María Cristina, ☎ 93/423–3101, ext.

8356); a small office with pamphlets and maps is at the **Ajuntament** (⊠ Plaça Sant Jaume, ☎ 93/402–7000, ext. 433; ☉ Summer, daily 9–8; and cultural information is available at the **Palau de la Virreina** (⊠ Rambla 99, ☎ 93/301–7775; ☉ Mon.–Sat. 9–9, Sun. 10–2).

American Visitors' Bureau (⊠ Gran Via 591 between Rambla de Catalunya and Balmes, 3rd floor, ☎ 93/301–0150 or 301–0032).

Consulates
U.S. (⊠ Pg. Reina Elisenda 23, ☎ 93/280–2227), **Canadian** (⊠ Via Augusta 125, ☎ 93/209–0634), **U.K.** (⊠ Diagonal 477, ☎ 93/419–9044).

Emergencies
Police: (National Police, ☎ 091; Municipal Police, ☎ 092; Main Police/Policía Nacional Station, ⊠ Via Laietana 43, ☎ 93/301–6666). **Medical emergencies:** (☎ 061). **Pharmacies:** (☎ 010). **Tourist Attention:** (⊠ La Rambla 43, ☎ 93/301–9060) is a 24-hour service offered by the police department to provide assistance to crime victims.

English Language Bookstores
Several bookstalls on the Rambla sell English guidebooks and novels, but the bookstore at the **Palau de la Virreina** (⊠ Rambla 99) has the best selection of books about Barcelona. Also try **Librería Laie** (⊠ Pau Claris 85), **Librería Francesa** (⊠ Passeig de Gràcia 91), or **Come In** (⊠ Provença 203).

Travel Agencies
American Express (⊠ Roselló 257, on the corner of Passeig de Gràcia, ☎ 93/217–0070), **WagonsLits Cook** (⊠ Passeig de Gràcia 8, ☎ 93/317–5500), **Viajes Iberia** (⊠ Rambla 130, ☎ 93/317–9320), and **Bestours** (⊠ Diputación 241, ☎ 93/487–8580).

Guided Tours

Orientation Tours
City sightseeing tours are run by **Julià Tours** (⊠ Ronda Universitat 5, ☎ 93/317–6454) and **Pullmantur** (⊠ Gran Viá de les Corts Catalanes 635, ☎ 93/318–5195). Tours leave from the above terminals, though it may be possible to be picked up at your hotel. The content and price of tours are the same with both agencies. A morning sightseeing tour visits the Gothic Quarter and Montjuïc; an afternoon tour concentrates on Gaudí and the Picasso Museum. Visits to Barcelona's Olympic sites are scheduled from May through October.

Excursions
These are run by **Julià Tours** and **Pullmantur** and are booked as above. Principal trips are a half-day tour to **Montserrat** to visit the monastery and shrine of the famous Black Virgin; a full-day trip to the **Costa Brava** resorts, including a boat cruise to the Medes Isles; and, from June to September, a full-day trip to **Andorra** for tax-free shopping.

Exploring Barcelona

Numbers in the margin correspond to points of interest on the Barcelona map.

Barcelona, capital of Catalonia, thrives on its business acumen and industrial muscle. Its hardworking citizens are proud to have and use their own language with street names, museum exhibits, newspapers, radio programs, and movies all in Catalan. A recent milestone was the realization of the long-cherished goal of hosting the Olympic Games, held in Barcelona in summer 1992. The Olympics were of singular importance to the city's modernization. The Games' legacy to Barcelona includes a vastly improved ring road and several other highways; four new beaches, and an entire new neighborhood in what used to be the rundown industrial district of Poble Nou; an adjoining marina; and a new sports stadium and swimming pools on the promontory of Montjuïc. This thriving metropolis also has a rich history and an abundance of sights. Few places can rival the narrow alleys of its Gothic Quarter for medieval atmosphere, the elegance and distinction of its Moderniste Eixample area, or the omnipresent fantasies of Gaudí's whimsical imagination.

It should take you two full days of sightseeing to complete the following tour. The first part covers the Gothic Quarter, the Picasso Museum, and the Rambla. The second part takes you to Passeig de Gràcia, the Sagrada Família, and Montjuïc.

★ **❶** Start on Plaça de la Seu, in front of the cathedral where on Sunday morning the citizens of Barcelona gather to dance the *Sardana*, a symbol of Catalan identity. Step inside the elaborate Gothic **cathedral** built between 1298 and 1450, though the spire and Gothic facade were not added until 1892. Highlights are the beautifully carved **choir stalls,** Santa Eulàlia's tomb in the crypt, the battle-scarred crucifix from Don Juan's galley in the naval battle of Lepanto in the **Lepanto Chapel,** and the cloisters. ☎ *93/315–1554.* ☞ *Free.* ☉ *Daily 7:45–1:30 and 4–7:45.*

❷ Around the corner is the **Museu Frederic Marès,** where you can browse for hours among the miscellany of sculptor/collector Frederic Marès. Displayed here is everything from polychrome crucifixes to hat pins, pipes, and walking sticks. ⊠ *Plaça Sant Iu 5,* ☎ *93/310–5800.* ☞ *450 ptas., Wed. 175 ptas., 1st Sun. of every month free.* ☉ *Tues.–Sat. 10–5, Sun. 10–2.*

NEED A BREAK? Don't pass up the chance for a quiet moment on the Mares terrace where you can sip a sherry or a cup of hot chocolate surrounded by stones placed there 2,000 years ago by Roman stonemasons. ⊠ *Plaça Sant Iu, 5-6.*

❸ The neighboring **Plaça del Rei** embodies the very essence of the Gothic Quarter. Following Columbus's first voyage to America, the Catholic Kings received him in the **Saló de Tinell,** a magnificent banqueting hall built in 1362. Other ancient buildings around the square are the **Lieutenant's Palace;** the 14th-century **Chapel of St. Agatha,** built right into the Roman city wall; and the **Padellás Palace,** which houses the **City History Museum.** (⊠ *Plaçdel Rei,* ☎ *93/315–1111,* ☞ *500 ptas. Tues.–Sat. 10–2; 4–8. Sun./Hol. 10–2.*)

★ **❹** Cross Via Laietana, walk down Princesa, and turn right into M Carrer Montcada, where you will come to one of Barcelona's most popular attractions, the **Museu Picasso.** Two 15th-century palaces provide a striking setting for the collections donated in 1963 and 1970, first by Picasso's secretary, then by the artist himself. The collection ranges from early childhood sketches to exhibition posters done in Paris shortly before his death. Of particular interest are his Blue Period pictures and his variations on Velázquez's *Las Meninas.* ⊠ *Carrer Montcada 1519,* ☎ *93/319–6310.* ☞ *750 ptas; Wed. half price, free 1st Sun. of every month.* ☉ *Tues.–Sat. 10–8, Sun. 10–3.*

NEED A BREAK? At the bottom of Montcada, on the left, is **La Pizza Nostra** (⊠ Arc de Sant Vicens 2, ☎ 93/319-9058), an ideal spot for a cup of coffee, a slice of cheesecake, or a pizza and a glass of wine. Or you may prefer the colorful **Xampanyet** tapas bar across the street. Carrer Montcada has several great watering spots. The **Museo de la Indumentaria** (Clothing Museum) across from the Picasso Museum has a lovely courtyard and café. Another good choice is the popular **Xampanyet** bar down at the far end of the street on the right at No. 22.

★ ⑤ **Santa Maria del Mar** is a wonderful example of Mediterranean Gothic architecture and is widely considered to be Barcelona's loveliest church. It was built between 1329 and 1383 in fulfillment of a vow made a century earlier by Jaume I to build a church for the Virgin of the Sailors. The structure's simple beauty is enhanced by a stunning rose window and magnificent soaring columns. ☉ *Mon.–Fri. 9–12:30 and 5–8; closed weekends.*

⑥ Continue up Carrer Argentería, cross Via Laietana, and walk along Jaume I till you come to **Plaça Sant Jaume,** an impressive square built in the 1840s in the heart of the Gothic Quarter. The two imposing buildings facing each other across the square are very much older. The 15th-century **Ajuntament,** or City Hall, has an impressive black and gold mural (1928) by Josep María Sert (who also painted the murals for New York's Waldorf Astoria) and the famous **Saló de Cent,** from which the Council of One Hundred ruled the city from 1372 to 1714. You can wander into the courtyard, but to visit the interior, you will need to arrange permission in the protocol office beforehand. The **Palau de la Generalitat,** seat of the Catalan Regional Government, is a 15th-century palace open to the public on Sunday mornings only.

⑦ Continue along the Carrer Ferrán, with its attractive 19th-century shops and numerous Moderniste touches, to the **Plaça Reial.** Here in this splendid 19th-century square, arcaded houses overlook the wrought-iron **Fountain of the Three Graces** and lampposts designed by a young Gaudí in 1879. Despite the preponderance of substance users, abusers, and peddlers here, Plaça Reial retains its elegance; the most colorful time to come is on a Sunday morning when crowds gather at the stamp and coin stalls and listen to soapbox orators.

NEED A BREAK?

Les Quinze Nits, Plaça Reial 6, will probably have a line of hopeful diners waiting for a shot at the Camós family's terrific price-value offer. Although not necessarily worth lining up for, this is indeed a bargain. **La Fonda,** another Camós operation, is a minute away at Escudellers 10.

⑧ Head to the bottom of the Rambla and take an elevator to the top of the **Monument a Colom** (Columbus Monument) for a commanding view of the city and port. Columbus faces out to sea, pointing, ironically, east toward Naples. (Nearby you can board the cable car to cross the harbor to Barceloneta or else catch it in the other direction up Montjuïc.) ◻ *350 ptas.* ☉ *Tues.–Sat. 10–2 and 3:30–6:30, Sun. 10–7.*

⑨ Our next stop is the **Museu Marítim** (Maritime Museum) housed in the 13th-century Drassanes Reiales, the old Royal Shipyards. The museum is packed with ships, figureheads, nautical paraphernalia, and several early navigation charts, including a map by Amerigo Vespucci, and the 1439 chart of Gabriel de Valseca from Mallorca, the oldest chart in Europe. ◻ *Plaça Portal de la Pau 1,* ☏ *93/318–3245.* ◻ *450 ptas., Wed. 200 ptas., 1st Sun. of every month free.* ☉ *Tues.–Sat. 10–2 and 4–7, Sun. 10–2.*

★ ⑩ Turn back up the Rambla to Nou de la Rambla. At No. 3 is Gaudí's **Palau Güell.** Gaudí built this mansion between 1885 and 1890 for his patron, Count Eusebi de Güell, and it's the only one of his houses open to the public. ◻ *450 ptas.* ☉ *Tues.–Sat. 10–1:30 and 4–7:30.*

980

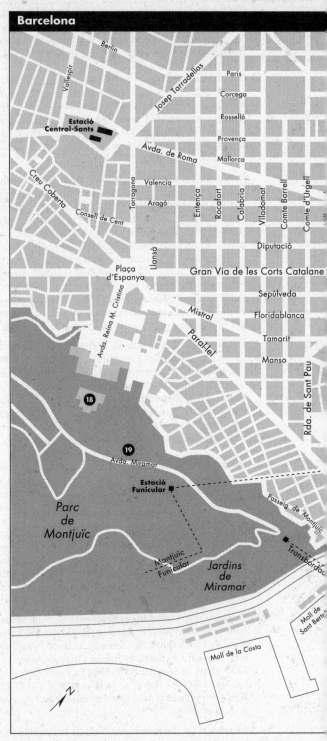

Barcelona

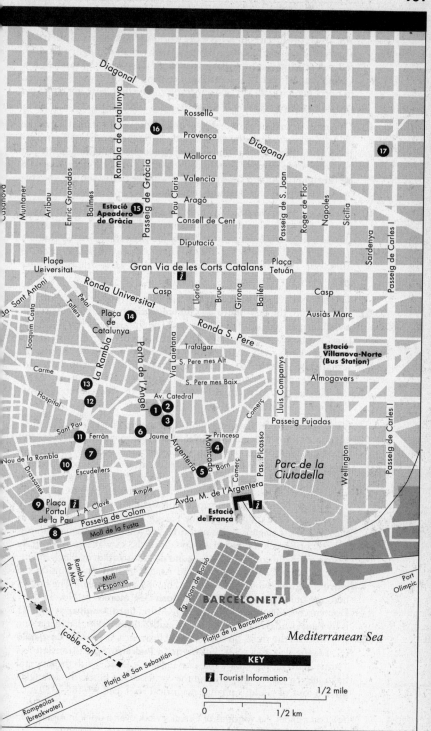

Diagonal

Rambla de Catalunya

Rosselló

Provença

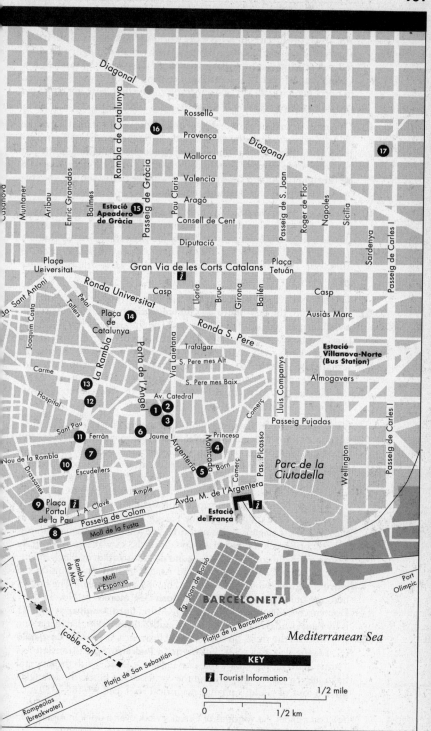 **16**

Mallorca

Diagonal

Valencia

Passeig de Gràcia

Pau Claris

Aragó

17

Passeig de S. Joan

Roger de Flor

Napoles

Sicilia

Sardenya

Passeig de Carles I

Estació
Apeadero
de Gràcia **15**

Balmes

Enric Granados

Aribau

Muntaner

Cusanova

Consell de Cent

Diputació

Plaça
Universitat

Gran Via de les Corts Catalans

Plaça
Tetuán

Ronda Universitat

Casp

Lloria

Bruc

Girona

Bailén

Casp

Ja. Sant Antoni

Joaquim Costa

Tallers

Pelai

Plaça
de
Catalunya **14**

Ausiàs Marc

Ronda S. Pere

Porta de l'Angel

La Rambla

Carme

Trafalgar

S. Pere mes Alt

Estació
Villanova-Norte
(Bus Station)

Hospital

S. Pere mes Baix

Almogavers

Av. Catedral

13

12

Via Laietana

1 **2**

3

Comerç

Lluis Companys

Passeig Pujadas

Sant Pau

11 Ferràn

6

Jaume I

Princesa

Wellington

Passeig de Carles I

Nou de la Rambla

7

10

Escudellers

Argenteria

Montcada

4

Born

Comerç

Pas. Picasso

Parc de la
Ciutadella

5

Ample

Drassanes

9 Plaça
Portal
de la Pau

J. A. Clavé

Avda. M. de l'Argentera

Estació
de França

Passeig de Colom

8

Moll de la Fusta

Rambla
de Mar

Pg. Joan de Borbó

Moll
d'Espanya

BARCELONETA

Port
Olímpic

(cable car)

Platja de la Barceloneta

Mediterranean Sea

Platja de San Sebastián

KEY

i Tourist Information

0 ——————— 1/2 mile

0 ——————— 1/2 km

Rompeolas
(breakwater)

⓫ Our next landmark, the **Gran Teatre del Liceu,** Barcelona's famous opera house, was tragically gutted by fire in early 1994. Built between 1845 and 1847, the Liceu claims to be the world's oldest opera house; it was also one of the world's most beautiful with ornamental gilt and plush red velvet fittings. Anna Pavlova danced here in 1930, and Maria Callas sang here in 1959. The Liceu is being restored and is expected to open again in 1997. *Visits to certain rooms that were not damaged can be arranged (☎ 93/318–9122).*

⓬ This next stretch of the **Rambla** is one of the most fascinating as the colorful paving stones on the Plaça de la Boquería were designed by Joan Miró. Glance up at the swirling Moderniste dragon and the Art Nouveau street lamps. Then take a look inside the bustling **Boquería Market** and the **Antiga Casa Figueras,** a vintage pastry shop on the corner of Petxina, with a splendid mosaic facade.

⓭ The **Palau de la Virreina** was built by a one-time Spanish viceroy to Peru in 1778. The building is now a major exhibition center, and you should check to see what's showing while you're in town. ⊠ *Rambla de les Flors 99,* ☎ *93/301–7775.* 🎫 *500 ptas., Wed. 250 ptas.* ☉ *Tues.–Sat. 10–2 and 4:30–9, Sun. 10–2, Mon. 4:30–9. Last entrance 30 mins before closing.*

⓮ The final stretch of the Rambla brings us past the lively bird market and out onto the busy **Plaça de Catalunya,** the frantic business center and transport hub of the modern city. The first stage of the tour ends here. You may want to head for the Corte Inglés department store across the square or for any of the stores on the nearby **Porta de l'Angel.** Alternatively, you can relax on the terrace of the ancient (although presently endangered by a construction project) **Café Zurich** on the corner of Pelai, or stop at the colorful beer hall, the **Cervecería,** opposite the Hotel Continental.

Above the Plaça de Catalunya you enter modern Barcelona and an elegant area known as the **Eixample,** which was laid out in the late 19th century as part of the city's expansion scheme. Much of the building here was done at the height of the **Moderniste** movement, a Spanish and mainly Catalan offshoot of Art Nouveau, whose leading exponents were the architects Gaudí, Domènech i Montaner, Puig i Cadafalch, and Antoni Gaudí. The principal thoroughfares of the Eixample are the Rambla de Catalunya and the Passeig de Gràcia, where some of the city's most elegant shops and cafés are found. Moderniste houses are one of Barcelona's special drawing cards, so walk up **Passeig de**
⓯ **Gràcia** until you come to the **Mançana de la Discòrdia,** or Block of Discord, between Consell de Cent and Aragó. Its name is a pun on the word *mançana,* which means both "block" and "apple." The houses here are quite fantastic: The floral **Casa Lleó Morera** at No. 35 is by Domènech i Montaner. The pseudo-Gothic **Casa Amatller** at No. 41 is by Puig i Cadafalch. At No. 43 is Gaudí's **Casa Batlló.** Farther along
★ **⓰** the street on the right, on the corner of Provença, is Gaudí's **Casa Milà** (⊠ Passeig de Gràcia 92), known as **La Pedrera,** which translates as "stone quarry." Its remarkable curving stone facade with ornamental balconies ripples its way around the corner of the block. To arrange a guided tour of Gaudí's phantasmagorical roof, call 93/488–3592.

NEED A
BREAK?

You can ponder the vagaries of Gaudí's work over a drink in **Amarcord,** a terrace café on the sidewalk in front of the Pedrera building at Provença 261. For a more sedate, old-world tearoom, head for the **Salón de Té Mauri** on the corner of Rambla de Catalunya and Provença.

★ **17** Now take the metro at Diagonal or walk 20 minutes to Barcelona's most eccentric landmark, Gaudí's **Temple Expiatori de la Sagrada Família** (Expiatory Church of the Holy Family). Far from finished at his death in 1926—Gaudí was run over by a tram and died in a pauper's hospital—this striking creation will cause consternation or wonder, shrieks of protest, or cries of rapture. In 1936 during the Spanish Civil War the citizens of Barcelona loved their crazy temple enough to spare it from the flames that engulfed all their other churches except the cathedral. An elevator takes visitors to the top of one of the towers for a magnificent view of the city. Gaudí is buried in the crypt. ☎ 93/455–0247. ▨ 900 ptas. ☉ Sept.–May, daily 9–7; June–Aug., daily 9–9.

Back across town to the south, the hill of **Montjuïc** was named for the Jewish cemetery once located on its slopes. Montjuïc is home to a castle, an amusement park, several delightful gardens, a model Spanish village, an illuminated fountain, the recently rebuilt Mies van der Rohe Pavilion, and a cluster of museums—all of which could keep you busy for a day or more. This was the principal venue for the 1992 Olympics.

★ **18** One of Barcelona's leading attractions is the **Museu Nacional d'Art de Catalunya** (National Museum of Catalan Art) in the Palau Nacional atop a long flight of steps up from the Placa Espanya. The collection of Romanesque and Gothic art treasures, medieval frescoes, and altarpieces, mostly from small churches and chapels in the Pyrenees, is simply staggering. Extensive renovations, directed by architect Gae Aulenti, who also remodeled the Musee d'Orsay in Paris, closed the museum for seven years; it reopened in early 1996. ☎ 93/423–7199.

★ **19** Nearby, on Avinguda de Miramar, is the **Fundació Miró** (Miró Foundation), a gift from the artist Joan Miró to his native city. One of Barcelona's most exciting contemporary galleries, it has several exhibition areas, many of them devoted to Miró's works. ☎ 93/329–1908. ▨ 800 ptas. ☉ Tues.–Sat. 11–7 (9:30 on Thurs.), Sun. 10:30–2:30.

Off the Beaten Path

If you're hooked on **Moderniste** architecture, you can follow a walking trail around the **Dreta de l'Eixample,** the area to the right of Rambla de Catalunya. Ask at a tourist office for a Gaudí or Modernisme trail brochure for the Eixample. Attend a concert at Domènech i Mon-

★ ★ taner's fantastic **Palau de la Música.** Make a trip to the **Parc Güell,** Gaudí's magical attempt at creating a garden city. ☉ May–Aug., daily 10–9; Sept.–Apr., daily 10–7.

Explore the **Gràcia** area, above the Diagonal. It's a small, once independent village within a large city, a warren of narrow streets, changing names at every corner, and filled with tiny shops where you'll find everything from old-fashioned tin lanterns to feather dusters.

Take a stroll around **Barceloneta,** the old fishermen's quarter built in 1755 below the Estació de França and the Ciutadella Park. There are no-frills fish restaurants on the Passeig Joan de Borbó and beach restaurants along the Passeig Marítim. Hike out to the end of the *rompeolas* (breakwater), extending 2½ miles southeast into the Mediterranean, for a panoramic view of the city and a few breaths of fresh air. The new port is home to the Aquarium, Europe's best; the Maregmagnum shopping center; the IMAX wide format cinema and numerous bars and restaurants. The 1992 Olympic Village, now a hot tapas and nightlife spot, is a mile to the north up the beach, easily identifiable by the enormous gold, Frank Gehry-designed fish sculpture next to the Hotel Arts.

Designed by American Richard Meier, the new contemporary art museum is an important addition to the city's treasury of art and architecture. Located several blocks to the right of the Rambla near the top of Barcelona's once (and still) rough and rundown Raval district, the **Museu d'Art Contemporani (MACBA)** and the neighboring **Contemporary Culture Center of Barcelona (CCCB)** have reclaimed important buildings and spaces as part of the city's renewal of its historic quarters and traditional neighborhoods. ⊠ *Plaça dels Àngels 1.* ☎ *93/412–0810.* ☉ *Tues.–Fri. 12–8, Sat.–Sun 10–3, Closed Mon.*

Shopping

Gift Ideas

There are no special handicrafts associated with Barcelona, but you'll have no trouble finding typical Spanish goods anywhere in town. If you're into fashion and jewelry, then you've come to the right place, as Barcelona makes all the headlines on Spain's booming fashion front. **Xavier Roca i Coll,** Sant Pere mes Baix 24, just off Laietana, specializes in silver models of Barcelona's buildings.

Barcelona and Catalonia have passed along a playful sense of design even before Antoni Gaudí began creating shock waves more than a century ago. Stores and boutiques specializing in design items (jewelry, furnishings, knickknacks) include **Gimeno** (⊠ Passeig de Gràcia 102), **Vinçon** (⊠ Passeig de Gràcia 96), **Bd** (Barcelona Design, at ⊠ Mallorca 291293), and **Dos i Una** (⊠ Rosselló 275).

Antiques

Carrer de la Palla and Banys Nous in the Gothic Quarter are lined with antiques shops where you'll find old maps, books, paintings, and furniture. An **antiques market** is held every Thursday, 10–8, in the Plaça del Pi. The **Centre d'Antiquaris** (⊠ Passeig de Gràcia 57), has some 75 antiques stores. **Gothsland** (⊠ Consell de Cent 331), specializes in Moderniste designs.

Boutiques

There are fashionable boutiques in the **Bulevard Rosa** on Passeig de Gràcia and Rambla de Catalunya. Others are on Gran Via between Balmes and Pau Claris; and on the Diagonal between Ganduxer and Passeig de Gràcia. **L'Illa** is another encyclopedic shopping opportunity on Diagonal between Numancia and Entenza, as is the **Les Glories** center near the square of the same name. **Maremagnum** in the port is another potential shopping spree. **Adolfo Domínguez,** one of Spain's top designers, is at Passeig de Gràcia 89 and Valencia 245; **Loewe,** Spain's top leather store, is at Passeig de Gràcia 35 and Diagonal 570; **Joaquín Berao,** a top jewelry designer, is at ⊠ Rosselló 277.

Shopping Districts

Elegant shopping districts are the Passeig de Gràcia, Rambla de Catalunya, and the Diagonal. For more affordable, more old-fashioned, and typically Spanish-style shops, explore the area between Ramblas and Via Laietana, especially around Carrer Ferran. The area around Plaça del Pi from Boquería to Portaferrisa and Canuda is recommended for young fashion stores and imaginative gift shops.

Department Stores

El Corte Inglés (⊠ Plaça de Catalunya 14 ☎ 93/302–1212; ⊠ Diagonal 617, near the María Cristina metro stop, ☎ 93/419–2828) is Spain and Barcelona's great consumer emporium.

Food and Flea Markets

The **Boquería Market** on the Ramblas between Carme and Hospital is a superb, colorful food market, held every day except Sunday. **Els Encants,** Barcelona's wild-and-woolly flea market, is held every Monday, Wednesday, Friday, and Saturday, 8–7, at the end of Dos de Maig on the Plaça Glòries Catalanes. **Sant Antoni Market,** at the end of Ronda Sant Antoni, is an old-fashioned food and clothes market, best on Sundays when there's a secondhand **book market** with old postcards, press cuttings, lithographs, and prints. There's a **stamp and coin market** in the Plaça Reial on Sunday mornings, and an **artists' market** in the Placeta del Pi just off the Rambla and Boquería on Saturday morning.

Bullfighting

Barcelona has two bullrings, the **Monumental** on Gran Via and Carles I, and the smaller **Les Arenes** on the Plaça d'Espanya, now almost exclusively used for rock concerts. Bullfights are held on Sundays between March and October; check the newspaper for details. The official ticket office, where there is no markup on tickets, is at Muntaner 24 (☎ 93/453–3821) near Gran Via. There's a **Bullfighting Museum** at the Monumental ring (☉ March–Oct., daily 10–1 and 5:30–7).

Dining

For details and price-category definitions, *see* Dining *in* Staying in Spain, *above.*

$$$$ ✕ **Beltxenea.** There is an air of intimacy in this redecorated Eixample apartment, now converted into a series of elegant dining rooms. In summer you can dine outside in the formal garden. Chef Miguel Ezcurra's excellent cuisine is one of Barcelona's top Basque dining opportunities; a specialty is his *merluza con kokotxas y almejas* (hake and clams fried in garlic then simmered in stock). ⊠ *Mallorca 275,* ☎ *93/215–3024. AE, DC, MC, V. No lunch Sat. Closed Sun., and July–Aug. No lunch Sat.*

$$$$ ✕ **Jean Luc Figueras.** Every restaurant Jean Luc Figueras has had anything to do with has shot straight to the top of the charts, so it is no surprise that the first to bear his name has done likewise. This one, installed in a Gràia town house that was once couturier Cristóbal Balenciaga's studio, may be the best of all. For the $20 more or so that it will cost, the taster's menu is the best solution. ⊠ *C. Santa Teresa 10,* ☎ *93/415–2877. Reservations essential. AE, DC, MC, V. Closed Sun. No lunch Sat.*

$$$ ✕ **Agut d'Avignon.** This venerable Barcelona institution takes a bit of finding; it's near the junction of Ferran and Avinyó in the Gothic Quarter. The ambience is rustic, and it's a favorite with businesspeople and politicians from the nearby Generalitat. The cuisine is traditional Catalan—the game specialties are recommended in season. ⊠ *Trinitat 3,* ☎ *93/317–3693. Reservations essential. AE, DC, MC, V.*

$$$ ✕ **La Cuineta.** This small intimate restaurant in a 17th-century house just off Plaça Sant Jaume and its sister location behind the cathedral specialize in Catalan nouvelle cuisine. The decor is elegant and traditional; the service, professional; and the cuisine, impeccable. ⊠ *Paradis 4,* ☎ *93/315–0111;* ⊠ *Pietat 12,* ☎ *93/315–4156. AE, DC, MC, V. Closed Mon.*

$$$ ✕ **Quo Vadis.** Located just off the Ramblas, near the Boquería Market and Betlem Church, is an unimpressive facade camouflaging one of Barcelona's most respected restaurants. Its much-praised cuisine includes delicacies like *hígado de ganso con ciruelas* (goose liver with plums). ⊠ *Carme 7,* ☎ *93/317–7447. AE, DC, MC, V. Closed Sun.*

$$$　✕ **TramTram.** With chef Isidro Soler at the helm in the kitchen and Reyes
★　Lizán as hostess and pastry chef, TramTram is one of Barcelona's culi-
nary stars. The excursion to the northwestern suburb of Sarrià is a de-
light. Order the taster's menu and let Isidro have his way with your
palate. You won't regret it. ✉ *Major de Sarrià 121,* ☎ *93/204–8518.
AE, MC, V. Closed Sun. and Dec. 24–Jan. 6.*

$$　✕ **Can Culleretes.** This picturesque old restaurant began life as a pastry shop in 1786—today it is one of the most atmospheric and reason-
able finds in Barcelona. Located on an alleyway between Ferran and
Boquería, its three dining rooms are decorated with photos of visiting
celebrities. It serves real Catalan cooking and is very much a family concern; don't be put off by the street life that might be raging outside. ✉
Quintana 5, ☎ *93/317–3022. AE, MC, V. No lunch Sun. Closed Mon.*

$$　✕ **Los Caracoles.** Just below the Plaça Reial is Barcelona's best known
tourist haunt, crawling with Americans having a terrific time. Its walls
are hung thick with photos of bullfighters and visiting celebrities; its
specialties are mussels, paella and, of course, *caracoles* (snails). ✉ *Es-
cudellers 14,* ☎ *93/309–3185. AE, DC, MC, V.*

$$　✕ **Set Portes.** With plenty of old-world charm, this delightful restau-
★　rant near the waterfront has been going strong since 1836. The cook-
ing is Catalan, the portions enormous, and specialties are paella *de
pescado* (with seafood) and *zarzuela Set Portes* (a mixed grill of
seafood). The restaurant serves non-stop from 1 PM to 1 AM. ✉ *Passeig Isabel II 14,* ☎ *93/319–3033. AE, DC, MC, V.*

$$　✕ **Sopeta Una.** Dining in this delightful small restaurant with old-fash-
★　ioned decor and intimate atmosphere is more like eating in a private
home. All the dishes are Catalan, and the atmosphere is very genteel
and middle class. For dessert, try the traditional Catalan *música,* a plate
of raisins, almonds, and dried fruit served with a glass of muscatel. It's
near the Palau de la Música; don't be put off by the narrow street. ✉
Verdaguer i Callis 6, ☎ *93/319–6131. V. Closed Sun.*

$　✕ **Agut.** Simple, hearty Catalan fare awaits you in this unpretentious
★　restaurant in the lower reaches of the Gothic Quarter. Founded in 1924,
its popularity has never waned. There's plenty of wine to wash down
the traditional home cooking, along with a family warmth that always
makes the place exciting. ✉ *Gignàs 16,* ☎ *93/315–1709. AE, MC, V.
Closed Sun. evening, Mon. and July.*

$　✕ **Egipte.** This small, friendly restaurant hidden away in a very con-
★　venient location behind the Boquería Market—though it's far better
known to locals than to visitors—is a real find. Its traditional Catalan
home cooking, huge desserts, and swift personable service all contribute
to its popularity and good value. ✉ *Jerusalem 12,* ☎ *93/301–6208.
Reservations not accepted. AE, DC, MC, V.Closed Sun.*

Lodging

Hotels around the Rambla and in the Gothic Quarter have plenty of
old-world charm, but are less strong on creature comforts; those in the
Eixample are mostly '50s or '60s buildings, often recently renovated;
and the newest hotels are found out along the Diagonal or beyond, in
the residential districts of Sarrià and Pedralbes, with the exception of
the Hotel Arts in the Olympic Port. There are hotel reservation desks
at the airport and Central Station.

For details and price-category definitions, *see* Lodging *in* Staying in Spain,
above.

$$$$　🏨 **Condes de Barcelona.** As this is one of Barcelona's most popular
★　hotels, rooms must be booked well in advance. The decor is stunning,
with marble floors and columns, an impressive staircase, and an out-

standing bar area. Guest rooms are on the small side. ✉ *Passeig de Gràcia 75, 08008,* ☎ *93/484–8600;* FAX *93/488–0614. 183 rooms with bath. Restaurant, bar, parking. AE, DC, MC, V.*

$$$$ 🏨 **Hotel Arts.** This luxurious skyscraper, a Ritz-Carlton property, overlooks Barcelona from the new Olympic Port, providing unique views of the Mediterranean, the city, and the mountains behind. A short taxi ride from the center of the city, the hotel is virtually a world of its own. Rooms are ultra-modern with pale wood, Bang & Olufsen CD players, and Frette linens. The hotel has three restaurants that respectively serve Mediterranean cuisine, Californian cooking, and tapas, like *gambas al ajillo* (baby shrimp fried in garlic). ✉ *C. de la Marina 1921, 08005,* ☎ *93/221–1000,* FAX *93/221–1070. 455 rooms and suites with bath. 3 restaurants, bar, pool, beauty salon, beach, shops, parking. AE, DC, MC, V.*

$$$$ 🏨 **Hotel Claris.** Widely considered Barcelona's best hotel, the Claris is a fascinating melange of design and tradition. The rooms come in 60 different layouts, all decorated in classical 18th-century English style. Wood and marble furnishings and decorative details are everywhere, along with a Japanese water garden, a first-rate restaurant, and a rooftop pool—all close to the center of Barcelona. ✉ *Carrer Pau Claris 150, 08009,* ☎ *93/487–6262,* FAX *93/215–7970. 124 rooms and suites with bath. Restaurant, bar, pool, garden. AE, DC, MC, V.*

$$$$ 🏨 **Princesa Sofía.** The Barcelona hotel most convenient to the airport, the Sofía is somewhat far from the hue and cry of downtown. For business and convenience, though, it's one of the city's best guarantees. ✉ *Plaça Pius XII 4, 08028,* ☎ *93/330–7111,* FAX *93/411–2106. 505 rooms with bath. 3 restaurants, 2 pools, sauna, exercise room, shops. AE, DC, MC, V.*

$$$$ 🏨 **Ritz.** Founded in 1919 by César Ritz, this is still the grand old lady
★ of Barcelona hotels. Extensive refurbishment has now restored it to its former splendor. The entrance lobby is awe-inspiring, the rooms spacious, and the service impeccable. ✉ *Gran Via 668, 08010,* ☎ *93/318–5200,* FAX *93/318–0148. 158 rooms with bath. Restaurant, bar. AE, DC, MC, V.*

$$$ 🏨 **Colón.** This cozy, older hotel has a unique charm and intimacy rem-
★ iniscent of an English country hotel that recent refurbishing has left intact. It's in an ideal location right in the heart of the Gothic Quarter, and the rooms on the front overlook the cathedral and square. It was a great favorite of Joan Miró. ✉ *Avda. Catedral 7, 08002,* ☎ *93/301–1404,* FAX *93/317–2915. 147 rooms with bath. Restaurant, bar. AE, DC, MC, V.*

$$$ 🏨 **Regente.** This smallish hotel on the corner of Valencia has a rooftop pool, plenty of style and charm, and a wonderful Modernista lobby. ✉ *Rambla de Catalunya 76, 08008,* ☎ *93/215–2570,* FAX *93/487–3227. 78 rooms with bath. 2 restaurants, bar, pool. AE, DC, MC, V.*

$$ 🏨 **España.** This hotel with modern, large bedrooms—the best and quietest overlook the bright interior patio—has stunning Art Nouveau public rooms. The high-ceiling downstairs has a breakfast room decorated with mermaids, elaborate woodwork, and an Eusebio Arnau Art Nouveau sculpted chimney in the cafeteria. The rooms have been recently refurbished, and the neighborhood is seedy but safe. ✉ *Sant Pau 911, 08001,* ☎ *93/318–1758,* FAX *93/317–1134. 76 rooms with bath. Restaurant, breakfast room, cafeteria. AE, DC, MC, V.*

$$ 🏨 **Gran Via.** Architectural features are the special charm of this 19th-century mansion, close to the main tourist office. The original chapel has been preserved, and you can have breakfast in a hall of mirrors, climb its Moderniste staircase, and make calls from elaborate Belle Epoque phone booths. ✉ *Gran Via 642, 08007,* ☎ *93/318–1900,* FAX

93/318–9997. 53 rooms with bath. Breakfast room, parking. AE, DC, MC, V.

$$ 🏨 **Oriente.** Barcelona's oldest hotel opened in 1843. Its public rooms
★ are a delight—the ballroom and dining rooms have lost none of their 19th-century magnificence—though the bedrooms have undergone a rather bland renovation. It's located just below the Liceu, and its terrace café is the perfect place for a drink. ⊠ *Rambla 45, 08002,* ☎ *93/302–2558,* 𝐅𝐀𝐗 *93/412–3819. 142 rooms with bath. Restaurant, bar. AE, DC, MC, V.*

$ 🏨 **Continental.** Something of a legend among cost-conscious travelers, this comfortable hostel with canopied balconies stands at the top of Ramblas, just below Plaça Catalunya. The rooms are homey and comfortable, the staff is friendly, and the location's ideal. Buffet breakfasts are a plus. ⊠ *Rambla 138, 08002,* ☎ *93/301–2508,* 𝐅𝐀𝐗 *93/302–7360. 35 rooms with bath. Breakfast room. AE, DC, MC, V.*

$ 🏨 **Jardí.** With views over the adjoining traffic-free and charming
★ squares, Plaçdel Pi and Plaça Sant Josep Oriol, this hotel's renovated bedrooms have white-tile floors, pine furniture, and powerful showers. Exterior rooms are the quietest. ⊠ *Plaça Sant Josep Oriol 1, 08002,* ☎ *93/301–5900,* 𝐅𝐀𝐗 *93/318–3664. 40 rooms with bath. Bar, breakfast room. AE, DC, MC, V.*

Bars and Cafés

Cafés and Tearooms

Zurich (⊠ Plaça de Catalunya 1), at the head of La Rambla, on the corner of Pelai, is one of the oldest and most traditional cafés, perfect for watching the world go by. Its fate is at present uncertain however, as the whole block is being reurbanized (i.e., demolished). Near the Picasso Museum, don't miss the hip **Textil Café** in the Museu Textil's lovely medieval courtyard (⊠ Montcada 1214). The **Croissant Show** (⊠ Santa Anna 10 just off the Rambla) is a small coffee and pastry shop, ideal for a quick midmorning or afternoon break. **Salón de Té Mauri,** on the corner of Rambla de Catalunya and Provença, and **Salón de Té Libre i Serra** (⊠ Ronda Sant Pere 3) are both traditional tearooms with a good selection of pastries. **Carrer Petritxol** (from Portaferrissa to Plaça del Pi) is famous for its *chocolaterías*, hot chocolate, and tearooms.

Tapas Bars

Alt Heidelberg (⊠ Ronda Universitat 5) has German beer on tap and German sausages; **Cal Pep** on Plaça de les Olles (near Santa Maria del Mar) is another popular spot, as is **Casa Tejada** at Tenor Viñas (near Plaça Francesc Macià).

Cocktail Bars

The two best areas are the **Passeig del Born,** which is near the Picasso Museum and very fashionable with the affluent young, and the **Eixample,** near Passeig de Gràcia. A bar called **Dry Martini** (⊠ Aribau 162) has more than 80 different gins; **Ideal Cocktail Bar,** (⊠ Aribau 89) has good malt whiskeys. **El Paraigua,** on Plaça Sant Miquel, in the Gothic Quarter behind the city hall, serves cocktails in a stylish setting with classical music.

Champagne Bars

Xampanyerías, serving sparkling Catalan cava, are something of a Barcelona specialty. Try **Brut** (⊠ Trompetas 3), in the Picasso Museum area; **La Cava del Palau** (⊠ Verdaguer i Callis 10), near the Palau de la Música; or **La Folie** (⊠ Bailén 169), one of the best.

Special Cafés

Els Quatre Gats (⌧ Montsiò 5, off Porta de l'Angel) is a reconstruction of the original café that opened in 1897—it's a real Barcelona institution. Literary discussions, jazz, and classical music recitals take place in this café where Picasso held his first show. **Café de l'Opera** (⌧ Ramblas 74), opposite the Liceu, is a longstanding Barcelona tradition, ideal for a coffee or drink at any time of day.

The Arts

To find out what's on in town, look in the daily papers or in the weekly *Guía del Ocio*, available from newsstands all over town. *Actes a la Ciutat* is a weekly list of cultural events published by the Ajuntament and available from its information office on Plaça Sant Jaume or at the Virreina at La Rambla 99.

Concerts

Catalans are great music lovers, and their main concert hall is the **Palau de la Música** (⌧ Sant Francesc de Paula 2, ☎ 93/268–1000). The ticket office is open weekdays 11–1 and 5–8 and Saturday 5–8 only. Its Sunday morning concerts are a popular tradition. Tickets are reasonably priced and can usually be purchased just before the concert.

Dance

L'Espai de Dansa i Mùsica de la Generalitat de Catalunya (⌧ Travessera de Gràcia 63, ☎ 93/414–3133), usually listed simply as "L'Espai" (the Space), is now Barcelona's prime venue for ballet and contemporary dance. **El Mercat de les Flors** (⌧ Lleida 59, ☎ 93/426–1875), not far from Plaça d'Espanya, continues to offer its traditionally rich program of modern dance and theater, as does the **Teatre Victoria** (⌧ Avda. Parallel 67, ☎ 93/443–2929).

Theater

Most theater performances are in Catalan, but Barcelona is also known for its experimental theater and for its mime troupes such as **Els Joglars** and **La Claca.** The best-known modern theaters are the **Teatre Lliure** (⌧ Montseny 47, in Gràcia, ☎ 93/218–9251), **El Mercat de les Flors** (☞ Dance, *above*), **Teatre Romea** (⌧ Hospital 51, ☎ 93/317–7189), **Teatre Tívoli** (⌧ Casp 10, ☎ 93/412–2063), and **Teatre Poliorama** (⌧ Rambla Estudios 115, ☎ 93/317–7599).

Film

Many theaters show foreign movies in their original languages—indicated by "v.o," or *versión original*. The **Filmoteca** (⌧ Avda. Sarrià 33, ☎ 93/430–5007) often includes English films in its schedule. The **Verdi** (⌧ Verdi 32, in Gràcia) and the **Rex** (⌧ Gran Via 463) always have recent v.o. releases.

Nightlife

Cabaret

Belle Epoque (⌧ Muntaner 246, ☎ 93/209–7385) is a beautifully decorated music hall with sophisticated shows. **El Mediévolo** (⌧ Gran Via 459, ☎ 93/243–1566) has medieval feasts and entertainment; it's all geared to tourists but fun.

Casino

The **Gran Casino de Barcelona** (☎ 93/893–3866), 42 kilometers (26 miles) south in Sant Pere de Ribes, near Sitges, also has a dance hall and some excellent international shows in a 19th-century atmosphere. Jacket and tie essential.

Discos

Two top discos are **Otto Zutz** (⌧ Lincoln 15, ☎ 93/238–0722), just below Via Augusta, and **Up and Down** (⌧ Numancia 179, ☎ 93/280–2922) ask for "ñpendow." **Oliver and Hardy** (⌧ Diagonal 593, next to the Barcelona Hilton, ☎ 93/419–3181) is kind to persons over 35; **La Tierra** (⌧ Aribau 230, ☎ 93/200–7346) and **El Otro** (⌧ Valencia 166, ☎ 93/323–6759) also accept postgraduates.

Flamenco

The best place is **El Patio Andaluz** (⌧ Aribau 242, ☎ 93/209–3378). **El Cordobés** (⌧ Ramblas 35, ☎ 93/317–6853) is aimed at tour groups but can be fun. **Los Tarantos** (⌧ Plaça Reial 17, ☎ 93/318–3067) is presently the hippest flamenco venue.

Jazz Clubs

Try **L'Auditori** (⌧ Balmes 245); **La Cova del Drac** (⌧ Vallmajor 33, ☎ 93/200–7032); or the Gothic Quarter's **Harlem Jazz Club** (⌧ Comtessa Sobradiel 8, ☎ 93/310–0755).

Ports and Beaches

The Barcelona waterfront has undergone a major overhaul since 1992. The **Port Vell** (Old Port) now includes an extension of the Rambla, the **Rambla de Mar,** crossing the inner harbor from just below the Columbus Monument. This boardwalk connects the Rambla with the **Moll d'Espanya,** where a shopping mall, a dozen restaurants, aquarium, cinema complex, and Barcelona's two yacht clubs are located. A walk around the Port Vell leads past the marina to Passeig Joan de Borbó, both lined with restaurants that have outdoor tables. From here, you can go south out to sea along the *rompeolas*, or breakwater, a two-mile excursion, or north (left) down the San Sebastián beach to the Passeig Maritim that leads to the **Port Olympic.** Except for the colorful inner streets of Barceloneta, the traditional fisherman's quarter, all of this new construction is largely devoid of character. Take the Golondrina boat (☞ Getting Around By Boat, *above*) to the end of the breakwater and walk in to Barceloneta for some paella.

The beaches that stretch down to and past the Port Olympic are much improved although generally somewhat dusty and crowded; water quality is erratic.

MOORISH SPAIN

Stretching from the dark mountains of the Sierra Morena in the north, west to the plains of the Guadalquivir valley, and south to the mighty snowcapped Sierra Nevada, Andalucía rings with echoes of the Moors. In the kingdom they called Al-Andalus, these Muslim invaders from North Africa dwelt for almost 800 years, from their first conquest of Spanish soil (Gibraltar) in 711 to their expulsion from Granada in 1492. And to this day the cities and landscapes of Andalucía are rich in their legacy. The great Mosque of Córdoba, the magical Alhambra Palace in Granada, and the Giralda tower, landmark of Seville, were the inspired creations of Moorish architects and craftsmen working at the behest of Al-Andalus's Arab emirs. The brilliant white villages with narrow streets and sturdy-walled houses clustered round cool inner patios, the whitewashed facades with heavily grilled windows, and the wailing song of Andalucía's flamenco, so reminiscent of the muezzin's call to prayer, all stem from centuries of Moorish occupation.

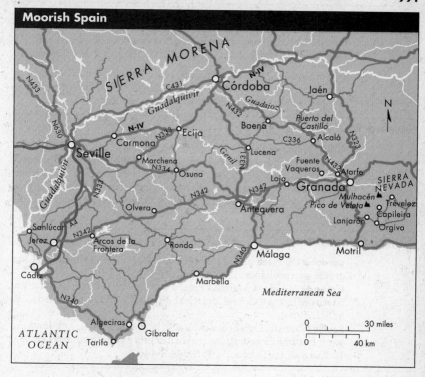

Moorish Spain

Getting There from Madrid

Seville, Córdoba, and Granada all lie on direct train routes from Madrid. Service is frequent from both Chamartín and Atocha stations in Madrid, and includes overnight trains (to Seville and Granada), slower day trains, and express talgos. In addition, the high-speed AVE train connecting Seville and Atocha Station began service in 1992 on entirely new track; it's more expensive but it's a pleasurable ride and has cut traveling time on that route from 5½–6 hours to about 2½ hours. Most bus service from Madrid to Moorish Spain operates out of the Estación del Sur (☞ Arriving and Departing *in* Madrid, *above*). If you drive, follow the N-IV, which takes you through the scorched orange plains of La Mancha to Córdoba, then along the Guadalquivir River to Seville. The N323 road, which splits from the N-IV at Bailén, takes you past lovely olive groves and rolling hills to Granada.

Getting Around

Seville and Córdoba are linked by direct train service. Buses are a better choice between Seville and Granada, and between Córdoba and Granada, as trains are relatively slow and infrequent and often involve a time-consuming change. **Seville's** older bus station, Estación del Prado de San Sebastián (☎ 95/441–7111) is between José María Osborne and Manuel Vazquez Sagastizabal; a new bus station, Estación Plaza de Armas, located on Arjona, next to the Cachorro Bridge, is closer to downtown (☎ 95/490–8040). Check with the tourist office to determine which one you'll need. The city also has a new train station, Santa Justa, built in conjunction with the 1992 International Exposition, located on Avda. Kansas City, (☎ 95/454–0202). In **Granada,** the main bus station is Alsina Gräells (✉ Camino de Ronda 97, ☎ 958/251–358). The train station is at the end of Avenida Andaluces;

the RENFE office is located at ⊠ Reyes Católicos 63, ☎ 958/271272.
Córdoba has no central bus depot, so check at the tourist office for the
appropriate company. The train station is on the Glorieta Conde de
Guadalorce (RENFE office: ⊠ Ronda de los Tejares 10, ☎ 957/475884).

Driving in Moorish Spain, long anathema to travelers, has been largely
transformed by improvements made for the 1992 festivities. If you enjoy
winding roads and gorgeous landscapes, consider renting a car.

Guided Tours

Guided tours of Seville, Córdoba, and Granada (del) are run by **Julià
Tours** (☎ 91/571–8696), **Pullmantur** (☎ 91/541–1807), and **Trapsatur**
(☎ 91/542–6666), both from Madrid and resorts of the Costa del Sol;
check with travel agents. Local excursions may be available from
Seville to the sherry bodegas and the equestrian museum of Jerez de
la Frontera.

Visitor Information

Córdoba (⊠ Plaza de Judá Leví, ☎ 957/200522, and Palacio de Con-
gresos y Exposiciones, ⊠ Torrijos 10, ☎ 957/471235).
Granada (⊠ Plaza Mariana Pineda 10, ☎ 958/226688, and the less
useful office at Corral del Carbón, ⊠ C. Mariana Pineda, ☎
958/225990).
Seville (⊠ Avda. Constitución 21(del), ☎ 95/422–1404, just down the
street from the cathedral, and the smaller office at Costurero de la Reina,
⊠ Paseo de las Delícias 9, ☎ 95/423–4465).

Exploring Moorish Spain

The downside to a visit here, especially to Seville, is that petty crime,
much of it directed against tourists, is rife. Purse snatching and thefts
from cars, frequently when drivers are in them, are depressingly familiar.
Always keep your car doors *and* trunk locked. *Never* leave any valuables in your car. Leave your passport, traveler's checks, and credit cards
in your hotel's safe, *never* in your room. Don't carry expensive cameras or wear jewelry. Take only the minimum amount of cash with you.
There comes a point, however—if your windshield is smashed or your
bag is snatched, for example—when all the precautions in the world
will prove inadequate. If you're unlucky, it's an equally depressing fact
that the police, again especially in Seville, have adopted a distinctly casual attitude to such thefts, and often combine indifference to belea-
guered tourists with rudeness in about equal measure.

Seville

*Numbers in the margin correspond to points of interest on the Seville
map.*

Lying on the banks of the Guadalquivir River, **Seville**—Spain's fourth-
largest city and capital of Andalucía—is one of the most beautiful and
romantic cities in Europe. Here in this city of the sensuous Carmen and
the amorous Don Juan, famed for the spectacle of its Holy Week processions and April Fair, you'll come close to the spiritual heart of
★ ❶ Moorish Andalucía. Begin your visit in the **cathedral,** begun in 1402,
a century and a half after St. Ferdinand delivered Seville from the
Moors. This great Gothic edifice, which took just more than a century
to build, is traditionally described in superlatives. It's the biggest and
highest cathedral in Spain, the largest Gothic building in the world,
and the world's third-largest church after St. Peter's in Rome and St.
Paul's in London. And it boasts the world's largest carved wooden altarpiece. Despite such impressive statistics, the inside can be dark and

Seville

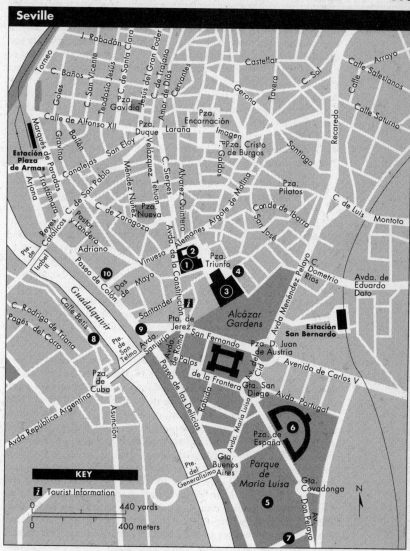

gloomy with too many overly ornate Baroque trappings. But seek out the beautiful Virgins by Murillo and Zurbarán and reflect on the history enshrined in these walls. In a silver urn before the high altar rest the precious relics of Seville's liberator, St. Ferdinand. You'll want to pay your respects to Christopher Columbus, whose mortal vestiges are enshrined in a flamboyant mausoleum in the south aisle. Borne aloft by statues representing the four medieval kingdoms of Spain, it's to be hoped that the great voyager has found peace at last, after the transatlantic quarrels that carried his body from Valladolid to Santo Domingo and from Havana to Seville. ⊠ *Plaza Virgen de los Reyes,* ☎ *95/421–4971* 🎫 *Cathedral and Giralda 600 ptas.* ⊘ *Mon.–Sat. 11–5, Sun. 2–4. Cathedral also open for Mass.*

Every day the bell that summons the faithful to prayer rings out from a Moorish minaret, relic of the Arab mosque whose admirable tower of Abu Yakoub the Sevillians could not bring themselves to destroy. Topped in 1565-68 by a bell tower and weather vane and called the ★ ❷ **Giralda,** this splendid example of Moorish art is one of the marvels of Seville. In place of steps, 35 sloping ramps climb to the viewing platform 230 feet from the ground. St. Ferdinand is said to have ridden his horse to the top to admire the view of the city he had conquered. Seven centuries later your view of the Golden Tower and shimmering Guadalquivir will be equally breathtaking. Try, too, to see the Giralda at night when the floodlights cast a new magic on this gem of Islamic art. 🎫 *Giralda and cathedral 600 ptas.* ⊘ *Mon.–Sat. 11–5, Sun. 10–2 (Giralda only) and 2–4.*

★ ❸   The high fortified walls of the **Alcázar** belie the exquisite delicacy of the palace's interior. It was built by Pedro the Cruel—so known because he murdered his stepmother and four of his half-brothers—who lived here with his mistress, María de Padilla, from 1350 to 1369. Don't mistake this for a genuine Moorish palace, as it was built more than 100 years after the reconquest of Seville; rather, its style is Mudéjar—built by Moorish craftsmen working under orders of a Christian king. The Catholic Kings (Ferdinand and Isabella), whose only son, Prince Juan, was born in the Alcázar in 1478, added a wing to serve as the administrative center for their New World empire, and Charles V enlarged it further for his marriage celebrations in 1526. Pedro's Mudéjar palace centers around the beautiful **Patio de las Doncellas** (Court of the Damsels), whose name pays tribute to the annual gift of 100 virgins to the Moorish sultans whose palace once stood on the site. Resplendent with lacelike stucco and gleaming *azulejo* (tile) decorations, it is immediately reminiscent of Granada's Alhambra, and is in fact the work of Granadan artisans. Opening off this patio you will find the Salón de Embajadores, where in 1526 Carlos V married Isabel of Portugal, and the apartments of María de Padilla.

The fragrant **Alcázar Gardens** are planted with jasmine and myrtle; there's also an orange tree said to have been planted by Pedro the Cruel and a lily pond well stocked with fat, contented goldfish. The end of your visit brings you to the **Patio de las Banderas** for an unrivaled view of the Giralda. ⊠ *Plaza del Triunfo,* ☎ *95/422–7163.* 🎫 *Palace and gardens 600 ptas.* ⊘ *Tues.–Sat. 10:30–5, Sun. 10–1.*

★ ❹   The **Barrio de Santa Cruz,** with its twisting alleyways, cobbled squares, and whitewashed houses, is the perfect setting for an operetta. Once the home of Seville's Jewish population, it was much favored by 17th-century noblemen and today boasts some of the most expensive properties in Seville. All the romantic images you've ever had of Spain will come to life here: Every house gleams white or deep ocher yellow;

wrought-iron grilles adorn the windows, and every balcony and patio is bedecked with geraniums and petunias. Ancient bars nestle side by side with antiques shops. Don't miss the famous **Casa Román** bar in Plaza de los Venerables Sacerdotes with its ceilings hung thick with some of the best hams in Seville, or the **Hostería del Laurel** next door, where in summer you can dine in one of the loveliest squares in the city. Souvenir and excellent ceramic shops surround the **Plaza Doña Elvira,** where young Sevillanos gather to play guitars around the fountain and azulejo benches. And in the **Plaza Alianza,** with its well-stocked antiques shops and **John Fulton Gallery** (Fulton is the only American ever to qualify as a full-fledged bullfighter), stop a moment and admire the simplicity of the crucifix on the wall, framed in a profusion of bougainvillea.

⑤ Take a cab, or better still, hire a horse carriage from the Plaza Virgen de los Reyes, below the Giralda, and visit **Parque de María Luisa** (María Luisa Park), whose gardens are a delightful blend of formal design and wild vegetation, shady walkways, and sequestered nooks. In the 1920s the park was redesigned to house the 1929 Hispanic-American exhibition, and the impressive villas you see here today are the **⑥** fair's remaining pavilions. Visit the monumental **Plaza de España,** whose grandiose pavilion of Spain was the centerpiece of the exhibition. At the opposite end of the park you can feed the hundreds of white **⑦** doves that gather round the fountains of the lovely **Plaza de América;** it's a magical spot to while away the sleepy hours of the siesta.

⑧ An early evening stroll along the **Calle Betis** on the far side of the Guadalquivir is a delight few foreigners know about. Between the San Telmo and Isabel II bridges, the vista of the sparkling water, the palm-**⑨** lined banks, and the silhouette of the **Torre de Oro** (Tower of Gold), a 12-sided tower built by the Moors in 1220, is simply stunning. During the day you can enjoy a nice view from the tower itself, which also houses a small naval museum. ☎ 95/422–2419, ▭ 100 ptas., ☉ Tues.–Fri. 10–2, weekends 11–2.

For those that want to take in a bit of the bullfighting history that this region is famous for, a short walk up the *Paseo de Colón* from **⑩** the Torre de Oro will lead you to the **Maestranza Bullring,** one of Spain's oldest and most beautiful. ⊠ *Paseo de Colón,* ☎ *95/422–4577.* ▭ *Plaza tours and bullfighting museum 250 ptas.,* ☉ *Mon.–Sat. 10–1:30.*

Thirty kilometers (19 miles) from Seville, the N-IV brings you to **Carmona.** This unspoiled Andalucían town of Roman and Moorish origin is worth a visit, either to stay at the parador or the spectacular Casa de Carmona hotel (one of the finest in all of Spain) or to enjoy its wealth of Mudéjar and Renaissance churches, and its streets of whitewashed houses of clear Moorish influence. Most worthwhile is the **Church of San Pedro,** begun in 1466, whose extraordinary interior is an unbroken mass of sculptures and gilded surfaces, and whose tower, erected in 1704, is an unabashed imitation of Seville's famous Giralda. Carmona's most moving monument is its splendid **Roman Necropolis,** where in huge underground chambers some 900 family tombs dating from the 2nd to the 4th century AD have been chiseled out of the rock. ⊠ *C. Enmedio,* ☎ *95/414–0811.* ▭ *250 ptas.* ☉ *Tues.–Sat. 8:30–2:30, Sun. 10–2.*

Córdoba

Numbers in the margin correspond to points of interest on the Córdoba map.

Ancient **Córdoba,** city of the caliphs, is one of Spain's oldest cities and the greatest embodiment of Moorish heritage in all Andalucía. From the 8th to the 11th centuries, the Moorish emirs and Caliphs of the West held court here, and the city became one of the Western world's greatest centers of art, culture, and learning. Moors, Christians, and Jews lived together in harmony within its walls. It is for its famous

★ ❶ **Mezquita** (mosque), one of the finest built by the Moors, that Córdoba is known. Its founder was Abd ar-Rahman I (756–788), and it was completed by Al Mansur (976–1002) around the year 987. As you step inside you'll face a forest of gleaming pillars of precious marble, jasper, and onyx, rising to red-and-white horseshoe arches, one of the most characteristic traits of Moorish architecture. Not even the heavy Baroque cathedral that Charles V so mistakenly built in its midst—and later regretted—can detract from the overpowering impact and mystery wrought by the art of these Moorish craftsmen. The Mezquita was indeed a fitting setting for the original copy of the Koran and a bone from the arm of the Prophet Mohammed, holy relics once housed in the Mezquita that were responsible for bringing thousands of pilgrims to its doors in the great years before St. Ferdinand reconquered Córdoba for the Christians in 1236. The mosque opens onto the **Patio de los Naranjos** (Orange Tree Courtyard) and the bell tower, which served as the mosque's minaret. It's well worth climbing the uneven steps to the top for the view of the Guadalquivir River and the tiled rooftops of the old city. ⊠ *Torrijos and Cardinal Herrero,* ☎ *957/470512.* 🖃 *700 ptas.* ☉ *Daily May–Sept., 10–7; Oct.–Apr., 10–5.*

Near the mosque, the streets of Torrijos, Cardenal Herrero, and Deanes are lined with tempting souvenir shops specializing in local handicrafts, especially the filigree silver and embossed leather for which Córdoba
❷ is famous. In her niche on Cardenal Herrero, the **Virgen de los Faroles** (Virgin of the Lanterns) stands demurely behind a lantern-hung grille.
❸ Now make your way westward to the old **Judería,** or Jewish quarter.
❹ On the **Plaza Judá Leví** you'll find the municipal tourist office.

❺ Overlooking the Plaza Maimónides (or Bulas) is the **Museo Taurino** (Museum of Bullfighting), housed in two delightful old mansions. You'll see a well-displayed collection of memorabilia, paintings, and posters by early 20th-century Cordoban artists, and rooms dedicated to great Cordoban *toreros*—even the hide of the bull that killed the legendary Manolete in 1947. ☎ *957/472000, ext. 211.* 🖃 *400 ptas.* ☉ *Tues.–Sat. 9:30–1:30 and 5–8 (4–7 in winter), Sun. 9:30–1:30.*

❻ A statue of the great Jewish philosopher **Maimónides** stands in the Plaza
❼ Tiberiades. A few paces along Judíos, you come to the only **synagogue** in Andalucía to have survived the expulsion of the Jews in 1492. It's one of only three remaining synagogues in Spain—the other two you saw in Toledo—built before 1492, and it boasts some fine Hebrew and Mudéjar stucco tracery and a women's gallery. ⊠ *C. Judíos,* ☎ *957/298133.* 🖃 *75 ptas.* ☉ *Tues.–Sat. 10–2 and 3:30–5:30, Sun. 10–1:30.*

Across the way is the courtyard of El Zoco, a former Arab souk, with some pleasant shops and stalls, and sometimes a bar open in summer.

As you leave Córdoba and head for Granada, the N432 climbs from the Guadalquivir valley up into the mountains of central Andalucía. It is 63 kilometers (39 miles) to **Baena,** a picturesque Andalucían town of white houses clustered on the hillside, where you may want to stop for a drink and wander the narrow streets and squares as yet largely untouched by tourism. Mountain views line the route as the road twists toward its highest point, 3,000-foot Puerto del Castillo, before

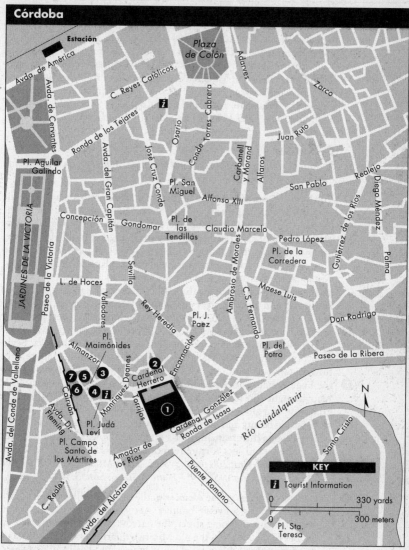

Córdoba

Estación

Plaza de Colón

Avda. de América

Avda. de Cervantes

C. Reyes Católicos

Adarves

Zarco

Ronda de los Tejares

Osario

Conde Torres Cabrera

Juan Ruto

Avda. del Gran Capitán

José Cruz Conde

Pl. Aguilar Galindo

Pl. San Miguel

Carbonell y Morand

Alfaros

San Pablo

Realejo

Diego Méndez

Concepción

Gondomar

Alfonso XIII

Pl. de las Tendillas

Claudio Marcelo

Pedro López

Gutiérrez de los Ríos

Palma

JARDINES DE LA VICTORIA

Paseo de la Victoria

Sevilla

Valladares

L. de Hoces

Rey Heredia

Pl. J. Paez

Ambrosio de Morales

Pl. de la Corredera

Maese Luis

C.S. Fernando

Don Rodrigo

Pl. Maimónides

Almanzor

Montíquez Desues

Encarnación

Pl. del Potro

Paseo de la Ribera

Avda. del Conde de Vallellano

Cairuán

7 5 3

2 Cardenal Herrero

6 4 i

Pl. Judá Leví

1

Cardenal González

Ronda de Isasa

Río Guadalquivir

Santo Crisio

N

Avda. Dr. Fleming

Pl. Campo Santo de los Mártires

Amador de los Ríos

KEY

i Tourist Information

C. Reales

Avda. del Alcázar

Puente Romano

0 _____ 330 yards
0 _____ 300 meters

Pl. Sta. Teresa

dropping down onto the *vega* (fertile plain) of Granada. At Pinos Puente, you can take a short detour to the village of **Fuente Vaqueros** where Federico García Lorca was born on June 5, 1898. In 1986, to commemorate the 50th anniversary of his assassination in Granada at the outbreak of the Civil War, his birthplace was restored as a museum. The nearby village of Valderrubio inspired his *Libro de Poemas* and *La Casa de Bernarda Alba*. ⊠ *Museo de Lorca,* ⊘ *Jan., Feb., and July–Sept., Tues.–Sun. 10–1 and 6–8; Apr.–June, Tues.–Sun. 10–1 and 5–7; Oct.–Dec. and Mar., Tues.–Sun. 10–1 and 4–6. Tours every hr on the hr.*

Granada

Numbers in the margin correspond to points of interest on the Granada map.

The city of **Granada** rises majestically on three hills dwarfed by the mighty snowcapped peaks of the Sierra Nevada, which boasts the highest roads in Europe. Atop one of these hills, the pink-gold palace of the Alhambra, at once splendidly imposing yet infinitely delicate, gazes out across the rooftops and gypsy caves of the Sacromonte to the fertile vega rich in orchards, tobacco fields, and poplar groves. Granada, the last stronghold of the Moors and the most treasured of all their cities, fell finally to the Catholic Kings in January 1492. For Ferdinand and Isabella, their conquest of Granada was the fulfillment of a long-cherished dream to rid Spain of the Infidel, and here they built

★ ❶ the flamboyant **Capilla Real** (Royal Chapel) where they have lain side by side since 1521, later joined by their daughter Juana la Loca. Begin your tour in the nearby Plaza de Bib-Rambla, a pleasant square with flower stalls and outdoor cafés in summer, then pay a quick visit to

❷ the huge Renaissance **cathedral** commissioned in 1521 by Charles V who thought the Royal Chapel "too small for so much glory." A grandiose and gloomy monument, not completed until 1714, it is far surpassed in beauty and historic value by the neighboring Royal Chapel, which, despite the great emperor's plans, still houses the tombs of his grandparents and less fortunate mother. ☎ *958/229239.* ▭ *Royal Chapel and cathedral 200 ptas.* ⊘ *Mar.–Sept., Mon.–Sat. 10:30–1 and 4–7; Oct.–Feb., Mon.–Sat. 11–1 and 3:30–6, Sun. 3:30–6.*

❸ The adjacent streets of the **Alcaicería,** the old Arab silk exchange, will prove a haven for souvenir hunters. Across the Gran Vía de Colón, Granada's main shopping street, the narrow streets begin to wind up

❹ the slopes of the **Albaicín,** the old Moorish quarter, which is now a fascinating mixture of dilapidated white houses and beautiful *cármenes,* luxurious villas with fragrant gardens. Few visitors find their way to

★ ❺ the **balcony** of **San Nicolás Church,** which affords an unforgettable view of the Alhambra, particularly when it is floodlit at night.

★ ❻ The Cuesta de Gomérez climbs steeply to the **Alhambra precincts,** where the Duke of Wellington planted shady elms and Washington Irving tarried among the gypsies from whom he learned the Moorish legends so evocatively recounted in his *Tales of the Alhambra*. Above the

❼ **Puerta de la Justicia,** the hand of Fatima, her fingers evoking the five laws of the Koran, beckons you inside the mystical Alhambra, the most imposing and infinitely beautiful of all Andalucía's Moorish monuments.

❽ The history of the **Alhambra** is woven through the centuries. Once inside its famous courts the legends of the Patio of the Lions, the Hall of the Two Sisters, and the murder of the Abencerrajes spring to life in a profusion of lacy walls, frothy stucco, gleaming tiles, and ornate dome ceilings. Here in this realm of myrtles and fountains, festooned arches and mysterious inscriptions, every corner holds its secret. Here the emirs installed their harems, accorded their favorites the most lav-

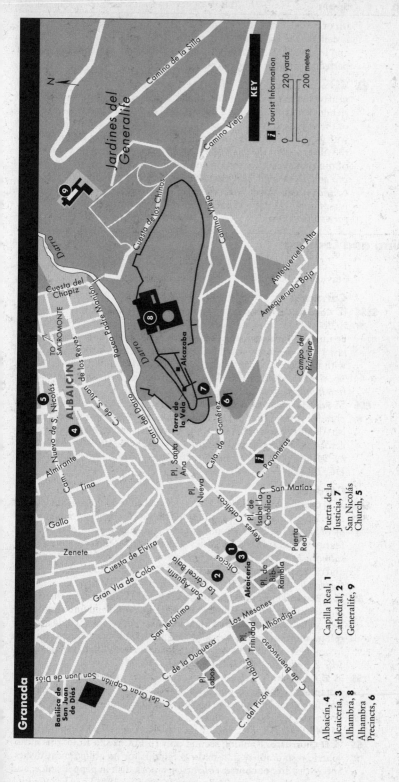

Granada

Basílica de San Juan de Diós

ALBAICIN

Jardines del Generalife

KEY
ℹ Tourist Information
0   220 yards
0   200 meters

Albaicín, **4**
Alcaicería, **3**
Alhambra, **8**
Alhambra
Precincts, **6**

Capilla Real, **1**
Cathedral, **2**
Generalife, **9**

Puerta de la
Justicia, **7**
San Nicolás
Church, **5**

ish of courts, and bathed in marble baths. In the midst of so much that is delicate the Baroque palace of Charles V seems an intrusion, heavy and incongruous, were it not for the splendid acoustics that make it a perfect setting for Granada's summer music festival.

⑨ Wisteria, jasmine, and roses line your route to the **Generalife,** the nearby summer palace of the caliphs, where crystal drops shower from slender fountains against a background of stately cypresses. The view of the white clustered houses of the Albaicín, the Sacromonte riddled with gypsy caves, and the imposing bulk of the Alhambra towering above the tiled roofs of the city will etch on your memory an indelible image of this most beautiful setting and greatest Moorish legacy. ⊠ *Alhambra and Generalife 625 ptas., free Sun. after 3. ⊙ Nov.–Feb., daily 9–6, Mar.–Oct., daily 9–8. Floodlit visits Tues., Thurs., and Sat. 10 PM–midnight (Sat. 8–10 PM in winter). Ticket office closes 45 mins before closing times.*

Dining and Lodging

For details and price-category definitions, *see* Dining *and* Lodging *in* Staying in Spain, *above.*

Carmona

$$$$ 🏨 **Casa de Carmona.** If you want to relax royal-style, this is the place
★   to do it: The Carmona is one of the most stunning properties in all of Spain. The 16th-century Lasso de la Vega Palace was renovated in the late 1980s and today you'll find beautifully furnished rooms, decorated with fine art, rich fabrics, and antiques. ⊠ *Plaza de Lasso 1, 41410,* ☎ *95/414–3300,* ℻ *95/414–3752. 30 rooms with bath. Restaurant, bar, minibars, pool, health club. AE, DC, MC, V.*

$$$ 🏨 **Parador Alcázar del Rey Don Pedro.** The beauty of this modern
★   parador is its splendid, peaceful setting in the ruins of the old Moorish Alcázar on top of the hill above Carmona, and its magnificent views across the vast fertile plain below. ⊠ *Alcázar, 41410,* ☎ *95/414–1010,* ℻ *95/414–1712. 63 rooms with bath. Restaurant, bar, pool. AE, DC, MC, V.*

Córdoba

$$$ ✕ **El Caballo Rojo.** The Red Horse, located close to the mosque, is Cór-
★   doba's most outstanding restaurant, famous throughout Andalucía and all of Spain. The decor resembles a cool Andalucían patio, and the menu features traditional specialties such as *rabo de toro* (bull's tail); *salmorejo,* a local version of gazpacho with chunks of ham and egg; and other exotic creations inspired by Córdoba's Moorish heritage. ⊠ *Cardenal Herrero 28,* ☎ *957/475375. AE, DC, MC, V.*

$$ ✕ **El Blasón.** Under the same management as El Caballo Rojo, this charming restaurant is fast gaining a name for fine food and unbeatable ambience. In an old inn with a pleasant tapas patio and a whole array of restaurants upstairs, its specialties include *salmón con naranjas* (salmon in oranges) and ternera *con salsa de alcaparrones* (in caper sauce). ⊠ *José Zorrilla 11,* ☎ *957/480625. AE, DC, MC, V.*

$$ ✕ **El Cardenal.** Close to the mosque, beside the Marisa hotel, this restaurant in the heart of Córdoba's tourist center offers a stylish setting for lunch or dinner. A marble staircase with Oriental rugs leads up to the second-floor dining room. ⊠ *Cardenal Herrero 14,* ☎ *957/480346. AE, DC, MC, V. Closed Mon. in winter, no dinner Sun.*

$$ ✕ **El Churrasco.** Ranking second only to El Caballo Rojo, this atmo-
★   spheric restaurant with a patio is famous for its grilled meat dishes. Specialties are, of course, *churrasco,* a pork dish in pepper sauce, and an excellent salmorejo. ⊠ *Romero 16,* ☎ *957/290817. AE, DC, MC, V. Closed Aug.*

$$ ✕ **La Almudaina.** This attractive restaurant is in a 15th-century house and former school that overlooks the Alcázar at the entrance to the Judería. It has an Andalucían patio, and the decor and cooking are both typical of Córdoba. ✉ *Campo Santo de los Mártires 1,* ☎ *957/474342. AE, DC, MC, V. No dinner Sun.*

$$$–$$$$ 🏨 **Conquistador.** This delightful contemporary hotel on the east side
★ of the mosque is built in Andalucían Moorish style with a charming patio and ceramic decor. The hotel itself has no restaurant, but guests can dine in the attractive Mesón del Bandolero in Calle Torrijos on the opposite side of the mosque. ✉ *Magistral González Francés 15, 14003,* ☎ *957/481102,* ⒻⒶⓍ *957/475079. 100 rooms with bath, 3 suites. Bar, sauna. AE, DC, MC, V.*

$$ 🏨 **Marisa.** This hotel is in a charming old Andalucían house whose location is in the heart of the old town overlooking the mosque's Patio de los Naranjos is its prime virtue. You'll find the decor quaint and charming, and the rates reasonable. ✉ *Cardenal Herrero 6, 14003,* ☎ *957/473142,* ⒻⒶⓍ *957/474144. 28 rooms with bath. MC, V.*

Granada

$$$ ✕ **Baroca.** Located one block above the Camino de Ronda, the locals
★ consider this Granada's best restaurant. The menu favors international cuisine; desserts are especially good. Service is professional and the ambience agreeable. ✉ *Pedro Antonio de Alarcón 34,* ☎ *958/265061. AE, DC, MC, V. Closed Sun. and Aug.*

$$$ ✕ **Carmen de San Miguel.** This is a restaurant to visit for its superb setting in a villa with an outdoor terrace and magnificent views over Granada. Located on the Alhambra hill beside the Alhambra Palace hotel, the setting is unbeatable; the food is average Continental-style cuisine. ✉ *Paseo Torres Bermejas 3,* ☎ *958/226723. AE, DC, MC, V. No dinner Sun.*

$$$ ✕ **Cunini.** In the center of town, close to the cathedral, Cunini has long been famous for the quality of its seafood. ✉ *Pescadería 9,* ☎ *958/250777. AE, DC, MC, V. Closed Mon.*

$$ ✕ **Sevilla.** This is a very atmospheric, colorful restaurant in the Alcaicería beside the cathedral. There's a superb tapas bar at the entrance, and the dining room is picturesque but rather small and crowded. The menu can be rather tourist-oriented, but try their *sopa Sevillana* (fish soup). ✉ *Oficios 12,* ☎ *958/221223. AE, DC, MC, V. Closed Sun.*

$ ✕ **Los Manueles.** This old inn is one of Granada's long-standing traditions. The walls have ceramic tiles, and the ceiling is hung with hams. There's lots of atmosphere, good old-fashioned service, and plenty of traditional Granadan cooking. ✉ *Zaragoza 2,* ☎ *958/223413. AE, DC, MC, V.*

$$$$ 🏨 **Parador de San Francisco.** Magnificently located in an old convent within the Alhambra precincts, the parador was where Queen Isabella was entombed before the completion of the Royal Chapel. It's one of Spain's most popular hotels, and you need to book at least four months in advance. ✉ *Alhambra, 18008,* ☎ *958/221440,* ⒻⒶⓍ *958/222264. 38 rooms with bath. Restaurant, bar. AE, DC, MC, V.*

$$$–$$$$ 🏨 **Alhambra Palace.** This flamboyant ocher-red Moorish-style palace
★ was built about 1910 and sits halfway up the hill to the Alhambra. The mood is more harried than at the more isolated parador. Though recently renovated, it remains a conversation piece with rich carpets, tapestries, and Moorish tiles. Rooms overlooking the town are preferable. The terrace is the perfect place for an early evening drink as the sun sets over the Sierra Nevada. ✉ *Peña Partida 2, 18009,* ☎

958/221468, FAX *958/226404. 123 rooms with bath, 9 suites. Restaurant, 2 bars. AE, DC, MC, V.*

$$ 🏨 **América.** This is a simple but charming hotel within the Alhambra precincts. It's very popular so you'll need to reserve a room months ahead. The location is magnificent, and guests can linger over breakfast on a delightful patio. ⊠ *Real de la Alhambra 53, 18009,* ☎ *958/227471,* FAX *958/227470. 14 rooms with bath. Restaurant. No credit cards. Closed Nov.–Feb.*

$$ 🏨 **Victoria.** An absolute gem of an old-world hotel, it overlooks the
★   Puerta Real—from which noise might be a disadvantage. Carpeted bedrooms have dark polished furniture. ⊠ *Puerta Real 3, 18005,* ☎ *958/257700,* FAX *958/263108. 66 rooms with bath, 3 suites. 2 restaurants, 2 bars. AE, DC, MC, V.*

$ 🏨 **Inglaterra.** Set in a period house just two blocks above the Gran Vía de Colón in the heart of town, this is a hotel that will appeal to those who prefer old-world charm to creature comforts, though accommodations are perfectly adequate for the reasonable rates. ⊠ *Cetti Meriem 6, 18010,* ☎ *958/221559,* FAX *958/221586. 36 rooms with bath. AE, DC, MC, V.*

Seville

$$$ ✕ **Egaña-Oriza.** This is currently one of Seville's most fashionable
★   restaurants. Basque specialties include *merluza con almejas en salsa verde* (white fish and clams in green sauce) and *tostón de hígado de oca gratinada* (goose liver on toast au gratin). It's opposite the old tobacco factory, now Seville University. ⊠ *San Fernando 41,* ☎ *95/422–7271. AE, DC, MC, V. No lunch Sat. Closed Sun. and Aug.*

$$$ ✕ **La Albahaca.** Set in an attractive old house in the heart of the Barrio Santa Cruz, the Albahaca offers plenty of style and atmosphere and original, imaginative cuisine. Specialties of the chef, who was formerly in the Hotel Alfonso XIII, are *suprema de lubina con almejas negras* (sea bass with venus clams) and *filetitos de ciervo con salsa de hongos* (venison with wild mushroom sauce). ⊠ *Plaza Santa Cruz 12,* ☎ *95/422–0714. AE, DC, MC, V. Closed Sun.*

$$$ ✕ **La Isla.** In the center of town between the cathedral and the Convent of La Caridad, La Isla has long been famous for its superb seafood and paella. ⊠ *Arfe 25,* ☎ *95/421–5376. AE, DC, MC, V. Closed Aug.*

$$$ ✕ **San Marco.** The brothers Ramacciotti serve Italian-influenced cuisine in an 18th-century mansion with a classic Andalucían patio—a wonderful spot for a summer meal. Try the ravioli *rellenos de lubina en salsa de almejas* (stuffed with sea bass in a clam sauce), cordero relleno *de espinacas y setas* (with spinach and forest mushrooms), or any of a delectable array of desserts. ⊠ *Cuna 6,* ☎ *95/421–2440. AE, DC, MC, V. Closed Mon. and Aug.*

$$ ✕ **La Judería.** This bright, modern restaurant near the Hotel Fernando
★   III is fast gaining recognition for the quality of its Andalucían and international cuisine and reasonable prices. Fish dishes from the north of Spain and meat from Ávila are specialties. Try cordero lechal asado (roast baby lamb) or *urta a la Roteña* (a fish dish unique to Rota). ⊠ *Cano y Cueto 13,* ☎ *95/441–2052. Reservations essential. AE, DC, MC, V. Closed Sun. in Aug.*

$$ ✕ **Mesón Don Raimundo.** In an old convent close to the cathedral, the
★   Mesón has an atmosphere and decor that are deliberately Sevillian. Its bar is the perfect place to sample some splendid tapas, and the restaurant, when not catering to tour groups, is one of Seville's most delightful. ⊠ *Argote de Molina 26,* ☎ *95/422–3355. AE, DC, MC, V. No dinner Sun.*

$–$$ ✕ **El Bacalao.** This popular fish restaurant, opposite the church of Santa Catalina, is in an Andalucían house decorated with ceramic tiles. As its name suggests, the house specialty is bacalao; try it *con arroz* (with rice) or al pil-pil. ⊠ *Plaza Ponce de León 15,* ☎ *95/421–6670. AE, MC, V. Closed Sun., and end of July through beginning of Aug.*

$ ✕ **Mesón Castellano.** This recently refurbished old house opposite the church of San José is an ideal place for lunch after a morning's shopping on Calle Sierpes. Specialties are Castilian meat dishes. ⊠ *Jovellanos 6,* ☎ *95/421–4028. AE, DC, MC, V. Lunch only. Closed Sun.*

$$$$ ▣ **Alfonso XIII.** This ornate Mudéjar-style palace was built for King
★ Alfonso XIII's visit to the 1929 exhibition. It is worth a visit for its splendid Moorish decor, including the beautiful stained glass and colorful ceramic tiles typical of Seville. Much of the hotel was renovated for Expo 92. ⊠ *San Fernando 2, 41004,* ☎ *95/422–2850,* FAX *95/421–6033. 128 rooms with bath and 18 suites. 2 restaurants, bar, pool, shops, meeting rooms. AE, DC, MC, V.*

$$$$ ▣ **Colón.** The rooms and suites have been modernized to a high de-
★ gree of comfort while retaining much of their old-fashioned style. It's right in the heart of town, close to the main shopping center. You can dine in the elegant El Burladero restaurant or in the more casual La Tasca. ⊠ *Canalejas 1, 41001,* ☎ *95/422–2900,* FAX *95/422–0938. 204 rooms with bath and 14 suites. 2 restaurants, 2 bars, beauty salon, meeting rooms. AE, DC, MC, V.*

$$$ ▣ **Doña María.** Close to the cathedral, this is one of Seville's most charming hotels. Some rooms are small and plain; others are tastefully furnished with antiques. Room 310 has a four-poster double bed, 305 has two single four-posters, and both have spacious bathrooms. There's no restaurant, but a breakfast buffet is served. There's also a rooftop pool with a good view of the Giralda, just a stone's throw away. ⊠ *Don Remondo 19, 41004,* ☎ *95/422–4990,* FAX *95/421–9546. 70 rooms with bath. Pool. AE, DC, MC, V.*

$$ ▣ **Bécquer.** Conveniently located near the main shopping areas, this relatively modern hotel prides itself on attentive service. It's one of the best mid-range bets, with comfortable rooms decorated in traditional Spanish style. There's also a parking garage. ⊠ *Reyes Católicos 4, 41001,* ☎ *95/422–8900,* FAX *95/421–4400. 120 rooms with bath. Bar, breakfast room, parking. AE, DC, MC, V.*

$$ ▣ **Giralda.** Recently modernized and extensively renovated, this is a comfortable, functional hotel with spacious, light rooms decorated in typical Castilian style. In a cul-de-sac off Avenida Menéndez Pelayo, it lies on the edge of the old city and caters largely to tour groups. Rooms on the fifth floor are best. ⊠ *Sierra Nevada 3, 41003,* ☎ *95/441–6661,* FAX *95/441–9352. 96 rooms with bath, 5 suites. Restaurant, bars, meeting rooms. AE, DC, MC, V.*

$$ ▣ **Murillo.** This picturesque hotel in the heart of the Barrio Santa Cruz was redecorated in 1987. The rooms are simple and small, but the setting is a virtue. You can't reach the hotel by car, but porters with trolleys will fetch your luggage from your taxi. ⊠ *Lope de Rueda 7, 41004,* ☎ *95/421–6095,* FAX *95/421–9616. 57 rooms with bath or shower. Bar, breakfast room. AE, DC, MC, V.*

$ ▣ **Internacional.** If you are looking for an inexpensive alternative, this old-world, family-run hotel lies in the narrow streets of the old town near the Casa de Pilatos. The rooms are very plain, but the service is friendly. ⊠ *Aguilas 17, 41003,* ☎ FAX *95/421–3207. 26 rooms with bath. AE, DC, MC, V.*

The Arts and Nightlife

Granada

FLAMENCO

There are several "impromptu" flamenco shows in the caves of the Sacromonte, but these can be dismally bad and little more than tourist rip-offs. Go only if accompanied by a Spanish friend who knows his way around or with a tour organized by a local agency. **Jardines Neptuno** (⊠ C. Neptuno, ☎ 958/522533) is a regular but colorful flamenco club that caters largely to tourists. **Reina Mora** (⊠ Mirador de San Cristóbal, ☎ 958/272228), though somewhat smaller than Jardines Neptuno, offers regular flamenco shows known as *tablaos*.

Seville

FLAMENCO

Regular flamenco clubs cater largely to tourists and cost a little more than 3,000 ptas. per person, but their shows are colorful and offer a good introduction for the uninitiated. **El Arenal** (⊠ Rodo 7, ☎ 95/421–6492) is a flamenco club in the back of the picturesque Mesón Dos de Mayo. **Los Gallos** (⊠ Plaza Santa Cruz 11, ☎ 95/421–6981) is a small intimate club in the heart of the Barrio Santa Cruz offering fairly pure flamenco. There are shows of flamenco and other regional dances nightly at **El Patio Sevillano** (⊠ Paseo de Colón, ☎ 95/421–4120), which caters largely to tour groups.

BULLFIGHTS

Corridas take place at the Maestranza bullring on Paseo de Colón, usually on Sunday from Easter through October. The best are during the April Fair. Tickets can be bought in advance from the windows at the ring (one of the oldest and most picturesque in Spain) or from the kiosks in Calle Sierpes (these charge a commission). The ring and a bullfighting museum may be visited year-round. ☎ 95/422–4577. ☜ 250 ptas. ☺ Mon.–Sat. 10–1:30.

COSTA DEL SOL

What were impoverished fishing villages in the 1950s are now retirement villages and package-tour meccas for northern Europeans and Americans. Behind the hideous concrete monsters you'll come across old cottages and villas set in gardens that blossom with jasmine and bougainvillea. The sun still sets over miles of beaches and the lights of small fishing craft still twinkle in the distance. Most of your time should be devoted to indolence—sunbathing and swimming. When you need something to do, you can head inland to the historic town of Ronda and the perched white villages of Andalucía. You can also make a day trip to Gibraltar or Tangier.

Getting There

Daily flights on Iberia and Aviaco connect Málaga with Madrid and Barcelona. Air Europa and Spanair also schedule wallet-friendly flights. Iberia (☎ 95/213–6166 or 213–6167), British Airways, and charter airlines such as Dan Air offer frequent service from London; most other major European cities also have direct air links. You'll have to make connections in Madrid for all flights from the United States. Málaga Airport (☎ 95/224–0000) is 12 kilometers (7 miles) west of the city. City buses run from the airport to the city every 30 minutes (150 ptas., 6:30 AM–midnight); the Portillo bus company (☎ 95/236–0191) has frequent service from the airport to Torremolinos. A suburban train serving Málaga, Torremolinos, and Fuengirola also stops at the airport

every half hour. From Madrid, Málaga is easily reached by a half dozen rapid trains a day.

Getting Around

Buses are the best means of transportation on the Costa del Sol (as well as from Seville or Granada). Málaga's long-distance station is on the Paseo de los Tilos (☎ 95/235–0061); nearby, on Muelle de Heredía, a smaller station serves suburban destinations. The main bus company serving the Costa del Sol is **Portillo** (offices at the bus station, ☎ 95/236–0191). **Alsina Gräells** (at the station, ☎ 95/231–8295) has service to Granada, Córdoba, Seville, and Nerja. The train station in Málaga (✉ Explanada de la Estación, ☎ 95/236–0202) is a 15-minute walk from the city center, across the river. The **RENFE** office (✉ Strachan 2, ☎ 95/221–4127) is more convenient for tickets and information.

Guided Tours

Organized one- and two-day excursions to places such as Seville, Granada, Córdoba, Ronda, Gibraltar, and Tangier are run by **Julià Tours, Pullmantur,** and numerous companies from all the Costa del Sol resorts and can be booked through your hotel desk or any travel agent.

Visitor Information

The most helpful tourist offices, by far, are in Málaga and Marbella. The Málaga office covers the entire province.

Estepona (✉ Paseo Marítimo Pedro Manrique, ☎ 95/280–0913).
Fuengirola (✉ Avda. Jesús Santos Rein 6, ☎ 95/246–7457).
Gibraltar (✉ Cathedral Square, ☎ 9567/74950).

Málaga (✉ Pasaje de Chinitas 4, ☎ 95/221–3445, and at the airport in both national and international terminals).
Marbella (✉ Glorieta de la Fontanilla, ☎ 95/277–1442).
Nerja (✉ Puerta del Mar 2, ☎ 95/252–1531).
Ronda (✉ Plaza de España 1, ☎ 95/287–1272).
Torremolinos (✉ Plaza Pablo Ruiz Picasso, s/n, (below the Town Hall) ☎ 95/237–1159).

Exploring the Costa del Sol

Nerja

Nerja is a small but expanding resort that so far has escaped the worst excesses of the property developers. Its growth to date has been largely confined to villages such as El Capistrano, one of the showpieces of the Costa del Sol. There's pleasant bathing here, though the sand is gray and gritty. The **Balcón de Europa** is a fantastic lookout, high above the sea. The famous **Cuevas de Nerja** (a series of stalactite caves) are off the road to Almuñecar and Almería. A kind of vast underground cathedral, they contain the world's largest known stalactite (203 feet long). ☎ 95/252–9520. 🎟 450 ptas. ☉ Daily summer 10:30–6, winter 10:30–2 and 3:30–6.

Málaga

Málaga is a busy port city with ancient streets and lovely villas set among exotic foliage, but it has little to recommend it to the overnight visitor. The central Plaza de la Marina, overlooking the port, is a pleasant place for a drink. The main shops are along the Calle Marqués de Larios.

The **Alcazaba** is a fortress begun in the 8th century when Málaga was the most important port of the Moorish kingdom. The ruins of the Roman amphitheater at its entrance were uncovered when the fort was restored. The inner palace dates from the 11th century when, for a short period after the breakup of the Caliphate of the West in Córdoba, it became the residence of the Moorish emirs. Today you'll find the **Archaeological Museum** here and a good collection of Moorish art. ✉ Entrance on Alcazabilla, ☎ 95/221–6005. 🎟 150 ptas. ☉ Mon.–Sat. 11–2 and 5–8 (4–7 in winter), Sun. 10–2.

Energetic souls can climb through the Alcazaba gardens to the summit of **Gibralfaro.** Others can drive by way of Calle Victoria or take the parador minibus that leaves roughly every 1½ hours from near the cathedral on Molina Lario. The Gibralfaro fortifications were built for Yusuf I in the 14th century. The Moors called it Jebelfaro, which means "rock of the lighthouse," after the beacon that stood here to guide ships into the harbor and warn of invasions by pirates. Today the beacon is gone, but there's a small parador that makes a delightful place for a drink or a meal and has some stunning views.

Torremolinos

As you approach **Torremolinos** through an ocean of concrete blocks, it's hard to grasp that as recently as the early 1960s this was an inconsequential fishing village. Today, this grossly overdeveloped resort is a prime example of 20th-century tourism run riot. The town center, with its brash Nogalera Plaza, is full of overpriced bars and restaurants. Much more attractive is the district of La Carihuela, farther west, below the Avenida Carlota Alexandra. You'll find some old fishermen's cottages here, a few excellent seafood restaurants, and a traffic-free esplanade for an enjoyable stroll on a summer evening.

Benalmádena, Fuengirola, and Mijas

Head west from Torremolinos, toward the similar but more staid resorts of **Benalmádena** and **Fuengirola,** both retirement havens for British and American senior citizens. A short drive from Fuengirola up into the mountains takes you to the picturesque and over-photographed ★ village of **Mijas.** Though the vast tourist-oriented main square may seem like an extension of the Costa's tawdry bazaar, there are hillside streets of whitewashed houses where you'll discover an authentic village atmosphere that has changed little since the days before the tourist boom of the 1960s. Visit the bullring, the nearby church, and the chapel of Mijas's patroness, the Virgen de la Peña (to the side of the main square), and enjoy shopping for quality gifts and souvenirs.

Marbella

Marbella is the most fashionable and sedate resort area along the coast. It does have a certain Florida land boom feel to it, but development has been controlled, and Marbella will, let's hope, never turn into another Torremolinos. The town's charming old Moorish quarter may be crowded with upmarket boutiques and a modern, T-shirt-and-fudge section along the main drag; but when people speak of Marbella they refer both to the town and to the resorts—some more exclusive than others—stretching 16 kilometers (10 miles) or so on either side of town, between the highway and the beach. If you're vacationing in southern Spain, this is the place to stay. There are championship golf courses and tennis courts, fashionable waterfront cafés, and trendy shopping arcades.

Ojén

A short drive up into the hills behind Marbella brings you to the village of **Ojén.** Its typical streets are a far cry from the promenades of the coastal resorts. Look out for the traditional pottery sold here and for the picturesque cemetery, with its rows of burial-urn chambers.

Back on the coastal highway, Marbella's Golden Mile, with its mosque, Arab banks, and residence of King Fahd of Saudi Arabia, proclaims the ever-growing influence of wealthy Arabs in this playground of the rich. In **Puerto Banús,** Marbella's plush marina, with its flashy yachts, fashionable people, and expensive restaurants, the glittering parade outshines even St. Tropez in ritzy glamour.

Ronda

Ronda is reached via a spectacular mountain road from San Pedro de Alcántara. One of the oldest towns in Spain and the last stronghold of the legendary Andalucían bandits, Ronda's most dramatic feature ★ is its ravine, known as **El Tajo,** which is 915 feet across and divides the old Moorish town from the "new town" of El Mercadillo. Spanning the gorge is the **Puente Nuevo,** an amazing architectural feat built between 1755 and 1793, whose parapet offers dizzying views of the River Guadalevin way below. Ronda is visited more for its setting, breathtaking views, and ancient houses than for any particular monument. Stroll the old streets of **La Ciudad;** drop in at the historic **Reina Victoria** hotel, built by the English from Gibraltar as a fashionable resting place on their Algeciras-Bobadilla railroad line; and visit the **bullring,** one of the oldest and most beautiful rings in Spain (and recent site of singer Madonna's videos). Here Ronda's most famous native son, Pedro Romero (1754–1839), father of modern bullfighting, is said to have killed 5,600 bulls during his 30-year career; and in the **Bullfighting Museum** you can see posters dating back to the very first fights held in the ring in May 1785. The ring is privately owned now, but three or four fights are still held in the summer months. Tickets are exceedingly difficult to come by (☎ 95/287–4132; 🖅 Bullring and museum

250 ptas. ⊙ Daily 10–5:30, until 7 in summer). Above all, don't miss the clifftop walk and the gardens of the **Alameda del Tajo,** where you can contemplate one of the most dramatic views in all of Andalucía.

Estepona

Returning to the coast road, the next town is **Estepona,** which until recently marked the end of the urban sprawl of the Costa del Sol. Estepona lacks the hideous high-rises of Torremolinos and Fuengirola, and, set back from the main highway, it's not hard to make out the old fishing village this once was. Wander the streets of the Moorish village, around the central food market and the **Church of San Francisco,** and you'll find a pleasant contrast to the excesses higher up the coast.

Casares

Nineteen kilometers (11¾ miles) northwest of Estepona, the mountain village of **Casares** lies high in the Sierra Bermeja. Streets lined with ancient white houses perch on the slopes beneath a ruined Moorish castle. Admire the view of the Mediterranean and check out the village's thriving ceramics industry.

Between Estepona and Gibraltar, the highway is flanked by prosperous vacation developments known as *urbanizaciones.* The architecture here is much more in keeping with traditional Andalucían style than the concrete blocks of earlier developments. The new **Puerto de Sotogrande** near Manilva is one of the showpieces of the area.

Gibraltar

To enter **Gibraltar,** simply walk or drive across the border at La Línea and show your passport. In theory car drivers need an International Driver's License, insurance certificate, and registration book; in practice, these regulations are usually waived—play it safe, however, to avoid a possible hefty fine and bring these documents with you. It is also possible to fly into Gibraltar on daily flights from London but, as yet, there are no flights from Spanish airports. There are, however, plenty of bus tours from Spain. **Juliá Tours, Pullmantur,** and many smaller agencies run daily tours (not Sunday) to Gibraltar from most Costa del Sol resorts. Alternatively, you can take the regular Portillo bus to La Línea and walk across the border. In summer, Portillo runs an inexpensive daily tour to Gibraltar from the Torremolinos bus station. Once you reach Gibraltar the official language is English and the currency is the British pound sterling, though pesetas are also accepted.

The Rock of Gibraltar acquired its name in AD 711 when it was captured by the Moorish chieftain Tarik at the start of the Arab invasion of Spain. It became known as Jebel Tariq (Rock of Tariq), later corrupted to Gibraltar. After successive periods of Moorish and Spanish domination, Gibraltar was captured by an Anglo-Dutch fleet in 1704 and ceded to the British by the Treaty of Utrecht in 1713. This tiny British colony, whose impressive silhouette dominates the straits between Spain and Morocco, is a rock just 5⅘ kilometers (3⅗ miles) long, ¾ kilometers (½ mile) wide, and 1,394 feet high.

On entering Gibraltar by road you have to cross the airport runway on the narrow strip of land that links the Rock with La Línea in Spain. Here you have a choice. You can either plunge straight into exploring Gibraltar town, or opt for a tour around the Rock. Several minibus tours are readily available at this point of entry.

Numbers in the margin correspond to points of interest on the Gibraltar map.

The tour around the Rock is best begun on the eastern side. As you enter Gibraltar, turn left down Devil's Tower Road, and drive as far

① as **Catalan Bay,** a small fishing village founded by Genoese settlers in the 18th century, and now one of the Rock's most picturesque resorts.

The road continues on beneath water catchments that supply the

② colony's drinking water, to another resort, **Sandy Bay,** and then plunges through the Dudley Ward Tunnel to bring you out at the Rock's most

③ southerly tip, **Punta Grande de Europa** (Europa Point). Stop here to admire the view across the straits to the coast of Morocco, 22½ kilometers (14 miles) away. You are standing on what in ancient times was called one of the two Pillars of Hercules. Across the water in Morocco, a mountain between the cities of Ceuta and Tangier formed the second pillar. Plaques explain the history of the gun installations here, and,

④ nearby on Europa Flats, you can see the **Nun's Well,** an ancient Moor-

⑤ ish cistern, and the **Shrine of Our Lady of Europe,** venerated by sailors since 1462.

⑥ Europa Road winds its way high on the western slopes above **Rosia Bay,** to which Nelson's flagship, HMS *Victory,* was towed after the Battle of Trafalgar in 1805. Aboard were the dead of the battle, who are now buried in Trafalgar Cemetery on the southern edge of town, and the body of Admiral Nelson himself, preserved in a barrel of rum. He was then taken to London for burial.

⑦ Continue on Europa Road as far as the **casino** (Europa Rd., ☎ 9567/ 76666, ⊙ daily 9 PM–4 AM) above the Alameda Gardens. Make a sharp

⑧ right here up Engineer Road to **Jews Gate,** an unbeatable lookout point over the docks and Bay of Gibraltar to Algeciras in Spain. Here you can gain access to the **Upper Nature Preserve,** which includes St. Michael's Cave, the Ape's Den, the Great Siege Tunnel, and the Moor-

⑨ ish Castle (☞ *below*). Queens Road leads to **St. Michael's Cave,** a series of underground chambers adorned with stalactites and stalagmites, which provides an admirable setting for concerts, ballet, and drama. ▨ *Preserve, including all sites £5.00 adults, plus £1.25 per vehicle.* ⊙ *Daily 10–6.*

⑩ Drive down Old Queen's Road to the **Apes' Den** near the **Wall of Charles V.** The famous Barbary apes are a breed of cinnamon-color, tailless monkeys, natives of the Atlas Mountains in Morocco. Legend holds that as long as the apes remain, the British will continue to hold the Rock. Winston Churchill himself issued orders for the maintenance of the ape colony when its numbers began to dwindle during World War II.

⑪ Passing beneath the cable car that runs to the Rock's summit, drive up to the **Great Siege Tunnel** at the northern end of the Rock. These huge galleries were carved out during the Great Siege of 1779–83. Here, in 1878, the Governor, Lord Napier of Magdala, entertained ex-President Ulysses S. Grant at a banquet in **St. George's Hall.** From here, the **Holyland Tunnel** leads out to the east side of the Rock above Catalan Bay.

⑫ The last stop before the town is at the **Moorish Castle** on Willis Road. Built by the successors of the Moorish invader Tarik, the present **Tower of Homage** was rebuilt by the Moors in 1333. Admiral Rooke hoisted the British flag from its top when he captured the Rock in 1704, and here it has flown ever since. The castle has been closed to the public and can be seen only from the outside.

⑬ ⑭ Willis Road leads steeply down to the colorful, congested town of Gibraltar where the dignified Regency architecture of Britain blends with the shutters, balconies, and patios of southern Spain. Apart from the attraction of shops, restaurants, and pubs on Main Street, you'll want to visit some of the following: the **Governor's Residence;** the **Law**

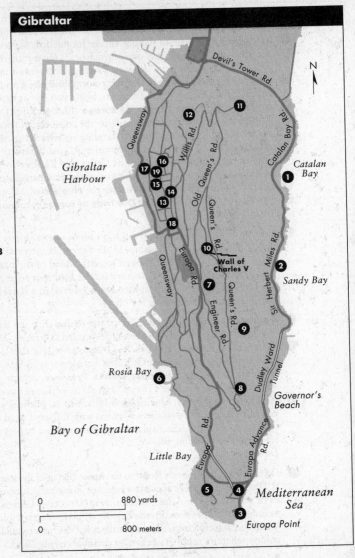

Gibraltar

⑮ ⑯ **Courts,** where the famous case of the *Mary Celeste* sailing ship was heard
⑰ in 1872; the Anglican **Cathedral of the Holy Trinity;** the Catholic **Cathedral of St. Mary the Crowned;** and the recently refurbished **Gibraltar Museum,** whose exhibits recall the history of the Rock throughout the ages. ⊠ *Gibraltar Museum, Bomb House La.,* ☎ *9567/74289.* 🎫 *£1.75.* ⊙ *Weekdays 10–6, Sat. 10–2.*

⑱ Finally, the **Nefusot Yehudada Synagogue** on Line Wall Road is worth a look for its inspired architecture, and, if you're interested in guns,
⑲ the **Koehler Gun** in **Casemates Square** at the northern end of Main Street is an impressive example of the type of gun developed during the Great Siege.

Dining and Lodging

For details and price-category definitions, *see* Dining *and* Lodging *in* Staying in Spain, *above.*

Estepona

$$$ 🏠 **El Molino.** In an old windmill, this restaurant has offered classic French cuisine for some three decades. Try the lubina al hinojo or the delicious Chateaubriand steak. ✉ *Carretera N340 at km 166,* ☎ *95/288–2135. AE, DC, MC, V. No lunch. Closed Sun., Tues., and Jan.*

$$–$$$ ✗ **Alcaría de Ramos.** José Ramos, winner of the National Gastronomy Prize, opened this restaurant outside town in 1990, and it has quickly garnered a large and loyal following. Try the *ensalada de lentejas con salmón ahumado* (lentil salad with smoked salmon), followed by cordero asado and the chef's justly famous fried ice cream.✉ *Rte. N340, km 167,* ☎ *95/288–6178. MC, V. No lunch. Closed Sun., and June 15–July 15.*

$$ 🏠 **Santa Marta.** This is a small, quiet hotel with just 37 rooms in chalet bungalows set in a large, peaceful garden. Some rooms are a little faded after 30 years, but the tranquil setting is a plus. Good lunches are served by the pool. ✉ *Rte. N340, km 167, 29680,* ☎ *95/288–8177,* FAX *95/288–8180. 37 rooms with bath. AE, MC, V. Closed Oct.–Mar.*

Gibraltar

$$$ ✗ **La Bayuca.** One of the Rock's best-established restaurants, La Bayuca is renowned for its onion soup and Mediterranean dishes. Prince Charles and Prince Andrew have dined here while on naval service.✉ *21 Turnbull's La.,* ☎ *9567/75119. AE, DC, MC, V. No lunch Sun. Closed Tues.*

$$–$$$ ✗ **Country Cottage.** Opposite the Catholic cathedral, this is the place to go for a taste of Old England. Enjoy steak and kidney pie, Angus steak, and roast beef, by candlelight. ✉ *13 Giro's Passage,* ☎ *9567/70084. AE, MC, V. Closed Sun.*

$$$ 🏠 **The Rock.** The Rock has undergone a massive refurbishment pro-
★ gram with the aim of bolstering its reputation as Gibraltar's supreme luxury hotel. You'll find a comfortable, old-fashioned English atmosphere, along with a pool, sun terrace, and gardens. Located on Gibraltar's western slopes, the hotel overlooks the town and harbor. ✉ *3 Europa Rd.,* ☎ *9567/73000,* FAX *9567/73513. 143 rooms with bath, 10 suites. Restaurant, bar, pool, beauty salon. AE, DC.*

$$ 🏠 **Bristol.** This colonial-style hotel is just off Gibraltar's main street, right in the heart of town. Rooms are large and comfortable, and the tropical garden is a real haven for those guests who want to relax in peaceful isolation. ✉ *10 Cathedral Sq.,* ☎ *9567/76800,* FAX *9567/77613. 60 rooms with bath. Breakfast room, bar, pool. AE, DC, MC, V.*

Málaga

$$$ ✗ **Café de Paris.** The owner of this stylish restaurant in the Paseo Marítimo area was a chef at Maxim's in Paris and La Hacienda in Marbella. The *menú de degustación* (tasting menu) lets you try a little of everything. Specialties include *rodaballo con espinacas* (turbot and spinach). ✉ *Vélez Málaga 8,* ☎ *95/222–5043. AE, DC, MC, V. Closed Sun.*

$$ ✗ **Casa Pedro.** It's crowded and noisy, but Malgueños have been flocking to this no-frills fish restaurant for more than 50 years. In the seaside suburb of El Palo, the restaurant has a huge, bare dining room that overlooks the ocean. Try joining the hordes of local families who come here for lunch on Sundays. It's quieter at other times. ✉ *Quitapenas 121, El Palo beach (Bus 11),* ☎ *95/229–0003. AE, DC, MC, V. Closed Nov. No dinner Mon.*

$$ ✗ **Rincón de Mata.** This is one of the best of many restaurants in the pedestrian shopping streets between Calle Larios and Calle Nueva. The menu is more original than most, with house specialties such as *tunedor* (calf in sauce). In summer there are tables outside on the sidewalk. ✉ *Esparteros 8,* ☎ *95/222–3135. AE, DC, MC V.*

$ ✕ **La Cancela.** This is a colorful restaurant in the center of town, just off Calle Granada. Dine indoors or alfresco. ⊠ *Denís Belgrano 5,* ☎ *95/222–3125. AE, DC, MC, V.*

$$$ 🏨 **Los Naranjos.** This small hotel in the Luz chain is on a pleasant avenue in a residential district 1 kilometer east of the city center. There's a small garden in front but rooms overlooking the street, though soundproofed, can be noisy if you prefer sleeping with the windows open. ⊠ *Paseo de Sancha 35, 29016,* ☎ *95/222–4317,* ᖴᴬˣ *95/222–5975. 41 rooms with bath. Breakfast room, bar. AE, DC, V.*

$$$ 🏨 **Parador de Gibralfaro.** In a small wood on top of Gibralfaro moun-
★ tain 3½ kilometers (2 miles) above the city, this cozy parador offers spectacular views over the city and bay. Recent renovations have added a swimming pool and more than doubled the number of rooms without subtracting from the charm of this comfortable retreat. ⊠ *Apdo. de Correos 274, Gibralfaro, 29016,* ☎ *95/222–1903,* ᖴᴬˣ *95/222–1904. 38 rooms with bath. Restaurant, bar, pool, meeting rooms. AE, DC, MC, V.*

$$ 🏨 **Las Vegas.** In a pleasant, though somewhat tumultuous, part of town, just east of the center, this conveniently located hotel has a dining room overlooking the Paseo Marítimo, a pool, and a large leafy garden. Rooms at the back enjoy a good view of the ocean. ⊠ *Paseo de Sancha 22, 29016,* ☎ *95/221–7712,* ᖴᴬˣ *95/222–4889. 107 rooms with bath. Restaurant, bar, pool. AE, DC, MC, V.*

$ 🏨 **Victoria.** This small, renovated hostel in an old house just off Calle Larios offers excellent budget accommodations in a convenient central location. ⊠ *Sancha de Lara 3, 29015,* ☎ ᖴᴬˣ *95/222–4223. 13 rooms with bath. AE, V.*

Marbella

$$$$ ✕ **La Hacienda.** This restaurant, owned by the family of the late Paul
★ Schiff, former chef, belongs to the Relais Gourmand group and is one of the highest rated dining establishments in Spain. The menu reflects the influence of both Schiff's native Belgium and his adopted home, Andalucía, a combination of European and Spanish cuisine presently orchestrated by chef Francisco Galvez. The menú de degustación at around 7000 ptas. will enable you to sample the very best creations of this famous restaurant. ⊠ *Las Chapas, Rte. N340, km 193, 12 km (7 mi) east of Marbella on the road to Málaga;* ☎ *95/283–1116,* ᖴᴬˣ *95/283–3328. Reservations essential. AE, DC, MC, V. Closed Mon., Tues., midday July and Aug., and mid-Nov.–mid-Dec.*

$$$$ ✕ **La Meridiana.** Another of Marbella's most outstanding restaurants and a favorite with the local jet set, La Meridiana is located just west of town, toward Puerto Banús, and is famous for its original Bauhaus-type architecture and the superb quality and freshness of the ingredients. ⊠ *Camino de la Cruz,* ☎ *95/277–6190. Reservations essential. AE, DC, MC, V. Closed Mon. No lunch Tues., no lunch in summer.*

$$$ ✕ **La Fonda.** In a beautiful 18th-century house with antique furniture,
★ and in one of the loveliest old squares in Marbella, La Fonda is owned by one of Madrid's leading restaurateurs. Its cuisine combines the best of Spanish, French, and Austrian influences. A delightful patio filled with potted plants makes a perfect setting for summer dining. ⊠ *Plaza del Santo Cristo 9,* ☎ *95/277–2512. AE, DC, MC, V. No lunch. Closed Sun. and mid-Jan.–mid-Feb.*

$$–$$$ ✕ **La Tricycleta.** In an old house on a narrow alley in the center of town, English-owned La Tricycleta has become an institution. You can have a predinner drink in the downstairs bar, which is heated by a log fire in winter, and then dine upstairs or outside on the covered rooftop patio. A longstanding favorite is the duck in beer sauce. ⊠ *Buitrago 14,* ☎ *95/277–7800. AE, MC, V. Closed Sun.*

$ ✕ **Mesón del Pollo.** This small, charming "house of chicken" illustrates how Marbella, despite tourism, remains truly Spanish. Porcelain lamp shades, azulejo tiles, a dozen tables, and the scent of roasting chicken fill this popular lunch spot. Try the pollo *a la sevillana* (with squid, fried potatoes, salad, and cider) dinner or *fritura malagueña* (Málaga's famous fried fish), or sample tapas of octopus or meatballs. ⊠ *Antonio Martín, across from the El Fuerte Hotel, no phone. Reservations not accepted. No credit cards.*

$$$$ ⊞ **Los Monteros.** Situated 2½ kilometers (1½ miles) east of Marbella,
★ on the road to Málaga, this deluxe hotel offers all the facilities of a top hotel, including golf, tennis, pools, horseback riding, and gourmet dining in its famous El Corzo Grill restaurant. This is the third most expensive hotel in Spain, after the Ritz and Villa Magna in Madrid. Eighty percent of the guests are British, which may explain the somewhat starched formality of the rooms. ⊠ *Urb. Los Monteros, 29600,* ☎ *95/277–1700,* ℻ *95/282–5846. 161 rooms with bath. 2 restaurants, 1 indoor and 2 outdoor pools, beauty salon, sauna, 10 tennis courts, exercise room, horseback riding, squash, shops, nightclub. AE, DC, MC, V.*

$$$$ ⊞ **Marbella Club.** The grande dame of Marbella tends to attract an older clientele. The bungalow-style rooms run from cramped to spacious, and the decor varies considerably; specify the type you prefer, but ask for a room that's been recently renovated. The grounds are exquisite. Breakfast is served on a patio where songbirds flit through the vegetation. *Rte. N340, km 178, 29600,* ☎ *95/282–2211,* ℻ *95/282–9884. 76 rooms with bath. Restaurant, bar, nightclub, 2 pools, beauty salon, sauna, tennis, exercise room. AE, DC, MC, V.*

$$$$ ⊞ **Puente Romano.** A spectacular, modern hotel and apartment com-
★ plex of low, white-stucco buildings located 3¼ kilometers (2 miles) west of Marbella on the road to Puerto Banús. The "village" has a Roman bridge in its beautifully landscaped grounds as well as two pools, a tennis club, squash courts, and a disco. ⊠ *Rte. N340, km 177, 29600,* ☎ *95/282–0900,* ℻ *95/277–5766. 216 rooms with bath. 2 restaurants, 2 swimming pools(one heated), tennis, paddle tennis, squash, shops, nightclub. AE, DC, V.*

$$–$$$ ⊞ **El Fuerte.** This is the best of the few hotels in the center of Marbella, with simple, adequate rooms. It's in a 1950-style building in the midst of a large garden with an outdoor pool. ⊠ *Avda. El Fuerte s/n, 29600,* ☎ *95/286–1500,* ℻ *95/282–4411. 263 rooms with bath. Indoor and outdoor pools, tennis, paddle tennis, squash. AE, DC, V.*

Mijas

$$$ ✕ **Valparaíso.** *Pato* (duck) a la naranja is one of the specialties served in a pleasant villa with garden and terrace on the road from Fuengirola to Mijas. ⊠ *Carretera de Mijas km. 4,* ☎ *95/248–5996. AE, MC, V. No lunch. Closed Sun. Nov.–May.*

$$ ✕ **Mirlo Blanco.** Here you can try Basque dishes such as *txangurro* (crab) and *merluza a la vasca* (hake with asparagus, eggs, and clam sauce). ⊠ *Plaza Constitución 13,* ☎ *95/248–5700. AE, DC, MC, V.*

$$$$ ⊞ **Byblos Andaluz.** In this new luxury hotel set in a huge garden of
★ palms, cypresses, and fountains, you'll find every comfort. Its Le Nailhac restaurant is famous for its French cuisine; special low-calorie meals are also available. ⊠ *Mijas-Golf, Fuengirola, 29640,* ☎ *95/247–3050,* ℻ *95/247–6783. 144 rooms with bath. Indoor and outdoor pools, beauty salon, sauna, spa, 18-hole golf course, tennis, exercise room, shops. AE, DC, MC, V.*

Nerja

$$ ✕ **Casa Luque.** This is one of the most authentically Spanish of Nerja's restaurants, in a charming old Andalucían house behind the Balcón de Europa church. ⊠ *Plaza Cavana 2,* ☎ *95/252–1004. AE, DC, MC, V. Closed Mon. and Feb.*

$$ ✕ **Udo Heimer.** A genial German is your host at this Art Deco villa. His menu is a combination of traditional German dishes and local produce. Try ham-stuffed pumpkin or prawns wrapped in bacon and served in a curried banana sauce. ⊠ *Pueblo Andaluz 27,* ☎ *95/252–0032. AE, DC, MC, V. No lunch. Closed Wed. and Jan.–Feb.*

$$$ ▥ **Mónica.** Opened in 1986, the Mónica is spacious and luxurious, with cool, Moorish-style architecture and lots of marble. Popular with package tours, it's within walking distance of the center of town. ⊠ *Playa Torrecilla, 29780,* ☎ *95/252–1100.* 🖷 *95/252–1162. 234 rooms with bath. Restaurant, bar, pool, tennis, nightclub. AE, DC, MC, V.*

$$$ ▥ **Parador.** All the rooms in this small parador a little to the east of
★   the center of Nerja have balconies that overlook the sea. There's a pleasant leafy garden and outdoor pool, and an elevator takes you down to the beach. ⊠ *Almuñecar, 8, Nerja 29780,* ☎ *95/252–0050,* 🖷 *95/252–1997. 73 rooms with bath. Restaurant, outdoor pool. AE, DC, MC, V.*

Ronda

$$$ ✕ **Don Miguel.** Near the bridge over the Tajo gorge, the restaurant's terrace offers spectacular views of the ravine. Baby lamb, asado de cordero lechal Don Miguel, reared on the owner's farm, is a specialty. ⊠ *Villanueva 4,* ☎ *95/287–7410. AE, DC, MC, V. Closed Sun. and Wed. in June, July, Aug. and mid-Jan.–mid-Feb.*

$$ ✕ **Pedro Romero.** Located opposite the bullring, this restaurant is, not surprisingly, packed with colorful taurine decor. The restaurant serves traditional regional recipes; the *tocino del cielo al coco* (sweet caramel custard flavored with coconut) is a treat. ⊠ *Virgen de la Paz 18,* ☎ *95/287–1110. AE, DC, MC, V.*

$$–$$$ ▥ **Reina Victoria.** A spectacularly situated old-world hotel with a distinctly British air, the Reina Victoria sits atop the very rim of the gorge. Its views and style are tops, but its facilities are often overwhelmed by tour groups. ⊠ *Jerez 25, 29400,* ☎ *95/287–1240,* 🖷 *95/287–1075. 89 rooms with bath. Restaurant, pool. AE, DC, MC, V.*

$$ ▥ **Polo.** A cozy, old-fashioned hotel in the center of town, Polo is a reasonably priced restaurant. The staff is friendly and the rooms simple but comfortable. ⊠ *Mariano Soubiron 8, 29400,* ☎ *95/287–2447,* 🖷 *95/287–2449. 33 rooms with bath. Restaurant. AE, DC, V.*

Torremolinos

$$ ✕ **Casa Guaquin.** Casa Guaquin is widely known as the best seafood restaurant in the region. Changing daily catches and menu stalwarts such as *coquillas al ajillo* (sea cockles in garlic sauce) are served on a seaside patio. ⊠ *Paseo Maritimo 63,* ☎ *95/238–4530. AE, MC, V. Closed Thurs. and mid.-Dec.–mid-Jan.*

$$ ✕ **El Atrio.** This small, stylish restaurant is in the Pueblo Blanco. Its cuisine is predominantly French. In summer, you can dine on the terrace. ⊠ *Casablanca 9,* ☎ *95/238–8850. AE, MC, V. No lunch. Closed Sun. and Dec.*

$$ ✕ **Europa.** A short walk from the Carihuela, this villa in a large garden has leafy dining in pleasant surroundings. It's best on Sundays, when local families flock here for a leisurely lunch. ⊠ *Via Imperial,* ☎ *95/238–8022. AE, MC, V.*

$$ ✕ **Juan.** This is a good place to enjoy seafood in summer, with a sunny outdoor patio facing the sea. The specialties include the great Costa del Sol standbys: *sopa de mariscos* (shellfish soup), *dorada al horno* (oven-roasted giltheads), and fritura malagueña. ✉ *Paseo Marítimo 29, La Carihuela,* ☎ *95/238–5656. AE, DC, MC, V.*

$$$ 🏨 **Cervantes.** This busy cosmopolitan hotel in the heart of town has comfortable rooms, good service, and a well-known dining room on its top floor. ✉ *Las Mercedes s/n, 29620,* ☎ *95/238–4033,* FAX *95/238–4857. 396 rooms with bath. Restaurant, 2 pools (one heated), beauty salon, sauna, shops, nightclub. AE, DC, MC, V.*

$$ 🏨 **Tropicana.** Located on the beach at the far end of the Carihuela is a comfortable, relaxing resort hotel with several good restaurants nearby. ✉ *Trópico 6, 29620,* ☎ *95/238–6600,* FAX *95/238–0568. 86 rooms with bath. 2 restaurants, pool. AE, DC, MC, V.*

$ 🏨 **Miami.** Set in an old Andalucían villa in a shady garden to the west ★ of the Carihuela, this is something of a find amid the ocean of concrete blocks. ✉ *Aladino 14, 29620,* ☎ *95/238–5255. 26 rooms with bath. Pool. No credit cards.*

EXCURSION TO MOROCCO

The crossing to Morocco, just 14 kilometers (9 miles) across the Strait of Gibraltar, may be the longest short trip on the globe. A 90-minute cruise from Algeciras to Tangier replaces late 20th-century Europe with timeless North Africa.

Islam is the state religion and Arabic is the official language, but French, Berber, Spanish, and English are also spoken. Berbers, Romans, Vandals, and Arabs inhabited Morocco in the country's early history: Incessant conflict between Arabs and Berbers left Morocco ripe for invasion. Spain and Portugal, after expelling the Moors from the Iberian Peninsula, attacked the Moroccan coast. European countries, including Germany, France, and Spain, fought over the country's aegis until 1956, when all foreign rights were relinquished, except for those to the Western Sahara, which is still disputed territory.

Essential Information

You will not need a visa; the water is potable; and the time is usually one hour behind Spain. Women traveling alone or without men will have difficulty: Hire a reputable guide, wear conservative clothing, and be on guard at all times.

Getting Around

BY BOAT

From Algeciras to Tangier, **Transmediterranea** (in **Algeciras,** ✉ Recinto del Puerto s/n, ☎ 956/663850; in **Madrid,** ✉ C. Pedro Muñoz Seca 2, ☎ 91/431–0700; in **Tangier,** ✉ 31 Ave. de la Resistance, ☎ 212/994–1101) has a 90-minute hydrofoil and a two-hour car ferry. The slow boat is bigger, more stable, and offers better views than the somewhat claustrophobic hydrofoil. Having your passport stamped and getting your yellow exit card before you leave the boat can save you an hour or more.

BY BUS

Bus stations: **Casablanca** (✉ 303 Blvd. Brahim, ☎ 212/225–2901), **Fez** (✉ Ave. Mohammed V, ☎ 212/562–2041), **Marrakesh** (✉ Bab Doukkala, ☎ 212/443–4518), **Tangier** (✉ Place d'Espagne, ☎ 212/994–6682).

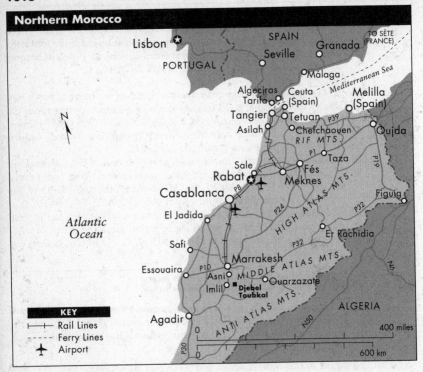

BY CAR

Moroccan roads are free-for-alls: In addition to the poor surfaces, there is a bumpercar, helter-skelter confusion from which, miraculously, most people emerge unscathed. If you choose to brave the roads in search of freedom from set schedules, international car-rental agencies are well represented. Agencies in **Casablanca:** Budget (⌧ Torres de los Habous, Ave. des F.A.R., ☎ 212/231–4027) and Hertz (⌧ 25 Rue Foucault, ☎ 212/231–2223); **Fez:** Avis (⌧ 50 Blvd. Chefchaouen, ☎ 212/562–6746), Budget (⌧ Bureau Grand Hotel, Av Chefchaouen, ☎ 212/562–0919), and Hertz (⌧ Hotel de Fez, Ave. des F.A.R., ☎ 212/562–2812); **Marrakesh:** Budget (⌧ 213 Ave. Mohammed V, ☎ 212/443–4604) and Hertz (⌧ 154 Ave. Mohammed V, ☎ 212/443–4680); **Tangier:** Budget (⌧ 79 Ave. du Prince, Moulay Abdallah, ☎ 212/993–7994) and Hertz (⌧ 36 Ave. Mohammed V, ☎ 212/993–3322).

BY PLANE

Royal Air Maroc (in the U.S., ☎ 800/344–6726 [outside NY], 212/750–6071 [in NY]; in Madrid, ☎ 91/541–1288) and **Iberia Airlines** (in the U.S., ☎ 800/772–4642; in Madrid, ☎ 91/261–9100) fly to Casablanca from Madrid in 90 minutes. The former has comprehensive domestic service.

BY TRAIN

Trains from Tangier to Casablanca leave at 4 PM and arrive six hours later. There are two stations in **Casablanca,** the Gare du Port (also called Casa–Port, ☎ 212/222–3011) and the Gare des Voyageurs (also called Casa–Voyageurs, ☎ 212/224–3818). The latter serves Marrakesh and the south. The stations in **Fez** (☎ 212/562–5001), **Marrakesh** (☎ 212/443–4518), and **Tangier** (☎ 212/993–1201) do not have proper names that are used locally.

Guided Tours

Most Moroccan cities have a swarm of very insistent, unofficial "guides." The best way to get rid of these volunteers, who may falsely assure you that all hotels are full and take you to shops where they get commissions on purchases, is to ignore them and seem to know exactly where you are going. If you do want a guide, hire a cheaper and better one at the local tourist office.

Visitor Information

United States (✉ 20 E. 46th St., Suite 1201, New York, NY 10017, ☎ 212/557–2520), **United Kingdom** (✉ 205 Regent St., W1R 7DE, London, ☎ 44171/437–0073), **Madrid** (✉ C. Quintana 2, 28008, ☎ 91/541–2995), **Casablanca** (✉ 55 Rue Omar Slaoui, ☎ 212/222–1177), **Fez** (Place de la Resistance, ☎ 212/562–3460), **Marrakesh** (✉ 176 Blvd. Mohammed V, ☎ 212/443–2097; ✉ Place Abdel–Moumen ben Ali, ☎ 212/444–8906), **Tangier** (✉ 29 Blvd. Pasteur, ☎ 212/994–8661).

Exploring

In **Tangier,** walk up the Rue Portugal, just right of the port entrance, skirting the left-hand edge of the medina. Continue up the hill through a small gate in the medina wall to the **Fondouk** (caravanserai) **Market,** where you will be surrounded by the color and vitality—men and women with bright *djellabas* (full-length robes with pointed hoods)— that inspired Delacroix, Regnault, Fortuny, and so many others to make Morocco a leitmotif. A left on Rue de la Liberté leads up to Place de France and the sumptuous **French consulate.** Another left on Boulevard Pasteur takes you down past a belvedere to the **tourist office.**

Walk down the **Grand Socco** (large market) through the pointed archway to the **Petit Socco** (small market) into the heart of Tangier's old city and artisan district. Uphill to the left is the **Place de la Kasbah,** where a belvedere has views over the port across to Tarifa.

Casablanca, a booming metropolis of 3.5 million inhabitants, is bound to disappoint cineasts and romantics expecting to bump into Ingrid Bergman and Humphrey Bogart at the counterfeit **Rick's Bar** in the Hyatt Regency (where waiters take orders in trench coats and fedoras). The **Grand Mosquée Hassan II,** however, will not disappoint. Opened in 1994, the mosque has room for 20,000 worshipers inside, where the glass floor reveals the ocean below, and 80,000 in the courtyard. The 200-meter minaret is Morocco's tallest structure, while the mosque itself is second only in size to the one in Mecca. Casablanca's **Corniche** is a pleasant promenade, and the **spice market** in the medina is another attraction.

The tumultuous and panoramic **Djemâa el Fna** (Assembly of the Dead) **square,** the highlight of a visit to **Marrakesh,** is a sensorial feast. Great clouds of aromatic smoke from the outdoor kitchens in the center of the square combine with the sounds of Berber musicians and storytellers, the eerie call to prayer of the muezzin, the flutes of snake charmers, and water vendors' bells; scribes and clients are tucked intimately in the shade of umbrellas, tooth pullers are surrounded by even rows of molars, the snowcapped Atlas peaks rise behind the Kotoubia minaret; and the warmth of the fires meets the cool evening breeze from the mountains (Marrakesh is equidistant from the Atlantic and the Sahara).

Traditionally considered Morocco's intellectual and spiritual capital, **Fez** can at first seem almost too quiet after tumultuous Marrakesh. Whereas the latter is a crossroads between the Berber Sahara and black Africa on the one hand and Islam and the Orient on the other, Fez is more refined, Andalucían, Mediterranean, and Islamic. The 9th-century medina of **Fez el Bali** (Old Fez) is a labyrinth of mosques (360 of them) and *medersas* (medieval residential colleges), shops, and artisans. Nowhere in Morocco is a good guide more indispensable.

The architectural treasures here are many: carving and tilework, the **water clock,** the **Kairaouine Mosque,** and **Kairaouine University,** which, founded in the 9th century, predates Bologna's university by 200 years and Oxford's by 300. The souks and fondouks are all hauntingly ancient and aesthetically perfect.

The 5 PM or 7 PM return ferry from Tangier to Algeciras sails as the sun sets, spotlighting the Spanish coast. North Africa behind you seems almost peaceful at this safe remove.

Great Itinerary

In addition to the following itinerary, which affords the most complete Moroccan experience on a constricted time budget, visit the elegant beach town of **Asilah,** south of Tangier; the capital at **Rabat;** the beach at **Essouaira** on the Atlantic coast, south of Casablanca; and the imperial city of **Meknes,** next to Fez, if time allows. Also, the trip over the High Atlas range to **Ouarzazate** is spectacular, as is the southern desert.

Day 1: Algeciras-Tangier-Casablanca. Take the boat to Tangier for the day, and the train to Casablanca for the first night.

Day 2: Casablanca-Marrakesh. After a morning tour of Casablanca's spectacular Mosquée Hassan II and the spice market, take the afternoon express to Marrakesh.

Days 3 and 4: Marrakesh. Explore Djemâa el Fna square and visit the Koutoubia minaret, the Majorelle and Menara Gardens, the souks, the Saadian Tombs, the Palais el Bahia, and the El Badi Palace.

Day 5: Marrakesh-Fez. Flying from Marrakesh to Fez is safest and fastest; otherwise, rent a car or take an eight-hour bus ride.

Day 6: Fez. See Fez el Bali, the water clock, the Kairaouine Mosque and Kairaouine University, the souks and fondouks.

Day 7: Fez-Tangier-Algeciras. Take the 7 AM train back to Tangier and a sunset ferry across the strait.

Dining and Lodging

For details and price-category definitions *see* Dining *and* Lodging *in* Staying in Spain, *above.*

Casablanca

$$ ✕ **Al Mounia.** The best spot in Casablanca for authenticity and value, Al Mounia serves the classic Moroccan specialties: *pastilla* (pigeon pie), *harira* (lentil, chickpea, and meat soup), *tajines* (meat or fish stewed in almonds, plums, and/or vegetables), *mechoui* (roast lamb), and couscous. ⊠ *95 Rue du Prince Moulay Abdallah,* ☎ *212/222–2669. AE, DC, MC, V. Closed Sun.*

$$$$ ✕🏨 **Royal Mansour.** One of Morocco's top hotels, the Royal Mansour's extras are a treat: fabulous food served in a lush garden courtyard accompanied by live Cole Porter tunes, and a rooftop *hammam* (Turkish bath). ⊠ *27 Ave. des F.A.R.,* ☎ *212/231–3011,* 🖷 *212/231–2583. 159 rooms with bath, 23 suites. 3 restaurants, piano bar, sauna, Turkish bath, meeting rooms. AE, DC, MC, V.*

$$ 🏨 **Hotel Moussafir.** New, impeccably clean, and well situated near the Casa–Voyageurs train station, the Moussafir is about one-tenth as expensive as the Royal Mansour and not nearly as far removed in quality. ⊠ *Blvd. Bahmir,* ☎ *212/240–1984,* 🖷 *212/240–0799. 99 rooms with bath. Restaurant, bar. AE, DC, MC, V.*

Fez

$$ ✕ **Al Andalus.** This excellent spot on the airport road in the modern part of town is a local secret. Owner Hilali Fouad's collection of curios and antiques is as enticing as the food. ✉ *34 Rte. d'Immouzzer,* ☎ *212/560–3162, AE, DC, MC, V.*

$$$$ ✕⌂ **Hotel Merinides.** This spectacular hotel is usually booked well in advance. The views over Fez el Bali from the pool, nicely raised above the fray, are unique. ✉ *Borj Nord,* ☎ *212/564–6040,* FAX *212/564–5225. 90 rooms with bath. 2 restaurants, 2 bars, pool. AE, DC, MC, V.*

$$–$$$$ ⌂ **Palais Jamai.** This elegant palace, built 120 years ago, was once the residence of the Vizir Jamai. There are views over the medina, and it is close to the old part of Fez. ✉ *Bab Guissa,* ☎ *212/563–4331,* FAX *212/563–5096. 145 rooms with bath. 2 restaurants, pool, tennis. AE, DC, MC, V.*

Marrakesh

$$$$ ✕ **Dar Marjana.** Diners here feel like they've walked into a Delacroix painting. Excellent cuisine, beautiful surroundings, Nubian waiters uniformed in rich greens, belly dancing, and folk music make for a true tour de force. ✉ *15 Derb Sidi Ali Tair, Bab Doukkala,* ☎ *212/444–5773. MC, V. Closed Tues.*

$$$$ ✕⌂ **La Mamounia.** Everyone from Winston Churchill to Bryan Ferry has loved this unique oasis within an oasis. One of the most famous hotels in the world, La Mamounia is worth every one of the many nickels it costs. The hotel is walking distance from Djemâa el Fna square; its grounds, facilities, service, and taste are sensational. ✉ *Ave. Bab Jdid,* ☎ *212/444–8981,* FAX *212/444–4940. 171 rooms with bath, 64 suites, 3 villas. 5 restaurants, 5 bars, pool, beauty salon, massage, sauna, Turkish bath, tennis, squash, billiards, shops, meeting rooms. AE, DC, MC, V.*

Tangier

$$$$ ✕⌂ **El Minzah Hotel.** Ask any native where the best place in town is, for both dining and lodging, and the immediate answer will be the El Minzah. Lovely studded wooden doors, hotel staff in Ottoman costumes, and fine views over the Mediterranean to the Iberian Peninsula prove them right. ✉ *85 Rue de la Liberté,* ☎ *212/993–5885,* FAX *212/993–4546. 100 rooms with bath. Restaurant, bar, pool. AE, MC, DC, V.*

$$ ⌂ **Hotel Continental.** Overlooking the port from the edge of the medina, this wonderful palace built in 1888 is the best buy in town for aesthetes and romantics (who else goes to Morocco anyway?). Bertolucci stayed in Room 108 while shooting *The Sheltering Sky.* Monsieur Abdessalam is a gracious host. ✉ *36 Rue Dar el Baroud,* ☎ *212/993–1024,* FAX *212/993–1143. 15 rooms with bath, 30 rooms share 10 baths. Bar, tearooms. AE, DC, MC, V.*

$ ⌂ **Hotel Muniria.** William Burroughs wrote *Naked Lunch* in Room 9, now the home of Madame Rabia, the lovely owner. Room 8 overlooks the Bay of Tangier. Rue Magellan can be tricky to find. ✉ *2 Rue Magellan,* ☎ *212/993–5337. 6 rooms with bath, 2 rooms share a bath. Bar. No credit cards.*

CANARY ISLANDS

Traditionally a popular spot for winter holidays, Spain's Canary Islands are becoming a year-round destination favored by sun-seekers and nature lovers alike. The Canaries lie 70 miles off the coast of southern Morocco in the Atlantic Ocean and enjoy mild, sunny weather throughout the year, except for the north coast of Tenerife, which has above-average rainfall for the Canaries and below-average temperatures, year-round. Each of the seven volcanic islands in the archipelago is distinct. Some have lush tropical vegetation, poinsettias as tall as trees, and banana plantations, while others are arid and resemble an exotic moonscape of lava rock and sand dunes. Mt. Teide (12,198 feet), Spain's highest peak and snowcapped for much of the year, is here. The islands are also home to six national parks and dozens of other protected ecological zones in which visitors can hike through mist-shrouded forests of virgin laurel trees, eat food cooked by nature over volcanic craters, or scuba dive off long stretches of unspoiled coastline.

Important Addresses and Numbers

Visitor Information

Each of the Canary Islands has its own tourist offices that are generally open 9 to 2.

Tenerife (⊠ Plaza de España 1, Santa Cruz, ☎ 922/605592).
Gran Canaria (⊠ Parque Santa Catalina, Las Palmas, ☎ 928/264623).
Lanzarote (⊠ Parque Municipal, Arrecife, ☎ 928/813792).
La Palma (⊠ Palacio Salazar, C. O'Daly 22, Santa Cruz de la Palma, ☎ 922/411957).

Arriving and Departing

By Plane

Iberia and its sister carrier **Aviaco** have several direct flights a day to Tenerife, Gran Canaria, and Lanzarote from most cities in mainland Spain. **Air Europa** and **Spanair** fly to the Canary Islands from Madrid and Barcelona at slightly lower prices.

From the United States, **Air Europa** (☎ 212/888–7010) flies once a week directly to Tenerife.

By Boat

Transmediterranea (☎ 91/431–0700) operates a slow, comfortable ferry service between Cádiz and the Canary Islands.

Getting Around

By Plane

All the Canary Islands are served by air except La Gomera. Tenerife has two airports: Reina Sofía is in the south, and Los Rodeos is in the north. As a general rule, long-distance flights arrive at the southern terminal and interisland flights use the northern one. Driving time from one airport to the other is 1½ hours.

Airport information: Tenerife (⊠ Reina Sofía, ☎ 922/759200; ⊠ Los Rodeos, ☎ 922/635800), Gran Canaria (☎ 928/579000), Lanzarote (☎ 928/811450), Fuerteventura (☎ 928/851250), and La Palma (☎ 922/411540).

Interisland flights are handled by **Iberia** and its regional subsidiary, **Binter Airlines.**

By Boat

Transmediterranea operates interisland car ferries. Trips often take all night; ferries have sleeping cabins. The company also runs passenger-only hydrofoil service three times a day between Las Palmas and Tenerife. One hydrofoil a day links southern Fuerteventura with Las Palmas and Tenerife.

By Bus

In Tenerife, buses meet all arriving Iberia flights at Reina Sofía airport and transfer passengers to the bus terminal in the outskirts of Santa Cruz de Tenerife. Buses also meet the Gomera hydrofoil and ferry.

By Car

Most visitors rent a car or jeep for at least part of their stay—it is by far the best way to explore the countryside. Reservations for car rentals are necessary only during the Christmas and Easter holidays. **Hertz** and **Avis** have representatives in all the islands, though better rates can be obtained from the Spanish company **Cicar** (☎ 928/802790), located at all the airports.

Guided Tours

One-day tours of Tenerife and sightseeing excursions to other islands can be arranged through **Viajes Insular** (☎ 922/380262), which has branches on every island except La Gomera and El Hierro.

Exploring the Canary Islands

Tenerife

Of all the Canary Islands **Tenerife** is the most popular and has the greatest variety of scenery to offer visitors. Its beaches are small, though, with volcanic black sand or sand imported from the Sahara Desert.

The south coast resort of **Playa de las Americas,** built chock-a-block with hotels, is where the majority of tourists stay. Located in the most arid and barren zone of the island, it offers little apart from sprawling hotel swimming pools and sizzling nightlife.

An hour northeast by superhighway is the pleasant provincial capital, **Santa Cruz,** known as the site of Spain's wildest fiesta, the prelenten Carnival, which takes place the weekends before and after Ash Wednesday. The **Museo Arqueológico Provincial** (Provincial Archeology Museum, ⌧ Bravo Murillo 5, ☎ 922/242090) contains ceramics and mummies from the stone-age culture of the Guanches, the native people who inhabited the islands before they were conquered and colonized by the Spanish in the 15th century. The best thing to visit in Santa Cruz is the colorful weekday morning market, **Mercado de Nuestra Señora de Africa,** which sells everything from tropical fruits and flowers to canaries and parrots. (⌧ Avenida de San Sebastín; ⊘ 5 AM–noon, Mon.–Sat.).

North of Santa Cruz are the university town of La Laguna and the island's first resort village, **Puerto de la Cruz.** High-rise hotels and hawkers of plastic bananas are encroaching on the small-town feel of the village, but it still retains a tropical flower-filled central square.

Inland the road rises through banana plantations, almond groves, and pine forests to the entrance to ★**Mt. Teide National Park** (visitors center ⊘ Daily 9–4). Before arriving at the foot of the mountain, you pass through a stark landscape called Las Cañadas del Teide, a violent jumble of rocks and minerals created by millions of years of volcanic activity. A cable car (⌫ 1,000 ptas.; ⊘ Daily 9–5, last trip leaves at 4) will take you within 534 feet of the top of Mt. Teide, where there are good views of the southern part of the island and neighboring Gran Canaria.

Also worth a visit are the north coast towns of **Icod de los Vinos,** which boasts a 3,000-year-old, 57-foot-tall dragon tree once worshipped by the ancient Guanches and a plaza surrounded by typical wood-balconied Canarian houses; and farther west, **Garachico,** the most peaceful and best-preserved village on this touristy isle.

Gran Canaria

The "in" spot of the '60s and '70s, **Gran Canaria** has better beaches than Tenerife. Most visitors base themselves in the south coast resorts of **Playa del Inglés** and **Maspalomas,** where the white sand beach extends for 4 kilometers (2½ miles).

The central highlands of Gran Canaria provide a glimpse of rural island life. The road passes through numerous villages, and it is common to see farmers walking along the road laden with burlap sacks of potatoes. The **Parador Cruz de Tejada** specializes in traditional Canarian cuisine. Twenty-one kilometers (13 miles) beyond the parador is the **Mirador Los Pechos,** the highest viewpoint on the island.

Gran Canaria's capital, **Las Palmas,** is a vibrant Spanish city with an interesting old quarter called La Vegueta. Here you can wander cobblestone streets and visit the **Casa Museo Colón** (Columbus House and Museum, ⊠ Colón 1; ☎ Free), where the great navigator is said to have stayed when he stopped to repair the mast on the *Pinta* before leaving and discovering America. The real jewel of the capital, however, is **Las Canteras beach,** a sparkling-clean strand of white sand perfect for swimming or strolling.

Lanzarote

Stark and dry, with landscapes of volcanic rock, **Lanzarote** enjoys good beaches and tasteful architecture—low-rise with a green-and-white color scheme—the latter due to the efforts of the late artist, César Manrique, a Lanzarote native who is all but worshipped for single-handedly saving the island from mass development. The **Jameos del Agua** (Water Cavern, ⊠ Rte. GC710, 21 km/13 mi north of Arrecife) is a natural wonder created when molten lava streamed through an underground tunnel and hissed into the sea. The site features an auditorium with fantastic acoustics for concerts and a restaurant and bar.

★ The **Parque National Timanfaya,** popularly known as the "fire mountains," takes up much of the southern part of the island. Here you can have a camel ride, take a guided coach tour of the volcanic zone, and eat lunch at one of the world's most unusual restaurants, **El Diablo,** where meat is cooked over the crater of a volcano using the earth's natural heat.

Fuerteventura

The island of **Fuerteventura** was only recently discovered by tourists—mostly Germans—who come to windsurf and to enjoy the dunes of **Corralejo** and the endless white sand beaches of the **Sotovento** coast. Diving is good along the lengthy and lonely **Jandía Peninsula,** while the arid interior is largely the domain of goatherds.

La Palma

Called the garden isle, **La Palma** has luxuriant foliage, tropical storms, rainbows, and black crescents of beach, the best known of which is
★ **Los Cancajos.** Its capital, **Santa Cruz de la Palma,** was burned to the ground by pirates in 1533. It was rebuilt with assistance from the king of Spain and today remains one of the most beautiful and harmonious examples of Spanish colonial architecture.

Dining and Lodging

For price-category definitions *see* Dining *and* Lodging *in* Staying in Spain, *above.*

Gran Canaria

$$ ✕ **Tenderete II.** Canarian cuisine is cherished at this unassuming little restaurant in a shopping center. Typical soups and stews are al-

ways available for the first course, and it is one of the only restaurants in the islands that serves *gofio*, a traditional corn and barley pudding. The main course is always fish, grilled or baked in rock salt. ⊠ *Avda. de Tirajan, Edificio Aloe, Maspalomas,* ☎ *928/761460. AE, DC, MC, V.*

$$$ ⊞ **Hotel Palm Beach.** The Palm Beach, one of the most sophisticated and luxurious hotels in the Canary Islands, is in the middle of a 1,000-year-old palm oasis at the edge of Maspalomas Beach. Spacious rooms have dark bamboo furniture, large marble baths, and terraces that overlook the sea or pool area. ⊠ *Avda. del Oasis s/n, Maspalomas, 35106,* ☎ *928/140806,* FAX *928/141808. 358 rooms with bath. Restaurant, bar, pool, tennis, shops, nightclub. AE, MC, V.*

Lanzarote

$-$$ ✕ **La Era.** One of only three buildings that survived the eruption of the volcano that wiped out the town of Yaiza in 1730, this farmhouse restaurant offers simple dining rooms with blue-and-white check tablecloths arranged around a center patio. This is a great place to try regional dishes such as goat stew, or Canarian cheeses. ⊠ *Barranco 3, behind city hall (Ayuntamiento), Yaiza,* ☎ *928/830016. AE, DC, MC, V.*

$$$$ ✕⊞ **Meliá Salinas.** A stunning hotel built around an interior tropical garden, the Melia Salinas offers a chance to rub elbows with vacationing business and political leaders from all over Europe. Rooms have a tropical feel thanks to louvered closets and doors, and all include large, flower-filled terraces that face the sea. The hotel's restaurant, **La Graciosa,** Lanzarote's swankiest dining spot, overlooks the garden. A German chef prepares international cuisine with fresh island ingredients such as giant prawns, duck breast in plum sauce, and halibut wrapped in chard. ⊠ *35509 Costa Teguise, 35509,* ☎ *928/590040,* FAX *928/590390. 310 rooms with bath. 2 restaurants, 2 bars, pool, beauty salon, sauna, 5-hole golf course, tennis, archery, basketball, exercise room, squash, shops. AE, DC, MC, V.*

Tenerife

$$$ ✕ **Mesón El Drago.** In the village of El Socorro halfway between Santa Cruz and Puerto de la Cruz, this green-and-white 18th-century farmhouse with its brick floors and flower-filled patio has been converted into a showcase of typical Canarian cookery. Among the best dishes are *puchero canario* (a tangy stew of vegetables and meats) and fish casserole. ⊠ *Urbanización San Gonzalo, El Socorro,* ☎ *922/543001. AE, MC, V.* ☺ *Tues.–Sun. for lunch, Fri. and Sat. for dinner.*

$$ ✕ **La Masia del Mar.** There's no menu here; you simply point and choose from a vast array of fresh fish and shellfish in a big refrigerated case. Add a salad and a bottle of white wine to the order, and then find a seat on a wide terrace that overlooks Las Caletas cove (about 5 kilometers [3 miles] west of Playa de las Americas), and enjoy a simple feast of the best food the Canary Islands has to offer. ⊠ *Caleta de Adeje,* ☎ *922/710241. MC, V.*

$$$ ⊞ **Gran Hotel Bahía del Duque.** This sprawling hotel is a jumble of pastel-color houses and palaces, with Renaissance windows, loggias, and quiet courtyards. Rooms have oversize beds, summery wicker and pine furnishings, and rich architectural details such as scalloped plaster work and hand-painted ceramics. ⊠ *38660 Adeje, 38670,* ☎ *922/713000,* FAX *922/712369. 362 rooms with bath. 5 restaurants, bar, 4 pools, beauty salon, sauna, tennis, exercise room, squash. AE, MC, V.*

$$ ⊞ **Hotel Monopol.** One of the town's first inns, this hotel has been lodging tourists for more than a century. Before that it was a private home built in 1742 in the Canarian patio style. Tropical plants fill the center courtyard. Rooms are simple but have good views of the sea or main plaza. ⊠ *Quintana 15, Puerto de la Cruz, 38400,* ☎ *922/ 384611,* FAX *922/370310. 110 rooms with bath. Restaurant, 2 bars, pool. AE, MC, V.*

27 Sweden

Stockholm

Uppsala and the Folklore District

The West Coast and the Glass Country

SWEDEN'S STUNNING NATURAL ASSETS—wild forests, sparkling lakes and rivers, glaciered mountains, and unspoiled archipelagoes—occupy a land area daunting to the visitor in its far-flung diversity. Stretching nearly a thousand miles from the barren Arctic north to the fertile plains of the south, the country is Europe's fourth largest, yet its 173,665 square miles are home to only 8.7 million people (less than a million more than the population of New York City). The train line that runs 2,128 km (1,322 miles) from Trelleborg, in the far south, through desolate moorland and endless birch forests to Riksgransen, in the north, is the world's longest stretch of continuously electrified railroad. Even with its superbly efficient infrastructure of air, road, and rail transport, however, the considerable distances involved should temper your ambition to see too much in one trip.

This is a land of contrasts: long, warm days of summer followed by exceedingly dark, cold winters; ancient Viking rune stones in sight of steel-and-crystal skyscrapers; collective socialism and flag-waving royalism; introspective conformity and ebullient farcical humor; trim grandmothers in hats and gloves strolling past graphic billboard advertisements for safe sex. While their shop windows may be full of the latest in consumer goods, Swedes are reluctant urbanites: their hearts and souls are in the forests and among the islands; there they faithfully retreat for summers and weekends, picking berries, fishing, or just listening to the silence. Still, right in the center of Stockholm, thanks to a cleanup program in the 1970s, you can fish for salmon or go for a swim. In Göteborg's busy harbor, you can lean over the rail of your ferry and watch fish jump out of the water; in downtown Malmö, startlingly large hares hop around in the parks. It is this pristine quality of life that can make a visit to Sweden such a relaxing break from the modern world.

Once the dominant power of the Nordic region, Sweden has had a tradition of looking mostly inward for political solutions. During the cold war, it was largely successful in steering its famous "Middle Way" between the two superpowers. In response to the economic recession of the late 1980s, Sweden started making adjustments to its all-embracing welfare state. When the country developed one of Europe's largest budget deficits, the fragile conservative coalition that had defeated the long-incumbent Social Democrats in 1991 attempted further cutbacks. The populace reinstated the Social Democrats in 1994, hoping to recapture their cradle-to-grave social services, but the world economy hasn't cooperated and the deficit remains. Most recently, in a radical break with tradition and a very closely contested decision, Sweden joined the European Union (EU) in January 1995. While the domestic benefits of this move have yet to be determined, Sweden's history of even-handed adoption of the best of both socialism and capitalism has helped make it an influential and respected arbiter between clashing interest groups within the EU.

ESSENTIAL INFORMATION

Before You Go

When to Go

In an attempt to encourage visitors from abroad, Sweden has extended the main tourist season to run from mid-May through mid-September. Bear in mind, however, that many attractions close in late August,

Sweden

when the Swedes' own vacation season ends and children return to school. The weather can be magnificent in the spring and fall, and many visitors prefer sightseeing when fewer people are around.

The concentrated nature of the Swedes' own vacation period—the country virtually closes up shop for the entire month of July—can sometimes make it difficult to get hotel reservations during July and early August. On the other hand, the big city hotels, which cater mainly to business travelers, reduce their rates drastically in summer, when their ordinary clients are on vacation. (If you're traveling fall through spring, the high season for business travel, be forewarned that prices are high.) Ask your travel agent about special discounts offered by the major hotel groups, or contact the tourist information center, **Next Stop Sweden** (⌧ Box 3030, 103 61 Stockholm, ☎ 08/725–5500, ℻ 08/725–5531).

CLIMATE

Like the rest of northern Europe, Sweden has unpredictable summer weather, but, as a general rule, it is more likely to be rainy on the west coast than on the east. The country rarely gets hot; when the sun shines, the climate is usually agreeable. In Stockholm it never really gets dark in midsummer, while in the far north, above the Arctic Circle, the sun doesn't set between the end of May and the middle of July.

The following are the average daily maximum and minimum temperatures for Stockholm.

Jan.	30F	– 1C	May	58F	14C	Sept.	60F	15C
	23	– 5		43	6		49	9
Feb.	30F	– 1C	June	67F	19C	Oct.	49F	9C
	22	– 5		51	11		41	5
Mar.	37F	3C	July	71F	22C	Nov.	40F	5C
	26	– 4		57	14		34	1
Apr.	47F	8C	Aug.	68F	20C	Dec.	35F	3C
	34	1		55	13		28	– 2

Currency

The unit of currency in Sweden is the krona (plural kronor), which is divided into 100 öre and is written as SKr, SEK, or kr. Coins come in values of 50 öre and 1, 5, or 10 kronor; bills in denominations of 20, 100, 500, and 1,000 kronor. Traveler's checks and foreign currency can be exchanged at banks all over Sweden and at post offices displaying the NB EXCHANGE sign. At press time (spring 1996), the exchange rate was 6.9 kronor to the U.S. dollar, 5.1 kronor to the Canadian dollar, and 11.39 kronor to the pound sterling.

What It Will Cost

Sweden is seen as an expensive country but, in recent years, hotel prices have fallen in line with the European average. As in most countries, the most expensive hotels are found in major cities. Restaurant prices are generally high, but there are bargains to be had: Look for the *dagens rätt* (dish of the day) in many city restaurants. This costs about SKr 40–SKr 65 and can include a main dish, salad, soft drink, bread and butter, and coffee.

Many hotels have special low summer rates and cut prices on weekends in winter. Because of heavy taxes and excise duties, liquor prices remain among the highest in Europe. It pays to take in your maximum duty-free allowance (although prices for wine in Systembolaget, the state liquor stores, are not unreasonable). Value-added tax (known as *Moms* in Swedish) is imposed on most goods and services at a rate of 25%, with the exception of a 21% Moms on food, hotels, restaurants, and transportation. You can get a refund for most of the tax on goods if you take advantage of the tax-free shopping service offered at more than 13,000 stores throughout the country (☞ Shopping *in* Staying in Sweden, *below*).

SAMPLE PRICES
Cup of coffee, SKr 15–SKr 200; glass of beer, SKr 30–SKr 45; Coca-Cola, SKr 20–SKr 25; ham sandwich, SKr 25–SKr 50; 1-mile taxi ride, SKr 70–Skr 100 (depending on the taxi company).

Customs on Arrival

Travelers from the United States may import duty-free: 1 liter of liquor or 2 liters of fortified wine; 2 liters of wine; 15 liters of beer; 200 cigarettes or 100 cigarillos or 50 cigars or 250 grams of tobacco; 50 grams of perfume; 0.25 liter of aftershave; and other goods up to the value of SKr 1,700. Travelers from the United Kingdom or other European Union countries may import duty-free: 1 liter of liquor or 3 liters of fortified wine; 5 liters of wine; 15 liters of beer; 300 cigarettes or 150 cigarillos or 75 cigars or 400 grams of tobacco; and other goods, including perfume and aftershave, of any value. Duties are applied according to the traveler's point of origin, not citizenship—for example, if a U.S. citizen traveling from New York to Sweden were to break the trip for a few days in London, then the more generous U.K. limitations would be applied. There are no limits on the amount of foreign currency that can be imported or exported.

Language

Virtually all Swedes you are likely to meet will speak English, as it is a mandatory subject in all schools—though some of the older people you encounter in the rural areas may not be so familiar with English.

Getting Around

By Car

ROAD CONDITIONS
Sweden has an excellent network of more than 80,000 kilometers (50,000 miles) of highways. The fastest routes are those with numbers prefixed with an *E* (for "European"), some of which are the equivalent of American superhighways or British motorways—for part of the way, at least. Road E4, for instance, covers the entire distance from Helsingborg, in the south, to Stockholm, and on to Sundsvall and Umeå, in the north, finishing at Haparanda, on the Finnish border. All main and secondary roads are well surfaced, but some minor roads, particularly in the north, are gravel.

RULES OF THE ROAD
You drive on the right and, no matter where you sit in a car, you must wear a seat belt. You must also have at least low-beam headlights on at all times. Signs indicate five basic speed limits, ranging from 30 kph (19 mph) in school or playground areas to 110 kph (69 mph) on long stretches of *E* roads.

PARKING
Park on the right-hand side of the road, but if you want to park overnight, particularly in suburban areas, be sure not to do so on the night the street is being cleaned; circular signs with a red border indicate when this occurs —for example, MON 0–6 means no parking between midnight Sunday and 6 AM Monday. Parking meters and, increasingly, timed ticket machines, operate in larger towns, usually between 8 AM and 6 PM. The fee varies from about SKr 4 to SKr 20 per hour. Parking garages in urban areas are mostly automated, often with machines that accept credit cards; LEDIGT on a garage sign means

space is available. On the street, a circular sign with a red border and a red diagonal on a blue background means parking is prohibited; a yellow rectangle with a red border means restricted parking. Beware: fines for parking tickets are extraordinarily high in Sweden. City "Trafikkarta" maps, available at gas stations, include English explanations of parking signs and systems.

GASOLINE

Sweden has some of the highest gasoline prices in Europe, about SKr 7.85 per liter, depending on the grade. Lead-free gasoline is readily available. Gas stations are self-service: pumps marked SEDEL are automatic and accept SKr 20 and SKr 100 bills; pumps marked KASSA are paid for at the cashier; the KONTO pumps are for customers with Swedish gas credit cards.

BREAKDOWNS

The **Larmtjänst** organization, run by a confederation of Swedish insurance companies, provides a 24-hour breakdown service. Its phone numbers are listed in all telephone books. A toll-free emergency number (☎ 020/910040) is also available.

By Train

Sweden's rail network, mostly electrified, is highly efficient, and trains operate frequently, particularly on the main routes linking Stockholm with Göteborg and Malmö. First- and second-class cars are provided on all main routes, and sleeping cars are available in both classes on overnight trains. Most long-distance trains have either a buffet or dining car. Seat reservations are advisable, and on some trains—indicated with *R*, *IN*, or *IC* on the timetable—they are compulsory. Reservations can be made right up to departure time at a cost of SKr 30 per seat (☎ 020/757575). In addition, the Swedish rail network operates several daily high-speed trains called the X2000 from Stockholm to Gothenburg, Falun, Malmö, and Sunsvall, and from Gothenburg to Malmö.

FARES

On "Low price" or "Red" departures, fares are reduced by 50%, but careful planning and a Reslust discount card, which costs SKr 150, are necessary. Passengers paying low fares cannot make stopovers, and the tickets are valid for only 36 hours.

By Plane

Sweden's domestic air network is highly developed. Most major cities are served by **SAS** (☎ 020/727000). From Stockholm, there are flights to about 30 points around the country. SAS offers cut-rate round-trip "Jackpot" fares every day of the week on selected flights; these are available on most routes during the peak tourist season, from late June to mid-August. Some even more favorable offers on domestic flights are frequently available from the end of June through early August and during the Christmas and Easter seasons.

By Bus

Sweden has an excellent network of express bus services that provides an inexpensive and relatively speedy way of getting around the country. An information and booking office is at the front of Stockholm's Cityterminalen, the central bus terminal at Klarabergsviadukten. **Swebus** (☎ 08/237190 or 020/640640) and **Wasatrafik** (☎ 08/727–9020 or 020/656565) offer daily bus service from most major Swedish cities to various parts of Sweden. Other private companies operate weekend-only service on additional routes. In the far north, postal buses delivering mail to remote areas also carry passengers, providing an offbeat and inexpensive way to see the countryside.

By Boat

The classic boat trip in Sweden is the four-day journey along the Göta Canal between Gothenburg and Stockholm, operated by **Göta Canal Steamship Company** (✉ Box 272, 401 24 Gothenburg, ☎ 031/806315, FAX 031/158311; also N. Riddarholmshamnen 5, S–111 28 Stockholm, ☎ 08/202728). Children must be at least 8 years old to ride aboard the steamship.

By Bicycle

Cycling is popular in Sweden, and the country's uncongested roads make it ideal for extended bike tours. Bicycles can be rented throughout the country; inquire at the local tourist information office. Rental costs average around SKr 80 per day or SKr 400 per week. The **Swedish Touring Club** (STF) in Stockholm (✉ Kungsgatan 2, Box 25, 101 20, ☎ 08/463–2210, FAX 08/201332) can give you information about cycling packages that include bike rental, overnight accommodations, and meals. **Cykelfrämjandet** (✉ Torsgatan 31, Box 6027, 102 31 Stockholm, ☎ 08/321680, FAX 08/310503) has an English-language guide to cycling trips.

Staying in Sweden

Telephones

LOCAL CALLS

Sweden has plenty of pay phones, and there are also special offices marked TELE or TELEBUTIK from which you can make calls. To call from a pay phone, you'll need either SKr 1 or SKr 5 coins, since a local call costs SKr 2. You can also purchase a *telefonkort* (telephone card) from a Telebutik, hospital, or *Pressbyrån* store for SKr 30, SKr 55, or SKr 95. The card can be a savings if you plan to make numerous domestic calls, and indispensable when you're faced with one of the many public phones that accept only cards. Telephone numbers beginning with 020 are toll-free within Sweden.

INTERNATIONAL CALLS

These can be made from any pay phone. For calls to the United States and Canada, dial 009, then 1 (the country code), then wait for a second dial tone before dialing the area code and number. When dialing the United Kingdom, omit the initial zero on area codes (for Central London you would dial 009 followed by 44, wait for the second tone, then dial 171 and the local number). You can also make international calls from Telebutik offices. To reach an **AT&T** long-distance operator, dial 020/795611; for **MCI**, dial 020/795922; and for **Sprint,** 020/799011.

OPERATORS AND INFORMATION

For international calls, the operator assistance number is 0018; directory assistance, which costs SKr 11.25 per minute, is 07977. Within Sweden, dial 90130 for operator assistance and 07975 for directory assistance (this service is free if called from a public phone).

COUNTRY CODE

If you're calling Sweden from another country, the country code is 46.

Mail

POSTAL RATES

Airmail letters and postcards to the United States and Canada weighing less than 20 grams cost SKr 7.50. Postcards and letters within Europe cost SKr 6.

RECEIVING MAIL

If you're uncertain where you will be staying, have your mail addressed to "poste restante" and sent to S-101 10 Stockholm. Collection is at the Central Post Office, Vasagatan 28–32, ☎ 08/781–2040. American Express (☞ Important Addresses and Numbers *in* Stockholm, *below*) offers a poste-restante service free to its clients and for a small fee to others.

Shopping

Swedish goods have earned an international reputation for elegance and quality, and any visitor to the country should spend some time exploring the many impressive shops and department stores. The midsummer tourist season is as good a time as any to go shopping, as many stores have their annual sales at that time. Best buys are glassware, stainless steel, pottery and ceramics, leather goods, and textiles. You will find a wide selection of goods available in such major stores as **NK, Åhléns,** and **PUB,** which have branches all over the country.

High-quality furniture is a Swedish specialty, and it is worthwhile to visit one of the many branches of **IKEA,** a chain famous for its well-designed and affordable self-assembled furnishings. These are usually located on the outskirts of major towns. For glassware at bargain prices, head for the Kingdom of Crystal (☞ The West Coast and the Glass Country, *below*). All the major glassworks, including **Orrefors** and **Kosta Boda,** have large factory outlets where you can pick up seconds at only a fraction of the normal retail price. For clothing, the best center is Borås, not far from Gothenburg. Here you can find bargains from the leading mail-order companies. In rural areas, head to the local **Hemslöjd** craft centers for high-quality clothing, woodwork and needlework.

VAT REFUNDS

About 13,000 Swedish shops—1,000 in Stockholm alone—participate in the tax-free shopping program for visitors, enabling you to claim a refund of most of the value-added tax (Moms) that you have paid. Shops taking part in this service display a distinctive black, blue, and yellow sticker in the window. (Some stores offer the service only on purchases amounting to more than SKr 200.) The store will wrap and seal your purchase and give you a "Tax-Free Shopping Check" equivalent to the tax paid, minus a handling charge. This check can be cashed when you leave Sweden and show your unopened packages, either at the airport or aboard ferries. If you're packing your purchases in a suitcase, you can show them at the "Tax-Free" counter at Arlanda airport's check-in lobby and get your refund before you check your luggage. You should have your passport with you when making your purchase and claiming your refund.

Opening and Closing Times

Banks are open weekdays 9:30–3; some stay open until 5:30 in larger cities. Banks at Stockholm's Arlanda Airport and Gothenburg's Landvetter Airport are open every day, with extended hours. **Forex** and **Valuta Specialisten** currency-exchange offices operate in downtown Stockholm, Gothenburg, and Malmö, also with extended hours.

Museum hours vary widely, but most are open weekdays 10–4 or 10–5. Many are also open on weekends but may close on Monday.

Shops are generally open weekdays 9 or 9:30–6 and Saturday 9–1 or 9–4. Some department stores remain open until 8 or 10 on certain evenings, and some are also open Sunday noon–4 in major cities. Many supermarkets open on Sunday.

National Holidays

January 1; January 6 (Epiphany); March 28 (Good Friday); March 30 (Easter Monday); May 1 (Labor Day); May 8 (Ascension); May 27 (Whit Monday); June 22 (Midsummer Day); November 1 (All Saints' Day);

December 25–26. Hotels and restaurants may close for some of these holidays and for the week between Christmas and New Year's.

Dining

Swedish cuisine has recently gone cosmopolitan. The inevitable fast-food outlets, such as McDonald's and Burger King, have come on the scene, as well as Clock, the homegrown version of Pizza Hut. But there is also a good range of more conventional restaurants, from top-class establishments to less expensive places where you can pick up a cheaper lunch or snack. Snacks can also be enjoyed in a *konditori,* which offers inexpensive sandwiches, pastries, and pies with coffee, tea, or soft drinks. A cross between a café and a coffee shop, the konditori can be found in every city and town. The yellow pages of major towns' phone books include a *Restaurangguiden* that lists restaurants by type of cuisine, with cross-references to the city maps found in the phone book's red pages.

Many restaurants all over the country specialize in *husmanskost*—literally "home cooking"—which is based on traditional Swedish recipes.

Sweden is best known for its *smörgåsbord,* a word whose correct pronunciation defeats non-Swedes. It consists of a tempting buffet of hot and cold dishes, usually with a strong emphasis on seafood, notably herring, prepared in a wide variety of ways. Authentic smörgåsbord can be enjoyed throughout the country, but the best is found in the many inns in Skåne, where you can eat as much as you want for about SKr 300. Many Swedish hotels serve a lavish smörgåsbord-style breakfast, often included in the room price. Do justice to your breakfast and you'll probably want to skip lunch!

MEALTIMES

Swedes eat early. Restaurants start serving lunch around 11 AM, and outside the main cities you may find that they close quite early in the evening (often by 9) or may not open at all for dinner. Don't wait too long to look for someplace to have a meal. In major cities, especially on weekends, it's advisable to make reservations for dinner.

WHAT TO WEAR

Except for the most formal restaurants, where a jacket and tie are preferable, casual—or casual chic—attire is perfectly acceptable in restaurants in all price categories. Swedish dress, however, like other Europeans', tends to be a bit more formal and a bit less flamboyant than that of Americans.

RATINGS

Prices are per person and include a first course and main course, but no drinks. Service charges and Moms are included in the check, so there is no need to tip.

CATEGORY	COST
$$$$	over SKr 350
$$$	SKr 250–SKr 350
$$	SKr 120–SKr 250
$	under SKr 120

Lodging

Sweden offers accommodations from simple village rooms and campsites to hotels of the highest international standard. Except at the major hotels in the larger cities that cater mainly to a business clientele, rates are fairly reasonable. Prices are normally on a per-room basis and include all taxes and service and usually breakfast. Apart from the more modest inns and the cheapest budget establishments, private baths and showers are standard features, although it is just as well to double-check when making your reservation. Whatever their size, virtually all Swedish hotels provide scrupulously clean accommodations and courteous service. In Stockholm, there is a hotel reservation office—**Hotellcentralen**—at the central train station (☎ 08/240880, FAX 08/791–8666) and at the Stockholm Tourist Center in Sweden House. In other areas, local tourist offices will help you with reservations.

HOTELS

You can get a good idea of the facilities and prices at a particular hotel by consulting the official annual guide, "Hotels in Sweden," free at the Swedish Travel and Tourism Council (✉ Box 101 34, 121 28 Stockholm–Globen, ☎ 08/725–5500, FAX 08/725–5531). There is a good selection of hotels in all price categories in every town and city, though major international chains such as Sheraton and Best Western have made only small inroads in Sweden thus far. The main national chains are Scandic and RESO. The Sweden Hotels group has about 100 independently owned hotels and offers a central reservation service (☎ 08/789–8900). The group also has its own classification scheme—A, B, or C—based on the facilities available at each establishment. **Countryside Hotels** (✉ Box 69, 830 13 Åre, ☎ 0647/51860, FAX 0647/51920) is a group of 35 handpicked resort hotels, some of them restored manor houses or centuries-old inns.

HOUSE-RENTAL VACATIONS

In Sweden these are popular among other Europeans, particularly the British and Germans. There are about 250 chalet villages with amenities such as grocery stores, restaurants, saunas, and tennis courts. You can often arrange such accommodations on the spot at local tourist information offices. An alternative is a package, such as the one offered by **Scandinavian Seaways,** that combines a ferry trip from Britain across the North Sea with a stay in a chalet village. Scandinavian Seaways is based in the United Kingdom at Parkeston Quay, Harwich, Essex (☎ 01255/240240), with a second office in London (☎ 0171/409–6060). Their number in Gothenburg is 031/650600.

CAMPING

Camping is also popular in Sweden. About 750 officially approved sites dot the country, most next to either the sea or a lake and offering such activities as windsurfing, riding, and tennis. They are generally open between June 1 and September 1, though some are available year round. A free but abbreviated list of sites is published in English by the **Sveriges Campingvårdernas Riksforbünd** (Swedish Campsite Owners' Association; ✉ Box 255, 451 17 Uddevalla, ☎ 0522/39345, FAX 0522/33849).

RATINGS

Prices are for two people in a double room, based on standard rates; tax and breakfast are included.

CATEGORY	COST
$$$$	over SKr 1,200
$$$	SKr 970–SKr 1,200
$$	SKr 725–SKr 970
$	under SKr 725

Tipping

Swedes seldom expect tips, though in hotels it is customary to tip the porter about SKr 5 per item. Taxi drivers do not expect a tip. A consistent feature of the Swedish restaurant scene is that you must often dispose of your coat or sports jacket, whether you want to or not; the fee for leaving a coat in the checkroom is between SKr 6 and SKr 15.

STOCKHOLM

Arriving and Departing

By Plane

All international flights arrive at Arlanda Airport, 40 kilometers (25 miles) north of the city. The airport is linked to Stockholm by a major highway. For information on arrival and departure times, call the individual airlines.

BETWEEN THE AIRPORT AND DOWNTOWN

Buses leave from both the international and domestic terminals every 10–15 minutes between 6:30 AM and 11 PM, and run to Cityterminalen, at Klarabergsviadukten, next to the central train station. The ride costs SKr 50 per person. A bus-taxi package is available from the bus driver for SKr 120 per person inside city limits and SKr 180 anywhere in the Stockholm area; additional passengers in a group pay only the bus portion of the fare. For bus information, call **SL** at 08/670–1010. A taxi directly from the airport will cost around SKr 300 (be sure to ask the driver if he offers a "fixed-price" airport-to-city rate before you get into the taxi), but a possible alternative if you are not traveling alone is the SAS limousine service to any point in greater Stockholm. It operates as a shared taxi at SKr 274 per person. If two or three people travel together in a limousine to the same address, only one pays the full rate; all others pay SKr 130. The Moms will be deducted if the limousine is booked ahead of time through a travel agent in connection with an international arrival.

By Train

Major domestic and international trains arrive at Stockholm Central Station on Vasagatan, a main boulevard in the heart of the city. This is also the hub for local commuter services. For train information and ticket reservations 6 AM–11 PM, call 020/757575. At the station there is a ticket and information office where you can make seat or sleeping-car reservations. An automatic ticket-vending machine is also available. Couchette reservations on the regular train cost SKr 85 and beds from SKr 165.

By Bus

All major bus lines arrive at Cityterminalen, just beside the train station. Bus tickets are also sold at the railroad reservations office.

By Car

The two main access routes from the west and south are the E20 main highway from Gothenburg and the E4 from Helsingborg, the latter continuing as the main route to Sundsvall, the far north, and Finland. All routes to the CENTRUM (city center) are well marked.

Getting Around

The most cost-effective way to get around Stockholm is to use the **Stockholmskortet** (Key to Stockholm card). Besides unlimited transportation on city subway, bus, and rail services, it offers free admission to 60 museums and several sightseeing trips. The card costs SKr 175 for 24 hours, SKr 350 for two days, and SKr 525 for three days. It is available from the tourist information centers at Sweden House and the Kaknästornet (TV tower), and at the Hotellcentralen accommodations bureau at the central train station.

Maps and timetables for all city transportation networks are available from the Stockholm Transit Authority (SL) information desks at Sergels

Torg, Stockholm Central Station, and Slussen in Gamla Stan. You can also obtain information by phone (☎ 08/600–1000).

By Bus and Subway

The SL operates both the bus and subway systems. Tickets for the two networks are interchangeable. The subway system, known as T-banan (the *T* stands for tunnel), is the easiest and fastest way to get around the city. Station entrances are marked with a blue T on a white background. The T-banan has about 100 stations and covers more than 60 route-miles. Trains run frequently between 5 AM and 2 AM.

The fare system on buses and the subway is based on zones. The basic fare is SKr 13, good for travel within one zone, such as downtown, for one hour. You pay more if you travel in more than one zone.

Single tickets are available at station ticket counters, but it is cheaper to buy the SL Tourist Card, a significant savings. The card, valid on both buses and the subway and also providing free admission to a number of sights and museums, can be purchased at Pressbyrån newsstands and SL information desks. A card for the entire Greater Stockholm area costs SKr 54 for 24 hours or SKr 107 for 72 hours. Travelers under 18 or over 65 pay SKr 33 for one day and SKr 70 for three days. Also available from the Pressbyrån newsstands are SKr 85 coupons, good for at least 10 bus or subway rides in the central zone.

The Stockholm bus network provides service not only within the central area but also to out-of-town points of interest, such as Waxholm, with its historic fortress, and Gustavsberg, with its porcelain factory. In greater Stockholm, a few buses run through the night.

By Train

SL operates conventional train service from Stockholm Central Station to a number of nearby points, including Nynäshamn, a departure point for ferries to the island of Gotland. Trains also run from the Slussen station to the fashionable seaside resort of Saltsjöbaden.

By Taxi

Typically, a trip of 10 kilometers (6 miles) will cost SKr 93 between 9 AM and 4 PM on weekdays, SKr 103 on weekday nights, and SKr 110 on weekends—all including Moms. Major taxi companies are Taxi Stockholm (☎ 08/150000), Taxikurir (☎ 08/300000), and Taxi 020 (☎ 020/850400).

Important Addresses and Numbers

Embassies

U.S. (⊠ Strandvägen 101, ☎ 08/783–5300). **Canadian** (⊠ Tegelbacken 4, ☎ 08/613–9900). **U.K.** (⊠ Skarpögatan 6–8, ☎ 08/671–9000).

Emergencies

Police (☎ 08/769–3000; emergencies only: 90000); **Ambulance** (☎ 90000); **Doctor** (Medical Care Information, ☎ 08/644–9200); travelers can get hospital attention in the district where they are staying or can contact the private clinic, **City Akuten** (☎ 08/411–7102); **Dentist** (8 AM–9 PM ☎ 08/654–1117, 9 PM–8 AM ☎ 08/644–9200); **24–hour Pharmacy** (C. W. Scheele ☎ 08/218934; all pharmacies display the sign APOTEK).

English-Language Bookstores

Most bookstores have a good selection of English books. **Akademibokhandeln** (Mäster Samuelsgatan 32, ☎ 08/613–6100), one of a chain of bookstores, has the widest selection of paperbacks, dictionaries, and maps in many languages.

Travel Agencies

American Express (⊠ Birger Jarlsgatan 1, ☎ 08/679–5200, FAX 08/611–6214).

Visitor Information

The main tourist information office is the Stockholm Tourist Center at **Sweden House** (⊠ Kungsträdgården, Hamngatan 27, ☎ 08/789–2490). During the peak tourist season (June through August), it is open weekdays 8–6, weekends 9–5. Its current off-season hours are 9–6 and 10–3, respectively. Besides providing information, it handles tickets for sightseeing excursions. There are additional information centers at Stockholm Central Station, at City Hall (summer only), and in the Kaknästornet (TV Tower). When planning to visit any of the tourist attractions in Stockholm, be sure to call ahead, as opening times and prices are subject to change.

Guided Tours

Orientation

Some 30 different tours—by foot, boat, bus, or a combination of these—are available during the summer. Some take only 30 minutes, others an entire day. A popular three-hour bus tour, costing SKr 230, runs daily at 9:45 AM. The tour includes Stadshuset (City Hall), Storkyrkan (the Cathedral in Gamla Stan), the Vasa Museum, and the Kungliga Slott (Royal Palace), among other stops. Tickets can be purchased from the Excursion Shop at Sweden House.

Boat

You'll find a bewildering variety of tours available at Stockholm's quay. The **Waxholm Steamship Company** (☎ 08/679–5830) operates scheduled service to many islands in the archipelago on its white steamers. Trips range from one to three hours each way. Popular one-day excursions include Waxholm, Utö, Sandhamn, and Möja. Conventional sightseeing tours include a one-hour circular city tour run by the **Strömma Canal Company** (☎ 08/233375). It leaves from the Nybroplan quay every hour on the half-hour between 10:30 and 5:30 in summer.

Special-Interest

A number of special-interest tours are available in the Stockholm area, especially in summer. You can choose to spend a weekend at a chalet in the archipelago, rent of a small fishing boat, or visit the Gustavsberg porcelain factory just outside Stockholm, which has a retail shop. Several outstanding 17th-century villas and estates within an hour or two of Stockholm have been converted into quaint, high-quality hotels, such as the stately Ulvhälls Herrgård in Strängnäs, on Lake Mälaren. Contact the Tourist Center at Sweden House for details.

Excursions

Don't miss the boat trip to the 17th-century palace of **Drottningholm,** the private residence of the Swedish royal family and a smaller version of Versailles. Trips depart every hour on the hour from 10 to 4 and at 6 PM during the summer from City Hall Bridge (Stadshusbron). Another popular trip goes from Stadshusbron to the ancient towns of Sigtuna and Skokloster. By changing boats you can continue to Uppsala to catch the train back to Stockholm. Information is available from the **Strömma Canal Company** (☎ 08/233375) or the Tourist Center at Sweden House.

Personal Guides

Contact the **Guide Center** at the **Stockholm Information Service** (☎ 08/789–2496).

Exploring Stockholm

Numbers in the margin correspond to points of interest on the Stockholm map.

Because Stockholm's main attractions are concentrated in a relatively small area, the city itself can be explored in a few days. If you're planning any full-day excursions, you might want to devote a full week to your visit.

Stockholm, built on 14 small islands separated by open bays and narrow channels, is a handsome, civilized city, full of parks, squares, and airy boulevards, yet it is also a bustling, modern metropolis. Glass-and-steel skyscrapers abound, but in the center you are never more than five minutes' walk from twisting, medieval streets and water views.

The first written mention of Stockholm dates from 1252, when a powerful regent named Birger Jarl is said to have built a fortified castle here. This strategic position, where the calm, fresh waters of Lake Mälaren meet the salty Baltic Sea, must have prompted King Gustav Vasa to take over the city in 1523, and King Gustavus Adolphus to make it the heart of an empire a century later.

During the Thirty Years' War (1618–48), Sweden gained importance as a Baltic trading state, and Stockholm grew commensurately. But by the beginning of the 18th century, Swedish influence had begun to wane, and Stockholm's development slowed. It did not pick up again until the Industrial Revolution, when the hub of the city moved north from the Old Town area.

City Hall and the Old Town

Anyone with limited time should give priority to a tour of Stockholm's
★ **Gamla Stan** (Old Town), a labyrinth of narrow medieval streets, alleyways, and quiet squares on the island just south of the city center. From the Central Station, take Vasagatan down to the waterfront. Ideally, you should devote an entire day to this district, but it's also nice to start with a detour along the quay and across Stadshusbron to the
★ ❶ modern-day **Stadshuset** (City Hall), constructed in 1923 and now one of the symbols of Stockholm. Lavish mosaics adorn the walls of the **Golden Hall,** and the **Prince's Gallery** features a collection of large murals by Prince Eugen, brother of King Gustav V. Take the elevator halfway up, then climb the rest of the way to the top of the 348-foot tower for a magnificent view of the city. ✉ *Hantverkargatan 1,* ☎ *08/785–9074.* 🎟 *SKr 30.* ☾ *Tours daily at 10 and noon; also at 11 and 2 in summer.* 🎟 *Tower: SKr 15.* ☾ *May–Sept., daily 10–4:30.*

Retrace your steps across the Stadshusbron and head for the stairway leading up from the quay onto the Gångbro (footbridge). Crossing into
❷ the Old Town, the first thing you'll see is the magnificent **Riddarholms Kyrka** (Riddarholm Church), where a host of Swedish kings are buried. ✉ *Riddarholmen, Gamla Stan,* ☎ *08/789–8500.* 🎟 *SKr 10.* ☾ *May–Aug, daily 10–3; Sept., Wed. and weekends noon–3.*

★ ❸ Proceed across Riddarhusbron to the **Kungliga Slott** (Royal Palace), preferably by noon, when you can watch the colorful changing of the guard. The smartly dressed guards seem somewhat superfluous, as tourists wander at will into the palace courtyard and around the grounds. Several distinct attractions are open to the public. Be sure to visit the **Livrustkammaren** (Royal Armory), with its outstanding collection of weaponry and royal regalia. The **Skattkammaren** (Treasury) houses the Swedish crown jewels, including the regalia used for the coronation of King Erik XIV in 1561. You can also visit the **Representationsvän** (State Apartments), where the king swears in each successive government. ⊠ *Gamla Stan,* ☎ *08/789–8500.* ⊞ *SKr 50 for Armory; SKr 30 for Treasury; SKr 30 for State Apartments.* ☉ *Hours subject to change; call ahead.*

4
5 From the palace, follow Källargränd past the **Storkyrkan,** the 15th-century Gothic cathedral, to **Stortorget,** the historic square where a massacre ordered by King Christian II in 1520 triggered a revolt and the founding of the sovereign state of Sweden. Leave the square by the opposite corner and turn left to stroll down **Västerlånggatan,** one of the main streets in the Old Town. This popular shopping area brims with boutiques and antiques shops. Walk down to the Skeppsbron waterfront, then head back toward the city center over the Ström bridge, where anglers cast for salmon. From here you can turn right and fol-
6 low the waterfront around to the **Nationalmuseum,** Stockhom's national art gallery. ⊠ *Södra Blasieholmshamnen,* ☎ *08/666–4250;* ☉ *Wed., Fri.-Sun. 11-5, Tue., Thu. 11-8.*

7 If you turn left you will see the **Operan** building with its terrace bistro. By now you may wish to rest; if so, cross straight ahead into the park,
8 the **Kungsträdgården.** Originally built as a royal kitchen garden, the property was turned into a public park in 1562. In summer, you can watch people playing open-air chess with giant chess pieces. In winter, the park has a skating rink.

Djurgården

★ Be sure to spend at least a day visiting the large island of **Djurgården.** Although it's only a short walk from the city center, the most pleasant way to approach it is by ferry from Skeppsbron, in the Old Town. Or you might want to take the streetcar that runs from Norrmalmstorg,
9 near the city center, to **Waldemarsudde,** (☎ *08/662–2800*), an art museum in what was once the summer residence of Prince Eugen. Whichever way you take to Djurgården, you will not want to miss the spectacu-
★ **10** lar **Vasamuseet,** which opened in 1990. The *Vasa,* a restored 17th-century warship, is one of the oldest preserved war vessels in the world and has become Sweden's most popular tourist attraction. It sank ignominiously in Stockholm Harbor on its maiden voyage in 1628, reportedly because it was not carrying sufficient ballast. Recovered in 1961, the ship has been restored to its original appearance. The museum in which it is housed also has film presentations and displays. ⊠ *Galärvarvet,* ☎ *08/666–4800.* ⊞ *SKr 45.* ☉ *Thurs.–Tues. 10–5, Wed. 10–8.*

11 Another of the island's chief attractions is **Gröna Lund Tivoli,** Stockholm's version of the famous Copenhagen amusement park. It is a family favorite, with rides and attractions well marked for all age groups. ⊠ *Djurgårdesvägen,* ☎ *08/670–7600.* ☉ *late Apr.–early Sept. Prices and hours are subject to change: call ahead.*

★ **12** Just across the road is **Skansen,** a large, open-air folk museum showcasing 150 reconstructed traditional buildings from Sweden's various regions. Here you can see a variety of handicraft displays and demonstrations. There is also an attractive zoo—with many native Scandinavian species, such as lynxes, wolves, reindeer, and brown bears—as well as an excellent aquarium and carnival rides for children. ⊠ *Djurgårdsslätten 49-51,* ☎ *08/442–8000.* ☉ *Call ahead for prices and times; they're subject to change.*

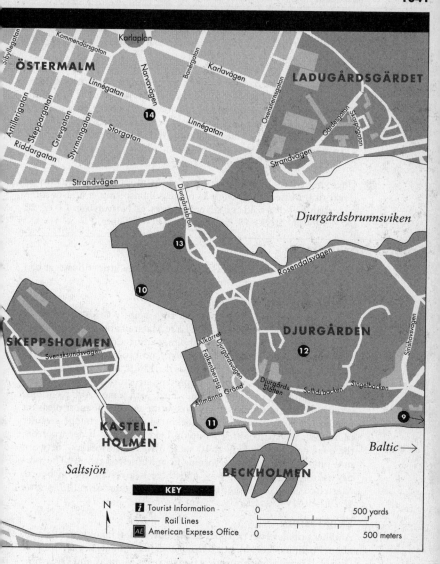

ÖSTERMALM

Sibyllegatan
Kommendörsgatan
Karlaplan
Narvavägen
Banérgatan
Karlavägen

LADUGÅRDSGÄRDET

Linnégatan

Artillerigatan
Skeppargatan
Grevgatan
Styrmansgatan
Storgatan
Riddargatan

Linnégatan

Oxenstiernsgatan

Gärdesgatan
Stanggatan

Strandvägen

Strandvägen

Djurgårdsbron

Djurgårdsbrunnsviken

Rosendalsvägen

SKEPPSHOLMEN

Svensksundsvägen

Alkärret
Falkenbergsg.
Djurgårdsvägen

DJURGÅRDEN

Sirishovsvägen

KASTELL-
HOLMEN

Allmänna Gränd

Djurgårds
Slätten
Sollidsbacken
Singelbacken

Saltsjön

BECKHOLMEN

Baltic →

KEY

i Tourist Information
— Rail Lines
AE American Express Office

N

0   500 yards
0   500 meters

NEED A
BREAK? For a mediocre snack but a great view, try the **Solliden Restaurant**
(☎ 08/660–1055) at Skansen. Skansen also offers a selection of open-
air snack bars and cafés; Gröna Lund has four different restaurants and
many snack bars.

⟲ **⑬** From Skansen, head back toward the city center. Just before the bridge,
the Djurgårdsbron, you come to the **Nordiska Museet** (Nordic Museum).
Like Skansen, the museum shows how the Swedes have lived over the
past 500 years, with displays of peasant costumes, folk art, and Sami
culture. Families with children should visit the delightful "village life"
play area on the ground floor. ⊠ *Djurgårdsvägen 6-16,*
☎ *08/666–4600.* ⊠ *SKr 40.* ⊘ *Tues.–Sun. 11–5.*

⑭ Once you're back on the "mainland," drop into the **Historiska Museet**
(Historical Museum). Though its name is uninspiring, it houses some
remarkable Viking gold and silver treasures. ⊠ *Narvavägen 13-17,* ☎
08/783-9400. ⊠ *SKr 55.* ⊘ *Tues.–Sun. 11–5, Thurs. 11–8.*

Around Stockholm

The region surrounding Stockholm offers many attractions that can
easily be seen on day trips from the capital.

Gripsholm and the *Mariefred*

★ One "must" is a trip to the majestic 16th-century **Gripsholm Slott** at
Mariefred, on the southern side of Lake Mälaren about 64 kilometers
(40 miles) from Stockholm. Gripsholm, with its drawbridge and four
massive round towers, is one of Sweden's most romantic castles. There
had been a castle on the site as early as the 1380s, but it was destroyed,
and King Gustav Vasa built the present structure in 1577. It now
houses the state portrait collection, which, with some 3,400 paintings,
is one of the largest portrait galleries in the world. The most pleasant
way to reach Gripsholm from Stockholm is on the vintage steamer
Mariefred, the last coal-fired ship on Lake Mälaren. It departs from
the quay next to City Hall at 10 AM daily (except Monday), between
mid-June and late August, returning from Mariefred at 4:30. The journey takes 3½ hours each way, and there is a restaurant on board.
Mariefred ☎ *08/669–8850.* ⊠ *Round-trip fare, SKr 140. Castle*
☎ *0159/10194.* ⊠ *SKr 30.* ⊘ *Apr.–Sept., Tue.–Sun. 10–3.*

Skokloster

Another popular boat trip goes to **Skokloster Slott** (Skokloster Palace),
about 70 kilometers (44 miles) from Stockholm. Boats depart from the
City Hall Bridge (Stadshusbron) daily, except Monday and Friday, between early June and mid-August. The route follows the narrow in-
lets of Lake Mälaren along the "Royal Waterway" and stops at **Sigtuna,**
an ancient trading center. You can get off the boat here to visit the town,
which has medieval ruins and an 18th-century town hall, then catch
the boat again on its return journey. Or you can continue on to Skokloster, an impressive palace dating from the 1650s. Built by the Swedish
field marshal Carl Gustav Wrangel, it contains many of his trophies
from the Thirty Years' War. Other attractions include what is thought
to be the largest private collection of arms in the world, as well as some
magnificent Gobelin tapestries. Next door to the palace is a motor museum housing Sweden's largest collection of vintage cars and motorcycles. The round-trip boat fare is SKr 165, and there are a restaurant
and a cafeteria on board. ⊠ *Strömma Canal Company,* ☎ *08/233375.*
Palace ☎ *018/386077.* ⊠ *Palace: SKr 40; motor museum: SKr 35.* ⊘
daily noon–6.

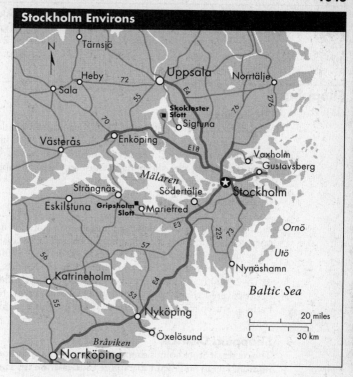

Stockholm Environs

Archipelago

★ Lovers of the sea could easily spend an entire week cruising among the 24,000 islands in **Stockholms Skärgården** (archipelago). The **Båtluf-farkortet** (Inter-Skerries Card), available from early June to mid-August, gives you 16 days' unlimited travel on Waxholmsbolaget (Waxholm Steamship Company) boats, which follow scheduled routes throughout the archipelago. The card is sold in the Excursion Shop at Sweden House and at the Waxholm Steamship Company terminal at Strömkajen, in front of the Grand Hotel. It costs SKr 230.

Off the Beaten Path

Just over 508 feet tall, the **Kaknästornet** (the Kaknäs TV Tower) at Gärdet is the tallest structure in Scandinavia. From the top you can enjoy a magnificent view of the city and the surrounding archipelago. Facilities include a cafeteria, a restaurant, and a gift shop. ⊠ *Ladugårds-gärdet,* ☎ *08/667–8030. Admission: SKr 20. Open Apr., daily 9–6; May–Aug., daily 9–8; Sept.–May, daily 10–5.*

You can admire the world's largest display of water lilies at the **Bergian-ska Botaniska Trädgården** (Bergianska Botanical Garden), just north of the city center. One variety has leaves more than 7 feet in diameter. ⊠ *Frescati,* ☎ *08/162853. Admission: SKr 10 to the garden, free to the park. Greenhouse open daily 11–5; herbal garden open daily 8–5; Victoria House open May–Sept., daily 11-5; park always open.*

A group of four secluded islands known as **Fjäderholmarna** (the Feather Islets), only 20 minutes by boat from downtown, has been open to the public only since the early 1980s. Formerly this was a restricted military zone; now it's a worthwhile destination, with a museum depicting life in the archipelago, as well as Scandinavia's largest aquarium. The latter has countless species of Baltic marine life, as well as a cafeteria, handicraft studios and shops, a restaurant (✉ Fjäderholmarnas Krog, ☎ 08/718–3355), and an unusual pirate-ship playground. Boats leave from Slussen, Strömkajen, and Nybroplan (Apr. 29–Sept. 17). *✉ Strömma Canal Co., ☎ 08/233375. Fjäderholmarna information, ☎ 08/718–0100.*

Shopping

Gift Ideas
Stockholm is an ideal place to find the best in Swedish design and elegance, particularly glass, porcelain, furs, handicrafts, home furnishings, and leather goods. Quality is uniformly high, and you can take advantage of tax-free shopping in most stores (☞ Shopping *in* Staying in Sweden, *above*).

Department Stores
The largest is **NK** (✉ Hamngatan 18–20, ☎ 08/762–8000), where you can find just about anything in the impressive number of independently operated boutiques, including a large selection of Swedish crafts. Two other major stores are **PUB** (✉ Hötorget, ☎ 08/791–6000), which was completely rebuilt in 1995, and **Åhléns City** (✉ Klarabergsgatan 50, ☎ 08/246000). All three are open on Sunday. **Sturegallerian** is an elegant covered shopping gallery built on the site of the former public baths at Stureplan. There are about 50 shops, plus a number of restaurants.

Shopping Districts
The center of Stockholm's shopping activity is the wide boulevard **Hamngatan.** Here you'll want to explore the **Gallerian** (✉ Hamngatan 37, ☎ 08/796–9340), a huge covered shopping complex. The **Old Town** area is best for handicrafts, antiquarian bookshops, and art galleries.

Food and Flea Markets
One of the largest flea markets in northern Europe, the **Loppmarknaden,** is held in the parking garage of the **Skärholmen** shopping center, a 20-minute subway ride from downtown. Market hours are weekdays 11–6, Saturday 9–3, and Sunday 10–3, with an entry fee of SKr 10 on weekends. Superior food markets selling such Swedish specialties as marinated salmon and reindeer can be found at Östermalmstorg's **Saluhall** and at Hötorget's underground market.

Glassware
For the best buys, try **Nordiska Kristall** (✉ Kungsgatan 9, ☎ 08/104372). **Arioso** (✉ Västerlånggatan 59, ☎ 08/213810), in the Old Town, is good for modern crystal and ceramics. **Duka** (✉ corner of Kungsgatan and Sveavägen, ☎ 08/104530), specializes in crystal as well as porcelain.

Handicrafts
A good center for all kinds of Swedish handicrafts in wood and metal is **Svensk Hemslöjd** (✉ Sveavägen 44, ☎ 08/232115), which also sells embroidery kits and many types of weaving and knitting yarn. For elegant home furnishings and timeless fabrics, Stockholmers tend to favor **Svenskt Tenn** (✉ Strandvägen 5A, ☎ 08/670–1600), best known for its selection of designer Josef Franck's furniture and fabrics. **Svenskt Hantwerk** (✉ Kungsgatan 55, ☎ 08/214726) has a wide selection of Swedish folk costumes and handicraft souvenirs from different parts of Sweden.

Dining

$$$$ ✕ **Operakällaren.** Situated in the elegant Opera House, this is one of Stockholm's best-known traditional restaurants, featuring both Scandinavian and Continental cuisine. It is famed for its smörgåsbord, available from June 1st onward, with seasonal variations, through Christmas. In summertime you can dine on the veranda, which faces the Kungsträdgården, the waterfront, and the Royal Palace. ⊠ *Operahuset,* ☎ *08/676–5801. AE, DC, MC, V. Main dining room closed July.*

$$$$ ✕ **Paul and Norbert.** A very cozy, 32-seat restaurant on Stockholm's most elegant avenue, Paul and Norbert is noted for its French-style cuisine based on indigenous wild game such as reindeer, elk, partridge, and grouse, as well as fish. Its furnishings are rustic but refined. ⊠ *Strandvägen 9,* ☎ *08/663–8183. Reservations essential. AE, DC, MC, V. Closed weekends. Call for yearly closing dates.*

$$$$ ✕ **Ulriksdals Värdshus.** Top-notch service, a beautiful location—in a castle park on the outskirts of town—and a noteworthy Swedish and international menu highlighting a lunchtime smörgåsbord all make this worth a splurge. Built in 1868, the restaurant was once a country inn, and it hasn't lost a bit of its country hospitality. ⊠ *Ulriksdals Slottspark,* ☎ *08/850815. AE, DC, MC, V. No dinner Sun.*

$$$ ✕ **Clas på Hörnet.** Just outside the city center, Clas på Hörnet is a small,
★ intimate establishment occupying the ground floor of a restored 200-year-old town house, now a hotel (☞ Lodging, *below*). It offers a choice of international and Swedish cuisine. ⊠ *Surbrunnsgatan 20,* ☎ *08/165136. AE, DC, MC, V. Closed July.*

$$$ ✕ **Den Gyldene Freden.** Once a favorite haunt of Stockholm's artists
★ and composers, this restaurant, dating from 1722, has an Old Town ambience. Every Thursday, the Swedish Academy meets for lunch on the second floor. The menu presents a tasteful combination of French and Swedish cuisines. ⊠ *Österlånggatan 51,* ☎ *08/249760. AE, DC, MC, V. Closed Sun.*

$$$ ✕ **Stallmästaregården.** This historic old inn with an attractive court-
★ yard and garden sits in Haga Park, just north of Norrtull, about 15 minutes by car from the city center. In summer, fine French and Swedish cuisine is served in the courtyard overlooking Brunnsviken Lake. A prix-fixe business lunch is available. ⊠ *Norrtull, near Haga,* ☎ *08/610–1300. AE, DC, MC, V. Closed Sun.*

$$$ ✕ **Wedholms Fisk.** Serving only fresh fish and shellfish, this open, high-ceilinged restaurant is in Berzelii Park, across from the Royal Dramatic Theater. The tartare of salmon and the grilled sole are noteworthy. Portions are generous. The Scandinavian artwork on display is part of the owner's personal collection. ⊠ *Nybrokajen 17,* ☎ *08/611–7874. AE, DC, MC, V. Closed Sun. and July.*

$$ ✕ **Bakfickan.** The name means "hip pocket" and is appropriate, as the
★ restaurant is tucked around at the back of the Opera House complex. It's a budget-price alternative to the nearby Operakällaren and is particularly popular at lunchtime, offering Swedish home cooking and a range of daily specials. Counter and table service are both available. ⊠ *Operahuset, Gustav Adolfs Torg,* ☎ *08/207745. Reservations not accepted. AE, DC, MC, V. Closed Sun.*

$$ ✕ **Eriks Bakficka.** A favorite among locals, Eriks is a block from the elegant waterside street Strandvägen, a few steps down from street level. The restaurant serves a wide variety of Swedish dishes, and there's a lower-priced menu is in the pub section. The same owner operates Eriks in Gamla Stan, one of Stockholm's most exclusive restaurants. ⊠ *Frederikshovsgatan 4,* ☎ *08/660–1599. AE, DC, MC, V. Closed weekends in July.*

$$ ✕ **Gondolen.** Suspended under the gangway of the Katarina elevator at Slussen, Gondolen offers a magnificent view over the harbor, Lake Mälaren, and the Baltic. The cuisine is international, and a range of prix-fixe menus is available. ⊠ *Stadsgården 6,* ☎ *08/641–7090. AE, DC, MC, V. Closed Sun.*

$$ ✕ **Martini.** This central and highly popular Italian restaurant is a great place for people-watching; patrons line up to get a seat during the summer, when the terrace is open. The main restaurant is below street level, but light colors and a bustling atmosphere make it a cheerful place. ✉ *Norrmalmstorg 4,* ☎ *08/679–8220. AE, DC, MC, V.*

$$ ✕ **Nils Emil.** Frequented by members of the Swedish royal family, this elegant but unpretentious restaurant is noted for its delicious Swedish cuisine and generous helpings. Walls are decorated with paintings of the Stockholm archipelago, birthplace of chef-owner Nils Emil. ✉ *Folkungagatan 122, Södermalm,* ☎ *08/640–7209. Reservations essential. AE, DC, MC, V. Closed July. No lunch Sat.*

$$ ✕ **Sturehof.** Opened before the turn of the century, Sturehof is Sweden's oldest fish restaurant, with an unpretentious, nautical ambience. It also has an English-style pub. ✉ *Stureplan 2,* ☎ *08/679–8750. AE, DC, MC, V.*

$ ✕ **Open Gate.** This popular, trendy, art deco Italian-style trattoria is
★   near the Slussen locks, on the south side of Stockholm Harbor. Pasta dishes are the house specialty. ✉ *Högbergsgatan 40,* ☎ *08/643–9776. Reservations not accepted. AE, DC, MC, V. Closed Sun.*

$ ✕ **Örtagården.** This vegetarian, no-smoking restaurant is one floor up from the Östermalmshallen market hall. It offers an attractive buffet of soups, salads, hot dishes, and homemade bread—not to mention a five-kronor bottomless cup of coffee—in a turn-of-the-century atmosphere. ✉ *Nybrogatan 31,* ☎ *08/662–1728. AE, MC, V.*

Lodging

Stockholm has plenty of hotels in higher price brackets, but summer rates—some as much as 50% off—can make even very expensive hotels affordable. The major chains also offer a number of bargain plans on weekends throughout the year and weekdays in summer.

More than 50 hotels offer the "Stockholm Package," providing one night's lodging at between SKr 360 and SKr 760 per person and including breakfast and a Key to Stockholm card (☞ Getting Around, *above*). The package is available June through mid-August, at Christmas and Easter, and Thursday–Monday year-round; get details from the **Stockholm Information Service** (✉ Excursion Shop, Box 7542, 103 93, ☎ 08/789–2415). The package can also be reserved through travel agents or through **Hotellcentralen** (✉ Central Station, 111 20, ☎ 08/240880, FAX 08/791–8666).

If you arrive in Stockholm without a hotel reservation, **Hotellcentralen** will also arrange accommodations for you. The office is open November–March, weekdays 8–5 and weekends 8–2; April and October, daily 8–5; May and September, daily 8–7; and June–August, daily 7 AM–9 PM; telephone reservations can be made after 9 AM. There is a reservations office in Sweden House (☞ Important Addresses and Numbers, *above*) as well. A small fee is charged for each reservation, but advance telephone reservations are free. **Hotel Booking** (☎ 08/116–0380) is an independent agency that can reserve at no cost to you in any Swedish hotel. Or phone one of the central reservations services operated by the major hotel groups: RESO (☎ 08/720–8880), Scandic (☎ 08/610–5050), Sweden Hotels (☎ 08/789–8900), Best Western (☎ 08/330600 or 020/792752), or Radisson SAS (☎ 020/797592).

$$$$ 🏨 **Amaranten.** Only five minutes' walk from the central train station, Amaranten is a large, modern hotel built in 1969. Rooms with air-conditioning and soundproofing are available at a higher rate. Guests can enjoy the brasserie and a piano bar. ✉ *Kungsholmsgatan 31, 104 20,* ☎ *08/654–1060,* FAX *08/652–6248. 360 rooms with bath; 50 rooms with* *bath, air-conditioning, and soundproofing. Restaurant, piano bar, no-smoking rooms, indoor pool, sauna, meeting rooms. AE, DC, MC, V.*

$$$$ ⊞ **Continental.** In the city center, across from the Central Train Station, the Continental is popular with American visitors. It was opened
★ in 1966 and was renovated in 1992.⊠ *Klara Vattugränd 4, 101 22,* ☎ *08/244020,* FAX *08/411–3695. 268 rooms with bath. Restaurant, no-smoking rooms, sauna, meeting rooms. AE, DC, MC, V.*

$$$$ ⊞ **Diplomat.** This elegant hotel within easy walking distance of Djurgården and Skansen offers magnificent views over Stockholm Harbor. The
★ den and Skansen offers magnificent views over Stockholm Harbor. The building itself is a turn-of-the-century town house that accommodated foreign embassies in the 1930s and was converted into a hotel in 1966. The Teahouse Restaurant is a popular spot for light meals. ⊠ *Strandvägen 7C, 104 40,* ☎ *08/663–5800,* FAX *08/783–6634. 133 rooms with bath, including 24 with harbor view. Restaurant, no-smoking rooms, sauna. AE, DC, MC, V.*

$$$$ ⊞ **Grand.** Opposite the Royal Palace on the waterfront in the center of town, the Grand is a large, gracious, Old World–style hotel dating from 1874. Most rooms have waterfront views, and guests are entitled to relax at the nearby Sturebadet health spa. The two restaurants—French and Swedish—offer harbor views, and the bar serves light snacks. ⊠ *Blasieholmshamnen 8, 103 27,* ☎ *08/679–3500,* FAX *08/611–8686. 319 rooms with bath. 2 restaurants, bar, no-smoking rooms, sauna, meeting room. AE, DC, MC, V.*

$$$$ ⊞ **Lady Hamilton.** As charming, desirable, and airily elegant as its namesake, the Lady Hamilton opened in 1980 as a modern hotel inside a
★ 15th-century building, so close to the Royal Palace in Gamla Stan that some rooms afford a view of the changing of the guard. Swedish antiques accent the light, natural-toned decor in all the guest rooms and common areas. Romney's "Bacchae" portrait of Lady Hamilton hangs in the foyer, where a large, smiling figurehead from an old ship supports the ceiling. The breakfast room looks out on the lively cobblestone street, while the subterranean sauna rooms, in whitewashed stone, provide a chance to take a dip in the building's original, medieval well. ⊠ *Storkyrkobrinken 5, 111 28,* ☎ *08/234680,* FAX *08/411–1148. 34 rooms with shower. Bar, no-smoking rooms, sauna, meeting rooms. AE, DC, MC, V.*

$$$$ ⊞ **Radisson SAS Strand.** This gracious, Old World hotel was built in 1912 but was modernized in 1983. No two rooms are the same, but all are furnished with antiques. The Piazza is an indoor restaurant with an outdoor feel to it; its specialty is Italian cuisine, and it has a superb wine list. An SAS check-in counter for business-class travelers adjoins the main reception area. ⊠ *Nybrokajen 9, 103 27,* ☎ *08/678–7800,* FAX *08/611–2436. 148 rooms with bath. Restaurant, no-smoking rooms, sauna, meeting rooms. AE, DC, MC, V.*

$$$$ ⊞ **Reisen.** This 17th-century building, on the waterfront in the Old Town, has been a hotel since 1819; it has a fine restaurant, a grill, tea and coffee service in the library, and possibly the best piano bar in town. The swimming pool was installed beneath surviving medieval arches in the structure's foundations. ⊠ *Skeppsbron 12–14, 111 30,* ☎ *08/223260,* FAX *08/201559. 114 rooms with bath. 2 restaurants, piano bar, no-smoking floor, indoor pool, sauna, library, meeting rooms. AE, DC, MC, V.*

$$$$ ⊞ **Scandic Crown.** A modern hotel with a panoramic view of the Old Town and City Hall, the Scandic Crown is on Stockholm's increasingly trendy south side. Two big draws on the property are the Couronne d'Or, a French eatery, and a cellar with wines for tasting, some dating from 1650. ⊠ *Guldgränd 8, 104 65* ☎ *08/702–2500,* FAX *08/642–8358. 264 rooms with bath. 2 restaurants, piano bar, no-smoking rooms, indoor pool, beauty salon, sauna, meeting rooms. AE, DC, MC, V.*

$$$$ 🏨 **Stockholm.** You can't get much closer to the center of Stockholm than in this modern yet traditionally furnished hotel, which occupies the sixth and seventh floors of an office building on one of the city's main squares. It's a clean, efficient lodging intended for those who want to spend their waking hours shopping, sightseeing, or on business. ⊠ *Norrmalmstorg 1, 111 46,* ☎ *08/678–1320,* 🖷 *08/611–2103. 92 rooms with shower or bath. No-smoking rooms, meeting room. AE, DC, MC, V.*

$$$ 🏨 **Birger Jarl.** A short bus ride from the city center, the Birger Jarl is a contemporary, conservative, thickly carpeted refuge for business travelers, catered conferences, and tourists requiring unfussy comforts. Breakfast is an extensive buffet just off the lobby, but room service is also available. Rooms are not large, but they are well furnished; there are heated towel racks in the bathrooms and bathtubs for all double rooms. Four family-style rooms have extra floor space and sofa beds. ⊠ *Tulegatan 8, 104 32,* ☎ *08/151020,* 🖷 *08/673–7366. 225 rooms with bath. Coffee shop (closed summer), no-smoking rooms, sauna, meeting rooms. AE, DC, MC, V.*

$$$ 🏨 **City.** A large, modern-style hotel built in the 1940s but completely rebuilt in 1984, the City is near the city center and Hötorget market. Since it's owned by the Salvation Army, no alcohol is served. Guests take breakfast in the Winter Garden atrium. ⊠ *Slöjdgatan 7, 111 81,* ☎ *08/723–7200,* 🖷 *08/723–7209. 293 rooms with bath. Restaurant, no-smoking rooms, sauna, meeting rooms. AE, DC, MC, V.*

$$$ 🏨 **Clas på Hörnet.** An 18th-century inn converted into a small hotel
★   in 1982, Clas på Hörnet is just outside the city center. Its rooms, furnished with antiques of the period, go quickly. If you can't reserve a night's lodging, at least have a meal in the excellent restaurant (☞ Dining, *above*). ⊠ *Surbrunnsgatan 20, 113 48,* ☎ *08/165130,* 🖷 *08/612– 5315. 10 rooms with bath. Restaurant. AE, DC, MC, V.*

$$$ 🏨 **Gamla Stan.** This quiet, cozy hotel is in one of Old Town's 17th-century houses. Each room is uniquely decorated. ⊠ *Lilla Nygatan 25, 111 28,* ☎ *08/244450,* 🖷 *08/216483. 51 rooms with shower. No-smoking floor, meeting rooms. AE, DC, MC, V.*

$$$ 🏨 **Prize.** This sleek hotel appeals to train lovers; the ultramodern rooms are as compactly efficient as train compartments. Some have no windows, but are fitted with backlit shoji screens to simulate daylight. The hotel occupies part of the World Trade Center, above one end of the Central Train Station, but a shock-absorbent base eliminates noise and vibrations from the trains below. Breakfast is available for SKr 55. ⊠ *Kungsbron 1, 111 22,* ☎ *08/149450,* 🖷 *08/149848. 158 rooms with shower. No-smoking rooms. AE, DC, MC, V.*

$$$ 🏨 **Tegnérlunden.** A quiet city park lies across from this modern hotel a 10-minute walk from the downtown hub of Sergelstorg, with the shops of Sveavägen along the way. Rooms, though small and sparely furnished, are clean and well maintained. The lobby is bright with marble, brass, and greenery, as is the sunny rooftop breakfast room. ⊠ *Tegnérlunden 8, 113 59,* ☎ *08/349780,* 🖷 *08/327818. 103 rooms with shower. No-smoking rooms, sauna, meeting room. AE, DC, MC, V.*

$$ 🏨 **Aldoria.** Clean, modern, and simply furnished, the Aldoria has a loyal clientele of business travelers and academics who appreciate the convenient location at Fridhemsplan. The hotel occupies two floors of an office building in a busy commercial neighborhood on Kungsholmen; rooms overlooking the courtyard are spared the street noise. ⊠ *St. Eriksgatan 38, 112 34,* ☎ *08/654–1885,* 🖷 *08/652–2963. 22 rooms with shower. No-smoking rooms. AE, DC, MC, V.*

$$ 🏨 **Alexandra.** In the Södermalm area, to the south of the Old Town, the Alexandra is only five minutes by subway from the city center. Small and modern, the hotel opened in the early 1970s. ⊠ *Magnus Ladulås-*

gatan 42, 118 27, ☎ 08/840320, FAX 08/720–5353. 75 rooms with bath. No-smoking rooms, sauna. AE, DC, MC, V.

$$ ⌂ **Arcadia.** On a hilltop near a large waterfront nature preserve, this converted dormitory is still within 15 minutes of downtown by bus or subway, or 30 minutes on foot along pleasant shopping streets. Rooms are furnished in a spare, neutral style, with plenty of natural light. The adjoining restaurant serves meals on the terrace in summer. ⌧ *Körsbärsvägen 1, 114 89, ☎ 08/160195, FAX 08/166224. 82 rooms with shower. Restaurant, no-smoking rooms, sauna, meeting rooms. AE, DC, MC, V.*

$$ ⌂ **August Strindberg.** A narrow, frescoed corridor leads from the street to the flagstone courtyard, into which the Strindberg's restaurant expands in summertime. New parquet flooring and high ceilings distinguish the rooms, which are otherwise plainly furnished. Kitchenettes are available to all guests; some rooms can be combined into family apartments. With four floors and no elevator, this may not be appropriate for older travelers, but there is one large room on the ground floor. ⌧ *Tegnérgatan 38, 113 59, ☎ 08/325006, FAX 08/209085. 19 rooms with shower. Restaurant, bar. AE, DC, MC, V.*

$$ ⌂ **Långholmen.** This former prison, built in 1724, was converted into a combination hotel and hostel in 1989. It sits on the island of Långholmen, which has popular beaches and a prison museum. The Inn, next door, serves Swedish home cooking, the Jail Pub offers light snacks, and a garden restaurant operates in the summertime. ⌧ *Långholmen, Box 9116, 102 72, ☎ 08/668–0500, FAX 08/720–8575. 101 rooms with shower. 3 restaurants, meeting room. AE, DC, MC, V.*

$$ ⌂ **Örnsköld.** Just behind the Royal Dramatic Theater in the heart of
★ the city, this hidden gem has the atmosphere of an old private club, with a brass-and-leather lobby and Victorian-style furniture in the moderately spacious, high-ceilinged rooms. Breakfast is served in the rooms; those over the courtyard are quieter, but those facing the street—not a busy one, in any case—are sunnier. The hotel is frequented by actors appearing at the Royal Theater. ⌧ *Nybrogatan 6, 114 34, ☎ 08/667–0285, FAX 08/667–6991. 30 rooms with shower. AE, MC, V.*

$ ⌂ **Gustav af Klint.** A "hotel ship" moored at Stadsgården quay, near Slussen subway station, the Gustav af Klint is divided into two sections—a hotel and a hostel. You can dine on deck in summer. Breakfast, at SKr 40, is not included in the hostel rates. ⌧ *Stadsgårdskajen 153, 116 45, ☎ 08/640–4077, FAX 08/640–6416. 14 cabins with showers; 80 hostel beds. Restaurant, cafeteria. AE, MC, V.*

The Arts

Stockholm's main theater and concert season runs from September through May or June, so there are not many major performances during the height of the tourist season. For a list of events, pick up the free monthly booklet "Stockholm This Week," available from hotels and tourist information offices. For tickets to theaters and shows try **Biljettdirekt** at Sweden House (☞ Visitor Information, *above*) or any post office.

Concerts

The city's main concert hall is the **Konserthuset** (⌧ Hötorget 8, ☎ 08/786–0200), home of the Stockholm Philharmonic Orchestra. The season runs from mid-September to mid-May. In addition to full-scale evening concerts, there are occasional lunchtime performances. In summer, many city parks have free concerts; listings appear in the "Events" section of "Stockholm This Week."

Opera

The season at the **Operan** (Royal Opera House; ☎ 08/248240), just across the bridge from the Royal Palace, runs from mid-August to early June and offers world-class performances. From May to early September, there are performances of opera, ballet, and orchestral music at the exquisite **Drottningholm Court Theater** (☎ 08/660–8225), which was the setting for Ingmar Bergman's film *The Magic Flute*. The original 18th-century stage machinery is still used in these productions. You can get to Drottningholm by subway and bus or by special theater-bus (leaving from the Grand Hotel or opposite the Central Train Station).

Theater

Stockholm has about 20 top-rank theaters—including **Dramaten,** the Royal Dramatic Theater with its great gilded statues at Nybroplan. If you feel you cannot follow a dramatic performance in Swedish, you might choose a musical instead; musicals are regularly staged at several city theaters. Productions by the English Theatre Company are occasionally staged at **Södra Teatern** (⊠ Mosebacketorg 1, ☎ 08/644–9900).

Film

English and American films predominate, and they are screened with the original soundtrack and Swedish subtitles. Programs are listed in the local evening newspapers, though movie titles are usually given in Swedish. Movie buffs should visit **Filmstaden Sergel** (⊠ Hötorget, ☎ 08/840500), where 18 cinemas under one roof show a variety of films from noon until midnight. Bear in mind that most, if not all, cinemas take reservations over the phone; it's best to make one or you may find a show sold out well ahead of time. Another item of cinematic interest is Stockholm's annual Film Festival, which takes place in early November and includes new and classic films from all over the world.

Nightlife

Cabaret

Stockholm's biggest nightclub, **Börsen** (⊠ Jakobsgatan 6, ☎ 08/787–8500), offers high-quality Swedish and international cabaret shows. Another popular spot is the **Cabaret Club** (⊠ Barnhusgatan 12, ☎ 08/411–0608); although it can accommodate 450 guests, reservations are advised.

Bars and Nightclubs

Café Opera (⊠ Operahuset, Gustav Adolfs Torg, ☎ 08/411–0026) is a popular meeting place for young and old alike; at the waterfront end of Kungsträgården, it has the longest bar in town, plus dining, roulette, and dancing after midnight. **Riche** (⊠ Birger Jarlsgatan 4, ☎ 08/611–8450) is another popular watering hole in the city center. Piano bars are also an important part of the Stockholm scene; try the **Anglais Bar** at the Hotel Anglais (⊠ Humlegårdsgatan 23, ☎ 08/614–1600). The **Clipper Club** at the Hotel Reisen, (⊠ Skeppsbron 12–14, ☎ 08/223260) is another good spot. Not to be forgotten is the renovated restaurant/bar **Berns' Salonger** (⊠ Berzelii Park 9, ☎ 08/614–0550); the Red Room, on the second floor, is where playwright August Strindberg once held court. **Sture Compagniet** (⊠ Sturegatan 4, ☎ 08/611–7800) is a popular club. **Café Victoria** (⊠ Kungsträdgården, ☎ 08/101085) draws club lovers as well.

Irish pubs are trendy among the happy-hour crowd. **Limerick** (⊠ Tegnérgatan 10, ☎ 08/673–4398) has the right atmosphere. **Dubliner** (⊠ Birger Jarlspassagen, ☎ 08/679–7707) attracts Irish beer lovers. **Bagpiper's Inn** (⊠ Rörstrandsgatan 21, ☎ 08/311855) is another current hit.

Jazz Clubs

Fasching (⊠ Kungsgatan 63, ☎ 08/216267) is Stockholm's largest, with a jazz lunch weekdays and soul music Saturday nights. Get to **Stampen** (⊠ Stora Nygatan 5, ☎ 08/205793) in good time if you want a seat, but call first to make sure it hasn't been reserved for a private party.

Dancing

Penny Lane (⊠ Birger Jarlsgatan 29, ☎ 08/201411) pulls in all ages with music from the seventies. **Downtown** (⊠ Norrlandsgatan 5A, ☎ 08/411–9488) is a popular spot in the middle of a shopping mall. **La Isla** (⊠ Fleminggatan 48, ☎ 08/654–6043), on Kungsholmen, offers salsa disco on weekends.

UPPSALA AND THE FOLKLORE DISTRICT

The Swedish region known as the "Folklore District"—essentially the provinces of Dalarna (sometimes called Darlecarlia in English) and Värmland—is easily accessible from Stockholm. It's the best place in which to see some of the country's enduring folk traditions. One popular option is to approach Dalarna through the ancient city of Uppsala, returning to Stockholm through the Bergslagen region, the heart of the centuries-old Swedish iron industry.

Getting Around

This route can be covered entirely by train; the ride from Stockholm to Uppsala takes only 50 minutes, and service is fairly frequent. For information on bus travel in the region, call Dalatrafik (☎ 020/232425). A car will give you the flexibility to explore some of the attractions not so easily accessible by public transportation; the drive, via the E4, is about 71 km (44 miles).

Guided Tours

Uppsala is compact enough to explore on foot, and guided sightseeing tours are available; you can book a tour in advance by calling the Guide Service (Uppsala Tourist Information office, ☎ 018/274818).

Visitor Information

Falun (⊠ Stora Torget, ☎ 023/83637); **Ludvika** (⊠ Fredsgatan 10, ☎ 0240/86050); **Mora** (⊠ Ångbåtskajen, ☎ 0250/26550); **Örebro** (⊠ Slottet, ☎ 019/212121); **Rättvik** (⊠ Torget, ☎ 0248/70200); **Uppsala** (⊠ Fyris Torg 8, ☎ 018/117500 and 018/274800; also at Uppsala Castle in summer).

Exploring Uppsala and the Folklore District

As the cradle of Swedish civilization, Uppsula is well worth exploring for a day or two. If you opt for a guided tour of the city you should first stop by **Gamla Uppsala** (Old Uppsala), which is dominated by three huge burial mounds dating from the 5th century AD. The first Swedish kings, Aun, Egil, and Adils, were all buried here. The church next to the burial mounds was the seat of Sweden's first archbishop, built on the site of a former pagan temple. At the adjacent Odinsborg restaurant you can sample local mead brewed from a 14th-century recipe. Check all prices and times listed below with the local tourist office, as they are subject to change.

★ In **Uppsala** itself, your first stop should be the enormous **cathedral**, whose twin towers dominate the city skyline. The cathedral has been the seat of the archbishop of the Swedish church for 700 years. Its present appearance owes much to major restoration work completed during the late 19th century. Make a point of visiting the **Cathedral Museum** in the north tower, where you can see one of Europe's finest collections of ecclesiastical textiles. ⊠ *Cathedral open daily 8–6.* ☎ *Museum: SKr 10.* ☉ *May–Aug., daily 9–5; Sept.–Apr., Sun. 12:30–3.*

Nearby, in a strategic position atop a hill, is **Uppsala Castle.** This impressive structure was built during the 1540s by King Gustav Vasa. Having broken his ties with the Vatican, the king was eager to show who was actually running the country; he even arranged to have the cannons aimed directly at the archbishop's palace. ☎ *SKr 35.* ☉ *mid-Apr.–mid-June, daily 11–3; mid-June–mid Aug., daily 10–5.*

Uppsala is also the site of Scandinavia's oldest university, founded in 1477. Be sure to visit one of its most venerable buildings, the **Gustavianum,** near the cathedral. Beneath its cupola is the anatomical theater, where public dissections of executed convicts were a popular 17th-century tourist attraction. ⊠ *Akademigatan 3,* ☎ *018/182500.* ☎ *SKr20.* ☉ *June–Aug. daily 11–3.*

One of Uppsala's most famous sons was Carl von Linné, known as **Linnaeus.** A professor of botany at the university during the 1740s, he developed the system of plant and animal classification still used today. You can visit the **gardens** he designed, as well as his former residence, now a **museum.** *Svartbäcksgatan 27,* ☎ *018/109490.* ☎ *Garden: SKr 10.* ☉ *May–Aug., daily 9–9; Sept., daily 9–7.* ☎ *Museum: SKr 10.* ☉ *June–Aug., Tue.–Sun. noon–4; May and Sept., weekends noon–4.*

From Uppsala, the train heads northwest through pleasant farming country into the province of Dalarna, passing through **Säter,** one of the best-preserved wooden villages in Sweden. The best nearby overnight option is Falun, Dalarna's capital. By car, take Route 72 from Uppsala to Route 70, then Route 60 to Falun, about 169 km (105 miles).

Falun is known for its huge hole in the ground, referred to as the **"Great Pit."** The hole has been there since 1687, when an abandoned copper mine collapsed. Other mines on the site are still being worked. You can take a guided tour (wear your boots) down into some of the old shafts and hear the gruesome story of 17th-century miner Fat Mats, whose body was perfectly preserved in brine for 40 years following a cave-in. A museum tells the story of the local mining industry. ☎ *Mine: SKr 55.* ☉ *May–Aug., daily 10–4:30; Sept.–mid-Nov. and Mar.–Apr., weekends 12:30–4:30.* ☎ *Museum: free with mine tour, or SKr 5.* ☉ *May–Aug., daily 10–4:30, Sept.–Apr., daily 12:30–4:30.*

★ Just outside Falun, at **Sundborn,** is the former home of Swedish artist Carl Larsson. Here, in an idyllic lakeside setting, you can see a selection of his paintings, which owe much to local folk-art traditions. His great-grandchildren still use the house on occasion. ☎ *SKr 55.* ☉ *May–Sept., daily 10–5; Oct.–Apr. Tues. at 11; guided tours only, in groups of 15 every 10 minutes (may be a wait in summer).*

The real center of Dalarna folklore is the area around **Lake Siljan,** by far the largest of the 6,000 lakes in the province. By car, take Route 80 from Falun to Route 70, and begin your tour either at the attractive lakeside village of **Tällberg,** in the south, or at **Mora,** toward the north end of the lake. In the neighboring village of **Rättvik,** hundreds of people wearing traditional costumes arrive in longboats to attend Midsummer church services. Mora itself is best known as the home of

★ the artist **Anders Zorn.** His **house** and a **museum** exhibiting his paintings are open to the public. ⊠ *Vasagatan 36,* ☎ *0250/16560.* ☎ *Mu-*

Uppsala and the Folklore District

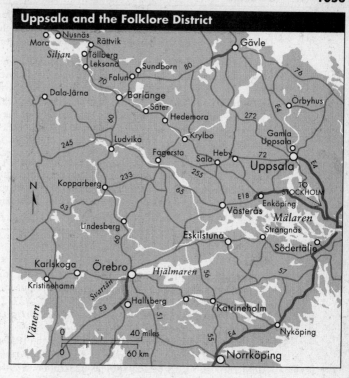

seum: SKr 25. ☉ May 15–Sept.15, Mon.–Sat. 9–5, Sun. 11–5; Sept. 16–May 14, Mon.–Sat. 10–5, Sun. 1–5. ⌂ House: SKr 30, guided tours only. ☉ May 15–Sept. 15, Mon.–Sat. 10–4, Sun. 11–4; Sept. 16–May 14, Mon.–Sat. 12:30–4, Sun. 1–4.

Near Mora is the village of **Nusnäs.** Here you can visit two of the biggest workshops producing the famous, brightly colored Dalarna wooden horses, known as **Dalahäst.**

Heading south again (by car, take Route 70 to Route 60, about 143 km/89 mi), you'll come to **Ludvika,** an important center of the old Bergslagen mining region, stretching from the forests of Värmland in the west to the coastal gorges in the east. Ludvika has a notable open-air mining museum, the **Gammelgården.** Check times and prices with the Ludvika tourist office. There is also a **Railway Engine Museum** that showcases three steam turbine–driven engines once used to pull trains filled with iron ore, the only ones of their kind in the world. ⌂ SKr 20. ☉ June 1–Sept. 3, daily 10–6.

Another local attraction is **Luosa Cottage.** The poet Dan Andersson lived here in the early part of the century, in order to experience the rigorous life of the local charcoal burners. Music and poetry festivals are held in Andersson's memory in nearby towns; check with the Ludvika tourist office. ⌂ Cottage: SKr 20. ☉ mid-May–Aug., daily 11–5.

Continuing south from Ludvika, about 119 km (74 miles) via Route 60, you'll come to **Örebro,** a sizable town at the western edge of **Lake Hjälmaren.** The lake is linked to Lake Mälaren and the sea by the Hjälmare Canal. Örebro received its charter in the 13th century and developed as a trading center for the farmers and miners of the Bergslagen region. Rising from a small island in the Svartån River, right in the center of town, is an imposing **castle,** parts of which date from the 13th century. The castle is now the residence of the regional governor. Guided tours run from mid-June to the end of August; check with the Örebro tourist office for details. There's an excellent restaurant inside.

To get a feel for the Örebro of bygone days, wander around the **Wadköping** district, where a number of old houses and crafts workshops have been painstakingly preserved. At the north end of town is the **Svampen** (Mushroom), a 193-foot-tall water tower. If you take the elevator to the top, you can enjoy a magnificent view of the surrounding countryside. There is also a cafeteria and a tourist office. ☉ *Tower: Apr. 30–May 31, daily 10–10; June 1–Sept. 4, daily 10–8.*

Direct train service from Örebro back to Stockholm operates at two-hour intervals, and the journey takes just under three hours. You can also take the hourly train to Hallsberg and change there to the frequent Gothenburg–Stockholm service. By car, it's about 196 km (122 miles) via the E18 and E20.

Dining and Lodging

Falun

$$$ 🍴 **Bergmästaren.** In the town center, this is a small, cozy hotel built in traditional Dalarna style and filled with antique furnishings. ✉ *Bergskolegränd 7, 791 26,* ☎ *023/63600,* FAX *023/22524. 88 rooms, most with bath. Restaurant, no-smoking rooms, hot tub, sauna, meeting room. AE, DC, MC, V.*

$$ 🍴 **Hotel Falun.** This medium-size hotel built in the 1950s is in the center of town. The front desk closes at 9 PM. ✉ *Centrumhuset, Trotzgatan 16, 791 71,* ☎ *023/29180,* FAX *023/13006. 27 rooms, 17 with shower. No-smoking rooms, meeting rooms. AE, DC, MC, V.*

Ludvika

$$$ 🍴 **Grand.** A medium-size, modern-style hotel, the Grand enjoys a central location. ✉ *Eriksgatan 6, 771 31,* ☎ *0240/18220,* FAX *0240/611018. 102 rooms with bath. Restaurant, no-smoking rooms, sauna, nightclub, meeting rooms. AE, DC, MC, V.*

$ 🍴 **Rex.** The Rex is a basic, modern hotel near the city center. It was built in 1960. Its restaurant serves breakfast only. ✉ *Engelbrektsgatan 9, 771 30,* ☎ *0240/13690. 28 rooms, 15 with shower. Breakfast room. AE, DC, MC, V. Closed 1 wk in summer.*

Mora

$$ 🍴 **Siljan.** Taking its name from the nearby lake, the Siljan is a popu-
★ lar, small but up-to-date hotel. ✉ *Moragatan 6, 792 01,* ☎ *0250/13000,* FAX *0250/13098. 43 rooms with shower, 2 with WC only. Restaurant, bar, no-smoking floor, sauna, exercise room, nightclub, meeting room. AE, DC, MC, V.*

Örebro

$$$ ✕🍴 **Scandic Grand.** In the heart of town, the Grand is the city's largest hotel. It was built in 1985 and offers all the modern comforts. ✉ *Fabriksgatan 23, 700 08,* ☎ *019/150200,* FAX *019/185814. 219 rooms with shower. 2 restaurants, no-smoking rooms, sauna, meeting rooms. AE, DC, MC, V.*

$$$ ✕🍴 **Stora Hotellet.** Across the street from the castle on the Svartån River, this Best Western hotel is one of the oldest in Sweden, dating from 1858. It has a cozy 13th-century cellar restaurant, the Slottskällaren, and an English pub, the Bishop's Arms. ✉ *Drottninggatan 1, 701 45,* ☎ *019/124360,* FAX *019/611–7890. 103 rooms with bath or shower. Restaurant, pub, no-smoking rooms, sauna, meeting rooms. AE, DC, MC, V.*

Tällberg

$$
★ 🏨 **Åkerblads.** Near the shores of Lake Siljan, the Åkerblads offers a genuine experience of rural Sweden. Occupying a typical Dalarna farmstead, parts of which date from the 16th century, it is run by the 19th generation of the Åkerblad family. A hotel since 1910, it was modernized in 1987. ✉ Sjögatu, 793 70, ☎ 0247/50800, FAX 0247/50652. 58 rooms with bath, 6 rooms with shared WC/shower. Restaurant, pub, no-smoking rooms, sauna, meeting rooms. AE, DC, MC, V.

Uppsala

$$$
★ ✕ **Domtrappkällaren.** One of the city's most popular restaurants, Domtrappkällaren is in a 14th-century cellar near the cathedral. The menu includes both French and Swedish fare. ✉ St. Eriksgränd 15, ☎ 018/130955, FAX 018/101740. Reservations essential. AE, DC, MC, V.

$$$$ 🏨 **Gillet.** Now operated by the Sweden Hotels group, this centrally located, medium-size hotel was opened in 1971 and renovated most recently in 1994. ✉ Dragarbrunnsgatan 23, 751 42, ☎ 018/155360, FAX 018/153380. 170 rooms with bath. Restaurant, brasserie, no-smoking rooms, indoor pool, sauna, meeting rooms. AE, DC, MC, V.

$$ 🏨 **Grand Hotel Hörnan.** An Old World, medium-size hotel opened in 1906, the Grand Hotel Hörnan is in the city center near the train station, with a view of the castle and the cathedral. ✉ Bangårdsgatan 1, 753 20, ☎ 018/139380, FAX 018/120311. 37 rooms with shower. No-smoking rooms, meeting room. AE, DC, MC, V. Closed July.

THE WEST COAST AND THE GLASS COUNTRY

Gothenburg is the point of entry for many visitors traveling to Sweden by ferry. If somehow you landed first in Stockholm, consider scheduling a side trip to this great shipping city and Sweden's scenic western coast. One option is to combine a western visit with a trip through the Glass Country to the medieval fortress town of Kalmar, on the east coast.

Getting Around

This route can be followed by either car or train. By car, it's 478 km (297 miles), following the E20 all the way. Regular trains for Gothenburg depart from Stockholm's Central Train Station about every hour, and normal travel time is about 4½ hours. There are also daily high-speed trains (the X2000) between the two cities, which take only about three hours, but these require a supplementary fare. First-class seats on the X2000 include breakfast, lunch or dinner, depending on departure time. Seat reservations are compulsory on all trains to Gothenburg. There are also hourly flights to Gothenburg from Stockholm's Arlanda Airport between 7 AM and 10 PM on weekdays, slightly fewer on weekends. The trip by air takes 55 minutes.

As for getting around the city of Gothenburg itself, the best option is the **Göteborgskortet** (Key to Gothenburg card), similar to one available in Stockholm. It provides free travel on all public transportation, free parking, and free admission to the Liseberg amusement park and all city museums. Prices for the card are SKr 120 for one day, SKr 200 for two days, and SKr 250 for three days. Cards for children under 18 are SKr 60 for one day, SKr 100 for two days, and SKr 140 for three days.

Guided Tours

In summer, sightseeing tours of Gothenburg leave regularly from the city tourist office on Kungsportsplatsen (reserve tickets at the office in advance). Tour boats run frequently in summer (☞ Exploring the West Coast and the Glass Country, *below*).

Visitor Information

Gothenburg (⊠ Kungsportsplatsen 2, ☎ 031/100740); **Jönköping** (⊠ Djurläkartorget, ☎ 036/105050); **Kalmar** (⊠ Larmgatan 6, ☎ 0480/15350); **Malmö** (⊠ Central Station, Skeppsbron, ☎ 040/300150); **Växjö** (⊠ Kronobergsgatan 8, ☎ 0470/41410).

Exploring the West Coast and the Glass Country

Vacationers traveling by car often drive straight through **Göteborg** (Gothenburg) in their eagerness to reach the coast. But this attractive harbor city is well worth a stop. A quayside jungle of cranes and warehouses attests to the city's industrial might, yet within a 10-minute walk of the waterfront is an elegant, modern city of broad avenues, green parks, and gardens. Most major attractions are within walking distance of one another, and there is an excellent streetcar network. In summer, you can take a sightseeing tour on a vintage open-air streetcar.

British merchants were largely responsible for the development of Gothenburg in the 19th century, when it acquired the nickname "Little London." A more accurate name would have been "Little Amsterdam," for the city was in fact laid out in the 17th century by Dutch architects, who gave it its extensive network of straight streets divided by canals. Only one major canal survives, but you can explore it on one of the popular sightseeing boats. The Swedes fondly refer to these boats, built short and squat so that they can pass under the city's 20 low bridges, as *paddan* ("toads"). Passengers embark for the one-hour tour at the **Paddan terminal** at Kungsportsplatsen. ⌑ *Fare: SKr 60.* ☉ *Departures: late Apr.–late June and mid-Aug.–early Sept., daily 10–5; late June–mid-Aug., daily 10–9; early Sept.–Oct. 1, daily 12–3; closed Oct.–Apr.*

★ The hub of Gothenburg is **Kungsportsavenyn,** commonly called simply Avenyn ("the Avenue"). It is a broad, tree-lined boulevard flanked with elegant shops, restaurants, and sidewalk cafés, and has a distinctly Parisian air, especially in summer. The Avenue ends at **Götaplatsen,** around which are grouped the municipal theater, concert hall, art museum, and library. (The library has an excellent selection of English-language newspapers.) Just off the Avenue is **Trädgårdsföreningen** (The Garden Association), an attractive park with a magnificent Palm House, built in 1878 and recently restored, and a Butterfly House (☎ 031/611911) containing 40 different species. ⌑ *Park: SKr 10; Palm House and Butterfly House: SKr 25 each.* ☉ *Apr., Tue.–Sun. 10–4; May and Sept., daily 10–4; June–Aug., daily 10–5; Oct.–Mar., Tue.–Sun. 10–3.*

If you're interested in shopping, the best place to go is **Nordstan,** a covered complex of shops near the train station. Many of its businesses participate in the tax-free shopping service.

The new **Maritime Center** (⊠ Packhuskajen 8, ☎ 031/101035), at the harbor near the Nordstan shopping complex, provides a chance to explore a number of historic vessels, among them a destroyer, a lightship, a trawler, and several tugboats. ⌑ *SKr 35.* ☉ *Mar.–Apr. and Sept.–Nov., daily 10–4; May–June, daily 10–6; July–Aug., daily 10–9.*

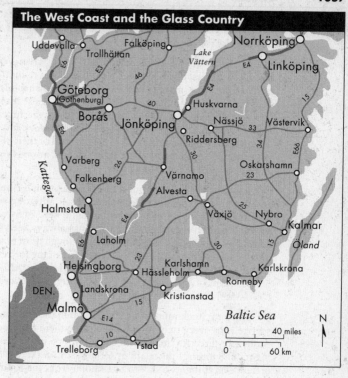

The West Coast and the Glass Country

Uddevalla · Falköping · Norrköping
Trollhättan · Lake Vättern · Linköping
Göteborg (Gothenburg)
Borås · Jönköping · Huskvarna
Nässjö · Västervik
Riddersberg
Varberg · Värnamo · Oskarshamn
Falkenberg · Alvesta
Kattegat · Halmstad · Växjö · Nybro · Kalmar
Öland
Laholm
Helsingborg · Karlshamn · Karlskrona
Hässleholm · Ronneby
DEN. · Landskrona · Kristianstad
Malmö
Baltic Sea · N
E14
Trelleborg · Ystad · 40 miles · 60 km

To reach Jönköping, the next stop on the journey, take the train from Gothenburg's Central Train Station and change at Falköping, or follow Route 40 by car, about 149 km (93 miles).

Jönköping is an attractive town on the southern shore of **Lake Vättern,** Sweden's second-largest lake. The town is distinguished not only by its age—it celebrated the 700th anniversary of its founding in 1984— but also by its history as the birthplace of the match-manufacturing industry, established here in the 19th century. The **Tändsticksmuseet** (Matchstick Museum), built on the site of the first factory, has exhibits on the development and manufacture of matches. ☎ *036/105543.* ✉ *SKr 25.* ☉ *June–Aug., Mon.–Fri. 10–5, weekends 10–3; Sept–May, Tues.–Thurs. 12–4, weekends 11–3.*

To the southeast of Jönköping, 120 km (75 miles) via E4 and Route 27, lies **Växjö,** the chief town in Kronoberg County and the best place from which to explore Sweden's Glass Country. Some 10,000 Americans visit Växjö each year, drawn here by a desire to see the area from which their ancestors emigrated during the last century. The **Emigrants' House** (☎ 0470/20120), in the town center, tells the story of the migration period, when close to a million Swedes—a fourth of the entire population—set sail for the promised land across the sea. The museum's exhibits detail the rigors of their journey, and those of Swedish descent can research their ancestry in an archive and research center. On the second Sunday in August, Växjö celebrates "Minnesota Day." Swedes and Swedish-Americans come together to commemorate their common heritage with American-style square dancing and other festivities.

Many of Sweden's most famous glassworks are within easy reach of Växjö. There is no regular local bus service around the area, however, so touring by car is most convenient—especially if you plan to take advantage of the deep discounts on seconds at the factory shops. Otherwise you can usually find an organized tour of the facilities through the tourist office.

Swedish glass manufacture dates from 1556, when Venetian glass-blowers were first invited to the Swedish court—yet another 200 years passed before glassmaking became a major Swedish industry. The area between Växjö and Kalmar was chosen for its dense forest, which offered an unlimited supply of wood for firing the furnaces. All the

★ major Swedish glass companies, including **Orrefors** and **Kosta Boda**, still do their manufacturing in this area, and all of their plants are open to the public. ☉ *weekdays 9–6, Sat. 9–3, Sun. noon–4 (no glass manufacturing on weekends in winter).*

Driving east 109 km (68 miles) on route 25, you'll come to **Kalmar,**

★ an attractive coastal town dominated by an imposing seaside **castle.** The town was once known as the "lock and key" of Sweden: Situated on the kingdom's southern frontier, it has always been subject to attacks. The castle dates back 800 years, although most of what one sees today reflects King Gustav Vasa's rebuilding of the fortress in the 16th century. 🎫 *SKr 40.* ☉ *June 15–Aug. 15, Mon.–Sat. 10–6, Sun. 12–6; Apr.–June 14 and Aug. 16–Oct., weekdays 10–4, weekends 12–4; Nov.–Mar., Sun. 1–3.*

To return to Stockholm from Kalmar, catch the train to Alvesta (the service runs every two hours) and change there for Stockholm. Two trains run direct to Stockholm each day, one in the daytime, one at night. The journey takes about 6½ hours. **SAS** (☎ 020/727000) operates several flights a day to Stockholm from the Kalmar airport, 5 kilometers (3 miles) from the town center. The trip takes about 45 minutes. By car, take the E22 to the E4; it's about 408 km (254 miles) to Stockholm.

Dining and Lodging

Gothenburg

$$$$ ✕ **Sjömagasinet.** In a renovated 200-year-old shipping warehouse,
★ this waterfront restaurant has a view of the harbor and the suspension bridge; in summer an outdoor terrace provides even better views. The regular menu features seafood, and there's a less expensive prix-fixe menu as well. ⊠ *Klippanskulturreservat,* ☎ *031/246510,* 🆖 *031/245539. Reservations essential. AE, DC, MC, V.*

$$$ ✕ **Åtta Glas.** A casual, lively restaurant in what was formerly a barge, Åtta Glas offers excellent views of the river and of the Kungsportsbron, a bridge spanning the canal in the center of town. The two standard specials—ox fillet and grilled salmon—are the best deals at SKr 69, and a children's menu, which includes ice cream, is popular with families. The second floor houses a bar, which draws a younger crowd on weekends. ⊠ *Kungsportsbron,* ☎ *031/136015,* 🆖 *031/711–2124. AE, DC, MC, V.*

$$$ ✕ **Räkan.** A popular, informal restaurant, Räkan makes the most of an
★ unusual gimmick. The tables are arranged around a long tank, and if you order shrimp, the house specialty, they arrive at your table in radio-controlled boats you navigate yourself. Less expensive prix-fixe menus are available. ⊠ *Lorensbergsgatan 16,* ☎ *031/169839,* 🆖 *031/186418. Reservations essential. AE, DC, MC, V. No lunch weekends.*

$$ ✕ **Weise.** A centrally located restaurant with a German beer-cellar atmosphere, Weise was once a haunt of local painters and intellectuals and retains an old, bohemian ambience: The tables and chairs date from 1892. The traditional Swedish menu includes such dishes as pork and brown beans. ✉ *Linnégatan 54,* ☎ *031/131402. AE, DC, MC, V.*

$$$$ 🏨 **Sheraton Hotel and Towers.** Opened in 1986, the Sheraton Hotel
★ and Towers is Gothenburg's most modern and spectacular international-style hotel. It wraps around an atrium lobby and a restaurant renovated in 1995. Guests receive a 20% discount at the well-appointed health club on the premises. ✉ *Södra Hamngatan 59–65, 401 24,* ☎ *031/806000,* FAX *031/159888. 344 rooms with bath. Restaurant, bar, no-smoking rooms, beauty salon, convention center, travel services. AE, DC, MC, V.*

$$$ 🏨 **Eggers.** Dating from 1859, the Best Western Eggers has more Old
★ World character than other hotel in the city. It is near the train station and is doubtless where many emigrants to the United States spent their last night in Sweden. Most rooms are furnished with antiques. ✉ *Drottningtorget, 401 25,* ☎ *031/806070,* FAX *031/154243. 67 rooms with bath. No-smoking rooms, meeting rooms. AE, DC, MC, V.*

$$$ 🏨 **Liseberg Heden.** Not far from the famous Liseberg amusement park, the Liseberg Heden is a popular, modern, family hotel. ✉ *Sten Sture-gatan, 411 38,* ☎ *031/200280,* FAX *031/165283. 159 rooms with bath. Restaurant, no-smoking rooms, sauna, meeting rooms. AE, DC, MC, V.*

Jönköping

$$ ✕ **Mäster Gudmunds Källare.** This particularly inviting restaurant is
★ cozily nestled beneath the vaults of a 16th-century cellar and is only two minutes from the train station. The cuisine is international. ✉ *Kapell-gatan 2,* ☎ *036/100640. AE, DC, MC, V.*

$$$ 🏨 **John Bauer Hotel.** This modern, family-run Best Western in the center of town overlooks Munksjön. It was named for a local artist famous for his fairy-tale depictions of trolls and mystical landscapes. ✉ *Södra Strandgatan 15, 550 02,* ☎ *036/100500,* FAX *038/712788. 100 rooms with shower or bath. Restaurant, bar, no-smoking rooms, sauna, billiards, meeting room. AE, DC, MC, V.*

$$$ 🏨 **Stora Hotellet.** Stora Hotellet is an old-fashioned establishment opened in 1861 and most recently renovated in 1995. ✉ *Hotellplan, 551 12,* ☎ *036/100000,* FAX *036/719320. 114 rooms with shower or bath. 3 restaurants, bar, no-smoking rooms, sauna, meeting rooms. AE, DC, MC, V.*

Kalmar

$$$$ 🏨 **Slottshotellet.** Occupying a gracious old house on a quiet street, Slottshotellet faces a waterfront park and is a few minutes' walk from both the train station and Kalmar Castle. Inside, you'll find a host of modern facilities wrapped in a 19th-century atmosphere. Only breakfast is served except in summer, when full restaurant service is offered on the terrace. ✉ *Slottsvägen 7, 392 33,* ☎ *0480/88260,* FAX *0480/88266. 36 rooms with shower. Restaurant, bar, no-smoking rooms, sauna, meeting room. AE, DC, MC, V.*

$$$ 🏨 **Stadshotellet.** This Best Western in the city center is a large, Old World hotel. The main building dates from 1907. ✉ *Stortorget 14, 392 32,* ☎ *0480/15180,* FAX *0480/15847. 139 rooms with bath or shower. Restaurant, bar, no-smoking rooms, sauna, meeting rooms. AE, DC, MC, V.*

Växjö

$$$ 🏨 **Statt.** A conveniently located, traditional hotel, this Best Western is popular with tour groups. The building dates from 1853, but the

rooms themselves are modern, and the hotel has a cozy Irish pub and two restaurants. ⊠ *Kungsgatan 6, 352 33,* ☎ *0470/13400,* FAX *0470/44837. 124 rooms with bath or shower. Restaurant, pub, sauna, meeting rooms. AE, DC, MC, V.*

$ 🖭 **Esplanad.** This small, central, family hotel offers the basic amenities. ⊠ *Norra Esplanaden 21A, 352 31,* ☎ *0470/22580,* FAX *0470/26226. 27 rooms, most with shower. No-smoking rooms. MC, V.*

28 Switzerland

Zürich

Geneva

Luzern

Lugano

Bern

Zermatt

THE SWISS KEEP THEIR COZINESS under strict control: An electric eye beams open a sliding glass door into a room lined with carved wood, copper, and old-fashioned rafters. That is the paradox of the Swiss, whose primary decorative impulses pitch high-tech urban efficiency against rustic Alpine comfort. Fiercely devout, rigorously clean, prompt as their world-renowned watches, the Swiss are a people who drink their eau-de-vie in firelit *Stübli* (cozy little pubs)—but rarely on Sunday. Liquors here are measured with scientific precision into glasses marked for one or two centiliters, and the local wines come in graduated carafes reminiscent of laboratory beakers. And as for passion—well, the "double" beds have separate mattresses and sheets tucked firmly down the middle. (Foreigners with more lusty Latin tastes may request a French—that is, a standard—double bed.) Politically isolated, culturally self-contained, Switzerland remains economically aloof . . . even Europhobic. As their neighbors pull their wagons in a circle, sweeping away borders so as to present a unified front to the world, the Swiss continue to choose their apples from bins marked *Inländ* (domestic), leaving the *Ausländ,* or imported, varieties to rot humbly beside them. Yet Switzerland itself is many different countries. Not far from the hum of commerce in the streets of Zürich you can listen to the tinkle of cowbells on the slopes of the Klewenalp. While befurred and bejeweled socialites shop in Geneva, the women of Appenzell, across the country, stand beside their husbands on the Landsgemeinde-Platz, raising their hands to vote—a right they won only in 1990.

Switzerland combines most of the attractions of its larger European neighbors—Alpine grandeur, urban sophistication, ancient villages, exhilarating ski slopes, and all-around artistic excellence. It's the heartland of the Reformation, the homeland of William Tell; its cities are full of historic landmarks, its countryside strewn with castles. Its varied cuisine reflects French, Italian, and German influences.

All these assets have made Switzerland a major tourist destination, and the Swiss are delighted to pave the way. A welcoming if reserved people, many of them well versed in English, they have earned their age-old reputation for hospitality. Their hotels and inns are famous for cleanliness and efficiency, and the notorious prices—rivaling the highest in the world—are somewhat offset by the knowledge that what you're paying is an accurate reflection of what you're getting.

ESSENTIAL INFORMATION

Before You Go

When to Go

Switzerland attracts visitors year-round. Winter sports begin around Christmas and usually last until mid-April, depending on snow conditions. The countryside is a delight in spring, when wildflowers are in bloom, and foliage colors in fall rival those in New England. In the Ticino, or the Italian-speaking region, and around Lake Geneva (Lac Léman), summer stays late: There is often sparkling weather in September and October, and popular resorts are less crowded. But beware: in November, as in May, resorts throughout the country may close up altogether. Always check with the local tourist office.

Switzerland

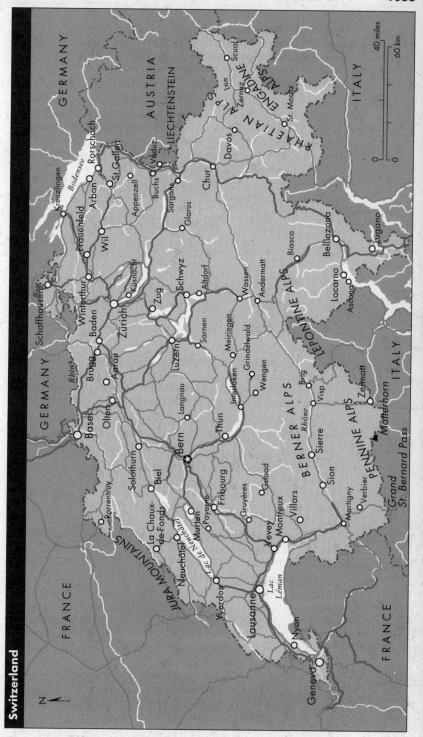

CLIMATE

Summer in Switzerland is generally warm and sunny, though the higher you go, the cooler it gets, especially at night. Winter is cold everywhere: In low-lying areas the weather is frequently damp and overcast; in the Alps, days are brilliantly clear but invariably cold and snowy—especially above 4,600 feet.

Summer and winter, some areas of Switzerland are subject to an Alpine wind that blows from the south and is known as the *Föhn*. It brings with it clear but somewhat oppressive weather, which the Swiss claim causes headaches. The only exception to these more general weather patterns is the Ticino; protected by the Alps, it has a positively Mediterranean climate—even in winter.

The following are the average daily maximum and minimum temperatures for Zürich.

Jan.	36F	2C	May	67F	19C	Sept.	69F	20C
	26	− 3		47	8		51	11
Feb.	41F	5C	June	73F	23C	Oct.	57F	14C
	28	− 2		53	12		43	6
Mar.	51F	11C	July	76F	25C	Nov.	45F	7C
	34	1		56	14		35	2
Apr.	59F	15C	Aug.	75F	24C	Dec.	37F	3C
	40	− 4		56	14		29	− 2

Currency

The unit of currency is the Swiss franc (SF), divided into 100 rappen (known as centimes in French-speaking areas). There are coins of 5, 10, 20, and 50 rappen and of 1, 2, and 5 francs. Bills come in denominations of 10, 20, 50, 100, 500, and 1,000 francs.

At press time (spring 1996), the Swiss franc stood at 1.15 to the U.S. dollar, 1.20 to the Canadian dollar, and 1.68 to the pound sterling.

All banks change money, though many impose a minimum and a slight fee. Traveler's checks get a better exchange rate, as do cash advances against major credit cards. Main airports and train stations have exchange offices (bureaux de change) that are open longer hours than banks and often offer equally good rates of exchange. Most hotels and some restaurants will also change money, but usually at a far less favorable rate. Most major credit cards are generally, though not universally, accepted at hotels, restaurants, and shops. Travelers checks are almost never accepted outside banks.

What It Will Cost

A high standard of living means that Switzerland is generally expensive: If it's luxury you're after, you'll pay more for it here than in almost any other European country. Though annual inflation has been less than 2% for years, the Swiss currency has gained appreciably against the U.S. dollar, resulting in price increases of up to 25%. You'll find plenty of reasonably priced hotels and restaurants, however, if you look for them.

As in any other European country, cities are more expensive than the smaller towns. Zürich and Geneva are the priciest, followed by Basel, Bern, and Lugano. Holiday resorts—especially the better-known Alpine ski centers—rival the cities for high prices. Elsewhere, prices drop appreciably, particularly off the beaten track and in the northeast.

Cup of coffee, 3 SF; bottle of beer, 3.50 SF; soft drink, 3.50 SF; sausage and *Rösti* (hash-brown potatoes), 16 SF; 1-mile taxi ride, 12 SF (more in Geneva, Lugano, or Zürich).

Customs on Arrival

There are two levels of duty-free allowance for visitors to Switzerland. Residents of non-European countries may import 400 cigarettes or 100 cigars or 500 grams of tobacco, plus 2 liters of alcoholic beverage below 15% and 1 liter of alcoholic beverage in excess of 15%. Residents of European countries may import 200 cigarettes or 50 cigars or 250 grams of tobacco, plus 2 liters of alcoholic beverage below 15% and 1 liter of alcoholic beverage in excess of 15%. These allowances apply only to those age 17 and above.

There are no restrictions on the import or export of any currency.

Language

French is spoken in the southwest, around Lake Geneva, and in the cantons of Fribourg, Neuchâtel, Jura, Vaud, and the western portion of Valais; Italian is spoken in the Ticino, and German is spoken everywhere else—in more than 70% of the country, in fact. The Romance language called Romansh has regained a firm foothold throughout the Upper and Lower Engadine regions of the canton Graubünden, where it takes the form of five different dialects. English, however, is spoken widely. Many signs are in English as well as in the regional language, and all hotels, restaurants, tourist offices, train stations, banks, and shops have at least a few English-speaking employees.

Getting Around

By Plane

Swissair connects the cities of Zürich, Basel, and Geneva. The airline's in-house tour operator, **Swisspack,** arranges flexible packages (✉ 106 Calvert St., Hamson, NY 10528, ☎ 800/688–7947) for the independent traveler who flies at least one way between North America and Europe on Swissair or Delta. "The Swiss Travel Invention" allows visitors to tailor-fit their Swiss holiday to include hotels, car rentals, rail vacations, and guided tours at great savings. **Crossair** is Switzerland's domestic airline, flying between local airports and bringing in visitors from various Continental cities as well, including Rome, Barcelona, Berlin, Amsterdam, and London.

By Car

ROAD CONDITIONS

Swiss roads are usually well surfaced but wind about considerably—especially in the mountains. Don't plan to achieve high average speeds. When estimating likely travel times, look carefully at the map: There may be only 32.3 kilometers (20 miles) between one point and another, but there could also be a mountain pass along the way. There is a well-developed highway network, though some notable gaps still exist in the south along an east–west line, roughly between Lugano and Sion. Under some mountain passes, there are tunnels through which cars are transported by train while passengers remain inside—an experience not unlike riding through the world's longest car wash.

A combination of steep or winding routes and hazardous weather conditions may close some roads during the winter, especially over mountain passes. Dial 120 or 163 for bulletins and advance information on road conditions.

Driving is on the right. In built-up areas, the speed limit is 50 kph (30 mph), and on main highways, it's 120 kph (75 mph). On other roads outside built-up areas, the limit is 80 kph (50 mph). Fines for speeding are exorbitant and foreigners are required to pay on the spot—in cash.

Children under 12 are not permitted to sit in the front seat. Driving with parking lights is prohibited, and the use of headlights is mandatory during heavy rain and in road tunnels.

To use the main highways, you must display a disk or *vignette,* which you can buy for 40 SF from Switzerland Tourism before you leave home or at the border stations when you enter the country. Cars rented within Switzerland already have these disks.

Traffic going up a mountain has priority, except for postal buses coming down. Signs showing a yellow post horn against a blue background indicate that postal buses have right-of-way.

During the winter, snow chains are advisable—sometimes mandatory. They can be rented in all areas, and snow-chain service stations have signs reading SERVICE DE CHAÎNES À NEIGE or SCHNEEKETTENDIENST.

PARKING

Parking areas are clearly marked. Parking in public lots normally costs about 1 SF per hour.

GASOLINE

Sans plomb or *bleifrei* (lead-free) gas costs 1.14 SF per liter, and super costs 1.30 per liter. Leaded regular is no longer available.

BREAKDOWNS

Assistance is available through the telephone exchange: Ask for *Autohilfe.* The Touring Club Suisse has a 24-hour breakdown service. Useful organizations are the **Automobile Club de Suisse** (⊠ ACS, Wasserwerkegasse 39, Bern, ☎ 022/342–2233) and the **Touring Club Suisse** (⊠ TCS, 9 rue Pierre Fatio, Geneva, ☎ 022/737–1212), both of which have branches throughout Switzerland.

By Train

Swiss trains are swift (except through the mountains), immaculate, and unnervingly punctual. Don't linger between international connections: The Swiss don't wait for languorous travelers. If you plan to use the trains extensively, get a comprehensive timetable (*Offizieles Kursbuch* or *Horaire*), which costs 20 SF, or a portable, pocket version called the *Fribo* for 10.80 SF. A useful booklet "Switzerland by Train," available from Switzerland Tourism, describes passes, itineraries, and discounts available to rail travelers. Apply for tickets through your travel agent or **Rail Europe** (☎ 800/438–7245).

Trains described as Inter-City or Express are the fastest, stopping only at principal towns. A *Regionalzug* is a local train, often affording the most spectacular views. Meals, snacks, and drinks are provided on most main services. Seat reservations are useful during rush hours and high season, especially on international trains and in second class.

FARES

There are numerous concessions for visitors. The **Swiss Pass** is the best value, offering unlimited travel on Swiss Federal Railways, postal buses, lake steamers, and the local bus and tram services of 30 cities. It also gives reductions on many privately owned railways, cable cars, and funiculars. Available from Switzerland Tourism and from travel agents outside Switzerland, the card is valid for four days (210 SF second class, 316 SF first class), eight days (264 SF second class, 378 SF first class), 15 days (306 SF second class, 442 SF first class), or one month (420 SF second class, 610 SF first class). There is also a new three-day **Flexi Pass** (210 SF second class, 316 SF first class), which offers the same unlimited travel options as a regular Swiss Pass for any three days within a 15-day period.

Within some popular tourist areas, **Regional Holiday Season Tickets**, issued for 15 days, give five days of free travel by train, postal buses, steamers, and mountain railways, with half fare for the rest of the validity of the card. Central Switzerland offers a similar pass for seven days, with two days of free travel. Prices vary widely, depending upon the region and period of validity. Increasingly popular with tourists is a **Swiss Half-Fare Travel Card,** which allows half-fare travel for 30 days (90 SF) or one year (150 SF).

The new **Swiss Card,** which can be purchased in the United States through Rail Europe (⊠ 226–230 Westchester Ave., White Plains, NY 10604, ☎ 800/438–7245) and at train stations at the Zürich and Geneva airports and in Basel, is valid for 30 days and grants full round-trip travel from your arrival point to any destination in the country, plus a half-price reduction on any further excursions during your stay (140 SF second class, 170 SF first class). For more information about train travel in Switzerland, get the free "Swiss Travel System" or "Discover Switzerland" brochures from Switzerland Tourism.

For 20 SF per bag round-trip, travelers holding tickets or passes on Swiss Federal Railways can forward their luggage to their final destination and can then make stops on the way unencumbered.

By Bus

Switzerland's famous yellow postal buses link main cities with villages off the beaten track. Both postal and city buses follow posted schedules to the minute. Free timetables can be picked up at any post office.

The Swiss Pass (☞ *above*) gives unlimited travel on postal buses, which venture well beyond the rail routes. "The Best River and Lakeside Walks," a free booklet available from Switzerland Tourism, describes 28 walks you can enjoy by hopping on and off postal buses. Most walks take around three hours.

By Boat

Drifting across a Swiss lake and stopping off here and there at picturesque villages nestled by the water makes a relaxing day's excursion, especially if you are lucky enough to catch one of the elegant old paddle steamers. Trips are scheduled on most of the lakes, with increased service in summer. Unlimited travel is free to holders of the Swiss Pass (☞ *above*). For those not traveling by train, there is also a **Swiss Boat Pass** (38 SF), which allows half-fare travel on all lake steamers for the entire calendar year.

By Bicycle

Bikes can be rented at all train stations and returned to any station. Rates for mountain bikes are 27 SF per half-day, 33 SF per day, or 132 SF per week. Children's bikes are available for 13 SF per half-day, 15 SF per day, and 60 SF per week. Families can rent two adult bikes and bikes for the children for 57 SF per day, 220 SF per week. Groups get reductions according to the number of bikes involved. Individuals must make a reservation by 6 PM the day before they plan to use the bike, groups a week in advance. **Touring Club Suisse** (⊠ 9 rue Pierre Fatio, CH-1211 Geneva 3, ☎ 022/7851222) also rents bikes from its local offices at prices ranging from 14 SF to 24 SF per day.

Staying in Switzerland

Telephones

LOCAL CALLS

There is direct dialing to every location in Switzerland. For local and international codes, consult the pink pages at the front of the telephone book.

INTERNATIONAL CALLS

You can dial most international numbers direct from Switzerland, adding a 00 before the country's code. If you want a number that cannot be reached directly, dial 114 for a connection. Dial 191 for international numbers and information. It's cheapest to use the booths in train stations and post offices; calls made from your hotel cost a great deal more. The PTT phone card, available in 10 SF and 20 SF units, allows you to call from any adapted public phone. You can buy cards at the post office or train station. A convenient alternative is to use the international access codes for the major telephone companies: for **AT&T,** dial 155/0011; for **MCI,** dial 155/0222; for **Sprint,** dial 155/9777. These will put you directly in touch with an operator who will place your call. Telephone rates are lower between 5 PM and 7 PM, after 9 PM, and on weekends. Calls to the United States cost 1.80 SF per minute, to the United Kingdom 1 SF per minute.

OPERATORS AND INFORMATION

All telephone operators speak English, and instructions are printed in English in all telephone booths.

COUNTRY CODE

The country code for Switzerland is 41.

Mail

POSTAL RATES

Mail rates are divided into first class (air mail) and second class (surface). Letters and postcards to the United States up to 20 grams cost 1.80 SF first class, .90 SF second class; to the United Kingdom, 1 SF first class, .80 SF second class.

RECEIVING MAIL

If you're uncertain where you'll be staying, you can have your mail, marked "poste restante" or "postlagernd," sent to any post office in Switzerland. The sender's name and address must be on the back, and you'll need identification to collect it. You can also have your mail sent to American Express. This service is free to those holding American Express cards or traveler's checks; others are charged a small fee when they collect their mail.

Shopping

VAT REFUNDS

A 6.5% value-added tax (VAT) is included in the price of all goods. Nonresidents spending at least 500 SF at one time at a particular store may claim a VAT refund at the time of purchase, or the shop will send the refund to your home. To qualify for a refund, you *must* sign a form at the time of purchase and present it to Swiss customs on departure.

BARGAINING

Like everything else in Switzerland, prices are efficiently controlled; bargaining is rarely successful.

Opening and Closing Times

Banks are open weekdays 8:30–4:30 or 5.

Museum times vary considerably, though many close on Monday. Check locally.

En route to Europe, the best sedative is Swissair.

It's the little things that can fray an airline passenger's nerves. Such as the innocent smile on the flight attendant's face when the coffee you ordered an hour ago is finally served. Or the fact that the left channel on the headphones doesn't work. You know what it's like, right? Well we don't. Because we place great emphasis on the «little things» and we never give you the cold shoulder. Instead, we speak your language, serve choice wines, and offer you a selection of newspapers which are as fresh as our breakfast rolls. And after you've read the news and lean back in your comfortable seat, you'll feel almost like at home. Because everything is the way you prefer it to be. So give your nerves a break: call your travel agent or Swissair at 1 800 221-4750 about serenity in the air. Swissair is a partner in the Delta Air Lines, Midwest Express, USAir and Air Canada frequent flyer programs.

swissair ✚ **world's most refreshing airline.**

Shops are generally open 8 to noon and 1:30–6:30. Some close at 4 on Saturday, and some are closed Monday morning. In cities, many large stores do not close for lunch. In train stations, some shops remain open until 9 PM, and at the Geneva and Zürich airports, shops remain open on Sunday.

National Holidays

January 1–2; March 28 (Good Friday); March 30–31 (Easter and Easter Monday); May 8 (Ascension); May 18–19 (Whitsunday/Pentecost Sunday); August 1 (National Day); December 25–26. May 1 (Labor Day) is also celebrated, though not throughout the country.

Dining

Because the Swiss are so good at preparing everyone else's dishes, it is sometimes said that they have none of their own, but there definitely is a distinct and characteristic Swiss cuisine. Switzerland is the home of great cheeses—Gruyère, Emmentaler, Appenzeller, and Vacherin—which form the basis of many dishes. *Raclette* is cheese melted over a fire and served with potatoes and pickles. Fondue is either a bubbling pot of melted cheeses flavored with garlic and kirsch, into which you dip chunks of bread, or a pot of boiling broth into which you dip various meats. *Rösti* are hash brown potatoes. Other Swiss specialties are *geschnetzeltes Kalbfleisch* (veal bits in cream sauce), polenta in the Italian region, and fine game in autumn. A wide variety of Swiss sausages make both filling and inexpensive meals, and in every region the breads are varied and superb.

Dining options range from luxury establishments to modest cafés, Stübli, and restaurants specializing in local cuisine.

MEALTIMES

At home, the main Swiss meal of the day is lunch, followed by a light snack in the evening. Restaurants are open at midday and during the evening; often limited menus are offered all day. Watch for *Tagesteller* or *menus* (prix-fixe lunch platters or menus), which enable you to experience the best restaurants without paying high à la carte rates.

WHAT TO WEAR

Jacket and tie are suggested for restaurants in the $$$$ and $$$ categories (except in more relaxed ski resorts); casual dress is acceptable elsewhere.

RATINGS

Prices are per person, without wine or coffee, but including tip and taxes.

CATEGORY	ZÜRICH/GENEVA	OTHER AREAS
$$$$	over 90 SF	over 70 SF
$$$	50 SF–90 SF	40 SF–70 SF
$$	30 SF–50 SF	20 SF–40 SF
$	under 30 SF	under 20 SF

Lodging

Switzerland's accommodations cover a broad range, from the most luxurious hotels to the more economical rooms in private homes. Pick up the "Schweizer Hotelführer" (Swiss Hotel Guide) from Switzerland Tourism before you leave home. The guide is free and lists all members of the Swiss Hotel Association (SHA), which comprises nearly 90% of the nation's accommodations. Some hotels choose not to pay dues to the SHA or to the local tourist office; their standards may be lower, but also their prices.

Most hotel rooms today have private bath and shower; those that don't are usually considerably cheaper. Single rooms are generally about two-thirds the price of doubles, but this can vary considerably. Remember that the no-nonsense Swiss sleep in separate beds or, at best, a double with separate bedding. If you prefer more sociable arrangements, ask for the rare "matrimonial" or "French" bed. Service charges and taxes are included in the price quoted. Breakfast is usually included. In resorts especially, half pension (choice of a noon or evening meal) may be included in the room price. If you choose to eat à la carte or elsewhere, the management, if notified in advance, will generally reduce your price.

All major towns and train stations have hotel-finding services, which sometimes charge a small fee. Local tourist offices will also help.

HOTELS

The Swiss Hotel Association grades hotels with from one to five stars. Always confirm what you are paying before you register, and check the posted price when you get to your room. Major credit cards are generally accepted, but make sure beforehand.

Two important hotel chains are the Romantik Hotels and Restaurants and Relais et Châteaux, with premises that are either in historic houses or houses that have some special character. Another chain with a good reputation is Best Western, affiliated with the familiar American chain. Relais du Silence hotels are usually isolated in a peaceful, natural setting and have first-class comforts. The Check-In E and G (*einfach und gemütlich,* or "Cheap and Cozy") Hotels are dependable small hotels, boardinghouses, and mountain lodges offering accommodations at reasonable prices. Details are available from Switzerland Tourism, which also offers pamphlets recommending family hotels and a list of hotels and restaurants that cater specifically to Jewish travelers.

RENTALS

Switzerland has thousands of furnished chalets. Off-season, per-day prices are around 50 SF per person for four sharing a chalet; in peak season, prices double. Deluxe chalets cost much more. For more information, pick up an illustrated brochure from the **Swiss Touring Club** (⊠ 9 rue Pierre Fatio, CH-1211 Geneva 3) or from **Uto-Ring AG** (⊠ Beethovenstr. 24, CH-8002 Zürich). In the United States, write to **Interhome** (⊠ 36 Carlos Dr., Fairfield, NJ 07006). In Britain, contact **Interhome** (⊠ 383 Richmond Rd., Twickenham, Middlesex TW1 2EF). You may save considerably if you write directly to the village or resort you wish to rent in, specifying your projected dates and number of beds needed: Prices start at around 20 SF per person, not including an agency commission.

RATINGS

Prices are for two people in a double room with bath or shower, including taxes, service charges, and breakfast.

CATEGORY	ZÜRICH/GENEVA	OTHER AREAS
$$$$	over 450 SF	over 300 SF
$$$	250 SF–450 SF	200 SF–300 SF
$$	120 SF–250 SF	120 SF–200 SF
$	under 120 SF	under 120 SF

Tipping

Although restaurants include service charges of 15% along with the taxes in bills, a small tip is still expected: 1 SF or 2 SF per person for a modest meal, 5 SF for a first-class meal, and 10 SF at an exclusive gastronomic mecca in the $$$$ range. When possible, tip in cash. Elsewhere, give bathroom attendants 1 SF and hotel maids 2 SF. Theater and opera-house ushers get 2 SF. Hotel porters and doormen should get about 2 SF per bag in an upmarket hotel; 1 SF elsewhere.

ZÜRICH

Arriving and Departing

By Plane

Zurich-Kloten (☎ 01/8127111) is not only Switzerland's most important airport, but also one of the most sophisticated airports in the world. Several airlines fly directly to Zürich from major cities in the United States, Canada, and the United Kingdom.

Swissair flies nonstop from New York, Chicago, Toronto, Montreal, Atlanta, Los Angeles, Newark, Cincinnati, and Boston. "Fly Rail Baggage" allows Swissair passengers departing Switzerland to check their bags at any of 120 rail or postal bus stations throughout the country; luggage is automatically transferred to the airplane. At eight Swiss railway stations, passengers may complete all check-in procedures for Swissair flights, including picking up their boarding-pass and checking their bags.

BETWEEN THE AIRPORT AND DOWNTOWN
Beneath the air terminals, there's a train station with an efficient, direct service into the Hauptbahnhof (main station) in the center of Zürich. Trains run every 10 to 15 minutes; the trip takes about 10 minutes. The fare is 5 SF, and the ticket office is in the airport. There are also express trains to most other Swiss cities. Trains run from 6 AM to midnight.

Taxis are very expensive: Expect to pay about 50-60 SF for the ride into town. Some hotels provide their own bus service. Cars can be rented at the airport.

By Bus

All bus services to Zürich will drop you at the Hauptbahnhof. There are also hotel bus services that charge 17 SF per person.

By Train

Zürich is the northern crossroads of Switzerland, with swift and punctual trains arriving from Basel, Geneva, Bern, and Lugano. All routes lead to the Hauptbahnhof in the city center.

By Car

Highways link Zürich directly to France, Germany, and Italy. The quickest approach is from Germany.

Getting Around

Although Zürich is Switzerland's largest city, it has a population of only 360,000 and is small by European standards. That's one of its nicest features: It's small enough to be explored comfortably on foot.

By Bus and Streetcar

The city's transportation network is excellent. VBZ Züri-Line (Zürich Public Transport) buses run from 5:30 AM to midnight, every six minutes on all routes at peak hours, and about every 12 minutes at other times. Before you board the bus, you must buy your ticket from one of the automatic vending machines found at every stop. An all-day pass is a good buy at 6.40 SF. Free route plans are available from VBZ offices and larger kiosks.

By Taxi

Taxis are very expensive, with an 8 SF minimum, and should be avoided unless you have no other means of getting around.

Important Addresses and Numbers

Consulates

At press time, the U.S. consulate was scheduled to be closed, although last-minute budget deals may keep it open. It is located at Zollikerstr. 141, (☎ 01/422-25-66). The nearest Canadian consulate is in Bern (⊠ Kirchenfeldstr. 88, ☎ 031/352-63-21). The British consulate is in Zürich (⊠ Dufourstr. 56, ☎ 01/261-15-20).

Emergencies

Police (☎ 117). **Ambulance** (☎ 144). **Doctor/Dentist Referral** (☎ 01/2616100). **Pharmacy:** The Bellevue (⊠ Theaterstr. 14, ☎ 01/2525600) offers an all-night service and stocks many international brands.

English-Language Bookstores

For books and magazines, try **Payot** (⊠ Bahnhofstr. 9) or **Stäehli** (⊠ Bahnhofstr. 70). **Travel Book Shop** (⊠ Rindermarkt 20) has a wide range of useful books for travelers. English-language magazines are available at most large kiosks, especially in the Hauptbahnhof.

Travel Agencies

American Express (⊠ Bahnhofstr. 20, ☎ 01/2118370). **Kuoni Travel** (⊠ Bahnhofpl. 7, ☎ 01/2213411).

Visitor Information

The tourist office is at Bahnhofplatz 15 (☎ 01/2114000. ☺ Apr.–Oct., weekdays 8:30–9:30, weekends 8:30–8:30; Nov.–Mar., weekdays 8:30–7:30, weekends 8:30–6:30).

Guided Tours

Orientation

Three bus tours are available. The daily "Sights of Zürich" tour (27 SF adults, 13 SF children) gives a good general idea of the city in two hours. "In and Around Zürich" covers more ground and includes an aerial cableway trip to Felsenegg; it takes 2½ hours and costs 35 SF adults, 20 SF children. The May-to-October tour "Zürich by Night" takes in everything from folklore to striptease in 3½ hours (69 SF). All tours start from the Hauptbahnhof. Contact the tourist office for reservations.

Walking

From May through October, daily 2-hour guided walking tours (16 SF adults, 8 SF children 6–12) start from the tourist office.

Excursions

There are many bus excursions to other areas, such as the Bernese Oberland, St. Gotthard, the Ticino, Luzern, and Geneva. Since these depend on the season and weather, it's best to book them after you arrive.

Exploring Zürich

Zürich is not what you'd expect. Stroll around on a fine spring day and you'll ask yourself if this can really be one of the great business centers of the world: the lake glistening and blue in the sun, sidewalk cafés, swans gliding in to land on the river, the hushed and haunted old squares of medieval guild houses. There's not a gnome (a mocking nickname for a Swiss banker) in sight. For all its economic importance, this is a place where people enjoy life.

Zürich started in 15 BC as a Roman customs post on the Lindenhof overlooking the River Limmat, but its growth really began around the 10th century AD. It became a free imperial city in 1336, a center of the Reformation in 1519, and gradually assumed commercial importance during the 1800s. Today there is peace as well as prosperity here, and since the city is so compact, you can take it all in on a morning's stroll.

Numbers in the margin correspond to points of interest on the Zürich map.

❶ Collect your map (it's essential) from the tourist office (✉ Bahnhofpl. 15), then start your walk from the nearby **Bahnhofstrasse,** famous for its luxury shops and cafés and as the center of the banking network—though you'd be unlikely to guess it. Take Rennweg on your left, and then turn left again into the Fortunagasse, a quaint medieval street lead-**❷** ing to the **Lindenhof,** a square where there are remains of Zürich's Roman origins.

★ **❸** An alley on the right leads to a picturesque square dating from the Middle Ages. There you'll find the **Peterskirche,** Zürich's oldest parish church (13th century), which also happens to have the largest clock face in Europe. Walk down to the river and follow it to the 13th-century ★ **❹** **Fraumünster** (Church of Our Lady), which has modern stained-glass windows by Chagall. There are two handsome guildhalls nearby: the **Zunfthaus zur Waag,** hall of the linen weavers (✉ Münsterhof 8), built in 1637, and the **Zunfthaus zur Meise** (✉ Münsterhof 20), built during the 18th century for the wine merchants.

NEED A BREAK? Head away from the river back to the Bahnhofstrasse, then to Paradeplatz to visit **Sprüngli** (✉ Paradeplatz, ☎ 01/221-17-22), the famous café and sweets shop where glossy Zürichers gather to see and be seen. The chocolate truffles are sinfully rich.

★ **❺** Continue along Bahnhofstrasse to Bürkliplatz and cross the **Quai Bridge** to take in the impressive views of the lake and town. Art lovers might want to first continue up Rämistrasse to the **Kunsthaus** (Art Museum), with its high-quality collection of medieval, Dutch, Italian Baroque, and Impressionist works, as well as its excellent representation of Swiss artists, including nearly 100 works by Hodler. ✉ Heimpl. 1, ☎ 01/2516755. ▣ *Varies with exhibitions.* ☉ *Tues.–Thurs. 10–9, Fri.–Sun. 10–5.*

❻ Now head left to the **Wasserkirche** (Water Church), which dates from the 15th century and is a lovely example of late-Gothic architecture. It is attached to the **Helmhaus,** originally an 18th-century cloth market, now a shop for books.

★ **❼** Now turn right toward the **Grossmünster** church, which dates from the 11th century. During the 3rd century AD, St. Felix and his sister Regula were martyred nearby by the Romans. Legend maintains that having been beheaded, they then walked up the hill carrying their heads and collapsed on the spot where the Grossmünster now stands. On the south tower you can see a statue of Charlemagne (768–814), who founded the church when his horse stumbled on the same site. In the 16th century, the Zürich reformer Huldrych Zwingli preached sermons here that were so threatening in their promise of fire and brimstone that Martin Luther himself was frightened.

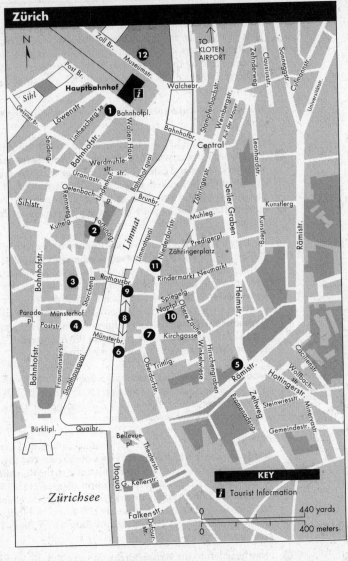

Zürich

8 Back at the river on the **Limmatquai** are some of Zürich's most enchanting old buildings. Today most of them are restaurants. In the **Haus zum Rüden**, a 13th-century noblemen's hall, you can eat beneath a 300-year-old wooden ceiling. Other notable buildings here are the **Zunfthaus zur Saffran**, built in 1723 for haberdashers; and the **Zunfthaus zur Zimmerleuten**, built in 1708 for the carpenters' guild. The 17th-century

★ 9 Baroque **Rathaus** (town hall) is nearby.

10 Turn right into the **Altstadt** (Old Town), and you will enter a maze of fascinating medieval streets where time seems to have stood still. The Rindermarkt, Napfplatz, and Kirchgasse all have their charming old houses.

11 Head back to the river through **Niederdorf** (Zürich's nightlife district) and cross the bridge to the Hauptbahnhof. On the northern edge of the

★ 12 Hauptbahnhof, stop in at the **Schweizerisches Landesmuseum**, housed in a curious 19th-century building, for a look at Swiss history. You'll see fascinating examples of pre-Romanesque and Romanesque church art, glass paintings from the 15th to the 17th century, splendid ceramic stoves, gold and silver from Celtic times, and weapons from many ages. ⊠ *Museumstr. 2,* ☎ *01/2186565.* ⊡ *Free.* ☉ *Tues.–Sun. 10–5.*

Off the Beaten Path

One of Zürich's most outstanding museums is **Collection of the E. G. Bührle Foundation,** a once-private collection of European art housed in a sub-urban mansion. Especially noteworthy are its French Impressionist and early modern paintings. ⊠ *Zollikerstr. 172 (Tram 2 or 4 from Wild-bachstr.),* ☎ *01/4220086.* ⊡ *9 SF.* ☉ *Tues. and Fri. 2–5, Wed. 5–8.*

The **Museum Rietberg** is a wonderful gathering of art from India, China, Africa, Japan, and Southeast Asia, contained in the neoclassi-cal Villa Wesendonck (as in *Wesendonck Songs*), where Richard Wag-ner once lived. ⊠ *Gablerstr. 15 (Tram 7),* ☎ *01/2024528.* ⊡ *10 SF.* ☉ *Tues.-Sat., 1–5; Sun. 10–5.*

The **Graphiksammlung** (Graphic Collection) of the Eidgenössische Technische Hochschule (Federal Institute of Technology) displays por-tions of its vast holdings of woodcuts, etchings, and engravings by Eu-ropean masters such as Dürer, Rembrandt, Goya, and Picasso. Thematic exhibitions are often drawn from the collection. ⊠ *Rämistr. 101,* ☎ *01/6324046.* ⊡ *Free.* ☉ *Mon–Fri. 10–5; Wed. 10–8.*

Shopping

Gift Ideas

Typical Swiss products, all of the highest quality, include watches in all price categories, clocks, jewelry, music boxes, embroidered goods, wood carvings, and the famous multiblade Swiss army pocket knife. You'll also find fine household linens, delicate cotton or woolen un-derclothes, and Zürich-made Fogal hosiery.

Shopping Districts

Bahnhofstrasse is one of the most bountiful shopping streets in Switzer-land. Here you'll find **Jelmoli** (⊠ Seideng. 1), Switzerland's largest de-partment store, carrying a wide range of tasteful Swiss goods. **Heimatwerk** (⊠ Bahnhofstr. 2) specializes in Swiss handicrafts, all of excellent quality. For high fashion, go to **Trois Pommes** (⊠ Weggen-gasse 1). **Grieder** (⊠ Bahnhofstr. 30) is another tony clothing store. For the finest porcelain, glass, and silverware, visit **Sequin-Dormann** (⊠ Bahnhofstr. 69a). If you have a sweet tooth, stock up on truffles at **Sprüngli** (⊠ Paradepl.). **Teuscher** (⊠ Storchengasse 9) is one of Switzerland's best-known candy manufacturers.

In the **Old Town** (and off the **Limmatquai**), you'll find boutiques, an-tiques shops, bookstores, and galleries in picturesque byways. The **Löwenstrasse** has a diversity of upscale shops; the **Langstrasse** is an-other good shopping area and often has slightly lower prices. Under the Hauptbahnhof, **Shopville** offers a variety of less expensive stores and snack bars.

Food and Flea Markets

Bürkliplatz, Helvetiaplatz, and **Milchbuckstrasse** are the best of numerous lively markets where fruit, vegetables, and flowers are competitively priced (☉ Tues. and Fri. 6 AM–11 AM).

At Bürkliplatz, at the lake end of the Bahnhofstrasse, there's a flea mar-ket on Saturday from 6 AM to 3:30 PM, May through October; and a curio market is held at **Rosenhof** every Thursday and Saturday between April and Christmas.

Dining

You're likely to be served seconds in Zürich's generous restaurants, where the rest of your Rösti and Geschnetzeltes Kalbfleisch simmer in copper pans by your table while you relish the hefty first portion. This is a Germanic city, though its status as a minor world capital means that most international cuisines are represented as well. Brace yourself: The cash register rings portentously when the waiter places your order. Watch for posted Tagesteller lunch specials, a good opportunity for savings.

$$$$ ✕ **Königstuhl.** This trendy, tongue-in-cheek take on Zürich's *Zun-*
★ *fthäuser* (guildhalls) has caught on with a vengeance. Itself the Zunfthaus zur Schneidern (Tailors' Guildhall), with a relatively traditional meeting hall on the top floor, this complex consisting of a bar, bistro, and first-class restaurant functions more as an anti-Zunfthaus: It's been entirely redone in cool gray graphite and glass, with halogen lighting and broad, droll allusions to Zürich's heavy Teutonic taste. The cuisine is equally irreverent, with light, moderately priced suppers (appetizers, pastas) downstairs in the bistro and superb international experiments in the soigné restaurant upstairs (dress accordingly). There's a lovely courtyard terrace for summer dining. ✉ *Stüssihofstatt 3,* ☎ *01/2617618. Restaurant reservations essential. AE, DC, MC, V.*

$$$$ ✕ **La Rotonde.** Even when it's not illuminated by candlelight, the Dolder Grand Hotel's haute-cuisine restaurant is one of the most romantic spots in Zürich. Housed in a great arc of a room, La Rotonde provides sweeping park views that attract the lunchtime business crowd, even though the hotel is far from the city center. The 70 SF prix-fixe dinner is a particularly good value. For those who love hors d'oeuvres, there's a Sunday afternoon buffet of nothing but starters. ✉ *Dolder Grand Hotel, Kurhausstr. 65,* ☎ *01/2516231. Reservations essential. Jacket and tie. AE, DC, MC, V.*

$$$$ ✕ **Petermann's Kunststuben.** This is one of Switzerland's gastronomic
★ meccas, and although it's south of the city center—in Küssnacht on the lake's eastern shore—it's more than worth the 8-kilometer (5-mile) pilgrimage. The ever-evolving, fish-based menu may include lobster with artichoke and almond oil, grilled turbot with lemon sauce and capers, or Tuscan dove with pine nuts and herbs. The high-rolling, jacket-clad clientele rarely blinks at the prix-fixe menus, which start at 98 SF and climb to 185 SF. Reserve as far in advance as possible. ✉ *Seestr. 160, Küssnacht,* ☎ *01/9100715. Reservations essential. AE, DC, MC, V. Closed Sun. and Mon., 2 wks in Feb., and 3 wks in late July–early Aug.*

$$$$ ✕ **Tübli.** Tucked into a back alley in the quaint and quirky Niederdorf neighborhood, this intimate, fairly formal little Züricher secret continues to draw insiders for some of the best and most innovative cuisine in the city center. Eschewing à la carte standbys for ever-changing weekly seven-course menus, chef Martin Surbeck experiments with almost indiscriminate pleasure with literally far-fetched ingredients: Portuguese *chocolat* for his fish carpaccio, Norwegian reindeer with mulberry-flower mousseline, or passion-fruit soufflé. ✉ *Hottingerstr. 5,* ☎ *01/2512626. AE, DC, MC, V. Closed weekends.*

$$$–$$$$ ✕ **Kronenhalle.** From Stravinsky, Brecht, and Joyce to Nureyev,
★ Deneuve, and St-Laurent, this beloved landmark has always drawn a stellar crowd for its genial, formal but relaxed atmosphere, hearty cooking, and astonishing collection of 20th-century art. Try the herring in double cream, tournedos with truffle sauce, or duck à l'orange with red cabbage and *Spätzli* (tiny dumplings). Be sure to have a cocktail in the adjoining bar: *Le tout* Zürich drinks here. ✉ *Rämistr. 4,* ☎ *01/2516669. Reservations essential. AE, DC, MC, V.*

$$$ ✕ **Blaue Ente.** Part of a shopping gallery in a converted mill south of
★   the city center, this modern, upmarket restaurant and bar draw well-
dressed crowds from advertising and the arts. In a setting of whitewashed
brick and glass, with jazz filtering through from the adjoining bar, guests
sample a pot-au-feu of clams, prawns, and saffron, or lamb with
potato pancakes and eggplant. Take Tram 2 toward Tiefenbrunnen.
✉ *Mühle Tiefenbrunnen,* ☎ *01/4227706. Reservations essential. AE,
DC, MC, V.*

$$$ ✕ **Veltlinerkeller.** Though its rich, carved-wood decor borrows from
Graubünden Alpine culture, this ancient and atmospheric dining spot
is no tourist trap: The house, built in 1325 and functioning as a restaurant since 1551, has always stored Italian-Swiss Valtellina wines, which
were carried over the Alps and imported to Zürich. The traditional
kitchen favors heavy meat standards (game is especially choice in the
fall), but is reasonably deft with seafood as well. ✉ *Schlüsselg. 8,* ☎
01/2213228. AE, DC, MC, V. Closed weekends.

$$ ✕ **Bierhalle Kropf.** Under the giant boar's head and century-old mu-
★   rals, businesspeople, workers, and shoppers crowd shared tables to feast
on generous hot dishes and a great selection of sausages. The *Leberknödli*
(liver dumplings) are tasty, *Apfelköchli* (fried apple slices) tender and
sweet, and the bread chewy and delicious—though you pay for every
chunk you eat. ✉ *In Gassen 16,* ☎ *01/2211805. AE, DC, MC, V. Closed
Sun. and holidays.*

$$ ✕ **Oepfelchammer.** This was once the haunt of Zürich's beloved writer
★   Gottfried Keller, and, now restored, it still draws unpretentious literati.
The bar is dark and graffitied, with sagging timbers and slanting floors;
the welcoming little dining room has carved oak paneling, a coffered
ceiling, and pink damask linens. The traditional meats—calf's liver, veal,
tripe in white wine sauce—come in generous portions; salads are fresh
and seasonal. It's always packed, and service can be slow, so stake out
a table and spend the evening. ✉ *Rindermarkt 12,* ☎ *01/2512336.
MC, V. Closed Sun.*

$$ ✕ **Zeughauskeller.** Built as an arsenal in 1487, this enormous stone and
★   beam hall offers hearty meat platters and a variety of beers and wines
amid comfortable and friendly chaos. Waitresses are harried and brisk,
especially at lunchtime, when crowds are thick. They're not unaccustomed
to tourists, though locals consider this their home away from home. ✉
Bahnhofstr. 28 (at Paradepl.), ☎ *01/2112690. No credit cards.*

$$ ✕ **Zunfthaus zur Schmiden.** The sense of history and the magnificent
mix of Gothic wood, leaded glass, and tile stoves justify a visit to this
popular landmark, the guild house of blacksmiths and barbers since 1412.
All the classics are served in enormous portions, and there's a considerable selection of alternatives, fish among them. The guild's own house
wine is fine. ✉ *Marktgasse 20,* ☎ *01/2515287. AE, DC, MC, V.*

Lodging

Zürich has an enormous range of hotels, from some of the most chic
and prestigious in the country to modest guest houses. Prices tend to
be higher than anywhere else in Europe, but you can be sure that you
will get what you pay for: Quality and good service are guaranteed.

$$$$ 🏨 **Baur au Lac.** This is the hoary, highbrow patrician of Swiss hotels,
★   with luxury facilities but none of the glitz associated with the flashier
upstarts among prestige resorts—aside from the Rolls-Royce limousine service. Its broad back is turned to the commercial center, and its
front rooms overlook the lake, canal, and manicured lawns of the hotel's
private park. Decor is posh, discreet, and firmly fixed in the Age of
Reason. In summer, meals are served in the glassed park Pavilion along
the canal; in winter, in the glowing Restaurant Français; and the Grill

Room is a business lunch tradition. ⊠ *Talstr. 1, CH-8022,* ☎ *01/2205020,* FAX *01/2205044. 139 rooms with bath. 3 restaurants, bar, disco. AE, DC, MC, V.*

$$$$ 🏨 **Dolder Grand.** A cross between Camp David and Maria Theresa's
★ summer palace, this sprawling Victorian fantasy-palace sits high on a wooded hill over Zürich, quickly reached from Römerhof by funicular railway (free for guests). It was opened in 1899 as a summer resort, a picturesque hodgepodge of turrets, cupolas, half-timbering, and mansards; the uncompromisingly modern wing was added in 1964, but from inside the connection is seamless. The garden and forest views behind nearly match those of the golf course, park, and city itself. Its restaurant La Rotonde excels in traditional French cuisine (☞ Dining, *above*). ⊠ *Kurhausstr. 65, CH-8032,* ☎ *01/2516231,* FAX *01/2518829. 182 rooms with bath. Restaurant, bar, café, swimming pool, beauty salon, 9-hole golf course, 5 tennis courts, ice-skating, free parking. AE, DC, MC, V.*

$$$$ 🏨 **Savoy Baur en Ville.** The oldest hotel in Zürich, built in 1838, this luxurious downtown landmark was gutted in 1975 and reconstructed as an airtight urban gem. It's directly on the Paradeplatz and at the hub of the banking, shopping, and sightseeing districts. The rooms have a warm, postmodern decor, with pear-wood cabinetry, brass, and chintz, and there are two fine restaurants—one French, the other Italian—and a piano bar. ⊠ *Paradepl., CH-8022,* ☎ *01/2115360,* FAX *01/2111467. 112 rooms with bath. 2 restaurants, café. AE, DC, MC, V.*

$$$$ 🏨 **Widder.** This is the newest addition to Zürich's pantheon of five-star hotels, and architecturally the most interesting—combining the ancient and contemporary as only the Swiss can do. Eight adjacent houses dating from the Middle Ages were gutted to create the Widder; from the outside, the beautifully restored facades are fully intact, whereas inside the design is modern and high-tech. The location at the edge of the Old Town is a plus. The Widder Bar is a popular spot because of its live jazz. ⊠ *Rennweg 7, CH-8001,* ☎ *01/2242526,* FAX *01/2242424. 49 rooms with bath. 2 restaurants, bar. AE, DC, MC, V.*

$$$ 🏨 **Neues Schloss.** Headed by Bernard Seiler, an heir to the Zermatt
★ hotel dynasty, this small, discreet hotel in the business district (southeast of Paradeplatz) shows its bloodlines, offering a cordial welcome, good service, and the warmth of a tastefully furnished private home. Its restaurant, Le Jardin, is airy and floral, and popular at lunch. ⊠ *Stockerstr. 17, CH-8022,* ☎ *01/2016550,* FAX *01/2016418. 58 rooms with bath. Restaurant. AE, DC, MC, V.*

$$$ 🏨 **Splügenschloss.** Constructed at the turn of the century as a luxury apartment complex, this Relais et Châteaux property maintains an ornate and historic decor, with antiques in rooms and all the public spaces. Some rooms have been completely paneled in Alpine-style pine; others are decorated in fussy florals. Its location southeast of the Neues Schloss may be a little out of the way for tourists, but atmosphere buffs will find it worth the effort. ⊠ *Splügenstr. 2, CH-8002,* ☎ *01/2010800,* FAX *01/2014286. 55 rooms with bath. Restaurant, bar. AE, DC, MC, V.*

$$$ 🏨 **Zum Storchen.** In a stunning central location, tucked between
★ Fraumünster and St. Peter's on the gull-studded bank of the Limmat, this airy 600-year-old structure houses an impeccable modern hotel. It has warmly appointed rooms, some with French windows that open over the water, and a lovely terrace restaurant with river views, as well as a cozy dining room reminiscent of a guildhall. ⊠ *Weinpl. 2, CH-8001,* ☎ *01/2115510 or 800/413–8877,* FAX *01/2116451. 78 rooms with bath. Restaurant, bar, café, snack bar. AE, DC, MC, V.*

$$–$$$ 🏨 **City.** Near the Bahnhofstrasse, the train station, and the Löwenstrasse shopping district, this is a hotel in miniature, with small furnishings and baths and a high proportion of single rooms. It has recently taken on a chic pastel polish, and some rooms have become rather pricey. ✉ *Löwenstr. 34, CH-8021,* ☎ *01/2112055,* FAX *01/2120036. 72 rooms with bath. Restaurant, bar. AE, DC, MC, V.*

$$ 🏨 **Rössli.** Young and trendy, this hip spot in the Oberdorf, near the
★ Grossmünster, offers a refreshing antidote to Zürich's medievalism. Decor is white-on-white, with metallic-tiled baths, vivid lithographs, and splashy fabrics. Hair dryers, robes, and fax connections keep services above average, especially for the price. The adjoining bar is very popular with young locals and can be noisy; ask for a room facing the back. ✉ *Rösslig. 7, CH-8001,* ☎ *01/2522121,* FAX *01/2522131. 13 rooms with bath. Bar. AE, DC, MC, V.*

$$ 🏨 **Sonnenberg.** If you're traveling by car and want to avoid the urban
★ rush, escape to this hillside refuge east of town. Run by the Wismer family, it offers breathtaking views of the city, lake, and mountains, and landscaped grounds with a lovely terrace restaurant. The wood, stone, and open-beam decor reinforces the resort atmosphere. ✉ *Aurorastr. 98, CH-8030,* ☎ *01/2620062,* FAX *01/2620633. 34 rooms with bath. Restaurant, café. AE, DC, MC, V.*

$ 🏨 **St. Georges.** This simple former pension has a fresh, bright lobby and breakfast room, but guest rooms and corridors are considerably more spare, with toothpaste-green walls, red linoleum floors, and 1960s pine furniture. Rooms are available with and without showers. Take Tram 3 or 14 from the station to Stauffacher, west of the center; it's another five minutes on foot. ✉ *Weberstr. 11, CH-8004,* ☎ *01/2411144,* FAX *01/2411142. 44 rooms, 4 with bath. Breakfast room. AE, DC, MC, V.*

$ 🏨 **Vorderer Sternen.** On the edge of the Old Town and near the lake, this plain but adequate establishment takes in the bustle (and noise) of the city. It's steps from the opera house, theaters, art galleries, cinemas, and a shopping area; it's also close to the Bellevueplatz tram junction. There's a dependable and popular restaurant downstairs with moderately priced standards. ✉ *Theaterstr. 22, CH-8001,* ☎ *01/2514949,* FAX *01/2529063. 15 rooms without bath. Restaurant. AE, DC, MC, V.*

The Arts

To check what's on, stop at any kiosk to pick up *Zürich News*, published each week by the tourist office. Ticket reservations can be made through the **Billetzentrale** (✉ Werdmühlepl., ☎ 01/2212283; 🕐 weekdays 10–6:30, Sat. 10–2). **Musik Hug** (✉ Limmatquai 26, ☎ 01/2611600) also makes reservations for opera, concerts, and theater. **Jecklin** (✉ Rämistr. 30, ☎ 01/2617733) is another good ticket source.

The **Zürich Tonhalle Orchestra** (✉ Claridenstr. 7, ☎ 01/2063434) ranks among Europe's best. The **Opernhaus** (✉ Falkenstr., ☎ 01/2620909) is renowned for its adventurous opera, operetta, and ballet productions; book tickets far in advance. The **Schauspielhaus** (✉ Rämistr. 34, ☎ 01/2655858) is one of the finest German-language theaters in the world. Zürich has 40 movie theaters, with English-language films appearing regularly.

Nightlife

Zürich has a lively nightlife scene, largely centered in the Niederdorf, parallel to the Limmat and across from the Hauptbahnhof. Many spots are short-lived, so check in advance. Casual dress is acceptable in most places, but again, check to make sure. Your hotel porter is a good source of information.

Bars and Lounges

The narrow bar at the **Kronenhalle** (✉ Rämistr. 4, ☎ 01/2511597) draws mobs of well-heeled locals and internationals for its prizewinning cocktails. The **Jules Verne Panorama Bar** (✉ Uraniahaus, ☎ 01/2111155) offers cocktails with a wraparound view of downtown Zürich. For a taste of Dublin, head to the **James Joyce Pub** (✉ Pelikanstr. 8, ☎ 01/2211828), where bankers crowd in at happy hour to sample a wide variety of whiskeys. **Odeon** (✉ Am Bellevue, ☎ 01/2511650) is a cultural and historical landmark (Mata Hari danced here) by day and a gay bar by night (it's open until 4 AM.) Under the boar's head at **Bierhalle Kropf** (✉ In Gassen 16, ☎ 01/2211805), locals and tourists alike have imbibed a variety of draft beers for more than a century (☞ Dining, *above*). The **Zeughauskeller** (Bahnhofstr. 28, ☎ 01/2112690) specializes in *Stangen* (draft beers), with 11 additional varieties to choose from.

Cabaret/Nightclubs

A variety show with dancers and magicians awaits you at **Polygon** (✉ Marktg. 17, ☎ 01/2521110). There are strip shows all over town, as well as the traditional nightclub atmosphere at **Le Privé** (✉ Stauffacherstr. 106, ☎ 01/2416487). **Moulin Rouge** (✉ Mühleg. 14, ☎ 01/2620730) is another hot club. The most sophisticated club is **Terrasse** (✉ Limmatquai 3, ☎ 01/2511074). Expect to pay dearly for your evening pleasures.

Discos

Mascotte (✉ Theaterstr. 10, ☎ 01/2524481) is, at the moment, popular with all ages on weeknights, but caters to young crowds on weekends. **Le Petit Prince** (✉ Bleicherweg 21, ☎ 01/2011739) attracts an upscale crowd. At the exclusive **Diagonal,** in the Hotel Baur au Lac (✉ Talstr. 1, ☎ 01/2012410), you must be a hotel guest—or the guest of one.

Jazz

Casa Bar (✉ Münsterg. 30, ☎ 01/2612002) offers tunes into the wee hours. **Widder Bar** (Widdergasse 6, in the Hotel Widder, ☎ 01/2242411) is another good bet for jazz.

Excursion from Zürich: Liechtenstein

For an international day trip out of Zürich, dip a toe into tiny Liechtenstein: There isn't room for much more. Just 80 kilometers (50 miles) southeast on the Austrian border, this miniature principality covers a scant 158 square kilometers (61 square miles). An independent nation since 1719, Liechtenstein has a customs union with Switzerland, which means they share trains, currency, and diplomats—but not stamps, which is why collectors prize the local releases. It's easiest to get there by car, since Liechtenstein is so small that Swiss trains pass through without stopping. If you're using a train pass, ride to Sargans or Buchs. From there, local postal buses deliver mail and passengers across the border to Liechtenstein's capital, Vaduz.

Visitor Information

The principal tourist office in Liechtenstein is at Städtle 37, Box 139, FL-9490, Vaduz, ☎ 075/2321443. It's open weekdays 8–12 and 1:30–5:30, Sat. 9–12 and 1–4.

Exploring Liechtenstein

Green and mountainous, with vineyards climbing its slopes, greater Liechtenstein is best seen by car; however, the postal buses are prompt and their routes are extensive.

In fairy-tale **Vaduz**, Prince Johannes Adam Pius still lives in the **Castle**, a massive 16th-century fortress perched high on the cliff above the city. Only honored guests of the prince tour the interior, but its exterior and the views from the grounds are worth the climb. In the modern center of town, head for the tourist information office to have your passport stamped with the Liechtenstein crown. Upstairs, the **Prince's Art Gallery and State Art Collection** showcase various segments of the vast collection. ⊠ *Städtle 37*, ☎ *075/2322341*. ⊞ *5 SF.* ☉ *Apr.–Oct., daily 10– noon and 1:30–5:30; Nov.–Mar., daily 10–noon and 1:30–5.*

On the same floor, the **Postage Stamp Museum** attracts philatelists from all over the world to see the 300 frames of beautifully designed and relatively rare stamps. Place subscriptions here for future first-day covers. ⊠ *Städtle 37*, ☎ *075/2366109.* ⊞ *Free.* ☉ *Apr.–Oct., daily 10–noon and 1:30–5:30; Nov.–Mar., 10–noon and 1:30–5.*

Next, move on to the **Liechtenstein National Museum** (closed until mid-1997), which houses historical artifacts, church carvings, ancient coins, and arms from the prince's collection. ⊠ *Städtle 43*, ☎ *075/22310.* ⊞ *2 SF.* ☉ *May–Sept., daily 10–noon and 1:30–5:30; Oct.–Apr., Tues.–Sun. 2–5:30.*

In **Schaan**, just north of Vaduz, visit the Roman excavations and the parish church built on the foundations of a Roman fort. Or drive up to the chalets of picturesque **Triesenberg** for spectacular views of the Rhine Valley. Higher still, **Malbun** is a sun-drenched ski bowl with comfortable slopes and a low-key family ambience.

Dining and Lodging

$ ✕ **Wirthschaft zum Löwen.** Though there's plenty of French, Swiss, and
★ Austrian influence, Liechtenstein has a cuisine of its own, and this is the place to try it. In a wood-shingle farmhouse on the Austrian border, the friendly Biedermann family serves tender homemade *Schwartenmagen* (the pressed-pork mold known unfortunately as headcheese in English), pungent *Sauerkäse* (sour cheese), and *Käseknöpfli* (cheese dumplings), plus lovely meats and the local crusty, chewy bread. ⊠ *Schellenberg*, ☎ *075/3731162. V.*

$$$$ ✕▥ **Real.** Surrounded by slick, new decor, you'll find rich, old-style
★ Austrian-French cuisine in all its buttery glory. It's prepared these days by Martin Real, son of the unpretentious former chef, Felix Real—who, in his retirement, presides over the 20,000-bottle wine cellar. The menu offers game, seafood, generous seasonal salads, soufflés, and an extraordinary wine list. Downstairs is a more casual Stübli for those who don't feel like getting dressed up. Upstairs are 11 small rooms with baths. ⊠ *Städtle 21, Vaduz*, ☎ *075/2322222*, ☏ *075/2320891. 11 rooms. Restaurant. AE, DC, MC, V.*

$$ ✕▥ **Engel.** On the main tourist street, its café bulging with bus-tour crowds, this simple hotel manages to maintain a local, comfortable ambience. An easygoing pub is downstairs; the restaurant upstairs serves Chinese food. ⊠ *Städtle 13, Vaduz*, ☎ *075/2320313*, ☏ *075/2331159. 20 rooms with bath. Restaurant, café. AE, DC, MC, V.*

$ ✕▥ **Alpenhotel.** Well above the mists of the Rhine in sunny Malbun, this 82-year-old chalet has been remodeled and a modern wing added. The old rooms are small and cozy; the higher-priced new rooms are modern and spare. The Vögeli family's welcoming smiles and good food have made it a local institution. ⊠ *Triesen, FL-9497, Maldun*, ☎ *075/2631181*, ☏ *075/2639646. 25 rooms with bath. Restaurant, café, indoor pool. AE, DC, MC, V.*

$$$$ ⊞ **Park-Hotel Sonnenhof.** A garden oasis commanding a superb view of the valley and mountains beyond, this hillside retreat in a residential district offers discreet luxury minutes from downtown Vaduz. Some rooms open directly onto the lawns; others have balconies. The excellent restaurant, open only to guests, offers a five-course tasting menu for 100 SF, as well as more modest entrés. ⊠ *Mareestr. 29, Vaduz FL-9490,* ☎ *075/2321192,* FAX *075/2320053. 29 rooms with bath. Restaurant, indoor pool, sauna. AE, DC, MC, V.*

GENEVA

Arriving and Departing

By Plane
Cointrin (☎ 022/7993111), Geneva's airport, is served by several airlines with direct flights from New York, Washington, Toronto, or London. Swissair also has flights from Chicago and Los Angeles. Check with individual airlines for their schedules.

Swissair ticket holders departing from Cointrin can check their luggage through to the airplane from 120 rail and postbus stations, and also get their boarding passes at eight train stations.

BETWEEN THE AIRPORT AND DOWNTOWN
Cointrin has a direct rail link with Cornavin (☎ 022/7316450), the city's main train station in the center of town. Trains run about every 10 minutes from 5:30 AM to midnight. The trip takes about six minutes, and the second-class fare is 5 SF.

There is also regular city bus service from the airport to the center of Geneva. The bus takes about 20 minutes, and the fare is 3 SF. Some hotels provide their own bus service.

Taxis, though plentiful, are very expensive, charging at least 30 SF to the city center. Tips are expected only for luggage.

By Train
All services—domestic and international—use Cornavin Station in the center of the city. For information, dial 022/1573333, a schedule and reservation number taxed at 1.40 SF per minute.

By Bus
Long-distance buses generally use the bus station at Place Dorcière, behind the English Church in the city center.

By Car
Since Geneva sits on the border of the French Alps, near Annecy and not far from Lyon, entry from the French autoroutes is very convenient. From within Switzerland, enter from the north via Lausanne.

Getting Around

By Bus and Streetcar
There are scheduled services by local buses and trains every few minutes on all routes. Before you board, you must buy your ticket from one of the vending machines at the stop (they have English instructions). For 2.20 SF you can use the system for one hour, changing as often as you like. Save money and buy a ticket covering unlimited travel all day within the city center for 8.50 SF. If you have a **Swiss Pass,** you can travel free (☞ Getting Around Switzerland by Train, *above*).

By Taxi

Taxis are extremely expensive; use them only if there's no alternative. There is a 5 SF minimum charge per passenger just to get into the cab, plus a 2 SF-per-kilometer charge.

Guided Tours

Orientation

Bus tours around Geneva are operated by **Key Tours** (☎ 022/7314140). They leave from the bus station in place Dorcière, behind the English Church, at 2 (also at 10 AM in high season). These tours, which involve some walking in the Old Town, last about two hours and cost 27 SF for adults, 14 SF for children under 14.

Special-Interest

The United Nations organizes tours around the Palais des Nations. Take Bus 8 or F past Nations to the Appia stop. Enter by the Pregny Gate in the avenue de la Paix. Tours, lasting about an hour, are given regularly from January through March and November to mid-December, weekdays 10–noon and 2–4; April through June, September, and October, daily 10–noon and 2–4; July and August, daily 9–6. They cost 8.50 SF for adults, 4 SF for children 6–18.

The tourist office offers a series of two-hour guided group walks following varying itineraries, from "Historic Edifices" to "International Geneva." Tours depart at 2:30 daily from the Hotel de Ville, June 15-September 30, and cost 35 SF per person (minimum two). The tourist office also provides audio-guided tours (in English) of the Old Town, covering 26 points of interest, complete with map, cassette, and player; rental is 10 SF. A refundable deposit of 50 SF is required.

Excursions

There are bus excursions from Geneva to Lausanne, Montreux, the Mont Blanc area, the Jura, and the Bernese Oberland. They vary considerably according to the weather and time of year, so inquire locally.

Boat excursions vary for the same reasons. When the weather is fine, take one of the delightful day trips that stop at some of the villages on the vineyard-fringed lake; some trips also pass by or stop at the 13th-century Château de Chillon, the setting for Byron's *Prisoner of Chillon*. Full details are available from **Mouettes Genevoises** (☎ 022/7322944), **Swissboat** (☎ 022/7324747), **Compagnie de Navigation** (☎ 022/3112521), or from the tourist office.

Visitor Information

The **Office du Tourisme de Genève** (✉ Cornavin Station, ☎ 022/7385200; open mid-Sept.–mid-June, Mon.–Sat. 9–6; mid-June–mid-Sept., weekdays 8–8, weekends 8–6). There is also an information booth at place du Molard 4, on the left bank (☎ 021/3119827). For information by mail, contact the administration (✉ rte. de l'Aèroport 10, Case Postale 1215, Genève 15, ☎ 022/7880808, FAX 022/788–81–70).

Exploring Geneva

Draped at the foot of the Jura and the Alps on the westernmost tip of Lake Geneva (or Lac Léman, as the natives know it), Geneva is the most cosmopolitan and graceful of Swiss cities and the stronghold of the French-speaking region. Just a stone's throw from the French border and 160 kilometers (100 miles) or so from Lyon, its grand mansarded mansions stand guard beside the River Rhône, where yachts bob, gulls dive, and Rolls-Royces purr beside manicured promenades. The combination of Swiss efficiency and French savoir faire gives the city a chic polish, and the infusion of international blood from the United Nations adds a heterogeneity that is rare in cities with a population of only 160,000.

Headquarters of the World Health Organization and the International Red Cross, Geneva has always been a city of humanity and enlightenment, offering refuge to writers Voltaire, Hugo, Dumas, Balzac, and Stendhal, as well as to religious reformers Calvin and Knox. Byron, Shelley, Wagner, and Liszt all fled from scandal into Geneva's sheltering arms.

A Roman seat for 500 years (from 120 BC), then home to early Burgundians, Geneva flourished under bishop-princes into the 11th century, fending off the greedy dukes of Savoy in conflicts that lasted into the 17th century. Under the guiding fervor of Calvin, Geneva rejected Catholicism and became a stronghold of Protestant reforms. In 1798 it fell to the French, but joined the Swiss Confederation as a canton in 1815, shortly after Napoleon's defeat. The French accent remains nonetheless.

Numbers in the margin correspond to points of interest on the Geneva map.

★ ❶ Start your walk at Gare de Cornavin (Cornavin Station), heading down the rue du Mont-Blanc to the **Pont du Mont-Blanc,** which spans the westernmost point of Lac Léman as it squeezes back into the Rhône. From the middle of the bridge you can see the snowy peak of Mont Blanc itself, and from March through October you'll have a fine view of the **Jet d'Eau,** Europe's tallest fountain, gushing 475 feet into the air.

❷ Back at the foot of the bridge, turn right onto quai du Mont-Blanc to reach the **Monument Brunswick,** the high-Victorian tomb of a duke of Brunswick who left his fortune to Geneva in 1873. Just north are the city's grandest hotels, overlooking a manicured garden walk and the embarkation points for excursion boats. If you continue north through elegant parks and turn inland on the avenue de la Paix, you'll reach ★ ❸ the enormous **International Complex,** where the **Palais des Nations** houses the European seat of the United Nations. (You can also reach it by taking Bus 8 or F from the train station. For guided tour information, ☞ Special-Interest Tours, *above*.)

❹ Or turn left from the Pont du Mont-Blanc and walk down the elegant quai des Bergues. In the center of the Rhône is the **Ile Rousseau** (Rousseau Island), with a statue of the Swiss-born philosopher. Turn ❺ left onto the **Pont de l'Ile,** where the tall Tour de l'Ile, once a medieval prison, guards the two banks. Turn left again and cross the place Bel-Air, the center of the business and banking district, and follow the rue ❻ de la Corraterie to the **place Neuve.** Here you'll see the **Grand Théâtre,** which hosts opera, ballet, and sometimes the Orchestre de la Suisse Romande (it also performs at nearby Victoria Hall), and the **Conservatoire de Musique.** Also at this address is the **Musée Rath,** with topnotch changing exhibitions. ✉ Pl. Neuve, ☎ 022/3105270. ✇ Up to 10 SF. ⊙ Hours vary with exhibition; check local listings.

★ ❼ Above the ancient ramparts on your left are some of the wealthiest old homes in Geneva. The University of Geneva is situated in the Parc des Bastions, behind imposing gates. Keep left until you see the famous **Monument de la Réformation,** which pays homage to such Protestant pioneers as Bèze, Calvin, Farel, and Knox. Passing the uphill ramp and continuing to the farther rear gate, take the park exit just beyond the monument and turn left on the rue St-Leger, passing through the ivy-covered arch and winding into the **Vieille Ville,** or Old Town.

★ **8** When you reach the ancient place du Bourg-de-Four, once a Roman forum, turn right on rue des Chaudronniers and head for the **Musée d'Art et Histoire,** with its fine collection of paintings, sculpture, and archaeological finds. ⊠ *2 rue Charles-Galland,* ☎ *022/3114340.* ⊑ *Free.* ☉ *Tues.–Sun. 10–5.*

★ **9** **10** Just beyond are the spiraling cupolas of the **Eglise Russe** (Russian Church) and the **Collection Baur,** which features of Oriental arts. ⊠ *8 rue Munier-Romilly,* ☎ *022/3461729.* ⊑ *5 SF.* ☉ *Tues.–Sun. 2–6.*

★ **11** Alternatively, from the place du Bourg-de-Four head left up any combination of narrow streets and stairs toward the **Cathédrale St-Pierre,** with its schizophrenic mix of Classical and Gothic styles. Hidden beneath its nave (entrance outside) is one of the biggest **archaeological digs** in all of Europe, a massive excavation of the cathedral's early Christian precursors, now restored as a stunning maze of backlit walkways over mosaics, baptisteries, and ancient foundations. ☎ *022/7385650.* ⊑ *Site: 5 SF.* ☉ *Tues.–Sun. 10–1 and 2–6.*

12 Calvin worshiped in the cathedral, but he made the **Temple de l'Auditoire,** an austere Gothic church just south of the cathedral toward place du Bourg-de-Four, into his lecture hall, where he taught missionaries his doctrines of reform. ⊠ *Place de la Taconnerie,* ☎ *022/7385650.* ☉ *Oct.–May, Tues.–Sat. 2–5; June–Sept., Tues.–Sat. 2–6.*

13 Behind the Temple de l'Auditoire, on the rue de l'Hôtel de Ville, is the 16th-century **Hôtel de Ville,** where in 1864, in the Alabama Hall, the Geneva Convention was signed by 16 countries, laying the foundations for the International Red Cross. ⊠ *4 rue de l'Hôtel de Ville,* ☎ *022/3272209.* ☉ *Individual visits by request. Guided group tours by prior arrangement.*

The winding, cobbled streets leading from the cathedral down to the modern city are lined with antiques shops, galleries, and unique but often expensive boutiques. The medieval Grand' Rue is the oldest in Geneva, the rue de l'Hôtel de Ville features lovely 17th-century homes, and the rue Calvin has noble mansions from the 18th century (No. 11 stands on the site of John Calvin's house). At No. 6 rue du Puits-St-Pierre is

★ **14** the **Maison Tavel,** the oldest building in town, presenting a vivid, intimate re-creation of daily life and urban history. ⊠ *6 rue du Puits-St-Pierre,* ☎ *022/3102900.* ⊑ *Free.* ☉ *Tues.–Sun. 10–5.*

Down the hill, plunge back into the new city and one of the most luxurious shopping districts in Europe, stretching temptingly between the quai Général-Guisan, rue du Rhône, rue de la Croix d'Or, and rue du Marché. It's tough enough to resist top-name *prêt-à-porter* (ready-to-wear clothing), dazzling jewelry and watches, luscious chocolates, and luxurious furs and leathers, but the glittering boutiques of the new three-

15 story **Confédération-Centre**—where all the above are concentrated with a vengeance—could melt the strongest resolve. Escape across the

16 quai, head back toward the lake, and come to your senses in the **Jardin Anglais,** where the famous floral clock will tell you that it's time to stop.

Dining

Perch fresh from Lac Léman, cream-sauced *omble chevalier* (a kind of salmon trout), Lyonnaise *cardon* (a celerylike vegetable often served in casseroles), pigs' feet, and the famous cheese fondue are specialties

1086

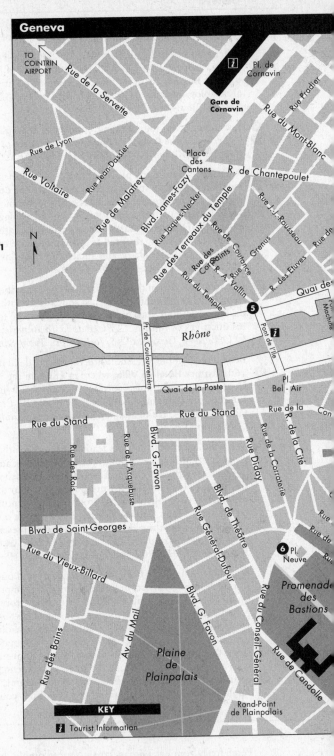

Geneva

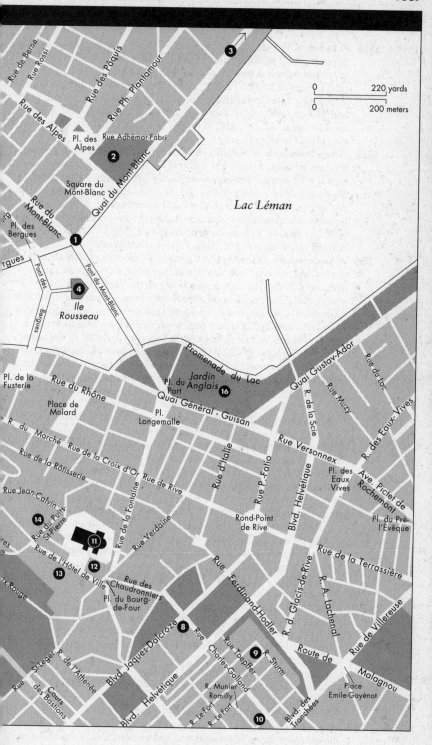

220 yards
200 meters

Lac Léman

Rue de Berne
Rue Rossi
Rue des Pâquis
Rue Ph. Plantamour
Rue des Alpes
Pl. des Alpes
Rue Adhémar-Fabri
Quai du Mont-Blanc
Square du Mont-Blanc
Rue du Mont-Blanc
Pl. des Bergues
Pont des Bergues
Pont du Mont-Blanc
Ile Rousseau

Promenade du Lac
Quai Gustav-Ador
Rue du Lac
Pl. de la Fusterie
Rue du Rhône
Pl. du Port
Jardin Anglais
Quai Général - Guisan
R. de la Scie
Rue Muzy
Place de Molard
Pl. Longemalle
R. du Marché
Rue de la Croix d'Or
Rue de Rive
Rue de la Rôtisserie
Rue d'Italie
Rue P.-Fatio
Rue Versonnex
R. des Eaux-Vives
Rue Jean-Calvin
Rue de la Fontaine
Blvd. Helvétique
Pl. des Eaux Vives
Ave. Pictet de Rochemont
Rue du Puits St-Pierre
Rue Verdaine
Rond-Point de Rive
Pl. du Pré-l'Évêque
Rue de l'Hôtel de Ville
Rue des Chaudronniers
Rue Ferdinand-Hodler
R. d. Glacis-de-Rive
R. A. Lachenal
Rue de la Terrassière
Pl. du Bourg-de-Four
Rue de Villereuse
R.-Rouge
St-Léger
R. de l'Athénée
Blvd. Jaques-Dalcroze
Rue Toepffer
Rue Charles-Galland
R. Sturm
Route de
Malagnou
Cours des Bastions
Blvd. Helvétique
R. Munier Romilly
R. Le-Fort
R. Le-Fort
Blvd. des Tranchées
Place Emile-Gayénot

of this most French of Swiss cities. Be warned: Many restaurants close on weekends.

$$$$ ✕ **Le Béarn.** This elegant and formal little Empire-style restaurant, dressed up with pretty porcelain and crystal, features modern, light, and creative cuisine: ravioli stuffed with Scottish salmon and oysters, preserved rabbit in green mustard sauce, and any number of truffle specialties, including a spectacular truffle soufflé. There are also excellent Swiss and French wines. ⊠ *4 quai de la Poste,* ☎ 022/3210028. *Reservations essential. AE,DC, MC, V. Closed Sun., Sat. lunch Oct.–Apr.; summer, closed weekends.*

$$$$ ✕ **Les Continents.** It's often a shock to find exceptional restaurants in modern business hotels, but this one, at the base of the Inter-Continental's 18 stories, serves contemporary French cuisine prepared by Irish super-chef Tommy Byrne. Try the sole sautéed in pistou, pigeon pie, or veal kidney with shallots and sweetbreads. All the international heads of state have met here during the peace conferences of the past 25 years. ⊠ *7–9 ch. du Petit-Saconnex,* ☎ 022/9193350. *Reservations essential. AE, DC, MC, V. Closed weekends.*

$$$ ✕ **La Cassolette.** In the heart of Carouge, the picturesque *cité sarde* (Sar-
★ dinian city) of old houses, tiny streets, and ancient courtyards, this modern and colorful upscale bistro features the imaginative cuisine of young chef Réné Fracheboud. Novel specialties—salmon and zucchini with dried tomatoes and curry oil, or veal sweetbreads and duck liver in bitter cocoa and Arabian coffee—are served on Miami-bright triangular platters, in high contrast to the very pink decor. ⊠ *31 rue Jacques Dalphin, Carouge,* ☎ 022/3420318. *No credit cards. Closed weekends.*

$$$ ✕ **La Mère Royaume.** Only in Geneva could you find good, classic French cooking served in a pseudo-historic setting under the careful direction of a charming Italian couple. Even the name is Genevois: La Mère Royaume was a local Joan of Arc, who in 1602 repulsed the army of the duke of Savoy by dumping hot soup on the soldiers' heads. The formal main restaurant serves French standards—foie gras sautéed in raspberry vinegar, rack of lamb with garlic confit—but the rustic bistro offers inexpensive plats du jour. ⊠ *9 rue des Corps-Saints,* ☎ 022/7327008. *AE, DC, MC, V. Closed Sun. No lunch Sat.*

$$ ✕ **Boeuf Rouge.** In a kitsch-packed fin-de-siècle setting, this cozy and
★ popular spot delivers the real thing: rich, unadulterated Lyonnaise cuisine. Try the down-home preserved-duck-gizzard salad; hand-stuffed pistachio sausage with warm lentil salad; *boudin noir* (blood sausage) with apples; or *andouillettes* (spicy pork sausages) in mustard sauce—followed by an authentic tarte tatin. There's proud service, a chic clientele after 9, and a good house Beaujolais. ⊠ *17 rue Alfred-Vincent,* ☎ 022/7327537. *AE, MC, V. Closed weekends.*

$$ ✕ **La Favola.** Run by a young Ticinese couple from Locarno, this
★ quirky little restaurant may be the most picturesque in town. The tiny dining room, at the top of a vertiginous spiral staircase, strikes a delicate balance between rustic and fussy, with its lace window panels, embroidered cloths, polished parquet, and rough-beamed ceiling sponge-painted ochre and rust. The food finds the same delicate balance between country simple and city chic: carpaccio with olive paste or white truffles, rabbit in Gorgonzola, and venison *bollito* (the Italian version of boiled beef) braised in Barolo wine. ⊠ *15 rue Jean Calvin,* ☎ 022/3117437. *MC, V. Closed weekends.*

$$ ✕ **Le Pied-de-Cochon.** This old bistro, facing the Palais de Justice in the old town, serves lawyers, artists, and workers alike. Crowded, noisy, smoky, and lively, with original beams and a zinc-top bar, it serves good, simple fare. *Pieds de cochon* (pigs' feet)—either grilled, with mushrooms, with lentils, or *désossés* (boned)—are the staple; there are also andouillettes, tripes, and salads. ✉ *4 pl. du Bourg-de-Four,* ☎ *022/3104797. AE, DC, MC, V. Closed Sun. May–Sept.*

$ ✕ **Les Armures.** In the picturesque and historic hotel at the summit of
★ the Old Town (☞ Lodging, *below*) and across from the Hôtel de Ville, this atmospheric restaurant has several dining halls, all decorated with authentic arms from the Middle Ages. The broad menu of Swiss specialties ranges from fondue to choucroute (sauerkraut) to Rösti, but some of the dishes are pure Genevois. There also are inexpensive pizzas and a good selection of salads and fruit tarts. Everyone comes here, from workers to politicians. ✉ *1 rue du Puits-St-Pierre,* ☎ *022/3103442. AE, DC, MC, V.*

$ ✕ **Taverne de la Madeleine.** Tucked into the commercial maze between
★ the Rue de la Croix d'Or and the Old Town, next to l'Eglise de la Madeleine, this casual, alcohol-free café claims to be the oldest eatery in Geneva. It's run by the city's temperance league, and thus loses the businesspeople who insist on a pitcher of Fendant with their meals: All the more room for you to relax over homemade choucroute, perch, or fresh-baked fruit tarts in the charming Victorian dining room upstairs. There are big, fresh salads, vegetable plates, and a variety of loose-leaf teas. Hot food is served until 7 PM in summer, only until 4 PM in winter. ✉ *20 rue Toutes-âmes,* ☎ *022/3106070. No credit cards.*

Lodging

$$$$ 🏨 **Beau-Rivage.** Hushed and genteel, this grand old Victorian palace has been largely restored to its 1865 splendor: It's all velvet, parquet, and frescoes, and there's a marble fountain in the lobby. Front rooms take in magnificent Right Bank views, as does the terrace restaurant on the second floor, over the prestigious French restaurant Le Chat Botté. In 1898, Empress Elizabeth of Austria died here after being stabbed only 300 feet away. ✉ *13 quai du Mont-Blanc, CH-1201,* ☎ *022/7310221,* FAX *022/7389847. 97 rooms with bath. 2 restaurants, bar, café, in-room VCRs. AE, DC, MC, V.*

$$$$ 🏨 **Le Richemond.** Under the management of the Armleder family since
★ 1875, this Right Bank luxury landmark maintains its Victorian presence without looking like a museum. Nor does it feel like one: It's a lively, thriving, contemporary inn, proud of recent guests (Michael Jackson) as well as past ones (Colette, Miró, Chagall). Only the restaurant Le Gentilhomme indulges in museumlike conservatism: Amid pompous red velvet, crystal, and gilt, you can indulge in a meal Escoffier would have relished. There's classic but showy French cuisine, old wines, brandy, cigars, and your share of the 8 kilos of caviar they serve every day. ✉ *Jardin Brunswick, CH-1211,* ☎ *022/7311400,* FAX *022/7316709. 98 rooms with bath. 2 restaurants, bar, café, beauty salon. AE, DC, MC, V.*

$$$ 🏨 **Les Armures.** In the heart of the Old Town, this 17th-century ar-
★ chitectural treasure has been restored; now its charming original stonework, frescoes, and stenciled beams vie with impeccable modern comforts. Its few rooms are intimate, combining appropriate Old World furnishings with slick marble baths. Its casual restaurant is an Old Town must (☞ Dining, *above*). Approach by car can be difficult, and the nearest parking is three blocks away. ✉ *1 rue du Puits-St-Pierre, CH-1204,* ☎ *022/3109172,* FAX *022/3109846. 28 rooms with bath. Restaurant, bar, in-room VCRs. AE, DC, MC, V.*

$$$ 🏨 **Metropole.** Built in 1855, hosting Franz Liszt, Richard Wagner, and
★ Hector Berlioz *en passage,* this grand old hotel was lent to the city of Geneva as a clearinghouse for Red Cross archives of prisoners of World War II. Restored to its original dignity inside and out in 1982 by its management of more than 30 years, the Metropole has as much

riverside splendor as its Right Bank sisters—at a lower price. There's a relaxed, unfussy ambience despite the grand scale, with leather and hunting prints mixed in with discreet pastels. Riverside rooms are noisier, over traffic, but the view compensates; ask for the quieter third or fourth floors. It's seconds from the best shopping and minutes from the Old Town. ⌧ *34 quai Général-Guisan, CH-1204,* ☎ *022/3111344,* FAX *022/3111350. 140 rooms with bath. 2 restaurants, bar, café. AE, DC, MC, V.*

$$ 🏨 **Strasbourg-Univers.** A stylish oasis in the slightly sleazy train-station neighborhood, this mid-level retreat was fully renovated in 1992 and now offers sleek decor (marble and faux burled wood), convenience, and four-star quality at a three-star price. ⌧ *10 rue Pradier, CH-1201,* ☎ *022/7322562,* FAX *022/7384208. 52 rooms with bath or shower. Restaurant, bar, café. AE, DC, MC, V.*

$$ **Touring-Balance.** Renovations have given this 19th-century hotel a
★ modern, contemporary look; ask to stay in the slick, solid, high-tech rooms on the higher floors, which are adorned with gallery-quality lithographs. The restaurant offers a straightforward French menu, with entrées around 45 SF. You can't beat this location for shopping and sightseeing. ⌧ *13 pl. Longemalle, CH-1204,* ☎ *022/287122,* FAX *022/3104045. 64 rooms with bath. Restaurant, café. AE, DC, MC, V.*

$ 🏨 **De la Cloche.** This once-luxurious walk-up has tidy, tasteful new decor
★ that hasn't altered its period details, and the courtyard setting is so quiet you can hear birds in the garden. Good-size rooms with high ceilings share baths down the hall. The prices, which include breakfast, are still the lowest in town. ⌧ *6 rue de la Cloche, CH-1201,* ☎ *022/7329481. 8 rooms without bath. Breakfast room. No credit cards.*

$ 🏨 **Des Tourelles.** Once worthy of a czar, now host to the backpacking crowd, this fading Victorian offers enormous bay-windowed corner rooms, many with marble fireplaces, French doors, and views over the Rhône. Several rooms have been renovated to include a modern shower and toilet, and those on the street side have double-glazed windows to keep the street noise out. The staff is young and friendly, and the breakfast—included in the rate—is an all-you-can-eat backpacker's delight. ⌧ *2 blvd. James-Fazy, CH-1201,* ☎ *022/7324423,* FAX *022/7327620. 25 rooms, some with shower. Breakfast room. AE, DC, MC, V.*

LUZERN

Arriving and Departing

By Plane

The nearest international airport is **Kloten** in **Zürich,** approximately 54 kilometers (33 miles) from Luzern. **Swissair** flies in most often from the United States and the United Kingdom. Easy rail connections, departing hourly, whisk you on to Luzern within 50 minutes.

By Car

It's easy to reach Luzern from Zürich by road, approaching from the national expressway N3 south, connecting to the N4 via the secondary E41, in the direction of Zug, and continuing on N4 to the city (roads are well-marked). Approaching from the southern St. Gotthard Pass route, or after cutting through the Furka Pass by rail ferry, you'll descend below Andermatt to Altdorf, where a view-stifling tunnel sweeps you through to the shores of the lake and on to the city. Arriving from Basel in the northwest, it's a clean sweep on the N2 into Luzern.

By Train

Luzern functions as a rail crossroads, with express trains connecting hourly from Zürich and every two hours from Geneva, the latter with a change at Bern. For rail information, call the Swiss Federal Railways (☎ 1573333).

Getting Around

Luzern's modest scale allows you to explore most of the city easily on foot, but you will want to resort to mass transit to visit far-flung attractions like the Verkehrshaus (Swiss Transport Museum) and nearby Alpine viewpoints.

By Bus
The city bus system offers easy access to sights throughout the urban area. If you're staying in a Luzern hotel, you will be eligible for a special **Guest-Ticket,** offering unlimited rides for two days for a minimal fee of 5 SF.

By Taxi
Given the small scale of the Old Town and the narrowness of most of its streets, taxis can prove a pricey encumbrance.

By Boat
It's a crime to see this city and the surrounding mountainous region only from the shore; some of its most impressive landscapes can be seen from the deck of one of the cruise ships that ply the Vierwaldstättersee (Lake Luzern). The boats of the Schiffahrtsgesellschaft des Vierwaldstättersees (☎ 041/3676767) operate on a standardized, mass-transit-style schedule, crisscrossing the lake and stopping at scenic resorts and historic sites. Both the Swiss Pass and the Swiss Boat Pass (☞ Getting Around in Switzerland, *above*) entitle you to free rides.

Important Addresses and Numbers

Emergencies
Police (☎ 117). **Medical, dental, and pharmacy referral** (☎ 111). **Auto breakdown:** Tourist Club of Switzerland (☎ 140), Swiss Automobile Club (☎ 041/2100155).

Visitor Information
The City Tourist Office, near the Bahnhof (⊠ Frankenstr. 1, ☎ 041/4107171), offers information April–October, weekdays 8:30–6, Saturday 9–5; May–October, Sunday 9–1 as well; and November–March, weekdays 8:30–noon and 2–6, Saturday 9–1. Another tourist information center is at Schweizerhofquai 2, open May and Oct., weekdays 9–noon and 1–7, Sat. 9–noon and 1–4; June–Sept., weekdays 9–5, Sat. 9–4; it has an accommodations service.

Guided Tours

Orientation
The Luzern tourist office offers a two-hour guided walking tour of Luzern, departing from the office daily at 9:30; from May through September, there are 2 PM tours as well. The 15 SF price includes a drink.

Excursions
★ You may want to take a high-altitude day trip to **Mount Pilatus, Mount**
★ **Rigi,** or—if you're bound for the highest—the **Titlis,** above Engelberg. All can be accomplished by means of a combination train and cog-railway, though to mount the Titlis you must complete the journey by riding a series of cable cars. For information, check at the Central Switzerland Tourism Association (⊠ Verkehrsverband Zentralschweiz, Alpenstr. 1, Luzern, ☎ 041/4101891) or at the City Tourist Office. Boat
★ and bus trips to William Tell country—**Altdorf** and **Bürglen**—make the most of both scenery and local legend.

Exploring Luzern

Luzern's Old Town straddles the waters of the River Reuss where it flows out of the Vierwaldstättersee, its more concentrated section occupying the river's right bank. To get a feel for its riverfront center, ★ start at the right-bank end of the landmark **Kapellbrücke,** with its flanking water tower. Stay on this side for the moment and head down the **Rathausquai,** lined with hotels and cafés on the right and bordered by a sloping reinforced embankment on the left. Facing the end of a modern bridge (the Rathaus-Steg) stands the **Altes Rathaus** (Old Town Hall), built between 1599 and 1606 in the late-Renaissance style.

Numbers in the margin correspond to points of interest on the Luzern map.

❶ Just to the right of the Rathaus, the **Am Rhyn-Haus** contains an impressive collection of late paintings by Picasso. ⊠ *Furreng.,* ☎ *041/ 4101773.* ☑ *6 SF.* ☉ *Apr.–Oct., daily 10–6; Nov.–Mar., daily 11–1 and 2–4.*

Turn right and climb the stairs past the ornately frescoed **Zunfthaus zur Pfistern,** a guildhall dating from the late 15th and early 16th centuries, to the Kornmarkt, once the site of the local grain market. Cross the square and cut left into the **Weinmarkt,** the loveliest of Luzern's several squares. The Gothic fountain in the center depicts St. Mauritius, patron saint of warriors, and its surrounding buildings are flamboyantly frescoed in 16th-century style.

★ **❷** Leave the square from its west end, turn right on Kramgasse, and cross Mühlenplatz to the **Spreuerbrücke,** a weathered, narrow covered wooden bridge dating from 1408. In its interior gables there is a series of eerie, well-preserved paintings (by Kaspar Meglinger) of the Dance of Death; they date from the 17th century, though their style and inspiration—tracing back to the plague that devastated Luzern and all of Europe in the 14th century—is medieval.

❸ At the other end of the bridge, on the left bank, stands the stylish **Historisches Museum** (Historical Museum). Its exhibits of city sculptures, Swiss arms and flags, and reconstructed rooms depict both rural and urban life. The late-Gothic building was constructed as an armory, and dates from 1567. ⊠ *Pfisterg. 24,* ☎ *041/2285424.* ☑ *4 SF.* ☉ *Tues.–Fri. 10–noon and 2–5, weekends 10–5.*

NEED A BREAK?
Follow Baselstrasse west to a funicular that will carry you up (2 SF) to the **Château Gütsch,** where you can have a drink on the panoramic terrace and take in a bird's-eye view of the old town, the river, and the fortification walls—a must for photographers.

★ **❹** From the end of the Spreuerbrücke, cut back upstream along Pfistergasse and turn left onto Bahnhofstrasse to reach the Baroque **Jesuitenkirche** (Jesuit Church), constructed 1667–78. Its symmetrical entrance is flanked by two onion-domed towers, added in 1893. Do not fail to go inside: Its vast interior, restored to mint condition, is a rococo explosion of gilt, marble, and epic frescoes.

❺ Continue past the Rathaus-Steg bridge, but before you enter the **Kapellbrücke** (Chapel Bridge), take a look at its exterior from the right. It snakes diagonally across the water and, when first built in the early 14th century, served as the dividing line between the lake and the river. Its shingled roof and grand stone water tower (now housing a souvenir stand) are to Luzern what the Matterhorn is to Zermatt—but considerably more vulnerable, as was proved by a fire in 1993. Almost 80%

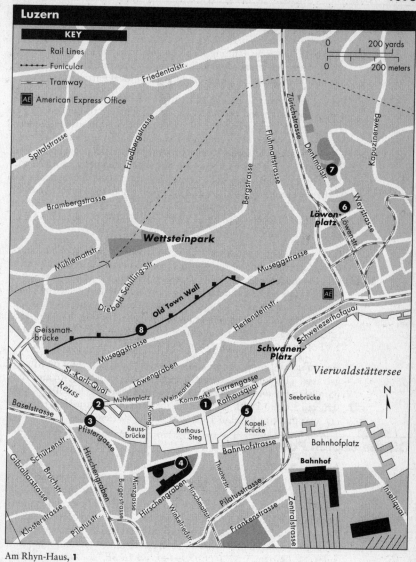

Luzern

KEY
— Rail Lines
••••• Funicular
═╪═ Tramway
AE American Express Office

0 — 200 yards
0 — 200 meters

Friedentalstr.

Spitalstrasse

Brambergsstrasse

Friedbergstrasse

Mühlemattstr.

Diebold Schilling-Str.

Wettsteinpark

Bergstrasse

Fluhmattstrasse

Zürichstrasse

Denkmalstr.

Kapuzinerweg

7

6
Löwen-platz

Weystrasse

Löwenstr.

Museggstrasse

Old Town Wall

Hertensteinstr.

AE

Geissmatt-brücke

8

Museggstrasse

Schweizerhofquai

Löwengraben

Schwanen-Platz

St.-Karli-Quai

Vierwaldstättersee

Reuss

Baselstrasse

2

Mühlenplatz

Weinmarkt

Kornmarkt

1

Furrengasse

Rathausquai

Seebrücke

N

Pfistergasse

Reuss-brücke

Krama

Rathaus-Steg

5

Kapell-brücke

Schützenstr.

Bahnhofstrasse

Bahnhofplatz

Gibraltarstrasse

Bruchstr.

Hirschengraben

Burgerstrasse

Münzgasse

4

Hirschengraben

Hirschmattstr.

Theaterstr.

Pilatusstrasse

Bahnhof

Zentralstrasse

Inseliquai

Klosterstrasse

Pilatusstr.

Winkelriedstr.

Frankenstrasse

Am Rhyn-Haus, **1**
Bourbaki-
Panorama, **6**
Historisches
Museum, **3**
Jesuitenkirche, **4**
Kapellbrücke, **5**
Löwendenkmal, **7**
Spreuerbrücke, **2**
Zytturm, **8**

of this fragile monument was destroyed, including many of the 17th-century paintings inside; the original 111 gable panels painted by Heinrich Wägmann in the 17th century have been replaced with polychrome copies. The paintings depict scenes from the history of Luzern and Switzerland, legendary exploits of the city's patron saints—St. Leodegar and St. Mauritius, and coats of arms of local patrician families.

Now break away from the old town and work your way through dense pedestrian and bus traffic at Schwanenplatz to Haldenstrasse. Turn left on Zürichstrasse or Löwenstrasse and continue to **Löwenplatz,** which is dominated by an enormous conical wooden structure that looks like a remnant of some Victorian world's fair. That's what it was

❻ meant to be: The **Bourbaki-Panorama** was created between 1876 and 1878 as a genuine, step-right-up tourist attraction. The conical roof shelters a sweeping, wraparound epic painting of the French Army of the East retreating into Switzerland at Verrières—a famous episode in the Franco-Prussian War. ⊠ *Löwenpl.,* ☎ *. 041/4109942.* ☑ *3 SF.* ☉ *May–Sept., daily 9–6; Mar.–Apr. and Oct., daily 9–5.*

Just beyond lies yet another 19th-century wonder, a Luzern landmark that is certainly one of the world's most evocative public sculptures:

★ **❼** the **Löwendenkmal** (Lion Monument). Designed by Danish sculptor Berthel Thorvaldsen and carved out of a sheer sandstone face by Lucas Ahorn of Konstanz, it's a simple image of a dying lion, his chin sagging on his shield, a broken stump of spear in his side. It commemorates the 760 Swiss guards and their officers who died defending Louis XVI of France at the Tuileries in Paris in 1792.

Return down Löwenstrasse and, at Löwenplatz, turn right on Museggstrasse. This long street cuts through an original city gate and runs parallel to the **watchtowers** and **crenellated walls** of Old Luzern, con-

❽ structed around 1400. The clock in the **Zytturm,** the fourth of the towers, was made in Basel in 1385 and still keeps time.

Off the Beaten Path

★ Not easily included in a walking tour of central Luzern but one of the city's (if not Switzerland's) greater attractions, the **Verkehrshaus** (Swiss Transport Museum) can be reached by steamer, car, or city bus. It's almost a world's fair in itself, with a complex of buildings and exhibits both indoors and out, including dioramas, live demonstrations, and a "Swissorama" (360-degree screen) film. Every mode of transportation is covered, from stagecoaches and bicycles to jumbo jets and space capsules. ⊠ *Lidostr. 5,* ☎ *041/3704444.* ☑ *15 SF.* ☉ *Mar.–Oct., daily 9–6; Nov.–Feb., weekdays 10–4, Sun. 10–5.*

Shopping

Although Luzern no longer produces embroidery or lace, one can find here a wide variety of Swiss crafts of the highest quality, and watches in all price categories.

Luzern offers a good representation of general Swiss goods: At **Sturzenegger** (⊠ Schwanenpl. 7, ☎ 041/4101958), you'll find St-Gallen-made linens and embroidered niceties. At **Mühlebach & Birrer** (⊠ Kapellpl., ☎ 041/4106673) there's a selection of Alpen-style (although Austrian-made) Geiger clothing (boiled-wool jackets, edelweiss-embroidered sweaters) as well as Swiss-made handkerchiefs. **Schmid-Linder** (⊠ Denkmalstr. 9, ☎ 041/4104346) sells a comprehensive line of Swiss kitsch: cuckoo clocks, cowbells, embroidery, and a large stock of wood carvings from Brienz, in the Berner Oberland. **Innerschweizer Heimatwerk** (⊠ Franziskanerpl.14, ☎ 041/2106944) sells nothing but local crafts—mostly contemporary, rather than traditional—from handwoven items to ceramics and wooden toys. One enormous patriarch of the unusually competitive watch business is **Gübelin** (⊠ Schweizerhofquai, ☎ 041/4105142), the exclusive source for Audemars Piguet, Patek Philippe, and its own house brand. **Bucherer** (⊠ Schwanenpl., ☎ 041/3697700) represents Piaget and Rolex. Like Gübelin, it advertises heavily and offers inexpensive souvenirs to lure shoppers into its luxurious showroom. An abundance of small shops carry Tissot, Rado, Corum and others–but prices are controlled by the manufacturers. Watch for close-outs on out-of-date models.

Dining

Rooted in the German region of Switzerland and surrounded by farmland, central Switzerland has a native cuisine that's best described as down-home and hearty. Luzern takes pride in its *Kügelipaschtetli,* puff pastry nests filled with tiny veal meatballs, mushrooms, cream sauce, occasionally raisins, and bits of chicken, pork, or sweetbreads. Watch for lake fish such as *Egli* (perch), *Hecht* (pike), *Forelle* (trout), and *Felchen* (whitefish). Though most often served baked or fried, a Luzern tradition offers them sautéed and sauced with tomatoes, mushrooms, and capers. After your meal here, have a steaming mug of coffee laced with *Träsch,* a harsh schnapps blended from the dregs of other eaux-de-vie; the locals leave their spoons in their cups as they drink.

$$$$ ✕ **Wilden Mann.** You may choose between the ancient original Bürg-
★ erstube, all dark beams and family crests, already a carriage stop for travelers bound for the St. Gotthard pass in 1517, or the more formal Liedertafel dining room next to it, with wainscoting, vaulting, and candlelight. On either side, the menu and prices are the same (with additional soup, salad, and sausage options in the Stube)—and the cooking is outstanding. ⊠ *Bahnhofstr. 30,* ☎ *041/2101666. AE, DC, MC, V.*

$$$–$$$$ ✕ **La Vague (Hotel des Balances).** This chic, upscale restaurant cum ca-
★ sual bistro offers soigné decor, a shimmering riverside view, and adventuresome, worldly cuisine that features local fish. A typical three-course dinner may include salmon carpaccio marinated with herbs, followed by duck with port and fig sauce, and topped off with a kirsch-doused chestnut parfait. A house specialty is light, fresh fish fondue for two. ⊠ *Metzgerrainle 7 (Weinmarkt),* ☎ *041/4103010. AE, DC, MC, V.*

$$ ✕ **Galliker.** Step past the ancient facade into an all-wood room roar-
★ ing with local action, where Luzerners drink, smoke, and bask in their culinary roots. Brisk, motherly waitresses serve the dishes Mutti used to make: Fresh *Kutteln* (tripe) in rich white wine sauce with cumin seeds; real *Kalbskopf* (chopped fresh veal head) served with heaps of green onions and warm vinaigrette; authentic Luzerner Kügelipaschtetli; and their famous simmered-beef pot-au-feu, served only on Tuesday, Wednesday, and Saturday. ⊠ *Schützenstr. 1,* ☎ *041/2401002. AE, MC, V. Closed Sun., Mon., and mid-July–mid-Aug.*

$$ ✕ **Rebstock/Hofstube.** Across from the Hofkirche and at the opposite end of the culinary spectrum from Galliker, this up-to-date kitchen offers modern, international fare, including rabbit, lamb, and organic vegetarian specialties. The lively bentwood brasserie hums with locals lunching by the bar, while the more formal, old-style restaurant glows with wood and brass under a low-beamed herringbone-patterned ceiling. On warm summer days you can sit in the garden or on the terrace. ⊠ *St.-Leodegarstr. 3,* ☎ *041/4103581. AE, DC, MC, V.*

$ ✕ **Zur Pfistern.** One of the architectural focal points of the Old Town waterfront, this floridly decorated former guildhall, whose origins can be traced back to 1341, offers a good selection of moderately priced meals in addition to higher-priced standards. Lake fish and *pastetli* (Cornish pasty-like meat pies made with puff pastry) are good local options. In summer the small first-floor balcony may provide the best seat in town for a picture-postcard waterfront view. ⊠ *Kornmarkt 4,* ☎ *041/4103650. AE, DC, MC, V.*

Lodging

Luzern serves as a convenient home base for those exploring the Vierwaldstättersee and the surrounding region. Unlike most Swiss cities, it has its high and low seasons, and drops prices considerably in winter.

$$$$ 🏨 **Château Gütsch.** Any antiquity in this "castle" built as a hotel in 1888 is strictly contrived, but honeymooners, groups, and determined romantics in search of a storybook Europe enjoy the Disneyland-like experience: the turrets and towers worthy of Mad Ludwig of Bavaria, the cellars, crypts, and corridors lined with a hodgepodge of relics—not to mention the magnificent hilltop site above Luzern and the private forest beyond. An extravagant renovation, reducing the number of fantasy-style rooms but enlarging them considerably, has bumped this lodging-attraction into the deluxe category. ⊠ *Kanonenstr., CH-6003,* ☎ *041/2490272,* 𝖥𝖠𝖷 *041/2490252. 49 rooms. Restaurant, pool. AE, DC, MC, V.*

$$$$ 🏨 **Palace.** Brilliantly refurbished and subtly modernized to take in broader lake views, the Palace now wears a classic look with a touch of the postmodern. Built in 1906 and regularly updated, the hotel has a recently renovated fifth floor, and an entire sixth floor consists of spacious new rooms with views of the lake and the mountains. ⊠ *Haldenstr. 10, CH-6002,* ☎ *041/4100404,* 𝖥𝖠𝖷 *041/4101504. 185 rooms. Restaurant, bar, health club, 2 saunas, steam room, parking. AE, DC, MC, V.*

$$$ 🏨 **Des Balances.** Restored and refurbished outside and in, this river-
★   front property built in the 19th century on the site of an ancient guildhall gleams with style. State-of-the-art tile baths, up-to-date pastel decor, and one of the best locations in town make it the slickest in its price class. Nearly every window frames a period scene outdoors, including the Chapel Bridge and the Jesuit Church. ⊠ *Metzgerrainle 7, CH-6003,* ☎ *041/4103010,* 𝖥𝖠𝖷 *041/4106451. 57 rooms with bath. 2 restaurants, piano bar. AE, DC, MC, V.*

$$$ 🏨 **Wilden Mann.** Living up to its reputation, the city's best-known hotel
★   offers its guests a gracious and authentic experience of Old Luzern. Joining several old structures that once were part of the town wall, it has been carefully renovated in such a way as to maintain its Reformation ambience, with stone, beams, brass, hand-painted tiles, and burnished wood everywhere. Standard rooms have a prim 19th-century look. ⊠ *Bahnhofstr. 30, CH-6003,* ☎ *041/2101666,* 𝖥𝖠𝖷 *041/2101629. 43 rooms. 2 restaurants. AE, DC, MC, V.*

$$ 🏨 **Des Alpes.** With a terrific riverfront location in the bustling heart of the Old Town, this historic hotel has been completely renovated inside to look like a laminate-and-vinyl chain motel. Rooms are generously proportioned, tidy, and sleek; front doubles, several with balconies, overlook the water and the promenade. Cheaper back rooms face the Old Town. ⊠ *Rathausquai 5, CH-6003, 041/4105825,* 𝖥𝖠𝖷 *041/4107451. 45 rooms with bath. Restaurant, café. AE, DC, MC, V.*

$$ 🏨 **Zum Weissen Kreuz.** Now refurbished and upgraded, this former
★   bargain hotel on the waterfront is slick, bright, and airtight, with tile, stucco, oak, and pine to soften the modern edges. Some rooms face the lake, others the Old Town. The restaurant, Al Forno, serves pasta and pizzas. ⊠ *Furreng. 19, CH-6003,* ☎ *041/4104040,* 𝖥𝖠𝖷 *041/4104060. 22 rooms with bath. Restaurant. AE, DC, MC, V.*

$ ☷ **Schlüssel.** On the Franziskanerplatz, with several rooms overlooking the Franciscan church and fountain, this spare, no-nonsense little lodging attracts young bargain hunters. It's a pleasant combination of tidy new touches (quarry tile, white paint) and antiquity: You can have dinner in a low, cross-vaulted "crypt" and admire the fine old lobby beams. ⊠ *Franziskanerpl. 12, CH-6003,* ☎ *041/2101061,* 𝔽𝔸𝕏 *041/2101021. 11 rooms, most with bath. Restaurant. MC, V.*

$ ☷ **SSR Touristen.** Despite its friendly collegiate atmosphere, this cheery
★ dormlike spot is anything but a backpackers' flophouse. It has a terrific setting on the Reuss, around the corner from the Old Town. Sleep in a dormitory room with 10 beds, or in one of several four-bed rooms—some with bath, some without. ⊠ *12 St. Karli Quai, CH-6003,* ☎ *041/4102474,* 𝔽𝔸𝕏 *041/4108414. 100 beds. AE, DC, MC, V.*

The Arts

Luzern hosts the **International Music Festival** for three weeks in August every year. Performances take place at the **Kunsthaus** (⊠ Frohburgstr. 6, ☎ 041/233880). For more information, contact Internationale Musikfestwochen (⊠ Postfach, CH-6002, Luzern, ☎ 041/2103562). **The Allgemeine Musikgesellschaft Luzern** (AML), the local orchestra in residence, offers a season of concerts from October through June. These are also held in the Kunsthaus (⊠ Frohburgstr. 6, ☎ 041/2103880).

Nightlife

Bars and Lounges

The **Des Balances** hotel has a hip, upscale piano bar (⊠ Metzgerrainle 7, ☎ 041/4103010). **Château Gütsch** (⊠ Kanonenstr. ☎ 041/2490272) draws a sedate dinner-and-dancing crowd. **Mr. Pickwick** (⊠ Rathausquai 6, ☎ 041/4105927) is a Swiss version of an English pub.

Casinos

The most sophisticated nightlife in Luzern is found in the **Casino** (⊠ Haldenstr. 6, ☎ 041/4185656), on the northern shore by the grand hotels. You can play *boules* in the Gambling Room (5 SF federally imposed betting limit), dance in the **Babilonia** club, watch a strip show in the **Red Rose,** or have a Swiss meal in **Le Chalet** while watching a folklore performance.

Discos

Flora Club (⊠ Seidenhofstr. 5, ☎ 041/2297979) mixes dancing with folkloric shows.

Folklore

The **Stadtkeller** (⊠ Sternenpl. 3, ☎ 041/4104733) transports you to the Valais Alps for cheese, yodeling, and dirndled dancers. **Nightboat** (⊠ Landungsbrücke 6, ☎ 041/3676767) sails every evening May through September at 8:45, offering drinks, meals, and a mid-cruise folklore show. The Casino and Flora Club are two other options.

LUGANO

Arriving and Departing

By Plane

There are short connecting flights by **Crossair**—the Swiss domestic network—to Lugano Airport (☎ 091/6101212) from Zürich, Geneva, Basel, and Bern, as well as from Paris, Nice, Rome, Florence, and Venice. The nearest intercontinental airport is at Milan, Italy, about 56 kilometers (35 miles) away.

BETWEEN THE AIRPORT AND DOWNTOWN

There is no longer regular bus service between the local airport and central Lugano, 7 kilometers (4 miles) away; taxis, costing about 30 SF to the center, are the only option.

By Train

There's a train from Zürich every hour; the trip takes about three hours. If you're coming from Geneva, you can catch the Milan express at various times, changing at Domodossola and Bellinzona. Daytimes, there's a train every hour from Milan's Stazione Centrale; the trip takes about 1½ hours. Always keep passports handy and confirm times with the Swiss Federal Railways. For train information in Lugano, phone 091/1753333.

By Car

There are fast, direct highways from both Milan and Zürich. If you are planning to drive from Geneva, check weather conditions with the automobile associations beforehand.

Getting Around

By Bus

Well-integrated services run regularly on all local routes. Buy your ticket from the machine at the stop before you board.

By Train

The **Regional Holiday Season Ticket** gives unlimited free travel for seven consecutive days on most rail and steamer routes and a 50% or 25% discount on longer trips in Lugano. Available at the tourist office, they cost 96 SF for adults (88 SF for Swiss Pass holders) and 45 SF for children 6–16. They can be used with or without a Swiss Pass. The newest version offers any three out of seven days free on most routes, with 50% or 25% reductions on the remaining four days. It costs 70 SF for adults, 62 SF for Swiss Pass holders, and 30 SF for children.

By Taxi

Though less expensive than in Zürich or Geneva, taxis are still not cheap, with a 10 SF minimum. To order a cab, call 091/9712121 or 091/9719190.

By Boat

The **Navigation Company of Lake Lugano** (☎ 091/971-52-23) offers cruise-boat excursions around the bay to the romantic fishing village
★ of **Gandria** and to the Villa Favorita. You may use these like public transit, following a schedule and paying according to distance, or look into special tickets: Seven consecutive days' unlimited travel costs 50 SF, three days' within a week costs 44 SF; an all-day pass costs 30 SF.

Guided Tours

The tourist office is the best source of information about hiking tours into the mountains surrounding Lugano; it offers several topographical maps and suggested itineraries. There are bus trips to Locarno, Ascona, Lake Como, Lake Maggiore, Milan, Venice, St. Moritz, Florence, the Alpine passes, and the Italian market in Como. A free guided walking tour of Lugano leaves the tourist office every Tuesday at 9:30 AM from April through October.

Visitor Information

Ente Turistico Lugano (✉ Riva Albertolli 5, CH-6901, ☎ 091/9214664; ☉ Oct.–June, weekdays 9–6; July–Sept., weekdays 9–6:30; April–Oct., Saturday 9–5).

Exploring Lugano

Because of its beautiful, sparkling bay of the Lago di Lugano and dark, conical mountains rising up on either side, Lugano is often referred to as "the Rio of the Old World." The largest city in the Ticino—Switzerland's Italian-speaking region—Lugano has not escaped some of the overdevelopment inevitable in a successful resort town. There's bumper-to-bumper traffic, right up to the waterfront, much of it manic Italian style; and concrete high-rise hotels crowd the waterfront, with balconies skewed to a view no matter what the aesthetic cost.

Even so, the view from the waterfront is unforgettable, the boulevards are fashionable, and the Old Quarter is still reminiscent of sleepy old towns in Italy. And the sacred *passeggiata*—the afternoon stroll to see and be seen that winds down every Italian day—asserts the city's true personality as a graceful, sophisticated Old World resort—not Swiss, not Italian . . . just Lugano.

Numbers in the margin correspond to points of interest on the Lugano map.

Start your walk under the broad porticoes of the tourist office and cross over to the tree-lined promenade, where you can stroll along the waterfront and take in stunning mountain views. Head left into the **Parco Civico,** with its cacti, exotic shrubs, and more than 1,000 varieties of roses. There's an aviary, a tiny "deer zoo," and a fine view of the bay from its peninsula. The **Villa Ciani,** temporarily closed for renovations, contains paintings and sculptures from Tintoretto to Giacometti.

❷ Also in the Parco Civico is the **Museo Cantonale di Storia Naturale** (Cantonal Museum of Natural History), with exhibits on the region's animals, plants, and mushrooms. ⊠ *Viale Cattaneo 4,* ☎ *091/9237827.* ☞ *Free.* ☺ *Tues.–Sat. 9–noon and 2–5.*

❸ If you continue left along the waterfront, you'll come to the **Lido,** with a stretch of sandy beach, several swimming pools, and a restaurant. ☞ *5 SF.*

★ ❹ Or follow the promenade to the right until you reach the **Imbarcadero Centrale,** where steamers set out into the bay, and turn inland to the **Piazza della Riforma,** stronghold of Lugano's Italian culture, where the modish locals socialize in outdoor cafés. From here, enter the **Old Town** and follow the steep, narrow streets lined with chic Italian clothing shops and small markets offering pungent local cheeses and porcini mushrooms.

❺ On the street of the same name, you'll find the **Cathedral San Lorenzo,** with its graceful Renaissance facade and noteworthy frescoes inside.

★ ❻ Then shop your way down the Via Nassa until you reach the **Church of Santa Maria degli Angioli,** in Piazza Luini, dating from 1455. Inside, you'll find splendid frescoes of the *Passion* and *Crucifixion* by Bernardino Luini (1475–1532).

❼ Across the street, the waterfront **Giardino Belvedere** (Belvedere Gardens) set off 12 modern sculptures with palms, camellias, oleanders, and magnolias. At the far end there's **public bathing** on the Riva Caccia. ☞ *Bathing: 5 SF.* ☺ *mid-May–mid-Sept.*

If you want to see more of Lugano's luxurious parkland, take the funicular from the Old Town to the train station: Behind the station, deer **❽** greet you as you enter the floral **Parco Tassino.** Or take Bus 2 east to **❾** the San Domenico stop in Castagnola to reach the **Parco degli Ulivi** (Olive Park), where you can climb the olive-lined slopes of Monte Brè for views of the surrounding mountains.

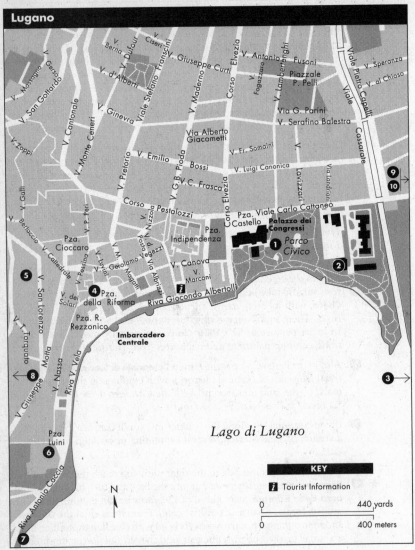

Lugano

Lago di Lugano

KEY

i Tourist Information

| 0 | 440 yards |
| 0 | 400 meters |

Cathedral San
Lorenzo, **5**

Church of Santa
Maria degli Angioli, **6**

Giardino Belvedere, **7**

Lido, **3**

Museo Cantonale di
Storia Naturale, **2**

Parco Civico, **1**

Parco Tassino, **8**

Parco degli Ulivi, **9**

Piazza della
Riforma, **4**

Villa Favorita, **10**

★ ⑩ The dust has finally settled at the **Villa Favorita,** owned by the Baron Heinrich von Thyssen-Bornemisza, and you'll find the villa not only completely renovated but also with a portion of its magnificent art collection back on the walls. Among the artists represented are Thomas Hart Benton, Giorgio de Chirico, Frederic Church, Lucien Freud, Edward Hopper, Franz Marc, Jackson Pollock, and Andrew Wyeth. ✉ *Strada Castagnola,* ☎ *091/9721741.* ▣ *12 SF.* ☉ *Easter–Oct., Fri.–Sun. 10–5; during special exhibitions, Tues.–Sun. 10–5.*

Dining

The Ticinese were once poor mountain people, so their cuisine shares the earthy delights of the Piemontese: polenta, gnocchi, game, and mushrooms. But as in all prosperous resorts, the mink-and-Vuarnets set draws the best in upmarket international cooking. Prix-fixe lunches are almost always cheaper, so dine as the Luganese do—before your siesta. That way you can sleep off the fruity local merlot wine before the requisite passeggiata.

$$$$ ✕ **Al Portone.** With silver and lace dressing up the stucco and stone,
★ the settings are formal, but the ambience is strictly easy. Chef Roberto Galizzi creates *nuova cucina* (nouvelle cuisine, Italian-style) with ambition and flair, putting local spins on classics such as roast veal kidneys with balsamic vinegar, pasta with white beans and lobster, seafood carpaccio, or simple and luxurious creamed potatoes with white truffles. ✉ *Viale Cassarate 3,* ☎ *091/9235511,* ℻ *091/9716505. Reservations essential. AE, DC, MC, V. Closed Sun. and Mon.*

$$$$ ✕ **Santabbondio.** Ancient stone and terra-cotta blend with pristine pas-
★ tels in this upgraded grotto, where superb and imaginative new Franco-Italian dishes are served in intimate, formal little dining rooms and on a flower-filled terrace. Watch for lobster risotto, eggplant ravioli, or scallops in orange-basil sauce to confirm what locals assert—that chef-owner Martin Dalsass is the region's best. It's a cab ride from town, toward the airport, but worth the trip. ✉ *Via ai Grotti di Gentilino, Lugano/Sorengo,* ☎ *091/9932388,* ℻ *091/9943237. AE, DC, MC, V. Closed Mon. and first wk in Jan. No lunch Sat., no dinner Sun.*

$$$ ✕ **Galleria.** Though the setting aspires to formal hauteur, with contemporary appointments, modern art, and jacket-clad guests, family warmth and vigor peek through the chinks in the facade, and in the end this is a comfortable place for good, middle-class Italian cooking. ✉ *Via Vegezzi,* ☎ *091/9236288. AE, DC, MC, V. Closed Sun.*

$$$ ✕ **Locanda del Boschetto.** The grill is the first thing you see in this no-
★ nonsense restaurant specializing in simple but sensational seafood *alla griglia* (grilled). Crisp linens contrast with rustic wood touches, and the low-key service is helpful and down-to-earth. ✉ *Via Boschetto 8,* ☎ *091/9942493. AE, DC, MC, V. Closed Mon.*

$$ ✕ **Al Barilotto.** Despite its generic pizzeria decor and American-style
★ salad bar, this restaurant draws local crowds for grilled meats, homemade pasta, and wood-oven pizza. Take Bus 10 from the center. ✉ *Hôtel de la Paix, Via Calloni 18,* ☎ *091/9949695. AE, DC, MC, V.*

$ ✕ **La Tinera.** This tiny tavern crowds loyal locals, tourists, and fami-
★ lies onto wooden benches for authentic regional specialties, hearty meats, and pastas. It's tucked down an alley off Via Pessina in the Old Town. Regional wine is served in traditional ceramic bowls. ✉ *Via dei Gorini 2,* ☎ *091/9235219. AE, DC, MC, V.*

$ ✕ **Sayonara.** There's nothing Japanese about it: This is a modern urban pizzeria with several rooms that are crowded at lunchtime with a mix of tourists and shoppers. The old copper pot automatically stirs polenta, which is offered in several combinations, one of them with mountain hare. ✉ *Via F. Soave 10,* ☎ *091/9220170. AE, DC, MC, V.*

Lodging

There are few inexpensive hotels in the downtown area, but a brief drive into the surrounding countryside increases your options. Since this is a summer resort, many hotels close for the winter, so call ahead.

$$$$ ⊞ **Ticino.** This warmly appointed 16th-century house, a member of the
★   Romantik Hotels group, is in the heart of the Old Town, just steps away from the funicular to the station. Shuttered windows look out from every room onto a glassed-in garden and courtyard, and vaulted halls are lined with art and antiques. ⊠ *Piazza Cioccaro 1, CH-6901,* ☎ *091/9227772,* 🖷 *091/9236278. 23 rooms with bath. Restaurant. AE, DC, MC, V.*

$$$$ ⊞ **Villa Principe Leopoldo.** With exorbitant prices to match its Old World
★   service and splendor, this sumptuously appointed Relais et Château garden mansion sits on a hillside high over the lake. There is free transportation to the airport and the town, and a 19-hole golf course 5 kilometers away. ⊠ *Via Montalbano 5, CH-6900,* ☎ *091/9858855,* 🖷 *091/9858825. 24 suites. Restaurant, bar, pool, hot tub, massage, sauna, tennis courts, health club, free parking. AE, DC, MC, V.*

$$$ ⊞ **Alba.** This solid little hotel, surrounded by landscaped grounds and
★   with an interior that is lavish in the extreme, is ideal for lovers with a sense of camp or honeymooners looking for romantic privacy. Mirrors, gilt, plush, and crystal fill the public areas, and the beds are all ruffles and swags. ⊠ *Via delle Scuole 11, CH-6902,* ☎ *091/9943731,* 🖷 *091/9944523. 25 rooms with bath. Restaurant, bar. AE, DC, MC, V.*

$$$ ⊞ **Du Lac.** This discreet and simple hotel offers you more lakefront luxury for your money than the glossier Grand Eden down the same beach. All rooms face the lake, but the sixth floor is the quietest. The hotel has a private swimming area on the lake. ⊠ *Riva Paradiso 3, CH-6902,* ☎ *091/9941921,* 🖷 *091/9941122. 53 rooms with bath. Restaurant, bar, pool, massage, sauna. AE, DC, MC, V.*

$$$ ⊞ **International au Lac.** This is a big, old-fashioned, friendly city hotel, half a block from the lake, with many lake-view rooms. It's next to Santa Maria degli Angioli, on the edge of the shopping district and the Old Town. The restaurant serves primarily Italian fare, with a smattering of continental dishes. ⊠ *Via Nassa 68, CH-6901,* ☎ *091/9227541,* 🖷 *091/9227544. 86 rooms with bath. Restaurant, pool. AE, DC, MC, V. Closed Nov.–Mar.*

$$$ ⊞ **Park-Hotel Nizza.** This former villa, modernized in 1974 and re-
★   furbished every winter, affords panoramic views from its perch on the lower slopes of San Salvatore; high above the lake, it's an uphill hike from town. The mostly small rooms are decorated with antique reproductions; there is no extra charge for lake views. An ultramodern bar overlooks the lake, and a good restaurant serves vegetables from its own garden and even wine from its own vineyards—al fresco, when weather permits. There's a weekly barbecue with the owners presiding. A shuttle provides service to Paradiso. ⊠ *Via Guidino 14, CH-6902,* ☎ *091/9941771,* 🖷 *091/9941773. 30 rooms with bath. Restaurant, bar, outdoor pool. AE, DC, MC, V. Closed Nov.–Mar.*

$$ ⊞ **San Carlo.** The San Carlo offers one of the better deals in this high-priced town: It's small, clean, newly furnished, and right on the main pedestrian shopping street a block from the waterfront. It's also 150 yards from the funicular that takes you to the railway station. There are no frills, but the atmosphere is friendly. ⊠ *Via Nassa 28, CH-6901,* ☎ *091/9227107,* 🖷 *091/9228022. 22 rooms with bath. Breakfast room, free parking.*

$ ⊞ **Flora.** Though it's one of the cheapest hotels in town, this 70-year-
★   old family-owned lodging has been reasonably well maintained. Room decor is minimal, a holdover from the 1960s (red-orange prints,

wood-grain Formica), and the once-elegant dining hall has seen better days. But some rooms have balconies, and there's a sheltered garden terrace for balmy nights. ✉ *Via Geretta 16, CH-6902,* ☎ *091/9941671,* FAX *091/9942738. 33 rooms with bath. Restaurant, bar, pool. AE, DC, MC, V.*

$ 🖭 **Zurigo.** Ideally situated behind the tourist office and handy to parks, shopping, and promenades, this spartan hotel near the Palais Congrès offers quiet comfort at rock-bottom rates, even in high season. Several rooms have full bathrooms. ✉ *Corso Pestalozzi 13, CH–6900,* ☎ *091/9234343* FAX *091/9239268 25 rooms. Breakfast room. No credit cards.*

BERN

Arriving and Departing

By Plane
Belp (☎ 031/9615516) is a small airport, 9 kilometers (6 miles) south of the city, with flights to and from most European capitals. A bus from the airport to the train station costs 12 SF, a taxi about 35 SF.

By Train
Bern is a major link between Geneva, Zürich, and Basel, with fast connections running usually every hour from the enormous central station. The high-speed French **Train de Grande Vitesse** (TGV) gets to Paris in 4½ hours.

By Car
The Geneva-Zürich expressway runs by Bern, with crossroads leading to Basel and Lugano as well.

Getting Around

By Bus and Tram
Bern is such a small, concentrated city that it's easy to get around in on foot. There are 6½ kilometers (4 miles) of covered shopping arcades in the center. If you don't feel like walking, however, the bus and tram service is excellent; fares range from 1.50 SF to 2.40 SF. Buy individual tickets from the dispenser at the tram or bus stop; the posted map will tell you the cost. Tourist cards for unlimited rides are available at 5 SF for one day, 7 SF for two, and 10 SF for three. Buy them at the tourist office in the Bahnhof (train station) or at the public-transportation ticket office in the subway leading down to the main station (take the escalator in front of Loeb's department store and turn right through the Christoffel Tower). A Swiss Pass (☞ Getting Around in Switzerland, *above*) allows you to travel free.

By Taxi
This extravagant alternative to walking costs between 6 SF and 15 SF across town.

Important Addresses and Numbers

Embassies
U.S. (✉ Jubiläumsstr. 93, ☎ 031/3577011). **Canadian** (✉ Kirchenfeldstr. 88, ☎ 031/3526381). **U.K.** (✉ Thunstr. 50, ☎ 031/3525021).

Emergencies
Police (☎ 117). **Ambulance** (☎ 144). **Doctor/Dentist** (☎ 3119211). **All-night pharmacy** (☎ 3112211).

Visitor Information

The tourist office is on Bahnhofplatz (☎ 031/3116611); it's open June–Sept., daily 9–8:30; Oct.–May, Mon.–Sat. 9–6:30 and Sun. 10–5.

Guided Tours

Walking

A two-hour tour around the Old Town, covering all the principal sights, is offered for 20F by the tourist office from May to October, daily at 10 and 2; from November to March, Saturday at 2; and in April, Monday to Saturday at 2.

Excursions

Bern prides itself on its central location, and offers easy access to Zürich and Geneva as well as to the remote farmlands of the Bernese Mittelland, where you can visit the Emmental Valley. The most popular (though expensive) outing is up into the heights of the Jungfrau in the Alpine Bernese Oberland. The train passes through Interlaken, Lauterbrunnen, Wengen, and Kleine Scheidegg on its way to the Jungfraujoch, which, at 11,525 feet, has the highest rail station in Europe.

Exploring Bern

No cosmopolitan nonsense here: Local specialties are fatback and sauerkraut, the annual fair features the humble onion, and the president takes the tram to work. Walking down broad, medieval streets past squares teeming with farmers' markets and cafés full of shirt-sleeved politicos, you might forget Bern is the federal capital—indeed, the geographic and political hub—of a sophisticated and prosperous nation.

It earned its pivotal position with a combination of muscle and influence dating from the 12th century, when the Holy Roman Emperor Berchtold V established a fortress on this gooseneck in the River Aare. By the 15th century the Bernese had overcome the Burgundians to expand their territories west to Geneva. Napoléon suppressed them briefly—from 1798 until his defeat in 1815—but by 1848 Bern was back in charge as the capital of the Swiss Confederation.

Today it's not the massive Bundeshaus (House of Parliament) that dominates the city, but the perfectly preserved arcades, fountains, and thick, sturdy towers from the Middle Ages. They're the reason UNESCO granted Bern World Cultural Heritage status, ranking it with the Pyramids and the Taj Mahal.

Numbers in the margin correspond to points of interest on the Bern map.

①② Start on the busy **Bahnhofplatz** in front of the grand old Schweizerhof hotel, facing the station. To your left is the **Heiliggeistkirche** (Church of the Holy Spirit), finished in 1729 and at odds with both the modern and the medieval in Bern. Head to the right up Bollwerk and turn

★ ③ right into Kleeplatz and Hodlerstrasse, where you'll come to the **Kunstmuseum Bern** on your left. Established for the promotion of Swiss artists, it houses an exceptional group of works by Ferdinand Hodler, including some enormous, striking allegories; there are landscapes and portraits as well. The museum's pride—and its justified claim to fame—is its collection of more than 2,000 works by Paul Klee, who lived in Bern. ⊠ *Hodlerstr. 8–12,* ☎ *031/3110944* FAX *031/3117263.* ☞ *6 SF.* ☉ *Tues. 10–9; Wed.–Sun. 10–5.*

Bern

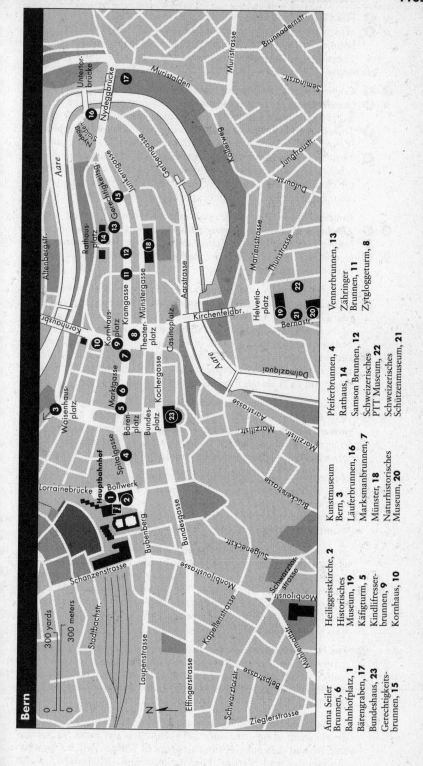

Anna Seiler
Brunnen, **6**
Bahnhofplatz, **1**
Bärengraben, **17**
Bundeshaus, **23**
Gerechtigkeits-
brunnen, **15**

Heiliggeistkirche, **2**
Historisches
Museum, **19**
Käfigturm, **5**
Kindlifresser-
brunnen, **9**
Kornhaus, **10**

Kunstmuseum
Bern, **3**
Läuferbrunnen, **16**
Marksmanbrunnen, **7**
Münster, **18**
Naturhistorisches
Museum, **20**

Pfeiferbrunnen, **4**
Rathaus, **14**
Samson Brunnen, **12**
Schweizerisches
PTT Museum, **22**
Schweizerisches
Schützenmuseum, **21**

Vennerbrunnen, **13**
Zähringer
Brunnen, **11**
Zytgloggeturm, **8**

★ **4**
★ **5** Head for the **Pfeiferbrunnen** (Bagpiper Fountain), the first of the city's many signature fountains, erected between 1539 and 1546, and the **Käfigturm** (Prison Tower), which dates from the 13th and 14th centuries. There's a small museum of economic and cultural life inside. ⊠ *Marktgasse 67* ☎ *031/3112306.* ☞ *Free.* ☉ *Tues.–Fri. 9–1 and 2–6.*

6 **7**
★ **8** Continue down Marktgasse past the **Anna Seiler Brunnen** and **Marksmannbrunnen** to the **Zytgloggeturm** (clock tower), built as a city gate in 1191 but transformed by the addition of an astronomical clock in 1530.

9
10 To your right is the Theaterplatz, to your left the **Kindlifresserbrunnen** (Ogre Fountain) and Kornhausplatz, where you will see the imposing 18th-century **Kornhaus** (granary), the magnificent vaulted cellar of which is now a popular beer hall. Now walk past the clock tower and observe the clock from the east side. At four minutes before the hour, you can see the famous mechanical puppet bears perform their ancient dance.

11 **12**
13
★ **14** Continue down Kramgasse, past fine 18th-century houses and the **Zähringer Brunnen** and **Samson Brunnen.** Turn left at the next small intersection and head for Rathausplatz, with its **Vennerbrunnen** (Ensign Fountain) and late-Gothic **Rathaus** (City Hall), seat of both the city and cantonal governments.

15 Head back to the main thoroughfare, here named Gerechtigkeitsgasse, and continue past the **Gerechtigkeitsbrunnen** (Justice Fountain) and lovely patrician houses. Artisans' shops, galleries, and antiquaries line this leg of the endless arcades. Turn left at the bottom and head down the steep Nydegg Stalden through one of the city's oldest sections, past the

16 **Läuferbrunnen** (Messenger Fountain), to the River Aare. Here you come upon the **Nydeggkirche** (Nydegg Church), on the right, built between 1341 and 1571 on the foundations of Berchtold V's ruined fortress.

★ **17** Cross the river by the **Untertorbrücke** (Lower Gate Bridge), then turn right and climb up to the **Nydeggbrücke.** Here are the famed **Bärengraben** (Bear Pits), where Bern keeps some of its live mascots. According to legend, Berchtold named the town after the first animal he killed while hunting—a bear, since the woods were thick with them.

★ **18** Now cross the bridge and head back into town, turning left up Junkerngasse to the magnificent Gothic **Münster** (cathedral), begun in 1421. It features a fine portal (1490) depicting the Last Judgment, recently restored and repainted in extravagant hues. There are also stunning stained-glass windows, both originals and period reproductions.

★ **19** Arty boutiques line the Munstergasse, leading to the **Casino,** which houses a concert hall and restaurants, but no casino. If you head even farther south (across the river yet again), you'll find Helvetiaplatz, a historic square surrounded by museums. The **Historisches Museum** (Historical Museum) has a prehistoric collection, 15th-century Flemish tapestries, and Bernese sculptures. ⊠ *Helvetiapl. 5,* ☎ *031/3511811* ℻ *031/3510663.* ☞ *5 SF.* ☉ *Tues.–Sun. 10–5.*

20 The **Naturhistorisches Museum** is one of Europe's finest museums of natural history. It features enormous wildlife dioramas and a splendid collection of Alpine minerals. ⊠ *Bernastr. 15,* ☎ *031/3507111* ℻ *031/350-7499.* ☞ *3 SF (Sun. free).* ☉ *Mon. 2–5, Tues.–Sat. 9–5, and Sun. 10–5.*

21 The **Schweizerisches Schützenmuseum** (Swiss Rifle Museum) traces the development of firearms since 1817 and celebrates Swiss marksmanship beyond the apple-splitting accuracy of William Tell. It's between the History and Natural History museums. ⊠ *Bernastr. 5,* ☎ *031/3510127,* ℻ *031/351-0804.* ☞ *Free.* ☉ *Tues.–Sat. 2–4, Sun. 10–noon and 2–4.*

㉒ **The Schweizerisches PTT Museum** (Swiss Postal and Telecommunications Museum), now housed in its striking new building behind the Historical Museum, has detailed documents, art, and artifacts of early technology relating to the history of the mails in Switzerland. ⊠ *Helvetiastr. 16*, ☎ *031/3387777,* ⍚ *031/3387777.* ⌦ *2 SF.* ☉ *Tues.–Sun. 10–5.*

★ ㉓ Alternatively, head back from the Casino on Kochergasse past the enormous domed **Bundeshaus** (Capitol). By night, be sure to stick to Kochergasse instead of the river-view promenade behind the capitol building; some visitors have been annoyed by obvious drug trafficking.

Dining

Although Bern teeters between two cultures politically, Teutonic conquers Gallic when it comes to cuisine. Dining in Bern is usually a down-to-earth affair, with Italian home cooking as a popular alternative to the local standard fare of meat and potatoes. Specialties include the famous *Bernerplatte* (sauerkraut with boiled beef, fatty pork, sausages, ham, and tongue), *Buurehamme* (hot smoked ham), and *Ratsherrentopf* (Rösti with roast veal, beef, liver, and sausage). Coffee and *Kuchen* (pastry) are the four-o'clock norm.

$$$$ ✕ **Bellevue-Grill.** When Parliament is in session, this haute-cuisine
★ landmark is transformed from a local gourmet mecca to a political clubhouse. It's where the movers and shakers put their heads together over healthy portions of updated classics such as chopped veal liver Geschnetzeltes with raspberries. ⊠ *Kochergasse 3–5,* ☎ *031/3204545.* AE, DC, MC, V.

$$$$ ✕ **Schultheissenstube.** The intimate, rustic dining room, with a club-
★ like bar in the center and an adjoining all-wood Stübli, looks less like a gastronomic haven than a country pub, and the folksy music furthers the delusion. Yet the cooking is sophisticated, international, and imaginative—duck breast in hazelnut vinaigrette, oyster-and-champagne risotto, seafood lasagna with saffron, Cornish hen with goose-liver sauce. ⊠ *Hotel Schweizerhof, Bahnhofpl. 11,* ☎ *031/3114501. Jacket and tie in dining room.* AE, DC, MC, V. *Closed Sun.*

$$$ ✕ **Jack's Brasserie.** Locally known as the "Stadt Restaurant," this brasserie in the Hotel Schweizerhof has high ceilings, wainscoting, roomy banquettes, and an airy, bustling mood. It's frequented by shoppers, Parliament members, and businesspeople who enjoy its urbane, slightly formal atmosphere. You can enjoy a drink here by day or settle in at mealtime for a smartly served menu of French classics with a light touch. ⊠ *Hotel Schweizerhof, Bahnhofpl. 11,* ☎ *031/3114501.* AE, DC, MC, V.

$$$ ✕ **Zum Rathaus.** Across from the Rathaus in the Old Town, this atmospheric, all-wood landmark has been a restaurant since 1863, though the row house dates from the 17th century. Downstairs, the setting is casual and comfortable, while the upstairs "Marcuard-Stübli" is considerably more formal; during the summer, opt for the outdoor café on the Rathausplatz. The cooking ranges from local meat standards to game, salmon, and hearty pastries. ⊠ *Rathauspl. 5,* ☎ *031/3116183.* AE, DC, MC, V. *Closed Sun. and Mon.*

$$ ✕ **Della Casa.** You can stay downstairs in the steamy, rowdy Stübli,
★ where necktied businessmen roll up their sleeves and play cards, or head up to the restaurant, where they leave their jackets on. It's an unofficial Parliament headquarters, with generous local and Italian specialties. ⊠ *Schauplatzg. 16,* ☎ *031/3112142.* DC, MC, V. *No credit cards downstairs. Closed Sun. No dinner Sat.*

$$ ✕ **Harmonie.** Run by the same family since 1900, this leaded-glass and old-wood café-restaurant serves inexpensive basics alongside pricier heavy-

meat dinners: sausage-and-Rösti, *Käseschnitte* (cheese toast), *Bauer-nomelette* (farm-style, with bacon, potatoes, onions, and herbs), and fondue. It's lively and a little dingy, very friendly, and welcoming to foreigners. ⊠ *Hotelg. 3*, ☎ *031/3113840*, FAX *031/3114012. No credit cards.*

$$ ✕ **Lorenzini.** In a town where the cozy or stuffy holds sway, this hip, ★ bright spot stands apart. Delicious homemade pasta and changing menus representing the specialties of different Italian regions are served with authentic, contemporary flair. The clientele is a mix of voguish yuppies; the café-bar downstairs draws the young and even more seriously chic. ⊠ *Marktgasse-Passage 3*, ☎ *031/3117850. DC, MC, V.*

$$ ✕ **Zunft zur Webern.** Built as a weavers' guildhall in 1704, this classic building has been renovated on the ground floor in a slick but traditional style, with gleaming new wood and bright lighting. The cuisine reflects the sophisticated decor, with generous portions of such upgraded standards as lamb stew with saffron. ⊠ *Gerechtigkeitsg. 68*, ☎ *031/3114258*, FAX *031/3122067. MC, V. Closed Sun. and Mon.*

$ ✕ **Brasserie zum Bärengraben.** Directly across from the bear pits, this ★ popular, easygoing little local institution, with the thinnest veneer of a French accent, serves inexpensive lunch specials to shoppers, tourists, businesspeople, and retirees, who settle in with a newspaper and a *dezi* (deciliter) of wine. The menu offers many old-style basics—Kalbskopf vinaigrette, pigs' feet, stuffed cabbage—and wonderful pastries. À la carte dining can be more expensive. ⊠ *Muristalden 1*, ☎ *031/3314218. No credit cards.*

$ ✕ **Klötzlikeller.** A cozy, quiet, muraled wine cellar, this is much more ★ intimate than the famous Kornhauskeller and just as lovely. Its history as a wine bar dates back to 1635, when there were as many as 250 of them in Bern. True to its heritage, the Klötzlikeller is able to secure the limited wine of Bern, which is sold by the glass. There's also a good, if limited, menu of meat specialties. ⊠ *Gerechtigkeitsg. 62*, ☎ *031/3117456*, FAX *031/3119710. AE, MC, V. Closed Sun. and Mon.*

$ ✕ **Kornhauskeller.** This spectacular vaulted old wine cellar, under the ★ Kornhaus granary, is now a popular beer hall with live music on weekends. Drinkers and revelers take tables in the upstairs galleries while diners in the vast main hall below gaze up at the ceiling frescoes. The Swiss fare satisfies the largest of appetites, but the historic ambience is the real reason to come. ⊠ *Kornhauspl. 18*, ☎ *031/3111133*, FAX *031/3123950. AE, DC, MC, V. Closed Sun. and Mon.*

Lodging

$$$$ 🏨 **Bären/Bristol.** These neighboring properties have been twinned as dependable business-class hotels, with modern interiors and first-class comforts. The Bärenbar, where bears figure heavily in the decor, serves drinks and snacks. ⊠ *Schauplatzg. 4–10, CH-3001*, ☎ *031/3113367*, FAX *031/3116983 (Bären)*; ☎ *031/3110101*, FAX *031/3119479 (Bristol). 149 rooms, 91 with bath. Bar/café, in-room VCRs, sauna. AE, DC, MC, V.*

$$$$ 🏨 **Bellevue Palace.** This is a palace indeed, with a view that gives it an advantage over its friendly rival in luxury, the Schweizerhof. It is 75 years old, with Art Nouveau details that include a sweeping staircase and a spectacular stained-glass ceiling in the lobby. Room decor varies greatly, but all are deluxe. Rooms in the back face the river and the distant snowcapped Alps, including the Eiger and the Jungfrau. Right next to the Parliament building, the Bellevue hosts its fair share of politicos. ⊠ *Kocherg. 3–5, CH-3001*, ☎ *031/3204545*, FAX *031/3114743. 155 rooms with bath. 2 restaurants, bar, café, grill. AE, DC, MC, V.*

$$$$ 🏨 **Schweizerhof.** The quarters are roomy and luxuriously appointed (most double rooms are the size of junior suites and, starting at 350

SF, represent a great value); halls are decorated with antiques from the collection of the Gauer family, the hotel's owners; and service is excellent. The brasserie of this grand, graceful landmark by the Bahnhof is a great place for meeting friends. ⊠ *Bahnhofpl. 11, CH-3001,* ☎ *031/3114501,* FAX *031/3122179. 94 rooms with bath. 3 restaurants, bar, café, deli, nightclub, meeting rooms. AE, DC, MC, V.*

$$$ ★ 🏨 **Belle Epoque.** This relatively new hotel with period furnishings is more suggestive of fin de siècle Paris than you might expect in Germanic Bern: Every inch of the arcaded row house is filled with authentic Art Nouveau and Jugendstil antiques. Despite the historic look, amenities, including white-tile baths and electric blinds, are state-of-the-art. The bar, off the lobby, is a congenial place for a rendezvous. ⊠ *Gerechtigkeitsg. 18, CH-3011,* ☎ *031/3114336,* FAX *031/3113936. 17 rooms with bath. Breakfast room, piano bar. AE, DC, MC, V.*

$$$ 🏨 **Bern.** Behind a spare and imposing neoclassical facade, this onetime theater and formerly modest hotel has been transformed into a sleek, modern gem, with an air-shaft garden "courtyard" lighting the better rooms. ⊠ *Zeughausg. 9, CH-3011,* ☎ *031/3121021,* FAX *031/3121147. 96 rooms with bath. 2 restaurants, café, piano bar. AE, DC, MC, V.*

$$$ 🏨 **Innere Enge.** Opened in December 1992, this renovated early 18th-century inn has been transformed into a slick, deluxe business hotel. Spacious, light, and airy thanks to generous windows that face the Bernese Alps, it's outside the city center. Marian's Jazzroom, in the Louis Armstrong Bar, features top jazz acts. Take Bus 21 ("Bremgarten") from the train station. ⊠ *Engestr. 54, CH-3012,* ☎ *031/3096111,* FAX *031/3096112. 26 rooms with bath. Restaurant, café, piano. AE, DC, MC, V.*

$$ ★ 🏨 **Goldener Adler.** From the outside, this 1764 building looks like a magnificent patrician town house, but its interior is modern and modest, with linoleum baths and severe Formica furniture. The ambience is comfortable and familial nonetheless: Peter Balz runs the kitchen while his wife Verni manages the front. Simple Continental fare is served in the restaurant; for value, take the menu of the day for 15 SF. ⊠ *Gerechtigkeitsg. 7, CH-3011,* ☎ *031/3111725,* FAX *031/3113761. 16 rooms with bath. Restaurant (closed Sun.), café. AE, DC, MC, V.*

$$ ★ 🏨 **Krebs.** A small, classic Swiss hotel, the Krebs is impeccable and solid, managed with an eye for every detail. The spare decor is warmed with wood and made comfortable by the personal, friendly service of the Buri family. A handful of inexpensive rooms without bath offer excellent value. ⊠ *Genferg. 8, CH-3001,* ☎ *031/3114942,* FAX *031/3111035. 44 rooms, 41 with shower. Restaurant. AE, DC, MC, V.*

$ 🏨 **Glocke.** Though it's very plain and shabby in spots, the Bell has a young, friendly management team and two lively restaurants, one a "Swiss Chalet," with dancing and folklore shows, the other an Italian trattoria with a small group of musicians. The rooms have a fresh paint job, tile baths, and homey, unmatched towels. A few rooms without baths cost less. ⊠ *Rathausg. 75, CH-3011,* ☎ *031/3113771,* FAX *031/3111008. 20 rooms, some with bath. 2 restaurants. AE, DC, MC, V.*

$ 🏨 **Goldener Schlüssel.** This is a bright, tidy spot with wood, crisp linens, and tiled baths. It's in the heart of the Old Town, so the rooms are quieter in the back. Two good restaurants serve Swiss and international specialties. ⊠ *Rathausg. 72, CH-3011,* ☎ *031/3110216,* FAX *031/3115688. 29 rooms, some with shower. 2 restaurants. DC, MC, V.*

$ ★ 🏨 **Hospiz zur Heimat.** The elegant 18th-century exterior belies the dormitory gloom inside, but the baths are new and the rooms are immaculate. It's in an excellent Old Town location. ⊠ *Gerechtigkeitsg. 50, CH-3011,* ☎ *031/3110436,* FAX *031/3123386. 40 rooms, some with bath. Breakfast room. AE, DC, MC, V.*

$ 🏨 **Jardin.** In a commercial neighborhood far above the Old Town, this is a solid, roomy, middle-class hotel with fresh decor and baths in every room. It's easily reached by Tram 9 to Breitenrainplatz. ✉ *Militärstr. 38, CH-3014,* ☎ *031/3330117,* ⨳ *031/3330943. 17 rooms with bath. Restaurant. AE, DC, MC, V.*

$ 🏨 **Marthahaus.** Take Bus 20 over the Kornhaus Bridge to this spare, old-style pension in a residential neighborhood north of the Old Town, where rates are low and service is friendly. ✉ *Wyttenbachstr. 22a, CH-3014,* ☎ *031/3324135. 20 rooms, 6 with bath. Breakfast room. MC, V.*

ZERMATT

Lying at an altitude of 5,300 feet, Zermatt offers the ultimate Swiss-Alpine experience: spectacular mountains, a roaring stream, state-of-the-art transport facilities, and a broad range of high-quality accommodations—some of them bursting with rustic atmosphere—plus 230 kilometers (143 miles) of downhill runs and 7 kilometers (4 miles) of cross-country trails. But its greatest claim to fame remains the **Matterhorn** (14,690 feet), which attracts swarms of package-tour sightseers pushing shoulder to shoulder to get yet another shot of this genuine wonder of the Western world.

Arriving and Departing

Zermatt is a car-free resort isolated at the end of the Mattertal, a rugged valley at the eastern end of the Alpine canton of Valais. A good mountain highway and the Brig-Visp-Zermatt Railway cut south through the valley from Visp, the crossroads of the main Valais east–west routes. The airports of Zürich and Geneva are roughly equidistant from Brig, but by approaching from Geneva you can avoid crossing mountain passes.

By Train

The Brig-Visp-Zermatt Railway, a private narrow-gauge system, runs from Brig to Visp, connecting on to Zermatt. All major rail routes connect through Brig, whether you approach from Geneva or Lausanne in the west, from the Lötschberg line that tunnels through from Kandersteg and the Bernese Oberland, or from the Simplon Pass that connects from Italy.

By Car

You can drive up the Mattertal as far as Täsch, but there you must abandon your car in a large parking lot and catch the train for the cogwheel climb into Zermatt.

Getting Around

Because Zermatt permits no private cars, electric taxi shuttles operated by hotels are the only means of transportation. The village is relatively small and easily covered on foot.

By Cable Car and Mountain Rail

Hiking and skiing are Zermatt's raisons d'être, but you can get a head start into the heights by riding part of the sophisticated network of cable cars, lifts, cog railways, and even an underground metro that carry you above the village center into the wilderness. Excursions to the Klein Matterhorn and Gornergrat are particularly spectacular.

Important Addresses and Numbers

Visitor Information

The main tourist office, the **Verkehrsbüro Zermatt,** is across from the train station (✉ Bahnhofpl., CH-3920 ☎ 027/9661181).

Emergencies
Police (☎ 027/605656). **Ambulance** (☎ 027/9672000).

Exploring Zermatt

Zermatt lies in a hollow of meadows and trees ringed by mountains—among them the broad **Monte Rosa** (14,940 feet) with its tallest peak, the **Dufourspitze** (at 15,200 feet, the highest point in Switzerland), of which visitors hear relatively little, so all-consuming is the cult of the Matterhorn. But the Matterhorn deserves idolatry: Though it has become an almost self-parodying icon, like the Eiffel Tower or the Statue of Liberty, this distinctive, snaggle-tooth pyramid thrusting upward in solitary splendor is even more impressive than the photographs suggest.

Despite its celebrity mountain, Zermatt remains a resort with its feet on the ground. It is as protective of its regional quirks as it is of its wildlife and its tumbledown *mazots* (little grain-storage sheds raised on mushroomlike stone bases to keep the mice away), which hunker between the glass-and-concrete chalets like old tenements trapped between skyscrapers. Streets twist past weathered wood walls, flower boxes, and haphazard stone roofs until they break into open country that inevitably slopes uphill.

The cog railway between Visp and Zermatt began disgorging summer tourists with profitable regularity in 1891, but it was not until 1927 that it also plowed through in wintertime. What had drawn the first tourists and made Zermatt a household word was Edward Whymper's spectacular—and catastrophic—conquest of the Matterhorn in 1865. Whymper and his band of six managed to reach the summit, but then tragedy struck. On the treacherous descent, four of the men lost their footing and snapped their safety rope, pulling each other 4,000 feet to their death. The body of one of them was never recovered, but the others lie in the grim little cemetery behind the church in the village center.

If you want to experience the exhilaration of standing on top of the world without risking life or limb, take the trip up the Gornergrat—the train is used for excursions as well as ski transport. Part of the rail system completed in 1898 and the highest exposed rail system in Europe (the train to the Jungfraujoch, though higher, bore through the face of the Eiger), it connects out of the main Zermatt station and climbs slowly up the valley to the **Riffelberg,** which at 8,471 feet offers wide-open views of the Matterhorn. From **Rotenboden,** at 9,248 feet, a short downhill walk leads to the **Riffelsee,** with its postcard-perfect reflections of the famous peak. At the end of the 9-kilometer (6-mile) line, passengers pour onto the observation terraces of the **Gornergrat** (10,269 feet), to take in majestic views of Gorner glacier, the Matterhorn, Monte Rosa, and scores of other peaks. There are departures every 24 minutes between 7 AM and 7 PM. The round-trip fare is 58 SF. Or you can take a one-way ticket for 34 SF and either ski back down to the village or hike down on relatively easy trails (bring warm clothes, sunglasses, and sturdy shoes).

Dining

Perched at the German end of the mostly French canton of Valais, Zermatt offers a variety of French and German cooking, from veal and Rösti to raclette and fondue. Specialties often feature pungent mountain cheese: *Käseschnitte,* for instance, are substantial little casseroles of bread, cheese, and often ham, baked until the whey saturates the crusty bread and the cheese browns to gold. Air-dried beef is another Valais treat: The meat is pressed into a dense brick and dried in mountain breezes, then ultimately served in thin, translucent slices, with gherkins and crisp pickled onions. Alas, McDonald's has infiltrated this once-isolated retreat, and you now have to climb or ski to find memorable, cut-above dining outside the hotels. Since Zermatt is for the most part a one-street town, street addresses are not always used.

$$ ✕ **Findlerhof.** Whether for long lunches between sessions on the slopes,
★ for the traditional wind-down après-ski, or for a panoramic meal-break on an all-day hike, this mountain restaurant in tiny Findeln, between the Sunnegga and Blauherd ski areas, is de rigueur with hip young Brits and Americans. The Matterhorn views from the wraparound dining porch are astonishing, the winter dining room cozy with pine and stone, and the food surprisingly fresh and creative. Franz and Heidi Schwery tend their own Alpine garden to provide spinach for the bacon-crisped salad, and rhubarb and berries for their hot desserts. Rösti and cream-sauced pastas round out the menu. It's about 20 minutes' walk down from the Sunnegga Express stop, and another 20 minutes back down to Zermatt. ✉ *Findeln,* ☎ *027/9672588. No credit cards. Closed May–mid-June, mid-Oct.–Nov.*

$$ ✕ **Zum See.** Beyond Findeln, in a tiny village by the same name, Zum
★ See has become something of an institution, serving light meals of a quality and level of inventiveness that would merit acclaim even if the restaurant weren't in the middle of nowhere at 5,794 feet. In summer its shaded picnic tables draw hikers who reward themselves with home-made pasta and fresh-cranked sorbet at the finish of a day's climb; in winter its low, cozy log dining room gives skiers a glow with a fine assortment of brandies. ✉ ☎ *028/672045. No credit cards. Closed May–June, Oct.–mid-Nov.*

$ ✉ **Elsie's Bar.** Directly across from the church, this popular, central après-ski haunt looks like a log cabin inside. Its barroom draws an international crowd in search of cocktails, American-style. Light meals include cheese specialties and snails. ✉ ☎ *027/9672431. AE, DC, MC, V.*

Lodging

At high season—Christmas and New Year's, Easter, and late summer—Zermatt's high prices rival those of Zürich and Geneva. But read the fine print carefully when you plan your visit: Most hotels include half pension in their price, offering breakfast and your choice of a noon or evening meal. Hotels that call themselves "garni" do not offer pension dining plans.

$$$$ 🏠 **Mont Cervin.** One of the flagships of the Seiler dynasty, this is a sleek,
★ luxurious, and urbane mountain hotel. Built in 1852, it's unusually low-slung for a grand hotel, with dark beams and classic decor; a few rooms are full of rustic stucco and carved blond wood. Jacket and tie are required in the guests' dining hall, and for the Friday gala buffet, it's black tie only. The new "Residence," across the street through a handy tunnel, offers chic, luxurious apartments. ✉ *CH-3920,* ☎ *027/9668888,* FAX *027/9672878. 143 rooms with bath. Restaurant, grill, indoor pool, sauna, health club, disco. AE, DC, MC, V. Closed May–mid-June and mid-Oct.–Nov.*

$$$$ 🏠 **Zermatterhof.** The Cervin's rival for five-star luxury, this 19th-century hotel has recently undergone major renovations to better emphasize its rustic beginnings. Some of the suites now have fireplaces and whirlpool tubs; many also have balconies facing the Matterhorn. There's a formal restaurant, a more casual rotisserie, and a garden lunch room. ✉ *CH-3920,* ☎ *027/9670101,* FAX *027/9674842. 93 rooms with bath. 2 restaurants, indoor pool, sauna, health club. AE, DC, MC, V.*

$$$ ⊞ **Hotel Simi.** Run by the Biner-Simon family, the Simi is a friendly, inn-style hotel where creature comforts are taken seriously: Guests are encouraged to linger in the sauna, in the intimate bar, or over the huge buffet breakfast. The location, on a quiet side street in the center of town, is ideal. Rooms are simply furnished, with pine-paneled walls, twin beds, and light-color fabrics; the lobby lounge has comfortable couches and a small bar. ⊠ *CH-3920,* ☎ *027/9674656,* FAX *027/9674861. 45 rooms with bath. Lobby lounge, sauna. MC, V.*

$$$ ⊞ **Monte Rosa.** This was the first inn in Zermatt, and the home base
★ of Edward Whymper when he conquered the Matterhorn in 1865. Behind its graceful shuttered facade you will find flagstone floors, brass, stained and beveled glass, honey-gold pine, fireplaces, and an elaborate Victorian dining hall, fully restored. Dinner is a five-course candlelight affair that could have been styled by Merchant Ivory. The bar is an après-ski must. Guests have access to the Mont Cervin sports facilities and all Seiler restaurants on the members' "Dine-Around" plan. ⊠ *CH-3920,* ☎ *027/9661131,* FAX *027/9671160. 49 rooms with bath. Restaurant, sauna. AE, DC, MC, V.*

$$$ ⊞ **Pollux.** Constructed in 1978 and renovated in 1989, this simple but chic modern hotel is on the main pedestrian shopping street. If you're hoping for quiet, reserve a room at the back; the front rooms are good for people-watching. An appealing old-fashioned Stübli draws locals with its low-price lunches, snacks, and Valais cheese specialties; the terrace café fronts directly on the busy street. ⊠ *CH-3920,* ☎ *027/9671946,* FAX *027/9675426. 32 rooms with bath. Restaurant, Stübli, sauna, disco. AE, DC, MC, V.*

$$$ ⊞ **Julen.** Its 1937 chalet-style construction, knotty-pine decor, and im-
★ peccable 1981 renovation qualify this lodge for membership in the Romantik chain, which assures guests of authentic regional comforts. The main restaurant offers excellent regional menus (at reasonable prices for non-guests, too) in a refined, candlelit atmosphere, and the welcoming Stübli downstairs serves unusual lamb specialties from locally raised flocks. ⊠ *CH-3920,* ☎ *027/9672481,* FAX *027/9671481. 37 rooms with bath. Restaurant, café, sauna. AE, DC, MC, V.*

$$$ ⊞ **Romantica.** Among the scores of anonymous modern hotels around Zermatt, this modest structure stands out with an exceptional location, directly above the town center. Its tidy gardens and flower boxes, game trophies, and old-style stove soften the cookie-cutter look, and its plain rooms benefit from big windows and balconies. Views take in the mountains (though not the Matterhorn) over a graceful clutter of stone roofs. ⊠ *CH-3920,* ☎ *027/9671505,* FAX *027/9675815. 14 rooms with bath. Bar. AE, MC, V.*

$ ⊞ **Alphubel.** Although it's surrounded by other hotels just steps from the main street, this modest, comfortable pension feels off the beaten track, and it offers large sunny balconies in its south-side rooms. The interior—a little institutional—lets you know that the place was built in 1954, but there's a sauna in the basement available to guests for a slight surcharge. ⊠ *CH-3920,* ☎ *027/9673003,* FAX *027/9676684. 32 rooms, 16 with bath. Restaurant, sauna. AE, MC, V.*

$ ⊞ **Mischabel.** This slightly stuffy old budget pension—run by the same
★ family for 40 years—provides comfort, atmosphere, and a central location few places can match at twice the price, with balconies on the south side framing a perfect Matterhorn view. Creaky, homey, and covered with knotty pine aged to the color of toffee, its rooms have sinks only, though you'll find linoleum-lined showers on every floor. ⊠ *CH-3920,* ☎ *027/9671131,* FAX *027/9676507. 28 rooms without bath. Restaurant. MC, V.*

$ ⊞ **Touring.** Its reassuringly traditional architecture and snug, sunny,
★ all-pine rooms, not to mention its location above the town with excellent Matterhorn views, make this an appealing choice for travelers
hoping to avoid the chic scene below. Built in 1958 and tastefully updated in 1989, it's family-run, and rooms with Matterhorn views cost
only 2 SF extra. There's a sunny, enclosed playground with lounge chairs
for parents. ⊠ *CH-3920,* ☎ *027/9671177,* FAX *027/9674601. 28
rooms, 10 with bath. Restaurant, Stübli. MC, V.*

29 Turkey

Istanbul

The Aegean Coast

The Mediterranean Coast

Central Anatolia and Cappadocia

TURKEY IS ONE PLACE TO WHICH THE PHRASE "East meets West" really applies, both literally and figuratively. It is in Turkey's largest city, Istanbul, that the continents of Europe and Asia meet, separated only by the Bosporus, which flows 29 kilometers (18 miles) from the Black Sea to the Sea of Marmara. On the vibrant streets of this city of 12 million people, miniskirts and trendy boots mingle with head scarves and prayer beads. People from as far away as Ghana, Sri Lanka, and the Philippines, and as nearby as the Central Asian republics and the former Soviet Union make their way to Istanbul in search of better lives.

Although 97 percent of Turkey's landmass is in Asia, Turkey has faced West politically since 1923, when Mustapha Kemal, better known as Atatürk, founded the modern republic. He transformed the remnants of the shattered Ottoman Empire into a secular state with a Western outlook. So thorough was this changeover—culturally, politically, and economically—that in 1987, 49 years after Atatürk's death, Turkey applied to the European Community (EC) for full membership. It has been a member of the North Atlantic Treaty Organization (NATO) since 1952.

For 16 centuries Istanbul, originally known as Byzantium, played a major part in world politics: first as the capital of the Eastern Roman Empire, when it was known as Constantinople, then as capital of the Ottoman Empire, the most powerful Islamic empire in the world, when it was renamed Istanbul. Atatürk moved the capital to Ankara at the inception of the Turkish Republic.

The legacies of the Greeks, Romans, Ottomans, and numerous other civilizations have made the country a vast outdoor museum. The most spectacular of the reconstructed classical sites are along the western Aegean coast and the southwest Mediterranean coast, which are lined with magnificent sandy beaches and sleepy little fishing villages, as well as busy holiday spots with sophisticated facilities for travelers.

For those with more time—an extra five to seven days—an excursion inland to central Anatolia and the eroded lunar valleys of the Cappadocia area will show some of the enormous diversity of the landscapes and people of Turkey.

ESSENTIAL INFORMATION

Before You Go

When to Go

The height of the tourist season runs from April through October. July and August are the busiest and warmest months. April through June and September and October are the best months to visit archaeological sites or Istanbul and the Marmara area because the days are cooler and the crowds are smaller.

CLIMATE

The Mediterranean and Aegean coasts have mild winters and hot summers. You can swim in the sea from late April through October. The Black Sea coast is mild and damp, with a rainfall of 228 centimeters (90 inches) a year.

The following are the average daily maximum and minimum temperatures for Istanbul.

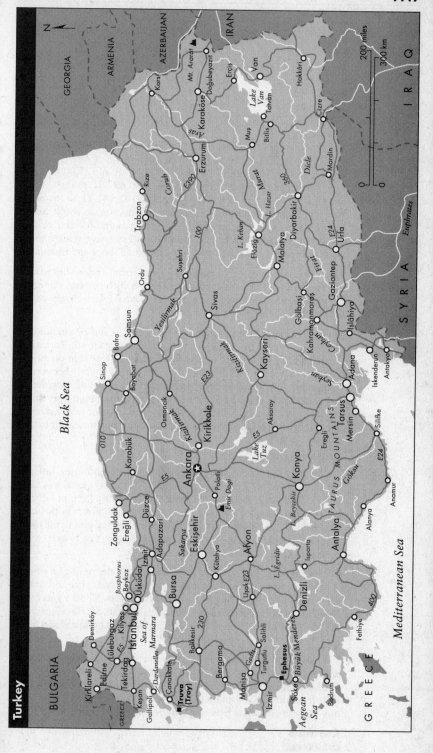

Jan.	46F	8C	May	69F	21C	Sept.	76F	24C
	37	3		53	12		61	16
Feb.	47F	9C	June	77F	25C	Oct.	68F	20C
	36	2		60	16		55	13
Mar.	51F	11C	July	82F	28C	Nov.	59F	15C
	38	3		65	18		48	9
Apr.	60F	16C	Aug.	82F	28C	Dec.	51F	11C
	45	7		66	19		41	5

Currency

The monetary unit is the Turkish lira (TL), which comes in bank notes of 20,000, 50,000, 100,000, 250,000, and 500,000. Coins come in denominations of 500, 1,000, 2,500, 5,000, 10,000, and 25,000. At press time (spring 1996), the exchange rate was 66,697 TL to the U.S. dollar, 48,282 TL to the Canadian dollar, and 101,841 TL to the pound sterling. These rates are subject to wide fluctuation, so check close to the time of your departure. Major credit cards and traveler's checks are widely accepted in hotels, shops, and expensive restaurants in cities and resorts, but rarely in villages and small shops and restaurants.

There are no problems changing money back from Turkish lira to other currencies. But because the value of Turkish currency can sometimes fall significantly over a very short period, it is advisable to change enough money for only a few days at a time.

Foreign exchange bureaus are now widespread in Turkey's major cities and tourist resorts (they usually have a sign saying DÖVIZ, Turkish for "Foreign Exchange"). Exchange rates can usually be seen on an electronic display just inside the door. Rates may vary slightly between exchange bureaus but are always better than bank rates and considerably more attractive than rates offered in hotels. Exchange bureaus are usually open from 9:30 or 10 AM to 6 PM and, in areas where there are many tourists, remain open on Saturdays and sometimes, though not always, on Sundays.

What It Will Cost

Turkey is the least expensive of the Mediterranean countries. Inflation, which has hovered between 50% and 70% for many years, was nearly 80% in 1995, but frequent devaluations of the lira keep prices fairly stable when measured against foreign currencies. Prices in this chapter are quoted in U.S. dollars, which indicate the real cost to the tourist more accurately than do the constantly increasing lira prices.

SAMPLE PRICES

Coffee can range from about 30¢ to $2.50 a cup, depending on whether it's the less expensive Turkish coffee or American-style coffee and whether it's served in a luxury hotel or a café; tea, 20¢ to $2.50 a glass; local beer, $1–$3; soft drinks, $1–$4; lamb shish kebab, $1.50–$7; taxi, less than $1 for 1 mile (prices are 50% higher between midnight and 6 AM).

Visas

U.S. citizens not arriving on a cruise line need visas. These are most easily obtained at the port of entry—just be sure to have cash (U.S. $20). Canadian tourists do not need visas. Visas are required for visitors from the U.K.—obtain them at the port of entry for £10 or from any Turkish consulate (the rate will be somewhat higher).

Customs

ON ARRIVAL

Turkish customs officials rarely look through tourists' luggage on arrival. You are allowed to bring in 400 cigarettes, 50 cigars, 200 grams of tobacco, 1.5 kilograms of instant coffee, 500 grams of tea, and 2.5

liters of alcohol. An additional 600 cigarettes, 100 cigars, or 500 grams of tobacco may be imported if purchased at the Turkish duty-free shops on arrival. Register all valuable personal items in your passport on entry. Items at duty-free shops in airports are usually less expensive here than in duty-free shops in other European airports or in in-flight offerings.

ON DEPARTURE

You must keep receipts of your purchases, especially for such items as carpets, as proof that they were bought with legally exchanged currency. Also, it cannot be emphasized strongly enough that Turkey is extremely tough on anyone attempting to export antiques without authorization or on anyone caught with illegal drugs, regardless of the amount.

Language

Atatürk launched language reforms that replaced Arabic script with the Latin-based alphabet. English and German are widely spoken in cities and resorts. In the villages or in remote areas, you'll have a hard time finding anyone who speaks anything but Turkish. Try learning a few basic Turkish words; the Turks will love you for it.

Getting Around

By Car

ROAD CONDITIONS

Turkey has excellent main roads—25,000 miles of well-maintained, paved highways—but signposts are few, lighting is scarce, and city traffic is chaotic. City streets and highways are jammed with vehicles operated by high-speed drivers who constantly blast their horns. In Istanbul, it's safer and faster to drive on the modern highways. Avoid the many small one-way streets, since you never know when someone is going to barrel down one of them in the wrong direction. Better yet, use public transportation or take taxis. Parking is a big problem in the cities and larger towns.

RULES OF THE ROAD

The best way to see Turkey is by car, but be warned that it has one of the highest accident rates in Europe. In general, Turkish driving conforms to Mediterranean customs, with driving on the right and passing on the left. But watch out for drivers passing on a curve or on the top of a hill. Other hazards are peasant carts and motorcycles weaving in and out of traffic. Archaeological and historical sites are indicated by yellow signposts.

GASOLINE

Throughout the country Mobil, Shell, and British Petroleum, as well as two Turkish oil companies, have gas stations that are open 24 hours on the main highways. Others are open from 6 AM to 10 PM.

BREAKDOWNS

Before you start out, check with your hotel or a tourist information office about how, in case of an emergency, to contact one of the road rescue services available on some highways. Turkish mechanics in the villages will usually manage to get you going again, at least until you reach a city for full repairs. In the cities, entire streets are given over to car-repair shops. Prices are not high, but it's good to give a small tip to the person who does the actual repair work. If you're not in the shop during the repairs, take all the car documents with you. **The Touring and Automobile Club (TTÖK,** ☎ 212/282–8140) gives information about driving in Turkey and has a repair service.

By Train

Although there are express trains in Turkey, the term is usually a misnomer. These trains ply several long-distance routes, but they tend to be slow. The best daily trains between Istanbul and Ankara are the Başkent Expres and the Faith Expres. The overnight Yatakli Ankara Expres has luxurious sleeper cars while the Anadolu Expres offers cheaper bunk beds. There are overnight trains to Pamukkale as well as daily trains to Edirne from Sirkeci station in Istanbul. Dining cars on some trains have waiter service and serve surprisingly good and inexpensive food.

FARES

Train fares tend to be less expensive than bus fares. Seats on the best trains, as well as those with sleeping berths, should be reserved in advance. There are 10% student discounts (30% Dec.–May) and 30% discounts for groups of 24 or more. In railroad stations, buy tickets at windows marked ANAHAT GISELERI. Travel agencies carrying the TCDD (State Railways) sign and post offices sell train tickets, too.

By Bus

Buses, which are run by private companies, are much faster than trains and provide excellent, inexpensive service. Buses are available, virtually around the clock, between all cities and towns. They are fairly comfortable and many are air-conditioned. Companies have their own fixed fares for different routes. Istanbul to Ankara, for instance, varies from $8 to $13; Istanbul to İzmir varies from $11 to $16. *Şişe suyu* (bottled water) is included in the fare. You can purchase tickets at stands in a town's *otogar* (central bus terminal) or at branch offices in city centers. All seats are reserved. There are small variations in fares among the different companies, but it is usually worth paying the 3%–5% extra for companies such as Varan, Ulusoy, and Pamukkale. Many buses between major cities are double-deckers and all of those operated by the larger companies have toilets. Companies such as Varan, Ulusoy, and Pamukkale offer no-smoking seating. For very short trips or getting around within a city, take minibuses or a *dolmuş* (shared taxi). Both are inexpensive and comfortable.

By Plane

Turkish Airlines (THY) operates an extensive domestic network. There are at least nine flights daily on weekdays between Istanbul and Ankara. During the summer, many flights between the cities and coastal resorts are added. Try to arrive at the airport at least 45 minutes before your flight because security checks, which are rigidly enforced without exception, can be time-consuming. Checked luggage is placed on trolleys on the tarmac and must be identified by boarding passengers before it is put on the plane. Unidentified luggage is left behind and checked for bombs or firearms.

THY offers several discounts on domestic flights: 10% for families; 50% for children under 13; 90% for children under two; and 50% for sports groups of seven or more. The THY sales office is at Taksim Square (☎ 212/252–1106; reservations by phone, ☎ 212/663–6363).

By Boat

Turkish Maritime Lines operates car ferry and cruise services from Istanbul. Cruises are in great demand, so make your reservations well in advance, either through the head office in Istanbul (✉ Rihtim Cad. 1, Karaköy, ☎ 212/249–9222) or through **Sunquest Holidays Ltd.** in London (✉ Aldine House, Aldine St., London W12 8AW, ☎ 0181/800–5455).

The **Black Sea Ferry** sails from May through September from Istanbul to Samsun and Trabzon and back, from Karaköy Dock in Istanbul. One-way fares to Trabzon are about $30 for a reclining seat, $38 to $94 for cabins, and $50 for cars. The Istanbul-to-İzmir car ferry departs three days a week. The price of a one-way ticket with no meals included varies between $38 and $122, and $40 for a car.

Staying in Turkey

Telephones

Note: All telephone numbers in Turkey now have seven local digits plus three-digit city codes. Intercity calls are preceded by 0.

Pay phones are yellow, push-button models. Most take *jetons* (tokens) although an increasing number, particularly in large cities, take phonecards. Multilingual directions are posted in phone booths.

LOCAL CALLS

Jetons can be purchased for 7¢ at post offices and, for a couple of cents more, at street booths. If you need operator assistance for long-distance calls within Turkey, dial 131. For intercity automatic calls, dial 0, then dial the city code and the number. Jetons are available for 25¢ and 80¢ for long-distance calls. Far more practical than the jetons are telephone cards, available at post offices for $2 for 30 units, $3.50 for 60 units, and $5 for 100 units.

Telephone numbers in European and Asian Istanbul have been assigned different codes: the code for European Istanbul (for numbers beginning with 2, 5, or 6) is 0/212; for Asian Istanbul (for numbers that start with 3 or 4), dial 0/216.

INTERNATIONAL CALLS

For all international calls dial 00, then dial the country code, area or city code, and the number. You can use the higher-price cards for this, or reach an international operator by dialing 132. To reach an **AT&T** long-distance operator, dial 00800-12277, for **MCI**, dial 00800-11177, and for **Sprint**, 00800-14477. The country code for Turkey is 90.

Mail

Post offices are painted bright yellow and have PTT (Post, Telegraph, and Telephone) signs on the front. The major ones are open Monday–Saturday from 8 AM to 9 PM, Sundays from 9 to 7. Smaller branches are open Monday–Saturday 8:30–5.

RECEIVING MAIL

If you're uncertain where you'll be staying, have mail addressed to "post restante" and sent to Merkez Postanesi (central post office) in the town of your choice.

Shopping

BARGAINING

The best part of shopping in Turkey is visiting the *bedestans* (bazaars), all brimming with copper and brass items, hand-painted ceramics, alabaster and onyx goods, fabrics, richly colored carpets, and relics and icons trickling in from the former Soviet Union. The key word for shopping in the bazaars is "bargain." You must be willing to bargain, and bargain hard. It's great fun once you get the hang of it. As a rule of thumb, offer 50% less after you're given the initial price and be prepared to go up by about 25% to 30% of the first asking price. It is often advisable to get up to leave, as the best price is invariably the one called after you as you disappear around the corner. You can always think about it for two minutes and, if you are happy about it, return and accept. It's both bad manners and bad business to underbid grossly or to start bargaining if you're not serious about buying. Outside the bazaars prices are usually fixed, although in resort areas some shopkeepers may be willing to bargain if you ask for a "better price." Part of the fun of roaming through the bazaars is having a free glass of *çay* (tea), which vendors will offer you whether you're a serious shopper or just browsing. Beware of antiques: Chances are you will end up with an expensive fake, but even if you do find the genuine article, it's illegal to export antiques of any type.

VAT REFUNDS

Value-added tax (VAT) is nearly always included in the price. You can claim back the VAT if you buy articles from authorized shops. The net total value of articles subject to VAT on your invoice must be more than a specified amount, depending on the nature of the goods, and these articles must be exported within three months of purchase. The invoice must be stamped by customs. Otherwise, mail the stamped invoice back to the dealer within one month of departure and the dealer will send back a check.

Opening and Closing Times

Banks are open weekdays, 8:30–noon and 1:30–5, although a few banks remain open at lunchtime. Foreign exchange bureaus normally remain open from 9:30 or 10 AM to 6 PM.

Mosques are usually open to the public, except during *namaz* (prayer hours), which are observed five times a day. These times are based on the position of the sun, so they vary throughout the seasons between the following hours: sunrise (5–7), lunchtime (noon–1), afternoon (3–4), sunset (5–7), bedtime (9–10). Prayers last 30–40 minutes.

Museums are generally open Tuesday–Sunday, 9:30–4:30, and closed Monday. **Palaces,** open the same hours, are closed Thursday instead of Monday.

Most **shops** are closed all day Sunday, although small grocery stores and a few other stores in the main shopping areas remain open seven days a week. Generally shops are open Monday–Saturday, 9:30–1 and 2–7. There are some exceptions in the major shopping areas in large cities and resort areas, where shops stay open until 9 PM.

National Holidays

January 1; February 9–11 (Şeker Bayram, "sugar feast," a three-day celebration marking the end of Ramadan); April 23 (National Sovereignty and Children's Day); April 18-21 (Kurban Bayram, an important sacrificial feast celebrating Abraham's willingness to sacrifice his son to God); May 19 (National Youth and Sports Day); August 30 (Victory Day); October 28–29 (Republic Day); November 10 (Atatürk's Commemoration).

Dining

The Turkish people are justly proud of their cuisine. In addition to the blends of spices used, the food is also extremely healthful, full of fresh vegetables, yogurt, legumes, and grains, not to mention fresh seafood, roast lamb, and kebabs made of lamb, beef, or chicken. The old cliché about it being hard to find a bad meal in Paris more aptly describes dining in Istanbul, where even the tiniest little hole-in-the-wall serves delicious food. Because Turkey is predominantly Muslim, pork is not readily available. But there's plenty of alcohol, including local beer and wine, which are excellent and inexpensive. Particularly good wines are Villa Doluca and Kavaklidere, available in *beyaz* (white) and *kirmizi* (red). The most popular local beer is Efes Pilsen. The national alcoholic drink, raki, is made from grapes and aniseed. Turks mix it with water or ice and sip it throughout their meal or serve it as an aperitif.

Hotel restaurants have English-language menus and usually serve a bland version of Continental cuisine. Far more adventurous and tasty are meals in *restorans* and in *lokantas* (Turkish restaurants). Most lokantas do not have menus because they serve only what's fresh and in season, which varies daily. At lokantas, you simply sit back and let the waiter bring food to your table, beginning with a tray of mezes. You point to the dishes that look inviting and take as many as you want. Then you select your main course from fresh meat or fish—displayed in glass-covered refrigerated units—which is then cooked to order, or from a steam table laden with casseroles and stews. For lighter meals there are *kebabcis,* tiny restaurants specializing in kebabs served with salad and yogurt, and *pidecis,* selling *pides,* a pizzalike snack of flat bread topped with butter, cheese, egg, or ground lamb and baked in a wood-burning oven.

MEALTIMES

Lunch is generally served from noon to 3 and dinner from 7 to 10. In the cities you can find restaurants or cafés open virtually anytime of day or night, but in the villages, finding a restaurant open at odd hours can be a problem.

WHAT TO WEAR

Except for the pricier restaurants, where formal dress is appropriate, informal dress is acceptable at restaurants in all price categories.

PRECAUTIONS

Although tap water is heavily chlorinated, it is not safe to drink in cities and resorts. It's best to play it safe and drink *maden suyu* (bottled mineral water) or regular şişe suyu, which is better tasting and inexpensive.

RATINGS

Prices are per person and include an appetizer, main course, and dessert. Wine and gratuities are not included.

CATEGORY	MAJOR CITIES	OTHER AREAS
$$$$	over $40	over $30
$$$	$25–$40	$20–$30
$$	$12–$25	$10–$20
$	under $12	under $10

Lodging

Hotels are officially classified in Turkey as HL (luxury), H1 to H5 (first- to fifth-class); motels, M1 to M2 (first- to second-class); and P, *pansiyons* (guest houses). The classification is misleading because the lack of a restaurant or a lounge automatically relegates the establishment to the bottom of the ratings. A lower-grade hotel may actually be far more charming and comfortable than one with a higher rating. There are also many local establishments that are licensed but not included in the official ratings list. You can obtain their names from local tourist offices.

Accommodations range from international luxury chains in Istanbul, Ankara, and İzmir to comfortable, family-run pansiyons. Plan ahead for the peak summer season, when resort hotels are often booked solid by tour companies. Turkey does not have central hotel reservations offices.

Rates vary from $10 to more than $200 a night for a double room. In the less expensive hotels, the plumbing and furnishings will probably leave much to be desired. You can find very acceptable, clean double rooms with bath for between $30 and $70, with breakfast included. Room rates are displayed in the reception area. It is accepted practice in Turkey to ask to see the room in advance.

Prices are for two people in a double room, including 20% VAT and a 10–15% service charge.

CATEGORY	MAJOR CITIES	OTHER AREAS
$$$$	over $200	over $150
$$$	$100–$200	$100–$150
$$	$60–$100	$50–$100
$	under $60	under $50

Tipping

Except at the cheapest restaurants, a 10% to 15% charge is added to the bill. Since the money does not necessarily find its way to the waiter, leave an additional 10% on the table or hand it to the waiter. In the top restaurants, waiters expect tips of between 10% and 15%. Hotel porters expect between $2 and $5, and the chambermaid, about $2 a day. Taxi drivers don't expect tips, although they are becoming accustomed to foreigners giving them something. Round off the fare to the nearest 5,000 TL. At Turkish baths, the staff that attends you expects to share a tip of 30% to 35% of the bill. Don't worry about missing them—they'll be lined up expectantly on your departure.

ISTANBUL

Arriving and Departing

By Plane

All international and domestic flights arrive at Istanbul's Atatürk Airport. For arrival and departure information, call the individual airline or the airport's information desk (☎ 212/663–6400).

BETWEEN THE AIRPORT AND DOWNTOWN

Shuttle buses run from the airport's international and domestic terminals to the Turkish Airlines (THY) terminal in downtown Istanbul, at Meşrutiyet Caddesi, near the Galata Tower. Buses depart for the airport at the same address every hour from 6 AM to 11 PM. After that, departure time depends on demand. Allow at least 45 minutes for the bus ride. Plan to be at the airport two hours before your international flight because of the lengthy security and check-in procedures. The ride from the airport into town takes from 30 to 40 minutes, depending on traffic. Taxis charge about $15 to Taksim Square and $11 to Sultanahmet.

By Train

Trains from the west arrive at Sirkeci station (☎ 212/527–0050 or 0051) in Old Istanbul. Eastbound trains to Anatolia depart from Haydarpasa station (☎ 216/348–8020 or 216/336–0475) on the Asian side.

By Bus

The destination for buses arriving in Istanbul is the newly built Esenler terminal northwest of the city center. From the terminal, the major bus companies offer free minibus service to centers such as Sultanahmet, Taksim, and Aksaray. There is also the Hizli Tren (rapid train) connecting the terminal to Aksaray, though this is often very crowded and can be extremely hot in summer. A few buses from Anatolia arrive at Harem terminal, on the eastern shore of the Bosporus. If you arrive with baggage, it is much easier to take a taxi, which will cost about $8 to Taksim from the Esenler terminal and about $5 to Old Istanbul.

By Car

If you drive in from the west, take the busy E5 highway, also called Londra Asfalti, which leads from Edirne to Atatürk Airport and on through the city walls at Cannon Gate (Topkapı). E5 heading out of Istanbul leads into central Anatolia and on to Iran and Syria. An alternative to E5, when leaving the city, is to take one of the numerous car ferries that ply the Sea of Marmara and the Dardanelles from Kabataş Dock, or try the overnight ferry to İzmir, which leaves from Sarayburnu.

Getting Around

The best way to get around the magnificent monuments in Sultanahmet in Old Istanbul is to walk. They're all within easy distance of each other, along streets filled with peddlers, shoe-shine boys, children playing, and craftsmen working. To get to other areas, you can take a bus or one of the many ferries that steam between the Asian and European continents; *deniz otobüsü* (sea buses) running between the continents, as well as to destinations such as the Princes' Islands, are fast and efficient. Dolmuş vehicles and taxis are plentiful, inexpensive, and more comfortable than city buses. A new tram system runs from Topkapı, via Sultanahmet, to Sirkeci. Subway system construction is underway between Taksim and Levent, and there is the Tünel, a tiny underground train that's handy for getting up the steep hill from Karaköy to the bottom of Istiklâl Caddesi. It runs every 10 minutes and costs about 25¢.

By Bus

Buy a ticket before boarding a bus. You can buy tickets, individually or in books of 10, at ticket stands around the city. Shoe-shine boys or men on the street will also sell them to you for a few cents more. Fares are about 25¢ per ride. On the city's orange privatized buses (Halk Otobüsü) as well as on the city's double-deckers, pay for tickets on the bus. The London-style double-deckers operate along a scenic route between Sultanahmet and Emigran on the Bosporus.

By Dolmuş

These are shared taxis operating between set destinations throughout the city. Dolmuş stops are indicated by a blue and white sign with a large D. The destination is shown either on a roof sign or a card in the front window. Many of them are classic American cars from the 1950s but are gradually being replaced by modern minibuses.

By Taxi

Taxis are inexpensive. Since most drivers do not speak English and may not know the street names, write down the street you want, the nearby main streets, and the name of the area. Taxis are metered. Although tipping is not expected, you should round off the fare to the nearest 5,000 TL.

By Boat

For a fun and inexpensive ride, take the *Anadolu Kavaği* boat along the Bosporus to its mouth at the Black Sea. The boat leaves year-round from the Eminönü Docks, next to the Galata Bridge on the Old Istanbul side, at 10:30 AM and 1:30 PM, with two extra trips on weekdays and four extra trips on Sundays from April to September. The fare is $6 (round-trip). The trip takes 1¾ hours one way. You can disembark at any of the stops and return by land if you wish. Regular ferries depart from Kabataş Dock, near Dolmabahçe Palace on the European side, to Üsküdar on the Asian side; and also from Eminönü Docks 1 and 2, near Sirkeci station.

Important Addresses and Numbers

Visitor Information

Official tourist information offices are at **Atatürk Airport** (☎ 212/663–6400); the **Hilton Hotel** (☎ 212/233–0592); **Karaköy Yolcu Salonu,** International Maritime Passenger Terminal (☎ 212/249–5776); and in a pavilion in the **Sultanahmet** district of Old Istanbul (⊠ Divan Yolu Cad. 3, ☎ 212/518–1802 and 518-8754).

Consulates

U.S. (⊠ Meşrutiyet Cad. 147, Tepebaşi, Beyoğlu, ☎ 212/251–3602).
Canadian (⊠ Büyükdere Cad. 107/3, Bengün Han, ☎ 212/272–5174).
U.K. (⊠ Meşrutiyet Cad. 34, Tepebaşi, Beyoğlu, ☎ 212/293–7540).

Emergencies

Tourism Police (☎ 212/527–4503) They are well-equipped for dealing with travelers' problems. **Ambulance** (☎ 112). **Doctors:** For an English-speaking doctor, call the American Hospital (⊠ Güzelbahçe Sok. 20, Nişantaşi, ☎ 212/231–4050/69) or the International Hospital (Yesilyurt, ☎ 212/663–3000). **Pharmacies:** There is one on duty 24 hours in every neighborhood; call 118 for details. Consult the notice in the window of any pharmacy for the name and address of the nearest all-night shop. One that's centrally located is **Taksim** in the Taksim district (⊠ Istiklal Cad. 17, ☎ 212/249–2252).

English-Language Bookstores

Dünya Aktuel Bookshop (⊠ Istiklal Cad. 469, ☎ 212/249–1006) has several branches, including one each in the Hilton and the Swissôtel. **Net** (⊠ Yerebatan Cad. 15/3, Sultanahmet, ☎ 212/520–8406) publishes tourism guides and **ABC Bookshop** (⊠ Istiklâl Cad. 461, ☎ 249–2414) sells English-language books and magazines. **Robinson Crusoe** (⊠ Istiklal Caddesi 389, Tunel, ☎ 212/293–6968 or 293–6977) carries books in major European languages. For English speakers, there is a fiction section and many coffee-table books about Turkey.

Travel Agencies

Most are concentrated along Cumhuriyet Caddesi, off Taksim Square, in the hotel area. They include **American Express** (⊠ Hilton Hotel, Cumhuriyet Cad., Harbiye, ☎ 212/241–0248 or 212/241–0249); **Intra** (⊠ Halaskargazi Cad. 111/2, Harbiye, ☎ 212/247–8174 or 212/240–3891); **Setur** (⊠ Cumhuriyet Cad. 107, Harbiye, ☎ 212/230–0336); and **Vitur** (⊠ Cumhuriyet Cad. 269/4, Harbiye, ☎ 212/230–0895). **Istanbul Vision** (⊠ Cumhuriyet Cad. No: 12/C, Elmadağ, ☎ 212/241–3935) offers a range of tours around Istanbul and into Anatolia; **Fest** (⊠ Dikilitaş, Tenigelin Sok., Meksan Binasi, No. 1, 7th Floor, Beşiktaş, ☎ 212/258–2589 or 258–2573) specializes in expeditions to less-touristed sections of the city.

Guided Tours

Tours are arranged through travel agencies (☞ Travel Agencies, *above*). Choices include a half- or full-day "Classical Tour." The full-day guided "Classical Tour" by private car costs between $60 and $90 per person. The half-day tour costs $25 and includes Hagia Sophia, the Museum of Turkish and Islamic Arts, the Hippodrome, Yerebatan Saray, and the Blue Mosque; the full-day tour costs $50, and, in addition to the above sights, includes Topkapı Palace, the Süleymaniye Mosque, the Covered or Egyptian Bazaar, and lunch. The "Bosporus Tour" costs $25 for a half day or $50 for a full day, and includes lunch at Sariyer and visits to the Dolmabahçe and Beylerbeyi palaces. The

"Night Tour" costs $50 and includes dinner and drinks at Kervansaray or Galata, where there is a show.

Exploring Istanbul

Istanbul is noisy, chaotic, and exciting. Spires and domes of mosques and medieval palaces dominate the skyline. At dawn, when the muezzin's call to prayer rebounds from ancient minarets, many people are making their way home from the nightclubs and bars, while others are kneeling on their prayer rugs, facing Mecca.

Day and night, Istanbul has a schizophrenic air to it. Women in jeans, business suits, or elegant designer outfits pass women wearing the long skirts and head coverings that villagers have worn for generations. Donkey-drawn carts vie with old Chevrolets and Pontiacs or shiny Toyotas and BMWs for dominance of the loud, narrow streets, and the world's most fascinating Oriental bazaar competes with Western boutiques for the time and attention of both tourists and locals.

Ironically, Istanbul's Asian side is filled with Western-style sprawling suburbs, while its European side contains Old Istanbul—an Oriental wonderland of mosques, opulent palaces, and crowded bazaars. The Golden Horn, an inlet 6½ kilometers (4 miles) long, flows off the Bosporus on the European side, separating Old Istanbul from New Town. The center of New Town is Beyoğlu, a district filled with a combination of modern and turn-of-the-century hotels, banks, and shops grouped around Taksim Square. There are three bridges spanning the Golden Horn: the Atatürk, the Galata, and the Haliç. The historic Galata Bridge, which has been replaced by a modern drawbridge, is a central landmark and a good place to get your bearings. From here, you can see the city's layout and its seven hills. The bridge will also give you a taste of Istanbul's frenetic street life. It's filled with peddlers selling everything from pistachio nuts and spices to curly-toed slippers fancy enough for a sultan; fishermen grill their catch on coal braziers and sell them to passersby. None of this sits well with motorists, who blast their horns constantly, usually to no avail. If you want to orient yourself in a quieter way, take a boat trip from the docks on the Eminönü side of the Galata Bridge up the Bosporus.

Old Istanbul (Sultanahmet)

Numbers in the margin correspond to points of interest on the Istanbul map.

★ ❶ The number-one attraction in Istanbul is **Topkapı Saray** (Topkapı Palace) on Seraglio Point in Old Istanbul, known as Sultanahmet. The palace, which dates from the 15th century, was the residence of a number of sultans and their harems until the mid-19th century. To avoid the crowds, try to get there by 9 AM, when the gates open. If you're arriving by taxi, tell the driver you want the Topkapı *Saray* in Sultanahmet, or you could end up at the remains of the former Topkapı bus terminal on the outskirts of town.

Sultan Mehmet II built the first palace during the 1450s, shortly after the Ottoman conquest of Constantinople. Over the centuries, sultan after sultan added ever more elaborate architectural fantasies, until the palace eventually ended up with more than four courtyards and some 5,000 residents, many of them concubines and eunuchs. Topkapı was the residence and center of bloodshed and drama for the Ottoman rulers until the 1850s, when Sultan Abdül Mecit moved with his harem to the European-style Dolmabahçe Palace farther up the Bosporus coast.

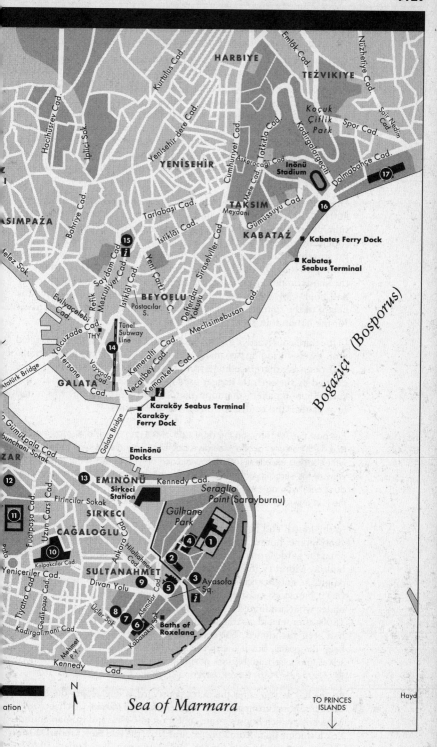

HARBIYE

TEŽVIKIYE

Küçük Çiflik Park

Spor Cad.

YENISEHIR

İnönü Stadium

TAKSIM
Meydani

KABATAŚ

16

Kabataş Ferry Dock

ŚIMPAŻA

BEYOĞLU

15

Kabataş Seabus Terminal

Tünel Subway Line

GALATA

14

Karaköy Seabus Terminal
Karaköy Ferry Dock

Galata Bridge

Eminönü Docks

Boğaziçi (Bosporus)

12

13   EMİNÖNÜ
Sirkeci Station

Kennedy Cad.

Seraglio Point (Sarayburnu)

11

SİRKECİ

Gülhane Park

ÇAĞALOĞLU

10

SULTANAHMET

Divan Yolu

4   1

9

2

3   Ayasofya Sq.

5

8   7

6

Baths of Roxelana

ation

N

Sea of Marmara

TO PRINCES ISLANDS

Hayd

② In Topkapı's outer courtyard are the **Aya Irini** (Church of St. Irene), open
③ only during festival days for concerts, and the **Court of the Janissaries**
(Merasim Avlusu), originally for members of the sultan's elite guard.

Adjacent to the ticket office is the **Bab-i-Selam** (Gate of Salutation),
built in 1524 by Süleyman the Magnificent, who was the only person
allowed to pass through it. In the towers on either side, prisoners were
kept until they were executed beside the fountain outside the gate in
the first courtyard. In the second courtyard, amid the rose gardens, is
the **Divan-i-Humayun,** the assembly room of the council of state, once
presided over by the grand vizier (prime minister). The sultan would
sit behind a latticed window, hidden by a curtain so no one would know
when he was listening, although occasionally he would pull the curtain aside to comment.

One of the most popular tours in Topkapı is the **Harem,** a maze of nearly
400 halls, terraces, rooms, wings, and apartments grouped around the
sultan's private quarters on the west side of the second courtyard. Forty
rooms are restored and open to the public. Next to the entrance are
the quarters of the eunuchs and about 200 of the lesser concubines,
who were lodged in tiny cubicles, as cramped and uncomfortable as
the main rooms of the Harem are large and opulent. Tours begin every
half hour. Only a limited number are taken on each tour. During the
height of the tourist season it is often advisable to try to buy a ticket
for the harem tour soon after entering the palace.

In the third courtyard is the **Hazine Dairesi** (Treasury), four rooms filled
with jewels, including two uncut emeralds, each weighing 3½ kilograms
(7.7 pounds), that once hung from the ceiling. Here, too, you will be
dazzled by the emerald dagger used in the movie *Topkapı* and the 84-
carat "Spoonmaker" diamond that, according to legend, was found
by a pauper and traded for three wooden spoons.

NEED A
BREAK?

Just past the Treasury, on the right side of the courtyard, are steps leading
to a 19th-century rococo Mecidiye pavilion, now the **Konyali Restaurant,**
which serves excellent Turkish food (lunch only) and has a magnificent
view of the seraglio and the Golden Horn. On a terrace below is an outdoor café with an even better view. Go early or reserve a table to beat
the tour-group crush. ☎ *212/513-9696.* ☾ *Wed.–Mon.*

In the fourth and last courtyard of the Topkapı Palace are small, elegant summer houses, mosques, fountains, and reflecting pools scattered
amid the gardens on different levels. Here you will find the **Rivan Köşk,**
built by Murat IV in 1636 to commemorate the successful Rivan campaign. In another kiosk in the gardens, called the **Iftariye** (Golden
Cage), the closest relatives of the reigning sultan lived in strict confinement under what amounted to house arrest. The custom began during the
1800s after the old custom of murdering all possible rivals to the throne
had been abandoned. The confinement of the heirs apparently helped
keep the peace, but it deprived them of any chance to prepare themselves for the formidable task of ruling a great empire. ✉ *Topkapı Palace,*
☎ *212/512–0480.* ▦ *$4, harem $1.* ☾ *Wed.–Mon. 9:30–5:30.*

★ **④** To the left as you enter the outer courtyard, a lane slopes downhill to
three museums grouped together: the **Arkeoloji Müzesi** (Archaeological
Museum), which houses a fine collection of Greek and Roman antiquities, including finds from Ephesus and Troy; the **Eski Şark Eserleri Müzesi**
(Museum of the Ancient Orient), with Sumerian, Babylonian, and Hit-
tite treasures; and the **Çinili Köşk** (Tiled Pavilion), which houses ceramics from the early Seljuk and Osmanli empires. The admission price covers
all three museums. ☎ *212/520–7740.* ▦ *$2.* ☾ *Tues.–Sun. 9:30–5.*

★ ❺ Just outside the walls of Topkapı Palace is **Hagia Sophia** (Church of the Divine Wisdom), one of the world's greatest examples of Byzantine architecture. Built in AD 532 under the supervision of Emperor Justinian, it took 10,000 men five years to complete and was the third church to be built on the site. The first one was built in 360; both it and its successor were destroyed by fire. The dome of the current church was the world's largest until the dome at St. Peter's Basilica was built in Rome 1,000 years later. Hagia Sophia was the cathedral of Constantinople for nearly 1,000 years, surviving earthquakes and looting Crusaders until 1453, when it was converted into a mosque by Mehmet the Conqueror. Minarets were added by succeeding sultans. Hagia Sophia originally had many mosaics depicting Christian scenes, which were plastered over by Süleyman I, who felt they were inappropriate for a mosque. In 1935, Atatürk converted Hagia Sophia into a museum. Shortly after that, American archaeologists discovered the mosaics, which were restored and are now on display.

According to legend, the **Sacred Column,** in the north aisle of the mosque, "weeps water" that can work miracles. It's so popular that over the centuries believers have worn a hole through the marble and brass column. You can stick your finger in it and make a wish. ⊠ *Ayasofya Meyd.,* ☎ *212/522-1750.* ▧ *$4.25.* ☉ *Tues.–Sun. 9:30–5.*

❻ Across from Hagia Sophia is the **Blue Mosque** (Sultan Ahmet Cami), with its shimmering blue tiles, 260 stained-glass windows, and six minarets, as grand and beautiful a monument to Islam as Hagia Sophia was to Christianity. Mehmet Aga, also known as Sedefkar (Worker of Mother of Pearl) built the mosque during the reign of Sultan Ahmet I in eight years, beginning in 1609, nearly 1,100 years after the completion of Hagia Sophia. His goal was to surpass Justinian's masterpiece, and many in the world believe he succeeded.

Press through the throngs and enter the mosque at the side entrance that faces Hagia Sophia. Remove your shoes and leave them at the entrance. Immodest clothing is not allowed, but an attendant will lend you a robe if he feels you are not dressed appropriately. ▧ *Free.* ☉ *Daily 9–5.*

The **Carpet and Kilim museums** (Hünkar Kasri) are in the mosque's stone-vaulted cellars and upstairs at the end of a stone ramp, where the sultans rested before and after their prayers. ☎ *212/518–1330.* ▧ *$1.50.* ☉ *Tues.–Sat. 9–4.*

❼ The **Hippodrome** is a long park directly in front of the Blue Mosque. As a Byzantine stadium with 100,000 seats, it was once the focal point for city life, including chariot races, circuses, and public executions. Disputes between rival groups of supporters of chariot teams often degenerated into violence. In 531, 30,000 people died in the Hippodrome in what came to be known as the Nike riots. The original shape of the Hippodrome is still clearly visible. The monuments that can be seen today—the **Egyptian Obelisk** (Dikilitas), the **Column of Constantinos** (Örme Sütun), and the **Serpentine Column** (Yilanli Sütun) taken from the Temple of Apollo at Delphi in Greece—formed part of the central barrier around which the chariots raced.

On the western side of the Hippodrome is **Ibrahim Paşa Palace,** the grandiose residence of the son-in-law and grand vizier of Süleyman the Magnificent. Ibrahim Paşa was executed when he became too power-
❽ ful for Süleyman's liking. The palace now houses the **Türk Ve Islâm Eserleri Müzesi** (Museum of Turkish and Islamic Arts), which gives a superb insight into the lifestyles of Turks of every level of society, from the 8th century to the present. ⊠ *Şifahane Sok, across from the Blue*

Mosque, in line with the Serpentine Column, ☎ 212/518–1385 or
212/518–1805. ⊠ $2.50. ☉ Tues.–Sun. 9:30–5.

★ ❾ Walk back along the length of the Hippodrome and cross the busy main
road, Divan Yolu. Turn left onto Hilaliahmer Caddesi. On your left is
the **Yerebatan Saray** (Sunken Palace), also known as the Cistern Basilica. This underground cistern was probably first excavated by Emperor
Constantine in the 4th century and then enlarged by Emperor Justinian
in the 6th century. It has 336 marble columns rising 8 meters (26 feet)
to support Byzantine arches and domes. The cistern was always kept full
as a precaution against long sieges. Its echoing vastness and the reflections of the columns in the dark water give it a haunting, cathedral-like
beauty, and it is a welcome relief from the heat and noise above ground.
⊠ Yerebatan Cad., ☎ 212/522–1259. ⊠ $2. ☉ Wed.–Mon. 9–5.

NEED A BREAK?	For a real treat, spend an hour in a Turkish bath. One of the best is **Cağaloğlu Hamamı,** near Hagia Sophia in a magnificent 18th-century building. This establishment also offers luxurious massages, and you can nibble or sip something at the bar as you mellow out after your bath. ⊠ Ismail Gürkan Cad. 34, ☎ 212/522–2424. ⊠ $8 for self-service bath, $15 for full service, $24 for deluxe Ottoman massage. ☉ Daily 8–8 for women; 7 AM–10 PM for men.

★ ❿ The shopper's paradise, the **Grand Bazaar** (Kapali Çarşışı) lies about
¼ mile northwest of the Hippodrome (a 15-minute walk or 5-minute
taxi ride). Also called the Covered Bazaar, this maze of 65 winding,
covered streets hides 4,000 shops, tiny cafés, and restaurants, believed
to be the largest number under one roof anywhere in the world. Originally built by Mehmet the Conqueror in the 1450s, it was ravaged by
two modern-day fires, one in 1954 that virtually destroyed it, and a
smaller one in 1974. In both cases, the bazaar was quickly rebuilt. It's
filled with thousands of curios, including carpets, fabrics, clothing, brass
ware, furniture, icons, and gold jewelry. ⊠ Yeniçeriler Cad. and Fuatpaşa Cad. ⊠ Free. ☉ Apr.–Oct., Mon.–Sat. 8:30–7; Nov.–Mar.,
Mon.–Sat. 8:30–6:30.

⓫ When you leave the bazaar, cross Fuatpaşa Caddesi and walk around
★ ⓬ the grounds of **Istanbul University,** which has a magnificent gateway
facing Beyazit Square. Follow Besim Ömer Paşa Caddesi, the western
border of the university, to the right to the 16th century **Süleymaniye
Cami** (Mosque of Süleyman). The mosque was designed by Sinan, the
architectural genius who masterminded more than 350 buildings and
monuments under the direction of Süleyman the Magnificent. This is
Sinan's grandest and most famous monument, and the burial site of
both himself and his patron, Süleyman. ⊠ Free. ☉ Daily outside
prayer hours.

★ ⓭ The Grand Bazaar isn't the only bazaar in Istanbul. Another one worth
visiting is the **Egyptian Bazaar** (Misir Çarşışı). You reach it by walking down Çarşi Caddesi to Çakmakçilar Yokuşu and Firincilar Sokak,
and then into Sabunchani Sokak, where you will see the back of the
bazaar. It was built in the 17th century as a means of rental income
for the upkeep of the Yeni Mosque. The bazaar was once a vast pharmacy, filled with burlap bags overflowing with herbs and spices for
folk remedies. Today, you're more likely to see bags full of fruit, nuts,
Royal Jelly from the beehives of the Aegean coast, and white sacks spilling
over with culinary spices. Some shopkeepers will offer you tastes of
energizing pastes, such as *macun*, as well as dried fruits or other Turkish delights. Nearby are equally colorful fruit and fish markets. ⊠ Next
to Yeni Cami. ☉ Mon.–Sat. 8–7.

Frenetic Pandeli serves savory food underneath domed alcoves. Try the
kağitta levrek (paper-wrapped grilled sea bass). It is up two flights of stairs
over the arched gateway to the Egyptian Bazaar. ✉ *Misir Carsişi, Em-
inönü,* ☎ *212/527–3909. AE, DC, MC, V. Lunch only. Closed Sun. $$*

New Town

New Town is the area on the northern shore of the Golden Horn, the
waterway that cuts through Istanbul and divides Europe from Asia.
14 The area's most prominent landmark is the **Galata Tower,** built by the
Genoese in 1349 as part of their fortifications. In this century, it served
as a fire lookout until 1960. Today it houses a restaurant and night-
club (☞ Nightlife, *below*), and a viewing tower. ✉ *Büyük Hendek Cad.*
☎ *$1.* ☉ *Daily 9–8.*

15 North of the tower is the **Çiçek Pasaji** (Flower Arcade), off Istiklâl Cad-
desi, a lively blend of tiny restaurants, bars, and street musicians.
Strolling further on Istiklâl Caddesi is an experience in itself. The busy
pedestrian road is lined with shops, restaurants, banks, and cafés in turn-
of-the-century buildings. The restored original 19th-century tram still
carries people from Tunel to Taksim Square. On the side streets you'll
find Greek and Armenian churches, bars, and other establishments; in
the narrow, poorer residential alleys, you'll see laundry hanging between
the old buildings, as you dodge through the children at play.

Next head for Dolmabahçe Mosque and Dolmabahçe Palace, which
are reached by following Istiklâl Caddesi to Taksim Square and then
taking Inönü (Gümüssuyu) Caddesi around the square downhill to a
★ **16** junction. You will see the **Dolmabahçe Mosque** on your right and the
clock tower and gateway to Dolmabahçe Palace on your left. The
mosque is a separate building from the palace. It was founded by
Valide Sultan Bezmialem, mother of Abdül Mecit I, and was completed
in 1853. ☎ *Free.* ☉ *Daily outside prayer hours.*

17 The **Dolmabahçe Palace** was also built in 1853 and, until the decla-
ration of the modern republic in 1923, was the residence of the last
sultans of the Ottoman Empire. It was also the residence of Atatürk,
who died here in 1938. The palace, floodlit at night, is an extraordi-
nary mixture of Hindu, Turkish, and European styles of architecture
and interior design. Queen Victoria's contribution to the lavishness was
a chandelier weighing 4½ tons. Guided tours of the palace take about
80 minutes. ✉ *Gümüssuyu Cad.,* ☎ *212/258–5544.* ☎ *$5.* ☉ *Apr.–Oct.
9–4; Nov.–Mar. 9–3. Closed Mon.*

Shopping

Gift Ideas

The **Grand Bazaar** (☞ Exploring Istanbul, *above*) is a what it sounds
like: a smattering of all things Turkish—carpets, brass, copper, jewelry,
textiles, and leather goods. Tünel Square, a quick short metro ride up
from Karaköy, is a quaint group of stores with old prints, books, and
artifacts.

Stores

Stores and boutiques are found in New Town on such streets as **Istik-
lâl Caddesi,** which runs off Taksim Square, and **Rumeli, Halaskargazi,**
and **Valikonagi Caddeleri,** north of the Hilton Hotel. Two streets in the
Kadiköy area with good shops are **Bağdat** and **Bahariye Caddeleri.** In
Altunizade on the Asian side, **Capitol,** a new and slick mall, has movies
and entertainment, too. **Ataköy Shopping and Tourism Center** is a large
shopping and leisure mall near the airport, while **Akmerkez,** the newest
of the malls in Etiler, draws those who like luxury and designer wear.

Markets

Balikpazari (fish market) is in Beyoğlu Caddesi, off Istiklâl Caddesi. Despite its name, you will find anything connected with food at this market. A **flea market** is held in Beyazit Square, near the Grand Bazaar, every Sunday from about 10 AM, where Turkish traders are now joined by new arrivals from the former Soviet Union, has everything from cheap electronic goods to former Soviet army boots and hats. A crafts market, with street entertainment, is open on Sundays along the Bosporus at Ortaköy. A weekend crafts market is also held on Bekar Sokak, off Istiklal Caddesi.

Dining

Most major hotels have dining rooms serving bland international cuisine. It's far more rewarding to eat in Turkish restaurants. For details and price-category definitions, *see* Dining *in* Staying in Turkey, *above.*

$$$$ ✕ **Körfez.** The specialty here is seafood dishes such as bass baked in salt. The garden setting on the waterfront is very romantic. The restaurant boat ferries guests across the Bosporus from Rumeli Hisari. ⊠ *Kanlica,* ☎ *216/413–4098. AE, DC, MC, V. Closed Mon. and Nov.–Apr.*

$$$$ ✕ **Tugra.** This spacious and luxurious restaurant in the historic Çirağan Palace serves the most delectable of long-savored Ottoman recipes, including stuffed bluefish and Circassian chicken. The Bosporus view is framed by the palace's marble columns; high ceilings carry dazzlingly crafted glass chandeliers. ⊠ *Cirağan Cad. 84, Beşiktaş,* ☎ *212/258–3377, ext. 7684. AE, DC, MC, V.*

$$$$ ✕ **Ulus 29.** Seafood is the specialty at this chic restaurant tucked away in a park in the upscale Ulus district. The terrace has spectacular views spanning both Bosporus bridges. In the summer, guests are ferried across to the Bosporus site, Çubuklu 29, which is reminiscent of a Roman villa. ⊠ *Ahmet Adnan Saygun Cad., Ulus Park,* ☎ *212/265–6181 in spring, fall, and winter; Paşabahçe Yolu, Çubuklu,* ☎ *216/322–3888 in summer. Reservations essential. Dinner only. AE, DC, MC, V.*

$$$ ✕ **Divan.** You'll enjoy gourmet Turkish and international cuisine, elegant surroundings, and excellent service at this restaurant in the Divan hotel. ⊠ *Cumhuriyet Cad. 2, Elmadağ,* ☎ *212/231–4100. AE, DC, MC, V. Closed Sun.*

$$$ ✕ **Gelik.** This restaurant in a two-story, 19th-century villa is usually packed, often with people who want to savor its specialty: various meats cooked in deep wells. ⊠ *Sahil Yolu, Ataköy,* ☎ *212/560–7284. AE, DC, MC, V.*

$$$ ✕ **Urcan.** A dramatic array of fresh fish and lobsters welcome you to this Bosporus fish restaurant, one of the finest in town. It's one of those places where locals bring visitors they want to impress, so you may see some visiting dignitary or celebrity. The decor is heavily nautical. ⊠ *Orta Ceşme Cad., 2/1, Sariyer,* ☎ *212/242–0367. AE, DC, V.*

$$ ✕ **Borsa Lokantasi.** This unpretentious restaurant serves some of the
★ best food in Turkey. The baked lamb in eggplant purée and the stuffed artichokes are not to be missed. ⊠ *Yaliköskü Cad. Yaliköskü Han 60–62, Eminönü,* ☎ *212/522–4173. No credit cards. Closed Sun. Lunch only. Another branch at Halaskargazi Cad. 90/1, Osmanbey,* ☎ *212/232–4200. AE, DC, MC, V.*

$$ ✕ **Dünya.** The frenetic traffic of the adjacent Ortaköy Square and waiters balancing appetizer trays is countered by the picturesque Bosporus view, which on summer nights includes many passing pleasure boats. The grilled *cupra* (breem) is a must, while mezes are always fresh and sumptuous. ⊠ *Salhane Sok. 10, Ortaköy,* ☎ *212/258–6385. No credit cards.*

$$ ✕ **Four Seasons.** Located within a large Victorian building, Dört Mevsim is noted for its blend of Turkish and French cuisine and for its owners, Gay and Musa, an Anglo-Turkish couple who opened it in 1965. On any given day, you'll find them in the kitchen overseeing such delights as shrimp in cognac sauce and baked marinated lamb. ⊠ *Istiklâl Cad. 509, Beyoğlu,* ☎ *212/293–3941. AE, DC, MC, V. Closed Sun.*

$$ ✕ **Hanedan.** The emphasis is on kebabs, all kinds, all excellent; there are better-than-average mezes, too. The setting is lively, by the Besiktas ferry terminal. ⊠ *Çiğdem Sok. 27, Besiktas,* ☎ *212/260–4854. AE, MC, V.*

$ ✕ **Hacibaba.** This is a large, cheerful-looking place with a summer ter-
★ race overlooking an old Greek church. Fish, meat, and a wide variety of vegetable dishes are on display for your selection. Before you choose your main course, you'll be offered a tray of mezes that can be a meal in themselves. ⊠ *Istiklal Cad. 49, Taksim,* ☎ *212/244–1886. AE, DC, MC, V.*

$ ✕ **Haci Salih.** This tiny, family-run restaurant has only 10 tables, so
★ you may have to line up and wait—but it's worth it. Traditional Turkish food is the fare here, with special emphasis on vegetable dishes and lamb. Alcohol is not served, but you can bring your own. ⊠ *Anadolu Pasaju 201, off Istiklâl Cad., Beypğlu,* ☎ *212/243–4528. No credit cards. Closed Sun. Lunch only.*

$ ✕ **Rejans.** Founded by two Russians and a Crimean fleeing the Bolshevik revolution, this restaurant offers excellent Russian food and lemon vodka, as well as Turkish dishes. The decor of the Rejans has remained virtually unchanged since the 1930s. ⊠ *Istiklav Cad., Olivo Gecidi 15, Galatasaray,* ☎ *212/244–1610. V. Closed Sun.*

$ ✕ **Yakup.** This cheery hole-in-the-wall is smoky and filled with locals rather than tourists, and it can get loud, especially if there is a football (soccer) match on television. From the stuffed peppers to the *tereyağli borek* (buttered pastries) and octopus salad, the mezes are above average. ⊠ *Asmali Mescit Sok. 35–37, Beyoğlu,* ☎ *212/249–2925. AE, MC, V.*

Lodging

The top hotels are mainly around Taksim Square in New Town. Hotels generally include the 15% VAT and a service charge of 10% to 15% in the rate. Modern, middle-range hotels usually have a friendly staff but bland architecture and interiors. In Old Istanbul, the Aksaray, Laleli, Sultanahmet, and Beyazit areas have many conveniently located, inexpensive small hotels and family-run pansiyons. Istanbul has a chronic shortage of beds, so plan ahead. For details and price-category definitions, *see* Lodging *in* Staying in Turkey, *above.*

$$$$ 🏨 **Çirağan Palace.** This 19th-century Ottoman palace is the city's
★ most luxurious—and expensive—hotel. The swimming pool is right at the edge of the Bosporus. Guest rooms in the palace have a view of the new hotel and the rooms in the new hotel have a view of the palace (and are cheaper). ⊠ *Çirağan Cad. 84, Beşiktaş,* ☎ *212/258–3377,* FAX *212/259–6687. 295 rooms with bath and 27 suites. 4 restaurants, bar, pool, beauty salon, Turkish bath, health club, shops, casino. AE, DC, MC, V.*

$$$$ 🏨 **Hilton.** Recently redecorated with Turkish rugs and large brass urns, this is one of the best Hiltons in the chain. Ask for a room overlooking the Bosporus. ⊠ *Cumhuriyet Cad., Harbiye,* ☎ *212/231–4646,* FAX *212/240–4165. 510 rooms with bath. Restaurant, bar, pool, beauty salon, spa, Turkish baths, tennis, squash, shop, casino, meeting rooms. AE, DC, MC, V.*

$$$$ 🏨 **Hyatt Regency.** This massive but tasteful pink building, reminiscent of Ottoman splendor, houses one of the city's newer five-star hotels. Many rooms have views of the Bosporus. The interior has plush carpeting and the decor is a combination of earth tones in many textures. The restaurants serve a range of Asian, Turkish, and Italian foods. ⊠ *Taşkişla Cad., Taksim,* ☎ *212/225–7000,* ℻ *212/225–7007. 360 rooms with bath. 2 restaurants, bar, café, pool, 1 tennis court, health club, baby-sitting, business services. AE, DC, MC, V.*

$$$$ 🏨 **Pera Palace.** A grand hotel with a genuinely Turkish feel, the Pera
★   Palace was built in 1892 to accommodate guests arriving on the *Orient Express.* Although it has been modernized for comfort, the hotel has retained its original Victorian elegance. Many old features, such as a magnificent old lift, are still in working order. The likes of Atatürk, Agatha Christie, Mata Hari, and even Greta Garbo once slept here. ⊠ *Meşrutiyet Cad. 98, Tepebaşi,* ☎ *212/251–4560,* ℻ *212/251–4089. 139 rooms with bath. Bar, patisserie. AE, DC, MC, V.*

$$$$ 🏨 **Swissôtel.** Superbly located near the city center in a hilltop wood,
★   the hotel has views across the Bosporus and beyond to the Sea of Marmara, together with all the lavish facilities one would expect from a five-star hostelry, including excellent sports facilities and a range of French, Turkish, Japanese, Chinese, and Swiss cuisine. ⊠ *Bayıldim Cad. 2, Maçka,* ☎ *212/259–0101,* ℻ *212/259–0105. 600 rooms with bath. 7 restaurants, 5 bars, air-conditioning, minibars, indoor and outdoor pools, 3 tennis courts, health club. AE, DC, MC, V.*

$$$ 🏨 **Ayasofia Pansiyons.** These guest houses are part of an imaginative project undertaken by the Touring and Automobile Club to restore a little street of historic wooden houses along the outer wall of Topkapı Palace. One of the houses has been converted into a library and two into pansiyons, furnished in late Ottoman style, with excellent dining rooms. During the summer, tea and refreshments are served in the gardens to guests and nonguests alike. ⊠ *Soğukçeşme Sok., Sultanahmet,* ☎ *212/513–3660,* ℻ *212/512–3669. 63 rooms with bath. Restaurant, café, bar, Turkish bath. AE, MC, V.*

$$$ 🏨 **Divan.** Quiet, but close enough to Taksim Square, this old hotel has recently been renovated; some rooms have private terraces overlooking the Bosporus. The restaurant here is renowned for impeccably prepared Turkish and international dishes. ⊠ *Cumhuriyet Cad. 2, Şişli,* ☎ *212/231–4100,* ℻ *212/248–8527. 169 rooms with bath, 11 suites. Restaurant, bar, tea shop, beauty salon. AE, DC, MC.*

$$$ 🏨 **Yeşil Ev (Green House).** Practically next door to the Blue Mosque,
★   this 19th-century building is decorated in old-fashioned Ottoman style with lace curtains and latticed shutters. Its high-walled garden restaurant is a verdant and peaceful oasis in the midst of frenetic Istanbul. ⊠ *Kabasakal Sok. 5, Sultanahmet,* ☎ *212/517–6785,* ℻ *212/517–6780. 20 rooms with bath. Restaurant. AE, MC, V.*

$$ 🏨 **Barin.** Modern, clean, and comfortable, with good, friendly service, the Barin caters to business travelers as well as tourists. ⊠ *Fevziye Cad. 7, Şehzadebaşi,* ☎ *212/513–9100,* ℻ *212/526–4440. 65 rooms with bath. AE, DC, MC, V.*

$$ 🏨 **Barut's Guesthouse.** Quiet and secluded and in the heart of Old Is-
★   tanbul, Barut's has a peaceful roof terrace overlooking the Sea of Marmara. The hotel also has a modern art gallery in its foyer. ⊠ *Ishakpaşa Cad. 8, Sultanahmet,* ☎ *212/516–0357,* ℻ *212/516–2944. 23 rooms with bath. MC, V.*

$$ 🏨 **Büyük Londra.** This is another Victorian hotel, similar to the Pera Palace—not quite as grand—that has grown old gracefully. ⊠ *Meşrutiyet Cad. 117, Tepebaşi,* ☎ *212/293–1619 or 249–1025,* ℻ *212/245–0671. 54 rooms with bath. Restaurant, bar. AE, MC, V.*

$$ ▩ **Richmond.** A turn-of-the-century building on Istiklâl Caddesi was renovated to create this comfortable hotel. Downstairs is the Lebon patisserie, which is a remake of the 19th-century pastry shop that once operated there and an excellent place from which to watch the world pass by along Istiklâl Caddesi. ⊠ *Istiklâl Cad. 445,* ☎ *212/252–5460,* FAX *212/252–9707. 101 rooms with bath. Restaurant, bar, café. AE, V.*

$ ▩ **Berk Guest House.** An English-speaking couple, Güngör and Nevin Evrensel run this tidy little inn. Two rooms have balconies overlooking a garden. ⊠ *Kutlugün Sok. 27, Cankurtaran, Sultanahmet,* ☎ *212/516–9671,* FAX *212/517–7715. 7 rooms with bath. No credit cards.*

$ ▩ **Hotel Empress Zoe.** Named after an empress who ruled Byzantium in the 11th century, this unusual property is decorated with murals and paintings in that era's style. Rooms, which are of varying configurations, are brightened with colorful embroidered textiles—some have views. The American owner, Ann Nevans, is a graceful manager and can help out with personalized itineraries of the nearby Sultanahmet sights and beyond. ⊠ *Akbik Cad., Adliye Sok. 10, Sultanahmet,* ☎ *212/518–2504,* FAX *212/518–5699. 12 rooms with bath. MC, V.*

The Arts

Entertainment in Istanbul ranges from the **Istanbul International Festival**—held late-June through mid-July and attracting internationally renowned artists and performers—to local folklore and theatrical groups, some amateur, some professional. Because there is no central ticket agency, ask your hotel for help. You can also pick up tickets at the box office or through a local tourist office.

For tickets to the Istanbul International Festival, apply to the **Istanbul Foundation for Culture and Arts** (⊠ Kültür ve Sanat Vakfi, Yildiz, Besiktaş, ☎ 212/260–4533). Tickets can also be purchased at the Marmara Hotel in Taksim Square (☎ 212/251–4696). Performances, which include modern and classical music, ballet, opera, and theater, are given throughout the city in historic buildings, such as the Church of St. Irene and Rumeli Castle. The season at the city of Istanbul's **Cemal Resit Rey Concert Hall** (☎ 212/248–9404 or 212/248–5392) runs from September through May and includes classical, jazz, and rock music, as well as ballet performed by visiting and local groups.

Concerts

Tickets for performances at the main concert hall, **Atatürk Kültür Merkezi,** are available from the box office at Taksim Square (☎ 212/251–5600), where you can also buy tickets for concerts at the Cemal Resit Rey Concert Hall. From October through May, the **Istanbul State Symphony** gives performances at the Atatürk Kültür Merkezi. Ballet and dance companies also perform at this hall.

Nightlife

Bars and Nightclubs

Bebek Bar (⊠ Bebek Ambassadeurs Hotel, Cevdet Paşa Cad. 113, Bebek, ☎ 212/263–3000) has views over the Bosporus. The crowd here includes locals from the neighborhood and nearby Bosporus University. Open daily until 1 AM.

Beyoğlu Pub (⊠ Istiklâl Cad. 140/7, Beyoğlu, ☎ 212/252–3842) is behind an arcade off Istiklal with a pleasant first-story garden open in the warmer months and a discrete indoor bar frequented by moviegoers, expatriates, and quietly sophisticated Istanbullites.

Kemancı Rock-Bar (⊠ Taksim Sitesi, Sıraselviler, ☎ 212/245-3048) is a three-story rock bar with live rock and blues bands. One of the first such bars in Istanbul, it's still a firm favorite, often loud, lively, and crowded on weekends.

Orient Express Bar (⊠ Pera Palace Hotel, Meşrutiyet Cad. 98, Tepebaşi, ☎ 212/251–4560). Its fin-de-siècle decor distills the atmosphere of old Istanbul with the lingering presence of the rich, powerful, and famous (from Atatürk to Italian King Victor Emmanuel to Josephine Baker) who once played here.

Tribunal (⊠ Istiklâl Cad. Muammer Karaca Cikmazi 3, ☎ 212/249–7179) once served as a French court and retains the original inlaid brick ceiling. Live bands perform authentic gypsy, Greek, or Latin music after 11 PM. On weekends, the bar is open until 4 AM.

A well-established nightclub is **Kervansaray** (⊠ Cumhuriyet Cad. 30, Elmadağ, ☎ 212/247–1630), where you can dine, dance, and watch belly-dancing shows every evening until midnight. Two other good places for floor shows are **Balim** (⊠ Kemerhatun Mah. Hamalbaşi Cad. 8, Beyoğlu, ☎ 212/249–5608) and **Olimpia** (⊠ Acar Sok. Tomtom Mah., off Istiklâl Cad., ☎ 212/244–9456). **Galata Tower** (⊠ Kuledibi, ☎ 212/245–1160) serves dinner between 8:30 and 10, with a Turkish show and dancing from 10 PM to 1 AM.

Jazz

Hayal Kahvesi (⊠ Büyük Parmakkapi Sok. 19, Beyoğlu, ☎ 212/244–2558) is a bohemian side-street bar with wooden furniture and lace curtains. Local groups perform jazz, blues, and rock; Tuesday and Friday are jazz nights.

Tepe Bar Lounge (⊠ Marmara Hotel, Taksim Square, ☎ 212/251–4696) is on the top floor of the Marmara Hotel and has a 360-degree view of Istanbul. Local and visiting musicians play every evening from 11 to 1 AM.

Discos

Memo's (⊠ Salhane Sok. 10, Ortaköy, ☎ 212/261–8304), near hopping Ortaköy square, is home to a faithful yuppie clientele. The disco gets rolling around 11 PM. **Hayal Khavesi** (⊠ Burunbahçe, Çubuklu, ☎ 216/413-6880), a huge, restaurant/bar/disco complex on the Asian shore of the Bosporus, hosts dancing to live jazz or rock on Fridays or Saturdays. **Cities** (⊠ Sabancıı Korusu, Yeniköy, ☎ 212/223–8424), a posh and trendy bar decorated Viennese style, turns into a disco after 11 PM. **Çubuklu 29** (⊠ Bahçeburun, Çubuklu, ☎ 216/322–2829), situated by the Bosporus on the Asian side, is open from mid-June through September. **Şaziye** (⊠ Eytam Cad. 21, Maçka ☎ 212/232–4155 or 212/231–1401) turns into a popular disco after 11:30 PM.

THE AEGEAN COAST

Some of the finest reconstructed Greek and Roman cities, including the fabled Pergamum, Ephesus, Aphrodisias, and Troy, are found in this region of Turkey. Bright yellow road signs pointing to historical sites or to those currently undergoing excavation are everywhere here. There are so many Greek and Roman ruins, in fact, that some haven't yet been excavated and others are going to seed.

Grand or small, all the sites are steeped in atmosphere and are best explored early in the morning or late in the afternoon, when there are fewer crowds. You can escape the heat of the day on one of the sandy beaches that line the coast.

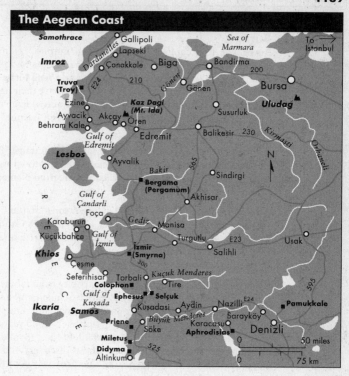

The Aegean Coast

Getting Around

The E24 from Çanakkale follows the coast until it turns inland at Kuşadası to meet the Mediterranean again at Antalya. All the towns on the itinerary are served by direct bus routes, and there are connecting services to the ancient sites.

Guided Tours

The travel agencies in all the major towns offer tours of the historical sites. **Troy-Anzac Tours** (☎ 286/217–5849 or 286/217–5847), in central Çanakkale, has guided tours of the battlefields at Gallipoli. The tour takes about four hours and costs about $10 per person, including breakfast. Travel agencies along Teyyare Caddesi in Kuşadası offer escorted tours to Ephesus; Priene, Miletus, and Didyma; and Aphrodisias and Pamukkale.

Visitor Information

Contact the tourist office in each town for names of travel agencies and licensed tour guides.

Ayvalık (⊠ Yat Limanı Karşısi, ☎ 266/312–2122).
Bergama (⊠ Hükümet Binası, Zemin Kat, B Blok, ☎ 232/633–1862).
Bursa (⊠ Ulu Cami Parkı, Atatürk Cad. 1, ☎ 224/221–2359).
Çanakkale (⊠ Iskele Meyd. 67, ☎ 286/217–1187).
Çeşme (⊠ Iskele Meyd. 8, ☎ 232/712–6653).
İzmir (⊠ Atatürk Cad. 418, Alsancak, ☎ 232/422–0207; Gaziosmanpaşa Bul. 1/C, ☎ 232/484–2147).
Kuşadası (⊠ Iskele Meyd. ☎ 256/614–1103).

Exploring the Aegean Coast

Bursa

★ **Bursa,** the first capital of the Ottoman Empire, is known as Yeşil (Green) Bursa, not only because of its many trees and parks but also because of its **Yeşil Cami** (Green Mosque) and **Yeşil Türbe** (Green Mausoleum). Both the mosque and mausoleum derive their names from the green tiles that line their interiors. They are across from each other on Yeşil Caddesi (the appropriately named "Green Avenue"). ✎ *Free.* ◷ *Daily outside prayer hours.*

Bursa is also the site of **Uludağ** (the Great Mountain), Turkey's most popular ski resort. To fully appreciate why the town is called Green Bursa, take a ride on the *teleferik* (cable car) from Namazgah Caddesi up the mountain for a panoramic view.

The town square is called **Heykel,** which means "statue," and is named for its statue of Atatürk. Off Heykel, along Atatürk Caddesi, is the **Ulu Cami** (Great Mosque) with its distinctive silhouette of 20 domes. ✎ *Free.* ◷ *Daily outside prayer hours.*

Troy

Long thought to be simply an imaginary city from Homer's *Iliad*, **Troy** was excavated in the 1870s by Heinrich Schliemann, a German amateur archaeologist who also found the remains of nine successive civilizations, one on top of the other, dating back 5,000 years. Considering Troy's fame, the site is surprisingly small. It's best to take a guided tour to appreciate fully the significance of this discovery and the unwavering passion of the man who proved that Troy was not just another ancient myth. ✎ *$2.50.* ◷ *Daily 8–7.*

★ The E24 highway leads around the **Gulf of Edremit,** a glorious area of olive groves, pine forests, and small seaside resorts. **Ayvalık,** 5 kilometers (3 miles) off the main bus route, between Çanakkale and İzmir, is an ideal place to stay while visiting the ruins of ancient Pergamum, 40 kilometers (24 miles) away. From Ayvalık you can take boats to **Ali Bey Adası,** a tiny island with pleasant waterfront restaurants, and to the Greek island of Lesbos.

Pergamum

★ **Pergamum** is reached by driving southeast along E24 following the signs toward **Bergama,** the modern-day name of the ancient Greek-Roman site. If you're traveling by bus, be certain it is going all the way to Bergama, or you'll find yourself dropped off at the turn-in, 8 kilometers (5 miles) from the site.

Because the ruins of Pergamum are spread out over several miles, it's best to take a taxi from one site to the next. The most noteworthy places are the Asklepieion, the Ethnological Museum, the Red Hall, and the **Acropolis.** ✎ *$2.50.* ◷ *Apr.–Oct., daily 8:30–6:30; Nov.–Mar., daily 8:30–5:30.*

Pergamum's glory peaked during the Greek Attalid dynasty (241–133 BC), when it was one of the world's most magnificent architectural and artistic centers—especially so under the rule of Eumenes II, who lavished his great wealth on the city. Greek rule continued until 133 BC, when the mad Attalus III died, bequeathing the entire kingdom to Rome.

The most famous building at the acropolis is the **library,** which once contained a collection of 200,000 books, all on papyrus. The library's collection was second only to the one in Alexandria, Egypt.

İzmir

The coastal area between Bergama and **İzmir**, 104 kilometers (64 miles), was once thick with ancient Greek settlements. Today only İzmir remains. Called Smyrna by the Greeks, it was a vital trading port that was often ravaged by wars and earthquakes. İzmir was almost completely destroyed by a fire in 1922 during the final stages of Turkey's War of Independence against Greece.

The city was quickly rebuilt, and it then became known by its Turkish name, İzmir. It's a lively, modern city filled with wide boulevards and apartment houses and office buildings. The center of the city is **Kültürpark**, a large green park that is the site of İzmir's industrial fair from late August to late September (a time when most hotels are full).

On top of İzmir's highest hill is the **Kadifekale** (Velvet Fortress), built in the 3rd century BC by Lysimachos. It is easily reached by dolmuş and is one of the few ancient ruins that was not destroyed in the fire. At the foot of the hill is the restored **Agora**, the market of ancient Smyrna. The modern-day marketplace is in **Konak Square**, a maze of tiny streets filled with shops and covered stalls. ⊘ *8–8. Closed Sun.*

Kuşadası

Kuşadası, about 80 kilometers (50 miles) south of İzmir on Route 300, has grown since the late 1970s from a fishing village into a sprawling, hyperactive town geared to serving thousands of tourists who visit the nearby ruins and beaches. Still, the busy town maintains an easy pace.

Ephesus

★ The major attraction near Kuşadası is **Ephesus**, a city created by the Ionians in the 11th century BC and now one of the grandest reconstructed ancient sites in the world. It is the showpiece of Aegean archaeology. Ephesus was a powerful trading port and the sacred center for the cult of Artemis, Greek goddess of chastity, the moon, and hunting. The Ionians built a temple in her honor, one of the Seven Wonders of the Ancient World. Later the city received a visit from St. Paul, who spent two years preaching there and established one of the first Christian communities on the Aegean coast. Over the centuries heavy silting of the old port finally led to the city being abandoned and the ancient site now lies two miles inland.

Allow yourself one full day for Ephesus. The city is especially appealing out of season when it can seem like a ghost town with its shimmering, long, white marble road grooved by chariot wheels.

Some of the splendors you can see here include the two-story **Library of Celsus;** houses of nobles, with their terraces and courtyards; a 25,000-seat **amphitheater,** still used today during the Selçuk Ephesus Festival of Culture and Art; remains of the municipal baths; and a brothel. ▤ *$5; $1.20 (houses on the slopes).* ⊘ *Daily 8:30–6 (summer), 8:30–5 (winter).*

Selçuk

On Ayasoluk Hill in **Selçuk**, 4 kilometers (2½ miles) from Ephesus, is the restored **Basilica of St. John** (St. Jean Aniti), containing the tomb of the apostle. Near the entrance to the basilica is the **Ephesus Museum**, with two statues of Artemis. The museum also has marvelous frescoes and mosaics among its treasures. ▤ *$2.50.* ⊘ *Basilica and museum Tues.–Sun. 8:30–6.*

St. Paul and St. John preached in both Ephesus and Selçuk and changed the cult of Artemis into the cult of the Virgin Mary. **Meryemana,** 5 kilometers (3 miles) from Ephesus, has the **House of Mary,** thought by some to have been the place where St. John took the mother of Jesus after

the crucifixion and where some believe she ascended to heaven. 🖼 *$1.20.*
🕐 *Daily 7:30–sunset.*

Priene, Miletus, and Didyma

Priene and Miletus, 40 kilometers (25 miles) from Kuşadası, are sister
cities, also founded by the Ionians in the 11th century BC. Nearby is
★ **Didyma,** a holy sanctuary dedicated to Apollo. **Priene,** on top of a steep
hill, was an artistic and cultural center. Its main attraction is the **Temple of Athena,** a spectacular sight with its five fluted columns and its
backdrop of mountains and the fertile plains of the Meander River. You
can also see the city's small amphitheater, gymnasium, council chambers, marketplace, and stadium. 🖼 *$1.20.* 🕐 *Daily 8:30–6.*

Nearby, **Miletus,** once a prosperous port, was the first Greek city to
use coins for money. It also became an Ionian intellectual center and
home to such philosophers as Thales, Anaximander, and Anaximenes,
all of whom made contributions to mathematics and the natural sciences. The city's most magnificent building is the **Great Theater,** a remarkably intact 25,000-seat amphitheater built by the Ionians and kept
up by the Romans. Climb to the highest seats in the amphitheater for
a view across the city to the bay. 🖼 *Ruins $1.20, museum $1.20.* 🕐
Tues.–Sun. 8:30–6.

Didyma

The temple of **Didyma** is reached by a 32-kilometer (20-mile) road called
the **Sacred Way,** starting from Miletus at the bay. The temple's oracles
were as revered as those of Delphi. Under the courtyard is a network of
corridors whose walls would throw the oracle's voice into deep and ghostly
echoes. The messages would then be interpreted by the priests. Fragments
of bas-relief include a gigantic head of Medusa and a small statue of Poseidon and his wife, Amphitrite. 🖼 *$1.20.* 🕐 *Daily 8:30–6.*

Pamukkale

★ East of Kuşadasıı, 215 kilometers (133 miles) away, is **Pamukkale,** which
first appears as an enormous chalky white cliff rising some 330 feet
from the plains. Mineral-rich volcanic spring water cascades over
basins and natural terraces, crystallizing into white stalactites—curtains of solidified water seemingly suspended in air. The hot springs in
the area were popular with the ancient Romans, who believed them
to have curative powers. You can see the remains of Roman baths among
the ruins of nearby **Hierapolis.** The village of Pamukkale has many small
hotels surrounding the hot springs, which are used today by people who
still believe that they cure a variety of problems, including rheumatism.
Farther down in the village are inexpensive pansiyons, some also with
hot springs. It's best to stay in Pamukkale overnight before heading
★ on to the ruins of **Aphrodisias,** a city of 60,000 dedicated to Aphrodite,
the Greek goddess of love and fertility. It thrived from 100 BC to AD
500. Aphrodisias is reached via **Karacasu,** a good place to stop for lunch;
fresh trout is the local specialty. Aphrodisias is filled with marble
baths, temples, and theaters, all overrun with wild blackberries and
pomegranates. Across a field sprinkled with poppies and sunflowers
is a well-preserved **stadium,** which was built for 30,000 spectators.

Dining and Lodging

For details and price-category definitions, *see* Dining *and* Lodging *in*
Staying in Turkey, *above.*

Ayvalık

$$ 🏨 **Büyük Berk.** Part of a larger complex, this modern hotel sits on
Ayvalık's best beach, about 3¼ kilometers (2 miles) from the center of

town. ✉ *Sarimsakli Mev.*, ☎ *266/324–1045,* 𝖥𝖠𝖷 *266/324–1194. 180 rooms with bath. Restaurant, outdoor pool, dance club.*

$ 🏨 **Ankara Oteli.** Located on Sarimsakli beach, just a few feet from the surf, the Ankara Oteli gives excellent value for the money. ✉ *Sarimsakli Mev.*, ☎ *266/324–1195 or 266/324–1048,* 𝖥𝖠𝖷 *266/324–0022. 104 rooms with bath. Restaurant, café, bar. No credit cards.*

Bergama

$$ 🏨 **Hotel Iskender.** This establishment is plain, modern (air-conditioning against the hot summers) and conveniently situated in the center of town. An outdoor restaurant serves tasty fresh mezes and grilled foods. ✉ *İzmir Cad. Ilica Önü Mevkii,* ☎ *232/633–1245,* 𝖥𝖠𝖷 *232/633–1245. 60 rooms with bath. 2 restaurants, bar. No credit cards.*

$$ 🏨 **Tusan Bergama Moteli.** The rooms here are simple, clean, and just off the main road to Bergama. While the location is not that convenient if you don't have a car, the facilities are enough for a one-night stay. The real draw, though, is a pool fed by hot springs. ✉ *İzmir Yolu, Çati Mev.,* ☎ 𝖥𝖠𝖷 *232/633–1938. 42 rooms with bath. Restaurant, swimming pool. No credit cards.*

Bursa

$$ ✕ **Cumurcul.** A converted old house has become a local favorite, where grilled meats and fish are both attentively prepared. ✉ *Çekirge Cad.,* ☎ *224/235–3707.* V.

$ ✕ **Kebabcı Iskender.** Bursa is famous for the dish served here, *Iskender Kebab* (Alexander's kebab), slivers of skewer-grilled meat served with tomato sauce and yogurt. ✉ *Ünlü Cad. 7, Heykel,* ☎ *224/221–4615. No credit cards.*

$$$ 🏨 **Celik Palace.** After guests have indulged at the hotel's restaurant,
★ casino, and clubs, they can enjoy the crowning luxury: a dip in the domed, Roman-style pool fed by hot springs. ✉ *Çekirge Cad. 79,* ☎ *224/233–3800,* 𝖥𝖠𝖷 *224/236–1910. 173 rooms with bath. Restaurant, bar, pool, casino, nightclub, dance club, meeting room. AE, DC, MC, V.*

$$ 🏨 **Ada Palas.** As at many properties in this region, guests here have use of a thermal pool. This comfortable hotel is just a short walk from the shore and is near Kültür Park, the center of town. ✉ *Murat Cad. 21,* ☎ *224/236–3990,* 𝖥𝖠𝖷 *224/236–4656. 39 rooms with bath. Restaurant. V.*

Çanakkale and Troy

$$ 🏨 **Akol.** This modern hotel is perched on the waterfront in Çanakkale; ask for a room with a terrace overlooking the Dardanelles. ✉ *Kordonboyu,* ☎ *286/217–9456,* 𝖥𝖠𝖷 *286/217–2897. 138 rooms with bath. Restaurant, bar, outdoor pool, disco, meeting room. AE, MC, V.*

$$ 🏨 **Büyük Truva.** Near the center of Çanakkale, the Truva is an excellent base for sightseeing. ✉ *Kordonboyu,* ☎ *286/217–1024,* 𝖥𝖠𝖷 *286/217–0903. 66 rooms with bath. Restaurant, bar. No credit cards.*

$ 🏨 **Tusan.** Along the beachfront north of Troy at Güzelyali, and framed by a pine forest, the Tusan is one of the most popular hotels in the area. Be certain to reserve well in advance. ✉ *Güzelyali,* ☎ *286/232–8210 or 286/232–0646,* 𝖥𝖠𝖷 *286/232–8226. 64 rooms with bath. Restaurant, bar, disco. MC, V. Closed Oct.–Feb.*

Çeşme

$$$ 🏨 **Altıın Yunus Çeşme.** Low, bright-white cuboid buildings curl around a white sand beach edging a cove dotted with sailboats at this large, holiday resort with a full range of facilities. Rooms are decorated Mediterranean style, with lots of white and ocean blue, plush carpets, and big beds; all have air-conditioning and minibars. ✉ *Boyalıık Mevkii,* ☎ *232/723–1250,* 𝖥𝖠𝖷 *232/723–2252 or 232/723–2242. 514*

*rooms with bath. 8 restaurants, 7 bars, indoor pool, 2 outdoor pools,
sauna, health club, 5 tennis courts, beach. AE, DC, MC, V.*

İzmir

$$$$ 🏨 **İzmir Hilton.** At 34 stories, the Hilton is one of the Aegean coast's
tallest buildings. Striking and modern, the structure looms over the city
center. From the 10-story atrium to the rooftop restaurant, the public
spaces are suitably grand. Guest rooms are plush with their thick floral comforters and matching drapes. ⊠ *Gazi Osman Pasa Bul. 7,* ☎
232/441–6060, 🆁🅰🆇 *232/441–2277. 381 rooms with bath. 4 restaurants,
2 bars, pool, shops, casino, business services. AE, DC, MC, V.*

$$ 🏨 **Kismet.** Tastefully decorated, the Kismet is a quiet, comfortable hotel
with friendly service. ⊠ *1377 Sok. 9,* ☎ *232/463–3853,* 🆁🅰🆇 *232/421–
4856. 68 rooms with bath. Restaurant, bar, sauna. AE, MC, V.*

Kuşadası

$$$ ✕ **Sultan Han.** Full of atmosphere, with excellent food to boot, Sul-
★   tan Han is an old house built around a courtyard, where the focal point
is a gigantic tree. You can dine in the courtyard or upstairs in small
rooms. One of the specialties is fresh seafood, which you select from
platters piled high with fish and shellfish of every possible variety. Ask
to have your after-dinner coffee served upstairs, where you can sit on
cushions at low brass tables. ⊠ *Bahar Sok. 8,* ☎ *256/614–6380,* 🆁🅰🆇
256/614–6381. Reservations essential. No credit cards.

$$ ✕ **Ali Baba Restaurant.** With a peaceful view of the bay, this water-
front spot engages a simple style, with starched white tablecloths and
wooden chairs. The focus is on fish: Try the marinated octopus salad
or the fried calamari, followed by a grilled version of whatever has just
been caught. ⊠ *Belediye Turistik Carsisi,* ☎ *256/614–1551. Reser-
vations essential. MC, V.*

$ ✕ **Nil Restaurant.** Not as scenic as some of its waterfront rivals, the
Nil more than compensates with its nautical atmosphere and fine food.
You can make your own selection from the appetizers on display, fol-
lowed by any of a number of seafood dishes. The house specialties are
fish baked in salt and *bugulama* (stewed fish with spices). ⊠ *Türkmen
Mah., 50. Yıil Caddesi 3,* ☎ *256/614–8063. AE, V.*

$$$ 🏨 **Club Kervansaray.** A refurbished 300-year-old caravansary, this
hotel in the center of town is decorated in the Ottoman style and loaded
with charm and atmosphere. Its restaurant has a floor show and there's
dancing after dinner in the courtyard, where the camels were once
kept. ⊠ *Atatürk Bul. 2,* ☎ *256/614–4115,* 🆁🅰🆇 *256/614–2423. 40
rooms with bath. Restaurant, bar, café, nightclub. AE, DC, MC, V.*

$$$ 🏨 **Kismet.** Although it's a small hotel, Kismet is run on a grand scale,
★   surrounded by beautifully maintained gardens on a promontory over-
looking the marina on one side and the Aegean on the other. Ask for
rooms in the garden annex. Its popularity makes reservations a must.
⊠ *Akyar Mev., Tükmen Mahallesi,* ☎ *256/614–2005,* 🆁🅰🆇 *256/614–
4914. 98 rooms with bath. Restaurant, private beach. AE, MC, V. Closed
Nov.–Mar.*

$ 🏨 **Liman Hotel.** Opened in 1993, this whitewashed building is dramatic,
with black cast-iron balconies and black window frames. The upstairs
summer terrace is a nice place to cool off and watch the town and port.
The front rooms also offer panoramic views. ⊠ *Kibris Cad., Buyral
Sok. 4,* ☎ *256/614–7770,* 🆁🅰🆇 *256/614–6913. 16 rooms with shower.
Café, bar. No credit cards.*

Pamukkale

$$ 🏨 **Tusan.** The best feature of the Tusan is its pool, one of the most inviting in the area. The rooms are basic and comfortable. The one-story

building is at the top of a steep hill. ⊠ *Pamukkale, Denizli,* ☎ *258/272–2010,* ⨎ *258/272–2059. 47 rooms with bath. Restaurant, outdoor pool. AE, DC, MC, V.*

Selçuk

$ ⊞ **Hülya.** This is a pleasant, family-run pansiyon, where one of the family members is a fisherman who sometimes brings in some of his daily catch. Rooms are typically bare. There's a kitchen where you can cook if necessary. The down-to-earth owners serve meals in the lemon blossom-scented courtyard. ⊠ *Atatürk Cad., Özgür Sok. 15,* ☎ *232/892–2120. 8 rooms with bath. No credit cards.*

$ ⊞ **Kale Han.** In a refurbished stone building is one of the nicest hotels in town, managed by a very welcoming family. Rooms are simple, with bare, whitewashed walls and dark timber beams. The restaurant serves excellent food around the clock. ⊠ *Atatürk Cad. 49,* ☎ *232/892–6154,* ⨎ *232/892–2169. 52 rooms with shower. Restaurant, pool. MC, V.*

THE MEDITERRANEAN COAST

Until the mid-1970s, Turkey's southwest coast was inaccessible to all but the most determined travelers—those intrepid souls in four-wheel-drive vehicles or on the backs of donkeys. Today well-maintained highways wind through the area and jets full of tourists arrive at the new Dalaman Airport.

Thanks to strict developmental control, the area has maintained its Turkish flavor, with low, whitewashed buildings and tiled roofs. The beaches are clean, and you can swim and snorkel in turquoise waters so clear that it is possible to see fish 20 feet below. There are excellent outdoor cafés and seafood restaurants in which to dine, and there's no shortage of bars, discos, or nightclubs.

Getting Around

By Car

Although the highways between towns are well maintained, the smaller roads are usually unpaved and very rough.

By Boat

There are many coves and picnic areas accessible only by boat. For a small fee, local fishermen will take you to and from the coves; also, you can take one of the many water taxis. Or charter a small yacht, with or without skipper, at the marinas of Bodrum and Marmaris. Many people charter boats and join small flotillas that leave the marinas daily for sightseeing in the summer. One of the most enjoyable ways to see the coast is to take a one- or two-week **Blue Voyage** cruise on a *gulet,* a wooden craft with a full crew. There are also three-night mini Blue Voyage trips for scuba divers and snorkelers. For information, contact the following Blue Voyage agencies: in the United States, **Club Voyages** (⊠ Box 7648, Shrewsbury, NJ 07702, ☎ 908/291–8228); in the United Kingdom, **Explore** (⊠ 1 Frederick St., Aldershot, Hants GU11 1LQ, ☎ 012/5231–9448), **Simply Turkey** (⊠ 8 Chiswick Terrace, Acton La., London W4, ☎ 0181/747–1011), and **Falcon Sailing** (⊠ 13 Hillgate St., London W8, ☎ 0171/727–0232).

Guided Tours and Visitor Information

Local tourist offices list all the guided tours for the area and will also arrange for local guides.

1146

The Mediterranean Coast

Bodrum (✉ Baris Meyd. 12, ☎ 252/316–1091).
Dalaman (✉ Dalaman Airport, ☎ 252/692-5291).
Datça (✉ Iskele Mah. Hükümet Binasi, ☎ 252/712–3163 or 252/712–3546).
Kaş (✉ Cumhuriyet Meyd. 5, ☎ 242/836–1238).
Marmaris (✉ Iskele Meyd. 2, ☎ 252/412–1035).

Exploring the Mediterranean Coast

Bodrum

Sitting between two crescent-shaped bays, **Bodrum** has for years been the favorite haunt of the Turkish upper classes. Today the elite are joined by thousands of foreign visitors, and the area is rapidly filling with hotels and guest houses, cafés, restaurants, and discos. Many compare it to St. Tropez on the French Riviera. Fortunately, it is still beautiful and unspoiled, with gleaming whitewashed buildings covered with bougainvillea and magnificent unobstructed vistas of the bays. People flock to Bodrum not for its beach, which is a disappointment, but for its fine dining and nightlife. You'll find beautiful beaches in the outlying villages on the peninsula—**Torba, Türkbükü, Yalikavak, Turgutreis, Akyarlar, Ortakent, Bitez,** and **Gümbet.** Easy to reach by minibus or dolmuş, these villages are about an hour's drive away and have clean hotels and plenty of outdoor restaurants. One of the outstanding sights in Bodrum is **Bodrum Castle,** known as the **Castle of St. Peter.** Located between the two bays, the castle was built by crusaders in the 11th century. It has beautiful gardens and a **Museum of Underwater Archaeology.** ✉ $2.50 (castle and museum). ☉ Tues.–Sun. 8:30–noon and 1–5.

The peninsula is downright littered with ancient Greek and Roman ruins, although getting to some of them involves driving over rough dirt roads. Five kilometers (3 miles) from Bodrum is **Halikarnas,** a well-preserved

10,000-seat Greek amphitheater built in the 1st century BC and still used for town festivals. 🎫 *Free.* ☉ *Daily 8:30–sunset.*

Marmaris

Another beach resort between two bays is **Marmaris,** which has some of the best sailing on the Mediterranean. It is 178 kilometers (111 miles) from Bodrum via Muğla along Route 400. You'll climb steep, winding mountain passes, with cliffs that drop straight into the sea. The final 30 kilometers (19 miles) into Marmaris is a broad boulevard lined with eucalyptus trees. Marmaris, like Bodrum, is a sophisticated resort with boutiques, elegant restaurants, and plenty of nightlife. Nearby are quiet villages that are easy to reach by boat or taxi. One of these ★ is **Cnidos,** where you can see the ruins of Aphrodite's circular temple and an ancient theater. By road, Cnidos is a very rough 108 kilometers (67 miles) from Marmaris. It's easier and quicker to take a boat. Another town is **Turunç,** worth a day's visit, especially for its beaches.

Freshwater **Lake Köyceğiz** can be reached by boat through the reed beds of the **Dalyan delta.** This entire area is a wildlife preserve, filled with such birds as kingfishers, kestrels, egrets, and cranes. Köyceğiz and **Dalyan** villages, both 20 minutes' drive from Dalaman Airport, are good stopping-off places for exploring the area. It costs about $20 to rent a boat with a boatman to sail from Dalyan to the ruins and beach.

Ölü Deniz

★ One of Turkey's greatest natural wonders is **Ölü Deniz,** an azure lagoon flanked by long, white beaches. The area is about 145 kilometers (90 miles) from Koyceğiz. There are a few wooden chalets in camping grounds and one beachfront hotel. Opposite the beach, you'll find small restaurants with rooftop bars, many with live music that goes on all night.

Southeast of Fethiye, near Route 400, are several ancient sites, including the ruins of **Pinara,** one of the most important cities of the former Roman province of Lycia. Near Pinara, up a steep and strenuous dirt road, you'll find nearly 200 Roman tombs cut honeycomb-fashion into the face of the cliffs. 🎫 *$1.20.* ☉ *Daily 8:30–sunset.*

Xanthos

Return to Route 400 and head 18 kilometers (11 miles) south toward the village of Kinik. At Kinik leave the main highway and take a mile-long bumpy road to **Xanthos,** another major city of ancient Lycia. It was excavated in 1838; much of what was found here is now in the British Museum in London. What's left is still well worth the bumpy ride: the acropolis, the Tomb of Harpies, some plaster-cast reliefs, and ruins of some Byzantine buildings. 🎫 *$1.20.* ☉ *Daily 8:30–sunset.*

Patara and Kalkan

★ Ten minutes from Xanthos is **Patara,** once the city's port. Here you'll find ruins scattered around the marshes and sand dunes. The area's long, wide beaches remain unspoiled despite the fact that they attract hundreds of Turkish families and tourists. The nearest place to stay is **Kalkan,** a fishing village 20 minutes away by minibus.

Kaş

★ **Kaş,** 30 kilometers (18 miles) from Kalkan, is another fishing village that has become a popular resort and is also developing into a major yachting center. Although luxury hotels have replaced many of the tiny houses on the hills, there are still plenty of old-fashioned pansiyons for those on a budget. One of the attractions here is a day trip by boat to the underwater city of **Kekova,** where you can look overboard and see ancient Roman and Greek columns that were once part of a thriving city before the area was flooded. Kekova is especially popular with scuba divers and snorkelers, but to scuba dive or fish in this area, a permit must be obtained from the directorate of the harbor and from the directorate of the ministry of tourism. Boats leave daily at 9:30 and cost about $15.

For romantic ruins it would be hard to beat **Phaselis.** The Roman agora, theater, aqueduct, and a necropolis with fine sarcophagi are scattered throughout the pine woods that surround the Temple of Athena. Overgrown streets descend to the translucent water, which is ideal for swimming.

Kemer is the center of intensive tourist development, with hotels and restaurants, a well-equipped marina, and club-style holiday villages that make you forget you're in Turkey. The remaining 35 kilometers (26 miles) are increasingly occupied by villas and motels along the smooth pebbles of Konyalti Beach, which stretches to the outskirts of Antalya.

Antalya

The resort of **Antalya,** on the Mediterranean, is a good base for several worthwhile excursions. The city is on a restored harbor and is filled with narrow streets lined with small houses, restaurants, and pansiyons. On the hilltop are tea gardens where you can enjoy tea made in an old-fashioned samovar and look across the bay to the Taurus Mountains, which parallel the coast. To the right of the port is the 13th-century **Yivli Minare** (Fluted Minaret). The Hisar Café, Tophane tea garden, and Mermerli tea garden all overlook Antalya's harbor.

Dining and Lodging

For details and price-category definitions, *see* Dining *and* Lodging *in* Staying in Turkey, *above.*

Antalya

$–$$ ✕ **Hisar Restaurant.** Built into the 700-year-old walls of an old fortress, the Hisar is hard to beat for atmosphere. The inside is dominated by wood paneling through which it is possible to get a glimpse of the city wall and a view of the harbor. The mezes are above average and even the standard items are served with a twist: Try the tenderized steak rolled in cheese, mushrooms, and ham. ⊠ *Cumhuriyet Meydani,* ☎ *242/241–5281. AE, V.*

$$$$ 🏨 **Talya.** This is a luxurious resort hotel with its own beach that you
  ★   reach by taking an elevator down the side of the cliff. From every angle there's a view of the sea. It gets booked up quickly in high season. ⊠ *Fevzi Çakmak Cad.,* ☎ *242/248–6800,* FAX *242/241–5400. 204 rooms with bath. Restaurant, pool, exercise room, beach, dance club. AE, DC, MC, V.*

$$ 🏨 **Tütav Türk Evleri.** Part of the old Kaleiçi district, this hotel consists of a row of tastefully restored Turkish houses joined together. There are well-tended gardens surrounding the inn and its popular restaurant, which is known for its delectable fish stew. ⊠ *Mermerli Sok. 2,* ☎ *242/248–6478,* FAX *242/241–9419. 20 rooms with bath. Restaurant, bar, pool, sauna. AE, MC, V.*

$ 🏨 **Natali Pansiyon.** Each room is different in this small, odd pansiyon in the Kaleiçi district, but if you're feeling game, ask for the one with the enormous tiled bathroom (which is bigger than the bedroom). Breakfast is served on a terrace with a view over the old town. ⊠ *İzmir Ali Efendi Sok. 13, Kaleiçi,* ☎ *242/247–7821. 7 rooms, 3 with bath. No credit cards.*

Bodrum

$$$ ✕ **Club Pirinç.** This restaurant has a pleasant bar, nine guest rooms, a swimming pool, and serves Turkish-French cuisine. ✉ *Akçabuk Mev., Kumbahçe,* ☎ *252/316–2902. No credit cards.*

$$$ ✕ **Restaurant No. 7.** Octopus casseroles are a specialty at this eatery. ✉ *Eski Banka Sok. 7.,* ☎ *252/316–2042. No credit cards.*

$$ ✕ **Balik Restaurant.** Specialties here include fish, meat, and chicken kebabs. ✉ *Yeniçarşi 28,* ☎ *252/316–1454. No credit cards.*

$$ ✕ **Korfez Restaurant.** This seaside fish restaurant with white tablecloths and candles overlooks the bay. Try the calamari and octopus salad. ✉ *Cumhuriyet Cad. 32,* ☎ *252/316–1300 or 316–1241. AE, V.*

$$$ 🏨 **Manastır Hotel.** The hotel's name comes from the fact that part of it was once a monastery. The atmosphere is Aegean, with the pink and green of bougainvillea blowing against whitewashed walls. The restaurant serves grilled fish and spectacular Turkish salads. At peak times you may have to pay half-board. ✉ *Bariş Sitesi Mevkii, Kumbahçe,* ☎ *252/316–2854,* ⅀ *252/316–2722. 59 rooms with bath. 2 restaurants, 2 bars, pool, sauna, 1 tennis court, meeting rooms. AE, MC, V.*

$ 🏨 **Hotel Anka.** This hilltop hotel, just a mile from the city center, has commanding views of the Bodrum bay. Rooms with balconies in whitewashed bungalows are simple and clean, and the staff is warm. ✉ *Eskiçeşme Mah. Asarlik Mevkii, Gümbet,* ☎ *252/316–8217,* ⅀ *252/316–6194. 85 rooms with bath. Restaurant, 2 bars, pool, beach, dance club. AE, D, MC, V.*

Dalyan

$ ✕ **Yalı Restaurant.** This is a waterside eatery reached by a short boat ride from Dalyan. It's also a good stopping-off point if you're planning a walk to the Kaunos ruins. ☎ *252/284–2150. No credit cards.*

$$ 🏨 **Dalyan Hotel.** Comfortable and clean with views across Lake Köyceğiz to the tombs, the Dalyan is set among trees on the shore of the lake. It has an excellent restaurant and a friendly, attentive staff. ✉ *Yalii Sokak, Maras Mahalli,* ☎ *252/284–2239,* ⅀ *252/284–2240. 20 rooms with shower. 2 restaurants, 2 bars, pool. V.*

Kalkan

$$ 🏨 **Kalkan Han.** A rambling old house in the back part of the village, the Kalkan Han has a special treat for visitors: a roof terrace with sweeping views of the bay, a perfect place to enjoy breakfast. ✉ *Köyiçi Mev.,* ☎ *242/844–3151,* ⅀ *242/844–2048. 16 rooms with bath. Restaurant, bar. No credit cards. Closed Nov.–Apr.*

$ 🏨 **Balikçi Han.** This delightful pansiyon is in a converted 19th-century inn, directly on the waterfront. ✉ *Yalı Mahallesi Boyu,* ☎ *242/844–1075. 7 rooms with bath. No credit cards.*

Kaş

$$ ✕ **Mercan.** On the eastern side of the harbor, the Mercan serves good, basic Turkish food in an attractive open-air setting. The water is so close you can actually hear fish jumping. The menu includes whole lamb on a spit, fish, and lobster, as well as vegetarian choices. ✉ *Hukumet Cad.,* ☎ *242/836–1209. MC, V.*

$$ 🏨 **Kaş Oteli.** There's good swimming off the rocks in front of the hotel, or you can laze in the sun with drinks and snacks from the bar or restaurant. There are also wonderful views of the Greek island of Kastellorizo. ✉ *Hastane Cad. 15,* ☎ *242/836–1271,* ⅀ *242/836–1368. Restaurant, bar. No credit cards. Closed Nov.–Apr.*

$$ ☒ **Mimosa.** Conveniently located on a hill near the bus station, this small property has plain but perfectly adequate rooms, all with balconies and views. ⊠ *Elmali Cad.,* ☎ *242/836–1272,* FAX *242/836–1272. 26 rooms with bath. Pool. No credit cards.*

$ ☒ **Medusa Hotel.** Set on a cliff overlooking the sea, this picturesque hotel is also a diving school. Front rooms have expansive ocean views, while back rooms face the mountains. ⊠ *Küçükçakil,* ☎ *242/836–1440,* FAX *242/836–1368. 40 rooms with bath. 2 restaurants, 2 bars, pool. No credit cards.*

Köyceğiz

$$$ ☒ **Hotel Özay.** This lakeside hotel is quiet, modern, and efficiently run. The setting is smothered in lush greenery and palm trees. Daily boat tours of the lake are available and Turkish belly-dancing shows take place at night. ⊠ *Kordon Boyu 11, Köyceğiz,* ☎ *252/262–4300,* FAX *252/262–2000. 34 rooms with bath. Restaurant, bar, pool. AE, DC, MC, V.*

$ ☒ **Kaunos Hotel.** Ask for front rooms with lake views at this small, modern hotel set right on the water. ⊠ *Cengiz Topel Cad.,* ☎ *252/262–4288,* FAX *252/262–4836. 44 rooms with bath. Restaurant, bar, pool, dance club. No credit cards.*

Ölü Deniz

$$$$ ✕ **Beyaz Yunus.** Wicker chairs and wooden floors fill this domed
★ restaurant, whose name means "white dolphin." The most elegant restaurant in the area, it's situated on a promontory near Padirali and serves Continental and Turkish cuisines imaginatively prepared and presented. ☎ *252/616–6036. No credit cards.*

$ ✕ **Kebabcı Salonu.** You can grill meat at your table in this outdoor restaurant, where tables and chairs are clustered around trees in a field. Meals are served with mezes, salad, and wine. ⊠ *Behind Han Camp, no phone. No credit cards.*

$$ ☒ **Meri Oteli.** Located on a steep incline above the lagoon, this is a series of bungalows, with rooms a bit down-at-the-heel but clean. These are the only accommodations at the lagoon. ☎ *252/616–6060,* FAX *252/616–6456. 75 rooms with bath. Restaurant. AE, DC, MC, V.*

CENTRAL ANATOLIA AND CAPPADOCIA

Cappadocia, an area filled with ruins of ancient civilizations, is in the eastern part of Anatolia and has changed little over the centuries. People still travel between their farms and villages in horse-drawn carts, women drape their houses with strings of apricots and paprika for drying in the sun, and nomads pitch their black tents beside sunflower fields and cook on tiny fires that send smoke billowing through the tops of the tents.

Getting Around

By Car

There are good roads between Istanbul and the main cities of Anatolia—Ankara (the capital of Turkey), Konya, and Kayseri. The highways are generally well maintained and lead to all the major sites. Minor roads are full of potholes and are very rough. On narrow, winding roads, look out for oncoming trucks.

By Bus

There is a good interlinking bus network between most towns and cities, and fares are reasonable.

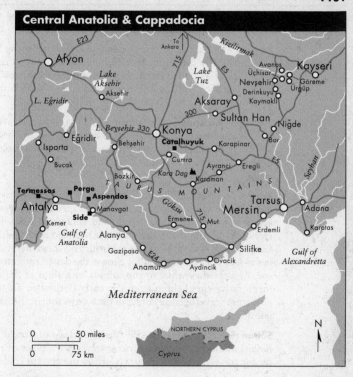

Central Anatolia & Cappadocia

By Train
Though there are frequent trains between the main cities, they are almost nonexistent between small towns. It's much quicker to take a bus.

By Taxi
Drivers are usually willing to take you to historical sites out of town for reasonable fares.

Guided Tours

As the Cappadocia area is so vast, you'll need at least two days to see the main sights. If you are driving, consider hiring a guide for about $15–$30 a day. Local tourist offices and hotels will be able to recommend guides and excursions.

Visitor Information

Check with local tourist offices for names of travel agencies and English-speaking guides.

Aksaray (⊠ Ankara Cad. Dinçer Apt. 2/2, ☎ 382/213–2474).
Ankara (⊠ Gazi Mustafa Kemal Bul. 121, Tandoğan, ☎ 312/229–2631).
Kayseri (⊠ Kagni Pazari 61, ☎ 352/222–3903).
Konya (⊠ Mevlana Cad. 21, ☎ 332/351–1074).
Nevşehir (⊠ Atatürk Cad. Hastane Yani, ☎ 384/213–1137).
Ürgüp (⊠ Kayseri Cad. 37, ☎ 384/341–4059).

Exploring Central Anatolia and Cappadocia

An hour's drive, 30 kilometers (19 miles), to the northwest of Antalya is **Termessos,** which has an almost complete Roman amphitheater built on a mountainside, and the unexcavated remains of a Roman city

on the other side of the mountain. There are organized tours to Termessos from Antalya. ☎ *Free.* ☺ *Daily 9–5:30.*

Perge, 19 kilometers (11 miles) east of Antalya, has many Roman ruins
to explore. You can climb up a 22,000-seat amphitheater, walk down
a restored colonnaded street, visit well-preserved thermal baths and a
Roman basilica, and see the spot where St. Paul preached his first ser-
mon in AD 45. ☎ *$2.50.* ☺ *Daily 9–5:30.*

★ Nearby is **Aspendos,** 44 kilometers (23 miles) to the east of Antalya,
which contains Turkey's best-preserved amphitheater. The acoustics are
so fine that modern-day performers don't need microphones or am-
plifiers. *Admission: $2.50. Open daily 9–5:30.*

Konya
Konya, home of the Whirling Dervishes, is reached by driving 427 kilometers (267 miles) northeast of Antalya past **Lake Beyşehir.** There is
also a longer and more difficult road via **Lake Eğridir.** The Whirling
Dervishes belong to a religious order founded in the 13th century by
Celaleddin Rumi, or Mevlana, a Muslim mystic, who said, "There are
many ways of knowing God. I choose the dance and music." You can
see the dervishes whirl to the sounds of a flute at the annual commemorative rites held in Konya in early December. Tickets are available from travel agencies or from the Konya tourist information office
(☞ *above*).

Sultan Han, 95 kilometers (59 miles) northeast of Konya, is Anatolia's
largest and best-preserved caravansary, once a place of rest and shelter for travelers and their camels plying the ancient trade routes.

Cappadocia
Cappadocia roughly forms the triangular area between **Kayseri,**
Nevşehir, and **Niğde.** Most of the main sights are within an even
smaller triangular area linked by Ürgüp, Göreme, and Avanos. **Ürgüp**
is the center from which to explore the villages and the best place to
shop, as well as to arrange tours.

The softness of the rock in this area was ideal for hollowing out cave
dwellings and forming defenses from invading armies. The Cappado-
cians carved out about 40 underground cities, with some structures as
deep as 20 stories underground. The largest of these cities housed
20,000 people. Each had dormitories, dining halls, sewage disposal systems, ventilation chimneys, a cemetery, and a prison. Large millstones
sealed off the entrances from enemies. Two of these cities are open to
the public, one at **Derinkuyu,** 21 kilometers (13 miles) south of Nevşehir,
★ and the other at **Kaymakli,** 30 kilometers (19 miles) south of Nevşehir.
☎ *$2.50.* ☺ *Daily 8–sunset.*

The Christians also hid in these underground cities when the Islamic
forces swept through Cappadocia in the 7th century. Some of the earliest relics of Christianity are to be found in the **Göreme Valley,** a few
miles east of Nevşehir. There are dozens of old churches and monas-
★ teries covered with frescoes. For a history of the area, visit the **Göreme
Open-Air Museum,** 1 kilometer (½ mile) outside of Göreme village on
the Ürgüp road. ☎ *Free.* ☺ *Daily 8:30–5:30.*

Dining and Lodging

For details and price-category definitions, *see* Dining *and* Lodging *in*
Staying in Turkey, *above.*

Avanos

$ ⊞ **Zelve.** This is a small modern hotel in the center of town. ⊠ *Hükümet Meydani,* ☎ *384/511–4524,* 𝖥𝖠𝖷 *384/511–4687. 29 rooms with bath. Restaurant, bar. AE, DC, MC, V.*

Göreme

$ ✕⊞ **Ataman Hotel.** Run by tourist guide Abbas and his wife Şermin, this atmospheric hotel and restaurant is built into the face of a rock facing the lush Göreme valley. The large restaurant specializes in seafood and French cuisine. The cozy rooms have been decorated in Seljuk style, with mother-of-pearl candle sconces, fireplaces, and tile decorations hanging on the walls. ⊠ *Göreme,* ☎ *384/271–2310,* 𝖥𝖠𝖷 *384/271–2313. 38 rooms with bath. 2 restaurants. MC, V.*

Konya

$ ✕ **Ali Baba Kebapçısı.** This restaurant serves good kebabs and is famous for its Firin kebab, cooked over an open charcoal fire. ⊠ *Eski Avukatlar Sok. 11/A,* ☎ *332/351–0307. No credit cards.*

$ ✕ **Bolu Restaurant.** You can eat dishes here for which Konya is renowned: *etli ekmek* (flat bread with ground lamb) and tereyağli borek. ⊠ *Pürçüklü Mah. 31/c,* ☎ *332/352–4533.*

$$ ⊞ **Balikçilar Hotel.** Conveniently located across from Konya's main sight, Mevlana, this hotel has air-conditioned and spare but comfortable rooms. Many of the employees are trainees from tourism schools and can be helpful in planning local outings. ⊠ *Mevlana Karşisi 1,* ☎ *332/350–9470,* 𝖥𝖠𝖷 *332/351–3259. 48 rooms with bath. 2 restaurants, 2 bars, Turkish bath, meeting room. MC, V.*

Ürgüp

$$ ✕ **Hanedan.** In the cellar of an old Greek house, the Hanedan is on a hill a short distance from town. You can sit on the terrace and watch the sun set across the plains toward the mountains. The food is very good and is presented with flair. ⊠ *Nevşehir Yolu Üzeri,* ☎ *384/341–4266.* 𝖥𝖠𝖷 *384/341–8866. Group reservations essential. DC, MC, V.*

$$ ⊞ **Büyük Almira.** This centrally located hotel, renovated and expanded in 1994, has comfortable rooms overlooking an outdoor swimming pool. The biggest and most popular disco in town is also here. ⊠ *Kayseri Cad. 43,* ☎ 𝖥𝖠𝖷 *384/341–8999. 101 rooms with bath. 2 restaurants, 3 bars, pool, dance club, meeting room. MC, V.*

$ ⊞ **Hitit.** The family-run Hitit is a comfortable, small hotel with a restaurant that serves basic but enjoyable food. ⊠ *Dumlupinar Cad. 54,* ☎ *384/341–1481. 15 rooms without bath. No credit cards. Closed Nov.–Mar.*

INDEX

1170

Index

NOTES

NOTES

NOTES

NOTES

NOTES

NOTES

NOTES

NOTES

NOTES

NOTES

NOTES

NOTES

NOTES

NOTES

NOTES

NOTES

Escape to ancient cities and

journey to  *exotic islands with*

CNN Travel Guide, a wealth of valuable advice. Host

Valerie Voss will take you to

all of your favorite destinations,

 *including those off the beaten*

path. Tune-in to your passport to the world.

CNN TRAVEL GUIDE
SATURDAY 12:30 PMET   SUNDAY 4:30 PMET

CNN✈
Airport Network

Your
Window
To The
World
While You're
On The
Road

Keep in touch when you're traveling. Before you take off, tune in to CNN Airport Network. Now available in major airports across America, CNN Airport Network provides nonstop news, sports, business, weather and lifestyle programming. Both domestic and international. All piloted by the top-flight global resources of CNN. All up-to-the minute reporting. And just for travelers, CNN Airport Network features two daily Fodor's specials. "Travel Fact" provides enlightening, useful travel trivia, while "What's Happening" covers upcoming events in major cities worldwide. So why be bored waiting to board? TIME FLIES WHEN YOU'RE WATCHING THE WORLD THROUGH THE WINDOW OF CNN AIRPORT NETWORK!

lor's Travel Publications

ailable at bookstores everywhere, or call 1–800–533–6478, 24 hours a day.

Gold Guides

U.S.

Alaska	Florida	New Orleans	Santa Fe, Taos, Albuquerque
Arizona	Hawai'i	New York City	Seattle & Vancouver
Boston	Las Vegas, Reno, Tahoe	Pacific North Coast	The South
California		Philadelphia & the Pennsylvania Dutch Country	U.S. & British Virgin Islands
Cape Cod, Martha's Vineyard, Nantucket	Los Angeles		
	Maine, Vermont, New Hampshire	The Rockies	USA
The Carolinas & the Georgia Coast		San Diego	Virginia & Maryland
	Maui & Lāna'i	San Francisco	Washington, D.C.
Chicago	Miami & the Keys		
Colorado	New England		

Foreign

Australia	Europe	Montréal & Québec City	Scotland
Austria	Florence, Tuscany & Umbria	Moscow, St. Petersburg, Kiev	Singapore
The Bahamas			South Africa
Belize & Guatemala	France	The Netherlands, Belgium & Luxembourg	South America
Bermuda	Germany		Southeast Asia
Canada	Great Britain		Spain
Cancún, Cozumel, Yucatán Peninsula	Greece	New Zealand	Sweden
	Hong Kong	Norway	Switzerland
Caribbean	India	Nova Scotia, New Brunswick, Prince Edward Island	Thailand
China	Ireland		Tokyo
Costa Rica	Israel		Toronto
Cuba	Italy	Paris	Turkey
The Czech Republic & Slovakia	Japan	Portugal	Vienna & the Danube
	London	Provence & the Riviera	
Eastern & Central Europe	Madrid & Barcelona		
	Mexico	Scandinavia	

Fodor's Special-Interest Guides

Caribbean Ports of Call	Halliday's New Orleans Food Explorer	Sunday in New York	Where Should We Take the Kids? Northeast
The Complete Guide to America's National Parks	Healthy Escapes	Sunday in San Francisco	
		Walt Disney World, Universal Studios and Orlando	Worldwide Cruises and Ports of Call
Family Adventures	Kodak Guide to Shooting Great Travel Pictures		
Gay Guide to the USA	Net Travel	Walt Disney World for Adults	
Halliday's New England Food Explorer	Nights to Imagine	Where Should We Take the Kids? California	
	Rock & Roll Traveler USA		

Special Series

Affordables

Caribbean
Europe
Florida
France
Germany
Great Britain
Italy
London
Paris

Fodor's Bed & Breakfasts and Country Inns

America
California
The Mid-Atlantic
New England
The Pacific Northwest
The South
The Southwest
The Upper Great Lakes

The Berkeley Guides

California
Central America
Eastern Europe
Europe
France
Germany & Austria
Great Britain & Ireland
Italy
London
Mexico
New York City
Pacific Northwest & Alaska
Paris
San Francisco

Compass American Guides

Arizona
Canada
Chicago
Colorado
Hawaii
Idaho
Hollywood
Las Vegas

Maine
Manhattan
Montana
New Mexico
New Orleans
Oregon
San Francisco
Santa Fe
South Carolina
South Dakota
Southwest
Texas
Utah
Virginia
Washington
Wine Country
Wisconsin
Wyoming

Fodor's Citypacks

Atlanta
Hong Kong
London
New York City
Paris
Rome
San Francisco
Washington, D.C.

Fodor's Español

California
Caribe Occidental
Caribe Oriental
Gran Bretaña
Londres
Mexico
Nueva York
Paris

Fodor's Exploring Guides

Australia
Boston & New England
Britain
California
Caribbean
China
Egypt
Florence & Tuscany
Florida

France
Germany
Ireland
Israel
Italy
Japan
London
Mexico
Moscow & St. Petersburg
New York City
Paris
Prague
Provence
Rome
San Francisco
Scotland
Singapore & Malaysia
Spain
Thailand
Turkey
Venice

Fodor's Flashmaps

Boston
New York
San Francisco
Washington, D.C.

Fodor's Pocket Guides

Acapulco
Atlanta
Barbados
Jamaica
London
New York City
Paris
Prague
Puerto Rico
Rome
San Francisco
Washington, D.C.

Mobil Travel Guides

America's Best Hotels & Restaurants
California & the West
Frequent Traveler's Guide to Major Cities
Great Lakes
Mid-Atlantic

Northeast
Northwest & Great Plains
Southeast
Southwest & South Central

Rivages Guides

Bed and Breakfasts of Character and Charm in France
Hotels and Country Inns of Character and Charm in France
Hotels and Country Inns of Character and Charm in Italy
Hotels and Country Inns of Character and Charm in Paris
Hotels and Country Inns of Character and Charm in Portugal
Hotels and Country Inns of Character and Charm in Spain

Short Escapes

Britain
France
New England
Near New York City

Fodor's Sports

Golf Digest's Best Places to Play
Skiing USA
USA Today The Complete Four Sport Stadium Guide

Fodor's Vacation Planners

Great American Learning Vacations
Great American Sports & Adventure Vacations
Great American Vacations
Great American Vacations for Travelers with Disabilities
National Parks and Seashores of the East
National Parks of the West

WHEREVER YOU TRAVEL, *H*ELP IS NEVER FAR AWAY.

From planning your trip to

providing travel assistance along

the way, American Express®

Travel Service Offices are

always there to help.

American Express Travel Service
Offices are found in central locations
throughout Europe.

Travel

http://www.americanexpress.com/travel